Managing Access to Medicines and Health Technologies

MDS-3

Managing Access to Medicines and Health Technologies

Kumarian Press
An Imprint of Stylus Publishing

msh
Management Sciences for Health

Published 2013 by Kumarian Press, an imprint of Stylus Publishing, LLC
22883 Quicksilver Drive, Sterling, VA 20166-2102

Management Sciences for Health
Attn: Managing Drug Supply
4301 North Fairfax Drive, Suite 400
Arlington, VA 22203 USA
Tel.: +1-703-524-6575
Fax: +1-703-524-7898
E-mail: mds@msh.org
Website: www.mds-online.org

Library of Congress Cataloging-in-Publication Data
MDS-3 : managing access to medicines and health technologies / Management Sciences for Health, Inc. ; editor, Martha Embrey. — 3rd ed.
     p. ; cm.
Managing drug supply
Includes bibliographical references and index.
ISBN 978-1-56549-586-9 (cloth : alk. paper) — ISBN 978-1-56549-587-6 (pbk. : alk. paper) — ISBN 978-1-56549-588-3 (library networkable e-edition) — ISBN 978-1-56549-589-0 (consumer e-edition)
I. Embrey, Martha A., 1961- II. Management Sciences for Health (Firm) III. Title: Managing drug supply.
[DNLM: 1. Drug Industry—economics. 2. Developing Countries. 3. Drugs, Essential—supply & distribution. 4. Health Services Accessibility. 5. Technology, Pharmaceutical. QV 736.1]
362.17'82—dc23
2012045295

Acknowledgments
The development of this edition of *MDS-3: Managing Access to Medicines and Health Technologies* was largely supported through the Strategies for Enhancing Access to Medicines grant from the Bill & Melinda Gates Foundation. The opinions expressed herein are those of the authors and do not necessarily reflect the views of the Gates Foundation.

Recommended citation
Management Sciences for Health. 2011. *MDS-3: Managing Access to Medicines and Health Technologies*. Sterling, Va.: Kumarian Press.

Technical Writer and Editor
Martha Embrey

Managing Editor
Marian Ryan

Designer
Edna Jamandre

Copyeditor
Laura Glassman

Proofreaders
Karen Weller-Watson
Robin O. Surratt

Reference Reviewer
Karen Frenchu

Illustrators
Eustace Githonga
Uto Hogerzeil
Tony Namate

Cover Photo Credits
(from top to bottom)
Michael Paydos (Tanzania)
Martha Embrey (Kenya)
David Lee (Vietnam)
Saul Kidde (Uganda)
Mark Morris (Afghanistan)

Printed in the United States of America.
All first editions printed on acid-free paper that meets the American National Standards Institute Z39-48 Standard.

THIRD EDITION, 2013
10   9   8   7   6   5   4   3   2   1

Contributors by Chapter

This list shows the technical contributors to each chapter and their professional affiliations and locations at the time of their contribution—not necessarily their current affiliation and location. Contributors are listed alphabetically, not in relation to the proportion of material they contributed. Many chapters retain a substantial proportion of text from the first two editions of this book. Authors from earlier editions are indicated by an asterisk. Authors who contributed to both the current and previous editions are indicated with a dagger.

1. Toward Sustainable Access to Medicines
Martha Embrey, MSH, USA
*Graham Dukes, Euro Health Group, Norway
*Jonathan D. Quick, MSH, USA

2. Historical and Institutional Perspectives
†Graham Dukes, University of Oslo, Norway
Helena Walkowiak, MSH, USA
*Ronald W. O'Connor, MSH, USA

3. Intellectual Property and Access to Medicines
Sisule Musungu, South Centre, Switzerland

4. National Medicine Policy
†Graham Dukes, University of Oslo, Norway
*Pascale Brudon, World Health Organization (WHO), Switzerland

5. Traditional and Complementary Medicine Policy
Torkel Faulkenberg, Karolinska Institutet, Sweden

6. Pharmaceutical Legislation and Regulation
Enrique Fefer, Consultant, USA
*Graham Dukes, Euro Health Group, Norway
*Marcelo Vernengo, Universidad de Belgrano, Argentina
*Robert L. Watt

7. Pharmaceutical Production Policy
Martha Embrey, MSH, USA
*John Holley, Integral Development Associates, USA
*Paul J. N. Lamberts, Deventer Hospital Pharmacy, The Netherlands
*Ronald W. O'Connor, MSH, USA
*Robert L. Watt

8. Pharmaceutical Supply Strategies
Malcolm Clark, MSH, Australia
*Jonathan D. Quick, MSH, USA
*James R. Rankin, MSH, USA
*Germán Velásquez, WHO, Switzerland

9. Pharmaceutical Pricing Policy
David Henry, University of Newcastle, Australia
Andrew Searles, University of Newcastle, Australia

10. Economics for Pharmaceutical Management
†David Henry, University of Newcastle, Australia
*Kara Hanson, Harvard School of Public Health, USA
*Jonathan D. Quick, MSH, USA
*Germán Velásquez, WHO, Switzerland

11. Pharmaceutical Financing Strategies
Martha Embrey, MSH, USA
*William Newbrander, MSH, USA
*Jonathan D. Quick, MSH, USA
*Catriona Waddington, Overseas Development Administration, UK

12. Pharmaceutical Benefits in Insurance Programs
John Chalker, MSH, UK

13. Revolving Drug Funds and User Fees
Martha Embrey, MSH, USA
*Margaret Hume, MSH, USA
*Jennie I. Litvack, World Bank, USA
*Jonathan D. Quick, MSH, USA

14. Global and Donor Financing
Logan Brenzel, World Bank, USA
*Enrique Fefer, Pan American Health Organization, USA
*Margaret Hume, MSH, USA
*Irene Klinger, Pan American Health Organization, USA

15. Pharmaceutical Donations
Malcolm Clark, MSH, Australia
Martha Embrey, MSH, USA
*Christel Albert
*Hans Hogerzeil, WHO, Switzerland

16. Managing Medicine Selection
Christopher Olson, MSH, USA
*Hans Hogerzeil, WHO, Switzerland

17. Treatment Guidelines and Formulary Manuals
Christopher Olson, MSH, USA
*Chris Forshaw, WHO, Malawi
*Hans Hogerzeil, WHO, Switzerland

18. Managing Procurement
Andrew Barraclough, MSH, Thailand
Malcolm Clark, MSH, Australia
*David Lee, MSH, USA
*Jonathan D. Quick, MSH, USA

19. Quality Assurance for Pharmaceuticals
Thomas Layloff, MSH, USA
*David Lee, MSH, USA
*Jonathan D. Quick, MSH, USA

20. Quantifying Pharmaceutical Requirements
Laila Akhlaghi, MSH, USA
*Christopher Olson, MSH, USA
*James R. Rankin, MSH, USA

21. Managing the Tender Process
Malcolm Clark, MSH, Australia
Ned Heltzer, MSH, USA
James Rankin, MSH, USA
*Johan van Haperen, Danida, Denmark

22. Managing Distribution
Malcolm Clark, MSH, Australia
*Anthony Battersby, Feilden Battersby Health Systems
Analysts, UK
*James Bates, MSH, USA
*Andrew Garnett, Feilden Battersby Health Systems
Analysts, UK

23. Inventory Management
Vimal Dias, MSH, Sri Lanka
*Jonathan D. Quick, MSH, USA
*James R. Rankin, MSH, USA

24. Importation and Port Clearing
†Hilary Vaughan, Crown Agents, UK
*Vimal Dias, MSH, Sri Lanka
*John Ellery, Greenshields Cowie, UK

25. Transport Management
Gabriel Daniel, MSH, USA
*Anthony Battersby, Feilden Battersby Health Systems
Analysts, UK
*Andrew Garnett, Feilden Battersby Health Systems
Analysts, UK

26. Kit System Management
Henk den Besten, IDA Solutions, The Netherlands
*Miguel de Clerck, Médecins sans Frontières,
Switzerland
*Jean-Pierre de Lamalle, Médecins sans Frontières,
Switzerland
*Myriam Henkens, Médecins sans Frontières,
Switzerland
*Hans Hogerzeil, WHO, Switzerland
*Ignacio J. Packer, Médecins sans Frontières,
Switzerland

27. Managing for Rational Medicine Use
John Chalker, MSH, UK
*Richard O. Laing, MSH, USA
*Budiono Santoso, Gadjah Mada University, Indonesia

28. Investigating Medicine Use
Lloyd Matowe, MSH, USA
*Dennis Ross-Degnan, Harvard University, USA

29. Promoting Rational Prescribing
John Chalker, MSH, UK
*Richard O. Laing, MSH, USA
*David Ofori-Adjei, University of Ghana Medical
School, Ghana
*Christopher Olson, MSH, USA
*Budiono Santoso, Gadjah Mada University, Indonesia

30. Ensuring Good Dispensing Practices
†Paul Spivey, Consultant, UK

31. Community-Based Participation and Initiatives
Jane Briggs, MSH, Guatemala
*Aida Girma, United Nations Children's Fund
(UNICEF), USA

32. Drug Seller Initiatives
Malcolm Clark, MSH, USA
Ned Heltzer, MSH, USA
Keith Johnson, MSH, USA
Robert Staley, MSH, USA

33. Encouraging Appropriate Medicine Use by Consumers
Keith Johnson, MSH, USA
*Daphne A. Fresle, WHO, Switzerland

Reviewers

Reviewers provided feedback on one or more chapters. Reviewers' professional affiliations and locations are from the time of their review—not necessarily their current affiliation and location. Their input does not necessarily reflect the views of their employers.

Frances Aboagye-Nyame	MSH, USA
Syed Rizwanuddin Ahmad	USA
Samvel Azatyan,	WHO, Switzerland
Guitelle Baghdadi-Sabeti	WHO, Switzerland
Andrew Barraclough	MSH, Thailand
Hare Ram Bhattarai	MSH, Nepal
Tina Brock	MSH, USA
Malcolm Bryant	MSH, USA
Robert Burn	MSH, USA
Edelisa Carandang	WHO, Switzerland
Peter Carrasco	WHO, Switzerland
John Chalker	MSH, UK
Malcolm Clark	MSH, Australia
Peter Cross	MSH, USA
Gabriel Daniel	MSH, USA
Vimal Dias	MSH, Sri Lanka
Alex Dodoo	University of Ghana Medical School, Ghana
Alison Ellis	MSH, USA
Marthe Everard	WHO, Switzerland
Julie Frye	MSH, USA
Michael Gabra	MSH, USA
Louis Garrison	University of Washington School of Pharmacy, USA
Natalie Gaul	MSH, USA
Nigel Gericke	Consultant, South Africa
Raj Gonsalkorale	Consultant, Australia
Ned Heltzer	MSH, USA
Suzanne Hill	WHO, Switzerland
Hans Hogerzeil	WHO, Switzerland
Kathleen Holloway	WHO, Switzerland
Keith Johnson	MSH, USA
Mohan Joshi	MSH, USA
Charles Kagoma,	MSH, Tanzania
Grace Kahenya	MSH, Zambia
Richard Laing	WHO, Switzerland

Rama Lakshminarayanan	World Bank, USA
David Lee	MSH, USA
Evan Lee	MSH, France
Andrew Marsden	MSH, France
Lloyd Matowe	MSH, USA
Thomas Moore	MSH, USA
Gail Naimoli	MSH, USA
Bannet Ndyanabangi	MSH, USA
William Newbrander	MSH, USA
Christopher Olson	MSH, USA
Patricia Paredes,	MSH, USA
Alain Prat	WHO, Switzerland
Jonathan Quick	MSH, USA
James Rankin	MSH, USA
Steve Reed	MSH, USA
Andreas Seiter	World Bank, USA
John Sheptor	MSH, USA
Rima Shretta	MSH, USA
Anthony So	Duke University, USA
Robert Staley	MSH, USA
Helen Tata	WHO, Switzerland
Linda Tawfik	MSH, USA
Dat Tran	MSH, USA
Anita Wagner	Harvard University, USA
Helena Walkowiak	MSH, USA
Hella Witt	MSH, USA
Andre Zagorski	MSH, USA
Xiaorui Zhang	WHO, Switzerland

Contents

Preface

It is my great pleasure to present *MDS-3: Managing Access to Medicines and Health Technologies.* In the thirty years since the original publication of *Managing Drug Supply,* the world has experienced remarkable changes as the global health context has evolved. Think, for example, about the profound impact that HIV/AIDS alone has had. Advances in science and medicine, donor funding for vast global health initiatives, the advent of innovative information technologies, and a greater focus on building strong health systems have fundamentally affected our work. What has not changed over the years is MSH's commitment to identifying problems in access to and use of medicines and designing and implementing relevant, effective responses. We hope that *MDS-3* will be a valuable tool in the effort to ensure universal access to quality medicines and health technologies and their appropriate use.

The new and updated information in *MDS-3* reflects the dramatic changes in the public health landscape. Nearly 100 experts from a wide range of disciplines and virtually every corner of the world have contributed to this third edition. In addition to new country studies, references, and extensive revisions, *MDS-3* offers new chapters on areas such as pharmaceutical benefits in insurance programs, pricing, intellectual property, drug seller initiatives, and traditional and complementary medicine. The revisions and new chapters echo the wide variety of issues that are important to health practitioners and policy makers today. Even the book's new title depicts the need to broaden our focus from medicines to include *health technologies,* such as test kits and laboratory supplies, and to embrace the concept of *access.* Too often people assume that if medicines and technologies are available, positive health outcomes will naturally result. Access, however, encompasses not only product availability, but also the need to provide medicines and pharmaceutical services that are safe, efficacious, cost-effective, and high quality. Equally important are affordability and acceptability, including cultural and personal preferences.

We hope that *MDS-3* will be used widely by those with an interest in improving access to medicines and health technologies. To make the book accessible to as many users as possible, we are making the content available in several formats in addition to this print version. The easiest way to access *MDS-3* is online at http://www.mds-online.org. The entire book can be searched online, and individual chapters can be downloaded. *MDS-3* is also available directly from MSH on flash drive or CD-ROM for those without reliable Internet access or who prefer these media.

As users of *MDS-3,* you are vital to ensuring that it remains a valuable and dynamic resource. Your suggestions for enriching and updating the information and improving its presentation are greatly welcome. We will update individual chapters as needed to provide new material in a timely manner. Please send suggestions to us at mds@msh.org.

We acknowledge with great appreciation all the authors, reviewers, and others whose efforts are reflected in *MDS-3.* Any contribution that *MDS-3* makes is a direct result of their knowledge, experience, and deep dedication—and of the hard work of those around the world who each day strive to help their countries and their programs realize the full health impact of ensuring access to medicines and health technologies for all.

Jonathan D. Quick, MD, MPH
President and Chief Executive Officer
Management Sciences for Health
February 2012

How to Use *MDS-3*

This manual may seem intimidating, but you do not need to read it from cover to cover. Instead, we have organized it to provide a sequential overview of major topics and within each section, more detailed explanations of fundamental concepts, definitions of basic terms, and practical ideas for designing and implementing effective changes in pharmaceutical management systems.

The following features make the material accessible to readers looking for information in specific areas.

Overview chapters. Starting with Part II on Pharmaceutical Management, overview chapters introduce each element in the pharmaceutical management framework: selection (Chapter 16), procurement (Chapter 18), distribution (Chapter 22), use (Chapter 27), and management (Chapter 37). These overview chapters provide background information that leads into more detailed discussions of specific topics in the following chapters.

Chapter summaries. Each chapter begins with a summary of the chapter's contents. Those readers who are interested in a rapid overview of an area or of all aspects of managing access to medicines can read the summaries for that particular area.

Country studies. Reports of experiences in various countries illustrate points in the text. Although conditions in some countries may have changed since these country studies were written, they provide useful examples of the ways in which the pharmaceutical management process can operate and in some cases, how it should not operate.

Boxes. Boxes are used to make information such as the steps of a process easy to locate and use. In addition, some boxes contain general experiences or descriptions of relevant initiatives or resources.

Glossaries. Glossaries are included for the chapters on intellectual property (Chapter 3), insurance (Chapter 12), selection (Chapter 16), procurement (Chapter 18), distribution (Chapter 22), use (Chapter 27), management (Chapter 37), analyzing expenditures (Chapter 40), financial management (Chapter 41), storage facilities (Chapter 42), and computers (Chapter 51).

References and further readings. Each chapter contains a list of references that are cited in the text or that relate to topics the chapter covers. Particularly useful references are marked with a star.

Chapter annexes. Annexes provide sources of additional information and samples of pharmaceutical management forms currently in use in various parts of the world.

CHAPTER 1

Toward sustainable access to medicines

SUMMARY

Most leading causes of death and disability in developing countries can be prevented, treated, or at least alleviated with cost-effective essential medicines. Despite this fact, hundreds of millions of people do not have regular access to essential medicines. Many of those who do have access are given the wrong treatment, receive too little medicine for their illness, or do not use the medicine correctly.

MDS-3 addresses practical ways in which government policy makers, essential medicines program managers, nongovernmental organizations (NGOs), donors, and others can work to ensure that high-quality essential medicines are available, affordable, and used rationally. Medicines are of particular importance because they can save lives and improve health, and they promote trust and participation in health services. They are costly, and special concerns make medicines different from other consumer products. Moreover, substantive improvements in the supply and use of pharmaceuticals are possible.

Within a decade after the first modern pharmaceuticals became available, efforts began to ensure their widespread availability. From the mid-1950s to the mid-1970s, basic pharmaceutical management concepts began to evolve in countries as diverse as Cuba, Norway, Papua New Guinea, Peru, and Sri Lanka.

In 1975, the World Health Organization (WHO) defined *essential medicines* as those medicines that meet the health needs of the majority of the population. In 1982, Management Sciences for Health published the first edition of *Managing Drug Supply,* which incorporated the essential medicines concept and has become known as the seminal guide to managing pharmaceuticals in developing countries. Over the last thirty years, countries have acquired considerable experience in managing pharmaceutical supply. Broad lessons that have emerged from this experience include the following—

- National medicine policy provides a sound foundation for managing pharmaceutical supply.
- Wise medicine selection underlies all other improvements.
- Effective management saves money and improves performance.
- Rational medicine use requires more than medicine information.
- Systematic assessment and monitoring are essential.

Although much has been achieved, challenges remain—

- Achieving financial sustainability through greater efficiency and financing mechanisms that increase availability while ensuring equity (financing options include public financing, health insurance, voluntary and other local financing, and donor financing)
- Improving efficiency in public pharmaceutical supply through strategies that build on public-sector strengths while incorporating greater flexibility and competitiveness
- Changing the behavior of providers, patients, and the public to promote effective, safe, and economical prescribing, dispensing, and patient use of medicines
- Reorienting the role of government to improve the availability, affordability, and rational use of medicines in the private sector, which supplies 60 to 90 percent of the medicines consumed in many developing countries
- Regulating safety, efficacy, and quality through adoption and enforcement of legislation and regulations that ensure that all medicines meet basic quality standards

MDS-3 is organized around the four basic functions of the pharmaceutical supply management framework—

- Selection
- Procurement
- Distribution
- Use

These functions are supported by a core of management support systems—

- Planning and administration
- Organization and management
- Information management
- Human resources management

Effective pharmaceutical management rests on a policy and legal framework that establishes and supports the public commitment to essential medicines supply and is influenced by economic issues (Part I of this manual). Other major sections of the manual are devoted to each of the main functions of the pharmaceutical management framework (Part II) and management support (Part III).

This manual provides concepts and approaches that can produce measurable health improvements through greater access to and more rational use of medicines. Governments, private organizations, donors, and others who use this manual must provide the will and the resources to put these concepts and approaches into action.

1.1 Introduction

Interest in human health and illness is as old as humanity. Scientific study of human anatomy and human diseases can be traced to the Greek physician Hippocrates and earlier. Yet as recently as one hundred years ago, the best that medicine could offer was a handful of demonstrably effective preparations. Penicillin, one of the first antibiotics, and chloroquine, the first modern antimalarial, are about seventy years old. Medicines for common conditions such as diabetes are only fifty years old. Oral contraceptives have been generally available for only forty years.

In industrialized countries, the age of modern pharmaceuticals has eliminated or dramatically reduced mortality from most common infections, allowed families to plan their growth, extended the lives of millions of people suffering from chronic illnesses, and provided relief from pain and suffering for hundreds of millions more people. From the first mass production of penicillin in the 1940s has grown a pharmaceutical industry valued at 600 billion U.S. dollars (USD) annually. The research efforts of that industry continually provide safer, more effective products. The industry's distribution networks ensure ready access to thousands of products for people throughout the industrialized world.

In many other parts of the world, however, people have not fully benefited from these medical advances. In the late 1970s, 60 to 80 percent of people in developing countries were estimated as lacking regular access to even the most essential medicines. By 2003, WHO estimated that less than half the citizens in 32 percent of the world's poorest countries lacked regular access to essential medicines, which improved on 1999 access estimates (WHO 2006c). Lack of access is directly related to income—81 percent of the countries with the lowest access to medicines also had the lowest incomes (WHO 2006c).

The large share of the world's population that does not benefit from simple, safe, effective pharmaceuticals—and the millions of children and adults who die each year from common conditions that can be prevented or treated with modern medicines—signal a fundamental failure of health care systems.

Those who do have access to essential medicines often receive the wrong medicine, the wrong dosage, or a quantity insufficient for their needs. In some countries, many modern medicines are dispensed without prescription by untrained and unlicensed drug sellers. Even when patients and consumers receive the correct medicine, half do not consume it correctly (WHO 2002).

MDS-3 is concerned with practical ways in which government policy makers, essential medicines program managers, NGOs, donors, and others can work to close the huge gap between the need for essential medicines and public access to them—between the vast number of people who could benefit from modern pharmaceuticals and the much smaller number of people who actually do benefit. This manual is also concerned with closing the gap between the availability of medicines and their rational use.

This chapter focuses on the role of medicines in health care and health policy. It describes the essential medicines concept, reviews major lessons in pharmaceutical management since the 1980s, and summarizes major challenges still facing the pharmaceutical sector.

1.2 Why worry about medicines?

To clinicians facing the sick and injured on a daily basis, the importance of medicines is obvious. Nonetheless, summarizing the reasons that ministers of health, directors of health programs, donors, and others involved in the health sector should be concerned with medicines is useful. Accessible health services and qualified staff are necessary components of any health care system, but medicines have special importance for at least five reasons—

- Medicines save lives and improve health.
- Medicines promote trust and participation in health services.
- Medicines are costly.
- Medicines are different from other consumer products.
- Substantive improvements in the supply and use of medicines are possible.

These observations were the primary motivation for preparing this manual. The following chapters focus on the richness and diversity of opportunities for practical, effective improvements in pharmaceutical supply and use.

Medicines save lives and improve health

Most leading causes of discomfort, disability, and premature death can be prevented, treated, or at least alleviated with cost-effective essential medicines. Although the relative frequencies of specific conditions vary among countries, outpatient services throughout the world are presented with a fairly common set of health problems for which essential medicines have an important role: acute infections, skin diseases, gastrointestinal complaints, musculoskeletal conditions, and injuries.

Mortality figures across developing regions (see Table 1-1) reflect a huge burden of illness that can be substantially reduced if carefully selected, low-cost pharmaceuticals are available and appropriately used. Essential medicines significantly affect the common causes of morbidity and mortality, including acute respiratory infections, diarrheal diseases, HIV/AIDS, measles, malaria, maternal

Table 1-1 Mortality from infectious, chronic, and other conditions in WHO member countries worldwide and in select WHO regions, 2004

Conditions	All WHO member countries	Africa	Southeast Asia
Respiratory infections	4,259	1,437	1,416
Diarrheal diseases	2,163	1,005	684
Tuberculosis	1,464	405	519
Malaria	889	806	36
HIV/AIDS	2,040	1,651	206
Other infections and parasites	2,963	982	1,229
Nutritional deficits	487	159	179
Cardiovascular disease	17,073	7,175	3,875
Diabetes mellitus	1,141	172	280
Malignant neoplasms	7,424	480	1,195
Maternal and perinatal conditions	3,707	1,236	1,367

Source: WHO 2008a.

and perinatal mortality, tuberculosis, and cardiovascular and other chronic diseases (see Box 1-1).

Not only are essential medicines effective against common health problems, they are also cost-effective. Undeniably, long-term health gains can be made by investing in prevention through health education and other programs to improve nutrition, sanitation, water supply, housing, environment, and personal health habits. At the same time, essential medicines provide a direct, low-cost response for many diseases.

Medicines promote trust and participation in health services

The credibility of health workers depends on their ability to save a dying village elder with a course of penicillin, to restore life to a limp child with oral rehydration, or to relieve an irritating skin infection with a simple ointment. In addition to the direct effect on health, the availability of essential medicines attracts patients, who can then also receive preventive and public health messages. The provision of essential medicines is one element of primary health care that families everywhere take an interest in and that brings them to health facilities.

Over the years, household and patient surveys around the world have found that pharmaceutical availability is a major determinant of where patients go for health care and how satisfied they are with that care. Availability of medicines and supplies also affects the productivity of health staff. When pharmaceutical supplies fail to arrive, patient volume drops, and health workers are left idle. Irregular pharmaceutical supply can be a greater constraint on program effectiveness than inadequate numbers or inadequate training of health workers.

Medicines are costly

Although medicines are cost-effective, they can be quite costly for an individual, a household, a government health system, or a country.

At the individual and household levels, medicines represent the major out-of-pocket health expenditure; 60 to 90 percent of household health spending may go toward medicines (WHO 2000). In northern India, at least 57 percent of a family's average out-of-pocket cost of a newborn's illness was for medicines (Srivastava et al. 2009). The trend of private spending by households as the principal source of worldwide pharmaceutical spending increased during the 1990s (WHO 2004c). In addition to those direct costs, income is lost when family members are sick, and this loss reinforces the poverty-illness cycle. Women are especially vulnerable because they are usually the main family caregivers.

For ministries of health in most developing countries, expenditures on medicines are second only to those made on staff salaries and benefits, which can cost up to half of total health expenditures (WHO 2006d). Payment of personnel costs is largely unavoidable as long as staff are employed. Medicine expenditures, therefore, represent the largest expenditure over which ministries have year-to-year discretionary control. This fact makes medicine expenditures both extremely important and extremely vulnerable—particularly to fluctuations in the availability of public funding as well as to various political and economic pressures, such as rampant inflation and currency fluctuations.

At the national level, pharmaceuticals represent 10 to 20 percent of health expenditures for leading industrialized countries. But for most developing countries, they may

Box 1-1
Impact of essential medicines on common causes of morbidity and mortality

HIV/AIDS still kills about 2 million people per year, even though global initiatives to combat the epidemic have increased dramatically. The widespread treatment of HIV/AIDS with antiretrovirals (ARVs) in resource-limited settings is relatively new, and prices for treatment have dropped dramatically in recent years making it available to far more people. Even with the increase in ARV treatment, however, medicines to treat opportunistic infections are still an important aspect of treating patients with HIV/AIDS.

Respiratory infections, which accounted for more than 4.25 million deaths in 2004, are usually cured readily with inexpensive oral antibiotics. About 20 percent of all deaths in children under five years of age are caused by acute lower respiratory infections (pneumonia, bronchiolitis, and bronchitis); 90 percent of these deaths are caused by pneumonia.

Diarrheal diseases, a top cause of childhood mortality, can be prevented through improved water and sanitation. Diarrhea can be treated in the home with simple oral rehydration solution and selective use of antimicrobial medicines. Recent case management advances such as reformulated oral rehydration solution and zinc supplementation have helped significantly decrease mortality caused by diarrhea.

Measles, another leading cause of childhood mortality, is preventable through immunization. But when immunization is missed, much of the resulting mortality can still be eliminated through the treatment of respiratory, diarrheal, and other potentially fatal complications.

Malaria threatens almost half the world's population and is responsible for nearly 1 million deaths each year; over 80 percent of fatal cases are in African children under four years of age. Early diagnosis and treatment with effective medicines can cure infections and save lives.

Maternal and perinatal mortality can be reduced through prenatal care and nonmedicine interventions such as high-risk case management. Postpartum hemorrhage can be avoided with the use of oxytocic drugs, and maternal anemia, a major contributing factor to maternal and perinatal morbidity and mortality, can be reduced with preventive doses of iron folate preparations. In addition, spacing the birth of children through family planning (using largely oral, injectable, and implanted contraceptives) improves both maternal and neonatal outcomes.

Tuberculosis (TB), once on the decline, is now a leading cause of death worldwide from an infectious disease. Although drug resistance is growing and second-line TB drugs are costly, short-course chemotherapy is curative, and the investment is highly cost-effective. Other strategies to bring TB under control include testing for TB drug resistance and treating TB/HIV co-infection.

Cardiovascular and other chronic diseases are rapidly increasing in developing countries as socioeconomic development, immunization, and other improvements increase life expectancy. In some countries, such as Russia, life expectancy has declined because of cardiovascular disease. Health services are facing a growing demand for essential medicines to treat hypertension, ischemic heart disease, diabetes, and other chronic diseases.

Sources: Jamison et al. 2006; WHO 2008b.

---

represent 20 to 40 percent of total public and private health expenditures (WHO 2006b).

In absolute figures, the sums that countries spend on pharmaceuticals vary tremendously. In 2000, the world's population in low-income countries spent an average of USD 4.4 per capita per year, whereas the population in high-income countries spent an average of USD 396 per capita (WHO 2004c). For example, Afghanistan spent USD 9 on pharmaceuticals, Cambodia spent USD 11, and Haiti spent USD 3; for industrialized countries in the same year, the figure ranged from USD 272 in Norway and USD 253 in the United Kingdom to USD 382 in Switzerland and USD 528 in Japan (WHO 2004c) (Table 1-2). In general,

medicine expenditures increase with gross national product (GNP).

Medicines are different from other consumer products

Because pharmaceuticals are produced by a competitive industry that responds primarily to economic demand, one might expect their production and sale could be left almost wholly to the play of market forces (see Chapter 10). In that case, politicians and lawmakers would have only the same sorts of concerns that apply to other forms of trade—prevention of fraud, protection of trademarks, and so forth.

Table 1-2   Per capita pharmaceutical and health expenditures in selected developing countries, 1990 and 2000

| | Per capita expenditures (USD) | | | |
| | 1990 | | 2000 | |
Country	Medicines	Health	Medicines	Health
Bangladesh	2	6	5	14
Brazil	16	146	61	265
Chile	30	100	46	328
China	7	11	20	45
Costa Rica	37	132	42	280
Ghana	10	15	4	11
India	3	21	3	23
Indonesia	5	12	5	20
Kenya	4	16	7	30
Mexico	28	89	8	327
Morocco	17	26	20	54
Mozambique	2	5	2	12
Pakistan	7	12	5	18
Philippines	11	16	15	34
Turkey	21	76	58	150

Sources: Ballance, Pogány, and Forstner 1992; Murray and López 1994; WHO 2004c.

But medicines are different and require special attention, because—

- The consumer (patient or parent) often does not choose the medicine—it is prescribed by a clinician or recommended by pharmacy staff.
- Even when the consumer chooses the medicine, he or she is not trained to judge its appropriateness, safety, quality, or value for money.
- Neither the average medical practitioner nor the average pharmacist is equipped to independently assess the quality, safety, or efficacy of each new medicine.
- Fear of illness can lead patients to demand costly medicines from health workers, or to buy such medicines for themselves, when cheaper medicines—or no medicines—would achieve the same result.
- The consumer often cannot judge the likely consequences of not obtaining a needed medicine. This problem is most troublesome when the decision maker is a parent and the patient is a child.

These knowledge gaps, anxieties, and uncertainties associated with both acute and chronic illnesses create special concerns about the supply and use of medicines.

The issues that make medicines different from other consumer products also help make the pharmaceutical sector a likely target for mismanagement, bribery, and fraud. Contributing factors to this vulnerability to corrup-

tion include knowledge gaps and information imbalances between manufacturers, regulators, health care providers, and consumers; a lack of legislation or regulation or enforcement mechanisms; and the high value and volume of medicines in the marketplace (see Cohen 2006 and WHO 2009).

Substantive improvements are possible

In most health systems, the potential for improving the supply process is tremendous, reflecting in part the magnitude of current inefficiencies and waste.

Figure 1-1 shows a hypothetical program in which an annual expenditure of USD 1 million on pharmaceutical supply results in only USD 300,000 worth of therapeutic benefit to the patient. Lack of careful selection, incorrect quantification, high prices, poor quality, theft, improper storage, expiration of medicines, irrational prescribing, corruption, and incorrect medicine use by patients cause losses totaling 70 percent of the original expenditure.

However, much can be accomplished with substantial effort, a moderate amount of know-how, and relatively little additional funding. Some pharmaceutical management improvements require an initial investment in systems development, training, physical infrastructure, and other development initiatives, but the potential cost reductions and therapeutic improvements are dramatic. Even small improvements, when made in a number of related areas of

Figure 1-1   Waste in pharmaceutical management and potential for improvement

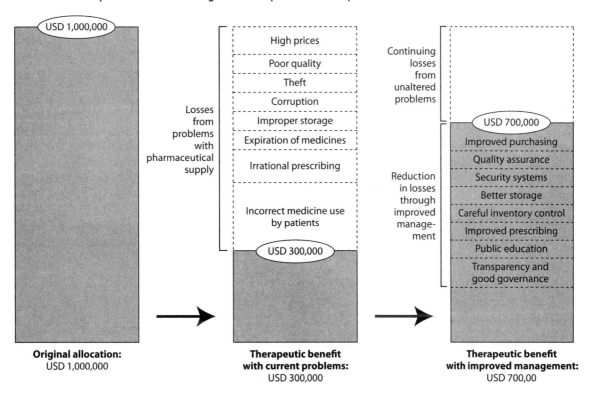

pharmaceutical management, can yield substantial overall savings.

1.3   Public health objectives and the essential medicines concept

Public health programs are concerned with using available resources to achieve maximum health improvements for the population. The perspective is not that of the individual patient, who may well benefit from a costly medicine, but of the entire community or population, which will benefit most if safe, effective medicines are accessible to all who need them.

Within a decade after the first modern pharmaceuticals became available, efforts began to ensure their widespread availability. From the mid-1950s to the mid-1970s, basic medicine management concepts began to evolve in countries as diverse as Cuba, Norway, Papua New Guinea, Peru, and Sri Lanka. In 1975, WHO defined *essential medicines* as "indispensable and necessary for the health needs of the population. They should be available at all times, in the proper dosage forms, to all segments of society." In 1978, the International Conference on Primary Health Care at Alma-Ata, Kazakhstan, recognized essential medicines as one of the eight elements of primary health care. (See Chapter 2 for additional historical background.)

The first WHO Model List of Essential Drugs, containing about 200 products and a description of the essential medicines concept, was published in 1977. Since 1977, the WHO model list has been revised every two to three years, and as of 2007, at least 156 countries had adopted essential medicines lists (WHO 2007a).

Consistent with a public health perspective, the essential medicines concept embraces the following guiding principles—

- The vast majority of health problems for most members of the population can be treated with a small, carefully selected number of medicines.
- In practice, most doctors and other health professionals routinely use a small fraction of medicines produced. Training and clinical experience should focus on the proper use of these few medicines.
- Procurement, distribution, and other supply activities can be carried out most economically and most efficiently for a limited list of pharmaceutical products.
- Patients can be better informed about the effective use of medicines when the number of medicines they are confronted with is limited.

Implementation of these principles occurs through the adoption of national medicine policies and through practical pharmaceutical management initiatives. The major goals of such initiatives are outlined in Box 1-2.

1.4 A paradigm for defining and improving access to medicines

Access to health care, including essential medicines, is a fundamental human right. Realization of this right may involve various combinations of public and private financing and service provision. The public health challenge is to work with the private sector and NGOs to achieve universal access to essential medicines and rational use of medicines. This work involves building mutual understanding, constructive partnerships, and the right incentives.

Access to health care can be defined as a construct that encompasses distinct dimensions, which are distinguished by sets of specific relationships (CPM 2003) (Figure 1-2). Four dimensions of access have particular relevance to essential medicines, vaccines, and other health commodities—

- *Availability,* defined by the relationship between the type and quantity of product or service needed, and the type and quantity of product or service provided
- *Affordability,* defined by the relationship between prices of the products or services and the user's ability to pay for them
- *Accessibility,* defined by the relationship between the location of the product or service and the location of the eventual user of the product or service
- *Acceptability* (or satisfaction), defined by the relationship between the user's attitudes and expectations about the products and services and the actual characteristics of products and services

In addition, a cross-cutting characteristic of access is—

- *Quality of products and services,* an essential component of access cutting across all the dimensions, but which specifically applies to products in terms of their safety, efficacy, and cost-effectiveness

Indicators for measuring these dimensions of access are described in Chapter 36.

The pharmaceutical management framework (Figure 1-3) provides the underpinning for improving access to medicines as described in the paradigm above. Pharmaceutical management involves four basic functions: selection, procurement, distribution, and use. Selection involves reviewing the prevalent health problems, identifying treatments of choice, choosing individual medicines and dosage forms, and deciding which medicines will be available at each level of a health care system. Procurement includes quantifying medicine requirements, selecting procurement methods, managing tenders, establishing contract terms, assuring pharmaceutical quality, and ensuring adherence to contract terms. Distribution encompasses clearing customs, stock control, stores management, and delivery to drug depots and health facilities. Use comprises diagnosing, prescribing, dispensing, and proper consumption by the patient.

In the pharmaceutical management framework (Figure 1-3), each major function builds on the previous function and leads logically to the next. Selection should be based on actual experience with health needs and medicine use, procurement requirements follow from selection decisions, and so forth. A breakdown in one part of the framework leads to

---

Box 1-2
Goals for national medicine policies and pharmaceutical management initiatives

Health-related goals

- Make essential medicines physically available and geographically accessible to the entire population.
- Ensure the safety, efficacy, and quality of medicines manufactured and distributed in the country.
- Increase attendance at health facilities by increasing the credibility and acceptance of the health system.
- Promote rational prescription, dispensing, and patient use of medicines.

Economic goals

- Lower the cost of medicines to the government, other health care providers, and the public.

- Reduce foreign exchange expenditures for pharmaceuticals without reducing the supply.
- Attain sustainable financing through equitable funding mechanisms such as government revenues or social health insurance.
- Provide jobs in pharmaceutical supply and possibly production.

National development goals

- Increase skills of personnel in management, pharmacy, and medicine.
- Improve internal communication systems.
- Create reliable supply systems that incorporate a mix of public and private supply services.

Figure 1-2   Increasing access framework

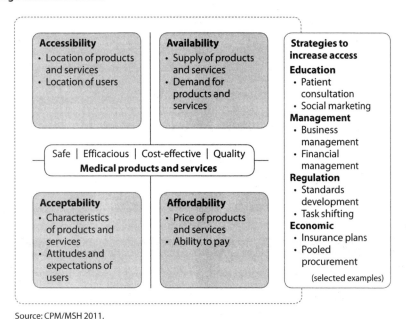

Source: CPM/MSH 2011.

failure of the whole pharmaceutical management process. Costs rise, shortages become common, and patients suffer when the separate tasks are performed not as part of a system but independently and disjointedly.

At the center of the pharmaceutical management framework is a core of management support systems: organization, financing and sustainability, information management, and human resources management. These management support systems hold the pharmaceutical management framework together. Although individual parts of the framework may function independently for a short time, the framework as a whole will soon cease to operate, and patient care will suffer without a functional organizational structure, adequate financing, reliable information management, and motivated staff.

Finally, the entire framework relies on policies, laws, and regulations, which when supported by good governance, establish and support the public commitment to essential medicine supply.

1.5   Lessons learned in pharmaceutical management

Since the 1980s, countries have acquired considerable experience in managing pharmaceutical supply. Although many important lessons have emerged from this experience, five broad themes capture the most important insights—

- National medicine policy (NMP) provides a sound foundation for managing pharmaceutical supply.

- Wise medicine selection underlies all other improvements.
- Effective management and good governance save money and improve performance.
- Rational medicine use requires more than just the dissemination of medicine information.
- Systematic assessment and monitoring are essential.

These five broad areas contain many specific lessons, some of which follow and most of which are covered in detail in the rest of the manual.

National medicine policy provides a sound foundation for managing pharmaceutical supply

A national medicine policy is a guide for action; it is generally a document containing the goals set by the government for the pharmaceutical sector and the main strategies for reaching those goals. It provides a framework to coordinate activities by the various actors in the pharmaceutical sector: the public sector, NGOs, the private sector, donors, and other interested parties (see Chapter 4).

The NMP concept began receiving support during the 1980s, when piecemeal approaches to policy were leaving important problems unsolved. A focused NMP, suited to the needs of the particular country and with clear priorities, was found to significantly affect the availability and use of pharmaceuticals in such countries as Australia, Bangladesh, Colombia, and the Philippines.

Comprehensive, officially adopted policies can focus efforts to improve access to medicines, medicine use, and

Figure 1-3   Pharmaceutical management framework

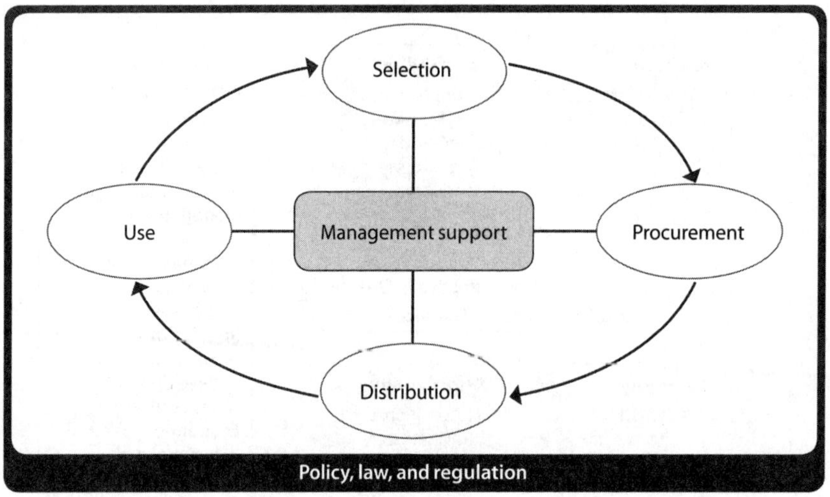

Source: CPM/MSH 2011.

medicine quality. Sometimes, however, the policy formulation process engenders such strong opposition that all energy becomes focused on the policy, effectively stalling other useful but less controversial efforts to improve the availability and use of medicines.

Formal NMPs provide a sound foundation for managing essential medicines programs. Of equal or greater importance, however, is the underlying strategic planning process: What are the long-term goals for the pharmaceutical sector? What strategies should be involved? How can key stakeholders be engaged in the process? The experiences of the last three decades suggest that governments and programs with clear objectives and strategies can make progress in the pharmaceutical sector.

Wise medicine selection underlies all other improvements

Establishing and using a limited list of carefully selected essential medicines is perhaps the single most cost-effective action that any health care system or health care provider can take to promote regular supply and rational use of medicines (Chapter 16).

As mentioned, more than 150 countries reported having adopted national essential medicines lists (WHO 2007a). In contrast, in the mid-1970s, few countries had selective medicine lists organized by generic name. Many of the national formularies that did exist were unselective and often contained more than one thousand products. Ministry of health procurement lists were commonly dominated by brand-name medicines.

Studies of the economic effect of essential medicines lists and formulary lists demonstrate that considerable savings can be achieved, primarily through careful choices for those few high-unit-cost and high-volume items that consume

the major share of the pharmaceutical budget. Chapter 40 describes how to analyze medicine expenditures.

An essential medicines list or formulary list that identifies medicines by level of care becomes the basis for training in therapeutics; for estimating pharmaceutical requirements; for competitive procurement by generic name; for planning distribution to health facilities; and for efforts to promote rational, cost-effective medicine use. The national essential medicines list or formulary list can also guide public education efforts, local production, and private-sector medicine management. The list, based on WHO criteria, should be updated regularly (usually every two to three years), divided by level of care, and accompanied by a clear policy on its application for procurement, distribution, and use of medicines (see Chapter 17).

Changing national policies to add or substitute a new treatment or diagnostic tool is a complex decision for a country's ministry of health. Major policy changes, such as switching to artemisinin-based combination therapy (ACT) for malaria, require intensive preparation and planning that involve multiple national and international stakeholders. For example, fluctuations in the demand for ACTs as countries changed their first-line treatment policies, then a delay in implementation, resulted in a global shortage of medicine that could have been allayed with better planning and communication.

Effective management and good governance save money and improve performance

Effective management and good governance make a vital difference in all aspects of pharmaceutical supply, especially with respect to the procurement and distribution of essential medicines. The basic principles of efficient procurement and distribution have been known for several decades, but the view of the public sector as the lead player in a country's pharmaceutical supply has evolved. Countries are increasingly adopting the concept of multisector collaboration among public, NGO, and private entities to improve efficiencies in supplying pharmaceuticals.

Examples of the positive consequences of good management at the national level include savings in pharmaceutical costs through competitive procurement in El Salvador, Ghana, and the eastern Caribbean; improved medicine availability as a result of better quantification in Namibia and Kenya; and more reliable delivery as a result of redesigned distribution systems in South Africa.

Good pharmaceutical procurement practices include restriction of purchases to the essential medicines list (national formulary list), determination of order quantities based on reliable needs estimation, competitive tendering from qualified suppliers, separation of key functions, prompt payment, regular audits, and a formal system of supplier qualification and monitoring (Chapter 18). WHO has developed an assessment to measure transparency and governance in a country's pharmaceutical sector, including procurement procedures; for example, an assessment showed that four Southeast Asian countries all used an objective quantification method and that the post-tender system to monitor and report suppliers' performance was effective. However, WHO recommended that the appeals process for rejected tender applicants be instigated or strengthened, and noted that the procurement auditing process was weak (WHO 2006a).

Effective distribution management comes from—

- Defining appropriate roles in the distribution system for the public and private sectors
- Designing an efficient network of storage facilities with the fewest number of levels appropriate to the country's geography
- Selecting the appropriate strategy for delivery
- Keeping reliable records of medicine stocks and consumption
- Allocating supplies based on actual workload and treatment needs
- Maintaining accountability procedures and secure storage at each level of the system
- Constructing or renovating facilities appropriate for storing medicines
- Managing storage facilities to maintain pharmaceutical quality and efficiently serve health units
- Making reliable transport arrangements
- Reinforcing reporting and supervision arrangements

As mentioned, the most efficient system may result from collaboration among the public, private, and NGO sectors. Kit system distribution has both benefits and costs; it should be used only when necessary to ensure that supplies reach lower levels of the system. Chapter 26 describes how kit systems are used to distribute pharmaceuticals.

Rational medicine use requires more than medicine information

Although 50 percent or more of pharmaceutical expenditures may be wasted through irrational prescribing, dispensing, and patient use of medicines, many methods for promoting rational medicine use have never been scientifically evaluated (Le Grand, Hogerzeil, and Haaijer-Ruskamp 1999). Among those methods that have been properly studied, not many have had much measurable effect on medicine use when implemented individually (Arnold and Straus 2005).

The actual use of pharmaceuticals is influenced by a wide range of factors, including pharmaceutical availability, provider experience, economic influences, cultural factors, community belief systems and patient attitudes, and the complex interactions among these factors. Medicine use patterns reflect human behavior and must be viewed from a social-science perspective rather than a biomedical perspective.

Pharmaceutical companies succeed in changing the habits of doctors and patients because they understand what influences these habits. Interventions to promote rational medicine use often fail because they are based on the notion that simply improving knowledge will improve medicine use. Examples of interventions that are likely to fail include dull medicine bulletins that drily present "the facts," standard treatment manuals distributed to health staff without an active orientation, withdrawal of dangerous or ineffective products with no advice for prescribers on substitutions, and campaigns to discourage injection use that do not address the reasons why many patients prefer injections.

Fortunately, we have learned much in recent years about principles for promoting rational medicine use. These principles involve informed, focused, active, and engaging approaches for changing medicine-use practices by prescribers, dispensers, and patients (Laing, Hogerzeil, and Ross-Degnan 2001). Box 1-3 lists WHO's recommended interventions to promote the rational use of medicines.

Systematic assessment and monitoring are essential

One of the most basic, yet most significant, advances in pharmaceutical management has been the introduction of objective standard indicators for assessing, comparing, and monitoring medicine policies and management effectiveness. Since their introduction in the early 1990s, medicine-use indicators have been developed to assess virtually all key aspects of pharmaceutical management and NMPs. Examples of standard indicators include the percentage of government pharmaceutical purchases conforming to the national essential medicines list, the ratio of local

---

Box 1-3
Recommended interventions to promote the rational use of medicines

- Establishing a mandated multidisciplinary national body to coordinate policies on medicine use and monitor their impact
- Formulating and using evidence-based clinical guidelines for training, supervision, and supporting critical decision making about medicines
- Selecting on the basis of "treatments of choice" lists of essential medicines that are used in drug procurement and insurance reimbursement
- Setting up drug and therapeutics committees in districts and hospitals and giving them the authority to improve the use of medicines
- Promoting problem-based training in pharmacotherapy in undergraduate curricula
- Making continuing in-service medical education a requirement of licensure

- Promoting systems of supervision, audit, and feedback in institutional settings
- Providing independent information (including comparative data) about medicines
- Promoting public education about medicines
- Eliminating perverse financial incentives that lead to irrational prescribing
- Drawing up and enforcing appropriate regulation, including that of promotional activities for medicines
- Reserving sufficient governmental expenditure to ensure equitable availability of medicines and health personnel

Source: WHO 2006c.

---

pharmaceutical prices to world market prices, the number of medicines per patient prescription, and the percentage of key medicines available at health facilities (see, for example, MSH/RPM 1995; CPM 2003; WHO 2007b).

Measured at one point in time, such indicators allow a program to compare itself to a target level of performance, to identify areas of relative strength and weakness, and to make comparisons with other programs for which data are available. Measured over time, such indicators can be used to set and monitor performance targets for pharmaceutical sector improvements.

Systematic assessment and monitoring based on standard indicators are a routine part of planning, program management, and donor evaluation in the field of essential medicines and pharmaceutical management. For example, the Global Fund to Fight AIDS, Tuberculosis and Malaria requires that grantees meet targets on certain indicators to receive additional funds. Each country and program needs to select, develop, and adapt indicators to suit local circumstances and needs, but the basic concept of objective indicators should be incorporated into any essential medicines program (see Chapter 48).

1.6 Challenges for pharmaceutical management

Major challenges for policy makers and managers include achieving financial sustainability; improving efficiency in public pharmaceutical supply; changing the perceptions and behaviors of providers, patients, and the public; reorienting the role of government and the private sector to improve access to medicines; and regulating safety, efficacy, and quality, which may be the biggest challenge of all.

Achieving financial sustainability

Financial sustainability is achieved only when expenditures and financial resources balance and are sufficient to support a given level of demand. If demand for medicines exceeds the available resources, the health system is left with only four options: improve efficiency, increase financial resources, reduce demand, or accept a decline in quality of care. When the components of financial sustainability are not in balance, it simply defies economic reality to promise constant availability of high-quality essential medicines without improving efficiency, increasing financing, or limiting demand.

Efficiency means getting the most benefit from available resources. Much of this manual is devoted to improving therapeutic efficiency through better selection and use of medicines and improving operational efficiency through better organization, procurement, and distribution of medicines.

To achieve financial sustainability, policy makers and managers of essential medicines programs must become familiar with economic concepts and methods related to cost containment, efficiency, cost-effectiveness analysis, public expenditure decisions, the roles of the public and private sectors, and the economics of regulation. High-income countries increasingly rely on economic methods and perspectives. Countries with more limited resources must also make maximum use of the insights offered by the field of pharmaco-economics.

Health-sector reform is concerned with improving efficiency through changes in the organization and allocation of health care resources. It is also concerned with health care financing.

People pay for health care in different ways: collectively, through national health insurance or through the taxes they pay on goods, services, or income; in groups, through premiums paid for voluntary health insurance; or individually, through user fees at government facilities or private out-of-pocket health expenditures. In most countries, the primary burden for health financing falls directly or indirectly on the people of the country; the proportion of health care that is paid out of pocket actually increases in many low-income countries, where more than 60 percent of the total health spending comes from out of pocket (Gottret and Schieber 2006).

Local funding for recurrent health expenditures is often supplemented by external development assistance. In fact, the poorest countries may find it impossible to provide certain basic health services, including essential medicines, without some external assistance. External funding is a growing source of financing in low-income countries, especially in sub-Saharan Africa and South Asia. Although health aid increased from USD 2.6 billion in 1990 to USD 10 billion in 2003, experts are calling for increases in external assistance ranging from USD 25 billion to 70 billion a year to reach the UN Millennium Development Goals and other, disease-specific treatment goals (Gottret and Schieber 2006). For example, the U.S. Institute of Medicine estimated that instituting ACT for malaria worldwide would require USD 300 million to 500 million each year (Committee on the Economics of Antimalarial Drugs 2004), which would clearly be impossible for developing countries to cover with local funds.

Public financing provides an essential foundation for a country's health system and, in particular, for health promotion and preventive services. But providing free medicines through public resources has proved unsustainable in many developing as well as developed countries. Government budgets are squeezed, and donor funds are directed to a variety of other worthy causes. The policy of free medicines is often, in practice, a policy of shortages. Although global initiatives to provide ARVs to people in developing countries have brought free HIV/AIDS treatment to many, the sustainability of this arrangement is unknown. Most agree that, even with the introduction of lower-priced ARVs, HIV/AIDS treatment in developing countries will continue only as long as external funding continues.

Full or partial cost recovery through user fees is one way to supplement public financing. Revolving pharmaceutical funds and community medicine schemes linked to strengthening primary health care have been tried in countries in Africa, Asia, and Latin America. Some programs have led to a serious decline in utilization, with no visible improvement in pharmaceutical availability. Yet some user-fee programs increased both equity of access and quality. Some global development organizations have called for the abolition of user fees as a barrier to access to poor people (UNMP 2005), but others point out that if the removal of user fees is not compensated for by other funding, patients may be forced to spend more on medicines or health care services in the private sector (Gottret and Schieber 2006).

Social health insurance (compulsory health insurance or social security), private health insurance, and community health insurance schemes finance pharmaceutical supply for a small but growing portion of the population in developing countries. People in most high-income countries are already covered by some form of public or private health insurance; however, the median coverage is only 35 percent in Latin America, 10 percent in Asia, and 8 percent in Africa (WHO 2004a). Health insurance coverage that includes pharmaceuticals has expanded access to medicines in many countries, including Argentina, China, Egypt, South Africa, and Vietnam (WHO 2004b). WHO has committed to promoting the provision of medicines benefits through social health insurance and prepayment schemes (WHO 2004b). Chapter 12 discusses health financing through insurance in detail.

In the face of changing epidemiologic patterns, increasing demand for modern health care, and growing populations, the challenge for countries is to implement those pharmaceutical financing strategies that best ensure equity of access and a continuous supply of medicines. For many countries, reaching this goal means taking a pluralistic approach—one that uses different ways to serve different needs and different groups and that combines the benefits of public financing, health insurance, voluntary financing mechanisms, and donor support.

Improving governance and efficiency in public pharmaceutical supply

Aside from the problem of financing, public-sector pharmaceutical supply in many countries continues to be plagued by ineffective management systems. They often lack sufficient qualified human resources and are characterized by systems that are not transparent and do not promote accountability. As such, they become susceptible to political pressures, fraud, and abuse.

In fact, corruption is increasingly recognized as a barrier to social and economic development, and many governments and international development organizations are placing the issue high on development and health agendas. For example, in 2004, WHO launched its program on good governance in pharmaceutical systems (see Box 1-4); the United Nations Convention Against Corruption became effective in 2005; Transparency International's Global Corruption Report for 2006 focused on health systems; and the Medicines Transparency Alliance came together in

2007. Figure 1-4 shows a framework for improving governance and accountability.

The international donor community has recognized and is addressing the need to increase access to lifesaving medicines: new funding sources, such as the U.S. President's Emergency Plan for AIDS Relief, the President's Malaria Initiative, UNITAID, and the Global Fund to Fight AIDS, Tuberculosis and Malaria, are making unprecedented sums of money available to procure medicines for deadly diseases. However, the two greatest threats to successfully increasing access to medicines are weak and vulnerable pharmaceutical supply systems and the worsening human resources crisis. The scope of the challenge to countries in terms of the drastic effect the new funding is having on pharmaceutical systems is unparalleled.

Sustainability is the extent to which a program will continue to achieve its policy and pharmaceutical supply objectives without additional outside financial or technical support. Key factors for program sustainability, in addition to financing, are motivated, capable staff; effective management systems; and political support. Low pay, inadequate training, lack of incentives, inappropriate recruitment, and ineffective disciplinary measures undermine staff performance, which is already decimated in many countries by the loss of trained human resources from "brain drain" and HIV/AIDS.

Box 1-4
WHO's Good Governance for Medicines program

The pharmaceutical sector is highly vulnerable to corruption and unethical practices, in part because pharmaceuticals have a high market value; regulating and procuring pharmaceuticals is complex; and the sector involves many international, national, and local entities.

Poor governance in the pharmaceutical system can lead to severe health and economic consequences. For example, corruption in the regulatory system can result in approval of medicines that are inappropriate because of safety, efficacy, quality, or price. Similarly, if inspection, postmarketing surveillance, or quality-control systems are corrupt, counterfeit and substandard medicines can easily enter the marketplace, causing harm or even death. Waste associated with corruption can also be a major drain on the public budget and decrease the resources available not only to buy medicines but also to pay health care workers. Corruption affects the public's trust in the government as well as in the whole health profession.

Recognizing how these problems affect the health sector negatively, WHO initiated the Good Governance for Medicines program in late 2004. The program offers a technical-support package for governments to tackle unethical practices in the public pharmaceutical sector. The goal of the program is to curb corruption in pharmaceutical systems by applying transparent and accountable administrative procedures and promoting ethical practices among health professionals.

Tackling corruption in the pharmaceutical sector requires a long-term strategy. WHO has identified a three-step approach—

1. Assess the level of transparency and vulnerability to corruption of key functions in national pharmaceutical regulation and management systems.

2. Use a national consultation process to develop a national program on good governance for medicines that increases transparency and accountability in the pharmaceutical sector and promotes ethical practices.

3. Implement and promote the national good governance for medicines program.

From 2004 to 2007, WHO gradually introduced the project in ten countries: Bolivia, Cambodia, Indonesia, the Lao People's Democratic Republic, Malawi, Malaysia, Mongolia, Papua New Guinea, the Philippines, and Thailand. National assessors used the WHO transparency assessment tool to measure the level of transparency in national medicines regulation and public-sector pharmaceutical procurement systems.

Information collected from the first four countries where the program was introduced—the Lao People's Democratic Republic, Malaysia, the Philippines, and Thailand—revealed that although they have different public-sector procurement and medicines regulation profiles, they have some common strengths and weaknesses. For example, all have publicly available standard operating procedures for procurement, but none requires members of the registration or selection committees to fill out a conflict-of-interest form.

WHO will continue to work with governments and WHO regional offices to select new countries and activities related to the Good Governance initiative.

For additional information, access WHO's Good Governance website at http://www.who.int/medicines/ggm/en/index.html.

Figure 1-4   Governance framework

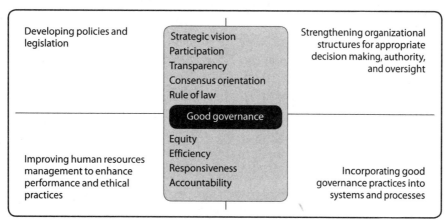

Source: Adapted from United Nations Development Programme (UNDP), *Governance for Sustainable Human Development,* http://mirror.undp.org/magnet/policy/ (Geneva, 1997).

Growing pressure to scale up access to medicines, combined with the influx of funds mentioned above, is exposing weaknesses in how developing countries procure and distribute pharmaceuticals to their citizens. Examples abound in which the conventional central medical stores (CMS) approach to pharmaceutical procurement and distribution continues to result in chronic medicine shortages—even after considerable investment has been made in training, management systems, and physical infrastructure. Public-sector supply systems in affected countries—primarily in Africa—have to adapt existing systems to manage hugely increased volumes of medicines and commodities. Alternative strategies for public pharmaceutical supply are attracting interest. They include formation of an autonomous supply agency, direct delivery, the primary distributor system, various privatized models, and mixed systems. Successful scaling up will require a dramatic transformation of the systems traditionally used for procurement and supply of medicines. Alternative strategies for public pharmaceutical supply have been implemented with varying degrees of success in countries such as Benin, Botswana, Colombia, Guatemala, South Africa, Tanzania, and Zambia.

With an autonomous supply system, an autonomous or semi-autonomous agency manages bulk procurement, storage, and distribution. With the direct delivery (non-CMS) system, the government tenders to establish prices and suppliers for essential medicines, which are then delivered directly by suppliers to districts and major health facilities. With the primary distributor system (another non-CMS system), the government pharmaceutical procurement office establishes a contract with a single primary distributor as well as separate procurement contracts with pharmaceutical suppliers. The primary distributor is contracted to manage pharmaceutical distribution by receiving medicines from the suppliers and then storing and distributing them to districts and major facilities. In fully privatized models, public administration of pharmaceutical supply is minimized, with independent pharmacies or other mechanisms providing medicines within or outside government facilities; various financing and reimbursement arrangements can be used. Chapter 8 covers supply strategies in detail.

Selection, procurement, and distribution can each be carried out in centralized, partially decentralized, or fully decentralized systems. Decentralization aims to improve the responsiveness, quality, and efficiency of health services. Improvements are far from certain, however. Problems with attempts to decentralize pharmaceutical management functions have included lack of local management and supervisory capacity, increased costs (caused by loss of savings from bulk purchasing), lack of local staff trained in pharmaceutical management, inadequate financial resources, self-interested interference by local officials, and poor pharmaceutical quality (caused by difficulty in selecting and monitoring suppliers).

For managing pharmaceutical supply, a task-specific approach to decentralization may be useful. Examples of tasks that may be better performed centrally include development of essential medicines lists, preparation of standard treatment guidelines, management of competitive tenders, selection and monitoring of suppliers, quality assurance, and development of training programs in rational medicine use. Tasks that can be decentralized include those that do not require uncommon technical skills. Decentralization is advisable when local information is required, local circumstances are important and variable throughout the country, and local interests favor improved performance. Examples of such tasks include adapting medicine lists or standard treatments to local needs, quantifying medicine requirements, coordinating local distribution, conducting training

Country Study 1-1
Working with the private sector to improve malaria outcomes in Tanzania, Ghana, and Nigeria

In many African countries, informal medicine sellers are the first point of contact for caregivers seeking treatment for childhood illnesses. These individuals typically have little or no health training and frequently misdiagnose malaria, provide inappropriate treatment, give an incorrect dose, and/or give inaccurate advice. Several programs designed to improve practices among this group for treating childhood illnesses have shown promising results.

Tanzania

Management Sciences for Health's Strategies for Enhancing Access to Medicines (SEAM) Program, in collaboration with the Tanzanian government, created a new category of accredited drug dispensing outlet (ADDO) to improve access to affordable, quality medicines and pharmaceutical services in retail drug outlets in rural or peri-urban areas where there are few or no registered pharmacies. To achieve this goal, the SEAM Program took a holistic approach that combined changing the behavior and expectations of individuals and groups who use, own, regulate, or work in retail drug shops as well as that of community members. Major program activities included changing behavior of dispensing staff through training, education, and supervision; improving awareness of community members regarding quality and the importance of treatment adherence through marketing and public education; and focusing on regulation and inspection and improving local regulatory capacity.

Postintervention assessment results showed that—

- Thirty-two percent of malaria treatment encounters at ADDOs included the sale of an appropriate first-line antimalarial, compared with only 16 percent at baseline. Twenty-four percent of encounters were dispensed exactly according to standard treatment guidelines, compared with 6 percent at baseline.

- The average availability of antimalarials increased from 74 to 90 percent in the ADDO region compared with 71 percent availability in the control region.

After the SEAM Program ended, the government of Tanzania adopted the ADDO program and announced the program's nationwide rollout.

Ghana

The strategy in Ghana involved implementing a franchise system called CAREshops among participating chemical sellers' shops to establish uniform standards, train personnel, monitor adherence to franchise standards, and create business incentives for adherence to those standards. The goal of this initiative was to improve access to reasonably priced, quality-assured essential medicines and health supplies and high-quality dispensing services in underserved rural areas. Other key elements of the franchising program include a ten-week, five-module training program, including appropriate dispensing practices in malaria management, designed and delivered to the selected group of licensed chemical sellers.

Postintervention assessment results showed that—

- At endline, there was an increase from 50 percent to 62 percent in dispensing any antimalarial to simulated malaria clients at CAREshops (compared with a decrease from 58 percent to 55 percent in the control regions).
- However, only 18 percent of CAREshop facilities dispensed the antimalarial exactly according to treatment guidelines at endline, compared with 10 percent and 13 percent of chemical sellers in two control regions. Clearly, additional training, supervision, and monitoring are still necessary.

in rational medicine use, and monitoring medicine use at health facilities.

The effectiveness of the pharmaceutical supply system in achieving a reliable supply of essential medicines must be continually and objectively assessed. Fundamental restructuring of pharmaceutical supply arrangements challenges the status quo and may threaten a variety of interests. But continuing to support an ineffective supply system wastes precious resources and denies patients access to lifesaving essential medicines.

Changing the perceptions and behaviors of providers, patients, and the public

One of the greatest challenges is to change the way in which providers, patients, and the public view and use pharmaceuticals. Major problems, noted earlier, include prescribing and dispensing incorrect, harmful, or unnecessary medicines; failure by patients to use needed medications correctly; and wasteful or harmful self-medication practices.

However, three years after implementation, the franchise organization had not reached the break-even point and continued to lose money, although many shops were independently performing well. Discussions between the original implementing organization and an outside organization to restructure the franchise business plan were unsuccessful, and by the end of 2008, the head of the implementing organization said that the franchise was in serious financial peril.

Nigeria

The Basic Support for Institutionalizing Child Survival (BASICS) Program designed an intervention in Nigeria that combined a short, highly focused training for private-sector patent-medicine vendors with the promotion of age-specific, color-coded, prepackaged antimalarials for children under five. These activities were supported by a comprehensive social marketing and behavior-change strategy, which included mass media promoting the new prepackaged antimalarials and medicine sellers displaying shop identifiers from the training. More than eight hundred patent-medicine vendors were trained in a two-month period at the relatively low cost of approximately USD 8 each. Training materials focused on immediate treatment of children under five with fever using an appropriate-dose (preferably prepackaged) antimalarial.

Postintervention assessment results showed that—

- The number of patent-medicine vendors giving the correct antimalarial and dose increased from 9 percent to 53 percent.
- Patent-medicine vendor knowledge about the need to use insecticide-treated nets tripled (from 21 percent to 65 percent) between pre- and postintervention surveys.

Sources: Greer et al. 2004; MSH/SEAM 2008a; 2008b

Given the huge share of public and private pharmaceutical expenditures that may be wasted through irrational medicine use, governments, NGOs, and others must continue to explore effective, sustainable ways of improving medicine-use patterns. For example, the International Conferences on Improving the Use of Medicines in 1997 and 2004 brought together leading national and international policy makers, program managers, researchers, clinicians, and other stakeholders to produce state-of-the-art consensus on interventions to improve medicines use in nonindustrialized countries, to define evidence-based recommendations for program implementation, and to generate global research agendas to fill gaps in knowledge (www.icium.org). See also Chapters 29 and 33, which address rational prescribing and use by the public.

Reorienting the role of government

Access to health care, including essential medicines, is a fundamental human right. Realization of this right may involve various combinations of public and private financing and service provision. In high-income countries, public financing of pharmaceuticals predominates. In low- and middle-income countries, the public-private mix varies remarkably, from over 90 percent public provision of medicines in Slovakia and the Solomon Islands to roughly 90 percent private market supply and financing of pharmaceuticals in Cambodia and Georgia (WHO 2004c).

From a public health perspective, therefore, the specific concerns with improving access to medicines in the private pharmaceutical market are improving the availability, geographic accessibility, affordability, and acceptability of quality medicines and related services. Measures to improve *availability* include certification and training of pharmacy aides and other drug sellers; focus on efficiency in the supply chain, including the private sector; licensing and incentives for wholesalers, pharmacies, and other drug outlets; and community-based medicine schemes. Innovative franchising and accreditation initiatives have been used successfully to increase the quality of medicines and pharmaceutical services from retail drug sellers, which are often more *geographically accessible* and therefore people's first source of health care (Country Study 1-1). *Affordability* can be improved with greater insurance coverage, better price information, competitive procurement and price competition through generic substitution, regulation of producer and resale prices, and modification of retail sales margins. *Acceptability* can be promoted by regulating medicine information and marketing; including essential medicines concepts in basic medical education; providing focused continuing education for health professionals; and actively educating the public and patients. Finally, *quality* of services is increased by enforcing licensing requirements for doctors, pharmacists, and other health professionals, and *quality* of products is improved by putting into place good procurement practices, such as using prequalified suppliers, and an effective regulatory system that includes monitoring, testing, and enforcement (Chapter 6).

The public health challenge is to work with the private sector and NGOs to achieve universal access to essential medicines and rational use of medicines. This work involves building mutual understanding, constructive partnerships, and the right incentives.

Regulating safety, efficacy, and quality

Regulatory control, often neglected in the pharmaceutical sector of developing countries, is an indispensable foundation for ensuring the safety, efficacy, and quality of pharmaceuticals in a country. Governments must ensure that all pharmaceuticals available on the local market meet basic standards. Moreover, the same quality standards applied to the open market must be applied to medicines procured through the public sector. Pharmaceutical legislation and regulation should also establish basic professional standards in both the public and the private sectors.

In industrialized countries, regulatory capacity has developed in phases over many decades. Most developing countries also will require time to develop effective regulatory capacity. Such capacity requires a firm legislative basis, trained personnel, specific technical resources, adequate funding, and—perhaps most important—public commitment to establishing and enforcing basic standards (Chapter 6).

1.7 Managing pharmaceutical sector improvements

This manual is meant to provide policy makers and managers with practical, accessible advice on a wide range of topics relevant to managing pharmaceutical supply. The basic functions of management are planning, implementation, and monitoring. Effective planning requires thoughtful reflection on basic goals, systematic assessment of the current situation, identification of root causes of problems, creative consideration of all reasonable strategies for improvement, and selection of strategies based on defined criteria.

Program implementation is an interactive process that involves organizing people, finances, and other resources to achieve the desired results. The test of any policy or plan is in its implementation. Gradual phasing-in of new initiatives can help build management systems, which can then support full-scale implementation. Active decision making and problem solving are fundamental to the implementation process.

Finally, ongoing monitoring and periodic evaluation are needed to measure progress, to adjust implementation plans, and to assess the effect of pharmaceutical management improvements. Objective indicators and specific program targets provide concrete measures against which actual performance can be compared. Without such indicators, judging the success and, therefore, the value of human and financial investments in pharmaceutical sector improvements is difficult.

The experiences of countless countries and programs demonstrate that substantive, sustainable improvements in the supply and use of medicines are possible. But an equal or greater number of negative experiences demonstrate that success is by no means assured. Clear goals, sound plans, effective implementation, and systematic monitoring of performance are essential ingredients in pharmaceutical sector development. ∎

References and further readings

★ = Key readings.

Arnold, S. R., and S. E. Straus. 2005. Interventions to Improve Antibiotic Prescribing Practices in Ambulatory Care. *Cochrane Database of Systematic Reviews,* Issue 4. Art. no. CD003539.

Ballance, R., J. Pogány, and H. Forstner. 1992. *The World's Pharmaceutical Industries: United Nations Industrial Development Organization Document.* Brookfield, Vt.: Ashgate Publishers.

Cohen, J. C. 2006. Pharmaceuticals and Corruption: A Risk Assessment. In *The Global Corruption Report 2006: Corruption and Health,* Transparency International, ed. <http://www.transparency.org/publications/gcr/gcr_2006>

Committee on the Economics of Antimalarial Drugs, Board on Global Health; K. J. Arrow, C. Panosian, H. Gelband, eds. 2004. *Saving Lives, Buying Time: Economics of Malaria Drugs in an Age of Resistance.* Washington, D.C.: National Academy Press. <http://www.nap.edu/openbook.php?record_id=11017&page=R1>

CPM/MSH (Center for Pharmaceutical Management/Management Sciences for Health). 2011. *Center for Pharmaceutical Management: Technical Frameworks, Approaches, and Results.* Arlington, Va.: CPM.

★ CPM (Center for Pharmaceutical Management). 2003. *Defining and Measuring Access to Essential Drugs, Vaccines, and Health Commodities: Report of the WHO-MSH Consultative Meeting, Ferney-Voltaire, France, December 11–13, 2000.* Prepared for the Strategies for Enhancing Access to Medicines Program. Arlington, Va.: Management Sciences for Health. <http://www.msh.org/seam/reports/Access_Meeting_Ferney_Voltaire_1.pdf>

Dumoulin, J., M. Kaddar, and G. Velásquez. 1991. *Access to Drugs and Finance: Basic Economic and Financial Analysis.* Geneva: World Health Organization. <http://whqlibdoc.who.int/hq/1991/WHO_DAP_91.5.pdf>

★ Gottret, P., and G. Schieber. 2006. *Health Financing Revisited: A Practitioner's Guide.* Washington, D.C.: World Bank. <http://siteresources.worldbank.org/INTHSD/Resources/topics/Health-Financing/HFRFull.pdf>

Greer, G., A. Akinpelumi, L. Madueke, B. Plowman, B. Fapohunda, Y. Tawfik, R. Holmes, et al. 2004. *Improving Management of Childhood Malaria in Nigeria and Uganda by Improving Practices of Patent Medicine Vendors.* Arlington, Va.: BASICS II for the United States Agency for International Development. <http://www.m-mc.org/spotlight/nigeria_malaria/ManagementofMalaria.pdf>

Jamison, D. T., J. G. Breman, A. R. Measham, G. Alleyne, M. Claeson, D. B. Evans, P. Jha, A. Mills, and P. Musgrove. 2006. *Disease Control Priorities in Developing Countries, Second Edition.* Washington, D.C., and Oxford: World Bank and Oxford University Press. <http://www.dcp2.org/pubs/DCP>

*Laing, R. O., H. V. Hogerzeil, and D. Ross-Degnan. 2001. Ten Recommendations to Improve Use of Medicines in Developing Countries. *Health Policy and Planning* 16(1):13–20.

Laing, R. O., B. Waning, A. Gray, N. Ford, and E. 't Hoen. 2003. Twenty-Five Years of the WHO Essential Medicines Lists: Progress and Challenges. *Lancet* 361(9370):1723.

Le Grand, A., H. V. Hogerzeil, and F. M. Haaijer-Ruskamp. 1999. Intervention Research in Rational Use of Drugs: A Review. *Health Policy and Planning* 14(2):89–102.

MSH/RPM (Management Sciences for Health/Rational Pharmaceutical Management Project). 1995. *Rapid Pharmaceutical Management Assessment: An Indicator-Based Approach.* Arlington, Va.: MSH/RPM. <http://erc.msh.org/newpages/english/toolkit/rpma.pdf>

MSH/SEAM (Management Sciences for Health/Strategies for Enhancing Access to Medicines). 2008a. *Ghana: Creating a Franchise System for Drug Sellers—CAREshops®.* Arlington, Va.: MSH/SEAM. <http://www.msh.org/seam/reports/seam_ghana_careshops.pdf>

———. 2008b. *Tanzania: Accredited Drug Dispensing Outlets—Duka la Dawa Muhimu.* Arlington, Va.: MSH/SEAM. <http://www.msh.org/seam/reports/SEAM_Final_Report_Summary-Tanzania_ADDOs.pdf >

Murray, C. J. L., and A. D. López, eds. 1994. *Global Comparative Assessments in the Health Sector: Disease Burden, Expenditures, and Intervention Packages.* Geneva: World Health Organization.

PriceWaterhouseCoopers. 2007. *Pharma 2020: Challenging Business Models.* <http://www.pwc.com/gx/en/pharma-life-sciences/pharma-2020-business-models/index.jhtml>

Srivastava, N. M., S. Awasthi, and G. G. Agarwal. 2009. Care-seeking Behavior and Out-of-Pocket Expenditure for Sick Newborns among Urban Poor in Lucknow, Northern India: A Prospective Follow-up Study. *BMC Health Services Research* 9:61. <http://www.biomedcentral.com/content/pdf/1472-6963-9-61.pdf>

★ UNMP (United Nations Millennium Project). 2005. *Prescription for Healthy Development: Increasing Access to Medicines.* Report of the Task Force on HIV/AIDS, Malaria, TB, and Access to Essential Medicines, Working Group on Access to Essential Medicines. Sterling, Va.: Earthcscan. <http://www.unmillenniumproject.org/documents/TF5-medicines-Complete.pdf>

WHO (World Health Organization). 2010a. *Continuity and Change: Implementing the Third WHO Medicines Strategy—2008–2013.* Geneva: WHO. <http://apps.who.int/medicinedocs/pdf/s16821e/s16821e_lo.pdf>

★ ———. 2010b. *Measuring Transparency to Improve Good Governance in the Public Pharmaceutical Sector: Assessment Instrument.* Geneva: WHO.

———. 2009. *Corruption and Pharmaceuticals.* Fact Sheet No. 335. Geneva: WHO. <http://www.who.int/mediacentre/factsheets/fs335/en/index.html>

———. 2008a. *Global Burden of Disease Summary Tables.* Geneva: WHO. <http://www.who.int/evidence/bod>

———. 2008b. *The Top Ten Causes of Death.* Fact Sheet No. 310. Geneva: WHO. <http://www.who.int/mediacentre/factsheets/fs310_2008.pdf>

———. 2007a. *Medicines: Essential Medicines.* Fact Sheet No. 325. Geneva: WHO. <http://www.who.int/mediacentre/factsheets/fs325/en>

———. 2007b. *WHO Operational Package for Assessing, Monitoring and Evaluating Country Pharmaceutical Situations: Guide for Coordinators and Data Collectors.* Geneva: WHO. <http://www.who.int/medicines/publications/WHO_TCM_2007.2.pdf>

———. 2006a. *Measuring Transparency in Medicines Registration, Selection and Procurement: Four Country Assessment Studies.* Geneva: WHO. <http://whqlibdoc.who.int/hq/2006/WHO_PSM_PAR_2006.7_eng.pdf>

———. 2006b. *Rational Use of Medicines: Progress in Implementing the WHO Medicines Strategy.* Report by the Secretariat. Geneva: WHO. <http://apps.who.int/gb/ebwha/pdf_files/EB118/B118_6-en.pdf>

★ ———. 2006c. *Using Indicators to Measure Country Pharmaceutical Situations: Fact Book on WHO Level I and Level II Monitoring Indicators.* Geneva: WHO. <http://www.who.int/medicines/publications/WHOTCM2006.2A.pdf>

———. 2006d. *The World Health Report 2006: Working Together for Health.* Geneva: WHO. <http://www.who.int/whr/2006/en/index.html>

★ ———. 2004a. *Equitable Access to Essential Medicines: A Framework for Collective Action.* Geneva: WHO. <http://whqlibdoc.who.int/hq/2004/WHO_EDM_2004.4.pdf>

———. 2004b. *WHO Medicines Strategy: Countries at the Core 2004–2007.* Geneva: WHO. <http://whqlibdoc.who.int/hq/2004/WHO_EDM_2004.2.pdf>

★ ———. 2004c. *The World Medicines Situation.* Geneva: WHO. <http://whqlibdoc.who.int/hq/2004/WHO_EDM_PAR_2004.5.pdf>

———. 2002. *Promoting Rational Use of Medicines: Core Components.* Geneva. WHO. <http://whqlibdoc.who.int/hq/2002/WHO_EDM_2002.3.pdf>

———. 2000. *Global Comparative Pharmaceutical Expenditures with Related Reference Information.* Geneva: WHO

★ WHO/EMP (World Health Organization/Department of Essential Medicines and Pharmaceutical Policies). 2009. *A Framework for Good Governance in the Public Pharmaceutical Sector: Working Draft for Field Testing and Revision.* Geneva: WHO/EMP. <http://www.who.int/medicines/areas/policy/goodgovernance/GGMframework09.pdf>

World Bank. 1993. *World Development Report 1993: Investing in Health.* New York: Oxford University Press. <http://files.dcp2.org/pdf/WorldDevelopmentReport1993.pdf>

| Part I: Policy and economic issues | Part II: Pharmaceutical management | Part III: Management support systems |

Policy and legal framework
1 Toward sustainable access to medicines
2 Historical and institutional perspectives
3 Intellectual property and access to medicines
4 National medicine policy
5 Traditional and complementary medicine policy
6 Pharmaceutical legislation and regulation
7 Pharmaceutical production policy
8 Pharmaceutical supply strategies
Financing and sustainability

CHAPTER 2

Historical and institutional perspectives

SUMMARY

Concerns about medicines—or lack of medicines—can be traced back for centuries. The discovery of "wonder drugs" about the time of World War II, however, was a milestone in pharmaceutical management. The dramatic effectiveness of some new pharmaceuticals and the intensive marketing of many others combined to catalyze widespread use of modern medicines. A rapidly growing and profitable industry, together with an enthusiastic but largely uninformed public and an often inadequately regulated marketplace, resulted in excesses of promotion and consumption, along with substantial levels of expenditure that necessitated new policy measures.

Despite the advent of wonder drugs, however, it had become clear by the 1970s that the least-advantaged nations were not even meeting the basic needs of their people for essential lifesaving and health-promoting medicines. Through the 1970s and 1980s, governments and international organizations such as the World Health Organization (WHO) began to redress this imbalance, with support from nongovernmental organizations (NGOs), largely through the promotion of essential medicines programs.

In the 1990s and 2000s, the devastation caused by the HIV/AIDS pandemic specifically helped draw attention to the plight of people living in resource-limited areas—especially sub-Saharan Africa—and the increased interest in health care and funding for treatment in developing countries spawned a number of significant global initiatives to address inequities and increase access to health care and essential medicines in the most-affected countries. As the world responds with dramatically increased financial assistance to provide affordable medicines for HIV/AIDS, tuberculosis (TB), and malaria, there has been growing recognition that the effectiveness of these multimillion-dollar initiatives is limited by the capacity of health care and pharmaceutical supply systems at the national and local levels. Constraints to improving access to medicines include inadequate infrastructure in facilities and a lack of trained staff and equipment for those facilities.

Although differences have always existed between the way pharmaceutical policies have developed in industrialized countries, on the one hand, and developing countries, on the other, many elements of pharmaceutical policy are applicable everywhere. The increasingly globalized economy is driving more uniform approaches to pharmaceutical policy, especially as the many parties engaged in the pharmaceutical arena work together in global programs for the benefit of all.

2.1 The discovery of miracle medicines

During and soon after World War II, new and powerful medicines began to emerge in rapid succession from laboratories around the world. Penicillin was isolated and first used clinically in 1941; chloroquine, first investigated in the mid-1930s, was released for trial against malaria in 1943; and streptomycin followed in 1944 as the first effective medicine for tuberculosis. Adding to the earlier benefits of smallpox and typhoid immunizations, diphtheria and tetanus toxoid vaccines were first adopted during the war for use in large military populations. Tetracycline and chloramphenicol were introduced in 1948, isoniazid in 1951, and erythromycin in 1952. Chlorpromazine signaled a new era of mental health medicine therapy in the same year. In 1954, the sulfonylureas became the first oral preparations for treating diabetes, and nystatin emerged as an antifungal agent. In 1955, field trials of oral contraceptives took place in Puerto Rico, leading to a virtual revolution that enabled women to begin to effectively control family size.

In just over a decade, the whole field of therapeutics was revolutionized, putting into the hands of practitioners and consumers new pharmaceutical compounds that could cure or control problems in ways largely unknown in earlier times. As both scientific and anecdotal evidence spread, practitioners and patients demanded, and were willing to pay for, the innovative and powerful products that the pharmaceutical industry was patenting and producing.

2.2 The increasing gap in access to medicines

In this exciting period during the middle of the twentieth century, many authors of popular books on pharmaceuticals wrote of the revolution in medical care that modern medicines had made possible: antibiotics seemed on the verge of controlling deadly infections such as pneumonia and septicemia; cortisone had arrived to suppress painful inflammation; asthma was yielding to isoprenaline; one vaccine after another was appearing to stop fatal epidemics. *Miracle* was the word many authors used to describe these effects.

From the global perspective, however, such miracles were for the minority. Affluent countries stood in stark contrast to the rest of the world, where entire populations had little access to medicines or were struggling to cope with a maze of competitive products, many of which were obscure, overpriced, outdated, ineffective, or, frankly, dangerous. In many countries, two contrasting problems existed side by side: no medicines at all in the countryside, but hundreds or thousands of medicines competing for prescribers' and customers' attention in the cities. Medical and nursing staff in some areas worked without the medicines they needed, while practitioners in other areas faced a flood of expensive products about which they had no reliable information or that their patients could not afford.

2.3 The rise of the essential medicines concept

An idea gradually emerged: why not concentrate first on a basic list of reliable medicines to meet the most vital needs—understanding them, finding ways to pay for them, supplying them to the people? The idea of working with a limited range of medicines had long been used in places where no alternative existed; doctors had learned to carry twenty vital medicines in their bags, oceangoing ships commonly carried 100 or fewer medicines, and in later years, some airlines designed medicine kits for use in emergencies on long-distance flights.

The idea was first applied on a national scale before World War II in Norway, which was then a poor country. Norway decided to limit its list of approved medicines to those most needed in medical practice and most affordable for the population, avoiding unnecessary duplication. In the developing world, Papua New Guinea had a policy based on "essential drugs" by the early 1950s, Sri Lanka followed in 1959, and Cuba had a list of essential medicines by 1963.

How many medicines were needed for such a list? Sri Lanka chose 500, similar in number to Norway's original list. Whatever choice was made, it provided a starting point; one day, money might be available for more. Newly independent countries, committed to providing universal health care yet desperately short of resources, saw an essential medicines policy as a means of moving ahead despite stubborn obstacles.

It became clear that focusing on an essential medicines list could also make better use of limited financial resources. The most basic medicines were often well established through longtime use, and because patents on many of them had expired, several competing manufacturers were making them and selling them at lower prices. Often, a low-cost medicine was as good as a newer product being sold at a cost ten or fifty times higher.

By the mid-1970s, the essential medicines concept had evolved into a practical policy suitable for worldwide use, with one important modification. Rather than the view that only essential medicines should be allowed on the market, the view was now that any safe and efficacious medicine should be allowed for sale, but that essential medicines

should be given priority. At this point WHO adopted the concept. In 1975, WHO's Director General defined essential medicines as "those considered to be of utmost importance and hence basic, indispensable, and necessary for the health needs of the population. They should be available at all times, in the proper dosage forms, to all segments of society."

Two years later, WHO issued its first model list of 224 "essential drugs" (including vaccines). By then, many countries were finding the cost of medicines a concern; for example, the government of Bangladesh was spending 60 percent of its entire public health budget on medicines, yet much of the poor population could still not get access to affordable treatment. Often, pharmaceuticals and raw materials had to be imported from high-cost countries, and their prices were further inflated by substantial markups imposed by importers, wholesalers, and retailers. In addition, thousands of brand-name combination products, often of questionable efficacy and safety, were flooding the private sector. Now, realizing that a limited list of essential medicines could help solve most of those problems, public health services could base their purchasing, supply, and training primarily on items that were most needed and most affordable.

The pharmaceutical industry grew rapidly in the postwar era. Substances that cured, prevented, or ameliorated many problems were formulated into products that were protected by patents, giving producers a long period in which to establish a dominant market presence and accumulate profits. Sophisticated production and testing methods allowed the formation of efficient, largely automated, high-volume manufacturing processes, resulting in large profits that could be plowed back into new-product research and the acquisition of smaller firms. These forces created an increasingly concentrated multinational industry.

Developing countries had another reason to give priority to essential medicines. The rush to get new products to the market resulted in inadequately tested medicines and many cases of serious or fatal medicine-induced diseases. In 1960, the introduction in Europe of the sleeping aid thalidomide resulted in the birth of thousands of deformed children. In 1973, clioquinol, used to suppress diarrhea in Japan, was found to cause blindness and paralysis. Even some widely used and valuable medicines brought unexpected problems. For example, the antibiotic chloramphenicol, misused widely in Latin America, caused aplastic anemia. These examples generated a growing recognition that pharmaceuticals often brought problems as well as great promise.

UN agencies and WHO lead the way

Although WHO's role in promoting the idea of essential medicines was historic, it was only the starting point for a much broader trend involving other international organizations. By the 1970s, UN member states were urging international agencies to take up the problems of imbalances in growth, inequities, and redistribution of resources in developing countries. In 1974, the International Labor Office adopted the idea of defining and meeting "basic needs" in the developing world as a whole, not limited to medicines alone. WHO also urged a broader approach aimed at improving the health of rural and peri-urban populations. In Alma Ata in 1978, the WHO/UN Children's Fund (UNICEF) Conference on Primary Health Care adopted the essential medicines concept as one of its basic tools. In Geneva, the Division of Drug Policy and Management came into being to develop the concept as part of national pharmaceutical policy for member states. Important backing also came from an interagency task force set up by the United Nations (UN), which by 1979 recommended the adoption of national medicines lists using generic names.

By this time, other UN agencies were also focusing on medicines. The UN Conference on Trade and Development (UNCTAD) supported the use of generic names, competitive procurement, and cooperative purchasing arrangements. The UN Industrial Development Organization (UNIDO) emphasized local and regional cooperative production. UNICEF, long active in directly providing medicines through its supply division, embraced the essential medicines idea with WHO in the late 1970s. Finally, the mutually supportive role of such UN agencies became more visible and eventually more coherent when a series of conferences and task forces created a rough division of labor: UNICEF would concentrate on supply, WHO on health policy, UNCTAD on trade, and UNIDO on industrial development.

The emergence of generic pharmaceuticals

By the 1980s, the patents on many medicines developed in the two decades after World War II began to expire, opening the way for worldwide production and distribution. Southeast Asia, especially, had a growing number of new pharmaceutical firms with low overhead costs that began to manufacture generic versions of well-known medicines and sell them at a fraction of the original price. Because they were working in countries where foreign patents were not recognized, some of these manufacturers had long-term experience in copying pharmaceutical products; not all maintained high standards of quality, however. Nevertheless, public pharmaceutical supply systems found that they could obtain much better prices by procuring the new, low-cost generic versions of familiar medicines.

The movement accelerates

WHO's Action Programme on Essential Drugs grew vigorously in the early 1980s. By 1984, large amounts of extrabudgetary funds from European donors were provided specifically to support projects in each region of the world for strengthening medicine selection, procurement, and distribution. Issues of pharmaceutical financing were tackled, and standards were set for pharmaceutical information and training. In 1985, the WHO Conference of Experts in Nairobi broadened the approach with a new emphasis on the need to use medicines rationally. That same year, the *Essential Drugs Monitor,* an international newsletter advocating an essential medicines policy in all its forms, began publication. Such initiatives were heavily backed by voluntary efforts from the outside, notably by Health Action International (HAI), an international coalition of NGOs from some fifty countries with a special interest in pharmaceuticals.

The industry's reaction

As they gained momentum, these dramatic developments provoked mixed reactions from the international pharmaceutical industry. Major multinational corporations had reaped substantial profits from selling their new products in the industrialized world. However, even given the fierce competition among multinational pharmaceutical firms, a low-cost solution to the problem of access to medicines in the developing world had not evolved. One explanation was that the industry had grown accustomed to serving affluent populations, where buyers generally accepted high prices in exchange for the newest products, which they assumed were the best. To cultivate that market, companies focused on marketing and promoting their new products. Selling a relatively small volume of pharmaceuticals to the most affluent part of the population was simpler and more profitable than trying to meet the needs of larger populations with limited ability to pay.

Despite the limited coverage of the people in the developing world by the multinational pharmaceutical industry, these countries constituted a potentially lucrative market, with promise for the future. As developed countries introduced stricter systems of pharmaceutical regulation and were forced by the economic recession of the 1970s to look critically at their own medicine costs, the largely unregulated countries of the rest of the world provided a new prospect for profitability. The fact that the UN and WHO were encouraging restrictive policies and beginning to formulate ethical criteria for pharmaceutical marketing in the developing world seemed to threaten the multinationals' future prospects. Where the new generic manufacturers now saw an opportunity, the traditional multinationals saw a threat. One reaction of the producers of originator products was to demand better patent protection, which came to fruition with the World Trade Organization's Agreement on Trade-Related Aspects of Intellectual Property Rights in 1994 (see Chapter 3).

The pharmaceutical industry's direct reactions to essential medicines policies varied from hostile to mixed, with representatives declaring on occasion that the concept was completely unacceptable. The Geneva-based International Federation of Pharmaceutical Manufacturers and Associations (IFPMA) suggested that the adoption of an essential medicines list "would result in substandard rather than improved medical care and might well reduce health standards already attained." The federation was heavily backed in its protests by the U.S. Pharmaceutical Manufacturers Association, which by 1985 was arguing that the imposition of additional and arbitrary criteria involving "essentiality" or "medical interest" would clearly be contrary to the public interest. In retrospect, one major problem was probably the failure to communicate to the industry and practitioners what "essential medicines" really meant. As noted, the essential medicines concept was not a question of reducing access to medicines for those who already enjoyed it, but of providing access for those who had otherwise been without.

Subsequently, having accepted that for poorer countries the essential medicines approach might be "practical, even if regrettable," the research-based segment of the pharmaceutical industry turned to limiting its application, insisting that the concept applied only in the public sectors of the least-developed countries. This segment of the industry simultaneously discouraged WHO's other policy initiatives, notably those involving advertising standards, and continued to promote the view that generic medicines were likely to be substandard and even dangerous.

Since 1985, however, the research-based multinational industry and the trade as a whole have largely come around to the view that they can earn a fair profit by providing low-cost medicines—whether brand-name or generic—on a large scale to essential medicines programs, with high sales volume compensating for low profit margins. On some fronts, the IFPMA has collaborated with essential medicines programs, with WHO, and with donors. Tensions between pharmaceutical manufacturers and international organizations have shifted from the essential drug concept to other issues, such as intellectual property and parallel importing.

The campaign for rational use of medicines

After access to essential medicines is addressed, proper use remains a challenge, because waste by both prescribers and users is common. The notion that if one medicine is good, two are better (and three ideal) dies hard, and both prescribers and users are prone to overuse. The quantities of medicines prescribed for a given illness are often far more than what is reasonably needed. Medicines are often prescribed when none is needed at all, because patients expect or demand a pill or an injection, or because physicians or medical assistants are anxious to be seen as doing something. In some cases, half of medicines reaching the periphery are

wasted by irrational prescribing and by inappropriate use by patients, who fail to follow the instructions given by prescribers.

The notion that all pharmaceutical policies need to promote the "rational use of medicines" was only slowly accepted. Pharmaceutical policies had always centered on medicines, not on patients. Pharmaceutical policies had been the concern largely of administrators and pharmacists, whereas medicine use was largely in the hands of physicians and paramedical staff. The medical profession in particular resented any suggestion that it might be acting irrationally as a group or that it might be in need of guidance or control. Medical personnel often insisted on the "right" to prescribe the medicine of their choice.

The rational use of medicines concept developed momentum after WHO's 1985 Nairobi Conference of Experts used it as its central theme. The conference emphasized the need for the public to understand and use medicines better, particularly in view of all that was known about nonadherence to treatment. In many cases, neither the prescriber nor the patient was to blame for irrational use; the fault often resulted from lack of proper information and training, compounded in some cases by fear, carelessness, or misleading persuasion from the seller or others. With much of a nation's pharmaceutical supply potentially being wasted because of irrational use, the effort to promote proper use, although time-consuming, is vital to any effective health policy and any well-managed economy.

Basic data on how medicines are actually being used in a particular country and situation, why errors are made, and the types of intervention that may improve the situation are important aids in understanding and modifying medicine use. WHO's Collaborating Centre on Drug Utilization Research developed methods—including some that can be applied simply and quickly—for studying these matters, and those methods have now been used in many parts of the world (see WHO 2003). In 1989, the International Network for the Rational Use of Drugs (INRUD) was formed to bring together developing-country teams composed of decision makers in ministries of health, researchers, health care professionals, social scientists, and support groups. INRUD continues to serve as a forum for joint country-level efforts to investigate medicine-use problems, test strategies to change providers' and consumers' behavior with regard to specific problems, implement large-scale behavior-change efforts, and share national experiences internationally with colleagues. The International Conferences on Improving Use of Medicines (www.icium.org) in 1997 and 2004 have played a large role in the evolution of paradigms for promoting rational use of medicines.

In 2001, WHO launched the Global Strategy for Containment of Antimicrobial Resistance, which recognizes antimicrobial resistance as a global problem that must be addressed in all countries (WHO 2001b). No country, however effective it is at containing resistance within its borders, can protect itself from the importation of resistant pathogens through travel and trade. Poor prescribing practices and irrational use in any country now threaten to undermine the potency of vital antimicrobials around the world. In addition, the U.S. Agency for International Development has recognized the critical importance of the issue and supports a variety of programs that help contain the spread of antimicrobial resistance.

The evolution of malaria treatment is an example of how irrational use has created major problems with drug resistance. During the past century, antimalarial drugs were used on a large scale, generally as monotherapies, introduced in sequence, and were used continually, despite unacceptably high levels of resistance. In addition, many people have typically sought care for malaria through the private sector—antimalarial medications are often available at retail drug outlets. Private prescribers and dispensers, however, are less likely to follow standard treatment guidelines, and patients will generally pay for and take only the medications needed to feel better—not necessarily what constitutes the recommended dose; for example, anecdotal evidence suggests that some people prescribed artemisinin-based combination therapy (ACT) take only the artemisinin-based drug because it is the one that makes them feel better, a practice that negates the purpose of taking a combination of medicines to slow the spread of drug resistance.

As discussed in Chapter 51, the lack of trained health professionals in many countries makes it difficult to adequately monitor rational medicine use, especially in the case of antiretrovirals (ARVs), which patients must take for the duration of their lives. This gap in human resources makes it that much more crucial to educate patients as well as the entire community about the importance of adherence and medicine use and to explore the effectiveness of community-based interventions (see Chapters 31 and 33).

2.4   Global focus on AIDS, tuberculosis, and malaria

The devastation caused by the HIV/AIDS pandemic helped draw attention to the plight of people living in resource-limited areas—especially sub-Saharan Africa. The WHO's "3x5" initiative was the first to declare a global target to provide three million people living with HIV/AIDS in low- and middle-income countries with antiretroviral therapy (ART) by the end of 2005, with the ultimate goal of making treatment accessible to all people. An additional incentive for specific action has been the establishment of the UN Millennium Development Goals; Goal 6 targets the end of the spread of HIV by 2015 and universal treatment by 2010. By 2010, however, new infections were still outstripping gains made in treatment coverage (UN 2010).

The increased interest in health care and funding for treatment in developing countries has spawned a number of significant global initiatives to address inequities and increase access to health care and essential medicines in the most-affected countries.

Large-scale funding initiatives include the following—

- *The Global Fund to Fight AIDS, Tuberculosis and Malaria* is a large multilateral funding program that approved grants for over USD 3 billion in its first two years of existence. Of that money, more than 60 percent has been distributed in Africa and almost 50 percent has gone to procure medicines and commodities.
- *The U.S. President's Emergency Plan for AIDS Relief (PEPFAR),* announced in 2003, made a contribution of USD 19 billion to sixteen countries—including twelve in Africa. In 2009, PEPFAR became part of the Global Health Initiative, which responds to a broad range of global health needs. In response to the evolving global HIV/AIDS situation, PEPFAR now places more emphasis on overall health systems' strengthening and sustainability rather than emergency action.
- *UNITAID,* whose funding comes from taxes on airline tickets in six countries and from country and foundation contributions, was established to support the health-related Millennium Development Goals. UNITAID's model is based on long-term funding commitments and the purchase of high volumes of medicines and diagnostics used to leverage price reductions. It disburses funds to international partners working in health commodities procurement, such as the William J. Clinton Health Action Initiative and UNICEF.

Prominent partnerships and initiatives include the following—

- *The AIDS Medicines and Diagnostics Service* is a network to support increased access to good quality and effective treatments for HIV/AIDS by improving supply of ARVs and diagnostics in developing countries.
- *The Stop TB Partnership's Global Drug Facility* helps TB programs get quality-assured TB medicines at the best prices, store them properly, distribute them in a timely manner, and use them rationally.
- *The Stop TB Partnership's Green Light Committee* works to assure access to preferentially priced second-line medicines for multidrug-resistant TB.
- *The Roll Back Malaria Partnership,* established in 1998, has a goal of achieving the malaria-specific Millennium Development Goal, which is to halt and begin to reverse the incidence of malaria, by 2015, through a coordinated global approach toward prevention and treatment, including the establishment

of the Malaria Medicines and Supplies Service, which facilitates access to affordable antimalarial medicines and commodities such as insecticide-treated mosquito nets, rapid diagnostic tests, and insecticides. Also, the Global Fund's Affordable Medicines Facility–Malaria Initiative seeks to increase access to affordable ACTs subsidies. Instituting subsidies for ACTs will allow prices to be brought into line with those of cheap, yet ineffective medicines, such as sulfadoxine-pyrimethamine, eventually driving them out of the market.

The role of advocacy groups and community-based organizations

Increased advocacy from various groups, such as multilateral organizations, bilateral donors, nongovernmental organizations from all levels, and civil society organizations, has resulted in pressure to change policies and push pharmaceutical issues onto national and international health care agendas. Issues highlighted by these groups include the need for new health technologies and medicines for the three diseases, such as more sensitive TB diagnostics and pediatric formulations of ARVs. The response to HIV/AIDS, in particular, put into motion an advocacy movement that has profoundly influenced issues on a global scale.

The extreme impact of the AIDS pandemic fostered a unique alliance of activists and people living with the infection acting as advocates within the community. In 1983, an advocacy group in Brazil created a nongovernmental organization to fight AIDS, a year after the first case had been diagnosed there, and more groups followed. In addition to increasing prevention and treatment in poor and remote communities, Brazilian activists are credited with assuring adequate funding for ARVs and contributing to the country's successful pricing negotiations with pharmaceutical manufacturers (Homedes and Ugalde 2006). In 1987 in New York City, the AIDS Coalition to Unleash Power (ACT UP) was formed as an activist group dedicated to influencing AIDS-related policy. ACT UP was the most visible example of how involvement at the community level and from people living with HIV/AIDS could greatly affect public policy and issues such as ARV access and affordability, demonstrating an impact that ranged far beyond the group's New York roots. Since 1998, the Treatment Action Campaign and its allies in South Africa have led a lengthy and highly visible public campaign to improve access to ART through the public health sector.

Today, organizations around the world strive to mobilize community support and action not only to improve the lives of local families touched by HIV/AIDS, but to keep AIDS issues—especially access to ARVs—high on the public agenda. For example, the International HIV/AIDS Alliance (www.aidsalliance.org), which was founded in 1993, works with community organizations in more than forty developing countries to strengthen the local response to HIV-related disease, including building community knowledge of and demand for ART. The HIV/AIDS Alliance produces a range of resources and tools to improve the effectiveness of the community effort.

Lack of systems to support access to medicines for HIV/AIDS, TB, and malaria

As the world has responded with increased financial assistance to provide affordable medicines for HIV/AIDS, TB, and malaria, there is a growing recognition that the effectiveness of these large initiatives is limited by the capacity of health and pharmaceutical supply systems at the national and local levels. Indeed, this challenge was borne out by the findings of a UN Millennium Project task force with a mandate to combat HIV/AIDS, malaria, TB, and other diseases and improve access to essential medicines. The task force concluded that attempting to address individual diseases through global programs cannot succeed without the allocation of more resources for strengthening entire health systems, noting that "existing approaches to combating AIDS, tuberculosis, and malaria, although imperfect, are adequate to greatly reduce the effect of these three diseases. However, the woeful state of health systems in most developing countries prevents these effective interventions from reaching those in greatest need, even where resources are available . . . Reliable provision of essential drugs is a strong indicator of the effectiveness of the health system" (Ruxin et al. 2005).

Although the additional financial commitment for medicines to treat these diseases is welcomed and necessary, funding is never the only constraint and is now, often, not the major constraint. Other constraints to improving access to medicines include inadequate infrastructure in facilities such as clinics, hospitals, pharmacies, and laboratories and a lack of trained staff and equipment for those facilities.

2.5 Current organizational roles in essential medicines

Organizations that are active in the essential medicines field may be useful points of contact. Numerous organizations in the public and private sectors offer a range of experience in advocacy, in public policy development, and in education and technical assistance. Several of these organizations are discussed briefly in the following sections. Organizations (such as the World Bank, the regional development banks, the Global Fund to Fight AIDS, Tuberculosis and Malaria, and aid agencies in Europe and the United States) that primarily finance development projects, including pharmaceutical programs, are discussed in Chapter 14.

WHO and other UN agencies

WHO's Department of Essential Medicines and Pharmaceutical Policies has played a leading role in promoting the essential medicines concept. WHO publishes documents on practices and methods as well as the *Essential Medicines Monitor* newsletter on current developments around the world. It convenes expert committees, holds workshops and training sessions worldwide, and has supported some country-specific pharmaceutical management programs, largely with funds provided by interested donors.

WHO's Department of Essential Medicines and Pharmaceutical Policies is also responsible for promoting pharmaceutical quality, providing information on safety and efficacy, and convening an expert committee that revises the Model List of Essential Medicines every two to three years, and now another list specifically for children's medicines. It is responsible for the quality certification scheme and good manufacturing practices standards. In addition, its prequalification program plays a major role in promoting quality medicines through evaluation and inspection activities and by building national capacity for sustainable manufacturing and quality monitoring.

Other WHO programs dealing with specific health areas, such as diarrhea, immunizations, and HIV/AIDS, have interests in essential medicines. The WHO regional offices and individual country programs often have additional technical staff in advisory positions.

The Pan American Health Organization is WHO's regional office for the Americas. Its technical pharmaceutical management staff collaborates with ministries of health, social security agencies, and other governmental and nongovernmental institutions to strengthen national and local health systems. Other regional offices, in the Eastern Mediterranean, Africa, Europe, the Western Pacific, and South East Asia, contribute to supporting and managing essential medicines activities in their regions.

UNICEF is actively involved in program and project development internationally and at the country level. Headquarters activities include technical supervision, design, and support of country-level programs ranging from large-scale procurement (through its Supply Division, based in Copenhagen) to strategies for the purchase, distribution, and use of medical supplies. In some countries, UNICEF coordinates medicine procurement and distribution for public health programs receiving Global Fund grants.

The Interagency Pharmaceutical Coordination Group includes senior pharmaceutical advisers from WHO, the World Bank, the Joint UN Programme on HIV/AIDS (UNAIDS), the UN Population Fund (UNFPA), and UNICEF. The group, which meets every six months, coordinates the pharmaceutical policies underlying their technical advice to partner countries and plans and coordinates the preparation of interagency statements and technical documents.

In 2002, the UN Secretary-General commissioned the UN's Millennium Project to develop an action plan for the world to achieve the Millennium Development Goals, which were established in 2000. The eight Millennium Development Goals, which have a target date of 2015, range from halving extreme poverty to promoting gender equality. The goals were agreed to by the world's countries and have formed the basis for a remarkable worldwide effort to improve the lives of those living in extreme poverty. Pharmaceutical management is a prominent component in achieving several of the goals, such as reducing child mortality, improving maternal health, and combating HIV/AIDS and other diseases.

Nongovernmental organizations

Health Action International is an association of NGOs founded in 1982 "working to increase access to essential medicines and improve their rational use." HAI and local and regional affiliates, such as Acción Internacional para la Salud, are focal points for campaigns on essential medicines action by governments and UN agencies and against industry products and practices that counter the concept.

Healthy Skepticism, previously known as the Medical Lobby for Appropriate Marketing, was formed in 1983 in Australia. The organization tracks inappropriate and misleading promotion of pharmaceutical products in developed and developing countries and encourages the use of accurate and consistent information about pharmaceuticals to improve health-related decision making. The organization's AdWatch program publicizes techniques used in pharmaceutical advertising. Healthy Skepticism has been a stimulus for other groups to monitor advertising and promotion of pharmaceuticals and other medical products. It has also influenced multinational corporations to modify their promotional practices.

The International Network for the Rational Use of Drugs works through national groups representing individuals from ministries of health, universities, NGOs, and private-sector institutions to understand local medicine-use problems and create reproducible activities that improve medicine use. INRUD's interdisciplinary focus links clinical and social sciences and emphasizes the behavioral aspects of medicine use, particularly as they concern providers and consumers, the promotion of well-designed research studies, and the sharing of experiences and technical expertise among participating individuals. INRUD also promotes cooperation among donors interested in funding activities that contribute to these objectives. The INRUD secretariat at Management Sciences for Health (MSH) is the coordinating body for the country core groups and publishes an annual newsletter, *INRUD News* (www.inrud.org).

The International Society of Drug Bulletins (ISDB) is an association of independent and official medicine information bulletins that provides the medical community with the most current information on individual medicines free from funding and the influence of the pharmaceutical industry. ISDB helps countries develop independent, unbiased medicine information bulletins and facilitates cooperation among countries in promoting independent medicine information (see Chapter 34).

Through its Center for Pharmaceutical Management, the nonprofit organization MSH is involved in pharmaceutical sector assessments and analysis, research, technical assistance, training, and publications to improve health through the rational use of medicines. MSH staff members work with international agencies and other NGOs, as well as directly with the public and private sectors in many countries. MSH produces training materials, software for pharmaceutical management, and publications such as this manual and the widely recognized *International Drug Price Information Guide*.

The International Pharmaceutical Federation (FIP) is a global organization comprised of 122 national associations of pharmacists and pharmaceutical scientists and 4,000 individual members. FIP advocates globally on behalf of the role of the pharmacist in the health care system. FIP is active in promoting good pharmacy practice and pharmacy education and gathering and disseminating important data on the profession; a key resource is the *2009 FIP Global Pharmacy Workforce and Migration Report*.

The U.S. Pharmacopeia (USP) is the official public standards–setting authority for prescription and over-the-counter medicines manufactured or sold in the United States. USP sets standards for the quality, purity, strength, and consistency of these products, which are recognized and used in more than 130 countries. USP also works in developing countries to improve pharmaceutical quality and the information available on medicines.

Médecins Sans Frontières (MSF), the humanitarian medical organization, started its Campaign for Access to Essential Medicines in 1999 to advocate for better access and lower prices of essential medicines at the local, national, and international levels. An example of MSF's work is the annual update of *Untangling the Web of Price Reductions: A Pricing Guide for the Purchase of ARVs for Developing Countries*.

As noted in Chapter 8, missions and other NGOs provide a substantial portion of health care and pharmaceutical supply services in many countries. The Ecumenical Pharmaceutical Network (EPN) works to strengthen the medicine-related activities of faith-based health care organizations in Africa. At the international level, the EPN acts as an advocate for access to medicines and a clearinghouse for information.

Regulatory bodies

The International Conference of Drug Regulatory Authorities is a biennial forum of officials from national regulatory authorities. Its principal concerns include mechanisms to guard against substandard, counterfeit, and dangerous products. It also supports WHO's certification scheme and guiding principles for small regulatory authorities.

The International Conference on Harmonization (ICH) of Technical Requirements for Registration of Pharmaceuticals for Human Use is a collaborative effort by the regulatory authorities of the European Union, the United States, and Japan to harmonize technical issues related to the registration of pharmaceuticals in these countries. The conference also makes recommendations on how to achieve greater harmonization around the world in the interpretation and application of related technical guidelines and requirements. The ICH norms do not always fully reflect the needs and capabilities of developing countries; however, WHO promotes developing-country interests by serving in an observer capacity, and the ICH Global Cooperation Group works with drug regulatory authorities in nonmember countries to facilitate the harmonization process in all countries.

Industry organizations

Most countries have individual national associations that represent manufacturers, distributors, and private pharmacies. These associations are intended primarily to protect members' interests, but they provide support to selected activities, such as training, local publications, and community medicine outlets in some countries. The IFPMA is an international advocacy group formed of many national and regional pharmaceutical manufacturers' associations and companies; it prepares position papers for the industry, testifies before international organizations, acts as a public-relations resource for the industry, and occasionally undertakes educational projects, such as quality-control training for developing-country staff. The International Federation of Pharmaceutical Wholesalers plays a similar role with respect to pharmaceutical distributors.

2.6 Clients, governments, producers, and beyond: changes in the pharmaceutical field

A review of the changes in the pharmaceutical field over the last forty years may suggest that a new symmetry among its players is on the horizon; however, a look at the future suggests a continuing process of evolution.

The evolving pharmaceutical industry

As noted previously, the multinational pharmaceutical industry has become less hostile toward some national and international pharmaceutical policy initiatives in recent decades, while focusing more on intellectual property issues. One reason for the shift in industry strategy has been the declining rate of pharmaceutical product innovation. Research-based companies are less confident that they can build their future on a regular flow of innovative new medicines; regulatory authorities have more difficulty approving new medicines to be marketed in their countries; and some medicines have been withdrawn from the market because of safety issues, such as the anti-inflammatory drug Vioxx (rofecoxib). For example, although the U.S. Food and Drug Administration (FDA) approved an average of eighty-three new medicines per year between 1998 and 2002, only one-third were new chemical entities. Over that same period, the FDA granted priority review to no more than seven medicines per year that represented a treatment advance, and the only real "breakthroughs" were usually "last-ditch treatments" for rare conditions not responding to other therapy (Angell 2004). Such medicines were likely to be used only occasionally and would not provide a significant income for the innovator company. As for safety issues, of thirteen new medicines that were removed from the U.S. market for safety reasons over a decade, not one left a significant therapeutic gap (Sigelman 2002). In the case of Vioxx, estimates are that it led to between 88,000 and 139,000 heart attacks in the United States that would not otherwise have occurred (Graham et al. 2005). With fewer new medicines emerging that carry the promise of major revenues, and with the occasional safety disaster, the industry today hesitates to rely on product innovation alone to assure a robust future as much as it once did. As a result, most major pharmaceutical developers are evaluating their research and development practices and are considering changing their current development paradigm (Kaitin 2010).

Another reason for a shift in industry policy is that developed countries have become increasingly critical of pharmaceutical prices and expenditure. Many countries have imposed rigid price controls on medicines or limits on the permitted cost of a course of treatment or instituted other interventions to control medicine prices (see Chapter 9 on pharmaceutical pricing policies). Pharmaceutical companies now must not only persuade doctors to prescribe their products but also convince critical therapeutics committees and pharmacy benefit managers that their medicines are sufficiently cost-effective to merit a place in treatment manuals and reimbursement lists—examples of the principle of essential medicines in practice.

New industry attitudes have also come as a result of structural changes in the pharmaceutical industry itself. Seeking to develop new business models to compensate for market obstacles in industrialized countries, many companies have entered once unfamiliar areas; for example, some research-based companies have started (or restarted) producing generic medicines, either by diversifying their own activities or by acquiring established generic manufacturers.

Intellectual property laws

The issue of access to medicines for HIV/AIDS, TB, and malaria has had an impact on international trade activities. Activists working to improve affordability of ARVs in developing countries first highlighted the negative implications of the World Trade Organization's Agreement on Trade-Related Aspects of Intellectual Property Rights (TRIPS) for access to essential medicines in developing countries, resulting in the development of the Doha Declaration, which addresses the right of all countries to protect the health of their citizens (see Chapter 3).

The TRIPS agreement may make it difficult for resource-limited countries to get access to new medicines at affordable prices. Although certain flexibilities were included in the agreement to help countries circumvent the intellectual property restrictions and accommodate their public health needs, without the necessary technical expertise, countries have found it difficult to interpret the laws and implement the appropriate policy mechanisms; however, governments are addressing this issue. For example, the regional group representing countries of East, Central, and Southern Africa created a model national pharmaceutical policy that addresses ways for member countries to incorporate these flexibilities into their policies.

Public-private pharmaceutical initiatives

For a long time, the private and public pharmaceutical sectors worked in relative isolation from each another; contact was formal, critical, and sometimes hostile. In the final years of the twentieth century, however, a number of international public-private partnerships were developed to create positive and innovative collaboration in research, development, and distribution, especially in serving the needs of developing countries. Promising advances are emerging, particularly through initiatives under the auspices of the United Nations and its specialized agencies, such as WHO. Examples include the Global Alliance for TB Drug Development and the Medicines for Malaria Venture. More time is needed to determine the long-term value of these partnerships, but increasing evidence suggests that such public-private initiatives can be productive.

Globalization and the Internet

No more than fifty years ago, the world remained rigidly divided into nation-states, each with its own specific approach to its own specific problems; however, the process of globalization has quickly broken down that compartmentalization. Many companies now operate worldwide, developing policies and conducting activities that can only partially be controlled by national governments; in fact, some corporations have greater financial resources than many of the governments with which they do business.

The Internet is an example of a worldwide activity that largely escapes national control. On the one hand, the Internet allows users to circumvent undesirable practices such as government censorship, but on the other hand, it facilitates activities that hurt society at large, for example, the dishonest advertising and sale of ineffective and dangerous medicines. Drug regulatory authorities and others have been working to address the issue of pharmaceuticals being sold through the Internet, as well as on ways to increase access to reliable information through the Internet (for example, see WHO/IMPACT 2009; WHO 2001a, 2002).

Ongoing policy changes

The changes in the political and economic environment discussed in this chapter mean that pharmaceutical management must also adapt to new opportunities and challenges.

Of the tools and concepts described throughout *MDS-3*, some originated in industrialized countries, others in the developing world, and others in the international community. Many have outgrown their origins, and the ideas and experiences are increasingly becoming common ground for solving important pharmaceutical management issues throughout the world while continuing to evolve as that world changes.

Although death and disability are always tragic, the rationale for national concern and action on essential medicines is driven by the large gap remaining between what we know and what we do. We know how medicines can help eliminate unnecessary and preventable deaths and disability, yet millions continue to die of TB, which is essentially curable with medical therapy. People living with HIV/AIDS can now extend their lives with ARV medicines, but more than half of those in need of treatment do not have access (UNAIDS 2009). Malaria, pneumonia, diarrhea, and hypertension are manageable with basic medicines, yet they continue to kill millions. Children are born unwanted and into poverty merely because low-cost family-planning supplies are unavailable.

The clear public health challenge is to continue to lead public policy makers and managers toward a consistent approach to essential medicines. The primary activity is to identify and attack the major problems that are amenable to solution with available resources. The strategies of many national pharmaceutical programs in less advantaged nations, and increasingly among decision makers in more-advantaged settings, are converging: first, to ensure that the basic medicines that save lives and improve health are available to all; second, to ensure that they are used appropriately; and third, to logically deal with the many medicines that are not essential to public health, but may play a limited or specialized role in health care. ∎

References and further readings

★ = Key readings.

Angell, M. 2004. *The Truth about the Drug Companies.* New York: Random House.

Foster, S. D. 1991. Supply and Use of Essential Drugs in Sub-Saharan Africa: Some Issues and Possible Solutions. *Social Science and Medicine* 32:1201–18.

Graham, D. J., D. Campen, R. Hui, M. Spence, C. Cheetham, G. Levy, S. Shoor, and W. Ray. 2005. Risk of Acute Myocardial Infarction and Sudden Cardiac Death in Patients Treated with Cyclo-oxygenase 2 Selective and Non-selective Non-steroidal Anti-inflammatory Drugs. *Lancet* 365(9458):475–81.

Homedes, N., and A. Ugalde. 2006. Improving Access to Pharmaceuticals in Brazil and Argentina. *Health Policy and Planning* 21(2): 123–31.

Kaitin, K. I. 2010. Deconstructing the Drug Development Process: The New Face of Innovation. *Clinical Pharmacology and Therapeutics* 87(3):356–61.

★ Laing R., B. Waning, A. Gray, N. Ford, and E. 't Hoen. 2003. 25 Years of the WHO Essential Medicines Lists: Progress and Challenges. *Lancet* 361:1723–9.

Mangham, L. J., and K. Hanson. 2010. Scaling Up in International Health: What Are the Key Issues? *Health Policy and Planning* 25:85–96.

Quick, J. D., H. V. Hogerzeil, G. Velasquez, and L. Rago. 2002. Twenty-five Years of Essential Medicines. *Bulletin of the World Health Organization* 80(11):913–4. <http://www.who.int/bulletin/archives/80(11)913.pdf>

Ruxin J., J. E. Paluzzi, P. A. Wilson, Y. Tozan, M. Kruk, and A. Teklehaimanot. 2005. Emerging Consensus in HIV/AIDS, Malaria, Tuberculosis, and Access to Essential Medicines. *Lancet* 365(9459):618–21.

Sigelman, D. W. 2002. Dangerous Medicine. *The American Prospect* (Online) 13(17). <http://www.prospect.org/cs/articles?article=dangerous_medicine>

Smith, M. K., and S. Tickell. 2003. The Essential Drugs Concept Is Needed Now More Than Ever. *Transactions of the Royal Society of Tropical Medicine and Hygiene* 97(1):2–5.

UN (United Nations). 2010. *The Millennium Development Goals Report 2010.* New York: UN.

UNAIDS (Joint United Nations Programme on HIV/AIDS). 2009. *AIDS Epidemic Update 2009.* Geneva: UNAIDS. <http://data.unaids.org/pub/Report/2009/JC1700_Epi_Update_2009_en.pdf>

★ UN Millennium Project. 2005. *Prescription for Healthy Development: Increasing Access to Medicines. Report of the Task Force on HIV/AIDS, Malaria, TB, and Access to Essential Medicines Working Group on Access to Essential Medicines.* Sterling, Va.: Earthcscan. <http://www.unmillenniumproject.org/documents/TF5-medicines-Complete.pdf>

★ WHO (World Health Organization). 2009. *Report of the 17th Expert Committee on the Selection and use of Essential Medicines: 23 to 27 March 2009.* Geneva: WHO. <http://www.who.int/selection_medicines/committees/expert/17/en/>

———. 2007. *The Selection and Use of Essential Medicines: Report of the WHO Expert Committee, 2007 (Including the 15th Model List of Essential Medicines).* Geneva: WHO. <http://www.who.int/medicines/publications/essentialmeds_committeereports/en/>

★ ———. 2004a. *The World Medicines Situation.* Geneva: WHO. <http://www.searo.who.int/LinkFiles/Reports_World_Medicines_Situation.pdf>

———. 2004b. *WHO Medicines Strategy: Countries at the Core 2004–2007.* Geneva: WHO. <http://whqlibdoc.who.int/hq/2004/WHO_EDM_2004.5.pdf>

———. 2003. *Introduction to Drug Utilization Research.* Geneva: WHO. <http://www.who.int/medicines/areas/quality_safety/safety_efficacy/Drug%20utilization%20research.pdf>

———. 2002. WHO and Top Publishers Today Launch "Access to Research" Internet Initiative for Developing Countries. Press Release WHO/7. Geneva: WHO. <https://apps.who.int/inf/en/pr-2002-07.html>

———. 2001a. *Pharmaceuticals and the Internet: Drug Regulatory Authorities' Perspective.* Geneva: WHO. <http://whqlibdoc.who.int/hq/2001/a74987.pdf>

———. 2001b. *WHO Global Strategy for Containment of Antimicrobial Resistance.* Geneva: WHO. <http://www.who.int/csr/resources/publications/drugresist/WHO_CDS_CSR_DRS_2001_2_EN/en/>

WHO/IMPACT (World Health Organization/International Medical Products Anti-Counterfeiting Taskforce). 2009. Overview of IMPACT Working Groups' Documents and Activities. Geneva: WHO. <http://www.who.int/impact/activities/overviewofIMPACTworkingdocs.pdf>

Annex 2-1   Useful contact information

Affordable Medicines Facility–Malaria
Global Fund to Fight AIDS, Tuberculosis and Malaria
Chemin de Blandonnet 8
1214 Vernier
Geneva, Switzerland
Telephone: +41 58 791 17 00
Fax: +41 58 791 17 01
E-mail: amfmconsult@theglobalfund.org
http://www.theglobalfund.org/en/amfm

AIDS Medicines and Diagnostics Service
HIV/AIDS Department
World Health Organization
20 Avenue Appia
CH 1211 Geneva 27 Switzerland
Telephone: +41 22 791 21 11
Fax: +41 22 791 31 11
E-mail: amds@who.int
http://www.who.int/hiv/amds/en

Alliance for the Prudent Use of Antibiotics
75 Kneeland Street
Boston, Massachusetts 02111 USA
Telephone: +1 617 636 0966
Fax: +1 617 636 3999
E-mail: apua@tufts.edu
http://www.tufts.edu/med/apua

Campaign for Access to Essential Medicines
Médecins Sans Frontières
Rue de Lausanne 78
P.O. Box 116
CH 1211 Geneva 21 Switzerland
Telephone: +41 22 849 84 05
Fax: +41 22 849 84 04
E-mail: access@msf.org
http://www.msfaccess.org

Clinton Health Access Initiative
William J. Clinton Foundation
55 W. 125th Street
New York, New York 10027 USA
Telephone: +1 212 348 8882
Fax: +1 212 348 5147
http://www.clintonfoundation.org/what-we-do/clinton-hiv-aids-initiative

Consumers International
24 Highbury Crescent
London N5 1RX United Kingdom
Telephone: +44 20 7226 6663
Fax: +44 20 7354 0607
Additional offices in Africa, Malaysia, and Chile
http://www.consumersinternational.org

Ecumenical Pharmaceutical Network
P.O. Box 738-00200
Nairobi, Kenya
Telephone: +254 20 444 4832/444 5020
Fax: +254 20 444 1090
Mobile: +254 72 430 1755
E-mail: info@epnetwork.org
http://www.epnetwork.org

Euro Health Group
Tinghøjvej 77
2860 Søborg, Denmark
Telephone: +45 3969 6888
Fax: +45 3969 5888
E-mail: eurohealth@ehg.dk
http://ehg.dk

Global Drug Facility
Green Light Committee (Stop TB Partnership)
Stop TB Partnership Secretariat
World Health Organization
HTM/STB/TBP
20 Avenue Appia
CH 1211 Geneva 27 Switzerland
Telephone: +41 22 791 46 59
Fax: +41 22 791 48 86
E-mail: gdf@who.int
http://www.stoptb.org/gdf
E-mail: glc_secretariat@who.int
http://www.who.int/tb/challenges/mdr/greenlightcommittee/en/index.html

Global Fund to Fight AIDS, Tuberculosis and Malaria
Geneva Secretariat
Chemin de Blandonnet 8
1214 Vernier
Geneva, Switzerland
Telephone: +41 58 791 17 00
Fax: +41 58 791 17 01
E-mail: info@theglobalfund.org
http://www.theglobalfund.org/

Health Action International Africa
Kabarnet Lane
P.O. Box 66054-00800
Nairobi, Kenya
Telephone: +254 20 386 0434/5/6
Fax: +254 20 386 0437
E-mail: info@haiafrica.org
http://www.haiafrica.org

Health Action International Europe
Overtoom 60/II
1054 HK Amsterdam, The Netherlands
Telephone: +31 20 683 3684
Fax: +31 20 685 5002
E-mail: info@haiweb.org
http://www.haiweb.org

Health Action International Latin America
(Acción Internacional para la Salud)
Apdo 41-128 Urb Javier Prado
Calle Mario Florian Mz 3 Lote 22, San Borja
Lima 41 Peru
Telephone/fax: +51 1 346 1502
E-mail: infoais@aislac.org
http://www.aislac.org

Healthy Skepticism
34 Methodist Street
Willunga, South Australia 5172 Australia
Telephone/fax: +61 8 8557 1040
http://www.healthyskepticism.org

HIV/AIDS Alliance
UK Secretariat / International HIV/AIDS Alliance
1st and 2nd Floors, Preece House
91-101 Davigdor Road
Hove BN3 1RE United Kingdom
Telephone: +44 1273 718 900
Fax: +44 1273 718 901
E-mail: mail@aidsalliance.org
http://www.aidsalliance.org

International Conference on Harmonization (ICH) of Technical Requirements for Registration of Pharmaceuticals for Human Use
ICH Secretariat
c/o IFPMA
15 Chemin Louis-Dunant
P.O. Box 195
CH 1211 Geneva 20 Switzerland
Telephone: +41 22 338 32 06
Fax: +41 22 338 32 30
E-mail: admin@ich.org
http://www.ich.org/index.xl

International Federation of Pharmaceutical Manufacturers and Associations (IFPMA)
15 Chemin Louis-Dunant
P.O. Box 195
CH 1211 Geneva 20 Switzerland
Telephone: +41 22 338 32 00
Fax: +41 22 338 32 99
E-mail: info@ifpma.org
http://www.ifpma.org

International Network for the Rational Use of Drugs
c/o Management Sciences for Health
4301 N. Fairfax Drive, Suite 400
Arlington, Virginia 22203 USA
Telephone: +1 703 524 6575
Fax: +1 703 524 7898
E-mail: inrud@msh.org
http://www.inrud.org

International Pharmaceutical Federation (FIP)
Andries Bickerweg 5
2517 JP The Hague, The Netherlands
Telephone: +31 70 302 1970
Fax: +31 70 302 1999
E-mail: fip@fip.org
http://www.fip.org

International Society of Drug Bulletins
103 Hertford Road
London N2 9BX United Kingdom
http://www.isdbweb.org

Karolinska Institutet
Department of Public Health Sciences
Division of International Health (IHCAR)
SE-17177 Stockholm, Sweden
Telephone: +46 8 524 800 00
Fax: +46 8 31 11 01
http://www.phs.ki.se/ihcar

Management Sciences for Health
Center for Pharmaceutical Management
4301 N. Fairfax Drive, Suite 400
Arlington, Virginia 22203 USA
Telephone: +1 703 524 6575
Fax: +1 703 524 7898
E-mail: cpm@msh.org
http://www.msh.org

Médecins Sans Frontières
Rue de Lausanne 78
CP 116-1211 Geneva 21 Switzerland
Telephone: +41 22 849 84 00
Fax: +41 22 849 84 04
http://www.msf.org

Medicus Mundi International Network
Murbacherstrasse 34
CH 4013 Basel, Switzerland
Telephone: +41 61 383 18 11 (Monday–Wednesday)
E-mail: office@medicusmundi.org
http://www.medicusmundi.org

Pan American Health Organization
WHO Regional Office for the Americas
525 23rd Street, N.W.
Washington, D.C. 20037 USA
Telephone: +1 202 974 3000
Fax: +1 202 974 3663
http://www.paho.org

Roll Back Malaria Partnership
(Secretariat hosted at WHO)
20 Avenue Appia
CH 1211 Geneva 27 Switzerland
Telephone: +41 22 791 58 69
Fax: +41 22 791 15 87
E-mail: inforbm@who.int
http://www.rollbackmalaria.org

UNAIDS
20 Avenue Appia
CH 1211 Geneva 27 Switzerland
Telephone: +41 22 791 36 66
Fax: +41 22 791 41 87
http://www.unaids.org/en

UNICEF
UNICEF House
Essential Drugs Unit
2 United Nations Plaza
New York, New York 10017 USA
Telephone: +1 212 326 7000
Fax: +1 212 887 7465
http://www.unicef.org

UNITAID
UNITAID Secretariat
World Health Organization
20 Avenue Appia
CH 1211 Geneva 27 Switzerland
Telephone: +41 22 791 55 03
Fax: +41 22 791 48 90
E-mail: unitaid@who.int
http://www.unitaid.eu

U.S. Pharmacopoeia
12601 Twinbrook Parkway
Rockville, Maryland 20852 USA
Telephone: +1 301 881 0666
http://www.usp.org

U.S. President's Emergency Plan for AIDS Relief
Office of the Global AIDS Coordinator
SA-29, 2nd Floor
2201 C Street, N.W.
Washington, D.C. 20522 USA
Telephone: +1 202 663 2440
http://www.pepfar.gov

World Bank's Multi-Country HIV/AIDS Program
The World Bank
1818 H Street, N.W.
Washington, D.C. 20433 USA
Telephone: +1 202 458 0606
Fax: +1 202 522 7396
E-mail: actafrica@worldbank.org
http://go.worldbank.org/I3A0B15ZN0

World Health Organization Collaborating Centre for Drug Statistics Methodology
Norwegian Institute of Public Health
P.O. Box 4404 Nydalen
N-0403 Oslo, Norway
Telephone: +47 21 07 81 60
Fax: +47 21 07 81 46
E-mail: whocc@fhi.no
http://www.whocc.no

World Health Organization Department of Essential Medicines and Pharmaceutical Policies
HSS/EMP
20 Avenue Appia
CH 1211 Geneva 27 Switzerland
Telephone: +41 22 791 21 11
Fax: +41 22 791 47 30
E-mail: empinfo@who.int
http://www.who.int/medicines/en

World Health Organization Eastern Mediterranean Regional Office
Abdul Razzak Al Sanhouri Street
P.O. Box 7608, Nasr City Cairo 11371 Egypt
Telephone: +20 2 2276 5000
Fax: +20 2 2670 2492
E-mail: inf@emro.who.int
http://www.emro.who.int

World Health Organization Regional Office for Africa
Cité du Djoué, P.O. Box 06
Brazzaville, Republic of Congo
Telephone: +47 241 39100 or +242 770 02 02
Fax: +47 241 39503
E-mail: regafro@afro.who.int
http://www.afro.who.int

World Health Organization Regional Office for Europe
Scherfigsvej 8
DK 2100 Copenhagen Ø Denmark
Telephone: +45 3917 1717
Fax: +45 3917 1818
E-mail: postmaster@euro.who.int
http://www.euro.who.int

World Health Organization Regional Office for South East Asia
World Health House
Indraprastha Estate
Mahatma Gandhi Marg
New Delhi 110 002 India
Telephone: +91 11 2337 0804
Fax: +91 11 2337 0197
E-mail: registry@searo.who.int
http://searo.who.int

World Health Organization Regional Office for the Western Pacific
P.O. Box 2932
1000 Manila, Philippines
Telephone: +63 2 528 8001
Fax: +63 2 521 1036
E-mail: pio@wpro.who.int
http://www.wpro.who.int

| Part I: Policy and economic issues | Part II: Pharmaceutical management | Part III: Management support systems |

Policy and legal framework
1 Toward sustainable access to medicines
2 Historical and institutional perspectives
3 Intellectual property and access to medicines
4 National medicine policy
5 Traditional and complementary medicine policy
6 Pharmaceutical legislation and regulation
7 Pharmaceutical production policy
8 Pharmaceutical supply strategies
Financing and sustainability

CHAPTER 3

Intellectual property and access to medicines

SUMMARY

In an era of increasingly globalized trade, pharmaceutical patents play a key role in the availability and affordability of medicines, as shown by the conflict over access to anti-retroviral medicines for people living with HIV/AIDS in resource-limited countries. Patent protection can also be a contentious issue in high-income countries, when high medicine prices impede access to effective treatment.

Governments grant intellectual property rights as an incentive to produce inventions that will benefit society as a whole. The varied extent of protection and enforcement of these around the world became a source of tension in international economic relations, leading to international negotiations within the World Trade Organization (WTO). These negotiations resulted in the Agreement on Trade-Related Aspects of Intellectual Property Rights (TRIPS), which is a set of trade rules meant to introduce a global system to monitor and enforce the protection of intellectual property rights among WTO members.

TRIPS covers five essential issues—

- How to apply basic principles of the trading system and other international intellectual property agreements
- How to give adequate protection to intellectual property rights
- How to enforce such rights adequately in a country's own territories
- How to settle disputes on intellectual property among members of the WTO
- What special transitional arrangements to apply during the period when the new system is being introduced

Developing countries expressed concerns regarding the possible effect of TRIPS, including the following—

- TRIPS treats medicines like any other commodity, but medicines are not ordinary consumer products.
- Prices will likely be higher for new medicines in countries with no previous patent protection.
- Generic competition will be delayed in countries with a previous patent term less than twenty years.
- The local pharmaceutical industry could be weakened, and dependence on developed countries may increase.
- TRIPS may not improve research and development (R&D) decisions regarding treatments for the diseases common in poor countries.

The minimum standards required by TRIPS resulted in developing countries losing some capacity to regulate pharmaceutical patents and control the cost of medicines; however, the agreement left some flexibility for them to take measures to protect public health. Because the provisions relating to patents and pharmaceutical regulation are confusing and contentious, regulators must acquire the relevant technical expertise to use these flexibilities within TRIPS to improve access to medicines.

The international rules regarding intellectual property are evolving quickly. Developing countries must actively participate in discussions of the future of the intellectual property system to ensure its appropriateness for countries at very different levels of development. As the rules evolve, their impact must be properly understood if policies are to be based on relevant evidence.

3.1   The global pharmaceutical market

The international trade in pharmaceuticals has expanded dramatically since 1980. During the 1990s, trade grew substantially faster than production. High-income industrialized countries used to dominate international trade in pharmaceuticals. In 1999, they accounted for 93 percent of global exports by value. Between 1980 and 1999, middle-income countries' share of world exports fell, while the export share of some low-income countries, such as India, Pakistan, and Indonesia, more than doubled, from 1.1 percent to 2.9 percent. High-income countries also dominated imports. During the same period, their shares increased, and the shares of both low- and middle-income countries in world imports dropped significantly (WHO 2004).

With the exception of Japan, the countries that contribute most to world trade are also the world's major producers: the United States, the United Kingdom, Germany, and France. Japan, the world's second-largest producer, continues to produce primarily for its domestic market.

Sales figures by value from 2005 indicate that North America, Japan, and Europe accounted for almost 90 percent of the world's pharmaceutical purchases (IMS Health 2006). So although sub-Saharan Africa, for example, represents a huge proportion of the disease burden relative to the rest of the world, its global pharmaceutical market share is only 1 to 2 percent (Scheffler and Pathania 2005; CIPIH 2006), which generally makes it an unattractive target market for manufacturers. However, the number of emerging pharmaceutical markets increased from seven in 2006 to seventeen in 2010, with China expected to become the third-largest market by 2011—up from eighth-largest in 2006 (Campbell and Chui 2010).

Categories of pharmaceuticals

The world pharmaceutical market consists of several categories, characterized by different degrees of market competition. Innovative pharmaceutical products that are patented (*original brands*) are protected from competition for the life of the patent in the countries that recognize the patent. Legal competition is limited to medicines that are *therapeutically equivalent* (used to treat the same clinical indication) but that have either a different composition or a different manufacturing process from the original brand. At the other end of the spectrum are pharmaceuticals known as *generics*. Generally, generic pharmaceutical products are the chemical equivalent of the original brand product that are usually manufactured without a license from the originator company. This large category includes pharmaceuticals whose patents or other exclusivity rights have expired, pharmaceuticals that have never been patented, and copies of patented pharmaceuticals in countries where the drug is not patented or where a compulsory license has been granted (see Section 3.2). The legality of copying patented products depends on the manufacturing country's patent legislation.

Generic medicines are usually sold under their generic names and may be manufactured and marketed by many companies. This market is highly price competitive because buyers can choose among several sources of chemically identical medicines. On the manufacturing side, the distinction between originator companies and generics manufacturers is often blurred. In some cases, major research-based international companies have generics manufacturing subsidiaries producing "branded generics." For some medicines, these products account for a large share of the world's market in generics.

Another category comprises traditional or complementary medicine, which includes herbal medications. The use of herbal products has increased, especially in developed countries; however, regulation governing the quality, sale, and use of such medicines varies widely. Countries are recognizing the large role that traditional medicine plays in health care, and more countries are addressing the challenges of including traditional medicine in national health policy, including protecting indigenous knowledge and applying intellectual property rights. Chapter 5 discusses traditional and complementary medicines.

Role of patents in the pharmaceutical sector

In an era of increasingly globalized trade, pharmaceutical product patents play a key role in the availability and affordability of medicines, as shown by the conflict over access to antiretroviral medicines for people living with HIV/AIDS in resource-limited countries. Patent protection can also be a contentious issue in high-income countries, when high prices for branded medicines impede access to effective treatment.

A *patent* is an exclusive right that a government gives to an inventor, preventing others from making, using, offering to sell, selling, or importing an invention or inventive process for a defined period. The patent does not give an inventor the right to make, use, or sell the invention. The inventor may have to comply with other laws and regulations to make use of the claimed invention. For example, a pharmaceutical company may obtain a patent on a new medicine, but it will be unable to market the medicine in a country without the government's regulatory approval.

The patent gives the inventor the opportunity to recoup his or her investment in R&D in exchange for publicly disclosing the underlying information about the invention. The concept behind patenting medicines is that the exclusive marketing rights provided by a patent allow high prices during the patent term, which generate profits that fund the R&D necessary to create and bring new pharmaceutical products to the market. Therefore, patients who buy patented pharmaceuticals (or their employers, their insurers, or their governments) pay a premium that is in theory designed to support the research process. When a patent expires, generic products enter the market and force prices down through competition.

One of the functions of a patent is to serve as a financial incentive for creators of inventions that benefit society (CIPIH 2006). However, people living in developing countries and their governments have little purchasing power, which removes real incentive to the global private sector to invest in developing medicines that treat diseases endemic in developing countries—also known as tropical and neglected diseases. Section 3.5 discusses R&D issues.

Developing countries and nongovernmental organizations have argued that patents on pharmaceuticals in the developing world raise prices and thereby reduce access to lifesaving treatment. In contrast, the research-based pharmaceutical industry and many developed countries have argued that the larger problem in resource-limited countries is an insufficient health service infrastructure.

3.2 Globalization of intellectual property standards and access to medicines

Ideas and knowledge are increasingly important parts of trade. Most of the value of new medicines and other high-technology products lies in the amount of invention, innovation, research, design, and testing involved. Creators can be given the right to prevent others from using their inventions, designs, or other creations—and to use that right to negotiate payment in return from others using such intellectual property rights. These intellectual property rights, which include not only patents but also copyrights and trademarks, reward the results of innovation and creativity in many areas, including music, science, and authorship.

Governments give creators intellectual property rights as incentive to produce inventions that will benefit society as a whole. The extent of protection and enforcement of these rights varied widely around the world, and as the focus on intellectual property in trade intensified, these differences became a source of tension in international economic relations. New, internationally agreed-upon trade rules for intellectual property rights were viewed as a way to introduce more order and predictability and to settle disputes more systematically.

History and evolution of intellectual property rights for pharmaceuticals

Intellectual property rights were important to chemical firms in nineteenth-century Europe and to U.S. and European pharmaceutical companies in the twentieth century. Because these companies particularly wanted patent protection, they began lobbying governments on the design of such protection. Large companies focused more and more on the use of intellectual property rights as part of their business strategy, which gave them an increasingly greater incentive to influence how such rights evolved.

World Trade Organization agreements. In the 1980s, this context gave rise to collaboration among U.S., European, and Japanese companies, including pharmaceutical and chemical companies, in campaigning for the inclusion of an agreement on intellectual property rights in the WTO's Uruguay Round of Multilateral Trade Negotiations. (See Box 3-1 for information on the WTO.) Those negotiations produced the Agreement on Trade-Related Aspects of Intellectual Property Rights and the Agreement on Technical Barriers to Trade. From its origin in 1989 until it was finalized in 1994, TRIPS evolved into a detailed international agreement containing industrialized-country standards of intellectual property protection, requiring multilateral trade negotiations among all WTO members. The Agreement on Technical Barriers to Trade seeks to ensure that technical standards, testing, and certification procedures do not create unnecessary obstacles to trade. This agreement can affect the development of production capabilities in developing countries by affecting their ability to export.

WTO agreements, including TRIPS, are treaties that create international obligations among the members. TRIPS

Box 3-1
World Trade Organization

The World Trade Organization (WTO) is the international organization that deals with the rules of trade between nations at a global or near-global level. At the center of the organization are the agreements that the members comprising the majority of the world's trading countries or customs unions (158 members as of July 2008) negotiate and sign. These agreements provide the legal ground rules for international commerce. WTO membership requires nations to adopt the terms of the twenty-six existing agreements and mandates that members' national laws conform to the global standards. The content of the WTO's twenty-six agreements covers many aspects of national law related to trade in goods, services, and intellectual property.

The majority of the WTO's current agreements come from the 1986–94 negotiations called the Uruguay Round and earlier negotiations under the General Agreement on Tariffs and Trade. Although difficult to achieve with so many diverging points of view, the WTO generally makes decisions based on member consensus. The highest decision-making authority within the WTO is the Ministerial Conference, composed of members' ministers of trade, who meet at least once every two years to negotiate any matter under any of the multilateral trade agreements. Other meetings involving various committees, working groups, and special sessions occur between full meetings. The Council for Trade-Related Aspects of Intellectual Property Rights, which deals with TRIPS-related issues, reports directly to the WTO General Council. The World Health Organization (WHO) has an observer-status seat on the TRIPS council.

The WTO is unique as an international organization in that it has a dispute settlement body, the decisions of which are final and binding on members. This capacity gives the WTO the power to enforce trade rules.

Because many of the agreements have important implications for public health, WHO has established a new department called Trade, Foreign Policy, Diplomacy, and Health to promote greater policy coherence between trade and health policy, so that international trade and trade rules maximize health benefits and minimize health risks, especially for poor and vulnerable populations.

introduced intellectual property rules into the multilateral trading system for the first time and attempted to narrow the gaps in the way these rights are protected around the world and to bring them under common international rules. Consequently, TRIPS globalizes a set of intellectual property principles and harmonizes intellectual property regulation by establishing minimum levels of protection that each government has to give to the intellectual property of other WTO members. To the chemical and pharmaceutical companies that had been promoting it, TRIPS was a major step in the globalization of standards of protection for patents, copyrights, trade secrets, and trademarks.

Previously, patenting essential public goods such as medicines and food was considered contrary to the public interest. When the WTO launched the Uruguay Round of trade negotiations in 1986, more than fifty countries were not granting product patents on pharmaceuticals. After TRIPS, all WTO member countries had to reform their domestic intellectual property laws to conform to the new obligations of the agreement.

Many questions arose regarding the (mainly developing) countries that seemingly had little to gain by agreeing to these terms of trade. Lacking intellectual property experts in their WTO delegations, most developing states did not have a clear understanding of the ramifications of the TRIPS negotiations. Some countries were interested in agreeing to TRIPS in exchange for concessions that would expand their exports of agricultural or textile products. However, because TRIPS required countries to recognize patents on pharmaceutical products—often for the first time—it had implications for both the cost of patented medicines and the long-term outlook of the generics industries in those countries. In addition, TRIPS covers many more issues relevant to public health, including traditional medicines, biotechnology, genetic materials, medical devices, and technology transfer.

The Doha Declaration. Although one of TRIPS' stated goals was to reduce tensions arising from intellectual property protection, patent protection for pharmaceuticals and its effects on public health—and particularly access to medicines—has remained a highly controversial issue. Debate in developing countries reflected growing concerns about the implications of TRIPS regarding access to medicines, which were seen as signs of the conflict between the recognition of intellectual property rights and essential public health objectives.

Developing countries expressed concerns regarding TRIPS' possible effect that included the following—

- TRIPS treats medicines like any other commodity, but medicines are not ordinary consumer products.
- Prices will likely be higher for new medicines in countries with no previous patent protection.

- Generic competition will be delayed in countries with previous patent terms less than twenty years.
- The local pharmaceutical industry could be weakened, and dependence on developed countries may increase.
- TRIPS may not improve R&D decisions regarding treatments for the diseases common in poor countries.

The medicine access issue and related advocacy resulted in the Declaration on TRIPS and Public Health at the WTO Ministerial Conference in Doha in November 2001. The Doha Declaration, as it is known, affirms the right of developing countries to protect the health of their populations, declaring that TRIPS "can and should be interpreted and implemented in a manner supportive of WTO members' right to protect public health and, in particular, to promote access to medicines for all." The right to health is embedded in international, regional, and national human rights instruments, including the constitution of WHO, the United Nations Universal Declaration of Human Rights, and various national constitutions.

Despite initial resistance by some developed countries, the Doha Declaration was adopted by consensus. It is one of the important benchmarks in trade history, because it is regarded as elevating public health above trade with respect to national intellectual property law. In addition, the Doha Declaration resulted from the success of civil society in focusing attention on these issues and from developing countries' solidarity in standing up collectively for their concerns about the intellectual property regime under TRIPS.

The Doha Declaration was not intended to amend TRIPS. Rather, it aims to clarify the relationship between TRIPS and public health policies of WTO member countries and to confirm the rights retained under the agreement, particularly by defining the flexibility allowed in certain key policy areas. The declaration can make it easier for developing countries to adopt measures necessary to ensure access to health care without the fear of legal consequences. However, the Doha Declaration is not self-executing, and countries therefore need to make the legal amendments necessary to implement it. Developing countries in particular should be encouraged (and provided the relevant technical assistance) to review their legislation to ensure that they incorporate into national laws any flexibilities allowed by TRIPS to address public health concerns.

Key concepts related to TRIPS

TRIPS covers five essential issues—

- How to apply basic principles of the trading system and other international intellectual property agreements
- How to give adequate protection to intellectual property rights

- How to enforce those rights adequately in a country's own territories
- How to settle disputes on intellectual property among members of the WTO
- What special transitional arrangements to apply during the period when the new system is being introduced

TRIPS includes an enforcement mechanism through economic sanctions for countries that fail to comply with the minimum standards for protecting intellectual property rights. When intellectual property disputes between countries arise because of differences in the interpretation of TRIPS, the WTO provides a dispute settlement process that includes negotiation, dispute settlement decision making, and an appeal process. Trade sanctions may be imposed only if the dispute settlement process has run its course and the losing country has failed to comply with the decision.

As mentioned, TRIPS introduced minimum standards for protecting and enforcing nearly all forms of intellectual property rights, including those for pharmaceuticals. As a minimum-standards agreement, however, TRIPS allows members to protect intellectual property more extensively if they choose. Members are free to determine how best to implement the provisions of the agreement within their own legal system and practice (see Correa 2000). The key concepts for pharmaceuticals are described in the following subsections.

Patent protection. Under TRIPS, member countries must provide patent protection for a minimum of twenty years from the filing date of a patent application for any pharmaceutical product or process that fulfills the criteria of novelty, inventiveness, and usefulness. National legislation and practices define what can be patented, and countries must establish their own criteria for what constitutes a "new" and "inventive" product.

Countries should recognize that patentability standards that are too broad can contribute to extending the patent life of a new medicine through designating new or inventive uses as described above or different dosages. This practice is called *evergreening*. To limit this extension of rights to original patent holders, national patent legislation needs to ensure that public health needs are taken into account. Similarly, incremental innovation, or "me-too" drugs, is within the same chemical class as one or more other pharmaceutical products already on the market; however, the pharmaceutical industry feels that me-too drugs advance safety and efficacy and support the development of novel products (Wertheimer and Santella 2009).

Transitional arrangements. TRIPS provides transitional periods during which countries must bring their national legislation and practices into conformity with its provisions. The compliance dates for WTO members were 1996 for developed countries; 2000 for developing countries; 2005 for developing countries that had not introduced patents for pharmaceuticals before joining the WTO, such as India; and 2016 (for medicines only) and July 2013 for least-developed countries (LDCs) in recognition of these countries' economic, financial, administrative, and technological constraints to conforming.

Generic medicines. After a patent expires (or a license is issued), copies of a medicine can legally be made. These are called multisource medicines—or generics—and should be chemically equivalent to the original brand medicine. Promoting generic medicines within a country requires appropriate legislation and regulations, reliable quality-assurance capacity, professional and public acceptance of generic medicines, and economic incentives and information for both prescribers and consumers.

Under the TRIPS regime, a different manufacturing process for a chemically equivalent pharmaceutical product would be blocked if the originator company still held a product patent on the chemical entity. Currently, a different chemical entity may pose therapeutic competition to an existing medicine, and a different company may hold such a patent. In some cases, however, an originator company will place a patent not only on the chemical entities in the ingredients, but also on the resulting metabolite that produces the desirable therapeutic effect (Correa 2000). Such metabolite patents may block pharmaceuticals in the same therapeutic category if they share a common metabolic pathway.

Trade liberalization can increase competition and reduce prices for generic medicines that are already on the market. But inappropriately implementing TRIPS-compliant national legislation can delay new generic products, which can result in large economic costs. The prompt introduction of generic medicines can be facilitated by drafting appropriate legislation and regulations on patentability, such as using exceptions to permit early testing and approval of generics and compulsory licensing (see following subsections).

As an alternative to promoting generics, some brand-name pharmaceutical manufacturers have volunteered to lower their prices in certain markets (for example, selling certain medicines in developing countries at greatly reduced prices compared to prices in major markets); however, such programs usually feature multiple restrictions. Some companies have gone further by donating medicines for particular programs (see Chapter 15).

Compulsory licensing (TRIPS Article 31). As a provision of TRIPS, compulsory licensing occurs when a government authorizes the production of a patented product or the use of a patented process without the patent holder's consent as long as certain conditions are met, such as the license being used predominantly (that is, 51 percent) for the domestic market. The patent holder, however, retains intellectual property rights and "shall be paid adequate remuneration" according to the circumstances. In other words, compulsory licensing allows local manufacturers in resource-limited countries to make close-to-marginal-cost versions of patented medicines to address public health needs, if they give a royalty payment to the patent holder. Generally, the grant of a compulsory license requires prior negotiation with the patent holder. However, grounds for governments to grant compulsory licenses without any previous negotiation may include public interest, national emergencies such as epidemics, public noncommercial use, or remedying anticompetitive practices.

In the pharmaceutical sector, compulsory licenses have been used to stimulate price-lowering competition and to ensure the availability of needed medicines. For example, if a new product introduced to the market were to play an important role in public health, such as a vaccine against HIV/AIDS or malaria, a country's national law could grant a compulsory license under Article 31 of TRIPS. Compulsory licensing, however, is not always a solution for resource-limited countries. For instance, when prior authorization from the patent owner is required, as is the normal case, negotiations can be lengthy and complicated, and a country may not have the necessary legal expertise. In addition, the manufacturing process for a pharmaceutical product may be protected under a separate patent or as a trade secret. Finally, countries may lack the technical expertise or facilities necessary to copy and manufacture the product or to attain the economies of scale that make such a decision feasible (see Chapter 7 on production policy).

Despite the constraints, a country's comprehensive patent legislation should adequately provide for granting compulsory licenses to strengthen its position, even if the country rarely uses the provision. Now, most developed countries and many developing countries include compulsory licensing in their national legislation; for example, in 2010, Colombia successfully used the threat of compulsory licensing to reduce by two-thirds the price of Kaletra, an antiretroviral, while the United States has used the threat to mitigate anticompetitive situations.

Figure 3-1 shows the exact text from a compulsory license granted in Zambia in 2004.

Voluntary licensing (TRIPS Article 40). A voluntary license is an agreement negotiated between the patent holder and another company for manufacturing and marketing. TRIPS Article 40 authorizes the regulation of anticompetitive features of voluntary licenses. Regulation could favor export and regional production, nonexclusivity, technology-transfer requirements, access to confidential test data, and disclosure of reasonable royalty rates. Usually, efforts must first be made to obtain a voluntary license on reasonable terms and conditions before a party obtains a compulsory license (see Country Study 3-1).

Parallel importation (TRIPS Article 6). Parallel importation occurs when a third party, without the consent of the patent holder, imports a medicine that has already been put on the market abroad more cheaply by the patent holder or a licensee. The practice is based on the principle that the patent holder has been compensated through the first sale of the product and that further control over the resale of the product would unreasonably restrain trade and competition. In other words, having been paid, the patent holders are said to have "exhausted" their rights. If the importing country's patent system provides that the patent holder's right has been exhausted when the patented product has been placed on the market in another country, the patent holder cannot prevent parallel importation into the importing country. TRIPS permits WTO members to determine their own rules regarding exhaustion—international exhaustion permits parallel trade and may permit importation of a medicine produced under compulsory license in another country.

Because most pharmaceutical companies set prices for the same products at different levels in different countries, parallel importation promotes competition for the patented product by allowing the importation of equivalent patented products marketed at lower prices in other countries. However, companies have been pressuring governments not to import medicines from countries that produce generic versions, claiming that the practice is a breach of the TRIPS agreement. Article 6 of TRIPS explicitly states that practices relating to parallel importation cannot be challenged under the WTO dispute settlement system, provided that no discrimination exists on the basis of the nationality of the persons involved; however, preexisting or new "TRIPS-plus" legislation (see below) often specifies national exhaustion. Here, the patent holder has exclusive marketing rights, and resale is permitted only within the country after first sale. Preferential pricing offers are frequently linked to the prevention of parallel importation between developing and developed markets.

Exceptions to rights conferred (including Bolar exception) (TRIPS Article 30). TRIPS specifies the rights given to a patent owner but allows limited exceptions, subject to specified conditions in Article 30. Of particular interest regarding access to medicines is the so-called Bolar exception to patent rights that allows a country to complete all of the procedures and tests that are necessary to register a generic product before the patent expires on the original medicine. Allowing generics manufacturers to conduct the tests needed to prepare their applications for regulatory approval during the term of the patent enables them either to market their products immediately upon expiration of the patent or, for example, to apply for a compulsory license during the term of the patent.

Protection of undisclosed test data (TRIPS Article 39.3). In many countries, national regulatory agencies require originator pharmaceutical companies to submit extensive data showing the safety and efficacy of a new product before it is approved for the market. These data

Figure 3-1 Compulsory license granted in Zambia

Republic of Zambia
MINISTRY OF COMMERCE, TRADE AND INDUSTRY

The Government of Zambia, conscious that the HIV/AIDS pandemic constituted a serious handicap in the national struggle against hunger, illness, under development and misery;

and taking into consideration that high rates of morbidity and mortality have put Zambia among the ten countries in Africa most hit by this disease. Current estimates are that, at the end of 2003, over **917,718** Zambians were infected by HIV of whom an unestimated number are suffering from full-blown AIDS. The AIDS death toll is so far in excess of **835,904** and about **750,504** children have been orphaned by this pandemic, creating a situation where 75% of households in Zambia are caring for at least one orphan and that children aged below 14 years headed more than 130,000 poverty stricken households out of a total of 1,905,000, and that;

in spite of the multiplicity and diversity of vigorous prevention campaigns, the spread of the virus is still on an upward trend as shown by the high number of infections;

Taking into account the gravity of the situation being faced by most African Countries, including Zambia, the need to ensure access to drugs at affordable prices, while respecting the protection of intellectual property, is well recognised. For this reason;

On 14 November, 2001 the World Trade Organisation, while recognising Members' commitment to the TRIPS Agreement, declared the right of each Member State to take measures aimed at protecting public health and in particular to promote access to medicines for all, by utilising to the full, the flexibilities in the TRIPS Agreement relating to among others, the granting of compulsory licences, in cases which constitute a national emergency or other circumstances of extreme urgency and of public health crisis including those relating to HIV/AIDS, tuberculosis, malaria or other epidemics which can represent a national emergency or other circumstances of extreme urgency.

Considering further that;

A triple compound of Lamivudine, Stavudine and Nevirapine has proved, in the last few years to be one of the most effective and economical anti-retroviral treatment, but that the three different international owners of such single drugs failed to reach an agreement to produce this combination, and therefore;

The Ministry of Commerce, Trade and Industry of the Republic of Zambia making use of the provisions of Section forty of the Patent Act, Chapter 400 of the Laws of Zambia, and Statutory Instrument No 83 of 2004 titled "The Patents (Manufacture of Patented Antiretroviral Drugs) (Authorisation) Regulations, 2004" Regulation 3, has decided to grant a Compulsory Licence No. CL 01/2004 to PHARCO LTD, a company incorporated in Zambia, which has already presented a project proposal for the local manufacture of the mentioned triple compound under the names of Normavir 30 and Normavir 40.

It is further understood that the use or vending of the above mentioned drugs is subject to Regulation 4 of Statutory Instrument No 83 of 2004, titled "The Patents (Manufacture of Patented Antiretroviral Drugs) (Authorisation) Regulations, 2004" and therefore cannot be exported to any place outside Zambia.

Communication of this decision will be given to the applicant and to the patent right holders.

In consideration that the mentioned product, a triple combination of drugs, is not marketed in Zambia by the International Patent owners and that it is in the national interest to keep the final price as low as possible, the total amount of royalties due to the patent right owners shall not exceed 2.5% of the total turnover of the mentioned products at the end of each financial year of PHARCO LTD.

The Ministry of Commerce, Trade and Industry shall in accordance with Section forty one of the Patent Act notify the concerned parties of the expiration of the present Compulsory Licence as soon as conditions of national emergency and extreme urgency created by the HIV/AIDS pandemic will come to an end, or upon expiry of the period of emergency stipulated in Statutory Instrument No 83 of 2004 titled "The Patents (Manufacture of Patented Antiretroviral Drugs) (Authorisation) Regulations 2004."

The Government of the Republic of Zambia reserves the right to review the Compulsory Licence should the conditions and circumstances under which it is granted change.

Dipak K. Patel, MP	Ref: MCT/104/1/1c
MINISTER	Date: 21/09/04

Source: www.cptech.org/ip/health/c/zambia/zcl.html

Country Study 3-1
Using voluntary licenses in sub-Saharan Africa to produce antiretroviral medicines

A number of companies in Africa have obtained voluntary licenses from originator pharmaceutical producers (in some cases through advocacy efforts) to locally manufacture antiretroviral medicines for HIV/AIDS. South Africa led the way with several generics pharmaceutical companies receiving voluntary licenses from patent holders of antiretroviral medicines. Aspen Pharmacare, which is South Africa's largest pharmaceutical manufacturer, and Cipla Medpro are two of the companies that secured the rights to distribute generic HIV/AIDS medicines to other countries in sub-Saharan Africa. Voluntary licenses from several different patent holders allow the generics companies to produce medications that combine multiple products into one tablet (fixed-dose combination), which helps patients adhere to treatment. In addition, the U.S. Food and

Drug Administration qualified Aspen Pharmacare, which allowed U.S.-government-funded organizations in Africa to purchase generic antiretrovirals for the first time.

In Kenya, Cosmos Limited was the first producer to receive voluntary licenses from GlaxoSmithKline and Boehringer Ingelheim to produce generic versions of lamivudine, zidovudine, and nevirapine. One of the benefits of producing the products locally is that the packaging will include instructions printed in both English and Kiswahili, but more important, the supply and availability should become more reliable, and prices are expected to fall. As part of the voluntary licensing agreements, Cosmos will be able to sell the generic medicines to five other sub-Saharan countries.

---

are the result of many years of research and are sometimes very expensive for the originator company to produce. Sometimes, such as in the case of the cancer medicine paclitaxel, a government has underwritten much of the product's R&D. In addition, a multinational company may simply acquire the innovation from an academic institution or biotechnology company.

TRIPS Article 39.3 obliges member countries to protect this confidential test data from "unfair commercial use" including disclosure, except where necessary to protect the public. Countries vary in how they implement the requirements of Article 39.3. Whereas some countries permit pharmaceutical regulatory authorities to rely on the original test data to register generic equivalents, others, such as the United States and European Union countries, grant the originator company a time-limited period that excludes regulatory authorities from using existing test data to register generic products without consent. These laws are known as data exclusivity laws.

The originator company is unlikely to consent to its data being used to register a generic equivalent to its product, and although generic competitors could replicate clinical trials at considerable cost, another significant barrier relates to the ethics of conducting redundant trials on patients. Therefore, data exclusivity laws provide a form of market protection for the originator company.

Consequently, controversy exists about how Article 39.3 should be implemented to ensure the protection of public health. The disagreement centers on whether the phrase "unfair commercial use" means that regulatory agencies can use original data to assess generic product applications,

as long as they do not disclose the data to the competitor. This interpretation would imply that Article 39.3 does not require data exclusivity. On the contrary, the research-based pharmaceutical industry and some trade representatives have argued for the alternative interpretation that Article 39.3 does require data exclusivity.

Exclusive marketing rights (TRIPS Article 70.9). As noted, when TRIPS was launched in 1996, many countries did not offer patents for pharmaceutical products. These countries were given a transition period to phase in patent protection for pharmaceuticals. However, TRIPS Article 70.9 says these countries have to accept patent applications for pharmaceuticals, even though they are not obligated to examine the applications or grant any patents until the end of the transition period.

In cases where the country takes advantage of the transition period, Article 70.9 requires that when a patent application has been filed for a product in that country, the WTO member must grant exclusive marketing rights to the patent applicant for a period of five years after obtaining marketing approval, as long as the product has been patented and received marketing approval in another WTO member country. The rights can expire before the end of the five years if either a patent is granted (in which case the patent holder would rely on the patent instead of the exclusive marketing rights) or the patent application is rejected. Exclusive marketing rights, therefore, are considered a mechanism for the patent applicant to obtain payment for use of the product until the patent is granted.

Least-developed countries have been granted a waiver to Article 70.9—extending the transition period until 2016.

Decision on the implementation of paragraph 6 of the Doha Declaration. Although developing countries have the right to exercise the flexibilities under TRIPS, they often find using these flexibilities in public health policy a challenge. For example, paragraph 6 of the Doha Declaration recognized that while developing countries can issue compulsory licenses, TRIPS did not take into account the difficulties they faced because of a lack of manufacturing capacity. Many developing countries and LDCs cannot produce either active ingredients or formulations because of lack of technology, equipment, human resources, or other domestic production capacity. Although these countries may issue compulsory licenses to import generic versions of patent-protected medicines, TRIPS rules constrain the ability of countries that do have the capacity to manufacture generics, such as India, to export such products. Manufacture must be primarily for the domestic market. Therefore, countries without sufficient manufacturing capacity in pharmaceuticals could issue a compulsory license for the importation of products they cannot manufacture, but they may not be able to find sources for importing affordable new medicines.

Consequently, after the adoption of the Doha Declaration, WTO members spent almost two years in negotiations that culminated in the Decision on Implementation of Paragraph 6. That decision is intended to permit all LDCs (as designated by the United Nations) and developing countries with insufficient or no manufacturing capacity to import a particular medicine to make effective use of compulsory licensing. The Paragraph 6 Decision allows nonproducing countries to issue a compulsory license to import medicines in accordance with a special compulsory license for export issued in the exporting country. However, making use of this flexibility is a complex process, and both importing and exporting countries will need to pass the legislation to make it possible.

The terms of the Doha decision were made a permanent feature of TRIPS through an amendment including a new article, 31*bis*. Essentially, the Paragraph 6 Decision and the amendment eliminate the requirement that pharmaceutical products manufactured under a compulsory license be "predominantly for the supply of the domestic market." In addition, to prevent duplicating payment to the patent holder, the amendment eliminates the need to remunerate the patent holder in the importing country if the patent holder in the exporting country has already been remunerated.

A publication from WHO gives more information on how countries can implement the Paragraph 6 Decision (Correa 2004).

Decision on the implementation of paragraph 7 of the Doha Declaration. Paragraph 7 permits LDCs to extend the transition period for pharmaceutical patents beyond what is defined in TRIPS to the year 2016. Part of the motivation for paragraph 7 concerns the rights of LDCs to promote technology transfer by giving them additional time to build a technological base for their pharmaceutical sectors. In addition, Article 66.2 seeks to provide benefits specific to LDCs by requiring developed countries to offer incentives to private companies and other institutions in their territories to engage in technology-transfer activities.

Practically, however, the only LDCs that can take advantage of the extension in paragraph 7 are those that do not grant patents for pharmaceuticals. For example, Angola and Eritrea are the only countries of thirty African LDCs that do not grant patents for pharmaceuticals (Correa 2002). To take advantage of the benefit, other LDCs that already grant pharmaceutical patents must amend their legislation and not grant product patents until 2016.

Another consequence of paragraph 7's transition extension concerns the requirement to grant exclusive marketing rights (TRIPS Article 70.9). After the Doha Declaration, ambiguity existed regarding whether a transition extension for pharmaceuticals applied to exclusive marketing rights as well as to patents. To clarify the situation, WTO members approved a waiver that exempts LDCs from having to provide exclusive marketing rights for any new medicines during the period without patent protection.

3.3 Constraints to establishing health-sensitive intellectual property laws

Although the adoption of the TRIPS minimum standards resulted in developing countries losing some policy flexibilities in regulating pharmaceutical patents and controlling the cost of medicines, the agreement left some room for countries to take measures to protect public health. Furthermore, at Doha, WTO members reaffirmed the right of each member to fully use the provisions of the agreement that provide flexibility for protecting public health; however, the provisions relating to patents and pharmaceutical regulation are confusing even to specialists in the field of intellectual property law and medicine regulation. Therefore, countries with little capacity for interpreting and acting on international trade agreements are most at risk in terms of losing access to medicines. Regulators and legislators must acquire the relevant technical expertise to use the flexibilities, such as compulsory licensing and parallel importation, to improve access to medicines in their countries.

Substantial legal and administrative obstacles exist to introducing and implementing these complex provisions. Several constraints that developing countries face at the national level in their efforts to use TRIPS flexibilities are mentioned below, but countries can address many of these constraints by adopting complementary policy and legal measures.

Country Study 3-2
Countries in Asia, Latin America and the Caribbean, and Africa that are using TRIPS flexibilities

Although TRIPS establishes minimum standards that WTO members must follow related to intellectual property rights, certain flexibilities in the agreement allow exemptions to developing countries, especially regarding pharmaceutical patents. However, taking advantage of these flexibilities requires that the eligible countries amend their national intellectual property rights legislation.

An analysis of forty-nine countries in Asia, Latin America and the Caribbean, and Africa looked at the extent to which countries have incorporated the TRIPS flexibilities affecting pharmaceuticals and public health. Updated use of flexibilities in selected African countries is also available (Munyuki and Machemedze 2010; UNAIDS, WHO, and UNDP 2011).

National law provisions	Countries implementing selected TRIPS flexibilities		
	Asia (n = 13)	Latin America/ Caribbean (n = 19)	Africa (n = 17)
Pharmaceutical products are patentable	10 (77%)	18 (95%)	11 (65%)
Data protection	6 (46%)	16 (84%)	6 (35%)
Government or noncommercial use allowed	7 (54%)	9 (47%)	17 (100%)
Exhaustion of rights			
• National exhaustion	2 (15%)	4 (21%)	6 (35%)
• International exhaustion (allowing parallel importation)	6 (46%)	13 (68%)	7 (41%)
• No exhaustion	3 (23%)	1 (5%)	1 (6%)
Early working exception	4 (31%)	6 (32%)	5 (29%)
Compulsory licensing grounds			
• Failure to work/exploit	10 (77%)	14 (74%)	15 (88%)
• Anticompetitive practice	5 (38%)	14 (74%)	5 (29%)
• Dependent patents	7 (54%)	10 (53%)	10 (59%)
• Demand not met on reasonable terms	3 (23%)	5 (32%)	13 (76%)
• Public interest	10 (77%)	15 (79%)	8 (47%)
• National emergency	5 (38%)	11 (58%)	6 (35%)
• No provision	2 (15%)	0 (1 unknown)	0

Source: Musungu and Oh 2006.

Lack of technical expertise to incorporate TRIPS flexibilities into national law

Countries can use the flexibilities offered by TRIPS only if they incorporate them into their legislation; however, many developing countries have not done so for various reasons, including a lack of technical expertise and information on best practices. Resource-limited countries are generally not aware of the measures undertaken by their counterparts around the world. As a result, countries within a region with similar access problems may adopt different strategies, with varying degrees of success. Country Study 3-2 summarizes the extent to which TRIPS flexibilities are being used in forty-nine different countries. For example, while 100 percent of the countries surveyed in Africa provided for government or noncommercial use in their laws, less than half the countries in Asia or Latin America/Caribbean had done so.

Insufficient domestic research and manufacturing capacities

Most developing countries have limited pharmaceutical research and manufacturing capacities. The challenge for these countries is how to enlarge their capacity for research through increased investment in basic sciences, R&D, and technological innovation. As technology evolves and becomes an important tool for development, it also becomes more of a means of gaining competitive advantage.

Developing countries face significant barriers that may block their own R&D efforts or opportunities for collaboration with other countries, such as insufficient numbers of trained researchers and inadequate research support at local universities or institutions. In addition, an individual country's interest in bolstering indigenous, national manufacturing capacity may limit regional, multicountry collaboration

Country Study 3-3
Differences between bilateral trade agreements and TRIPS

Many countries that trade with the United States are members of the WTO and therefore are obligated to abide by the TRIPS provisions. However, they may enter into bilateral trade agreements that commit them to more stringent intellectual property rules than TRIPS (TRIPS-plus) in exchange for concessions in other areas of trade—often access to the U.S. market for agricultural or manufactured goods. Evaluating the implications of bilateral trade agreements on public health can be difficult. The benefits and costs associated with protecting pharmaceutical patents vary by country, and these agreements will take many years to take full hold. The public health community has raised concerns regarding these bilateral agreements and their possible effect on access to medicines, especially how they may limit the availability of generic medicines in developing countries.

The following are key differences in intellectual property provisions between bilateral trade agreements and TRIPS:

Use of compulsory licenses. Under TRIPS, governments may issue a compulsory license to obtain generic medicines by temporarily overriding a patent. Compulsory licensing is an important tool for governments to protect the public interest or to remedy anticompetitive behavior. Four bilateral agreements now limit the use of compulsory licensing to emergencies, antitrust remedies, and cases of public noncommercial use.

Test data protection. Getting approval to market medicines requires a company to submit test data to regulatory authorities to prove a medicine's safety and efficacy. The protection of such data differs from country to country. TRIPS requires only that test data be protected against "unfair commercial use." However, most bilateral

agreements require governments to guarantee exclusive use of test data for pharmaceutical products for five years, which is the U.S. standard. Furthermore, some free-trade agreements require an additional data exclusivity period for new uses of already approved medicines, and some go even further by prohibiting generic manufacturers from using test data submitted to a regulatory authority in another territory—even outside the trade agreement territory. These new test data provisions may be an obstacle for governments using compulsory licensing.

Patent terms. Bilateral agreements mandate the extension of patent protection beyond the current twenty-year limit mandated in TRIPS to compensate for procedural delays in granting patents or in securing marketing approval for pharmaceuticals.

Use of parallel imports. Parallel importation allows a government to import pharmaceuticals that have been placed on the market more cheaply in foreign markets, which can help reduce medicine prices. TRIPS allows WTO members to establish their own national policies regarding whether to permit parallel importation of patented medicines. By contrast, many bilateral agreements allow patent holders to prevent parallel importation.

Bolar exception. TRIPS does not limit generics companies from starting the process of entering a new market before a patent has expired. Generics producers often take this action so they can be ready to sell their product immediately after the patent expires. Most bilateral agreements prevent marketing approval of a generic medicine during the patent term without the consent of the patent holder, which could make compulsory licenses an ineffective way to allow competition from generics manufacturers.

to produce medicines unless the benefits of investment in R&D and procurement of locally manufactured products can be shared across the region.

Insufficient capacity for medicine registration and regulation

Pharmaceutical registration is the process by which a country's regulatory authority assesses the safety, quality, and efficacy of medicines to approve their use. Countries normally require that all medicines offered for sale in their territories be registered locally. Although the ultimate role of medicine

regulation is to protect public health, national regulatory authorities in developing countries often lack the facilities and expertise needed to review medicines destined for their national markets.

Regulatory authorities handle applications for new chemical entities, generic medicines, new fixed-dose combination products, and even herbal medicines. Innovative new products, including important antimalarials and antiretroviral medicines for HIV/AIDS, require more complex assessment than their generic equivalents; therefore, most countries carry out a fast-track review based on prior approval by U.S. or EU regulatory agencies. Where a comparable product is

Country Study 3-3
Differences between bilateral trade agreements and TRIPS (continued)

Differences between bilateral trade agreements and TRIPS: specific examples

Intellectual property provisions	U.S.-Vietnam (2001)	U.S.-Jordan (2001)	U.S.-Singapore (2003)	U.S.-Chile (2003)	U.S.-Morocco (2004)	U.S.-Australia (2004)	U.S.-DR-CAFTA[a] (2005); U.S.-Bahrain (2006)
Patent term	Extension given for delays caused by regulatory approval process.	Extension given for delays caused by regulatory approval process.	Extension given for delays caused by regulatory approval process. In addition, extension given when a delay in the granting of the patent exceeds four years from the filing of the application (five years for U.S.-Chile) or two years after a request for examination (three years for U.S.-Chile).			Same as U.S.-Singapore.	TRIPS standards apply.
Grounds for issuing compulsory licenses	Compulsory licenses limited to national emergencies, and for public noncommercial use.		TRIPS standards apply, as antitrust				
Link between patent status and pharmaceutical marketing approval	No specific provision.	Patent owner must be notified when marketing approval is sought during the patent term.	Marketing approval of a generic medicine is prohibited during the patent term, unless authorized by the patent owner. In addition, the patent holder must be notified of the identity of the generic company requesting marketing approval.				
Test data protection for pharmaceutical products	Data exclusivity for a "reasonable" period, normally not less than five years.	TRIPS standards apply. In addition, length of protection should be the same as in the originator's country.	Data exclusivity for five years. In addition, where pharmaceutical regulators rely on foreign marketing approvals, data exclusivity applies automatically at home.	Data exclusivity for five years.	Data exclusivity for five years. Additional three-year data exclusivity triggered by "new clinical information."	Data exclusivity for five years. In addition, data exclusivity applies in all free-trade agreement member countries, once first obtained in another territory. In the case of U.S.-Bahrain, additional three-year data exclusivity triggered by "new clinical information" (with equivalent provisions on cross-border application).	
Parallel imports	No specific provision.	TRIPS standards apply.	Patent holders may limit parallel imports of pharmaceutical products through licensing contracts.	TRIPS standards apply.	Patent holders may limit parallel imports through licensing contracts.		TRIPS standards apply.

Source: Fink and Reichenmiller 2005.

[a] Dominican Republic, Costa Rica, El Salvador, Guatemala, Honduras, and Nicaragua.

already on the market, the assessment of generic medicines tends to take place at the national level (see Chapter 6).

When a country's pharmaceutical regulatory process is unwieldy, that can delay the entry of needed medicines in a particular market and act as a barrier to access as well as to growth of the local pharmaceutical industry. Many developing countries have no reliable fast-track procedure for registering new essential medicines, such as antiretroviral medicines. The requirement for local clinical trials can also deter and delay registration. With growing demand for rapid registration of new and more complex medicines, pharmaceutical regulatory capacity needs to develop in a way that also protects public health.

Procurement is also affected. A country's procurement agency must determine whether a medicine is locally under patent before it can import a generic version of the medicine; however, finding this information can be complicated and difficult (Tayler 2004). The procurement agency can ask the national patent office to help, but staff may not have the capacity to undertake such a request. Professional firms will search for patents, but the fees may be prohibitive. Médecins Sans Frontières has published the patent landscapes for HIV/AIDS medicines in developing countries, although it notes that it cannot promise complete accuracy. WHO's AIDS Medicines and Diagnostics Service maintains a drug regulatory database and additional information related to HIV/AIDS products (http://www.who.int/hiv/amds/patents_registration/en/index.html). Other organizations have called for the creation of a global patent database, including the World Health Assembly in its *Global Strategy and Plan of Action on Public Health, Innovation and Intellectual Property* (WHO 2008).

TRIPS-plus provisions

"TRIPS-plus" refers to the incorporation into national legislation of intellectual property rights that are stricter than those mandated by TRIPS. This includes efforts to extend patent life beyond the twenty-year TRIPS minimum, limit compulsory licensing in ways not required by TRIPS, limit exceptions that facilitate the prompt introduction of generics, and extend the period of data exclusivity. Because the public health effect of TRIPS requirements has yet to be fully assessed, WHO recommends that developing countries be cautious about enacting legislation that is more stringent than the TRIPS requirements. From a public health perspective, countries that are not bound by TRIPS should evaluate TRIPS requirements and incorporate into national legislation and trade-related practices those elements that clearly benefit national public health interests.

Existing intellectual property protection in many resource-limited countries is often stronger than the minimum required by TRIPS; so in countries such as Kenya and Malawi, the existing legislation is already considered TRIPS-plus (DFID 2004). These countries will not be able to use TRIPS-compliant flexibilities unless they amend their national legislation. Moreover, almost all developing countries will need to change their legislation to take advantage of the import/export mechanisms in the Paragraph 6 Decision.

Free-trade agreements. One form of TRIPS-plus is bilateral and regional free-trade agreements that have intellectual property components. Most developing-country members face difficulties in trade negotiations, where they are asked to accept obligations in the public health sector in exchange for concessions in areas such as market access for agricultural products, which may be important to their economies (see Country Study 3-3). For example, both Vietnam and Cambodia entered into bilateral trade agreements with the United States that contain intellectual property requirements, including compliance with TRIPS standards, when these countries were not members of the WTO.

International patent law harmonization. An indirect influence on the evolution of TRIPS-plus provisions is the World Intellectual Property Organization (WIPO) Patent Agenda initiative. WIPO is a specialized agency of the United Nations whose primary objective is the promotion of creative intellectual activity and the facilitation of the transfer of technology to developing countries. The WIPO Patent Agenda initiative comprises a set of interrelated activities designed to harmonize the international patent system by building a legal framework that would create something comparable to a global patent. Such a system would, in essence, reduce the need for countries to have national patent offices, but more important, it would eliminate the flexibilities permitted by the TRIPS agreement that allow developing countries exceptions to rules on patents—essentially creating TRIPS-plus standards for everyone. A WIPO forum in 2006 allowed stakeholders to present their arguments both for and against the harmonization efforts and how such efforts might affect public health (WIPO 2006). Opinions on the benefits of harmonization have been sharply divided, and as of 2011, the WIPO standing committee was still trying to finalize recommendations for an international patent system.

3.4 Access to medicines in the TRIPS era

The globalized intellectual property system is one factor among many that affects access to pharmaceuticals in developing countries. Sometimes, countries may adopt policies that adversely influence access, such as applying tariffs or taxing medicines. Other restraints include a lack of human and financial resources, reliance on the public sector, and absence of an adequate infrastructure to supply and administer medicines effectively. For example, in sub-Saharan Africa, medicines for HIV/AIDS treatment are increasingly available from multiple sources: Indian-manufactured copies of patented antiretrovirals, generic purchases, brand-name purchases, and donations from pharmaceutical companies; bilateral and multilateral programs provide funding for procurement. Still, less than half the patients who need treatment are getting it, in part because of weak pharmaceutical management infrastructures and too few trained health professionals.

As intellectual property rights are strengthened globally, the cost of medicines in developing countries is likely to increase unless effective steps are taken to facilitate their availability at lower costs. Moreover, countries need to adopt a range of policies to improve access to medicines. Additional resources to improve services, supply mechanisms, and infrastructure are critical. Countries need to ensure that their intellectual property protection legislation does not run counter to public health policies and that other economic policies are in harmony with health policy objectives.

Box 3-2 includes a list of issues for country-level policy makers to keep in mind regarding intellectual property rights and access to medicines.

Using available resources to develop expertise

A lack of clarity often exists about the options available on the patent status of medicines and importing generic medicines from foreign producers. Within developing-country governments, experience in implementing TRIPS and its flexibilities is limited, and the political will to act is often low. Making changes to a country's intellectual property regime requires effective cooperation between different government departments, including health, trade, and industry, which may have limited experience in developing common policy.

The international rules regarding intellectual property are developing quickly. Active participation by developing countries in discussions of the future of the global intellectual property system is essential to ensure both

---

Box 3-2
Issues on intellectual property and pharmaceuticals for policy makers

Governments should—

- Avoid provisions in bilateral trade agreements that could reduce access to medicines in developing countries
- Increase funding for research projects run by public-private partnerships and by developing countries, and make that funding more sustainable
- Develop advance-purchase schemes for vaccines, medicines, and diagnostics
- Incorporate digital libraries of traditional medical knowledge into their patent offices' data to ensure that data contained in them are considered when patent applications are processed
- Make available reliable information on the patents they have granted
- Amend their laws to allow compulsory licensing for export consistent with TRIPS
- Eliminate tariffs and taxes on health care products

Governments of developing countries should—

- Identify a trade and pharmaceuticals focal point within the ministry of health
- Establish contacts, perhaps a working group, with trade and other key ministries
- Obtain reliable specialized legal advice
- Develop a mechanism to monitor the health effect of new trade agreements

- Promote health research that is in line with public health needs
- Promote the use of research exemptions as part of their patent law
- Invest appropriately in health-delivery infrastructure
- Improve financing of the purchase of medicines and vaccines
- Make use of compulsory licensing provisions where they will promote innovation or access to medicines

National patent and related legislation should—

- Promote standards of patentability that take health into account
- Establish process and product patents for twenty years
- Incorporate exceptions, trademark provisions, data exclusivity, and other measures to support generic competition
- Permit compulsory licensing, parallel importation, and other measures to promote availability and ensure fair competition
- Permit requests for extension of the transitional period for TRIPS implementation, if needed and if eligible
- Carefully consider national public health interests before instituting TRIPS-plus provisions

Sources: WHO 2001; CIPIH 2006.

the legitimacy of standard setting and its appropriateness to countries at very different levels of development. As the rules evolve, their impact must be properly understood if policies are to be based on relevant evidence.

Box 3-3 contains a list of organizations and resources that provide information on intellectual property rights and public health.

Regional collaboration

The constraints on national efforts to implement TRIPS flexibilities to improve public health show that developing countries need significant additional resources and technical assistance. One way to provide such support is through regional mechanisms that can complement national efforts. A regional approach to using the TRIPS flexibilities creates better policy conditions for addressing the challenges of implementing TRIPS flexibilities, which can be daunting for each individual country. Politically, a collective regional position on matters of public health and access to medicines can provide bargaining advantage for developing countries in their negotiations within WTO and with developed-country trading partners.

A regional approach to the use of TRIPS flexibilities could enable similarly situated countries to address their constraints jointly by drawing on each other's expertise and experience and by pooling and sharing resources and information. Policies that are likely to benefit significantly from regional collaboration in implementing TRIPS flexibilities include those related to production of pharmaceuticals, regulatory approval of medicines, market surveillance and maintenance of quality standards, and import rules and competition issues (Musungu, Villanueva, and Blasetti 2004).

3.5   Intellectual property and R&D for new medicines

Patent protection is an incentive for R&D for new medicines. The patent-holding company has exclusive rights over the product for a defined period, protecting it from competition in the country where the patent is recognized. Patent protection allows the manufacturer to set prices according to what the market will bear, which is likely to be well above production cost for medicines that treat widespread and severe illnesses in high-income markets. The temporary monopolies that patents create reward firms for taking expensive risks in developing new medicines.

Trends in new medicine innovation

Following years of rapid innovation from 1980 to the mid-1990s, evidence suggests an overall decline in the output of global R&D into new medicines. Although R&D spending tripled between 1990 and 2000, the annual number of new medicines approved fell from its peak of more than fifty in 1996 to thirty-two in 2000, the lowest output in more than twenty years (WHO 2004). The increasing costs of R&D and the decrease in productivity have been factors in encouraging mergers between pharmaceutical companies. Rising R&D costs are also prompting manufacturers to develop strategic alliances with small research companies, particularly biotechnology companies, reflecting the emerging commercial potential of genomics-based discoveries.

In general, patents are most effective at attracting investment in products that have commercial prospects, leaving important gaps where R&D is the most commercially risky. The diseases and conditions that affect people in the world's major markets largely determine where the pharmaceutical industry's investments go. Of the 1,393 new chemical entities developed between 1975 and 1999, only 16 were for the treatment of tropical diseases and tuberculosis (Trouiller et al. 2002). The Global Forum for Health Research highlights the fact that only 10 percent of R&D spending is directed to the health problems that account for 90 percent of the global disease burden—the so-called 10/90 gap (see http://www.globalforumhealth.org). For example, no new class of anti-tuberculosis medicine had been developed in almost twenty years, despite the high global burden of this disease. Therefore, the debate centers around how to reach a balance between meeting the high costs of pharmaceutical R&D and creating incentives to stimulate access to those medicines in poor and developing countries.

Encouraging R&D in neglected diseases

Various initiatives are being used to encourage R&D into medicines for neglected diseases. Public-sector or donor funds or research mandates often address gaps in research that are not adequately provided for by intellectual property rights incentives. Some "push" mechanisms work by reducing costs and risks, including tax credits, grants, and support for clinical trials. "Orphan" medicine laws are examples of this type of mechanism. Another mechanism, called a "pull" initiative, creates a market for medicines or increases their profitability; for example, when a company develops a medicine for a neglected disease and in return gets the right to extend the patent on one of its more profitable products. Another type of proposal to tackle the problem of R&D for these forgotten medicines is the creation of public-private partnerships that mobilize expertise, capacity, and funding from both the public and private sectors (see Box 3-4). In fact, recent research has shown that two-thirds of projects developing medicines for neglected diseases involve these sorts of public-private collaborations (Moran 2005).

Box 3-3
Sources of information on intellectual property rights and public health

Business and Industry Advisory Committee to the OECD (BIAC). BIAC is the business community's representative to the Organisation for Economic Co-operation and Development (OECD). BIAC's members are the major business organizations in the OECD member countries. BIAC ensures that business and industry needs are adequately addressed in OECD policy decisions. *http://www.biac.org*

Commission on Intellectual Property Rights. The British government set up the commission to look at how intellectual property rights might work better for developing countries. The commission's final report (in seven languages) and supporting documents are available on its website. *http://www.iprcommission.org*

Commission on Intellectual Property Rights, Innovation and Public Health. The World Health Assembly (WHO's highest body) set up this independent commission in 2003 to collect and analyze data and proposals on intellectual property rights, innovation, and public health. The commission presented its final report in April 2006. Documents relating to the commission's work are available on its website. *http://www.who.int/intellectualproperty/en*

Knowledge Ecology International. Knowledge Ecology International is a nonprofit organization that focuses on issues related to intellectual property and health care. Its website includes links to many intellectual property documents and several related listservs. *http://www.keionline.org*

Health Action International/WHO Drug Prices Project. This project seeks to gather and publicize accurate data on pharmaceutical price structure as a first step to negotiation, management, and policy to bring prices down and make medicines more affordable. *http://www.haiweb.org/medicineprices*

Intellectual Property Watch. This nonprofit, independent news service reports on the interests and activities that influence the design and implementation of international intellectual property policies. *http://www.ip-watch.org/index.php*

International Federation of Pharmaceutical Manufacturers and Associations (IFPMA). IFPMA is a global organization that represents research-based pharmaceutical, biotechnology, and vaccine companies and national industry associations in developed and developing countries. *http://www.ifpma.org*

International Generic Pharmaceutical Alliance (IGPA). IGPA is a network of associations representing manufacturers of generic medicines; it comprises the generic medicine associations of Canada, Europe, India, Japan, and the United States, with Brazil, Jordan, Taiwan, and South Africa having observer status. *http://www.egagenerics.com*

IPRsonline.org. IPRsonline.org is an Internet portal containing a selection of online documents and resources related to intellectual property rights and sustainable development, including discussion papers from various organizations, a calendar of related events, latest news on intellectual property rights, and links to listservs and relevant institutions. *http://www.IPRsonline.org*

Médecins Sans Frontières Campaign for Access to Essential Medicines. The campaign is an advocacy effort to promote policies to lower medicine prices and push for increased research into neglected diseases. *http://www.accessmed-msf.org*

Pharmaceutical Research and Manufacturers of America (PhRMA). This industry organization represents the United States' leading pharmaceutical research and biotechnology companies. *http://www.phrma.org*

Science and Development Network. This Internet-based network, also known as SciDev.Net, provides up-to-date information on science- and technology-related issues that affect developing countries, including news, policy briefs, key documents, and feature articles. It includes a section devoted to intellectual property. *http://scidev.net*

South Centre. South Centre is an intergovernmental organization that promotes the interests of developing countries by analyzing development problems and experience and providing intellectual and policy support on global issues including trade, development, and intellectual property rights. *http://www.southcentre.org*

World Health Organization (WHO). In 2006, WHO member states established an Intergovernmental Working Group (IGWG) on Public Health, Innovation and Intellectual Property. The working group's mandate was to prepare a global strategy and plan of action on public health, innovation and intellectual property to address conditions disproportionately affecting developing countries. Documents related to IGWG activities can be found on its website *http://www.who.int/phi/documents/en/*. In addition, the website of WHO's unit on Trade, Foreign Policy, Diplomacy and Health includes an updated list of related publications and links to other WHO sites related to globalization. *http://www.who.int/trade/en*

World Intellectual Property Organization (WIPO). This specialized agency of the United Nations administers twenty-three international treaties dealing with different aspects of intellectual property protection. It also provides technical assistance to member countries needing help with developing national systems for intellectual property. *http://www.wipo.org*

World Trade Organization (WTO). This international organization deals with the rules of trade between nations at a global or near-global level. See Box 3-1 for a detailed discussion. *http://www.wto.org*

Box 3-4
Using public-private partnerships to develop medicines for neglected diseases

Some partnerships act like pharmaceutical companies that develop their own medicines, whereas others act more like funding agencies. An example of the former type of partnership is the Drugs for Neglected Diseases Initiative, started by Médecins Sans Frontières, with the support of several ministries of health, research institutes, and pharmaceutical manufacturers—including partnerships with southern research centers. Initially focused on treatment for sleeping sickness, leishmaniasis, and Chagas disease, this nonprofit research organization develops or adapts medicines for patients suffering from several different diseases with little profit-making potential. The initiative's first commercial development, in collaboration with Sanofi-Aventis SA, is a new antimalarial medicine. This inexpensive, fixed-dose combination of artesunate and amodiaquine was launched in 2007 and by 2011, more than 80 million treatments had been distributed.

The Medicines for Malaria Venture, founded in 1999, is a public-private partnership concerned with the discovery, development, and registration of new medicines for the treatment and prevention of malaria; similarly, the Global Alliance for TB Drug Development is committed to delivering new anti-tuberculosis medicines; it has three medicine candidates in clinical trials, including moxifloxicin, which is the nearest to approval. Moxifloxicin should

shorten the treatment duration for drug-sensitive, adult tuberculosis cases. The business model of the nonprofit pharmaceutical company Institute for One World Health is to take promising leads on new medicines that lack a profitable market and complete the development process. The company then collaborates with other companies and nonprofit hospitals and organizations in the developing world to conduct medical research and to manufacture and distribute the newly approved therapies.

In the vaccines area, the International AIDS Vaccine Initiative researches and develops HIV vaccine candidates by directing and financing partnerships with private companies and academic and government agencies, including those in developing countries; the Malaria Vaccine Initiative operates in a similar fashion for malaria vaccine projects. Further downstream in the R&D process, the Global Alliance for Vaccines and Immunization works to enhance the commercial attractiveness of vaccines by stimulating demand in developing country markets, strengthening infrastructure, and guaranteeing some product purchase. The idea is that a strong advance commitment to purchasing safe and effective vaccines will reduce the financial risks faced by private-sector manufacturers and help redirect research toward the vaccines that are a priority for resource-limited countries.

These mechanisms fill some important gaps between the opportunities that face commercial medicine manufacturers, on the one hand, and the global burden of disease, on the other. Strong public-sector involvement is needed to ensure that new medicines are created to address priority health problems in developing countries. To help address such issues, WHO created an intergovernmental working group to develop a framework that identifies and prioritizes needs-based research for diseases that disproportionately affect developing countries. As a result of the group's work, in 2008 the sixty-first World Health Assembly adopted Resolution WHA 61.21: Global Strategy and Plan of Action on Public Health, Innovation and Intellectual Property. In 2009, the World Health Assembly adopted Resolution WHA 62.16: Final Agreement on Stakeholders in the Plan of Action on Public Health, Innovation, and Intellectual Property. The global strategy and plan of action comprises eight elements, which are designed to promote innovation, build capacity, improve access, and mobilize resources. Additional information and materials are available at

WHO's website: http://www.who.int/phi/implementation/phi_globstat_action/en/index.html.

Technology transfer

Technology transfers involve knowledge sharing between developed and developing countries. TRIPS recognizes that "the protection and enforcement of intellectual property rights should contribute to the promotion of technological innovation and to the transfer and dissemination of technology" and suggests that developed-country members introduce incentives to encourage technology transfer by private companies.

As encouraged by TRIPS, the transfer of technology is potentially an important source of growth in developing countries. One of the reasons that developing countries do not use the compulsory licensing mechanism in TRIPS is because of a lack of mechanisms for technology transfer. Although compulsory licensing permits an invention to be used without the consent of the patent holder, it does not guarantee that the country will have the appropriate technology available, including facilities for manufacturing.

Increasingly, technology transfer is a component in non-profit initiatives and public-private partnerships that involve developing-country governments and the private sector. For example, several R&D companies are linking with industry partners in India, China, and elsewhere to increase the supply of patented medicines. In the cases of South Africa and Kenya, advocacy efforts on the part of governments and civil society resulted in patent holders granting voluntary licenses to local manufacturers. WHO, international philanthropic groups, and nongovernmental organizations are brokering collaborations between R&D and generics companies.

In all of these partnerships, both the research-based company and the developing country stand to benefit. For example, a company benefits from being seen as committed to corporate social responsibility, and developing-country partners get increased access to scientific technology and skills, new products for new markets, and experience in working with international standards.

Alternative paradigms in R&D of pharmaceuticals

In addition to public-private partnerships, a different R&D paradigm for pharmaceuticals is the use of an open collaborative model, such as the Human Genome Project's successful international effort to sequence the human genome, which used a nonproprietary system sanctioned by the governments of six major countries. One of the innovative aspects of this model is the publicly available results, which has been a growing trend in biomedical research (see additional discussion in Chapter 34). The collaborative and transparent nature of this kind of openly accessible research is appealing, but its application to pharmaceutical R&D is still unclear.

Others have suggested creating a global decision-making process to name targets for R&D funding, with each individual country deciding how it will meet those targets (Hubbard and Love 2004). The theory is that to meet the R&D targets, some countries will choose public-sector management of investments, while others will rely on a more private (profit or nonprofit) approach. Most will choose mixed approaches. Another idea is to set up a global fund to pay for research into medicines for neglected diseases; such medicines would then be supplied free or at greatly discounted prices to resource-limited countries. One R&D paradigm or another is unlikely to be chosen explicitly. Box 3-5 illustrates how some developing countries are approaching R&D for new medicines.

UNITAID is working to establish an international patent pool that would, in theory, increase access to patents and promote the development of more affordable medicines in developing countries. The concept of the pool is for patent holders to give up their patents and allow their intellectual

---

Box 3-5
How developing countries are approaching R&D

Only 4 percent of the entire global spending on health research is by low- or middle-income countries, and the majority is public-sector funded. Researchers in all but the most technologically advanced countries find developing new and innovative pharmaceutical products difficult without adequate infrastructure or equipment, and few countries have the regulatory framework to oversee the process of ensuring pharmaceutical quality, efficacy, and safety. However, developing and transitional countries such as India, Indonesia, South Africa, and Brazil have created successful industries specializing in the manufacture of generic medicines, while a few countries have even developed new medicines.

For example, in the 1970s, Pliva, a small Croatian company, developed a new antibiotic called azythromycin, which looked promising in animal trials. Pliva did not have the resources necessary to mass produce and market the new medicine in the world market. It patented the product globally, which led to a licensing agreement with the U.S. pharmaceutical giant Pfizer to market the medi-cine worldwide, while Pliva retained marketing rights in Eastern Europe. Zithromax became one of Pfizer's top antibiotic products.

Although this kind of R&D success may not be realistic for every small company, other ways exist to make progress. For instance, the generic pharmaceutical industry in India was the first to create a fixed-dose combination of antiretroviral medicines for HIV/AIDS, which is less expensive, and by simplifying the dosage improves patients' ability to adhere to their treatment. Scientists in other countries, such as South Africa and China, are focusing their R&D efforts on taking centuries-old herbal preparations used in traditional medicine and creating modern medicines. Some of these R&D efforts are advancing with the help of public-private partnerships, with large pharmaceutical companies providing the technology and expertise, and some are using a combination of state and private financing or nonprofit foundation funding to develop their pharmaceutical sectors.

Source: Fleck 2005.

property rights to be managed by the pool under certain conditions. By giving up a period of exclusive marketing rights, patent holders receive royalties from the pool in exchange for a license to produce the medicine in a developing country (UNAIDS 2009). WHO's Expert Working Group on Research and Development Financing rated the patent pool model high for operational efficiency, feasibility, and impact on health in developing countries. As it is based on the voluntary donation of intellectual property, however, questions remain about the quantity and quality of intellectual property that patent holders would choose to donate, particularly outside the area of HIV/AIDS. For the pool to work well, a minimum critical mass is needed, and it is not clear whether this would be achieved voluntarily for many diseases (WHO 2010). ∎

References and further readings

★ = Key readings.

Abbott, F. M. 2001. *The TRIPS Agreement, Access to Medicines and the WTO Doha Ministerial Conference.* Geneva: Quaker United Nations Office. <http://www.quno.org/geneva/pdf/economic/Occassional/Access-to-Medicine7.pdf>

Baker, B. 2004. *Processes and Issues for Improving Access to Medicines: Willingness and Ability to Utilise TRIPS Flexibilities in Non-Producing Countries.* London: Department for International Development (DFID) Health Systems Resource Centre. <http://www.iprsonline.org/resources/docs/Baker_TRIPS_Flex.pdf>

Campbell, D., and M. Chui. 2010. *Pharmerging Shake-Up: New Imperatives in a Redefined World.* Norwalk, Conn.: IMS Health. <http://www.imshealth.com/pharmergingreport2010>

CIPIH (Commission on Intellectual Property Rights, Innovation and Public Health). 2006. *Public Health, Innovation and Intellectual Property Rights.* Geneva: World Health Organization. <http://www.who.int/intellectualproperty/documents/thereport/en/index.html>

Commission on Intellectual Property Rights. 2002. *Integrating Intellectual Property Rights and Development Policy.* London: Commission on Intellectual Property Rights. <http://www.iprcommission.org/papers/pdfs/final_report/CIPRfullfinal.pdf>

Correa C. M. 2004. *Implementation of the WTO General Council Decision on Paragraph 6 of the Doha Declaration on the TRIPS Agreement and Public Health.* Geneva: WHO. <http://whqlibdoc.who.int/hq/2004/WHO_EDM_PAR_2004.4_(2).pdf>

———. 2002. *Implications of the Doha Declaration on the TRIPS Agreement and Public Health.* Geneva: World Health Organization. <http://whqlibdoc.who.int/hq/2002/WHO_EDM_PAR_2002.3.pdf>

———. 2000. *Integrating Public Health Concerns into Patent Legislation in Developing Countries.* Geneva: The South Centre. <http://www.southcentre.org/index.php?option=com_docman&task=doc_download&gid=13&Itemid=&lang=en>

★ DFID (U.K. Department for International Development). 2004. *Access to Medicines in Under-Served Markets: What Are the Implications of Changes in Intellectual Property Rights, Trade and Drug Registration Policy?* London: DFID Health Systems Resource Centre. <http://www.dfid.gov.uk/pubs/files/dfidsynthesispaper.pdf>

DFID and the *Lancet.* 2007. *The Bigger Access to Medicine Picture: Life beyond TRIPS.* Proceedings of the Access to Medicines Workshop, London, April 19–20. London: DFID.

★ Fink, C., and P. Reichenmiller. 2005. *Tightening TRIPS: The Intellectual Property Provisions of Recent US Free Trade Agreements.* Washington, D.C.: World Bank. <http://siteresources.worldbank.org/INTRANETTRADE/Resources/Pubs/TradeNote20.pdf>

Fleck, F. 2005. Developing Countries Take a Creative Approach to R&D. *Bulletin of the World Health Organization* 83(1):1–80. <http://www.who.int/bulletin/volumes/83/1/feature0105/en/index.html>

Ford, N., D. Wilson, O. Bunjumnong, and T. von Schoen Angerer. 2004. The Role of Civil Society in Protecting Public Health over Commercial Interests: Lessons from Thailand. *Lancet* 363:560–3.

Ghauri, P. N., and P. M. Rao. 2009. Intellectual Property, Pharmaceutical MNEs and the Developing World. *Journal of World Business* 44(2):206–15.

Hubbard, T., and J. Love. 2004. A New Trade Framework for Global Healthcare R&D. *PloS Biology* 2(2):0147–50. <http://biology.plosjournals.org/archive/1545-7885/2/2/pdf/10.1371_journal.pbio.0020052-S.pdf>

IMS Health. 2006. *World Markets: New Products and Markets Fuel Growth in 2005.* Norwalk, Conn.: IMS Health.

Kyle, M., and A. McGahan. 2009. *Investments in Pharmaceuticals before and after TRIPS.* Cambridge, Mass.: National Bureau of Economic Research.

Moran, M. 2005. *Fast Track Options as a Fundraising Mechanism to Support R&D Into Neglected Diseases.* Geneva: World Health Organization. <http://www.who.int/intellectualproperty/submissions/en/Mary.Moran2.pdf>

MSF (Médecins Sans Frontières). 2001. *Fatal Imbalance: The Crisis in Research and Development for Drugs for Neglected Diseases.* Geneva: MSF Access to Essential Medicines Campaign and the Drugs for Neglected Diseases Working Group. <http://www.msf.org/source/access/2001/fatal/fatal.pdf>

Munyuki, E., and R. Machemedze. 2010. *Implementation of the TRIPS Flexibilities by East and Southern African Countries: Status of Patent Law Reforms by 2010.* Harare: EQUINET. <http://www.equinetafrica.org/bibl/docs/Diss80TRIPSupdate2010.pdf>

★ Musungu, S. F., and C. Oh. 2006. *The Use of Flexibilities in TRIPS by Developing Countries: Can They Promote Access To Medicines?* Geneva: South Centre and World Health Organization. <http://www.who.int/entity/intellectualproperty/studies/TRIPSFLEXI.pdf>

Musungu, S. F., S. Villanueva, and R. Blasetti. 2004. *Utilizing TRIPS Flexibilities for Public Health Protection through South-South Regional Frameworks.* Geneva: South Centre. <http://www.southcentre.org/index.php?option=com_docman&task=doc_download&gid=9&Itemid=&lang=en>

Roberts, M. J., A. G. Breitenstein, and C. S. Roberts. 2002. The Ethics of Public-Private Partnerships. In *Public-Private Partnerships for Public Health,* ed. M. R Reich. Cambridge, Mass.: Harvard Center for Population and Development Studies. <http://www.hsph.harvard.edu/faculty/michael-reich/files/Partnerships_book.PDF>

Scheffler, R. M., and V. Pathania. 2005. Medicines and Vaccines for the World's Poorest: Is There Any Prospect for Public-Private Cooperation? *Globalization and Health* 1:10. <http://www.ncbi.nlm.nih.gov/pmc/articles/PMC1200561/pdf/1744-8603-1-10.pdf>

Smith, R., D. C. Correa, and C. Oh. 2009. Trade, TRIPS, and Pharmaceuticals. *Lancet* 373(9664):684–91.

Sonderholm, J. 2010. *Intellectual Property Rights and the TRIPS Agreement: An Overview of Ethical Problems and Some Proposed Solutions.* Washington, D.C.: World Bank.

Tayler, Y., ed. 2004. Battling HIV/AIDS: *A Decision Maker's Guide to the Procurement of Medicines and Related Supplies.* Washington, D.C.: World Bank.

★ 't Hoen, E. F. M. 2009. *The Global Politics of Pharmaceutical Monopoly Power: Drug Patents, Access, Innovation and the Application of the WTO Doha Declaration on TRIPS and Public*

Health. Diemen, Netherlands: AMB Publishers. <http://www.soros.org/initiatives/health/focus/access/articles_publications/publications/aem_20090312/politics_20090312.pdf>

Trouiller, P., P. Olliaro, E. Torreele, J. Orbinski, R. Laing, and N. Ford. 2002. Drug Development for Neglected Diseases: A Deficient Market and a Public Health Policy Failure. *Lancet* 359:2188–94.

UNAIDS, WHO, and UNDP (Joint United Nations Programme on HIV/AIDS, World Health Organization, and United Nations Development Programme). 2011. *Using TRIPS Flexibilities to Improve Access to HIV Treatment: Policy Brief.* Geneva: UNAIDS, WHO, and UNDP.

UNCTAD-ICTSD (United Nations Conference on Trade and Development–International Centre for Trade and Sustainable Development). 2005. *Resource Book on TRIPS and Development: An Authoritative and Practical Guide to the TRIPS Agreement.* Cambridge, UK: Cambridge University Press.

UNITAID. 2009. *The Medicines Patent Pool Initiative.* Geneva: UNITAID. <http://www.unitaid.eu/images/projects/PATENT_POOL_ENGLISH_15_may_REVISED.pdf>

Wertheimer, A. I., and T. M. Santella. 2009. *Pharmaceutical Evolution: The Advantages of Incremental Innovation in Drug Development.* Washington, D.C.: Competitive Enterprise Institute. <http://cei.org/issue-analysis/2009/04/07/pharmaceutical-evolution>

WHO (World Health Organization). 2010. *Report of the World Health Organization Expert Working Group on Research and Development Financing.* Geneva: WHO. <http://www.who.int/phi/documents/ewg_report/en/index.html>

———. 2008. *Global Strategy and Plan of Action on Public Health, Innovation and Intellectual Property.* 61st World Health Assembly. <http://apps.who.int/gb/ebwha/pdf_files/A61/A61_R21-en.pdf>

———. 2005. Access to Medicines: Intellectual Property Protection: Impact on Public Health. *WHO Drug Information* 19(3):236–41.

———. 2004. *The World Medicines Situation.* Geneva: WHO. <http://www.searo.who.int/LinkFiles/Reports_World_Medicines_Situation.pdf>

———. 2001. *Globalization, TRIPS and Access to Pharmaceuticals.* Geneva: WHO. <http://apps.who.int/medicinedocs/en/d/Js2240e/>

WHO/EDM (World Health Organization/Essential Drugs and Medicines Policy). 2004. *Determining the Patent Status of Essential Medicines in Developing Countries.* Geneva: WHO/EDM. <http://whqlibdoc.who.int/hq/2004/WHO_EDM_PAR_2004.6.pdf>

WIPO (World Intellectual Property Organization). 2006. Open Forum on the Draft Substantive Patent Law Treaty, Geneva, March 1–3. [Web page containing transcripts of remarks and presentations made by participants.] Geneva: WIPO. <http://www.wipo.int/meetings/en/2006/scp_of_ge_06/scp_of_ge_06_inf1.html>

WTO (World Trade Organization). 2006. TRIPS and Pharmaceutical Patents. Fact Sheet. Geneva: WTO. <http://www.wto.org/english/tratop_E/TRIPS_e/tripsfactsheet_pharma_2006_e.pdf>

Glossary

Bioequivalence: Two pharmaceutical products are bioequivalent if they are pharmaceutically equivalent and the rate and extent of bioavailability are similar to such a degree that their effects can be expected to be essentially the same.

Bolar (early working) exception: An exception to patent rights allowing a third party to undertake, without the authorization of the patentee, acts in respect of a patented product necessary for the purpose of obtaining marketing approval for the sale of a product.

Compulsory license: A license to exploit a patented invention granted by the state upon request of a third party.

Data exclusivity: A legal provision that data collected (for example, the results of clinical trials) for obtaining marketing approval may not be used for a specified period by the regulatory authorities to grant approval to a generic equivalent.

Data protection: An obligation imposed on third parties to protect test data, such as the results of clinical trials, that are usually collected to comply with government regulations on the safety, efficacy, and quality of a broad range of products (for example, drugs, pesticides, medical devices). For example, TRIPS provides for the protection of such data against unfair commercial use.

Differential pricing: The practice of setting different prices for different markets, typically higher prices in richer markets and lower prices in poorer markets.

Doha Declaration: The Declaration on the TRIPS Agreement and Public Health agreed upon at the Doha WTO Ministerial Meeting in 2001.

Downstream research: Applied research usually directed at the development of a product or process with a potential commercial application.

Evergreening: A term popularly used to describe patenting strategies that are intended to extend the patent term on the same compound.

Exhaustion of rights: Principle whereby the right holder's intellectual property rights in respect of a product are considered exhausted (that is, he or she can no longer exercise any rights) when that product has been put on the market by the right holder or by an authorized party.

Incremental innovation: Innovation that builds incrementally on previous innovation, as compared with "breakthrough" innovation, which is a completely novel means to prevent, treat, or cure a particular disease.

Intellectual property rights: Rights awarded by society to individuals or organizations over inventions, literary and artistic works, symbols, names, images, and designs used in commerce. They give the titleholder the right to prevent others from making unauthorized use of their property for a limited period.

Interchangeability: A pharmaceutical product that is therapeutically equivalent to a comparator (reference) product.

Parallel imports: The purchase of a patented medicine from a lawful source in an exporting country and its importation without seeking the consent of the "parallel" patent holder in the importing country.

Patent: An exclusive right awarded to an inventor to prevent others from making, selling, distributing, importing, or using the invention, without license or authorization, for a fixed period of time. In return, the patentee discloses the invention to the public. Three requirements usually exist for patentability: novelty; inventive step or nonobviousness (knowledge not obvious to one skilled in the field); and industrial applicability or utility.

Patent pools: An agreement between two or more patent owners to license one or more of their patents to one another or third parties.

Source: Adapted from CIPIH 2006.

| Part I: Policy and economic issues | Part II: Pharmaceutical management | Part III: Management support systems |

Policy and legal framework
  1 Toward sustainable access to medicines
  2 Historical and institutional perspectives
  3 Intellectual property and access to medicines
  4 National medicine policy
  5 Traditional and complementary medicine policy
  6 Pharmaceutical legislation and regulation
  7 Pharmaceutical production policy
  8 Pharmaceutical supply strategies
Financing and sustainability

CHAPTER 4

National medicine policy

SUMMARY

A national medicine policy (NMP) is a political commitment and a guide for action that shows how the government will ensure that efficacious and safe medicines of good quality are affordable, accessible, and rationally used. The NMP provides a framework for coordinating the activities of all the parties involved, such as the public and private sectors, nongovernmental organizations (NGOs), donors, and other interested stakeholders; it also defines the role that the public itself should play.

The medicine policy of one country may be similar in many ways to the medicine policies of other countries, but because their starting situations will vary, the policies will likely differ in what they emphasize and in how problems can best be tackled. A national government will be the principal agency responsible for creating the overall NMP and putting it into practice; however, collaboration will be needed with prescribers, dispensers, consumers, and those who make, market, distribute, and sell medicines. Sometimes, disagreements among the parties will be unavoidable because their interests differ, but ideally a wide partnership will develop, because an effective medicine policy is ultimately in the best interests of all.

This chapter examines the components of an NMP. Countries must choose the elements most relevant to their situation and most realistic, given their available human and financial resources. At the outset, governments will need to give priority to solving current problems, such as a lack of relevant laws and regulations and

difficulty in implementing and enforcing laws and regulations that already exist; issues of finance, supply, cost, and pricing; and rational use of medicines. Less pressing matters may be addressed later.

This chapter reviews the main steps in formulating an NMP including—

- Organizing the process
- Identifying and analyzing problems
- Setting goals and objectives
- Drafting the policy
- Seeking wide agreement on the policy
- Obtaining formal endorsement of the policy
- Launching the policy

Formulating a policy is one thing; putting it into effect is another. No single, best way to implement an NMP exists, but this chapter shares the approaches that some countries have taken.

Experience shows that the essential medicines concept is central to a successful national medicine policy. The core of the concept is using an established list of essential medicines based on standard treatment guidelines, leading to a better supply of medicines, more rational prescribing, and lower costs. Finally, the success of an NMP will depend heavily on political commitment by the government and support from all stakeholders in the pharmaceutical sector.

4.1 Introduction

For many decades, pharmaceutical policies were developed in a piecemeal fashion, where they existed at all. At one moment, a country may have developed a regulation on pharmaceutical advertising—at another moment, a decree on the places where medicines can be sold. One country might concentrate on sound manufacturing practice—another country on the problem of providing very poor populations with access to medicines. Only gradually did people come to realize that the issue of medicines and their proper place in society needed to be looked at as a whole. If a policy covered only select issues in the pharmaceutical sector, problems could soon arise with other issues; in fact, a one-sided approach might actually make a situation worse.

In the 1970s, for example, efforts were made in certain countries to solve problems involving pharmaceutical procurement and distribution without examining the ways in

which medicines were being prescribed or used by patients. The result in some instances was that access to medicines improved, but people did not know how to use them rationally. Similarly, essential medicines policies developed for the public sector only were ineffectual because they did not address how the private and public sectors could complement each other. More recently, some East African countries' difficulties in collecting direct taxes have led to a heavier reliance on import duties and manufacturing taxes, including those from medicines. This policy makes imported pharmaceuticals more expensive and discourages local production, resulting in the availability of fewer low-cost medicines in the marketplace.

These experiences suggested that pharmaceutical problems might be better tackled within a common framework created through the development of a comprehensive national medicine policy. The overall goal of an NMP should be to promote equity and sustainability of the pharmaceutical sector (WHO 2003). Its general objectives can be simply

Figure 4-1   Structure of a complete national medicine policy

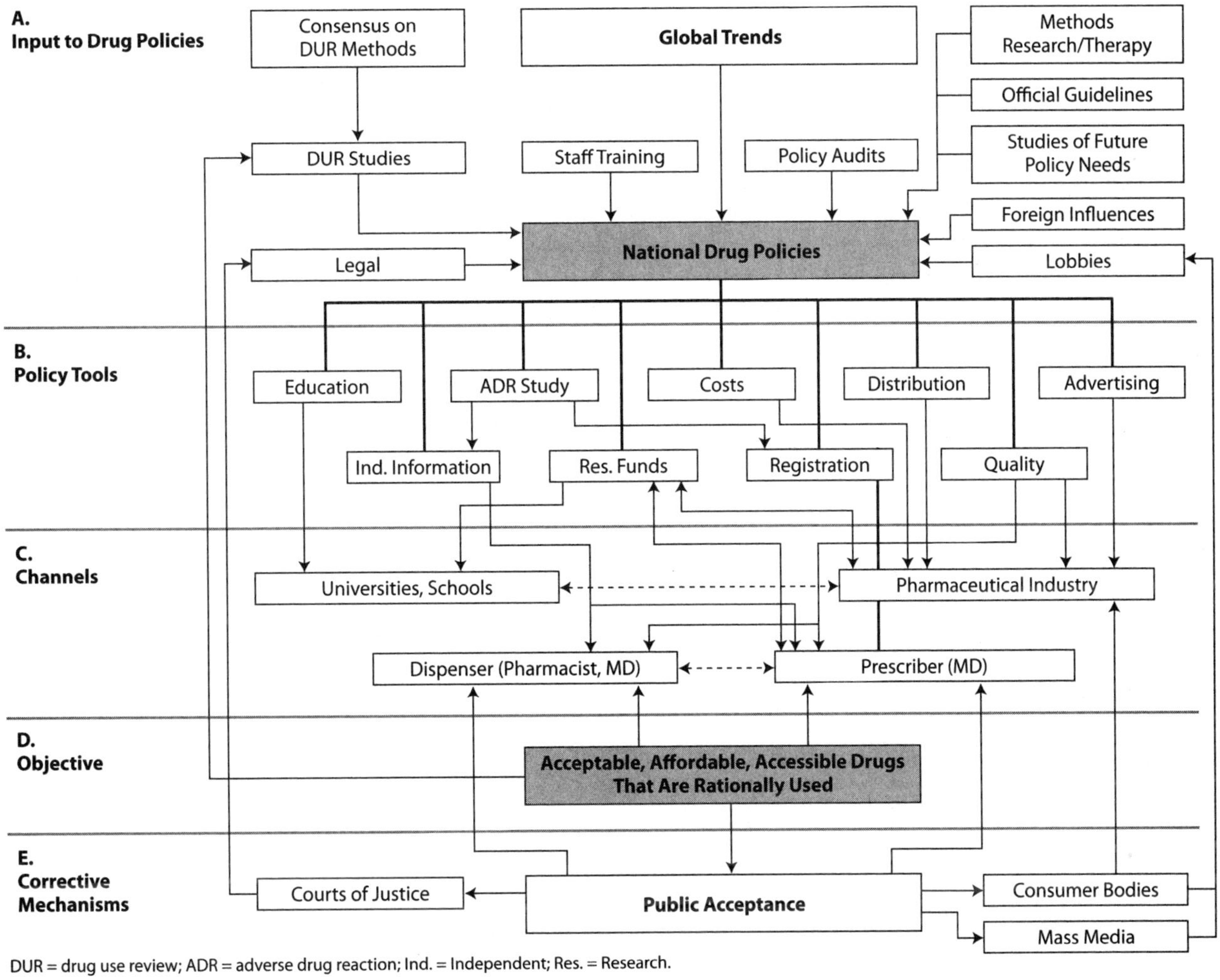

DUR = drug use review; ADR = adverse drug reaction; Ind. = Independent; Res. = Research.

This figure shows how many different elements are linked in the construction of a national medicine policy. No individual country's policy is likely to be structured in exactly the same way, and many national medicine policies are simpler. The chart can, however, be useful in analyzing the situation and looking for solutions. For example, the area of rational prescribing can be analyzed by examining the linkages illustrated. The figure shows that the prescriber is likely to receive information, advice, and persuasion from various sources: the institution where he or she was educated, the drug regulatory agency, formularies, industry representatives, and others. Can the quality of influencing sources be improved? Do they reinforce or contradict one another? Is some better form of guidance needed if the prescriber is to improve rational prescribing practices?

stated: a national medicine policy should ensure that *effective* and *safe* medicines of *good quality* are *accessible* and *affordable* to the entire population and that they are *rationally used*.

The 1980s saw the idea of an NMP emerging as a positive concept, and the World Health Organization (WHO) and World Bank became active in developing the idea further. Now the idea that every country should try to achieve optimal availability, quality, and use of medicines for patients and consumers is widely accepted. By 2007, more than 130 countries had formulated NMPs, about 60 percent of which had an updated implementation plan in place (WHO 2010).

4.2   What is a national medicine policy?

An NMP is a political commitment to a goal and a guide for action. It is a written document specifying the medium- to long-term goals set by the government for the pharmaceutical sector, their relative importance, and the main strategies for attaining them. Moreover, it provides a framework for coordinating activities of the pharmaceutical sector: the public and private sectors, NGOs, donors, and other interested parties. (Figure 4-1 illustrates the structure of a national medicine policy.) The NMP should be incorporated into the national health system to ensure that NMP goals and objectives are addressed in broad national health plans, including disease-specific programs, and that resources are allocated efficiently. An NMP should also express the government's commitment to promoting good governance practices, including increased transparency and accountability.

In the developed world, most countries do not have written NMPs, yet many are successful in pursuing pharmaceutical sector goals. However, even in those countries, some experts advocate drawing up a document that clearly outlines the objectives of an NMP; for example, Australia launched an official NMP in 1999. In countries where resources are severely limited, an integrated approach to solving problems helps make the best use of limited resources.

What should a medicine policy accomplish?

The overall purpose of an NMP is usually expressed in general terms, without necessarily touching on every aspect of the policy. The purpose stresses the most important objectives in the simplest way. In Nigeria, the medicine policy states that the goal is "to make available at all times to the Nigerian populace adequate supplies of drugs that are effective, affordable, safe and of good quality; to ensure the rational use of such drugs; and to stimulate increased local production of essential drugs" (Federal Ministry of Health, Nigeria/WHO 2005). In Ghana, the overall goal of the policy is "to improve and sustain the health of the population of Ghana by ensuring the rational use and access to safe, effective, good quality and affordable pharmaceutical products" (Ministry of Health, Ghana, 2004).

Although specific objectives differ according to the priorities recognized by the government, the most common follow the essential medicines concept and are directly *health related*—

- To make essential medicines available and affordable to those who need them
- To ensure the safety, efficacy, and quality of all medicines provided to the public
- To improve prescribing and dispensing practices and to promote ethical practices among health professionals and the correct use of medicines by health workers and consumers

The core of the essential medicines concept is that the use of a limited number of medicines that have been carefully selected based on agreed standard treatment guidelines leads to a better supply of medicines and more rational prescribing, as well as to lower medicine costs.

The national medicine policy may also include economic goals (for example, to reduce the use of foreign exchange for pharmaceutical imports, or to provide jobs in areas such as dispensing, prepackaging, or production of pharma-

ceuticals) and national development goals (for example, to improve internal transportation and communication systems, develop national pharmaceutical production, or to take a stand on intellectual property rights in this particular field). Regardless of a country's specific circumstances, a comprehensive NMP should clearly specify the roles of both the public and the private sectors.

In addition, the policy should be concerned with *efficiency* (delivery of the maximum level of services given a certain level of resources); *equity* (fairness in access); *sustainability* (the ability to provide continued benefits into the future without relying on external support); and *transparency*, with clear lines of accountability. Finally, the NMP should address the issue of access to essential medicines as part of the government's obligation to fulfill its citizens' right to health (see Section 4.4).

What approaches should be used?

In addition to indicating the broad political choices that the government has made regarding the pharmaceutical sector, a general medicine policy should define some specific objectives—outcomes to achieve within a given time frame. Each objective must be linked to some clear ideas about how it will be obtained. For instance, the supply of essential medicines can be improved in the public sector by increasing the pharmaceutical budget, introducing cost-sharing mechanisms, or allocating more resources to underserved populations. Pharmaceutical supply can also be increased through the private sector by introducing economic incentives for pharmaceutical manufacturing and distribution. Some of these strategies can be introduced in the national policy document, whereas others may need to be worked out separately, after additional research and consultation. Including too much detail in the national policy may make it difficult to read and understand. The optimal solution is likely to involve applying different approaches in the private and public sectors. This combination of different approaches and strategies forms the core of an NMP.

Why do medicine policies differ by country?

Objectives and strategies may differ from country to country for various reasons. Differences may exist in the structure of the health care system, the number of trained pharmacists and physicians, the capacity of the drug regulatory authority, the way in which pharmaceuticals are distributed, or the level of funding available for pharmaceuticals. The biggest differences in the scope of medicine policies lie between industrialized countries and least developed countries.

In most industrialized countries, health care coverage is broad, and access to medicines per se is not a prominent issue (although cost is likely to be a concern). The annual public and private expenditure on medicines is high, perhaps 500 U.S. dollars (USD) per person or more (WHO 2004b). The role of the government here is to set up rules for the operations of the private sector without becoming directly involved in medicine provision or in the pharmaceutical industry. This model requires the existence of an active private sector that is capable of developing, manufacturing, marketing, and distributing medicines to the entire population. Therefore, in these settings, pharmaceutical policies are oriented heavily toward containing costs while ensuring rational use in the interests of both public health and the economy, and the regulations should focus on the quality assurance of pharmaceutical products and services as well as on cost containment.

Although many middle-income countries have experienced improvements in indicators that measure pharmaceutical access, WHO estimates that almost one-quarter of the population in middle-income countries still lacks access to essential medicines (WHO 2004b). Whereas least developed countries are afforded equity pricing for some medicines, such as those for HIV/AIDS, middle-income countries that are ineligible for such discounts pay higher prices; however, in 2009, only one-third of these countries were instituting economic policies that could help make medicines more affordable (Stevens and Linfield 2010).

In the least developed countries, total spending on pharmaceuticals is less than USD 5 per person per year (WHO 2004b). The private sector has traditionally failed to supply affordable, high-quality medicines to the majority of the population. Consequently, governments have attempted to supply and distribute essential medicines through the public sector, often with donor support. In addition, policies often focus on such matters as ensuring the proper use of a basic range of essential medicines and encouraging the private sector to play a more constructive role in supplying those medicines.

Who are the main participants in developing and implementing a national medicine policy?

The national government is the essential driving force in designing and implementing medicine policies. Through its medicine policy, the state seeks to guarantee the availability and accessibility of effective, high-quality essential medicines for the population and to ensure that they are properly used. This goal holds true whether the government is directly involved in procurement and distribution of medicines, empowers parastatal or private institutions to carry out this function, or acts mainly as a regulatory authority for a largely private pharmaceutical market.

The government is not, however, the only actor involved with the NMP. A partnership is required, involving government ministries of health, finance, and industry; health

professionals, including doctors and other prescribers and pharmacists; public and private wholesalers and retailers; academia; NGOs and consumer groups; and the pharmaceutical industry (national and multinational). Consulting with provincial and district personnel and traditional medicine practitioners is important. In addition, governmental agencies, such as the drug regulatory authority and government-sponsored health care and insurance schemes, must be involved. The involvement of such diverse groups and conflicting interests means that development and implementation of a sustainable NMP is not easy. Reaching full agreement with all the parties on every matter is ideal but not always possible. With patience and goodwill, however, an environment conducive to success can be created.

The ministry of health should establish a specific office that is responsible for coordinating the NMP review and implementation process. The office should arrange regular NMP stakeholder committee meetings to assess implementation and policies. Working groups may be needed to analyze the effect of the NMP on specific areas. In addition, the NMP office should be given the capacity to monitor and evaluate the implementation process and coordinate necessary action plans with stakeholders.

The consultations and national discussions that lead to the production of the medicine policy document are very important because they create a mechanism to bring all parties together and achieve a sense of collective ownership of the final policy. This "buy-in" is crucial in view of the national effort that will later be necessary to implement the policy. The policy *process* is just as important as the policy *document* (WHO 2001). (Box 4-1 lists all of the stakeholders involved with the most recent revision of Ghana's National Medicine Policy.)

The development and implementation of an NMP is a highly political process, requiring careful analysis to understand who the advocates are, who the opponents are, and what each group's strategies are. Mobilizing alliances and coalitions and creating constituents inside and outside the government are necessary to mobilize political will during the process.

4.3 Components of a national medicine policy

The areas of pharmaceutical policy unavoidably overlap, but the main components include legislation and regulation, choice of medicines, supply and financing policies, and a means of encouraging rational medicine use. Some countries also have a tradition of local production (or they have ambitions in this area), and that factor can also be a key issue in a national medicine policy. These components form the basic framework, with other components added according

---

Box 4-1
List of stakeholders who provided input in the 2004 revision of Ghana's National Medicine Policy

- Accra Metropolitan Health Directorate
- Association of Ghana Industries
- Customs, Excise and Preventive Service
- Dangme West District Administration, Greater Accra
- Danish International Donor Agency
- Department for International Development
- European Union, Ghana Delegation
- Faculty of Law, University of Ghana
- Faculty of Pharmacy, Kwame Nkrumah University of Science and Technology
- Food and Drugs Board
- General Practice Pharmacist Association
- Ghana Registered Nurses' Association
- Ghana Standards Board
- Government and Hospital Pharmacists Association
- Greater Accra Regional Directorate of Pharmaceutical Services
- KAMA Health Services, Accra
- Komfo Anokye Teaching Hospital

- Lady Pharmacists Association
- Ministry of Environment, Science and Technology
- National Centre for Pharmacovigilance
- National Drug Information Centre
- Pharmaceutical Manufacturers Association of Ghana
- Pharmaceutical Society of Ghana
- Pharmacy Council of Ghana
- Pharmacy Department, Korle-Bu Teaching Hospital
- Save the Children Fund, UK (Ghana Office)
- School of Medical Sciences, Kwame Nkrumah University of Science and Technology
- The World Bank, Ghana Office
- United Nations Population Fund
- University of Ghana Medical School, Korle-Bu
- Upper West Regional Directorate of Pharmaceutical Services
- Veterinary Council of Ghana
- Volta Regional Health Administration
- World Health Organization Headquarters, Geneva

---

to local conditions. Each component is essential but not sufficient in itself to ensure access. Box 4-2 summarizes these basic components of a national medicine policy, which are discussed further in the following sections.

Legislative and regulatory framework

The formulation of a medicine policy should be followed by the enactment of appropriate legislation and the introduction of regulations to provide a legal basis for the policy and make it enforceable. An NMP is usually a declaration of intent rather than a law, so the strategies set out in the policy may need to be supported by appropriate laws and regulations. In the Philippines, for example, one policy objective was to extend the use of generic medicines, and many activities related to that objective were reinforced by a new law on generics.

Legislation should provide the basis for ensuring that pharmaceutical products are of acceptable quality, safety, and efficacy and specify an agency to be responsible for this. Regulations, which are more flexible than legislation, should define the actors in the system and their responsibilities: regulations should state who can produce or import pharmaceuticals, who can prescribe them, and which medicines can be sold without the need for a prescription. Regulations should also state who can store and sell pharmaceuticals, and which institution is responsible for monitoring and enforcing regulations. Several legislative models and structures have been devised for the regulation of medicines, as discussed in Chapter 6.

As noted, making a policy, or even a law or regulation, provides no guarantee that it will be implemented. Too often, laws and regulations are not enforced, and the penalties and sanctions that the law provides are not imposed. Sometimes this failure results from lack of resources or lack of political will; sometimes an element of corruption exists. Although a commitment to good governance and the need to fight corruption should be included as a cross-cutting item throughout the NMP, some countries may also have a separate component that specifically defines how a good governance program will be implemented (Anello 2006). Another reason for failure may be that the government's rules are impractical or difficult to enforce. In this case, a careful review of the main regulations applying to the pharmaceutical sector may lead to proposals to amend them so that they are better adapted to local realities and can be better enforced.

Appropriate legislation and regulation should be accompanied by a functioning quality assurance system; pharmaceuticals of low quality, either imported or locally produced, should never reach the patient. Quality assurance calls for a transparent pharmaceutical registration system and a well-organized and -trained inspection administration that is independent of commercial pressures and a system of quality control backed by one or more laboratories (see Chapter 19).

Box 4-2
Components of a national medicine policy

Legislative and regulatory framework

- Legislation and regulations
- Drug regulatory authority
- Medicine registration and licensing
- Pharmaceutical quality assurance, including inspection and enforcement
- Pharmacovigilance
- Regulation of prescription and distribution
- Infrastructure for good governance in medicines

Choice of essential medicines

- Principles of essential medicine selection
- Selection process (market approval and selection based on national morbidity patterns)
- Selection criteria (sound and adequate evidence, cost-effectiveness)
- Use of essential medicines lists
- Traditional and herbal medicines

Supply

- Local production
- Supply system strategies and alternatives, including mix of public and private sectors
- Procurement mechanisms
- Inventory control, including prevention of theft and waste
- Distribution and storage
- Disposal of unwanted or expired medicines

Rational use of medicines

- Multidisciplinary national body to coordinate medicine use policies
- Standard treatment guidelines as the basis for selecting essential medicines and training health professionals
- Independent medicine information
- Rational medicine use training for health personnel
- Education about rational use of medicines for consumers
- Promotional activities

Affordability

- Taxes or tariffs on essential medicines
- Distribution margins and pricing

- Measures to encourage competition through generics and price information and negotiation
- Trade-related intellectual property mechanisms

Financial strategies for medicines

- Role of government in the pharmaceutical market
- Pharmaceutical financing mechanisms (public financing, user charges, health insurance, donor assistance)
- Measures to improve efficiency and cost-effectiveness

Human resources development

- Role of health professions
- Role of government in planning and overseeing training and development of human resources for the pharmaceutical sector
- Human resources management and development plan
- Education, training, and courses, including minimum requirements for each cadre of professional staff
- National and international collaborating networks
- Motivation and continuing education
- Ethical framework and code of conduct

Monitoring and evaluation

- Responsibilities and commitment
- Baseline survey of the whole country
- Indicators for monitoring
- Periodic monitoring
- Independent external evaluation every two to three years

Research

- Operational research
- Pharmaceutical development and clinical research

Technical cooperation among countries

- Information sharing
- Harmonization

Sources: Adapted from WHO 1995 and WHO 2003.

Choice of essential medicines

The selection of essential medicines to meet the health needs of the population and the registration of safe, high-quality, and effective medicines are important features of an NMP. Adoption of and political commitment to the essential medicines concept should guide selection and reimbursement decisions. Essential medicines are those considered most vital for saving lives and alleviating serious and common diseases in the majority of the population. WHO created the first Model List of Essential Drugs in 1977 and encouraged countries to use it as an example for making their own lists. Such national essential medicines lists have, in many countries, become the basis of public pharmaceutical supply systems. Hospital and outpatient practice formularies commonly guide prescribing in both the private and the public sectors. The principles, criteria, and process of medicine selection are described in Chapter 16.

In a wealthy country, any medicine that meets standards of quality, safety, and efficacy can be sold, and several thousand registered pharmaceutical products may be available on the market. Where resources are limited, however, an essential medicines list can limit the number of unnecessary or inappropriate purchases. For example, more than a hundred medicines are available to treat rheumatism and arthritis, but many are similar and some are unnecessarily expensive; three or four such medicines that are proven efficacious and affordable may be all that are needed to adequately treat patients. This selective approach is likely to save money and enable a resource-limited pharmaceutical management system to concentrate on essential medicines.

Medicines may also be selected using other criteria. For example, some countries have been hesitant to add fixed-dose combination products to lists that already include the individual components. Sometimes, a drug regulatory authority may be willing to accept a product only if its price is competitive with that of similar medicines already on the market. Some countries have accepted only medicines for which they believe a "medical need" exists—for example, where the medicines have special advantages over other products. This criterion is unpopular with manufacturers, and it is difficult to apply, but many insurance schemes now use the principle to determine for which medicines they are willing to make reimbursements. The NMP can define procedures to periodically update the national essential medicines list and address the selection of traditional and herbal medications.

Supply

In many developing countries, availability of essential medicines is the most pressing concern of the NMP. To ensure that high-quality medicines are available to all, governments not only need to select their priority medicines but also to define policies in production, procurement, and distribution, as well as to provide a mechanism for financing, which can be a key limitation. Such policies should take into account what is feasible in the short term and what is necessary for sustainable systems in the long term and under special circumstances, such as when transport is likely to be impeded during the rainy season.

In most countries, the private sector operates in the pharmaceutical supply system to some degree, including commercially based producers, importers, wholesalers, pharmacies, and other retail drug sellers. Private-sector products are often relatively expensive, with the costs covered either from the patient's pocket or refunded from a private or public insurance system. In less affluent countries, however, a public pharmaceutical supply system procures and distributes medicines and makes them available to consumers at either low or no cost. These public systems were set up in part because private-sector activities were concentrated in urban areas, prices put products out of reach of the poor, and no universal health insurance systems existed. The rationale for many of these state-supported systems persists, but they often require improvements in organization, management, and financing to carry out their mandate.

Another type of supply system is operated by NGOs, such as Christian or Islamic missions. Their goal is largely to supply the needs that are not met by the commercial private sector or the public sector, especially among the poor and in rural areas. Often their role is explicitly recognized by government and incorporated into the NMP and public health strategies.

Both government and NGO health services can be supplied through a variety of alternative arrangements that incorporate components of private-sector flexibility and efficiency (see Chapter 8).

Pharmaceutical production policy (see Chapter 7) is an important aspect of pharmaceutical supply. For many years, countries have been interested in developing their own local manufacturing capacity and a degree of national self-sufficiency. Unfortunately, the difficulties of local production have frequently been underestimated. Local production in developing countries is not necessarily a low-cost venture; although wages and some other costs are likely to be lower than in industrialized countries, pharmaceutical constituents and even packaging materials have to be imported, and maintenance of machinery is costly. Many factors influence the feasibility of local production, and a range of policy options exists. When formulating an NMP, the most important objective should be to get good-quality, therapeutically useful medicines to the people who need them, at prices they can afford—policies related to industrial production should not interfere with policies related to health care.

Affordability

Affordable prices are necessary to ensure access to medicines in both the public and private sectors. Newer medicines, such as those to treat HIV/AIDS and the newer artemisinin-based combination therapies for malaria, are very expensive. Possible mechanisms to increase affordability to essential medicines in all sectors include selecting cost-effective treatments, comparing price information, promoting price competition through generic substitution, regulating producer prices and retail margins (see Chapter 9, on pharmaceutical pricing policy), limiting tariffs on pharmaceuticals, and taking advantage of trade-related intellectual property measures such as compulsory licensing and parallel imports (see Chapter 3, on intellectual property and access to medicines).

Financing strategies

Ensuring stable and adequate financing for medicines is a major challenge. Public financing of medicines for government health services to increase access to medicines is accepted as a legitimate policy in most countries and by most institutions, and indeed, funding initiatives such as the Global Fund to Fight AIDS, Tuberculosis and Malaria have dramatically altered the pharmaceutical financing context in many developing countries. In addition, financing mechanisms such as user fees are used in the least developed countries to increase financial resources, but they are difficult to manage in a way that protects the poorest members of the population. Public and private health insurance schemes are becoming more common, and including reimbursement for medicines should be promoted. Financing policies should be designed to maximize resources for pharmaceuticals while keeping prices as low as possible. These issues are discussed in Chapter 11.

Rational medicine use

Medicines should be used appropriately, safely, and only when needed. Irrational medicine use includes overuse, underuse, and inappropriate use, caused by such factors as lack of adequate regulatory systems; shortages of essential medicines and availability of nonessential medicines; lack of sound, objective medicine information; and the considerable influence of medicine promotion on both prescribers and consumers.

An NMP should specify major activities and responsibilities for promoting rational prescribing, dispensing, and patient medicine use. A wide variety of approaches has been developed in an effort to promote rational prescribing and dispensing (Chapters 29 and 30). Medicine prescribing and use have been improved in certain institutional settings. Although not yet widely implemented, programs focused on rational medicine use can help improve medicine use in the public and private sectors. Pre- and in-service training can also promote rational medicine use.

Inadequate training of health professionals, lack of control of medicine promotion, and dispensing of medicines by untrained persons all promote irrational use of medicines. Strategies for public medication education should provide individuals and communities with the information, skills, and confidence necessary to use medicines in an appropriate, safe, and judicious way (see Chapter 33).

Human resources, monitoring, evaluation, and research

Implementing an NMP depends on people; they must be trained, motivated, and retained through competitive salaries and other incentives. Human resources management is therefore an important element of the policy. The roles of different health professions should be clear. The policy should lead to a human resources management plan that identifies education, training, continuing education requirements, and other elements necessary to develop and sustain an adequate supply of skilled professionals who are motivated to perform at a high level (Chapter 51).

The implementation of an NMP should be routinely monitored, and its effect should be evaluated at regular intervals. Provisions for monitoring and evaluation need to be included in the policy itself, and adequate staff and budget need to be allocated. Appropriate use of indicators helps quantify progress and needed improvements (Chapter 36).

Research is essential for health service and health care improvements. NMPs are particularly concerned with operational research aimed at constantly improving and adapting the selection, procurement, distribution, and use of existing medicines. The Lao People's Democratic Republic (P.D.R.) incorporated operational research into the monitoring and evaluation plan of its NMP (see Country Study 4-1). NMPs may also include specific provisions for clinical research and the development of new medicines, especially using local resources, such as indigenous plants.

Finally, many NMPs address technical cooperation among countries. Cooperation among countries within the same region and the same economic area has become increasingly common. There are examples of cooperation in virtually every aspect of pharmaceutical policy and management.

4.4 Setting priorities

When the basic components of a policy have been identified, choices must be made about the most appropriate strategies and activities to achieve policy objectives at each

Country Study 4-1
Using operations research to develop and implement the Lao P.D.R. National Drug Policy

The Food and Drug Department of the Ministry of Health in the Lao People's Democratic Republic introduced a National Drug Policy (NDP) in 1993 with the goal of ensuring the availability and rational use of high-quality medicines at a low cost, with a focus on vulnerable populations in remote areas. Over the initial ten years, the Food and Drug Department implemented the policy in three phases—

- Phase I (1993–95): Develop a draft NDP, train inspectors, and create an information, education, and communication strategy on the rational use of medicines
- Phase II (1996–2000): Implement the NDP in five pilot provinces, including building individual and institutional capacity, developing related laws and standard treatment guidelines (STGs), and initiating and evaluating operations research projects
- Phase III (2001–2003): Consolidate NDP achievements and revise the policy, roll out policy implementation to the rest of the country, further strengthen pharmaceutical management capacity, and continue operations research

The success of the Lao P.D.R.'s NDP implementation is due in part to the emphasis placed on health systems research, which began during Phase II. Operations research was built into the pilot program design to improve implementation by bridging the gap between policy and practice and to provide evidence for policy making. The six operations research areas included—

- Use of public health messages to reduce irrational use of antibiotics
- Use of traditional medicine in Champassack province
- Knowledge, attitudes, and perceptions about quality of drugs among customers and health care providers (including drug sellers)
- Effectiveness of "feedback" for improving treatment based on STGs
- Methods used to effectively implement the NDP

- Regulation of private pharmacies in Savannakhet province

When results of a mid-program evaluation in 2000 showed the success of the NDP pilot program, policy makers revised the NDP to broaden its scope to include three new components: health systems research, human resources development, and overall management and coordination. In addition, recommendations were made to adapt the Lao NDP model for use elsewhere in the region.

Building research into the design of the Lao P.D.R.'s NDP yielded two strategic benefits. First, the results of this research guided the revision of the NDP in 2001 and showed policy makers how to more efficiently scale up the NDP nationwide. Second, building a research component into the NDP framework made monitoring and evaluation possible; the choice to pilot the implementation in only five districts made evaluating the NDP's effect by comparing pilot districts to control districts easier. In fact, research results showed that the pilot provinces performed significantly better in several aspects of quality and rational use of medicines. Research on the effectiveness of communications that promoted the rational use of medicines found that consumers still self-medicated with antibiotics, even after hearing medicines information on the radio and receiving advice from the doctor. This finding indicated that policy makers needed to adjust the information, education, and communication strategy regarding rational use of medicines.

Seeing the value of this research-based evaluation, policy makers made operations research a permanent component in the 2001 NDP. However, a solid operations research component alone is not enough to ensure a NDP's successful implementation. Research must be coupled with effective communication and dissemination of results, strong political will, and technical competence in the pharmaceutical sector.

Sources: Tomson et al. 2005; Lao P.D.R. Food and Drug Department 2003; Paphassarang et al. 2002.

level of the system. For example, to improve the supply system for essential medicines, many possible solutions exist: developing the central medical stores (CMS) further or transforming the CMS into a parastatal organization (as in Tanzania), decentralizing pharmaceutical procurement (as in Cameroon), or developing incentives for the private sector to manage supply and distribution. Activities

can then be undertaken to implement the approaches selected—for example, using restrictive or competitive tenders, buying only from the essential medicines list, negotiating contracts with the private sector, and so forth. A series of interventions can be undertaken to increase rational prescribing and use of essential medicines, but depending on the country, some of these strategies will

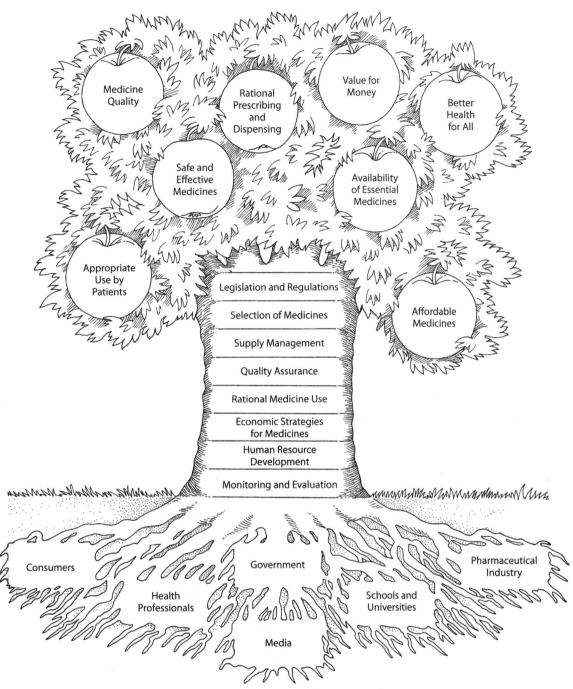

Medicine Quality

Rational Prescribing and Dispensing

Value for Money

Better Health for All

Safe and Effective Medicines

Availability of Essential Medicines

Appropriate Use by Patients

Legislation and Regulations

Selection of Medicines

Supply Management

Quality Assurance

Rational Medicine Use

Economic Strategies for Medicines

Human Resource Development

Monitoring and Evaluation

Affordable Medicines

Consumers

Government

Pharmaceutical Industry

Health Professionals

Schools and Universities

Media

NATIONAL MEDICINE POLICY—A TREE THAT BEARS FRUIT

be more cost-effective than others. Options may involve training medical students, providing independent medication information to all prescribers, or using programs for the ongoing review of medicine use to identify opportunities for improvement.

The range of strategies and activities that can be successfully implemented depends on the pharmaceutical situation and the socioeconomic conditions of the country. If resources are insufficient without external input, a set of priority activities should be identified that can be executed within existing means.

Initially, considering the following questions may be helpful—

- Is this approach based on scientific evidence, and has it proved to be effective in other countries?
- Is this approach or activity really needed to improve the situation in a particular area?

- Does it address the greatest needs?
- Are other approaches or activities available that might be more effective?

Policy elements may have to be set aside that—however successful they may have been in another country—would be no more than expensive luxuries in the local context, or would not work because too few technical and financial resources exist.

The combination of pharmaceutical policies that can be successfully implemented in a particular country over the short to medium term is closely linked to the structure of the pharmaceutical distribution systems, pharmaceutical spending levels, the presence or absence of health insurance schemes, the number of trained people available, and the capacity of the drug regulatory authority.

4.5   Formulating a national medicine policy

Formulating and implementing a national medicine policy are highly political processes. A policy should promote equity of access to health care by making the pharmaceutical sector more efficient, cost-effective, and responsive to health needs. Such responsiveness may involve the redistribution of goods and power, leading to increased competition among the groups affected by reform.

As mentioned, given the diverse interests and the economic importance of the issues involved, designing or revising an NMP requires complex negotiations with all stakeholders: the national and international pharmaceutical industry, the medical profession, retail drug sellers, NGOs, the government bureaucracy, and international donors. The challenge is to identify the main elements of an appropriate pharmaceutical policy and then construct a process that will bring the diverse groups together.

The pharmaceutical sector represents many varied interests that do not always run parallel; opposition to a new policy and sometimes even legal confrontations must be expected. Therefore, identifying political allies and maintaining their support throughout the process is important. Strategies to identify and deal with opponents should be developed, ways of working with them must be identified, and steps must be taken to resolve disputes. Differences may be resolved through effective communications, a collaborative approach, and careful monitoring of the policy formulation process. Decisions and priorities touching on the interests of various stakeholders must be balanced by estimating gains and losses. Nothing can be left to chance, particularly if the proposed policy seeks to change in an important way structures, historical practices, or the behavior of people. The more significant the proposed changes, the more the process of policy formulation should involve all stakeholders, taking account of their needs and fears and

encouraging them to take an active part in the new policy. No simple formula exists, but political will and leadership, and effective communication and collaboration are the main components for success.

Step 1. Organize the policy process

The ministry of health (MOH) is usually the most appropriate agency to take the lead in developing an NMP. The first step is to decide how formulation of the policy will be achieved, who will be involved at the various stages, and how the necessary finances will be obtained. A plan outlining the process and the final output can be drawn up by the pharmaceutical department in the ministry, with the support of a small committee. The more changes the policy seeks to produce, the more different stakeholders will need to be involved. This factor should be considered from the beginning, because it helps to determine the resources needed. The need for external assistance from WHO or other countries with experience in developing an NMP should also be assessed at this stage.

Step 2. Identify and analyze problems

The second task when formulating a policy is performing a thorough analysis of the main problems so that attainable objectives can be set (see Chapter 36). The best way to begin is to bring together a small team of experts, including some who have performed similar studies in other countries. The national experts should not come only from the MOH; they may be from the health professions, from trade and industry, and from other agencies of government (particularly the treasury). The group's function is to examine the situation systematically, identify problems and root causes, recommend what must and can be done, and suggest approaches that might be taken. Recommendations can be formulated and discussed in a multidisciplinary workshop to prepare advice for the government. Ghana followed a similar process, which led to the drafting of an NMP in 2004 by a team of experts representing diverse interests, including consumer rights, law, traditional medicine, trade, and manufacturing.

However ambitious it may seem in the early stages of medicine policy development, the situation in the country as a whole needs to be systematically reviewed so as to identify viable reforms. This objective may be best achieved through a detailed situational analysis. For example, in countries where a poor national economic situation is a major factor leading to unsatisfactory pharmaceutical supply, basing reforms on demands for more government money makes no sense because such funds are not available. The ultimate solution must take these structural constraints into account. Not everything can be done at once, and for some urgently needed changes, reliance on donor help may be necessary while a longer-term national solution is developed.

Step 3. Set goals and objectives

After high-priority problems and related goals have been defined, primary objectives can be identified. (See Box 4-3 for a list of the objectives of Malawi's NMP.) For instance, if one of the priority problems is the availability of poor-quality medicines, one of the primary objectives should be to ensure that they are replaced by products of good quality. The selection of the strategies or approaches is more complex and should come from the situational analysis in step 2 or perhaps in a workshop with key people asking some key questions: Where do these poor-quality medicines come from and why are they here? Would good-quality medicines necessarily be more expensive? What incentives would encourage improvements? After objectives and strategies are outlined, key participants can work out a strategy for improvement, which can then be discussed in a larger workshop to reach consensus among all the main participants.

However, not all the parties are likely to agree immediately on the strategy. Representatives of the pharmaceutical industry may be suspicious, fearing loss of profit; doctors and pharmacists may have different points of view and may worry about losing freedom; any party that feels secure in the status quo may feel threatened by change. Not uncommonly, one government agency will disagree with another on objectives, approaches, or timetables. To move forward, it is important to establish as much trust as possible, identify matters on which consensus and compromise are possible, and use those matters as the basis on which to proceed.

Step 4. Draft the policy

After a thorough analysis of the situation and an outline of the main goals, objectives, and approaches have been completed, a draft of the NMP should be written. It should state the general goal of the policy; in most countries, the goal will be to ensure that high-quality medicines are accessible and affordable to the entire population and that they are used rationally. Then the NMP should describe specific objectives and the strategy or strategies to be adopted for meeting each. For example, to ensure that essential medicines are available in health facilities (objective), the policy might propose the creation of an autonomous procurement unit and the strengthening of pharmaceutical management in health facilities (strategies).

This drafting of the policy can be done by the small committee of experts set up in step 2, with the support of the people who performed the situational analysis. The group should remain small, because a big group is difficult to manage and will have problems drafting a coherent text. The group may find that examples of NMP documents from other countries are helpful.

The draft policy should be assessed for its approach to human rights issues. Human rights concern the relationship between the state and the individual, generating individual rights and state obligations. Box 4-4 includes a list of questions to ask when assessing health programs for their attention to the right to health.

Step 5. Circulate and revise the policy

To get full support from all sectors, the document should be widely circulated for comments, first within the MOH

Box 4-3
Objectives of Malawi's 2009 National Medicine Policy

Broad objective of the NMP

To develop within the available resources the potential that medicines have to control common diseases and alleviate suffering.

Specific objectives of the NMP

- To ensure ready and constant availability (universal access) of essential medicines and medical supplies to the community
- To rationalize use of these essential medicines through the provision of improved medicine utilization information
- To educate the public on appropriate medicine use and storage

- To improve supply management, prescribing, dispensing practices, and patient adherence
- To ensure continuing education and professional development for pharmaceutical and other relevant health workers
- To institute a sustainable financing mechanism to ensure continuous availability of adequate quantities of the required essential medicines
- To ensure effective regulation of pharmaceuticals
- To strengthen partnership at the national, regional, and international levels in ensuring the full implementation of NMP through utilization of available resources, knowledge, and expertise

Source: Government of Malawi 2009.

Box 4-4
Access to essential medicines as part of the fulfillment of the right to health

The basic principles of what is called the "rights-based approach" include participation, accountability, non-discrimination, attention to vulnerable groups, and explicit linkage to human rights instruments. Five simple questions are presented here to assess the medicines policy in a specific country or program.

1. Which essential medicines are covered by the right to health? Although WHO provides guidance on essential medicine lists, exactly which medicines are regarded as essential remains a national responsibility and, therefore, the national list of essential medicines should be used to define the minimum needs. If no such national list exists, the first step is to develop one. For situations outside the scope of national governments, such as ships and refugee camps, specific lists of essential medicines have been developed by WHO and relevant stakeholders.

2. Have all beneficiaries of the medicine program been consulted? True participation means that the beneficiaries of national medicines policies and programs are consulted in decisions that affect them. Besides the usual stakeholders, such as the government, universities, and professional associations, other important beneficiaries to be consulted are rural communities, nongovernmental organizations, patients and consumer groups, and representatives of the vulnerable groups listed in item 4.

3. Do mechanisms exist for transparency and accountability? The objectives of the medicines policy and program should be clear and include government obligations to respect, protect, and fulfill the right to health in line with any applicable international treaties. The policy should identify indicators and targets to monitor progress toward universal access to essential medicines. The national medicines policy should specify the roles and responsibilities of all stakeholders, with mechanisms in place to hold each of them accountable.

4. Do all vulnerable groups have equal access to essential medicines? How do you know? The main vulnerable groups to be considered are children (especially girls), women, people living in poverty, rural communities, indigenous populations, national (ethnic, religious, linguistic) minorities, internally displaced persons, the elderly, those with disabilities, and prisoners. Ensuring equality starts with collecting disaggregated access statistics for each of these groups. Such statistics are essential to create awareness among policy makers, to identify vulnerable groups that need special attention, and to monitor progress toward universal access. The minimum effort should consist of gender-disaggregated statistics and surveys specifically aimed at vulnerable groups.

5. Are safeguards and redress mechanisms in place in case human rights are violated? Access to essential medicines is best ensured by the development and implementation of rights-based medicines policies and programs; however, when progress is unjustifiably slow, mechanisms for redress and appeal are needed as a last resort. A WHO study has shown that targeted litigation is an additional means to encourage governments to fulfill their constitutional and international treaty obligations regarding the right to health and access to essential medicines.

Sources: Hogerzeil et al. 2006; Hogerzeil 2006.

---

and then in other government departments and agencies. Endorsement by ministries or departments, such as planning, finance, education, and commerce, is of particular importance, because the success of decisions regarding registration, foreign exchange allocations, and human resources development depends on the support of government officials outside the health sector. After this wide consultation is completed, the document can be finalized. Although the formulation of the policy should reflect broad participation by the community, health workers, the pharmaceutical industry, and universities, ultimate responsibility for producing the policy remains with the MOH and the government.

Step 6. Obtain formal endorsement for the policy

In some countries, the document can then go to the cabinet or parliament for formal endorsement. In others, it can be an administrative document that serves as a basis for the implementation plans and for changes in pharmaceutical laws, which are often needed. In certain cases the NMP document becomes a law—for example, in Uganda, where it was called the National Drug Policy and Authority Statute; however, the MOH found that arrangement made the implementation and revision of the NMP unwieldy, so the revised NMP was separated from the statute in 2002. Although creating a law can demonstrate strong commitment on the part of the government, it is not always advantageous, because legislation is difficult to pass and difficult to change once enacted. Incorporating select components of the NMP into a law, such as was done with the Generics Act in the Philippines, may be more useful. When a national medicine policy was drafted in 2000 in newly independent East Timor, the policy was written as a simple text that could be printed in the media and posted on health facility walls for all to read, so that it became the property of the people as a nation.

Step 7. Launch the policy

Launching an NMP is a political task rather than merely a technical one. It requires as much attention as any other political campaign. Promotion should be based on good information, top-level political support, mobilization of highly qualified people, and securing of international support. The policy should be promoted through a clear and well-designed campaign that disseminates information through a variety of channels to reach different target groups. The policy needs to be explained in a way that allows the media and the public to become involved in discussions.

4.6   Implementing a national medicine policy

Policy implementation—the execution of approaches included in the policy through specific plans and programs—is a critical step; the policy itself is worthless if it is not implemented. Each NMP requires an overall implementation plan or master plan. Given the multisectoral nature of pharmaceutical issues, the MOH should develop, as early as possible, a consensus with other government agencies on action plans dealing with specific issues of economics and finance (including foreign exchange), commerce, industry, and education. The implementation plan roughly outlines for each component of the policy what needs to be done and who is responsible, estimates the budget requirement, and proposes an estimated time frame. The implementation plan allows coordination of donor input and assists in monitoring the policy implementation and intervening where necessary to keep the process moving.

The master plan should then be broken down into annual workplans, which should be carefully developed with the various agencies involved in implementation. The workplans should outline the specific approaches and activities for each component, specifying in detail who is responsible, listing the major tasks, and describing the target output, the detailed time frame, and the exact budget. (See Chapter 38 for more information on developing plans.)

Countries take different approaches to implementation (see Country Study 4-2 for Australia's approach). In all cases,

if the policy is to succeed, government officials must be proactive and committed. A number of strategies are summarized below.

Use appropriate timing, and a combination of approaches and methods of implementation. Not everything can be done at the same time. In the Philippines, the rules for generic labeling and promotion had to be put in place before generic prescribing and dispensing could be implemented. In practice, a one-year interval was necessary between the issuance of the rules on generic labeling and the issuance of those on dispensing. In this way, by the time doctors and pharmacists were required to switch to generics, the products in the pharmacies had already been generically labeled.

Start implementation in relatively easy-to-change areas to ensure initial high-visibility success. Perception of success is an important consideration; if the policy is perceived to have yielded significant positive results, it is likely to continue to receive support from important sectors.

Adopt a flexible policy. In certain cases, an activity may have to be postponed because the timing is not right. If, for example, the policy proposes imposing strict rules on pricing, waiting until pharmacists have received an explanation about why the rules will be to everyone's advantage may be better than imposing the rules immediately and being met with resistance. Consensus building should always be balanced against compromising too much on key points. If the initial planning process has been carried out properly, valid objections should already have been addressed, and there should be no need to compromise later.

Use experts to vouch for the policy's technical soundness. It is important that the most qualified people in the medical and pharmaceutical fields support the policy (for example, clinical pharmacologists or specialists in the main hospitals and universities). Those who have been involved in developing the policy are likely to be its strongest advocates and its most useful allies as it is introduced and implemented.

Mobilize consumers, the media, or other key groups. Although such mobilization has been successful in the Philippines and Australia, this approach has not been common in Africa, because of the lack of a well-organized consumers' movement.

Create constituencies that support the policy both inside and outside the government. After suspicions have been allayed, such constituencies may be found in any sector. Even within the private sector, support will develop when people realize that a healthy public sector will complement rather than undermine the private sector. Having constituencies in all sectors is critical to the success of the implementation and the long-term sustainability of the policy.

Country Study 4-2
Innovative approaches in formulating and implementing a national medicine policy in Australia

In 1985, WHO called the Conference of Experts on the Rational Use of Drugs, which resulted in a document known as the *Revised Drug Strategy*. The 39th World Health Assembly, held in 1986, adopted this strategy, which calls on governments to implement a national medicinal drug policy. Australia, as a participant at this assembly, contributed to the development of this strategy. The need for a national medicine policy was further illustrated in the *Health for All Australians* document issued jointly by all Australian state and territorial health ministers in 1988.

Initially, in 1991, the government formed two advisory groups. The Australian Pharmaceutical Advisory Council (APAC) was a council of representatives from the major organizations involved, which would raise issues and make recommendations across the gamut of medicine policy. APAC represented an opportunity for all interested parties to contribute positively on a multilateral and consensus basis to the development and conduct of the policy.

The second group was the Pharmaceutical Health and Rational Use of Medicines (PHARM) working party, which advised the ministry on a policy for the use of medicines and a strategy for its implementation. PHARM drew on the best available knowledge and relevant concepts to establish a coherent framework for tackling the complex set of problems involved in the way medicines are used. The group also drew on research in behavioral change and health education; espoused principles of community ownership, participation, and consultation; and acknowledged the importance of media advocacy.

In 1992, this collaborative approach led to adoption of a draft national medicine policy. The approach was to—

- Use consumer and professional education as a primary tool
- Stimulate partnerships among the major players
- Identify—
  - What will empower consumers to use drugs well and encourage health professionals to help them do this?
  - What constitutes effective education?
  - What combination of information, skills, and motivation will be effective for different groups?
  - What will work in practice?
  - What standards should apply, and who should set them?

After policies were developed and implemented over several years, the government conducted a major review during 1999. What had evolved were four good but separate programs for improving the availability, quality, and quality use of medicines and the viability of the national pharmaceutical industry. In late 1999, the revised policy bringing these four programs together into one document was launched with government-wide support.

The 2000 National Medicines Policy has four objectives based on active partnerships, taking into account elements of social and economic policy—

- *Timely access to the medicines that Australians need, at a cost individuals and the community can afford.* The Commonwealth Government's Pharmaceutical Benefits Scheme helps improve the health of all Australian residents by ensuring they have timely access to necessary and lifesaving medicines at an affordable price.
- *Medicines meeting appropriate standards of quality, safety, and efficacy.* The Therapeutic Goods Administration provides a national framework for regulating therapeutic goods in Australia. It also ensures their quality, safety and efficacy.
- *Quality use of medicines.* Australia's National Strategy for Quality Use of Medicines (QUM) is central to the National Medicines Policy. The National Strategy for QUM is intended to assist the QUM partners, health care consumers, health practitioners and educators, health care facilities, the medicines industries, the media, health care funders and purchasers, and governments in becoming more aware of the QUM framework and approach.
- *Maintaining a responsible and viable medicines industry.* The chairs of the National Medicines Policy groups—the Pharmaceutical Health and Rational Use of Medicines Committee; the Australian Pharmaceutical Advisory Council; the Pharmaceutical Benefits Advisory Committee; and the National Prescribing Services—meet regularly to discuss issues of importance to the National Medicines Policy.

Each partner shares responsibility to various degrees for achieving each of these objectives, and all partners consider these central objectives in any relevant initiatives. The policy also recognizes the fundamental role consumers have in reaching these objectives, and all partners have committed to consult with consumer representatives. As of 2010, the policy still served as the framework for Australia's pharmaceutical sector.

Sources: Hodge 1993; Australian Government 1999.

There is no single, perfect way to implement an NMP. In most countries, the implementation process is launched and maintained directly through the pharmacy department of the MOH, as in Guinea, Tanzania, and Zimbabwe. Such a department is generally supported by committees that continue to deal with different aspects of the policy. The problem with this approach is the policy's lack of visibility; often, the limited human and financial resources of these departments prevent them from being proactive and coordinating all the actors, and physicians may not accept the promotion of rational medicine use if it comes from the MOH pharmacy department. In addition, the department may focus too much on pharmacological issues rather than on the broad public health aspects that should inform the NMP. The policy's central leadership needs to smooth out these differences and facilitate implementation; for example, by having the rational use component of the policy come from the medical department or an NGO. Country Study 4-3 illustrates how implementation can go wrong.

Regional cooperation can be useful in implementing medicine policies. Countries, institutions, and organizations can share information, expertise, skills, and facilities. Exchanging experiences helps ensure that best practices are promoted, that mistakes are not repeated, and that limited resources are used effectively. The East, Central, and Southern Africa Health Community of fourteen member countries has developed a template for a national pharmaceutical policy that its members can use as a resource for creating or revising their own national policies. The WHO Regional Office for Africa has a website with country profiles that include documents related to national medicine policy in African countries (http://www.afro.who.int/en/clusters-a-programmes/hss/essential-medicines/edm-country-profiles.html). These various documents can be used as resources and bases for comparison for any country developing or implementing an NMP.

4.7   Monitoring and evaluating a national medicine policy

Monitoring is a form of continuous review that allows senior managers to assess the progress toward achieving defined targets in each policy area and adjust strategies accordingly. It can be carried out using a combination of methods, including supervisory visits and both routine and sentinel reporting.

Evaluation is a way of analyzing progress toward meeting objectives and goals. It should build on and use monitoring systems. At the start of a program, evaluation is used to provide a clear assessment of needs. A midterm evaluation can provide valuable information about how well the program is working. Final evaluation allows a complete review of program achievements from which lessons can be drawn for the future.

A system for monitoring and evaluation serves as a management tool that enables continuous assessment of progress and helps officials make management decisions in response to problems identified. The findings, results, and recommendations of the monitoring and evaluation team should be discussed with national stakeholders and should serve as the basis for identifying problems, finding solutions, and improving performance. A monitoring and evaluation sys-

---

Country Study 4-3
When things go wrong with national medicine policies: The case of Yemen

From 1995 to 2002, the Republic of Yemen received technical help in developing a national medicine policy. An important element included the creation of an effective public pharmaceutical supply system to serve the 30 percent of the population unable to afford private-sector medicines.

Initially funded by donors, the system was intended to rely partly on government funding and partly on patient contributions. By late 2005, the system had virtually collapsed, and in an attempt to improve the situation, the government "nationalized" the system and declared that all medicines would be supplied free of charge from then on; however, no evident improvement occurred. By early 2006, donors were helping the government determine why the system had failed while instituting an emergency supply program.

The situational analysis showed that the revolving fund proposal had never been adequately implemented through a detailed plan of action, that expectations of patient contributions had been too optimistic in view of widespread poverty, that successive governments had shown too little commitment to funding, and that corruption had played a major role.

In such situations, bringing together the original players and seeking their views on the failure and on a recovery plan are vital. In Yemen, a small-scale emergency scheme was set up to restore faith in the system, to be followed by a longer-term (five-year) recovery plan.

tem also provides transparency and accountability and creates a standard by which comparisons can be made between countries and areas and over time. All this information may produce the necessary evidence that progress is being made (or not) to support the policy in discussions with interested parties and policy makers.

Indicators for monitoring national medicine policies have been developed by WHO and are discussed in Chapters 36 and 48. Indicators may need to be developed, adapted, or deleted to match particular national contexts. For example, countries may have additional objectives beyond those included in the WHO manual, such as development of national medicine production. In any case, a formal monitoring system is needed; ideally, this system would be integrated with the health information system. A lack of understanding about the value of monitoring and feedback can be a limitation that results in the inadequate allocation of human and budgetary resources. Therefore, this institution-building process requires the commitment of senior policy makers, but effective monitoring can be carried out even in countries with limited resources.

4.8 Constraints and facilitating factors

Formulating and implementing an NMP should be manageable, yet few countries have succeeded in implementing all aspects of their planned policies. Why? Some of the main reasons are clear—

Lack of political will: Many governments hesitate to create policies that might antagonize industry and other groups, particularly if opposition is known to exist. Building support even in potentially hostile sectors is important at the start of the process and as implementation progresses.

Lack of resources: Often, understanding or documentation of the problems, their causes, and solutions in the pharmaceutical sector is not sufficient to persuade national governments to devote scarce resources to building and implementing NMPs. The MOH will need to be persuasive in its communication with other ministries and departments to avoid these problems; the essential message is that a national medicine policy contributes to improving people's health and therefore to strengthening the economy and the nation.

Opposition: Frank opposition to medicine policies often comes from those who benefit from a laissez-faire approach. Doctors fear interference with their freedom to prescribe. Importers and manufacturers are commonly earning large profits on precisely the medicines or pharmaceutical practices that they fear would be threatened by policy changes, such as price controls or better procurement procedures. Retail pharmacists may oppose policy initiatives that would threaten their earnings.

Corruption: Corruption can be an issue in the pharmaceutical sector, where a great deal of money flows and where demand, as a rule, greatly exceeds supply. No easy solution exists; corrupt practices in a country usually extend well beyond the pharmaceutical sector. However, as the pharmaceutical sector balances the roles of public and private services, corruption is likely to decrease.

None of these impediments is easily overcome, but a number of factors can facilitate the policy process—

Support of domestic and international interest groups: Some of the domestic groups whose support is needed include political parties, industry groups, physicians and other health care professionals, consumers, and consumer activist groups. International interest groups include foreign governments, multilateral organizations, multinational corporations, and international lending agencies. Their support is required for successful policy formulation, even if it is sometimes necessary to enter into bargains and trade-offs to win such support. The consequences of each trade-off in the formulation and implementation of pharmaceutical policies should be carefully considered.

Shared values: The extent to which a congruence of interests exists among groups is another important predictor of the success of an NMP. The interests of a politically weak group (for example, poor consumers) can often be protected if its goals coincide, at least partially, with those of more powerful interest groups (for example, retail pharmacists who want to sell more medicines and are willing to handle generic products because the higher volume of sales can compensate for lower unit earnings).

The macroeconomic situation: Improvements in the efficiency of the pharmaceutical system may help countries cope with the consequences of macroeconomic shocks. For instance, the devaluation of the franc in West Africa pushed countries in the region to strengthen their essential medicines policies in the public sector and to introduce mechanisms to promote the sale of medicines under generic names in the private sector alongside more expensive branded products.

Technical expertise: The existence of technical expertise and capabilities within ministries of health, as well as access to data on patent-related issues and pharmacological, legal, and economic policy (including the policies of other countries), are key to the formulation of a sound and workable policy. WHO has a cadre of medicine advisers located in its country offices who can provide technical expertise (http://www.who.int/medicines/areas/coordination/medicinesadvisers/en/index.html). Donors and international organizations can also sup-

ASSESSMENT GUIDE

National medicine policy development and content

- Does an official NMP document exist? Has it been updated in the past ten years?
- Does the document contain objectives and strategies based on priority problems?
- Does it cover issues such as legislation, essential medicines list, registration of pharmaceuticals, supply of essential medicines, financing and pricing policies, and rational use of medicines?
- If no official NMP document exists, do any unofficial documents set objectives and strategies for the pharmaceutical sector?
- Do laws exist that specify the government's responsibility in ensuring equitable access to essential medicines?
- Does the national constitution or any other national law recognize the right of everyone to the enjoyment of the highest attainable standard of health?
- Were patients' organizations and rural communities consulted when the NMP and program were developed?

NMP implementation

- Is the NMP used as a guide for action by policy makers and senior management officers in the ministry of health?
- Does the NMP describe the obligations of the various stakeholders?
- Does the pharmaceutical legislation provide a legal basis for enforcement of the NMP?
- Does an implementation plan exist to put the policy into practice?
- Is the policy monitored regularly? If so, how is it monitored? Are baseline and target data available on access to essential medicines against which progress can be measured?
- Does any evaluation take place of the performance and outcome of the NMP in terms of attaining its objectives?
- Are legal mechanisms available to file complaints about lack of access to essential medicines? If so, have they been used?
- Is the NMP highly visible in the ministry of health and the government?

port the emergence and revision of medicine policies in developing countries through planning and technical assistance.

The presence of committed people in the MOH: In the United Kingdom in 1968, Bangladesh in 1982, the Philippines in 1986, Guinea in 1992, and Uganda in 1993, the development of these countries' first medicine policies was sustained by individuals and institutions that were persuaded of the need for it and worked toward its realization.

Each country must shape its own NMP in accordance with its needs and resources. The goals outlined at the beginning of this chapter provide a policy focus. Experiences in countries show that success in terms of public health is linked to the essential medicines concept, with an emphasis on a list of essential medicines. Strategies vary among countries, and in the end, the impact of a country's NMP depends on political commitment from the government and the support of doctors and other health professionals. ∎

References and further readings

★ = Key readings.

Anello, E. 2006. *Ethical Infrastructure for Good Governance in the Public Pharmaceutical Sector.* Working Draft for Field Testing and Revision. Geneva: World Health Organization/Department of Medicines Policy and Standards. <http://www.who.int/entity/medicines/areas/policy/goodgovernance/Ethical_Infrastructure.pdf>

Australian Government, Department of Health and Ageing. 1999. *National Medicine Policy 2000.* Canberra: Commonwealth of Australia. <http://www.health.gov.au/internet/main/publishing.nsf/Content/0241A32640D477CACA256F18004685E4/$File/nmp2000.pdf>

Brudon, P. 1997. *Comparative Analysis of National Drug Policies.* Geneva: World Health Organization.

★ Brudon, P., J.-D. Rainhorn, and M. R. Reich. 1999. *Indicators for Monitoring National Drug Policies: A Practical Manual.* 2nd ed. Geneva: World Health Organization. <http://whqlibdoc.who.int/hq/1999/WHO_EDM_PAR_99.3_pp1-114.pdf>

★ Dag Hammarskjöld Foundation. 1995. Making National Drug Policies a Development Priority: A Strategy Paper and Six Country Studies (Norway, Sri Lanka, Bangladesh, Australia, India, Mexico). *Development Dialogue* 1:1–240. <http://www.dhf.uu.se/pdffiler/95_1.pdf>

Dukes, M. N. G. 2005. "The Industry and the Developing World." In *The Law and Ethics of the Pharmaceutical Industry.* London: Elsevier.

Federal Ministry of Health Nigeria/WHO. 2005. National Drug Policy. Abuja: Federal Ministry of Health. <http://collections.info collections.org/whocountry/collect/whocountry/pdf/s6865e/s6865e.pdf>

Government of Malawi. 2009, National Medicine Policy Malawi. Lilongwe: Ministry of Health.

Hodge, M. M. 1993. Australia Focuses on the Quality Use of Medicines: Policy and Action. *Essential Drugs Monitor* 15:12–3.

Hogerzeil, H. V. 2006. Essential Medicines and Human Rights: What Can They Learn from Each Other? *Bulletin of the World Health Organization* 84:371–5.

———. 2004. The Concept of Essential Medicines: Lessons for Rich Countries. *BMJ* 329:1169–72.

Hogerzeil, H. V., M. Samson, J. Casanovas, and L. Rahmani-Ocora. 2006. Is Access to Essential Medicines as Part of the Fulfilment of the Right to Health Enforceable through the Courts? *Lancet* 368:305–11.

Lao P.D.R. Food and Drug Department of the Ministry of Health. 2003. National Drug Policy Programme 1993–2003. Vientiane: Ministry of Health.

Ministry of Health, Ghana. 2004. National Drug Policy. 2nd ed. Accra: Ministry of Health.

Paphassarang, C., R. Wahlström, B. Phoummalaysith, B. Boupha, and G. Tomson. 2002. Building the National Drug Policy on Evidence: A Cross-Sectional Study on Assessing Implementation in Lao P.D.R. *Southeast Asian Journal of Tropical Medicine and Public Health* 33(3):647–53.

Peltzer, K., N. Phaswana-Mafuya, G. Mohlala, S. Ramlagan, A. Davids, K. Zuma, and N. Mbelle. 2006. *Impact of the National Drug Policy on Pharmaceuticals in Two Provinces in South Africa.* Pretoria: Human Sciences Research Council. <http://www.hsrc.ac.za/Research_Publication-19478.phtml>

Phanouvong, S., S. Barraclough, and K. Harvey. 2002. How to Implement National Drug Policies Successfully. *Essential Drugs Monitor* 31:26–7.

★ Rainhorn, J.-D., P. Brudon-Jakobowicz, and M. R. Reich. 1994. Priorities for Pharmaceutical Policies in Developing Countries: Results of a Delphi Survey. *Bulletin of the World Health Organization* 72:257–64. < http://whqlibdoc.who.int/bulletin/1994/Vol72-No2/bulletin_1994_72(2)_257-264.pdf>

★ Seiter, A. 2010. *A Practical Approach to Pharmaceutical Policy.* Washington, D.C.: The World Bank. <http://issuu.com/world.bank.publications/docs/9780821383865>

Stevens, P., and H. Linfield. 2010. *Death and Taxes: Government Mark-ups on the Price of Drugs.* London: International Policy Network. <http://www.policynetwork.net/sites/default/files/Death&Taxes web.pdf>

Tomson, G., C. Paphassarang, K. Jonsson, K. Houamboun, K. Akkhavong, and R. Wahlstrom. 2005. Decision-Makers and the Usefulness of Research Evidence in Policy Implementation—A Case Study from Lao PDR. *Social Science & Medicine* 61:1291–9.

WHO (World Health Organization). 2010. *Continuity and Change: Implementing the Third WHO Medicines Strategy—2008–2013.* Geneva: WHO. <http://apps.who.int/medicinedocs/pdf/s16821e/s16821e_lo.pdf>

———. 2009. *WHO Model List of Essential Medicines.* 16th ed. Geneva: WHO. (Updated every two years.) <http://www.who.int/selection_medicines/committees/expert/17/sixteenth_adult_list_en.pdf >

★ ———. 2006. *Using Indicators to Measure Country Pharmaceutical Situations: Fact Book on WHO Level I and Level II Monitoring Indicators.* Geneva: WHO. <http://www.who.int/medicines/areas/rational_use/AMU_Surveillance/en/>

———. 2004a. *WHO Medicines Strategy 2004–2007: Countries at the Core.* Geneva: WHO. <http://whqlibdoc.who.int/hq/2004/WHO_EDM_2004.2.pdf>

———. 2004b. The World Medicines Situation. *Geneva: WHO.* <http://whqlibdoc.who.int/hq/2004/WHO_EDM_PAR_2004.5.pdf>

★ ———. 2003. How to Develop and Implement a National Drug Policy. *WHO Policy Perspectives on Medicines* 6:1–6.

★ ———. 2001. *How to Develop and Implement a National Drug Policy.* 2nd ed. Geneva: WHO. <http://whqlibdoc.who.int/publications/924154547X.pdf>

———. 1995. *Report of the WHO Expert Committee on National Drug Policies.* Geneva: WHO. <http://whqlibdoc.who.int/hq/1995/WHO_DAP_95.9.pdf>

WHO/EDM (World Health Organization/Essential Medicines). 2002. "National Drug Policy Monitoring and Evaluation." Presentation available in *Course Report on Drug Policy Issues for Developing Countries.* Geneva: WHO.

WHO/WPRO (World Health Organization/Regional Office for the Western Pacific). 2004. *Enhancing Health Policy Development: A Practical Guide to Understanding the Legislative Process.* Manila: WHP/WPRO. <http://www.wpro.who.int/publications/pub_9290610859.htm>

World Bank. 1993. *World Development Report 1993: Investing in Health.* New York: Oxford University Press.

CHAPTER 5

Traditional and complementary medicine policy

SUMMARY

For thousands of years, traditional medicine (TM) has been an important source of health care for much of the world, and many populations use and value TM not only as the source of their primary health care but also as part of their spiritual and cultural belief systems. Meanwhile, people in Europe, Australia, and North America have increasingly embraced TM, also referred to as complementary and alternative medicine (CAM), by using herbal medications to complement their standard health care.

Attractive features of TM practices include greater accessibility in many parts of the world, cultural acceptance in low- and middle-income countries, comparatively low cost and, often, a lesser need for modern technology. In developed countries, CAM is used for preventing disease and maintaining wellness, in addition to complementing conventional care for chronic and acute health conditions.

Although TM/CAM has a great influence on health care practices, there is wide variation from country to country in policies, laws, and regulations governing the safety, quality, and efficacy of TM/CAM therapies. Many consumers use herbal products to treat themselves—often without a health practitioner's knowledge or advice.

Consumers and practitioners may not be adequately informed about potential adverse effects, drug interactions, and how to use herbal medicines safely. Lack of regulations on quality standards and evaluation for safety and efficacy of these products may cause problems, resulting in the marketing of unsafe or ineffective TM/CAM products.

Countries that already have a strong pharmaceutical regulatory structure in place should adapt their existing systems to include herbal medications, and countries that lack regulatory standards should work toward setting up a national system that encompasses both pharmaceuticals and herbal medicines. All countries should have some framework in place to review and monitor herbal medicines, including a regulatory agency, a national advisory committee, and a system to monitor adverse reactions from herbal medicines.

Expanding the credibility and integration of TM/CAM will require developing an evidence base for safety and efficacy, which means consolidating data from existing national and international studies and supporting new research to fill evidence gaps.

5.1 The changing role of traditional and complementary medicine in health care

For thousands of years, traditional medicine has been an important source of health care for much of the world, and many populations use TM not only as the source of their primary health care but also as part of their spiritual and cultural belief systems. Meanwhile, people in Europe, Australia, and North America have increasingly embraced alternative and complementary practices, such as the use of herbal medications, to supplement their standard health care.

The growing attention focused on TM has introduced a number of public health issues in developing and developed countries alike, including policy, safety and quality, efficacy, access, and appropriate use. Regulations that ensure the quality and safety of TM products and procedures are often lacking, and because herbal medicines are now marketed across regions and internationally, these issues have evolved from being local in scale and are now of global concern.

Definitions of traditional and complementary medicine

The World Health Organization (WHO) defines *traditional medicine* as—

Diverse health practices, approaches, knowledge and beliefs incorporating plant, animal, and/or mineral based medicines, spiritual therapies, manual techniques and exercises applied singularly or in combination to maintain well-being, as well as to treat, diagnose or prevent illness (WHO 2002, 7).

Traditional medicine is a comprehensive term that refers to forms of medicine long-established in a country, whether developed or developing. Health care practices that are not part of a country's own tradition and that are not well established within the country's conventional health care system are often referred to as *complementary* and *alternative* medicine. Sometimes, the terms *complementary medicine* or *alternative medicine* are used interchangeably with *traditional medicine,* but CAM may include more recently developed technologies, unlike TM.

TM/CAM therapies are considered medication based if they use herbal medicines, animal parts, minerals, or homeopathic remedies. Herbal medicines include herbs, herbal materials, herbal preparations, and finished herbal products that contain therapeutically active ingredients that are plant based. Therapeutic interventions that are not based primarily on medications are procedure based. These therapies may include acupuncture; manual therapies, such as massage and chiropractic, heat, or exercises; and qigong, tai chi, yoga, meditation, or spiritual practices. Box 5-1 includes a list of definitions developed by WHO related to TM/CAM and herbal medications.

Increasing popularity of traditional and complementary medicine

Traditional medicine has been used continuously in developing countries for centuries, but more recently, alternatives to conventional medicine have become increasingly popular in developed countries. TM and CAM have also attracted more attention within the context of the globalization of the health care sector, health sector reform, and health care provision. The popularity of TM/CAM is reflected in its worldwide economic importance: the global market for herbal medicines is estimated to be over 60 billion U.S. dollars (USD) and growing 10 to 20 percent a year (UNCTD 2000).

Traditional and complementary medicine usage is widespread. For example, according to WHO, up to 80 percent of people in Africa and Asia use TM as part of their primary health care; in China, traditional herbs make up 30

Box 5-1
WHO definitions related to traditional medicines

Traditional medicine. *Traditional medicine* is the sum total of the knowledge, skills, and practices based on the theories, beliefs, and experiences indigenous to different cultures, whether explicable or not, used in the maintenance of health as well as in the prevention, diagnosis, improvement, or treatment of physical and mental illness.

Complementary/alternative medicine. The terms *complementary medicine* and *alternative medicine* are used interchangeably with *traditional medicine* in some countries. They refer to a broad set of health care practices that are not part of that country's own tradition and are not integrated into the dominant health care system.

Herbal medicines. *Herbal medicines* are defined as plant-derived material or preparations with therapeutic or other human health benefits, which contain either raw or processed ingredients from one or more plants. In some traditions, material of inorganic or animal origin may also be present. Specific elements of herbal medicines are defined as discussed here.

- *Herbs,* including crude plant material such as leaves, flowers, fruit, seed, stems, wood, bark, roots, rhizomes, or other plant parts, which may be entire, fragmented, or powdered.
- *Herbal materials,* including, in addition to herbs, fresh juices, gums, fixed oils, essential oils, resins, and dry powders of herbs. In some countries, these materials may be processed by various local procedures, such as steaming, roasting, or stir-baking with honey, alcoholic beverages, or other materials.
- *Herbal preparations* are the basis for finished herbal products and may include comminuted or powdered herbal materials, or extracts, tinctures, and fatty oils of herbal materials. They are produced by extraction, fractionation, purification, concentration, or other

physical or biological processes. They also include preparations made by steeping or heating herbal materials in alcoholic beverages and/or honey, or in other materials.
- *Finished herbal products,* consisting of herbal preparations made from one or more herbs. If more than one herb is used, the term *mixture herbal product* can also be used. Finished herbal products and mixture herbal products may contain excipients in addition to the active ingredients. However, finished products or mixture products to which chemically defined active substances have been added, including synthetic compounds and/or isolated constituents from herbal materials, are not considered to be herbal.

Traditional use of herbal medicines. This refers to the long historical use of these medicines. Their use is well established and widely acknowledged to be safe and effective, and may be accepted by national authorities.

Therapeutic activity. This refers to the successful prevention, diagnosis, and treatment of physical and mental illnesses; improvement of symptoms of illnesses; as well as beneficial alteration or regulation of the physical and mental status of the body.

Active ingredients. These are ingredients of herbal medicines with therapeutic activity. In herbal medicines where the active ingredients have been identified, the preparation of these medicines should be standardized to contain a defined amount of the active ingredients, if adequate analytical methods are available. In cases where it is not possible to identify the active ingredients, the whole herbal medicine may be considered as one active ingredient.

Sources: Adapted from WHO 2002, 2000.

to 50 percent of total medicine consumption; and 90 percent of Germans, 70 percent of Canadians, and 50 percent of Swedes have used a natural remedy at some time (WHO 2008b; Hanssen et al. 2005).

Even with the long history of TM use in most countries, however, and a sharp increase in TM/CAM in developed countries, a schism remains between traditional and conventional medical practice. Typically, both traditional and conventional practitioners are unaware or even suspicious of what the other can offer in terms of health care and services. In addition, patients can be reluctant to admit to health care providers that they are using both types of treatment, creating what could be a potentially alarming risk—especially for those patients taking certain herbal medications in combination with pharmaceuticals.

But barriers to addressing issues related to TM/CAM appear to be weakening in some areas, such as government recognition. More countries are considering ways to integrate TM/CAM into their national health care system, as some Asian countries, including China and South Korea, already do (Holliday 2003). For example, a recent report notes that increasing numbers of U.S. hospitals and physicians are offering CAM therapies; more insurers are covering alternative treatments; and integrative medicine centers now exist, many of which have ties to medical schools and teaching hospitals (IOM 2005). Developing countries, too, are acting on the need to officially recognize TM; for example, the government of Uganda has begun to integrate TM into its health system, and South Africa now legally recognizes traditional healers as health care professionals (Bianchi 2004).

5.2 Why people use traditional and complementary medicines

Positive features that attract people to TM/CAM include diversity, flexibility, greater accessibility in many parts of the world, extensive acceptance in developing countries, comparatively low cost, and a lesser need for modern technological capability.

Accessibility

Traditional medicine therapies are commonly used in developing countries because they are often more widely available and more affordable than conventional therapies. In addition, because TM practices are, often, woven into everyday life and belief systems, and because traditional healers are trusted members of the community, TM is often the first source of health care at the community level. Conventional health care may be a last resort, especially if the nearest primary health care facility is some distance from the community.

In resource-limited countries, especially in rural areas, there are usually fewer conventional health care practitioners than TM practitioners. In India, TM is the only available source of health care for a large part of the rural population (WHO 2002). This situation has been aggravated as large numbers of trained and licensed conventional health care workers leave their native countries for better opportunities elsewhere (the "brain drain" phenomenon); sub-Saharan Africa has been particularly hard hit (see Chapter 51).

In developed countries, patients have become more informed about their health and use print media, television, and the Internet to get information on which to base their health decisions. As a result, alternative therapies are appealing because they are perceived as more natural and therefore safer compared to "manufactured" pharmaceutical products (WHO 2004a). A perceptual difference between cultures may be that people in developing countries are more likely to view TM as their primary source of medical care, whereas people in developed countries generally view alternative treatments as complementary to, rather than competitive with, conventional medicine.

Affordability

Most poor people in developing countries buy their medicines out of pocket; even if the public health sector offers medicines at no charge, essential medicines may not be reliably stocked, or health facilities may be too far away. The rural poor often cannot afford the transportation costs to get to a public health facility. Herbal medicines in developing countries are often cheap, and the TM practitioner may accept a trade in-kind or offer a sliding payment scale. In addition, many herbal medications are available for purchase in stores, so patients may buy and take medication without ever incurring the cost of seeing a practitioner. A cost comparison of malaria treatments in Ghana showed that clinic treatment cost USD 1.60, self-treatment with medicines bought from a private drug shop (both chloroquine and herbal) was USD 0.35, and self-treatment with herbs cost USD 0.10 (Ahorlu et al. 1997). Recent evidence also suggests that the rising cost of conventional medicine in some developed countries is contributing to increased use of alternative medicines (Pagan and Pauly 2005).

Perceived safety

TM/CAM therapies are also popular because of the lower rate of adverse effects compared with some pharmaceutical-based therapies. For example, St. John's wort taken to treat mild depression generally causes fewer side effects than antidepressive pharmaceuticals; capsaicin cream, derived from hot *Capsicum* peppers and used to treat osteoarthritis, does not cause the gastrointestinal effects that nonsteroidal anti-inflammatory medications do. Evidence suggests that some patients may choose an herbal medication over a conventional medication specifically to avoid adverse effects (Fraenkel et al. 2004). Although consumers may perceive herbal products as natural and therefore less likely to cause problems, these products are not without risk and are not necessarily safer than conventional pharmaceuticals.

Potential for treating disease

People also use TM/CAM because of its perceived efficacy, both in general (Sydara et al. 2005) and in particular for treatment of chronic, debilitating diseases that defy conventional pharmaceuticals. Indeed, plant extracts have been proved to have pharmacological effects on many conditions, both acute and chronic. Moreover, analysis from U.S. National Cancer Institute researchers showed that more than two-thirds of all drugs discovered in the previous quarter-century were derived from natural products, such as plants (Newman and Cragg 2007); for example, aspirin (salicylic acid) uses a compound derived from the white willow tree, and paclitaxel, a chemotherapy agent, is made using a substance found in the Pacific yew tree. As long-time treatments for the most severe form of malaria have become ineffective because of antimicrobial resistance, artemisinin compounds from *Artemisia annua,* an herb native to Asia, are now the first-line treatment for malaria in most countries.

Although research projects have investigated the effectiveness of herbal medicines to treat HIV/AIDS, thus far no equivalent to artemisinin for malaria has been found for HIV/AIDS. However, traditional healers have been targeted as essential partners in efforts to educate their communities and provide support for people living with HIV/AIDS (see Country Study 5-1), and many Africans use traditional herbal medications to treat AIDS symptoms and manage opportunistic infections (UNAIDS 2000, 2002). TM/CAM is also important to HIV/AIDS patients in developed countries; more than eighty percent of a sample of people living with HIV/AIDS in the United States reported regular use of alternative medicine therapies (Sparber et al. 2000).

5.3   Risks associated with herbal medications

Many people believe that, because herbal medications are "natural," or have been used in some parts of the world for generations, they must be safe. But, like modern pharmaceuticals, herbal medications can cause adverse effects (Farah et al. 2000). The causes of such adverse reactions are diverse: the use of inherently toxic herbal medicines or an overdose of herbs, conventional drug–herbal medicine interactions, and idiosyncratic reactions such as allergies. Most countries have no adverse drug reaction surveillance (pharmacovigi-lance) system for medicines at all, or the existing system may exclude herbal medicines.

Poor quality

A lack of strict standards for the production and manufacture of herbal medications can cause quality problems, such as adulteration, misidentification of ingredients, substitution of one herb with another, inclusion of pharmaceuticals without identification on the labels, contamination, and variability in the amount of active ingredient. For example, an analysis of different red yeast rice products on the market showed levels varying by 100-fold across ten products, and four were contaminated with a mycotoxin (ConsumerLab 2009). Heavy metals, fumigation agents, microbial toxins, and pharmaceutical substances have all been found in toxic concentrations in TM/CAM medications (Ernst 2001; Huang et al. 1997; Ko 1998). In 2009, a manufacturer recalled its herbal weight-loss product, which was found to actually contain the unlabeled prescription drug sibutramine, which can substantially increase blood pressure, and phenolphthalein, a suspected cancer-causing chemical that is not approved for marketing in the United States (FDA 2009).

Incorrect usage

Incorrect usage of herbal medication therapies can have fatal outcomes. The inappropriate long-term use of kava kava (*Piper methysticum*), for example, has been associated with serious cases of liver damage (Stevinson et al. 2002), and *Ginkgo biloba,* which stimulates circulation, may cause excessive bleeding during surgery (Ang-Lee et al. 2001). The U.S. Food and Drug Administration recalled all botanical products, marketed for a variety of ailments, that contained aristolochic acid, from the plant *Aristolochia,* after reports of adverse events showed a relationship with kidney failure. Problems also occur, when TM therapies are marketed and used in different cultures, with potentially hazardous changes in indicated uses and doses. *Ma huang (Ephedra sinica),* which contains ephedrine, has long been used in traditional Chinese medicine for respiratory symptoms, but its marketing at higher doses in the United States as a weight-loss product led to a number of severe effects and deaths (Ang-Lee et al. 2001).

Lack of information

Many consumers in both developed and developing countries use herbal products to treat themselves without a health practitioner's advice because of the availability and relatively inexpensive cost of such products. Consumers who treat themselves, however, may be uninformed about potential adverse effects and the safe use of herbal medicines.

Country Study 5-1
Using traditional practitioners in HIV/AIDS activities in sub-Saharan Africa

Kenya

Women Fighting AIDS in Kenya (WOFAK) is a non-profit support organization started in 1994 by ten women affected by HIV/AIDS. WOFAK has incorporated traditional medical practices into its program because of a concern that conventional medicine is too expensive for WOFAK clients. WOFAK works to sustain and promote various forms of traditional medicine and beneficial cultural practices throughout the country, and it supports the exploration of traditional therapies for HIV and associated opportunistic infections.

To further its objectives, WOFAK established a collaboration with the Kenya Forestry Research Institute (KEFRI) to grow, process, and conduct safety assessments and analyses of medicinal herbs. Although collaboration between conventional and traditional practitioners in Kenya is rare, WOFAK encourages such partnerships to improve the quality of health services to people living with HIV/AIDS. For example, a KEFRI herbalist worked part-time at the WOFAK drop-in center treating clients with herbal medicine. The center has two clinic rooms—one for traditional medicine and one for conventional medicine—and the center employs one community nurse, one traditional healer, one part-time doctor, and two herbal nurses. Cross-referrals occur between the conventional health practitioners and the traditional medicine practitioners, according to the condition, the medicine available, or the patient's preference. Conventional screening methods are used to determine the problem before treatment begins. In addition, WOFAK conducts training sessions for traditional healers in HIV/AIDS issues, including patient counseling, the role of traditional healers in AIDS control, and the identification of herbs for treatment of opportunistic infections.

Tanzania

The Tanga AIDS Working Group (TAWG) was begun in 1990 after a traditional healer successfully used herbal medicines to treat a patient in a government hospital in the Tanga region of Tanzania. The doctors were so impressed that they initiated collaboration with healers to better provide services for their patients with HIV/AIDS. One of the first TAWG activities was to work with local healers to develop three herbal remedies to treat a variety of HIV/AIDS-related conditions. From that activity evolved a home-care service for patients and their families, a type of service that patients often pre-

fer because it is more confidential than hospital-based services. These home visits are used to monitor general health, administer traditional therapies, and provide counseling services. Many hospital staff members refer patients to TAWG for HIV testing because they know that TAWG staff members have been trained as counselors on how HIV/AIDS is contracted, spread, and prevented.

In addition to home-based counseling, HIV testing services are provided at TAWG facilities. For patients who are hospitalized, TAWG prescribes herbal medicines collected by a healer and distributed by the hospitals, a process that allows patients to be monitored by conventional health care providers. TAWG's success is due to the trusting and collaborative relationship between clients, staff members, traditional healers, and conventional health practitioners.

Uganda

In the early 1990s, when the prevalence of HIV/AIDS in Uganda was among the highest in the world, the National AIDS Control Program, the Uganda AIDS Commission, and two nongovernmental organizations launched Traditional and Modern Health Practitioners Together Against AIDS and Other Diseases (THETA). THETA's first project was a collaborative clinical study to evaluate traditional herbal medicines for their effectiveness against HIV/AIDS-related symptoms, and its second project aimed to determine whether traditional healers could be trained as effective counselors on sexually transmitted infections and HIV/AIDS.

THETA's clinical studies showed that local herbal medications were just as efficacious in treating herpes zoster, which is especially problematic for people living with HIV/AIDS, as the conventional drug acyclovir. To increase access to these local products, THETA started an herbal processing-and-packaging demonstration laboratory, and grows medicinal herbs in a garden in Kampala. THETA also developed a Resource Center for Traditional Medicine and AIDS, which includes a library and a speakers bureau. To facilitate the exchange of information, the center has published booklets, training kits, educational videos, and a newsletter.

In addition, THETA's training program for traditional healers has been so successful that it has expanded to several districts. Healers who have gone through the intensive, two-year training and certification program serve as HIV/AIDS trainers for other traditional healers and fill a gap in providing counseling services in geographic areas where counseling would not otherwise be available. Healers have been recognized for their unique education methods, which include song, dance, storytelling, and drama. Part of the training process includes workshops with conventional health practitioners to promote collaboration between traditional healers and health care providers.

> *I work together with fellow healers to educate the communities. When there are many of us, we can handle all the questions.*
>
> —Trained healer from Kiboga

South Africa

In South Africa, an estimated 80 percent of people regularly see *sangomas,* or traditional healers. The Nelson R. Mandela School of Medicine at the University of KwaZulu-Natal (KZN) in Durban has developed the Biomedical and Traditional Healing Collaboration Against HIV/AIDS to improve collaboration with traditional healers caring for people with HIV/AIDS. In 2003, a memorandum of understanding was signed between the school and the KZN Traditional Healers' Council (including the Ethekwini Traditional Healers' Council), as well as two other traditional healers' organizations, Mwelela Kweliphesheya and the Umgogodla Wesizwe Trust. The provincial health department helps run the project.

The project has trained hundreds of traditional healers on HIV/AIDS awareness, voluntary counseling and testing, home-based care, and antiretroviral therapy awareness. Membership in one of the councils is required for participation in the program. Traditional healers are recognized as effective counselors, and the project is developing strategies that use *sangomas* to deliver HIV prevention messages and behavioral counseling.

Sangomas are already treating many patients with HIV/AIDS while they are on the waiting list for antiretroviral therapy. They not only treat people's opportunistic infections, but also encourage patients' behavioral changes and advise them on good nutrition and healthy living. The project is working to improve two-way communication and referral between *sangomas* and conventional health practitioners. The *sangomas* already refer patients to health care facilities, but they feel that they do not receive reciprocal referrals because of hostility on the part of the conventional practitioners. The project is working with all parties to clarify patient confidentiality issues, which should help improve communication and information exchange.

In addition, the project supplies the traditional healers, who do not have the resources to buy supplies such as rubber gloves, with home-based care kits and helps them incorporate record keeping into their practices, which, although advocated by the healer councils, is challenging because of low literacy. Record keeping is seen as an important element of successful collaboration between the traditional and conventional health systems.

Biomedical and Traditional Healing Collaboration Against HIV/AIDS recognizes that the integration of traditional healers into care for patients with HIV/AIDS will help reduce workload, improve patient care, and give the HIV/AIDS treatment program partners within patients' communities.

Sources: Kenya, Tanzania, Uganda: UNAIDS 2002; South Africa: Smart 2005; IRIN PlusNews 2010.

Often, the labeling of herbal preparations contains inadequate or unclear information about usage or possible adverse effects, leading to improper use by consumers. In a fatal example, the label on a bottle of Chinese wintergreen oil indicated that it was primarily for external use but could be taken orally for enhanced efficacy, even though ingesting as little as 4 mL can be fatal. An elderly consumer seeking relief from arthritis drank the entire contents of the 60 mL bottle that she purchased in a grocery, resulting in her death (Hofman et al. 1998).

Another problem is that most people do not communicate with their health care providers about other medications they are taking. Studies show that up to 70 percent of people use TM/CAM therapies simultaneously with conventional medicine without telling their health care providers (Eisenberg et al. 2001). This lack of com-

munication puts consumers at risk of suffering serious adverse effects caused by the interaction between herbal medicines and conventional medicines (Ernst 2001; Fugh-Berman 2000). Problems with herbal medicine–conventional medicine interactions can be prevented through improved communication between patients and health care providers and, in the case of self-treatment, better consumer information.

Clearly, issues related to herbal safety, herb-drug interactions, and health care provider and consumer education and communication are increasingly important for national and international authorities to address, given the growing popularity of herbal products in both developed and developing countries. WHO has published guidelines on developing consumer information for TM and CAM that discuss many of these issues (WHO 2004a).

5.4   Meeting the challenges of traditional medicine

Although TM has a great influence on health care practices worldwide, little reliable information exists regarding the safety, quality, and efficacy of TM/CAM medications, in part because most country governments do not regulate or officially recognize TM/CAM therapies. In the countries that do recognize TM, the scope of regulations varies considerably because of differences in history, culture, and product use. Some countries classify herbal products as medicines and some as food, and regulate accordingly. Generally, countries do not register herbal and other TM products the same way as conventional medicines, and evidence of quality, efficacy, and safety may not be required before marketing. Governments will continue to take different approaches in recognizing and classifying TM/CAM preparations unless an international framework is established for evaluating and regulating these products (Bast et al. 2002).

TM therapies have the potential to contribute to a better health care system in many places; however, a number of challenges must be met to avoid the emergence of more costly and less safe and effective health care (see Box 5-2). WHO has developed strategies to address these challenges through recent resolutions and through the publication of the *WHO Traditional Medicine Strategy: 2002–2005*. This overarching strategy includes four major objectives: (1) framing government policy; (2) ensuring safety, efficacy, and quality; (3) enhancing access; and (4) promoting proper use of TM/CAM, including herbal medicines (WHO 2002).

To share experiences and support the adoption of TM/CAM strategies, more than 1,500 representatives from member states and interested stakeholders attended the first WHO Congress on Traditional Medicine in 2008 in Beijing. Attendees shared national experiences and information on national TM/CAM policy, regulation of traditional and herbal medicines and TM/CAM practice, TM in primary health care, and research. The resulting Beijing Declaration calls on WHO member states and other stakeholders to take steps to integrate TM/CAM into national health systems (WHO 2008a).

Government policy on traditional medicine

TM is used widely to prevent, diagnose, treat, and manage disease, but considering TM's popularity, the development of regulation and legislation of the herbal medicines market has generally been inadequate. Public policies on TM differ significantly because countries and regions have diverse priorities; for example, the Chinese and Indian governments want to use TM to strengthen primary health care in remote areas; in Africa, many countries are looking for the best ways to use local TM resources and make TM an integrated part of minimal health care packages; and in Europe, licensing providers and creating standards of training and priorities for research have become crucial issues.

Box 5-2
Traditional, complementary, and alternative medicine challenges

National policy and regulatory frameworks

- Lack of official recognition of TM/CAM and TM/CAM providers
- TM/CAM not integrated into national health care systems
- Lack of regulatory and legal mechanisms
- Equitable distribution of benefits of indigenous TM knowledge and products
- Inadequate allocation of resources for TM/CAM development and capacity building

Safety, efficacy, and quality

- Lack of research methodology
- Inadequate evidence base for TM/CAM therapies and products
- Lack of adequate regulation and registration of herbal medicines
- Lack of registration of TM/CAM providers
- Inadequate support for research

Access

- Lack of data measuring access levels and affordability
- Need to identify safe and effective therapies and products
- Lack of official recognition of role of TM/CAM providers
- Lack of cooperation between TM/CAM providers and conventional practitioners
- Unsustainable use of medicinal plant resources

Rational use

- Lack of training for TM/CAM providers as well as for conventional practitioners on TM/CAM
- Lack of communication between TM/CAM and conventional practitioners, and between conventional practitioners and consumers
- Lack of information for public on appropriate use of TM/CAM

Source: WHO 2002.

Countries create policies that help characterize the role of TM in the national health care system and ensure that regulatory and legal mechanisms promote good practice, equitable access, and assurance of quality, safety, and efficacy. Unfortunately, a 2003 WHO survey found that only forty-five countries reported having enacted a national TM policy (WHO 2005). Fifty-one additional countries, however, reported having such policies in development. Without relevant policies, TM/CAM is practiced with little government oversight and without patient or consumer protection. Therefore, national policies should encompass legislation and regulation of practice and products; education, training, and licensing of providers; and research and development.

Before a country develops a national TM policy, it should assess TM use and practices and evaluate how TM can be used to improve the existing health care system. A national policy on TM/CAM must ensure the safety, efficacy, and quality of TM/CAM products and practices; at the same time, such a policy is not useful if it unduly hinders patient treatment options or leads to higher health care costs.

Although national TM policies have been, initially, slow to take shape, countries are increasingly aware of the importance of ensuring the safety and efficacy of TM, and those with some sort of regulations on herbal medicines increased from fourteen in 1988 to fifty-three in 2003 (WHO 2005). Another survey showed that eleven of twenty-six drug regulatory authorities in sub-Saharan Africa actually registered TMs (WHO 2010a). But, again, because national priorities differ, government approaches to legislation and regulations lack consistency (see Country Study 5-2).

Integration into national health care systems

The integration of TM within the national health care system generally follows four approaches (Bodeker 2001; WHO 2008a).

A *tolerant* health system is based on conventional Western medicine, but allows some TM/CAM practitioners to practice in some capacity. In the United Kingdom, only the practice of osteopathy and chiropractic are protected by statute; Canada's provinces individually regulate CAM practitioners, resulting in some CAM practitioners being regulated in some provinces but not others; in the United States, provider training, credentialing, and licensure requirements vary from state to state. Few national credentialing and licensing bodies are available to determine qualifications for a particular practice.

An *inclusive* system recognizes TM practices but does not fully integrate them into health care delivery, education, or regulation. Nigeria and Mali are examples of inclusive systems, where the governments have a national TM policy, but there is otherwise little regulation of products or practices. In some countries, such as Norway, Zimbabwe, and South Africa, authorities are giving substantial recognition to TM/CAM providers through national efforts designed to increase the integration of TM/CAM and conventional medical systems.

A *parallel* health care system has both conventional and TM as separate components of the national health system. For example, the government of India officially recognized the Ayurvedic and Unani medical systems through the Indian Medicine Central Council Act of 1970. More than 700,000 registered traditional medical practitioners are active in India and almost 500 colleges of Ayurvedic and other traditional medicine education exist (Joshi 2008).

An *integrated* system integrates conventional and TM systems at the level of medical education and practice. Integrative measures include government regulation and registration to control the safety, efficacy, and quality of herbal medicine products; registration of traditional healers and herbalists; and establishment of specialized hospitals, colleges, and universities. Worldwide, only China, the Democratic People's Republic of Korea, the Republic of Korea, and Vietnam are considered to have fully integrated systems (WHO 2002). The Association of Southeast Asian Nations recently committed to promoting the integration of TM/CAM into its members' national health care services, including drafting an Action Plan and Declaration on Traditional Medicine (ASEAN 2009).

Ensuring quality, safety, and efficacy

Many developing countries have a weak regulatory infrastructure for conventional pharmaceuticals, and most countries have no national regulations governing the quality, safety, and efficacy of herbal medications. To be registered as medicines, herbal products must undergo scientific study to assure their safety and efficacy, composition, dosage form, and claimed indications. However, in some countries, such as the United States, herbal products are regulated as foods rather than as medicines; manufacturers are not required to conduct safety or efficacy tests on their products and thus have little incentive to invest in research. Under U.S. law, the onus is on the Food and Drug Administration to prove toxicity in order to remove a product from the market.

Countries that do have a strong pharmaceutical regulatory structure in place should adapt their existing systems to include herbal medications, and countries that lack regulatory standards should work toward setting up a national system. All countries should have some framework in place to review and monitor herbal medicines, including a coordination agency, a national advisory committee, and a pharmacovigilance system for herbal medicines. WHO and its Regional Office for the Western Pacific have published a number of references and guidelines on assessing traditional therapies, and specifically herbal medicines, for use by government authorities and researchers. They are available

Country Study 5-2
The regulatory status of traditional medicine in eight countries

The creation of a national TM policy helps define the role of traditional medicine in a national health care system by putting mechanisms in place for ensuring availability, accessibility, safety, quality, efficacy, and appropriate use. Although more countries are recognizing and addressing the legal and policy issues surrounding TM and CAM, their efforts vary considerably in scope and approach. The following table summarizes the status of regulations, training, and insurance coverage in eight countries as of 2005 or before.

Country	Regulations and laws	Official training and education
Bolivia	• Regulation of herbal medicines was instituted in 1982; they are regulated in their own category as over-the-counter medications. • There are 52 registered herbal medicines. • A postmarketing survelliance system is planned. • Practice of TM was legally recognized in 1985. • TM practitioners must have a government license, although no registry exists. • No official program exists to integrate TM and conventional medicine.	• Ministry of Health established a training program for TM practitioners at conventional medical schools in 1982. • KUSKA, a research organization, runs two TM schools. • Formal courses, workshops, and seminars in TM are available through the government health sector.
Ethiopia	• Health, Drug, Science and Technology Policy of 1999 covers TM national policy. • Ethiopia does not regulate herbal medicine, and no regulatory status exists for herbal medicine. • There are no restrictions on the sale of herbal medicines. • Ethiopian Traditional Healers Association reviews practitioner qualifications in the absence of regulations.	None
Gambia	• No laws or regulations regarding TM exist, but a national policy is under development. • There are no restrictions on the sale of herbal medicines. • There is a licensing process for TM practitioners. • Some TM practitioners are involved in the primary health program.	• There is a training program for TM for health workers.
Kenya	• TM was incorporated into national health policy in the 1970s. • Herbal medicines are not regulated, and there are no restrictions on their sale. • TM practitioners must be registered. • Patent law was revised in 1999 to include protection for TM. • In 2004, Kenya announced that it would develop a national action plan on regulating and promoting TM. • A postmarketing surveillance plan is under development.	• Some training is available for traditional birth attendants.
Netherlands	• There is no national policy on TM/CAM. • Herbal medicines are regulated under the same laws as conventional pharmaceuticals. • There is no registration system for herbal medicines. They are sold in pharmacies and other outlets as over-the-counter products. • As of 1997, CAM practitioners can legally practice medicine, except for specific medical acts reserved for conventional physicians. • Legal registers exist for various categories of nonconventional practitioners who have satisfied specific requirements. Registration gives them the right to practice under a protected title, to ensure they are qualified in a specific field of health care.	• CAM institutions have organized training courses, developed standards of training and professionalism, and established national registration systems. • Most members of CAM organizations are trained as conventional physicians or nurses. • Courses on CAM are offered at conventional medical schools. • Three-year programs are offered in homeopathy, separate from conventional medical school curricula.
Philippines	• National policy on TM was established in 1997. • There is a TM division within the Department of Health. • Herbal medicines are regulated as over-the-counter medications, separate from conventional pharmaceuticals; medical claims may be made for herbals with supporting scientific proof. • The postmarketing surveillance system includes conventional and herbal medicines. • Traditional and Alternative Medicine Act signed in 1997 seeks to integrate TM into the national health care delivery system. • Philippines Institute of Traditional and Complementary/Alternative Health Care was created to promote research and integration of TM.	• Training in TM for conventional practitioners is a government priority.

Country	Regulations and laws	Official training and education
United Kingdom	• Herbal medicines can be licensed or unlicensed; if licensed, they must meet the same manufacturing and safety requirements as conventional medicines. Unlicensed herbal products are not required to meet any specific quality or safety standards, but that may change in accordance with new EU directives. • The postmarketing surveillance system was expanded to include herbals in 1996. • CAM practitioners without a conventional medical degree are tolerated by law but not officially recognized. • No restrictions exist on registered physicians who also practice CAM if they have the required skills and/or qualifications.	• The British Medical Association recommends incorporating CAM into the undergraduate curriculum of medical schools and making accredited postgraduate training available. • Many professional CAM associations offer training in their specialties. • The Institute of Complementary/Alternative Medicines is working to establish national standards of training.
Vietnam	• A national TM/CAM policy is under development. • Laws and regulations on herbal medicines were established in 1989. They are regulated as prescription and over-the-counter medicines. • More than 1,500 herbal medicines are registered. • Safety requirements for herbal medicines include traditional use without demonstrated harmful effects and reference to documented scientific research on similar products. • The postmarketing surveillance system integrates conventional and herbal medicines. • Vietnam's constitution, as well as various laws and regulations, outlines the integration of conventional and traditional health care. Promotion of these objectives is a shared responsibility of the Ministry of Health, Vietnamese Traditional Medicine Association, and the Viet Nam General Union of Medicine and Pharmacy. • Regulations from 1991 specify qualifications for TM practitioners as well as procedures they are permitted to use. • The government entrusts an assessing committee with issuing licenses to TM practitioners.	• Government programs train community health workers to use TM methods to treat common diseases. • No college or university of traditional medicine exists, although the government plans to create one. • Hanoi Medical University has a department of traditional medicine. • Two secondary schools are the main seats of learning in TM.

Sources: WHO: 2001, 2005.

online at http://www.who.int/medicines/areas/traditional/en/index.html.

Expanding the credibility of TM will depend on developing an evidence base for safety and efficacy, which means consolidating existing national and international studies and supporting new research to fill evidence gaps. The increasing number of national TM/CAM research institutes in developed and developing countries is an encouraging sign that more research and collaboration is under way. Examples are found in China, Germany, Ghana, India, Indonesia, Mali, Nigeria, Norway, Thailand, the United States, and Vietnam.

Evaluating quality. Correct botanical identity is a critical step in ensuring the quality of herbal medicine. Formal procedures are needed, including retaining botanical voucher specimens for each raw material batch and using simple organoleptic tests. Increasingly, thin-layer chromatography and qualitative and quantitative high-performance liquid chromatography methods are being used to confirm the identity and quality of raw materials. Other strategies that help ensure the quality of herbal products include developing standard operating procedures for cultivation and manufacturing, quality standards, and assays for determining the pharmacological activity of the product.

Evaluating or even establishing quality standards for herbal medications is difficult because the properties of plants vary drastically according to the plants' genetic makeup and variability; where they are grown, climatic conditions, and time of harvest or collection; and post-harvesting treatment. Some products share more properties with food products, whereas others are potent medicines, and each plant may have hundreds of natural constituents that contribute to its therapeutic qualities.

Without any sort of manufacturing standard, herbal products range in composition from products that are virtually unprocessed, to extracts, to mixtures that include other chemicals. Given their natural complexity and the differences in formulation, isolating and identifying key active ingredient(s), establishing dosage levels, determining mechanisms of action, and weighing risks against benefits often prove difficult. Overall, the general lack of regulations governing quality-control standards and consistency among herbal products hinders the ability of health professionals to guide patients on product selection and use, as well as the ability of researchers to conduct studies that could further clarify product efficacy and appropriate uses.

To ensure that herbal products marketed to consumers are of adequate and consistent quality, national drug regulatory authorities must establish guidance on all elements of quality assurance, including standard operating procedures, such as Good Agricultural and Collection Practices (GACPs), Good Manufacturing Practices (GMPs), and Good Laboratory Practices (GLPs). Guidelines have been published related to these standards, such as WHO's *Quality Control Methods for Medicinal Plant Materials*. These guidelines not only facilitate the technical work of drug regulatory authorities but also encourage countries to establish quality-control procedures for herbal medicines.

Evaluating clinical efficacy. A report from the U.S. Institute of Medicine (IOM 2005) stated that conventional and complementary medical treatments should be held to the same standards for demonstrating clinical effectiveness and that investigators should use common methods, measures, and criteria to generate and interpret the evidence necessary for making decisions about the use of complementary medicines. Because TM/CAM practices have developed within different cultural and regional contexts, there have been only limited efforts at parallel development of standards and methods—either national or international—for undertaking the type of evaluation that exists for conventional pharmaceuticals. Importantly, scientific research has increased on the chemistry and pharmacology of raw herbal materials and constituent phytochemicals. Despite this increase, however, many natural products on the global market lack clinical proof of safety and efficacy. Table 5-1 lists some herbal medicines that have been evaluated for clinical efficacy.

Additionally, TM/CAM practitioners often focus on the overall condition of the individual patient, rather than on the particular ailment or disease from which the patient is suffering. This more holistic approach to health care makes TM attractive to many people; to be evaluated, however, it requires an evidence base that uses innovative scientific approaches to include the many patient health factors, both specific and nonspecific, considered by TM practitioners. Therefore, the debate continues concerning the appropriateness of applying and combining accepted research methodologies to evaluations of TM/CAM.

Pharmacovigilance. Insufficient safety and efficacy research has hindered the development of national surveillance systems for monitoring and evaluating adverse reactions from herbal medicines. Pharmacovigilance needs to incorporate instruments to identify adverse reactions experienced by patients, studies to determine adverse reactions in specific settings, and a postmarketing quality surveillance system for herbal medicines.

Any adverse reaction reporting must document the product's specific batch number, identify the botanical ingredients present, and include other relevant information, when available. For example, an adverse reaction recorded for a product labeled "ginseng" could be incorrectly assumed to be caused by *Panax quinquefolius* (American or Western ginseng), whereas the product may actually be made from *Pfaffia paniculata,* which is sold as Brazilian ginseng. Monitoring adverse drug reactions requires some technical sophistication to differentiate crude-milled herbal material in tablet or capsule form from concentrated extracts; the latter may contain solvent residue that may be the cause of an adverse reaction, rather than the plant. Similarly, simultaneous conventional pharmaceutical and illicit drug use should be documented to help clarify causality.

In cases where a national pharmacovigilance system for conventional pharmaceuticals exists, it should be enhanced and broadened in ways that will include surveillance of herbal medicines. Knowledgeable researchers and practitioners of TM should be consulted during the development of such systems. WHO has published guidelines on how to include herbal medicine monitoring in pharmacovigilance systems (2004b). Chapter 35 provides more information on pharmacovigilance monitoring.

Enhancing access

Poor countries are the most in need of inexpensive, effective treatments for diseases and access to essential medicines. In these regions, some form of TM is often the most widely available and affordable source of health care. Creating linkages between traditional and conventional medicine through collaboration and communication may help improve health care access and services for all people, and especially for those in resource-limited, rural areas. Such linkages may also promote the acceptance of TM as part of the overall health care system.

Other access issues relate to the protection of TM knowledge and intellectual property rights and the sustainable use of natural resources. Many methods can be used to protect TM knowledge, such as creating a national policy on protecting indigenous knowledge and formalizing the record of information on medicinal plants.

Promoting acceptance of TM in the health care system. One strategy is to develop local professional organizations of TM/CAM practitioners that can form the basis of future national organizations. A strong organization of TM/CAM practitioners will help create better mechanisms for self-regulation and contribute to enhanced professional standards and increased consumer trust and safety. Establishing such professional organizations also facilitates outreach and communication within the health care community.

Countries in Asia that have better-integrated health care systems experience more professional information exchange and cooperation between the TM and conventional health sectors, partly through links in their educational systems (Holliday 2003). Recognizing the effect that TM has on the lives of most Africans, Uganda has added traditional healing studies to its university curriculum to

Table 5-1   Select examples of clinical effectiveness based on meta-analyses of clinical TM/CAM therapy research

Therapy	Medical condition	Conclusion
Artemether	Severe malaria	Equally effective as quinine, but more effective in quinine-resistant areas
Ginkgo biloba	Peripheral arterial disease	More effective than placebo
St. John's wort	Mild depression	More effective than placebo, as effective as (and safer than) synthetic antidepressants
Kava kava	Anxiety	More effective than placebo
Saw palmetto	Prostate hyperplasia	Effective in relief of symptoms
Horse chestnut *(Aesculus hippocastanum L)* seed extract	Chronic venous insufficiency	Effective in short term at reducing leg pain and swelling
Glucosamine sulfate	Osteoarthritis	Decreased pain and increased function

Sources: Ernst 2001; Pittler and Ernst 2008, 1999; Schneider 1992; Towheed et al. 2008.

show that TM has a role in the health care system. In some countries, more informal links are being made between TM practitioners and primary health care providers—especially through efforts to increase access to HIV/AIDS treatment and counseling (Kaboru et al. 2006). But in many other countries, the two types of health care providers work in isolation from each other. Creating opportunities to improve cooperation between TM practitioners and conventional medicine practitioners may allow patients to use both TM and conventional therapies to best meet their needs while improving patient safety. WHO has published the results of a workshop on how to help traditional health practitioners become more involved in primary health care (WHO 2009a).

Protecting medicinal plants. A key to guaranteeing access to traditional medicines is the protection and sustainable use of medicinal plant resources. Raw materials for herbal medicines are often collected from wild plant populations, and overharvesting for local use or to meet export demand is a growing problem. For example, when countries affected by chloroquine-resistant malaria began turning to artemisinin-based antimalarials, China, which exports raw material and extracts of the source plant, *Artemisia annua,* could not fulfill the need. Fortunately, *Artemisia annua* can readily be grown from seed as an annual crop, and many countries, including Kenya, Nigeria, and Tanzania, are establishing commercial plantations.

To help protect its resources, Kenya has banned the export of an endangered tree, *Prunus africana,* that has medicinal properties. The Republic of Kiribati is promoting resource management, conducting agricultural research on medicinal plants to help improve crops and yield, as well as offering registered traditional healers seeds and advice on growing conditions (B. Snell, *E-drug,* Feb. 7, 2005). As part of national TM strategies, other countries are compiling national inventories of medicinal plants to help focus efforts on natural resource management and sustainability.

Protecting indigenous knowledge and intellectual property. Use of herbal medicines requires access not only to biological resources, but also to community knowledge about plants' therapeutic properties. However, rights to indigenous knowledge and resources have, for the most part, been overlooked by Western intellectual property systems, where the components of TM have been treated as part of the public domain and available to anyone. Although research into TM is essential to ensuring access to safe and effective treatments, the knowledge of TM practices and products can be a source of substantial economic benefit to companies and research institutes.

Currently, TM knowledge is being appropriated, adapted, and patented by scientists and industry, with little or no compensation to its original creators or holders, and without their informed consent. Because of such appropriation and because of the focus on intellectual property rights and pharmaceuticals in general, growing attention is being paid to the issue of protecting TM knowledge and products. But, because intellectual property rights are usually given to individuals or organizations, whereas indigenous knowledge is community based, determining what can and should be protected may be difficult.

Country Study 5-3 describes a unique collaboration between the University of California, Berkeley, and Samoa that is designed to protect indigenous knowledge while exploiting modern research and development capabilities.

WHO encourages countries to adopt systems that compile a national inventory of medicinal plants and create records to preserve TM knowledge and enable its correct and continuous use over generations. For example, the Ministry of Health in Côte d'Ivoire has conducted a knowledge survey among traditional practitioners and recorded more than 2,000 traditionally used plants (WHO 2002); traditional healers, lawyers, and scientists are some of the stakeholders in Zambia working to create a national policy specifically to protect and document knowledge and biological resources (Ngandwe 2005); and India has developed a digital library of knowledge and formulations used in Ayurveda that is organized to help international patent offices to avoid granting inappropriate patents. Other countries, such as China, are

---

Country Study 5-3
Innovative indigenous knowledge research agreement: Samoa and the University of California, Berkeley

In the 1980s, an ethnobotanist from the United States was searching for a cure for breast cancer among the flora in Samoa. As part of the project, he interviewed two *taulasea* (traditional healers) who had used the bark of the indigenous mamala tree (*Homalanthus nutans*) as a treatment for hepatitis. Later tests of mamala showed that it contained prostratin, a previously known substance that showed powerful effects against HIV in the laboratory. The hope is that prostratin will become an effective treatment for HIV/AIDS. However, the supply of prostratin is limited to mamala tree bark, found wild in Samoa and a few other South Pacific islands. To make prostratin more widely available without endangering its source in the rain forest, researchers at the University of California, Berkeley (UC Berkeley), are using genetic engineering to clone the tree's genes and insert them into microbes to mass-produce the substance.

This research is conducted under an innovative agreement between the university and the nation of Samoa, which asserts national sovereignty over the gene sequence. The intellectual property agreement was made after scientists visited tribal chiefs to give a presentation on genetic engineering. The contract gives Samoa and UC Berkeley equal shares of any royalties that the university might ultimately derive from the use of the genes. Samoa's portion will be allocated to the government, villages, and the families of the *taulasea* who first showed the American ethnobotanist how to use the plant. In addition, if the research results in a marketable product, UC Berkeley and Samoa will establish a distribution process that will allow access to developing countries at a cost including no or minimal profit.

A separate agreement was established in 2001 between the Samoan government and the AIDS Research Alliance (ARA), allowing clinical research on prostratin, with 20 percent of the ARA's profits to be returned to the Samoan people. ARA planned to finish its preclinical trials in 2010, paving the way to begin human clinical trials.

Sources: ARA 2010; Black 2004.

---

using the Indian database as a template for developing their own knowledge libraries (Hepeng 2005). The information generated by these inventories should be used by national patent offices worldwide to evaluate the novelty and innovation of patent applications. In South Africa, the Patents Amendment Act of 2005 requires that every patent application state whether the invention is based on or derived from traditional knowledge.

Promoting rational use

As with the rational medicine use concept promoted for conventional pharmaceuticals (Chapter 27), appropriate use of TM and herbal medicines is dependent on qualified practitioners, proper prescribing and use of high-quality products, and reliable information and guidance for practitioners and patients. The degree to which traditional or alternative medicine is integrated into the conventional health care system will affect the type of information about TM/CAM needed in the community. In many countries, additional work is needed to raise awareness of safe and appropriate use of TM, but unfortunately there is a shortage of organized networks of traditional practitioners to help promote safe TM practices.

Reliable information based on results from high-quality scientific studies is crucial in guiding TM/CAM practitioners, conventional health care providers, and the public in the most appropriate use of herbal medicines. The *WHO Monographs on Selected Medicinal Plants* is an important reference for national health authorities, scientists, and pharmaceutical companies, providing technical information on the safety, efficacy, and quality control of widely used medicinal plants (WHO 1999, 2004, 2007, 2009).

Proper use by providers. Training for TM practitioners should ensure that their knowledge and qualifications are adequate in their area of expertise. Without appropriate training or accompanying qualification and licensing schemes, it is difficult for national authorities and consumers alike to identify qualified TM providers. In the few countries that integrate TM and conventional medicine into one health care system, TM practitioners benefit from university education, which should include study of both TM and conventional medicine. Subsequently, these practitioners can become part of staff at hospitals of conventional medicine, promoting the use of TM in combination with conventional medicine practices. In the absence of formal education, TM practitioners or healers who receive basic training in primary health care can help disseminate important health information, especially in areas where people rely predominantly on TM.

Also, because TM/CAM use is becoming more widespread, all doctors, nurses, pharmacists, and other conventional health care providers should receive education about TM treatments during their professional education. Parallel

ASSESSMENT GUIDE

TM/CAM national policy, laws, and regulations

- Is there a national policy on TM/CAM?
- Are there any laws or regulations relating to TM/CAM? How are the laws enforced?
- Do any laws or regulations pertain specifically to herbal medicines?
- If so, are herbal medicines regulated separately from conventional medicines? Are they classified as prescription or over-the-counter, or are they given another status, such as food?
- Is there a national program or expert advisory group that has responsibility for TM/CAM issues?

Evaluating the quality, safety, and efficacy of herbal medicines

- What regulatory requirements apply to the manufacturing of herbal medicines?
- What are the regulatory requirements for the safety assessment of herbal medicines?
- What type and level of evidence, if any, is required to prove the efficacy of herbal medicines?
- Is there a registration system for herbal medicines?
- Is there a postmarketing surveillance system for herbal medicines? Does it include reporting for adverse reactions?

TM/CAM research

- Is there a national research institute devoted to TM/CAM?

- Are there any policies in place to compile an inventory and/or protect traditional medicine resources, such as endangered plants? Is there any system to document indigenous knowledge and resources?

Integration of TM/CAM into the conventional health system

- Is TM/CAM officially recognized by the government as part of the health care system? Is there any integration with the national health care system? Are there any herbal medicines on the national essential medicines list?
- Is the practice of TM/CAM regulated both for health care providers and TM/CAM providers?
- Are there any training programs for TM/CAM practices?

Use of TM/CAM

- How do consumers typically use herbal medicines? Where do they buy herbal medicines? From pharmacies or other medicine outlets? From licensed or unlicensed practitioners?
- How are consumers informed about the benefits and risks of herbal medicines? Are there any regulations related to medical or health claims or labeling?

education helps TM providers and conventional health care professionals understand how their roles can complement each other for the benefit of the patient.

Proper use by consumers. Because many consumers use herbal medicines without consulting a health care professional, they must have access to reliable information and product labeling to make informed decisions on the safe use of herbal medicines. Without knowledge of the potential for adverse reactions, patients may fail to inform their doctors about the TM/CAM products they are using, and doctors may fail to ask.

Public information about TM/CAM helps spread knowledge about the health benefits as well as the possible risks, but the information must be reliable and adapted to the specific local context. An information campaign on herbal medicines should consider the local social, cultural, religious, and spiritual contexts, because medical concepts and understanding can vary significantly. Consequently, efforts to ensure that consumers use TM/CAM properly

must involve a range of stakeholders, including government representatives, health authorities, professional and consumer organizations, and TM/CAM researchers. An important resource related to consumer education is *Guidelines on Developing Consumer Information on Proper Use of Traditional, Complementary and Alternative Medicine* (WHO 2004a).

Currently, few standards exist to control the labeling and advertising of herbal medicines. The regulatory framework for TM/CAM products should include guidelines on how to educate the public, including restrictions on information and advertisements. Such regulations can be issued either by national authorities, in the form of enforceable controls, or by local organizations, such as professional groups, in the form of voluntary controls. These kinds of regulations help secure the trustworthiness of the information, prevent false health claims and misleading advertisements, and ensure the appropriate labeling of TM/CAM products.

Consumers also need to be reminded that information on the Internet is not easily controlled or regulated and that special attention is needed when evaluating online information (see Chapter 34). Some countries have special regulations to control the publication of health information on the Internet, but product marketing and advertising are mostly unrestricted. ■

References and further readings

★ = Key readings.

Ahorlu, C. K., S. K. Dunyo, E. A. Afari, K. A. Koram, and F. K. Nkrumah. 1997. Malaria-Related Beliefs and Behaviour in Southern Ghana: Implications for Treatment, Prevention and Control. *Tropical Medicine and International Health* 2(5):488–99.

Ang-Lee, M., J. Moss, and C. Yuan. 2001. Herbal Medicine and Perioperative Care. *Journal of the American Medical Association* 286:208–16.

ARA (AIDS Research Alliance). 2010. AIDS Research Alliance Gains Exclusive Rights to New Technology from Stanford University. <http://www.prweb.com/releases/2010/02/prweb3532854.htm>

ASEAN (Association of Southeast Asian Nations). 2009. *ASEAN Bulletin,* August. <http://www.aseansec.org/23107.htm#Article-11>

Bast, A., R. F. Chandler, P. C. Choy, L. M. Delmulle, J. Gurenwald, S. B. A. Halkes, K. Keller, et al. 2002. Botanical Health Products, Positioning and Requirements for Effective and Safe Use. *Environmental Toxicology and Pharmacology* 12:195–211.

Bianchi, F. 2004. "New Tradition for African Healthcare." *Christian Science Monitor,* October 13. <http://www.csmonitor.com/2004/1013/p06s02-woaf.html>

Black, H. 2004. "Samoa to Benefit from AIDS Drug." *The Scientist,* October 1. <http://www.the-scientist.com/news/20041001/02>

★ Bodeker, G. 2001. Lessons on Integration from the Developing World's Experience. *BMJ* 322:164–7.

★ Bodeker, G., and G. Burford, eds. 2007. *Traditional, Complementary and Alternative Medicine: Policy and Public Health Perspectives.* London: Imperial College Press.

Bodeker, G., C. K. Ong, C. Grundy, G. Burford, and K. Shein. 2005. *WHO Global Atlas of Traditional, Complementary and Alternative Medicine.* Geneva: WHO Press.

ConsumerLab.com. 2009. Product Review: Red Yeast Rice Supplements. <http://www.consumerlab.com/reviews/Red_Yeast_Rice_Supplements-Lovastatin_Monacolin/Red_Yeast_Rice/>

De Silva, T., T. Bahorun, M. Sahu, and L. M. Huong. 2009. *Traditional and Alternative Medicine: Research and Policy Perspectives.* Dehli: Daya Publishing House.

Eisenberg, D. M., R. C. Kessler, M. I. Van Rompay, T. J. Kaptchuk, S. A. Wilkey, S. Appel, and R. B. Davis. 2001. Perceptions about Complementary Therapies Relative to Conventional Therapies among Adults Who Use Both: Results from a National Survey. *Annals of Internal Medicine* 135(5):344–51.

Ernst, E. 2001. Research into Complementary/Alternative Medicine: An Attempt to Dispel the Myths. *International Journal of Clinical Practice* 55(6):376–9.

Farah, M. H., R. Edwards, M. Lindquist, C. Leon, and D. Shaw. 2000. International Monitoring of Adverse Health Effects Associated with Herbal Medicines. *Pharmacoepidemiology and Drug Safety* 9(2):105–12.

Farnsworth, N. R., O. Akerele, A. S. Bingel, D. D. Soejarto, and Z. G. Guo. 1985. Medicinal Plants in Therapy. *Bulletin of the World Health Organization* 63(6):965–81.

FDA (U.S. Food and Drug Administration). 2009. FDA's MedWatch Safety Alerts: November 2009. Rockville, Md.: U.S. Department of Health and Human Services. <http://www.fda.gov/ForConsumers/ConsumerUpdates/ucm192103.htm>

Fraenkel, L., S. T. Bogardus Jr., J. Concato, and D. R. Wittink. 2004. Treatment Options in Knee Osteoarthritis: The Patient's Perspective. *Archives of Internal Medicine* 164(12):1299–304.

Fugh-Berman, A. 2000. Herb-Drug Interactions. *The Lancet* 355(9198):134–8.

Hanssen, B., S. Grimsgaard, L. Launsø, V. Fønnebø, T. Falkenberg, and N. K. R. Rasmussen. 2005. Use of Complementary and Alternative Medicine in the Scandinavian Countries. *Scandinavian Journal of Primary Health Care* 23(1):57–62.

Hepeng, J. 2005. "Chinese Medicine Set for Protection." Science and Development Network, January 14. <http://www.scidev.net/en/news/chinese-medicine-set-for-protection.html>

Hofman, M., J. Diaz, and C. Marella. 1998. Oil of Wintergreen Overdose. *Annals of Emergency Medicine* 31:793–4.

Holliday, I. 2003. Traditional Medicines in Modern Societies: An Exploration of Integrationist Options through East Asian Experience. *Journal of Medicine and Philosophy* 28(3):373–89.

Huang, W. F., K. C. Wen, and M. L. Hsaio. 1997. Adulteration by Synthetic Therapeutic Substances of Traditional Chinese Medicines in Taiwan. *Journal of Clinical Pharmacology* 37:224–350.

Hussain, K., M. T. Majeed, Z. Ismail, A. Sadikun, and P. Ibrahim. 2009. Complementary and Alternative Medicine: Quality Assessment Strategies and Safe Usage. *Southern Med Review* 2(1):19–23.

IOM (Institute of Medicine). 2005. *Complementary and Alternative Medicine in the United States.* Washington, D.C.: National Academy Press.

IRIN Plus News. 2010. South Africa: Traditional Healers Extend Healthcare. 1 April. <http://www.plusnews.org/report.aspx?ReportID=88655>

Joshi, K. 2008. Indian Herbal Sector. In *India Science and Technology 2008.* New Delhi: National Institute of Science Technology and Development Studies.

Kaboru, B. B., T. Falkenberg, J. Ndulo, M. Muchimba, K. Solo, E. Faxelid, and The Bridging Gaps Project's Research Team. 2006. Communities' Views on Prerequisites for Collaboration between Modern and Traditional Health Sectors in Relation to STI/HIV/AIDS Care in Zambia. *Health Policy* 78(2–3):330–9.

Ko, R. 1998. Adulterant in Asian Patent Medicines. *New England Journal of Medicine* 339(12):839–41.

★ Newman, D. J., and G. M. Cragg. 2007. Natural Products as Sources of New Drugs Over the Last 25 Years. *Journal of Natural Products* 70(3):461–77.

Ngandwe, T. 2005. "Zambia Moves to Protect Traditional Knowledge." Science and Development Network, March 18. <http://www.scidev.net/en/news/zambia-moves-to-protect-traditional-knowledge.html>

Pagan, J. A., and M. V. Pauly. 2005. Access to Conventional Medical Care and the Use of Complementary and Alternative Medicine. *Health Affairs* 24(1):255–62.

Pittler, M. H., and E. Ernst. 2008. Horse Chestnut Seed Extract for Chronic Venous Insufficiency. *Cochrane Database of Systematic Reviews.* Issue 3.

———. 1999. Artemether for Severe Malaria: A Meta-Analysis of Randomised Clinical Trials. *Clinical Infectious Diseases* 28:597–601.

Schneider, B. 1992. [Ginkgo biloba extract in peripheral arterial diseases. Meta-analysis of controlled clinical studies.] [German.] *Arzneimittelforschung* 42(4):428–36.

Smart, T. 2005. Traditional Healers Being Integrated into HIV Care and Treatment in Kwazulu-Natal. *AIDSmap.com,* News, June 13.

Sparber, A., J. C. Wootton, L. Bauer, G. Curt, D. Eisenberg, T. Levin, and S. M. Steinberg. 2000. Use of Complementary Medicine by Adult Patients Participating in HIV/AIDS Clinical Trials. *Alternative and Complementary Medicine* 6(5):415–22.

Stevinson, C., A. Huntley, and E. Ernst. 2002. A Systematic Review of the Safety of Kava Extract in the Treatment of Anxiety. *Drug Safety* 25:251–61.

Sydara, K., S. Gneunphonsavath, R. Wahlström, S. Freudenthal, K. Houamboun, G. Tomson, and T. Falkenberg. 2005. Use of Traditional Medicine in Lao PDR. *Complementary Therapies in Medicine* 13(3):199–205.

Towheed, T. E., T. P. Anastassiades, B. Shea, J. Houpt, V. Welch, and M. C. Hochberg. 2008. Glucosamine Therapy for Treating Osteoarthritis. *Cochrane Database of Systematic Reviews.* Issue 4.

★ UNAIDS (Joint United Nations Programme on HIV/AIDS). 2002. *Ancient Remedies, New Disease: Involving Traditional Healers in Increasing Access to AIDS Care and Prevention in East Africa.* Geneva: UNAIDS. <http://data.unaids.org/Publications/IRC-pub02/jc761-ancientremedies_en.pdf>

———. 2000. *Collaboration with Traditional Healers in HIV/ AIDS Prevention and Care in Sub-Saharan Africa: A Literature Review.* Geneva: UNAIDS. <http://data.unaids.org/Publications/ IRC-pub01/jc299-tradheal_en.pdf>

UNCTD (United Nations Conference on Trade and Development). 2000. *Systems and National Experiences for Protecting Traditional Knowledge, Innovations and Practices. Background Note by the UNCTAD Secretariat.* Geneva: UNCTD. <http://www.unctad.org/ en/docs/c1em13d2.en.pdf>

WHO (World Health Organization). 2011. *Quality Control Methods for Herbal Materials.* Geneva: WHO. <http://apps.who.int/medicine docs/documents/h1791e/h1791e.pdf>

———. 2010a. Regulatory Harmonization: Updating medicines Regulatory Systems in Sub-Saharan African Countries. *WHO Drug Information* 24(1):6–20.

———. 2010b. *Safety Issues in the Preparation of Homeopathic Medicines.* Geneva: WHO.

———. 2009a. *Report of the WHO Interregional Workshop on the Use of Traditional Medicine in Primary Health Care: Ulaanbaatar, Mongolia 23–26 August 2007.* Geneva: WHO. <http://apps.who.int/ medicinedocs/documents/s16202e/s16202e.pdf>

———. 2009b. *Sixty-second World Health Assembly: Resolution on Traditional Medicine.* Geneva: WHO.

———. 2008a. *Beijing Declaration: Adopted by the WHO Congress on Traditional Medicine, Beijing, China, 8 November 2008.* Geneva: WHO.

★ ———. 2008b. *Traditional Medicine.* Fact Sheet no. 134. Geneva: WHO. <http://www.who.int/mediacentre/factsheets/fs134/en>

★ ———. 2007a. *WHO Guidelines for Assessing Quality of Herbal Medicines with Reference to Contaminants and Residues.* Geneva: WHO.

———. 2007b. *WHO Guidelines on Good Manufacturing Practices (GMP) for Herbal Medicines.* Geneva: WHO.

★ ———. 2005. *National Policy on Traditional Medicine and Regulation of Herbal Medicines: Report of a WHO Global Survey.* Geneva: WHO. <http://apps.who.int/medicinedocs/pdf/s7916e/ s7916e.pdf>

★ ———. 2004a. *Guidelines on Developing Consumer Information on Proper Use of Traditional, Complementary and Alternative Medicine.* Geneva: WHO. <http://apps.who.int/medicinedocs/en/ d/Js5525e/#Js5525e>

★ ———. 2004b. *WHO Guidelines on Safety Monitoring of Herbal Medicines in Pharmacovigilance Systems.* Geneva: WHO. <http:// whqlibdoc.who.int/publications/2004/9241592214_eng.pdf>

★ ———. 2002. *WHO Traditional Medicine Strategy 2002–2005.* Geneva: WHO. <http://whqlibdoc.who.int/hq/2002/WHO_EDM_ TRM_2002.1.pdf>

———. 2001. *Legal Status of Traditional Medicine and Complementary/ Alternative Medicine: A Worldwide Review.* Geneva: WHO. <http:// whqlibdoc.who.int/hq/2001/WHO_EDM_TRM_2001.2.pdf>

★ ———. 2000. *General Guidelines for Methodologies on Research and Evaluation of Traditional Medicine.* Geneva: WHO. <http:// whqlibdoc.who.int/hq/2000/WHO_EDM_TRM_2000.1.pdf>

———. 1999, 2004, 2007, 2009. *WHO Monographs on Selected Medicinal Plants.* Vols. 1–4. Geneva: WHO.

★ ———. 1996. *Guidelines for the Assessment of Herbal Medicines.* WHO Technical Report Series no. 863. Geneva: WHO.

★ ———. 1995. *Guidelines for Training Traditional Health Practitioners in Primary Health Care.* Geneva: WHO. <http:// whqlibdoc.who.int/hq/1995/WHO_SHS_DHS_TRM_95.5.pdf>

WHO/WPRO (World Health Organization/Regional Office for the Western Pacific). 1998. *Guidelines for the Appropriate Use of Herbal Medicines.* Western Pacific Series no. 23. Manila: WHO Regional Office for the Western Pacific. <http://apps.who.int/medicinedocs/ en/d/Jh2945e/#Jh2945e>

———. 1993. *Research Guidelines for Evaluating the Safety and Efficacy of Herbal Medicines.* Manila: WHO Regional Office for the Western Pacific. <http://whqlibdoc.who.int/wpro/-1993/ 9290611103.pdf>

CHAPTER 6

Pharmaceutical legislation and regulation

SUMMARY

Realistic and effective laws and regulations are needed for the pharmaceutical sector because—

- Pharmaceuticals concern the whole population
- Many parties are involved: patients, health providers, manufacturers, and salespeople
- Serious consequences, including injury and death, can result from the lack or misuse of medications
- The consumer has no way to determine product quality
- Informal controls are insufficient

Countries may choose to develop new legislation or to revise existing laws. When starting afresh, it is useful to prepare a general law. Models exist, and expert assistance is readily available. After the law is passed, regulations made under it can bring its various provisions into operation, one by one, as the necessary resources and experience are acquired.

In drafting or revising legislation, a country should—

- Inventory the laws and regulations already in force
- Determine what type of legislative instrument is required
- Involve both legal and health experts
- Keep all interested parties informed

National drug legislation generally includes provisions relating to the manufacturing, importing, distribution, marketing, prescribing, labeling (including language), dispensing, and sometimes pricing of pharmaceutical products, as well as the licensing, inspection, and control of personnel and facilities. A regulatory authority is usually established for administrative control. Medicine registration is often a major element in legislation, to ensure that individual products meet the criteria of efficacy, safety, and quality.

Countries that need to introduce comprehensive legislation can seek guidance from the experiences of others and from WHO (2001a) guidelines.

6.1   The role of pharmaceutical legislation and regulation

The role of pharmaceuticals has become more prominent on international agendas as health indicators have been increasingly linked with a country's successful development. In addition, the legal and economic issues that surround pharmaceuticals have become more complex and politicized because of the increase in global trade.

Why pharmaceutical laws and regulations are necessary

The use of ineffective, poor-quality, or harmful medicines can result in therapeutic failure, exacerbation of disease, resistance to medicines, and sometimes death. It also undermines confidence in health systems, health professionals, pharmaceutical manufacturers, and distributors. To protect public health, governments need to approve comprehensive laws and regulations and to establish effective national regulatory authorities to ensure that the manufacture, trade, and use of medicines are regulated appropriately and that the public has access to accurate information on medicines.

Differences between pharmaceutical laws, regulations, and guidelines

Laws today are usually written in fairly general terms to meet present and possibly future needs. Laws usually have language that enables the government to issue regulations based on the law. Passing new laws may require a lengthy process, with the country's legislative branch giving final approval. Regulations can be passed more rapidly and simply than laws, sometimes requiring, for example, only the approval of a single government minister on the advice of experts. They can also be altered more easily. After approval, a regulation has the same power as the law itself. Guidelines, which do not carry the force of law, can be more easily modified and updated and offer informal information on what the government's thinking is regarding the best way to implement regulations. Following guidelines will help avoid misinterpretation of and facilitate compliance with laws and regulations.

Pharmaceuticals involve many parties, including patients, doctors, other health workers, salespeople, and manufacturers. The field also involves important risks: people can suffer or die not only from a lack of medicines, but also from drugs that are impure, wrongly prescribed, or used incorrectly. Thus, it is easy to see why laws and regulations are needed. However, some argue that medicines—like many other commodities—should be subject only to the control of the ultimate user. But medicines are indeed different, as discussed in Chapter 1.

Additionally, informal controls are insufficient: charlatanism or quackery (that is, the deliberate sale of remedies known to be worthless) is centuries old, and firm action may be needed to put a stop to it; however, as discussed later in the chapter, the Internet presents new challenges in controlling deceitful drug promotion. Counterfeiting, also, has been on the rise in developed and developing countries. U.S. customs officials, for example, report that pharmaceuticals are one of the fastest-growing categories of counterfeit goods coming into the country illegally. Pharmaceuticals accounted for 10 percent of total seizures in 2008 to become the third-largest category, compared to 6 percent in 2007 (Mui 2009).

The approach to pharmaceutical regulation should not be simply punitive: rules creating a positive situation tend to be more effective. Finally, laws and regulations are effective only to the extent that they meet society's needs.

Evolution of policy and law

There may be a long preparatory period before the sort of consensus develops that can form the basis for a law. It is sometimes preferable to work for a while with informal agreements among parties or with government guidelines, so that generally accepted rules of behavior can develop in practice; the law then serves to confirm and formalize them (see Country Study 6-1).

Whether or not a national drug policy exists, countries need effective, enforceable legislation and regulation. These legislative acts may take the form of a single national drug law that deals with all the issues or a series of complementary laws, each introduced when the time is right. In some countries, certain aspects of the pharmaceutical sector are governed by national laws, and other aspects, such as pharmacy and medical practice, are governed by state or provincial laws. This chapter focuses on a single, comprehensive drug law at the national level. Most of the issues discussed are also applicable in situations where legal responsibility is divided between national and state or provincial governments.

A law on medicines must, first and foremost, clearly define what all the parties—manufacturers, doctors, pharmacists—are required to do, so that no serious misunderstanding is possible. Medicine registration laws and regulations, for example, make clear what a manufacturer needs to do to obtain a license to sell a product. They define how a registration agency should assess both the manufacturer and the product to determine if they meet society's needs.

A good law also creates administrative bodies to put rules into practice—for example, a national drug regulatory authority with broad competence, or separate organs to deal with the various aspects of pharmaceutical regulation such as practice of pharmacy, inspection of factories, and advertising of medicines.

Trying to achieve too much, too quickly, can be tempting. It took more than a hundred years for pharmaceutical policies and laws to evolve to current levels in the industrialized world. Sensible questions to ask are—

- What are the most important goals to achieve within five, ten, and fifteen years?
- What means are available to achieve them?
- In which order can they best be tackled?
- What help is available?

The answers to these questions provide a good starting point in developing both policies and the laws needed to support them.

Laws and regulations are intended to be used together to achieve their objective. It is appropriate to begin with passing a broad law, emphasizing the requirement that pharmaceutical products be safe and effective. The various provisions of the law are then brought into operation through regulation, step by step, addressing the most important things first. For instance, in resource-constrained countries, setting up a new pharmaceutical distribution system may be urgently necessary, but pharmaceutical registration can wait for several years, while procuring essential medicines in the meantime through reputable channels where product quality is controlled.

Globalization and harmonization

Laws and regulations evolve within countries over time, but in recent years, the trend has been toward the globalization of pharmaceutical issues, which affects national legislation. This globalization, exemplified through changes in international trade, patent protection, and pricing, has resulted in a number of initiatives that must be considered by countries developing pharmaceutical regulations. Some examples of these initiatives follow.

TRIPS Agreement. The TRIPS Agreement (Agreement on Trade-Related Aspects of Intellectual Property Rights) of the World Trade Organization (WTO) has greatly affected international pharmaceutical regulation. TRIPS is an attempt to reduce gaps in the way intellectual property rights are protected around the world and to bring them under common international rules; however, the implications of the agreement's provision on patents caused concerns in developing countries. In response to those concerns, at the Doha Conference in 2001, WTO members adopted a special affirmation—known as the Doha Declaration—on issues related to TRIPS and public health. The declaration affirms that the TRIPS Agreement should be implemented in ways that protect public health and promote access to medicines. Chapter 3 on intellectual property and access to medicines goes into more detail on these issues.

Driven by the increase of global trade in pharmaceutical products and the subsequent complexity of technical regulations related to medicine safety and quality, several initiatives have been established to promote the harmonization of international pharmaceutical guidelines and regulations by intergovernmental organizations at regional and inter-regional levels.

International Conference on Drug Regulatory Authorities. Organized by WHO, the International Conference on Drug Regulatory Authorities (ICDRA) provides officials from the drug regulatory authorities from all WHO member states with a forum to work on strengthening cooperation and collaboration. Held since 1980, the annual conferences promote the exchange of information and provide a platform to develop international consensus on pharmaceutical regulation. The conferences are a unique forum that assemble all drug regulatory authorities, regardless of their organizations' stage of development. The ICDRA has been instrumental in guiding regulatory authorities on how the harmonization of regulation can improve the safety, efficacy, and quality of medicines.

International Conference on Harmonisation. The International Conference on Harmonisation of Technical

---

Country Study 6-1
The evolution of pharmaceutical legislation

Venezuela's first medicine-related law was issued in 1883 as the Ordinance of the Council of Physicians on Secret Medicines and Patents. Pharmaceutical laws have been revised regularly; a significant number of pharmaceutical laws were adopted over the course of the twentieth century. The law that established the medicine registration system—the Law on the Exercise of the Pharmacy—was passed in 1928, before the Ministry of Health was set up in 1936. The National Institute of Hygiene was established in 1938 to serve as the nation's national regulatory agency. Over the years, new rules and organizations have been created to expand the scope of regulation and to add capacity for executing the laws. The section on pharmacological advice, the Laboratory for Pharmacological Analysis, and the Center for Pharmacological Surveillance were established in 1944, 1946, and 1962, respectively. Rules for good manufacturing practices (GMP) were drawn up in 1990. A pharmaceutical law was approved in 2000 that addressed certain concepts for the first time, such as generic and essential medicines.

Tunisia first introduced pharmaceutical regulation in 1942, in the form of a decree on medical and pharmaceutical promotion and medicine control. All finished pharmaceutical products, whether manufactured in Tunisia or imported, must undergo a technical committee review and obtain a certificate of approval from the Ministry of Health before they may be placed on the market. Registration is also required for homeopathic drugs, and some herbal medicines are registered with the status of allopathic medicines. Key legislation includes the 1961 Law on Inspection of Pharmacies and Manufacturers, the 1969 Poisonous Drug Law, and the 1985 Law on Production of Drugs for Human Use. Between 1985 and 1991, several legal texts were promulgated concerning GMP, clinical trials, medical and scientific information, procedures to obtain licensing of manufacturing and registration. New organizations were also created by law, for example the Pharmacy and Medicines Directorate in 1981, the National Pharmacovigilance Center in 1984, and the National Medicines Control Laboratory in 1990.

In the **Netherlands,** the legal basis for licensing of pharmaceutical manufacturing and distribution was established in 1956. The Medicines Act of 1958 thereafter regulated the admission of medicines to the Dutch market through the Medicines Evaluation Board. But the board started to operate only after 1963, triggered by the thalidomide disaster of 1961. European pharmaceutical regulation is now playing a growing role. In 1995, the European Medicines Evaluation Agency was founded to coordinate the tasks of the drug regulatory authorities of European Union member states. Certain aspects of the Netherlands' pharmaceutical regulation now follow European Union rules. For example, GMP inspection is based on the 1983 European Union guidelines for GMP. Since January 1, 1995, a European procedure for registration has operated in the Netherlands. Now two types of trade licenses exist: a European license and a national license. Products with a European license may be sold throughout the European Union, while the national licenses are valid only for the country in which the license was issued by means of the national registration procedure.

Estonia's drug regulatory framework began to take shape only over the two decades since the country gained independence. However, the pace of regulatory development has been rapid. The Licensing Board of Pharmaceutical Activities and the Center of Medicines were both created in 1991. Registration and licensing were introduced that year. In 1993, the State Agency of Medicines was created to become the Drug Regulatory Authority. The main legislation—the Medicinal Products Act—came into force in 1996.

Source: Ratanawijitrasin and Wondemagegnehu 2002.

Requirements for Registration of Pharmaceuticals for Human Use (ICH) is a project that brings together the regulatory authorities and experts from the pharmaceutical industry of Europe, the United States, and Japan to discuss scientific and technical aspects of product registration. The purpose is to promote harmonization in the application of technical guidelines and requirements for new product registration in order to reduce the duplication of and facilitate the evaluation of testing carried out during the research and development of new medicines. Harmonization conserves resources and increases the availability of new medicines, while maintaining regulatory obligations to safeguard the products. Although intended for new products, ICH guidelines are also being used to register existing products. The guidelines, formally produced by and for ICH member countries, reflect the technical capabilities of their well-developed regulatory agencies and pharmaceutical industries. Thus, other countries should consider their local situations before trying to apply ICH guidelines. However, the ICH guidelines do end up affecting all countries, particularly as they relate to the quality specifications of medicinal products, including generic medicines, the

---

Country Study 6-2
Harmonization efforts in the Americas

Although subregional harmonization activities have been under way in a number of countries in the Americas (for example, Mercosur, the Andean Community, NAFTA), no overarching mechanism existed for exchanging information and promoting harmonization in the Americas.

In 1999, a hemispheric forum was established, with the Pan American Health Organization (PAHO) as its secretariat, to communicate about pharmaceutical regulation among the different subregions. The resulting organization, known as the Pan American Network for Drug Regulatory Harmonization (PANDRH), has a steering committee that represents the drug regulators of subregional groups active in the pharmaceutical regulatory harmonization process and formulates recommendations on how to promote coordination among the countries. PANDRH includes all representatives involved in addressing the problems connected with pharmaceuticals: regulatory authorities, industry (domestic and multinational), consumers, and professional associations.

In addition, PANDRH has formed a number of working groups to address issues of importance to pharmaceutical regulations including good manufacturing practices, bioequivalence, good clinical practices, drug counterfeiting, pharmacopoeias, and external quality control. Examples of working group activities include harmonizing good manufacturing practices guidelines for inspectors and making the guidelines easily available on the PANDRH website (http://new.paho.org/hq/index.php?option=com_content&task=view&id=1054&Itemid=513); developing specific criteria to prioritize necessary bioequivalence studies; and developing inspection guidelines for audits on good clinical practices, including establishing legal penalties for noncompliance.

The PANDRH steering committee adopted statutes in 2009, which are available on the website.

As PANDRH secretariat, PAHO supports the member countries with—

- Information on pharmaceutical legislation
- Collection and dissemination of documents, experiences, and procedures on drug regulatory harmonization in each country and subregion
- Research to document compliance with existing harmonization agreements
- Definition of the analytical methodology for addressing common problems
- Exchange of information among the harmonization efforts of the different integration processes

Subregional and technical meetings are held often, and PAHO convenes periodic conferences that bring together all the groups to share information and advance harmonization efforts. The Pan American Conference is a meeting open to all interested stakeholders, including consumers, industry representatives, and nongovernmental organizations. Providing an open forum helps ensure the successful adoption and implementation of harmonized outcomes.

One of the major issues of concern to PANDRH members is the recognition that serious limitations exist in some subregions, such as Central America, where no legal framework exists to authorize and operationalize the commitments made by technical groups; therefore, PANDRH takes the particular needs of each subregional bloc and the different degrees of development of their constituent countries into account to implement the subregional agreements. This specificity means that the agreements must be implemented gradually.

Sources: PAHO 2005; PANDRH Steering Committee 2009.

requirements for which vary considerably across countries (Gray 2004). WHO, with its observer status on the ICH steering committee, is expected to act as a link between ICH and non-ICH countries (through the ICDRA) and to disseminate information to non-ICH countries. The ICH has also established a Global Cooperation Group that promotes ICH guidelines by acting as an information resource for nonmembers.

Country Study 6-2 discusses regulatory harmonization efforts in the Americas.

Pharmacopoeias. Pharmacopoeias are documents that outline technical information, manufacturing and testing procedures, and standards for active pharmaceutical substances and products. Some countries, such as Germany and Thailand, also have pharmacopoeias specifically for herbal products. A pharmacopoeia is usually recognized as part of a country's national pharmaceutical laws; therefore, the standards and procedures are legally enforceable. WHO has also developed an international pharmacopoeia that, unlike other pharmacopoeias, has no legal status, but is meant as a reference for member countries that may adapt it and incorporate it into their national legislation. Because of the extensive resources required to produce and maintain these complex documents, most countries do not have national pharmacopoeias and rely on one or more internationally recognized pharmacopoeias, such as those from the United States, the European Union, Japan, or WHO. The organizations that publish pharmacopoeias, pressured by the need to facilitate international trade, are actively working to harmonize their requirements.

Drafting and revising pharmaceutical legislation and regulations

Regulatory authorities are continually faced with new issues—such as globalization and extension of free trade—while increased responsibilities from market expansion and the sophistication and new categories of products place heavy demands on regulatory systems. The development of cutting-edge technologies and health care techniques and the extensive use of the Internet as a source of information and commerce impose further complex challenges.

As a first step before drafting any new law, it is important to inventory the laws and regulations already in force. Even if no general drug law exists, pieces of legislation are likely to touch on the field—for example, laws on narcotics and the licensing and responsibilities of pharmacists. An out-of-date general drug law may exist that should be replaced rather than merely amended. Determining the extent to which existing laws and regulations contribute to attaining the national policy objectives is essential. Because concepts of pharmaceutical policy are modern, legislation more than twenty years old may not be relevant; starting over may be simpler.

The second step is for drafters and experts to meet to decide what type of legislative instrument is required. The most straightforward model is likely to be a comprehensive law that deals in outline with all the relevant issues, each main section taking up a particular matter. Sections can then be implemented one at a time, through the passage of regulations.

In countries with a long history of regulation, laws on pharmacists and the registration of medicines as well as regulations on prices and costs are likely to be separate, because they came into being at different times. In starting afresh, however, and particularly if the laws on these matters are outdated or incomplete, it may be easier to pull together all relevant elements into a single law.

Ideally, the task of writing or revising the law should be entrusted to a group of legal and health experts who are familiar with all the issues, but not all countries can assemble such a group. Rather than solving the problem by copying laws from abroad, countries with limited expertise can obtain assistance from international and bilateral agencies to draft new pharmaceutical legislation that meets the country's own needs. International and regional meetings of drug regulatory authorities (for example, ICDRA) also provide opportunities for learning how to approach the problem and identifying expert colleagues who can be called on for advice. In addition, WHO has a number of publications that can assist countries in developing national medicine policies (available at http://apps.who.int/medicinedocs/en/cl/CL1.1.1.1.2/clmd,50.html#hlCL1_1_1_1_2).

At all stages of the process, it is important to discuss early drafts of the law with all interested parties, including the health professions, trade and industry groups, other concerned government departments (such as those handling commerce and education), and consumer groups. The greater the consensus, the greater is the chance that a law will be passed and will work in practice. Sometimes, countries react to a crisis by rushing through the enactment of a new law without putting it through a consensual process or carefully evaluating its effect on other sectors. However, this attempt to respond quickly may backfire if the law is not carefully thought through.

When the law is approved, regulations are developed to guide the implementation of the law. Regulations can be modified more easily than laws as the local situation evolves. When a regulation is revised, it is important to research and take into account what other laws will be affected by the revision. Declaring that a revision nullifies all previous laws and regulations in conflict, without making sure what those previous laws cover, can result in confusion. It is easier to track revisions when a country's laws are well codified, such as in the *U.S. Code of Federal Regulations*. Following the adoption of regulations, guidance documents may be developed to provide more flexible and detailed information on how to comply with regulations.

Box 6-1
Elements of a comprehensive drug law

A. General provisions

1. Title*
2. Purposes*
3. Territorial extent
4. Application of other laws
5. Definitions*

B. Control of availability and marketing

1. Drug registration*
2. National essential medicines list/national formulary
3. Scheduling prescription, and dispensing authority*
4. Labeling*
5. Generic labeling, manufacturing, and substitution
6. Pharmacovigilance
7. Information and advertising*
8. Public education
9. Imposition of fees
10. Price control
11. Special products (herbal medicines, medicines for clinical trials, orphan drugs)

C. Control of supply mechanisms

1. Importation of medicines*
2. Exportation of medicines*

3. Controls, incentives, disincentives for local manufacture
4. Control of distribution, supply, storage, and sale*

D. Drug control administration

1. Organization and function*
2. Appeals against decisions of the drug control authority*

E. Powers of enforcement

1. Prohibition of specified activities*
2. Penalties for each offense based on magnitude and occurrence*
3. Legal procedures for offenses*

F. Powers to make rules and regulations

1. Who has authority*
2. Under which circumstances*

G. Repeals and transitional provisions

1. Repeal of sections of existing laws in conflict with the act
2. Transitional period to implementation*

H. Exemptions from provisions of the law*

* Elements for which model legislation has been developed by WHO.
Sources: Adapted from WHO 1998b, 1999c.

6.2 Basic elements of national pharmaceutical legislation

A well-defined set of elements constitutes the initial requirements for a strong and comprehensive national pharmaceutical law. These elements, though basic, are sufficiently wide and varied in their scope to meet most of the objectives of a national pharmaceutical policy. Box 6-1 presents a model for national pharmaceutical legislation, showing the various key elements. This model can be adapted to support the efforts of small national drug regulatory authorities in countries where only one or two professionals are available to deal with pharmaceuticals and related products.

6.3 Key provisions of national pharmaceutical legislation

Because a consumer cannot independently assess the safety, efficacy, or quality of pharmaceuticals, these products are universally recognized as being different from ordinary items of commerce, such as clothing or household appliances, and therefore in need of handling by specially trained health professionals. These requirements make pharmaceuticals subject to numerous controls at all levels, and legal authority is granted to regulate their manufacture, distribution, marketing, prescribing, labeling, dispensing, and related activities, such as pricing.

An effective national pharmaceutical law is a primary means of ensuring that pharmaceutical policy goals are achieved while the unique character of pharmaceutical products, personnel, and facilities is preserved. The law may specify what products can legally be imported—for example, those included on the national medicines list and possessing a WHO-type certificate of quality—and which individuals are legally qualified to prescribe and dispense them, thus promoting certain national pharmaceutical policies.

Likewise, control of the manufacture, storage, distribution, and sale of pharmaceutical products enables a government to better ensure compliance with a national policy of having essential medicines of appropriate quality, safety, and efficacy available for their intended purposes. The processes of licensing and registration can grant authorization only to those personnel, products, and facilities that conform to the national pharmaceutical law. For example, counterfeit or dangerous medicines can be taken off the market, and sanctions can be taken against those responsible for introducing them illegally.

In addition, countries that host clinical trials to test new medicines should incorporate regulations on how the studies should be conducted, including an application process that explains the purpose and protocol of the intended research and the creation of an ethics committee to approve and monitor any study protocol that includes human participants. For countries needing assistance in this area, WHO publishes guidelines on good clinical practices (WHO 2005b).

The promulgation of regulations, the collection of licensing and registration fees, and the enforcement of the national law and its regulations are legally delegated to an agency—usually called the national drug regulatory authority—headed by a commissioner or director who is responsible to a cabinet-level person, such as the minister of health. For example, in the United States, the basic national pharmaceutical law is called the Federal Food, Drug, and Cosmetic Act, which is enforced by the Food and Drug Administration. For controlled substances, additional restrictions are imposed by the Drug Enforcement Administration. In the United States, wholesale distributors, pharmacy practice, and medical practice are regulated by individual states.

Defining the roles of various parties

Because so many parties are involved with medicines, the laws need to clearly state the roles, responsibilities, and rights of each, ranging from practitioners, auxiliaries, nurses, and pharmacists to importers, manufacturers, and distributors. Countries approach prescribing and dispensing differently, depending on their circumstances; for example, in Canada, a physician must be the medicine prescriber, but in areas where physicians are scarce, legal authority may be granted to nurses or other health practitioners to prescribe essential medicines. The legislation should establish the qualifications required for those handling medicines, or it must state who has the authority to set these standards by passing appropriate regulations (for example, a government minister).

Licensing, inspection, and quality control

The law should create mechanisms to ensure that relevant parties are licensed and inspected so the community can have confidence in them. Doctors and nurses may be covered by other laws, but the medicine law needs to ensure that the people who import, distribute, and sell medicines are properly qualified, approved, registered, and inspected.

Pharmaceuticals themselves require a special form of inspection. An inspector visiting a pharmacy or warehouse may have reason to suspect that medicines are not of sufficient quality or in good condition: they may be damp, dirty, or disintegrating. More often, samples need to be obtained for testing in the quality-control laboratory, an essential part of the inspection system.

Some countries have their own quality-control laboratories, either specifically for medicines or shared with other commodities (such as foods). A number of countries use regional laboratories, such as the ones serving sub-Saharan Africa or the Caribbean. Whatever the structure, the pharmaceutical law needs to designate a quality-control laboratory that has the capacity and equipment to do the job.

Countries that have pharmaceutical manufacturing operations should enforce good manufacturing practices (GMP), which is a system to ensure that products are consistently produced and controlled according to quality standards. GMP covers all aspects of production from the starting materials, premises, equipment, and quality testing to the training and personal hygiene of staff. WHO has established detailed guidelines for good manufacturing practice, and many countries have formulated their own requirements based on WHO's GMP. Other regions, such as the Association of Southeast Asian Nations and the European Union, have harmonized their GMP requirements.

Although important, GMP monitoring sometimes receives more resources than the inspection of distribution channels; however, the consumer's interest is not served by manufacturing a product under GMP but then storing and distributing it under adverse conditions. Inspection of distribution channels, including the importation of pharmaceuticals, should also be emphasized, particularly in countries where the distribution system has several intermediate levels or the climate is unfavorable. WHO has produced guidelines relating to good storage practices for pharmaceuticals (WHO 2003a).

Chapter 19 has more information on quality-control and inspection procedures.

Pharmacovigilance

The law should also provide a basis for a pharmacovigilance (that is, postmarketing surveillance) system to report problems with adverse reactions and product quality. *Pharmacovigilance* is defined by WHO (2002a) as "the science and activities relating to the detection, assessment, understanding and prevention of adverse effects or any other drug-related problems."

Pharmacovigilance is an overarching concept that encompasses any system used to monitor medicine safety, use, and efficacy. For example, adverse drug reaction monitoring as part of a product's postmarketing surveillance contributes to the assessment of benefit, effectiveness, and risk of medicines. A pharmacovigilance system is difficult—if not impossible—to implement in an unregulated market that allows the importation and sale of pharmaceuticals through informal channels or the sale of powerful medicines without prescription. Drug regulatory agencies should have access to information from the WHO Programme for International Drug Monitoring (http://www.who.int/medicines/areas/quality_safety/safety_efficacy/Joining WHOProgrammeforInternationaDrugMonitoring.pdf),

---

Box 6-2
Adverse drug reaction monitoring

An adverse drug reaction (ADR) is a harmful and unexpected reaction to a drug taken at a normal dosage. The research done on medicines before they are allowed on the market is incomplete; generally fewer than 5,000 people have been exposed to the medicine in premarket tests, an insufficient number to detect less common ADRs. In addition, information on chronic toxicity and reactions in special groups, such as pregnant women and children, is often unavailable from this premarket research, because these groups are usually not included as subjects in clinical trials. Postmarketing surveillance, therefore, allows for the detection of rarer, but possibly critical ADRs. In addition, postmarketing monitoring may detect counterfeit or substandard products. Often, a country's national drug regulatory authority is responsible for ADR monitoring and reporting.

To facilitate information gathering, the drug regulatory authority should provide case report forms to health providers on adverse drug reactions. The completed case report form is then sent to the national or regional ADR center or to the manufacturer of the product. These forms vary by locale, but should include the following minimum information.

Patient information—

- Patient identifier
- Age at time of event or date of birth
- Gender
- Weight

Adverse event or product problem—

- Description of event or problem
- Date of event
- Date of report
- Relevant tests/laboratory data
- Other relevant patient information/history
- Outcomes attributed to adverse event

Suspected medication(s)—

- Name (international nonproprietary name and brand name)

- Dose, frequency, and route
- Therapy date
- Diagnosis for use
- Event abated after use stopped or dose reduced
- Batch number
- Expiration date
- Event reappeared after reintroduction of the treatment
- Concomitant medical products and therapy dates

Reporter—

- Name, address, telephone number
- Specialty and occupation

It can take years or even decades before adverse events are linked to the use of particular medicines. For example, several years passed before certain birth defects were associated with thalidomide use by pregnant women; decades passed before aspirin was linked to gastrointestinal problems. In some cases, medicines are withdrawn from the market, as was the case with bromfenac, terfenadine, and encainide after they were connected to serious health outcomes. In other cases, labeling is changed to include the new information on effects, contraindications, or dosage as a result of information received through postmarketing surveillance.

Clearly, the usefulness of a postmarketing surveillance program depends on cooperation from health professionals. All health care providers, including physicians, pharmacists, nurses, dentists, and others, should report ADRs as part of their professional responsibility. Even when some doubt exists about the relationship between the product and the ADR, all suspected ADRs, especially related to new medicines, should be reported as soon as possible. Many countries provide an easy system for reporting ADRs to their drug regulatory authorities, such as a dedicated phone line as provided in Ghana and a special reporting website as in Brazil.

Source: WHO 2002c.

which provides a clearinghouse for the millions of adverse drug reaction reports received from almost 100 countries. International pharmacovigilance activities have had a notable effect on international drug regulation. Box 6-2 describes the elements that comprise an adverse drug reaction program, and Chapter 35 has more information on implementing a pharmacovigilance program.

Advertising and promotion

Although many countries have rules to ensure that advertising is not misleading, these rules are generally not sufficient to cover pharmaceuticals. With consumer products, a certain degree of exaggeration is often tolerated as the normal practice of the marketplace. But for medicines that have the capacity to kill or cure, and with claims that people cannot easily verify, it is important that advertising to health professionals and to consumers be objective and reliable; misleading and extravagant pharmaceutical advertising claims may pose significant risks to the public.

For these reasons, most laws on pharmaceuticals now include a clause empowering regulation on advertising. In many countries, it is illegal to advertise to consumers medicines intended to be prescribed by health professionals. However, direct promotion of pharmaceutical products through the Internet is practically impossible to control; therefore, the national regulatory agency should educate consumers on identifying reliable sources of information, preferably in collaboration with national consumer and professional organizations. All advertising and labeling must be consistent with the information verified when the pharmaceutical product was registered or approved for marketing, with modifications required by the regulatory authority on the basis of postmarketing experience.

Useful guides to the principles that should underlie honest pharmaceutical promotion have been issued by WHO and separately by manufacturers (WHO 1988, 1999b).

Sanctions

Because constant vigilance is needed if the public is to be protected, pharmaceutical laws must be properly enforced with appropriate penalties for violators. There is no use establishing that medicine quality is poor, a warehouse is rat infested or damp upon inspection, or an advertisement is untruthful unless something is done about it. The drug regulatory agency must use its authority to impose appropriate penalties when necessary: sanctions may be penal (fines, imprisonment, or both) or simply corrective (banning the drug, closing down the warehouse). Sometimes a party has contravened the law so seriously that the appropriate sanction is determined to be loss of license to prescribe, manufacture, import, or distribute. On occasion, all of the penalties may be imposed.

To be effective, the drug regulatory authority must be able to apply sanctions on a timely basis, so it must have either the legal staff to ensure compliance or the necessary links with the relevant government department charged with enforcement. Therefore, the law governing pharmaceutical products must give legal authority to the appropriate personnel to carry out any necessary enforcement activities.

In addition, because the pharmaceutical sector is vulnerable to corruption, a country should not only include an anticorruption mechanism in its regulatory framework, but also have sanctions in place for bribery, fraud, collusion, and other dishonest acts (WHO/PSM 2006). Many countries have specific laws that address corruption in the public sector or provisions in their procurement regulations to ensure transparency and provide sanctions against, for example, bribery.

6.4 Medicine registration, licensing, and marketing authorization

The licensing and inspection of manufacturers and importers, although important, do not provide assurance about the products. Many countries have evolved systems of drug registration to ensure that individual products approved for sale meet the following criteria—

Efficacy: The medicine should be shown to be effective for the indications claimed. However, note that no product is ever 100 percent effective for all users. In practice, efficacy means that in a majority of cases the product meets its therapeutic claim.

Safety: The medicine should not present risks that are disproportionate to its benefits. Some patients may suffer severe reactions even to medicines shown to be safe in clinical studies. However, in the great majority of cases, adverse effects are minor or very infrequent.

Quality: The medicine should be well made, as specified in the official pharmacopoeia chosen as a standard. If not listed in an official pharmacopoeia, the product's manufacturing should comply with the quality documentation submitted by the applicant that demonstrates its safety and efficacy.

Clinical use information: All the clinical information needed to use the medicine properly, including indications, doses, precautions, and adverse effects, should be provided as part of the packaging, in language understandable to the health professional or patient, as appropriate.

Medicine registration, also referred to as licensing or marketing authorization, is often a major element in national pharmaceutical law. In its fully developed form, however, it is costly and labor intensive. Establishing a drug registration system is generally not justified until a country has a

Box 6-3
Stages in the evolution of a medicine
registration system

Stage 1: Notification procedure. Standard information is obtained on all pharmaceutical products currently marketed in the country and entered into a register. No judgment is made at this time regarding the appropriateness of the drugs for sale in the country.

Stage 2: Basic authorization procedure. Products listed in the register are provisionally authorized to remain on sale. All other drugs that are to be sold require a license, which is issued after an appropriate assessment of the efficacy, safety, and quality and a review of truth and completeness of packaging and labeling information.

Stage 3: Full registration or licensing procedure. Full evaluation of individual products is conducted by examining detailed data submitted by the manufacturer and obtained from the literature to assess their quality, safety, and efficacy.

Stage 4: Reevaluation of older drugs. All older pharmaceutical products on the market are systematically reassessed for compliance with the standards.

significant volume of private-sector pharmaceutical sales. The primary concern of many resource-limited countries is ensuring a reliable flow of essential generic drugs from reputable suppliers into the public health system.

As a country's economic development proceeds and more resources become available, priorities may change. The private sector may become more active, and local and multinational firms may begin actively promoting their new products to prescribers and even to the public. At this point the need for a medicine registration system arises.

As proposed in the WHO (1999c) guidelines for small drug regulatory authorities, a medicine registration system can best be developed in stages, starting with an inventory of all pharmaceutical products on the market, followed by a provisional authorization that allows products to continue to be sold until they complete the full registration procedure as shown in Box 6-3. Country Study 6-3 shows how Namibia maximized its resources by streamlining its medicine registration system.

In stage 1, the information requested initially may be simply the international nonproprietary name; product trade name, if any; name of the manufacturer; and country of origin. Later, this can be expanded to include composition, including inactive ingredients; pharmacological action; therapeutic classification; and claims made in the package insert. Having a complete register of what is on sale in the marketplace allows the regulatory agency to evaluate information from other countries or from WHO about problems with a particular medicine (for example, toxicity, contamination, evidence of inactivity), to determine whether the product is on sale in their country, and what actions might be taken.

Stage 2 requires assessment for new pharmaceutical products. Because this procedure is costly and time-consuming, countries can rely on decisions made in other countries with well-developed regulatory agencies, such as those that are members of the ICH. Is the drug approved for sale in its home country? If so, what claims have been made for it? Does it carry a WHO-type certificate indicating that it is manufactured under satisfactory conditions? The firm wishing to import the product must provide documented answers to these questions. Regulatory authorities may consult other countries directly before deciding to accept or reject a product. WHO and other bodies hold international and regional meetings of regulatory authorities from different countries, which helps create trust across borders and facilitates informal work sharing. Approval of locally manufactured pharmaceuticals requires inspection of the manufacturing premises and staff.

The task of full registration described in stage 3 should never be taken up lightly—even a large regulatory agency can be overwhelmed by the vast amount of material that needs to be examined. Some groups of countries handle assessment jointly; others look at where else in the world the medicine is licensed, and under what conditions. Countries that have the resources to handle registration and licensing independently can often obtain technical advice and practical help from WHO and support from other countries with well-developed regulatory agencies.

Stage 4, the reevaluation of older products on the market, is the final stage in the development of a registration system and is very ambitious. Few industrialized countries have yet managed to complete it.

If a medicine is intended to be generically equivalent to another already on the market, regulations must stipulate the evidence needed to support their equivalence (see Box 6-4). WHO has a resource for countries without a fully functioning system for premarket evaluation and market authorization that wish to assess and authorize multisource (generic) pharmaceutical products (WHO 1998b). WHO also makes available findings from assessment reports generated as part of its program to prequalify medicines for HIV/AIDS, tuberculosis, and malaria, including information based on product data showing compliance with international standards for quality, safety, and efficacy, bioequivalence (for generic products), and findings resulting from inspections of production sites according to GMP standards (see http://mednet3.who.int/prequal/). The WHO prequalification process should be useful to

Country Study 6-3
Revising registration procedures in Namibia

In its first fifteen years of independence, Namibia developed very comprehensive pharmaceutical regulatory procedures, considering its small population and limited resources. Unfortunately, human resources capacity did not keep pace with administrative requirements, and the number of medicine registration applications quickly created a huge backlog of about 1,000 medicines awaiting marketing approval, including antiretroviral (ARV) medicines. At that time, forty-nine ARVs were on the market, but the backlog prevented access to valuable fixed-dose combinations and pediatric products. One estimate showed that at the current capacity, it would take eighteen years to review all outstanding applications.

The Rational Pharmaceutical Management (RPM) Plus Program worked with the government on interventions to streamline the registration process. Key was a policy change allowing the Medicines Control Council (MCC) to give priority to ARVs for registration and create a proxy evaluation process to quickly accept products already registered in International Conference on Harmonisation countries or South Africa; for example, the new policy permits the MCC to accept certain quality requirements that have already been approved by recognized authorities, such as through WHO's prequalification program. Other interventions included training nonprofessional staff to take on some application processing responsibilities and creating a drug registration database.

Within a year after RPM Plus's intervention began, 1,392 applications for new medicines were evaluated. Of those, fourteen ARVs and twenty-four generic ARVs were reviewed and approved (which increased the number of ARVs on the market by 75 percent). The fourteen approvals included much-needed pediatric dosage forms and fixed-dose combinations; the addition of generic products helps reduce prices.

Source: Pereko and Nwokike 2006.

Box 6-4
Interchangeability

New multisource (generic) pharmaceutical products must be of good quality and at least as safe and efficacious as existing products. The need for interchangeability arises when a patient changes from one brand to another, for example, when—

- Physicians prescribe by generic name
- Generic substitution is permitted by national legislation
- The same brand is not always available, for example, in remote areas of the country
- Patients in hospitals are given whatever brand the hospital has in stock, and sometimes different brands on different occasions
- Patients receive a different brand after discharge from the hospital

A number of features are important to interchangeability, although the science behind demonstrating interchangeability is still evolving: compliance with appropriate quality standards and at least compliance with relevant pharmacopoeial standards; stability; possible differences in sensitizing potential caused by the use of different excipients; therapeutic equivalence in terms of, as appropriate, bioequivalence, pharmacodynamic studies, clinical studies, or in vitro dissolution rate; and product information and labeling.

By their nature, different brands of modified (sustained-, continuous-, prolonged-, slow-) release products are more likely not to be equivalent than are different brands of immediate, conventional-release products. Some drug regulatory agencies take the view that such products should never be considered interchangeable, while others define a series of studies that should be conducted, including in some circumstances comparative clinical trials. For delayed-release products, such as enteric-coated tablets, interchangeability is more easily demonstrated.

Source: WHO 1998b.

Figure 6-1   Resources for medicine registration in twenty-six African countries

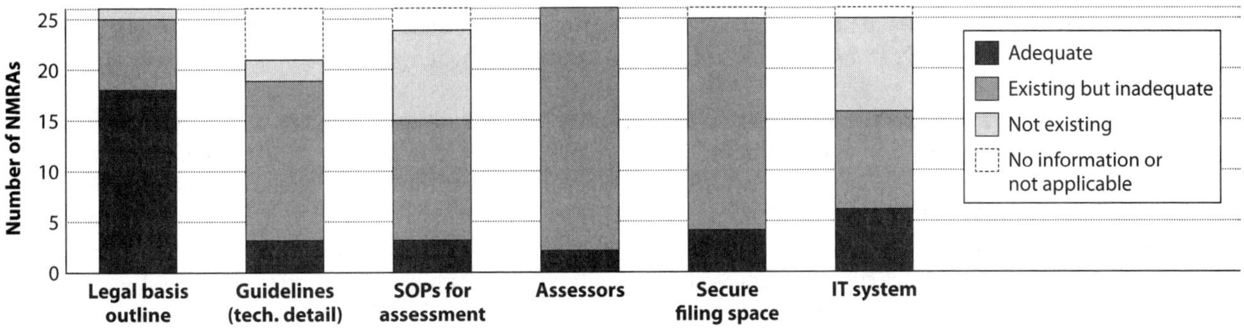

NMRAs = national medicine regulatory authorities; SOPs = standard operating procedures; IT = information technology.
Source: Adapted from WHO 2010b.

developing-country regulatory authorities that do not have sufficient capacity to fully assess products and determine their acceptability before licensing.

The registration systems of many African countries are still lagging. For example, in twenty-six countries surveyed, the technical standard of evaluations, if they existed, were not in line with WHO standards; only 11 percent had adequate standard operating procedures for assessment, 85 percent did not have enough space to store data securely, and only one-quarter of the countries had functioning computerized registration systems (WHO 2010b) (see Figure 6-1).

Classifying pharmaceuticals for dispensing

As part of the marketing authorization process, the national drug regulatory agency is also responsible for classifying each pharmaceutical product in terms of how it is dispensed and sold. For example, prescription-only medicines require a directive from an authorized health practitioner; pharmacist-only medicines are available without prescription, but only under a pharmacist's supervision; and over-the-counter medicines are available without a prescription in retail outlets besides the pharmacy, such as a grocery or licensed drug seller. This classification affects the product's availability and appropriate use. Factors to consider in the classification include—

- The safety of the active ingredient
- The need for professional counsel before use
- The nature of the ailment or symptoms the medicine is intended to treat
- The risk/benefit ratio (TGA 2003)

Consideration should also be given to the restrictions for prescribing and dispensing controlled drugs as provided in the international drug control treaties, namely the 1961 Single Convention on Narcotic Drugs and the 1971 Convention on Psychotropic Substances. The list of narcotic

and psychotropic drugs is available from the International Narcotics Control Board (http://www.incb.org).

Regulating traditional and herbal medicines

As discussed in Chapter 5, countries are increasingly recognizing the large role that traditional and complementary medicine plays in their health care systems. An important challenge is the evaluation and assurance of the quality, safety, and efficacy of herbal and traditional medicines. Since the earliest days of humankind, herbal medicines have been applied in health care throughout the world. Many are still widely used and have become important in international trade. Significant quantities of herbal products are now imported by countries in the European Union, North America, and Asia. However, the use and production of herbal products remains largely unregulated, and their safety and therapeutic value cannot always be guaranteed.

Recognition of the clinical, pharmaceutical, and economic value of herbal medicines is growing, although the level of official recognition through legislation varies widely among countries. WHO published a reference on the national experiences of fifty-two countries in formulating policies on traditional and herbal medicinal products and in introducing measures for their registration and regulation (WHO 1998c). WHO also published a summary of the legal status of traditional and complementary medicines in 141 countries (WHO 2005c) and guidelines on how to develop national policies on the safety, efficacy, and quality of herbal medicines (WHO 1998a).

6.5   Controlling alternative and informal distribution channels

In some countries, unregulated, informal, or even illegal distribution (including sales in marketplaces and on streets) and smuggling of medicines are widespread. Another major problem is that medicines may be traded through several intermediaries and free-trade zones and are sometimes repackaged and relabeled to hide their true source or identity, leading to the circulation of substandard and counterfeit medicines.

As the volume of expensive medicines such as for HIV/AIDS and malaria increases in formal distribution channels, there will be an increase in leakage of these medicines to informal channels. A WHO study of regulations in ten countries (Ratanawijitrasin and Wondemagegnehu 2002) showed that pharmaceuticals distributed through the informal sector received little regulatory attention from governments compared with those distributed through the formal sector. Products of substandard quality and incorrect information—especially exaggeration about efficacy—are often found in the informal sector.

It is important for countries to assess the influence of alternative and informal distribution channels on their health care systems. If citizens purchase most of their medicines from informal dealers, they may be getting substandard-quality products, which may adversely affect public health. Medicine regulation can be used to promote quality criteria for medicines and health commodities by establishing and enforcing standards for all distribution channels and encouraging the public to be careful about where they buy pharmaceutical products. Chapter 32 discusses how initiatives can improve the quality of products and services from private-sector drug sellers. Country Study 6-4 describes how

the government in the Lao People's Democratic Republic (P.D.R.) has instituted regulations to improve the quality of private pharmacies.

Another challenge to drug regulators that has emerged in recent years is the widespread use of the Internet to sell uncontrolled pharmaceuticals across national borders (WHO 2003b). Regulation and enforcement can deter illegal practices, although it requires cooperation among national agencies such as those handling drug regulations, customs, and the postal service. Because of the transnational nature of e-commerce, international cooperation in its control is also needed.

6.6 Substandard and counterfeit medicines

Substandard medicines are products whose composition and ingredients do not meet the correct scientific specifications and consequently may be ineffective, dangerous to the patient, or both. Substandard products may occur as a result of negligence, human error, insufficient human and financial resources, or counterfeiting.

Counterfeit medicines are considered a subset of substandard medicines, but the difference is that they are deliberately and fraudulently mislabeled regarding their identity or source. Counterfeiting can apply to both branded and generic products, and counterfeit medicines may include products with the correct ingredients but fake packaging,

---

Country Study 6-4
Regulatory interventions in Lao P.D.R.

In Lao P.D.R., private pharmacies make up the majority of the retail market for medicines. However, little or no control of private pharmacies existed until 1996, when such regulation was incorporated into the National Drug Policy. District pharmacists became responsible for inspecting and monitoring private pharmacies, and a special unit was created at the provincial level to oversee the regulations. Inspectors made sure that the pharmacies had up-to-date regulatory documents. In addition, the central drug regulatory authority instituted a number of policies to improve the quality assurance system in the country. These included the development of a good manufacturing practices regulation with associated training, improvements in the medicine registration system, and the institution of fines and sanctions to enforce the new regulations.

In 1997, a baseline assessment was conducted in 115 of 214 licensed private pharmacies in Savannakhet province before the new regulations had fully taken hold.

A follow-up study in 1999 used the same indicators to assess the effect of the new policies and activities on private pharmacy services. The results showed significant improvement in almost all indicator values, including the organization in the pharmacy; availability of essential medicines and essential materials for dispensing, such as a hygienic counter; and information given to the customers. Analysis of samples from the 115 pharmacies showed a decrease in the proportion of substandard medicines—from 46 percent in 1997 to 22 percent in 1999—still high, but substantially better.

Before the regulatory interventions, the quality of pharmaceutical service was low in Savannakhet province. The development of a regulatory framework with regular inspections and enforcement through sanctions was not only possible to initiate in a resource-limited country, but also appeared to be an important catalyst for better quality medicines and pharmacy practices.

Sources: Stenson et al. 2001; Syhakhang et al. 2001.

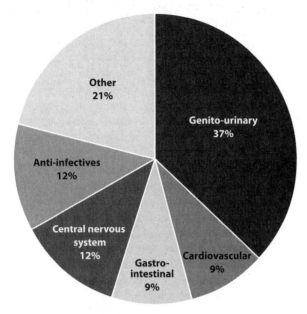

Figure 6-2   Reports of counterfeit medicines by therapeutic class received in 2007

Total number of cases: 1,513. One case reflects at least one production lot (e.g., thousands of tablets, capsules, or other forms).
Data from the Pharmaceutical Security Institute (http://www.psi-inc.org).

with the wrong ingredients, without active ingredients, or with insufficient active ingredients.

In wealthier countries, the most frequently counterfeited medicines are new, expensive lifestyle medicines. In developing countries, the most counterfeited medicines are those used to treat life-threatening conditions such as malaria, tuberculosis, and HIV/AIDS. Figure 6-2 gives the number of reports of counterfeit medicines, by therapeutic class, submitted in 2007 and shows that the highest percentage reported concerned genito-urinary medicines.

Trade in these medicines is more prevalent in countries with weak pharmaceutical regulatory control and enforcement, scarce or erratic supply of basic medicines, unregulated markets, and unaffordable prices. Governments need to develop strategies and put appropriate legislation and sanctions into place to reduce corruption and criminal activity. As in the case of e-commerce, enforcement of these laws requires cooperation among regulatory authorities, police, customs services, and the judiciary to control more effectively the pharmaceutical market.

6.7   Establishing effective administrative control

In many countries, medicine legislation and regulation are not regularly updated or are imported from other countries and do not reflect national realities. Countries can draw

guidance from the experiences of others, but problems have arisen when overly complex provisions were adopted. Legislation and administrative practices must be attuned to available resources, and every opportunity must be taken to understand and use the information provided by regulatory authorities in other countries (WHO 1990). The example of approving microbicides to control HIV infection shows the regulatory difficulties faced by resource-constrained countries (Box 6-5).

Required resources

To perform effectively, national regulatory authorities must have the necessary political support, legal power, human and financial resources, and independence in decision making. They also must have strong public support and proper management. Where national regulatory authorities have a high profile within the government, they are organized as a commission, board, statutory authority, or department, with the legal power from government to acquire and use resources, including hiring qualified full-time staff at a salary scale that discourages corruption and conflicts of interest.

Ideally, one central, autonomous agency should be accountable for the overall effectiveness of pharmaceutical regulation. In countries whose regulatory functions are split among two or more agencies, the fragmentation can lead to duplication of effort, lapses in implementation, inconsistent regulation, and wasted resources. In recent years, several countries (for example, Argentina and Brazil) have successfully established such centralized agencies to regulate food, medicines, and consumer products. However, a survey of twenty-six countries in sub-Saharan Africa showed that most countries' regulatory systems were uneven—with gaps and overlaps in responsibilities spread over several bodies other than the drug regulatory authority, including the ministries of trade and health, pharmaceutical councils, and regional authorities, especially for licensing and inspection (WHO 2010b).

Table 6-1 details the resources required to achieve effective administrative control; at a minimum, these needs include a drug regulatory authority with staff, a team of inspectors to visit warehouses and retailers, and access to a laboratory capable of performing quality-control testing.

Personnel are the key resource for making effective pharmaceutical regulation possible. Because of the technical nature of their work, the law often prescribes that inspectors be pharmacists or have other relevant education and training. Others can be trained to undertake licensing, registration, and enforcement duties. Depending on the size of the country and the degree of pharmaceutical development, the entire staff may consist of only a few individuals. Sometimes contracting out specific duties may be appropriate; however, it is important for the contractor not to have any conflicts of

> **Box 6-5**
> **Regulatory hurdles in the development of microbicides for HIV/AIDS**
>
> More women than men account for new HIV infections in many parts of the world. In certain places, women's lack of power means they cannot insist on condom use to protect themselves, and even if they have a single partner or husband, they are still at risk. This situation has resulted in much interest in the development of microbicides—a topical medicine used vaginally to prevent HIV transmission—that gives women control of usage.
>
> A major obstacle to the approval of an effective microbicide is the fact that those now in clinical testing are new medicines that have not been on the market yet. Many developing countries do not have the resources or regulatory framework available to perform the testing and review of new medicines themselves, so they rely on product reviews from the United States or Europe to determine acceptability for their countries. However, because microbicides will be marketed primarily in developing countries, developed countries have no incentive to review and license them for their own markets.
>
> To help fill the gaps, the European Parliament approved an initiative for the European Medicines Agency (formerly known as the European Medical Evaluation Agency) to scientifically assess products such as microbicides that are proposed for use primarily in developing countries. The drug regulatory agencies in developing countries would then use the scientific assessments to make decisions about licensing. Other steps that could help overcome these regulatory hurdles would be collaboration between regulatory authorities in developing and industrialized countries to jointly review product profiles and to help resource-limited countries develop the capacity to make drug registration decisions autonomously.
>
> Although results of clinical trials of microbicides for HIV have been mixed, research continues, and the European assessment mechanism is one that could be used with other similar products.
>
> Sources: Coplan, Mitchnick, and Rosenberg 2004; Davis 2009; Fox, Beasley, and Kelland 2010.

interest, such as an ongoing consultancy with a pharmaceutical company that could specifically benefit from the contracting arrangement.

Computer software now greatly simplifies many of the administrative tasks of the regulatory agency. Personnel should have access to the latest scientific and technical information to facilitate their work.

Financing

The law must provide a realistic mechanism for funding regulatory functions. Funds may be provided from general tax income and from charges levied on the manufacturers, importers, and distributors to cover the bulk of the costs of the pharmaceutical control system. The level of charges may be set from year to year, but the nature of the charges can be defined in the law. For example, the law may set lower fees for essential medicines; importers can be required to pay a fee when they submit a new medicine application to the regulatory authority for consideration, a supplementary fee when the license is issued, and an annual fee for as long as the medicine remains on sale; and manufacturers might be required to relicense their products periodically (for example, every five years).

Fees and charges substantially fund the cost of operating the national regulatory agencies in most developed and some developing countries. In Canada, the United Kingdom, and the United States, the agencies recover 70 percent, 100 percent, and about 50 percent, respectively, of their regulation costs (WHO 2003b). Because of their large markets, developed countries tend to charge higher fees than developing countries. In addition, in developing countries, fee revenues are often added to the general treasury rather than being assigned specifically to the drug regulatory agency, which makes it hard to adequately finance regulation. However, regulatory agencies should not be completely dependent on fees to fund all of their activities; they should receive some financial support from their governments to help ensure their independence and ability to carry out basic responsibilities. Most of the twenty-six drug regulatory authorities surveyed in Africa get their funding from more than one source (e.g., fees, government, donors); however, none had sufficient or sustainable operating funds (WHO 2010b).

Guiding principles for small national drug regulatory authorities

Regulation is not the only component of pharmaceutical policy, and sometimes in resource-limited settings, it is not even the most pressing one. Nonetheless, the existence of a well-functioning national drug regulatory authority to help ensure medicine quality, safety, and efficacy is the best guarantee that the public is getting the medicines it deserves. A national regulatory authority needs a clear mission statement including goals and objectives to direct its work. Goals

Table 6-1   Resources required for effective administrative control

Resources required	Specific function or purpose
Personnel	• Regulatory activities (licensing, registration, and so forth) • Monitoring, inspection, and surveillance • Enforcement
Physical and infrastructure	• Office space for regulatory and enforcement personnel • Access to appropriate analytical laboratory resources • Computers, software, sampling equipment, and office equipment • Vehicles for distribution, inspection, and enforcement activities
Technical	• Preservice and in-service training • Knowledge of pharmaceutical manufacturing processes, packaging, and so forth • Collation of data • Dissemination of information • Reference library (books, journals, bulletins)
Financial	• Capital and recurrent expenditures • Technical programs • Payments for patents and royalties • Payments for consultants • Payments for quality-control samples • Publications (forms, licenses, pharmacopoeia) • Travel for inspection and enforcement activities

Source: Adapted from Jayasuriya 1985.

usually include protecting public health by ensuring the safety, efficacy, and quality of medicines and their appropriate use. Plainly outlined objectives provide a measure to evaluate how well the agency is functioning.

Primary pharmaceutical regulation activities should not be compromised by other nonregulatory tasks with which the national regulatory authority may be charged. If the authority responsible for pharmaceutical regulation has nonregulatory functions, such as manufacturing, procurement, or service delivery, conflicts of interest may occur regarding mandates and resource allocation.

When a country is ready to introduce pharmaceutical regulation, work by WHO (1990) provides useful guidance for authorities with limited human, financial, scientific, and technological resources. To be effective, a small drug regulatory authority needs to operate within the national pharmaceutical laws and policies that have been established and must relate to other interested bodies, including organizations responsible for pharmaceutical procurement in the public sector and the national formulary committee. As mentioned, effectively enforcing pharmaceutical legislation requires national regulatory authorities and other government enforcement agencies, such as customs, police, and prosecutors, to work together. National regulatory agencies should also seek the cooperation of health professionals, pharmaceutical and consumer associations, and other interested parties through stakeholder workshops, meetings addressing specific issues, or other venues open to the public.

A drug regulatory authority's objectives can be accomplished effectively only if a mandatory system of licensing

products, manufacturers, importing agents, and distributors is in place. A small authority has limited capacity to undertake these tasks. For imported pharmaceutical substances, a small authority is dependent on information generated in the exporting country. The WHO certification scheme on the quality of pharmaceutical products moving in international commerce (WHO 2000) was designed to provide this information, although recommendations have been made on how to update the scheme (WHO 2008). As discussed in Chapter 19, this scheme must be supplemented by direct contacts with international agencies and other regulatory agencies to obtain necessary information; however, the certification scheme is only as good as the certifying authority. WHO's prequalification program provides information on approved sources for products related to HIV/AIDS, malaria, tuberculosis, and reproductive health.

Many national regulatory authorities do not make publicly available their regulatory policies, administrative procedures, guidelines, and criteria for decisions. Lack of transparency means that communication is probably lacking on medicine regulation between national regulatory authorities and their stakeholders. Moreover, transparency is required to make the agency accountable for its actions and to limit the influence of political pressures and personal favors in the decision-making process. Transparency will also contribute to the credibility and authority of communications between the agency and those affected by its actions: manufacturers, importers, distributors, health professionals, and consumers. An assessment tool is available to measure transparency in the pharmaceutical sectors (WHO 2009a) and a report describes the assessment of four countries' pharmaceutical registration, selection, and procurement systems: Lao P.D.R., Malaysia, Philippines, and Thailand (WHO 2006a).

To increase the amount of information and communication, WHO is helping drug regulatory authorities develop websites with information on—

- Lists of approved medicines
- National pharmaceutical regulations
- Methods to ensure safe, efficacious, and rational use of specific medicines
- Lists of approved companies and their authorized activities
- Details of persons and institutions with responsibility for pharmaceutical regulation

WHO resources available for drug regulatory authorities include—

- A model website for drug regulatory authorities that aims to enhance communication and transparent dialogue among national drug regulatory authorities, industry, consumers, and health professionals (http://www.who.int/medicines/areas/quality_safety/regulation_legislation/model_site/en)
- A list of recognized drug regulatory authorities' websites (http://www.who.int/entity/medicines/areas/quality_safety/regulation_legislation/ListMRAWebsites.pdf)
- A tool to assess regulatory authorities (http://www.who.int/medicines/areas/quality_safety/regulation_legislation/assesment/en/index.html)
- Practical guidance for conducting a review (based on the WHO Data Collection Tool for the Review of Drug Regulatory Systems) (http://www.who.int/medicines/areas/quality_safety/regulation_legislation/GuideAssessRegSys.pdf)
- A drug regulatory status database (http://www.who.int/hiv/amds/patents_registration/en/index.html)

In summary, the regulatory authority should be vested with legal powers to—

- Issue, vary, and revoke licenses for pharmaceutical products on grounds of quality, safety, and efficacy
- Ensure the safe and effective use of each product by controlling, through the terms of the license, the content of all labeling (including package inserts, associated prescribing information, and advertising) and the channels through which the product may legitimately be supplied
- Inspect and license all manufacturing premises, importing agents, wholesalers, distributors, hospital dispensaries, independent pharmacies, and other retail outlets to ensure that they comply with prevailing regulations and guidelines

To implement these responsibilities, the authority must have the power to order that certain things be done and to prosecute those who disregard the law. To retain public confidence and respect, the authority must be seen as operating in an independent, authoritative, and impartial manner. It should be concerned exclusively with the determination of standards and the implementation of controls. Although it needs to work closely with the body responsible for public pharmaceutical procurement, it should not be responsible for procurement and should remain independent in its operations and decisions.

6.8 Evaluating the effectiveness of pharmaceutical legislation

Evaluating the effectiveness of pharmaceutical legislation and accompanying regulations is not always easy. The process of evaluation depends on the types of performance indicators and criteria used and on the availability of adequate data. The questions in the Assessment Guide at the end of this chapter provide a framework.

The most important factor in the effectiveness of pharmaceutical laws and regulations is the extent to which the legislative framework is in tune with national policy and the existing situation in the pharmaceutical sector. Changes in policy need to be reflected in the legislation and in its implementation.

Measuring the effectiveness of a law on pharmaceuticals is easier for certain elements than for others. For instance, the registration process can be evaluated in relation to quantitative targets and time schedules to see whether the agency is on schedule.

The degree of noncompliance with a law or regulation may suggest not only the need to take action against those responsible but also the desirability of identifying the causes of noncompliance: it may be related to technical defects in the law or in its wording, or to operational problems of implementation, such as lack of transparency or poor communication, which can be resolved. Enforcement personnel should periodically report on their perception of how the law functions and the types of problems encountered to facilitate any necessary revisions. Many legislative and regulatory provisions can be improved and updated when the legislation is sufficiently flexible to allow for modifications by the regulatory agency.

Responsibility for evaluating the effectiveness of a drug law often falls on the regulatory authority established by law for policy making, implementation, or both. The level of accountability and transparency under which the drug regulatory authority operates can be evaluated by examining reporting requirements, external reviews of performance, processes involved with lodging complaints, and appeals procedures. Periodic self-evaluation to identify weaknesses in policy making and implementation activities is important. The body must devise its own systems to judge whether it receives sufficient feedback and whether its operational effectiveness can be improved. ∎

References and further readings

★ = Key readings.

Coplan, P. M., M. Mitchnick, and Z. F. Rosenberg. 2004. Regulatory Challenges in Microbicide Development. *Science* 34:1911–2.

Davis, S. 2009. Microbicide Hopes Fade with Poor Trial Results. *Science and Development Network* 16 December. <http://www.scidev.net/en/news/microbicide-hopes-fade-with-poor-trial-results-1.html>

Feeley, R., B. O'Hanlon, A. Stene, and Y. Sezgin. 2009. *Finding Middle Ground: Making Better Use of the African Private Health Sector Through More Effective Regulations.* Bethesda, Md.: Private Sector Partnerships (PSP)-*One*, Abt Associates. <http://www.globalhealthlearning.org/assets/filelib/076/file_FINAL_Leg_Reg_Report.pdf>

Fox, M., D. Beasley, and K. Kelland. 2010. AIDS Gel with Gilead Drug Protects Women in Study. 20 July. Vienna: Reuters. <http://www.reuters.com/article/idUSTRE66I49G20100720?pageNumber=1>

★ Gray, A. 2004. *Resource Guide on Drug Regulation in Developing Countries.* London: UK Department for International Development Health Systems Resource Centre. <http://www.bvsde.paho.org/bvsacd/cd65/Gray.pdf>

Hayashi, Y., and R. Palop. 2002. Harmonization. In *Proceedings of the Tenth International Conference of Drug Regulatory Authorities (ICDRA)*, Hong Kong, China, 24–27. Geneva: World Health Organization.

Hill, S., and K. Johnson. 2004. *Emerging Challenges and Opportunities in Drug Registration and Regulation in Developing Countries.* London: UK Department for International Development Health Systems Resource Centre. <http://www.hlsp.org/LinkClick.aspx?fileticket=0TXMdaAk5KA%3D&tabid=1643>

Jayasuriya, D. C. 2002. Medicinal Products and the Law in Developing Countries—Concepts, Issues and Approaches. New Delhi: Har-Anand Publications.

Jayasuriya, D. C. 1985. *Regulation of Pharmaceuticals in Developing Countries.* Geneva: World Health Organization.

Kaplan, W., and R. Laing. 2003. Paying for Pharmaceutical Registration in Developing Countries. *Health Policy and Planning* 18:237–48.

Mui, Y. Q. 2009. "Crackdown Targets Counterfeit Drugs: Fake Medicines a Growing Enterprise." 20 November. *Washington Post.*

PAHO (Pan American Health Organization). 2005. *Proceedings of IV Pan American Conference on Drug Regulatory Harmonization.* Boca Chica, Dominican Republic, March 2–4.

PANDRH Steering Committee (Pan American Network for Drug Regulatory Harmonization). 2009. Statutes. Washington, D.C.: Pan American Health Organization.

Pereko, D., and J. Nwokike. 2006. "Improving the Availability of ARVs in Namibia by Using Policy Change to Streamline the Drug Registration Process." Paper presented at the XVI International AIDS Conference, Toronto, August 13–18.

Ratanawijitrasin, S., and E. Wondemagegnehu. 2002. *Effective Drug Regulation: A Multicountry Study.* Geneva: World Health Organization.

Stenson, B., L. Syhakhang, C. S. Lundborg, B. Eriksson, and G. Tomson. 2001. Private Pharmacy Practice and Regulation: A Randomized Trial in Lao P.D.R. *International Journal of Technology Assessment in Health Care* 17(4):579–89.

Srivastava, D. 2008. *A Country Level Report on the Pharmaceutical Sector in India. Part One: Institutions Involved in Pharmaceutical Regulation.* London: UK Department for International Development.

Syhakhang, L., B. Stenson, R. Wahlström, and G. Tomson. 2001. The Quality of Public and Private Pharmacy Practices: A Cross-Sectional Study in the Savannakhet Province, Lao PDR. *European Journal of Clinical Pharmacology* 57:221–7.

TGA (Therapeutic Goods Administration). 2003. *Australian Regulatory Guidelines for OTC Medicines.* Woden, A.C.T., Australia: TGA. <http://www.tga.gov.au/industry/otc-argom.htm>

★ TCM/HTP/WHO (Department of Technical Cooperation for Essential Drugs and Traditional Medicine/Health Technology and Pharmaceuticals/World Health Organization). 2007. *Report of the WHO Consultation on Regulatory Technical Package and Model for Regulatory Decision Making, WHO Headquarters, Geneva 27–29 November 2006.* <http://www.who.int/medicines/publications/ReportWHOconsultationNov06.pdf>

WHO (World Health Organization). 2010a. Medicines: Counterfeit Medicines. Fact Sheet No. 275. Geneva: WHO. <http://www.who.int/mediacentre/factsheets/fs275/en>

————. 2010b. Regulatory Harmonization: Updating Medicines Regulatory Systems in Sub-Saharan African Countries. *WHO Drug Information* 24(1):6–20.

★ ————. 2009a. *Measuring Transparency in the Public Pharmaceutical Sector: Assessment Instrument.* Geneva: WHO. <http://apps.who.int/medicinedocs/documents/s16732e/s16732e.pdf>

————. 2009b. Annex 3: Procedure for Prequalification of Pharmaceutical Products. In *WHO Expert Committee on Specifications for Pharmaceutical Preparations.* 43rd Report. <http://www.who.int/medicines/publications/pharmprep/pdf_trs953.pdf#page=164>

————. 2008. WHO Certification Scheme on the Quality of Pharmaceutical Products Moving in International Commerce. *WHO Drug Information* 22(3):207–18.

★ ————. 2007a. *Practical Guidance for Conducting a Review.* [Based on the WHO Data Collection Tool for the Review of Drug Regulatory Systems.] Geneva: WHO. <http://www.who.int/medicines/areas/quality_safety/regulation_legislation/GuideAssessRegSys.pdf>

★ ————. 2007b. WHO Data Collection Tool for the Review of Drug Regulatory Systems. [To Be Used Jointly with *Practical Guidance for Conducting a Review.*] Geneva: WHO. <http://www.who.int/medicines/areas/quality_safety/regulation_legislation/ENdatacollectiontool.pdf>

————. 2006a. *Measuring Transparency in Medicines Registration, Selection and Procurement: Four Country Assessment Studies.* Geneva: WHO. <http://apps.who.int/medicinedocs/documents/s14096e/s14096e.pdf>

————. 2006b. Annex 7: Multisource (Generic) Pharmaceutical Products: Guidelines on Registration Requirements to Establish Interchangeability. In *WHO Expert Committee on Specifications for Pharmaceutical Preparations.* 40th Report. Geneva: WHO. <http://whqlibdoc.who.int/trs/WHO_TRS_937_eng.pdf>

————. 2005a. Annex 5: Guidelines for Registration of Fixed-Dose Combination Medicinal Products. In *WHO Expert Committee on Specifications for Pharmaceutical Preparations.* 39th Report. Geneva: WHO. <http://apps.who.int/prequal/info_general/documents/TRS929/WHO_TRS_929_annex5FDCs.pdf>

————. 2005b. *Handbook for Good Clinical Research Practice (GCP): Guidance for Implementation.* Geneva: WHO. <http://apps.who.int/medicinedocs/documents/s14084e/s14084e.pdf>

ASSESSMENT GUIDE

Policy, legislation, and regulation

- Is there a national medicine policy approved by the government? Is the policy suitable to regulate the market? When was it last updated?
- Is there a comprehensive medicine law? Is it appropriate? Is it a new law or a revision of an existing law? When was it last updated?
- Is the legislation flexible in allowing for the passage and revision of regulations in response to new scientific information and market changes?
- Is there a drug regulatory authority responsible for the promulgation of regulations and for enforcement? Does the necessary political will and funding exist to support it?
- Are regulatory policies, procedures, and criteria for decisions available to all stakeholders?

Medicine selection and registration

- Is there a system for medicine registration? Is this a notification procedure? A basic authorization procedure? A full registration procedure? Is periodic renewal required?
- Is medicine registration based on an assessment of a medicine's efficacy, safety, quality and truth of packaging information? Are pharmacological or therapeutic standards used?
- Are there different registration procedures for essential medicines, generic products, multisource drugs, or imported products from selected countries?
- Is the WHO certification scheme on the quality of pharmaceutical products moving in international commerce used systematically for the registration of imported medicines?
- Are relevant medicines procured from suppliers prequalified by WHO?
- Is there a system for the collection of data regarding the efficacy and safety (adverse effects) of marketed medicines?

Licensing, inspection, and control

- Do mechanisms exist for the licensing, inspection, and control of pharmaceutical personnel and for manufacturing, distribution, and dispensing facilities?
- Do inspectors use a checklist for inspecting different types of pharmaceutical establishments?
- How many inspections were made during each of the last three years for the different types of pharmaceutical establishments?
- Is there an audit system to evaluate the inspection system?

Advertising and promotion

- Is there any specific regulation regarding therapeutic claims in drug labeling and promotion?
- Is there any legal provision for the compulsory use of generic names in medicine labeling and promotion?
- Are there controls on pharmaceutical promotion, and are these consistent with the WHO ethical criteria for medicinal drug promotion?

Compliance and enforcement

- What measures exist for enforcement of pharmaceutical laws and regulations? Are they enforceable administratively or through court actions? Are statistics available about compliance and enforcement?
- During the last three years, how many pharmaceutical products were eliminated from the register? How many batches of pharmaceutical products were recalled from the market?
- Is there a system for reporting pharmaceutical product problems? What types of and how many complaints were registered in the past three years, and what corrective measures were taken?
- How many violations have occurred with regard to pharmaceutical advertising and promotion in the past three years? What corrective measures were taken?
- Are there any statistics about the reaction of the industry and consumers to regulatory actions?

———. 2005c. *National Policy on Traditional Medicine and Regulation of Herbal Medicines—Report of a WHO Global Survey*. Geneva: WHO. <http://apps.who.int/medicinedocs/pdf/s7916e/s7916e.pdf>

———. 2003a. Annex 9: Guide to Good Storage Practices for Pharmaceuticals. In: *WHO Expert Committee on Specifications for Pharmaceutical Preparations*. 37th Report. Geneva: WHO.

★ ———. 2003b. *WHO Policy Perspectives on Medicines 7—Effective Medicines Regulation: Ensuring Safety, Efficacy and Quality.* Geneva: WHO. <http://apps.who.int/medicinedocs/pdf/s4921e/s4921e.pdf>

———. 2002a. Annex 3: Good Practices for National Pharmaceutical Control Laboratories. In *WHO Expert Committee on Specifications for Pharmaceutical Preparations*. 36th Report. <http://apps.who.int/medicinedocs/en/d/Jh3009e/16.html>

———. 2002b. *The Importance of Pharmacovigilance: Safety Monitoring of Medicinal Products*. Geneva: WHO. <http://whqlibdoc.who.int/hq/2002/a75646.pdf>

———. 2002c. *Safety of Medicines: A Guide to Detecting and Reporting Adverse Drug Reactions*. Geneva: WHO. <http://whqlibdoc.who.int/hq/2002/WHO_EDM_QSM_2002.2.pdf>

★ ———. 2001a. *How to Develop and Implement a National Drug Policy.* 2nd ed. Geneva: WHO. <http://whqlibdoc.who.int/publications/924154547X.pdf>

———. 2001b. *Pharmaceuticals and the Internet: Drug Regulatory Authorities' Perspective: Meeting Report, September 24–25, 2001, Copenhagen, Denmark*. Geneva: WHO. <http://whqlibdoc.who.int/hq/2001/a74987.pdf>

———. 2000. *WHO Certification Scheme on the Quality of Pharmaceutical Products Moving in International Commerce*. Geneva: WHO.

———. 1999a. *Effective Drug Regulation: What Can Countries Do?* Geneva: WHO. <http://whqlibdoc.who.int/hq/1999/WHO_HTP_EDM_MAC(11)_99.6.pdf>

———. 1999b. *Medical Products and the Internet*. Geneva: WHO. <http://whqlibdoc.who.int/hq/1999/WHO_EDM_QSM_99.4.pdf>

★ ———. 1999c. Annex 8: National Drug Regulatory Legislation: Guiding Principles for Small Drug Regulatory Authorities. In *WHO Expert Committee on Specifications for Pharmaceutical Preparations*. Thirty-Fifth Report. Geneva: WHO.

———. 1998a. *Guidelines for the Appropriate Use of Herbal Medicines.* Manila: WHO Regional Office for the Western Pacific. <http://whqlibdoc.who.int/wpro/-1993/9290611103.pdf>

★ ———. 1998b. *Marketing Authorization of Pharmaceutical Products with Special Reference to Multisource (Generic) Products: A Manual for Drug Regulatory Authorities.* Geneva: WHO. <http://whqlibdoc.who.int/hq/1998/WHO_DMP_RGS_98.5.pdf>

———. 1998c. *Regulatory Situation of Herbal Medicines: A Worldwide Review*. Geneva: WHO. <http://whqlibdoc.who.int/hq/1998/WHO_TRM_98.1.pdf>

———. 1990. Guiding Principles for Small National Drug Regulatory Authorities. In *WHO Expert Committee on Specifications for Pharmaceutical Products*. Technical Report Series, no. 790. Geneva: WHO.

———. 1988. *Ethical Criteria for Medicinal Drug Promotion*. Geneva: WHO.

WHO/IMPACT (World Health Organization/International Medical Products Anti-Counterfeiting Taskforce). 2008. *Counterfeit Drugs Kill!* Geneva: WHO. <http://www.who.int/impact/FinalBrochure WHA2008a.pdf>

★ WHO/PSM (World Health Organization/Department of Medicines Policy and Standards). 2006. *Ethical Infrastructure for Good Governance in the Public Pharmaceutical Sector: Working Draft for Field Testing and Revision*. Geneva: WHO/PSM. <http://www.who.int/medicines/areas/policy/goodgovernance/Ethical_Infrastructure.pdf>

★ WHO/QSM (World Health Organization/Quality Assurance and Safety of Medicines). 2004. WHO Medicines Regulatory Package. <http://www.who.int/medicines/areas/quality_safety/regulation_legislation/reginfo/en/index.html>

WHO/WPRO (World Health Organization/Regional Office for the Western Pacific). 2004. *Enhancing Health Policy Development: A Practical Guide to Understanding the Legislative Process.* Manila: WHO/WPRO. <http://www.wpro.who.int/publications/pub_9290610859.htm>

| Part I: Policy and economic issues | Part II: Pharmaceutical management | Part III: Management support systems |

Policy and legal framework
1 Toward sustainable access to medicines
2 Historical and institutional perspectives
3 Intellectual property and access to medicines
4 National medicine policy
5 Traditional and complementary medicine policy
6 Pharmaceutical legislation and regulation
7 Pharmaceutical production policy
8 Pharmaceutical supply strategies
Financing and sustainability

CHAPTER 7

Pharmaceutical production policy

SUMMARY

Policy makers must be concerned about pharmaceutical production for the same reasons that underlie other policy and legal decisions: pharmaceuticals can be dangerous as well as lifesaving. Health professionals and patients have no ready way of making judgments about medicines without public surveillance as a guide.

The potential for national or local production of quality-assured, low-cost pharmaceuticals to meet national needs is an issue that has been debated and discussed for several decades. The justifications for local production have included the problems of lack of access, high prices for imported pharmaceuticals, and poor pharmaceutical quality. These challenges prompted public and political interest in considering local production to promote self-sufficiency, achieve independence from international suppliers, develop local industrial capacity, and create jobs. The changing landscape in the global pharmaceutical market, however, has made local production of pharmaceuticals in many countries unlikely as a viable option, except under certain circumstances, such as the existence of a large national market or a need to address specific requirements within a local market. Furthermore, self-sufficiency in pharmaceutical supply has proved to be a myth; because most active pharmaceutical ingredients are now sourced globally, even the most developed countries cannot be considered wholly self-sufficient in pharmaceutical production.

The globalization of the pharmaceutical sector and the advent of worldwide public health funding initiatives have led to a more competitive market for generic pharmaceuticals, resulting in significant decreases in the prices of some essential medicines. Domestic production operations have had difficulty achieving the high quality expected in the market at prices that compete with those of large-scale international producers, and many countries have limited capacity to monitor and regulate pharmaceutical production activities. Decisions regarding producing or importing pharmaceuticals are complex and involve health policy, industrial policy, a country's national development strategy, and related political pressures. Despite the argument that actual production decisions should be left to private-sector and market forces, policy makers must sometimes respond to pressures to become more involved in decisions about pharmaceutical production. The principal policy question now is often not whether to make or buy pharmaceuticals, but rather what pharmaceuticals to buy and where to buy them.

Three important points related to decision making about local pharmaceutical production guide this chapter—

- Pharmaceuticals are potentially lifesaving and life-threatening. Pharmaceutical production requires precise standards, quality control, a highly skilled labor base, capital, national regulatory capacity, and management. Modern pharmaceutical production often uses raw materials that are most economical in the international market, which means that high-quality, low-cost medicines are not likely to be produced from the raw materials stage in countries that do not have the required market size and resources in terms of skilled people, technology, and quality control.

- Section 7.1 describes several types of pharmaceutical manufacturers that operate in low- and middle-income countries, ranging from subsidiaries of multinational firms to small, hospital-based operations that repackage medicines into course-of-therapy packs. Policy makers must assess the feasibility for the range of production options, from the primary manufacture of raw materials to the packaging of finished products.

- Because consumers are unable to judge medicine quality on their own, policy makers must be concerned about regulating the production quality of medicines from either international or domestic sources. Regulatory policy should focus on assuring that manufacturers who supply products to the national market follow good manufacturing practices. Whether policy makers take an active or a passive role, they must recognize that the regulations and incentives existing in a country always affect pharmaceutical production. The most constructive stance is to shape policies and regulations that promote the goal of reliable access to effective, safe, and inexpensive medicines rather than to focus on where the production takes place. If preferences are given to locally produced medicines, the sick may pay directly or indirectly for these preferences through higher prices or poorer quality.

7.1 Levels and types of local production

Most countries are part of the global pharmaceutical market, but few try to be entirely self-sufficient. Raw materials, which form the backbone of the industry, are produced and traded as commodities worldwide. Almost all countries, even the largest ones, actively acquire at least some raw materials, machinery, and packaging goods abroad—at the most economical prices and at different stages of production—and then complete the process at home. It is a matter of competitive advantage, not imaginary independence, in an increasingly globalized economy.

Production standards known as good manufacturing practices (GMPs) are quality requirements that have been adopted as guidelines by the industry and the World Health Organization (WHO). The GMP system ensures that products are consistently produced according to quality standards appropriate to their intended use and as required by the product specification. Some countries require more-exacting standards to further ensure quality, and any hope for an export market increasingly requires compliance with international GMP standards.

The three different levels of production are primary, secondary, and tertiary.

Primary production

Primary production is the processing of raw materials to create active pharmaceutical ingredients (APIs) and ancillary substances used in pharmaceutical formulations. The final API, which is the biologically active compound in the pharmaceutical that produces the therapeutic effect, should meet pharmacopoeial or similar requirements. Primary manufacturing may involve either chemical or biological processes requiring different types of production facilities, technologies, skills, and knowledge. The manufacture of active ingredients is the most expensive aspect of pharmaceutical production because of the necessary investment in capital equipment, process development, and quality assurance systems.

The more modern or sophisticated the products, the more skills and greater capability are needed to develop and maintain the production processes. Few middle- to low-income countries will have all the infrastructure needed, including a pool of skilled workers (scientists and engineers), industrial technology, a research and development base, quality-control experience, capital, and reliable utilities—as well as the potential market size—to make primary production an initial goal. Rather, because these basic commodities are most efficiently produced in large volumes—much greater than the markets could absorb in many countries—they tend to be traded and bought as are other international commodities, such as steel, some foods, and other chemicals.

Secondary production

Secondary production is the large-scale processing of finished dosage forms, such as tablets, capsules, or injections, from raw materials or intermediate products, often from both local and imported sources. Production of sterile preparations (such as injections, antibiotics, and intravenous fluids) and nonsterile preparations (oral solids, liquids, and topical preparations) can be carried out with either locally produced or imported packing materials. Although less technically demanding than primary production, this stage must be completed to precise specifications. It requires modern, high-speed, precision equipment to produce pills, capsules, and liquids, often in large quantities and at very low unit costs, which are targets that small facilities find difficult to achieve, especially while also meeting international GMP standards.

Tertiary production

Tertiary production includes packaging and labeling finished products from primary and secondary sources into bulk packs, smaller dispensing packets, bottles, or course-of-therapy units for individual use. The initial quality of the pharmaceutical product established in the earlier phases of production must be maintained in the tertiary and final step, so ensuring high quality standards through rigorous operational procedures is important. This type of production can be developed first in many countries as a positive contribution that also builds industrial skill and experience. Tertiary production also addresses specific local needs for certain formulations, labeling, and packaging.

7.2 Trends in local production

During the 1970s and 1980s, some international organizations and governments were promoting the idea of creating or strengthening the pharmaceutical manufacturing capacity of developing countries under the assumptions that such initiatives would—

- Increase countries' self-sufficiency in pharmaceutical supply
- Improve medicine quality
- Produce foreign exchange through exports of domestically manufactured medicines
- Create new jobs

However, even with the enthusiasm about the potential role of pharmaceutical production in the developing world, a 1986 World Bank report (Lashman 1986) concluded that the economies of scale and technological requirements for manufacturing medicines made local production an unrealistic option for most countries. The exceptions were countries with large local markets and the capacity to produce APIs, including Argentina, Brazil, China, Egypt, India, Mexico, and Thailand.

At that time, the pharmaceutical industry in most developing countries depended on production by multinational affiliates and the licensed production of generic products; very few developing countries were able to initiate any systematic pharmaceutical export (Balance, Pogany, and Forstner 1992). In addition, the increased market for generic medicines plus greater price competition led to significant decreases in the prices of many essential medicines. This market shift worked against domestic manufacturers, who were largely unable to produce medicines at prices that were competitive with those of large-scale international pharmaceutical producers. These factors led to a trend away from the promotion of local pharmaceutical production and toward more emphasis on quality-control and procurement issues (Kaplan and Laing 2005).

In a 2004 report, the World Health Organization estimated the worldwide pharmaceutical production capacity of 188 countries, which had changed little from the 1992 statistics—

- Ten countries had a sophisticated pharmaceutical industry and a significant research base (eight Western European countries, plus Japan and the United States). These countries—led by the United States and Japan—were responsible for 84 to 88 percent of the world's pharmaceutical production value.
- Sixteen countries had innovative capabilities: a sound production capacity and at least one new molecular entity marketed between 1961 and 1990 (including several European countries, Argentina, Australia, Canada, China, India, Israel, Mexico, and the Republic of Korea). India and China had seen huge growth in their pharmaceutical production over the preceding decade. India, in fact, had developed highly specialized manufacturing capabilities and had become one of the largest exporters of API raw materials for the production of generics (World Bank 2005).
- Thirteen countries produced both active ingredients and finished products (including Brazil, Egypt, Indonesia, Norway, and Turkey).
- Eighty-four countries from virtually every continent only produced finished products from imported ingredients.
- Forty-two countries and areas had no pharmaceutical industry (primarily low-income African and Asian countries).

Moving from one category to the next requires substantial technical and financial resources, and still, no country is completely self-sufficient in pharmaceutical production.

Even countries that export more pharmaceuticals than they import still rely on imports of some finished products, APIs, or other materials.

Currently, several types of pharmaceutical manufacturers, with different business models, operate manufacturing facilities in low- and middle-income countries (World Bank 2005)—

- *Subsidiaries of large multinational companies* that manufacture patent-protected, branded products for local and regional markets.
- *Global manufacturers of generics* that focus on developed markets in the United States, Europe, and large middle-income markets such as India and China. Some have manufacturing operations in smaller developing countries or joint ventures with local manufacturers.
- *Generics companies with predominantly national operations* that focus on the domestic market with occasional exports into neighboring countries. Their ability to comply with good manufacturing practices varies.
- *Small-scale local manufacturers* that usually make a limited number of products, including traditional medicines, to serve local or regional markets. Most are not able to meet GMP standards.

In addition, most hospitals repackage medications in smaller, unit-dose containers and may compound specialty items, such as creams with special formulations, for their own patients and for satellite facilities. The type of small-scale production of pharmaceuticals in a hospital pharmacy could include secondary production from existing raw materials that are usually imported and the packaging or repackaging of finished goods into smaller dispensing packs and course-of-therapy packages (see Chapter 45).

National manufacturers vary widely in the scope of their operations. Some in larger markets may have substantial capabilities in primary and secondary manufacturing activities and extensive pharmaceutical distribution networks. Smaller countries may be limited to a few major companies that do basic manufacturing or formulation and packaging. Many developing countries may have only one or two local importing distributors who represent all the international manufacturers. Multinational manufacturers of proprietary medicines have used this pathway to globalize their operations, and as multinational generic producers grow, they will likely follow the same expansion model (Guimier, Lee, and Grupper 2004). Country Study 7-1 profiles three types of manufacturers operating in West Africa.

Finally, one of the most important global trends has been the rapid growth of active-ingredient manufacturing companies in India and China. India, especially, led the way in developing highly specialized manufacturing capabilities that cover a large range of medicines, from antibiotics to antiretrovirals. Leading companies have invested in manufacturing facilities that meet the highest international standards for GMPs. Technical advances in China have caught up as it has entered into joint ventures with pharmaceutical manufacturers in developed countries as a way of acquiring technological expertise. China and India will probably maintain a competitive production advantage because of their skilled labor forces, low resource costs, and large, high-volume domestic markets, which will help them keep their pharmaceutical prices low (Attridge and Preker 2005).

7.3 The effect of globalization on local production

The creation of high-profile international initiatives, such as the Global Fund to Fight AIDS, Tuberculosis and Malaria, and increased funding for public health treatment programs

are part of the growing momentum to increase access to medicines in developing countries (see Chapter 2). In addition, initiatives to reduce pharmaceutical prices, such as the Clinton Foundation's negotiations with multinational producers and global procurement mechanisms, such as the Global Fund's voluntary pooled procurement system, are expanding the number of procurement options for these countries. As a result, the market is growing for pharmaceuticals that treat diseases that disproportionately affect poor countries. In addition, the scale-up of public health treatment programs, such as antiretroviral therapy, is creating a large demand for pharmaceuticals in the public sector. Countries that are tempted to add to or expand their production of pharmaceuticals to fulfill the needs of such targeted public health programs must carefully evaluate the cost-effectiveness of global production compared with that of their procurement options. Global funding mechanisms require that products either be prequalified by WHO or approved by a stringent regulatory authority. So far, mainly

---

Country Study 7-1
Profiles of three pharmaceutical facilities operating in West Africa

A 2004 study looked at the pharmaceutical production capacity in West Africa using data available from interviews with key stakeholders and field visits to Ghana and Côte d'Ivoire. The following profiles illustrate the similarities and differences of three different types of pharmaceutical production operations.

The first firm is an owner-operated company that started small and grew into an operation employing more than 300 people, with production lines for tablets, liquids, capsules, syrups, and powders. The company sells most of its products to private-sector customers, but some sales go to the public sector. The firm does not export its products but has developed a large sales and distribution network covering the entire country. The company funded its expansion using sales profits that were supplemented by loans from commercial banks. Because the company already had significant domestic market share, it was looking for new markets and new products, including medicines to treat HIV/AIDS and malaria. Although the company's owner-operated status has probably helped keep costs manageable, strict control by the owners could discourage the recruitment of talented workers from outside the firm whose expertise could help the firm expand into a large-scale, international player.

Large European multinational pharmaceutical companies own the majority of the second firm, and it operates under licensing agreements with them and other international partners. The company's structure allows

it to benefit from both the financial support and technical expertise of these experienced partners. However, because the firm buys most of its APIs through its parent companies, costs are higher than what the firm could achieve by procuring through open international tenders. Consequently, the prices of imported medicines from Asia are generally lower. The company is not planning on producing any new medicines to treat HIV/AIDS, tuberculosis, or malaria.

The third company is privately owned but run by professional expatriate managers brought in by the principal investors, who are based outside the country. On one hand, the company benefits from easier access to international financing and management expertise, but on the other hand, the expatriate management team is costly. The company is looking to expand its reach to export markets throughout West Africa and is planning to add an artemisinin-based combination therapy (ACT) product to its production portfolio.

The structure of each of these firms offers advantages and disadvantages to operating pharmaceutical production facilities in West Africa. The first and third companies, however, which plan on adding antiretrovirals and ACTs to their production, may have a difficult time meeting WHO prequalification requirements.

Source: Guimier, Lee, and Grupper 2004.

large, well-established companies have been able to achieve prequalification standards.

An additional factor affecting the globalization of the pharmaceutical sector is the World Trade Organization's Agreement on Trade-Related Aspects of Intellectual Property Rights (TRIPS). TRIPS allows countries affected by a public health crisis such as HIV/AIDS to bypass patent laws and issue a voluntary or compulsory license to a company to manufacture or import a particular medicine to ease the crisis. However, the consensus is that many smaller middle- and low-income countries lack the necessary infrastructure to take advantage of this mechanism by investing in and successfully operating pharmaceutical plants (although they may issue compulsory licenses to import such products). This situation may be changing, however. In 2010, WHO founded Quality Chemical Industries, Ltd., of Kampala, to be the first manufacturer in a least-developed country in compliance with GMPs—moving a step closer to achieving prequalification status in the WHO system.

7.4 Issues that affect local production decisions

In some countries, national pharmaceutical policies promote local pharmaceutical production as a way of improving access to medicines and achieving national self-sufficiency. But decisions regarding which pharmaceuticals and how many should be imported or locally produced are complex and involve health policy, industrial policy, and a country's national development strategy. Sometimes, a health policy with the goal of increasing access to affordable and quality-assured medicines is pitted against an industrial policy with the goal of promoting a local industry whose products may be more expensive than those on the international market (see Country Study 7-2). Countries should consider their economic conditions and health services infrastructure when deciding on investments in the local pharmaceutical industry.

The greatest challenge for policy makers is often not the creation of a comprehensive policy on local production, but rather the creation of policy elements that function as constructive next steps and build on existing conditions and local institutional capacities. Many countries are limited in their capacity to monitor, supervise, and regulate pharmaceutical production. Policies need to take into account a country's capacity to implement and enforce appropriate regulations.

The Assessment Guide for this chapter lists many of the factors and policy issues that affect production decisions. Each issue contains elements that may favor or hinder the production decision or leave it unaffected. In general, policy makers should concentrate on promoting guidelines that

Country Study 7-2
Health policy versus industrial policy: Rifampicin in India

The international market for rifampicin, an essential antituberculosis medicine, presented an example of rivalry between the pharmaceutical production sectors in China and India. In India, the cost of imported rifampicin from China, at 40 U.S. dollars (USD) per kilogram, was lower than the cost of Indian manufacturers, at USD 70 per kilogram. However, Indian manufacturers questioned the quality of the Chinese medicine and demanded that their government place restrictions on these imports. India already had an overcapacity for rifampicin manufacturing; therefore, this situation illustrates a typical schism between health policy goals and industrial policy goals. Because India was estimated to have 25 percent of the world's tuberculosis cases, the government had to decide which was more important: getting the cheapest rifampicin from China, which would presumably make the medicine more affordable for patients, or sustaining and developing national rifampicin manufacturers.

Source: Attridge and Preker 2005.

support the essential medicines concept: improving the prospects of access to low-cost, quality-assured, effective medicines. Producers can make their own decisions about what and how much to make, and essential medicines program managers can concentrate on choosing to buy from the best sources, whether they are domestic or international.

Human and physical infrastructure

A primary issue in many countries, especially low-income countries, is the ability to find experienced and skilled staff, particularly scientists and engineers. Managing the issues of quality assurance, including regulatory compliance and meeting GMP standards, is key to ensuring high quality. In the current market, technical expertise to produce complex formulations, such as fixed-dose combinations, is critical. In the short term, human resources can be supplemented from external sources, but production decisions are long-term investments that require sustainable, local staffing.

In addition to human resources, the reliability of water, power, and environmental controls are central to the production decision. If materials, equipment, and spare parts are not available, items will have to be imported from countries with established pharmaceutical industries.

Market factors

Population size and distribution combine with per-capita income to determine how many potential customers in the national market will be able to buy medicines. Although aspirations for health are high, difficult economic times can lead to falling real personal incomes and low government capacity to provide health services, both of which limit actual market size in many countries. The national markets of most developing countries are too small to absorb all the outputs of domestic production if done at scale; therefore, a manufacturer producing essential medicines at a scale adequate to lower unit production costs to competitive levels will often have to consider exporting its products, which requires a more sophisticated distribution network and the ability to ensure that its products meet international quality standards.

Other local competitors and importers also need to be taken into account, along with the possibility of a preference in the public-sector market for local production. Barriers to importation of finished products may help local producers initially, but they will increase local prices paid by consumers (and public health organizations) and make the national producers uncompetitive internationally.

Regulatory and legal provisions

As discussed in Chapter 6, pharmaceutical registration requirements are rules that prohibit dangerous, unproven, or useless items and promote the availability of quality-assured and effective medicines. However, a cumbersome or corrupt registration process can limit a producer's incentives to offer a product. From the producer's viewpoint, the important issues related to registration are the transparency, speed, fairness, and expense of the process.

With the globalization of the pharmaceutical sector, an increasing movement exists to establish and enforce GMPs as common high standards for quality. The enforcement of these standards is through regular inspection of manufacturing facilities by authorities. Therefore, a strong regulatory agency in the home country facilitates an export business, because it provides a credible proof of quality.

A manufacturer's adherence to GMPs can add significantly to investment and operating costs. If the national drug regulatory authority is not strong enough to enforce GMPs, facilities may be tempted to relax their practices. Given the shift toward globalized quality standards in pharmaceutical production, however, the rationale for local production at some lower quality standard has shrunk, and such second-tier products will be exposed in the world market. Currently, developing countries vary greatly in their capacity to monitor GMPs, and pharmaceutical manufacturing should be encouraged only in countries that have an effective regulatory agency to enforce them.

Economic incentives and disincentives

Pharmaceutical production involves a worldwide marketplace, and the raw materials that constitute about half of production costs are traded widely as competitive commodities. Reliable, rapid access to foreign exchange is essential. The pharmaceutical industry is commonly one of the most price-controlled industries, which can help as well as distort a local production decision; price controls, by definition, distort the marketplace. (See Chapter 9 for more information on pharmaceutical pricing policies).

Tax treatment and local development incentives can affect the cost of production start-ups through direct subsidies, assisted capitalization schemes, training support, or tax abatement. However, evidence suggests that legislated incentives to promote exports from local production do not affect developing-country production: by 1999, less than 5 percent of low-income country pharmaceuticals were exported on average, a figure that had been on the decline for two decades (WHO 2004).

Duties and import controls

Differential taxation of pharmaceutical materials, both imported and local, can significantly affect the production decision. If the public-policy goal is to create a level playing field for producer decisions on what and where to produce, there should be no difference in the tax treatment of raw materials, both active and inactive ingredients, and finished

Table 7-1   Distribution by country groups of tariff rates for finished pharmaceutical products, 2009

Tariff rate (%)	Number of countries (n = 136)	Low-income countries	Low–middle-income countries	Upper–middle-income countries	High-income countries
0	62	16	13	12	21
0–5.0	32	9	14	6	3
5.1–10.0	28	5	9	12	2
10.1–20.0	13	3	5	2	3
> 20.0	1	0	1	0	0

Source: Stevens and Linfield 2010.

products. Heavy taxation of packaging materials and production will deter local industrial development.

The Organisation for Economic Co-operation and Development (OECD) countries have an agreement to impose zero tariffs on specified lists of active ingredients for medicines, which has facilitated internal OECD pharmaceutical trading. Average tariff rates have been decreasing; however, in a 2009 analysis, 54 percent of countries were applying import tariffs, down from 61 percent in 2005 (Stevens and Linfield 2010). As Table 7-1 shows, for many middle-income and low-income countries, substantial tariff barriers remain.

Many pharmaceuticals are classified as chemicals, with tariffs that have been levied to protect and promote a national chemical industry. Many countries, including India, use nontariff barriers to protect national industries from cheaper pharmaceutical-related imports, which may decrease their consumers' and health systems' access to inexpensive products. Such barriers include antidumping regulations, onerous systems of certification of origin and quality, and legislation requiring local pharmaceutical manufacture (see, for example, Olcay and Laing 2005).

To increase pharmaceutical access, countries may be better off focusing on reducing or eliminating their tariffs and taxes on pharmaceuticals. Markups added throughout the pharmaceutical distribution system may be far greater than import tariffs; additionally, such internal distribution tariffs could outweigh any price benefits achieved through local production. Chapter 9 discusses the effects of taxes and tariffs within the pharmaceutical distribution system.

Collaboration and public-private partnerships

The use of public-private partnerships in the research and development of pharmaceuticals has been growing. Efforts such as the Drugs for Neglected Diseases Initiative are described in Chapter 3. In addition, public-private partnerships and joint ventures can be mechanisms for developing countries to gain some of the benefits of local production, such as the acquisition of technical expertise, without taking on business risk. In fact, partnering with international companies is often the most common form of local production support, with joint ventures and majority or minority ownership shares depending on the strength of the local economy and the political and market potential. The potential for profit repatriation by the external partners is critical.

As pharmaceutical markets become more globalized on many levels, suppliers may be more likely to form alliances and partnerships that increase their capability to compete in the world market. Likewise, multinational pharmaceutical producers have developed a better awareness of the need to consider the social implications of their business practices, and as a result, to be more open to entering into collabora-

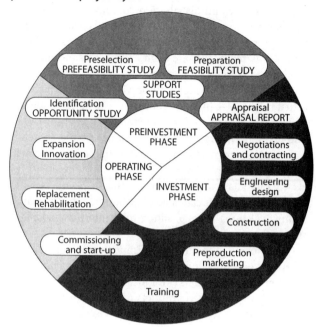

Figure 7-1   Preinvestment, investment, and operating phases of the project cycle

tive arrangements that promote technology transfer in low-income countries (Chapter 3).

In addition to benefiting from collaboration between large multinational companies and smaller enterprises, small country markets can coordinate or join together to create economies of scale. Some African governments have adopted policies that favor local industrial development and investment and have created trading blocs in an effort to harmonize tariffs, currency, and medicine registration processes (Guimier, Lee, and Grupper 2004).

7.5   Assessing the feasibility of local production

Despite the argument that production decisions should be left to private-sector and market forces, policy makers must sometimes respond to pressures to become more involved in decisions about pharmaceutical production. A feasibility study may serve either to warn against a hasty decision to consider manufacturing locally or, if the decision is made to go forward, to establish an appropriate framework, timetable, and resource plan for analysis. Figures 7-1 and 7-2 illustrate the project investment cycle and the complexity of the analysis process *only* for the feasibility stage. The issues to be considered in a careful investigation include marketing analysis, raw materials and supplies, location, engineering and technology, organization and overhead costs, human resources, implementation planning and budgeting, financial analysis, and investment appraisal.

Figure 7-2   Information flow for an industrial feasibility study

Revenues and marketing costs	Operating costs	Investment costs	Financial analysis
Sales program and revenue	Production program	Land, site	Fixed investment
Marketing costs	Raw materials and factory supplies	Civil engineering	Preproduction expenditures
Marketing personnel	Production personnel	Environmental protection costs	Net working capital
Wages, salaries	Wages, salaries	Technology	Total investment
	Land, site, related annual costs	Machinery, equipment	Source of finance
	Technology costs	Cash flow (working capital)	Balance sheet
	Factory overheads		Net income statement
	Administrative overhead costs		Net present value, internal rate of return
	Total costs of products sold		

Source: Behrens and Hawranek 1991.

When a project feasibility analysis is carried out in the public sector, many different government agencies (ministries of treasury, industry, and commerce, as well as the ministry of health) must be involved to appraise the forces and issues that will determine the outcome of the analysis. The complexity of these negotiations means substantial time commitments from senior analysts and policy makers. Nevertheless, the vast majority of worldwide production is done by private companies that have learned from experience how to manage the process efficiently. Country Study 7-3 illustrates the difficulties encountered by some public-sector production programs.

A feasibility assessment of how well sub-Saharan African countries could use local production to increase access to medicines concluded that a few countries appeared to meet the criteria for developing a successful pharmaceutical production industry; however, long-term financial viability was unknown because of major factors out of the companies' control, such as the price they would have to pay to import APIs and the stability of their market share (Guimier, Lee, and Grupper 2004).

As mentioned, new global public health initiatives have greatly influenced the pharmaceutical marketplace. Countries' desire to increase access to antiretrovirals, artemisinin-based combination therapies for malaria, and other essential medicines have renewed their interest in assessing the feasibility of local production, based on the assumption that domestically manufactured medicines would be cheaper than those bought from a foreign manufacturer. The World Bank (2005) points out that local manufacturing has the potential to strengthen political support for public

health treatment programs and institute pride in a national industry. Under the challenging conditions for developing and maintaining a successful domestic production enterprise, however, national stakeholders will have to consider whether scarce resources should support local pharmaceutical production or be used to improve the health system infrastructure or other areas of pharmaceutical management, such as the distribution system and the pharmaceutical regulatory system. Investments in local medicine production will be cost-effective only if domestic pharmaceuticals can be produced more cheaply than they can be imported on the open market (Guimier, Lee, and Grupper 2004). For example, the institutions and governments that buy recommended medicines to treat HIV/AIDS, tuberculosis, and malaria must follow the procurement guidelines of their major donors. Therefore, domestic producers must meet international quality standards, such as WHO's prequalification standards, as well as be price competitive with large international competitors. If the cost of developing local production capacity is too high or the quality of the products is doubtful, local production must be viewed as probably not justifiable.

WHO, the United Nations Conference on Trade and Development, and the International Centre for Trade and Sustainable Development are collaborating on a project to promote local production of medical supplies and related technology transfer in developing countries. Started in 2009, the project is working to identify the challenges and obstacles of local production and make evidence-based recommendations on their feasibility and sustainability (WHO n.d.). ∎

Country Study 7-3
Local public-sector production problems

- The Social Security Agency (CSS) laboratory in Panama had produced a number of pharmaceutical products for decades. The government gave the laboratory a permit to operate, but it did not require registry of the laboratory's products, which would entail instituting some quality-control measures. In 2006–2007, more than 120 people died after taking cough syrup contaminated with diethylene glycol, an industrial solvent, and the CSS treated more than 50,000 patients exposed to the contaminated medicines. The director of CSS explained that analyses are performed on the medications to guarantee quality, "but unfortunately in this case they did not detect the toxic substance." The laboratory was closed. Investigation showed that adulterated glycerin (which contained over 20 percent diethylene glycol) that a local firm sold the laboratory had come from China via Spain. More than a dozen people in Spain and Panama (but not China) were charged with crimes related to the incident.

- One Latin American ministry created an "in-house" pharmaceutical factory to produce essential medicines for its own system. Production had little connection with the ministry market, however, and the product line drifted into over-the-counter preparations and beauty aids, largely missing its original purpose.

- In another semi-autonomous government laboratory, production of essential medicines is usually two to three years behind schedule, throwing ministry purchasing into turmoil and resulting in higher prices because of emergency purchases.

- A parastatal company in East Africa faced multiple problems in producing pharmaceuticals at competitive prices. Inadequate capitalization and inadequate foreign-exchange allocation left the firm unable to purchase enough raw materials to operate at the break-even level of 60 percent capacity. For the pharmaceuticals that were produced, containers of inadequate quality—metal tins without aluminum coating—were all the local suppliers had, and these had to be lined with polyethylene bags, adding to production costs. Plastic containers were tried, but the lids fit poorly because a proper mold could not be obtained locally at reasonable cost. The cardboard used for boxes to pack intravenous fluids collapsed when stacked, and the containers broke when transported over rough roads. When the government attempted to purchase pharmaceuticals on tender from the company, it could not meet the competitive prices on the market, and as a result of a structural adjustment program, the company was put up for sale.

- For political reasons, a Latin American government was obligated to purchase a nonfunctional private facility as a means of expanding its production capacity. Originally constructed to produce small quantities of a large number of sterile injectable products, it had never functioned because of an inadequate water supply, which rendered it useless as a production facility. In addition, the plant lacked the production capacity, types of equipment, and storage capacity to produce the priority items required by the ministry.

References and further readings

★ = Key readings.

★ Attridge, C. J., and A. S. Preker. 2005. *Improving Access to Medicines in Developing Countries: Application of New Institutional Economics to the Analysis of Manufacturing and Distribution Issues.* Washington, D.C.: World Bank. <http://siteresources. worldbank.org/HEALTHNUTRITIONANDPOPULATION/ Resources/281627-1095698140167/AttridgeImprovingAccessFinal. pdf>

Balance, R., J. Pogany, and H. Forstner. 1992. *The World's Pharmaceutical Industries: An International Perspective on Innovation, Competition, and Policy.* Brookfield, Vt.: Ashgate Publishers.

Bate, R. 2008. *Local Pharmaceutical Production in Developing Countries: How Economic Protectionism Undermines Access to Quality Medicines.* London: International Policy Network. <http:// www.policynetwork.net/health/publication/local-pharmaceutical- production-developing-countries>

Behrens, W., and P. M. Hawranek. 1991. *Manual for the Preparation of Industrial Feasibility Studies.* Vienna: United Nations Industrial Organization.

CVI (Children's Vaccine Initiative). 1992. *Local Vaccine Production: Issues of Quality and Viability.* Geneva: World Health Organization. <http://whqlibdoc.who.int/hq/1999/CVI_99.02.pdf>

★ Guimier, J-M., E. Lee, and M. Grupper. 2004. *Processes and Issues for Improving Access to Medicines: The Evidence Base for Domestic Production and Greater Access to Medicines.* London: DFID Health Systems Resource Centre. <http://www.who.int/3by5/capacity/4) processes_issues_improvingaccess.pdf>

★ Kaplan, W., and R. Laing. 2005. *Local Production of Pharmaceuticals: Industrial Policy and Access to Medicines.* Washington, D.C.: World Bank. <http://siteresources.worldbank.org/HEALTH NUTRITIONANDPOPULATION/Resources/281627-1095698 140167/KaplanLocalProductionFinal.pdf>

Lashman, K. H. 1986. *Pharmaceuticals in the Third World: An Overview.* Population, Health and Nutrition Technical Note 86-31. Washington, D.C.: World Bank.

ASSESSMENT GUIDE

Human and physical resources

- Are technical specialists available?
- Are skilled production staff available?
- Is there an educational system that can supply trained workers?
- What are the cost and reliability of water, power, construction, equipment, and other resources?
- Are there financial resources available to retain skilled workers and to support the maintenance of infrastructure?

Market factors

- What are the population size, geographic distribution, and income levels in the country?
- Is there existing local production capacity (competition)?
- What are the barriers to imported products (degree of protection)?
- Can the size, reliability, and preference of the public-sector market ensure economies of scale?
- Is there predictable demand for medicines?

Regulatory environment

- What is the status of laws on pharmaceutical registration?
- What is the status of product and process patent protection?
- Does the regulatory agency have systems and capacity to assure product quality through GMPs and enforcement of standards?

- Are there generic labeling, prescribing, and dispensing laws and practices?

Investment and industrial development environment

- How strong is the country's financial sector (banking and nonbanking activities)?
- Is there sufficient access to capital?
- Are tax or other investment incentives available?
- Are industrial development funds available (access to start-up capital)?
- What are the ownership requirements (limits on foreign ownerships, requirements of local ownership)?
- Are there restrictions on repatriation of profits (foreign investors)?

Economic incentives

- Does the government enforce price controls?
- Is there access to foreign exchange?
- Are there export incentives?

Duties and import controls

Are there duties or import controls on—

- Active pharmaceutical ingredients (versus finished products)?
- Inactive pharmaceutical ingredients and other raw materials?
- Packaging materials?
- Specialized pharmaceutical equipment?
- Nonspecialized equipment?

Mohammed, N. 2009. The Role of Local Manufacturers in Improving Access to Essential Medicines: The Case of Uganda. *Africa Health* November 2009:40–2. <http://www.medicinestransparency.org/fileadmin/uploads/Documents/MeTA-Uganda_AfricaHealth.pdf>

MSH (Management Sciences for Health). 2008. *International Drug Price Indicator Guide* (updated annually). Cambridge, Mass.: MSH. <http://erc.msh.org/mainpage.cfm?file=1.0.htm&module=DMP&language=English>

Olcay, M., and R. Laing. 2005. *Pharmaceutical Tariffs: What Is Their Effect on Prices, Protection of Local Industry and Revenue Generation?* <http://www.who.int/intellectualproperty/studies/TariffsOnEssentialMedicines.pdf>

Stevens, P., and H. Linfield. 2010. *Death and Taxes: Government Markups on the Price of Drugs.* London: International Policy Network. <http://oi.org.mk/upload/Death-and-Taxes-web.pdf.>

UNIDO (United Nations Industrial Development Organization). 2003. *UNIDO's Manuals on Preparing Industrial Feasibility Studies.* Vienna: UNIDO.

World Health Organization (WHO). 2007. *Quality Assurance of Pharmaceuticals: Compendium of Guidelines and Related Materials: Good Manufacturing Practices and Inspection.* 2nd ed. Vol. 2. Geneva: WHO. <http://whqlibdoc.who.int/publications/2007/9789241547086_eng.pdf>

————. 2006a. *WHO Basic GMP Training Modules.* Geneva: WHO. <http://apps.who.int/prequal/trainingresources/pq_pres/gmptraining/GMPBasicTraining.htm>

————. 2006b. *A WHO Guide to Good Manufacturing Practice (GMP) Requirements: Part 3, Training.* Geneva: WHO. <http://whqlibdoc.who.int/hq/2006/WHO_IVB_05.24_eng.pdf>

————. 2004. *The World Medicines Situation.* Geneva: WHO. <http://whqlibdoc.who.int/hq/2004/WHO_EDM_PAR_2004.5.pdf>

————. 2003. Good Manufacturing Practices for Pharmaceutical Products: Main Principles. *WHO Expert Committee on Specifications for Pharmaceutical Preparations: Thirty-Seventh Report.* Annex 4. Geneva: WHO. <http://apps.who.int/medicinedocs/pdf/s5517e/s5517e.pdf>

————. 2002. Guidelines on Packaging for Pharmaceutical Products. *WHO Expert Committee on Specifications for Pharmaceutical Preparations: Thirty-Sixth Report.* Annex 9. Geneva: WHO. <http://whqlibdoc.who.int/trs/WHO_TRS_902.pdf>

————. 1997a. *A Guide to WHO Good Manufacturing Practice (GMP) Requirements: Part 1, Standard Operating Procedures and Master*

Formulae. Geneva: WHO. <http://whqlibdoc.who.int/hq/1997/WHO_VSQ_97.01.pdf>

————. 1997b. *A Guide to WHO Good Manufacturing Practice (GMP) Requirements: Part 2, Validation.* Geneva: WHO <http://whqlibdoc.who.int/hq/1997/WHO_VSQ_97.02.pdf>

————. n.d. *WHO Project on Improving Access to Medicines in Developing Countries through Local Production and Related Technology Transfer.* Geneva: WHO. <http://www.who.int/phi/implementation/TotLCProject.pdf>

★ World Bank. 2005. *Pharmaceuticals: Local Manufacturing.* Washington, D.C.: World Bank. <http://siteresources.worldbank.org/HEALTHNUTRITIONANDPOPULATION/Resources/281627-1109774792596/HNPBrief_3.pdf>

CHAPTER 8

Pharmaceutical supply strategies

SUMMARY

The basic goals of national medicine policies and public-sector pharmaceutical supply systems are to provide access to needed medicines and supplies, promote the rational use of medicines, and ensure the quality, safety, and efficacy of medicines. Various strategies exist to achieve these goals through different combinations of public and private involvement in the pharmaceutical management cycle. National systems vary with respect to public and private roles in financing, distribution, and dispensing of pharmaceuticals, ranging from fully public to fully private systems.

At least five alternatives have traditionally existed for supplying medicines and supplies to governmental and nongovernmental health services—

- *Central medical stores (CMS):* Traditional public-sector pharmaceutical supply system, in which medicines are procured and distributed by a centralized government unit.
- *Autonomous supply agency:* An alternative to the CMS system, managed by an autonomous or semi-autonomous pharmaceutical supply agency.
- *Direct delivery system:* A decentralized, non-CMS approach in which medicines are delivered directly by suppliers to districts and major facilities. The government pharmaceutical procurement office selects the supplier and establishes the price for each item, but the government does not store and distribute medicines.
- *Primary distributor (or prime vendor) system:* Another non-CMS system in which the government pharmaceutical procurement office establishes a contract with one or more primary distributors as well as separate contracts with pharmaceutical suppliers. The contracted primary distributor receives medicines from the suppliers and then stores and distributes them to districts and major facilities.
- *Primarily private supply:* An approach used in some countries that allows private pharmacies in or near government health facilities to provide medicines for public-sector patients. With such an approach, measures are required to ensure equity of access for the poor, medically needy, and other target populations.

These systems vary considerably with respect to the role of the government, the role of the private sector, and incentives for efficiency. Mixed systems in which different categories of pharmaceuticals are supplied through different mechanisms are frequently seen, and countries that take advantage of the capacities in both the public and private sectors usually have systems that are more effective; they also tend to be more resistant to shock from disaster events.

In many countries, missions, charities, and other not-for-profit, nongovernmental organizations (NGOs) provide an important share of health care. NGOs in some countries have established not-for-profit essential medicines supply agencies to provide high-quality, low-cost pharmaceuticals for their health facilities. Some of these have been very successful, but the model has not worked in all countries.

In most countries, the commercial sector is able to provide a range of services that can enhance public access to essential medicines. In general, this sector would potentially respond well to new opportunities for providing supply services; however, the private commercial sector is not always sufficiently well developed or motivated to provide critical supply services to the public sector and should not be seen as a cure-all remedy for solving problems with existing systems.

The commercial sector also plays a vital role in providing access to many people, especially in rural and underserved urban areas where retail drug outlets are the first stop to treat common illnesses. Because these outlets operate in a relatively uncontrolled environment, improving and monitoring the quality of products and services is challenging, and drug sellers generally lack qualifications or training in pharmaceutical management. Much work remains to be done to solve these problems, although strategies that engage the interests of shop owners, dispensers, the government, and the public have recently been developed and tested with some success. Chapter 32 covers drug seller initiatives.

In many countries—especially in countries that have been rolling out large-scale HIV/AIDS programs—the relative roles of the public and private sectors in pharmaceutical supply management are undergoing change in both the pharmaceutical sector and the overall health sector. Changes in public and private roles need to be designed to account for the planned magnitude of scale-up and to promote accessibility to medicines and rational medicine use.

Perspectives on the role of government in health care vary from a solidarity, or social welfare, approach (which holds that the state should provide all health and other social services except when it is unable to do so) to a self-help, or market-economy, approach (which holds that the private market should provide most health services). This chapter does not argue for or against either approach but advocates that, for most countries, the best strategy is a balanced approach drawing on the strengths and capabilities of both public and private sectors.

This chapter provides an overview of systems and strategies for organizing pharmaceutical supply for public health services and issues related to health-sector reform, including the decentralization of pharmaceutical management functions. Issues and options related to meeting public health needs through the private pharmaceutical sector are also considered, including the potential contribution of private nonprofit essential medicines services. In the context of rapidly growing programs to treat critical diseases, such as HIV/AIDS, the chapter outlines approaches for addressing supply problems. Finally, the chapter summarizes different government roles, including periods of transition from one model of service delivery to another.

8.1 Systems for pharmaceutical financing and distribution

Approaches to pharmaceutical supply can be described in terms of public and private roles in financing, wholesale distribution, and retail distribution. The six main approaches range from fully public to fully private, as summarized in Table 8-1.

1. *Fully public:* The classic public system follows a CMS approach, in which a centralized government unit finances, procures, and distributes medicines. The state is the owner, funder, and manager of the entire supply system. Many countries in Africa, Asia, Europe, and Latin America have made this their standard strategy.

2. *Private supply to government health services:* Through direct delivery or prime distributor contracts (described later in this chapter), private channels are used to provide publicly funded medicines to government-operated health facilities. Although most common in North America, where it is known as a prime vendor system, this approach can also be found in Africa, Asia, and Latin America.

3. *Social health insurance systems:* Public funding from central budgets and social health insurance premiums can be used to reimburse pharmacies or patients themselves for medicines that are provided through private pharmacies. Australia, many countries in Western Europe, and North America have followed this approach in recent years.

4. *Private financing and public supply:* Government medical stores or state-owned wholesalers may supply medicines that are dispensed by government health facilities but paid for (in whole or in part) by patient fees. Many former socialist economies followed this approach. In the 1990s, it was being used by China and by government health services in Asia, Africa, and Latin America that implemented user fees for pharmaceuticals but continued to operate government medical stores. China specifically has shifted its health financing scheme from a socialized system to a market-oriented one. Some countries, such as Uganda, have eliminated user fees and increased public spending, whereas others are working toward instituting social health insurance systems in place of user fees (WHO 2003; WHO/WPRO n.d.).

5. *State wholesale monopoly:* At least through the 1980s, in parts of Europe and Africa, pharmaceuticals were imported and distributed by a state monopoly that supplied private pharmacies as well as government

Table 8-1   Systems for financing and distributing medicines

Financing	Distribution	
	Wholesale	Retail
Public		
Fully public	Public	Public
Private supply to government health services	Private	
Social health insurance systems	Private	Private
Private		
Private financing and public supply	Public	Public
State wholesale monopoly	Public	Private
Fully private	Private	Private

Figure 8–1   Supply chain management framework

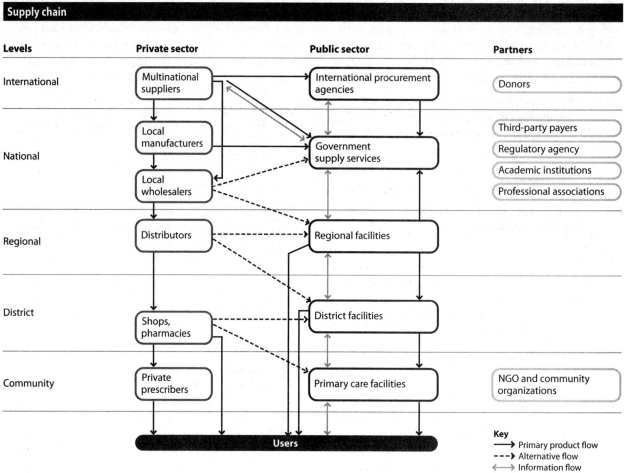

Source: CPM/MSH 2011.

health services in some cases. Although this model has historical significance, it is rarely seen now.

6. *Fully private:* Patients pay the entire cost of medicines and purchase them from private retail pharmacies and drug sellers, which now exist in nearly every country in the world and account in some cases for a large percentage of pharmaceutical distribution. Outside the market economies that have high levels of social and private health insurance, this approach is also the major source of prescription medicines in many countries, including many of those that nominally provide free pharmaceutical services.

The context of financing public health in resource-limited countries has changed because of global funding initiatives to combat specific diseases—primarily HIV/AIDS and malaria. The Global Fund to Fight AIDS, Tuberculosis and Malaria; the Global Drug Facility; the U.S. President's Emergency Plan for AIDS Relief; and others are dramatically changing the public health financing paradigm for

these programs, with a particular emphasis on pharmaceuticals. More information on these donor initiatives can be found in Chapters 2 and 14.

Public financing includes government budgets (central, regional, and local) and compulsory social health insurance programs. Private financing includes out-of-pocket payments by individuals and households, private health insurance, community medicine schemes, cooperatives, employers, and financing through other nongovernmental entities. Chapter 11 includes more information on financing, and Chapter 12 covers pharmaceutical benefits in insurance.

Public distribution includes wholesale distribution and retail dispensing by government-managed pharmaceutical supply and health services as well as distribution through state-owned enterprises (state corporations). Private distribution includes private for-profit wholesalers, retailers, and nonprofit essential medicines supply services. Figure 8–1 illustrates a pharmaceutical supply chain framework featuring the public and private sectors and possible partners.

REASON FOR GOVERNMENT ACTION   CONSTRAINTS ON GOVERNMENT EFFECTIVENESS

8.2 Perspectives on the role of the state in health care

Different perspectives on the role of the state in providing health care result in differences in assigning the responsibility for pharmaceutical supply. The debate over the proper role of government is as old as government itself. This debate has been heightened, on the one hand, by the failure of centrally planned economies to ensure economic security for their populations and, on the other hand, by the inability of some market economies to ensure access to basic social services such as health care. Two views of the role of government can be identified—

- *Social welfare perspective:* the government should provide all health and other social services, except in specific instances when it is unable to do so.
- *Market economy perspective:* the private market should be left to provide all health and other social services, except when the private market fails to do so and the state can be expected to achieve better outcomes.

Such totally divergent views may exist in theory, but in practice, neither approach sufficiently provides adequate access to health services for all population groups. Increasingly, countries recognize that they must strike a balance between public and private control to create the most efficient service delivery system, and each country's context for making these decisions differs.

Governments everywhere, regardless of level of economic development, are subject to a common set of constraints. These include—

- Inefficiency in service delivery, which may result from lack of individual incentives for good performance, bureaucratic inflexibility, and overemployment
- Interest-group pressures from political supporters, business partners, members of one's local community, or concerned parties, which may lead to inefficient or inequitable use of public resources

- Lack of good governance, which may manifest itself in self-interested manipulation of the medicine selection process, corruption in the award of tenders, nepotism in the appointment of key staff, or theft of pharmaceutical products by health staff

Although government effectiveness has its limits, leaving the supply of pharmaceuticals entirely to the market economy may also fail to achieve public health objectives. Issues that must be considered include—

Equity: Because of the relatively high cost of medicines compared with incomes, without government involvement, the poor and medically needy may be denied access to necessary and often lifesaving medicines.

Information failure: Patients and some health professionals do not have full information about the quality, safety, efficacy, value for money, and appropriateness of individual medications.

Competition failure: Patents and brand names may establish a virtual monopoly for some products, and cumbersome or obstructive registration procedures, combined with the high initial investment required to build manufacturing facilities and develop new medicines, may limit the number of new competitors.

Externalities: Health services such as vaccination and treatment of contagious tuberculosis or sexually transmitted infections benefit people besides those who receive the services.

Chapter 10 has more information on pharmacoeconomic issues.

The remaining sections of this chapter discuss major areas of public involvement in pharmaceutical supply: organizing pharmaceutical supply for government and NGO health services, decentralization and pharmaceutical management, and use of private channels to meet needs for essential medicines and health commodities.

Government action in each of these areas should be informed by a realistic assessment of the appropriate role

Table 8-2   Comparison of basic pharmaceutical supply systems

Model	Contracting suppliers	Storage and delivery	Monitoring medicine quality	Advantages	Disadvantages
Central medical stores Conventional supply system; medicines procured and distributed by centralized government unit	CMS	CMS	CMS, DRA	• Maintains government control over entire system • Is easy to monitor	• High capital cost for offices, storage, and transport facilities • Recurrent cost of staff, transport, other operating costs • Limited incentive for efficiency • Open to political and other interference
Autonomous supply agency Bulk procurement, storage, and distribution managed by autonomous or semi-autonomous agency	Autonomous agency	Autonomous agency	PPO and autonomous agency, DRA	• Maintains advantages of centralized system • Flexibility in personnel and management systems may improve efficiency • Is less open to interference • Separate finances facilitate revolving drug funds	• Cost and effort of establishing supply agency • May retain some constraints of CMS • Limited competitive pressure for efficiency if operated as monopoly
Direct delivery system Decentralized approach; tenders establish the supplier and price for each item; medicines delivered directly by supplier to districts and major facilities	PPO	Suppliers	PPO, DRA	• Eliminates cost of government-operated storage and distribution • Decentralized order quantities and delivery help adjust to variations in seasonal and local demand • Maintains price benefits of centralized tendering • Reduces inventory costs and expiration for high-cost, low-volume medicines	• Coordination and monitoring of deliveries, payments, and quality are demanding • Feasible only where adequate private infrastructure exists • Suppliers limited to those able to ensure local distribution (may reduce competition, increase cost) • Direct delivery by multiple suppliers (especially to remote areas) is inefficient, may raise costs
Primary distributor system PPO establishes contracts with pharmaceutical suppliers and separate contract with a single primary distributor, which warehouses and distributes medicines to districts and major facilities	PPO	Primary distributor	PPO and primary distributor	• Maintains advantages of single distribution system • Potential primary distributors compete on service level and cost	• Monitoring of service level and pharmaceutical quality is demanding • Competition depends on well-developed private distribution system
Primarily private supply Private sector manages all aspects of pharmaceutical supply	Procurement and distribution by private enterprises	Procurement and distribution by private enterprises	DRA	• Least demanding and least costly for the government	• Does not ensure equity of access for poor, medically needy, or other target groups • Medicine quality is more difficult to monitor

CMS = central medical stores; DRA = national drug regulatory authority; PPO = pharmaceutical procurement office (ministry of health or other government office).

of the state, given the country's circumstances. Whatever a society's expectations or a government's promises, constraints exist to government involvement, and dangers arise in an unregulated market approach to pharmaceutical supply. Government supervision of the private pharmaceutical market involves complex and often contentious issues. Public health objectives may conflict with short-term commercial interests. Ideological or political considerations not directly related to either public health or commercial perspectives may further cloud discussions.

8.3   Basic pharmaceutical supply systems

Of all the decisions policy makers and managers face, the most complex and costly often concern the financing and supply of medicines for government health services. In some countries, public-sector pharmaceutical supply is well financed and administratively efficient. In other countries, the pharmaceutical supply system is unreliable and shortages are common; such systems suffer from inadequate funding, outdated procedures, interference of various sorts, and a variety of other problems.

The pharmaceutical management framework—including all aspects of procurement and distribution—is the subject of Part II of this book. Before confronting the particulars of the pharmaceutical management framework, however, the basic structure of the supply system must be established, and pharmaceutical and supply chain management practices should be applied to achieve maximum efficiency.

Although many variations exist, five basic approaches are used for organizing pharmaceutical supply for public health services (see Table 8-2)—

- Central medical stores
- Autonomous supply agency
- Direct delivery system
- Primary distributor system (also known as prime vendor system)
- Primarily private system

A mixed system is frequently seen in practice, where different approaches are used for different levels of health facilities or different categories of products. Sometimes, separate supply systems for disease-specific programs operate parallel to the primary supply system; these *vertical supply systems* are discussed in Section 8.6.

This discussion speaks primarily from a government perspective. However, the mechanisms described here are equally relevant to faith-based and other nonprofit health services, private hospital purchasing groups, for-profit health systems, and other institutional health services. This is particularly true for the autonomous agency, direct delivery, and primary distributor approaches.

Central medical stores

The traditional approach to public-sector pharmaceutical supply is the CMS, in which medicines are financed, procured, and distributed by the government, which is the owner, funder, and manager of the entire supply system. The government handles selection, procurement, and distribution—usually through a unit within the ministry of health. Financing is usually from central treasury allocations and donors, although this model can be adapted to a revolving drug fund (see Chapter 13). In countries that have decentralized budgeting and procurement, lower-level units, such as districts, may have the authority to purchase directly from the CMS.

With the CMS approach, problems with financial management, quantification of requirements, management of tenders, warehouse management, transport, and security of pharmaceuticals are common. These problems often arise from political or administrative interference; civil service constraints on discipline or dismissal of poorly performing or dishonest staff; overall inadequacy of financial resources; procurement constraints arising from the treasury payment cycle, erratic release of ministry of health funds, or slow payment from districts; and transport difficulties resulting from the need to maintain a large vehicle fleet. In Malawi, for example, regulations force the CMS to continue shipping medicines to districts that have not paid, which provides a disincentive for districts and creates decapitalization in the CMS.

One way to address some of these constraints is to contract out (or outsource) specific aspects of the supply system (see Section 8.4). Outside contractors that specialize in certain services may be able to provide them at lower cost and higher quality. Port clearing, warehouse management, and transport are among the services that are sometimes contracted out to the private sector.

Autonomous supply agency

Problems with CMS systems have led some governments to establish systems that place the responsibility for bulk procurement, quality assurance, storage, distribution, and financial management in the hands of an autonomous or semi-autonomous supply agency. This model has been tried in several countries, particularly in Africa and Latin America (Country Study 8-1).

Autonomous supply agencies are often established as parastatals, either under the ministry of health or as independent organizations with a board of directors with representatives from several government ministries and sometimes from the private and nonprofit sectors. These supply agencies operate like the nonprofit essential medicines supply services described in Section 8.7, except that their primary client is the government's health services. The

Country Study 8-1
An autonomous medical supply service: Medical Stores Department in Tanzania

Before 1994, Tanzania functioned with a traditional CMS model for procurement, storage, and distribution. Throughout the 1980s, CMS management became increasingly ineffective, and operational and financial sustainability were major issues. Recognizing the seriousness of the situation, the Ministry of Health made reforming the CMS a cornerstone of its 1992 Pharmaceutical Master Plan. The reforms resulted in the development of an autonomous Medical Stores Department (MSD) to procure, store, distribute, and sell health commodities to the public sector and authorized private organizations. The department had a mandate to make available essential medicines and supplies on a nationwide basis, to be financially self-sustaining, and to base decision making on "sound commercial principles." Although MSD is still a government-owned institution, it has autonomous status and makes its own rules, regulations, and procedures.

Now MSD is the predominant single distributor of pharmaceuticals and medical supplies in Tanzania. It operates a self-sustaining revolving drug fund with eight zonal stores. MSD serves national referral hospitals, regional health facilities, district health facilities, health centers and dispensaries, faith-based health facilities, and approved NGOs.

MSD improved the supply of essential medicines and health commodities to the public sector compared with the CMS, but major increases in workload in recent years have stretched MSD's physical and managerial capacity. At one time, MSD had a virtual monopoly on distributing pharmaceuticals and supplies to all public-sector and mission or faith-based health facilities. Now, however, because of decentralization, districts and hospitals have control over their own budgets and can procure medicines and supplies from sources other than MSD. A 2007 survey showed that only 33 percent of health facilities procured exclusively from MSD, whereas most also procured medicines and supplies from private pharmaceutical wholesalers and private pharmacies. The government provides no guidelines to health facilities on when they should procure from private sources. Between 2000 and 2007, the number of private wholesalers had doubled to almost 200. Although facilities may not use MSD as their exclusive supplier, MSD sales turnover has been steadily increasing (see table).

MSD Total sales and percentage markups: 2004–2006

	2004	2005	2006
Sales in U.S. dollars	38,417,481	52,000,000	86,980,000
Percent markup of total sale	17.0	17.0	15.5

Storage space and general stock availability from MSD have been problematic. In a 2001 assessment, on average, MSD was able to supply less than 80 percent of items requested, with some zonal stores achieving less than 70 percent. A spot assessment in 2003 showed that the MSD facilities had an average of 49 percent of vital medicine items available, although its target is to have 100 percent availability for these medicines. In 2007, however, the availability of tracer items in the MSD zonal stores was only about 50 percent when measurement included buffer stock; not surprisingly, primary health facilities received only 67 percent of their orders from MSD. MSD and its zonal stores reported product delivery delays and insufficient forecasting as the main problems resulting in stockouts; product rationing at different levels of the supply chain distorts the perception of demand. The assessment did find good practices in place for storage and stock management operations at the central and regional stores. At every MSD warehouse visited, stocks were secure, protected from light, in properly ventilated areas, and well organized. The information technology stock management system was functioning.

A major concern in 2007 was the effect of vertical program supply systems, which, because of their large value relative to the essential medicines supply system, distort health priorities. The assessment concluded that government-funded essential medicines were being "crowded out" by the disproportionate funding and attention given to vertical programs. In addition, the report noted that vertical systems caused duplication and overburdened staff, who have to manage parallel information and funding flows. Evidence also suggests that MSD receives only a fraction of what it is owed for distributing vertical program goods.

Sources: CPM 2003; Euro Health Group and MSH Tanzania 2007; MoHSW 2007.

successful transition from a CMS system to an autonomous supply system requires substantial time and resources to upgrade and develop infrastructure, such as a pharmaceutical information system. Moreover, political commitment is needed to support the wide-ranging changes in government regulations and laws that are often required to ensure the necessary autonomy for the new system.

For example, Zambia's pharmaceutical distribution agency is a parastatal called Medical Stores Limited (MSL). MSL is publicly financed but is an independent entity with its own management and board. Because it has management and operational flexibility, MSL has instituted practices that are more often seen in the private sector, such as creating performance incentive schemes for its staff and workers and investing in technologically advanced systems for warehouse management and fleet tracking. MSL also outsources its senior operational management to Crown Agents, Ltd., under a fixed-term contract, which requires Crown Agents to build local management capacity using global best practices in warehousing, inventory management, and distribution (Dalberg Global Development Advisors/MIT-Zaragoza International Logistics Program 2008).

Autonomous supply services are established to achieve the efficiency and flexibility associated with private management while maintaining sufficient public-sector supervision to ensure that the services provide essential medicines, at reasonable prices, with adequate quality control. The basic concept is that, under the right conditions, a well-constituted management board or board of directors will appoint qualified senior managers, who will ensure an efficient, accountable supply service. In practice, however, finding and retaining qualified senior management staff are often difficult, which can result in poorly managed autonomous agencies. In addition, success relies on sufficient human and financial resources to create and maintain the needed infrastructure and management systems.

Pharmaceutical supply agencies may be established in the context of a public-sector revolving drug fund or in a system in which government institutions purchase medicines with centrally allocated treasury funds. In either system, funds are best used to purchase medicines on a cash-and-carry basis; not extending credit is a key to sustainability.

Experience to date, though limited, suggests that the following features are necessary to establish a successful autonomous supply agency (see Figure 8-2)—

Figure 8–2   Checklist for evaluating an autonomous essential medicines supply agency

Essential medicines and public health mandate
☐ Medicines limited to those on the national essential medicines list or formulary?
☐ Dressings, diagnostic agents, and other medical supplies included in range of products?
☐ Distribution restricted to government facilities?

Legal status
☐ Operating unit under the ministry of health? Parastatal? Fully private agency?
☐ Status established by ministry directive? Legal notice? Act of law? Other measure?
☐ For-profit or nonprofit organization?

Management board (board of directors)
☐ Membership: How appointed? How representative? How independent?
☐ Role and authority: How broad? How independent?
☐ Chairperson: How selected? How independent?

Senior managers
☐ Recruitment: By whom? Approval by board required?
☐ Job descriptions and required qualifications clearly spelled out in writing?
☐ Authority to manage: Hire and fire? Set salary and benefit packages?

Personnel system
☐ Civil service system?
☐ Parastatal system with some civil service characteristics?
☐ Private-sector flexibility, incentive structure, and controls?

Supply management and quality assurance
☐ Professional personnel experienced in supply chain management and supervision?
☐ Professional pharmacists involved in management and supervision?
☐ Adequate quality assurance procedures in place and enforced?

Capital financing (working capital needed for infrastructure, replacing vehicles)
☐ Source: Central government allocation, donor, development bank, commercial bank?
☐ Type: Grant, "soft" development loan, commercial loan?
☐ Adequacy: Capital sufficient for current size and anticipated growth of supply demands?

Recurrent financing (working capital for the purchase of medicines and payment of suppliers may come from a mix of sources)
☐ Medicines financed from district or facility central allocations?
☐ Medicines financed through user fees?
☐ Medicines financed through insurance?
☐ Salary and other recurrent operating costs financed through central allocations? Through markup on medicines distributed by the agency? Through fixed supply fee?

Financial control and accountability
☐ Able to maintain its own bank accounts?
☐ Annual independent public audit required?
☐ Annual report to ministry of health and central government required?
☐ Protection from decapitalization through unfunded distribution, distribution during emergency situations, credit sales?

- Sufficient autonomy to allow efficient operations that are free from political interference
- Oversight by an independent management board
- Professional pharmaceutical supply managers with substantive decision-making powers
- Good personnel management and adequate salaries for staff
- Adequate financing
- Public accountability and sound financial management
- Continued focus on essential medicines (rather than "profitable" alternatives)
- Focus on quality assurance of both products and services
- High-quality storage, distribution, and information technology infrastructure

An autonomous supply agency may achieve value for money and improved pharmaceutical availability through more efficient management. The two important questions are: Does the agency have the flexibility to be efficient? Does the agency have the incentive to be efficient? Such agencies are likely to improve pharmaceutical supply only if they are structured to overcome the constraints of the CMS approach. Competitive pressure encourages efficiency.

Difficulties can be anticipated if any of the following occur—

- Senior managers are political appointees rather than professional managers appointed by an independent management board.
- The government retains the authority to require distribution of medicines without charge or on a credit basis (without ensuring payment).
- Special interests outside the agency influence medicine procurement.
- The agency is required to retain staff members regardless of their ability or performance.
- A well-functioning agency is expected to handle additional responsibilities beyond its capacity.
- The agency acts as a monopoly, with no pressure to maintain low prices, reliable service, and high quality.

Professional managers should have full authority to make decisions regarding hiring and firing, set terms and conditions of employment, and create or revise in-house policies and regulations. Finally, countries considering an autonomous supply agency should recognize that this approach will not solve problems related to overall lack of funding for medicines.

Direct delivery system

CMS and autonomous supply services involve bulk procurement and distribution from a central warehouse. The costs and logistical problems associated with central storage and distribution are substantial. An alternative may be a direct delivery system in situations where suppliers have that capacity.

In this non-CMS model, a government procurement office tenders to establish prices and suppliers for each essential medicine, but the suppliers deliver the medicines directly to individual regional stores, district stores, or major health facilities. Variations of direct delivery contracts have been implemented in many countries.

Besides its general use for supply of essential medicines and commodities, direct delivery can be used successfully in very specific situations, such as the supply of nonstandard equipment (for example, X-ray machines), where a central procurement office contracts with a supplier that delivers, installs, and commissions expensive capital equipment.

Direct delivery contracts may specify fixed quantities with scheduled deliveries or estimated quantity tenders with orders placed by the local warehouses or health facilities as needed. Financing arrangements can be tricky. Debts can quickly accumulate if pharmaceutical supplies are not balanced against available funds. Separate accounts must be maintained for each supply point (if funding is from central allocations) or all supplies must be paid for at the time of delivery. Like most procurement systems, direct delivery contracts require a sole-source commitment—that is, for the tender medicines, the local warehouses and facilities order from the supplier that holds the tender contract. The local purchasers are free to order medicines that are not on the tender from any supplier. (See Chapters 21 and 39 for details related to preparing and tendering direct delivery contracts.)

Direct delivery supply agreements depend on and encourage further development of private-sector distribution systems. In principle, they reduce storage and transport requirements for the government by specifying in procurement contracts that medicines are to be delivered directly to district stores and major health facilities. The government only has to store medicines at the district level and deliver them to health centers and peripheral health units.

Direct delivery contracts can preserve the benefits of centralized selection (the essential medicines list), bulk procurement (suppliers offer favorable prices to get all the business for the products they are awarded), and centralized quality control. Hospitals and districts benefit from being able to manage their own funds and determine the exact quantities needed. Finally, the problems of security, central storage, and transport are shifted from the ministry to the private suppliers.

With a direct delivery system, however, district-level and facility-level pharmaceutical management responsibilities are much greater, because they can include ordering, receiving, and paying for medicines. Success depends on adequate financing and management systems and the ability and willingness of staff to undertake the increased responsibilities.

Primary distributor system

The primary distributor system (also known as the prime vendor system) often involves the public procurement agency tendering for two types of contracts. First, the public procurement agency contracts with any number of suppliers to establish the source and price for each medicine, but the medicines are not delivered by the suppliers directly; instead, a separate contract is negotiated (through tender, if feasible) with one or more private-sector distributors, the primary distributors. In some cases, a single primary distributor serves the whole health system. In larger systems, different primary distributors may serve different regions or different levels of the health system. Another variation is to contract with private or NGO systems to supply only a particular geographic area or a specific group of health facilities, thus easing the burden of the public-sector system (Country Study 8-2).

The suppliers deliver tender medicines to the primary distributors, which are responsible for maintaining sufficient stock to fill orders from regional warehouses, district stores, or health facilities. The local warehouses and health facilities order medicines from the designated primary distributor, and the primary distributor fills the orders from medicines

---

Country Study 8-2
Developing a prime vendor pharmaceutical supply system for the Tanzanian mission sector

Church-owned hospitals, health centers, and pharmaceutical dispensaries in Tanzania are principally located in rural areas, where 70 percent of the population resides. Historically, they had no central pharmaceutical procurement body and relied mostly on the Medical Stores Department, international donations, and private-sector pharmacies for medicines and supplies. However, church hospitals reported dissatisfaction with services provided by the MSD, such as unacceptable out-of-stock rates. The Mission for Essential Medical Supplies (MEMS), a not-for-profit organization established by the Evangelical Lutheran Churches in Tanzania, had a history of providing laboratory services and supplies to health facilities. These facilities asked MEMS to expand its supply list to include pharmaceuticals and medical supplies.

The Strategies for Enhancing Access to Medicines (SEAM) Program agreed to help MEMS develop and implement a private-sector prime vendor pharmaceutical supply system that would improve medicine quality, supply, availability, and affordability for participating not-for-profit hospitals. The system would use pooled procurement to purchase from a single supplier and offer participating health facilities supplementary services from MEMS, such as purchase requisition review, a strategy for pharmaceutical quality assurance, training in rational use and pharmaceutical management, and medicine information services. The contractual requirements were for the prime vendor to stock and supply more than 500 items, initially to twelve rural hospitals and expanding to forty hospitals as the project progressed. The contracted delivery time was either ten or twenty-one days, depending on the goods. The prices of the goods were fixed for twelve months, starting in November 2004.

From November 2004 until April 2005, fourteen hospital orders were received electronically from ten health facilities. The prime vendor made twenty-nine deliveries, with an average of two deliveries per order (and a range of one to six). Despite considerable procurement experience, however, the contracted prime vendor (Diocare/Crown Agents) had difficulty meeting the terms of the contract, mainly because it underestimated the complexity and costs of the program: substantial variations occurred in stock demand from the health facilities, warehouse systems were overstretched, and contract expectations were unclear. Although the prime vendor worked to resolve its own infrastructure and inventory deficiencies and worked with MEMS to address supply chain management issues extending from the distributor to the end user, the negatives—out-of-stock situations, partial shipments, and poor service—outweighed the positives, and the parties agreed to discontinue the contract in late 2005.

Even with the failure of the original prime vendor relationship, MEMS continued with much of the original strategy developed during the SEAM Program, including quantifying requirements for pharmaceuticals and medical supplies for church hospitals, pooling procurement requirements, and using a prime vendor as its principal supplier (a local wholesaler, Pyramid Pharma, in collaboration with an international supplier, the International Dispensary Association). The network of hospitals grew; as of August 2008, MEMS coordinated routine pharmaceutical and medical supply procurement for thirty faith-based hospitals serving over 4 million rural Tanzanians. In addition, through the palliative care project of Evangelical Lutheran Churches in Tanzania, Interchurch Medical Assistance, and Catholic Relief Services, MEMS extended its services of procurement coordination to thirty-seven other hospitals, including public hospitals.

Source: SEAM 2008.

Figure 8-3   Public- and private-sector roles in pharmaceutical supply

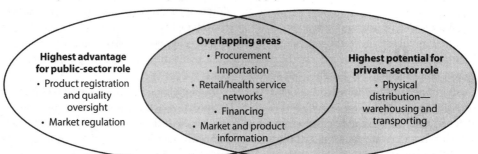

Source: Dalberg Global Development Advisors/MIT-Zaragoza International Logistics Program 2008.

▨ Potential intervention areas with private sector.

in stock. Primary distributors may maintain their own vehicle fleets or subcontract with other firms for transportation.

In some cases, a group of providers, such as hospitals, pool their resources to benefit from bulk purchasing, but instead of taking on the responsibility for selection, price negotiation, and quality assurance, the group contracts with a primary distributor that takes over these additional tasks, leaving the group to merely administer the contract.

Like other private-sector contracts, this system depends on sole-source commitment for the medicines under tender contract, although districts and health facilities may be allowed to purchase nontender medicines from any source. The system also requires the availability of good information, and performance monitoring and compliance by both health system staff and the contracted distributors.

The primary distributor is paid a fee for storage and delivery services. In some industrialized countries, this fee is typically less than 2 percent. Primary distributors are able to achieve such low margins by distributing very large volumes of goods and by generating revenue through the "float" in money markets or bank interest. This income is generated through a difference in payment terms: the primary distributor pays the supplier after thirty to sixty days but requires health facilities to pay within fifteen days, thus giving the primary distributor access to the equivalent of fifteen to forty-five days' cash turnover.

The primary distributor system may appear to add an extra intermediary and extra costs, but experience has shown that the cost of a primary distributor can be more than offset in some situations by savings from increased efficiency. Competitive awards of primary distributor contracts and enforcing contract terms are important to achieve this efficiency.

Primarily private system

National policy, insufficient financing, or management problems have led some countries to avoid taking on the responsibility for providing hospitals and health centers with even essential medicines. In some systems, commercial pharmacies are established within ministry facilities; such pharmacies may be part of a parastatal pharmaceutical enterprise, or they may be independent enterprises. In other cases, the government may contract with commercial pharmacies to provide medicines to public-sector patients. Pharmacies established in government health facilities may operate on a nonprofit or for-profit basis, depending on the arrangement with the government. Often, such pharmacies are limited to the sale of essential medicines. In some cases, private pharmacies operate in parallel with government pharmacies in the same institution.

In countries where pharmaceutical procurement has been decentralized to the regional, district, or even health facility level, procurement officers may be quick to fill their supply orders through a private wholesaler if they perceive that the public-sector supplier is undependable or slow. Not only is this practice more expensive, but also the quality of products in the private-sector supply chain is generally not monitored as closely, if at all. In addition, unreliable orders cripple the public-sector supplier by rendering forecasts useless, resulting in overstocks and expiries. Moreover, without the purchasers to make the public sector's revolving funds revolve, decapitalization results. An added complication occurs when legislation forces the public supplier to continue to ship orders to districts that do not pay or when districts allow debts to build up and then quit placing orders with the CMS rather than pay off accumulated debt, as was the case in Ghana (Seiter and Gyansa-Lutterodt 2009).

In many countries, the relative roles of the public and private sectors in public health and pharmaceutical supply are undergoing change. Changes in public and private roles must be designed to promote accessibility to medicines and rational medicine use (Figure 8-3). As with revolving drug funds operated by the government, the greatest concern with a mainly private supply system is equity of access for the poor, children, patients with communicable diseases, and other target groups.

8.4 Contracting for pharmaceutical supply services

The direct delivery system, the primary distributor system, and in some instances, the autonomous supply agency system involve management or service contracts (see Chapter 39). Important differences exist between contracting for pharmaceutical products and contracting for services. Contract terms are different, and a different approach is needed for monitoring.

Contracting out or outsourcing in health care has most commonly been used for nonclinical services such as equipment maintenance, laundry, and food services. Contracting out services is common in the private sector. Often, companies find that outside contractors who specialize in specific services such as managing cafeterias or repairing computers can provide those services at lower cost and higher quality than companies can provide in-house.

In pharmaceutical supply, primary distributor systems, transport contracts, port-clearing services, and other private-sector involvement require contracting for services in contrast to contracting for products (for example, medicines). However, contracting out activities requires the skills of writing, negotiating, and monitoring contracts. The contract must include specific performance indicators with a time frame for when those indicators will be met. Even experienced companies can run into problems by underestimating the necessary financial and human resources to fulfill the contract requirements. In the case of pharmaceutical supply, for example, a lack of reliable data from health facilities on medicine use and demand makes estimating order quantities difficult, resulting in overages or stockouts. All parties to the contract need to have a clear understanding of any limitations that may affect performance.

The outsourcing process functions most effectively where potential competition exists, as with any tendering process. Contracting out also demands a commitment to pay the contractors according to the terms of the contract. Government officials must develop special skills to prepare and monitor such contracts.

8.5 Comparison of basic supply systems

The five basic supply systems are compared in Table 8-2. The models vary with respect to the role of the state and the degree of private-sector involvement. The CMS approach demands the most of the central government in terms of human and physical resources, because it operates virtually the entire distribution system. With an autonomous supply agency, direct delivery system, or primary distributor system, the role of the government changes from direct operations to a combination of direct operations and contract management coordination and monitoring. Some direct delivery or primary distributor systems do not require a large central government distribution infrastructure, but depending on where the responsibility for procurement lies, such systems may require a pharmaceutical procurement office or an equivalent department with oversight responsibility to manage contracts and monitor performance effectively. A CMS or autonomous supply agency approach may be required when the local private sector is not sufficiently developed to support the efficient operation of a direct delivery or primary distributor system.

Ghana and Zambia provide examples of different types of systems in terms of the role of the private sector. In Ghana, private-sector wholesalers provide a substantial portion of sales and delivery of medicines to public regional medical stores, hospitals, and NGO facilities. In Zambia, however, almost all of the public and NGO facilities receive medicines through international suppliers and procurement agents; medicines are then distributed through the public-sector supply chain (Dalberg Global Development Advisors/MIT-Zaragoza International Logistics Program 2008).

Pharmaceutical supply systems need to achieve three main objectives: (a) high service level, as measured by low rates of shortages and stockouts; (b) efficiency, as measured by having low total costs for a given level of service; and (c) the ability to cope with disaster situations (see Chapter 15 for examples of pharmaceutical supply management issues in emergencies). Autonomous supply agencies, direct delivery contracts, and primary distributor systems offer different approaches to create the flexibility, competition, and clear performance targets that help achieve these objectives.

Historically, options for handling public supply have been presented as a choice between various stand-alone alternatives (for example, CMS, autonomous store, or primary distributor). However, with growing demand for products and services, individual organizations and companies, whether public or private, will undoubtedly struggle to satisfy all needs. Against this background, a multifaceted approach using the full range of resources, including a combination of public- and private-sector strategies that spread the burden and risk, will increasingly be required.

Some countries may choose to join forces with others in their region to increase efficiency in their pharmaceutical sectors. These regional partnerships could range from sharing information on pricing and suppliers to formal pooled procurement schemes, where one central body procures medicines and commodities for a regional group of countries (see Chapter 18 on procurement). Some countries may consider setting up similar alliances for storage and distribution or contracting with a private company to provide regionwide services to multiple countries. Some regional organizations are exploring options for collaborating in pharmaceutical supply, and experiences from the eastern Caribbean and the Gulf states demonstrate the potential savings and sustainability of such arrangements (Kanavos et al. 2010); however, strong political commitment and a shared cultural outlook and language appear to be required for success.

8.6 Vertical supply systems

Public health programs that focus on targeted interventions, such as family planning or tuberculosis control, may operate vertical pharmaceutical supply systems that are set up outside a country's regular health and pharmaceutical supply system. With the dramatic increase in global health initiatives, multiple vertical supply systems have become the norm in many countries. For donors, particularly, vertical programs can be appealing because they show quick results and they are easier to manage than inclusive, horizontal programs. However, many government and donor policy makers in developing countries see vertical programs as diverting human and financial resources from already resource-constrained health systems and as undermining sustainability of the pharmaceutical sector in general. An analysis of the effect of global health initiatives on country health systems found that, in some places, the resulting vertical supply systems duplicated or displaced the countries' existing systems and that lack of coordination between vertical and essential medicines systems caused stock excesses and deficits (WHO Maximizing Positive Synergies Collaborative Group 2009).

International vertical supply programs include the Global TB Drug Facility, which works to provide inexpensive, quality-assured tuberculosis medicines for DOTS programs worldwide. The World Health Organization (WHO) created a similar program for HIV/AIDS-related medicines and commodities; however, unlike the Global TB Drug Facility, the AIDS Medicines and Diagnostic Service does not procure medicines directly but rather provides resources and assistance to countries in procuring quality medicines at the best prices and managing the distribution of those medicines. Other large vertical programs include the President's Malaria Initiative; the U.S. President's Emergency Plan for AIDS Relief and its supply mechanism, the Supply Chain Management System project; and the Global Fund to Fight AIDS, Tuberculosis and Malaria's procurement mechanism. Some large-scale vertical supply programs are based on donated medicines, such as the ivermectin distribution program for onchocerciasis.

Efforts are being made in some countries, such as Uganda, to integrate supply systems for vertical programs into essential medicines programs. Resource-intensive functions such as procurement, quality assurance, storage, and physical distribution may be integrated under the essential medicines program, whereas financing, quantification, and monitoring may stay under the control of the vertical program. Integration can provide savings and benefits but is reliant on strong government commitment to the process.

The initial experiences with integrating vertical program supply systems may not be a reliable guide to the potential for incorporating mature HIV/AIDS programs into broader public health supply systems—even ones that are efficient and well managed. Integrating HIV/AIDS programs into a country's general essential medicines program may be very difficult because of the sheer difference in scale compared with previously integrated programs, such as those for family planning. Typically, integrating a vertical program involves the absorption of a smaller supply system into a larger one, which can be reasonably achieved when the larger system functions well and has sufficient spare capacity. However, a supply system for a country's HIV/AIDS program may be as large as or larger than its essential medicines supply program; under such circumstances, integration of the two systems would require a strategic redesign and restructuring of the entire pharmaceutical supply system.

8.7 Meeting health needs through private channels

As mentioned, changes in national policy, declining government financial resources, or other trends may lead to an increased role for the private sector, including for-profit and not-for-profit entities, in providing access to medicines. Governments' inability to provide regular medicines and supplies may push more health facilities to purchase medicines from private wholesalers, and patients to purchase medicines from retail drug sellers.

Not-for-profit pharmaceutical services

Nonprofit health care providers, including faith-based and charitable health services and other NGOs, play an important role in the financing and provision of health services in many countries. The share of health services provided through the private nonprofit health sector varies considerably among countries, but in low-income countries it can be large, especially in rural areas; for example, the Christian Health Association of Malawi provides up to 40 percent of services in the country overall, with 90 percent of its facilities located in rural areas (UN 2007). NGOs can play an important role in promoting the concept of essential medicines and in supplying essential medicines.

To the extent that NGOs target their services to rural populations, mothers and children, the urban poor, and other underserved groups, encouraging the growth and development of such organizations can be in the government's interest. Government incentives and subsidies for NGOs may include annual lump-sum grants, temporary assignment of ministry health personnel, payment of NGO staff, permission to purchase pharmaceuticals from government stores, exemption from import duties (sometimes limited to products on the national essential medicines list), and payment of retirement benefits. Providing access to government medical stores and exemption from import duties are particularly important in encouraging NGOs to supply essential medicines for their patients. Some countries have allowed specific NGOs to purchase medicines from government medical stores—in some cases, at subsidized prices.

Beginning in the late 1970s, coincident with WHO's introduction of the essential medicines concept, mission or other nonprofit health associations in some countries began to create their own agencies to procure and distribute essential medicines. These NGOs generally develop their own essential medicines list, often based on the WHO model. NGOs obtain pharmaceutical products from the national parastatal (where one exists), local manufacturers, international nonprofit suppliers, or other foreign suppliers. Financing usually comes from a combination of external donations, local donations, and fees. Ghana, India, Kenya, Nepal, Nigeria, and Uganda are among the countries in which NGOs operate essential medicines supply services. Country Study 8-3 describes the origin and operation of Kenya's Mission for Essential Drugs (MEDS) and Uganda's Joint Medical Stores (JMS). Despite financial and organizational difficulties, some NGO essential medicines services have been very successful. Furthermore, in some countries where public-sector systems have experienced problems, demands on NGO services have increased as they try to fill service gaps.

For NGOs that lack the capital or organizational capacity required to establish their own central store, the direct delivery or primary distributor system offers a means to obtain more favorable prices on a limited range of locally procured essential medicines.

For-profit pharmaceutical services: retail pharmacies and drug sellers

On the consumer side, when public facilities are not located where people can easily access them, or if their supply of medicines is unreliable, people will turn to retail drug outlets as their first source of health care. Such outlets often offer questionable product and service quality at higher prices. In these examples, patients are left to buy virtually all medicines on their own from the private sector. This situation usually results from lack of funds within the government rather than any official pharmaceutical management plan. Private pharmacies and other private drug outlets exist in virtually every country in the world. In addition, doctors, other clinicians in private practice, and practitioners in the informal health sector commonly dispense pharmaceuticals, often deriving more income from pharmaceuticals than from consulting fees.

The percentage of total pharmaceutical expenditures that pass through the private sector varies from under 10 percent in some small, relatively isolated countries to over 90 percent in countries with a well-developed private sector and limited public-sector pharmaceutical supply. By retail value,

---

Country Study 8-3
NGO essential medicines services in East Africa

Two mission-run pharmaceutical supply services that are generally considered success stories are Kenya's Mission for Essential Drugs and Uganda's Joint Medical Stores. A WHO-commissioned report presented the findings of an analysis of key factors for success and obstacles faced in running NGO pharmaceutical supply systems. Both systems are now largely self-sustaining, but they required—and continue to require to some degree—an enormous amount of multidonor support. Although operating in similar environments, MEDS, established in 1986, and JMS, established in 1979, differ in where they source their products, either locally or internationally, and what clients they serve, but both have efficient systems, producing 90 percent availability rates and competitive prices. Kawasaki and Patten (2002) said in their analysis, "The most important point is that both organizations maintain high staff motivation levels, and provide a reliable pharmaceutical supply

system for their customers. Both organizations voice a strong commitment to serving the poor in their respective countries, and achieve this goal through efficiency and maintaining their purpose. Both organizations are beginning to supply significant amounts of products to organizations in neighboring countries."

Although MEDS and JMS are clearly effective in contributing to increased access to medicines in their respective countries, this success evolved from and depended on decades of sustained commitment—financial, technical, and political—from supportive donors. However, as it has for other essential medicine supply services in the region, the increase in demand for products has pushed MEDS and JMS to the limit of their current capacities, which will test their ability to maintain quality services.

Source: Kawasaki and Patten 2002.

the majority of pharmaceuticals in many developing countries flow through the private sector (including the private nonprofit or faith-based sector).

For many common medical problems, such as malaria and diarrhea, a variety of factors encourage people to diagnose themselves or their children, then purchase medications from retail drug sellers before visiting a government health facility. These factors include distance to the health facility; perceived seriousness of the illness; medicine availability in the public facility; cash availability; and perceptions of privacy and quality of the health care providers, health facilities, and medicines.

Because pharmacies are mainly located in urban areas, whereas many people live in rural and peri-urban communities, these informal shops are often the most convenient retail outlet from which to buy medicines. Moreover, when public primary health care facilities have unreliable supplies of medicines, patients will turn to private shops to obtain pharmaceuticals prescribed by the government health worker.

Given the absence of pharmacy services in rural areas and the shortage in poor urban areas, retail drug outlets play an important role in providing access to essential medicines for a significant proportion of the population in many developing countries; however, experience (CPM 2003) shows that access through retail drug outlets can be characterized by a number of problems including—

- Authorization to sell only a limited list of medicines, not including basic essential prescription medicines
- Illegal availability of prescription medicines that are prohibited for sale in drug shops
- Quality of medicines that cannot be assured
- Difficulty in finding reliable and legal sources of medicines and other health care commodities
- Lack of adequate facilities for storing medicines properly
- Dispensing staff who lack basic qualifications and training
- High prices charged to consumers
- Inadequate regulation and supervision

Because informal retail drug outlets generally operate in an uncontrolled environment, improving and monitoring the quality of products and services is a challenge; however, groundbreaking initiatives aimed at the informal private sector have been introduced successfully. Chapter 32 describes programs that have created accreditation and franchising schemes to provide incentives to drug shop owners to maintain standards of quality medicines and services. Such initiatives are innovative approaches to improving products and services in the commercial sector, but they are complex, costly, and time-consuming undertakings that require extensive commitment and resources.

Other, less complex approaches aimed at improving dispensing by private-sector providers include interventions such as vendor-to-vendor education programs (Tavrow et al. 2003), face-to-face drug seller training (Ross-Degnan et al. 1996), and combined drug retailer and community education programs (Marsh et al. 2004) that often focus on one condition, such as diagnosing and treating childhood malaria. Knowledgeable dispensers are more likely to ask questions and give instructions and advice to customers rather than simply sell the medicine that the customer requests (Brieger et al. 2004).

8.8 Health systems strengthening, decentralization, and pharmaceutical supply management

The various mechanisms for buying and distributing pharmaceuticals must be couched in the context of ongoing efforts to strengthen health systems, which is a unifying theme for many global health organizations and initiatives, including WHO, the Global Fund to Fight AIDS, Tuberculosis and Malaria, and the U.S. President's Emergency Plan for AIDS Relief. Changes to strengthen the supply system may include incorporation of competitive mechanisms within the public sector, decentralization of health service provision, contracting out specific services, and expanding the role for private or NGO sectors.

Selection, procurement, and distribution can, in principle, be effectively managed in centralized, partially decentralized, or fully decentralized systems. In a fully decentralized public-sector system, each authorized level, typically a province or a district, is responsible for independently procuring and supplying its own medicines. More commonly, in mixed systems, centers, provinces, and sometimes districts each supply a different set of medicines. Of the four main functions in the pharmaceutical management cycle, only local distribution and medicine use are, by their nature, decentralized. Most other functions could be performed at the national, provincial, district, or local level.

Much attention has been given to decentralization. But what is meant by decentralization? The term is used to describe at least three different approaches to transferring power from central authorities: delegation, devolution, and privatization. These can be described as follows—

Delegation describes the assignment of responsibility for specific tasks to lower-level units within the health system, with overall control remaining at the central level. For example, selection and quantification can be delegated to hospitals, while tendering, compiling pharmaceutical orders, and determining final order quantities remain central functions.

Country Study 8-4
Decentralization's effect on the supply of essential medicines in Indonesia

In Indonesia, the public-sector pharmaceutical supply situation was complex before decentralization occurred. Numerous vertical programs were managing program-specific commodity and medicine supply. A centralized procurement mechanism existed, but supply was locally administered for some essential medicines. The decentralization of the health system led to disruption and confusion because traditional lines of communication and authority were dislocated, and opinions conflicted on determining levels of responsibility. The laws and regulations relating to decentralization were unclear, and program managers were making new, often inconsistent, interpretations of the existing regulations. In addition, different provinces and districts responded in different ways, developing and using differing methods and procedures, which resulted in conflicting information, sometimes even from within the same organization. The nature of the conflicting information made direct comparisons and data analysis difficult. However, even with the problems that were associated with Indonesia's decentralization process, evidence indicated that in 2004, medicine availability had not decreased.

Devolution refers to the transfer of power (responsibility, authority, and accountability) to lower-level units, which are then outside the direct control of the central level.

Privatization is properly defined as the transfer of ownership from the public to the private sector. But the term is also applied, less precisely, to contracting government services to the private sector (as with direct delivery contracts) or introducing private-sector features into the public sector (as with government-owned but semi-autonomous supply agencies). As mentioned in Section 8.4, contracting requires skillful management and careful monitoring.

Decentralization in any of these forms is intended to improve the responsiveness, quality, and efficiency of health services. Decentralization aims to achieve these benefits through greater local involvement, more direct public accountability, increased flexibility to adjust to local circumstances, more rapid and more accurate communication, and quicker adaptation to changing conditions. Improvements are far from certain, however. The loss of scale and purchasing power and the general lack of technical and managerial skills at the regional and district levels hinder decentralized systems from achieving efficient and effective supply management. This can be seen in the example from Indonesia in Country Study 8-4. Problems that have occurred with attempts to decentralize pharmaceutical management functions include—

Lack of capacity: Decentralization of pharmaceutical management responsibility may be implemented without ensuring that sufficient local staff and management capacity are present to sustain services.

Lack of financial resources: Responsibility is sometimes decentralized without providing an adequate budget or financing system at the levels where responsibility is placed. In this case, decentralization simply becomes abandonment of responsibility.

Increased corruption: Because of the money involved, interference for personal gain is common in pharmaceutical supply systems. Although decentralization is meant to improve accountability, it sometimes creates opportunities for local officials or other special interests to profit.

Increased cost: Decentralization of procurement usually means smaller order quantities. It can result in higher prices for essential medicines, although this problem can be overcome with central contracts coupled with decentralized ordering. Districts or facilities with purchasing power that choose to purchase from the private sector pay more for medicines.

Decreased product quality: Selecting reliable suppliers and monitoring medicine quality are difficult at the local level if no unified national system exists or if public entities are buying from unmonitored private-sector sources.

Untested private-sector providers: Private companies that have limited experience with providing large-scale health care services may underestimate the level of effort and resources necessary to fulfill the need, or the contracting authority may make the same mistake in assessing the capacity of the vendor.

In managing a pharmaceutical supply system, thinking in terms of a task-specific approach to decentralization is useful. Tasks better performed centrally include those that require specialized skills, involve economies of scale, or depend on extensive or rapidly changing technical information. Examples of such tasks include development of essential medicines lists, preparation of standard treatments, management of competitive tenders, selection and monitoring of suppliers, quality assurance, and development of training programs on rational medicine use.

Tasks that can be decentralized include those that do not require uncommon technical skills and those for which local information is required. Decentralization is appropriate when local circumstances vary significantly throughout the country and local interests favor improved performance. Examples of such tasks include adaptation of medicines lists or standard treatments to local needs, quantification of medicine requirements, coordination of local distribution, training in rational medicine use, and monitoring of medicine use at health facilities.

In the Philippines, the province of Pangasinan's approach to pooled procurement by government hospitals provides an example of a task-specific approach. Procurement is based on the national medicine formulary, treatment guidelines, and morbidity and mortality data, and hospital procurement plans must be approved by the provincial therapeutic committee. Suppliers are selected from those that have been prequalified. Tendering is centralized at the level of the General Services Office to obtain lower bulk prices, and all deliveries are made directly to the hospitals. Quantification of medication requirements, budgeting, receipt and storage, and supervision of medicine quality and use are all decentralized to the level of the individual hospital.

8.9 Analyzing options for supplying essential medicines

The following considerations are important in developing an appropriate strategy for drawing on the combined strengths of both public and private pharmaceutical sectors—

Analysis of the national policy framework: Within the context of economic, development, and industrial policy, what is the overall government approach to the roles of the public and private sectors? What have been the experiences in other sectors with the mix between private and public provision and financing of services?

Analysis of the legal framework: Is the legislation related to pharmaceuticals up-to-date? Is the drug regulatory authority adequately staffed, financed, and equipped? Does a national commitment exist to implement the measures necessary to ensure pharmaceutical quality, safety, and efficacy?

Pharmaceutical-sector analysis: What is the current status of the public pharmaceutical sector with respect to financing, human resources, physical infrastructure, management systems, and overall performance? What is the current status of the private sector with respect to these elements?

Comparative advantages of public and private pharmaceutical sectors: Given the current level of development in the public and private sectors, what are the advantages of promoting one over the other? Are clear benefits likely to result from changing the status quo?

Costs versus benefits of expanded private-sector involvement: Any change involves costs and benefits. Do the potential economic and health benefits of expanded private-sector involvement outweigh the costs of such expansion?

Phasing-in of changes in the pharmaceutical sector: Even if good information and sound judgment lead to the conclusion that the public role in the pharmaceutical sector should change, planners should not assume that such a shift can occur immediately and in one step. Phasing-in of changes may lead to a smoother transition.

Monitoring of changes: Finally, the objectives of government action must be clearly specified, and indicators need to be identified and monitored to determine whether the objectives are being met. Such monitoring is especially important if changes are being made in phases and if an opportunity exists to hasten, delay, or modify implementation based on experience.

Clarifying public-sector roles in essential medicines programs should be a central concern in the development and review of national medicine policies. From a public health perspective, the objectives for government involvement with all pharmaceutical sectors, public and private, are to provide access to medicines by ensuring—

- Physical availability
- Affordability
- Geographical accessibility
- Acceptability (or satisfaction)
- Quality of products and services

Chapter 36 provides information on how to assess a pharmaceutical system.

Ultimately, the role a government assumes in providing essential medicines depends on the circumstances of the individual country. The spectrum of responsibility in supplying pharmaceutical products ranges from entirely public to primarily private. Most countries operate under a paradigm somewhere in between. Generally, countries that take advantage of the capacities of both their public and private sectors have better access to medicines. As mentioned, increasing challenges to pharmaceutical supply may encourage the formation of regional partnerships to increase the resource capacity for participating countries.

8.10 Implementing sustainable changes in pharmaceutical supply systems

Pharmaceutical availability and affordability are of particular concern when government health services do not exist or are not able to provide medicines for poor, medically needy, geographically isolated, or otherwise underserved populations. In countries where a large proportion of the population is poor and government health services lack sufficient resources, ensuring universal access to medicines is particularly challenging.

These considerations must now be placed into a new and evolving context resulting from dramatic changes in public health care—especially in the pharmaceutical market—related primarily to HIV/AIDS but also to changes in treatment guidelines for malaria and other diseases. For example, from its founding in 2003 through 2010, the U.S. President's Emergency Plan for AIDS Relief is estimated to have contributed approximately 32 billion U.S. dollars (USD) through partnerships with more than 30 countries. In 2009, almost 14 percent of the budget was used to procure antiretrovirals. The Global Fund to Fight AIDS, Tuberculosis and Malaria approved grant proposals for over USD 19.2 billion through Round 9. Through Round 7, almost 60 percent of grants had been distributed in Africa, and 45 percent had gone to medicines and commodities (PEPFAR 2010; Global Fund n.d.).

For many countries, this increase in pharmaceutical funding has dramatically affected the size of their pharmaceutical market not only for these products but also for all pharmaceuticals. In addition, the high value of HIV/AIDS medicines and artemisinin-based combination therapies for malaria, as well as the sheer volume of products, will make security in the supply chain a much larger concern (see Chapter 43).

A key message is that a country cannot easily or quickly make major changes in the way it supplies medicines and health commodities; developing and implementing sustainable improvements is a complex and expensive process. A clear policy, legal, and regulatory framework must underpin planned changes, which requires the support and buy-in of stakeholders at all levels of the system. Substantial and sustained investments will be needed in a range of activities and technical areas, such as advocacy, information systems, logistics, infrastructure, and human resources development. Because the time frame for implementation will be years, changes must be addressed in phases, with appropriate technical assistance throughout. In addition, efficient decision making and project management must be in place to avoid delays in implementation.

The goal should be not only a more cost-efficient and effective supply system that maximizes access to pharmaceuticals, but also a system that—once in place—is able to function with minimum external support. Technical assistance and leadership, as well as donor and government funding and private investment, will be integral in countries that are implementing changes to their pharmaceutical supply systems, but the empowerment of stakeholders from the national level down to the local levels will help foster self-reliance and reduce dependence on outside support.

Each country must assess its own situation to determine which strategies appear best suited to its circumstances. The concepts tried in other countries and their experiences

of challenges and success should provide a framework for identifying options and making choices while keeping the key public health objectives in mind: increasing the availability and affordability of essential medicines, promoting rational use of medicines, and ensuring acceptable medicine quality. ∎

References and further readings

★ = Key readings.

Brieger, W. R., P. E. Osamor, K. K. Salami, O. Oladepo, and S. A. Otusanya. 2004. Interactions between Patent Medicine Vendors and Customers in Urban and Rural Nigeria. *Health Policy and Planning* 19(3):177–82.

★ CPM (Center for Pharmaceutical Management). 2003. *Access to Essential Medicines: Tanzania, 2001.* Prepared for the Strategies for Enhancing Access to Medicines Program. Arlington, Va.: Management Sciences for Health. <http://www.msh.org/seam/reports/access_to_medicines_tanzania.pdf>

CPM/MSH (Center for Pharmaceutical Management/Management Sciences for Health). 2011. *Center for Pharmaceutical Management: Technical Frameworks, Approaches, and Results.* Arlington, Va.: CPM.

Dalberg Global Development Advisors/MIT-Zaragoza International Logistics Program. 2008. *The Private Sector's Role in Health Supply Chains: Review of the Role and Potential for Private Sector Engagement in Developing Country Health Supply Chains.* <http://apps.who.int/medicinedocs/documents/s16323e/s16323e.pdf>

Euro Health Group and MSH Tanzania. 2007. *The United Republic of Tanzania Drug Tracking Study: Final Report.* Søborg, Denmark: Euro Health Group. <http://hdptz.esealtd.com/fileadmin/documents/Key_Sector_Documents/Tanzania_Key_Health_Documents/Tanzania_Drug_tracking_study_final_report.pdf>

Global Fund to Fight AIDS, Tuberculosis and Malaria. No date. Grant Portfolio. <http://portfolio.theglobalfund.org/en/Home/Index>

Kanavos, P., P. Das, V. Durairaj, R. Laing, and D. O. Abegunde. 2010. *Options for Financing and Optimizing Medicines in Resource-Poor Countries.* Geneva: WHO.

Kawasaki, E., and J. P. Patten. 2002. *Drug Supply Systems of Missionary Organizations Identifying Factors Affecting Expansion and Efficiency: Case Studies from Uganda and Kenya.* Geneva: World Health Organization/Essential Drugs and Medicines Program.

Lalvani, P., P. Yadav, K. Curtis, M. Bernstein, and N. Ooman. 2010. *Increasing Patient Access to Antiretrovirals: Recommended Actions for a More Efficient Global Supply Chain.* Washington, D.C.: Center for Global Development.

Marsh, V. M., W. M. Mutemi, A. Willets, K. Bayah, S. Were, A. Ross, and K. Marsh. 2004. Improving Malaria Home Treatment by Training Drug Retailers in Rural Kenya. *Tropical Medicine and International Health* 9(4):451–60.

McPake, B., and E. Ngalande-Bande. 1994. Contracting Out Health Services in Developing Countries. *Health Policy and Planning* 9(1):25–30.

MoHSW (Ministry of Health and Social Welfare [Tanzania]). 2008. *Mapping of Partners and Financial Flows in the Medicines Supply System in Tanzania.* Dar es Salaam: MoHSW. <http://apps.who.int/medicinedocs/documents/s16504e/s16504e.pdf>

———. 2007. *In-Depth Assessment of the Medicines Supply System in Tanzania.* Dar es Salaam: MoHSW.

MSF (Médecins Sans Frontières). 2009. *Untangling the Web of Price Reductions: A Pricing Guide for the Purchase of ARVs for Developing*

ASSESSMENT GUIDE

National pharmaceutical financing and distribution

- Which pharmaceutical financing sources are used (government budgets, private out-of-pocket purchases, insurance, other sources)?
- What is the structure of the pharmaceutical distribution system (state wholesale monopoly, private wholesale distributors, NGO pharmaceutical supply agency, centralized distribution for government facilities, other distributors)?
- What is the national health care delivery context (decentralization, rapidly expanding demand for pharmaceuticals caused by rollout of artemisinin-based combination therapy for malaria)?

Pharmaceutical supply for government health services

- What system is currently used (central medical stores, autonomous supply agency, direct delivery, primary distributor, primarily private supply)?
- Is a kit system in place? Do current plans include kits, or is the goal to shift to an ordering system?
- Which alternative supply systems were considered?
- How well is the current system performing (see notes)?

Autonomous pharmaceutical supply agency (if applicable)

- Does the agency have an independent and effective management board?
- What are the qualifications of the senior managers?
- What measures to ensure efficiency and monitor performance are in place?
- Are financing and financial controls adequate?
- How is the system performing in terms of cost and delivery (see notes)?

Direct delivery and primary distributor contracts (if applicable)

- Does the legal framework permit outsourcing of services?
- Are contracts effectively monitored?
- Is competition sufficient to ensure low prices and good service?
- Are financing and financial controls adequate?
- How is the system performing in terms of cost and delivery (see notes)?

Performance indicators for pharmaceutical supply

- Are indicator medicines currently available at health facilities?
- What is the frequency of stockouts for indicator medicines at health facilities?
- What is the average duration of stockouts for indicator medicines at health facilities?
- What is the average time between order and delivery for indicator medicines for regular orders?
- What percentage of supplier medicine prices are the average distribution costs (administration, storage, transport)?

Measures affecting private supply channels

- How mature is the commercial pharmaceutical sector (how many companies, how large, how long in business)?
- Are companies interested in expansion? Do they have access to capital for investment? Are they prepared to take risks to enlarge their business?
- What is the capacity of NGOs that are providing health care services?
- What is the geographic reach of each company or NGO? Are they limited to urban distribution?
- Would additional supply responsibilities be easily absorbed, or would such responsibilities overwhelm their capacity?
- What licensing provisions and incentives are in place to increase geographic access through private wholesalers and retailers?
- Does the law permit the sale of any essential prescription medicines in nonpharmacy drug outlets?
- Can the drug regulatory authority ensure the quality of privately sourced medicines?
- Does the current supply system result in a greater reliance on the private sector for access to medicines?
- What kind of training and certification exists for pharmacy aides and other drug sellers?
- What types of policies, legislation, and regulations on clinician dispensing exist?

Notes: Supply system performance should be measured at least annually. Most indicators can be measured at regional and other supply depots as well as at health facilities. Whenever possible, annual figures should be compared for the most recent year and two preceding years (three years total). See Chapter 48 for a discussion of indicator medicines. See assessment guides for Chapters 18 and 22 for additional procurement and distribution indicators, respectively.

Countries. 12th ed. Geneva: Campaign for Access to Essential Medicines/MSF. Updated regularly and available online at http://utw.msfaccess.org.

MSH (Management Sciences for Health). *International Drug Price Indicator Guide* (updated annually). Arlington, Va.: Center for Pharmaceutical Management/MSH. <http://erc.msh.org>

PEPFAR (U.S. President's Emergency Plan for AIDS Relief). 2010. Making a Difference: Funding. <http://www.pepfar.gov/documents/organization/80161.pdf>

Ross-Degnan, D., S. B. Soumerai, P. K. Goel, J. Bates, J. Makhulo, N. Dondi, Sutoto, D. Adi, L. Ferraz-Tabor, and R. Hogan. 1996. The Impact of Face-to-Face Educational Outreach on Diarrhoea Treatment in Pharmacies. *Health Policy and Planning* 11(3):308–18.

Sarley, D., L. Allain, and A. Akkihal. 2009. *Estimating the Global In-Country Supply Chain Costs of Meeting the MDGs by 2015: Technical Brief.* Arlington, Va.: USAID/DELIVER PROJECT. <http://pdf.usaid.gov/pdf_docs/PNADP080.pdf>

★ SEAM (Strategies for Enhancing Access to Medicines Program). 2008. *Tanzania: Developing a Prime Vendor Pharmaceutical Supply System.* Arlington, Va.: SEAM/Management Sciences for Health. <http://www.msh.org/seam/reports/SEAM_TANZANIA_Prime_Vendor.pdf>

Seiter, A., and M. Gyansa-Lutterodt. 2009. *Policy Note: The Pharmaceutical Sector in Ghana.* Washington, D.C.: World Bank. <http://apps.who.int/medicinedocs/documents/s16765e/s16765e.pdf>

Tavrow, P., J. Shabahang, and S. Makama. 2003. Vendor-to-Vendor Education to Improve Malaria Treatment by Private Drug Outlets in Bungoma District, Kenya. *Malaria Journal* 2:10.

UN (United Nations). 2007. "WHO Regional Director Appeals for Political Leadership and Adequate Resources to Tackle the TB Emergency in Africa." Press release, March 27.

UNICEF Regional Office for West and Central Africa/GIP ESTHER. 2008. *Evaluation of ARV Procurement and Supply Management Systems in West and Central Africa Region.* Dakar, Senegal: UNICEF Regional Office for West and Central Africa. <http://apps.who.int/medicinedocs/documents/s16466e/s16466e.pdf>

WHO (World Health Organization). 2004. *Perspectives and Practice in Antiretroviral Treatment: Mission for Essential Drugs and Supplies, Kenya.* Geneva: WHO.

———. 2003. *The World Health Report 2003: Shaping the Future.* Geneva: WHO. <http://www.who.int/whr/2003/en/>

———. 1994. *Public/Private Collaboration for Health: National Health Systems and Policies.* Geneva: WHO.

WHO/DAP (World Health Organization/Action Programme on Essential Drugs). 1998. *Collaboration between NGOs, Ministries of Health and WHO in Drug Distribution and Supply.* Geneva: WHO. <http://apps.who.int/medicinedocs/en/d/Js2237e/#Js2237e>

———. 1997. *Public-Private Roles in the Pharmaceutical Sector: Implications for Equitable Access and Rational Drug Use.* Geneva: WHO/DAP. <http://whqlibdoc.who.int/hq/1997/WHO_DAP_97.12.pdf>

★ ———. 1994. *Indicators for Monitoring National Drug Policies.* Geneva: WHO/DAP.

★ WHO/EPN (World Health Organization and Ecumenical Pharmaceutical Network). 2006. *Multi-Country Study of Medicine Supply and Distribution Activities of Faith-Based Organizations in Sub-Saharan African Countries.* Geneva: WHO/EPN. <http://whqlibdoc.who.int/hq/2006/WHO_PSM_PAR_2006.2_eng.pdf>

WHO/WPRO (World Health Organization/Western Pacific Region). No date. "Country Profile on Financing Health Services, WPRO." <http://www.wpro.who.int/NR/rdonlyres/EF30E961-890C-4E2C-B6DA-93037EFA09BD/0/countprofile.pdf>

★ World Health Organization Maximizing Positive Synergies Collaborative Group. 2009. An Assessment of Interactions between Global Health Initiatives and Country Health Systems. *Lancet* 373:2137–69.

Yadav, P. 2010. "In-Country Supply Chains." *Global Health: The Magazine.* Winter. <http://www.globalhealthmagazine.com/cover_stories/supply_chains>

CHAPTER 9

Pharmaceutical pricing policy

SUMMARY

In a market economy, the interaction of producers and consumers determines the price of goods and services. Understanding the theory of supply and demand helps explain how prices are determined, and this theory also explains how responsive (elastic) both supply and demand are to changes in price. For example, medicines that are not considered essential and that the buyer could credibly refuse to purchase will have more elastic prices, whereas the prices of medicines that are considered essential and that the buyer must obtain will be inelastic, meaning buyers will be less sensitive to higher prices.

Factors that interfere with the ability of the market to efficiently produce and allocate goods and services are said to result in "market failure." An example of market failure is when buyers do not have the same level of knowledge; for example, some buyers might pay more than others for the same medicines because they are unaware of what everyone else is paying.

When buyers or sellers have market power (monopoly or monopsony), they can distort how the market price mechanism works. For example, in absolute monopolies (one seller) and oligopolies (a few sellers), the seller has significant ability to set prices, because the consumer has limited choices. This distortion allows the seller to command a price that is higher than would have prevailed under more competitive situations. In a monopsony, where the government has market power as the only large buyer in the market, the government acts on behalf of consumers to obtain better prices.

In addition to these economic theories of price determination, prices for medicines are influenced by the fact that medicines have certain traits that set them apart from other consumer products. For example, consumers need expert advice to make rational choices between using and not using a medicine and about what kind of medicine to use. This advice is provided by prescribers, who may not know or even care about the price of medicines. Medicines also serve as an investment in future health, which may be difficult for the consumer to value.

The literature unanimously concludes that medicine price differences exist between countries, even when comparing between or within the strata of industrialized, middle-, and low-income countries. Price variation within countries is more likely in less price-regulated markets, such as the United States; however, prices vary in other countries, where public, private, and nongovernmental (not-for-profit) sectors procure medicines separately. Variable prices for medicines within and between countries often result from—

- The pharmaceutical manufacturer selling the same product for different prices
- Intra- and intercountry differences in the margins charged in the postmanufacturing supply chain by wholesalers, distributors, and pharmacists, as well as taxes and co-payments levied by the state

Conducting pharmaceutical price comparisons is challenging, but such assessments can identify price variations and provide valuable information on their source and on interventions that can help reduce medicine prices. For example, margins and taxes charged along the pharmaceutical supply chain can add significantly to the final price of medicines; however, governments can control these markups by enacting price-control policies and eliminating tariffs and taxes. In addition, buyers of pharmaceuticals should assess their own position in the marketplace and use tactics such as price negotiations, pooled procurement, and information sharing to increase their market power.

9.1 The theory of determining prices

The history of economics, and therefore much of economic thought, is dominated by discussion of the theory of prices and how they are determined. This theory is underscored by the behavior of market participants—buyers and sellers. As noted in Chapter 10, a scarcity of resources requires that buyers and sellers make choices about how resources will be used, whereas abundance allows limitless production and consumption. However, resources *are* always limited, and using a resource in one way means it is no longer available for alternative uses.

In competitive markets, producers need to decide, for a given amount of resources, what and how much to produce, while consumers, with a given amount of income, need to choose what and how much they will buy. Producers and consumers come together in the marketplace, and under certain assumptions, their interaction determines market prices.

Demand and supply

Demand is generated by consumers, while the supply is provided by producers. Critical to the theory is an understanding of what drives each group, because consumers and producers are not driven by the same forces.

Demand: Market theory places the consumer in the lead role for determining what will be produced. Consumers want to maximize their welfare through the total bundle of goods and services they buy with their income. The bundles of goods that consumers choose to buy at given prices tell producers what to produce. In theory, consumers make rational choices as to what is included in the bundle of goods; however, nothing in the theory suggests that these preferences are equitable or socially desirable, only that they represent choices. Prices of complementary products or substitute products affect demand, as does the number of consumers in the market and their desire—for example, if a consumer prefers to buy a branded medicine over a generic and is willing to pay more. Associated with the role of creating demand is the consumer's ability to vote—with money—on what will be produced. Therefore, individuals with greater income have proportionally more votes (Bannock et al. 1984).

Supply: Producers want to maximize their profit. Profits are determined by the cost of production and the firm's total revenue (or sales). To maximize profit, the seller has an incentive to use resources in the production process in the least costly way. In a perfectly competitive marketplace, firms receive "normal profits"; that is, they cover the cost of all production costs plus the minimum return required to keep them in business. If the firms' returns were greater than this minimum, new firms would be encouraged to enter the market, and the competition would drive profits downward until normal profits were reached. If the returns were less than the minimum, low profitability would encourage firms to leave the market, raising the profits of the remaining businesses until they achieved normal profits. Other factors that affect the supply curve include the number of producers, which increases competition; technology, which can initially represent a cost to the producer but ultimately increases efficiency; and the cost of inputs.

Elasticity of prices

The intersection of supply and demand provides the tool for understanding price determination. However, a further aspect of supply and demand helps explain behavior, that is, how responsive each is to changes in price.

Elasticity of demand: On the demand side, if consumers really need a product to the extent that a significant price increase has little effect on the quantity demanded, demand is nonresponsive to price and is said to be *price inelastic.* The reverse situation is where demand is very responsive to price, such that a slight rise in price causes a proportionally larger fall in demand. Pharmaceutical demand varies across countries. It is also relatively *income inelastic,* meaning that a person's income affects pharma-

ceutical purchases less than other factors (OECD 2008). The four determinants of price elasticity of demand are substitutability, proportion of income committed to the purchase, whether the item is a luxury or a necessity, and market timing (see Box 9-1).

Elasticity of supply: On the supply side, if suppliers do not respond to price changes, they are price inelastic, whereas suppliers who do respond are said to be price elastic. The determinants of the price elasticity of supply depend on timing (Jackson and McConnell 1989). In the immediate market period, say on the day of a significant price rise, producers may not be physically able to increase production. However, over time and assuming demand is maintained, suppliers will seek to increase production by using existing excess capacity and ultimately by expanding their production capabilities by increasing capital and labor.

9.2 The reality of competition in a market-based economy

An *economic market* is defined as a trade of goods or services between two independent players: (a) buyers and (b) sellers or producers. Price carries information about the value of the goods or services, with the buyers' willingness to pay defined as *demand,* and the sellers' willingness to produce the goods being the *supply.* The market is where the buyers and sellers interact, and the interaction of supply and demand determines price.

Most economic theory starts with an assumption of a perfectly competitive market where buyers demand goods and services until the marginal value of each is equal to their price, and producers adjust the supply until the marginal cost of each unit is equal to the market price. This interaction allows demand and supply to fluctuate until they are in equilibrium. When price equilibrium exists between demand and supply, then the resulting allocation of resources for the goods or services of that market is also in equilibrium. Such a market is perfectly competitive. The necessary conditions of a perfectly competitive market include—

- A large number of buyers and sellers or suppliers to form the market
- Buyers that have excellent information, act rationally, and have the time and ability to compare the prices of various suppliers
- Suppliers or producers that have free entry and exit from the market
- Homogenous products of known quality offered by different producers

A review of these characteristics shows that health care is not an example of a perfectly competitive market. Buyers do not have perfect information—patients must rely on health

---

Box 9-1
Factors that influence elasticity of demand

The degree to which the product can be substituted with another

For example, aspirin is produced by many companies. In a situation where the consumer sees no major difference between each firm's brand of aspirin, a rise in price by one firm will result in a proportionally greater fall in the quantity purchased. For example, if firm A decides to increase its price by 20 percent, the level of demand for A's aspirin line is likely to fall by a larger proportion (by more than 20 percent) because consumers will purchase the equivalent and cheaper products from firms B, C, or D. This scenario exemplifies *price elasticity*. However, where the product has no or few direct substitutes, demand will be less responsive to price changes. For example, a newly patented, innovative medicine that has no therapeutic equivalent (a single-source drug), which is also considered to be essential, will have demand that is *price inelastic*: that is, a 20 percent rise in price might not affect demand at all.

Proportion of income

If a product costs only a small proportion of income, it is likely to be price inelastic. For example, if the price of over-the-counter analgesics sold by all sellers, such as paracetamol and aspirin, increases by 20 percent, the level of demand is only likely to fall slightly, because the price represents a small fraction of the consumer's average weekly income.

Luxuries and necessities

As their names suggest, the demand for necessities is likely to be price inelastic because consumers cannot live without them, whereas the demand for luxuries will vary significantly with price. Essential medicines are necessities.

Time

Time makes demand more price elastic as information spreads about alternatives and because firms making alternatives find starting to produce identical or similar products profitable. For example, the manufacturer of a patented, innovative medicine that has no therapeutic alternative will be able to reap monopoly profits. However, these profits will encourage other manufacturers to look for other ways to obtain the same therapeutic outcome with a different (nonpatented) technique (such as the development of "me-too" drugs). The arrival of me-too drugs makes demand more elastic.

---

care providers to give them information about treatment. Furthermore, the suppliers—health providers—do not have easy market entry because of various factors such as licensing and regulatory requirements. Finally, health care is not homogenous in that quality varies among health providers. The result is often a noncompetitive market with market failures, as described in the remainder of this section.

The best possibility for the seller to charge higher prices and earn larger profits is in the extreme situation of an absolute monopoly. In an *absolute monopoly,* a product has only one seller with no alternative. This situation prevails with many patented medicines, particularly if no effective alternative treatments exist.

Oligopolistic competition occurs when only a few sellers operate in the market, so each seller can still influence price. *Monopolistic competition* involves multiple sellers, but they reduce the competition by allowing products to be differentiated (for example, by advertising); a single seller still has some influence over price or at least is able to vary prices without losing all sales. Similar descriptions apply to buyers in the market. Where a market has only one large buyer, which sometimes happens when governments purchase or subsidize pharmaceutical products, it is a *monopsony*. In this case, the government acts on behalf of consumers to obtain better prices.

Figure 9-1 illustrates the range of buyer and seller market positions from perfect competition to monopoly and monopsony. Sellers in pharmaceutical markets are focused at the oligopoly and monopoly end of the supply spectrum. Depending on the influence of buyers, they can be located anywhere on the spectrum, from perfect competition to monopsony.

Market failure

Factors that interfere with the ability of the market to efficiently produce and allocate goods and services are said to result in market failure. Price distortions occur when the market fails to recognize and appropriately value important aspects of society, such as public goods. As noted in Chapter 10, public goods are those goods and services that people cannot be prevented from using, such as local roads, and goods and services whose costs do not vary if additional people use them, such as radio broadcasts. The price system cannot properly evaluate public goods because it has no means to value the level of each individual's demand for the

Figure 9-1   Market structures for buyers and sellers

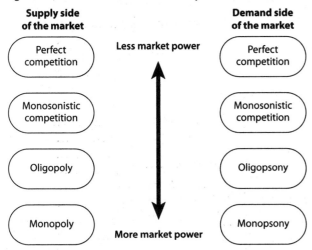

Source: Jackson and McConnell 1989.

good or service and no means of excluding those who claim not to use the good or service.

For example, the evaluation of the safety of pharmaceuticals before human use, which is undertaken by a publicly funded body, is a public good because most individuals do not have the resources to conduct these assessments. Once the evaluation has been undertaken, the cost of sharing this information is almost zero: use of this information by one individual does not reduce anyone else's ability to use it. When consumers cannot be excluded from using the good or service, the market finds determining a price difficult, because potential consumers have an incentive to use the good or service without paying for it. Left alone, the free market would undersupply this information.

Pharmaceutical regulation, which can be considered a public good, can nevertheless contribute to market failure by creating a high barrier to companies that want to enter the market. Only large companies have the staff and resources to satisfy regulatory requirements, which reduce the number of companies that can compete in this market.

Market failure also occurs because of *externalities,* which are the benefits or costs associated with production or consumption that accrue to others. Immunization is one example: the benefits of disease prevention accrue not only to the person who is immunized, but also to others in the community who are exposed to a lower risk of infection. Externalities are not valued by the price mechanism because the individual who is to be immunized will assess only the benefit he or she directly receives, not the benefit received by others. When such externalities create public goods, governments may be willing to subsidize these prices.

Another type of market failure occurs when buyers do not have the same level of knowledge; buyers do not always know what others are paying for the same product, and the seller has an interest in keeping these prices hidden. That is, buyers pay more when they assume everyone else is paying the same price. For example, some large health care organizations in the United States negotiate deals with pharmaceutical manufacturers but do not make the purchase prices publicly available (Dougherty 2004). Alternatively, complex pricing arrangements can be set up that hide the ultimate price paid by the buyer (Country Study 9-1). In South Africa, the government has made such practices illegal in the private sector. Medicines have a single "exit price," which includes logistics fees; legislation also determines the markup and dispensing fee charged by the pharmacist. The intention is to make the pricing process transparent to consumers.

Country Study 9-1
Lack of transparency in medicine markets in New Zealand

Buyers commonly do not know the true price paid for individual products. For example, in New Zealand, a pharmaceutical company sells a range of medicines, including highly priced patented medicines. The public-sector buyer and the company negotiate a price for a bundle of medicines. The pharmaceutical company provides significant discounts to the buyer, but the company does not want other buyers to know that it will discount the patented medicines to make a sale. In the absence of an enforceable confidentiality agreement between the buyer and seller, what options does the pharmaceutical company have to maximize its profits? One way would be to make an agreement with the buyer to purchase the patented medicine at the stated market price in exchange for a rebate at the end of some stipulated period. Alternatively, the company could hide the true price paid for a patented medicine by providing substantial discounts on other, possibly off-patent medicines sold by the company. This way, a buyer appears to be paying the market price requested by the company for the patented medicine, but in reality, the buyer is paying a much lower price for the basket of medicines. Naturally, the seller would prefer not to offer any discounts to anyone; however, if the buyer is in a position to exercise its own market power and negotiate lower prices, the seller will not want this price information to be freely available.

Source: McNee 2006.

So, to some degree, market failure in the pharmaceutical market is a price consumers pay for effective regulation. However, information asymmetry, high barriers to market entry, and monopolistic behavior have led to high prices for many patented medicines, which have made them unaffordable in many settings. Government intervention has been used to correct these distortions. Section 9.7 covers many approaches to price reduction.

Market power

Participants that exert market power can distort how the market price mechanism works. For example, in absolute monopolies (one seller) and oligopolies (a few sellers), the seller has significant ability to set prices, because the consumer has fewer choices. This distortion allows the seller to command a price that is higher than would have prevailed under more competitive situations (Jackson and McConnell 1989).

The same profit motive that drives sellers to seek new and more efficient means of production is also an incentive for them to form collectives where they can exert more power in the market. Antitrust and antimonopoly legislation aims to counter this anticompetitive tendency of markets. However, even strong, enforced legislation is no guarantee that firms will operate competitively. In 2006, five pharmaceutical companies were charged in Britain with colluding to set high prices (Dyer 2006). Despite the risk and cost of being caught, the large potential profits from price setting are a potent incentive to collude.

Sellers are not alone in their ability to influence the market. The strongest buying power is obtained from a monopsony buying position, that is, where a market has only one buyer. The most effective monopsony will have multiple sources for the product. In pharmaceutical markets, this situation translates into one buyer purchasing from several sellers of equivalent medicines. In this setting, the monopsonist can credibly purchase medicines from different sources, which creates a significant incentive for sellers to offer the best possible price. The least effective setting for a monopsony will be for patented, innovative medicines for which no alternatives are available (single-source medicines).

Negotiating with a monopoly removes some of the monopsonist's market power. However, even in this setting, the monopsony will have stronger buying power than several buyers (oligopsony) in negotiating with a single seller and even stronger power than when many buyers are negotiating with a single seller.

The extent to which the monopsony can offset monopoly pricing power will also depend on how necessary the medicine is. The offset will be strongest for medicines that are not considered essential and that the buyer could credibly refuse to buy. These medicines will have some elasticity of demand, and buyers will be price sensitive. The offset will be weak-est for medicines that are considered essential and that the buyer must purchase. The demand for these medicines will be inelastic, and the need for the medicines will make buyers less price sensitive.

In some circumstances, a buyer emerges that has significant buying power. Examples of such large-scale buyers with purchasing power include health maintenance organizations in the United States (private sector) and, as shown in Country Study 9-2, the Pharmaceutical Benefits Scheme in Australia (public sector, monopsony). Although regulation is a critical factor influencing prices, compared to large procurement agencies, smaller buyers have little leverage and will likely pay higher prices. However, buyers can form cooperatives or join to increase their market power, which is the theory behind pooled procurement, discussed in Chapter 18.

It is intuitive to think that large buyers will have strong market positions to negotiate prices, if not by being the sole source of demand, then by the volume of the product they are expected to purchase. However, this association between a large buyer and low prices does not always hold true; the World Health Organization (WHO) reports that some government procurement operations are effective in obtaining low medicine prices, while others are not—usually because they purchase brand-name pharmaceuticals that are no longer under patent rather than lower-priced generic alternatives (Gelders et al. 2006). The buyer should be continually aware of the availability of generics entering the market.

The concern that a single large buyer can adversely affect producers appears uncommon in the area of pharmaceuticals but has been seen in some sectors of low-income countries. For instance, a large, powerful buyer can force down the prices of produce, such as fruit or coffee, to the extent that smaller producers suffer genuine hardship.

9.3   Economic characteristics of pharmaceuticals

Aside from the obvious characteristic of having health benefits, medicines have certain traits that set them apart from most other consumer products (see also Chapter 1).

First, when patients purchase a medicine, they do not gain an "asset" in an economic sense. In most countries, the patient cannot legally resell the medicine; its value rests in the knowledge that went into its development and the testing that determined the correct way to use it, such as dose, course of treatment, and contraindications. Particularly for recently introduced innovative medicines, the economic value of the pharmaceutical to the producer lies in this intellectual property rather than in the chemical constituents of the product.

Second, the patient is not a consumer in the traditional sense. She or he is usually directed by a third party, a doctor or other health professional, to purchase a medicine. The

Country Study 9-2
Australia's pharmaceutical benefits scheme

The Australian Pharmaceutical Benefits Scheme (PBS) requires consumers to make a maximum co-payment of 33.30 Australian dollars (AUD) for all medicines listed on the national formulary (as of 2010). Disadvantaged citizens in the community pay only AUD 5.40, and a safety net exists for people who exceed a maximum amount per year. Medicines not listed with the PBS may still be sold in Australia (provided safety and quality requirements are met), but at an unsubsidized price. However, since few patients will purchase full-price medications, particularly if a therapeutically equivalent medicine is available with a PBS subsidy, the Australian system operates as a monopsony, with the PBS as sole gatekeeper to medicines sold in the country. Pharmacists also receive an incentive each time they dispense a generic medicine to decrease the use of originator brands.

The Australian system of providing affordable access to medicines relies on public-private interactions. The public sector, through the PBS, determines what medicines will be subsidized by the government and at what level of subsidy. The government negotiates the agreed price with pharmaceutical manufacturers and the dispensed price with the Pharmaceutical Guild of Australia, including the markups and dispensing fees. Private-sector doctors are largely responsible for prescribing, and private-sector pharmacists are largely responsible for dispensing the medicine to the patient and collecting the co-payment at the point of sale.

The Australian Productivity Commission compared pharmaceutical prices in a range of industrialized nations. The commission found that—

- Prices for patented, innovative medicines in the United States were 104 percent higher than in Australia. While Australian prices were at the lower end of the price spectrum, prices in Spain were even lower.
- The price of me-too medicines was at least 57 percent more expensive in Canada, Sweden, the United Kingdom, and the United States than in Australia. However, Australian prices were similar to those in New Zealand and Spain.
- The price of generics was at least 40 percent more expensive in Canada, Sweden, the United Kingdom, and the United States than in Australia, but lower prices were recorded in New Zealand and Spain.

In general, countries with less price control (such as the United States) had higher medicine prices than those in the more controlled Australian system. Although the report could not identify specific causal factors explaining why prices tended to be lower in Australia, it was thought to be related to the policy environment and specific features of Australia's cost containment techniques—reference pricing, in particular. Overall, prices in Spain and New Zealand were close to those in Australia. All three countries have predominantly public coverage of medicines for all residents.

Sources: Australian Government Department of Health and Ageing 2010; Australian Productivity Commission 2001; Sansom 2004; Sweeney 2007.

doctor, as gatekeeper to the pharmaceutical market, does not pay for the medication and may not even know how much the prescribed medication will cost the patient. Thus, transmission of price signals between those who initiate demand for the medicine and those who supply it is blurred.

Third, without the expert advice of an intermediary, few consumers have sufficient information to make rational choices between using and not using a medicine, using a brand-name medicine versus a generic, or using a prescription medicine versus an alternative (nonpharmaceutical) therapy. This asymmetry of information affects the pricing mechanism because the consumer is not in a position to make informed choices. The pricing mechanism can be further distorted if the intermediary is influenced by pharmaceutical promotions.

Fourth, health services are a form of investment: investing in health services today is expected to have a return later (Grossman 1972; Johnson 2001). Medicines are a form of investment because people do not receive their benefits until some point in the future. Furthermore, some individuals' pharmaceutical investments may have no obvious return at all, as in the case of vaccines. These characteristics make estimating the monetary value of medicines difficult for the individual. For example, statin drugs can reduce the risk of heart disease in later life. In terms of seeing these medicines as an investment, individuals must assess the benefits of this protection without experiencing what the heart disease actually feels like, and they must judge the possible consequences of *not* taking the statin drugs.

The level of competition among different pharmaceutical product categories is important in understanding medicine pricing strategies. The three main product categories are patented medicines, generic medicines, and branded off-patent medicines.

Patented medicines

This group can be further categorized into—

- Patented, innovative, essential medicines, where no alternative medicine or intervention can provide the same therapeutic outcome, sometimes referred to as *single-source* medicines (such as Herceptin for the treatment of breast cancer)
- New medicines protected by patents, but for which alternative therapies are available (such as Tamiflu for the treatment of influenza)

The distinction between the two types is important because it reflects the degree of market power held by the seller and the price elasticity of demand. Demand for single-source medicines that are considered essential is likely to be inelastic, and combined with patent protection, the seller is in a strong market position compared to situations where alternative therapies are available.

A recent example is the breast cancer drug Herceptin. Because alternatives to this drug do not currently exist, the manufacturers have set a very high price in the knowledge that patients and their insurers (including governments) will be under heavy pressure to pay. This is a classic example of a single-source product with price inelasticity because of patent protection.

The effect of patents on the market stems from monopoly rights that, to varying degrees, are conferred for the life of the patent. These rights allow the monopolist to charge higher prices than would be possible under more competitive conditions, although the extent of the monopolist's price-setting power is not unlimited. For example, the state can counter the monopolist's price-setting power by establishing price regulations, forming a monopsony to purchase medicines on behalf of all residents, issuing a compulsory license to another producer, or using policy instruments such as restrictions on pharmaceutical company profits. More details on these techniques follow in Section 9.7.

Markets can also limit the monopolist's price structure. The potential profits the monopolist stands to make from an essential single-source patented medicine should stimulate other firms to develop medicines that have the same health outcome because patents are granted for the chemical compound rather than the therapeutic indication. The arrival of competitor products restricts the price-setting power of the monopolist, but their arrival on the market is not necessarily immediate. In the United States, competitor medicines are estimated to arrive between one and six years after the original medicine is introduced to the market (Congressional Budget Office 1998).

When a large number of competitor products enters a particular market segment—more than is needed to satisfy clinical need and introduce genuine price competition—the term *me-too* medicines is often applied. Many examples exist, including gastric acid inhibitors, statins, and angiotensin-receptor antagonists. Although a degree of competition is desirable, the development and aggressive marketing of patented me-too medicines may consume pharmaceutical budgets and divert resources and development efforts away from treatments for less common diseases. From a societal point of view, whether the incremental benefit from me-too medicines is worth the cost of development is questionable.

Generic medicines

Generic or multisource medicines are not under patent and can be produced using the same compounds found in the originator product using either the same or a different process. Multisource pharmaceutical products are pharmaceutically equivalent products that may or may not be therapeutically equivalent; products may not be therapeutically equivalent because differences in the excipients or the manufacturing process can lead to differences in product performance.

Because patents are country specific, some countries can produce generic medicines using compounds that are still protected by patents in other countries. Where patents operate, generic medicines are allowed to enter the market only when the patent expires. Under special circumstances, such as a public health emergency, countries are allowed to manufacture patented medicines under compulsory licenses, which are sanctioned by the World Trade Organization's Agreement on Trade-Related Aspects of Intellectual Property Rights. Producers may also enter into voluntary licensing agreements with local companies. (See Chapter 3.) Some countries in sub-Saharan Africa are using voluntary licenses to manufacture antiretroviral medicines to improve access to inexpensive treatment for HIV/AIDS.

In general, the absence of patent protection lowers the barrier to entry into the market because generic companies do not have to bear the high costs of research and development (R&D), including rigorous clinical trials to prove safety and efficacy of the medicine. Reduced R&D costs enable multiple companies to enter the market, resulting in a high level of competition. However, the expiration of patents does not mean that barriers to market entry disappear. As noted, the originator company develops significant marketing leverage while protected by the patent, which must be overcome by new generic medicines. Buyers may not always be aware of the availability of lower-priced generic medicines, they may be persuaded by promotional efforts not to change medicine

Figure 9-2   The effect of generic competition on the prices of antiretrovirals in Brazil

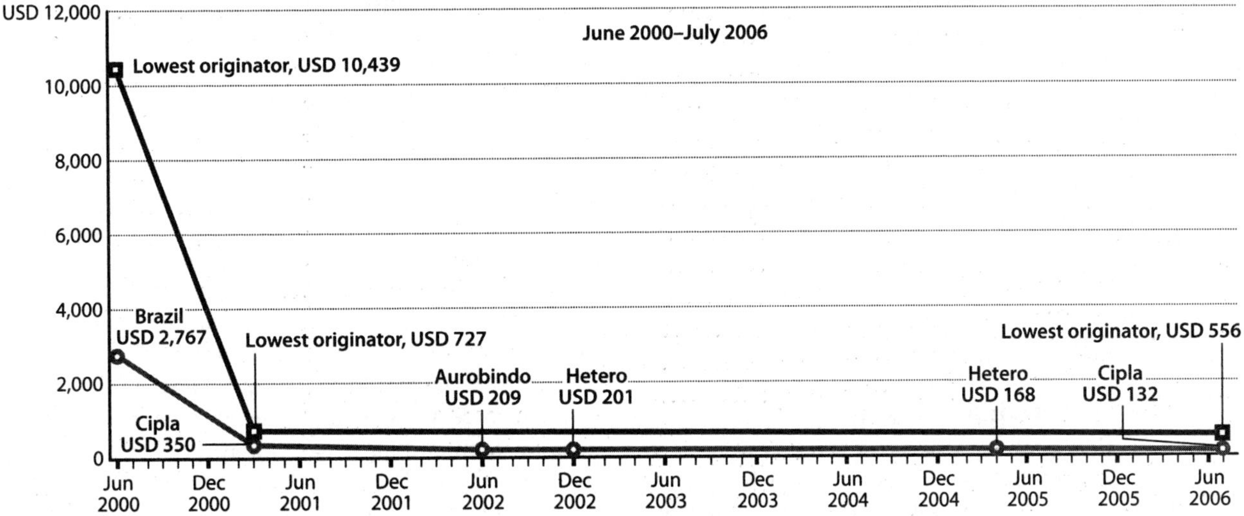

Source: MSF 2006.
USD = U.S. dollars.

brands, or they may view the generic product as inferior or of poor quality. For example, Malaysian buyers appear to prefer higher-priced branded medicines to cheaper generics (Babar et al. 2005).

Although the absence of patent protection can encourage the entry of generic medicines, strict regulation of medicine prices has been associated with a lower penetration of generic medicines into the market, because reduced profitability keeps generic firms from covering the costs of market entry. In countries with relatively little price regulation, such as Germany and the United States, generics have a greater market share than in the more heavily regulated markets of Australia (Lofgren 2004), France (Königbauer 2006), and Italy.

The entry of generics can be delayed for other reasons. Patent holders use a number of techniques to extend their period of market exclusivity, including making legal challenges to generic manufacturers trying to enter the market and developing minor variations in product characteristics that are sufficient to generate a new patent (known as *evergreening*). Another approach is for governments to grant data exclusivity rights to the manufacturers who introduced the pharmaceutical product. Such rights prevent pharmaceutical regulators from using the originator's data to make registration decisions about generic equivalents for a defined period (such as five years), thereby slowing the introduction of generic competition. Increasingly, such provisions are being guaranteed as part of bilateral trade agreements. Chapter 3 covers these issues in more depth.

The process of allowing generic medicines onto the market differs among countries. The United States passed a law designed to allow faster entry of generic medicines when patents expire. However, it also provides a significant penalty if generic companies enter the market too early. In Europe, the entry of generics was made easier by forgoing the requirement of trials demonstrating safety and efficacy as long as the generic medicine is the bioequivalent of the originator and the originator is sold in the same market. Some patent-holding companies responded by removing the patented medicines from the market before the entry of the generic and then releasing a modified form of the original drug. This strategy effectively prevents generics from claiming bioequivalence of an existing medicine sold in the European market, thereby delaying entry of the generic product (Australian Productivity Commission 2001).

In general, introducing generic competition is the most effective way to lower medicine prices. The effect is not only because of the lower-priced generic products but also because originator companies often respond by lowering prices of their patented products. This effect has been very evident in the pricing trend of antiretroviral medicines for HIV/AIDS. According to Médecins Sans Frontières (MSF 2006), in 2000, when Brazil first introduced a generic antiretroviral medicine, the lowest originator price to treat one patient for a year was 10,439 U.S. dollars (USD). By July 2006, the generic version of the same drug cost USD 132, while the lowest price branded version cost USD 556 (see Figure 9-2). However, for increased competition to result in lower prices, purchasers must be informed about their medicine choices.

Branded off-patent medicines

A complicating issue in the generic market is when well-known branded medicines go off patent and the originator company produces generic versions of its own products and retains the brand names that are recognizable through extensive marketing campaigns. Apparently, when the brand-name generic has a larger share of the generic market, the brand-name medicine will be more expensive; in addition, a higher market share held by the brand-name generic will result in higher generic medicine prices—among all companies (Hollis 2005). The market entry of brand-name generic medicines, if combined with a large market share for the manufacturer, will prevent prices falling to levels reached with more diverse competition. Therefore, by entering both branded and generic segments, large companies can exercise considerable market power.

9.4   Variable pricing for medicines

The literature unanimously concludes that medicine price differences exist between countries, even when the comparison is made between or within the strata of industrialized, middle-, and low-income countries. For example, price information compiled by WHO's Global Price Reporting Mechanism shows clear differences in prices paid by low- and middle-income countries for medicines treating HIV/AIDS. Importantly, low-income countries did not always obtain the lowest prices for medicines; as shown in Table 9-1, the 2009 cost of stavudine 30 mg in low-income countries was 37 percent more than the price paid in middle-income countries.

Price variation within countries is more likely in less price-regulated markets, such as the United States; however, prices vary in other countries, where public, private, and nongovernmental (not-for-profit) sectors procure medicines separately. An example is South Africa, where the public sector achieves low prices through tendering; in contrast, medical insurance funds and individuals paying out of pocket typically pay higher prices, although government legislation has been introduced that aims to control medicine prices in the private sector.

Variable prices for medicines within and between countries often result from one of the following—

- The pharmaceutical manufacturer sells the same product for different prices.
- The margins charged in the postmanufacturing supply chain by wholesalers, distributors, and pharmacists, as well as taxes, duties, and co-payments levied by the state, differ intra- and intercountry.

Differential pricing by the pharmaceutical company

Price differentiation (also known as tiered pricing) occurs when a firm sells the same product at a different price to different groups of people. It is known as *equity pricing* when the intention is to improve the affordability of medicines in low-income settings. The groups of people could be populations in different countries or subpopulations within a single country. From the buyer's perspective, tiered pricing may appear to be a form of market failure, particularly for those who pay the higher prices, but for the seller, it is another method of maximizing profits by ensuring each buyer group pays according to its willingness and ability to pay.

A seller can price differentiate if—

- It has monopoly rights over the product.
- Willingness and ability to pay are different among groups of buyers (varying price elasticities).
- Buyers cannot trade the item among themselves. That is, buyers who negotiate a low price do not resell the item, thereby undercutting the seller in markets that are able and willing to pay a higher price (Wagner and McCarthy 2004).
- An agreement exists to achieve more equitable access to essential medicines through differential pricing for needy populations. Examples of such agreements exist for medicines for HIV/AIDS, some vaccines, insulin, oral contraceptives, and some antimalarial medicines.

A common misperception is that the price paid by consumers reflects the cost of production plus a margin. In reality, manufacturers want to charge the highest price that the consumer will pay to maximize profits. Therefore, in terms of upward movements in price, the price paid by the buyer need not have any relationship to the cost of production. Evidence confirms that the relationship between production costs and medicine price is tenuous (Loff and Heywood 2002). In Brazil, South Africa, and Thailand, pharmaceutical companies have responded to pressure from court actions, government interventions, and the introduction of generic medicines by significantly reducing their originator medicine prices, which suggests that little relationship exists between medicine prices and the cost of production.

Differential pricing caused by supply chain factors

The pathway from manufacturing, transporting, storing, and then distributing medicines to the patients who need them is complex. Margins and taxes charged along this supply path can add significantly to the final price of medicines. Therefore, a pharmaceutical pricing policy must acknowledge the potential for the supply chain to significantly reduce the affordability of essential medicines to consumers.

As an example, a pharmaceutical pricing study in Ghana (Sarley et al. 2003) showed that although government policy limited margins on pharmaceuticals in the public-sector supply chain to a cumulative 40 to 50 percent, the actual margins averaged 100 percent and in some cases exceeded 300 percent by the time the medicines got to the patients. High markups occurred throughout the supply chain, but

Table 9-1   Median price paid by low- and middle-income countries for selected first-line antiretroviral formulations, 2005 and 2009

Antiretroviral medicine	USD per patient per year, 2005		USD per patient per year, 2009	
	Low-income countries	Middle-income countries	Low-income countries	Middle-income countries[a]
Stavudine (d4Tt) 30–40[b] mg	58	44	30	19
Lamivudine (3TC) 150 mg	73	80	38	—
Zidovudine (ZDV) 300 mg	153	146	100	94
Nevirapine (NVP) 200 mg	102	102	42	43
Efavirenz (EFV) 600 mg	346	372	132	103
3TC/ZDV 150/300 mg	241	241	114	153
d4T/3TC/NVP 30–40[b]/150/200 mg	168	211	83	93

Sources: WHO/GPRM 2005; 2009.
Note: — = not available.
[a] Upper-middle income.
[b] WHO recommendation changed from 30 mg to 40 mg.

dispensing facilities reported pricing their products slightly below those in private local pharmacies—no matter what the margin increase—because they perceived that patients would pay at least this amount.

Developing pharmaceutical pricing policies requires more than just an understanding of the supply chain, although that is clearly a good start. Prices, margins, and taxes change over time, and even unintentional adjustments throughout the supply chain can enormously affect medicine affordability. For this reason, stages in the supply chain should be continually monitored, so that changes in costs can be assessed and, if needed, acted upon to remedy unacceptable increases.

A key report from the advocacy group Health Action International (HAI) and WHO (Levison 2006) describes pricing throughout the pharmaceutical supply chain—

Supply chain, stage 1: the price from the manufacturer.
Called the manufacturer's selling price, if the manufacturer is located in the same country as the buyer, no further costs are added at this stage. If the medicine is imported, the price from this stage is the manufacturer's selling price, plus freight and transit insurance. The determinants of the price negotiated between the buyer and the manufacturer will be—
- The level of competition applying to the medicine (whether it is single source or multisource)
- The quantity sought by the buyer
- The number of alternative buyers in the same country for the same medicine (a single buyer will have stronger purchasing power than multiple smaller buyers)
- Pricing regulations and controls
- The price negotiated with the manufacturer

Supply chain, stage 2: the landed price. These are the fees and charges required to deliver the medicine to the

wholesaler. Determinants of the price at this stage will be—
- The fees, charges, and profits levied by transporters, insurers, and warehouses
- The level of taxes levied by the state (for example, stamp duty; value-added tax, or VAT; and goods and services tax, or GST)
- Tariffs on imported medicines and ingredients for locally manufactured medicines

Supply chain, stage 3: the wholesale selling price. This price is the landed price plus the wholesaler's costs of storage, transport, insurance, and profit margin. The wholesaler could be a private (for-profit) operation; a public operation; or a not-for-profit, nongovernmental organization. Increasingly, wholesalers are being replaced by distributors who have a relationship with suppliers and work with lower margins because they do not own the stock.

Supply chain, stage 4: the retail selling price. This is the wholesaler's price plus all costs associated with transporting medicines to the retailer, including transit insurance. Retailers could be a private, for-profit operation, a public operation, or a nongovernmental organization. After delivery to the retailer, storage and stock insurance are required. The retailer also adds a profit margin and sometimes a professional dispensing fee. Sizable markups can occur in the retail stage, especially in the private sector and from dispensing doctors; a WHO study of thirty countries concluded that although pharmaceutical availability tended to be better in the private sector, it was also associated with higher medicine prices and therefore lower affordability (Gelders et al. 2006). Compared with international reference prices, private-sector prices were between three and one hundred times more.

Supply chain, stage 5: the dispensed selling price. The state can impose additional taxes such as VAT or GST on top of the retail price; such taxes are controllable by the government. A European study of nine countries showed that nations applying VAT or GST to medicines ultimately had higher medicine prices, even if they had comparatively lower wholesale prices (Martikainen et al. 2005). Other studies have shown that significant reductions in price are possible with the removal of these taxes. For example, estimates for Peru indicate that the removal of VAT on medicines would reduce prices by 18 percent (Ewen and Dey 2006).

Country Study 9-3 describes an analysis of supply chain markups in Malaysia.

9.5 Monitoring medicine prices by performing price comparisons

Although the literature shows that price variation exists within and between countries (Wagner and McCarthy 2004; Scherer 2004; Waning et al. 2010), the methodology used for many of these comparisons has been criticized because of the difficulties in validating the results (Danzon 2004).

Challenges related to price comparisons

Comparing pharmaceutical prices between countries is complicated: The same medicine is often sold in different countries in different strengths, pack sizes, and with various modes of administration; in addition, any assessment must determine whether the product is being sold in the public or private health care system and account for differences in tariffs, taxes, and other markups. Comparability is even more of a problem if the assessment is based on a basket of medicines. For this reason, comparing individual medicines

that have high usage and limited ranges of doses and modes of administration may be better.

Selecting which price to use as the basis for comparison is critical. Should it be the price paid by the patient, the third-party insurer, or in the case of a state purchaser, the government? Some argue that the price paid by the consumer is the most important because it represents the patient's out-of-pocket expense (Wagner and McCarthy 2004). The advantage of using this payment is that it includes all of the add-on costs after manufacture, such as margins paid to wholesalers, distributors, and pharmacists. The final price paid by the consumer can be more than doubled by the additional costs encountered in the postmanufacturing supply chain (Ewen and Dey 2006). Moreover, understanding the components of the final price identifies potential targets for price reductions. However, a disadvantage of relying solely on price as a measure of affordability is that a low price for a medicine in a low-income country does not make it affordable. Sometimes, a further measure is required, such as the number of days the country's lowest paid worker must work to pay for the medicine. This is one of the measures used in studies conducted by HAI and WHO.

Determining which price to use for comparison will ultimately depend on the intended use of the analysis. In many comparisons, the manufacturer's or wholesaler's price is the basis for measurement, and this can be a useful tool to improve procurement practices. The common resource for international reference prices is the *International Drug Price Indicator Guide*, which provides an indication of pharmaceutical prices on the international market. The guide includes actual prices paid by government agencies, pharmaceutical suppliers, and international development organizations for almost a thousand pharmaceuticals (see Box 9-2). The Global Fund requires principal recipients to submit

---

Box 9-2
International Drug Price Indicator Guide

Produced in collaboration with the WHO, Management Sciences for Health's *International Drug Price Indicator Guide* provides an indication of pharmaceutical prices on the international market. Updated annually, the guide contains a spectrum of prices from pharmaceutical suppliers, international development organizations, and government agencies. The 2008 edition has more than 1,100 items and prices from 30 sources.

Lower prices can be obtained through bulk purchasing, competition, skillful price negotiations, and sound supply management. The guide makes price information more widely available to improve procurement of medicines of assured quality for the lowest possible price.

Readers can use the guide to—

- Locate new supply sources
- Assess the efficiency of their procurement systems
- Determine the probable cost of pharmaceutical products for their programs
- Compare current prices paid to those available on the international market
- Assess the potential financial impact of changes to a medicine list
- Support rational drug use education

The *International Drug Price Indicator Guide* can be accessed at http://erc.msh.org/priceguide.

Country Study 9-3
Examples of supply chain markups: Malaysia

A price survey in Malaysia using the WHO/HAI methodology compared median price ratios of medicines distributed in the private and public sectors with international reference prices. Despite the expectation that the prices of medicines in the public sector would be relatively low, in some cases, public-sector prices were higher than the international reference price. The study also found that the postmanufacture margins charged in the supply chain were significantly driving prices upward in both the public and private sectors. The authors concluded that the lack of a coherent government policy to regulate medicine prices allowed excessive profits and reduced medicine affordability.

The survey also found substantial price differences within the private sector between dispensing doctors and pharmacies. Compared with pharmacies, brand-name medicines tended to be cheaper when purchased from a dispensing doctor, but generic medicines were more expensive. Overall, the study found that dispensing doctors had excessive profit margins, particularly on some lower-priced generic medicines. This finding has been consistent in the literature: dispensing doctors, who benefit financially from the consultation and the prescription, have perverse incentives to prescribe expensive medicines and then charge a higher margin on these products. Because patients have little information about medicines, they have little recourse about taking the doctor's advice about the choice of treatment. This asymmetry of knowledge supports the argument that without regulation, doctors should not be allowed to sell the medicines that they prescribe to their patients.

The following table illustrates the percentage of markups encountered after medicine was purchased from the manufacturer for the public sector and for retail pharmacies and dispensing doctors in the private sector. Overall, the data confirm an expectation that public-sector prices tend to be lower than those offered by the private sector. Yet the supply chain analysis highlights several critical points where application of taxes, charges, and margins causes medicine prices to increase dramatically.

Percentage supply chain markups for generic and branded atenolol in the public and private sectors

Supply chain stage	Generic	Branded
Public sector		
Stage 1 MSP + insurance and transport	Price paid in stage 1 = MYR 7.78	Price paid in stage 1 = MYR 33.63
Stage 2 Customs and port charges	+ 22.2%	+ 5.6%
Stage 3 Distributor wholesale markup	+ 20.0%	+ 20.0%
Stage 4 Retailer or dispensing doctor markup	NA	NA
Stage 5 Other charges	NA	NA
Total markup over stage 1 price	**46.5%**	**26.7%**
Private sector: retail pharmacies		
Stage 1 MSP + insurance and transport	Stage 1 price = MYR 9.62	Stage 1 price = MYR 40.05
Stage 2 Customs and port charges	+ 17.9%	+ 20.4%
Stage 3 Distributor wholesale markup	+ 5.8%	+ 19.1%
Stage 4 Retailer or dispensing doctor markup	+ 100.0%	+ 25.4%
Stage 5 Other charges	NA	NA
Total markup over manufacturer's price	**149.5%**	**79.8%**
Private sector: dispensing doctor		
Stage 1 MSP + insurance and transport	Stage 1 price = MYR 9.58	Stage 1 price = MYR 41.17
Stage 2 Customs and port charges	+ 18.0%	+ 18.0%
Stage 3 Distributor wholesale markup	+ 15.0%	+ 11.1%
Stage 4 Retailer or dispensing doctor markup	+ 146.2%	+ 76.0%
Stage 5 Other charges	NA	NA
Total markup over stage 1 price	**234.0%**	**129.0%**

Sources: Babar et al. 2005; Gelders et al. 2006.
Note: MSP = manufacturer's sale price; MYR = Malaysian ringgit; NA = not applicable.

prices paid for medicines purchased with fund resources, which are made public. Other multinational resources for price comparisons include Médecins Sans Frontières' guide to antiretroviral prices in developing countries (http://utw. msfaccess.org) and WHO's Global Price Reporting Mechanism and website for medicine price information (http:// www.who.int/hiv/amds/gprm/en). A new resource focuses on prices and sources for children's medicines (UNICEF/ WHO 2010).

The WHO/HAI methodology for monitoring medicine prices

The goals of conducting a pricing survey include the ability to compare home-country prices with international reference prices, and to make intracountry price comparisons of medicines provided by different sectors, such as the government, nongovernmental organizations, and private facilities. The WHO/HAI methodology for comparing medicine prices (outlined in WHO/HAI 2008a) is based on simple techniques that have been field-tested and validated in many countries (see Country Study 9-4 for some examples). The methodology is available to governments, nongovernmental organizations, and researchers and is designed to facilitate intra- and intercountry comparisons of medicine prices and ultimately to identify which sector delivers the best medicine prices to patients. Documentation in English is freely available from http://www.haiweb.org/medicineprices. Documentation in French, Russian, and Spanish is also available on the HAI website.

Selecting locations. The first location of the survey's sample is the major central urban center—usually the capital city. In addition, three other locations are randomly selected from a list of all areas that can be reached in one day of travel from the urban center. In each location, at least five public health centers are sampled, including the main public hospital. Five private-sector pharmacies are also included based on their proximity to the public health centers. If the country has private nongovernmental organizations or dispensing doctors that provide medicines to patients, five from each category are selected using the same methodology.

Selecting medicines. The surveyors collect price data at each facility for a list of core and supplementary medicines. WHO identifies the core medicines based on the global burden of disease, medicine availability and importance, and patent status. Supplementary medicines are selected based on the health issues in the survey country. To prevent the collected data from being distorted by medicines that might be counterfeit or of poor quality, the methodology stipulates the sampling of only registered medicines or those with market authorization.

Categorizing medicines. Price data are categorized by the innovator brand (which is or was under patent), the highest-volume generic sold, and the lowest-priced generic.

A generic drug can fall into both the highest-volume and the lowest-priced medicine categories. The brand name of the innovator product may vary by country, but unless licensed, generic equivalents cannot be labeled with brand names; for example, Valium is the name of the innovator product, and although generic medicines cannot use this name, they may use their own brand name or the nonproprietary name of the active ingredient, diazepam.

In countries where a medicine is under patent, only the innovator brand should be available. Exceptions might occur, for example, when the innovator brand is produced under license or where the country allows the sale of equivalent generics. If a patent is not in force, multiple generic equivalents for the innovator may be available. The WHO/ HAI methodology defines generic medicines as those intended to be the equivalent of the innovator brand and that are produced after the expiration of patents or other exclusivity periods. The definition implies that the same active ingredient is used in the generic and the innovator. Medicines cannot be categorized as generic if they are produced under license to the innovator.

Analyzing price data. Prices are ultimately presented as a ratio of the median price in the surveyed country to the international reference price, provided by Management Sciences for Health's *International Drug Price Indicator Guide*. The ratio is called the median price ratio. To simplify data entry and analysis, WHO/HAI provide a computer program that facilitates data entry and automatically provides the outcomes from analysis. Apart from information on prices, the analysis reports on the availability, affordability, and components of medicine prices, which are the charges and markups that contribute to the final price. The methodology also provides instructions on presenting results so the findings can be effectively disseminated.

9.6 Obtaining value in pharmaceutical markets: buyer strategies

As mentioned in Section 9.1, the determination of price is related to factors influencing both supply and demand. Supply-side strategies target the seller and ensure the lowest possible medicine price is paid by the patient. The following strategies focus on the supply side with emphasis on pharmaceutical manufacturers and the pharmaceutical supply chain.

Demand-side strategies focus on the use of medicines: Are medicines being prescribed appropriately? Are generic medicines being substituted for more expensive brand-name products? Has promotion and advertising created patient demand that exceeds clinical demand? Demand-side questions are equally as important to medicine pricing as the supply-side pricing issues, but they are the topic of other chapters. Nevertheless, the development of a compre-

Country Study 9-4
Measuring medicine value: WHO/HAI survey methodology to compare prices and affordability in multiple countries

Price surveys using the WHO/HAI methodology have been undertaken in several countries, including China, India, Kuwait, Malaysia, the Philippines, Tajikistan, and Thailand. The surveys determined comparative prices in these countries and identified medicine prices that were different from the international reference price and by how much. Rather than using actual currency units for comparing prices, the surveys used ratios that identified the relative price in the target country compared with an international reference price.

Within each country, the surveys also compared prices in the public and private sectors, which facilitated policy recommendations, such as encouraging the use of generic medicines, increasing private-sector competition when only small price differences existed between innovator brands and equivalent generics, or reducing price markups in the supply chain.

Examples of medicine price survey findings for China's Shandong Province, Kuwait, the Philippines, Tajikistan, and Thailand follow.

Shandong Province, China

- In the private sector, innovator brands were 14 times more expensive than lowest priced generics.
- In the public sector, the difference was 4 times more than the lowest priced generics.
- Comparing public-sector procurement prices and public-sector patient prices for core medicines revealed that patients paid an additional 75 percent of the procurement price for generics and 22 percent for innovator brands.

Kuwait

- Private-sector procurement prices of medicines were 18.3 (innovator brands), 16.1 (most popular generic), and 15.9 (lowest priced generic) times the international reference price.
- Public-sector prices for innovator brands were 5

times the international reference prices and generic equivalents were 1.2 times the international reference prices.

Philippines

- Generic products markups ranged up to 355 percent at the retail level and 117 percent at the distributor level.
- VAT significantly increases the price of medicines in the country.

Tajikistan

In the private sector—

- Some innovator brands were 43 times the international reference price.
- The most popular generic equivalent and the lowest priced generic equivalent were 2.3 times the international reference price.

In the public sector—

- Prices tended to be slightly higher than those in the private sector: innovator brands in the public sector were 49 times the international reference price.
- The most popular generic equivalent and the lowest priced generic equivalent were 2.3 and 2.4 times the international reference price, respectively.
- The "brand premium" innovator product price was up to 20 times the price of the generic.

Thailand

- Public sector prices were higher than the international reference price: 32 percent for innovator brands and 75 percent for generics.
- In the private sector, patients paid 3.9 times more overall for originator brands than for the lowest price generics.

Sources: Ball et al. 2005; Drug Information Center Project ZdravPlus/ USAID 2005; Qiang 2005; WHO/HAI 2006, 2008c.

hensive policy to contain the cost of medicines should consider strategies that correct distortions in both supply and demand as well as the government's role.

Assess the circumstances

The buyer strategies outlined below are used in different countries, with varying degrees of success. Any strategy used on its own is unlikely to provide the best possible outcomes for reducing medicine prices. The best possible outcomes will require an assessment of which buying technique best suits the circumstances for each purchase of medicines and a clear understanding of the buyer's own position in the marketplace.

Examples of issues a buyer should address in an assessment include—

- The ability to join with others to purchase medicines (pooled procurement). Are cultural or political barriers preventing buyers from joining forces? Can these differences be resolved? Saving money can be a powerful motivator for tolerance.
- Whether the buyer is in the public or private sector and whether the buyer can influence government policy. For example, a public-sector buyer may be able to influence government policy to mandate the use of reference or differential pricing.
- The type and volume of medicine being purchased. Although the least powerful market position will be associated with buying single-source essential medicines compared to nonessential and multisource medicines, some large buyers have successfully negotiated price discounts on patented, single-source medicines. Successful negotiations can result from the size and certainty of the order and the effect on reducing the seller's risk (see maximizing buying power below). The seller's risk is reduced when the purchaser makes reliable payments.
- Whether the purchasing group has access to good advice on efficacy and cost-effectiveness of medicines in the country. A careful, independent assessment of the comparative performance of a new medicine can be a powerful tool when negotiating with a manufacturer or supplier.

Monitor prices

Knowing what prices other buyers paid for medicines helps buyers evaluate the value of their own medicine purchases. Although comparing medicine prices is not a straightforward task, without knowing what a medicine really costs to produce, comparing prices paid by other buyers is the next best measure. In addition, ongoing price monitoring is preferable to a one-time comparison, because markets continually change, and new products, new clinical data, or new treatments can mean that medicines that are a good value today can be overpriced tomorrow.

Analyze pharmaco-economics

Pharmaco-economic techniques, such as cost-effectiveness, cost-benefit, and cost-utility analysis, are of value to some pharmaceutical and health commodity buyers, but are labor intensive. The analyses do not set prices but assess the costs and outcomes from using certain medicines. The evaluator must decide whether the medicine or commodity represents good value at the price offered and then use this information in price negotiations. Pharmaco-economic and related medicine expenditure analyses, such as ABC and VEN (vital-essential-nonessential), are described in Chapters 10 and 40.

Maximize buying power

As identified in Figure 9-1, market power for sellers increases as the spectrum moves from a competitive market to an oligopoly and monopoly. Buyers can exert corresponding buying power as oligopsonies and monopsonies; therefore, buyers that pool their procurement can potentially lower prices by providing the seller more stable levels of demand, certainty of payment, and lower administrative costs compared with selling to multiple small buyers. In addition, the development of medicine insurance schemes that cover many members (such as the Australian PBS) and the use of a common formulary help shift the purchaser's buying power to this stronger market position.

Examples of organizations that combine buying power include the International Dispensary Association Foundation and the Clinton Health Access Initiative. For example, the Clinton initiative reports price reductions for antiretroviral medicines of 50 percent for first-line treatments and 90 percent for pediatric formulations (Clinton Health Access Initiative 2010).

Negotiate prices

Price negotiation models apply to large public- and private-sector buyers that have some degree of buying power. Examples are government programs purchasing medicines on behalf of the public and third-party payers, such as private health insurers. Formularies can be used as a bargaining tool (for example, lower prices exchanged for including more of a single pharmaceutical company's medicines on the formulary) and as a list used by prescribers to select the lowest-priced medicine available within a therapeutic class. Clearly, the formulary must include generics. The strength of these negotiation models might diminish when dealing with essential, single-source medicines, because there are no alternatives to negotiate.

Techniques used for price negotiations include—

Tendering, where the buyer issues a tender seeking price offers from different pharmaceutical suppliers. An initiative to introduce joint tendering in El Salvador resulted in lower medicine prices (SEAM 2007). Through improved tendering and other practices, New Zealand's Pharmaceutical Management Agency has saved; for example, the price of generic medicines in New Zealand is estimated at less than a quarter of the price of those in Canada (Cumming et al. 2010). However, supplier performance must be monitored to ensure the quality and reliability of supply. (See also Chapter 21.)

Package agreements, which comprise contracts negotiated for multiple products from one company. These arrangements can entail rebates on the entire package or large discounts on out-of-patent medicines in return for purchasing full-price patented medicines. These agreements tend to work best when a credible alternative is available, such as another supplier from which the package could be purchased (McNee 2006). Package agreements that include hidden discounts are attractive to the purchaser because of the immediate cost savings; however, the true price of the medicine is hidden from the consumer making the final purchase. Such arrangements are open to abuse (including fraud), and they may hamper attempts to create a uniform pricing structure for a pharmaceutical class or to introduce genuine competition, if key information is hidden from other suppliers.

Price/volume agreements, which work when uncertainty exists about the level of demand for a medicine. Under these agreements, when a certain threshold volume is reached, the manufacturer's price falls. This threshold can be determined by population and economic modeling. For example, a medicine may appear to be a cost-effective treatment at a certain price for individuals with a severe form of a disease but be cost-ineffective when used to treat less severe cases. The estimated number of individuals with severe disease represents a threshold volume of use above which the price automatically falls to a level where the medicine is considered cost-effective for less severe cases. Australia uses this technique to maintain the cost-effective use of medicines and protect against unintended use that can be encouraged by excessive promotion of medicines (Sansom 2004).

Rebates, which are payments that the pharmaceutical manufacturers make to the buyer. Rebates can, for example, be related to sales volumes, so that when a certain volume is reached, the manufacturer provides a rebate to the buyer. Rebates are sometimes required by legislation, usually for public-sector buyers, or included in private-sector contracts with the pharmaceutical company. As is the case with discounting, such arrangements should be completely transparent.

9.7 Government intervention in the pharmaceutical market

Government intervention in pricing is a controversial topic because market economists feel strongly that the market should be left to its own devices. However, as noted previously, market failure is common in the pharmaceutical sector. In theory, the market can efficiently determine prices for many goods and services. However, the price of medications can determine quality of life or when or if people die. In reality, an uncontrolled market can lead to the most vulnerable people paying the most for medicines—if they can afford them at all. In general, and particularly for single- or limited-source medicines, an unregulated medicine market is unlikely to provide acceptable outcomes in terms of achieving public health equity.

More general government intervention in pharmaceutical markets should include the establishment of an essential medicines list and the development of policies that encourage the purchase of low-priced, quality generic medicines. The government should encourage the entry of generic products into the market, even if legislative changes are required to streamline the registration process for these medicines. If generic competition is weak or nonexistent, as in the case of an innovator brand that is still under patent, governments can consider regulating prices or requiring compulsory licenses (Gelders et al. 2006).

Some countries favor minimal regulation of pharmaceutical pricing, allowing suppliers, health sectors, and patients to determine an equilibrium. Most industrialized countries favor more intervention, with governments either subsidizing medicines or providing them free to their citizens (Henry and Lexchin 2002). Other forms of governmental interventions include price controls or limits on pharmaceutical profitability. For example, several countries of the Organisation for Economic Co-operation and Development require manufacturers to limit prices in exchange for receiving subsidies through country reimbursement schemes, which can cover a large percentage of the population (OECD 2008).

Countries that intervene take the view that providing affordable medicines is too important to be left to the market—that medicines are more than just consumables to be traded for the highest possible price. However, instituting price-control regulations takes substantial political will and can produce unexpected consequences; for example, some claim that price control of medicines in the Philippines is thwarting the market for generics (Hookway 2010).

The arguments against government interventions tend to focus on the potential negative effect on R&D of new pharmaceutical products. Most notably, regulations that restrict market-determined prices reduce profitability, which, in turn, can restrict research into new and innovative medicines. Several studies have shown that regulation of medicine prices, differential pricing of medicines, and profitability of pharmaceutical companies are associated with the level of R&D undertaken by a pharmaceutical firm (Danzon and Towse 2003; Scherer 2001; Vernon 2005). However, these findings do not suggest that, in the absence of price controls, R&D will increase for medicines for neglected diseases that affect health in the developing world. Profitable medicine lines are those that sell in large volumes in industrialized nations, which can afford to pay more.

The ethical question is whether medicine prices should be the main determinant of pharmaceutical R&D. Incentives other than high medicine prices that are used to encourage R&D include tax concessions and public grants. These incentives are discussed in Chapter 3 on intellectual property and access to medicines.

Government-imposed price controls can be used at different points in the supply chain, but probably the two most important broad stages can be defined as prices from the manufacturer and prices in the supply chain. Methods identified by the WHO that governments can use to influence the manufacturer's price (Dukes et al. 2003) are discussed in the following sections.

Price controls on the manufacturer

These price controls usually take the form of governments restricting medicine prices to the cost of production plus a profit margin (also called cost-plus pricing). However, accurate cost information from the manufacturer is difficult to obtain. The information might be more readily available from local manufacturers without production units in other countries, but the listing of R&D in the cost structure is likely to be controversial and almost impossible to obtain from multinational organizations.

As an example, under the United Kingdom's Pharmaceutical Price Regulation Scheme, the government has the right to refuse a pharmaceutical company's application to increase the prices of existing medicines. In addition, the government can (and has) demanded price reductions for medicines purchased by its National Health Service (ABPI and DOH 2009).

Profit controls on the manufacturer

Although profit controls are not widely used internationally, the United Kingdom caps the profits pharmaceutical companies can earn from sales to the National Health Service (ABPI and DOH 2009). Within this cap, companies are allowed to price freely. From a single country's perspective, multinational operations still have the ability to shift costs throughout their operations, leaving the reported profitability subject to a degree of manipulation. Profit controls in the United Kingdom have been criticized for being open to manipulation and having an allowable profit level that is set too high (Earl-Slater 1997).

Reference pricing and brand premiums

Reference pricing allocates a medicine to a therapeutic group of medicines that are considered equivalent on the basis of safety, efficacy, and outcome. Prices of all medicines in the group are tied to that of the lowest—or in some cases, the average—price. The reference price does not necessarily become the market price for all medicines in the same therapeutic class, but rather a benchmark price. Manufacturers can set prices higher than the reference, but in doing so, they need to compete against equivalent, lower-priced

medicines. Although typically a government intervention, large, private-sector buyers use it as well.

Brand premiums are often used in conjunction with reference pricing. They are used when a third party, such as an insurance company or the government, pays for medicines to which patients contribute a co-payment. The brand premium operates by reimbursing all medicines in a therapeutic class up to a certain amount—where the reimbursement is determined by the price of the least expensive generic (or an average of all medicines in the class). Patients pay the smallest co-payment if they purchase the medicine priced at the reference price, but if the patient buys a higher-priced medicine (say a branded generic), the patient pays the co-payment plus the difference between the reference price and the selected medicine's price (Sansom 2004). The two advantages of this technique are that price competition between supplying pharmaceutical companies is encouraged and patients have an incentive to switch to lower-priced medicines.

Comparative pricing controls (international benchmarking)

This technique compares the prices in one country with those in reference countries. The government limits price increases of existing medicines to the average increase recorded in a set of reference countries, and new medicines are priced at the average (or lowest) of the reference countries. The difficulties with comparative pricing are the same issues encountered when comparing prices in different countries. Strengths, pack sizes, and active ingredients tend to differ among countries, and unit prices are lowest when products are purchased in bulk. Additionally, the point in the supply chain at which the price is compared (manufacturer, wholesaler, retailer, patient) introduces further intercountry differences in terms of margins and taxes.

A given product may have several selling prices (public-tender price, private-sector uninsured price, etc.), so one has to be selected for the comparison. Choosing benchmark countries can also be difficult; for example, including countries at a similar stage of economic development may seem sensible, but such countries may not have an effective system for setting prices. Nevertheless, the Netherlands, Portugal, and Romania all use international benchmarking, and the Netherlands reported an average 20 percent decrease in the cost of pharmaceuticals when it introduced the comparative pricing technique in 1996 (Dukes et al. 2003).

Eliminating tariffs and taxes

As mentioned, sizable price increases can occur throughout the supply chain, some of which are imposed by governments in the form of taxes and tariffs. WHO estimates that high tariff structures in selected low-income countries increase the price of medicinal ingredients by 23 percent and the price of finished medicines by over 12 percent (WHO 2004). Although tariffs and taxes provide the opportunity for raising state revenue, their effect on medicines is to reduce affordability and substantially erode public health objectives. Sometimes the argument for tariffs is to protect emerging local industries until they become established; nonetheless, the effect on medicine affordability is the same. In terms of pricing policy, governments must minimize unnecessary add-on costs and should not impose revenue-raising charges on essential items such as medicines (Global Health Council 2007).

In addition to introducing price control measures and eliminating taxes and tariffs on pharmaceuticals, WHO has identified the following methods by which governments can influence medicine prices by controlling the margins charged by the retail pharmacy, and in some countries, by dispensing doctors (Dukes et al. 2003).

Fixed margins

These margins are a fixed percentage of the wholesale price. Commonly used in the United States and Europe, fixed margins tend to average about 30 percent of the wholesale price. Problems include the tendency for pharmacists to negotiate rebates and other discounts directly with the wholesaler that do not get passed on to the consumer. In some countries (for example, Denmark), these discounts are illegal (Dukes et al. 2003).

Digressive markups

These margins are a shifting percentage of wholesale prices: lower-priced medicines have a proportionally larger margin than more expensive medicines. This system tries to encourage the dispensing of less expensive medicines by using the pharmacist's profit-maximizing behavior as a driver.

Capitation systems

The pharmacist is reimbursed with a fixed sum based on the number of patients per year or a fixed fee per prescription. The system's goal is to keep pharmacists from benefiting from either the price or volume of medicines dispensed, but the system is open to manipulation if the pharmacist continues to add a margin on to the wholesale price.

9.8 Influence of globalization on pharmaceutical prices

As noted previously, the international system to protect intellectual property rights tends to keep the prices of patented medicines high. Countries can take some actions to lower the cost of medicines under the World Trade Organization's Agreement on Trade-Related Aspects of International Property Rights (see Chapter 3). For example, compulsory licenses can be used in national emergencies or when a country needs a supply of a medicine for government use. If the required medicine is under patent, the patent may be broken to allow the medicine to be locally manufactured. If the country does not have the capacity to manufacture the medicine, it can be imported from another country where it is not already protected by patent. The granting of the license requires that the patent holder be paid a "reasonable" fee. Compulsory licensing is not an option that is available only to low-income countries. During an anthrax emergency in 2001, the U.S. government considered invoking this right to bring down the price of ciprofloxacin (Bradsher and Andrews 2001).

Parallel importation is common in the European Union, although it represents only about 2 percent of the European market (OECD 2008). A branded medicine may be sold relatively cheaply in one member state and then be imported into another country and sold below the usual domestic selling price. Such arrangements are attractive to the importing country, but parallel importation can undermine efforts to achieve equitable international pricing of essential medicines when manufacturers shy away from offering cheaper versions of their products in low-income countries for fear they will appear on the European market and undercut those prices. In addition, a study concluded that the bene-ttfit of parallel trade goes to the traders themselves, rather than to patients in the form of cheaper medicines and better access (Kanavos et al. 2004).

Voluntary price reductions offered by major pharmaceutical corporations (often under pressure from advocacy groups) have reduced the cost of antiretroviral therapy available in low-income countries dealing with HIV/AIDS epidemics. These pricing structures have resulted in significant price decreases but have not necessarily translated into improved access. Other factors, such as the inability of health systems to deliver medicines to those who need them, also hinder access. For example, despite the reduction in prices of antiretroviral medicines for HIV/AIDS, only an estimated 31 percent of the world's low- and middle-income populations living with HIV have access to treatment (WHO/UNAIDS/UNICEF 2009).

The Affordable Medicines Facility–malaria (AMFm) initiative is piloting a program to increase access to artemisinin-based combination therapies (ACTs) by paying a large proportion of the cost of ACTs to the manufacturers so the public and private sectors can buy the products at a greatly subsidized price (about USD 0.05 per treatment). The idea is that the subsidy will trickle down to the end user, resulting in a price reduction from about USD 6–10 per treatment to about USD 0.20–0.50. At that cost, ACTs would be cheaper than monotherapies, which would theoretically be crowded out of the market. Social marketing strategies have used similar approaches to increase the availability of products such as contraceptives and bed nets. Launched in 2010 by the Global Fund to Fight AIDS, Tuberculosis and Malaria, the AMFm will be independently evaluated in 2012 in the nine pilot countries.

9.9   Conclusion

The international and domestic systems that determine the selling prices of pharmaceutical products are extremely complex. Although covering all the issues in depth is difficult, one can draw a number of important conclusions—

- Patented medicine prices tend to be high, and a competitive market for generic products is the most important mechanism for ensuring the affordability of essential medicines.
- Governments can intervene effectively in the pharmaceutical market by becoming large purchasers on behalf of their communities and by regulating the different markups along the supply chain, which can greatly affect the costs to consumers. Governments can also eliminate or reduce taxes on important medicines. To encourage the supply of generic medicines, governments can work to minimize barriers to their entry into the market.
- Health insurance that covers a core list of essential medicines with minimal consumer co-payments can be a major force in improving access to essential medicines. An insurer can use purchasing power and other techniques that reduce medicine prices. Chapter 12 discusses different types of health insurance schemes.
- A number of mechanisms exist to control pharmaceutical prices, including tendering, generic substitution, reference pricing, international benchmarking, and pharmaco-economic analysis. No *one* mechanism will meet all of a country's needs, and the country must determine which mechanisms are best, based on assessing the context and monitoring it for change over time. Within a particular country, different methods may be appropriate for different market segments (for example, public versus private procurement).
- The total costs of medicines depend not only on selling prices but also on volumes of use. Unnecessary medicine use contributes to both costs and adverse clinical outcomes. The demand side of the pharmaceutical market is just as important as the supply side. ∎

References and further readings

ABPI and DOH (Association of the British Pharmaceutical Industry and Department of Health [UK]). 2009. *The 2009 Pharmaceutical Price Regulation Scheme.* London: DOH. <http://www.dh.gov.uk/en/Healthcare/Medicinespharmacyandindustry/Pharmaceuticalpriceregulationscheme/2009PPRS/index.htm>

Australian Government Department of Health and Ageing. 2010. "Pharmaceutical Benefits Scheme." <http://www.pbs.gov.au/html/home>

Australian Productivity Commission. 2001. *International Pharmaceutical Price Differences.* Research Report. Canberra: AusInfo. <http://www.pc.gov.au/_data/assets/pdf_file/0018/18153/pbsprices.pdf>

Babar, Z.-U.-D., M. I. M. Ibrahim, H. Singh, and N. I. Bukhari. 2005. *A Survey of Medicine Prices Availability, Affordability and Price Components in Malaysia Using the HAI/WHO Methodology.* Malaysia: University College Sedaya International and Universiti Sains Malaysian in collaboration with the World Health Organization and Health Action International. <http://www.haiweb.org/medicineprices/surveys/200410MY/survey_report.pdf>

Ball, D., K. Tisocki, and N. Al-Saffar. 2005. *Medicine Prices in the State of Kuwait: Report of a Survey on Medicine Prices in Kuwait.* Amsterdam: Health Action International Europe in collaboration with the World Health Organization, Kuwait University, and the Kuwait Ministry of Health. <http://www.haiweb.org/medicineprices/surveys/200406KW/survey_report.pdf>

Bannock, G., R. E. Baxter, and R. Rees. 1984. *The Penguin Dictionary of Economics.* 3rd ed. Middlesex: Penguin Books.

Bradsher, K., and E. L. Andrews. 2001. "U.S. Says Bayer Will Cut Cost of Its Anthrax Drug." *New York Times Business,* October 24.

Cameron, A., M. Ewen, D. Ross-Degnan, D. Ball, and R. Laing. 2009. Medicine Prices, Availability, and Affordability in 36 Developing and Middle-Income Countries: A Secondary Analysis. *Lancet* 373:240–9. <http://www.haiweb.org/medicineprices/news/31122008/MedPrices%20-%20Word2.pdf>

Clinton Health Access Initiative. 2010. "What We've Accomplished." <http://www.clintonfoundation.org/what-we-do/clinton-health-access-initiative/what-we-ve-accomplished>

Congressional Budget Office. 1998. *How Increased Competition from Generic Drugs has Affected Prices and Returns in the Pharmaceutical Industry.* Washington, D.C.: Congressional Budget Office. <http://www.cbo.gov/ftpdocs/6xx/doc655/pharm.pdf>

Cumming, J., N. Mays, and J. Daubé. 2010. How New Zealand Has Contained Expenditure on Drugs. *BMJ* 340: c2441.

Danzon, P. 2004. Price and Availability of Pharmaceuticals: Evidence from Nine Countries. *Health Affairs Web Exclusive* W3:521–36. <http://knowledge.wharton.upenn.edu/papers/1210.pdf>

Danzon, P. M., and A. Towse. 2003. Differential Pricing for Pharmaceuticals: Reconciling Access, R&D and Patents. *International Journal of Health Care Finance and Economics* 3:83–205.

Dougherty, R. H. 2004. "Behavioural Pharmacy Benefit Management: Case Studies." Hamilton, N.J.: Centre for Health Care Strategies, Inc.

Dukes, M. N. G., F. M. Haaijer-Ruskamp, C. P. de Joncheere, and A. H. Rietveld, eds. 2003. *Drugs and Money: Prices, Affordability and Cost Containment.* 7th ed. Amsterdam: IOS Press for World Health Organization Regional Office for Europe. <http://www.euro.who.int/document/e79122.pdf>

Dyer, O. 2006.Nine Company Chiefs Are Charged with Conspiracy to Defraud NHS. *BMJ* 332:872.

Earl-Slater, A. 1997. The Pharmaceutical Price Regulation Scheme. *Financial Accountability and Management* 13(1):35–54.

Ewen, M., and D. Dey. 2006. Medicines: Too Costly and Too Scarce. Briefing paper, World Health Organization and Health Action

ASSESSMENT GUIDE

- Describe the buyers and sellers in the pharmaceutical sector. Is there one dominant buyer? Does one dominant seller have negotiating power in the market?
- Does the government have a policy regarding the promotion of generic medicines?
- What is the regulatory process that allows generic medicines into the market?
- For the three categories of medicines in the market, patented, generic, and branded off-patent, what is their percentage of use by volume and value? Are prescribers and patients more likely to use generic products if they are available?
- Do any data exist showing the variation of medicine prices in the public, private, and nonprofit sectors? For innovator products and lowest price generics?
- How do pharmaceutical prices in public and private sectors compare to those in other countries or to international reference prices?
- What are the markups on medicines throughout the supply chain? Does the government regulate any of the markups? Does the government or other authorities impose markups in the form of tariffs or taxes?
- Have pharmaceutical buyers used any strategies to maximize their power in the market, such as monitoring prices, negotiating prices, or pooling procurement?
- Does the government impose price controls at the dispensing level, such as fixed margins or banning or regulating the practice of dispensing doctors?

International Project on Medicine Prices. <http://www.haiweb.org/medicineprices/2005/PricingbriefingpaperFINAL.doc>

Feldstein, P. J. 2004. *Health Care Economics.* 6th ed. Albany, N.Y.: Delmar Cenage Learning.

Ford, N. 2004. Patents, Access to Medicines and the Role of Non-Governmental Organisations. *Journal of Generic Medicines* 1(2):137–45.

Frank, R. G. 2001. Prescription Drug Prices: Why Do Some Pay More Than Others Do? *Health Affairs* 20(2):115–28.

Gelders, S., M. Ewen, N. Noguchi, and R. Laing. 2006. *Price, Availability and Affordability: An International Comparison of Chronic Disease Medicines.* WHO-EM/EDB/068/E. Cairo: World Health Organization Regional Office for the Eastern Mediterranean and Health Action International. <http://www.haiweb.org/medicineprices/08092008/EDB068final.pdf>

Global Health Council. 2007. *The Impact of Tariff and Non-Tariff Barriers on Access to Essential Drugs for the Poorest People. Policy Brief.* Washington, D.C.: Global Health Council. <http://apps.who.int/medicinedocs/documents/s16764e/s16764e.pdf>

Grace, C. 2003. *Equitable Pricing of Newer Essential Medicines for Developing Countries: Evidence for the Potential of Different Mechanisms.* London: London Business School. <http://apps.who.int/medicinedocs/en/m/abstract/Js18815en/>

Grossman, M. 1972. On the Concept of Health Capital and the Demand for Health. *Journal of Political Economy* 80(2):223–55.

Henry, D., and J. Lexchin. 2002. The Pharmaceutical Industry as a Medicines Provider. *Lancet* 360:1590–5.

Hollis, A. 2005. How Do Brands' "Own Generics" Affect Pharmaceutical Prices? *Review of Industrial Organization* 27:329–50.

Hookway, J. 2010. "Philippine Price Controls Hamper Rise of Generics." *Wall Street Journal,* June 18.

Jack, W. 1999. *Principles of Health Economics for Developing Countries.* World Bank Institute Development Studies. Washington, D.C.: World Bank.

Jackson, J., and C. R. McConnell. 1989. *Economics.* 3rd ed. New York: McGraw-Hill.

Johnson, D. 2001. Economic Issues in Health Policy. *Australian Economic Review* 34(3):295–311.

Kanavos, P., J. Costa-i-Font, S. Merkur, and M. Gemmill. 2004. *The Economic Impact of Pharmaceutical Parallel Trade in European Union Member State: A Stakeholder Analysis.* Special Research Paper,

LSE Health and Social Care. London: London School of Economics and Political Science. <http://archives.who.int/prioritymeds/report/append/829Paper.pdf>

Königbauer, I. 2006. Advertising, Generic Competition and Price Regulation in Pharmaceutical Markets. *CESifo Economic Studies* 52(3):565–86.

Levison, L. 2006. *Investigating Price Components: Medicine Costs between Procurement and Point of Delivery: Draft Report on Initial Country Field Studies.* Geneva: World Health Organization and Health Action International.

Loff, B., and M. Heywood. 2002. Patents on Drugs: Manufacturing Scarcity or Advancing Health. *Journal of Law, Medicine and Ethics* 30: 621–9.

Lofgren, H. 2004. Generic Drugs: International Trends and Policy Developments in Australia. *Australian Health Review* 27(1):39–48.

Martikainen, J., I. Kivi, and I. Linnosmaa. 2005. European Prices of newly Launched Reimbursable Pharmaceuticals—A Pilot Study. *Health Policy* 74(3):235-46.

McNee, W. 2006. *PHARMAC: National Formularies and Generic Pricing.* Paper presented at Toward a National Pharmaceuticals Strategy, February 9–10, Vancouver, Canada.

Mendis, S., K. Fukino, A. Cameron, R. Laing, A. Filipe Jr., O. Khatib, J. Leowski, and M. Ewen. 2007. The Availability and Affordability of Selected Essential Medicines for Chronic Diseases in Six Low- and Middle-Income Countries. *Bulletin of the World Health Organization* 85(4):279–88. <http://www.who.int/bulletin/volumes/85/4/06-033647.pdf>

MSF (Médecins Sans Frontières) Campaign for Access to Essential Medicines. 2006. *Untangling the Web of Antiretroviral Price Reductions.* 9th ed. Geneva: MSF. Updated regularly. Available at http://utw.msfaccess.org.

MSH/WHO (Management Sciences for Health/World Health Organization). Updated annually. *International Drug Price Indicator Guide.* Cambridge, Mass.: MSH. <http://erc.msh.org/priceguide>

OECD (Organisation for Economic Co-operation and Development). 2008. *Pharmaceutical Pricing Policies in a Global Market.* Paris: OECD. <http://www.oecd.org/document/44/0,3746,en_2649_37407_41382764_1_1_1,00.html>

Olcay, M. and R. Laing. 2005. *Pharmaceutical Tariffs: What is Their Effect on Prices, Protection of Local Industry and Revenue Generation?* Prepared for: The Commission on Intellectual Property

Rights, Innovation and Public Health, Geneva: World Health Organization. <http://www.who.int/intellectualproperty/studies/ TariffsOnEssentialMedicines.pdf>

Qiang, S. 2005. *A Survey of Medicine Prices, Availability, Affordability and Price Components in Shandong Province, China*. Geneva: World Health Organization and Health Action International. <http://www. haiweb.org/medicineprices/surveys/200411CN/survey_report. pdf>

Rice, T. 2002. *The Economics of Health Reconsidered*. 2nd ed. Chicago: Health Administration Press.

Sansom, L. 2004. The Subsidy of Pharmaceuticals in Australia: Process and Challenges. *Australian Health Review* 28(2):194–205.

Sarley, D., H. Abdallah, R. Rao, P. Gyimah, J. Azeez, and B. Garshong. 2003. *Ghana Pharmaceutical Pricing Study: Policy Analysis and Recommendations*. Arlington, Va.: John Snow, Inc./DELIVER, for the U.S. Agency for International Development. <http://www.who. int/hiv/amds/en/country2.pdf>

Scherer, F. M. 2001. The Link between Gross Profitability and Pharmaceutical R&D Spending. *Health Affairs* 20(5):216–20.

Scherer, F. M. 2004. The Pharmaceutical Industry—Prices and Progress. *New England Journal of Medicine* 351(9):927–32.

SEAM (Strategies for Enhancing Access to Medicines Program). 2007. *El Salvador: Improving Pharmaceutical Procurement*. Arlington, Va.: Management Sciences for Health. <http://www.msh.org/ seam/reports/SEAM_El_Salvador_Improving_Pharmaceutical_ Procurement.pdf>

Sweeny, K. 2007. *Key Aspects of the Australian Pharmaceutical Benefits Scheme*. Working Paper no. 35. Melbourne: Centre for Strategic Economic Studies. <http://www.cfses.com/documents/pharma/35-Key_aspects_of_PBS_Sweeny.pdf>

Tajikistan State Drug Information Center. 2005. *Medicine Prices in the Republic of Tajikistan: Survey Report*. Amsterdam: Health Action International, Project ZdravPlus/U.S. Agency for International Development, World Health Organization, and Tajikistan Ministry of Health. <http://www.haiweb.org/medicineprices/ surveys/200502TJ/survey_report.pdf>

UNICEF/WHO (United Nations Children's Fund/World Health Organization). 2010. *Sources and Prices of Selected Medicines for Children*. 2nd ed. New York and Geneva: UNICEF/WHO.

Vernon, J. 2005. Examining the Link between Price Regulation and Pharmaceutical R&D Investment. *Health Economics* 14(1):1–16.

Wagner, J. L., and E. McCarthy. 2004. International Differences in Drug Prices. *Annual Review of Public Health* 25:475–95.

Waning, B., W. Kaplan, M. P. Fox, M. Boyd-Boffa, A. C. King, D. A. Lawrence, L. Soucy, S. Mahajan, H. G. Leufkens, and M. Gokhale. 2010. Temporal Trends in Generic and Brand Prices of Antiretroviral Medicines Procured with Donor Funds in Developing Countries. *Journal of Generic Medicines* 7(2):159–75.

WHO (World Health Organization). 1993. *Evaluation of Recent Changes in the Financing of Health Services: Report of a WHO Study Group*. Who Technical Report Series no. 829. Geneva: WHO.

———. 2003. *Guidelines for Price Discounts of Single-Source Pharmaceuticals*. Geneva: WHO. <http://apps.who.int/medicine docs/pdf/s4884e/s4884e.pdf>

———. 2004. *The World Medicines Situation*. Geneva: WHO. <http:// www.searo.who.int/LinkFiles/Reports_World_Medicines_ Situation.pdf>

———. 2009. *Priority Interventions: HIV/AIDS Prevention, Treatment and Care in the Health Sector*. Geneva: WHO.

WHO/AFRO (World Health Organization Regional Office for Africa). 2007. *AFRO Essential Medicines Price Indicator*. Brazzaville, Congo: WHO/AFRO. <http://www.afro.who.int/index.php?option=com_ docman&task=doc_download&gid=904>

WHO/GPRM (World Health Organization/Global Price Reporting Mechanism). 2009. *Transaction Prices for Antiretroviral Medicines and HIV Diagnostics from 2008 to October 2009*. Geneva: WHO. <http://www.who.int/hiv/amds/GPRMsummaryReportNov2009. pdf>

———. 2005. *Global Price Reporting Mechanism for ARVs in Developing Countries: 1st Quarterly Summary Report, September 2005*. Geneva: WHO. <http://www.who.int/hiv/amds/gprm_quarterly report_0905.pdf>

WHO/HAI (World Health Organization/Health Action International). 2006. *Thailand: Medicine Prices, Availability, Affordability and Price Components*. Geneva: WHO and HAI. <http://www.haiweb.org/ medicineprices/surveys/200610TH/sdocs/Thailand-summary-report-FINAL.pdf>

———. 2008a. *Measuring Medicine Prices, Availability, Affordability and Price Components*. 2nd ed. Geneva: WHO and HAI. <http:// apps.who.int/medicinedocs/documents/s14868e/s14868e.pdf>

———. 2008b. *Medicine Prices, Availability, Affordability and Price Components: A Synthesis Report of Medicine Price Surveys Undertaken in Selected Countries of the WHO Eastern Mediterranean Region*. WHO-EM/EDB/089/E. Cairo: WHO. <http://www.emro. who.int/dsaf/dsa964.pdf>

———. 2008c. *Philippines: Components of Medicine Price*. Geneva: WHO/HAI. <http://www.haiweb.org/medicineprices/ surveys/200807PHC/sdocs/summary_survey_report.pdf>

WHO/UNAIDS/UNICEF (World Health Organization/Joint United Nations Programme on HIV/AIDS/United Nations Children's Fund). 2009. *Towards Universal Access: Scaling Up Priority HIV/ AIDS Interventions in the Health Sector*. Geneva: WHO. <http:// www.who.int/hiv/pub/tuapr_2009_en.pdf>

CHAPTER 10

Economics for pharmaceutical management

Summary   10.2

10.1 Economics as a tool for making choices   10.2

10.2 Some basic economic concepts   10.3

10.3 Economics of the public sector   10.4
Goals of public expenditure

10.4 Understanding the private sector   10.5
Markets and competition • Ethics and business

10.5 Government interaction with the private sector   10.7
Market failure • Types of government interventions • Challenges to government interventions

10.6 Efficiency concepts   10.9
Allocative efficiency • Technical efficiency

10.7 Economic evaluation of pharmaceutical products   10.10
Cost-minimization analysis • Cost-effectiveness analysis • Cost-utility analysis • Cost-benefit analysis • Steps for conducting a cost-effectiveness evaluation • Conducting pharmaco-economic evaluations

References and further readings   10.14

ILLUSTRATIONS

Table 10-1   Examples of resource-allocation decisions at different levels of government   10.3

Table 10-2   Using economic analysis methods to make choices   10.12

BOX

Box 10-1   Types of costs   10.13

COUNTRY STUDY

CS 10-1   Australia: ten years of using pharmaco-economics in decision making   10.8

SUMMARY

Economics can help managers make difficult resource-allocation decisions by providing a framework and a set of concepts and tools for evaluating alternatives in terms of their costs and benefits. Key economic concepts include—

Scarcity: the fact that resources are always limited
Opportunity cost: the benefits that are given up in choosing one option over the next-best alternative
Marginal costs and marginal benefits: the additional costs incurred and additional benefits gained by increasing output
Incentives: the factors related to both monetary and nonmonetary rewards or to penalties that influence the behavior of individuals or organizations

Considerable debate exists about the appropriate role of government in the health sector. The "social welfare" perspective argues for broad government involvement, whereas the "market economy" perspective holds that government should become involved only when the market system fails. General support exists for the government to provide public goods, which are available for the benefit of everyone. Prominent examples include goods and services with positive externalities, such as immunization, and merit goods, such as health education, which private markets tend not to provide in sufficient quantities.

Policy makers must also be concerned with distribution issues—who pays for and who benefits from publicly supported services. Through the use of subsidies, governments can encourage the consumption of health services beyond what individuals would pay for on their own.

The private sector is actively involved and often predominant in health care and especially the pharmaceutical sector. Government involvement with the private sector is often justified as a means of correcting "market failure," which may result from equity considerations, failure of competition, information failure, and externalities. Governments are not always successful in correcting the failure.

Efficiency means getting the most output for a given quantity of resources. The tools of pharmaco-economic evaluation can help pharmaceutical managers identify the most efficient options. Different methods include cost-minimization analysis, cost-effectiveness analysis, cost-utility analysis, and cost-benefit analysis.

These methods are demanding and labor intensive, and although widely used in pharmaceutical access programs in high-income countries, their applicability is more limited in low- and middle-income countries. Essential medicines lists, standard treatment guidelines, generic substitution, tendering and reference pricing, and tariff and tax minimization can be more effective instruments for improving pharmaceutical purchasing and improving affordability.

Pharmaco-economic analysis can be very helpful, but should be used selectively, for instance, in assessing an entire public health program (such as childhood vaccination) or when an important product is expensive and available from only one source.

10.1 Economics as a tool for making choices

Health economics is about understanding both medical and nonmedical resource-allocation decisions that affect health under conditions of scarcity and uncertainty (Drummond et al. 2005). Pharmaco-economics is the area of health economics that focuses on the economic evaluation of medicines. Because budgets are never large enough, health managers must constantly decide which of several courses of action to follow. They may make choices among programs, among program goals or objectives, or among strategies or activities for achieving specific goals. This chapter introduces the concepts of health economic analysis and shows how these concepts can be applied to the selection of medicines.

Evidence-based medicine and pharmaco-economic analysis play a much greater role in medicine selection now than they did ten years ago, because program managers are under increasing pressure to show that they are obtaining value for their purchases or subsidies. These methods have been used most effectively within health insurance/pharmaceutical subsidy schemes in high-income countries (Birkett et al. 2001; Hjelmgren et al. 2001; Pearson and Rawlins 2005), but the basic principles are relevant to low- and middle-income countries.

As covered in other chapters, pharmaceutical management is characterized by a complex series of processes, involving (a) research and discovery, (b) product development, (c) safety and efficacy testing, (d) manufacture, (e) distribution, (f) prescription, (g) dispensing, and (h) consumption. The first four elements constitute the costs incurred before the manufacturer's distribution to wholesalers. The prices the manufacturer charges are usually many times the marginal cost of production and are set in order to recover all of these costs and generate a profit margin. The patent system allows manufacturers to behave as monopolists, charging what the market will bear. Retail prices depend on this system and the last four processes listed. Therefore, the application of health economics methods to the selection of medicine must consider the complexity of these processes and the often conflicting roles of the different stakeholders.

Program managers can use economic analysis as a useful tool to augment, but not fully replace, experience and common sense. Economic analysis can lay out, sometimes in stark detail, the costs and consequences of different courses of action. However, real-world decision making must consider political, professional, and commercial realities. Achieving optimal value for money with every purchase or subsidy is a worthy but unattainable goal; however, judiciously and consistently applying appropriate pharmaco-economic methods will help deliver greater value for money in the longer term.

An important caveat is that health economics, done appropriately, is a rigorous, demanding discipline. Many problems with pharmaco-economic analyses arise because of limitations or biases in available clinical data, which result in unrealistic assumptions about clinical benefits and cost-effectiveness of medicines (Hill et al. 2000; Rennie and Luft 2000; Bell et al. 2006). Therefore, organizations must have access to clinicians, epidemiologists, statisticians, and economists to conduct pharmaco-economic analyses well. Because these professionals are often in short supply and expensive, many countries do not have the necessary resources. Regional cooperation is likely necessary to achieve widespread proficiency in the application of these methods.

In most low- and middle-income countries, complex health economic analyses of each individual medicine product are not necessary; rather, they are selectively applied to public health programs, such as childhood immunization, or to expensive products from a single source. In fact, formal pharmaco-economic evaluations of pharmaceutical classes should be aligned with the basic elements of pharmaceutical management policy, including maintaining essential medicines lists, establishing generic medicines policies, ensuring efficient pharmaceutical procurement and distribution systems, minimizing tariffs and taxes, and encouraging rational use of medicines.

10.2 Some basic economic concepts

Economics provides methods for evaluating choices in terms of their costs and benefits. Table 10-1 lists examples of resource-allocation decisions that can benefit from using economic tools, moving from a more macro, or health system, level to the micro level of individual products.

Highlighting a few basic economic concepts critical for understanding issues in public health may be useful. They are scarcity, opportunity cost, marginal benefits and costs, and incentives.

Scarcity. Resources are never sufficient to do everything. Choices have to be made about the best ways to use the resources that are available. Resources are not limited to money; time is a scarce resource as well, as every busy program manager knows.

Opportunity cost. Choices that entail opportunity costs go beyond money alone. They take into account potential benefits that are given up in order to follow a chosen course of action—benefits that could be derived from committing resources to the next-best alternative. For example, if running a training course in inventory management means that another course in rational medicine use cannot be conducted, the forgone course is the

Table 10-1   Examples of resource-allocation decisions at different levels of government

Central government	Central ministry of health	Pharmaceutical program managers
How much should the public sector spend for all recurrent budgets?	How much should be allocated to primary, secondary, and tertiary care?	How much should be spent on pharmaceuticals, training, and storage?
How much should be allocated to the different ministries?	How much should be allocated to different program activities?	What methods can be used to plan for international pharmaceutical purchases when the value of local currency is falling?
	How much should be spent on pharmaceuticals, personnel, and other operating costs?	
	How much should be allocated to different geographic jurisdictions?	Which pharmaceutical distribution strategy will deliver medicines to health facilities most efficiently?
	How much should be allocated to urban compared to rural, dispersed populations, for whom unit costs of services are higher?	Which medicines should be purchased and at what prices; to whom should they be given?

opportunity cost of running the inventory management course. The concept of opportunity cost is helpful in evaluating alternatives by looking explicitly at the trade-offs they involve.

Marginal benefits and costs. When resource-allocation decisions are made, the question is often not whether to allocate all or nothing to a particular activity, but whether to spend a bit more or a bit less. The additional costs of doing a bit more are called marginal or incremental costs, and the additional benefits that result are called marginal benefits. The relationship between the additional costs and benefits is usually called the incremental cost-effectiveness ratio.

For example, ministries of health are rarely faced with decisions about whether or not to provide vaccinations; however, a program manager might have to decide whether to keep the clinic open for another hour at the end of the day. To make this decision, the manager would estimate the marginal cost of keeping the facility open (in terms of extra salaries, utilities, and so forth) and compare this cost to the marginal benefit (in terms of numbers of additional children who would be vaccinated during the extra hour). The incremental cost-effectiveness ratio would be expressed as the cost per extra child vaccinated. The opportunity cost of keeping the clinic open for another hour would be the activities forgone as a result: for example, resources may no longer be sufficient to conduct an educational outreach session.

Incentives. An incentive is some kind of compensation (a reward or penalty that is monetary or otherwise) that influences the behavior of individuals or organizations. For example, governments may provide a financial incentive to parents to ensure that their children are fully immunized. Governments have an incentive to provide preventive health care because it should reduce the demand for and thus the cost of providing more expensive curative care. In practice, however, patients and communities strongly demand curative care. Governments can also create incentives to influence the behavior of individuals or organizations. In charging fees, for example, they can discourage individuals from making unnecessary visits to health facilities for minor complaints. This assumed tendency to overuse facilities if they are made available free of charge is known as "moral hazard." However, many studies have shown that user fees reduce care-seeking behavior among poor patients, which may have negative health outcomes.

The carrot-or-stick approach can be extended to industry. For instance, by levying fines for the distribution of substandard products, governments can encourage pharmaceutical producers to maintain the quality of their products. By establishing certain kinds of controls and incentives, government can influence consumers and providers to choose lower-priced medicines.

10.3 Economics of the public sector

The appropriate role of the government in the health sector, as well as in the broader economy, has been debated for centuries by philosophers, economic theorists, and political thinkers. Since the 1980s, the debate has been heightened by a two-pronged dilemma. On the one hand, centrally planned economies have generally failed to ensure economic security for their populations; on the other hand, some market-focused economies have shown notable inability to ensure universal access to basic social services such as health care.

In appraising the role of government, considering the two extreme positions in this debate is useful. One can be called the social welfare perspective; it supports the vision of an active central government that provides virtually all social services and participates actively in the production of goods and services throughout the economy. This perspective assumes without question that education, health, and other social services will be fully provided by the government. What can be called the market economy perspective, at the other extreme, holds that the government should intervene only if and when the market system performs imperfectly. The economist's perspective on the appropriate degree of government involvement is to weigh benefits against costs; in other words, both governments and markets can be imperfect, and the appropriate mix needs to be assessed on a sector-by-sector basis.

Goals of public expenditure

Historically, the role of the public sector has been undisputed for certain activities. Traditionally, these areas have included maintenance of law and order and national security; investment in infrastructure, such as roads, electricity, and communications networks; and provision of certain types of goods and services. Technically, these activities are termed *public goods, externalities,* and *merit goods.* However, none of these areas is now invulnerable to change, and many governments have experimented with privatizing areas previously regarded as the sole province of the public sector.

Public goods. Services that are widely agreed to be essential and that are consumed collectively (for example, national defense and policing), certain types of utilities and amenities (such as street lighting, sewage systems, and parks), and public health services (such as aerial spraying for vector control) are termed *public goods.* Public goods are often referred to as nonexcludable, meaning that they cannot be provided to some and withheld from others, and nonrival, meaning that no competition exists for the goods; consumption by one person does not reduce its availability to others (Cowen 2008). Because of these factors, public goods are often not sold in the market, and relying on the private sector to provide them may be impractical.

In practice, these definitions have limited applicability, and in recent years, governments have explored ways to engage the private sector in some forms of public infrastructure. For example, power and water companies, which are traditional public entities, have been privatized in many countries, and new highways are often built through partnerships between the public and private sectors. Currently, the overall effects of these policies are unclear, but they do represent a clear shift in government thinking about providing public goods.

Externalities. External effects, sometimes called social costs or benefits, extend beyond the party directly involved in the production or use of a good or service (Musgrove 1996). Examples of goods with positive externalities are immunization and communicable disease control; all members of the community enjoy the benefits of immunization or treatment because their chances of contracting these diseases are reduced as a result. Because private markets tend to underprovide public goods with positive externalities, governments usually take responsibility for funding public goods or subsidizing their use.

Merit goods. Merit goods are things that are good in themselves and include, for example, providing health services for the poor. If left to the market, merit goods would be underprovided. Populations want these services to be provided, but private markets tend not to take care of this group.

Government activity often extends beyond these three types of goods and services. Many people look to government to create a supportive environment for the private sector by encouraging stability and ensuring the availability of basic infrastructure to enforce laws and legally binding contracts. Arguments for a more active public sector are often most forcefully made in developing countries, where levels of private investment may be low, and the private sector is consequently less well developed. Nevertheless, the governments there are sometimes much less developed and can have issues with corruption and lack of transparency.

The roles that governments can play in the pharmaceutical sector are discussed in Chapter 8 and range from total control and provision of all pharmaceutical services (increasingly rare) to minimal government intervention, with pharmacy services provided mostly by the private sector, without government support or interference.

10.4 Understanding the private sector

In contrast with the public sector, private-sector resource allocation decisions are determined largely by the interaction of buyers and sellers in the marketplace, mediated by price. Health program managers in the public sector sometimes think of the private sector as greedy, unscrupulous, unethical, and concerned only with profit at the expense of equity and quality. They often see consumers as unable to judge the quality of health services and therefore vulnerable to manipulation by the private sector. However, the private sector usually plays a significant role in the health sector in the production, distribution, and sale of pharmaceuticals as well as in the direct provision of a significant proportion of health services through private clinical practices, private hospitals, and retail drug sellers. This fact alone is an important reason for better understanding the private sector, which, some believe, has advantages over the public sector in certain circumstances and for certain activities. Appreciating both the strengths and the weaknesses of the public and the private sectors is essential to good public-sector decision making.

Markets and competition

The private sector is characterized by buyers and sellers in the marketplace negotiating the exchange of goods and services through the mechanism of price. In the pharmaceutical sector, the sellers of medicines may be manufacturers, wholesalers, pharmacies, or retail drug sellers. Purchasers may be government, private, or nongovernmental health facilities, or individual consumers. When multiple suppliers act independently and large numbers of purchasers exist, markets are described as "competitive." Through the use of prices as signals, competitive markets are able to allocate resources efficiently, making sure that resources get to the people who are willing and able to pay for them.

Suppliers enter the market when they see an opportunity to make a profit, that is, to earn revenues in excess of costs. With this incentive, they are willing to invest their own money and take a risk as they engage in new activities, expand into new markets, and respond to consumer demand. Under competitive conditions, suppliers can be expected to earn a reasonable level of profit; if they try to increase their profits above this level, another supplier will likely offer a lower price and take away their business. In this way, the price system functions as a control, or discipline, mechanism. Suppliers do not compete on the basis of price only; they may compete on quality (providing a higher quality for the same price), reliability, service, or capacity.

In practice, this type of competitive market is sometimes hard to achieve with pharmaceutical products. Because information is a public good, private markets will tend to underprovide it. The scientific advances that underlie innovative pharmaceuticals are an example of this phenomenon. Various mechanisms have been developed to encourage research and development in medicines and vaccines for neglected diseases. For example, an advance market commitment, a contract from a government or donor, guarantees a viable market for a new medicine or vaccine that would otherwise be too financially risky to develop—such as a product that would benefit developing countries. In 2009, five countries and the Bill & Melinda Gates Foundation activated the first advance market commitment of USD 1.5 billion to speed the development of a vaccine for pneumococcal disease (GAVI Alliance 2009).

The intellectual property system, notably patents, also tries to address this shortcoming by giving innovators a time-limited monopoly in exchange for revealing the nature of their invention. Monopolies, in general, lead to higher prices and suboptimal use in the short run, but the intended trade-off (not always realized) is that this system produces a greater rate of innovation in the long run. Thus, the situation is far more complex than a simple competitive market.

In most countries, patents are now granted for twenty years, although the effective patent period of medicines is eight to fourteen years, because of the time development takes. After the patent on a medicine expires, generic suppliers are able to compete, and prices typically plummet to become much closer to the marginal cost of production. For both patented and generic products, the pharmaceutical marketplace is also distorted by the presence of public and private insurance.

In most developed countries, the government negotiates prices with pharmaceutical suppliers in an effort to provide a counteracting force (monopsony or single-buyer power) to offset the single-seller power of monopolists. Government intervention is the rule rather than the exception, especially in rich countries. The theoretically competitive model of multiple suppliers and multiple purchasers is often replaced by a more pragmatic model of multiple monopolistic suppliers of products and one or a few large purchasers (government or nongovernmental organizations) who can exercise considerable purchasing power. (See Chapter 9 on pharmaceutical pricing policies.)

Economies of scale. In competitive markets, suppliers have an incentive to produce goods and services as efficiently as possible, using the least-cost combination of inputs. In some cases, the private sector is able to generate efficiency gains because of the size and diversity of its operations. Economies of scale occur when the production of larger quantities leads to lower average costs. For example, a plant that produces 4 million tablets a day is likely to do so at a lower cost per tablet than one that produces only 10,000 a day. Beyond some level of output, however, additional machinery or equipment may need to be bought, or more resources may need to be spent in supervising production, which may increase average costs.

Economies of scope. Economies of scope result when combining a number of different activities enables them to be done at lower average cost. Private distribution networks may benefit from economies of scope by combining the delivery of pharmaceuticals with the delivery of other goods and services.

Ethics and business

As previously mentioned, both nongovernmental organizations and public-sector groups have tended to attribute unethical and unscrupulous motives to the private sector. Although examples exist of suppliers that brazenly cheat by providing substandard medicines, for example, the long-term interests of private providers do not encourage engaging in this type of activity. As long as there is the prospect of a continued, profitable relationship with a purchaser, the supplier has an incentive to retain customers by providing good-quality services.

Much of the criticism of the last decade has been directed at manufacturers of patented pharmaceuticals. The main arguments have centered on the price at which they sell their products, particularly in poorer countries, and their lack of involvement in the development of new medicines for some diseases that are major causes of morbidity and mortality in those countries (Trouiller et al. 2002). With the help of intense lobbying from advocacy groups, however, the pharmaceutical industry appears to be recognizing its wider global responsibilities and is addressing its damaged reputation. As a result, modest progress is being made in some areas to provide greater access to some previously unaffordable medicines (for example, antiretroviral medicines for HIV/AIDS) and in the development of medicines for neglected diseases. In theory, many pharmaceutical suppliers will be quite happy to sell medicines at "differential" (lower) prices in poor countries, as long as those prices are above their marginal costs of production and distribution and prohibitions against reexporting to higher-priced markets (parallel trade) are enforceable (Danzon and Towse 2003).

Encouraged by the World Health Organization and the World Bank, some research-based companies have been using differential prices to sell their products on different markets (WHO and WTO 2001). This subject is discussed in more detail in the chapter on medicine pricing (Chapter 9). Products that have been the subject of differential pricing include contraceptives, vaccines, and antiretroviral medicines (GAVI n.d.).

In addition, nonprofit organizations are developing new medicines for conditions such as tuberculosis, malaria, leishmaniasis, and trypanosomiasis. Some are part of large international initiatives (Medicines for Malaria Venture, Drugs for Neglected Diseases Initiative, TB Alliance), and much funding has come from the private sector (for example, the Bill & Melinda Gates Foundation). Several initiatives are public/private-sector partnerships, involving pharmaceutical manufacturers (see Chapter 3 on intellectual property and access to medicines). The result has been considerable blurring of the traditional barriers between the public and private sectors in pharmaceutical research, development, and distribution.

10.5 Government interaction with the private sector

Governments interact with the private sector in many different ways. In its simplest form, this interaction consists of government purchases of pharmaceuticals and supplies from private pharmaceutical companies. In theory and in relation to pharmaceutical products, much government involvement is motivated by a desire to correct "imperfect" private markets.

Market failure

A number of potential market failures exist in the medical marketplace in general, and the pharmaceutical marketplace in particular, that distort outcomes away from the efficiencies that would be expected under the simple competitive ideal—

- Insurance means that patients, and physicians as their agents, do not face the social costs of their decisions to use health care.
- Information is a public good, but the adoption of the patent system as compensation creates monopoly power, which can be abused.
- In general, purchasers do not have good information about the price and quality of the health care services they buy. This information asymmetry can work to the benefit of sellers.
- Regulatory requirements create high barriers for new manufacturers entering the market, which lessens competition.

Patients' inability to assess the quality, safety, or efficacy of pharmaceuticals means they must rely on the clinicians who prescribe them, on pharmaceutical producers to maintain production quality standards, and on governments to intervene with regulatory activities. Inspection of medicines, registration and licensing of pharmacists, and medicine registration processes are all ways in which governments attempt to protect consumers from dangerous, ineffective, and poor-quality medicines (see Chapters 6 and 19). These demanding safety standards, although necessary, make entering the market difficult for new companies.

Achieving economic efficiency in the presence of market failure is one of the principal aims of pharmaco-economics; techniques for achieving efficiency are discussed later in this chapter. Efficiency in pharmaceutical management requires that the medicines are effective and affordable, represent value for money, and are used appropriately. But governments are not concerned only with efficiency. Most also try to achieve a degree of equity in the distribution of funds and services. Lack of access to essential medicines discriminates against those with the least ability to pay, leading to avoid-

able mortality, suffering, resentment, and in some cases, economic decline. Governments are in the best position to correct these inequities, and access to essential medicines is now regarded by some as a human right. Because private-sector decision making is driven more by profit than by equity considerations, equity is often the first motivation for government involvement in essential medicines programs. The relatively high cost of pharmaceuticals compared to that of other goods suggests that without government involvement, the poor would be denied access to lifesaving medicines. This probability is especially high in remote areas, where cash incomes are usually lower and delivery costs higher.

Types of government interventions

In a broad sense, arguments are that government interventions are needed to correct market imperfections, ensure the safety and efficacy of medicines, and improve access and affordability. These aims can be advanced by various types of legislation; in addition, governments can influence prices by becoming large purchasers (or subsidizers) of medicines and using their extensive purchasing power. Pharmaco-economic analysis can facilitate the use of this approach as a tool for calculating social willingness to pay, as discussed below.

The term *regulation* refers to the set of tools that governments use to ensure that private-sector actions are consistent with the broader welfare of society. The objectives of regulation are usually improvements in quality, efficiency, or equity. Pharmaceutical legislation and regulation are discussed further in Chapter 6.

With pharmaceuticals, the instruments used to regulate the private sector (for example, manufacturers, distributors, pharmacies) include controls on medicine and service quality through mandatory inspection programs; controls on imports (restricting imports of dangerous products or permitting the import of only essential medicines); and registration and licensure of pharmacists. Restrictions have also been widely imposed on the prices at which pharmaceuticals can be sold. For example, in Australia, a section of the National Health Act prevents the national medicines selection body (the Pharmaceutical Benefits Advisory Committee) from listing a new product on the schedule at a higher price than the comparators unless it offers better efficacy or safety (see Country Study 10-1).

A number of issues should be considered in evaluating the potential effect of regulation: the extent of coverage (for example, does it include both public and private sectors?), the capacity of government to monitor compliance, the extent of enforcement and exemptions, and the extent to which the private sector can circumvent or evade regulations (for example, through the emergence of an uncontrolled parallel market for nonessential or banned medicines).

Country Study 10-1
Australia: Ten years of using pharmaco-economics in decision making

In Australia, the federal government subsidizes the use of pharmaceuticals through the maintenance of a "positive" formulary, called the Pharmaceutical Benefits Schedule (PBS). Recommendations to list new medicines on the PBS are made to the health minister by a Pharmaceutical Benefits Advisory Committee (PBAC), based on the importance of the medicine, the need for it in the community, its efficacy and safety compared to other medicines or treatments for the condition, and, since 1993, its cost-effectiveness. In addition, the committee considers the financial implications of adding the medicine to the formulary.

The PBAC analyzes the relative clinical performances and costs of both the potential new medicine and comparable medicines already listed on the PBS. The PBAC bases its decisions on the principle that if a medicine is no better than a comparable product, it should not cost more. If the product is superior to existing therapies but more expensive (a common situation), and funds are available, any extra expenditure should represent "value for money." Costs are not limited to each product's acquisition cost, but can include savings in other areas—for instance, decreased use of other medicines or fewer consultations, tests, and hospital admissions.

Incremental cost-effectiveness ratios for the new medicine compared to existing medicines are then developed. These economic data inform decision making, but no formal "threshold" exists for what is cost-effective. Other issues, including clinical need and social values, are influential. Decisions projected to cost more than 10 million Australian dollars (AUD) per year must be approved by the cabinet of the federal government.

More than ten years' experience in using pharmaco-economic evaluations in PBAC decision making has resulted in several observations. The processes have survived multiple technical and ethical challenges, notably but not exclusively from industry. A government productivity commission criticized the PBAC about the level of disclosure in its decision making. In 2002, the Department of Health and Aging began publishing summaries of PBAC's positive recommendations on its website, but so far full details of the assessment process are still not provided.

No evidence suggests that Australia has been denied access to important medical advances by the demand that a new medicine demonstrate "value for money," with the PBS subsidizing a comprehensive range of medicines for patients. The PBS is a positive formulary, in that the PBAC does not seek to limit choice or restrict the numbers of medicines within a classification. However, pressures on the system are real; for example, patient advocacy groups with particular clinical needs continue to seek relaxation of decision-making criteria that affect them.

As in most other countries, the costs of medicines are a concern, and the viability of the PBS has been questioned. To curtail growth in pharmaceutical costs, the PBAC increasingly relies on restricting subsidies by defining eligibility criteria that target patients in whom the new medicine has been demonstrated to be cost-effective. During the decade in which the PBAC has used pharmaco-economic analyses, expenditure on the PBS has risen from about AUD 1 billion per year in the early 1990s to about AUD 6 billion in 2005. This increase does not mean that the use of economic information in decision making has been a failure—rather, it suggests that the other side of the cost equation, the demand side, has been less well managed. Prescribers often ignore restrictions, and the use of new medicines for indications and patient populations in which the medicine has not been shown to be cost-effective has contributed to the rapid growth in PBS costs.

Using pharmaco-economic analyses in decision making is not a panacea for rising pharmaceutical budgets. However, such techniques do make the trade-offs between the costs and benefits of the medicine more transparent. Although considerable progress has been made in the technical aspects of the conduct of pharmaco-economic analyses, progress on managing prescribing practices has been notably less successful. The challenge ahead is how to use the available information on cost-effective medicine use to influence how medicines are prescribed and used in the Australian community.

Source: Birkett et al. 2001; Hailey 2009.

When regulations are in place, they should be regularly evaluated to determine whether they are achieving the desired effects or, as is frequently the case, the government intervention has had unforeseen and negative consequences.

Legislation designed to improve the affordability of medicines is harder to implement when the government does not subsidize medicines and thus is unable to use its extensive purchasing powers. For example, since 1997, South Africa has tried to regulate medicine prices in the private sector, but it has met stiff resistance from stakeholders, including pharmaceutical manufacturers, wholesalers, and retail pharmacists (Republic of South Africa 1997). To achieve greater control over prices and improve affordability and access, the South African government plans to introduce a form of national health insurance before 2014 (*ANC Today* 2009).

The capacity required to implement and monitor the effects of regulations—and the costs of monitoring them—needs to be carefully weighed against the proposed benefits.

Challenges to government interventions

Arguments in favor of government involvement often contrast private-market failure with "perfect" government intervention, but this result is never achieved in practice. The private market may fail, but government intervention also fails sometimes. Governments in all countries at all levels of development are subject to threats to their effectiveness. Informed decisions about public involvement in essential medicines programs must acknowledge the sources of government ineffectiveness, including inefficiency in service delivery, inequities in revenue collection, interest-group pressures, lack of good governance, and widespread corruption.

Inefficiency in service delivery arises from a lack of individual incentives for good performance, bureaucratic inflexibility, and political pressure to create employment. Overexpenditure on staff and underexpenditure on pharmaceuticals, for example, could result in having idle staff who are unable to meet the needs of patients. Inefficiencies in government accounting systems that cause lengthy delays in payments may result in suppliers' raising their prices or deciding not to bid at all on government contracts.

Inequities in revenue collection can result in a reduction in health services, which is felt most acutely by lower-income groups, which are most dependent on them. If the more affluent members of society succeed in avoiding taxes and other government levies, the financial burden for government activity falls on those with fewer means and options.

Even honest, well-meaning politicians and officials are subject to interest-group pressures. Political supporters, members of the same ethnic group, and concerned business organizations can influence bureaucrats to allocate services and resources in ways that do not promote equity. Generally, the more affluent are able to exert such pressures; ironically, the less well-off may lose directly and indirectly—by paying more in taxes as well as by receiving fewer services.

Finally, lack of good governance and corruption can be revealed in self-interested manipulation of the medicine selection process, corruption in the award of tenders, nepotism in the appointment of key staff, sales of medicines on the outside by health staff, and other destructive practices. Indeed, the World Bank has identified corruption as one of the greatest obstacles to a country's economic and social development (see http://www.worldbank.org/anticorruption).

10.6 Efficiency concepts

Efficiency concepts form the basis for understanding the use of pharmaco-economic analysis. Whereas effectiveness concerns the degree to which services are provided or outputs are produced (for example, how well does a medicine work in practice?), efficiency can be understood as getting the most output for a given quantity of resources committed or, alternatively, achieving a given level of output at minimum cost. In this field, efficiency is usually referred to as "cost-effectiveness" (Drummond et al. 2005).

Several types of efficiency concepts exist, with a variety of definitions that are characterized by some lack of agreement. Generally, *economic efficiency* refers to economic systems that can provide more goods and services to society without using more resources. *Scale efficiency* occurs when the production costs are reduced because of higher production volume. *Productive efficiency* in a health system refers to maximizing health outcome for a given cost, or the minimizing cost for a given outcome. Because types of efficiency relate to the pharmaceutical sector, this chapter takes a pragmatic approach by referring to the concepts of allocative efficiency and technical efficiency. *Allocative efficiency* is the broad concept of undertaking the best combination of activities to achieve the greatest net benefit to the community; for example, should we spend money on preventing cardiovascular deaths or childhood illness? Or should we spend money on education or health? *Technical efficiency* is concerned with determining the right quantities of different inputs and the least-expensive combination of inputs to achieve a given outcome; for example, what is the most cost-effective way to reduce cardiovascular deaths? The concepts of allocative and technical efficiency are closely linked and in real life cannot be separated.

Allocative efficiency

Allocative efficiency has relevance to pharmaceuticals, not least because medicines can consume 25 to 65 percent of entire health budgets in some low-income countries (WHO

2010). In some countries, 20 to 30 percent of pharmaceutical expenditure is for products that have no relevance to the main health problems of the population—clearly an inefficient allocation of scarce resources, which might be better used in public health programs or education (WHO 2010).

Decisions affecting allocative efficiency are most often made at the policy level, for example, deciding whether to allocate additional funds to the ministry of health or the ministry of education. Within the ministry of health, decisions involve how much to spend on primary, secondary, and tertiary care or whether to spend additional program funds on controlling tuberculosis or treating sexually transmitted infections. Such allocative decisions can have unintended and undesirable effects; a decision to reduce spending on pharmaceuticals and supplies in order to pay salaries could lead to inefficiency if staff are then underused because of other shortages (for example, a surgeon who cannot perform operations because the operating-room equipment has not been maintained or because anesthetics are in short supply).

Technical efficiency

Technical efficiency means obtaining the maximum physical output from the physical inputs in pursuit of a particular goal, such as reducing deaths from HIV/AIDS by increasing the number of individuals receiving and adhering to effective antiretroviral medicines. Technical efficiency includes not only the cost-effectiveness of the medicines, but also the system that selects, procures, distributes, and dispenses the medicines to consumers.

Selection of medicines should consider the medicines' comparative efficacy and cost-effectiveness, measured in terms of the money spent in achieving an adequate and sustained suppression of the AIDS virus, for example.

In procurement, the use of competitive international tendering has advantages. As discussed in Chapter 9 on medicine pricing, improving the efficiency of the tendering process can result in substantial price reductions. Determining the appropriate quantities of medicines to buy also affects efficiency: overstocking brings risks of expiry, and stockouts reduce program output and lead to expensive emergency orders.

In pharmaceutical distribution, when not enough transportation is available or vehicles are often inoperative, personnel may be underused. The same output could be achieved with fewer personnel, or output could be dramatically increased with a slightly greater expenditure on vehicle maintenance. A program manager might consider the costs and benefits of changing from using a fleet of program vehicles to contracting delivery to a commercial transportation firm in an effort to increase efficiency.

Rational use of medicines has the potential to improve efficiency; for example, prescribing excessive courses of antibiotics is inefficient, because the same outcome could be achieved using fewer. Similarly, a subtherapeutic medicine dose fails to achieve the desired clinical outcome and wastes resources because the patient is likely to return for further treatment. Polypharmacy leads to lower rates of adherence to treatment and is inefficient; resources are consumed, but the desired clinical outcome is not achieved.

Program managers can control only some of the factors that affect technical efficiency. For example, program managers may not have control over the allocation of funds among different line items, such as personnel and fuel, making it difficult to use inputs in the most efficient combinations. Incentives and management structures are important. If a more efficient use of resources leads to tangible benefits for health workers, they are more likely to make more efficient choices. If they are penalized (for example, if underspending a budget leads to less money being allocated next year with no offsetting incentives), health workers are unlikely to behave in an efficient and cost-saving manner.

Information is important in increasing technical efficiency: managers and health care providers who have information about the costs of alternatives are more likely to make efficient use of their resources than those who do not. Formulary manuals, standard treatments, and therapeutic guidelines are intended to provide such information to health workers. Relatively simple performance indicators have been developed using information that should be available to most supply system managers; such indicators can be used to monitor supply system efficiency on a routine basis (see Chapter 48).

Health care decision makers can use information on efficiency to improve the current situation and make better plans related to performance, costs, and staff utilization. In addition, efficiency is an important economic concept because demonstrating that existing resources are being used efficiently provides powerful support to requests for additional resources. But achieving both allocative and technical efficiency depends on access to information on both costs and outcomes of competing treatment programs. Exploring the relationships between costs and benefits lies at the center of economic evaluation.

10.7 Economic evaluation of pharmaceutical products

Although concepts of efficiency are vital to all aspects of pharmaceutical management, including procurement, distribution, and dispensing, as well as to the selection of essential medicines for formularies and reimbursement lists, pharmaco-economics is defined as the analysis of the costs and benefits of medicine therapy to health care systems and society (ISPOR 2003).

The essential characteristic of pharmaco-economic analyses is that they involve *comparisons*—usually a new medicine is compared with the best existing treatment; therefore, decisions are almost always made "on the margin." The best analyses are those that are based on high-quality clinical studies (Birkett et al. 2001).

The term *economic evaluation* refers to a set of analytical tools that can help identify which of several alternative treatments offers the greatest benefit compared with its cost. These analytical tools can help address questions such as: What medicines should be included on the formulary? What are the patient outcomes of various treatment modalities? How do two options for providing pharmacy services compare?

Four methods of economic analysis are commonly distinguished and are described here in increasing order of methodological and practical difficulty (Drummond et al. 2005).

1. *Cost-minimization analysis (CMA):* calculating the cost of two or more alternatives that have the same outcome to identify the lowest-cost option
2. *Cost-effectiveness analysis (CEA):* measuring both costs and benefits of alternatives to find the strategy with the best ratio of benefits, measured in therapeutic (clinical) or program effects, per money unit of expenditure
3. *Cost-utility analysis (CUA):* same as cost-effectiveness analysis, except that benefits are measured in "utility" units, which in theory can be compared across different disease states
4. *Cost-benefit analysis (CBA):* comparing the costs and benefits of an intervention by translating the health benefits into a monetary value, so that both costs and benefits are measured in the same unit

The distinctions among these four methods mainly concern the benefits of intervention.

Cost-minimization analysis

In cost-minimization analysis, the benefits have to be measured in the same or equivalent units, and all the alternatives considered need to produce the same quantity of benefits. The choice (which appears deceptively simple) is to identify the lowest-cost alternative, and the analysis is limited to calculation of the costs. For example, if two medicines have the same therapeutic benefits, have the same safety profile, and are of equivalent quality, the medicine with the lower cost would be selected.

In practice, CMA can be more demanding than it appears. The first challenge is to define an acceptable degree of therapeutic equivalence before comparing the costs of two regimens. Generally, *noninferiority* is the term used to define equivalence (Djulbegovic and Clarke 2001). In other words,

a new treatment should be no worse than an existing medicine. A noninferiority boundary is set during the statistical analysis, to represent the tolerable maximum level of inferiority that will be allowed (for example, 10 percent); the statistical confidence interval around the difference between the two treatments must lie below this level. The costs of the medicines can be compared on that basis. Because the costs of medicines tend to vary somewhat with dose, the doses at which the products can be considered equivalent must be determined. These equivalent-effective doses are then used to establish the relative price of the new product. The costs of administration must also be included. An oral medication replacing an intravenous form with identical efficacy and safety will have the advantage of not requiring nursing time and injection equipment.

Cost-effectiveness analysis

With cost-effectiveness analysis, the unit of output of the alternatives is the same, but the quantities of output, or effectiveness of the strategy, differ. The outcomes are often described in natural units; for instance, resolution of pneumonia or cases of malaria prevented must be consistent for the treatments being compared. CEAs of this type are useful in judging technical efficiency. Sometimes the outcome measured is deaths avoided or life years gained by the use of a new treatment compared with an existing therapy. The challenge is to identify the option with the lowest cost per unit of benefit gained. For example, different vaccination strategies (fixed point, outreach, campaign) may reach different numbers of children and have varying levels of effectiveness, but cost-effectiveness analysis can help identify the one that has the lowest cost per fully immunized child.

Cost-effectiveness must be considered alongside therapeutic effectiveness. Generally, but not always, the new treatment is considered superior to the old one. Occasionally, it is less effective but much cheaper. If the budget is fixed, purchasing the lower-cost medicine may enable more patients to be treated and more lives to be saved, although the medicine is less efficacious. When working with a fixed budget, comparing the cost-effectiveness ratios of each medicine with no treatment is important. Usually, the medicine with the lowest ratio of cost to units of health gained is preferable. If the budget is not fixed and some growth is possible, the incremental cost-effectiveness ratio, which compares the new (more effective) medicine with existing treatment, should be used to commit additional funds.

CEA's main challenge is to compare different therapies: Is 5,000 dollars per heart attack avoided or 50 dollars per symptom-free period for asthma patients a better deal? Or is spending 1,000 dollars per life-year gained by reducing disability from a stroke or 5,000 dollars per life year gained for a breast cancer survivor better? In the latter instance, although the "outcomes" seem to be the same, they are not,

Table 10-2   Using economic analysis methods to make choices

Type of analysis	Medicine therapy choice: antibiotic A versus antibiotic B for treating childhood pneumonia	Transportation scheme choice: program fleet versus contracted private firm
Cost minimization	Of two medicines with equal effectiveness, which is the least expensive?	Assuming that both options are identically effective, which is the least expensive?
Cost-effectiveness	Two medicines have different degrees of effectiveness: What is the cost per child cured using antibiotic A versus antibiotic B (allowing for different efficacy of drugs A and B)?	The two options have different performances with respect to on-time delivery: What is the cost per medicine kit delivered using program transport versus a contracted firm? (Perpetually late deliveries are factored in as a smaller level of desired output.)
Cost utility	What is the cost per QALY saved of treating childhood pneumonia with drug A versus treating tuberculosis with short-course chemotherapy? (Note: This method is controversial for comparing medicine therapies.)	Because the outcome of interest is the same in both cases (that is, medicines delivered on time), no need exists to use a specially constructed measure of output.
Cost benefit	What is the cost-benefit ratio (value of costs per value of life saved) for treating childhood pneumonia versus the cost-benefit ratio for saving lives through improved road lighting? (Note: This method is normally not used to compare alternative therapies.)	Because the outcome of interest is the same in both cases (that is, medicines delivered on time), no need exists to use a specially constructed measure of output.

because quality of life will differ between stroke and breast cancer survivors. For this reason, health economists have sought different metrics that enable them to make comparisons across different disease states.

Cost-utility analysis

Cost-utility analysis is cost-effectiveness analysis conducted with the program outcomes measured in utility units. The most common utility measures are the quality-adjusted life-year (QALY) and the disability-adjusted life-year (DALY), which is more commonly used in studying developing countries (Drummond et al. 2005).

The DALY is a measure of health outcome used to compare interventions with different types of output (Murray 1994). This approach is useful for making decisions about allocative efficiency because it enables comparisons of treatments for different conditions, such as malaria, depression, and heart disease. DALYs combine mortality and morbidity (or disability) into a single measure by weighting the life-years saved by the amount of disability associated with a specific outcome.

For example, diagnosis and treatment of African trypanosomiasis costs 15 dollars per DALY saved; treatment for zinc deficiency costs 73 dollars per DALY saved; and measles vaccination costs 4 dollars per DALY saved (Laxminarayan et al. 2006). By contrast, interventions such as cancer treatment and environmental control of dengue fever both cost thousands of dollars per DALY saved. The 1993 *World Development Report* (World Bank 1993) was the first major analysis to use this outcome measure.

QALYs are similar to DALYs in that they calculate program benefits in terms of life-years saved, except that in the case of QALYs, the years are weighted by the "quality" of those years when they are lived in less-than-perfect health. Like DALYs, QALYs also allow comparison of interventions with different outputs. QALYs are controversial because individual qualities of life and preferences are difficult to compare. Furthermore, survey-based quality-of-life scales are not perfect measures, nor are they easily translated into QALYs.

Cost-benefit analysis

In cost-benefit analysis, both costs and outcomes are measured in financial units. Cost-benefit analysis is rarely undertaken in the health sector because of the difficulty and equity implications of assigning a monetary value to life-years saved (Drummond et al. 2005). Its main advantage is that it allows the comparison of programs with different outcomes—for example, investment in health versus investment in education.

Table 10-2 shows how each of these tools can be applied to make a range of choices, for instance, between alternative medicine therapies or alternative transportation schemes.

Steps for conducting a cost-effectiveness evaluation

Conducting a cost-effectiveness evaluation has six key steps.

Step 1. Define the objective. For example, in terms of program output—

- Which medication regimen should be the therapy of choice for the treatment of childhood pneumonia?
- What is the best approach to transporting essential medicines to health facilities?

Step 2. Enumerate the different ways to achieve the objective. For example—

- Short-course chemotherapy with more expensive medicines (option 1), versus traditional long-course chemotherapy with cheaper medicines (option 2)
- Purchase of program vehicles for delivery of medicines to health facilities (option 1) versus a contract with a private transport firm for delivery of medicines (option 2)

Step 3. Identify, measure, and value the benefits of each option. In the step 2 medicine-choice example, benefits could be measured in DALYs, which would require measures of therapeutic effectiveness and epidemiological data on the course of illness without treatment. For the transport example, an indicator of performance could be used, such as on-time delivery of pharmaceutical consignments to a health facility.

In the clinical arena, the benefits of competing treatments are usually measured in controlled clinical trials. The highest level of clinical evidence to use in economic analysis is a systematic review and meta-analysis of all available high-quality trials that compare interventions. Failure to use high-quality clinical data often leads to suboptimal pharmaco-economic analyses.

Step 4. Identify, measure, and value the costs of each option. All the inputs required for each option should be identified and the costs determined. Capital as well as recurrent costs should be included. Box 10-1 lists different types of costs that should be considered (see also Chapter 41). During this process, defining a relevant timeframe for these analyses is important. For instance, the efficacy of statins in the prevention of heart attacks and strokes has to be measured over years, not weeks or months.

Step 5. Calculate and interpret the cost-effectiveness of each option. The incremental cost-effectiveness ratio is the difference in total cost between the intervention and comparison options, divided by the difference in the number of units of output. Better overall efficiency is indicated by a lower cost per unit of output.

Step 6. Perform sensitivity analysis on the conclusions. Sensitivity analysis measures how various assumptions made in the course of estimating costs and outputs affect the conclusions. Sensitivity analysis deals with uncertainty in assumptions that underlie the analysis or with problems of imprecise measurement. In practice, sensitivity analysis identifies the values or assumptions about which uncertainty exists; determines their likely range of values; and recalculates study results based on a combination of the "best guess," most conservative, and least conservative estimates of these key values. The question of interest is whether the conclusions of the analysis would be changed with these extreme values.

Although certain costs or benefits cannot be measured accurately, it may be possible to show that the results of the analysis do not change over any reasonable range of cost or benefit. Alternatively, the difficulties in measurement may indicate that the results are very sensitive to error in measurement and that caution should be used in interpreting the results of the study. Sensitivity analysis is easy to do and is essential to properly use and defend study results.

Conducting pharmaco-economic evaluations

As noted, conducting full pharmaco-economic analyses that deal adequately with all of the sources of uncertainty is very demanding of time and resources. For the analyses to be valid and error-free, they must draw on the skills of epidemiologists, biostatisticians, and economists. Given the need to integrate a variety of information of varying quality, pharmaco-economic analysis can be prone to errors—and even manipulation—that can make any product look more economically attractive than it really is. To guard against this possibility, systematic checklists (see Drummond et al. 2005) are helpful for critical review. The principles of economic analysis are best understood by further reading and through exercises that involve the calculation and interpretation of cost-effectiveness ratios (see References

Box 10-1
Types of costs

Recurrent cost: The cost of goods that are consumed or used up over the course of a year (for example, staff, pharmaceuticals, fuel).

Capital cost: The cost of goods that are intended to last for longer than a year (such as buildings, vehicles, medical equipment).

Annualized capital cost: Capital cost per year of useful life for a building, vehicle, or other capital item.

Fixed cost: Cost that does not change with the level of output (for example, building, equipment, salaries to a certain extent).

Variable cost: Cost that changes, depending on the amount of services delivered (for instance, pharmaceuticals and supplies).

Total cost: The sum of recurrent costs and annualized capital costs.

Average cost per unit: Total cost divided by the number of units produced (for example, cost per patient treated, per immunization given, per cure dispensed).

Marginal cost: The cost of producing or providing one additional unit.

and Further Readings). In addition, the World Health Organization has published *Introduction to Drug Utilization Research* and *Drugs and Money: Prices, Affordability and Cost Containment* (WHO 2003; Dukes et al. 2003), which contain practical advice and exercises in cost-effectiveness analysis and a review of cost-containment measures. ∎

References and further readings

★ = Key readings.

ANC (African National Congress) Today. "A Unified, Equitable and Integrated National Health System that Benefits all South Africans." July 24, 2009. <http://www.polity.org.za/article/anc-today-statement-by-african-national-congress-outlining-the-proposed-national-health-insurance-scheme-25072009-2009-07-25>

Bell, C. M., D. R. Urbach, J. G. Ray, A. Bayoumi, A. B. Rosen, D. Greenberg, and P. Neumann. 2006. Bias in Published Cost-Effectiveness Studies: Systematic Review. *BMJ* 332:699–703.

Birkett, D. J., A. S. Mitchell, and P. McManus. 2001. A Cost-Effectiveness Approach to Drug Subsidy and Pricing in Australia. *Health Affairs* 20(3):104–14.

★ Bootman, J. L., R. J. Townsend, and W. F. McGhan. 2004. *Principles of Pharmacoeconomics.* 3rd ed. Cincinnati, OH: Harvey Whitney Books.

Carrin, G. 1984. *Economic Evaluation of Health Care in Developing Countries.* London: Croom Hel.

Cowen, T. 2008. "Public Goods." In: *The Concise Encyclopedia of Economics.* 2nd ed. David R. Henderson (ed.). Indianapolis, Ind.: Library of Economics and Liberty. <http://www.econlib.org/library/Enc/PublicGoods.html>

Danzon, P. M., and A. Towse. 2003. Differential Pricing for Pharmaceuticals: Reconciling Access, R&D and Patents. *International Journal of Health Care Finance and Economics* 3(3):183–205.

DiMasi, J. A., and C. Paquette. 2004. The Economics of Follow-on Drug Research and Development: Trends in Entry Rates and the Timing of Development. *Pharmacoeconomics* suppl 2:1–14.

Djulbegovic, B., and M. Clarke. 2001. Scientific and Ethical Issues in Equivalence Trials. *Journal of the American Medical Association* 285:1206–8.

★ Drummond, M. F., M. J. Sculpher, G. W. Torrance, B. J. O'Brien, and G. L. Stoddart. 2005. *Methods for the Economic Evaluation of Health Care Programmes.* 3rd ed. Oxford: Oxford University Press.

Dukes, M. N. G., F. M. Haaijer-Ruskamp, C. P. de Joncheere, and A. H. Rietveld (eds.). 2003. *Drugs and Money: Prices, Affordability and Cost Containment.* 7th ed. Amsterdam: IOS Press on behalf of WHO Regional Office for Europe. <http://www.euro.who.int/document/e79122.pdf>

Feldstein, P. J. 2004. *Health Care Economics.* 6th ed. Albany, N.Y.: Delmar Cenage Learning.

Folland, S., A. Goodman, and M. Stano. 1997. *The Economics of Health and Health Care.* 2nd ed. Upper Saddle River, N.J.: Prentice Hall.

GAVI Alliance (Global Alliance for Vaccines and Immunization). No date. *Key Concepts: Tiered Pricing.* Geneva: GAVI. <http://www.who.int/entity/immunization_financing/options/en/briefcase_pricing-tiers.pdf>

———. 2009. *GAVI Partners Fulfil Promise.* Geneva: GAVI Alliance. <http://www.gavialliance.org/library/news/amc-updates/gavi-partners-fulfil-promise/>

Hailey, D. 2009. The History of Health Technology Assessment in Australia. *International Journal of Technology Assessment in Health Care* 25 suppl. 1: 61–7.

Hill, S., A. S. Mitchell, and D. A. Henry. 2000. Problems with Pharmacoeconomic Analyses. *Journal of the American Medical Association* 283:2116–21.

Hjelmgren, J., F. Berggren, and F. Andersson. 2001. Health Economic Guidelines—Similarities, Differences and Some Implications. *Value in Health* 4:225–50.

ISPOR (International Society for Pharmacoeconomics and Outcomes Research). 2003. *Health Care Cost, Quality, and Outcomes: ISPOR Book of Terms,* M. L. Berger, K. Bingefors, E. C. Hedblom, C. L. Pashos, and G. W. Torrance (eds.). Lawrenceville, N.J.: ISPOR.

———. 2010. *Pharmacoeconomic Guidelines Around the World.* <http://www.ispor.org/PEguidelines/index.asp>

Jack, W. 1999. *Principles of Health Economics for Developing Countries.* World Bank Institute Development Studies. Washington, D.C.: World Bank.

Laxminarayan, R., J. Chow, and S. A. Shahid-Salles. 2006. "Intervention Cost-Effectiveness: Overview of Main Messages." In: *Disease Control Priorities in Developing Countries.* 2nd ed. D. T. Jamison, J. G. Breman, A. R. Measham, G. Alleyne, M. Claeson, D. B. Evans, P. Jha, A. Mills, and P. Musgrove (eds). Washington, D.C.: Disease Control Priorities Project. <http://files.dcp2.org/pdf/DCP/DCP02.pdf>

Murray, C. J. 1994. Quantifying the Burden of Disease: The Technical Basis for Disability-Adjusted Life Years. *Bulletin of the World Health Organization* 72(3):429–45.

★ Musgrove, P. 1996. *Public and Private Roles in Health: Theory and Financing Patterns.* HNP Discussion Paper. Washington, DC: World Bank. <http://siteresources.worldbank.org/HEALTHNUTRITIONANDPOPULATION/Resources/281627-1095698140167/Musgrove-PublicPrivate-whole.pdf >

Palmer, S., and D. J. Torgerson. 1999. Definitions of Efficiency. *BMJ* 318(7191):1136.

Pearson, S. D., and M. D. Rawlins. 2005. Quality, Innovation, and Value for Money: NICE and the British National Health Service. *Journal of the American Medical Association* 294(20):2618–22.

Rennie, D., and H. S. Luft. 2000. Pharmaco-economic Analyses: Making Them Transparent, Making Them Credible. *Journal of the American Medical Association* 283:2158–60.

Republic of South Africa. 1997. Act No. 90, Medicines and Related Substances Control Amendment Act, 1997. *Government Gazette,* no. 18505, December 12, 1997. <http://www.info.gov.za/view/DownloadFileAction?id=70836>

Rice, T. 2002. *The Economics of Health Reconsidered.* 2nd ed. Chicago: Health Administration Press.

Roberts, M., W. Hsiao, P. Berman, and M. Reich. 2004. *Getting Health Reform Right: A Guide to Improving Performance and Equity.* New York: Oxford University Press.

Trouiller, P., P. Olliaro, E. Torreele, J. Orbinski, R. Laing, and N. Ford. 2002. Drug Development for Neglected Diseases: A Deficient Market and a Public-Health Policy Failure. *Lancet* 359:2188–94.

WHO (World Health Organization). 2010. Essential Medicines. <http://www.who.int/medicines/services/essmedicines_def/en/index.html>

———. 2003. *Introduction to Drug Utilization Research.* Geneva: WHO. <http://www.who.int/medicines/areas/quality_safety/safety_efficacy/Drug%20utilization%20research.pdf >

———. 1993. *Evaluation of Recent Changes in the Financing of Health Services: Report of a WHO Study Group.* Geneva: WHO.

WHO and WTO (World Health Organization and World Trade Organization Secretariats). 2001. *Report of the Workshop on Differential Pricing and Financing of Essential Drugs, 8–11 April 2001, Høsbjør, Norway.* <http://whqlibdoc.who.int/hq/2001/a73725.pdf>

World Bank. 1993. *World Development Report 1993: Investing in Health.* New York: Oxford University Press.

CHAPTER 11

Pharmaceutical financing strategies

SUMMARY

Medicines save lives and improve health, but they are costly. Nevertheless, they are necessary to make effective use of staff and other health resources. Financial sustainability requires establishing a balance among the demand for medicines, the cost of meeting this demand, and the available resources. Otherwise, shortages result and quality of care declines.

A pharmaceutical financing strategy should begin with efforts to make better use of available funds. If improved efficiency in selection, procurement, distribution, and use of medicines does not create the necessary balance, options for increasing funding include making the case for greater government funding of medicines, introducing or strengthening health insurance coverage for medicines, or obtaining donor assistance.

In recent years, the increase in the international community's commitment to global health and access to pharmaceuticals has resulted in global health initiatives, private foundations, and public-private partnerships playing much larger roles in financing the health sector in developing countries. However, many countries have a hard time absorbing additional resources because of a lack of human and infrastructure capacity, and donor funding presents problems because of its unpredictability, making planning difficult for countries.

Globally, 57 percent of health care is publicly financed, with the share increasing with national income. For health care, and especially for medicines, private spending usually represents a higher share of health financing in lower-income countries. Expanding private and nongovernmental organization (NGO) health services, including providing essential medicines, can shift demand away from overstretched public resources. But quality of care and equity must be ensured.

Public financing through national and local government budgets is a major but sometimes inadequate source of financing for essential pharmaceuticals. The case for public financing of pharmaceuticals can be strengthened through better quantification of medicine needs, per capita pharmaceutical budgets, demonstration of medicines' effect on health, recognition of political benefits, improved management, expenditure trend analysis, and comparative expenditure analysis. Efforts should be made to ensure that available public resources are targeted to those most in need.

User charges may exist in the form of government revolving drug funds (RDFs), community medicine schemes, and retail purchase of medicines. Experience indicates that user charges pose many difficulties, but countries need to have an alternative funding strategy in place to make up the difference before discontinuing user-fee programs.

Health insurance covers a small but growing portion of the population in most developing countries. Important elements of insurance include risk sharing and prepayment. Plans vary in the extent of and mechanisms for insurance coverage for medicines. National social insurance schemes, private voluntary insurance, and community prepayment schemes can increase access to essential medicines. Insurance programs can be designed to encourage cost control and rational medicine use.

Voluntary and other local financing can contribute to improving the overall health care and pharmaceutical financing situation. Donor financing and development loans can help a country develop more efficient pharmaceutical supply systems and alternative financing approaches. For the poorest countries, some external financing for medicines may be needed to ensure universal access to essential medicines. And countries that are scaling up access to antiretroviral therapy for HIV/AIDS or changing first-line malaria treatment to artemisinin-based combinations must rely on external funders, such as the Global Fund to Fight AIDS, Tuberculosis and Malaria (Global Fund) and the U.S. President's Emergency Plan for AIDS Relief.

Financing mechanisms can be compared in terms of access to medicines, rational medicine use, efficiency, equity, sustainability, and administrative requirements. Financial sustainability may require a pluralistic approach in which needs are met through a combination of financing mechanisms, and no one strategy will be applicable to all countries.

11.1 Why pharmaceutical financing is important

In 2000, at the United Nations Millennium Summit, world leaders agreed to a set of measurable targets for combating poverty, hunger, disease, illiteracy, environmental degradation, and discrimination against women. Known as the Millennium Development Goals (MDGs), they provide a framework for the United Nations system and other global and national stakeholders and donors to work collaboratively (UN Millennium Project 2005). Because three of the eight goals concern health, the MDGs have put financing for health systems and pharmaceuticals in a brighter spotlight. In addition, large global health initiatives and increased spending by private sources, such as the Bill & Melinda Gates Foundation, are making unprecedented funds available for health systems in general and pharmaceuticals in particular.

Besides the major role medicines play in the MDGs and other large global health initiatives, financing of pharmaceuticals is a critical issue for several reasons. First, because medicines save lives and improve health, pharmaceutical financing must ensure access to essential medicines for all segments of the population. Second, medicines are costly. For most ministries of health, medicines represent the largest expenditure after staff salaries. Most low-income households spend over half of their health expenditures on medicines, and in some countries, over 80 percent of a household's health-related spending is on medicines (Hammond et al. 2007). In contrast, medicines commonly represent about 20 percent of total public and private health expenditures in developing countries (WHO 2004c). Third, inadequate funding for medicines means that expenditures for staff salaries and other health care costs may be used inefficiently or simply wasted.

This chapter considers the factors that determine financial sustainability, sources of health care financing, and strategies to achieve financial sustainability of pharmaceutical supplies.

11.2 Balancing the financial sustainability equation

Financial sustainability, as illustrated in Figure 11-1, is achieved only when resources are in balance with costs and are sufficient to support a basic quality of care for a given level of health care demand. If demand for medicines exceeds available resources, the health system is left with only four options—

1. Improve efficiency.
2. Reduce demand.
3. Increase financial resources.
4. Accept a decline in quality of care.

In most settings, promising high-quality services and constant availability of essential medicines without also ensuring a high level of efficiency, achieving adequate financing, and controlling demand for medicines defies economic reality.

The same financial sustainability equation applies to NGOs. When demand surpasses available resources, they face the same choices: improve efficiency, control demand, increase financial resources, or accept a decline in quality of care.

For all sectors—public, for-profit private, and not-for-profit private—pharmaceutical financing should not be approached simply as a question of where do we get the money? It must be approached in terms of methods to improve efficiency and to ensure that demand is appropriate.

Improving efficiency

Two broad categories of efficiency were defined in Chapter 10: allocative and technical efficiency. *Allocative efficiency* applies to the distribution of services within the population. Spending the majority of a country's pharmaceutical budget on essential medicines for primary health care, rather than on specialized medicines for national referral hospitals, is likely to save more lives and thereby results in allocative efficiency.

Technical efficiency is achieved if resources are used to produce a given output at the lowest possible cost or to produce greater outputs for the same cost. Pharmaceutical financing decisions are concerned mostly with technical efficiency, which has two components: therapeutic efficiency (improved selection and use) and operational efficiency (improved management of procurement and distribution).

Efforts to balance the financial sustainability equation should always emphasize finding ways to improve efficiency.

Controlling demand

Because the demand for health care services may be virtually unlimited, something always controls demand. In practice, health systems control demand—by intent or by neglect—through combinations of six possible measures—

1. Increase cost to the patient.
2. Impose rationing or other administrative controls.
3. Provide attractive alternatives.
4. Increase waiting time.
5. Decrease quality of services.
6. Provide targeted education.

Figure 11-1   Financial sustainability equation

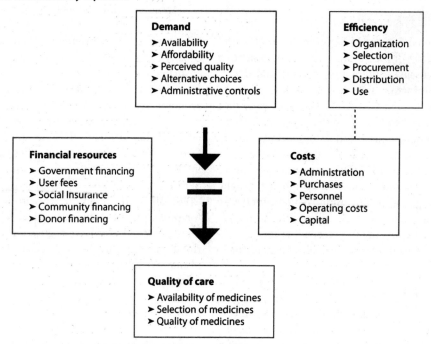

Some health services unintentionally control demand through a combination of long waiting times and poor quality (medicine shortages, for example). In the worst examples of user-fee programs, fees are introduced without quality improvements. Not surprisingly, increased cost—added to long waiting times and low quality—further reduces use. User fees can both increase financial resources and reduce demand, but measures needed to ensure access for the poor are difficult to implement successfully.

Increasing financial resources

The components of financial sustainability can be brought into better balance by increasing financial resources. The remainder of this chapter considers ways to maintain or increase financial resources through public financing, user charges, health insurance, community and other voluntary financing, donor financing, and development loans.

11.3   Health and pharmaceutical financing

Pharmaceutical financing must be viewed in the overall context of health financing. Funding for recurrent operating costs and long-term development costs of health services comes from public sources (national and local government budgets and national social health insurance); private sources (direct payment by patients, private health insurance, employers, and NGOs); and external development aid.

Health expenditures among countries

The relative importance of each funding source varies dramatically among regions and among countries within a region and evolves over time. Health expenditure data categorized by region and income level are shown in Table 11-1. Data in this section are quoted from the World Health Organization (WHO 2009b), unless otherwise noted. Several observations can be made about levels and sources of financing for health.

Health expenditures vary widely among regions and countries. Total per capita health expenditures vary tenfold among regions. Among developing countries, annual health expenditures vary from less than 10 U.S. dollars (USD) per capita in Madagascar, Myanmar, Niger, and several other countries to more than USD 100 per capita in several countries in Latin America, the Caribbean, and southern Africa.

Total health spending depends on economic output, but some countries spend more than others. Health expenditures are directly related to national economic output as measured by gross domestic product (GDP). Developing-country health spending is lower than that of developed countries (with a global average of 8.7 percent of GDP), but some developing countries spend relatively less on health (for example, 2.1 percent of GDP for Congo and 2.5 percent for Indonesia), and others spend more (for example, 7.0 percent for Uganda and 6.4 percent for Bolivia).

As a share of the total, public-sector spending increases as national incomes rise. Globally, health expenditures are

Table 11-1   Composition of health expenditures by country income level and region, 2006

Country income level and region	Per capita health expenditures (USD)	Total health expenditures (% of GDP)	Government health expenditures (% of total health expenditures)	Social security expenditures (% of total government expenditures)	Private expenditures (% of total health expenditures)	Out-of-pocket expenditures (% of private health expenditures)	External expenditures (% of total health expenditures)
Country income level							
Low	22	4.3	36.2	7.0	63.8	85.4	16.9
Lower middle	74	4.5	43.2	40.3	56.8	85.7	0.8
Upper middle	412	6.3	55.1	40.4	44.8	70.0	0.2
High	4,012	11.2	60.7	41.6	39.3	36.2	0.0
Region							
Africa	58	5.5	47.1	7.6	52.9	49.8	10.7
Americas	2,636	12.8	47.7	27.7	52.3	30.6	0.1
Southeast Asia	31	3.4	33.6	8.5	66.4	88.3	1.9
Europe	1,756	8.4	75.6	49.2	24.4	70.8	0.1
Eastern Mediterranean	116	4.5	50.9	19.7	49.1	87.0	2.0
Western Pacific	361	6.1	61.0	63.1	39.0	80.7	0.2
Global	716	8.7	57.6	41.1	42.4	49.3	0.4

Source: Data adapted from WHO 2009b.

about 57 percent public and 42 percent private in origin. Excluding the United States (where private spending is 54 percent of the total spent on health), about 70 percent of health costs are publicly supported in established market economies. But in developing countries, private spending (generally out of pocket) is a higher proportion, rising to about 80 percent in the Lao People's Democratic Republic and about 86 percent in Guinea. In addition, low-income countries have more difficulty collecting revenue; for example, in the early 2000s, high-income countries collected about 32 percent of their GDP in revenue (for example, taxes), compared with an average of 18 percent for low-income countries (Schieber et al. 2006).

Developing countries devote a lower share of public spending to health. Total government spending as a share of GDP is higher among high-income countries. Lower public health spending in developing countries reflects the lower share of health expenditures in the national budget: about 15 percent of government spending in Europe is on health, whereas in Africa, the share is close to 9 percent and less than 5 percent in Southeast Asia. However, governments in low-income countries recognize the need to devote more resources to public health. African leaders vowed to increase spending to 15 percent of their overall budgets in the 2001 Abuja Declaration on HIV/AIDS, Tuberculosis, and Other Related Infectious Diseases (Schieber et al. 2006); however, as mentioned, collecting the needed revenue is challenging.

The combined result of lower proportional allocations to health and lower overall income is that government spending on health in low-income countries is roughly USD 8 per capita, compared with USD 225 in the upper-middle-income countries and almost USD 2,500 in high-income countries.

Developing countries have a high disease burden but low health expenditures. Developing countries have over 80 percent of the world's population and carry 90 percent of the global disease burden, but they spend only about 12 percent of the global total on health (Lopez et al. 2006). In contrast, the thirty member countries of the Organisation for Economic Co-operation and Development make up less than 20 percent of the world's population but spend 90 percent of the world's resources on health.

Insurance coverage increases with income. People in most high-income countries are covered by some form of public or private health insurance; however, the median coverage is only 35 percent in Latin America, 10 percent in Asia, and 8 percent in Africa (WHO 2004c). This differential coverage creates significant variation in out-of-pocket health spending, which is 90 percent of total private health spending in low-income countries, compared with 15 percent in high-income countries (Schieber et al. 2007.)

Foreign aid is a major contributor in certain regions. Foreign sources account for more than 20 percent of health expenditures in almost half of the countries in the WHO's African region (Kirigia and Diarra-Nama 2008). Moreover,

Table 11-2   Pharmaceutical expenditures by country income, 2000

Country income level	Per capita pharmaceutical expenditures (USD)			Share of world total (%)	Share of expenditure on health (%)
	Minimum	Maximum	Average		
WHO member states	0.60	549.00	74.00	100.0	15.2
High income	84.00	549.00	396.00	78.7	11.8
Middle income	4.00	198.00	31.00	18.8	24.8
Low income	0.60	26.00	4.40	2.4	19.2

Source: Adapted from WHO 2004a.

although many countries have recently seen large increases from disease-focused funding and global health initiatives, the United Nations Millennium Project estimates that an additional USD 74 billion will be needed by 2015 to meet the MDGs (Schieber et al. 2006).

Private health expenditures in Table 11-1 include those derived from voluntary, religious, and other NGOs as well as spending by individuals and private companies. NGOs play an important role in financing and providing health services in many countries.

Thus, the relative contributions of public and private spending, external aid, and health insurance differ considerably among regions and countries. Level of economic development has a significant influence. But national policy, commitment to health, political and historical factors, and other influences result in substantial differences among countries within the same region and countries at similar levels of development.

Pharmaceutical expenditures among countries

Data on pharmaceutical expenditures are much less complete than data on overall health expenditures. Regional pharmaceutical expenditures as of 2000 based on WHO (2004c) figures are shown in Table 11-2, from which the following observations can be made—

Per capita medicine consumption varies widely among regions and countries. Pharmaceutical expenditures vary greatly among regions. Like total per capita health expenditures, pharmaceutical expenditures vary up to tenfold among countries within a region.

Spending on pharmaceuticals depends on country income level. Spending on pharmaceuticals is related to the country's income level. In 2000, high-income countries accounted for almost 80 percent of the global expenditures on pharmaceuticals, whereas low-income countries accounted for only about 2 percent. The share of high-income countries decreased from 1990, because middle-income countries increased their share from 17.1 to 18.8 percent.

Private spending represents a greater share of total spending on pharmaceuticals in developing countries. Among established market economies, private spending on medicines averages over 40 percent of total pharmaceutical spending; the remaining pharmaceutical costs are paid through public budgets and social insurance. In contrast, less than one-third of pharmaceutical expenditures is publicly funded in developing countries for which estimates are available. In many countries of Latin America and Asia, a large proportion of pharmaceutical expenditures are privately financed. Exceptions include countries such as Papua New Guinea and island nations in the South Pacific, where private-sector coverage is low and public supply predominates.

Spending on pharmaceuticals accounts for a greater share of total health expenditures in lower-income countries. In high-income countries, pharmaceuticals account for an average of 9.8 percent of total health expenditures. In low-income countries, however, the proportion of government spending dedicated to pharmaceuticals has significantly decreased: in 1990, the average was 21.5 percent, whereas in 2000, the figure was down to 16 percent. Countries most affected included those that carried a high debt burden, major disease burdens, such as HIV/AIDS epidemics, or both.

Therefore, overall spending on pharmaceuticals is related to economic development. In lower-income countries, pharmaceuticals consume a higher share of total health expenditures, although large global initiatives, such as the Global Fund, are accounting for larger shares of pharmaceutical spending in select countries. Private expenditures play a major role in overall pharmaceutical financing.

Financing options for essential medicines

Funding options for pharmaceuticals are essentially the same as those for health care in general: government revenues (national and local); direct payment by patients (fee for service); health insurance (national social insurance or voluntary insurance); community, employer, and other vol-

---

Box 11-1
Funding mechanisms for essential medicines

Public financing (government budgets)

- National government
- Local government

User fees

- Public-sector RDFs
- Community pharmaceutical schemes
- Direct private medicine purchases (out-of-pocket purchases)

Health insurance (prepaid health schemes)

- Social insurance (compulsory health insurance or social security)
- Private insurance (indemnity insurance that is voluntary or through an employer)
- Community health insurance
- Health savings accounts

Voluntary and other local financing

- Private voluntary (NGOs)
- Voluntary community mechanisms
- Cooperatives
- Employer-provided health care

Donor financing

- Bilateral grants
- Multilateral grants
- Private foundations
- Global health initiatives

Development loans

- World Bank
- Regional development banks

---

untary local financing; donor financing; and development loans (see Box 11-1).

Financing arrangements affect the relationships among patients, providers, and the payers or financiers of health services (Figure 11-2). With direct purchase of medicines by consumers, for example, the relationship is primarily between the patient, who is paying for the medicines, and the pharmacy, which is providing the medicines. The government's role is to regulate pharmaceutical quality and sales outlets.

With managed care, the provider and payer (insurer) are closely linked, if not a single organization. Although this arrangement may help control health care costs, it creates a potential conflict of interest between cost control and quality of care. Public supervision and competition are important to promote quality of care.

With each financing arrangement, the role of the government is different. Governments must adapt policies as the mix of financing arrangements in the country changes.

11.4 Private-sector financing: medicine sales and user fees

The most common form of pharmaceutical sale is the direct purchase of medicines by consumers from commercial pharmacies, licensed and unlicensed drug sellers, and other retail medicine outlets. Excluding high- and middle-income countries with large social or private health insurance coverage, retail purchase is the most common source of medicines.

For government, NGO, or community health care programs, user fees for medicines are often part of an RDF or community pharmaceutical scheme. In an RDF, revenues from medicine fees are used to replenish pharmaceutical supplies. Many different forms of RDFs exist, but the common element is a direct link between fees charged and medicines dispensed. Often, an RDF is simply one component of a comprehensive system of fees for publicly provided health services, which may include fees for outpatient consultation, laboratory investigations, and inpatient care. Over the past decade, the debate over user fees has intensified within the context of a global call for increased access to medicines: many in the international health community are calling for all user fees to be abolished; however, eliminating existing user fees in resource-limited countries does not necessarily improve access to medicines and services unless sufficient resources are available to take up the slack and ensure equitable access.

Although many countries offer free medicines for targeted populations (most commonly for tuberculosis or indigent patients), few countries offer all medicines at no cost through their public health facilities (see Table 11-3).

In the context of community health initiatives (see Chapter 31), community medicine-sales schemes often have broader objectives. These may include furthering health education; providing preventive services such as immunization; and raising sufficient revenue from medicine fees to help finance salaries, medical supplies, or other costs.

Public-sector RDFs and community medicine-sales schemes are distinguished from private medicine outlets by

Figure 11-2   Relationships in health care financing

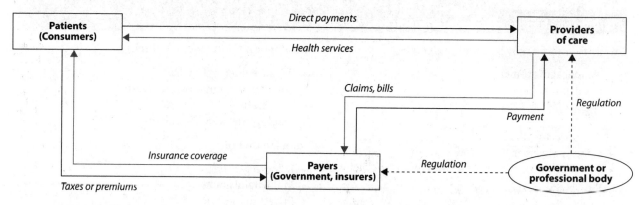

Source: Adapted from WHO 1993.

an emphasis on providing essential medicines, a concern with affordability, and a direct connection between diagnosis by a health worker and appropriate medicine treatment. Proponents of user charges for health care believe the following—

- Revenue can be raised by user fees.
- Medicine availability and the quality of care are improved.
- Equity is promoted because limited public resources can then be targeted to those most in need.
- Decentralization is reinforced through local control of resources.
- Efficiency is fostered by fees, which reinforce the use of local rather than referral services.

In contrast, opponents of user fees believe as follows—

- Net revenue collection is often very low, considering the additional administrative costs of collecting fees.
- Medicine availability and quality of care often show no improvement.
- User charges replace, rather than supplement, government funding.
- People are dissuaded from seeking essential health care, especially the very poor.
- Incentives are created for overprescribing.

Considerable experience with RDFs and broader user-fee programs provides examples that support both proponents and opponents of user charges. Programs that have implemented high fees with no preparation of the public and little improvement in quality have seen significant decreases in use; programs designed with little attention to management and accounting systems have seen substantial abuse and little revenue compared with the cost of fee collection; RDFs established without a reliable source of low-

cost medicines have quickly ceased to revolve; and some schemes with medicine charges have had problems with overprescribing.

Chapter 13 provides additional information on RDFs. In summary, RDFs and community pharmaceutical schemes are not easy to implement. Many factors can undermine their intended benefits, and large-scale successes in government health services are limited.

11.5   Public financing through government budgets

Health officials and managers of essential medicines programs argue for increasing expenditures for pharmaceuticals, sometimes without appreciating the dynamics of public expenditure. Public financing of pharmaceuticals can occur through national and local government budgets or through compulsory programs such as social security and national social insurance schemes. This discussion focuses on central government funding of pharmaceuticals; public funding through insurance is covered in Chapter 12.

Determinants of public pharmaceutical expenditures

Actual public expenditures for pharmaceuticals are determined by a combination of economic factors, national budget decisions, and internal decisions by health ministries. Major factors include—

- National economic output (GDP)
- The share of GDP collected in taxes as revenue for government expenditures (average of about 15 percent in low- and lower-middle-income countries)
- The share of government spending devoted to health (5 to 10 percent in most developing countries)
- The relative share of government health spending

Table 11-3   Medicines provided at no cost in public health facilities, 2003

Types of medicines	Country income level					
	Low		Middle		High	
	Number of countries	Percentage of countries	Number of countries	Percentage of countries	Number of countries	Percentage of countries
All medicines	12	21.8	40	67.8	2	15.4
Malaria medicines	19	37.3	36	81.8	1	9.1
Tuberculosis medicines[a]	50	96.2	45	93.8	9	75.0
Medicines for sexually transmitted diseases	17	34.0	38	79.2	2	18.2
HIV/AIDS-related medicines	16	35.6	37	78.7	7	58.3
All medicines for those who cannot afford them	30	58.8	31	72.1	5	41.7
Medicines for children under five years of age	19	38.0	34	77.3	3	23.1
Medicines for pregnant women	19	37.3	34	79.1	1	8.3
Medicines for elderly persons	12	22.2	18	35.3	4	28.6
None[a]	8	14.8	2	3.1	2	11.1

Source: Adapted from WHO/TCM 2006.

[a] Inconsistencies in reporting noted.

devoted to recurrent operating expenses compared to long-term development

- The relative share of recurrent health expenditures for salaries, medicines, utilities, supplies, and other expenses
- Variations in exchange rates, which determine the international purchasing power of local currency allocations
- Unexpected fluctuations in the national economy caused by devaluations, global changes in commodity prices, political factors, or other events
- The level of corruption in the health and pharmaceutical sector (an estimated 10 to 25 percent of public expenditure in the health sector is lost to corruption; WHO 2009a)

Government economic and development policies influence GDP growth and, to an even greater extent, the share of GDP collected as revenue for government operations. Within the government, resource allocation decisions result from a combination of historical precedent, local political forces, external pressures such as those from donors or development banks, and systematic program planning. Development banks have instituted debt-relief initiatives (Chapter 14), but those measures do not necessarily result in more resources or make reallocation of existing country resources to health easier (Gottret and Schieber 2006).

Arguments for expenditures on essential medicines

The case for increasing expenditures on essential medicines can be made in the ministry of health or the ministry of finance. Obtaining a higher share of the budget for pharmaceuticals requires changing the balance between staff and nonstaff expenditures or between curative health services that depend on essential medicines and preventive services such as immunization and health education. Managers must be prepared to respond to the argument that, with limited resources, expenditures on preventive services are more cost-effective than pharmaceutical treatment, even at the primary level.

In addition to demands from the health sector, public treasuries are faced with demands from education, other social services, industry, agriculture, national development, and defense. Because pharmaceuticals often constitute such a large and visible share of health expenses, the case for increased expenditure on pharmaceuticals can sometimes be taken directly to the ministry of finance.

Arguments and approaches that can be used to support central government spending on essential medicines include—

Health impact: As noted in Chapter 1, pharmaceuticals are a highly cost-effective component of health care. This point is sometimes lost when policy makers focus on symptomatic pharmaceutical treatments. The case for pharmaceutical allocations is strengthened by emphasizing the vital role of medicines in reducing morbidity and mortality from acute respiratory infection, diarrhea, HIV/AIDS, malaria, tuberculosis, and other common killers. For example, appropriate treatment of sexually transmitted infection greatly reduces transmission of HIV/AIDS, and simple prenatal iron-folate preparations reduce maternal and neonatal morbidity.

Quantification of medicine needs: Systematic documentation of specific medicine needs has convinced ministries in some countries to increase allocations for essential medicines (see Chapter 20).

Expenditure trend analysis: Budget allocations are typically based on a percentage increase in the budget from the previous year. This method may be reasonable for salaries and local currency expenses, but because of the high foreign exchange component for pharmaceuticals, the last-year-plus approach may lead to a steady decline in purchasing power over time. Appropriate adjustments for both inflation and exchange rates (see Chapter 41) are needed simply to purchase the same quantities of pharmaceuticals.

Budget gap analysis: Combining quantification of pharmaceutical needs and expenditure trends reveals any gap between need and historical budgets and expenditures.

Per capita pharmaceutical budgets: Population size and patient utilization rates for public facilities are major determinants of pharmaceutical requirements. Per capita pharmaceutical budgets establish a fixed amount per person per year—for example, USD 0.50 per capita. Each year, the per capita amount is adjusted for purchasing power (inflation and exchange rate fluctuations), and the total pharmaceutical budget is calculated by multiplying the adjusted per capita figure by the current population estimate.

Effect on use: When medicines are out of stock, patient attendance rates drop, reducing the use and effect of all health services.

Political visibility: The public often equates pharmaceutical availability at government health facilities with quality of services. Pharmaceutical shortages make for bad press; an adequate supply of medicines makes for good press.

Transparency assessment: Countries can assess the level of transparency and potential vulnerability to corruption of some key components in medicine procurement. WHO suggests that the national assessment be carried out by independent national investigators using the standardized WHO assessment instrument (WHO/EMP/MAR 2009). Results can provide a basis for developing and institutionalizing a national infrastructure of transparent procedures and ethical practices that by addressing corruption can decrease the loss of health resources available for pharmaceuticals and boost public trust in the health system.

Improved management: Central pharmaceutical supply units sometimes have a history of inefficiency and susceptibility to influence. Restructuring central pharmaceutical supply services, improving management, and strengthening accounting control can help convince officials to increase government pharmaceutical allocations.

Comparative expenditure analysis: Measured in absolute or percentage terms, some governments spend much less on essential medicines than others. Relevant regional comparisons by ministry officials and essential medicines program managers may help strengthen the case in countries that are underspending on pharmaceuticals relative to other countries.

Program managers should carefully consider which of the preceding approaches, adapted to the local situation, will be most convincing in their own circumstances.

Management of public pharmaceutical expenditures

Securing an adequate budget for essential medicines is important, but proper financial management is also necessary. Common problems include difficulty gaining access to budgeted amounts, often due to shortfalls in government revenues; inability to spend budgeted amounts as a result of delays in the procurement process; increasing the transparency of the pharmaceutical and distribution process; and difficulty obtaining adequate foreign exchange, even if sufficient local funds are available. Although developing countries are generally moving toward decentralizing their health systems, this process has been slow to include pharmaceutical financing (Enemark et al. 2005).

Financial planning and management are discussed in Chapter 41. Problems of disbursement of government funds and foreign exchange may be reduced with autonomous central supply agencies (see Chapter 8).

11.6 Health insurance

Decisions that affect the availability of health insurance in a country are important to all aspects of health service delivery but are largely outside the control of national medicine policies and essential medicines programs.

WHO recommends that countries include a prepayment mechanism as part of a health care financing strategy with a goal of achieving universal health care coverage (WHO 2005c). Therefore, as insurance assumes a greater role in health care in many countries, understanding health financing, and specifically insurance concepts, becomes increasingly important.

Insurance concepts

The basic purpose of insurance is risk sharing. If an individual suffers serious illness, the cost of treatment can pose a large financial hardship. So individuals find sharing the risk through regular payment of insurance premiums worthwhile to protect themselves from ever having to pay the full cost of a catastrophic illness. Insurance spreads the burden of payment for illness among all the members of the scheme whether they are ill or healthy, poor or not.

In principle, risk sharing through insurance is most worthwhile when the event insured against is largely unpredictable, infrequent, costly as well as unwanted, unplanned, and uncontrollable by the insured. These principles apply most clearly to life, fire, and car insurance. However, applying this traditional view of insurance to medical care presents some difficulties: people can control some aspects of use; some services are low cost; some conditions are frequently or continuously experienced (for example, chronic illness); illness is difficult in some cases to define; people sometimes want to incur the hazard (for example, pregnancy); and the availability of insurance increases the use of services. Despite these difficulties, the concept of risk sharing through insurance has become highly developed in the health sector. Four categories of health insurance can be described—

1. *Social health insurance:* The most typical understanding of social health insurance is that membership is compulsory for a designated population; financial contributions into the system, which are often deducted directly from wages, link to the receipt of benefits; cross-subsidization occurs between high- and low-risk groups and high- and low-income groups; and management usually has some degree of independence from the government.
2. *Private health insurance:* Voluntary private indemnity insurance is provided through employers, mutual societies or cooperatives, or directly by companies. Hospital and physician services are usually covered, but limited or no benefits may be available for preventive services, primary care, or outpatient medicines. Voluntary health insurance contributes to less than 5 percent of the health expenditures in developing countries and usually supplements care for middle- and high-income sectors (Gottret and Schieber 2006).
3. *Community prepaid schemes:* In many countries in Asia, Africa, and Latin America, prepayment plans based on the concept of pooling risk and resources have been developed for rural populations, groups in informal employment, or others without access to other health insurance. Such schemes are based on community affiliation, and the community is highly involved in managing the system. However, evidence suggests that most community-based systems cover a small percentage of people and do not reach the poorest members of the community (Schieber et al. 2006).
4. *Health or medical savings accounts:* Not strictly a form of insurance, medical savings accounts encourage individuals, often by providing tax advantages or subsidies, to save for the expected costs of medical care, enlist health care consumers in controlling costs, and mobilize additional funds for health systems. Only a few countries, including China, Singapore, and the United States, use the concept of health savings accounts.

Insurance systems face several problems that can undermine the potential benefits of prepayment and risk sharing—

Moral hazard: When members of a health insurance scheme use services or consume medicines more frequently than if they were not insured, the phenomenon is called "moral hazard." Deductibles and co-payments are commonly used to avert this problem.

Adverse selection: This term describes the tendency for people at greatest health risk and people with chronic illnesses to join voluntary insurance programs, whereas the healthiest people, whose premiums should be used to pay the bills of the sicker members, avoid joining.

Skimming: This problem occurs when insurers use various screening measures to avoid insuring people at greatest health risk (and therefore greatest expense to them). Skimming reduces the equity benefits of insurance by excluding those who are most in need.

Cost escalation: Rising costs can result from improvements in or greater use of technology, increased use (greater demand caused by insurance coverage), and increases of both the population in general and older populations.

In addition to these problems, insurers, particularly in developing countries, frequently have to deal with the public's and health providers' lack of understanding of the insurance concept. Members may think that premiums are like deposits in a savings account, which leads to unrealistic demands that everyone receive at least as much as he or she has paid in. Insurance is not sustainable in this environment, because no risk sharing occurs. Other members may avoid using their insurance because they believe that they can claim only as much as they have contributed in premiums. Considerable effort may be needed to educate members, the general public, and health providers.

Many countries see the initiation or promotion of one or more insurance schemes as a way to address health financing issues. Yet the complexity of the issues involved is often poorly understood. Ideally, insurance schemes should be designed in the context of an overall health policy and health financing strategy. Issues to address when designing a health insurance scheme include policy objectives, population coverage, benefits to be included (outpatient, inpatient, medicines, and so forth), organization of health services, premium calculation and payment mechanisms, utilization and cost-control measures, and administrative arrangements.

Provision of pharmaceutical benefits

Should social health insurance, private health insurance, or community prepaid health care schemes include pharmaceuticals in their list of benefits? At least three strong arguments favor including medicines in insurance schemes.

First, pharmaceuticals are an essential component of modern health care. Second, early treatment of acute illnesses such as malaria and treatment of chronic illnesses such as diabetes can reduce costly care for complications and hospitalizations. Third, because medicines make up such a large share of household health costs in many countries, their inclusion in an insurance program will make the program more acceptable and desirable.

Chapter 12 discusses health financing through insurance in detail.

11.7 Voluntary and other local financing

The cost of providing health care, including essential medicines, may be supported by a variety of community, employer, or other local financing sources.

NGOs play a significant role in the health services of some countries. NGOs often attract foreign and local donations of pharmaceuticals, medical supplies, equipment, and cash. Direct user charges often provide the major share of financing for these services, and markups on pharmaceuticals often subsidize salaries, immunizations, or other NGO costs.

NGOs that are able to provide significant amounts of health care and remain financially viable help balance the overall national sustainability equation (see Figure 11-1). Thus, as described in Chapter 8, facilitating NGOs' efforts to provide essential medicines as part of their overall package of services is in the interest of governments.

Aside from community pharmaceutical schemes and other Bamako Initiative–type programs, a host of voluntary community mechanisms exists in different countries to help support local health services (see Chapter 31). In some countries, villages maintain sick funds to pay the health costs, including medicines, of the poorest members of the village. Monies come from periodic assessments or special fund-raising events. Aside from structured insurance-like schemes, however, informal community fund-raising has not been able to sustain the supply of medicines for entire communities.

In many countries, some private companies and cooperative societies (coffee growers or mining companies, for example) provide health care for employees or members by maintaining a company health service, by reimbursing local private health providers ("self-insurance"), or by contributing to private insurance for employees. Companies may also work with local government health facilities, supplementing government funding with company funding for medicines, medical supplies, or other expenses.

Such arrangements also help balance the financial sustainability equation. They should be supported with information about the essential medicines concept, with copies of the national essential medicines list and standard treatment guidelines, and perhaps, on a selective basis, with access to public supply services.

11.8 Donor financing and development loans

As mentioned previously, the landscape of donor development assistance has been changing dramatically. Traditionally, donor assistance has come from multilateral institutions such as WHO, the United Nations Children's Fund, and development banks; from bilateral arrangements with donor governments; or from charitable organizations, other NGOs, and foundations. In recent years, the international community's commitment to global health and access to pharmaceuticals has increased—almost fourfold from 1990 to 2007 (Ravishankar et al. 2009). As a result, in addition to traditional sources of funding from bilateral and multilateral institutions, global health initiatives, private foundations, and public-private partnerships are playing much larger roles as resources to improve health in developing countries; for example, global health initiative resources have contributed to an aggregate increase in overall health financing (WHO Maximizing Positive Synergies Collaborative Group et al. 2009). Because funding for health comes from out-of-pocket sources in many developing countries, donors are being called on to finance health system scale-up to reach the MDGs.

Many developing countries have a hard time absorbing additional resources, however, because of a lack of human and infrastructural capacity, and donor funding presents problems because of its unpredictability, making planning difficult for countries (Hecht and Shah 2006). Funding that goes through a country's administrative structure rather than through independent initiatives can help build national financial capacity (Hecht and Shah 2006).

Development assistance has typically been targeted toward long-term health-sector development, often concentrating on specific areas such as primary health care, essential medicines, or immunization. Since the late 1990s, donor funding has been directed more toward the entire health sector as part of a sector-wide approach to aid or toward the national government budget instead of toward specific programs or interventions, which means that health program managers may have to take additional steps to get access to funding for specific health programs or pharmaceuticals. In addition, development banks now require countries to use poverty reduction strategy papers as a mechanism to coordinate funding in a way that contributes to an overall development strategy. Chapter 14 has more information.

Multilateral and bilateral organizations generally do not support recurrent costs for personnel, regular supplies of essential medicines, and other operating costs. International and local religious organizations and NGOs have supported recurrent costs, but such funding has become more difficult to obtain. Loans may be used for the long-term development of health care systems, human resources, and physical infrastructure. They may provide working capital to establish an RDF. But loans generally should not be used to finance the current cost of personnel, medicines, medical supplies, or other routine operating expenses.

For essential medicines, donor assistance has been used effectively in many countries to provide short- and long-term staff training, to develop and implement national medicine policies, to improve storage and transport systems, to improve supply management, to promote rational medicine use, and to strengthen pharmaceutical regulatory and quality assurance capacity. In addition, large initiatives, such as the U.S. President's Emergency Plan for AIDS Relief and the Global Fund, have provided resources to introduce and scale-up antiretroviral treatment programs, including procuring antiretrovirals, and to roll out artemisinin-based combination therapies for malaria. With an increasing global emphasis on strengthening health systems, more funding is available for long-term initiatives that will use systems strengthening as a way to increase access to medicines and commodities; for example, the GAVI Alliance has an innovative grant program designed to help countries clear health system bottlenecks that decrease immunization coverage, such as work force, management, and supply chain issues (WHO 2007). The grant funding is contingent on meeting performance outcomes.

In the poorest countries—with minimal foreign exchange earnings, limited cash income among the population, and no local production capacity—combined public and private resources may be insufficient to provide all essential medicines needs, even with the best selection, procurement, distribution, and use of medicines, especially in those countries that have a high HIV/AIDS or drug-resistant malaria burden. For such countries, outside assistance may be needed to fund some basic essential medicines requirements and is certainly needed to fund expensive antiretrovirals and new, expensive antimalarials.

Nevertheless, long-term human, financial, and institutional sustainability is an essential consideration in all development projects. Intensive financial support and large teams of advisers may achieve short-term success, but to achieve sustained success, a realistic transition to local staffing and financing must be planned from the outset.

Finally, governments can coordinate assistance from donors by establishing national health and pharmaceutical policies, by inviting donors to participate in the development of a master plan as a framework for action, and by convening regular donor coordination meetings (see Chapter 14). Sector-wide approaches, medium-term expenditure frameworks, and poverty reduction strategy papers help provide countries a framework for development planning, but donors need to harmonize procedures and reporting requirements to help countries handle multiple external funding streams. Also, donors are encouraged to make long-term commitments to assistance in the form of predictable on-budget financing (Hecht and Shah 2006).

11.9 Comparing financing mechanisms

Few health systems rely on a single funding mechanism. Political, economic, and social factors influence options for health financing. But financing mechanisms should meet certain stated policy objectives, and discussions about financing should be informed by a clear understanding of the choices.

Criteria for evaluating financing mechanisms

Access to medicines, rational medicine use, efficiency, equity, sustainability, and feasibility are among the most common and important criteria for evaluating funding mechanisms for pharmaceuticals.

Access to medicines: Are the availability and affordability of medicines improved? With user charges, for example, medicines may become more available but less affordable. In the end, are more people receiving the essential medicines they need?

Rational medicine use: Does the financing mechanism create incentives for overuse, underuse, or misuse of medicines? Patient demand is high when medicines are free, but provider-induced demand may be high if revenue from medicine charges is used for staff salaries. An insurance plan may achieve a uniquely effective balance if it stimulates patient demand by expanding access, uses cost controls to contain demand, and promotes standard treatments by providers.

Efficiency: Does the financing mechanism encourage the maximum output or health benefit from available resources? As noted earlier and in Chapter 10, two broad categories of efficiency exist—allocative and technical. Pharmaceutical financing decisions often try to improve technical efficiency related to pharmaceutical management.

Equity: Who benefits, and who pays for services? Equity in health care means that essential care is provided according to need and financed according to ability to pay. Equity implies universal access (availability and affordability) to basic health services, including medicines, regardless of income level.

Sustainability: Will a reasonable level of funding be maintained over time? Both the amount of revenue generated and the reliability of funding over time are important. A major problem with relying on donor funding is its volatility.

Administrative requirements: What are the administrative and managerial requirements to make the funding mechanism operational? For instance, managing a viable RDF is many times more demanding than managing a system in which medicines are free. Insurance programs require a host of new administrative arrangements. In contrast, government financing systems are usually well established, and donor administrative requirements, though often tedious, are usually well defined.

Other criteria that may be used to evaluate health financing options include acceptability, community involvement, flexibility, and health impact. Acceptability refers to the balance of support and resistance from the public, providers, and politicians. With financing mechanisms that meet other criteria, acceptance often grows with experience and understanding. Community involvement may be valued for its own sake, but it is often considered with the other criteria because it may contribute to efficiency, equity, and sustainability. Flexibility is the extent to which funds can be used for various purposes. Donor funds tend to have the greatest restrictions, and community financing schemes have greater flexibility. Improved health impact is the ultimate objective of pharmaceutical financing reforms, but data that directly link funding and impact are scant. Access to essential medicines becomes a more immediate measure of potential impact.

Application of the criteria for evaluating funding mechanisms

Using these evaluation criteria helps structure the comparison of funding mechanisms. Experience, local circumstances, and degree of subjectivity affect the way individual criteria are applied to financing mechanisms. Table 11-4 provides an illustrative comparison of funding mechanisms according to the preceding evaluation criteria. Several overall observations can be made.

Stereotyping and oversimplification should be avoided. Free government services may appear equitable, unless (as in some countries) political forces result in public pharmaceutical supplies being concentrated at national and regional referral hospitals in urban areas. User fees for poor rural populations may appear inequitable, but equity is actually improved if a situation of constant shortages requiring out-of-pocket purchase in the private sector at high prices is replaced by a community pharmaceutical scheme providing a reliable supply of low-cost medicines. Some national social health insurance programs provide health benefits so that low-income members are actually subsidizing high-income members. For example, in some countries, social security taxes are imposed only on wages below a certain level, so those with higher earning capacity do not have to pay taxes on much of their income. These wealthier people are often city dwellers who have the greatest access to, and make the most use of, government health services, thereby benefiting disproportionately from the payments of those with lower incomes.

Examples of common misperceptions about access, rational use, efficiency, sustainability, and administrative requirements could also be cited. The point is that comparisons of financing mechanisms should be based on clear analysis, experience, and the best available information, rather than on untested assumptions or stereotyped thinking.

Evaluation often depends on effectiveness of implementation. Proponents of RDFs cite their potential for financing a sustainable supply of low-cost medicines. Opponents cite numerous programs that generate minimal revenue with much effort, and nonfunctioning exemption programs for the poor. As noted earlier, the financial performance and health impact of a user-fee program are highly dependent on the way the program is managed and monitored.

Similarly, insurance programs are complex undertakings. A successful insurance plan must organize the registration of members and dependents, the definition of services covered, accurate projections of payments to set premiums, collection of premiums, handling of claims, payment to providers, utilization review, quality monitoring, and cost control. Bad planning or poor implementation of different elements can result in a program that is inefficient, inequitable, unsustainable, and administratively chaotic.

In short, it is important to distinguish between a financing mechanism that is inappropriate for a given setting and one that might be appropriate but is ineffectively implemented.

Seek improvement, not perfection. Policy makers sometimes discard a new financing alternative because it has certain limitations, potential inequities, or other undesirable features. The question is not whether a specific financing mechanism meets all criteria—none do. The question is whether it will, on balance, improve the pharmaceutical financing situation.

Doing nothing about pharmaceutical financing is often the easiest course for an uncertain policy maker or a nervous manager. But if financial resources are inadequate, access and quality of care will decline. Analysis of financing mechanisms should aim at identifying actions that will lead to significant improvements, not at finding perfect solutions.

11.10 Developing a pharmaceutical financing strategy

Because pharmaceutical financing is part of health financing, in many countries, complementary financing arrangements are evolving for different health care needs and population groups. Although each financing mechanism has benefits and limitations, the net effect of the pluralist

Table 11-4   Comparison of funding mechanisms by evaluation criteria

Funding mechanism	Access to essential medicines	Appropriate medicine use	Efficiency	Equity	Sustainability	Administrative requirements
Public financing (government budgets)	⇑ If budget sufficient and management adequate	⇑ With good selection and prescribing	□ No incentive for improvement	⇑⇓ Depends on who pays taxes and who receives services	⇑⇓ Depends on economic growth and government revenues	□ No new requirements
User fees						
Government RDFs	⇑ Access decreases for poor unless exemptions and other protections in place	⇑⇓ Fees may discourage overuse or lead to underuse; may encourage overprescribing if revenue for staff	⇑ Success depends on supply management improvements	⇑⇓ Higher-income contribute more; poor benefit if supply improved; exemption plans rarely work	⇑ With good management, reliable pharmaceutical supply	⇑ Much more demanding than free system
Community pharmaceutical schemes	⇑ Same as RDFs	⇑⇓ Same as RDFs	⇑ Same as RDFs	⇑ Local control and targeting support equity	⇑ Same as RDFs	⇑ Improvements require significant local management capacity
Direct private medicine purchases	⇑ Primarily benefits urban and higher-income people	⇑ Prices create affordability problem, which often leads to inadequate doses	⇑ Strong financial incentive	⇓ Poor cannot afford essential medicines	⇑ For population that can afford medicines	⇑⇓ Systems exist in private sector
Health insurance						
Social	⇑ If pharmaceutical benefits included in benefit package	⇑⇓ Appropriate use if insurance cost controls in existence; inappropriate use if patients exert pressure on provider for medicines	□ No efficiency incentive	⇑ Should be very equitable	⇑ Requires good management, adequate premiums	⇑ Substantial administrative requirements for new system; requires fraud and abuse controls
Private	⇑ Same as social insurance	⇑⇓ Same as social insurance	⇑ Some incentive	⇑⇓ Increased equity depends on membership	⇑ Requires good management, sufficient number of members to maintain sustainability	⇑ Same as social insurance
Community financing (different mechanisms have different effects)	⇑⇓	⇑⇓	⇑	⇑	⇑	⇑⇓
Donor financing						
Bilateral and multilateral grants	⇑	⇑⇓ Similar to public financing	□ Similar to public financing	⇑ Usually involves transfer from richer countries	⇓ Not sustainable	⇑ Reporting requirements
Development loans	⇑	⇑⇓ Same as grants	□ Same as grants	⇑⇓ Depends on terms and sources of funds for repayment	⇓ Not sustainable	⇑ Reporting requirements

Note: ⇑ = increases; ⇓ = decreases; ⇑⇓ = may increase or decrease; □ = no change.

approach is to distribute the burden of health financing across several sectors. No one health financing strategy will fit all countries—each country's context must dictate the best approach.

If the essential medicine supply is adequate, the challenge for policy makers and essential medicines program managers is to maintain the funding, pharmaceutical supply system, and medicine use patterns that ensure this adequacy. If the supply of essential medicines is inadequate, efforts should be made to use available funds better through more efficient selection, procurement, distribution, and use of medicines. Efforts to balance public resources and the demand for health care may also include measures to encourage private and NGO health providers.

When efforts to improve therapeutic and operational efficiency and to moderate demand for medicines do not balance the sustainability equation, additional funding is needed. Managers can make the case for greater government funding of pharmaceuticals, introduce or strengthen user fees for medicines, introduce or expand health insurance coverage for medicines, or seek donor assistance. In each case, efforts should be made to ensure that available public resources are targeted to those most in need.

The challenge for policy makers, essential medicines program managers, NGO managers, and others concerned with pharmaceutical financing is to make optimal use of every available source of financing. Success depends on political commitment, adaptation of financing mechanisms to local circumstances, good leadership and management, and modification of financing systems based on experience. Equity of access, quality of medicines, and rational use remain key objectives for any financing strategy. ■

References and further readings

★ = Key readings.

Carrin, G., M.-P. Waelkens, and B. Criel. 2005. Community-Based Health Insurance in Developing Countries: A Study of Its Contribution to the Performance of Health Financing Systems. *Tropical Medicine and International Health* 10(8):799–811.

Enemark, U., A. Alban, E. C. Seoane-Vasquez, and A. Seiter. 2005. Purchasing Pharmaceuticals. In *Spending Wisely: Buying Health Services for the Poor*, A. S. Preker and J. C. Langenbrunner, eds. Washington, D.C.: World Bank.

Ensor, T., and S. Cooper. 2004. Overcoming Barriers to Health Service Access: Influencing the Demand Side. *Health Policy and Planning* 19(2):69–79.

★ Gottret, P., and G. Schieber. 2006. *Health Financing Revisited: A Practitioner's Guide*. Washington, D.C.: World Bank. <http://siteresources.worldbank.org/INTHSD/Resources/topics/Health-Financing/HFRFull.pdf>

Gottret P., G. J. Schieber, and H. R. Waters, eds. 2008. *Good Practices in Health Financing: Lessons from Reforms in Low- and Middle-Income Countries*. Washington, D.C.: World Bank.

Hammond, A. L., W. J. Kramer, R. S. Katz, J. T. Tran, and C. Walker. 2007. *The Next 4 Billion: Market Size and Business Strategy at the Base of the Pyramid*. Washington, D.C.: World Resources Institute and International Finance Corporation. <http://www.wri.org/publication/the-next-4-billion>

★ Hecht, R., and R. Shah. 2006. Recent Trends and Innovations in Development Assistance for Health. In *Disease Control Priorities in Developing Countries*. 2nd ed. D. T. Jamison, J. G. Breman, A. R. Measham, G. Alleyne, M. Claeson, D. B. Evans, P. Jha, A. Mills, and P. Musgrove, eds. Washington, D.C.: World Bank and Oxford University Press.

James, C. D., K. Hanson, B. McPake, D. Balabanova, D. Gwatkin, I. Hopwood, C. Kirunga, et al. 2006. To Retain or Remove User Fees? Reflections on the Current Debate in Low- and Middle-Income Countries. *Applied Health Economics and Health Policy* 5(3):137–53.

Kirigia, J. M., and A. J. Diarra-Nama. 2008. Can Countries of the WHO African Region Wean Themselves off Donor Funding for Health? *Bulletin of the World Health Organization* 86(11):889–95. <http://www.ncbi.nlm.nih.gov/pmc/articles/PMC2649560/pdf/08-054932.pdf>

Kirigia, J. M., A. Preker, G. Carrin, C. Mwikisa, and A. J. Diarra-Nama. 2006. An Overview of Health Financing Patterns and the Way Forward in the WHO African Region. *East African Medical Journal* 83(8) (Suppl.):1–28. <http://www.who.int/health_financing/documents/eamj-health_financing_africa.pdf>

Lagarde, M., and N. Palmer. 2008. The Impact of User Fees on Health Service Utilization in Low- and Middle-Income Countries: How Strong Is the Evidence? *Bulletin of the World Health Organization* 86(11):839–48. <http://www.who.int/bulletin/volumes/86/11/07-049197.pdf>

Lopez, A. D., C. D. Mathers, M. Ezzati, D. T. Jamison, and C. J. L. Murray, eds. 2006. *Global Burden of Disease and Risk Factors*. Washington, D.C.: World Bank and Oxford University Press. <http://www.dcp2.org/pubs/GBD>

McIntyre, D. 2007. *Learning from Experience: Health Care Financing in Low- and Middle-Income Countries*. Geneva: Global Forum for Health Research.

Palmer, N., D. H. Mueller, L. Gilson, A. Mills, and A. Haines. 2004. Health Financing to Promote Access in Low Income Settings—How Much Do We Know? *Lancet* 364:1365–70.

★ Preker, A. S., and J. C. Langenbrunner, eds. 2005. *Spending Wisely: Buying Health Services for the Poor*. Washington, D.C.: World Bank.

★ Ravishankar, N., P. Gubbins, R. J. Cooley, K. Leach-Kemon, C. M. Michaud, D. T. Jamison, and C. J. L. Murray. 2009. Financing of Global Health: Tracking Development Assistance for Health from 1990 to 2007. *Lancet* 373(9681):2113–24.

Roberts, M., W. Hsiao, P. Berman, and M. Reich. 2004. *Getting Health Reform Right: A Guide to Improving Performance and Equity*. New York: Oxford University Press.

★ Schieber, G., C. Baeza, D. Kress, and M. Maier. 2006. Financing Health Systems in the 21st Century. In *Disease Control Priorities in Developing Countries*. 2nd ed. D. T. Jamison, J. G. Breman, A. R. Measham, G. Alleyne, M. Claeson, D. B. Evans, P. Jha, A. Mills, and P. Musgrove, eds. Washington, D.C.: World Bank and Oxford University Press. <http://www.dcp2.org/pubs/DCP>

Schieber, G., P. Gottret, L. Fleisher, and A. Leive. 2007. Financing Global Health: Mission Unaccomplished. *Health Affairs* 26:921–34.

Sekhri, N., and W. Savedoff. 2005. Private Health Insurance: Implications for Developing Countries. *Bulletin of the World Health Organization* 83(2):127–34. <http://www.who.int/entity/bulletin/volumes/83/2/en/index.html>

UN (United Nations) Millennium Project. 2005. *Investing in Development: A Practical Plan to Achieve the Millennium Development Goals; Overview*. New York: UN Millennium Project. <http://www.unmillenniumproject.org/reports/index_overview.htm>

ASSESSMENT GUIDE

Pharmaceutical financing policy and needs

- Is pharmaceutical financing included in national health and national medicine policy?
- Has a comprehensive estimate been made of pharmaceutical financing needs?
- Has a formal budget gap analysis been done recently?

National economic and health financing indicators

- What is the per capita GDP?
- What is the total national health expenditure (public and private) per capita?
- What is the total national health expenditure as a percentage of the GDP?
- What are total government expenditures as a percentage of the GDP?
- What percentage of total public expenditures do health expenditures represent?
- What is the percentage breakdown of health spending by source (public, private, NGO, donor)?

National pharmaceutical financing indicators

- What is the total per capita pharmaceutical consumption (from all sources)?
- What percentage of total health expenditures (from all sources) do pharmaceuticals represent?
- What is the percentage breakdown of pharmaceutical spending by source (public, private, NGO, donor)?

Public pharmaceutical financing indicators

- What is the total public expenditure on pharmaceuticals?
- What is the per capita public expenditure on pharmaceuticals?
- What is the percentage breakdown of public health expenditures (personnel, medicines, other)?

Efficiency of public pharmaceutical expenditures

- Allocative efficiency: Is the pharmaceutical budget appropriately distributed to ensure a supply of essential medicines, address priority health problems, and serve groups most in need?
- What percentage of the public pharmaceutical budget is used for national and referral hospitals?

- Therapeutic efficiency: Are an essential medicines list and standard treatments used? Is medicine use rational?
- Operating efficiency: Are procurement and distribution well managed?

User charges for medicines (see Chapter 13)

- Are user fees charged for medicines and services at government facilities?
- Is revenue used as a revolving fund specifically to resupply medicines?
- What percentage of government pharmaceutical expenditures is recovered through user charges?

Health insurance (see Chapter 12)

- What types of health insurance presently exist: compulsory, voluntary, community?
- What percentage of the population is covered by health insurance?
- What percentage of those insured have policies that cover pharmaceuticals?
- What methods exist for supply and payment for pharmaceutical benefits?

Donor financing (see Chapter 14)

- What percentage of total government health expenditures is represented by international assistance?
- What is the total value of international aid for pharmaceuticals?
- What are the major sources of donor funding for the pharmaceutical sector?

Effects of current pharmaceutical financing arrangements

- What is the availability of medicines in the public and private sectors?
- How affordable are pharmaceuticals in the public and private sectors?
- How equitable is access to medicines for rural, poor, and medically needy populations?
- What are the incentives for rational or irrational medicine use?

Note: It is preferable to compare budgets and expenditures in terms of local currency, U.S. dollars, and international dollars. Data for the three most recent years should be used to show expenditure trends. Both budgeted and actual expenditure data should be included. Price basis for pharmaceuticals should be clarified (producer, wholesale, retail).

WHO (World Health Organization). 2009a. Medicines Strategy and Policies: Good Governance for Medicines Program. *Who Drug Information* 23(2):122–6. <http://whqlibdoc.who.int/druginfo/23_2_2009.pdf>

———. 2009b. *World Health Statistics 2009*. (Updated annually). Geneva: WHO. <http://www.who.int/whosis/whostat/en/>

———. 2007. *The Global Fund Strategic Approach to Health System Strengthening; Report from WHO to the Global Fund Secretariat*. Geneva: WHO. <http://www.who.int/healthsystems/GF_strategic_approach_%20HS.pdf>

★ ———. 2005a. Achieving Universal Health Coverage: Developing the Health Financing System. Geneva: WHO Department of Health Systems Financing, Health Policy. <http://www.who.int/health_financing/documents/pb_e_05_1-universal_coverage.pdf>

———. 2005b. Designing Health Financing Systems to Reduce Catastrophic Health Expenditure. Geneva: WHO Department of Health Systems Financing, Health Policy. <http://www.who.int/health_financing/documents/pb_e_05_2-catastrophic.pdf>

———. 2005c. Sustainable Health Financing, Universal Coverage and Social Health Insurance. World Health Assembly Resolution 58.33, Executive Board Resolution. Geneva, WHO. <http://www.who.int/health_financing/documents/cov-wharesolution5833/en/index.html>

———. 2004a. *Equitable Access to Essential Medicines: A Framework for Collective Action*. Geneva: WHO. <http://whqlibdoc.who.int/hq/2004/WHO_EDM_2004.4.pdf>

———. 2004b. *Reaching Universal Coverage via Social Health Insurance: Key Design Features in the Transition Period*. Geneva: WHO. <http://whqlibdoc.who.int/hq/2004/EIP_FER_DP_04.2.pdf>

———. 2004c. *The World Medicines Situation*. Geneva: WHO. <http://apps.who.int/medicinedocs/collect/medicinedocs/pdf/s6160e/s6160e.pdf>

———. 1993. *Evaluation of Recent Changes in the Financing of Health Services: Report of a WHO Study Group*. Geneva: WHO.

WHO/EMP/MAR (World Health Organization Departments of Essential Medicines and Pharmaceutical Policies & Ethics, Equity, Trade and Human Rights). 2009. *Measuring Transparency in the Public Pharmaceutical Sector: Assessment Instrument*. Geneva: WHO <http://apps.who.int/medicinedocs/documents/s16732e/s16732e.pdf>

WHO Maximizing Positive Synergies Collaborative Group et al. 2009. An Assessment of Interactions between Global Health Initiatives and Country Health Systems. *Lancet* 373(9681):2137–69.

WHO/TCM (World Health Organization/Technical Cooperation for Essential Drugs and Traditional Medicine). 2006. *Using Indicators to Measure Country Pharmaceutical Situations: Fact Book on WHO Level I and Level II Monitoring Indicators*. Geneva: WHO. <http://apps.who.int/medicinedocs/documents/s14101e/s14101e.pdf>

World Bank. 1993. *World Development Report 1993: Investing in Health*. New York: Oxford University Press. <http://files.dcp2.org/pdf/WorldDevelopmentReport1993.pdf>

CHAPTER 12

Pharmaceutical benefits in insurance programs

Summary   12.2

12.1 The challenge of providing universal health coverage   12.2

12.2 What is health insurance?   12.3

12.3 Main components of health insurance financing   12.4
Revenue collection • Risk pooling • Prepayment • Purchasing health care services

12.4 Potential problems with insurance systems   12.5

12.5 Provider payment mechanisms   12.6
Cost sharing through co-payment • Capitation payment • Fee for service • Case payment • Payment for performance (incentive payments) • Budget transfer • Salary

12.6 Including medicines as part of insurance benefits   12.8
Controlling the costs of medicines through insurance programs • Access to medicines and rational medicine use

12.7 Social health insurance   12.11
Challenges of social health insurance systems

12.8 Community-based health insurance   12.12
Community-based management • Challenges with community-based health insurance

12.9 Private health insurance   12.14
Expansion of private health insurance

12.10 Health or medical savings accounts   12.16
Challenges with medical savings accounts

12.11 Implementing an appropriate insurance scheme   12.17

Assessment guide   12.19

Glossary   12.19

References and further readings   12.20

ILLUSTRATIONS

Table 12-1   Countries with medicines covered by health insurance in 1999 and 2003   12.9
Table 12-2   Organizational features of selected community-based health insurance schemes in West Africa   12.13

BOX

Box 12-1   Assessing a country's enabling environment for insurance reform   12.18

COUNTRY STUDIES

CS 12-1   Financing maternal and child health services in Bolivia   12.7
CS 12-2   Patterns of medicine use by senior citizens in the United States   12.10
CS 12-3   The effect of HIV/AIDS on a community-based health program in Tanzania   12.12
CS 12-4   Strengthening and sustaining community-based health insurance schemes in Uganda   12.15
CS 12-5   Percentage of insurance in health care spending in twenty-six countries: social insurance versus private insurance   12.16
CS 12-6   Medical savings accounts in Singapore   12.17

SUMMARY

Health insurance is a mechanism for spreading the risks of incurring health care costs over a group of individuals or households, protecting the individual from a catastrophic financial loss in the event of a serious illness. Insurance, therefore, spreads the burden of payment for illness among all the members of the scheme whether they are ill or healthy, poor or rich. By their very nature, insurance schemes act as financing agents: they receive funds from employers, households, and the government and use these funds to purchase health care for their beneficiaries. Therefore, the main components of insurance schemes are collecting revenue, pooling resources and risks, and purchasing quality goods and services.

Many countries see the initiation or promotion of one or more insurance schemes as a way to address health financing issues and achieve universal health care coverage for citizens. Health insurance is appealing to governments because it takes the entire financial burden and spreads the total cost of insured health care among various partners. However, when governments consider instituting health insurance, they need to be aware of the realities of implementation; the complexity of the issues involved is often poorly understood. No one, widely accepted model of universal health insurance would be accepted in all societies, and how best to develop one in a resource-poor setting is still a matter of considerable debate. Whatever type of health financing mechanism a country decides to adopt, the transition to universal coverage may require several years, even decades.

This chapter covers four models of health insurance—

- Social or public health insurance
- Private health insurance
- Community-based health insurance
- Health or medical savings accounts

Any health insurance model may or may not cover medicines. Some insurance schemes incorporate medicines as part of a comprehensive care package, others compensate for them separately, and others do not cover them at all. However, strong arguments favor including medicines in insurance schemes because proper use of medicines can help prevent serious illness and death, and because pharmaceuticals make up such a large share of out-of-pocket spending in countries around the world.

Health insurance coverage for medicines offers significant potential to reduce the burden of disease and poverty. Using their power as large-scale purchasers, health insurance programs with pharmaceutical benefits can expand access to medicines at affordable prices to vulnerable populations and enforce better prescribing by clinicians and more cost-effective use by consumers. Furthermore, carefully designed insurance-based financing for medicines is both scalable and sustainable.

In part because of the pervasive potential for "moral hazard" (which in this case refers to more frequent use of services or medicines by members of an insurance scheme than would occur were they not insured), well-managed health insurance programs—whether public or private, mandatory or voluntary—are always looking for ways to manage costs efficiently. Public and private insurance programs control pharmaceutical expenditures through measures related to payment, management, prescribing patterns, dispensing practices, and use. Such programs can therefore profoundly affect the quality of prescribing by making reimbursement depend on adherence to treatment guidelines or restricted formularies. Ultimately, cost-control measures should aim to optimize access to and rational use of essential medicines, which remain a highly cost-effective element of health care, particularly for vulnerable populations.

12.1 The challenge of providing universal health coverage

In many countries, especially those with the fewest resources, poor people are often caught in a vicious cycle of poverty that causes ill health, and ill health in turn sustains poverty. Much of health care in developing countries is financed out-of-pocket, a system that places the largest burden on the poorest people. For example, household spending accounts for more than 60 percent of total health spending in low-income countries (Gottret and Schieber 2006), of which 60 to 90 percent may be spent on medicines

(WHO 2000). In addition to those direct costs, income is lost when family members are sick, and this loss reinforces the poverty-illness cycle. Women are especially vulnerable, because they are usually the main family caregivers.

The objective of universal health coverage is to ensure that all of a country's citizens have access to adequate and affordable health care. Traditionally, governments have provided a national health service for all citizens with financing through tax revenue. Many of these health systems have not worked well or consistently provided needed medicines, a gap that has led to increased out-of-pocket spending for health care services and medicines in the private sector, thereby worsening household poverty. Evidence from multiple countries has shown that a lack of health insurance is a key condition related to catastrophic household spending for health care (Xu et al. 2003). In an attempt to make health financing systems more equitable and increase coverage to the entire population, many low- and middle-income countries are exploring ways to strengthen such systems, including through various health insurance models.

People in most high-income countries are already covered by some form of public or private health insurance; however, the median coverage is only 35 percent in Latin America, 10 percent in Asia, and 8 percent in Africa (WHO 2004a). Health insurance coverage that includes pharmaceuticals has expanded access to medicines in many countries, including Argentina, China, Egypt, South Africa, and Vietnam (WHO 2004b).

Health insurance schemes appeal to both citizens and their governments because they help manage the financial burden by spreading the total cost of insured health care among various partners. In addition, donors and international financial institutions, such as the World Bank, are finding health insurance to be an increasingly feasible health financing mechanism for developing countries. Nevertheless, no one model of universal health insurance would be widely accepted in all societies, and although universal health coverage—where no citizens face the risk of losing their life savings because of catastrophic medical expense—is a highly desirable goal, how best to achieve it in a resource-poor country with underdeveloped private or public insurance schemes is still being debated.

This chapter presents an overview of how health insurance plays a role in financing health services, in general, and medicines, in particular. The chapter describes the main components of health insurance and potential problems with insurance systems. Four common types of health insurance schemes are described, with examples of how they are operating in different countries. Finally, although this chapter describes many options and potential paths, the right direction to take will depend greatly on the context of cultural expectations and the status and existence of other legal, financial, and regulatory institutions.

12.2 What is health insurance?

Health insurance is a mechanism for spreading the risks of potential health care costs over a group of individuals or households, with the goal of protecting the individual from a catastrophic financial loss in the event of serious illness. Insurance, therefore, spreads the burden of payment for illness among all the participants of the scheme, whether they are ill or healthy, poor or rich.

In principle, risk sharing through insurance is most worthwhile when the event insured against is largely unpre-

dictable, infrequent, costly, unwanted, and uncontrollable by the insured. A good example is insuring a house against fire. The event is unlikely and unpredictable but would be very costly if it occurred. Many people are prepared to pay a regular premium for a lifetime to gain peace of mind against a catastrophe that they hope will never happen.

Applying this traditional view of insurance to medical care presents some difficulties: people can control some aspects of use; some services are low cost; some conditions are frequently or continuously experienced (for example, medicines needed for chronic conditions); in some cases illness is difficult to define; people sometimes want to incur the risk (for example, pregnancy); and the presence of insurance increases the use of services. Despite these difficulties, the concept of risk sharing through insurance has become highly developed in the health sector.

The principal aims of well-managed insurance schemes are to reduce catastrophic financial loss in the event of a serious illness and to guarantee the funds or access needed to secure necessary, if expensive, medical services. Health insurance provides this financial protection by evening out household health expenditures. In addition, purchasing, payment, and monitoring mechanisms within health insurance schemes can contribute to efficient use of resources and improved quality of care (Eichler and Lewis 2000); for example—

- Access and affordability can be improved by removing financial barriers and by giving providers incentives to serve the covered population.
- Equity can be improved if higher-income people contribute more than lower-income people and relatively healthy people subsidize those who consume more system resources and are relatively sick (risk pooling).
- Efficiency can be improved if incentives are incorporated into the system to encourage appropriate use of resources.
- Quality can be improved if the system is structured to reward providers who deliver high-quality services and penalize those who do not.

This chapter covers four models of health insurance, defined below. Any model may or may not cover medicines as part of its benefit package.

Social or public health insurance: The most typical understanding of social health insurance is that membership is compulsory for a designated population; financial contributions into the system, which are often deducted directly from wages, link to the receipt of benefits; cross-subsidization occurs between high- and low-risk groups and high- and low-income groups; and management usually has some degree of independence from the government (Gottret and Schieber 2006). Social health insurance schemes have existed in different parts of the world for some time, especially in Western Europe; Germany launched its program in 1883 (Carrin and James 2005).

Private health insurance: Private indemnity insurance is (usually) paid for by voluntary contributions from employers, mutual societies, cooperatives, or individuals. In high-income countries, private health insurance either replaces or supplements public coverage. The Netherlands has the greatest proportion of population covered by some sort of private health insurance, while the United States and Uruguay are countries with the highest private health insurance expenditures relative to total health expenditures (Sekhri and Savedoff 2005).

Community-based health insurance: In many countries in Asia, Africa, and Latin America, prepayment plans based on the concept of pooling risk and resources have been developed for rural populations, groups in informal employment, or others without access to other health insurance. Such schemes are based on community affiliation, and the community is highly involved in managing the system.

Health or medical savings accounts: Not strictly a form of insurance, medical savings accounts (MSAs) encourage individuals, often by providing tax advantages or subsidies, to save for the expected costs of medical care, enlist health care consumers in controlling costs, and mobilize additional funds for health systems. Only a few countries, including Singapore, China, and the United States, use the concept of health savings accounts.

12.3   Main components of health insurance financing

Decisions that affect the availability of health insurance in a country are important to all aspects of health service delivery but are largely outside the control of national medicine policies and essential medicines programs. As insurance assumes a greater role in health care in many countries, however, understanding health financing, and specifically insurance concepts, becomes increasingly important.

By their very nature, insurance schemes act as financing agents: they receive funds from employers, households, and the government, and they use those funds to purchase health care for their beneficiaries. Therefore, the main components of insurance are collecting revenue, pooling resources and risks, and purchasing goods and services (Gottret and Schieber 2006; WHO 2000).

Generally, insurance can be classified as using either a *single payer* or *multiple payer*. In *single-payer systems,* one organization (usually the government) collects and pools revenues and purchases health services for the whole population. All citizens are included in a single risk pool, and single-payer

insurers have powerful influence as the only buyer of health services (a situation known as monopsony). In *multiple-payer systems,* several different organizations perform all functions for specific parts of the population. Their insurance pools have different levels of risk, and consumers may be able to choose their own insurer.

Other basic issues related to sources of health care financing and achieving financial sustainability for pharmaceutical supplies are covered in Chapter 11.

Revenue collection

Revenue collection is the process by which the health system receives money (usually taxes or premiums) from households, organizations, and companies, as well as from donors. Health systems have a limited set of mechanisms for collecting revenue, such as general taxation, mandated social health insurance contributions (usually salary related and almost never risk related), voluntary private health insurance contributions (usually risk related), or out-of-pocket payments from individuals.

Most high-income countries rely on either general taxation or mandated social health insurance contributions. As a country's income increases, so does the proportion of revenue that its government collects. Estimates show that in the early 2000s the average percentage of gross domestic product (GDP) collected by central governments as revenues was related to wealth (Gottret and Schieber 2006; Gupta et al. 2004). Therefore, low- and middle-income countries struggle to collect enough revenue to finance basic health services equitably and efficiently. In general, low-income countries depend far more on out-of-pocket financing, because of their low levels of income (resulting in a limited tax base), large informal sectors, and weak administrative capacity (Schieber and Maeda 1997).

Risk pooling

Risk pooling spreads the financial risk associated with health care among large groups. Pooling requires some transfer of resources (or cross-subsidization) from healthy people to sick people and from rich to poor. Without such pooling, poor people are exposed to serious financial hardship when they get sick; the more extensive the risk pooling in a health financing system, the less individuals will have to bear the financial consequences of their own health risks, and the more they are likely to have access to the care they need (Carrin and James 2004).

In a successful pooling scheme, contributions, whether through tax or insurance premiums, are not based on risk but based on the ability to pay. If the pooling is voluntary, high-risk people and poor people will join the pool because they see personal benefit, while healthier and richer people see less value for themselves (known as "adverse selection").

Fragmentation of the pool, or the involvement of too many small organizations in revenue collection, pooling, and purchasing, restricts the efficiency of all three tasks. In fragmented systems, the number of existing pools and purchasers does not matter, but rather the issue is that many of them are too small to be sustainable. Large pools are better than small ones because they have a bigger share of contributions that can be allocated exclusively to health services. A large pool can take advantage of economies of scale in administration and purchasing and reduce the level of the contributions required to protect against uncertain needs, while still ensuring that funds are sufficient to pay for services without any risk sharing.

When all payments for health care services and pharmaceuticals are made out-of-pocket, this situation represents the highest degree of pool fragmentation. In this case, each person constitutes a pool and thus has to pay for his or her own health services.

Prepayment

Prepayment is a feature of all types of health insurance. Because it unlinks expected health expenditures from the ability to pay, prepayment is a critical mechanism for attaining health care equity. Without prepayment, consumers pay entirely out-of-pocket for health care, purchasing it, like any other service, whenever it is needed. The fairness of health financing is often measured by the amount of prepayment required, because any out-of-pocket spending opens the consumer to financial risk (WHO 2000).

Risk pooling coupled with prepayment redistributes health spending between high- and low-risk individuals (risk subsidies) and high- and low-income individuals (equity subsidies). Pool members pay for expected costs in advance, which relieves them of uncertainty and ensures compensation should a loss occur. However, few systems are able to meet the entire cost of health care from the prepaid and pooled funds. Most require some type of co-payment for the use of health services or the purchase of medicines, which households must pay out of pocket.

Prepayment without pooling simply allows for advance purchase of health services or purchase on an installment basis, such as in the example of health or medical savings accounts, which is presented later.

Purchasing health care services

Purchasing is the process by which pooled funds are paid to providers to deliver health goods and services. All health financing systems face similar challenges in choosing which health services to buy or provide, who should provide them, and which payment mechanisms are used. The fact that a government takes responsibility for collecting revenues for the health system does not necessarily mean that it should also provide care. To provide services, most health systems use a variety of methods involving a mix of public, private for-profit, and private not-for-profit providers.

The advantages of using pooled resources to purchase services include not only economies of scale but also strengthened capacity to bargain with providers regarding price, quality, and opportunity of services. Purchasing agreements can provide incentives for health service providers—including the promotion of rational medicine use—through contracting, budgeting, and payment mechanisms (see Section 12.5). The purchasing process should include an ongoing search for the most cost-effective services to purchase, the most cost-effective providers to purchase from, and the most efficient mechanisms and contracting arrangements to pay for such services.

Three categories describe the financial relationship between the insurer and the service providers in health insurance. The first is *reimbursement,* where providers are paid after they deliver the services. An example of the reimbursement approach is called *indemnity insurance,* where no contractual arrangements exist between insurers and providers, and the provider is paid a fee for the service. The second is *contracting,* where the insurers negotiate payment agreements with certain doctors, hospitals, and health care providers, to supply a range of services and possibly medicines at reduced cost to those insured. This method can free the patient from the need to pay for health care up front and also helps contain costs and control quality by giving the insurers direct purchasing power over providers. Third is *integration with providers,* when the roles of health care purchasers and providers are under one organizational umbrella (such as a government). One example is a health maintenance organization, where the providers are salaried employees of the insurer (OECD 2004).

12.4 Potential problems with insurance systems

Market failure is the term used by economists to describe circumstances that constrain the smooth operation of the market (Normand and Weber 1994). Economists generally agree that governments need to develop structures and policies to counter the effects of market failure. In the case of health services, the major sources of market failure are the monopoly power of providers and ignorance and uncertainty among consumers (Normand and Weber 1994).

Monopoly power of providers: To protect the public and ensure a basic level of competence, entry into the health care professions is restricted by licensing and other rules that govern access to health care. Thus, the health care professions exercise monopoly power, limited to some degree if providers must compete against one another. A country's health policy should ensure that this monopoly power does not work against the interests of the patient. In addition to the power exercised by professionals, a "natural monopoly" occurs when only one service provider is available in a particular area who can provide care efficiently. In the case of access to medicines, people in rural areas may have little choice but to buy pharmaceuticals from a retail drug seller or a dispensing doctor if other sources are too far away.

Ignorance and uncertainty among consumers: Consumers depend on health care professionals to inform them of which services are appropriate and also to provide those services. This asymmetry of information further reinforces the monopoly power of professionals. In addition, the time at which any one person will need access to health services or medicines is usually very uncertain. When uncertainty and ignorance about the need or options for health care are combined with the high cost of specific types of care, market failure often results.

In addition, insurance only works if some people pay more in contributions than they take out in services, to compensate for those whose care costs the scheme more than they pay in. An insurance contribution is not a payment for a service but rather the price for insuring a particular risk (Normand and Weber 1994). Therefore, insurance systems face several problems that can undermine the potential benefits of prepayment and risk sharing—

Moral hazard: When members of a health insurance scheme use services or consume medicines more frequently than if they were not insured, the phenomenon is called "moral hazard." Deductibles and co-payments are commonly used to avert this problem. Moral hazard can be overcome by clearly describing the benefit package and trying to coordinate the co-payments and the provider payment methods with incentives for necessary care only.

Adverse selection: This term describes the tendency for people at greatest health risk and people with chronic illnesses to join voluntary insurance programs, whereas the healthiest people, whose premiums should be used to pay the bills of the sicker members, avoid joining. The effect of adverse selection is to raise costs and reduce the risk-sharing effect of insurance, which makes financial sustainability much more difficult to achieve; for example, in Senegal, unstable insurance schemes showed evidence of adverse selection compared with financially stable schemes that registered a larger proportion of household members—both healthy and unhealthy (Atim et al. 2005).

Skimming: This problem occurs when insurers use various screening measures to avoid insuring people at greatest health risk (and therefore of greatest expense to them). Skimming reduces the equity benefits of insurance by excluding those who are most in need.

Cost escalation: Rising costs can result from improvements in or greater use of technology, increased use (greater demand caused by insurance coverage), and increases of both the population in general and older populations. Private indemnity insurance suffers from the tendency toward cost escalation because the insurer usually has no contractual relationship with the provider. Thus the tendency is both for insureds to increase their use of medicines and services and for providers to overprovide services. The other models allow for greater cost controls.

Unrealistic expectations: In addition to these problems, insurers, particularly in developing countries, frequently have to deal with misunderstanding of the insurance concept by the public and by health providers. Members may think that premiums are like deposits in a savings account: "If I have paid 10 dollars each month in premiums this year, I must be sure to receive 120 dollars' worth of health services in a year." This belief leads to unrealistic demands that everyone should receive at least as much as he or she has paid in. Insurance is not sustainable in such an environment, because no risk sharing occurs. Other members may avoid using their insurance because they believe that they can claim only as much as they have contributed in premiums. Considerable effort may be needed to educate the insured, the general public, and health providers.

Country Study 12-1 shows some of the problems experienced with a new insurance scheme in Bolivia that targeted women and children. Experienced public and private insurance organizations have developed measures to counter moral hazard, adverse selection, skimming, cost escalation, and lack of familiarity with insurance. Policy makers, government insurance regulators, and insurers need to work together to implement these measures.

12.5 Provider payment mechanisms

Methods of provider payment are a crucial part of the design of all insurance schemes. Each method affects the administrative costs of the scheme according to the complexity of approving claims and making payments. Similarly, all payment methods include incentives that may reduce or increase demand for treatment or medicines by the insured and reduce or increase costs and quality of care by the provider. It is most important that, whichever method of provider payment is chosen, mechanisms are incorporated to contain costs while maintaining needed access and quality of care for the sick.

Country Study 12-1
Financing maternal and child health services in Bolivia

Bolivia has higher maternal and child mortality rates than any other country in Latin America. Most of those deaths occur in the poorest sectors of society and are preventable with adequate health care. In 1996, Bolivian officials began the National Insurance for Mothers and Children (SNMN) program in an effort to lower economic barriers to health care for mothers and children.

Through the program, women and children under five years of age receive free medical care and medicines for certain medical conditions that are common causes of maternal and child mortality, such as unattended births for women, and diarrhea and acute respiratory illnesses for children. All levels of care are covered in the program, including primary care facilities and hospitals.

Since the implementation of the SNMN program, use of health services covered by the program, especially among the poor, increased. However, this increase lowered the motivation levels of health workers because of the influx of patients, which was unaccompanied by an increase in remuneration. As a result, SNMN patients were reportedly being treated unfairly in medical facilities, and amenities received, length of stay, and even treatment prescribed have reportedly all been used to discriminate against insured patients.

In 1999, SNMN was expanded to become the Basic Health Insurance plan, which expanded coverage to other additional health priorities that had previously been addressed by vertical public health programs, such as tuberculosis. New changes in 2002 doubled the financing, expanded the benefit package, revised reimbursement schedules, and introduced performance agreements between the different levels of the Ministry of Health's decentralized system.

Results suggest that the reforms further increased coverage of priority maternal and child services; for example, between 1998 and 2002, pneumonia and diarrhea coverage for children under five years increased from 69 percent to 100 percent and 29 percent to 43 percent, respectively. Despite these increases, however, after a few years, coverage rates began tapering off and even decreasing. In addition, despite the introduction of public health insurance, households remain an important source of financing for the sector, with out-of-pocket expenditures contributing 30 percent of national health spending.

To encourage additional gains, the government added a matching grant program with conditions to encourage mothers to use health services for themselves and their children; however, this program does not target certain populations, a situation that could exacerbate stubborn rural-urban coverage gaps.

Sources: Partnerships for Health Reform n.d.; Camacho et al. 2003; Narváez 2009.

Designing payment mechanisms for medicines is more challenging because insurers find it more difficult to establish reimbursement schemes that cover all the places that sell medicines, such as pharmacies, clinics, and informal drug sellers, than to administer payments to hospitals for inpatient care, for example.

Cost sharing through co-payment

One of the most common methods used to reduce excessive demand for services and pharmaceuticals, as discussed more fully below, is to have consumers share costs through co-payments or user fees, so that choosing treatment has a personal financial consequence, thereby reducing excess demand and moral hazard as well as increasing revenue levels. If co-payment charges are too high, however, they can discourage people from seeking timely care, which can negatively affect health and longer-term costs. Of course, cost sharing is also likely to be detrimental to poor people's access to care and medicines.

As an incentive to encourage rational medicine use and lower costs to the system, co-payments for medicines can be set at different levels depending on whether the medicine is on an essential medicines list or formulary, or whether it is generic or brand name (see Section 12.6 for a more detailed discussion of tiered payments).

Another cost-sharing mechanism is a *deductible*—a set amount that each person in the insurance scheme must pay each year before he or she can tap into the benefits of the plan.

Capitation payment

A capitation payment is where providers receive a prospective, fixed payment for each person served under the scheme for a particular period of time. Administration is relatively simple and inexpensive. Specific health services are often not explicitly defined, meaning that providers have some flexibility in terms of what they provide. In this system, no incentive exists to provide excessive health care. In fact, the incentives are actually to provide minimal care and to needlessly transfer patients to higher levels of care. Competition among providers can decrease the tendency to underproduce, because poor service may cause patients to change providers.

Fee for service

Fee for service is a payment mechanism in which the insurer pays providers for each service provided to a patient. Its perceived strength is in encouraging providers to provide health services—particularly preventive care. Administrative costs are likely to be high, because of the costs of billing and reimbursement as well as monitoring fees.

However, this method of payment may also encourage an overdelivery of health services (supplier-induced demand). The same effect can be seen on pharmaceutical sales. Wherever fees depend on medicine sales, the number of medicines prescribed increases. The potential overdelivery can be counteracted by combining fee for service with maximum budgets or by adjusting fees after a specified quantity of services is exceeded. Some co-payment by the patient may decrease the demand and counteract the overdelivery of services.

Case payment

An important example of a case payment is the diagnosis-related group payment method, wherein health facilities or providers are paid an inclusive flat sum for a patient's treatment (including medicines) according to the diagnosed condition. Case payments can be easier to administer than reimbursement from an itemized list, and requiring documentation of adherence to treatment according to guidelines to receive payment can have a positive effect on the use of medicines.

Payment for performance (incentive payments)

In a variation on fee for service or as an adjunct to capitation, doctors or health facilities may be paid or partly paid based on whether they achieve predetermined quality-based performance indicators. Such indicators may include appropriate prescribing of antibiotics, immunization coverage, blood pressure screening, or cervical smears. Performance can also include appropriate management of people with chronic conditions such as HIV/AIDS (based on CD-4 counts) or diabetes (measured through blood sugar levels).

Budget transfer

Many countries use a budget to pay for public health services; for example, in Central Asian countries, governments provide annual budgets to tuberculosis hospitals (Liu and O'Dougherty 2005). Budgets can be set for providers, which, if strictly fixed, can help contain costs. Budgets can also be earmarked specifically for medicines and supplies. Similar to what happens with use of capitation, savings occur because no link exists between the quantity and mix of health services given to the individual and the amount received by providers. Providers' ability to contain overall costs, though, is limited if the budget is insufficient and results in others having to provide the necessary care. Focusing on the pharmaceutical budget alone, however, without considering the interaction with other service providers—known as the "silo mentality"—can result in suboptimal health care or cost shifting (Drummond and Jonsson 2003).

Salary

Health workers employed by institutions are usually paid a salary. Salaries provide a neutral incentive to providers' actions—what services the provider recommends and what he or she prescribes is based on the needs of the patient, the knowledge of the provider, and the availability of resources (Liu and O'Dougherty 2005). However, as with both budgets and capitation, salaried employees can suffer from low motivation and underproduction, especially when salaries are perceived as low. When the institution is part of the government health system, low motivation can influence providers to seek better remuneration in the private sector or to moonlight in the private sector. To improve productivity, performance-related conditions and incentives can be implemented in addition to salaries.

12.6 Including medicines as part of insurance benefits

Should insurance schemes include medicines in their list of benefits? According to the insurance concepts previously discussed, pharmaceuticals might not be a top priority for insurance coverage: common illnesses for which medicines are needed occur frequently, patients and providers may reinforce overprescription and overuse of medicines, and the potential for fraud and abuse is substantial. Some insurance schemes will incorporate medicines as part of a comprehensive care package, others will compensate for them separately, and others will not cover them at all. Table 12-1 shows that the number of countries with private health insurance that covers medicines has increased from 1999 to 2003.

However, there are strong arguments for including medicines in insurance schemes. First, pharmaceuticals are an essential component of modern health care. Second, early treatment of acute illnesses, such as malaria, and treatment of chronic illnesses, such as diabetes, can reduce costly care for complications and hospitalizations (for both patients and systems). Third, because pharmaceuticals make up

Table 12-1   Countries with medicines covered by health insurance in 1999 and 2003*

	Country income level					
	Low-income		Middle-income		High-income	
	Number of countries (%)		Number of countries (%)		Number of countries (%)	
Medicines coverage	1999	2003	1999	2003	1999	2003
Public health insurance	8/23	8/23	27/35	26/35	8/9	7/9
	(34.8)	(34.8)	(77.1)	(74.3)	(88.9)	(77.8)
Private health insurance	8/17	13/17	16/29	24/29	5/6	6/6
	(47.1)	(76.5)	(55.2)	(82.8)	(83.3)	(100.0)

Source: WHO/TCM 2006.
* For countries with data on both years.

such a large share of household health costs in many countries, their inclusion in an insurance program will make the program more acceptable and desirable and help prevent catastrophic expenditures that increase poverty. Fourth, it is possible to pay only for medicines included in standard treatment guidelines or essential medicines lists, thereby significantly reinforcing the quality use of essential medicines.

Country Study 12-2 shows how extensively a lack of insurance coverage for medications affects the elderly in the United States.

Inpatient pharmaceutical supplies for insured individuals are usually provided by the hospital as part of routine inpatient care. Insurance coverage for outpatient medications may be provided through private pharmacies, insurer-affiliated pharmacies, in-house pharmacies, or pharmaceutical benefits management schemes (see below). The pharmaceutical supply mechanism depends in part on whether the insurer functions only as the financier of services or whether, as with managed care, insurance is linked to specific health providers.

When private pharmacies are used, insurers either reimburse members after they have purchased medicines or reimburse the pharmacy directly. This system provides flexibility for the member but has high administrative costs and is open to considerable fraud and abuse. Insurers may require that prescriptions be filled only at specific insurer-affiliated pharmacies that have a contract or working agreement with the insurer. The member's choice is limited, but administrative costs are less, and abuse is easier to control.

Managed-care organizations and polyclinics often maintain their own in-house pharmacies. Pharmacy staff may be on salary, or the entire pharmacy service may be contracted out. In either case, the insurer-provider can exert greater control over which medicines are available and what prices are charged.

Pharmaceutical benefits management (PBM) schemes contract with insurers to manage pharmacy services. The PBM provider negotiates pharmaceutical prices with suppliers, sets the formulary of medicines to be used, reviews and adjudicates claims, reviews patterns of use by patients and providers, audits the program to prevent fraud and abuse, and implements programs to make medicine use more rational. PBM may provide such services through subcontracts with local pharmacies and through mail-order pharmacy services. Although unheard of in most countries, purchase of medicines by mail—especially medicines for chronic diseases—has existed for many years in North America and is widely accepted. Although PBM appears to add another middleman and additional expense, successful PBM schemes reduce costs to insurers.

Controlling the costs of medicines through insurance programs

Well-managed insurance programs—whether public or private, mandatory or voluntary—always look for ways to control costs while ensuring quality. Controlling the cost of individual services allows an insurance scheme to keep premiums down, expand benefits, or (for commercial insurers) increase profits. Public and private insurance programs control pharmaceutical expenditures through measures related to payment, management, prescribing patterns, and use. Control methods can be used separately or in combination.

1. Control of payment
   - Co-payments are payments made by the member, such as a charge of 1 U.S. dollar (USD) per item for generic medicines and USD 2 per item for brand-name medicines. Co-payments are intended to prompt the patient to consider carefully whether the medication is useful or not; however, they may discourage poor patients from taking needed medications.
   - Tiered co-payments require patients to pay different amounts for their prescriptions, depending on how the medicines are classified. A simple tiered plan will include generics and brand-name medicines (as above). Other tiers may include preferred branded versus nonpreferred branded or even a mail-order program.

Country Study 12-2
Patterns of medicine use by senior citizens in the United States

The social health insurance system for older citizens in the United States, Medicare, did not include pharmaceutical benefits until 2006. In anticipation of the addition of medicines as a benefit, a nationwide survey of over 17,000 older Americans looked at issues that included patterns of medication usage and adherence, current pharmaceutical insurance coverage (from a supplemental plan to Medicare), and out-of-pocket costs.

Results showed that almost 90 percent of those in the survey took prescription medications, even though three-quarters of them had no prescription insurance coverage. Nearly half reported taking five or more prescription medications. Not surprisingly, out-of-pocket costs were high—nearly one-third spent over USD 100 per month for their prescription medications—and 37 percent of seniors without prescription insurance coverage reported not adhering to their regimen because of cost (for example, not filling a prescription, skipping doses, or taking smaller doses).

In another study, researchers looked at middle-age and elderly groups who reported taking less medication than prescribed for chronic conditions because of cost. In the two to three years of follow-up, more of the patients who restricted their medication use reported a significant decline in their health status, such as those with cardiovascular disease having suffered higher rates of angina, nonfatal heart attacks, and strokes. Therefore, patients not adhering to treatment regimens because of lack of insurance coverage for medicines may suffer worse health outcomes.

Sources: Safran et al. 2005; Heisler et al. 2004.

- Co-insurance is a specified percentage to be paid by the member—for example, 25 percent for drugs used in serious and chronic illnesses, 50 percent for most other pharmaceuticals, and 75 percent for symptomatic treatments for minor illnesses.
- A deductible is a specified initial amount the insured must pay before services are covered. It is usually a set amount per quarter or per year.
- Maximum allowable cost or maximum reimbursement price (benefit capping) specifies the highest reimbursement amount for each item to control medicine charges, encourage generic substitution, or establish co-payment levels.

2. Control of prescribing patterns
   - Provider pharmaceutical budgets encourage providers to work within a total pharmaceutical budget for a patient population. Prescribers may be offered a financial incentive for meeting budget targets.
   - Prior authorization requires the insurer to approve the individual prescription before it can be dispensed. This control can be used to enforce adherence to a formulary or essential medicines list or to limit the use of a certain class of medicines.
   - Step therapy restricts a patient from receiving the most expensive therapy first without trying the less expensive alternatives.
   - Selective reimbursement of medicines on formulary lists or essential medicines lists encourages compliance. The use of other products or therapeutic categories, including nonprescription medications, vitamins, and minerals, can be discouraged by lack of reimbursement.
   - Voluntary or mandatory prescribing or dispensing of generic equivalents lowers costs if the brand-name premium is significant.
   - Standard treatment guidelines are recommended to prescribers, especially in managed care programs, for common or high-cost diseases.

3. Control of use
   - Prior authorization by the insurer is sometimes mandated for all prescriptions but is more common for specific medicines or medicine categories, such as "lifestyle" medicines, vitamins, or over-the-counter medications. Alternatively, coverage could be limited to people with a specific condition (for example, making Cox-2 inhibitors available only to those with documented gastrointestinal problems).
   - Caps on services may be instituted, such as limits on the quantities dispensed, number of items given at one time, frequency of refills, or total expenditures. Commonly, insurance schemes will limit the amount of medication per prescription, such as a thirty-day supply or 100 units. In the case of expenditure limits, the scheme may cover only a certain amount of money's worth of medicines per month or year; however, this control method penalizes those most in need of medications, resulting in higher medical costs overall (Hoadley 2005).
   - Use review identifies overprescription or other forms of inappropriate prescribing or dispensing.

This control examines the specific prescriptions for inappropriate use rather than overall usage patterns; for example, identifying a prescription that should not be dispensed to a pregnant woman.

Reference price systems for pharmaceuticals are a cost-containment method introduced in the late 1980s. The basic premise is that a cluster of similar medicines is associated with one specific price accepted by the government for reimbursement purposes. Should a physician prescribe a product priced above this reference price, it is the patient who pays the difference. This policy is meant to increase the cost-consciousness of patients and to incite them to demand reference-priced medicines. For more information on reference pricing, see Chapter 9 on pharmaceutical pricing policies.

These cost-control measures vary in terms of their administrative complexity, effect on access to medicines, effect on rational use of medicines, and acceptability to members and health care providers. Schemes that fail to ensure service quality *and* control costs are not likely to be sustainable.

Access to medicines and rational medicine use

Cost-control measures must not reduce access to essential medicines, which are a highly cost-effective element of health care. Yet insurers, particularly those in new programs and low-income countries, are wary of the costs of overuse and fraud. In an extreme response to this problem, one Latin American country in the mid-1990s proposed omitting medicines entirely from its national health insurance scheme.

Unfortunately, those most in need are often the most affected by cost-control measures. Experience in developed countries has demonstrated that overly restrictive cost-control measures can reduce medicine use but increase total health care costs because of deferred treatment and increases in hospitalization and other costs. A study of Medicare beneficiaries in the United States showed that a cap on medicine benefits resulted in a 31 percent savings in pharmaceutical costs, but that those savings were offset by poorer clinical outcomes and increased hospitalization rates and visits to the emergency department (Hsu et al. 2006).

Rational medicine use in the context of insurance schemes requires a careful balance between controlling costs and ensuring access to needed medications. As mentioned previously, control measures can be used to provide financial incentives for prescribers, dispensers, and patients to follow standard treatment guidelines, formularies, and essential medicines lists, as part of a strategy to promote rational medicine use. Furthermore, a group of members of an insurance scheme serve as a defined population for implementing such rational-use strategies and can also provide data to monitor the effects of these strategies. Essential medicines

or formulary lists, standard treatment guidelines, prescriber and dispenser training, public and patient education, and other measures described in Part III are relevant to improving medicine use in the context of insurance schemes.

12.7 Social health insurance

Social health insurance is a compulsory system, such as a social security fund or national health insurance fund, that includes members of a designated population. Payments to the system are linked to the receipt of health benefits, so only members of the designated population may access services. Key features of a successful social insurance plan include (WHO/SEARO 2003)—

- Compulsory or mandatory membership
- Prepayment contributions from payroll deductions based on income and not risk
- Cross-subsidization and coverage of a large proportion of the population
- Benefit based on need
- Arrangement of social assistance to cover vulnerable populations
- Collected revenue administered by a quasi-independent body

Financial contributions into the social health insurance system can come from workers, employers, the self-employed, and the government—either as an employer of civil servants or as a subsidizer for people not in the formal employment sector. Workers and employers generally contribute based on the worker's salary, while the self-employed make contributions based on estimated income or a flat rate. The government may pay for the unemployed, elderly, or others who cannot afford to pay into the system. These schemes typically contract with a mix of public and private providers to offer a specified benefit package. Social health insurance funds may cover preventive and public health care, or the ministry of health may retain these responsibilities.

One of the fundamental principles of social health insurance is that contributions are not based on risk but are instead based on ability to pay, reflecting an objective of equal access to health care and opting for a certain degree of equity in financing. Countries are relatively successful at collecting wage contributions from people employed in medium and large firms. However, care must be taken to ensure that imposing deductions on wages for health insurance will not distort the labor market by increasing tax evasion or reducing the size of the formal sector. Collecting from the informal sector, from small businesses, and from independent workers has proven to be extremely difficult, and countries should include within their system framework mechanisms to protect the poor.

Services may be provided through government facilities, insurer-operated facilities, private facilities, or a combination of these. Medicines may be provided through contracts with pharmacies. Often, the schemes have an independent agency that manages the health insurance fund, thereby separating the financing of care from the provision of care.

Challenges of social health insurance systems

Low-income countries often find generating enough tax revenue to finance social health insurance difficult. Economic growth may be too modest and compliance among the income earners may be insufficient. These countries also have difficulty introducing or enlarging a social health insurance plan because it requires consensus among disparate partners to accept that those with similar health care needs should receive similar health service benefits, regardless of their level of contribution—an acute issue when countries have a significant disparity between rich and poor.

Moreover, governments need a strong organizational and managerial framework to support a social health insurance scheme because of the complexity of the collection and purchasing activities, which can generate huge funds. Therefore, good governance and transparent practices are extremely important. Often, the challenge is compounded by communication and infrastructure problems such as inadequate roads, telecommunications, and banking facilities that inhibit the scheme from collecting contributions and organizing reimbursements, managing revenues and assets, and monitoring the related health and financial information. A lack of adequate human resources with the necessary expertise can also result in management weaknesses and increased costs. WHO provides useful guidance for the design of social insurance schemes (Carrin and James 2004; Normand and Weber 1994).

Finally, social health insurance requires strong political support, which can be impossible in countries with political instability or economic insecurity. For many low-income countries, social insurance may not be feasible because "the fundamental problem in these countries is not ineffective financing. The real problems are the systems of political governance that regularly under-finance health care services or spend public funds inefficiently. Under such conditions, even the best-designed social insurance system will fail" (Savedoff 2004, 184).

12.8 Community-based health insurance

Low-income countries often have large populations that live in rural areas and work in informal sectors, which limits how well the government can effectively collect taxes to fund social health insurance or other tax-based health funds. Because of this difficulty reaching certain groups, community-based health insurance schemes (also known as mutual health organizations or *mutuelles de santé*) have been one way to fill government gaps and protect marginalized population groups against the cost of illness. According to one analysis (Preker et al. 2002b), community-based health financing (CBHF) schemes appear to extend cover-

---

Country Study 12-3
The effect of HIV/AIDS on a community-based health program in Tanzania

The Community Health Fund (CHF) is a voluntary prepayment scheme that entitles members to access health care for a year, without restriction based on their health status. However, the scheme was designed without considering the effect that HIV/AIDS would have on the community. A study was conducted in the Hanang district to measure the level and costs of HIV/AIDS-related services that CHF members and nonmembers sought during 2002.

Results showed that CHF members used outpatient services 2.5 times per year compared with 2.1 visits for nonmembers; however, although the overall numbers of visits did not vary much, CHF members with HIV/AIDS used outpatient services on a more regular basis, suggesting that membership created a culture of seeking health care more expediently. As a result, the difference in the number of inpatient visits between members and nonmembers was dramatic: CHF members were 40 percent less likely to be hospitalized than nonmembers, resulting in a sizable cost savings. In addition, when members were hospitalized, their stays were significantly shorter than the stays of nonmembers. Because the region had been experiencing shortages of hospital beds, this result benefited all patients in the district, not just those with HIV/AIDS. Overall, the study concluded that CHF members were managing their HIV/AIDS conditions better through regular outpatient services than nonmembers and that a focus on identifying HIV-positive patients and getting them into treatment earlier would result in further benefits to the community.

Source: Chanfreau et al. 2005.

Table 12-2   Organizational features of selected community-based health insurance schemes in West Africa

CBHF scheme and region	Premium per person per month (USD) (2003)	Co-payment percentage	Benefit package
And Faggaru Thiès, Senegal	0.35 per person per month + 1.72 one-time membership fee	0	• Pre- and postnatal care • Family planning • Delivery • Primary health care • Medicines • Hospitalization
Fissel Thiès, Senegal	0.17 per person per month + 0.86 one-time membership fee	20	• Deliver • Hospitalization (only medicines) • Medicines (outpatient) • Primary health care • Transport
Darou Mousty Louga, Senegal	0.17 per person per month + 1.72 one-time membership fee	Hospitalization: 0 All other services: 50	• Delivery hospitalization (only medicines) • Medicines (outpatient) • Primary health care • Prenatal care
Nkoranza, Nkoranza, Ghana	0.10 per person per month	0	• Excludes outpatient care, except snakebites • Hospitalization includes: medical consultations, admission fees, complicated delivery, lab analysis, X-ray, medicines, and referral
Dodowa, Dangme West, Ghana	0.09 per person per month	0	• Outpatient services • Basic laboratory services • Pre- and postnatal care • Family planning • Delivery • Child welfare services, immunization • Ambulance services

Source: PHR*plus* 2004.

age to a large number of rural and low-income populations that would otherwise be excluded from collective arrangements to pay for health care.

Membership in community-based health insurance schemes is usually voluntary, and the organizations are always nonprofit and based on the concepts of mutual aid and social solidarity. Membership may be based around geographical entities (villages or districts), trade or professional groupings (such as trade unions or agricultural cooperatives), or health care facilities. Such schemes have been around for many years, but recently they have attracted increased interest; for example, in Ghana, the number of community-based health financing schemes increased to 159 from only four in about two years. Estimates place the numbers of these schemes worldwide in the hundreds or even thousands (PHR*plus* 2004).

All community-based health insurance schemes share the goal of finding ways for communities to meet their health financing needs through pooled revenue collection and resource-allocation decisions made by the community. Like all insurance schemes, they allow members to pay smaller premiums on a regular basis to offset the risk of having to pay large health care fees upon falling sick. This system also removes the financial barrier at the time of need, so people are more likely to seek health care services earlier. Country Study 12-3 shows how people living with HIV/AIDS in

Tanzania have improved their health-seeking behavior with the help of a community-based health insurance plan.

Community-based management

Unlike other insurance plans, community-based health insurance schemes usually depend upon members to help manage and run the scheme; therefore, the fund managers are accountable to the interested households rather than to the government. Perhaps the most fundamental role of management is to administer the scheme's resources and activities to ensure that income is sufficient to cover the fund's expenses each year. The plan managers need to discern the community's needs and preferences and take them into account in the scheme design.

Most community schemes make a collective decision on what to purchase. Schemes cover different levels of care depending on the needs and preferences of the scheme members, their ability to pay, and the availability of services in the area. The more extensive the package of services offered by the scheme, the larger the premium needed to sustain the scheme, reaching cost levels that may discourage people from joining. Contributions have to be set low to encourage people to join but also have to be balanced against the expected benefits. Table 12-2 shows how selected community-based schemes are organized in West Africa.

Community-based management can certainly be cost-effective, but it can be difficult to do well. A recent assessment of twenty-seven community schemes in Thiès, Senegal, concluded that, overall, financial performance was poor (Atim et al. 2005). The main reasons for this poor performance were adverse selection, low dues recovery, unrecovered loans, frequent changes to benefit packages without changes to premiums, and limited use of financial tools.

Because the schemes are normally voluntary, if households do not trust those managing the fund they may withdraw their membership. Evidence shows that people are more likely to enroll if client households are directly involved in the design and management of the schemes, whereas top-down interference with the design and management of the schemes appears to stunt their sustainability (Preker et al. 2002a).

Challenges with community-based health insurance

Community-based health insurance schemes are small in size, a condition that affords them the benefits of social regulation mechanisms by peer pressure, solidarity, and the neighborhood nature of social control. Their small size is also their main challenge; financial reserves tend to be small because of the low income of the contributing population. Schemes that share risk only among the poor and sick deprive their members of much-needed cross-subsidies from healthier groups with higher incomes. In addition, schemes that operate outside of formal health systems may limit their members' access to a more comprehensive range of care.

A Nigerian study in rural, urban, and peri-urban communities showed that fewer than 40 percent of the people were willing to pay for community-based health insurance; the figure was less than 7 percent in the rural community (Onwujekwe et al. 2010). Even if premiums are minimal, the poorest people may find community-based health insurance plans difficult to join. Cash-poor households may be excluded because few schemes allow payment in kind (because of the added complexity of management). Governments and donors can help by subsidizing premiums for the poorest segment of the population; some schemes set aside a certain percentage of total funds to pay for care for the indigent (PHR*plus* 2004). For example, in Rwanda, the government and more than ninety community-based schemes have decided to subsidize premiums for the poor to access a defined package of services (Gottret and Schieber 2006).

Although mutual health organization membership in Ghana, Mali, and Senegal offered protection against catastrophic expenditures related to hospitalization, membership did not affect how much members paid for medicines, which represented the largest proportion of the cost of outpatient care (Chankova et al. 2008).

Country Study 12-4 shows the results and recommendations from an assessment of the sustainability of community-based insurance schemes in Uganda.

A proposed solution to the size issue is to create an organization that offers "reinsurance" to several community-based health insurance schemes, thereby spreading the risk among multiple programs. The management of such an organization remains a challenge, but this approach could be a way of protecting several schemes against catastrophic liabilities while maintaining the advantages of community stewardship (see Fairbank 2003 for an extensive discussion).

12.9 Private health insurance

Private health insurance refers to schemes that are financed through private health premiums, which are usually (but not always) voluntary. With private insurance, the money can be paid directly to the insurance company either through employers or communities or individually. The insurance company may be either for profit or not-for-profit.

Although the government often regulates this type of insurance, the pool of financing is not usually channeled through the general government. In developing countries, private insurance schemes are offered primarily by employers, but the proportion of the population covered by private insurance tends to be very small.

One frequently cited characteristic of private insurance is that premiums are risk related; meaning that if the client is older or has a chronic disease, the premiums will be higher than if the client is young and healthy. Sometimes, an insurer will use historical data on a community or employment group to determine the risk of future claims compared with those of other communities or employment groups.

Worldwide, varied private insurance models exist, with some arrangements blurring the boundaries between public and private insurance. A recent proposal for a taxonomy of health insurance (OECD 2004) classified four types of private insurance, each of which has a different way of determining contributions—

Private mandatory health insurance: Insurance is legally mandated and premiums may or may not be risk related.
Private employment group health insurance: Insurance is a benefit of employment and is usually not risk related.
Private community-rated health insurance: Policies are voluntarily taken up by individuals or groups, and insurers are legally required to apply community-related rather than risk-related calculations for premiums (no discrimination based on age, health status, claims history, or other factors).
Private risk-related health insurance: Policies are voluntarily taken up by individuals or groups, and insurers apply risk-related premiums.

Country Study 12-4
Strengthening and sustaining community-based health insurance schemes in Uganda

An assessment of fourteen community-based health insurance schemes in Uganda investigated activities and best practices that were contributing to the schemes' financial stability and sustainability.

Findings and recommendations included—

Quality of life: Scheme members reported a significant improvement in quality of life as a result of membership. The addition of local outpatient clinics to the package of covered benefits allowed more convenient and cheaper access to primary care for some members.

Management and governance: Management and governance structures varied across schemes; each scheme should include a community-based representative as part of the decision-making process.

Financial management and viability: A larger number of members was a better predictor of cost recovery than the amount of premium payments; therefore, an increase in premiums could result in a loss of members, which would be detrimental to cost recovery. Schemes need to improve accounting mechanisms and improve the financial management skills of scheme managers.

Risk management: Schemes used different ways to manage financial risk, such as co-payments to decrease moral hazard and membership restrictions to avoid adverse selection. Some of these control mechanisms may have limited the growth of membership and thus the size of the risk pool, and the effectiveness of these measures depended on how well the members understood and supported them. Schemes are strengthened when their members are informed about insurance concepts.

Marketing and membership incentives: Schemes with more members are financially more secure, so schemes must always be recruiting new members and working to retain current members. Marketing research improves the ability to enroll new scheme members. Some schemes successfully used insecticide-treated net subsidies as an incentive to recruit new members.

By the mid 2000s, community-based health insurance schemes had lost much of their momentum in Uganda. While about a dozen schemes continued, with approximately 30,000 people enrolled, few new schemes had been launched since the late 1990s. An evaluation carried out on two schemes found explanations from both the supply and demand side.

Demand-side problems included—

Lack of understanding: Members and potential members did not understand the basic principles of community-based health insurance schemes.

Lack of trust: There was widespread mistrust of financial institutions among Ugandans due to the collapse of some financial institutions in the 1990s.

Inability to pay premiums: Eight out of ten people interviewed cited inability to afford the required contribution.

Supply-side problems included—

Limited interest or knowledge: Health care providers and managers were often unaware of or unexperienced with community-based health insurance.

Lack of coherent government framework: Uganda had no specific procedures in place regarding community-based health insurance, despite mentioning such programs specifically in health policy documents.

Sources: Derriennic et al. 2005; Basaza et al. 2007.

The main market imperfections of private insurance models are the insurers' incentives to avoid insuring people at greatest health risks (skimming). Conversely, because private insurance plans are usually voluntary, people at greatest health risk and people with chronic illnesses have an incentive to join the program and the healthiest have an incentive to avoid joining (adverse selection). Adverse selection raises costs and reduces the risk-sharing effect of insurance.

Expansion of private health insurance

Some think that the development of a private insurance market may form the foundation for the future evolution of social insurance by creating capacity within a country (Pauly et al. 2006). In countries with limited public resources, health insurance allows tax revenues to be targeted at services to provide health care for the poor. However, close government regulation is critical, and regulatory capacity is often weak in developing countries; in the worst-case scenario, governments may take resources from the poor to support the establishment of the health insurance system.

Private insurance can exist alongside single-payer systems, such as social health insurance, by substituting for social health insurance, by complementing it by covering services not otherwise included, or by supplementing it by providing improved coverage to what is already covered (for example, providing access to elective surgery without

Country Study 12-5
Percentage of insurance in health care spending in twenty-four countries: Social insurance versus private insurance

An analysis of insurance in twenty-four countries in three regions showed that Latin America and the Caribbean had the most developed social insurance markets, whereas in East and Central Africa, neither social nor private insurance funds a significant proportion of health expenditures. In the Middle East and North Africa, social insurance schemes generally covered civil servants and those employed in the formal sector.

Region and country	Social insurance	Private insurance
Latin America/Caribbean		
Bolivia	37.7	2.5
Dominican Republic	4.8	7.5
Ecuador	21.5	10.3
El Salvador	20.5	1.1
Guatemala	27.8	3.9
Mexico	34.3	1.4
Nicaragua	10.5	Not available
Peru	24.6	3.1
Average	*22.7*	*4.3*
East/Central/South Africa		
Ethiopia	0.0	0.0
Kenya	4.0	3.0
Malawi	0.0	1.0
Mozambique	0.0	0.0
Rwanda	0.0	0.0
South Africa	1.0	41.0
Tanzania	0.0	3.0
Uganda	0.0	0.0
Zambia	0.0	0.0
Average	*1.0*	*5.0*
Middle East/North Africa		
Djibouti	20.0	0.0
Egypt	12.4	<1.0
Iran	19.0	1.0
Jordan	0.0	<4.0
Lebanon	16.0	15.0
Morocco	2.6	16.2
Tunisia	35.0	5.0
Average	*13.0*	*6.0*

Source: Nandakumar et al. 2004.

waiting on a list) (Anderson and Hussey 2005). Although all citizens wishing to access private coverage for one of these purposes are eligible to buy it, where it is available, only high-income individuals are likely to take the opportunity, creating an equity gap in access to health care (Anderson and Hussey 2005). Country Study 12-5 shows the extent of coexistence of social and private health insurance in twenty-four countries.

A number of countries have encouraged the expansion of private health insurance; for example, South Africa has a tax-based public system that primarily serves the low-income population, but it is supplemented by a private insurance system that mostly higher-income people purchase to supplement the public system. The government has increased regulation of the private insurance market to increase the equity between the public and private systems (Anderson and Hussey 2005).

12.10   Health or medical savings accounts

Health or medical savings accounts are individual accounts established to encourage consumers to save for expected costs of medical care, enlist health care consumers in controlling costs, and mobilize additional funds for health systems. MSAs are not considered a form of insurance because no pooling of risk occurs between healthy and sick and rich and poor. Because individual savings alone generally cannot protect someone from the financial risk incurred through catastrophic illness or long-term chronic disease, MSAs, in practice, have been used in conjunction with social insurance schemes. They may be administered by public organizations, as in China and Singapore, or by private entities, as in the United States and South Africa.

Medical savings accounts were introduced in Singapore in 1984; elsewhere, experience is limited to few countries, and mainly in the form of demonstration or pilot projects. Even in Singapore, government budget and out-of-pocket payments still play the predominant role in health spending, with MSAs accounting for only a small proportion (see Country Study 12-6).

Contributions may be mandatory or voluntary. If MSAs are voluntary, other benefits—such as tax exemption—are usually included to create incentives for participation. In this case, maximum contribution levels may be required to prevent the program from being used purely as a tax shelter. Singapore has instituted a compulsory minimum level of contribution with the aim of ensuring that individuals accumulate enough funds to cover health care in their older age.

An alternative model proposed in Canada is for third parties, such as the government, to fund savings accounts. Local health authorities would pay equal amounts into each individual's medical savings account instead of purchasing health care services for the entire population.

Challenges with medical savings accounts

The theory behind MSAs is that they will help control health costs by creating an incentive for consumers to purchase health services wisely, because money left in the account can be used for future health care needs. Proponents argue that with comprehensive health insurance, neither doctors nor patients have incentives to consider the cost-effectiveness of proposed treatments. But the counterargument is that moral hazard arises more among providers than among consumers because of the information asymmetry between service providers and patients. From this perspective, the existence of money in a person's MSA influences providers much like the existence of third-party insurance (Hanvoravongchai 2002).

Another concern about the MSA model is that it is less equitable than comprehensive benefit systems. Those who are indigent or suffer from chronic illnesses are unlikely to be able to accumulate enough savings to cover their needs.

MSA schemes that include high deductibles can also prevent the poor from accessing health services.

Increasing an individual's resources may improve access to needed medicines; however, with the issue of supplier-induced demand and where a provider's income depends partially or totally on profits from pharmaceutical sales, an incentive exists to prescribe multiple medicines (polypharmacy) and to use brand-name as opposed to generic medicines. These tendencies can be combated by strategies that restrict prescribing to an essential medicines list (China) or through large co-payments (United States).

12.11 Implementing an appropriate insurance scheme

Many countries see the initiation or promotion of one or more insurance schemes as a way of addressing health financing issues progressively and equitably. The concept of

---

Country Study 12-6
Medical savings accounts in Singapore

In 1984, Singapore adopted a system of compulsory, individually owned medical savings accounts to help people pay for their medical expenses. The government implemented three different health financing programs depending on need: Medisave, Medishield, and Medifund. The funds are invested and managed by the government; private insurance is not encouraged.

The Medisave program is a national health care savings program. Citizens begin contributing 6 to 8 percent of their wages, which increase according to their age. These funds can then be used to pay for specified inpatient (at both public and private hospitals) and certain expensive outpatient services, such as renal dialysis. Primary care and medicines cannot be paid for from this account. Medisave accounts are not taxed and earn tax-free interest.

The Medishield program was established in 1990 as a catastrophic insurance program to supplement Medisave accounts, which alone are not sufficient to pay for prolonged hospitalizations and treatment for chronic illnesses, especially for low-income workers who contribute less to their accounts. Premiums vary, increasing with age.

The Medifund program was established in 1993 for low-income workers whose medical bills still may not be covered by the other two programs. The government funds this program from the budget surplus, so it is not

guaranteed, reinforcing the government's position that health care is not an entitlement. Funds are distributed on a case-by-case basis.

The combination of subsidies and MSAs appears to provide a safety net, yet the system still has many limitations. In 2002, out-of-pocket spending still accounted for one-third of total health spending in Singapore, while Medisave, Medishield, and Medifund combined accounted for less than 10 percent. The remaining 60 percent came from government health spending on subsidies and from employer-provided benefits.

This limited role of the MSA thus far can be attributed to strict spending criteria, such as caps on per day cost of hospital stays and surgical procedures, and high deductibles and co-payments. The high co-payments in the Medishield program can still be a financial barrier for some people. The extent of this burden, and possibly a sign of the inequality of the system, is seen in the increase in applications for assistance from Medifund. The number rose from 58,000 in 1997 to 91,000 in 2000. Nevertheless, the MSA system is estimated to have contributed to Singapore's relatively low spending on health care (3.3 percent of GDP in 2006). A more extensive evaluation will not be available until 2030, when the system is expected to achieve full implementation.

Sources: Gottret and Schieber 2006; Massaro and Wong 1996; Hanvoravongchai 2002; WHO 2009.

cross-subsidization of the young for the old and the well for the sick is a valuable way to expand the pool of those covered and to maximize risk sharing. However, when governments are considering instituting health insurance, they need to consider the realities of implementation; the complexity of the issues involved is often poorly understood.

When examining the implications of various insurance proposals, it is critical to consider the "enabling environment" of the country (Eichler and Lewis 2000). These factors include all circumstances of the country that affect the health sector, such as the economy, the government's ability to assume leadership and regulatory roles, the realities of the current health financing and delivery system, and cultural factors (such as the acceptance of social responsibility). Assessing the enabling environment reveals existing constraints and points to interventions that might be needed to facilitate reform (see Box 12-1).

Besides the immediate issue of deciding who and what will be covered under the insurance plan, other crucial issues to address include policy objectives, organization and geographic availability of health services, premium calculation and payment mechanisms, use and cost control measures, and administrative arrangements. In the case of medicine coverage, questions that policy makers need to answer include—

- Who receives a medicines benefit?
- Which medicines are covered (limited to formularies or generics over brand names)?
- In which settings are medicines covered (inpatient, outpatient, emergency)?

- What will the cost be to the member, the member's family, the insurance program?
- How can the insurance program influence access to and quality use of medicines?
- What are the desired and undesired effects of medicine policies in insurance, and how can these be routinely monitored?

The ability to administer the health insurance scheme efficiently is a central element of sustainability. The requirements for an active management system to ensure revenue collection, determine co-payments that optimize efficiency and quality care, and manage the benefit package are crucial and demanding. Any insurance system lacking an effective monitoring system that allows frequent changes to accommodate differing circumstances is likely to become insolvent or fail to provide adequate service.

An initial factor to consider when designing or reforming a health insurance scheme is the potential for building on existing successful institutions. For example, if a country already has a well-run tax-based health care system, continuing with this approach may be appropriate. Or if a tradition of community-based health insurance exists, the country may decide to build on it. In all cases, government stewardship and a strong political will to undertake the necessary health financing reform are essential.

The overall structure of the social health insurance scheme should be laid down in a health insurance law. Details that may be subject to frequent change can be established in regulations. Appropriate legislation should specify issues of membership and population coverage; organization, responsibilities, and decision-making authority; the method of financing; and the relationship with providers and the benefits provided by health insurance. Including legislation to protect consumers is particularly important if public faith in the schemes is to be maintained. Therefore, honest and fair marketing regulations need to be put in place and a transparent process for reporting, investigating, and resolving disputes needs to be ensured.

Whatever type of health financing mechanism a country decides to adopt, the transition to universal coverage may take several years, even decades. For example, in Japan, thirty-six years elapsed between the enactment of the first law related to health insurance and the final law implementing universal coverage (Carrin and James 2005). ∎

Box 12-1
Assessing a country's enabling environment for insurance reform

What obstacles and facilitating elements exist in the "enabling environment" of the health sector?

- National income is a constraint.
- Governments lack the capability to effectively collect taxes.
- National reforms such as decentralization affect the health sector.
- Laws and regulations may seriously limit the range of feasible insurance reform options.
- The legal and regulatory framework for the health sector may be inadequate.
- The government may not be ready to assume a leadership and regulatory role.
- Powerful interest groups must be considered.

Source: Eichler and Lewis 2000.

ASSESSMENT GUIDE

General health financing

- What is the country's GDP per capita?
- What is the total national health expenditure (public and private) per capita?
- What is the total national health expenditure as a percentage of GDP?
- What is the percentage breakdown of health spending by source (public, private, nongovernmental organization, donor)?
- What percentage of health care costs is paid out of pocket?
- Does the country already have an efficient tax-based health care system that might form the basis for a tax-based insurance program?
- Does a tradition of community-based insurance exist in the country or region that might facilitate the introduction or expansion of this sort of scheme?
- Are national laws or regulations related to health insurance in place?
- Is there a plan for universal health coverage through insurance?
- Is the government's organizational and managerial framework strong enough to support its role in administering a health insurance scheme?

Insurance systems

- What types of health insurance currently exist: social, private, community? Are existing plans compulsory or voluntary?
- What percentage of the population is covered by each form of health insurance?
- What are the benefit packages? Do limitations exist, such as co-payments and deductibles?
- What are the characteristics of the covered populations: formally employed? high-income?
- What percentage of those insured has policies that cover medicines? What medicines are covered and what restrictions exist on medicines?
- What are the premiums for each form of insurance? Are the premiums calculated on degree of risk?
- What conditions are covered by each form of insurance?
- Is reimbursement dependent on insurance company treatment guidelines or a medicine list for each form of insurance?
- How are providers chosen and reimbursed for each form of insurance?

Glossary

Adverse selection: The tendency for people at greatest health risk to join voluntary insurance programs, while the healthiest people, whose premiums should be used to cross-subsidize the bills of the sicker members, avoid joining.

Capitation payment: A prospective, fixed payment to providers for each person served under the scheme for a particular period of time.

Case payment: An inclusive flat sum paid to health facilities or providers for a patient's treatment (including medicines) according to the diagnosed condition.

Co-insurance: A specified percentage to be paid by the member for the service or medicine; for example, 25 percent for medicines used in serious and chronic illnesses, 50 percent for most other pharmaceuticals, and 75 percent for symptomatic treatments for minor illnesses.

Community-based health insurance (also known as mutual health organizations): A usually voluntary prepayment plan to pool risk and resources centered on the concepts of mutual aid and social solidarity. Membership may be based on geographical entities, trade or professional groupings, or health care facilities.

Co-payment: Cost-control measure in insurance schemes in which the member pays a set charge per item received; co-payments may be lower for generic medicines, higher for brand-name medicines.

Cross-subsidization: A risk-sharing concept, where the healthy subsidize the ill and the rich subsidize the poor.

Deductible: A set amount that each person in the insurance scheme must pay each year before he or she can tap into the benefits of the plan.

Exemption: A release from payment of fees for specific population groups or disease or medicine types, employed in many revolving drug fund schemes to promote access to services.

Fee for service: A payment mechanism where the insurer pays providers for each service provided to a patient.

Health insurance: A financing scheme characterized by risk sharing, in which regular payments of premiums are made by or on behalf of members (the insured). The insurer pays the cost or a set portion of the cost for covered health services.

Health maintenance organization (HMO): A type of managed care organization that provides health insurance that is fulfilled through hospitals, doctors, and other providers with which the HMO has a contract. Unlike traditional indemnity insurance, care provided in an HMO generally follows a set of care guidelines.

Health or medical savings accounts: Not strictly a form of insurance, medical savings accounts encourage individuals, often by providing tax advantages or subsidies, to save for the expected costs of medical care.

Indemnity insurance: A type of insurance where no contractual arrangements exist between insurers and providers and the provider is paid a fee for the service.

Managed care: Insurance systems in which the insurer plays an active role in overseeing the utilization and quality of service, for example, through health maintenance organizations (HMOs), preferred provider organizations (PPOs), and managed indemnity insurance.

Market failure: A term used by economists to describe circumstances that constrain the smooth operation of the market (Normand and Weber 1994).

Maximum allowable cost (MAC) or maximum reimbursement price (MRP): Cost-control measure in insurance schemes that specifies the highest amount that will be reimbursed for each pharmaceutical item dispensed.

Moral hazard: In the context of health financing, when members of a health insurance scheme use services or consume medicines more frequently than if they were not insured.

Multiple-payer system: Where several different organizations collect and pool revenues and purchase health services for specific parts of the population.

Mutuelles de santé: Term used in West Africa for community-based health insurance plans.

Out-of-pocket spending: When a person pays a nonreimbursable fee directly to a health service provider at the time of service or to a dispenser for a medicine or other health commodity.

Payment for performance (or incentive payments): A variation on fee for service in which doctors or health facilities are paid based on whether they achieve predetermined quality-based performance indicators.

Pharmaceutical benefits management scheme: Mechanism in which organizations contract with insurers to provide pharmacy services, often through subcontracts with local pharmacies and through mail-order pharmacy services.

Premium: In private insurance schemes, the money that is regularly paid to the insurance company for health insurance coverage.

Prepayment: A payment made in advance that guarantees eligibility to receive a service when needed at limited or no additional cost. Prepayment is a feature of all types of health insurance.

Prior authorization: Cost-control measure in insurance schemes in which the insurer retains the right to approve medicine use before medicines are dispensed to the patient.

Private health insurance: A scheme that is usually paid for by voluntary contributions from employers, mutual societies, cooperatives, or individuals.

Purchasing: The process by which pooled funds are paid to providers to deliver health goods and services.

Reference price systems: A cost-containment method for pharmaceuticals where a cluster of similar medicines is associated with one specific price accepted by the government for reimbursement purposes.

Reimbursement: A system where providers are paid after they deliver the services.

Reinsurance: When a direct insurer contracts with a second insurer to share risks that the direct insurer has assumed for its members. Often associated with small community-based plans, reinsurance protects the direct insurer from catastrophic liabilities.

Risk pooling: A method that shares the financial risk associated with health care among large groups. Pooling requires some transfer of resources (or cross-subsidization) from healthy people to sick people and from rich to poor.

Single-payer system: Where one organization (usually the government) collects and pools revenues and purchases health services for the whole population.

Skimming: A problem that occurs when insurers use various screening measures to avoid insuring people at greatest health risk (and therefore greatest expense).

Social or public health insurance: A compulsory system, for civil servants, people in the formal employment sector, and certain other groups through programs such as social security funds, national health insurance funds, and other systems. Premiums are often deducted directly from salaries or wages.

Step therapy: A restriction on a patient from receiving the most expensive pharmaceutical therapy without first trying the less expensive alternatives.

Tiered co-payments: The different payments that patients make for their prescriptions, depending on which tier the medicine falls in; for example, generic or brand name.

Universal health coverage: The concept of ensuring that all of a country's citizens have access to adequate and affordable health care.

User fee: An out-of-pocket payment made by the patient at the time a health service is provided.

References and further readings

★ = Key readings.

Anderson, G. F., and P. S. Hussey. 2005. Single-Payer Health Insurance. In *Spending Wisely: Buying Health Services for the Poor*, A. Preker and J. C. Langenbrunner, eds. Washington, D.C.: World Bank.

Atim, C., F. Diop, and S. Bennett. 2005. *Determinants of the Financial Stability of Mutual Health Organizations: A Study in the Thiès Region of Senegal*. Bethesda, Md.: Partners for Health Reform*plus* Project/ Abt Associates.

Basaza, R., B. Criel, and P. Van der Stuyft. 2007. Low enrolment in Ugandan Community Health Insurance Schemes: Underlying Causes and Policy Implications. *BMC Health Services Research* 7:105. <http://www.biomedcentral.com/content/pdf/1472-6963-7-105.pdf>

Brenzel, L., and W. Newbrander. 2002. Linking Ability and Willingness to Contribute to Micro-insurance. In *Social Re-Insurance: A New Approach to Sustainable Community Health Financing*, D. Dror and A. Preker, eds. Washington, D.C., and Geneva: World Bank and International Labour Office.

Camacho, S., N. Schwab, and R. P. Shaw. 2003. *Bolivia's Reform to Improve Maternal and Child Mortality*. Washington, D.C.: World Bank. <http://info.worldbank.org/etools/docs/library/48615/oj%5Fbolivia.doc>

Carapinha, J. L., D. Ross-Degnan, A. T. Desta, and A. K. Wagner. 2011. Health Insurance Systems in Five Sub-Saharan African Countries: Medicine Benefits and Data for Decision Making. *Health Policy* 99:193–202.

★ Carrin, G. 2003. *Community-Based Health Insurance Schemes in Developing Countries: Facts, Problems and Perspectives*. Geneva: Department of Health System Financing, Expenditure and Resource Allocation, World Health Organization. <http://whqlibdoc.who.int/hq/2003/EIP_FER_DP.E_03.1.pdf>

Carrin, G., and P. Hanvoravongchai. 2003. Provider Payments and Patient Charges as Policy Tools for Cost-Containment: How

Successful Are They in High-Income Countries? *Human Resources for Health* 1(1):6.

Carrin, G., and C. James. 2005. Social Health Insurance: Key Factors Affecting the Transition towards Universal Coverage. *International Social Security Review* 58(1):45–64.

———. 2004. *Reaching Universal Coverage via Social Health Insurance: Key Design Features in the Transition Period.* Geneva: Department of Health Systems Financing and Resource Allocation, World Health Organization.

Carrin, G., I. Mathauer, K. Xua, and D. B. Evans. 2008. Universal Coverage of Health Services: Tailoring Its Implementation. *Bulletin of the World Health Organization* 86:857–63.

Chanfreau, C., S. Musau, and L. Kidane. 2005. *Costing HIV/AIDS Services for Community Health Fund Members and Non-Members in Hanang District, Tanzania.* Bethesda, Md.: Partners for Health Reform*plus* Project/Abt Associates. <http://www.healthsystems 2020.org/content/resource/detail/1615/>

Chankova, S., S. Sulzbach, and F. Diop. 2008. Impact of Mutual Health Organizations: Evidence from West Africa. *Health Policy and Planning* 23:264–76.

Derriennic, Y., K. Wolf, and P. Kiwanuka-Mukiibi. 2005. *An Assessment of Community-Based Health Financing Activities in Uganda.* Bethesda, Md.: Partners for Health Reform*plus* Project/Abt Associates. <http://www.healthsystems2020.org/files/1482_file_ Tech060_fin.pdf>

Doetinchem, O., G. Carrin, and D. Evans. 2009. *Thinking of Introducing Social Health Insurance? Ten Questions.* Geneva: World Health Organization. <http://www.who.int/health_financing/documents/ cov-pb_e_09_04-10qshi/en/index.html>

Drechsler, D., and J. Jüttig. 2005. *Private Health Insurance for the Poor in Developing Countries?* Paris: Development Centre, Organization for Economic Cooperation and Development. <http://www.oecd. org/dataoecd/25/14/35274754.pdf>

Dror, D. M., and A. S. Preker, eds. 2002. *Social Reinsurance: A New Approach to Sustainable Community Health Financing.* Washington, D.C., and Geneva: World Bank and International Labour Office.

Drummond, M. F., and B. Jonsson. 2003. Moving Beyond the Drug Budget Silo Mentality in Europe. *Value in Health* 6(Suppl. 1):74–7.

Eichler, R., and E. Lewis. 2000. *Social Insurance Assessment Tool.* Cambridge, Mass.: Management Sciences for Health. <http://erc. msh.org/toolkit>

Faden, L., C. Vialle-Valentin, D. Ross-Degnan, and A. Wagner. 2011. Active Pharmaceutical Management Strategies of Health Insurance Systems to Improve Cost-Effective Use of Medicines in Low- and Middle-Income Countries: A Systematic Review of Current Evidence. *Health Policy* 100:134–43.

Fairbank, A. 2003. *Sources of Financial Instability of Community-Based Health Insurance Plans: How Could Social Reinsurance Help?* Bethesda, Md.: Partners for Health Reform*plus* Project/Abt Associates. <http://www.healthsystems2020.org/files/1542_file_ Tech024_fin.pdf>

★ Gottret, P., and G. Schieber. 2006. *Health Financing Revisited: A Practitioner's Guide.* Washington, D.C.: World Bank. <http://site resources.worldbank.org/INTHSD/Resources/topics/Health-Financing/HFRFull.pdf>

★ Gottret P., G. J. Schieber, and H. R. Waters, eds. 2008. *Good Practices in Health Financing: Lessons from Reforms in Low- and Middle-Income Countries.* Washington, D.C.: World Bank

Gupta, S., B. Clements, A. Pivovarsky, and E. Tiongson. 2004. Foreign Aid and Revenue Response: Does the Composition of Aid Matter? In *Helping Countries Develop: The Role of Fiscal Policy*, S. Gupta, B. Clements, and G. Inchauste, eds. Washington, D.C.: International Monetary Fund.

Hanvoravongchai, P. 2002. *Medical Savings Accounts: Lessons Learned from International Experience.* Geneva: World Health Organization.

<http://www.who.int/healthinfo/paper52.pdf>

Heisler, M., K. M. Langa, E. L. Eby, A. M. Fendrick, M. U. Kabeto, and J. D. Piette. 2004. The Health Effects of Restricting Prescription Medication Use Because of Cost. *Medical Care* 42(7):626–34.

★ Hoadley, J. 2005. *Cost Containment Strategies for Prescription Drugs: Assessing the Evidence in the Literature.* Menlo Park, Calif.: Kaiser Family Foundation. <http://www.kff.org/rxdrugs/upload/Cost-Containment-Strategies-for-Precription-Drugs-Assessing-The-Evidence-in-the-Literature-Report.pdf>

Hsiao, W. C., and P. R. Shaw, eds. 2007. *Social Health Insurance for Developing Nations.* Washington, D.C.: World Bank.

Hsu, J., M. Price, J. Huang, R. Brand, V. Fung, R. Hui, B. Fireman, J. P. Newhouse, and J. V. Selby. 2006. Unintended Consequences of Caps on Medicare Drug Benefits. *New England Journal of Medicine* 354(22):2349–59.

International Labour Organisation–Universitas Programme. 2002. *Extending Social Protection in Health Through Community Based Health Organizations: Evidence and Challenges.* Geneva: International Labour Organisation. <http://cristian-baeza.com/ Papers%20in%20the%20WEB/Final%20CBHO%20Study%20 Universitas,%20Julio%2011,%202002.pdf>

Kelley, A. G., F. Diop, and M. Makinen. 2006. *Approaches to Scaling Up Community-Based Health Financing Schemes.* Bethesda, Md.: Partners for Health Reform*plus* Project/Abt Associates. <http:// www.healthsystems2020.org/files/1172_file_prim2.pdf>

Liu, X., and S. O'Dougherty. 2005. Paying for Public Health Services: Financing and Utilization. In *Spending Wisely: Buying Health Services for the Poor*, A. Preker and J. C. Langenbrunner, eds. Washington, D.C.: World Bank.

Massaro, T. A., and Y. Wong. 1996. *Medical Savings Accounts: The Singapore Experience.* Dallas, Tex.: National Center for Policy Analysis. <http://www.ncpa.org/pdfs/st203.pdf>

Mtei, G., and J. Mulligan. 2007. *Community Health Funds in Tanzania: A Literature Review.* Ifakara, Tanzania: Igakara Health Research and Development Centre. <http://www.tgpsh.or.tz/uploads/media/ CHF_DESK_STUDY_IFAKARA_RC.pdf>

Nandakumar, A. K., M. Bhawalkar, M. Tien, R. Ramos, and S. De. 2004. *Synthesis of Findings from NHA Studies in Twenty-Six Countries.* Bethesda, Md.: Partners for Health Reform*plus* Project/Abt Associates.

Narváez, R. 2009. Public Health Insurance in Bolivia and Gaps Between Rural and Urban Areas. *FOCALPoint* 8(7):4–6. <http:// focal.ca/pdf/focalpoint_october2009.pdf>

Newbrander, W., and L. Brenzel. 2002. Creating a Favorable Market Environment for Micro-insurance at the Community Level. In *Social Re-Insurance: A New Approach to Sustainable Community Health Financing*, D. Dror and A. Preker, eds. Washington, D.C., and Geneva: World Bank and International Labour Office.

Normand, C., and A. Weber. 1994. *Social Health Insurance: A Guidebook for Planning.* Geneva: World Health Organization.

OECD (Organization for Economic Cooperation and Development) Health Project. 2004. *Proposal for a Taxonomy of Health Insurance.* Paris: OECD. <http://www.oecd.org/dataoecd/24/52/31916207. pdf>

Onwujekwe, O., E. Okereke, C. Onoka, B. Uzochukwu, J. Kirigia, and A. Petu. 2010. Willingness to Pay for Community-Based Health Insurance in Nigeria: Do Economic Status and Place of Residence Matter? *Health Policy and Planning* 25(2):155–61.

Partnerships for Health Reform. No date. *Reducing Maternal and Child Mortality in Bolivia.* Bethesda, Md.: Partnerships for Health Reform/Abt Associates. <http://www.healthsystems2020.org/files/ 811_file_ess1.pdf>

Pauly, M. V., P. Zweifel, R. M. Scheffler, A. S. Preker, and M. Bassett. 2006. Private Health Insurance in Developing Countries. *Health Affairs* 25(2):369–79.

★ PHR*plus* (Partners for Health Reform*plus* Project). 2004. *21 Questions on CBHF: An Overview of Community-Based Health Financing.* Bethesda, Md.: PHR*plus* Project/Abt Associates.

★ Preker, A., and G. Carrin, eds. 2004. *Health Financing for Poor People: Resource Mobilization and Risk Sharing.* Washington, D.C., and Geneva: World Bank, World Health Organization, and International Labour Office.

Preker, A. S., G. Carrin, D. Dror, M. Jakab, W. Hsiao, and D. Arhin-Tenkorang. 2002a. Effectiveness of Community Health Financing in Meeting the Cost of Illness. *Bulletin of the World Health Organization* 80:143–50. <http://www.ncbi.nlm.nih.gov/pmc/articles/PMC2567719/pdf/11953793.pdf>

———. 2002b. The Role of Communities in Resource Mobilization and Risk Sharing: A Synthesis Report. In *Health Care Financing for Rural and Low-Income Populations,* A. Preker, ed. Washington, D.C., and Geneva: World Bank and World Health Organization.

Ron, A., and X. Scheil-Adlung, eds. 2001. *Recent Health Policy Innovations in Social Security.* New Brunswick, N.J.: Transaction Publisher.

Safran, D. G., P. Neuman, C. Schoen, M. S. Kitchman, I. B. Wilson, B. Cooper, A. Li, H. Chang, and W. H. Rogers. 2005. Prescription Drug Coverage and Seniors: Findings from a 2003 National Survey. *Health Affairs* Jan–Jun (Suppl.) Web Exclusive, April 2005, W5-152–W5-166.

Savedoff, W. 2004. Is There a Case for Social Insurance? *Health Policy and Planning* 19(3):183–4.

Schieber, G., and A. Maeda. 1997. A Curmudgeon's Guide to Health Care Financing in Developing Countries. In *Innovations in Health Care Financing: Proceedings of a World Bank Conference, March 10–11, 1997,* G. Schiber, ed. Washington, D.C., World Bank.

Schneider, P. 2004. Why Should the Poor Insure? Theories of Decision-Making in the Context of Health Insurance. *Health Policy and Planning* 19(6):349–55.

★ Sekhri, N., and W. Savedoff. 2005. Private Health Insurance: Implications for Developing Countries. *Bulletin of the World Health Organization* 83(2):127–34. <http://whqlibdoc.who.int/bulletin/2005/Vol83-No2/bulletin_2005_83(2)_127-134.pdf>

★ Sekhri, N., W. Savedoff, and S. Thripathi. 2005. *Regulation Private Health Insurance to Serve the Public Interest: Policy Issues for Developing Countries.* Geneva: World Health Organization. <http://whqlibdoc.who.int/hq/2005/EIP_HSF_DP_05.3.pdf>

Shaw, R., and C. Griffin. 1995. *Financing Health Care in Sub-Saharan Africa through User Fees and Insurance.* Washington, D.C.: World Bank.

WHO (World Health Organization). 2009. *World Health Statistics 2009.* <http://www.who.int/whosis/whostat/2009/en/index.html>

———. 2005a. *Achieving Universal Health Coverage: Developing the Health Financing System.* Geneva: WHO. <http://www.who.int/health_financing/documents/pb_e_05_1-universal_coverage.pdf>

———. 2005b. *Designing Health Financing Systems to Reduce Catastrophic Health Expenditure.* Geneva: WHO. <http://www.who.int/health_financing/documents/pb_e_05_2-catastrophic.pdf>

———. 2004a. *Equitable Access to Essential Medicines: A Framework for Collective Action.* Geneva: WHO.

———. 2004b. *WHO Medicines Strategy: Countries at the Core 2004–2007.* Geneva: WHO.

———. 2000. *Global Comparative Pharmaceutical Expenditures with Related Reference Information.* Geneva: WHO.

WHO/SEARO (World Health Organization/Regional Office for South-East Asia). 2005. *Social Health Insurance: Selected Case Studies from Asia and the Pacific.* Manila: WHO. <http://whqlibdoc.who.int/searo/2005/9290222395_eng.pdf>

———. 2003. *Social Health Insurance: Report and Documentation of the Technical Discussions Held in Conjunction with the 40th Meeting of CCPDM, New Delhi, 4–5 September 2003.* New Delhi: WHO/SEARO.

WHO/TCM (World Health Organization/Technical Cooperation for Essential Drugs and Traditional Medicine). 2006. *Using Indicators to Measure Country Pharmaceutical Situations: Fact Book on WHO Level I and Level II Monitoring Indicators.* Geneva: WHO.

Xu, K., D. B. Evans, K. Kawabata, R. Zeramdini, J. Klavus, and C. J. Murray. 2003. Household Catastrophic Health Expenditure: A Multicountry Analysis. *Lancet* 362(9378):111–7.

Zerda, A., G. Velásquez, F. Tobar, and J. E. Vargas. 2002. *Health Insurance Systems and Access to Medicines: Case Studies from: Argentina, Chile, Colombia, Costa Rica, Guatemala and the United States of America.* Washington D.C.: Pan American Health Organization. <http://apps.who.int/medicinedocs/en/d/Jh3012e/#Jh3012e>

CHAPTER 13

Revolving drug funds and user fees

SUMMARY

Many governments, nongovernmental organizations, and community health programs have implemented user fees to fund or partially fund the cost of pharmaceuticals or other health services. Many different forms of revolving drug funds (RDFs) exist. Their common element is that fees are charged for medicines dispensed. In the context of the Bamako Initiative, community pharmaceutical schemes often have cost-recovery objectives that include the financing of health education, immunization, and other aspects of primary health care.

During the 1990s and early 2000s, the debate over user fees intensified within the context of a global call for increased access to medicines: evidence supports arguments from both sides, and opinions still differ about the feasibility of creating and sustaining an equitable cost-recovery system based on user fees (Meessen et al. 2006). Supporters assert that RDFs can raise substantial revenue, improve pharmaceutical availability and quality of care, promote equity by making pharmaceuticals more accessible to the poor while charging those who can afford to pay, reinforce decentralization through local control of resources, and encourage efficiency in pharmaceutical management and medicine use. Others caution that collection costs may exceed revenue collected, no improvement may occur in pharmaceutical availability or other quality measures, user charges are a form of "sick tax" that substitutes for public spending, people are dissuaded from seeking essential health care, and incentives are created for overprescribing. Note that some critics judge RDFs separately from health system user fees (for example, Save the Children 2002).

Planning and implementing an RDF require simultaneous commitment to public health goals and sound business management. A number of steps are involved—

Feasibility: Determine whether the concept of an RDF is politically acceptable, economically viable, and realistic in terms of managerial requirements.

Organizational structure and legal status: Decide which RDF functions will be centralized and which decentralized. Seek government or legal endorsement for such issues as retention of revenue at the facility or district level. Community involvement is often essential for the acceptability, credibility, and accountability of RDFs.

Pricing and exemptions: Establish policies that ensure access to services and also maintain the financial integrity of the RDF. Determine fee collection mechanisms as well as fee levels. Consider willingness to pay and cost data in setting pharmaceutical prices.

Financial planning: Ascertain initial capitalization requirements and recurrent costs. The availability of government and donor subsidies helps determine the RDF's cost-recovery objectives.

Supply management: Consider management requirements because weaknesses in any area can threaten the RDF's service performance and financial viability.

Public communications: Tailor target audiences, messages, and media to each stage of RDF implementation.

Monitoring and supervision: Put in place recording, reporting, supervisory, and other measures to monitor effect on patients, financial performance, pharmaceutical availability, and medicine use.

Establishing and sustaining RDFs have been difficult in practice. Improved pharmaceutical availability, equity, and efficiency are more likely with local control and retention of revenue; reliable supply of low-cost essential medicines; locally appropriate fee schedules; protection mechanisms to ensure equitable access; continued or increased levels of government funding for health; businesslike orientation to personnel, financial management, and supply management; strict measures to ensure accountability; and implementation in phases or through a well-conceived pilot approach.

13.1 Introduction

Revolving drug funds (RDFs) are difficult to implement. Examples of successful large, national RDFs are limited. Revenues are often much less than expected. Use of health services and, therefore, equity of access often decrease. Reliable pharmaceutical supply, management, accountability, and rational medicine use are challenges for any RDF.

Countries and programs that implement RDFs should do so with a full understanding of the problems other programs have faced and the solutions that have succeeded elsewhere. (Country Study 13-1 illustrates the number of years and tremendous political commitment needed to establish an RDF in the Sudan.)

At the same time, many countries providing "free" health services have found that public resources are insufficient to

Country Study 13-1
Establishing a successful revolving drug fund in Sudan

With initial capitalization and technical support from Save the Children, the Ministry of Health in Sudan's Khartoum state phased in an RDF from 1989 to 1996. A 2006 evaluation included record review and interviews with policy makers, health care practitioners, patients, and households in the catchment area of facilities operating under the RDF. A control group comprised facilities not affected by the RDF.

The results showed that the RDF facilities had a higher level of medicine availability (97 percent) compared with controls (86 percent). Clients reported the medicines to be affordable—the average cost of a prescription amounted to only 2 percent of the lowest monthly government salary.

Key success factors included autonomy that allowed the RDF managers to keep their funds separate from other government accounts, government tax and licensing exemptions, and an innovative currency swap agreement that allowed the RDF to access hard currency at official rates.

The table below lists the lessons learned in Khartoum's RDF experience. Based on the results, the Ministry of Health is expanding the RDF to the rest of the country in phases—by the end of 2006, nineteen of twenty-five states were part of the RDF.

Lessons learned from the RDF in Khartoum state

	Factor for success	Components/results
1	Substantial investments	• Helping RDF to absorb devaluation loss • Allowing RDF to mature until sustainable
2	Gradual implementation	• Allowing time for necessary preparation • Testing of drug supply and cash collection systems • Proper staff training
3	Management style	• Adopting transparency • Flexible organization structure • Business-oriented management • Joint management between national Ministry of Health and expatriate Save the Children staff
4	Political commitment	• Tax and import duty exemptions • Independent account • Import license exemption • Monopoly
5	Currency swap agreement	• Safeguard against devaluation • Permitting importation of low-cost and quality medicines • High markup on cost covering the RDF operating expenses while keeping retail prices lower
6	Price revision	• Protecting the RDF against devaluation • Keeping pace with market prices • Maintaining users' ability to pay
7	Community acceptance	• Increasing RDF turnover • Permitting replenishment of exhausted stocks • Avoiding the tie-up of funds • Ensuring revenue available to cover RDF operating expenses
8	Focus on common diseases	• Short list for treatment of common diseases • Avoiding the wastage of limited resources • Increasing coverage by purchasing large quantities
9	Reliable supply system	• Regular availability of medicines • Low-cost medicines • Maximizing RDF sales • Allowing RDF to make medicines regularly available
10	Supervision	• Prohibiting medicine leakage • 100% cash collection rates • Reducing losses due to expiration and deterioration of medicines

Sources: Ali 2009; Hamed and Ibrihim 2009.

meet rising costs and increasing demand. When funds are limited, provision of essential medicines is among the first components of health care to suffer: medicine shortages become common even when selection, procurement, distribution, and use are efficient and rational.

On the basis of research showing that user fees can easily cause a decrease in the use of preventive health care services, most international agencies discourage implementing user fees for preventive care, including the World Bank and World Health Organization (WHO). (Nevertheless, even when preventive services are free, they are still underused in both developed and developing countries, as reported by Liu and O'Dougherty 2005.) In addition, many in the international health community are calling for all user fees to be abolished; however, eliminating existing user fees in resource-limited countries does not necessarily improve access to medicines and services unless sufficient resources are available to take up the slack and ensure equitable access. For example, the elimination of medicine fees at public facilities may result in more stock-outs, leading patients to pay more in private pharmacies that have reliable stock (James et al. 2006; Xu et al. 2006). Although user fees can contribute to budgets for services and pharmaceuticals that would otherwise not be available, evidence shows that fees are usually a major detriment to access to the poorest people in the community, because exemption plans that are supposed to act as a safety net for needy patients are often nonfunctional (Gottrett and Schieber 2006).

Proponents on both sides of the issue recognize the challenges of providing sustainable financing for pharmaceuticals that maximizes equitable access, especially for long-term treatment, such as that for HIV/AIDS. WHO now promotes minimizing fees for health care and medicines and encourages countries to use taxes or insurance schemes to finance health expenses (Foster et al. 2006). Ghana is one country whose government decided to abolish its national "cash-and-carry" system of financing health services and replace it with a national health insurance system while maintaining local facilities' autonomy in managing their RDFs. Chapter 12 discusses health insurance in detail.

Cost sharing through medicine fees is one of several pharmaceutical financing strategies described in Chapter 11. That chapter is concerned with programs in which medicine fees are used to finance essential medicines at the national level, at the district level, at individual institutions such as teaching and referral hospitals, or through community pharmaceutical schemes.

Medicine fees may be simply one component of a broader program of user fees. Although such programs may not think of themselves as RDFs, this chapter should be useful for any program involved in setting medicine fees and using the revenue to resupply medicines.

13.2 The revolving fund concept

What is a revolving drug fund?

In an RDF, a sum of money (contributed by the government, donors, or the community) is used to purchase an initial stock of essential and commonly used medicines to be sold, ideally at a price sufficient to replace the stock of medicines and ensure a continuous supply (see Figure 13-1). Reasons usually given for establishing an RDF are—

- Essential medicines are a critical component of effective preventive and curative care.
- Patients perceive the increased availability of pharmaceuticals as a real improvement in the quality of care.
- Pharmaceuticals are tangible, and most patients are willing to pay for them.
- The public spends significant amounts of money for pharmaceuticals from the private sector, often buying inadequate quantities at high prices. Medicines supplied through an RDF are generally more affordable.
- Patients may attach greater value to medicines for which they have paid. A potential result is improved patient adherence to treatment.
- RDFs linked to essential medicines programs offer the potential for increasing the efficiency of pharmaceutical services as well as generating additional revenue.
- Increased price awareness by prescribers and patients may result in improved use of medicines.

Whereas the primary objective of private pharmacies is to maximize profit, the objective of RDFs is to maximize access. If current public financing is sufficient to ensure universal access to essential medicines without charge, medicine fees are unnecessary. If current financing is inadequate, an RDF can provide supplementary resources to make low-cost essential medicines more accessible (Uzochukwu and Onwujekwe 2002; Xu et al. 2006).

Experiences with RDFs

There are numerous examples of experiences with user-fee programs and, in particular, with RDFs. From these experiences, proponents of user charges suggest the following—

- Substantial revenue can be raised by user fees, which add to central allocations.
- Pharmaceutical availability and quality of care are improved with the additional revenue.
- Equity is promoted because limited public funds can be targeted to the most needy while the rest pay.
- Decentralization is reinforced through local control of resources.

Figure 13-1 The RDF cycle

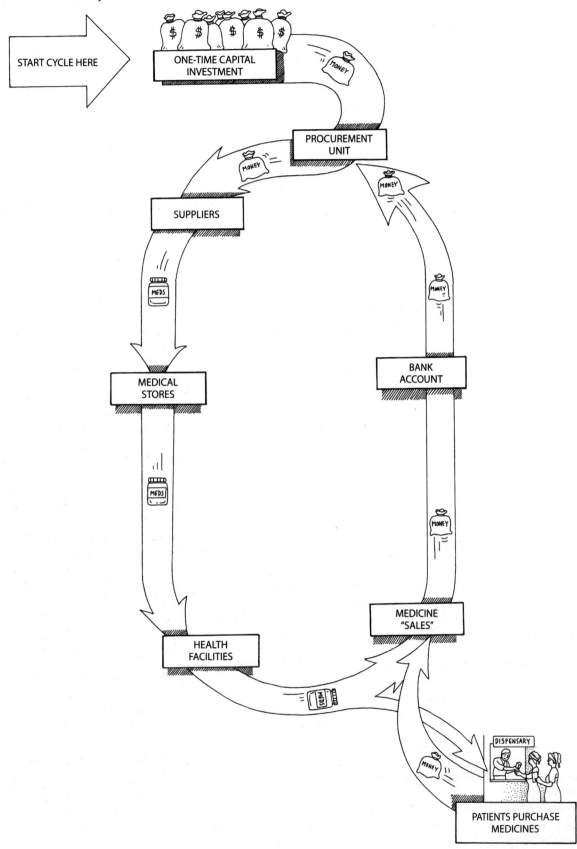

• Efficiency is fostered through lower fees at first-level facilities to reinforce the referral system and through higher fees at higher-level hospitals to reduce the disproportionately large expenditures typically made on pharmaceutical supply for referral hospitals.

Not all governments or health financing experts favor user fees for medicines. Opponents observe the following—

• Collection costs may exceed revenue collected when the full cost of developing the system and all additional administrative costs are considered.
• No improvement may take place in pharmaceutical availability and other quality measures (as has occurred in some user-fee programs).
• User charges may become a form of "sick tax," substituting for rather than supplementing central allocations.
• People, particularly the poor and other target groups, are dissuaded from seeking essential health care.
• Incentives for overprescribing are created if revenue is used to support staff salaries.

Decades of experience with RDFs and user fees for services demonstrate the need for thoughtful design that includes community involvement, careful implementation associated with quality improvement, and good management. However, experience also shows that cost-recovery programs are rarely able to achieve these standards in the long term.

Programs that have implemented large fees with no preparation of the public and little improvement in quality have seen significant decreases in use; programs designed with little attention to management and accounting systems have resulted in abuse and generated little revenue compared with the cost of fee collection; programs that have not reinvested revenues to improve quality have resulted in a decline in public confidence and use; RDFs without a reliable source of low-cost medicines have quickly ceased to revolve, and some schemes with pharmaceutical charges have led to overprescribing.

Steps for planning and implementing an RDF

The planning and implementation of a successful RDF require simultaneous commitment to public health goals and sound business management principles. Each of the following steps requires careful attention—

• Carry out a situation analysis and feasibility assessment.
• Prepare a financial plan that considers cost-recovery objectives, capitalization requirements, and long-term financial needs.

• Determine the organizational structure, staffing, and legal status of the RDF.
• Develop an implementation plan.
• Determine pricing and exemption policies.
• Develop the necessary systems for pharmaceutical management and financial management.
• Prepare public communications for introducing the RDF.
• Monitor impact and adjust the program accordingly.

13.3 Situation analysis and feasibility assessment

Governments considering whether to introduce cost recovery must address questions of political, economic, and managerial feasibility, given local circumstances (see Figure 13-2).

Similarly, governments that are considering discontinuing such programs must take measures and have the resources in place to handle the consequences of losing revenue, such as increased medicine stockouts and upsetting health care providers who have come to rely on fees to supplement income (Gilson and McIntyre 2005).

Political issues

Three political issues are key in establishing an RDF: acceptance of the user fee concept, local retention of fee revenue, and political and administrative decentralization.

Acceptance of user fees. Although many believe strongly in the concept of universal access to health care, a policy of free medicines is worth little if medicines are unavailable. When RDFs have been proposed in settings where pharmaceuticals at health facilities have been scarce, public reaction has generally been positive. Moreover, when an RDF has resulted in a noticeable increase in the availability of pharmaceuticals, public acceptance has been much greater than government officials anticipated. Studies have shown that the public's willingness to pay for government health services is closely tied to people's perception of quality and the value that they are getting for their money (Shaw 1995). Conversely, if people have experienced a steady supply of medicines provided free of charge by the government, they are more likely to oppose any introduction of fees. In this setting, the need for an RDF should be carefully considered.

Local retention of fee revenue. The "law of the treasury" often requires that revenues earned by any arm of government be remitted to the central government. RDFs will not revolve, however, unless the facilities that collect medicine fees can retain this revenue to replenish their pharmaceutical supplies. Reinvestment of revenues in the collecting facility also promotes a sense of community ownership, which further protects and strengthens the RDF. Facilities

Figure 13-2   Cost-recovery potential determined by patients and costs, not by policy

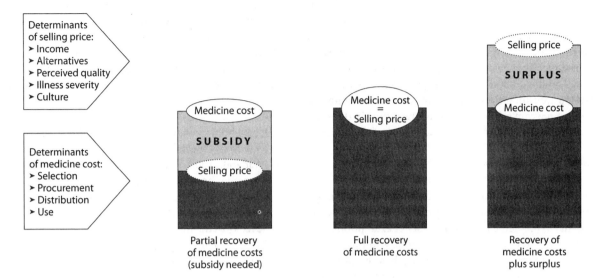

in a pilot project area are often permitted to retain revenues, but replication on a broader scale requires permanent changes in government policy.

Political and administrative decentralization. The question of local involvement and autonomy can be politically sensitive. Successful revolving drug funds often involve community participation and supervision, which ensures financial sustainability and greater community interest in the local health facility. Local empowerment must be accepted and supported by higher levels of government (which must give department or provincial authorities the authority and flexibility to design policies appropriate for their areas). An RDF's local autonomy in the Lao People's Democratic Republic provided financial flexibility and allowed it to avoid decapitalization during a period of rapid inflation (Murakami et al. 2001).

Economic issues

Can sufficient funds be recovered to justify the effort required to make an RDF successful? The answer to this question depends on national and local economic strength, patients' ability and willingness to pay, "competition" from other sources of supply, the availability of capital, policies on exemptions and subsidies, and the program's overall ability to balance public health and economic objectives. All these issues should be carefully considered. Household and patient surveys that ask people about their choice of health services and health care expenditures can reveal a great deal about both willingness and ability to pay for health treatment.

Economic feasibility is also influenced by the level at which fees are introduced. Should RDF implementation be top-down, starting first in hospitals, or bottom-up, begin-

ning in the community? Each approach has advantages and disadvantages.

Despite the many concerns related to economic feasibility, health service use and equity may actually improve with medicine fees (Murakami et al. 2001). A brief explanation of the economic underpinning of this observation may be illuminating. Although opponents of cost sharing often speak about the increase in cost, purchasing medicines locally often avoids the high travel and time costs of seeking care elsewhere, and paying a fee for a medicine as part of an RDF may cost less than paying for it in the private sector (Xu et al. 2006). The key lesson is that price must be examined from the perspective of the patient.

Managerial issues

Given the human and physical infrastructure, can a cost-recovery system be made to operate? Accountability, a businesslike orientation, supply management capacity, and human resources capacity are especially critical when a revolving drug fund is initiated at the community level, because management systems and capacity may need to be developed.

Demonstrated commitment by the government (and often by the donor) is essential. Is support available to help maintain the fund until self-sufficiency is reached?

13.4 Financial planning

RDF financial planning involves defining the cost-recovery objective, the roles of government and external funding, the capitalization requirements, and foreign exchange issues. Because the goal of an RDF is to maintain steady pharmaceutical supply while serving as many people as possible, careful analysis is necessary of both recurrent costs and regular government and donor contributions. Pharmaceutical sales must make up any shortfall between these costs and revenues. Many countries that are eager to commence cost-recovery programs fail to do a careful financial analysis before embarking on such programs. As a result, a well-intentioned RDF may quickly decapitalize; some revenues are raised, but a direct relationship does not necessarily exist between revenues and stock replacement.

Cost-recovery objective

The cost-recovery objective for an RDF may be set by policy, but the actual level of cost recovery depends on the response of patients to medicine fees, the number of exemptions, and collection efficiency, among other factors. Although some programs attempt to cover all primary health care costs through user fees, many countries have found recovering full costs on a large scale extremely difficult.

Cost-recovery alternatives. The level of cost recovery reflects the relationship between the total operating costs and the total revenues collected. Possible cost-recovery objectives include—

- Partial recovery of pharmaceutical costs, which require continued subsidy from government or other sources
- Full recovery of pharmaceutical costs
- Full recovery of pharmaceutical costs plus some local operating costs
- Full recovery of all pharmaceutical costs and local operating costs

Tension between public health and financial objectives is inherent in the RDF concept. Because RDF fees are intended to increase the availability of essential medicines at the local level, they must not serve as financial barriers to people receiving needed services. The RDF must improve total access to service, not decrease it. Yet the fees must be high enough to ensure replenishment of supplies and financial sustainability of the RDF.

Establishing a realistic cost-recovery objective depends on striking a balance among operating costs, revenue collection, and government and other funding.

Operating costs. Pharmaceutical costs should be calculated based on the full replacement cost of medicines. This cost includes the original purchase price (with insurance and freight), price increases caused by inflation and currency fluctuations, and the cost of losses caused by expiration, spoilage, and pilferage. Other recurrent costs include management of the procurement office, transportation, storage at various levels, and perhaps repackaging. In addition to pharmaceutical costs, local operating costs include health

workers' salaries, fuel for vehicles, consumable items such as dressings, cold-chain costs, and utilities (see Chapter 41).

Revenue collection. Revenue collection in RDFs is determined by patients' willingness to pay, exemption rates, and collection efficiency; it is often far below target levels.

The price at which most patients will buy medicines at a government health facility, which is a reflection of their willingness to pay, depends on several factors—

- Household income, which can vary dramatically by season, especially in rural areas
- Availability and cost of alternative sources of medicines and health care (the "competition")
- Perceived quality of the pharmaceuticals and associated health care services
- Severity of the illness
- Cultural factors, such as the priority given to health care for men, women, and children

Basing RDF prices only on actual costs sometimes leads to a dramatic and dangerous decline in health facility use. Because of differences in access, perceived quality, and usual quantities of pharmaceuticals purchased, direct comparison with private-sector prices can be misleading. Estimates of willingness to pay can be made using the techniques described in Section 13.7 on pricing.

Exemption rates are another major determinant of actual revenue collections. In cost-recovery programs with broad exemption criteria, over 50 percent of patients do not pay; a high level of cost recovery is difficult, if not impossible, in such circumstances. Exemption criteria, administrative arrangements, and mechanisms for financing exemptions are considered later in this chapter.

Finally, total revenue reflects collection efficiency: What share of expected revenues is actually collected? When the number of patients treated, quantity of medicines dispensed, pharmaceutical prices, and exemption rates are considered, how much money should have been collected, and how much money actually was? It is not unusual to find that actual collections are less than two-thirds—sometimes as little as one-third—of expectations.

Reasons for collection inefficiency include simple laxity in implementing fees, unofficial ("backdoor") exemptions, and pilferage of medicines and cash. A high collection rate depends on sound pharmaceutical management systems, well-developed financial management and accountability measures, regular monitoring and supervision, and when necessary, vigorous use of disciplinary and legal measures. Collection inefficiency is a major threat to RDFs.

Role of government and external funding

Government and external funding are often necessary to plan and implement an RDF and to cover the cost of exemptions, subsidize high-cost medicines, and fund other health system costs not financed through user fees.

Maintaining government funding. If continued government funding is needed for pharmaceuticals, how can it be secured? What strategies can ensure that RDF revenue supplements, rather than substitutes for, central treasury allocations?

The simple but vague promise of "continued funding at present levels" may be difficult to monitor and enforce in practice. Trends in government revenues, allocations among ministries and within the ministry of health, local inflation, and foreign exchange fluctuations (which usually have a major effect on pharmaceutical purchasing power) all make increases or decreases in pharmaceutical budgets difficult to predict.

At least three budgeting strategies exist: (1) maintaining an annual per capita pharmaceutical budget; (2) establishing a budgeting formula and an agreed-upon list of groups of patients or treatments for public support (for example, children, prenatal supplements, tuberculosis treatment); and (3) excluding RDF revenue entirely from all national or local budget information and expenditure analysis.

The last approach has been implemented in one East African country by showing user-fee revenue as a nominal amount in official budget figures and excluding it from historical comparisons and budget analyses. As a result, rising user-fee and insurance revenue has not measurably affected central government allocations for health.

Funding from donors and development loans. Grants and development loans can be instrumental in planning and implementing an RDF. This category of funding may include financing of start-up capital, development costs, and price subsidies during the first few years of operation. Such funding should not be relied on for long-term subsidy, however, because it puts the RDF's financial sustainability at risk.

In an RDF, donated medicines should normally be sold through health facilities at regular RDF prices, and the revenues from such sales should be used to support health services, as determined by the community. Distributing donated medicines without charge creates confusion for health staff and patients. Medicines provided to support programs such as leprosy or tuberculosis control, which are often included in the list of exempt health conditions, would be an exception.

Start-up financing

Starting or expanding a revolving drug fund requires working capital, support for the development of management systems, and sometimes partial subsidy of pharmaceutical costs.

Capitalization requirements. Capitalization means filling the RDF pipeline—from central warehouses through peripheral medicine stores—with appropriate inventories at each level before pharmaceutical sales begin. Only when the pipeline is filled is the drug fund able to revolve. Gaps in the pipeline result in missed deliveries from one level to the next and eventual stockouts at the point of service delivery.

The central government or an external donor may provide seed stock for RDF capitalization, or it may be contributed at the local level by the community. Pipeline calculations for an RDF are illustrated in Box 13-1. The pipeline is affected by inventory management decisions (Chapter 23), distribution system design (Chapter 22), and cost-saving measures related to pipeline management (Chapter 40).

Overcapitalizing RDFs wastes money, but RDFs that are undercapitalized quickly break down—for example, when fees are collected from pharmaceutical sales, but funds are inadequate to replenish pharmaceutical stocks. When revenues intended for pharmaceutical purchases are inadequate to purchase all necessary medicines, funds may be used for emergency purchases of small quantities at higher-than-expected prices or to pay other expenses, further decapitalizing the fund.

Development and implementation of management systems. Support may be needed to develop pharmaceutical and financial management systems and for training, community orientation, monitoring, and other implementation activities.

Price subsidies. Lower prices and broader exemptions may be needed at the beginning to gain acceptance for the system. The total development cost of an RDF, therefore, may need to include funds to partially subsidize prices for the first few years.

Foreign exchange

Foreign exchange is an extremely important issue that requires support and cooperation from government groups outside the health sector. Where local currency is not freely convertible and the demand for foreign exchange exceeds supply, government commitment is required to provide the foreign exchange necessary to replenish pharmaceutical supply on a regular basis. Because revolving drug funds are designed by health policy makers but foreign exchange allocations are made outside the health sector, often by the ministry of finance, central bank, or national planning ministry, the issue of foreign exchange can be problematic. Coordination among different arms of government is difficult but essential to ensure the sustainability of supply.

Liberalization of foreign exchange markets has greatly improved the situation in many countries. Even where governments continue to allocate foreign exchange for government ministries, an RDF may be able to obtain a waiver for foreign exchange on the open market.

Box 13-1
Pipeline calculations for capitalizing an RDF

A revolving drug fund must have sufficient working capital (pharmaceuticals and cash) to start revolving and keep revolving. Working capital depends on the amount of pharmaceuticals and cash in the pipeline. The length of the pipeline is measured in numbers of months. It is determined by the number of levels in the distribution system, the safety stock at each level, and the average working stock (which depends on the delivery interval—see Chapter 23). The diameter of the pipeline is determined by the final outflow—the total value of pharmaceuticals dispensed per month.

The following example illustrates a pipeline calculation for establishing an RDF to serve a network of 210 community pharmacies. It includes a central supply agency, district stores, and community pharmacies.

The pipeline for the proposed pharmaceutical sales program begins with the disbursement of funds for procurement and ends at the point where funds are collected and made available for purchasing replenishment supplies. The pipeline can be broken down into a number of segments, as illustrated below.

Average monthly sales. The number of low-, medium-, and high-volume community pharmacies and the average monthly sale per pharmacy are estimated in the table opposite.

Capital requirements. With an average pipeline length of sixteen months and an average consumption for all 210 pharmacies of 65,000 U.S. dollars (USD) per month, total capital requirements would be as follows—

$$16 \times USD\ 65,000 = USD\ 1,040,000$$

Sources of capital and possible cost savings. Working capital can be supplied from various sources: the purchase pipeline and safety stock could be financed by donations, the working stock for central and district levels by government allocations, and the community pharmacy funds from community fund-raising efforts. Improved procurement payment terms, more rapid flow of medicines through the system (faster turnover), and more efficient bank transfers could shorten the pipeline and reduce capitalization costs.

Cash and pharmaceuticals in the pipeline	Months
Purchase pipeline: In this example, it is assumed that roughly 50 percent of pharmaceuticals will be purchased from international sources and 50 percent from local sources. For international purchases, an average of six months will elapse between the provision of a letter of credit and the receipt of the pharmaceuticals at the central supply agency. For domestic purchases, payment will be made upon receipt. Therefore, the average purchase pipeline will be three months.	3
Central supply agency safety stock: A three-month safety stock will be maintained at the central supply agency.	3
Central supply agency working stock: The supply agency will tender once a year but will receive deliveries every four months, which implies a maximum working stock of four months and an average working stock of two months.	2
District safety stock: The district medical stores of the supply agency will maintain a two-month safety stock.	2
District working stock: The district medical stores will receive shipments from the central supply agency every two months, implying a maximum working stock of two months and an average working stock of one month.	1
Community pharmacy safety stock: The community pharmacies will maintain a one-month safety stock.	1
Community pharmacy working stock: The community pharmacies will be resupplied once a month, implying a maximum working stock of one month and an average working stock of half a month.	0.5
Community pharmacy cash on hand: The community pharmacies will use their revenues once a month when they purchase their resupplies from the district medical stores. On average, these funds will have been held half a month by the community pharmacies.	0.5
District to center cash transfer: Money received by the district medical stores will be deposited within the week at the local branch of the national bank. On average, this money will take one month to be credited to the account of the supply agency.	1
Cash on hand: In general, purchases made by the supply agency will represent one-third of its annual turnover. As a result, money will sit in the agency's central account up to four months, or an average of two months, before being used to make a purchase.	2
Total pipeline =	16

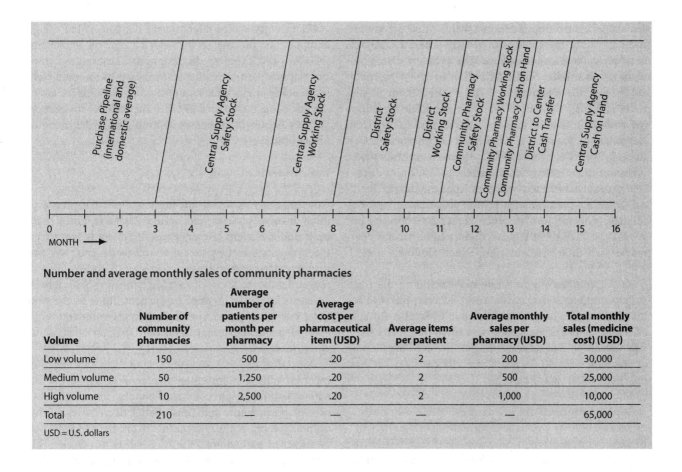

Number and average monthly sales of community pharmacies

Volume	Number of community pharmacies	Average number of patients per month per pharmacy	Average cost per pharmaceutical item (USD)	Average items per patient	Average monthly sales per pharmacy (USD)	Total monthly sales (medicine cost) (USD)
Low volume	150	500	.20	2	200	30,000
Medium volume	50	1,250	.20	2	500	25,000
High volume	10	2,500	.20	2	1,000	10,000
Total	210	—	—	—	—	65,000

USD = U.S. dollars

13.5 Organizational issues

Organizational issues for RDFs include their structure, pharmaceutical supply system, need for a multidisciplinary team, community involvement, and legal matters.

Organizational structure

RDFs can be managed through a highly centralized structure, a decentralized approach, or a mixed approach in which different functions are managed at different levels. Centralized systems have the potential advantages of a standardized medicine list, bulk purchasing, and national uniformity in pricing policies. Decentralized price setting, determination of exemption policies, and adjustments in the medicines list, however, may make an RDF more responsive to local circumstances.

In practice, many RDFs combine the two approaches. For example, procurement may be centralized, and policies with regard to prices and exemptions may be determined locally. Or the central government may provide training and supervision, and all other management systems, including procurement and distribution, may be decentralized. The important issue is to identify the key requirements for RDF implementation and to clarify where responsibility lies for each. Major routine functions include—

- Product selection (review and revision of the essential medicines list)
- Procurement and distribution
- Price setting
- Determination of exemption policies
- Audit and financial oversight
- Local representation and oversight

Pharmaceutical supply system

RDF survival depends on a regular supply of low-cost, high-quality medicines; if procurement and distribution are not reliable, the RDF will quickly stop functioning. RDFs may be established as part of a major effort to revitalize government pharmaceutical supply systems, including central medical stores (CMS), or in conjunction with the establishment of an autonomous pharmaceutical supply agency.

RDFs may also be supplied through a direct-delivery system, in which tenders establish the supplier and price for each item and suppliers deliver medicines directly to districts and major facilities. Pharmaceuticals may be supplied through a primary distributor system, in which the government establishes a contract with a single private distributor (or prime vendor) as well as separate contracts with pharmaceutical suppliers. The primary distributor manages pharmaceutical distribution by receiving medicines from the suppliers and distributing them to districts and major facilities. Finally, some RDFs that have the authority (that is, they are not required to buy from the public-sector supplier) may procure pharmaceuticals through the local private sector, especially in cases where the government supply is unreliable. The Nyamira district RDF in Kenya normally procures from the district medical store; however, it uses a private procurement agent to fill gaps (Enemark, Alban, and Vazquez 2004). In the Lao P.D.R., the RDF often buys medicines from private pharmacies, which are also its competition (Murakami et al. 2001).

Pharmaceutical supply strategies—including the CMS system, autonomous agencies, direct delivery, and primary distributors—are described in detail in Chapter 8. Because a reliable supply of medicines is essential to the success of RDFs, decision makers and managers involved in planning or implementing RDFs must carefully consider the best pharmaceutical supply strategy.

Multidisciplinary team

Just as an immunization program needs staff specialized in cold-chain maintenance, epidemiology, and community mobilization, RDFs need staff specialized in certain areas. In addition to staff with clinical and pharmacy training, RDFs need staff with skills in economics, business, and accounting. Such skills are often found in other ministries and in the nongovernmental sector. Recruitment of some specialized staff may be needed.

Community involvement

Community involvement is essential for the acceptability, credibility, and accountability of RDFs. Informal involvement may include advising on program development and the collection and use of revenue and participating in public awareness campaigns. Formal involvement may include participation in generating start-up funds, setting fees, determining who receives exemptions, ensuring accountability, and monitoring the use of revenues. For example, cases in sub-Saharan Africa showed that by involving communities in initial cost-sharing strategies, the community-based management committees were empowered to make more complicated management decisions down the road (Shaw 1995). Also, rural districts in Uganda where communities owned and managed funds from user fees had improved service quality and increased usage, while urban districts, which had little community involvement, saw decreases in service usage (Kipp et al. 2001).

Community stakeholders must be a part of the design and planning process, so that they become owners of and therefore advocates for the program. Garnering community support and providing information to the public are particularly important at the outset, when user charges are just being introduced or when major program changes occur. Chapter 31 discusses community participation in greater detail.

Legal aspects

Government-run RDFs and broader user-fee programs often involve policies and actions that are not strictly legal under current law or whose legal status is unclear. Examples include the policy that user-fee revenue will add to, not replace, central government allocations; retention of revenue at the facility or district level; opening of local bank accounts; carrying forward of unspent funds to the next fiscal year (as opposed to returning funds to the treasury); and independent external audits of RDF financial accounts and stocks.

Depending on local conventions and the policy or action involved, official endorsement may require various combinations of ministry circulars, legal notices, cabinet approval, acts of parliament, and presidential decrees (executive orders). Generally, the more cumbersome the method (such as an act of parliament), the harder it is to reverse. This fact can provide a degree of protection from future political whim. Therefore, if some principles are vital to the success of the RDF (such as local retention of fees or additivity to treasury allocations), the effort to have these principles endorsed through legal notice or even an act of parliament may be worthwhile.

13.6 Implementation planning

Implementation planning involves decisions about bottom-up versus top-down implementation, phasing and pilot testing, and development of RDF procedures.

Bottom-up versus top-down implementation

Bottom-up versus top-down development of user charges is both a policy question and an implementation question. Introducing fees at all levels at the same time is rarely feasible. Therefore, should fees be introduced first at the hospital level or at the community level?

Arguments favoring starting at the top include the following (Griffin 1988; Blakney, Litvack, and Quick 1989)—

Equity: Higher-level facilities generally serve populations that are better able to pay for services and have access to other health providers.

Reinforcement of referral system: Introducing charges at higher levels encourages the use of cost-effective lower-level services.

Revenue potential: Higher-level facilities provide large volumes of more costly pharmaceuticals and other services.

Administrative capacity: Senior managers, pharmaceutical management staff, accountants, and other necessary staff may be better equipped to undertake the additional administrative burden.

Impact evaluation: The health care and financial effect of user fees is easier to monitor at a smaller number of more accessible facilities.

Arguments favoring starting at the level of the community or primary care facilities include the following—

Demand: Communities are actively interested in ensuring a regular supply of essential medicines.

Lack of alternatives: Rural populations often have fewer choices in health care; if the government or community cannot provide medicines, they may go without.

Support for prevention: Increasing pharmaceutical availability at the primary health care level also attracts people for essential preventive services.

Community involvement: A bottom-up approach provides greater opportunity for community involvement. Also, government or donor start-up funds may be supplemented by community contributions.

The relative strength of the case for bottom-up versus top-down implementation varies with local circumstances. Too often, however, the choice is strongly influenced by local political pressures or donor interests rather than by the merits of each approach.

Experience and careful monitoring can help determine the viability of an RDF at each level. The cost of establishing and maintaining user fees at the lowest level may be greater than the revenue collected.

Phasing and pilot testing

Most countries find implementing an RDF at all levels and in all parts of the country at the same time unworkable. Success depends on developing and testing fees, pharmaceutical supply procedures, and financial management systems. It is best done through pilot testing or phased implementation.

Pilot testing an RDF in one province or one district before it is implemented nationally enables systems to be developed and monitored under close supervision. In countries such as Nepal, Nigeria, and Liberia, different approaches to RDFs in different parts of the country allowed cross-fertilization of experience.

Pilot tests can be misleading, however, if they are conducted only in more accessible, better organized areas; if they are conducted with much more intensive technical and financial support than could be expected with national implementation; or if they result in systems suitable to the pilot area but less suitable to other parts of the country. Circumstances can also change; for example, Azerbaijan successfully piloted RDFs in populations of refugees and internally displaced persons. The pilot experience showed that RDFs were feasible and relatively sustainable. However, plans to expand the funds were canceled when market prices of pharmaceuticals dropped lower than what the RDF would have to charge to recoup procurement and overhead charges (Holley, Akhundov, and Nolte 2004).

Phased implementation, beginning at the higher levels of the system, offers the advantage of firmly establishing effective pharmaceutical supply, financial management, pricing, exemption, and accountability systems at each level before proceeding to the next level. A phased approach can help build public acceptance, test and revise fee structures, develop management capacity, and train staff over a reasonable period of time.

With phased implementation, the high-level facilities in each area serve as training and demonstration centers for the next level: provincial hospitals establish their systems, then become training sites for district hospitals; district hospitals develop their systems and become training sites for health centers; health centers become training sites for health posts or community health workers. It may take six to eighteen months to develop, implement, and reinforce RDF management systems at each level.

With either a pilot or a phased approach, an RDF cannot expand any faster than the capacity of the supply system to provide a steady supply of essential medicines.

Development of RDF procedures

An essential aspect of any approach is the development of procedures for pharmaceutical and financial management. Normally, a procedural manual or set of manuals should be developed. Shorter versions of these manuals, including one-page checklists, can be prepared to address the information needs of specific levels and functions.

13.7 Pricing and equity of access

RDF pricing and exemption policies are critical for ensuring that patients in need of essential medicines and medical supplies receive them and that the RDF does not decapitalize. These two requirements pull in opposite directions, creating a constant tension. Prices, as well as the accompanying policies with regard to exemptions, are the mechanism by which the necessary balance is achieved.

Pricing strategies

Pricing for RDFs involves two related questions: what type of medicine fees should be charged, and what should the level of fees be?

Types of medicine fee. Alternatives include course-of-therapy fee, prescription fee, item fee, multilevel item fee (price bands), and variable item fee (see Table 13-1). These mechanisms can be compared with respect to the following criteria—

Effect on prescribing practices: Does the fee create incentives for prescribing more medicines or fewer medicines, higher-cost or lower-cost medicines?

Effect on patients: Is the fee likely to dissuade patients from buying needed medicines, or does it create incentives for patients to use medicines more cost-effectively? Will patients feel they have paid a fair price?

Ease of collection and accounting: How easily can health staff calculate the required payment, make change, and keep accurate payment records?

Balancing pharmaceutical costs and revenues: How closely do the fees received for individual medicines balance the actual cost of medicines dispensed? Can fund managers easily ensure that the collected funds are sufficient to resupply the medicines dispensed?

The effect of fees on prescribing practices is not shown in Table 13-1 because that correlates with whether health staff salaries or bonuses depend on revenue derived from medicine fees. Like private practitioners, government and community health care providers are likely to prescribe more medicines and more costly medicines if their income depends on pharmaceutical sales.

Course-of-therapy fees, multilevel item fees, and variable item fees can all differ for individual medicines. In such instances, the fees charged to patients can be based on the actual cost of the medicine, an assessment of the health impact of the medicine, or a combination of these factors. Pricing can be based on the VEN (vital, essential, nonessential) system (see Chapter 40): for example, the equivalent of USD .10 per item for vital medicines, USD .20 per item for essential medicines, and USD .30 per item for nonessential medicines. With this approach, vital medicines may be sold at prices lower than their replacement cost.

With the variable item fee, the price can be based on a fixed percentage markup over cost, a variable percentage markup, actual cost plus a fixed dispensing fee, or another formula (see the discussion of retail margins in Chapter 9). For example, higher-cost medicines or medicines with a greater health impact may have a lower markup.

Ease of collection and accountability are important considerations, because administrative and accountability

Table 13-1   Comparison of types of medicine fees

Type of fee	Example	Effect on patients[a]	Ease of collection and accounting[b]	Balancing pharmaceutical costs and revenue[c]
Course-of-therapy fee Fixed fee for diagnosis based on standard treatment	USD .20 for one course of malaria treatment; USD .30 for one of pneumonia treatment; USD 1 for one month of hypertension treatment	• Promotion of standard treatments • No incentive to overuse or underuse medicines	+++	0
Prescription fee Standard medicine fee per visit	USD .40 per visit (regardless of number, amount, or type of medicines)	• Patient pressure for more medicines • No incentive for cost consciousness	+++	0
Item fee Standard fee per medicine	USD .20 per item (regardless of amount or type of medicines)	• Patient pressure for high-cost medicines • Incentive to use fewer medicines	++	+
Multilevel item fee Three to five levels or price bands	Fee based on pharmaceutical category: A USD .10 per item B USD .20 per item C USD .30 per item	• Preference to buy low-cost medicines • Incentive to use fewer medicines	+	++
Variable item fee Variable fee per medicine, based on type or cost of medicine	Medicine cost plus 20 percent for all items	• Preference to buy low-cost medicines • Incentive to use fewer medicines • More cost consciousness	0	+++

[a] Medicine prescribing is influenced by whether the prescriber's salary depends on pharmaceutical revenues (see text).
[b] 0 to +++ = range from hardest to easiest for collection and accounting.
[c] 0 to +++ = range from hardest to easiest to balance pharmaceutical costs and revenues.

problems are major constraints on the success of RDFs. Unfortunately, course-of-therapy and prescription fees—which are the easiest to implement and are in some respects the most equitable—make it difficult to ensure that revenues collected are sufficient to pay for medicines dispensed.

One approach is to begin with fees that are easy to implement and then move to more complex but financially sustaining fees as the program evolves. More complex fees require more staff training and more sophisticated accounting systems, which can be implemented over time.

Level of medicine fee. What level of fee is appropriate? With an item fee, for example, should the fee be the equivalent of USD .10 per item, USD .15 per item, or USD .20 per item? If the system is introduced first at rural hospitals, prices can be set on the low side, and patient response can be monitored. Prices can be adjusted accordingly during the first year or two, before moving to the next level.

For RDFs, as in business, there are two basic approaches to price setting: (1) the willingness-to-pay, or market, approach and (2) the cost-based, or accounting, approach. Pricing decisions should draw on information gained through both approaches.

In the willingness-to-pay approach, price levels can be set by using any feasible combination of the four methods used by private companies—

- *Consumer opinion:* Survey questionnaires and focus groups ask community members what they would be willing to pay for specific services.
- *Expert opinion:* The most efficient way to set prices is by asking someone who really knows the product and the population. The expert must have firsthand knowledge of the population being served and how people value medicines. Ministry officials and essential medicines program managers are usually not expert at price setting.
- *Comparative pricing:* Surveying private facilities, mission hospitals, retail pharmacies, patent medicine sellers, and other nongovernmental providers to find out their medicine charges may be useful. However, results must be interpreted in light of differences in income level and perceived value of services.
- *Test pricing:* Companies sometimes use early experience in a small area to establish national prices; the response to initial prices can be used to adjust subsequent prices.

In the cost-based approach, prices are established according to the cost-recovery objectives. Because RDF revenues are used to purchase replacement stocks, a factor for inflation and anticipated stock losses must be built into the calculation of sales price. Some programs include a factor for "stock replacement reserve" and "general reserves," and

any program offering exemptions must adjust for them (see Chapter 41). In the cost-based approach to pricing, the markup percentage must also be determined. Many programs use a fixed percentage, with the more expensive medicines thus producing higher revenues. Other programs use variable markups.

In determining pricing strategies, it must be remembered that the sustainability of the RDF depends on covering some or all of the costs of the system. (What that portion is, and exactly which costs are to be covered, may vary.) The objective is not to maximize profits but to maximize service delivery at a certain basic quality level. Willingness to pay is usually as important as cost data in determining pharmaceutical prices. For example, before the RDF is introduced, estimated sales prices for all pharmaceutical items should be compared with those of similar medicines sold by the private sector. If, after accounting for the replacement costs of pharmaceuticals and exemptions, RDF prices are higher than private-sector prices, the whole RDF strategy must be reconsidered.

Pricing decisions must be made in full recognition of the tension between cost-recovery objectives and social policies regarding access to care. At the same time, administrative requirements for collecting fees must be considered. Most experiences in pharmaceutical cost recovery suggest that when equity-oriented exemption policies and administrative realities are considered, simply recovering the full replacement cost of pharmaceuticals and delivery is often a struggle. Ultimately, cost-recovery potential is determined by patients' willingness and ability to pay for medicines, and not by a policy that mandates a specified markup (see Figure 13-2).

Financial sustainability of RDFs depends on keeping medicine fees in line with changes in the cost of medicines. During periods of high local inflation and foreign exchange fluctuation, frequent price adjustments may be required. Fee increases may present a short-term hardship to patients, but unless certainty exists that the government or a donor will finance the shortfall, such increases are imperative for the survival of the RDF.

Ensuring equity of access

Protection mechanisms—a safety net—are needed to ensure continued access to essential medicines for the poor, the medically needy, and other target groups.

Many programs would like to establish generous exemption policies. But if the RDF is to be viable over the long run, the revenues collected, along with budget subsidies, must be sufficient to purchase replacement pharmaceutical stocks.

As illustrated in Figure 13-3, calculation of the anticipated cost of exemptions leads to determination of the "base" for cost recovery: the total costs that must be recovered

Figure 13-3   Effect of multiple exemptions on the cost-recovery base of an RDF

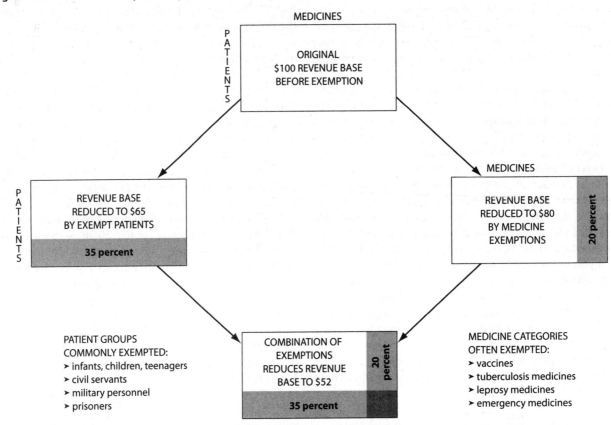

Note: Reducing the patients to 65 percent of original and the medicines to 80 percent of original leaves a revenue base of .80 x .65 = .52 of $100 = $52.

to ensure that the RDF does not decapitalize. Assessment of total costs to be recovered and government subsidies available determines cost-recovery targets (that is, what percentage of total costs must be recovered from paying patients). This, in turn, suggests various pricing strategies.

As Figure 13-3 shows, the lower the pharmaceutical subsidy provided by the government, the greater the burden of generous exemption policies on the local community. Because of this burden, local communities should contribute to the discussion on establishing exemption policies.

Types of protection mechanisms. Exemption from payment, partial exemption (sliding scale), and differential prices are the most common protection mechanisms. Differential pricing is the setting of different price levels by type of patients, level of the health system, or type of pharmaceuticals. Fee levels may be higher for adults than for children, for example. Pharmaceutical and service fees also may be graduated by level of care, with referral hospitals charging the highest fee for a given medicine or service, district hospitals charging lower fees, health centers charging even lower fees, and community health workers charging the lowest fees. In addition to reinforcing referral patterns,

this approach seeks to improve equity by making pharmaceuticals more affordable through community health workers and lower-level health facilities. Differential pricing by the VEN classification helps make the most essential medicines available at the lowest prices.

The type of fee may also provide some protection. Registration or consultation fees paid before seeing a clinician may dissuade people from seeking needed care, even if they would have been exempt from payment. But when medicine fees are in effect, the most acutely ill patients will have been identified before the issue of payment arises.

Exemption criteria. Criteria used to grant full or partial exemptions fall into three main categories—

- *Poverty:* people below a certain income or standard of living
- *Personal factors:* children (usually those under five), the elderly, the disabled, prisoners, and some categories of students
- *Health conditions:* pregnancy, to encourage proper prenatal care; communicable diseases, such as tuberculosis, HIV/AIDS, and sexually transmitted infections, to encourage treatment or control their spread

For political reasons, user-fee programs sometimes begin with broad exemptions that include civil servants, teachers, members of the military, war veterans, older children, and other groups that are able to pay and for which no equity or public health arguments exist for exemption. Financial sustainability depends on narrowing the list of exemptions as the RDF gains acceptance and as systems develop to target those truly in need.

Administering exemptions. The practicalities of administering exemptions often present the greatest barrier to ensuring equity in RDFs. Procedures should be administratively feasible, exempt the correct groups, and prevent abuse by those who do not meet exemption criteria. An assessment of the Ghana pharmaceutical sector showed that reimbursement delays and exemptions management have substantially contributed to the decapitalization of RDFs (MOH Ghana 2002).

Exemptions and differential pricing based on objective criteria, such as pregnancy, age, or diagnosis, are easier to implement than more subjective criteria. Even verification of age can be difficult, however. Exempting children under five years of age (who are usually known to the staff of well-child clinics) is easier to enforce than exempting children under fifteen years of age (who may be difficult to distinguish from young adults).

Although policy makers usually agree that the poor should be exempt, defining who is poor is difficult, particularly in noncash economies. Measures used to assess poverty level include type of employment, household income (cash and noncash), household expenditures (for example, total cash and noncash expenditures during the last month), and wealth (housing, land, livestock, and other personal holdings).

Verifying poverty or other exemption criteria may not be difficult in a local dispensary where patients are well known to staff. But in a busy, less personal health center or hospital outpatient department, it can be quite difficult. For example, at a hospital in Ghana, only 2 of almost 42,000 patients were identified to receive "pauper" exemptions (Nyonator and Kutzin 1999). Involving the community in deciding who should receive waivers has been successful in some settings (Holley, Akhundov, and Nolte 2004; Jacobs and Price 2006).

Experiences from many countries have shown that exemption plans are rarely effective or functional—either because the system is not well understood or because pressure is great to generate revenue in the facility—and that even if a user-fee system is well organized, the lack of waivers will likely entail a trade-off between financial sustainability and access to the poor (Nyonator and Kutzin 1999; Xu et al. 2006).

Financing the cost of exemptions

An effective system of exemptions and other protection mechanisms is essential to ensure equity of access. Unless someone pays the cost of these exemptions, however, an RDF will soon cease to revolve. Exemptions can be financed through any combination of the following—

- Central government recurrent budget allocations
- Higher markups on medicines for patients who can pay
- Community contributions
- Local or external donors

A certain level of government financial support is usually necessary to ensure equitable access for the poor and other target groups; otherwise, prices for paying patients must be increased to cover the cost of exemptions. In practice, using higher markups for paying patients to finance exempt patients usually fails, unless the proportion of exempt patients is low and collection efficiency is high. In community pharmaceutical schemes, village health committees sometimes maintain "poor funds" to pay for those who cannot afford medicine fees. In Cambodia, some public hospitals established health equity funds for poor people that used a community-based third-party-payer arrangement to administer the scheme. These hospitals saw an increase in services given to the poor (Jacobs and Price 2006).

Finally, exemptions may be financed by local or external donors, but few are willing to provide long-term subsidies. In some cases, however, donors support exemptions through in-kind contributions (medicines for acute respiratory infection, diarrheal disease, or nutritional support), with the understanding that treatment will be dispensed without charge if the patient meets established exemption criteria. As discussed in Chapter 15, country program managers and policy makers, rather than donors, should decide how donations will be handled in cost recovery.

13.8 Management of pharmaceuticals and money

RDFs face much more demanding management requirements than free systems. The concepts of service performance and cost control must pervade the management of RDFs.

Pharmaceutical supply management

Selection, procurement, quality assurance, distribution, management information, and medicine use are all handled somewhat differently in the context of an RDF.

Selection. The essential medicines list for the RDF (its "product line") must be based on essential medicines selection criteria (see Chapter 16), but provider perspectives and patient preferences must also be considered. For example, if two medicines are therapeutically equivalent and similar in price, the more popular ("sellable") one should normally be purchased. Supplying high-cost, low-volume medicines with limited health effect is probably best left to the private sector, because such medicines can tie up working capital and result in losses caused by expiry.

Procurement. Regardless of the level at which procurement is managed, a reliable source for the purchase of resupplies is essential. Turning to local distributors or private pharmacies to cover delayed shipments from normal sources often raises costs beyond what can be recovered through sales. Even if the RDF is managed by a government entity (as opposed to a parastatal or private organization), the procurement cycle must be freed from the treasury cycle to ensure that pharmaceuticals can be bought when needed and tenders are not automatically canceled between fiscal years. Procurement must ensure maximum bulk discounts (such as one-year competitive contracts) while controlling inventory-holding costs (for example, by arranging three or four deliveries per year of high-volume items).

Quality assurance. Quality assurance procedures must ensure both the reality and the appearance of quality. For example, dispensing containers should protect the medicine, but their appearance may also influence whether patients feel they have paid a fair price for the medicine inside.

Distribution and inventory control. Distribution must be through a "pull" system, based on actual demand. Inventory records must be accurate to ensure the purchase of correct quantities. Underestimates result in lost sales and gaps in health service for clients, and overestimates can lead to costly expirations. Transport arrangements must ensure steady supply.

Management information. Giveaway systems can sometimes afford not to know what happens to medicines after they are distributed, but RDFs need good information on which products are in demand and which ones are not. Information on stockouts is needed from facilities because inventory records at distribution depots may not fully reflect undersupply problems.

Rational use. If health workers benefit directly from pharmaceutical sales, monitoring must ensure that workers are not irrationally catering to patient demands (for more injections, for example) or overprescribing. Prescribers and dispensers must ensure that poorer patients, who cannot afford to buy everything prescribed, know which are the necessary, curative medicines (for example, co-trimoxazole for pneumonia) and which are the optional, symptomatic medicines (such as paracetamol). Dispensing staff must guard against patients buying subtherapeutic quantities of all pharmaceuticals prescribed, rather than therapeutic quantities of only the curative medicines.

Financial management and accountability

Traditional accounting systems for governments and not-for-profit organizations are designed primarily to account for funds spent. RDFs require systems that ensure reliable collection of fees, safekeeping of revenue, and proper expenditure of revenue.

Systems and procedures. Standard procedures must be implemented for fee collection, stock control and valuation, reporting, banking, auditing, and control of expenditures. Potential sources of theft, fraud, and abuse must be monitored to minimize losses.

Examples of accountability problems include clerks who charge patients the full fee but record only half the fee and pocket the difference; dispensing staff who give a patient ten tablets, record having issued twenty tablets, and keep the difference; accounting staff who record and deposit less than the full amount collected; and procurement staff who authorize payment to suppliers for pharmaceuticals never received and share the payment with the supplier.

Chapter 41 describes procedures and systems for financial management and accounting in the context of RDFs. In government-operated RDFs, procedures must be consistent with the law. In Ghana, for example, although the law defines standard markups for pharmaceuticals, actual fees varied dramatically by district and facility—patients paid from 11 to 275 percent over the approved prices (Nyonator and Kutzin 1999). It is therefore important that governments make the fee schedules transparent and that accounting officials review and endorse RDF accounting procedures.

Enforcement. Even the best-designed systems for financial management and accountability require enforcement. At each level, regular supervision should focus on areas of potential abuse. Disciplinary procedures provide a range of possible responses, from warnings through dismissal, depending on the severity and frequency of the offense. RDF managers should be prepared to invoke disciplinary procedures and to bring criminal charges when necessary. Government procedures on misuse of public funds must be visibly and vigorously applied to ensure full collection and proper expenditure of revenue. Well-publicized prosecution of one prominent offender can be a highly effective method for improving overall adherence to procedures.

13.9 Preparing health staff, patients, and the public

Introducing or expanding an RDF requires building support from health staff, patients, and the public through orientation programs, training, and good communication.

Orientation and training for health staff

For RDFs at the national, institutional, or community level, orienting senior officials to the objectives and organization of the program is important. Even if most such officials will have no direct program responsibility, their work may be indirectly affected and, in practice, their support (formal or informal) may be needed.

Training should consider the information needs of pharmacy, pharmaceutical management, accounting, and other staff directly involved in the RDF, as well as the needs of health workers and unskilled staff whose cooperation is necessary. Training should focus on new knowledge, skills, and attitudes needed by each group. In addition, all staff should receive basic orientation that will enable them to correctly inform patients and the community about the RDF.

Communications for the public and patients

Public and patient acceptance are vital for the implementation and further development of RDFs. A communications strategy should systematically address the following issues:

Target audiences: Target groups include national leaders, community leaders, local opinion leaders (who may be different from official community leaders), health workers, patients currently attending facilities, and the general public.

Opinion survey: A "market survey" using questionnaires, in-depth interviews, or focus group discussions can help assess how high-priority target groups might respond to fees, and how much pricing elasticity may exist.

Messages: Building on the positive aspects of user fees, without making promises that cannot be kept, is important. Clarifying exemptions, such as for maternal and child health, is good public relations and good public health policy. If the RDF fees are for pharmaceuticals only, promote this: "The doctor is still free." Community participation and management, if appropriate, can be important concepts to convey.

Media and methods: Choice of media for communication depends on local availability and practices. Print media, radio, television, and local meetings are all appropriate options. In countries such as Nigeria, Kenya, and the Philippines, where newspapers have good coverage, stories of small successes can be distributed regularly as press releases at low cost to the program (through print media, radio, local meetings).

After the preceding issues have been addressed, an effective communication plan can be developed to support the implementation plan for the RDF. Chapter 33 is aimed primarily at public and patient communications for improved medicine use, but it also provides useful information for preparing an RDF communication plan.

13.10   Monitoring and supervision

Regular monitoring and supervision are essential to assess the effect of RDFs on patients and financial performance. Supervisory visits should focus on patients' responses to user fees, implementation of exemption procedures, pharmaceutical availability, and key aspects of the collection and accounting system. A supervision checklist can help ensure that critical functions are reviewed. Routine reporting systems must be adapted to handle financial and pharmaceutical supply information, as well as health care information. Some systems have a community-based management committee that monitors operations. In cases where a lack of human resource capacity makes monitoring and supervision difficult, a larger community role can ease the burden on the system.

Visits should be targeted to facilities whose reports indicate poor performance or for which routine reports are not available. An RDF in the Caribbean uses routine reports to classify community pharmacies as red, yellow, or green and to direct supervision efforts accordingly. In East Africa, a national cost-sharing program uses routine reports similarly, to classify districts for the purpose of targeted supervision.

With new RDFs, major new fees, or other major changes, supervisory visits should be as frequent as possible, and a reporting system should be used to identify and address early problems. Sentinel sites and special studies may be needed to guide the development of the program and to assess its effect. Chapter 48 describes these and other relevant aspects of monitoring, and Chapter 49 discusses information system design. Key issues for RDF monitoring appear in the assessment guide at the end of this chapter.

Decapitalization must be avoided, because it quickly leads to failure and loss of community confidence. Each health center operating an RDF should be visited every month or two to ensure that procedures are being followed and that the RDF will not become decapitalized.

If possible, a formal evaluation should be planned within the first three years of a new program to assess its overall impact, equity, sustainability, efficiency, and long-term prospects. Chapters 36 and 48 describe methods for such an evaluation.

13.11   Common pitfalls and lessons of RDFs

Although the concept of RDFs is simple, the successful establishment and long-term sustainability of such schemes have been fraught with difficulty. Often, the monies

Table 13-2   Effect of introducing user fees in health care

Change in service level	Outpatient medicine fees	Inpatient medicine fees	Who retains funds	Exemption	Effect on quality
Service usage decreased					
Burkina Faso	Yes	Yes	40 percent at hospitals	No	No improvement
Ghana	Yes	No	Distributed between district, ministry of health (MOH), and treasury	Yes	Medicine shortages persisted
Kenya	Yes	No	75 percent facility/25 percent district	Yes	Improved rating in provincial hospitals
Lesotho	Yes	Yes	MOH	Yes	Equivocal
Mozambique	Yes	Yes	Unknown	Yes	Equivocal
Zimbabwe	Yes	Yes	100 percent at national hospital/ other facilities to treasury	Yes	No evidence
Service usage increased					
Benin	Yes	Yes	75 percent facility	Yes	Improved medicine availability in public health centers
Burundi	Yes	Yes	100 percent community	Yes	Improved medicine availability in public health centers
Cameroon	Yes	Yes	100 percent health centers/ 50 percent hospitals	No	Improved medicine availability in public health centers
Guinea	Yes	Variable	100 percent facility	No	Improved public perception
Mauritania	Yes	Yes	Unknown	Yes	Improved medicine availability in public health centers
Senegal	Yes	Yes	Unknown	Yes	No evidence
Sierra Leone	Yes	Yes	Majority to RDF/remainder at facility	No	Improved medicine availability in public health centers
Togo	Yes	Yes	100 percent facility	No	Improved medicine availability in public health centers
Service usage response mixed					
Gambia	Yes	Yes	MOH or RDF	Yes	Improved medicine availability
Guinea Bissau	Yes	Yes	National facilities to MOH/Bamako Initiative related to community, facility, region	No	Improved medicine availability in some facilities
Mali	Yes	Yes	Unknown	Yes	Improved medicine availability
Nigeria	Variable	Variable	Variable from facility to state level	No	Improved medicine availability
Uganda*	Variable	No	100 percent community	No	Variable improvement
Zaire (D.R. Congo)	Yes	Unknown	100 percent community	Yes	Variable improvement

* The government of Uganda eliminated user fees in 2001.
Source: Singh 2003.

collected are insufficient to replenish the original stocks, and the fund soon becomes depleted. An important factor in RDF failure is a resistance to thinking of the fund in business terms. A lack of careful economic and financial analysis in planning the fund, or weaknesses in financial management or in management of the supply system, can lead to failure.

Table 13-2 illustrates the experiences in twenty African countries that instituted user fees, including RDFs. Results shown include the effect on health care service usage.

Common pitfalls

Specific causes for RDF decapitalization include the following (see Figure 13-4)—

- Unanticipated increases in procurement cost caused by inflation or changes in exchange rates
- Underestimation of the capitalization costs of the supply system

Figure 13-4   Cycle of terrors: Causes of RDF decapitalization

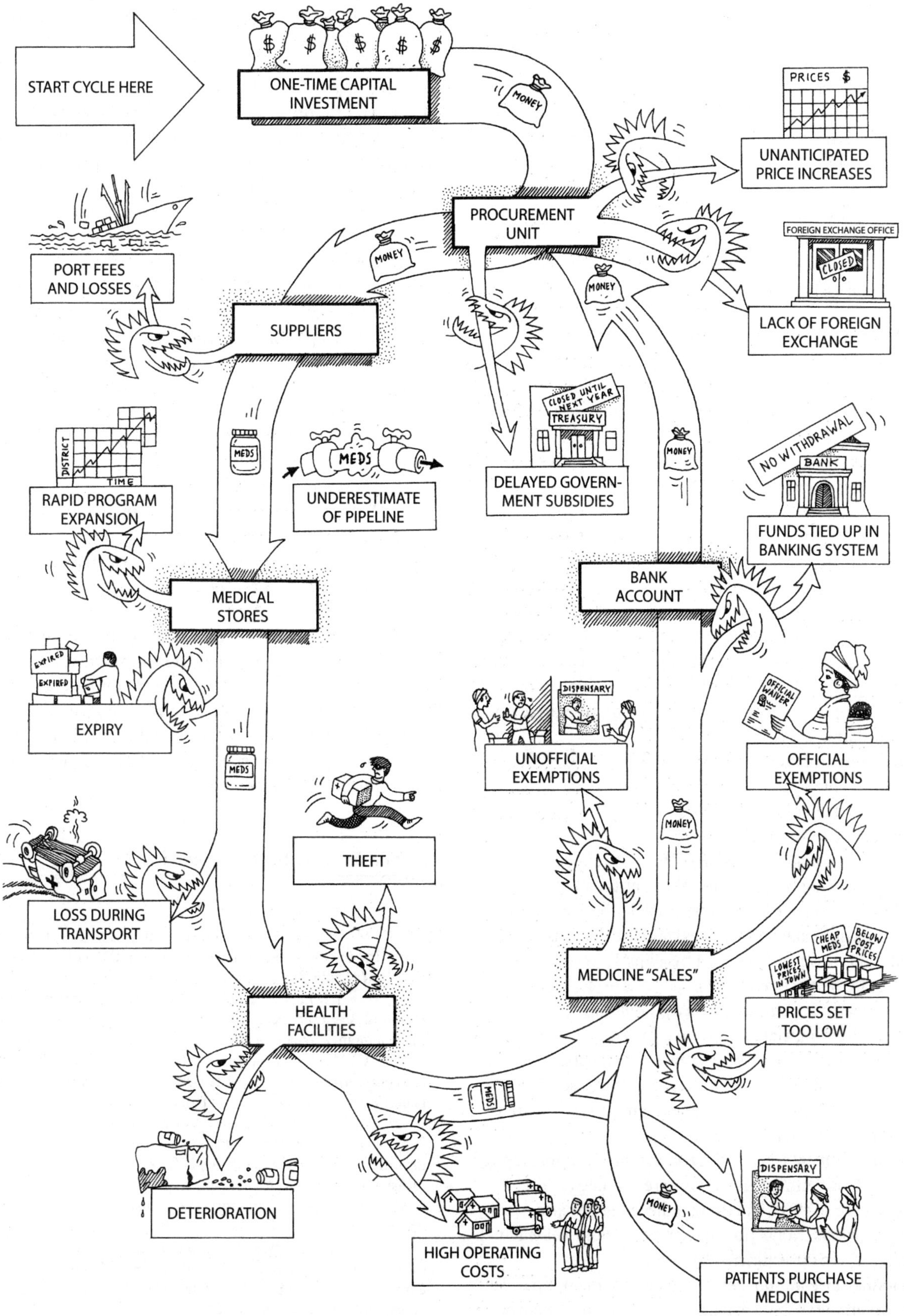

- Rapid program expansion for which additional capital funds are not made available
- Unanticipated losses of pharmaceuticals through theft, deterioration, or expiry
- High operating costs that exceed budget amounts
- Prices set too low for intended level of cost recovery
- Too many exemptions that are not subsidized
- Funds tied up in the national banking system or ministry accounting systems
- Delays in collecting subsidies and other payments from government agencies
- Foreign exchange limitations that restrict international purchases for resupply

Guidelines from RDF experiences

No guaranteed strategies exist for designing and implementing an RDF. However, experience with RDFs suggests some guidelines that may increase the chance that an RDF will improve pharmaceutical availability, ensure equity of access, and promote greater efficiency.

Local control and retention of revenue: Keeping the money locally creates an incentive for revenue collection and promotes the use of revenue to improve quality. When fees are remitted to a general government account, there is little incentive to collect fees and virtually no visible improvement occurs in the supply of pharmaceuticals or the quality of care. Community supervision of an RDF is important to ensure its proper management and accountability.

Reliable supply of low-cost essential medicines: RDFs require a dependable source of medicines. Some governments have established independent pharmaceutical services specifically to supply RDFs.

Locally appropriate fee schedules: The types and levels of charges cannot be determined simply as a matter of policy. Pricing decisions must consider both the cost of pharmaceuticals (and services) and the demonstrated willingness to pay. Fees must be adjusted regularly to reflect increases in real costs.

Protection mechanisms to ensure equitable access: Exemptions, partial exemptions, and other protection mechanisms are necessary to ensure that patients are not denied essential services. Lower fees or free services at the lowest levels of health care encourage patients to use local facilities first.

Continued or increasing levels of government funding for health: Government allocations are still needed for preventive services and to subsidize the poor and other target groups. Collection of user fees should not lead to a reduction of government allocations.

Businesslike orientation: Personnel management, financial management, supply management, and "customer rela-

tions" systems provide built-in checks and balances. Qualified staff must be explicitly assigned to RDF activities. District and facility managers must set collection targets, monitor performance against targets, and take corrective action. Active community involvement is important for the acceptability, credibility, and accountability of RDFs. Public communications should explain the program and ensure that charges and protection mechanisms are understood.

Strict measures to ensure accountability: In addition to systems for the control of pharmaceuticals and revenues, dependable monitoring (often with local community involvement) is important: spot checks, periodic independent audits, and vigorous use of legal and disciplinary mechanisms when abuses are uncovered. Systems that fail to respond effectively to theft of pharmaceuticals are unlikely to fare any better when cash starts disappearing. Government procedures on the misuse of public funds must be visibly and vigorously applied to ensure full collection and proper expenditure of revenue.

Planned implementation: Phased implementation or a well-conceived pilot approach can help build public acceptance and develop management capacity before the system expands to cover the entire country.

Implementation of RDFs depends on a host of issues and, ultimately, on good management. Government and, in many cases, donor commitment are necessary for several years to ensure that sustainable organizational arrangements, financial management, and pharmaceutical supply management systems are in place. The success of an RDF lies in the details of planning and implementation. ∎

References and further readings

★ = Key readings.

Ali, G. K. M. 2009. How to Establish a Successful Revolving Drug Fund: The Experience of Khartoum Atate in the Sudan. *Bulletin of the World Health Organization* 87:139–42.

Blakney, R. B., J. I. Litvack, and J. D. Quick. 1989. *Financing Primary Health Care: Experiences in Pharmaceutical Cost Recovery.* Boston: Management Sciences for Health/PRITECH.

Enemark, U., A. Alban, and E. C. S. Vazquez. 2004. *Purchasing Pharmaceuticals.* Health, Nutrition and Population Discussion Paper. Washington, D.C.: World Bank.

Foster, S., R. Laing, B. Melgaard, and M. Zaffran. 2006. Ensuring Supplies of Appropriate Drugs and Vaccines. In *Disease Control Priorities in Developing Countries,* D. T. Jamison, J. G. Breman, A. R. Measham, G. Alleyne, M. Claeson, D. B. Evans, P. Jha, A. Mills, and P. Musgrove, eds. Washington, D.C.: Disease Control Priorities Project.

Gilson, L., and D. McIntyre. 2005. Removing User Fees for Primary Care in Africa: The Need for Careful Action. *BMJ* 331:762–5.

★ Gottret, P., and G. Schieber. 2006. *Health Financing Revisited.* Washington, D.C.: World Bank.

ASSESSMENT GUIDE

Policy, organization, and implementation

- Are key functions related to pricing, exemptions, supervision, and other aspects of pharmaceutical management and financial management clearly assigned and effectively performed?
- Are central, district, facility, and community roles clearly and appropriately identified and communicated to all concerned?
- Are policy or legal clarifications needed with regard to exemptions, local retention of revenue, or banking and accounting procedures?
- Are policy makers oriented, have health staff been trained, and has the public been adequately informed about the RDF?

Pharmaceutical management and financial management systems

- Does the RDF have a reliable source of pharmaceuticals through the CMS, an autonomous supply agency, or some other pharmaceutical supply mechanism?
- What types of medicine fees are used: course-of-therapy fee, prescription fee, item fee, multilevel item fee, variable item fee? Should the type of fee be revised to create incentives for more rational use of medicines or to improve accountability?
- Are fee levels set on the basis of medicine costs, assessment of ability to pay, or a combination of the two factors?
- Is there a system for regular supervision at each level and a supervision checklist?
- Are revenues, expenditures, stock levels, and other measures reported and reviewed on at least a quarterly basis?
- Are financial management systems backed up by administrative and legal actions to ensure accountability?

Effect on patients and households

- Is the number of patients decreasing, or are people being dissuaded from seeking necessary care?
- What is the effect of medicine fees on the poorest households? Is access increasing or decreasing? Are expenditures on other household essentials such as food being affected?
- What are the expected and actual percentages of patients exempted from payment? Do specific exemption criteria exist, and are they implemented as intended to ensure equity of access?
- Is the availability of essential medicines, and therefore the quality of care, increasing?
- Are medicines being rationally prescribed and bought? Are health staff overprescribing or underprescribing? Are patients overpurchasing or underpurchasing?

Financial performance

- What costs were intended to be covered by medicine fees: a portion of medicine costs, full medicine costs, or medicine costs plus a surplus to cover other recurrent costs?
- What percentage of the cost-recovery objective is being achieved?
- What percentage of MOH pharmaceutical expenditures is funded by user fees? What level of continued government funding has been planned, and what level is actually being provided?
- How is the cost of exemptions, different prices, and other protection mechanisms being funded? Can protection mechanisms be sustained to ensure access to the poor and other target groups?
- Is the current level of capitalization sufficient to ensure a steady supply of pharmaceuticals?

Note: This assessment guide assumes that an RDF exists. Section 13.3 discusses feasibility assessment when an RDF does not exist.

Griffin, C. C. 1988. *User Charges for Health Care in Principle and in Practice.* Economic Development Institute Seminar Paper 37. Washington, D.C.: World Bank.

Hamed, M. M., and M. I. B. M. Ibrihim. 2009. Do Systems Contribute to the Sustainability of the Revolving Drug Fund (RDF) in Sudan? *Sudanese Journal of Public Health* 4(2):288–95. <http://www.sjph.net.sd/files/vol4i2/SJPH-vol4i2-p288-295.pdf>

Holley, J., O. Akhundov, and E. Nolte. 2004. *Health Care Systems in Transition.* Copenhagen: World Health Organization Regional Office for Europe on behalf of European Observatory on Health Systems and Policies. <http://www.euro.who.int/document/E84991.pdf>

Jacobs, B., and N. Price. 2006. Improving Access for the Poorest to Public Sector Health Services: Insights from Kirivong Operational Health District in Cambodia. *Health Policy and Planning* 21(1):27–39.

★ James, C. D., K. Hanson, B. McPake, D. Balabanova, D. Gwatkin, I. Hopwood, C. Kirunga, et al. 2006. To Retain or Remove User Fees? Reflections on the Current Debate in Low- and Middle-Income Countries. *Applied Health Economics and Health Policy* 5(3):137–53.

Kipp, W., J. Kamugisha, P. Jacobs, G. Burnham, and T. Rubaale. 2001. User Fees, Health Staff Incentives, and Service Utilization in Kabarole District, Uganda. *Bulletin of the World Health Organization* 79:1032–7.

Knippenberg, R., F. Traore Nafo, R. Osseni, Y. Boye Camara, A. El Abassi, and A. Soucat. 2003. *Increasing Clients' Power to Scale Up Health Services for the Poor: The Bamako Initiative in West Africa.* Background paper to the *World Development Report.* Washington, D.C.: World Bank.

Lagarde, M., and N. Palmer. 2008. The Impact of User Fees on Health Service Utilization in Low- and Middle-Income Countries: How Strong Is the Evidence? *Bulletin of the World Health Organization* 86:839–48.

Liu, X., and S. O'Dougherty. 2005. Paying for Public Health Services: Financing and Utilization. In *Spending Wisely: Buying Health Services for the Poor,* A. S. Preker and J. C. Langenbrunner, eds. Washington, D.C.: World Bank.

★ Meessen, B., W. Van Damme, C. Tashobya, and A. Tibouti. 2006. Poverty and User Fees for Public Health Care in Low-Income Countries: Lessons from Uganda and Cambodia. *The Lancet* 368:2253–7.

MOH Ghana (Ministry of Health, Republic of Ghana). 2002. *An Assessment of the Pharmaceutical Sector in Ghana.* Accra: MOH. <http://whqlibdoc.who.int/hq/2002/a87429_eng.pdf>

Murakami, H., B. Phommasack, R. Oula, and S. Sinxomphou. 2001. Revolving Drug Funds at Front-Line Health Facilities in Vientiane, Lao PDR. *Health Policy and Planning* 16(1):98–106.

Newbrander, W., D. Collins, and L. Gilson. 2001. *User Fees for Health Services: Guidelines for Protecting the Poor.* Boston: Management Sciences for Health.

———. 2000. *Ensuring Equal Access to Health Services: User Fee Systems and the Poor.* Boston: Management Sciences for Health.

Nyonator, F., and J. Kutzin. 1999. Health for Some? The Effects of User Fees in the Volta Region of Ghana. *Health Policy and Planning* 14(4):329–41.

Preker, A., and G. Carrin, eds. 2004. *Health Financing for Poor People: Resource Mobilization and Risk Sharing.* Washington, D.C., and Geneva: World Bank and World Health Organization and International Labour Office.

Save the Children. 2002. *Selling out Rights: How Policy Affects Access to Health Services in East and Central Africa.* London: Save the Children UK.

Shaw, R. P. 1995. User Fees in Sub-Saharan Africa: Aims, Findings, Policy Implications. In *Financing Health Services through User Fees and Insurance: Case Studies from Sub-Saharan Africa,* R. P. Shaw and M. Ainsworth, eds. Discussion Paper 294. Washington, D.C.: World Bank.

Singh, A. 2003. *Building on the User-fee Experience: The African Case.* Geneva: World Health Organization.

Uzochukwu, B., and O. Onwujekwe. 2005. Healthcare Reform Involving the Introduction of User Fees and Drug Revolving Funds: Influence on Health Workers' Behavior in Southeast Nigeria. *Health Policy* 75(1):1–8.

Uzochukwu, B., O. E. Onwujekwe, and C. O. Akpala. 2002. Effect of the Bamako-Initiative Drug Revolving Fund on Availability and Rational Use of Essential Drugs in Primary Health Care Facilities in South-East Nigeria. *Health Policy and Planning* 17(4):378–83.

Xu, K., D. B. Evans, P. Kadama, J. Nabyonga, P. O. Ogwal, P. Nabukhonzo, and A. M. Aguilar. 2006. Understanding the Impact of Eliminating User Fees: Utilization and Catastrophic Health Expenditures in Uganda. *Social Science & Medicine* 62(4):866–76.

CHAPTER 14

Global and donor financing

SUMMARY

The international community's commitment to global health and access to pharmaceuticals has been increasing; in addition to traditional sources of funding from bilateral and multilateral institutions, such as development banks and United Nations (UN) agencies, private foundations and public-private partnerships are playing much larger roles as resources to improve health in developing countries. The types of assistance available include—

- Financial assistance (loans or grants)
- Commodities
- Technical expertise
- Training, study tours, and fellowships
- Research funding

Some donor funding is being directed toward the entire health sector as part of a sector-wide approach (SWAp) to aid or toward the national government budget instead of to specific programs or interventions, which means that health program managers must take additional steps to get access to funding for specific health programs. Ministries of health need to collaborate with other government ministries, which are likely to carry out negotiations with donor agencies. Ministries of health must be able to justify the demand for additional funding for pharmaceutical management activities.

Challenges associated with donor assistance include a country's inability to use donor funds effectively because of limited infrastructure, the unpredictability of donor assistance from year to year, and the complex monitoring and evaluating requirements that vary by donor. In recognition of some of these challenges, donors and recipient countries have been working together to improve collaboration and harmonize funding requirements. Performance-based funding is another trend being used to improve the effectiveness of development aid.

With heavy demand for assistance funds, proposals must satisfy donors' concerns about consistency with government policies, government commitment, health care reform, project impact, and sustainability. Many donors follow a two-stage proposal process, requiring the submission and approval of a project profile or letter of intent, followed by a more detailed project proposal. Project documents often include—

- Project goals (development objectives)
- Project purpose (immediate objectives)
- Outputs
- Activities
- Inputs and resources

Private foundations tend to follow more flexible procedures for reviewing grant proposals and overseeing grant-funded projects, but most donors require periodic progress reports and evaluation.

14.1 The role of donors in development

The resource requirements for meeting the health needs of populations in developing countries are increasing significantly because of the introduction of new technologies, the dual burden of addressing communicable and chronic disease patterns, and the growth and aging of populations; as populations age, demand for higher-cost medical treatment increases. As a result, the need for additional resources in the health sector is growing faster than government health expenditures. In addition, the health spending patterns and health needs of rich and poor countries vary greatly: developing countries account for 84 percent of the world's population and 90 percent of the global disease burden, but they represent only 12 percent of global health spending. High-income countries spend 100 times more than low-income countries spend on health (Gottret and Schieber 2006).

As a result of globalization, the international community's commitment to the Millennium Development Goals (MDGs), and emerging health threats such as severe acute respiratory syndrome and avian influenza, global health is becoming a more important part of the international policy arena. Along with this increased focus on global health, new foundations and public-private partnerships have emerged that are committed to contributing to solutions to the world's health problems. These partnerships are funded by donor governments and private foundations such as the Bill & Melinda Gates Foundation and the United Nations Foundation.

Governments have a few options for expanding available resources for health. One option is to reprioritize health care activities toward lower-cost and more cost-effective programs and services within the ministry of health budget. A second option is to increase the allocation of total government expenditures to the health sector. A third option is for countries to identify new and innovative sources of financing, such as taxes earmarked for health. A final approach is to expand the number of resources through additional external funding. For low-income countries, external sources of financing account for almost one-fifth of total health expenditures (WHO 2010, Table 7: Health expenditure). Expanding resources for the health sector is sometimes referred to as expanding the resource envelope, or expanding fiscal space.

International development assistance, also called external cooperation, can provide the necessary funds and technical expertise to complement national efforts. Development assistance can serve as a catalyst for major health system reforms that would otherwise be difficult to accomplish. Policy makers and managers can strengthen their health initiatives and programs by understanding where to obtain such assistance, the criteria that must be met, and the ongoing commitments that must be fulfilled to establish and maintain fruitful relationships with donor and funding agencies.

Traditionally, donor funding has come directly to specific programs or interventions in the form of grants, commodities, or technical assistance. Although global funding initiatives that focus on a specific disease, such as HIV/AIDS, have changed the landscape of health-related development funding, the trend is for external funding to be directed more toward the entire health sector or toward the national government budget. This trend results in additional steps that policy makers and program managers must take to access funding and technical assistance for specific health programs and interventions. The process is illustrated in Figure 14-1. The ministry of health needs to work in cooperation with ministries of planning, external relations, and finance, which are likely to carry out negotiations with donor agencies. Ministries of health must be able to justify the need for additional funding and for expanding their resource envelope.

Health programs and projects supported by external assistance will continue to include activities related to pharmaceuticals that range from the straightforward (procurement of medicines for a specific program, such as malaria control) to the complex (reorganization of the public-sector supply system). The funding for these activities is expected to grow in parallel with the growth in overall funding for health projects.

14.2 Development assistance challenges

Development assistance comes with challenges. Project support is typically outside the regular health budget, making it difficult for the government and its partners to monitor and evaluate. As a result, ministries of health often do not know the extent and intended priorities of donor funding. In addition, ministries of finance strive to roll development assistance into national budgets, to improve transparency and accountability and to strengthen national planning efforts. In countries where the health budget is constrained,

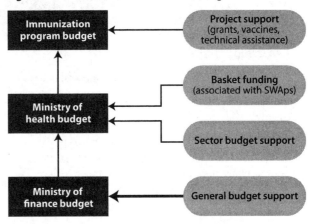

Figure 14-1 Modalities of donor financing

SWAps = sector-wide approaches.

the addition of donor funding forces ministries of health to make better decisions about funding priorities, because usually some donor assistance replaces rather than adds to budget resources.

In addition, countries may have limited absorptive capacity. In other words, they cannot use donor funding effectively because of a lack of human resources or infrastructure, or the level of donor funding may be too high relative to how quickly a country can spend it, either because of bureaucratic procedures in procurement or disbursement, or because of *fungibility,* which refers to the country's limited capacity to use the funds for their intended purposes.

Countries also face multiple reporting, procurement, and monitoring requirements for each donor. The High Level Forum on Aid Effectiveness was created to improve government and donor coordination, alignment, and harmonization for scaling up the MDGs. In a series of three meetings, senior government policy makers in developing countries and donor agencies developed a set of principles to improve harmonization of requirements that donors and global partnerships are committed to implementing (see Box 14-1). The "Three Ones" principles aim to build a coordination framework for HIV/AIDS funding among governments, donors, international organizations, and civil society (UNAIDS 2005). In addition, the International Health Partnership Plus (IHP+) was established to improve coordination of development assistance in health in 2007. IHP+ seeks to strengthen national health systems and to achieve better health results by mobilizing donor countries and other development partners around a single-country-led national health strategy. Eight of the largest institutions in health—including the World Health Organization (WHO); the Global Alliance for Vaccines and Immunization (GAVI); the Global Fund to Fight AIDS, Tuberculosis and Malaria (Global Fund); and the Gates Foundation—agreed to collaborate within the context of the IHP+ processes.

Box 14-1
Best practice principles for engagement of global health partnerships at the country level

Ownership

1. To respect partner country leadership and help strengthen their capacity to exercise it.

Alignment

2. To base their support on partner countries' national development and health-sector strategies and plans, institutions, and procedures. Where these strategies do not adequately reflect pressing health priorities, to work with all partners to ensure their inclusion.

3. To progressively shift from project to program financing.

4. To use country systems to the maximum extent possible. Where use of country systems is not feasible, to establish safeguards and measures in ways that strengthen rather than undermine country systems and procedures.

5. To avoid, to the maximum extent possible, creating dedicated structures for day-to-day management and implementation of global health partnership (GHP) projects and programs.

6. To align analytic, technical, and financial support with partners' capacity development objectives and strategies; make effective use of existing capacities; and harmonize support for capacity development accordingly.

7. To provide reliable indicative commitments of funding support over a multiyear framework and disburse funding in a timely and predictable fashion according to agreed schedules.

8. To rely, to the maximum extent possible, on transparent partner government budget and accounting mechanisms.

9. To progressively rely on country systems for procurement when the country has implemented mutually agreed standards and processes; to adopt harmonized approaches when national systems do not meet agreed levels of performance; to ensure that donations of pharmaceutical products are fully in line with *WHO Guidelines for Drug Donations.*

Harmonization

10. To implement, where feasible, simplified and common arrangements at the country level for planning, funding, disbursement, monitoring, evaluating, and reporting to government on GHP activities and resource flows.

11. To work together with other GHPs and donor agencies in the health sector to reduce the number of separate, duplicative missions to the field and diagnostic reviews assessing country systems and procedures. To encourage shared analytical work, technical support, and lessons learned and to promote joint training.

12. To adopt harmonized performance assessment frameworks for country systems.

13. To collaborate at the global level with other GHPs, donors, and country representatives to develop and implement collective approaches to cross-cutting challenges, particularly in relation to strengthening health systems, including human resource management.

Managing for results

14. To link country programming and resources to results and align them with effective country performance-assessment frameworks, refraining from requesting the introduction of performance indicators that are not consistent with partners' national development strategies.

15. To work with countries to rely, as far as possible, on countries' results-oriented reporting and monitoring frameworks.

16. To work with countries in a participatory way to strengthen country capacities and demand for results-based management, including joint problem solving and innovation, based on monitoring and evaluation.

Accountability

17. To ensure timely, clear, and comprehensive information on GHP assistance, processes, and decisions (especially decisions on unsuccessful applications) to partner countries requiring GHP support.

Source: Adapted from High Level Forum on the Health MDGs 2005.

A final challenge related to donor assistance for health is the predictability, volatility, and fragmentation of the funding, because donor funding for the health sector fluctuates widely from year to year. In 2006–07, more than two-thirds of health aid commitments were for less than 500,000 U.S. dollars (USD), and significant portions were earmarked (Norad-AHHA 2009). Under these conditions, governments find both planning their own funding for the sector and influencing how donor funds are spent difficult.

14.3 Sources of international assistance for health

Government donations and concession loans that include at least a 25 percent nonreimbursable component (in effect, a 25 percent donation) are referred to as *official development assistance,* and they are the major source of external funding for the health sector in the developing world. Total development assistance for health increased from USD 5.6 billion in 1990 to USD 21.8 billion in 2007 (Ravishankar et al. 2009). About 40 percent of assistance was allocated to Africa and almost 30 percent to Asia in 2006–07 (OECD DAC 2009). Much of this increase came from new global partnerships and foundations, and the funds targeted specific diseases, such as AIDS, tuberculosis, malaria, and vaccine-preventable diseases; for example, funds mobilized by UN agencies and development banks decreased, whereas funds provided by the Global Fund, the GAVI Alliance, and the Gates Foundation all increased substantially (Ravishankar et al. 2009). The fastest-growing segment of health assistance has benefited HIV/AIDS programs, which grew from 25 percent to 39 percent of global development assistance between 2000 and 2006 (OECD DAC 2009). HIV prevalence is the biggest predictor of health aid to low-income countries, and countries with low HIV prevalence but high mortality are disadvantaged by the inequity; for example, Zambia receives USD 20 per person for health, whereas Chad receives USD 1.59 (Norad-AHHA 2009).

The Gates Foundation is the largest single source of private health funding, but much of its funding is disbursed to other channels, including the GAVI Alliance, the Global Fund, and UN agencies. In addition, government donations to health increased from 2002 to 2007, with the United States representing the biggest share. Governments use different mechanisms to channel their funds; some use multilaterals (for example, Finland, France, and the Netherlands), while others such as the United Kingdom and the United States use bilaterals or nongovernmental organizations (NGOs) (Ravishankar et al. 2009).

The major sources of international assistance to support health and pharmaceutical activities and projects include multilateral institutions, bilateral agencies, NGOs, foundations, and public-private partnerships (see Figure 14-2).

Figure 14-2   Major channels for funding development assistance for health, 2007

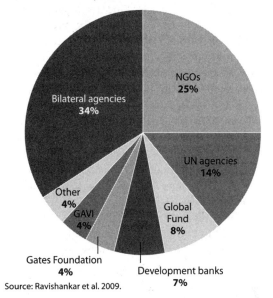

Source: Ravishankar et al. 2009.

Multilateral institutions

Multilateral institutions pool resources from many donors and provide technical and commodity assistance globally or regionally through cash grants, commodity transfers, technical assistance, or loans. They are focused around sector areas of work, such as health or economic development. Multilateral institutions include the World Bank, the regional development banks, and the UN agencies, including the United Nations Children's Fund (UNICEF), the United Nations Development Programme (UNDP), the United Nations Population Fund, and WHO.

Bilateral agencies

Bilateral agencies are linked to national governments and involve government-to-government exchanges of goods and funding on a grant basis. Examples of bilateral agencies include the Norwegian Agency for Development Cooperation, the Swedish International Development Cooperation Agency, the U.K. Department for International Development, and the U.S. Agency for International Development (USAID). Bilateral agencies may work in countries through contracted organizations to provide technical assistance to projects.

Nongovernmental organizations

NGOs can operate not for profit or for profit and may be affiliated with religious institutions or other groups or agencies. Although development funds have traditionally been provided to recipient governments, an alternative mechanism is to target funds directly to NGOs, particularly those based in the community. The role of NGOs as conduits for health aid has increased substantially—increasing from 13 percent in 1990 to 25 percent in 2006 (Ravishankar et al. 2009).

The objectives of NGOs tend to be targeted to specific diseases and population groups. The procedures these organizations follow tend to be less stringent than those of bilateral and multilateral agencies; in addition, in the approval process, NGOs favor an affinity of mission or ideology between donor and recipient organizations and the existence of a positive, ongoing relationship. This funding mechanism, which has gained acceptance as a way to ensure that resources reach target populations at the local level, tends to be favored by NGOs and foundations in developed countries. Bilateral and multilateral agencies are generally more reluctant to become directly involved in small projects because of the high costs of reviewing, supervising, and evaluating such initiatives.

Private foundations

Foundations now account for a significant share of total health assistance to developing countries, usually through cash grants. For instance, in 2004, total health assistance from the Bill & Melinda Gates Foundation was nearly equal to total health lending by the World Bank, and the Gates Foundation's endowment is expected to increase from USD 29 billion to USD 60 billion, making it the world's largest charitable organization. Private foundations sometimes follow more flexible procedures for reviewing grant proposals and overseeing grant-funded projects.

Public-private partnerships

In addition to these major sources of donor assistance, global public-private partnerships that tend to focus on specific diseases or health conditions have proliferated. Examples include the GAVI Alliance; the Global Fund; the Medicines for Malaria Venture; the Partnership for Maternal, Newborn & Child Health; Roll Back Malaria (RBM); Stop TB Partnership; and the Millennium Challenge Corporation. Box 14-2 describes some of the major health alliances.

Despite rapid increases in development assistance for health, the resources available are still short of the funding needed to achieve the health MDGs, which is estimated to range from an additional USD 25 billion to 70 billion per year (World Bank 2006b) up to USD 135 billion by 2015

Box 14-2
Selected global public-private partnerships in health

GAVI Alliance
http://www.gavialliance.org

The GAVI Alliance is a public-private partnership focused on increasing children's access to vaccines in poor countries. Partners include the GAVI Fund, governments, UNICEF, WHO, the World Bank, the Bill & Melinda Gates Foundation, the vaccine industry, public health institutions, and NGOs. GAVI provides countries with resources to strengthen routine immunization and health systems services; finances the introduction of new and underused vaccines, such as those for hepatitis B, Hib disease, and yellow fever; and supports safe injection practices through safe injection commodity assistance. Although the GAVI Alliance procures only selected vaccines for countries, its funding helps strengthen immunization systems overall, which increases a country's capacity to deliver all necessary vaccines to children.

Seventy-two of the poorest countries, containing half the world's population, are eligible to apply for support from the GAVI Alliance, and as of 2008, seventy-one had received GAVI support. The GAVI Alliance has made commitments of USD 4 billion to seventy-five countries between 2000 and 2015.

Global Fund to Fight AIDS, Tuberculosis and Malaria
http://www.theglobalfund.org

The Global Fund is a partnership among governments, civil society, the private sector, and affected communities. Its purpose is to attract, manage, and disburse resources to fight AIDS, tuberculosis, and malaria, including the procurement of pharmaceuticals and commodities. The Global Fund does not implement programs directly but rather relies on the knowledge of local experts. As a financing mechanism, the Global Fund works closely with other multilateral and bilateral organizations involved in health and development issues to ensure that newly funded programs are coordinated with existing programs. The Global Fund finances programs only when it is assured that its assistance does not replace or reduce other sources of health funding; it actively seeks to complement other donor funds and to use its own grants to catalyze additional investments by donors and by recipients themselves.

Since 2002, the Global Fund has approved USD 19.3 billion in funding to support more than 572 programs in 144 countries.

The Partnership for Maternal, Newborn & Child Health
http://www.who.int/pmnch

The Partnership for Maternal, Newborn & Child Health was created to support sixty countries' efforts to achieve MDGs related to maternal and child health. The partnership works to promote and harmonize national, regional, and global action to improve maternal, newborn, and child health. The partnership is made up of a broad constituency of more than 300 members representing partner countries, UN and multilateral agencies, NGOs, health professional associations, bilateral donors and foundations, and academic and research institutions. The partnership supports country-led efforts to provide complete coverage of essential interventions for maternal, newborn, and child health by focusing on country support; advocacy; promoting the assessment, scaling up, and implementation of cost-effective interventions; and monitoring and evaluating stakeholders to ensure they meet their financial and policy commitments.

Roll Back Malaria
http://rbm.who.int

The global RBM effort was announced by the heads of WHO, UNICEF, UNDP, and the World Bank in November 1998. The RBM partnership consists of malaria-affected countries, UN agencies, the private sector, industry, countries of the Organisation for Economic Co-operation and Development, development banks, community-based organizations, research entities, and the media. The initiative aims to reduce global malaria mortality by 50 percent by the year 2010. Partners are working together to scale up malaria-control efforts at the country level, coordinating their activities to avoid duplication and fragmentation and to ensure optimal use of resources. The strategy to achieve this goal relies on six core elements: (1) early detection, (2) rapid treatment, (3) multiple means for prevention, (4) well-coordinated action, (5) a dynamic global movement, and (6) focused research.

One initiative of RBM is the Malaria Medicines and Supplies Services (MMSS), which works to support procurement and supply management efforts for nets, insecticides, medicines, and diagnostics that are needed to achieve malaria-related health goals. MMSS collects, consolidates, and disseminates information on the demand and supply of medicines and other commodities and helps advise countries on how to procure medicines efficiently. MMSS does not procure itself, but it establishes links with procurement agencies.

Stop TB Partnership
http://www.stoptb.org

The Stop TB Partnership, established in 2000, involves a coalition of 517 governments, national and international NGOs, and public and private donors committed to controlling and eventually eliminating tuberculosis (TB) as a global public health problem. Partners work in seven specific areas: DOTS expansion; TB/HIV; multi-drug-resistant TB; new TB medicines; new TB vaccines; new TB diagnostics; and advocacy, communications, and social mobilization.

Stop TB Partnership's Global Drug Facility
http://www.stoptb.org/gdf

The Global Drug Facility (GDF) was established in response to difficulties that countries had in finding and funding stable TB medicine supplies to support DOTS expansion. The GDF uses a combination of grants and direct pharmaceutical procurement to eligible countries. The mechanism links demand for medicines to supply, competitively outsources all services to partners, uses product packaging to simplify pharmaceutical management, and links grants to TB program performance. Besides procuring quality TB medicines, the GDF provides technical assistance in TB pharmaceutical management and monitoring of TB medicine use.

UNITAID
http://www.unitaid.eu

The founding countries of Brazil, Chile, France, Norway, and the United Kingdom, with the backing of international organizations such as WHO, UNAIDS, UNICEF, the Global Fund, and NGOs and private foundations, such as the Clinton Foundation, have launched an international drug purchase facility called UNITAID. The facility is funded by an innovative financing mechanism—a levy on airline tickets—to help scale up access to treatment for HIV/AIDS, malaria, and tuberculosis in developing countries. By 2010, UNITAID had twenty-eight supporting countries plus the Gates Foundation. In three years, the levy had contributed USD 1.3 billion to UNITAID's assistance fund.

The goal of UNITAID is to provide multiyear contributions for a long-term and predictable supply of medicines and diagnostics by leveraging price reductions and increasing the availability and supply of medicines. The program initially focused on funding pediatric formulations for TB and HIV/AIDS, scaling up second-line antiretroviral medicines and artemisinin-based combination therapies, and supporting the WHO prequalification program to ensure quality pharmaceuticals.

(UN Millennium Project 2005). Governments have committed to increasing official development assistance to up to 0.7 percent of their respective gross domestic products by 2015 to support scaling up to achieve the MDGs (UN General Assembly 2002). New and innovative financing mechanisms, such as the airline ticket levies used by UNITAID, are being developed to raise the necessary additional resources.

14.4 Types of assistance

The types of assistance offered (and the conditions attached) can vary widely—

- Financial assistance (loans or grants)
- Commodities
- Technical expertise
- Study tours and fellowships
- Research funding

In negotiating development assistance of any type, governments are advised to ensure that the assistance supports their national health priorities rather than diverts attention from them. Information describing the level, duration, and type of assistance available, as well as the timing for presentation of proposals, is generally available at the country level through development banks, embassies, and offices of UN agencies. Table 14-1 lists major donors to international health and their websites.

Financial assistance

Loans issued by the World Bank are one of the largest sources of financial assistance in the health sector. Lending for health and nutrition averaged USD 825 million a year over the first decade of the 2000s (World Bank 2010b). In fiscal year 2010, lending to developing countries totaled over USD 72 billion. The bank itself comprises two development institutions that are owned by 187 member countries—the International Bank for Reconstruction and Development (IBRD) and the International Development Association (IDA). The IDA and IBRD, as well as their regional counterparts, such as the Asian, African, or Inter-American Development Banks, provide low-interest loans, interest-free credit, and grants to developing countries for education, health, infrastructure, and communications. The IBRD

Table 14-1   Major international donors involved in health

Bilateral donors	
Country, acronym or abbreviation	**Agency name, website**
Australia, AusAID	Australian Agency for International Development, http://www.ausaid.gov.au
Austria, ADA	Austrian Development Agency, http://www.ada.gv.at
Belgium, DGD	Belgian Development Cooperation, http://diplomatie.belgium.be/en/policy/development_cooperation/index.jsp
Canada, CIDA	Canadian International Development Agency, http://www.acdi-cida.gc.ca
Denmark, Danida	Danish International Development Agency, http://www.um.dk
European Commission	European Commission, http://ec.europa.eu
France, AFD	Agence Française de Développement (French Development Agency), http://www.afd.fr
Germany, GIZ	German Agency for International Cooperation, http://www.giz.de/en
Ireland	Irish Aid, http://www.irishaid.gov.ie
Italy, DGCS	Italian Development Cooperation, http://www.cooperazioneallosviluppo.esteri.it/pdgcs
Japan, JICA	Japan International Cooperation Agency, http://www.jica.go.jp/english/index.html
Netherlands, DGIS	Dutch Development Cooperation Program, http://www.minbuza.nl/en/key-topics/development-cooperation/development-cooperation.html
New Zealand, NZAid	New Zealand's International Aid and Development Agency, http://www.nzaid.govt.nz/
Norway, Norad	Norwegian Agency for Development Cooperation, http://www.norad.no
Spain, AECID	Spanish Agency for International Development Cooperation, http://www.aecid.es
Sweden, Sida	Swedish International Development Cooperation Agency, http://www.sida.se
Switzerland, SDC	Swiss Agency for Development and Cooperation, http://www.deza.ch
United Kingdom, DfID	Department for International Development, http://www.dfid.gov.uk
United States, USAID	U.S. Agency for International Development, http://www.usaid.gov

Key UN agencies and multilateral donors

Acronym or name	Organization and website
ADB	Asian Development Bank, http://www.adb.org
AfDB	African Development Bank, http://www.afdb.org
—	Clinton Foundation, http://www.clintonfoundation.org
EuropeAid	EuropeAid Co-operation Office, http://ec.europa.eu/comm/europeaid
GAVI	Global Alliance for Vaccines and Immunizations, http://www.gavialliance.org
—	Global Fund to Fight AIDS, Tuberculosis and Malaria, http://www.theglobalfund.org
IADB	Inter-American Development Bank, http://www.iadb.org
MMV	Medicines for Malaria Venture, http://www.mmv.org
PMI	President's Malaria Initiative, http://www.fightingmalaria.gov
UNAIDS	Joint United Nations Programme on HIV/AIDS, http://www.unaids.org
UNDP	United Nations Development Programme, http://www.undp.org
UNFPA	United Nations Population Fund, http://www.unfpa.org
UNICEF	United Nations Children's Fund, http://www.unicef.org
UNIDO	United Nations Industrial Development Organization, http://www.unido.org
UNITAID	http://www.unitaid.eu
WHO	World Health Organization, http://www.who.int
World Bank	http://worldbank.org

Selected foundations that support international health

Foundation	Website
African Development Foundation	http://www.adf.gov
Aga Khan Foundation	http://www.akdn.org/akf
Bill & Melinda Gates Foundation	http://www.gatesfoundation.org
Henry J. Kaiser Foundation	http://www.kff.org
Izumi Foundation	http://www.izumi.org
John D. and Catherine T. MacArthur Foundation	http://www.macfound.org
The Nippon Foundation	http://www.nippon-foundation.or.jp
Open Society Institute (OSI) and the Soros Foundations Network	http://www.soros.org
The Rockefeller Foundation	http://www.rockfound.org
Wellcome Trust	http://www.wellcome.ac.uk
W. K. Kellogg Foundation	http://www.wkkf.org

Resources for international grant seekers

Institution	Website
European Foundation Centre	http://www.efc.be
Foundation Center	http://foundationcenter.org
Grantmakers Without Borders	http://www.internationaldonors.org
The Grantsmanship Center	http://www.tgci.com
World Initiatives for Grantmaker Support	http://www.wingsweb.org

focuses on middle-income countries needing capital investment and advisory services, while the IDA helps the poorest countries of the world increase economic growth. The IDA is mostly funded through contributions from the governments of richer member countries. Box 14-3 describes the initiative that the World Bank has put in place to help relieve the debt of the poorest countries.

World Bank assistance has focused on strengthening health systems, with some targeted programs aiming at population, nutrition, and other priority public health areas. Approximately 200 World Bank projects between 1991 and 2002 have had some type of pharmaceutical component—funding for procurement of pharmaceuticals and vaccines, strengthening of the pharmaceutical sector, or improving regulatory frameworks and institutional capacity. Total lending over this period amounted to nearly USD 3 billion, which represents about USD 250 million per year over the twelve-year period.

Loans are also provided on a government-to-government basis as part of bilateral agreements that, in turn, reflect political commitments. Such loans are much more favorable than those from commercial banks: interest rates are lower, repayment schedules are adjusted to a country's financial capabilities, and loans frequently have a nonreimbursable grant component.

Because these loans become part of the national debt and must be repaid by future government administrations, they should be accepted only after thorough study of the costs and benefits. In general, loans should be used for investment—for the development of infrastructure and national capability—and not to cover recurrent health expenditures or to pay for consumables, such as pharmaceuticals. In addition, a bank's internal procedures may raise the real cost of the loan (for example, by including the total cost of preproject planning expenses, as well as the time and travel of bank representatives and consultants, which can be substantial). Concessionary loans with low interest rates and lengthy repayment periods, however, often end up being the equivalent to a grant when inflation outstrips the interest rate.

Grants, which do not require repayment, are a much sought after source of assistance. However, the Global Fund, for example, requires recipients to reach specific targets throughout the life of the grant. Many countries that have not been able to meet their performance goals have had funding cut off, which can cause programmatic challenges. Other costs are not always obvious. For example, a grant can include a requirement that the recipient demonstrate commitment to the work by the assignment of counterpart resources (staff and infrastructure) to complement those of the grant. Such commitments can siphon scarce resources from other, more important health programs. National priorities can become distorted if disproportionate attention is given to an issue simply because it is the fashionable "cause of the year" and can attract grant money or loans.

Commodities

Funds are often made available for the purchase of commodities such as pharmaceuticals, medical supplies, laboratory reagents, equipment, or computers. The conditions for commodity purchase should be subject to negotiation to ensure not only that price and quality are acceptable but also that the commodities meet country needs and do not lead to an unacceptable level of dependence on a foreign source. Pharmaceutical products should correspond to those on the national list of essential medicines and should be labeled in a language understood in the country.

Only as a last resort should loans be used to buy pharmaceuticals. This essential, recurring expenditure should be within the national financial capacity.

Some assistance agreements limit the provision of critical supplies to periods of economic crisis or emergencies caused by natural disasters. The guidelines for donations included in Chapter 15 are relevant not only for donated commodities but also for those purchased through grants or loans.

Technical expertise

Donors can provide funds to obtain the managerial or technical expertise required for project execution, both short term (for example, two weeks to set up a laboratory instrument and to train staff in its use) or long term (for example, management of a four-year project). The work must be carried out with in-country counterparts to transfer technical competence to the recipient country and not perpetuate a relationship of dependence.

Training, study tours, and fellowships

Study tours, fellowships, and other forms of training are important investments in a country's professional capacity and are attractive to the individuals who benefit directly. Such opportunities can provide a powerful incentive to improve job performance, particularly for officials and employees receiving low government salaries. Arrangements should be in place, however, to ensure that individuals who have benefited from this assistance return to share their knowledge and skills with fellow workers and that they remain in their jobs for a sufficient length of time to justify the investment.

Research funds

Funds are increasingly available for operational research and evaluation. This is in recognition of the fact that a project's chances of success are enhanced by a clear under-

> **Box 14-3**
> **The Debt Relief Initiative for Heavily Indebted Poor Countries**
>
> Economic crises in the 1980s resulted in many low-income countries becoming overwhelmed with huge debts that they were unlikely to ever be able to pay back. In 1996, the International Development Association and the International Monetary Fund launched the Debt Relief Initiative for Heavily Indebted Poor Countries (HIPC) as a way to help the poorest countries get out from under the debt burden that was stifling poverty-reduction efforts. The HIPC Initiative calls for all creditors—multilateral, bilateral, and commercial—to voluntarily forgive a specified percentage of debt to countries that meet certain qualifications. A country is potentially eligible for HIPC status if it meets criteria related to per capita income and level of indebtedness. In 2006, 40 countries were potentially eligible (World Bank 2006b). A series of steps begins the process whereby countries put policies in place to reduce poverty and create a plan to clear any arrears from foreign creditors. The last step leads to the *completion point*, where the country has shown satisfactory performance in its strategies and in other indicators such as improvements in health, education, and governance. At the completion point, the debt relief from participating creditors becomes irrevocable. As of 2010, 30 of 40 countries had reached the completion point (IMF 2010).
>
> To supplement the HIPC Initiative, additional relief is available in the form of the Multilateral Debt Relief Initiative (MDRI), which was implemented in 2006. Under the MDRI, countries that have successfully reached the completion point of the HIPC Initiative are then eligible to have forgiven 100 percent of their debt owed to the IDA, the African Development Fund, and the International Monetary Fund. Although eligible countries do not have to meet any new conditions to benefit from the MDRI, they may have to show that their performance has not deteriorated since they reached the completion point of the HIPC Initiative. The three institutions together will forgive more than USD 50 billion over 40 years. To compensate for the resources lost through the debt forgiveness program, donors have agreed to contribute additional funds to ensure IDA's financial capacity.
>
> To avoid the need for future debt relief initiatives, the World Bank has instituted a debt sustainability framework for low-income countries that puts loan responsibilities on both the borrowers and the lenders. Countries seeking loans must take measures to strengthen their ability to manage debt, and lenders must consider long-term debt projections and economic analyses as part of the loan process.
>
> Sources: World Bank 2006a, 2006b; IMF 2010.

standing of the environment in which the project is to take place, by ongoing monitoring during project implementation, and by an impact evaluation after completion. Well-designed research proposals may be a prerequisite for funding approval.

14.5 Improving aid effectiveness by working with the donor community

Since the 1990s, health projects and vertical health programs funded by donors at the country level have proliferated. Donor assistance can be critical to a country's ability to deliver high-priority health services. Therefore, the efficient use of this assistance is vital. Too often, donor-supported projects are developed and negotiated independently, and their funding remains largely outside the official government budget. Donors often work in selected areas within countries, resulting in overlap in some program areas and expanding gaps in others. These factors have led to an increasing lack of accountability of governments to their

constituencies and reduced managerial control over support to the health sector by countries. In addition, the lack of fiduciary management has resulted in a misallocation of scarce government resources.

Sector-wide approaches to aid

One important advance has been the creation of sector-wide approaches for the health sector. Although no standard definition of a SWAp exists, it is generally characterized by a strong and well-articulated health-sector plan that is then supported financially and technically by the government and its development partners through one "market basket." External aid is moved on budget and roles and responsibilities are clearer, allowing the ministry of health to direct and manage the health sector as a whole.

Ministries of health are in a powerful position to influence donor cooperation. Although they may be motivated by a desire to reduce duplication of effort, they may also find an important opportunity to build support and momentum for health program priorities such as essential medicines

Country Study 14-1
Attempting to meet financial goals through a health-sector SWAp in Mozambique

The government of Mozambique, in consultation with its donor partners, established a SWAp for health programming in 2000. Following a lengthy civil war, what was left of the health system was highly fragmented and oriented toward urban areas. As the country began to rebuild, development partners often took responsibility for providing health services in some areas, which exacerbated the fragmentation. When the SWAp was established, the goal was to coordinate external assistance and develop a transparent and collaborative relationship between the Ministry of Health and donor partners to share a set of common principles, objectives, and working arrangements that included the following—

- Health-sector strategic plan endorsed by partners, which prioritizes funding and interventions
- Code of conduct describing the basic arrangement with partners
- Set of working arrangements for communication and consensus building
- Sector financing framework
- Mechanisms to evaluate health-sector progress

The SWAp's financial goals were to increase government health expenditure and to raise the proportion of external funding going to common funding and budget support rather than through vertical programs. Mozambique achieved those goals. Between 2001 and 2005, the government more than doubled its total health expenditures; however, funds to vertical programs also increased (primarily because of global HIV/AIDS programs).

The gains in common funding enabled the Ministry of Health to fund government priorities that were described in operational plans and budgets. Progress in the areas of financial management and planning resulted in Mozambique being the first country to integrate resources from the Global Fund to Fight AIDS, Tuberculosis and Malaria into the SWAp's common fund. In addition, better financial harmonization has allowed the SWAp to become more efficient in its health procurement. The Ministry of Health was also given the full responsibility to manage the funds for procuring medicines.

By 2009, Mozambique had twenty-eight development partners supporting the health sector, and fifteen partners had signed a memorandum of understanding to support the sector through pooled funding (the fund is called Prosaude). Although the government's financial contributions to the health sector had been increasing under the SWAp, the trend leveled off. Donor fragmentation was still a problem, and donors were still channeling vertical funds according to their defined priorities through a network of implementing NGOs—even those who had signed the memorandum of understanding. This arrangement undermined Ministry of Health ownership by creating a parallel network through NGOs instead of strengthening the Ministry of Health. In addition, assessing the effectiveness of these contributions was difficult, and the predictability and disbursement of the funds did not always follow the government budget cycle.

Sources: Martinez 2006; WHO/AFRO 2009.

programs. Donors such as USAID, however, do not contribute to a SWAp market basket because of the perceived loss of control over how governments use the funds. Country Study 14-1 describes Mozambique's experiences with establishing a SWAp.

Concomitant to development of a SWAp for the health sector, many countries have moved toward improving public expenditure management through the development of a medium-term expenditure framework (MTEF). An MTEF is usually a three-year rolling budget that is built on individual sector budget proposals, such as health, relative to an overall budget ceiling. The MTEF seeks to harmonize the recurrent and development aspects of the budget, as well as to generate greater transparency by rolling development assistance on budget. Countries with an MTEF face an added challenge in accepting additional donor funding when the value may replace rather than add to the government budget.

Poverty reduction strategy papers

Poverty reduction strategy papers (PRSPs), which were initiated by the International Monetary Fund and the World Bank in 1999, describe a country's macroeconomic, structural, and social strategies to promote growth and reduce poverty, as well as the country's external financing needs. Governments prepare PRSPs in collaboration with civil society and development partners—striving to promote national ownership of the strategy through broad-based participation. The goal of the PRSP approach is to link national policies and programs, donor support, and the development outcomes needed to meet the MDGs. PRSPs also serve as the guide for International Monetary Fund and World Bank lending and for debt-relief initiatives mentioned in Box 14-3 (IMF 2010).

Health authorities may find finance and planning agents difficult to convince that financing the health sector is an investment in the economy rather than a consumption good. Including health-sector priorities in the PRSP provides the basis for resource-allocation judgments at the national level, thus making the PRSP the national planning and resource-allocation document and the lens through which development assistance is viewed and evaluated.

Performance-based funding

One of the trends in improving donor aid effectiveness is the notion of performance-based funding, or results-based management. Donors are increasingly requiring that programs achieve quantitative targets before renewing aid to them. The popularity of this approach comes from its objectives of helping donors focus resources on programs that are effective, identifying problems early in the program implementation and making modifications, and improving future programs (Radelet 2006). Box 14-4 describes an innovative mechanism to forgive loans using performance-based objectives.

As mentioned previously, the Global Fund approves initial grants for two years, then uses performance-based guidelines to make decisions regarding continued funding (Global Fund 2003). The indicators that the Global Fund uses to measure performance are categorized along a continuum of (1) short-term, (2) medium-term, and (3) long-term expectations—

1. *Process indicators*: These are what need to be completed to achieve improvements; for example, "training program for antiretroviral treatment (ART) adherence established."

2. *Coverage indicators:* These track changes in key variables that demonstrate that individuals in target groups are being reached and are benefiting; for example, "percentage of patients achieving 95 percent adherence to ART (% target against baseline)."

3. *Impact indicators*: These measure changes in morbidity and mortality or the burden of disease in the target population that indicate that the primary objectives of the interventions have been achieved; for example, "Percentage of treatment failure among population taking antiretroviral medicines (% target against baseline)."

Multiple donors requiring monitoring and evaluation based on multiple indicators can be a huge challenge to recipient countries, however, because of the amount of time meeting these requirements takes away from already overstretched personnel. The Global Fund encourages its grantees to use existing systems for monitoring and reporting to avoid duplicate reporting whenever possible.

14.6 Securing donor interest

Health authorities should take the initiative to approach appropriate donor agencies regarding their interest in supporting specific program areas, such as essential medicines. Even at an early stage, a donor appreciates receiving a written proposal, however preliminary and general it may be, to determine if sufficient interest exists to proceed further.

Box 14-4
The Investment Partnership for Polio: An innovative financing mechanism

The Investment Partnership for Polio, comprising the World Bank, the Bill & Melinda Gates Foundation, Rotary International, and the United Nations Foundation, is a program to fund immunization of children in polio-endemic countries. As part of the partnership, the International Development Association created an innovative credit buy-down system in which the partnership "buys down" a country's IDA loans after the project successfully reaches agreed performance goals—in this case, the completion of the country's polio eradication program. In this way, the loans ultimately revert to grant funding. To fund the buydowns, the partnership established a trust fund with USD 50 million. The first two countries to take advantage of the loan buy-down mechanism were Nigeria and Pakistan.

The buy-down mechanism is designed to enhance the efficiency of the IDA's assistance in priority areas; to mobilize additional resources from other partners; and to focus the attention of governments, partners, and World Bank staff on clearly defined performance objectives. Ultimately, countries are rewarded for contributing to the worldwide effort to eradicate polio.

In Pakistan, the partnership approved two projects for USD 42.71 million in 2003 and for USD 74.27 million in 2006 to purchase the oral polio vaccine and help the country's Polio Eradication Initiative. The number of polio cases decreased from 1,147 in 1997 to 31 in 2007. After the project was completed, a credit of USD 42 million was converted into a grant and written off for the government of Pakistan.

Sources: Investment Partnership for Polio 2003; World Bank n.d.

Information describing the level, duration, and type of assistance available, as well as the timing for presentation of proposals, is generally available at the country level through development banks, embassies, and offices of UN agencies. Table 14-1 lists major donors to international health and their websites.

As demand for assistance funds increases, donor agencies have become more selective about the project proposals they will consider. Proposals must meet general criteria regarding government policies and commitment, private-sector involvement, impact, and sustainability to satisfy the concerns of donors.

The conditions for assistance may require recipient governments to take steps toward reforming or even restructuring the health sector. Where pharmaceuticals are concerned, this requirement may mean profound changes in how the pharmaceutical supply is managed. For example, it may mean moving from a centralized government agency that handles all aspects of procurement, warehousing, and distribution to a system that limits central government involvement to coordination and supervision and delegates operational aspects to provincial and local levels or to the private sector.

Government policies

Project proposals must be consistent with the priorities of the recipient country and, most important, with the PRSP. Pharmaceutical projects should refer to official policies in this area, particularly if the country has a national medicines policy and action plan to improve the availability of essential medicines and to promote the rational use of medicines.

Government commitment

The commitment of the recipient government to the objectives of the proposal should be reflected in its assignment of staff, space, and equipment to these objectives. The external contribution is generally intended to complement the counterpart contribution, not the other way around.

Health care reform

Extensive health system reforms are under way in many countries. Their aim is to restructure the organization, financing, and provision of health services to achieve greater equity, efficiency, and quality using available resources. This reform often includes stimulation of competition and greater involvement by the private sector. Donors may require that pharmaceutical reforms be undertaken as part of health care reform. Thus, representatives of the health professionals' associations and of the local pharmaceutical industry may be included in the formulation of a project

and in the identification of strategies for its implementation. Private-sector involvement in pharmaceutical supply is discussed in Chapter 8.

In addition, several major global health initiatives, such as the GAVI Alliance, the Global Fund, and the U.S. President's Emergency Plan for AIDS Relief, have shifted some focus and funding from disease-specific activities to strengthening countries' overall health systems. Evidence indicates that these efforts have resulted in some successes, including increases in overall health financing and improved health system governance and accountability (WHO Maximizing Positive Synergies Collaborative Group 2009). In the area of pharmaceutical management, the accomplishments in HIV/AIDS programs, in particular, have enhanced the pharmaceutical sector overall in areas such as pharmaceutical development, procurement, and distribution as well as human resource and information management systems (Embrey, Hoos, and Quick 2009).

Impact

The expected impact of a project should be explicitly stated in the proposal; donors are wary of projects that simply propose to do more of what is already being done. They are interested in supporting initiatives that will noticeably change the status quo at the policy-making or operational levels or both. How will the project improve existing conditions? Will it result in an integrated and intersectoral program that will be more cost-effective than the present one? Although the effect of a single project may be difficult to quantify, an effort should be made to explain its expected impact.

Sustainability

Donors are increasingly interested in the sustainability of their investments. Even at the proposal stage, they want assurance that achievements will not disappear after external funding has ended. In numerous examples, project funds have been used unwisely to support unusually high salaries or luxurious offices; when the funding for these salaries and offices ends, so does the interest in the activities launched.

To prevent such backlash, project activities should be designed to be carried out as much as possible within normal structures and working environments. Also, arrangements should be in place before the project ends to institutionalize the project's achievements, that is, to provide the funds for the staff, infrastructure, and supplies required to continue the activities started. Special attention is required in projects that include the purchase of essential medicines as a central element: in these cases, financial mechanisms must be installed to ensure that the medicines continue to be available when external aid has ended.

14.7 Obtaining grants from private foundations

Private foundations are an important source of international assistance, especially for NGOs whose philosophies, missions, and values correspond with those of the donors. Foundations' procedures for reviewing and approving grant proposals and for overseeing grant-funded projects tend to be considerably more flexible than those of bilateral and multilateral agencies. Nonetheless, four important steps should be followed.

Step 1. Identify potential foundations

Funding groups and directories identify foundations of potential interest, describe the interests and funding priorities of individual foundations, and provide broad guidelines and criteria for application. Foundation websites often have a section with information for those seeking grants.

Step 2. Target selected foundations

Reviewing annual reports of the foundations under consideration for information about their programs, geographic areas of interest, monetary range of grants, and proposal guidelines is useful. This review can help grant seekers develop a list of foundations whose funding criteria fit their interests.

The development of foundation proposals takes time, persistence, and the cultivation of personal relationships: introduction to foundation staff, discussion of mutual areas of interest with program officers, and making a case for support are all necessary before a proposal is formally submitted.

Step 3. Develop proposal

A foundation proposal should generally include the following key elements. The guidelines for proposals will designate the page number limit.

- Description of the organization
- Problem to be addressed
- Proposed solution
- Statement of objectives and methodology
- Plan for project management
- Timeline
- Evaluation plan
- Budget

A cover letter summarizes the proposal and provides a strategic link between the proposal and the foundation's mission and interests. In addition, the letter makes a specific request for funding the proposed activities.

Step 4. Submit proposal and follow up

Foundations do not generally have deadlines for submission of proposals but review them on a rolling basis. Staff members look at the proposal whenever it is received to determine its compatibility with the foundation's current interests and priorities, its technical merit, and the financial and management capacity of the submitting organization.

If a proposal is deemed appropriate, the board of trustees reviews it for final consideration and approval. Meetings of the board are usually scheduled quarterly. The review process can take up to six months to complete.

When an award is made, the foundation presents a payment and reporting schedule to the grantee. Grant funds are restricted to those activities outlined in the proposal. At the end of each grant period, a narrative and a financial report on the specific use of funds are usually required.

14.8 Project formulation documents

Many donors follow a two-stage proposal process for new projects, requiring submission and approval of a project profile or letter of intent, followed by a more detailed project document. Donors may be willing to assist in preparing these documents, or governments may request assistance through local offices of WHO, UNICEF, or UNDP.

The project profile

The project profile or letter of intent should contain sufficient information for preliminary discussion and decision making. It should describe and reflect broad agreement within the government or the requesting organization regarding the problem to be solved, the proposed solution, and the estimated cost. Requirements to include at the project profile stage are the problem analysis, goals, objectives, and activities, including expected results and a time frame. Other elements can be outlined, and a skeleton budget should be included. Often, donors will require that the proposal show in-kind support from in-country partners. Quantitative information should be included, if possible. Annex 14-1 contains the instructions for submitting a letter of inquiry to the Bill & Melinda Gates Foundation.

All parties that may be affected or involved in the project must be included in early planning discussions to avoid the sense that a particular project belongs to a specific official or unit. Such an attitude discourages the participation of other individuals or institutions and limits the coordination required to ensure that project goals are pursued in an appropriate manner.

The project profile is submitted for review to the donor agency. Months may go by before a response is received. The response, even if highly positive, almost always contains recommendations for changes or additions to ensure that the proposal complies with donor requirements, some of which, at first sight, may not seem relevant. The recommendations, however, should not be overlooked. More likely than not, they reflect a political decision of the donor country or institution that any project to be funded must address certain issues of national or global interest. The issues vary according to the source of funds, but common ones include environmental protection, the role of women, alleviation of poverty, and human rights.

Once the donor institution is satisfied that its concerns will be addressed in the project and confirms its support, the complex work involved in preparing the project document begins.

The proposal document

The proposal document is more detailed than the profile because it is intended to guide project implementation and to serve as the reference for monitoring and evaluation. It often serves as the legal basis for the commitments assumed by the donor and recipient.

Donor agencies usually require that the project design be systematic and comprehensive; many favor the logical framework approach, which is described in Chapter 38 and in the World Bank's *Logframe Handbook* (World Bank 2005). The Logframe uses a hierarchy of key elements to design the project—

- Project goals (development objective)
- Project purpose (immediate objective)
- Outputs
- Activities
- Inputs and resources

Like the project profile, the proposal document is submitted to the funding agency for review. Once donor comments and recommendations have been received and the recipient has satisfactorily responded, donor approval of the project follows. Disbursement of funds for each project year is approved after submission of an annual workplan, which should include an introduction, specific objectives and strategies, planned activities, and a budget.

14.9 Use of local and international consultants and advisers

Regardless of funding source, expert advice can be required at various stages of a project, such as design, implementation, specialized problem solving, and external evaluation. If the donor or recipient does not have the required expertise available in-house, the donor or recipient commonly contracts with outside professionals. In some cases, the donor may require the use of an external consultant, to ensure that the appropriate technical expertise is applied and to provide a degree of independence from local political pressures. Recipients, whether governments or NGOs, may seek outside consultants who are respected for their technical or managerial competence and who can provide impartial input to overcome the objections of special-interest groups and support new or controversial initiatives.

Clear and early identification of what is expected from a consultant is crucial. This is done with clear terms of reference that define what is to be produced, a specific time frame, and supervision and reporting responsibilities.

Consultants' education and experience (qualifications) should also be spelled out. For a specific, highly technical, and short-term assignment, such as training government inspectors in good manufacturing practices, five years of experience as an inspector in a well-established regulatory agency, plus knowledge of the local language, may be sufficient. A consultant who will be managing a four-year project to develop a national essential medicines program should have extensive experience in similar projects internationally; counterparts in the host country will benefit from the consultant's experience in other parts of the world.

The process of selecting a consultant can vary from an informal interview for a short-term job to a highly structured process for a project manager or specialist who will serve for one year or longer. In the latter case, the donor, the host government, and any participating agencies often work together to advertise the search and ensure the prompt review of applications by a selection committee. Although a formal process may take six months or longer, it provides legitimacy and authority to those selected for key project posts. The hiring process needs to be transparent and competitive—all qualified consultants should be given an opportunity to compete for the position. The World Bank has guidelines on selecting and employing consultants (World Bank 2010).

The selection of consultants for specific short-term assignments (for example, advising warehouse staff on good storage practices) should be carried out in a much shorter time. This can be achieved with the cooperation of international and bilateral organizations such as WHO, UNICEF, USAID, and the Danish Agency for Development Assistance; they have rosters of specialized consultants who have worked with them and for whom they can provide references.

Government-to-government requests for expert assistance are also common and are promoted by international agencies through technical cooperation among countries (TCC) projects. In the TCC process, countries work together to develop human resources or technical capacity through cooperative exchanges, which may include experts or consultants. The expert exchanged is not a consultant per se but a professional who does the same job in his or her own country. Under a TCC project, the host government covers travel and local expenses, and the cooperating government continues to pay the official's salary. Ideally, TCC activities should be managed by the governments with the participation of public and private institutions and organizations.

Joint consultancies with an international and a local consultant should be considered. They combine the advantages of the international consultant's insights from similar projects in other parts of the world and the local consultant's knowledge of the environment and local contacts. A positive side effect is the mutual transfer of knowledge, allowing both consultants to further their professional development.

14.10   Progress reports and evaluations

Donors' demands may increase as the project progresses, because funding officials need to know whether their investment is resulting in the positive changes envisioned in the project plan. Toward this end, donors may request a semiannual status report and an annual report accompanied by a financial statement. Reports provide the project manager with an opportunity to describe the project's achievements, problems encountered and actions taken to overcome them, and any discrepancies between the original workplan and actual implementation. Any potential changes in project objectives should be discussed and approved in advance by the funding agency. As mentioned, efforts are under way to harmonize reporting requirements between governments and donors.

Project evaluation provides a structured environment for donor-recipient interaction, whether carried out midway through the project or as a final exercise. The mission of the evaluation team, which includes donor representatives, is to determine whether planned objectives were achieved and the reasons for successes and failures. The project document serves as the basic guide in this work, and the value of having developed clear objectives, clarified the assumptions and risks, and selected manageable indicators becomes evident. (See Chapter 36 for a more detailed discussion of indicators for pharmaceutical-sector assessment.)

Before the evaluation team arrives, the project manager should prepare a summary of major project accomplishments; the more specific it is the better. Arrangements should be made for evaluators to visit sites where project activities have taken place. Presentations on the results achieved should be made by those directly responsible for the activity or, better yet, by those benefiting from it.

Providing the evaluation team with information about achievements as well as difficulties that were overcome is in the project manager's interest. The government's commitment to the project should also be highlighted, in part by quantifying the administrative support and space provided and the staff and resources assigned. The most convincing

evidence is documented changes in government policies that would lead to institutionalization of the goals pursued by the project.

A favorable evaluation facilitates future discussion with the donor agency regarding extension of the present project or preparation of new initiatives. However, successful completion of the original project should not lead a recipient country to assume that continuing funding is assured and that an expanded or new project can be launched. A major goal of donor agencies is to promote greater self-reliance, and after a certain period of external support, donors expect recipients to absorb the costs for consolidating and expanding the gains achieved under the project. Donor's priorities also change, often for reasons that may have little or nothing to do with the recipient country. This further emphasizes the importance of staying up-to-date regarding what sectors and program areas are priorities for international development assistance. ■

References and further readings

★ = Key readings.

Baum, W. C. 1982. *The Project Cycle.* Washington, D.C.: World Bank.

Bill & Melinda Gates Foundation. 2010. "How to Apply for a Global Health Grant." Global Health Letter of Inquiry Instructions. <http://www.gatesfoundation.org/grantseeker/Pages/how-to-apply-global-health.aspx>

Embrey, M., D. Hoos, and J. Quick. 2009. How AIDS Funding Strengthens Health Systems: Progress in Pharmaceutical Management. *Journal of Acquired Immune Deficiency Syndrome* 52(Suppl.):34–7.

Global Fund (Global Fund to Fight AIDS, Tuberculosis and Malaria). 2003. "Guidelines for Performance-Based Funding, July 1, 2003." <http://www.searo.who.int/LinkFiles/Strategic_Alliance_and_Partnerships_13f_Guidelines_on_performance_based_funding.pdf>

Gottret, P., and G. Schieber. 2006. *Health Financing Revisited: A Practitioner's Guide.* Washington, D.C.: World Bank. <http://siteresources.worldbank.org/INTHSD/Resources/topics/Health-Financing/HFRFull.pdf>

Greco, G., T. Powell-Jackson, J. Borghi, and A. Mills. 2008. Countdown to 2015: Assessment of Donor Assistance to Maternal, Newborn, and Child Health between 2003 and 2006. *Lancet* 371:1268–75.

★ Hecht, R., and R. Shah. 2006. "Recent Trends and Innovations in Development Assistance for Health." In D. T. Jamison, J. G. Breman, A. R. Measham, G. Alleyne, M. Claeson, D. B. Evans, P. Jha, A. Mills, and P. Musgrove, eds. *Disease Control Priorities in Developing Countries,* 2nd ed. Washington, D.C.: World Bank and Oxford University Press. <http://www.dcp2.org/pubs/DCP>

High Level Forum on the Health MDGs. 2005. *Best Practice Principles for Global Health Partnership Activities at Country Level.* Report of the Working Group on Global Health Partnerships, Paris, November 14–15. <http://www.hlfhealthmdgs.org/Documents/GlobalHealthPartnerships.pdf>

International Monetary Fund. 2010. "Debt Relief under the Heavily Indebted Poor Countries (HIPC) Initiative: A Factsheet." Washington, D.C.: International Monetary Fund. <http://www.imf.org/external/np/exr/facts/pdf/hipc.pdf>

ASSESSMENT GUIDE

Sources and types of assistance

- Describe current development assistance received from international sources. Is the assistance provided through official development assistance or through bilateral agencies, multilateral institutions, NGOs, foundations, or public-private partnerships?
- Does the international assistance support national health priorities and programs? To what extent is it useful in catalyzing health system reforms that would otherwise be difficult to accomplish?
- Does funding coincide with a sector-wide approach to aid or does it follow a poverty reduction strategy paper?
- What types of international assistance are provided—for example, funds (loans or grants), commodities, technical assistance, training?
- When loans are provided, are they used for investment purposes rather than to cover recurrent health expenditures?
- Is the country eligible for the Debt Relief Initiative for Heavily Indebted Poor Countries?
- When the assistance is provided in the form of commodities, are purchase terms negotiated to ensure appropriate products, price, and quality?

Ministry of health involvement

- Have health-sector priorities been clearly articulated to support national development policies?
- Does the ministry of health take an active role in identifying sources and types of assistance and representing its interests to the ministries of planning, external relations, and finance, which are likely to carry out negotiations with donors?
- Does the ministry of health facilitate the cooperation of multiple donors by communicating national policies and programs, inviting donors to participate in the development of a master plan, hosting regular donor coordination meetings, or giving periodic progress reports to donors?

Project development

- Are project proposals written in a way that is consistent with government policies, specifically the national medicine policy (if one exists)?
- Is government commitment reflected in the assignment of staff, space, and equipment to project objectives?
- Do project proposals include plans for monitoring and evaluating impact and sustainability and other issues of concern to donor agencies?
- Does each proposal include a description of the problem to be addressed? Are project goals, purposes, and strategies clearly stated? Are outputs, activities, and inputs specified?
- Are all involved parties included in project planning?
- Are external consultants employed in project design, implementation, or evaluation to provide specific technical expertise and independence from local political pressures? Has the consultant been hired using competitive and transparent procedures?

Investment Partnership for Polio. 2003. *Financial Innovation Will Buy Polio Vaccine to Help Eradicate Polio Worldwide.* Washington, D.C., April 29. <http://go.worldbank.org/BZDWNYS0N0>

Kaijage, F. J., ed. 1993. *Management Consulting in Africa: Utilizing Local Expertise.* West Hartford, Conn.: Kumarian Press.

KIT/IDRC (Royal Tropical Institute, Amsterdam/International Development Research Centre). 2003. Designing and Conducting Health Systems Research Projects. In C. M. Varkevisser, I. Pathmanathan, and A. Brownlee, eds. *Proposal Development and Fieldwork.* Ottawa: IDRC. <http://www.idrc.ca/EN/Resources/Publications/Pages/IDRCBookDetails.aspx?PublicationID=210>

Kubr, M. 1993. *How to Select and Use Consultants: A Client's Guide.* Geneva: International Labour Office.

Lu, C., C. M. Michaud, K. Khan, and C. J. Murray. 2006. Absorptive Capacity and Disbursements by the Global Fund to Fight AIDS, Tuberculosis and Malaria: Analysis of Grant Implementation. *Lancet* 368:483–8.

Martinez, J. 2006. *Implementing a Sector Wide Approach in Health: The Case of Mozambique.* London: HLSP Institute. <http://www.hlsp.org/LinkClick.aspx?fileticket=zoJzXKwmB%2b4%3d&tabid=1706&mid=3369>

Michaud, C. M. 2003. *Development Assistance for Health (DAH): Recent Trends and Resource Allocation.* Paper prepared for the Second Consultation of the Commission on Macroeconomics and Health, World Health Organization, Geneva, October 29–30. <http://www.who.int/macrohealth/events/health_for_poor/en/dah_trends_nov10.pdf>

★ Norad-AHHA (Norwegian Agency for Development Cooperation–Global Health and AIDS Department). 2009. *The Global Health Landscape and Innovative International Financing for Health Systems: Trends and Issues.* Oslo: Norad.

OECD DAC (Organisation for Economic Co-operation and Development, Development Assistance Committee). 2009. "Measuring Aid to Health." Technical note. DAC: Paris. <http://www.oecd.org/dataoecd/44/35/44070071.pdf>

★ Radelet, S. 2006. *A Primer on Foreign Aid.* Washington, D.C.: Center for Global Development. <http://www.cgdev.org/content/publications/detail/8846/>

Ravishankar, N., P. Gubbins, R. J. Cooley, K. Leach-Kemon, C. M. Michaud, D. T. Jamison, and C. J. L. Murray. 2009. Financing of Global Health: Tracking Development Assistance for Health from 1990 to 2007. *Lancet* 373(9681):2113–24.

UNAIDS (Joint United Nations Programme on HIV/AIDS). 2005. *The "Three Ones" in Action: Where We Are and Where We Go from Here.* Geneva: UNAIDS. <http://data.unaids.org/publications/irc-pub06/jc935-3onesinaction_en.pdf>

UNDP/UNFPA/WHO/(United Nations Development Programme/United Nations Population Fund/World Health Organization)/World Bank Special Programme of Research, Development and Research Training in Human Reproduction. 2000. *Preparing a Research Project Proposal: Guidelines and Forms.* 3rd ed. Geneva: WHO. <http://whqlibdoc.who.int/hq/2000/WHO_HRP_PP_2000.pdf>

United Nations General Assembly. 2002. *Follow-up Efforts to the International Conference on Financing for Development: Report of the Secretary-General.* New York: United Nations.

United Nations Millennium Project. 2005. *Investing in Development: A Practical Plan to Achieve the Millennium Development Goals: Overview.* New York: UN Millennium Project. <http://www.unmillenniumproject.org/reports/index_overview.htm>

WHO (World Health Organization). 2010. *World Health Statistics 2010.* Geneva: WHO. <http://www.who.int/entity/whosis/whostat/EN_WHS10_Full.pdf>

———. 2003. How to Develop and Implement a National Drug Policy. *WHO Policy Perspectives on Medicines.* No. 6. Geneva: WHO. <http://apps.who.int/medicinedocs/pdf/s4869e/s4869e.pdf>

WHO/AFRO (World Health Organization/Regional Office for Africa). 2009. *WHO Country Cooperation Strategy 2009–2013: Mozambique.* Brazzaville: WHO/AFRO.

WHO Maximizing Positive Synergies Collaborative Group. 2009. An Assessment of Interactions between Global Health Initiatives and Country Health Systems. *Lancet* 373(9681):2137–69.

WHO/PAHO (World Health Organization/Pan American Health Organization). 2000. *Standardized Format for PAHO Project Documents and Profiles.* Washington, D.C.: WHO/PAHO. <http://www.paho.org/English/DEC/Standardized_Format.pdf>

World Bank. 2010a. *Guidelines: Selection and Employment of Consultants by World Bank Borrowers.* Washington, D.C.: World Bank. <http://siteresources.worldbank.org/INTPROCUREMENT/Resources/ConGuid-10-06-RevMay10-ev2.doc>

———. 2010b. *Helping Country Health Systems Deliver Results in a New Global Context.* Washington, D.C.: World Bank. <http://siteresources.worldbank.org/IDA/Resources/73153-128527143242 0/IDA_AT_WORK_Health_2010.pdf>

———. 2006a. "Multilateral Debt Relief Initiative Fact Sheet." Washington, D.C.: World Bank. <http://siteresources.worldbank.org/INTDEBTDEPT/Resources/mdri_eng.pdf>

———. 2006b. News and Broadcast, "Debt Relief." <http://go.worldbank.org/KNZR2IIQG0>

———. 2005. *The Logframe Handbook: A Logical Framework Approach to Project Cycle Management.* Washington, D.C.: World Bank. <http://go.worldbank.org/7DN9H8Q0Q0>

———. No date. "Pakistan: Ten Things Worth Knowing about the World Bank in Pakistan." <http://go.worldbank.org/FXROC21KF0>

World Bank/UNICEF/UNFPA/Partnership for Maternal, Newborn and Child Health. 2009. *Health Systems for the Millennium Development Goals: Country Needs and Funding Gaps; Background Document for the Taskforce on Innovative International Financing for Health System; Working Group 1 Technical Report: Constraints to Scaling Up and Costs.* UN-Edited Conference Version, October 29–30. <http://www.internationalhealthpartnership.net//CMS_files/documents/wb,_unicef,_unfpa,_pmnch,_background_to_constraints_to_scaling_up_and_costs_EN.pdf>

Annex 14-1   Bill & Melinda Gates Foundation Global Health Letter of Inquiry Instructions

Formatting

Please use 10-point font and 1-inch margins. Page size must be set to U.S. letter standard 8.5 x 11.0 inches.

Instructions

Please provide the legal name of the organization that will manage the proposed project, the submission date, the project title, and the name and email address of the person who can answer questions about the proposed project.

General Questions
Please answer the questions to the best of your ability. Your answers to these questions will help the foundation to determine how to appropriately route your LOI for internal review and have no bearing on whether the foundation will decide to approve or decline your request. This section will not count against your four-page limit.

Response to the following sections is limited to a total of four pages

I. Project Purpose and Background
Describe the purpose of the project and how it will impact the health problem being addressed. Provide a brief overview of the prior work leading to your project. Describe how the proposed project relates to the broader context of ongoing activities in the field.

II. Project Framework
The foundation uses a modified logical framework model to help you present your project in a clear, concise, and logical way. The Project Framework is not intended to show every detail of the project or to limit its scope. It is simply a convenient, systematic summary of the key factors from which foundation staff will assess how your project aligns with foundation priorities. In the event you are requested to submit a full proposal the Project Framework will form the basis of your dialogue with foundation staff and you will be required to fully elaborate on the details of your plan.

Using the table provided, please build your framework accordingly:

Step One – Building from the top down
Strategic Area – From the list provided identify the foundation strategic area to which your project will directly contribute. If other strategic areas are applicable or secondarily relevant, please describe.
Project Goal – Identify the ultimate impact your project will have if you achieve your stated objectives. This should be a clear, singular goal.
Objectives – List a small number of objectives or major components of the project required to achieve the project goal and a brief summary of your approach to achieving the objectives. *In the event you are requested to submit a full proposal you will be required to identify the actual activities or tasks that will be needed to meet the stated objectives.*

Step Two – Working across the framework
Indicators of Success – What will success of the project look like? Identify the quantitative or qualitative ways of measuring or assessing: the impact of the project on the strategic area; progress toward the project goal; and progress toward achieving the stated objectives. Indicators of success can be either outputs or outcomes. Outputs are direct, tangible products or services of the project (e.g., reports produced). Outcomes reflect changes or benefits measuring the impact expected to occur as a result of the project (e.g., performance gains through application of new knowledge, health benefits). *Please note: you are not expected to quantify or specify specific measures at this time; only to indicate the methods that will be used.*
Monitoring and Evaluation – Identify the methods and sources by which you will measure and evaluate the progress and impact on the strategic area, project goal and stated objectives. *Please note: monitoring and evaluation may not be relevant at the strategic area level for your project.*

III. General Approach
Describe in general how you plan to approach this project. Provide a summary of the activities required to support achievement of the stated objectives.

IV. Major Assumptions
Describe any external factors that could influence the success of the project but are likely beyond your direct control.

V. Budget
Provide a preliminary project budget by the stated objective(s) and by year using the table provided. In addition, please indicate the total organization revenue for the most recent financial year. If applicable, indicate whether additional support (in-kind or financial) will be provided for this project by other organizations. All financial figures must be provided in U.S. dollars.

Please refer to the foundation's Indirect Cost Policy when building the preliminary budget. Projects chosen to submit a full proposal will be required to adhere to the policy.

VI. Organizational Experience and Collaborative Partnerships
Briefly describe the relevant experience and comparative advantage your organization brings to accomplishing the targeted objectives of the project. If the project will involve a consortium or collaborative partnership, please provide this information for each organization along with a rationale for your selection of collaborators. The rationale should include how the work will be distributed, how duplication will be avoided, and how the efficiency of the collaboration will be maximized.

VII. Certification
By submitting this letter of inquiry, you certify to the Bill & Melinda Gates Foundation that you are authorized to apply for this project on behalf of your institution.

Additional Information

Global Access
A principal goal of most activities funded by the foundation within the Global Health Program is to ensure that innovations (and related rights) are managed and public health solutions are optimized for the purpose of facilitating (i) the broad and prompt dissemination of data and information to the scientific community (as further described below in the section entitled "Data Sharing and Publication") and (ii) the access (in terms of price, quantity, and functionality) to affordable health solutions for the benefit of people most in need within the developing world. We refer to the goal of these two objectives as achieving "Global Access." We believe that the achievement of Global Access is a critical component to achieving the fundamental aim of reducing health inequities in the developing world.

With respect to your proposed project, ensuring that disadvantaged markets and populations in developing countries can one day readily access or otherwise directly benefit from the intended health solutions, should they prove effective and be commercialized (as applicable), is of paramount importance. Similarly, the other results of your work, such as incremental technological advances or discoveries, as well as data and other information arising out of the project, may also ultimately prove critical to addressing global health concerns.

While the science is and will continue to be the principal focus of the foundation, an essential aspect of your work is to identify and shape the path forward in managing the complex technologies and collaborations, fostering the necessary relationships with various sectors of the global health community, and in developing the intended project outcomes – all in a manner that facilitates the furtherance of the Global Access Objectives. The foundation believes strongly that, regardless of the nature or stage of your project, reasonable steps can and must be taken to help assure that you and your collaborators (as applicable) have provided for the achievement of these objectives.

Data Sharing and Publication
The generation of new evidence-based knowledge, technologies and practices that will result in significant improvements in the health of the populations of developing countries are among the most important charitable goals of projects supported by the foundation. Recognizing the possibility of securing intellectual property, grantees will be expected to prepare findings for timely publication and dissemination. You must consider publication strategies that will maximize the probability of your work reaching both the scientific and civil society communities in the developing world. The costs involved with making data widely available may be included in the proposed budget and will be subject to review and approval.

This document is subject to the Gatesfoundation.org. Privacy and Terms of Use policies.

Source: Bill & Melinda Gates Foundation 2010.

| Part I: Policy and economic issues | Part II: Pharmaceutical management | Part III: Management support systems |

Policy and legal framework
Financing and sustainability
  9 Pharmaceutical pricing policy
  10 Economics for pharmaceutical management
  11 Pharmaceutical financing strategies
  12 Pharmaceutical benefits in insurance programs
  13 Revolving drug funds and user fees
  14 Global and donor financing
  15 Pharmaceutical donations

CHAPTER 15

Pharmaceutical donations

SUMMARY

Most pharmaceutical donations are given with the best of intentions but can nevertheless create problems at the receiving end. Often, donated pharmaceuticals are not relevant to the needs of the recipient, or they arrive unsorted or close to expiry. They may be labeled with a brand name or in a language that is not understood. Many pharmaceutical donations counteract government policies or violate national regulations of the recipient country and can be expensive for the country to store or destroy.

Guidelines for pharmaceutical donations are needed for a number of reasons. Donors and recipients do not communicate on equal terms, and recipients often need assistance in formulating their needs. Many donors do not understand the potential difficulties at the receiving end and need guidance. Medicines require special regulations because they are different from other donated items. Pharmaceutical donations that occur without input from the recipient countries should be discouraged.

The four core principles for a useful pharmaceutical donation are—

1. A donation benefits the recipient to the maximum extent possible.
2. A donation should be given with full respect for the wishes and authority of the recipient.
3. Items that are not acceptable in the donor country for quality-related reasons are also not acceptable as donations: there should be no double standards in quality.
4. Effective communication between the donor and recipient is necessary before any donation.

These principles have been translated into a set of guidelines for pharmaceutical donations. First, recipients should review and adopt these guidelines and present them officially to the donor community. Only then can they be implemented and enforced. Second, recipients should develop and publish administrative procedures for pharmaceutical donations. Third, recipients should indicate to the donors, as clearly as possible, how they want to be helped, specifying the medicines they need, the quantities, and the priorities. Donors should inform the recipients well in advance which pharmaceutical donations are coming, and when.

15.1 Introduction

In the face of disaster the natural impulse is to reach out and help those in need. Donations of medicines can alleviate peoples' suffering, and international relief efforts benefit enormously from donations by private individuals, groups, and organizations. Organizations may donate pharmaceuticals or medical supplies for a variety of reasons. Some may seek tax deductions that can result from charitable donations; some may be seeking positive publicity; while others may want to dispose of unwanted products without having to pay for destruction. Unfortunately, many pharmaceutical donations have caused problems instead of helping.

This chapter summarizes the problems with inappropriate pharmaceutical donations, describes a set of guidelines for donations, and offers some practical recommendations for recipients and donors.

15.2 Problems with pharmaceutical donations

Many different types of pharmaceutical donations exist, and each has its own set of specific problems. The types covered in this section are—

- Pharmaceutical donations in emergency situations
- Pharmaceutical donations between governments as part of development aid
- Donations of returned or unwanted pharmaceuticals

Pharmaceutical donations in emergency situations

A sizable disaster does not always lead to an objective assessment of the emergency medical needs, based on hard facts and past experience. Frequently, an emotional appeal for massive medical assistance is issued. In times of emergency, the term "medical supplies" has special emotional connotations that can impede an objective approach. Although Country Study 15-1 provides examples of targeted emergency donations guided by quickly published lists of needs (e.g., in Haiti and Lebanon), more often than not, emergency pharmaceutical donations are inappropriate, which is why donors are often urged to respond to a disaster with cash rather than products (Pinheiro 2008). The main problems can be summarized as follows—

- Donated pharmaceuticals are often not relevant for the emergency situation, for the disease pattern, or for the level of care that is available.
- Health workers and patients are not always familiar with the donated pharmaceuticals.
- The pharmaceuticals are often not registered for use in

the recipient country and may not comply with local treatment guidelines.

- The pharmaceuticals that arrive are frequently unsorted, difficult to identify, unknown in the recipient country, labeled with brand names, or labeled in a language that is not locally understood.
- The quality of the pharmaceuticals does not always comply with standards in the donor country. Donated pharmaceuticals may have expired or may expire before they reach the patient; they may be returned pharmaceuticals (half-finished packages that have been returned to the pharmacy or free samples given to health professionals) (see Ette 2004); or they may be unwanted by the donor because they are close to expiration or the product is being discontinued (donating such products is also known as *drug dumping*). Donations may spoil or become damaged, which may be impossible to detect in the recipient country.
- The distribution plan often ignores normal administrative procedures. For example, the distribution system may bypass the central government stores or otherwise conflict with the plan of the national authorities.
- Donated pharmaceuticals may have a high declared value reflective of the market value in the donor country rather than the world market price. This valuation may result in high import taxes and overheads for storage and distribution in the recipient country, and the inflated value of the donation may be deducted from the recipient government's pharmaceutical budget.
- Pharmaceuticals may be donated in the wrong quantities or be otherwise unusable, and some stocks may have to be destroyed. Disposing of pharmaceuticals is not only wasteful; it is expensive for the recipient to safely destroy pharmaceutical stock.

There are several underlying causes for these problems. The most prominent cause is probably the common but mistaken belief that any type of pharmaceutical is better than nothing at all or, similarly, that expired pharmaceuticals are good enough for people in need. Second, pharmaceutical donations are often made despite the lack of a stated need or prior clearance by the recipient. Third, in many donor countries, donated pharmaceuticals are tax-deductible (at full market price). This last factor is why so many donated pharmaceuticals arrive close to or past their expiry date and why such products are typically not high-use, high-volume items. Pharmaceutical donations initiated by pharmaceutical manufacturers in exchange for tax breaks are likely to consist of medicines and supplies that are not commonly viewed as essential.

Inappropriate pharmaceutical donations create logistical problems because the donated products must be sorted, stored, and distributed, sometimes using precious human resources and transport volume in disaster areas or war zones. Or they may pose an environmental threat if they have to be destroyed. Often, the total transport costs are higher than the value of the pharmaceuticals. Stockpiling of unused pharmaceuticals can encourage pilfering and black-market sales.

Even donations that are appropriate in every other way can cause problems when they far surpass the quantities that are needed. For example, a World Bank analysis of pharmaceutical donations during emergencies indicated that in Gujarat, India, after an earthquake in 2001, 95 percent of the donations received were deemed appropriate, but exceeded what was needed by 1,178 tons (Autier et al. 2002).

Pharmaceutical donations as part of development aid

Most of the problems noted above may also apply to large pharmaceutical donations between governments given as part of development (commodity) aid. The situation is usually better than with emergency aid, however, as there is more time to plan for the donations. Generally, the recipient is more involved in specifying what is needed.

The ideal situation occurs when the recipient country can indicate specific medicines and quantities needed, without any restriction on the selection and country of origin of the pharmaceuticals. Unfortunately, these conditions seldom apply. The choice is often restricted to manufacturers or suppliers in the donor country. Even if the medicines are listed generically on the national list of essential medicines in the recipient country, the donated items are often brand-name products or different formulations that may not be registered in the recipient country. The donation may then interfere with the implementation of national registration, quality assurance, and inspection schemes. If the selection of medicines is restricted by the donor, the donation may not be in accordance with national programs promoting standard treatment guidelines and rational medicine use.

Donations of returned pharmaceuticals

Many nongovernmental groups in developed countries collect unused medicines (returned medicines or free samples) and send these products in emergency situations or, on a regular basis, to institutions in developing countries. At the receiving end, such donations can frustrate all efforts to manage and administer pharmaceutical stocks in a rational way. Donating returned medicines is a clear example of double standards: in no developed country would the use of such products be permitted. In addition, these medicines are a problem for doctor and patient. The prescriber is forced to use countless different medicines and brands in ever-changing dosages; patients on long-term treatment suffer because the same medicines may not be consistently available. For

Country Study 15-1
Multicountry experiences with pharmaceutical donations

Bosnia and Herzegovina, 1997. During the war in Bosnia and Herzegovina, many areas became dependent on foreign donations of medicines and medical supplies. An estimated 27,800 to 34,800 metric tons of medical materials were brought into the area between 1992 and mid-1996. Three types of donations were identified, each inappropriate to some degree. The first type of donation conformed to WHO's interagency guidelines for pharmaceutical donations, but approximately 5 percent of the 13,200 metric tons of this donation were considered inappropriate, because it consisted of prepackaged kits that were not fully applicable to local health needs. The second type of donation consisted of small amounts of miscellaneous medicines that were largely delivered unsorted, unidentifiable, or expired, and were frequently items not useful for the local health problems. The third type of donation comprised large quantities of useless or unusable medicines—what is known as drug dumping. In total, 50 to 60 percent of all the medical supplies donated to Bosnia and Herzegovina were deemed inappropriate (Berckmans and Autier 1997).

Croatia, 1991. Starting in 1991, war and political instability affected countries that were part of the former Yugoslavia, prompting large amounts of pharmaceutical donations from the international community. In Croatia, 2,700 tons of inappropriate donations of foreign origin classified as "pharmaceutical wastes" were stored in 250 warehouses. USD 4 million was budgeted to ensure its safe disposal (World Bank 1999; Stritof and Vrhovac 1997, cited in Autier et al. 2002).

East Timor, 1999. When East Timor declared independence from Indonesian rule, a militia-led campaign of destruction ensued. Seventy-five percent of the population of 850,000 was displaced, and almost 70 percent of the country's infrastructure was destroyed. Assessments estimated that inappropriate donations to East Timor comprised about 10 percent (by volume) of the total donations received during the emergency phase, and less than 5 percent of donations after March 2000. Although the pharmaceutical donations in East Timor had some problems, several reasons why the donations were generally acceptable included—

- Direct connections by air or water to the island are difficult, so supplies went through Australia, which facilitated surveillance.
- The United Nations coordinated significant donations, which came in the form of New Emergency Health Kits, which helped limit ad hoc donations.

- Media coverage was scant.
- Pharmaceutical companies were willing to make donations that complied with WHO's donation guidelines.

The East Timor experience suggests that the WHO donation guidelines can positively affect pharmaceutical donations in emergency and postemergency situations (Autier et al. 2002).

El Salvador, 2001. Two earthquakes hit El Salvador in 2001, affecting at least 25 percent of the total population and up to 75 percent of the population in specific areas. Immediately following the disasters, pharmaceutical donations began to arrive in the country. Although a government-led coordination body managed the donations, the effectiveness of the system was diminished because of a lack of coordination with the agencies sending out the medicines, and lack of classification skills within the country for medicine sorting. Total pharmaceutical donations approximated 882 tons. Approximately 37 percent of the total volume of donated medicines was defined as inappropriate, and an additional 12.9 percent was defined as "mixed unusable drugs giving rise to suspicion of dumping" (Autier et al. 2002).

Eritrea, 1993. During the war for independence, despite careful wording of appeals, much time and energy had to be spent sorting pharmaceutical consignments. Examples of inappropriate donations included seven truckloads of expired aspirin tablets that took six months to burn, a whole container of unsolicited cardiovascular-related medicines with two months to expiry, and 30,000 half-liter bottles of expired amino-acid infusion that could not be disposed of anywhere near a settlement because of the smell.

Gujarat State (India), 2001. A major earthquake occurred in the state of Gujarat in 2001 in an area that was already experiencing a severe drought. India has an established natural disaster management system with a defined chain of command from the central to peripheral level. Officers were stationed at checkpoints to facilitate arrival and movement of supplies and donated goods, and the government had a coordination committee to synchronize the activities of various donors. The result was that the majority of pharmaceutical donations to the area appeared to be appropriate and clearly labeled, and had expiry dates that were at least one year from the time of arrival in India (Autier et al. 2002).

Haiti, 2010. A 7.0 earthquake struck Haiti on January 12, 2010. From January 16–21 alone, approximately 530 tons of pharmaceutical supplies arrived at the Port-au-Prince airport (PAHO/WHO 2010b), and another 810 tons of medical supplies were donated before February 6 (PAHO/WHO 2010a). PROMESS (the Program on Essential Medicine and Supplies), Haiti's central pharmaceutical store, was responsible for organizing the donations. With the assistance of the Pan American Health Organization and the U.S. government, PROMESS staff worked with medical personnel to help receive, sort, and check the expiration dates of the pharmaceutical donations, so that the items could be shelved. They also dealt with the challenges of providing security for the donations and the PROMESS facility. The Ministry of Public Health and Population waived any fees for essential medicines until four months after the disaster to assure maximum access to medicines.

Lebanon, 2006. During a Middle East humanitarian crisis, more than a quarter of the Lebanese population was displaced, and 50 to 70 percent of health facilities were partially or completely destroyed in the affected border regions. In addition, the supply of fuel, medicines, and medical supplies was disrupted. WHO posted a list of needed medicines and supplies—mostly for chronic diseases and surgical interventions—to guide donations. The local WHO coordinator said, "Lebanon needs medicines, but it needs the right kind. Every box of medicines or other supplies donated has to be checked, sorted, stored, and shipped to the right places." Reports indicated that most of the donations that came in were exactly what the country needed (WHO 2006b).

Lithuania, 1993. Eleven women in Lithuania temporarily lost their eyesight after using a medicine that had been provided through pharmaceutical donations. The medicine, closantel, was an anthelmintic that should be used only in veterinary medicine but was mistakenly given for the treatment of endometritis. The donation had been received without product information or package inserts, and doctors had tried to identify the product by matching the name on the box with the names on leaflets of other products.

Mozambique, 2000. In 2000, Mozambique was hit by the worst floods ever recorded in the country, resulting in 700 deaths and displacing more than 500,000 people. As news of the disaster spread, a huge volume of aid cargo was sent, but delivery was chaotic. One person involved reported that "[a]t least 71 shipments arrived during 45 days, most without warning, many with no documentation or packing list" (Christie and Hanlon 2001). Overall, the international community donated 514 tons of medicines, but only 130 tons, or 25 percent, corresponded to requests issued by the ministry of health; three-quarters were considered inappropriate (Autier et al. 2002).

Rwanda, 1994. At the peak of the refugee crisis, a large international pharmaceutical company donated six million units of Ceclor CD, a sophisticated antibiotic. The refugee workers had no experience with this medicine, so it was not used. Part of this donation was returned to the donor, and the remainder expired and had to be destroyed (Purvis 1996 in Autier et al. 2002).

Sudan, 1990. A large consignment of pharmaceuticals was sent from France to war-devastated southern Sudan. Each box contained a collection of small packets of medications, some partly used. All were labeled in French, a language not spoken in Sudan. Most were inappropriate; some could be dangerous. Items included contact lens solution, appetite stimulants, monoamine oxidase inhibitors (dangerous in Sudan), X-ray solutions, drugs against hypercholesterolemia, and expired antibiotics. Of fifty boxes, twelve contained products that could be of use. It would have been much better to have used the money spent on transport to purchase penicillin and other essential medicines in Kenya, which could then have been sent to Sudan.

Source: WHO/DAP 1999 unless otherwise noted.

these reasons, this type of donation is generally discouraged and even forbidden in some countries. The immense effort required to sort such donations is largely wasted because most of the products are unusable.

Disposal of unwanted pharmaceuticals

The best way to avoid having to dispose of unwanted pharmaceutical donations is to stop inappropriate donations from occurring; unfortunately, however, even with increased recognition of problematic donations in the face of large-scale disasters, such as the 2004 South Asian tsunami, disposal remains an important issue. The same international coalition that developed the WHO Drug Donation Guidelines has collaborated on guidelines for the safe disposal of pharmaceuticals. These guidelines were based on experiences during the war in Bosnia and Herzegovina, where an estimated 1,000 to 17,000 metric tons of unused medicines were stockpiled, requiring disposal at a quoted cost of USD 2.20–4.10 per kilogram (WHO 1999). There have been calls for donors to take responsibility for paying for disposal of unused donations (Ciment 1999).

The need for guidelines

The examples of inappropriate donations discussed above illustrate the need for international guidelines for pharmaceutical donations. In summary, guidelines are needed because—

- Donor and recipient do not communicate on equal terms; recipients, therefore, need assistance in specifying how they want to be helped.
- Many donors mean well but do not realize the difficulties at the receiving end and need guidance.
- Pharmaceutical needs vary by country and situation. Donations should be based on an analysis of actual needs, and selection and distribution must fit within pharmaceutical policies and administrative systems. Inappropriate donations frustrate the implementation of national pharmaceutical policies and programs to promote rational medicine use.
- Medicines are different from other donated items. Medicines can be harmful, they require labels and written information, they need special storage conditions and adequately trained personnel to be used effectively, they may expire, and they may have to be destroyed in a particular way.

15.3 Chronology of existing guidelines for pharmaceutical donations

In 1988, the Christian Medical Commission (CMC) of the World Council of Churches in Geneva was the first organization to issue guidelines for pharmaceutical donations. This carefully worded document was specifically intended to make more rational the many donations that are made to individual church-related hospitals by well-intentioned but ignorant groups or individuals.

In 1990, the WHO Action Programme on Essential Drugs, in collaboration with major international emergency aid agencies, issued a set of guidelines for donors that was included in *The New Emergency Health Kit,* which was updated in 1998, and again in 2006 (WHO 2006a). As with those of the CMC, these guidelines stress that donations should be based on a specific request by the recipient and should, in all cases, be cleared before dispatch. Minimum labeling and outside packaging information standards are also specified.

In 1994, the WHO office in Zagreb issued detailed guidelines for humanitarian assistance for the former Yugoslavia, where WHO acts as a clearinghouse for all donations of medicines and medical supplies (WHO 1994). The guide-lines are specific for the situation, listing criteria for the acceptance of donations and for necessary documentation, labeling, and packaging.

In 1996, WHO concluded a worldwide consultative process with more than 100 participants to develop *Guidelines for Drug Donations,* in close collaboration with the United Nations High Commissioner for Refugees (UNHCR), United Nations Children's Fund (UNICEF), the Red Cross, and nongovernmental organizations. The Partnership for Quality Medical Donations, which is a coalition of industry and relief groups, also supports the guidelines.

15.4 Guidelines for pharmaceutical donations

WHO carried out an assessment of first-year experiences with the 1996 guidelines (WHO 2000a) and published revised guidelines in 1999. Although the assessment was positive for the most part, concerns were expressed about the clarity of the specific guideline on the shelf life of donated medicines, which was revised in the new edition (WHO/DAP 1999). The new guideline allows for direct donations of pharmaceuticals with a remaining shelf life of less than one year to specific health facilities, provided assurance can be given that the pharmaceuticals can be used prior to expiration. This requirement addresses the concern that legitimate donations were being delayed because of confusion in the original clause related to expiry.

The many problematic donations received during the aftermath of the 2004 tsunami in South Asia, as outlined in Country Study 15-2, indicate, unfortunately, that many donors are not heeding the guidelines.

Core principles

The first and paramount principle is that a donation should be intended only to assist the recipient, and all efforts should be made to maximize its positive effect. This principle implies that all donations should be based on an expressed need by the recipient and that unsolicited donations are to be discouraged. The second principle is that a donation should be given with full respect for the authority of the recipient and be supportive of existing government policies and administrative arrangements. The third principle is that no double standards should be applied: if the quality of an item is unacceptable in the donor country, it is also unacceptable as a donation. The fourth principle is that effective communication must be maintained between the donor and the recipient; donations should be based on expressed need and should not be sent unannounced.

If these core principles are adhered to, donations will usually be helpful rather than harmful, providing the specific guidelines on medicines selection, quality, presentation, packaging, and labeling in Box 15-1 are followed.

Country Study 15-2
Tsunami-related donations of medicines and supplies

On December 26, 2004, a massive earthquake measuring 9.3 on the Richter scale triggered a tsunami that devastated eleven countries in South Asia. International donors were quick to respond with aid; however, as with previous humanitarian crises, the lack of coordination and knowledge about the actual needs of the population decreased the effectiveness of emergency aid and generated additional challenges to public health efforts rather than easing what might have been the biggest crisis the area had ever experienced.

In Indonesia, pharmaceutical donations seemed to cause more problems for government authorities than they helped the population. Although the government asked for no medicines, more than 4,000 tons of pharmaceuticals were received for a population of 2 million, according to an assessment conducted by Pharmaciens Sans Frontières Comité International. Of these donations, most were deemed inappropriate: 60 percent of the medicines were not on the Indonesian national list of essential medicines; 70 percent were labeled in a foreign language; and 25 percent had an inadequate expiry date. Of the medicines that were appropriate, some arrived in extremely large quantities that would not be used before they expired. Approximately 661 tons of the donated medicine needed to be destroyed at an estimated cost of EUR 2.4 million. Countries are often hesitant to refuse donations because of a fear of offending donors, which only perpetuates the problem.

In Sri Lanka, relief workers requested a donation of intravenous antibiotics to treat infected wounds. Although the pharmaceutical manufacturer shipped the antibiotics quickly to a nonprofit consolidator working in Colombo, the shipment was initially delayed by bureaucratic procedure at the airport, and then it took additional time to get the medicines on their way to those in need. By the time any of the shipment made it into the affected regions, the perceived need had not materialized—perhaps because patients had died already or because of the difficulty in assessing the need in the midst of chaos. Although the Sri Lankan officials were grateful to receive "an antibiotic that can treat horrible infections you can't treat with normal antibiotics," concern existed about what would happen when the stockpile expired.

The Pharmaciens Sans Frontières assessors in Banda Aceh, Indonesia, concluded that in the years after the first publication of the *Guidelines for Drug Donations*, the quality of pharmaceutical donations in emergency situations had not improved. During disasters where resources and capacity are limited, donations can be not only useless, but even detrimental to the health of peoples affected and the economy of the recipient country.

Sources: Chase and Barta 2005; Mason 2005; PSFCI 2005.

Special guidelines for pharmaceutical donations in emergency situations

In emergency situations, it may not be practical for potential donors to wait for a specific request from the recipient. In any case, however, all proposed donations should be approved by the recipient before they are sent.

In the acute phase of an emergency, or in the case of refugee populations without any medical care, sending a range of medicines and medical supplies that is specifically designed for the circumstances is preferable. The Interagency Emergency Health Kit, which has been widely used since 1990, contains medicines, disposable supplies, and basic equipment for a population of 10,000 for three months. Its contents are based on a consensus among the major international aid agencies (WHO, UNICEF, UNHCR, Red Cross organizations, Médecins Sans Frontières, and OXFAM). It is permanently stocked by several major international suppliers (for example, UNICEF and the International Dispensary Association) and can be available within forty-eight hours.

From the recipients' point of view, a donation in cash for the local purchase of essential medicines is usually much more welcome than a donation in kind (assuming the local market is functional). Apart from being supportive of the activities of the local coordinating body, a cash donation is usually more cost-effective and also supports local industry. In addition, local prescribers and patients are usually more familiar with locally available medicines. A donation in cash also avoids the problem of the coordinating body having to prioritize long lists of needs according to what might or might not arrive.

Special guidelines for donations as part of development aid

When pharmaceuticals are donated as part of development aid, more time is usually available to specify needs and to follow guidelines on pharmaceutical donations. Special care should be taken that the medicines and their specifications comply with the national pharmaceutical policy and are

Box 15-1
Guidelines for pharmaceutical donations

These guidelines, developed by WHO and updated from the original 1996 guidelines, reflect consensus among the major international agencies active in humanitarian emergency relief: WHO, Caritas Internationalis, Churches' Action for Health of the World Council of Churches, International Committee of the Red Cross, International Federation of the Red Cross and Red Crescent Societies, International Pharmaceutical Federation, Joint United Nations Program on HIV/AIDS, Médecins Sans Frontières, Office of the United Nations High Commissioner for Refugees, OXFAM, Pharmaciens Sans Frontières, UNICEF, United Nations Development Programme, United Nations Population Fund, and the World Bank.

Many different scenarios exist for pharmaceutical donations. They may take place in acute emergencies or as part of development aid in nonemergency situations. They may be corporate donations (direct or through private voluntary organizations), aid by governments, or donations to single health facilities. And although there are legitimate differences among these scenarios, the basic rules for an appropriate donation apply to all. The guidelines describe this common core of good donation practices.

The guidelines aim to improve the quality of pharmaceutical donations, not to hinder them. They are not international regulations but are intended to serve as a basis for national or institutional guidelines, to be reviewed, adapted, and implemented by governments and organizations dealing with pharmaceutical donations.

Selection of medicines

1. All pharmaceutical donations should be based on an expressed need and be relevant to the disease pattern in the recipient country. Pharmaceuticals should not be sent without prior consent by the recipient.

2. All donated pharmaceuticals or their generic equivalents should be approved for use in the recipient country and appear on the national list of essential medicines, or, if a national list is not available, on the WHO *Model List of Essential Medicines*, unless specifically requested otherwise by the recipient.

3. The presentation, strength, and formulation of donated pharmaceuticals should, as much as possible, be similar to those commonly used in the recipient country.

Quality assurance and shelf life

4. All donated pharmaceuticals should be obtained from a reliable source and comply with quality standards in both donor and recipient country. The WHO Certification Scheme on the Quality of Pharmaceutical Products Moving in International Commerce (WHO 2000c) should be used.

5. No medicines that were issued to patients and then returned to a pharmacy or elsewhere, or that were given to health professionals as free samples, should be donated.

6. Upon their arrival in the recipient country, all donated pharmaceuticals should have a remaining shelf life of at least one year. An exception may be made for direct donations to specific health facilities, provided that the responsible professional at the receiving end acknowledges that he or she is aware of the shelf life, and that the quantity and remaining shelf life allow for proper administration prior to expiration. In all cases, the date of arrival and the expiry date of the medicines should be communicated to the recipient well in advance.

Presentation, packing, and labeling

7. All pharmaceuticals should be labeled in a language that is easily understood by health professionals in the recipient country; the label on each individual container should contain at least the international nonproprietary name (INN, or generic name), batch number, dosage form, strength, name of manufacturer, quantity in the container, storage conditions, and expiry date.

8. As much as possible, donated pharmaceuticals should be presented in larger-quantity units and hospital packs.

9. All pharmaceutical donations should be packed in accordance with international shipping regulations, and be accompanied by a detailed packing list that specifies the contents of each numbered carton by INN, dosage form, quantity, batch number, expiry date, volume, weight, and any special storage conditions. The weight per carton should not exceed 50 kilograms. Pharmaceuticals should not be mixed with other supplies in the same carton.

Information and management

10. Recipients should be informed of all pharmaceutical donations that are being considered, prepared, or actually under way.

11. In the recipient country, the declared value of a pharmaceutical donation should be based upon the wholesale price of its generic equivalent in the recipient country, or, if such information is not available,

on the wholesale world-market price for its generic equivalent.

12. Costs of international and local transport, warehousing, port clearance, and appropriate storage and handling should be paid by the donor agency, unless specifically agreed otherwise with the recipient in advance.

Source: WHO/DAP 1999.

in accordance with national treatment guidelines or common practice in the recipient country. Administratively, the pharmaceuticals should be treated as if they were procured: they must be approved for importation and use by the drug regulatory authority in the country, probably through the same simplified procedure that would apply for government tenders. They should be entered into the inventory and distributed through the existing distribution channels. If cost-sharing procedures exist, the donated pharmaceuticals should not automatically be distributed free of charge, and the donor should not insist on free distribution. A good example of a successful integration of donated pharmaceuticals into the regular pharmaceutical supply system is described in Country Study 15-3.

Special guidelines for donations of medical and laboratory equipment and supplies

The same core principles and general guidelines that apply to donating pharmaceuticals also apply to donating medical and laboratory equipment and supplies. A key factor to consider is whether the recipient truly needs the equipment and has the expertise and the means to operate and maintain it. Generally, capital equipment should not be donated in emergency situations, unless the emergency situation is expected to be prolonged.

A donation implementation plan should include the availability of trained personnel for operation and maintenance as well as support for other resources for operation (manuals, reagents, and supplies) and maintenance (technical documentation and spare parts). In addition, plans must include detailed installation and commissioning procedures. Finally, any special requirements for the equipment should be communicated to the recipient. Such requirements may include air or water cooling; electrical power; water quality; mechanical layout or radiation or acoustic shielding requirements; or specialized software needed to install, operate, or maintain the equipment. Periodic inspection, maintenance, and calibration should be carried out. WHO offers guidelines that cover equipment and supply donations (WHO 2000b).

15.5 Implementation of a policy for pharmaceutical donations

In managing pharmaceutical donations, both recipients and donors need to act to ensure that appropriate donations are received and that good use is made of them.

Management of pharmaceutical donations by the recipient

Recipient governments must play a role in managing donations. No matter how disastrous the situation, failure to be involved may make things worse. National guidelines and administrative procedures need to be defined, and any requirements need to be specified in as much detail as possible.

Define national guidelines for pharmaceutical donations. Recipients find refusing a donation that is already under way notoriously difficult. For this reason, prevention is better than cure. The key point is that recipients should indicate to their (future) donors what kind of assistance they are likely to need and how they would like to receive it. If this information is provided in a rational and professional way, most donors appreciate it and will comply. Therefore, recipients should first formulate their own guidelines for pharmaceutical donations based on the CMC or WHO guidelines or the summary given above. These guidelines should then be officially presented to the donor community. Only after the guidelines have been presented and published can they be enforced. The preparation and implementation of the national donation guidelines should include stakeholders at all levels of the country's pharmaceutical management system to ensure that local officials are informed about the guidelines.

Define administrative procedures for pharmaceutical donations. It is not enough for recipients to adopt and publish general guidelines on the selection, quality, and presentation of donations. Administrative procedures need to be developed by recipients for defining needs, receiving donations, distributing, budgeting, and perhaps refusing or destroying some goods. Procedures need to be developed to carry out the following actions—

- Define needs
- Prioritize among requirements
- Coordinate all pharmaceutical donations
- Decide what documentation is needed when a pharmaceutical donation is being proposed, and who should receive these papers
- Establish criteria for accepting or rejecting a donation
- Coordinate reception, storage, and distribution of donated pharmaceuticals
- Agree on whether the donor or the recipient will pay for transportation, warehousing, port clearing, and similar costs before the donation shipment arrives
- Agree on how donations are to be valued in budget and expenditure records
- Agree on charging for donated pharmaceuticals in the context of a public user-fee program
- Deal with donated pharmaceuticals not registered or included in the national essential medicines list in the country
- Supervise the distribution of donated medicines and supplies to prevent them from being diverted for export, for commercial sale, or to illicit channels
- Dispose of worthless donations

Specify the needs for donated pharmaceuticals. Recipients must also provide donors with as much specific information on medicine needs as possible. This requirement puts the onus on the recipient to prepare requests carefully, indicating quantities required and prioritizing the items. The more information that is given, the better. Openness about donations that are already in the pipeline, or anticipated, is helpful to donors. It is always greatly appreciated and pays off in the long term. Recipients are entitled to the same openness from donors with regard to pharmaceutical donations that are in the pipeline.

Good practices for donors

Donors should always respect the four core principles listed in section 15.4. Donors should also respect the guidelines issued by the recipients and respond to the priority needs they have indicated. Donor-driven donations should always be discouraged, particularly donations that are initiated by international pharmaceutical companies to obtain tax advantages or donations of returned medicines or samples.

Country Study 15-3
Integrating pharmaceutical donations into the Mongolian supply system

After the collapse of the former Soviet Union, Mongolia became one of the countries where a large proportion of medicine consumption is covered by pharmaceutical donations. Such donations are treated as regularly procured pharmaceuticals.

Upon the arrival of a donation, all papers are sent to the Ministry of Health for clearance of the import. If the medicines are accepted, an import price is decided on by a special unit in the ministry. This price is normally equal to the last tender price for the same product or a price taken from Management Sciences for Health's *International Drug Price Indicator Guide*. Many donors are valuing their donations at a much higher price—for example, retail price in the donor country—but this price is not accepted as a reference. If a product that is not on the Mongolian essential medicines list is accepted, it is given a price equivalent to that for a similar medicine on the list, irrespective of the price in the donor country.

The value of the pharmaceutical consignment is entered into the accounts of Mongol Emimpex, the state wholesaler. Then a selling price is set for each medicine by adding a 15 percent markup for the wholesaler and 23 percent for the pharmacist. These markups cover all expenses for control and distribution. The (assigned) import value is kept on a separate account and transferred to a fund controlled by the Ministry of Health for future pharmaceutical procurement.

The main benefit of this system is that it is sustainable and not destructive to the existing pharmaceutical supply system. In many other countries, uncontrolled sales of donated pharmaceuticals are well known to take place, and the money is pocketed by health personnel. In Mongolia, the system is completely transparent. All pharmaceuticals coming into the country are for sale, and the donors are assured that their import value goes back to the revolving fund.

The only drawback of the system is that even the neediest customers—patients or health institutions—have to pay for donated pharmaceuticals, and they may not be able to do so. However, the case would be the same with normal pharmaceutical procurement and has to be solved by health insurance systems or specific government support to the needy.

Source: WHO/DAP 1999.

DONATIONS CAN THEMSELVES BE A DISASTER AREA

The public at large in the donor country is usually not aware of common problems with pharmaceutical donations. The government should therefore make some effort to create more public awareness of donors' responsibilities. The best moment for this publicity is probably at the time of the public appeal through the media, when the government is requesting funds.

At the country level, would-be donors are usually counseled to choose a "lead donor" among themselves to coordinate their actions and sometimes also to act as a central contact point in discussions with the recipient government. Some organizations act as coordinators/consolidators for international pharmaceutical donations. For example, the German association of research-based pharmaceutical companies matches requests from ministries of health and international relief agencies with donations from German pharmaceutical companies to maximize the usefulness and efficiency during emergency situations.

As previously mentioned, the recipient country should supply as much information as possible on requested and approved donations. But the donors themselves should also inform the recipient well in advance and in detail about what donations are coming, and when. This information will greatly assist the coordinating body in the recipient country in planning for the proper reception of the donations and in identifying the need for additional supplies. Although the landscape of pharmaceutical donations is complex, assessments have shown that, when handled with care, the donation process can help satisfy local medical needs (Reich 1999).

15.6 Donations as part of public-private partnerships

Although the focus of pharmaceutical and medical supply donations is on cases of disaster or other emergency, a number of public-private partnerships are built on using existing products to address specific health conditions. Examples of such programs include the albendazole donation program to fight lymphatic filariasis and the Zithromax program to prevent blindness from trachoma. The Axios Foundation administers such programs for pharmaceutical companies, providing technical assistance to facilities in least-developed countries (see, for example, http://www.accesstotreatment.org and http://www.pmtctdonations.org). Although pharmaceutical companies generally sponsor donation partnerships to help get a particular medicine to those who need it, the partnerships are also part of the companies' goal to publicize social responsibility through philanthropy.

Pharmaceutical companies have spent millions of dollars on donations, and although countries can certainly benefit from the additional resources for targeted programs, the partnerships are not trouble-free. For example, costs are associated with pharmaceutical donation programs, such as distribution, storage, and training health workers. The public sector may be expected to handle those costs, possibly at the expense of other health programs, including the diversion of human resources. In addition, a partnership that targets only a specific country or commits to a specific time period may be depriving other needy countries or patients who will not have access to the medicines after the partnership commitment is completed. Product-based donation programs are generally difficult to sustain without an open-ended commitment or a commitment to eradicate a containable disease, and such programs often fill only a small part of the actual need.

Merck's Mectizan program operates in all countries where onchocerciasis is endemic and where filariasis is co-endemic and is supplying the medicine until the diseases are eradicated. Because onchocerciasis is limited in geography, has a simple treatment protocol, and can be eradicated, an open-ended donation program is feasible. On the other hand, most disease-specific initiatives target only select countries where the disease is endemic and usually commit to a limited initial time frame (Buse and Walt 2000b).

The Malarone donation program in Kenya is an example of a public-private partnership undermined by dissatisfaction among stakeholders about how well their individual interests were represented. Eventually, the partners clashed over accountability and ownership of the program (Shretta et al. 2001). Furthermore, incorporating the donated Malarone into the public health treatment guidelines and national pharmaceutical policy caused confusion and conflict. Ultimately, there was concern that the failure of the Malarone donation program could discourage other corporate philanthropy and taint the view of public-private partnerships.

When entering into public-private health programs based on pharmaceutical donations, recipient countries must be fully involved with the planning and implementation of the program (Buse and Walt 2000a), and the donor organizations should follow the core principles of donating pharmaceuticals or medical supplies. ∎

References and further readings

★ = Key readings.

Autier, P., R. Govindaraj, R. Gray, R. Lakshminarayanan, H. G. Nassery, and G. Schmets. 2002. *Drug Donations in Post-Emergency Situations.* Washington, D.C.: World Bank.

Berckmans, P., and P. Autier. 1997. Inappropriate Drug-Donation Practices in Bosnia and Herzegovina, 1992 to 1996 [letter]. *New England Journal of Medicine* 337(25):1842–5.

Buse, K., and G. Walt. 2000a. Global Public-Private Partnerships: Part II—What Are the Health Issues for Global Governance? *Bulletin of the World Health Organization* 78(5):699–709.

———. 2000b. Global Public-Private Partnerships: Part I—A New Development in Health? *Bulletin of the World Health Organization* 78(4):549–61.

Chase, M., and P. Barta. 2005. "Antibiotics without Patients: Drug Shipment's Long Road to Treating Tsunami Victims Illustrates Obstacles to Aid." *Wall Street Journal,* February 2, p. B1.

Christie, F., and J. Hanlon. 2001. *Mozambique and the Great Flood of 2000,* p. 95. Bloomington, Ind.: The International African Institute and Indiana University Press.

Ciment, J. 1999. Study Finds That Most Drug Donations to Developing Countries Are Appropriate. *BMJ* 319:942.

Ette, E. I. 2004. Conscience, the Law, and Donation of Expired Drugs. *Annals of Pharmacotherapy* 38:1310–3.

Hechmann, R., and A. Bunde-Birouste. 2007. Drug Donations in Emergencies: The Sri Lankan Post-Tsunami Experience. *Journal of Humanitarian Assistance.* <http://sites.tufts.edu/jha/archives/54>

Hogerzeil, H. V., M. R. Couper, and R. Gray. 1997. Guidelines for Drug Donations. *BMJ* 314:737.

Mason, P. 2005. Tsunami Relief: Same Mistakes Repeated. *Pharmaceutical Journal* 274(7335):178.

MSH (Management Sciences for Health). *International Drug Price Indicator Guide.* Cambridge, Mass.: MSH. (Updated annually.) <http://erc.msh.org>

PAHO/WHO (Pan American Health Organization/World Health Organization). 2010a. Emergency Operations Center Situation Report #21: Haiti Earthquake. Washington, D.C.: PAHO. <http://new.paho.org/disasters/index.php?option=com_docman&task=doc_download&gid=767&Itemid=>

———. 2010b. Promess Warehouse: Matching the World's Medical Donations to Haiti's Needs. Washington, D.C.: PAHO. <http://new.paho.org/hq/index.php?option=com_content&task=view&id=2412&Itemid=1926>

Pinheiro, C. P. 2008. Drug Donations: What Lies Beneath. *Bulletin of the World Health Organization* 86 (8): 580–1. <http://www.who.int/bulletin/volumes/86/8/07-048546.pdf>

PQMD (Partnership for Quality Medical Donations). "Seven Key Components in the Comprehensive Management of Medical Product Donations." <http://www.pqmd.org>

PSFCI (Pharmaciens Sans Frontières Comité International). 2005. *Study on Drug Donations in the Province of Aceh in Indonesia: Synthesis.* Clermont-Ferrand, France: PSF-CI. <http://www.acfid.asn.au/what-we-do/docs_what-we-do/docs_humanitarian-and-emergencies/docs_tsunami/drugdonationsaceh.pdf>

Purvis, A. 1996. "The Goodwill Pill Mess." *Time,* April 29.

Reich, M. R., ed. 1999. *An Assessment of US Pharmaceutical Donations: Players, Processes, and Products.* Cambridge, Mass.: Harvard School of Public Health. <http://www.hsph.harvard.edu/faculty/reich/donations>

Shretta, R., G. Walt, R. Brugha, and R. W. Snow. 2001. A Political Analysis of Corporate Drug Donations: The Example of Malarone® in Kenya. *Health Policy and Planning* 16(2):161–70.

Snell, B. 2001. Inappropriate Drug Donations: The Need for Reforms. *Lancet* 358:578–80.

Stritof, M., and B. Vrhovac. 1997. *Report on the Receipt and Storage of Donations and Evaluation of Drug Distribution during and after Croatian Patriotic War from August 12th, 1991, to August 12th, 1996.* Zagreb: Center for the Receipt and Distribution of Drugs and Medical Supplies, Croatian Ministry of Health and State Institute of Health Insurance, Zagreb University Hospital.

Surian, A. 2000. "Drug Donations and Awareness Raising." *Drug Donations.* <http://www.drugdonations.org/eng/eng_awareness.html>

ASSESSMENT GUIDE

Indicators of policy

- Is there a national policy on donations of pharmaceuticals and medical and laboratory equipment and supplies?
- What are the differences between the national policy and the WHO policy on pharmaceutical donations?
- Is there a set of administrative procedures for managing pharmaceutical donations?
- Do pharmaceutical donations comply with the national list of essential medicines?
- Does the ministry of health have control over which medicines and supplies will be accepted?

Extent of pharmaceutical donations

- What is the value of international aid received for pharmaceuticals (cash and in-kind donations) compared with the value of the public pharmaceutical budget spent?

Implementing pharmaceutical donations

- Who coordinates all pharmaceutical donations?
- Which documents are needed when a donation is planned; who should receive them?
- What are the criteria for accepting or rejecting a donation; who makes the final decision?
- What procedure is used when donations do not follow the guidelines?
- Who coordinates reception, storage, and distribution of the donated pharmaceuticals?
- How are donations valued and entered into the budget/expenditure records?

- How will inappropriate donations be disposed of?

Problems with pharmaceutical donations

- What are the main problems with pharmaceutical donations?

Needs assessment for donors in an emergency

- What is the nature of the event, its effects, expected duration, expected amount of time the population will be displaced or affected?
- What are the demographics and socioeconomic status of affected populations?
- What is the status of the existing health care infrastructure and availability of transportation to existing health care sites?
- Are human resources available to take responsibility for and to appropriately dispense prescription medication?
- What are the recipients' customary modes of treating diseases?
- What are the affected area's location, accessibility, climatic conditions, and security status?
- What are the rules and regulations of local recipient governments?
- Are contacts in place for key ministry of health or other country personnel?
- How receptive are local authorities to foreign humanitarian operations in their country?

Sources: Hogerzeil et al. 1997; PQMD 2002.

Wemos Foundation. 2000. *Guide for Improving the Quality of Drug Donations for Individuals and Organisations That Want to Donate Pharmaceutical Materials.* Amsterdam: Wemos Foundation. <http://www.drugdonations.org/eng/eng_gooddonationpractice.html>

WHO (World Health Organization). 2006a. *The Interagency Emergency Health Kit 2006.* Geneva: WHO. <http://whqlibdoc.who.int/hq/2006/WHO_PSM_PAR_2006.4_eng.pdf>

———. 2006b. Notes for the Media: WHO Advises on the Right Drug Donations for Lebanon. <http://www.who.int/mediacentre/news/notes/2006/np19/en/>

———. 2000a. *First-Year Experiences with the Interagency Guidelines for Drug Donations.* Geneva: WHO.

———. 2000b. *Guidelines for Healthcare Equipment Donations.* Geneva: WHO. <http://www.who.int/medical_devices/publications/en/Donation_Guidelines.pdf>

———. 2000c. *WHO Certification Scheme on the Quality of Pharmaceutical Products Moving in International Commerce.* Geneva: WHO.

———. 1994. *Medical Supplies Donor Guidelines for WHO Humanitarian Assistance for Former Yugoslavia.* Zagreb, Yugoslavia: WHO.

———. 1999. *WHO Interagency Guidelines on Safe Disposal of Unwanted Pharmaceuticals in and after Emergencies.* Geneva: WHO. <http://whqlibdoc.who.int/hq/1999/WHO_EDM_PAR_99.2.pdf>

★ WHO/DAP (World Health Organization/Department of Essential Drugs and Other Medicines). 1999. *Guidelines for Drug Donations.* 2nd ed. Geneva: WHO.

WHO/EPN (World Health Organization/Ecumenical Pharmaceutical Network). 2006. *Multi-Country Study of Medicine Supply and Distribution Activities of Faith-Based Organizations in Sub-Saharan African Countries.* Geneva: WHO.

World Bank. 1999. *Project Appraisal Document on a Proposed Loan in the Amount of US$29.0 Million to the Republic of Croatia for a Health System Project.* Washington, D.C.: World Bank.

Part I: Policy and economic issues   Part II: Pharmaceutical management   Part III: Management support systems

Selection
  16 Managing medicine selection
  17 Treatment guidelines and formulary manuals
Procurement
Distribution
Use

CHAPTER 16

Managing medicine selection

SUMMARY

The rationale for selecting a limited number of essential medicines is that it may lead to better supply, more rational use, and lower costs. Essential medicines are those that are deemed to satisfy the health care needs of the majority of the population and that should be available in the appropriate dosage forms and strengths at all times. Because selection of medicines has a considerable impact on quality of care and cost of treatment, it is one of the most cost-effective areas for intervention.

A list of essential medicines may be selected for use in one or more health facilities or for the public sector as a whole. In the latter case, the list usually indicates the level of the health care system where each medicine may be used. It can also be considered a supply list. A formulary system is part of the medicine selection process. The system includes a formulary list, which is ideally based on an essential medicines list, and a formulary manual, which contains summary information on each medication on the formulary list. Standard treatment guidelines are systematically developed statements that assist prescribers in deciding on appropriate treatments for specific clinical problems. Whereas a formulary manual is medicine centered, treatment guidelines are disease centered, presenting treatment alternatives and recommending a treatment of first choice.

The process of selecting essential medicines begins with defining a list of common diseases for each level of health care. The treatment of first choice for each health problem is the basis for the list of essential medicines, the national formulary system, and the treatment guidelines. The supply system should then supply the medicines that have been selected, based on this series of steps.

Essential medicines should be selected on the basis of (1) relevance to the pattern of prevalent diseases, (2) proven efficacy and safety, (3) adequate scientific data and evidence of performance in a variety of settings, (4) adequate quality, (5) favorable cost-benefit ratio, (6) desirable pharmacokinetic properties, (7) possibilities for local manufacture, and (8) availability as single compounds. The drugs should be identified by the International Nonproprietary Name (INN), sometimes referred to as the generic name.

General acceptance of an essential medicines list can be promoted by wide consultation with senior specialists and experts, including professional organizations and academic institutions, on the list's development and use. An open and transparent system of regular updates is an absolute prerequisite for maintaining the authority and acceptance of an essential medicines list or formulary list. The essential medicines concept can be applied in any country, in the public and private sectors, and in rural areas as well as at referral hospitals.

16.1 Introduction

Pharmaceuticals may constitute as much as 40 percent of the health care budget in developing countries, yet large portions of the population may lack access to even the most essential medicines. The limited funds available are frequently spent on ineffective, unnecessary, or even dangerous medications.

As much as 70 percent of pharmaceuticals on the world market are duplicative or nonessential. Many are minor variations of a prototype drug product and offer no therapeutic advantage over other medicines that are already available. Some are medications that show high toxicity relative to their therapeutic benefit. In some cases, new medicines are released without sufficient information on efficacy or toxicity. Finally, new products often are for therapeutic indications not relevant to the basic needs of the population. In all of these cases, the newer medicines are nearly always more expensive than existing medicines.

With so many different pharmaceutical products available, prescribers often find it impossible to keep their knowledge up-to-date and to compare alternatives. In addition, the variety of available products may contribute to inconsistent prescribing within the same health care system or even in the health facility. With regard to procurement, purchasing power is significantly lessened by the large number of duplicative and nonessential pharmaceutical products on the market.

In short, pharmaceuticals can provide great benefits, but their cost is substantial. The selection of medicines has a considerable impact on the quality of care and the cost of treatment, and it is therefore one of the areas where intervention is most cost-effective.

16.2 Practical implications of the essential medicines concept

The World Health Organization (WHO) has defined essential medicines as those that satisfy the needs of the majority of the population and therefore should be available at all times. The rationale for the selection and use of a limited number of essential medicines is that it leads to an improved supply of medicines, more rational prescribing, and lower costs; in fact, the appropriate use of essential medicines is one of the most cost-effective strategies a country can enact.

The essential medicines concept is a global concept that can be applied in any country, in the private and public sectors, in referral hospitals as well as primary health care units, and in both urban and rural areas. However, the decision about exactly which medicines should be considered as essential should be a national-level responsibility. By 2007, 86 percent of countries had national essential medicines lists, of which at least 69 percent had been updated in the previous five years. Some have state or provincial lists as well (Kathleen Holloway, personal communication, March 2010).

Under optimal circumstances, the registration of medicines for the private and public sectors should be based on an evaluation of efficacy, safety, and quality. In some countries, cost and need are also criteria for medicine registration. In such cases, the selection of essential medicines takes place during medicine evaluation, approval, and registration and is therefore applicable to both the public and private sectors.

More commonly, the selection and use of essential medicines are limited to public-sector health facilities. However, many private-sector facilities and health insurance systems have limited formulary lists, which can serve the same function. For each level of health care in the public sector, a limited list of essential medicines is prepared as the basis for supplying pharmaceuticals, for prescribing in the public sector, and for training of health workers—which is why such lists should be closely related to standard treatment guidelines for clinical health care practice. This correlation is especially relevant for medical and paramedical training institutions and teaching hospitals, because they have an important influence on the prescribers of the future.

There are many reasons to support the use of a limited essential medicines list. First, fairness dictates that basic health services be accessible to everyone before more expensive services are made available to a small, usually urban proportion of the population.

Second, no public-sector or health insurance system can afford to supply or reimburse all medicines that are available on the market. Therefore, essential medicines lists guide not only the procurement and supply of medicines in the public sector, but also schemes that reimburse medicine costs as well as what medicines it makes sense for local manufacturers to produce. Because the availability of pharmaceuticals in the public sector is erratic in many countries, a regular supply of most products on the essential medicines list would result in a real improvement in public health and would increase the public's confidence in the health care system. Many international organizations, including the United Nations Children's Fund (UNICEF) and international nonprofit supply agencies, have adopted the essential medicines concept for their supply systems.

Third, when the limited list of essential medicines represents prescribers' consensus on pharmaceutical treatments of first choice, its use may improve the quality of care by ensuring that patients receive the treatment of choice as well as similar treatment from different providers. It also allows prescribers to become more familiar with a smaller number of medicines. This restricted number of possibilities contributes to improved recognition of actual benefits and limitations of specific medicine therapy, as well as to the detection and prevention of adverse drug reactions.

Fourth, improved effectiveness and efficiency in patient treatment reduce health care costs. Therefore, lack of funds in developing countries is not the only reason to limit treatment selection to essential medicines, nor does such a policy necessarily compromise quality of care. In fact, the essential medicines concept is increasingly being accepted as a universal tool to promote both quality of care and cost control.

Fifth, for public-sector supply programs, advantages exist in concentrating procurement and logistics efforts on a limited number of medicines, including reduction in the number of different products that must be stocked, distributed, and monitored. Essential medicines are usually available from multiple suppliers. With increased competition, more favorable prices can be negotiated. In addition, limiting the number of different medicines used to treat a particular clinical problem means larger quantities of the selected medicine will be needed, creating potential opportunities to achieve economies of scale. Ensuring the quality of a small number of pharmaceutical products is easier, which is another reason why many national pharmaceutical programs base their medicine donation policies on the national essential medicines list.

Finally, the selection of a limited number of essential medicines facilitates efforts to provide drug information and education, both of which advance rational prescribing and use. Objective drug information and training materials are so scarce in most developing countries that their provision is considered very beneficial by physicians and other health care workers. Thus, although the number of pharmaceutical products for public health use may be limited by an essential medicines list, the practical availability of medicines and corresponding drug information and training materials may be increased. Patient education and efforts to promote proper use of medicines by patients can also be enhanced by focusing on these medicines.

The potential advantages of using a limited list of essential medicines are summarized in Table 16-1. These advantages do not, however, follow automatically. The essential medicines list is only a starting point, not an end in itself. For

Table 16-1   Advantages of a limited list of essential medicines

Major objective	Challenge
Supply	• Easier procurement, storage, and distribution • Lower stocks • Better quality assurance • Easier dispensing
Prescribing	• Training more focused and therefore simpler • More experience with fewer medicines • Nonavailability of irrational treatment alternatives • Reduction of antimicrobial resistance • Focused drug information • Better recognition of adverse drug reactions
Cost	• Lower prices, more competition
Patient use	• Focused education efforts • Reduced confusion and increased adherence to treatment • Improved medicine availability

countries to realize its advantages, the selection of essential medicines must be followed by other actions outlined in this book, including the promotion of the essential medicines list by use of a formulary manual and standard treatment guidelines, improvements in procurement and distribution, and efforts to promote rational medicine use.

With the continuing impact of infectious diseases such as malaria, tuberculosis, and HIV/AIDS, as well as widespread increases in antimicrobial resistance, the application of the essential medicines concept is more appropriate than ever. In developing countries, antimicrobial resistance has resulted in the use of new and far more expensive treatments for malaria and tuberculosis, while the scale-up of treatment for HIV/AIDS is straining limited health care resources. Developed countries, too, have experienced large increases in pharmaceutical expenditures. The use of the essential medicines concept in both developed and developing countries can promote the most efficient use of resources as well as help combat the spread of antimicrobial resistance.

16.3 Selection criteria

Although there are many different settings in which a national list of essential medicines can be used, the criteria for selection are basically the same in each. For a national essential medicines list to be credible and widely accepted, the criteria must be defined and published. The final selection criteria should be based on thorough discussions and acceptance by a multidisciplinary committee of experts. Specialists within the selection committee can interpret data and evaluate the safety of medicines in their areas of expertise.

Box 16-1 summarizes the criteria used by the WHO Expert Committee on the Selection and Use of Essential Medicines, which were the result of extensive deliberation. The WHO criteria are frequently adopted and modified to fit local requirements.

Determining the safety and efficacy of specific pharmaceutical products requires access to relevant, up-to-date, and unbiased information, such as summaries of relevant clinical guidelines, systematic literature reviews, important references, and quality assurance standards. Personal observations should not be used as justification for selecting a medication, nor should selection be based on sales figures or a medicine's popularity in the market. Sources of objective information can include a national drug information center; many useful references are available in the WHO Essential Medicines Library (http://www.who.int/medicines/publications/en). See also Section 16.8 and Chapter 34.

The choice of medicines depends on the capacity of health care staff to use them effectively. Consequently, it is important to have thorough knowledge of the extent of staff training and the availability of support facilities for each level of the health care system before deciding where individual medicines will be made available. For example, cancer medicines are expensive, have serious side effects, and require frequent laboratory monitoring. Therefore, such medicines might be limited to a few designated cancer treatment centers. In addition, selection should take into account potential staff confusion and medication errors that could be caused by including sound-alike or look-alike products and various concentrations of liquid preparations for the same drug.

In choosing among medicines of similar safety and efficacy, the total cost of treatment should be considered. Care must be taken, however, in making the comparison. For example, ampicillin may be cheaper than amoxicilline in a tablet-to-tablet comparison but more expensive in a course-of-therapy comparison, because ampicillin must be taken more often. Because pharmaceutical costs vary from country to country, cost comparisons should be country-specific.

Decision making becomes more complicated when more expensive medicines are also more effective, as in the case of certain antibacterial, antitubercular, or antimalarial medicines for resistant organisms. In such cases, the cost of cure may actually be lower for medicines that are more expensive, based on a tablet-to-tablet (dose-to-dose) comparison. Chapters 10 and 17 discuss how cost-effectiveness analysis can guide such decisions.

Thus, although all selection criteria may appear reasonable and almost self-evident, considerable room exists for discussion about the relative merits of individual medicines. Before such a discussion occurs, members of the selection committee should review, discuss, and come to a common understanding of the selection criteria and the quality of the evidence to support the choices.

16.4 Use of International Nonproprietary (generic) Names

Each drug product on the market has a chemical name (for example, 6-{D(-)-, a-amino-a-phenylacetamido}-penicillinic acid) and an International Nonproprietary Name, or generic name (ampicillin). The INN is the medicine's official name, regardless of what company or organization manufactures or markets it. A proprietary, commercial, trade, or brand name is chosen by the manufacturer to facilitate recognition and association of the product with a particular firm for marketing purposes. For most common medicines, there are several branded products that all contain the same active ingredient and therefore share the same INN.

INNs are intended for use in pharmacopoeias, labeling, product information, advertising and other promotional material, pharmaceutical regulation, and as a basis for generic product names. INNs are assigned through WHO, following a well-established procedure. Official INN listings are in Latin, English, French, Spanish, and Russian. Their use is normally required by national or, as in the case of the European Union, international legislation. As a result of ongoing collaboration, national names such as British Approved Names (BAN), Japanese Adopted Names (JAN), and U.S.-Accepted Names (USAN) are usually the same as the INN. WHO offers guidance on the use of INNs (see http://www.who.int/medicines/services/inn/en).

The use of generic names for pharmaceutical purchasing as well as prescribing carries considerations of clarity, price, and quality. Proponents of generic drug purchasing and prescribing point out that—

- Generic names are more informative than brand names and facilitate the purchase of products from multiple suppliers, whether as brand-name or generic products.
- Generic drug products are often cheaper than products sold by brand name.
- Generic prescribing facilitates product substitution, whenever appropriate.

With regard to clarity, the generic name helps identify the class of medication. The common stem of the INN usually indicates a "family" of drugs. For example, the names of all benzodiazepines end with -zepam (diazepam, temazepam, nitrazepam), and beta-blockers share the stem -olol

---

Box 16-1
WHO criteria for selection of essential medicines

Essential medicines are those that satisfy the health care needs of the majority of the population; they should therefore be available at all times in adequate amounts and in the appropriate dosage forms.

The choice of such medicines depends on many factors, such as the pattern of prevalent diseases; treatment facilities; the training and experience of available personnel; financial resources; and genetic, demographic, and environmental factors.

Only medicines for which sound, adequate data on efficacy and safety are available from clinical studies, and for which evidence of performance in general use in a variety of medical settings has been obtained, should be selected.

Each selected medicine must be available in a form in which adequate quality, including bioavailability, can be ensured; its stability under the anticipated conditions of storage and use must be established.

When two or more medicines appear to be similar in the above respects, the choice between them should be made on the basis of a careful evaluation of their relative efficacy, safety, quality, price, and availability.

In cost comparisons between medicines, the cost of the total treatment, not only the unit cost of the medicine, must be considered. The cost-benefit ratio is a major consideration in the choice of some medicines for the list. In some cases, the choice may also be influenced by other factors, such as pharmacokinetic properties, or by local considerations, such as the availability of facilities for manufacture or storage. In 2002, WHO began to view and evaluate affordability as a consequence of a selection rather than as a precondition for selection; for example, antiretroviral medicines for HIV/AIDS are now included in the WHO Model List, although they are expensive. Including these medicines on the list implies that they should become affordable enough for any patient to have them.

Most essential medicines should be formulated as single compounds. Fixed-ratio combination products are acceptable only when the dosage of each ingredient meets the requirements of a defined population group and when the combination has a proven advantage over single compounds administered separately in terms of therapeutic effect, safety, or patient adherence to treatment.

Source: WHO 2007.

Table 16-2   Example of level-of-use categories, Ethiopia Essential Drugs List, fifth edition, 2007

Therapeutic class and item description in national list		Sublists by level of care					
		Zonal hospital	District hospital	Health station	Community pharmacy	Drug shop	Rural drug vendor
OP.300 Anti-infectives, ophthalmic							
OP.301 Antibacterials							
Chloramphenicol	Ointment, 1%, 5% Solution, 0.4%, 0.5%, 1%, 5%	×	×	×	×	×	×
Erythromycin	Ointment, 0.5%	×			×	×	
Gentamicin	Solution, 0.3%	×			×	×	
Neomycin sulfate	Ointment, 0.5%, 2%	×			×	×	
Oxytetracycline hydrochloride	Ointment, 0.5%	×	×	×	×	×	
Polymixin B+ bacitracin	Ointment, 100,000 units + 500,000 units	×			×		
Rifamycin	Solution, 1%	×			×		
Silver nitrate	Solution, 1%	×	×	×	×	×	
Tetracycline	Ointment, 1% Solution, 1%	×	×	×	×	×	×
Tobramycin	Solution, 0.3%	×			×		

Source: Drug Administration and Control Authority of Ethiopia, 2007.

(propranolol, atenolol, metoprolol). In addition, students and prescribers should find learning one generic name rather than a host of different brand names much easier. Nevertheless, many students initially may find memorizing a brand name easier, because such names are usually designed to sound attractive. The confusion comes later, when the students are confronted with many different names for the same medicine.

With regard to price, the patents on many common medicines have expired, allowing various manufacturers to produce and market equivalent products by the medicines' generic names. These generic products are usually sold at a lower price than that of branded equivalents. Therefore, the use of the generic name introduces elements of price competition. If a prescription is written using the generic name of the medicine, the pharmacist may dispense an equivalent product with a price that is more attractive to the consumer but that also meets quality standards. The concept of generic substitution is accepted in an increasing number of countries: even if the prescription is made under a brand name, the pharmacist may substitute a generic equivalent unless the prescriber specifically indicates that this should not be done, by writing "do not substitute" on the prescription. This measure may lead to large savings in pharmaceutical costs.

Opponents to generic prescribing argue that the quality of generic medicines is inferior to that of brand-name products. Quality control and naming of medicines are completely separate issues. Generic medicines from reliable suppliers are as safe, effective, and high quality as medicines with well-known brand names. At the same time, brand-name medicines from a manufacturer with inadequate procedures for quality control can be of poor quality, despite the brand name. Also, although any medicine can be counterfeited, there are more incentives for counterfeiting brand-name medicines. In countries with strong drug regulatory systems, drug products sold by generic name have the same low rate of recall as brand-name products. Some pharmaceutical companies also sell their branded products under the generic name, for a much lower price.

Bioequivalence is often misused as an argument against the use of generic equivalents. For many medicines, the variation in bioavailability among individual patients is much larger than the variation among products of different manufacturers. In fact, bioavailability is clinically relevant for only a relatively small number of medicines. (Medicine quality and bioequivalence are discussed in Chapter 19.)

16.5 Essential medicines lists in context

An essential medicines list names the medicines considered optimal treatment choices to satisfy the health care needs of a given population. In its simplest form, it is used for one health facility (for example, a hospital) or for a group of health facilities to indicate which medicines should be procured and prescribed. For practical purposes, the lists can be considered supply lists, defining the range of medicines for the different levels of care and indicating dosage form and, sometimes, pack size and other specifications. A sample page of a list, organized by levels of use, is reproduced in Table 16-2.

Lists of registered medicines

Adoption of a national list of essential medicines, usually limited to the public sector, does not necessarily mean that no other medicines are available in the private sector. In many countries, the marketing of pharmaceutical products requires prior evaluation, approval, and licensing by the national drug regulatory authority. The criteria for approval and licensing include efficacy, safety, and quality, but some countries also consider cost and need. Registration of medicines is discussed in greater detail in Chapter 6. The list of registered medicines includes all drug products that have been licensed.

The number of drug products that are licensed may be many times greater than the number of drug products on the essential medicines list, for two reasons. First, equivalent drug products produced by different manufacturers are registered separately (the product is registered, not the active substance). Second, medicines may not be considered essential for use in the public sector, yet their efficacy, safety, and quality are such that they can be available in the private market. For example, in the United Kingdom, the list of medicines available free of charge through the National Health Service contains several laxatives; if a particular patient wants another brand, it is available for sale but without reimbursement. Figure 16-1 illustrates the relationship between the list of essential medicines and the list of registered medicines.

Formulary manuals

The term *formulary* can be confusing. It is useful to distinguish between the formulary list as a selection tool, the formulary manual as a source of medicine information, and the formulary system as a pharmaceutical management process.

A *formulary list* is a list of pharmaceutical products approved for use in a specific health care setting. It may be a national formulary list, a provincial list, a hospital list, or a list indicating products reimbursed by a health insurance program. In the public sector of most developing countries, the formulary list is synonymous with essential medicines list.

A *formulary manual* contains summary drug information. It is not a full textbook, nor does it usually cover all medicines on the market. Instead, it is a handy reference that contains selected information that is relevant to the prescriber, dispenser, nurse, or other health worker. It commonly includes the generic name of a medicine, indications for use, dosage schedules, contraindications, side effects, and important information that should be given to the patient. A formulary manual is drug centered—it is based

Figure 16-1   The essential medicines target

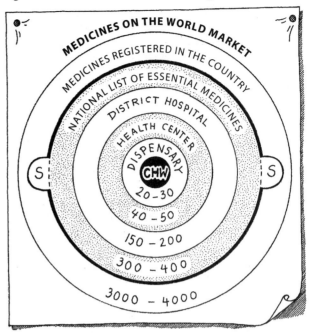

Notes: S = specialist medicines available to special hospitals and departments in the public sector; CHW = community health worker, who typically has an essential medicines list of 12 to 18 items.

on monographs for individual drugs or therapeutic groups. Formularies may or may not contain evaluative statements or comparisons of medicines. Some national formularies include options for therapeutic substitution; for example, in Panama the official medicines list includes three interchangeable drugs—astemizol, cetirizine hydrochloride, and loratadine—under the category of "nonsedating antihistamines." Some formularies include comparative price information, which can help guide prescribing decisions.

A *national formulary manual* is based on the national list of essential medicines. The *British National Formulary* includes most of the medicines registered for use in the United Kingdom, and even though medicine selection is not as limited there as in developing countries, the beginning of each section in the manual contains general evaluative statements, and the formulary indicates the medicines whose costs are not reimbursed through the National Health Service. The development of a formulary manual is discussed in Chapter 17.

Finally, the term *formulary system* is used in some settings to encompass the whole system for developing, updating, and promoting the formulary (essential medicines) list. A fully developed formulary system usually includes, in addition to the formulary list and formulary manual, regular newsletters or bulletins, guidelines for the use of nonformulary medicines, and methods for evaluating the need for changes in the formulary list or manual. The formulary system in the hospital setting is discussed in Chapter 45.

Treatment guidelines

Treatment guidelines (standard treatment guidelines [STGs], treatment protocols, clinical guidelines) are systematically developed statements that assist prescribers in deciding on appropriate treatments for specific clinical problems. These guidelines usually reflect the consensus on the optimal treatment options within a health facility or health system. The information is disease centered, emphasizing the common diseases and complaints and the various treatment alternatives. Information on medicines is usually limited to strength, dosage, and duration. Most guidelines indicate a treatment of first choice. Some include diagnostic criteria for starting the treatment or for choosing among treatment alternatives. The development of treatment guidelines is discussed in Chapter 17.

The key difference between a formulary manual and treatment guidelines is that the former is drug centered, concentrating on drug information and usually not providing comparisons of different medicines, whereas the latter are disease centered, listing treatment alternatives and indicating treatments of choice.

16.6 Approaches to developing essential medicines lists, formularies, and treatment guidelines

Essential medicines lists, formularies, and treatment guidelines are interdependent and should be developed in a systematic way (see Figure 16-2). The most logical approach is based on the needs of patients and on the job descriptions of health workers. The first step is to prepare a list of common health problems. A first-choice treatment for each health problem on the list may be limited to one or more medicines or to various forms of nondrug treatment. This choice of treatment can be the basis for two important documents: the list of essential medicines for the specific level of care, which is a direct result of the selection; and a set of treatment guidelines for that level of care, which requires additional clinical information (diagnostic signs and symptoms and treatment algorithms).

This approach works best for the primary health care level. The number of diseases and conditions may be too many or too complex to be practical for a hospital, although the approach could be applied at the departmental level and is commonly used at the specialist level. An example of the latter is cancer treatment, in which following an STG provides a way of evaluating outcomes and improving treatment.

In practice, some sort of medicines list is already available in most settings and can serve as a starting point. This list is critically reviewed by therapeutic group, and, as in the WHO Model List of Essential Medicines, first-choice medi-

cines and alternative or complementary medicines may be indicated.

The lists of essential medicines for each level of care should be combined into one national list of essential medicines. This list is the basis for developing the national formulary system. This approach ensures that the supply of medicines, which is based on the national list of essential medicines, is consistent with the treatment guidelines in public-sector facilities and training institutions and that summary drug information is available for all medicines supplied in the public sector.

Using another approach, the list of registered medicines can be critically reviewed for selection of a much shorter national list of essential medicines. Using this shortened list, drug and therapeutics committees in individual health facilities can choose a treatment of first choice for that facility or district. Medicine selection at the facility level is especially valuable when the national list of essential medicines is too extensive to be practical for individual facilities. In addition, facility-level medicine selection ensures the maximal involvement, acceptance, and compliance of the prescribers concerned (see Country Study 16-1).

For most countries, medicine selection by committee is the preferred approach because it minimizes the opportunity for private interests to influence the decision-making process. Furthermore, the judicious selection of committee members with relevant backgrounds, previous experience, and no conflicts of interest can ensure the transparency of the decision-making process and thereby facilitate the rational selection of medicines (see Country Study 16-2).

At the national level, an officially appointed committee or regional or local officials can select essential medicines for the public sector. One advantage of national-level selection is the potential for improved efficiency and economy of central procurement; regional or local staff members should be included in the committee. In large countries, regional selection and procurement may be more appropriate.

The greatest efficiency is possible when medicine selection is coordinated with other activities in the supply process. This coordination can be achieved, in part, by including representatives from the ministry of health, the purchasing department, and regional and local health facilities, including medical and paramedical prescribers. Technical experts should include one or more clinical pharmacologists, an internist, an infectious diseases specialist, a pediatrician, a surgeon, one or more hospital and district pharmacists, a hospital director, and other specialists as needed. Representatives of disease control programs (such as malaria, tuberculosis, and HIV/AIDS programs) can be co-opted to attend certain meetings. Committee members should serve for several years with staggered terms, so that the committee retains some experienced members each year. Committee members should be known for their integrity, honesty, and dedication; ide-

Figure 16-2   Common health problems guide selection, training, supply, and medicine use

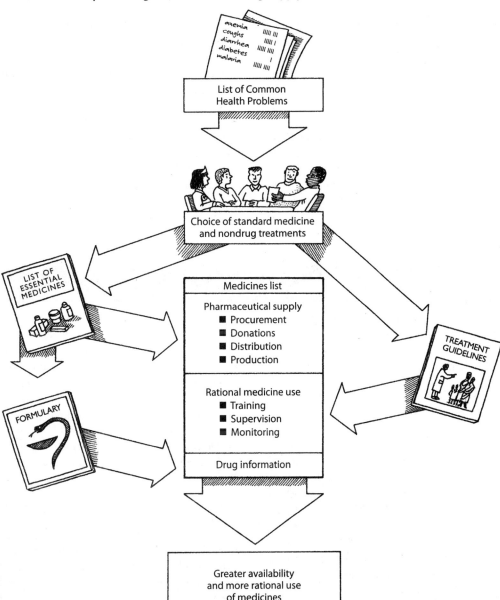

ally, they should not have relationships with any pharmaceutical manufacturer or distributor, or be closely related to any person who does.

The most practical approach to drawing up an essential medicines list for the first time is to have it prepared by one or two experts, preferably using the WHO Model List of Essential Medicines and the WHO criteria for selection (see Box 16-1). The full committee can then review the draft and finalize the list. After first publication of the national list, the committee should meet at least every two years to update it. The committee's decisions should again follow the established criteria. Using a revision form may facilitate rational

additions and deletions (Figure 16-3). It provides a mechanism for prescribers to participate constructively in the selection process, and because the form requires a certain amount of effort on the part of the petitioner, it may reduce requests for items that are not really needed.

The same basic principles apply at the hospital level. The selection of medicines should be made on the basis of the national list of essential medicines, using similar criteria. The list should be made by a hospital drug and therapeutics committee that, ideally, is convened by a clinical pharmacologist, with senior clinicians and the hospital pharmacist as members. This committee may also advise on prescribing policies and should, from time to time, review the prescribing patterns in the facility through simple prescription surveys (see Chapter 28). Such committees are now mandatory in several countries. In countries where the numbers of qualified staff members are limited, the first priority is establishing such committees in the teaching hospitals to serve as models for the rest of the country and for future generations of prescribers. Chapter 45 describes in detail medicine management in a hospital setting.

Lists of essential medicines and treatment guidelines should also be drawn up for the lower levels of health care, such as health centers and dispensaries. Paramedical workers and teaching staff such as nurse tutors should be involved in the process, which is usually coordinated at the national level.

16.7 Therapeutic classification systems

Essential medicines lists and national formularies are best organized according to therapeutic category. In addition, analyses of medicine requirements, medicine consumption, or medicine prices are often facilitated by listing medicines according to their therapeutic class. Countless therapeutic classification systems are in use throughout the world. Some, such as the British National Formulary system, are organized by target organ or disease condition (for example, eye infections). Others, such as the American Hospital Formulary Service Drug Information system, are organized by pharmacologic-therapeutic action. The Nordic ATC system combines anatomic, therapeutic, and chemical criteria to classify medicines.

Country Study 16-1
Approaches to updating essential medicines and formulary lists

Ethiopia. The first edition of Ethiopia's national essential drugs list was published in 1980, and with the establishment of the first national drug policy in 1993, the government confirmed its commitment to the essential medicines concept. The fourth edition of the list, which was revised in 2002, includes sublists appropriate for different levels of health care: health centers, which include community health stations; district hospitals; and zonal hospitals (see Table 16-2). The revised edition was initially prepared by two committees assigned by the oversight agency, Ethiopia's Drug Administration and Control Authority (DACA). The committees presented the original list at a three-day workshop that included stakeholders from many disciplines, such as representatives from academia, professional associations, research institutions, the Ministry of Health, and consumer organizations. The revised version of the list was drawn up by a technical committee designated at the workshop. DACA sees the national medicines list as the product of an ongoing process, subject to continual deletion and addition as new medicines with better risk/benefit ratios replace less effective products.

Organisation of Eastern Caribbean States.
The Organisation of Eastern Caribbean States Pharmaceutical Procurement Service (OECS/PPS) is a group purchasing service for nine small Caribbean countries. Procurement is limited primarily to the OECS/PPS Regional Formulary. Medicines are selected by the OECS/PPS Technical Advisory Subcommittee (TAC), which consists of one member appointed by each participating country (generally, the chief medi-

cal officer or a comparable ministry appointee) and the central stores managers from each country. The OECS/PPS managing director is a nonvoting member of the TAC. The formulary list is subject to continual review; in the sixth edition (2002–05), twenty-nine pharmaceutical products were removed from the list and eighty-nine were added. The sixth edition also includes a new section on managing HIV/AIDS, including the addition of antiretroviral medicines. Changes are based on the evaluation and approval of written requests (see Figure 16-3).

World Health Organization. Since publication of the first Model List of Essential Drugs in 1977, the list has been updated every two to four years. The list is updated using a systematic approach, similar to that recommended for developing STGs. An expert advisory committee consisting primarily of clinical pharmacologists and physicians evaluates the latest clinical evidence, and decisions are made through a transparent process involving several rounds of external review. A major change that occurred with the 1985 list was the introduction of complementary medicines, which allowed substitution of therapeutic equivalents. In the first fifteen years, the number of medicines on the list increased slightly, but most changes involved replacement of one preparation with a more therapeutically appropriate or cost-effective preparation. For example, amoxicilline replaced ampicillin, and doxycycline replaced tetracycline. Nevertheless, the seventeenth Essential Medicines List, published in 2011, contains more than 350 active ingredients and is divided into a core list and a complementary list.

Country Study 16-2
Updating the National Essential Medicines List of Kenya

Kenya was one of the first African countries to recognize the importance of the essential medicines concept and developed its own essential medicines list in 1981, based on the WHO model. In 1992, the Ministry of Health decided to intensify its efforts to rationalize the pharmaceutical sector. Those efforts included updating the essential medicines list, rigorously implementing the list as the basis for pharmaceutical management in the public sector, and developing clinical treatment guidelines.

It was decided early on that the review of the essential medicines list and the development of clinical guidelines should be done in tandem. Draft treatment guidelines for the most common diseases and conditions had been prepared by the Ministry of Health, in consultation with university teachers and specialists at provincial hospitals, and distributed widely for comments. Review of the essential medicines list was begun by comparing the drugs from the 1981 national list with those mentioned in the draft treatment guidelines, alongside the 1992 WHO Model List of Essential Medicines.

It was decided to hold two national workshops simultaneously at the same location, one for refining the treatment guidelines and the other for revising the list. This process facilitated interaction between the two development committees and ensured that the new essential medicines list was in keeping with national clinical practice.

The participants in the medicines list workshop were mainly government pharmacists from various departments, joined by a professor of clinical pharmacology and a clinical pharmacist from the University of Nairobi, a senior nursing officer, and the head of the Kenya Essential Drugs Programme. The group based its deliberations on the WHO criteria for the selection of essential medicines (see Box 16-1) and consulted frequently with the clinical guidelines group. Emphasis was placed on medicines required to meet the health care needs of the majority of the population.

The two workshops concluded with a final joint session in which a revised list conforming to WHO criteria was approved. This list included 195 drugs in 256 dosage forms and strengths (fewer than the 1981 version) and was divided into seven levels of care. The process that was followed resulted in a common base of understanding and commitment toward both the essential medicines list and the treatment guidelines.

The revised essential medicines list was printed in a twenty-eight-page booklet, which included background information, selection criteria, and listings by therapeutic category and level of care, as well as an alphabetical listing with store codes and packing units. This booklet was distributed to all public-sector hospitals, missions, professional associations, and local manufacturers. In the newest edition, published in 2002, the Ministry of Health combined the essential medicines list and the national standard treatment guidelines into one document.

The national drug policy adopted in September 1993 stated that the essential medicines list would be used for (1) public education and information; (2) public-sector procurement, prescribing, and dispensing; (3) paramedical and medical graduate education; (4) in-service training programs for health professionals; (5) preferential import duties and value-added taxes on drugs; (6) selective support for the local pharmaceutical industry; (7) pricing policies; and (8) controlling donations of medicines.

In the late 1980s and 1990s, the government of Kenya turned its focus to managing the HIV/AIDS epidemic. Initially its strategy was centered on behavior change and prevention, but lowered prices and increased access to antiretroviral medicines made treatment a reality for people living with HIV/AIDS in Kenya. The Ministry of Health gathered stakeholders comprising senior clinicians and pharmacists from the government, academic, and private sectors to collaborate on a standard treatment protocol for HIV/AIDS, and clinical guidelines for antiretroviral treatment were published in 2001; the second edition was published in 2002 (NASCOP 2002).

The process for establishing the most appropriate HIV/AIDS treatment regimens was based on an evaluation of clinical efficacy, cost, and the need for a second line of treatment in case of antimicrobial resistance, adverse effects, or treatment failure. The antiretrovirals established as first- and second-line treatments have been added to the Kenya Essential Medicines List.

Figure 16-3 Sample form for proposing revisions in essential medicines lists

ADDITION/DELETION/SPECIAL AUTHORIZATION FORM

√ Formulary Addition ___ Deletion
___ Request for Special Authorization

Section A
To be completed by doctor

Ciprofloxacin
Name(s) of medication (generic and brand) _____ Name of manufacturer
Desired dosage: √ Tablet ___ Capsule ___ Injection
___ Other (specify): _____
Estimated usage: √ Routine ___ Emergency ___ Clinical Evaluation
Is similar-acting medication stocked now in pharmacy? ___ Yes √ No
If yes, please explain advantages of this medication:

Ndowa N. _____ Guc-Harare
Name of requesting medical/dental officer _____ Clinic/hospital
Ndowa _____ January 16, 1998
Signature _____ Date
Forward completed form to attention of:
Chairman, National Formulary Committee

Section B
To be completed by medical supplies officer

Central Medical Stores Report

Cost of requested medication: 32-65 (250 mg Tab)
Cost of similar-acting item stocked: N/A
Remarks (advantages, disadvantages):
Ciprofloxacin has been added to the WHO Model List of
Essential Drugs (1995, Tech. Rep. Series 850)

Gerritt Dawee _____ February 12, 1998
Medical Supplies Officer _____ Date

Section C
To be completed by formulary committee

Formulary Committee Report

Determination: ___ Rejected √ Approved: S (Specialist Use)
_____ Level of Use
Reasons:
LEAST COSTLY ORAL MEDICATION PROVIDING 95% CURE RATE
IN THESE SEXUALLY TRANSMITTED INFECTIONS
(NB—RESTRICTED TO THESE INDICATIONS ONLY).

Vanyaganya, F. _____ March 14, 1998
Formulary Committee (Chairman) _____ Date

(Formulary Addition/Deletion & Special Authorization / Page 2)
Pertinent Pharmacological Data on Medication

Therapeutic Action and Indications for Use:

As a third-line treatment of chancroid and/or gonorrhea
Note: (A) First-line drugs are now marginally efficacious. (1)
(B) Prolonged courses of erythromycin (second-line treatment of
chancroid-haemophilis ducreyi) do not heal ulcers.

Side Effects, Toxicity, and Precautions:

Side effects:
CNS stimulation; hypersensitivity reactions; interstitial nephritis;
photosensitivity; dizziness or lightheadedness; headache; nervousness;
insomnia; gastrointestinal disturbances.
Relative contraindications:
Hypersensitivity; renal function impairment.
Caution: There is limited experience of the effect of concurrent HIV infection
on adverse effects profiles.
(2)

Dosages (Maximum and Minimum):

500 mg as a single dose in adults.

References:

(1) Ndowa et al., "Efficacy of STD Treatment Regimens in a Genito-Urinary Clinic
in Harare." Centr. Afr. J. Med. 3, 1995, pp. 36–40.
(2) USP-DI 1994 and manufacturer's product data sheet.

Existing therapeutic classification systems also differ in their complexity; some systems may have five or six levels of subdivision. The level of complexity should be appropriate to the intended use of the system. In general, public pharmaceutical supply programs should strive for a noncomplex therapeutic classification system that is readily understood by midlevel medical workers and trained supply clerks as well as by pharmacists and physicians.

Increasingly, essential medicines programs are adopting the Anatomical Therapeutic Chemical (ATC) classification scheme used in the WHO Model List of Essential Medicines. In the ATC system, medicines are divided into different groups based on the body organ or system on which they act and their chemical, pharmacological, and therapeutic properties (WHO Collaborating Centre for Drug Statistics Methodology 2009). The searchable website is http://www. whocc.no/atc_ddd_index. This relatively straightforward system has been adopted by UNICEF and by most international nonprofit suppliers of essential medicines. Therefore, national and local programs will find price comparisons and ordering are easier if this system is adopted.

16.8 Sources of information

In most developing countries, the sources of current information available for medicine selection decisions are limited. (Chapter 34 discusses sources of drug information and how to assess them.)

Many academicians prefer to base the selection of essential medicines on information from original research articles, which requires compiling articles from journals for comprehensive review. The randomized controlled trial is becoming the "gold standard" both to establish medicine efficacy and to determine the comparative efficacy of different medicines for the same clinical problem. Results from such studies are not easily obtainable, unfortunately, so selection decisions must usually be made on the basis of the best available evidence.

Many respected reference texts and periodicals, such as drug bulletins, critically assess and synthesize the best available evidence. Of the many valuable resources that may be consulted, *Martindale: The Extra Pharmacopoeia* is particularly useful because it contains summaries on more than 5,300 medicines and information on the composition of 70,000 medicinal preparations. Other publications, such as the *British National Formulary*, contain comparative evaluations of individual drugs or of therapeutic groups. Independent drug bulletins, such as the *Medical Letter on Drugs and Therapeutics and the Drug and Therapeutics Bulletin*, regularly prepare comparative reviews of medicines and therapeutics.

The WHO Model List of Essential Medicines is a useful reference, derived from the consensus of recognized international experts and updated every two to four years. In 2007, WHO published the first Model List of Essential Medicines for children, revising it in 2008 and 2011 to include missing medicines for children, using evidence-based clinical guidelines. The medicines on this list are widely acknowledged to be safe, efficacious, cost-effective, and of acceptable quality. Consulting essential medicines lists from other countries may also be useful. Many drug regulatory authorities post essential medicines lists and formularies on their websites.

Sufficient information on efficacy, safety, and dosages—particularly for risk groups such as children, pregnant women, and the elderly—is often difficult to obtain for newer drug products. Because the relative merits of newly marketed pharmaceuticals are unknown until clinical experience has accumulated or appropriate comparative trials with other medicines are undertaken, it is advisable to delay the inclusion of such medicines until sufficient information is available from reliable independent sources.

16.9 Implementing and updating essential medicines lists

The development and use of lists of essential medicines have enormous implications for pharmaceutical procurement, local production, supply, training, prescribing, and supervision. However, many essential medicines lists, treatment guidelines, and formulary manuals have been developed, printed, and forgotten. There are many reasons for such failures.

Reasons for failure

Probably the most common reason for failure is not involving as wide a group of national experts and policy makers as possible. Lists and guidelines developed by individuals, departments, or institutions operating in isolation are bound to fail, as are those that are not updated regularly. They lack credibility, and other interested parties will not accept them. Another common mistake is a lack of both a purpose and a medicine policy framework. Such weaknesses provide an opportunity for pressure groups to defeat the endeavor. Also, if the whole selection process lacks openness and transparency, or if no procedure exists for incorporating suggestions and additions, the lists and guidelines are likely to fail. Last, failure can result if selections are perceived as unrealistic (for example, listing sophisticated medicines for lower health care levels in resource-poor settings).

Gaining acceptance of essential medicines lists

The development and use of a national list of essential medicines are cornerstones of a national medicine policy. The formulation and acceptance of a national medicine policy are, in most cases, based on the concept of essential medicines and entail the development of a list. An essential medicines list can be developed without a medicine policy, but it

Table 16-3 Key factors in successfully developing and implementing an essential medicines program

Key factor
• Establish a transparent process for creating and updating the list of essential medicines, providing a voice for key stakeholders but ensuring a scientific, evidence-based process.
• Link the essential medicines list to clinical guidelines for diagnosis and treatment, involving both specialists and primary care providers.
• Actively engage support from medical opinion leaders, senior clinicians, training institutions, professional organizations, nongovernmental organizations, and the public.
• Make the list of essential medicines, formulary manuals, and standard treatment guidelines widely available in all health care facilities and to all health care providers in both printed and electronic versions.
• Consider launching new or revised lists with the involvement of senior government officials, such as the minister of health or the president, and intensive press coverage.
• Make clear the specific legal or administrative authority of the essential medicines list for training, procurement, reimbursement, and public information.
• Consider establishing an administrative or budgetary mechanism to allow the limited supply and use of nonlisted medicines (for example, by certain specialist units).
• Regularly update the list so that it reflects therapeutic advances and changes in cost, antimicrobial resistance patterns, and public health relevance.

Source: WHO 2002.

cannot be developed without wide agreement on the purpose and use of the list.

In developing a national list of essential medicines, it is important to obtain the support of professional organizations, such as the national medical and pharmaceutical associations. They should be consulted from the start and should be informed about the reasons for developing a list and the selection criteria. The same is true for senior clinicians and teachers from medical and pharmacy schools, who are often leading national figures involved in the process of medicine registration. Arguments in favor of the essential medicines concept and the advantages of a limited list of medicines (see Table 16-1) should be discussed with those individuals. The acceptance of the list by senior specialists and other health care workers can be further enhanced by their involvement in the development of the list, treatment guidelines, and formulary manual (see Chapter 17) and by generous acknowledgment of their contributions. The obvious advantages of a consistent set of training and information materials and a corresponding system of pharmaceutical supply offset most professional resistance.

When the list is completed and printed, it is important to give it national prominence and credibility through a launching campaign. This step should involve the highest level of government officials, such as the minister of health

ASSESSMENT GUIDE

Management structure of the National Essential Medicines List (NEML)

- Has an NEML been officially adopted and distributed countrywide?
- Is there an official medicines committee whose duties include updating the NEML?
- Has the NEML been updated and distributed countrywide in the past five years?
- Is there a national medicine policy statement to promote and define the use of the NEML?
- What are the selection criteria for the NEML?

Outcome of the selection process

- What are the total number of medicines on the NEML (in dosage forms and strengths) and the number of medicines per level of health care?
- Is there duplication of therapeutically equivalent products on the NEML?

Use of the NEML (public sector)

- Is procurement in the public sector limited to medicines on the NEML?

- What is the value of medicines from the NEML out of the total value of medicines procured?
- What percentage of health facilities has a copy of the NEML available?
- What is the number of medicines from the NEML out of the total number of medicines prescribed?
- Do pharmaceutical donations comply with the NEML?
- Is the concept of essential medicines part of the curriculum in the basic training of health personnel?

Use of the NEML (private sector)

- Is the NEML used to promote national pharmaceutical production?
- Is there at least one major incentive for selling essential medicines at low cost?
- Are essential medicines sold under INNs in private drug outlets?
- Of the fifty best-selling medicines in the private sector, how many are on the NEML?

---

or the president, and intensive press coverage. A national conference can emphasize points such as the advantages of the list, the national consensus in defining the health needs of the population at large, and the cost-effective use of limited resources.

Authority of essential medicines lists

Specifying the purpose of the list at an early stage is critical. Will procurement and distribution of medicines in the public sector be limited to products on the list? Is a change in legislation or regulation needed for enforcing the use of a list, or perhaps a decree? Will exceptions to the list be allowed? If so, on what grounds and by which authority?

Pressure will be brought to provide patients with medicines not on the essential medicines list. Exceptions to the official list must be controlled by administrative or budgetary methods. Health services often require a written request for special authorization of nonlisted medicines (for example, the form in Figure 16-3) and have procedures for evaluating and approving such requests. A budgetary maximum may also be used for such exceptions—a maximum of 5 to 10 percent of the pharmaceutical budget, for example. Such a budget for nonlisted medicines is usually effective in ensuring acceptance of the list by district authorities and clinical specialists; without such a safety valve, many lists are

perceived as too rigid and are likely to be undermined. In addition, if certain nonformulary medicines are commonly ordered, they may be considered for inclusion when the list is revised.

Finally, an open and transparent system of regular updates is an absolute prerequisite to maintain the authority and acceptance of an essential medicines or formulary list. Table 16-3 lists the factors that are important in developing and implementing the elements of an essential medicines program. ■

References and further readings

★ = Key readings.

NASCOP (National AIDS and STD Control Programme [Kenya]). 2005. *Guidelines for Antiretroviral Drug Therapy in Kenya.* Nairobi: NASCOP.

OECS/PPS (Organisation of Eastern Caribbean States/Pharmaceutical Procurement Service). 2002. *Regional Formulary and Therapeutics Manual.* 6th ed. Castries, St. Lucia: OECS/PPS.

Savelli, A., H. Schwarz, A. Zagorskiy, and A. Bykov. 1996. *Manual for the Development and Maintenance of Hospital Drug Formularies.* Submitted to the U.S. Agency for International Development by the Rational Pharmaceutical Management Project. Arlington, Va.: Management Sciences for Health. <http://erc.msh.org/mainpage.cfm?file=2.3.1.htm&module=drugs&language=english>

★ WHO (World Health Organization) 2002. *WHO Policy Perspectives on Medicines: The Selection of Essential Medicines.* Geneva: WHO. <http://whqlibdoc.who.int/hq/2002/WHO_EDM_2002.2.pdf>

———. 2007. *Proposed Procedure to Update and Disseminate the WHO Model List of Essential Medicines.* Technical Report Series 946 (Annex 5). <http://www.who.int/medicines/publications/essential meds_committeereports/TRS946_EMedLib.pdf >

WHO (World Health Organization) Collaborating Centre for Drug Statistics Methodology. 2009. *Guidelines for ATC Classification and DDD Assignment 2010.* Oslo: WHO Collaborating Centre for Drug Statistics Methodology. <http://www.whocc.no/filearchive/publications/2010guidelines.pdf>

WHO/DAP (World Health Organization/Action Programme on Essential Drugs). 1994. *National, Regional, and International Essential Drugs Lists, Formularies, and Treatment Guides.* Geneva: WHO/DAP. <http://whqlibdoc.who.int/hq/1994/WHO_DAP_94.2.pdf> A list of published essential drugs lists, formularies, and treatment guidelines.

★ WHO (World Health Organization) Expert Committee on the Selection and Use of Essential Medicines. 2008. *The Selection and Use of Essential Medicines. Report of the WHO Expert Committee, October 2007 (Including the Model List of Essential Medicines for Children)* Geneva: WHO. (Updated every two years.) <http://www.who.int/medicines/publications/essentialmeds_committeereports/TRS_950.pdf>

WHO (World Health Organization) Expert Committee on Specifications for Pharmaceutical Preparations. 2009a. *WHO Expert Committee on Specifications for Pharmaceutical Preparations.* 43rd report. Geneva: WHO. <http://www.who.int/medicines/publications/pharmprep/PDF_TRS953_WEB.pdf>

★ ———. 2009b. *WHO Model List of Essential Medicines.* 16th ed. WHO: Geneva. <http://www.who.int/selection_medicines/committees/expert/17/sixteenth_adult_list_en.pdf>

WHO/GPE (World Health Organization/Global Programme on Evidence for Health Policy). 2003. *Guidelines for WHO Guidelines.* Geneva: WHO/GPE.

Glossary

Bioavailability: The rate and extent of availability of an active ingredient from a dosage form as measured by the concentration/time curve in the systemic circulation or its excretion in the urine.

Branded generics: Generic pharmaceutical products marketed under brand names.

Drug: Any substance in a pharmaceutical product that is used to modify or explore physiological systems or pathological states for the benefit of the recipient.

Drug product: A unique combination of drug(s), strength, and dosage form (for example, ampicillin 500 mg capsule).

Efficacy: The ability of a medicine to produce the purported effect, as determined by scientific methods.

Formulary list: A list of medicines approved for use in a specific health care setting.

Formulary manual: A manual containing clinically oriented, summary pharmacological information about a selected number of medicines. The manual may also include administrative and regulatory information pertaining to medication prescribing and dispensing.

Formulary system: The principles, criteria, procedures, and resources for developing, updating, and promoting the formulary (essential medicines) list.

Generic name: The locally approved or nonproprietary name of a drug. It is generally the International Nonproprietary Name given by WHO.

Generic pharmaceutical products: Products marketed by any producer under nonproprietary or locally approved names.

International Nonproprietary Name (INN): A globally recognized name developed by WHO to facilitate the identification of pharmaceutical substances or active pharmaceutical ingredients. A nonproprietary name is also known as a generic name.

Multisource pharmaceutical products: Pharmaceutically equivalent products, available from different manufacturers, that may or may not be therapeutically equivalent.

Pharmaceutical equivalents: Products that contain the same amount of the same active substance(s) in the same dosage form, meet the same or comparable standards, and are intended to be administered by the same route.

Pharmaceutical product: A dosage form containing one or more drugs along with other substances included during the manufacturing process.

Therapeutic equivalents: Pharmaceutically equivalent products whose effects with respect to both safety and efficacy are essentially the same, when administered in the same molar dose, as can be derived from appropriate studies (bioequivalence, pharmacodynamic, clinical, or in vitro studies).

| Part I: Policy and economic issues | Part II: Pharmaceutical management | Part III: Management support systems |

Selection
16 Managing medicine selection
17 Treatment guidelines and formulary manuals
Procurement
Distribution
Use

CHAPTER 17

Treatment guidelines and formulary manuals

Summary   17.2

17.1 Need for local reference manuals   17.2
Treatment guidelines • Formulary manual

17.2 Treatment guidelines   17.3
*Establishment of a guideline development committee •
Information in treatment guidelines • Use of treatment
guidelines*

17.3 Formulary manuals   17.10
*Information in a formulary manual • Developing
a formulary manual • Practical issues in formulary
manual development • Hospital formularies*

17.4 Production and distribution issues   17.14

17.5 Implementing and maintaining treatment guidelines
and formulary manuals   17.14

Assessment guide   17.16

References and further readings   17.16

ILLUSTRATIONS

Figure 17-1 Sample page from *WHO Model Formulary,*
2008   17.13

Table 17-1 Summary of the standard treatment guideline
development process   17.6

BOXES

Box 17-1 Potential benefits of standard treatment
guidelines   17.3

Box 17-2 Cost-effectiveness analysis for choosing standard
treatments   17.8

Box 17-3 Using monitoring systems to evaluate the
appropriateness of standard treatment
guidelines   17.10

Box 17-4 Information in a formulary manual   17.11

COUNTRY STUDIES

CS 17-1 Production and use of treatment guidelines   17.5
CS 17-2 Improving compliance with standard treatment
guidelines in Indonesia   17.9
CS 17-3 Availability and knowledge of HIV/AIDS-related
treatment guidelines in Rwanda   17.15

SUMMARY

Treatment guidelines are disease oriented and reflect a consensus on the treatments of first choice for a range of medical conditions. A formulary manual is drug oriented and contains summary drug information on a selected number of medicines, sometimes combined with practical prescribing and dispensing information. They can both be developed for various levels of health care.

The process of developing these publications (the formulary process) is a continual effort, not limited to the one-time production of a set of treatment guidelines or a formulary manual. The process includes gaining acceptance of the concept, preparing a text on the basis of wide consultation and consensus building, implementing an introductory campaign and training activities, and undertaking regular reviews and updates.

Treatment guidelines can be made for one institution, such as a hospital; for one level of care, such as all health centers; or for a region or nation. Treatment guidelines are powerful tools to promote rational prescribing, provided they are based on extensive involvement of the end users. Their development is a good opportunity to integrate technical advice from various disease programs into an overall training program. Treatment guidelines should be used as the basis for undergraduate medical and paramedical training, for in-service training, for supervision, and for medical audit. The range of medicines included should be limited to those on the national list of essential medicines.

A formulary manual, whether at a national or facility level, should be developed by a formulary subcommittee of the national drug committee or the facility's drug and therapeutics committee. Both committees should ensure the full participation of prominent specialists and health opinion leaders in the process. One or two editors should be commissioned to draft and edit the formulary manual.

To maintain the credibility of the information, a system for regular updates and for incorporation of accepted amendments into the next edition is essential for both formularies and treatment guidelines.

This chapter builds on concepts introduced in Chapter 16, which should be read first.

17.1   Need for local reference manuals

After standard treatment guidelines (STGs) for a country's common conditions and complaints have been agreed upon and adopted, the next step is the development of a national essential medicines list and a formulary manual.

The procedures for developing an essential medicines list, a set of treatment guidelines, and a formulary manual are all similar; together, they can be called the formulary process. Standard treatment guidelines are disease oriented, whereas formulary manuals are very much drug-oriented documents. These two documents are the cornerstone of rational medicine therapy. General information on the selection of medicines and the development and maintenance of a list of essential medicines is given in Chapter 16. In this chapter, the specific aspects of the formulary process are outlined in relation to developing treatment guidelines or a formulary manual.

Treatment guidelines

The terms *standard treatment guidelines*, *treatment protocols*, and *clinical guidelines* are all used to indicate systematically developed statements that help practitioners or prescribers make decisions about appropriate treatments for specific clinical conditions. Treatment guidelines exist for various levels of health care, ranging from general prescribing guidelines for paramedical workers in rural areas to detailed protocols for tertiary health care centers in wealthy urban areas and teaching hospitals.

Standard guidelines benefit health officials, supply management staff, health care providers, and patients (Box 17-1). Together with a national list of essential medicines, treatment guidelines are powerful tools in promoting the rational use of medicines, and they are integral in strategies to reduce antimicrobial resistance. They offer an opportunity to ensure that the training of health workers is based both on a logical approach to treatment and on a consensus about the selection of essential medicines. Comprehensive treatment guidelines are a logical starting point for integrated training and an excellent basis for pharmaceutical supply in the public sector. Treatment guidelines should be used for in-service training, supervision, and medical audit. They can also assist in the standardization (and rationalization) of prescribing patterns in countries with large numbers of foreign-trained medical graduates. STGs, when properly developed and implemented, will improve the patient's clinical outcome at a lower total cost (Grimshaw et al. 2004).

Formulary manual

A formulary manual contains summary information on a selected number of medicines. It is drug centered, and the information is usually organized in therapeutic groups. In

---

Box 17-1
Potential benefits of standard treatment guidelines

For health officials

- Permits identification of cost-effective treatments for common health problems
- Provides basis for assessing and comparing quality of care
- Identifies most effective therapy in terms of quality and combats antimicrobial resistance
- Provides information for practitioners to give to patients concerning the institution's standards of care
- Is a vehicle for integrating special programs (control of diarrheal disease, acute respiratory infection, tuberculosis, malaria, and so on) at the point of the primary health care provider

For supply management staff

- Identifies which medicines should be available for the most commonly treated problems
- Facilitates prepackaging of course-of-therapy quantities of commonly prescribed items

- Makes medicine demand more predictable, so forecasting is more reliable

For health care providers

- Provides expert consensus on most effective, economical treatment for a specific setting
- Gives providers the opportunity to concentrate on correct diagnosis
- Sets a quality-of-care standard
- Provides a basis for monitoring and supervision

For patients

- Encourages adherence to treatment through consistency among prescribers at all locations within the health care system
- Ensures most cost-effective treatments are provided
- Improves availability of medicines
- Improves treatment and outcomes

---

most developing countries, the national formulary list is limited to medicines on the national list of essential medicines. A *therapeutic formulary* includes detailed and comprehensive therapeutic information on each of the medicines listed and may also include guidelines on rational prescribing and dispensing; here, the distinction between a formulary and treatment guidelines becomes less clear, as is the case with the *British National Formulary* (BNF).

Although there are several available reference texts that include comprehensive drug information, they may not be appropriate for all settings. A national formulary manual concentrates on medications relevant to a particular country. For example, it would exclude information on medicines that are not available in the country or that are overly expensive. It would also put less emphasis on uncommon, irrelevant, or minor side effects. But it should include information that may be missing in other texts on nationally important medicines, such as those used for tropical conditions or for locally common diseases that may be rare in other countries. It would also include information on specific treatment considerations (for example, G6PD deficiency, sickle cell anemia, HIV infection). Recommended dosage schedules can be adapted to national requirements, special storage guidelines may be added, and specific national problems (such as overuse of injections or polypharmacy) can be addressed.

The World Health Organization (WHO) launched its first model formulary in 2002, with electronic versions available on its website and on CD-ROM. The *WHO Model Formulary* presents independent information on the more than 300 medicines on the *WHO Model List of Essential Medicines* and is updated periodically, along with the essential medicines list. Each section of the formulary starts with a comparative overview of various therapeutic alternatives, while each medication entry has information on use, dosage, adverse effects, contraindications, and warnings. The formulary is intended to be a model for national governments and institutions to use as a basis for developing their own national formularies. It is particularly relevant for developing countries, where commercial and promotional materials are often the only available source of drug information to health workers, prescribers, and patients.

17.2 Treatment guidelines

In developing standard treatment guidelines, the starting point is a list of common diseases and complaints. Next, the standard treatment of choice is defined for each diagnosis or problem. In terms of selection of health problems to be addressed, formatting standard treatment guidelines can be approached in different ways—

- Individual—Standard treatments are established for only one problem or set of problems, such as only diarrheal disease, only acute respiratory infection (ARI), or only malaria.

- Selective—Standard treatments are established for a small number of high-priority problems, perhaps six to twelve, for example, a "package" of treatments for diarrheal disease, ARI, antenatal care, immunization screening, malaria, and tuberculosis.
- Comprehensive—Standard treatments are established for 30, 50, 100, or an even greater number of common health problems. When published, such standard treatment guidelines become more like textbooks than basic references.

Technical advice from various vertical disease-oriented programs (malaria, diarrheal diseases, schistosomiasis, tuberculosis, sexually transmitted infections, HIV/AIDS, and many others) can be integrated into one set of national treatment guidelines; however, separate funding sources for vertical programs can result in the independent publication of disease-specific STGs, which may be appropriate for facilities that function primarily to treat one condition (for example, HIV/AIDS).

The number of treatment guidelines developed should be appropriate to the specific situation. But developing individual treatment guidelines one by one may result in a missed opportunity to use the process to integrate several special programs. At the other extreme, comprehensive standard treatment guidelines risk overwhelming health workers with new information, thus reducing the chance that *any* of the standard treatments—even those for common, high-priority problems—will be followed. There may be situations where it is appropriate to target different levels of the health system with manuals containing differing amounts of information.

Information on local disease patterns should also be considered. Seldom do primary care clinics have access to clinical laboratories. But results from surveys using available district, regional, or national laboratory facilities can be used to make scientifically based selections of preferred medicines for certain types of diarrhea, ARI, malaria, tuberculosis, and other infectious diseases. Dynamic standard treatment guidelines are periodically updated to reflect changes in treatment patterns.

Any treatment guideline should include only medicines on the national list of essential medicines. This limitation ensures that the supply system, based on the list of essential medicines, supports the treatment guidelines. Ideally, a formulary list should be developed after the appropriate treatment guidelines for common diseases have been identified or developed.

Unlike the drug information in a national formulary manual, which tends to be noncontroversial, treatment guidelines may generate considerable differences of opinion among prescribers. Reaching consensus is much more difficult, and the developmental process takes much more time. To the extent possible, treatment selection should be evidence based and take into account the local economic situation. Wide consultation is a key condition for acceptance and impact.

The process of developing treatment guidelines is similar to that of developing an essential medicines list or formulary manual (see Country Study 17-1), and only those aspects specific to treatment guidelines are discussed here (see Table 17-1 for an overview of the process).

Establishment of a guideline development committee

For national treatment guidelines, the guideline development committee can be a subcommittee of the national drug and therapeutics committee and is likely to differ from the national formulary committee. The committee should include one or two leaders who have final responsibility for the guidelines and who can lead the group through the process; clinical specialists in the fields under study; other experts as needed, such as a nutritionist or a health economist; several end users (general practitioners, medical assistants, nurses); patient/caregiver advocates; and other stakeholders who should have input. Sometimes focus groups are used to provide patient and caregiver feedback. Not all medical specialties need to be represented on the committee, but they can be co-opted to prepare or review the relevant chapters. The group should also have technical and administrative support.

Before starting the work, and especially before inviting other experts to write chapters or sections, the guideline development committee must make several important decisions on target groups, choice of authors, and editing and reviewing of the manuscript.

Targeting different levels of care. The length and format of the publication depend on the target group and the level of detail. A key question is: should all information for all levels of health workers be presented in one publication, or should different publications be issued for different levels of care? One publication for all levels can serve as a complete reference for all recommended treatments. It also allows practitioners at the lower levels to read about treatments that are recommended at the higher levels, which may be an advantage in emergency cases and is, at the least, educational. In addition, the production process is easier, and the publishing costs are reduced.

In contrast, separate guidelines for different levels of health care can recommend treatments focused on medicines supplied to that level, so that no unavailable medicines are recommended. Several developing countries with large proportions of paramedical prescribers have produced separate national treatment guidelines for general practitioners and for paramedical prescribers (such as clinical officers, medical assistants, and nurses). The former are pocket-size

Country Study 17-1
Production and use of treatment guidelines

Australia. Started as a hospital-based initiative, the Antibiotic Guidelines were first issued in Victoria in the late 1970s. They were used as a teaching document for medical students and interns and, more important, as an audit standard against which prescribing patterns in the wards could be compared. More and more hospitals became involved, and subsequent editions of the guidelines booklet were increasingly used in other regions of the country. New editions were introduced with marketing campaigns that were professional and inventive, using posters, advertisements, drug use studies, and face-to-face education. These campaigns, together with the widening range of professionals involved in subsequent editions, greatly improved the acceptance of the guidelines.

As the administrative requirements of producing, promoting, and evaluating a comprehensive set of therapeutic guidelines increased, the series was turned over to a nonprofit organization, Therapeutic Guidelines Limited, which expanded the range of titles and converted them to electronic format. The guidelines now cover ten areas, including analgesic, antibiotic, cardiovascular, gastrointestinal, psychotropic, and respiratory medicines, and provide up-to-date therapeutic information for a range of diseases. The guidelines are developed by expert writing groups composed of about twelve people, including a chair, an editor, experts in relevant medical specialties, a general practitioner, and a pharmacist. Although the text is drafted by individual members of the writing groups, all group members devote many days to meetings and workshops to discuss and reach agreement on the final guidelines. At that point, the manuscript is reviewed by ten to twenty outside experts. The time taken to produce each book, from the first writing group meeting to publication, is twelve to fourteen months. Each booklet is updated every two to three years. Although the guidelines are used primarily in Australia, several other countries, including Japan and China, have adapted and translated individual guidelines for use locally.

Nicaragua. A series of therapeutic guidelines existed in Nicaragua; however, although they were technically sound, their presentation was unattractive and the language was more appropriate for doctors than for paramedical workers. In addition, the material was spread over several booklets, and many health facilities did not have a complete set.

Development of new guidelines for rural health workers included a three-day workshop attended by health workers who were stationed alone in ten "sentinel" health posts as well as nurses, physicians, and pharmacists from the surrounding areas. The group identified the most common diseases treated in the health posts and drew up a corresponding list of essential medicines. The resulting draft booklet was widely field-tested. It was then decided to revise and expand the handbook for the national level with a bottom-up approach, again calling on the experience of end users. The national-level draft was also reviewed by a multidisciplinary group of specialists at the regional, provincial, and university levels. The product was an extensive, illustrated, 440-page learning and action guide for local health workers, *Buscando remedio* ("Seeking a Remedy"). The sixth edition was published in 2010.

Ghana. In 2004, Ghana's National Drugs Program published the fifth edition of the Standard Treatment Guidelines (STGs) and Essential Medicines List (EML). The STG 2004 is an update of the 2000 version. The fifth edition is based on the best-available medical evidence and includes ratings of the quality of evidence associated with each recommendation. The new STG lists 530 drug products, a number that reflects eighty-three deletions and forty-eight additions since the 2000 edition. Changes to the list of medicines are partly the result of changes in the *WHO Model List of Essential Medicines* and the addition of antiretroviral medicines for HIV/AIDS. In addition, the British Approved Names used in the previous edition have been replaced with the recommended International Nonproprietary Names.

Ghana's publication of the updated STG and EML 2004 coincided with the nationwide implementation of the National Health Insurance Scheme (NHIS). The STG and EML 2004 govern the standards of care under the NHIS, and the NHIS list of medicines for reimbursement is based on the national EML. The introduction of the new health insurance scheme gives Ghana the opportunity to make the STG 2004 widely available and facilitates adherence monitoring.

Table 17-1   Summary of the standard treatment guideline development process

Key action	Tasks
Recruit guideline development group chair	• Advertise • Interview • Train
Prepare scope	• Identify clinical issues • Search literature • Draft scope • Hold stakeholder workshop • Finalize scope with workshop input

Form the Guideline Development Group	• Select members
	  – Health care professionals
	  – Patients/caregivers
	  – Technical experts
	  – Technical/administrative support

Formulate the review questions	• Structure questions • Use patient experiences • Agree on review protocols and economic plan
Identify the evidence	• Develop search strategy for each question • Search relevant databases and information sources • Ensure validity • Consider stakeholder input
Review the evidence	• Select relevant studies • Assess quality of studies • Summarize evidence and present results
Create guideline recommendations	• Develop recommendations based on clinical and cost effectiveness • Prioritize recommendations for implementation • Formulate research recommendations
Agree on format and style and share writing guidelines with authors	
Write the first draft of the guideline	
Edit draft and send it to a wide circle of stakeholders for review	• Consult and respond to stakeholder comments
Revise draft based on comments	
Prepare final guideline	• Launch and publish the guideline
Review and update within a specified time frame	• Decide on update schedule • Correct errors

Source: Adapted from NICE 2009.

books with treatment guidelines in a condensed format; the latter use simpler language, are extensively illustrated, and recommend only medicines that are available at rural health facilities. One set of guidelines is usually sufficient in countries where primary health care is delivered mainly by physicians.

Identifying and assessing the clinical evidence. The first step in identifying the evidence is for the group to formulate the clinical questions to answer. The PICO guide (NICE 2009) provides a framework based on patients, intervention, comparison, and outcome—

Patients/population: Which patients or population of patients are we interested in? How can they be best described? Are there subgroups that need to be considered?

Intervention: Which intervention, treatment, or approach should be used?

Comparison: What is/are the main alternative/s to compare with the intervention?

Outcome: What is really important for the patient? Which outcomes should be considered: intermediate or short-term measures; mortality; morbidity and treatment complications; rates of relapse; late morbidity and readmission; return to work, physical and social functioning and other measures such as quality of life; general health status; costs?

A systematic review of the evidence involves identifying and evaluating information to answer the questions based on the best available evidence in the relevant area. This process should be transparent and involves four major steps: selecting relevant studies; assessing their quality; synthesizing the results; and grading the evidence. The evidence may include primary scientific papers, systematic reviews from the Cochrane Collaboration, reviews published in well-known journals, and guidelines developed by other credible organizations.

Many resources exist on how to assess clinical information (see, for example, NICE 2009, Shekelle et al. 1999, and SIGN 2008). Chapter 34 includes more detail on evaluating pharmaceutical information.

Drafting the guidelines. The most practical approach is to invite a number of authors to draft first texts of separate chapters. The authors should be recruited from the level of prescribers for which the guidelines are intended. For example, inviting a university specialist to write treatment guidelines for dispensing nurses may not be practical; a nurse-tutor would be better equipped for that task, although the author can consult relevant specialists and have them review the draft text. Several production issues—for example, the specifications for text and presentation (see Section 17-4)—should be addressed early in the process. A key to the successful acceptance of treatment guidelines is involving well-respected opinion leaders in the development process.

Reviewing and editing the draft. The editors of the guidelines should unify the draft chapters into one consistent document before sending the draft text out for review by a large number of stakeholders. As mentioned, reaching consensus on a treatment of first choice is usually more difficult than agreeing on the factual drug information that is included in a national formulary manual. In addition, more opposition is bound to arise after the guidelines have been published. Several rounds of consultation, involving an increasing number of experts, professional associations, patient/caregiver advocates, and other stakeholders can do a great deal to resolve objections. If consensus cannot be reached, the guidelines should indicate it.

Adapting existing guidelines. Many health care organizations and some ministries of health do not have the resources necessary to develop treatment guidelines from scratch. In this case, existing guidelines can be adapted for local use. Policy makers should focus on the guidelines that are most important, based on local disease patterns. It may be difficult to identify appropriate guidelines to evaluate, as they may not be easily accessible; however, some organizations post their guidelines on the Internet (see References and Further Readings). Other resources may be leveraged through partnerships and collaboration with other stakeholders.

Once a guideline development group identifies existing guidelines that correspond with their treatment priorities, they must still use as rigorous an evaluation method as possible, given the resources available. The task of the group that adapts existing guidelines, then, is not to identify and analyze the available literature, but rather to ensure that the adaptation and its recommendations are locally relevant and likely to be adopted by health care providers. A guideline assessment tool can be used to evaluate its usability and

validity. The Joint United Nations Programme on HIV/AIDS includes such a tool in its publication on developing treatment guidelines (UNAIDS 1999).

Information in treatment guidelines

Treatment guidelines are disease oriented (in contrast to formularies, which are drug oriented). This focus means that the treatment of choice is presented for each common health problem, together with basic information needed by the prescriber. Any appropriate nondrug treatments should always be included. Alternative treatments may be listed, with an indication of when they should be used. Comparisons of the costs of various treatments may also be included in the analysis, with the "best" treatment dependent on circumstances (such as antimicrobial resistance) or selection criteria (Box 17-2).

Some STGs, for example, those of Ghana, also include a section on the level of evidence for the recommended treatment. The evidence is rated as supported by either (A) randomized controlled trials; (B) well-conducted clinical studies; or (C) expert committee recommendations.

Treatment guidelines necessarily repeat some information that is also presented in the national formulary manual. It is not necessary, however, to include all drug information—only that which is needed to make rational treatment decisions.

Diagnostic criteria. Diagnostic criteria are especially important when a disease may present in different stages of severity (for example, dehydration). They must indicate when treatment is needed and when it is not, such as in the treatment of fever or cough. Required investigations may be included.

Treatment of first choice. The section on the first-choice treatment (drug or nondrug) contains the most information for the prescriber. It should include the choice of medicine, its usual dosage schedule, and, when needed, adapted dosage schedules for children, for patients with concurrent liver or renal diseases, for pregnant patients, for the elderly, and for other high-risk groups.

Cost of treatment. Information on the cost of treatment is useful if alternatives are proposed. However, including such information means that the guidelines must be updated regularly. The information can also be presented as price ranges, such as "cheap," "moderate," and "expensive"; these types of categories are unlikely to change substantially.

Important contraindications and side effects. The section on contraindications and side effects should list both relative and absolute contraindications; groups at special risk (the elderly, and patients who are pregnant, breastfeeding, or have liver or renal disease) must be highlighted. Side effects should be broken down into reactions that are self-limiting and those that may require a change in therapy.

Box 17-2
Cost-effectiveness analysis for choosing standard treatments

Even when funds are limited, the cheapest treatment for a specific health problem may not be the best treatment. A cost-effectiveness analysis (CEA, see Chapter 10) may help to organize cost and effectiveness information to guide decisions about first- and second-line treatments. Including indirect costs beyond the price of the medicine in the analysis provides a clearer picture. Indirect costs might include program costs, such as health staff, program administration, laboratory reagents, hospitalization costs, and vehicle costs. A CEA may be particularly helpful when higher-cost treatments are also more effective, such as for certain antibacterial, antitubercular, or antimalarial drugs for which drug resistance is high. A CEA can also be useful in establishing standard treatment guidelines for chronic diseases, such as hypertension, and for antibiotic prophylaxis for surgery.

Below is a real-life example of how two different kinds of thrombolytic agents for the treatment of myocardial infarction were compared from the point of view of effi-

cacy and cost-effectiveness in Australia. The usual treatment of myocardial infarction was compared with usual treatment plus the use of either streptokinase or tissue plasminogen activator.

Comparison was done in terms of (a) total treatment costs, (b) death rates, and (c) cost per life saved (or death averted). The treatment costs included all the direct and indirect costs.

A CEA may be carried out using only information on cure rates and medicine costs. However, a truer picture may emerge if broader measures of effectiveness are used (morbidity, including disability, as well as mortality) and if all costs are included. For example, in an area of moderate resistance, a more effective second-line antimalarial may not be more cost-effective when only medicine costs are considered, but it may prove more cost-effective when additional costs are considered, such as hospitalization of patients who fail to respond to first-line treatment.

Economic analysis of two thrombolytics in acute myocardial infarction in Australia
A review of the literature was conducted in Australia to determine the cost-effectiveness of different thrombolytics to treat myocardial infarction (MI). The evaluation included the cost of the treatments and the mortality rate following MI.

Cost of treatment and mortality rates
Usual care (UC) of MI: 3.5 million Australian dollars (AUD)/1,000 cases, 120 die
UC of MI + streptokinase (SK): AUD 3.7 million/1,000 cases, 90 die
UC of MI + tissue plasminogen activator (tPA): AUD 5.5 million/1,000 cases, 80 die

Comparison of the different treatments
Difference between SK and UC of MI:
Cost of treatment = AUD 3.7–3.5 million/1,000 cases = AUD 0.2million/1,000 cases = AUD 200 per case
Number of deaths that will be prevented = 120–90 = 30 deaths/1,000 cases treated
Cost-effectiveness of SK = AUD 0.2 million/30 lives = AUD 6,700 per life saved

Difference between tPA and usual care of MI
Cost of treatment = AUD 5.5–3.5 million/1,000 cases = AUD 2.0 million/1,000 cases = AUD 2,000 per case
Number of deaths that will be prevented = 120–80 = 40 deaths/1,000 cases treated
Cost-effectiveness of tPA = AUD 2.0 million/40 lives = AUD 50,000 per life saved

Difference between tPA and SK treatments for MI
Cost of treatment = AUD 2.0–0.2 million/1,000 cases = 1.8 million/1,000 cases = AUD 1,800 per case
Number of deaths that will be prevented = 90–80 = 10 deaths/1,000 cases treated
Increased cost-effectiveness of tPA over SK = AUD 1.8million/10 lives = AUD 180,000 per life saved

If one has a budget of only AUD 500,000, which medicine should one use?
For SK: number of cases that can be treated = 500,000/200 = 2,500 cases
Number of lives that can be saved = (30/1000) × 2500 = 75 lives
For tPA: number of cases that can be treated = 500,000/2000 = 250 cases
Number of lives that can be saved = (40/1000) × 250 = 10 lives

Conclusion
This study concluded that although tPA had slightly better efficacy and saved marginally more lives, when cost was taken into account, more patients could be treated and more lives saved using SK. In other words, the extra cost-effectiveness of tPA over SK was so high (AUD 180,000 per life saved) that fewer people could be treated, and fewer lives saved, using tPA as compared to SK, with the limited budget available.

Source: Aylward 1996, cited in RPM Plus/WHO 2007a.

Important drug information, warnings, and precautions. This section highlights the information that the patient should be given by both the prescriber and the dispenser.

Referral criteria. These criteria describe when to refer the patient to a higher level of care. For example: If the patient's condition does not improve within four hours, refer the patient to a hospital.

Index. Although treatment guidelines are usually disease centered, many prescribers also use them to check on specific drugs or dosage schedules. For this reason, an index with both drug names and health problems makes the manual more useful.

Use of treatment guidelines

Treatment guidelines should be used for basic training of health workers, in-service training, supervision, reference, and medical audit. They are potentially valuable in promoting the rational use of medicines, because many prescribers recognize them as useful references. Because they are related to the list of essential medicines, they should also serve as the basis for the supply of essential medicines.

It was originally hoped that the availability of guidelines would change irrational prescribing patterns. However, it has become apparent that sending treatment guidelines to all prescribers is not enough to bring about an improvement in prescribing practices. To be effective, guidelines must be properly introduced to the prescribers, and their use should be monitored (see Country Study 17-2).

All relevant health workers should have their own copies of the guidelines, and training courses should be organized to introduce the guidelines and teach health workers how to use them. Treatment guidelines for paramedical prescribers are usually well received and are common in developing countries, as is also true of national treatment guidelines for general doctors. National guidelines for tertiary care are rare, but general care guidelines are often used in tertiary institutions. In South Africa, three separate STGs exist: one each for adult and pediatric patients in the hospital setting and a combined version for primary health care, which also includes the national essential medicines list. In developed countries, treatment protocols are usually drawn up for specific diseases (hypertension, diabetes, certain types of

---

Country Study 17-2
Improving compliance with standard treatment guidelines in Indonesia

Acute respiratory infection (ARI) is the leading cause of morbidity and mortality of children under five years old in Indonesia. Despite the widespread availability of standard treatment guidelines in health centers, evidence suggested that health professionals did not always comply with the STGs and that the use of nonstandard medicines for ARI, such as antibiotics, antihistamines, corticosteroids, and phenobarbital, was common. An intervention study was carried out in twenty-four health centers with the aim of reducing the use of nonstandard medicines for under-five ARI patients.

Twenty-four health centers from two districts were randomly assigned to receive the intervention (Group A) or act as controls (Group B). The intervention consisted of a two-hour small group discussion about ARI STGs, followed by two self-assessment discussions (after one month and two months) to discuss prescribing habits. Finally, both the intervention and control groups participated in a feedback seminar where the results of the study were presented. The level of compliance with the STGs was measured by analyzing thirty prescriptions a month from each health center that had ARI as a single diagnosis, and looking at the number and costs of prescriptions and how many prescriptions included antibiotics, antihistamines, or corticosterioids.

	Baseline/4 weeks postintervention	
Outcome measures	Group A (n = 12)	Group B (n = 12)
Medicines prescribed per encounter	4.0/3.1	3.8/4.0
Percentage antibiotics	63/22	67/67
Percentage antihistamines	79/23	75/64
Percentage corticosteroids	21/6	22/24
Average prescription costs (rupiahs)	1,123/750	1,296/1,151

As the results in the table show, in Indonesia, small-group interactive seminars followed by two self-assessment meetings were effective in improving health center staff compliance with STGs for ARI. In addition, after presentation of the study results to both groups, the control health centers experienced significant improvements on all outcome measures. So, even though these centers did not experience the entire intervention, a low level of feedback was instructive.

Source: Hidayati and Munawaroh 2004.

> **Box 17-3**
> **Using monitoring systems to evaluate the appropriateness of standard treatment guidelines**
>
> Integral to the success of instituting and promoting the use of standard treatment guidelines is establishing a monitoring and evaluation system to guide updates and revisions. Monitoring programs can focus specifically on the issue of treatment failure, and reports of high rates of clinical failure should prompt a thorough investigation and evaluation. For example, are there problems in the treatment guidelines themselves or in the implementation of the treatment guidelines? Are quality medications available and used properly by patients? Investigations should document clinical failure rates, physician compliance with STGs, patient compliance with prescriptions, drug quality, and antimicrobial resistance estimates. If the evaluation finds high rates of clinical failure despite compliance with STGs, a review of the official recommendations is essential.
>
> In several countries, monitoring programs for formal treatment failure have been established for certain conditions, such as malaria and tuberculosis, and results have been used to modify existing treatment guidelines. Many malaria-endemic countries have changed their national malaria treatment policy after antimicrobial resistance monitoring indicated that chloroquine or sulfadoxine-pyrimethamine was no longer effective in the country. For most infectious diseases, however, formal monitoring systems are not usually in place. Yet, mechanisms should exist for health care providers to report their experiences in using national STGs, and in turn, national authorities should have a procedure in place for responding to concerns by conducting studies or investigations.
>
> Source: APUA 2003.

cancer) or for single hospital departments (prescribing policies in the pediatrics department of a teaching hospital, for example).

Treatment guidelines have the strongest long-term impact if they are frequently updated, widely distributed, integrated into the basic curriculum of medical and paramedical teaching institutions, and used for audit—especially when the turnover and transfer of field staff is so frequent that the effect of in-service training is quickly diluted. The first edition of guidelines should be reviewed and updated after one year to rectify errors and ambiguities; after that, revisions should occur every two to three years, or as indicated by new evidence to support changes (see Box 17-3).

17.3 Formulary manuals

As noted in Chapter 16, the term *formulary* can be applied to a simple formulary list, the formulary manual (the subject of this discussion), or a fully developed formulary system. A formulary system develops from the essential medicines or formulary list and the formulary manual. It includes drug information and other resources to support good pharmaceutical management and the rational use of medicines. Formulary manuals provide on-the-spot information with a particular scope of use in mind—for example, national versus facility-specific—as well as a focus on a particular level of health care practice. As with treatment guidelines, the production of a formulary manual is one step in an ongoing process, and formulary manuals should periodically be reviewed and updated.

Information in a formulary manual

The information is usually presented in the form of drug information sheets or drug monographs. Such sheets can also be used as the basis for developing drug package inserts for locally manufactured drugs targeted at either prescribers or patients.

In most developing countries, the medicines included in the national formulary list are limited to those on the national list of essential medicines. However, a formulary manual may also include some information on commonly used medicines whose use is not recommended, stating exactly why these medicines are not recommended and discouraging their use.

Box 17-4 outlines information that may be included in a formulary manual. Acknowledgments should list all persons or agencies that contributed to the formulary; this background enhances its authority and credibility. The introduction should briefly describe the development process and the manual's intended use.

Basic information for each medication should be easy to read and complete but concise. The format and wording should be carefully chosen so that the information can be easily understood.

If cost information is included, the formulary manual must be updated regularly. Price information may be presented as treatment cost per day or as cost per course of treatment. This information may be presented in tables or bar charts. If the manual includes information that prescribers or dispensers should give to patients to ensure the correct use of the drug, this information should be specific.

Box 17-4
Information in a formulary manual

Introductory information

- Acknowledgments (individuals and agencies that contributed, explanation of how drug information is presented in manual)
- List of approved abbreviations
- Introduction (development of manual, intended uses)
- Formulary policies and procedures

Basic information for each drug

- Generic name, common synonyms, or brand names
- Dosage form(s) and strength(s)
- Main indications (diseases and conditions for which a drug is given)
- Pharmacology (may include pharmacokinetic data)
- Contraindications (reasons not to give the drug)
- Precautions (such as pregnancy, breast-feeding, certain health conditions)
- Side effects (major and minor, with estimated frequency)
- Dosage schedule (dosage form, frequency, duration, pediatric dosage, dosage adjustments for the elderly and for those with renal or liver disease)
- Instructions and warnings
- Drug, food, lab interactions (most common or severe)

Supplementary information on each drug

- Price
- Level-of-use code
- Regulatory category (prescription only, over-the-counter, controlled narcotic drugs)
- Storage guidelines
- Patient counseling information
- Labeling information

- National essential medicines list reference number
- Stores catalog number

Prescribing and dispensing guidelines

- Rational prescribing
- Principles of prescription writing
- Use of placebos
- Special requirements for inpatient prescriptions
- Guidelines on quantities to be supplied
- Special requirements for controlled drug prescriptions
- Prevention and reporting of adverse drug reactions
- Dispensing guidelines (correct dispensing practices, patient counseling)
- List of cautionary and advisory labels
- Table of drug interactions (highlighting most common and most severe)

General drug use advice (optional)

- Use of intravenous (IV) additives (general guidance, table with recommended quantities)
- Prescribing in special situations (pregnancy, breast-feeding, renal or liver disease, the elderly, children, terminal care)
- Poisoning (general information, antidotes for common poisons, telephone for poison center if one exists)
- Treatment of snakebites, insect stings

Other components

- Metric conversion scales and tables
- Adverse drug reaction reporting form
- Formulary revision form
- Indexes (by generic name, brand name, therapeutic category)
- Abbreviations

Cautionary and advisory labels may be mentioned as a letter code (for example, *A*: Do not use alcohol).

A section on prescribing and dispensing guidelines can help promote rational medicine use. For example, general points to consider before writing a prescription include the use of International Nonproprietary (generic) Names, the importance of nondrug treatment and simple advice, suggestions for dealing with patients' demands for injections and other expensive dosage forms, and the limited usefulness of combination drugs (see Box 35-3 on safe medication practices, in Chapter 35). Dispensing guidelines may include correct dispensing practices and types of information to be given in counseling patients (see Chapters 30 and 33). A list of cautionary and advisory labels can be included. Each of these can be numbered and cross-referenced in the drug sheets.

A comprehensive index of all drug groups and drug names (including brand names in italics, where appropriate) should be provided at the end of the publication. A good index greatly enhances the usefulness of the formulary manual and the accessibility of its information.

The first edition of the formulary manual will generate many comments. It is worthwhile to invite and structure such comments by including a formulary revision form, containing a request for supporting references.

Developing a formulary manual

The production and maintenance of a formulary manual are major tasks requiring discussion and planning. A clear, systematic process for the development, printing, and distribution of the manual should be agreed upon, with sufficient time, personnel, and resources allocated.

Many aspects of the formulary process have already been described, in discussions of essential medicines lists (Chapter 16) and standard treatment guidelines (in this chapter). The process for developing a formulary manual or national formulary list is not very different, and only some specific aspects are discussed here. WHO has published a practical guide on how to develop a national formulary based on the *WHO Model Formulary* (WHO 2004).

Establish a national formulary committee. The formulary committee could be the national drug committee itself or a smaller subcommittee of it. Ideally, the formulary committee should include a clinical pharmacist or pharmacologist, a physician, and additional prominent medical specialists, as required, to prepare or review sections related to their areas of expertise for accuracy and completeness.

Secure agreement on the content, structure, and format of the formulary. The formulary committee should propose the content, structure, general arrangement of the information, and layout for approval by the national drug committee. The committee should use models such as the *WHO Model Formulary* to save time and effort. Specific issues to be addressed regarding the nature, content, and format of the formulary manual are summarized in the next section.

Appoint an editor. One person (or a maximum of two coeditors) should be appointed to draft the text of the formulary manual. The editor should have an understanding of the pharmaceutical, pharmacological, and clinical aspects of the information required and of the level of language appropriate for the target audience.

Review the draft. When the first draft has been produced, it should be presented to the formulary committee for review. The committee should call upon other experts to resolve issues in dispute or to assist in the review of sections on specialized drugs or topics. Future users of the manual, such as doctors, nurses, pharmacists, and other health care workers, can comment on local practices and customs that may affect how the formulary is accepted. The accepted amendments are then incorporated into the text. This second draft should be widely circulated among the members of the national drug committee and any other invited reviewers for further comment.

A special national meeting involving committee members and stakeholders, including future users of the formulary manual, should then be called to discuss any outstanding issues and gain final approval of the form and content of the document. It is important for the credibility and accept-ability of the formulary manual that all relevant opinions be considered and that key health policy makers be included in the process, even when their expected contributions may be minimal. With this approach, all participants will consider the formulary as partly their own creation and thus will be more committed to ensuring its acceptance and widespread use. Finally, it is important to keep the process ethical. The formulary system must not tolerate influence or pressure from pharmaceutical manufacturers or suppliers concerning any product being considered for addition to or deletion from the formulary.

Revise and produce new editions. As therapeutic practices change and amendments are made to the national list of essential medicines, these must be reflected in the formulary manual, along with proposed revisions submitted by users. When a sufficient number of revisions has been received and accepted, the development process must be repeated to produce a new edition. Producing new editions regularly is important for maintaining the usefulness and credibility of the formulary.

Between editions, new information can be disseminated through circulars or drug bulletins. Prior to the production of a second edition, readers' opinions on the general usefulness, design, and layout of the manual may be sought through a survey.

Practical issues in formulary manual development

In developing a formulary manual, consideration needs to be given to such issues as sequencing, presentation of the information, which information to include, ease of use, inclusion of brand-name drugs (see Figure 17-1), and pricing choices.

Sequence of drug monographs. Structuring drug information by therapeutic class is often preferred to alphabetical order. This format places each medicine in its therapeutic context and helps minimize duplicate listing of medicines. The therapeutic classification of the national list of essential medicines (Chapter 16) should be used. If the manual is organized by therapeutic class, each new section (by therapeutic class) could begin with applicable STGs (for example, guidelines for antiretroviral therapy at the beginning of the listings for the antiretroviral therapeutic class).

Presentation of drug information. Information on drugs can be presented in text or tables. Tables are useful if the information is brief and aid comparisons among medicines. When information is relatively extensive, however, text is more appropriate.

Information on medicines not on the national list of essential medicines. Should information be included on medicines that are not recommended but are used in some settings or that complement medicines on the list? Alternatively, information on these medicines can be provided through a drug information circular or drug bulletin,

Figure 17-1   Sample page from *WHO Model Formulary, 2008*

2.   Analgesics, antipyretics, NSAIMs, DMARDs

Codeine

Tablet: 30 mg (phosphate)

> Drug subject to international control under the Single Convention on Narcotic Drugs (1961).

Uses: mild to moderate pain; diarrhea (section 17.5.3).

Contraindications: respiratory depression, obstructive airways disease, acute asthma attack; where risk of paralytic ileus.

Precautions: renal impairment (Appendix 4) and hepatic impairment (Appendix 5); dependence; pregnancy (Appendix 2) and breastfeeding (Appendix 3); overdosage: section 4.2; interactions: Appendix 1.

Dose: Mild to moderate pain, by mouth, ADULT, 30–60 mg every 4 hours when necessary; maximum, 240 mg daily; CHILD, 1–12 years, 0.5–1 mg/kg every 4–6 hours when needed; maximum, 240 mg daily.

Adverse effects: constipation particularly troublesome in long-term use; dizziness, nausea, vomiting; difficulty with micturition; ureteric or biliary spasm; dry mouth, headaches, sweating, facial flushing; in therapeutic doses, codeine is much less liable than morphine to produce tolerance, dependence, euphoria, sedation, or other adverse effects.

NSAIMS = nonsteroidal anti-inflammatory medicines; DMARDS = disease-modifying antirheumatic drugs.

as well as through training of prescribers. Including private-sector medicines that are not on the national list of essential medicines makes the formulary manual more comprehensive and of interest to a wider audience. However, inclusion of these medicines means that many more monographs must be prepared, making the publication much larger and not easily produced in portable form. And including information that is not relevant to the public sector may induce an unwanted demand for items that are not on the national list of essential medicines.

Size of the publication. A formulary manual may be pocket size for day-to-day use or a larger, desktop reference for occasional use. If used daily, durability is a key consideration. Size is determined primarily by intended use. If the focus is on individual drugs, the formulary is probably most useful as a desktop reference. If the focus is more comparative and evaluative, with information on indications, dosages, and cost—including medicines of first choice—it should probably be pocket size. A loose-leaf edition is not recommended, because with this format, pages tend to disappear and updates are not always properly inserted.

Ease of use. Consideration should be given to promote fast and easy access to the information in the manual, for example by using color-coded pages for each section, edge indexes, and headers. A quick reference listing of commonly used topics can be included on the back cover.

Inclusion of brand-name drugs. Although the drug monographs should always appear under the generic name of the drug, listing common brand names may be useful. If these names are included, they should appear in italics, both in the main text and in the index, so that they are easily identifiable. This method enables prescribers who are not yet familiar with generic names to locate the required monograph easily. Cross-references are helpful.

Provision of national formularies free of charge. The production of a formulary manual is time-consuming and costly, and recovering some of these costs may be necessary. It may be possible to provide the formulary free to public-sector health workers and students and to charge the full price to users in the private sector. Ideally, the formulary manual should be distributed without charge to everyone in the target audience.

Hospital formularies

In many countries, especially those with highly developed health systems, hospitals develop their own formulary manuals. The advantage is that the formulary can be tailored to fit the particular requirements of the hospital and to reflect departmental consensus on first-choice treatments from the national list of essential medicines. In many countries, national STGs are in place, which can be used as a starting point when developing a hospital formulary list or local STGs.

The process is similar to that previously discussed. A hospital formulary committee is given responsibility for producing and subsequently revising the formulary list and manual. Additional information presented in hospital formulary manuals may include details of recommended hospital procedures, hospital antibiotic policy, and guidelines for laboratory investigations and patient management. Hospital formularies usually reflect consensus on the treatment of first choice and thus are not always distinct from treatment guidelines.

17.4 Production and distribution issues

Production issues for treatment guidelines and formulary manuals are similar. In addition to the information in Section 17-3, the following practical advice is useful for producing local reference manuals. The Malawi Essential Drugs Programme documented its experience in a WHO document that includes useful tips and descriptions of how problems were solved (WHO/DAP 1994).

It is important to define a standard style for chapters, tables, and monographs before requesting outside experts to write sections of a publication (treatment guidelines or formulary manual). If standards are not set, large differences in approach, level of detail, and style (for example, for headings, abbreviations, and use of bullets) can be expected. Correcting those differences at a later stage is cumbersome, time-consuming, and expensive. It is a good idea to include one or two examples and a few sample pages along with instructions to the writers. When the manual is ready to be printed, the page proofs should be checked very carefully. A typographical error in a dosage, for example, could be fatal.

The manual can be designed using an in-house computer and word-processing program or contracted out to a graphic designer and printing company. In estimating the number of copies required, consider whether the target audience is likely to increase in the time between editions. The number of copies required is commonly underestimated. Because increasing the number of copies is usually relatively cheap, including an extra margin of at least 10 to 20 percent is recommended.

A clear, systematic, and realistic distribution plan should be drawn up before the manual is printed. Apart from government mail, distribution may be carried out through workshops, professional associations, or sales, or by adding the manuals to regular pharmaceutical supply deliveries. The use of advanced technology in developing countries will affect how health care providers access information such as STGs and formularies (see Chapter 50). More and more formularies and guidelines are being made available online, especially those related to HIV/AIDS (for example, in Brazil, India, Namibia, Nepal). In addition, personal digital assistants (PDAs) and smart phones, which are gaining popularity in developed and developing countries, are another platform for medicine information; the *British National Formulary* is available in PDA format, and the *WHO Model Formulary* will also be PDA-accessible. The U.S. Guideline Clearinghouse has a list of guidelines that are downloadable to a PDA (www.guideline.gov). Whatever distribution method is chosen, the introduction and distribution costs should be included in the budget. A procedure should be set up to monitor distribution and to handle requests for additional printed copies.

17.5 Implementing and maintaining treatment guidelines and formulary manuals

The most common failure in implementing treatment guidelines and national formularies is a lack of credibility and acceptance, caused by failure to involve a wide range of national experts and established training institutions in their production. The greater stakeholders' involvement in the development process, the more likely they are to accept, use, and defend the outcome. Therefore, it is important to involve health workers at various levels, including rural health care and training institutions, in both the development and the review process. A broad range of opinions on the proposed content and format of a first edition and subsequent revisions should be solicited.

After the treatment guidelines manual or formulary manual has been developed and distributed, work is still required to ensure its acceptance and widespread use. Which interventions are the most effective to maximize usage in the health care community will vary depending on the local environment; however, studies show that all interventions should include paper-based or computerized reminders (Grimshaw et al. 2004). The quality of the materials also contributes to their acceptance. A common mistake with treatment guidelines is the selection of medications that are too sophisticated, too expensive, or not generally available at the relevant level of health care. However, acceptance can be improved by ensuring that medicine availability matches the guidelines, by using the materials for teaching and examination at all levels of training, and by using the manual to set standards for drug utilization review. If possible, free copies should be made available to all health workers and all types of students (nursing, pharmacy, paramedical, and medical) and the material should be officially adopted in training institutions. Finally, treatment guidelines and formulary manuals need to be publicized, so health care professionals know they are available (see Country Study 17-3).

The following are important elements for a plan to implement standard treatments—

- Printed reference materials
- Official launch
- Initial training
- Reinforcement training
- Monitoring
- Supervision

Printed reference materials may include manuals, posters, and training materials. Depending on the number of treatments involved, printed references may be in the form of wall charts, pocket handbooks, or larger, "shelf-size" reference books.

Country Study 17-3
Availability and knowledge of HIV/AIDS-related treatment guidelines in Rwanda

The Rwandan government has developed standard treatment guidelines for a number of illnesses, including HIV/AIDS, tuberculosis, and malaria. However, health providers at different levels of care do not necessarily have copies of the guidelines on hand—and indeed may not even know they exist. A 2003 survey focused on the availability of various Rwandan HIV/AIDS guidelines, including those for antiretroviral therapy (ART), opportunistic infections (OIs), sexually transmitted infections (STIs), and voluntary counseling and testing (VCT). Of the forty-nine public and mission facilities surveyed, staff at less than one-third knew that these documents existed,

with awareness being highest at referral facilities and lowest at district pharmacies (see table below).

Despite the government's efforts to develop a variety of guidelines to help health care providers mitigate the effects of the HIV/AIDS epidemic, stronger efforts are needed to improve awareness, demand, and distribution of STGs throughout the health care sector. To support correct usage of the HIV/AIDS guidelines, the survey authors' recommendation was that all staff involved in HIV/AIDS patient management, including pharmacists and pharmacy staff, receive training.

Availability of HIV/AIDS-related documents in public and mission health facilities

Document	All facilities (n = 49)	Level of care			
		Referral hospital	District pharmacy	District hospital	Health center
Awareness of existence of documents	27%	67%	21%	29%	23%
Guidelines for ART, adult and child	10%	67%	0%	6%	15%
Guidelines for ART and monitoring	18%	100%	0%	12%	31%
Guidelines for prescription of ARV drugs	16%	67%	0%	24%	15%
Guidelines for clinical management of HIV/AIDS patients	11%	100%	0%	6%	15%
Guidelines for medical management of HIV/AIDS, including OI	24%	67%	7%	24%	38%
Standard operating procedure for OIs	27%	67%	7%	29%	38%
Guidelines for STIs	57%	67%	29%	65%	85%
Correct manual for corresponding level of care	8%	33%	7%	0%	15%
Guidelines for VCT	39%	67%	7%	59%	46%
Guidelines for home-based care of HIV/AIDS	4%	33%	0%	0%	8%

Source: Lijdsman et al. 2004.

After the materials are distributed, a careful introduction campaign is needed to promote their general acceptance and use. This campaign may include the official launch of the publication by an upper-level official, press reviews, introductory workshops in key educational institutions, articles in drug information circulars and drug bulletins, or a competition for the design of the cover or formulary logo. The cost of such a campaign should be included in the planning.

To maintain formularies and STGs, regularly scheduled meetings must be established and attended by expert committee members who are responsible for updates. The committee reviews and evaluates the latest evidence regarding treatment of diseases and conditions as well as therapeutic drug classes, and considers which medicines should be added to or deleted from the formulary list. A monitoring and evaluation system that tracks treatment failure can

also inform this updating process (see Box 17-2). Any new medicines offering an advantage over the current selections should be considered for addition, and medicines that are no longer used or for which there is insufficient evidence of efficacy, safety, or quality should be recommended for deletion. Although the task of regularly maintaining STGs and formularies is time-consuming, it is critical.

As with the list of essential medicines (Chapter 16), the credibility and acceptability of the treatment guidelines and formulary manual can be maintained only if a transparent process for reviewing and updating them is in place. Especially for treatment guidelines, a second edition will be needed soon after the first. Mistakes will undoubtedly have occurred that need correction, and comments and proposals for change are bound to be received from people who may not have taken the trouble to comment on the first draft. ∎

ASSESSMENT GUIDE

Management structure

- Is there a national committee responsible for managing the formulary process?
- Are there drugs and therapeutics committees in major hospitals?

Outcome of the formulary process

- Is there a national therapeutic guide with standardized treatments? When was the last update?
- Is there a national formulary manual with basic drug information? When was the last update?
- Are the treatment guidelines and formulary manual consistent with the national list of essential medicines?
- Do the treatment guidelines cover common problems such as acute respiratory tract infections, diarrheal diseases, sexually transmitted infections, tuberculosis, leprosy, hypertension, diabetes, and epilepsy?

Use of treatment guidelines and formulary manual

- Is there a national drug policy statement to encourage the use of the treatment guidelines and formulary manual?
- Are the treatment guidelines and formulary manual used for basic and in-service training of health personnel?
- What percentage of public-sector health facilities has a copy of the treatment guidelines and/or formulary manual?
- What percentage of prescriptions in public-sector health facilities complies with the treatment guidelines?
- Is a process in place to ensure that treatment guidelines and formulary manuals are periodically evaluated and updated?

References and further readings

★ = Key readings.

APUA (Alliance for the Prudent Use of Antibiotics). 2003. *Framework for Use of Antimicrobial Resistance Surveillance in the Development of Standard Treatment Guidelines.* Boston: APUA. <http://www.tufts.edu/med/apua/policy/apua_action_3_144427577.pdf>

Bahtsevani, C., G. Uden, and A. Willman. 2004. Outcomes of Evidence-based Clinical Practice Guidelines: A Systematic Review. *International Journal of Technology Assessment in Health Care* 20(4):427–33.

Feder, G., M. Eccles, R. Grol, C. Griffiths, and J. Grimshaw. 1999. Using Clinical Guidelines. *BMJ* 318:728–30.

Grimshaw J. M., and I. T. Russell. 1993. Effect of Clinical Guidelines on Medical Practice: A Systematic Review of Rigorous Evaluations. *Lancet* 342(8883):1317–22.

★ Grimshaw, J. M., R. E. Thomas, G. MacLennan, C. Fraser, C. R. Ramsay, L. Vale, P. Whitty, et al. 2004. Effectiveness and Efficiency of Guideline Dissemination and Implementation Strategies. *Health Technology Assessment* 8(6).

Hidayati, S., and S. Munawaroh. 2004. "Small Group Discussion among Paramedics at the Health Center Level to Improve Compliance with Standard Treatment Guidelines for Acute Respiratory Infections." Paper presented at the International Conference on Improving Use of Medicines, March 30–April 2, Chiang Mai, Thailand.

Lijdsman, C., C. Onyango, A. Gatera, S. Saleeb, B. Tarrafeta, and M. Gabra. 2004. *Assessment of the Health Commodity Supply Sector in Rwanda, September 2003.* Submitted to the U.S. Agency for International Development by the Rational Pharmaceutical Management Plus Program. Arlington, Va.: Management Sciences for Health. <http://www.who.int/3by5/amds/en/country8.pdf>

MSF (Médecins sans Frontières). 2010. *Essential Drugs: Practical Guidelines.* 3rd ed. Paris: MSF. <http://www.refbooks.msf.org/msf_docs/en/Essential_drugs/ED_en.pdf>

National Health and Medical Research Council [Australia]. 1999. *A Guide to the Development, Implementation and Evaluation of Clinical Practice Guidelines.* Canberra: Commonwealth of Australia. <http://www.nhmrc.gov.au/_files_nhmrc/file/publications/synopses/cp30.pdf>

New Zealand Guidelines Group. 2001. *Handbook for the Preparation of Explicit Evidence-based Clinical Practice Guidelines.* Wellington: New Zealand Guidelines Group. <http://old.nzgg.org.nz/download/files/nzgg_guideline_handbook.pdf>

NHS CRD (National Health Service Centre for Reviews and Dissemination). 2008. *Systematic Reviews: CRD's Guidance for Undertaking Reviews in Health Care.* York, UK: NHS Centre for Reviews and Dissemination. <http://www.york.ac.uk/inst/crd/pdf/Systematic_Reviews.pdf>

———. 2001. *Undertaking Systematic Reviews of Research on Effectiveness: CRD's Guidance for Those Carrying Out or Commissioning Reviews.* CRD Report Number 4. 2nd ed. York: NHS Centre for Reviews and Dissemination.

★ NICE (National Institute for Health and Clinical Excellence). 2009. *The Guidelines Manual.* London: NICE. <http://www.nice.org.uk>

RPM Plus and WHO (Rational Pharmaceutical Management Plus Program and World Health Organization). 2007a. *Trainer's Guide.* Drug and Therapeutics Committee Training Course, Session 6: Evaluating the Cost of Pharmaceuticals. Arlington, Va.: Management Sciences for Health. <http://www.msh.org/projects/rpmplus/Documents/upload/06-TG_Evaluating-drug-costs_final-08.pdf>

———. 2007b. *Trainer's Guide; Participant's Guide.* Drug and Therapeutics Committee Training Course, Session 10: Standard Treatment Guidelines. Arlington, Va: Management Sciences for Health. <http://www.msh.org/projects/rpmplus/Resources/TrainingInitiatives/All-DTC-Training-Guides.cfm>

———. 2007c. *Trainer's Guide; Participant's Guide.* Drug and Therapeutics Committee Training Course, Session 2: Developing and Maintaining a Formulary. Arlington, Va.: Management Sciences for Health. <http://www.msh.org/projects/rpmplus/Resources/TrainingInitiatives/All-DTC-Training-Guides.cfm>

Shekelle, P. G., S. H. Woolf, M. Eccles, and J. Grimshaw. 1999. Developing Guidelines. *BMJ* 318: 593–6.

SIGN (Scottish Intercollegiate Guidelines Network). 2008. *SIGN 50: A Guideline Developers' Handbook.* Edinburgh: SIGN. <http://www.sign.ac.uk/guidelines/fulltext/50/index.html>

UNAIDS (Joint United Nations Programme on HIV/AIDS). 1999. *Developing HIV/AIDS Treatment Guidelines.* Geneva: UNAIDS. <http://data.unaids.org/Publications/IRC-pub03/developingkm_en.pdf>

★ WHO (World Health Organization). 2004. *How to Develop a National Formulary Based on the* WHO *Model Formulary: A Practical Guide.* Geneva: WHO. <http://whqlibdoc.who.int/hq/2004/WHO_EDM_PAR_2004.8.pdf>

WHO/DAP (World Health Organization/Action Programme on Essential Drugs). 1994. *Producing National Drug and Therapeutic Information: The Malawi Approach to Developing Standard Treatment Guidelines.* Geneva: WHO/DAP. <http://apps.who.int/medicinedocs/pdf/whozip24e/whozip24e.pdf>

★ WHO/GPE (World Health Organization/Global Programme on Evidence for Health Policy). 2003. *Guidelines for WHO Guidelines.* Geneva: WHO/GPE. <http://whqlibdoc.who.int/hq/2003/EIP_GPE_EQC_2003_1.pdf>

Woolf, S. H., R. Grol, A. Hutchinson, M. Eccles, and J. Grimshaw, J. 1999. Potential Benefits, Limitations, and Harms of Clinical Guidelines. *BMJ* 318: 527–30.

Formularies and treatment guidelines

★ Joint Formulary Committee [Great Britain]. *British National Formulary.* London: British Medical Association and the Royal Pharmaceutical Society of Great Britain. [Updated every six months.] <http://www.bnf.org>

★ Ministry of Health/Ghana National Drugs Programme. 2004. *Standard Treatment Guidelines.* 5th ed. Accra: Ministry of Health/Ghana National Drugs Programme. <http://collections.info collections.org/whocountry/en/d/Js6861e/>

★ MSF (Médecins sans Frontières). 2010. *Clinical Guidelines: Diagnostic and Treatment Manual for Curative Programmes in Hospitals and Dispensaries: Guidance for Prescribing.* Paris: MSF. <http://www.refbooks.msf.org/msf_docs/en/Clinical_Guide/CG_en.pdf>

National Department of Health [South Africa]. 2008. *Standard Treatment Guidelines and Essential Drugs List for South Africa: Primary Health Care.* Pretoria: National Department of Health. <http://flagshipcourse.sarpam.net/wp-content/uploads/group-documents/13/1310473918-STGEMLPHC2008.pdf>

Organisation of Eastern Caribbean States Pharmaceutical Procurement Service (OECS/PPS). 2006. *Regional Drug Formulary, Seventh Edition, 2006–2007.* Castries, St. Lucia: OECS/PPS. <http://www.oecs.org/pps/documents-a-reports/cat_view/36-health/37-pharmaceutical-procurement/39-oecspps-regional-formulary>

PAHO (Pan American Health Organization). 2004. *Guía para el tratamiento de las enfermedades infecciosas (PAHO Guide for the Treatment of Infectious Diseases)* [Spanish]. Washington, D.C.: PAHO. <http://www.paho.org/Spanish/AD/DPC/CD/amr-guia-tratamiento.pdf>

SIGN (Scottish Intercollegiate Guidelines Network). *Quick Reference Guides and Full Guidelines.* <http://www.sign.ac.uk/guidelines/index.html>

★ Therapeutic Guidelines Limited [Australia]. <http://www.tg.com.au>

WHO links to international antiretroviral treatment guidelines and reports can be accessed at http://womenchildrenhiv.org/wchiv?page=cp-01-02

★ WHO (World Health Organization). 2008. *WHO Model Formulary.* Geneva: WHO. <http://www.who.int/selection_medicines/list/WMF2008.pdf>

———. 2006a. *Antiretroviral Drugs for Treating Pregnant Women and Preventing HIV Infection in Infants in Resource-Limited Settings: Towards Universal Access: Recommendations for a Public Health Approach.* 2006 revision. Geneva: WHO. <http://whqlibdoc.who.int/publications/2006/9789241594660_eng.pdf>

★ ———. 2006b. *Antiretroviral Therapy for HIV Infection in Adults and Adolescents: Recommendations for a Public Health Approach.* 2006 revision. Geneva: WHO. <http://whqlibdoc.who.int/publications/2006/9789241594677_eng.pdf>

CHAPTER 18

Managing procurement

SUMMARY

This chapter focuses primarily on best practices for health systems that manage procurement in-house. An effective procurement process seeks to ensure the availability of the right medicines in the right quantities, at reasonable prices, and at recognized standards of quality. Pharmaceuticals may be acquired through purchase, donation, or manufacture.

The procurement cycle involves the following steps—

- Mobilize procurement team and key players
- Review medicine selections
- Specify quality standards
- Determine quantities needed
- Reconcile needs and funds
- Choose procurement method
- Locate and select suppliers
- Specify contract terms
- Monitor order status
- Receive and check medicines
- Make payment
- Distribute medicines
- Collect consumption information

The major procurement methods used by health systems are open tender, restricted tender, competitive negotiation, and direct procurement, which vary with respect to their effect on price, delivery times, and workload of the procurement office. In recent years, some public-sector procurement systems (particularly in Latin America) have introduced e-procurement (Internet tendering) and more specifically the "reverse auction" approach, although these methods have not been widely used to procure pharmaceuticals. Funding sources (governments and donors) often dictate which procurement method to use. Finally, some developing-country health systems purchase medicines and health commodities directly from international procurement agents, many of which are based in Europe.

Key principles of good pharmaceutical procurement for health systems include—

- Reliable payment and good financial management
- Procurement by generic name
- Clear specification of a recognized pharmaceutical quality standard
- Limitation of procurement to the essential medicines list
- Increasing procurement volume by aggregating demand
- Formal supplier qualification and monitoring
- Competitive procurement
- Monopsony commitment
- Order quantities based on reliable estimate of forecasted actual need
- Transparency and written procedures
- Separation of key functions
- Product quality assurance program
- Annual audit with published results
- Regular reporting of procurement performance indicators

As described in Chapter 8, different systems for managing supply chains for public health systems include the central stores system, autonomous supply agency system, direct delivery system, primary distributor system, private pharmacy system, or often a mix of these systems. All involve pharmaceutical procurement.

Procurement may proceed under different purchasing models—annual purchasing, scheduled purchasing, or perpetual purchasing. Different combinations of these models may be used at different levels of the system or for different medicines.

Effective procurement is a mechanism for managing the buyer-seller relationship to ensure transparent and ethical transactions that result in the buyer receiving the correct goods and the seller receiving timely payment. A collaborative process is needed between the procurement office, with requirements for trained staff and appropriate management systems, and technical and policy committees, which may make final decisions as to which medicines to buy, in what quantities, and from which suppliers.

Key considerations for financial sustainability include reliable access to funds for pharmaceutical purchase and support of the procurement office, access to foreign currency exchange for international procurement, and reliable payment mechanisms.

18.1 Introduction

The pharmaceutical procurement system is a major determinant of pharmaceutical availability and total pharmaceutical costs. In most developing countries, pharmaceutical purchases represent the single largest health expenditure after personnel costs. Pharmaceuticals also consume the major share of health-related foreign currency exchange.

An effective procurement process should—

- Seek to manage the buyer-seller relationship in a transparent and ethical manner
- Procure the right medicines in the right quantities
- Obtain the lowest practical purchase price
- Ensure that all pharmaceuticals procured meet recognized standards of quality
- Arrange timely delivery to avoid shortages and stockouts
- Ensure supplier reliability with respect to service and quality
- Set the purchasing schedule, formulas for order quantities, and safety stock levels to achieve the lowest total cost of purchasing at each level of the system
- Achieve these objectives in the most efficient manner possible

Given the impact of procurement activities on the operation and effectiveness of health services, it is essential that these activities be performed by competent staff using sound procedures, working in adequate offices with good communications, and with access to reliable inventory and consumption information. Good procurement management also demands medical, pharmaceutical, managerial, financial, and often political expertise.

Some developing countries have relatively successful public-sector procurement programs, but in many countries, pharmaceutical procurement continues to be less successful, in spite of extensive reform efforts and substantial financial assistance from aid agencies.

When a health system sets up a centrally managed pharmaceutical procurement program, it is, in effect, developing a form of a pooled procurement system serving health regions, districts, and individual health facilities. The purchases may be financed centrally through government allocations or donor contributions, in a decentralized way through medicines fees, or through some combination of financing alternatives. Procurement may be managed through any of several organizational arrangements described in Chapter 8 and discussed later in this chapter.

Over the last twenty years, formal pooled procurement programs have become common in some industrialized countries (known in the United States as group purchasing organizations), and the factors that make them successful are known. Regional approaches to multicountry pooled procurement have had mixed results, although there are some long-standing regional programs that have achieved some successes. At the global level, United Nations agencies such as UNICEF, United Nations Population Fund, and United Nations Development Programme have long functioned as pooled procurement systems serving their country programs. In recent years, a number of new global procurement mechanisms have emerged, such as the Stop TB Global Drug Facility, the U.S. President's Plan for Emergency AIDS Relief (PEPFAR)–funded Supply Chain Management System (SCMS), and the Global Fund to Fight AIDS, Tuberculosis and Malaria's voluntary pooled procurement system.

Although the procurement chapters in this manual are written primarily with public-sector procurement programs in mind, the principles and procedures can be applied to either public or private procurement at any level, from a rural aid post to a national health program. The details of procurement at various levels may be slightly different, but the basic steps are the same.

18.2 The procurement cycle

The procurement cycle includes most of the decisions and actions that determine the specific medicine quantities obtained, prices paid, and quality of medicines received.

Procurement is defined here as the process of purchasing supplies directly from national or multinational private or public suppliers; purchasing through global agencies and procurement mechanisms or regional procurement systems; or purchasing from international procurement agents. These sources may be used individually or in combination to meet the entire range of pharmaceutical needs.

Steps in the procurement cycle are illustrated in Figure 18-1 and discussed in Chapters 9–15 and 18–21.

18.3 Factors influencing pharmaceutical prices and total costs

Given the limited budgets of virtually all health programs, pharmaceutical procurement costs must be a concern of all policy makers, senior officials, essential medicines program managers, and procurement staff. Pharmaceutical procurement costs include several different components; some costs are obvious and some are not.

Unit prices

What determines the tender price of a container of 1,000 amoxicilline tablets or ten ampoules of adrenaline? There are many considerations involved in pharmaceutical pricing by manufacturers and distributors, and many factors that

Figure 18-1   Procurement cycle

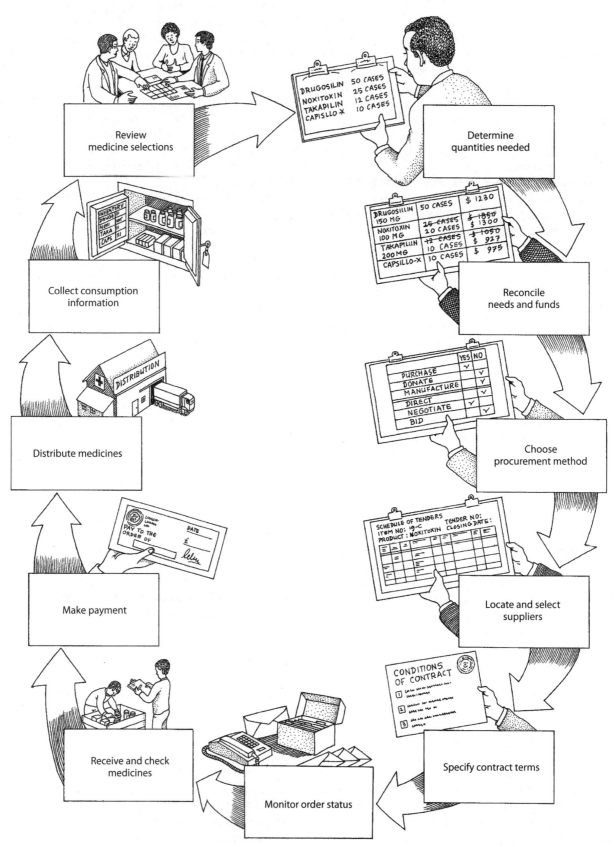

cause prices to vary from country to country. A fundamental principle is that increasing competition among suppliers and products usually decreases pharmaceutical prices.

Several factors influence competition and pricing in any pharmaceutical market. One issue is how many different drug products and different generic versions of the same product are on the market. The "rule of five" in pharmaceutical pricing says that in general the lowest competitive prices are available when five or more generic alternatives for a particular product are available or when, in a tender, there are at least five bids per item (WHO 1999).

These factors can be influenced by government policies on registration, licensing for manufacturing and distribution, authority to prescribe and dispense, generic substitution, and price control. In some markets, even sole-source suppliers may offer discount pricing to the public sector that is not necessarily related to purchase volume to establish or maintain market share or to negotiate with international development entities. As discussed in Section 18.4, the type of procurement method used greatly influences how much competition there is among potential suppliers. The strategies and issues discussed in Section 18.5 also directly or indirectly influence the degree of competition and the degree of discount pricing available to the health system.

Reorder frequency and the total cost of purchasing

Pharmaceutical acquisition prices are only one part of the total cost of pharmaceutical purchasing; the other important components are the costs associated with holding inventory, the costs of operating the purchasing system, and the extra costs incurred when stockouts occur (shortage costs).

Although procurement offices typically concern themselves mainly with pharmaceutical acquisition costs, the other cost components may increase the total purchasing cost by 50 percent or more of the acquisition costs. For each country's situation, total purchasing costs can be minimized by choosing the optimal reorder frequency model, as defined by the—

- Interval between orders—options include annual (one order per year), scheduled (periodic orders, for example, every three months), and perpetual (orders placed whenever stock falls to a specified level)
- Safety stock targets, which vary according to supplier lead times, patterns of consumption, and service-level objectives
- Formula used for calculating the order quantity, which may be a fixed or variable quantity

The choice of reorder frequency models is discussed in Chapter 23; these are not always simple decisions. Systems minimize costs by striking the right balance between the various elements—less frequent ordering decreases pro-

curement process costs, but increases stock-holding costs. The reorder frequency model may differ from one level of the supply system to another or from one type or class of drug product to another. For example, consider a supply system with a central medical store (CMS) and several regional warehouses that serve hospitals and major health centers, which then distribute to primary care facilities. The CMS might purchase most items through annual tender; however, most countries can achieve lower total costs by purchasing at least some items more frequently. The regional stores might order from the CMS on a quarterly basis for most items. The health centers and hospitals might order most items monthly, with a weekly supplemental order, and so forth.

The reorder frequency influences the types of procurement methods and purchasing contracts that can be used (see Section 18.4). However, this works both ways; individual country circumstances (typically storage conditions and space availability) or laws and funding regulations, especially from donors, may dictate one sort of procurement method or contract, which then limits the options for choosing the reorder frequency. For example, if only fixed-quantity tenders are allowable under local laws, implementing a perpetual purchasing model will be difficult. If all pharmaceuticals are imported and average lead times are six to nine months, avoiding an annual purchasing system for most items will be a challenge.

The systems and formulas used to estimate needs and define order quantities vary with the purchasing model and with the availability of information on past consumption. The procedures for estimating annual procurement needs are discussed in Chapter 20; with scheduled or perpetual purchasing, order quantity can usually be determined by one of the formulas from Chapter 23. However, some situations may require the use of a procedure such as morbidity-based forecasting to estimate needs for procurement (Chapter 20).

Chapter 40 presents total cost analysis as a method for compiling and analyzing the total costs of inventory management: pharmaceutical acquisition, inventory holding, purchasing operations, and shortage costs. Total cost analysis examines stable and variable costs for potential savings and helps managers evaluate potential changes in supply chain structure, and in procurement and distribution policy and procedure, in terms of the likely impact on total operating costs.

Visible and hidden costs

As discussed above, the total procurement cost has four components—pharmaceutical acquisition prices, inventory-holding costs, purchasing operations costs, and shortage costs. Some of these costs are easily visible to managers—the total expenditures for pharmaceutical acquisition or the salaries of procurement staff. However, the costs associated with shortages and poor supplier performance are not so obvious; hidden costs associated with poor performance by the supplier or the procurement office include—

- Increased acquisition costs due to emergency procurement, such as when a vital medicine is ordered too late or usage exceeds estimates or the supplier fails to deliver on time
- Replacement costs when goods are lost or must be discarded because of poor packaging, improper shipping conditions, rapid spoilage, or short shelf life
- Replacement costs for short shipments, incorrect concentrations of liquid preparations, wrong dosage forms, and so on
- Storage, port charges, and administrative expenses due to inefficient clearing procedures or lack of funds or proper documentation
- Health and economic costs of stockouts resulting from delay or default on delivery

The potential impact of hidden costs on the total cost is illustrated in Figure 18-2. In this example, supplier A has quoted a lower price, but additional expenses resulting from poor performance ultimately raise the total cost above that quoted by supplier B. In a competitive tender, a large number of suppliers with varying technical and commercial backgrounds may submit bids, and their quoted prices will vary considerably. Because no cost adjustments for performance are permitted to be considered during the tender assessment process, once tender bidding has begun, the prequalification of suppliers based on past performance can help minimize the impact of hidden costs.

Many of the hidden costs mentioned above can be minimized through careful procurement practices, such as avoiding last-minute orders due to a lack of planning; however, other hidden costs are imposed or regulated by the government, which may be more difficult for the procurement office to work around. Country Study 18-1 shows examples of hidden costs of medicines that are controlled through national pharmaceutical policy. See also Chapter 9 on pharmaceutical pricing.

18.4 Overview of procurement methods

There are numerous mechanisms by which governments, nongovernmental organizations (NGOs), and other organizations manage their in-house procurement of pharmaceuticals. Pharmaceutical procurement methods, at any level of a health system, generally fall into a few basic categories: open tender; restricted tender; competitive negotiation, including international or local shopping; and direct procurement. Each of these methods can be used with any of the standard

Figure 18-2   Impact of hidden cost on total cost

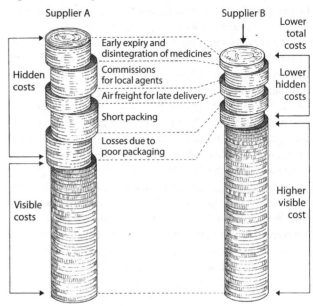

TOTAL COST = VISIBLE COST + HIDDEN COST

reorder frequency models—annual, scheduled, or perpetual review—given the right sort of procurement contract.

Open tender: Open tendering is a formal procedure by which quotes are invited from any supplier's representative on a local or worldwide basis, subject to the terms and conditions specified in the tender invitation. International competitive bidding, as specified in World Bank (2000; 2004b) guidelines, is a tender open to all interested international manufacturers from World Bank member countries.

Restricted tender: In a restricted tender, interested suppliers must be approved in advance, often through a formal prequalification process that considers adherence to good manufacturing practices, past supply performance, financial viability, and related factors. The prequalification process is often open to any supplier that wishes to apply.

E-procurement and reverse auction: E-procurement is Internet-based tendering. In the reverse auction approach (which is a variation of restricted tenders), qualified bidders submit an initial offer; the lowest offer received is posted publicly without naming the bidder after the first round; and then qualified bidders are invited to offer lower prices than that posted low price. The process continues round-by-round until no more prices are submitted; then the lowest posted bid wins the contract. This approach has rarely been used for pharmaceutical procurement (with most experience in Latin America); however, it may gain traction as global Internet capacity and use increase. Pharmaceutical quality assurance requirements and related factors may limit the use of this model, at least in its current form.

Competitive negotiation: In competitive negotiation, the buyer approaches a limited number of selected suppliers (typically at least three) for price quotations. Buyers may also bargain with these suppliers to achieve specific price or service arrangements. This procurement method is used primarily in the private sector, because public-sector procurement organizations are generally forbidden from negotiating or bargaining with suppliers. For example, global organizations such as UNICEF, the Clinton Foundation, and SCMS have successfully negotiated reduced prices of antiretroviral (ARV) medicines with manufacturers.

International or local shopping: As with competitive negotiation, in international or local shopping, the buyer obtains at least three quotes from suppliers; however, bargaining or negotiation of any kind are generally not permitted.

Direct procurement: The simplest, but usually most expensive, method of procurement is direct purchase from a single supplier, either at the quoted list price or at a negotiated standard discount off the list price. For single-source medicines (generally those under patent

with no licensing agreements that allow other firms to manufacture the medicine), the buyer basically has three choices—negotiated procurement, direct procurement, or selection of an alternative drug product.

International open tenders usually attract the largest number of competitive offers and potentially the lowest prices. International tenders for pharmaceuticals are limited to primary manufacturers and commercial suppliers or to international procurement agencies.

Virtually all professionally managed pharmaceutical procurement offices (that is, international procurement agencies and successful government pharmaceutical procurement units) purchase most large-volume items by either restricted tender or competitive negotiation from a limited list of reliable suppliers, such as private companies and global procurement mechanisms such as SCMS, the Global Fund's voluntary pooled procurement, or UNICEF.

Some procurement offices use a combination of methods: open or restricted tender for large-volume items, and competitive negotiation or direct procurement for lower-volume or emergency supplies.

In many country situations it may not be feasible or cost-effective to satisfy demand for medicines and obtain

Country Study 18-1
Hidden costs in the procurement process: Examples from nine countries

Understanding the many component costs related to procuring medicines is an important step in reducing overall costs. Improving procurement practices can help decrease hidden costs, but many costs result from government policies. In a study of the hidden costs of essential medicines, information on such government-influenced tariffs and charges was collected from the literature and through personal communication. The table below shows the extensive variation and potential impact that these types of costs can have on prices of essential medicines—which may be passed along to patients.

Source: Adapted from Levison and Laing 2003.

Percentage added to prices of essential medicines

Hidden cost	Sri Lanka	Kenya	Tanzania	South Africa	Brazil	Armenia	Kosovo	Nepal	Mauritius
Import tariff	0	0	10		11.7	0	1	4	5
Port charges	4	8	1				4		
Clearance and freight		1	2					1.5	5
Preshipment inspection		2.75	1.2						
Pharmacy board fee			2						
Importer's margins	25						15	10	
Value added tax					14	18	20	0	
State government tax					6				
Wholesaler	8.5	15	0	21.2	7	25	15	10	14
Retail	16.25	20	50	50	22	25	25	16	27
Total markup	**63.97**	**54.22**	**74.3**	**74.05**	**82.38**	**87.5**	**73.64**	**48.08**	**59.26**

> **Country Study 18-2**
> **Pooled procurement through the Organisation of Eastern Caribbean States/**
> **Pharmaceutical Procurement Service**
>
> The Pharmaceutical Procurement Service (PPS) (origi-
> nally known as the Eastern Caribbean Drug Service) was
> established in 1986, with U.S. Agency for International
> Development (USAID) support, to manage the pro-
> curement process on behalf of member countries of the
> Organisation of Eastern Caribbean States (OECS).
>
> Before the OECS/PPS, the pharmaceutical supply
> systems of OECS member countries were beset with
> problems: disorganized procurement and management
> functions and poorly trained staff contributed to chronic
> medicine shortages in health facilities. Because of fiscal
> constraints, countries were slow to make payments to
> suppliers and incurred large surcharges. The pharma-
> ceutical prices paid by OECS states ranged 30 percent
> or more above those paid by other countries of the
> Caribbean, such as Barbados.
>
> Design of the OECS/PPS procurement program incorpo-
> rated a number of key features—
>
> **Selective list:** Procurement under OECS/PPS is based
> on the *Eastern Caribbean Regional Drug Formulary and
> Therapeutics Manual,* compiled from individual country
> medicine lists representing large-volume items for which
> demand is consistently high. The OECS/PPS procures
> approximately 80 percent of public-sector pharmaceuti-
> cals and medical supplies. Country-level purchasing offi-
> cers may purchase nontender items independently.
>
> **Pooled quantities:** Each year, the nine participating
> countries project their expected purchases of formu-
> lary items and forward these estimates to OECS/PPS,
> where management and technical staff review them. The
> individual projections are then aggregated into a single
> tender list.
>
> **Competitive bidding:** Suppliers are prequalified for the
> OECS/PPS restricted tenders. Prequalification is based
> on submission of a vendor registration form and refer-
> ence checks with international agencies and procurement
> agencies that are listed as references. A single contract
> award is made for each tendered product to a primary
> and a secondary supplier. Unless quality or performance
> issues are a concern, the lowest tender price receives the
> primary award. Tenders are not split.
>
> **Supplier monitoring and quality assurance:** The per-
> formance of all contract suppliers (lead times, partial
> shipments, quality problems) is monitored and reviewed
> annually to determine which suppliers should continue
> as registered participants. OECS/PPS solicits oral and
> written reports from member countries concerning
> potential product problems and follows up with testing at
> the Caribbean Regional Drug Testing Laboratory.
>
> **Variable purchase quantities by group members:**
> OECS/PPS estimates of purchase volume are not bind-
> ing on individual countries or on OECS/PPS, and no

competitive pricing entirely through locally managed procurement. There are global as well as some regional procurement sources that can be accessed to augment, or if needed,
to replace locally managed procurement for a selected set of
products.

At the global level, United Nations agencies such as
UNICEF have long operated pooled procurement systems
primarily serving their own country programs. In recent
years, several other global pooled procurement mechanisms
have emerged along with the large increase in funding for
procurement through financing mechanisms such as the
Global Fund, UNITAID, and PEPFAR. Moreover, a number
of nonprofit procurement agencies serve as suppliers to public and NGO health systems in developing countries; while
these are not pooled procurement mechanisms per se, they
do offer relatively small-scale purchasers access to "global"
pricing.

Generally, three types of these global procurement mechanisms exist—

Integrated "local-to-global" supply chain systems: These
mechanisms work directly with countries to coordinate
demand and manage tenders and competitive negotiations to establish best prices; manage global freight and
logistics systems to coordinate distribution; and operate
in-house product quality assurance programs. The best
known such mechanism is probably the UNICEF system. In addition, SCMS now provides HIV-related commodities and services to countries that receive PEPFAR
funding.

Donor-supported global procurement agencies: Examples
include the Stop TB/WHO Global Drug Facility, which
purchases and distributes both first-line and second-line
TB medicines, and the Global Fund's voluntary pooled
procurement mechanism, which purchases and delivers
medicines and other health commodities to Global Fund
principal recipients.

Nonprofit procurement agencies: These agencies purchase
and distribute medicines and other health commodities

fixed procurement quantity or delivery schedule exists. All OECS member states are charged the same contract price, regardless of volume, for the duration of the contract period. All tender prices are CIF (cost, insurance, and freight) direct to the member country.

Monopsony commitment: Member countries are required to purchase items listed in OECS/PPS contracts solely through the PPS system, from contracted suppliers. OECS/PPS monitors this requirement annually.

Reliable payment mechanism: Payments to suppliers are managed by the Eastern Caribbean Central Bank (ECCB), where each participating country maintains a special revolving drug account. Suppliers are paid directly by the ECCB from the purchasing country's drug account, and the individual countries reimburse their accounts when they receive their shipments. An important element in PPS's initial success in pooling procurement was its ability to pay suppliers promptly in foreign exchange within sixty days of receipt in country. However, in recent years, some OECS countries have been slow to reimburse their country drug accounts, resulting in suppliers withholding shipments to both the late and the on-time payers. An additional consequence has been the dwindling number of suppliers competing in the tendering process, which can discourage the lowest prices in competitive bidding.

Thirteen-percent fee to group members: With each order, an administrative fee of 13 percent of the payment amount is made by ECCB to the PPS account. (The fee was originally 15 percent.) This fee covers all PPS operating expenses; no additional budget allocations have been required. OECS/PPS became financially self-supporting in 1989.

The results of the OECS/PPS procurement program have been extremely positive. After initial success with pharmaceuticals, the PPS has expanded its list of tendered products to include medical supplies, contraceptives, and x-ray consumables. It includes 700 items—about 70 percent of them pharmaceuticals. Participating countries benefited from an average 44 percent reduction in acquisition price for tender products in the first OECS/PPS tender cycle (1987–88) and an average of 37 percent between 1998 and 2002. Between 1997 and 2006, the value of annual purchases increased by more than 100 percent.

The main challenges include late payments by member countries, the opposition and influence of suppliers, countries making purchases outside of the cartel, managing donations, poor forecasting, and small purchase orders.

Sources: Burnett 2003; WHO 2007.

to public sector and NGO health systems in developing countries. Such agencies are often, but not always, donor financed. Examples include Action Medeor, IDA Foundation, MissionPharma, and Trimed.

Regional multicountry pooled procurement has been attempted over the years in different parts of the world, but has rarely proven sustainable. However, some regional systems have achieved successes over time, including the Pooled Procurement Service (PPS) of the Organisation of Eastern Caribbean States (OECS), the Gulf Cooperation Council group purchasing program, and the Pan American Health Organization (PAHO) regional programs for purchasing vaccines and ARVs.

Undoubtedly, the primary consideration in developing a pooled procurement system is political commitment; without it, the system will never succeed. But even with political commitment, several aspects of procurement need to be harmonized for successful implementation of multicountry pooled procurement mechanisms. They include laws, regulations, and operational processes related to—

- Medicines regulation and registration of products
- Procurement processes and local preference issues
- Financial mechanisms and payment to vendors
- Standard currency

The difficulty in harmonizing these processes should not be discounted, and some issues also affect global pooled procurement mechanisms. For example, the lack of harmonization among national registration requirements often limits the capacity of a global pooled procurement system to establish supply contracts that will serve all target countries, because the best-value supplier may not have registered its products in all of the countries. Over the years, regional groups, such as the Association of Southeast Asian Nations and the Pan American Network for Drug Regulatory Harmonization have worked to formalize pharmaceutical harmonization initiatives, often focused on pharmaceutical registration, and sometimes on procurement policies and regulations (see Country Study 18-2).

Four models of procurement collaboration include informed buying, coordinated informed buying, group contracting, and central contracting and purchasing (MSH/CPM 2002). Regional pooled procurement does not have to start with a full-fledged pooled procurement system. The first step might be simple information sharing between national or subnational procurement agencies. If

Country Study 18-3
Assessing regional collaboration of procurement activities to increase access to HIV/AIDS medicines and commodities in sub-Saharan Africa

Sub-Saharan Africa faces challenges in increasing access to high-quality, affordable pharmaceuticals for treating people living with HIV/AIDS. Even when antiretroviral treatment is available, its effectiveness is undermined by lack of access to a constant and uninterrupted supply of antiretroviral medicines. Groups of countries in different parts of the developing world have had success in pooling their resources to more efficiently procure essential medicines and supplies. Regional collaboration for the procurement of HIV/AIDS-related pharmaceuticals and commodities was proposed as a way to increase access to these products in the fourteen countries belonging to the Commonwealth Regional Health Community (CRHC) of East, Central, and Southern Africa.

Regional collaboration for procurement

Collaborative procurement covers a range of options, from simple information sharing to pooling of resources, combined with contracting and purchasing by an agency acting on behalf of a group of facilities, health systems, or countries. The four models of collaboration assessed are informed buying, coordinated informed buying, group contracting, and central contracting.

Information sharing		Pooled procurement	
Informed buying	**Coordinated informed buying**	**Group contracting**	**Central contracting and purchasing**
Member countries share information about prices and suppliers.	Member countries undertake joint market research, share supplier performance information, and monitor prices.	Member countries jointly negotiate prices and select suppliers. Member countries agree to purchase from selected suppliers.	Member countries jointly conduct tenders and awards contracts through an organization acting on their behalf.
Countries conduct procurement individually.	Countries conduct procurement individually.	Countries conduct purchasing individually.	Central buying unit manages the purchase on behalf of countries.

all the requirements to sustain an effective and efficient formal pooled procurement system can be met, the group can progress to pooling resources combined with joint contracting and purchasing carried out by an agency acting on behalf of a group of facilities, health systems, or countries. Country Study 18-3 summarizes an assessment of countries in sub-Saharan Africa that was done to determine if a regional collaboration model for procurement was feasible.

In many countries, laws and government regulations or the funding sources (that is, donors) dictate the procurement method to be used, often based on the value of the goods being purchased. Chapter 21 focuses on the tender process and compares the most common procurement methods.

18.5 Good pharmaceutical procurement practices

Pharmaceutical procurement practices vary widely from country to country. However, decades of experience with essential medicines programs and many more years of experience with large government-run pharmaceutical supply

services in a number of countries, as well as with regional and global pooled procurement schemes, have suggested a number of key principles, which Box 18-1 summarizes. These practices are applicable to individual procurement agencies as well as to pooled procurement systems serving multiple health systems.

Reliable payment and good financial management

Prompt, reliable payment of suppliers has the single greatest influence on bringing down pharmaceutical prices and keeping those prices as low as possible (see Country Study 18-2), but this area often receives inadequate attention. Given greater needs and limited resources, donors and funding agencies are increasingly disbursing funds more readily to health programs with a history of strong financial management, and in some cases, *only* to countries that have strong financial management records.

Financial mechanisms such as decentralized, dedicated pharmaceutical purchasing accounts may allow the procurement cycle to operate independently from the treasury cycle. Revolving pharmaceutical funds can help achieve this separation by establishing their own bank accounts and their own working capital.

Assessment

The Rational Pharmaceutical Management (RPM) Plus Program of Management Sciences for Health administered a questionnaire to assess the structure of public-sector pharmaceutical management to support pooled procurement in eleven CRHC member states: Kenya, Lesotho, Malawi, Mauritius, Mozambique, Seychelles, Swaziland, Tanzania, Uganda, Zambia, and Zimbabwe. Before this study, no standardized approach had been used to guide groups of countries in selecting the best model for collaboration. The methodology identifies favorable conditions that point a group of countries toward a particular model, based on the group's characteristics.

Assessment results

The assessment results showed that three countries—Lesotho, Tanzania, and Zimbabwe—representing 27 percent of countries studied, appeared ready to initiate coordinated informed buying. This method of collabo-

ration for procurement requires dedicated human resources and a budget to conduct market research on pharmaceutical suppliers. A number of countries do not currently have the needed resources, resulting in the small proportion of countries ready to start this mode of collaboration.

Coordinated informed buying strategy

- Creating a mechanism for the collection, analysis, storage, and dissemination of information on HIV/AIDS-related pharmaceuticals and commodities
- Creating awareness of coordinated informed buying among decision makers and other relevant bodies
- Developing capacity within member states to conduct informed buying-related market research
- Setting up and operating a coordinated informed buying system within the CRHC member states
- Monitoring program execution

Source: MSH/RPM Plus 2004.

Readiness of countries to undertake coordinated informed buying

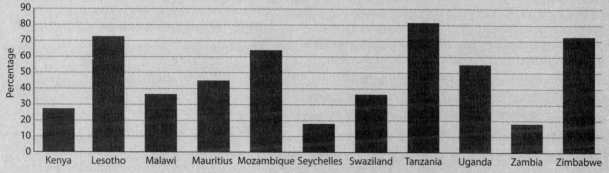

Efficient financial management systems are especially important if funds are limited and procurement priorities must be closely managed. Being able to order pharmaceuticals when needed and to pay for them on time reduces both prices and stockouts.

Procurement by generic name (International Nonproprietary Name)

Procurement by generic name—formally known as the International Nonproprietary Name (INN)—has become the standard for purchasing pharmaceuticals that are available from multiple companies. Brand-name suppliers may compete, but their bids should be by generic name; they may offer lower prices for certain medicines than generic competitors, because they wish to keep their public-sector market share. Perhaps the most impressive achievement in recent years is the dramatic reduction in worldwide prices of ARVs, which has led to a surge in patients who can receive

life-saving treatment. This price reduction has largely been driven by procurement of generics, which has been well documented (Holmes et al. 2010). All pharmaceuticals supplied to the health system should be labeled with the INN featured prominently, in addition to any brand name that may be on the label. For more information on INNs see http://www.who.int/medicines/services/inn/en.

Procurement limited to essential medicines list or formulary list

Virtually no health program can afford to purchase all pharmaceuticals available on the market. A limited medicine list or formulary, defining which medicines will be purchased, is one of the most effective ways to control procurement costs. It simplifies other supply management activities and reduces inventory-holding costs as well (see Chapter 23).

The first step is to avoid generic duplication; after this, two main options exist for reducing the procurement list. The

Box 18-1
Good pharmaceutical procurement principles

Reliable payment and good financial management

- Develop mechanisms for prompt, reliable payment, which might bring down pharmaceutical prices more than bulk discounts.
- Establish financial mechanisms with separate pharmaceutical accounts (for example, revolving drug funds) to allow the procurement cycle to operate on a separate schedule from the treasury cycle.

Procurement by generic name

- Use generic names (International Nonproprietary Names) for fair competition.
- Specify quality standards, not specific brands, for medicines with bioavailability problems.

Procurement limited to essential medicines list or formulary list

- Select safe, effective, cost-effective medicines.
- Use formal approval procedures for procurement of nonlisted medicines.

Procurement in large volume

- Concentrate purchases on limited list to increase quantities, reduce price.
- Specify divided deliveries

Formal supplier qualification and monitoring

- Use formal supplier qualification based on pharmaceutical quality, service reliability, and financial viability.
- Approve suppliers before tendering (prequalification) or after (postqualification).
- Use a formal monitoring system to ensure continued supplier qualification.

Competitive procurement

- Use competitive bidding on all but very small or emergency purchases to obtain the best prices.
- Allow only prequalified suppliers to compete in restrictive tenders.
- Evaluate suppliers after submission of bids in open tenders.

Monopsony commitment

- Procure all contracted pharmaceuticals from winning supplier.

- Enter into no separate deals with noncontracted suppliers.

Order quantities based on reliable estimate of actual need

- Develop reliable consumption records and morbidity data.
- Adjust systematically for past surpluses, shortages, stockouts.
- Adjust for expected program growth and changing disease patterns.

Transparency and written procedures

- Develop and follow written procedures for all procurement actions.
- Make information on the tender process and results public to the maximum extent possible.

Separation of key functions

- Separate key functions that require different expertise.
- Functions that involve different committees, units, or individuals may include selection, quantification, approval of suppliers, and award of contracts.

Product quality assurance program

- Establish and maintain a formal system for product quality assurance.
- Include quality assurance product certification, inspection of shipments, targeted laboratory testing, and reporting of suspect products.

Annual financial audit with published results

- Conduct an annual financial audit to assess compliance with procurement procedures, promptness of payment, and related factors.
- Present results to the appropriate public supervising body.

Regular reporting on procurement performance

- Report key procurement performance indicators against targets at least annually.
- Use key indicators such as ratio of prices to world market prices, supplier lead times, percentage of purchases made through competitive tendering, and planned versus actual purchases.

first combines the standard formulary process (Chapter 16) with therapeutic category analysis (Chapter 40). For example, a program that regularly purchases cimetidine, famotidine, and ranitidine (all therapeutically similar anti-ulcer medicines) might save substantial sums by restricting the formulary to one of these medicines and combining the estimated purchase volume into a single, much larger quantity of the selected medicine.

The second approach takes formulary selection and therapeutic category analysis one step further through competitive tender within a selected therapeutic subcategory (Chapter 40). The medicine selection committee determines which subcategories are appropriate for category-based tendering and which medicines in those subcategories are acceptable equivalents. The tender request specifies only the therapeutic category rather than individual drug products. This strategy has been used for several years in some purchasing groups in the United States and in the OECS and is similar to strategies used in Europe for establishing reimbursement prices.

Any change from one therapeutically similar product to another should be carefully considered, particularly for medicines used in chronic treatment; patients using these medicines need to be monitored during the changeover, which can generate significant costs for care and treatment.

Efforts to limit the medicine list by reducing therapeutic duplications will meet resistance both from pharmaceutical suppliers whose products are removed from the procurement list and from some doctors and some patients who prefer a wider range of choices. Suppliers may issue dire public warnings of adverse impact on public health and patient care if their pharmaceuticals are not purchased. The health system needs to be prepared to counter these claims with carefully designed information campaigns.

Resistance from doctors can often be overcome by documenting the cost savings possible with the restricted procurement list and pointing out the benefits of year-round access to the limited list rather than sporadic access to a larger list of medicines.

Increasing procurement volume by aggregating demand

One of the essential characteristics of pooled procurement is pooling the relatively small demand for a product from each health unit to create a single larger procurement volume for that product. Increasing the total procurement volume for any product increases the likelihood of favorable prices and contract terms as long as there is sufficient competition in the market. Moreover, increasing procurement volume typically increases the number of potentially interested suppliers who wish to win the business, and increases the loyalty and responsiveness of suppliers who win contracts. When the market is tight for a particular product or set of prod-

ucts and available supplies are not adequate to meet global demand, the larger purchasers typically get first preference from suppliers.

However, simply increasing procurement volume may not necessarily assure low prices; one recent analysis of global pricing of ARVs did not correlate volume and price for nineteen of twenty-four dosage forms (Waning et al. 2009), and a study of e-procurement reverse auctions (although not pharmaceutical procurement) also could not link product volume with reduced pricing (Shalev and Asbjornsen 2010). However, in most circumstances, when procuring generically available medications with multiple suppliers, greater procurement volume will attract more competitive offers.

At the national or subnational levels, pooling procurement volume from many facilities or from several states or countries, restricting the medicine list, and eliminating duplication within therapeutic categories lead to higher volumes for single items. In addition, the commitment to awarding a single contract for the entire volume of each item raises suppliers' interest in bidding and provides an incentive for them to offer their most competitive prices.

A contract award to a single supplier does not mean that the entire volume must be shipped at once. Many procurement services specify divided deliveries over the period of the contract as part of the contract terms, sometimes to multiple delivery points. As discussed in Chapter 21, many supply systems use estimated quantity tenders, with orders placed throughout the contract period as needed, using either a scheduled or perpetual purchasing model (see Chapter 23). These strategies allow optimal use of available storage and transport capacity, reduce inventory-holding costs, and ease cash flow constraints.

The potential pricing benefits from a single-supplier award must be compared to the risks to commodity security in the event of unforeseen events (supplier failure, war/civil unrest, industrial disruption, weather events, and other instances of force majeure). In some cases, especially for critical medicines, a risk analysis calls for a secondary supply source. Moreover, when the volume of procurement for individual items represents a significant percentage of the total market for those items, it may be wiser to split contract awards or negotiated contracts among multiple suppliers to preserve future competition and to assure the availability of reliable supply sources if the primary contractor is unable to perform.

Formal supplier qualification and monitoring

All suppliers should be qualified through a process that considers product quality, service reliability and delivery time, and financial viability. The process for evaluating new suppliers can include formal registration, reference checks with past clients and international agencies, test purchases in small quantities, and informal local information gathering (see Chapter 21). The global procurement mechanisms such as SCMS and Global Fund voluntary pooled procurement may insist that suppliers and their products either be registered by a "stringent regulatory authority" or approved by the WHO prequalification system (Chapter 19).

Although both prequalification (qualifying suppliers before the tender process) and postqualification (qualifying suppliers after bids have been received) have been used in international pharmaceutical procurement, increasingly, health systems and the donors that finance procurement prefer prequalification. In a postqualification system, the procurement office evaluates the suppliers after it receives the bids. Once the tenders are opened, the time window to evaluate and award a contract is limited, which can lead to rushing through the postqualification process. Qualifying suppliers before the tender submission allows enough time for a thorough evaluation. And by first eliminating substandard suppliers from the tender process, prequalification results in a more efficient process by automatically qualifying the lowest-priced bidder.

No matter which supplier qualification model the health system uses, the procurement office needs to make vigorous efforts to assure that purchases come only from suppliers that are known to provide quality products.

Successful procurement operations ensure continued good performance by suppliers through a formal monitoring system that tracks lead time, compliance with contract-pricing terms, partial shipments, remaining shelf life, compliance with packaging and labeling instructions, and compliance with other contract terms. A data file for each supplier, which may be electronic or manual or a combination, should have copies of registration papers, references, special correspondence, complaints, and other anecdotal information. The information system should track the number and value of tender contracts awarded chronologically and the value of total purchases from the supplier by year.

Procurement programs using restricted tenders should make special efforts to seek out potential new suppliers at least every two to three years to maintain competitive pressure on established suppliers.

Competitive procurement

As discussed in Section 18.4, the main methods for purchasing pharmaceuticals are restricted and open tenders, competitive negotiations, and direct purchase from a single-source supplier. Supplier competition is key to favorable pricing, and most modern procurement regulations require competitive procurement in the public sector; therefore, if the needed products have multiple suppliers, then public-sector programs should use competitive bidding for all but very small or emergency purchases. This would not be required when purchasing through a regional or global pooled procurement mechanism because the global or regional procurement office would manage competition.

Monopsony and pooled procurement

A monopsony refers to a situation involving one buyer with many sellers. This is the cornerstone of a pooled procurement system—the group members act as one buyer.

Maintenance of the procurement monopsony will be most feasible when there is strong political will or when all members of the procurement group are voluntarily and enthusiastically participating. Perhaps the single most important factor in the twenty-five-year survival of the multicountry pooled procurement system serving the OECS has been political will and commitment of member governments, although maintaining the monopsony remains a challenge that they must address constantly (see Country Study 18-2).

A review of the two other successful regional pooled procurement programs—the Gulf Cooperation Council and PAHO's vaccine and ARV programs—identified voluntary commitment as a critical factor of their success (DeRoeck et al. 2006). Each program has some flexibility. In the PAHO system, countries choose to participate or not on a yearly basis, and in the Gulf Cooperation Council system, countries are allowed to purchase up to 40 percent of their vaccines outside of the system. But the major point is that once members have committed to purchase a certain percentage or quantity, they are expected to honor that commitment.

On the other hand, the lack of political will to sustain the monopsony commitment is one reason the CARICOM (Caribbean Community) purchasing program for the public sector was unsuccessful in the early 1980s, and it was a major factor in the failure of the FORMED system, which was tried in Central America in the 1990s.

The monopsony commitment should be monitored and enforced. Frequently, local, regional, or multinational suppliers will offer low prices on a short-term basis to individual group members in an attempt to break the purchasing group. A transitory small benefit to one critical group member will adversely affect all other group members, so they must resist these offers; otherwise, suppliers will lose interest in the pooled procurement tenders, the group will fail, and prices overall will rise. Decentralization in some countries has complicated the procurement issue by providing budget funds to lower levels of the health system, to procure their own pharmaceuticals, in addition to the centrally allocated procurement budget. This leads health facilities to purchase from more expensive, but in some cases, more reliable private-sector sources, which leaves the central procurement system with a severe financial shortage because of lost procurement volume (MOH Uganda 2008).

Order quantities based on reliable estimate of actual need

Accurate estimates of procurement volume are needed to avoid stockouts of some pharmaceuticals and overstocks of others in the case of guaranteed quantity contracts. In addition, suppliers are most apt to compete for an estimated-quantity supply contract if they believe that the quantities specified are reasonably accurate.

The most reliable way to quantify future pharmaceutical demand is to start with accurate past-consumption data from all units being supplied, assuming the supply pipeline has been consistently full. These data should be tempered by known or expected changes in morbidity patterns, seasonal factors, service levels, formulary changes or changes to prescribing patterns, and patient attendance. Unfortunately, in many countries, past consumption data are incomplete or do not reflect real need because the supply pipeline has never been full. In such cases, the morbidity-based and adjusted consumption techniques discussed in Chapter 20 may be needed to estimate procurement demand.

Expert technical assistance in quantification may be useful in initial phases of the procurement program, with local officials participating to gain an understanding of the methodology, particularly when applying the morbidity or adjusted consumption methods.

When funds are not available to purchase all the pharmaceuticals listed in estimates, reducing the list according to health system resources is required. The following three tools, discussed in more detail in Chapter 40, can help with prioritization—

VEN (vital, essential, nonessential) analysis classifies medicines in two or three categories, according to how critical the medicines are for treating commonly encountered diseases. Priority is given to vital medicines.
Therapeutic category analysis applies economic analysis of therapeutic choices to help select the best medicines for treating common diseases while minimizing overall cost to the health system.
ABC analysis assembles data from recent or projected procurements to determine where procurement money has actually been spent, allowing managers to focus first on high-cost and high-use items when considering ways to reduce procurement costs.

Transparency and written procedures

The appearance and reality of open and fair competition are essential to attract the best suppliers and the best prices. Fair competition can be achieved by maintaining transparent tender procedures: formal written procedures should be strictly followed throughout the tender, and formal, explicit criteria should be used to make procurement decisions.

Broad-based committees should have the sole authority to make contract awards. Information on the tender process and results should be public, to the extent permitted by law and regulation. At a minimum, both bidders and health units should have access to information on the suppliers and the prices for all winning contracts.

When the pharmaceutical tender process is secretive, it tends to be perceived as corrupt or unfair. There may be charges of cronyism. Whether true or not, such charges are damaging in that suppliers, health care providers, and patients lose confidence in the system. Unsuccessful suppliers may feel that they have no chance to win and consequently withdraw from future tenders or submit only token bids. As the pool of potential suppliers decreases to a small set, price competition decreases and procurement prices will be much higher than necessary.

Advocates for increasing the use of e-procurement systems, and particularly e-procurement-mediated reverse auctions, cite transparency and the potential for reduced tender management costs as primary benefits; however, as noted, their effectiveness in widespread application for pooled procurement of pharmaceuticals remains to be seen. One study of public e-procurement in Chile (including all products, not just pharmaceuticals) did not try to compare relative transparency of e-procurement compared with other methods, but it did show a minimal decrease of less than a half of 1 percent in administrative costs when compared with standard methods and less than 3 percent savings through overall price reductions (Singer et al. 2009).

Separation of key functions

There are several key procurement functions, which typically require different expertise. In general, these functions should be handled by different individuals, units, committees, or subcommittees. Such functions include—

- Selection of medicines
- Quantification of pharmaceutical requirements
- Preparation of product specifications and quality standards
- Approval of suppliers (prequalification or post-qualification)
- Adjudication
- Award of tender

Without appropriate separation of functions, the procurement process is much more susceptible to influence by special interests. Suppliers or procurement personnel may be able to bias medicine selection, manipulate orders to increase the quantities of certain medicines, prejudice supplier qualification decisions, manipulate the final award of tender, and slant product specifications to limit competition, for example, by selecting less common dosage forms.

Separation of key functions contributes to professionalism and accountability. Section 18.6 describes ways in which a procurement system can be organized to separate these functions.

Product quality assurance program

An effective procurement program must ensure that the medicines purchased and distributed are of the specified quality, according to specified standards, which are clear and recognized. Chapter 19 discusses three categories of procedures to establish an effective quality assurance system—

- Ensuring that only medicine products that meet current standards for quality are bought
- Verifying that shipped goods meet the specifications
- Monitoring and maintaining the quality of pharmaceuticals from the moment they are received until the medicine is finally consumed by the patient

When managing pharmaceutical procurement by generic name and introducing new suppliers whose products are not familiar in the country, the procurement program must be particularly alert to product quality issues.

Some products vary substantially in formulation and bioavailability from supplier to supplier. When this difference is therapeutically significant, purchasers should be cautious about making changes in supplier from year to year, and particularly in accepting unknown suppliers.

Even when new products are completely equivalent in content and effect, changes in dosage form can be problematic, requiring patient and provider re-education. For medicines used primarily in chronic therapy, changes should only be made to effect a significant cost savings.

Annual audit with published results

At least once a year, the procurement unit should undergo a financial and procurement audit, which is a formal examination and verification of books and records by accountants who specialize in financial audit procedures. *Internal audits* are conducted by auditors from within the government (for the public sector) or the organization managing the health system (for the nonpublic sector). *External audits* are conducted by auditors from outside the managing organization and are generally considered less potentially biased and therefore more credible, even if the process and findings are the same.

The annual external or statutory audit, conducted by a registered or licensed auditor, should include tests to ensure that the organization's assets are safeguarded and accounted for, that the systems of internal controls and procedures are adequate to account for all the organization's income and expenditures, and that the organization is complying with its constitution, rules and regulations, and management.

This includes compliance with procurement procedures, promptness of payment, and inventory control.

The auditor should issue a statutory audit report in accordance with legal regulations of the jurisdiction and, in addition, should issue a detailed letter of comment to the management of the organization and to the appropriate public supervisory body.

Regular reporting on procurement performance

Using standard *indicators* to monitor performance and program implementation (see Chapters 36 and 48) significantly improves pharmaceutical management. Standard indicators allow comparison of actual performance with targets, over time and among countries. Some indicators use a standard list of ten to twenty *indicator medicines*, which are also called tracer medicines or a market basket of medicines (Chapter 48).

The procurement office should be required to report on key procurement performance indicators at least annually. The Assessment Guide at the end of this chapter suggests some procurement indicators. Indicators such as average supplier lead time and percentage of key medicines in stock should be used to assess performance on a continuing basis. These indicators should not be limited to the public sector but can be used by all organizations including faith-based pharmaceutical services, NGOs, and private health institutions seeking to control their pharmaceutical costs and improve their performance. Figure 18-3 provides actual indicator data from several countries.

18.6 Organization and management of the procurement and distribution functions

One important policy issue facing senior managers is how to structure the procurement program and supply chain system and how to divide the responsibilities. Chapter 8 describes five different supply chain systems currently being used by governments to supply pharmaceuticals to their health services—

Central stores system: Conventional CMS approach, in which pharmaceuticals are procured and distributed by a centralized government unit.

Autonomous supply agency system: Bulk procurement, storage, and distribution managed by an autonomous or semi-autonomous supply agency, *not* directly managed by the government (although government is often part of the agency's governing board).

Direct delivery system: A "non-CMS" approach, in which tenders establish prices and suppliers for each essential medicine, which is delivered directly by suppliers to individual districts and major facilities.

Figure 18-3   Comparison of two procurement indicator results for six countries

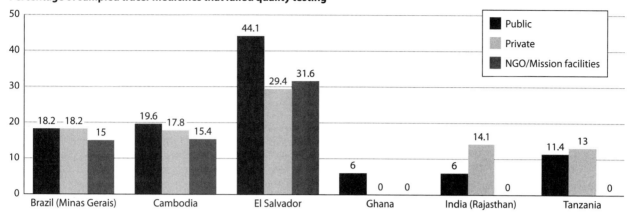

Percentage of sampled tracer medicines that failed quality testing

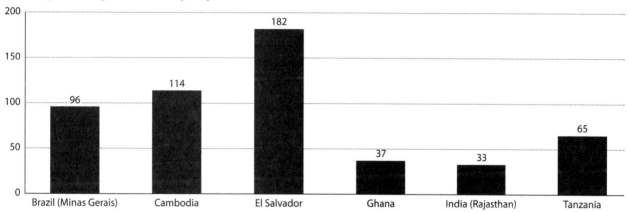

Percentage of average international price paid for set of indicator medicines

Sources: CPM 2003a, 2003b, 2003c, 2003d, 2003e, 2003f.

Primary distributor system (also known as prime vendor system): contract for pharmaceutical pricing is negotiated with suppliers, and a separate contract is negotiated with one or more primary distributors, who warehouse and distribute pharmaceuticals to districts and major health facilities.

Primarily private supply: Public-sector patients obtain pharmaceutical services from private pharmacies. Government may or may not reimburse the cost of those services, and may also set maximum reimbursable prices including a dispensing fee, minus any co-payments. Reimbursement may go directly to the pharmacy-based on claims submitted, or to the patient (meaning that the patient pays the pharmacy and submits a reimbursement claim).

The important point to a public health system in adapting these alternative supply chain models is to retain the advantages of pooled procurement to the extent feasible. Generally, two common variations exist on managing the

purchasing transactions in pooled procurement programs. In both, a single agency manages tenders and contract negotiations on behalf of the group. Then, in a centralized purchasing model the central office also manages the purchasing transactions on behalf of group members, while in a decentralized purchasing model the group members purchase individually from the suppliers who hold the contracts that were centrally negotiated. (See Country Studies 18-2 and 18-3 for examples of group purchasing systems.)

Centralized management of both the purchasing and contracting functions offers some potential advantages—

- Economies of scale reduce the cost of managing procurement offices.
- Sustaining an effective program is easier with only one procurement unit to staff and manage.
- A single procurement list for a large group of facilities increases volume, promotes reduced prices, and improves market presence, which leads to better supply security and quality.

- Better-managed systems of finance and payment may encourage suppliers to compete for contracts and to perform well.

A centralized purchasing system also has potential drawbacks—

- If it does not function well, all group members suffer: although the prices may be theoretically better than with individual members doing the purchasing, the system may not be as responsive and may not provide the medicines needed in time to provide continuous care to patients.
- Without significant input from the participating facilities, centralized purchasing services will likely not meet users' needs very well.
- If the central agency has substantial corruption, the program will never function effectively.

Pharmaceutical purchasing and distribution systems have traditionally been heavily centralized in many developing countries, with little management input from lower levels. Many of these countries are now decentralizing procurement to the regional, state, or even local facility level, either by choice or because the central system has collapsed.

However, decentralized procurement management has proved challenging in many countries. Problems encountered include significantly higher prices (if the decentralized managers select their own suppliers), potential product quality issues, irrational purchasing patterns based on the whims of prescribers or local procurement offices, and overall erratic supply because of local inefficiencies, lack of access to funds, or poor management.

Supervision by senior management

Without political commitment to efficiency and active supervision by senior management, the procurement system will not function efficiently, regardless of its organization. The lack of modern financial management, accounting systems, and supervisory responsibility has doomed many pharmaceutical systems to chronic failure.

To manage the pharmaceutical supply chain, senior managers should demand and use regular reports from procurement and distribution agencies and from health facilities on expenditures, purchases, stock levels, order status, lead times, and budget status. If a system lacks the capacity to produce these reports in a timely manner, introduction of the tools to provide them should be top priority. Senior managers should also maintain regular communications with facilities and staff; systems do not work very well if the senior managers have never visited any facilities outside the capital.

Many operations-level procurement managers have not had formal management training and may fail to appreciate the importance of setting such realistic and quantifiable procurement objectives as—

- Acquiring quality supplies at the best possible price
- Ensuring prompt and dependable delivery
- Following procedures that are transparent and not influenced by special interests
- Maintaining a procurement pattern that produces an even workload and constant supply to clients
- Achieving efficiency through use of appropriate systems and procedures
- Limiting total procurement operating costs
- Ensuring that revenue is adequate to support the office, and that finances are managed effectively
- Filling key positions with well-trained and motivated staff
- Maintaining effective working relationships with senior management and with clients

Senior management is responsible for assuring that these considerations are properly addressed and particularly for enforcing transparency and equity in the purchasing process.

Responsibilities in the procurement process

Effective procurement is a collaborative process between the procurement office, which manages many of the steps, and technical and policy committees, which should usually make the decisions about which medicines to buy, in what quantities, and from which suppliers. In a complex setting such as a procurement program at the national level, the following division of responsibilities may be appropriate.

Procurement office. The procurement office, which may be part of the government or independent, collates information on medicine needs, develops a proposed procurement list based on clients' requirements, manages the tendering process, manages and arranges supply contracts unless there is a separate tender board, and monitors performance of suppliers and of clients.

Staff of the procurement office should not have the sole deciding voice in determining which products are purchased and which suppliers receive contracts; these decisions should be made by committees that include representatives from other administrative sections or stakeholders, including client facilities. This separation of powers helps ensure broad ownership of the system and avoids conflicts of interest. If the procurement office is independently operated, it is important that its operations be supervised by a board of directors that includes senior health-policy makers.

Tender board. In many countries, tendering and contract negotiation are done according to law by a government tender board, which either reports to the finance ministry or is independent of any ministry. In such situations, the procurement office prepares the list of requirements, and the tender board may monitor the tender process. The prime task of the tender board is to make the award decision; in some cases, this will be an absolute decision, while in others, the tender board will make recommendations to health officials. Whichever system is followed, it is essential that the health system provide technical input into the contract award decision.

Medicine selection committee. Often the same as the formulary committee or pharmacy and therapeutics committee, the medicine selection committee should comprise knowledgeable practitioners and other health professionals who evaluate competing drug products in various therapeutic categories and select products that are most essential to the health system. A senior physician frequently chairs the committee, and a pharmacist generally serves as organizing secretary. The committee reviews requests for additions to the procurement list, compares the cost effectiveness of medicines on the list, and recommends which medicines to purchase, and when necessary, which medicines to delete. The committee also determines which therapeutic categories, if any, are suitable for open tender by therapeutic class. The committee needs access to current, unbiased drug information and members who can synthesize such information to make appropriate selection decisions.

Procurement/tender committee. Whether or not a government tender board is in charge of tendering, the health system should establish a procurement committee to make final decisions or to make the recommendations for such decisions to the tender board on medicine selection, procurement quantity, and supplier selection, and approve the exact specifications for product description, packaging and labeling, and quality assurance standards. The committee should base those decisions on recommendations from technical committees and subcommittees. It reviews information on suppliers and determines which should participate in tenders, if a restricted tender is used, and which suppliers should receive contracts, unless such decisions are made by a separate tender board. The procurement committee should include senior officials from the highest level of government served by the procurement system as well as officials from user facilities. For example, a federal government program that serves teaching hospitals and regional health systems might include two or three representatives of the ministry of health, two or three regional representatives, and one or two teaching hospital representatives.

In some countries, separate subcommittees develop product specifications and investigate suppliers' qualification for participation in tenders.

Procurement office staffing and management systems

The structure of the procurement office depends on the scope of the program, the availability of funds, and whether the office is managed as a government entity or as an independent agency.

Staffing requirements. In general, the procurement office needs a director, an assistant director, and experienced technical staff members, with at least one pharmacist or physician to provide sound technical input for the development and refinement of procurement lists.

Accounting and finance officers are needed to manage the accounts and in some systems manage payment to suppliers. Automated offices need data processors and at least one information technology professional. Also needed are one or more clerical managers, one or more secretaries or clerks, a receptionist or telephone operator, maintenance staff, and, in some systems, a driver and security staff.

Staff in key procurement and distribution positions must be well trained and highly motivated, with the capability to manage the procurement process effectively. Unfortunately, in many countries, people are transferred just as they become competent in a position, and a new cycle of training and time lag between appointment and competence must begin again.

Salaries for procurement staff. When procurement office salaries are too low to support an individual or a family, or much lower than for equivalent work in the private sector, corrupt practices and neglect of duties are much more likely to occur. These kinds of problems increase funding requirements to replace the resulting theft and waste. Paying reasonable salaries in the first place and implementing tough controls is more cost-effective.

In some countries, restructuring the procurement office as an independent parastatal or privatized unit may be the only way to pay adequate salaries to staff.

Communications and market information. To succeed in the international market, procurement programs need two sorts of critical information: comparative price and availability data on products in the national and international pharmaceutical market and information about suppliers' capacity, reliability, and quality. Health system procurement agencies without access to price information or to the performance record of international suppliers operate in a vacuum and are essentially at the mercy of the marketplace.

Access to information depends on communications capacity. An Internet and e-mail connection and

GOOD COMMUNICATION IS ESSENTIAL TO THE PROCUREMENT PROCESS

external telephone line are essential in modern procurement, even if all procurement is done through local suppliers. For international procurement, direct access to an overseas line is mandatory. Countries have sources of comparative price information including the *International Drug Price Indicator Guide* (MSH, published annually), the annual source and price guide for HIV/AIDS medicines and commodities (WHO/UNICEF/UNAIDS/MSF 2005), the Global Fund's price and quality reporting tool (http://www.theglobalfund.org/en/procurement/pqr/), and other national and multicountry resources that WHO makes available on its website (http://www.who.int/medicines/areas/access/ecofin/en/index.html) and through its Procurement & Supply Management Toolbox (http://www.psmtoolbox.org). Chapter 21 discusses options for obtaining and evaluating information about pharmaceutical suppliers. A central repository of international information on worldwide supplier performance and tender pricing would be useful but has not yet proved feasible.

Tracking performance of the procurement system. A reliable management information system (MIS) is one of the most important elements in procurement. Lack of a functioning MIS or the inability to use it appropriately is a primary cause of program failure.

The MIS must be used to track all orders placed, the number and status of shipments and receipts, compliance with contract pricing, lead time of each order, payments made by the office or by group members, performance bond status, and the results of any investigations related to product quality.

The information system should also track the performance of health system units, number of orders placed, payments made, quantities actually purchased compared with estimates, purchases from all contract suppliers, and if possible, pharmaceutical purchases from noncontract suppliers. In all but the smallest procurement systems, the MIS should be computerized.

Computerized procurement information systems depend on appropriate software (Chapter 50). Key staff must be familiar with the software, and competent data entry personnel must be available.

Procurement manuals and technical assistance. Achieving and sustaining an efficiently functioning procurement system are complex and demanding jobs. Using written policies and procedures that spell out how the procurement process should be managed and how the procurement system should operate is critical. A comprehensive procedures manual can be time-consuming to develop, but worthwhile if actively used to orient and manage staff.

The Global Fund to Fight AIDS, Tuberculosis and Malaria publishes policy guidelines for procurement through its program (Global Fund 2009). For purchasing through World Bank–financed loans, the World Bank's *Standard Bidding Documents for Procurement of Health Sector Goods* (World Bank 2004b) and *Procurement of Health Sector Goods Technical Note* (World Bank 2000) are essential references. A recently developed procurement system assessment tool, funded by the World Bank, includes transparency indicators in its evaluation (see Country Study 36-3).

When starting a new procurement system or revamping a poorly functioning system, outside technical assistance may help local managers in design and implementation. A number of organizations offer materials and technical support to help procure pharmaceuticals and commodities; for example, WHO has procurement assistance programs specifically for medicines and supplies related to HIV/AIDS, malaria, and tuberculosis (AIDS Medicines and Diagnostics Service, Roll Back Malaria's Commodity Services, and Global TB Drug Facility). WHO also provides other types of technical assistance on procurement issues in addition to its supplier prequalification program. The U.S. Agency for International Development funds several global and local programs that provide assistance to country-level pharmaceutical procurement programs. Other bilateral agencies, such as the U.K. Department for International Development, the Danish International Development Agency, and others, fund support to focus countries and regions, and major development banks and United Nations agencies such as UNICEF and the United Nations Development Programme provide procurement support in some countries (see the Glossary and References and Further Readings sections for more information).

18.7 Financial sustainability

Procurement programs cannot function effectively when funds are chronically inadequate. Traditionally, many countries have relied totally on the public budget to support pharmaceutical procurement, with medicines provided free to both inpatients and outpatients. In some countries, pharmaceutical purchases have consumed 20 to 40 percent of the total public health budget. The reality is that few countries

have sufficient budget capability to purchase enough medicines to cover the needs of all patients, without supplementing the budget with some sort of cost recovery or donor support.

An epic occurrence in international health and development was the advent in the 2000s of global financing mechanisms such as the Global Fund, PEPFAR, and UNITAID, discussed in Chapter 14. These initiatives provide large-scale financing for countries to procure medicines and essential commodities, and in some cases, support global procurement mechanisms that make a limited range of commodities directly available to countries, such as the SCMS and Global Fund voluntary pooled procurement programs described earlier. Despite the increasing scope of these initiatives, financing issues still require the attention of health systems managers.

Sources of funds for pharmaceutical procurement

Primary sources of funds for pharmaceuticals include government financing, user fees, health insurance, community cofinancing, and donor financing. Chapter 11 describes these options in terms of their efficiency, equity, feasibility, and sustainability.

The most important considerations for procurement are regular access to and availability of funds and adequate access to foreign exchange. Government and donor funds are sometimes released irregularly throughout the financial year, and regulations often specify that funds must be spent in the year in which they are allocated or be returned to the treasury. Together, these factors may make it difficult to operate proper procurement systems and to obtain the best prices.

Strategies such as decentralized financial management and various types of revolving drug funds have been used to separate pharmaceutical procurement from the annual treasury cycle. This separation also often requires some form of cost recovery, which the decentralized mechanism manages.

Uncoupling the procurement cycle from the treasury cycle has substantial management advantages. Inventory management improves when medicines can be ordered when needed rather than at an arbitrary point in the government fiscal year. When suppliers know that orders will be placed promptly after tendering and that payment will be made according to contract terms, prices will be much more competitive.

Pharmaceutical financing issues that affect the procurement system are discussed in Chapters 9–14. These issues include the actual revenue potential of user-fee programs, equity aspects of user fees, management and accountability requirements for successful user-fee programs, the role of health insurance and other social financing mechanisms, the role of donor financing, and related issues. For donor financing, grants and loans should be clearly distinguished:

loans may be necessary to finance the start-up capital for a revolving drug fund or for a major emergency, but are an undesirable mechanism for financing the recurrent costs of supplying medicines.

Access to foreign currency exchange

Pharmaceutical procurement almost always requires the health system's largest outlay of foreign currency exchange. Shortage of foreign exchange can constrain international procurement and be a country's rationale for seeking donor support for pharmaceutical purchases. In situations where foreign exchange is constrained, procurement and pharmaceutical management systems should be as efficient as possible, so that they make the best use of local supply sources of products meeting established quality standards and obtain the best possible prices in international procurement. Sound documentation of actual needs and of economical use of funds may help justify increases in foreign currency exchange allocation from the ministry of finance or central bank. For example, in the Organisation of Eastern Caribbean States' Pharmaceutical Procurement Service, the Eastern Caribbean Central Bank handles the program's currency exchange from Eastern Caribbean dollars and pays suppliers in U.S. dollars at no charge to participating countries (Burnett 2003).

Reliable payment mechanism

As discussed earlier, sustained low pharmaceutical prices are possible only when a procurement program can guarantee prompt payment in full according to contract terms.

One example of sustainable financing is the revolving drug fund described in Country Study 18-2. However, revolving drug funds work only if the political will and financial capacity exist to replenish deposits in the fund each time purchases are made. Otherwise, the fund will soon vanish. Examples are numerous: one cautionary tale comes from Central America, where a European donor provided capital for revolving funds in several countries. Within a few years, all but one of the funds were totally decapitalized. That one country continued with the program for an additional year, but it experienced periodic problems with replenishing the account after purchases were made, resulting in delays in procurement and stockouts in health facilities; eventually the system ended.

Financial support for the procurement office

Procurement services may be part of the warehouse and distribution operation or be set up as a separate procurement office. In either case, salaries and operational costs of the procurement function must be covered. For typical public procurement systems, the only existing funding source for the procurement office is support through the government budget.

For pooled procurement programs that have a centralized procurement office that is not a formal government office, options may include—

- A periodic percentage payment to the office from group members, based on the invoice value of shipments
- A percentage payment from group members at the beginning of the procurement cycle, based on the projected value of the total procurement, or at the end of the cycle, based on the actual value of total shipments
- Payment from group members in the form of a flat annual fee, based on total expenses divided by the total number of areas and independent institutions served

The proper choice depends on the situation. The risk in tying a procurement office's reimbursement to the value of purchases by user facilities is the possible incentive for the procurement office to increase, rather than decrease, prices and total purchases. Therefore, if this approach is used, checks and balances must be put in place, such as using budget price volume instead of actual buy price or requiring that user representatives make all major procurement decisions. ∎

Glossary

ABC value analysis: Method by which medicines are divided, according to their annual usage (unit cost times annual consumption), into Class A items (the 10 to 20 percent of items that account for 75 to 80 percent of the funds spent), Class B items (with intermediate usage rates), and Class C items (the vast majority of items with low individual usage, the total of which accounts for 5 to 10 percent of the funds spent). ABC analysis can be used to give priority to Class A items in procurement, inventory control, and port clearing.

Active pharmaceutical ingredient (API): That portion of a drug product that has therapeutic properties.

AIDS Medicines and Diagnostics Service (AMDS): A WHO-sponsored network to provide resources and technical assistance to countries buying pharmaceuticals and diagnostics for HIV/AIDS programs (http://www.who.int/hiv/amds/en).

Annual purchasing: A periodic inventory control system in which pharmaceutical requirements are determined and orders are placed once a year.

Back order: An order for a product that is currently out of stock. Back orders are filled when a new supply of the product becomes available.

Basic unit: The smallest unit in which a medicine can be conveniently dispensed or administered. It is used in quantification, reorder formulas, and comparison of prices of different-sized bottles or vials. Typical basic units are tablet or capsule, mL (for liquids), and g (for ointments and creams).

ASSESSMENT GUIDE

Procurement performance indicators

- Percentage by value of ministry of health (MOH) medicines purchased through a central procurement system
- Percentage of average international price paid for last regular procurement (indicator medicines)
- Percentage by value of MOH pharmaceutical purchases that are on the essential medicines list or national medicines formulary
- Percentage by value of MOH medicines purchased through competitive tender
- Percentage by value of medicines purchased from local manufacturers
- Average lead time for a sample of orders (calculated separately for all suppliers, local manufacturers, foreign suppliers)
- Average time for payment for a sample of orders (calculated separately for all suppliers, local manufacturers, foreign suppliers)
- Percentage of pharmaceuticals (batches) subjected to quality-control testing compared with target percentage to be tested
- Percentage of pharmaceuticals (batches) that failed quality-control testing

Procurement system procedures

- What type of system is used to supply medicines to public facilities (CMS, autonomous agency, direct delivery, primary distributor, private pharmacies)?
- What type(s) of purchasing models are used at each level of the supply system (annual, scheduled, or perpetual)?
- How are order and tender quantities determined at each level of the system?
- How are suppliers selected for tender or negotiation—does a formal qualification process exist?
- Is procurement done using generic names, brand names, or a mix?
- Are therapeutic equivalent medicines purchased through therapeutic subcategory tendering?
- How are lead times factored into ordering formulas and safety stock requirements?

- Are purchases limited to items on the formulary or essential medicines list?
- What constraints limit successful procurement in the public-sector pharmaceutical supply system?

Procurement system responsibilities

- Which agency or office is responsible for procurement of medicines and, if different, vaccines, contraceptives, diagnostics, and medical supplies?
- How are procurement responsibilities divided for medicine selection, needs estimation, tender management, and contract awards?
- Are written procedures for tenders and contract awards in place and regularly followed? Is the tender process transparent?
- What type of procurement management information system is used, and what kinds of reports are produced?
- How does the purchasing office obtain information on comparative prices and new supplier performance?
- What kinds of computers and computer applications are used to manage procurement?
- Is information available to carry out ABC, VEN, or total variable cost analyses?
- What procedures are used for monitoring supplier performance and enforcing procurement contracts?

Procurement finance

- What are the usual payment terms, payment lead times, and current debts owed to local and international suppliers?
- Does a problem exist with currency-exchange status in the public sector? If so, what impact does this situation have on pharmaceutical procurement?
- Are funds available as needed or is a fixed schedule used for the release of funds (and what approvals are needed)?
- Do cost recovery or drug revolving funds contribute significantly to procurement financing?
- To what degree is procurement financed by donors or by loans from development banks?

Batch: The quantity of a pharmaceutical produced in one production run.

Bid bond: A form of financial guarantee provided when a bid is submitted. The bond is forfeited if the successful bidder withdraws the offer or refuses to agree to the announced contract requirements.

Bulk purchasing: Procurement of pharmaceuticals in large quantities in order to obtain lower unit prices. Generally done in a bid system in which all medicines are identified by their generic (INN) name.

Call for offers: A publicized invitation to bid. Used in tender or bid purchasing. Includes product specifications, required delivery date, closing date for submitting offers, and other requirements of participation.

Certificate of manufacture: A document accompanying a commercial invoice that is presented to the buyer's bank—usually one of the requirements of a letter of credit—certifying that the products have been manufactured, are ready for shipment, and are in safekeeping.

CIF (cost, insurance, freight): When a seller quotes CIF, the costs of goods, marine insurance, and transportation to the named destination point are included.

Competitive negotiation: A procurement method by which the buyer approaches a small number of selected potential sellers and bargains with them directly to achieve specific price or service arrangements (used primarily in the private sector).

Compound: To mix together the ingredients of a prescription or pharmaceutical formula. Generally refers to a manual process performed for individual orders by a dispenser or pharmacist.

Consumption: The rate at which items are issued to clients or patients. This is also called demand (which is, in strict terms, the rate of requests or orders). Consumption is usually measured in terms of units consumed within a specific period.

Consumption-based estimate: Prediction of future pharmaceutical requirements on the basis of historical information on pharmaceutical consumption.

Direct procurement: The simplest but usually most expensive method of procurement, in which an item is purchased from a single supplier at its quoted price.

Disintegration: The breaking up of a tablet or capsule into granules or aggregates in an aqueous fluid.

Dissolution: The breaking down of fine particles into molecules or ions homogeneously dispersed in an aqueous fluid.

Estimated-quantity contract: A supply contract for a fixed period that stipulates an estimated total quantity, with the actual total quantity determined by orders placed as needed at the contract price during the contract period.

Excipient: An inert substance used to give a pharmaceutical preparation a suitable form or consistency.

Expiry date: The date appearing on a drug product and established by the manufacturer beyond which the manufacturer will not guarantee the potency, purity, uniformity, or bioavailability of the product.

External packaging: The case, crate, carton, or other container in which individual packages are placed.

FAS (free alongside ship): Used to indicate only the cost of transporting the goods to a ship are included by the seller. Carriage and freight are specifically excluded.

Financial guarantees: Deposits in the form of earnest money, bid bonds, performance bonds, or retention money required of suppliers to guarantee their participation once they have submitted bids or to ensure the complete fulfillment of contractual obligations by the supplier that wins the bid.

FOB (free on board): Used to indicate only the cost of transporting the goods to and on board a ship are included by the seller. Carriage and freight are specifically excluded.

Freight: The fee charged for carrying goods. The term is also applied to the items to be carried although the correct term for them is *cargo*.

GDF (Global Drug Facility): An organization that currently both supplies and acts as a procurement agent for anti-tuberculosis drugs for developing countries (http://www.stoptb.org/GDF/default.asp).

Global Fund to Fight AIDS, Tuberculosis and Malaria: An international, independent public-private partnership designed to attract and manage significant funding to finance the fight against AIDS, tuberculosis, and malaria (http://www.theglobalfund.org).

GMPs (good manufacturing practices): Performance standards for pharmaceutical manufacturers established by WHO and many national governments; they include criteria for personnel, facilities, equipment, materials, manufacturing operations, labeling, packaging, quality control, and, in most cases, stability testing.

GPP (good procurement practice): The internationally recognized concept of using best-practice principles in procurement, marked by openness and transparency.

Group purchasing: Purchasing done by one procurement office on behalf of a group of facilities, health systems, or countries. Group members agree to purchase certain medicines exclusively through the group.

Hidden costs: Costs in addition to the contract price that are not paid to the supplier but are real costs to the supply system. These include costs associated with poor quality, late deliveries, defaults on deliveries, short packing, and other factors.

Identity: Presence of the correct active ingredient in a drug product.

Immediate container (package): The individual jar, bottle, box, blister pack, or other container in which a single group of items is packed.

International procurement services: Organizations such as UNICEF, IDA Foundation, SCMS, and other groups that supply medicines on a nonprofit basis.

Inventory: The sum of all items held in stock.

Inventory-holding cost: Also known as *carrying cost*. The cost of holding one unit of an item in stock for a year. It may be expressed as a monetary amount or a percentage of purchase cost. This includes capital costs, costs associated with storage space, utilities, handling costs, losses due to waste and theft, and storehouse administrative costs. These costs may be 20 to 40 percent of the purchase price for a year.

Inventory value: The sum of the number of units of each item on hand or in storage in the system multiplied by the current unit price of each item.

IQC (Indefinite quantity contract): A contract that provides for an indefinite quantity, within stated limits, of specific supplies or services to be furnished during a fixed period with deliveries to be scheduled by placing orders with the contractor.

Issue unit: The quantity or size of each item counted in the stock records. For example, in some supply systems, the unit for tetracycline capsules might be one bottle of 100 capsules, and in others it might be one capsule. This is not necessarily the same as the basic unit or comparison unit, although they may be the same (see Chapter 50 for a discussion of units).

Item: A unique product for inventory purposes. In pharmaceutical supply, an important issue is whether generic equivalent items are treated as the same item or whether different brands of the same generic product are treated as different items. The item is sometimes called a stock-keeping unit (SKU), which is *not* the same as an *issue unit*.

Lead time: The time interval needed to complete the procurement cycle. It begins at the time the need for new stock is recognized and ends when that stock is received and available for issue.

Lead-time analysis: A systematic study of the components of lead time, aimed at discovering areas in which lead time can be reduced.

Line item: A product listed on an order or invoice. Each separate product on the document is one line item, no matter what quantity of the product is listed.

Make or buy: A management decision that involves the analysis of the cost and potential benefits of manufacturing a product rather than buying it on the open market.

Monopsony: A monopsony is a market with only one buyer. The buyer's-side analogy is a monopoly, in which there is only one seller in a market.

Open tender: The formal procedure by which quotations for the supply of pharmaceuticals under their generic names are invited from any local or international manufacturer or representative, subject to the terms and conditions specified in the tender invitation.

Opportunity cost of inventory: The cost of monies tied up in inventory. If average inventories increase, then capital invested in inventory increases proportionally. Since these funds invested in inventory could be used for other expenditures, they should be valued at current bank interest rates.

Order quantity: The amount of stock to be ordered (or that has already been ordered) via requisition or purchase order from a supplier or supply point.

Order status: The position of an order with respect to the specific tasks that must be performed for the order to be delivered to the buyer.

Payment terms: The conditions arranged between a buyer and a seller regarding the method of reimbursement. Letters of credit and commercial or deferred terms are the most common.

Performance bond: A form of financial guarantee that the supplier deposits when accepting the contract. This amount is forfeited if the supplier defaults on the contract.

Perpetual purchasing: A procurement model in which stock levels are reviewed continually, and orders are placed whenever stock levels fall below designated or calculated reorder points.

Pooled procurement: Another name for group purchasing.

Population-based estimate: Prediction of future pharmaceutical requirements based on the demographic composition of the population, disease patterns, and norms for treatment.

Port clearing: The process of locating items in port, obtaining the proper import documentation, paying the necessary fees, and inspecting the pharmaceuticals for damage during transit.

Potency: The extent to which a medicine contains the specified amount of the active ingredient.

Procurement: The process of acquiring supplies, including those obtained by purchase, donation, and manufacture.

Procurement period: The period of time between an order to a supplier and the next scheduled order.

Product file: A card or ledger file that records the technical specifications and performance of suppliers for each product.

Purchasing costs: All costs involved in placing and monitoring an order, including communication costs, the cost of preparing an order or tender and of subsequent negotiations, the staff time involved in routine checking of inventory levels, costs of receiving goods, any related special fees, and administrative costs. In practice, the cost of each order is estimated by dividing the total annual direct and indirect costs of the purchasing department by the number of orders placed in the year.

Purity: The extent to which medicines are free from potentially harmful contaminants, significant quantities of other medicines, bacteria, or other microorganisms.

Quality assurance: The management activities required to ensure that the medicine that reaches the patient is safe, effective, and acceptable to the patient.

Quality control: The testing of medicine samples against specific standards of quality.

Quantification: Estimation of the quantities of specific medicines needed. Financial requirements for purchasing the quantities are also calculated.

Restricted tender: Procurement procedure in which participation in bidding is limited to suppliers that meet certain prerequisites or have previously registered as suppliers.

Retention money: See **Performance bond.**

Roll Back Malaria Partnership's Commodity Services: A unit to support the procurement and supply management efforts for nets, insecticides, medicines, and diagnostics. The commodity service does not procure products itself, but it publishes market data, distributes forecast information, and fosters collaboration to address bottlenecks. (http://www.rollbackmalaria.org/psm/index.html)

Scheduled purchasing: Procurement model in which stock levels are reviewed periodically at set times during the year and orders are placed as necessary.

Secondary manufacture: The processing of medicinal substances, usually together with excipients, to produce a pharmaceutical dose form.

Shelf life: The length of time a material may be stored without affecting its usability, safety, purity, or potency.

Shortage cost: If emergency supplies are purchased to address a stockout, any increment in purchase price is a shortage cost. This cost is more difficult to quantify than holding cost but may still be significant. Loss of customers, decreased goodwill, and decreased sales are also real shortage costs if pharmaceuticals sales are involved.

Specifications: A precise description of an item to be procured, including any special requirements.

Stock: The items stored in a warehouse or facility (or health system). There are several types of stock:

Pipeline stock: Stock that is in transit at various stages of the purchasing and distribution cycles.

Quarantine stock: Stock that has been physically received in the storage facility but is held separately and not available for issue. There may be a need to confirm product quality or compliance with the contract, or the transfer to working stock might be delayed pending completion of necessary documents.

Safety stock: The buffer or minimum stock that is kept on hand to protect against stockouts. If there is no safety stock, stockouts will occur when deliveries are delayed or when there is an unexpected increase in demand. In theory, the safety stock is separate from the working stock, but in practice there is no separation of the two, and safety stock sometimes must be issued.

Seasonal stock: Stock that is acquired with the expectation that it will be needed to satisfy seasonal demand—for example, cough and cold medications in the winter. This stock is also part of the working stock once it is in the warehouse.

Vertical program stock: Stock that is not available on open request but is held for sole use by a vertical program, such as family planning or the Expanded Programme on Immunization (EPI). This stock may also be separated into working stock and safety stock.

Working stock: Stock that is on hand in the warehouse or storeroom and is shipped to requesting operating units. Working stock fluctuates as orders are filled and new stock arrives.

Other stock: Stock that is not usually issued but may be needed for purposes such as shipping or repackaging. May include items such as shipping tape, boxes, and labels.

Supplier: Any individual or company that agrees to provide medications, regardless of whether that party is the manufacturer.

Supplier file: A record kept for each supplier indicating when orders were placed, when they were received, what kind of service the supplier provided, and the quality of the product provided.

Supplier reliability: The past performance of a supplier in terms of medicine and packaging quality, timeliness of delivery, and level of service provided.

Supply Chain Management System (SCMS): A U.S. government initiative to procure and distribute HIV/AIDS-related pharmaceuticals and other commodities in countries supported by PEPFAR (www.pfscm.org).

Tendering: The procedure by which competing bids are entered for a particular contract.

Trade terms: A set of standard terms to describe the buyer's and seller's responsibilities in international trade—a list is found in Chapter 39.

VEN system: A system of setting priorities for purchasing pharmaceuticals and keeping stocks in which medicines are divided according to their health impact into vital, essential, and nonessential categories.

Wholesaler: A dealer who purchases supplies from a manufacturer and resells them to the ultimate buyers.

References and further readings

★ = Key readings.

Burnett, F. 2003. Reducing Costs through Regional Pooled Procurement. *Essential Drugs Monitor* 32:7–8.

Center for Pharmaceutical Management. 2003a. *Access to Essential Medicines: Cambodia, 2001.* Prepared for the Strategies for Enhancing Access to Medicines Program. Arlington, Va.: Management Sciences for Health. <http://www.msh.org/seam/reports/cambodia_assessment_report.pdf>

———. 2003b. *Access to Essential Medicines: El Salvador, 2001.* Prepared for the Strategies for Enhancing Access to Medicines Program. Arlington, Va.: Management Sciences for Health. <http://www.msh.org/seam/reports/el_salvador_final.pdf>

———. 2003c. *Access to Essential Medicines: Ghana, 2001.* Prepared for the Strategies for Enhancing Access to Medicines Program. Arlington, Va.: Management Sciences for Health. <http://www.msh.org/seam/reports/ghana_final.pdf>

———. 2003d. *Access to Essential Medicines: State of Minas Gerais, Brazil, 2001.* Prepared for the Strategies for Enhancing Access to Medicines Program. Arlington, Va.: Management Sciences for Health. <http://www.msh.org/seam/reports/brazil_final.pdf>

———. 2003e. *Access to Essential Medicines: State of Ratjasthan, India, 2001.* Prepared for the Strategies for Enhancing Access to Medicines

Program. Arlington, Va.: Management Sciences for Health. <http://www.msh.org/seam/reports/Rajasthan-SEAMAssessment-2001.pdf>

———. 2003f. *Access to Essential Medicines: Tanzania, 2001.* Prepared for the Strategies for Enhancing Access to Medicines Program. Arlington, Va.: Management Sciences for Health. <http://www.msh.org/seam/reports/access_to_medicines_tanzania.pdf>

DeRoeck, D., S. A. Bawazir, P. Carrasco, M. Kaddar, A. Brooks, J. Fitzsimmons, and J. Andrus. 2006. *International Journal of Health Planning and Management* 21:23–43.

Global Fund (Global Fund to Fight AIDS, Tuberculosis and Malaria). 2010. *Information Note: Procurement Support Services Voluntary Pooled Procurement and Supply Chain Management Assistance.* Geneva: Global Fund.

———. 2009. *Guide to the Global Fund's Policies on Procurement and Supply Management.* Geneva: Global Fund. <http://www.theglobalfund.org/en/procurement>

Holmes, C. B., W. Coggin, D. Jamieson, H. Mihm, R. Granich, P. Savio, M. Hope, et al. 2010. Use of Generic Antiretroviral Agents and Cost Savings in PEPFAR Treatment Programs. *Journal of the American Medical Association* 304(3):313–20.

HAI/WHO (Health Action International /World Health Organization). No date. "Medicine Prices, Availability, Affordability and Price Components." [How to conduct a pharmaceutical price survey and survey results from countries.] <http://www.haiweb.org/medicineprices/>

Levison, L. and R. Laing. 2003. The Hidden Costs of Essential Medicines. *Essential Drugs Monitor* 33:20–1.

MOH (Ministry of Health) Uganda. 2008. *Health Sector Strategic Plan 2005/06–2009/10 Mid-Term Review Report.* Kampala: Government of Uganda.

MSF (Médicins Sans Frontières) 2010. *Untangling the Web of Antiretroviral Price Reductions: A Pricing Guide for the Purchase of ARVs for Developing Countries.* 12th ed. (Updated regularly.) <http://utw.msfaccess.org/>

———. 2003. *Surmounting Challenges: Procurement of Antiretroviral Medicines in Low- and Middle-Income Countries: The Experience of MSF.* <http://apps.who.int/medicinedocs/en/d/Js4892e>

★ MSH (Management Sciences for Health). 2010. *International Drug Price Indicator Guide.* Arlington, Va.: MSH. [Updated annually.] <http://erc.msh.org/mainpage.cfm?file=1.0.htm&module=DMP&language=English>

MSH/CPM (Management Sciences for Health/Center for Pharmaceutical Management). 2002. *Regional Pooled Procurement of Drugs in Sub-Saharan Africa.* Submitted to the Rockefeller Foundation. Arlington, Va.: MSH/CPM.

MSH/RPM Plus (Management Sciences for Health/Rational Pharmaceutical Management Plus Program). 2009. *HIV Test Kits Listed in the USAID Source and Origin Waiver: Procurement Information Document.* 5th ed. Arlington, Va.: MSH/RPM Plus Program. <http://www.msh.org/projects/rpmplus/Documents/upload/HIV-Test-Kits_5thEd_final.pdf >

———. 2004. *Increasing Access to Quality Pharmaceuticals and Other Commodities for the Treatment, Care, and Support of HIV/AIDS Patients: A Case for Regional Collaboration for Procurement.* Presented at the XV International AIDS Society Conference, July 11–16, Bangkok, Thailand.

———. 2002. *Requesting USAID Approval to Procure HIV Test Kits and Other HIV/AIDS-Related Pharmaceutical Products: Guidance and Sources of Information.* Arlington, Va.: MSH/RPM Plus Program. <http://www.msh.org/projects/rpmplus/documents/upload/HIV_Test_Kits_Complete.pdf>

Ombaka, E. 2009. Current Status of Medicines Procurement. *American Journal of Health-System Pharmacy* 66(5[Suppl. 3]):20–8. <http://www.ajhp.org/cgi/reprint/66/5_Supplement_3/s20.pdf>

Shalev, M., and S. Asbjornsen. 2010. Electronic Reverse Auctions and the Public Sector: Factors of Success. *Journal of Public Procurement* 10:428–52.

Singer, M., G. Konstantindis, E. Roubik, and E. Beffermann. 2009. Does e-Procurement Save the State Money? *Journal of Public Procurement* 9(1):58–78.

UNICEF. 2004a. *HIV AIDS Care and Support Procurement of Antiretrovirals for ART and PMTCT.* Copenhagen: UNICEF.

———. 2004b. *Procurement Services.* Brochure. Copenhagen: UNICEF. <http://www.unicef.org/supply/files/PSleaflet.pdf>

Waning, B., W. Kaplan, A. C. King, D. A. Lawrence, H. G. Leufkens, and M. P. Fox. 2009. Global Strategies to Reduce the Price of Antiretroviral Medicines: Evidence from Transactional Databases. *Bulletin of World Health Organization* 87:520–8.

Waning, B., M. Kyle, E. Diedrichsen, L. Soucy, J. Hochstadt, T. Bärnighausen, and S. Moon. 2010. Intervening in Global Markets to Improve Access to HIV/AIDS Treatment: An Analysis of International Policies and the Dynamics of Global Antiretroviral Medicines Markets. *Globalization and Health* 6:9. <http://www.globalizationandhealth.com/content/6/1/9>

WHO (World Health Organization). 2010a. *Good Procurement Practices for Artemisinin-Based Antimalarial Medicines.* Geneva: WHO. <http://whqlibdoc.who.int/publications/2010/9789241598927_eng.pdf>

———. 2010b. WHO Prequalification of Medicines Programme: Inspection of Finished Pharmaceutical Product Manufacturers to Increase Quality of Medicines. *WHO Pharmaceuticals Newsletter* 2:16–8. <http://www.who.int/medicines/publications/newsletter/2010news2_1.pdf>

———. 2009a. Prequalification of Medicines Programme. *WHO Drug Information* 24 (1):3. <http://www.who.int/medicines/publications/druginformation/DrugInfo2010_Vol24-1.pdf>

———. 2009b. *The Selection and Use of Essential Medicines.* Geneva: WHO. <http://apps.who.int/medicinedocs/documents/s17060e/s17060e.pdf>

———. 2007. *Multi-Country Regional Pooled Procurement of Medicines: Identifying Key Principles for Enabling Regional Pooled Procurement and a Framework for Inter-Regional Collaboration in the African, Caribbean, and Pacific Island Countries.* Geneva: WHO. <http://www.who.int/medicines/publications/PooledProcurement.pdf>

★ ———. 1999. *Operational Principles For Good Pharmaceutical Procurement.* Geneva: WHO.

———. No date. *Guidelines on the Implementation of the WHO Certification Scheme on the Quality of Pharmaceutical Products Moving in International Commerce.* Geneva: WHO. <http://www.who.int/medicines/areas/quality_safety/regulation_legislation/certification/guidelines/en/index.html>

WHO/AMDS (World Health Organization/AIDS Medicines and Diagnostics Service). No date. Procurement & Supply Management Toolbox. [Updated regularly.] <http://www.psmtoolbox.org/en/>

WHO/UNICEF/UNAIDS/MSF (World Health Organization/United Nations Children's Fund/Joint United Nations Joint Programme on HIV/AIDS/Médecins Sans Frontières). 2005. *Sources and Prices of Selected Medicines and Diagnostics for People Living with HIV/AIDS.* 6th ed. Geneva: WHO. <http://apps.who.int/medicinedocs/pdf/s8112e/s8112e.pdf>

WHO/UNICEF/UNDP/UNFPA/WB (World Health Organization/United Nations Children's Fund/United Nations Development Programme/United Nations Population Fund/World Bank). 2007. *A Model Quality Assurance System for Procurement Agencies: Recommendations for Quality Assurance Systems Focusing on Prequalification of Products and Manufacturers, Purchasing, Storage and Distribution of Pharmaceutical Products.* Geneva: WHO. <http://apps.who.int/medicinedocs/documents/s14866e/s14866e.pdf>

WHO/WPRO (World Health Organization/Regional Office for the Western Pacific). 2002. *Practical Guidelines on Pharmaceutical Procurement for Countries with Small Procurement Agencies.* Manila: WHO/WPRO. <http://apps.who.int/medicinedocs/en/d/Jh2999e>

World Bank. 2004a. *Battling HIV/AIDS: A Decision Maker's Guide to the Procurement of Medicines and Related Supplies.* Washington, D.C.: World Bank. <http://go.worldbank.org/F0IITA9BR0>

★ ———. 2004b. *Standard Bidding Documents for Procurement of Health Sector Goods: Pharmaceuticals, Vaccines and Condoms.* Revised August 2008. Washington, D.C.: World Bank. <http://go.worldbank.org/R557PHPNU0>

★ ———. 2000. *Technical Note: Procurement of Health Sector Goods.* Revised May 2006. Washington, D.C.: World Bank. <http://siteresources.worldbank.org/INTPROCUREMENT/Resources/health-tn-ev3.doc>

CHAPTER 19

Quality assurance for pharmaceuticals

SUMMARY

The purpose of quality assurance in pharmaceutical supply systems is to help ensure that each medicine reaching a patient is safe, effective, and of acceptable quality. A comprehensive quality assurance program includes both technical and managerial activities, spanning the entire supply process from pharmaceutical selection to patient use.

Established quality standards are published periodically in pharmacopoeias and in some government publications. For the purposes of primary health care, the most important characteristics of a pharmaceutical product are identity, purity, strength, potency, uniformity of dosage form, bioavailability, and stability.

Pharmaceutical quality is affected by starting materials, manufacturing process, packaging, transportation and storage conditions, and other factors; these influences may be cumulative.

If a pharmaceutical does not meet established quality standards, passes its expiration date, or has been degraded by storage conditions, the possible consequences are—

- Lack of therapeutic effect, leading to prolonged illness or death
- Toxic and adverse reactions
- Waste of limited financial resources
- Loss of credibility of the health care delivery system

A comprehensive quality assurance program must ensure the following—

- Pharmaceuticals selected have been shown to be safe and efficacious for their intended use, are presented in an appropriate dosage form, and have the longest possible shelf life.
- Suppliers with acceptable quality standards are selected.
- Pharmaceuticals received from commercial suppliers and donors meet specified quality standards at the time of delivery.
- Packaging meets contract and usage requirements.
- Repackaging activities and dispensing practices maintain quality.
- Storage and transportation conditions do not compromise product quality.
- Product quality concerns reported by prescribers, dispensers, and consumers are properly cataloged and addressed.
- Product recall procedures are implemented to remove defective products.

A quality assurance program should include training and supervision of staff members at all levels of the supply process and a suitable information system. Often, public officials must balance the costs of establishing and maintaining quality assurance systems against the benefits of having safe and effective medicines.

19.1 Pharmaceutical quality

As in most manufacturing processes, the quality of a final pharmaceutical product is determined by the starting materials, equipment, and technical know-how that go into producing and packaging it. Unlike a steel bolt or a tailored suit, however, a medicine is a dynamic product whose color, consistency, weight, and even chemical identity can change between manufacture and ultimate consumption. A medicine that passes all laboratory tests upon receipt may be useless within a few months if the packaging, storage, and transportation conditions are not maintained properly.

The purpose of quality assurance in pharmaceutical supply systems is to help ensure that each medicine reaching a patient is safe, effective, and of appropriate quality. The quality of pharmaceutical products is ensured by the technical and managerial activities of the quality system, which includes evaluating pharmaceutical product documentation, performing or reviewing quality-control laboratory tests, and monitoring product performance. Managerial activities include selecting reliable suppliers, preparing contract terms, monitoring supplier performance, and performing inspection procedures throughout the distribution network (Figure 19-1).

Note that quality assurance in pharmaceutical supply is not the same as quality control in manufacturing.

Pharmaceutical quality assurance framework

The following five elements are critical to achieving the expected treatment outcome. Using a pharmaceutical product to treat a patient presumes that the—

1. Active pharmaceutical ingredient (API) has been shown to be safe and effective for this treatment
2. Product is of suitable quality to provide an effective outcome
3. Prescriber has accurately identified the need for the treatment

Figure 19-1   Quality assurance framework

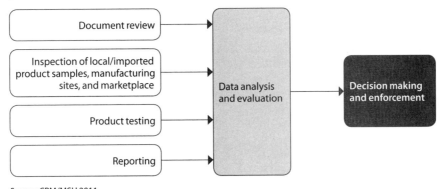

Source: CPM/MSH 2011.

4. Prescriber or dispenser has properly instructed the patient on how to use the product
5. Patient complies with the prescribed regimen correctly

The first two items are product-specific issues, which are the most easily addressed technically, whereas items three and four are practitioner-specific and depend on the practitioners' education, knowledge, and skill as well as the rigorous enforcement of performance standards. Item five is a patient-specific issue that depends on the patient's knowledge and commitment and the patient's access to services.

The safety and effectiveness of an API may be established either through a review of historical usage, such as in the case of digoxin's evolution from the foxglove plant (*digitalis purpurea*), or through complex procedures established for new chemical entities, such as those described by the International Conference on Harmonisation of Technical Requirements for Registration of Pharmaceuticals for Human Use (ICH).

After the safety and effectiveness of an API has been approved for marketing in an ICH market region, other regions of the world follow with little or no additional assessment. The ICH economic zones (European Union, Japan, United States) perform almost 100 percent of the pharmaceutical research and consume over 85 percent (by value) of the pharmaceutical products in the world. These regions allocate large amounts of resources to ensure the safety and effectiveness of APIs granted market authorization in their zones. Once the safety and efficacy have been established through these procedures, other regions do not have to expend the same level of resources to establish these attributes. However, other product-quality issues, including bioavailability and bioequivalence, content uniformity, impurities and degradation, and medicine safety (pharmacovigilance), should be monitored on an ongoing basis in all market zones.

The complexity of globalized pharmaceutical markets and the difficulty in ensuring quality of imported products,

including API, have been illustrated in headlines about deaths caused by adulterated products such as cough syrup in Peru and heparin in the United States—both tied to ingredients from China. As a result, the U.S. Food and Drug Administration (FDA) seeks to increase its global presence to make monitoring foreign manufacturers easier and to strengthen its involvement with harmonization of pharmaceutical standards (FDA 2010). In addition, the FDA wants to help build regulatory capacity in foreign counterparts. As part of that international effort, the agency has opened permanent offices in a number of cities around the world and has entered into dozens of agreements with other drug regulatory authorities (DRAs) to share inspection reports and other private information that can help improve the quality of pharmaceutical products worldwide.

The pharmaceutical regulatory and quality assurance processes that should be addressed by a country's DRA include (WHO 2004b)—

- Product registration: assessing and authorizing products for market entry and monitoring their safety and effectiveness after entry
- Regulation of manufacturing, importation, and distribution
  - Quality of manufacturing (good manufacturing practices)
  - Procurement integrity (assuring the qualifications of suppliers)
  - Quality of medicines in the distribution system (including product and premises inspection and product screening and testing)
- Regulation of medicine promotion and information: including postmarketing pharmacovigilance and consumer education

Of course, a country's quality assurance system is only as effective as its ability to monitor and enforce regulations. A country should address all issues at some level as part of a basic pharmaceutical quality assurance infrastructure;

however, in a resource-constrained setting, the risks to patients for each process must be assessed so resources can be allocated to focus on the most significant health threats.

Defining and assessing pharmaceutical quality

Pharmaceutical quality can be defined and tested in many ways. Quality standards are published periodically in pharmacopoeias and in some government publications, which provide detailed descriptions of pharmaceutical characteristics and analytical techniques. Standards may vary slightly from one pharmacopoeia to another, so a particular pharmaccutical may meet the standards of one pharmacopoeia and not those of another. When public standards have not been established, as is generally the case for newly marketed pharmaceuticals, analytical methods developed by the manufacturer and submitted as a part of the tender or marketing authorization requirements are usually applied.

The major pharmaceutical manufacturing and exporting countries publish their own pharmacopoeias, and on a regional basis, the *European Pharmacopoeia* establishes standards that are enforced by the governments of the European Union and others that adopt them. The *International Pharmacopoeia*, published by the World Health Organization (WHO), the *U.S. Pharmacopeia,* and the *British Pharmacopoeia* are used frequently by public-sector pharmaceutical supply programs in developing countries.

One important limitation of the *European Pharmacopoeia* is that it provides few specifications for individual dosage forms. The WHO *International Pharmacopoeia* (WHO 2008a) includes monographs on finished dosage forms, including antiretrovirals and newly developed antimalarial medicines. Analytical procedures in the *U.S. Pharmacopeia* tend to use complex and expensive technology, which may be beyond the reach of many developing countries. The European, Japanese, and U.S. pharmacopoeias are engaged in ongoing efforts to harmonize some of their standards, but progress is slow. Until common standards are finally achieved, purchasers must specify which dosage form standards are acceptable.

For pharmaceutical procurement organizations, pharmaceutical quality is assessed as the product's compliance with specifications concerning identity, purity, strength, potency, and other characteristics. Uniformity of the dosage form, bioavailability, and stability are important characteristics that are also considered in the specifications.

Identity. The identity test should confirm the existence of the active ingredient(s) indicated on the label. This characteristic is generally the easiest to check.

Purity. In addition to the API, most pharmaceuticals are made with ingredients added for bulk, consistency, or color that should not contain potentially harmful contaminants or microorganisms. The product should not have significant quantities of other products from cross-contamination.

Strength or potency. The medicine should contain the declared amount of API. Harmful by-products of degradation must be absent or should be below defined limits. Most pharmacopoeias specify an average content range, such as 90 to 110 percent of the amount written on the label, rather than an exact amount. To ensure a long shelf life, manufacturers often produce pharmaceuticals with the maximum allowable amount (for example, 110 mg rather than 95 mg), which provides a margin of safety for slight losses in strength or potency over time.

Uniformity of dosage form. The consistency, color, shape, and size of tablets, capsules, creams, and liquids should not vary from one dose to the next. Any lack of uniformity may suggest problems with other quality parameters such as identity, purity, or strength or potency. Lack of dosage uniformity may not influence the safety or effectiveness of a medicine, but it does reflect a lack of good manufacturing practices, which could influence the acceptability of a product to pharmacists, medical practitioners, and patients.

Bioavailability. *Bioavailability* refers to the speed and completeness with which a pharmaceutical administered in a specific form (tablet, capsule, intramuscular injection, subcutaneous injection) enters the bloodstream. The bioavailability of a product may depend on the other ingredients used in the formulation, such as solvents, binders, coloring agents, and coatings, or how ingredients are combined.

The comparative bioavailability of two pharmaceuticals is particularly important when a product that is usually purchased from one manufacturer is replaced with a product containing the same drug substance in the same dosage form, and in the same amount, but manufactured by a different firm. Even though the products both contain the correct amount of the API, the preparations may not give the expected therapeutic result if the API is released too quickly, too slowly, or incompletely when they are compared. Two pharmaceuticals are said to be *bioequivalent* and may be used interchangeably if both are absorbed into the bloodstream at the same rate and to the same extent.

Human bioequivalence studies are required for a number of medicines. Box 19-1 lists some medicines documented to have problems in bioavailability that require studies to determine the bioequivalence of products. Guidelines are available for the study of bioavailability, as well as specific bioavailability protocols for a small number of medicines (WHO/EURO 1988; USP 2007).

If purchasing is done through established and reliable suppliers, the bioavailability of most brand-name and generic medicines used in primary health care is sufficient to ensure that the patient receives the intended effect. Deciding which pharmaceuticals have a potential bioavailability problem is important, because manufacturers cannot supply clinical studies for all products, and government procurement programs generally cannot perform bioequivalence test-

Box 19-1
Some substances exhibiting potential bioavailability problems in conventional oral forms

API

- Aminophylline
- Ampicillin
- Carbamazepine
- Chloramphenicol
- Chloroquine
- Chlorpromazine
- Digitoxin
- Digoxin
- Dihydroergotamine
- Ergotamine
- Erythromycin

- Estrogens, conjugated or esterified
- Furosemide
- Glibenclamide
- Glyceryl trinitrate
- Griseofulvin
- Hydrochlorothiazide
- Iron sulfate
- Isosorbide dinitrate
- Levodopa
- L-thyroxine
- Methotrexate

- Methyldopa
- Nitrofurantoin
- Phenytoin
- Prednisolone
- Prednisone
- Quinidine
- Rifampicin
- Spironolactone
- Theophylline
- Warfarin

Source: WHO/EURO 1988.

ing. The Biopharmaceutical Classification System can help identify potential bioavailability problem products (Kasim et al. 2004). Where pharmaceutical registration systems exist, manufacturers or suppliers should be required to supply data on clinical studies whenever needed. Procurement agencies should also work with country DRAs and use their information in making decisions.

Stability. To be useful, a pharmaceutical must retain its properties within specified limits, such as particular storage conditions. The manufacturer and, in some cases, a country's DRA establish the time that a pharmaceutical's stability is under warranty, which ends with the expiration date. A product's stability depends on the active ingredient, which can be affected by its formulation and packaging. Improper storage and distribution can lead to physical deterioration and chemical decomposition, reduced potency, and occasionally, formation of toxic by-products of degradation. These effects are more likely to occur under tropical conditions of high temperature and humidity.

WHO has published a list of pharmaceutical substances that are less stable and therefore require particular attention (WHO 1990). However, few data are available on the stability of medicines under true field conditions. The ICH,

whose members comprise experts from the major pharmaceutical manufacturing countries, has established guidelines on quality testing and storage in tropical regions (ICH 2003). WHO has been updating its stability guidelines with input from member country DRAs and in cooperation with ICH (WHO 2010d, 2009b). Several studies have examined the stability of a small number of essential medicines under tropical conditions of excessive temperature (over 40°C), high humidity, and inappropriate storage conditions (Gammon et al. 2008; Hogerzeil et al. 1991; Hogerzeil, Walker, and de Goeje 1993). Table 19-1 lists the medicines that have been found to have problems under tropical and high-temperature conditions.

Consequences of poor pharmaceutical quality

A poor-quality medicine is one that does not meet specifications. The use of poor-quality products may have undesirable clinical and economic effects, as well as affect the credibility of the health delivery system. Clinical effects can include prolonged illness or death or adverse reactions. On the economic side, limited financial resources may be wasted on poor-quality medicines.

Table 19-1   Medicines found to have stability problems under tropical or high-temperature conditions

Oral solids (tablets)	Oral liquids (syrups)	Inhalation	Injections/injectables
Acetylsalicylic acid	Paracetamol	Ipratropium	Ergometrine
Amoxicilline			Lidocaine
Ampicillin			Methylergometrine
Diltiazem			Succinylcholine
Lopinavir/ritonavir			Naloxone
Penicillin V			
Retinol			

Sources: Gammon et al. 2008; Hogerzeil et al. 1991; Hogerzeil et al. 1992; Hogerzeil, Walker, and de Goeje 1993; Pau et al. 2005.

Figure 19-2   Determinants of pharmaceutical quality

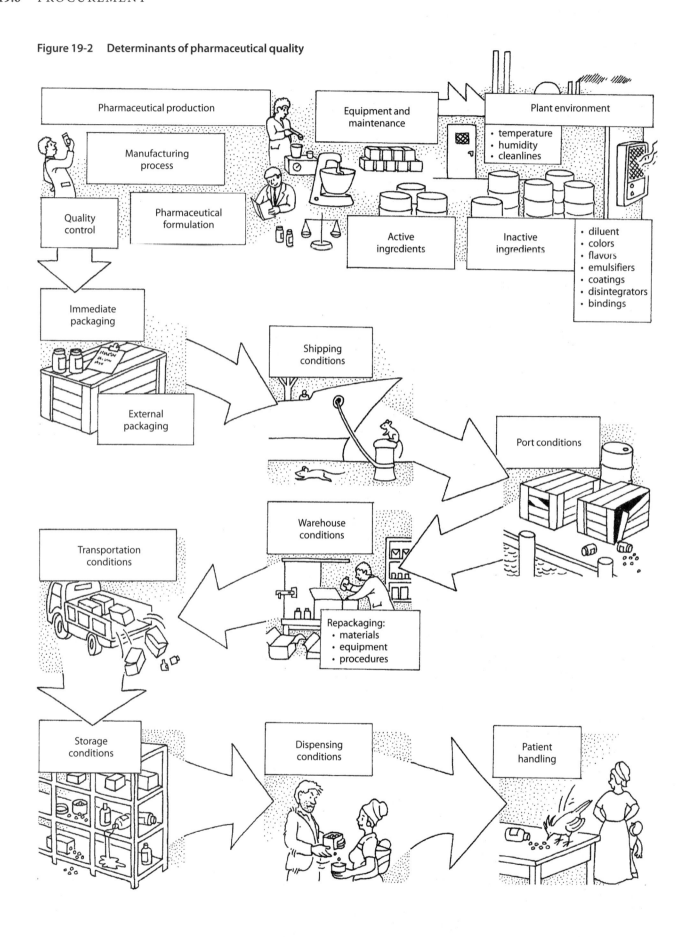

Lack of therapeutic effect may lead to prolonged illness or death. Poor pharmaceutical quality can sometimes lead to serious health consequences and death—for example, the use of poor-quality cardiac medicines and medicines for seizures and asthma. With others, such as cold remedies and minor painkillers, a reduction of up to 50 percent in the content of the active ingredient may not have serious consequences apart from ineffectiveness, although the best procurement policy requires all products to meet specifications.

Poor-quality pharmaceuticals may induce toxic or adverse reactions. When some products expire or are exposed to adverse climatic conditions (for example, excessive heat and humidity), they may undergo physical or chemical changes that can result in the formation of possibly toxic degradation products. Although fear of toxic pharmaceutical degradation in tropical climates is prevalent, tetracycline is the only common medicine in which it is known to occur. Excessive active ingredients may also lead to toxic or adverse reactions.

A much more frequent problem is contamination with microorganisms, usually bacteria or fungi. The consequences of this lack of sterility can be quite severe, particularly in the case of injectable medicines or in patients who are immunocompromised. Contamination of creams, syrups, and other medicines in jars and tubes is especially common in tropical environments, but the consequences vary, depending on the type of organism and the pharmaceutical involved. Errors in formulation and product contamination are uncommon with manufacturers who strictly comply with internationally accepted procedures and good manufacturing practices (GMPs). In practice, however, adherence to GMPs may vary from country to country, from manufacturer to manufacturer, or even between production runs at the same manufacturer. When contaminants are highly toxic or when toxic substances are inadvertently included in the product, the result can be catastrophic.

Poor pharmaceutical quality wastes money. Ineffective care or the need to treat adverse drug reactions resulting from poor product quality leads to more costly treatments. Poor pharmaceutical packaging casts doubts on product quality, leading to rejection by health personnel and patients. These products will then expire on the medical stores' shelves, wasting limited financial resources.

Poor pharmaceutical quality may seriously affect health system credibility. Patients and providers may suspect the quality of medicines when therapeutic failure or adverse drug reactions occur. Changes in product appearance, such as discoloration, crumbling of tablets, and hardening of oral suspensions, or changes in taste and smell rightly influence patients' perceptions of product quality. Patients may be discouraged from using health facilities, and worker morale may be affected, particularly if medicine shortages are also common.

Determinants of pharmaceutical quality

The quality of a medicine product coming off the production line is determined by the start-up materials, plant environment, manufacturing equipment, and technical know-how invested in developing and manufacturing the pharmaceutical. The medicine that ultimately reaches the patient, however, is further affected by packaging and by transportation and storage conditions.

These influences, especially factors in the manufacturing process, can be cumulative. For example, the excipient substances used to give tablets bulk and consistency may not affect the color, texture, or chemical quality of a pharmaceutical until the immediate container is opened in a hot, humid environment. Then, depending on the ingredients, the tablet may remain firm and dry or become moist and crumble within a matter of days. Factory humidity during packaging may also affect quality. If oral rehydration sachets are not packaged in a very low-humidity environment, moisture enters the sachet and may result in chemical or physical changes in the mixture that make it difficult to use. Similarly, the amount of grinding, thoroughness of mixing, choice of packaging, maintenance of packaging equipment, and other factors can have an effect that may not appear until the medicine reaches the point of consumption. Figure 19-2 summarizes these influences.

The dynamic nature of pharmaceuticals and the cumulative effects of the production process, right through to packaging, handling, transport, and storage conditions, require quality assurance at all levels in the pharmaceutical supply system (see *A Model Quality Assurance System for Procurement Agencies* [WHO/UNICEF/UNDP/UNFP/World Bank 2007]).

Prevalence of poor-quality pharmaceuticals

Data summarized in Table 19-2 indicate the extent of the pharmaceutical quality problem, as detected by pharmaceutical quality testing in the public, private, and nongovernmental organization (NGO) sectors of six countries.

In recent years, national and international authorities have recognized the emergence of counterfeit medicines as a serious problem. In most industrialized countries with effective regulatory systems and market control, the incidence of counterfeit medicines is an estimated 1 percent of market value (WHO 2010b). Therefore, most counterfeiting cases occur in developing countries—especially in Asia, where many of the counterfeit medicines are produced, and in Africa, where poverty and loose regulatory oversight make marketing of counterfeit products easier (see Box 19-2). However, counterfeiting is an increasing problem in all countries, including developed countries, where Internet purchases are popular. Over half of Internet medicine purchases from illegal websites are counterfeit (WHO 2010b).

Table 19-2   Percentage of tracer medicines that failed quality testing in the public, private, and NGO sectors

Country	Number of medicines	Number of samples	Public facilities	Private facilities	NGO facilities
Brazil (Minas Gerais)	8	64	13.6	9.1	10.0
Cambodia	14	132	13.0	9.6	7.7
El Salvador	10	87	50.0	28.6	27.3
Tanzania	10	110	12.9	13.0	0
Ghana	7	103	6.3	2.9	0
India (Rajasthan)	9	125	6.0	12.7	0

Source: CPM 2003a, 2003b, 2003c, 2003d, 2003e, 2003f.

Global quality-monitoring options

Currently, no global pharmaceutical quality standards exist, even for the APIs used in worldwide pharmaceutical product formulation, which are produced by only a few countries. However, the ICH processes to establish GMPs for APIs were more inclusive than any of the previous processes; for example, besides the usual ICH parties, representatives from the generics industry, the self-medication industry, and the Pharmaceutical Inspection Convention and Pharmaceutical Inspection Co-operation Scheme were included in the deliberations (ICH 2000).

These GMP standards are the world's first harmonized standards and have been adopted by the ICH regions and the Pharmaceutical Inspection Convention and Pharmaceutical Inspection Co-operation Scheme, in addition to WHO and many other countries. This harmonization implies that any DRA could perform an inspection of an API manufacturer and expect it to conform to these consensus GMPs. However, because almost all sovereign nations or market zones protect their local production of pharmaceutical products through selective tariffs and other mechanisms, no incentive exists for the development of a worldwide quality standard for APIs (Chapter 7). Some pharmacopoeias, including the *European Pharmacopoeia* and WHO's *International Pharmacopoeia,* have regional quality standards for many APIs; however, these pharmacopoeial standards have not been harmonized, resulting in varying specifications for APIs among regions (see Chapter 6 for more information on pharmacopoeias).

Because of the lack of harmonized standards, no basis exists for a pharmaceutical product common market with universal recognition of quality standards. The dearth of internationally recognized specifications leaves each market zone to establish its own specifications. Among the major pharmacopoeias, only the *British Pharmacopoeia* and the *U.S. Pharmacopeia* have standards for a significant number of products, and even they have essentially no specifications for products under patent protection in their markets.

19.2 Practical approaches to quality assurance

The procedures to establish a comprehensive quality assurance program can be divided into three categories—

1. Procedures to ensure that only medicine products that meet current standards for quality are bought. These include—
   - Careful product selection
   - Careful supplier selection
   - Certificate of analysis for each batch of product
   - Certification of good manufacturing practices
   - Batch certification (WHO-type certificate of a pharmaceutical product)
   - Inclusion of detailed product-quality specifications in the contract
2. Procedures to verify that shipped goods meet the specifications. These include—
   - Pre- and postshipment inspection
   - Analytical pharmaceutical testing
3. Procedures to monitor and maintain the quality of pharmaceuticals from the moment they are received until the medicine is finally consumed by the patient. These involve—
   - Proper storage and distribution procedures
   - Appropriate dispensing
   - Instructions to the patient on proper use of medications
   - Product defect and pharmacovigilance reporting programs

Few pharmaceutical management programs can effectively manage all the possible quality assurance activities for all the medicines that are procured. Consequently, realistic goals must be set to identify the combination of managerial and technical quality assurance activities that will be most effective under existing conditions. The critical elements in quality assurance for pharmaceutical procurement are listed in Figure 19-3, and Country Study 19-1 discusses how the Tanzania Food and Drugs Authority

Box 19-2
Counterfeits and diversion from legal channels

Recent examples of dangerous counterfeit medicines in the marketplace in countries worldwide include—

Southeast Asia: Of 391 samples of artesunate, 50 percent had little or no active ingredient and a wide range of wrong ingredients, including banned pharmaceuticals (Newton et al. 2008).

Madagascar, Senegal, and Uganda: Of 197 antimalarial samples from the public and private sectors that underwent full laboratory quality-control testing, the failure rates from Senegal, Madagascar, and Uganda were 44 percent, 30 percent, and 26 percent, respectively (USP and USAID 2009).

United States: The FDA warned consumers about 24 websites selling counterfeit medicines (FDA 2007).

Democratic Republic of Congo: The antidepressant fluvoxamine and the muscle relaxant cyclobenzaprine HCl had been labeled and sold as commonly prescribed antiretrovirals for HIV/AIDS treatment (Ahmad 2004).

Niger: Up to 2,500 people reportedly died after being given a fake meningitis vaccine (WHO 2003).

WHO defines counterfeit medicines as those that are "deliberately and fraudulently mislabeled with respect to identity and/or source" (WHO 2010c). Within this broad definition, it is useful to consider different categories of counterfeiting activities—

- Professional counterfeit organizations have modern production facilities capable of manufacturing products and labeling strikingly similar to the authentic products. They operate in the most lucrative markets—mostly developed countries.
- Mediocre counterfeit organizations produce poorly made look-alike products that in a side-by-side comparison can be discerned from legitimate products.

- Minor relabelers distribute to only a few outlets in an attempt to preserve the value of their outdated inventory by relabeling expired products with valid expiration dates and the same product name.
- More advanced or major petty relabelers deal in a secondary pharmaceutical market for outdated products primarily obtained from legitimate sources in developing and developed countries but distributed mostly in developing countries.
- Substitution counterfeiters place lower-priced finished dosage forms into more expensive packaging for marketing at higher prices. These relabeled outdated products may be distributed in developing or developed countries.

Formulating counterfeiters generally do not include the active pharmaceutical ingredient in the formulation. Substitution counterfeiters generally use the wrong medicine, whereas the relabelers generally have the right API present in about the right amount. Therefore, relabelers are the most difficult to detect, if their labeling is well done. Generally, most counterfeits have flawed labels that can help identify them as substandard. If the pharmaceutical product is provided without its original label, however, this feature may not always be helpful in identifying counterfeit products. Local or within-country counterfeit marketing depends on astute practitioners and consumers for detection and a good internal communication system to support prompt legal action.

The different characteristics of counterfeiters can be roughly summarized as follows in the table below.

In 2006, WHO launched the International Medical Products Anti-Counterfeiting Taskforce, which is WHO's primary channel for anti-counterfeit activities.

Category	API[a]	Distribution scale	Product quality[b]	Label quality[c]	Detection
Professional	No	Large; frequently international	Very good	Excellent	Testing, side-by-side comparisons
Hack	No	Generally within a country or a limited region of a country	Poor	Good	Testing, physical examination
Minor petty	Yes?	Generally a few privately held stores	Very good	Good	Label examination
Major petty	Yes?	Generally a limited market segment in a given country	Excellent	Good	Label examination
Substitution	No	Generally a few privately held stores	Good	Good	Testing, examination

[a] In general, only the relabelers may have the correct product.
[b] Physical appearance, uniformity.
[c] Print quality, color.

Figure 19-3 Critical elements in quality assurance for pharmaceutical procurement

1. Product selection
- products with longer shelf life (for example, powders for reconstitution rather than oral suspensions)
- avoidance of products with bioavailability problems, when possible

2. Product certification
- supplier prequalification
- recent GMP inspection reports from national drug authorities
- formal supplier-monitoring system
- limitation of purchases from new suppliers to noncritical products

3. Product certification
- GMP certificate from drug regulatory authority (prequalification)
- certificate of pharmaceutical products (WHO-type) for all new products, new suppliers
- batch certificate (WHO-type) for problem drugs only

4. Contract specifications
- acceptable pharmacopeial standards
- language, labeling requirements
- minimum shelf life
- packaging standards

5. Inspection of shipments
- physical inspection of all shipments
- sampling for analysis of suspect products

6. Targeted laboratory testing
- therapeutically critical drugs
- drugs with known bioavailability problems
- new suppliers
- suppliers with quality difficulties in the past

7. Product problem reporting system
- system for reporting suspect or problem products

approached the design of its pharmaceutical quality assurance program.

Because resources are limited, countries should target priorities for quality assurance activities. The VEN (vital, essential, nonessential) method (Chapter 40) helps identify a small group of medicines that have the greatest health impact. Vital lifesaving medicines (antibiotics, cardiac medications, and intravenous solutions) warrant greater attention than other important but not lifesaving medications, such as analgesics. ABC analysis (Chapter 40) can be used to identify those medicines that have the greatest budgetary effect if their quality is unacceptable. The choice of medicines to monitor closely is based on the following criteria—

- Medicines with a narrow therapeutic window
- Medicines with inherent bioavailability problems
- Modified-release preparations
- Products from new suppliers and suppliers with problems in the past
- Medicines that require stable dosage forms and appearance

19.3 Obtaining good-quality pharmaceuticals

Obtaining medicines of good quality involves careful selection of suppliers and products, compliance with GMPs, reliance on appropriate pharmaceutical product or batch certificates, and detailed contract specifications.

Careful product selection

In many systems, therapeutic medicine formulary committees first assess the safety and efficacy of selected medicines on the basis of evidence from clinical trials (Chapter 16). Specific product selection involves assessing the technical documentation provided by the supplier on the pharmaceutical characteristics of the dosage form. Dosage forms that may offer longer shelf life include—

- Powders for reconstitution instead of injectable liquids
- Powders for reconstitution instead of oral suspensions
- Tablets instead of capsules

When appropriate, request and review product-specific stability studies from the manufacturer. For a few medicines, such as certain heart, asthma, and seizure medicines, studies that demonstrate bioequivalence among different manufacturers' products may also be necessary.

Select products with packaging that can withstand rough transport and extreme climatic conditions. Plastic containers may be better than glass bottles for intravenous solutions, oral liquids, and disinfectants. Avoid metal tins that will rust. In some countries, unit-of-use packages (blister packs) and containers with smaller quantities (for example, 100 tablets rather than 1,000 tablets) may be cost-effective. These measures aim to avoid quality loss after the containers are opened or as a result of frequent handling. The increased costs should be weighed against the wastage and contamination that may occur with bulk containers, plus the costs of any repackaging.

Careful supplier selection

This step may be the most critical in quality assurance (see Chapter 21). Suppliers can be selected competitively by restricted tender with prequalification, through open ten-

der with postaward qualification, or in some cases, through less formal procedures (see Chapters 18 and 21). Standard procedures should include requiring certifications, gathering information on supplier reliability and product quality, inspecting product samples, and if necessary, conducting laboratory testing of pharmaceuticals with high potential for bioavailability or stability problems. Country procurement offices obtained a major resource for helping assure quality pharmaceutical purchases when WHO launched its medicine prequalification program in 2001. Box 19-3 has more information on the program.

Contacts with DRAs and purchasing groups (for example, the United Nations Children's Fund and IDA Foundation)

Country Study 19-1
Building quality assessment infrastructure in Tanzania

Substandard pharmaceuticals circulating in the market are a problem in many countries. As part of a 2001 assessment, the Strategies for Enhancing Access to Medicines (SEAM) program took 110 samples of ten different medicines and found that 12.9 percent of the samples from public facilities and 13 percent from private pharmacies were substandard. A further measure of the quality of medicines in the marketplace is the percentage registered with the Tanzanian Food and Drugs Authority (TFDA). Only 26 percent of the medicines surveyed in the thirty-nine *duka la dawa baridi,* which are private drug shops, were registered, while a further 24 percent were notified. The quality of notified and unregistered medicines cannot be assured, since they have not passed through the registration process, which would include almost three-quarters of medicines sampled at the *duka la dawa baridi.*

SEAM collaborated with the TFDA to establish a comprehensive national quality assurance program that can ensure that both imported and locally manufactured pharmaceutical products meet approved quality standards. The main focus of the intervention was on product examination and testing at ports of entry and surveillance and testing of products circulating in the market. Market surveillance requires routine inspection of facilities and sampling of products in the marketplace, including distributors and retail outlets. This strategy required enhancing inspection and pharmaceutical testing capacity within the TFDA, which involved developing and incorporating a number of tools and activities, among them the following—

- Flow charts and standard operating procedures for structured inspection activities at ports of entry and facilities, such as warehouses, hospital dispensaries,

retail pharmacies, and over-the-counter drug shops. The flow charts and procedures have been compiled into a *Level One Drug Inspectors' Handbook.*
- A thin-layer-chromatography-based program to screen pharmaceutical products (initially targeted at antimalarial medicines, then selected antibiotics and antiretrovirals).
- Quality assurance protocols and training materials based on a combination of visual inspection and non-laboratory-based testing (using thin-layer-chromatography Minilab). School of Pharmacy faculty at the Muhimbili University College for Health Sciences collaborated on the development and oversight of the inspectors' training.
- Support for TFDA inspectors' training, and monitoring and evaluation.
- Personal digital assistants to standardize the inspection process and allow computer downloads of inspection results for management review.

Working closely with stakeholders and sensitizing them to quality requirements helped get the quality assurance program established in 2002. Since then, improved efficiencies have resulted in a doubling of the number of pharmaceutical products screened and a quadrupling of the number of premises inspected—all with relatively few inspectors. The new quality assurance program has resulted in many product confiscations and importation refusals, in addition to closures of premises and improvements in standards. In summary, the quality assurance activities were conducted with relatively modest resources yet increased the presence of the TFDA in the marketplace, providing a significant deterrent to the marketing of substandard and counterfeit products.

Source: SEAM 2007.

> **Box 19-3**
> **WHO's prequalification of medicines program**
>
> In 2001, WHO, in partnership with the United Nations Joint Programme on HIV/AIDS, the United Nations Children's Fund, and the United Nations Population Fund, and with support from the World Bank, launched its prequalification of medicines program to assess and approve manufacturers of medicines to treat HIV/AIDS, malaria, and tuberculosis. Since then, the program has added medicines and commodities related to reproductive health, and it also prequalifies quality-control laboratories. The program evaluates data on medicine safety, efficacy, and quality and inspects facilities for compliance with GMPs. Inspection activities have expanded to include manufacturers of selected APIs as well as clinical sites and contract research organizations. In addition, the program offers training workshops on how to meet prequalification requirements, assess multisource interchangeable medicines, and conduct and assess stability studies.
>
> In 2009, the program prequalified 44 products, for a total of 237 products manufactured in sixteen countries (WHO 2010c). The program also prequalified three new quality-control laboratories to bring the total to eleven.
>
> Originally intended for United Nations procurement agencies, the program has become a valuable resource for any purchaser, including countries themselves.
>
> More information on the prequalification program is on WHO's website at http://apps.who.int/prequal/. The website lists all product and manufacturing site requirements, standards used in evaluating the product, and the profile of the inspection teams. It also includes the list of prequalified medicines and their manufacturers.
>
> Source: WHO 2010c.

and product-quality testing laboratories can help with reference checks and exchanges of information on problem products. Publications by medicine information services and professional organizations, such as the U.S. Pharmacopeia, the FDA, and the American Society of Health-System Pharmacists, provide information on the bioequivalence of pharmaceuticals as well as on pharmaceutical recalls (see Annex 19-1).

A procurement office or agency needs to analyze information on suppliers' performance and develop and apply operational definitions and criteria to assess the reliability of suppliers and avoid subjectivity. Lack of explicit definitions and criteria provides rejected suppliers with the opportunity to question the integrity of the procurement process.

For products from new suppliers, visual inspection of samples of the product, packaging, and labeling is important. Some programs send samples for laboratory testing on a routine basis; others do so only when concerns arise about specific products. Although prepurchase testing may detect defective products, bear in mind that the samples are provided by the supplier, which will make every effort to ensure that the samples meet the standards. The samples may not, however, be representative of what is actually delivered.

Chapter 21 discusses the need for an information system that provides the procurement office and tender committee with feedback on suppliers' compliance with contracts. Keeping a record of condition of received goods, compliance with contract terms, and timeliness of delivery is essential.

This information, and that from the adverse drug reaction and product-quality reporting system, should be considered when assessing offers and awarding supply contracts.

Product certification

WHO has established GMPs for pharmaceutical products, similar to those enforced by the national pharmaceutical control agencies in industrialized countries. They include criteria for personnel, facilities, equipment, materials, manufacturing operations, labeling, packaging, quality control, and in most cases, stability testing.

In countries with effective pharmaceutical control agencies, adherence to GMPs is enforced by a system of inspections and regulatory controls, often specific to individual medicine dosage forms. A manufacturer may have acceptable standards for solid dosage forms but not for sterile injectable preparations. Recent reports of GMP inspections and pharmaceutical recall histories can be obtained by writing to national pharmaceutical control agencies. Often, a supplier must approve or at least expedite requests for performance reports from national pharmaceutical control agencies, and failure to obtain such reports for the buyer makes past performance suspect.

Buyers with pharmaceutical staff trained in GMP inspection may perform their own inspections of local manufacturers that are potential suppliers, if funds are available to do so.

Countries that participate in the scheme agree to certify that pharmaceuticals are registered in the exporting country and that manufacturers' facilities have been inspected and comply with GMPs. However, a WHO study (1995) showed that very few importing countries actually request pharmaceutical product certificates for registration or procurement purposes.

This certification scheme provides some assurance, based on inspection of the manufacturing facilities for GMPs by the competent authority of the exporting country. For the procurement office, it is an inexpensive means to help ensure the quality of purchased products. Through the certification scheme, the procurement office should be able to obtain the following information—

- Whether a product is legally marketed in the exporting country, and if not, the reasons why
- Whether the supplier manufactures the dosage forms, packages, and/or labels a finished dosage form manufactured by an independent company, or is involved in none of these activities
- Whether the manufacturer of the product has been inspected and the periodicity of inspection
- Whether the certificate is provisional, pending technical review
- Whether the information submitted by the supplier satisfies the certifying authority on all aspects of manufacture of the product undertaken by another party

The reliability of the pharmaceutical product certificates issued under the WHO scheme and access to them depend largely on the—

- Reliability and responsiveness of the exporting country's authority
- Capability of the exporting country's authority to make adequate GMP inspections
- Capability of the importing country's authority to assess the authenticity or validity of the certificate of a pharmaceutical product submitted, especially when it is submitted through the manufacturer or importing agent

Therefore, product certification under the WHO scheme is only as reliable as the agency performing it, and WHO estimates that only about 20 percent of member countries have a national drug regulatory system that can ensure the quality of medicines circulating in their national markets (WHO 2008b). For this reason, certificates should be accepted with caution unless the national DRA's competence to fulfill the scheme is known. In addition, although national pharmaceutical-control agencies in the major pharmaceutical-exporting countries are generally conscientious in their assessments, receiving reports may take some time. Agencies in some countries have been found to be less reliable and responsive.

WHO recognizes that today's pharmaceutical manufacturing sector looks much different from when the scheme was formulated decades ago under the assumption that a pharmaceutical product would be sold directly from the country of manufacture to the country of final destination. Pharmaceutical manufacturing and trade have become far more globalized in that different stages of manufacturing take place in different countries before the product reaches the final destination. Because of this evolution and other identified problems, WHO has proposed revising the scheme (WHO 2008b).

Product pedigrees

The purpose of a pharmaceutical pedigree is to establish a chain of custody from the manufacturer to the dispenser by documenting all parties that have handled a particular unit of a pharmaceutical as it travels through each step in the supply chain. Pharmaceutical wholesalers who provide fraudulent or no product pedigrees may help divert counterfeits into legitimate distribution systems. Failure to comply with the pedigree requirements is against the law in the United States.

Implementing a pharmaceutical pedigree process can be done with paper or electronic records. For example, affixing radio frequency identification (RFID) or bar codes to packaging would help maintain supply chain integrity and improve inventory control (see Section 19.4). Although electronic tracking is likely more efficient and secure, it requires expensive technology and training. Paper-based systems may be executed quickly but in the long run may be more time-consuming and more susceptible to forgery.

Batch certificates

Reliable pharmaceutical manufacturers may comply with GMPs by routinely conducting batch analyses. Local manufacturers that do not have their own quality-control laboratories may contract quality-control testing services from other manufacturers, private testing facilities, or national reference laboratories.

Some pharmaceutical procurement offices request other certificates, such as the certificate of free sale, the certificate of origin, or the certificate of licensing status (see Table 19-3). These certificates do not provide important information regarding compliance with GMPs, or results of laboratory testing of samples from individual batches. For this reason, the WHO-type certificate of a pharmaceutical product and batch certificate are preferred.

DRAs and the procurement market today

In many countries, DRAs and procurement offices do not work together effectively, nor are integrated information

Table 19-3   Comparison of certificates used in pharmaceutical procurement

Type of certificate	Uses	Limitations
WHO-type certificates		
Certificate of pharmaceutical product		
• Issued by DRA in exporting country • Provides licensure status of product • Provides inspection status of manufacturer	• Essential for product licensure • Ideally required for all new products • Prequalification of suppliers • Screening of new suppliers	• Is only as reliable as issuing DRA • Does not provide batch-specific information
Statement of licensing status		
• Issued by DRA in exporting country • States that product is licensed	• Prequalification of suppliers • Screening of new suppliers	• Does not provide batch-specific information
Batch certificate		
• Issued by manufacturer or DRA in exporting country • Confirms that individual batches conform to specifications • Linked to certificate of pharmaceutical product	• Usually requested for antibiotics • May be required for problem medicines	• Issued by few DRAs • Easily falsified • Many require additional expense
Non-WHO-type certificates		
Free-sale certificate		
• Issued by DRA in exporting country • Confirms product is sold in the country of origin	• Commonly used for licensure	• No indication that product has been evaluated for safety and efficacy • No indication that product is registered for use in country of origin
GMP certificate		
• Issued by DRA in exporting country	• Prequalification of suppliers	• Only as reliable as issuing DRA
Analytic batch certificate		
• Issued by manufacturer • Contains results of analytical tests • Not linked to certificate of pharmaceutical product	• Postqualification of suppliers	• Manufacturers' certificates may be falsified • Does not necessarily conform to specifications approved at time of product licensure

systems in place. Ideally, when a DRA exists and the medicine registration system is operational, procurement by government agencies should be limited to medicines registered by the DRA. Procurement offices should seek information from the DRA and strive for closer cooperation with the authority. To facilitate registration of generic medicines, the evaluation and approval process should not be complicated. Clinical trial data, except for bioequivalence data, are not normally required, allowing the submission of an abbreviated application by the manufacturer or distributor. WHO recommends that all medicines on the public or private market in a country, whether they are imported or locally manufactured, be subject to the same standard of control, including medicine registration.

The standard of control varies from country to country. In some exporting countries, medicines are registered and freely sold but not rigorously evaluated for efficacy. In other countries, which do evaluate efficacy, certain medicines may have been registered before evidence of efficacy was legally required. Moreover, in some countries, manufacturers may produce exclusively for export; the exporting country's DRA may not closely scrutinize these manufacturing plants. Procurement offices still need to request certificates from the DRA of the exporting country, as recommended by WHO.

Contract specifications

Detailed specifications to help ensure that high-quality products are bought and received include the following—

• Analytical methods and source of reference materials or documented evidence of suitability for the material used to assess product-quality attributes and certificate of analysis.
• Portions of manufacturers' reference materials to be used in product-quality assessments. For these reference materials, the manufacturers will supply either the API used in the manufacture of the product or a purified portion of the API. Because the reference material is used to assign qualitative and quantitative properties, its identity must be assured and its

purity must be suitable to perform the assessments at an appropriate confidence level for the intended use of the material. The identity of a reference material is generally assessed by infrared spectral comparisons and quantitative assessments performed by ultraviolet-visible spectral measures, either directly or in conjunction with chromatographic procedures. However, for most pharmaceutical measurements, the identity and quality of solid materials can be assessed by melting point/mixed melting point measurements, while liquids can be assessed by refractive index measurements.

- Language for the product label and package insert, which should be the language or languages common to the country.
- Minimum information required on the label (generic or International Nonproprietary Name, dosage form, strength, quantity, expiration date, manufacturer, batch number).
- Additional information, such as the product registration number and date of manufacture.
- Standards for packaging that will withstand the specific storage and transport conditions (for example, corrugated boxes with specifications for dividers, maximum size, and maximum weight).

To reduce theft and resale, some programs may require labeling and logos to indicate that the product is solely for distribution within a particular health care program (for example, ministry of health, social security fund).

Contract specifications are discussed in detail in Chapter 39.

19.4 Verifying the quality of shipped products

The quality of products received should be verified as soon as possible by physically inspecting each shipment and testing selected products in the laboratory as required by regulation. In addition, more advanced product-tracking technologies have been introduced to help ensure the integrity of the pharmaceutical supply chain.

Product identification technology

The traditional approach to assuring product integrity is labeling with batch number and expiration date. Unfortunately, this labeling is easily duplicated. To make fraud more difficult, several approaches are available that use overt or covert systems. *Overt technologies* are visible to the eye, and *covert technologies* require devices for detection. Because each step up in identification technology costs more, the most advanced technologies are used on high-value products or in large-quantity inventory control.

Bar coding: The simplest and least expensive technology for product tracking is the bar code, which has been adopted widely in many industries. Its uses range from tracking shipping containers to individual dosage units. The airline industry makes extensive use of this technology to track and direct baggage, and the retail industry has made bar coding the standard to track inventory and sales. Because of their widespread use and simplicity, bar-code detecting devices are relatively inexpensive.

Radiofrequency identification: The RFID tag is a radiofrequency transponder chip with a permanent unique identification code and the ability to be programmed with product information, such as batch number and expiration date. The combination of product information and identification code provides a high level of security against counterfeiting. RFID can be used overtly or covertly—either visible on the product or hidden in the packaging. Another advantage of the RFID technology is the ability to detect several different items at the same time, unlike visual bar-code readers, which must have each tag visible and separate for reading. However, until this RFID technology matures and becomes more widespread, it will remain much more expensive than the traditional bar-code technology.

Holograms: Hologram technology provides visual authentication that can be very difficult to counterfeit or remove (although instances of fake holograms have been found on counterfeit antimalarial products in Southeast Asia). However, the technology is not easily automated and optimally requires an authentic label or accurate image for visual comparison.

Other technologies that have been developed for product authentication include color-shifting inks, ultraviolet printing, and embedded chemical markers and infrared tags. As the technologies mature, several will likely be used to assure different aspects of the supply chain. The continuing adoption of these authentication technologies will make product counterfeiting more difficult and expensive, but unfortunately will not likely eliminate it.

Inspection of shipments

Regardless of other quality assurance procedures in use, each pharmaceutical shipment should be physically inspected. This means verifying adherence to contract specifications and order completeness as well as inspecting samples of all items to spot any major problems. Training competent receiving staff can be an economical means of ensuring pharmaceutical quality and reducing losses from supplier negligence or fraud.

Inspection in the exporting country before shipment can be arranged through an independent agency (for example, the Société Générale de Surveillance), for early detection of noncompliance with contract terms or defective products.

Tiered pharmaceutical quality assessments

As mentioned earlier in the chapter, the safety and efficacy of an API is the most critical attribute of a pharmaceutical product. The safety and efficacy of new APIs in the European Union, Japan, and the United States are determined in accordance with exhaustive ICH consensus guidelines that have been incorporated into the laws and regulations of those sovereign areas.

When the safety and efficacy of an API have been established, the dosage regimen is set so the minimum therapeutic level is attained without exceeding the maximum tolerated dose. That level of efficacy is called the "therapeutic window" (see Box 19-4). Pharmaceutical quality assessments may include bioavailability testing to ensure that the API falls within the therapeutic window.

Three tiers of product-quality assessment differ by cost and levels of precision, accuracy, and sensitivity—

1. *Minilab® screening assessments:* The Global Pharma Health Fund developed the Minilab to rapidly assess whether products are grossly substandard and to detect counterfeit products with no API or the wrong ingredients (see http://www.gphf.org/web/en/minilab for more information). The Minilab uses a thin-layer-chromatography method that does not require standard laboratory resources, so it can be used in the field, such as at ports of entry, while providing a good level of quality assurance. The Minilab has methods available for more than fifty pharmaceutical products and is regularly incorporating more.

2. *Validated laboratory assessments or legal reference method assessments:* These methods are used to assess assays, content uniformity, known impurities, and API dosage release. For medicines with a narrow therapeutic index, such as warfarin sodium, or for pharmaceuticals that fail the first-tier screening assessment, more accurate laboratory assessment technologies are required to support litigation concerning quality standards violations. Legal reference methods are methods of analysis that have been adopted into law and are suitable for use in litigation; however, Minilab screening and validated assessments are generally quicker, less labor intensive, and less expensive than legal reference methods, which are the gold standard.

3. *Specialized instruments:* Methods such as high-performance liquid chromatography coupled with

---

Box 19-4
Therapeutic window

Fortunately, the overwhelming majority of pharmaceutical products have a large therapeutic window, which is a great advantage for manufacturers and consumers. A wide therapeutic window allows the production of fewer dosage levels, which reduces production, supply, and inventory costs and allows consumers to more easily take a dose of a medicine that is efficacious and well tolerated. Products with a narrow therapeutic window require strict monitoring of the patient's therapeutic response; for example, patients taking the anticoagulant warfarin sodium must have their individual coagulation times strictly monitored to determine the ideal dose. A further indicator of the critical dosing requirement for this product is the large number of tablets available containing 1, 2, 2.5, 3, 4, 5, 6, 7.5, or 10 mg. These dosing levels contrast markedly with those of acetaminophen (paracetamol), which has a wide therapeutic window. In the United States, acetaminophen is often marketed as a 325-mg dosage unit, whereas in Europe the dosage unit generally is 500 mg. The dosing instructions for both products instruct the user to take one or two units up to four times per day.

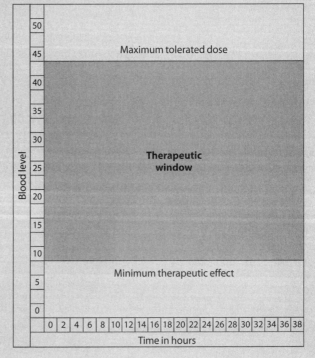

mass spectrometry may be used to determine unknown impurities and metabolites. Generally, these technologies are expensive and require highly trained individuals to operate them and interpret the data.

In summary, wide-therapeutic-index products may be screened rapidly to assess their quality clearance with minimal risk of compromising their safety and efficacy. Narrow-therapeutic-index products and those that fail the rapid screening technologies should be assessed by validated technologies that are fast and efficient. Products that fail the validated technologies may require further assessments by the legal reference methods of the sovereign state to support litigation or with specialized instrumentation to litigate untoward or unexpected contamination.

Laboratory testing

Upon arrival after shipment, batch samples may be laboratory tested routinely or "by exception." Most programs test selected samples from only some of the batches. Testing by exception means that analyses are done only when a supplier or a particular product is suspect.

Laboratory testing is costly in terms of technical human resources, equipment, and reagents. Guidelines should target sampling to products that (a) have the greatest potential for bioavailability and stability problems, (b) are from new or questionable suppliers, and (c) have been the source of complaints. With new suppliers, a probationary testing period—for example, testing the first three shipments, then shifting to intermittent sampling—is useful. Suppliers whose failure rates are unacceptable are dropped from future tenders. Sampling from well-established suppliers is done much less frequently, often only for at-risk products.

Programs that require routine testing of samples for all products prior to distribution to health facilities often produce significant delays in product availability at the health-facility level. The need for laboratory testing of products reported to have problems should be carefully assessed; many problems with quality are detectable on visual inspection and do not require laboratory testing. For example, verified observations of tablets that crumble before their expiry date, oral suspensions that harden, or injectable solutions that contain particles are enough to justify recalling the product without testing.

The tests that should be performed depend on the pharmaceutical and the reason for testing. Basic chemical analyses are done to verify the identity of the medicine and under extenuating circumstances to look for degradation, chemical contamination, or adulteration. WHO advocates a system of economical, less technically demanding basic tests for commonly used medicines (WHO 1998) that can be done in simple laboratories. A complete analysis of tablet and capsule forms includes tests for identity, strength or potency, uniformity, impurities, disintegration, and dissolution.

Biological testing is more specialized and can be performed only in established facilities with staff trained to use microbiological and pharmacological methods. Microbiological tests include sterility tests for injectable medicines and eye preparations and microbiological assays of antibiotics and vitamins. Pharmacological tests include the pyrogen test; toxicity tests; hormone assays, such as for insulin and pituitary derivatives; and tests to determine the bioavailability of selected pharmaceuticals.

Construction of a quality-control laboratory where one does not already exist should be considered with caution. It may not be cost-effective for some countries to establish a sophisticated national pharmaceutical control laboratory for a number of reasons, including—

- Low projected volume of work
- Insufficient financial resources for land purchase, facility construction, testing equipment, furniture, supplies, equipment maintenance, salaries, training, and other operating costs
- Lack of trained personnel, such as microbiologists, pharmacologists, laboratory technicians, and animal caretakers
- Lack of local capacity for maintenance and repair of equipment, difficulty in obtaining spare parts, irregular and unstable power supply

In some countries, a college of pharmacy or an independent laboratory may have some of the required testing facilities. Also, many international quality-control laboratories provide pharmaceutical analyses at a relatively reasonable price. If analyses are performed by foreign laboratories, foreign exchange and billing problems may be reduced by requiring the suppliers to pay the laboratory directly, with the arrangement clearly described in the purchase contract. In addition, chain-of-custody and legal standing of the testing laboratory in the importing country may be at issue.

19.5 Maintaining pharmaceutical quality

Maintaining medicine quality requires careful attention to storage conditions and transport, as well as to dispensing practices and use.

Appropriate storage and transport

Procedures to help maintain pharmaceutical quality begin with proper storage conditions at the port and prompt release. Storage activities are discussed in Chapters 42, 44, and 46, and proper transport conditions are addressed in Chapter 25.

Appropriate dispensing and use

Inappropriate dispensing procedures contribute to pharmaceutical product deterioration and contamination or medication errors. The following procedures help maintain the quality of pharmaceutical products—

- Use only proper dispensing containers (for example, airtight containers, light-resistant bags or vials); the paper envelopes often used for end-user dispensing do not protect tablets and capsules.
- Require clear labeling of dispensed medicines, and enforce procedures to label products with the patient's name, the medicine's name, its strength, its expiration date, and instructions for its use and storage.
- Write information and instructions in the local language, avoiding the use of abbreviations, or use symbolic instructions.

The prescriber and the dispenser should counsel the patient on the proper use of medications, explaining *what* the medicine is, *why* the patient needs it, *how* to take it, and *where* and *how* to store it until treatment is completed, in addition to possible contraindications and adverse reactions (see Chapter 30).

Pharmaceutical product presentations: treatment kits, co-packaging, and fixed-dose combinations

Medicines can be packaged according to therapeutic regimens or for delivery to dispensing sites or individual patients to facilitate and reduce the costs of inventory management and distribution systems. For example, a tuberculosis treatment kit could include enough antimicrobial products for a particular number of patients. Broader-based treatment kits for poorly served areas may include a selection of essential medicines that supplements the national supply system (see Chapter 26 for more information).

Co-packaging or co-blistering is a method commonly used to deliver multiple medicines for a specific treatment regimen such as tuberculosis. These packages are prepared from individual pharmaceutical products, so their quality assessments should be based on each product's individual standards, including stability testing.

Fixed-dose combination (FDC) products have more than one active ingredient formulated into one product—for example, the anti-tuberculosis medicines isoniazid and rifampin are available as single products or as an FDC in one pill. FDCs simplify the prescription of medicines and the management of pharmaceutical supply, improve patient adherence, and may also limit the risk of treatment-resistant infections caused by inappropriate medicine selection and monotherapy, as is the case with artemisinin-based combination therapies. WHO recommends FDCs be developed for antiretroviral pharmaceutical products to simplify HIV/AIDS treatment regimens and to improve patient adherence. From a regulatory standpoint, FDCs are treated as new pharmaceutical entities in which the individual APIs must be shown to be stable and bioavailable in this composite product (WHO 2003).

19.6 Monitoring pharmaceutical quality

Despite every effort, defective products occasionally slip through, and the quality of even the best-manufactured product may deteriorate. Furthermore, health care personnel and patients alike may have erroneous perceptions that only brand-name products from innovator firms are of good product quality, especially when generic products are not well known and accepted.

Product problem reporting system

Establishing a national product problem reporting system is important so that health workers can report suspected or confirmed problems with specific pharmaceutical products. Product problem reporting should be part of an overall pharmacovigilance system, which also includes monitoring and reporting adverse drug events and medication errors. Chapter 35 covers those areas of pharmacovigilance in detail.

Figure 19-4 is a sample medicine and supplier evaluation form that pharmacy staff and health care providers at all levels can use to report suspected lapses in pharmaceutical or packaging quality. Standard procedures for product problem reporting should specify—

- Who should report the perceived product quality problem
- How to fill in the reporting form
- Where and to whom the reporting form should be sent
- What additional measures need to be taken, such as sending samples or information concerning the quantities involved
- What follow-up information should be provided to the person or facility that reported the problem

Quality assurance program staff should carefully analyze all reports, using laboratory testing as required, and take appropriate actions. The reporter should be informed about the results and the actions taken, even if products are

Figure 19-4   Sample medicine and supplier evaluation form

Organization of Eastern Caribbean States
Eastern Caribbean Drug Service

MEDICINE AND SUPPLIER EVALUATION FORM

Submitted by: _____

Country: _____ Date: _____

Sample Location:
☐ CMS _____
☐ Other _____
(specify)

Address communications to:

ECDS
PO Box 3093
La Clery
Castries
St. Lucia
Telephone: (809-45) 25058/25895

Medicine Description: Generic Name, Strength, Form,	Brand Name	Medicine or Supplier	Lot Number or Batch Number	Expiration Date	Comments

Suggested criteria for medicine evaluation:

1. Physical characteristics — e.g., hardness, color, mixing ease for reconstitution
2. Packaging — expiry date, lot or batch number, package insert
3. Labeling — language (English vs. French), legibility (especially ampoules)
4. Patient acceptability — taste, color, size of tablet, etc.
5. Health care provider acceptability — e.g., is the ampoule easy to break?

Guidelines for medicine sampling:

1. Take samples from previously unopened containers.
2. Minimum sample size: tablets/capsules—200; injections—40 ampoules; liquids—40 mL.
3. Tablets/capsules must be tightly packed in plastic/glass vial (DO NOT USE PAPER OR PLASTIC ENVELOPES).
4. Enclose COMPLETE LABEL (generic name, strength, quantity, manufacturer and supplier names, lot/batch number, expiry date, date of manufacture).
5. Print label legibly, and double check lot number for accuracy.

not defective, to encourage continued participation in the program. Product problem reports and results should be recorded to provide information for future procurement.

Product recalls

Pharmaceutical products found to be defective should be recalled quickly. The quality assurance unit in the country's DRA should develop standard procedures for carrying out the recall. Rapid action helps avoid unnecessary exposure once the problem has been detected. The central distributor's inventory control system should include information on all batches that have been received. Because tracking individual batches to the health facility is often either impractical or fraught with uncertainty, recall notices have to be sent to all health facilities that received any of the products in question to check their shelves and return the products to the central distribution point.

Recalls may be classified according to the degree of risk to the consumer: (a) serious illness or death, (b) temporary or mild illness, or (c) no adverse clinical effect. The level of recall is determined by both the degree of risk and the extent of distribution of the product and may be directed at the patient, the health facility, or the medical stores level.

After issuing a recall, the quality assurance program should monitor its progress to ensure complete compliance. The supplier should be notified and required to replace defective products. The procurement office should pursue other remedies specified in the contract, such as withholding payment or obtaining reimbursement for or replacement of the defective products.

19.7 Personnel and training in the supply system

Central to the operation of most well-run pharmaceutical supply systems is at least one qualified pharmacist with some training or experience in industrial pharmacy and procurement. Such an individual can be invaluable in establishing and overseeing quality-control practices suited to local requirements. This person should participate in—

- Selecting medicines
- Setting technical specifications for pharmaceutical contracts
- Reviewing supply offers and selecting suppliers
- Reviewing storage and transportation facilities
- Coordinating any pharmaceutical quality testing and helping to train the inspectors who check pharmaceutical shipments

In some government systems, qualified pharmacists are employed at all levels, including the district hospitals, and they are expected to oversee local storage and transportation conditions. In addition, they report problems or questions concerning individual medicines to the main office. In other countries, locally trained dispensers are responsible for much of the day-to-day work and must be trained to detect and report quality problems. Some countries must rely on staff that has not received any technical training in pharmaceutical management.

In addition to pharmacists and pharmaceutical assistants, other staff members involved in quality assurance need training and supervision as a part of quality assurance efforts.

- Physicians, health administrators, and health system officials must know about the factors that influence pharmaceutical quality to make informed decisions about supply sources and to monitor and promote quality assurance in their facilities.
- Port-clearing personnel should be trained to identify the categories of pharmaceuticals requiring special storage and transport conditions.
- Clerks responsible for inspecting pharmaceutical shipments should receive formal training in inspection procedures.
- Pharmaceutical inspectors must be familiar enough with pharmaceutical labeling and packaging materials to determine whether contract conditions regarding pharmaceutical dosage, packaging, and labeling have been met.
- Staff involved with local repackaging should be trained to ensure pharmaceutical quality and to follow good practices, especially regarding label control.
- Physicians, nurses, and paramedical personnel handling pharmaceuticals throughout the health system need to know about the factors that influence pharmaceutical quality and what they can do to ensure that the medicines dispensed to patients are safe and effective.

Quality assurance is a widely shared responsibility. Within a supply system, the organizational structure needs to establish the responsibilities for the review and preservation of pharmaceutical quality at all levels. If a pharmaceutical becomes ineffective or unsafe by the time it reaches the patient, then all the other activities of the supply system have been in vain. ∎

ASSESSMENT GUIDE

Quality assurance structures

- Are there stated policies and practices aimed at ensuring pharmaceutical quality?
- Who is responsible for monitoring pharmaceutical quality?
- In what laboratories is quality-control testing done?
- Does a formal system exist for reporting product quality complaints?

Quality assurance procedures

- Is the WHO Certification Scheme on the Quality of Pharmaceutical Products Moving in International Commerce used systematically?
- Are favorable GMP inspections required for all suppliers, including local manufacturers?
- Is a physical inspection made of all pharmaceuticals received?
- Are all pertinent documents and labeling, including patient inserts, reviewed for accuracy and compliance with standards?
- How many laboratory analyses were performed during the past year of the total number of products or batches procured?
- To whom are results of analyses of suspected or confirmed defective products communicated?

- Are the test results of substandard medicines recorded for use in future procurement assessments?
- Is information on pharmaceutical stability and problem pharmaceuticals used in evaluating suppliers and pharmaceutical products?
- Are storage conditions periodically evaluated at the ports of entry? At the central warehouse? At district and regional stores? In hospital pharmacies? At health centers and rural health posts?
- Are transport conditions maintained to ensure product quality?
- Are good dispensing practices followed in the health facilities or pharmacies?
- Are the various levels of health workers adequately trained to carry out their respective roles in quality assurance?

Outcome of quality assurance

- In the previous year, how many reports were submitted on pharmaceutical product problems?
- What number of pharmaceuticals or batches failed quality-control testing of the total number of pharmaceuticals or batches tested in the previous year?

References and further readings

★ = Key readings.

Ahmad, K. 2004. Antidepressants Are Sold as Antiretrovirals in DR Congo. *Lancet* 363:713.

Bogdanich, W. 2007. "Chinese Chemicals Flow Unchecked onto World Drug Market." *New York Times,* October 31. <http://www.nytimes.com/2007/10/31/world/asia/31chemical.html>

CPM (Center for Pharmaceutical Management). 2003a. *Access to Essential Medicines: Cambodia, 2001.* Prepared for the Strategies for Enhancing Access to Medicines Program. Arlington, Va.: Management Sciences for Health.

———. 2003b. *Access to Essential Medicines: El Salvador, 2001.* Prepared for the Strategies for Enhancing Access to Medicines Program. Arlington, Va.: Management Sciences for Health.

———. 2003c. *Access to Essential Medicines: Ghana, 2001.* Prepared for the Strategies for Enhancing Access to Medicines Program. Arlington, Va.: Management Sciences for Health.

———. 2003d. *Access to Essential Medicines: Minas Gerais, Brazil, 2001.* Prepared for the Strategies for Enhancing Access to Medicines Program. Arlington, Va.: Management Sciences for Health.

———. 2003e. *Access to Essential Medicines: Rajasthan, India, 2001.* Prepared for the Strategies for Enhancing Access to Medicines Program. Arlington, Va.: Management Sciences for Health.

———. 2003f. *Access to Essential Medicines: Tanzania, 2001.* Prepared for the Strategies for Enhancing Access to Medicines Program. Arlington, Va.: Management Sciences for Health.

CPM/MSH (Center for Pharmaceutical Management/Management Sciences for Health). 2011. *Center for Pharmaceutical Management: Technical Frameworks, Approaches, and Results.* Arlington, Va.: CPM.

FDA (U.S. Food and Drug Administration). 2010. Office of International Programs website. <http://www.fda.gov/AboutFDA/CentersOffices/OC/OfficeofInternationalPrograms/default.htm>

———. 2007. "FDA Warns Consumers about Counterfeit Drugs from Multiple Internet Sellers." FDA news release P07-76, May 1. <http://www.fda.gov/NewsEvents/Newsroom/PressAnnouncements/2007/ucm108904.htm>

Gammon, D. L., S. Su, J. Jordan, R. Patterson, P. J. Finley, C. Lowe, and R. Huckfeldt. 2008. Alteration in Prehospital Drug Concentration after Thermal Exposure. *American Journal of Emergency Medicine* 26(5):566–73.

Hogerzeil, H. V., G. J. A. Walker, and M. J. de Goeje. 1993. *Stability of Injectable Oxytocics in Tropical Climates: Results of Field Surveys and Simulation Studies on Ergometrine, Methylergometrine and Oxytocin.* Geneva: World Health Organization.

Hogerzeil, H. V., A. Battersby, V. Srdanovic, and N. E. Stjernstrom. 1992. Stability of Essential Drugs during Shipment to the Tropics. *British Medical Journal* 304:210–2.

Hogerzeil, H. V., A. Battersby, V. Srdanovic, L. V. Hansen, O. Boye, B. Lindren, G. Everitt, and N. E. Stjernstrom. 1991. *WHO/UNICEF Study on the Stability of Drugs during International Transport.* Geneva: WHO/UNICEF. <http://whqlibdoc.who.int/hq/1991/WHO_DAP_91.1.pdf>

Hussain, K., P. Ibrahim, Z. Ismail, M. T. Majeed, and A. Sadikun. 2009. Traditional and Complementary Medicines: Quality Assessment

Annex 19-1   Resource organizations

Crown Agents
St. Nicholas House
St. Nicholas Road
Sutton, Surrey SM1 1EL
United Kingdom
http://www.crownagents.com

European Directorate for the Quality of Medicines (EDQM)
European Pharmacopoeia
7, Allée Kastner, CS 30026
F67081 Strasbourg
France
http://www.pheur.org

European Free Trade Association (EFTA)
9–11, Rue de Varembé
CH 1211 Geneva 20
Switzerland
http://secretariat.efta.int

European Medicines Agency (EMA)
7 Westferry Circus
Canary Wharf
London E14 4HB
United Kingdom
http://www.ema.europa.eu

International Conference on Harmonisation of Technical Requirements for Registration of Pharmaceuticals for Human Use (ICH)
15, Chemin Louis-Dunant
P.O. Box 195
CH 1211 Geneva 20
Switzerland
http://www.ich.org

IDA Foundation
Slochterweg 35
1027 AA Amsterdam
P.O. Box 37098
1030 AB Amsterdam
The Netherlands
http://www.idafoundation.org

U.S. Food and Drug Administration (FDA)
Many of FDA's materials are available on its website: http://www.fda.gov. Specific categories of information are available—

- CDERLearn at http://www.fda.gov/cder/learn/CDERLearn/default.htm is the site with educational tutorials.
- The Orange Book lists U.S.-approved medicines and their therapeutic equivalence. It is available at http://www.fda.gov/cder/ob/default.htm.
- Drugs@FDA at http://www.accessdata.fda.gov/scripts/cder/drugsatfda/ presents approval data and labeling information.
- The FDA Office of Regulatory Affairs at http://www.fda.gov/ora has publications and training materials available on inspection, compliance, and laboratory operations.
- The FDA Office of International Programs at http://www.fda.gov/InternationalPrograms/default.htm describes FDA's activities in other countries.

World Health Organization
Essential Medicines and Pharmaceutical Policies Department
Avenue Appia 20
CH 1211 Geneva 27
Switzerland
http://www.who.int/medicines/en

Strategies and Safe Usage. *Southern Med Review* 2(1):19–23. <http://apps.who.int/medicinedocs/documents/s16460e/s16460e.pdf>

ICH (International Conference on Harmonisation of Technical Requirements for Registration of Pharmaceuticals for Human Use). 2003. *ICH Harmonised Tripartite Guideline Stability Testing of New Drug Substances and Products Q1A(R2) (Second Revision): Current Step 4 Version.* 6 February. Geneva: ICH. <http://www.ich.org/fileadmin/Public_Web_Site/ICH_Products/Guidelines/Quality/Q1A_R2/Step4/Q1A_R2__Guideline.pdf>

————. 2000. *ICH Harmonised Tripartite Guideline: Good Manufacturing Practice Guide for Active Pharmaceutical Ingredients Q7: Current Step 4 Version.* 10 November. Geneva: ICH. <http://www.ich.org/fileadmin/Public_Web_Site/ICH_Products/Guidelines/Quality/Q7/Step4/Q7_Guideline.pdf>

Kasim, N. A., M. Whitehouse, C. Ramachandran, M. Bermejo, H. Lennerna, A. S. Hussain, H. E. Junginger, et al. 2004. Molecular Properties of WHO Essential Drugs and Provisional Biopharmaceutical Classification. *Molecular Pharmaceutics* 1(1):85–96.

Newton, P. N., F. M. Fernández, A. Plançon, D. C. Mildenhall, M. D. Green, L. Ziyong, E. M. Christophel, et al. 2008. A Collaborative Epidemiological Investigation into the Criminal Fake Artesunate Trade in South East Asia. *PLoS Medicine* 5(2):e32.

Pau, A. K., N. K. Moodley, D. T. Holland, H. Fomundam, G. U. Matchaba, and E. V. Capparelli. 2005. Instability of Lopinavir/Ritonavir Capsules at Ambient Temperatures in Sub-Saharan Africa:

Relevance to WHO Antiretroviral Guidelines. *AIDS* 19(11):1233–4.

Promoting the Quality of Medicines Program. 2010. *Matrix of Medicine Quality Reports Affecting USAID-Assisted Countries.* (Updated regularly.) Rockville, Md.: United States Pharmacopeial Convention. <http://www.usp.org/pdf/EN/dqi/ghcDrugQualityMatrix.pdf>

SEAM (Strategies for Enhancing Access to Medicines). 2007. *Tanzania: Product Quality Assurance Program.* Arlington, Va.: Management Sciences for Health. <http://www.msh.org/seam/reports/SEAM_TANZANIA_Quality_Assurance.pdf>

Seiter, A. 2005a. *Pharmaceuticals: Counterfeits, Substandard Drugs and Drug Diversion.* HNP Brief #2. Washington, D.C.: World Bank. <http://siteresources.worldbank.org/HEALTHNUTRITIONANDPOPULATION/Resources/281627-1109774792596/HNPBrief_6.pdf>

————. 2005b. *Pharmaceuticals: Quality Assurance in the Distribution Chain.* Washington, D.C.: World Bank. <http://apps.who.int/medicinedocs/documents/s16759e/s16759e.pdf>

USP (United States Pharmacopeia). No date. *US Pharmacopeia–National Formulary.* Updated annually. Rockville, Md.: United States Pharmacopeial Convention. <http://www.usp.org/USPNF/>

————. 2007. *Ensuring the Quality of Medicines in Resource-Limited Countries: An Operational Guide.* Rockville, Md.: United States Pharmacopeial Convention. <http://www.usp.org/pdf/EN/dqi/ensuringQualityOperationalGuide.pdf>

USP and USAID (U.S. Pharmacopeia and U.S. Agency for International Development). 2009. *Survey of the Quality of Selected Antimalarial*

Medicines Circulating in Madagascar, Senegal, and Uganda. Rockville, Md.: United States Pharmacopeial Convention. <http://www.usaid.gov/our_work/global_health/hs/publications/qamsa_report_1109.pdf>

WHO (World Health Organization). 2010a. *Guidelines for Implementation of the WHO Certification Scheme on the Quality of Pharmaceutical Products Moving in International Commerce.* <http://www.who.int/medicines/areas/quality_safety/regulation_legislation/certification/guidelines/en/index.html>

———. 2010b. *Medicines: Counterfeit Medicines.* Fact sheet 275. Geneva: WHO. <http://www.who.int/mediacentre/factsheets/fs275/en/index.html>

———. 2010c. Prequalification of Medicines Success in 2009. *WHO Drug Information* 24(1):3–6. <http://www.who.int/medicines/publications/druginformation/DrugInfo2010_Vol24-1.pdf>

———. 2010d. *WHO Expert Committee on Specifications for Pharmaceutical Preparations.* 44th Report. Geneva: WHO. <http://whqlibdoc.who.int/trs/WHO_TRS_957_eng.pdf>

———. 2009a. Prequalification of Quality Control Laboratories. *WHO Drug Information* 23(4):300–5. <http://whqlibdoc.who.int/druginfo/23_4_2009.pdf>

———. 2009b. Stability Testing of Active Pharmaceutical Ingredients and Finished Pharmaceutical Products. Annex 2 to *WHO Expert Committee on Specifications for Pharmaceutical Preparations.* 43rd Report. Geneva: WHO. <http://apps.who.int/medicinedocs/documents/s16236e/s16236e.pdf>

———. 2008a. *The International Pharmacopoeia.* 4th ed. Geneva: WHO. <http://www.who.int/medicines/publications/pharmacopoeia/overview/en/>

———. 2008b. WHO Certification Scheme on the Quality of Pharmaceutical Products Moving in International Commerce. *WHO Drug Information* 22(3):211–9. <http://whqlibdoc.who.int/druginfo/22_3_2008.pdf>

———. 2007a. General Guidelines for the Establishment, Maintenance and Distribution of Chemical Reference Substances. Revision. Annex 3 to *WHO Expert Committee on Specifications for Pharmaceutical Preparations.* 41st Report. Geneva: WHO. <http://apps.who.int/medicinedocs/documents/s14139e/s14139e.pdf>

———. 2007b. *Quality Assurance of Pharmaceuticals: A Compendium of Guidelines and Related Materials.* Good Manufacturing Practices and Inspection, 2nd updated ed. Vol. 2. Geneva: WHO. <http://apps.who.int/medicinedocs/documents/s14136e/s14136e.pdf>

———. 2004a. Stability Testing for Hot and Humid Climates. *WHO Drug Information* 18(2):113–6. <http://whqlibdoc.who.int/druginfo/18_2_2004.pdf>

———. 2004b. *The World Medicines Situation.* Geneva: WHO.

———. 2003. Regulation of Fixed-Dose Combination Products. *WHO Drug Information* 17(3):174–7.

★ ———. 1998. *Basic Tests for Drugs: Pharmaceutical Substances, Medicinal Plant Materials and Dosage Forms.* Geneva: WHO. <http://whqlibdoc.who.int/publications/1998/9241545135.pdf>

★ ———. 1997a. *Certification Scheme on the Quality of Pharmaceutical Products Moving in International Commerce.* Geneva: WHO. <http://whqlibdoc.who.int/hq/1997/WHO_PHARM_82.4_Rev.5.pdf>

———. 1997b. *Quality Assurance of Pharmaceuticals: A Compendium of Guidelines and Related Materials.* Vol. 1. Geneva: WHO.

———. 1995. *Use of the WHO Certification Scheme on the Quality of Pharmaceutical Products Moving in International Commerce.* Geneva: WHO.

★ ———. 1994. *WHO Guidelines on Stability Testing of Pharmaceutical Products Containing Well-Established Drug Substances in Conventional Dosage Forms.* Geneva: WHO. <http://whqlibdoc.who.int/hq/1994/WHO_PHARM_94.565_rev.1.pdf>

———. 1990. *WHO Expert Committee on Specifications for Pharmaceutical Preparations.* 31st Report. Geneva: WHO.

———. 1986. *Accelerated Stability Studies of Widely Used Pharmaceutical Substances under Simulated Tropical Conditions.* Geneva: WHO. <http://whqlibdoc.who.int/hq/1985-86/WHO_PHARM_86.529.pdf>

WHO/EURO (World Health Organization Regional Office for Europe). 1988. *The Investigation of Bioavailability and Bioequivalence.* (Draft.) Copenhagen: WHO/EURO.

WHO/UNICEF/UNDP/UNFP/World Bank (World Health Organization, United Nations Children's Fund, United Nations Development Programme, United Nations Population Fund, World Bank). 2007. *A Model Quality Assurance System for Procurement Agencies: Recommendations for Quality Assurance Systems Focusing on Prequalification of Products and Manufacturers, Purchasing, Storage and Distribution of Pharmaceutical Products.* Geneva: WHO. <http://apps.who.int/medicinedocs/documents/s14866e/s14866e.pdf>

CHAPTER 20

Quantifying pharmaceutical requirements

Summary   20.2

20.1   Methods of quantification   20.3
     Major options for quantification • Relative predictive
     accuracy of quantification methods

20.2   Applications of quantification   20.4

20.3   Issues to consider in quantification   20.5
     Preparing an action plan for quantification • Using
     centralized or decentralized quantification • Using manual
     or computerized methods for quantification • Estimating
     the time required • Developing and organizing the
     medicines list • Filling the supply pipeline • Estimating
     the procurement period • Considering the effect of
     lead time • Estimating safety stock • Adjusting for
     losses and other changes • Cross-checking the results
     of quantification • Estimating total procurement
     costs • Adjusting and reconciling final quantities

20.4   Consumption method   20.15
     Example • Steps in the quantification

20.5   Morbidity method   20.18
     Example • Steps in the quantification

20.6   Proxy consumption method   20.24
     Example • Steps in the quantification

20.7   Service-level projection of budget
     requirements   20.26
     Example • Steps in the quantification

References and further readings   20.28

Assessment guide   20.29

ILLUSTRATIONS

COUNTRY STUDIES

BOXES

SUMMARY

Quantification is the first step in the procurement process (see Chapter 18). In general terms, quantification is the process used to determine how much of a product is required for the purpose of procurement. But more specifically, quantification involves estimating not only the quantities needed of a specific item, but also the financial means required for purchasing the item. Needs are estimated for a given context, and the analysis must include contextual factors, such as available funds, human resources capacity, storage space capacity, and capacity to deliver services.

The methods and strategies described in this chapter can be used as tools to—

- Prepare and justify a pharmaceutical budget
- Plan for new and expanding programs
- Optimize pharmaceutical budgets based on priority health problems to be treated and the most cost-effective treatment approaches
- Calculate emergency needs for disaster relief and epidemics
- Resupply an existing supply network that has become depleted of products
- Compare current medicine consumption/demand with public health priorities and usage in other health systems

The quantification method must be chosen in light of the resources and information available.

The consumption method, which uses data on medicine consumption, gives in many instances the most accurate prediction of future needs. Large, well-established pharmaceutical supply systems rely primarily on the consumption method. To be reliable, the consumption data must come from a stable supply system with a relatively uninterrupted supply and a full supply pipeline. Consumption data may or may not reflect rational prescribing and use of medicines or actual demand for medicines.

The morbidity method quantifies the theoretical quantity needed for the treatment of specific diseases. This method requires reliable data on morbidity and patient attendances (visits to health facilities) and uses standard treatment guidelines to project medicine needs. This method is the most complex and time-consuming, and it can produce major discrepancies between projections and subsequent use. Nevertheless, this method is often useful for new and expanding programs and may be the most convincing approach for justifying a budget request.

If no reliable information is available on past consumption or morbidity, use can be extrapolated from data for other facilities, regions, or countries. The proxy consumption method is flexible enough to apply to various situations and can be either population or service based. Service-level quantification of budget requirements can be applied when only budget requirements, and not specific medicine quantities, are needed. It provides a clear, logical, one-page justification of pharmaceutical financing requirements.

Several critical issues are common to all methods. The medicines list is the central component and must be produced in a format suitable to the type of quantification. In a new supply system, or one in which shortages have been widespread, quantification estimates must be adjusted because the supply pipeline must be filled. The lead time has a major effect on quantities required for safety stocks. In virtually all supply systems, adjustment is necessary for losses caused by wastage and theft.

Quantification estimates can be cross-checked by combining different methods. No matter which method is used, a gap may exist between the initial estimates of medicine needs and the allocated budget. The quantification process itself may help justify an increase in the budget, but often the quantification estimates must be adjusted and reconciled to match available funds. The choice between manual and computerized quantification may be dictated by circumstances, but the process is much easier with computer assistance. Quantification can be centralized, or it can be decentralized to staff of peripheral warehouses and health facilities. The personnel and time requirements depend on the quality and accessibility of source data and on the type and scope of quantification.

20.1 Methods of quantification

Quantification is the first step in the procurement process (see Chapter 18). In general terms, quantification is the process used to determine how much of a product is required for the purpose of procurement. But more specifically, quantification involves estimating not only the quantities needed of a specific item but also the financial means required for purchasing the item. Needs are estimated for a given context, so the analysis must include contextual factors, such as available funds, human resources capacity, storage space capacity, and capacity to deliver services. Often, the terms *quantification* and *forecasting* are used interchangeably. For purposes of this chapter, forecasting refers to the projection of future needs beyond the next purchase order.

Medicine needs can be quantified by using one or a combination of four standard methods. Quantification involves estimating the quantities of specific medicines or supply items needed for a procurement. Most quantification exercises also estimate the financial requirements to purchase the medicines. The quantification methods described in this chapter are normally used to quantify needs for an annual or semiannual procurement. They are not usually used to calculate routine order quantities in an established supply system that uses scheduled purchasing (periodic orders) or perpetual purchasing (orders placed whenever need arises). In such situations, one of the reorder formulas presented in Chapter 23 is used to calculate the optimal order quantity and order interval for each item. The goal is to maintain the most cost-effective balance between service levels and inventory costs.

Major options for quantification

The four general methods discussed in this chapter are—

1. Consumption method
2. Morbidity method
3. Proxy consumption method
4. Service-level projection of budget requirements

The *consumption method* uses records of past consumption of individual medicines (adjusted for stockouts and projected changes in medicine use) to project future need (see Section 20.4).

The *morbidity method* estimates the need for specific medicines based on the expected number of attendances, the incidence of common diseases, and standard treatment patterns for the diseases considered (see Section 20.5). Box 20-1 describes the morbidity method used when a program is scaling up.

The *proxy consumption method* uses data on disease incidence, medicine consumption, demand, or use, and/or pharmaceutical expenditures from a "standard" supply system and extrapolates the consumption or use rates to the target supply system, based on population coverage or service level to be provided (see Section 20.6).

Box 20-1
Estimating for programs that are scaling up care for patients requiring continuous treatment

In the following example, the program is scaling up with ten new patients per month requiring continuous treatment. The number of patient-months of medicines that can be expected to be consumed from January to April is 10 + 20 + 30 + 40 = 100 patient-months.

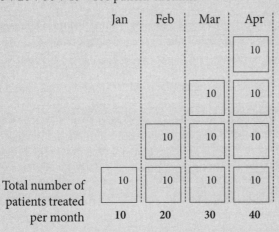

A formula used to determine number of patient-months is—

$$P\left(\frac{n(n+1)}{2}\right)$$

P = average number of patients added each month
n = number of months covered

For the preceding example the calculation would be—

$$10\left(\frac{4(5)}{2}\right) = 100 \text{ patient-months for the period of January to April}$$

Service-level projection of budget requirements uses the average medicine cost per attendance or bed-day in different types of health facilities in a standard system to project medicine costs in similar types of facilities in the target system (see Section 20.7). This method does not estimate quantities of individual medicines.

Relative predictive accuracy of quantification methods

Quantification of pharmaceutical requirements is inherently imprecise because of the many variables involved. Useful results depend as much on "art," or human judgment, as on science.

In many instances, the most precise method for quantifying pharmaceutical usage is the consumption-based approach, provided the source data are complete, accurate, and properly adjusted for stockout periods and anticipated changes in demand and use. This method does not normally address the appropriateness of past consumption patterns, which may or may not correspond with public health priorities and needs. Thus, irrational medicine use may be perpetuated by total reliance on the consumption method. If stockouts have been widespread for long periods, applying this method accurately may be impossible, which is why capturing actual demand is the most accurate approach.

Morbidity-based quantification is the most complex and time-consuming method. In many countries, assembling valid morbidity data on more than a defined set of diseases is very difficult; therefore, some needs will be overlooked in the quantification. Data on patient attendance are often incomplete and inaccurate, and predicting what percentage of prescribers will actually follow the standard treatment regimens used for quantification is difficult. Despite these constraints, this method may remain the best alternative for planning for procurement or for estimating budget needs in a supply system or facility in which a limited range of health problems accounts for virtually all medicine consumption, such as a small primary care system; a special-purpose hospital; a new program with no previous consumption history, such as HIV/AIDS programs rolling out antiretroviral therapy (ART); or changes in standard treatment guidelines.

Proxy consumption is the method generally used if neither the consumption-based nor the morbidity-based method is feasible. This method is most likely to yield accurate projections when used to extrapolate from one set of facilities to another set that serves the same type of population in the same type of geographic and climatic environment. If the method is applied by drawing standard data from another country, the results will be only a rough estimate of need. Even when target and standard facilities are closely matched, quantification estimates are suspect, because it is a big leap to assume that disease incidence, utilization pat-

terns, and prescribing habits will be essentially the same in both settings. Still, this method may be the best alternative in the absence of suitable data required for the consumption- or morbidity-based method. The proxy consumption method is also useful for cross-checking projections made with other methods.

Service-level projection of budget requirements produces a rough estimate of financial needs for pharmaceutical procurement and not the quantity of products. The method relies on two assumptions: (1) that the "standard" system (used for comparison) and the target system are comparable in terms of patient attendance and bed-days per type of facility, and (2) that the patterns of medicine use are roughly the same in both systems. Despite its limitations, this method can be useful in predicting medicine costs in a new system or in a system in which no data are readily available. Table 20-1 summarizes the applications and limitations of the four major quantification methods.

20.2 Applications of quantification

Quantification is normally applied for—

Calculating order quantities for procurement: Formal quantification may be necessary before each scheduled procurement. These estimates need to be accurate to avoid stockouts, emergency purchases, and overstocks and to maximize the effect of procurement funds. The consumption method is the first choice, cross-checked to assess the appropriateness of usage and demand patterns. When consumption data are unreliable or unavailable, such as in new programs, the morbidity method, the proxy consumption method, or both, may need to be applied for an initial quantification, switching to the consumption method when reliable data can be compiled or the program has stabilized.

Estimating budget requirements: In many countries, the annual pharmaceutical procurement budget is determined by adding a fixed percentage to the previous year's request or allocation to allow room for contingencies, such as expected cuts by the ministry of finance, population growth, or expansion of services. Both budget requests and cuts are frequently prepared without reliable estimates of actual needs. This cycle can be broken with rational, well-documented quantification. Although consumption-based quantification is the best guide to probable expenditures, the morbidity-based method may be the most convincing documentation for a budget request. Proxy consumption is useful for checking and justifying either consumption or morbidity methods. When budget requirements do not need to be justified by specifying order quantities, the service-level method can be used as an alternative.

Table 20-1   Comparison of quantification methods

Method	Uses	Essential data	Limitations
Consumption	• First choice for procurement quantifications, given reliable data • Most reliable predictor of future consumption	• Reliable inventory records • Records of supplier lead time • Projected pharmaceutical costs	• Must have accurate consumption data • Can perpetuate irrational use
Morbidity	• Estimating need in new and scaling-up programs or disaster assistance • Comparing use with theoretical needs • Developing and justifying budgets	• Population and patient attendances • Actual or projected incidence of health problems • Standard treatments (ideal, actual) • Records of supplier lead time • Projected pharmaceutical costs	• Morbidity data not available for all diseases • Standard treatments may not really be used • Accurate attendance difficult to predict
Proxy consumption	• Procurement quantification when other methods are unreliable • Comparing use with other supply systems	• Comparison area or system with good per capita data on consumption, patient attendance, service levels, and morbidity • Number of local health facilities by category • Estimates of local user population broken down by age	• Questionable comparability of patient populations, morbidity, and treatment practices
Service-level projection of budget requirements	• Estimating budget needs	• Use by service levels and facility type • Average medicine cost per attendance	• Variable facility use, attendance, treatment patterns, supply system efficiency

Developing procurement quantities for new programs: When medicines are needed for launching a new full-service health system or vertical program (such as HIV/AIDS programs or DOTS), quantification serves two purposes: to establish funding requirements for procurement and to develop the initial procurement list. In most situations, the consumption-based method is not feasible, and some combination of morbidity-based and proxy consumption methods must be used for the initial quantification.

Developing procurement quantities for scaling-up programs: Scaling up is the term used to describe an incremental increase or growth in the number of patients being treated over a period of time. Patient-months can be used to estimate needs for scaling up, where one "patient-month" is the quantity of a product needed to treat one patient for one month. The total number of patients treated over an incremental period of time in patient-months is often used in this situation for estimating needs for chronic conditions. For example, programs may not be able to serve all the patients needing ART at the start of an HIV/AIDS program but are able to scale up slowly as they receive additional donor funds, human resources, and training and address other access barriers (see Box 20-1 for an example of a scaling-up calculation).

Quantifying for assistance projects: A donor organization may undertake ad hoc quantification studies to plan procurement needs in the context of a development project. When local consumption data are not sufficiently reliable for quantification, the morbidity or proxy consumption method should be used, either singly or in combination.

Estimating pharmaceutical requirements for emergency relief situations: In emergencies such as floods or earthquakes, the first step is to provide emergency kits quickly (Chapter 26). As local health problems become clear, a morbidity-based method can be used to project requirements in the short and medium term, until the regular supply system can resume services. Country Study 20-1 describes quantification for a cholera epidemic.

Comparing actual medicine consumption with theoretical need: In most functional supply systems, the regular procurement quantification is based on past consumption. However, periodic comparison of consumption with theoretical demand based on public health priorities is a useful practice. The morbidity-based method provides the most informative comparison, but simply comparing consumption data from different systems is worthwhile because significant differences in medicine use can help identify irrational prescribing patterns or persistent inventory problems.

20.3 Issues to consider in quantification

Several issues must be addressed in any quantification process—

• Preparing an action plan for quantification
• Using centralized or decentralized quantification
• Using manual or computerized methods for quantification

- Estimating the time required
- Developing and organizing the medicines list
- Filling the supply pipeline
- Estimating the procurement period
- Considering the effect of lead time
- Estimating safety stock
- Adjusting for losses and other changes
- Cross-checking the results of quantification
- Estimating total procurement costs
- Adjusting and reconciling final quantities
- Preparing for possible program expansion (scaling up)

Preparing an action plan for quantification

Perhaps the most critical step in any large-scale quantification is preparing and then following a sound action plan through each step of the quantification. Country Study 20-2 shows the Dominican Republic's quantification experience when scaling up its national TB program. Essential points in planning for quantification include—

- Naming the official or office that will manage the process and define roles and responsibilities

---

Country Study 20-1
The morbidity method and a cholera epidemic in a Latin American country

A cholera epidemic in Latin America spread rapidly to most regions of one country within six months. A quantification was carried out to determine pharmaceutical supply needs to treat cholera patients.

Target coverage. All cholera patients requiring treatment through hospitals, clinics, and community health workers were to be covered.

Medicines list. The medicines to be included were not clear, because average treatment practices were not known and standard treatment guidelines had not yet been developed. A team collected data from sample patient charts and focused surveys to determine current treatment practices.

Source of supply. Products were to be purchased from both local and international suppliers. All cost estimates were converted to U.S. dollars for purposes of consistency.

Data. Because demand had increased dramatically for medicines used to treat cholera, stockouts were common and consumption data were not reliable. Fairly accurate morbidity data were readily available, reported weekly by fax to the central level.

Resources for quantification. A team of local and international specialists collected and analyzed data on disease incidence and current treatments and developed a computer spreadsheet for quantification.

Quantification. The morbidity method was used to calculate supply needs based on current epidemiological data, with two alternatives for treatment: current average treatment practices, and WHO treatment guidelines. The accompanying graph illustrates the projected annual supply costs for both calculations. Note the huge difference in total costs of the alternative treatment regimens. Total medicine costs were more than two times higher with current treatment practices, with the excess almost exclusively caused by overuse of lactated Ringer's IV solution when oral rehydration solution (ORS) could be safely substituted.

Results and follow-up. The results of calculations were presented to the national cholera committee, which agreed to a switch to WHO guidelines. Policy makers used the comparative cost information in educational activities to improve prescribing practices.

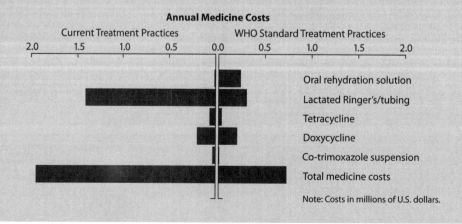

Annual Medicine Costs

Current Treatment Practices — WHO Standard Treatment Practices

Oral rehydration solution
Lactated Ringer's/tubing
Tetracycline
Doxycycline
Co-trimoxazole suspension
Total medicine costs

Note: Costs in millions of U.S. dollars.

- Forming a working group to coordinate activities of the offices, departments, and facilities involved
- Defining the objectives and coverage of the quantification
- Examining the availability of data and choosing the best quantification method according to objectives and available data and resources (personnel, funding, computer capacity)
- Developing medicines lists and data collection forms

- Determining standard treatments used in quantification
- Training staff members in the applicable quantification method and in data collection and analysis
- Developing a workplan and timeline for quantification, with realistic deadlines for each phase
- Managing quantification according to plan (adjusting for inevitable delays and unexpected constraints)
- Communicating results to relevant committees or

Country Study 20-2
Using consumption data to quantify medicines for the national TB program in the Dominican Republic

The morbidity method is usually recommended for quantifying tuberculosis (TB) medicines and supplies. The advantage of this method is that the necessary information, either the number of cases in previous years or the expected number of respiratory symptomatic cases (expected RS), is usually available in most TB programs. Since implementing the DOTS strategy in 2002, the Dominican Republic has used the expected RS–morbidity method to estimate the needs of TB medicines and commodities. However, as in most countries in the initial phases of implementing DOTS, the Dominican Republic National TB Program (DR-NTP) identified many fewer cases than expected. So in the program's initial years, the quantifications were overestimated, and deficiencies in the inventory reporting systems prevented corrections, leading to large surplus stocks. When a national financial crisis in 2004–05 slowed the public procurement process, the surplus TB medicine was used as safety stock.

In 2004, the DR-NTP pilot-tested a pharmaceutical information system based on consumption. The data showed a progressive depletion of the safety stocks in the health facilities in the pilot areas and overstocks of some medicines in certain other health facilities. Based on this information, the DR-NTP redistributed medicines from health facilities with overstocks to those with limited safety stocks to reduce the risk of interrupting or delaying the start of DOTS treatment. Furthermore, because of devaluation of the local currency, resources to procure TB medicines were insufficient to meet demand. Using data generated by the system, RPM Plus showed that the cost of a course of treatment for a new patient had increased from USD 32 in 2004 to USD 155 in 2005. RPM Plus presented the price analysis to Ministry of Health and TB program authorities and recommended they procure lower-priced, quality medicines through international agencies. As a result, a ministerial decree was pro-

mulgated that required TB medicines to be procured through the Global Drug Facility (GDF). The annual savings were estimated at about USD 775,000.

Although the information system was running in just two pilot areas, the data proved valuable for decision making. The staff endorsed the new system because the time it took to fill out the forms was less than the time it took to take physical counts of the medicines. Staff members also appreciated having an updated register of the availability of medicines in health facilities and warehouses at any given time. In addition, the daily consumption form provides an overview of medicine use in the health facilities, showing data on the start of new treatments, the completion of treatments, and treatment defaulters.

The consumption-based information system relies on four basic forms—

- A daily consumption form filled out in health facilities
- A quarterly report on consumption and availability (which is a requisition form, as well) filled out in health facilities and sent to the provincial authorities
- A quarterly report on distribution and availability (which is a requisition form, as well) filled out by the provinces and sent to the national authorities
- A quarterly national summary that is prepared at the national level

By 2010, the scaled-up information system was generating data routinely on stock levels at facilities. In addition to allowing program managers to respond promptly to the stock crisis, the information on prices paid allowed the national TB program to make important decisions about procurement methods to maximize the efficient and effective use of public resources.

Source: Management Sciences for Health/Rational Pharmaceutical Management Plus Program and Strengthening Pharmaceutical Systems Program.

managers to determine final assumptions and quantities
- Adjusting estimated quantities as needed
- Evaluating the quantification process and planning improvements to resolve problems encountered

The WHO manual *Estimating Drug Requirements* (WHO/DAP 1988) discusses how to develop a good action plan and manage the quantification process.

Countries that are faced with the major challenge of rapidly scaling up ART programs have special quantification issues to address. Country Study 20-3 describes how some African countries have worked to improve the quantification process for their ART programs.

Using centralized or decentralized quantification

Most supply systems have traditionally managed quantification at the central level. The increasing trend toward decentralizing this responsibility adds significantly to ownership of the results at health facilities and, if managed properly, can improve the accuracy of the results. However, a centralized approach is generally more efficient when the supply system is in equilibrium, with adequate supply to all levels.

Country Study 20-3
Quantification challenges in sub-Saharan countries scaling up antiretroviral therapy

An increase in funding from global initiatives such as the Global Fund to Fight AIDS, Tuberculosis and Malaria and the U.S. President's Emergency Plan for AIDS Relief has resulted not only in greater access to antiretrovirals (ARVs) in developing countries, but also in political pressures to increase the number of patients receiving ART. Previous methods used for quantifying pharmaceuticals clearly were not effective in the context of the unprecedented level of scale-up of HIV/AIDS programs, and new methods and tools were required to help countries and facilities determine their ARV needs.

Besides the scope and speed of the scale-up efforts, a key difference to address was the chronic nature of ART—lasting for the lifetime of a patient. A concern that continues to vex HIV/AIDS programs is quantification for pediatric ART. Issues include inappropriate pack sizes, the lack of fixed-dose combination products that are suitable for children, and the need to accommodate a child's growth patterns when calculating dose and consumption. (See Chapter 2 discussion of HIV/AIDS, tuberculosis, and malaria.)

Management Sciences for Health's Rational Pharmaceutical Management (RPM) Plus Program worked with a number of countries in sub-Saharan Africa in developing effective ways to quantify their needs for scaling up ART programs—

Data collection. Often, data collected at the clinics do not meet the needs of pharmacy staff for quantification; for example, data may not represent patients who actually collect their medicines from the dispensary. Mechanisms and tools, such as the Electronic Dispensing Tool (MSH/SPS n.d.), were put into place to collect data at the dispensary. The tool has been used in Côte d'Ivoire, Kenya, Namibia, Rwanda, Tanzania, and Zambia. The data collection activities were developed in collaboration with the facility staff members who collect and use the data themselves, resulting in more consistent collection and better quality data. Good quality data at the facility level is forwarded to the national program to use for national quantification purposes and results in more accurate forecasts and assumptions.

Quantification tools and related training. Facility-level tools were developed to determine quantification needs for ARVs. A manual and electronic version of the tool is used by facility staff to determine order quantities from the central medical stores. Quantimed, a quantification tool for larger programs, includes the capability to perform quantification for programs that are scaling up. Training for staff at central medical stores and ministries of health focuses on how to use Quantimed to estimate the amount of pharmaceuticals needed for procurement purposes and also to plan budgets and reports to donors. More information on Quantimed can be found in Box 20-2.

Coordination mechanisms. Kenya, Namibia, and Rwanda established committees under their national AIDS control programs to regularly discuss procurement and quantification activities for HIV/AIDS programs. The committees include representatives from donors, central medical stores, and ministries of health as well as ART providers. The committees track growth trends, monitor data collection, and evaluate the assumptions used in national quantifications on a quarterly basis. The committees' key role is to identify problems in the quantification process and make recommendations to remedy them.

A common approach in decentralizing quantification is to have each responsible office or facility compile its own estimates, based on a common list of approved medicines. The list can be sent directly to the procurement office, which compares the list with past consumption, clarifies any questions directly with the client, and compiles the master list for procurement. Reviews at the district and provincial levels before submission to the procurement office may increase the validity and ownership of estimates, at the cost of adding time to the process.

It is important to make sure that consumption is not double counted: that is, if all medicines come to facilities through a central warehouse, and a needs estimate is submitted by both the central warehouse and the client facilities that order from the warehouse, the total estimate for each medicine should be either the total of all facility estimates (plus central warehouse safety stock) or the central warehouse estimate, whichever is deemed more accurate.

Using manual or computerized methods for quantification

Conducting an accurate pharmaceutical quantification without computerization is possible; however, computers

---

Box 20-2
Quantimed: Pharmaceutical quantification and cost estimation tool

Quantimed is a Microsoft Access–based tool, developed by Management Sciences for Health, that facilitates the calculation of pharmaceutical needs using one of three primary quantification methods—past consumption, morbidity (including scaling-up patterns), and proxy consumption—or any combination of these. With appropriate data, Quantimed determines needs for a single health facility, a national public health program, or a group of geographic or administrative areas.

Quantifying needs for HIV/AIDS-related medicines and other commodities is particularly challenging in rapidly expanding prevention of mother-to-child transmission (PMTCT) and antiretroviral therapy (ART) programs that do not have data history to drive conventional model estimates. Quantimed's scaling-up function facilitates calculations of pharmaceutical requirements and costs for programs that are expanding, and allows comparisons of different scaling-up scenarios.

The primary users of the Quantimed tool are program managers of public or private programs and government planners, all of whom can gain information useful for strategic and program planning, pharmaceutical rationalization, and financial planning.

Quantimed is designed to—

- Quantify requirements and calculate estimated cost of pharmaceuticals needed for a short course of treatment or long-term treatment for chronic conditions, such as HIV/AIDS
- Develop caseload estimates for each type of health service or intervention for a given target population, using morbidity-based, consumption-based, and/or proxy consumption–based methods

- Determine pharmaceutical requirements for a new or expanding public health program
- Compare the costs of alternative treatment regimens and pharmaceutical products
- Compare alternative expansion models to enable the user to determine the possible extent and speed for scaling up a program with given resources
- Calculate percentages of the patient population receiving various therapies for a program with limited treatment data
- Calculate the estimated total cost of medicines, medical supplies, laboratory supplies, and reagents needed to provide services for a given target population, or for an estimated number of patients
- Calculate order quantity, based on the best estimate of requirements for each pharmaceutical, according to user-defined procurement and inventory factors
- Assist program managers in comparing medicine and other health commodity prices from local and international suppliers
- Provide cost estimates in local currency and international currencies, as well as conversions between currencies

Users should be aware that Quantimed is only a tool; it cannot reason for itself. All results must be analyzed and interpreted using human judgment. Quantimed cannot be used to distinguish between accurate and erroneous data, or for distinguishing between rational and irrational therapy, determining which pharmaceuticals should be ordered, or making management decisions. A user's guide is available (MSH/RPM Plus 2006).

For more information on Quantimed, see http://www.msh.org/projects/sps/Resources/Software-Tools/Quantimed.cfm.

using spreadsheet or database software make the process much easier. The examples of quantification tables in this chapter were constructed with a standard spreadsheet. One database software tool developed to ease the process of quantification is called Quantimed. For more information on Quantimed, see Box 20-2.

Computerized quantification has three major advantages: speed, accuracy, and flexibility. The process is much faster because the formulas can be programmed into the software, and after the data for basic assumptions are entered, the calculations are done automatically. The computer itself will not make errors in computation; if the data are entered correctly and the formulas are correct, the calculated answer will be correct. Speed and accuracy are especially useful for very complicated calculations such as those used to determine the number of patient-months of treatment for programs that are scaling up.

Finally, it is much easier to do "what if" analysis, where the user makes changes in quantities of various items to see what happens to the total procurement costs. Tables constructed manually need to be retyped or rewritten, and all sums need to be recalculated each time a change is made. With a computer, the recalculation and reprinting are done at the touch of a key. When a computerized medicines list and quantification model have been developed, they can be reused repeatedly.

Estimating the time required

Quantification is time-consuming, and a realistic time frame must be established for all the steps in the quantification plan. The time frame depends largely on how many levels of the supply system are involved and on the quality and type of data available. In multilevel systems in which data are incomplete, several months will almost certainly be required to produce a useful quantification.

Developing and organizing the medicines list

The medicines list is the central component of any quantification process. The quantities needed cannot be calculated until it is known which products are needed. Specifications for each medicine on the list should include the following elements—

- Medicine description, generic name, or International Nonproprietary Name (INN)
- Dosage form, such as tablet, suppository, ampoule for injection
- Strength/concentration—for example, 250 mg, 95 percent, 10 mg/mL
- Basic unit, such as tablet, tube, milliliter, bottle
- Package size in basic units
- Projected purchase price per basic unit or per package

In computerized quantification, data management is easiest when a separate field is provided for each of these specifications (see Chapter 50).

The medicines on the list need to be sorted according to the type of quantification and the type of facilities and personnel that will be recording data. The list must be provided in a form useful for retrieving information quickly and correctly. For example, if medicines are stored and records are arranged by dosage form (all tablets and capsules together, all injections together), the list should be organized by dosage form. If items are stored by therapeutic class, the list should be organized by therapeutic class, and so on. If the process involves decentralized data collection, the list should be distributed on data collection forms to each level and facility responsible for quantification at least three months before the estimates are needed for procurement.

For decentralized quantification, all facilities should submit estimates directly on the list (by hard copy or electronically). This procedure allows the compilation of one master list in a reasonable time, comparison of estimated quantities among facilities, and verification of estimates and adjustment if necessary. Dosage forms and strengths should match those included in the appropriate standard treatment guidelines and those available from likely sources of supply. For example, if 500 mg tablets are quantified but suppliers offer only 300 mg tablets, making a conversion will be difficult.

Medicines lists for quantification are often derived from past procurement or formulary or essential medicines lists. Procurement lists from previous purchases may contain specifications and the last prices paid, but they may not represent rational medicine selection or comply with the formulary or essential medicines list. Essential medicines lists or medicine formulary lists that have been regularly updated should be the basis for the quantification list, because they reflect medicines needed for current morbidity patterns (see Chapters 16 and 17).

Filling the supply pipeline

The supply pipeline refers to stock levels within the supply system and the number of supply points at each level, as discussed in Chapter 23. The number of levels, the frequency of requisition and delivery, and the amount of safety stock at each level all influence the amount of pharmaceuticals needed to fill the pipeline and, hence, the amount that must be procured when a program is started or expanded. Underestimation of stock in the pipeline is a common cause of program failure, particularly when a revolving drug fund has been planned. Quantification for a depleted pipeline should include the safety stock levels required at each level of distribution, not just the central level.

Estimating the procurement period

The procurement period covers the time from one order until the next regular order will be placed. In a scheduled system, this period might be multiples of one month; in a perpetual system, it could be counted in days or weeks for the purposes of quantifying. Note that the quantity ordered plus the safety stock must cover the time until the next order is received, which is the procurement period plus the lead time (see below). Procurement periods are influenced by funding and storage space availability as well as by expiry and stability of the stock being ordered.

Considering the effect of lead time

The procurement order quantity should be sufficient to last until the next procurement cycle is completed. The steps of the procurement process needed to place an order may take several months. In addition, after an order is placed, several more months are often required for the pharmaceuticals to arrive in the country, clear customs, and reach the central warehouse. The waiting period from the time an order is prepared until it arrives in the country is the lead time (Chapter 23). The lead time can vary for each product and/or supplier. When lead times are underestimated, the likely results are shortages and more expensive emergency purchases.

When quantifying for a program that is scaling up, the quantity required to cover the lead time will also need to be scaled up.

Estimating safety stock

Safety stock is the amount of stock that is kept in reserve in case an item is unavailable from the supplier or for a sudden increase in demand.

$$\text{Safety stock} = C_A \times LT$$

C_A = Average monthly consumption, adjusted for stockouts (see Section 20.4)
LT = Average lead time (for projected supplier or worst case), in months

Any length of time can be used for the lead time in the preceding equation, but the period should be at least as long as the lead time period, while taking financial resources and storage space into consideration.

When a lead time is unreliable, safety stock should be increased. With a variable lead time, use the following formula—

$$DD_E = DD_P + (OD \times OD\%)$$

DD_E = expected delivery date
DD_P = promised delivery date
OD = average overdue period in days
$OD\%$ = percentage of orders overdue

When quantifying for a program that is scaling up, the quantity required for safety stock will also need to be scaled up.

Adjusting for losses and other changes

Inevitably, some medicines will be lost because of damage, spoilage, expiration, and theft. If such losses are not considered in quantification and procurement, stockouts are likely to result. To prevent shortages, a percentage can be added to allow for losses when quantifying requirements. Many systems need to allow at least 10 percent for losses.

Not all medicines are equally at risk for loss—for example, some are more attractive to thieves than others, such as valuable antiretrovirals and artemisinin-based antimalarials. The medicines that are most at risk may vary from country to country. If they can be identified, adjusting the quantities for those items by a higher percentage may be feasible, rather than applying the same adjustment to all items. One strategy is to allow a loss percentage only for vital items, accepting the risk of stockouts for other items. If losses have already been accounted for as part of a consumption-method quantification, there is no need to make a loss adjustment.

Clearly, the best interests of the health system are served by making every effort to control loss and wastage. Options for controlling theft are discussed in Chapter 43; Chapter 40 offers tips for analyzing expiry dates in a large pharmaceutical inventory; and Chapters 45 and 46 provide suggestions for managing stock to avoid wastage.

In a supply system in which patient use or the number of facilities is growing, assuming that medicine consumption will increase is reasonable. In such situations, estimated quantities can be increased by a percentage corresponding to the rate of growth.

Cross-checking the results of quantification

Because there will be some imprecision in the estimates no matter how rigorously the appropriate quantification methods are followed, checking the estimates with a different quantification method is always useful. Ideally, the estimates would produce very similar results, but in practice this rarely happens. The two sets of data can then be evaluated to see which appears to be more realistic, considering the reliability of source data used for the two estimates. Box 20-3 provides guidelines for how to evaluate and compare consumption-based versus morbidity-based estimates. These quantities will likely need to be adjusted to fit

Box 20-3
Comparing morbidity- and consumption-based estimate results

The following scenarios include suggested actions to take based on the results of each method and depending on confidence in the data used. For the consumption method, the pharmaceutical management information system should accurately and reliably maintain data on *consumption* (not on stock movement, which may include losses and expired stock). A crucial factor to consider in any analysis of results is the possible irrational use of medicines in the system.

Consumption-based estimate greater than morbidity-based estimate

If the consumption-based estimate is 50 percent greater than the morbidity-based estimate, conduct a more detailed investigation of the data before proceeding with the quantification. Were the data entry and transcription done correctly? Was the correct population and morbidity information obtained? Is there a possibility of large-scale leakage and/or diversion of supplies? When the data have been verified, or for discrepancies less than 50 percent, proceed as follows—

If **not confident in the quality of either** the consumption or morbidity data—

- Consider an overall system assessment, then strengthening of the health management information system and pharmaceutical management information system.
- Seek comparative facilities, regions, or countries with reliable information systems and use their data as proxy data.
- Try to estimate the percentage of confidence in the accuracy, completeness, or reliability of the data and adjust the results accordingly.

If **more confident in the consumption data** than the morbidity data—

- Examine the morbidity data for underestimation of disease incidence.
- Make sure the population data are current. Ask whether any large movement of population into the area has occurred, such as refugees, seasonal workers, or employees of new industries.
- Determine whether standard treatment guidelines are followed.
- Investigate whether pharmaceuticals are used in other programs or for other purposes.

If **more confident in the morbidity data** than the consumption data—

- Consider whether pilferage, expiration, or stock leakage is high.
- Investigate whether pharmaceuticals are used in other programs or for other purposes.
- Ask whether stockouts of related pharmaceuticals caused higher consumption of this item.

If **confident in the quality of both** the consumption and morbidity data—

- Use the consumption-based estimate to avoid the problem of ordering too few pharmaceuticals and supplies.

Morbidity-based estimate greater than consumption-based estimate

If **not confident in the quality of either** the consumption or morbidity data—

- Consider an overall system assessment, then strengthening of health management information system and pharmaceutical management information system.
- Seek comparative facilities, regions, or countries with reliable information systems and use their data as proxy data.
- Try to estimate the percentage of confidence in the accuracy, completeness, or reliability of the data and adjust the results accordingly.

If **more confident in the consumption** data than the morbidity data—

- Examine the morbidity data for overestimation of disease incidence.
- Ask whether a change in population has occurred as a result of exodus caused by war, unrest, drought, famine, migration of seasonal workers, or departure of refugees.
- Determine whether standard treatment guidelines are followed.
- Investigate whether pharmaceuticals are used for other programs or for other purposes.
- Consider whether program coverage is low and/or support services or diagnostics for health conditions are inadequate.

If **more confident in the morbidity** data than the consumption data—

- Consider whether the management information system is poor.
- Ask whether the budget has been sufficient to meet the full needs of the population or if a proportion has gone untreated.
- Consider whether program coverage is low and/or support services or diagnostics for health conditions are inadequate, and whether access to these services

has been limited by unrest, strikes, or transport problems.

- Determine whether medicines are being supplied from multiple sources not included in the quantification.

If **confident in the quality of both** consumption and morbidity data—

- Use the morbidity-based estimate to avoid ordering too few pharmaceuticals and supplies.

the budget as well. Table 20-2 illustrates how three different quantification methods produced different estimates for the same supply system in a Latin American country.

Cross-checking is a fundamental step in reconciling procurement quantities with available funds. It is also useful to cross-check consumption with theoretical demand to get an idea of the rationality of pharmaceutical therapy in the system. If the supply system usually bases purchases on past consumption, cross-checking for high-volume, high-cost medicines using another method may reveal targets for interventions to promote more rational medicine use. For example, in one quantification conducted for intrauterine devices (IUDs), the quality of the issues data (quantities distributed from a storage point) were considered good, and indeed they were an accurate record of the stocks given out. However, enough IUDs had been issued for every man, woman, and child in the province. A comparison of the population and morbidity data highlighted the problem of leakage and/or resale of the IUDs outside the country. This comparison produced a more accurate quantification for next year's supply.

Estimating total procurement costs

When estimating the cost of medicines on a quantified list, the critical issue is determining the next purchase prices. Using the last purchase prices is not adequate, because in most cases, doing so results in an underestimate of the actual next purchase prices, leading to insufficient funds when the time comes to place orders.

Two basic ways exist to estimate the next purchase price of a medicine; both are usually needed to estimate the cost for the full list of medicines.

The first option is obtaining data on current medicine prices in the market where the medicines will be purchased. As discussed in Chapter 21, sources for price data include local suppliers, international procurement agencies, and references such as Management Sciences for Health's *International Drug Price Indicator Guide,* which is updated annually.

Table 20-2 Comparison of quantification results in a Latin American country

Medicine	Consumption estimate	Morbidity estimate	Proxy consumption estimate
ORS 1 L package	11,290,000	18,650,000	14,850,000
Chloroquine 300 mg tablet	1,230,000	2,233,000	2,005,000
Paracetamol 500 mg tablet	20,960,000	14,010,000	22,320,000

The other option for estimating next purchase price is to adjust the last purchase price for factors such as—

- International inflation for products bought internationally
- Devaluation of local currency for products purchased internationally (if relevant)—this percentage is added to the price for medicines purchased on the international market
- Local inflation for products purchased on the local market, adding the appropriate percentage based on the current local situation

After price estimates are obtained, percentages for shipping and insurance of pharmaceuticals obtained from international sources (usually 15 to 20 percent) and any known fees, such as those paid to a tender board or for local customs duties, must be added.

Adjusting and reconciling final quantities

Difficult decisions must often be made to reduce the number of medicines or the quantities of medicines or both until the estimated quantities and costs correspond with the available budget. These reductions may require policy decisions regarding priority diseases, priority age groups, priority facilities to be supplied, selection of less expensive

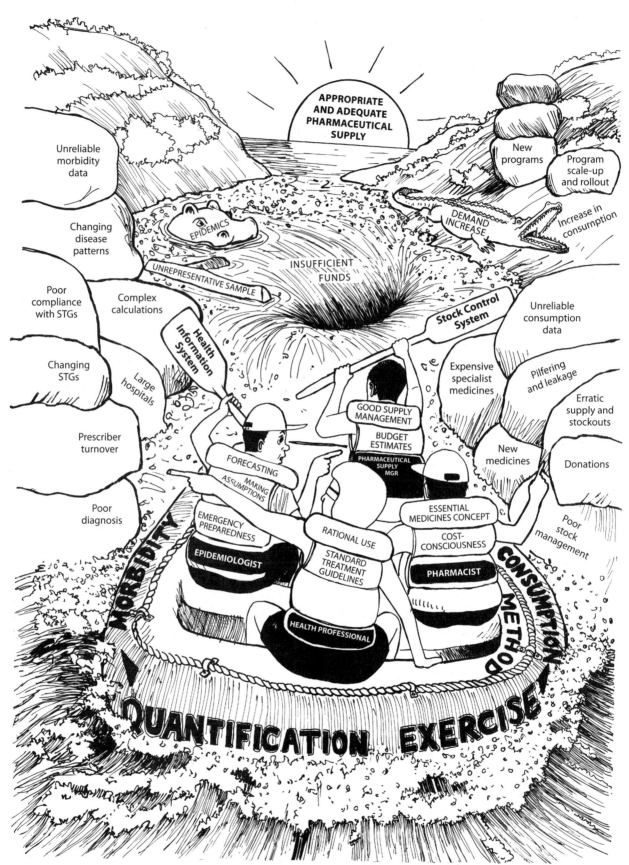

SUCCESSFUL PHARMACEUTICAL QUANTIFICATION REQUIRES A TEAM EFFORT AND A MIX OF METHODS

therapeutic alternatives, and changes to standard treatment guidelines. Chapter 40 discusses several approaches for making reductions rationally, using specific tools such as VEN (vital, essential, nonessential) categories, ABC analysis, and therapeutic category analysis. Another way of providing a foundation for reduction is to cross-check the quantification with another method to find out where the quantified estimate is much higher than necessary based on known morbidity and attendance data or much higher than that in a comparable health system.

Eliminating adjustments for expected losses may be a tempting first step in reducing quantities, but it is a false economy unless losses will in fact be eliminated. If the losses are likely to occur, they must be incorporated into the final quantification, or stockouts will almost certainly result. Cutting the overall percentage allowed for losses may be possible by targeting the allowance to those items most at risk and/or eliminating the adjustment for nonvital medicines, with the expectation that some stockouts will result for medicines that are not covered.

20.4 Consumption method

In the consumption method, a list is prepared of all medicines eligible for procurement, and the most accurate inventory records of past consumption are used to calculate the quantities needed for each medicine.

Consumption during a recent period of six to twelve months is adjusted for stockouts to obtain the average monthly consumption. A percentage for increase in projected use is added to the projected monthly consumption. Then the average monthly consumption is multiplied by the number of months to be covered by the procurement. Safety stock and lead time levels (in months) are also multiplied by the projected monthly consumption. These three figures are added to obtain the gross needs during the period, subtracting the usable stock on hand and any stock on order from the gross estimate, to derive the quantity to purchase. This quantification formula is the same as the consumption-based reorder formula described in Chapter 23. An adjustment is then made for losses.

The anticipated unit cost for each medicine (not the last unit cost) is multiplied by the number of units to be purchased to obtain the expected purchase value for the entire quantity. All purchase values for individual medicines are added to obtain the total expected procurement cost. If this cost is greater than the budget, adjustments are made, as described in the previous section.

Example

Table 20-3 shows a sample consumption-based quantification from an eastern Caribbean country. This sample is not the complete quantification list, but it illustrates the estimates for nineteen medicines. Box 20-4 provides a summary of calculations used in consumption-based quantification.

Steps in the quantification

Step 1. Prepare a list of medicines to be quantified. The medicines list should be prepared as described in Section 20.3, sorted into the order that will best facilitate data collection, and distributed to those officials and facilities that will enter consumption data.

Step 2. Determine the period of time to be reviewed for consumption. If the procurement is to cover a twelve-month period, the consumption data for the past twelve months should be reviewed (if a full year's useful data are available). A twelve-month review may also be used for a procurement covering six months, but if seasonal variations are significant, such as with malaria, using the same six-month period from the preceding year may be preferable. A short review period, such as three months, is inadequate to plan a procurement to cover twelve months, unless the three months reviewed reflect a steady state of consumption for the entire year.

Step 3. Enter consumption data for each medicine. For each medicine on the list, enter—

- The total quantity used during the review period, in basic units
- The number of days in the review period that the medicine was out of stock (if the number of days out of stock cannot be determined with accuracy, the estimated number of months out of stock during the period can be entered)
- The lead time for the last procurement (or the average from the last several procurements)

Using the most accurate and current records available is important. The likely sources for data on consumption and lead time are—

- Stock records and distribution reports from a central distribution point
- Stock records and reports from regional or district warehouses
- Invoices from suppliers
- Dispensing records from health facilities

If projected pricing data are available at this stage, entering prices while entering consumption data (see step 10) may save time.

Step 4. Calculate the average monthly consumption. The average monthly consumption is a key variable in the quantification formula and should be as accurate as

Table 20-3 Consumption-based quantification for an eastern Caribbean country

Medicine	Strength	BU	Pack size	C_T Total consumption in period (BU)	D_OS Days out of stock	C_A Adjusted average monthly consumption (BU)	C_P Projected average monthly consumption (BU)	S_I Stock on hand (BU)	S_O Stock on order (BU)	SS Safety stock level (BU)	Q_O Suggested quantity to order (BU)	Q_A Adjusted order quantity	Order quantity (packs)	Probable pack price (USD)	Value of proposed order (USD)
Ampicillin	500 mg	Capsule	1,000	59,500	0	9,917	10,413	32,000	42,000	31,239	50,956	56,052	57	46.50	2,650.50
Ampicillin	250 mg	Capsule	1,000	89,000	34	18,218	19,129	81,000	58,000	57,387	90,548	99,603	100	24.70	2,470.00
Ampicillin sodium injection	500 mg	Ampoule	100	3,879	0	647	679	111	7,600	2,037	437	481	5	17.03	85.15
Ampicillin suspension 100 mL	125 mg/5 mL	Bottle	1	4,128	0	688	722	1,513	3,000	2,166	4,151	4,566	4,567	0.57	2,603.19
Antihistamine decongestant elixir	250 mL	Bottle	1	853	29	169	177	351	929	531	844	928	929	1.57	1,458.53
Antihistamine decongestant	(Any)	Tablet	500	50,000	0	8,333	8,750	0	62,500	26,250	42,500	46,750	94	12.00	1,128.00
Bacitracin antibiotic ointment	—	Tube	1	2,414	31	484	508	3,400	100	1,524	2,596	2,856	2,856	0.54	1,542.24
Bendrofluazide	5 mg	Tablet	500	141,500	30	28,208	29,618	142,000	50,000	88,854	163,416	179,758	360	4.60	1,656.00
Benzathine benzyl-penicillin injection	2.4 MU	Ampoule	50	1,318	0	220	231	1,486	0	693	1,286	1,415	29	12.10	350.90
Cephradine injection	500 mg	Ampoule	100	2,695	0	449	471	2,300	1,100	1,413	2,252	2,477	25	75.00	1,875.00
Chlorhexidine gluconate solution (Hibitane)	5%	Liter	5	302	0	50	53	433	0	159	203	223	45	3.90	175.50
Chlorhexidine/cetrimide (Savlon)	5 liter	Liter	5	438	0	73	77	418	250	231	256	282	57	14.70	837.90
Chlorpropamide	250 mg	Tablet	1,000	162,000	0	27,000	28,350	169,000	0	85,050	171,200	188,320	189	27.90	5,273.10
Cimetidine (Tagamet) inj.	200 mg	Ampoule	10	1,090	0	182	191	2,580	0	573	0	0	0	2.49	0.00
Cimetidine	400 mg	Tablet	1,000	24,000	0	4,000	4,200	23,500	25,000	12,600	1,900	2,090	3	17.90	53.70
Cloxacillin suspension 100 mL	125 mg/5 mL	Bottle	1	882	0	147	154	1,446	0	462	402	442	443	1.00	443.00
Co-trimoxazole suspension 100 mL	200/40 mg/5 mL	Bottle	1	1,152	0	192	202	374	1,930	606	120	132	132	0.75	99.00
Co-trimoxazole	400/80 mg	Tablet	1,000	81,000	0	13,500	14,175	82,000	0	42,525	88,100	96,910	97	21.00	2,037.00
Dextrose in saline (IV) 1,000 mL	5%/0.9%	Bottle	1	1,525	32	308	323	0	2,288	969	1,588	1,747	1,747	1.35	2,358.45
													Total order cost:		**27,097.16**

Note: BU = basic unit; USD = U.S. dollars; MU = mega-unit; consumption period = 6 months; procurement period = 6 months; lead time = 3 months; use adjustment for 6 months = 5%; loss adjustment = 10%.

Box 20-4
Consumption-based calculations

Formula number	Objective of formula	Calculations
1	Adjusted average monthly consumption (preferred)	$C_A = C_T \div [R_M - (D_{OS} \div 30.5)]$
2	Adjusted average monthly consumption (alternative)	$C_A = C_T \div (R_M - M_{OS})$
3	Projected average monthly consumption	$C_P = C_A + (C_A \times A_U)$
4	Basic safety stock requirements	$C_A \times LT$
5	Quantity to order	$Q_O = C_A \times (LT + PP) + SS - (S_I + S_O)$
6	Quantity to order adjusted for losses	$Q_A = Q_O + (Q_O \times A_L)$

C_A = Average monthly consumption, adjusted for stockouts
C_T = Total consumption during review period, in basic units
R_M = Total consumption review period, in months
D_{OS} = Number of days an item was out of stock during the review period
M_{OS} = Estimated number of months an item was out of stock during the review period
C_P = Projected average monthly consumption
A_U = Use adjustment

SS = Quantity needed for safety stock
LT = Average lead time (for projected supplier or worst case), in months
Q_O = Quantity to order in basic units, before adjustment for losses or program change
PP = Procurement period (number of months to be covered by order)
S_I = Stock now in inventory, in basic units
S_O = Stock now on order, in basic units
Q_A = Quantity to order adjusted for losses or program change
A_L = Loss adjustment

possible. The simple approach is to divide total consumption by the number of months reviewed. If stockouts occurred during that period, the average must be adjusted to include the consumption that would have occurred if stock had been available.

Two ways exist of accounting for stockouts when computing average monthly consumption. The recommended method is illustrated in Box 20-4 as formula number 1. Enter the total consumption and divide this number by the number of months in the review period minus (the total number of days out of stock in the same period divided by 30.5 to convert to months). For example, see the entry for ampicillin 250 mg capsules in Table 20-3, which shows consumption-based quantification for a Caribbean country. Total consumption for a six-month review period was 89,000 capsules. The medicine was out of stock for thirty-four days in the six-month period. Therefore, the average monthly consumption is—

$$C_A = 89{,}000 \div [6 - (34 \div 30.5)],$$
$$\text{or } 89{,}000 \div 4.8852 = 18{,}218$$

An alternative method, which is simpler but less precise, is shown as formula number 2 in Box 20-4. It uses the estimated number of months out of stock for adjusting consumption, omitting the step of converting days to months. Using the same medicine from Table 20-3, the medicine was in stock for about five of the six months, leaving about one month out of stock. Therefore, the average monthly consumption is—

$$C_A = 89{,}000 \div (6 - 1) = 89{,}000 \div 5 = 17{,}800$$

Step 5. Calculate projected average monthly consumption for expected changes in consumption pattern. When using the example of ampicillin 250 mg capsules in Table 20-3, if use is expected to increase by 5 percent in the coming year, adjusting the average monthly consumption by 5 percent would be reasonable, which would raise the expected monthly need by 911 capsules, bringing the total to 19,129 capsules.

Some changes in consumption may be independent of trends in overall patient use. One example is predictable seasonal variation in the consumption of cough and cold remedies. A potential spike in an unpredictable epidemic disease such as cholera is another example. If such variation is anticipated or is part of the consumption data, increasing or decreasing estimates for medicines such as oral rehydration solution, parenteral solutions, and some antibiotics would be sensible; however, this variation does not mean that the need for all medicines will increase or decrease by the same factor.

If a new formulary medicine is known to be replacing an older medicine in the formulary, the estimate for the older medicine should be reduced. If an initiative is being launched to alter prescribing patterns, anticipating at least some success by reducing the expected need for targeted medicines by a small percentage would be reasonable. When a turnover occurs in prescribing staff members, the new prescribers may have different ways of treating common conditions that could substantially affect medicine needs in some therapeutic categories. If such changes can be anticipated, adjusting the forecasts would be wise to avoid spending resources on medicines that will not be as popular as in the past.

Step 6. Calculate the safety stock needed for each medicine. Safety (buffer) stock is needed to prevent stockouts, although high levels of safety stock increase inventory holding costs and should be avoided (see Chapter 23). In some supply systems, the safety stock is set for each item at a fixed quantity or a fixed number of months' worth of consumption. However, the preferred method is to calculate the safety stock based on the projected average consumption and the expected lead time (see formula number 3 in Box 20-4). The projected average consumption from step 5 is multiplied by the average lead time. This safety stock level should avoid stockouts, assuming that the item is reordered when only the safety stock remains, the supplier delivers within the projected lead time, and consumption is no greater than average. Using formula number 3 in Box 20-4, the safety stock for ampicillin 250 mg capsules in the example is $19{,}129 \times 3$ months = 57,387.

For vital items identified from a VEN analysis (see Chapter 40), adjusting the safety stock may be necessary to cover variations in consumption or lead time. Several options can be used for adjusting safety stock levels (see Chapter 23). The simplest method multiplies the basic safety stock by an adjustment factor. For example, an adjustment factor of 1.5, or 50 percent, would increase the safety stock of ampicillin 250 mg capsules in Table 20-3 to 86,081 capsules. If this sort of adjustment is done for all items, the cost of safety stock will increase substantially; therefore, adjustments should be made only when true uncertainty exists about the lead time or consumption.

Step 7. Calculate the quantity of each medicine required in the next procurement period. The suggested formula for calculating the quantity to order is shown as formula number 5 in Box 20-4. The calculation is done in three main steps. First, the projected average consumption is multiplied by the sum of the lead time and the procurement period, yielding the total needs before considering safety stock, stock on hand, or stock on order. The second step is to add the quantity needed for safety stock. Finally, the quantity of usable stock on hand and the stock on order are added together, and then subtracted from the previous total. Using the example of ampicillin 250 mg capsules from Table 20-3, the quantity to order is—

$$Q_O = 19{,}129 \times (3 + 6) + 57{,}387 - (81{,}000 + 58{,}000) = 90{,}548$$

Because the ampicillin capsules are purchased in bottles of 1,000, ninety-one bottles should be ordered.

Step 8. Adjust for losses. To avoid stockouts, one should adjust quantification estimates to allow for losses, as discussed in Section 20.3. If the supply system from Table 20-3 averaged 10 percent per year in losses, and this percentage was applied to ampicillin 250 mg capsules, the allowance would add 9,055 capsules to the estimate from step 7, bringing the total purchase quantity to 99,603, or 100 bottles of 1,000 capsules.

Step 9. Compile decentralized quantifications (if applicable). In a decentralized quantification, staff members at each facility or storage point enter their own consumption quantities and stockout information following the preceding steps, and the estimates of the individual facilities are totaled and compiled on the master quantification list.

Step 10. Estimate costs for each medicine and total costs. In order to estimate procurement costs, multiply the quantities estimated for each medicine by the most accurate prediction of the expected next purchase price (not the last one), as discussed in Section 20.3.

After the expected price has been entered for each medicine, multiply the price by the estimated quantity needed to obtain the total procurement value for each medicine. Table 20-3 uses the package price as the basis for making these projections, but in many cases using the unit price is preferable, because combining information from different sources to arrive at an average allows more flexibility. The basic unit price is also preferable if the package sizes that will be ordered are not known or if projections are based on average international prices from a source such as the annual *International Drug Price Indicator Guide*.

After the estimated procurement value has been calculated for each medicine, the final step in the basic quantification process is to add the estimated procurement values for all medicines to obtain the total expected cost for the procurement.

Step 11. Compare total costs with budget and make adjustments. If the total expected procurement cost exceeds the available budget, only two choices exist: either obtain more funds or reduce the number of medicines and/or the quantities ordered. Section 20.3 discusses rational ways to adjust the estimates.

20.5 Morbidity method

The morbidity method uses data on patient use (attendances at health facilities) and morbidity (the frequency of common health problems) to project the need for medicines based on assumptions about how the problems will be treated. Readers who plan to undertake a morbidity-based quantification can refer to the WHO manual *Estimating Drug Requirements* (WHO/DAP 1988), which provides a more detailed discussion of the steps in this type of quantification.

The morbidity method requires a list of common health problems, an essential medicines list that includes therapy for the problems, and a set of standard treatments for quantification purposes (based on either average current practices or "ideal" treatment guidelines). For most health problems, at least two alternative treatments exist, and a percentage must be assigned based on how frequently each regimen is used. Then, the expected incidence (number of treatment episodes) of each health problem must be estimated. The incidence of a health problem can be estimated from total patient contacts or from a subgroup, for example, "number of HIV-infected patients" or "number of women attending antenatal clinic services."

The quantification formula involves multiplying the quantity of each medicine included in standard treatments for each health problem by the number of treatment episodes expected for the health problem. The expected total need for each medicine is the sum of the estimates from all treatment regimens in which the medicine is included. Then the estimates are adjusted to fill the supply pipeline, allowing for losses caused by theft and wastage. Finally, the expected cost is calculated on the basis of the expected purchase price of each medicine, and estimates are reconciled with available funds.

Because of the limited data likely to be available on morbidity patterns and the difficulty in defining standard treatments that are meaningful for quantification, applying this method to every health problem is difficult. This difficulty limits the method's utility for a complex health system with many types of health problems and several levels of health facilities. In general, the morbidity method is most useful in estimating for a relatively small number of different health problems, for example, in primary care and special-purpose facilities and programs.

Because a limited number of health problems are likely to be addressed in most morbidity-based quantification procedures, the resulting estimates for each medicine must be adjusted to cover health problems not considered in the quantification, usually using some variant of proxy consumption (see Section 20.6). Adjustments may also be required to fill the supply pipeline, to account for losses, and, in most cases, to reconcile the quantities needed with the funds available.

In a simple quantification exercise for one health problem, such as cholera (see Country Study 20-1), or for a small group of health problems and medicines, the process can be done manually (although it is easier with a computer). A spreadsheet program or specialized quantification software, such as Quantimed, is virtually required to conduct a complicated morbidity-based quantification covering a large number of health problems and medicines (see Box 20-2).

Figure 20-1 is a flow diagram that illustrates how the data inputs on population, percentage of coverage, health problems, standard treatments, and unit costs are used to calculate the quantities needed and projected procurement costs.

Example

Table 20-4 is an example of morbidity-based quantification. The table shows a number of health problems for which medicines are to be procured, morbidity estimates for a

Figure 20-1 Morbidity method

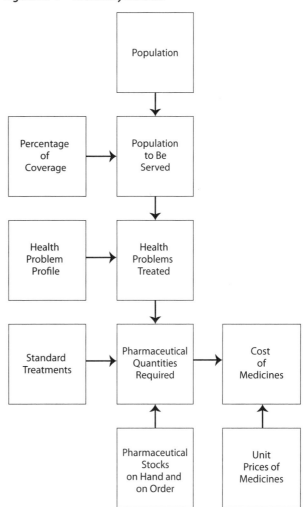

one-year period, and sample standard treatment regimens expected to be prescribed for the health problems. The medicine needs for the health problems are calculated in basic units. All this information, together with projections for losses, adjustments made to reflect available funds, and quantities required to fill the supply pipeline, is used to produce a procurement list. Table 20-4 follows steps 1–6 in the next section. Box 20-5 provides a summary of calculations used in morbidity-based quantification.

Steps in the quantification

Step 1. Specify the list of problems. List the major specific health problems encountered (see Table 20-4). If an existing information system reports on diseases, those disease codes should be used; if no coding system exists, the International Classification of Diseases (ICD) system can be used. (See http://www.who.int/classifications/icd/en for more information.)

Table 20-4 Pharmaceutical needs based on morbidity

Problem	Severity	Age group	F — Episodes per 1,000 contacts	C_E — Expected number of contacts	E_T — Projected number of episodes	Number of regimen	P_T — % Cases treated with regimen	Pharmaceutical product	Basic unit	D_CU — Basic units per dose	N_D — Doses per day	L_D — Number of days	Q_E — Basic units per episode	Q_T — Total basic units needed
Malaria	1	<5	364	3,279,578	1,193,767	1	100	Artesunate 50 mg	Tablet	1	1	3	3	3,581,301
						1	100	Amodiaquine 150 mg	Tablet	1	1	3	3	3,581,301
						2	80	Paracetamol solution 120 mg/5 mL	mL	1.50	4	10	60	57,300,816
		>5	278	3,279,578	911,723	1	100	Artesunate 50 mg	Tablet	4	1	3	12	10,940,676
						1	100	Amodiaquine 150 mg	Tablet	4	1	3	12	10,940,676
						2	80	Paracetamol 500 mg	Tablet	2	4	5	40	29,175,129
	2	<5	65	3,279,578	213,173	1	100	Quinine injection 300 mg/mL	mL	0.50	3	1	1.5	319,759
						1	100	Quinine 300 mg	Tablet	0.50	3	6	9	1,918,553
						2	100	Paracetamol solution 120 mg/5 mL	mL	1.50	4	10	60	12,790,356
		>5	61	3,279,578	200,054	1	100	Quinine injection 300 mg/mL	mL	2	3	1	6	1,200,326
						1	100	Quinine 300 mg	Tablet	2	3	6	36	7,201,954
						2	100	Paracetamol 500 mg	Tablet	2	4	10	80	16,004,343
Conjunctivitis	—	<5	53	3,279,578	173,818	1	100	Tetracycline 1% eye ointment	5 g tube	1	3	7	1	173,818
		>5	38	3,279,578	124,624	1	100	Tetracycline 1% eye ointment	5 g tube	1	3	7	1	124,624
Otitis media	—	<5	106	3,279,578	347,635	1	100	Co-trimoxazole suspension	mL	5	2	10	100	34,763,531
						2	100	Paracetamol solution 120 mg/5 mL	mL	1.50	4	10	60	20,858,119
						3	80	Pseudoephedrine syrup	mL	2.50	4	5	50	13,905,412
		>5	29	3,279,578	95,108	1	100	Co-trimoxazole 800/160 mg	Tablet	1	2	10	20	1,902,155
						2	100	Paracetamol 500 mg	Tablet	2	4	5	40	3,804,311
						3	80	Pseudoephedrine 60 mg	Tablet	1	4	5	20	1,521,724
Acute tonsillitis	—	<5	72	3,279,578	236,130	1	100	Penicillin VK 125 mg/5 mL liquid	mL	5	4	5	100	23,612,964
						2	100	Paracetamol solution 120 mg/5 mL	mL	1.50	4	10	60	4,167,779
		>5	33	3,279,578	108,226	1	100	Procaine penicillin 3 MU injection	Vial	1	1	1	1	108,226
						2	100	Penicillin VK 250 mg	Tablet	1	4	5	20	2,164,522
						3	100	Paracetamol 500 mg	Tablet	2	4	5	40	4,329,043
Gastritis, heartburn	—	<5	11	3,279,578	36,075	1	100	Antacid suspension	mL	5	4	5	100	3,607,536
		>5	77	3,279,578	252,528	1	70	Antacid suspension	mL	10	4	5	200	35,353,855
						2	30	Cimetidine 300 mg	Tablet	1	4	5	20	1,515,165

Note: Based on 3,123,408 contacts in the past year; 5 percent expected rate of increase; MU = mega-unit.

The health problem list should not be broken down into too much detail but should be defined according to the diagnostic capacity and health problems treated at each type of health facility. At the lowest level of the system, only a limited number of problems are recognized and treated; the range of problems diagnosed and treated normally increases at the health center, district hospital, and referral hospital levels.

Because treatments differ markedly for adult and pediatric patients, at least two categories (under five years and over five years) need to be included for most problems. Although it may be tempting to establish several categories (under five, five to twelve, thirteen to sixty-five, and over sixty-five), it is best to avoid overcomplicating the development of treatment guidelines (see below) and the process of compiling data on treatment episodes.

Step 2. Establish the list of medicines to be quantified. The objective here is a list of essential medicines that covers the major health problems and forms the basis for standard treatment schedules (see Table 20-4). A current and appropriate national or health system formulary or essential medicines list should be used when available. If no official list exists, one needs to be developed (see Chapter 17); it may grow out of the process of developing standard treatments.

The medicines list must be available in two formats—one organized in alphabetical order by generic name (INN) and one by therapeutic categories. The therapeutic category list is most useful in developing standard treatment schedules, and the list organized by generic name is used for the procurement list.

Step 3. Establish standard or average treatments. Standard or average treatment regimens are required for each health problem to forecast medicine needs, as in Table 20-4. Developing this information is the most complicated part of using the morbidity method. Two basic options exist for developing standard treatments: average actual treatments or ideal standard treatments. The components are the same,

but an important difference exists between the approaches: average regimens are based on observed or reported practices and are more likely to predict what will actually happen, whereas ideal regimens define what should happen if prescribers follow the ideal guidelines. Country Study 20-1 illustrates how different the results can be between average current treatments and standard treatments.

Which should be used? Perhaps both, in a combination approach. For example, if one treatment regimen is viewed as ideal but another is commonly used, include both regimens in the guidelines for quantification and estimate the percentage of treatment episodes that will receive each of the two regimens.

For some health problems, particularly with severely ill patients, the duration of treatment varies significantly between individual patients, depending on their treatment response. Expert advice should be used to help estimate average treatment duration. The same applies for preventive treatment, where adherence to treatment can significantly influence treatment duration.

In most quantification exercises, developing (or modifying) the treatment guidelines is necessary (see Chapter 17). Ideally, standard treatment guidelines should be developed by expert committees (with additional expert assistance, if needed). Unless reliable information is available on medicine use and prescribing patterns, a special study may be needed to determine average actual treatment patterns; this study can be combined with a study to determine morbidity patterns and incidence of health problems (see step 4).

Whichever option is used, the same information must be compiled (see Section 20.3)—

- The percentage of treatment episodes in which the medicine will be prescribed
- The name of each medicine and strength/concentration with separate treatments listed for age (or weight) level, as appropriate

---

Box 20-5
Morbidity-based calculations

Formula number	Objective of formula	Calculations
1	Quantity of medicines needed per treatment episode	$Q_E = D_{CU} \times N_D \times L_D$
2	Expected total number of contacts (in thousands)	$C_E = C + (C \times A_U)$
3	Expected treatment episodes	$E_T = C_E \times F$
4	Total quantity of medicines needed	$Q_T = E_T \times Q_E \times P_T$

Q_E	= Quantity of each medicine needed for each treatment episode	C_E	= Expected total number of contacts
D_{CU}	= Basic units per dose	F	= Frequency of health problem (per thousand)
N_D	= Number of doses per day	E_T	= Expected treatment episodes
L_D	= Length of treatment in days	Q_T	= Total quantity required
C	= Past total number of contacts	P_T	= Percentage of cases expected to be treated
A_U	= Utilization adjustment		

- The basic unit
- The number of basic units in each average dose for the health problem in question
- The average number of doses of each medicine per day for the problem
- The average number of days of treatment for each medicine per episode

These components are combined to project the quantity of each medicine needed for each treatment episode (Q_E) in each standard treatment regimen. This projection is made by multiplying the basic units per dose (D_{CU}) by the number of doses per day (N_D). This result is multiplied by the length of treatment per episode, in days (L_D). The entire formula is—

$$Q_E = D_{CU} \times N_D \times L_D$$

In the example from Table 20-4, three different medicine products are prescribed for otitis media for both age groups; the medicines are the same, but the dose and dosage form differ. The quantity of co-trimoxazole suspension needed to treat otitis media in patients under five years old is calculated as—

$$Q_E = 5\,\text{mL} \times 2\,\text{doses/day} \times 10\,\text{days} = 100\,\text{mL}$$

Generally, this calculation is done for all medicines in all the standard treatment regimens; however, the formula may not be appropriate for all formulations, such as in pediatric solutions, because patients may receive an entire bottle rather than the exact volume needed for a treatment course. Using the average consumption over the course of treatment (or monthly, for chronic conditions) may be more accurate. Similarly, for conjunctivitis in Table 20-4, the basic unit used in the treatment is one tube of eye ointment, but one dose would not comprise one tube—a tube should last throughout the course of treatment.

If different treatment regimens (perhaps with multiple medicines) are used for the same disease according to its severity, separate standard regimens must be considered and assigned for each. This situation is illustrated by the malaria treatment guidelines in Table 20-4, which include two levels of severity. Patients who are categorized as severity 2 could have started on this regimen directly or have been put on this regimen after first-line treatment failed.

For each regimen, the proportion of patients with each disease who will be treated with each different therapy is estimated. From Table 20-4, in patients over five years old with gastritis, 70 percent are expected to be treated with antacid and 30 percent with cimetidine. In some situations, depending on treatment practices, allocating 70 percent for antacid and 50 for cimetidine (because some patients will receive both medicines) might be appropriate. Thus, the cumulative percentage may exceed 100 percent for a particular health problem.

If major differences exist in the way that health conditions are treated by different level and/or prescribers, estimating how many (or what percentage of) treatment episodes of each disease will be managed by each category of prescriber may be useful; then specify separate treatment regimens common for each prescriber category.

Practitioners involved in developing standard treatment guidelines for quantification should understand that the guidelines are for quantification only and that a prescriber's freedom will not necessarily be curtailed as a result. In one West African country, a committee was formed to develop standard treatment guidelines for quantification, with the assistance of an outside expert. The committee met but decided that standard treatment guidelines would restrict doctors' freedom to choose a therapy and instead produced a simple therapeutics manual. When the external quantification team arrived in the country, no lists had been produced of common diseases with guidelines for quantification, and the process ultimately failed to produce a useful list for procurement.

Step 4. Collect morbidity data for each health problem treated. This step estimates the expected number of treatment episodes for each health problem from step 1. A treatment episode is "a patient contact for which a standard course of drug treatment is required" (WHO/DAP 1988, Module 6, Section 1). Table 20-4 shows one way of organizing morbidity data for the health problems from step 1 and estimating the number of treatment episodes.

Information from the regular health information system on morbidity patterns and treatment episodes can be used for quantification. In many cases, however, this information is not available, and a special study is needed in sentinel facilities, from which data can then (with caution) be extrapolated. The study can take two forms: a retrospective review of records in selected facilities (if those records are relatively accessible, complete, and accurate), or a prospective study in a sample of health facilities. The study must be completed before actually starting the quantification. Some key issues in conducting these studies include—

- Both the number of contacts and the number of treatment episodes must be obtained in the study of sample facilities. In new programs or during scale-up, treatment episodes could take the form of target treatment figures, rather than historical figures from actual patients.
- Only patient contacts that normally result in pharmaceutical treatment should be counted, separate from those that do not (such as well-child programs).
- The sample data should specify the frequency of each health problem in terms of a common denominator, such as 1,000 inpatients or 1,000 outpatient visits (for

example, number of acute diarrhea cases per 1,000 outpatient contacts). The health problem data can also be presented as a percentage of the population (cases out of 100); for example, 20 percent of child visits are for diarrhea.

- Separate frequencies must be developed for all age groups specified in the standard treatment guidelines. Table 20-4 shows one format for doing so.
- Separating curative from noncurative contacts may not be possible in a retrospective review of records. Even for curative contacts, not all patients who come to facilities with health problems receive pharmaceutical therapy (although the vast majority does if medicines are in stock). If this factor is thought to be important, the proportion of cases that will be treated with pharmaceuticals can be estimated.
- Also, some health problems will require short-term treatment, while others, such as HIV/AIDS, will require lifelong ART, which makes distinguishing between acute and chronic treatments important.
- If discrete types of prescribers (such as doctors compared with paramedical staff) use different treatment regimens, the number of treatment episodes must be compiled separately for each prescriber type.
- The sample data should also specify the number of patient contacts per total population in the area served by the sample facilities. For example, if the total population in the sample area was 3.9 million, and 3,123,408 patient contacts took place per year (as in Table 20-4), on average 0.8 patient contacts occurred per inhabitant. This average could be used to project the number of contacts in another area, as described in Section 20.6 on the proxy consumption method.

Estimating Drug Requirements (WHO/DAP 1988) provides guidelines for surveying health facility records, doing a prospective study of morbidity, and constructing morbidity projections. Chapter 28 of this manual provides guidance for studying medicine use in health facilities.

Step 5. Calculate the number of treatment episodes for each health problem. Two options exist for calculating the number of treatment episodes. If the number of expected patient contacts (outpatient contacts, inpatient admissions, or both) can be estimated directly in the target facilities, the calculations are done in one step based on the number of contacts. If the information on contacts is not reliable, it must be estimated from the population in the area served and the frequency of contacts per inhabitant in the target population.

First, the number of treatment episodes must be adjusted for expected changes in patient use. In Table 20-4, the 3,123,408 contacts from the previous year are separated into two categories: under five years of age and over five years of age. A 5 percent increase is expected (A_U). Therefore, the

estimated number of treatment episodes for each age group and each health problem is multiplied by 1.05.

$$C_E = C + (C \times A_U)$$
$$C_E = 3,123,408 \times 1.05$$

Next, multiply the expected total number of contacts (C_E) by the expected frequency of the problem (F) to obtain the number of treatment episodes (E_T) based on the previous year's data. The estimated total number of patient contacts for the past year is divided by 1,000, so that the denominators of contacts and treatment frequency are the same. (The frequency of treatment episodes is usually expressed in treatment episodes per 1,000 contacts.) This calculation must be done separately for each discrete age range used in the process. If multiple levels of treatment are used, the number of treatment episodes at each level must also be estimated—

$$E_T = C_E \times F$$

In the Table 20-4 example, there were 3,279,578 expected contacts, and in the past year there were 364 episodes of malaria per 1,000 patients under five years old. Therefore, the calculation is—

$$E_T = 3,279,578 \times 364 \div 1,000$$

Step 6. Calculate the quantity of medicines needed for each health problem. For each health problem, the projected number of treatment episodes from step 5 (E_T) is multiplied by the quantity of basic units (Q_E) specified in the guidelines for each age group (and each level of disease severity from step 3). This result is then multiplied by the percentage of cases that are expected to be treated (P_T). The full formula is—

$$Q_T = E_T \times Q_E \times P_T$$

In Table 20-4, 80 percent of patients under age five with malaria, severity level 1, are expected to be treated with paracetamol solution. Therefore, the calculation is—

$$Q_T = 1,193,767 \times 60 \text{ mL} \times 0.8$$

This calculation yields a total of 57,300,816 mL needed for this treatment regimen.

Step 7. Combine the estimates for each medicine from the various health problems into a master procurement list. This step combines the estimated quantities from different treatment regimens into one master list for procurement. For example, in Table 20-4, paracetamol solution is included in four different treatment guidelines (malaria severity 1 and severity 2, otitis media, and tonsillitis). For the master procurement list, the four separate estimated quantities must be added to yield the total number of milliliters of paracetamol needed. Master list quantities usually then need to be adjusted to cover factors such as health problems not considered in the basic estimates, shortages in the supply pipeline, and losses caused by theft and wastage.

Step 8. Adjust quantities to cover other health problems. The reliability of morbidity-based quantification increases as the number of health problems addressed increases, but getting reliable data or estimates for all major health problems is rarely feasible. In this situation, the morbidity-based quantification cannot predict total pharmaceutical needs, and medicine needs must be adjusted to cover health problems not addressed in the quantification. Otherwise, stockouts will occur.

Because reliable consumption data from the target system are not available for comparison (or that method would probably have been used for the quantification), the proxy consumption method described in Section 20.6, or "expert opinion," may be used to estimate what percentage adjustment should be made to the morbidity-based estimates.

If data on medicine use are available from another similar health system, extrapolating requirements for twenty or thirty commonly used medicines might be possible, and then determining the average percentage difference between the estimates produced by each method. For example, if the extrapolated method produces estimates that average 10 percent higher than those produced by the morbidity method, the quantities of all medicines could be increased by 10 percent.

An alternative is surveying local experts to determine what percentage of overall patient contacts have been captured in the list of health problems used for morbidity quantification. For example, if local experts agree that about 90 percent of the medicine needs are covered in the standard treatments, estimated quantities could again be increased by 10 percent.

Step 9. Adjust for filling the pipeline and current stock position. So far, the calculations assume that the supply pipeline (see Section 20.3) is relatively intact and that the procurement is only replacing medicines that are being consumed. If major stockouts have occurred that need to be corrected, additional stock will be necessary to fill the pipeline.

If applicable, make adjustments for stock on hand, stock on order, lead time, and safety stock as described in the consumption method (see Section 20.4, step 6) to finalize the preliminary estimates. Because no average monthly consumption data are available to calculate lead time and safety stock, estimate the projected monthly consumption by dividing the total quantity required by the number of months it is to be used. This estimate could be plugged into the formula used to determine safety stock and lead time in the consumption method.

Step 10. Adjust quantities for expected losses. This procedure is discussed in Section 20.3. In most supply systems, losses are a reality, and unless they are considered in the quantification process, stockouts will be unavoidable.

Step 11. Estimate costs for each medicine and total costs. With adjustments made to cover needs for additional health problems, losses, and filling the pipeline (if necessary), the total estimated quantity can be divided by the purchase pack size to determine the number of packs to be ordered. For example, in Table 20-4, 23,612,964 mL of penicillin VK solution are the estimated need. If this medicine is produced in 100 mL bottles, 236,130 bottles should be ordered.

If the basic unit price is used as the basic estimate of cost, multiply it by the expected package size to determine the expected package price. If the available prices are based on package price, enter it directly.

To calculate the estimated procurement value, multiply the expected pack price by the estimated number of packages to be purchased. The prices used in the estimate should be the expected next purchase price, not the last purchase price (see Section 20.3).

Step 12. Compare total costs with budget and make adjustments. Reduce the estimated quantities or the number of medicines or both to conform to budget realities, if necessary. The morbidity-based method lends itself to considering the relative therapeutic value of pharmaceuticals on the list. In the example illustrated by Table 20-4, one might determine that because pseudoephedrine has not proved to be useful in otitis media, the percentages allotted for this medicine could be reduced. The important point is that when reductions are required, they should be made rationally, with the goal of maximizing the therapeutic benefit of expenditures.

20.6 Proxy consumption method

Many supply systems face a severe information deficit, which limits accurate quantification. When neither consumption nor morbidity methods are feasible, the best option is extrapolating from consumption data from another region or health system. The proxy consumption method uses known consumption data from one system, called the standard, to estimate the medicine needs in a similar or expanded system, known as the target.

This method can be population based, defining medicine use per 1,000 population, or service based, defining medicine use per specified patient case, inpatient admission, or rural health center. A complete quantification may use a combination of the two methods, with different denominators for different products.

Table 20-5　Proxy consumption

Pharmaceutical product	Strength	Basic unit	Standard system consumption: 50,000 inhabitants, 32,500 outpatient contacts						Target system extrapolation: 80,000 inhabitants, unknown outpatient contacts				
			Total usage in 6-month period (BU)	Days out of stock	Adjusted average monthly usage (BU)	Adjusted annual usage (BU)	Usage per 1,000 inhabitants	Usage per 1,000 outpatient contacts	Projected requirements in BUs based on 80,000 inhabitants	Pack size	Order quantity (packs)	Probable pack price (USD)	Value of proposed order (USD)
Ampicillin	500 mg	Capsule	59,500	0	9,917	119,000	2,380	3,662	190,400	1,000	191	46.50	8,881.50
Ampicillin	250 mg	Capsule	89,000	34	18,218	218,617	4,372	6,727	349,788	1,000	350	24.70	8,645.00
Ampicillin suspension 100 mL	125 mg/5 mL	Bottle	4,128	0	688	8,256	165	254	13,210	1	13,210	0.57	7,529.70
Antihistamine decongestant elixir 250 mL	—	Bottle	853	29	169	2,027	41	62	3,244	1	3,244	1.57	5,093.08
Bacitracin antibiotic ointment	—	Tube	2,414	31	484	5,813	116	179	9,300	1	9,301	0.54	5,022.54
Bendrofluazide	5 mg	Tablet	141,500	30	28,208	338,490	6,770	10,415	541,584	500	1,084	4.60	4,986.40
Benzathine benzyl-penicillin injection	2.4 MU	Ampoule	1,318	0	220	2,636	53	81	4,218	50	85	25.00	2,125.00
Chlorpropamide	250 mg	Tablet	162,000	0	27,000	324,000	6,480	9,969	518,400	1,000	519	27.90	14,480.10
Cimetidine	400 mg	Tablet	24,000	0	4,000	48,000	960	1,477	76,800	1,000	77	17.90	1,378.30
Co-trimoxazole	400/80 mg	Tablet	81,000	0	13,500	162,000	3,240	4,985	259,200	1,000	260	21.00	5,460.00
Erythromycin	250 mg	Tablet	80,500	0	13,417	161,000	3,220	4,954	257,600	500	516	14.50	7,482.00
Ferrous salt/folic acid	200/.04 mg	Tablet	353,000	0	58,833	706,000	14,120	21,723	1,129,600	1,000	1,130	2.30	2,599.00
Fluphenazine decanoate injection 10 mL	25 mg/mL	Vial	324	0	54	648	13	20	1,037	1	1,037	8.63	8,949.31
Indomethacin	25 mg	Capsule	167,000	0	27,833	334,000	6,680	10,277	534,400	1,000	535	3.30	1,765.50
Insulin lente	100 IU/mL	Vial	4,504	0	751	9,008	180	277	14,413	1	14,413	3.91	56,354.83
Methyldopa	500 mg	Tablet	191,000	32	38,579	462,954	9,259	14,245	740,726	500	1,482	30.00	44,460.00
Nystatin skin cream 30 g	100,000 IU	Tube	1,815	0	303	3,630	73	112	5,808	1	5,808	0.67	3,891.36
Oral rehydration salts	—	Sachet	6,820	0	1,137	13,640	273	420	21,824	1	21,824	0.06	1,309.44
Paracetamol elixir 150 mL	120 mg/5 mL	Bottle	2,934	0	489	5,868	117	181	9,389	1	9,389	0.65	6,102.85
Paracetamol	500 mg	Tablet	319,000	0	53,167	638,000	12,760	19,631	1,020,800	1,000	1,021	3.90	3,981.90
Penicillin VK suspension 100 mL	125 mg/5 mL	Bottle	1,447	0	241	2,894	58	89	4,630	1	4,631	0.71	3,288.01
Salbutamol liquid 150 mL	2 mg/5 mL	Bottle	1,063	0	177	2,126	43	65	3,402	1	3,402	0.83	2,823.66
Tetracycline HCl	250 mg	Capsule	62,000	0	10,333	124,000	2,480	3,815	198,400	1,000	199	12.00	2,388.00
Vitamins, multiple	—	Tablet	259,000	0	43,167	518,000	10,360	15,938	828,800	1,000	829	3.80	3,150.20
												Total order cost:	212,147.68

Note: BU = basic unit; USD = U.S. dollars; MU = mega-unit; IU = international unit.

Example

Table 20-5 illustrates the proxy consumption method of extrapolating consumption of outpatient pharmaceuticals from a standard health system to the target health system. The data in Table 20-5 do not represent any particular country.

Steps in the quantification

Step 1. Select the standard system for comparison and extrapolation. The standard facilities should, if feasible, closely resemble the region or country for which the estimate is made in terms of geography and climate, patient population served, morbidity patterns, prescribing practices, standard treatment guidelines, essential medicines lists, and pharmaceutical supply status. Representative standard facilities should be selected at each level of health care that has a different medicines list, morbidity patterns, or prescribing practices. They should have an adequate and uninterrupted pharmaceutical supply (but not greatly overstocked), fairly rational prescribing practices, and complete and accurate records of patient contacts and pharmaceutical inventory movement. Of course, finding an ideal standard may not be possible, but an effort should be made to select the best standard data available.

Step 2. Develop the medicines list. See Section 20.3 for a discussion of issues.

Step 3. Establish the period to be covered in review. Determine the number of months' worth of data to be reviewed in the standard system. See Section 20.4 for a discussion of these issues.

Step 4. Review records from the standard system to compile contact or population data. Use available reports on patient contacts in the standard system; if reports with suitable data are not already compiled, a survey of standard facilities can be done to determine the number of patient contacts during the period established. A similar survey might be carried out in the target system, but if the target system has had a severe problem with stockouts, the attendance data may not reflect the number of contacts that can be expected when medicines are available.

Step 5. Establish the denominator for extrapolation. The denominator used to extrapolate consumption can be either population in the area served or number of patient contacts, depending on the data obtainable through step 4. Whichever one is used, the denominator is usually thousands of patient contacts or thousands of inhabitants in the region (as in Table 20-5). In very large systems, using tens of thousands or even millions of contacts or inhabitants might be preferable.

Step 6. Determine the consumption rate in the standard system. For each medicine, produce an adjusted average monthly consumption (see Section 20.4). The average monthly consumption is multiplied by twelve to obtain the adjusted annual consumption (or by the applicable number of months for any other period that was determined in step 3). Then divide the adjusted annual consumption by the number of thousands of contacts or inhabitants to establish the consumption rate.

Step 7. Extrapolate the standard system's consumption rate to the target system. Multiply the standard consumption rate for each medicine by the estimated number of thousands of contacts or inhabitants in the target system to yield the projected requirements in the target system.

Step 8. Adjust for expected losses. Because these estimates are very rough and the percentages of losses that were experienced in the standard system may be unclear, adjusting for losses may not be realistic. However, if known losses exist, add a percentage allowance, at least for vital medicines (see Section 20.3).

Step 9. Estimate costs for each medicine and total costs and make adjustments. Multiply the projected quantities for each medicine by the most accurate prediction of the next procurement cost and reconcile that product with available funds, as discussed in Section 20.3.

20.7 Service-level projection of budget requirements

This method is used to estimate financial requirements, not specific medicine quantities, for pharmaceutical procurement on the basis of costs per patient treated at various levels of the same health system or, with great caution, data from other health systems. It does not forecast needs for specific medicines but provides a clear, logical, one-page justification of pharmaceutical financing requirements. Generalizing from one region in a country to another region in the same country is more reliable than extrapolating data to a different country.

Like the proxy consumption method, this extrapolation method produces rough estimates because significant, but not always apparent, variations may exist between the target health system and the system used as a source of standard data. Possible sources of error include prescribers in the target system using a different mix of medicines from those in the source system, variability in disease frequency and the number of patient attendances per facility, and differences in the effectiveness of procurement and financial management systems in the two settings.

The main requirement for this method is a fairly reliable estimate of average medicine cost per patient attendance and average numbers of patient attendances at various levels of the standard health system. This information may not be readily available, but it can be compiled through a special study in one part of a health system where pharmaceutical

Table 20-6   Service-based budgeting of essential medicines requirements

Type of facility and patient (1)	Number of facilities (2)	Average annual workload per facility (3)	Average cost per attendance or bed-day from sample facilities (USD) (4)	Annual pharmaceutical needs (USD) (5)
Provincial general hospitals	13			
Inpatients		176,000 bed-days	0.55	1,258,400
General outpatients[a]		195,000 attendances	0.55	1,394,250
Prenatal patients		19,500 attendances	0.15	38,025
District hospitals	42			
Inpatients		57,000 bed-days	0.50	1,197,000
General outpatients		85,000 attendances	0.50	1,785,000
Prenatal patients		11,000 attendances	0.15	69,300
Subdistrict hospitals	35			
Inpatients		21,500 bed-days	0.45	338,625
General outpatients		60,000 attendances	0.50	1,050,000
Prenatal patients		7,500 attendances	0.15	39,375
Rural health training centers	38			
Inpatients		20,000 bed-days	0.40	304,000
General outpatients		40,000 attendances	0.45	684,000
Prenatal patients		5,000 attendances	0.15	28,500
Health centers	315			
Inpatients		1,500 bed-days	0.20	94,500
General outpatients		32,000 attendances	0.40	4,032,000
Prenatal patients		4,000 attendances	0.15	189,000
Dispensaries	1,114			
General outpatients		18,000 attendances	0.30	6,015,600
Subtotals				
Provincial general hospitals				2,690,675
District and subdistrict hospitals				4,479,300
Rural health training centers				1,016,500
Health centers and dispensaries				10,331,100
Total				18,517,575
Per capita requirement				0.686

Source: Adapted from Ministry of Health, Government of Kenya. 1992. Workload-Based Annual Budget for Pharmaceuticals and Non-Pharmaceuticals.
Note: USD = U.S. dollars. The exchange rate used is Kenya shillings 60 to USD 1. Population equals 27 million (estimate for 1993).
[a] This category includes (for all levels) adult and pediatric general outpatients, casualty, and specialty clinics.

supplies are consistent and where treatment practices are considered to be representative. The following data must be compiled—

- The average number of curative and noncurative outpatient attendances and inpatient bed-days and/or other type of patient contact for each type of facility in the source health system
- The average cost per outpatient curative and noncurative attendance and per bed-day and/or other type of patient contact in each type of facility in the source health system

Example

Table 20-6 shows the method applied to estimate financial requirements for pharmaceutical procurement in Kenya.

Steps in the quantification

Step 1. Establish the categories of facilities and determine the number in each category. List each type of facility to be quantified for in the first column. The number of facility categories used depends on the size and scope of the target health system. Table 20-6 shows six significant levels, ranging from provincial general hospitals to dispensaries (see column 1). The number of facilities in each category is entered in the second column.

Step 2. Determine the patient contact denominators for each type of facility, and compile or estimate the average number of patient contacts of each type at each category of facility. These data can be obtained from centrally available information or from a special-purpose survey to determine the average number of patient contacts for each category of facility. For each category, several different types of patient contact may result in pharmaceutical costs. Minimally, inpatient and outpatient costs and contacts should be separated.

In the example in Table 20-6 (column 3), in all but the lowest-level facility (dispensaries) contacts were separated into three types: inpatient, with bed-days as the common denominator; and general outpatient and prenatal visits, each with attendances as the denominator.

Step 3. Calculate the average cost per contact. The average cost per attendance and/or bed-day is derived by dividing the total pharmaceutical purchases for the sample facility or facilities that are providing the source of data for extrapolation in the class by the total attendances or bed-days. In facilities with both inpatients and outpatients, the fraction of total procurement costs attributable to inpatients, outpatients, and noncurative visits must be estimated. Column 4 in Table 20-6 shows the average cost data based on the source data from the sample facilities.

Step 4. Calculate the total projected pharmaceutical costs. Multiply the average number of patient contacts for each facility (column 3 in Table 20-6) by the number of facilities (column 2). This result is then multiplied by the average pharmaceutical cost for that type of patient in that type of facility (column 4), which estimates total financial requirements for each type of attendance in each type of facility (column 5). These totals are then summed to produce the total financial requirements. The result is an estimate of the probable pharmaceutical costs, on average, for each type of facility and for the system as a whole. The results are not necessarily applicable to any specific facility. ∎

References and further readings

★ = Key readings.

Allers, C., and Y. Chandani. 2006. *Guide for Quantifying ARV Drugs.* Arlington, Va.: DELIVER for the U.S. Agency for International Development. <http://pdf.usaid.gov/pdf_docs/PNADG486.pdf>

Chandani, Y., L. Teclemariam, D. Alt, C. Allers, and L. Lyons. 2006. *Guide for Quantifying HIV Test Kits.* Arlington, Va.: DELIVER, for the U.S. Agency for International Development. <http://pdf.usaid.gov/pdf_docs/PNADG490.pdf>

Hogerzeil, H. V. 1986. Estimating Drug Requirements: Standardized Supply of Essential Drugs in Ghana. *Tropical Doctor* 16:155–59.

MSH (Management Sciences for Health). 2010. *International Drug Price Indicator Guide.* (Updated annually.) Cambridge, Mass.: MSH. <http://erc.msh.org>

MSH/RPM Plus (Management Sciences for Heatlh/Rational Pharmaceutical Management Plus Program). 2008. *A Commodity and Management Planning Guide for the Scale-Up of HIV Counseling and Testing Services.* Arlington, Va.: MSH/RPM Plus. <http://www.msh.org/projects/rpmplus/Documents/upload/HIV-Testing-Commodity-Guide-VCT_final.pdf>

———. 2006. *Quantimed User's Guide,* Version 1.2. Arlington, Va.: MSH/RPM Plus. <http://www.msh.org/projects/rpmplus/Documents/upload/Quantimed_English_Final.pdf>

MSH/SPS Program (Management Sciences for Health/Strengthening Pharmaceutical Systems Program). No date. Electronic Dispensing Tool. <http://www.msh.org/projects/sps/SPS-Documents/upload/edt_flyer_english.pdf>

Osore, H. 1989. Estimating Drug Requirements Using Morbidity Data-Based Method: Cumulative Country Experience. *Tropical Doctor* 19:90–94.

Soeters, R., and W. Bannenberg. 2009. *The Selection and Use of Essential Medicines: Report of the WHO Expert Committee, March 2009.* Geneva: WHO. <http://whqlibdoc.who.int/trs/WHO_TRS_958_eng.pdf>

———. 1988. Computerized Calculation of Essential Drug Requirements. *Social Science and Medicine* 27:955–70.

★ WHO/DAP (World Health Organization/Action Programme on Essential Drugs). 1988. *Estimating Drug Requirements: A Practical Manual.* Geneva: WHO/DAP. <http://whqlibdoc.who.int/hq/1988/WHO_DAP_88.2.pdf>

ASSESSMENT GUIDE

Availability of data

- Do the medical stores and health facilities have current and accurate records of medicine usage?
- What data and reports are maintained centrally (or at other levels of the health system) on outpatient attendances, inpatient bed-days, or other counts of patient contacts?
- For how many diseases does reliable information exist on numbers of cases reported or treated annually?
- Are there official standard treatment guidelines for certain diseases? If so, how many diseases are covered, and how is compliance monitored?

Management of quantification

- Do a formal workplan and schedule for quantification exist?
- Does a quantification committee exist with representatives from health facilities (prescribers and pharmacy staff), government (heads of special disease programs and health information systems staff), central medical store (or other group handling pharmaceutical distribution), and donors?
- Is quantification done manually or by computer? If computers are used, which offices have computers, and what software program is used for quantification? Which levels of warehouses and facilities have computerized procurement and inventory records?

- Is quantification decentralized or managed centrally? Which offices and levels of the system are responsible for quantification?
- If quantification is decentralized, what training is or has been provided to responsible staff members at peripheral facilities?
- Are preprinted quantification and/or data-collection forms distributed to the facilities?

Quantification methods

- What quantification methods are used to forecast pharmaceutical and budget needs?
- Are actual procurement quantities and costs compared at the end of each year against the initial quantification estimates?
- Is the supply system pipeline functioning well, or have pharmaceutical shortages been frequent or widespread? If shortages have occurred, do only certain medicines present problems, or do shortages exist for many different medicines?
- What information is used to predict procurement costs? If last year's prices are used, how are they adjusted?
- What standard formulas are used to calculate order quantities?
- Is there an essential medicines list or health system medicine formulary that is used for quantification? Is procurement limited to medicines on the list?
- What techniques are used to adjust initial estimates to conform to budget realities?

CHAPTER 21

Managing the tender process

SUMMARY

The primary function of a procurement office is to obtain the required items at the right time, in the correct quantities, and at the most favorable prices. The procurement office compiles a list of requirements, identifies potential suppliers, selects the most cost-effective supplier for each product, secures firm supply contracts, and makes sure that the suppliers and the health system comply with contract terms. Competitive tenders are recommended for most pharmaceutical procurement in public-sector pharmaceutical systems, so this chapter addresses the principles of efficient tender management, focusing on the most common tendering models.

To maximize the benefit of pharmaceutical purchases, corruption and favoritism in procurement must be minimized. Equally important is avoiding the appearance of favoritism, so the tender process should be as transparent as possible under national procurement laws.

A formal tender process includes medicine selection, quantification, preparation of tender documents and contracts, notification and invitation to bid, formal bid opening, collation of offers, adjudication and supplier selection, contract award, performance monitoring of suppliers and clients, and enforcement of contract terms if necessary. Reliable suppliers are the cornerstone of effective procurement, and a prequalification process is recommended; tender adjudication and selection of suppliers is the critical step that determines the costs of medicines and defines the integrity of the procurement process. Adjudication should be based on formal written criteria and must be free from influence by special interests.

Accurate and timely information is critical at each stage of the process, and lack of effective information systems is a main cause of procurement delays and inefficiencies. The information system must be able to—

- Produce information for quantification and tender documents
- Collate offers for adjudication
- Issue notifications of award and purchase orders
- Track order status and compliance with contract terms
- Manage communications with contract suppliers
- Track suppliers' performance for future tenders

21.1 Introduction to tender management

Many of the major policy and management issues relevant to pharmaceutical procurement were covered in Chapter 18. Several types of procurement methods are used for pharmaceuticals, but the procurement method chosen for each medicine should—

- Obtain the lowest possible purchase price for high-quality products
- Ensure suppliers' reliability, in terms of both quality and service
- Maintain transparency in the process and minimize the opportunity for illicit influences on procurement decisions
- Achieve these objectives with the least possible professional and clerical staff time and within the shortest possible lead time

Table 21-1 summarizes the most frequently used methods to purchase pharmaceuticals.

This chapter focuses on the management of competitive tenders. Some global procurement mechanisms, such as the United Nations Children's Fund (UNICEF), the Supply Chain Management System, and the Global Fund's voluntary pooled procurement system, use negotiation as a primary tactic to establish contracts on high-use and high-cost items; as discussed in Chapter 18, these large procurement systems need to ensure multiple source options to assure steady supply and to be certain that multiple suppliers stay in the particular market. However, most modern laws and regulations covering public-sector procurement require competitive procurement methods. Negotiation can be legitimate when only a few suppliers are available for a particular product, but negotiation is not generally recommended when using public funds.

Country Study 21-1 shows how El Salvador lowered costs by making its tendering process more efficient.

This chapter discusses the best practices in managing the standard tender processes used to purchase pharmaceuticals. Historically, the tender process has been an annual cycle in most public-sector health systems. In some situations, tenders are conducted two or three times per year; however, some procurement offices have begun entering into multiyear framework contracts to reduce the administrative burden of managing frequent tender cycles. Global procurement systems such as UNICEF and USAID's Supply Chain Management System also use these sorts of framework contracts for selected products.

As discussed in Chapter 18, Internet-based approaches, including "e-procurement" with "reverse auctions," have been advocated for public-sector procurement, with the most experience occurring in Latin America. These methods, however, have not yet been proven for pharmaceutical procurement.

The standard steps in the normal tender cycle are—

1. Determine the tender format and scope.
2. Define requirements—select and quantify medicines and supplies.
3. Select suppliers to participate in the tender.
4. Prepare and send tender documents.
5. Receive and open offers.
6. Collate offers for adjudication.
7. Adjudicate the tender.
8. Issue contracts to winning bidders.
9. Monitor performance and product quality.
10. Enforce contract terms as needed.

Each of these steps requires informed decisions about which of several possible procedures best fits the particular situation. In most countries, options will be limited by procurement laws and regulations, but even in the most restrictive legal settings, the procurement program has several choices to make. The goal of this chapter is to provide

information to help procurement managers make the best choices for their own situations.

21.2 Determining the tender format and scope

Some countries have procurement regulations that specify the tender format for pharmaceutical purchasing. The World Bank and some bilateral donors may mandate specific tender formats for procurement financed by loans or donated funds (see References and Further Readings). However, in many cases, flexibility exists in structuring the tender; in those situations, options include—

- Restricted versus open tender
- Local or international scope
- Estimated or fixed tender quantities
- Split or single tender awards
- Primary/secondary contracts or rebids
- Required or optional use of local agents in international tenders
- Annual or biannual tenders versus multiple tenders during the year

Table 21-1   Comparison of procurement methods

Procurement method	Brief description	Effect on price	Procurement lead time	Workload for procurement office	Need for evaluating suppliers	Conditions favoring use
Open tender	Bidding is open for all interested suppliers	Usually lowest prices	Moderate to long	High	High	• When many reputable suppliers are available and likely to be interested • If prequalification is not feasible or not allowed by regulation or donor's provisions
Restricted tender	Participation of suppliers is limited to those who have registered with the government or who have prequalified	Favorable	Moderate to long	High	High	• When substantial list of registered suppliers has been developed • When capacity exists to manage prequalification and supplier monitoring
Competitive negotiation	The buyer approaches a small number of potential suppliers and negotiates for specific price or service arrangements	Can be favorable	Short to moderate	Moderate	High	• Experienced purchasing office with good access to market intelligence • Low-price or small-volume items • When there are few suppliers • When special terms or specifications are required by the buyer for items not widely available • Emergency purchases to supplement tender
Direct procurement	Purchase is made directly from a single supplier at the quoted price	Usually highest prices	Short to moderate	Low	High	• Emergency purchases when negotiation is not possible • Purchase of single-source pharmaceuticals • Low-price or small-volume items

> ### Country Study 21-1
> ### El Salvador: Improving efficiency through joint tendering
>
> In El Salvador, the Strategies for Enhancing Access to Medicines (SEAM) Program's 2001 assessment found that some essential medications were lacking in both public health care facilities and those of nongovernmental organizations (NGOs). At the Ministry of Public Health and Social Welfare (MSPAS, from its initials in Spanish), purchasing had been decentralized, decreasing the ability to negotiate prices for pharmaceuticals in large volumes and providing little management capacity for inventory management. Although the NGO sector was small, these organizations provided services in rural areas that did not have access to MSPAS services. Because they bought small volumes, the NGOs could not negotiate favorable prices for their medicines, which limited the availability of essential medicines.
>
> On the basis of the SEAM assessment and recommendations, MSPAS authorities developed a pharmaceutical procurement system based on joint tendering for medicines from the national Essential Medicines List to select products, their suppliers, and unit prices for the thirty hospitals and 362 public and NGO health units.
>
> From late 2002 to 2005, MSPAS held three joint tender processes. The 2003 purchases resulted in a lower number of tenders, a 45 percent decrease in the median unit prices for the medicines, and greater efficiency in spending on medications and use of the budget appropriation.
>
> The three-year experience showed that a joint bidding program based on the national Essential Medicines List could be implemented, and the following lessons were learned—
>
> - The active participation of hospitals in the program's design contributed to its acceptance and to ensuring transparency in the evaluation of tender bids.
> - Joint tendering within the network of public hospitals resulted in greater efficiency in spending on medications, a reduction in the number of tender processes, and improved quality assurance of medicines.
> - To optimize the benefits of joint purchasing, an effective logistics system must accompany it.

Restricted or open tender

One of the most important decisions to make is whether the tender will be restricted to suppliers who are prequalified because they have demonstrated reliability, or whether the tender will be open to any supplier who is interested. This decision is required whether the tender is local or international.

A restricted tender with *prequalification* involves developing a list of registered suppliers based on past performance, references from previous clients, and documentation of product quality. Then, only those registered suppliers may participate in tenders. This process avoids the necessity of trying to decide whether the lowest bidder is eligible to be awarded the contract. With prequalification, by definition, the lowest bidder should be qualified for the contract.

When prequalification works well, substandard suppliers are kept out of the tender process entirely. Prequalification is not beneficial, however, if it protects favored suppliers from competition. In some countries, a new supplier finds surviving the prequalification process virtually impossible, no matter how reliable the new supplier may actually be.

Prequalification can be extremely time-consuming, especially if policy requires that suppliers be prequalified separately for each medicine. This problem can be mitigated through ABC analysis and prequalifying only high-demand, category A medicines while prequalifying low-demand products by lot (see Chapter 40 for details). As noted below, however, proper postqualification requires just as much time. The policy question is where the time should be allocated in the tender process.

To help countries procure quality pharmaceuticals, the World Health Organization (WHO) operates a prequalification program for HIV/AIDS, tuberculosis, and malaria medicines. See Box 21-1 for more information. Many international donors that provide procurement funding accept WHO prequalification or documentation of a supplier's or product's approval by a so-called stringent regulatory authority as evidence that the supplier is eligible for prequalification in a tender (see Chapter 19).

Although a country's laws may require that a pharmaceutical supplier and its products be registered in the procuring country, procurement managers may wish to follow WHO's international standards for prequalifying potential bidders first and then add a requirement that successful bidders must register their products locally.

An open tender with *postqualification* makes the tender available to all interested bidders. Suppliers' bids and documentation are solicited, received, and reviewed with respect to registration status, product quality, technical and financial capacity, and past performance.

An open tender can arguably increase the pool of prospective suppliers, but complications and delays in postqualification often occur. In addition, a well-managed prequalification process can generate good competition. Pharmaceuticals are unlike some other commodities, in that product quality is both crucial and difficult to ensure. Therefore, the success of open tenders with postqualification depends on the capacity of the procurement program to winnow out unqualified suppliers and poor-quality products after bids have been received, in some cases, from all over the world. The procurement office must go through a process similar to that used in prequalification. The difference is the need to screen many more suppliers and products. Moreover, bids are usually submitted with a time limit on price validity (see Chapter 39). Screening all suppliers and products after bid opening and within the period of price validity may be difficult. In one Indian state, for example, price validity was specified as 180 days, while the contract award typically took twelve to fifteen months (Heltzer et al. 2008). If delays like this occur, prices have to be reconfirmed, and in some cases, rebidding may be needed.

Poorly defined criteria for postqualification can also exclude qualified bidders, especially when the criteria favor developing local industry over assuring medicine quality. Finally, postqualification may be used for fraudulent purposes, if, for example, someone in the procurement agency wants to tilt business toward preferred companies.

Prequalification is generally accepted as an essential procurement practice. The *Interagency Guidelines for Establishing a Model Quality Assurance System* specifically state that prequalification is a key element in ensuring product quality (WHO et al. 2007). Following this lead, many countries have formally incorporated prequalification and restricted tendering into their procurement regulations; for example, Tanzania's Public Procurement and Regulatory Authority has published regulations and bid documents for use in the health sector that explicitly provide for restricted, prequalification-based tendering. Such practices have also been a feature of many successful pharmaceutical procurement programs around the world.

As these arguments make clear, the eventual goal of most procurement programs should be tenders limited to registered, prequalified suppliers. Prequalification avoids wasting time on suppliers that do not perform according to contract and helps minimize the possibility of introducing substandard products. However, aggressively seeking out potential new suppliers that may wish to become registered is important for maintaining competitive pressure on established suppliers.

International versus local procurement

In most developing countries, the national pharmaceutical industry produces only a limited range of products.

Box 21-1
WHO's prequalification program

The World Health Organization set up the Prequalification of Medicines Progamme in 2001 to facilitate access to quality medicines for HIV/AIDS, malaria, and tuberculosis. Originally, the program was intended to give UN procurement agencies, such as UNICEF, a range of quality medicine suppliers from which to choose. Over time, the program has become a useful tool for anyone purchasing medicines on a large scale, including countries themselves. For example, the Global Fund to Fight AIDS, Tuberculosis and Malaria disburses money for medicines that have been prequalified through the WHO process.

Manufacturers applying to the program must present extensive information on their product to allow qualified assessment teams to evaluate its quality, safety, and efficacy. The manufacturer must also open its manufacturing sites to an inspection team that assesses working procedures for compliance with WHO good manufacturing practices. The assessment teams work with regulators from the developing countries where the medicines

will be used to make sure that the process is transparent and trusted by the end users. The program also prequalifies quality-control laboratories.

WHO's prequalification process takes a minimum of three months if the product meets all the required standards. When products do not meet the appropriate standards, the process can be longer and ultimately result in no prequalification for a product. WHO also carries out random quality-control testing of prequalified medicines that have been supplied to countries.

Medicines on the prequalification list include both brand-name and generic products. Since 2001, reproductive health products and zinc (for childhood diarrhea) have been added to the program. Also included are fixed-dose combinations, which are assessed based on the same principles used by the European Agency for the Evaluation of Medicinal Products and the U.S. Food and Drug Administration.

Source: WHO 2010b.

Therefore, most products must be procured via international markets. Nevertheless, countries with a local industry often require that public tenders give it some preference, such as following the World Bank example of granting a 15 percent price preference to locally manufactured products. However, greater price preferences make it difficult to achieve value for money—which is critical when national pharmaceutical budgets are limited. In all cases, the quality assurance requirement must be maintained. A strong national drug regulatory authority uses its product registration process to assure quality.

For many items, an international competitive tender, whether open or restricted, almost always results in lower prices than a tender limited to the local market. For some inexpensive items that cost a lot to ship, such as parenteral solutions, purchasing locally may be cheaper if the manufacturing plant meets acceptable quality standards. Facility licensing through a strong, independent drug regulatory authority is crucial.

In countries with a large pharmaceutical industry, such as India, international tendering is largely unnecessary; however, some countries that have an enormous number of companies licensed to manufacture pharmaceuticals may only have a few that meet international production and quality assurance standards. In such circumstances, establishing sufficiently stringent prequalification criteria to assure product quality while supporting national economic development demands is a challenge. Failure in this difficult balancing act can result in substandard products entering the health system.

One common constraint on international procurement is pharmaceutical registration. Countries with pharmaceutical registration systems normally require that all medicines purchased through public tender be registered locally. Both restricted and open tenders can be limited to products registered in the purchasing country. This requirement may limit or eliminate international procurement if the registration process is complicated and time-consuming, but in most countries, some flexibility is available to assure access to essential medicines.

Some countries expedite or even waive registration for new medicines that are considered vital to public health, such as antiretroviral medicines. In many cases where registration is waived, a donor is financing the purchase and helps make the case for a waiver.

Countries in some regions, particularly Latin America, have attempted to move toward regional harmonization of pharmaceutical registration, with virtually automatic registration granted if the product is either registered within the region or originates from a country recognized as having effective pharmaceutical regulatory systems. In an example of such harmonization, Namibia accepted products already registered in International Conference on Harmonization countries or South Africa to streamline its registration of antiretrovirals. However, regional harmonization generally faces many barriers, including concerns that products from the region's stronger economies could have an unfair advantage.

In sum, much has been debated about regional harmonization, but the discussions have not advanced very far. Time will determine whether meaningful harmonization can be achieved.

Estimated- versus fixed-quantity contract

Two basic options exist for defining purchase quantity: the traditional *fixed-quantity, scheduled-delivery* purchasing contract, and the *estimated-quantity, periodic-order* contract.

The *fixed-quantity contract* specifies guaranteed quantities (with a small variation sometimes allowed) and delivery in either one large shipment or smaller, separate shipments over the life of the contract. The purchaser accepts the risk that quantities for specific items may be too high (resulting in overstocks) or too low (resulting in shortages). If the purchaser actually needs more than the projected quantity (plus permitted variation), the price may be adjusted for additional quantities, depending on the contract.

With the second type of contract—the *estimated-quantity, periodic-order (draw-down) system*—the tender quantity is just an estimate rather than a firm order. A contract price is negotiated for each medicine, and the purchaser or members of the purchasing group order periodically from contract suppliers at the contract price throughout the contract term. In a pooled procurement system, orders can be placed directly by group members or channeled to the supplier through a central procurement office. Purchasers order only the quantities of each item needed, regardless of the quantity stipulated in the original tender estimate.

The supplier delivers to purchasers at the contract price throughout the term of the contract, regardless of the variation between projected and actual total quantity purchased under the contract. The supplier takes the risk that actual quantities will differ from those estimated: if the quantities are higher, it is not a problem (assuming the supplier has the necessary capacity), but if purchases are significantly lower than estimates, the supplier may not participate in future tenders. This system benefits the purchaser, because the purchaser's financial liability is limited to each order, and if demand changes, the purchaser is not burdened with unneeded stock or pressed to cover shortages. However, in the interest of maintaining a mutually beneficial relationship with a supplier, the purchaser must make every effort to reliably estimate demand and should communicate any significant changes—either increases or decreases—in projected order quantities.

Pharmaceutical tenders for most developing countries have been made for many years as fixed-quantity, scheduled-delivery tenders, and suppliers serving these procurement programs might be expected to resist the change to estimated-quantity contracts. However, many large-scale procurement programs serving developing countries successfully use the estimated-quantity, drawdown contract.

When the draw-down system is used, prices should be guaranteed for the entire period of the contract. If possible, prices should be negotiated as CIF (cost, insurance, and freight) or CIP (carriage and insurance paid), with no extra charges for freight and insurance (see Chapter 39).

In the 1970s and 1980s, when inflation was a persistent problem around the world, tendering more than once a year or including an escalator clause effective after a certain number of months, based on inflation, was often necessary. Although inflation is no longer a severe problem in most places, circumstances in some countries, such as Yugoslavia in the mid-1990s and Zimbabwe in the 2000s, can warrant adding an inflation factor to tender agreements. In such contexts, a guaranteed-quantity tender or a procurement system policy to make most purchases at the lowest contract price possible (that is, before an escalator clause takes effect) may produce the best results for the health system. Guaranteed access to foreign currency greatly helps to manage procurement in high inflationary situations.

In countries where access to funds and foreign exchange is sporadic and uncertain, tendering on a periodic basis, as funds become available, may be necessary. This procedure almost always requires a fixed-quantity, scheduled-delivery tender format.

Similarly, if most products must be imported and lead times are extremely long, fixed-quantity, scheduled-delivery contracts are best, because the drawdown system requires reasonable access to contract suppliers. This type of contract functions acceptably with lead times of up to four to five months, but it would be difficult to manage where lead times are routinely greater than one year. One option is to limit tender participation to suppliers that can provide shorter lead times (assuming such sources are available). This strategy might produce an overall price increase but could potentially reduce waste. A total cost analysis exercise (described in Chapter 40) would help model the potential impact of such a change.

In some situations, combining the formats might be best: negotiating fixed-quantity contracts for products that can be purchased most cost-effectively in large single quantities and using estimated-quantity contracts for other products.

Splitting tender awards

Some procurement programs routinely split contract awards among two or three suppliers, with the rationale of maintaining capacity with several suppliers or avoiding dependence on one supplier for a critical medicine. However, any health system procurement program that routinely splits tenders is almost certainly not getting the best possible pricing, and the opportunity exists for "bid rigging"—suppliers agreeing beforehand what bids will be offered, with the realization that all will benefit from a share of the pie.

Split tenders may be desirable in some circumstances—for example, when a country is making one huge annual purchase of essential medicines, the risk of supplier default is real, and the public health consequences will be severe if default occurs and the medicines are not available. In addition, large global procurement programs may determine that split awards are needed to modulate the global market and maintain competition and assure access to essential products (Chapter 18).

Primary/secondary contracts versus rebids

When a supplier defaults, delays in receiving medicines have usually already occurred by the time the problem is understood. Rebidding contracts through the entire tender procedure will likely result in stockouts or high-priced emergency purchases, or both. A primary/secondary contract system can avoid rebidding delays by providing an immediate option if the contract winner cannot perform. This sort of system is used by the Organisation of Eastern Caribbean States (OECS) Pharmaceutical Procurement Service and is common to many pharmaceutical purchasing groups.

In a primary/secondary system, two contract awards are made, with the primary award to the bidder offering the lowest price and the secondary award to the second-lowest bidder, provided that the secondary supplier is one that is expected to be able to supply under all conditions. The secondary contract should be used only when the primary supplier is unable to perform.

Primary/secondary awards are useful *only* if two requirements are met: the second-lowest price is reasonably close to the lowest and thus worth locking in, and a reliable secondary supplier is prepared to accept that status and guarantee the price in case the primary supplier defaults. If either condition is not met, a secondary award is not worthwhile.

Some countries have regulations prohibiting these types of contracts, requiring that a new tender be made in the case of default. World Bank international competitive bidding tender procedures call for rebids when a supplier defaults, but some flexibility for local purchasing and local competitive bidding usually exists in such cases.

Use of local agents in international procurement

Multinational manufacturers and exporters are commonly represented by local representatives in developing countries. The decision to require, encourage, or avoid buying through local agents in international tenders affects the range of foreign suppliers, the efficiency of communication between the buyer and the supplier, and the choice of trade and

Box 21-2
Advantages and disadvantages of buying through local agents

Potential advantages

1. *Speeds and improves communication.* Local agents may be authorized to make decisions without a special contact with the foreign supplier. When necessary, the local agent may be better able to contact the appropriate person at the foreign supplier's office.
2. *Locates least-expensive acceptable supplies.* In competitive tenders, the interest of the local agents lies in locating inexpensive suppliers, including sources that might not otherwise have come to the attention of the purchaser.
3. *Facilitates payment.* Local agents can sometimes accept local currency and allow deferred payment. Currency conversions can be troublesome, and some countries specify that payments be made in local currency to local agents.
4. *Expedites delivery.* Local agents often handle port clearing. For instance, when port-clearing fees require negotiation, local agent knowledge and experience can frequently save money and time.
5. *Speeds receipt of emergency supplies.* Local agents often maintain stocks within the country, which speeds receipt of emergency supplies and may reduce the amount of warehouse space required.
6. *Affords greater legal recourse.* The presence of an in-country agent affords greater opportunity for legal action if the supplier defaults.
7. *Introduces new products.* Occasionally, new products or formulations are introduced that are cost-effective alternatives to existing products. The agent is necessarily biased but may provide scientific articles in support of the product. Other information sources

should be sought to supplement the introductory information provided by the agent.
8. *May offer potential for using primary distributor.* In some countries, government warehousing and distribution costs possibly may be eliminated by implementing a prime vendor contract with a local distributor that will warehouse and distribute medicines directly to public health facilities.

Potential disadvantages

1. *May slow and confuse communication.* If untrained, unmotivated, poorly supervised, or part time, a local agent may lengthen and confuse arrangements with the foreign supplier. In addition, if the purchaser requires specific product information, a local agent may impede communication.
2. *May increase cost.* Local agents may add as much as 15 to 30 percent to the visible cost, even though their commission is often much less. Higher unit prices are also paid for low-volume purchases through local agents, compared to direct purchase.
3. *Serves as a source of black-market pharmaceuticals.* Licensed importers can be a major source of pharmaceuticals for illicit use, and local agents need to be regulated through licensure and regular inspection of records and stocks.
4. *May completely default on an order.* Local agents who are not financially stable may go out of business and disappear. Two or three local suppliers should be kept available as backup for emergency tenders.
5. *Attempts to increase medicine consumption.* Local agents employ detail men or company representatives to visit health system physicians to encourage product use, as well as to request new medicines.

---

payment terms. Major advantages and disadvantages of buying through local agents are listed in Box 21-2.

Chapters 8 and 39 further discuss the potential for contracting with local distributors to provide warehousing and transport services.

Tender frequency and timing

Tender planning must take into account the time required for each step. The time required to develop or revise a tender list, including medicine selection and quantification, varies widely, but may require two to six months in some settings. The time required to select suppliers for tender participa-

tion can also be considerable; in one African country, the first prequalification process took more than one year.

If standard documents are not available, preparing documents for tender can take at least a month after quantification is completed. Some countries, such as Tanzania and Uganda, have overcome this problem by developing standard bidding documents. The time spent waiting for tender offers depends on geographic scope (local versus international) and in some cases on regulations of the government or the funding agency. A reasonable response time for local tenders is likely to be fifteen to twenty days, and for international tenders, forty-five to sixty days. Collating offers is quicker with computerized systems, but at least one month

Figure 21-1   Example of a timetable for an annual tendering system

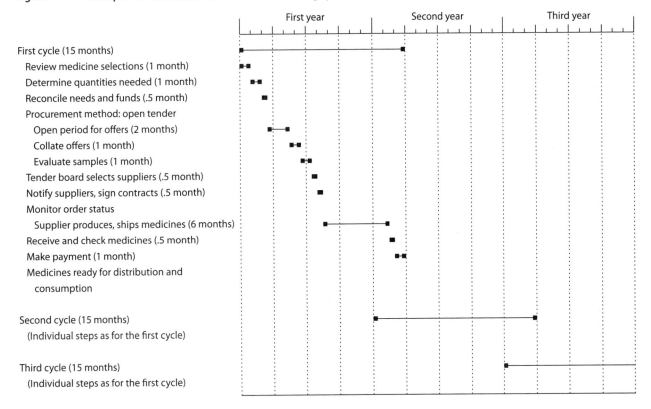

should be allowed for this process. Some online tendering systems capture supplier bids through the procurement agency's Web portal, which can greatly facilitate collection and collation of bids (note that this is not the same process as in e-tendering with reverse auction). Adjudication and contract award should also be faster in computerized systems, but again, one month should be allowed, and at least two months with manual systems. After contracts are awarded, the lead time between orders to the supplier and initial deliveries may be a month or less with local tenders, but international suppliers' lead times usually range from three months to one year, and on occasion even longer.

Efficient procurement offices spread the tender workload throughout the year, with overlap from one tender cycle to the next; when contracts have been awarded for the first cycle, planning for medicine selection for the next cycle should begin. Frequent communication with clients and with suppliers is needed to make sure that the tender proceeds according to schedule. Many procurement offices use spreadsheets to simplify tender tracking, but all procurement staff members need to use a common spreadsheet format to avoid misunderstandings that can result from different people developing their own. Figure 21-1 illustrates an annual tender cycle of fifteen months, with overlap.

The frequency of tendering should be attuned to the funding cycle, and for international tenders, to the availability of foreign exchange (particularly if inflation is an issue). Tendering once a year is not appropriate when funds, including foreign exchange, are released in monthly installments, because bids will expire before the funds for the actual awards become available. This can also be a problem where funds are released late from the government treasury but revert back if not spent by the end of the fiscal year.

21.3 Defining needs

As discussed in Chapter 18, restricting the number of pharmaceuticals on a procurement list can increase effective procurement volume for those pharmaceuticals. A central agency will usually be more efficient than a large number of health facilities operating independently when it comes to selecting a restricted list of essential medicines. If selection is totally decentralized, the benefits of group purchasing will be lost. On the other hand, if the health facilities do not have real input into which medicines are selected, they will not feel that their needs are being served and will lose a feeling of ownership, which may result in facilities making direct purchases outside the tender contracts, undermining the integrity of the system. A balance needs to be struck between centralized and decentralized elements of procurement.

Selection of medicines for the tender

The medicine selection committee (see Chapter 16), which is often known as the formulary committee, should meet before each tender to finalize the list of medicines. If, for example, a tender is scheduled for June and quantification takes three months plus one month for clarification and tender document preparation, the medicine selection committee would meet in January.

Requests for additions or changes to the procurement list should be compiled throughout the year by the procurement agency, the selection committee, or both. Often, provisions are in place to obtain special approval for purchasing items not included on the essential medicines list.

Requests for additions to the list should be made in writing with justification for the addition and (if applicable) the name of the product to be replaced. Members of the technical staff of the procurement agency or medicine selection committee should compile information from the medical literature on the new product (and on the therapeutic category the product represents) for the selection committee. Some procurement programs require that for each addition to the list a similar product be deleted, unless the proposed addition represents a new therapeutic category. Usually, however, the list of products continues to grow, which can present problems in both managing and financing procurement.

Analyses of past procurements using methods such as VEN (vital, essential, nonessential), ABC, and therapeutic category analysis (see Chapter 40) should be compiled before the meeting of the medicine selection committee to focus deliberations and help in rationally limiting the procurement list.

After the selection committee has met, the procurement office develops a list of the approved medicines for quantification. In computerized procurement agencies, this process may take one or two weeks.

Quantification

As discussed in Chapter 20, the procurement office is responsible for producing a reasonably accurate estimate of pharmaceutical requirements for each tender, but much of this responsibility can be decentralized. Some health systems ask each level with decision-making authority to compile its own list of estimated quantities required for medicines on the procurement list. The central procurement office then compares the lists with past consumption, checks for any known changes affecting demand, clarifies questions directly with the client, and compiles the overall list for procurement.

Quantification can consume considerable time in programs that are decentralized but require multiple layers of review. With four levels of management authority (health area, regions/districts, provinces, and national) involved in reviewing estimates, developing a list of medicine needs for procurement may take six to nine months. If the quantification process extends to six months or more, a full year may pass by the time the pharmaceuticals are actually received. In that time, needs may change, and money is wasted if the pharmaceuticals purchased no longer match current needs.

Methods for procurement quantification—consumption-based, morbidity-based, and proxy consumption—are discussed in Chapter 20. The choice of method is based largely on the type and reliability of data on medicine usage, patient use, and morbidity patterns.

Countries should avoid making one major effort to quantify medicines and then relying on the same data for several years thereafter. No matter how accurate the original quantification may have been, given changes from year to year, the earlier projections become increasingly unreliable guides to later procurement needs.

When the quantification has been completed, the responsible committee (it may be a tender board or a special procurement committee) should review and approve the list of medicines and the quantities proposed. Having the procurement office estimate the actual cost before the list is sent to the committee for review, and definitely before the actual tendering is executed, is important. If cost estimates are not done, the subsequent evaluation of tender offers may indicate that costs exceed funding.

21.4 Selecting suppliers for tender participation

The selection of suppliers has a profound effect on the quality and cost of pharmaceuticals acquired. Inadequate safeguards in supplier selection may result in the purchase of medicines that are ineffective, unsafe, or even deadly. As discussed in Chapter 18, hidden costs resulting from late deliveries, complete default on confirmed orders, losses caused by poor packaging, or short expiration dates—common problems with unreliable suppliers—may raise the actual medicine cost to several times the original contract cost.

New suppliers are constantly coming into the market, while others are changing to new fields, merging, or going out of business altogether. New companies may have difficulties with quality control and packaging for export during their first years of production but later become reliable, low-cost producers. At the same time, a company long known for high-quality products and prompt service may become seriously deficient as a result of changes in management or regional distributors. A multinational company offering an attractive price may provide excellent service in one country and poor service in a nearby country, solely because of its choice of in-country representatives.

An efficient procurement office must therefore be able to closely monitor supplier performance and consider the relevant information during both prequalification or postqualification.

Types of potential pharmaceutical suppliers

Government pharmaceutical factories, local private manufacturers, and foreign manufacturers are *primary* sources of pharmaceuticals, because these companies do the manufacturing themselves. Donors, international procurement services, independent foreign exporters, and local importers and distributors are *secondary* sources; they obtain pharmaceuticals from manufacturers for resale.

As discussed, both donor financing and national procurement laws and regulations may determine the options for supplier selection.

Pharmaceutical manufacturers. Pharmaceutical manufacturers can be classified as *research-based* and *non–research-based* producers. The well-known multinational pharmaceutical companies are research based in that their reputation and, to a large extent, their profitability depend on new pharmaceuticals developed through research. These pharmaceuticals are patented and vigorously promoted by brand name. Nevertheless, many such firms also produce a line of pharmaceuticals that they sell by generic name at a lower price than their brand-name products. These pharmaceuticals are often made on the same production line and sometimes in the same batch as the brand-name product. Quality standards are identical; only the packaging and appearance of the medicine are different.

Non–research-based firms range from small, one-factory, local companies to large national or multinational generic pharmaceutical manufacturers that frequently market pharmaceuticals only by their nonproprietary names. Although they may have less name recognition, many generic manufacturers produce products equal in quality to those of any brand-name company.

International procurement services. International procurement services are sometimes nonprofit companies or arms of international agencies. Sometimes these services operate as private, for-profit entities. They provide services from one or more warehouses, and they vary with regard to selection of medicines, prices, means of quality assurance, payment terms, restrictions placed on the buyer, and nature and timeliness of service provided. Some well-established international procurement agencies are listed in the annual *International Drug Price Indicator Guide* (MSH). Some procurement agencies, such as Crown Agents, do not maintain inventory but are ad-hoc purchasing agents that must go through the sometimes lengthy process of negotiating prices with individual manufacturers and then arranging shipment from the manufacturer to the purchaser.

These agencies can play a valuable role in international tenders, providing competitive international prices for a range of products and access to small quantities of pharmaceuticals—sales that may not interest primary manufacturers. Their proposals should be evaluated by the same criteria used for other sources of supply, and they should specify the name of the manufacturer and the mechanism for quality assurance, like any commercial distributor.

Independent international wholesale exporters. Independent international wholesale exporters—sometimes known as "jobbers"—purchase pharmaceuticals from a variety of manufacturers for resale. Many of these companies around the world specialize in exports to developing countries. Most exporting countries exercise less strict control over jobbers than over manufacturers, a practice that can open purchasers to risk of procuring poor-quality products. Hence, it is essential to get the name of the primary manufacturer and make sure that the distributor provides bona fide quality assurance documents and certifications from the exporting-country regulatory agency with each registration request, tender offer, and shipment. Forged certification documents have been received in some countries from less reliable foreign exporters. WHO has developed prequalification procedures related specifically to wholesalers. Procurement offices should consider adapting the WHO procedures when qualifying wholesalers as suppliers.

Local importers and distributors. Local importers and distributors—also known as wholesalers—are often major forces in the local pharmaceutical market, both financially and politically. Like foreign distributors, these companies may not closely examine the quality of the products supplied by the manufacturers with which they work. In many countries, these companies have exclusive rights to represent certain manufacturers, and tender offers for these manufacturers' products come through the local distributor. Again, the procurement office may wish to adapt and apply the WHO wholesaler prequalification criteria when qualifying this type of supplier.

Locating and contacting qualified suppliers

Generally, identifying qualified suppliers should be done through a systematic prequalification process or by advertising an open tender followed by a rigorous postqualification evaluation.

Open public tenders can be publicized through local newspaper notices and Internet tender portals, such as dgMarket (http://www.dgmarket.com). Increasingly, procurement agencies are posting tender notices to their own websites (for example, Tamil Nadu Medical Services Corporation and Tanzania's Medical Stores Department). Notices can be sent to international newspapers, trade directories, and journals with wide circulation. The World Bank has published guidelines on e-tendering for programs that it finances (World Bank 2009).

Agencies that are required to purchase only from pre-qualified suppliers may still publicize their intent to purchase through an international notice, in addition to contacting prequalified suppliers directly. This "safeguard" practice informs the prequalified suppliers and may also arouse the interest of new suppliers.

Even when all foreign suppliers in a tender are represented by local agents, notice through international channels may be faster and more reliable than depending on local agents to alert foreign suppliers. Earlier notification allows suppliers more time to prepare offers and thus increases the probability of competitive offers.

Contacts with international agencies. Contacts with international agencies may be an effective way for a procurement office with little international experience to identify potential suppliers. This arrangement may be especially useful in places without central government authority, such as in the early days of East Timor's independence, when UNICEF procured pharmaceuticals on behalf of the interim government.

The WHO prequalification scheme can guide countries to suppliers that provide quality-assured products, and the Global Fund's voluntary pooled procurement mechanism also helps countries access quality products at competitive prices. Other global initiatives, such as Stop TB and the Global Drug Facility, Roll Back Malaria and the Affordable Medicines for Malaria program, and WHO's AIDS Medicines and Diagnostics Service, offer information on suppliers of specialized products, and in some cases, on comparative pricing.

Contacts with other procurement offices. As discussed in Chapter 18, even where a formal, regional multicountry pooled procurement system is not realistic, countries in a region may be able to develop a coordinated information-sharing process among their national procurement offices—sharing information on prices and supplier performance.

Information on international prices. To know whether potential suppliers are offering competitive prices, procurement offices need a point of reference or sufficient experience in the market to make accurate cost estimates. One such reference for international prices for essential medicines, the annual *International Drug Price Indicator Guide,* contains the catalog prices from several international procurement agencies and actual tender prices received by developing-country procurement agencies. The Global Fund's Global Price Reporting Mechanism is an important source of comparative pricing data from countries that purchase medicines through Global Fund grants. Reference prices can also come from one of the nonprofit international procurement agencies, and most of them provide a price catalog on request. The global initiatives discussed above can provide pricing information related to their specific

mandates. Chapter 18 lists various price-reporting references.

Evaluating new suppliers

When considering contract awards to previously unknown suppliers, establishing how product quality will be assured is essential. If the procurement office does not have a way to test products, it may argue against an award to a foreign supplier whose products are either not approved through the WHO prequalification process or not registered by a stringent regulatory authority. As noted, procurement laws, regulations, or policies may require that national suppliers be given preference (or at least access to the tender), but in many cases, these suppliers do not have international certification. The procurement office is still responsible for excluding substandard suppliers from the tender.

In addition to deciding whether a supplier is generally reliable, which of the supplier's products are of acceptable quality must be determined. Some suppliers may produce good-quality liquids but not tablets or injections. A supplier may have difficulty producing certain medicines because of a lack of quality raw materials or a lack of certain equipment.

Some procurement programs establish a list of critical medicines for which potential quality issues exist and limit suppliers for those products. Trying to qualify each supplier separately for each medicine on the tender list certainly will add substantial time to the pre- or postqualification process. In a West African country that decided to prequalify suppliers separately for each medicine, the prequalification process for one tender took nearly eighteen months.

Procurement staff must develop a formal system of determining suppliers' reliability to eliminate suppliers that are substandard. Two aspects are involved: evaluating potential new suppliers (for pre- or postqualification) and rating the performance of current and past suppliers.

Evaluation of new (unknown) suppliers should be approached through formal prequalification and through testing products received when feasible, followed by performance monitoring.

Formal prequalification. As mentioned, prequalification is the process of developing a list of registered suppliers based on past performance, references from previous clients, and documentation of product quality before they are invited to submit bids on tenders. Although establishing an initial list of prequalified suppliers can be time-consuming, it expedites the tender evaluation because every bidder is qualified. A rigorous prequalification process will include references from past clients and inspections of manufacturing sites by quality experts (WHO 1999).

Annex 21-1 lists information one should check when considering a new supplier. Sample registration forms used by the international nonprofit procurement agencies can be requested from the agencies.

Test performance on trial purchases. As part of their monitoring process, procurement programs should, if possible, test samples of products received. Products from new suppliers should be tested more often than products from established, trusted suppliers. Purchasers should generally not procure products that are needed to treat critical illness or that absolutely require timely delivery from completely new suppliers. For example, an unknown supplier might be awarded a contract for vitamin B complex, but not for gentamicin.

Monitoring and evaluating supplier performance

After a contract is awarded, monitoring the supplier's service and quality should provide the basis for decisions regarding future purchases. In many countries, monitoring is done informally and without written records, which makes assembling data for review by procurement committees difficult. Successful purchasing agencies use a formal monitoring system, as described in Section 21.9 on procurement information.

In general, suppliers that have performed poorly should be excluded from the next tender. Some procurement agencies give a probationary re-approval to suppliers that have had problems, such as too many partial shipments or excessive lead times, but offer high-quality products at competitive prices. If problems recur, the nonperforming suppliers are then barred from the next tender. If a supplier's problems are sufficiently grave, it can be barred for a two-year period and then be forced to prequalify again.

Some procurement offices use a point system, assigning values to performance criteria such as those shown in Annexes 21-1 and 21-2. The relative weights of each category vary; for example, in some situations, the lead time may be very important and be given a high weight; in other situations, it may be a minor factor. In countries with strong regulatory control of the pharmaceutical market, product quality may be given a low weight, because all registered products are assumed to be of acceptable quality.

Rating systems offer two options for ranking applications: in one, a minimum passing score is used; in the other, suppliers are ranked from top to bottom overall, and contract preference is given to higher-ranked suppliers when prices are equivalent. A supplier with a much higher rank might get the contract despite a competitor's offer of lower prices.

Because ratings of supplier reliability and quality have a tremendous effect on the number and quality of suppliers that participate in a tender, the ratings must be as impartial as possible, with criteria written into the tender adjudication process. Ratings will always be subjective to some extent, so to ensure impartiality, the entire procurement committee, or at least a multiperson team, should be responsible for assigning supplier ratings.

21.5 Preparing and issuing tender documents

After selection, quantification, and preparation of the tender list are completed, bid packages are sent out to suppliers or posted on a website. For restricted tenders, packages are made available to all prequalified bidders; in open tenders, they are made available to all interested bidders. The tender package typically includes the documents discussed below. (See References and Further Readings for sources of tender documents that can be adapted.)

Invitation to bid. This describes the scope of the procurement, the purchasing group that is soliciting offers, the conditions under which bids will be accepted, the address for submission, the date and time bids are due, and the dates to be covered by the contract.

Instructions to bidders. These cover how to submit documents, including how to state prices; dates of bid validity; what currencies to use; what documents are required in addition to bid forms; bid and performance bonds (if applicable; see Chapter 39); precautions against undue contact with procurement office staff; format for submitting offers; domestic preference (if any); criteria for bid evaluation; and procedures involved in adjudication, award, and notification. Forms should be appended for performance and bid bonds and for documenting domestic preference and value added, if applicable.

In addition, the procurement manager should indicate in the tender document itself how suppliers' offers will be evaluated. This step shows all suppliers the importance of the various requirements specified in the tender. Figure 21-2 shows an evaluation matrix introduced by Papua New Guinea to assess the potential suppliers for pharmaceutical tenders.

Bidding documents usually include a statement indicating that the procurement committee may reject any or all bids. Rejection of all bids is justified when no effective competition exists or bids are not substantially responsive.

Conditions of contract. These discuss general conditions in the contract that will be signed with successful bidders and any special conditions applicable to the current procurement (see Chapter 39).

General technical specifications. These provide information on good manufacturing practices (GMP) standards, pharmacopoeial standards, nomenclature and description required for each product, shelf life and expiration date parameters, labeling instructions, packaging instructions, GMP and quality assurance certificates required, and other evidence of product quality to be submitted with the tender and with each shipment.

Specific pharmacopoeial standards should be listed for each product; if any of a range of standards is adequate (*British Pharmacopoeia, U.S. Pharmacopeia, European Pharmacopoeia,* or *International Pharmacopoeia*), it

Figure 21-2   Papua New Guinea pharmaceutical tender

TENDER EVALUATION SHEET		
Indicator	**Weight**	**Comment**
1. Financial	**30%**	
1.1 Form of bid	30%	Lowest
2. Performance	**30%**	
2.1 Delivery	5%	Within specified time—5%
2.2 Years experience supplying Papua New Guinea (PNG)	5%	2 years or more—5%
2.3 Past contracts	5%	PNG—3%; developing countries—2% (within last 5 years)
2.4 Packaging	5%	As specified in tender—5%
2.5 Financial capacity	5%	Acceptable bid bond supplied—5%
2.6 Evidence of financial capacity	5%	Banker's details and financial records—5%
3. Quality	**40%**	
3.1 Product documentation submitted as per conditions of bid	15%	Documents submitted for all pharmaceutical and medical equipment products—15% > 80% required documentation—10% 60–80% required documentation—7.5% 30–60% required documentation—5% 0–30% required documentation—0%
3.2 Manufacturer's certifications submitted as per form of bid	15%	Manufacturer's certifications received for all pharmaceutical and medical equipment products—15% > 80% required documentation—10% 60–80% required documentation—7.5% 30–60% required documentation—5% 0–30% required documentation—0%
3.3 Manufacturer's labeling submitted as per form of bid	10%	Manufacturer's labeling received for all pharmaceutical and medical equipment products—15% > 80% required documentation—10% 60–80% required documentation—7.5% 30–60% required documentation—5% 0–30% required documentation—0%

should be noted. If special packaging or labeling is required for a subset of products, this requirement should be indicated on the schedule of requirements (see below), but a generic statement of packaging and labeling applied to all products should be included in the general technical specifications. Instructions about labeling (contents and language) and package inserts can be included in the technical specifications, unless specific requirements exist for a subset of products. These should be indicated on the tender list.

If all products are to be shipped to the same destination, on the same delivery schedule, by whatever means is most efficient and cost-effective, this specification can be stated in the conditions of contract. If different instructions apply to certain products, they should be stipulated in the schedule of requirements.

Schedule of requirements, or tender list. This provides a concise description of each product and the quantity required, along with any technical specifications unique to that item. If it can be printed with sufficient space for suppliers to enter offers, having suppliers use this space for bids greatly simplifies the collation of offers. Sufficient space should be provided so that the supplier can enter all relevant information, including the name of the original manufacturer.

The schedule of requirements should include the International Nonproprietary Name (INN), or generic name (for combination products, the name of each generic component), the strength in metric units for each component, the basic unit (tablet, capsule, vial, bottle), the package size, and the number of packages needed. Some tenders list both the total number of packages and the total number of basic units needed, to avoid misunderstanding and to allow for the possibility that a supplier may offer a different (but acceptable) package size representing the same number of basic units. The tender should specify whether the listed package sizes are the only ones acceptable; some procurement agencies request offers on all package sizes available.

Each unique product should have a separate inventory code number, used only for that product. This code is useful in compiling product catalogs and is essential for computerized information systems. It can also be helpful in making sure that all parties are referring to the same item when clarifying issues with client facilities or with suppliers. For therapeutic category analysis, a supplementary code can be used to assign each drug product to a therapeutic category (see Chapter 40).

To simplify future procurements and make sure that all staff use the same terminology in procurement and tender functions, compiling all information about each tender product into a procurement catalog is useful. With a computerized system, developing a catalog is simple; updating a product catalog manually is more difficult, but the effort may be worthwhile to save time in compiling future tender lists.

21.6 Adjudicating the tender

The most important aspect of adjudication is that it is an open and transparent process that assures all participants that the tender was conducted fairly. Tender adjudication involves several separate activities and stages—

- Prepare for adjudication during the open period.
- Receive and open bids.
- Collate bids for adjudication.
- Adjudicate offers and award contracts.

Preparing during the open period

The length of the open period (time between the invitation to tender and the closing date) typically varies from four to eight weeks. A longer open period lengthens the total lead time for obtaining pharmaceuticals but may also increase the number of offers received. The procurement agency should prepare for receipt of documents, collation, and adjudication during the open period.

Some suppliers may request clarification about product description, package size, pharmacopoeial standard, labeling, or packaging requirements. If clarification is needed because of a mistake or omission in the tender package, it should be provided to all participating bidders. Similarly, if one supplier is given approval to offer a product or package that is similar to but not the same as that listed in the schedule of requirements, all bidders should be informed that such an exception is approved.

Receiving and opening tender offers

To ensure confidentiality and to avoid accusations of price fixing or undue influence on decisions, the procurement agency must adhere strictly to the closing date and time. No bids should be opened before the date and time specified. A written record should be kept of all bids received, documenting the date received and the person who received the bid. The unopened bids should be stored in a locked, secure area until the closing date. The date of bid receipt should also be entered into the procurement management information system to track the response to tenders. If due dates are approaching and suppliers—particularly those known to be reliable, low-cost sources—have not responded, the procurement agency can remind *all* suppliers of the approaching deadline by telephone, fax, or e-mail.

At the specified date and time, the bids should be formally opened, with at least one member of the procurement committee and bidder representatives (if they choose to be present) in attendance. Specifics of how the bids are opened and documented vary by country—with some procedures mandated by national regulations. Details such as the bidder's name and address, and required documentation such as bid form and bid security for each opened bid, are often read aloud. If the bid security has not been deposited, an immediate disqualification usually results.

Each opened bid should be logged in a ledger and numbered for future reference. If possible, writing the number of enclosed pages on the outside of the tender envelope may be useful to avoid confusion during adjudication. Often, a note taker documents the meeting proceedings, and at the end of the meeting, attendees sign the draft minutes, which everyone will receive for record-keeping purposes.

Collating offers for adjudication

The first step in collating offers is to determine which offers, if any, are nonresponsive to tender conditions. Suppliers that have not met the basic requirements related to bidder qualification, medicine description, strength, pack size, quality requirements, and delivery date are nonresponsive. If required information has not been provided, the bid is nonresponsive. If the tender documents require the supplier's signed acceptance of contract terms and the supplier has not signed, the bid is nonresponsive.

Information from all responsive bids should be compiled in an adjudication report to allow side-by-side comparison of the offers. Nonresponsive bids should not be entered into the collated adjudication report, but the problems should be documented in writing for review by the procurement committee.

Prices must be converted to a common currency and adjustments made for differences in trade terms (for example, adding freight costs to those bids that do not include freight expenses). If local or domestic preference is considered in the adjudication, the adjudication report should separate offers eligible for the local preference margin, so that they can be fairly compared with offers that are not eligible.

Spreadsheets are now commonly used to simplify the collation of information and the preparation of an adjudication report. In addition, specialized procurement software is available that automates all of the processes related to collecting bids, collating offers, and ranking them according to predetermined criteria (see Section 21.10). Figure 21-3 illustrates an adjudication report prepared by a specialized computer program.

Managing the adjudication process

The authority to adjudicate tenders and award contracts should be confined to the procurement committee (or government tender board). Procurement office staff should assemble information for the tender board or procurement committee and make technical recommendations, but they should not have a vote in the contract decision.

As discussed in Chapter 18, the adjudication process must be free from influence by special interests; it should be open and transparent, with written rules for the process, including evaluation, award, any special criteria, and the appeal period for rejected bidders. Results of adjudication, including the winning bidder and the contract price, should be available to all participating bidders. In countries where pharmaceutical procurement has fallen into disrepute, credibility can be rebuilt by broadening participation in the tender board or procurement committee and making sure that it has final authority for approving all pharmaceutical procurement and for enforcing transparency in the tender process.

Evaluation of offers. For restricted tenders that do not involve split contract requirements, this process can be quick. The procurement committee reviews the collated bid information and normally selects the lowest bidder for each product. Contracts are then developed. Disqualification of low bidders should be documented and become part of the tender record.

For open tenders, supplier evaluation does not begin until bids are received, and adjudication is a two-stage process: a tender evaluation committee is formed for ranking the bids according to standard evaluation criteria, and then beginning the postqualification supplier evaluation process. When the postqualification analysis has been completed, the procurement committee meets to review the recommendations of the tender evaluation committee and determine whether the lowest evaluated bid should receive the contract. If not, the next-lowest evaluated bid is considered, and so forth.

The responsible procurement committee or tender board should carefully consider each item on the tender list and make an award for each item, unless no responsive bids were received. If the primary/secondary supplier system is used, equal care is needed in selecting secondary suppliers, because they will automatically be used if the primary supplier defaults.

Written bid evaluation criteria should be applied rigorously and without exception. Tender contracts should be awarded to the lowest bidder that has the capacity to supply products that meet the standards required (considering local preference, if applicable). This award should be mandatory unless the lowest bidder has not performed in prior procurements.

In local tenders, Incoterms, such as cost, insurance, and freight (CIF) and carriage and insurance paid (CIP), are generally not applicable. Delivered price, which includes landed cost, overheads, and profit margin, is more common and is an adequate standard for comparing costs. Letters of credit are normally not used to pay local suppliers; other mechanisms, such as deferred payment, may be beneficial and should be considered if stated in the evaluation criteria and in instructions to bidders. When the health procurement agency sells its products and receives payment from health facilities, it should try to arrange supplier payment terms that are longer than those provided to health facility customers. For example, if health facilities are given thirty days to pay, then thirty-to-sixty-day payment terms to suppliers can help cash flow.

Local and foreign suppliers may offer different trade terms (CIP to purchaser's warehouse, or CIF to purchaser's main port). To make these two prices comparable, all duties, fees, handling, and transportation costs to the purchaser's warehouse must be added to the CIF price.

Delivery dates should be compared in terms of past suppliers' performance rather than promised delivery date. If the lowest acceptable bidder's expected delivery is beyond the required date, then the effect of a shortage must be considered in light of the cost of alternative treatments or of a special air shipment to cover the interim period.

Special criteria. Special criteria are sometimes applied, such as a local preference margin calculated by adding a percentage to the value of foreign bids, before they are compared with local bids. World Bank–financed international competitive bidding (ICB) procurements allow local preference, to a maximum of 15 percent. Although pricing is the accepted means of granting local preference, some countries have more explicit requirements to grant local companies preference in contract awards to foster industrial development. This approach, however, can put the procurement office at risk of having to accept lower local standards of service or product quality. In any event, all procurement agencies should use supplier performance as the basis for purchasing decisions.

Some programs try to maintain as broad a supplier base as possible to protect against loss of a primary supply source.

Figure 21-3 Sample tender adjudication report by item by supplier

Quotations from All Suppliers

Central Medical Stores		
Run Date : 21/11/2011 16:28:22		Tender Number : 42
		Report ID : OR4968_PPS
		Page No : 1 of 5

Bid Transaction Code : BIT-55	Bid Opening Date : 27/01/2005	Tender Category : Open Tender
Bid Transaction Date : 24/01/2005	Tender Number : 42	Tender Currency : USD
From Item Code : 0	To Item Code : zzzzzzzzzzzzz	
From Supplier Code : 0	To Supplier Code : zzzzzzzzzzz	
From DMO Classification : 0	To DMO Classification : zzzzzzzzzzz	
From DMO Sub Classification : 0	To DMO Sub Classification : zzzzzzzzzzz	
From Therapeutic Class : 0	To Therapeutic Class : zzzzzzzzzzz	
From Therapeutic Sub Class : 0	To Therapeutic Sub Class : zzzzzzzzzzz	

Quotations from All Suppliers

Central Medical Stores		
Run Date : 21/11/2011 16:28:22		Tender Number : 42
		Report ID : OR4968_PPS
		Page No : 3 of 5

Supplier	Brand	Supplier's	Air Shipment			Sea Shipment			Manufacturer	Remarks
			CIF Landed /	Price / Adj	Lead	CIF Landed /	Price / Adj	Lead		
Glaxo Wellcome Inc.	BWEBRAND	P100	180.00	1.8000	2	160.00	1.6000	1	BWEMAN	

Item Code : 01019 / Benzatropine 2mg TAB ORAL TAB

Adjudication Unit : TAB

Supplier	Brand	Supplier's	CIF Landed /	Price / Adj	Lead	CIF Landed /	Price / Adj	Lead	Manufacturer	Remarks
American Hospital Supply	AHSBRAND	P1000	42.00	0.0420	5	10.00	0.0100	14	AHSMAN	
Alcon Pharmaceuticals Ltd.	ALCBRAND	P100	3.50	0.0350	5	1.20	0.0120	10	ALCMAN	
Biomedical International Corp	BIOBRAND	TAB	0.02	0.0200	5	0.01	0.0150	7	BIOMAN	
Glaxo Wellcome Inc.	BWEBRAND	P1000	160.00	0.1600	2	120.00	0.1200	1	BWEMAN	Countries Forecast : 70,000 TAB

Item Code : 01012 / Carbamazepine 100 MG TAB ORAL TAB

Adjudication Unit : TAB

Supplier	Brand	Supplier's	CIF Landed /	Price / Adj	Lead	CIF Landed /	Price / Adj	Lead	Manufacturer	Remarks
American Hospital Supply	AHSBRAND	P500	7.00	0.0140	5	6.00	0.0120	14	AHSMAN	
Alcon Pharmaceuticals Ltd.	ALCBRAND	P1000	15.00	0.0150	5	12.50	0.0125	10	ALCMAN	
Biomedical International Corp	BIOBRAND	P1000	17.00	0.0170	5	13.00	0.0130	7	BIOMAN	
Glaxo Wellcome Inc.	BWEBRAND	P500	32.00	0.0640	2	28.00	0.0560	1	BWEMAN	Countries Forecast : 60,000 TAB

In insecure regions, maintaining a geographic and political distribution of suppliers can mitigate supply disruptions due to war, natural disasters, or international political problems.

Appeal period for rejected bidders. Some countries allow an appeal period during which rejected suppliers may request reconsideration by the tender board. The appeal process varies greatly according to national regulations; the time to resolve appeals according to law may be less than a week or many months, but ideally, the appeal period should be no more than one month, to avoid delays in procurement. Ultimately, the other bidders should be notified and given information about the winning bid.

21.7 Issuing contracts to winning bidders

When tender awards are made, contracts must be established with successful bidders (see Chapter 39).

A list of all contracts awarded, specifying for each item the supplier, price, and total value, should be made available to all responsive bidders; if necessary, the name of the successful bidder can be omitted from the public document.

If winning bidders decline to accept the contract, bid bonds or other types of security (if used) are forfeited. In the primary/secondary system, the secondary supplier is contacted immediately. In other cases, the item must be rebid; depending on the volume, local competitive bidding may be the preferred method.

21.8 Laws governing international agreements

Almost all procurement laws and regulations are based on previous laws developed in and for the country, although some countries, such as Tanzania and Uganda, have based their procurement regulations and laws on World Bank standards. With more people and goods moving from one country to another, questions about which system of law applies often arise. If, for example, the Medical Stores Department of Tanzania signs a contract to buy medicines from France, will the agreement fall under Tanzanian law or French law? The matter becomes particularly important if a disagreement arises. For example, suppose some of the goods arrive damaged, but when the contract was written, no specification of legal jurisdiction was included. Which court should adjudicate the matter?

The legal system in the country of one of the parties signing the agreement is usually chosen, or perhaps the country where the goods currently are or where payment is to be made. National procurement laws and regulations may dictate the choice of "prevailing law," but otherwise choosing the system that seems most relevant to the situation and to the risks is advisable. If, for example, goods are being imported and the concern is that the supplier may not deliver, involvement of the courts in the supplier's country may be the best way of ensuring delivery. Goods transported in boats or trains belonging to a third country are not necessarily well protected, and the laws of that country may not safeguard the goods. This fact does not alter the fact that the seller should be responsible for ensuring that the goods arrive. No guarantee exists that the courts of the country selected will agree to adjudicate any case that arises, but if the choice has been a commonsense one, it will probably be respected.

An alternative is to indicate some other body to settle disputes. In commercial contracts with some countries, the chamber of commerce may be asked to act as arbitrator. Arbitration is often a quicker and less expensive way of settling disputes than court proceedings, which may be costly and take many years. Finding a suitable arbitrator who is fair, sufficiently expert in the field concerned, and trusted by both parties is important.

One word of warning: international disputes are often not effectively settled by the courts, or even by arbitration. An unscrupulous foreign seller of a dangerous or defective product may expect to be able to escape liability because of the time and expense involved in bringing an international action. The supplier can change its name, address, domicile, and legal or corporate form and be out of reach of the courts. The law may be unclear. Even between industrialized countries with a long history of personal-injury litigation, claiming compensation for drug injury from a foreign manufacturer of a bad product remains difficult. Dealing with a firm of good reputation may be worth paying a somewhat higher price.

21.9 Monitoring performance and product quality

The procurement office is responsible for monitoring performance and compliance with contract terms by suppliers and facilities that order pharmaceuticals. The office must actively track suppliers' lead time, delivery status, compliance with contract pricing and terms, shelf life, and packaging of products. In decentralized procurement systems, central procurement authorities find it difficult to monitor local government procurement activities. Resulting problems can include high prices, poor service and product quality, irrational supplier and product selection, and poor payment practices, all of which undermine patient services. Therefore, monitoring local government and facility procurement performance becomes vitally important. Are they ordering according to schedule, in reasonable quantities, and are they paying for their purchases according to the contract? Are total purchases roughly equal to estimated needs? In some countries, governments have concluded that recentralizing procurement is the best way to achieve desired procurement outcomes.

Maintaining an active program to ensure product quality before procurement and after receipt and distribution is crucial (see Chapters 18, 19, and 35). Reports of problems from prescribers, dispensers, consumers, and purchasing managers must be recorded in the product and supplier files and reviewed as part of the monitoring and evaluation of suppliers, and suppliers need to be made aware of any problems related to the quality of the products they supplied.

When testing is available, it is not necessary to test every drug from every supplier, but products that have been reported as suspect should always be tested. Testing should be done periodically for random samples of medicines known to be subject to degradation in questionable storage conditions, medicines that have a low therapeutic index (see Chapter 19), and pharmaceuticals received from suppliers of questionable or unknown reputation.

Chapter 39 discusses supply contracts and enforcement provisions. Enforcement is the key: there is no point in an elaborate contract unless it will be enforced when necessary. The reality is that unless substantial performance bonds are required as a condition of the contract, there may be limited recourse in the case of problems with foreign suppliers other than canceling outstanding orders and withholding payment.

21.10 The procurement information system

The most important tool in the procurement office is its management information system (MIS). The MIS can be computerized, manual, or a combination; computerized systems make it much easier to develop reports, and they speed up procurement processes such as prequalification and collation of tender offers for adjudication.

Procurement offices can probably get the greatest benefit from specialized computer software programs for procurement. Companies that sell off-the-shelf tender software include ActiveCost, Bloochip, mSupply, and Orica. The development and use of standard bidding documents can drastically decrease the time needed to prepare tender documents and contracts. The skills exist in most countries, if not in the procurement agencies themselves, to develop spreadsheet programs that can effectively accomplish most other tasks. Posting tenders and associated documents on an agency website and other Internet sites, such as dgMarket, can also help manage aspects of the tender process, such as sending out tender documents and related information, although certain tasks still require hard-copy documentation.

This section describes the information that should be tracked and used; the method of storing and retrieving the information is secondary. The information system includes several different types of records: those on products, tendering and ordering, suppliers, clients, quality assurance, accounts receivable and payable for pharmaceutical orders, and accounting records for the procurement office itself (see Chapters 41 and 49).

Product records

Product files record the standard technical specifications for a specific item and the performance of past suppliers of the product. Detailed product records are particularly important when quality is critical. A sample product card for a manual system is shown in Figure 21-4. Product records can also be maintained in a special-purpose, procurement software system or a spreadsheet. Producing a catalog of all items that can be used to compile quantification lists, tender lists, adjudication forms, and notices of awards may be useful.

Records related to tendering and ordering

A record of each year's procurement, tracking the total quantity estimated and actually purchased of each item (along with the contract supplier and price), facilitates the estimation of future prices and is essential in assembling future quantifications and checking quantity estimates from clients in decentralized ordering systems.

An ongoing record of the order status and shipments pending can be made using separate folders for orders outstanding, orders received as partial shipments, and orders completed.

Another simple manual system uses a ledger to track each order (the order number, date ordered, date received, dates additional shipments were received, and dates payments were made), organized chronologically or by purchase order number. With systems that do not use purchase order numbers, keeping track of outstanding orders may be difficult.

A computerized information system can provide standard reports on order status, organized by product, purchase order number, or supplier. Figures 21-5 and 21-6 illustrate order status reports available from a typical information system.

Records to monitor supplier and facility performance

Supplier performance monitoring has two parts. First, the system should track lead time, compliance with contract pricing terms, partial shipments, remaining shelf life, compliance with packaging and labeling instructions, and compliance with other contract terms. This record should track the number and value of tender contracts awarded chronologically and the value of total purchases from the supplier by year. Second, a file on each supplier should contain copies of all registration papers, references, special correspondence, complaints, and anecdotal information.

The facility performance monitoring system tracks total purchases compared with estimated quantities for each procurement cycle, purchases from noncontract suppliers, lead time for payment to suppliers (if that is the facilities' responsibility), compliance with deadlines for quantification, complaints about product quality and supplier service problems, and results of follow-up of complaints and requests for action.

Quality assurance records

A chronological record of all product-quality complaints, with documentation on the results of follow-up, should be separate but linked to a record that documents all quality assurance tests performed, the reason, and the results. These records should be linked to or entered into both product and supplier records.

Accounts receivable and payable

The procurement office should have a record of each order placed with contract suppliers, the dates payments were made against the outstanding amount, and the total amount still owed. A separate purchase order number for each purchase simplifies record keeping and accounting. By using individual purchase order numbers, records can be

Figure 21-4   Sample product card

Side one / product specifications

Generic name: Paracetamol		Category: Analgesic	
Trade names: Calpol, Panadol, Tylenol			Code number: 02-4600
Form: Tablet	Dosage: 500 mg		Package size: 1,000 tabs
Acceptable pharmacopeial standards: IP / USP / EP / BP			
Additional technical specifications: Standard specifications (Schedule A) plus: (1) Double-scored tablet, imprinted with unique identifiers (our logo) (2) Shrink-wrapped in packaging units of 10 x 1,000			

Side two / supplier history

Purchase order number	Supplier	Quantity	Unit price	Date promised	Date delivered	Comments
085/10	Generix	5,000	20.25	01/11	02/11	
086/10	Novapharm	10,000	21.80	01/11	12/10	
003/11	Generix	5,000	20.25	04/11		Revised date 05/11
004/11	Novapharm	10,000	21.80	04/11	03/11	
046/11	Novapharm	15,000	23.00	07/11		

Figure 21-5 Sample pending purchase orders by item report

Pending Purchase Order By Item

Central Medical Stores
User ID   : ORION
Run Date   : 21/11/2011

Report ID : OPR012
Page No   : 1 of 2

From Order Type	:	PON
From Order No	:	0
From Order Date	:	21/11/2009
From Item Code	:	0
From Supplier Code	:	0

To Order Type	:	PON1
To Order No	:	99999999999999999999
To Order Date	:	21/11/2011
To Item Code	:	zzzzzzzzzzzzzzzzz
To Supplier Code	:	zzzzzzzzzzz

Item Code			Item Name								
PO No	Date	Supplier Code and Name	UOM	Order Quantity	Delivered Quantity	Balance Quantity	Price	Discount%	Order Value	Delivered Value	Balance Value
01000			Lamivudine 10 MG TAB ORAL TAB								
PON-5	************	AAL A.A. Laquis Ltd	TAB	9 - 0	5 - 0	4 - 0	10.00	4.00	86.40	48.00	38.40
PON-6	************	AAL A.A. Laquis Ltd	TAB	9 - 0	0 - 0	9 - 0	10.00	4.00	86.40	.00	86.40
PON-6	************	AAL A.A. Laquis Ltd	TAB	50000 - 0	0 - 0	50000 - 0	35.00	3.00	1,697,500.00	.00	1,697,500.00
					Total / Balance				1,697,672.80	48.00	1,697,624.80
01002			ACETAZOLIMIDE 250mg TAB ORAL TAB								
PON-106	************	AHS American Hospital Supply	TAB	1100 - 0	0 - 0	1100 - 0	.44	0.00	484.00	.00	484.00
					Total / Balance				484.00	.00	484.00
01010			Amoxicillin								
PON-6	************	AAL A.A. Laquis Ltd	TAB	10 - 0	0 - 0	10 - 0	12.00	2.00	117.60	.00	117.60
PON-6	************	AAL A.A. Laquis Ltd	TAB	4000 - 0	0 - 0	4000 - 0	25.00	2.00	98,000.00	.00	98,000.00
					Total / Balance				98,117.60	.00	98,117.60
01020			Bisacodyl								
PON-107	************	APO Apotex Inc.	TAB	30000 - 0	15000 - 0	15000 - 0	.00	0.00	60.00	30.00	30.00
					Total / Balance				60.00	30.00	30.00

Figure 21-6   Sample pending purchase orders by supplier report

Pending Purchase Order By Supplier

Central Medical Stores
User ID   : ORION
Run Date   : 21/11/2011

Report ID : OPR011
Page No   : 1 of 4

From Order Type	: PON	To Order Type	: PON1
From Order Date	: 21/11/2009	To Order Date	: 21/11/2011
From Delivery Date	: 21/11/2009	To Delivery Date	: 21/11/2011
From Item Code	: 0	To Item Code	: zzzzzzzzzzzzzzzzz
From Supplier Code	: 0	To Supplier Code	: zzzzzzzzz
From Order Number	: 0	To Order Number	: 99999999999999999999
From Tender Code	:	To Tender Code	:

PO No	Date	Currency				Exchange Rate					
Item Code	Item Short Name	UOM Code	Order Qty	Price	Discount%	Order Value	Delivered Qty	Delivery Value	LC No Balance Qty		Balance Value

Supplier Code : AAL   Name : A.A. Laquis Ltd

PO No / Item Code	Item Short Name	UOM Code	Order Qty	Price	Discount%	Order Value	Delivered Qty	Delivery Value	Balance Qty	Balance Value
PON-5	01/04/2010	USD			2.64					
01000	Lamivudine 10 MG TAB ORAL TAB	TAB	9 - 0	10.00	4.00	86.40	5 - 0	48.00	4 - 0	38.40
	Total / Balance					86.40		48.00		38.40
PON-6	01/04/2010	USD			2.64					
01000	Lamivudine 10 MG TAB ORAL TAB	TAB	50000 - 0	35.00	3.00	1,697,500.00	0 - 0	.00	50000 - 0	1,697,500.00
01000	Lamivudine 10 MG TAB ORAL TAB	TAB	9 - 0	10.00	4.00	86.40	0 - 0	.00	9 - 0	86.40
01010	Amoxicillin	TAB	4000 - 0	25.00	2.00	98,000.00	0 - 0	.00	4000 - 0	98,000.00
01010	Amoxicillin	TAB	10 - 0	12.00	2.00	117.60	0 - 0	.00	10 - 0	117.60
42017	Plaster, Dressing Strip	STRIP	10200 - 0	15.00	1.00	151,470.00	0 - 0	.00	10200 - 0	151,470.00
	Total / Balance					1,947,174.00		.00		1,947,174.00
	A.A. Laquis Ltd Total					1,947,260.40		48.00		1,947,212.40

Table 21-2   Standard procurement reports

Report name	Contents
Reorder report	Suggested order quantities, sorted by item or supplier
Purchase orders pending	Outstanding orders, by item or supplier
Physical stock status	Summary list of quantities for all items in inventory, by name or code, with nearest expiry date
Stock detail report	List of all items in stock, with quantity by batch (lot number) and expiry date
Expired stock	All expired stock and stock without expiry date
Expiry risk	Stock at risk of expiry—stock quantity, expiry date, average use, and quantity and value of stock at risk
Out of stock	All items out of stock
Stock count form	Stock count list, by name, dosage form, location, or code
Inventory adjustment	List of items for which the stock count and records differ
Inventory variance	Changes made to stock balances outside normal process
Suppliers	List of all suppliers, with contact information
Accounts payable	Aged list of debts to suppliers
Facilities	List of all client facilities, with contact information
Accounts receivable	Aged list of debts from facilities
Summary of warehouse activity	Purchases and sales, year to date and month to date
Tender request	List of items needed, with specifications
Tender offers	Bid details for each tender offer
Tender status	Tender contract status and price amendment history
Adjudication report	Bids received by item, ranked by total cost
Tender award list	List of contracts awarded
Currency exchange history	Report on exchange rates by currency
Financial transactions	Financial transactions, by date and account code
Requisition forms	Purchase requisition form and pending purchase requisitions
Stock transactions	List of all shipments to facilities, by item or facility, with total value
Purchases/receipts	List of all purchases and other receipts, by item or source, with total value
ABC analysis	ABC analysis of warehouse consumption, and analysis for each client facility
Supplier performance	Comparison of stated versus actual lead times, adherence to contracted price and delivery terms

arranged by either purchase order number or supplier. The procurement office should include the relevant purchase order number in every communication to the supplier, including the initial order, the tender contract, and any subsequent communications related to the purchase.

If the procurement office is based in a warehouse that also sells pharmaceuticals to clients, accurate records should be kept of amounts owed by clients and fees charged for procurement services. A separate transaction number assigned to each shipment or charge for services makes tracking easier.

Reporting

As discussed throughout this chapter, the procurement information system will be called upon to issue periodic reports for pharmaceutical and supplier selection, quantification, and tender collation and adjudication, as well as status reports on orders or payments. Standard reports, such as those listed in Table 21-2, are much more easily produced by a computerized information system, but even a manual system should be organized enough to produce the reports fairly regularly. ∎

ASSESSMENT GUIDE

For additional indicators and procurement assessment information, see the *Methodology for Assessing Procurement Systems* (OECD/DAC 2010) and procurement system assessments from Tanzania (PPRA 2007) and Uganda (PPDA 2007). See also Country Study 36-3 on developing a procurement system assessment in India.

Quantitative indicators

- Percentage by value of ministry of health (MOH) pharmaceuticals purchased through a central procurement system
- Percentage of average international price paid for last regular procurement (indicator medicines)
- Percentage by value of MOH pharmaceutical purchases that are on the essential medicines list or national drug formulary
- Percentage by value of MOH pharmaceuticals purchased through competitive tender
- Percentage by value of pharmaceuticals purchased from local manufacturers
- Average lead time for a sample of orders (calculated separately for all suppliers, local manufacturers, foreign suppliers)
- Average time period for payment for a sample of orders (calculated separately for all suppliers, local manufacturers, foreign suppliers)

Procurement responsibility

- Is procurement managed centrally, or is authority decentralized?
- How much time is normally required to complete the following steps (and who is responsible for managing the step): selection, quantification, preparation of tender documents, tender adjudication, and contract award?
- Have the persons responsible for procurement been trained in this field?
- Is there a written procurement procedures manual? If so, do practices conform to the written procedures?
- What type of procurement method is normally used?
- Who determines the procurement method for a specific procurement?
- Are the methods based on law or written policies?
- How many different suppliers currently supply medicines to the health system?
- Are suppliers bilateral aid programs, international procurement services, multinational companies, or local import agents?

- Does a single supplier or small group seem to win most of the supply contracts for the system?
- Who is responsible for selecting potential suppliers?
- On what basis are the suppliers selected for tender participation?
- Are suppliers prequalified?
- Is a formal rating system used for evaluating suppliers' suitability?
- Are supplier selection criteria documented and closely adhered to?
- What role do local agents play in locating, selecting, and conducting business with pharmaceutical suppliers?
- Who has the authority to award contracts to suppliers?
- Are there written procedures for committee actions, and are they followed?
- Are written minutes made of procurement committee meetings?
- What kinds of influences are brought to bear on the individuals who select the suppliers and award contracts?

Tender and contract methods

- Do tenders and supply contracts specify a fixed quantity and delivery schedule or an estimated quantity, with orders placed as needed?
- If both systems are used, what is the approximate percentage by value of pharmaceuticals purchased under each system?
- What are the procedures for placing orders to suppliers?
- What is the average time required to get an order approved?
- Who approves the order?
- Is there an effective policy limiting MOH pharmaceutical procurement to drugs on the national drug formulary list or essential medicines list? If so, is it effective?
- Is there an effective policy limiting MOH pharmaceutical procurement to medicines registered with the drug regulatory authority? If so, do procedures exist for granting exemptions?
- For competitive tenders, does the schedule of requirements list medicines by generic name or brand name?
- Are any medicines or groups of medicines tendered by therapeutic group (for example, oral first-generation cephalosporin) instead of by individual medicine in the group?

- Does the tender document specify pharmacopeial standards, WHO certification, specific packaging, specific labeling on packaging, specific labeling on individual dosage form, specific labeling language, delivery or order schedule, limit on back orders or number of partial shipments, minimum shelf life, replacement of goods damaged in shipment, samples submitted with bid?
- Are domestic companies allowed a local preference margin on bids? If so, what percentage?
- Is value added required for local preference? If so, what percentage is required, and how is value added determined?
- What is the usual basis for selecting the contract supplier? Is it the lowest price with no exceptions, the lowest price from a prequalified vendor, the lowest price of products deemed to be of acceptable quality, or some other standard policy?
- If product quality is a factor in tender awards, how is quality determined?
- What circumstances prompt split tender awards, if any?
- Are secondary supplier awards routinely made in case the primary supplier fails to perform? If so, do secondary suppliers normally agree to honor original tender prices?
- What circumstances warrant switching to the secondary supplier?
- Are constraints experienced in the use of secondary suppliers?
- Are bid bonds required? If so, what percentage of procurement value is required?
- Are performance bonds required after contracts are awarded? If so, what are the usual amounts or percentage of procurement value required?
- Is a fee charged to vendors that request tender documents? If so, what is the amount?
- Does the tender contract provide for penalties if the vendor does not perform? If so, are these penalties enforced?
- Are contract terms to which suppliers are expected to adhere clearly specified?
- Do these terms provide sufficient protection from common difficulties, such as late deliveries, inade-

quate medicine labeling, short shelf life, and poor quality?
- Are trade terms, payment terms, delivery schedules, and payment methods clearly specified?

Payment to suppliers

- Are there problems with timely access to procurement funds or foreign exchange? If so, how do they affect the procurement timetable?
- What are the usual payment terms for international purchases and for domestic purchases?
- What are the usual real lead times for payment for credit purchases (both international and local purchases)?
- What is the total debt owed to domestic vendors and to international vendors for pharmaceuticals and supplies?

Procurement information system

- Is there a systematic method for monitoring the status of outstanding orders and for providing information to other units regarding the status of outstanding orders?
- Do suppliers frequently refuse to supply an item for which they have won the contract, or do they default on an order?
- Are there frequent problems with suppliers' performance?
- What system is used to monitor the performance of suppliers and of health units that order pharmaceuticals?
- What reports are prepared on performance, and how are these reports used?
- Are computers used in the tender management and procurement information system? If so, what kinds of software are used?
- Are the software and hardware suited to the purpose?
- Are personnel who use the computers trained in the use of the software?
- Does the computerized information system produce reliable information on consumption and performance?
- Is a reliable system in place for maintaining and supporting the hardware and software?

References and further readings

★ = Key readings.

EuropeAid Cooperation Office. 2008. *Practical Guide to Contract Procedures for EU External Actions*. Brussels: European Commission. <http://ec.europa.eu/europeaid/work/procedures/implementation/practical_guide/index_en.htm>

Heltzer, N., A. Shrivastav, and M. Clark. 2008. *Developing an Assessment System for Procurement Agencies in Health Sector in India*. Submitted to the World Bank by the Center for Pharmaceutical Management. Arlington, Va.: Management Sciences for Health.

International Chamber of Commerce. 2010. *Incoterms 2010: ICC Rules for the Use of Domestic and International Trade Terms*. ICC Publication no. 715. Paris: ICC Publishing.

★ MSH (Management Sciences for Health). 2010. *International Drug Price Indicator Guide: 2009 Edition*. Cambridge, Mass.: MSH. (Updated annually.) <http://erc.msh.org/priceguide>

OECS/PPS (Organisation of Eastern Caribbean States/Pharmaceutical Procurement Service). 2009. "Supplier Pre-Qualification Form." <http://oecs.org/doc-lib/doc_details/431-supplier-prequalification?fontstyle=f-larger>

OECD/DAC (Organisation for Economic Cooperation and Development/Development Assistance Committee). 2010. *Methodology for Assessing Procurement Systems*. Paris: OECD. <http://www.oecd.org/dataoecd/50/33/45181522.pdf>

PPDA (Public Procurement and Disposal of Public Assets Authority). 2007. *A Report on the Compliance and Performance Indicators for the Uganda Procurement System*. Kampala: PPDA. <http://www.oecd.org/dataoecd/55/59/41050415.pdf>

PPRA (Public Procurement Regulatory Authority [Tanzania]). 2007. *Assessment of the Country's Procurement System: Final Report*. Dar es Salaam: PPRA.

WHO (World Health Organization). 2010a. *Good Procurement Practices for Artemisinin-Based Antimalarial Medicines*. Geneva: WHO. <http://whqlibdoc.who.int/publications/2010/9789241598927_eng.pdf>

———. 2010b. *Prequalification of Medicines by WHO*. Fact sheet no. 278. Geneva: WHO. <http://www.who.int/mediacentre/factsheets/fs278/en/index.html>

———. 2010c. WHO Prequalification of Medicines Programme: Inspection of Finished Pharmaceutical Product Manufacturers to Increase Quality of Medicines. *WHO Pharmaceuticals Newsletter* 2:16–18. <http://www.who.int/medicines/publications/newsletter/2010news2_1.pdf>

———. 2009. Prequalification of Medicines Programme. *WHO Drug Information* 24 (1):3. <http://www.who.int/medicines/publications/druginformation/DrugInfo2010_Vol24-1.pdf>

———. 2007. *Multi-Country Regional Pooled Procurement of Medicines: Identifying Key Principles for Enabling Regional Pooled Procurement and a Framework for Inter-Regional Collaboration in the African, Caribbean and Pacific Island Countries*. Geneva: WHO. <http://apps.who.int/medicinedocs/documents/s14862e/s14862e.pdf>

———. 1999. *Operational Principles for Good Pharmaceutical Procurement*. Geneva: WHO. <http://apps.who.int/medicinedocs/pdf/whozip49e/whozip49e.pdf>

———. No date. *Guidelines on the Implementation of the WHO Certification Scheme on the Quality of Pharmaceutical Products Moving in International Commerce*. Geneva: WHO. <http://www.who.int/medicines/areas/quality_safety/regulation_legislation/certification/guidelines/en/index.html>

WHO/WPRO (World Health Organization/Regional Office for the Western Pacific). 2002. *Practical Guidelines on Pharmaceutical Procurement for Countries with Small Procurement Agencies*. Manila: WHO/WPRO. [Includes model tender invitation document, model bid form, model invitation to bid and contract form.] <http://apps.who.int/medicinedocs/en/d/Jh2999e/>

World Bank. 2009. *E-Tendering Requirements for MDB Financed Procurement*. Washington, D.C.: World Bank. <http://siteresources.worldbank.org/INTPROCUREMENT/Resources/E-Tendering_Requirements_for_MDB_Loans-Grants_and_Credits_November_2009.pdf>

★ ———. 2004. *Standard Bidding Documents for Procurement of Health Sector Goods: Pharmaceuticals, Vaccines and Condoms*. Revised August 2008. Washington, D.C.: World Bank. <http://go.worldbank.org/R557PHPNU0>

———. 2002. *Standard Prequalification Document: Procurement of Health Sector Goods. Trial Edition*. Washington, D.C.: World Bank. <http://go.worldbank.org/MKC98ZYT80>

★ ———. 2000. *Technical Note: Procurement of Health Sector Goods*. Washington, D.C.: World Bank. <http://siteresources.worldbank.org/INTPROCUREMENT/Resources/health-tn-ev2-a4.doc>

World Health Organization, United Nations Children's Fund, United Nations Development Programme, United Nations Population Fund, World Bank. 2007. *A Model Quality Assurance System for Procurement Agencies: Recommendations for Quality Assurance Systems Focusing on Prequalification of Products and Manufacturers, Purchasing, Storage and Distribution of Pharmaceutical Products*. Geneva: WHO. <http://www.who.int/medicines/publications/ModelQualityAssurance.pdf>

Annex 21-1 Prequalifying new suppliers

WHO published guidelines related to pharmaceutical procurement that include a section on prequalifying suppliers (WHO/WPRO 2002). The guidelines note that the primary activities for a prequalification system include—

- Obtaining supplier information through the use of questionnaires
- Using the WHO Certification Scheme
- Seeking information from the drug regulatory authority of the exporting country
- Exchanging information with other drug regulatory authorities
- Evaluating product samples
- Monitoring and recording supplier performance

The WHO procurement guidelines also include a model questionnaire for suppliers. The World Bank (2002) also has a prequalification document for its vendors, which may be a useful resource. In addition, an example of the Organisation of Eastern Caribbean States Pharmaceutical Procurement Service's supplier prequalification form is available (OECS/PPS 2009).

Questions to ask as part of a prequalification process include the following. Annex 21-2 lists questions related to supplier performance monitoring.

Status

- Is the supplier a primary manufacturer or a distributor?
- If a manufacturer, does the supplier manufacture all products in-house?
- If the supplier does not manufacture all products in-house, who is the primary manufacturer for each product offered?

Quality control

- Does the supplier use good manufacturing practices (GMPs)?
- Does the supplier have an on-site quality control laboratory or arrangements with an immediately accessible laboratory?
- What tests—chemical, biological, stability, accelerated stability, or others—are routinely performed during and after the manufacturing process?
- Are special tests performed for stability in tropical environments?

Inspection

- What official government agencies or reputable international organizations have inspected the manufacturing facilities?

- What are the results of the most recent inspections?
- What certification documents are available from the regulatory agency concerning the supplier's status and compliance with GMPs?

Personnel and facilities

- What are the qualifications of key production and quality-control personnel?
- What is the capacity of the supplier's plant(s)?
- Does the supplier have the capacity to supply all the required quantities?
- Will the supplier have to subcontract portions of large awards?

Trade references

- What other local or foreign public procurement programs and hospitals buy from the supplier?
- How long has the supplier served the above groups?
- What is the experience of these customers with regard to the supplier's quality and service?

Financial status

- Is the supplier financially stable?
- Will the supplier remain in existence for the entire contract period?

Corporate associations

- Is the supplier a subsidiary, a parent company, or in some other way formally associated with any known supplier? If so, what is the reliability of the known supplier?
- Is the supplier producing certain products under a supervised licensing agreement with a known supplier?
- How long has the supplier been supplying the goods under consideration?

Local reputation

- How is the supplier regarded by knowledgeable physicians and pharmacists?
- How are products of the supplier regarded by knowledgeable physicians and pharmacists?
- Is any information available from public sources (such as newspapers or trade journals) concerning the supplier's performance in other countries?

Annex 21-2   Criteria for evaluating suppliers

SERVICE

Participation record

- Has the supplier attempted to alter or withdraw bids after submitting them?
- Has the supplier accepted an award of a bid and subsequently failed to deliver the product?

Response to inquiries

- Has the supplier adequately responded to all inquiries from the purchaser within a reasonable period of time?
- Did the supplier provide regular information regarding the status of outstanding orders?

Delivery time

- What was the supplier's average promised lead time? What was the actual lead time for the last procurement cycle?
- What percentage of shipments was late? How many days (weeks, months) late?
- What additional costs were incurred because of late shipments?

Adherence to delivery instructions

- Did shipments arrive under the proper shipping conditions (for example, cold storage for vaccines)?
- Did shipments arrive at the correct port?
- Did the supplier send full shipments as requested, or were there partial shipments? How many partial shipments on average?

Provision of documents

- Did the supplier provide advance copies of documents according to contract terms?
- Did shipments arrive with all required documents correctly and completely filled out and signed?
- If required documents were omitted, how did the supplier correct the problem?

Packing and labeling

- Did the supplier always ship the correct dosage form, the correct package size, the correct quantity in each package? Were short shipments frequent?
- Was labeling complete and adequate for proper use? Was it in the correct language?

Product shelf life

- Did all products shipped comply with contractual terms for remaining shelf life? If not, how many products were shipped with a shelf life less than that called for in the contract?
- Did the supplier promptly replace any items shipped that did not have an acceptable remaining shelf life or allow the return for credit or exchange of products nearing their expiration date (one standard is within three months of expiration date)?
- Did the supplier analyze samples of products approaching their expiration date to determine whether longer shelf lives can be applied to the products? Was there a charge?

Compliance with contract financial terms

- Did all invoices comply with contract pricing terms? Were any problems promptly rectified?
- Were all shipments correctly insured and shipped according to financial terms in the contract?
- Were there any problems obtaining compensation or reimbursement for lost or damaged goods?

Information available from supplier

- Did the supplier make suggestions concerning ways in which the purchaser could reduce costs (for example, by combining or splitting orders or altering delivery schedules)?
- Did the supplier provide information on purchases and payments for use in reconciling accounts?
- Did the supplier provide information on purchases broken down by products and/or therapeutic categories?

QUALITY

Pharmaceutical product

- Have complaints been received concerning product quality for this supplier? If so, what were the results of follow-up?
- Have products supplied conformed to specified pharmacopeial standards with regard to identity, purity, potency, physical appearance, dissolution, and other attributes?
- Have any products failed quality assurance testing conducted by the purchaser?
- Did the supplier provide requested batch analyses with each shipment?
- Does the supplier cooperate in making samples available and paying for quality-control tests performed by independent quality assurance agencies?
- Were there documented product problems that the supplier refused to acknowledge and rectify?
- Did the products last throughout the period of their stated shelf life?
- Was any discoloration or disintegration reported?

Packaging materials

- Were there specific examples of loss due to breakage or damage to packaging during shipments? If so, what was the extent or value?
- Did packaging meet standards appropriate to the climate of the purchasing country?
- Was external packaging sufficiently rugged to ensure arrival in the country in good condition?
- Did the external packaging protect the product from damage during transport within the country? For example, were vials sufficiently padded to withstand long trips on extremely rough roads?
- Was the immediate container able to withstand rough in-country transportation, heat, and humidity? For example, did pressure-sealed lids on tins shake loose on rocky roads?

Part I: Policy and economic issues

Part II: Pharmaceutical management

Part III: Management support systems

Selection
Procurement
Distribution
22 Managing distribution
23 Inventory management
24 Importation and port clearing
25 Transport management
26 Kit system management
Use

CHAPTER 22

Managing distribution

Summary   22.2

22.1 Goals of distribution management   22.3

22.2 The distribution cycle   22.4

22.3 Distribution system design   22.6
Basic design features • Distribution network • Push and pull systems • Resupply interval • Storage • Delivery systems versus collection systems • Transport • Delivery schedules

22.4 Resources for distribution management   22.14
Logistics managers • Staffing levels • Information systems • Communications

22.5 Cost analysis and performance monitoring   22.16
Calculating costs • Collecting and analyzing cost and performance data

22.6 The private-sector option   22.17

22.7 Considering improvement and replacement   22.18
Example 1. Poor administration • Example 2. Seasonal variations • Example 3. Major transport problems • Example 4. Increased volume

Glossary   22.18

Assessment guide   22.20

References and further readings   22.21

ILLUSTRATIONS

Figure 22-1 Typical pharmaceutical distribution system   22.4

Figure 22-2 The distribution cycle   22.5

Figure 22-3 Design characteristics of distribution networks   22.7

Figure 22-4 Comparison of four distribution networks   22.10

Figure 22-5 Stock volume in store design   22.13

Figure 22-6 Planning for monthly requisitions and deliveries   22.15

Table 22-1 Comparison of three-level and four-level distribution hierarchies   22.9

Table 22-2 Comparison of delivery and collection systems   22.14

COUNTRY STUDIES

CS 22-1 TB medicine distribution challenges in mountainous terrain   22.8

CS 22-2 Transition from primary health kits to a direct requisition system in Tanzania   22.11

CS 22-3 Improving pharmaceutical management using an imprest system in a clinic in Ghana   22.12

SUMMARY

The primary distribution management goal is to maintain a steady supply of pharmaceuticals and supplies to facilities where they are needed, while ensuring that resources are being used in the most effective way. Distribution costs, which include costs related to storage and transportation, are a significant component of the expense of running a public health supply system. Transportation costs alone can represent a significant percentage of the value of medicines distributed to remote locations. Designing a system for storing and distributing pharmaceuticals, medical supplies, and equipment is complex and important.

Effective pharmaceutical distribution relies on good system design and good management. A well-designed and well-managed distribution system should—

- Maintain a constant supply of medicines
- Keep medicines in good condition throughout the distribution process
- Minimize medicine losses caused by spoilage and expiry
- Maintain accurate inventory records
- Rationalize medicine storage points
- Use available transportation resources as efficiently and effectively as possible
- Reduce theft and fraud
- Provide information for forecasting medicine needs
- Incorporate a quality assurance program

The distribution cycle begins when pharmaceuticals are dispatched by the manufacturer or supplier. It ends when medicine consumption information is reported back to the procurement unit.

The distribution cycle includes the following steps—

- Port clearing (for imported products)
- Receipt and inspection
- Inventory control
- Storage
- Requisition of supplies
- Delivery
- Dispensing to patients
- Reporting consumption

Designing a new distribution system or, as is more likely in practice, evaluating and planning improvements to an existing system, requires systematic cost-effectiveness analysis and operational planning. The basic characteristics of a distribution system include its degree of centralization, the number of levels in the system, and the geographic or population coverage.

A distribution system has four major elements—

1. *System type* (geographic coverage, population coverage, or both; number of levels in the system; push versus pull system; degree of centralization)
2. *Information system* (inventory control, records and forms, consumption reports, information flow)
3. *Storage* (selection of sites, building design, materials-handling systems, order picking, layout)
4. *Delivery* (collection versus delivery, in-house versus third party, dedicated or shared arrangements, choice of transport, vehicle procurement, vehicle maintenance, routing and scheduling of deliveries)

Whenever a new system is designed or an existing one is modified, cost analysis (comparing the total costs of using various options) can help ensure that available storage, transport, and human resources are used effectively. After implementation, a program of performance monitoring should ensure that the distribution system works as intended.

Centralized distribution is one option; some countries procure and distribute medicines regionally, and some use commercial supply systems, which often exist in parallel with public systems. Collaboration between private and public systems may occur at any level.

Operational planning and logistics skills are the key to developing a cost-effective and efficient distribution system. It is therefore important to have a logistics management staff composed of qualified professionals.

The steps in planning a distribution system are as follows—

1. Determine whether distribution operations would be carried out most effectively in the public or private sector, or a combination of both
2. Determine whether a push or pull system is to be used
3. Plan store locations and delivery routes—
   - Map the demand for medicines and estimate future demand based on population growth or program scale-up
   - Locate supply entry points
   - Rationalize primary storage points
   - Plan primary distribution routes and locate new intermediate stores, as necessary
   - Plan secondary distribution routes, if necessary
   - Size the stores
4. Plan delivery schedules and the required transport infrastructure

5. Establish staffing levels
6. Establish information flow

In some countries, private or parastatal distribution companies can provide cost-effective alternatives for the storage and distribution of medicines, especially at the national and regional levels. Contracting out to such a company involves—

- Assessing the cost of the existing system
- Determining what functions to contract out
- Specifying service requirements for the contract
- Preparing tender documents
- Evaluating the tender participants
- Agreeing to and signing a contract
- Monitoring the contractor's performance

22.1 Goals of distribution management

The primary distribution management goal is to maintain a steady supply of pharmaceuticals and supplies to facilities where they are needed while ensuring that resources are used in the most effective way. Distribution costs, including storage and transportation costs, are a significant expense of running a public health supply system, often second only to personnel costs. Transportation costs alone may exceed the value of the medicines distributed to some locations, especially in countries with low population densities that cover large geographical areas. Reducing these costs can mean that more money is available for medicine purchases and clinical care. A good distribution system is a *cost-effective* system that provides an acceptable level of service.

Public health authorities are rarely in a position to create a pharmaceutical distribution system from the ground up; rather, the challenge is to evaluate and improve existing systems.

In many public health systems, senior officials do not consider pharmaceutical distribution a high priority; it is too often placed in the hands of poorly trained and inexperienced staff members who are given responsibility but little authority. Under such circumstances, management tends to react to problems and crises rather than take a long-term, strategic view. For example, to save money, a decision may be made to close an apparently costly warehouse, without considering the potential result of increased costs in other areas, such as transportation.

In planning distribution systems to maximize service while minimizing total cost, it is important not to fall into the trap of improving one part of the system to the detriment of the overall system. In the example above, reducing the number of warehouses will decrease operating and inventory costs. However, with fewer warehouses, transport costs for both the central medical stores and hospitals are likely to increase because of the greater distance to travel to either deliver or collect supplies; therefore, the distribution planner will want to ensure that warehouse and inventory savings are not negated by the increase in transport costs. The effect on customer service will also have to be considered. Inventory costs may be reduced, but if customers must wait longer to receive supplies or if availability deterio-

rates, broader health system objectives will be undermined. This concept of trade-offs and searching for overall system improvement is important for distribution system planners to understand and apply.

Ideally, a public sector with inefficiencies in its distribution system would perform a wholesale evaluation of the existing structure to find solutions that would be optimal for the entire supply and broader health system. To do this, however, requires that the government deem the distribution function important and make available sufficient financial and expert human resources to conduct the technically demanding strategic reviews. Whereas in some situations existing management will be able to conduct such reviews, in many cases management will have neither the time nor the required expertise to carry them out; therefore, public health authorities may find it more efficient to appoint specialized consultants.

Health programs are frequently managed by well-qualified health personnel who lack logistics experience. *Logistics* is defined here as the "science (and art) of getting the right amounts of the right things to the right places at the right time" (Foster 1990, 207). Warehouse and transport managers, storekeepers, and drivers may possess these skills but may have little influence on decision making. The best way to use their knowledge and skills is to make them part of a logistics team that manages the system design process.

A well-run distribution system should—

- Maintain a constant supply of medicines
- Keep medicines in good condition
- Minimize medicine losses caused by spoilage and expiry
- Rationalize pharmaceutical storage points
- Use available transport as efficiently as possible
- Reduce theft and fraud
- Provide information for forecasting medication needs
- Incorporate a quality assurance program

Senior management should regularly monitor the cost and performance of the distribution system as important indicators of the health care system's operations. Major alterations in the system should be introduced only after careful evaluation and planning, taking into account available human

Figure 22-1 Typical pharmaceutical distribution system

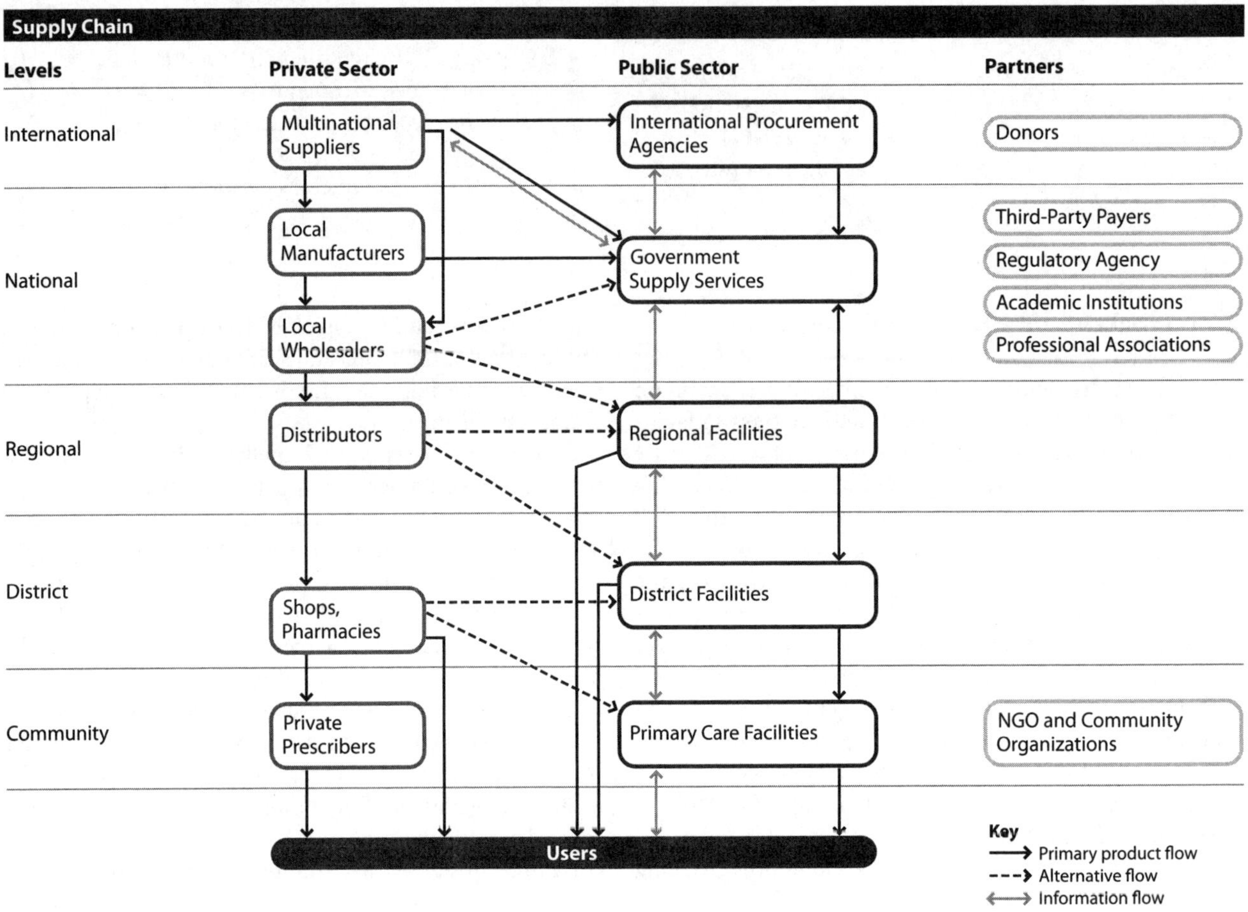

and material resources. A strategic review should begin with evaluating the following factors (which do not, however, comprise an exhaustive list of considerations)—

- Underlying assumptions and strategy of the medical stores organization
- Current and future customer service needs (products, service)
- Basic structure, costs, and performance of logistics system: processes, location and number of warehouses, movement of stock between warehouses
- Product range and sources
- Operating efficiency
  - Space utilization—area, cube, seasonality, pharmaceutical storage requirements
  - Equipment and vehicle use—time, capacity, seasonality
  - Staff performance—throughput per warehouse staff, sales per employee
  - Inventory—stock turn, availability, expiry
  - Order processing—volume of orders, costs, processing time

The key to an effective strategic review is exercising rigor in considering all of these areas but not getting mired in precisely analyzing each factor. Appropriate tools to use as part of a strategic review include ABC analysis focusing on order frequency (Chapter 40) and a weighted distribution analysis that identify the most cost-effective distribution strategies using global positioning system (GPS)–based mapping.

Following a review, the alternative options should be evaluated for suitability (main problems are solved, strengths of organization are exploited, option fits with organization and health-sector objectives); feasibility (available funding, skills and operational capacities available, technology available and supportable); and acceptability (preferred solution meets wider expectations and meshes with culture).

22.2 The distribution cycle

The distribution cycle begins when pharmaceuticals are dispatched by the manufacturer or supplier. It ends when medicine consumption information is reported back to the

Figure 22-2   The distribution cycle

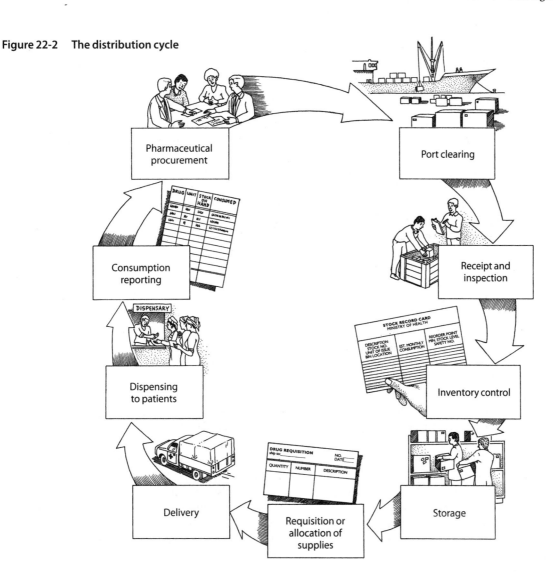

procurement unit. Figure 22-1 illustrates a typical public-sector pharmaceutical distribution system and its interactions with the private sector.

The major activities of the distribution cycle are summarized in Figure 22-2. They include—

Pharmaceutical procurement (see Chapters 18–21): The distribution sequence intersects the procurement process at the point at which medicines and commodities are available for delivery to the health facilities.

Port clearing (see Chapter 24): Unless the medicines are acquired locally or the international supplier takes responsibility for port clearing, it is the purchaser's first step in making medicines available for distribution. Port clearing involves identifying shipments as soon as they arrive in port, processing all importation documents, completing any customs requirements, storing medicines properly until they leave the port, surveying the shipment for losses and signs of dam-

age, and collecting the medicines as soon as they have been cleared. Port clearing may be managed directly or through a separate contract with a port-clearing agent.

Receipt and inspection (see Chapter 44): Central stores staff must carry out a complete inspection of every shipment as soon as it is received from the port or local supplier. The shipment must be kept separate from other stock until this inspection has been completed. Inspectors should check for damaged and missing items and for compliance with the contract conditions concerning drug type, quantity, presentation, packaging, labeling, and any special requirements. Prompt and accurate inspection of all shipments is essential to ensure that suppliers fulfill their contracts. Insurance companies will demand an accurate record of any losses incurred before settling a claim.

Inventory control (see Chapters 23, 44, and 46): Establishing and maintaining effective inventory records and procedures are the basis for coordinating the flow of pharmaceuticals through the distribution system and the primary protection against theft and corruption. The inventory control system is used for requisitioning and issuing medicines, for financial accounting, and for preparing the consumption and stock balance reports necessary for procurement. Record keeping must be sufficiently detailed to provide an "audit trail" that accurately traces the flow of medicines and funds through the system. This audit trail must be designed to satisfy the requirements of government auditors (and sometimes donor agencies) as well as program managers. An appropriate inventory management system should be adapted to suit the capacity and needs of personnel at all levels in the health program. Inventory records must be monitored regularly by supervisors to ensure accuracy and to avoid or detect losses. Careful inventory control is a key to providing a cost-effective and responsive distribution system.

Storage (see Chapters 42, 44, and 46): Storage facilities may range from large mechanized warehouses at the national level to small wooden boxes sitting in health centers or carried by community health workers. Proper location, construction, organization, and maintenance of storage facilities help maintain medication quality, minimize theft and loss through damage, and maintain regular supply to health facilities.

Requisition of supplies (see Chapters 23, 44, and 46): Pharmaceutical supply systems may operate under a push or a pull system (see Section 22.3). The forms and procedures for requisition are a key part of the inventory control system. They may vary from country to country and from one level to another within the same country. The requisition system may be manual or computerized or a combination of both, but it should always be designed to simplify distribution by facilitating inventory control, providing an audit trail for tracing the flow of medicines, assisting in financial accounting, and listing medicines issued.

Delivery (see Chapter 25): Medicines may be delivered by warehouse staff or collected by health facility staff. Transport may involve air, water, railway, or on- and off-road vehicles, porters, or a combination of means. Cost-effective choices between public- and private-sector carriers need to be made. Transport managers should select methods of transportation carefully and schedule deliveries realistically and systematically to provide punctual and economic service. Vehicle breakdowns; availability of fuel, lubricants, and spare parts; seasonal variations in access routes; safety along specific supply lines; the availability of private-sector services; and other local factors must all be considered in transport planning.

Dispensing to patients (see Chapter 30): The distribution process achieves its purpose when medicines reach hospital wards, outpatient clinics, health centers, or community health workers and are appropriately prescribed and dispensed to patients.

Consumption reporting (see Chapters 20 and 23): The closing link in the distribution cycle is the flow of information on consumption (which takes into account actual demand—that is, what would have been consumed if not stocked out) and stock balances back through the distribution system, to the procurement office, for use in quantifying procurement needs. When adequate inventory and requisition records are kept, compiling consumption reports is straightforward.

22.3 Distribution system design

Designing a new distribution system or, as is more likely in practice, evaluating and planning improvements to an existing system, requires systematic cost-effectiveness analysis and operational planning. Some guiding principles include—

- Managing and evaluating distribution and logistics as an integrated activity (for example, receipt, storage, distribution, and customer service operating together as a single system rather than as self-contained micro-systems unconnected to one another)
- Ensuring distribution system operations are linked to the overall objectives of the medical stores and the broader public health system
- Ensuring customer service needs are understood and accommodated
- Balancing the trade-offs between costs and service (for example, although every hospital might like to have a medical store on its premises, the increases in inventory-holding and operating costs are unlikely to make such an option cost-effective)
- Keeping stock moving
- Minimizing lead times, inventory, and costs
- Analyzing ways to improve effectiveness (for example, reduce number of warehouses, contract out transport, invest in new information systems) as well as efficiency (for example, ensure full transport loads, minimize inventory, mechanize materials-handling, automate order processing)
- Minimizing the steps in storage and handling, which decreases the opportunity for damage and loss

When the system is in place, regular performance monitoring is needed to ensure that the system functions as intended. The major design characteristics for a distribution network (see Figure 22-3) are considered in detail in subsequent chapters and are mentioned only briefly here.

Figure 22-3 Design characteristics of distribution networks

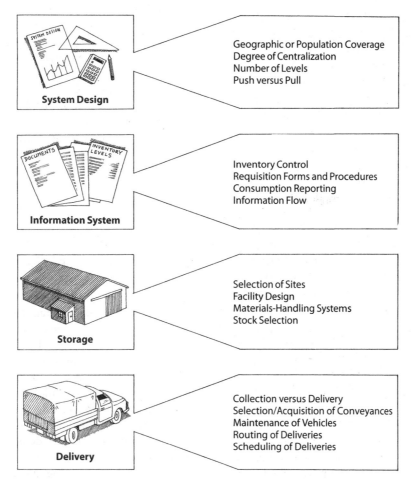

System Design
- Geographic or Population Coverage
- Degree of Centralization
- Number of Levels
- Push versus Pull

Information System
- Inventory Control
- Requisition Forms and Procedures
- Consumption Reporting
- Information Flow

Storage
- Selection of Sites
- Facility Design
- Materials-Handling Systems
- Stock Selection

Delivery
- Collection versus Delivery
- Selection/Acquisition of Conveyances
- Maintenance of Vehicles
- Routing of Deliveries
- Scheduling of Deliveries

Basic design features

The basic characteristics of a distribution system include its degree of centralization, the number of levels in the system, and the geographic or population coverage. Country Study 22-1 highlights the challenges of supplying tuberculosis (TB) medicines in the sparsely populated, mountainous country of Nepal. Comparable problems are faced by small island states, such as those in the Pacific, and geographically large countries with small, partially nomadic populations, such as Mongolia.

In a typical central supply model, pharmaceutical procurement and distribution are coordinated at the national level. Medicines received at the central medical stores (CMS) are distributed to lower-level warehouses and onward to the health facilities. In a decentralized system, the districts or regions are responsible for receiving, storing, and distributing medicines according to their needs; in some cases, they may also be responsible for procurement. Chapter 8 discusses various options for providing medicines to the public sector, some of which require in-house storage and some of

which eliminate part or all of public-sector supply system warehousing.

In designing a distribution system or redesigning an existing system, the following important steps have to be taken—

1. Determine the number of storage levels in the system
2. Determine the location of storage sites
3. Decide at which level of the supply system decisions will be made concerning orders
4. Fix resupply intervals or frequency of placing orders
5. Select a collection or delivery method for distributing medicines to user units
6. Select an appropriate mode of transport
7. Determine the amount of inventory to be held at each level in the system
8. Develop a set of feasible and economical delivery routes and work out a practical delivery schedule and appropriate modes of transport to service these routes; determine whether it is more efficient to keep and maintain vehicles or contract out the delivery service

In the mountain kingdom of Nepal, the government is succeeding in treating TB and preventing thousands of deaths a year. Starting with four pilot projects in 1996, the DOTS program has been extended to reach all institutions (including primary health care centers, health posts, and 99 percent of sub–health posts), and treatment success rates more than doubled during the program expansion. But success has not been easy. Much of Nepal is remote mountainous and hilly terrain, and many areas are sparsely populated, making pharmaceutical distribution extremely difficult. Medicines are distributed from the central level to regional stores and then supplied to the district, usually by vehicle or plane. From there, the medicines have to be carried by bicycle or on foot to some remote treatment centers. In some areas, additional lower-level health posts are used to provide DOTS to maximize population coverage. Patients can be treated there and only have to go to a larger, more distant health center for occasional monitoring.

Sources: WHO n.d.; SEARO 2010.

9. Estimate the operating costs and assess the cost-effectiveness of contracting for storage and transport at one or more levels
10. Establish a warehouse management system based on a set of standard operating procedures

Distribution network

A public pharmaceutical distribution system may require several layers of stores, each with distinct functions.

In a typical three-level distribution system, purchases from a supplier are received by one or more *primary stores,* which generally serve a whole country or region and may or may not supply health facilities directly. The physical size of the primary stores is determined by national or regional demand for medicines and by the supply frequency. In some countries, this level has been eliminated, with direct delivery from suppliers to intermediate stores.

Medicines are distributed from the primary to the *intermediate stores.* Their size is determined by the demand of the area health facilities and the frequency of supply by the primary stores. Intermediate stores may be independent but are often on the site of a regional or district hospital. Intermediate stores distribute medicines to individual *health facility stores.* This would be a four-level system.

Sometimes two layers of intermediate stores are needed, with first-level intermediate stores supplying second-level intermediate stores. For example, a regional store might supply district stores. Determining the optimum number of levels should be done individually according to program needs and resource constraints, weighing benefits against cost considerations. Some countries eliminate both intermediate levels of store in favor of direct delivery to facilities from suppliers or a primary distributor (see Chapter 8). Having fewer warehouses can decrease the opportunity for losses, and enhances control. Additional factors to consider in determining the number of storage levels are—

- Geography
- Population
- Availability of storage space
- Staff
- Availability and cost of transport
- Political and other resource constraints

Table 22-1 compares the three- and four-level systems in terms of management complexity, setup costs, operating costs, inventory costs, and applicability according to location and density of clinical facilities. Three-level systems are easier to manage and may be less expensive to set up and operate. However, when clinical facilities are widely dispersed and travel times are long, the four-level system may provide better service and may even prove less expensive to operate when all costs are considered.

Figure 22-4 gives examples of four different distribution networks and shows how the quantity and, therefore, the value of stock held in the system tend to increase as more levels are added. Note that the relationships between costs and number of levels are not always as direct as shown in the figure; efficient inventory management in a CMS system might result in lower total inventory costs than would be found in a regional stores network with less efficient inventory management.

No foolproof method exists for establishing the optimal number of levels and facilities in the distribution system, but the following steps may provide a useful way of arriving at the best hierarchy for an individual country or program—

1. Diagram the existing distribution hierarchy (include all clinical and storage facilities and the supply lines connecting them).
2. Diagram three or four feasible alternative hierarchies (include patterns based on different linkages between existing facilities as well as patterns that require additional facilities).
3. For each of these alternatives, estimate as accurately as possible the values for the factors listed in Table 22-1 (management complexity, setup costs, operating costs, inventory-holding costs, delivery times, and so forth).

Table 22-1   Comparison of three-level and four-level distribution hierarchies

Factors	Three-level	Four-level	Comments
Management complexity	Less complex	More complex	Four-level systems are more likely to have problems with transport, communications, and performance monitoring.
Setup costs • Buildings • Equipment • Vehicles	Lower	Higher	In regions where clinical facilities are relatively numerous or widely dispersed, the costs of a four-level system may be justified.
Operating costs • Personnel • Utilities • Fuel • Expendable supplies	Lower	Higher	The same observation as above.
Inventory-holding costs	Lower	Higher	If a four-level system results in more dependable delivery, lower safety stock is needed, and inventory-holding costs are not as high as expected.
Distribution of clinical facilities	Preferable with denser distribution	Often useful with sparser distribution	Distance can be measured in kilometers (miles), time, or transportation costs. Thus, an area that is small in square kilometers but is burdened with long travel times may benefit from a four-level system.
Quality of service • Number of stockouts • Ratio of interim and emergency to regular deliveries	Variable, depending on the location of storage and clinical facilities and the reliability of transportation between facilities		Inventory control and delivery are harder to manage in extended systems, but with good management, such systems are more responsive to the needs of remote facilities.

Total cost analysis is a good way to model these costs (see Chapter 40).

4. Diagram the current and proposed information flows.
5. Select and implement the system that provides the best quality service with available funds.

This systematic approach may identify previously unrecognized possibilities for improving distribution. Furthermore, the information generated can be used to substantiate requests to senior officials or external aid sources for additional funds, to implement a more costly, but more effective, plan.

Push and pull systems

Distribution schemes can be defined by which levels of the system order medicines and which, if any, passively receive medicines distributed from higher levels. The two basic alternatives are—

1. *Pull system:* Each level of the system determines what types and quantities of medicines are needed and places orders with the supply source (which may be a warehouse in the system or a commercial supplier). This type of system is sometimes called an independent demand or a requisition system.
2. *Push system:* Supply sources at some level in the system determine what types and quantities of medicines will be delivered to lower levels. A delivery plan is made at

the beginning of a planning period, usually a year, and supplies are delivered according to the plan. This type of system is also known as an allocation or a ration system—the best-known example in pharmaceutical supply is the ration kit system (see Chapter 26).

When using a pull system, managers of operational units are expected to work out their own demand estimates and buffer stocks and submit requisitions to central stores indicating their requirements. In a push system, operational units are expected to supply certain stock and consumption information to the supply source so that issuing officers can plan allocations.

As discussed in Chapter 26, pull systems are preferred whenever the capacity exists to manage them effectively. However, a push system can be useful in certain situations, such as for disaster relief and when the supply pipeline does not function at all levels of the system. Some countries use a mix of push and pull, with primary health medicines being supplied routinely in a kit, while district and regional hospitals determine their own needs. Making the transition from a push to a pull system may be the ideal, but it is not an easy undertaking and can involve complex and demanding changes in inventory management, warehouse operations, and distribution. Country Study 22-2 shows the challenges Tanzania is facing as it moves from supplying essential medicines kits to a direct requisition system.

Conditions that tend to favor push and pull distribution systems are presented below.

Figure 22-4   Comparison of four distribution networks

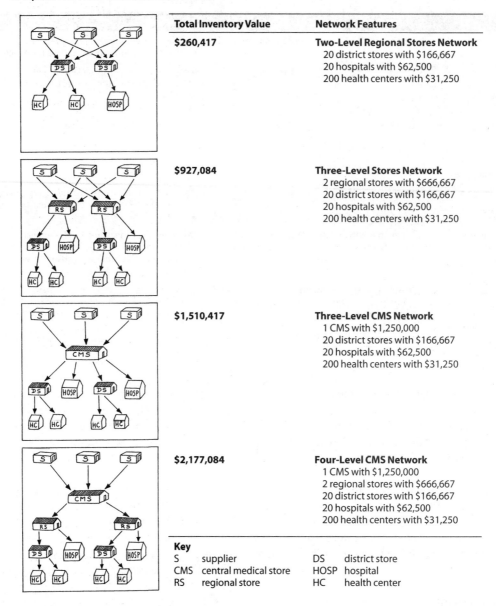

Total Inventory Value	Network Features
$260,417	**Two-Level Regional Stores Network** 20 district stores with $166,667 20 hospitals with $62,500 200 health centers with $31,250
$927,084	**Three-Level Stores Network** 2 regional stores with $666,667 20 district stores with $166,667 20 hospitals with $62,500 200 health centers with $31,250
$1,510,417	**Three-Level CMS Network** 1 CMS with $1,250,000 20 district stores with $166,667 20 hospitals with $62,500 200 health centers with $31,250
$2,177,084	**Four-Level CMS Network** 1 CMS with $1,250,000 2 regional stores with $666,667 20 district stores with $166,667 20 hospitals with $62,500 200 health centers with $31,250

Key

S	supplier	DS	district store
CMS	central medical store	HOSP	hospital
RS	regional store	HC	health center

Conditions favoring a pull system. Conditions favorable to a pull system of inventory management include—

- Lower-level staff members are competent in assessing needs and managing inventory.
- Sufficient supplies are available at supply sources to meet all program needs.
- A large range of products is being handled.
- Field staff members are regularly supervised, and performance is monitored.
- Good data are available to decision makers.

Conditions favoring a push system. Conditions favorable to a push system of inventory management include—

- Lower-level staff members are not competent in inventory control.
- Demand greatly exceeds supply, making rationing necessary.
- A limited number of products is being handled.
- Disaster relief is needed, or the situation calls for short-term supply through prepacked kits (see Chapter 26).

Resupply interval

The resupply interval determines whether deliveries are made to user units quarterly, monthly, weekly, or at any other time. If deliveries are made weekly, average stock levels will

The Tanzanian Ministry of Health (MOH) is instituting a policy of replacing essential medicine kits with an indent (direct requisition) system in order to tailor medicine orders to fit the needs of each particular health facility and to reduce waste. The MOH introduced a pilot project in the Morogoro region in 1999, where health facilities placed their orders with the medical stores department (MSD) through the District Medical Officer. The pilot has since been rolled out to five of the country's twenty regions.

The scaling up of the indent system is placing MSD operations under some strain, contributing to a slower rollout than planned. Inventory management, warehousing, and picking and packing operations all need to be re-engineered. The primary health care kits comprise four prepacked stock items that require only simple block stacking in the warehouse. Replacing the kits with the indent system means that instead of distributing more than 3,000 prepacked kits every month, MSD has to pick, pack, and deliver items according to customized orders, which is having a significant impact on the size and nature of MSD's inventory, storage, and distribution operations.

Source: SEAM 2003.

be low and the likelihood of stockouts will decrease, but transport costs will be very high. If deliveries are made only once a year, transport costs will be low, but the average stocks and storage costs will be high. See Chapter 23 for discussion of the relationship between delivery frequency and stock levels (and associated costs). (See Country Study 22-3 on how an imprest system of resupply is being used in Ghana.)

The optimum resupply interval should be worked out to suit individual program needs. Most public programs use intervals of one to three months. The following are helpful factors to consider before making a decision—

- Storage capacity at each level of the system
- Availability, order size, carrying capacity, and cost of transport
- Seasonal factors that influence transport reliability
- Staffing levels and competence of staff at each level of the system
- Other factors, such as expiration dates, security against pilferage, cash flow, and other locally relevant concerns

Storage

Geographic distribution of population and health facilities determines where medicines are needed. Storage planning starts with an analysis of existing and future supply requirements to establish the type and quantity of medicines required by each facility and the overall volume to be handled by the distribution system. Suitable locations and sizes for the central and intermediate stores can then be determined. Store locations should be chosen to make the most cost-effective use of existing public and private transport networks. Chapter 42 covers planning for storage facilities in detail.

Buildings can be renovated, purchased, rented, or built. The design of large storage buildings should take into account the storage conditions required for different products and the need to move large volumes of material efficiently. Stores at health facilities may consist of a simple storeroom with shelving. However simple the store, storage facilities should always protect against theft and damage by water, pests, or fire.

Another type of facility that can play a role in the distribution system is the regional cross-docking center (or stockless distribution center). As can be inferred, the centers do not hold or manage stock. They can serve primarily as data warehouses to collect, assure the quality of, and report on inventory and order information. They also receive picked and packed orders for each health facility in the region from the central supply and deliver the orders within the prescribed time frame.

Well-sited stores are vital to the success of a distribution system. However, no such thing as a perfect site exists. Needs often conflict: a location may be close to a good road but too far from the health centers it must serve. It is the responsibility of the logistics team to balance these needs. The following steps will facilitate the decision-making process.

Map the demand for medicines. Map the geographical distribution of medicines demand. Where are the hospitals, clinics, and aid posts? Which ones serve the most people? Estimate the volume and weight of each facility's annual pharmaceutical requirements using morbidity data, medicine requisitions, and delivery records. Plan for expansion. Where are new or expanded health facilities likely to be located? Are new public health programs going to be scaled up? Are any recommended treatments changing? How will these changes affect the geographical relationship between existing facilities and storage sites?

Country Study 22-3
Improving pharmaceutical management using an imprest system in a clinic in Ghana

The adoption of a top-up system of pharmaceutical supply has improved the pharmaceutical supply management at the Bank of Ghana Clinic, a parastatal outpatient health facility in Accra. A top-up system is a type of imprest system where running stock is replenished with quantities equal to those used. With the top-up system, the total responsibility for supply is given to the supplier, in this case, the clinic's pharmacy unit.

The maximum (imprest) level of stocks is agreed upon with the department in charge. The content of the list of stocks to be held is based on the regularly used medicines, and the final list is agreed on by the user and the pharmacy. The stock level of each medicine is based on the known average use of the medicine and the interval between stock replacements. In the Bank of Ghana Clinic, an initial survey determined the actual weekly consumption pattern of injectable medicines, with a 10 percent safety margin added. This information was the basis of the maximum weekly stock levels (imprest levels). New supply forms were designed to provide data on quantity used, top-up quantity, and expiry dates. At the beginning of the week, the nursing staff fills in the current stock levels and sends the forms to the pharmacy, where the technician notes how much of each medicine is needed to make the stock up to the imprest level. The pharmacy staff then delivers the items to the department.

In this system, there is no need for the department staff to order; the stock is automatically renewed by the pharmacy. After the clinic instituted this new supply system, their trend toward overstocking was reversed, and there was a significant reduction in inventory value, and therefore, expenditure. The success of the clinic's initial trial with injectables was expanded to other medications and commodities. A successful system depends on good communication and trust between user and supplier.

Source: Marfo 1998.

Locate supply entry points. Most countries have a limited number of entry points capable of handling pharmaceutical imports. These include major seaports and international airports, railway terminals, and cross-border customs posts. The logistics team should decide which points are the most appropriately located and best equipped for handling pharmaceutical shipments. Some countries have several suitable entry points for medicines, and it may be efficient for pharmaceuticals to be delivered through more than one port to more than one primary store. Multiple primary storage points may be justified in large countries or where physical barriers exist, such as mountain ranges or wide rivers without bridges.

Another option to consider is a regional distribution center, which uses regional warehouses as a consolidation point to regulate the flow of pharmaceuticals into a country's central supply. Using a regional distribution center reduces the risk of holding large amounts of stock, such as expiry, damage, or theft (SCMS 2010).

Select primary storage points. Review the location of the existing primary stores and consider whether they are well placed for current and future needs. The most suitable location for a primary store depends on geographic, demographic, and communications factors. A good choice is a point on the national transport network centered in the region with the highest population density. Using this location will help reduce overall transport costs. It is not essential for the primary store to be located in or near a major city. A city location may be administratively convenient but logistically inefficient.

The location of in-country pharmaceutical manufacturers and suppliers may affect the location of stores. Medicines received from those sources are generally delivered directly to primary or intermediate stores, and the transport portion of the pharmaceutical prices can be reduced if stores are located near a large concentration of local suppliers.

Plan primary distribution routes and locate intermediate stores. Good transport routes between the primary and intermediate stores (including any second-level intermediate stores) are crucial. These routes handle the largest quantities of medicines and must be reliable. Intermediate stores should therefore be located on good, all-weather roads or close to railway stations or navigable waterways.

Depending on the volume of pharmaceuticals to be delivered, a supply route that serves two or more intermediate stores on a circuit is usually cheaper than a route that serves only one. However, lengthy primary delivery circuits should be avoided where roads are bad, where overnight security is a problem, or where quality of medicines may be at risk through long exposure to unacceptable temperatures (see Chapter 25).

Plan secondary distribution routes. Secondary distribution routes link intermediate stores to health facilities. The planning of these routes requires detailed knowledge of rural road conditions, travel times, and available transport. Local input is essential. Medicines can be delivered from the intermediate store, collected from the intermediate store, or collected from a convenient health facility on a delivery circuit. The most practical solution for each health facility will vary.

Figure 22-5   Stock volume in store design

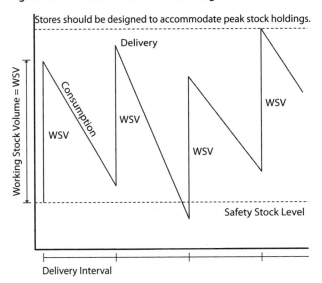

Size the stores. The previous steps establish which of the existing primary and intermediate stores are suitably located (or cannot be relocated) and where new stores are required. The volume of medicines to be held in each store can be estimated as described in Chapter 42. The maximum volume to be held depends on supply frequency: programs that receive single annual medicine deliveries require larger primary stores than those supplied more frequently. Estimates for maximum stock levels must also take into account the safety stock volume. However, deliveries do not always arrive exactly on time, and consumption is not entirely predictable (as shown in Figure 22-5). Available storage capacity should always be greater than the calculated maximum stock holding to allow for emergencies and for program expansion.

The capacity of each existing store should be assessed. If the existing storage capacity is insufficient, five possible solutions are available—

1. Reorganize the store by changing the shelving, changing the layout, or introducing pallet racking (see Chapters 42 and 44).
2. Build or rent additional warehouse space. This option involves capital costs for warehouse construction or recurrent costs for warehouse rental.
3. Increase the supply frequency to eliminate the need for additional storage space, probably at some increase in administrative costs. Suppliers may also charge extra for more frequent delivery. If the supply interval is already short, decreasing it may not be practical.
4. Upgrade one or more underused lower-level stores to higher-level status.
5. If insufficient space at the primary level is the problem,

consider holding larger stocks at the intermediate level, assuming the capacity exists. A system based on regular transfer of stock between stores at the same level should be avoided in most cases, because it is difficult to record such movements. However, some supply systems can manage redistribution, depending on the qualifications and motivation of the personnel involved.

Delivery systems versus collection systems

Basically, supplies are moved between the warehouse and the receiving facility in two ways: collection or delivery. In the case of a collection system, the receiving facility takes on the responsibility of collecting supplies from the warehouse. In a delivery system, the warehouse is responsible for delivering supplies by either in-house transport or a private-sector contract, or a combination of both. In planning a public health distribution system, considering all transport costs incurred in getting supplies to health facilities is important—not only the costs incurred by the medical store, but also those of each hospital and health facility that sends staff to collect supplies from a medical store depot or is responsible for distribution to lower levels. Although modifying medical stores' distribution systems might reduce costs, the financial impact on hospitals or local health authorities should also be considered before making final decisions.

Each method has advantages and disadvantages; the choice should be based on individual program needs and constraints. General advantages and disadvantages associated with collection and delivery are shown in Table 22-2.

Transport

Transport is frequently the least reliable link in the distribution system and is often a source of great frustration. Transport planning requires the selection of appropriate means of transport and the procurement and maintenance of vehicles or other conveyances. Issues to be considered include—

- Using private-sector alternatives
- Evaluating fleet capacity
- Planning transport system improvements
- Acquiring and disposing of vehicles
- Managing vehicle use
- Maintaining vehicles
- Maintaining medicine quality during transport

Transport managers should make the best use of available transport through careful route planning and delivery scheduling, and should carefully consider private-sector alternatives; these issues are addressed in Chapter 25.

Table 22-2 Comparison of delivery and collection systems

System	Advantages	Disadvantages
Delivery	• If proper delivery routes, order intervals, and delivery schedules are in place, the total cost of transport will be less. • Deliveries of supplies can be combined with other important scheduled and compulsory visits to the field. Also offers an opportunity to supervise fieldwork. • Medicine selection, assembly, and packing operations can be scheduled and accomplished efficiently. • Security and control can be enhanced by a well-managed, well-maintained transport fleet.	• Needs reliable transport facilities. Outright purchase or leasing of vehicles gives rise to high capital and operating costs. • If the delivery route is long, there is the possibility of breakage and loss of quality. • Security lapses may occur because of a lack of a responsible officer accompanying goods in many instances. • Health facilities may be closed when the delivery truck arrives, or a responsible officer may not be on hand to receive supplies. • The delivery truck may be in a hurry to get to the next destination, making it difficult to check for short shipments, damage, and other problems before the truck departs. • Not always possible to make economic use of larger vehicles if delivering to individual hospitals and health facilities.
Collection	• Provides an opportunity for issuing personnel to meet people from the field and discuss common problems, and for field officers to meet and exchange ideas among themselves. • Frees central-level staff from providing transport facilities to the field. • Provides greater incentive to obtain supplies regularly, since the facility is responsible for collecting supplies. • Allows field personnel to attend to other business in town. • Offers the possibility of a greater choice of methods of transport. • Allows for better checking, handling, and security of goods received.	• Takes up a lot of health facility staff time. • Time may be wasted waiting for assembly of supplies, or supplies might not be ready for collection on the first visit. • Total cost of transport may be high. • Health center personnel may tend to increase the frequency of visits for various reasons. • Health staff might become frustrated with the supply system if they find stockout situations at the end of a long trip to the sales depot.

Delivery schedules

Good planning is needed to ensure that each facility receives supplies regularly and on time. For example, an intermediate store may be responsible for forty clinical facilities with a delivery interval of one month. The total time required to supply all these facilities using available resources must not exceed one month. If analysis shows that a longer period is required to supply all facilities, then the delivery schedule must be changed or additional transport resources acquired. Figure 22-6 illustrates this concept.

When determining the appropriate delivery intervals for each store and health facility, consider the following factors.

Storage capacity of primary, intermediate, and health facility stores. Deliveries must never exceed the holding capacity of any store. This situation is more likely to occur with irregular or infrequent deliveries. Analysis of product throughput and delivery frequency can address this issue.

Increased transport costs per unit supplied for deliveries to small, remote facilities. An obvious solution is to supply these areas infrequently. The disadvantage is that this policy increases maximum stock levels at these facilities and

may also increase the risk of stockouts in places where environmental conditions make storage for extended periods difficult or expensive.

Efficient vehicle usage. If delivery intervals are too frequent, vehicles may travel half empty. If delivery intervals are long, large vehicles will be needed. Vehicles owned by the health service may stand idle for much of the time.

Climatic factors. Delivering to some facilities at certain times of the year may be impossible. Delivery frequency and volume must be scheduled to work around interruptions caused by rainy seasons or other recurring climatic constraints.

22.4 Resources for distribution management

Logistics managers

Under the traditional CMS supply paradigm, transport and warehouse managers and other officers with responsibility for logistics often had low professional status, and their skills and experience were frequently undervalued, if not

Figure 22-6 Planning for monthly requisitions and deliveries

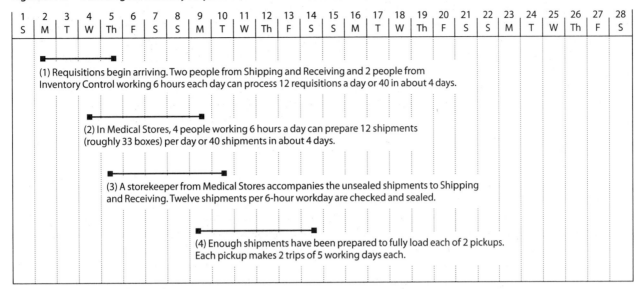

ignored. However, as the importance of pharmaceutical supply management to health programs has become more apparent, many countries are undertaking serious reforms (for example, shifting toward more autonomous, commercially oriented systems) and are recognizing the need for experienced professionals. Therefore, logistics systems are now more often being run by well-trained, experienced professionals than previously.

Experienced professionals should be responsible for the operational planning, implementation, and monitoring of the tasks described in this chapter. In large countries, regional cadres may be more appropriate than a single group of national experts. Logistics managers must stress the importance of improving medicine availability and reducing distribution costs wherever possible. Major decision making may benefit from specialized providers of technical assistance.

To ensure efficient and effective management and planning, the logistics managers or planning team must be vested with sufficient status to resist political pressures; for example, to resist building a store in an area where one is not justified on operational grounds.

Staffing levels

The logistics managers must determine the staffing levels required to administer and operate the pharmaceutical distribution system effectively. Are sufficient staff members available? Are they appropriately trained? Are funds available to recruit and train additional personnel if necessary? The most well-designed distribution system will not work unless there are enough suitably qualified staff members to run it.

Information systems

Reliable management information is vital for coordinating the distribution network. Medicine consumption information flows up and down the network. The information system consists of forms and procedures to record inventory levels, cost and sale prices, and receipt and issue of medicines. The system may be manual, computerized, or both.

It is easy to visualize the one-way flow of medicines through the supply pipeline from CMS to regional or district stores and, finally, to hospitals, health centers, and community health workers. It is more difficult to understand and manage the complementary flow of forms and reports needed to coordinate pharmaceutical distribution.

Forms, records, and reports form the core of the supply information system. Forms are documents that move from one unit to another, carrying specific information about pharmaceutical needs, movements of medicines, and associated financial transactions. Copies of forms filed at various points in the distribution network comprise the audit trail to trace the flow of medicines and funds. Records may be maintained in computer databases, as card files, in ledgers, or in folders. Reports should be prepared regularly to summarize medicine consumption and expenditures. Individual health facilities report to district offices, which report to regional offices, which report to the central office. Such reports are used to project medicine needs, monitor trends in use, revise budgets, and assess medicine use.

The forms shown in Chapters 44 and 46 can be adapted by any supply system to suit its requirements. Some forms may be usable as is, some forms may need modification, and additional forms may be required to suit special information needs.

When a new pharmaceutical supply program is initiated or an existing one is adapted, a complete information system should be established as part of the basic planning process (see Chapter 49). All necessary forms should be available, and all staff members should be trained in the use of these forms before pharmaceuticals start moving through the system. Without this type of preparation, the process of recording medicine consumption and forecasting medicine needs quickly breaks down.

Communications

Good communications are essential to a pharmaceutical distribution system. Where reliable telecommunications networks and postal services do not exist, especially in rural areas, staff often must travel long distances to deliver or collect reports and requisitions. These journeys should be combined with supervisory activities if possible.

Good telecommunications reduce the need for travel, save staff time, increase security, and reduce wear and tear on vehicles. Maximum use should be made of the telecommunications resources available, and appropriate investments in communications technology should be made. Providing a facility with a radio transmitter or a fax machine may help avoid unnecessary travel costs. Increasingly, the Internet may be used for electronic communications, saving resources and improving information delivery times. Other technologies include VSAT (very small aperture terminal) satellite systems and mobile phone technology, which provides a cost-effective communication mechanism, even in remote areas. Mobile phones are being used in many places to report inventory data from the field.

Products with a high market value are at greater risk from diversion and theft than those with a lower market value. Antiretroviral products and artemisinin-based combination therapies, for example, may be at heightened risk; therefore, distribution security will be of increased concern. To track vehicles, onboard computers in delivery vehicles can communicate with a central location (such as the CMS) via GPS, global system for mobile communications (GSM), and short message service (SMS) without any input from the driver. Other wireless communications options to communicate with drivers, such as high-frequency radio and cellular telephones, are becoming more commonly used as a means of managing distribution and protecting pharmaceutical supply systems. Chapters 25 and 43, focusing on transport and security, respectively, cover these issues in more detail.

22.5 Cost analysis and performance monitoring

When designing or revising a distribution system, compiling and analyzing data on current operating costs are crucial,

especially for modeling the potential cost impact of various alternatives. Total cost analysis, described in Chapter 40, is one method for analyzing costs and modeling alternatives in a supply system. This section gives an overview of the variable costs that apply to the distribution component of supply systems.

Cost analysis is not usually a continuous activity and should not be confused with performance monitoring (see Chapter 48), which should be carried out regularly using appropriate indicators to ensure that system performance is maintained.

Calculating costs

The first tasks in an evaluation of options are to calculate the *in-house costs* of the distribution system and then to estimate the costs of other alternatives for comparison. In-house costs include storage space, stores operation, equipment, staffing, holding and transport, administration and management, upgrading, and costs of contracting out (see Chapter 41).

Storage space includes the annual cost of rent paid to private warehouse owners and the annual amortized cost of warehouses owned by the health care service.

Operation costs include local building taxes and utility costs (electricity, gas, water, and insurance).

Equipment costs are annual amortized costs for equipment such as forklifts, for security equipment such as fire alarms and fire extinguishers, for specialized equipment such as cold rooms, for computer equipment used in stock control, and for other similar items. Costs should be amortized for items that are expected to have a useful life of more than one year.

Distribution staff costs include overhead and wages paid to storekeepers, drivers, mechanics, and laborers.

Holding stock (carrying cost) is the real cost associated with maintaining stock in inventory, as discussed in Chapter 23. Sufficient inventory must be kept to protect against stockouts and to take full advantage of bulk purchasing agreements. Holding too much stock increases storage costs and locks up funds; a good distribution system balances these two factors.

Transport includes all distribution charges not covered by the supplier's contract, which may end at the factory gate, at the dockside, or at the client's own warehouse (see Chapter 25). Transport costs may include—

- Air freight or shipping
- Insurance
- Demurrage
- Port clearing
- Transferring goods between forms of transport
- Distributing pharmaceuticals within the country
- Packing and unpacking

If government vehicles are used for medicines distribution, the costs include fuel, vehicle repair and maintenance, salaries and daily expenses for drivers, and vehicle amortization. Where financial management and accounting systems are not strong or are integrated into the general ministry of health accounting system, estimating the costs related to the in-house service may be difficult. When parastatal or private haulers are used, fixed and variable transport costs are more transparent.

In most cases, some costs (such as insurance and port-clearing fees) are outside the control of the pharmaceutical program. However, freight charges depend on the volume, value, and/or weight of the supplies ordered, as well as the fees charged by the shipping agent. Shipping costs are important considerations when evaluating pharmaceutical tenders. It is easiest to compare costs from competing suppliers when prices are CIF (cost, insurance, and freight) or CIP (carriage and insurance paid) (see Chapter 39).

Administrative overhead comprises all administrative costs incurred by, or allocated to, the distribution system.

Losses caused by poor management include the following direct costs—

- Damage from incorrect storage or transport conditions
- Theft of stock
- Misdirection of stock
- Unnecessary supplies in stock
- Supplies that expire before they can be used

Costs are also attributable to stock shortages. Extra costs are usually incurred when emergency purchases are made. When medicines are not available, it may be necessary to keep patients in the hospital for a longer period, thereby increasing nursing costs and making beds unavailable for other patients. When patients cannot be treated properly, they may infect others. These indirect losses are difficult to calculate, but they may be estimated using techniques of cost-effectiveness analysis (see Chapter 10).

Upgrading may require additional expenditures to bring an in-house distribution system to an acceptable level of efficiency. These costs must be compiled and included with other in-house costs for comparison with alternatives.

Contracting out incurs costs for private storage and distribution that should be estimated so that a comparison can be made with existing expenditures. These costs can be estimated by assessing private-sector capacity (see Chapter 36) and conducting a nonbinding tender to determine the costs of private-sector services (see Chapter 39).

Collecting and analyzing cost and performance data

In order to calculate costs accurately, collecting data from in-house accounting and reporting systems and from other sources is necessary. Data should be collected from natural cost centers; for example, if the system is organized on a regional basis, analysis of the costs by region will indicate how each region is performing.

Skilled staff or consultants are needed to design and carry out cost surveys, analyze data from survey questionnaires, and make useful inferences from imperfect data sets. The most informative survey collects field-based information from stock and vehicle maintenance records and from discussions with local staff. Chapter 36 discusses the management of an ad hoc assessment. Chapter 40 discusses data collection for total cost analysis. Chapter 48 addresses general principles of monitoring and evaluation, both valuable considerations when designing and implementing performance monitoring of the distribution system. In monitoring schemes, the same data should be collected from more than one source so that results can be cross-checked to assess the accuracy of existing record-keeping and reporting procedures.

22.6 The private-sector option

Pharmaceutical shortages are a common feature of government health services in many countries, even where such supplies are available through the formal and informal private sector. This situation is especially prevalent in major towns and cities. This private availability in the midst of public shortage suggests that, in these countries, the private sector is able to distribute pharmaceuticals more effectively than the public sector.

As discussed in Chapter 8, alternatives exist in many countries to a government-run storage and distribution system. With a well-developed private sector, contracting out both storage and distribution to a private company may be possible and appropriate. The first step should always be to identify local private-sector capacity. Determining the appropriate combination of private and public systems is then possible. A health service can contract all distribution services to the private sector, or may find that some combination of private and public systems is the most appropriate.

In many countries, the private sector can offer a comprehensive and effective distribution service only to the regional or district level. In small or low-income countries, very few private-sector distribution companies may be available, and when competition is limited, a contracted service may not be cheaper or better than the public sector (Bennett 1992).

Many formerly socialist economies have parastatal pharmaceutical distribution companies. Under the pressures of structural adjustment, these organizations are now forced to operate in the market economy. Parastatals can be well placed to provide distribution and transport services where a clear contractual (quasi–private sector) relationship between the parties incorporates performance targets and penalties for noncompliance.

The decision to use contracted services must be carefully considered because properly managing a contractor's work requires considerable staff time and expertise. To decide whether private provision of distribution systems is truly cheaper, the cost of the existing transport and distribution system must be assessed. Comprehensive tender documents must be prepared, specifying contractual and performance requirements precisely and unambiguously. It is then necessary to assess the capabilities and financial stability of the tender participants. After the contract is signed, the performance of the contractor must be carefully monitored. Contracting is discussed in Chapter 39.

22.7 Considering improvement and replacement

Most health services already have a pharmaceutical distribution network, but needs and systems evolve. For instance, a program might begin by using medicine kits and then wish to move to a requisition-based system, which is more complex and usually increases the number of individual items handled (see Chapter 26).

A distribution system may be outdated; storage points chosen long ago may not suit the present situation, or record keeping may be inadequate. Data may be inaccurate, out-of-date, or not available in a clear, user-friendly form.

If the distribution system does not meet current needs, changes are necessary. The problems might be solved by improving the present system, but sometimes a complete and radical change is the best solution, although it may be difficult to carry out. Even a good system requires frequent minor adjustments to respond to changing needs.

The four examples that follow illustrate typical distribution problems and the types of action that may be appropriate to solve them.

Example 1. Poor administration

Problems in this system include failure to comply with standard operating procedures, inadequate reporting of shortages by peripheral health facilities, and excessive losses due to theft.

Action: Review and strengthen supervision, administrative procedures, and reporting standards. It may be necessary to change personnel, to provide incentives to improve performance, or both.

Example 2. Seasonal variations

Medicine shortages occur because roads are closed during periods of heavy rain or snow.

Action: Review delivery intervals and delivery quantities to take account of predictable weather hazards. Deliver more supplies when the weather is good. Check storage capacity.

Example 3. Major transport problems

Major transport problems, such as lack of fuel or lack of vehicles in working order, arise.

Action: Are the causes of these transport problems local or general? Local problems may be solved by providing more spare parts or installing a fuel depot. General, widespread problems may be a sign of structural weakness, necessitating more radical solutions. Contracts with private-sector or parastatal organizations may be a more cost-effective way to manage all or part of the transport system.

Example 4. Increased volume

New or expanding health programs may result in greatly increased distribution volumes.

Action: Evaluate existing storage and transport capacity and performance and determine how easy it would be to expand the existing in-house system. Existing systems may already be working close to capacity, and expansion might be constrained by limited human resources and management systems. Evaluate the capacity and interest of the private sector to provide a cost-effective service. Determine the optimum mix of public- and private-sector services. Contract accordingly.

Successfully implementing new distribution systems or modifying existing ones depends on many factors. Some of the most important factors include—

- Active commitment of management and staff
- Human resource readiness—having prepared staff members in all departments and at all levels
- Management's full understanding of its own organization
- Willingness at all levels to change and adapt—learn new skills, do new jobs, accept new responsibilities
- Openness to new ideas and creativity
- Continuous, institutionalized effort to improve ■

Glossary

Bin card: Card that records receipts, issues, and balances held in the stores. The bin card is kept in the warehouse with the physical stock.

Card file: A stock record based on the use of cards stored in a file box or a plastic, visible-edge record tray (Kardex).

Cold chain: A system of freezers, refrigerators, cold boxes, and other devices needed to maintain the proper temperature for vaccines (and other perishable supplies) from the point of manufacture to the point of administration.

Collection system: Pharmaceutical distribution system in which the health facilities are responsible for providing transport of supplies from the warehouse to the health facility. Compare *delivery system.*

Delivery system: Pharmaceutical distribution system in which the warehouse is responsible for providing transport of supplies from the warehouse to the health facilities. Compare *collection system.*

Demurrage: A charge assessed by shippers to purchasers that fail to unload and return containers. It can also apply when carriers are unable to off-load shipments because of delay through the fault of the purchaser.

Distribution system: A system of administrative procedures, transport facilities, storage facilities, and user facilities through which supplies move from a central point to the user facilities.

Double-shelf system: A system for stock control in which the stock of each item is physically separated onto two shelves. When the stock on one shelf is expended, the stock from the other shelf is used, and an order for replacement stock is placed.

First-expiry/first-out procedure (FEFO): A method of inventory management in which products with the earliest expiry date are the first products issued, regardless of the order in which they are received. This method is more demanding than *FIFO* but should be used for short-dated products such as vaccines.

First-in/first-out procedure (FIFO): A method of inventory management in which the first products received are the first products issued. This method generally minimizes the chance of drug expiration.

Holding costs: The costs of carrying inventory, usually expressed as a percentage of the average inventory. These costs include both the capital costs and the storage costs.

Imprest system: A form of periodic inventory control in which stocks are replenished up to a pre-established level. No running stock records are kept. The only stock control document is a pre-printed sheet showing each item, its description, the unit of issue, and the imprest level. Generally used only at small facilities.

Indent system: A type of pull distribution system where facilities make direct requisitions for stock rather than receive pre-allotted quantities from a central facility.

Inventory: The total stock kept on hand at any storage point to protect against uncertainty, permit bulk purchasing, minimize waiting time, increase transportation efficiency, and buffer against seasonal fluctuations.

Inventory control: The function of supply management that aims to provide sufficient stocks of medicines at the lowest costs possible.

Inventory models: Systems of inventory control that determine how much stock is bought and how often it is bought. See Chapter 23 for a discussion.

Inventory taking: A periodic activity in which a physical count is made of the stock and compared with inventory control records. Also known as *physical stock count.*

Issue: To distribute a specific amount of an item to an intermediary stocking facility or a health facility.

Lead time: The time between the initiation of a purchase order and receipt at the warehouse from the supplier.

Lead-time demand: The number of units demanded and issued during the lead time.

Order picking: The systematic extraction of items from warehouse shelving to fill a client's order. Staff work from a picking list that defines the quantity and location of each item required.

Pallet: A transportable flat storage base, with or without sides, designed to hold goods and to permit handling by mechanical aids such as pallet trucks and forklifts.

Pipeline: The total storage capacity that must be filled in a pharmaceutical supply system, including the central medical stores, regional warehouses, district warehouses, and all regional facilities.

Pipeline analysis: The systematic diagramming of the supply system and calculation of the amount of stock held at each point in the system. The analysis determines the amount of stock actually needed and the amount of stock to be held at each storage point.

Prepacked kits: Also known as *ration kits* or *set packs.* An assortment of medicines and medical supplies to cover a set number of patient attendances, which are distributed unopened to health facilities.

Preventive maintenance: A series of maintenance and service activities performed regularly by a technician or operator and designed to prevent the breakdown of vehicles and other equipment. This form of maintenance is the least expensive.

Pull system: Pharmaceutical distribution system in which each peripheral facility determines the medicine quantities to be requisitioned from the procurement unit or warehouse. Compare *push system.*

Push system: Pharmaceutical distribution system in which the procurement unit or warehouse determines what medicine quantities are to be issued to the peripheral facilities. Compare *pull system.*

Receiving report: A document indicating when items were received, from whom, the total quantity in the shipment, the invoice price, and the amount of damaged or lost stock.

Routing: Determining the order in which facilities will receive their deliveries, based on the geographic location of facilities and an attempt to minimize delivery costs.

Safety stock: The buffer, cushion, or reserve stock kept on hand to protect against stockouts caused by delayed deliveries or markedly increased demand.

Service level: Most commonly defined as the percentage of items requested that are supplied, in the quantity requested, by a supplier or warehouse in one delivery. This term is sometimes used to describe the percentage of demand that is met from stock on hand.

Stock: Goods and materials stored for future use.

Stock count/physical inventory: The process of inventory taking, in which a physical count is made of all items in inventory and compared with the written record.

Stock numbers: Sequential numbers designating each item in inventory.

Stock position: All stock now available and soon to be available, including stock on hand and outstanding orders. This is sometimes called the *total inventory.*

Stock records: A generic term that applies to bin cards, Kardex records, stock ledgers, and computer files. These provide basic information for inventory management by recording all transactions for an item, including receipts, issues, orders placed, orders received, and stock losses.

ASSESSMENT GUIDE

Pharmaceutical distribution system

- Which levels of the supply system order pharmaceuticals from suppliers?
- Is distribution through a push or a pull system?
- Does the system include semi-autonomous vertical distribution components, such as EPI?
- How many levels are there in the distribution hierarchy? How many stores, clinical facilities, or pharmacies are at each level? How many levels of warehouses are needed (for example, central, provincial, district)?
- What are the catchment populations of warehouses, stores, clinical facilities, or pharmacies? Map the geographical distribution of each.
- Is the current distribution system based on collection or delivery?
- How many warehouses are needed? Where should they be? What geographic areas should they serve? What products should they store?
- What volume of medicines is distributed to each warehouse, store, clinical facility, and pharmacy per year? How often is each supplied? What is the physical capacity of each store? Is physical capacity ever exceeded? Map the current demand distribution.
- What criteria are used to calculate the resupply quantities at each level in the system?
- What changes in demand distribution are anticipated in the future?
- What mode of transport is used for each link in the distribution chain? What alternatives are available? What are the travel times for each link?

Supply sources

- What percentages in terms of bulk, value, and number of items do overseas and in-country suppliers contribute annually?
- Which ports of entry are used by each of the overseas suppliers? Which ports clear imports most efficiently and with the least loss?
- Where are the in-country pharmaceutical supply sources located?

Communications

- What methods of communication are available and actually used between each node in the distribution system (telephone, fax, radio link, physical visit)?

Performance indicators

- Cost of stock held as a percentage of stock turnover
- Percentage of health facilities submitting requisitions on time

- Frequency of delivery
- Number of emergency deliveries
- Number of items supplied out of total requested by clients (service level)
- Average stock position in months (quantity on hand and on order, divided by average monthly consumption)
- Stockout frequency for indicator medicines
- Percentage availability of indicator medicines at each level
- Quantity and value of expired items in stock
- Losses caused by damage and theft
- Distribution costs per ton per kilometer
- Vehicle availability and frequency of breakdowns
- Vehicle fuel availability in different parts of the country (a good indicator of the transport system's ability to make deliveries)
- Mechanical breakdown frequency for vital temperature control equipment such as cold rooms and air-conditioners
- Staff attendance rate and sick time used
- Variation between actual and recorded inventory level
- Currency of record maintenance
- Supplier and warehouse lead time

Monitoring and evaluation

- Are there effective systems for monitoring and evaluating distribution system costs and performance? If not, which elements are missing?
- How much can demand forecasts change without affecting the distribution system? For example, what would be the effect of a 50 percent increase in demand?
- What is the annual operating cost of the distribution system as a percentage of pharmaceuticals distributed? Are there significant regional variations?
- What are the costs of private-sector alternatives to in-house services?

Private-sector alternatives

- What private-sector pharmaceutical distribution systems exist? Identify the location of private-sector pharmacies within catchment areas of clinical facilities or pharmacies.
- Who are the private-sector storage and transport providers? Assess whether they are capable of handling medicines and delivering services to areas where they are needed.
- How would contracting out any services to the private sector affect customer service or costs?

Stocking cost: The cost of maintaining stock, including the capital and storage costs.

Stockout: Complete absence of an item that is normally expected to be on hand. In many cases, this indicator can be misleading, because a warehouse may always reserve a small stock—the warehouse is not literally out of stock, but a functional stockout exists because the warehouse will not issue the reserved stock.

Tachograph: A device that records comprehensive details of every journey and can provide a check on the accuracy of a driver's log.

Trans-shipment: Shipment of supplies to an intermediate location, from which they are forwarded by another means of transport to a facility.

Two-bin inventory control: Same as *double-shelf system,* except that two physically separate bins rather than shelves are used.

Unique identifiers: Techniques by which medicines can be identified as originating within the government supply system. Unique identifiers include labels with a program logo, reserved batch numbers, and imprinting of tablets and capsules.

Visual inventory system: A no-paper inventory control method in which the need to order is determined simply by looking at the inventory on the shelf. This system usually provides acceptable performance only in small facilities with a limited number of items in stock.

Working stock: That part of the inventory that is expected to be issued or consumed. It fluctuates between zero and the order quantity. The other component of inventory is the safety stock.

References and further readings

★ = Key readings.

Adam, T., R. Baltussen, T. Tan Torres, D. Evans, R. Hutubessy, A. Acharya, and C. J. L. Murray. 2003. *Making Choices in Health: WHO Guide to Cost-Effectiveness Analysis.* Geneva: World Health Organization. <http://www.who.int/choice/book/en>

Beenhakker, H. L., S. Carapetis, L. Crowther, and S. Hertel. 1987. *Rural Transport Services: A Guide to Their Planning and Implementation.* London: Intermediate Technology Publications.

Bennett, S. 1992. Promoting the Private Sector: A Review of Developing Country Trends. *Health Policy and Planning* 7(2):97–110.

★ Christopher, M. 2005. *Logistics and Supply Chain Management: Creating Value-Added Networks.* 3rd ed. New York: Prentice Hall.

★ Christopher, M., and H. Peck. 2003. *Marketing Logistics.* 2nd ed. Oxford: Butterworth-Heinemann.

Dalberg Global Development Advisors and the MIT-Zaragoza International Logistics Program. 2008. *The Private Sector's Role in Health Supply Chains: Review of the Role and Potential for Private Sector Engagement in Developing Country Health Supply Chains.* Technical Partner Paper 13. New York: Rockefeller Foundation. <http://apps.who.int/medicinedocs/documents/s16323e/s16323e.pdf>

Dawson, J., and I. Barwell. 1993. *Roads Are Not Enough: New Perspectives on Rural Transport Planning in Developing Countries.* London: Intermediate Technology Publications.

Foster, S. D. 1990. "Logistics and Supply." In *Why Things Work: Case Histories in Development,* ed. J. B. Halstead and J. A. Walsh. New York: Rockefeller Foundation.

★ Gattorna, J., ed. 2003. *Gower Handbook of Supply Chain Management.* 5th ed. Aldershot, Hampshire, UK: Gower Publishing Limited.

★ Johnson, J. C., D. F. Wood, D. L. Wardlow, and P. R. Murphy Jr. 2007. *Contemporary Logistics.* 9th ed. Upper Saddle River, N.J.: Prentice Hall.

Marfo, D. S. 1998. How "Topping-up" Improved Drug Management at a Small Clinic in Ghana. *Essential Drug Supply* 25/26:4.

McMahon, R., E. Barton, and M. Piot. 1992. *On Being in Charge: A Guide to Management in Primary Health Care.* 2nd ed. Geneva: World Health Organization. <http://whqlibdoc.who.int/publications/9241544260.pdf>

SCMS (Supply Chain Management System). 2010. *Regional Distribution Centers and Inventory Management.* Arlington, Va.: SCMS. <http://scms.pfscm.org/scms/docs/papers/tech_brief_RDCs_OCT.pdf>

SEAM (Strategies for Enhancing Access to Medicines). 2003. *Access to Essential Medicines: Tanzania, 2001.* Prepared for the SEAM Program. Arlington, Va.: Management Sciences for Health. <http://www.msh.org/seam/reports/CR022304_SEAMWebsite_attach1.pdf>

SEARO (World Health Organization Regional Office for South-East Asia). 2010. *Tuberculosis Control in the South-East Asia Region: The Regional Report 2010.* New Delhi: WHO. <http://www.searo.who.int/LinkFiles/TB_Day_Kit_SEA-TB-315.pdf>

Simchi-Levi, D., P. Kaminsky, and E. Simchi-Levi. 2007. *Designing and Managing the Supply Chain.* 3rd ed. New York: McGraw-Hill/Irwin.

Slack, N., S. Chambers, and R. Johnston. 2010. *Operations Management.* 6th ed. Upper Saddle River, N.J.: Prentice Hall.

Starkey, P., S. Ellis, J. Hinem, and A. Ternell, eds. 2002. "*Improving Rural Mobility: Options for Developing Motorised and Non-Motorised Transport in Rural Areas.*" Technical Paper 525. Washington, D.C.: World Bank. <http://ifrtd.gn.apc.org/new/proj/Improving%20Rural%20Mobility%20Paper.pdf>

WHO (World Health Organization). 2010. "Quality Assurance—Distribution and Trade of Pharmaceuticals." In *WHO Expert Committee on Specifications for Pharmaceutical Preparations.* 44th report. Geneva: WHO. <http://whqlibdoc.who.int/trs/WHO_TRS_957_eng.pdf>

———. 2002. *Guidelines for Establishing or Improving Primary and Intermediate Vaccine Stores.* Geneva: WHO. <http://whqlibdoc.who.int/hq/2002/WHO_V&B_02.34.pdf>

———. n.d. "Preventing TB Deaths in One of the World's Poorest Countries." <http://www.who.int/inf-new/tuber4.htm.>

WHO and EPN (World Health Organization/Ecumenical Pharmaceutical Network). 2006. *Multi-Country Study of Medicine Supply and Distribution Activities of Faith-based Organizations in Sub-Saharan African Countries.* Geneva: WHO/EPN. <http://whqlibdoc.who.int/hq/2006/WHO_PSM_PAR_2006.2_eng.pdf>

Wolff, J., R. Cushman, F. Kweekeh, E. McGrory, and S. Binzen, eds. 1990. *Beyond the Clinic Walls: Case Studies in Community-Based Distribution.* West Hartford, Conn.: Kumarian Press.

| Part I: Policy and economic issues | Part II: Pharmaceutical management | Part III: Management support systems |

Selection
Procurement
Distribution
  22 Managing distribution
  23 Inventory management
  24 Importation and port clearing
  25 Transport management
  26 Kit system management
Use

CHAPTER 23

Inventory management

SUMMARY

This chapter discusses inventory management—the management of the routine ordering process. Seven basic issues must be considered for effective, efficient inventory management—

- The supply system's purpose and the type of distribution system
- The records and reports that will provide the foundation for inventory management
- The selection of items to be stocked
- The balance between service levels, including stockout costs, ordering costs, and stock-holding costs
- The policy on when to order
- The policy on how much to order and methods for determining reorder quantities or reorder intervals
- The control of costs associated with inventory management (ordering, stockout, and stock holding)

The type of inventory management system needed depends first on the context—different systems are used for dependent demand systems (manufacturing) and independent demand systems (distribution of finished goods). Similarly, a different system may be needed in a push system as opposed to a pull system (see Chapter 22), although ordering has to be done in both push and pull systems. Clearly, most inventory management for pharmaceutical supply concerns the distribution of finished goods.

Accurate and current stock records are essential to good inventory management. They are the source of information used to calculate needs, and inaccurate records produce inaccurate needs estimations (and problems with stockouts and expiry). Each inventory system should monitor performance with indicators and produce regular reports on inventory and order status, operating costs, and consumption patterns.

The primary reason for holding stock in a pharmaceutical supply system is to ensure availability of essential items almost all the time. The selection of items to stock should be based on their value to public health and on the regularity and volume of consumption. VEN (vital, essential, nonessential) and ABC analyses are useful tools for defining which items on the formulary list must be held in stock (see Chapter 40). Although ABC analyses are often based on the value of the medicines, for inventory management, ABC analyses based on order frequency and volume are also important.

Key issues in inventory management are service level and safety stocks. The *service level* is the measurement of service from a supplier or from a warehouse, with the goal of never having stockouts. The principal determinant of service level is safety stock—the higher the level of safety stock in the warehouse, the higher the service level. However, excessive safety stocks cause excessive inventory-holding costs. The basic method for setting safety stock is multiplying the lead time by the average monthly consumption, but adjustments may be needed to cope with variations in consumption and lead-time patterns. The other key determinant is the turnaround time with the supplier or the warehouse, that is, the time taken to fill and deliver an order once it is received by the supplier or the warehouse. This turnaround time is a component of the overall lead time that is used by the user-level stockholder to determine inventory levels.

The ideal inventory model is the optimal stock movement pattern, in which inventory levels are as low as possible (without risking stockouts) and optimized, consumption patterns are consistent, and suppliers always deliver on time—but this model is rarely achieved in practice. As described in Section 23.6, the three common inventory models used in pharmaceutical supply systems are defined by how often regular orders are placed with suppliers—

- Annual purchasing (one regular order per year)
- Scheduled purchasing (periodic orders at set times during the year)
- Perpetual purchasing (orders are placed whenever stock becomes low, or when stock levels reach predetermined reorder levels)

Average inventory levels (and holding costs) are expected to decrease with more frequent orders.

The basic formulas for calculating order quantity are relatively simple; two useful formulas are minimum-maximum and consumption based. Both incorporate several essential factors—

- Average monthly consumption
- Supplier/warehouse lead time
- Safety stock
- Stock on order
- Stock in inventory
- Stock back-ordered to lower levels

The more complicated mathematical formulas, such as economic order quantity and exponential smoothing of demand, do not necessarily lead to better services than the simpler approaches and are not recommended for most pharmaceutical supply systems.

Whichever formulas are used, purchase quantities should be adjusted to take into account factors such as seasonal demand, expiry dates, expected changes in use or prices, currency fluctuation, and availability of storage space.

Key ways of minimizing total costs include—

- Lowering order processing, purchase, or delivery costs through efficient procurement
- Lowering stock-holding costs through good store-keeping practices
- Controlling stock levels and minimizing stockouts by using effective inventory control techniques
- Minimizing financial costs through use of attractive financing methods

Primary considerations in promoting efficiency are the costs of purchasing and holding stock in inventory. A regular and accurate stock count and standard methods for valuing the inventory are needed to determine the base inventory value. Other relevant costs are the operating costs associated with procurement and with holding inventory.

The objective of good inventory management is to maintain a steady supply to operating units (and patients) while minimizing the costs of holding inventory and managing procurement. Compiling information on the total costs of inventory management (pharmaceutical acquisition costs, inventory-holding costs, purchasing operations costs, and shortage costs) allows managers to evaluate strategies for reducing costs.

23.1 Introduction

Inventory management is the heart of the pharmaceutical supply system; in fact, the nonspecialist might say that inventory management *is* pharmaceutical management. That would be simplistic, as the other chapters of this book demonstrate, but without a healthy inventory management system, the pharmaceutical supply system as a whole will not be viable.

Inventory management for pharmaceutical supply sounds easy—all that must be done is to order, receive, store, issue, and then reorder a limited list of items. In reality, the task is difficult, and in many countries, poor inventory management in the public pharmaceutical supply system leads to waste of financial resources, shortages of some essential medicines or overages of others resulting in expiration, and decline in the quality of patient care.

"Sick" inventory management systems generally feature subjective, ad hoc decisions about order frequency and quantity, inaccurate stock records, and a lack of systematic performance monitoring. These problems are directly related to lack of knowledge and appreciation of what inventory management means as well as to ineffective management. In many cases no systematic procedures and rules exist to guide staff, a problem compounded by lack of understanding of the basic issues of proper inventory management on the part of managers.

Seven basic issues must be carefully considered when an inventory management system is being initially designed or upgraded—

1. Definition of the context in which the inventory management system must function
2. Determination of the types of stock records and inventory reports needed

3. Selection of items to be stocked as standard items
4. Maintenance of appropriate service levels for different classes of items
5. Adoption of a decision rule or a model for determining when to reorder
6. Adoption of a decision rule or a model for determining how much to reorder
7. Identification and control of inventory management costs using product classification systems such as ABC analysis, VEN analysis, level of use, and other cost-minimizing techniques. (See Chapter 40 for further details on minimizing costs.)

To address these issues, managers may use mathematical formulas and models to set policies concerning stock levels, reordering frequency, and reorder quantity. Because inventory management is so vital in maintaining supply systems—public or private—a number of formulas have been developed over the years, some fairly simple and others using complex mathematical models that not only are difficult to construct, but also are hard to solve. In the great majority of pharmaceutical supply situations, the simple models, formulas, and methods work as well as the complex models, so the simple approach is emphasized in this chapter.

One goal of inventory management is to achieve a reasonable balance between holding costs, on the one hand, and purchasing and shortage costs, on the other. In order to maintain this balance, the relevant costs need to be identified and quantified and then examined for how they interrelate. This analysis allows managers to see the "big picture" in the system and consider the effect of potential changes. Chapter 40 illustrates different approaches to controlling costs in pharmaceutical management.

23.2 The context of an inventory management system

Before defining rules for inventory management, the context in which an inventory management system operates must be defined. Two factors are relevant—independent versus dependent demand, and the use of "push" versus "pull" systems for distribution.

One factor that defines the context is whether the inventory system supports a supply system in which clients (health facilities) order finished products from a warehouse or other supply source, or whether the system supports primarily internal manufacturing; this factor determines whether the system is an independent demand system or a dependent demand system. The fundamental inventory management concepts and resulting procedures are quite different for the two systems.

Independent demand systems are applicable to the management of procurement and distribution of finished goods. The order intervals and quantities are derived from forecasts based on historical consumption by clients, tempered by knowledge of expected changes in consumption. Inventory levels are set to provide a defined level of service to clients, at an acceptable cost.

Dependent demand systems manage inventory requirements for raw materials and supplies based on what is needed for production in a manufacturing or repackaging operation. They are also known as *materials requirement planning systems*. Ordering intervals and quantities as well as inventory levels depend on projected production schedules. The just-in-time system is an example of inventory management in this context.

Because a typical pharmaceutical supply system is involved mainly in the procurement and distribution of finished pharmaceutical products, this chapter focuses on the independent demand system. However, in some pharmaceutical supply situations (such as local manufacturing or repackaging), a dependent demand system would be more appropriate. Readers who need information on dependent demand systems can find sources in References and Further Readings (Dear 1990; Waters 2003).

The other factor that defines the inventory management context is whether the distribution system is a pull system or a push system. In the *pull system*, operating units order medicines from a warehouse or supplier according to local determination of need. In the *push system*, a central authority orders medicines from suppliers and determines the quantities that will be shipped to the operating unit, based on the annual distribution plan and on information transmitted to the warehouse about need at the operating unit. The best-known example of a push system in pharmaceutical supply is the ration kit system, discussed in Chapter 26. Note that a push system has some features of a dependent demand system—a plan is set for distribution to operating units, and procurement is done to carry out that plan.

The inventory management methods discussed in this chapter can be applied in either a pull or a push system. In certain complex systems involving multiple levels of storage located, for example, at central, provincial, district, and health facilities, both push and pull systems may be at work in different levels of the system. Both systems may possibly be used at the same time for limited periods, for example, when introducing a limited push system to supplement supplies while addressing inefficiencies in the pull system.

Before readers go further, they may find reviewing the procurement glossary at the end of Chapter 18 useful. It contains commonly used terms that have a specific meaning in the discussion of inventory management.

23.3 Stock records and standard reports

This section discusses the types of stock records and reports that form the foundation of effective inventory management.

Stock records

Stock records are the core records in the inventory management system. They are the primary source of information used in the various reordering formulas discussed later in this chapter; they are also the source of data used to compile performance reports discussed in this section. Stock records can be either manual or computerized. Commonly used manual stock records include—

Vertical file cards: File cards are stored vertically in alphabetical or numerical order in a card file or drawer.
"Kardex" system: File cards are stored in a visible-edge record-tray system, with names and stock numbers on the lower edge, overlapped to provide an index.
Bin cards: File cards are physically kept with the stock. This system makes a visual check easy, serves as a reminder to keep records, and serves as a backup to records previously described. If a product has two different batches with two different batch numbers and expiry dates, two sets of bin cards should be maintained. However, only one stock card containing information on both batches needs to be used.
Ledger system: Records are kept on ledger sheets in a bound or loose-leaf book.

Many supply systems maintain two stock records for each item to improve accuracy and accountability. Typically, a bin card is kept with the stock, combined with a ledger, Kardex, or computer system kept in the central office. The use of these record systems in a large warehouse is discussed in

Chapter 44, and the maintenance of stock records in health facilities is treated in Chapter 46. Examples of manual and computerized stock records can be found in those chapters.

In most supply systems, computerization is desirable if the local situation can afford and support automation. Use of computers is an efficient way to manage inventory with perpetual or periodic purchasing; moreover, a good software program, properly used, makes information retrieval and reporting much easier than a manual system (see Chapter 50). However, much depends on the type of software program used, how well the system is operated, and the accuracy of data entry. In most pharmaceutical supply environments, stock can still be controlled with manual records, if necessary.

The key point about stock records, whether manual or computerized, is that they must be current and accurate. Managing the reordering process well is impossible if stock movement cannot be tracked.

Several factors contribute to inaccurate stock records; some are entirely avoidable, but some are not—

- High-volume, repetitious entries lead to occasional entry errors just by the nature of the task.
- Medicine names and descriptions are similar—ten items may be different forms of the same medicine, and an entry may be made for the wrong form, or different strengths of the same item may be confused.
- Duplicate entries for receipts or issues may be caused by duplicate paperwork provided separately to different clerks.
- Spoiled or junk stock may be destroyed but not written off the records.
- Theft produces inaccurate records, except when they are deliberately altered to conceal the theft.
- Physical stock counts may be rarely or never taken, they may be inaccurate, or the records may not be reconciled after stock counts.
- Sloppy storekeeping and warehouse practices may make carrying out accurate stock counts difficult and prevent reconciliation of physical stock with recorded stock, especially when stock of the same item is stored in different locations.
- Clerical and stock management staff may be poorly paid, poorly trained, and poorly motivated.
- Supervision of warehouse staff or clerical staff is often minimal, and management may make limited or no effort to reconcile discrepancies.

Automation and newer technologies, such as bar coding, reduce some of the problems related to inaccurate data entries, but this technology is still expensive to implement and does not solve all the problems. The best way to promote greater accuracy is better training and closer supervision, with spot checks of records and stock status by supervisors.

Stock counts are important, both for reordering purposes and for determining the inventory value. Some pharmaceutical supply systems still never count stock and rely totally on inventory records, but most systems have a policy of conducting stock counts at least annually (although they may not really be carried out every year). The best approach to tracking the quantity actually in stock is *cyclic counting*.

In cyclic counting (sometimes known as continuous counting or perpetual inventory), the entire inventory is divided into counting groups, and one group is counted each week (or each month), with reconciliation of discrepancies; another group is counted the next week (or next month), and so forth. A cyclic counting program provides for every item in the inventory to be counted at least once a year and for a reconciliation to be carried out between physical and recorded stock. A regular, cyclic stock-counting procedure is generally accepted as superior to an annual stock count. Two main reasons account for the change to cyclic counting—

1. With an annual stock count, a whole warehousing and distribution operation is shut down for a day or two to a week or more. This procedure disrupts the supply system and causes frustration for warehouse and financial staff, who must rush to get the whole process completed as quickly as possible.
2. When discrepancies are found in an annual count, tracing exactly where the problem arose during the year is difficult, so the records are simply corrected to reflect actual stock, and any losses are written off.

Cyclic counting, in contrast, can take place without interrupting normal operations. With more frequent counting, tracking down the source of discrepancies may be possible. Moreover, more frequent counting may make it harder for staff to pilfer stock.

One method of cyclic counting is to assign the counting frequency and timing by ABC category (defined in Section 23.4), counting A items three or four times a year, B items twice, and C items once; any B or C items that are prone to disappear may be worth adding to the A category.

For best results, the staff members who perform the stock counts should not be the ones to reconcile discrepancies; a system of rotating different staff members through both functions helps maintain the integrity of the process.

Activity reports and performance monitoring

The most accurate stock records have little value if the information in them is not compiled in reports for use by the managers who make purchasing and stock management decisions. Two similar but separate types of reports are useful: periodic analyses and routine reports.

The inventory management system's health can be measured periodically using standard performance indicators. Box 23-1 lists performance indicators commonly used by commercial firms. The assessment guide at the end of the chapter cites indicators that have been tested in public supply systems.

Routine reports on purchasing and inventory management activities should be produced monthly to quarterly in a computerized system and at least annually in a manual system. The following lists illustrate the types of reports that are useful for improving inventory management.

Storage facilities should report on—

- Stock position—stock on hand and on order, globally and by item, reported as absolute quantities and in terms of months' worth of consumption; listing inventory by descending stock value and also by descending (or ascending) number of available months of consumption is also useful
- Beginning and ending inventory value, and the average inventory-holding costs
- Value of all supplies received and issued during the reporting period
- Changes in inventory value and any discrepancies noted during stock counts
- Value of stock adjustments carried out during reconciliation

- Consumption patterns for all stock items and an ABC analysis of consumption—with computer assistance, this analysis can be done globally and for each operating unit
- Service level from suppliers to medical stores and from medical stores to health facilities
- Medicines at risk of expiry in inventory and an estimate of how much stock is likely to expire before it can be used
- Quantity and value of obsolete stock waiting for disposal and stock destroyed or junked

Purchasing and financial departments should report on

- Budget status—year-to-date expenditures versus targets, and amount remaining
- Purchases and expenditures, broken down by supplier and by operating unit
- Summaries of accounts payable to suppliers
- Status of outstanding orders
- Comparison of expected and actual lead times for completed orders
- Supplier performance
- Comparison of actual purchase price and projected cost
- Comparison of actual items purchased and original needs projections

---

Box 23-1
Performance indicators used by commercial firms

Inventory management performance indicators are used in commercial companies throughout the world to measure how effectively inventory is being managed; these indicators can and should be used in public pharmaceutical supply systems when data are available.

Net sales to inventory (also called *inventory turnover*): The total value of medicines distributed, minus write-offs, divided by the value of the inventory. The higher the ratio, the lower the average inventory level (and average holding cost). Most private companies would expect a turnover ratio of twelve or higher; in public pharmaceutical supply systems, the ratio is dictated to some extent by the purchasing model, but a ratio of at least six is realistic in most cases.

Inventory shrinkage: The sum of beginning inventory value plus purchases, minus the sum of the cost of goods sold, plus ending inventory value. Ideally, this figure would be zero, but any value less than 10 percent of inventory value is within expectations in most public pharmaceutical supply systems.

Expense ratio: Total operating expenses divided by net sales (or value of medicines distributed). In one view, the lower this ratio, the more efficiently services are being managed.

Service level: The percentage of items ordered or requested that is filled from stock by the supplier or warehouse. From the public health viewpoint, the higher the service level, the better, as long as inventory costs do not rise to insupportable levels.

Average inventory-holding cost: The average cost of holding inventory as a percentage of average inventory value. In a public pharmaceutical supply system, 30 to 40 percent is a reasonable target.

Incremental ordering cost: The average incremental cost of placing each order. In a private company in an industrialized country, this might be 100 to 200 U.S. dollars per order. It should be considerably lower in most public pharmaceutical supply systems.

- Operating costs attributable to stock management and to purchasing

Accurate reporting is possible with either a manual or a computerized information system, but the information is much more readily compiled with computer assistance. Again, source data for the reports—stock records and purchasing records—must be maintained accurately and kept up-to-date. The key is for senior managers to demand these sorts of reports, use them in making policy decisions, and take corrective action when reports are not produced.

23.4 Selection of items to be held in stock

Stock must be held for several reasons—

To ensure availability: In the typical pharmaceutical supply system, one cannot forecast demand with complete accuracy or be certain about suppliers' performance. Proper inventory management allows the absorption of fluctuations in supply and demand and reduces the risk of stockouts.

To maintain confidence in the system: If stockouts occur regularly, patients and staff lose confidence in the system, and patient use drops for both curative and preventive services.

To reduce the unit cost of medicines: Ordering medicines in bulk allows quantity discounts from suppliers and reduces shipping and port-clearing costs.

To avoid shortage costs: If emergency orders are needed to cope with stockouts, the unit cost is likely to be much higher than for a regular order. Also, when a pharmaceutical sales program is operating, stockouts result in lost revenue, because clients go elsewhere for medicines.

To minimize ordering costs: Purchasing costs increase when items are ordered frequently. These costs include salaries and benefits for purchasing and accounting staff members, office space costs, utilities, supplies, and other costs associated with tenders and regular orders.

To minimize transport costs: Medicines can be delivered less frequently, enabling transport resources to be used more economically.

To allow for fluctuations in demand: Changes in demand for specific medicines are often unpredictable, and an adequate inventory allows the system to cope with demand fluctuations.

Obviously, pharmaceutical supply systems need to hold a certain level of inventory; however, holding high stock levels has disadvantages (see Figure 23-1). Substantial capital can be tied up in inventory and thus be unavailable for other purposes. As inventories become larger, the costs for personnel, utilities, insurance, storage facilities, and other costs

of holding stock increase. High inventory levels also increase the likelihood of losses caused by spoilage, expiry, obsolescence, and theft. These adverse effects of high stock levels compel managers to practice proper inventory management by balancing stock-holding costs, ordering costs, and stockout costs; otherwise, supply systems would simply hold large quantities of stock at all levels so that no chance of shortages would exist.

Most pharmaceutical supply systems try to regularly stock all items that are on the formulary or essential medicines list (see Chapter 16). In many cases, items that are not on the approved list but that are regularly requested by physicians are also routinely held in stock. Often no differentiation is made between vital and nonessential items, between high-cost and low-cost items, or between items that move quickly and those that are rarely used. This lack of discrimination often leads to an accumulation of slow-moving stock and excess capital tied up in inventory.

One way to decide which items should be stocked is to look at records of stock movement in and out of the storage facilities and identify the high-volume items that definitely need to be stocked, as well as items that have shown little or no movement in the past year. A good tool for reviewing stock movement is ABC analysis, which categorizes items by the volume and value of consumption during a specific period of time, usually one year. Class A items—10 to 20 percent of items, representing 75 to 80 percent of expenditures—are mostly high-volume, fast-moving medicines. Class B items are usually 10 to 20 percent of items, and 15 to 20 percent of expenditures. Class C items often represent 60 to 80 percent of the items but only about 5 to 10 percent of the total expenditures; these are the low-volume, slow-moving items. Thus, class C is a good place to look for items that might not be needed in stock at all times.

The VEN system is another method for categorizing stock, as vital (V), essential (E), or nonessential (N). This system is sometimes modified to two categories—V and N. VEN analysis is often used to prioritize procurement when not enough funds exist to purchase all items requested. The system can also help determine which items should be kept in stock and which can be ordered when needed. Clearly, V medicines would be more likely to be regular stock items than N medicines. Both ABC and VEN analyses are discussed in detail in Chapter 40.

Not all medicines have to be stocked at each level of the system. One way of classifying stock versus nonstock items is according to the approved level of use. For example, a medicine such as aspirin would be a stock item at all levels of the system, but a third-generation cephalosporin or a drug used in cancer chemotherapy might be a stock item only in tertiary-care hospitals. Classifying medicines according to their eligibility for routine use at each level helps minimize stock levels and ensure that only qualified staff members prescribe dangerous or expensive

Figure 23-1   Balancing benefits and costs in inventory management

BENEFITS
- Minimize life-threatening shortages
- Facilitate bulk purchasing
- Increase transportation efficiency
- Protect against seasonal fluctuations

COSTS
- Capital cost
- Expiration
- Spoilage
- Obsolescence
- Storage
- Pilferage

medicines. Another option is to stock slow-moving items only at the central level, then consolidate orders and distribution.

Finally, the issue of local availability must be kept in mind. If a medicine is vital to patient care (even if rarely used) and it cannot be obtained quickly when needed, that medicine will probably need to be kept as a stock item. When no local sources of supply exist and all medicines are imported, with long lead times, all medicines need to be held in stock somewhere in the system. In most countries, however, opportunities exist to purchase some medicines as needed from local sources, and considering which of those items need to be constantly held in stock is worthwhile.

Whichever approaches are used to designate stock and nonstock items, some scheme is needed for periodically reevaluating the stock status. If the system is computerized, the software can be programmed to automatically recategorize items at specified intervals based on recent patterns of stock movement.

23.5   Service level and safety stock

After the decision has been made about which items will be routinely held in stock and which will be ordered only when they are needed, the discussion turns to how much stock should be held at each level of the system. Different points of view are likely to exist: stock controllers and clinical staff

may feel that inventory levels should be high, to avoid shortages; financial managers, however, hope to minimize inventory levels to hold down costs.

One of the most common ways to measure the performance of a commercial supplier or public warehouse is to calculate the service level provided to clients. Suppliers try to balance service level and the costs of holding stock. The single most important factor in establishing that balance is the average stock held by the supplier and, in particular, the safety stock.

Service level to operating units

The *service level*, in its most simple form, is the percentage of individual items ordered from a supplier or warehouse that is issued from stock on hand. It is measured by counting the total number of items issued and dividing by the total number of items requested.

Service level = (# items issued ÷ # items requested) × 100

If twenty products are listed on a request, and ten units of each product are requested, 200 items are on the order; if only 170 items are issued, the service level is 85 percent. When assessing the annual service level of a supplier, the key is the total number of items requested on all requisitions and how many of those items were supplied from stock on hand at the supplier's warehouse.

Some commercial suppliers (and public warehouses) are prone to making partial shipments. When an order is received, an initial shipment is made with part of the request; later, one or more additional shipments are made with the remainder of the order quantity. For purposes of measuring the service level, only the initial shipment after each order should count.

In some supply systems, counting all items requested and issued is too time-consuming, and a count of line items (the number of different products ordered, disregarding order quantities) is used. This scheme makes it hard to decide how to count line items when only part of the request was shipped. Suppliers would argue that any of an item shipped should count as a full shipment for service-level measurement, but many clients would disagree. Systems have evolved to measure line-item service level in categories, for example, the percentage of line items that falls into the categories "none issued," "part issued," and "issued in full."

Other ways to measure service level include—

- The percentage of individual items or line items requested that are *delivered* within the promised lead time (this can be useful when delivery times vary).
- The value of all items shipped from stock as a percentage of the value of all items ordered.
- The percentage of full orders completely filled from stock. Two variations exist—in one, either the whole order is shipped or not; in the other, performance is categorized as discussed for the line-item method.
- The percentage of time that a product was found to be in stock during a period of one year. For example, if a product was found to be out of stock for 36 of 365 days in a year, the service level could be calculated as (365 − 36) × 100 ÷ 365, equal to a service level of 90 percent.
- The percentage of *products* that are supplied (e.g., if 100 products are ordered and 70 are supplied in any quantity, the product service level is 70 percent).
- The percentage of *units* supplied (e.g., if 100 boxes of ampicillin vials were ordered and 70 were supplied, the unit service level is 70 percent).
- A strong overall measure of service combines product service and unit service (e.g., 70 percent × 70 percent equals a 49 percent service level).

Whatever measure is used, what is meant by a reasonable service level? Many private-sector pharmaceutical wholesalers promise 95 percent service levels to customers (although they do not always fulfill this promise). Is this level sufficient? The point to remember is that every percentage point decrease in service level by a supplier or warehouse represents a corresponding increase in shortages at the client facility. If a supplier promises a 95 percent service level, 5 percent of the requested items are not expected to be shipped immediately (implying a potential 5 percent stock-

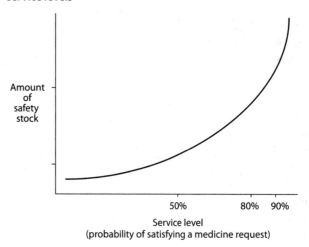

Figure 23-2   Safety stock requirements to maintain various service levels

out at the receiving facility). If the level drops to 90 percent, it follows that 10 percent of the items are not being shipped when they are needed. A public-sector pharmaceutical supply system should strive for a 100 percent service level, at least for vital items; setting lower goals might be reasonable for nonessential medicines and supplies.

Service level is directly determined by the average inventory level, and particularly by the average level of safety stock, held by the supply source. Figure 23-2 illustrates the typical relationship between safety stock and service level from a supply source (either commercial or public).

Note in Figure 23-2 that although the safety stock requirements increase as the service level increases, the relationship is not linear. As the service level increases above 80 percent, the amount of additional safety stock needed to produce a further increase in service level rises steeply. The amount of safety stock required to achieve a 99 percent service level may be double that required to achieve a 95 percent service level. For example, where a safety stock of 2,000 units is needed to achieve a service level of 95 percent, 4,000 units may be needed to raise the service level to 99 percent.

For both the supplier and the client, the balance between cost and service is really a matter of trade-offs. If the supplier cannot or will not maintain adequate inventory levels to sustain an acceptable service level, the client will either have to change suppliers or have to increase safety stock levels at the receiving units. For the supplier, the trade-off is between incurring higher inventory costs to maintain the promised service level and running the risk of shortage costs, as clients go elsewhere for service.

In commercial enterprises, safety stock levels are set using standard formulas that incorporate knowledge about demand patterns, inventory costs, sales income lost from stockouts, and other factors. If a stockout occurs, it is normally accepted as the cost of tight inventory control. In

Box 23-2
Estimating safety stock

The minimum safety stock needed to avoid a stockout is the quantity of stock used on average during the average lead time from the supplier. Thus, if an order is placed as soon as the stock level falls to the safety stock level, if demand is no greater than average during the lead time, and if the supplier delivers within the average lead time, a stockout will be avoided.

The most common method for estimating safety stock needs is to determine the average lead time for each item from the current supplier and the average consumption (per month or per week). If stockouts occurred, consumption must be adjusted to what would have been used, as described in Chapter 20, Section 20.4.

In calculating the amount of safety stock, it is also important to consider warehouse storage capacity. It is no use to order the appropriate amount of safety stock if the warehouse does not have the space for it.

The formula for setting the basic safety stock (SS) level is lead time (LT) multiplied by the average consumption (C_A)—

$$SS = LT \times C_A$$

For example, if the average lead time is three months and the average monthly consumption is 1,000 units, the minimum safety stock would be 3,000 units.

Unfortunately, consumption patterns are not always smooth, and suppliers do not always deliver within the average lead time, so most supply systems increase the basic safety stock—at least for critical items—to cope with variations in consumption and lead time.

The simplest approach for coping with varying consumption and lead time is adding an arbitrary multiplier to the basic formula for safety stock; member countries in the Organisation of Eastern Caribbean States Pharmaceutical Procurement Service, for example, multiply the basic safety stock by 1.5 for vital items, to protect against stockouts.

Another simple way of adjusting the safety stock for variable consumption is to review a one-year period and determine the maximum quantity consumed during the average lead-time period for the current supplier of the item and the average quantity consumed during that same lead-time period. For the example cited above, the average consumption during the three-month average lead-time period was 3,000 units; suppose that for any three-month period during the year, the highest consumption was 4,000 units. Using this method, the minimum stock level would be 3,000 units, and the additional safety stock allotment would be 1,000 units.

The information from lead-time analysis (see Chapter 40) can be used to predict the next lead time, as follows—

$$DD_E = DD_P + (OD \times OD\%)$$

where—

DD_E = expected delivery date
DD_P = promised delivery date
OD = average overdue period in days
$OD\%$ = percentage of orders overdue

Chapter 40 cites an eastern Caribbean supplier that had a contract lead time of 45 days but was late on 50 percent of shipments, with an average delay of 43 days. According to the formula above, this supplier has an expected delivery date of 66.5 days, calculated as—

$$DD_E = 45 + (43 \times 50\%) = 66.5$$

When calculating safety stock needs for products from this supplier, using a lead time of 66.5 days would be safer than using 45 days.

When both consumption and lead times are highly variable, some commercial firms use a mathematical approach using the standard deviation of the average consumption and the average lead time to set safety stock levels (see Section 23.9).

Note that all these adjustments tend to increase inventory-holding costs by increasing the safety stock level; therefore, it is important to monitor consumption and lead-time patterns continuously and adjust safety stock to the lowest levels compatible with current patterns. In a computerized inventory control system, this adjustment should be done automatically by the software.

Figure 23-3   Ideal inventory control model

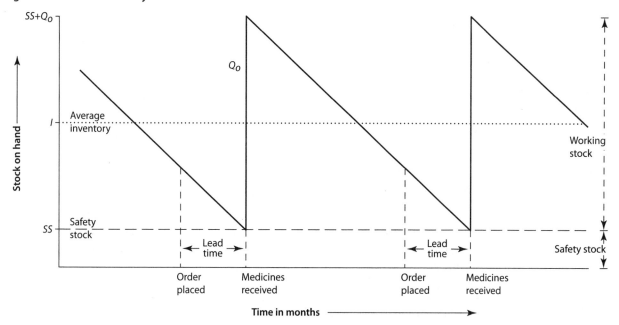

public pharmaceutical systems, the cost of additional safety stock must be weighed against the potential adverse health and political effects of stockouts.

When one designs or restructures an inventory management system, safety stock policy is an important consideration. The policy may differ at each level of the system, between products, or between different facilities at the same level (depending on VEN and ABC classification systems, lead times, and consumption patterns). The objective is to provide maximum service levels throughout the supply system with minimum necessary *total* safety stock.

Methods for setting safety stock levels

Many ways exist of estimating the level of safety stock required to achieve specific service levels. All consider two major factors: average consumption and average lead time. Box 23-2 discusses simple methods for estimating safety stock needs. In most supply systems, the more complex mathematical models for estimating safety stock needs will probably not provide any significant advantage over simple methods (see Section 23.9).

23.6 Inventory control models and reorder frequency

The ideal inventory control model is shown in Figure 23-3. In this ideal model, pharmaceuticals are issued in response to demand, but stockouts are not permitted; the stock on hand steadily declines until the point at which an order

must be placed. The stock on hand consists of two components, the working stock and the safety stock (SS). In the ideal model, the supplier performs according to plan, the shipments arrive on time, the quantity ordered (Q_O) is received, and the inventory level is back to its starting maximum point (Q_O + SS). Working stock varies from zero to the quantity ordered and represents the stock used to satisfy demand between deliveries. Note that in the ideal model, the average working stock is half of the order quantity—

$$\text{Average working stock} = \tfrac{1}{2}\,Q_O$$

The average inventory (I) or average stock on hand is the safety stock plus the average working stock—

$$I = SS + \tfrac{1}{2}\,Q_O$$

To reduce the average inventory and thereby reduce the inventory-holding costs, the working stock, the safety stock, or both should be lowered. When medicines are used at a constant rate, the line in Figure 23-3 representing stock on hand declines with a constant slope. Large, infrequent orders lead to high average inventory levels. The average working stock can be reduced by placing smaller orders more frequently. The average inventory can also be reduced by cutting the safety stock, but this method increases the chance of stockouts. Alternatively, stock-holding costs could be reduced by minimizing the individual cost components that make up inventory-carrying costs, as illustrated in Figure 23-1. These improvements would be possible through improved storekeeping practices and better financial management.

As illustrated in Figure 23-3, any inventory control model used to manage purchasing must address the following issues—

1. Safety stock—how much stock will be kept in reserve to prevent stockouts
2. Reorder frequency—the period of time between each order for an item (also known as the procurement period)
3. Reorder quantity—the number of units specified when an order is placed

In addition, storage capacity—the amount of space available for storage—needs to be considered when determining target stock levels and ordering and replenishment frequency. As is made clear in Figure 23-4, the policy on reorder frequency has a major influence on average stock levels and inventory-holding costs, as well as on service level.

Different inventory control models based on reorder frequency have been developed to fit various situations. Two ways to classify these models are—

1. *Periodic review model:* In periodic review models, orders can be placed only at specified intervals, and the item is ordered at every interval.
2. *Perpetual review model:* In perpetual review models, orders can be placed at any time; the user (or a minimum stock level) determines when to order and how much to order.

In pharmaceutical supply systems, the most common inventory control models are—

- Annual purchasing—a periodic review model with the interval set at once a year
- Scheduled purchasing—a periodic review model in which orders are placed at prescribed intervals (such as weekly, monthly, quarterly, biannually)
- Perpetual purchasing—a model in which stock levels are reviewed each time stock is issued (or at least weekly) and orders are placed whenever stock falls below a minimum level
- Draw-downs from framework contracts

Annual purchasing

With annual purchasing (which is actually a form of scheduled purchasing), procurement is carried out once each year for all items. Order quantities are normally calculated by a large-scale quantification process (see Chapter 20).

After quantification is done, a tender or competitive negotiation (see Chapters 18 and 21) is used to purchase

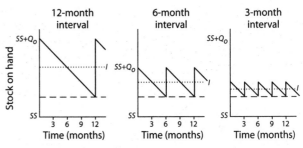

Figure 23-4   Impact of reorder interval on average inventory

Key: I = average inventory Q_O = order quantity SS = safety stock

the entire annual amount (or as much as can be afforded). Contracts with suppliers may provide that deliveries be spaced throughout the year if problems exist with local storage space, storage conditions, or security. In virtually all supply systems using annual purchasing, mechanisms exist to make supplementary purchases during the year. Countries use annual purchasing for the following main reasons—

- Financial regulations and realities may dictate the choice.
- A single procurement can be easier to manage than more frequent purchasing, depending on staff capacities and availability of information.
- Pharmaceutical purchase prices per unit are usually lower when large-volume purchases are made. This consideration can be important when inflation or local currency devaluation is significant and progressive. In such cases, committing the funds at discounted prices and prevailing exchange rates is preferable.
- Tradition and inertia may promote continuance of annual purchasing just because it has always been done that way.
- Greater purchase volumes result in lower prices and can be accompanied by staggered deliveries to facilitate storage and distribution management, as well as a more even cash flow arrangement.

Several disadvantages stem from using annual purchasing as the sole purchasing model for the supply system—

- Actual consumption is often different from the annual forecast or the actual demand, leading to shortages and surpluses; expensive emergency orders are required to cope with shortages, and surplus stock may spoil or expire.
- Average stock levels and inventory-holding costs are higher with this model (see Figure 23-4).
- Local suppliers that win annual tender contracts may find coping with huge, single deliveries difficult.
- More storage space is required, unless deliveries from suppliers can be spaced throughout the year.

- The necessary funds to pay for the single annual purchase may be difficult to obtain, particularly if hard currency is required.
- Workload in the procurement office and main receiving points is uneven.

In general, annual purchasing is best suited to new programs, which have no existing system for inventory management. Annual purchasing may be mandatory in countries where local sources of supply are limited and lead times from foreign suppliers average several months. Annual purchasing may also be preferred when donors support pharmaceutical purchases. Even in systems that use mainly scheduled or perpetual purchasing, some items may be best purchased annually.

Scheduled purchasing

In this periodic review model, specific ordering windows are determined, and regular orders can be placed only at the scheduled intervals—for example, once each month, each quarter, or every six months. Orders are placed at the scheduled order date for quantities large enough to cover average needs until the next order is scheduled plus stock needed during the lead time for that order (plus replenishment of safety stock, if needed).

One variation on this model is staggered review, in which the procurement office reviews one group of medicines (or medicines from one group of suppliers) at one interval, another group at the next interval, and so forth. In this manner, the workload in the procurement office and the financial requirements for pharmaceutical purchasing are spread out during the year, while still limiting the number of orders placed to each supplier (which can be an important issue in supply contracts).

The ordering frequency can also be varied according to ABC category, so that more expensive, faster-moving items are ordered more frequently and other items less frequently (this system is discussed below).

Scheduled purchasing with a review period of six months can operate in much the same way as annual purchasing, but shorter intervals require one of the options for calculating order quantities described in Section 23.9. Normally, an emergency ordering system is used when stock runs low between scheduled orders or when a supplier's shipment is delayed.

In scheduled purchasing, supply contracts can be negotiated anew at each interval, or longer contracts can be negotiated at the beginning of the year, with the provision that orders will be placed as needed at the specified ordering intervals (the estimated-quantity contract; see Chapter 21).

In most supply systems, a new order is customarily placed only after the previous one is received. However, some programs use tandem ordering, with overlapping orders and different expected times of arrival, if estimated lead times are reliable.

Scheduled purchasing has several benefits—

- An estimated-quantity rather than fixed-quantity contract can be supported.
- A scheduled system may be preferable to local suppliers because it allows them to spread their demand over the year.
- Inventory-holding costs are less than with annual purchasing (see Figure 23-4).
- Less space is needed in warehouses than with annual purchasing.
- Items with variable demand can be purchased more frequently in smaller lots, reducing overstocking and costly emergency orders.
- The procurement unit can respond more rapidly to program needs and make better use of a limited pharmaceutical budget.
- In many countries, funds and foreign exchange are easier to obtain for making smaller, more frequent purchases.
- The procurement and port-clearing workload is fairly evenly spread over the year.
- Because many products need reordering at scheduled points, procurement costs are better controlled, especially in instances where the procurement process is lengthy and cumbersome.
- It supports pooled procurement systems, where orders from all partners are joined and placed as a single order. See Country Study 23-1.

One potential difficulty is that when orders are placed late in the fiscal year, the purchasing cycle will not be complete before the end of the year. This schedule may result in a conflict with regulations regarding spending time limits. Shortages caused by poor forecasting or changes in demand are less likely with this model than with annual purchasing, but they can still occur with scheduled review periods three to six months apart.

If progressive inflation and devaluation are problems, an escalator clause may be required in annual estimated-quantity contracts; if a separate contract is negotiated at each ordering interval, prices are likely to increase throughout the year. In such cases, the best strategy may be to procure as many essential items as possible, along with any items likely to increase in price, in the first part of the year.

Scheduled purchasing works most effectively when consumption patterns are relatively stable, at least for the duration of the period between orders. If needs fluctuate widely from month to month, perpetual purchasing would be preferable, assuming that it is logistically feasible.

> **Country Study 23-1**
> **Scheduled purchasing in the eastern Caribbean**
>
> Scheduled purchasing is used in the Pharmaceutical Procurement Service (PPS) pooled procurement program. PPS is an agency serving the nine member countries of the Organisation of Eastern Caribbean States (OECS). The OECS/PPS operates a centralized, restricted international tendering system in which all approved suppliers are prescreened by a vendors' registration questionnaire. Prequalification is necessary to assess the quality standards, technical competence, and financial viability of competing suppliers. The supply contracts are awarded every eighteen months based on estimates of needs submitted by the nine member countries and compiled by the OECS/PPS. The pooled procurement list represents large-volume class A and B items for which demand is consistently high in the participating countries.
>
> The countries use a scheduled purchasing system in which orders are placed every February, July, and October; some countries order from all suppliers at each interval, and others use a staggered method. The reorder quantity is calculated using the consumption-based forecasting formula.
>
> In this scheme, each country has a revolving drug fund at the Eastern Caribbean Central Bank; the country can order pharmaceuticals only up to the value of their allocated national budget during any order interval. Emergency purchases are made when shortages occur because of delayed shipments, or when unusual demand depletes stock before another order is due to be placed with a contract supplier. If the primary contract supplier defaults, an order is placed immediately with an alternative supplier.
>
> The contract suppliers that are located in the region allow for more frequent orders in some cases, are frequently used as secondary contract suppliers, and are used as the primary source for emergency purchases.
>
> Source: F. Burnett, personal communication.

Scheduled purchasing is probably the best choice as an alternative to annual procurement in countries that do not have immediate access to suppliers. The major requirements for managing scheduled purchasing are an inventory information system that can produce reliable information on consumption, stock levels, and outstanding orders, and the management and financial capacity to place all necessary orders according to the schedule.

Perpetual purchasing

In this model, a perpetual inventory record is maintained for each item. The inventory position (stock on hand and on order) is reviewed on a regular basis (usually with every transaction, but at least weekly); whenever the stock position falls below a designated reorder point, an order is initiated. As will be discussed later, the order quantity may be predetermined or variable.

Safety stocks and average inventories are much lower with this model than with either scheduled or annual purchasing, but some safety stock is still needed. The chief advantage of perpetual purchasing over scheduled and annual purchasing is the ability to rapidly respond to sudden changes in consumption, because the inventory position is reviewed continuously and orders are placed frequently.

In some systems that use perpetual purchasing, orders are batched—that is, an order is not placed with a supplier until several different items are needed from that supplier. If batching is used, safety stocks must be adequate to cover periods when a needed item is on hold for batching.

Perpetual purchasing is used by most hospitals and health systems in industrialized countries, where lead times for virtually all items are one or two days. In the United States, perpetual purchasing normally takes place in a prime vendor distribution system, whereby a commercial distributor supplies all contract items on short notice (see Chapter 8). This system avoids the batching issue, because all or virtually all items are ordered from the same supplier. However, in many developing countries, government regulations and difficulty in employing suitable primary distributors may make this method challenging.

If applied appropriately, perpetual purchasing produces an even workload for procurement, warehousing, and port clearing. Depending on the supply system's budgeting and financial policies, perpetual purchasing with frequent small orders may be useful in spreading cash requirements throughout the year.

Despite the many benefits of a perpetual system, it is not suitable for all public-sector pharmaceutical supply systems. Several potential constraints exist. If lead times are not relatively short (one month or less), perpetual purchasing will be difficult to use without maintaining large safety stocks (thereby defeating its purpose). If the supply system cannot maintain current and accurate stock records, the perpetual purchasing model will fail because by the time transactions are posted, vital items may be out of stock. If formal approval from the ministry of health or ministry of finance must be obtained for each purchase and for foreign exchange permits, the time needed for approval may make perpetual purchasing awkward.

The more frequent purchases in perpetual purchasing will drive up incremental purchasing costs and perhaps total purchasing costs, but any increase in incremental purchasing costs may be offset by decreased inventory-holding costs. Perpetual purchasing may be comparatively harder to fit into public health objectives and budgetary limits, because all the small purchases must be tracked for compliance with guidelines.

Potential applications for perpetual purchasing exist in many pharmaceutical supply systems even if the entire purchasing system cannot be converted to this method. For example, perpetual purchasing might be considered for fast-moving items that can be ordered at competitive prices from local sources. A perpetual system might be used by lower-level stores and facilities that order from a larger warehouse; this could be done whether or not the main warehouse uses perpetual purchasing, so long as the ordering cycles can be coordinated.

The main requirements for perpetual purchasing are—

- Stock records that are current and accurate
- A computer with suitable software to manage an inventory of more than a few items (see Chapter 50)
- Good access to and communication with suppliers and user units, with lead times of one month or less
- Ready access to funds, unless suppliers are prepared to wait for payment
- An estimated-quantity contract that allows ad hoc orders, or a purchasing environment where formal contracts are not used

Drawing down from framework contracts

A framework contract establishes the essential terms and conditions of the procurement agreement, such as time frame, product specifications, prices, quantities, and conditions of supplier performance. During the framework contract term, the supplier holds the stock until it receives orders for specific purchases. Each order is itself a separate contract that follows the broad framework terms with specific terms added, such as delivery date.

Combinations of annual, scheduled, and perpetual purchasing

Although establishing one inventory control model for all pharmaceuticals may be simplest from a management perspective, it may not be the most cost-effective solution.

A thorough review of options may reveal that some medicines are best purchased annually—for example, imported medicines in a country where local currency devaluation is a major problem, or low-priced, infrequently used medicines. Other medicines might be most effectively purchased through scheduled purchasing—for example, relatively slow-moving but regularly used items. High-volume medicines and very expensive medicines may be most effectively purchased with a perpetual model, if logistically feasible.

ABC analysis can be used to examine the effect of variations in order frequency on average inventory value for class A, B, and C items. Table 23-1 shows the relationships among the average order interval, the average inventory level, and the service level for class A, B, and C medicines in a large public-sector pharmaceutical supply system. This projection is based on an average lead time of nine months. Note the difference in average inventory value needed to maintain a 95 percent service level with the various permutations of order frequency for class A, B, and C items.

Although the lowest average inventory cost is obtained in the example by increasing the frequency of ordering for all classes, this strategy may increase the procurement workload and the costs of purchasing significantly, particularly if formal tenders are required. Changing the tender frequency for class A items to twice, rather than once, a year and changing the order quantity from twelve months' to six months' usage reduce the average inventory value by almost half, while still maintaining the desired service level; this change should not increase the cost of purchasing to unacceptable levels (although a total cost analysis should be performed to check the potential effect).

Dear (1990) describes a reordering system that builds on ABC analysis, called ABC/FS. In this system, the A, B, and C items are further broken down into three categories—fast turnover (F), slow movement (S), and no movement in the past year (class C items that might be reclassified as D for dead).

Using a mixed model of annual, scheduled, and perpetual purchasing, the purchasing office in this system concentrates on the fast-moving and expensive stock items, which have the most effect on inventory costs. Vital (V) and nonessential (N) classification can be combined with ABC/FS, with interesting implications for inventory management. For example, a class A, slow-moving item that is also a vital medicine (ASV) might be accorded a higher safety stock than a class A, fast-moving, nonessential item (AFN). An AFN item might be ordered only for specific patients as needed, or a class C, slow-moving, nonessential item (CSN) might be considered for nonstock status and ordered only as needed. Clearly, combinations of annual, scheduled, and perpetual purchasing can be used in many different ways if the supply system can manage such flexibility.

Table 23-1   Value of average inventory by service level and procurement pattern

Procurement pattern and ABC category—order interval	Value of inventory (USD thousands)				
	Service level				
	99%	98%	95%	90%	85%
Pattern A A products—12 months B products—12 months C products—12 months	10,801	9,730	8,204	7,394	7,394
Pattern B A products—6 months B products—12 months C products—12 months	8,766	7,750	6,902	5,217	4,606
Pattern C A products—6 months B products—6 months C products—12 months	8,365	7,360	5,927	4,788	4,056
Pattern D A products—6 months B products—6 months C products—6 months	8,103	7,104	5,661	4,507	3,697
Pattern E A products—4 months B products—6 months C products—12 months	7,820	6,862	5,476	4,392	3,738
Pattern F A products—4 months B products—4 months C products—4 months	7,380	6,471	5,086	3,982	3,275

Source: Adapted from Quick 1982.

23.7 Factors to consider in calculating reorder quantity

When the basic inventory control model has been established, the final question is how much should be ordered at each order interval. This section examines the factors that must be taken into account; Section 23.8 shows how the factors are integrated into a reordering formula.

Factors in the reorder formula

Depending on the reorder formula used, any or all of the following factors may be essential variables.

Average consumption. Sometimes called *demand,* the average consumption expected in the next purchasing cycle is the key variable that determines how much stock should be ordered. Future consumption is the great unknown of inventory management, so it is given special attention in this section. However, the other factors are equally important. Even if consumption is accurately predicted, stockouts will occur if the lead time is badly underestimated or if another factor is overlooked or miscalculated.

Lead time. Lead time is the time between initiation of a purchase order and receipt at the warehouse from the selected supplier. If a distinct trend exists in that supplier's performance, the average should be weighted toward recent performance with a moving average. However, if the pattern fluctuates—for example, two months, six months, two months, six months—it is best to apply lead-time analysis (Chapter 40) or calculate the standard deviation as discussed in Section 23.9.

Safety stock. Safety stock is the stock that should always be on hand to prevent stockouts. When lead times and consumption are predictable and stable, the reorder level does not necessarily need to include safety stock; however, when consumption patterns and lead times are highly variable, additional safety stock will be needed, as discussed in Section 23.5.

Reorder level. The reorder level is the quantity of remaining stock that should trigger a reorder of the item. In the minimum-maximum ordering system, this level is called the *minimum stock level.* The standard way to set the reorder level in a basic purchasing formula is to multiply the average lead time by the average quantity consumed during the lead time. This stock level may or may not be the same as the safety stock level, as discussed above, and in fact, may include a separate quantity of stock as a safety stock.

Maximum stock level. In most reordering formulas, this level is the target stock level, which is the stock needed to satisfy demand until the next order after the current one is received.

Stock position. Stock position is the sum of stock on hand (working and safety stock) and stock on order, minus any stock back-ordered to clients. Overstocks may occur if several months' worth of stock are on hand or on order when a new order is placed. Stockouts may result if significant quantities from an upcoming order are on back-order to lower-level facilities and this amount is not factored into the reorder quantity.

Procurement period. The procurement period covers the time until the next regular order will be placed. In a scheduled system, the period might be in multiples of one month; in a perpetual system, it could be counted in days or weeks for the purposes of forecasting. Note that the quantity ordered plus the safety stock must cover the time until the next order is received, which is the procurement period plus the lead time.

It should be noted that in all previous cases, stock levels are dependent on accurately estimating medicine demand. If estimates are not based on accurate stock-keeping records, then stock-level computations will also be inaccurate, and health institutions will run the risk of mismanaging procurements, resulting in stockouts or overstocks.

Projecting demand

Ordering rationally requires forecasting future needs, the least predictable variable in a reordering formula. Four different methods can be used for forecasting demand—

1. *Projective:* forecasts using past consumption to predict demand (in pharmaceutical supply systems, the method most likely to produce reasonably accurate forecasts)
2. *Causal:* forecasts based on external factors such as market conditions, epidemics, changes in health system size and structure
3. *Judgmental:* forecasts based on subjective estimates of purchasing staff and advice from other staff (the least demanding method, and often the least accurate, if used alone)
4. *Morbidity:* forecasts based on the incidence of disease and the use of standard treatment guidelines

Generally, a reordering formula should be based primarily on projective forecasting, derived from average monthly consumption. The other methods can be used as appropriate to adjust actual purchase quantities. Unfortunately, although past demand is the best source of data for projection, a stable pattern or trend may not exist. In a series of observations of monthly consumption for a twelve-month period (called a time series), several components may be part of the observed demand pattern—

Base rate: demand that may be fairly stable from month to month

Trend: a steady pattern of increasing or decreasing demand, for example, increased usage caused by gradually increasing patient attendances

Seasonality: relatively predictable changes, such as increase in demand for malaria drugs during the rainy season

Cyclic demand: demand that ebbs and flows, for example, with a country's economic cycle

Random noise: unexplained variations in demand; for example, in one month, 100 bottles of amoxicilline suspension were consumed, with a pattern of thirty, ten, eighty, and twenty bottles in succeeding months, with no obvious reason for the variation

Adjustment is relatively easy for a definite trend toward higher (or lower) use or seasonality (if it is predictable). Cyclic use patterns can also be dealt with if they are apparent. The real problem is random noise, and in many consumption series at the item level, random noise seems to be the dominant component.

Fairly complex mathematical models have been developed for smoothing forecasts—exponential smoothing, seasonal indexes, and other methods. Some of these models are discussed later in the chapter. Most incorporate factors such as trend and seasonality while attempting to cope with random noise. However, the more complex models have limited value in most pharmaceutical supply situations; the following methods of tracking average consumption (to forecast demand) are suitable for most pharmaceutical supply systems—

- *Simple average consumption:* the average monthly consumption over the past twelve months (or less, such as six months, if no seasonal changes exist in consumption)
- *Seasonal average consumption:* the average consumption in the last comparable season or epidemic cycle for specific medicines
- *Moving average consumption:* the average monthly consumption in the most recent months—for example, the past two or three months

The key variables in these methods are which months and how many months (or weeks or days) are included in the review period for which consumption is averaged. Note that consumption in the three methods is stated in monthly terms, but it could be daily or weekly for a perpetual system, or yearly for annual purchasing.

Whichever review period is used, if the item was out of stock for part of the period, the consumption must be adjusted to what it would have been if no stockouts had occurred. One good method for making such adjustments is described in Chapter 20, Section 20.4.

When consumption patterns during the year are fairly stable or unpredictable variations (random noise) exist, simple average consumption provides adequate results, adjusting safety stock levels to cope with variations in consumption.

When big differences exist in seasonal demand, use of simple average consumption may produce stockouts in peak demand seasons (and simultaneously set stock levels too high in nonpeak seasons). Therefore, the seasonal average is used to adjust reorder and stock levels for each season. The review period is set to the number of periods in a season. For example, if the malaria season lasts four months, look at consumption patterns for sulfadoxine-pyrimethamine in the four-month malaria season last year rather than the past twelve months to predict needs for this year's season.

Moving averages are suitable for use when a definite trend exists in consumption, up or down, in recent months and reasons exist to expect the trend to continue. Both moving averages and seasonal averages fit well with scheduled purchasing, but they can be applied (with caution) to perpetual purchasing as well.

Integrating experience and other factors

No matter how precise the reordering formula is, external factors may force an adjustment of the quantity suggested by a reordering formula. In most supply systems, the reordering formula suggests quantities, but the purchasing manager makes the final decision. If the reordering formulas are appropriate, relatively few formula recommendations should be overruled by the manager (certainly fewer than 10 percent). However, if the manager knows about an external factor, such as those cited below, or believes that the formula is producing nonsense (perhaps because reordering factors have not been properly entered), experience and local judgment should be the deciding factors.

The key is for responsible officials to understand and accept the reordering formula, so that managers are not looking for reasons to override suggested quantities. One way to ensure this acceptance is to involve operations-level managers in developing and approving the reorder formula that will be used. Examples of factors that might affect reorder quality follow.

Budget status. Most supply systems operate under a specified budget ceiling. Budget management has two basic approaches. In one, the supply system develops a purchasing budget for each item, specifying the quantity budgeted for the year. Then the orders during the year are tracked against this line-item budget. In order to increase the total annual quantity for any item, the quantity for another item must be reduced (or more funds must be located). In the other budget management approach, all procurement funds are lumped together, and orders are placed for whatever items

are perceived to be needed until funds are gone. With either budgeting approach, managers need to monitor the items and quantities on each purchase order and cumulative purchases to make sure that the budget is not overspent.

Access to funds. Even if funds are theoretically budgeted, they may not be available at the time to place an order; if funds are insufficient to purchase all the items suggested by the standard reordering formula, adjustments need to be made (see Chapters 20 and 40).

Pack size and minimum order. The order quantity often needs to be adjusted so that even pack sizes are ordered. For example, if the formula suggests ordering 900 capsules, it might be possible to order nine bottles of 100 capsules. However, if the contract price is based on bottles of 1,000, the order would be placed for one bottle of 1,000. Similarly, if the formula suggests ten bottles of 100 capsules but the supplier's contract specifies a minimum order of twelve bottles, then twelve bottles must be ordered (such minimums should be avoided in supply contracts, if possible).

Expected changes in use. If a change is anticipated within the next purchasing cycle in the number of health facilities or in the formulary or essential medicines list, allowances need to be made in reordering schemes, particularly in annual and scheduled purchasing models.

Expected price increase. If managers know that prices will rise significantly for a medicine or group of medicines before the next ordering cycle, they may decide that ordering unusually high quantities will be cost-effective if consumption patterns indicate that the higher quantities will be used before expiry (or loss or deterioration).

Rising delivery costs. If shipping costs are a major factor in total pharmaceutical costs and they are expected to increase significantly, the approach is similar to the one used for rising prices. The medicines affected should be ordered in higher quantities, with the same precaution concerning capacity to use the entire quantity.

Quantity discounts. Some suppliers routinely offer quantity discounts—for example, 10 percent off with a certain total monetary order, or one item free if twelve are ordered. In such cases, particularly for fast-moving items that will definitely be used, the reordering system should be flexible enough to take advantage of the discounts, within funding limits. Again, the main limitation is the capacity to use the item before expiration or loss.

Excess stock of slow-moving products. If senior managers discover an excessive average inventory level, the temptation is to order a cutback in all purchasing. But this policy will only lead to shortages of fast-moving items, with no reduction for most of the problem stock. Strategies to promote the use of slower-moving items by substitution for other medicines (as appropriate), close review of reorder levels and quantities, and careful monitoring of the ordering procedures, without a purchasing freeze, are better alternatives.

Losses to theft and wastage. If losses are significant, they need to be considered in the order quantity (see Chapter 20).

Storage space. In the case of certain bulky products, order quantities may need to be reduced to accommodate storage space limitations.

Short-dated products. Certain pharmaceutical products come with a very limited shelf life. In such cases, order quantities should be limited in relation to the expected monthly consumption rate to prevent risk of medicine expiry.

23.8 Standard reordering formulas

The previous section discussed factors that need to be incorporated into the reordering formula. This section looks at two approaches to the question of how much to order—

1. Minimum and maximum stock levels
2. Consumption-based reordering formulas

Minimum and maximum stock-level formula

This formula is often used in scheduled purchasing with set order intervals. Using this approach, one defines a theoretical maximum stock for each item to provide sufficient, but not excessive, stock to last from one order to the next, as well as a minimum stock level or reorder level that determines at what point an order should be placed. Safety stock may be included in the minimum stock level, or an additional quantity may be assigned to protect against variations in demand and supplier performance.

Some supply system managers set the minimum and maximum stock levels arbitrarily for all items, but better inventory control is obtained with a flexible calculation for each item, based on standard reorder parameters—

- Average monthly consumption, adjusted for stockouts (C_A)
- Supplier lead time (LT)
- Procurement period—time until the next order will be placed (PP)
- Safety stock—additional stock to cope with variability in consumption and lead time (SS)
- Stock on hand in inventory (S_I)
- Stock now on order from a supplier but not yet received (S_O)
- Quantity of stock back-ordered to lower levels (S_B)

The basic formula for setting the minimum stock level is the average consumption multiplied by the lead time, plus any additional safety stock. Times are usually expressed in months, and stock quantities, in basic units (see the glossary at the end of Chapter 18). Options for setting safety stock levels were discussed in Section 23.5; any safety stock needed in addition to the minimum stock level might be defined arbitrarily or by calculating the difference between average and maximum consumption. The equation for calculating the minimum stock (S_{MIN}) is—

$$\text{Minimum stock} = (LT \times C_A) + SS$$

The maximum (target) stock level (S_{MAX}) can be calculated as the minimum stock plus the procurement period multiplied by the average consumption; the equation is—

$$(S_{MAX}) = (S_{MIN}) + (PP \times C_A)$$

An example of minimum-maximum level calculations is a case in which the lead time for tetracycline capsules is two months, the average monthly consumption (adjusted for stockouts) is 1,000 capsules, and the additional safety stock allocated is 2,000 capsules. For a procurement period of six months, the following minimum and maximum quantities would be set—

$$S_{MIN} = (2 \times 1,000) + 2,000 = 4,000 \text{ capsules}$$
$$S_{MAX} = 4,000 + (6 \times 1,000) = 10,000 \text{ capsules}$$

When the stock level is found to be at or below the minimum level, the order quantity (Q_O) is calculated as the maximum stock plus stock back-ordered to clients, minus the sum of stock on hand and stock on order. The formula is—

$$Q_O = (S_{MAX} + S_B) - (S_I + S_O)$$

In the example above, suppose 3,000 tetracycline capsules are in stock and another 2,000 are on order. Because the tetracycline has been in stock, there are no back orders to health facilities. The quantity to order would be calculated as—

$$Q_O = 10,000 - (3,000 + 2,000) + 0 = 5,000$$

Some variation of this system is used in many different countries. As long as the minimum and maximum quantities reflect current lead times, consumption patterns, safety stock needs, and order intervals, this system works as well as any other basic reorder formula. The key is regular updating of the minimum and maximum levels. Otherwise the original minimum and maximum levels will become obsolete, because average consumption and lead times usually change with time for many items. Then the formula will produce shortages of items that are moving faster than when the levels were set and overstocks of the items that are moving slower than before.

These problems are most likely to occur when the levels were set for each item by hand in one massive effort, with no formal plan for reviewing and updating the quantities. If several thousand items are used, at least one full-time worker is needed to keep the minimum and maximum quantities updated using a manual review system. Any supply system that uses this reorder formula to manage a large inventory would be well advised to obtain computer software that does the minimum-maximum quantity updating automatically, according to a formula similar to those above. In addition, by using an ABC analysis of all items, managers can prioritize the setting and reviewing of minimum and maximum quantities for items by class A, B, and C.

A supply system using the minimum-maximum method needs supplementary orders to cover situations in which the stock for an item has not sunk to the minimum when regular orders are placed but does so in the middle of the interval between orders, or when the order is not placed as soon as the reorder level is reached. In those situations, the stock will not last until the next regular order has been placed and received, unless safety stocks have been set very high.

One way to deal with emergency orders in a minimum-maximum system is called *modified optional replenishment*. With that system, there is a reorder level, which is the same as the standard definition for minimum level, as well as a second minimum stock level, which might be called the *emergency warning level*. If the stock position is above the reorder level at the reorder date, no order is placed. If the stock level falls to the emergency warning level between scheduled orders, an emergency order is placed.

Although the terminology can vary, this sort of emergency warning level can be useful in any supply system. Of course, emergency purchases must be closely monitored by managers. Some temptation may exist to disregard the regular system and rely mostly on emergency orders (which can be ruinously expensive).

Consumption-based reordering formula

This formula bypasses the step of setting (or calculating) minimum-maximum levels and instead calculates the proposed reorder quantity directly. The formula recommended here is basically the same as the formula for consumption-based quantification in Chapter 20 (except for back orders, which are normally not an issue in large-scale forecasting). The suggested next order quantity is calculated for each item based on the average consumption, lead time, desired safety stock level, stock position, and period to be covered by the purchase. The safety stock level in this formula serves a function equivalent to the minimum stock level in the previous formula, in that it is the level that warns of possible stockouts if an order is not placed. However, with this formula, an order quantity can be calculated at any time without waiting to reach the safety stock level.

Note that the variables are the same as those used in the maximum-minimum method; in fact, the proposed reorder

quantity should be the same with both formulas, assuming the same variable values. This formula facilitates management of scheduled purchasing, because the formula always suggests an order quantity whenever stock is not enough to cover the next procurement period, without regard to any predetermined reorder level. Another advantage with this formula is that when emergency orders are needed in a scheduled purchasing system, the same formula is used to compute emergency order quantity as would be used for a regular order.

This consumption-based reordering formula is suitable for perpetual purchasing, assuming that computer software is available that recalculates suggested order quantity on command, ideally after each transaction. Country Study 23-1 shows how scheduled purchasing is managed with this formula in the Organisation of Eastern Caribbean States.

The variables in the recommended formula are—

- Average monthly consumption, adjusted for stockouts (C_A)
- Supplier lead time (LT)
- Procurement period—time until the next order will be placed (PP)
- Safety stock (SS)
- Stock in inventory (S_I)
- Quantity of stock now on order from a supplier but not yet received (S_O)
- Quantity of stock back-ordered to lower levels (S_B)

In this formula, the minimum safety stock (which can be modified as discussed in Section 23.5) should be the lead time multiplied by the average consumption during the lead time: $C_A \times LT$.

The complete formula to calculate the quantity to order (Q_O) for each item (without considering intrasystem back orders) is the adjusted average consumption, multiplied by the sum of lead time and procurement period, plus safety stock, minus the sum of stock on hand and stock on order. The symbolic formula is—

$$Q_O = C_A \times (LT + PP) + SS - (S_I + S_O)$$

If the supply system uses back orders internally, and quantities are outstanding to operating units that must be filled when an order is received, the formula would add back orders (S_B) to the projected demand requirements in the formula (as was the case for the minimum-maximum formula), yielding—

$$Q_O = C_A \times (LT + PP) + SS + S_B - (S_I + S_O)$$

For example, suppose (because of an epidemic of cholera) no tetracycline capsules are in stock, and 2,000 are back-ordered to lower-level facilities at the time scheduled for reordering. One order is outstanding to the supplier for 3,000 capsules. The lead time for this supplier is two months, the average monthly consumption is 1,000 capsules, the safety stock is calculated as 2,000 capsules, and the procurement period is six months. The quantity to order is calculated as—

$$Q_O = 1,000 \times (2 + 6) + 2,000 + 2,000 - (0 + 3,000) = 9,000$$

23.9 Mathematical models for reordering

The goal of inventory management is a system that responds to what patients actually need, not one based on the results of modeling. The most advanced commercial supply systems are moving toward using technology to track what customers buy, then reporting the information throughout an integrated supply chain to the manufacturer. However, until those technologies become the norm for pharmaceutical supply, many authoritative sources agree that simple models to determine product orders, such as those presented in Section 23.8, are preferable to more complex models in most situations. Objections to complex models include (1) that the refinements gained in controlling stock even in the best cases are not substantial in comparison to minimum-maximum and consumption-based formulas; (2) that in most cases, the information fed into the equations is only an estimate, leading to results that are not precise despite the air of precision lent by sophisticated calculations; and (3) that in many cases, staff members do not understand the more complex models, do not trust the results, and make their own subjective determinations of order quantities and desired stock levels.

Mathematical models have been developed to address most aspects of inventory management. The most widely known of these models is the economic order quantity (EOQ), but others are worth mentioning, such as the economic order interval (EOI) and some of the mathematical approaches for smoothing forecasts of demand and lead time and for estimating safety stock requirements. EOQ and EOI are illustrated in some detail here, followed by brief discussions of some of the other models.

Economic order quantity

The EOQ concept has been around for more than fifty years and is widely applied in commercial firms that use a perpetual purchasing model. The basic idea is that an ideal order quantity exists for any item, which strikes an optimum balance between inventory-holding costs and incremental ordering costs (see Box 23-3 and Chapter 40).

With its precise outputs, EOQ seems very sophisticated. EOQ might appear to be exactly what is needed in all pharmaceutical supply systems, or at least those that use per-

petual purchasing. In fact, the need to order by package means that some deviation from the true EOQ will occur for many items. Another limitation is that the EOQ formula assumes that lead times and consumption rates are predictable, orders are received instantaneously, and stockouts are not permitted. Because that is obviously not true, additional calculations are required to establish the appropriate safety stock level, which introduces uncertainty even if the basic EOQ calculation is exact.

Some have contended that EOQ is really "the square root of two times a guess, times a scientific guess, divided by a precise guess, times management's guess." Nevertheless, the EOQ is still a reasonable choice for estimating order quantities in a perpetual purchasing system in which access to suppliers and funds is such that orders can be placed at any time. The quantities calculated using the model should, however, be treated as guidelines and not absolutes.

When other reordering formulas are used to manage inventory, calculating the EOQ periodically for high-use, high-value items (class A) may be useful for comparing the theoretical ideal order quantity with current practice.

Economic order interval

A concept related to EOQ is EOI—the theoretical ideal interval for spacing orders placed for the EOQ. As is the case with EOQ, the EOI changes, depending on the values of the individual variables; with a much higher acquisition cost, the EOI decreases (more orders per year), and so forth. Also, like EOQ, the EOI formula produces recommendations that must be rounded.

Although EOI has its main application in systems that use EOQ to set the order quantity, EOI can be used in pharmaceutical supply systems to check the theoretical ideal ordering intervals for scheduled purchasing and then to group items that would best be ordered monthly, quarterly, semiannually, and so forth. The EOI is also illustrated in Box 23-3.

Exponential smoothing

Exponential smoothing is a common technique for coping with variation in consumption or lead-time patterns. In this technique, a smoothing constant (called *alpha*) is used to adjust the observed average consumption or lead-time values.

One application of exponential smoothing calculates the projected demand (D) by factoring in the average consumption from the three-month lead time (C_L), the consumption from the past month (C_A), and the smoothing factor alpha (α), which for these purposes is usually set between 0.1 and 0.2. The equation is—

$$D = C_L + [\alpha \times (C_A - C_L)]$$

**Box 23-3
Economic order quantity and order interval**

EOQ

Although many variations exist, the most basic formula for the EOQ is—

$$\text{EOQ} = \sqrt{(2 \times U \times O) \div (H \times C)}$$

where—

U = annual use, in units
O = incremental ordering cost
H = average holding cost (percentage of average inventory value)
C = projected net acquisition cost

Considering an example of dextrose bags for IV injection, assume a projected annual use of 25,000 bags at an average acquisition price of USD 2 per bag. Also assume that the estimated incremental ordering cost is USD 70 per order placed, and the average inventory-holding cost is 40 percent. The calculation proceeds as follows—

Step 1: $2 \times 25,000 \times 70 = 3,500,000$ $(2 \times U \times O)$
Step 2: $2 \times 0.4 = 0.8$ $(H \times C)$
Step 3: $3,500,000 \div 0.8 = 4,375,000$
   $([2 \times U \times O] \div [H \times C])$
Step 4: Square root = 2,091.65

Thus, according to the EOQ model, dextrose bags should be ordered in quantities of 2,091.65 bags. Before going further, the reader should consider what happens when the individual variables go up or down. For example, if the item's acquisition cost is USD .20 (with all other variables the same), the EOQ would be 6,614.38 bags; if the price is USD 20, the EOQ would be 661.44 bags. If only consumption changes, annual use of 5,000 bags produces an EOQ of 935.41 bags, and annual use of 50,000 bags yields an EOQ of 2,958.04 bags. When incremental costs of purchasing go up, the EOQ goes up (to decrease the ordering frequency); as the holding cost percentage goes up, the EOQ goes down, to increase order frequency and decrease stock levels.

EOI

The formula for calculating the EOI uses the same variables as the EOQ but combines them as follows—

$$\text{EOI} = \sqrt{(2 \times O) \div (U \times H \times C)}$$

where—

U = annual use in units
C = projected net acquisition cost
O = ordering cost
H = holding cost

The EOI produces its result as fractions of a year (assuming that consumption is based on a year). For the EOQ example above, the EOI for orders of 2,091.65 bags would be 0.084 years, which converts to 1.004 months, 4.35 weeks, or 30.5 days. The calculation is—

Step 1: $(2 \times 70) \div (25,000 \times 0.4 \times 2)$
Step 2: $140 \div 20,000 = .007$
Step 3: $\sqrt{.007} = 0.08366$ years

If, for example, an item had averaged 150 units consumed per month over the last three months but 200 were used in the last month, the smoothed average using an alpha value of 0.1 would be—

$$D = 150 + [0.1 \times (200 - 150)] = 155$$

Clearly the difference between the simple average and the smoothed average would be greater with larger consumption values and with a higher alpha factor.

This equation is not complex in itself, but choosing the value for the alpha factor is tricky (most authorities recommend trial runs using various values, then observing results and trying again). The higher the alpha, the more "adaptable" the forecast is to recent trends; however, the higher the alpha factor, the lower the reliability when a large random noise factor is present in the consumption pattern.

Standard deviation of consumption and lead time

The standard deviation of consumption and of lead time can be used in mathematical models to adjust forecasts when variation (random noise) in the consumption or lead-time pattern is considerable. Standard deviation is basically an estimate of how much an individual value is likely to vary from the average of all values in a series (see Rowntree 2003 for methods for calculating standard deviation).

The following equation illustrates how the standard deviation of lead-time consumption (SD_{LTC}) is calculated, for use in setting safety stocks—

$$SD_{LTC} = \sqrt{(LT \times SD_C{}^2) + (C_A{}^2 \times SD_{LT}2)}$$

where—

C_A = average monthly consumption

LT = average lead time
SD$_C$ = standard deviation of consumption
SD$_{LT}$ = standard deviation of lead time

For example, if consumption of an item averages 1,000 units per month with a standard deviation of 100, and the lead time averages three months with a standard deviation of 0.75 months, the average consumption during the lead time period is 3,000 units, and the standard deviation of that lead time consumption is calculated as—

$$\sqrt{[3 \times (100 \times 100)] + [(1,000 \times 1,000) \times (0.75 \times 0.75)]} = 769.74$$

Most values in any series of observations show a normal distribution pattern around the mean (average) value. (For example, in a population of men who average 6 feet in height, about half the men will be taller and about half will be shorter rather than exactly 6 feet.) Normal distributions characteristically demonstrate that the standard deviation times about two will encompass 95 percent of the values clustered above and below the average (see Rowntree 2003). Thus, in the example here, 95 percent of the time, the monthly consumption will fall within two times the standard deviation of monthly consumption.

This calculation could be used with any reordering formula to assign safety stock in order to theoretically achieve a 95 percent service level. For the example given above, 2 × 770 equals 1,540 units needed as safety stock, in addition to average lead-time consumption. In a minimum-maximum formula, the minimum level would be 3,000 units (C$_A$ × LT), and the added safety stock would be 1,540 units. In a consumption-based formula, the total safety stock would be 4,540 units. ■

References and further readings

★ = Key readings.

★ Burt, D. N., S. Petcavage, and R. Pinkerton. 2009. *World Class Supply Management*. 8th ed. New York: McGraw-Hill.

★ Dear, A. 1990. *Inventory Management De-mystified*. Dordrecht, The Netherlands: Kluwer Academic Publishers.

Downes, J., and J. Goodman. 2010. *Dictionary of Finance and Investment Terms*. 8th ed. Hauppauge, N.Y.: Barron's Educational Series.

Quick, J. 1982. Applying Management Science in Developing Countries: ABC Analysis to Plan Public Drug Procurement. *Socio-Economic Planning Sciences* 16(1):39–50.

★ Rowntree, D. 2003. *Statistics Without Tears: A Primer for Non-mathematicians*. Upper Saddle River, N.J.: Pearson Allyn & Bacon Publishers.

Warren, C., J. Reeve, and J. E. Duchac. 2008. Inventories. In *Accounting*. 23rd ed. Cincinnati, Ohio: South-Western College Publishing.

★ Waters, C. D. J. 2003. *Inventory Control and Management*. 2nd ed. Chichester, England: John Wiley & Sons.

Performance indicators

As discussed in Chapters 36 and 48, indicators have been developed expressly for use in public-sector pharmaceutical supply systems. Some of them should be considered as tools to measure inventory management performance, although no standards exist yet for the acceptable range of performance. These indicators include—

- Average percentage of inventory variation in the stock record-keeping system, at a sample of warehouses and facilities
- Percentage of stock records that correspond with physical counts, at a sample of warehouses and facilities
- Percentage of a specified set of indicator medicines that are in stock at a sample of warehouses and facilities
- Average percentage of time out of stock for the set of indicator medicines
- Average lead time from suppliers and from warehouses to facilities

Context for inventory management

- Are all supply system operations related to finished goods, or does the system also manufacture pharmaceuticals?
- At what levels of the system are pharmaceutical orders placed, either to suppliers or to other levels of the system?

Selection of items for stock status

- How do managers and operations personnel determine which items should be held in stock and which (if any) should be ordered only as needed?

Costs associated with inventory and purchasing operations

- How is inventory valued, and what procedures are used to physically count stock and reconcile records?
- How many months' worth of stock is on hand at central storage facilities? At regional and district facilities? At hospital pharmacies, health centers, dispensaries, and other clinical facilities?
- What information is available on inventory values, operating costs of warehouses, operating costs of the purchasing department, and costs associated with shortages? If such information is available, how is it used?
- Are techniques such as ABC value analysis, VEN analysis, and total variable cost analysis used in for-

mulating inventory management strategies? If so, in what areas?

Stock records and routine reports

- What inventory needs exist at each level of the health care system? How accurate and how current are the records? Do they supply the information needed for procurement and distribution decisions?
- If a computerized information system is in use, is it a general purpose inventory management package or a special-purpose package developed for managing public-sector pharmaceutical supply systems? Does it automatically calculate minimum and maximum quantities or consumption-based order quantities?
- What standard reports are produced on inventory status, procurement operations, and consumption patterns? How is the information used?

Safety stocks and service levels

- How are safety stock levels calculated at each level of the system?
- What adjustments in safety stocks are made for variations in consumption and lead-time patterns?
- What percentage service levels are normally achieved by warehouses supplying lower levels of the system? What percentage service levels are provided by major suppliers to the system?

Purchasing model

- How frequently are pharmaceutical orders placed at each level that places orders? Is the same model used for all items?
- What percentage of orders are routine and what percentage are emergency orders?
- Do any special factors dictate the choice of inventory management strategies, such as government financial and administrative regulations, staff, existing management information systems, supplier access, or contract procedures?

Reorder formulas

- What reordering formulas are used to determine purchase quantities? Is the same formula used at all levels and all facilities?
- What source data are used in the formulas?
- How much weight is given to the manager's experience and judgment? What other factors are considered?

CHAPTER 24

Importation and port clearing

SUMMARY

The purpose of an effective and efficient importation and port-clearance process is to ensure that pharmaceuticals and related health supplies are cleared from a land, sea, or airport with the least possible delay after their arrival.

Port delays can have costly consequences, such as—

- Reduced shelf life or, for vaccines and other very temperature-sensitive items, possibly a complete loss of potency
- Deterioration of product
- Damage to product cartons and other packaging or damage to outer identification
- Increased chance of theft
- Storage fees (demurrage), which can result in prohibitively high costs
- Stockouts, resulting in emergency purchases made at higher unit cost and with the potential for unassured quality
- Cash flow problems caused by pharmaceutical products being tied up for indefinite periods in port

The port-clearing process consists of—

- Managing preshipment issues, such as documentation, which are often required for the clearance process
- Identifying and anticipating the arrival of shipments
- Locating the shipments and the particular consignments
- Obtaining the documents needed for clearing before the arrival of supplies at a port, and ensuring that the documents are in accordance with the country's port and customs requirements
- Making timely payments relating to the clearance process
- Ensuring that appropriate storage space is available to receive the shipment and that transport is available immediately
- Delivering goods to the warehouse or other storage facility as appropriate

Expediting port clearing is an important function, requiring either a well-organized, paper-based activity-monitoring system or a computerized information system, as well as suitably trained human resources.

Port clearing may be slowed by government customs and import regulations, and inefficiencies within agencies that import goods. Private companies are sometimes able to achieve more rapid port clearance than government agencies. Two private-sector choices are available: either the supplier can be made responsible for the port-clearing process and delivering goods to a nominated warehouse, or the task can be contracted out to a clearing and forwarding agent. Retaining the services of experienced and well-trained staff can significantly improve the port-clearing process. A cost/benefit analysis should be carried out to establish the most suitable method for managing port clearance—either in-house or outsourced to the private sector. In addition, any changes to clearance formalities must be monitored continuously to prevent unnecessary delays when new regulations come into force.

Losses and damage in transit can be substantial. In order to recover insured losses, the import unit must lodge insurance claims systematically and expeditiously, because insurance companies usually have specific periods within which claims must be made.

24.1 Managing importation

This chapter discusses systems and procedures to improve the efficiency of port clearing. The port-clearing process is vital to the efficient operation of a public pharmaceutical supply program, whether it is performed by public employees or contracted out.

In many countries, clearing pharmaceutical consignments from airports and other ports is an inefficient and time-consuming activity that leads to financial losses. Unlike products that are nonperishable or indestructible, medicines and medical supplies can be damaged by poor handling and inadequate or poor storage conditions. They are also highly attractive to thieves. Thus, there is a critical need to clear pharmaceuticals and other temperature-sensitive and high-value products, such as HIV test kits, as quickly as possible after delivery to any port. The speed of this process is particularly important in landlocked countries, where goods may travel long distances overland, subject to unexpected delays, in less than desirable storage conditions.

Financial losses caused by poor port-clearing management, such as the following, can be extensive and are often proportional to the delay in the port.

- Shelf life can be affected when products are kept in the port under incorrect storage conditions. In the case of vaccines and other temperature-sensitive products, the product may be rendered unusable or extra costs may be incurred to test the potency of the items.

- The likelihood of theft and product deterioration or damage is increased, especially when cartons are damaged by poor handling or are handled multiple times.
- Storage fees (demurrage) can result from delays in clearing; such fees are often substantial.
- Port-clearing delays result in longer delivery lead times. Unless funds are invested to increase safety stocks, stockouts may occur at storage and dispensing facilities, leading to extra expenditures on emergency purchases and supply chain disruption.
- Capital funds are tied up by port-clearing delays, which worsen cash flow problems in programs operating a revolving drug fund.

In many countries, the efficiency and economy of port clearing are hindered by cumbersome, bureaucratic, or obsolete regulations and by the poor systems and procedures used by customs and port authorities. The resulting delays for importers are substantial, yet improving performance can be difficult. The common practice adopted by private companies and individual importers is to obtain the services of a private clearing agent on a contract basis. An experienced agent has the best chance of negotiating the regulatory labyrinth in the shortest possible time.

24.2 Using a clearing and forwarding agent

Importation and customs clearance is a specialized area of work. Unless the pharmaceutical program already has an experienced team with clearing and forwarding skills, contracting with a specialized clearing and forwarding agent is strongly recommended.

If a private-sector agent is used, tenders for these services should be obtained from several companies, particularly if a large volume of business is involved. Any tender must clearly specify the service levels required and request pharmaceutical handling experience and references from current and previous clients. Tenderers should be asked to specify all charges and rates and to clearly identify the duties they will perform (see Box 24-1). Before an agent is appointed, it is important to obtain satisfactory business references from other clients and verify documents that have been submitted with the tender offers. The agent's offices and warehouses should also be inspected to ensure that good business and materials-handling practices are observed. Pharmaceuticals require special handling, and the agent should show an understanding of the problems associated with such commodities and demonstrate the ability to deal with these problems.

The import agency must have a broad understanding of the regulations and procedures related to customs and

---

Box 24-1
Contracting for port clearing

The following list includes the main features of a contract for port-clearing and forwarding services. Professional advice should be sought to ensure that terms and conditions are locally appropriate, legally enforceable, and realistic.

Scope of work

- Dealing with customs formalities
- Arranging clearance from the port or airport
- Arranging transport to the agent's warehouse or the consignee's premises
- Reviewing existing warehousing and identifying any potential problems in terms of capacity, security, ease of access, and availability of handling equipment
- Providing safe and secure warehousing prior to delivery, if required
- Arranging for delivery to final destinations, if required, which may include ensuring that lists of authorized signatories for taking over goods are available to maintain security
- Specifying documentation to be provided by the

supplier and by the consignee (for example, shipping advisory, bill of lading, air waybill, packing list)

Performance standards

- Time periods allowed for each stage in the import and port-clearing process
- Procedures for regular performance monitoring

Service requirements

- Reporting
- Quoting for individual consignments
- Payment arrangements
- Penalties for poor performance
- Security
- Dealing with defective shipments in a timely manner
- Restrictions on the sublease of services to other companies

Payment terms

- Port or airport charges itemized in detail
- Agent's costs itemized in detail

port clearance, whereas the clearing agent must be familiar with key local officials and understand local rules, practices, and culture to help the recipient through the routines required. For example, differences in standard work weeks because of cultural or religious customs could make clearance and delivery procedures unfeasible on particular days of the week (for instance, arrivals should not be scheduled in Muslim countries on Fridays). The agent should obtain documentation from the import agency in advance of the arrival of goods in port to avoid storage charges, and should also assist in obtaining relevant permits, waivers, or bonds. The agent must also be up-to-date with current legislation and promptly notify the principals of any changes.

The agent must take full responsibility for ensuring that the cargo is cleared and delivered with minimal delay, in a secure and appropriate way, and at the lowest cost (or at a cost consistent with the contracted rate). Even if this system is in place, it is critically important for the recipient to understand all the stages of the importation and port-clearing process.

24.3 Organizing an import unit

An alternative to contracting with a private-sector clearing agent is to empower an import unit in the supply system to handle port-clearance responsibilities. This unit's responsibility should be specifically defined and include standard operating procedures, and the responsible officials should be accountable to the pharmaceutical supply program for prompt, reliable port clearance. The unit should have one or more experienced clearing agents on staff. Before the decision is made to organize an in-house import unit, its cost-effectiveness should be compared with that of using a contract with a private clearing agent. Chapter 44 discusses the responsibilities of an import unit attached to medical stores.

24.4 The port-clearing process

The most important steps in the port-clearing process are discussed in this section. Shippers and their forwarding agents must check conditions at the relevant port at each end of the journey. This step includes establishing any limitations on the use, size, and availability of containers and container-handling equipment; determining storage conditions in warehouses or storerooms in the port; and ascertaining the availability and functionality of refrigeration equipment to store vaccines and other temperature-sensitive products.

Notify buyer of expected arrival date of shipments

As soon as a consignment of medicines is shipped (in the case of air freight, preferably twenty-four hours ahead of dispatch), the seller has the responsibility of telling the buyer the name of the carrying vessel, aircraft, or vehicle and its expected time of arrival at the buyer's port. This step is often done by e-mail or fax. The seller then dispatches to the buyer copies of all the documents mentioned in Figure 24-1 and Box 24-2. When the buyer receives these documents, the local agents for the shipper or carrier can be contacted to obtain exact arrival details.

Locate shipments

The shipper's local agent provides final details specifying the quay, airport, or land destination where the shipment will arrive. Typically, a land destination will be a customs-bonded warehouse that can be publicly or privately owned (often by the importer) and is often located right at the port of entry, which minimizes handling and therefore risk. Subsequently, the agent provides details of the specific port or customs warehouse to which the consignment will be cleared. During the time that goods are parked in a bonded warehouse, duties do not have to be paid. Duty is not due until the product is taken from the bonded warehouse to sell or consume; if the products are reexported or destroyed, then duties will not have to be paid at all. Storage in a bonded warehouse also allows time for pharmaceuticals to be quality-tested before being released to the market. Such warehouses require adequate security to prevent theft or diversion of pharmaceutical shipments and also should have the capacity to store medicines at the right conditions, including appropriate temperature, to prevent damage.

Obtain documents needed for clearing

The port authorities require the original copies of the documents described in Box 24-2 to permit clearance by the buyer or its authorized clearing agent. Having an established list of duly authorized persons able to sign for goods helps ensure full security and accountability. Along with the original documents described in Box 24-2, the buyer or the clearing agent prepares customs and port authority entries. The drug regulatory authority may also inspect the shipment to make sure that the pharmaceuticals are registered, have been imported by a licensed importer, and any charges have been fully paid. After these steps are completed, customs duties (if applicable) as well as port authority and other charges must be paid before the consignment of medicines is removed from the custody of the customs and port authorities. When import agencies do not make advance preparations to have the required funds ready, clearance is delayed and storage fees accumulate.

Deliver to warehouse

Except in the case of medicines requiring special storage conditions—for example, a cold room or a dark location—the consignment is kept in a general-purpose port or customs warehouse until delivery. Such warehouses should be checked to ensure that they have appropriate handling and storage facilities for medicines in addition to straightforward container handling. The loading of the consignment onto trucks must be supervised by wharf officers from the import agency or its authorized clearing agent. To avoid delays at the delivery site, drivers should be told precisely where the consignment is to be delivered and informed of any particular timing issues related to warehouse closures or lack of receiving staff.

24.5 Expediting port clearing

Port facilities in many countries are inefficient. Nevertheless, the port-clearing department or port-clearing agent can improve the situation by adopting better systems and procedures. Typical problems experienced by an import unit, and some methods for expediting work, are discussed in this section.

Use of an activity monitoring system

One of the greatest problems experienced by the manager of an import unit or port-clearing department is the supervision of staff engaged in clearing shipments of medicines at the port. Unlike the staff of other departments, such as procurement and inventory control, many of the personnel involved in clearing medicines spend much of their time outside the office. Hence, supervision, assignment of duties, and progress monitoring are difficult. Careful selection of appropriate staff for port-clearing positions and consistent communication via radios or wireless telephones are important.

Figure 24-1 Processing of import documents

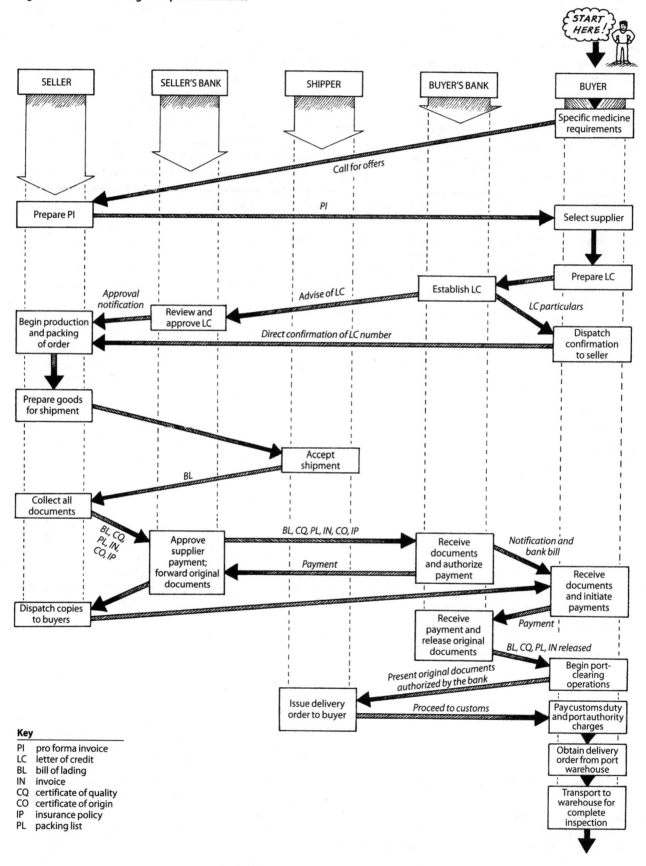

Key

PI pro forma invoice
LC letter of credit
BL bill of lading
IN invoice
CQ certificate of quality
CO certificate of origin
IP insurance policy
PL packing list

Box 24-2
Documents used in port clearing

Air waybill (AWB). Document prepared by the shipper that provides details about the contents of the shipment, the route and carrier, and the shipping charges.

Bank bill (BB). A bill presented by the buyer's bank to the buyer that covers the total cost of goods received and any bank charges for processing the order (cable charges, interest on letter of credit, fees).

Bank guarantee (BG). In certain circumstances, the lack of necessary documents may make it impossible for the buyer to clear a consignment of medicines that has arrived at the port. In such instances, a bank guarantee from the buyer's bank can facilitate port clearing.

Bill of lading (BL). A document certifying that the goods are in the charge of the carrying vessel and dated on or before the last date for shipment as given in the letter of credit. The document is issued by the shipper and signed by the master of the vessel.

Certificate of origin (CO). Document stating that the product under consideration has been produced by the manufacturer in the country concerned. Such a certificate should be obtained from a national chamber of commerce or similar institute of the exporter's country.

Certificate of quality (CQ). A buyer usually insists on certification from the supplier, such as batch certificates and a WHO-type certificate of a pharmaceutical product from the exporting country's drug regulatory authority (see Chapters 19 and 39).

Insurance policy (IP). Pharmaceutical consignments are generally insured against damage, pilferage, and complete loss. The insurance policy indicates that a certain sum of money has been paid as a premium to cover the consignment of medicines. This document normally provides information about the nature and extent of coverage provided and the terms and conditions under which it is valid.

Invoice (IN). Document provided by the supplier indicating costs, freight, insurance, and any other payment due on the order.

Letter of credit (LC). An interbank document issued by the buyer's bank. It states that a certain sum of money is available for the seller to claim from the bank as soon as a consignment is shipped and the required documents are presented, as specified in the letter of credit. It becomes irrevocable when appropriated and numbered by the bank.

Packing list (PL). Prepared by the seller, this document describes in detail the contents of each package in a consignment of medicines, including strength, pack size, number of packs per carton, and number of cartons per package. This information helps the buyer check whether medicines actually shipped are in accord with the packing list and the purchase contract.

Pro forma invoice (PI). Provided to the buyer by the supplier. It includes information such as the price of the product, shipping and insurance charges (if applicable), total value, a detailed description of the product offered, and terms of payment. In some cases, the PI must be authorized by the country's drug regulatory authority before clearing can be completed. The PI can also form the basis of assessing the fee payable to the drug regulatory authority by the importer.

Registration documents (RD). In some countries, the customs department or the drug regulatory authority requires registration documentation before pharmaceuticals can enter the system.

Under such conditions, the import manager may also find it helpful to maintain an information system that is capable of monitoring current port-clearing activities, causes of delays, and assignment of personnel and equipment. This system should also be able to expedite clearance of urgently needed consignments. In some instances, an information system includes the issue of logbooks for all officers, whether in-house or contracted, who are responsible for customs and port clearance, to record their activities. Logbooks can be used to identify possible causes for delays and solutions for avoiding them.

Information and documentation for expected consignments

Another major problem is lack of information on expected shipments. Commonly, the import unit spends a great deal of time checking with shipping agents to ascertain whether goods have arrived. In many instances, the import unit learns of the arrival of consignments only after the goods have actually landed. In some cases, high port-storage charges have already been incurred and goods requiring special storage may have been delayed or damaged by the

Table 24-1   Flow of importation documents

Document	Who generates?	By when?	How transmitted?	Who receives?
Purchase order	NGO distributor	Within 2 weeks of contract approval	Scanned copy sent by e-mail or regular mail	Supplier
Pro forma invoice	Supplier	1 week from receipt of purchase order	E-mail or fax	NGO distributor
Import permit	Ministry of health	3 days after receipt of pro forma invoice	Collection by NGO distributor	NGO distributor
Import declaration form	National revenue authority at ministry of finance	3 days after receipt of import permit	Collection by NGO distributor	NGO distributor, through clearing/forwarding agent
Invoice	Supplier	Within 3 days of receipt of Import declaration form	Scanned copy sent by e-mail	NGO distributor and then to clearing/forwarding agent
Packing slip	Supplier	Within 3 days of receipt of import declaration form	Scanned copy sent by e-mail	NGO distributor and then to clearing/forwarding agent
Ocean bill of lading	Suppliers' agent	Within 1 week of shipment	Scanned copy sent by e-mail	NGO distributor and then to clearing/forwarding agent
Air waybill	Suppliers' agent	Within 1 day of shipment	Scanned copy sent by e-mail	NGO distributor and then to clearing/forwarding agent

time notification is received. Table 24-1 shows an example of a nonprofit distributor's importation document flow.

Excessive delays in port clearing and high port-storage charges are usually caused by a breakdown of communication between the supplier and the purchasing department. As described in Chapter 39, the procurement contract should clearly specify the number of copies of invoices, shipping documents, and any other supporting documentation needed, such as product registration papers or import licenses. One copy of the shipping document must be sent to the purchasing office by fax or other expeditious means when the shipment leaves the supplier's warehouse.

Often, the documents needed for clearing are not received on time from the supplier or too few copies are sent, resulting in additional delay and expense. Overcoming this problem requires the maintenance of good communication among the supplier, the freight forwarder, the consignee, and all other parties; a good practice is to use established, detailed document requirements that are agreed on by all parties involved in the process. In addition, reports of supplier inefficiency should be incorporated into the general merit-rating system for suppliers (see Chapter 21).

Country Study 39-2 describes how Papua New Guinea has addressed delays in port clearance by awarding contracts that require suppliers or their agents in the buyer's country to be responsible for customs, port clearance, and delivery of goods to warehouses designated by the buyer. In such cases, the seller is motivated to clear consignments and make the delivery immediately, because payment is not made to suppliers until receipt of the shipment.

24.6 Lodging insurance claims

When damaged goods or short shipments are identified, completing the insurance claim quickly is important. Recovery of insured losses depends on the existence of a thorough, systematic routine for inspecting all shipments when they are accepted at the port or at the central warehouse (see Chapter 44), and submission of claims within the time stipulated by the insurance company. Consistent recovery of insured losses also depends on the assignment of qualified staff members to carry out claims processing. An effective monitoring system reduces the chance that claims will be forgotten or unduly delayed. This function should be part of the system used for monitoring the port-clearing process. ■

References and further readings

★ = Key readings.

★ Durgavich, J. 2009. *Customs Clearance Issues Related to the Import of Goods for Public Health Programs*. Task Order 1. Arlington, Va.: USAID /DELIVER Project, Task Order 1. <http://pdf.usaid.gov/pdf_docs/PNADP583.pdf>

★ International Chamber of Commerce. 2010. *Incoterms 2010: ICC Official Rules for the Interpretation of Trade Terms*. [In 31 languages.] Paris: ICC Publishing.

Nelson, C. A. 2009. *Import/Export: How to Take Your Business Across Borders*. New York: McGraw-Hill.

Rushton, A., J. Oxley, and P. Croucher. 2010. *Handbook of Logistics and Distribution Management*. 4th ed. London: Kogan Page.

Weiss, K. D. 2007. *Building an Import/Export Business*. 4th ed. New York: John Wiley & Sons.

ASSESSMENT GUIDE

Existing arrangements

- Which air, sea, and land ports are used? What proportion of total supplies comes through each port?
- What is the average time to clear goods from each port?
- Do any particular problems exist at each site, and how do they affect the clearance process?

Port conditions and clearance procedures

- Are cold rooms, freezers, and locked warehouses available? Do they have appropriate temperature controls? Are security personnel on duty at all times? Does security include fenced areas, alarms, or other controls? Are medicines damaged by climatic conditions?
- What are the causes of recent port losses?
  - Physical damage
  - Theft
  - Poor storage conditions
  - Lost shipments caused by crowding or disorganized port management
  - Delayed port clearance
  - Lack of human resources
  - Lack of appropriate handling equipment
- Who is responsible for port clearing?
  - Central medical stores staff
  - Ministry of health or government import unit
  - Private import agents
- Do port-clearing staff members know in advance when and where a shipment is due? Is this information used to speed port clearance? Do the same problems recur regularly, and if so, are remedial procedures being implemented?
- Are port-clearing staff members trained in import documentation and port-clearing procedures?
- Does the import unit workload vary significantly throughout the year? If so, when? Does this variation cause any difficulties?
- Do port authorities assign priority to pharmaceutical and other "sensitive" shipments?

- Do customs and import control regulations affect port-clearing efficiency? Do other agencies assist or impede port clearing? If the latter, can this situation be rectified?
- Are storage fees regularly incurred, and are they justified? Can they be avoided through remedial action?
- Are adequate and secure procedures in place for receiving and checking pharmaceuticals?
- Is adequate and suitable transport for distribution available?

Private clearing agents

- Are private clearing agents available? Are they competent to handle pharmaceutical shipments?
- How do charges for contracting with a private agent compare with the cost of existing arrangements?

Communications

- Does the import unit or agency have direct access to a reliable overseas telephone line and e-mail access? Does it have a fax machine and a computer?

Monitoring and evaluation

- What is the average time needed to clear shipments from the port or airport?
- Are effective systems in place for monitoring and evaluating import procedures? If not, which elements are missing?
- What is the annual cost of port losses as a percentage of the value of pharmaceuticals received? Do significant variations exist between ports? Why?
- If delays in port clearance are chronic, what are the causes?
  - Poor procedures by the buyer
  - Bureaucratic delays at the port
  - Inadequate communications
  - Lack of human resources
  - Missing or incomplete documentation
  - Lack of funds to clear goods

| Part I: Policy and economic issues | Part II: Pharmaceutical management | Part III: Management support systems |

Selection
Procurement
Distribution
  22 Managing distribution
  23 Inventory management
  24 Importation and port clearing
  25 Transport management
  26 Kit system management
Use

CHAPTER 25

Transport management

SUMMARY

Unreliable transport for pharmaceutical supplies is a major problem in many health care programs. Good transport practice demands reliability, efficiency, safety, accountability, timeliness, affordability, and sustainability.

Transport is difficult to plan and manage well. Politicians and senior program managers generally assign greater priority to other, more visible, aspects of health care delivery. However, policy makers and administrators need to appreciate that effective and responsive health service depends on always having medicines available when and where they are needed, which requires the secure and proper transport of pharmaceuticals and medical supplies. If the pharmaceutical sector has to compete with other services for planned and emergency logistics, the consequences may be critical to public health.

Transport is provided for pharmaceuticals and related supplies either by the subject facility, by the supplier, or by an outsourced transport service. The type, volume, frequency, and duration of transport services required are determined by the nature of the health service. For practical purposes, main stores or central medical stores require major transport when moving pharmaceuticals from port to warehouse. If the store has branches in different parts of the country, it will need to transport the supplies to the branches. Facility-level transport requires a sophisticated transport network, involving in-house vehicles, rental services, or supplier delivery.

When planning transport system improvements, managers must—

- Thoroughly review and understand the existing transport system
- Select suitable vehicles
- Ensure adherence to standard operating procedures
- Ensure that vehicles are used for their intended purpose
- Maintain vehicles properly
- Replace vehicles before they wear out or become too expensive to operate
- Provide funds for vehicle maintenance and replacement
- Consider the formation of a vehicle pool system
- Consider alternatives, such as third-party and private-sector contracts

Major determinants of the transport system, which require special attention, are the vehicles and their operation and management. The costs of purchasing, running, and maintaining vehicles are high. If funding is inadequate, transport services will not be sustainable.

Transport services require effective management, which is particularly difficult to achieve in countries where transport is challenging and the pool of qualified managers is relatively small. When a shortage of transport exists, health service vehicles are frequently misused for the personal benefit of health service staff. Strong management is necessary to eliminate abuses and to ensure that vehicles are used appropriately. Although cost is a limiting factor, the logistics needs of the pharmaceutical sector can be adequately met if vehicle costs are shared with other services.

In many countries, the burden of managing transport and transport maintenance services can be reduced by contracting out these services to private or parastatal companies that specialize in such operations and are able to provide competitive rates. Before taking such action, the private or parastatal sector must be assessed based on its capacity and past performance, and existing operating costs must be accurately assessed so that a realistic cost comparison can be made. Transport contractors should then be carefully selected and monitored, and contract terms should be clearly drawn up and enforced. These measures also make monitoring transport costs easier.

Contracting out transport services will be inevitable where air transport, and to a large extent, sea or river distribution is involved. However, in many developing countries with scarce transport resources, efficient private-sector transportation companies are still evolving and may not be sufficiently competitive or efficient. In such situations, regional and interregional cooperation and collaboration among various government agencies, nongovernmental organizations (NGOs), donors, and the private sector can help maximize available transport resources.

Effective quality assurance procedures are needed to ensure that pharmaceuticals are correctly handled before, during, and after transit, to avoid damage.

25.1 Planning in-house transport systems

The existing transport system should be thoroughly reviewed to make efficient and rational use of existing resources. Current operating costs should be accurately assessed and compared with the projected cost of alternative systems. This section examines the issues that must be considered when planning improvements in a transport system.

Understand the existing transport system

To understand the existing transport system and its problems, one needs an assessment to provide a clear understanding of the health system's purpose and organization. This assessment requires a determination of—

- Frequency, type, and payload of transport needed according to the nature of the health service, including the amount of inventory holding, which determines the frequency of resupply.
- Location and scope (mapping) of transport needs of all warehouses and health facilities.
- Performance record of the existing pharmaceutical transport system. A detailed inventory must be made of vehicles in use at every level in the distribution system, listing age, condition, operational status, and actual versus intended use. Obtaining this information is an essential starting point for any transport assessment and should be carried out thoroughly. The data collected may be used to determine whether the existing transport fleet, in its current state, is capable of satisfying program needs.
- Estimated costs for the repair of defective vehicles.
- Location and availability of spare parts, and vehicle servicing capacity.
- Location and availability of fuel.
- Geographical, climatic, and political factors that affect transportation.
- Population distribution. Transport costs per capita are much higher in sparsely populated areas than in areas of high population density. This factor is important to take into account so that funds can be targeted in a balanced manner.
- The condition, capacity, and limitations of road, rail, air, water, and other transportation networks.
- Alternative transportation resources at every level. These resources include vehicles belonging to other government agencies, to NGOs, and to private-sector carriers. Vehicle sharing between programs is often a good option for reducing costs and improving reliability. Public transport should also be considered where suitable. Unconventional forms of transport such as bicycles or boats may be highly cost-effective, particularly for smaller-volume distribution in rural areas. For low-volume, time-critical, and high-value products, an international commercial shipper is a useful and dependable alternative. Such services are available in bigger towns.
- The annual cost of the existing transportation system. A crude index of performance can be obtained by considering this cost as a percentage of the value of pharmaceuticals delivered.
- Staff management issues related to transport, including the availability of key staff and management time available to devote to transport management.

If information is not already available, it should be collected using a structured survey (see Chapter 36). Total cost analysis is a good method for compiling cost data (see Chapter 40). Most information requires regular updating if it is to remain useful. Some data, such as vehicle breakdown reports, are required at monthly to quarterly intervals. Other data, such as road improvement information, need only occasional updating.

Plan routes and schedules

Pharmaceutical delivery routes should be planned at every level to make the best use of available resources. The following guidelines should be adopted—

- Arrange delivery routes and schedules so that vehicles start each journey fully loaded. Using a large vehicle to deliver small quantities of medicines is inefficient. Unless full loads are being dropped off at a single delivery point, a delivery circuit may be cheaper to operate than a series of trips back and forth.
- Always seek out a return load to maximize vehicle use, or alternatively, try to combine deliveries with supervisory visits.
- Make maximum use of good roads. Shortcuts along poor roads may save fuel and time, but driving on good roads improves vehicle life. Isolated travel routes also pose security concerns.
- Use vehicles that are appropriate to the route. Using four-wheel-drive vehicles on surfaced roads is a waste of resources.
- Arrange routes so that the vehicle can be parked in a secure compound during overnight stops.
- Plan routes to take account of fuel availability. If fuel is scarce, carrying fuel drums or fitting vehicles with long-range fuel tanks may be necessary. This need will reduce the space available for carrying supplies.
- Consult experienced drivers before deciding on the route. Drivers often have the best knowledge of local road conditions, fuel availability, weather, and security hazards. Their advice can be extremely valuable.

Country Study 25-1
Determining the appropriate fleet mix needed to transport pharmaceuticals in Zambia

The following analysis uses three sets of data from Zambia to plan a transport fleet based on deliveries from the Medical Stores Ltd. (MSL) to district health management teams (DHMTs) and hospitals. Below is an example of a schedule, for Route A.

Route A		Delivered at (departure date plus x days)	CYCLE 1			CYCLE 2			CYCLE 3		
			Order to stores	Truck departs stores	Delivery at health facility	Order to stores	Truck departs stores	Delivery at health facility	Order to stores	Truck departs stores	Delivery at health facility
	Drop Point 1	1	23-Dec-04	3-Jan-05	4-Jan-05	20-Jan-05	31-Jan-05	1-Feb-05	17-Feb-05	28-Feb-05	1-Mar-05
	Drop Point 2	1	23-Dec-04	3-Jan-05	4-Jan-05	20-Jan-05	31-Jan-05	1-Feb-05	17-Feb-05	28-Feb-05	1-Mar-05
	Drop Point 3	1	23-Dec-04	3-Jan-05	4-Jan-05	20-Jan-05	31-Jan-05	1-Feb-05	17-Feb-05	28-Feb-05	1-Mar-05
	Drop Point 4	2	23-Dec-04	3-Jan-05	5-Jan-05	20-Jan-05	31-Jan-05	2-Feb-05	17-Feb-05	28-Feb-05	2-Mar-05
	Drop Point 5	2	23-Dec-04	3-Jan-05	5-Jan-05	20-Jan-05	31-Jan-05	2-Feb-05	17-Feb-05	28-Feb-05	2-Mar-05
	Drop Point 6	3	23-Dec-04	3-Jan-05	6-Jan-05	20-Jan-05	31-Jan-05	3-Feb-05	17-Feb-05	28-Feb-05	3-Mar-05
	Drop Point 7	3	23-Dec-04	3-Jan-05	6-Jan-05	20-Jan-05	31-Jan-05	3-Feb-05	17-Feb-05	28-Feb-05	3-Mar-05
	Drop Point 8	3	23-Dec-04	3-Jan-05	6-Jan-05	20-Jan-05	31-Jan-05	3-Feb-05	17-Feb-05	28-Feb-05	3-Mar-05
	Drop Point 9	4	23-Dec-04	3-Jan-05	7-Jan-05	20-Jan-05	31-Jan-05	4-Feb-05	17-Feb-05	28-Feb-05	4-Mar-05
	Drop Point 10	4	23-Dec-04	3-Jan-05	7-Jan-05	20-Jan-05	31-Jan-05	4-Feb-05	17-Feb-05	28-Feb-05	4-Mar-05
	Drop Point 11	4	23-Dec-04	3-Jan-05	7-Jan-05	20-Jan-05	31-Jan-05	4-Feb-05	17-Feb-05	28-Feb-05	4-Mar-05
	Drop Point 12	5	23-Dec-04	3-Jan-05	8-Jan-05	20-Jan-05	31-Jan-05	5-Feb-05	17-Feb-05	28-Feb-05	5-Mar-05

The next set of data outlines the number and weight of cartons for each drop on the route and establishes a minimum and maximum loading weight. For example, the spreadsheet below shows that information for Chiengi DHMT. Combine with the route timing information above to develop fleet mix data for each route with the times for each delivery.

Station	Jan-04 No	Jan-04 Wt	Feb-04 No	Feb-04 Wt	Mar-04 No	Mar-04 Wt	Apr-04 No	Apr-04 Wt	May-04 No	May-04 Wt	Jun-04 No	Jun-04 Wt	Totals No	Totals Wt	Average No	Average Wt	Max No	Max Wt	Min No	Min Wt
Chadiza DHMT	61	878	154	1,089	98	1,014	16	608	60	840	52	612	441	5,041	74	840	154	1,089	16	608
Chama DHMT	113	959	155	1,213	183	1,262	37	956	93	1,680	31	316	612	6,386	102	1,064	183	1,680	31	316
Chavuma DHMT	103	968	6	228	119	838	10	328	105	742	23	233	366	3,337	61	556	119	968	6	228
Chavuma Mission H					3	6			4	6	86	1,023	93	1,035	16	173	86	1,023	3	6
Chibombo DHMT	104	1,601	119	1,052	132	1,720	51	1,246	189	2,181	33	1,021	628	8,821	105	1,470	189	2,181	33	1,021
Chiengi DHMT	80	386			88	407	74	814	35	448	38	304	315	2,359	53	393	88	814	35	304

The weight for each route will determine the payload required for each vehicle. The payloads (shaded) are not large, but they help to create the appropriate fleet mix. Other information to consider in the calculation includes the average time the driver spends waiting at delivery and whether the facility accepts deliveries on Sunday.

From	Location	Station	Average Boxes	Average Kg	Driving Time Dry	Driving Time Rain
Route A						
MSL	Mkushi	Mkushi DHMT	85	861	5	5
Mkushi	Serenje	Serenje DHMT	96	704	2	2
Serenje	Milengi	Milengi DHMT	30	409	14	16
Serenje	Samfya	Samfya DHMT	80	1,244	6	6
	Chilubi (leave at Samfya)	Chilubi DHMT	29	495		
Samfya	Lubwe	Lubwe Mission H	19	142	8	10
Lubwe	Kasaba	St. Margret H	30	272	3	4
Kasaba	Mansa	Mansa DHMT	169	1,696	9	10
		Mansa GH	135	1,112		
Mansa	Mwense	Mambilima H	36	124	2	2
	Mwense	Mwense DHMT	74	1,252	1	1
Mwense	Mbereshi	Mbereshi H	34	307	2	2
Mbereshi	Kawambwa	Kawambwa DHMT	93	974	1	1
Kawambwa	Nchelenge	Nchelenge DHMT	69	904	2	2
		St. Pauls H	95	819	0	0
Nchelenge	Chiengi	Chiengi DHMT	53	393	4	5
Chiengi	**MSL**				23	23
	Total		**1,127**	**11,708**	**79**	**86**
					106	**113**

- Compare the costs of alternative combinations of routes and vehicles before making a final choice. Country Study 25-1 describes Zambia's approach to vehicle selection. Transport cost assessment is described in Section 25.5.
- In the case of air transport, consider periodic deliveries (for example, monthly or quarterly), and select air transport contractors through public tenders, when applicable.
- Where sea or river distribution is involved, periodic deliveries to or collections by health facilities may be arranged by using boats owned or hired by the health facilities.

Analyze transport alternatives

The following are major transport options—

- Trucks, vans, and cars are the most common means of transporting medicines and supplies, but there are many other potential forms of transport.
- Air transport is frequently used for delivering emergency, costly, or heat-labile products, such as vaccines. Commercial air-freight charges are high, although packaging costs may be lower than with land transport. Theft may also be less common where airport security is good. In some settings, such as countries with many islands or challenging terrain, air transport may be not only the most cost-effective option, but also the only option for routinely transporting medicines. Light aircraft may be used to transport medicines and health workers to remote and otherwise inaccessible outposts and in emergency relief situations.
- Boats are appropriate in some areas with island communities, coastal settlements, navigable rivers, or large lakes. Pharmaceuticals transported by boat must be packaged and stored to protect them against water damage.
- Railways are an excellent and cheap means of transport, provided the service is reliable. Rail transport is particularly suitable for bulk shipments between major depots. One disadvantage is that the supplies usually need to be transferred to another form of transport at the end of the rail journey. Trans-shipment increases the risk of theft and damage.
- Private-sector trucking companies can offer a cost-effective delivery service, especially between major population centers. This issue is discussed in Section 25.6.
- Box trailer units increase load-carrying capacity without the need to buy additional trucks. Small trailers, towed behind cars or pickup trucks, can also be used to transport medicines in rural areas.

- Buses, minibuses, and other means of local passenger transport can be used by health workers for transporting small quantities of medicines.
- Transport resources owned or accessed by other government, nongovernmental, or donor agencies can be shared.

Many programs also use so-called intermediate transport to augment the major transport mechanisms. Table 25-1 compares the capacity and daily range of common intermediate transport mechanisms.

Prepare a transport plan

After the existing transport system has been analyzed and the transport alternatives assessed, the logistics team should choose among the various options and balance sometimes conflicting priorities. A detailed transport plan should then be prepared that describes how all warehouses and facilities will be served. Figure 25-1 shows an example of a multisite transport plan. Such a plan must include resource ownership; transportation routes and schedules; schedules of people, transportation equipment, and related sources; information on movement of vehicles, people, and goods; distances from the source to the delivery points; overnight stops; people driving and accompanying deliveries; fuel needs; per diem and contingency funds; alternative routing in emergencies; and accompanying documents, such as waybills, travel permits, logbooks, and vehicle and driver details.

Any arrangement including items held in a duty-free bond—at an airport or shipping port, for example—introduces a new set of variables to plan for, including securing the release of the shipments and transporting them by the client or forwarding agent to their required destination.

An inventory of special environmental and legal route-use requirements must be maintained for trip planning; for example, weigh stations, seasonal blockage by rain, security-restricted routes, security checkpoints, and toll roads. If a national security office exists, it can supply information to ensure safe driving through certain security-sensitive areas, such as recommending joining a convoy if the situation dictates.

Transportation planning systems help calculate the volume that needs to be transported to a certain location and at what time. Transportation planning systems provide management with details on multiple routes, schedules, operators, and the type and volume of loads. Such a system can be maintained manually or electronically, and it can be used to analyze transport operations and costs. A global positioning system (GPS) makes possible the monitoring of physical movement and location of vehicles.

Table 25-1   Performance characteristics and relative costs of some intermediate forms of transport

Vehicle	Maximum number of people carried[a]	Supplies carried (kg/m³)	Maximum speed (km/hr)	Maximum range (km)	Route limitations	Relative cost[c]
Porter	—	25–35 0.25 m³	5	20	Unlimited	0–10
Standard bicycle	1	20[b] 0.25 m³	20	60	Reasonably flat	50–90
Load-carrying bicycle	1	25–100[b] 0.35 m³	10–15	30–40	Reasonably flat	60–100
Bicycle and trailer	1	150 0.5 m³	10–15	30–40	Reasonably flat, wide track	90–150
Bicycle and sidecar	1	150 0.4 m³	10–15	30–40	Reasonably flat, wide track	90–150
Tricycle	1	150 0.5 m³	10–15	30–40	Reasonably flat	150–200
Pack animal	—	50–200[b] Varies	5	20	Unlimited	Variable
Animal-drawn cart	Varies	500–3,000 Varies	5	20	Reasonably flat, wide track	100–180
Motorcycle	1	50–75[b] 0.25 m³	40–90	100–200	Steep hills	250–600
Motorcycle and sidecar/tricycle	1	200–300[b] 0.5–1.0 m³	30–60	80–150	Moderate hills, wide track	350–800
ATV (quad bike)[d]	1	50–75[e] 0.5 m³	30–60	60	Rough, hilly terrain	750–1,500
Single-axle tractor and trailer	Varies	1,500 Varies	15–20	50	Steep hills, wide track	1,500
Utility vehicle	Varies	500–1,000 2.0 m³	60	60	Steep hills, wide track	3,000

Source: Adapted from Hathaway 1985.

[a] Number of people carried with full load of goods.
[b] The maximum load weights for these intermediate modes of transport are 50 percent of the values quoted by Hathaway (1985). Figures have been reduced to take account of the risk of damage to valuable commodities if unstable vehicles fall over when heavily loaded. In many cases, the volume carried, not the weight, is the limiting factor.
[c] Typical ranges are quoted. These are relative costs—no specific currency is implied.
[d] All-terrain vehicle, two-wheel drive and four-wheel drive.
[e] Payload given is without trailer. Trailers can be attached to all-terrain vehicles

25.2 Vehicle acquisition and disposal

This section examines various methods of vehicle procurement, policy options for vehicle replacement, the process of selecting appropriate vehicles, and methods for disposing of broken or obsolete vehicles.

Select method of vehicle procurement

A health program can procure vehicles, boats, or aircraft in four ways: purchase, donation, lease, or rental from the private sector. Contracting out transport to a private carrier should be considered as an alternative to procurement.

Purchase. Health programs generally acquire vehicles through purchasing, which involves capital expenditure. This method builds the capital base of the institution and makes the vehicle readily available. Recurrent costs include vehicle insurance, servicing, and maintenance. A cost-recovery system can be introduced that makes the vehicle available for contracting out or personal use for a mileage-based fee when not needed by the program.

Donation. Vehicle donations are useful in some situations; in some countries, donations are the main source of vehicles. This arrangement usually does not involve capital expenditure, although importation taxes and duties may still need to be budgeted. There may be disadvantages, however. Donors may not fund insurance, servicing, and maintenance, and the health program will have to pay these expenses. Donors may wish to supply vehicles manufactured in the donor country, whether or not spare parts and maintenance skills are locally available, which can lead to serious problems. Careful analysis of the advantages and disadvantages should be made before soliciting or accepting vehicle donations. It is important to keep in mind that

Figure 25-1 Multisite transport plan

Plan 1: Start of trip from central store (A) to first destination site (B).
Continue to sites B1 and B2 and return to central store (A) after completing delivery.

Plan 2: Start of trip from central store (A) to first destination site (C).
Continue to sites C1, C2, and C3 and return to central store (A) after completing delivery.

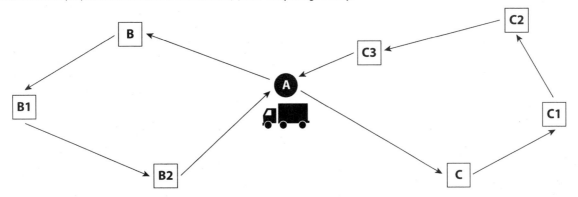

Distribution plan	Route	Schedule	Mileage	Travel time	Vehicle tag	Driver/assistant
1	A to B	Depart A on Mon 12 May at 8.00 Arrive B on Mon 12 May at 10.00 Deliver at B at 10.30 Continue to site B1	45 km	2 hrs	XD 23401	Bob Ray/Mike Todd
1	B to B1	Depart B on Mon 12 May at 13.30 Arrive B1 on Mon 12 May at 15.00 Deliver at B1 at 15.30 Overnight at B1	30 km	1.5 hrs	XD 23401	Bob Ray/Mike Todd
1	B1 to B2	Depart B1 on Tue 13 May at 8.00 Arrive B2 on Tue 13 May at 12.00 Deliver at B2 at 14.00 Overnight at B2	70 km	4 hrs	XD 23401	Bob Ray/Mike Todd
1	B2 to A	Depart B2 on Wed 14 May at 8.00 Arrive A on Wed 14 May at 12.00	65 km	4 hrs	XD 23401	Bob Ray/Mike Todd
2	A to C	Depart A on Mon 12 May at 8.00 Arrive C on Mon 12 May at 13.30 Deliver at C at 14.00 Overnight at C	85 km	5.5 hrs	XD 10002	Bill Ryan/Ted Able
2	C to C1	Depart C on Tue 13 May at 8.00 Arrive C1 on Tue 13 May at 10.30 Deliver at C1 at 11.00 Continue to C2	25 km	2.5 hrs	XD 10002	Bill Ryan/Ted Able
2	C1 to C2	Depart C1 on Tue 13 May at 11.30 Arrive C2 on Tue 13 May at 13.00 Deliver at C2 at 14.00 Continue to C3	25 km	1.5 hrs	XD 10002	Bill Ryan/Ted Able
2	C2 to C3	Depart C2 on Tue 13 May at 14.30 Arrive C3 on Tue 13 May at 16.30 Overnight at C3	40 km	2 hrs	XD 10002	Bill Ryan/Ted Able
2	C3 to A	Deliver at C3 on Wed 14 May at 8.00 Depart C3 on Wed 14 May at 8.30 Arrive A on Wed 14 May at 11.00	50 km	2.5 hrs	XD 10002	Bill Ryan/Ted Able

Notes: Time for meals and rest must be taken into consideration. The recipient facilities must be given advance notice of the delivery so that they can make receipt arrangements prior to the arrival of the delivery van.

sustainability is the key issue, whereas donor agreements are of limited duration. The health system may not have the capacity to maintain vehicles; if it does not, the donated vehicles will have a limited life.

Lease or rental. If an in-house transport system is to be maintained, the costs of leasing and purchasing should be compared. Leasing or rental companies provide vehicles on a short- or long-term basis and may also be able to supply drivers for an additional charge. An advantage of leasing or rental is that additional vehicles can be obtained readily, and broken-down vehicles can be replaced as part of the contract agreement at no cost to the system.

Contracting out. Private or parastatal trucking companies may have better transport management capacity than government agencies. Trucking companies are likely to be most competitive on the major routes. Contracting out the major routes means that the health service does not need to acquire and manage heavy vehicles, nor does it need to train drivers and maintenance staff for these vehicles. However, when outsourcing transportation services, managers need to have the skills to administer and monitor the contracts (see Chapter 39).

Establish vehicle replacement policy

Implementing a transport plan is only the first step; in-house transport systems quickly collapse if there is no vehicle replacement policy.

Reviewing the transport plan regularly and analyzing vehicle operating costs carefully are essential. Most important of all is to negotiate adequate funding to maintain the system. As vehicles get older, the cost of servicing and repairing them increases. Eventually, they will have to be replaced. The balance between capital and recurrent expenditures therefore changes from year to year. This fluctuation can pose a problem, particularly when many new vehicles are suddenly acquired from a donor. These vehicles will deteriorate at similar rates and will need to be replaced at about the same time.

Four basic policy options are available for vehicle replacement—

1. A target life is set for each category of vehicle. All vehicles in a category are replaced when they reach this set age, regardless of mileage or condition.
2. A target mileage is set for each category of vehicle. All vehicles in a category are replaced when they reach this mileage, regardless of age or condition.
3. Vehicles are replaced, regardless of age or mileage, when they exceed a preset maintenance cost.
4. Vehicles are replaced when their operational availability (reliability) falls below a defined level. The aim should always be to operate a dependable fleet with a manageable number of breakdowns to address.

Figure 25-2   Replacement policy graphs

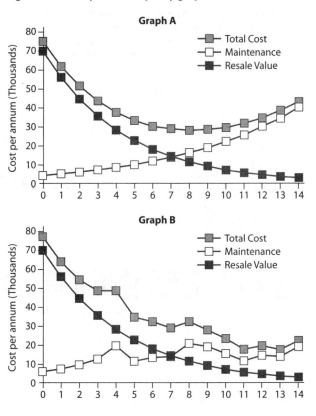

In practice, some combination of these four alternatives will probably be needed. For instance, a policy could be based on target life and mileage. Replacement occurs when one or the other of the two targets is exceeded. The chosen approach depends on the availability of funds and patterns of vehicle use. Commercial organizations have to operate their fleets as profit centers. Traditionally, government organizations and NGOs view their transport fleets as cost centers. Institutions that lease or rent vehicles from the private sector should follow similar replacement policies, because dependability and safety are also concerns for these vehicles.

Figure 25-2 shows two graphs indicating the decline in resale value compared to the rise in maintenance costs over time. Graph A illustrates an idealized model for determining the best time to replace a vehicle. If this model is used, vehicles are replaced as soon as annual maintenance costs exceed the capital value of the vehicle—in this example, after seven years. In practice, vehicle resale value is difficult to predict accurately over a long period, especially when operating conditions are harsh, and the resale value of older vehicles is determined more by condition than by age. Moreover, maintenance costs do not rise in a smoothly increasing curve over time; rather, the maintenance cost curve is "lumpy," as illustrated in Graph B, with peaks occurring whenever major components have to be replaced. Maintenance costs still exceed capital value after seven years, but by a smaller and fluctuating amount. Moreover, a significant proportion of these maintenance costs are fixed costs: preventive maintenance, tire replacement, and other costs that cannot be avoided, whatever the age of the vehicle.

The replacement policy should be reviewed regularly, based on an analysis of real data obtained from vehicle maintenance costs and operational reliability records. The operational costs of vehicle breakdowns should also be taken into account. These costs can be controlled to some extent by carefully planned preventive maintenance, but as vehicles age, the risk of unforeseen failure increases.

The condition of every vehicle in the fleet should be reviewed annually and compared with its planned life span and replacement target. If a vehicle has to be replaced prematurely, it is important to understand why.

Transport plans should be adaptable to respond to changing circumstances. For example, when funds are short, a vehicle may be kept beyond its planned replacement life, provided the vehicle is reliable and spare parts are still available.

Select appropriate vehicles

Over the years, programs often acquire a random mix of vehicles from a wide range of manufacturers, which complicates maintenance and support. Selecting vehicles wisely is essential, whether they are purchased or donated. Vehicle type, fuel, spare parts, temperature control, and need for refrigeration are critical issues.

Determining the size and mix of the transport fleet must be done based primarily on the weight of the shipments that the fleet must carry for each established route, as well as the basic characteristics of those routes, including the number of days needed to complete a route and any restrictions, such as the working hours at health facilities. Country Study 25-1 shows how to analyze data to determine the appropriate mix.

Vehicle type. Limit the variety of vehicles to simplify maintenance and enable vehicles to be interchanged within the distribution system. Choose vehicles that are in common use throughout the country. Nationwide availability of spare parts and maintenance capacity are the most important considerations in choosing a vehicle. If feasible, choose the same type of vehicles as other programs use. This strategy allows spare parts and servicing skills to be shared among programs.

Choose vehicles that are simple in design, robust, easy to maintain, and suited to local road conditions. Buying or securing four-wheel-drive vehicles is an ineffective use of resources if they will be used exclusively on paved roads. Choose vehicles that have interchangeable components, particularly items such as tires, batteries, engines, and transmissions. If an emergency arises, or if a vehicle is badly damaged, vehicles with interchangeable components can be used as sources of spare parts for others in the fleet. Vehicles that are tropicalized hold up better in difficult tropical and underdeveloped areas. Tropicalized vehicles are outfitted to withstand adverse climatic and road conditions such as excess heat, humidity, and rain. Features of a tropicalized vehicle may include heavy-duty tires and high traction to manage rough roads and mud, an extra fuel tank for long-distance driving, flood lighting for dark driving, air-conditioning, and a dust guard.

If possible, choose vehicle manufacturers that do not redesign models frequently. This strategy helps ensure the continuous availability of spare parts. In addition, assessing a vehicle's reliability is easier if it has been sold for a number of years, and maintenance personnel need less retraining.

Fuel. Diesel-powered vehicles are usually more cost-effective than gasoline-powered vehicles. They are more expensive to buy and maintain, but they are more fuel efficient and may be more reliable and longer lasting. However, at temperatures below −5° to −10°C, diesel vehicles can be difficult to operate unless fuel-line heaters or special low-temperature fuel is available. If fuel quality is a problem, select vehicles that can be adjusted to run on low-octane or adulterated fuel. If transport distances are long and fuel availability is unstable in rural areas, buying cars with an extra, built-in fuel tank is advisable.

Accessories and spare parts. Every vehicle should carry a tool kit, first-aid kit, fire extinguisher, and spare tires. Purchasing an adequate supply of spare parts, including oil filters, tires, and batteries, is essential. The quantity purchased will depend on future funding arrangements. If adequate funds for recurrent expenditures are ensured, the stock of spare parts can be renewed annually. If availability of such funds is not assured, vehicles should be purchased with several years' worth of spare parts. This precaution should be taken particularly with donated vehicles.

Temperature control. Vehicles should be painted white to reduce internal temperatures during hot weather (where applicable). They may also need to be fitted with ventilator units. In India, unrefrigerated but insulated vehicle bodies have been used to control transport temperatures. Most pharmaceuticals should not be stored for prolonged periods at temperatures above 30°C. Even in temperate climates, this temperature can be exceeded when a vehicle is parked in the sun. Some medicines, vaccines, and blood products can be damaged by exposure to temperatures even well below 30°C. These items should be transported in cold boxes or refrigerated vehicles.

In very cold climates, blood products and some pharmaceuticals and vaccines need protection against freezing during transport. Goods compartments may need to be heated; alternatively, products can be transported for limited distances using vaccine cold boxes fitted with "warm packs."

Refrigerated vehicles. Refrigerated vehicles are more difficult to maintain than conventional vehicles and should be used only in countries with a good maintenance infrastructure. Rather, it may be best to choose vehicles that have independent body units. The refrigerated body lasts longer than the vehicle to which it is attached and may be transferred to a new chassis.

Refrigeration units that can be powered by an independent engine will continue to operate even if the vehicle itself breaks down. All units should have electrical backup power units for use during overnight stops, and suitable power outlets should be provided at the stopping points.

When refrigerated vehicles break down, the shipment can be exposed to unacceptable temperatures within a few hours. It is important to ensure that adequate contingency plans (such as extra cold boxes) exist for this hazard.

In countries with cold winters, refrigerated vehicles should be fitted with a heating circuit to prevent sensitive products from freezing.

Manage vehicle disposal

As a general rule, any vehicle that has been broken for six months should be discarded. Most countries have committees that are responsible for deciding when to dispose of obsolete vehicles and equipment, which is the most accountable and transparent method. However, this procedure can be cumbersome, and large numbers of broken vehicles can be left to accumulate. These vehicles can be used to advantage in some countries. For example, they can be sold or dismantled for spare parts. The main constraint on sales is that proceeds usually accrue to the finance ministry rather than to the health ministry. Arranging for this money to be reallocated to the health service may be difficult.

25.3 Vehicle use

This section examines the issues involved in managing vehicles efficiently, safely, and cost-effectively and suggests ways to minimize system abuse.

Use onboard computers

The use of onboard computers helps a central transport operation to manage and monitor its vehicle fleet. Such technology is probably only worthwhile for large fleets that cover long routes. A system that uses GPS and short message service (SMS) allows the fleet manager to communicate directly with the driver and track the vehicle in real time.

System capabilities include—

- Alarms
- Engine monitoring (e.g., oil pressure, water level)
- Vehicle abuse monitoring (e.g., engine over-revving, harsh braking, speed violation)
- Tracking based on time or route

Prevent vehicle misuse

In-house transport systems often fail because the system is abused. Government vehicles are frequently used for private purposes, particularly by drivers and senior managers, and especially in countries where vehicles and fuel are scarce or salaries are low.

Planning and managing vehicle use and controlling misuse are difficult, but these activities are the key to sustaining a successful transport operation. Leadership and support are required from those people who have the authority to control negligent management practices.

The transport manager should control vehicle use, allocate transport resources, and be accountable for operational failures. Standard operating procedures to which drivers and users subscribe will help ensure adherence to proper use of vehicles and other transport resources. Transport should be planned and managed to achieve the following goals—

- Allocation of transport resources to meet the needs of the organization rather than those of the individual
- Prevention of unauthorized vehicle use
- Assignment of the most appropriate vehicle and driver for each purpose
- Use of alternatives, such as public transport, where appropriate and cost-effective
- Clear definitions of allowable uses by program staff and managers, to be respected by all users
- Assignment of vehicles to the primary user department, so that the department will be accountable and protect their use

Regular users should prepare written schedules of their transport needs at least a month in advance. The transport manager can then prepare a plan that makes the best use of available resources. Time for preventive maintenance should be allocated in the plan. When possible, journeys should be combined so that vehicles travel full and do not make wide detours. A detailed weekly or monthly plan should be prepared and later compared with the actual course of events, with analysis and follow-up of discrepancies. Health department lettering and insignia should be painted legibly on the vehicle to discourage unauthorized usage.

Methods of monitoring for abuses include—

- Checking the mileage recorded on the odometer every week and comparing this reading with the driver's official log.
- Requiring that the primary user/passenger sign a ledger kept by the driver when initiating and terminating a trip.
- Instituting a waybill system to document movement of the vehicles, involving the authorizing person at the point of origin and the receiving officer at destination.

- Assigning one operator to a vehicle and requiring that any transfer to another operator be accompanied by a handover note that details mileage, condition, inventory of parts, and similar details.
- Installing tachographs. These devices are legally required in European countries, but larger vehicles everywhere should be equipped with them. They record comprehensive details of every journey and can provide a check on the accuracy of the driver's log. The tachograph record also shows whether adequate rest stops have been taken.
- Introducing incentives for health facilities to prevent abuse by implementing good monitoring methods.

Misuse of motorcycles, light vans, and other small vehicles is more difficult to control, especially when vehicles are allocated to facilities in remote areas. Staff members may be encouraged to purchase motorcycles and other small vehicles from the health service at low cost; this strategy reduces vehicle abuse, generates income for vehicle replacement, and gives staff an incentive to maintain vehicles properly. An approach adopted in Zimbabwe was to sell vehicles to health workers on extended repayment terms and then to pay a mileage allowance. The health worker was free to use the vehicle for private purposes but also had an incentive to maintain it. After five years, the vehicle became the worker's property.

When vehicle misuse is discovered, the problem must be dealt with firmly and quickly. Allowing an abuse to continue ensures that it will become part of the system.

Train drivers and motorcycle riders

Drivers play a critical role in the optimal operation of transport services. Well-trained drivers and motorcycle riders have fewer accidents and better vehicle maintenance than those who are poorly trained. Driver-training modules are available from a number of sources. A driver or rider should—

- Drive or ride carefully and without aggression toward other road users
- Inspect the vehicle carefully at least once a day and after every stop for signs of damage, wear, and accidents
- Know which passengers are allowed in accordance with legal and corporate policies
- Drive within the allowable speed limit
- Be able to carry out preventive maintenance, minor servicing, and emergency repairs
- Be thoroughly knowledgeable about the routes and well informed about road and weather conditions and the location of service and refueling facilities
- Know what to do in case of an accident (requirements for immediate reporting, documentation, how to ensure the safety and security of the load)
- Be capable of administering basic first-aid treatment

Employing drivers with many years of experience and knowledge of the local road conditions will positively affect the performance and life of vehicles. Driver-mechanics (drivers with additional technical training) have the added skills to perform preventive maintenance and handle minor problems on the road.

It is important to ensure that drivers have a legal, active license, that their vision is tested regularly, and that vehicles are duly registered and carry current ownership, insurance, and inspection documents. Taking strong disciplinary action against those who drive after consuming alcohol or taking drugs is also important; vehicle damage often results from accidents caused by driving under the influence.

Ensure vehicle security

Vehicle security is a serious problem in many countries. Vehicles are stolen for resale or for spare parts, and pharmaceuticals may be stolen in transit. Precautions to take include—

- Keeping vehicles in locked compounds or garages.
- Employing security guards.
- Planning delivery routes so that vehicles can be securely parked during overnight stops.
- Instructing drivers never to leave vehicles unattended during transit.
- Avoiding driving at night, especially in countries where vehicles are poorly maintained or have no lights. Security problems are often worse after dark.
- Installing burglar alarms, immobilization devices, or both. Fit security dead bolts on cab doors and goods compartments. Where security is extremely difficult, it may be necessary to fit grilles around the cab interior.
- Buying vehicles with sleeping compartments for drivers if long delivery trips are required.
- Ensuring that every vehicle is fitted with a fire extinguisher. Tools and spare parts should be carried so that the driver can make simple repairs without having to leave the vehicle unattended.
- Installing a mobile communication radio for communication with the base.
- Ensuring that the vehicle and goods are checked at the start of a trip and at every point along the route for any suspicious devices that could be used by saboteurs.
- Engraving vehicle registration details onto windshields.

Ideally, all vehicles carrying valuable loads should have a second driver or a driver's assistant. On long journeys, a second driver is necessary to reduce the risk of the driver's falling asleep. If a breakdown or an accident occurs, one person can guard the vehicle while the other gets help.

25.4 Vehicle maintenance

Planned maintenance is an essential aspect of the transport system. It includes ensuring availability of spare parts, managing repairs—whether for land vehicles or boats—and disposing of waste products.

Provide spare parts and consumable supplies

Vehicles cannot be serviced and repaired without an adequate supply of spare parts and consumables—lubricants, brake fluid, tires, batteries, and oil filters. If vehicles are not serviced, they quickly become unreliable.

Senior logistics managers are responsible for emphasizing that pharmaceutical deliveries cannot be guaranteed without adequate funding for spare parts and consumables. Politicians and budget control officers must be persuaded to understand the importance of adequate recurrent funding or to consider contract alternatives to in-house transport.

Manage vehicle maintenance

A consistently high standard of maintenance increases the fleet's reliability; this standard can be achieved only if the maintenance policy is clearly defined, enforced, costed, and monitored.

Vehicle maintenance can be divided into four levels—

1. Preventive maintenance, as defined in the manufacturer's service manual, includes lubrication, oil changes, replacement of oil filters and brake pads, tire changes, and other measures that keep the vehicle operating safely and efficiently. All these can be foreseen and planned for.
2. Overhauls involve the dismantling or replacement of major components, such as engines, clutch linings, or transmissions. The mileage at which a specific overhaul is required varies from vehicle to vehicle, but overhauls can be foreseen and planned for.
3. Minor repairs include replacement of broken headlights and minor body work. They do not require the tools or skills of a specialist. Many of these will be unforeseen but can be managed if parts are available.
4. Major repairs are needed in the case of crash damage or other unforeseen problems that require specialized tools and skills.

Preventive maintenance and minor repairs can be carried out in simply equipped workshops by relatively unskilled mechanics, and require only a small selection of frequently used spare parts and consumables. Preventive maintenance for every vehicle should be scheduled in advance as part of the management of vehicle use. Major repairs and overhauls must be carried out in well-equipped workshops by skilled mechanics, and require access to a comprehensive stock of spare parts.

A health program often needs a combination of maintenance levels. For instance, the health program can perform preventive maintenance and minor repairs in its own workshops, and major repairs and overhauls can be contracted out to a central government workshop or a private garage.

The following examples indicate the range of options for organizing maintenance services. These options are based on the assumption that the health program is government run, but they are also relevant to NGOs.

Workshops operated and funded by the health program. The main advantage of this option is that workshops, maintenance staff, and the stock of spare parts are directly controlled by the health program. The main disadvantages are that transport maintenance services may be duplicated among government agencies, often when few trained staff members are available, and that the health program may have trouble tracking the true costs to make meaningful comparisons. Duplication wastes funds and can result in maintenance units that lack proper staff or are too small to operate cost-effectively. This result is less likely if only preventive maintenance and minor repairs are carried out.

Workshops operated and funded by another government agency. A network of vehicle maintenance workshops operated by the ministry of works can be used to maintain all government vehicles. This is a traditional administrative solution. It can be satisfactory, provided that workshops are fully equipped, staff members are well trained, and the government is committed to upgrading equipment and retraining staff as vehicle technology changes. A disadvantage is that the health program has no direct control over the quality of service, and no sanctions can be applied if the service is unsatisfactory.

Privatized government maintenance services. Workshop services owned and operated by government may be transferred or franchised to a parastatal organization or to a private company. Government agencies can then buy back the service at a rate that is periodically renegotiated. Privatization of government services has been widely advocated and has been adopted in many countries. Disadvantages include the possibilities of overcharging and corrupt and abusive pricing and billing practices.

Tendered maintenance contracts with private companies. An arrangement involving private maintenance contracts that run for one or more years has several advantages—

- The health program does not have to provide workshops or maintenance staff or hold stocks of spare parts. Capital investment is thus reduced, and the health program can concentrate on core activities.
- Cost control may be better: the service contract can set a flat rate per year for maintaining each vehicle, which includes the cost of normal spare parts. Only unforeseeable items (such as accident repairs) need to be paid for, on the basis of individual invoices.
- Quality assurance clauses can be built into the contract. These can impose financial penalties whenever the service quality fails to meet set targets. Bonus payments to the contractor may also be justified if reliability exceeds target norms.

Contracts of this kind succeed only in countries with well-developed private vehicle-maintenance sectors. Tenderers must use sophisticated costing techniques if they are to offer realistic quotes, and they must have well-equipped workshops and reliable sources of spare parts and consumables. Government must have good monitoring, reporting, and accounting procedures. Otherwise, unsatisfactory service or corrupt practices may go undetected.

Private workshops run by agents of the vehicle manufacturer. These workshops may be more expensive, but they are more reliable than other private workshops because the agents have a greater sense of responsibility to maintain the manufacturer's reputation. However, such workshops may be restricted to larger urban areas, with no accessibility to them in rural or remote areas.

Private workshops with services paid by invoice. This option has advantages but provides no cost certainty or quality assurance. It is generally used only for emergency repairs or when no other maintenance facilities are available.

Ensure safe disposal of waste products

Vehicle servicing produces toxic waste products. Oil, lubricants, tires, and batteries must be disposed of safely to avoid creating public health risks. The health program should require that the vehicle service organization adopt a safe disposal policy that complies fully with local regulations.

25.5 Measuring transport performance using key indicators

Using a set of key performance indicators can help determine a transport system's efficiency.

Vehicle capacity usage

The volume that the fleet carries seriously affects costs. When calculating product costs, vehicle capacity must be maintained at the highest levels to minimize the unit cost of transporting the product. This indicator depends on the frequency and size of orders. For example, if the fleet's total pallet capacity is 240 for twelve vehicles, and the fleet carried 200 pallets on a day, the capacity usage for that day would be 83 percent. The capacity percentage varies each day, and a cumulative percentage helps determine if the size and mix of the vehicle fleet meets the system's needs.

Vehicle time usage

A vehicle costs money whether it is being used or not. Keeping the vehicle working as much as possible (consistent with good maintenance practice) is most efficient. This indicator identifies the proportion of hours that each individual vehicle is in use compared with the total fleet. For example, the fleet of twelve vehicles from the example above has an operating day of ten hours for each vehicle, or 120 hours for the fleet. If the actual number of operational hours recorded for all twelve vehicles is ninety, time usage is only 75 percent. In addition, if customers were encouraged to change their delivery times, the number of hours available for the fleet to operate would increase further. The more the vehicles work, the more efficient the system and the less cost per delivery. Transportation planners need to maximize the operation of the fleet while considering the realities of their environment.

This indicator can also identify individual vehicles that are being used less than needed because of recurring mechanical problems, driver and personnel problems, and so on.

Vehicle total usage

A critical measurement of the fleet's effectiveness is the combination of the above two indicators. If the whole fleet is used for four hours out of ten at 100 percent capacity for those four hours, most transport managers would be happy. However, overall usage would only be 40 percent because of the remaining six hours of operational time left in the day for the whole fleet. Combining the results of the previous two indicators, which individually appear to be good, can show a different result when combined. For example, capacity usage of 83 percent multiplied by time usage of 75 percent equals a total usage of 62 percent, which shows room for improvement.

Average drops per vehicle and cases per drop

The average number of shipment drops per vehicle can be used to calculate the cost per drop. And while the number of drops may be acceptable, if the number of cases per drop is small, then the cost per delivery may be too high. These indicators may lead to a review of delivery frequency, thresholds for order sizes that can be delivered, and charges for delivery.

Table 25-2   Comparison of commercial, government, and mixed fleets

Factor	Commercial fleets	Government fleets	Mixed fleets
Government capital expenditure on vehicles	No	Yes	Yes, but reduced
Government expenditure on maintenance, insurance, wages, supervision, and per diems	No	Yes	Yes, but reduced
Flexibility to meet demand peaks	Yes	No	Yes
Fast transport beyond normal commercial routes	No	Yes	Yes
Security of pharmaceuticals in transit	Can be expected to be good	Variable	Variable
Running costs	Lowest for large loads and long hauls	Lowest for stable requirements	Can provide an optimum mix
Flexibility to change route and schedule at short notice	No	Yes	Variable
Experience in and care of transporting special products	Limited, and may cost extra to add such elements	Yes	Variable

Vehicle operating cost

Because most work activities revolve around the number of orders to deliver and the case/tons/pallet volumes associated with each order, this indicator is important. The cost of processing an order and then delivering it helps determine the level at which inappropriately sized orders should be managed differently.

25.6   Contracting transport services

This section examines the advantages and disadvantages of contracting out transport services to private transport companies. It also presents the costing decisions that need to be made and details procedures for selecting, working with, and monitoring contractors.

Private-sector transport issues

Private transport companies in some countries can offer better and cheaper pharmaceutical delivery service than the government is able to provide. These advantages are most likely to be gained in countries with a well-developed infrastructure and a good range of well-managed private transport companies. Where choice is limited, competition may be insufficient to produce real cost savings.

Private carriers will probably be most competitive on routes between major population centers. On these routes, vehicles are likely to carry a return load, an efficiency that lowers overall costs. By contrast, private carriers may be comparatively expensive when delivering to remote areas, where there is no potential for return loads; however, this cost premium may not apply if existing delivery routes already serve these areas. The health program may be able to

enter into a joint agreement with another agency that needs transport arrangements from the periphery to the center. Agricultural cooperatives are one possibility.

Whenever possible, pharmaceutical deliveries should be organized so that the transport contractor is supplied with full loads. Low transport costs depend on maximum use of vehicle capacity. Contract transport may improve the security of pharmaceuticals, provided the contractor is made responsible for any losses in transit. The health program or facility must be proactive in requiring transport companies to ensure that pharmaceutical supplies are not damaged during transport and layovers. Many private transport services are small and individually owned and may not have the capacity to maintain quality service. In such cases, using larger and more economically viable companies is preferable.

Table 25-2 compares the advantages and disadvantages of private-sector, government, and mixed transport fleets.

The preceding remarks relate principally to road transport contractors, but rail, air, river, and sea transport services may also be used for pharmaceutical deliveries. The following issues apply equally to those forms of transport.

Cost assessment

A thorough cost analysis should be conducted before a decision is made to contract out transport services. A decision to introduce private-sector transport can have far-reaching implications. For instance, existing vehicles will have to be sold if they are no longer needed. If many vehicles are sold, government workshops may no longer have sufficient work to remain viable. Unless these issues are taken into account, the overall effectiveness and efficiency of the government transport operation may decline rather than improve. Country Study 25-2 provides a sample analysis of alternatives.

In-house transport costs

Any comparison of public- and private-sector transport alternatives requires a realistic assessment of public-sector vehicle operating costs. The annual operating costs for a vehicle are made up of the following elements—

- Fixed costs
  - Amortized cost of the vehicle over its anticipated lifetime
  - Interest costs
  - Transportation taxes
  - Insurance premiums
  - Wages and overhead for the drivers
- Variable costs, based on anticipated annual mileage
  - Fuel
  - Preventive maintenance (filters, lubrication, brake pads, tires)
  - Repairs
  - Per diem payments to drivers for meals and accommodation

- Carrying costs of public-sector transport
  - Cost of transport administration
  - Cost of parking and garaging

Total cost analysis (see Chapter 40) can be used to compile cost data. When costs have been calculated, they can be used to assess the delivery cost per ton on specific routes. This cost can then be compared with quoted rates for alternative forms of transport. If the preliminary assessment indicates that private-sector transport is more economical, formal tenders to provide services should be conducted, as described in Chapter 39.

25.7 Maintaining pharmaceutical quality

Transport managers are responsible for ensuring that pharmaceuticals are not damaged during transit. It is essential that medicines be properly packed (see Figure 25-3).

The pharmaceutical manufacturer's original outer packing should withstand normal handling and transportation,

---

Country Study 25-2
Contract-or-buy analysis in Zimbabwe

In Zimbabwe, the cost of running the drug delivery routes from the central medical stores (CMS) to the provincial stores using CMS vehicles was compared with the cost of using private-sector carriers. The results of the analysis were used to decide which routes should be contracted out to the private sector. The operating parameters and costs for CMS vehicles were as follows:

Payload of each truck	5 tons
Annual mileage of all vehicles	468,000 km
Fixed costs	USD 0.37 per km
Variable costs	USD 0.03 per km
Fixed + variable costs	USD 0.40 per km

These figures were used to calculate the cost of running each route using CMS vehicles and private carriers. Results are shown in the accompanying table, which reveals that for loads that are multiples of 5 tons, using CMS vehicles is cheaper. Although the cost differential decreases with increasing distance, using CMS vehicles remains cheaper even for distant destinations. The full cost advantage is obtained only if the trucks are hauling loads in both directions. An empty CMS truck costs the same per kilometer as a fully loaded one, but the private carrier does not charge for the return journey. If the CMS vehicle has no load to carry back, using hired transport to Gweru, Bulawayo, and Binga becomes more economical. The cost ratio in all three cases is less than 2.0.

Destination	Distance (km)	One-way cost of using own fleet (USD 0.40 per km)	Private-sector tariff (USD per 100 kg)	Cost of transporting 5 tons	Ratio of tariff cost to own costs per 5 tons If full for return	If empty for return
Chinhoyi	110	44.00	2.94	147.00	3.35	1.67
Gweru	275	110.00	3.94	197.00	1.80	0.89
Masvingo	292	116.80	5.16	258.00	2.22	1.10
Bulawayo	439	175.60	4.73	236.50	1.36	0.67
Binga	880	352.00	7.69	384.50	1.09	0.55

Figure 25-3 Transporting pharmaceuticals safely

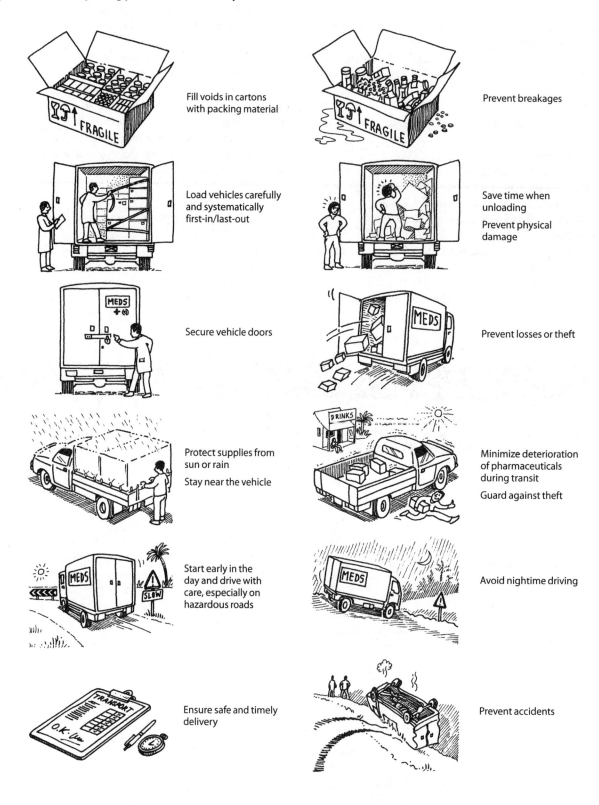

Fill voids in cartons with packing material

Prevent breakages

Load vehicles carefully and systematically first-in/last-out

Save time when unloading

Prevent physical damage

Secure vehicle doors

Prevent losses or theft

Protect supplies from sun or rain

Stay near the vehicle

Minimize deterioration of pharmaceuticals during transit

Guard against theft

Start early in the day and drive with care, especially on hazardous roads

Avoid nightime driving

Ensure safe and timely delivery

Prevent accidents

although standards may differ in developed countries, where palletized handling exists throughout the system. At the intermediate stores, this outer packing often must be removed to allow the assembly of small consignments; these must be repacked for transport in strong cartons or reusable crates. Empty spaces in partly filled cartons or crates should be filled with newspaper, straw, wood shavings, or other loose material to stop the contents from rattling about and prevent cartons from being crushed. If mechanical handling equipment is available, loads may then be assembled onto pallets.

Pallets, cartons, or crates should be carefully and systematically loaded into vehicles on a first-in/last-out basis. They must then be held secure by straps, nets, or other means. The vibration caused by travel over rough roads can damage tablets and other breakable products; long journeys over rough roads should be avoided whenever possible.

Delivery journeys in very hot or cold weather may damage temperature-sensitive products. Appropriate precautions must be taken, as discussed earlier in this chapter. Water damage during heavy rain can be avoided by ensuring that pharmaceuticals are unloaded directly into a building and not left standing outside. Make sure that vehicles have the necessary materials to protect loads from direct sun, dust, rain, and pilferage. Canvas covers and straps are as essential as spare tires and need to be carried at all times. ■

References and further readings

★ = Key readings.

★ Abdallah, H. 2004. *Guidelines for Assessing Costs in a Logistics System: An Example of Transport Cost Analysis.* Arlington, Va.: John Snow, Inc./DELIVER, for the U.S. Agency for International Development.

★ Archando-Callao, R. S., and A. Faiz. 1994. *Estimating Vehicle Operating Costs.* World Bank Technical Paper no. 234. Washington, D.C.: World Bank. <http://siteresources.worldbank.org/INTROADSHIGHWAYS/Resources/338993-1156667319236/1095944-1115669285546/wbtp-234.pdf>

Dawson, J., and I. Barwell. 1993. *Roads Are Not Enough: New Perspectives on Rural Transport Planning in Developing Countries.* London: Intermediate Technology Development Group.

Elsenaar, P., and S. Abouraad. 2005. *Road Safety Best Practices— Examples and Recommendations.* Geneva: Global Road Safety Partnership. <http://www.grsproadsafety.org/themes/default/pdfs/Road%20Safety%20Best%20Practices.pdf>

Hathaway, G. 1985. *Low-Cost Vehicles: Options for Moving People and Goods.* London: Intermediate Technology Development Group.

Hugos, M. H. 2006. *Essentials of Supply Chain Management.* 2nd ed. Hoboken, N.J.: John Wiley & Sons.

Rushton, A., J. Oxley, and P. Croucher. 2010. *Handbook of Logistics and Distribution Management.* 4th ed. London: Kogan Page.

Stroh, M. B. 2006. *A Practical Guide to Transportation and Logistics.* 3rd ed. Dumont, N.J.: Logistics Network.

Transaid. 2008. *Introduction to Transaid's Transport Management System Manual.* London: Transaid. <http://www.transaid.org/images/resources/TMS%20Consolidated%20Manual%20Revised%20Aug08.pdf>

WHO/EPI (World Health Organization/Expanded Programme on Immunization). 1994a. *Guidelines for Introducing Motorcycles into a Primary Health Care Programme.* Geneva: WHO/EPI. <http://whqlibdoc.who.int/hq/1994/WHO_EPI_LHIS_94.10.pdf>

———. 1994b. *Monitoring Vehicle Use: A Guide for Transport Officers.* Geneva: WHO/EPI. <http://whqlibdoc.who.int/hq/1994/WHO_EPI_LHIS_94.6.pdf>

———. 1994c. *Riders for Health: Manual for Motorcycle Instructors.* Geneva: WHO/EPI. <http://whqlibdoc.who.int/hq/1994/WHO_EPI_LHTM_94.1.pdf>

———. 2010. *Model Requirements for the Storage and Transport of Time- and Temperature-Sensitive Pharmaceutical Products.* Geneva: WHO/EPI.

★ WHO/V&B (World Health Organization/Vaccines and Biologicals). 2000. Transport. In *Product Information Sheets.* 12th ed. Geneva: WHO/V&B. <http://whqlibdoc.who.int/hq/2000/WHO_V&B_00.13.pdf>

ASSESSMENT GUIDE

Existing transport system

- Does the program have a transport management department?
- What are the major transport problems?
- Who provides the transport budget? (Compare the transport budget with actual expenditures.)
- What types of vehicles are used? (List all types used and the source, model, quantity, age, mileage, condition, and location of each.)
- Are vehicles shared with vertical programs, such as WHO's Expanded Programme on Immunization? Do availability and reliability vary among programs? If so, why?
- Do existing transport routes make effective use of vehicles?
- How are supervisory visits currently made?
- Is there a vehicle replacement policy? If so, how is replacement funded?
- Is there a policy for writing off broken-down vehicles? Is it implemented?
- Is there a preventive maintenance policy? Is it effective?
- What percentage of vehicles is in working condition? Describe by type and location of vehicle.
- Is there a policy to control and monitor vehicle use? Is it effective?
- Is there a driver training program? Is it effective?
- Is there a policy on transport security? Does it control losses?
- Are vehicles loaded correctly?
- What is the number of vehicles, compared to the number of drivers?

Transport alternatives

- What are the transportation terms for overseas and in-country suppliers? Could these be changed to require direct delivery to lower-level stores?
- Which of the following modes of transport are available?
  - Program vehicles
  - Motor pool vehicles
  - Buses
  - NGO vehicles
  - Intermediate forms of transport
  - Railways
  - Water transport
  - Commercial, government (including military), NGO flights

Private-sector transport alternatives and cost comparisons

- Do vehicle rental and leasing companies exist? What are the charges?
- Are commercial carriers available? Are they capable of transporting pharmaceuticals at rates equal to or lower than costs of in-house transport?
- Is the private transport alternative dependable? Does it have experience in transporting special products like pharmaceuticals?

Maintenance alternatives

- Are health program or other government workshops offered?
- Are privatized government workshops available?
- Are contracts with the private sector a possibility?

Monitoring and evaluation

- Are there effective systems for monitoring and evaluating transport costs and performance? If not, which elements are missing?
- Is a checklist used to ensure timely registration, licensing, and renewals?
- Are standard operating procedures (SOPs) in place for transport operation?
- Are vehicles checked regularly after making a long trip?
- Do the SOPs contain guidelines on what to do in the event of an accident?
- Are vehicles checked daily for safety using a checklist?

| Part I: Policy and economic issues | Part II: Pharmaceutical management | Part III: Management support systems |

Selection
Procurement
Distribution
   22 Managing distribution
   23 Inventory management
   24 Importation and port clearing
   25 Transport management
   26 Kit system management
Use

CHAPTER 26

Kit system management

SUMMARY

Pharmaceutical kits contain selected medicines and medical supplies, in predefined quantities, that are used for primary pharmaceutical supply, supplementary supply, or emergency supply. Emergency health kits are well standardized and widely used by the main international relief agencies, and they can prevent many common problems associated with pharmaceutical donations. Ration kits provide standard quantities of essential medicines for routine use in rural health care at dispensaries and health centers, and sometimes at hospitals. The relevance of pharmaceutical kits depends on a country's ability to manage its pharmaceutical supply system; using a kit system can help countries with weak capacity.

A pharmaceutical supply system based on kits has the following advantages—

- Selection of a limited range of essential medicines
- Simplified budgeting, procurement, storage, transport, and supply management
- Reduced risk of theft
- More reliable supply
- More rational prescribing
- Possible lower indirect costs

Ration kit systems have the following disadvantages—

- Less flexible contents than in an open-order system
- Difficulty adjusting the medicine list to suit seasonal or regional variations in morbidity
- Possibility of shortages and surpluses
- Special management skills and additional space and staff required for kit packing
- Discouragement of local development of distribution and inventory control skills
- Difficulty in monitoring expiry dates
- Lack of fit in a cost-sharing system
- Large payments when prepacked kits are procured
- Higher direct costs, such as additional handling and packing

Kits should be considered when—

- Pharmaceutical supply to rural areas needs to be drastically improved.
- Pharmaceutical supplies are required for an emergency or time-sensitive situation.
- Record keeping, drug ordering, and inventory control capacities are limited.
- Central medical store capacity is limited.
- Diversion and theft of medicines are common.
- Medicine needs are such that the number of different kits can be kept to a minimum.

A distribution system that is completely based on kits is usually viewed as a temporary solution to a logistics problem; however, changing from kits based on a push system to a requisition-based system can be difficult, and combining basic kit distribution with allowing limited ordering for some products may be necessary. Realistically, once a kit system is in place, its convenience paired with the challenges of a pull system often result in this temporary solution lasting much longer than originally planned. A flexible system for distributing medicines should be instituted as soon as the necessary managerial capacity and administrative structures can be created.

26.1 Pharmaceutical supply kits

Prepacked kits, also known as pharmaceutical ration kits, contain an assortment of medicines and medical supplies. The quantity, range, and purpose of kits vary according to situation. Some comprise essential medicines and supplies targeting various levels of health facilities. Others comprise special products to meet specific program needs. The medicines are packed centrally into sealed cartons and distributed unopened to the health facilities where they will be used. Typically, each kit is designed to supply a given number of patients (for example, 1,000).

The kit system is a typical example of an allocation, or "push," system. Supplies are distributed on the basis of a centrally estimated need and not on the basis of a specific request. This system is the opposite of a requisition, or "pull," system, in which health units order supplies on the basis of demand (see Chapter 22).

Different types of kits have been widely used in emergency relief efforts. Since the early 1980s, several countries have adopted kit systems like ration or supplementary kits for the routine supply of essential medicines and supplies to rural health care facilities, usually monthly or quarterly. These two major uses of kits, for emergency situations and for regular supply, are discussed separately.

26.2 Kits for emergency situations

In acute emergencies, medicines and medical supplies are often a first priority. Needs are difficult to assess on short notice; many of the large international relief agencies there-

Box 26-1
The Interagency Emergency Health Kit

This resource explains how to use standardized packages of essential medicines, supplies, and equipment after large-scale emergencies and disasters. The concept and contents of the kit were developed by the World Health Organization in collaboration with international and nongovernmental agencies. In the 1990s, the kit was called the WHO Emergency Health Kit; however, WHO was dropped from the name, recognizing that now the main contributors are organizations with greater emergency field experience. The Interagency Emergency Health Kit is geared mainly to relief agencies, but it also serves as a reference for national authorities and hospital managers interested in stockpiling medicines and supplies.

A complete emergency kit contains two separate sets of medicines and supplies for 10,000 people for approxi-

mately three months. The first set consists of ten identical packages of basic units containing medicines and supplies for 1,000 people each, intended for use by primary health workers with minimal training. The supplementary kit for 10,000 people contains medicines, renewable supplies, and equipment needed by well-trained health care workers working in referral health facilities.

All kits now provide medicines for malaria and for the prospective treatment of rape victims. In response to resistance of the malaria parasite to chloroquine and sulfadoxine-pyrimethamine in most places in the world, the kit contents were revised in 2006 to include artemether + lumefantrine fixed-dose combination tablets and artemether injections.

Source: WHO 2006.

fore rely on ready-made kits that contain a selection of the most commonly needed items.

The most popular kit is the Interagency Emergency Health Kit, which is now generally recommended for basic health care immediately after a disaster. Formerly known as the New Emergency Health Kit 98, the interagency kit was redesigned and updated through a collaborative process and finalized in 2006 (Box 26-1). Many international and nongovernmental organizations (NGOs) have agreed to use the same kit, and that agreement has made possible the maintenance of a permanent stock for immediate dispatch when an emergency arises. Thousands of kits are used every year in a variety of emergency situations (see Country Study 26-1). The kit contents and their intended use are described in a World Health Organization (WHO) information booklet (WHO 2006).

The kit measures about 4 cubic meters and weighs about 900 kilograms. It contains essential medicines, disposable supplies, and basic equipment for primary care up to the level of a health center. It can serve a population of 10,000 for three months (or about 10,000 consultation visits). The kit contains ten units for use by paramedical workers. It also contains a supplementary unit, with additional medications and supplies for minor medical and surgical care at the health center level.

This emergency health kit is adequate for the first phase of an emergency, when exact needs have not yet been established. When it is possible to define needs more precisely, some items in the standard kit may prove to be unnecessary, and other items may be insufficient or lacking. Most organizations then switch to other systems. Some of them—Médecins Sans Frontières (MSF) and the

Red Cross, for example—use different kits for the second phase.

MSF (www.msf.org) has created about forty medical kits, consisting of different modules. They include a basic dispensary module with simple treatment guidelines and modules containing dressings, surgical instruments, immunizations, intravenous infusions, and laboratory materials. The appropriate modules can be dispatched after MSF field staff have assessed local needs. Some MSF kits are specifically designed to address a particular health crisis—for example, Ebola kits, which include medications and protective gear, are used in outbreak locations.

The Red Cross organizations (www.icrc.org) use small kits to restock health facilities in emergency areas that are particularly busy. In addition to the hardware kit already available in these facilities, they may use a dispensary kit, a dressing kit, a pediatric kit, a sutures kit, an injection kit, and any others that are required.

The use of these kits prevents many of the problems with pharmaceutical donations that are discussed in Chapter 15.

26.3 Use of kits as a distribution strategy

In the early 1980s, the supply of essential medicines to rural facilities had become so unpredictable that several countries, including Kenya, Democratic Yemen, Tanzania, Uganda, and Bhutan, started to use ration kits for rural health care (see Country Study 26-2). The aim was to make a range of cost-effective essential medicines and supplies directly available to dispensaries and health centers, bypassing the district hospital. At that time, most of these programs were

Country Study 26-1
Emergency medicines after the Asian earthquake and Indian Ocean tsunami

On December 26, 2004, a powerful earthquake off the coast of Indonesia sparked a devastating tsunami in the Indian Ocean. The disaster resulted in hundreds of thousands of people dead and missing and more than a million people displaced in Asia and Africa—with the hardest-hit areas in Indonesia, Sri Lanka, and India.

An initial assessment of one of the hardest-hit areas of Indonesia, by WHO, the Indonesian government, the United Nations, and the U.S. military, showed that no master list existed that detailed the overall medical supplies and medicines being provided to interim health posts from various donations worldwide. One common complaint to the assessors was that aid groups brought in only enough supplies to treat clients and did not leave behind any supplies when they departed, rendering the community health care centers unable to treat patients. Initially, the temporary field hospitals met the acute needs of the population, but after the first few weeks, those affected most needed the restoration of primary health care and preventive services. The International Dispensary Association Foundation mobilized 350 Interagency Emergency Health Kits in two weeks for shipment and distribution to affected areas. The kits provided medicines and supplies sufficient for basic health care for 3.5 million people for three months and helped fill the gap until supply services could be reestablished.

Source: WHO 2005.

Box 26-2
Using patient kits to improve management and use of tuberculosis medicines

The Global Drug Facility (GDF) is an initiative to increase access to high-quality tuberculosis drugs for DOTS (directly observed treatment, short course) implementation. To help countries provide drugs to treat up to 10 million patients and reach TB control targets, the GDF's activities revolve around facilitating pharmaceutical management, increasing treatment adherence, and promoting rational medicine use. As part of this strategy, the GDF developed a TB patient kit, which was introduced in the Philippines in 2004. The patient kit contains enough medications, including two-drug and four-drug fixed-dose combinations (FDCs), for a full course of treatment for one patient.

The purpose of the kit is to improve the logistics of pharmaceutical supply, since fewer items will need to be ordered, distributed, and stocked in health facilities. In addition, the kit promotes rational medicine treatment because all medicines are available in the appropriate dosages and quantities when they are needed.

Two different kits conform to patient treatment guidelines for TB. The first is for newly diagnosed patients (Categories I and III) and contains all medications needed to treat one patient in the weight band (55–70 kg).

The recommended STOP TB Kit contains the following in two separate boxes—

1. Intensive phase: Six blisters of four-drug FDC tablets (FDC-4) (rifampicin/isoniazid/pyrazinamide/ethambutol 150/75/400/275 mg)
2. Continuation phase: Twelve blisters of two-drug FDC tablets (FDC-2) (rifampicin/isoniazid 150/75 mg)

Tablets are packed in blister sheets of seven rows of four tablets each.

The second kit is for patients who have relapsed or failed initial treatment (Category II), which contains all medicines needed to treat one patient in the weight band (55–70 kg).

The STOP TB Kit contains the following in three separate boxes—

1. Intensive phase: Nine blisters of four-drug FDC tablets (FDC-4) (rifampicin/isoniazid/pyrazinamide/ethambutol); fifty-six vials of streptomycin, water, syringes, and needles (S 1 g)
2. Continuation phase: fifteen blisters of three-drug FDC tablets (FDC 3) (rifampicin/isoniazid/ethambutol 150/75/275 mg)

Source: Stop TB Partnership/Global Drug Facility <http://www.stoptb.org/assets/documents/gdf/whatis/FS%20DP%20Brochure%20FINAL.pdf>

heavily supported by external donors; some of them still receive substantial external support.

The careful selection of medicines and the parallel development of treatment guidelines in the 1980s introduced the essential medicines concept to many national planners and rural health workers. The kit programs of the 1980s assisted in the dissemination of generic medicines and the promotion of the essential medicines concept in several countries.

A similar distribution strategy based on the kit concept is the use of patient packs for disease-specific treatment. A patient pack is essentially a medication kit for individual patients that includes the correct dose of the correct combination of medicines of assured quality. Box 26-2 discusses the development of patient packs for tuberculosis (TB) treatment. In Ethiopia, a kit for prevention of mother-to-child transmission of HIV/AIDS is composed of HIV test kits and antiretroviral medicines, which addresses the service and management needs of local prenatal care clinics.

The number of programs using kits for regular medicine supply has declined. The main reasons for this decrease are a reduction in long-term donor commitments, a general shift away from centralized public-sector funding for medicines, the incompatibility between kit systems and cost sharing, an increasing desire to implement more flexible requisition systems, and improved capacity in pharmaceutical supply management. However, countries with inadequate pull systems may opt to use kits as a supplement to their regular supply,

especially where challenging geography or a weak transportation system makes distribution difficult or where there is a lack of skilled human resources to properly maintain a well-functioning pull system (see Country Study 26-3).

26.4 Advantages and disadvantages of kit systems

The benefits of a kit system depend greatly on the quality of the planning and on the initial kit design. Advantages and disadvantages need to be carefully weighed before a decision is made to adopt the kit approach (see Figure 26-1 and Section 26.6).

Potential advantages of a kit system are—

- Rational selection of a limited range of essential medicines and medical supplies
- Simplified budgeting, procurement, storage, transport, and supply management, with reduced risk of diversion to hospitals and theft in transit
- Decreased handling needed at the central medical store level, which saves resources
- Scheduled supply intervals leading to more secure delivery to rural health units
- Better and more equitable availability of essential medicines and medical supplies at the primary health care level, which results in improved community confidence

---

Country Study 26-2
Use of the kit system as a distribution strategy in Kenya

Kenya has been distributing kits containing selected medicines and medical supplies to health facilities since the early 1980s as part of its regular pharmaceutical distribution system. The kit concept has helped promote the dissemination of generic medicines and has supported the growth of the pharmaceutical industry in Kenya.

The kits are designed to serve various levels of care, including provincial general hospitals, district hospitals, subdistrict hospitals, health centers, and dispensaries. Each box is expected to last a month for 1,000 patients at a particular facility; however, because the workload varies from facility to facility, distribution supervisors at the district level have the option to increase or decrease the supply of kits. The Medical Officer of Health can order additional medicines to supplement the kits, although because the use of kits has led to poor inventory control systems, additional medicine

orders may not be based on real consumption data, but rather on educated guesses as to the needs of the facilities. Another problem is that differing consumption patterns among the districts have resulted in overstock, which theoretically should be redistributed, but weak infrastructure and transportation problems have led to extra stock accumulating where it is not needed.

Consequently, the government of Kenya has begun to shift away from the kit concept. The change has occurred because of the disadvantages associated with kits and the restructuring of the distribution system to create an autonomous entity from which districts will requisition their supplies on a cash-and-carry basis. Hospitals will be expected to requisition medicines from a predefined list, but health centers and dispensaries will continue to receive kits during the transition, because the poor staffing levels in those facilities means they lack the capacity for more complicated inventory control.

- Support for the development of treatment guidelines and prescriber training programs, contributing to more rational prescribing
- Indirect savings

Disadvantages are—

- Less flexibility in the selection of essential medicines for specific health problems in different regions, climatic zones, or types of health units
- Resistance by senior prescribers because of the limited range of medicines in the kit
- Need for special management skills, space, and staff for central kit packing
- Requirement that all funds be available at once, assuming that contractors deliver kits in one installment
- Lack of flexibility in the quantities of medicines, leading to shortages or surpluses of certain items
- Need for multiple kit types to handle different usages at various levels of the health care system
- Difficulty in supplying or returning individual items, which may lead to wastage caused by expiry
- Difficulty in monitoring expiry dates
- Absence of information at the central level on the usage of individual medicines, which hurts the ability

to track consumption trends at the national level
- Negative effect on development of supply management systems and skills for inventory control, quantification, ordering, and distribution planning
- Added cost of kit packing
- Difficulty in combining kits with a cost-sharing program
- Difficulty in evaluating the quality of individual products, because the national drug regulatory authority may have to depend on information provided by the kit supplier
- Difficulty in transitioning to a pull system once the simpler kit system has functioned for a long time

The inflexibility of the kit system is its greatest problem. When kits are packed overseas (and they often are), a year may pass before a change in content reaches the rural facilities. In the meantime, stockouts of certain items may occur, while there may be surpluses of other items. This problem is frequently perceived as serious, yet a WHO evaluation (Haak and Hogerzeil 1991) showed that in most long-term governmental kit programs (as opposed to emergency or incidental external kit projects), stable kit content was reached in about two years. In the short term, the problem was sometimes solved by redistributing the accumulated

---

Country Study 26-3
Implementing a kit system in Papua New Guinea

In the 1990s, Papua New Guinea was experiencing serious shortages of essential medicines and supplies in its health centers. In 2000, the National Department of Health asked the AusAID-funded Health Services Support Program to design a health center kit to supplement the regular requisition supply system for two years, while the primary system was revamped. Two types of kits were introduced in 2001, a standard kit containing sixty-five essential medicines and medical supplies, and a supplementary kit with twenty prescription-only medicines. The standard kit was supplied to all health centers and provincial hospitals, while the supplementary kit was sent to health facilities that had a medical officer. The kit quantities were based on patient morbidity data and designed to meet the average patient-visit load in a small health center. The number of kits supplied to health centers varied depending on their average patient visits during a year. The kits were designed to meet 40 percent of the national demand, while the other 60 percent would continue to be met through the primary supply system.

Since mid-2001, thirteen rounds of kit distribution have been made every four months, with the distribution

from the capital of Port Moresby to the twenty provincial health offices outsourced to the private sector and distribution from the provincial capitals to health centers managed by the provincial health offices.

Although the initial kit supply period was two years, it was extended year by year through the end of 2008. The strategy to revamp the requisition supply system included a training program in pharmaceutical supply management for health center staff and for students of nursing and community health work. At the end of the five-year program, which began in 2003, expectations were that nationwide, skills of health center staff members in ordering, stock keeping, and stock-control practices would be adequate to return to a completely requisition-based system.

The experience in Papua New Guinea shows that improving a requisition system can be a long-term proposition that requires extensive, sustained training in pharmaceutical management at the grassroots level. The addition of a kit system can improve the availability of essential medicines by supplementing an ineffective primary pull system.

Figure 26-1   Weighing advantages and disadvantages of kit systems

ADVANTAGES		DISADVANTAGES

Rational selection of a limited range of essential medicines and medical supplies		Less flexibility in the selection of essential medicines for specific health problems in different regions, climatic zones, or types of health units; resistance by senior prescribers due to limited range of medicines in the kit
Simplified budgeting, procurement, storage, transport, and supply management, with reduced risk of diversions to hospitals and theft in transit		Need for special management skills; space and staff are needed for central kit packing; requirement that all funds be available at once
Scheduled supply intervals leading to more secure delivery to rural health units		Lack of flexibility in the quantities of medicines, leading to stockouts or surpluses of certain items
Better and more equitable availability of essential medicines and medical supplies at the PHC level		Difficulty in supplying or returning individual items, which may lead to wastage due to expiry; difficulty in monitoring expiry dates
Support for the development of treatment guidelines and prescriber training programs, contributing to more rational subscribing		Possible slow developments of supply management systems and skills for inventory control, quantification, ordering, and distribution planning
Possible indirect savings		Added cost of kit packing; difficulty in combining kits with a cost-sharing program

The primary health care program in Guinea grew rapidly and included a cost-sharing system from the start. Initially, the information system for monitoring pharmaceutical use did not function, and rural staff members were not trained in pharmaceutical management. A decision was made to introduce a kit system while keeping the cost-sharing system in place.

Although the kit contents were regularly modified, major disadvantages arose in combining the two systems

- Cost sharing reinforced the need for good-quality care and availability of medicines.
- New kits were opened as soon as one item in the previous kit had run out. This practice resulted in an accumulation of half-used kits. The facilities then had no cash to purchase more medicines. Medicines

could be procured only as part of a kit. Any "unsold" medicines remained in stock.
- Some medicines became heavily overstocked. However, a low-cost, efficient redistribution system, based on credits for future pharmaceutical procurement, avoided large-scale waste of expired medicines.
- Management committees and health workers resented paying for kit medicines they did not need.

Although the content of the kits was reviewed several times, and standardized treatment was considered a priority, discrepancies between need and supply remained. After a few years, the kit system was abandoned and replaced with a requisition system using a limited medicine list.

medicines; in the long run, it was addressed by adapting the kit content. The latter is easier if the kits are packed within the country. In some countries, the problem was solved by changing to kits with a smaller number of commonly used medicines and by supplying additional items through a requisition system. In addition, many countries have different kits for different levels of health facilities, with medicines and quantities that attempt to better meet the needs of the facility rather than a "one size fits all" system.

The most serious problems of mismatch between need and supply have occurred in kit projects that were badly planned or were operated in isolation from other supply structures. Some problems were directly related to poor performance by overseas suppliers.

Redistributing the accumulated surpluses is not always easy. When the same item has accumulated in most health units, redistribution does not make sense. However, most products that accumulated in the past were simple, commonly used, and very stable medicines. If the products were supplied free of charge, any surpluses could simply be taken back to the central store. In practice, surplus medicines are often returned to the nearest operating level with a requisition system, usually the district hospital. A special problem arises when the kit has been paid for, in which case returning surplus medicines may meet resistance, and some sort of credit system will have to be established. This reason is probably why kit systems and cost sharing do not go very well together. The combination was tried in Guinea, but the kit system was finally abandoned (see Country Study 26-4). In countries that have adopted decentralized pharmaceutical management, transferring

surplus stock from one place to another becomes impossible. In this case, the kit system's disadvantages outweigh its advantages.

26.5 Cost aspects of kit systems

The direct costs of a kit system are higher than those of a regular requisition system, for the following reasons. Most international suppliers add 3 to 5 percent to the price for packing the medicines in kits. If kits are packed locally, labor costs may be slightly lower, but certain investments are needed (for example, carton boxes and a strapping device). If kits are procured ready-made, the number of potential suppliers is restricted, and there is less possibility to benefit from competitive prices for individual medicines. Some waste (estimated at an average of 4 percent) is possible because of expiry of accumulating unused medicines (although this waste may not be more than with most requisition systems).

Several factors may result in reduced indirect costs. Waste is reduced because of decreased pilferage during transport and less frequent interception of medicines at the district level. A careful selection of kit contents implies that less money is wasted on items that are not cost-effective, not needed, or inappropriate. Because of the regular supply, less safety stock is needed at the facilities. The regular availability of essential medicines reduces the number of patients who refer themselves to higher levels of care, where average treatment costs are higher. Although such advantages would also be achieved by a good requisition system, the kit system has often been instrumental in realizing these improvements, but it is probably not needed forever to maintain them.

A pure cost comparison between a kit system and a requisition system leaves out the many qualitative aspects that are not related to costs and are much more difficult to measure. The ease of supply management and the better availability of essential medicines at the primary care level may justify some extra costs. The limited time of health care providers can be used more efficiently. The quality of care may also improve, and lives may be saved. Some overstock (and potential expiry and waste) of cheap but lifesaving medicines, such as oral rehydration salts and ergometrine injection, can be justified (whereas overstock of an expensive but noncritical drug such as praziquantel cannot).

26.6 Conditions for a successful kit program

A kit system is generally most useful when—

- Emergencies or special situations cannot be handled through the existing pharmaceutical supply system.
- Record keeping and pharmaceutical ordering capabilities are limited.
- Requisitioned medicines remain at the hospital level or at intermediate distribution points and do not pass down the system.
- Infrastructural and human capacity of the central medical store is limited.
- Theft in the distribution system is common.
- Pharmaceutical needs are similar throughout the area, and only a few different kits are needed.

Before a kit can operate properly, several conditions have to be met. First, medicines have to be selected (see Chapter 16), and quantities have to be estimated (see Chapter 20). Second, funding has to be secured; this condition requires a real political and financial commitment to satisfying the health needs of the rural population. A third condition is a well-trained and dedicated management team. Finally, a program for training prescribers is essential. If the prescribers do not follow the treatment guidelines on which the kit contents are based, a mismatch will exist between pharmaceutical supply and use, and patients' health may be at risk.

When should a kit system not be chosen? A kit system does not combine well with a cost-sharing program. A kit system is not needed when health facilities are close to the warehouse and when communications and transport facilities are good. Nor is it needed when the public sector has no pharmaceutical shortages and a well-managed and reliable requisition system already exists. In situations in which management deficiencies are present but the capacity exists to overcome them, developing a sustainable requisition system may be a better option. A kit system may become

very complicated if many different types of facilities exist or considerable regional or seasonal variations occur in the incidence of health problems. Generally, a kit-based supply system is successful when the overall supply system is poorly organized and pharmaceutical product availability is limited, conditions that are especially common in rural areas.

26.7 Implementing a kit program

Careful planning is required before a kit program is introduced (see Figure 26-2). After a program begins, changing it is difficult and may require a year or more. There are twelve steps to be taken in implementing a kit program.

Step 1. Assess the supply system: is a kit system appropriate?

The balance between advantages and disadvantages has been discussed. The situation should be carefully assessed (see Chapters 22 and 36) before choosing between a kit-based and a requisition-based system.

Step 2. Choose the types of health units to be supplied with kits

A kit distribution system is usually most suitable for smaller, poorly managed, poorly staffed facilities. Sometimes, a mixed distribution system may be an appropriate choice. In a district hospital, for example, kits may be used in the outpatient department, and a requisition system may be used to supply additional medicines for inpatients. There is a growing tendency to reduce the number of different kits and to supplement a limited kit system with a simple requisition system.

Step 3. Prepare a list of medicines and other items for each kit

Separate kits may be prepared for different types of health facilities; for example, one kit for dispensaries and one for health centers (see Chapter 16 and Table 26-1). Bulky products, liquid products, medicines with cold-chain requirements, and medicines with short shelf lives should be avoided whenever possible. If the kit system is being introduced following a long period of shortages, an additional starter kit may be designed that contains essential equipment to upgrade the facilities at the beginning of the program.

Step 4. Determine the quantities of medicines needed in each kit

Usually, kits are designed for a certain number of outpatient consultations (1,000 to 5,000). When this figure has been decided upon, the quantity of each item in the kit can be

Figure 26-2   Flow chart for kit program planning

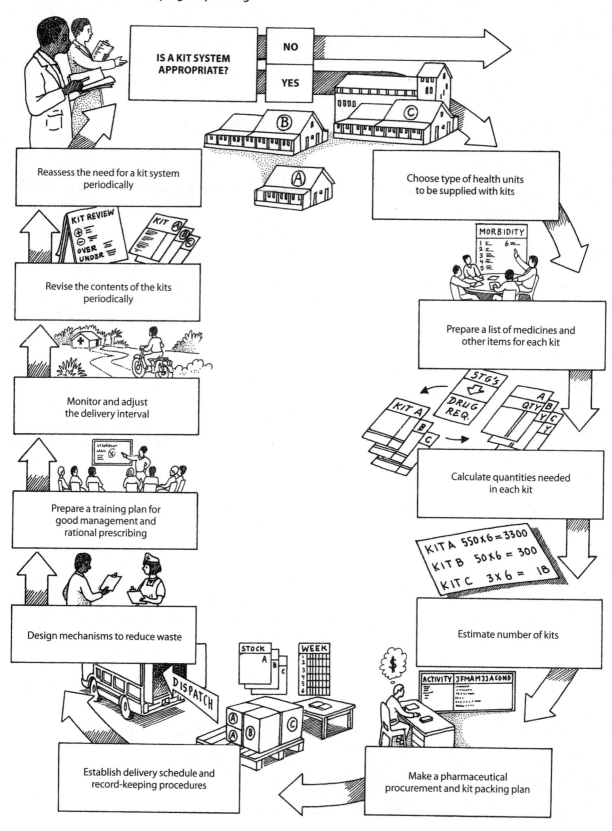

IS A KIT SYSTEM APPROPRIATE?

NO

YES

Reassess the need for a kit system periodically

Revise the contents of the kits periodically

Monitor and adjust the delivery interval

Prepare a training plan for good management and rational prescribing

Design mechanisms to reduce waste

Establish delivery schedule and record-keeping procedures

Choose type of health units to be supplied with kits

Prepare a list of medicines and other items for each kit

Calculate quantities needed in each kit

KIT A   550×6 = 3300
KIT B   50×6 = 300
KIT C   3×6 = 18

Estimate number of kits

Make a pharmaceutical procurement and kit packing plan

Table 26-1   Health center kit contents, Essential Medicines Program, Kenya

Item	Description	Unit of pack
1	Lignocaine hydrochloride injection BP 2%	Vial (30 mL)
2	Adrenaline acid tartrate injection BP 0.1% (requires cool storage)	Ampoule (1 mL)
3	Chlorpheniramine maleate injection BP 10 mg/mL	Ampoule (1 mL)
4	Chlorpheniramine maleate tablets BP 4 mg	1,000
5	Hydrocortisone sodium succinate injection BP (IV use) 100 mg base, with diluent	Vial
6	Phenobarbitone tablets BP 30 mg	1,000
7	Diazepam injection BP 10 mg/2 mL (IV & IM)	Ampoule (2 mL)
8	Albendazole tablets USP 400 mg	1,000
9	Aminophylline injection BP 250 mg/10 mL	Ampoule (10 mL)
10	Clotrimazole cream BP 1%	Tube (20 g)
11	Gentian violet crystals	Pack (5 g)
12	Hydrocortisone ointment BP 1% w/w	Tube (20 g)
13	Sodium hypochlorite solution BP 4% available chlorine	Bottle (5 L)
14	Compound magnesium trisilicate BP tablets chewable	100
15	Oral rehydration salts (WHO formula – 14 g to make 500 mL)	100 sachets
16	Tetracycline hydrochloride ophthalmic ointment USP 1%	Tube (5 g)
17	Ergometrine maleate injection BP – 500 mcg/mL (requires cool storage)	Ampoule (1 mL)
18	Chlorpromazine hydrochloride injection BP 25 mg/mL, 2 mL	Ampoule (2 mL)
19	Chlorpromazine hydrochloride tablets BP 25 mg, sugar coated	100
20	Salbutamol tablets BP 4 mg, scored	1,000
21	Griseofulvin tablets BP 500 mg	100
22	Griseofulvin tablets BP 125 mg	100
23	Metronidazole suspension 200 mg/5 mL	Bottle (60 mL)
24	Multivitamins/minerals supplement capsules	1,000
25	Multivitamins/minerals supplement syrup	Bottle (5 L)
26	Compound magnesium trisilicate + simethicone	100
27	Chloramphenicol ear drops	Bottle (10 mL)
28	Cough syrup (chlorpheniramine 1 mg, promethazine 2.5 mg, sodium citrate 4.5 mg, diphenhydramine 5 mg, ammonium chloride 90 mg, and ephedrine 5 mg)	Bottle (5 L)
29	Calamine lotion	Bottle (100 mL)
30	Povidone-iodine 10% standardized	Bottle (1 L)
31	Hydrogen peroxide 100 vol.	Bottle (1 L)
32	Lysol 12%	Bottle (5 L)
33	Chlorhexidine gluconate 4%	Bottle (5 L)
34	Methylated spirit	Bottle (5 L)

defined. Kit contents are normally intended to treat only the most commonly seen health problems, and all health facilities are assumed to see the same mix of problems per 1,000 attenders.

When a new kit program is to be started, the morbidity method is the best way to estimate requirements. This method helps determine both the types of medicines and their quantities, based on the expected number of attendances at a health facility (see Chapter 20). This first estimate can then be compared with the quantities used in other kit systems.

In the first years a kit system is operating, the consumption method can be used to adapt quantities to match actual consumption. Experienced kit suppliers can supply various kinds of kits and change kit contents with each order.

Step 5. Estimate the number of kits needed

The quantity of each type of kit is determined by the number of health units served and the estimated number of attendances at each health unit. If a kit distribution system starts after a period when pharmaceutical supplies have been reduced or are absent, increased patient attendance should be anticipated and allowed for. Taking into account long delivery times, most orders cover a period of nine to eighteen months.

Step 6. Make a pharmaceutical procurement and kit-packing plan

There are at least four ways to manage procurement and kit packing—

- Purchase prepacked kits from overseas
- Purchase prepacked kits on open tender, from local and/or overseas suppliers
- Contract a local company to pack all kits, using medicines purchased separately through local or international tender
- Set up kit packing at national or regional medical stores

The choice depends on cost, availability of staff, and availability of space at the medical stores. Kit suppliers should be prequalified as part of standard procurement procedures to avoid potential problems such as late shipments, incomplete kits, and poor-quality products. Prepacked kits are available through the United Nations Children's Fund (UNICEF), through international low-cost suppliers such as the International Dispensary Association (IDA), or from private companies. In some countries, such as Kenya, local suppliers compete in tenders for prepacked kits. Some programs begin by purchasing prepacked kits and concentrate on distribution and monitoring of consumption patterns. After the system is operating well at the periphery, the feasibility of establishing packing operations at central or regional medical stores can be considered.

Kits are usually procured by tender (see Chapter 21). Tender specifications for each medicine in the kit should be just as detailed as for individual medicine tenders. The specifications should describe how the kit is to be packed and stipulate the quality of the outer carton, the method of strapping, kit labeling, and any other relevant features. In addition, the buying agency should request sample checklists of kit contents along with expiry dates (for example, a sample checklist for every ten or twenty kits), and a buyer's representative should randomly sample kit contents by opening one in every twenty-five to fifty packed, sealed boxes. This type of quality control will help ensure that the contents and expiry dates meet the tender requirements.

Significant problems can arise in setting up a local packing operation. A kit cannot be packed until all items needed for the kit are available. If the supply of any item is delayed, the entire packing operation is held up, which may lead to stockouts at facilities. Because of this possibility, the period before expiry of the products must be as long as possible.

KIT CONTENTS MUST KEEP UP
WITH STANDARD TREATMENTS

Most programs pack or purchase kits in sturdy cardboard boxes sealed with tamper-proof tape or some other form of seal that will clearly reveal any attempt to open the box in transit. Lockable, reusable plastic containers are also available for locally packed kits. However, because kit distribution systems are used mainly where distribution conditions are difficult, the containers are unlikely to be returned to the central medical store.

One person from the supplier packing the kits should be assigned to check the contents of every kit to reduce the risk of theft during the packing process and to assure it has what it is supposed to have. A list of the contents should be made, signed, and dated, and a copy should be sealed into the kit. This list should also show the expiry date of whatever product is due to expire first, and that date should be marked on the outside of the carton as well.

Step 7. Establish delivery schedules and record-keeping procedures

The delivery schedule depends on the average number of patient visits to the facility. For example, when kits for 1,000 visits are used, a facility with 200 to 300 visits per month needs only one kit every three months.

A kit system simplifies record keeping but does not eliminate the need for it. At each level of the distribution chain, stock records should show the type, number, source, condition, and value of each kit received and issued. A periodic stock count must be done. In short, a kit should be treated in the same way as any other item as far as stock keeping is concerned. At a rural facility, a tally card or ledger should be used to keep a record of the number of kits received, opened, and in stock. As soon as a kit is opened, the contents should be entered into the item-by-item stock records at the facility. Where a kit system supplements a requisition-based system, a single record-keeping method should be used that bases demand figures on supplies made through both systems.

Step 8. Design mechanisms to minimize waste and stockouts

Actual medicine consumption should be analyzed regularly, particularly in the early stages of a kit program. Supervisors should use a simple checklist. Rural facilities need to supply the following information—

- Number of patient attendances per month
- Recent kit delivery dates
- The three medicines that are most often out of stock
- The three medicines that accumulate most often
- Proposals for changes in kit contents

Information on actual deliveries and receipts should be collected and given to planners to help monitor the program and to modify distribution plans as required. Details of stockouts, surpluses, and any proposals for change are particularly useful for adjusting the kit content.

Other mechanisms to prevent waste and stockouts are to—

- Allow individual requisitions for a few products whose consumption is variable (for example, antimalarials or

medicines for schistosomiasis)
- Assure that inventory control accounts for supplies in both the kit and requisition systems, if a mixed system is in use
- Create a simple system for returning unused stock
- Avoid containers with more than 1,000 tablets
- Specify maximum possible periods before expiry for medicines received from suppliers
- Instruct kit packers to mark the earliest expiry date on the outside of the kit carton
- Keep supply intervals as short as possible

Step 9. Prepare a training plan for good management and rational prescribing and dispensing

Staff members should be trained to use the standard treatment schedules on which the kit contents are based. A regular training schedule is important to ensure that new employees are aware of the supply system, its standard operating procedures, standard treatment schedules, and the kit composition, especially in areas where turnover in health care personnel is high, such as sub-Saharan Africa. As pharmaceutical supply improves, training and retraining in rational prescribing and dispensing are essential to prevent misuse of the medicines. Not only is in-service training necessary, but so are revisions to curricula in nursing and medical schools and for community health workers.

Step 10. Monitor and adjust delivery intervals

Any push system needs feedback, monitoring, and supervision if it is to operate effectively. Difficulties arise when

---

Country Study 26-5
Transition from primary health kits to a direct requisition system in Tanzania

The Tanzanian Ministry of Health and Social Welfare (MOHSW) is instituting a policy of replacing essential medicines kits with an indent (direct requisition) system in order to tailor medicine orders to fit the needs of each particular health facility and to reduce waste. The MOH introduced a pilot project in the Morogoro region in 1999, where health facilities placed their orders with the Medical Stores Department (MSD) through the District Medical Officer. It was then rolled out to five of the country's twenty-one regions.

The scaling up of the indent system put MSD operations under some strain, contributing to a slower rollout than planned. Inventory management, warehousing, and picking and packing operations all had to be reengineered. The primary health care kits comprise four prepacked

stock items that require only simple block stacking in the warehouse. Replacing the kits with the indent system means that instead of distributing more than 3,000 prepacked kits every month, MSD has to pick, pack, and deliver items according to customized orders, which is having a significant effect on the size and nature of MSD's inventory, storage, and distribution operations.

A 2007 assessment of the Tanzanian pharmaceutical distribution sector revealed that the MSD still shipped kits to some lower-level health facilities, and the rise in the number of vertical programs introduced additional program-specific kits. Staff in health facilities in only two of the six regions that had a direct requisition system had been trained in that system.

Sources: SEAM Program 2003; MOHSW 2008.

Country Study 26-6
Transition from a kit system to a modified optional replenishment system in Cambodia

An international organization committed itself to organizing the central medical store in Cambodia in 1992. NGOs had been supporting a large number of facilities throughout the country and had delivered continuous training in pharmaceutical management and rational prescribing. It was decided to introduce a three-phase pharmaceutical distribution system—

1. *Basic kit:* This kit contained fourteen different medicines in quantities considered minimal for functioning.
2. *Complete kit:* This kit contained forty-three different medicines in much larger quantities than the basic kit. The quantities were not, however, adapted to each particular facility, so surplus accumulations and shortages often occurred.
3. *Modified optional replenishment system:* The initial maximum consumption for three months was set to be equal to the standard consumption multiplied by the expected number of attendances at each facility. These maximum levels were to be revised once a year.

The kit systems allowed the health facilities to operate, although the delivered quantities did not completely match the prescribers' needs. When the modified optional replenishment scheme began to function properly, it did a better job of meeting prescribers' needs. A

reasonable level of procurement security existed at the central medical store.

Basic kits were supplied to health facilities, which had unqualified staff and no information on attendances and medicine consumption. Complete kits were supplied only after a qualified person had been appointed and the facility's information system had improved. Finally, the modified optional replenishment system was introduced when certain minimum standards of infrastructure, management, and staffing had been achieved. The supply system was downgraded if a health facility showed signs of irrational medicine prescribing or serious mismanagement of pharmaceuticals.

In 1996, the public sector reorganized the health system, including pharmaceutical distribution, resulting in the establishment of a centralized procurement and distribution system. In this system, orders flow up from public health centers to the operational district medical stores; are approved by the provincial health departments; are sent to the Essential Drugs Bureau, where they are consolidated and reviewed; and are then forwarded to the central medical stores. The medicines are procured by a private broker and distributed through central medical stores to the operational district medical stores, then directly to facilities. Kits are still used in rural communes.

---

a centrally planned delivery schedule is not regularly adjusted to conditions in the field, or when planned distribution schedules are incorrectly assumed to be followed. Receipt of the kits should always be confirmed. Stock levels at rural facilities should be reported regularly to spot any persistent stockouts or surpluses. Responsibility for monitoring and evaluation needs to be identified and assigned at the provincial or district level to provide feedback to the central authority responsible for kit design and distribution.

Step 11. Revise kit contents periodically

The items and quantities in each kit should be reviewed regularly. In stable, long-term kit programs, about two years are needed to get a reasonable balance between supply and demand for the individual items in a kit. Even then, changing disease patterns and changing prescription patterns make revising the kit contents periodically necessary. The system can also be refined by adding other kits or by changing to a mixed system.

Step 12. Reassess the need for a kit system periodically

At a certain stage, the program can change to other distribution methods, as described below.

26.8 Transition to other distribution systems

After a kit system has been functioning regularly for some time, pharmaceutical supply conditions will likely improve. More information on patient morbidity and medicine consumption will be available to planners and to rural health staff. Policy makers will get used to a limited range of essential medicines. Training of staff members should have improved their management capacities. At this point, moving to a more flexible distribution system may be possible, but only if the managerial and financial capacities exist to maintain sufficient product levels to fill the individual orders. In any case, a phased approach to transition will be essential.

In addition to the administrative issues previously mentioned, the transition to a requisition option demands that the facilities that have been handling the kit management and distribution (for example, central medical stores) reconfigure their physical capacity completely to accommodate a pick-and-pack operation. Planners should also consider the financial ramifications of the transition, including the possible costs related to renovations, new staff, additional training, and transportation. As seen in Country Study 26-5, in Tanzania, converting a kit-based pharmaceutical distribution system is fraught with challenges. Country Study 26-6 illustrates how Cambodia's supply program evolved.

Preparation for transition at the health facility level is mainly a matter of training followed by supportive supervision. A reliable and complete information system is also necessary, which is a challenge for all levels of the pharmaceutical system. At a minimum, the information system should monitor the number of patients treated, medicine consumption, and morbidity patterns. These data may also help determine whether sufficient management capacity exists to change to a requisition system based on real demand—a pull system—or to a more sophisticated push system. Notice regarding the change should be given to affected health facilities, and if the supply system is mixed, the quantities in the kit contents should be progressively reduced, so that the regular pull system can absorb the reduced quantities in the kits. Three possible stages to an open-order system are outlined below.

Fixed medicine allowance system

The first step may be to change from kits to a fixed medicine allowance system. This system also defines the selection and quantity of medicines in advance. However, the goods are not physically packed in a kit and are not necessarily dispatched at the same time. Provided that feedback is available from the health facilities, this system promotes a rapid and flexible response to changing needs.

Ordering within defined limits

The second step in the transition gives health workers some responsibility for ordering. Average medicine consumption is calculated for each facility, and these data are used to define maximum and minimum stock levels for each item. Health workers are then taught to order their medications within these limits.

Open requisitioning from a predefined list

The final stage in the transition makes health workers or pharmacy staff responsible for ordering the items and quantities they need from a predefined list, as described in Chapter 46. ∎

References and further readings

★ = Key readings.

★ Haak, H., and H. Hogerzeil. 1991. *Drug Supply by Ration Kits.* Geneva: World Health Organization.

★ ———. 1995. Essential Drugs for Ration Kits in Developing Countries. *Health Policy and Planning* 10:40–9.

MOHSW (Ministry of Health and Social Welfare) [Tanzania]. 2008. In-depth Assessment of the Medicines Supply System in Tanzania. Dar es Salaam: MOHSW. <http://apps.who.int/medicinedocs/documents/s16503e/s16503e.pdf>

SEAM (Strategies for Enhancing Access to Medicines) Program. 2003. *Access to Essential Medicines: Tanzania, 2001.* Arlington, Va.: Management Sciences for Health.

WHO (World Health Organization). 2005. Inter-Agency Rapid Health Assessment. West Aceh, Indonesia: WHO. <http://www.who.int/hac/crises/international/asia_tsunami/final_report/en/index.html>

———. 2006. *The Interagency Emergency Health Kit 2006: Medicines and Medical Devices for 10,000 People for Approximately 3 Months.* 3rd rev. ed. Geneva: WHO. <http://apps.who.int/medicinedocs/en/d/Js13486e>

ASSESSMENT GUIDE

Use of ration kits

- Which levels of health care and what percentage of facilities receive ration kits on a regular basis?
- How does actual distribution compare with the annual distribution plan?

Description of kits

- What are the kit contents, quantities, and intended number of patient contacts per kit?
- Are regional or seasonal kits in use? If so, what do they contain?
- What is the cost of each kit?
- What is the incremental cost for kit packaging versus open item procurement?

Financing, procurement, and distribution management

- Who pays for the kits (government or external donor)?
- Are kits prepared and packed locally or internationally?
- Is kit distribution integrated with the regular pharmaceutical supply system?
- On what basis are kits distributed (time interval, number of patient visits)?
- Does a procedure exist to order additional medicines or additional quantities?

- Which medicines are commonly out of stock before the next delivery of kits?
- What items are accumulating?
- Does a mechanism exist for transfer or exchange of products between facilities?
- What procedures are in place to deal with shortages? Are these procedures working?
- What procedures are in place to redistribute over-stock? Are these procedures working?

Monitoring and evaluation

- Is a procedure established to update the contents of the kit? When was this update last done?
- Is supervision of the kit program integrated with general supervisory activities?
- What is the effect of the kit system on availability of medicines and supplies?
- What is the effect of the kit system on prescription patterns?
- Are mechanisms in place to check actual distribution of kits to rural facilities against the planned distribution schedule?
- Is reporting on consumption done regularly?
- Are stock cards/bin cards maintained for each medicine?

CHAPTER 27

Managing for rational medicine use

Summary   27.2

27.1 Definition of rational medicine use   27.2

27.2 Examples of irrational medicine use   27.3
Polypharmacy • No medicine needed • Wrong medicines • Ineffective medicines and medicines with doubtful efficacy • Unsafe medicines • Underuse of available effective medicines • Incorrect use of medicines

27.3 Adverse impact of irrational medicine use   27.5
Impact on quality of medicine therapy and medical care • Impact on antimicrobial resistance • Impact on cost • Psychosocial impact

27.4 Factors underlying irrational use of medicines at various levels of the health system   27.6
Health system • Prescriber • Dispenser • Patient and community

27.5 Strategies to improve medicine use   27.9

27.6 Developing a strategy   27.10
Step 1. Identify the problem and recognize the need for action • Step 2. Identify underlying causes and motivating factors • Step 3. List possible interventions • Step 4. Assess resources available for action • Step 5. Choose an intervention or interventions to test • Step 6. Monitor the impact and restructure the intervention

Glossary   27.14

Assessment guide   27.15

References and further readings   27.15

ILLUSTRATIONS
Figure 27-1 The medicine-use process   27.3
Figure 27-2 Factors influencing prescribing   27.7
Figure 27-3 What countries are doing to promote the rational use of medicines   27.8
Figure 27-4 Framework for improving medicine use   27.10

BOXES
Box 27-1 Antimicrobial resistance global prevalence rates: 2000–2003 data   27.6
Box 27-2 Intervention strategies to improve medicine use   27.9
Box 27-3 Core strategies to promote rational use of medicines   27.12
Box 27-4 Useful organizations and websites on rational medicine use and antimicrobial resistance   27.14

COUNTRY STUDIES
CS 27-1 Overuse of therapeutic injections   27.4
CS 27-2 The practices of dispensing prescribers in Zimbabwe   27.8
CS 27-3 Building a national drug policy to improve the rational use of medicines: assessing implementation in Lao P.D.R.   27.11
CS 27-4 Chile's efforts to combat the overuse of antimicrobials   27.11

SUMMARY

This chapter defines rational medicine use and gives examples of irrational medicine use and the adverse effects that can result. It considers some of the factors underlying irrational medicine use and possible strategies to address the problem.

Rational use of medicines requires that "patients receive medications appropriate to their clinical needs, in doses that meet their individual requirements, for an adequate period of time, and at the lowest cost to them and their community" (WHO 1985).

Irrational medicine use occurs with polypharmacy (when more than one medicine is used unnecessarily), with the use of wrong or ineffective medicines, or with underuse or incorrect use of effective medicines. These actions negatively affect the quality of medicine therapy, raise health care costs, and may cause adverse reactions or negative psychosocial effects.

Prescriber lack of knowledge and experience is only one factor in irrational medicine use. Other underlying factors can affect the dispensing process, patient or community decisions and use, and the health system itself.

Strategies to address irrational medicine use can be characterized as educational, managerial, economic, or regulatory. Whichever method is selected, a successful intervention is likely to focus on key factors, target facilities with the poorest practices, and use credible sources

and communication channels. Personal contact (face-to-face meetings, for example) can sometimes be used to convey a limited number of key messages; these can be repeated and clarified using a variety of media.

When implementing an intervention strategy, the logical steps are to—

- Identify the problem
- Understand the underlying causes
- List possible interventions
- Assess available resources
- Choose an intervention
- Monitor and restructure the activity as necessary

Interventions should be based on an understanding of the cause of the problem and focus on active strategies to change behavior. Experience indicates that the most effective interventions are those that—

- Identify key influence factors
- Target individuals or groups with the worst practices
- Use credible information sources
- Use credible communication channels
- Use personal contact whenever possible
- Limit the number of messages
- Repeat key messages using a variety of methods
- Provide better medicine use alternatives to existing practices

27.1   Definition of rational medicine use

The aim of any pharmaceutical management system is to deliver the correct medicine to the patient who needs that medicine. The steps of appropriate selection, procurement, and distribution are necessary precursors to the rational use of medicines.

The Conference of Experts on the Rational Use of Drugs, convened by the World Health Organization (WHO) in Nairobi in 1985, defined rational use as follows: "The rational use of drugs requires that patients receive medications appropriate to their clinical needs, in doses that meet their own individual requirements, for an adequate period of time, and at the lowest cost to them and their community." Depending on the context, however, many factors influence what is considered rational. It may be rational, for example, for a drug seller to sell antibiotics without a prescription to earn enough income to survive.

This book uses the term *rational medicine use* in a biomedical context that includes the following criteria—

- Appropriate indication—that is, prescribing is based on sound medical considerations
- Appropriate medicine, considering efficacy, safety, suitability for the patient, and cost
- Appropriate dosage, administration, and duration of treatment
- Appropriate patient—that is, no contraindications exist, and the likelihood of adverse reactions is minimal
- Correct dispensing, including appropriate information for patients about the prescribed medicines
- Patient adherence to treatment

To conform to these criteria, prescribers should follow a standard process of prescribing, which starts with a diagnosis to define the problem that requires treatment. Next, the therapeutic goal should be defined. The prescriber must decide which treatment is required, based on up-to-date information on medicines and therapeutics, to achieve the desired goal for an individual patient. When the decision is made to treat the patient with medicines, the best drug for the patient is selected based on efficacy, safety, suitability, and cost. Then dose, route of administration, and duration of treatment are determined, taking into account the condition of the patient. When prescribing a medicine, the prescriber should provide proper information to the patient about both the medicine and the patient's condition. Finally, the prescriber should decide how to monitor the treatment, after considering the probable therapeutic and adverse effects of treatment.

Next, the medicine should be dispensed to the patient in a safe and hygienic manner, making sure that the patient understands the dosage and course of therapy; then the patient takes the medicine. Adherence occurs if the patient (and the community) understands and appreciates the value of using specific medicines for specific indications (see Figure 27-1 on the medicine use process).

27.2 Examples of irrational medicine use

Irrational medicine use occurs in all countries and in all settings for health care—from hospitals to homes. It involves cases in which no medicine is needed but is prescribed; cases in which the wrong medicines, or ineffective or unsafe medicines, are prescribed or dispensed; cases in which effective and available medicines are not used; and those in which medicines are used incorrectly by patients.

Polypharmacy

Polypharmacy occurs when patients use more medicines than are necessary; for example, a patient with an upper respiratory infection receiving prescriptions for antibiotics, cough remedies, analgesics, and multivitamins. Use of too many medicines may be a particular problem with prescribers who also dispense medicines, especially when they have a financial incentive; for example, dispensing prescribers in Zimbabwe tended to prescribe a medicine for every symptom reported by the patient, resulting in their prescribing more antibiotics, cough syrups, mixtures, and analgesics per patient than nondispensing prescribers (Trap and Hansen 2003). Polypharmacy is usually judged by measuring the average number of medicines per prescription.

No medicine needed

Many times, medications may be used unnecessarily. Use of medicines when none is needed involves many nontherapeutic uses. For example, in many countries—both developed and developing—the majority of children suffering from minor upper respiratory infections are treated with antibiotics, which are not needed. Overuse of antibiotics is not a problem limited to developing countries. France, for example, uses over three times more antibiotics per patient in primary care than does the Netherlands (Goossens et al. 2005).

Figure 27-1   The medicine-use process

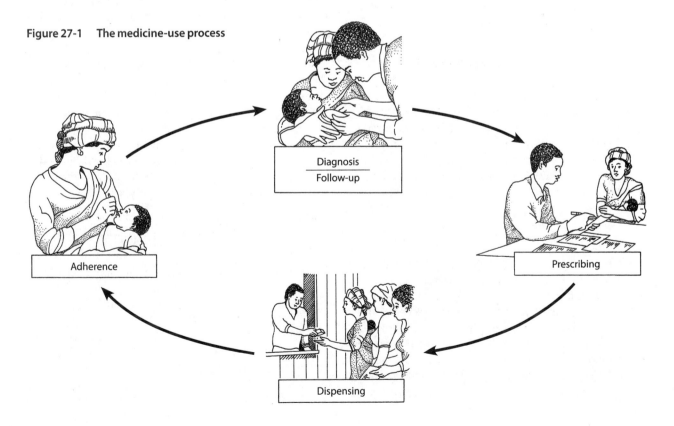

Wrong medicines

For various reasons, the wrong medicine may be prescribed and dispensed. Data from developing and transitional countries indicate that less than 40 percent of patients are treated according to standard treatment guidelines (WHO 2010). In some countries, for example, many children with acute diarrhea are indiscriminately prescribed and dispensed unnecessary and ineffective antimicrobials or antidiarrheals, instead of the recommended oral rehydration therapy (ORT). Also, because of spreading antimicrobial resistance (AMR), a medicine that was once efficacious may now be the wrong treatment choice; for example, chloroquine was once standard first-line treatment for malaria, but it is now largely ineffective in many areas of Asia, South America, and East Africa.

Ineffective medicines and medicines with doubtful efficacy

Medicines that are ineffective are sometimes given to patients because of common practice or because the patient thinks that the more medicines prescribed, the better. Excessive and unnecessary use of multivitamin preparations or tonics is an example of this prescribing pattern. A review of prescription quality at a pharmacy in India showed that in one week, 40 percent of prescriptions included multivitamin or tonic preparations (Patel et al. 2005).

Unsafe medicines

The likelihood of adverse reactions outweighs the therapeutic effects when unsafe medicines are prescribed. A common

---

Country Study 27-1
Overuse of therapeutic injections

Poor injection practices, especially in developing countries, include the prescription of unnecessary injections and the reuse of equipment without sterilization. Unsafe injections increase the risk of transmitting hepatitis B and C, HIV, and a number of other blood-borne pathogens. Although usage studies have shown a gradual trend toward lessened use of injections, progress still remains to be made in certain geographic areas—especially countries in the Middle East and Southeast Asia.

Egypt. In a household survey of 4,197 people in two regions of Egypt, more than 26 percent reported having received an injection in the previous three months. Overall, respondents reported receiving an average of 4.2 injections per year. Of those who had recently received an injection, 8 percent reported that the providers did not take the syringe from a sealed packet. Respondents reported receiving injections from public- and private-sector physicians, pharmacists, barbers, doctor's assistants, housekeepers, relatives, and friends (Talaat et al. 2003).

Mongolia. The Ministry of Health in Mongolia collected information on injection practices through interviews and observations of a sample of prescribers, injection providers, and members of the population. The sixty-five members of the population reported receiving an average of thirteen injections per year. All twenty health care facilities surveyed used single-use injection devices, but almost 30 percent of the providers admitted reusing infusion bottles. Observations of practices showed other breaks in infection-control procedure. Even with the high rate of injections, 90 percent of the prescribers and 49 percent of the population were aware of the potential risk of HIV transmission through unsafe injections (Logez et al. 2004).

Pakistan. A study of 198 adult patients in Karachi collected information on injection practices using a questionnaire about respondents' last interaction with a health care provider. It revealed that nearly one-half (49 percent) of respondents had been given an injection during their last visit; 91 percent of respondents reported that the doctor always recommended an injection; and 83 percent of respondents believed injections to be more powerful than alternatives. When treatments were equally effective, 83 percent of respondents preferred alternatives (pills or advice) to injections. Respondents reported that the nature of their complaint did not affect the likelihood of injection, and 30 percent had received ten or more injections in the previous year (Raglow et al. 2008).

Interventions to decrease the number of unnecessary injections and improve injection practices have shown that—

- Better communication between patients and providers can reduce injection overuse
- Increased access to single-use injection devices improves injection safety
- Managerial approaches (that is, restricting access to selected unnecessary and dangerous injectable medicines) can improve injection practices

example is the use of anabolic steroids for growth or appetite stimulation in children or athletes.

Underuse of available effective medicines

Several studies have shown that ORT was prescribed for only a small proportion of children with acute diarrhea. Regrettably, the underuse of effective oral rehydration therapy for acute diarrhea in children still occurs in many countries.

A large, multicountry survey conducted for WHO found that many people with serious mental disorders were not receiving any treatment, despite the availability of effective medicines. In developed countries, up to one-half of serious cases were untreated, while in less developed countries the figure was up to 85 percent (Demyttenaere et al. 2004).

Incorrect use of medicines

A frequent incorrect use of medicines is giving a patient only one or two days' supply of antibiotics rather than the full course of therapy. Patients may also take only as much medicine as needed to feel better, then save the remainder for a future illness; in addition, patients often self-medicate, using antibiotics or other prescription-only medicines bought from untrained drug sellers in retail drug outlets. Another common example of irrational use is overusing injectable preparations when using oral preparations would be easier and safer. This often occurs because prescribers and patients believe that injections are more efficacious than pills (see Country Study 27-1).

27.3 Adverse impact of irrational medicine use

The inappropriate use of medicines on a wide scale can have significant adverse effects on health care costs and the quality of drug therapy and medical care, as well as being a primary contributor to the spread of antimicrobial resistance. Other negative effects are the increased likelihood of adverse drug reactions and encouraging patients' inappropriate reliance on medicines.

Impact on quality of medicine therapy and medical care

Inappropriate prescribing practices can, directly or indirectly, jeopardize the quality of patient care and negatively influence the outcome of treatment. The underuse of ORT for acute diarrhea, for instance, can hinder the goal of treatment: namely, to prevent or treat dehydration and thus prevent death in children. Widespread ORT use has resulted in significant reductions in childhood death from diarrhea in the last twenty-five years; however, improvements could

THE VICIOUS CIRCLE THAT LEADS TO OVERUSE OF MEDICINE

still be made, as diarrhea remains the second-leading cause of mortality among children (WHO/UNICEF 2009).

The likelihood of adverse drug reactions increases when medicines are prescribed unnecessarily (see Chapter 35 on pharmacovigilance for a full discussion of the effects of adverse drug reactions and events). An overdosage of gentamicin, for example, can lead to permanent hearing problems. Misuse of injectable products raises the risk of transmitting HIV/AIDS, hepatitis B and C, and other blood-borne diseases.

Impact on antimicrobial resistance

A chronic use or underdosage of antibiotics and chemotherapeutic agents can contribute to the rapid emergence of resistant strains of bacteria or the malaria parasite. Health gains stemming from the discovery of antimicrobial agents are in jeopardy because of the spread of microbes that are resistant to inexpensive first-choice, or first-line, medicines. Resistance to antimicrobials is a natural biological phenomenon that can be amplified by a variety of factors, including human practices. The use of an antimicrobial in any dose and over any time period forces microbes to either adapt or die; the microbes that adapt and survive carry genes for resistance, which can be passed on. The bacterial infections in which microbial resistance is most evident are diarrheal diseases, respiratory tract infections, meningitis, sexually transmitted infections, tuberculosis, and hospital-acquired infections. The development of drug-resistant malaria and tuberculosis is of particular concern, as is the emergence of resistance to anti-HIV drugs. Box 27-1 lists the global prevalence rates of AMR for several infections.

When infections become resistant to first-line antimicrobials, treatment must be switched to second- or third-line medicines, which are almost always more expensive and sometimes more toxic. In many countries, the high cost of these replacement medicines is prohibitive, meaning that some diseases can no longer be treated in areas where resistance to first-line medicines is widespread. The economic cost of antimicrobial resistance in the European community is estimated to be 9 billion euros per year (SCORE 2004). Most alarming of all are diseases for which resistance is developing to virtually all available medicines.

Impact on cost

Overuse or incorrect use of medicines, even essential ones, causes both patients and the health care system to spend excessively on pharmaceuticals and waste financial resources. For example, in Nepal, up to half of total medicine costs in one study were related to inappropriate prescribing (Holloway et al. 2001). In many places, people buy medicines out-of-pocket—particularly antimalarials—and spending money on irrational treatment can dramatically affect household expenditure, especially in the poorest homes (Breman et al. 2006).

In many countries, expenditures on nonessential pharmaceutical products, such as multivitamins or cough mixtures, drain limited financial resources that could otherwise be allocated for more essential and vital products, such as vaccines or antibiotics. Inappropriate underuse of medicines at an early stage of a disease may also produce excess costs by increasing the probability of prolonged disease and eventual hospitalization.

As an example of the global impact of irrational medicine use on costs, the switch to artemisinin-based combination

therapies (ACTs) for malaria from ineffective antimalarials has had an enormous effect on the cost of malaria control. Estimates indicate that the additional annual costs of ACT range from 300 million U.S. dollars (USD) to USD 500 million globally, which does not include the resources required to strengthen health systems to effectively deliver ACTs, including the costs of improving pharmaceutical regulations, pharmacovigilance, diagnostics, and implementing different medicine policies for different population groups (Arrow et al. 2004).

Psychosocial impact

Overprescribing encourages patients to believe that they need medications for any and all conditions, even trivial ones. The concept that there is a pill for every ill is harmful. Patients come to rely on medicines, and this reliance increases the demand for them. Patients may demand unnecessary injections because during years of exposure to modern health services, they have become accustomed to having practitioners administer injections. Studies have also shown that patient demands and expectations can lead prescribers to prescribe unnecessary antibiotics for viral infections.

27.4 Factors underlying irrational use of medicines at various levels of the health system

Many interrelated factors influence medicine use (see Figure 27-2). The health system, prescriber, dispenser, patient, and community are all involved in the therapeutic process, and all can contribute to irrational use in a variety of ways.

Health system

Factors affecting the health system include unreliable supply, medicine shortages, expired medicines, and availability of inappropriate medicines, including substandard and counterfeit products. Such inefficiencies in the system lead to a lack of confidence in the system by the prescriber and the patient. The patient demands treatment, and the prescriber feels obliged to give what is available, even if the medicine is not the correct one to treat the condition. Financial incentives inherent in a health system can promote better use; for example, Kyrgyzstan implemented an outpatient drug benefit program that based prescription reimbursements on the use of standard treatment guidelines and generics (Kadyrova et al. 2004).

A government can show its commitment to rational medicine use by implementing key policies and regulations and by providing resources for rational-medicine-use programs and research (Figure 27-3). For example, less than one-third of low- and middle-income countries have either national AMR strategies or national AMR task forces (WHO/TCM 2006). In addition, health systems that fail to implement policies on standard treatment guidelines, essential medicines lists, and medicine formularies are missing out on well-proven methods to increase the rational use of medicines.

Prescriber

The prescriber can be affected by internal and external factors. He or she may have received inadequate training either preservice or in-service, or his or her prescribing practices may have become outdated because of a lack of continuing education and a poor supervisory system. Prescribing role models who are imitated may not prescribe rationally. Objective information on medicines may be lacking, and the information provided by supplier representatives may be unreliable. Temptation can be strong to generalize inappropriately about the effectiveness or side effects of medicines on the basis of limited personal experience. Externally, a heavy patient load and pressure to prescribe from peers, patients, and pharmaceutical company representatives all

complicate prescribing decisions. In India, doctors often prescribe ineffective tonics because many patients believe in them and will not return to a doctor who will not prescribe them, which impinges on the doctor's livelihood. Finally, profit may affect a prescriber's choice if the prescriber's income is dependent on medicine sales. Country Study 27-2 describes the prescribing practices of doctors who also dispense medicines.

Dispenser

The dispenser plays a crucial role in the therapeutic process. Dispensing quality may be affected by the training and supervision the dispenser has received and the medicine information available to the dispenser. A shortage of dispensing materials and short dispensing time caused by a heavy patient load may also have an adverse impact on dispensing. As with prescribers, dispensers, especially private drug sellers, may have a financial incentive to dispense irrationally. In addition, in some countries, drug sellers in retail outlets are rarely trained and there is little to no structure for monitoring or supervision. Finally, the low status of dispensers affects the quality of dispensing.

Figure 27-2   Factors influencing prescribing

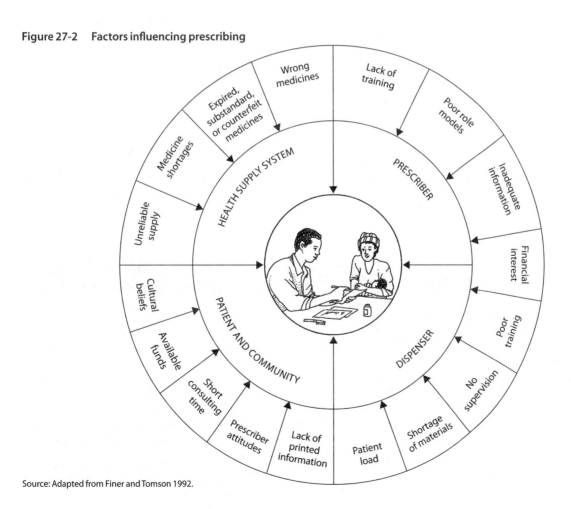

Source: Adapted from Finer and Tomson 1992.

Figure 27-3   What countries are doing to promote the rational use of medicines

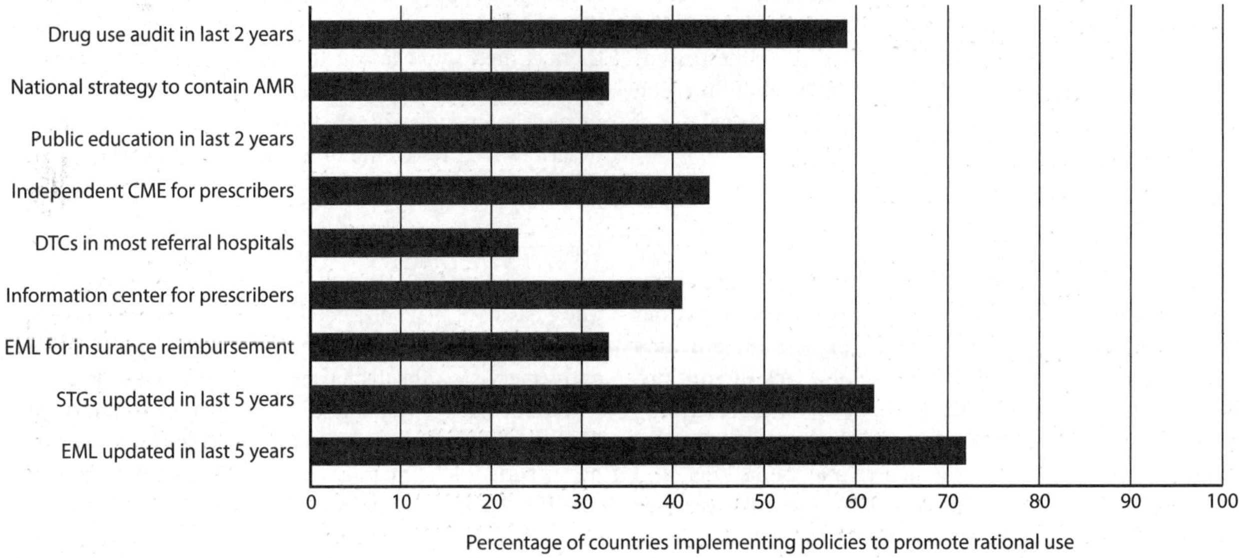

AMR = antimicrobial resistance; CME = continuing medical education; DTCs = drug and therapeutics committees; EML = essential medicines list; STGs = standard treatment guidelines
Source: Holloway 2005.

Patient and community

The individual's adherence to prescribed treatment is influenced by many factors, including cultural beliefs, the communication skills and attitudes of the prescriber and dispenser, the limited time available for consulting, the shortage of printed information, the affordability of treatment, and community beliefs about the efficacy of certain medicines or routes of administration. For example, patients may believe that injections are more powerful than capsules, or that capsules are more effective than tablets. In addition, many individuals practice self-medication, selecting and using medications on their own

for recognized illnesses. Self-medication often leads to irrational use and may include either over-the-counter or prescription medicines.

It is clear that, although the prescriber's knowledge and experience are important aspects influencing the use of medicines, they are not the only ones. As discussed above, there are many causes for irrational medicine use and many factors involved in the decision-making process.

These factors vary for each person and situation. Therefore, specific interventions to improve prescribing may work in some circumstances but not in others. Because of the complexity of factors involved, any single intervention is unlikely to work in every situation.

Country Study 27-2
The practices of dispensing prescribers in Zimbabwe

A study of twenty-nine randomly chosen private-sector dispensing doctors and twenty-eight private-sector nondispensing doctors in Harare investigated differences in prescribing practices. Data on prescribing for upper respiratory tract infections were collected from patient records and evaluated by a panel of experts based on standard treatment guidelines and the WHO/International Network for the Rational Use of Drugs (INRUD) rational drug-use indicators.

Results of the study showed major differences between the prescribing habits of dispensing and nondispensing physicians. Dispensing doctors prescribed significantly more medicines (35 percent more), antibiotics (33 percent more), and mixtures (72 percent more) per patient. The more symptoms reported by the patient, the more medicines he or she received. In addition, dispensing doctors prescribed three times more injections, and they prescribed subcurative doses of antibiotics almost 20 percent of the time.

Source: Trap and Hansen 2003.

27.5 Strategies to improve medicine use

Before attempting to change medicine use, the scale of the problem should be assessed and quantified. The underlying reasons for the problem behavior then need to be investigated. Quantitative and qualitative methods for assessing medicine use are described in Chapter 28. *It is a mistake to intervene before understanding the reasons for a problem behavior.*

Several choices exist for interventions to change medicine-use practices. These approaches can be characterized as educational, managerial, economic, or regulatory (see Box 27-2). Whichever approach is used, interventions should focus on specific problem behaviors and should target prescribers, dispensers, facilities, or the public, depending on where the assessment shows the problems lie. A single intervention rarely results in sustainable changes, so a combined strategy is preferred. Figure 27-4 shows a framework for improving uses.

Possible interventions for prescribers, such as training, accessing unbiased information, and using opinion leaders, are described in Chapter 29. After prescribing has been addressed, the next stage of medicine use is dispensing. This crucial aspect of the provider-patient relationship is often neglected or delegated to an untrained person. Chapter 30 describes ways to ensure good dispensing. The final stage of medicine use is when the patient takes the medicine. The patient is more likely to take medicines as advised if he or she understands how to take the medicine and if there is general community awareness of rational medicine use. Developing informational materials for patients and planning public education campaigns requires an understanding of cultural norms, values, and practices. These issues as well as those surrounding patient adherence are covered in Chapter 33.

Whatever problem is being addressed, health care providers and consumers need impartial drug and therapeutics information. Such information can serve as the basis for standard treatment guidelines or therapeutic standards. Information can be made available actively through drug bulletins or in a largely passive manner through drug information centers. However, in a 2003 survey, less than half of all countries—no matter what income level—had independent national drug information services for prescribers, dispensers, or consumers (WHO/TCM 2006). Medicine information is covered in Chapter 34.

No matter which point in the medicine-use process becomes the focus of an intervention strategy, there are

---

Box 27-2
Intervention strategies to improve medicine use

Educational strategies

Training of prescribers
- Formal education (preservice)
- Continuing education (in-service)
- Supervisory visits
- Group lectures, seminars, and workshops

Printed materials
- Clinical literature and newsletters
- Treatment guidelines and medicine formularies
- Illustrated materials (flyers, leaflets)

Approaches based on face-to-face contact
- Educational outreach
- Patient education
- Influencing opinion leaders

Managerial strategies

Monitoring, supervising, and feedback
- Hospital drug and therapeutics committees
- District health teams
- Government inspectorate
- Professional organizations
- Self-assessment

Selection, procurement, and distribution
- Limited procurement lists
- Drug use review and feedback
- Hospital and regional drug committees
- Cost information

Prescribing and dispensing approaches
- Structured medicine order forms
- Standard diagnostic and treatment guidelines
- Course-of-therapy packaging

Economic strategies
- Price setting
- Capitation-based budgeting
- Reimbursement and user fees
- Insurance

Regulatory strategies
- Medicines registration
- Limited medicine lists
- Prescribing restrictions
- Dispensing restrictions

Source: Adapted from Quick, Laing, and Ross-Degnan 1991.

Figure 27-4   Framework for improving medicine use

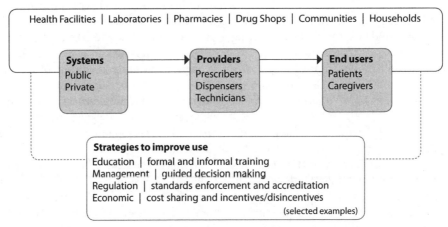

Source: CPM/MSH 2011.

common characteristics of effective interventions. These interventions—

Identify key influence factors. Use qualitative methods to understand why a person behaves in a certain way, and identify influences that can promote and prevent change.

Target individuals or groups with the worst practices. For the greatest impact, focus on these individuals or facilities.

Use credible information sources. Involve influential, respected authorities and ensure that resource materials are well referenced and authoritative.

Use credible communication channels. Enhance the message and acceptability of its content by communicating through existing, credible channels.

Use personal contact whenever possible. Communicate key messages most effectively with face-to-face individual or small-group meetings.

Limit the number of messages. Improve understanding by confining the intervention to a few key messages.

Repeat key messages using a variety of media. People learn in different ways—some learn visually from text or graphics, some learn through spoken messages, and some learn through a combination of media. Help reinforce key messages by repeating them using a variety of approaches.

Provide better alternatives. Whenever possible, give a positive message that encourages people to do something. Negative messages tend to alienate people. With an emphasis on the positive, the negative behavior can be excluded. For example, a positive message: DO treat diarrhea with ORT. Antidiarrheals are not necessary.

27.6   Developing a strategy

Six steps to follow in developing a strategy to promote rational medicine use are described below.

Step 1. Identify the problem and recognize the need for action

Within the facility, district, or country, a consensus must exist about the most important problems in medicine use. Recognition of the primary problems may come as a result of an indicator survey or drug use review, a disaster in which patients have been adversely affected, or an economic analysis of medicine expenditures. An effective response can be planned only after all the involved parties, including prescribers, patients, and health service managers, recognize that a problem exists. If an influential prescriber or politician refuses to accept that a specific problem exists, it will be very difficult to intervene effectively. Thus, compiling the evidence that clearly details the scope of the problem, establishing a consensus that action is needed, and securing support from all interested parties are important tasks. Country Study 27-3 shows how the Lao People's Democratic Republic approached the implementation of a national medicine policy to improve rational use.

Step 2. Identify underlying causes and motivating factors

As described in Section 27.4, many factors contribute to the irrational use of medicines. These factors must be investigated and understood before intervening. If this step has not been taken, the intervention is likely to fail. For example, a campaign to promote the use of generic medicines by hanging up posters in a health clinic will fail if the underlying reason for the lack of use is that the doctors do not know the generic names of the medicines. Also, a prescriber who is allowed to dispense and earn money from medication sales is going to be motivated to prescribe (and sell) more medicines and more expensive medicines, including brand-name products.

The National Drug Policy (NDP) of Laos was created in 1993 to improve the quality and use of medicines through developing drug legislation, quality control, guidelines, training, inspections, and health systems research. Since 1995, Lao P.D.R.'s National Drug Policy program has implemented the NDP through a pilot intervention program in five provinces. In each province in the assessment (pilot and control), four pharmacies at public hospitals and twenty private pharmacies were randomly selected.

The intervention comprised a number of activities in both the public and private sectors, including training private drug sellers and inspectors, developing standard treatment guidelines and indicators for rational medicine use, establishing drug and therapeutics committees, and implementing outreach to the general public on rational medicine-use concepts.

To measure the intervention outcome, researchers analyzed 110 prescriptions for children under five with simple diarrhea and 240 adult outpatient prescriptions based on twenty-nine indicators; in addition, twelve health care managers were interviewed on knowledge and attitudes. The results of the analysis showed that—

- Health care managers in the pilot province had better knowledge of NDP concepts.
- Significantly more essential medicines were available in the private pharmacies in the pilot province.
- The proportion of prescriptions of essential medicines in hospitals was higher in the pilot province (95 percent compared with 86 percent; p < 0.001).
- The management of simple diarrhea in children in the pilot province was significantly more likely to follow standard treatment guidelines.
- Fewer drugs were prescribed per patient in the pilot province (2.7 compared with 3.3; p < 0.001).

In conclusion, the pilot province performed significantly better in several aspects of rational medicine use. This operational research provided evidence to help the Lao Ministry of Health tailor the development and implementation of a national drug policy to its own context.

Source: Paphassarang et al. 2004.

In 1998, a study showing an alarming trend of increased sales and use of antibiotics in Chile was submitted to the Ministry of Health. The findings showed that in the previous ten years, sales of amoxicilline and oral fluoroquinolones had increased almost 500 percent, and sales of oral cephalosporins had increased more than 300 percent. Ministry of Health officials met with a number of stakeholders, including representatives from scientific and professional associations, the pharmaceutical regulatory agency, and consumer groups, to jointly develop a strategy to address the issue.

In September 1999, with stakeholder support, the Ministry of Health instituted measures to control the use of antibiotics by making them available only through pharmacists and only by prescription. The new policy was backed up with the distribution of informational leaflets, posters, and widespread media coverage.

Three months later, an evaluation of sales and use pre- and postintervention showed that consumption of amoxicilline had decreased by 36 percent, consumption of ampicillin had decreased by 56 percent, and consumption of erythromycin had decreased by 30 percent between the last quarter of 1998 and the last quarter of 1999. In addition, expenditures on antimicrobials in private pharmacies dropped by USD 6.5 million.

Chile's experience has shown that political commitment, stakeholder cooperation, and public education can be combined to save money and reduce the irrational use of antibiotics.

Source: Bavestrello and Cabello 2000.

Box 27-3
Core strategies to promote rational use of medicines

Evidence suggests that the following core policies, strategies, and interventions promote more rational use of medicines.

Establishing a mandated multidisciplinary national body to coordinate medicine-use policies. Ensuring rational medicine use requires many activities that need coordination among many stakeholders. Therefore, a national body is necessary to coordinate strategies and policy at the national level, in both the public and private sectors. This body should involve government, health professions, academia, the pharmaceutical industry, consumer groups, and the national regulatory authority.

Implementing procedures for developing, using, and revising standard treatment guidelines. Standard treatment guidelines (STGs) (or clinical guidelines or prescribing policies) are systematically developed statements to help prescribers make decisions about appropriate treatments for specific clinical conditions. STGs are made more credible through the use of evidence-based recommendations. They vary in complexity from simple algorithms to detailed protocols on diagnostic criteria, patient advice, and costs.

Implementing procedures for developing and revising an essential medicines list (or hospital formulary) based on treatments of choice. An essential medicines list makes pharmaceutical management easier at all levels: procurement, storage, and distribution are easier with fewer items, and prescribing and dispensing are easier for professionals. A national essential medicines list should be based on national STGs, and both should be revised regularly.

Establishing a drug and therapeutics committee in districts and hospitals, with defined responsibilities for monitoring and promoting rational use of medicines. This committee, also called a pharmacy and therapeutics committee, is responsible for ensuring the safe and effective use of medicines in the facility or area under its jurisdiction. The committee should operate independently, and members should represent all the major medical specialties and the administration. The primary tasks of the committee are to develop and revise institutional STGs (based on national guidelines) and to maintain an institutional essential medicines list or formulary.

Using problem-based training in pharmacotherapy based on national STGs in undergraduate curricula. The quality of basic pharmacotherapy training for undergraduate medical and paramedical students can significantly influence future prescribing habits. Training is most successful when it is problem based, concentrates on common conditions, takes into account students' level of knowledge, and is targeted to their future prescribing requirements. In most settings, rather than focusing on basic science, problem-solving skills should be promoted and interdisciplinary problem-based learning encouraged. If the existing focus is not on problem-based training in pharmacotherapeutics, national consultative workshops may help build awareness of the value of the approach.

Continuing in-service medical education as a licensure requirement and targeted educational programs by professional societies, universities, and the government. Unlike in developed countries, opportunities for continuing medical education in less developed countries are limited because continuing education is not required for licensure. Governments should support efforts by university departments and national professional associations to offer independent, unbiased continuing medical education courses to health professionals, including medicine dispensers. The most effective in-service training is likely to be problem based, repeated on multiple occasions, focused on practical skills, and linked to STGs.

Developing a strategic approach to improve prescribing in the private sector through regulation and collaborations with professional associations. Most efforts in improving use of medicines have focused on the public sector, but the private sector often provides greater access to pharmaceuticals. Changing practices in the private sector requires an understanding of the motivations of private prescribers. A range of strategies should be considered to improve rational medicine use, including licensing regulations with appropriate enforcement, accreditation and continuing education through professional associations, and financial incentives.

Monitoring, supervision, and using group processes to promote rational medicine use. Supervision that is supportive, educational, and face-to-face will be more effective with prescribers than inspection and punishment. Effective forms of supervision include prescription audit and feedback, peer review, and group processes of self-identifying medicine-use problems and solutions in a group of prescribing professionals. Group process interventions with practitioners and patients to improve prescribing practices have been effectively used to change prescribing behavior.

Training pharmacists and drug sellers to offer useful advice to consumers, and supplying independent medicine information. In many countries with shortages of trained health professionals, pharmacies and medicine shops are a major source of information for consumers. Interventions have shown that the skills of untrained prescribers and dispensers can be upgraded. In addition, sometimes the only information about medicines that prescribers receive is from the pharmaceutical industry, which may be biased. Pharmaceutical information centers and drug bulletins are two useful ways to disseminate independent, unbiased information. They may be administered by the government, a university teaching hospital, or a nongovernmental organization, under the supervision of a health professional.

Encouraging involvement of consumer organizations, and devoting government resources to public education about medicines. Governments have a responsibility to ensure the quality of information about medicines available to consumers. Without sufficient knowledge about the risks and benefits of medicine use, people will often fail to achieve their expected clinical outcomes and may even suffer adverse effects. Regulation of consumer advertising and promotion by pharmaceutical companies, as well as public education activities led by consumer organizations, may influence medicine use by the public.

Avoiding perverse financial incentives. Financial incentives may strongly promote rational or irrational use of medicines. Examples include the ability of prescribers to earn money from medicine sales; flat prescription fees that lead to overprescription; and dispensing fees that are calculated as a percentage of the cost of medicines, which encourages the sale of expensive medicines.

Ensuring sufficient government expenditure and enforced regulation. Appropriate regulation of the activities of all those involved in the use of medicines is critical to ensure rational medicine use. For regulations to be effective, they must be enforced, and the regulatory authority must be sufficiently funded and backed by the government's judiciary. Without sufficient competent personnel and finances, none of the core components of a national program to promote rational use of medicines can be carried out.

Sources: WHO 2002; Laing et al. 2001.

Step 3. List possible interventions

Educational, managerial, economic, and regulatory interventions can be used to address the problem of irrational use (see Chapter 29 for details). Whenever possible, a combination or sequence of interventions should be used, and there should be evidence that the interventions are effective in similar settings. As seen in Country Study 27-4, the government of Chile changed its regulations to restrict sales of antimicrobials to prescription only in the private sector, and supported the legal measure with a public and professional education and media campaign.

Step 4. Assess resources available for action

When deciding which intervention or combination of interventions to test, it is important to take stock of what resources are available. The most important limiting resource is usually human. Ask the following questions: Who will implement the intervention? Will that person have enough time to work on the intervention? Try to identify groups or individuals who would support the intervention. For example, manufacturers of generic medicines would support an intervention to popularize generics. Financial, transport, and material resources also need to be assessed.

Step 5. Choose an intervention or interventions to test

Factors to consider when choosing an intervention include the effectiveness with which it addresses the underlying causes of the problem; its previous success rate in similar situations, areas, or countries; its cost; and whether it can be sustained with available resources. Whichever intervention is chosen, it must be tested before widespread implementation. Again, if feasible, a strategy that combines a mix of interventions will be more effective and sustainable.

Step 6. Monitor the impact and restructure the intervention

During testing of the intervention, it is important to monitor related medicine use in order to evaluate the intervention's efficacy or unexpected and negative effect; for example, an intervention aimed at banning antidiarrheals may lead to an increased use of antibiotics. On completion of the intervention, evaluate the results to decide whether it should be expanded to involve a larger population. An intervention's effectiveness in a small area with a limited number of people does not guarantee widespread success.

Box 27-3 has a list of core strategies to promote the rational use of medicines.

The remaining chapters in this section address the task of improving medicine use. All these chapters should be reviewed before planning an intervention. In addition, Box 27-4 lists useful organizations and their websites, which provide further information on specific related topics. ■

Glossary

Adherence to treatment (also compliance): The degree to which patients adhere to medical advice and take medicines as directed. Adherence depends not only on the patient's acceptance of information about the health threat but also on the practitioner's ability to persuade the patient that the treatment is worthwhile and on the patient's perception of the practitioner's credibility, empathy, interest, and concern.

Antimicrobial resistance: A biological phenomenon where, as part of the natural selection process, microbes mutate and develop drug-resistant genes that can be passed on. Antimicrobial resistance can be amplified or accelerated by human behaviors, including the irrational use of medicines.

Clinical pharmacist: An individual trained in pharmacy, usually with the minimum of a bachelor's degree, who has had specialized training in the uses, side effects, contraindications, and dosages of medications for human use.

Clinical pharmacologist: A physician who has had specialized training in the uses, side effects, contraindications, and dosages of medications for human use.

Course-of-therapy prepackaging: Prepackaging of medicines in sealed plastic bags, each bag containing a complete course of treatment, as established by standard treatment guidelines. The package usually contains a complete label with instructions for use.

Dispense: To prepare and distribute to a patient a course of therapy on the basis of a prescription.

Dispenser: A general term for anyone who dispenses medicines. Also specifically used to mean an individual who is not a graduate pharmacist but who is trained to dispense medications, maintain stock records, and assist in procurement activities.

Generic substitution: Dispensing of a product that is generically equivalent to the prescribed product, with the same active ingredients in the same dosage form, and identical in strength, concentration, and route of administration.

Irrational prescribing: Prescribing that does not conform to good standards of treatment—for example, extravagant prescribing, overprescribing, incorrect prescribing, multiple prescribing, or underprescribing of medications.

Box 27-4
Useful organizations and websites on rational medicine use and antimicrobial resistance

APUA (Alliance for the Prudent Use of Antibiotics)
http://www.tufts.edu/med/apua

BUBL Catalogue of Internet Resources—Infectious Diseases
http://bubl.ac.uk/link/i/infectiousdiseases.htm

EARSS (European Antimicrobial Resistance Surveillance System)
http://www.ecdc.europa.eu/en/activities/surveillance/EARS-Net/Pages/index.aspx

Essentialdrugs.org
http://www.essentialdrugs.org

Infectious Disease News
http://www.infectiousdiseasenews.com

International Conference on Improving Use of Medicines (ICIUM 2011, ICIUM 2004, and ICIUM 1997)
http://www.icium.org

International Network for the Rational Use of Drugs
http://www.inrud.org

International Society for Infectious Diseases
http://www.isid.org

Promoting Rational Drug Use: A CD-ROM Training Program
http://archives.who.int/PRDUC2004/RDUCD/RDUCD.htm

Réseau Médicaments et Développement (Network of Medicines and Development)
http://www.remed.org

Therapeutics Initiative
http://www.ti.ubc.ca

United Kingdom Health Protection Agency ("Infectious Diseases")
http://www.hpa.org.uk/Topics/InfectiousDiseases

United Nations Children's Fund–United Nations Development Fund–World Bank–World Health Organization Special Programme for Research and Training in Tropical Diseases
http://www.who.int/tdr

U.S. Centers for Disease Control and Prevention ("Drug Resistance")
http://www.cdc.gov/drugresistance

World Health Organization ("Drug Resistance")
http://www.who.int/topics/drug_resistance/en

World Health Organization ("Essential Medicines and Pharmaceutical Policies")
http://www.who.int/medicines/en

World Health Organization ("Infectious Diseases")
http://www.who.int/topics/infectious_diseases/en

ASSESSMENT GUIDE

- Have studies been done to identify possible problems with rational medicines use? In the country? In the province? In the facility?
- If problems have been identified, what might be some of the underlying causes in the health system? With prescribers? With dispensers? With the public?
- Does the country have a national medicine policy or policies in place to promote rational medicine use, such as national standard treatment guidelines or an essential medicines list? Are there any regulations that seek to control medicine use? For example, restricting the sales of antibiotics to prescription only?
- Does the government have any campaigns to promote rational use in the public?

- Do prescribers follow a standard process of prescribing and monitoring treatment?
- What unbiased resources are available to prescribers regarding information on pharmaceuticals?
- At each level of the health care system, who is responsible for dispensing medicines? Are prescribers allowed to dispense medicines?
- Are injections a preferable way to deliver medicines with prescribers? With the public?
- Has an assessment been done to evaluate the level of antimicrobial resistance in the country?
- Have any interventions been designed and carried out to improve rational medicine use? What were the results? Were the results shared with other stakeholders?

Labeling: Placing written or symbolic instructions on the container in which medicine is dispensed to the patient.

Medicine use: The process of diagnosis, prescribing, labeling, packaging, and dispensing and of adherence to medicine treatment by patients.

Pharmacology: The study of medicines and their actions.

Polypharmacy: The practice of using too many medicines per patient.

Prescribing: The act of determining which medication the patient should have and writing the dosage, frequency, and duration of treatment on a form.

Self-medication: The selection and use of medicines by individuals to treat self-recognized symptoms.

Standard treatment guidelines: Agreed-upon treatment practices for a diagnosed illness; may include more than details of medicine treatment.

Symbolic labeling: A system of providing written instructions for patients, using sketches or other graphic representations.

Therapeutic substitution: Interchange of one drug product with another that differs in composition but is considered to have similar pharmacologic and therapeutic activities, in accordance with written protocols previously established and approved.

References and further readings

★ = Key readings.

Arrow, K. J., C. B. Panosian, and H. Gellband, eds. 2004. *Saving Lives, Buying Time: Economics of Malaria Drugs in an Age of Resistance.* Washington, D.C.: National Academy Press for Institute of Medicine.

Bavestrello, L., and A. Cabello. 2000. How Chile Tackled Overuse of Antimicrobials. *Essential Drugs Monitor* 28/29:13–4. <http://apps.who.int/medicinedocs/pdf/s2248e/s2248e.pdf>

Breman, J. G., A. Mills, R. W. Snow, J. Mulligan, C. Lengeler, K. Mendis, B. Sharp, et al. 2006. Conquering Malaria. In *Disease Control Priorities in Developing Countries,* 2nd ed, D.T. Jamison, J. G. Breman, A. R. Measham, and G. Alleyne, eds. Washington, D.C.: Disease Control Priorities Project.<http://files.dcp2.org/pdf/DCPFM.pdf >

CPM/MSH (Center for Pharmaceutical Management/Management Sciences for Health). 2011. *Center for Pharmaceutical Management: Technical Frameworks, Approaches, and Results.* Arlington, Va.: CPM.

Demyttenaere, K., R. Bruffaerts, J. Posada-Villa, I. Gasquet, V. Kovess, J. P. Lepine, M. C. Angermeyer, et al. 2004. Prevalence, Severity, and Unmet Need for Treatment of Mental Disorders in the World Health Organization World Mental Health Surveys. *Journal of the American Medical Association* 291(21):2581–90.

Finer, D., and G. Tomson, eds. 1992. *Essential Drug Information: The Story of a Workshop.* Stockholm: Karolinska Institutet.

Goossens, H., M. Ferech, R. Vander Stichele, and M. Elseviers for the ESAC Project Group. 2005. Outpatient Antibiotic Use in Europe and Association with Resistance: A Cross-National Database Study. *The Lancet* 365:579–87.

Hogerzeil, H., V. Bimo, D. Ross-Degnan, R. O. Laing, D. Ofori-Adjei, B. Santoso, A. K. Azad Chowdhury, et al. 1993. Field Tests for Rational Drug Use in Twelve Developing Countries. *Lancet* 342:1408–10.

Holloway, K. A. 2005. "Rational Use of Drugs: An Overview." Paper presented at the WHO/UNICEF Technical Briefing Seminar on Essential Medicines Policies, September 18–22, Geneva. <http://archives.who.int/tbs/tbs2005/holloway.ppt>

Holloway, K. A., B. R. Gautam, and B. C. Reeves. 2001. The Effects of Different Kinds of User Fee on Prescribing Costs in Rural Nepal. *Health Policy and Planning* 16:421–7.

Hutin Y. J. F., A. M. Hauri, and G. L. Armstrong. 2003. Use of Injections in Healthcare Settings Worldwide, 2000: Literature Review and Regional Estimates. *BMJ* 37(7423):1075–8.

★ INRUD (International Network for Rational Use of Drugs) Bibliography. No date. <http://www.inrud.org/Bibliographies/INRUD-Bibliography.cfm>
A searchable annotated database of published and unpublished articles, books reports, and other documents focusing on rational use of medicines, mainly in developing countries. Updated every six months.

Institute of Medicine. 2003. *The Resistance Phenomenon in Microbes and Infectious Disease Vectors: Implications for Human Health and Strategies for Containment: Workshop Summary.* Washington, D.C.: National Academies Press. <http://www.nap.edu/openbook. php?record_id=10651&page=1>

Kadyrova, N., B. Waning, and C. Cashin. 2004. "Kyrgyzstan Outpatient Drug (OPD) Benefit Program: Use of Automated Claims Data to Evaluate the Impact of the OPD Benefit Program on Rational Drug Prescribing by Physicians and Generic Drug Use by Patients." Paper presented at ICIUM 2004 Conference, March 30–April 2, Chiang Mai, Thailand.

Kardas, P. 2002. Patient Compliance with Antibiotic Treatment for Respiratory Tract Infections. *Journal of Antimicrobial Chemotherapy* 49(6):897–903.

★ Laing, R., H. V. Hogerzeil, and D. Ross-Degnan. 2001. Ten Recommendations to Improve the Use of Medicines in Developing Countries. *Health Policy and Planning* 16(1):13–20.

Logez, S., G. Soyolgerel, R. Fields, S. Luby, and Y. Hutin. 2004. Rapid Assessment of Injection Practices in Mongolia. *American Journal of Infection Control* 32(1):31–7.

Paphassarang, C., R. Wahlström, B. Phoummalaysith, B. Boupha, and G. Tomson. 2004. "Building the National Drug Policy on Evidence: Assessing Implementation in Lao P.D.R." Presented at ICIUM 2004 Conference, March 30–April 2, Chiang Mai, Thailand. <http://www.icium.org/icium2004/resources/ppt/AC092.ppt>

Patel, V., R. Vaidya, D. Naik, and P. Borker. 2005. Irrational Drug Use in India: A Prescription Survey from Goa. *Journal of Postgraduate Medicine* 51(1):9–12.

Quick, J. D., R. O. Laing, and D. Ross-Degnan. 1991. Intervention Research to Promote Clinically Effective and Economically Efficient Use of Pharmaceuticals: The International Network for Rational Use of Drugs. *Journal of Clinical Epidemiology* 44(Suppl. 2):57–65.

Radyowijati, A., and H. Haak. 2003. Improving Antibiotic Use in Low-Income Countries: An Overview of Evidence on Determinants. *Social Science and Medicine* 57(4):733–44.

Raglow, G. J., S. P. Luby, and N. Nabi. 2008. Therapeutic Injections in Pakistan: From the Patients' Perspective. *Tropical Medicine and International Health* 6(1):69–75. <http://www3.interscience.wiley.com/cgi-bin/fulltext/118999307/PDFSTART>

★ Ross-Degnan, D., R. O. Laing, J. D. Quick, H. M. Ali, D. Ofori-Adjei, L. Salako, and B. Santoso. 1992. A Strategy for Improved Pharmaceutical Use: The International Network for Rational Use of Drugs. *Social Science and Medicine* 35:1329–41.

SCORE (Strategic Council on Resistance in Europe). 2004. *Resistance: A Sensitive Issue.* Utrecht: SCORE.

Soumerai, S. B., S. Majumdar, and H. L. Lipton. 2005. "Evaluating and Improving Physician Prescribing." In *Pharmacoepidemiology*, 4th ed., B. Strom, ed. Chichester, England: John Wiley & Sons.

Stevenson, F. A., N. Britten, C. A. Barry, C. P. Bradley, and N. Barber. 2002. Perceptions of Legitimacy: The Influence on Medicine Taking and Prescribing. *Health* 6(1):85–104.

Talaat, M., S. el-Oun, A. Kandeel, W. Abu-Rabei, C. Bodenschatz, A. L. Lohiniva, Z. Hallaj, and F. J. Mahoney. 2003. Overview of Injection Practices in Two Governorates in Egypt. *Tropical Medicine and International Health* 8(3):234–41.

Trap, B., and E. H. Hansen. 2003. Dispensing Prescribers—A Threat to Appropriate Medicines Use? *Essential Drugs Monitor* 32:9.

★ Whyte, S. R., S. van der Geest, and A. Hardon. 2003. *Social Lives of Medicines.* Cambridge: Cambridge University Press.

★ WHO (World Health Organization). 2010. *Medicines: Rational Use of Medicines.* Fact Sheet No. 338. Geneva: WHO. <http://www.who.int/mediacentre/factsheets/fs338/en/>

★ ———. 2009. *Community-Based Surveillance of Antimicrobial Use and Resistance in Resource-Constrained Settings: Report on Five Pilot Projects.* Geneva: WHO. <http://whqlibdoc.who.int/hq/2009/WHO_EMP_MAR_2009.2_eng.pdf>

★ ———. 2007. *Progress in the Rational Use of Medicines.* Geneva: WHO. <http://apps.who.int/gb/ebwha/pdf_files/WHA60/A60_24-en.pdf>

———. 2005. *Containing Antimicrobial Resistance.* Geneva: WHO. <http://www.who.int/medicines/publications/policyperspectives/ppm_10_en.pdf>

———. 2004. *Safety of Injections: Global Facts and Figures.* Geneva: WHO. <http://www.who.int/injection_safety/about/resources/en/FactAndFiguresInjectionSafety.pdf>

★ ———. 2002. *Promoting Rational Use of Medicines: Core Components.* Geneva: WHO. <http://www.who.int/medicines/publications/policyperspectives/ppm05en.pdf>

———. 2001. *WHO Global Strategy for Containment of Antimicrobial Resistance.* Geneva: WHO. <http://apps.who.int/medicinedocs/index/assoc/s16343e/s16343e.pdf>

———. 1985. *The Rational Use of Drugs: A Review of the Major Issues.* Report of the Conference of Experts, November 22–29, Nairobi, Kenya. <http://whqlibdoc.who.int/hq/1985-86/WHO_CONRAD_WP_RI.pdf>

★ WHO and FIP (World Health Organization and International Pharmaceutical Federation). 2006. *Developing Pharmacy Practice: A Focus on Patient Care.* Geneva: WHO and FIP. <http://www.who.int/medicines/publications/WHO_PSM_PAR_2006.5.pdf>

WHO/TCM (World Health Organization/Technical Cooperation for Essential Drugs and Traditional Medicine). 2009. *Medicines Use in Primary Care in Developing and Transitional Countries: Fact Book Summarizing Results from Studies Reported Between 1990 and 2006.* Geneva: WHO. <http://whqlibdoc.who.int/hq/2009/WHO_EMP_MAR_2009.3_eng.pdf>

———. 2006. *Using Indicators to Measure Country Pharmaceutical Situations: Fact Book on WHO Level I and Level II Monitoring Indicators.* Geneva: WHO. <http://apps.who.int/medicinedocs/documents/s14101e/s14101e.pdf>

WHO/UNICEF (World Health Organization/United Nations Children's Fund). 2009. *Diarrhoea: Why Children Are Still Dying and What Can Be Done.* Geneva: WHO/UNICEF. <http://whqlibdoc.who.int/publications/2009/9789241598415_eng.pdf>

CHAPTER 28

Investigating medicine use

SUMMARY

Medicine-use researchers, health care providers, policy makers, and managers collect data to describe patterns of medicine use, to address medicine-use problems, and to monitor medicine use over time. They use two basic methods: quantitative methods, to measure what is being done, and qualitative methods, to provide information on why it is being done. Both methods are used to better understand the causes of problems before intervening to correct them. The intervention design must include outcome indicators that are meaningful, reliable, and measurable. Appropriate study sites and a relevant comparison group must be randomly selected; outcomes need to be measured before and after the intervention in both groups. If an appropriate comparison group cannot be identified, study designs that measure change over time (interrupted time series) may be used. Medicine-use data can also help evaluate the effect of interventions.

Reliably measuring medicine use requires standardized indicators to provide consistency. In 1993, the World Health Organization (WHO) and the International Network for the Rational Use of Drugs (INRUD) produced a manual that defines core medicine-use indicators and provides a methodology for measuring these indicators for general outpatients in health care facilities. Similar indicators are needed to measure pharmaceutical use in hospital inpatients, in private pharmacies, and for pharmacy benefits for insurance schemes, as well as to measure adherence to antiretroviral therapy (ART).

Sources of data differ according to the intended use and setting. Common sources of quantitative data include pharmaceutical supply orders, stock cards, patient registers, medical and prescription records, medicine-use databases, and patient exit surveys. For qualitative studies, data routinely come from patient interviews, questionnaire surveys, patient observation, and focus group discussions. Each method has strengths and weaknesses and is appropriate for different circumstances.

Medicine-use investigations can occur in public health care facilities, in private-sector facilities, and in the community. Methods for investigating use in different settings may differ; for example, mystery shoppers or simulated patients who pose as customers with specific health problems are useful for studying practices in private-sector pharmacies, whereas public health facilities may rely on readily available, routinely collected data.

After a medicine-use study, meetings to discuss the results help health care providers, managers, and policy makers identify specific problems related to the medicine-use process and design appropriate interventions to address them. The effectiveness of different interventions depends on a number of factors, including the intervention itself, the setting, and the implementation process. Evaluating interventions is necessary to assess the overall impact of the program or to compare the relative effectiveness of different interventions.

28.1   Reasons to investigate medicine use

Medicine-use researchers, managers, and policy makers collect data about medicine use for various reasons. These reasons can be grouped into three general categories—

1. To describe and compare current patterns of medicine use within a defined setting (for example, a health care facility or geographic area)—
   - Measuring consumption of particular medicines or therapeutic groups of medicines, such as acetylsalicylic acid versus paracetamol or acetaminophen
   - Comparing use by individual health facilities or prescribers
   - Deciding whether medicine use is clinically justified or cost-effective
   - Learning about the influence of prescribing on pharmaceutical costs

2. To identify and correct specific medicine-use problems—
   - Identifying the factors that cause specific problems related to medicine use
   - Designing interventions to address specific problems in prescribing, dispensing, or patient use
   - Measuring the effectiveness of behavior change interventions

3. To monitor medicine use over time—
   - Monitoring quality of care within a health facility or geographic area
   - Monitoring the efficiency and cost-effectiveness of prescribing
   - Monitoring the effect of drug regulatory interventions

A health manager who wishes to improve medicine use proceeds through a cycle of activities (Figure 28-1) that includes (a) assessing current patterns of medicine use,

Figure 28-1   Identifying and rectifying a medicine-use problem: An overview of the process

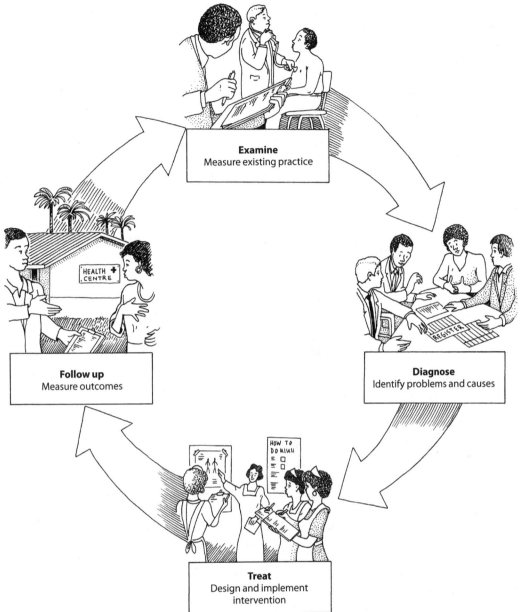

(b) identifying problems and their causes, (c) carrying out interventions to address specific problems, and (d) evaluating outcomes and monitoring subsequent practices. This process can be repeated to tackle increasingly complicated issues and to identify emerging problems.

The two main methods for gathering data on medicine use are quantitative and qualitative. Quantitative methods are better for answering the question *What is happening?* Qualitative methods are suited for answering the question *Why is it happening?*

Quantitative methods gather numerical data such as the number of antibiotics prescribed, the number of patients on antibiotics, or the cost of antibiotic therapy. Quantitative data can be used to create rates, averages, or other summary measures to describe the nature and extent of a medicine-use practice.

Qualitative methods, often in the form of observations, descriptions, opinions, or discussions, are frequently used to describe the beliefs and motivations that underlie particular practices. Without this information, it is difficult to determine why prescribers and patients act as they do and therefore how they can change their behavior. Qualitative studies can also be used to formulate appropriate questions for a quantitative survey.

28.2   Data sources and measurement issues

Health managers often need to describe the use of specific medicines or medicine classes or therapeutic categories; or compare use among different geographic areas, administrative units, or individual prescribers before or after certain interventions. Sources of data for such purposes differ, depending on the setting. A hospital administrator who wants to measure the use of expensive antibiotics requires different data from a program manager who needs to know how children in the community are treated for acute respiratory infection (ARI). Common sources of medicine-use data and their uses are outlined in Table 28-1.

Characteristics of medicine-use data

Medicine-use data differ in scope and level of aggregation. Researchers can look at previously collected data or records (retrospective) or collect specific data from one point in time forward.

Scope. Data may describe public-sector practices (in public facilities or administrative offices), private-sector practices (by private practitioners, pharmaceutical suppliers, or retail drug sellers), or community medicine use (practices in the community, independent of setting). Data on public-sector practices are the most readily available, because they flow out of routine record-keeping systems. Private-sector or community-based data are usually more expensive and time-consuming to collect.

Level of aggregation. Data on medicine use may be aggregated to measure consumption of specific medicines or medicine classes or therapeutic categories or may focus on patient-specific use. Data on patient-specific use are usually more informative, although aggregate consumption data may be sufficient to answer many cost-related questions.

Retrospective studies. These studies can be conducted using data from routine record keeping or past studies. Such existing data, although potentially incomplete, are less expensive to use. Retrospective studies can describe practices over a longer period of time.

Prospective studies. Prospective studies collect data, for example, from patient encounters. They provide information about the treatment setting, the diagnostic process, the communication between health providers and patients, or the time of consultation and dispensing.

Medicine-use encounters

A *medicine-use encounter* is the period of contact between a patient and a health care provider. Ideally, this encounter includes a number of components: history taking; the diagnostic process; selection of pharmacological and nonpharmacological treatment; prescription (and often dispensing) of treatment; and explanations about treatment, follow-up, or prevention. Medicine-use encounters that include one or more of these components occur in most settings with health care providers, who range from highly trained medical specialists to itinerant drug sellers.

Critical information on medicine-use encounters includes (a) the specific setting, provider, patient, and date of the encounter; (b) patient age and gender; (c) signs and symptoms (patient complaint) or diagnosis (by the health care provider); and (d) medicines prescribed or dispensed, including brand or generic name, strength, and route of administration (injection, oral, topical). Data on the total dose prescribed or dispensed (number of pills and duration of treatment), the instructions given, and the cost of the medicines dispensed are all valuable for specific purposes.

Studies in several settings have found that data collection forms need to allow for at least three diagnoses per encounter and at least ten medicines prescribed or dispensed. Data on total dose, duration of treatment, and medicine cost are often difficult to collect accurately and can add substantially to the cost of data collection. Unless specific reasons exist to collect this information, such as designing an intervention, medicine-specific data can be limited to brand or generic name, strength, and route of administration.

Measurement issues

Problems in identifying, classifying, and quantifying pharmaceuticals frequently occur when measuring medicine use. The same medicine is often available under different names and in many different dosages and forms. Identifying specific medicines and their ingredients, or grouping equivalent products, can be difficult and time-consuming. Similarly, grouping cases according to health problem can be difficult in environments where record systems are imprecise and diagnoses may be uncertain. Ways to overcome these common difficulties have been developed and are discussed below.

What is in a medicine? With hundreds or even thousands of products on the market, many medicine names are similar. When deciding which medicines to place in specific groups, the following steps may be taken—

- Use a list of generic medicines, such as the national essential medicines list or national formulary.
- If a system such as the Anatomical Therapeutic and Chemical (WHO Collaborating Centre 2009) or one of the other common systems is not used, develop a system of easy-to-recognize medicine codes based on medicine names and strengths (for example, "TET250T" for tetracycline 250 mg tablets). Coding systems are discussed in Chapters 16, 40, and 50.
- Use standard pharmaceutical references (MIMS, or the

Table 28-1   Sources of quantitative medicine-use data

Location of data	Sources of data (manual or computerized)	Potential uses of data
Public-sector administrative offices, medical stores	For retrospective studies: • Pharmaceutical supply orders • Stock cards • Shipping and delivery receipts	• Aggregate patterns of medicine use and expenditures • Comparative use of medicines within therapeutic classes • Comparative use by different facilities or areas
Health-facility clinical and medical record departments	For retrospective studies: • Patient registers • Health worker logs • Pharmacy receipts • Medical records For prospective studies: • Patient observations • Patient exit surveys • Inpatient surveys	• Aggregate patterns of medicine use and expenditures • Medicine use per case, overall, and by group (age, sex, health problem) • Provider-specific prescribing • Characteristics of patient-prescriber interactions
Health-facility pharmacies	For retrospective studies: • Pharmacy logs • Prescriptions retained in pharmacies For prospective studies: • Patient exit surveys • Patient observations	• Aggregate patterns of medicine use and expenditures • Dispensing practices • Characteristics of patient-dispenser interactions
Pharmacies and retail medicine outlets	For retrospective studies: • Prescriptions retained in pharmacies For prospective studies: • Customer exit surveys • Customer observations • Simulated patient visits	• Private-sector prescribing practices • Pharmaceutical sales without prescription • Self-medication practices • Characteristics of customer-salesperson interactions
Households	For retrospective studies: • Family medical records • Household surveys For prospective studies: • Household pharmaceutical audits • Family medical care logs	• Total community medicine use • Care-seeking behavior • Self-medication practices • Family medicine use patterns • Patient adherence to treatment

Monthly Index of Medical Specialities; *Martindale: The Extra Pharmacopoeia*; USP Drug Information; *British National Formulary*) to identify ingredients in brand-name medicines. Although expensive, the most useful single reference is probably *Martindale*. Free online references, such as http://www.drugs.com, are also available. Organize the medicines identified into therapeutic classes or categories, as relevant for analysis.

• Count combination products as single medicines (because of the difficulty in deciding which ingredients count as separate products).

Which medicines belong together? When attempting to place medicines in specific groups, beginning with an existing system of medicine categories, such as the WHO list of essential medicines or the more elaborate ATC, is useful. If necessary, the medicines can subsequently be reorganized into more useful local categories.

How many medicines are dispensed and how much do they cost? The following procedures can be helpful when encountering problems in estimating the amounts of medicines dispensed—

• Define the most common dispensing units (pills, milliliters, tubes, bottles) for every medicine, and be sure that enumerators record these units consistently when data from medication encounters are coded.

• Identify commonly used injections or liquids (for example, cough syrups) for which inconsistencies may occur in recording the correct basic unit (ampoule vs. mL, bottle vs. mL). Prepare a simple reference card for enumerators stating the correct units to be used for these medicines.

• For calculating medicine costs in public-sector studies, use a single, fixed set of unit costs (calculated per pill, per milligram, or per cubic centimeter; based on bulk purchase prices) for all health care facilities. This method ensures that any variations in cost are attributable to medicine selection and decisions about dosing.

How can cases be classified? When attempting to define reasons for treatment, it is important to develop explicit rules before data collection for classifying cases when only signs and symptoms are recorded and no diagnosis is made. In this way, health problems diagnosed as "malaria" can be distinguished from those recorded as "fever," or those diagnosed as "pneumonia" can be distinguished from "cough, fever, and difficulty in breathing." When possible, use the WHO *International Classification of Diseases, 10th Revision* (ICD-10) codes (WHO 2007). Separate categories can be developed for classifying frequently repeated clusters of problems (for example, ARI and otitis media, cough and fever).

How useful are standard treatment guidelines in measuring the quality of pharmaceutical use? One issue that frequently arises in medicine-use studies is how to apply information from standard treatment guidelines to measure the quality of prescribing. Because clinical guidelines are usually not developed as management tools, using them to measure quality of care introduces a number of practical problems. In the developing world, clinical guidelines frequently exist in the form of standard diagnosis and treatment protocols. These standard protocols are most commonly intended for use in primary health care facilities, although some countries have developed standards for secondary and tertiary care facilities as well.

Based on a given standard, some studies have tried to decide globally whether the use of medicines in a particular case is "correct" or "incorrect." In practice, this judgment is frequently difficult to make in a valid and reliable way. Local standard treatments may not be expressed in an explicit way that allows adherence to be accurately measured. Furthermore, standard guidelines are frequently difficult to apply for real patients with multiple health problems or problems that cannot be diagnosed accurately with available facilities.

A recommended approach for using standard treatments in medicine-use studies follows—

- Have local experts agree on explicit definitions of the standard diagnostic procedures and treatments for specific health problems.
- Define one or more explicit aspects of these standards as separate indicators rather than trying to measure global adherence. Example: Was oral rehydration solution (ORS), which should always be recommended to treat diarrhea with mild dehydration, given or not? Was an antidiarrheal, which should never be recommended to treat diarrhea with mild dehydration, given or not? Was the recommended dosage form of a pharmaceutical used—for example, oral ORS rather than injectable intravenous saline solution? Was the appropriate amount of the pharmaceutical used (daily dose times and duration of therapy)?

- Concentrate on measuring adherence to the most unambiguous aspects of the standard.

Unit of analysis. The *unit of analysis* is the basic entity being analyzed in the study. Depending on the focus of a medicine-use study, the patient, the prescriber, or the health facility can be the intended unit of analysis. For community-based surveys or studies of patient-level factors such as ability to pay for medicines, the patient may be the appropriate focus. The individual prescriber may be the best unit of analysis for studies of specific prescribing practices or influences on prescribing. In many health systems, the health facility is the appropriate study unit for examining medicine use in a geographic area or the reasons for differences in treatment practice. The geographic area may also be used as the unit of analysis for large-scale medicine-use studies.

Sample size. When measuring medicine use, the required sample size depends on which practices are being measured, how precise the measurements need to be, and the unit of analysis. A trade-off usually exists between the costs of collecting data and greater uncertainty. People carrying out scientific research usually need more precise data with larger samples than do managers or policy makers who measure medicine use to make decisions. Sample size must be planned accordingly.

Focusing on specific subgroups often improves the ability to make good decisions. When possible, the sample in a medicine-use study should be stratified to compare key groups. *Stratification* involves dividing a sample into homogeneous subsamples based on one or more characteristics of the population. For example, samples may be stratified by provider age or by area of practice; strata could be urban/rural, paramedic/physician, government/mission, or public sector/private sector. Where possible, the sample size should be greater in groups that are likely to have poor practices to learn more about the groups that are likely to be the focus of future interventions.

Ethical issues. Ethical issues must be considered in any study that measures individual behavior. Managers in a health system may have the right to examine performance, but these efforts are likely to be more favorably received if they involve representatives of the practitioners whose performance will be investigated—their supervisors, for example. Studies that deal with people directly should always include appropriate efforts to obtain informed consent from participants and to describe how the data will be used. Also, the protocols for all proposed medicine-use studies should be approved by institutional review boards or another competent health authority. In addition, efforts should be made to protect the privacy of all research participants, if applicable. Finally, emphasis should be placed on adequate and timely dissemination of findings for the benefit of those under study.

28.3 Measuring medicine use: quantitative methods

Medicine use encounters occur in many environments, including hospitals, health centers, private pharmacies or drug shops, and the home. Hospital medicine use is frequently studied by medicine-use review (described in Chapter 29). Although many different methods are used to investigate medicine use, this chapter emphasizes the methods published by WHO on investigating medicine use in health facilities (WHO/DAP 1993) and in the community (Hardon, Hodgkin, and Fresle 2004).

Studying medicine use in health care facilities using WHO indicators

Health managers and policy makers often need to know about the quality of medicine use in a group of health care facilities. To simplify and standardize the study of medicine use in these situations, WHO and INRUD produced the manual *How to Investigate Drug Use in Health Facilities* (WHO/DAP 1993; Hogerzeil et al. 1993). This manual describes in detail a set of reliable indicators to measure medicine use for general outpatients and a standard methodology to collect the data for these indicators. The major points of the manual are summarized here.

The WHO manual defines twelve core and seven complementary medicine-use indicators (see Box 28-1) that measure key aspects of pharmaceutical prescribing, patient care, and availability of pharmaceuticals and pharmaceutical information at outpatient facilities. The core indicators are highly standardized and do not require national adaptation.

Although not comprehensive, the core indicators provide a simple tool for quickly and reliably assessing a few critical aspects of medicine use. With these indicators, results should point to specific medicine-use problems that need to be examined in more detail. All the necessary data are collected from medical records or by direct observation at health care facilities.

The manual also defines a set of complementary indicators, which are less standardized and require defining variables specific to the country or location. One important complementary indicator measures adherence to treatment guidelines. This indicator requires clear, explicit criteria to be reliable and informative.

To measure medicine use, collect data from a sample of health care facilities. The number of health care facilities to include in the survey depends on the purpose of the survey. A regional or national medicine-use survey includes at least twenty facilities selected at random, with thirty medicine-use encounters sampled per facility, for a total of at least 600 encounters for the entire study. When the objective is to study medicine use by individual facilities or prescribers in a sample, at least 100 prescriptions should be obtained at each health facility or for each prescriber. When possible, the prescribing data are based on one year of retrospective encounters; prospective data can be collected if no

---

Box 28-1
WHO medicine-use indicators (outpatient facilities)

Core medicine-use indicators

Prescribing indicators

1. Average number of medicines per encounter
2. Percentage of medicines prescribed by generic name
3. Percentage of encounters with an antibiotic prescribed
4. Percentage of encounters with an injection prescribed
5. Percentage of medicines prescribed from essential medicines list or formulary

Patient care indicators

6. Average consultation time
7. Average dispensing time
8. Percentage of medicines actually dispensed
9. Percentage of medicines adequately labeled
10. Patients' knowledge of correct dosage

Health facility indicators

11. Availability of a copy of essential medicines list or formulary
12. Availability of key medicines

Complementary medicine-use indicators

1. Percentage of patients treated without medicines
2. Average pharmaceutical cost per encounter
3. Percentage of pharmaceutical costs spent on antibiotics
4. Percentage of pharmaceutical costs spent on injections
5. Prescription in accordance with treatment guidelines
6. Percentage of patients satisfied with the care they received
7. Percentage of health care facilities with access to impartial pharmaceutical information

Source: WHO/DAP 1993.

Table 28-2   Selected results of studies using WHO indicators

Country	Number of facilities	Number of medicines prescribed	Percentage antibiotics	Percentage injections	Percentage generics	Consulting time (minutes)	Percentage who know dosing	Percentage key medicines in stock
Africa								
Cameroon	20	3.0	51	41	58			
Ghana	20	4.3	47	56	59			
Malawi	72	1.8	34	19		2.3	27	67
Mozambique	26	2.2	43	18	99	3.7	82	87
Nigeria	20	3.8	48	37	58	6.3	81	62
Sudan	37	1.4	63	36	63			
Swaziland	20	3.0	54	38	63	6.1	87	92
Tanzania	20	2.2	39	29	82	3.0	75	72
Uganda	127	2.4	53	36	86	4.6	29	
Zimbabwe	56	1.3	29	11	94			
Asia								
Bangladesh	20	1.4	31	0			63	
Indonesia	20	3.3	43	17	59	3.0	82	
Nepal	20	2.1	43	5	44	3.5	56	90
Yemen	19	1.5	46	25				
Latin America and the Caribbean								
Eastern Caribbean	20	1.9	39	1	49			
Ecuador	19	1.3	27	17	37			38
El Salvador	20	2.2	32	7	72			
Guatemala	20	1.4	27	13	72			
Jamaica	20	2.4	30	4	40			

Source: Inrud Bibliography (http://www.inrud.org/Bibliographies/INRUD-Bibliography.cfm).

retrospective data are available. Data on patient care and facility indicators are always collected prospectively.

The principal use of an indicator survey is to obtain a snapshot of current medicine-use practices to contrast with surveys from other areas or with "optimal" values for the indicators. Data from an indicator study can be presented in a variety of ways. Table 28-2 presents selected results from twenty-one studies that used this basic methodology to study medicine use. Both similarities and differences in medicine-use patterns are apparent. At the time of these studies, Ghana and Nigeria showed a relatively high number of medicines per case (4.3 and 3.8, respectively); high injection use was evident in Uganda, Sudan, Nigeria, Swaziland, Cameroon, and Ghana (ranging from 36 to 56 percent); and Ecuador had low availability of essential medicines (38 percent). The rate of antibiotic use in primary care facilities was found to vary from 27 to 39 percent in Latin America and the Caribbean, from 31 to 46 percent in Asia, and from 29 to 63 percent in Africa. By focusing attention on specific areas of concern, the indicators can help identify priority areas for action.

Although a survey based on thirty encounters per facility mainly identifies overall patterns, performance in individual health care facilities can be contrasted. These facility-specific estimates can be unreliable because of low sample sizes, but interesting patterns often emerge (Figure 28-2). These estimates can show whether values of indicators are consistent or different across facilities and identify facilities that seem to have very low or very high values for specific indicators. By using qualitative methods, the reasons for these apparent differences can be explored in more depth before designing interventions. Box 28-2 describes a set of indicators used to measure facility-level treatment adherence for HIV/AIDS with the objective of identifying appropriate interventions and monitoring improvement.

Indicators can also be used to quantify the effects of an intervention. In 2004, researchers in Kenya evaluated the effect of two specific policy interventions on prescribing generic medicines, antibiotics, and injectables in a private hospital in Nairobi. Generics prescribing increased from 4 to 24 percent, the percentage of antibiotics prescribed decreased from 83 to 41 percent, and the proportion of

Figure 28-2   Comparison of facilities in indicator studies in Uganda and Indonesia

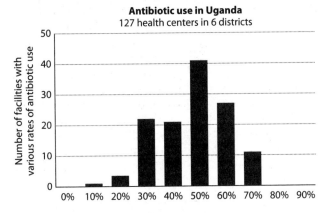

Antibiotic use in Uganda
127 health centers in 6 districts

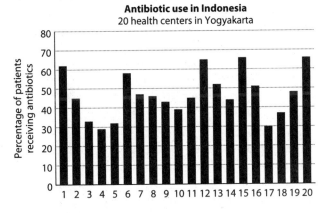

Antibiotic use in Indonesia
20 health centers in Yogyakarta

injectables fell from 17 to 7 percent following the intervention (Ojoo, Waning, and Maina 2004). In Ghana, a study assessing the effect of managerial and educational interventions for the treatment of lower respiratory tract infection showed the average number of medicines prescribed per patient as 3.8 in the intervention sites compared to 5.0 at control sites, indicating a marginal improvement (Ofei et al. 2004). In Uganda, a randomized, controlled, community-based trial was carried out in six districts, using the full set of WHO indicators as outcome measures (Kafuko, Zirabamuzaale, and Bagenda 1997). The study demonstrated that standard treatment guidelines plus prescriber in-service training resulted in significantly lower rates of overall medicine use, injection use, and antibiotic use compared to controls. Treatment guidelines alone did not result in any significant changes.

Medicine-use indicator studies have also been undertaken on inpatients (see Country Study 28-1). However, the interpretation of the results remains controversial, and consensus on a set of useful indicators is still needed. The WHO indicators were not designed for use with inpatients in hospitals or in specialty clinics, where medicine use patterns are more complex.

Finally, an indicator study can be a simple tool to motivate health personnel and policy makers. For example, before a nationwide prescriber training program in Malawi, each of twenty-four district medical officers surveyed three health care facilities in his or her own administrative area. This strategy was more effective for educating and motivating them than randomly surveying twenty facilities for the whole country for a baseline survey. While carrying out this survey, participants not only learned basic skills for measuring key aspects of quality of care but also became familiar with ideas about standards of practice and how their own areas conformed to these standards.

The WHO indicators can be used to study medicine use for specific problems, such as diarrhea, malaria, or ARI. Such research can be undertaken after an indicator study by selecting a limited number of common conditions for secondary analysis. This secondary analysis may highlight inappropriate treatment of common conditions (for example, antibiotics for the common cold or quinine injection for simple malaria).

WHO maintains a database of medicine-use surveys in developing and transitional countries to monitor the differences between different regions, provider types, public- and private-sector facilities, trends over time, and as a tool to identify effective interventions. The data have shown, for example, that over the sixteen years between 1990 and 2006, treatments for acute respiratory tract infection and malaria did not improve much; however, the use of generic and essential medicines in the public sector increased (WHO 2009).

Using aggregate data to measure medicine use

To understand how medicines are used to treat specific illnesses, researchers often have no alternative to collecting patient-specific data. However, these data may be expensive or difficult to obtain. Aggregate data on pharmaceutical consumption are often readily available from pharmaceutical procurement records, warehouse or pharmacy stock receipts, medicine-use databases (for example, IMS Health, or others), or even pharmaceutical importers' or manufacturers' records. Sometimes aggregate data can be used to answer specific questions about medicine use. Examples of questions about medicine use that might be answered using available aggregate data include—

What is the relative use of therapeutically substitutable products? For example, what is the relative use of paracetamol (acetaminophen) generic compared with branded products, or first-line recommended antimalarials compared with second- or third-line antimalarials?

What is the per capita use of specific medicines or medicine classes or therapeutic categories? For example, what is the per capita consumption of certain medicines that may

Box 28-2
Developing and implementing indicators to measure adherence to ART

Objectives of the INRUD Initiative on Adherence to Antiretrovirals include developing and validating a set of indicators that can be used to monitor adherence to ART and to investigate adherence rates and determinants for adherence for ART programs and individuals. During the initiative's first year, research teams in Ethiopia, Kenya, Rwanda, and Uganda tested the feasibility and reliability of a method to collect adherence data using routine pharmacy and clinic records. A validity study showed that the chosen adherence indicators correlated to increases in patients' CD4 counts and to weight gain. The five core indicators follow.

From pharmacy records for a sample of patients—

- Median percentage of days covered by ART dispensed over six months
- Percentage of patients with a thirty-day gap or more in medicines dispensed over six months
- Percentage of patients attending the clinic appointment set three months earlier on or before the scheduled appointment day
- Percentage of patients attending the clinic appointment set three months earlier within three days of the scheduled appointment day

From patient exit interviews—

- Percentage of patients who self-reported full adherence over the previous three days

On the basis of assessments using the indicators, national HIV/AIDS programs have helped clinics introduce interventions, such as appointment registers that assign blocks of time to patients and allow rapid identification of those who miss their appointments, protocols for calling or visiting patients who miss appointments, and the introduction of performance-based financing to compensate diligent staff.

Preliminary results show that these efforts have eased crowding and lessened waiting times at clinics. One clinic in Uganda reduced patients' average wait by more than an hour. These efforts have also enhanced teamwork among clinic staff, helped recruit new staff, and encouraged staff to start innovative programs for patients. One such program involved establishing groups of neighbors to share responsibility for picking up medicines so patients do not have to visit the clinics as often.

The indicators not only guide the development of appropriate interventions to address barriers to adherence, but also provide a useful way to measure facility performance both over time and in comparison with similar facilities.

Sources: Chalker et al. 2010; Ross-Degnan et al. 2010.

---

be widely overused, such as benzodiazepines or narcotic analgesics such as codeine?

What proportion of the pharmaceutical budget is spent on specific medicines or medicine classes or therapeutic categories? For example, how much is spent on ciprofloxacin or cephalosporins or on medicines to treat tuberculosis?

What proportion of specific medicines is being prescribed inappropriately? For example, what prescriptions contain contraindicated medicines or contraindicated medical conditions or lack of compliance with needed laboratory tests before or during therapy?

When aggregate data are used, similar products may not share a convenient unit of comparison. If the primary focus is cost, all pharmaceutical consumption data can be converted to monetary equivalents, using either actual or average purchase prices. However, if the focus is primarily clinical, this strategy will not work. Some researchers have established systems of therapeutic equivalence for particular medicine classes, such as antipsychotic agents.

One widespread system to deal with product equivalence is the system of defined daily doses (DDDs) (WHO Collaborating Centre 2009). A DDD is the "typical" dose of a medicine used to treat the most common medical problem for which the medicine is prescribed. The official DDD is usually the adult dose for the most common condition for which the medicine is used. Adjustments must be made to study pediatric medicine use. Converting aggregate quantities to DDDs indicates roughly how many potential treatment days of the pharmaceutical are procured or consumed. By using DDDs, pharmaceutical consumption in different settings or countries can be compared; for example, Table 28-3 compares patterns of use of narcotic analgesics in different countries, helping identify countries where potential overuse or underuse occurs. Because the comparison does not indicate which diseases medicines are being used to treat or in what dosages they are prescribed, these comparisons are inexact. Nonetheless, these analyses can be used to identify important medicine-use issues.

The use of appropriate denominators is important in interpreting analyses of aggregate data. Often the information sought is not how much of a medicine was used overall but how much was used per person, per visit, or

Table 28-3   Average medical consumption of narcotic medicines in Arab countries compared with three Western nations, 1996–2000 (DDDs/day/million inhabitants)

Country	Morphine	Fentanyl	Pethidine	Oxycodone	Codeine	Other	Average/ year	Cancer mortality/ million inhabitants
Syria	6	10	8		285	2,998 (Dextro)	3,307	61
Iran	19	8	4		1,051		1,082	481
United Arab Emirates	58	25	22		475		580	347
Lebanon	91	56	17		136		300	583
Bahrain	70	20	44		7		141	340
Egypt	12	3	5		46	46 (Dihydrocod)	112	205
Kuwait	38	18	37		12		105	227
Saudi Arabia	50	31	16	1	1	1 (Dextro)	100	411
Oman	39	12	19				70	316
Qatar	22	18	21			5 (Dihydrocod)	66	316
Jordan	27	14	25				66	389
Iraq	3	1	5				9	374
Yemen	1	0	1				2	402
United States	2,641	1,952	180	3,118	12	4,213 (Dextro)[a]	8,258	2,016
United Kingdom	1,860	930	53	21	13	9,347 (Dextro)[a]	2,901	2,612
Finland	736	895	13	525	137		2,307	19,63

Source: H. Enlund and L. Matowe, unpublished data.

Note: DDDs used in the calculations: morphine 30 mg, fentanyl 0.6 mg, pethidine 400 mg, oxycodone 30 mg, codeine 200 mg, dihydrocodeine 100 mg, dextropropoxyphene 250 mg.

[a] Consumption of exempt preparations (less than 135 mg/dosage unit).

per some other unit of analysis. The best denominator to use depends on the purpose of the analysis and the availability of data. Generally, the closer one can get to the population of concern, the better. For example, suppose the objective is to compare the use of ORS in one geographic area with its use in another area. One way would be to calculate packets of ORS used per child under five in each community. Another way would be to express use as ORS packets used per child visiting a health facility with a diagnosis of diarrhea; this method would control in part for possible differences in diarrhea incidence. For DDDs, the denominator is often per day per million inhabitants, as in Table 28-3.

Reviewing case records

Useful information can be obtained from case records at hospitals or health care facilities. The audit process can start with either a disease or a medicine. Criteria are usually defined for correct and incorrect treatment of a dis-

ease or correct and incorrect use of a medicine. Then case records of patients with the specified disease or who have received the medicine are identified and reviewed, and the treatment of the disease is recorded and classified as correct or incorrect. The cost of the treatment can also be determined. When records are selected by medicine, the use of the medicine can be classified as correct or incorrect. For example, if watery diarrhea is the diagnosis selected for study, ORS may be the correct treatment in most situations. Antidiarrheals, antibiotics, and injections would be incorrect. If a medicine such as procaine penicillin is the study medicine, its use would be correct for tonsillitis, skin infections, otitis media, and pneumonia, but incorrect for parasitic infections such as worms or malaria. Country Study 28-1 discusses the use of case records to investigate prescribing for hypertension in a Nigerian tertiary-care facility. Computerized case records make the data extraction process much easier.

When large numbers of records are surveyed, descriptive statistics can be generated, including the average number of medicines per contact, the average cost, and the percentage of patients receiving injections, antibiotics, or antidiarrheals. These indicators can be analyzed by specific diseases. A computer is required for studies in which a large number of records is surveyed and analyzed. Commercial software is available to analyze data on medicine use from large databases, but such programs are usually expensive. Spreadsheet software, such as Excel, is often used to generate such statistics. These descriptive statistics can form the basis for interventions focused on specific disease management or medicine use problems.

Investigating medicine use in the private sector

In many countries, pharmaceuticals are mostly prescribed and used in the private sector. Lack of access to data about private-sector medicine use prevents managers and policy makers from addressing problems in this area. The main method of collecting data on private-sector practices is through surveys conducted among private medical practitioners and retail medicine sales outlets. An example would be asking private doctors and other health care practitioners who prescribe medicines to provide information about their own practices. Private practitioners are often willing to share information about their behavior if they feel the reasons for collecting the data do not threaten them or their business. Private marketing companies in many countries have long collected these kinds of data from private doctors for use by pharmaceutical manufacturers and distributors; however, reported behavior is often rather different from actual behavior.

Surveys to investigate medicine use can also target retail outlets such as pharmacies, licensed drug shops, over-the-counter medicine sellers, and market vendors. Studies in many countries have found that persons selling medicines are often willing to explain what they know, to discuss their business, to have their interactions with customers observed, and even to keep records of the medicines they sell. To receive this kind of cooperation, persons collecting data must carefully explain the reasons for a study, show medicine sellers how they or their customers might benefit, and assure them of confidentiality. The *Community Drug Management for Childhood Illness: Assessment Manual* (Nachbar et al. 2003) includes techniques for assessing medicine use in retail outlets.

Many different methods can be used to collect quantitative data in retail pharmacy establishments. Some methods and the types of information they are best suited to collect include—

- Interviews with pharmacists or counter attendants to provide data about sales activity, knowledge and sources of information about medicines or clinical issues, and advising and sales practices
- Surveys of pharmaceuticals stocked or sold to measure product availability, retail cost, and sales volume
- Surveys of prescriptions received to describe the patterns of private-sector prescribing
- Observation of interactions with customers to examine customer demand, reasons for product selection, frequency of purchase without prescription, and communication about pharmaceuticals

- Exit interviews with customers to investigate knowledge about illness and medicines, care-seeking behavior, expectations, satisfaction with services, and reasons for product selection

Because reported practice is often much better than actual practice, a method for studying retail medicine use that deserves special attention is the simulated patient survey, or mystery shopper. This survey consists of visits to a sample of retail outlets by investigators posing as customers with specific types of health problems, for example, mothers of children with diarrhea (see Figure 28-3). These investigators are trained to seek advice about treatment and to respond in a standard way to questions asked by the counter attendant. They usually buy whatever medicines are recommended to complete the transaction. After leaving the shop, they record details of questions asked about signs and symptoms; advice given about medicines sold; and other advice given about case management, prevention, or referral.

Investigating medicine use in the community

Surveys of health care facilities, private practitioners, or drug retail outlets furnish information about medication decisions for cases seen by providers, but these studies do not tell much about medicine use from the community perspective. For example, studies of providers tell nothing about situations where people choose not to treat an illness or about failure to use medicines because of lack of knowledge, economic or geographic constraints, or other factors. Similarly, these studies tell little about the dynamics of care-seeking,

the use of multiple health providers, or the total pharmaceutical consumption in a community. Also, one cannot learn how patients actually consume the medicines they receive.

To learn about community medicine use, techniques must be used that differ from those already discussed. In the past, medical anthropologists or sociologists have carried out community medicine-use studies by using extensive ethnographic or participant observation methods. The WHO publication *How to Investigate the Use of Medicines by Consumers* (Hardon, Hodgkin, and Fresle 2004) describes a methodology that combines household interviews, surveys of pharmaceutical distribution channels such as health centers or pharmacies, and qualitative investigations using focus groups or in-depth interviews.

The core of any quantitative study of community medicine use is the cross-sectional household survey. The survey should include a minimum of 100 to 400 households, depending on the desired precision of the results and available resources. The sample of households is drawn so that all important groups in the community are represented. Different types of information can be collected from the households, depending on the purposes and duration of the survey. These include—

- Knowledge about medicines and illness, including sources of community information about medicines
- Reported care-seeking and medicine-use behavior in general or during specific episodes of illness
- Illness diaries, in which respondents record all episodes of perceived illness, the actions taken to deal with these problems, any medicines received for the illness, and how they took these medicines

Figure 28-3   What is reported in interviews may be very different from what is done in practice

- Pharmaceutical inventories to identify the type and source of all medicines present in the household
- Health care and pharmaceutical expenditures
- Adherence, including purchase of prescribed medicines and actual patterns of pharmaceutical consumption

A useful guide to conducting medicine-use assessments in the community is available through Management Sciences for Health (Nachbar et al. 2003). An example of how the assessment was used in Senegal is also available (Briggs, Nachbar, and Aupont 2003). Chapters 31 and 33 also discuss the importance of understanding community attitudes about medicine use.

28.4 Investigating the reasons for medicine-use problems: qualitative methods

The many factors that contribute to the irrational use of medicines are discussed in detail in Chapter 27. The best way to find out how factors such as knowledge, economic incentives, or attitudes and beliefs affect medicine use and to identify the most important constraints to changing specific behaviors is to use qualitative methods. These methods have been developed to investigate the causes of behavior and are helpful in identifying constraints to changes in behavior and opportunities for correcting the problem.

Quantitative methods are used to describe medicine-use patterns or to pinpoint specific problems that need attention, but they are usually not good for understanding why these patterns or problems exist. Qualitative techniques are better suited to examine the feelings, beliefs, attitudes, or motivations that underlie an observed problem. For example, focus group discussions with patients attending rural health facilities in Nepal revealed that patients felt they needed more medicines than they were prescribed or dispensed but said that they would be willing to accept advice from prescribers advocating fewer medications (Holloway et al. 2002).

Qualitative methods are based on talking to people at length and in depth or observing their behavior. When used in a formal way, these methods often involve highly trained interviewers or observers directed by an experienced researcher. Increasingly, managers and policy makers are using qualitative methods to rapidly assess the causes of a problem. Managers themselves do not necessarily need to know how to carry out qualitative research, but they do need to know what these methods are and when they may be useful.

Five useful techniques for collecting qualitative data on medicine use are focus group discussions, in-depth interviews, structured observation, questionnaires, and simulated patient surveys. These methods are outlined briefly in Figure 28-4, and their strengths and weaknesses are compared in Table 28-4. *How to Use Applied Qualitative Methods to Design Drug Use Interventions* (MSH/INRUD 1996) is a useful manual that provides more detail on qualitative methods.

28.5 Defining problems and designing interventions with medicine-use data

The best understanding of the origins of problems can often be obtained by using quantitative and qualitative methods together.

Defining problems and selecting interventions

The first step in improving medicine use is to measure existing practices and identify specific problems (see Figure 28-1). This step is usually done quantitatively, by carrying out an indicator study, for example. After narrowing attention to specific problems, one must identify why they occur—the motivations and constraints—and then suggest possible actions to address the problems. The objectives of this process are to—

- Identify the problem and describe it in greater detail
- Choose an intervention to address the identified problem and evaluate its feasibility
- Target the proposed intervention to specific patients, providers, and behaviors
- Define intervention messages that can motivate changes in behavior
- Choose the most suitable format and activities to implement the intervention

Interventions implemented without gathering this information are more likely to fail. Explicit questions should be formulated to guide this process. The goal is to identify a practical strategy to change behavior. Only questions that can help in the design of an effective intervention should be asked. For example, imagine that a survey finds that 64 percent of patients treated in one district received injections, but that the percentage varies from 11 to 93 percent in the twenty facilities studied. Questions to be answered during the investigation process might include the following—

- Are injections given more frequently to adults or to children, and are they given more often for specific health problems? (greater detail)
- Do facilities with low and high injection use differ in number of staff, percentage of staff who are paramedics, patient volume, distance from the district center, or frequency of pharmaceutical stockouts? (greater detail, targeting)

Figure 28-4   Five useful qualitative methods

Focus group discussion
- 1.5- to 2-hour discussion
- guided by trained moderator
- group of 6 to 10 similar respondents (age, gender, social status)
- focus on defined list of topics
- informal setting
- reveals beliefs, opinions, motives

In-depth interview
- semistructured extended interview with respondent
- interviewer uses predefined open-ended questions
- usually covers 10 to 30 topics
- reveals attitudes, beliefs, knowledge

Structured observation
- systematic observation of verbal and nonverbal behavior
- usually patient-provider interactions
- trained observers use structured recording form
- assesses actual behavior

Questionnaire
- fixed set of standardized questions
- large sample of respondents
- respondents systematically selected to represent a larger population
- quantifies frequency of attitudes, beliefs, knowledge

Simulated patient survey
- someone (the "simulated patient") poses as a patient or a relative of a patient
- simulated patient seeks care for specific health problem
- questions, advice, actions of health care provider recorded after encounter
- assesses actual behavior in a standardized way

Table 28-4   Comparison of qualitative methods

Method	Key points	Strengths	Weaknesses
Focus group discussion	• Small; equal participation • Homogeneous; shared point of view • Informal; free interaction and open sharing of ideas • Recorded; analysis at later time possible	• Good at eliciting the beliefs and opinions of a group • Richness and depth • Easy and inexpensive to organize	• Need for skilled moderator • Beliefs and opinions expressed may not represent true feelings • Potential bias in analysis
In-depth interview	• Open-ended and in-depth questions • Targets key informants or opinion leaders • Five to ten interviews; enough to explore important issues • If target group is diverse, five to ten held with each subgroup	• Unexpected insights or new ideas • Creation of trust between interviewer and respondent • Less intrusive than questionnaire • Useful with nonliterate respondents	• Time-consuming compared to questionnaires • Data analysis can be difficult • Bias toward social acceptability • Need for well-trained interviewers
Structured observation	• Data can be coded indicators or scales, list of events or behaviors, or diaries • To count frequency of behaviors, at least thirty cases per group • To understand typical features, a few cases in five or six settings may be enough	• Best way to study provider-patient interactions, including patient demand, quality of communication, or interaction time • Opportunity to learn about provider behavior in its natural setting	• Threatening to those observed • Observers must spend enough time to "blend in" • Behavior may not be natural • Need for skilled, patient observers • Not useful for rare behaviors
Questionnaire	• Fixed or open-ended responses • Sample size depends on sampling method, desired accuracy, and available resources • At least fifty to seventy-five respondents from each subgroup	• Best method to study range of knowledge, beliefs, opinions, population characteristics • Familiar to managers and respondents • Required skills often locally available	• Attitudes difficult to quantify • Respondents may answer questions even if they do not apply • Results sensitive to specific questions and wording • Large surveys can be expensive
Simulated patient survey	• Details of the condition are standardized • Simulated patient purchases what is recommended • Each facility should be visited by at least five simulated patients • At least twenty facilities should be visited	• Useful to compare knowledge and practices • Identification of different practices for rich/poor, male/female, rural/urban	• Ethical issues • Need for simulators who can speak local language and are credible purchasers in the setting

• Do patients expect to receive injections, and do they tend to go to prescribers who give injections more frequently? (targeting, feasibility)
• Are health providers and patients aware that injections can transmit hepatitis and HIV/AIDS and that they can cause anaphylactic shock? (intervention messages)
• Are health providers and patients aware that injections may increase the overall cost of treatment? (intervention messages)
• How do prescribers react when they are shown data from the indicator study on their use of injections in relation to their peers? (intervention format and activities)

Asking focused questions keeps the process oriented toward intervention design. The optimal number of questions depends on how much is already known about the problem and the target group. Country Study 28-2 lists the questions that guided the diagnostic process in an educational intervention to improve diarrhea treatment by physicians in a city in southern Brazil.

After asking a set of specific questions, a manager or policy maker must choose quantitative and qualitative methods to answer them. As described earlier, each method has strengths and weaknesses. Often, the best approach is trying to answer the same question using different methods. For example, suppose one objective is to determine whether patients' demand for injections helps explain why they are given so frequently. One way to do this is to observe a sample of clinical encounters to see how many times patients indicate verbally or nonverbally that they prefer injections. Patients can also be interviewed to see if they are satisfied with their treatment or if they plan to go elsewhere to look for different treatment. Finally, in-depth interviews or focus group discussions with prescribers can explore their feelings about patient demand and their perceptions about whether it affects their practice.

Country Study 28-2
Improving diarrhea treatment in Pelotas, Brazil

A review of health center records in Pelotas, Brazil, found problems in treating diarrhea in children. Before launching an educational intervention for physicians to improve practices, the study team used patient exit interviews, in-depth interviews of physicians and patients, and observations of treatment episodes to answer questions in five areas.

Describing the problem in greater detail

- Are practices the same in facilities managed by the municipality, the university, and the state government?
- Is lack of correct knowledge about diarrhea or its treatment a common problem among physicians and patients?
- Does a lack of knowledge exist about the causes and correct diagnosis of diarrhea? About the need for ORS? About the dangers of specific antidiarrheals? About the efficacy of antibiotics or antiparasitics?
- How do physicians think other physicians manage diarrhea?

Deciding whether an intervention is feasible

- How much do patients' expectations influence physicians' treatment choices?
- How satisfied are patients with different kinds of treatment for diarrhea?
- How important is patients' satisfaction to physicians?
- Do physicians feel that patients are capable of learning about diarrhea and its treatments?
- Would physicians or other staff have time to counsel patients about diarrhea or other health problems?

Targeting the intervention

- How often do mothers ask directly for specific types of treatment?

- Do mothers influence physicians' decision making in nonverbal ways?
- How do physicians respond when asked for certain treatments?
- Do physicians feel a group identity with colleagues at the health center?
- To which respected peers do physicians turn with questions about treatment?
- How often do physicians approach colleagues with medical questions?

Defining specific intervention messages

- How important to physicians is the self-image of being a knowledgeable scientist or powerful healer?
- When physicians have changed their practices in the past, what has caused them to do so, and how do they feel about these changes?
- What do physicians think about prototype materials developed to promote correct diarrhea treatment practices?

Deciding on the format and style of the intervention

- How do physicians get information about new health problems or medicines?
- Do they ever attend continuing education sessions, and are these useful?
- Do they read any journals (which ones)?
- Do they learn about medicines from pharmaceutical package inserts, advertisements, or pharmaceutical company representatives, and is this information valued?
- How do physicians respond when presented with summaries of the practices of their health center in relation to similar facilities?
- How do physicians feel about different models for continuing education: group seminars, visits by medical experts, visits by pharmacists?

Designing interventions

Quantitative and qualitative methods address different or complementary questions whose answers can then be used to design interventions. Country Study 28-3 shows how the managers of the Control of Diarrheal Diseases Program in the Kenya Ministry of Health used qualitative methods to design an intervention—questionnaires, a simulated patient survey, and focus groups—that explored the nature of problems in diarrhea treatment in private retail pharmacies. The results of these methods helped inform the design of

an intervention to train pharmacy attendants in appropriately treating diarrhea. Using the combined results of these methods, program managers targeted printed materials and training messages that proved effective in changing pharmaceutical sales and patient counseling behavior.

The intervention design process can begin with a synthesis meeting of everyone involved in the investigation process. If not everyone at the meeting is familiar with the studies, the first activity should be to present separate reports on each one. Each report should briefly cover the specific study questions addressed, the methods used, the results, and the conclusions. Written summaries of findings and tables or graphs should be distributed. Discussion of specific findings can take place after all the reports have been presented. Sometimes findings from two methods are complementary, but other times the results contradict each other. If the findings suggest important issues for discussion, these issues should be listed as they are raised and covered later in the integrated discussion.

After systematically answering all the questions, the meeting participants should have a solid idea about an intervention that might be effective. The specific behaviors to focus on will be more apparent, as will the specific target groups of prescribers or patients that are most likely to benefit from the intervention.

The synthesis meeting should then focus on designing an intervention. The process of synthesizing data to draw conclusions about intervention design can be difficult. Before attempting this synthesis, the group should be familiar with what is known from experience with the different intervention models and their relative effectiveness (see Chapter 29). Familiarization with these interventions will help facilitate effective implementation of new interventions.

Country Study 28-3
Assessing product availability and service quality in retail drug outlets in Uganda

As part of a program to introduce accredited drug shops in Uganda's Kibaale district, the East African Drug Sellers Initiative assessed the availability of medicines and services in retail drug shops in Kibaale and a control district, Mpigi, in 2008. The assessors used a combination of interviews with customers exiting the shops, mystery shoppers who pretended to need treatment for a child with fever, shop visits to determine medicine availability and prices for a list of tracer medicines, and household surveys to determine community health-seeking practices.

Thirty tracer medicines were available in 50 percent of the outlets in Mpigi and in 46 percent of the drug shops in Kibaale. Availability of individual medicines varied widely in each district; some medicines, such as paracetamol, were available in more than 90 percent of the drug shops, whereas other medicines, such as artemether/lumefantrine, were available in less than 10 percent of the facilities. Chloroquine tablets and sulfadoxine/pyrimethamine (SP) tablets were the most widely available antimalarial medicines, despite the change in antimalarial treatment policy to artemether/lumefantrine.

Data collectors interviewed customers as they left the shops to determine how much information they were given about the medicines dispensed. The upper table shows that most drug sellers asked about symptoms, but few gave any information on what danger signs to look for or when to seek care from a health professional.

In the mystery shopper component of the assessment, each data collector pretended to be the parent of a six-year-old child with symptoms of simple malaria. The lower table indicates the variety of treatments sold to the mystery shoppers.

Dispensing practices	Kibaale n = 16 (%)	Mpigi n = 20 (%)
Did the drug seller ask about the symptoms?	9 (56)	15 (75)
Did the drug seller ask about any other medicines the child may have taken?	5 (31)	8 (40)
Did the drug seller give instructions on how to take the medicines?	12 (31)	14 (70)
Did the drug seller give information on how to look for danger signs?	2 (13)	2 (10)
Did the drug seller recommend referral to a doctor or clinic?	1 (6)	0
Did the drug seller recommend referral to a doctor or clinic if danger signs arose?	1 (6)	3 (15)
Did the drug seller recommend returning if symptoms did not get better?	3 (19)	2 (10)

Medicines dispensed for malaria	Kibaale n =16	Mpigi n = 20
Amodiaquine	1	1
Amodiaquine and SP	0	1
Chloroquine	0	9
Chloroquine and SP	6	1
Paracetamol	0	2
Quinine	6	3
Quinine and SP	1	1
Referral	1	0
SP	1	2

The assessment will be repeated after an intervention combining dispenser training, supportive supervision, and government accreditation to measure changes in medicine availability and dispensing quality.

Source: East African Drug Seller Initiative/Management Sciences for Health, unpublished data.

28.6 Evaluating interventions

Evaluation is the process of collecting and analyzing information about the effectiveness and impact of an intervention. A more technical definition describes evaluation as attributing value to an intervention by gathering reliable and valid information about it in a systematic way and by making comparisons so more informed decisions can be made or causal relationships or general principles can be understood. Every policy maker or program manager wants to have an effective intervention—appropriate evaluations are necessary to determine the effect of specific interventions.

Selecting appropriate measures

Interventions should be evaluated by looking for both intended and unintended changes in specific outcomes. For all the outcomes of interest, indicators that are meaningful, reliable, and measurable must be selected. When choosing the most useful outcomes to measure, consider the following—

- Select the key behaviors targeted by the intervention and the most likely substitute behaviors.
- Select outcomes that can be clearly and explicitly defined.
- Select outcomes that can be reliably measured, preferably using routinely collected data.
- Focus on important outcomes rather than measuring all possible changes.
- Measure more than one dimension of success, especially if some changes are secondary—for example, changes in prescribing that follow changes in knowledge about specific medicines.

Steps to take when evaluating interventions

Techniques for evaluating interventions are covered in detail in other books, but every evaluation should include the four basic steps described below.

Step 1. Select the correct study unit. Because the behavior of patients and prescribers is affected by other people, the most appropriate study unit is often the health facility. If individual prescribers are chosen as the study unit, for example, the effect of their colleagues on their prescribing behavior may make attributing any observed changes to an intervention difficult. For interventions that involve changes in administrative procedures, a region or district may be used as the unit of study.

Step 2. If possible, randomly assign study units to intervention and comparison groups. An appropriate comparison group is the most important feature of a sound evaluation (see Figure 28-5). Random assignment of study units to intervention or comparison groups is not always possible. If it is not, choose a comparison group that is as similar as possible. In situations in which everyone will receive a particular intervention, early recipients may be compared with those who have not yet received the intervention.

Step 3. Measure outcomes before and after the intervention in both the intervention and the comparison groups. With at least two measurement points, both equality at baseline and changes in practice can be examined. Data must be collected in the same way in the comparison and intervention groups, because the process of being observed often causes changes in behavior.

Step 4. Measure effects over time. Short-term effects often disappear unless they are reinforced. To know whether an intervention really works, look at short- (one month), medium- (six months), and long-term (one year or more) effects.

Often, an appropriate comparison group cannot be identified. For example, a nationwide mass media campaign to reduce prescribing of antibiotics for common colds cannot suitably be controlled. When a control group cannot be found, interrupted time series analysis can be used to compare patterns of medicine-use before and after the intervention (see Figure 28-6).

In time series analysis, each time point should represent an equal interval (for example, one week or one month). Ideally, at least three time points should precede the intervention and the same number of time points should follow the intervention to reliably determine underlying trends. Finally, investigators must examine any major changes that could have affected the outcome (for example, changes in personnel can affect prescribing patterns, making it difficult to attribute any effects to the intervention).

Relative effectiveness of different interventions

The effectiveness of different interventions depends on many factors, including the type of intervention, the setting, and the implementation process. Generally, interventions are most effective when they target specific problem behaviors. A training program discouraging polypharmacy as a general problem is less likely to have an effect than training that targets specific commonly overused medicines or specific health problems in which polypharmacy is common. Interventions can target several problems at once. For example, an intervention to improve pneumonia treatment might combine training for health care workers in how to use a standard ARI treatment protocol with community-based education about case recognition and care-seeking. Interventions can also have unintended outcomes, such as interventions addressing the overuse of injections that unintentionally cause a decrease in immunizations.

Figure 28-5   Importance of a comparison group

This figure shows an apparent improvement in outcome score from about 40 measured at Time 1 to more than 60 at Time 2. With information only from the group that received an intervention between these two times, it is tempting to conclude that the intervention caused the improvement in outcome scores.

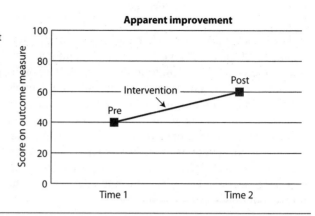

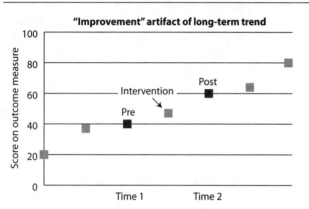

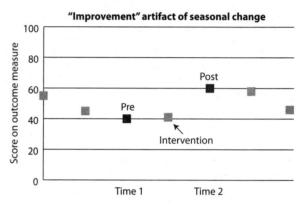

However, this conclusion can be misleading. The graph on the left shows that the intervention group has actually been experiencing a steady improvement in scores before, during, and after the intervention due to some external factor. On the right, the outcome seems to be seasonal, and it happened to be measured at a low point in the cycle at Time 1 and a high point at Time 2.

Only by using a comparison group can one guard against many possible incorrect conclusions about the effects of any intervention. Any reasons for change in outcomes outside of the intervention itself should affect both groups equally. Changes in the two groups can be compared to estimate the intervention's impacts.

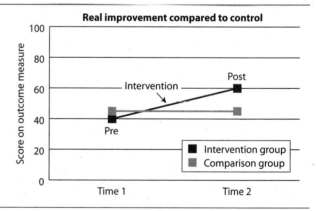

Research has shown that combining different types of interventions is more effective than using single interventions. However, multifaceted interventions tend to be more complex and may require more resources. Research has also shown that didactic lectures and passive distribution of educational material tend to have minimal effect, whereas supportive supervision and policy changes have been reported as generally effective. Chapters 27 and 29 describe examples of interventions to improve rational medicine use.

Researchers have used the techniques described in this chapter for many years. In a number of countries, managers of essential medicines programs have also used these methods to guide their decision making (see Country Study 28-4). The INRUD website has a searchable bibliography of more than 5,000 studies detailing the effect of various interventions to improve medicine use (http://www.inrud.org). Similarly, the website for the International Conferences on Improving Use of Medicines makes all conference presentations and abstracts accessible (http://www.icium.org). ∎

Figure 28-6   Using interrupted time series

Time series are a powerful method for investigating medicine use. Data that are routinely collected in many health systems about the use of different types of medicines can easily be displayed as time series. It is also possible to look at patient-specific information on medicine treatment in sample medical records. In most cases, these series are made more stable by dividing by a meaningful denominator, such as rate per 100 attendances or proportion of total antibiotic expenditures.

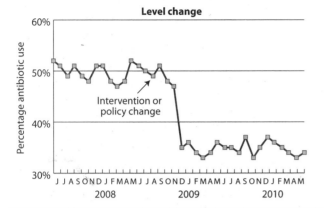

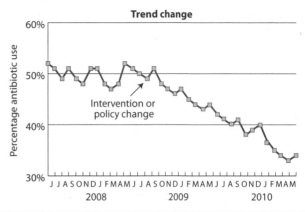

The figure on the left shows a sudden reduction in the level of antibiotic use following an intervention. The figure on the right shows a reduction in the trend rather than a drop in the level.

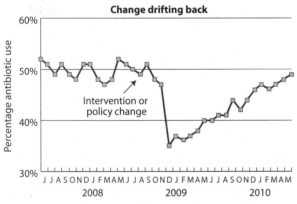

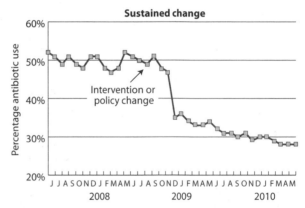

Frequently there is a drift back to the previous baselines after an intervention, as shown in the figure on the left. In some cases, there may be a level change, which can be sustained or increased over time, as shown in the figure on the right. Time series techniques allow one to assess the individual and cumulative effects of interventions over time.

Country Study 28-4
Investigative surveys undertaken as part of national essential medicines program management

In Indonesia, multiple studies have been undertaken using aggregate consumption data, indicator studies, and intervention studies. These have been used to guide national programs and World Bank–supported regional activities.

In Kenya, an indicator study was undertaken in five regions as part of the overall planning management and evaluation of the essential medicines program.

In Malawi, a national medicine use indicator survey was undertaken in every district, covering seventy-two facilities, before national training on standard treatments.

In Nepal, simulated patient studies have been used to investigate practices of drug sellers to assist in designing training programs to improve their practices.

In Uganda, researchers studied the effect of training prior to redesign of training programs.

In Zambia, a study was performed in the capital in which different training methods were evaluated by detailed record review, using drug use review techniques.

In Zimbabwe, an indicator-based baseline survey was performed before the first national policy and planning workshop. This survey is repeated every two years, and it was expanded to include urban facilities and the private sector.

References and further readings

★ = Key readings.

Bertoldi, A., A. J. D. Barros, A. Wagner, D. Ross-Degnan, and P. C Hallal. 2008. A Descriptive Review of the Methodologies Used in Household Surveys on Medicine Utilization. *BMC Health Services Research* 8:222. <http://www.biomedcentral.com/1472-6963/8/222>

Boyce, C., and P. Neale. 2006a. *Conducting In-Depth Interviews: A Guide for Designing and Conducting In-Depth Interviews for Evaluation Input.* Pathfinder International Tool Series: Monitoring and Evaluation—2. Watertown, Mass.: Pathfinder International. <http://www.pathfind.org/site/DocServer/m_e_tool_series_indepth_interviews.pdf?docID=6301>

———. 2006b. *Using Mystery Clients: A Guide to Using Mystery Clients for Evaluation Input.* Pathfinder International Tool Series: Monitoring and Evaluation—3. Watertown, Mass.: Pathfinder International. <http://www.pathfind.org/site/DocServer/m_e_tool_series_mystery_clients.pdf?docID=6303>

Briggs, J., N. Nachbar, and O. Aupont. 2003. *Community Drug Management for Childhood Illness: Senegal Assessment, September 2002.* Submitted to the U.S. Agency for International Development by the Rational Pharmaceutical Management Plus Program. Arlington, Va.: Management Sciences for Health. <http://www.msh.org/projects/rpmplus/Documents/upload/Senegal_C-DMCI_English.pdf>

Chalker, J., T. Andualem, L. N. Gitau, J. Ntaganira, C. Obuo, H. Tadeg, P. Waako, D. Ross-Degnan, and INRUD-IAA. 2010. Measuring Adherence to Antiretroviral Treatment in Resource-Poor Settings: The Feasibility of Collecting Routine Data for Key Indicators. *BMC Health Services Research* 10:43. <http://www.biomedcentral.com/content/pdf/1472-6963-10-43.pdf>

Chalker, J., N. T. K. Chuc, T. Falkenberg, N. T. Do, and G. Tomson. 2000. STD Management by Private Pharmacies in Hanoi: Practice and Knowledge of Drug Sellers. *Sexually Transmitted Infections* 76(4):299–302.

Chetley, A., A. Hardon, C. Hodgkin, A. Haaland, and D. Fresle. 2007. *How to Improve the Use of Medicines by Consumers.* Geneva: WHO. <http://apps.who.int/medicinedocs/documents/s14229e/s14229e.pdf>

★ Hardon, A., C. Hodgkin, and D. Fresle. 2004. *How to Investigate the Use of Medicines by Consumers.* Geneva: WHO and the University of Amsterdam. <http://whqlibdoc.who.int/hq/2004/WHO_EDM_PAR_2004.2.pdf>

★ Hogerzeil, H., V. Bimo, D. Ross-Degnan, R. O. Laing, D. Ofori-Adjei, B. Santoso, A. K. A. Chowdhury, et al. 1993. Field Tests for Rational Drug Use in Twelve Developing Countries. *Lancet* 342:1408–10.

Holloway, K. A., B. R. Gautam, T. Harpham, and A. Taket. 2002. The Influence of User Fees and Patient Demand on Prescribers in Rural Nepal. *Social Science & Medicine* 54(6):905–18.

Kafuko, J. M., C. Zirabamuzaale, and D. Bagenda. 1997. *Rational Drug Use in Rural Health Units of Uganda: Effect of National Standard Treatment Guidelines on Rational Drug Use.* Presentation at the International Conference on Improving Use of Medicines, April 1–4, Chiang Mai, Thailand. <http://archives.who.int/icium/icium1997/posters/2f3_text.html>

Le Grand, A., H. V. Hogerzeil, and F. M. Haaijer-Ruskamp. 1999. Intervention Research in Rational Use of Drugs: A Review. *Health Policy and Planning* 14(2):89–102.

★ MSH/INRUD (Management Sciences for Health/International Network for Rational Use of Drugs). 1996. *How to Use Applied Qualitative Methods to Design Drug Use Interventions.* Arlington, Va.: MSH/INRUD. <http://www.inrud.org/documents/upload/How_to_Use_Applied_Qualitative_Methods.pdf>

★ Nachbar, N., J. Briggs, O. Aupont, L. Shafritz, A. Bongiovanni, K. Acharya, S. Zimicki, S. Holschneider, and D. Ross-Degnan. 2003. *Community Drug Management for Childhood Illness: Assessment Manual.* Arlington, Va.: Management Sciences for Health.

Ofei, F., A. Forson, R. Tetteh, and D. Ofori-Adjei. 2004. *An Intervention to Improve Antibiotic Prescribing Habits of Doctors in a Teaching Hospital.* Presentation at the International Conference on Improving Use of Medicines, March 30–April 2, Chiang Mai, Thailand. <http://archives.who.int/icium/icium2004/resources/ppt/AD029.ppt>

Ojoo, M. A., B. Waning, and M. Maina. 2004. *Assessing the Effect of Two Policy Interventions on Treatment Costs and Drug Use Patterns in a Private Self Funding Healthcare Institution in Nairobi: The Case of Generic Prescribing and Generic Substitution.* Presentation at the International Conference on Improving Use of Medicines, March 30–April 2, Chiang Mai, Thailand. <http://www.icium.org/icium2004/resources/ppt/AC117.ppt>

Riegelman, R. 2004. *Studying a Study and Testing a Test: How to Read the Medical Evidence.* 5th ed. Philadelphia: Lippincott Williams & Wilkins.

Ross-Degnan, D., M. Pierre-Jacques, F. Zhang, H. Tadeg, L. Gitau, J. Ntaganira, R. Balikuddembe, J. Chalker, A. K. Wagner, and INRUD-IAA. 2010. Measuring Adherence to Antiretroviral Treatment in Resource-Poor Settings: The Clinical Validity of Key Indicators. *BMC Health Services Research* 10:42. <http://www.biomedcentral.com/content/pdf/1472-6963-10-42.pdf>

Varkevisser C. M., I. Pramanathan, and A. Brownlee. 2003. *Designing and Conducting Health Systems Research Projects.* Proposal Development and Fieldwork. Vol. 1. Ottawa: International Development Research Centre. <http://www.idrc.ca/en/ev-33011-201-1-DO_TOPIC.html#begining>

WHO (World Health Organization). 2009. *Medicines Use in Primary Care in Developing and Transitional Countries: Fact Book Summarizing Results from Studies Reported between 1990 and 2006.* Geneva: WHO. <http://whqlibdoc.who.int/hq/2009/WHO_EMP_MAR_2009.3_eng.pdf>

———. 2007. *International Statistical Classification of Diseases and Related Health Problems, 10th Revision.* 2nd ed. Geneva: WHO. <http://www.who.int/classifications/icd/en/>

★ ———. 2003. *Introduction to Drug Utilization Research.* Geneva: WHO. <http://whqlibdoc.who.int/publications/2003/924156234X.pdf>

WHO Collaborating Centre for Drug Statistics Methodology. 2009. *Guidelines for ATC Classification and DDD Assignment 2010.* 13th ed. Oslo: WHO. <http://www.whocc.no/filearchive/publications/2010guidelines.pdf>.

WHO/CDD (World Health Organization/Control of Diarrhoeal Diseases Programme). 1993. *Guide for Improving Diarrhoea Treatment Practices of Pharmacists and Licensed Drug Sellers.* Geneva: WHO/CDD.

★ WHO/DAP (World Health Organization/Action Programme on Essential Drugs). 1993. *How to Investigate Drug Use in Health Facilities: Selected Drug Use Indicators.* Geneva: WHO/DAP. <http://whqlibdoc.who.int/hq/1993/WHO_DAP_93.1.pdf>

———. 1992. *How to Investigate Drug Use in Communities: Guidelines for Social Science Research.* Geneva: WHO/DAP. <http://whqlibdoc.who.int/hq/1992/WHO_DAP_92.3.pdf>

Yusuff, K. B., and O. B. Balogun. 2005a. Pattern of Drug Utilization among Hypertensives in a Nigerian Teaching Hospital. *Pharmaco-epidemiology and Drug Safety* 14(1):69–74.

———.2005b. Physicians' Prescribing of Anti-Hypertensive Combinations in a Tertiary Care Setting in Southwestern Nigeria. *Journal of Pharmacy and Pharmaceutical Sciences* 8(2):235–42.

ASSESSMENT GUIDE

When assessing a country's or program's capacity to investigate medicine use, two main issues should be considered—

- Results of previous studies
- Technical capacity to undertake medicine-use investigations

Previous studies

- Have any studies been performed on facility medicine use using the WHO/DAP manual *How to Investigate Drug Use in Health Facilities*? If yes, what were the results?
- Have any special studies been undertaken to investigate specific medicine-use problems (such as injection use)? If yes, what were the results?
- Have any routine surveys such as census or household surveys included questions on pharmaceutical expenditures or use?

- Are pharmaceutical consumption data easily available for the public or private sector?
- What are the prevalent attitudes that will have a positive or negative effect on the use of health services and medicines?

Technical capacity

- Are any experienced researchers involved in studying medicine use or health-seeking behaviors?
- Can local experts assist in quantitative or qualitative surveys?
- Is a unit within the ministry of health dedicated to health systems research?
- Do the medical or pharmacy training schools undertake field research or offer student training in the field?
- What types of records are available in the public and private sectors that would facilitate research on medicine use?

| Part I: Policy and economic issues | Part II: Pharmaceutical management | Part III: Management support systems |

Selection
Procurement
Distribution
Use
   27 Managing for rational medicine use
   28 Investigating medicine use
   29 Promoting rational prescribing
   30 Ensuring good dispensing practices
   31 Community-based participation and initiatives
   32 Drug seller initiatives
   33 Encouraging appropriate medicine use by consumers
   34 Medicine and therapeutics information
   35 Pharmacovigilance

CHAPTER 29

Promoting rational prescribing

SUMMARY

The ultimate goals of studying and intervening in medicine use practices include—

- Improving quality of health care through effective and safe use of pharmaceuticals
- Improving cost-effectiveness of health care through economic and efficient use of pharmaceuticals

Before attempting an intervention to change medicine use practices, underlying reasons for problem behaviors must be understood. Interdisciplinary collaboration involving health and social science experts is of utmost importance in this task.

Strategies to improve rational prescribing can be characterized as targeted or system-oriented approaches. Targeted approaches include educational and managerial interventions, while system approaches include economic and regulatory interventions.

Educational strategies seek to inform or persuade and include—

- Training of prescribers (formal and continuing education, supervisory visits, group lectures, seminars, workshops)
- Printed materials (clinical literature and newsletters, treatment guidelines, medicine formularies, flyers, leaflets)
- Approaches based on face-to-face contact (educational outreach, patient education, influencing opinion leaders)

Managerial strategies seek to guide practice and include—

- Supervision, monitoring, and feedback
- Approaches to selection, procurement, and distribution (limited procurement lists, drug use review and feedback, hospital and regional drug and therapeutics committees, cost information)
- Prescribing and dispensing approaches (structured medication order forms, standard diagnostic and treatment guidelines, course-of-therapy packaging)

Economic strategies seek to promote positive financial incentives while removing perverse incentives for prescribers. These economic strategies include changes in how health care providers are reimbursed; disallowing medicine sales by prescribers removes the financial incentive for overprescribing.

Regulatory strategies seek to use laws and regulations to influence prescribing through restrictions and requirements. They include—

- Pharmaceutical registration
- Limited medicine lists
- Prescribing restrictions
- Dispensing restrictions

An intervention should be focused on a specific problem behavior and targeted at the facilities or people that have the greatest need for improvement. Interventions should be carefully selected with regard to efficacy, feasibility for implementation in the existing system, and cost. Before wide-scale implementation of an intervention, evaluating its effectiveness and cost in the existing health setting is imperative.

Programs to ensure rational use of medicines should be an integral part of health and medical care services. The responsibility for promoting rational use of medicines belongs to decision makers, administrators, and clinicians as well as health care professionals, consumers, educators, and pharmaceutical companies.

29.1   Improving prescribing: a conceptual framework

Inappropriate prescribing is a manifestation of irrational medicine use that occurs when medicines are not prescribed in accordance with guidelines based on scientific evidence to ensure safe, effective, and economic use. The underlying reasons for such practices on the part of prescribers and consumers need to be understood and addressed in any intervention.

Qualitative methods of research are useful in understanding why inappropriate prescribing behaviors occur (see Chapter 28). This approach makes it possible to design interventions relevant to a particular situation that form part of a systematic cycle directed at improving the quality of patient care. Most strategies for improving prescribing practices are mutually supportive.

The first step in developing a strategy to address irrational prescribing practices must be to consider who the prescribers are. In most developed countries, prescribers are doctors or other paramedical personnel who are highly trained. In many places, however, prescribers may include nurses, paramedics, and drug sellers. The latter, in particular, may have received little or no training in the use of medicines. A comprehensive policy should try to influence prescribing behavior at all levels of the system, focusing on the priority problems and targeting the prescribers involved. Box 29-1 has a list of core strategies to promote the rational use of medicines.

Box 29-1
Core strategies to promote rational use of medicines

Establishing a mandated multidisciplinary national body to coordinate medicine-use policies. Ensuring rational medicine use requires many activities that need coordination among many stakeholders. Therefore, a national body is necessary to coordinate strategies and policy at the national level, in both the public and private sectors. This body should involve government, health professions, academia, pharmaceutical industry, consumer groups, and the national regulatory authority.

Implementing procedures for developing, using, and revising standard treatment guidelines (STGs). Standard treatment guidelines (or clinical guidelines or prescribing policies) are systematically developed statements to help prescribers make decisions about appropriate treatments for specific clinical conditions. STGs are made more credible through the use of evidence-based recommendations. They vary in complexity from simple algorithms to detailed protocols on diagnostic criteria, patient advice, and costs.

Implementing procedures for developing and revising an essential medicines list (or hospital formulary) based on treatments of choice. An essential medicines list makes pharmaceutical management easier at all levels: procurement, storage, and distribution are easier with fewer items, and prescribing and dispensing are easier for professionals. A national essential medicines list should be based on national STGs, and both should be revised regularly.

Establishing a drug and therapeutics committee in districts and hospitals, with defined responsibilities for monitoring and promoting rational use of medicines. This committee, also called a pharmacy and therapeutics committee, is responsible for ensuring the safe and effective use of medicines in the facility or area under its jurisdiction. The committee should operate independently, and members should represent all the major medical specialties and the administration. The primary tasks of the committee are to develop and revise institutional STGs (based on national guidelines) and to maintain an institutional essential medicines list or formulary.

Using problem-based training in pharmacotherapy based on national STGs in undergraduate curricula. The quality of basic pharmacotherapy training for undergraduate medical and paramedical students can significantly influence future prescribing habits. Training is most successful when it is problem based, concentrates on common conditions, takes into account students' level of knowledge, and is targeted to their future prescribing requirements. In most settings, rather than focusing on basic science, problem-solving skills should be promoted and interdisciplinary problem-based learning encouraged. If the existing focus is not on problem-based training in pharmacotherapeutics, national consultative workshops may help build awareness of the value of the approach.

Continuing in-service medical education as a licensure requirement and targeted educational programs by professional societies, universities, and the government. Unlike in developed countries, opportunities for continuing medical education in less developed countries are limited because continuing education is not required for licensure. Governments should support efforts by university departments and national professional associations to offer independent, unbiased continuing medical education courses to health professionals, including medicine dispensers. The most effective in-service training is likely to be problem based, repeated on multiple occasions, focused on practical skills, and linked to STGs.

Developing a strategic approach to improve prescribing in the private sector through regulation and collaborations with professional associations. Most efforts in improving use of medicines have focused on the public sector, but the private sector often provides greater access to pharmaceuticals. Changing practices in the private sector requires an understanding of the motivations of private prescribers. A range of strategies should be considered to improve rational medicine use, including licensing regulations with appropriate enforcement, accreditation and continuing education through professional associations, and financial incentives.

Monitoring, supervision, and using group processes to promote rational medicine use. Supervision that is supportive, educational, and face-to-face will be more effective with prescribers than inspection and punishment. Effective forms of supervision include prescription audit and feedback, peer review, and group processes of self-identifying medicine-use problems and solutions in a group of prescribing professionals. Group process interventions with practitioners and patients to improve prescribing practices have been effectively used to change prescribing behavior.

Training pharmacists and drug sellers to offer useful advice to consumers, and supplying independent medicine information. In many countries with shortages of

---

trained health professionals, pharmacies and medicine shops are a major source of information for consumers. Interventions have shown that the skills of untrained prescribers and dispensers can be upgraded. In addition, the only information about medicines that prescribers receive is from the pharmaceutical industry, which may be biased. Pharmaceutical information centers and drug bulletins are two useful ways to disseminate independent, unbiased information. They may be administered by the government, a university teaching hospital, or a nongovernmental organization, under the supervision of a health professional.

Encouraging involvement of consumer organizations, and devoting government resources to public education about medicines. Governments have a responsibility to ensure the quality of information about medicines available to consumers. Without sufficient knowledge about the risks and benefits of medicine use, people will often fail to achieve their expected clinical outcomes and may even suffer adverse effects. Regulation of consumer advertising and promotion by pharmaceutical companies, as well as public education activities led by

consumer organizations, may influence medicine use by the public.

Avoiding perverse financial incentives. Financial incentives may strongly promote rational or irrational use of medicines. Examples include the ability of prescribers to earn money from medicine sales; flat prescription fees that lead to overprescription; and dispensing fees that are calculated as a percentage of the cost of medicines, which encourages the sale of expensive medicines.

Ensuring sufficient government expenditure and enforced regulation. Appropriate regulation of the activities of all those involved in the use of medicines is critical to ensure rational medicine use. For regulations to be effective, they must be enforced, and the regulatory authority must be sufficiently funded and backed by the government's judiciary. Without sufficient competent personnel and finances, none of the core components of a national program to promote rational use of medicines can be carried out.

Sources: WHO/EDM 2002; Laing et al. 2001.

The next step in improving prescribing practices is to identify the nature and scope of the problem. As described in Chapter 28, this step may be accomplished by using a number of methods, such as carrying out an indicator-based prescription survey or a drug use review (DUR); looking at aggregate medicine consumption data using such tools as ABC and VEN (vital, essential, nonessential) analysis or therapeutic classification; measuring defined daily dose (DDD) consumption; collecting adverse drug reaction (ADR) data; measuring infection rates; analyzing pharmaceutical management data; or observing a particular practice or event.

If the investigation confirms that the prescribing practices are a significant problem in the health system or facility, the underlying causes should be clearly defined in step three. This process is also described in Chapter 28.

The fourth step is to plan a package of interventions focused on specific problems and targeting specific actors: prescriber, patient, and community. Inputs from the target audience are important when formulating and implementing the package of interventions, because different sets of interventions may be applied to address inappropriate prescribing practices and prevent them from recurring. Each set of interventions must be monitored and evaluated to assess its impact. Evaluation of impact needs to be directed at the

specific prescribing pattern or prescribing behavior that the intervention is designed to improve. Clearly ineffective interventions can be dropped, and those that are partially effective can be revised to improve their efficacy. Effective interventions can then be incorporated and, if required, replicated on a wider scale in the health care system; therefore, producing timely monitoring data on the impact of the interventions is key. The complete cycle of medicine-use interventions is described in Chapter 28, and the required actions for each step are depicted in Figure 28-1.

29.2 Characterizing interventions

Interventions to improve prescribing in clinical practice can be characterized as either targeted directly toward the prescriber, such as education and managerial or administrative tactics, or system-directed, which emphasize policies, regulation, and economic strategies.

Targeted interventions

In *educational* interventions, prescribers are persuaded, by information or knowledge provided to them. These strategies may be implemented in the form of face-to-face

Figure 29-1   Facility-specific percentage of patients receiving antibiotics in Tanzania

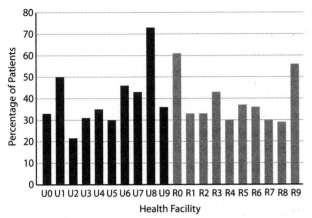

Source: WHO/DAP 1993.

education or training, seminars, and provision of written materials. A single-shot educational intervention without follow-up and monitoring is usually least effective, and the effect—if any—is not sustainable.

In *managerial* interventions, prescribers are guided in the decision-making process, through limiting lists for routine procurements, drug use review and feedback, supervision and monitoring, provision of treatment guidelines, and monitoring of prescribers' use of the guidelines.

System-oriented interventions

In *economic* interventions, prescribers are motivated by the promotion of positive financial incentives and the removal of perverse incentives. These economic strategies include changes in how health care providers are reimbursed, such as the institution of private or public patient-centered insurance plans, capitation-based reimbursement, and quality-based performance contracts. In addition, disallowing medicine sales by prescribers removes the financial incentive for overprescribing.

In *regulatory* interventions, prescribers are forced to restrict the decision-making process in prescribing. These strategies include policies encouraging use of generic pharmaceutical products, limitations on prescribing and dispensing, and withdrawal of questionable medicines from the market. These strong strategies are often unpopular with prescribers or consumers and may also bring about unintended effects, such as a change to other inappropriate prescribing practices.

A wide range of interventions is available to address irrational prescribing. These can be categorized as preventive or curative. Preventive approaches ensure that the prescriber starts off prescribing in an appropriate manner. Curative interventions attempt to reverse a pattern of irra-

tional prescribing. As is often true in medicine, prevention is often much easier than curing when it comes to prescribing problems.

Many interventions have a limited effect over time, and although temporary improvement may occur, prescribers may revert to their previous behavior if the intervention is not followed up. When interventions of different types are combined, the effect is likely to be synergistically increased; therefore, interventions should always be considered in sets.

Irrational prescribing is a universal problem. Considerable experience indicates which interventions are effective in high-income countries and in particular public health care systems, but those interventions cannot always be transferred to other settings. Therefore, it is important that a range of interventions be considered. Those that succeed in one country may not succeed elsewhere. Health care organizations, local communication channels, level of education, and other factors all influence the effectiveness of specific strategies in different environments.

29.3 Focus and target of interventions

For an intervention to be effective, it needs to be focused to achieve a specific goal and targeted at those prescribers who have a particular prescribing problem. For example, in a training intervention, a general lecture on pharmacology is unlikely to be effective in changing prescribing. A clearly focused presentation on the correct treatment of simple diarrhea—encouraging oral rehydration solution and discouraging antidiarrheals, antibiotics, and injections—or on the treatment of acute respiratory infections, and clearly specifying when an antibiotic is necessary is far more likely to achieve the desired results.

Quantitative surveys frequently find considerable variation among facilities. For example, a survey in Tanzania found that antibiotic use varied between 20 and 70 percent (Figure 29-1). Most facilities fell within the range of 20 to 40 percent. Only three facilities showed over 50 percent antibiotic use, and seven had over 40 percent use. These high-users would be the facilities to be targeted for any intervention. Both the potential impact and the cost-effectiveness of the intervention would be greater in these facilities.

29.4 Educational interventions

Educational interventions are the most common and are often disappointing in their sustainability and limited effect. Although the basic training of prescribers is essential for promoting rational use of medicines, educational components often need to be combined with managerial and regulatory interventions. Prescribers make many decisions concerning medicine use, and their training occurs in formal and informal ways throughout their careers. See Chapter 52 for discussion of various types of training programs.

Training of prescribers

Formal education (preservice). The training of doctors and paramedical staff differs in content and approach. Doctors control the use of scarce pharmaceutical resources not only through their own prescribing practices but also through their influence as instructors, supervisors, and trendsetters for the often larger force of paramedics. Thus, sound training of doctors in good prescribing practices can have a significant effect on the rational use of medicines.

The curricula of most health personnel training institutions contain segments that deal with medicine treatment. Because prescribing is often not taught in these curricula, students often learn prescribing from what they see during clinical "model" practices. For doctors and paramedical personnel, training on pharmaceuticals and how to use them should cover—

Basic pharmacology: Principal mechanisms of pharmaceutical action, metabolism, absorption, distribution, and elimination. In learning basic pharmacology, students gain knowledge about interactions between medicines and living systems at the theoretical level.

Clinical pharmacology: Study of the various classes of medicines with regard to clinical efficacy, risks, clinical pharmacokinetics, drug-drug interactions, drug-disease interactions, drug-genetics interactions, the concept of clinical trials, and pharmacoeconomics. In clinical pharmacology training, students learn how to use medicines properly and rationally at a more practical level.

Therapeutics: The use of pharmaceuticals to treat disease. Therapeutics is the practical application of basic and clinical pharmacology. It has traditionally received less attention than pharmacology in prescribers' formal education.

A number of educational programs have been developed to improve the teaching of pharmacotherapy. The World Health Organization (WHO) developed a manual (WHO/DAP 1994) for undergraduate medical students on the principles of rational prescribing, intended for use in developed and developing countries. The *Teacher's Guide to Good Prescribing* (Hogerzeil 2001) is its companion volume for university teachers. The *Guide to Good Prescribing* presents students with a normative model for pharmacotherapeutic reasoning. First, the students are taught to generate a standard pharmacotherapeutic approach to common disorders, resulting in a set of first-choice medicines, called "P[ersonal]-drugs." In the course of developing their P-drugs, the students are taught to consult existing national and international treatment guidelines, national formularies, pharmacology textbooks, and any other source of medicine information. Then they are shown how to apply this set of P-drugs to specific patient problems using a six-step problem-solving routine: (1) define the patient problem; (2) specify the therapeutic objective; (3) verify the suitability of your P-drug; (4) write a prescription; (5) inform and instruct the patient; and (6) monitor and/or stop the treatment.

The rationale behind this approach is that at some time in the course of their studies or early in their careers, medical students develop a set of medications that they will use regularly from then on. However, this choice is often made on irrational grounds, such as the prescribing behavior of their clinical teachers or peers, without really considering the alternatives or knowing how to choose among them. The manual not only helps students select P-drugs in a rational way but also teaches them to consult, understand, and use existing treatment guidelines in an intelligent way. For example, it teaches the students how to verify, for each individual patient, whether their P-drug is the most appropriate choice in this individual case and, if necessary, how to adapt the medicine, dosage form, dosage schedule, or duration of treatment. The training has been field-tested and evaluated in a number of medical schools, with a proven effect on the students (Country Study 29-1).

In addition to the safety and efficacy of a medicine, other important considerations for students include the use of generic names and attention to cost; supply logistics; and the effects of transportation, storage, and medicine quality on the availability and stability of medicines.

Experience shows that students usually learn about prescribing from their clinical tutors. The value of medical faculty trained in clinical pharmacology should not be underestimated. However, the task of incorporating and implementing the teaching of rational medicine use into the curricula is not solely the responsibility of clinical pharmacologists. It should become the concern and responsibility of staff from various disciplines involved in training, particularly clinicians.

In addition to giving increased attention to clinical pharmacology, medical faculties should increase their students' awareness of the importance of pursuing medicine information throughout their clinical training and practice. As part of their training in clinical pharmacology and therapeutics in Yogyakarta, Indonesia, medical students learn to critically assess medicine information and advertisements as well as reports of clinical trials published in a local medical journal. This training has proved helpful in improving their knowledge, skills, and critical attitudes.

In the public sector, paramedical personnel are commonly the first point of contact for patients in most rural areas and in some health facilities in urban areas. Improper use of medicines by these health workers can be dangerous and wasteful, whereas prompt and appropriate use of

Country Study 29-1
Impact of a short interactive training course in pharmacotherapy

The impact of a short interactive training course in pharmacotherapy, using the *Guide to Good Prescribing*, was measured in a controlled study with 217 under-graduate medical students in Groningen, Netherlands; Kathmandu, Nepal; Lagos, Nigeria; Newcastle, Australia; New Delhi, India; San Francisco, United States; and Yogyakarta, Indonesia. The course was composed of four half-day small group seminars combined with meetings after hours and group work. Students were taught how to develop their own P-lists of drugs for common conditions and how to choose drugs from their P-lists. In addition, they were taught how to write prescriptions and how to educate their patients.

The impact of the training course was measured by three tests, each containing both open and structured questions on the medicine treatment of pain, using patient examples. Tests were taken before the training, immediately after, and six months later.

After the course, students from the study group performed significantly better in all patient problems presented than the control students, who had received "normal" teaching. This finding applied to all old and new patient problems in the tests and to all six steps of the problem-solving routine. The students not only remembered how to solve a previously discussed patient problem (retention effect) but also could apply that knowledge to other patient problems (transfer effect). At all seven universities, both retention and transfer effects were maintained for at least six months after the training session. Students in the course were able to choose appropriate medicines to use, write correct prescriptions, and better counsel patients.

Source: WHO/DAP 1994.

medicines can save lives and prevent patients from becoming more debilitated. Paramedics and nurses in a number of developing countries are not legally allowed to prescribe. In reality, however, they see and prescribe for the majority of patients arriving at health centers. Where this practice is technically illegal, developing formal continuing education for paramedics can be difficult.

Many countries find that limiting the medicines paramedics can prescribe to a specific list and providing a pocket medicine reference manual and standard treatment guideline based on that list can be a useful tool (see Chapter 17). Medical workers are encouraged to use the manual rather than depend on recall for selecting medicines and medicine dosages for all but the most frequently treated conditions. Figure 29-2 illustrates the content and format of a standard treatment guideline used in Ghana. These workers do, however, need to be taught to diagnose so that they can use the appropriate treatment guidelines. Formal training in pharmacology and therapeutics provides a sound basis for paramedics to prescribe standard medicines and to understand the uses of new products that are added to their medicine lists.

In the private sector, prescribers, especially in resource-limited countries, may not be trained health practitioners at all, but instead employees or owners of informal medicine outlets where prescribing and dispensing may occur at the same time. Although countries may regulate the prescribing and dispensing practices or the level of education required in such outlets, clerks still do not often have knowledge or

training in the rational use of medicines (Rutta et al. 2009). This group is challenging to address through traditional interventions, although they are increasingly being recognized as playing probably the major role in medicine usage in resource-poor settings.

Continuing education (in-service). After their formal training is completed, prescribers develop their own prescribing practices, which are then influenced by whatever medicine information and commercial pressure they receive, the diagnostic facilities available to them, the expectations of the community, and medicine availability. Continuing education provides an opportunity for prescribers to keep informed on changes in the use of medicines.

In some areas, local associations of physicians or auxiliary medical workers have identified their need for continued training in therapeutics and have participated in seminars and other medical meetings designed to keep them up-to-date with current medicine information. Government health programs sometimes sponsor presentations for health personnel. In many countries, however, continuing education is not available for most prescribers, including those in teaching hospitals. Even when it does occur, it is often dominated by promotional messages from pharmaceutical companies that sponsor the events and are necessarily biased in favor of their products. Most prescribers are not trained to evaluate such information critically and tend to accept whatever they are told. They must also deal with the enticement of gifts and incentives proffered by pharmaceutical company representatives.

Figure 29-2   Excerpt from a Ghanaian standard treatment guidelines manual

Meningitis

Pharmacological Treatment (Evidence rating: A)

ADULTS:

Antibiotic treatment should be given for a total of 14 days. All treatment should be intravenous initially for a minimum of 7 days and should be started without delay. This may be subsequently changed to oral therapy with significant clinical improvement.

Benzylpenicillin, IV, 4 MU 4 hourly (subsequently amoxicilline, oral, 500 mg 8 hourly for remainder of treatment course)

PLUS

Chloramphenicol, IV, 1 g 6 hourly (subsequently chloramphenicol, oral, 500 mg 6 hourly for remainder of treatment course)

Alternatively, for all types of bacterial meningitis, ceftriaxone may be administered.

Ceftriaxone, IV, 2–4 g daily for 7 days (subsequently amoxicilline, oral, 500 mg 8 hourly for remainder of treatment course)

CHILDREN:

All treatment should be intravenous for a minimum of 10 days in children, and should be started without delay.

Benzylpenicillin, IV, 0.2 MU/kg body weight 6 hourly

PLUS

Chloramphenicol, IV, 25 mg/kg body weight 6 hourly

Alternatively, for all types of bacterial meningitis, ceftriaxone may be administered.

Ceftriaxone, IV, 50–60 mg/kg body weight once daily for 7 days

If cerebral spinal meningitis is suspected give benzylpenicillin, IV:

ADULTS: 4 MU 4 hourly for 14 days

CHILDREN: 0.2 MU/kg body weight 6 hourly for 14 days

PLUS Chloramphenicol, IV:

ADULTS: 1 g 6 hourly for 14 days

CHILDREN: 25 mg/kg body weight 6 hourly for 14 days

Prophylaxis for cerebrospinal meningitis

Prophylactic treatment is recommended for patients 2 days prior to discharge and also for their close contacts.

Ciprofloxacin, oral:

ADULTS: 500 mg as a single dose *(avoid in pregnancy)*

CHILDREN: 5–12 years: 250 mg as a single dose

OR

Ceftriaxone, IM:

ADULTS: 250 mg as a single dose

CHILDREN: > 12 years: 125 mg as a single dose

Source: Ministry of Health, Ghana National Drugs Programme, 2004.

Like their physician counterparts, paramedical staff members tend to become more routine in their prescribing habits after they have been practicing for several years, which may lead to illogical prescribing. Regular teaching and monitoring by senior paramedical staff members or medical officers, with attention to the medical workers' prescribing habits, are essential.

Rational prescribing among paramedical staff can be promoted by—

- Requiring them to keep a brief listing of patients seen and diagnoses made
- Devising and making available a limited list of specific medicines with which paramedics must be familiar
- Ensuring regular monitoring and supervision, with frequent on-site refresher training

Supervisory visits. Personal supervision and case reviews are often difficult or impossible to perform. Therefore, in many programs, if paramedical staff keep a list of patients seen, with diagnoses and treatments prescribed, their prescribing habits can be quickly reviewed, and suggestions for improved medicine therapy can be made. In-service refresher courses and discussion of cases by paramedical personnel can be organized locally, using the health center as a base and the visiting doctor as educator. In this way, supervision can be educational and supportive, not punitive.

Group lectures, seminars, and workshops. Lectures, seminars, or workshops given to a relatively large number of people are the most widely practiced activities for continuing education. They may be effective in improving prescribers' knowledge but are likely to be ineffective in changing prescribing behavior. When such seminars are focused on specific prescribing behavior, however, improvements can occur.

Printed materials

Printed materials carrying new information that is immediately relevant to the prescriber may help bring about a change in prescriber behavior. In general, however, printed materials may increase prescriber knowledge but rarely affect actual performance when used alone.

Printed materials are most useful when they are used in combination with other intervention strategies, especially those that involve active interaction between the party providing and the party receiving the information.

Clinical literature and newsletters. Many prescribers claim that they obtain information about therapeutics from medical journals. Unfortunately, many journals report research results that may not be directly applicable to daily practice. In addition, journals may overwhelm the prescriber with more information than can be digested, making it difficult to decide about the best prescribing choices.

Medical newsletters, such as the *Medical Letter* (www.medicalletter.com) or the *Drug and Therapeutics Bulletin* (www.dtb.org.uk), focus on a limited number of topics and provide summarized information in a form that is more immediately useful to the prescriber. Such information often compares and contrasts clinical choices and costs and provides recommendations about "optimal" treatments.

Treatment guidelines and medicine formularies. In many countries where an essential medicines list has been developed, treatment norms or guidelines have also been published (see Chapter 17). Such manuals are relatively inexpensive to produce and have several advantages over material from the pharmaceutical industry and sources from outside the country. They are not biased by commercial interest; include only those preparations available in the country; recommend doses that are appropriate for the local population; and provide special warnings that are relevant to local genetic, environmental, and epidemiological factors.

Consulting physicians and medical school faculty may oppose the preparation and distribution of reference manuals, fearing that they will lead to "cookbook" medicine. This fear seems to be largely unfounded, and physicians in the most prestigious medical schools in developed and developing countries are writing, using, and promoting such handbooks.

Illustrated materials (flyers, posters, and leaflets). Commercial pharmaceutical companies frequently use short, colorful, attractively printed materials to convey promotional messages. These materials usually contain only one or two ideas that are repeated in different ways, using text, drawings, tables, and charts. This type of material is often used in conjunction with face-to-face educational outreach or focused meetings.

Approaches based on face-to-face contact

The most effective means of changing behavior has consistently been face-to-face contact. The pharmaceutical industry uses this method through its representatives because it works!

Educational outreach. One method found to be effective in improving prescribing practices after completion of training is targeted outreach education to individuals or small groups of prescribers. The efficacy of this approach has been demonstrated by the marketing done by pharmaceutical companies, whose salespeople promote their products on a one-to-one basis to carefully targeted prescribers.

In this method, principles of communications theory and behavioral science are combined with conventional educational techniques to provide information to physicians or other prescribers about medicines that are often used inappropriately and to promote their replacement with more therapeutic alternatives. Trained educators or opinion leaders can provide this contact, and it can be incorporated into the existing supervision system of health care services.

Principles of educational outreach include—

- Focusing on specific problems and targeting the audience of prescribers
- Addressing the underlying causes of the prescribing problems: misleading beliefs, poor knowledge, false perceptions
- Allowing an interactive discussion and involving the targeted audience
- Using concise and authoritative materials based on credible scientific information
- Giving sufficient attention to solving practical problems encountered by prescribers in real settings

The face-to-face approach can be successful, especially when combined with other interventions. A review of thirteen studies on the prescribing practices of health professionals found that a personal visit by a trained person to a health care provider in his or her own setting resulted in positive prescribing practice changes in every case (Thomson et al. 2000). In all instances, the face-to-face interventions consisted of several components, including written materials and feedback sessions. Face-to-face approaches have worked with non–health care professionals also. In Kenya, a vendor-to-vendor outreach program had success in improving malaria knowledge, changing prescribing practices in private medicine shops and kiosks (Tavrow et al. 2003). This outreach program also included giving dispensers job aids to help them remember the appropriate medicines and dosages to recommend.

Patient education. Patient or consumer education plays an important role in promoting rational use of medicines. Inappropriate prescribing patterns may derive from the demands or misconceptions of patients, although such demands are often exaggerated by prescribers to justify their prescribing habits.

One way to educate patients about the rational use of medicines is through individual communication during the contact between prescriber and patient. This communication often cannot take place, however, because of time constraints and a heavy patient load. In health facilities in developing countries, the average patient contact time is often only one to three minutes—too short for effective communication. Another reason may be the prescriber's unwillingness to communicate with patients, or a lack of skill or interest in doing so. Prescribers are often not adequately trained in patient communication or are not sensitive to its importance.

Consumer education is carried out in many countries through mass campaigns by radio, television, or pamphlets and other printed materials (see Chapter 33).

Influencing opinion leaders

The attempt to train students in good prescribing practices can be frustrated by the environment in which they learn. For example, if a physician refers to medicines by their brand names during clinical training, the students will copy this practice and any other poor prescribing habits the physician may exhibit. Young doctors who have to prescribe according to the wishes of their senior colleagues can also pick up poor prescribing habits. One way of dealing with this situation is to identify the opinion leaders who influence the prescribing patterns of students and doctors in the establishment. Improving the prescribing practices of those leaders will indirectly influence the practices of the younger doctors and students.

29.5 Managerial interventions

Managerial interventions frequently require considerable effort to initiate and maintain. However, they can produce a sustained effect with small risk of adverse or unexpected consequences.

Monitoring, supervision, and feedback

Monitoring and supervision that are educational, conducted in person, and supportive—not punitive—will be more effective and better accepted by prescribers. Effective methods of supervision include prescription audit and feedback. Prescribers may be told how their prescribing compares with accepted guidelines or with that of their peers.

> **Box 29-2**
> **Responsibilities of a drug and therapeutics committee related to rational prescribing**
>
> - Developing, adapting, or adopting clinical guidelines for the health institution or district
> - Selecting cost-effective and safe medicines (for example, hospital or district medicine formulary)
> - Implementing and evaluating strategies to improve medicine use (for example, medicine-use evaluation, liaison with antibiotic and infection-control committees)
> - Providing ongoing staff education and training
> - Controlling access to staff by the pharmaceutical industry and its promotional activities
>
> Source: WHO/EDM 2002.

Involving peers in audits and feedback is particularly effective. Group processes include health professionals identifying a rational use issue and developing, implementing, and evaluating a strategy to correct the problem. This approach is used in the monitoring-training-planning methodology described in Chapter 52. Additional data can be used in behavior monitoring, such as facility-specific postoperative infection rates, morbidity rates, or, where available, local antimicrobial resistance rates.

Differences exist in carrying out monitoring and supervision activities in the public and private pharmaceutical sectors. Drug and therapeutics committees (DTCs) in health facilities and district health teams can serve as a feedback mechanism for rational medicine use in places like hospitals. In fact, governments may encourage hospitals to have DTCs by making it an accreditation requirement (see Box 29-2 for a list of DTC responsibilities).

Monitoring and supervision of prescription habits in the private sector, such as in retail medicine outlets, is difficult. Developing a method for monitoring, prescribing, and dispensing in such outlets remains a priority. The primary method is the use of simulated clients posing as patients with illnesses of public health importance (Madden et al. 1997).

Frequently, a formal inspection mechanism is legally mandated, but prescribing habits are rarely included in that inspection, and even then, resource limitations and a lack of good record keeping in private-sector operations make enforcing such inspection mandates difficult. Innovative public-private partnerships that use franchising and accreditation to improve services in private medicines outlets require rational medicine-use monitoring as part of the business model (see Chapter 32).

Selection, procurement, and distribution

Medicine use can be influenced by aspects of pharmaceutical management such as selection, procurement, and distribution. When the people responsible for these activities are consulted and informed, they are likely to cooperate in supporting rational prescribing.

Limited procurement list. The most common managerial intervention is selecting a limited list of medicines that will be routinely purchased. Other medicines may be made available, but require special approval (see Chapters 16 and 18). Managing a hospital formulary is therefore one of the key tasks of a DTC (see Chapters 16 and 17).

Drug use review and feedback. Drug use review is a tool to identify problems in the medication use process: medication prescribing, dispensing, administration, and monitoring. As problems are identified, strategies are developed and implemented to improve the use of medicines. If actions are successful, the result will be improved patient care and more efficient use of resources.

The approach to developing a program varies, but nine steps are important to follow—

Step 1: Establish responsibility for the DUR process. The DTC (or its equivalent) usually takes responsibility for the DUR program.

Step 2: Establish the scope for each study. A DUR focuses on the areas that show the most potential for improvement. A DUR may study one medication (such as ranitidine), a therapeutic class (H2 antagonists), or a particular age group or diagnosis (patients older than sixty-five years of age with duodenal ulcers). DUR might focus on one step in the medication-use process, such as prescribing, or include other aspects, such as pharmaceutical product labeling or medicine administration. Pharmacists, nurses, and physicians are a major source of suggestions for focusing DUR studies. Formal mechanisms for identifying problem areas include ADR reporting, medication error reporting, or ABC and VEN analysis (see Chapter 40). DUR usually focuses on medicines or therapies that are high use, high cost, high risk, or problem prone. Table 29-1 is a decision matrix

for selecting DUR studies to undertake. The higher the score, the more likely that this problem should be studied.

Step 3: Establish criteria or indicators, including benchmarks or thresholds. Criteria usually include the following components—

Uses: appropriate indications, treatment of underlying conditions, appropriate treatment of symptoms in treating underlying diseases
Selection: efficacy (comparative), safety, cost (total), duplicative therapy
Dosing: indication-specific dosing (age, diagnosis), indication-specific duration, dosing intervals
Interactions: disease, food, medicine, laboratory
Preparation and dispensing: labeling, dispensing time, stockouts, correct medicine, correct dose, correct dosage form
Administration: patient identification, handwashing, administration technique, documentation (correct patient, medicine, time, dose, and route)
Monitoring: clinical, laboratory
Outcome: therapeutic, safety

Thresholds or benchmarks are established for each indicator to define the expectations or goals for complying with the criteria.

Step 4: Collect and organize data. Data collection forms can be developed based on the criteria and configured into simple yes-or-no or fill-in-the-blank questions (see Figure 29-3). Depending on the complexity of interpretation required, the data collectors may or may not need a medical background. Pharmacists, nurses, or medical records personnel usually carry out data collection for hospital-based DUR studies. In hospitals where computers are used, the data collection may simply require printing a report from the computer databases.

The most common data sources are patient charts. Other sources are dispensing records, medication administration records, and laboratory reports. Focusing on specific indications related to the problem is important; avoid collecting too much data. A cumulative report should

Table 29-1   Selection matrix for drug use review*

Medication/health problem	High use	High cost	High risk	Problem prone	Total score
Paracetamol	1	0	0	0	1
Acute respiratory infections	2	0	1	1	4
Ceftriaxone	1	2	0	0.5	3.5
Warfarin	0.5	0	1	2	3.5
H2 antagonists	1	1	0	1	3
Surgical antimicrobial prophylaxis	1	1.5	0.5	1	4

* Each medicine or health problem is rated 0–2 on the basis of the use, risk, cost, and probability of problems. The highest total scores may be targeted for the DUR.

Figure 29-3   Sample form used in drug use review

Date:	Drug: ANTIBIOTIC USE IN SURGICAL PROPHYLAXIS		Data collector's initials:				
	Patient Chart No.						
	Diagnosis						
	Age/Sex/Weight						
	Date Treated						
CRITERIA AND INDICATORS	**Threshold**	**Observed**					
Justification for medicine being prescribed:			Yes No	Yes No	Yes No	Yes No	Yes No
1. Class of surgery: clean contaminated, dirty contaminated, ruptured, or gangrenous	100%						
2. Antibiotic on approved list for surgical prophylaxis	100%						
Process Indicators:			Yes No	Yes No	Yes No	Yes No	Yes No
3. Dose given only one time, and not more than 45 min. before incision	100%						
4. Antibiotic administered if surgery is prolonged, 4 or more hours later	100%						
5. Postoperative doses specified for no more than 24 hours	100%						
6. Antibiotic change recommended due to: (a) adverse reaction (b) decreased renal function (c) interaction (d) cost-effectiveness increased (e) documented infection	100%						
7. Nosocomial infection is documented prior to non-surgical prophylaxis use of antibiotic	100%						
Outcome Indicators: None*							

Source: Moore et al. 1997.

* In this case, the DUR focused on adherence to standard treatment guidelines. Outcome indicators that could be measured include postoperative infection rates or adverse drug reactions.

include data from at least thirty patients or at least 5 percent of the expected volume (whichever is greater).

Step 5: Analyze data. The data need to be tabulated and reported in a standard format for comparison with benchmarks.

Step 6: Develop conclusions. The DTC reviews the results of the data analysis and develops conclusions regarding reasons for differences between results and benchmarks.

Step 7: Make recommendations. The DTC recommends actions required to improve knowledge or change behavior. The committee may recommend a more focused study or a focus group to understand the issues more clearly.

Step 8: Take action. Implementation of recommendations must be part of every DUR.

Step 9: Follow up. Did the intervention achieve its objectives? Whenever an intervention is undertaken, a follow-up evaluation should assess the impact of actions taken and determine whether further action is required. Such action may include refining the criteria and thresholds or reanalyzing the causes of deficiencies and developing a new action plan.

Country Study 29-2 is an example of a DUR in a community hospital in the United States. Country Study 29-3 includes an example of a DUR in Kenya. The Kenya example is a variation of the methodology in Country Study 29-2 and a more appropriate application for that environment.

A self-monitoring program on medication use at health centers, based on the drug use indicators of WHO/International Network for Rational Use of Drugs, has been designed and implemented in a district day-to-day health management system in Gunungkidul district, Indonesia (Figure 29-4). With this program, prescribing indicators at the health centers are collected monthly. Prescribing data, based on these indicators, from different health centers are compared by the district health office and then fed back to the prescribers. The evaluation shows that such monitoring and feedback significantly improved prescribing patterns,

Figure 29-4 Changes in antibiotic and injection use with a self-monitoring program in Indonesia

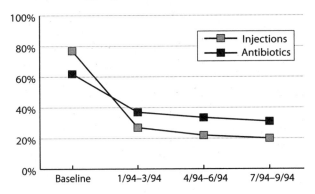

Source: Gunungkidul District Health Office, Yogyakarta, Indonesia.

Figure 29-5 Comparative daily cost of injectable and oral antibiotics in the eastern Caribbean

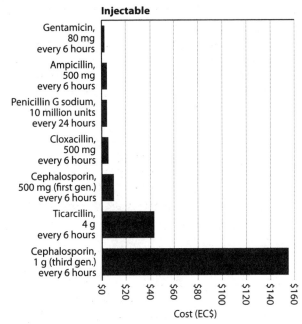

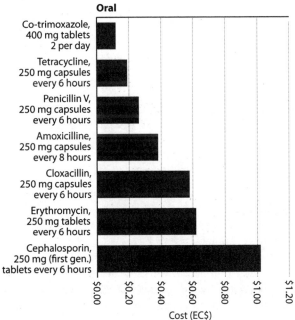

Source: Organisation of Eastern Caribbean States, Eastern Caribbean Drug Service 1993.

reducing polypharmacy and the use of antibiotics and injectable preparations. The average number of medications per prescription decreased from 4.2 to 3.1, and antibiotic and injection use also declined dramatically. The drug use indicators (WHO/DAP 1993) can themselves be used at the local level for self-audit and feedback.

Hospital and regional drug and therapeutics committees

Drug and therapeutics committees play an important role in improving prescribing practices at the national and regional levels, as well as at the district and institutional levels. Their role has expanded in some settings from selecting medicines for formularies to—

- Reviewing medication requisitions and revising them to fit budget allocations
- Determining which medicines should be made available to each type of health facility (if this determination is not made at the national level)
- Developing standard treatment norms for the common illnesses treated in the area or institution
- Establishing prescribing limitations aimed at controlling irrational medicine use (for example, limiting certain antibiotics to use only under the recommendation of a consultant)
- Limiting the amount dispensed at one time to curb abuse of particular medicines and reduce waste
- Reviewing antibiotic resistance patterns and revising guidelines for antibiotic use
- Stimulating medicine education activities among hospital staff
- Supervising and monitoring rational prescribing and safe medication-dispensing practices
- Developing and supervising an adverse drug event reporting system

Cost information

Medication cost is an underappreciated aspect of prescribing. Expensive, newer medicines are frequently used when comparable well-established and cheaper ones are available for the same condition. Several different mechanisms have been used to encourage physicians and paramedical staff to consider cost in their medicine selections. These include

Country Study 29-2
Drug use review at a U.S. hospital

At a small community hospital on the West Coast of the United States, the Pharmacy and Therapeutics (P&T) Committee is responsible for a DUR program that evaluates four to six medicines or medicine therapies per year. One December, the committee received a report from the quality assurance coordinator noting that the rate of postoperative infections for abdominal surgeries was significantly higher than the national average. The pharmacy director informed the committee of his observation that cefoxitin was often used for these patients, a costly and inappropriate choice. The committee decided to undertake a DUR for antibiotic prophylaxis in abdominal surgery wound infection.

The health problem met all indications for a DUR: high use, high cost, high risk, and problem prone. The chief of surgery was a member of the P&T committee. He concurred with the committee that the criteria should be developed from recently published recommendations in the *Medical Letter,* which included medicine selection, dosing, and timing of administration. The accompanying table is a summary of the DUR study. It illustrates the benchmark targets for each indicator; the actual percentage of compliance based on quarterly data collection; and the conclusions, recommendations, actions, and follow-up.

Abdominal surgery wound infection antibiotic prophylaxis

Collection period: January–December the following year

Total number of cases: 162

Date of report: January, 13 months after the initial letter

Number of cases reviewed: 120 (74%)

Criterion	Benchmark (%)	Indicator: % Compliance per quarter			
		1st	2nd	3rd	4th
1. Antibiotic selection (per *Medical Letter*)	100	70	85	94	100
2. Correct dose (per *Medical Letter*)	95	65	90	94	97
3. Preoperative dose 0–2 hours before surgery	95	30	52	89	94
4. Postoperative dose only for dirty surgery	98	78	89	82	91
5. No postoperative infection	96	90	93	96	100
6. No adverse reactions to medicines	97	97	100	87	97

Conclusions

Criterion 1. Surgeons are selecting antibiotics that are not considered the medicine of choice for the indicated procedure.

Criterion 2. Surgeons are prescribing unnecessarily high doses of antibiotics.

Criterion 3. Preoperative doses are delayed: current procedure is for pharmacy to send medicine to operating room rather than preoperative area. Turnaround time for dispensing from pharmacy often delays medicine administration.

Criterion 4. Surgeons order postoperative antibiotics for patients who do not meet criteria for dirty surgery.

Criterion 5. High rate of postoperative infections may improve with compliance with criteria.

Recommendations

1. Send letter to all surgeons with the following information—
   - Current postoperative infection rate versus national average
   - Criteria and recommendations from the *Medical Letter*
   - Results of the DUR data collection
   - Estimated cost impact of inappropriate medicine selection and unnecessary medicine use
2. Remove cefoxitin from formulary because of its disadvantages of short half-life and relative cost of therapy as compared with cefotetan.
3. Change procedures to administer preoperative doses in the preoperative area rather than the operating room. Instruct in-service nursing and pharmacy staff on new procedures.
4. Add approved antibiotics to floor stock in preoperative area for emergencies.

Actions

1. The chief of surgery informed the surgery committee about the DUR and the criteria in February of the implementation year.
2. A letter was sent to all surgeons in April.
3. Cefoxitin was removed from the formulary.

4. New procedures for administration were adopted in June, and in-service training of staff members began in July.

5. Antibiotics were added to preoperative floor stock in July.

Follow-up

Criterion 1. Met benchmark in fourth quarter. The education of surgeons contributed to an improvement in antibiotic selection.

Criterion 2. Met benchmark in fourth quarter. The education of surgeons contributed to an improvement in antibiotic dosing.

Criterion 3. Changes in procedures, floor stock, and in-service training of staff improved the timing of preoperative antibiotics but still not meeting benchmark. Benchmark is unrealistically high because of multitude of contributing factors for emergency procedures. Lower the benchmark to 93 percent.

Criterion 4. Education decreased unnecessary postoperative antibiotic prescribing for a short time, then surgeons began to return to old practices. P&T committee sent individual letters to specific surgeons, and the practice improved in the last quarter of the year, but it was still not meeting benchmark. Report cases of noncompliance to surgery committee for peer review and recommendations.

Criterion 5. Postoperative infection rate gradually improved throughout the year, meeting and exceeding the benchmark.

Criterion 6. Allergic reactions increased in the third quarter because of the change in floor stock procedures and preoperative nurse failure to screen for patient allergies. Previously, the pharmacy screened for allergies prior to dispensing. Nurses received in-service training for allergy screening, and the allergic reaction decreased in the last quarter, meeting benchmark.

using cost bar graphs, preparing facility pharmaceutical budgets, and printing prices in pharmaceutical manuals and on requisition forms.

Cost bar graphs. In many countries, diagrams or charts showing side-by-side comparisons of prices for alternative medicines have been circulated (for examples, see Figure 29-5). The intention is not to mandate that practitioners always choose the least expensive medicine but rather to encourage them to take cost into consideration.

Facility pharmaceutical budgets. In health programs that receive budgetary funds for pharmaceutical procurement, specific pharmaceutical budgets may be allocated to individual districts, hospital areas, or health centers. When annual estimates of pharmaceutical needs are made, or when regular requisitions for medicines are prepared, the expected acquisition cost of the medicines is compared with available funds. If reductions in medicine requests are necessary—and they usually are—the medical practitioners at the hospital or health center can participate in making the choices. This strategy puts the decision making closest to the point of medicine use. In some settings, this level of involvement by practitioners has helped create a cost consciousness that makes even their daily prescribing more cost-effective.

Printing prices in pharmaceutical manuals and on requisition forms. Even when practitioners are not required to make their medicine use conform to a specific budget, cost consciousness can be promoted by including recent pharmaceutical prices in therapeutics manuals, medicine lists, and other forms used in prescribing or requisitioning medicines. Alone, this measure may accomplish little, but in combination with some of the other measures described,

it may be quite helpful. Again, physicians and paramedical staff need not be required to pick the least expensive medicine in all cases, but the price list may encourage them to make inexpensive choices.

Prescribing and dispensing approaches

Managers can guide the prescribing and dispensing process by intervening at crucial points of the process.

Structured pharmaceutical order forms. For medicines that are frequently prescribed in hospitals, such as antibiotics, standard forms can be devised to optimize correct medicine use. The prescriber is provided with a medication order sheet containing a preprinted list of preferred medicines and dosage regimens for key medicines. Such forms have increased the cost-effectiveness of prescribing for hospital inpatients in the United States. For example, the form for antibiotics would specify correct standard dosages and an antibiotic review after seventy-two hours.

Standard diagnostic and treatment guidelines. Specific guidelines can be abstracted from formulary and therapeutics manuals (see Chapter 17). Guidelines for common conditions, such as postoperative pain, hypertension, diabetes, and various forms of cancer, can be agreed upon by the staff. Patients are treated in a standard manner according to the protocols. This approach has many benefits. Garnering agreement to follow the institutional guidelines may be time-consuming, but the active involvement of prescribers in this process can lead to significant changes in clinical practice. These guidelines can also be used as the basis of DUR and procurement lists.

Country Study 29-3
Antibiotic use review in Kenya

Antibiotics represent one of the most widely pre-scribed forms of medicine therapy. In some cases, the antibiotics prescribed may be inappropriate or too expensive. To ensure that antibiotics are prescribed appropriately and rationally, pharmacists have to review antibiotic usage periodically. The aim of antibiotic use review (AUR) is to determine the pattern (rates, appro-priateness, and costs) of antibiotic usage in a particular setting. The results of an AUR program are often com-municated to those concerned individually, through a memorandum, or through a general bulletin showing the norm and peer comparisons. The starting point of an AUR program is the formation of criteria by the drug and therapeutics committee (DTC). Prescriptions are checked for appropriateness of dosage, therapeutic indication, duration of treatment, and so on, according to the criteria. Deviant cases are recorded. AUR studies can be set up such that various clinicians, wards, and facilities can be compared.

The steps for performing an AUR are—

1. Select the subjects of the program.
2. Draft criteria and standards that define acceptable quality of care for subjects selected in step 1.
3. Obtain endorsement of the criteria and standards from the DTC.
4. Evaluate the quality of services in question using the criteria and standards.
5. Identify deficiencies in quality (if any).
6. Analyze the causes of deficiencies.
7. Formulate a plan for eliminating deficiencies.
8. Implement the plan.
9. Reevaluate the quality of services, as in step 4.
10. If usage is not acceptable, reanalyze the causes of defi-ciencies and devise a new plan for their elimination.

The worksheet for an AUR for amoxicilline is shown in the accompanying table, which considers ten patients from one prescriber in Kenya.

Review Criteria from DTC	Patients									
	1	2	3	4	5	6	7	8	9	10
Indications[a]	Tonsillitis	Otitis media	Urethritis	Bowel sterilization	Severe gram-negative meningitis	Boils/abscess	Severe cystitis	Surgical prophylaxis	Pneumonia	Severe wound infection
Appropriate indication?	Yes	Yes	Yes	No	No	Yes	Yes	Yes	Yes	Yes
Amoxicilline dosage[b]	250 mg tds	250 mg tds	250 mg tds	1,500 mg bd	500 mg tds	250 mg tds	500 mg tds	250 mg tds	250 mg tds	500 mg tds
Duration (usually 5 days)	5 days	7 days	7 days	1 day	10 days	7 days	5 days	5 days	5 days	7 days
Cost per capsule (KES)	30	30	30	30	30	30	30	30	30	30
Total cost[c]	470	650	650	380	1,800	650	920	470	470	1,280

[a] Acceptable indications are upper or lower respiratory tract infections; genitourinary tract infections; septicemia; surgical prophylaxis; skin and soft tissue infection; osteomyelitis; and peritonitis.

[b] Acceptable dosage is usually 250 mg tds. Dosage may be doubled in severe cases.

[c] Total cost for usual dosage for 5 days = 470 Kenya shillings (KES). This amount includes dispensing fee of KES 20.

Calculations

1. Calculate the frequency of inappropriate prescrib-ing—

$$2/10 \times 100 = 20\%$$

2. Total costs caused by inappropriate prescribing—
$$380 + 1,800 = KES\ 2,180\ (a\ loss)$$

Note: Only pharmaceutical costs are considered; medicines prescribed inappropriately are viewed as a waste.

Summary and comments

1. For patient #4: bowel sterilization would require a long-acting sulfonamide or neomycin tablets.

2. For patient #5: for severe gram-negative meningitis, patient would need a cephalosporin.

Source: Ministry of Health, Government of Kenya 1994.

Course-of-therapy packaging. Course-of-therapy (COT) packaging, often in the form of blister packs, has been widely used for oral contraceptives and, more recently, for tuberculosis therapy. Although such packaging adds to the cost of medicines, gains are experienced in convenience for both the dispenser and the patient. Comparative prices should be obtained before switching completely to COT; in many markets, the average difference between bulk and COT packaging is 10 percent or more. Prepacks (described in Chapter 30) are a form of COT packaging.

Country Study 29-4 shows how different sets of targeted interventions, including educational and managerial approaches, were used to improve rational medicine use among prescribers in four different countries.

29.6 Economic interventions

Financial incentives—both positive and negative—may strongly affect rational or irrational medicine use; for example, setting prices and changing the way fees are collected can result in different prescribing behaviors.

Price setting and fees

The price charged for pharmaceuticals can be used to encourage more rational use of them. For example, in cost-recovery programs, vital medicines (see Chapter 40) can be sold at prices below their real costs, and nonessential medicines can be sold at prices above their real costs. This cross-subsidization can encourage the use of vital effective medicines while discouraging the sale of nonessential, less effective medicines. Charging for a course of therapy rather than for each individual treatment (injection, tablet) encourages the patient to complete the prescribed therapy. Generic medicines are usually cheaper than their brand-name counterparts, making their use rational from a cost standpoint. Pricing incentives such as preferential markup on generics and reference pricing can be used to encourage generic substitution. (See Chapter 9 for more information on pricing policies.)

Flat prescription fees that cover all medicines within one prescription result in overprescribing; therefore, user charges should be made per medicine, not per prescription. Country Study 29-5 shows how prescription fee systems affected prescribing behavior in Nepal. Also, dispensing fees that are calculated as a percentage of the cost of the medicines promote the sale of more expensive medicines. A flat dispensing fee, not tied to the cost of the medication, is preferable.

Insurance

The concept of insurance is assuming a greater role in resource-limited countries. Insurance systems can be pro-

vided through the government (social health insurance), through private sources (for example, employers), and through community prepaid schemes. Not all insurance systems include pharmaceuticals in their list of benefits, but when they do, certain controls on payment, prescribing, and use can affect the rational use of medicines.

Capitation-based reimbursement

When a payment to health care providers is made by a third party, pharmaceutical costs are better controlled with a fixed per capita payment as compared to a per visit or per medicine reimbursement. But caution is needed to ensure that needed medicines are not underprescribed.

Medicine sales by prescribers

If the health worker receives the profit on medicine sales, as occurs in Japan and in some Bamako Initiative projects, there is an inducement to overprescribe and to prescribe more expensive medications. Although prescribers may deny this effect, the findings are consistent across cultures and countries: prescribers who benefit from medicine sales prescribe more than those who do not.

29.7 Regulatory approaches

Regulatory approaches aim to enforce decisions that are intended to improve prescribing. These methods are frequently used but sometimes have unintended or unexpected outcomes, which may result in extra costs or adverse patient consequences. Such effects have been noted in the United States (Country Study 29-6) with the use of a limit on the number of monthly prescriptions patients could receive. That study, however, does not rule out the use of carefully structured caps.

Although most countries have some sort of drug regulatory authority and legal requirements for registering medicines, a lack of resources can deplete their effectiveness. WHO estimates that fewer than one in six member states have well-developed pharmaceutical regulation and two in six have no or little pharmaceutical regulatory capacity (WHO 2004).

Pharmaceutical registration

Most countries have pharmaceutical regulations that limit pharmaceutical sales to registered pharmaceutical products. In countries where pharmaceutical registration is enforced, it limits the types and numbers of medicines available for prescribing. An effective registration process helps keep dangerous and ineffective medicines off the market. The requirements for registering new drug substances are

Country Study 29-4
Assessing the effect of targeted approaches in improving prescribing

Indonesia. Inappropriate prescribing at primary health centers (PHCs) has been a major public health concern in Indonesia. A study found that more than 90 percent of patients with acute respiratory infection (ARI) visiting health centers received antibiotics. Also, more than 85 percent of adult patients with muscle ache (myalgia) reportedly received unnecessary injections. An intervention featured interactive, systematic, problem-based training of physicians and paramedical personnel in 122 PHCs, which were compared with a control group of forty PHCs.

The intervention consisted of three sets of training modules: medication error, evidence-based medicine, and rational use of medicines, followed by self-monitoring, supervision, and feedback by a training team. The training evaluation on prescribing patterns was conducted six, twelve, and eighteen months following the intervention.

The use of antibiotics for ARI in the intervention group decreased significantly, from 92.3 percent before the intervention to 71 percent, 50 percent, and 30 percent, six, twelve, and eighteen months after the study (p < 0.05). No significant improvement was found in the control group. A significant decrease in antibiotic prescribing was also found in the treatment of diarrhea in the intervention group, from 90.3 percent before the study to 53 percent, 40 percent, and 26 percent, six, twelve, and eighteen months after the study (p < 0.05). No significant improvement was detected in the control group. Interactive, systematic problem-based training on rational use of medicines, followed by self-monitoring, supervision, and feedback, significantly improved prescribing patterns and resulted in significant cost savings.

Kenya. The Mission for Essential Drugs and Supplies (MEDS) conducts institutional training interventions in mission hospitals. These interventions consist of three phases: a baseline survey using the International

Network for the Rational Use of Drugs indicators, training, and a follow-up evaluation one year later. Some hospitals then complement the training with their own in-house continous medical education (CME) programs. A retrospective before/after study of three mission hospitals in Kenya with a comparison group assessed the effect of combining training with a CME program. A prescription review in each hospital looked at four prescribing indicators, including the percentage of cases prescribed antibiotics and injections. All three hospitals went through the MEDS training program, with one hospital instituting a regular, in-house CME program organized by the drug and therapeutics committtee.

The postintervention results showed that in one hospital, three of four indicators showed improvement, and one of four indicators deteriorated. In the second hospital, one of four indicators showed improvement, one of four did not change, and two of four deteriorated. In the third hospital, which had the CME program, all four indicators showed dramatic improvement, especially concerning antibiotic and injection use. Study researchers concluded that training by external facilitators had mixed success in improving prescribing habits, but a complementary CME program made for a much more successful educational intervention.

Lao P.D.R. In the Lao People's Democratic Republic (P.D.R.), standard treatment guidelines were introduced to all prescribers at provincial hospitals, but they were insufficient in improving treatment practices in malaria, diarrhea, and pneumonia. To evaluate the effects of an educational intervention, a randomized controlled trial was conducted in eight provincial hospitals, matched into four pairs. The hospital drug and therapeutics committees carried out the six-month intervention, which consisted of monthly audit sessions and feedback on treatment indicator scores.

---

stringent in some countries. In others, however, the facilities for assessing new products are not readily available, and monitoring and enforcement are unreliable.

Limited medicine lists

Limited medicine lists can be a managerial intervention, as described earlier, or a regulatory intervention, in which case certain medicines are completely banned. Limited medicine lists (formularies) have been used since the early

1970s to control costs and promote rational use in public- and private-sector pharmaceutical programs. In Tanzania, for example, *duka la dawa baridi* (private medicine shops) are legally restricted from selling most prescription medicines, although lax enforcement and a lack of alternatives mean that most do sell restricted products. In some cases, governments have gone further, banning certain medicines or pharmaceutical classes from both public and private markets. Limited medicine lists are the main mechanism to prevent the use of dangerous, ineffective, and

From the baseline assessment to six months postintervention, the total mean indicator score for all three diseases increased significantly more in the intervention group than in the control group. The individual scores for malaria and diarrhea also increased significantly more in the intervention group, but for pneumonia, the improvement was the same in both groups. Specific improvements in record keeping and rational prescribing were seen for all three diseases. Audit-feedback systems to improve quality of care can be feasible and effective in hospital settings in low-income countries.

Mexico. Most continuing medical education activities for primary care physicians in Mexico have not improved the quality of care provided, and physicians' practices are not always in accordance with updated clinical evidence. The Mexican Institute of Social Security conducted a nonrandomized prospective controlled study to evaluate the impact of a multifaceted educational intervention to improve case management in 175 primary care physicians divided into a study and control group. The study intervention consisted of three components over seven months: developing clinical guidelines; training clinical tutors; and a three-stage intervention including interactive workshops, individual tutorials, and roundtable peer-review sessions.

In the intervention group, improvement in medication prescribing was considerable: for acute respiratory infection, 32.7 percent of physicians improved their prescribing for antibiotics; for hypertension, 29.0 percent improved their antihypertension prescribing; and for type 2 diabetes, 25.2 percent improved their prescribing for hypoglycemic medicines or insulin. For all three, the changes were statistically significant (p < 0.01). No significant changes occurred in the control group.

Sources: Mexico: Reyes et al. 2004; Kenya: Kiambuthi 2004; Indonesia: Dwiprahasto and Kristin 2004; Lao P.D.R.: Kounnavong et al. 2004.

Country Study 29-5
Using an economic strategy to improve prescribing practices in Nepal

A study including looking at practices pre- and postintervention compared with a control group was conducted in thirty-three health facilities in three districts in eastern Nepal. At the baseline, all three districts charged the same flat fee per prescription, covering all medicines, in any amount. Later, two districts instituted new fee systems, while the third kept the same fee structure. One district started charging a single fee per medicine item (using a one-band item fee), no matter what the medicine was, and covered a full course of the medicine. The second district charged a higher fee per expensive item (for example, antibiotics and injections) and a lower fee per inexpensive item (for example, vitamins) (using a two-band item fee) and covered a full course of the medicine. All the fees for two drug products equaled about 25 percent of the average daily household income. Prescribing was monitored in all health facilities before and after the changes.

The table that follows shows that both types of item fee were associated with significantly better prescribing quality than the prescription fee. The percentage of patients receiving antibiotics decreased, and the proportion of prescriptions conforming to standard treatment guidelines increased in both districts using item fees, compared with the control district. The one-band fee was associated with a reduction in prescribing of cheap vitamins and tonics, and the two-band fee with a reduction in prescribing of expensive injections.

Source: Holloway and Gautam 2000.

Effects of user fees on prescribing quality in Nepal

Fee system	Control flat fee/prescription n=12		One-band fee/medicine item n=10		Two-band fee/medicine item n=11	
Average number of items/prescription	2.9 → 2.9	(0%)	2.9 → 2.0	(−31%)	2.8 → 2.2	(−21%)
Percentage of prescriptions with antibiotics	66.7 → 67.5	(+0.8%)	63.5 → 54.8	(−8.7%)	60.7 → 54.3	(−6.4%)
Percentage of prescriptions with injections	23.4 → 20.0	(−3.4%)	19.8 → 16.1	(−3.7%)	21.8 → 14.9	(−6.9%)
Percentage of prescriptions with vitamins or tonics	27.0 → 22.1	(−4.9%)	26.5 → 8.4	(−18.1%)	23.5 → 15.8	(−7.8%)
Percentage of prescriptions conforming to STGs	23.5 → 26.3	(+2.8%)	31.5 → 45.0	(+13.5%)	31.2 → 47.7	(+16.5%)
Average cost/prescription (NPR)	24.3 → 33.0	(+35.8%)	27.7 → 28.0	(+1.1%)	25.6 → 24.0	(−6.3%)

NPR = Nepalese rupee.

Country Study 29-6
Unintended effects of medicine restrictions

In the United States, poor patients' health care costs are covered by the Medicaid program. This program is administered by the states in different ways.

In 1992, New Hampshire decided to limit Medicaid outpatients to three medicines per month; another state, New Jersey, chose not to place limits. Researchers studied the medicine-use patterns and hospital and nursing home admissions for patients who had been taking more than three medicines per month.

As expected, the number of medicines per patient decreased by 35 percent, but the dosages of the medicines prescribed increased. The unexpected outcome was a 120 percent increase in nursing home admissions and a 20 percent increase in hospital admissions.

After eleven months, the three-medicine limit was withdrawn and replaced with a USD 1 co-payment scheme. Admission rates and medication levels returned to the levels that existed before the medicine limit. In general, the patients who were admitted to nursing homes were not discharged.

In retrospect, the behavior of the physicians who admitted their patients to nursing homes was quite rational.

No medicine limits applied for inpatients, and patients could continue to receive their medications by entering nursing homes. Thus, Medicaid saved a little on medicine costs, but the cost of extra admissions outweighed these savings.

The monthly proportion of patients in nursing homes is shown in the accompanying graph.

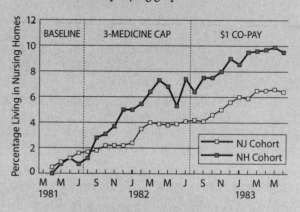

Source: Adapted from Soumerai et al. 1991.

---

unnecessarily expensive medicines. However, the danger exists that when safe but relatively ineffective medicines (such as kaolin for diarrhea) are withdrawn from the list, they may be replaced by effective medicines (metronidazole, for example) used inappropriately. This occurred in one country when antidiarrheals were banned. Metronidazole use increased from 10 percent to 65 percent in cases of watery diarrhea.

Prescribing restrictions

In theory, after a pharmaceutical is registered, it can be prescribed by all medically qualified prescribers. Health authorities often restrict paramedical staff to a limited number of medicines on the national essential medicines list. Those limitations are imposed to reduce wasteful prescribing and inappropriate use of expensive medicines. At the health facility level, the use of expensive or powerful medicines may be limited to the more experienced prescribers. In some hospitals, the use of third-generation cephalosporins is restricted to specialist prescribers. Prescriptions by junior staff members have to be countersigned by the specialist. In some settings, the junior prescriber can prescribe such medicines only for twenty-four- to forty-eight-hour

use; any extension requires the authorization of the specialist. Prescribing limitations may take the form of pharmaceutical registration, limited medicine lists (essential medicines lists), medicine formularies, or prescribing and dispensing privileges by level of use (facility level and competence level of prescriber). Another possible restriction is to limit the number of medicines prescribed to two or three per patient. However, this restriction is easily evaded by issuing two separate prescriptions.

Dispensing limitations

Limiting the amount of medicines to be dispensed has been applied in some countries to control wasteful or potentially dangerous dispensing. Examples of this approach follow.

- One Asian country established a system of three- and five-day limits for all outpatient prescriptions, except those for chronic diseases. Most antibiotics are given for five days, and all other medicines for acute illnesses are limited to three-day courses.
- In South America, one large rural health program established a system of prepackaging medicines in unit-of-use plastic bags containing the minimum

amount of drug product needed for one course of therapy.

- The government-supplied university hospital in one Southeast Asian country put dispensing limits on items that may be abused, tend to be prescribed indiscriminately, or are potentially dangerous. Maximum dispensing quantities have been established for codeine, diazepam, vitamin C tablets, and vitamin B complex, among others.

Such limitations can have adverse effects on the treatment of some diseases. For example, antibiotic treatment for typhoid typically requires more than five days. Patients with chronic diseases such as epilepsy or diabetes are forced to visit health centers frequently and may end up missing treatments. Therefore, when setting restrictions on duration of therapy or dispensing quantities, exceptions must be built in to cover chronic diseases and exceptional cases.

29.8 Developing an intervention strategy

When a problem has been identified and quantified and its causes have been determined, a set of interventions needs to be selected. A wide range of possible interventions has been indicated in Sections 29.4, 29.5, and 29.6.

Selecting an intervention

The first step in selecting a set of interventions is to clearly define the problem to be solved. The behaviors specific to the particular health problem, as well as factors causing variability in performance, need to be identified. Assessing the beliefs and motivations of the prescribers that may contribute to the observed behavior is also important. These assessments will require further studies involving qualitative investigational methods. When the problem has been defined, a package of interventions can be considered.

Cost-effectiveness has to be considered in the selection process. The implementation of the selected interventions needs to be carefully designed. The use of a control group enhances the detection of differences. Key outcomes must be defined beforehand. An evaluation of the impact versus the cost of the intervention is also necessary. The outcome of the intervention must be fed back to the participants to reinforce the changes that have occurred.

The selection of an appropriate set of interventions should consider its—

Likely effectiveness: What intervention is most likely to be effective in addressing the specific medicine use problems and their underlying causes? Do any previous stud-

ies or documented experiences exist about this specific intervention?

Feasibility: Is the intervention feasible to implement, taking into account the existing health care system and the available personnel?

Cost: What is the cost of the intervention? Can it be borne by the available resources?

Potential effect: If the intervention is effective, what effect will it have, and what will be its magnitude? Can beneficial effects outweigh the cost and possible adverse effects?

Unintended effects: What are the possible adverse effects of the intervention?

The framework for formative and intervention studies is described in Figure 29-6. The selected interventions need to be monitored carefully during implementation.

Combining interventions

Interventions can be combined. This approach was taken in Mexico, where the treatment of diarrhea was unsatisfactory. The first intervention was an educational workshop, which improved prescribing from 24.5 to 51.2 percent compliance with a treatment norm. This intervention was

Figure 29-6   Framework for formative and intervention studies

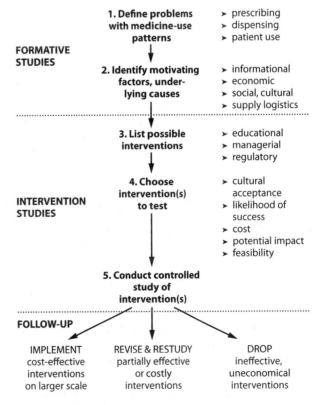

Source: Quick et al. 1991.

Figure 29-7 Combined intervention strategy: Prescribing for acute diarrhea in Mexico City

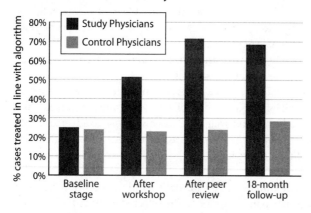

Source: Gutierrez et al. 1994.

followed by a managerial intervention—peer review—that further improved prescribing to 71.6 percent compliance with the same norm. Only minor changes occurred in the control group (see Figure 29-7). After eighteen months, the improvement had been maintained.

Combining different types of interventions is usually more effective. A mixture of large-group education and small-group education, combined with audit and feedback, is more likely to produce sustained changes than is a repetition of the same intervention. Innovative approaches include an online, blended learning program that focuses on clinicians' beliefs about their prescribing habits, feedback on their prescribing backed with their own patients' data on antimicrobial resistance, and an introduction to how to work with patients to reduce unnecessary antibiotic prescribing (Simpson et al. 2009).

In general, regulatory interventions should be carefully structured, and active surveillance is essential to detect unexpected or unintended effects. Many countries do not have the capacity to monitor or enforce regulations, limiting the effectiveness of regulatory approaches.

Social marketing of interventions

Implementing interventions without taking into account the level of understanding and acceptance of the prescribers or consumers carries the risk of failure or unintended effects; therefore, involving key stakeholders in the intervention design and implementation is critical. For instance, a policy of prescribing generic medicines is in place in public health facilities in many countries. When prescribers are not well informed about the advantages of generics, they may not comply with generic prescribing, and they may transfer their negative perceptions to their patients, which, in turn, further jeopardizes the implementation of the policy (see Chapter 16). Withdrawing popular medicines from

the market without giving proper information to the public can create confusion and anxiety for consumers, especially for routine users of the medicines. Whenever regulatory or managerial action is taken, informational and educational approaches need to be incorporated for prescribers as well as consumers.

Evaluating the effect of an intervention

Evaluation of whether an intervention has caused the desired effect—that is, improvement in prescribing behavior in a cost-effective manner—is often neglected. An intervention strategy is often implemented without prior field-testing to prove that it works in the existing system and is effective in influencing prescribing practices. Many countries have implemented countrywide training programs without proper design and evaluation. In these cases, the waste of resources such as funds, time, and energy will only further increase the burden on health care services. Some health managers falsely assume that if any intervention program takes place, the desired goals have been accomplished. Yet the production and dissemination of treatment guidelines to health care facilities, for example, does not necessarily lead to prescribers' using the guidelines or improving their prescribing practices.

Evaluation of effects should be regarded as an important component of any intervention strategy, and ongoing production of timely data to steer the intervention design is invaluable. The following points should be considered in designing an evaluation approach—

- An evaluation plan should be devised when planning an intervention. Before implementing a program on a wide scale, field-testing is imperative to find out whether the evaluation can be implemented feasibly in the existing health care setting and whether it is effective in influencing prescribing practices.
- Evaluation of the impact of an intervention program should focus primarily on the indicators targeted by the intervention messages. Secondary indicators can also be selected, as appropriate. Depending on the objectives and scope of the intervention, evaluation may include relevant aspects, such as knowledge of the targets, changes in perception about a specific practice of interest, the process of care, and cost of prescribing.
- Apart from relevance, the selection of indicators for impact evaluation should take into account reliability and feasibility of collecting data from the existing system.
- The evaluation of any intervention should use appropriate design and methodology, with adequate sample size, sampling, and use of control groups or interrupted time series.

ASSESSMENT GUIDE

Indicators of prescribing quality

- Average number of medicines per encounter
- Percentage of medicines prescribed by generic name
- Percentage of encounters in which an antibiotic is prescribed
- Percentage of encounters in which an injection is prescribed
- Percentage of medicines prescribed from the essential medicines list or formulary
- Average consultation time
- Prescription in accordance with treatment guidelines
- Percentage of patients treated without medicines
- Percentage of patients satisfied with the care they received

Indicators of prescription costs

- Average cost per encounter
- Percentage of pharmaceutical costs spent on antibiotics
- Percentage of pharmaceutical costs spent on injections

Targeted approaches

Educational interventions

- Is there an official continuing education system on rational use of medicines for prescribers and dispensers?
- How many training sessions on medicine use were given for prescribers in the last year?
- What percentage of prescribers surveyed attended at least one training session in the last year?
- Of all the training sessions organized in the past three years, what percentage was related to medicine use?

- Is the concept of essential medicines part of the curricula in the basic training of health personnel?

Managerial interventions

- Is there a national therapeutic guide with standardized treatments?
- Do hospital drug and therapeutics committees exist? And if so, do they undertake drug use studies? What results are available?
- What kinds of managerial interventions have been tried? Were their effects evaluated?

Systems-oriented approaches

Economic interventions

- How are prices for pharmaceuticals set in the country? How do the prices compare to other countries' pharmaceutical prices?
- What are the prescription and dispensing fee systems in place? Are they flat fees or based on a percentage of the cost of the prescription?
- Are prescribers also allowed to sell medicines?
- Are there insurance or cost-sharing schemes? If so, who do they cover and what benefits do they provide?

Regulatory interventions

- At what levels of the system are limited medicine lists used?
- What other regulatory interventions have been used?
- What evaluations have been undertaken of the effect of regulatory changes?

Note: Chapter 28 contains additional indicators and measures for assessing prescribing and the effect of interventions to promote rational prescribing.

- Measuring the long-term sustainability of the effect of any intervention is always desirable. Changes in prescribing behavior and practice observed immediately after an intervention often return to their baseline levels after a longer period of time. Experience shows that changes in prescribing usually return to pre-intervention levels after six months unless the intervention messages are continued. The use of time series analysis may be particularly useful in showing effects over time.

Measurements of medicine use, including measurements of the effect of intervention strategies, are discussed in more detail in Chapter 28. ■

References and further readings

★ = Key readings.

Brugha, R., and A. Zwi. 1998. Improving the Quality of Private Sector Delivery of Public Health Services: Challenges and Strategies. *Health Policy and Planning* 13:107–20.

Chalker, J. 2001. Improving Antibiotic Prescribing in Hai Phong Province, Vietnam: The "Antibiotic Dose" Indicator. *Bulletin of the World Health Organization* 79(4):313–20.

Chalker, J., S. Ratanawijitrasin, N. T. K. Chuc, M. Petzold, and G. Tomson. 2005. Effectiveness of a Multi-Component Intervention on Dispensing Practices at Private Pharmacies in Vietnam and Thailand—A Randomized Controlled Trial. *Social Science and Medicine* 60(1):131–41.

Chuc, N. T., M. Larsson, N. T. Do, V. Diwan, G. Tomson, and T. Falkenberg. 2002. Improving Private Pharmacy Practice: A Multi-

Intervention Experiment in Hanoi, Vietnam. *Journal of Clinical Epidemiology* 55(11):1148–55.

Dwiprahasto, I., and E. Kristin. 2004. *A Prospective Pharmaco-epidemiologic Study to Prevent Medication Error and to Improve Prescribing Patterns.* Paper presented at International Conference on Improving the Use of Medicines, March 30–April 2, Chiang Mai, Thailand.

General Medical Council. 2008. *Good Practice in Prescribing Medicines.* London: General Medical Council. <http://www.gmc-uk.org/static/documents/content/Good_Practice_in_Prescribing_Medicines_0911.pdf>

★ Grimshaw, J. M., L. Shirran, R. Thomas, G. Mowatt, C. Fraser, L. Bero, R. Grilli, E. Harvey, A. Oxman, and M. A. O'Brien. 2001. Changing Provider Behavior: An Overview of Systematic Reviews of Interventions. *Medical Care* 39(8 Suppl. 2):2–45.

★ Grol, R., and J. Grimshaw. 2003. From Best Evidence to Best Practice: Effective Implementation of Change in Patients' Care. *The Lancet* 362(9391):1225–31.

★ Gross, P., and D. Pujat. 2001. Implementing Practice Guidelines for Appropriate Antimicrobial Usage: A Systematic Review. *Medical Care* 39(8 Suppl. 2):55–69.

Gutierrez, G., H. Guiscafré, M. Bronfman, J. Walsh, H. Martinez, and O. Muñoz. 1994. Changing Physician Prescribing Patterns: Evaluation of an Educational Strategy for Acute Diarrhea in Mexico City. *Medical Care* 32:436–46.

Hogerzeil, H. V., ed. 2001. *Teacher's Guide to Good Prescribing.* Geneva: World Health Organization. <http://whqlibdoc.who.int/hq/2001/WHO_EDM_PAR_2001.2.pdf>

Holloway, K. A., and B. R. Gautam. 2000. Nepal: An Economic Strategy to Improve Prescribing. *Essential Drugs Monitor* 28/29:14.

Kiambuthi, J. 2004. *The Impact of Continuous Medical Education on Prescribing Habits in Mission Hospitals in Kenya.* Paper presented at International Conference on Improving the Use of Medicines, March 30–April 2, Chiang Mai, Thailand.

Kounnavong, S., B. Sisounthone, tA. Phanyanouvong, T. Southammavong, B. Eriksson, G. Tomson, and R. Wahlström. 2004. *Effectiveness of Feedback for Improving Case Management of Malaria, Diarrhea, and Pneumonia: A Randomized Controlled Trial at a Provincial Hospital in Lao PDR.* Paper presented at International Conference on Improving the Use of Medicines, March 30–April 2, Chiang Mai, Thailand.

★ Laing, R., H. Hogerzeil, and D. Ross-Degnan. 2001. Ten Recommendations to Improve Use of Medicines in Developing Countries. *Health Policy and Planning* 16(1):13–20.

Madden, J. M., J. Quick, D. Ross-Degnan, and K. K. Kafle. 1997. Undercover Care-Seeking: Simulated Clients in the Study of Health Care Provider Behaviour in Developing Countries. *Social Science and Medicine* 45:1465–82.

Ministry of Health, Ghana National Drugs Programme. 2004. *Standard Treatment Guidelines.* Accra: Ministry of Health Ghana.

Ministry of Health, Government of Kenya. 1994. *Good Management of Hospital Drugs and Supplies Manual.* Nairobi.

Moore, T., A. Bykov, T. Savelli, and A. Zagorskiy. 1997. *Guidelines for Implementing Drug Utilization Review Programs in Hospitals.* Submitted to the U.S. Agency for International Development by the Rational Pharmaceutical Management Project. Arlington, Va.: Management Sciences for Health. <http://erc.msh.org/newpages/english/dmpmodule/drugutil.pdf>

Obua, C., J. W. Ogwal-Okeng, P. Waako, O. Aupont, and D. Ross-Degnan. 2004. Impact of an Educational Intervention to Improve Prescribing by Private Physicians in Uganda. *East African Medical Journal* (Suppl.):17–24.

★ Oxman, A. D., M. A. Thomson, D. A. Davis, and R. B. Haynes. 1995. No Magic Bullets: A Systematic Review of 102 Trials of Interventions to Improve Professional Practice. *Canadian Medical Association Journal* 153(10):1423–31.

★ Quick, J. D., R. O. Laing, and D. Ross-Degnan. 1991. Intervention Research to Promote Clinically Effective and Economically Efficient Use of Pharmaceuticals: The International Network for Rational Use of Drugs. *Journal of Clinical Epidemiology* 44(Suppl. 2):57–65.

Radyowijati, A., and H. Haak. 2003. Improving Antibiotic Use in Low-Income Countries: An Overview of Evidence on Determinants. *Social Science and Medicine* 57(4):733–44.

Reyes, H., R. Pérez-Cuevas, S. Flores, P. Tomé, J. A. Trejo, and F. Espino. 2004. *A Multifaceted Continuing Medical Education Intervention Improves Primary Care Physicians' Performance in Mexico.* Paper presented at International Conference on Improving the Use of Medicines, March 30–April 2, Chiang Mai, Thailand.

Ross-Degnan, D., S. B. Soumerai, P. K. Goel, J. Bates, J. Makhulo, N. Dondi, Sutoto, D. Adi, L. Ferraz-Tabor, and R. Hogan. 1996. The Impact of Face-to-Face Educational Outreach on Diarrhoea Treatment in Pharmacies. *Health Policy and Planning* 11:308–18.

Rutta, E., K. Senauer, K. Johnson, G. Adeya, R. Mbwasi, J. Liana, S. Kimatta, M. Sigonda, and E. Alphonce. 2009. Creating a New Class of Pharmaceutical Services Provider for Underserved Areas: The Tanzania Accredited Drug Dispensing Outlet Experience. *Progress in Community Health Partnerships* 3(2):145–53.

Shankar, P. R., S. Palaian, S. Gyawali, P. Mishra, and L. Mohan. 2007. Personal Drug Selection: Problem-Based Learning in Pharmacology: Experience from a Medical School in Nepal. *PLoS ONE* 2(6):e524.

Simpson, S. A., C. C. Butler, K. Hood, D. Cohen, F. Dunstan, M. R. Evans, S. Rollnick, L. Moore, M. Hare, M. J. Bekkers, J. Evans, and the STAR Study Team. 2009. Stemming the Tide of Antibiotic Resistance (STAR): A Protocol for a Trial of a Complex Intervention Addressing the 'Why' and 'How' of Appropriate Antibiotic Prescribing In General Practice. *BMC Family Practice* 10:20. <http://www.biomedcentral.com/1471-2296/10/20>

Soumerai, S. B., D. Ross-Degnan, J. Avorn, T. J. McLaughlin, and I. Choodnovskiy. 1991. Effects of Medicaid Drug-Payment Limits on Admission to Hospitals and Nursing Homes. *New England Journal of Medicine* 325:1072–7.

Stenson, B., L. Syhakhang, C. S. Lundborg, B. Eriksson, and G. Tomson. 2001. Private Pharmacy Practice and Regulation: A Randomized Trial in Lao P.D.R. *International Journal of Technology Assessment in Health Care* 17(4):579–89.

Tavrow, P., J. Shabahang, and S. Makama. 2003. Vendor-to-Vendor Education to Improve Malaria Treatment by Private Drug Outlets in Bungoma District, Kenya. *Malaria Journal* 2:10.

★ Thomson O'Brien, M. A., A. D. Oxman, D. A. Davis, R. B. Haynes, N. Freemantle, and E. L. Harvey. 2000. Educational Outreach Visits: Effects on Professional Practice and Health Care Outcomes. *Cochrane Database System Review* 2000(2).

WHO (World Health Organization). 2009. *Community-Based Surveillance of Antimicrobial Use and Resistance in Resource-Constrained Settings: Report on Five Pilot Projects.* Geneva: WHO.

———. 2004. *The World Medicines Situation.* Geneva: WHO.

———. 2003. *Introduction to Drug Utilization Research.* Geneva: WHO. <http://apps.who.int/medicinedocs/pdf/s4876e/s4876e.pdf>

★ WHO/DAP (World Health Organization/Action Programme on Essential Drugs). 1994. *Guide to Good Prescribing: A Practical Manual.* Geneva: WHO/DAP. <http://whqlibdoc.who.int/hq/1994/WHO_DAP_94.11.pdf>

★ ———. 1993. *How to Investigate Drug Use in Health Facilities: Selected Drug Use Indicators.* Geneva: WHO/DAP. <http://apps.who.int/medicinedocs/pdf/s2289e/s2289e.pdf>

WHO/EDM (World Health Organization/Essential Drugs and Medicines Policy). 2002. *Promoting Rational Use of Medicines: Core Components.* Geneva: WHO/EDM.

CHAPTER 30

Ensuring good dispensing practices

SUMMARY

Good dispensing practices ensure that an effective form of the correct medicine is delivered to the right patient, in the correct dosage and quantity, with clear instructions, and in a package that maintains the potency of the medicine. Dispensing includes all the activities that occur between the time the prescription is presented and the time the medicine or other prescribed items are issued to the patient.

A safe, clean, and organized working environment provides a basis for good practice. Dispensing must be performed accurately and should be done in an orderly manner, with disciplined use of effective procedures. Care should be taken to read labels accurately. The dispenser must count and measure carefully and guard against contamination of medicines by using clean equipment and never allowing skin contact with the medicines.

Staff members who dispense must be trained in the knowledge, skills, and practices necessary to dispense the range of medicines prescribed at the facility. Their performance should be regularly monitored.

Prepackaging medicines can improve efficiency in dispensing. Dispensing can also be improved by routine procedures for safety checking before issuing medicines to patients.

Cost factors inevitably lead to the use of packaging that is less than ideal. The packaging used must be the best compromise between cost and the risk of waste, with regard to maintaining standards of cleanliness.

Labeling is also affected by cost. Labels should contain information about the medicine and its correct use. The style and language of labeling should be appropriate to the needs of the patient.

Ensuring patients' understanding of how to take their medicines is a primary responsibility of dispensers. Dispensers should check understanding by asking each patient to repeat instructions.

Good records, though sometimes neglected, are an essential part of dispensing; they facilitate good management and monitoring of services provided.

30.1   Introduction

Dispensing refers to the process of preparing and giving medicine to a named person on the basis of a prescription. It involves the correct interpretation of the wishes of the prescriber and the accurate preparation and labeling of medicine for use by the patient. This process may take place in a public or private clinic, health center, hospital, or in a shop or community pharmacy setting. It is carried out by many different kinds of people with a variety of training and backgrounds. No matter where dispensing is done or who does it, any error or failure in the dispensing process can seriously affect the care of the patient.

Dispensing is one of the vital elements of the rational use of medicines. Programs to improve rational use have often been concentrated on ensuring rational prescribing habits, overlooking dispensing and the patient's use of medicines.

Dispensing is commonly assumed to be a simple, routine process that cannot go wrong. Yet all the resources involved in patient care prior to dispensing may be wasted if dispensing does not result in the named patient receiving an effective form of the correct drug, in appropriate packaging, and with the correct dose and advice.

This chapter considers the factors that influence the process of dispensing and therefore are important in ensuring "correctly dispensed" medicine.

30.2   Dispensing environment

Dispensing environments must be clean, because most medicinal products are for internal use, making it important that they be hygienic and uncontaminated. The environment must also be organized so that dispensing can be performed accurately and efficiently. The dispensing environment includes—

- Staff
- Physical surroundings
- Shelving and storage areas
- Surfaces used during work
- Equipment and packaging materials

Staff members involved in dispensing must maintain good personal hygiene and should wear a uniform or other clean clothing.

The physical surroundings must be kept as free of dust and dirt as possible. Although the dispensary must be accessible to patients, care should be taken to locate it in a protected place and not beside, or open to, a road or other area where dust, dirt, and pollution are commonly present. Ideally, the dispensary should be designed so that access to the dispensing area itself is restricted to authorized personnel only.

Figure 30-1   Illustration of a stock container label

```
                    Tablets

                  PARACETAMOL
                    500 mg


                Batch no. 9312101
            Date of Manufacture: 12/06
               Expiry Date: 11/09
```

Maintaining a clean environment requires a regular routine of cleaning shelves, daily cleaning of floors and working surfaces, and daily removal of waste (garbage). A regular schedule should be in place for checking, cleaning, and defrosting the refrigerator. Spills should be wiped up immediately, especially if the liquid spilled is sticky, sweet, or attractive to insects and flies. Food and drink must be kept out of the dispensing area, and the refrigerator used strictly for medicines. Regular monitoring of the refrigerator temperature should be an established procedure, together with detailed actions to be taken to promptly repair the refrigerator if temperatures fall outside of acceptable limits (usually +2–8°C).

Dispensing equipment is used for measuring liquids, weighing solids, or counting tablets or capsules. Uncoated tablets normally leave a layer of powder on any surface they touch, which can easily be transferred to other tablets or capsules counted on the same surface. This process is called *cross-contamination* and can be dangerous if the contaminating substance (for example, aspirin or penicillin) is one to which a patient is sensitive. Cleaning any equipment used for handling different products, both between uses and at the end of the day, is essential.

The dispensing environment must be organized to create a safe and efficient working area. Space should be sufficient to allow for movement by staff members during the dispensing process. However, the distance that a dispenser must cover during the dispensing process should be minimized to maintain efficiency.

Stock containers and prepacked medicines must be stored in an organized way on shelves, preferably according to dosage forms (for example, tablets and capsules, syrups and mixtures) and in alphabetical order. All stock containers in use must be clearly and accurately labeled to ensure the safe selection of the correct preparation and to minimize the risk of error (see Figure 30-1).

In addition, a system of stock rotation should determine which items are to be used first, on either a first-in/first-out (FIFO) or first-expiry/first-out (FEFO) basis. Regular checking of expiry dates and removal of expired stock facilitates stock rotation, as does placing stock to be used first at the front of the shelf. Recommended storage conditions in terms of temperature, light, and moisture should be followed as closely as possible to maintain product quality. Stock bottles must be kept closed except when in use.

A limited range of preparations will be used with the greatest frequency, and these "fast movers" may be placed in the most accessible areas for the convenience of dispensers.

30.3 Dispensing person

A superficial look at dispensing suggests that it is a process of supplying goods to a patient on the basis of a written order, and that it can be done successfully by anyone who can read the prescription, count, and pour. As a result, dispensing is often delegated to any staff member who has nothing else to do, who then performs this function without any training or supervision. This situation is irrational and dangerous.

One major difference between supplying medicines or medical supplies and supplying other goods is that, with medicines or medical supplies, the recipient/patient usually does not know the correct use and is unable to judge the quality of the product he or she receives. Therefore, responsibility for the correctness and quality of medicines or products supplied lies entirely with the person dispensing them, and the patient must rely on the dispenser's ability. Consequently, in most countries, laws mandate that the distribution of medicines and important medical supplies to the general public be carried out by professional pharmacists. In many countries, however, where a shortage of qualified pharmacists or trained dispensers makes it difficult to achieve this level of service, medicines and related products are supplied by individuals who have no training in medicines and no knowledge about their safe use.

In addition to reading, writing, counting, and pouring, the dispenser or dispensing team needs specific additional knowledge, skills, and attitudes to complete the dispensing process. These include—

- Knowledge about the medicines being dispensed (common use, correct dose, precautions about the method of use, common side effects, common interactions with other medicines or food, storage needs)
- Good calculation and arithmetic skills
- Skills in assessing the quality of preparations
- Attributes of cleanliness, accuracy, and honesty
- Attitudes and skills required to communicate effectively with patients

The level of training needed for any particular dispensing task is determined by the range of medicines dispensed and the extent to which calculation and preparation are required.

Dispensing personnel must receive an appropriate level of training, which will enable them to correctly dispense the range of medicines prescribed in their facilities. This is true in both the private and the public sectors. At a basic health facility, where a limited range of medicines is used and the number of patients is small, dispenser training may be basic, highly structured, and built on the trainee's previous health care training. Dispensing assistants with this level of training may be employed at higher levels (for example, a district hospital) but should work under the guidance and supervision of trained pharmacy staff, such as a pharmacy technician or technologist. Dispensers in community pharmacy shops should also be trained in the basics of good dispensing practices and the handling of medicines. Dispenser training in medication counseling and adherence is especially important to the success of programs providing antiretroviral therapy for HIV/AIDS patients, which are rapidly increasing in resource-limited settings (see Country Study 30-1).

In areas where graduate pharmacists are scarce, they are more effectively employed as trainers and supervisors rather than as technicians performing the routine tasks of dispensing.

Country Study 30-1
Improving dispensing and counseling practices for antiretroviral therapy in Kenya

Starting in 2003, the government of Kenya initiated antiretroviral therapy (ART) for HIV/AIDS patients at four health facilities serving the Coast Province, including the Port Reitz District Hospital in Mombasa. Management Sciences for Health's Rational Pharmaceutical Management (RPM) Plus Program performed a facility assessment and identified several factors related to dispensing that needed to be addressed before the ART program was initiated—

- Prescriptions were written on unofficial pieces of paper, difficult to read, and often incomplete.
- Tablet counters were available, but staff used their hands to count.
- Labeling of medicines was inadequate.
- The facility was extremely hot and no fans were available.
- Only one dispensing window was available—access to the second window was restricted.
- Patients crowded at the windows, which was distracting to the dispensing staff and made confidential counseling impossible.
- Average length of a medication counseling session was twenty-two seconds.
- No reference books or guidelines of any type were available.
- The dispensary was used to store nonpharmacy items (for example, staff members had to maneuver around a wheelbarrow).

Before the ART program began, the newly appointed head pharmacist attended an RPM Plus Promoting Rational Drug Use course. Upon returning to the hospital, the pharmacist shared the results of the RPM Plus assessment with the dispensary staff, and the team worked to identify the underlying causes of problems and develop strategies to address each issue. The staff team—

- Prepared a code of good dispensing practice and hung it on the dispensary wall
- Collaborated with the medical staff to design an official prescription form that specified patient information
- Committed to using tablet counters—supportive supervision by the pharmacist in charge encouraged the behavior change
- Designed a preprinted stamp to clearly label medication envelopes
- Installed fans in the pharmacy
- Improved dispensing conditions and confidentiality by arranging for the installation of private counseling booths and freeing access to the second dispensing window
- Worked to apply their training in good dispensing practice and medication counseling for ART to improve the quality of dispensing and patient care for all medicines dispensed
- Made use of a set of key resource materials and national guidelines that were made available to them
- Cleared nonpharmacy items from the dispensary

In a review conducted one year later, staff members commented that reorganizing patient flow was key in facilitating the improvements in dispensing and that one of their greatest achievements was improving medication counseling for all patients. The new private booths at pharmacy windows provided a welcoming and secure atmosphere. The staff members saw the confidential nature of the booths as a valuable addition: "Before when I was dispensing pessaries to a patient there would be four heads listening." In addition, several of the dispensing staff members reported that they were applying their training on ART medication counseling to those patients taking medicines for the treatment of diabetes or hypertension.

Source: Pharmacist, Port Reitz District Hospital, personal communication.

Figure 30-2   The dispensing cycle

6. Issue medicine to patient with clear instructions and advice

1. Receive and validate prescription

2. Understand and interpret prescription

patient ✓
medicine ✓
dose ✓

Dispensing cycle

5. Record action taken

4. Make a final check

3. Prepare and label items for issue

30.4 Dispensing process

The consistent, repeated use of good dispensing procedures is vital in ensuring that errors are detected and corrected at all stages of the dispensing process. The term *dispensing process* covers all activities involved, from receiving the prescription to issuing the prescribed medicine to the patient.

The development and use of written standard operating procedures (SOPs) for the dispensing process will improve consistency and quality of work and can be used for training and reference. The framework for such SOPs may be based on the six major areas of activity (see Figure 30-2)—

1. Receive and validate the prescription
2. Understand and interpret the prescription
3. Prepare and label items for issue
4. Make a final check
5. Record the action taken
6. Issue medicine to the patient with clear instructions and advice

Step 1. Receive and validate the prescription

Upon receiving a prescription, the staff member responsible should confirm the name of the patient. This action is particularly important when the clinic is dealing with a large crowd of people and when there is any risk that staff

or patients may mix up prescriptions. Cross-checking the name and identity of the patient must also be done when issuing the medicines. (The use of matching numbers or symbols—one attached to the prescription and one given to the patient—can also contribute to making sure the right patient gets the right medicines and is especially helpful in situations where many people share the same surname.)

Step 2. Understand and interpret the prescription

Interpreting a prescription must be done by a staff member who can—

- Read the prescription
- Correctly interpret any abbreviations used by the prescriber
- Confirm that the doses prescribed are in the normal range for the patient (noting sex and age)
- Correctly perform any calculations of dose and issue quantity
- Identify any common drug-drug interactions

It is assumed that the prescription will be in written form. Verbal orders for medications should be given only in exceptional and emergency situations. In such cases, the order should be repeated back to the prescriber to ensure accuracy, and written confirmation should be supplied within an agreed-upon period. Computerized prescribing and dispensing systems are becoming more widespread, especially in large hospitals (see Chapter 45). If the person dispensing the medicine has any doubt about what is required by the prescriber, he or she must check with the prescriber. Illegible writing by prescribers has serious implications when many product names are confusingly similar. Checking a prescription may save a life (see Box 30-1).

All calculations should be double checked by the dispenser or counter-checked by another staff member. An arithmetical error could be fatal.

Step 3. Prepare and label items for issue

Preparation of items for issue is the central part of the dispensing process, and it must include procedures for self-checking or counter-checking to ensure accuracy. This part of the process begins after the prescription is clearly understood and the quantity has been calculated. It is good practice to write the label at this point as a form of self-check (see Figure 30-3).

Select stock container or prepack. A good dispenser selects the item by reading the label and cross-matching the product name and strength against the prescription. The dispenser should check the stock to make sure that it has not expired and choose the oldest stock (first-in/first-out) or first expiry, depending on the stock rotation method used. Most well-trained staff members deliberately read the container label at least twice during the dispensing process (see Figure 30-4). Selecting according to the color or location of

---

Box 30-1
Dispensing errors cost lives

A patient had been given a prescription for an antacid—something beginning with "D" and ending in "l." The prescription was poorly written, but the dosage of two tablets taken four times a day was clear. The dispenser at the shop was not sure about the drug name but knew of a product on the market with a trade name that began with "D" and ended with "l," and so dispensed it. That was how glibenclamide tablets (brand name Daonil) were dispensed at a level eight times the recommended daily dose, and the patient died of hypoglycemia. The prescriber who wrote out the prescription had the antacid Diovol in mind, but the handwriting was unclear. Although it is easy to see how this tragedy occurred, the fact remains that it should not have happened.

---

the container, without consciously reading the label, is poor dispensing practice and may have fatal consequences.

Another dangerous practice that should be discouraged is having many stock containers open at the same time. In this situation, product selection is frequently made only according to appearance, which could lead to errors. In addition, medicines continuously exposed to the air eventually deteriorate in quality. It is important to open and close containers one at a time.

Figure 30-3   Writing medicine labels

Figure 30-4   Selection from a shelf: Read the label every time

Figure 30-5   Position label upward when pouring liquids

RIGHT   WRONG

Figure 30-6   Counting methods

Measure or count quantity from stock containers.
Liquids must be measured in a clean vessel and should be
poured from the stock bottle with the label kept upward.
Using this technique avoids damage to the label from any
spilled or dripping liquid (see Figure 30-5).

Tablets and capsules can be counted with or without
the assistance of a counting device (see Figure 30-6). The
most important rule to follow is that the dispenser's hands
must not be in direct contact with the medicine. Using
the hands is bad practice for both hygienic and product
quality reasons. Counting should be done using one of the
following—

- Clean piece of paper and clean knife or spatula
- Clean tablet-counting device
- Lid of the stock container in use
- Any other clean, dust-free surface

Immediately after measuring or counting, the stock container lid should be replaced and the stock container label
should be rechecked for drug name and strength.

Pack and label medicine. Tablets or capsules should be
packed into a clean, dry container, such as a bottle, plastic
envelope, cardboard box, or paper envelope. Any of these
containers are satisfactory in a dry climate. During the rainy
season or in a humid climate, however, cardboard or paper
will not protect tablets and capsules from moisture in the
air, which can quickly ruin medicines and make them unfit
for use. Capsules and sugar-coated tablets are the most vulnerable to moisture. Section 30.6 and Table 30-1 cover packing and labeling in more detail.

Step 4. Make a final check

At this point, the dispensed preparation should be checked
against the prescription and against the stock containers
used. Although this step can be done as a self-check, it is
valuable to have the final check done by another staff member. The final check should include reading and interpreting
the prescription before looking at the dispensed medicines; checking the appropriateness of doses prescribed and
checking for drug interactions; checking the identity of
the medicine dispensed; checking the labels; and finally
countersigning the prescription.

Step 5. Record action taken

Records of issues to patients are essential in an efficiently
run dispensary. Such records can be used to verify the stocks
used in dispensing, and they will be required if a need arises
to trace any problems with medicines issued to patients.

Three different methods can be used to keep a record of
medicines dispensed. When the prescription is retained, the
dispenser should initial and annotate the prescription with
strength and quantities dispensed and either file it or enter
the details into a record book as soon as time is available.
When the prescription is returned to the patient, details
of the medicines dispensed must be entered into a record
book before the items are issued to the patient. The date, the
patient's name and age, the medicine name and strength, the
amount issued, and the dispenser's name should be entered
into the register. When dispensers use computers to record
the dispensing details, the computer program should retain

Table 30-1   Packaging materials for medicine dispensing

Category of packaging*	Package characteristics	Examples
Tablets/capsules		
Desirable	Clean, dry, plastic or glass container with tight-fitting cap or seal	Blister packages, plastic sachets, tightly sealing plastic or glass containers with screw or snap cap
Acceptable	Clean, dry container that provides protection from dirt and moisture	Zipper-lock plastic bags, glycine paper, tin with tight-fitting lid
Undesirable	Unclean absorbent paper, cotton, cardboard containers with no provision for closure	Unsealed plastic bags, paper bags, newspaper or other printed paper
Liquids (oral and topical)		
Desirable	Clean, dry, light-resistant glass container with tight-fitting cap	Amber or opaque bottle with screw cap
Acceptable	Clean, dry plastic or glass container with tight-fitting cap	Glass or plastic bottle with tight-fitting cap
Undesirable	Unclean paper, cardboard, metal, or plastic (not formed) container with no provision for closure	Previously used liquid-containing cartons, plastic-lined paper bags, plastic bags
Liquids (otic and ophthalmic)		
Desirable	Clean (preferably sterile), light-resistant glass or plastic container with a dropper incorporated into a tight-fitting cap or a top fitted with a dropper with a protective sleeve	Amber dropper bottle, opaque plastic dropper bottle
Acceptable	Clean, dry plastic or glass container with tight-fitting cap and a clean plastic/glass dropper (separate)	Glass or plastic bottle with tight-fitting cap, glass or plastic dropper with protective container (cardboard, zipper-lock, plastic, or paper)
Undesirable	Anything other than above	Anything else
Creams/ointments		
Desirable	Clean glass or porcelain wide-mouth jar with tight-fitting lid or collapsible plastic or metal tube	Wide-mouth jar with tight-fitting lid, cream or ointment tube with cap
Acceptable	Clean glass or porcelain jar with lid	Glass or porcelain jar
Undesirable	Anything other than above	Anything else

* *Desirable:* Packaging should meet listed requirements for a period greater than 30 days.
 Acceptable: Packaging should meet listed requirements for up to 30 days.
 Undesirable: Packaging provides no protection from dirt, moisture, or other contaminants, thus permitting rapid deterioration or contamination.

the information, which can then be recalled to generate summary reports.

Step 6. Issue medicine to the patient with clear instructions and advice

The medicine must be given to the named patient, or the patient's representative, with clear instructions and any appropriate advice about the medicine. The appopriate level of informational detail about possible side effects varies from patient to patient. Verbal advice is important, because illiteracy and poor labeling may both be problems. Country Study 30-2 shows data collected on how well dispensers instructed patients on medication use in six different countries.

Apart from information on the dose, frequency, length of treatment, and route of administration, priority should be given to providing information that will maximize the effect of the treatment. Advice should therefore concentrate on—

- When to take the medicine (particularly in relation to food and other medicines)
- How to take the medicine (chewed, swallowed whole, taken with plenty of water, etc.)
- How to store the medicine

Warnings about possible side effects should be given cautiously. Common but harmless side effects (nausea, mild diarrhea, urine changing color) should be mentioned to prevent a frightened patient from stopping the treatment. More serious side effects should be mentioned only with the agreement of the prescriber, who needs to take those risks into account when prescribing the medicine.

Every effort must be made to confirm that the patient understands the instructions and advice. This can be difficult to do if someone other than the patient is collecting items for the patient or for several patients, particularly when the same medicines are prescribed in different dosages. Whenever possible, the staff member dispensing

Country Study 30-2
The quality of medication counseling in three pharmaceutical service sectors

As part of an overall assessment of pharmaceutical management in six resource-limited countries, Management Sciences for Health's Strategies for Enhancing Access to Medicines (SEAM) Program used standard indicators to measure the quality of pharmaceutical services, including dispensing. The data on patients' knowledge of how to take their medicine came from interviews with patients exiting public and nongovernmental organization (NGO) facilities and from simulated patients at privately owned retail outlets. The exit survey did not aim to determine whether the patient's information about how to take the medicine was correct, but to determine if the patient was able to relate any information about the medicine's intended use, based on what they had been told by the dispenser. Simulated patients entered retail medicine outlets asking for help for their sick child. Results of the surveys are reflected in the tables below.

In general, attendants at all facilities and in all countries were lax about giving customers information on possible problems and side effects, but this finding was especially pronounced in private, for-profit outlets. The percentage of people receiving instructions on the purpose of their medication and how to take it varied, but was greatest in Cambodia and El Salvador. Of note are Cambodia's figures, where, in all three types of facilities, almost all those surveyed knew basic information on why and how to take their medications.

Sources: SEAM Program 2003a, 2003b, 2003c, 2003d, 2003e, 2003f.

Patients' knowledge of prescribed medicines at public facilities based on exit interviews

Indicator	Ghana n = 813	Tanzania n = 209	Cambodia n = varied	El Salvador n = 712	Brazil n = 178	India n = 1,391
% Patients who knew name of medicine	65	61	75	NA	60	9
% Patients who knew purpose of medicine	54	81	97	98*	80	63
% Patients who knew how long to take the medicine	40	76	100	98*	NA	81
% Patients who received other information about the medicine (including possible adverse effects)	35	20	48	NA	NA	8

* Patients were asked if they knew "how and why" the drugs are used. NA = not applicable.

Patients' knowledge of prescribed medicines at NGO facilities based on exit interviews

Indicator	Ghana n = 621	Tanzania n = 216	Cambodia n = varied	El Salvador n = 447	Brazil	India n = 373
% Patients who knew name of medicine	61	10	86	NA	NA	9
% Patients who knew purpose of medicine	46	70	98	98*	NA	61
% Patients who knew how long to take the medicine	35	80	100	98*	NA	78
% Patients who received other information about the medicine (including possible adverse effects)	35	80	45	NA	NA	3

* Patients were asked if they knew "how and why" the drugs are used. NA= not applicable.

Quality of dispenser services in simulated patient encounters in private, for-profit facilities

Indicator	Ghana n = 18	Tanzania n = 45	Cambodia n = 36	El Salvador n = 26	Brazil n = 21	India n = 48
% Encounters where attendant provided instruction on taking medication	14	87	100	89	42	60
% Encounters where attendant gave information on possible problems with medication	21	9	42	12	5	2
% Encounters where attendant provided information on care and how to treat fever	14	24	69	19	16	10

Figure 30-7   Ensuring understanding

Figure 30-8   Check routines, prevent mistakes

the medications should have the recipient repeat back the instructions (see Figure 30-7).

Every patient must be treated with respect. The need for confidentiality and privacy when explaining the use of some types of medicine must be recognized, and efforts should be made to structure medicine collection so that advice to patients can be as individual as possible. The person receiving the instructions may be feeling ill, and the success of treatment depends on the accuracy and effectiveness of the dispenser's communication with the patient.

30.5 Promoting efficient management in dispensing

Good dispensing practices are most threatened when dispensing staff face a crowd of patients demanding immediate attention. The need for speed must be balanced with the need for accuracy and care in the dispensing process. At this point, the patient's care, or even life, is in the hands of the dispenser. In dispensing, *accuracy is more important than speed*.

Prior agreement with the prescribers to prescribe only items that are available at the pharmacy or listed on the hospital or clinic formulary prevents unnecessary delay and confusion for the patient and improves efficiency in the dispensing process.

Organizing patient flow, such as establishing systems to receive payment and prescriptions and issue medicines, can reduce the potential for dispensing errors by removing the dispenser from the intense scrutiny of ten or more patients

anxiously waiting at the dispensary window. Strategies such as giving information on the current waiting time and issuing numbers linked to the order in which prescriptions will be dispensed can encourage patients to use the waiting time to access other hospital or clinic services, helps to prevent long queues and crowding at the dispensary window, and can improve patient satisfaction.

One good way to reduce dispensing time and improve safety is to prepackage and label commonly used medicines. This process also distributes some of the dispensing workload to less busy periods of the day. See Section 30.7 for a more detailed discussion of prepackaging.

Another way to prevent staff from making errors when under pressure is to organize the work so that more than one individual is involved in the dispensing process for each prescription. This method introduces a system of using counter-checks, which is a wise precaution in most situations (see Figure 30-8). One example of such a system assigns one person to receiving and checking prescriptions, another to preparing the medicines, and a third person to handing them to the patient with advice; the team members then rotate responsibility for these activities at regular intervals.

Techniques to ensure quality in dispensing include—

- Requiring that all staff work in accordance with written SOPs
- Maintaining records on what medicines and products have been issued
- Scheduling worker shifts to make best use of staff: providing more staff at peak hours, maintaining enough coverage to keep the dispensary open during breaks,

and coordinating shift starting/ending times with patient flow

- Involving the pharmacy staff in hospital/facility committees to identify and resolve problems involving patient flow, communication, and other areas

Regular inspection or auditing using a checklist, together with supportive supervision, may improve dispensing in a health facility (see Box 30-2).

A number of studies have investigated determinants, other than the management of the dispensing process, that influence dispenser behavior. Box 30-3 lists factors that have been cited as influential and may need to be addressed to improve the quality of the dispensing process.

30.6 Packaging and labeling of dispensed medicines

When products for dispensing have been collected from the shelf, they must be packaged so that they can be stored by the patient, and labeled to ensure patient understanding.

Containers for dispensed medicine

The purpose of a medicine container or packaging is to preserve the quality of the medicine up to the time of use, as well as to provide a surface for attaching or writing a label with identifying details and instructions for use. The container should not affect the quality of the medicine in any way or allow other contaminants to do so.

Ideally, such a container would match standard criteria per textbooks and international standards. These describe the nature and color of the container and its closure (cap or top), as well as the requirements for good labeling. Because many health systems cannot meet this ideal for financial or logistical reasons, it is important to seek the best possible solution, keeping in mind basic principles. Table 30-1 compares various options.

Liquids require clean bottles and effective caps or closures. Under no circumstances should two liquid medicines be mixed together for dispensing. They may interact chemically and become ineffective or dangerous. In many situations, suitable containers for dispensing liquids are difficult to obtain, and a policy of prescribing solid-dose preparations whenever possible is recommended. If patients bring their own bottles for liquid medicine, it is important to rinse and thoroughly drain the bottles before use.

The use of medicine reminder devices or medicine compliance aids as dispensing containers is becoming more popular as a tool for helping patients with complex medication regimens—especially elderly patients—take their medicines correctly at home. These devices typically hold seven days' supply of a patient's medicines in twenty-eight

---

Box 30-2
Sample inspection checklist

Environment

- ☐ Does the area appear clean and tidy?
- ☐ Is the refrigerator clean and tidy?
- ☐ What nonmedical items were found in the refrigerator?
- ☐ Is the temperature of the refrigerator checked regularly and maintained within an acceptable range?
- ☐ Are any spillages left unattended?
- ☐ Are stock containers in their proper place (or in use)?
- ☐ Are stock containers open but not in immediate use?
- ☐ Do any stock containers have incorrect or inadequate labeling?
- ☐ Are prepackaged medicines clearly labeled?
- ☐ Are sufficient counting aids or surfaces available?

General procedures

- ☐ Are all dispensed medicines checked by a second staff member before issue?
- ☐ What proportion of prescriptions are cross-checked for the patient's name at the point of receipt?
- ☐ Are dispensing containers cleaned before use?
- ☐ Are the required materials in the most efficient places?

Individual practices

- ☐ Are medicines counted into or out of dispensers' hands?
- ☐ Are there obvious self-checking routines for accuracy in calculation, selection, and labeling?
- ☐ Is equipment for measuring and counting cleaned between use for different medicines?
- ☐ What quality of advice is given to patients, and in what manner?
- ☐ Are patients able to repeat and remember vital instructions?

> **Box 30-3**
> **Factors that influence dispenser behavior**
>
> Pharmacies can often be a patient's first source of advice, and therefore, dispensers can greatly influence rational medicine use in the community. Many factors influence dispenser behavior—
>
> - Training and knowledge
> - Professional compensation (salary, prestige)
> - Economic incentives (markup and volume of sales)
> - Supply (cannot dispense what is not in stock)
> - Available product information
> - Availability of dispensing equipment (counting trays, vials, bottles, syringes, labels, and so on)
> - Public- versus private-sector promotional and marketing techniques
>
> - Social status of a dispenser and his or her role in the health care system
> - Dispenser-prescriber relationship
> - Lack of communication skills
>
> A review of the literature on determinants that affect antibiotic dispensing showed that dispensers most frequently cited the desire to meet customer demand, followed by economic incentives, such as dispensing according to what the customer could afford to pay. Other factors named included a lack of regulation and enforcement, marketing influences, and a lack of knowledge (Radyowijati and Haak 2003).

total compartments, four for each day. The use of reminder devices, however, has both advantages and risks (Nunney and Raynor 2001). The obvious advantage is that the patient is able to manage his or her medication schedule better, with fewer missed doses and less confusion. Risks include patients' difficulty with opening the compartments, little space available for appropriate labeling, the possibility of product deterioration in imperfect storage conditions, and the difficulty of cleaning the compartments. Moreover, the device cannot accommodate certain dose forms, such as liquids or drops. In addition, when tablets and capsules are separated from their original containers, patients may lose track of what medications they are taking and why. A card that provides the details of physical appearance of the contents of the device can help patients with identification.

Labeling of dispensed medicine

When there is a shortage of suitable containers, the labeling of medicines is frequently inadequate or even nonexistent. As a result, dispensed medicines are often used incorrectly and therefore do not provide the patient with the intended treatment. Studies have shown that, even in countries with the most sophisticated labeling practices, only about 50 percent of medicines are taken as intended by the prescriber.

Despite these discouraging statistics, however, labeling is important, and every effort should be made to provide information about the nature and contents of the preparation, the dosage regimen to be followed, and the identity of the intended patient (see Figure 30-9). This information is important to include even if the patient is illiterate; another family member may be able to read the instructions. In addition, if a patient is admitted to the hospital for acute care and is unconscious or unable to communicate fully, labels can provide vital information on the medication and dose for the treating clinician.

In some countries, small auxiliary labels are available with preprinted instructions, such as "Shake well before using," or cautions, such as "May cause drowsiness." Where such labels are available, they should be routinely used, as appropriate.

Prepackaged medicines should always be labeled with the name, strength, and quantity of the preparation and, where established courses of therapy exist, the dosage regimen. Such a label should leave a space for the patient's name to be added. It is important to avoid abbreviations, and unfamiliar expressions should not be used. If possible, the inclusion of the product batch number and expiry date is recommended.

Self-adhesive labels are unlikely to be available in many settings, but labels can be inserted into containers or stapled onto bags for tablets and capsules. Instruction labels may be preprinted, or the process can be simplified by having rubber stamps made for the common regimens (for example, "one to be taken three times a day"). If labels are handwritten, block capital letters should be used. Labels should be composed in the local language. If paper envelopes are used as containers, the instructions can be stamped onto them directly.

Where levels of illiteracy are high or where research has proved that written labels are not effective, consideration should be given to the additional use of pictorial or graphic labels, as illustrated in Figure 30-10. Graphic symbols should always be combined with written instructions. Before any large investment is made in printing such labels, however, they should be pretested to make sure that they communicate effectively. Pictorial language can be very culture specific.

The use of computers and printers to produce labels for dispensed medicine is now common in many countries. The

Figure 30-9   Dispensed medicine label

> JOHN TETTEH
> AMOXICILLINE CAP
> 500 MG
> TAKE 1 CAPSULE THREE TIMES A DAY
>
> *Daniel Piri   3/3/07*

Figure 30-10   Pictorial labeling

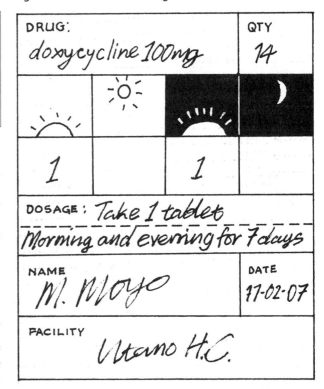

required software is designed for use on desktop personal computers, and this system may be considered where computers are available and affordable. Using computers can be very attractive and efficient, but the need for a continual supply of computer paper or labels and ink cartridges, as well as for a consistent electricity supply, must be considered.

30.7   Course-of-therapy prepackaging of medicines

The prepacking done at the local level differs from that done by the manufacturer, which includes preparing fixed-dose combinations of medicines and unit-dose blister packs. This chapter focuses on prepacking as a pharmacy-specific operation. However, blister cards and other unit-of-use packages created at the manufacturing level are useful to the dispenser because of the time saved and errors prevented by eliminating the need to count out tablets removed from a bulk package (Lipowski et al. 2002).

Local prepackaging of medicines for dispensing is valuable if the following conditions apply—

- Large numbers of patients come for medicines at the same time.
- A few medicines are prescribed frequently, and in the same quantities.
- The type of packaging used will provide protection from the environment until the patient uses the medicine.
- The package can be labeled with the drug name and strength.
- Prescribers are involved in the selection of packaging quantities and agree to prescribe the chosen quantities.

Benefits of course-of-therapy prepackaging

Course-of-therapy prepackaging has many advantages—

- Safer, easier, and faster distribution of medicines, with less room for error, which frees the dispenser from routine counting chores and allows more time for communication with patients

- Improved credibility among users, because of the attractiveness and cleanliness of the package, which can be comparable to that of commercially purchased medicines
- More accurate and efficient prescribing by all health workers because of the standard treatments chosen for prepackaging
- Simplified dispensing for multidrug therapies (for example, copackaging isoniazid, rifampicin, ethambutol, and pyrazinamide for tuberculosis treatment), resulting in improved patient adherence with recommended regimens
- Possibility for routine prepackaging to be done by untrained staff following clear procedures and subject to appropriate quality checks and controls
- Easier and more accurate recording of inventory, with better control over supplies and more accurate consumption data

Importance of controls in prepackaging process

Prepackaging of medicines is technically a "manufacturing" process, which must be done under strict controls reflecting good manufacturing practices. In particular—

- Only one kind and strength of medicine is prepacked at a time in one work area or on one surface.

- The supervisor checks beforehand that the "prepacker" has the correct labels and that the number of labels and containers is the same and corresponds to the number of tablets or capsules to be prepacked. For example, to prepack in amounts of twenty from a bulk container of 1,000 tablets, the packer requires fifty containers and fifty labels.
- The supervisor checks the product at the end of the process.
- A written record is kept of the details (name, strength, batch number, expiry date) of the preparation to be packed, the number of packs produced, the date packed, the name and signature of the packer, the name and signature of the supervisor, and the internal batch number for the prepackaged product.

Precautions and quality checks

Prepackaging is repackaging, and the legal responsibility for the quality and labeling of the newly packed medicine is transferred from the original manufacturer to the repacker. Repackaging of medicines may compromise the original manufacturer's expiry date, and generally an expiry date of six months, or the original expiry date if less, is given to repackaged medicines. Therefore, the quality of the product must be checked (at least a 10 percent sample) before and after prepacking. Package seals must also be checked on a regular basis to ensure that they close tightly and will protect the prepackaged medicine adequately.

The amount to be prepackaged depends on rate of use and the climatic conditions. In humid climates or during the rainy season, it may be best to prepack only an amount sufficient for a few days' needs, especially if the new packaging cannot be tightly closed. Repackaging is a waste of time and resources if the product becomes unfit for use. Chapter 7 provides more information on procedures for repackaging.

30.8 Aids in counting tablets and capsules

Aids for counting tablets and capsules include triangular or rectangular tablet counters, pan weighing scales, and electronic tablet counters.

Tablet counter

A tablet counter is a flat rectangle or triangle made of wood, metal, or plastic with raised edges along two sides. Metal or plastic is preferred because the surface can be easily cleaned or washed between uses for different products. The tablets are counted by first counting the number of rows of tablets in the counter and then pouring them into the container or package using a raised edge as a guide (see Figure 30-11).

Figure 30-11 Tablet counter in use

7 ROWS = 28 TABLETS

Key

Rows	4	5	6	7	8	9	10	11	12	13
Tablets	10	15	21	28	36	45	55	66	78	91

This simple device is good for counting small quantities of round compressed tablets, regardless of their size. The smaller the tablet, the more tablets can be counted at one time. With care, the counter can be used for sugar-coated round tablets. It is also useful as a surface on which to count any tablet or capsule, making the transfer to a container a simple process. The key for the number of rows and number of tablets is shown in Figure 30-11.

Pan weighing scales

Scales can be particularly useful when counting tablets or capsules during prepackaging. The balance must be free to move, and the pans must be clean. The required number of tablets or capsules is counted and placed on one of the scale pans. Equal quantities of the same tablet or capsule can then be counted by adding to the other scale pan until a balanced position is reached.

Electronic tablet counter

When prepackaging is done on a large scale, as in a teaching hospital for use in both the ward and outpatient department, the use of an electronic counter may be justified.

30.9 Pharmacy personnel

The availability of qualified pharmacy personnel varies widely throughout the world, and the status given to different levels of trained pharmacy staff is equally varied. These facts reflect the indeterminate role of trained pharmacy personnel in health care services.

Pharmaceuticals play such a prominent role in the provision and cost of health care that it is surprising how often the management of this resource is left to untrained and non-specialized staff. It is important to appreciate the value of an appropriately trained pharmacy workforce.

There are three recognized cadres of pharmacy staff: pharmacists, pharmacy technicians (also called technologists), and auxiliary or assistant staff. The first two normally receive their training in the formal educational sector.

Chapters 51 and 52 discuss in detail aspects of human resources and training related to pharmaceutical management.

Pharmacists

In most countries, a pharmacist is a professional who is registered with the appropriate national board or society after having obtained a university degree in pharmacy, frequently followed by a year of supervised work or apprenticeship.

Pharmacists are employed to practice in four main areas: regulation and control of medicines, hospital pharmacy, the manufacturing industry, and community (retail) pharmacy. The first two areas of practice are usually part of the public sector, and the latter two are usually part of the private sector, although manufacturers may be owned and operated by the public sector. Along with their practices, many pharmacists are also involved in teaching, training, and research.

The role of pharmacists in the supply of medicines has been altered significantly over the last twenty years. This change can be summarized as a move away from the care of pharmaceuticals (being product centered), and toward pharmaceutical care (being patient centered). A decrease in the need to compound medicines and an increase in the complexity and potency of available finished manufactured products have resulted in a change from concern about the preparation of medicinal products to involvement in the use of medicines by patients.

The training of pharmacists in industrialized countries reflects this change by providing more clinical and patient-oriented teaching, which prepares pharmacists to be participating members of the clinical team in hospitals and primary health care settings. Pharmacists are increasingly involved in deciding on and designing treatments, and are recognized by health professionals and the public as experts in medicine management and use. Their expertise and potential contribution to public and private health care have yet to be appreciated by many countries, which try to provide an effective supply of medicines and treatment without a trained pharmacist workforce of sufficient numbers.

Pharmacy technicians

Pharmacy technician training is usually a government-recognized vocational course provided on a full- or part-time basis through technical colleges or health training institutes. The length of training may vary according to the national education system. In most developing countries, courses are two to three years, whereas a course can be one year or less in industrialized countries. All courses emphasize practical skills and experience in dispensing medicines, and work experience is commonly a significant portion of the course. Basic teaching is given in pharmacology, pharmaceutics, microbiology, and related subjects. Course content always needs to be updated to meet evolving job requirements.

Pharmacy technicians are important members of the pharmaceutical care team, and they constitute the largest group of trained pharmacy personnel in many countries. Their training qualifies them to work effectively in dispensing and pharmaceutical supply activities. They have sufficient training to be involved in decision making and supervision of other staff members, and individuals with experience can be given significant responsibility. In countries where professional pharmacists are scarce, by default pharmacy technicians are often put in charge of managing pharmacies without pharmacist supervision.

Insufficient planning has been directed to developing attractive and rewarding career structures for pharmacy technicians so that those with experience and ambition can fulfill their potential.

Auxiliary or assistant pharmacy staff

Auxiliary staff complete a relatively short on-the-job training program to assist pharmacists and technicians in the routine work of dispensing and medicine supply. Such training should be oriented to the tasks of the work environment. Assistant staff should follow written protocols and need to be supervised in their work, especially if the products of that work are given directly to patients. These staff should not be expected to interpret prescriptions on their own. Their supervisors should recognize that, with experience, these assistants can develop higher skills in particular areas.

Untrained medicine sellers

Many people rely on private medicine shops and other retail outlets as their primary source of medicines and health care, and although regulations may prohibit access to certain medicines at these outlets, often a lack of enforcement means that restricted, prescription-only medications are sold without a prescription. Countries may not have any legal requirements for the training or education of these sellers; however, sellers are increasingly recognized as influential sources of information on illness and treatment in many areas. A number of interventions focused specifically on private-sector retail outlets have shown that training and incentive programs can improve dispensing habits among such sellers (see Chapter 32). ∎

References and further readings

★ = Key readings.

Beardsley, R. S., C. Kimberlin, W. N. Tindall. 2008. *Communication Skills in Pharmacy Practice: A Practical Guide for Students and Practitioners.* 5th ed. Baltimore, Md.: Lippincott Williams & Wilkins.

Berger, B. A. 2009. *Communication Skills for Pharmacists: Building Relationships, Improving Patient Care.* 3rd ed. Washington, D.C.: American Pharmacists Association.

Center for Pharmaceutical Management. 2003a. *Access to Essential Medicines: Cambodia, 2001.* Prepared for the Strategies for Enhancing Access to Medicines Program. Arlington, Va.: Management Sciences for Health. <http://www.msh.org/seam/reports/Cambodia_Assessment_Report.pdf>

———. 2003b. *Access to Essential Medicines: El Salvador, 2001.* Prepared for the Strategies for Enhancing Access to Medicines Program. Arlington, Va.: Management Sciences for Health. <http://www.msh.org/seam/reports/El_Salvador_final.pdf>

———. 2003c. *Access to Essential Medicines: Ghana, 2001.* Prepared for the Strategies for Enhancing Access to Medicines Program. Arlington, Va.: Management Sciences for Health. <http://www.msh.org/seam/reports/Ghana_final.pdf>

———. 2003d. *Access to Essential Medicines: Rajasthan, India, 2001.* Prepared for the Strategies for Enhancing Access to Medicines Program. Arlington, Va.: Management Sciences for Health. <http://www.msh.org/seam/reports/Rajasthan-SEAMAssessment-2001.pdf>

———. 2003e. *Access to Essential Medicines: State of Minas Gerais, Brazil, 2001.* Prepared for the Strategies for Enhancing Access to Medicines Program. Arlington, Va.: Management Sciences for Health. <http://www.msh.org/seam/reports/Brazil_final.pdf>

———. 2003f. *Access to Essential Medicines: Tanzania, 2001.* Prepared for the Strategies for Enhancing Access to Medicines Program. Arlington, Va.: Management Sciences for Health. <http://www.msh.org/seam/reports/CR022304_SEAMWebsite_attach1.pdf>

FIP (International Pharmaceutical Federation). 2001. *FIP Guidelines for the Labels of Prescribed Medicines.* The Hague: FIP. <http://www.fip.org/www/uploads/database_file.php?id=256&table_id=>

★ ———. 1998. *Good Pharmacy Practice (GPP) in Developing Countries: Recommendations for Step-wise Implementation.* The Hague: FIP. <http://www.fip.org/files/fip/Statements/latest/Dossier%20003%20total.PDF>

★ ———. 1997. *Standards of Quality for Pharmacy Services: Good Pharmacy Practice.* The Hague: FIP.

FIP Working Group on Pharmacists and HIV-AIDS. 2008. *Recommendations for Pharmacy Management and the Dispensing of Antiretroviral Medicines in Resource-Limited Settings.* The Hague: FIP. <http://www.fip.org/files/fip/HIV/eng/RecommendationsENG2008.pdf>

Institute for Safe Medication Practices. <http://www.ismp.org>

Lipowski, E. E., D. E. Campbell, D. B. Brushwood, and D. Wilson. 2002. Time Savings Associated with Dispensing Unit-of-Use Packages. *Journal of the American Pharmaceutical Association (Wash)* 42(4):577–81.

Nunney, J. M., and D. K. T. Raynor. 2001. How Are Multi-Compartment Compliance Aids Used in Primary Care? *Pharmaceutical Journal* 267:784–9.

Radyowijati, A., and H. Haak. 2003. Improving Antibiotic Use in Low-Income Countries: An Overview of Evidence on Determinants. *Social Science & Medicine* 57(4):733–44.

Royal Pharmaceutical Society of Great Britain. 2009. "Practice Guidance Documents." In *Medicines, Ethics and Practice: A Guide for Pharmacists.* London: Royal Pharmaceutical Society of Great Britain. <http://www.rpsgb.org/informationresources/download-societypublications> (Updated regularly.)

Shire Jama, A., L. Heide, and A. Petersen. 1985. Colour Coding of Labels for Essential Drugs. *Tropical Doctor* 15(4):195.

Wiedenmayer, K., R. S. Summers, C. A. Mackie, A. G. S. Gous, and M. Everard. 2006. *Developing Pharmacy Practice: A Focus on Patient Care.* The Hague: World Health Organization and International Pharmaceutical Federation. <http://fip.org/files/fip/publications/DevelopingPharmacyPractice/DevelopingPharmacyPracticeEN.pdf>

★ WHO (World Health Organization). 1997. *The Role of the Pharmacist in the Health Care System: Preparing the Future Pharmacist: Curricular Development. Report of a Third WHO Consultative Group on the Role of the Pharmacist, Vancouver, Canada, 27–29 August 1997.* Geneva: WHO. <http://whqlibdoc.who.int/hq/1997/WHO_PHARM_97_599.pdf>

ASSESSMENT GUIDE

Dispensing indicators

- *Average dispensing communication time.* This indicator measures the time the dispenser actually spends explaining how the medicines should be taken.
- *Percentage of prescribed items actually dispensed.* This indicator is primarily a stock indicator.
- *Percentage of prescribed medications that are adequately labeled as per standard operating procedure.* At a minimum, package labeling should indicate patient names, drug name, and when the medicine should be taken (dose and frequency).
- *Patients' knowledge of correct dosage.*

Dispensing regulation

- Does a licensing system regulate the sale and dispensing of pharmaceuticals (wholesalers, pharmacists, retailers)?
- Are pharmacists legally allowed to substitute generic products for brand-name products?

- Is there an official checklist for carrying out inspections in different types of pharmaceutical establishments?

Dispensing training

- At each level in the health care system, who is responsible for the dispensing of medicines? What training do these individuals have in the principles and practices of medicine dispensing? Are standard operating procedures for dispensing and medication counseling available?
- How much supervision do these individuals receive? What type of pharmaceutical training is available in the country? Are there standardized education curricula for pharmacy personnel? Are experience requirements for dispensers clearly defined, and are these reasonable, given the numbers and geographical distribution of individuals meeting, or eligible for meeting, these requirements?

Note: See also the checklist in Box 30-2.

CHAPTER 31

Community-based participation and initiatives

SUMMARY

Community participation in health care is important because of the recognized value of locally tailored approaches, as well as the need for increased community financing to supplement government expenditures. For example, the Alma Ata Declaration of 1978 focused on primary health care as the best way to achieve healthy communities, and the deployment of community health workers was viewed as a key component in that strategy. More recently, the concept of community case management has evolved to respond to international recommendations to deliver community-level treatment for common, serious childhood infections. Many activities of questionable value, however, carry the label of "community participation," which can reflect negatively on the whole field. This chapter summarizes the essential elements of a successful community participation program, with a focus on pharmaceutical management.

Community participation may involve—

- Contributing—community members contribute money, labor, or materials.
- Consulting—members are asked for their views and are informed of project plans.
- Managing—members actively participate in making decisions and in controlling resources.

When all three levels of participation are present, communities are full partners in providing services.

Full partnership in decision making means that health development is defined in terms of people's real needs and priorities; community economic, human, and organizational resources are mobilized; and mechanisms are created to increase people's access to information, knowledge, and skills and to help them make their goals and priorities known.

Community participation can improve pharmaceutical management through—

- Advocating for access to health care
- Promoting preventive health care
- Improving the availability of medicines and supplies
- Managing outreach services
- Managing facility-based health services
- Promoting appropriate medicine use

Formal health care professionals play a key role in facilitating community participation. They act as motivators; as supporters to the community in establishing strong organizations for community-based activities; as resource persons by establishing links between the community, government agencies, and other organizations; and as trainers and supervisors, building capacity within the community.

Community participation rarely emerges on its own. It succeeds best within an enabling environment, which includes—

- Political commitment to the concept of participation
- Interest in decentralization of health services
- Existence of a health structure
- Commitment to developing people's managerial capabilities

31.1 Introduction

The failure of traditional top-down development approaches to eradicate poverty and improve the living conditions of the poor has led to increased interest in popular participation in development. For the first decade or so after the Alma Ata World Conference on Primary Health Care, many governments in developing countries took initiatives to expand community participation in the promotion and delivery of basic health services, including medicines. This expansion represented a response to the increasing trend toward decentralization and recognition of the value of locally tailored approaches, as well as an acknowledgment of the need for increasing levels of community financing. In the 1990s, however, countries were finding it difficult to sustain community-based health programs, especially with the increased focus on centrally run vertical programs such as those focused on HIV/AIDS. But renewed interest in community-based approaches has resulted from countries seeking the most effective ways to accomplish the Millennium Development Goals.

Community participation can have an impact on health care, from policy to patient. At a higher level, community organizations and civil society groups have influenced policies—especially those related to the HIV/AIDS pandemic. At a more local level, a community-based focus creates a new form of governance for public health systems and alters the relationship between providers and users of health care services. Health professionals are being called upon to adopt new approaches and to work in partnership with communities: in sharing knowledge and skills, jointly deciding on plans for health care, and seeking to develop and strengthen the community's capacity to care for itself.

This chapter presents some of the key features of community participation in the promotion and delivery of basic health services, including pharmaceutical management. The chapter draws on the experiences of many community-based health programs, among them the Bamako Initiative, which promoted community management and financing of basic health services, including medicines, and the rise of community case management, which is a strategy to deliver community-level treatment for common, serious childhood infections. The chapter also describes how community volunteers and private-sector outlets can improve access to quality medicines and services. Although some of the interventions described are not specific to medicines, they relate to improving the availability and use of medicines to improve health outcomes.

Although many methods of community participation are possible, no clear-cut or universally applicable methods exist. Participation varies from one country to another and even from one community to another within the same country, depending on socioeconomic and political contexts. Because communities are not homogeneous, this chapter provides broad guidelines for increasing community participation. The terms *community, users, consumers,* and *beneficiaries* are used interchangeably.

31.2 The power of advocacy groups and community-based organizations

Increased advocacy from various groups, such as multilateral organizations, bilateral donors, nongovernmental organizations at all levels, and civil society organizations, has brought about pressure to change policies and push pharmaceutical issues onto national and international health care agendas. Issues that are receiving more attention include the need for new health technologies and medicines for tuberculosis (TB), malaria, and HIV/AIDS, including pediatric formulations of antiretrovirals (ARVs) and laboratory technologies, such as more sensitive TB diagnostics, that are suitable for developing countries. In particular, the HIV/AIDS pandemic put into motion an advocacy movement that has significantly influenced issues on a worldwide scale.

The profound impact of the AIDS pandemic resulted in a unique alliance of activists and people living with the infection acting as advocates within their communities. In 1983, an advocacy group in Brazil created a nongovernmental organization to fight AIDS, a year after the first case had been diagnosed there, and additional groups followed. In addition to increasing prevention efforts and treatment in poor and remote communities, Brazilian activists are credited with assuring adequate funding for ARVs and contributing to the country's successful pricing negotiations with pharmaceutical manufacturers (Homedes and Ugalde 2006). In 1987 in New York City, the AIDS Coalition

to Unleash Power (ACT UP) was formed as a community activist group dedicated to influencing AIDS-related policy. They were the most visible example of how involvement at the community level and from people living with HIV/AIDS could greatly affect public policy and issues such as ARV access and affordability that ranged far beyond their New York roots. Since 1998, the Treatment Action Campaign (TAC) and its allies in South Africa have led a lengthy and very visible public campaign to improve access to ART through the public health sector.

Today, organizations around the world work to mobilize community support and action not only to improve the lives of local families touched by HIV/AIDS, but to keep AIDS issues—especially access to ARVs—high on the public agenda. For example, the International HIV/AIDS Alliance (www.aidsalliance.org), which was founded in 1993, works with community organizations in more than forty developing countries to strengthen the local response to HIV-related disease, and includes supporting community engagement for antiretroviral therapy (ART). The HIV/AIDS Alliance produces many resources and tools to improve the effectiveness of the community effort. A resource is also available for how to involve communities in the national AIDS response (International Council of AIDS Service Organizations [ICASO], AfriCASO, and International HIV/AIDS Alliance 2007).

31.3 What does community participation mean?

Although wide consensus exists on the central role of community participation in primary health care, the concept has varying definitions and different interpretations. In its *World Health Report*, the World Health Organization (WHO) defined communities as "groups of people living near each other, or with various social connections, and often with a shared sense of purpose or need" (WHO 2004). In practice, however, "community" may be conceptualized differently depending on the context. In general, the definition includes clients or users of health services as well as the providers of health services and medicines in the locality. An analysis of community participation suggested that the definition of community differs according to the actual level of participation (Murthy and Klugman 2004).

Community participation is best defined as a cumulative process through which beneficiaries develop the managerial and organizational capacity to increase control over the decisions that affect their lives. Therefore, community participation means that members have a strong voice in all issues that affect the well-being of the community at large. A high level of community participation implies the involvement of difficult-to-reach population groups, as well as the nongovernmental organizations that represent their interests. The process of community participation can help these marginalized groups become better organized and more involved in decisions pertaining to their health.

When national government policies call for the decentralization of health-sector services, increased community participation is one way to help build capacity and ensure quality of services because management responsibility shifts to the local level. In this situation, however, civil society groups must advocate for the community to policy makers to ensure that the process of decentralized responsibility works effectively.

A community's full partnership in the decision-making process implies—

- Definition of health development in terms of local needs and priorities
- Mobilization of the community's economic, human, and organizational resources
- Creation of mechanisms that help people increase their access to information, knowledge, and skills; voice their opinions; and make their goals and priorities known

Three distinct approaches to community participation reflect different degrees of participation (Fox 1993)—

1. *Contributing:* Community members provide money, labor, or materials for health projects.
2. *Consulting:* Community members are asked for their views and are informed of project plans in order to secure their commitment and contributions to construction, operation, and maintenance.
3. *Managing:* Community members actively participate in decision making and in controlling community resources and are engaged in project identification, planning, organization, implementation, monitoring, and evaluation.

Many health professionals have seen community participation as mainly "contributing" to health projects; that is, the community assists the professionals with contributions of labor, materials, or money but only rarely with ideas. In both the contributing and the consulting modes, communities are regarded mainly as beneficiaries of assistance. When communities are involved with managing as well, the three concepts become synergistic; community members, in partnership with outside development workers, are able to use their heads and their voices—as well as their hands—in the development and operation of facilities and services they can genuinely call their own.

Community participation is best measured by its contribution to overall health outcomes, not only in terms of quantifiable project outputs but also in terms of the process of participation itself, including—

- Community involvement in needs assessment, planning, management of resources, implementation of project activities, monitoring, and evaluation
- People's capacity to manage and organize themselves
- People's access to new skills, knowledge, and information
- Community organization and solidarity
- Relationships between users and providers of health services
- Political will, leadership, commitment, and resources
- Transparency in project management and accountability of health services toward the public being served

31.4 Why promote community participation?

It is at the community level that women, men, and children get drinking water; that wastes are controlled to prevent disease; that nutritional deficiencies are identified and actions taken. It is in communities and in households that people choose health care providers, that families make decisions about the use of their resources, that patients obtain and decide how to use medicines. Therefore, projects aimed at improving access to and use of basic health services, including essential medicines, cannot achieve their objectives and ensure sustainability unless a genuine partnership exists with communities.

The concept of community participation in health is based on the following principles—

- Participation in one's own health care is a basic right to which all people are entitled.
- When health services are linked to local perceptions of needs and are managed with the support of local people, those services are more likely to achieve their objectives and be sustainable.
- By actively participating in project planning and decision making, people gain confidence in their ability to change their situation and better their health status.
- By solving their own problems, people become more self-reliant.
- Where public health institutions are weak, community participation in management and financing can improve efficiency, increase public accountability, restore users' confidence, mobilize additional resources to complement government resources, and improve the quality of services.
- By encouraging people to become involved, projects can benefit from local skills and resources.
- When people know from the start that a project is theirs, they show a greater sense of responsibility for the management and maintenance of services and facilities than when projects are controlled by "outsiders."

- The positive experience of planning, implementing, and managing a successful project leads to involvement in other development activities, resulting in a multiplier effect.
- Health, nutrition, and family planning outcomes can be significantly improved and sustained only when the strengthening of health services, including medicine supply, goes hand in hand with community awareness about public health issues and personal health care.

Community participation is crucial in promoting healthy lifestyles and better health management at the household and community levels.

31.5 Community participation and initiatives to improve pharmaceutical management

Community participation has a role in pharmaceutical management, including advocacy for health care as described in Section 31.2. Communities can also—

- Promote preventive health care
- Improve availability of medicines and supplies
- Manage outreach services
- Manage facility-based health services
- Promote appropriate medicines use

Promotion of preventive health care

Governments and households could save money if efforts were made to promote preventive health care as well as rational medicine use. Grassroots community networks can play a crucial role in promoting preventive care and encouraging therapy without medicines at home for minor illnesses.

The process by which health promotion is carried out, including the time and effort that go into developing a community's sense of ownership, is critical to a program's success. In Malawi, for example, as part of an effort to control malaria, village health committees began selling insecticide-treated nets (ITNs) for beds. The demand for ITNs was very high, and committees used the revenue to finance community improvements, such as drinking-water wells. In addition, malaria cases decreased by as much as half in some villages (Lewnes 2005).

Improvement of availability of medicines and supplies

In response to the problem of declining public resources for financing pharmaceutical and other recurrent costs, some communities have adopted cost-recovery and self-financing schemes in local health centers, dispensaries, and outreach services. The aim is to improve and extend services by gener-

ating sufficient income to cover some local operating costs, such as the supply of essential medicines, salaries of some support staff, incentives for health workers, and investment in community health activities.

Community cost sharing can be based on user fees, prepayment for services, local taxes, and various income-generating activities. Communities can also help pay health care costs by contributing labor or making direct financial contributions for the improvement and maintenance of health care infrastructure. Revolving drug funds are discussed in Chapter 13, while Chapter 12 covers community-based health financing.

Management of outreach services

Over the past thirty years, large numbers of community health workers (CHWs) have been trained in many countries as part of national strategies for primary health care, especially for children. CHWs can be general community health resources, or part of a specialized group, such as community medicine dispensers, traditional birth attendants, or HIV/AIDS communicators. All types of CHWs typically are trained in one or more health care functions, but have no formal professional certification (Haines et al. 2007).

CHWs have been shown to be an effective means of accelerating and extending the delivery of primary health care when they receive adequate training, are regularly supervised, are provided with adequate logistical support, and are linked to established district health systems for technical backup. CHWs can also be valuable in monitoring health in the community and as a referral point between health centers and the community. However, although CHWs are often seen as an extension of the health system, supervision is a challenge to implement and is often not carried out. Supervision should be an important focus of any CHW program in order to ensure the availability and rational use of medicines. Lessons learned about CHW programs (Haines et al. 2007) include—

- *Training and individual support:* Training alone is insufficient; supervision and support increase performance and sustainability.
- *Tasks and roles:* CHWs will probably perform better with clearly defined roles and a limited number of specific tasks to carry out.
- *Incentives:* Targeted incentives, monetary or otherwise, will probably reduce attrition and improve performance.
- *Community and policy support:* Consistent support can help sustain CHW programs; active involvement of communities ensures support is available and promotes the use of community workers by community members.

Figure 31-1   Framework for appropriate Community Drug Management for Childhood Illness

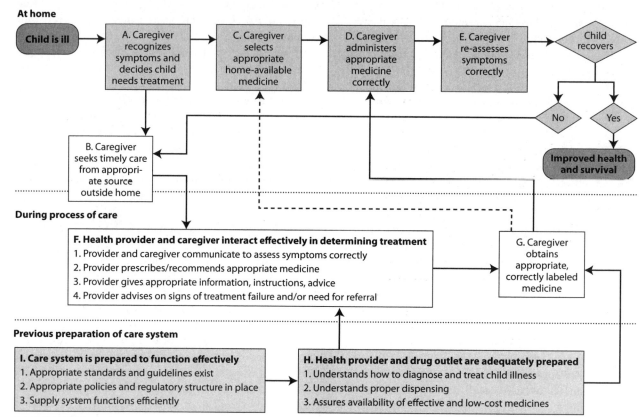

Source: Ross-Degnan et al. 2008.

To be successful, CHWs, who are sometimes volunteers, need to be fully trusted and supported in the community; for example, in Uganda, volunteers selected by community members to distribute ivermectin treatment for river blindness were far more successful than those selected by the local government, who may have been viewed with some suspicion. The annual dropout rate for the community-selected group was less than 2 percent, compared with 95 percent for the others (Katabarwa and Richards 2001).

A similar trust issue involves remuneration. Although monetary compensation to CHWs results in higher retention rates, it can also cause community members to view the volunteers as government employees rather than as true community advocates. Providing quality services in the community may earn the community health workers recognition and status, and they are often rewarded with payment in kind by community members. Research shows how incentives and disincentives affect the motivation and ultimately the retention of CHWs in the community (Bhattacharyya et al. 2001).

WHO's and UNICEF's Community Integrated Management of Childhood Illness (C-IMCI) initiative initially focused on prevention of childhood illness in the commu-

nity, with CHW responsibilities typically limited to education on sanitation, nutrition, family planning, child health, and immunizations. C-IMCI is evolving, however, and its focus has expanded to include community-based curative services or community case management of common conditions, such as malaria, diarrheal disease, and childhood pneumonia, in line with WHO and UNICEF recommendations in 2004 (WHO/UNICEF 2004). As a result, community case management through adequately trained and supervised community health workers is being increasingly promoted not only as a means of improving quality of care and rational use of medicines but also as a mechanism for increasing availability of medicines (Figure 31-1). Country Study 31-1 illustrates the success of community case management in Afghanistan, the Democratic Republic of Congo, and Nepal.

CHWs receive greater community support when they are empowered to provide curative services and medicines; however, an insufficient pharmaceutical supply can diminish the success of health volunteers. For community case management to succeed, medicines and supplies need to be available, managed appropriately, and used rationally (according to standardized treatment guidelines). Therefore, it is fundamental to pay attention to the supply management components of any community case management program. (See Country Study 31-2, which describes training community health workers in Senegal about appropriate use of medicines.)

Having informal health service providers in the community is being recognized as a means of enhancing primary health care by providing curative services. For example, in many resource-limited countries, community members often seek advice and medicines first from private drug sellers or medicine vendors; for various reasons they do not choose to seek care in the public sector—especially in rural areas, where public facilities may not be easy to reach. Chapter 32 covers initiatives to improve drug seller services in the community.

Management of facility-based health services

With the economic crisis of the 1980s, particularly in Africa, infrastructure deteriorated, pharmaceuticals were often unavailable, and civil servants went unpaid for long periods. In response, many governments began to involve communities in the management of public facility–based health services. Now, health care facilities from all sectors—public, nongovernmental, and faith based—benefit from community involvement.

Because essential medicines are necessary for integrated, high-quality, cost-effective basic health services, and because people perceive pharmaceuticals as a quality indicator, medicines have often served as a starting point for community co-financing and co-management of facility-based health services.

Locally elected health committees can participate in the day-to-day tasks of managing health facilities. Such committees can—

- Assist health staff in developing an appropriate payment mechanism or mechanisms (prepayment scheme, flat rate, or fee for service) and in pricing services, including medicines
- Establish procedures for procuring and managing medicines and other supplies
- Determine criteria and develop an administrative system for those who cannot afford to pay or who should be exempt from paying for other reasons
- Establish a system of internal control of receipts and expenditures that ensures financial viability, accountability, and transparency in managing the system
- Participate in the day-to-day financial management and bookkeeping and prepare the health center's budget

---

Country Study 31-1
Community case management successes

Afghanistan. After decades of war, Afghanistan's child survival rates were close to the world's worst. Geographic isolation, cultural strictures, and poor security blocked many women and children from accessing care at public health facilities, so the Afghan government trained 20,000 community health workers—half of them women and most nonliterate. Their jobs include providing Integrated Management of Childhood Illness and advice to mothers on child care and family planning. About half of all sick children are now seen by CHWs, and increased access has contributed to the 25 percent decline in child mortality seen over five years (Aitken et al. 2009).

Democratic Republic of Congo (DRC). Since 2005, the community case management (CCM) program in DRC has trained hundreds of CHWs to manage uncomplicated childhood conditions. A key component of the CCM strategy was managing medicines, and training included how to track inventory and calculate medicine needs. Initial program results showed that 90 percent of twenty randomly sampled CHWs dispensed the correct quantity of medicine; all said the medicine name and formulation and how to administer it; 90 percent asked

the caregiver to repeat the instructions to assure understanding; and stockouts were rare (Bukasa et al. 2008). Investing in pharmaceutical management from program initiation has encouraged positive results, including minimized stockouts and appropriate dispensing practices.

Nepal. The Ministry of Health in Nepal trains female community health volunteers (FCHVs) to provide some health services in their community. When FCHVs were given responsibility for managing childhood pneumonia using co-trimoxazole, some observers questioned the cadre's ability to correctly diagnose and treat pneumonia, especially those who were semiliterate. These concerns were addressed by using pictorial training materials to facilitate understanding. The intervention also includes regular refresher training for the FCHVs and community orientation to the concept. In the program's first decade, districts with FCHVs doubled the number of children who receive treatment—saving an estimated 6,000 lives a year. The intervention now covers about 80 percent of children, with plans for universal coverage in the next two years (Dawson et al. 2008; Global Health Council 2009).

Source: Embrey et al. 2010.

Country Study 31-2
Community health workers appropriately treat pneumonia in Senegal

The government of Senegal increased population access to health services by developing a network of health huts run by trained birth attendants (matrons) and community health workers. The Ministry of Health had used CHWs to treat malaria, diarrhea, and other minor ailments but had opposed their dispensing antibiotics because of fear of inappropriate use, which could contribute to drug resistance. Nevertheless, antibiotics were widely available in the market and were also inappropriately used in some health huts. In part on the basis of this information, the Ministry of Health agreed to operational research to test the feasibility of using CHWs to manage acute respiratory infection (ARI).

The research design was a nonrandomized controlled study with four intervention districts. Literate CHWs were trained for three days using a World Health Organization ARI algorithm in case management, followed by periodic one-day refreshers and ongoing supervision. Work tools included stopwatches, weighing scales, information materials, calculators, patient registers, and pharmaceutical stock cards. Co-trimoxazole was available in the health system through the national system's cost recovery, and its availability at the health hut was facilitated through store management training and supervision. Related educational activities and com-

munity mobilization were initially carried out by CHWs, who were joined by health promotion volunteers.

The training included 113 literate CHWs in ninety health huts. Postintervention tests showed marked improvement in CHW knowledge of ARI, unrelated to level of formal schooling. Under direct observation, nearly 90 percent of CHWs correctly evaluated, classified, and treated ARI cases, and more than 90 percent knew general danger signs. A record review showed that 95 percent of pneumonia cases were correctly classified, 97 percent were correctly treated, and 69 percent of severe cases were appropriately referred (an additional 22 percent received co-trimoxazole). Nearly twice as many pneumonia cases were treated in intervention areas than in control districts. The percentage of mothers knowing at least two danger signs increased from 33 percent in August 2003 to 65 percent in April 2004. Two CHWs inappropriately dispensed 552 tablets to older patients (of 36,800 tablets total), for a misuse rate of 1.5 percent. No stockouts of co-trimoxazole occurred during the study period. The study concluded that literate CHWs who are adequately trained and supported can correctly classify ARI, appropriately treat pneumonia with co-trimoxazole, and refer severe cases.

Sources: BASICS II 2004; Briggs et al. 2003.

- Carry out stock inventories of pharmaceuticals and other supplies and equipment
- Recruit and manage the support personnel hired with community funds (community pharmacy salespersons, guards, drivers, and so forth)

In some countries, health committees have a clear mandate to carry out evaluations of the performance of health staff and, if necessary, file complaints and propose disciplinary measures to district health offices.

Country Study 31-3 describes experiences with community participation within the Bamako Initiative framework in three different countries.

Promotion of appropriate medicine use

The inefficient and even unsafe treatment of illnesses through inappropriate medicine use is a problem in many settings (see Chapter 27). These problems are caused by irrational medicine prescribing practices on the part of providers (which may include non–health care professionals, such as informal drug vendors or caregivers). Other

causes include popular misconceptions and nonadherence to treatment on the part of patients. Advocacy by organized consumer groups and efforts to improve public access to information are effective ways to address these problems (see Chapter 34).

Consumer education helps improve adherence to recommended medicine therapies. As part of this process, consumers are able to provide feedback to prescribers on the effectiveness of medicines, undesirable side effects, and so on. Such a process is reinforced when personal links have been established between consumers and providers at the community level and when community members are organized and vocal in demanding quality health services, such as in some social-marketing programs discussed in Chapter 33.

An involved and informed community can also promote appropriate medicine use by helping to reduce disease stigma, such as for HIV/AIDS and tuberculosis, thereby encouraging early case detection and treatment adherence. For example, clinics can alert the community support group to trace a patient who has missed an appointment. Community members can also play a successful role in the treatment delivery process; for example, volunteers from the

Country Study 31-3
The Bamako Initiative in Benin, Guinea, and Mali

Since the late 1980s, the Bamako Initiative has been implemented to some degree in half the countries of sub-Saharan Africa. More than ten years later, experiences in Benin, Guinea, and Mali showed that communities were able to strengthen delivery of health services and ensure supply of essential medicines by forging a partnership between the state and organized community groups.

Before reforms were put in place, the vast majority of poor families in the three countries did not have access to affordable, quality health services or medicines, and the public health sector was in shambles. Immunization coverage was under 15 percent, and less than 10 percent of families made at least one visit per year to public health facilities. Although services were supposed to be free, patients often had to pay, and pharmaceuticals were often unavailable in the health unit. The only reliable source of medicines and care was usually in the informal private sector—mainly drug peddlers—where rural families typically spent 5 U.S. dollars per capita out of pocket per year.

In all three countries, the priority of the Bamako Initiative–related activities was to establish accountability and empower communities to take ownership of their health centers and services. A contractual arrangement between the state and communities promised delivery of basic professional health services by decentralizing decision making and management and instituting community cost sharing and co-management of health services. Communities were also involved in managing pharmaceuticals and revenue: The community pharmacies had double locks, requiring both the health center's chief nurse and a community representative to open; bank accounts required double signatures. Members of committees participated twice a year in the monitoring of health services—analyzing problems and helping to design new actions—and budgeting the use of these revenues, within clear national standard guidelines.

During the more than ten years of the Bamako Initiative in these three countries, access to community-based

health services was restored for more than 20 million people, use of services increased among children and women in the poorest segment of the population, and a sharper decline of mortality in rural areas compared to urban areas occurred in Guinea and Mali. Immunization levels increased in all three countries, with Benin averaging close to 80 percent, which is one of the highest levels of immunization among the poor in Africa (see figure below). Much of the success can be linked to ensuring the supply of affordable essential pharmaceuticals and commodities in health centers under the scrutiny of the committees and the involvement of communities in the planning and management of services, particularly immunization and maternal child health interventions.

The implementation of these initiatives were not without challenges. Top-down organization of health committees in the community tends to uphold elitism, and the rest of the population can feel marginalized. However, over time, the representation on committees improved, following guidelines from the policy makers. A remaining problem is the weak "voice" of the poorest citizens who have the least time to participate in meetings or other voluntary community support activities.

Steady improvements in immunization coverage in Benin, Guinea, and Mali

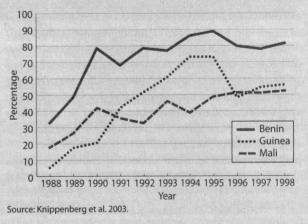

Source: Knippenberg et al. 2003.

community have been used as supporters for patients undergoing tuberculosis treatment in Cambodia and Peru (Thim et al. 2004; Shin et al. 2004), and worldwide, community-based groups have been established to support people living with HIV/AIDS.

When unregulated private markets offer pharmaceuticals of dubious quality, without prescription, and at exorbitant

prices, consumers must be sensitized to the health risks and costs involved. Community health workers, health committees, and networks at the grassroots level can, with increased access to information and technical support from health staff, serve as advocates to consumers for the promotion of reliable sources of local pharmaceutical procurement and the rational and correct use of medicines.

31.6 Health professionals' contribution to the process

Formal-sector health professionals play a key role in facilitating the process of community participation in health, and particularly in the supply and use of medicines. They serve as—

- Motivators who draw out people's untapped skills, experiences, and leadership potential
- Supporters who help the community establish strong and appropriate organizations for the planning, implementation, and management of community-based health activities
- Resource persons who establish links between the community, government agencies working in health and health-related areas, and other relevant organizations and services
- Trainers of community leaders, members of health committees, and community health workers who build on the knowledge and experiences that exist in the community
- Supervisors of community health workers who ensure delivery of quality health services

To fulfill these roles effectively and to create productive partnerships at the community level, health professionals must be able to—

- Communicate with the community and establish relationships with people, including community health workers and others who provide medicines
- Listen well and learn from the community
- Share skills and experiences with the community
- Respect people's ideas, skills, and wisdom
- Promote equity in male-female representation and in representation of the various social, economic, and age groups in local decision-making bodies
- Be aware of and respect the social practices, traditions, and culture of the community
- Foster collaboration with other projects, organizations, and services
- Promote a holistic or integrated approach to health development

31.7 Facilitating community participation in health programming

The participatory process for health programming includes community needs assessment, local decision making and participatory planning, community organization and leadership, and participatory monitoring. In the following sections, practical suggestions are given for each of these phases.

Community needs assessment

Conducting a needs assessment is the first step in initiating a community-based participatory health project. The purpose is to involve the project beneficiaries in determining their health problems, the causes of those problems, and their primary needs as the basis for planning community activities and for establishing baseline data against which progress can be measured in the future. Areas to be covered, the choice of method, and data analysis issues all need to be considered when planning such an assessment.

Key areas to be covered. Community participation in the needs assessment phase is fundamental. When undertaken as a joint exercise, a needs assessment can encourage dialogue between health professionals and community members, so that accurate and complete information is available to both parties when deciding on appropriate actions.

Basic community health needs: Assessing basic health needs begins with identifying and ranking problems, causes, cost of health care, health-seeking behavior, access to health services and medicines—including affordability of medicines and health care and use of medicines by the consumers and providers in the community. Specific needs in relation to problems identified, what the community would like to do to improve its health situation, and community resources that could be mobilized can then be considered.

Community decision-making process and power structures: How does the community work? What are the rules of the group? Who makes them? Who enforces them? How does power depend on sex, age, tribe, kinship, knowledge, money, education? Who makes decisions, and who controls resources at the household and community levels? What are the power relations between women and men, between basic service delivery systems and the community, between community and local authorities, between various socioeconomic and political groups? How do people feel about the decisions that affect their lives and the way these decisions are made?

Education and socialization: How do schooling and traditional education influence people's knowledge, attitudes, and behavior in dealing with health issues, in particular their choice of health care provider and their use of medicines?

Beliefs and values: How do beliefs, ideology, or religion affect people's understanding of health and development?

Basic population data: These data include population, number of households in the community, number of inhabitants living within five kilometers of the nearest health facility, and age and sex distribution.

Facilities and infrastructure: What community facilities (schools, churches, temples, markets), clinics, health posts, pharmacies, shops, drug shops, water supplies, street lighting, communications, and transport (such as roads or paths) exist?

Past and ongoing health and health-related projects: Are any past, ongoing, or planned projects or programs relevant? Achievements, approaches, constraints, resources, organization, and management of activities; services involved; and potential for coordinating efforts all need to be considered.

Methods. A community needs assessment is not necessarily a formal investigation. Common sense, creativity, and ingenuity can be used to determine the most appropriate methods, modify existing methods, or suggest new methods.

It is important to start by establishing contacts in the community and by identifying key informants who could be useful in providing information and in organizing and facilitating community meetings and group discussions. This information can be gathered in the following ways—

Door-to-door visits (household surveys): Conducting structured or informal interviews at a sample of households.

Group discussions: Holding casual, focused, or deliberately structured discussions at various levels of the community or neighborhood.

Individual discussions: Interviewing private providers and shopkeepers, for example.

Participatory mapping and modeling: Involving community members in making maps (social, demographic, health, water resources), using the ground, floor, or paper. (Box 31-1 provides some tips for participatory mapping. These tips can also be used in other interactions with the community.)

Role-playing: Helping community members describe their situation and needs by taking different roles.

Seasonal diagramming: Determining through discussion with community members, seasonal variation in illnesses, health care costs, access to health services, food availability or shortage, economic difficulties and impact effect on health, and coping mechanisms.

Secondary sources: Reviewing data from files, maps, project reports, population census reports, health center records, or articles.

Transect walks: Systematically walking with informants through an area and observing, asking, listening, discussing; identifying different zones, local technologies, introduced technologies, health-seeking behavior, average distance to nearest health facility, community-felt needs, perceived solutions, opportunities; and mapping and diagramming.

Many tools exist for situational analysis or needs assessment in the community. One example related to availability and use of medicines at the community level is

---

Box 31-1
Tips for helping in participatory mapping

- Help people get started by letting them do it themselves.
- Be patient. It's their map.
- Look, listen, and learn.
- Facilitate. Don't dominate.
- When community members are mapping, modeling, or diagramming, don't interfere.
- Sit back and watch. Or go away!
- Keep a permanent (paper) record, including mappers' names, to give them credit for their contributions.
- If necessary, suggest that sometimes a succession of maps works better.

Management Sciences for Health's Community Drug Management Assessment tool, which uses household surveys and individual interviewing techniques to study availability of medicines and their use by clients, drug sellers, or providers. This assessment manual is accompanied by an intervention guide to orient decision makers at a variety of levels on the best interventions to improve the availability and use of medicines in the community. Box 31-2 tells how the *Community Drug Management for Childhood Illness: Assessment Manual* can assess the practices of household caregivers or patients and their medicine providers.

Data analysis. When analyzing the data, bear in mind these key points—

Ranking of health problems and health-seeking behavior: Identify and rank the most important health problems and health-seeking behaviors for each of the major health problems identified and for vulnerable groups, such as children and pregnant women; the health care provider (traditional healer, health center, hospital, community health workers, drug sellers, self); and availability of medicines and average cost of treatment.

Wealth ranking: Identify clusters of households according to wealth, including those considered poorest and unable to pay for health care. Identify mechanisms to help the poor.

Analysis of differences: Seek opinions of all groups within the community and analyze differences in opinion by gender, age, social group, economic group, and occupation.

Trend analysis: Compare people's accounts of the past and the present; their reports of how things have changed (how health status has improved or worsened; changes in the size of families, the status of women, level of education, income, food, and nutrition); and the causes of these changes and trends.

Box 31-2
Assessing management of medicines for childhood illnesses and adult malaria in the community

The availability, appropriate management, and rational use of medicines are critical to the successful implementation of health programs. Child survival and malaria control programs have shown that identifying and treating patients early and appropriately in the community help prevent illnesses from worsening and reduce mortality. However, activities targeting only the public sector have limited impact because they may not reach households or private-sector providers, where most childhood illnesses and malaria cases are treated.

The Community Drug Management for Childhood Illness (C-DMCI) tool (Nachbar et al. 2003) has been developed to study the practices of household caregivers or patients and their medicine providers for childhood illnesses and adult malaria. This tool helps district health managers, program planners, and regional and national policy makers identify problems in pharmaceutical management in the community at the household and provider levels through a household survey and individual interviews with different providers of medicines in the community. The tool's survey questionnaires are designed to be administered by local community members such as schoolteachers, staff of nongovernmental organizations (NGOs), or others who are not health professionals. Data from the survey responses can then be analyzed by district health teams, national program staff, or NGO staff.

The C-DMCI uses an indicator-based approach to identify strengths and weaknesses of community pharmaceutical management, as well as to provide a systematic method of monitoring the effect of interventions targeting health providers, caregivers, and patients. The data collection instrument for assessing the products and services of drug sellers and health providers focuses on pharmaceutical availability, provider knowledge, and appropriate dispensing in both the private and public sectors. The instrument for assessing the practices of household caregivers and patients provides data on their behaviors and practices when choosing, purchasing, and administering medicines. An accompanying guide

(Ross-Degnan et al. 2008) can help decision makers prioritize problems and design appropriately targeted interventions to improve pharmaceutical management for childhood illnesses and adult malaria in the community.

In Senegal, the Ministry of Health, in collaboration with the Rational Pharmaceutical Management (RPM) Plus Program and the BASICS project, conducted an assessment using the newly developed C-DMCI assessment tool. The survey took place in 2002 in two districts.

Some key findings included—

- Oral rehydration solution (ORS), which is recommended as the first-line treatment for diarrhea, was not available in private pharmacies and was insufficiently available in the public sector.
- Only 56 percent of children with fever took the first-line antimalarial medicine, and fewer than 20 percent of children with pneumonia or diarrhea took the appropriate first-line treatment (co-trimoxazole and ORS, respectively).
- In general, the medicines were not correctly administered in the home, even when instructions were given to caregivers at the time of purchase; only about 60 percent of patients took chloroquine for three days.
- Only about 30 percent of caregivers took children with symptoms of pneumonia for care on the same day symptoms started.

Based on evidence showing wide misuse of antibiotics, the Ministry of Health introduced a policy permitting CHWs, with special training and close supervision, to treat cases of childhood pneumonia with co-trimoxazole. Evaluation showed that nearly 90 percent of workers correctly evaluated, classified, and treated acute respiratory illnesses, and there were no co-trimoxazole stockouts. In addition, nearly twice as many pneumonia cases were treated in intervention areas than in control districts. As a result, the Ministry of Health extended the community-based pneumonia treatment project nationwide.

Sources: Ross-Degnan et al. 2008; Senauer et al. 2008; Briggs et al. 2003; Nachbar et al. 2003.

Local decision making and participatory planning

Using the information collected in the needs assessment, community members, health professionals, and decision makers collaboratively decide what actions need to be taken, how, when, and with what means. The planning process should take place in a climate that fosters two-way communication and mutual learning, so that all stakeholders feel equally involved. The steps in participatory planning are shown in Box 31-3.

Community organization and leadership

Certain actions require collective efforts beyond the capacity of individuals, households, and even health committees and community health workers. The creation or strengthening of community organizational capacity is important for empowerment objectives. Creating organizational capacity can be laborious and time-consuming, but it is vital for ensuring the sustainability of community-based projects. The following tips for health professionals and community leaders can facilitate the process of community organization or group formation—

- Identify charismatic community leaders and strengthen their leadership skills.
- Ensure that the people involved are those who are genuinely concerned with community health.
- Clearly define the specific tasks to be performed by each community representative and health-service representative.
- Build on existing formal and informal functional grassroots structures that have credibility in the community, to the extent possible. These may include women's groups, youth groups, or religious groups.
- Ensure an equitable representation of women and various socioeconomic groups on village committees.

Participatory monitoring

Information is an essential tool for local decision making, and participatory monitoring offers ways to share information. Increasing beneficiaries' capacity to collect information and use it for action is important: information confers power. By having increased access to information, communities increase their ability to make decisions and gain greater control over their own development.

Participatory monitoring can serve as an educational process, a management tool, and a surveillance system. As an educational process, it increases participants' awareness and understanding of the various factors that affect their health and development in general. As a management tool, it helps measure progress, identify problems, and inform decisions aimed at improving efficiency in the delivery of essential health services, including medicines. Finally, as a surveillance system, participatory monitoring provides community members, health services, and other related services with vital quantitative and qualitative data on the status of community health and nutrition and on consumer behavior. For pharmaceutical management and use, this information might include data on household expenditures for medicines, sources and availability of medicines in the community, and consumer medicine use practices. If the purpose of monitoring is to assess the effectiveness of a particular intervention, then the indicator measured would relate to the intervention's objectives.

Box 31-3
Steps in participatory planning

1. Encourage community members to reflect on problems identified through the needs assessment.
2. Facilitate dialogue on possible solutions, including pros and cons for each solution.
3. Decide on priority areas that need community action.
4. Set clear and measurable objectives.
5. Establish qualitative and quantitative indicators.
6. Determine resources needed to achieve objectives.
7. Determine the ability and willingness of the community to contribute time, money, and labor; what forms of contribution are needed; and what cost-sharing mechanisms will be put in place.
8. Determine the division of responsibility between the community and health professionals (who will do what).
9. Determine mechanisms for monitoring progress, supervision, and technical backup.
10. Identify training needs for community members and health professionals.
11. Determine mechanisms for ensuring transparency in project management and accountability of health services and community-elected bodies to the public they serve.
12. Determine the frequency of community meetings and the most effective channels for reporting to the community on project activities, including the amount of revenue generated and expenditures.

Some of the methods listed for community needs assessment can also be used for monitoring; for example, the door-to-door survey is essential. The main difference between the two processes is that whereas community needs assessment is usually conducted at the beginning of a project, participatory monitoring is continuous.

When developing a community-based monitoring system, the following key components of participatory monitoring should be addressed—

- Organize community members around specific tasks: data collection and analysis, presentation of information for community and health-service feedback, communication of results, facilitation of the interaction about data issues, and coordination of the participatory planning exercise.
- Provide staff of health and health-related services continuous technical and methodological backup for the process. Use feedback sessions as platforms for maintaining a regular dialogue between service users and providers.
- Simplify the methodology for gathering and analyzing information, so that those with little formal education can actively participate.
- Develop a consensus as to what is the most essential information for action at the community and facility levels and what information is needed for monitoring.
- Focus on information as a powerful tool for local decision making and action and not simply on the generation of data.

- Link community-based planning and monitoring to facility-level planning and monitoring. Information at the community level and the dialogue between health staff and users often generate quantitative and qualitative information that can be vital to improving the performance of health facilities.

31.8 Creating an enabling environment

Community participation rarely emerges on its own without some external influence. It succeeds best within an enabling environment and with the support of appropriate mechanisms at all levels. Conditions that favor the development of community participation include the following (Oakley 1989)—

- Political commitment to community participation in health development and to the general notion of people's participation
- Interest in the decentralization of health services and the corresponding strengthening of district health systems that will serve as the basic health unit for community participation
- Existence of a minimum health structure that can serve as the basis for community participation in health care
- Development of people's managerial capabilities to take responsibility for a process of participatory health development

---

Country Study 31-4
Creating an enabling environment in the community to encourage tuberculosis treatment compliance

The Cambodian Health Committee, a nongovernmental organization, developed a community-based approach to TB case detection and treatment compliance in Svay Rieng, one of the poorest provinces in Cambodia. Barriers to TB treatment had included a lack of access to health facilities in rural areas and the economic burdens of time spent at and in travel to health centers. The program consisted of two components—one health center based and one home based. Both components relied on a set of interventions that included pretreatment patient education, patient supporters to supervise treatment, a treatment contract, food incentives, surprise home visits, and a microfinance project that established a network of village banks. The banks' low-cost loans to families involved in treatment and the food supplements provided to patients as an incentive to take their medication were special ways of reducing poverty in the

community and raising the public visibility of the TB treatment program.

The program resulted in some of the highest TB case-detection rates in the world; case-notification rates in the home-based program were over four times higher than the national rate of 144 per 100,000 people, and cure rates in new patients were over 90 percent for both health center– and home-based components. Both loan repayment and TB cure rates were close to 100 percent for the 590 families that participated in the village bank loans. The interest charged on the loans was used to train ninety-six village health agents to conduct community education and help with patient detection and follow-up. The use of food gifts as an incentive for treatment compliance was adopted nationwide as part of the Cambodian National TB Program.

Source: Thim et al. 2004.

An enabling approach requires training sessions for community representatives and leaders so that they can acquire basic managerial and organizational skills (group formation, leadership), basic financial management skills (budgeting and accounting), communication skills, and methodologies and skills for local information management (data collection, analysis, presentation of information, and feedback).

Health staff and other development agents can promote participation by providing technical support to—

- Develop local, community-based structures through which people can participate and hold health services accountable
- Maintain a continuous dialogue between service providers and community groups—consultation with communities should take place at all stages of the process, and health committees should work with other community leaders to find feasible mechanisms for regular interaction
- Improve local-level coordination among sectors so that the underlying basis of poor health can be understood
- Gain support from nongovernmental organizations, which can provide additional resources for health as well as play an important role in promoting community participation
- Supervise activities and provide feedback to the district level
- Create enablers and incentives to encourage community involvement in health care

An *enabler* is defined as a stimulus provided to a patient, caregiver, or health care provider to facilitate adherence to treatment; for example, a voucher to cover transportation expenses to attend clinics or to visit patients. An *incentive* is an added stimulus to encourage participation in treatment, such as monthly food baskets for patients if they adhere to treatment norms and make clinic visits, or food or other rewards to community treatment supervisors who properly supervise patients. Country Study 31-4 shows how a province in Cambodia created an enabling environment for a community-based tuberculosis program.

Finally, community initiatives and participation in health must be seen as part of the broader network of community participation in development and in all social services. ∎

References and further readings

★ = Key readings.

Aitken, I., F. Omar, A. Raza, A. Noorzada, and S. A. Alawi. 2009. "Pictorial C-IMCI Technology for Illiterate Community Health Workers in Afghanistan." Paper presented at the 36th Annual International Conference on Global Health, Washington, D.C., May 26–30.

Andersson, S., and B. Snell. 2010. *Where There Are No Pharmacists: A Guide to Managing Medicines for All Health Workers.* Penang, Malaysia: Third World Network and Health Action International Asia Pacific.

BASICS (Basic Support for Institutionalizing Child Survival Project) II. 2004. *CHWs in Senegal Can Appropriately Treat Pneumonia with Cotrimoxazole.* Prepared for the U.S. Agency for International Development. Arlington, Va.: BASICS II.

Bhattacharyya, K., P. Winch, K. LeBan, and M. Tien. 2001. *Community Health Worker Incentives and Disincentives: How They Affect Motivation, Retention, and Sustainability.* Arlington, Va.: Basic Support for Institutionalizing Child Survival Project (BASICS) II.

Briggs, J., N. Nachbar, and O. Aupont. 2003. *Community Drug Management for Childhood Illnesses: Senegal Assessment, September 2002.* Arlington, Va.: Rational Pharmaceutical Management Plus Program/Management Sciences for Health. <http://www.msh.org/projects/rpmplus/Documents/upload/Senegal_C-DMCI_English.pdf>

Bukasa, G., K. Senauer, J. Briggs, and G. Adeya. 2008. "Don't Forget the Medicines: Community Case Management, DRC." Paper presented at the 35th Annual International Conference on Global Health, Washington, D.C., May 27–31.

CORE Group, Save the Children, and U.S. Agency for International Development (USAID) (2010). *Community Case Management Essentials. Treating Common Childhood Illnesses in the Community: A Guide for Program Managers.* Washington, D.C.: CORE Group, Save the Children, and USAID.

Darmstadt, G. L., Z. A. Bhutta, S. Cousens, T. Adam, N. Walker, and L. de-Bernis. 2005. Evidence-Based, Cost-Effective Interventions: How Many Newborn Babies Can We Save? *Lancet* 365: 977–88.

Dawson, P., Y. V. Pradhan, R. Houston, S. Karki, D. Poudel, and S. Hodgins. 2008. From Research to National Expansion: 20 Years' Experience of Community-Based Management of Childhood Pneumonia in Nepal. *Bulletin of the World Health Organization* 86(5): 339–43.

Embrey, M., J. Briggs, and G. Adeya. 2010. Saving the Lives of Children by Improving Access to Essential Medicines in the Community. In *Routledge International Handbook of Global Public Health*, R. Parker and M. Sommer, eds. Oxford: Routledge.

Fox, J. 1993. "Rhetoric and Reality: A Commentary on the UNCHS Community Development Programmes in Ghana, Uganda, and Zambia." Paper presented at United Nations Centre for Human Settlements (Habitat) Seminar, Copenhagen, Denmark.

Global Health Council. 2009. "Female Community Volunteers Save Children from Pneumonia Deaths in Nepal." *Global Health.* <http://www.globalhealthmagazine.com/field_notes/nepal_female_community_health_volunteers_saving_children_from_pneumonia-rel>

★ Haines A., D. Sanders, U. Lehmann, A. K. Rowe, J. E. Lawn, S. Jan, D. G. Walker, and Z. qar Bhutta. 2007. Achieving Child Survival Goals: Potential Contribution of Community Health Workers. *Lancet* 369: 2121–31.

Homedes, N., and A. Ugalde. 2006. Improving Access to Pharmaceuticals in Brazil and Argentina. *Health Policy and Planning* 21(2): 123–31.

Hope, A., and S. Timmel. 2000. *Training for Transformation: A Handbook for Community Workers.* Vols. I–III. Rugby, Warwickshire, England: ITDG Publishing.

ICASO, AfriCASO (International Council of AIDS Service Organizations, African Council of AIDS Service Organizations), and International HIV/AIDS Alliance. 2007. *Coordinating with Communities—Guidelines on the Involvement of the Community Sector in the Coordination of National AIDS Responses.* Geneva: Joint United Nations Programme on HIV/AIDS. <http://www.

ASSESSMENT GUIDE

Enabling factors

- Is there political commitment to community participation in health development?
- Is there interest in the decentralization of health services and the corresponding strengthening of district health systems?
- Does a health structure exist?
- Is there a commitment to developing people's managerial capabilities to enable them to take responsibility?

Community participation indicators

- Do communities contribute money, labor, or materials to health projects or support community health workers?
- Are community members asked for their views and informed of project plans?
- Do community members actively participate in decisions and in the control of resources?
- What mechanisms exist to increase people's access to information, knowledge, and skills and to help them make their goals and priorities known?
- What organizational structures exist at the community level to facilitate participation?
- What community members provide health services or medicines or preventive health messages?

Community participation and pharmaceutical management

- Are community health workers used to help extend health care services to peripheral levels?
- Are they seen as part of the health care system? Are they volunteers?
- Who monitors them?
- What are the main sources of medicines and care in the community?

- What are the availability and use practices of key medicines in the community?
- Do mechanisms exist for consumers to provide feedback to prescribers on the effectiveness of medicines, undesirable side effects, and so on?
- Does community cost sharing exist to help cover the costs of health services and pharmaceutical supply?
- Are communities involved in the management of facility-based health services?

Involvement of health professionals

To what extent do health professionals—

- Establish relationships within the community?
- Share skills and experiences with and learn from the community?
- Ensure service quality through monitoring and supervising community health services?
- Respect people's ideas, skills, and wisdom?
- Promote equity in male-female representation and in the representation of various social, economic, and age groups in local decision-making bodies?
- Respect the social practices, traditions, and culture of the community?
- Foster collaboration with other projects, organizations, and services on behalf of the community?

Community participation in program planning

- Do communities participate in needs assessments?
- Do communities participate in the dissemination of the results?
- Do community members and health professionals plan together what actions need to be taken, how, when, and with what means?
- Are community members involved in monitoring project activities and results?

unaids.org/en/KnowledgeCentre/Resources/FeatureStories/archive/2007/20070611_coordinating_communities_guidelines.asp>

★ Kahssay, H. M., and P. Oakley, eds. 1999. *Community Involvement in Health Development: A Review of the Concept and Practices.* Geneva: World Health Organization. <http://whqlibdoc.who.int/pha/WHO_PHA_5.pdf>

Katabarwa, M. N., and F. O. Richards Jr. 2001. Community-Directed Health (CDH) Workers Enhance the Performance and Sustainability of CDH Programmes: Experience from Ivermectin Distribution in Uganda. *Annals of Tropical Medicine and Parasitology* 95(3):275–86.

Knippenberg, R., F. Traore Nafo, R. Osseni, Y. Boye Camara, A. El Abassi, and A. Soucat. 2003. *Increasing Clients' Power to Scale Up Health Services for the Poor: The Bamako Initiative in West Africa.* Background paper to the *World Development Report.* Washington, D.C.: World Bank.

Lehmann, U., and D. Sanders. 2007. *Community Health Workers: What Do We Know about Them? The State of the Evidence on Programmes, Activities, Costs and Impact on Health Outcomes of Using Community Health Workers.* Geneva: World Health Organization. <http://www.who.int/hrh/documents/community_health_workers.pdf>

Lewnes, A. 2005. "Insecticide-Treated Nets Help Malawi Communities Fight Malaria." <http://www.unicef.org/health/malawi_26146.html>

McPake, B., K. Hanson, and A. Mills. 1993. Community Financing of Health Care in Africa: An Evaluation of the Bamako Initiative. *Social Science and Medicine* 36:1383–95.

Morgan, L. M. 2001. Community Participation in Health: Perpetual Allure, Persistent Challenge. *Health Policy & Planning* 16(3):221–30.

Murthy, R. K., and B. Klugman. 2004. Service Accountability and Community Participation in the Context of Health Sector Reforms in Asia: Implications for Sexual and Reproductive Health Services. *Health Policy & Planning* 19(Suppl. 1):78–86.

★ Nachbar, N., J. Briggs, O. Aupont, L. Shafritz, A. Bongiovanni, K. Acharya, S. Zimicki, S. Holschneider, and D. Ross-Degnan. 2003. *Community Drug Management for Childhood Illness: Assessment Manual.* Arlington, Va.: Rational Pharmaceutical Management Plus Program/Management Sciences for Health. <http://erc.msh.org/toolkit/toolkitfiles/file/C-DMCI%20Assessment%20Manual%20English.pdf>

★ Oakley, P. 1989. *Community Involvement in Health Development: An Examination of the Critical Issues.* Geneva: World Health Organization.

Rifkin, S. B. 2009. Lessons from Community Participation in Health Programmes: A Review of the Post Alma-Ata Experience. *International Health* 1:31–6.

Ross-Degnan, D., K. Backes-Kozhimannil, A. Payson, O. Aupont, R. LeCates, J. Chalker, and J. Briggs. 2008. *Improving Community Use of Medicines in the Management of Child Illness: A Guide to Developing Interventions.* Arlington, Va.: Rational Pharmaceutical Management Plus Program/Management Sciences for Health.

Sanders, D. M., C. Todd, and M. Chopra. 2005. Confronting Africa's Health Crisis: More of the Same will not be Enough. *BMJ* 331: 755–8.

Schellenberg, J. A., C. G. Victora, A. Mushi, D. de Savigny, D. Schellenberg, H. Mshinda, and J. Bryce (Tanzania Integrated Management of Childhood Illness MCE Baseline Household Survey Study Group). 2003. Inequities Among the Very Poor: Health Care for Children in Rural Southern Tanzania. *Lancet* 361:561–6.

Senauer, K., J. Briggs, S. Saleeb, and G. Adeya. 2008. "Improving Child Health through Informed Policy Decisions and Targeted Interventions to Strengthen Medicine Management in the Community: The Example of Senegal." Paper presented at the 35th Annual International Conference on Global Health, Washington, D.C., May 27–31.

Shin, S., J. Furin, J. Bayona, K. Mate, J. Y. Kim, and P. Farmer. 2004. Community-Based Treatment of Multidrug-Resistant Tuberculosis in Lima, Peru: 7 Years of Experience. *Social Science and Medicine* 59(7):1529–39.

Special Programme for Research and Training in Tropical Diseases. 2004. *Community Participation and Tropical Disease Control in Resource-Poor Settings.* Geneva: World Health Organization on behalf of the Special Programme for Research and Training in Tropical Diseases. <http://whqlibdoc.who.int/hq/2004/TDR_STR_SEB_ST_04.1.pdf>

Thim, S., S. Sath, M. Sina, E. Y. Tsai, J. C. Delgado, A. E. Shapiro, C. E. Barry 3rd, P. Glaziou, and A. E. Goldfeld. 2004. A Community-Based Tuberculosis Program in Cambodia. *Journal of the American Medical Association* 292(5):566–8.

★ WHO (World Health Organization). 2004. Community Participation: Advocacy and Action. In *World Health Report.* Geneva: WHO. <http://www.who.int/whr/2004/chapter3/en/>

★ WHO/UNICEF (World Health Organization/United Nations Children's Fund). 2004. *WHO/UNICEF Joint Statement: Management of Pneumonia in Community Settings.* Geneva: WHO.

Part I: Policy and economic issues	Part II: Pharmaceutical management	Part III: Management support systems

Selection
Procurement
Distribution
Use
   27 Managing for rational medicine use
   28 Investigating medicine use
   29 Promoting rational prescribing
   30 Ensuring good dispensing practices
   31 Community-based participation and initiatives
   32 Drug seller initiatives
   33 Encouraging appropriate medicine use by consumers
   34 Medicine and therapeutics information
   35 Pharmacovigilance

CHAPTER 32

Drug seller initiatives

SUMMARY

Retail drug shops tend to constitute the largest group of recognized outlets for medicines in developing countries, and they are often seen as playing an important role in the community's health. Typically, however, drug sellers are untrained, regulations of shops are unenforced, and the quality of pharmaceuticals that shops sell is not assured.

Systematically improving the services and products offered by drug shops can significantly contribute to national and regional goals for improving public health. If drug shops have legal access to quality pharmaceuticals and well-trained dispensers, and regulatory standards are enforced, shops can help improve access to and appropriate use of medicines and other health care–related products to treat common conditions, particularly among underserved populations.

To develop a program that improves retail drug shops and their operations, an integrated approach is needed that is supported by national and local authorities as well as shop personnel. Certain components are also needed to establish shop standards, ensure pharmaceutical and service quality, improve the availability of essential medications, and establish mechanisms for monitoring adherence to program standards.

An integrated approach to improving retail drug shops using the accreditation model would typically include—

- Development of regulatory standards defining requirements for shop premises, personnel, and dispensing practices

- Training in dispensing and the medicines used for commonly presented medical conditions; continuing education for shop personnel to improve customer service and appropriate medicine use
- A list of essential medicines that can be dispensed legally by an appropriately trained drug seller, along with strict adherence to the standards, established with input from stakeholders, for the quality and types of medicines that are permitted to be stocked
- Incentives such as business training for owners
- Access to loans for improvement of shop premises and expanded inventory
- Establishment of record-keeping systems to allow shop owners to monitor sales, inventory, costs, and profits
- Improved monitoring and supervision mechanisms, including self-monitoring, and regular shop inspections by authorities for regulatory enforcement
- Consumer education to promote the appropriate use of medicines and public demand for quality medicines and competent services from recognized shops

Any approach to strengthen the quality of services offered at retail drug shops must focus on providing safe, affordable, appropriate, and effective pharmaceuticals to populations in need.

A website (http://www.drugsellerinitiatives.org) shares experiences and tools from drug seller initiatives to provide a resource for those in any country with an interest in improving access to quality pharmaceutical services and products provided by drug sellers.

32.1 Popularity of retail drug sellers in developing countries

Most people in developing countries get their medicines from retail drug sellers, which are often the most convenient source—for example, in Ghana, the chemical seller shop; in Uganda, the Class C drug shop; in Tanzania, *duka la dawa baridi* (DLDB). Although pharmacies in developing countries may have strong professional identities and well-trained staff to sell prescription medications, both pharmacies and trained pharmacy personnel are limited in number. Retail drug shops, in contrast, tend to be more numerous. They typically constitute the country's largest group of recognized (although historically unaccredited and often unregulated) outlets for nonprescription medicines. These drug outlets dot the countryside, and for those

who do not live in a city, they may be the only nearby place to buy medicines and get health advice on common illnesses such as malaria, acute respiratory infections, and diarrhea.

As small businesses, retail drug shops spring up to meet illness-related needs in their communities, providing over-the-counter medicines and other popular items. For example, caretakers often treat children at home, and retail drug sellers may be their only contact regarding their children's health (Gyapong and Garshong 2007). A review of literature looking at the role of drug sellers in Africa reported that the use of retail drug outlets during child illnesses ranged from 15 to 83 percent, with a median around 50 percent, and that caretakers used retail outlets even when cheaper alternatives existed, such as village health workers (Goodman et al. 2007).

32.2 Problems with retail drug shops

A problem with having retail drug sellers deliver health care is that they are often untrained, and therefore, customers are not counseled on or sold the proper medicines or dosages to treat common ailments. In addition, these shops frequently sell prescription medications that should be legally distributed only by licensed health centers or pharmacies. Not only is this practice unlawful, but it also likely results in incorrectly or inappropriately stored and dispensed medicines. As a result, consumers may receive medicines that are ineffective or dangerous for their condition. A 2001 assessment of Tanzania (CPM 2003b) found that few dispensers at DLDB dispensed malaria treatment according to guidelines, and other studies have found similar results (for example, Abuya et al. 2007).

Although governments recognize these dangers to public health, actions to shut down or punitively regulate retail drug shops have been almost universally unsuccessful. Most drug shops are seen as playing an indispensable role in their community's health system, especially in areas without licensed pharmacies. An increase in the number of drug sellers who legally dispense common medicines in an appropriate way would have the potential to help many people in many countries.

Overall, estimating precisely how many people could benefit from improving the quality of products and services through enhanced retail drug seller interventions is difficult; however, retail drug outlets are clearly far more accessible to populations in need than pharmacies or public health facilities. Country assessments (CPM 2003a, 2003b) estimated that Tanzania had more DLDB than all other health facilities—public and private—combined (4,627, compared with 4,288); Ghana had almost 1,000 pharmacies, located almost exclusively in urban areas, with almost 8,000 registered chemical sellers and possibly 2,000 more that were unregistered. A 2008 analysis of the pharmaceutical sector in Uganda estimated that the country had nearly 4,000 Class C drug shops (EADSI 2008). This scenario is common in many developing countries, and it illustrates the potentially broad effect of improving the quality of products and services in retail drug outlets and the huge impact closure of these shops would have on access to medicines.

Systematically improving the services and products offered by drug shops can contribute significantly to national and regional goals for improving public health. If drug shops can legally sell selected prescription medicines and have access to quality pharmaceuticals and better trained dispensers, and if regulatory standards are in place and enforced, then shops can improve access to and appropriate use of medicines and other health care–related products, particularly among underserved populations.

32.3 Strengthening the role of retail drug shops

Health managers, drug regulators, or policy makers who would like to expand access to quality pharmaceuticals should consider what role retail drug shops can play in the population. Licensed pharmacies need not be the only acceptable alternatives for improving access to and rational use of medicines. Although retail drug shops are often unregulated, consumers with longstanding habits of buying from these shops will continue to turn to them, even when such consumers have other choices to access medicines.

Taking a course of action and encouraging participation

Any approach to strengthen the quality of services offered at retail drug shops must focus on providing safe, affordable, appropriate, and effective pharmaceuticals to populations in need. The program must establish standards and requirements related to physical premises and operations before existing shops can be upgraded or new shops opened. Community-level input will help determine how to develop a drug shop initiative that best fits the specific context.

An integrated program to establish retail drug shops as a source for quality medicines must work with current drug shop owners to improve or upgrade existing retail drug shops. Consider the number of drug retail shops in the area and the quality of the services they offer, and explore incentives that may motivate existing owners to participate in a program. Many owners favorably perceive opportunities for developing new business and improving the quality of services. In addition, observing the successful conversion of an existing shop provides a powerful incentive for owners to join in. In a drug seller accreditation program in Tanzania, every DLDB owner in the pilot region of Ruvuma participated in the conversion process.

Relying on single-focus interventions for improving drug shops

Efforts to improve retail drug shops and increase access to quality medicines often rely on single-focus interventions. For example, some programs may try to improve access by educating people who dispense medicines. Others could focus on improving owners' management practices, strengthening regulations or regulatory agencies, or using social marketing for particular products. Some examples of the successes and limits of each type of intervention follow.

Educating dispensers. Educational interventions have trained dispensers to improve their knowledge and skills so they can provide appropriate treatment. Yet many factors other than knowledge guide dispensers in the private sector (for instance, the desire to make a profit from selling drugs). To improve their effectiveness, some educational interventions have used persuasive face-to-face discussions that focus on particular problem behaviors in interactions between dispensers and consumers, such as unclear messages about when to stop taking a medicine. Some interventions have successfully included peer group discussions to

educate participants on standards set by regulatory bodies or professional societies. Country Study 32-1 describes some drug seller education approaches and results in Africa.

Establishing regulations. Regulatory interventions may attempt to ban shops from selling prescription medicines without legally approved prescription authority. These efforts can prove counterproductive, especially in communities where unauthorized or unregulated shops pro-

---

Country Study 32-1
Retail drug seller education approaches and results in sub-Saharan Africa

Kenya

Approach: Conducting workshop training for groups of drug retailers combined with community information activities in rural Kenya. The initial drug seller training lasted four days, with annual one-day refresher workshops over the following years. Successful sellers were awarded certificates of satisfactory training in public ceremonies, and posters were displayed outside their shops showing that they had been accredited by the Ministry of Health. Public information activities to create awareness of the program focused on identifying trained retailers and giving information on the importance of early effective treatment for malaria in children, changes in malaria treatment policy, and situations for referrals. Trainers attended public gatherings (women's groups, school groups, and so on), handed out posters, and showed the program logo; local dance and drama groups conveyed program messages.

Results: The proportion of over-the-counter antimalarial medicines sold in an adequate dose rose from 8 percent to 64 percent in the intervention areas. In addition, the proportion of shop-treated childhood fevers receiving an adequate dose of a recommended antimalarial within twenty-four hours rose from 1 percent to 28 percent.

Approach: Training and equipping pharmaceutical wholesalers, both mobile drug vendors and wholesale counter attendants, to serve as volunteer outreach educators of new malaria guidelines to their drug retailer clients during normal business interactions ("vendor-to-vendor"). Components of the program included a shopkeeper job aid for a retailer to consult when selling antimalarial medicines; a client awareness poster to hang near the entrance of the outlet to generate consumer demand for the five approved brands of sulfadoxine-pyrimethamine (SP) and to communicate that SP was now available over the counter; orientation of wholesale owners; training and equipping of mobile vendors and wholesale counter attendants; and monitoring. Each

wholesaler trainee received a receipt book to record the names of the recipients of posters and to obtain their agreement to comply with the new guidelines. At the end of the training, all wholesalers received caps and shirts with the malaria dosage chart on the front.

Results: During the first six months, approximately 450–500 private drug outlets were reached. The intervention affected stocking patterns, malaria knowledge, and prescribing practices of shops and kiosks significantly, but not consistently for other types of outlets. About 32 percent of shops receiving job aids prescribed the approved first-line treatment, SP, compared to 3 percent of the control shops.

Nigeria and Uganda

Approach: The Basic Support for Institutionalizing Child Survival project designed an intervention in Nigeria that combined a short, highly focused training for patent medicine vendors with the promotion of age-specific, color-coded, prepackaged antimalarials for children under five. These activities were supported by a comprehensive social marketing and behavior change strategy, which included mass media promoting the new prepackaged antimalarials and display of shop identifiers from the training by patent medicine vendors. More than 800 medicine vendors were trained in a two-month period at the relatively low cost of about 8 U.S. dollars each. Training materials focused on immediate treatment of children under five with fever, using an appropriate dose (preferably prepackaged) of an antimalarial.

Results: Examples of postintervention assessment results showed that the number of patent medicine vendors giving the correct antimalarial and dose increased from 9 percent to 53 percent after the intervention. Also, knowledge of patent medicine vendors about the need to use insecticide-treated nets tripled (21 percent to 65 percent) between pre- and postintervention surveys.

Sources: Marsh et al. 2004; Tavrow, Shabahang, and Makama 2003; Greer et al. 2004.

vide the only available access to medicines. National or regional authorities can unilaterally introduce regulations, but enforcement may be sporadic, in part because limited resources often keep regulatory efforts from being consistent or sustainable.

Program managers need a balanced approach to developing regulations that will maintain consistent, reliable, and verifiable quality services. Program managers can create incentives that encourage shop owners to abide by regulations while making sure the owners understand what will happen if they do not comply.

Social marketing. Social marketing of condoms, contraceptives, and bed nets often uses techniques such as advertising campaigns to introduce new products through retail drug shops. For example, interventions have been used to help prevent the transmission of HIV by promoting the use of condoms and to help prevent malaria infection by encouraging the use of bed nets.

Although frequently implemented, single-focus interventions typically are less effective than programs that weave together multiple interventions as part of an integrated, holistic approach (Shah, Brieger, and Peters 2011).

32.4 Improving drug shops through an integrated approach

To develop a program that improves retail drug shops, an integrated approach that is supported by national and local authorities as well as shop personnel is needed. The program can include the proven single-focus practices that are consistent with the goals and resources available. Certain components are also needed to establish shop standards, ensure pharmaceutical and service quality, improve the availability of essential medications, and establish mechanisms for monitoring adherence to program standards.

Identifying the components of an effective integrated approach

An integrated approach to improving retail drug shops would typically include—

- Development of regulatory standards defining requirements for shop premises and dispensing practice
- Training in dispensing and the medicines used for commonly presented medical conditions; continuing education for shop personnel to improve customer service and appropriate drug use
- A list of essential medicines that can be legally dispensed by an appropriately trained drug seller, along with strict adherence to the standards, established with input from stakeholders, for the quality and types of medicines that are permitted to be stocked

- Incentives such as business training for owners to improve business practices, inventory control, marketing, and profitability
- Access to loans for improving shop premises and expanding inventory
- Availability of and training on the use of forms to help ensure accurate record keeping to allow shop owners to monitor sales, inventory, costs, and profits
- Improved monitoring and supervision mechanisms, including self-monitoring, and regular shop inspections by authorities for regulatory enforcement
- Consumer education to promote the appropriate use of medicines and public demand for quality medicines and competent services from recognized shops

National versus program standards

Many countries use a national drug regulatory authority or the ministry of health to establish national standards for essential medicine lists, treatment guidelines, and appropriate medicine use. If standards for pharmaceutical premises exist in a country, they should define the minimum required to operate a drug shop under the law. A national effort to strengthen drug shops and sellers to ensure expanded provision of quality products and services to the community would require review and revision of existing laws and regulations. For example, an accredited drug seller initiative might require new standards for training and shop premises that would have to be met and that would be enforced. Failure of a drug shop to comply would result in loss of accreditation or shop closure.

Individual shop owners or franchisees of shops can go beyond the minimum level required by law and regulations to set their operations and services apart from the competition. Individual or franchise standards, however, need to be consistent with existing national standards.

Stakeholder engagement

An integrated approach should include engagement not only with drug shop owners, dispensers, consumers, and health care providers, but also with other stakeholders concerned with public health issues, such as local government officials. Stakeholders need to work together to find ways to make drug shops and sellers effective and reliable partners in national health care delivery efforts. A successful program should seek to change the behaviors and expectations of individuals and groups that use, own, work in, or regulate drug shops.

Best practices

An integrated approach needs to encourage owners and dispensers to apply the following best practices.

Country Study 32-2
The drug shop accreditation process in Tanzania

The following example describes an integrated accreditation approach, adopted by a food and drug authority and ministry of health, that has improved retail drug shops and enhanced the availability and quality of the medicines that these shops sell.

The Tanzania Food and Drugs Authority (TFDA) had a plan to license nonpharmacy drug shops to improve public access to basic over-the-counter drugs in areas with few registered pharmacies. However, the drugs authority lacked the human and financial resources to make the plan succeed. Many drug shops, known as *duka la dawa baridi,* sold prescription drugs illegally; their dispensing staff often lacked basic dispensing training; and many operated without valid licenses from authorities.

Assessment of DLDBs

The Ministry of Health and Social Welfare assessed the DLDB in 2001 with assistance from the Strategies for Enhancing Access to Medicines (SEAM) Program (CPM 2003b) and found that the DLDB prices tended to be higher than those in all other outlets. Drugs in stock were frequently unregistered or purchased from unlicensed suppliers, so quality could not be assured. Many DLDB owners purchased illegal stock, including pharmaceuticals diverted from the public sectors of Tanzania and neighboring countries. Nonetheless, DLDB flourished. They were convenient, registered pharmacies were absent, and public health centers had stockout rates of 20 to 30 percent.

New approach

The TFDA and Ministry of Health and Social Welfare decided to explore new approaches to improve access to affordable, quality pharmaceuticals and services in rural or periurban areas. A pilot program, developed in collaboration with the SEAM Program, aimed at establishing a regulated system of accredited drug-dispensing outlets (ADDOs) to provide a limited list of essential prescription medicines in addition to nonprescription medications and other health supplies. The list of prescription medicines they could sell was based on the medicines authorized for public primary health care facilities.

The program formulated an integrated approach for the ADDOs to—

- Improve shop premises to provide better customer service and to ensure adequate storage and security for the expanded list of medicines approved for sale
- Help ensure access to financial resources, if needed, to improve shop premises and increase inventory
- Train dispensers in good dispensing practices, treatment guidelines, communication skills, and quality control
- Provide training in business skills, regulations, and business ethics for shop owners and dispensers
- Strengthen the ward, district, and regional systems under which all the drug shops operate, which include systems for processing accreditation applications, scheduling regular inspections, and reporting to TFDA

Use of formative research

Before any ADDOs opened, the program conducted research among consumers, shop owners, shop staff, community leaders, health care providers, and political authorities.

For owners—

- Provide quality medicines at affordable prices that are appropriate to local market needs.
- Meet all premises standards required, including maintenance of adequate storage facilities.
- Hire licensed, trained, and skilled dispensers (or work in the shop yourself as a licensed, trained, and skilled dispenser).
- Facilitate access to refresher training to upgrade dispensers' skills.
- Maintain accurate records of pharmaceuticals, financial transactions, patient information, and other useful data.

- Meet all regulatory, accrediting, and licensing standards and fulfill reporting obligations.
- Meet ethical standards and responsibilities.
- Work to ensure that essential, quality medicines are available at all times.

For dispensers—

- Listen to the customer's request, and serve or advise him or her appropriately, following established protocols.
- Provide appropriate information or advice about the medicines dispensed or, if needed, referral to a clinic for needed care.

The results indicated almost unanimous concern about the quality and origin of drugs sold by the DLDBs. All stakeholders wanted trained dispensers who could provide quality medications at reasonable prices. However, the owners preferred limited regulation by the government.

SEAM sponsored formal and informal discussions and consultations to foster broad support for the ADDO program strategy as well as ownership and partnership in the change process. Based on research and discussions, the final ADDO components balanced program objectives with measures to encourage DLDB owners' participation.

ADDO program components for standards and incentives

Component	Process or requirements
Accreditation application process	A Council Food and Drugs Committee is responsible for a four-part application process for shops: an application form, initial inspection of the existing facility, reinspection after any structural changes required for accreditation, and ongoing inspection after accreditation.
Incentives for owners	Owner incentives focus on improved shop profitability and approval to sell a range of prescription medications. Incentives for owners who commit to standards include access to microfinancing for stock purchases, a marketing campaign encouraging consumers to buy ADDO-provided products and services, and more reliable sources of affordable, quality wholesale pharmaceuticals.
Building/infrastructure	The standards provide instructions for premises, layout, identification, dispensing and services areas, storage, and security.
Staff qualifications	The minimum entry-level training for ADDO dispenser candidates is currently that of a nurse assistant, with plans to expand the qualifications to any secondary school graduate.
Medicine quality	The list of products approved for sale by ADDOs includes the full range of over-the-counter medicines and a limited list of prescription medicines, including common antibiotics and oral contraceptives. ADDOs may sell only those products registered with and approved by the TFDA.
Training and continuing education	All dispensers must be accredited by the TFDA, display their accreditation certificate at their place of employment, and wear their photo identification when working. Accreditation involves completing a TFDA-approved, module-based dispensers' course. Training topics include information on medicines that are authorized to be dispensed by ADDOs; symptoms of commonly encountered medical conditions and protocols for handling patients presenting with symptoms, including referral, when needed; treatment dosages, side effects, and patient information; laws governing dispensers' work; basic business management, record keeping, and ethics; and communication skills. Continuing education is a part of maintaining dispenser accreditation. Training for ADDO shop owners focuses on ethics, regulations, and improvement of business management skills.
Record keeping	ADDOs must account for all prescription drugs sold and their selling prices, financial and sales records, and expired medications. These records may be used for supervision purposes and must be available for review by inspectors.
Regulation, inspection, and sanctions	Local government officials receive a basic inspection training course from the TFDA and are certified as local TFDA inspectors. TFDA conducts a minimum of two inspections of each shop per year, and local inspectors inspect quarterly.
ADDO-restricted wholesalers	Approved wholesalers can receive a license to sell nonprescription and ADDO-approved prescription drugs under the supervision of a full-time pharmaceutical technician.

- Provide appropriate information or advice for self-care if a medicine is not required or recommended.
- Appropriately promote associated products or services connected to the customer's needs (for example, recommend insecticide-treated nets to families at risk of malaria).
- Refer customers to a qualified health provider for services beyond the scope of the shop.
- Communicate effectively with customers who demand inappropriate services or medicines by being firm and providing explanations as to why the service or product should not be used.
- Maintain a customer-oriented attitude that meets ethical standards and responsibilities.

32.5 Borrowing from accreditation and franchising

How can shop owners be encouraged to adopt best practices and cooperate with an improvement program? Accreditation and franchising can offer shop owners some positive incentives. Within the community context, consider elements from these approaches and incorporate the elements that best fit into the program.

Accreditation

Accreditation of drug shops includes certifying or licensing dispensers, identifying shops as members of a group that meets accreditation standards, and monitoring their ongoing adherence to standards. Accredited shops may become more acceptable to consumers than nonaccredited shops, but acceptance should be encouraged with a marketing campaign to inform consumers which shops are accredited and why this is important to them.

For example, the Tanzania Food and Drugs Authority (TFDA) and the Ministry of Health and Social Welfare developed a pilot program to establish a regulated system of licensed retail drug outlets, known as accredited drug-dispensing outlets (ADDOs), which has now been scaled up nationwide. The government accredits ADDOs to provide an expanded selection of drugs, including some prescription medicines, and other supplies. The program has provided ADDOs with links to organizations and agencies that provide financial support and reliable access to sources of quality wholesale goods. Country Study 32-2 describes this example in more detail.

Franchising

Franchising encourages existing or potential shop owners to invest in shops to meet franchise standards as well as government licensing criteria. Shop owners gain the right to operate under the franchise name as long as they meet and maintain the franchise standards. Box 32-1 describes how a franchise program works.

In Ghana, a for-profit group established the CAREshop® franchise, which sets its own standards in addition to meeting government licensure and operational requirements. The franchisor provided franchisee training and supervision and negotiated with suppliers for quality medicines at competitive prices. Table 32-1 summarizes the CAREshop franchise standards; note that the CAREshop franchise is no longer active, although individual shops remain in operation.

In Kenya, a nongovernmental organization called the HealthStore Foundation® developed a drug shop and clinic franchise. It consists of a network of Child and Family Wellness Shops (CFWshops™) and clinics, which are owned and managed by Kenyan community health workers and nurses. The franchisor provides franchisees with training, supervision, and access to microcredit. The franchisor also procures quality, essential pharmaceuticals for resale to franchisees at affordable prices. Country Study 32-3 describes the program in more detail.

How accreditation differs from franchising

Accreditation and franchising are not mutually exclusive. Governments can establish accreditation programs to reach

---

Box 32-1
How a franchise program works

Requirements

Franchising programs for drug shops operate within government pharmaceutical standards and regulations, under the authority of the ministry of health and other agencies charged with licensing and overseeing legal requirements for health care facilities and products. In addition, all franchising programs require—

- Commitment to performance standards that have been agreed upon and established so customers find quality pharmaceuticals and services in every shop
- Compliance with established standards, with monitoring through a system that reviews adherence and gradually increases self-regulation, which the franchisor verifies through periodic checks
- Fees for entering into the franchise and for remaining a member

Benefits to shop owners

In return for participation and fees, the franchisor provides benefits to owners and staff, including—

- Training, both initial and ongoing, for drug shop workers, supervisors, and owners

- Access to competitively priced quality drugs and health care supplies on a consistent basis
- Incentives such as business plans and franchisor backing that facilitates access to microfinancing and loans at market rates
- Designation as a franchise member
- Marketing of program standards and identity (brand marketing) that distinguish the quality of franchisee-provided medicines and services from those offered by competitors
- Opportunities for making a profit that is maintained or enhanced through ongoing participation and compliance

Benefits to consumers

Well-organized franchises of drug shops can benefit the public, particularly in underserved communities. Customers receive—

- Improved pharmaceutical services and steady supplies of medicine
- Quality, essential medicines at competitive prices

Table 32-1   Ghana CAREshop franchise standards and benefits

Operational area	Requirements	Benefits
Standards implemented by the shop owners in the franchise		
Building/infrastructure	• Paint exterior using the approved colors • Provide interior shelving and ventilation • Adhere to the cleanliness standards	• Franchise identification • Better customer service • Improved quality of services
Medicines in stock	• Procure only those drugs provided by the franchisor in compliance with the Pharmacy Council's approved list and have them delivered to the door	• Reduced cost of inventory • Assured availability of products
Minimum staff qualifications	• Meet all Pharmacy Council license requirements	• Better customer service • Improved rational drug use • Better pharmaceutical practices
Training and continuing education	• Complete a franchise training course in business, disease recognition, and record keeping • Participate in continuing education to maintain participation in the franchise	• Improved customer service • Improved rational drug use • Enhanced sustainability • New disease-related data for the ministry of health • Better business practices and improved services
Record keeping	• Keep standardized inventory, sales, and customer request records to track shop performance and create community health profiles	• Decreased stockouts of needed medicines • Improved profitability • Improved planning and decision making by the ministry of health
Standards implemented by the franchisor		
Medicine availability and quality	• Conduct quantification and tendering with suppliers on behalf of all shops • Buy only government-approved products from reliable sources	• Quality products at a competitive price • Consistent availability of drugs • Enhanced profitability
Supervision and inspection	• Supervise and inspect the shops to maintain the quality of services and ensure compliance to franchise standards	• Provision of quality care and products • Identification of problem areas • Improvement of performance

targeted areas underserved by pharmacies, while the private or nongovernmental organization sector can establish a franchising network for new or improved retail drug shops. In this way, both approaches can help fulfill the public health goals of access to and rational use of affordable, quality medicines.

Accreditation has many of the same requirements and benefits that franchising has, but with some important differences. Unlike franchisee shops, accredited shops generally remain small, independent businesses. They do not pay fees to a franchisor, nor do they receive the benefits of being part of a larger franchise system. The franchisor generally provides training and training updates to shops belonging to a franchise, whereas training for nonfranchise shop owners and dispensers to meet accreditation standards would have to come from outside organizations such as schools of pharmacy and regional training centers that offer routine, planned courses. Some franchise shops may seek additional training from outside agencies to address specific needs. Training agency courses typically are certified by an appropriate authority, and students pay course fees either directly or indirectly through their employer.

32.6 Taking steps to improve retail drug shops

A successful, integrated program requires that stakeholders' needs, interests, and expectations be taken into account. Typical stakeholders for drug shop accreditation or franchising programs include consumers, shop owners, shop dispensers, community leaders, health care leaders, and political and civic leaders. The availability of funding, partnerships, training, communications, and other resources must be determined. This section outlines the major steps involved in developing an improvement program including identifying stakeholder needs, expectations, and potential roles and formulating appropriate program components for the context.

Use formative research

As a first step, conduct research to gather local data for program planning and implementation. Formative research, which engages stakeholders through focus group discussions or other qualitative methods, can help gather information from stakeholders while involving them in the change process from the start. Failing to learn about stakeholder

Country Study 32-3
Improving pharmaceutical access and quality using franchising in Kenya

The majority of Kenyans living in rural areas get their basic essential medicines from shopkeepers in nearby markets. The Bamako Initiative established village pharmacies run by community health workers (CHWs) in certain districts. The high attrition rate in CHWs has been attributed to the difficulties they have in maintaining their activities without external support, including lack of sustained supervision or continuing education and the high cost of medicines they must purchase at wholesale pharmacies.

The Sustainable Healthcare Enterprise Foundation (now the HealthStore Foundation) established the Child and Family Wellness Shops (CFWshops™) in Kenya to engage CHWs and nurses working in their rural communities to provide access to essential health care commodities and services in a sustainable manner. The network targets the five to ten diseases causing 70 to 90 percent of morbidity and mortality among children and their families, while also providing basic health services and other products. It combines micro-enterprise and franchise principles to enable qualified CHWs and nurses to own and operate drug shops and medical clinics in underserved areas.

The franchise system provides standardized training in business and franchise management, medicine and client services management, and public health interventions in the community, including child survival interventions for malaria and acute respiratory infection. The franchisees receive a microloan that covers the costs of four-week training, initial pharmaceutical stock, and equipment and shop infrastructure. Once trained, the franchisees run drug shops or clinics in easily accessible market centers and receive ongoing supervision and mentoring support from field-based supervisors employed by the CFWshops organization. The franchisees are required to purchase their pharmaceutical supplies through the HealthStore Foundation to ensure quality and to adhere to franchise rules for service delivery. The franchisees are licensed by the Kenyan Ministry of Health and also receive continuing education from the HealthStore Foundation to adhere to national treatment guidelines.

The first eleven shops opened in April 2000, and by 2010, 76 shops had opened and served almost 500,000 patients that year. In 2003, the HealthStore Foundation added its first medical clinic to the network of CFWshops. The clinics are franchised like the drug shops but are owned and operated by nurses who can supply a wider range of medicines and health services than provided by the drug shops.

The franchised outlets provide their communities with a reliable source of quality-assured essential medicines, delivered by a trained health worker who adheres to certain standards of service prescribed by the franchise agreement. The franchisee runs a for-profit enterprise on a full-time basis, which provides him or her with an income that ensures sustainability of the initiative. Ongoing supervision support and continuing education also contribute to the sustainability of the venture.

See http://www.healthstore.org for more information.

interests not only can discourage stakeholder interest in joining or collaborating with the program, but also can handicap understanding of what is going to be required to make the program work and ultimately undermine adherence to any new or existing standards.

The keys to formative research are keeping an open mind and using good listening and recording skills to gather data. Formative research is a two-way street: learning from stakeholders while involving them in the improvement process. Stakeholders may be engaged several times during the research and planning process. A sample formative research process includes—

- Interviewing a few key individuals to learn their points of view

- Presenting preliminary ideas to small focus groups of stakeholders to hear what they think of your initial program proposal
- Developing broad stakeholder commitment to improvements by sharing the program design and implementation process through dissemination workshops

Focus group discussions are particularly effective for gathering information from stakeholders while at the same time raising awareness about health and related issues, such as licensing drug shops. A focus group typically brings together a group of five to twelve people who have something in common, for example, groups of consumers, pharmaceutical professionals, or new mothers. Information from focus group discussions can provide the basis for designing improved systems to meet as many different expectations as possible and developing communications and marketing plans to educate stakeholders and promote consumers' use of improved shops.

Establish key components with stakeholders

The second step of the design phase involves exploring with stakeholders the key components of the program, such as drug shop standards, incentives for shop owners, and ways to monitor and supervise drug shops' quality.

Every shop improvement program needs to establish standards in the following areas—

- Building/infrastructure
- Essential medicines lists
- Product quality
- Staff qualifications
- Training and continuing education
- Record keeping
- Regulation and inspection

Building/infrastructure. All participating retail drug shops in accreditation and franchising enterprises should arrange for the prominent display of signs and the logo of the enterprise. Some programs require owners to paint their shops with specific colors. Standards for the shops' interior and storage areas must include level of cleanliness and specifications for shelving, counters, and other physical requirements.

Essential medicines lists. National health authorities usually have an established list of essential medicines for primary health care centers, which can form the basis for a program list. If shops are to stock an expanded list of medicines, such as common antibiotics, close work with public health and regulatory authorities will be necessary to meet their regulations and standards and change the regulation, if necessary. For example, the program may need to train retail drug shop dispensers in the rational use of medicines and treatments for common illnesses and regularly supervise and monitor dispensers' performance to meet standards to dispense certain medicines. An understanding of how essential medicines are distributed is also required. In addition to keeping accurate records on essential medicines, the program should get a baseline estimate of how many and what types of unregistered health products are being sold.

Product quality. All programs require participating shops to purchase their medicines and supplies from approved sources of supply. Franchisees must purchase from the franchisor, while accredited shops need to purchase from licensed wholesalers. Programs should provide owners and dispensers with training in pharmaceutical procurement

and inventory management. Adhering to program standards and training is very important.

Staff qualifications. Although the ideal dispensers at retail drug shops are trained pharmacy providers, the program will need to consider local labor markets and other factors. Different programs may adopt various minimum certification requirements for dispensers that depend on their education, in-service training, the drugs they will dispense, and the level of skills that are generally available in the labor market. For example, in Tanzania, because of the shortage of pharmaceutical personnel, ADDO dispensers are required to be trained nurse assistants at a minimum. The program may want certification by a recognized board or authority. Most accredited programs insist that all dispensers display their accreditation certificate at work and may require them to wear identification cards with photographs.

Training and continuing education. Improvement programs need to provide training for both dispensers and owners. Data from focus group discussions can help develop training and continuing education programs that will encourage owners to join the program and improve their services and profitability. A professional organization, such as a school of pharmacy, or a regional training center may provide training. Programs ideally provide periodic continuing education and require participation for reaccreditation or ongoing franchising approval. Some programs tie continuing education topics and requirements to the results of supervisory visits.

Conveying good business practices to shop owners as well as what sort of price markups are commonly applied throughout the distribution system, from wholesalers to products for sale to consumers, is helpful. A simple price survey can compile pricing data.

Record keeping. Standards should include a record of drugs sold, with an emphasis on prescription medicines. Other data collected may include basic demographic information about customers, expired medicines, and medicine purchase and sale prices. Programs generally use standardized forms for recording all required information and train owners and dispensers in filling them out.

Regulation and inspection. Designing and implementing regular supervision and inspection helps motivate owners and dispensers to maintain the required standards, ensures a consistent level of quality across the network, and inspires customer loyalty. Inspection needs to cover all drug shops, not just accredited shops, to prevent nonaccredited shops from selling prescription medicines and undermining the incentive for accredited shops to maintain standards. All owners need to know that they will be inspected regularly and that they will suffer sanctions for violations.

Incentives. In a comprehensive program, a balance is necessary between standards, with which shop owners must comply, and incentives, which can motivate drug shop owners to participate in an improvement program, whether for accreditation or as part of a franchise. Make these incentives clear when recruiting owners to join the program.

Financial management. The most powerful retail incentives for shop owners are those that improve profitability, give the shops a competitive edge, and are exclusive to the shops. Shop owners can benefit from a more complete understanding of distribution systems and pricing methods. They also need to know the financial dimensions of related incentives, including—

- Legal approval to sell a range of prescription drugs
- Training for owners and dispensers
- Access to financing to purchase stock or implement building improvements
- A marketing campaign that promotes brand recognition and encourages consumers to buy drugs from network shops
- Access to convenient and reasonably priced wholesale services
- Reassessment of taxes and license fees, combined with fair and even-handed enforcement and collection, to accurately reflect shop revenue

Business ethics. Fulfilling a community social mission may motivate some owners. They may find that owning a business that provides a valuable service to the local population can give them status and a sense of personal satisfaction. Formative research will indicate whether this type of incentive will attract potential participants to the network. Over the long term, however, shop owners will remain in the network only if the financial benefits of participating are greater than the perceived costs. If their participation increases sales, customer volume, and technical skills while improving access to quality medicines without significantly increasing medicine costs, then the owners will be more likely to continue their participation.

Monitoring and supervision. Monitoring the performance of the drug shops participating in the network may be the most important supporting element of the program. It can foster a consistent level of excellence in the products and services at each shop. Monitoring or supervision activities that reinforce tangible improvement and practical training are less likely to be perceived by owners as burdensome or intrusive. Monitoring and supervision efforts in which inspectors, owners, and dispensers work together to identify problems and find solutions are more effective than efforts focused exclusively on identifying errors or noncompliance. At an accredited drug shop in Uganda, the drug seller said, "We used to run away from the inspectors because they used to come and close our shops and remove the medicines that we were not supposed to have. . . . Now that the National Drug Authority allows us to have antibiotics and other medicines, we don't keep these medicines hidden away or run from the inspectors like we used to do."

Marketing and communications

The last major step for developing the program requires planning ongoing communication with stakeholders, including shop owners and customers, who can help market the program and educate consumers. The program needs to motivate shop owners to join, to maintain established standards, and to monitor their own performance. Local monitors of the Accredited Drug Shop program in Uganda reported that owners and sellers in accredited shops were now watching out for and reporting unlicensed shops to authorities. The program also needs to motivate consumers to recognize the program's quality brand and purchase their medicines through "branded" shops. Educating consumers on what constitutes quality in retail drug shops and why visiting a branded shop can make a difference to their health is important to success.

Develop and implement a communication plan for general consumer awareness and the program's brand by carrying out a market analysis, developing key communication messages for different groups of customers, and identifying and implementing communication activities using print and other media, such as radio announcements and billboards.

Sustaining the quality of drug shops and services

As a comprehensive drug shop improvement program that uses accreditation or franchising measures is developed, a foundation should be laid to sustain the shops over the long term. If the program is successful on a small scale, pressure will arise to not only sustain the current operations but also to expand the program model. It is logical to assume that problem areas experienced during a pilot program will loom larger during scale-up. Consider sustainability within the context of growth, and prepare the program for the future by following through on carefully planned actions. These actions may not guarantee the program sustained success and growth, but they will put the program in a strong position to face future challenges. The following actions will help sustain the program—

- Touch base with stakeholder groups periodically and use their feedback to make program adjustments.
- Review lessons learned from the training program once a year, and revise materials as needed.
- Put reporting mechanisms in place to help track performance, and give feedback and support in a timely manner if performance fails to adhere to standards.
- Closely monitor the financial performance and stability of individual shops, including increases in

---

Box 32-2
Drug Shop Provider Association tool kit

As part of a project funded by the Rockefeller Foundation, Management Sciences for Health developed a tool kit to facilitate the expansion of ADDO associations in Tanzania; however, the tools can be adapted for use in any context. The tool kit was finalized through a consultative stakeholder workshop. It includes seven operational and management tools, which are available in English and Kiswahili—

- Roles, responsibilities, and benefits of ADDO provider associations
- How to form and register an ADDO provider association
- Basic components of a model constitution for ADDO provider associations
- How to plan and manage activities for ADDO provider associations
- How to mobilize financial resources for ADDO provider associations

- Institutional networking and coordination mechanisms for ADDO provider associations
- How to document, monitor, and evaluate activities

In addition, the tool kit includes additional promotional and orientation materials—

- Advocacy guide for the national-, regional-, and district-level stakeholders
- Promotional banners
- Presentation slides for provider association orientation
- A DVD produced by a local consultant, MediaNet, that ADDO providers can view to become familiar with the association concept

The tool kit is available in Appendix C of the project report: http://www.drugsellerinitiatives.org/DSI-PDF-Documents/upload/40-Rockefeller-ADDO-Association-Final-Report-MSH-Dec-2010.pdf.

---

profitability and the timeliness of meeting payment schedules.

- Develop solid wholesale operations or link to reputable established operations that will allow shops to more easily access affordable, quality pharmaceuticals, pass on savings to the consumer, and stay financially stable.
- Continue to use communication activities to influence consumer behavior and encourage shop owners and dispensers to adhere to standards.
- Solicit long-term support for networks of drug shops by encouraging providers and medical authorities to recognize the vital role that retail drug shops play in ensuring access to quality pharmaceuticals and services in areas that would not otherwise be served.
- Promote the establishment and strengthening of owner and dispenser associations as a mechanism to increase product and service quality and promote sustainability. Box 32-2 provides information on a provider association tool kit.

Country Study 32-4 describes how multiple national and international stakeholders contributed to the successful expansion of the ADDO program in Tanzania.

Management Sciences for Health (MSH) has put together a website (http://www.drugsellerinitiatives.org) whose purpose is to share initiative experiences and tools of drug sellers and others to provide a resource for those with an interest in improving access to quality pharmaceutical services and products provided by drug sellers in other countries. A drug seller initiative tool kit is a major component of the website. The tool kit identifies program components, such as regulation and monitoring, and then links tools and resources related to those components from experiences in Tanzania and Uganda. Stakeholders interested in initiating a drug seller initiative are encouraged to adapt the tools and resources for their own use. ∎

References and further readings

Abuya, T. O., W. Mutemi, B. Karisa, S. A. Ochola, G. Fegan, and V. Marsh. 2007. Use of Over-the-Counter Malaria Medicines in Children and Adults in Three Districts in Kenya: Implications for Private Medicine Retailer Interventions. *Malaria Journal* 6:57. <http://www.malariajournal.com/content/6/1/57>

Averbug, D., and M. Segall. 2008. *Best Practices in Training Private Providers.* Bethesda, Md.: Private Sector Partnerships (PSP)–One, Abt Associates Inc. <http://www.intrahealth.org/~intrahea/files/media/training-innovations-and-provider-performance/file_FINAL_Best_Practices_in_Training_Private_Providers_Primer.pdf>

Bennett, S., K. Hanson, P. Kadama, and D. Montagu. 2005. *Working with the Non-State Sector to Achieve Public Health Goals.* Making Health Systems Work. Working Paper No. 2. Geneva: World Health Organization. <http://www.who.int/management/working_paper_2_en_opt.pdf>

CPM (Center for Pharmaceutical Management). 2003a. *Access to Essential Medicines: Ghana, 2001.* Prepared for the Strategies for Enhancing Access to Medicines Program. Arlington, Va.: Management Sciences for Health. <http://www.msh.org/seam/reports/ghana_final.pdf>

Country Study 32-4
Multistakeholder contributions to ADDO program expansion

Many people in rural Tanzania seek health care and medicines from retail drug shops, called *duka la dawa baridi,* for reasons such as convenience. Historically, the TFDA authorized DLDB to provide nonprescription medicines. However, a 2001 assessment showed that many shops sold prescription medicines illegally and that the drug sellers were generally unqualified and untrained. In response, the SEAM Program collaborated with TFDA to develop and launch the ADDO program in 2003. The goal was to improve access to affordable, quality medicines and pharmaceutical services in retail drug outlets in areas where few or no registered pharmacies exist. To achieve this goal, SEAM took a holistic approach that combined training, accreditation, business incentives, and regulatory enforcement with efforts to increase consumer demand for quality products and services.

By the end of the SEAM Program in 2005, the TFDA had accredited more than 150 shops in Ruvuma. Results of the pilot in the Ruvuma region provided proof that ADDOs could improve access to quality medicines and pharmaceutical services. The next year, the Danish Agency for International Development Assistance

(Danida) funded an independent evaluation of the program and confirmed SEAM's findings. Based on the SEAM and Danida evaluations, the Ministry of Health and Social Welfare approved a plan to roll out the ADDO concept to mainland Tanzania.

As the program has taken off, many have recognized the potential of ADDOs not only to increase access to essential medicines, but also to serve as a platform for community-based public health interventions, such as improving child health. As a result, numerous organizations and programs have played a role in expanding both the services that ADDOs provide and their geographic reach—about 1,300 ADDOs are currently serving eight regions.

To be successful, nationwide scale-up of initiatives such as the ADDO program in Tanzania requires creative partnerships and solid commitment to productive collaboration. The following timeline illustrates the range of partners who have contributed to the success of Tanzania's ADDO program.

Tanzania ADDO timeline

2003	The SEAM Program and TFDA design and launch the ADDO program in the Ruvuma region.
2005	SEAM and TFDA evaluate the pilot program in Ruvuma.
2006	Danida sponsors an independent evaluation of the ADDO program in Ruvuma.
2006	The government of Tanzania, through the Ministry of Health and Social Welfare, approves a TFDA plan to roll out ADDOs throughout the Tanzanian mainland.
2006	The U.S. Agency for International Development, through MSH's Rational Pharmaceutical Management (RPM) Plus Program, funds the ADDO rollout in the Morogoro region using resources from the U.S. President's Emergency Plan for AIDS Relief.
2006	The government of Tanzania funds rollout in the Mtwara and Rukwa regions.
2006	The RPM Plus Program collaborates with the Basic Support for Institutionalizing Child Survival Project to add a child health component to ADDO services.
2006	The National Malaria Control Programme adopts the ADDO concept as part of its national strategy to increase access to malaria treatment.
2007	Tanzania's National Health Insurance Fund initiates a plan that allows members to fill prescriptions at ADDOs.
2007	MSH's Strengthening Pharmaceutical Systems Program uses President's Malaria Initiative funds to provide subsidized artemisinin-based combination therapy (ACT) through ADDOs.
2007	The Global Fund to Fight AIDS, Tuberculosis and Malaria agrees to fund ADDO rollout in six to eight high-impact malaria regions to improve access to ACTs for children under five; Danida also contributes funding for rollout.
2007	The Bill & Melinda Gates Foundation funds the East African Drug Seller Initiative to work with TFDA to review and revise the existing ADDO model to make nationwide scale-up more cost-efficient and to help ensure the long-term sustainability of ADDOs.
2008	The Gates Foundation provides the East African Drug Seller Initiative with supplemental funding to evaluate ADDO rollout in Tanzania and long-term sustainability in existing ADDO regions.
2008	The Prime Minister's Office for Regional Administration and Local Government mandates local governments to incorporate ADDO program implementation into their planning and budgets.
2009	The Rockefeller Foundation funds MSH to develop a strategy to promote program sustainability and quality through the establishment of ADDO owner and dispenser associations.
2009	Local governments in Arusha, Iringa, Kagera, Kilimanjaro, and Tabora mobilize to obtain funds to introduce ADDOs.
2009	The government of Tanzania starts rolling out ADDOs to six of the eight Global Fund– and Danida-supported regions and developing a strategy to open ADDOs in urban areas.
2009	The Clinton Foundation funds initial implementation activities in Shinyanga and Dodoma.
2009	A government of Tanzania regulation is revised to phase out unaccredited drug shops (*duka la dawa baridi*) by January 2011.

————. 2003b. *Access to Essential Medicines: Tanzania, 2001.* Prepared for the Strategies for Enhancing Access to Medicines Program. Arlington, Va.: Management Sciences for Health. <http://www.msh.org/seam/reports/CR022304_SEAMWebsite_attach1.pdf>

EADSI (East African Drug Seller Initiative). 2008. *Situational Analysis for the Pharmaceutical Sector and Access to Medicines in Uganda.* Arlington, Va.: Management Sciences for Health. <http://www.drugsellerinitiatives.org/DSI-PDF-Documents/upload/1-eadsi_uganda_pharmaceutical_sector_situational_analysis_2008.pdf>

Feeley, R., B. O'Hanlon, A. Stene, and Y. Sezgin. 2009. *Finding Middle Ground: Making Better Use of the African Private Health Sector Through More Effective Regulations.* Bethesda, Md.: Private Sector Partnerships (PSP)–*One,* Abt Associates Inc. <http://pdf.usaid.gov/pdf_docs/PNADP183.pdf>

Goodman, C., W. Brieger, A. Unwin, A. Mills, S. Meek, and G. Greer. 2007. Medicine Sellers and Malaria Treatment in Sub-Saharan Africa: What Do They Do and How Can Their Practice Be Improved? *American Journal of Tropical Medicine and Hygiene* 77(Suppl. 6):203–18.

Goodman, C., S. P. Kachur, S. Abdulla, P. Bloland, and A. Mills. 2007. Drug Shop Regulation and Malaria Treatment in Tanzania: Why Do Shops Break the Rules, and Does It Matter? *Health Policy and Planning* 22(6):393–403.

Greer, G., A. Akinpelumi, L. Madueke, B. Plowman, B. Fapohunda, Y. Tawfik, R. Holmes, et al. 2004. *Improving Management of Childhood Malaria in Nigeria and Uganda by Improving Practices of Patent Medicine Vendors.* Arlington, Va.: BASICS II for the United States Agency for International Development.

Gyapong, M., and B. Garshong. 2007. *Lessons Learned in Home Management of Malaria: Implementation Research in Four African Countries.* Geneva: World Health Organization on behalf of the Special Programme for Research and Training in Tropical Diseases.

IFC (International Finance Corporation). 2007. *The Business of Health in Africa: Partnering with the Private Sector to Improve People's Lives.* Washington, D.C.: World Bank. <http://www.ifc.org/ifcext/healthinafrica.nsf/Content/FullReport>

Marsh, V. M., W. M. Mutemi, A. Willetts, K. Bayah, S. Were, A. Ross, and K. Marsh. 2004. Improving Malaria Home Treatment by Training Drug Retailers in Rural Kenya. *Tropical Medicine and International Health* 9(4):451–60.

Mills, A., R. Brugha, K. Hanson, and B. McPake. 2002. What Can Be Done about the Private Health Sector in Low-Income Countries? *Bulletin of the World Health Organization* 80(4):325–30.

Palmer, N., A. Mills, H. Wadee, L. Gilson, and H. Schneider. 2003. A New Face for Private Providers in Developing Countries: What Implications for Public Health? *Bulletin of the World Health Organization* 81:292–7.

Patouillard, E., C. Goodman, K. Hanson, and A. Mills. 2007. Can Working with the Private-for-Profit Sector Improve Utilization of Quality Health Services for the Poor? A Systematic Review of the Literature. *International Journal for Equity in Health* 6:17.

Rooney, A., and P. van Ostenberg. 1999. *Licensure, Accreditation, and Certification: Approaches to Health Services Quality.* Bethesda, Md.: Quality Assurance Project, Center for Human Services. <http://pdf.usaid.gov/pdf_docs/PNACF510.pdf>

Ruster, J., C. Yamamoto, and K. Rogo. 2003. "Franchising in Health: Emerging Models, Experiences, and Challenges in Primary Care." *Public Policy for the Private Sector.* Note no. 263. World Bank. <http://rru.worldbank.org/documents/publicpolicyjournal/263Ruste-063003.pdf>

Rutta, E., B. Kibassa, B. McKinnon, J. Liana, R. Mbwasi, W. Mlaki, M. Embrey, et al. 2011. Increasing Access to Subsidized Artemisinin-Based Combination Therapy through Accredited Drug Dispensing Outlets in Tanzania. *Health Research Policy and Systems* 9:22. <http://www.health-policy-systems.com/content/9/1/22>

Rutta, E., K. Senauer, K. Johnson, G. Adeya, R. Mbwasi, J. Liana, S. Kimatta, M.Sigonda, and E. Alphonce. 2009. Creating a New Class of Pharmaceutical Services Provider for Underserved Areas: The Tanzania Accredited Drug Dispensing Outlet Experience. *Progress in Community Health Partnerships* 3(2):145–53.

Shah, N. M., W. R. Brieger, and D. H. Peters. 2011. Can Interventions Improve Health Services from Informal Private Providers in Low and Middle-Income Countries? A Comprehensive Review of the Literature. *Health Policy and Planning* 26(4):275–87.

Strategies for Enhancing Access to Medicines. 2007. *GHANA: Creating a Franchise System for Drug Sellers—CAREshops®.* Arlington, Va.: Management Sciences for Health. <http://www.msh.org/seam/reports/seam_ghana_careshops.pdf>

Tavrow, P., J. Shabahang, and S. Makama. 2003. Vendor-to-Vendor Education to Improve Malaria Treatment by Private Drug Outlets in Bungoma District, Kenya. *Malaria Journal* 2:10.

Part I: Policy and economic issues   Part II: Pharmaceutical management   Part III: Management support systems

Selection
Procurement
Distribution
Use
   27 Managing for rational medicine use
   28 Investigating medicine use
   29 Promoting rational prescribing
   30 Ensuring good dispensing practices
   31 Community-based participation and initiatives
   32 Drug seller initiatives
   33 Encouraging appropriate medicine use by consumers
   34 Medicine and therapeutics information
   35 Pharmacovigilance

CHAPTER 33

Encouraging appropriate medicine use by consumers

SUMMARY

Although prescribers play an essential role in the choice of medicines, the role of the consumer is equally important. Public knowledge, attitudes, and perceptions regarding the use of medicines influence the decision whether to seek health care, from whom, and whether to follow the proposed treatment. In some countries, most medicines can be bought directly over the counter, often from unauthorized sources, often in response to aggressive commercial marketing, and often through illegal sales of prescription-only medicine.

For consumers to use medicines appropriately, they need to know how to take them, what to avoid, and what negative effects to watch for. Communication is needed at a general level to give people a better understanding of what medicines are, how they act in the body, what their risks and benefits are, and what their role is in health care. At a more specific level, interventions are needed to tackle particularly serious problems of misuse. Relevant strategies, based on known facilitating factors and possible constraints, must be developed and implemented.

An increased focus on treating chronic diseases in developing countries, including HIV/AIDS, has resulted in research designed to promote treatment adherence. A major concern regarding poor adherence to treatment for infectious disease is the development of antimicrobial resistance; poor adherence is also costly in terms of the patient's quality of life, the subsequent increase in health care expenditure, and reduced productivity. Components to address in promoting adherence include—

- Communication between providers and patients
- Inadequate counseling
- Lack of resources for medicines and treatment
- Complexity and duration of treatment
- Availability of information

Strategies to encourage appropriate medicine use by the consumer can be public or patient centered, but they should always be culturally specific. A public-centered approach provides the community, or target populations within the community, with information on the role of medicines and on how to make appropriate health-seeking decisions at times of illness.

Seven steps toward more effective communication strategies are—

1. Describe medicine use and identify problems
2. Prioritize problems
3. Analyze problems and identify solutions
4. Select and develop intervention
5. Pretest intervention
6. Implement intervention
7. Monitor and evaluate intervention

Developing interventions in collaboration with the people whose medicine-use patterns have been targeted for change helps ensure that the cultural and social context in which beliefs and practices have developed is taken into account. A variety of approaches and resources improves the chance of the intervention's success and expands its capacity and reach.

33.1 The need to encourage appropriate medicine use

Although the prescriber's role in promoting rational medicine use is important, the patient, community, and cultural context cannot be ignored. The knowledge, attitudes, and education of the public in relation to disease etiology and treatment are critical determinants in the decision to seek health care, the choice of provider, the use of medicines, and the success of treatment—the patient or caregiver, therefore, is the final determinant of appropriate medicine use. Patients should be actively involved in the therapeutic encounter and treatment.

Often, the patient or caregiver decides whether to go ahead with a treatment, a choice frequently influenced by the views of family, close friends, and the community. People make a series of decisions before choosing a treatment.

First: People who are ill have to believe that their health status has changed and that something is wrong with them or that they need to take action to prevent illness. To some extent, a person's culture defines this perception. In the case of children, the knowledge and experience of the caregiver are critical determinants. This decision can be complicated by the lack of observable symptoms for some conditions.

Second: People or caregivers have to decide whether this change of health status is significant enough for them to seek help or whether the symptoms or potential health threat will go away without taking any action.

Third: After they decide to get help, people choose where to seek help: a hospital, a primary health care center, a private physician, a pharmacist, a market vendor or retail drug seller, a traditional healer, a relative, or some other community member. They may decide, rightly or not, that the symptoms are minor or that they have sufficient familiarity with the required treatment to take care of themselves with either a modern pharmaceutical or a traditional remedy.

Fourth: When they have a prescription or have received a recommendation for products from a pharmacy or drug shop, patients decide whether to buy the medicines, whether they are going to buy all or some of the items recommended, and which medicines to buy. Cost considerations may require a choice of which items to buy and which to ignore, and knowledge can help patients make rational choices within the context of medicine promotion and advertising, some of which may be unethical.

Fifth: Patients decide whether and when to take the medicines, how to take the medicines, whether to continue if side effects occur or symptoms disappear, and what to do with medicines that they do not use.

Consumers also need education on medicines and treatment because pharmaceuticals play such an important role in health care and because public education provides individuals and communities with information that enables them to use medicines in an appropriate, safe, and judicious way. Inappropriate medicine use has serious health and economic consequences for both individuals and the community. For example, development of antimicrobial resistance from the inappropriate use of antibiotics not only can harm an individual patient but also can harm the community when certain antibiotics become ineffective. Appropriate medicine use by consumers is an integral part of successful national pharmaceutical policies.

The 1978 Declaration of Alma-Ata, which focused on the need for primary health care, states that "people have the right and duty to participate individually and collectively in the planning and implementation of their health care," a principle that should be a cornerstone of national public health and hence of pharmaceutical policy. The World Health Organization (WHO) considers public information and communication on medicine as key elements in national pharmaceutical policy and as a prerequisite for consumers to be able to make sound decisions about health care. Despite the progress by some countries, however, governments seldom allocate the necessary human and financial resources for public education on medicine. Moreover, many training programs for health care providers do not adequately cover patient counseling, communication, and appropriate use of medicines. These topics are frequently given little priority—to be tackled only when the other elements of pharmaceutical policy are in place or when the training curriculum has an open slot.

Problems

Irrational medicine use includes overuse, underuse, and inappropriate use (see Chapter 27). Various factors contribute to these problems: lack of adequate regulatory systems, shortages of essential medicines, lack of objective medicine information for prescribers and consumers, poor communication between prescribers and patients, exclusion of patients from the information needed to become partners in therapy, and considerable influence of medicine promotion on both prescribers and consumers.

Most developing countries have public health problems of medicine misuse, including the following—

- Widespread availability of prescription medicines from informal sellers, market stalls, or unlicensed drugstores—WHO data indicate that two-thirds of antibiotics are dispensed without a prescription through the informal private sector (WHO 2011a).
- A culture of self-medication and lack of knowledge about the importance of following treatment guidelines (such as taking a full dose or course of therapy), which is integral to controlling antimicrobial resistance.
- Globalization and expansion of the private sector as a source of medicines, with a corresponding commercialization of pharmaceutical supply and promotion.

Benefits

Improving public understanding about medicines will not resolve all these issues, but—together with other activities to promote rational use—it will contribute to the development of better medicine use.

At an individual level, the benefits of improved public understanding include—

- Better knowledge of how to take medicines when needed
- Better appreciation of the limits of medicines and a lessening of the belief that "there is a pill for every ill"
- More balanced partnership between consumer-patients and health care providers
- More critical attitude toward advertising and other commercial information, which often fail to give objective information about medicines

At the community level, the benefits include—

- More understanding and support for pharmaceutical policy and measures to improve medicine use
- More efficient use of medicines and less waste of resources

- Improved confidence in health services and health care providers
- Increased success of measures to deal with public health problems
- Development of expectations about receiving quality medicines and pharmacy-related services
- Protection of the effectiveness of essential antibiotics by decreasing development of antimicrobial resistance

Communication is needed at a general level to give people a better understanding of what medicines are, how they act in the body, what their risks and benefits may be, and what role they play in health care. At a more specific level, interventions are needed to tackle particularly serious problems of misuse. Campaigns for the wiser use of specific medicines (for example, in malaria control programs) have proved effective in reducing morbidity and mortality and in reducing needless expenditures. Other campaigns have tackled particular medicine-related problems. For example, WHO launched Make Medicines Child Size to advocate for and address treatment issues specific to children. Box 33-1 provides more information on medicines and children.

33.2   Promoting treatment adherence and appropriate medicine use by patients

WHO defines adherence as "the extent to which a person's behavior—taking medication, following a diet, and/or executing lifestyle changes, corresponds with agreed recommendations from a health care provider" (WHO 2003, 3). The concept of adherence requires a trusting relationship between the patient and the health professional in which the patient agrees with the provider's recommendations.

A major concern regarding poor adherence to treatment for infectious disease is the development of antimicrobial resistance to the first-line medication, resulting in reliance on second- or third-line medicines that are expensive and may have higher levels of adverse drug reactions (see Chapter 35). Poor adherence is also costly in terms of the patient's quality of life, the subsequent increase in health care expenditure, and lost productivity (WHO 2003).

The scale-up of antiretroviral therapy (ART) in developing countries has brought greater attention to adherence among patients who must take antiretroviral medicines (ARVs) for the rest of their lives. Other conditions requiring long-term treatment adherence include noncommunicable, chronic diseases, such as diabetes, high blood pressure, and mental disorders. This point is important because WHO estimates that, globally, deaths from noncommunicable diseases will increase by 15 percent between 2010 and 2020—and over 20 percent in Africa, the eastern Mediterranean, and Southeast Asia (Holloway and van Dijk 2011). Many studies have shown that in developed countries, adherence to medicine regimens among patients with chronic diseases is mediocre, and the situation in developing countries is assumed to be worse because of the greater constraints to accessing affordable medicines and weaker health systems overall (WHO 2003). Poor adherence is a problem with any treatment regimen, but achieving a high rate of adherence and sustaining it over the long run is extremely difficult (Gill et al. 2005).

Reasons that patients do not follow prescribed short-term or chronic disease treatment include—

- Lack of ready access to care (for example, distance to clinic) or patient-unfriendly schedules (for example, limited hours of operation)
- Lack of appointments
- Poor communication between providers and patients
- Inadequate counseling
- Lack of resources for medicines and related treatment visits (for example, cost of travel)
- Complexity and duration of treatment, particularly in cases of chronic disease
- Lack of access to information

Communication between providers and patients

Patients are better able to adhere to their medication regimens when they have a strong relationship and enhanced communication with their health care provider (Osterberg and Blaschke 2005, WHO 2003). Lacking a trusting relationship, patients may hesitate to ask providers to clarify either their basic health condition or the treatment proposed. This hesitancy can be linked to fears of appearing foolish, to differences in social status and language, or to lack of encouragement by providers. Patients who have developed a trusting relationship with their health care provider, whether at a clinic or a drug shop, may be more likely to listen, to ask questions, and to follow advice.

Prescribers' and dispensers' communication skills can be weak: they tend to use complex terminology that patients cannot easily understand; they frequently lack knowledge of behavioral theory and practice; and they may have limited awareness of the scale, problems, and causes of patient nonadherence to treatment. The low priority given to communication skills in medical, paramedical, and pharmacy schools undoubtedly contributes to this situation. Fortunately, some medical and pharmacy schools—notably in Australia, Canada, Europe, and the United States—include communication techniques in their basic curricula, teaching behavioral theory and using role playing and video as learning tools. Audiovisual feedback to students markedly enhances their acquisition of such skills, and basic communication training should be an integral part of any prescriber's or dispenser's education and refresher training. These types of courses are gradually being incorporated into

---

Box 33-1
Pharmaceutical issues to consider in treating children

Product-related issues

Ability or willingness of children to swallow tablets and capsules and tolerate liquids: Generally, as children age, their ability and willingness to swallow tablets and capsules increases; however, age cannot be assumed to be a direct correlation. Liquid preparations are often preferred for younger children, but some treatment programs have reported that small children have difficulty swallowing large volumes of liquids (for example, zidovudine) and that the syrups taste bitter.

Limited product stability: Some products (for example, stavudine liquid) have a fixed expiry after reconstitution, thus making losses caused by expiration more of a problem and quantification of needs concomitantly more complex.

Fixed-dose combinations (FDCs): FDCs formulated for adults may not be suitable for use in children because the doses of one or more of the medicines combined into the product may not be appropriate for the child's age, weight, or body surface area. Using FDCs or portions of an FDC in children can therefore result in (a) underdosing, leading to treatment failure, resistance, or both, or (b) overdosing, which increases the potential for side effects. Some FDC products are not recommended or licensed to be cut or split by the manufacturer, for example, because the active constituents may not be evenly distributed throughout the preparation.

Losses through spillage or use: Losses from spillage or from sugary liquids and suspensions sticking to the bottle or oral syringe need to be considered when dispensing and monitoring adherence to liquid-based therapy.

Product availability of low-dose tablets or capsules and FDCs: Pediatric formulations for HIV/AIDS and tuberculosis (TB) are not readily available. The lack of pediatric dosage forms of most anti-TB and antiretroviral medicines necessitates using adult pills that must be broken into halves or quarters or crushing pills and

creating suspensions, which can result in wasted product and inaccurate measurement. The development of half-sized, scored pills would help provide practical treatment alternatives for children.

Treatment-related issues

Less detailed standard treatment guidelines (STGs) for children (mainly for HIV/AIDS treatment): Many countries have now developed STGs for ART; however, the focus is mainly on adults. The recommendations for children are generally less detailed, especially with regard to addressing product-related issues.

Complex quantification because a treatment regimen is not automatically translatable to specific products or dispensing quantities: For children, the product prescribed depends on dosage needed (such as a portion of the adult dose), the ability or willingness of the patient to swallow the product, and tolerance to a formulation. The selection will also depend on the range of products available for prescribing. The dose, and therefore the quantity to be dispensed, depends on the child's age, weight, or body surface area.

Adjustments needed for continuing growth and weight gain in children receiving long-term treatment: Once a child has started on long-term treatment, the dose will increase as the child gains weight or grows in height. Programs have reported that some uninformed providers have not changed the doses for children on ARVs to take their growth into account, which can result in resistance to treatment.

Access and adherence to treatment reliant on caregiver: Programs may need to use different approaches to promote adherence to and completion of a full course of treatment to a caregiver, especially when the caregiver is elderly or if the child is accompanied by different caregivers on each visit. The time that it takes to dispense medicines to children and their caregivers is typically much longer.

---

training programs in developing countries; for example, as part of a countrywide antimicrobial resistance containment initiative, the University of Zambia revised its medical curriculum to include antimicrobial resistance and rational medicines use (Joshi 2010).

Adherence to treatment is linked to the clarity of the prescriber's explanation: patients often feel that instructions are unclear or nonexistent. The timing and clarity of a message

powerfully affect how the consumer receives, understands, and retains it. Patients remember the first instructions presented the best; they recall instructions that are emphasized; and the fewer instructions given, the greater the proportion they remember. Thus, a message must not only be clear; it must also be succinct and then organized and delivered in a way that allows the patient to understand and process the information completely.

Although adherence to treatment depends on a patient's acceptance of information about the health threat itself, the practitioner must also be able to persuade the patient that the treatment is worthwhile. Adherence to treatment is linked to the patient's perception of the practitioner's friendliness, empathy, interest, and concern. Finally, in most circumstances, it is essential not only to specify the patient's precise actions (for example, taking two pills twice a day) but also to suggest how the patient can insert that action into the daily routine (for example, taking them at breakfast and dinner). To accomplish this, the health care provider must understand the patient's circumstances; for example, some patients may not be able to afford more than one meal a day or may have an atypical schedule, such as working at night and sleeping during the day.

A more fruitful patient-provider interaction can be encouraged if providers increase their sensitivity, patient and consumer organizations actively promote such interaction, and relevant campaigns are carried out to empower patients.

Inadequate counseling

WHO estimates that the average amount of time that a dispenser spends with a patient is less than one minute and that only about half of patients receive instructions on how to take the medicines they receive (Holloway and van Dijk 2011). Providers sometimes attribute lack of interaction with patients to the pressures of work and a lack of adequate staff. To help correct this problem, two things need to happen. First, health care facilities need to examine their patient care routines to increase efficiency and add time for more patient interaction. For example, many health centers and outpatient departments see all their patients during a few morning hours. One possibility to consider is extending this period so that each individual can receive more time with the prescriber and dispenser. Another possibility is to train staff to make better use of the time available and to ensure that patients do not fall into an "information gap": if the provider does not have the time to explain the treatment to the patient and ensure that the patient fully understands the instructions, the dispenser or nurse should receive training to do this. Second, health care providers must prioritize and effectively communicate critical information to patients under less-than-ideal circumstances. Staff must be encouraged to understand that effective communication with patients is not an unrealistic ideal but a core aspect of clinical practice.

Another common problem is a lack of space for confidential counseling. Pharmacy staff often must use a dispensing window that is crowded with customers to give information to one patient. The Rational Pharmaceutical Management Plus Program helped facilities in several countries, including Kenya and Ethiopia, to construct private dispensing booths where dispensers can counsel patients privately. Although the booths were constructed primarily to provide confidentiality to patients on ART, all patients, no matter what their condition, benefit from the dispensing booths.

Country Study 33-1 shows how an emphasis on counseling for ART in Kenya improved medication counseling for all patients at the facility.

Lack of resources for medicines and treatment

Patients in developing countries are more likely to pay out of pocket for the medicines they need—over 70 percent of medicine expenditures in low-income countries consist of consumer payments (Holloway and van Dijk 2011). When the patient bears part or all of the cost, he or she may not buy the medicine at all if it is too expensive. When more

---

Country Study 33-1
Medication counseling training for ART dispensers in Kenya

Beginning in 2003, the government of Kenya initiated ART for HIV-infected patients at four health facilities serving the Coast province. When the program began, pharmacy staff received training on rational medicine use specifically for ART and on how best to offer medication counseling to ART recipients. One sensitive issue for an ART program is ensuring patients a confidential location within the pharmacy to receive their medicines and counseling. Therefore, new booths at pharmacy windows were constructed to create private counseling areas that provide a welcoming and secure atmosphere. The staff members saw the confidential nature of the booths as a valuable addition: "Before, when I was dispensing pessaries to a patient there would be four heads listening."

When the pharmacy team later evaluated the ART program's first six months of operation, they felt that one of their main successes was using their training and the enabling environment of the booths to improve the quality of medication counseling, not only for ART, but also for their other patients. Several of the dispensing staff reported that they were applying their training on ART medication counseling to those patients taking diabetic or hypertensive medicine.

Source: RPM Plus Program 2004.

Figure 33-1   Improving adherence to treatment

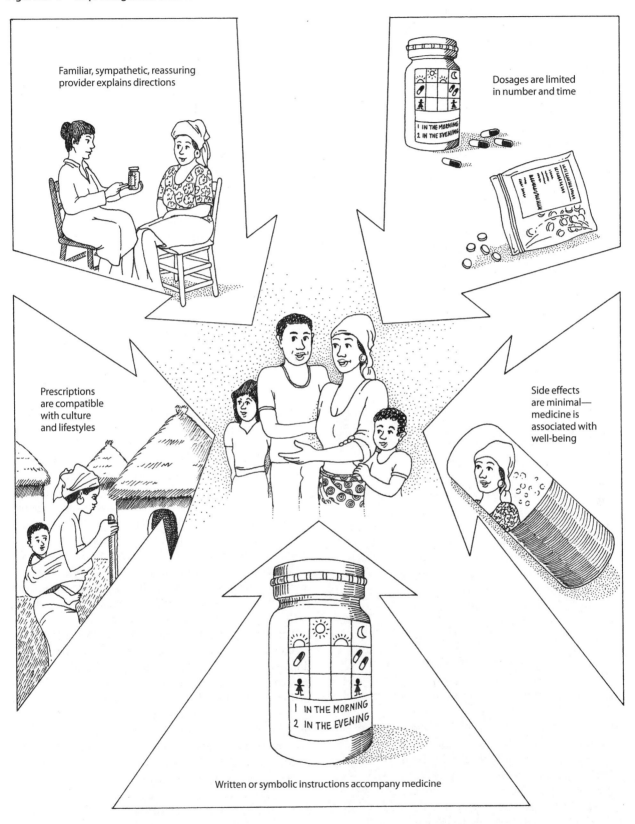

Familiar, sympathetic, reassuring provider explains directions

Dosages are limited in number and time

Prescriptions are compatible with culture and lifestyles

Side effects are minimal—medicine is associated with well-being

Written or symbolic instructions accompany medicine

than one medicine is prescribed (in some countries, the average number of medicines per prescription is five to six), the patient may be able to afford only one or two of the products listed and may choose the less important, relatively cheaper ones, such as vitamins, or buy only a partial treatment.

Providers need to know the approximate prices of medicines they prescribe, select the cheapest available generic medicines that are compatible with quality and therapeutic needs, and keep the number of products prescribed to a minimum. If the provider prescribes more than one medicine, he or she should indicate the most important ones to the patient.

Other economic factors may influence a patient's ability to access medicines. The patient may have enough money to buy the medicine but not enough to pay for the clinic visit. If the health care facility is too far away, the patient may not have enough money to pay for transportation. A lack of food can also affect treatment adherence; for example, in Tanzania, patients reported taking their ARVs only once a day instead of twice, because that was the only time they had food (Hardon et al. 2006). In some DOTS programs, food baskets provide incentives for clients to come in and take their medications.

Box 33-2
DOTS strategy for TB treatment

TB was the first disease for which an adherence strategy was developed and implemented on a large scale—DOTS, which originally stood for directly observed treatment, short-course. DOTS is considered one of the most cost-effective of all health interventions. The aspects directly related to patient adherence include using the most effective standardized, short-course regimens and FDCs to facilitate adherence; supervising treatment in a context-specific and patient-sensitive manner; and identifying and addressing physical, financial, social, cultural, and health system barriers to accessing TB treatment services.

Effective DOTS programs can help minimize the emergence of antimicrobial resistance to medicines; however, TB strains that are resistant to conventional therapy have been documented in almost every country. Countries that have the highest proportion of multidrug-resistant (MDR)-TB cases are in Eastern Europe, including Azerbaijan and Belarus (WHO 2011b). DOTS-Plus, designed to respond to MDR-TB, is a supplementary treatment strategy that builds on DOTS but focuses on the rational use of second-line TB medicines to treat MDR-TB cases.

Complexity and duration of treatment

The longer and more complex the treatment, the greater the likelihood that the patient will not follow it. Adherence to short-term treatments (less than two weeks) can be improved by clear instructions, special "reminder" pill containers and calendars, and simplified medicine regimens (see Figure 33-1). Adherence to long-term treatments is more difficult to achieve; the DOTS program was designed to increase adherence to onerous TB treatment (Box 33-2). Fixed-dose combinations of multiple medicines in one tablet or capsule simplify a treatment regimen as does prepackaging treatments, such as blister packs of artemisinin-based combination therapy. Although no single intervention is useful on its own, combinations of clear instructions, follow-up of patients missing appointments, patient self-monitoring, social support, cues for when to take the medicines, rewards, and group discussions are useful.

Availability of information

The availability of printed information in simple language to supplement a medicine's label may increase treatment adherence. (Labeling is covered in Chapters 30 and 34.) Such patient information leaflets need well-written text in the local language, effective graphic design, large print size, and clear layout to enhance legibility; a question-and-answer format may stimulate consumer involvement.

In many parts of the world, producing leaflets for individual patients is not feasible. High rates of nonliteracy in some countries also limit the value of such information. Yet simple instructions for the most commonly used and misused medicines could be printed on inexpensive paper. Simple booklets or posters for display in retail outlets and health centers can provide consumer information on the most common medicines. Even nonliterate patients can obtain information from such publications with help from family or community members. Figure 33-2 shows a poster used in Tanzania, translated from Swahili, to inform accredited drug-dispensing outlet customers about antimicrobial resistance.

Pictograms can provide reinforcing information about medicines. A setting and rising sun or moon to represent different times of the day for taking medicine have been used in a number of countries, although an evaluation in Bangladesh found that dispensers had to be trained in their use. The U.S. Pharmacopeia developed a series of pictograms for use on medicine labels (see Annex 33-1). The International Pharmaceutical Federation also has a pictogram project (http://www.fip.org/www/index.php?page=pp_sect_maepsm_pictogram).

A study in South Africa showed that images that had been developed locally were interpreted correctly more often than the U.S. Pharmacopeia images (Dowse and Ehlers 2004); therefore, each country needs to develop its own

Figure 33-2   Consumer education poster used in accredited drug-dispensing outlets in Tanzania

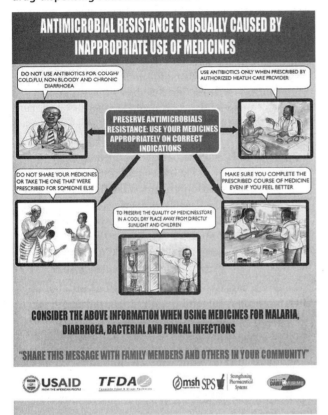

symbols using culturally recognizable objects. Pretesting is important, because patients need to understand the symbols without explanation. Research has shown that culturally appropriate icons can improve how well patients understand medicine labels and adhere to treatment but that inappropriate icons can be more confusing than words (Shrank et al. 2007).

33.3 Monitoring adherence in health care facilities

One particular challenge is how to measure and quantify adherence rates. No consensus exists for measuring adherence, and research reflects the variety of methods in practice (WHO 2003). A study of twenty-four health care systems serving more than 86,000 AIDS patients in East Africa showed that facilities used a wide range of methods to calculate treatment adherence. Fourteen different operational definitions of treatment defaulting existed, ranging from one day to six months following a missed appointment (Chalker et al. 2010).

Methods to measure adherence rates are subjective or objective: subjective measures include reporting by patients and health care providers, who tend to overestimate adherence. Objective measures include counting doses of medicine at clinic or home visits, but this method tends to overestimate adherence and does not reflect other adherence information, such as timing of doses and missed doses. Special medicine-bottle caps that record when a dose is removed are expensive and generally are used only for clinical trials. Relying on pharmacy records to see when prescriptions are filled and refilled is another method that is objective, but it does not indicate medicine use once the prescription has been filled. Directly observed treatment by a health care worker is the cornerstone of adherence for TB, but this approach is not practical for many long-term treatment regimens. Other objective methods use clinical monitoring, such as testing for blood sugar for diabetes or CD4 counts or viral load for HIV/AIDS.

The International Network for the Rational Use of Drugs Initiative on Adherence to Antiretrovirals has developed and validated a set of indicators that can be used to monitor adherence to ART either at the facility or HIV/AIDS program level. The indicators measure treatment adherence and defaulting by using routine pharmacy records and patient interviews to look at appointment keeping and days covered by dispensed medicine over a period of time. The indicators correlate with increases in patients' CD4 counts and weight (Ross-Degnan et al. 2010). The initiative published a manual and tools to measure adherence that offers a step-by-step guide on how to design and carry out a national or facility survey or a program adherence survey. The manual and tools can be downloaded for adaptation and use (http://www.inrud.org/ARV-Adherence-Project/Adherence-Survey-Tools-and-Manual.cfm).

33.4 Addressing determinants of adherence

Causes of poor adherence vary and are not well understood. WHO has defined five "dimensions" of adherence illustrating that adherence is not the responsibility of the patient alone (WHO 2003). They are (a) social and economic factors, (b) patient-related factors, (c) health care team and system factors, (d) therapy-related factors, and (e) condition-related factors. For example, patients may not have the money or transportation to access treatment, or they may have to wait for hours to pick up their medicines. Some patients, especially those with HIV/AIDS or mental illness, may feel stigmatized. Prescribers may not explain treatment clearly, or the treatment regimen may be difficult to follow or cause adverse reactions. A study in Ethiopia and Uganda showed that a positive and confidential partnership between patients and health care providers enhanced patients' satisfaction and feelings of trust in the treatment and helped overcome adherence barriers (Gusdal et al. 2009).

Strategies to increase patient adherence include the use of FDCs and prepackaged patient packs to simplify treatment (Country Study 33-2). WHO and the International Union against Tuberculosis and Lung Disease recommend FDCs to ensure proper treatment of TB (Blomberg et al. 2001). Another intervention often incorporated as part of DOTS is the use of incentives or enablers to positively influence the behavior of both providers and patients. An enabler might be a transportation voucher that helps the patient get to the treatment facility; an incentive could be a monetary bonus for a private provider who refers suspected TB patients to an accredited testing facility (Box 33-3). ART programs are instituting interventions to increase adherence, such as reducing waiting time, tracking appointment keeping and following up with patients, and using peer counselors as support (Gusdal et al. 2011). A TB program in Cape Town uses text messaging on cell phones to remind patients to take their medicines (Green 2003).

Interventions to promote adherence should address barriers at all levels of the health care system and not just focus on the patient alone. Like interventions to improve rational medicine use, a single-factor intervention probably has limited effectiveness compared with an approach that takes multiple factors into account. Box 33-4 shows some proven interventions related to the five dimensions of adherence.

The HIV/AIDS pandemic has focused attention on expanding the role of pharmacy staff in providing a full range of pharmaceutical care services to the patient, including medication counseling and adherence monitoring. However, as discussed in Chapter 51, the lack of trained health professionals in many countries makes adequately monitoring rational medicine use difficult, especially for chronic disease medications. This gap in human resources makes using other personnel, such as drug sellers, that much more crucial (see Chapter 32). In addition, educating patients as well as the entire community about the importance of adherence and medicine use and exploring the effectiveness of community-based interventions (see Chapter 31) become much more important.

33.5 Communicating with consumers about appropriate medicine use

Strategies to encourage appropriate medicine use by the consumer can be public or patient centered, but they should always be culturally specific. A public-centered approach provides the community, or target populations within the community, with information on the role of medicines and on how to make appropriate health-seeking decisions at times of illness.

Principles of public communication

The following principles should guide public education in appropriate medicine use—

Country Study 33-2
Using prepackaging to improve rational use of medicines

According to WHO, about half of patients who receive medicines fail to take them correctly, including taking less or more medication than necessary, taking antimicrobials for nonbacterial infections, and inappropriately self-medicating, often with prescription medications (WHO 2004b).

Several studies have shown that prepackaging medicines (particularly antimalarials) in daily doses can improve adherence, safety, and cost-effectiveness.

- One Ghanaian study showed that prepacking antimalarials into daily doses decreased costs by reducing the number of medicines prescribed, the amount of syrup consumed, and the number of injections given (WHO/TDR 1998). Prepackaging also improved adherence and reduced waiting times for treatment; moreover, patients found the packaging to be acceptable.
- A systematic review of fifteen studies of the effectiveness of FDC pills and unit-of-use packaging, such as blister packs, found that although more rigorous research was needed, both approaches are likely to improve adherence in a range of settings in both developed and developing countries (Connor, Rafter, and Rodgers 2004).
- A third study, conducted in the Brong Ahafo region of Ghana, examined the extent to which district health teams could reduce the burden of malaria in areas with severe resource constraints (Yeboah-Antwi et al. 2001). By prepackaging antimalarial medicines into unit doses, the teams were able to improve adherence by about 20 percent in both adults and children. In addition, the prepackaging intervention reduced costs to patients by 50 percent and decreased waiting time at dispensaries and medicine waste at facilities.

Sources: Conner, Rafter, and Rodgers 2004, WHO 2004b, Yeboah-Antwi et al. 2001, WHO/TDR 1998.

Box 33-3
Improving the efficacy of the DOTS strategy through the use of enablers and incentives

Treatment success in the 2009 worldwide DOTS cohort of 5.8 million patients was 86 percent on average, edging closer to the 90 percent target for 2015. However, treatment success was below average in the European region (67 percent) (WHO 2011b). WHO estimates that between 1995 and 2010, 6.8 million lives were saved because of the DOTS strategy.

To help improve the effectiveness of the DOTS strategy, many TB control projects and programs worldwide have adopted measures called *enablers* and *incentives* to motivate health care providers and patients. An enabler is something given to the patient or treatment provider that makes participation possible, practical, or easy. For example, providing bus tokens makes it easier for people to get to their appointments. An incentive is a stimulus designed to encourage stakeholders to behave in a certain way, such as providing food baskets to patients who show up to their appointments.

Unfortunately, the weak evidence base about enablers and incentives makes assessment of their effectiveness difficult. However, their potential role has been described in literature reviews, surveys of experiences, and mapping workshops.

Some examples of successful motivators include the following—

- In rural Bangladesh, patients sign a contract and pay a deposit of about 3.50 U.S. dollars upon initiation of TB treatment. At completion of therapy, patients receive back 37.5 percent of their original deposit, and the community-based supervisor receives the remainder. The "deposit" scheme was associated with significantly better TB treatment adherence and case detection compared to the national average.
- Targeting homeless and other vulnerable populations, the Czech Republic offers vouchers worth 4 to 5 euros for purchasing goods after TB diagnosis. As a result, case detection is five times higher among the homeless population receiving the incentive.
- Patients received travel support to attend a TB clinic in Romania for one year. During the pilot program, adherence to treatment increased to 95 percent, then fell back to 80 percent when the program ended.

Source: RPM Plus Program 2005.

- Medicine use should be viewed within the context of the society, community, family, and individual. Public communication on medicines should recognize cultural diversity in concepts of health and illness or notions about how medicines work. The different expectations surrounding conventional and traditional medicines need to be considered, as do preferences for injections or for tablets of a particular color because they are considered more potent. Social factors such as poverty, disadvantage, and power relations can also influence medicine use.
- School curricula should include education in the appropriate use of medicines, with different messages and educational approaches used for students of different ages (see, for example, Cebotarenco and Bush 2008).
- Public communication should encourage informed decision making by individuals, families, and communities on the use of medicines and on nonmedicine solutions.
- Public communication should be based on the best available scientific information about medicines, including their efficacy and side effects.

- To facilitate informed choices on medicine use, public communication should be accompanied by supportive legislation, such as regulating pharmaceutical advertising and promotion and controls on medicine availability. In addition, governments should ensure that over-the-counter medicines have adequate labels and include accurate and easily understood instructions.
- Nongovernmental organizations (NGOs), community groups, and consumer and professional organizations have important roles to play in public communication programs and should be involved, when possible, in the planning and implementation of communication activities.
- Effective public information about medicines requires a commitment to, and an understanding of the need for, improved communication between health care providers and patients. Educational and training curricula for providers should reflect this commitment.

Developing public communication strategies

Effective communication involves a process that is modified as new information on its effectiveness and need for improvements become evident and new communication methods and technologies become available (see Figure 33-3).

Public communication can aim to influence people's thinking in many ways, including—

- Organizing campaigns to promote the values and benefits of essential medicines
- Empowering the consumer to understand what a correct prescription should look like and to know what questions to ask a health care provider
- Providing young people with a general knowledge base about the actions and use of medicines on which they can draw as adult consumers
- Targeting a particular problem related to medicine use, such as home injections and the reuse of needles
- Working through pharmacies to offer information on specific medicines and treatment categories, as in the comprehensive information programs developed by the national corporation of Swedish pharmacists and the pharmaceutical society of Australia

Providing information is much easier than changing behavior. Many studies show that knowledge does not necessarily influence action. Changing people's behavior generally requires a long-term strategy undertaken after a careful analysis of the situation and identification of priority problems, with knowledge of the societal context in which the strategy will be carried out. Identification of target groups and pretested, culturally specific materials are necessary. These materials should always be evaluated for their effect not only on knowledge acquired but also on actual behavioral change. Repeat messaging is useful.

The steps shown in Figure 33-3 are discussed in the following sections.

Step 1: Describe medicine use and identify problems. Investigating how medicines are prescribed, dispensed, and used is the foundation for the communication process. Such an investigation should address the following issues—

Information already available: Reports of studies or from annual reports of organizations working in related fields can provide information about the problem.

Box 33-4
Selected areas of intervention to improve medication adherence

Social and economic

- Ensuring affordable prices for treatment and medicines
- Preparing family members to be supportive
- Providing other forms of social support
- Combating illiteracy
- Providing food and/or transportation vouchers
- Organizing peer and community support groups
- Creating patient organizations

Health care team and system

- Ensuring reliable pharmaceutical supply systems
- Improving communication between patients and health professionals
- Creating awareness and knowledge about the value of adherence
- Making convenient appointments for the patient
- Giving simple instructions about the treatment regimen
- Tracking patient appointment keeping and following up on no-shows
- Prescribing the simplest regimen possible

Condition

- Screening and treating patient depression or substance abuse

- Addressing condition-related stigma; for example, providing confidential pharmacy dispensing booths
- Educating the patient about the disease or condition and its treatment

Therapy

- Developing and prescribing FDC medicines
- Using prepackaging or course-of-therapy packaging
- Providing alternative medicines that are extended release or have a long half-life
- Minimizing adverse drug reactions

Patient

- Providing more information and skills related to self-management of treatment
- Addressing poor motivation and self-efficacy
- Providing adherence counseling
- Supporting behavioral changes
- Providing memory aids, such as special pill boxes or telephone reminders
- Providing treatment incentives and reinforcements

Sources: WHO 2003, Osterberg and Blaschke 2005.

Figure 33-3   Steps in an effective public communication intervention

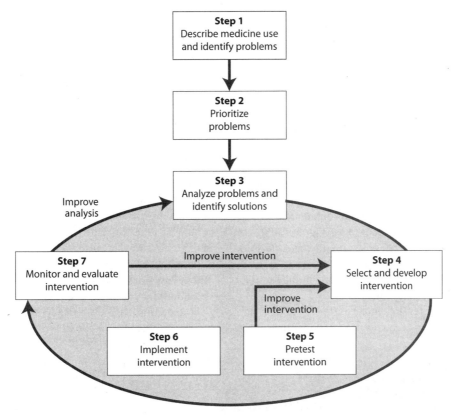

Source: Chetley et al. 2007.

New information needed: If it is not already available, information is needed on sources of medicines and on how health services and medicines are used in the community. The more data obtained on audience characteristics, the better: demographics, socioeconomic and literacy status, language patterns, community decision making and leadership processes, characteristics of prescribers and users, and local beliefs and practices relating to disease etiology and the use of medicines are all useful.

Communication networks: What sources of information about medicines, including nonmedical sources, are most credible to the target audience? What channels of information reach users most effectively? Do mass media channels play a role? What role can new technologies (for example, mobile phones) play?

Communication development: What resources exist in research, education and training, production and distribution of information, and social mobilization?

Researchers can combine quantitative and qualitative research methods to obtain the necessary data. Quantitative methods, such as household surveys, provide useful information on levels of knowledge and on the practices and beliefs prevalent in a population: they measure what is hap-

pening. Qualitative methods, such as focus group discussions and in-depth individual interviews, yield substantial information about specific behaviors, as well as the reasons and motivations underlying them: they explore how and why things are happening. These methods, described in Chapter 28, generate many ideas and provide language for communication materials. A handbook is also available on how to investigate consumers' use of medicines (Hardon, Hodgkin, and Fresle 2004).

Step 2: Prioritize problems. Policy makers or health professionals can prioritize medicine-use problems, but involving stakeholders through focus group discussions, for example, can increase community support for the process (Hardon, Hodgkin, and Fresle 2004). Questions to ask when prioritizing problems include the following: How many people are affected? Is the problem common or rare? How serious is the resulting adverse effect? Does the problem cost a lot of money? Does the community recognize the problem as serious? Will a community-based intervention solve the problem or does it require a different type of intervention, such as regulation? (Hardon, Hodgkin, and Fresle 2004). Once these questions are answered about the identified problems, the problems can be rated based on preselected criteria.

Step 3: Analyze problems and identify solutions. Initial research and prioritization of problems explore the causes of the problems, define the behaviors to be adopted or changed or knowledge to be acquired, and describe constraints and facilitating factors that will affect the planning process and the feasibility of possible objectives. Objectives for the analysis include identifying how stakeholders view the problems and possible solutions and identifying factors that can facilitate interventions (Hardon, Hodgkin, and Fresle 2004). All stakeholders, including community members, should have the opportunity to consider potential solutions to the problems. The target audience for the solution may be the entire population in the case of a broad-based national program; more often, however it will be a subsection of the community, such as schoolchildren, mothers of young children, the elderly, community leaders, or women's organizations. Problem analysis should also provide insight into the cultural context of behavior and beliefs and indications of useful language and expressions.

Step 4: Select and develop intervention. A critical part of the planning process is to clarify what the intervention should achieve. The intervention plan defines objectives and outlines how to reach them. The plan should include the elements discussed below.

Realistic and well-defined communication objectives:
Clear objectives make it easier to formulate activities that are likely to achieve the objectives and measure achievements. These objectives should focus on specific problems and target the people exhibiting the problem behavior. General campaigns may raise awareness, but they are unlikely to result in significant behavioral changes.

Approaches to change: Approaches can include either a campaign approach of short, high-intensity programs that focus on single issues (for example, injection misuse) or longer-term, sustained efforts integrated with other primary health care and educational activities (such as a literacy reader on medicine use, lesson outlines for the primary or secondary school curriculum, or routine health center education sessions).

The communication strategy may use a persuasive or social marketing approach to influence the target

---

Country Study 33-3
Using social marketing to promote the rational use of medicines and health commodities

Social marketing takes the concepts of commercial marketing and applies them to social issues. In a social marketing campaign, the needed product is made widely available and affordable to the target populations, and product availability is accompanied by a campaign to create demand by raising awareness of the product, often by using brand identification, and by promoting the use of the product to encourage some healthy behavior. Social marketing approaches use research to gain an understanding of the target audience and base marketing strategies on the population's perceptions, wants, and needs.

Social marketing is commonly used to promote the use of condoms and other reproductive health commodities, oral rehydration solution, nutritional supplements for children, water purification, insecticide-treated bed nets (ITNs), and voluntary counseling and testing services for HIV/AIDS.

PSI has long been involved with social marketing programs that promote ITNs in malaria-endemic areas, and since 2003, the organization has introduced social marketing of prepackaged treatment for malaria in Cambodia, Madagascar, Nigeria, and Myanmar. Because people most often treat malaria at home with products purchased in the private sector, where the quality of medicine is not assured and the level of knowledge and training in the vendor is low or nonexistent, focusing on these outlets to improve people's access to and proper use of antimalarials is important, especially in rural settings.

A special challenge with antimalarials comes with the shift to artemisinin-based combination therapy (ACT) as the recommended first-line treatment. PSI's social marketing campaign is designed to disseminate information on the new treatment regimen and emphasize the importance of adherence. Its PSI prepackaged medicines use blister packs that include country-specific, easy-to-follow instructions that are appropriate for people with low literacy. Packaging distinguishes between different age groups and the packs are color coded to facilitate adherence. In addition, retail outlets receive the products at a highly subsidized price, which is especially important in making the expensive ACTs affordable. Product branding focuses on the target population; for example, the children's product in Nigeria is called KidCare®, and the promotional materials include the tag line "Correct Malaria Medicine for Your Child." Initiatives are now ongoing to provide subsidized ACTs through private- and public-sector outlets in the additional countries of Democratic Republic of Congo, Kenya, Rwanda, Sudan, and Tanzania.

Sources: PSI 2005, n.d.

Box 33-5
Questions to ask when you get a new prescription medicine

- What is the name of the medicine, and what is it supposed to do?
- Is this the brand or generic name? (Is a generic version available?)
- When do I take the medicine—and for how long?
- Should I take this medicine on an empty stomach or with food?
- What should I do if I forget a dose?
- What foods, drinks, medicines, dietary supplements, or activities should I avoid while taking this medicine?
- What precautions should be taken?

  - By children
  - During pregnancy
  - When breast-feeding
  - While driving or operating machinery
  - If taking other medicines

- What are the possible side effects, and what do I do if they occur?
- When should I expect the medicine to begin to work, and how will I know if it is working?
- Will this new prescription work safely with the other prescription and nonprescription medicines I am taking?
- How should I store this medicine at home?

Source: National Council on Patient Information and Education, "Talk about Prescriptions" Planning Kit for October 2005. <http://www.talkaboutrx.org/questions_new_prescrip2005.jsp>

---

audience. Social marketing, often criticized as a top-down approach, can be an effective communication strategy, particularly in specifically targeted campaigns that take into account community needs, perceptions, and values (see Country Study 33-3). Alternatively, giving people the information and the problem-solving skills necessary to make their own decisions is ideal in the long run but much more difficult to implement and evaluate. With disadvantaged groups, it can also involve consciousness-raising and promoting awareness that they are empowered to make decisions and control their own lives. For example, consumers can be encouraged to act with authority and ask questions of the health care provider (see Box 33-5).

Communication channels to deliver messages: Ideally, a communication program should combine different channels, including interpersonal channels, to maximize exchange. Each channel has its own strength: what matters is that it be cost-effective and appropriate to the audience and the message. Possibilities include—

- Printed materials—posters, leaflets, textbooks, comics
- Mass media and electronic media—radio, television, newspapers, CD-ROMs, DVDs, the Internet, mobile technology, short-message service (SMS)
- Folk media—community theater, puppets, singing groups, and other such media (important traditional channels in many countries)
- Interpersonal (or face-to-face) encounters—health workers, schoolteachers, community leaders, shopkeepers, community organizations

Country Study 33-4 discusses a neighbor-to-neighbor communication strategy to improve the use of antimalarials in a district in Kenya.

Collaborating institutions: Collaborating with a wide range of institutions—NGOs; consumer organizations; religious, women's, youth, or social solidarity organizations; schools; development agencies such as WHO and the United Nations Children's Fund (UNICEF); and professional associations—enhances visibility, potentially increases impact, and can be used to promote rational use concepts and the national pharmaceutical policy. Religious groups provide a substantial proportion of health care and are potential partners in many countries. Country Study 33-5 illustrates a public education campaign launched through a collaboration of several French consumer and professional organizations.

Monitoring and evaluation (see Step 7 below): Milestones (for example, number of manuals produced or number of workshops completed) can help chart progress toward the objectives of the communication plan.

Timetable, budget, and source of financing: For each activity, the plan should define when it is to occur, who is responsible for it, and the funding source. A common method of displaying such information is a Gantt chart (see Chapter 38).

Step 5: Pretest intervention. Although frequently overlooked, pretesting materials is essential and saves time and money. Pretesting also often produces surprising results; for example, a patient may completely misunderstand a picture, particularly if it uses a stylized design in a society that is relatively inexperienced in interpreting graphic images.

Pretesting can help answer the following questions—

Country Study 33-4
Neighbor-to-neighbor education on antimalarials in Kenya

The Bungoma District Health Management Team in Kenya implemented a "neighbor-to-neighbor" (*jirani kwa jirani*) education program focused on caretaker purchase and consumption of antimalarial medicines. Forty government health workers received a one-day orientation on the approach and copies of two illustrated brochures explaining proper malaria treatment and recommended medicines, which they distributed in 112 villages. The health workers also organized thirty contests where village residents presented songs, dramas, or poems they had created to promote the use of effective antimalarial medicines.

About six weeks after launch, the neighbor-to-neighbor intervention had reached 53 percent of households in the intervention area through a brochure, song contest, or both. In addition, respondents in the intervention area, especially those with low education levels, were more likely than those in the comparison area to know the appropriate government-recommended antimalarial medicines and to report intention to use them, and people living in the intervention area were also twice as likely to have bought and taken the correct dose of the first-line antimalarial medicine, sulfadoxine-pyrimethamine.

Source: Tavrow and Rennie 2004.

- Does the target audience understand the materials?
- Do they feel that the materials apply to them?
- Do they find the materials attractive?
- Is anything offensive or culturally inappropriate?
- Is the message convincing? If not, why not?
- Do changes need to be made in the message or its format?

The WHO guide to improving consumers' medicine use (Chetley et al. 2007) points out that pretesting is also a way to open dialogue with the target audience on key issues, confirm research about the medicine use problem, and gather opinions on the planned intervention.

Step 6: Implement intervention. Unless other interventions have already been implemented and evaluated, the intervention usually serves as a pilot study, which makes evaluating the success of the intervention important, as well as gathering information on how it worked, so changes can be made later (Chetley et al. 2007).

Before beginning, ensure that all materials and people are ready, channels of distribution are organized, and everyone involved is fully informed about program goals and strategies. In addition, the monitoring and evaluation plan should be in place. Delays in program implementation will have implications for future planned activities.

Step 7: Monitor and evaluate intervention. Monitoring relates to how well the activities are being implemented as the intervention progresses, and evaluation assesses how well the objectives are being achieved (see Chapter 48). Monitoring and evaluation processes need to be planned at the beginning of a project, not addressed at the end of the intervention.

Once the program starts, a clear system of monitoring should be used to assess whether—

- Training has been sufficient and effective

- Target audiences are receiving program materials and messages
- Target audiences are using the materials and understanding the messages (in the case of radio programs, such an assessment might include a program log with transmission times, and tapes and listener interviews to determine whether the messages were understood)
- The program is on schedule (if not, why not?)

Monitoring produces feedback on how well the communication is working. It allows assessment and definition of what changes can or should be made as the intervention progresses. In face-to-face communication, for example, good communicators automatically monitor whether they are having the desired effect and then vary their style and content accordingly if necessary (Chetley et al. 2007).

Evaluating communication interventions is more challenging. An evaluation to determine whether the activities met program objectives should distinguish between attitude change, knowledge acquisition, and behavior change. One may occur without the other, but most educational interventions target more than one.

All study designs must measure change using key outcome measures that relate to the communication objectives (Chetley et al. 2007). One should—

- Review the intervention's communication objectives
- Identify in advance what behaviors are likely to be influenced because of the intervention and what changes in knowledge and attitudes are expected
- Limit the number of outcome measures: do not measure all possible changes
- Measure more than one dimension: decide whether the design will measure changes in attitudes, changes

in knowledge, or changes in medicine-use behavior, or any combination of these dimensions
- Choose outcome measures that can be clearly defined and reliably measured

Pre- and postintervention quantitative research are needed to measure effect on behavior. Defining some clear quantitative indicators, such as the percentage of respondents who self-treat a specific condition correctly or who never reuse disposable syringes, is also useful. Measures that can determine impact include—

- Exposure to project messages and materials
- Proportion of knowledge change
- Change in consumer satisfaction
- Change in medicine sales patterns
- Proportion of reported behavior change

- Use or adaptation of the program by other groups as a model in developing their own projects

When possible, compare results with those from a control group not exposed to the intervention.

Reassessment of procedures requires feedback on the following questions—

- What problems occurred in developing and implementing the program?
- Was the intervention acceptable to stakeholders?
- What factors outside the project (for example, change of legislation, increase or decrease in available medicines, support from the ministry of health) may have contributed to its success or lack of success?
- What factors within the project may have contributed to its success or lack of success?

Country Study 33-5
The INN—A medicine's true name: Promoting the use of International Nonproprietary Names

Concerned about the effect of what they viewed as advertising of prescription medicines disguised as "information" in Europe, several French organizations—Association Mieux Prescrire, Fédération Nationale de la Mutualité Française, and Union Fédérale des Consommateurs Que Choisir—collaborated on a public education campaign to encourage patients to recognize the International Nonproprietary Names (INNs) of medicines and use them in their dealings with health care professionals. The INN system allows health care professionals and patients to identify a medicine by its active ingredient and avoid potentially serious adverse effects caused by overdose when different brand names of the same generic medicine do not convey the product's active ingredient.

Launched by the Medicines in Europe Forum in France in 2005, the campaign targets consumers, patients, and health care professionals. The campaign has created a series of leaflets that it encourages pharmacies, surgeries, clinics, and hospitals to display. The information sheets were reprinted in each issue of *La revue Prescrire* and multiple press releases were sent to the media.

The text of two of the eleven leaflets follows.

The INN on drug packaging: practical and safe!

Anthony hands his prescription to the pharmacist.

"My doctor uses the INN—the international nonproprietary name—on prescriptions," says Anthony. "Could you give me a product where I can clearly see the INN on the box?"

"There you are. On this product the INN is clearly visible on the box, and it is also printed on each blister—the small plastic wells holding the tablets, under the aluminum film...That way, if you leave home with only part of the blister pack, you'll still know what drug it contains."

Anthony is happy: with the INN clearly visible at all times, he is sure of taking the right medicine at the right time.

Placing the INN on drug packaging reduces the risk of error.

Ask your doctor and pharmacist to explain the INN system.

A holiday trip ends in hospital

Marcelle and René are on a package tour to Thailand. But they have forgotten to bring their medicines with them, including their "blood pressure" drugs. It's not a problem for Marcelle. She knows the international nonproprietary name (INN) of the beta-blocker she has to take every day: metoprolol. The doctor in Bangkok has no trouble prescribing the right treatment for her. René remembers only the trade name of his medication, Avlocardyl®, and the Bangkok doctor has never heard of it. The same drug is marketed in Thailand, but under a dozen different trade names, none of which resembles Avlocardyl. The doctor prescribes another antihypertensive drug, but René reacts badly to it and has to be hospitalized. If only he'd known the INN...

The INN: one drug, one name, everywhere in the world

Source: *La revue Prescrire* 2007.

Box 33-6
Key components of a communication plan

- Communication objectives (awareness; increased knowledge; behaviors to be influenced, adopted, or changed); keep in mind that these may be phased or cumulative and may each involve different channels of communication.
- Intended audience(s) (include extent to which you will involve audience in program planning).
- Likely constraints (for each audience).
- Likely facilitating factors (for each audience).
- Approaches to change: power/sanctions, logic/facts, appeal/emotion, incentive/reward, facilitate/remove obstacles, fear or danger/emotion or combinations of these.
- Communication channels: a communications program should use a combination of channels, known as media mix, to maximize exchange; possibilities include visual aids: posters, flyers, pamphlets, brochures, video; mass media: radio, television, newspapers; folk media; mobile technology and SMS; interpersonal or face-to-face.
- Method for pretesting of materials or intervention.
- Collaborating institutions: collaborating with a wide range of institutions in communication activities enhances visibility, potentially increases impact, and acts as general advocacy for rational-use concepts and the national pharmaceutical policy.
- Monitoring and evaluation: this should include reporting and publications.
- Timeline (plan of activities).
- Budget, with identification of secure source of funding or potential funders to be approached.

Source: Chetley et al. 2007.

- What improvements could be made?
- What are the most important lessons for the future?

Fully documented communication activities are easier to monitor and evaluate, and help future program planners learn from the experience. Even when communication activities are carried out on a large scale, obtaining reports on them is often very difficult, particularly in developing countries. This difficulty leads to unnecessary duplication, loss of experience gained, and waste of resources. For example, a WHO study of twenty-eight developing and thirteen developed countries showed that public education interventions on rational medicine use were poorly documented (Fresle and Wolfheim 1997). In addition, most of the planning of the interventions was unstructured, with poorly defined objectives and broadly defined target groups, such as "general public." Also, the interventions generally suffered from a lack of consistent funding and little government or donor commitment, making it difficult for them to gain momentum and show success.

In summary, the preceding steps can be used for small educational interventions or large national programs. No single approach is the solution to all health communication problems; selecting from a tool kit of possibilities, based on an analysis of the situational context and the most appropriate approach to apply, is increasingly recognized as the best way to develop effective communication interventions (Chetley et al. 2007). Box 33-6 lists the key components of a communication plan.

Even if resources are sufficient only for a small-scale educational intervention, knowing why people act as they do is still important: no human behavior takes place in a vacuum; it is always "rational" within a given personal framework. Many beliefs about health care do not match a biomedical model, and recognition of both strengths and weaknesses of local traditions is needed. The credible channels of communication in a community should always be used to provide information. Materials must be pretested, because the perception of professionals will not be the same as those of a layperson whose formal education may be limited or nonexistent. Above all—and particularly when resources are limited—it is necessary to prioritize interventions in terms of the risk the problems pose to public health and then focus on the major problem behavior and target the main risk groups.

Country Study 33-6 illustrates innovative public education campaigns that focus on rational medicine use in three countries.

33.6   Facilitating and constraining factors in public communication

Many factors, which vary according to a country's level of development and health care infrastructure, affect public communication activities both positively and negatively. Factors that can facilitate public communication include the political will to increase medicine education and information, an understanding of people's health-seeking behavior, and expanded coverage by mass media. On the other hand, public education can be constrained by a lack of coherent policies on both medicine use and public education; commercial interests; professional interests; weak infrastructure; lack of resources; and economic, social, and cultural influences.

Facilitating factors

Facilitating factors stimulate, provide, or promote a fertile environment for public education. Identifying these factors can improve public communication campaigns.

Increased awareness of the need for public education on medicines. The democratic process, the growth of orga-nized consumer and public interest groups, especially in developing countries, access to information through the Internet, and the movement for individuals to take more responsibility for their own health care stimulate public interest in and demand for medicine and health information. Awareness of the level of patient nonadherence to treatment regimens has also grown along with the increasing emphasis on chronic conditions, including AIDS, in developing countries.

Increased networking allows government health services, NGOs, and community-based groups to share their public

---

Country Study 33-6
Innovative public education campaigns to improve medicine use

Ghana

The Pharmaceutical Society of Ghana introduced a television serial broadcast nationwide called "Let's Talk about Drugs," which focused on different medicine-use issues. Instead of a doctor or pharmacist answering questions or giving a presentation, the show dramatized issues brought up at the pharmacy and interspersed those dramatizations with local facts. Episodes focused on issues such as patient rights, irrational use of antibiotics, and generic medicines. A panel of pharmacists responded to questions called in by viewers—and the response was overwhelming. The pharmaceutical society had requests to translate the program into different local languages and to adapt it for radio broadcast.

Indonesia

A survey in Indonesia indicated that mothers who bought medicines for use at home were not knowledge-able enough to ensure safe and effective use. Generally, mothers knew only the brand-name products marketed for particular symptoms, and as a result, household medicine consumption patterns showed that multiple brand names with the same active ingredient were being used concurrently, which wasted money. In addition, the population knew little about contraindications or side effects from the medicines they had in their homes. The Department of Clinical Pharmacology at Gadjah Mada University designed an educational strategy called Cara Balajar Ibu Aktif (CBIA) (Mothers' Active Learning Method). The CBIA model used interactive discussions with small groups of six to eight people held in the context of regular meetings of women's grassroots organizations or other gatherings. Although mothers were the target population, teenagers and fathers also participated. Participants brought in all the medicines they had at home and worked with a tutor with a set of thirty to forty medicines to learn important facts about the active ingredients, the differences between products for adults and children, and how to interpret the package information. For example, the participants learned that brand names in different forms, such as syrups or tablets, have the same active ingredient, but syrups often cost ten times more. Also, brand names with "forte" or "plus" on the package are often more expensive, but the amount of active ingredient may be only slightly higher. In field tests, participants with CBIA experience were significantly more knowledgeable, and the number of brand-name medicines used in their households dropped dramatically. After journalists attended some of the sessions, stories about CBIA appeared in national newspapers and a popular women's magazine.

Nepal

A survey showed that mothers in Nepal were giving either inappropriate or inadequate antimicrobial home-based treatment to children for acute respiratory infection, as well as giving children antimicrobials to treat common colds; retail drug sellers had the same level of knowledge about appropriate medicine use as the mothers. A community-based education campaign used a child-to-child education program administered by teachers, using street theater performances in front of mothers' groups, followed by interactive group discussions with the mothers run by community health volunteers. In addition, community leaders and drug retailers were trained by paramedics on appropriate medicine use for acute respiratory infection. The main messages of the community education campaign were that young children with signs of severe infection must be taken to a health facility immediately and that medicines should be taken only on the advice of a health worker.

Sources: Boateng, Amporful, and Appiah 2005, Suryawati 2005, Karkee et al. 2004.

education experiences, so groups can learn from the experience of others.

As a response to both regulatory requirements and consumer pressures, some pharmaceutical companies are moving toward providing improved and user-friendly written patient information. In addition, some professional bodies (notably pharmacists) in Europe, the United States, and Australia have developed training programs for their members to promote communication skills and interaction with consumers. Many universities have also added such courses to their medical and pharmacy curricula.

Knowledge of social and behavioral theory. Research in the last decade has greatly expanded the knowledge base underlying health- and medicine-seeking behavior, particularly its cultural dimensions. Anthropologists have studied how medicine consumption is culturally mediated (van der Geest, Hardon, and Whyte 1990).

Expanded coverage by mass media and information technology. Communication technology has created powerful mechanisms to convey educational messages. Many people have access to radio and television, which open up new opportunities to reach large audiences, including nonliterate populations, with health-related messages. SMS and mobile technology have further expanded coverage. With new information technology such as the Internet, some health professionals and patients have greater access to information from online databases, websites, and e-mail (see Chapter 50). These resources have many potential benefits, including rapid access to objective information and low-cost sharing, pooling, and comparative evaluation of different communication methodologies.

Constraining factors

Implementers of public communication strategies need to recognize and evaluate inhibiting factors, because solutions vary according to the particular situation of each country. The successes and failures of others can help in developing a framework for effective action (see References and Further Readings).

Lack of coherent policies for both medicine use and public education. Many countries need to strengthen their national policies on medicine use and to incorporate public education in them. Without a clear policy, public communication cannot take place in a cohesive manner and receive adequate support. A fragmented approach can confuse the public with conflicting and competing messages.

The weak state of public education on medicines in many countries is partly the result of a lack of political commitment to public education in general. Within health services, public education is often a low priority and is consequently poorly financed and staffed. Sometimes NGOs fill this void; however, they usually depend on donor agencies for funding that can be withdrawn or reallocated. In some instances,

public education on medicines is a sensitive issue, because it may lead to community challenges of commercial and other vested interests. To improve the situation, a multisectoral approach involving key stakeholders both inside and outside the health sector is crucial.

Commercial interests. Commercial interests do not always match public interest. Particularly in developing countries, where control of pharmaceutical promotion may be nonexistent, weak, or unenforceable, industry may contribute to inappropriate medicine use by conducting promotional activities based on inaccurate information.

In retail drug outlets, where many people seek health care and buy pharmaceuticals for self-medication, the shop owner may or may not have any health care training or experience, and the counter attendants are typically untrained. Because the objective of these businesses is to make a profit, the drug sellers generally sell the medications that the customer requests, without providing any information. However, increased recognition that informal drug sellers play an important role in the public's rational use of medicines has led to the decision that they should also be a target of education campaigns. Chapter 32 covers drug seller initiatives to improve dispensing services.

Professional interests. Resistance to change within professional groups can constrain public education. Prescribers tend to hold influential and powerful positions, and they may not perceive the need for, or the importance of, public education. In turn, they often do not fulfill their professional role of providing advice on the appropriate use of medicines on either a personal or an organizational basis.

Public education can appear to conflict with existing values and power relationships, for example, by leading the public to challenge the traditional prescriber-patient relationship. Professional groups may oppose public education if they perceive it as a threat rather than a challenging opportunity arising from a new relationship with the community.

Weak infrastructure. Lack of infrastructure within the health system for implementation of pharmaceutical policies, including access to medicines and public education, can be a major constraint. Any effort to educate the public on appropriate medicine use can be undermined if necessary medicines are inconsistently available in the public or private sectors. Consumers then face the dilemma of reconciling public educational messages that motivate appropriate behavior with the reality of product availability in the public sector and the private-sector marketplace.

Lack of resources. Effective public education requires sufficient funding and the allocation of trained staff to enable targeting of population groups through appropriate strategies. Public education on medicines requires an extensive program to train health workers and other field staff in communication skills and appropriate medicine use.

Social, economic, and cultural factors. Lack of involvement and participation of the target groups often leads to problems. Support for public education programs may be withdrawn prematurely because of a failure to recognize that bringing about behavioral change is a slow and long-term process.

33.7 Understanding the importance of communication about appropriate medicine use

A need exists for consumer education in appropriate medicine use. Such programs—whether run by government, development organizations, NGOs, community groups, or professional bodies—merit support and encouragement. Public education should form an integral part of both national pharmaceutical policy and prescriber training. Policy makers, professional bodies, prescribers, dispensers, and educators have important advocacy and technical roles.

The reasons people decide to change (or not to change) their behaviors are almost always emotional; therefore, merely informing or educating about the change is necessary although not sufficient to prompt behavior change.

According to WHO (Chetley et al. 2007), research has shown the following—

- Combining strategies—such as education and communication with regulation—produces better results (see Chapter 29).
- Combining communication methods—face-to-face communication with mass media—produces better results.
- Using any single communication approach—print or radio or face-to-face communication—is rarely effective.
- Researching, planning, pretesting, and monitoring and evaluation are required.
- Involving the target audience is essential and leads to more practical and effective interventions.
- One-off communication interventions are not very effective, and their effect is not sustainable.

In addition, a coalition of resources improves the chance of the intervention's success and expands its capacity and reach. Smaller-scale programs can provide valuable experiences, and they may later serve as development models for more comprehensive strategies. Finally, and perhaps most critically, health care practitioners must be convinced of their core educational role. They must learn how to perform that role effectively and work to alter the all-too-common perception of patients as passive recipients of treatment.

Whether planning a campaign for promoting generic use of medicines (Chapter 29) or a national pharmaceutical policy (Chapter 4), or when starting a health insurance plan (Chapter 12), standard communication elements should be considered. These may involve a good logo, radio spots, a flyer or visual aid, a poster, and possibly folk media (Figure 33-4). Although every campaign does not need all of these elements, using several of these components helps vary the message's delivery. The communications elements described in Figure 33-4 can be used in such campaigns. ∎

References and further readings

General

Blomberg, B., S. Spinaci, B. Fourie, and R. Laing. 2001. The Rationale for Recommending Fixed-Dose Combination Tablets for Treatment of Tuberculosis. *Bulletin of the World Health Organization* 79(1):61–8. <http://www.who.int/bulletin/archives/79(1)61.pdf>

Boateng, F., E. Amporful, and B. Appiah. 2005. "Let's Talk about Drugs"—the Pharmaceutical Society of Ghana Takes to the Screen. *Essential Drugs Monitor* 34:13.

Brieger, W. R. 2003. *The Role of Patent Medicine Vendors in the Management of Sick Children in the African Region.* Arlington, Va.: BASICS II.

Cebotarenco, N., and P. J. Bush. 2008. Reducing Antibiotics for Colds and Flu: A Student-Taught Program. *Health Education Research* 23(1):146–57.

Chalker, J. C., T. Andualem, L. N. Gitau, J. Ntaganira, C. Obua, H. Tadeg, P. Waako, D. Ross-Degnan, and INRUD-IAA. 2010. Measuring Adherence to Antiretroviral Treatment in Resource-Poor Settings: The Feasibility of Collecting Routine Data for Key Indicators. *BMC Health Services Research* 10:43. <http://www.biomedcentral.com/1472-6963/10/43>

Chalker, J., T. Andualem, O. Minzi, J. Ntaganira, A. Ojoo, P. Waako, and D. Ross-Degnan. 2008. Monitoring Adherence and Defaulting for Antiretroviral Therapy in Five East African Countries: An Urgent Need for Standards. *Journal of the International Association of Physicians in AIDS Care* 7(4):193–9.

Connor, J., N. Rafter, and A. Rodgers. 2004. Do Fixed-Dose Combination Pills or Unit-of-Use Packaging Improve Adherence? *Bulletin of the World Health Organization* 82(12):935–9.

Dowse, R., and M. Ehlers. 2004. Pictograms for Conveying Medicine Instructions: Comprehension in Various South African Language Groups. *South African Journal of Science* 100:687–93.

Gill, C. J., D. H. Hamer, J. L. Simon, D. M. Thea, and L. L. Sabin. 2005. No Room for Complacency about Adherence to Antiretroviral Therapy in Sub-Saharan Africa. *AIDS* 19(12):1243–9.

Green, D. 2003. South Africa: A Novel Approach to Improving Adherence to TB Treatment. *Essential Drugs Monitor* 33:8.

Gusdal, A. K., C. Obua, T. Andualem, R. Wahlström, J. Chalker, and G. Fochsen on behalf of the INRUD-IAA project. 2011. Peer Counselors' Role in Supporting Patients' Adherence to ART in Ethiopia and Uganda. *AIDS Care* 23(6):657–62.

Gusdal, A. K., C. Obua, T. Andualem, R. Wahlström, G. Tomson, S. Peterson, A. M. Ekström, A. Thorson, J. Chalker, and G. Fochsen on behalf of the INRUD-IAA project. 2009. Voices on Adherence to ART in Ethiopia and Uganda: A Matter of Choice or Simply Not an Option? *AIDS Care* 21(11):1381–7.

Hardon, A., S. Davey, T. Gerrits, C. Hodgkin, H. Irunde, J. Kgatlwane, J. Kinsman, A. Nakiyemba, and R. Laing. 2006. *From Access to Adherence: The Challenges of Antiretroviral Treatment.* Geneva: World

Figure 33-4   Hints for selecting communication methods for public communication campaigns

A Good Logo

- is simple, not cluttered
- is immediately understandable and explicit, not abstract
- is related to the key program benefits and is a symbol of key data
- is easily reproducible
- works in different sizes and settings
- dramatizes the overall tone of the change approach
- is positive and uplifting

An Effective Radio Spot

- presents one idea
- begins with an attention getter
- is direct and explicit
- repeats the key idea at least two or three times
- asks listeners to take action
- makes the audience feel part of the situation
- maintains the same tone as the overall approach

A Useful Flyer or Visual Aid

- carries the information most likely to be forgotten
- uses visuals, not only words, to tell the story
- shows people doing key behaviors
- uses attractive images
- is concise
- maintains same tone as overall change approach
- is organized so that it favors a logical action sequence
- is designed for easy use as a visual aid
- matches graphic and language skills of a specific audience

An Effective Public Poster

- dramatizes a single idea
- attracts attention from at least 10 meters away
- uses visuals to carry the message
- is memorable
- models the behavior whenever possible
- shows the product's benefit to the audience
- is consistent with the tone of the overall change approach

Folk Media

- use local drama groups and musicians, who are often powerful vehicles for sharing health-related messages
- include traveling health fairs with puppet shows, musical acts, distribution of printed materials, and appearances by local celebrities
- stimulate interest in national and local programs, for example, through fairs that travel from village to village

Source: Adapted from Rasmuson et al. 1988.

ASSESSMENT GUIDE

- What are the problems related to current medicine prescribing, dispensing, and use, and what are the critical factors underlying these problems?
- What medicine prescribing, dispensing, and use practices are priorities for an intervention?
- What solutions are feasible to address the medicine prescribing, dispensing, and use problems that stakeholders support?
- Do public communication campaigns on medicine use already exist?
- What is the purpose of the campaign? What is it trying to achieve?
- Is medicine education included in the primary and secondary school curricula?
- What media are being used (for example, print, face-to-face, radio, theater)?

- What materials exist for public communication activities? How were these materials pretested? What evaluations of public education campaigns have occurred?
- Who is the audience for the campaign or the materials? What does this group know about the targeted medicine-use problem?
- What percentage of the public health or pharmaceutical budget is allocated to public communication on rational medicine use?
- What amount is spent on public communication campaigns on medicine use, and what percentage does this represent of the total amount spent on public health education campaigns?

Health Organization. <http://whqlibdoc.who.int/publications/2006/9241563281_eng.pdf>

Holloway, K., and L. van Dijk. 2011. *The World Medicines Situation 2011: Rational Use of Medicines*. 3rd ed. Geneva: WHO. <http://www.who.int/medicines/areas/policy/world_medicines_situation/WMS_ch14_wRational.pdf>

Joshi, M. 2010. *Reforming Pre-Service Curriculum as a Sustainable Low-Cost Intervention to Address Antimicrobial Resistance*. Paper presented at the American Public Health Association Annual Meeting, Denver, Colorado, November 6–10.

Karkee, S. B., A. L. Tamang, Y. B. Gurung, K. A. Holloway, K. K. Kafle, C. Rai, and R. Pradhan. 2004. *Community Intervention to Promote Rational Treatment of Acute Respiratory Infection in Rural Nepal*. Paper presented at the Second International Conference on Improving the Use of Medicines, Chiang Mai, Thailand, March 30–April 2.

Osterberg, L., and T. Blaschke. 2005. Adherence to Medication. *New England Journal of Medicine* 353(5):487–97.

PSI (Population Services International). No date. "About PSI Malaria Control." Washington, D.C. <http://www.psi.org/our-work/healthy-lives/malaria/about>

Rasmuson, M. R., R. E. Seidel, W. A. Smith, and E. M. Booth. 1988. *Communication for Child Survival*. Washington, D.C.: Academy for Educational Development for the U.S. Agency for International Development.

La revue Prescrire. 2007. "The INN—a Drug's True Name." <http://www.prescrire.org/cahiers/dossierDciAccueilEn.php>

Ross-Degnan, D., M. Pierre-Jacques, F. Zhang, H. Tadeg, L. Gitau, J. Ntaganira, R. Balikuddembe, J. Chalker, A. K. Wagner, and INRUD-IAA. 2010. Measuring Adherence to Antiretroviral Treatment in Resource-Poor Settings: The Clinical Validity of Key Indicators. 2010. *BMC Health Services Research* 10:42. <http://www.biomedcentral.com/1472-6963/10/42>

RPM Plus Program (Rational Pharmaceutical Management Plus Program). 2005. *Summary of Key I&E Experiences and Evidence*. Arlington, Va.: Management Sciences for Health/RPM Plus. <http://www.msh.org/projects/rpmplus/Documents/upload/TB_IE_Experiences_Evidence.pdf>

———. 2004. *Mombasa Antiretroviral Therapy Program: Report on the Six-Month Program Review of the Pharmaceutical Management System and Laboratory Services Conducted in November 2003*. Arlington, Va.: Management Sciences for Health/RPM Plus.

Shrank, W., J. Avorn, C. Rolon, and P. Shekelle. 2007. Effect of Content and Format of Prescription Drug Labels on Readability, Understanding, and Medication Use: A Systematic Review. *Annals of Pharmacotherapy* 41:783–801.

Suryawati, S. 2005. CBIA: Improving the Quality of Self-Medication through Mothers' Active Learning. *Essential Drugs Monitor* 32:22–3.

Tavrow, P., and W. Rennie. 2004. *Neighbor-to-Neighbor Education to Improve Malaria Treatment in Households in Bungoma District, Kenya: Operations Research Results*. Bethesda, Md.: Published for the U.S. Agency for International Development by the Quality Assurance Project. <http://pdf.usaid.gov/pdf_docs/PNADA546.pdf>

Van der Geest, S., A. Hardon, and S. R. Whyte. 1990. Planning for Essential Drugs: Are We Missing the Cultural Dimension? *Health Policy and Planning* 5:182–5.

WHO (World Health Organization). 2011a. *Global Status Report on Noncommunicable Diseases 2010: Description of the Global Burden of NCDs, Their Risk Factors and Determinants*. Geneva: WHO. <http://www.who.int/nmh/publications/ncd_report2010/en/>

———. 2011b. *Global Tuberculosis Control: WHO Report 2011*. Geneva: WHO. <http://www.who.int/tb/publications/global_report/2011/gtbr11_full.pdf>

———. 2004a. *Guidelines on Developing Consumer Information on Proper Use of Traditional, Complementary and Alternative Medicine*. Geneva: WHO. <http://apps.who.int/medicinedocs/pdf/s5525e/s5525e.pdf>

———. 2004b. *Rational Use of Medicines by Prescribers and Patients: Report by the Secretariat*. Geneva: WHO.

———. 2003. *Adherence to Long-Term Therapies: Evidence for Action*. Geneva: WHO. <http://apps.who.int/medicinedocs/en/d/Js4883e/7.2.html>

WHO/TDR (World Health Organization/Special Programme for Research and Training in Tropical Diseases). 1998. Advantages of Pre-Packaged Antimalarials. *Essential Drugs Monitor* 25–26:20.

Yeboah-Antwi, K., J. O. Gyapong, I. K. Asare, G. Barnish, D. B. Evans, and S. Adjei. 2001. Impact of Prepackaging Antimalarial Drugs on Cost to Patients and Compliance with Treatment. *Bulletin of the World Health Organization* 79(5):394–9.

Resources for planning public education programs

Most of the materials listed below are available free of charge to people in developing countries.

Chetley A., A. Hardon, C. Hodgkin, A. Haaland, and D. Fresle. 2007. *How to Improve the Use of Medicines by Consumers.* Geneva: WHO. <http://whqlibdoc.who.int/hq/2007/WHO_PSM_PAR_2007.2_eng.pdf>

Clift, E. 2001. *Information, Education and Communication: Lessons from the Past, Perspectives for the Future.* Geneva: WHO. <http://whqlibdoc.who.int/hq/2001/WHO_RHR_01.22.pdf>

EuroPharmForum. 2005. *Questions to Ask about Your Medicines (QaM): Campaign Proposal—March 1993 Including Guidelines—August 2004.* Copenhagen: World Health Organization Regional Office for Europe. <https://files.pbworks.com/download/KPFrDhaYAF/europharm/19341796/qam.pdf>

Fresle, D., and C. Wolfheim. 1997. *Public Education in Rational Drug Use: A Global Survey.* Geneva: World Health Organization/Action Programme on Essential Drugs. <http://whqlibdoc.who.int/hq/1997/WHO_DAP_97.5.pdf>

Hardon, A., C. Hodgkin, and D. Fresle. 2004. *How to Investigate the Use of Medicines by Consumers.* Geneva: WHO and University of Amsterdam. <http://apps.who.int/medicinedocs/pdf/s6169e/s6169e.pdf>

Hubley, J. 2004. *Communicating Health: An Action Guide to Health Education and Health Promotion.* 2nd ed. Oxford, U.K.: Macmillan. Available from Teaching-aids at Low Cost <http://www.talcuk.org> Explores the role of communication in improving people's health and discusses strategies for health education, health promotion, and empowerment of families and communities. Good chapter on pharmaceuticals.

Media/Materials Clearinghouse. <http://www.m-mc.org>
The clearinghouse has international health communication materials: pamphlets, posters, audiotapes, videos, training materials, job aids, electronic media, and other media and materials designed to promote public health.
- The Health Communication Materials Database offers access to a worldwide collection of health communication materials.
- The Health Communication Materials Network provides a forum for health communication specialists to share ideas, information, and samples of health communication materials with their colleagues, and to seek advice and suggestions from others working in this field.

National Cancer Institute at the National Institutes of Health. 2008. *Making Health Communication Programs Work.* <http://www.cancer.gov/cancertopics/cancerlibrary/pinkbook> A developed-country perspective, but still useful from a structured planning viewpoint.

O'Sullivan, G. A., J. A. Yonkler, W. Morgan, and A. P. Merritt. 2003. *A Field Guide to Designing a Health Communication Strategy.* Baltimore, Md.: Johns Hopkins Bloomberg School of Public Health/Center for Communication Programs. <http://www.jhuccp.org/sites/all/files/A%20Field%20Guide%20to%20Designing%20Health%20Comm%20Strategy.pdf>

Potter, L., and C. Martin. 2005. Tools to Evaluate Patient Education Materials. Health Literacy Fact Sheet. Hamilton, N.J.: Center for Health Care Strategies. <http://www.chcs.org/publications3960/publications_show.htm?doc_id=291711>

PSI (Population Services International). 2005. *Improving Home Based Management of Malaria Using the Private Sector.* Nairobi: PSI Malaria Control.

UNAIDS (Joint United Nations Programme on HIV/AIDS) and PSI. 2000. Social Marketing: Expanding Access to Essential Products and Services to Prevent HIV/AIDS and to Limit the Impact of the Epidemic. Brochure. <http://www.unaids.org/en/media/unaids/contentassets/dataimport/publications/irc-pub04/social_marketing_en.pdf>

WHO/CDD (World Health Organization/Diarrhoeal Diseases Control Programme). 1987. *Communication: A Guide for Managers of National Diarrhoeal Disease Control Programmes.* Geneva: WHO/CDD. <http://whqlibdoc.who.int/hq/1987/15475_%28part1%29.pdf> A good manual that is also valid for planning communication programs on controlling noncommunicable diseases.

WHO/DAP (World Health Organization/Action Programme on Essential Drugs). 1994. *Public Education in Rational Drug Use: Report of an Informal Consultation.* Geneva: WHO/DAP. <http://whqlibdoc.who.int/hq/1994/WHO_DAP_94.1.pdf> Outlines the rationale and principles of public education in drug use and identifies strategies for the development of DAP's activities in this area.

World Health Organization and Harvard Medical School and Harvard Pilgrim Health. 2009. *Medicines Use in Primary Care in Developing and Transitional Countries: Fact Book Summarizing Results from Studies Reported between 1990 and 2006.* Geneva: WHO. <http://apps.who.int/medicinedocs/documents/s16073e/s16073e.pdf>

WHO/SEARO (World Health Organization/Regional Office for South-East Asia). 2006. *The Role of Education in the Rational Use of Medicines.* New Delhi: WHO/SEARO. < http://www.searo.who.int/en/Section1243/Section1377/Section1740_12698.htm>

Younger, E., S. Wittet, C. Hooks, and H. Lasher. 2001. *Immunization and Child Health Materials Development Guide.* Seattle, Wash.: Bill & Melinda Gates Children's Vaccine Program at PATH (Program for Appropriate Technology in Health). <http://www.who.int/immunization_training/resources/en/CVP-Materials-Development-Guide.pdf> An excellent introduction to the development and testing of print radio, video, and computer-based materials for immunization and child health. Besides a focus on low-literate audiences, content also includes writing for policy makers, providers, field workers, and others targeted for training or advocacy efforts.

Organizations related to medicine use and safety for consumers

Ask about Medicines
<http://www.askaboutmedicines.org>
Ask about Medicines was an independent campaign to increase people's involvement in decisions about their use of medicines. Posters, action packs, leaflets, public relations tool kits, and fold-out medicine charts are available for free download at the website.

International Medication Safety Network (IMSN)
<http://www.intmedsafe.net/Contents/Home.aspx>
IMSN is a network of safe medication practice centers that aims to improve patient safety by minimizing preventable harm from medicine use. Its website includes contact information for members, position papers, and links to tools and resources from its member centers.

International Network for the Rational Use of Drugs (INRUD)
<http://www.inrud.org/index.cfm>
Established in 1989 and consisting of twenty-four groups from around the world, INRUD's goal is to "design, test, and disseminate effective strategies to improve the way drugs are prescribed, dispensed, and used, with a particular emphasis on resource poor countries." Its website provides details of its activities, bibliographies on the rational use of medicines, and a variety of resources available without cost.
- INRUD Bibliography on medicine use. <http://www.inrud.org/Bibliographies/INRUD-Bibliography.cfm>

National Council on Patient Information and Education
<http://www.talkaboutrx.org> Multiple campaigns on medicine, including "Educate before You Medicate," "Be MedWise," and "Your Medicine Information: Read It and Heed It." Posters, leaflets, radio spots, information folders, activity sheets.

U.S. Food and Drug Administration (FDA)
<http://www.fda.gov/Drugs/ResourcesForYou/Consumers/default.htm> The FDA has a website that provides information and resources on medicines specifically for consumers.

WHO's website on Rational Use of Medicines
<http://www.who.int/medicines/areas/rational_use/en> WHO's work on the rational use of medicines advocates twelve key interventions to aid in avoiding the health hazards and waste of resources resulting from the misuse of medicines. Its website explains these interventions and provides information resources, training courses, and publications.

Annex 33-1   Pictograms for use on medicine labels

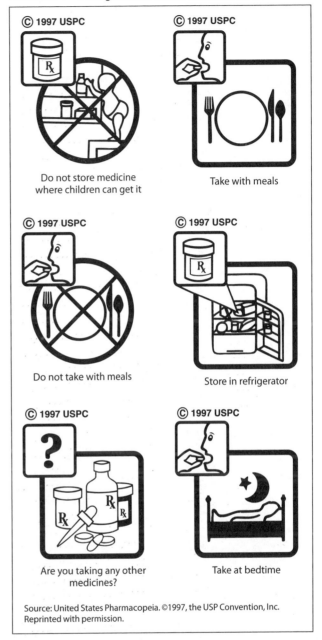

Source: United States Pharmacopeia. ©1997, the USP Convention, Inc. Reprinted with permission.

CHAPTER 34

Medicine and therapeutics information

SUMMARY

Prescribers, dispensers, and users of medicines all require information on medicines. The sources of this information can be classified as primary (articles or papers on original research), secondary (reviews of the primary literature), and tertiary (formulary manuals, standard treatment manuals, textbooks, and review articles, or pharmaceutical product information approved by drug regulatory agencies). Promotional literature has limited utility because it provides biased information designed to promote sales of commercial products.

The skills required to evaluate medicine information sources can be provided by a medicine information center (MIC); ideally, every country should have one. An MIC can be established in an accessible hospital or university department. The center should provide information proactively as well as respond to queries. The center requires trained staff with access to both text and computer information sources.

MIC activities include sending staff out to provide information; developing, producing, and disseminating a drug bulletin based on modern communication principles; and teaching.

Funding the center may be difficult, but diversified funding should be sought whenever possible. Funding from pharmaceutical companies may appear to affect the center's impartiality and should generally be used only for capital projects. Other problems that may affect the center include—

- Inadequate information sources
- Lack of acceptance
- Inadequate communication systems
- Lack of political will to establish or sustain the center

34.1   The important role of medicine and therapeutics information

Access to clinically relevant, up-to-date, user-specific, and objective information is required to make appropriate decisions for medicine prescribing, dispensing, and use. A health care system can provide access to the highest-quality medicines, but if those medicines are not properly used, they may have negligible, or even harmful, effects. Although access to good information about medicines does not guarantee appropriate decisions and use, it is a basic requirement for good decision making.

Medicine information comes in many forms, both printed and electronic, and the need for medicine information varies among different types of health care providers and patients. For example, physicians and pharmacists need access to the full range of information about generic and brand-name medicines, indications and contraindications for use, medicines of choice and therapeutic alternatives, dosing, precautions for use, drug interactions, side effects, adverse effects, clinical features and treatment of overdose, dosage forms and strengths, and cost of a course of treatment. Patients need basic instructions for using prescribed and self-care medicines. In addition, consumers increasingly expect, and are being provided with, more comprehensive medicine information as they become more involved in decisions regarding their own treatment and care (Chapter 33). This trend has accelerated with the growth of the Internet and the huge repositories of information that are easily accessible (see Box 34-1).

Identifying and accessing needed medicine information resources are important activities for a pharmaceutical management program. When limited funds do not allow the program to provide systemwide access to necessary information resources and individual practitioners are unlikely to be able to purchase information themselves, a centralized medicine information service should be considered.

The primary role of an MIC is to give clear and definitive information on medicines and promote their appropriate use. A secondary role of the center is to keep up-to-date with pharmacological and therapeutic advances and disseminate relevant information when it becomes available. This activity is particularly important to support a hospital's drug and therapeutics committee and the work it does in maintaining its formulary, treatment guidelines, and formulary manual (Chapter 17).

34.2   Types of medicine information

Information falls into three categories depending on its source—primary, secondary, or tertiary. Primary sources are the foundation on which all other medicine information resources are based. They provide original thinking and results of original research. Primary literature can be found as published articles or unpublished reports that provide detail on the research and its findings. Published information has typically gone through a peer-review process to assess scientific soundness and merit. Publications or reports would provide information on medicine-related subjects, such as clinical pharmaceutical trials, case studies, and pharmacological research.

Secondary sources are more difficult to define because interpretations vary as to what exactly they are. In essence, however, secondary resources function as a guide to or review of the primary literature and include, for example, indexing and abstracting services (for example, PubMed), commentaries on primary literature, review articles, drug bulletins, and meta-analyses or systematic reviews, such as Cochrane evaluations. Secondary sources are typically easy to access and use and to link to the primary literature.

Tertiary sources draw from primary and secondary literature and provide "processed" information that represents the interpretations and conclusions of the individuals or organizations doing the development. They are convenient and easily used but at the same time carry the risk of being less than objective. Examples include textbooks, general reference books, and pharmaceutical compendia. Obtain the most current edition available when using secondary or tertiary sources.

A selected list of medicine information sources that can be accessed online appears in Annex 34-1. All information sources have limitations, and medicine information users should recognize both their advantages and disadvantages.

Evaluation of information sources

Evaluating information sources is an important skill (see Box 34-2). The *Teacher's Guide to Good Prescribing* (Hogerzeil et al. 2001) contains a useful section on assessing literature. *Studying a Study and Testing a Test* (Riegelman 2004) is a valuable primer on evaluating medical literature.

Primary sources. Evaluating primary literature is difficult. The most reliable evidence comes from reports on randomized controlled clinical trials. Appropriate evaluation of these trials requires considerable time and experience, but they are by far the best source of objective information. To use primary literature effectively, the user needs a certain level of knowledge about research methodology and statistics. Keeping up with the volume of published information is also difficult. Thousands of journals are published regularly, with each containing many articles. Even if reading is limited to journals in a specific area of interest and expertise, the amount of information may preclude staying abreast of the latest findings. Therefore, many readers simply trust the journals' peer-review processes and assume that the process will identify any problems with the studies.

In judging published primary literature, the reader cannot assume that the results of a study or a research paper

---

Box 34-1
Medical products and the Internet

The Internet provides people with quick and easy access to vast amounts of information on practically any subject. It is a valuable source of health information on topics such as diseases, conditions, therapies, medical products, and health and medical organizations. The quality of information, however, varies, and consumers as well as health care professionals must be careful when using the Internet as a source of health information.

The World Health Organization (WHO) created a guide on medical products and the Internet to help people obtain reliable, independent, and comparable information. The guide has five key points—

1. The Internet is a valuable source of information, but the consulted source should be known and trusted. Consumers need to judge whether or not the information is reliable, complete, and up-to-date.
2. Determining and verifying the source of a website can be difficult, so consumers should look for the following—

   • Clear indication of the name and contact address of the website owner
   • Clear indication of funders, services, or other support to the website
   • Whether advertising or sponsorship is a source of funding
   • Intended audience (consumer, health professional, other)
   • Date of the last information update

3. When searching for and evaluating products, such as pharmaceuticals, if information sounds too good to be true, it probably is. Information should include active ingredients, other ingredients, side effects, interactions, how to use a product, how to store it, and contact information.
4. Consumers need to be cautious about buying medical products on the Internet. They can be illegal, risky, poor quality, a waste of money, and lacking in safety and efficacy assurance. Instructions for use may be inadequate.
5. Although the Internet can be a good source of information, consumers should not substitute it for an actual consultation with a health care provider.

Sources: WHO 2001, 1999.

Box 34-2
Evaluating information sources

Questions to ask when reviewing original clinical articles

- In which journal was the article published? What is the reputation of the journal? Is it known to have high standards for the acceptance of articles? Are articles peer reviewed?
- Who is the author, and what is his or her affiliation?
- Does the article report the results of a properly designed clinical study, or is it based on case reports or observations? If a clinical study, what was the sample size, and how were participants selected? Were controls used? Was the study prospective or retrospective? Is the report adequately referenced?
- Are reasonable conclusions drawn?
- Who funded the study? Does any potential exist for conflict of interest?

Questions to ask about bibliographic, abstracting, or indexing services

- What journals or information resources are covered by the service, and are these resources the ones that are essential for the particular purpose?
- What is the lag time between the publication of a journal and its inclusion in the service?
- How easily can the service be used? Are key words indexed? Are subject headings used?
- If abstracts are provided, who develops the abstracts, and how accurately do they reflect the primary source?

Questions to ask about consensus-generated documents

- How is consensus defined, and how are the individuals participating in the consensus definition process selected?

- How good is the consensus-generation process?
- Are references provided and accessible?
- Is the consensus process open to public review and comment?
- Is the information based on evidence published in peer-reviewed literature, or is it simply a compilation of use patterns reported as being accepted by the medical community?
- When was the consensus document published, and how frequently is the information updated?
- Who published the information, and what kind of reputation does the publisher have?

Questions to ask about secondary and tertiary references written by individuals or groups of individuals

- Who is the author, and what are his or her qualifications?
- Who is the publisher, and what is its reputation?
- Who paid for the development of the information? Does it come from a special-interest group? If the publication is reporting proceedings from a conference, who organized the conference, and do the organizers have a special interest?
- Has the information been peer reviewed? How good is the peer-review process?
- When was the information developed, and how current is it?
- Are references included in the article, or can the references be accessed by other means?

---

are valid simply because it has been accepted for publication. However, considering the source of a study or paper is useful when determining quality. A number of respected medical and pharmacy journals whose high standards for acceptance and publication make it unlikely that a research article containing erroneous, fraudulent, or misrepresented data would survive the editorial and review process. Annex 34-1 lists some English-language journals that have strong editorial policies and peer-review processes that include conflict-of-interest disclosure requirements to minimize the possibility of biased or unsupportable conclusions being reported. One way to monitor such problems is to read the

letters to the editor published in journals. If questionable conclusions survive the peer-review process, some reader will undoubtedly write to the journal editor and state his or her observations or concerns. Reputable journals readily share this type of correspondence, often allowing the authors of criticized articles the opportunity to respond.

Information published in journals without a strong review process needs to be more carefully scrutinized. "Throwaway" or controlled-circulation publications, provided free of charge, often by a special-interest group (a pharmaceutical manufacturer, for example), require careful review to determine what biases, if any, exist. Determining who is publishing these types of journals and what the peer-review process is, if any, for acceptance of an article is a good idea. In addition, note conflict-of-interest declarations.

Clinical trial databases and unpublished reports (known as gray literature) are also considered primary literature. Although not always readily available, this type of information can provide valuable insights. For example, some companies or researchers may elect not to publish results because the findings were negative. This decision presents an ethical problem in that negative findings, although potentially detrimental to the financial success of a particular product, are valuable in making evidence-based decisions on the use of a medicine. Finding information on clinical trials has been facilitated in recent years through the creation of clinical trial registries that are available online. For example, the Duke University Medical Library has a guide to searching the gray literature and clinical trials, including those on pharmaceutical company websites (http://guides.mclibrary.duke.edu/content.php?pid=224463&sid=1861375). The reader needs to carefully interpret unpublished data, however, because there may be negative underlying reasons why the data have not been published in peer-review journals.

Secondary and tertiary resources. Secondary and tertiary information resources are essentially derivations of

---

Box 34-3
The Cochrane Collaboration

The Cochrane Collaboration was established in 1993 in England to support the systematic, up-to-date review and synthesis of scientific research, which can be used to help people make well-informed decisions about health care. The collaboration is based on the ideas of Scottish doctor Archie Cochrane, who said in 1979 that health professionals should have an updated critical summary of all relevant randomized clinical trials (RCTs) to provide evidence-based care that is proven effective.

The Cochrane reviews are prepared mainly by health care professionals who follow an established methodology. The reviewers systematically study all reports of RCTs for treatment of a specific problem while focusing on identifying the benefits and risks of different interventions. The group often uses a technique called meta-analysis, which combines the results of different RCTs to get around problems of small sample sizes that can lead to statistical errors. After extensive peer review, the documents are published and updated periodically.

Cochrane reviews cover treatments for many different diseases. Specific groups of reviewers focus on particular subjects, such as eyes and vision, arthritis treatment, and neonatal health. An example of a Cochrane review is *Co-trimoxazole Prophylaxis for Opportunistic Infections in Children with HIV Infection,* published in 2006. The review found a significant reduction (33 percent) in mortality in HIV-positive children one to fifteen years of age taking co-trimoxazole versus a placebo. Co-trimoxazole is cheap and effective against a wide range of organisms that commonly cause opportunistic infections in children with HIV. The reviewers concluded that the use of co-trimoxazole prophylaxis was beneficial for HIV-infected children in Zambia, and whether this conclusion can be extrapolated to other resource-poor settings must be decided.

Although the Cochrane Collaboration has centers in Australia, Canada, Denmark, England, Italy, and the United States, it is beginning to influence far-reaching health policies in developing countries. Through its Developing Country Network, it encourages people from these countries to become reviewers and to register all RCTs throughout the world, so that the information is available and useful to researchers and the public. For example, the African Trials Register involves tracking down all controlled trials conducted in Africa by searching global and regional databases and hand-searching African journals. This project intends to ensure that trials conducted in Africa are documented so they can be used in Cochrane reviews.

The collaboration publishes its reviews in the Cochrane Library, primarily through CD-ROM and the Internet. Free access to abstracts and summaries of the reviews are available to the public, but most full-text documents require a subscription. Access to the reviews is steadily improving for people in low- and middle-income countries through free national subscriptions or global initiatives promoting free access to health care information, such as the HINARI Access to Research in Health Programme (http://www.who.int/hinari/en). Since it was established, the information disseminated by the Cochrane Collaboration is having a "significant impact on education, practice, research and policy" (Volmink et al. 2004).

E-mail: secretariat@cochrane.org

Web: http://www.cochrane.org

Sources: Grimwade and Swingler 2006, Volmink et al. 2004.

the primary literature. Some review articles summarize the results and conclusions of a number of reports from the primary literature (usually with comments by the reviewer). Systematic reviews of data from multiple trials addressing the same research question (meta-analyses) are particularly useful. The Cochrane Collaboration (see Box 34-3) undertakes this type of work.

Bibliographic, abstracting, or indexing services provide listings or compilations of published articles. Some list the addresses of the principal authors; others contain abstracts of articles, along with key words or subject headings to help users find the articles or references for which they are looking. Examples of such services include PubMed, Embase, International Pharmaceutical Abstracts, Index Medicus, Excerpta Medica, and the Iowa Drug Information Service. Different systems cover different journals and may, for instance, omit letters to the editor. A lag period exists between initial publication of a primary source and its inclusion in such secondary sources. Not relying entirely on one secondary source is therefore important.

Drug bulletins can be valuable in helping prescribers and supply system managers determine the relative merits of new medicines and keep up-to-date. Drug bulletins can have a variety of sponsors, such as government agencies, professional bodies, university departments, philanthropic foundations, and consumer organizations. They are published in many countries, sometimes free of charge, and many are highly respected because of their unbiased information. Examples in English are *Drug and Therapeutics Bulletin* (United Kingdom), *Medical Letter on Drugs and Therapeutics* (United States), and *Australian Prescriber* (Australia). *Prescrire International* is available in both French and English. National drug bulletins appear in many other countries, including Bukina Faso, Nepal, and Pakistan. The main advantages of national drug bulletins are that they can select topics of national relevance and use the national language.

Tertiary references, written by individuals or groups, are often developed with the input of consultant authors and reviewers and may be widely peer reviewed. In general, the more thorough the review process is, the more sound the information is likely to be. In many countries, the most widely available tertiary resources are formulary manuals and standard treatment manuals produced by the health system. These important resources are discussed in Chapter 17. Box 34-4 also lists selected tertiary sources.

Probably the most widely accepted secondary and tertiary information sources are those that report the consensus of experts, a process that involves a high level of scrutiny and feedback. A consensus statement is the closest one can come to agreement among experts. In most instances, consensus is defined as having addressed and considered all dissenting views so that, at a minimum, all disagreements have been publicly stated and considered. The consensus documents developed by the U.S. National Institutes of Health, such as the *NIH Consensus Development Conference Statement on the Management of Hepatitis B* from 2008, are good examples of this approach to information development.

Manufacturer-provided medicine information

Information provided by pharmaceutical companies is so commonly available and widely used that it warrants a separate discussion. This information can be technical, such as product labeling approved by a country's regulatory agency, textbooks, and journal reprints, or promotional information. Promotional information seeks to show how one company's product is better than another's or how a new product can treat a serious or not-so-serious medical condition. Although both technical and promotional information are ultimately intended to increase sales, the two differ greatly in

---

Box 34-4
Basic references for a medicine information library

- American Hospital Formulary Service medicine information
- *British National Formulary*
- Cochrane Library
- Medicine availability reference (specific for the country or region)
- *Dart, Medical Toxicology*, or another clinical toxicology or poisoning text
- *Goodman and Gilman, The Pharmacological Basis of Therapeutics*, or another basic pharmacology text
- *Index Nominum: International Medicine Directory*

- *Martindale: The Complete Drug Reference*
- National formulary or essential medicines list
- PubMed
- Price reference (specific for the country or region)
- *International Drug Price Indicator Guide*
- Textbook of internal medicine (such as *Harrison's Principles of Internal Medicine* or the *Oxford Textbook of Medicine*)
- Tropical medicine reference (in countries where appropriate)

Box 34-5
Medicine information and promotion: Educating medical and pharmacy students about medicine promotion

Understanding the relationship between health professionals and medicine promotional information produced by the pharmaceutical industry is important. Research has shown that doctors who rely more on industry promotional information tend to prescribe less appropriately, prescribe more often, and adopt new medicines more quickly; therefore, medical and pharmacy students need to be educated about recognizing medicine promotion and responding appropriately.

In 2005, an international cross-sectional survey, Educational Initiatives for Medical and Pharmacy Students about Medicine Promotion, examined the extent to which students are educated about the pharmaceutical industry and medicine promotion. The results are based on a survey of 228 pharmacy and medical school educators from sixty-four countries.

In the survey, nearly three-quarters of educators reported that education about medicine promotion is part of their required curriculum but that most students devoted less than one-half day to this topic. The regional breakdown is illustrated in the table below.

The survey reported what survey respondents felt were the main objectives of their medicine promotion curriculum—

- Of educators from all regions, 70 percent or greater, except the eastern Mediterranean (56 percent), said

the main objective of their curricula was to teach critical appraisal of medicine promotion.
- Of educators from all regions, 70 percent or greater said that the main objective was to increase students' use of independent resources.
- Only 14 to 26 percent of the educators felt that the main objective was to decrease students' use of medicine promotion.

Many pharmacy and medical educators have recognized the need for education about medicine promotion, but they frequently mention a lack of integration into the main curriculum and inadequate time allocation as barriers to a successful program.

In some cases, students themselves are taking an active role in opposing the influence of medicine promotion. In 2002, the American Medical Student Association launched its PharmFree campaign, which educates medical students about the influences of the pharmaceutical industry on medical training and the problems with using biased industry-based information to choose which medicines to prescribe. The association encourages students to refuse any gifts from pharmaceutical representatives as a way to show that they are not influenced by them, and they encourage the use of sources such as the *Medical Letter* to get unbiased evaluations of new medications.

Sources: Moghimi 2006, Mintzes 2005, Norris et al. 2005.

Educators' report of the role of medicine promotion in international pharmacy and medical school curriculum

Role of medicine promotion	Europe (%)	Americas (%)	Western Pacific (%)	Africa (%)	Eastern Mediterranean (%)	Southeast Asia (%)
Promotion is part of curriculum	81	83	67	86	70	91
Promotion is part of *required* curriculum	75	64	81	85	65	56
One-half day or less spent on promotion	30	32	39	25	20	20
Ten or more hours spent on promotion	40	34	32	50	45	44

terms of source and presentation. The information provided by pharmaceutical manufacturers varies considerably from country to country, depending on a government's regulatory requirements and its ability to effectively monitor and enforce those requirements. Box 34-5 covers an initiative to increase medical and pharmacy students' knowledge of medicine promotion.

Technical information. The information developed as part of a new medicine approval process by a country's drug regulatory authority has been thoroughly reviewed and should accurately reflect a product's basis for approval. It defines what information manufacturers are required by law to include with their product—that which is affixed to a bottle or package (the labeling) and more detailed information that needs to accompany the product (package insert). Approved product information guides prescribers, dispensers, and patients on use of a particular medicine and defines what the manufacturer can legally say (advertise) about its product. This information includes, for example, the medicine's approved indications for use, precautions, potential adverse effects, and dosing, as well as the product's strength, composition, and packaging and storage requirements. In addition, more and more countries are providing information for the patient in easy-to-read language on how to use the product correctly. Because this information is approved by the drug regulatory authority, it carries significant impact both clinically and legally.

Many health professionals and patients regularly use references that compile government-approved product information or brief descriptions of a product's physical characteristics and use that are based on approved product information. In the United States, the most common reference of this type is the *Physicians' Desk Reference,* where pharmaceutical companies pay to include their products (making it marketing focused). In the United Kingdom, the Association of the British Pharmaceutical Industry *Data Sheet Compendium* is commonly used; and in many other countries, the country-specific or regional edition of *MIMS* (*Monthly Index of Medical Specialties*) provides brief sets of information for products marketed in that country or region. The limitations of these types of publications must be kept in mind, particularly related to what is included (older, less-profitable products are more likely to be excluded) and the information omitted because of

---

Box 34-6
WHO ethical guidelines for medicine promotion

Since 1967, WHO has been concerned about improper pharmaceutical advertising. A new statement on ethical criteria for medicine promotion was adopted in 1988. At the 1997 Roundtable on WHO's Ethical Criteria for Promotion of Medicinal Drugs, participants agreed that inappropriate medicines promotion remained a problem both in developing and developed countries. The movement for a major project on pharmaceutical promotion originated at the May 1999 meeting of the WHO/public-interest nongovernmental organization, Roundtable on Pharmaceuticals.

Promotion of pharmaceuticals should support the national pharmaceutical policy. The WHO ethical criteria state that advertisements should be consistent with the approved scientific data sheet and should be fully legible. Advertisements to the public should be for nonprescription medicines only. Medical representatives should have appropriate training and should present information in an accurate and responsible manner, without offering incentives to prescribers or dispensers. They should make unbiased information on products available.

Under the criteria, free samples may be provided in modest quantities to prescribers. The criteria also state that providing free samples of nonprescription medicines is difficult to justify from a health perspective. When a pharmaceutical company sponsors a symposium or scientific meeting, its involvement should be clearly stated in advance at the meeting and in any publications.

The criteria recognize that postmarketing surveillance is important but caution that it should not be misused as a disguised form of promotion. The criteria also define standards in packaging and labeling, patient information, and promotion of exported medicines. Many, but not all countries and some companies have adopted these criteria as a guide for marketing practices.

Copies of the ethical criteria are available from WHO offices and have also been published in full in the *WHO Essential Drugs Monitor* 17 (1994).

Other helpful resources related to pharmaceutical promotion include—

- Health Action International has a website devoted to medicine promotion (http://www.haiweb.org/03_other.htm). It includes downloadable resources related to promotion to consumers, promotion in health education, and drug industry sponsorship.
- The organization Healthy Skepticism (http://www.healthyskepticism.org), formerly the Medical Lobby for Appropriate Marketing, is a nonprofit advocacy group that initially focused on revealing harmful medicine promotion activities in developing countries but now documents information from all countries. Its online library of medicine promotion information includes more than 19,000 items.
- *Understanding and Responding to Pharmaceutical Promotion: A Practical Guide* (WHO/HAI 2010) is designed to summarize medicine marketing and promotion issues for medical and pharmacy students (http://www.haiweb.org/10112010/DPM_ENG_Final_SEP10.pdf).

- Has the information been approved by the country's drug regulatory body?
- Are references to the medical literature provided or available? Do they come from peer-reviewed journals?
- Was the information unsolicited, or was it provided in response to a request or question?
- Does the information contain negative references to the use of other medicines that might be substitutes or therapeutic alternatives to the medicine in question? If so, are such negative references warranted?
- Do the claims for the medicine's effectiveness appear overly positive, sensational, or one-sided?
- Is the information balanced with the negative outcomes related to the use of a medicine (such as side effects or adverse effects)?
- Are cost comparisons included?
- Does the information included in the product insert or the labeling reflect current medical practice and standards?
- Are references dated and current?
- Is the information in a language suitable for the consumer?

space limitations. They are not comprehensive information sources.

Promotional information. Promotional materials developed by a pharmaceutical company typically present only favorable views of the sponsor's products, and the materials may not furnish adequate information to make good prescribing decisions. Although most countries have regulations defining acceptable pharmaceutical marketing, in practice, governments often have difficulty controlling what information companies provide. A multinational advocacy organization, Healthy Skepticism, monitors misleading advertisements, as does Health Action International. WHO has developed ethical guidelines for pharmaceutical promotion (see Box 34-6).

This does not mean that manufacturers' information is universally bad and should not be used at all, because manufacturers can supply very timely and useful medicine information. However, health care professionals or patients using manufacturer-supplied sources need to recognize the potential for bias and make a judgment about the materials' value (see Box 34-7).

34.3 Setting up a medicine and therapeutics information center

A medicine and therapeutics information center is a vital part of efforts to promote appropriate medicine use. In a small country with limited means, this center may be a small office in the national hospital with a shelf of books and WHO publications and where a hospital pharmacist is responsible for answering queries. Ideally, however, countries should develop formal MICs as part of their national health programs. An MIC should work closely with the national essential medicines program, provide support for development and maintenance of formulary and standard

treatment guidelines, and be involved in the production of national medicine-related materials.

To be successful, an MIC requires a stable location and environment, a philosophical commitment to providing needed medicine information, physical space to house the center, basic information references, staff, and equipment to support information access and dissemination.

An MIC and a poison control center are two different services, although they are often combined. Poison control is usually an emergency service requiring rapid response. A medicine information service deals with both urgent requests for therapeutic information and requests that require a more detailed review and synthesis of information.

Philosophical commitment

An MIC should be both reactive and proactive. Reactive or passive duties include providing information for people who call or come to the center with questions. Although this function is important, it certainly should not define the limits of a center's activities. A center's effect will be greater if it functions proactively by reaching out with medicine information for people who need it, in a format that is convenient and effective. This task will be easier if a medicine information service is based on a cooperative model, involving all health care disciplines and using existing resources to the greatest extent possible. The center not only should be driven by the needs and expectations of its users but also should work to create demand and raise expectations.

Site identification

Ideally, an MIC is in or near a major hospital or other major health care facility. Location within a hospital, university, or other academic institution provides a network of medical disciplines that can support and enrich the work, allowing

MEDICINE INFORMATION SHOULD BE RESPONSIVE TO CLIENTS' NEEDS

better access to medicine information and to libraries, research facilities, expertise, and academic and educational activities. Possible alternative sites include a facility within or adjacent to a medical or pharmacy association or a relevant governmental agency (such as the ministry of health, drug regulatory authority, pharmaceutical approval unit, or quality-control laboratory).

A secure location in one or two rooms allows space for office work, space for storage of references, and space for visitors to use the MIC's resources. Involving several institutions in the support of an MIC may be necessary. In some countries, a mutual agreement exists that the MIC at the university provides services on behalf of the ministry of health. In turn, the government covers some recurrent expenses.

Staffing and equipment requirements

An MIC needs dedicated staff who will not be diverted to other activities and duties and who can provide dependable coverage for the center's stated business hours. This need translates into one or two full-time employees, including a full-time clinical or hospital pharmacist who specializes in clinical pharmacology, therapeutics, or toxicology. Additional staffing may be required if activities other than information, such as pharmacovigilance, are part of the center's mission.

The training and experience of the staff must be clinically based. The user population for any information service is primarily clinicians, and expertise in pharmacotherapy is essential to communicate effectively with them. When an appropriately trained person is not available, every effort should be made to train someone to fill the position. Other relevant professionals—medical, paramedical, or non-medical—and specialists in information communication techniques may be required to help develop materials and provide specific information and services. When medicine information specialists are not available, a medical doctor with some training in clinical pharmacology should be considered to head the center. Ideally, the center should have qualified administrative staff to help establish, maintain, and update the information access and dissemination processes.

Proper photocopying, communications (including Internet access), and computer equipment are important in establishing a viable medicine information service. A computer, CD-ROM/DVD drive, printer, and appropriate software programs are highly desirable because access to electronic medicine and therapy databases is critical. However, small centers can provide important medicine information services using basic texts and other printed references if electronic access is not possible.

Basic information resources

The latest editions of the textbooks listed in Box 34-4 could form the core of a basic library for an MIC, along with journals and newsletters, WHO materials, and computer databases (see Annex 34-1). Although the most flexible and efficient of these resources are the computer databases, cost may limit their availability. Print resources, if kept up-to-date, can adequately cover basic information needs. Some print and electronic databases can be accessed free of charge.

Although subscriptions to medical and pharmacy journals and newsletters are expensive, some basic subscriptions should be considered if the funds are available. Many scientific journals are now available via open access or are free of charge. A list of many such journals can be found at the Directory of Open Access Journals (http://www.doaj.org). Because acquiring and updating information is costly, establishing a link to a medical library is very important. The addresses of organizations that produce widely accepted medicine newsletters or bulletins, which are inexpensive and useful sources of information, can be obtained from the International Society of Drug Bulletins (ISDB).

Electronic access to information is critical for an MIC because most databases and journals are online. If Internet access is unavailable or unreliable, however, or if the costs of online access are prohibitive, CD-ROMs might be an alternative resource. Databases to consider including in an MIC include—

- PubMed (online)
- British National Formulary (online)
- Cochrane Library (online and CD-ROM)
- DrugDex (online)
- Poisindex (online and CD-ROM)
- Martindale: The Complete Drug Reference (online and CD-ROM)
- AHFS Drug Information (online)
- International Pharmaceutical Abstracts (online)

- Embase (online)
- Iowa Drug Information Service (online, CD-ROM, and microfiche)

34.4 Managing a medicine information center

An MIC should provide a variety of services, from responding to patients' and doctors' queries to making proactive efforts such as publishing newsletters or drug bulletins, participating in clinical activities, and organizing formulary and treatment guideline committees (see Country Study 34-1). MIC staff members are also likely to be involved in training health professionals and regularly evaluating the performance of the center's staff. Although MICs tend to be small units, each one should have a well-developed annual plan.

Proactive outreach

Health care professionals in both the public and private sectors often have little time or funds to spend on medicine information resources. An MIC can fill this gap, but the service must be effectively marketed.

Medicine information professionals need to work to build credibility and improve perceptions of their accessibility and value to health care providers, specifically, and to the health care system overall. This can be done by—

Country Study 34-1
Therapeutics Information and Pharmacovigilance Center in Namibia

As the Namibian government began rolling out antiretroviral therapy, an assessment identified lack of a source of information about medicines and lack of a monitoring system for adverse drug reactions as critical gaps in Namibia's ability to deliver AIDS treatment. To fill this gap, the Rational Pharmaceutical Management Plus Program conceptualized a model that integrated medicines information and pharmacovigilance activities into one service unit called the Therapeutics Information and Pharmacovigilance Center (TIPC). Although most countries separate these activities, this integrated model was driven by the potential synergies between the two services, opportunities for leveraging resources, and human resource constraints. The model placed the TIPC under the Namibia Medicines Regulatory Council with existing Ministry of Health and Social Services committees serving as the advisory body.

The TIPC provides unbiased therapeutics information and serves as the official reference center for medicine safety monitoring in Namibia. It provides broad-based medicine-safety services, such as how to avoid potential drug interactions, and communicates point-of-care therapeutic information to health care providers and the public through a hotline, fax, and e-mail. Anyone can request medicine or therapeutics information by filling out a form on the TIPC website. The TIPC also publishes the *Namibia Medicines Watch*, a drug bulletin for health care providers and consumers.

The center implemented a nationwide system for spontaneous reporting of adverse drug reactions in 2007, through which it collects reports from health care providers and the public of adverse effects of medicines. The TIPC has also collaborated with partners to conduct trainings for health care workers in therapeutics information and pharmacovigilance and basic research methods.

Source: SPS Program n.d.

- Building alliances with the most influential clinicians, providing them with particular information they request, and involving them as consultants and reviewers
- Ensuring that they are readily accessible by telephone or in person and providing responses to queries promptly
- Making an extra effort to find answers for clinicians who have raised unusual medicine-related questions
- Participating in national essential medicines list committees, hospital drug and therapeutics committees, and standard treatment guidelines committees
- Preparing short, problem-oriented, practical bulletins on medicine-use problems specific to the country, district, or hospital
- Making patient rounds with doctors and other clinical staff
- Providing in-service training to health facility staff
- Making short presentations to outpatient groups
- Making presentations to community organizations

Drug bulletins

The development, production, and dissemination of newsletters or drug bulletins that address relevant medicine information issues often help develop the market for an MIC. These periodicals should promote rational medicine therapy and appear at regular intervals, ranging from weekly to quarterly, depending on their purpose and on the capacity of the MIC. Drug bulletins should provide impartial assessments of medicines and practical recommendations, based on a comparison of treatment alternatives and on the consensus of the main specialists in the field.

Drug bulletins are more likely to be effective if they take the following principles into account (see Figure 34-1)—

Understanding the reasons for prescribing behavior: As mentioned in Chapter 29, providing information alone does not change undesirable behavior. Understanding the reasons for the behavior is a necessary first step in developing appropriate messages.

Being oriented toward decisions and actions: Prescribers need information that is immediately useful in their daily work.

Emphasizing and repeating only a few key messages: If too many ideas are brought up in the bulletin, none will be absorbed. A few messages that are the focus of the bulletin and are repeated are more likely to be retained.

Capturing attention with headlines and visually appealing illustrations: An effective bulletin grabs the reader's attention with attractive graphics that emphasize key messages.

Keeping text brief and simple: Although readers of the bulletin may be well educated and knowledgeable, a bulletin should provide immediately accessible information.

Referencing the best research and having respectable sponsorship: The bulletin should be affiliated with a credible organization or institution such as a medical society or medical school. Key messages in each issue should be supported by a few well-chosen and respected references. Three references to the *Lancet, New England Journal of Medicine, British Medical Journal,* or *Journal of the American Medical Association* are better than twenty references to unpublished reports.

Being relevant: Materials in the bulletin should relate to clinical issues that affect the target audience and should discuss medicines that are available in the audience's country or health system.

The ISDB produces a regular newsletter, organizes regional workshops for international editors of bulletins and newsletters, and provides a forum for the exchange of high-quality information and ideas related to promoting effective dissemination of information. Box 34-8 includes information on starting or strengthening a drug bulletin.

Training

Training in the management of an MIC or a medicine information service is necessary for key personnel, as is training on medicine information retrieval, literature evaluation, publication development, and sustainability planning and funding. In addition, communications skills, including ability to write succinctly using language appropriate for the target audience, are critical. A large medicine information service should ideally have a career structure similar to those of academic or educational institutions. All staff members should have the opportunity for additional training and advancement within their own capabilities. When appropriate, professional staff should be encouraged to undertake relevant research activities.

Evaluation

Ongoing monitoring and evaluation is particularly important for services such as an MIC, where resources are limited and getting the most out of the available funding is essential. Monitoring should be built in from the start and should include documenting the questions asked, responses provided, references used, complaints and compliments received, timing of responses, and services provided (such as new medicine evaluations). The queries should be analyzed, and the results summarized in the annual report. In addition, periodic input from users of the medicine information service should be sought through personal contacts, questionnaires, or focus groups.

This information can help the center's manager make good decisions about future programs and budgeting. For example, if a certain inquiry has been made several times by

Figure 34-1   Example of a credible drug bulletin

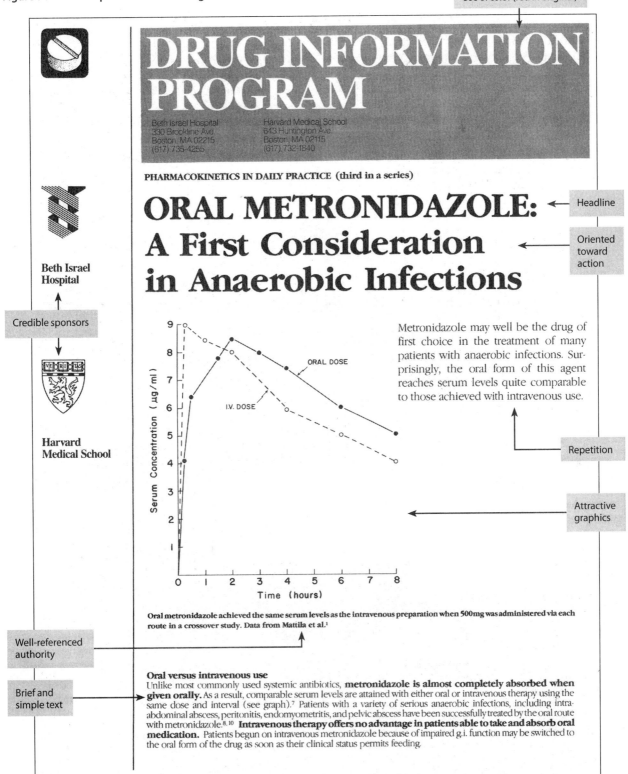

Use of color (red in original)

DRUG INFORMATION PROGRAM

Beth Israel Hospital
330 Brookline Ave.
Boston, MA 02215
(617) 735-4255

Harvard Medical School
643 Huntington Ave.
Boston, MA 02115
(617) 732-1840

PHARMACOKINETICS IN DAILY PRACTICE (third in a series)

ORAL METRONIDAZOLE: A First Consideration in Anaerobic Infections

Headline

Oriented toward action

Metronidazole may well be the drug of first choice in the treatment of many patients with anaerobic infections. Surprisingly, the oral form of this agent reaches serum levels quite comparable to those achieved with intravenous use.

Repetition

Attractive graphics

Beth Israel Hospital

Credible sponsors

Harvard Medical School

Oral metronidazole achieved the same serum levels as the intravenous preparation when 500mg was administered via each route in a crossover study. Data from Mattila et al.[1]

Well-referenced authority

Brief and simple text

Oral versus intravenous use

Unlike most commonly used systemic antibiotics, **metronidazole is almost completely absorbed when given orally.** As a result, comparable serum levels are attained with either oral or intravenous therapy using the same dose and interval (see graph).[7] Patients with a variety of serious anaerobic infections, including intra-abdominal abscess, peritonitis, endomyometritis, and pelvic abscess have been successfully treated by the oral route with metronidazole.[8,10] **Intravenous therapy offers no advantage in patients able to take and absorb oral medication.** Patients begun on intravenous metronidazole because of impaired g.i. function may be switched to the oral form of the drug as soon as their clinical status permits feeding.

different individuals, the question may be a good topic for an article in the medicine information newsletter or bulletin. If the same complaint about MIC service is made repeatedly, perhaps a review of the center's operations is in order. If a certain textbook or database is not frequently used, perhaps it should be replaced by another one.

Sources of help

Funding for the establishment of an MIC may come from government resources, donors supporting essential medicines projects, professional associations, university or other training programs, nongovernmental organizations, or a combination of several of these funding sources.

Several programs allow developing countries to more easily access health and medicine information and re-sources. For example, the International Pharmaceutical Federation's Pharmabridge program helps provide books, journals, and electronic resources to those who need them in developing countries (http://www.fip.nl/pharmabridge). WHO's HINARI Access to Research in Health Programme also allows developing countries to use a large collection of scientific and medical literature (http://who.int/hinari/en). WHO also has "blue trunk libraries" that have over 100 books arranged by topic, including essential medicines (www.who.int/ghl/mobile_libraries/bluetrunk/en). Blue trunk libraries are available in English, French, Portuguese, and Arabic. Collaboration between centers in developing and developed countries is very valuable and enables the exchange of information and staff for teaching and training. The ISDB is also a useful channel for support.

Box 34-8
Starting or strengthening a drug bulletin

Drug bulletins are a fundamental tool for promoting rational use of medicines, and locally produced bulletins are an effective approach to providing reliable and unbiased comparative information on medicines and therapies for prescribers, patients, and the public within the context of local needs and uses. The information should focus on using medicines safely and correctly and help people make better decisions about medicines.

WHO and the ISDB have worked together to develop guidelines called *Starting or Strengthening a Drug Bulletin: A Practical Manual,* which shows global experiences related to developing drug bulletins.

The objectives of the ISDB and WHO manual include—

- Illustrating what makes bulletins independent
- Reflecting the diversity found among drug bulletins
- Helping people make choices about what is appropriate for their bulletin
- Showing useful methods and models and helping people learn from the successes and failures of others
- Helping people decide whether to set up a bulletin, how to set up a bulletin, or how to strengthen their existing bulletin

The manual has sections on planning, production, and the editorial process, as well as a detailed discussion of books and journals that are good references for bulletins.

How drug bulletins provide unbiased information on pharmaceuticals in Kyrgyzstan

According to WHO, an underlying factor in irrational medicine use in Kyrgyzstan is the lack of access to inde-pendent medicine information. Working closely with the National Drug Committee, Kyrgyzstan's drug information center has taken on the important role of providing independent medicine information to health care providers. The center publishes a quarterly drug bulletin to disseminate unbiased and updated pharmaceutical information and to promote rational medicine use and information on health reform. Previously addressed topics include medical errors related to the name of medicines, medicine interactions, and modified-release preparations of pharmaceuticals.

How drug bulletins provide unbiased information on pharmaceuticals in Nicaragua

In Nicaragua, *Boletin AIS-COIME* is produced by a national nongovernmental organization, AIS-Nicaragua. It distributes free copies of its twelve-to-sixteen-page bulletins to all doctors working in public hospitals and primary health care units, pharmacy and medical students and teachers, nongovernmental organizations, and some private pharmacies. The bulletin is produced by a small team of three to four people and some volunteers. The team works together in a small room with access to a fax, photocopier, store, library, and meeting room. The country's drug information center provides them with information and reviews and helps with distribution of the bulletin.

Source: ISDB/WHO 2005.

ASSESSMENT GUIDE

Medicine information center

- Does a medicine information unit or center exist? If so, how is it funded and staffed?
- Does the medicine information unit or center (or another independent body) provide regular information on medicines to prescribers and dispensers?
- How many issues of independent drug bulletins are published each year?
- What percentage of prescribers receives copies of independent drug bulletins?
- What level of financial support did the medicine information center receive?
- How many queries did the medicine information center respond to in the past year?
- What current information resources are available? Which are most frequently used?

Local medicine information resources

- Has a national essential medicines list or formulary been officially adopted and distributed country-wide?
- Does a national publication (formulary bulletin or manual), revised within the past five years, provide objective information on medicines?
- Does a national therapeutic guide exist with standardized treatments for common diseases?
- What percentage of advertisements violates regulations on the ethical promotion of medicines, and how many sanctions have been implemented?
- What percentage of prescribers and dispensers has direct access to a (national) medicine formulary and standard treatment guidelines?

Funding issues

The source of funding may affect how an MIC functions. No matter how it is financed, the integrity of the unit is paramount. No special interests should be able to influence what information is or is not given out.

Obtaining initial capital funding from the sources listed previously may be possible. These organizations often provide funds for the purchase of items such as computers or photocopiers. For sustainability, it is wise to purchase a two- or three-year maintenance contract for such equipment as part of the initial capital costs.

Obtaining an adequate level of recurrent funding, particularly for staff salaries and journal, online database, or CD-ROM subscriptions, can be more difficult. Therefore, while establishing the center, every effort should be made to secure recurrent funding. For example, if a donor provides the start-up capital, the government may be persuaded to commit funding for a full-time pharmacist at the center. If a hospital is located near the center, it could be a source for long-term funding. In some countries, implementing user fees may be possible; however, this approach should be taken gradually, after the MIC has been accepted by users and they have given their input in determining services and fees.

Pharmaceutical companies may be willing to support a center, but this support should be considered cautiously. If medicine information critical of a sponsoring company's product is disseminated, the company may withdraw support. In general, funding from a pharmaceutical company should be used for discrete projects, such as replacement of a photocopier. Remember, however, that even the perception of bias toward a sponsoring company's products can harm an MIC's reputation.

Medicine information professionals in developing countries inevitably become fund-raisers to maintain activities. For example, in Cameroon, a consortium of donors was mobilized to share support for the drug bulletin. ■

References and further readings

General

★ = Key readings.

American International Health Alliance. 2003. *Learning Resource Center (LRC) Project Best Practices and Lessons Learned: A Guide to Improving Healthcare through Information and Communication Technology.* Washington, D.C.: American International Health Alliance. <http://www.aiha.com/resources/lrc_bestpract_eng.pdf>

★ FIP (International Pharmaceutical Federation). 2005. *Requirements for Drug Information Centres.* The Netherlands: FIP. <http://www.fip.org/files/fip/PI/RequirementsforDrugInformationCentres.pdf>

Garner, P., M. Meremikwu, J. Volmink, Q. Xu, and H. Smith. 2004. Putting Evidence into Practice: How Middle and Low Income Countries "Get It Together." *BMJ* 329:1036–9.

Grimwade, K., and G. H. Swingler. 2006. Cotrimoxazole Prophylaxis for Opportunistic Infections in Children with HIV Infection. *Cochrane Database of Systematic Reviews,* issue 1, art. no. CD003508. <http://www.cochrane.org/reviews/en/ab003508.html>

Healthlink Worldwide. 2003. *Resource Centre Manual: How to Set Up and Manage a Resource Centre.* London: Healthlink Worldwide. <http://www.asksource.info/support/manual/pdf/resource-centre-manual.pdf>

★ Hogerzeil, H. V., K. I. Barnes, R. H. Henning, Y. E. Kocabasoglu, H. Möller, A. J. Smith, R. S. Summers, and T. P. G. M. de Vries. 2001. *Teacher's Guide to Good Prescribing.* Geneva: World Health Organization/Department of Essential Drugs and Medicines Policy. <http://apps.who.int/medicinedocs/en/d/Js2292e/#Js2292e>

★ ISDB/WHO (International Society of Drug Bulletins and World Health Organization). 2005. *Starting or Strengthening a Drug Bulletin: A Practical Manual.* Geneva: ISDB/WHO. <http://www.who.int/medicines/areas/rational_use/startingstrengdrugbulletin.pdf>

Mintzes, B. 2005. *Educational Initiatives for Medical and Pharmacy Students about Drug Promotion: An International Cross-Sectional Survey.* Geneva: World Health Organization/Health Action International. <http://apps.who.int/medicinedocs/pdf/s8110e/s8110e.pdf>

Reggie, V., R. Balocco-Mattavelli, M. Bonati, I. Breton, A. Figueras, E. Jambert, C. Kopp, E. Montane, L. Rägo, and F. Rocchi. 2003. Prescribing Information in 26 Countries: A Comparative Study. *European Journal of Clinical Pharmacology* 59(4):263–70.

★ Riegelman, R. 2004. *Studying a Study and Testing a Test: How to Read the Medical Literature.* 5th ed. Philadelphia: Lippincott Williams & Wilkins.

SPS (Strengthening Pharmaceutical Systems) Program. No date. The Launch of Namibia's Therapeutics Information & Pharmacovigilance Center. Flyer. <http://www.msh.org/projects/sps/SPS-Documents/upload/namibia_featured_country_oct2008.pdf>

Volmink, J., N. Siegfried, K. Robertson, and A. M. Gülmezoglu. 2004. Research Synthesis and Dissemination as a Bridge to Knowledge Management: The Cochrane Collaboration. *Bulletin of the World Health Organization* 82(10):778–83.

WHO (World Health Organization). 2001. *Pharmaceuticals and the Internet: Drug Regulatory Authorities' Perspective.* Geneva: WHO. <http://whqlibdoc.who.int/hq/2001/a74987.pdf>

★ ———. 1999. *Medical Products and the Internet: A Guide to Finding Reliable Information.* Geneva: WHO. <http://apps.who.int/medicinedocs/en/d/Js2277e>

WHO/DAP (World Health Organization/Action Programme on Essential Drugs). 1995. Therapeutic Guidelines. *Essential Drugs Monitor* 19. Geneva: WHO. <http://apps.who.int/medicinedocs/fr/d/Js16518e/1.html>

★ Wiedenmayer, K., R. S. Summers, C. A. Mackie, A. G. S. Gous, and M. Everard, with D. Tromp. 2006. *Developing Pharmacy Practice: A Focus on Patient Care.* Geneva: World Health Organization/

International Pharmaceutical Federation. <http://www.who.int/medicines/publications/WHO_PSM_PAR_2006.5.pdf>

Medicine promotion and marketing

HAI (Health Action International). 1992. *Promoting Health or Pushing Drugs?* Amsterdam: HAI.

★ Healthy Skepticism. <http://www.healthyskepticism.org> An international nonprofit organization with the aim of improving health by reducing harm from misleading drug promotion. It maintains an online library of information related to drug promotion.

Mansfield, P. R., J. Lexchin, L. S. Wen, L. Grandori, C. P. McCoy, J. R. Hoffman, J. Ramos, and J. N. Jureidini. 2006. Educating Health Professionals about Drug and Device Promotion: Advocates' Recommendations. *PLoS Medicine* 3(11):e451.

Medicines and Healthcare Products Regulatory Agency [UK]. 2005. *The Blue Guide: Advertising and Promotion of Medicines in the UK.* 2nd ed. London: Stationery Office. <http://www.mhra.gov.uk/home/idcplg?IdcService=GET_FILE&dDocName=CON007552&RevisionSelectionMethod=LatestReleased>

Mintzes, B. 1998. *Blurring the Boundaries: New Trends in Drug Promotion.* Amsterdam: HAI-Europe. <http://haiweb.org/pubs/blurring/blurring.intro.html>

Moghimi, Y. 2006. The "PharmFree" Campaign: Educating Medical Students about Industry Influence. *PLoS Medicine* 3(1):e30.

Norris, P., A Herxheimer, J. Lexchin, P. Mansfield. 2005. *Drug Promotion: What We Know, What We Have Yet to Learn.* Geneva: World Health Organization/Health Action International. <http://whqlibdoc.who.int/hq/2005/WHO_EDM_PAR_2004.3_eng.pdf>

★ WHO (World Health Organization). 2002. *Essential Drugs Monitor* 31. Geneva: WHO. <http://apps.who.int/medicinedocs/pdf/s4937e/s4937e.pdf> Issue on drug promotion. Contains reports of studies on drug advertising, educating medical students about drug promotion, and a database on drug promotion.

★ WHO/HAI (World Health Organization/Health Action International). 2010. *Understanding and Responding to Pharmaceutical Promotion: A Practical Guide.* Amsterdam: HAI. <http://www.haiweb.org/10112010/DPM_ENG_Final_SEP10.pdf>

Annex 34-1   Information sources

Medical and therapeutic journals

Annals of Internal Medicine
http://www.annals.org

BMJ
http://bmj.bmjjournals.com

Journal of the American Medical Association
http://jama.ama-assn.org

Lancet
http://www.thelancet.com

New England Journal of Medicine
http://content.nejm.org

PLoS Medicine
http://www.plosmedicine.org

Drugs and toxicology information and pharmacology journals

British Journal of Clinical Pharmacology
http://www.blackwellpublishing.com/journal.asp?ref=0306-5251&site=1

Clinical Toxicology
http://informahealthcare.com/loi/ctx

European Journal of Clinical Pharmacology
http://www.springer.com/biomed/pharmaceutical+science/journal/228?changeHeader

Human and Experimental Toxicology
http://het.sagepub.com

International Journal of Clinical Pharmacology and Therapeutics
http://www.clinpharmacol.com

Pharmacy journals

American Journal of Health-System Pharmacy
http://www.ajhp.org

Annals of Pharmacotherapy
http://www.theannals.com

Journal of Clinical Pharmacy and Therapeutics
http://www.wiley.com/bw/journal.asp?ref=0269-4727

Pharmaceutical Journal UK
http://www.pjonline.com

Essential medicines lists, therapeutic formularies, and standard treatment guidelines

British National Formulary
http://www.bnf.org/bnf

Medicines Policy Documents from Selected African Countries, World Health Organization, 2005
http://collections.infocollections.org/whocountry/en

WHO Model Formulary 2008
http://apps.who.int/medicinedocs/en/m/abstract/Js16879e

WHO Model List of Essential Medicines: The Use and Selection of Drugs, 16th list (updated), March 2010
http://www.who.int/medicines/publications/essentialmedicines/en

Drug information newsletters

Australian Prescriber
http://www.australianprescriber.com

BTA (Boletín Terapéutico Andaluz) (Spanish)
http://www.easp.es/web/cadime/cadime_bta.asp?idCab=303&idSub=378&idSec=303

Butlletí Groc (Catalan)
http://www.icf.uab.es/ca/productes/bg/butlletigroc.html

Drug and Therapeutics Bulletin
http://dtb.bmj.com

FNT (Fichas de Novedad Terapéutica) (Spanish)
http://www.easp.es/web/cadime/cadime_fnt.asp?idCab=303&idSub=378&idSec=303

Medical Letter on Drugs and Therapeutics
http://www.medletter.com

La revue Prescrire/Prescrire International (French/English)
http://www.prescrire.org

Therapeutics Letter
http://www.ti.ubc.ca/TherapeuticsLetter

WHO Drug Information
http://www.who.int/medicines/publications/druginformation/en/index.html

WHO Pharmaceuticals Newsletter
http://www.who.int/medicines/publications/newsletter/en/index.html

Worst Pills, Best Pills
http://www.worstpills.org

Miscellaneous resources

Agency for Healthcare Research and Quality (US)
http://www.ahrq.gov

Cochrane Library
http://www.thecochranelibrary.com

electronic Medicines Compendium (UK)
http://emc.medicines.org.uk

International Network for the Rational Use of Drugs
  Tools and Resources
  http://www.inrud.org/Resources.cfm
  Bibliographies
  http://www.inrud.org/Bibliographies/index.cfm

U.S. Centers for Disease Control and Prevention
http://cdc.gov

U.S. Food and Drug Administration
http://www.fda.gov

U.S. National Institutes for Health
http://nih.gov

WHO Essential Medicines Teaching Resources
http://www.who.int/medicines/training/en

WHO Medicines Publications and Documentation
http://www.who.int/medicines/publications/en
http://apps.who.int/medicinedocs/en

CHAPTER 35

Pharmacovigilance

Summary   35.2

35.1 **What is pharmacovigilance and why is it important?**   35.2
Adverse drug reactions • Medication errors • Adverse drug events

35.2 **Designing a pharmacovigilance system**   35.6
Pharmacovigilance activities at the facility level • Pharmacovigilance activities at the national level • Pharmacovigilance activities as part of public health programs • Pharmacovigilance activities at the international level

35.3 **Data collection**   35.10
Passive data collection • Mandatory data collection • Active data collection • Data collection tools

35.4 **Data analysis and reporting**   35.11

35.5 **Taking actions for improvement**   35.15

References and further readings   35.16

Assessment guide   35.18

SUMMARY

Poor product quality, adverse drug reactions (ADRs), and medication errors greatly influence health care systems by negatively affecting patient care and increasing costs. Most of the statistics documenting the issues and highlighting the importance of pharmacovigilance come from developed countries, therefore low- and middle-income countries likely have greater problems because of the poorer state of their health system infrastructure, the unreliable supply and quality of medicines, the lack of adequately trained essential health care staff, and their limited access to communication and information technology.

Three areas of pharmacovigilance include—

- Product quality
- Adverse drug reactions
- Medication errors

Product quality problem reporting systems are covered in Chapter 19 on quality assurance. This chapter focuses on the importance of ADRs and medication errors and actions to take to minimize their impact. An ADR is a harmful response caused by the medicine after the patient has received it in the recommended manner; whereas, adverse drug events (ADEs) result from either the medicine itself or the medicine's inappropriate use or medication error.

Health professionals may still think of pharmacovigilance strictly in terms of identifying and reporting previously unknown and serious ADRs related to new products; however, pharmacovigilance activities are related to every sector of the pharmaceutical management framework: selection, procurement, distribution, use, management support, and the overarching policy and legal framework. Likewise, pharmacovigilance activities are carried out at the facility, national, and international levels and require collaboration among a wide range of partners with differing responsibilities. National governments are responsible for ensuring that medicines sold in their countries are of good quality, safe, and effective. An important component of a country's ability to monitor pharmaceutical safety is a national pharmacovigilance system that is supported by the drug regulatory authority. However, some countries have not included pharmacovigilance as part of their legal framework. Public health programs, such as those for treating HIV/AIDS and malaria, may have separate pharmacovigilance systems, while hospitals usually have the capacity to design and implement facility-based medication safety activities.

The major components of a pharmacovigilance system are data collection, which can be passive, active, or mandatory, and data analysis and reporting. When ADEs occur, they must be analyzed and reported and their significance must be communicated effectively to an audience that has the knowledge to interpret the information, including the national pharmacovigilance center, if one exists, and the World Health Organization (WHO) Programme for International Drug Monitoring. Based on the results of the analysis, actions should be carried out to reduce adverse drug events and thereby improve patient care. To encourage continued participation in the process, interventions should be shared with the data reporters. Follow-up data collection and analysis can then measure the effectiveness of the interventions.

The use of medicines involves a trade-off between benefits and the potential for harm. Pharmacovigilance can help minimize harm by ensuring that medicines of good quality are used rationally.

35.1   What is pharmacovigilance and why is it important?

WHO defines pharmacovigilance as "the science and activities relating to the detection, assessment, understanding and prevention of adverse effects or any other medicine-related problem" (WHO 2004, 1). Terms related to the science of pharmacovigilance are defined differently in different settings and by different organizations. The terms used in this chapter are defined in Table 35-1.

More and more evidence is showing the huge effect of poor product quality, ADRs, and medication errors on health care, but estimating the actual scale of this effect is almost impossible because most cases go undetected. Much of the documented evidence available on medicine quality and ADEs comes from industrialized countries. For example, in a bellwether report, the U.S. Institute of Medicine (IOM 2000) estimated that 7,000 or more people die each year from medication errors and ADRs and that the total costs may be between 17 billion U.S. dollars (USD) and USD 29 billion per year in hospitals nationwide. A follow-up report estimated that more than 1.5 million Americans are injured every year by medication errors in hospitals, nursing homes, and doctor's offices (IOM 2006). ADEs also are costly in terms of loss of trust in the health care system by patients.

Table 35-1   Definitions of terms related to pharmacovigilance

Terms	Definition	Example
Harm occurred		
Adverse drug event	Harm caused by the use of a drug	Heart arrhythmia from discontinuing atenolol (whether or not it was considered an error)
Adverse drug reaction	Harm caused by the use of a drug at normal doses	Skin rash from nevirapine
Harm may have occurred		
Medication error	Preventable event that may cause inappropriate use of a drug or patient harm	Failure to renew prednisone order on transfer to medical ward
Harm did not occur		
Potential adverse drug event	Circumstances that *could* result in harm by the use of a drug but did *not* harm the patient	Receipt of another patient's ampicillin, with no resulting effect

Source: Adapted from Nebeker, Barach, and Samore 2004.

Compared with that in high-income countries, the situation in low-and middle-income countries is likely more urgent because of the poorer state of health system infrastructure, the unreliable supply and quality of medicines, and the lack of adequately trained essential health care staff.

Three areas of pharmacovigilance include—

- Product quality
- Adverse drug reactions
- Medication errors

Quality issues relate to pharmaceutical products that are defective, deteriorated, or adulterated because of poor manufacturing practices, inadequate distribution and storage, poor labeling, or tampering. Counterfeit products would fall under this category, for example, as would medicines that have lost their potency after being stored at high temperatures. These quality assurance issues, including product problem reporting systems, are covered in detail in Chapter 19. In addition, pharmaceutical donations have

sometimes expired or are close to expiration or have been stored under conditions that adversely affect their quality. See Chapter 15 for more information about ensuring the quality of medicine donations.

This chapter focuses on the importance of ADRs and medication errors and actions to take to minimize them.

Adverse drug reactions

An ADR is a harmful response in the patient caused by the drug itself given in the recommended manner (dose, frequency, route, administration technique). Examples include allergic reactions, effects from withdrawal, or reactions caused by interactions with other medications. WHO defines a serious ADR as any reaction that is fatal, life-threatening, or permanently or significantly disabling; requires or prolongs hospitalization; or relates to misuse or dependence (WHO/UMC 2000).

When a new medicine is being developed, it goes through several phases of testing, first with animals, then with human

Table 35-2   Determining ADR probability using indicators

Probability scale: indicators	Yes	No	Don't know
1. Are there previous conclusive reports on this ADR?	+1	0	0
2. Did the ADR appear after the suspected drug was administered?	+2	−1	0
3. Did the ADR improve when the drug was discontinued or a specific antidote was administered?	+1	0	0
4. Did the ADR reappear when the drug was readministered?	+2	−1	0
5. Could alternative causes (other than the drug) have caused the ADR on their own?	−1	+2	0
6. Was the drug detected in the blood (or other fluids) in a concentration known to be toxic?	+1	0	0
7. Was the ADR more severe when the dose was increased or less severe when the dose was decreased?	+1	0	0
8. Did the patient have a similar ADR to the same or similar drugs in any previous exposure?	+1	0	0
9. Did any objective evidence confirm the ADR?	+1	0	0
Total score = _____ Possible = 0–4 Probable = 5–8 Definite = >9			

Source: Naranjo et al. 1981.

Figure 35-1   Analysis of medication errors in a U.S. hospital, 2005

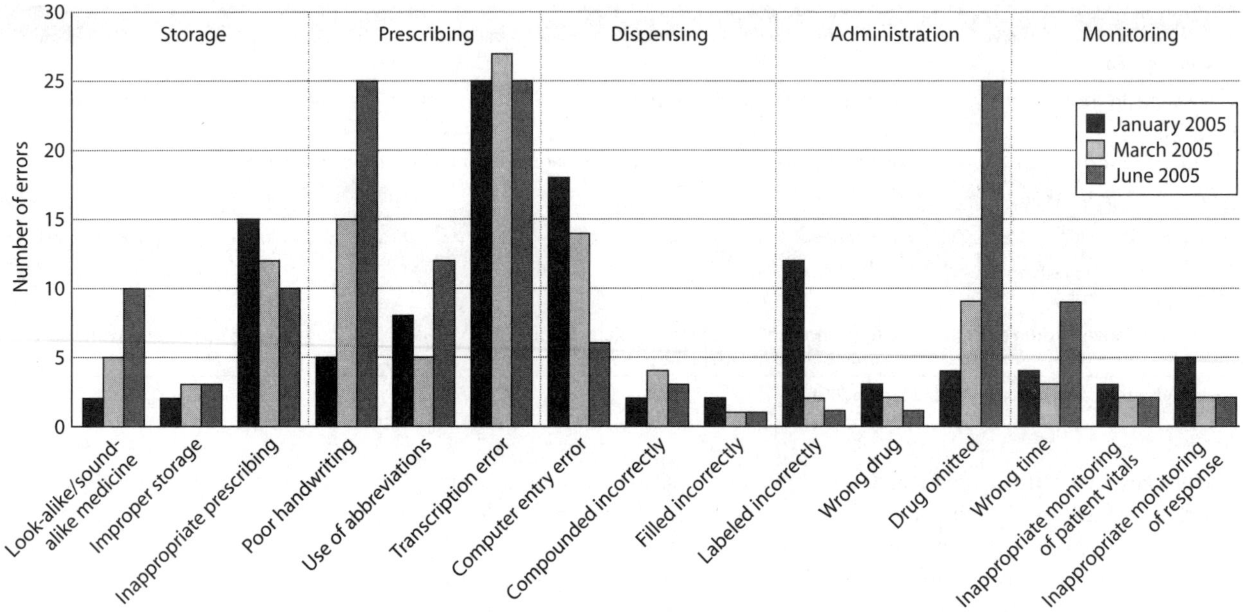

Source: Chris Olson, unpublished data.

volunteers, for safety and efficacy. However, when a product is approved, it may have been tested in only thousands of patients—many fewer than are likely to use the product once it is approved for sale on the market. Therefore, the information on effects generated in premarketing studies is incomplete relative to the full complement of likely users, making postmarketing surveillance an important tool for completing the safety and efficacy profile of a drug product (Ahmad 2003).

Because it includes so many more people than are included in the premarketing surveillance process, postmarketing surveillance should be able to detect rare but serious adverse reactions; chronic toxicity; effects in sensitive groups, such as children, pregnant women, and the elderly; and interactions with other pharmaceuticals, herbal medicines, or food. Often, however, linking an ADR with a specific medicine is difficult; for example, an ADR can occur long after a medication is administered, which makes confirming the cause a challenge. See Table 35-2 for ways to analyze probable causality.

Medication errors

The National Coordinating Council for Medication Error Reporting and Prevention defines medication error as "any preventable event that may cause or lead to inappropriate medication use or patient harm while the medication is in the control of the health care professional, patient, or consumer" (http://www.nccmerp.org/aboutMedErrors.html). Errors can be harmless or detrimental to the patient. A study

> **Box 35-1**
> **Medication error caused by sound-alike products**
>
> Nurses and pharmacists at a hospital reported two cases where RECOMBIVAX HB (hepatitis B vaccine, recombinant) was given to newborns instead of Comvax (hemophilus B conjugate vaccine with hepatitis B vaccine). When a telephone order was misunderstood, the wrong product was administered to the patients. Nurses in the unit felt this same error had probably occurred other times without anyone noticing. A safe medication practice to prevent sound-alike product name errors is to transcribe and read back verbal orders. Face-to-face verbal orders should be accepted only in emergencies or when the prescriber is physically unable to write the order.
>
> Source: ISMP 2003.

of thirty-six health care facilities in the United States showed that nearly one in five doses of medication was given in error, and 7 percent had the potential to cause patient harm (Barker et al. 2002).

Medication errors are caused by faulty systems, processes, and conditions that lead people to make mistakes or fail to prevent mistakes (Figure 35-1). For example, stocking wards in hospitals with certain concentrated solutions, even

Table 35-3   Dangerous abbreviations

Abbreviation	Intended meaning	Common error	Preferred term
U	Units	Mistaken as a 0 (zero) or a 4 (four), resulting in overdose. Also mistaken for cc (cubic centimeters) when poorly written.	Write *unit*.
µg	Micrograms	Mistaken for mg (milligrams), resulting in a one-thousand-fold overdose.	Write *mcg*.
Q.D.	Latin abbreviation for every day	The period after the Q has sometimes been mistaken for an I, and the drug has been given QID (four times daily) rather than daily.	Write *daily*.
Q.O.D.	Latin abbreviation for every other day	Misinterpreted as QD (daily) or QID (four times daily). If the O is poorly written, it looks like a period or an I.	Write *every other day*.
SC or SQ	Subcutaneous	Mistaken as SL (sublingual) when poorly written.	Write *subcutaneous* or *subcut*.
T I W	Three times a week	Misinterpreted as three times a day or twice a week.	Write specific days for administration, for example, MON., WED., and FRI.
D/C	Discharge; also discontinue	Patient's medications have been prematurely discontinued when D/C (intended to mean discharge) was misinterpreted as discontinue, because it was followed by a list of drugs.	Write *discharge* or *discontinue*.
HS	Half strength	Misinterpreted as the Latin abbreviation HS (hour of sleep).	Write *half strength*.
cc	Cubic centimeters	Mistaken as U (units) when poorly written.	Write *ml* or *mL* or *mls* for milliliters.
AU, AS, AD	Latin abbreviation for both ears; left ear; right ear	Misinterpreted as the Latin abbreviation OU (both eyes); OS (left eye); OD (right eye).	Write *ear*.
Lack of a leading zero (.X mg) or Use of a trailing zero (X.0 mg)		Decimal point is missed, resulting in a dosage error of tenfold or greater.	Always lead with a zero before a decimal point (0.X mg). Never follow a whole number with a decimal point and zero (X mg).
@	at	Mistaken as zero.	Write *at*.
MS, MSO4 MgSO4	Morphine sulfate, magnesium sulfate	Confused for each other.	Write *morphine sulfate* or *magnesium sulfate*.
IU	International Unit	Mistaken as IV (intravenous) or 10 (ten).	Write *international unit*.

Source: http://www.nccmerp.org/dangerousAbbrev.html.

though they are toxic unless diluted, has resulted in deadly errors. Other problems can result from illegible handwriting, use of dangerous abbreviations (Table 35-3), overlooked interactions with other medicines, and verbal miscommunications and sound-alike or look-alike products. Box 35-1 describes a case where the wrong medicine was administered to babies because of a misunderstood verbal order.

Medication errors, by definition, should be preventable through education and effective systems controls involving pharmacists, prescribers, nurses, administrators, regulators, and patients.

Adverse drug events

An ADE is a harmful response that is caused by a drug or the inappropriate use of a drug. Therefore, an ADR is always an ADE, but an ADE might include the result of an overdose because of a dispensing error or some other error occurring during the medication-use process. (See Figure 35-2.)

Medication-usage patterns strongly influence the incidence of ADEs. For example, injectable medications are more commonly used in developing countries, and they are more likely to be associated with ADEs (WHO/UMC 2002). In addition, self-medication, lack of regulatory control over the sale of medicines, and irrational prescribing all contribute to the incidence of ADEs.

ADEs are preventable when they are the result of a medication error (discussed below) or nonpreventable, as would be the result of an unknown allergy. A potential ADE could include an error that may or may not reach the patient but does not cause harm, such as a dispensing error that was discovered and avoided at the last minute. The documentation

Figure 35-2   Relationship of medication safety terms

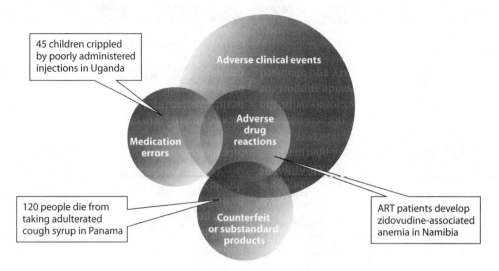

45 children crippled by poorly administered injections in Uganda

Adverse clinical events

Adverse drug reactions

Medication errors

120 people die from taking adulterated cough syrup in Panama

Counterfeit or substandard products

ART patients develop zidovudine-associated anemia in Namibia

Sources: SPS 2009, figure 1, adapted from Barker et al. 2002; Ferner and Aronson 2006; Nebeker, Barach, and Samore 2004.

of ADEs and ADRs is important—especially in new products—where such postmarketing information can result in changes to the recommended usage, product packaging or labeling, or even a recall. Identifying and documenting potential ADEs is useful because this can identify problem areas that might be corrected, such as a communication problem within the health facility or two medicines with similar names being stored next to and therefore confused with each other.

35.2 Designing a pharmacovigilance system

Health professionals may still think of pharmacovigilance strictly in terms of identifying and reporting previously unknown and serious ADEs related to new products; however, pharmacovigilance activities are related to every sector of the pharmaceutical management cycle. Figure 35-3 shows examples of the relationship between pharmacovigilance and pharmaceutical management.

Although many national pharmacovigilance programs are largely based on ADE reporting, a comprehensive system should encompass monitoring of medication errors and therapeutic ineffectiveness (related to poor treatment adherence, antimicrobial resistance, product quality problems, inappropriate use, or interactions); product quality problems; and communication of such information to health care professionals and consumers for risk-benefit decision making (SPS 2009). For example, as a pharmacovigilance system matures, it may expand from a program based strictly on passive ADE surveillance that relies on voluntary reports from health care providers or consumers to incorporate active surveillance methods to address

priority safety concerns, such as the use of registries, sentinel sites, and follow-up of defined patient cohorts. Other system expansion efforts can include establishing a link between pharmaceutical quality assurance and ADR monitoring and developing mechanisms to communicate medicine safety information to health care professionals and the public.

A country's pharmacovigilance system should incorporate activities and resources at the facility, national, and international levels and foster collaboration among a wide range of partners and organizations that contribute to ensuring medicine safety. Figure 35-4 illustrates the components of a comprehensive, ongoing pharmacovigilance system with functions for monitoring, detecting, reporting, evaluating, and documenting medicine safety data as well as intervening and gathering information from and providing educational feedback to the reporters—prescribers, health care workers, other health care professionals, and consumers. When the information has been collected, evaluators, such as epidemiologists or pharmacologists, should analyze it to determine the adverse event's severity, probable causality, and preventability.

Significant data must be communicated effectively to a structure or entity that has the authority to take appropriate action, whether at the facility, national, or even international level. The entity may be a hospital's drug and therapeutics committee, the national pharmacovigilance center, if one exists, or the WHO Programme for International Drug Monitoring. The final function in the framework is appropriate action. If data are collected, analyzed, and reported, but no one takes any action based on the data, the system is irrelevant. The risk reduction action may be regulatory (withdrawing marketing authorization, recalling a medica-

Figure 35-3 Pharmacovigilance and the pharmaceutical management framework

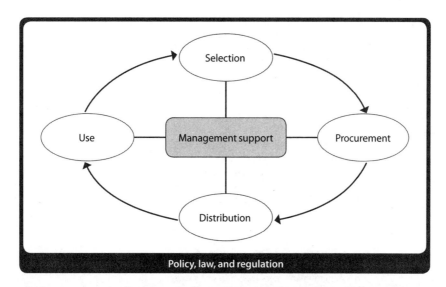

Pharmacovigilance activity	Detection within the pharmaceutical management framework	Prevention
Product quality	• Most product quality issues are detected in the *distribution* portion of the pharmaceutical management cycle. • Physical inspection is done at the time of receiving the product from the supplier and at other points of *distribution* to the patient. • Complaints about efficacy occur during *use*.	• Prequalify suppliers during *procurement*. • Establish a pharmaceutical quality assurance program. • Establish a *policy and legal framework* that addresses pharmaceutical quality. • Enforce laws and regulations related to product quality.
ADRs	• *Management support* functions, such as surveillance and monitoring systems, during *use* are the primary methods for detecting ADRs.	• Consider ADR information during the *selection* process to make formulary decisions and establish standard treatment guidelines. • Report ADRs to the appropriate parties at the facility, national, and international levels. • Train health professionals about ADRs. • Communicate with patients about ADRs.
Medication errors	• Errors can be detected in all phases of the pharmaceutical management cycle: ordering, storing, labeling, compounding, dispensing, transcribing, prescribing, administering, and monitoring.	Prevention strategies should focus on all processes— • Promote a culture of safety through a nonpunitive environment for reporting events. • Improve availability of drug information. • Train and educate staff. • Consider past and potential errors when selecting products or a formulary. • Issue prescribing guidelines. • Establish dispensing and administration procedures and safeguards. • Establish monitoring guidelines. • Improve written and oral communication. • Involve patient and family in care plan.

Source: CPM/MSH 2011.

tion); managerial (revising a hospital formulary, instituting distribution controls); or educational (teaching prescribers about medicine-medicine interactions or proper product handling). To encourage continued participation in the process, interventions should be shared with the data reporters as part of a feedback loop. Follow-up data collection and analysis will then measure the effectiveness of the interventions.

The outcome of a pharmacovigilance system should be decreased medicine-related problems with the ultimate effect being a reduction in morbidity and mortality.

As mentioned, pharmacovigilance activities are carried out at the facility, national, and international levels and require collaboration among a wide range of partners with differing responsibilities (Table 35-4). To plan for this information system, basic questions must be answered about

Figure 35-4   The pharmacovigilance framework

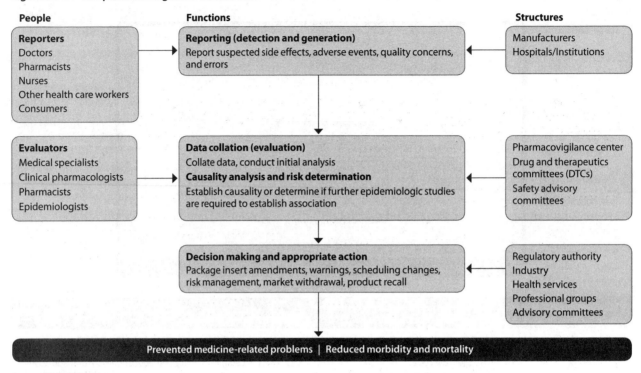

Source: CPM/MSH 2011.

whether the data flow will be separate for each area of pharmacovigilance or combined, who will be responsible for the data collection and reporting at each level of the health system, and whether vertical public health programs will be separated or integrated. For example, will the responsibility for pharmacovigilance fall under the drug and therapeutics committee (or pharmacy and therapeutics committee) at the facility level? How will pharmacovigilance drive decisions for formulary selection and treatment guidelines, changes in policies and procedures at different levels, and product approval and pharmaceutical regulation? These questions may be easier to answer if the country has a national pharmacovigilance system in place—or individual facilities developing their own systems may need to create the best information management system based on their own organization.

Pharmacovigilance activities at the facility level

Medication safety monitoring is an important part of high-quality health care in health facilities, especially hospitals. A U.S.-based study showed that ADEs in hospitalized patients resulted in significant health and economic consequences (Classen et al. 1997). Monitoring and reporting of medication errors and ADRs are important aspects of a hospital's safety system; consequently, most evidence of ADEs comes from hospitals, because the risks associated with hospital care are high and strategies for improvement are better documented. But many ADEs occur in other health care settings, such as physicians' offices, nursing homes, pharmacies, and patients' homes. However, underreporting of ADEs is a critical problem in all health care settings.

Even if a country lacks the infrastructure for coordinating national pharmacovigilance activities, hospitals usually have the capacity to design and implement a facility-based pharmacovigilance system. Effective systems for pharmacovigilance and promoting safe medication practices generally fall under the purview of the drug and therapeutics committee.

Hospital-based reports of ADRs make important contributions to clinical experience and improving the understanding of pharmacotherapy. In addition, the assessment of ADEs gives facilities the information necessary to reduce medication errors and improve health care for patients.

Pharmacovigilance activities at the national level

National governments are responsible for ensuring that medicines sold in their countries are of good quality, safe, and effective. An important component of a country's ability to monitor pharmaceutical safety is a national pharmacovigilance system that is supported by the drug regulatory authority (see Chapters 6 and 19).

Table 35-4   Roles and responsibilities of partners in pharmacovigilance

Partner	Responsibilities
Government	• Establish national pharmacovigilance system • Develop regulations for medicine monitoring • Provide up-to-date information on adverse reactions to professionals and consumers • Monitor effect of pharmacovigilance through indicators and outcomes
Industry	• Provide quality medicines of assured safety and efficacy • Assess and share ADRs that are reported
Hospitals	• Promote the incorporation of pharmacovigilance into procedures and clinical practice
Academia	• Teach, train, conduct research, and develop policy about pharmacovigilance • Include pharmacovigilance in curriculum
Medical and pharmaceutical professional associations	• Provide training and awareness to health professionals regarding pharmacovigilance
Poisons and medicines information centers	• Provide information on medication safety and pharmacovigilance • Collaborate with national pharmacovigilance centers, if applicable
Health professionals (including physicians, nurses, pharmacists, dentists)	• Detect, investigate, manage, and report ADRs, medication errors, and product quality concerns • Counsel patients about ADRs
Patients and consumers	• Understand to the extent possible their own health problems and participate in the treatment plan by following medication instructions • Report adverse reactions to health professionals as well as concomitant use of other medications, including traditional medicine
Media	• Create awareness in the community about the safe use of medicines

National pharmacovigilance centers are responsible for—

- Promoting the reporting of ADEs
- Collecting case reports of ADEs
- Clinically evaluating case reports
- Collating, analyzing, and evaluating patterns of ADEs
- Promoting policies and interventions that help prevent medication errors
- Determining what case reports constitute true adverse reactions to medications
- Recommending or taking regulatory action in response to findings supported by good evidence
- Initiating studies to investigate significant suspect reactions
- Alerting prescribers, manufacturers, and the public to new risks of adverse events
- Sharing their reports with the WHO Programme for International Drug Monitoring (WHO/UMC 2006)

A national pharmacovigilance system can be housed in a national pharmacovigilance center or in a tertiary or research-oriented hospital. In the traditional model, a pharmacovigilance system was strongly centralized and consisted of one national center collecting reports from health professionals around the country. Many countries are moving toward a more decentralized system with a national center functioning as a focal point for regional or facility-based centers (WHO/UMC 2000).

Pharmacovigilance activities as part of public health programs

Depending on how their public health systems are organized, countries may have public health initiatives that are disease-specific and operate separately from the primary health system (for example, HIV/AIDS, tuberculosis, malaria, vaccinations), also known as vertical health programs. Such vertical programs depend on good pharmacovigilance practices (WHO/UMC 2006). Monitoring ADRs is especially important when treatment is being scaled up, such as antiretroviral therapy (ART) for HIV/AIDS, or if a change is being made in the standard treatment guidelines, such as switching to artemisinin-based combination therapies for malaria.

The major aims of pharmacovigilance in public health initiatives are the same as those of the national pharmacovigilance system. The structure and organization of the existing national systems will help determine how the public health program pharmacovigilance efforts should be designed. In some cases, the country may not have a national pharmacovigilance system. In that case, the public health program's system takes on additional importance and may provide a model for the eventual establishment of a national system. In Kenya, as ART programs scaled up and developed facility-based ADR monitoring systems, the Ministry of Health recognized the importance of national-level coordination and added pharmacovigilance to its responsibilities—a good example of a bottom-up approach to incorporating pharmacovigilance into the health care system.

WHO has a good resource on using pharmacovigilance as a tool in public health treatment programs (WHO/UMC 2006).

Pharmacovigilance activities at the international level

The patterns of how people access and use pharmaceuticals are changing because of globalization, free trade, and increased use of the Internet (WHO 2004). These changing patterns require that pharmacovigilance activities around the world become more closely linked and therefore better able to respond to how medicines are being used in society.

At the international level, WHO initiated its Programme for International Drug Monitoring in 1968 to pool existing data on ADRs from ten countries. With its Uppsala Monitoring Centre, the WHO program now works with national pharmacovigilance programs in almost 100 countries (UMC 2010). The Uppsala Centre maintains the database of ADR reports—one of the largest in the world with more than 5 million case reports. The Uppsala Centre established standardized reporting by all national centers and facilitates communication between countries on medicine safety issues.

The Institute for Safe Medication Practices (http://www.ismp.org) has established a forum for individual health care providers and consumers in any country to confidentially share information on ADEs. Although the system was established for U.S.-based reporting, the institute welcomes reports from anywhere in the world. Health care professionals and consumers can submit reports and associated materials in confidence. After removing the identifiers, the information is shared with the U.S. Food and Drug Administration, the manufacturer, and others to inform them about pharmaceutical labeling, packaging, and nomenclature issues that may promote errors by their design.

Major components of a pharmacovigilance system are data collection, which can be voluntary or nonvoluntary, and data analysis and reporting.

35.3 Data collection

Passive data collection

Passive reporting of ADRs and medication errors (also known as voluntary case reporting) requires health care providers to be active participants in a culture of safety. Programs relying solely on voluntary, spontaneous reporting methods reveal only the tip of the iceberg, and calculated medication event rates are more an indication of reporting rates than actual occurrence rates. However, voluntary reporting should always be encouraged, because it helps

establish a team approach to improving patient care and reducing risks.

Barriers to voluntary reporting of medication events are—

- Fear of punishment by supervisors or fellow workers (in the case of an error)
- Fear of liability for the provider or facility
- Failure to recognize that an incident has occurred
- Unclear or cumbersome methods for reporting
- Poor track record of improvements by the institution
- Lack of time

The objective of a successful monitoring system is to learn from and correct sources of error rather than to punish offenders. In addition to driving out fear, facilities should try to improve error tracking through education programs that promote voluntary reporting and by communication to staff about the improvements resulting from medication events reported.

Mandatory data collection

Many country regulations require manufacturers and distributors of pharmaceuticals to report information on ADRs that they gather during postmarketing surveillance to health authorities. In addition, facilities seeking accreditation may be required to have an ADE collection system in place as part of the process to receive official recognition. Some countries require health care professionals to report ADEs, but the effectiveness of such legislation is unknown (WHO/UMC 2000).

Active data collection

Active data collection of medication events is carried out as a focused and structured activity and includes trigger tools, patient chart audits, and direct observation methods. Using a consistent methodology for active data collection provides more reliable calculated medication event occurrence rates and evidence of trends.

Trigger tools provide clues that an ADR occurred. Triggers are identified from either computerized reports or manual review methods to identify alerting orders, laboratory values, or clinical conditions. Further research into these triggers may help identify ADRs that have occurred or that are currently evolving—

Laboratory triggers are identified from defined parameters indicating an ADR might be associated (serum glucose under 50, white blood cell count below 3,000, platelets below 50,000, toxic drug levels, and the like).
Medication order triggers are prescription orders for antidotes or reversal agents such as dextrose 50 percent 50-mL injection, glucose tablets, diphenhydramine,

steroids, naloxone, epinephrine, or sudden change or stoppage of a patient's medication ("discontinue digoxin, quinidine, potassium chloride").

Clinical triggers are patient conditions often associated with ADRs, such as rash, falls, lethargy, or apnea.

Trigger detection methods yield more data than voluntary reports (Jha et al. 1998), and more sophisticated methods combine composite triggers (such as laboratory tests and medication orders) for better yields (Schiff et al. 2003).

Whereas trigger tools can help identify the patients and medications most likely implicated in an event, *chart review* is used to identify potential ADRs, medicine interactions, and medication errors. These reviews can be conducted prospectively, concurrently, or retrospectively. Retrospective reviews are often more convenient for data collection, although the time lapse since the event makes in-depth investigation difficult. Medical records classified by codes, such as ICD-10 (International Classification of Diseases, Tenth Revision) codes that indicate an ADR, provide a method to identify suspicious charts.

A prospective study might focus on recording any possible adverse event in every patient receiving a new medicine. For instance, the Ghana National Centre for Pharmacovigilance developed a simple form for facilities to document and report ADRs in pregnant women associated with a change in recommended treatment from chloroquine to sulfadoxine-pyrimethamine to prevent malaria (Dodoo 2005). Combined with their demographic information, the information collected on this cohort of patients can provide an effective way of identifying previously unrecognized ADRs (WHO/UMC 2000). Prospective and concurrent reviews can also detect potential adverse events before they happen or as they are evolving, so that patient harm can be avoided or minimized.

Direct observation provides an abundance of useful data on medication errors and helps to identify weaknesses in the medication-use process. Observers can be placed at any point in the medication-use process, but medication administration is often one of the most problematic areas and easiest to observe. If the data collection method is consistent, the resulting error rates are reliable and allow improvements to be measured. An example follows of the steps that could comprise data collection using direct observation of the medication administration process—

1. The observer follows randomly selected nurses as they administer medications to patients on a hospital ward. The observer collects data for a specified number of medications using preprinted forms. Figure 35-5 shows an example of an observation audit tool.
2. The observer verifies each medication on the original physician order in the patient chart, noting discrepan-

cies between the written order and the actual practice observed in terms of medication, dose, frequency, route, and so on.
3. The data are used to calculate error rates for a specific focus area, such as the ward or the facility. Rates or trends may help identify problematic procedures or areas for additional training.

A study comparing three methods for detecting errors—direct observation, chart review, or voluntary adverse event reporting—showed that direct observation was far more efficient and accurate in detecting medication errors (Flynn et al. 2002). Direct observation can also be used as a training and orientation tool for new employees by ensuring that new employees have a minimal level of competency and understand the facility's medication administration process.

Data collection tools

ADR and medication error data are usually collected by filling out a standardized form, thereby providing convenience and consistency. Data collection tools should be adapted from standards of practice and procedures, and the data fields on the form determined by how the data are eventually summarized and used. Ideally, if a country has a national pharmacovigilance program, the reporting form is standardized for use in all settings throughout the country.

For ADR data, identifying specifics about the patient is important. These include concomitant therapies and conditions, the patient's reaction to the medicine, and the medicine suspected of causing the reaction together with the manufacturer and batch number, if available. WHO gives guidance on what to include on a data collection form (WHO 2002) (see also Box 6-2 on adverse drug reaction monitoring in Chapter 6).

For medication error data, collecting information that can be analyzed for improvements to the medication-use system is important. Systems may have separate forms for tracking product quality problems, ADRs, and medication errors, or systems may use one form and process. Figure 35-6 shows a sample ADE reporting form that also combines reporting for product quality problems in Zambia.

35.4 Data analysis and reporting

After the ADR data have been collected, they should be analyzed to determine severity, probable causality, and preventability. Specific algorithms and classification systems have been developed for these analyses—

Severity (impact on the patient's health): Table 35-5 shows a classification for determining the severity of ADRs. It addresses both ADEs associated with medication error

Figure 35-5 Nonvoluntary data collection tool for pharmacovigilance

Medication Administration Audit Tool

Date: Unit: Name of Evaluator:

Checklist for medication administration	Patient #1		Patient #2		Comments
	Met	Not met	Met	Not met	
1. Washes hands before start of medication administration process, before and after each patient contact, and before preparing injectable medications.					
2. Performs and charts necessary pre-administration assessments for specific medicines (pulse, blood pressure, nausea, etc.).					
3. Notes allergies and compares to medicines to be administered.					
4. Correctly identifies patient. Compares name and/or ID# on MAR with patient ID band. Cannot use room number for identification.					
5. Correct medication (removes medications and verifies correct medication with the MAR).					
6. Correct dosage (including accurate measurement of liquids).					
7. Correct route of administration.					
8. Correct time of administration (administers within 1 hour before or after time ordered; considers relationship to meals and/or food; waits appropriate time between ophthalmic medicines, inhaled doses, etc.).					
9. Explains purpose of each medication; answers questions about the medication.					
10. Stays with patient until each medication has been safely swallowed.					
11. Properly administers medications (preps IV port, appropriate IV compatibility, administers over correct time interval).					
12. After medication administration, initials time of administration for each medication and signs appropriate document.					
13. Correct disposal of pharmaceutical waste; disposes of narcotics and dangerous drugs with applicable documentation.					
14. Maintains the security of the medications at all times (locked medicine cabinet or locked medication room door).					

Source: Feinberg 2001.

MAR = medication administration record.

Figure 35-6   Sample ADE/product quality problem form from Zambia

---

Zambia Pharmacovigilance Centre (ZPVC) in Lusaka
ADR Case Report Form
For adverse drug event and product quality problem reporting

In collaboration with the WHO International Drug Monitoring Programme

All information provided here will be treated as strictly confidential.

CLIENT INFORMATION

Name (or initials):		Age:	Weight (kg):
Sex: M F LMNP / / (if female) DOB: / /			Height (cm):

ADVERSE EVENT/PRODUCT QUALITY PROBLEM

Adverse event (Form Part 1)	And/or product quality problem (Form Part 2)	Date of onset of reaction: / /
		Time of onset of reaction: _____ h _____min

Description of reaction or problem (Include relevant tests/lab data, including dates):

1. MEDICINES/VACCINES/DEVICES (Include all medicines taken concomitantly.)

Trade Name and Batch No. (Asterisk Suspected Product)	Daily Dosage	Route	Date Started	Date Stopped	Reasons for Use

ADVERSE REACTION OUTCOME (Check all that apply.)

☐ Death	☐ Life-threatening event	Event reappeared on rechallenge:	Recovered: Y N
☐ Disability	☐ Hospitalization	Y N Rechallenge not done	Sequelae: Y N
☐ Congenital anomaly	☐ Other:	Treatment (of reaction):	Describe sequelae:
☐ Required intervention to prevent permanent impairment/damage			

COMMENTS: (e.g., relevant history, allergies, previous exposure, baseline test results, laboratory data)

2. PRODUCT QUALITY PROBLEM

Trade Name	Batch No.	Dosage Form and Strength	Expiry Date	Size/Type of Container

Product available for evaluation?   Y   N

REPORTING DOCTOR/PHARMACIST:

Name	Address
Telephone no.	
Qualifications	

Signature	Date

This report does not constitute an admission that medical personnel or the product caused or contributed to the event.

Source: Zambia Pharmacovigilance Centre, Lusaka, Zambia.
DOB = date of birth; LMNP = last menstrual period.

Table 35-5   Severity index for medication errors

Category	Description
Category A	Circumstances or events that have the capacity to cause error (note that these are *potential, not actual,* errors).
Category B	An error occurred but the error did not reach the patient (an "error of omission" *does* reach the patient).
Category C	An error occurred that reached the patient but did not cause patient harm.
Category D	An error occurred that reached the patient and required monitoring to confirm that it resulted in no harm to the patient or required intervention to preclude harm.
Category E	An event occurred that may have contributed to or resulted in temporary harm to the patient and required intervention.
Category F	An event occurred that may have contributed to or resulted in temporary harm to the patient and required initial or prolonged hospitalization.
Category G	An event occurred that may have contributed to or resulted in permanent patient harm.
Category H	An event occurred that required intervention necessary to sustain life.
Category I	An event occurred that may have contributed to or resulted in the patient's death.

Source: NCC MERP n.d.

and those not associated with error, so it can be applied to all medication events.

Probable causality (likelihood that the medicine's use or lack of use contributed to the ADR): Table 35-2 illustrates how to calculate the Naranjo Probability Score, a common method for determining whether a particular medicine was actually related to the ADR.

Preventability (Was an error associated with the event?): Box 35-2 is an algorithm used to help determine if the ADE was caused by a medication prescribing error, and therefore, preventable.

For ADEs that are considered preventable, identifying where the primary error occurred and what aspects contributed to the system breakdown is useful; therefore, analysis and reporting should facilitate this activity by identifying and targeting problem-prone areas, such as specific steps in the process (prescribing practices), medication types (injectables), disease states or patient types, employees (new employees, interns), patient care areas (surgery), and time of the day (night shift). For example, if data indicate that ADEs are caused by nurses giving the wrong dose of injectable medications, then focused activities for improvement should be developed. These activities might include educational activities and procedural changes, such as independent double-checks of all injectable medications. After implementing the interventions, the error rate can be checked for improvement.

Medication event data are organized on manual or electronic spreadsheets, which help summarize and sort data for reporting at the facility or regional level. National and international programs often use Internet-based ADR or medication error databases to collect and share data. (See References and Further Readings.)

ADRs should be reported to the national ADR program, if one exists, as well as to the pharmaceutical manufac-

> **Box 35-2**
> **Determining whether a medication error occurred**
>
> - Was the drug involved appropriate for the patient's clinical condition? (NO = Preventable)
> - Was the dose, route, or frequency of administration appropriate for the patient's age, weight, or disease state? (NO = Preventable)
> - Was required therapeutic pharmaceutical monitoring or other necessary laboratory tests performed? (NO = Preventable)
> - Was there a history of allergy or previous events to the drug? (YES = Preventable)
> - Was an interaction (medicine–medicine; medicine–food; medicine–herbal) involved in the ADR? (YES = Preventable)
> - Was a toxic serum drug concentration (or laboratory monitoring test) documented? (YES = Preventable)
> - Was poor compliance involved in the ADR? (YES = Preventable)
> - Was the error considered preventable because of deviations in procedures or standards of practice? (Yes = Preventable)
>
> Source: Adapted from Schumock and Thornton 1992.

turer; the latter is especially important if the ADR has not been reported previously in the literature or is not included on the product's label. Reporting the results of ADR and medical error analysis to the organizational body within a hospital or facility that has responsibility for medicine safety, such as the drug and therapeutics committee, is also important.

Country Study 35-1 shows how a research hospital in India established an ADR reporting system.

35.5 Taking actions for improvement

When ADEs occur, they must be analyzed and reported, and their significance should be communicated effectively to an audience that has the knowledge to interpret the information. National or even international actions that can result from the appropriate reporting of ADEs include—

- Pharmaceutical manufacturers sending out "Dear Doctor" letters to alert health care providers of newly discovered adverse reactions
- Pharmaceutical manufacturers revising medicine package inserts that reflect the new information
- Pharmaceutical manufacturers or national regulatory authorities instigating a medicine recall

At the clinical level, actions concerning serious or recurring ADEs include—

- Changing the medication formulary if necessary
- Implementing new prescribing procedures
- Implementing new dispensing procedures
- Modifying patient-monitoring procedures
- Educating professional staff (face-to-face; in-service education; bulletins; reports of collected ADRs)
- Educating patients

Most important at the clinical level, however, is taking action to improve medication safety and decrease medication events by developing a culture of safety in the health care organization (see Box 35-3). For example, the organization's leadership should maintain a clear commitment to safety by emphasizing that safety takes priority over production or efficiency; employee job descriptions and performance evaluations should include a component for participation in safety initiatives that are supported by recourses, rewards, and incentives; and the response to a problem should focus on improving system performance.

Country Study 35-2 illustrates the standard operating procedures and possible actions for addressing recurring ADRs in an ART program in Kenya. In a report on preventing medication errors, the Institute of Medicine (IOM 2006) urged that doctors, nurses, pharmacists, and other health care providers communicate more with patients about the risks, contraindications, and possible adverse reactions from medications and what to do if they experience an ADE. In addition, patients should be encouraged to take a more active role in their own medical care and should be given plenty of time to consult with health care providers about their medications (see also WHO's patient safety initiative, http://www.who.int/patientsafety/en).

In summary, the use of medicines involves a trade-off between benefits and potential for harm. Pharmacovigilance can help minimize the harm by ensuring that medicines of good quality are used rationally and that the expectations and concerns of the patient are taken into account when

Country Study 35-1
Implementing an ADR reporting system in India

ADR monitoring and reporting systems are uncommon at the local level in developing countries. Although India has a national ADR monitoring center in New Delhi, Kasturba Hospital, a 1,400-bed, tertiary care teaching hospital in Manipal had never had an ADR program before 2001. It established an ADR monitoring center not only to improve medication safety practices in the district, but also to provide a link between the region and the national center. The Kasturba Hospital program was launched and is maintained by the pharmacy department using established ADR-reporting centers in India as models.

The Kasturba Hospital system relies on physicians and pharmacists working together. When a physician detects an ADR, he or she fills out the reporting form and sends it to the pharmacy department, where a pharmacist follows up on the ward with an investigation of the incident.

Pharmacists may also report ADRs on their own. When the documentation is complete, the pharmacist analyzes the causality, preventability, and severity of the ADRs using various scales, then issues the results quarterly. Physicians who report ADRs may be given information on how to manage the reaction, and if it involves an allergy, the pharmacist counsels the patient and provides an alert card for the patient to give his or her health care provider. In the first year of the program, 142 ADRs were reported, including several rarely seen reactions, among them cisplatin-induced hiccups. As a result of the new program, the Kasturba Hospital staff saw an increase in the awareness of the importance of ADR monitoring and reporting and improved interactions between the physicians and the pharmacists.

Source: Mohan, Rao, and Rao 2003.

Box 35-3
Safe medication practices

- Encourage staff to report ADRs, errors, and unsafe conditions.
- Change the safety culture from punitive to participatory.
- Standardize abbreviations, and develop a list of dangerous abbreviations, acronyms, and symbols to avoid.
- Write or print clearly.
- Review medication orders for appropriateness before dispensing and administration.
- Clarify medication orders that are not clear or do not make sense for the patient's clinical condition.
- Provide health care providers with access to drug information.
- Read back and receive confirmation on all verbal and telephone orders.
- Identify look-alike and sound-alike products and take action to avoid mix-ups (for example, physically separate storage, clearly differentiate appearance, purchase alternatives, use generic versus brand name or vice versa to differentiate from sound-alike product).
- Label all medications in a standardized manner according to hospital policy.
- Dispense medications labeled for a specific patient and in the most ready-to-administer dosage form.
- Follow the five "rights" of drug administration: right patient, right drug, right time, right dose, and right route.
- Verify patient identification against labels and orders prior to medication administration.
- Develop a list of problem-prone or high-risk medications and implement strategies to minimize the risk.
- Standardize or limit the number of drug concentrations available in the organization.
- Remove high-risk medications from patient care areas (for example, concentrated electrolytes).
- Involve patients in their care: tell them the name of the medicine and its purpose before administration.

health care providers are making decisions about therapy. WHO (2004) lists the best ways to achieve these goals—

- Serving public health and fostering a sense of trust among patients in the medicines they use that also extends to confidence in the health service in general
- Ensuring that risks in medicine use are anticipated and managed
- Providing regulators with the necessary information to amend the recommendations on the use of medicines
- Improving communication between the health professionals and the public
- Educating health professionals to understand the effectiveness and risk of medicines that they prescribe. ∎

References and further readings

★ = Key readings.

Ahmad, S. R. 2003. Adverse Drug Event Monitoring at the Food and Drug Administration. *Journal of General Internal Medicine* 18(1):57–60.

AHRQ (Agency for Healthcare Research and Quality). 2001. *Making Health Care Safer: A Critical Analysis of Patient Safety Practices.* Rockville, Md.: AHRQ. <http://archive.ahrq.gov/clinic/ptsafety/>

ASHP (American Society of Health-System Pharmacists). 1993. ASHP Guidelines on Preventing Medication Errors in Hospitals. *American Journal of Hospital Pharmacists* 50:305–14.

Barker, K. N, E. A. Flynn, G. A. Pepper, D. W. Bates, and R. L. Mikeal. 2002. Medication Errors Observed in 36 Health Care Facilities. *Archives of Internal Medicine* 162:1897–903.

Bates, D. W., D. J. Cullen, N. Laird, L. A. Petersen, S. D. Small, D. Servi, G. Laffel, et al. 1995. Incidence of Adverse Drug Events and Potential Adverse Drug Events: Implications for Prevention. *JAMA* 274(1):29–34.

Classen, D. C., S. L. Pestotnik, R. S. Evans, J. F. Lloyd, and J. P. Burke. 1997. Adverse Drug Events in Hospitalized Patients: Excess Length of Stay, Extra Costs, and Attributable Mortality. *JAMA* 277(4):301–6.

CPM/MSH (Center for Pharmaceutical Management/Management Sciences for Health). 2011. *Center for Pharmaceutical Management: Technical Frameworks, Approaches, and Results.* Arlington, Va.: CPM.

Dodoo, A. 2005. Safety Challenges of Preventing Malaria During Pregnancy. *WHO Drug Information* 19(4):286–7.

Feinberg, J. L. 2001. *Med Pass Survey: A Continuous Quality Improvement Approach.* 2nd ed. Alexandria, Va.: American Society of Consultant Pharmacists.

Ferner, R. E., and J. K. Aronson. 2006. Clarification of Terminology in Medication Errors—Definitions and Classification. *Drug Safety* 29(11):1011–22.

Flynn, E. A., K. N. Barker, G. A. Pepper, D. W. Bates, and R. L. Mikeal. 2002. Comparison of Methods for Detecting Medication Errors in 36 Hospitals and Skilled-Nursing Facilities. *American Journal of Health-System Pharmacy* 59(5):436–46.

ICTDR (International Centers for Tropical Disease Research Network). 2003. *ICTDR Investigator Manual: Monitoring and Reporting Adverse Events.* Bethesda, Md.: U.S. National Institutes of Health. <http://www.icssc.org/Documents/Resources/ICTDR_AE_Manual_February_6_2003_final.pdf>

IOM (Institute of Medicine of the National Academies). 2000. *To Err Is Human: Building a Safer Health System,* L. T. Kohn, J. M. Corrigan,

Country Study 35-2
Standard operating procedures for aggregating ADR data and taking appropriate action in an ART program in Kenya

The Coast Provincial General Hospital in Mombasa, Kenya, was one of the first public facilities in the country to offer ART to AIDS patients. Hospital administrators and program managers realized the importance of monitoring and reviewing ADRs related to the use of these new, powerful antiretroviral medicines to ensure optimal treatment outcomes and patient safety. The ART program staff designed and implemented standard operating procedures for ADR monitoring for all staff involved with the ART program.

All ART patients' ADRs are reported on an ADR form. The forms are reviewed, compiled, examined for trends, and reported, and appropriate actions are taken in response to the ADR report. Actions can be taken at the individual patient level or, in the case of a noted trend, at the system level. A summary of the procedures for aggregating the individual ADR data follows.

Pharmacist in charge of the ART program—

1. Reviews the *ART ADR Forms* and *ART ADR Reports* and prepares the *ADR Summary Report* at the end of each month
2. Looks for unusual trends
3. Reviews the *Actions Taken* section of the reports submitted to ensure that appropriate actions have been taken as decided by the ART Eligibility Committee based on the outline in the following table
4. Presents the *ADR Summary Report* to the ART Eligibility Committee at the first meeting of each month
5. Reports on unusual trends
6. Reports on inappropriate actions taken

The ART Eligibility Committee—

1. Reviews the *ADR Summary Report* and, if necessary, the raw data
2. Decides to take appropriate actions in response to *ADR Summary Reports* or unusual trends or inappropriate actions taken (possible actions are outlined in the following table)
3. Forwards the *ADR Summary Reports* and presents the findings to the Scientific Committee

The Scientific Committee reviews the *ADR Summary Report* and decides on appropriate action to be taken.

Suggested trends and actions for the data fields appearing on the *ADR Summary Report* and the *ART ADR Form* appear in the following table. This table is not all inclusive; it merely provides a starting point for the ART Eligibility Committee, Scientific Committee, and Steering Committee to use when evaluating the *ART ADR Reports*.

ADR actions on an aggregate level

Trends	Possible actions
An increase in suspected or probable ADRs associated with a specific age group, gender, pregnancy status, drug class, or particular medicine	• Notify the Scientific Committee. • Medicine may be used cautiously in particular groups with extra patient monitoring (lab or clinic visits) required. • Medicine may not be given to particular groups. • Medicine may be removed from treatment plan. • ADR may be reported to the Pharmacy and Poisons Board by the Steering Committee on the recommendation of the Scientific Committee. Pharmacy and Poisons Board may inform the manufacturer. • ART Eligibility Committee or Scientific Committee will investigate possible causes of this increase and take appropriate corrective or preventive actions.
Serious ADRs associated with ADR probability category definite or probable • not listed in the product labeling or • occurring in medicines less than five years since first approved by the Pharmacy and Poisons Board	• Notify the Scientific Committee. • Medicine may be used cautiously with extra patient monitoring (lab or clinic visits) required. • Medicine may be removed from treatment plan. • ADR may be reported to the Pharmacy and Poisons Board by the Steering Committee on the recommendation of the Scientific Committee. Pharmacy and Poisons Board may inform the manufacturer.
Appropriate actions not being taken in response to suspected ADRs as decided by the ART Eligibility Committee	• Organize a training session. • Discuss with individual prescribers.

Source: Standard Operating Procedures for ART Pharmacy, Coast Provincial General Hospital, Mombasa, Kenya.

ASSESSMENT GUIDE

National activities

- Does the country address pharmacovigilance as part of its pharmaceutical legislation?
- Do any national policies and practices exist that are related to pharmacovigilance?
- Who is responsible for overseeing national pharmacovigilance activities?
- Does a national pharmacovigilance center exist? If so, where is it housed?
- Does the national pharmacovigilance program have a relationship with WHO's Programme for International Drug Monitoring?
- Does a national ADR monitoring and reporting system exist? If so, how many reports were submitted during the previous year? What is done with the reports?
- Is a system in place to report product quality problems? In the previous year, how many reports were submitted on medicine product problems?
- Are reports of medical errors collected and analyzed at the national level?
- Are the three areas—ADRs, product quality problems, and medication errors—combined in one reporting stream or separate streams?
- How is important information about ADRs communicated to health professionals? To the industry? To the media? To consumers?
- Is pharmacovigilance included in university curricula for health care professionals?

Public health program activities

- Do the country's public health programs (for example, HIV/AIDS, tuberculosis, malaria) have their own ADR reporting systems? If so, what is the reporting structure?
- Do the public health programs integrate their pharmacovigilance activities with national-level activities?

Facility activities

- Does the facility track information on ADRs in patients? Request an example of a recent report. Is reporting passive (voluntary) or active (nonvoluntary)?
- Does the facility track medication errors?
- What committee oversees the pharmacovigilance activities, and when did it last review a pharmacovigilance report?
- Does the facility have a culture of safety, that is, do employees feel comfortable reporting information on medication errors and ADRs? How many voluntary reports did the facility have in the last year?
- To whom are ADRs and medication errors reported? What is the mechanism?
- Does the organization have an internal mechanism to analyze and address problems with medication safety? Give examples of recent actions.

and M. S. Donaldson, eds. Washington, D.C.: National Academy Press. <http://www.nap.edu/books/0309068371/html/>

IOM Committee on Identifying and Preventing Medication Errors. 2006. *Preventing Medication Errors*, P. Aspden, J. A. Wolcott, J. L. Bootman, and L. R. Cronenwett, eds. Washington, D.C.: National Academy Press. <http://books.nap.edu/openbook.php?record_id=11623>

ISMP (Institute for Safe Medication Practices). 2003. Sound Alike Alert! *ISMP Medication Safety Alert* 8(6):3–4.

Jha, A. K., G. J. Kuperman, J. M. Teich, L. Leape, B. Shea, E. Rittenberg, E. Burdick, D. L. Seger, M. Vander Vliet, and D. W. Bates. 1998. Identifying Adverse Drug Events: Development of a Computer-Based Monitor and Comparison with Chart Review and Stimulated Voluntary Report. *Journal of the American Medical Informatics Association* 5(3):305–14.

Jha, N., O. Bajracharya, R. Shrestha, H. S. Thapa, and P. R. Shankar. 2009. Starting a Pharmacovigilance Program within a Teaching Hospital: Challenges and Experiences from Lalitpur, Nepal. *Southern Medical Review* 2(1):7–10

Mohan, N., P. G. Rao, and G. Rao. 2003. An Adverse Drug Reaction Reporting System at a Teaching Hospital in India. *American Journal of Health-System Pharmacy* 60:486–7.

Naranjo, C., U. Busto, E. M. Sellers, P. Sandor, I. Ruiz, E. A. Roberts,

E. Janecek, C. Domecq, and D. J. Greenblatt. 1981. A Method for Evaluating the Probability of Adverse Drug Reactions. *Clinical Pharmacology Therapeutics* 30(2):239–45.

NCC MERP (National Coordinating Council for Medication Error Reporting and Prevention). No date. NCC MERP Index for Categorizing Medication Errors. <http://www.nccmerp.org/pdf/indexBW2001-06-12.pdf>

Nebeker, J. R., P. Barach, and M. H. Samore. 2004. Clarifying Adverse Drug Events: A Clinician's Guide to Terminology, Documentation, and Reporting. *Annals of Internal Medicine* 140(10):795–801.

Pirmohamed, M., K. N. Atuah, A. N. O. Dodoo, and P. Winstanley. 2007. Pharmacovigilance in Developing Countries. *BMJ* 335(7618):462.

Schiff, G. D., D. Klass, J. Peterson, G. Shah, and D. W. Bates. 2003. Linking Laboratory and Pharmacy: Opportunities for Reducing Errors and Improving Care. *Archives of Internal Medicine* 163:893–900.

Schumock, G. T., and J. P. Thornton. 1992. Focusing on the Preventability of Adverse Drug Reactions. *Hospital Pharmacy* 27(6):538.

SPS (Strengthening Pharmaceutical Systems). 2009. *Supporting Pharmacovigilance in Developing Countries: The Systems Perspective.* Arlington, Va.: Management Sciences for Health. <http://www.msh.

org/projects/sps/SPS-Documents/upload/SPS_PV_Paper.pdf>

Uppsala Monitoring Centre (UMC). No date. *The Use of the WHO-UMC System for Standardised Case Causality Assessment.* Uppsala, Sweden: WHO. <http://who-umc.org/Graphics/24734.pdf >

———. 2010. *Report from the WHO Collaborating Centre for International Drug Monitoring: Activities July 2009–June 2010.* Uppsala, Sweden: WHO.

WHO (World Health Organization). 2009. *A Practical Handbook on the Pharmacovigilance of Antiretroviral Medicines.* Geneva: WHO. <http://apps.who.int/medicinedocs/documents/s16882e/s16882e.pdf>

———. 2007a. *Pharmacovigilance for Antiretrovirals in Resource-Poor Countries.* Geneva: WHO. <http://apps.who.int/medicinedocs/documents/s14234e/s14234e.pdf>

———. 2007b. *A Practical Handbook on the Pharmacovigilance of Antimalarial Medicines.* Geneva: WHO. <http://apps.who.int/

medicinedocs/documents/s16881e/s16881e.pdf>

———. 2004. Pharmacovigilance: Ensuring the Safe Use of Medicines. *WHO Policy Perspectives on Medicines* 9. Geneva: WHO.

★ ———. 2002. *Safety of Medicines: A Guide to Detecting and Reporting Adverse Drug Reactions.* Geneva: WHO.

★ WHO/UMC (World Health Organization/Uppsala Monitoring Centre). 2006. *The Safety of Medicines in Public Health Programmes: Pharmacovigilance an Essential Tool.* Geneva: WHO. <http://apps.who.int/medicinedocs/documents/s14085e/s14085e.pdf>

★ ———. 2002. *The Importance of Pharmacovigilance: Safety Monitoring of Medicinal Products.* Geneva: WHO. <http://whqlibdoc.who.int/hq/2002/a75646.pdf>

———. 2000. *Safety Monitoring of Medicinal Products: Guidelines for Setting up and Running a Pharmacovigilance Centre.* Uppsala, Sweden: WHO. <http://apps.who.int/medicinedocs/en/d/Jh2934e /#Jh2934e>

PART III

Management support systems

Planning and administration

36 Pharmaceutical supply systems assessment

37 Managing pharmaceutical programs

38 Planning for pharmaceutical management

39 Contracting for pharmaceuticals and services

40 Analyzing and controlling pharmaceutical expenditures

41 Financial planning and management

42 Planning and building storage facilities

Organization and management

43 Security management

44 Medical stores management

45 Hospital pharmacy management

46 Pharmaceutical management for health facilities

47 Laboratory services and medical supplies

Information management

48 Monitoring and evaluation

49 Pharmaceutical management information systems

50 Computers in pharmaceutical management

Human resources management

51 Human resources management and capacity development

52 Designing and implementing training programs

CHAPTER 36

Pharmaceutical supply systems assessment

SUMMARY

Pharmaceutical system assessments are useful to diagnose problems, plan major projects and interventions, monitor progress, and compare the performance of one system with that of another. Recent years have seen a growth in demand for such assessments because of the Global Fund to Fight AIDS, Tuberculosis and Malaria's policy to conduct procurement and supply management (PSM) assessments as a grant condition.

To produce useful results, all assessments should be structured. Two approaches may be useful—

- Comprehensive structured assessment, which generally involves a full-time, dedicated team using structured survey instruments to gather data through site visits, but may be done as a self-assessment exercise by managers
- Limited assessment, which uses interviews and document reviews

Four major categories of issues should be addressed in a comprehensive pharmaceutical sector assessment—

1. The functionality of the entire pharmaceutical system
2. The capacity of the private sector
3. "Political mapping" to understand the important actors and their attitudes and the feasibility of successfully implementing changes in the pharmaceutical system

4. Total operating costs of the existing pharmaceutical system and projected costs of potential alternative options

Special-purpose assessments, such as the Global Fund's PSM reviews, may be more limited in scope.

Specific information objectives should be set in advance, incorporating quantitative as well as qualitative data, performance indicators, and special-purpose analyses. The most important methods for collecting information are likely to be document review, key informant interviews, collection of data from existing records, and prospective observation.

Key issues in planning and managing the assessment are listed in this chapter, but readers should obtain one or more of the manuals mentioned throughout the chapter and in References and Further Readings for full details on organizing and conducting an assessment. When the data are in hand, they must be analyzed efficiently, and a user-friendly report should be produced, supplemented by presentations using graphic aids to help key decision makers absorb the findings. The assessment results must be used in developing new policies and procedures for the pharmaceutical system; otherwise, the process is a waste of resources.

36.1 Reasons for assessing pharmaceutical systems

High-level commitment to pharmaceutical sector improvements can be stimulated by discontent among health staff and the public about medicine shortages, concern in the ministry of finance about rising pharmaceutical expenditures, or publicity about poor pharmaceutical quality. Too often, however, the pressure resulting from this commitment leads to hasty assessments and inadequately developed plans for change. Sustainable improvements in the pharmaceutical sector depend on high-level national commitment to improvement, technically sound plans based on an accurate situation assessment, and the technical and financial resources to implement proposed changes.

This chapter proposes comprehensive structured assessments for accurately diagnosing problems in the pharmaceutical supply system, identifying their root causes, prioritizing the problems, analyzing options to determine feasible interventions, developing short- and long-term action plans, and providing indicators for monitoring progress. When a comprehensive structured assessment is carried out with full government commitment by an appropriate expert team (local or international), it enables the government to formulate a sound strategy for improving access, rational medicine use, and medicine quality. Figure 36-1 illustrates an options analysis framework.

A comprehensive assessment can be an invaluable input to the development of a national medicine policy (Chapter 4) or a strategic plan for pharmaceutical sector development (Chapter 38). It also provides government officials with a basis for coordinating donor involvement (see Chapter 14). Assessments may be required as a condition precedent for grants or other types of donor support, such as the PSM assessments that the Global Fund requires. The assessments discussed in this chapter do not take the place of an ongoing monitoring program (Chapter 48) or a management information system that tracks and reports on performance (Chapter 49). When good management information systems and monitoring programs are in place, the need for special-purpose assessment decreases, as does the effort and expense required to carry out an assessment when one is indicated.

Figure 36-1   Options analysis framework

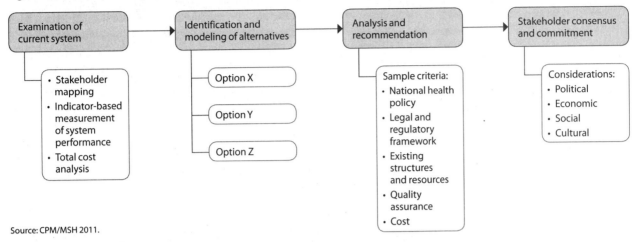

Source: CPM/MSH 2011.

Proposals for pharmaceutical sector assessments sometimes meet with resistance. Decision makers may believe that action is needed instead of another study. Managers may think they already know the nature and causes of problems. Government officials responsible for donor coordination may be weary from the seemingly innumerable visits from representatives of donors and technical assistance organizations who ask the same questions but leave little behind. And some donors may prefer action to research.

In such situations, the general nature of the problems may be evident, but the true causes are often not so clearly known, and the full range of solutions that could produce sustainable improvements has not been considered. An assessment is needed—but an assessment of a different nature from those previously experienced.

Accurate systematic assessment is a prerequisite for planning changes in the pharmaceutical sector and, in particular, in the pharmaceutical supply system. Pharmaceutical sector assessments can serve any of four main purposes—

- Diagnosing emergent problems in the system and analyzing options
- Planning a project or formulating a pharmaceutical policy
- Monitoring change in the pharmaceutical system
- Comparing the performance of the supply system with that of other systems

Diagnosing emergent problems and analyzing options

Accurate diagnosis and action are urgently needed when major problems exist: medicines are out of stock in the rural health facilities, patients and politicians are complaining, and money is short. The assessment in such cases must be done quickly, but it still needs to yield a thorough understanding of where the various subcomponents in the pharmaceutical system are functioning and where they are not, what factors are involved, and what sorts of interventions might be feasible and effective to address the problems. Country Study 36-1 shows how a rapid assessment approach was applied to help countries under pressure to scale up HIV/AIDS services analyze their pharmaceutical management situations and options.

Planning pharmaceutical management projects and formulating policies

Systematic assessments should be done before all major pharmaceutical management projects and certainly as part of the process of developing a national medicine policy (or making any significant legal or policy changes related to pharmaceuticals). In addition, the Global Fund requires grantees to develop PSM plans as a condition for funding. When a project is being planned, the preproject assessment should define precisely the problems to be addressed, the interventions and expected outcomes, and the resource requirements in terms of capital, equipment, infrastructure improvements, recurrent expenditures, and technical assistance.

Monitoring changes

After an intervention is undertaken or a policy put into place, it should be assessed periodically to measure progress toward achieving objectives and to determine whether strategy changes are warranted. At the end of the project, another assessment should look at process and outcome to determine the extent of change in the system, whether the reforms appear to be sustainable, and whether additional inputs are needed.

Country Study 36-1
Assessing pharmaceutical and commodity management for VCT, PMTCT, and ART programs: Ethiopia, Namibia, and Rwanda

With the increased focus of governments and donors to effectively scale up HIV/AIDS-related programs at the national level, supply systems for voluntary counseling and testing (VCT), prevention of mother-to-child transmission (PMTCT) of HIV, and antiretroviral therapy (ART) programs must work effectively. Governments and donors need to identify specific intervention options that will promote better commodity management practices among the VCT, PMTCT, and ART programs they support.

The Rational Pharmaceutical Management (RPM) project of Management Sciences for Health developed a rapid assessment approach for pharmaceutical management systems that identifies areas of improvement and provides intervention options for government agencies and donors to guide the scale-up of HIV/AIDS programs. Two phases result in a set of findings and recommended options for strengthening pharmaceutical and commodity management of HIV/AIDS services.

Phase 1: Situational diagnosis

- A country team gathers background information and reviews country data, reports, and strategic program plans for VCT, PMTCT, and ART.
- In-country, the team identifies local stakeholders' contributions to the pharmaceutical sector and maps the flow of medicines and commodities specifically for HIV/AIDS services, from the international level to the user level.
- Interviews are conducted with a variety of stakeholders, including government policy makers, pharmaceutical experts, central procurement units, central medical stores, donors, national AIDS commissions, stakeholders in the laboratory sector, pharmaceutical manufacturers (if any), pharmaceutical regulatory and professional agencies, private-sector wholesalers or distributors, and staff at service delivery sites.

Phase 1 provides critical information on the national policy and legal framework for pharmaceuticals. The assessment team looks at the availability of standard national treatment guidelines related to HIV/AIDS, staffing policies, quality assurance, distribution systems, inventory management and control procedures, availability of essential products, national practices for rational medicine use, and monitoring and evaluation systems. This

phase culminates in the identification of key strengths and weaknesses of the overall pharmaceutical system, as well as potential areas for improvement related to HIV/AIDS services.

Phase 2: Options analysis

- Assessors use Phase 1 data to select study areas and indicators and to generate options analysis matrices.
- In collaboration with country counterparts and donors, the team chooses study sites.
- Data are collected in-country over a period of two to three weeks. Data collection addresses pharmaceutical management system weaknesses and improvement options related to staff capacity, infrastructure, product selection, procurement, distribution, medicine availability, storage conditions, inventory control and management practices, medicine use, and management information and reporting systems.
- After analysis and interpretation of findings, the team compiles a full report with all assessment findings and the feasibility of improvement options.
- Local stakeholders attend an options analysis workshop where results are presented, priorities are proposed, and options are selected. The options constitute the basis upon which RPM Plus prepares its developmental action plans for improving pharmaceutical management for VCT, PMTCT, and ART programs.

Ethiopia

Assessment findings

Warehousing and distribution systems for PMTCT products at the central level were lacking. Pharmaceutical and laboratory structures at the facility level were limited in terms of space, storage, and handling capacity, thereby compromising product security and safety and patient confidentiality.

Assessment response

- Evaluated different options for the distribution of PMTCT supplies and started negotiations with PHARMID (a parastatal import and distribution company) to serve as a warehousing and distribution agent to PMTCT delivery sites.
- Conducted engineering and infrastructural assessments in more than ten target facilities and designed a renovation plan to ensure minimum operational

conditions. In five sites, renovations have been initiated to expand space, improve shelving, and ensure safety and security of PMTCT products.
- Developed standard operating procedures for the management of PMTCT supplies and providing training to pharmacy staff.

Namibia

Assessment findings

Inadequate capacity and information hampered procurement planning and quantification. Inventory control systems in the supply chain were weak.

Assessment response

- Developed and implemented systems to strengthen the procurement, storage, inventory control, and distribution functions of the central and regional medical stores
- Facilitated the quantification of rapid HIV test kits and antiretroviral drugs

- Developed standard operating procedures for pharmaceutical management for VCT, PMTCT, and ART programs in Namibia

Rwanda

Assessment findings

A lack of capacity existed to quantify and coordinate national needs for PMTCT and ART services.

Assessment response

- Facilitated links between the ministry of health, the central medical stores of Rwanda (CAMERWA), and VCT/PMTCT facilities
- Helped CAMERWA establish systems to collect data that will make quantification for procurement more accurate
- Developed standard operating procedures for VCT/ PMTCT and ART sites to facilitate operation and scale-up

Source: MSH/RPM Plus 2004.

Comparing the performance of different systems

An assessment may be needed to compare the effectiveness of one pharmaceutical management system with that of others. For example, an assessment might address two vertical distribution systems (such as essential medicines and HIV/AIDS-related products in the ministry of health) to ascertain how well each is functioning and whether opportunities exist for integrating them. Or the goal might be to compare the strengths and weaknesses of the public and private pharmaceutical sectors to determine what potential exists for collaboration.

36.2 Structure of the assessment

Every pharmaceutical system assessment should have a formal structure; otherwise, any observations, conclusions, and recommendations are wholly subjective, and the opinion of one expert (or assessment team) may be radically different from that of another expert or team that has visited the same offices and talked to the same people. García-Núñez (1992, 49) stresses the need for structure in assessment and project evaluation: "A person who visits a project and conducts a casual assessment of project activities is not conducting an evaluation. He/she is merely making observations. Individual unsubstantiated assessments should not be used as tools for decision making. Evaluations have to be conducted according to specific guidelines and procedures. Without a recognized frame-

work from which to draw conclusions, evaluation results are not credible."

Country Study 36-2 gives an example of an assessment using unstructured methods that failed to produce the necessary results; many others can be drawn from recent history around the world.

The primary questions to be answered when structuring a pharmaceutical system assessment are—

- What issues should be addressed in the assessment?
- What potential information sources exist?
- What information should be collected?
- What methods will be used to collect the information?
- What sort of team will do the assessment?
- What is the time frame and cost for the assessment?
- How will the study be managed?
- How will the results be presented for use by decision makers?

To fit the structure of the assessment to a specific purpose, many different combinations of answers might be appropriate. In some cases, the structure is defined and standardized by the funding agency. The rest of the chapter explores options that can be considered.

Prerequisites for assessment

Assessment approaches range from self-assessment by health system managers to assessment by a team of local

**Country Study 36-2
Unstructured assessments**

In one African country, several teams of international experts were given the responsibility of assessing the status of the public pharmaceutical supply system and quantifying resource needs for a World Bank loan. All the teams were experienced in the pharmaceutical management field, but none of the teams used a structured assessment approach—each team leader was free to develop his or her own methodology. The team responsible for identifying needs for equipment and infrastructure forgot to consider cold-chain equipment. Thus, the budget allocated for cold-chain equipment in the eventual project was a pure guess. The team assigned to evaluate treatment patterns and develop algorithms for morbidity-based quantification developed a treatment manual that was useless for quantification. Another team was assigned to look at the potential for private-sector collaboration in the public system; the team prepared a nice report on the issues that might be assessed but did not actually do the assessment. When decisions had to be made concerning what type of logistics system would be supported, no data were available on private-sector capacity. This gap was still in evidence five years later, when the country and the World Bank were again trying to figure out a way to salvage a viable pharmaceutical system.

experts to assessment by a full-time team of local and external experts doing extensive site visits. The approach should be tailored to the scope of the assessment and the quantity of data and quality of analysis needed for decision support. Four prerequisites for success exist with any of the approaches discussed in this section—

- Government commitment to the process
- A qualified assessment team
- A clear definition of objectives and procedures
- An unbiased approach

Government commitment. For a systematic assessment to be successful in public-sector programs, government commitment and active involvement are essential. If the study team is denied access to essential data or if key informants are never available, producing useful results will be difficult. Even if a report is produced, the likelihood of fruitful follow-up is greatly reduced without active senior-level commitment to using the assessment results for making policy decisions and instituting strategies for improvement.

Top management support must be translated into allocating both human and financial resources by making sure that operations staff members cooperate with the assessment and that health system staff assigned to the assessment actually participate fully in the process. Project budgets should include funding for scheduled assessments or for particular projects, at least a baseline and endline assessment.

Qualified assessment team. The team doing the assessment must be familiar with the intricacies of pharmaceutical systems in general and the local pharmaceutical sector in particular. The team also must be familiar with national administrative structures, the national health system, and local development experience. The team principals must be motivated and qualified to collect and analyze data and present the results in an organized fashion. The team should receive training to ensure the accuracy and validity of data collection and analysis. Outside experts are not always essential, but they can supplement local expertise by offering experience in comparable countries, a broader view, and an independent perspective.

Clearly defined objectives and procedures. Various assessment approaches and methods are discussed here; all have their place, but no matter which combination of methods is used, the goals, procedures, data to be collected, scope of the study, participants, and time frame should be clearly defined before the assessment begins. Once established, the structure should be followed within the bounds of normal constraints.

The assessment should be tailored to fit the purpose. The assessment may be broad in scope, to design a major essential medicines project, or it might have a limited focus, such as determining how many vehicles are needed for pharmaceutical distribution in a single region. Even in the latter example, the assessment should be structured broadly enough so that all potential options are identified (including contracts with the private sector).

The team should have a plan on how to analyze the data collected and how the assessment results will be presented to decision makers as well as disseminated to other stakeholders.

Unbiased approach. The assessment should be undertaken without preconceived notions as to what the findings will or should be. When a total lack of bias is not possible, all parties to the study should clearly understand what preconceptions exist.

A biased assessment may not identify the real causes of problems or consider all options for solution. For example, if an assessment is begun with the premise that all pharmaceutical services in the health system must be provided by government, it will probably overlook or downplay the potential for private-sector and nongovernmental organization (NGO) participation.

Assessment approaches

The two most common approaches to pharmaceutical system assessment are comprehensive structured assessment and limited assessment.

Comprehensive structured assessment. A comprehensive structured assessment gathers information from all levels of the pharmaceutical system. A specific team is responsible for making field visits to offices, warehouses, and health facilities and gathering multiple types of information through document review, interviews, data collection from records, and prospective observation. Preprinted survey instruments are used to collect data, which helps ensure that a standard set of information is collected at each field site.

The survey instruments are structured questionnaires and data collection forms; they may be designed for a specific assessment or adapted from manuals (see for example, MSH/RPM 1995, WHO 2007). This type of assessment is often done as a rapid, intensive exercise by a full-time, dedicated team in cooperation with pharmaceutical system counterparts, but it can also be done as a self-assessment exercise by managers in the health system.

Limited assessment. Limited assessments rely primarily on interviews and document review, with limited field visits and little if any primary data collection from records or

---

Country Study 36-3
Developing and testing a procurement system assessment in India

In 2008, the Indian government recognized that agencies procuring health commodities for central and state health projects lacked consistent practice standards. To improve states' efficiency in procuring health commodities for public and World Bank projects, MSH's Center for Pharmaceutical Management (CPM) developed a tool incorporating international best-practice standards to serve as a basis for identifying strengths and weaknesses of procurement agencies or departments. CPM piloted the assessment tool at the Tamil Nadu Medical Services Corporation (TNMSC), which procures for both government- and World Bank–sponsored programs.

The specific assessment tool modules included the following—

- General requirements
  - Physical resources
  - Organization, structure, and functions
- Transparency
- Procurement cycle management
  - Bidding documents
  - Pre- and postqualification of suppliers
  - Advertisement and sale of bid document
  - Communication during the bidding process
  - Receipt of bids and bid opening
  - Bid evaluation
  - Contract award
  - Contract administration
- Support and control systems (audit)
- Record keeping
- Human resources and personnel
- General risk assessment
- Private-sector supplier assessment

The tool format included columns for standards, compliance rating (range of zero for noncompliant to three for fully compliant), assessor observations and comments, and instructions for the assessor.

Five important points were kept in mind when conducting the assessment—

1. The correct composition of the assessment team is critical.
2. Advance communication is necessary.
3. Assessment is an iterative process—not just the physical application of the tool.
4. Willingness of the agency to share the information and introduce improvement is a must.
5. The assessment tool must remain dynamic.

The TNMSC did not meet the minimum total combined score for each of the assessment modules that was required to immediately start national or international procurements. A thorough analysis revealed that the TNMSC had significant weaknesses pertaining to transparency, record keeping, information technology, and quality assurance, but at the same time, it exhibited many strengths, including the capability to follow World Bank guidelines for procuring nonpharmaceutical commodities. The assessment team debriefed TNMSC management and discussed the broader strengths and weaknesses. The TNMSC team stated its readiness to close gaps identified by the assessment and adhere to guidelines for World Bank procurements.

For more information on the assessment or to receive a copy of the tool, contact cpm@msh.org.

Source: Heltzer, Shrivastav, and Clark 2008.

prospective observation. The assessment may be done by a small dedicated team or by a working group from the pharmaceutical system. The assessment normally has a scope of work and should follow a predefined assessment plan; however, because the scope is constrained and time is not needed to prepare and validate survey instruments, a limited assessment can usually be completed more quickly and less expensively than a comprehensive structured assessment. Country Study 36-3 describes a limited assessment of the pharmaceutical procurement system in India.

In some cases, a limited assessment obtains a great deal of information; the constraint is that the information tends to be whatever is provided by the officials interviewed. When a structured survey instrument is not used, the quantity and type of data obtained may not be consistent from site to site, which may hamper efforts to compile a valid picture of the whole system. The self-assessment option requires less incremental funding, but the usefulness of the results will depend on the willingness of officials to document and report problems.

Time frame and assessment costs

The financial and human resources required for an assessment obviously depend primarily on the assessment approach. A locally managed self-assessment can be done in two or three months at low incremental cost, although a few thousand dollars (or the equivalent) would probably be needed to cover travel costs, meeting expenses, forms, and communication costs.

A typical limited assessment involves two to six person-weeks for site visits, plus another person-week or so to develop a report (Box 36-1 shows an example of an assessment timetable used in Rajasthan, India). Costs depend on how many experts are involved, but an average might be 25,000 U.S. dollars (USD) to USD 50,000 to cover all costs.

Time requirements and costs for a comprehensive structured assessment vary considerably, according to the number of levels in the pharmaceutical system and the size of the country. An experienced two-person team of experts might be able to manage a structured field-visit survey of public-sector pharmaceutical programs in a small country with three weeks on site, one week beforehand for preparation, and two to three weeks after for analysis and report writing. This schedule assumes that local officials and counterparts are active supporters and participants and that the health system has no more than three levels to be covered: central, provincial, and district. In the same country, one more experienced person plus a counterpart would be needed to cover the private sector in detail, and an additional person would be needed if the public-sector system had more levels.

Larger countries and more complex pharmaceutical systems require more effort for a thorough assessment; this effort can be managed by adding more team members or more field time for existing members, but in any case, costs will increase because of the logistics of sending data collectors to multiple districts across a large country. If the principal assessment team includes international experts, which costs more, the total cost of a comprehensive struc-

---

Box 36-1
Sample pharmaceutical assessment timetable

April 23 (Monday) a.m.	Assessment team arrives in Jaipur
April 23 p.m	Meet with local NGO partner to discuss selection of districts and sample size
April 24	Adapt data collection forms and develop tracer drug list
April 25–27	Train field investigators and adapt questionnaires
April 26	Pilot instruments and make final adaptation of questionnaires
April 27	Photocopy and translate final data collection forms into Hindi
April 28 a.m.	Distribute forms and final instructions; review timetable for data collection in each district
April 28 p.m.	Field investigators leave for field
April 29–30	Data collection starts
May 1–4	Quality control teams leave for field
May 4–14	Use data collection forms at Jaipur SMS Hospital (state hospital and tertiary referral center)
May 14–15	Data collection complete
May 15–18	Input data and analyze

Source: CPM 2003e.

tured assessment of all sectors of a pharmaceutical system in a medium-sized country may still cost up to USD 250,000. Costs can be reduced by contracting with local companies for elements such as data entry, although a large-scale assessment is still going to be an expensive exercise. Nevertheless, a project or development loan to be based on the assessment might be worth tens of millions of dollars, making the expense worthwhile.

If only government budgetary resources are available, mounting a comprehensive structured assessment with external consultants may not be practical. However, multilateral or bilateral agencies may be prepared to support the assessment (and possibly provide experts). For example, the U.S. Agency for International Development (USAID) recognized the need for a comprehensive pharmaceutical assessment and options analysis in Uganda to frame its activities for a new system-strengthening project. Even if no donors are prepared to provide financial support or experts, advice and information may be available from international agencies such as the World Health Organization (WHO) and the United Nations Children's Fund (UNICEF); however, people with expertise in the area need to be involved for the assessment to prove valuable.

36.3 Defining the scope of the assessment

The issues that should be addressed in an assessment depend on its purpose; the issues that can be realistically addressed depend on the availability of information, the capacities of the assessment team, and the time frame allowed to collect information (discussed in the previous section). Issues of importance to the pharmaceutical system fall into one of three general categories—

1. Functionality of the pharmaceutical system
2. Private-sector capacity, including faith-based and other NGOs
3. Political situation and attitudes of major players and interest groups in the pharmaceutical sector

Understanding and solving widespread problems in a pharmaceutical system require a broad assessment covering all three categories. If the assessment is looking at only one vertical program or one aspect of the system (for example, HIV/AIDS commodity management in mission hospitals, see Country Study 36-4), the scope will be narrower, but many of the issues discussed in this section still need to be considered, if on a smaller scale.

Functionality of the pharmaceutical system

A comprehensive pharmaceutical system assessment needs to look at several subcategories of functions. Historically,

assessments focused mainly on the public-sector system; however, an inclusive view of access to pharmaceuticals in a country should encompass a range of operations, such as manufacturing, wholesaling, retailing, and providing health care services in both the public and private sectors, and the relationship between the different sectors. The Strategies for Enhancing Access to Medicines (SEAM) Program conducted comprehensive pharmaceutical sector assessments in six countries that included the private sector (Country Study 36-5). The functions of a pharmaceutical system can be categorized in many ways; the following list is drawn mainly from the indicator manuals discussed in Section 36.4—

Policy, legislation, and regulation: Are policies, laws, and regulations consistent, comprehensive, and current? Are they enforced?

Budget and finance: What sources of funds are available? Are the funds adequate to purchase all necessary medicines and to manage the pharmaceutical system effectively? Are the funds that are available effectively managed?

Medicine selection: How are medicines selected for use in the system? Do consistent policies and procedures exist, or is the choice up to each purchaser and prescriber?

Pharmaceutical procurement: Does an effective procurement system exist that gets good prices and manages to purchase medicines in the quantities and time frame needed?

Pharmaceutical logistics and availability: Are medicines well managed at storage facilities and available at the points where they are needed? Are major losses caused by expiration or theft?

Geographic accessibility: Are the locations of pharmaceutical products and services close enough for the people who need them to get access?

Affordability: Can the health system afford to procure and distribute adequate supplies to provide access to target users? Are users able to pay for pharmaceutical products or services?

Medicine use: Do prescribers, dispensers, and patients use medicines rationally, or do major problems exist with irrational use?

Acceptability (or satisfaction): Do users find pharmaceutical products and services acceptable to them?

Product quality assurance: Are the products that are purchased and used in the supply system of good quality? Are quality assurance programs adequate to ensure good product quality?

System management: Are management procedures fully transparent with clear lines of accountability? (See Country Study 36-6.) Does each level of the system have adequate quantities of well-trained managers and operations-level staff? Are modern human resources

---

Country Study 36-4
Information targets for an assessment in Tanzania

The following list is an excerpt of information targets set for a structured field-visit assessment of five missionary hospitals in Tanzania in 2006; the goal of the assessment was to collect information on existing needs and gaps in HIV/AIDS commodity management to develop a plan of action for strengthening pharmaceutical management systems for HIV/AIDS commodities in the mission sector. The complete set of information targets (and the structured survey instruments used to collect the data) can be obtained from MSH's RPM Plus Program.

- *Policies and guidelines for HIV/AIDS services delivery:* availability and implementation of guidelines for prevention of mother-to-child transmission, voluntary counseling and testing, and clinical management of HIV and AIDS; health sector strategy for HIV/AIDS; national policy on HIV/AIDS
- *Capacity and training of human resources:* numbers of staff from different cadres dispensing antiretrovirals (ARVs); number of staff trained in antiretroviral therapy commodity management; frequency of supportive supervision visits
- *Infrastructure supporting HIV/AIDS commodity management:* functionality of equipment (for example, refrigerator, dispensing trays, computers); availability of communications equipment (for example, telephone, fax machine, e-mail, Internet); number of burglar-proofed doors and windows; number of lockable cabinets; availability of cold room
- *Standard operating procedures (SOPs) that support HIV/AIDS commodity management:* availability and implementation of specific SOPs, such as requesting and ordering ARVs, medication use counseling for

ART, stock count discrepancy report for ARVs, disposal of ARVs
- *Supply procedures that support HIV/AIDS commodity management:* criteria used for medicine selection; pharmaceutical ordering process; data elements used to quantify needs; storage procedures for ARVs; procedures to manage medicine donations
- *Management information systems:* availability and use of records, such as ART Chart to Track the Expiry of ARV Drugs, Adverse Drug Reaction Form, Patient Log Book/Register; use of automated report systems (for example, computers, fax sheets, e-mail)
- *ART prescribing and dispensing practices:* number of reference books available in the pharmacy; adverse drug reaction monitoring and reporting system in place and functional for ARVs; mechanisms used to monitor ART adherence; adequate materials for labeling and packaging available
- *Monitoring and evaluation:* system in place for monitoring and evaluation at the pharmacy; list of indicators routinely tracked; percentage of ARVs whose physical count exactly match the records in the bin cards; current stock available and number of days that ARV medicines by type were out of stock during the last quarter
- *Commodity financing supporting HIV/AIDS services:* total budget of the hospital; percentage of budget spent on pharmaceuticals (current and previous three years); patient fees for any health service and how much

Source: Rutta, McCollum, and Mwakisu 2006.

---

management and training programs in place? Are salaries adequate to promote good performance?

Total operating costs: Do managers have information on the total costs associated with purchasing and inventory management needed to consider options for change in terms of their impact on total costs? (See Chapter 40.)

Monitoring and management information: Are effective monitoring programs in place at each level of the system? Does an effective management information system allow managers to track supplies and funds throughout the pharmaceutical system?

Assessment guides at the end of each chapter of this book contain suggestions about the information needed to answer these types of questions and, more important,

to understand why problems exist and what can be done about them.

When defining the scope of a particular assessment, one must determine what information will likely be available in that pharmaceutical system from government documents, records, and reports; from interviews with system managers and staff; and from officials in related government offices and ministries. If the assessment is to address the private sector in a meaningful way, a method is needed to obtain information about the current state of the private pharmaceutical sector—the current types and levels of service provided to clients in various parts of the country, the capacity for providing services to the public sector, the attitude toward public-private collaboration, and the constraints that would need to be resolved to establish a working

Country Study 36-5
Applying access indicators to the pharmaceutical sector in six countries

WHO and MSH organized a joint consultative meeting to identify an operational definition of access and propose testable indicators to measure it. Workshop participants developed a framework comprising seventeen key indicators to represent the four dimensions of access and the one cross-cutting characteristic. The SEAM Program used the framework to conduct an overall assessment of the pharmaceutical supply systems in six resource-limited countries: Brazil (State of Minas Gerais), Cambodia, El Salvador, Ghana, India (State of Rajasthan), and Tanzania. Local private, not-for-profit, and academic organizations collaborated in the adaptation of data collection instruments, sample selection, data collection, and analysis.

Select data came from public- and private-sector health care facilities—

- Public health facilities (clinics and hospital out-patient departments)
- Private not-for-profit clinics and hospitals (NGOs)
- Private for-profit facilities (hospitals and clinics)
- Private retail drug outlets (pharmacies, chemical sellers)

To gather data on these indicators, SEAM used prescription-dispensing records to measure the quality of medicine-dispensing activity from the previous year, interviewed patients as they exited facilities to gather information on their perceptions and experiences, and conducted an exercise where simulated patients went to private retail pharmacies and drug outlets to obtain information about the quality of the services provided. An example of the indicator results follows.

Sources: CPM 2003a, 2003b, 2003c, 2003d, 2003e, 2003f.

Prescribing indicators based on record review

Indicator	Ghana	Tanzania	Cambodia	El Salvador	Brazil	India[a]
Public facilities						
Average medicines per encounter	4.5	1.6	2.0	2.2	1.8	2.7
% by generic name	77	76	90	84	65	23
% on essential medicines list	70	NA	97	93	65	70
% antibiotics	56	41	56	33	18	45
% vitamins/tonics	NA	NA	37	31	0	9
Private, for-profit facilities						
Average medicines per encounter	4.7	1.8	3.8	2.2	1.8	3.2
% by generic name	63	66	42	57	26	11
% on essential medicines list	70	NA	58	70	49	63
% antibiotics	48	30	64	23	15	39
% vitamins/tonics	NA	NA	41	24	0	14
NGO facilities						
Average medicines per encounter	4.9	2.3	2.5	2.2	2.3	2.7
% by generic name	76	72	77	63	36	13
% on essential medicines list	66	NA	82	72	62	66
% antibiotics	52	20	51	28	25	40
% vitamins/tonics	NA	NA	30	31	2	12

NA = Data not available.
[a] According to patient exit interviews.

Country Study 36-6
Pharmaceutical sector transparency assessments in four Asian countries

WHO's Good Governance in Medicines initiative has created a tool for assessing the level of transparency in three functions of the public pharmaceutical sector—registration of pharmaceutical products, selection of essential medicines, and procurement. Assessors interview at least ten key informants for each function (at least thirty interviews for the country). The key informants, chosen using strict criteria, represent the public and private sectors, including civil society organizations.

When the interviews are complete, a rough quantification is used to characterize the level of transparency for each function—registration, selection and procurement—using a zero to ten scale. The interpretation represents the following degrees of vulnerability to corruption.

0.0–2.0	2.1–4.1	4.1–6.0	6.1–8.0	8.1–10.0
Extremely vulnerable	Very vulnerable	Moderately vulnerable	Marginally vulnerable	Minimally vulnerable

WHO used this methodology to assess four Asian countries: the Lao People's Democratic Republic (Lao P.D.R), Malaysia, the Philippines, and Thailand. The assessment

results showed that the four countries shared a number of strengths and weaknesses. For example, all four had information systems for the registration process of pharmaceutical products, an official national list of essential medicines, and SOPs for transparent procurement. A common weakness was the lack of a conflict of interest form or guidance for the members of committees responsible for registering pharmaceutical products or selecting essential medicines.

The following table lists the vulnerability scores calculated for the four assessment countries. WHO notes that the scoring indicates vulnerability to corruption based on procedures at the time of the survey and not that one country's system is more corrupt than another. The scoring system is meant to help countries monitor their progress in improving transparency and good governance practices. Assessment results will provide a starting point for countries to develop and implement a national strategy promoting good governance in regulation and procurement of medicines.

Source: WHO 2006.

Vulnerability scale scores in four-country assessment

Function	Lao P.D.R.	Malaysia	Philippines	Thailand
Registration	5.6 Moderate	6.8 Marginal	6.8 Marginal	7.0 Marginal
Selection	6.1 Marginal	5.7 Moderate	6.1 Marginal	8.0 Marginal
Procurement	6.9 Marginal	7.1 Marginal	8.5 Minimal	7.1 Marginal

relationship. Information access varies from country to country; access largely determines how detailed an assessment is feasible and sensible.

Private-sector capacity

Many countries are incorporating private-sector services into the public pharmaceutical system, particularly when problems in the public system seem intractable (Quick et al. 2005). Of course, private entities of all sorts—nongovernmental, faith based, for profit—operate in the pharmaceutical sector of any country, but the level of their intersection and relationship with the government vary. Any assessment that is done in the context of major problems in the public pharmaceutical system should investigate private-sector capacity and the potential for public-private collaboration

of the sort outlined in Chapter 8. Note that such assessments should encompass NGOs as well as the for-profit private sector.

The public sector may not have much reliable information on hand about the private sector, and establishing communication may be difficult if a history of mutual suspicion and hostility exists between the private and public sectors. For some countries, reports compiled by international companies that specialize in selling industry information can be obtained, but this information is expensive, not always detailed and current, and available for only a limited number of nonindustrialized countries. Most countries have associations that represent manufacturers, distributors, and pharmacies, but getting more than general information about the market and the member companies from these sources may be difficult.

Country Study 36-7
Data collection methodology for a pharmaceutical sector assessment in Tanzania

The Ministry of Health sponsored an assessment of the pharmaceutical sector in Tanzania to evaluate the situation in both public and private sectors and the viability of potential strategies for improving consumer access to essential medicines.

The pharmaceutical sector assessment, led by the Strategies to Enhance Access to Medicines (SEAM) Program, was based on two distinct sets of data collection efforts. First, a team of consultants worked with local counterparts to conduct key informant interviews, carry out site visits, and review documents (for example, policy documents, legislation and regulation relative to pharmaceuticals and public sector procurement, study reports, and financial reports).

Second, SEAM surveyed a sample of 104 facilities, including public, nongovernmental, and private hospitals; pharmacies; zonal medical stores; health centers; dispensaries; and *duka la dawa baridi,* or retail drugstores. The survey was conducted in six districts: Dodoma Urban, Njombe, Tanga Urban, Karagwe, Kilimanjaro Rural, and Masasi. Within each subsector, a representative sample included each relevant type of facility, focusing on outpatient care. Sampling issues for surveys were addressed and resolved in collaboration with local counterparts. Key issues considered included the existing information about the distribution of facilities and population, in particular the information's level of detail.

The following tasks were performed at each type of facility—

1. Public-sector facilities and private not-for-profit hospitals and clinics that also provide medicines to outpatients

   - Inspect and determine availability of a set of tracer essential medicines
   - Obtain prices charged for medicines (if relevant)
   - If possible, obtain prices paid by facility to its suppliers
   - Review inventory control record or bin card for tracer set of essential medicines

   - Conduct interviews of relevant staff to fill in facility survey form
   - Conduct patient or client exit interviews (minimum of ten patients)
   - Review medical records or prescriber logs to collect prescribing data (thirty consultations)
   - Obtain or purchase twenty units of a designated tracer essential medicine (for testing purposes)

2. Private for-profit hospitals and clinics

   - Inspect or determine availability of a set of tracer essential medicines
   - Obtain prices charged for medicines (if relevant)
   - If possible, obtain prices paid by facility to its suppliers
   - Review inventory control record or bin card for tracer set of essential medicines
   - If possible, review medical records or prescriber logs to collect prescribing data (thirty consultations)
   - Conduct interviews with relevant staff to fill in facility survey form
   - Purchase twenty units of a designated tracer essential medicine (for testing purposes)

3. Private drug outlets (pharmacies and other types of drug outlets)

   - Obtain a list of medicinal product names (brand or the manufacturer if generic) that are available for sale
   - Determine availability of a set of tracer essential medicines
   - Obtain prices for a set of tracer essential medicines; if possible, obtain prices paid by pharmacy or drug outlet to its suppliers
   - Conduct questionnaire-based interview of drug outlet attendant
   - Observe and record simulated patient or mystery client scenario
   - Purchase twenty units of a designated tracer essential medicine (for testing purposes)

Source: CPM 2003f.

In most situations, the best option for assessing the private sector's capacity to play an increased role in the pharmaceutical system and contribute more to national medicine policy objectives is by conducting a special survey of the various components of the sector (including associations and their member companies). The SEAM Program conducted detailed assessments of the private pharmaceutical sectors in six countries. Country Study 36-7 describes the methodology used in Tanzania; the other assessment reports describe the methodologies used in the other five countries (see http://www.msh.org/seam).

Political mapping

An assessment aimed at making significant changes in the pharmaceutical system needs to define the consequences of potential changes. The assessment should also determine which politically powerful individuals and groups are likely to support potential changes, which will be actively opposed to change, and which will be basically indifferent. This process, called political mapping, is also useful in evaluating the feasibility of successfully implementing options for change.

Defining the best sources of information to map interest groups, political feasibility, and attitudes is not always simple. In most countries, the assessment team will be able to assemble at least a rudimentary map of political issues; likely consequences of various options for change; supporters and opponents of change; and individuals, organizations, companies, and interest groups that are prominent in pharmaceutical management (public or private). Truly reliable political mapping requires the active cooperation of senior managers (or ex-managers) in the government who are knowledgeable about the various political issues and interest groups but who have no personal stake in the outcome of the assessment.

Political mapping is an essential component of pharmaceutical system assessment; for example, in most countries, the private pharmaceutical sector is hardly a monolith—often important differences in attitudes and interests exist between local and international manufacturers, manufacturers and distributors, chain and independent pharmacies, and so forth. As noted previously, NGOs are another part of the private sector that involves people with unique views, and the various NGOs active in the country are likely to have differences in interests and attitudes.

The mapping process, if done accurately, helps define the causes of problems in the pharmaceutical system, examine the likely consequences of various changes and interventions, and determine which options are feasible and sustainable. Brugha and Varvasovszky (2000) describe stakeholder analysis, and political mapping computer software called PolicyMaker is available to help organize and interpret information (http://polimap.books.officelive.com). Williams, Durrheim, and Shretta (2004) take a political mapping approach to decision making regarding malaria treatment policy.

36.4 Defining the information targets

When the issues to be addressed and the assessment approach and time frame have been determined, the next step is to define the specific set of qualitative and quantitative data targeted for collection. In many cases, these data are collected in the form of standard performance indicators and are later organized into tables that provide insight into the pharmaceutical system.

Quantitative and qualitative data

Quantitative data describe the what, where, and when of a situation—for example, the percentage of a list of essential medicines that is available in a sample of health facilities. Qualitative data provide insights into why and how the situation is as it is—for example, why key informants believe that essential medicines are not more widely available. Quantitative methods can be used to give precision to qualitative ideas. Therefore, qualitative research is often used initially to identify problems and define the scope of options and issues, whereas quantitative data can then define the magnitude of the problem and measure the changes over time. In-depth interviews, structured observation, and focus group discussions are qualitative methods that can be used to explore behavior, attitudes, practices, and causal factors. Some of the data collected by these methods may be quantified, but the analysis itself is a qualitative one.

Although a comprehensive assessment should include both qualitative and quantitative elements, collecting a valid sample of quantitative data from a widely varied sample can sometimes be more time consuming and involve more work than conducting a series of focused qualitative informant interviews (which are more informal than focus group discussions); therefore, many reports on country pharmaceutical systems contain very little quantitative data and many unsubstantiated observations from informants. When an assessment does not gather quantitative data for analysis and comparison, the magnitude of problems or how much a situation has changed over time is difficult to know. At the same time, qualitative information is essential to understanding quantitative data, the reasons that specific weaknesses and constraints exist, and what strategies might be effective in overcoming the problem.

As noted, a properly structured assessment gathers and interprets both quantitative and qualitative information; problems with imbalance usually result when an assessment has no formal structure. Chapter 28 discusses issues related to quantitative and qualitative data; for more information, see the starred entries in References and Further Readings.

Performance indicators

Performance indicators are standardized measurements that theoretically mean the same thing in every country; for that reason, they are widely used to compare the performance of different businesses, economies, and societies. A well-known set of indicators in international development is published annually by the World Bank in the *World Development Report*; the 1993 edition focused on health issues (World Bank 1993). In addition, the United Nations has drafted more than sixty indicators to measure progress toward the Millennium Development Goals, such as "the percentage of children under 5 years with fever being treated

---

Box 36-2
WHO pharmaceutical monitoring indicators for three levels of the pharmaceutical sector

WHO has developed a core indicator package to monitor and evaluate country pharmaceutical situations. By repeating the assessment at regular intervals, WHO supports ministries of health in assessing the current pharmaceutical situation and giving them access to information that they can use to determine priority areas for intervention, track progress, plan programs, assess program effectiveness, coordinate donors and raise funds.

The core indicator package has three levels of assessment.

Level I: *The Questionnaire on Structures and Processes of Country Pharmaceutical Situation* measures structures and processes at the level of national governments, including policies, regulations, quality-control measures, essential medicines lists, supply systems, financing, access, production, rational use, and intellectual property rights legislation. WHO's plan is to distribute the questionnaire every four years to all member states. WHO uses this questionnaire to assess the global pharmaceutical situation, evaluate progress achieved toward goals set in the WHO Medicines Strategy, and make plans and set targets for WHO work for the next four years.

Level II: *The WHO Operational Package for Monitoring and Assessing Country Pharmaceutical Situations* is a practical and cost-efficient survey tool used by ministries of health to assess outcomes, including access, quality and safety, and rational use of essential medicines, at public health facilities and their pharmacies; central and district warehouses; or private, NGO, and mission pharmacies, as appropriate to country situation and households. The tool provides an evidence base for prioritizing health programs, developing and implementing plans, tracking progress, coordinating donors, and raising funds. More than forty member states have used this tool at least once to date.

Level III: A series of detailed survey packages to assess specific aspects of the pharmaceutical sector, such as medicine prices, the supply system, or traditional medicines. A country may implement a Level III survey to learn more about a specific area of the medicine sector after the results of the Level II survey have pointed to an area as needing more analysis.

Sources: WHO/TCM and DACP 2006; WHO 2007.

---

with antimalarial drugs" (see the indicator website at http://unstats.un.org/unsd/mdg/Default.aspx).

Performance indicators should be the foundation for ongoing monitoring in the pharmaceutical system (see Chapter 48) and should be a fundamental part of any pharmaceutical system assessment. Indicators to assess and monitor public pharmaceutical systems are a relatively recent development, and the optimal indicators to measure system performance have not been fully determined. WHO has developed pharmaceutical indicators to measure important aspects of a country's pharmaceutical situation at three different levels (see Box 36-2). Several other sets of performance indicators for pharmaceutical management systems have been developed; Box 36-3 discusses four of them and lists performance indicator resources and tools for specific public health programs.

Defining information targets for a specific assessment

Three principles guide the setting of information targets for a specific assessment—

- Get all the information needed for the purpose, within time limitations, but do not gather data that are unnecessary (doing so wastes time and effort in two phases of the process—collection and analysis).
- Make sure that the data used in producing analyses and recommendations are as reliable as possible, and determine which data are likely to be reliable and which are not.
- Define information targets based on what is available, and do not try to collect information that is nonexistent or impossible to retrieve.

Country Study 36-4 shows some of the information targets for a pharmaceutical system assessment done in Tanzania in 2006.

36.5 Methods for collecting information

The basic methods of obtaining information in a pharmaceutical system assessment are—

- Document review
- Key informant interviews
- Collection of data from existing records
- Prospective studies

Box 36-3
Examples of indicators in pharmaceutical management

Working in collaboration with USAID, the International Network for the Rational Use of Drugs, the Harvard Drug Policy Research Group, and the Pan American Health Organization Essential Drugs Program, MSH's Drug Management Program developed and field-tested an initial list of thirty-three indicators plus methods for data collection in 1993. Under the auspices of the USAID-supported Rational Pharmaceutical Management project, this indicator set and manual were further tested and revised to include forty-six indicators for the rapid assessment of pharmaceutical systems. The manual that documents this rapid assessment method also provides practical guidelines for organizing and completing a structured field-visit assessment (MSH/RPM 1995).

In 1994, the WHO Action Programme on Essential Drugs published a manual that proposed a set of thirty-one background information indicators, fifty structural indicators, thirty-eight process indicators, and ten outcome indicators, primarily for countries to assess themselves on issues related to national medicine policy. The indicators were field-tested in twelve countries in 1995 and 1996. WHO published the second edition of the indicators in 1999 (Brudon, Rainhorn, and Reich 1999).

The Australian Department of Health and Ageing adapted the WHO indicator format to develop pharmaceutical policy indicators focused on medicine use. The second edition of the indicator manual was published in 2004 (Quality Use of Medicines and Pharmacy Research Centre 2004). This set has sixty-seven process indicators, fifty-seven impact indicators, and six outcome indicators. The indicators are used to monitor the implementation and effect of Australia's National Strategy for Quality Use of Medicines.

WHO and MSH organized a joint consultative meeting to identify an operational definition of access and propose testable indicators to measure it. Four dimensions of access emerged as being of particular relevance to essential drugs, vaccines, and other health commodities—physical availability, affordability, geographic accessibility, and acceptability (or satisfaction). In addition, the quality of products and services was identified as a cross-cutting dimension. Workshop participants developed a set of seventeen key indicators to represent the four dimensions of access and the one cross-cutting characteristic (CPM 2003g). The SEAM Program used the resulting framework to conduct an overall assessment of the pharmaceutical supply systems in six resource-limited countries: Brazil (state of Minas Gerais), Cambodia, El Salvador, Ghana, India (state of Rajasthan), and Tanzania (http://www.msh.org/seam).

Increasing access framework

Accessibility	Availability	Strategies to increase access
• Location of products and services • Location of users	• Supply of products and services • Demand for products and services	**Education** • Patient consultation • Social marketing **Management** • Business management • Financial management **Regulation** • Standards development • Task-shifting **Economic** • Insurance plans • Pooled procurement (selected examples)

Safe | Efficacious | Cost-effective | Quality
Medical products and services

Acceptability	Affordability
• Characteristics of products and services • Attitudes and expectations of users	• Price of products and services • Ability to pay

Source: CPM/MSH 2011.

Pharmaceutical system indicators and tools for specific public health programs

- *Compendium of Indicators for Monitoring and Evaluating National Tuberculosis Programs* (http://www1.msh.org/projects/rpmplus/Documents/upload/Compendium_Indicators_ME_NTB_Programs.pdf)
- *Pharmaceutical Management for Tuberculosis Assessment Manual* (RPM Plus 2005)

- *Pharmaceutical Management for Malaria Manual* (RPM Plus 2004)
- *Drug Management for Childhood Illness Manual* (Keene et al. 2000)
- *Community Drug Management for Childhood Illness: Assessment Manual* (Nachbar et al. 2003)

Source: Rational Pharmaceutical Management Plus Program (http://www.msh.org/rpmplus).

This chapter summarizes these methods (see also Chapter 28; INRUD 1996, WHO 2007, MSH/RPM 1995).

Country Study 36-7 illustrates the methodology used to assess the public and private sectors of the pharmaceutical system in Tanzania.

Document review

Most countries have conducted studies of problems in the pharmaceutical sector and have made attempts to correct them. When donors have been involved in improving pharmaceutical services, many relevant reports are likely to exist. Government agencies can provide budget reports and, in many cases, files of technical reports by various agencies on the pharmaceutical sector. Contacting international agencies such as WHO, UNICEF, or the World Bank, bilateral donors, and technical assistance organizations to obtain copies of relevant documents is also useful.

A review of the literature should be one of the first steps in any assessment. Failure to include this important step inevitably results in a waste of time and money to regather data that are already available and reinvent analyses and recommendations that duplicate those already made. Worse, interventions that have been unsuccessful in the past may be tried again, with similar lack of success.

Key informant interviews

Interviews are one of the quickest ways to learn about urgent problems, if the assessment team is able to identify the people who are most knowledgeable about the situation and if these people are prepared to discuss the situation frankly. Interviews may be misleading, however, if the informants are not fully frank because of fear of retribution or if they have some vested interest in hiding or distorting information. Nevertheless, interviews are essential for insight into the political and administrative processes, which are major determinants of whether assessments will lead to real action.

Interviews may be conducted with or without structure. In the unstructured format, the interviewer relies on personal experience to ask relevant questions and to ensure that

important issues are not overlooked, which means the interviewer should be knowledgeable and well trained. In the structured approach, the interviewer uses a written survey form listing the important questions and the qualitative and quantitative information to be solicited.

Each format has advantages and disadvantages. The unstructured interview allows a free flow of conversation and may promote a more revealing interview, but it is subject to bias. Overlooking important issues is also easy when the interview is unstructured, and collating and analyzing responses from a series of such interviews are difficult, particularly if different interviewers are involved. The structured interview is usually more formal but is more likely to ensure that all important issues are addressed by each interviewer and that the responses are ordered in a manner that facilitates analysis. An interviewer using a structured format can combine both approaches by asking more probing questions to investigate an issue more thoroughly, but then return to the interview guide once the probing has finished.

Data collection from retrospective record review

A record review is a critical step in all structured assessments and should be done at each site where reasonably well-organized, complete, and current records exist. Where records are totally disorganized and badly out-of-date, the information gained may not be worth the effort, and other methods will be needed.

Relevant records include government publications on budgets and expenditures, drug regulatory inspection reports, patient medical records, pharmacy dispensing records, records of procurement and accounts payable to suppliers, warehouse ledgers, bin cards and computer records, and accounting and finance records. Private-sector records to review may include company financial reports, balance sheets, sales and stock data, and customs and import data.

Data collection by prospective field observation

When needed information cannot be obtained from a retrospective review of records, it may be possible to use prospective observation to obtain the information. For example, one method of reviewing prescribing practices in a health facility is to examine clinical charts and dispensing records. If these records are not available, the team can observe patient encounters directly and record the prescribing in that manner (a patient exit survey).

Some types of data are best obtained by prospective methods. For example, to determine whether private pharmacies are selling prescription-only medicines without a prescription, the best method is a simulated purchase survey, where local data collectors visit a sample of pharmacies and actually attempt to purchase prescription medicines (see Boyce and Neale 2006b).

Other methods for collecting qualitative information

Other common methods for obtaining useful data include focus groups and household surveys, although both methods can be complex, technically demanding, and costly. These techniques, however, can be important tools in determining why attitudes and practices exist in one group or another (see Chapter 28), and sometimes they can be piggybacked onto other household surveys or reports from previous efforts can be used, such as national demographic and health surveys (see http://www.measuredhs.com).

36.6 Planning and managing the assessment

The key issues in planning most assessments are—

- Defining the assessment approach
- Defining and locating financial resources
- Defining management and technical responsibilities
- Developing a draft workplan

After these issues are resolved, the assessment leader and the team develop a management plan. The plan must cover these issues—

- Making logistics arrangements
- Preparing a system overview
- Selecting sites to be visited
- Selecting indicator medicines
- Defining data collection methods
- Developing and refining data collection forms
- Selecting and training data collectors
- Revising the workplan to its final form

These issues are relevant to most comprehensive structured assessments, and they are covered in great detail in *Rapid Pharmaceutical Management Assessment* (MSH/RPM 1995) and the *WHO Operational Package for Assessing, Monitoring and Evaluating Country Pharmaceutical*

Situations (WHO 2007), which are available without charge. Any country or supply system that is planning a pharmaceutical assessment should get these manuals to aid in its planning and execution.

Given proper preparation, the actual data collection process may go relatively smoothly and produce reliable data for evaluation. However, one can safely assume that the assessment will not proceed entirely according to the workplan, no matter how well it was thought out. Minor frustrations will occur, such as unavailability of some key team members, weather-related delays for some site visits, and unexpected absence of key informants. These can be worked around, as long as the assessment team maintains its flexibility and sense of humor. Major problems such as widespread work stoppages can shut down the entire public health system and require postponement of the assessment, if it has not started, or interrupt the study until facilities reopen.

The following are vital issues to consider when analyzing situations and options—especially for fast-track assessments—

- Ability to quickly identify and mobilize the lead team of assessors, once a country need has been identified
- Continuity of the team throughout the different phases of the approach and their solid understanding of the methodology
- Experienced, knowledgeable assessors to facilitate interviews with national policy makers and officials, interpret policy data, and develop and analyze improvement options
- Full engagement of local stakeholders throughout the different implementation phases
- A logistics system to support scheduling, recruitment, and training of data collectors and then data entry and analysis

Data analysis

When a large amount of quantitative data is available on costs, purchases, medicine consumption, and use patterns, it must be organized to facilitate analysis. Chapter 40 is devoted to the issue of analyzing data to understand and control costs in the pharmaceutical supply system; most of the analytical techniques in that chapter can and should be incorporated into assessment information targets, if necessary data are available. Several other chapters offer suggestions for organizing data to facilitate analysis during an assessment (see Chapters 28, 48, and 49).

To avoid confusion and haste at the end of an assessment, one should collate and prepare assessment data for analysis as they are collected (see Chapter 48). If a computerized program such as Epi Info (see Chapter 50) or even an Excel spreadsheet is used for collating survey results, data should ideally be entered at the end of each day by team members or a local data-entry person, or if teams are operating simultaneously in different parts of a country, then data should be collated at the end and entered into a system. Both team members and counterparts should play an active role in examining data that are recovered and considering what sorts of additional analyses may be appropriate beyond those prescribed in the assessment workplan.

Preparing the assessment report

Chapter 49 discusses how to interpret data from a pharmaceutical management information system. The issues are similar for interpreting results from assessments. No matter how well the assessment was designed, planned, and executed, the data obtained may not be totally reliable. Part of the job of the study team is to determine what sorts of biases, inaccuracies, or inconsistencies may exist and what precautions are necessary in interpreting the data. The report itself must be presented in a way that helps the decision makers who need to use the information; a clear outline and executive summary of not more than two pages, which includes a statement of the next steps, are important. The methodology and detailed results can be mentioned in the text and appended to keep the document concise for interested but nonspecialist readers.

Presentations and workshops

Many key decision makers may not have the time to read the whole report. Presentations and workshops are excellent ways to convey important results directly and may be useful before the final report is written, providing feedback for clarification. Charts and graphs are important visual aids to organize the presentation and ensure that key points are covered. Actual examples of graphic presentations of findings from a medicine use assessment are found in Chapter 28.

Using the assessment results

An assessment should be seen as only one of several steps involved in planning and implementing pharmaceutical system changes. The assessment may be part of the development process for a donor project proposal, a national pharmaceutical sector restructuring exercise, or a national five-year development plan.

If the assessment is leading to a donor project proposal, the assessment team should be aware of this goal from the outset. If possible, the prospective donor should contribute to the assessment design. As mentioned, some donors, such as the Global Fund, have standardized assessment protocols. To encourage a sense of involvement, the prospective donor might also be given an opportunity to participate at various

points in the assessment and report-writing process. The assessment team should be sure to collect all background information that may be needed. The content and format of the assessment should be compatible with what is needed for a project proposal. Depending on donor requirements, the assessment report may serve as a project proposal with little or no editing.

If the assessment is part of a national restructuring or planning exercise, key government officials must be involved from the beginning, as well as stakeholders from the private sector and the community. People are much more committed to implementing solutions that they have helped develop.

The whole assessment process will have been wasted if the report goes on a shelf and is not used to effect changes in policies and procedures. Follow-up may be tied to the development of national medicine policies, revisions in legislation and regulation, and consideration of public-private collaboration.

After the assessment is complete, a workshop to bring stakeholders together and work through the assessment results and related options will define next steps and stakeholder roles and responsibilities. The assessment results may suggest revised policies and procedures in pharmaceutical selection, procurement, distribution, and use. The assessment and subsequent stakeholder options workshop should guide the development of strategic plans for pharmaceutical systems (see Chapter 38) and monitoring programs, program planning, and management information systems. Country Study 36-8 looks at examples of how assessment results were used to address issues in pharmaceutical management for TB medicines in several countries. ■

References and further readings

★ = Key readings.

Boyce, C., and P. Neale. 2006a. *Conducting In-Depth Interviews: A Guide for Designing and Conducting In-Depth Interviews for Evaluation Input.* Watertown, Mass.: Pathfinder International. <http://www.pathfind.org/site/DocServer/m_e_tool_series_indepth_interviews.pdf?docID=6301>

————. 2006b. *Using Mystery Clients: A Guide to Using Mystery Clients for Evaluation Input.* Watertown, Mass.: Pathfinder International. <http://www.pathfind.org/site/DocServer/m_e_tool_series_mystery_clients.pdf?docID=6303>

★ Brudon, P., J-D. Rainhorn, and M. Reich. 1999. *Indicators for Monitoring National Drug Policies: A Practical Manual.* 2nd ed. Geneva: World Health Organization. <http://whqlibdoc.who.int/hq/1999/WHO_EDM_PAR_99.3_pp1-114.pdf>

Brugha, R., and Z. Varvasovszky. 2000. Stakeholder Analysis: A Review. *Health Policy and Planning* 15(3):239–46.

Conteh, L., and K. Hanson. 2003. Methods for Studying Private Sector Supply of Public Health Products in Developing Countries: A Conceptual Framework and Review. *Social Science & Medicine* 57(7):1147–61.

Country Study 36-8
Using assessment results to improve TB pharmaceutical management in three countries

The RPM Plus Program's indicator-based *Pharmaceutical Management for Tuberculosis Assessment Manual* (PMTB) helps users, primarily national tuberculosis (TB) programs, conduct studies that—

- Provide data on TB pharmaceutical management practices
- Identify ways to improve the national TB pharmaceutical management system, thereby promoting an uninterrupted supply of quality TB medicines
- Build country-based research capacity

Findings from an assessment can provide the basis for policy dialogue, strategic planning, program monitoring, and intervention design.

The PMTB has been used in Armenia, Azerbaijan, Cambodia, China, Congo (Brazzaville), the Dominican Republic, Ethiopia, Georgia, Moldova, India (Uttar Pradesh), and Romania. Highlights from Ethiopia, China, and Cambodia follow.

Field-testing of the PMTB in Ethiopia and impact of findings on policy

In 2004, RPM Plus field-tested the PMTB tool in Ethiopia to evaluate TB medicine availability and use. Key assessment findings included the following—

- Inventory records were not regularly updated, resulting in discrepancies between stock records and actual stock.
- Standard treatment guidelines (STGs) differed slightly from recommendations of WHO: for example, STGs for Category I patients included injections instead of tablets.
- Health care providers gave incorrect medicines 10 percent of the time.
- Of intensive-phase patients, 76 percent were observed taking their medicines (a primary element of the DOTS strategy).
- Only 32 percent of patients had adequate knowledge about how to take their medicines.

Following the assessment, Ethiopia's TB and Leprosy Prevention and Control Program took specific measures to address some of these problems, such as—

- Recruiting a logistics officer to oversee the details of TB medicines and supplies management
- Incorporating information on logistics management into the newest national TB program manual
- Providing training to pharmacy staff on how to

manage TB medicines and commodities, and supporting supervision to reinforce their training
- Using new methods to record and report on the consumption of TB medicines and stock status
- Conducting pharmaceutical supply management assessments throughout the year to monitor progress and identify areas that still need improvement
- Revising STGs to align with WHO recommendations

Using PMTB findings to introduce new pharmaceutical management systems in China

After adapting the PMTB tool to the Chinese setting, RPM Plus used the tool in two provinces—Shandong and Henan. On the basis of the findings, Henan province was chosen to update its TB pharmaceutical management system. In 2006, three sets of SOP manuals were prepared for use at provincial, prefecture, and county levels, and training in procedures was completed for thirty personnel. The SOPs have been modified in line with feedback to make them more user-friendly in the Chinese context. With positive results in seven pilot facilities in Henan since July 2006, the plan is to expand the new system's implementation to the rest of the province and throughout China, reaching more than 3,500 TB facilities.

Using the PMTB to evaluate policy change in Cambodia

The Japan International Cooperation Agency used the PMTB methodology and questionnaires to conduct TB pharmaceutical management assessments in Cambodia during 2003–04 and 2005–06. The first assessment established a baseline and illustrated key problems in pharmaceutical management, such as medicine availability and rational medicine use. The second assessment measured any improvement in TB pharmaceutical management practices after switching the national TB program's policy from an eight-month to a six-month treatment regimen and evaluated whether any change occurred in TB medicine availability in the private sector.

A comparison of findings from the two surveys revealed improvement in a few areas and highlighted the need for further interventions emphasizing the following areas: periodic supervision, on-the-job training for drug storekeepers and TB service providers, further expanding community DOTS, strengthening public-private collaboration, and exploring the possibility of procurement and use of four fixed-dose combination TB medicines or patient kits.

Source: MSH/RPM Plus 2006.

ASSESSMENT GUIDE

- What are the reasons that the pharmaceutical system is being assessed?
- What issues should the assessment address?
- Have any assessments of the pharmaceutical system been conducted in the past?
- Who is sponsoring the assessment? Who is actually conducting the assessment?
- If the assessment covers the public sector, is the government committed and involved in the assessment process?
- What other stakeholders should be involved in the assessment?
- What information related to the pharmaceutical system will likely be available for review?

- Is the scope of the assessment comprehensive (covering the entire system—both public and private sectors)? Or is the scope more focused (for example, one sector or one vertical program)?
- What are the qualitative and quantitative information targets to be collected as part of the assessment? Are the information targets based on standard performance indicators?
- What methods will be used to collect the information?
- What is the time frame and cost for the assessment?
- What are the qualifications of the assessment team?
- Who will analyze the results?
- How will the results be presented for use by decision makers?

CPM (Center for Pharmaceutical Management). 2003a. *Access to Essential Medicines: Cambodia, 2001.* Prepared for the Strategies for Enhancing Access to Medicines Program. Arlington, Va.: Management Sciences for Health. <http://www.msh.org/seam/reports/Cambodia_Assessment_Report.pdf>

———. 2003b. *Access to Essential Medicines: El Salvador, 2001.* Prepared for the Strategies for Enhancing Access to Medicines Program. Arlington, Va.: Management Sciences for Health. <http://www.msh.org/seam/reports/El_Salvador_final.pdf>

———. 2003c. *Access to Essential Medicines: Ghana, 2001.* Prepared for the Strategies for Enhancing Access to Medicines Program. Arlington, Va.: Management Sciences for Health. <http://www.msh.org/seam/reports/Ghana_final.pdf>

———. 2003d. *Access to Essential Medicines: Minas Gerais, Brazil, 2001.* Prepared for the Strategies for Enhancing Access to Medicines Program. Arlington, Va.: Management Sciences for Health. <http://www.msh.org/seam/reports/Brazil_final.pdf>

———. 2003e. *Access to Essential Medicines: Rajasthan, India, 2001.* Prepared for the Strategies for Enhancing Access to Medicines Program. Arlington, Va.: Management Sciences for Health. <http://www.msh.org/seam/reports/India_Assessment_Report.pdf>

———. 2003f. *Access to Essential Medicines: Tanzania, 2001.* Prepared for the Strategies for Enhancing Access to Medicines Program. Arlington, Va.: Management Sciences for Health. <http://www.msh.org/seam/reports/CR022304_SEAMWebsite_attach1.pdf>

★ ———. 2003g. *Defining and Measuring Access to Essential Drugs, Vaccines, and Health Commodities: Report of the WHO-MSH Consultative Meeting, Ferney-Voltaire, France, December 11–13, 2000.* Arlington, Va.: Management Sciences for Health. <http://www.msh.org/seam/reports/Access_Meeting_Ferney_Voltaire_1.pdf>

CPM/MSH (Center for Pharmaceutical Management/Management Sciences for Health). 2011. *Center for Pharmaceutical Management: Technical Frameworks, Approaches, and Results.* Arlington, Va.: CPM.

García-Núñez, J. 1992. *Improving Family Planning Evaluation.* West Hartford, Conn.: Kumarian Press.

Hardon, A., P. Brudon-Jakobowicz, and A. Reeler. 1992. *How to Investigate Drug Use in Communities: Guidelines for Social Science Research.* Geneva: World Health Organization. <http://whqlibdoc.who.int/hq/1992/WHO_DAP_92.3.pdf>

★ Heltzer, N., A. Shrivastav, and M. Clark. 2008. *Developing an Assessment System for Procurement Agencies in Health Sector in India.* Submitted to the World Bank by the Center for Pharmaceutical Management. Arlington, Va.: Management Sciences for Health.

★ INRUD (International Network for the Rational Use of Drugs). 1996. *How to Use Applied Qualitative Methods to Design Drug Use Interventions* (Working Draft). INRUD Secretariat. Arlington, Va.: Management Sciences for Health. <http://www.inrud.org/documents/upload/How_to_Use_Applied_Qualitative_Methods.pdf>

Keene, D., P. Ickx, and J. McFadyen. 2000. *Drug Management for Childhood Illness Manual.* Published for the U.S. Agency for International Development by the Rational Pharmaceutical Management Project. Arlington, Va.: Management Sciences for Health.

Keene, D., and T. Moore. 2000. *Drug Management for Childhood Illness: Data Collector's Guide.* Published for the U.S. Agency for International Development by the Rational Pharmaceutical Management Project. Arlington, Va.: Management Sciences for Health.

Kruk, M. E., and L. P. Freedman. 2008. Assessing Health System Performance in Developing Countries: A Review of the Literature. *Health Policy* 83(3):263–76.

★ MSH/RPM (Management Sciences for Health/Rational Pharmaceutical Management Project). 1995. *Rapid Pharmaceutical Management Assessment: An Indicator-Based Approach.* Arlington, Va.: MSH/RPM. <http://erc.msh.org/newpages/english/toolkit/rpma.pdf>

MSH/RPM Plus (Management Sciences for Health/Rational Pharmaceutical Management Plus Program). 2006. *Assessing Pharmaceutical Management Systems to Ensure Availability and Rational Use of Essential TB Medicines.* Arlington, Va.: MSH/RPM Plus. <http://www.msh.org/projects/rpmplus/documents/upload/07-035-PMTB_FINAL-format.pdf>

———. 2004. *Defining a Rapid Assessment Approach to Improve Medicine and Commodity Management for VCT, PMTCT, and ART Programs.* Poster presented at the XV International AIDS Conference, July 11–16, Bangkok. <http://www.who.int/hiv/amds/en/PMTCTRapidAssessment-Final.pdf>

Nachbar, N., J. Briggs, O. Aupont, L. Shafritz, A. Bongiovanni, K. Acharya, S. Zimicki, S. Holschneider, and D. Ross-Degnan. 2003.

Community Drug Management for Childhood Illness: Assessment Manual. Submitted to the U.S. Agency for International Development by the Rational Pharmaceutical Management Plus Program. Arlington, Va.: Management Sciences for Health. <http://erc.msh.org/toolkit/Tool.cfm?lang=1&CID=2&TID=101>

Quality Use of Medicines and Pharmacy Research Centre, University of South Australia. 2004. *Measurement of the Quality Use of Medicines Component of Australia's National Medicines Policy: Second Report of the National Indicators.* Canberra: Australian Government Department of Health and Ageing. <http://www.health.gov.au/internet/main/publishing.nsf/Content/AC9F1C85C978FB0CCA256F1800468E76/$File/qumnmp.pdf>

Quick, J. D., N.-A. Boohene, J. Rankin, and R. J. Mbwasi. 2005. Medicines Supply in Africa. *BMJ* 331:709–710.

RPM Plus (Rational Pharmaceutical Management Plus Program). 2005. *Pharmaceutical Management for Tuberculosis Assessment Manual.* Zagorskiy A., C. Owunna, and T. Moore, eds. Submitted to the U.S. Agency for International Development by the RPM Plus Program. Arlington, Va.: Management Sciences for Health. <http://www.msh.org/projects/rpmplus/documents/upload/FINAL-PMTB-Manual-for-Web.pdf>

———. 2004. *Pharmaceutical Management for Malaria Manual.* Prepared by Malcolm Clark 2002 and revised by Rima Shretta 2003. Submitted to the U.S. Agency for International Development by the Rational Pharmaceutical Management Plus Program. Arlington, Va.: Management Sciences for Health. <http://erc.msh.org/toolkit/Tool.cfm?lang=1&CID=2&TID=225>

Rutta, E., J. McCollum, and S. Mwakisu. 2006. *Rapid ART Pharmaceutical Management Assessment in Five Mission Hospitals in Tanzania.* Submitted to the U.S. Agency for International Development by the Rational Pharmaceutical Management Plus Program. Arlington, Va.: Management Sciences for Health.

Uganda Ministry of Health. 2008. *Pharmaceutical Situation Assessment Level II: Health Facilities Survey in Uganda: Report of a Survey Conducted July–August 2008.* Kampala: Uganda Ministry of Health. <http://apps.who.int/medicinedocs/documents/s16377e/s16377e.pdf>

WHO (World Health Organization). 2009. *Measuring Transparency in the Public Pharmaceutical Sector: Assessment Instrument.* Geneva: WHO. <http://apps.who.int/medicinedocs/documents/s16732e/s16732e.pdf>

———. 2007. *WHO Operational Package for Assessing, Monitoring and Evaluating Country Pharmaceutical Situations: Guide for Coordinators and Data Collectors.* Geneva: WHO. <http://www.who.int/entity/medicines/publications/WHO_TCM_2007.2.pdf>

———. 2006. *Measuring Transparency in Medicines Registration, Selection and Procurement: Four Country Assessment Studies.* Geneva: WHO.

———. 2004. *The World Medicines Situation.* Geneva: WHO.

★ WHO/DAP (World Health Organization/Action Programme on Essential Drugs). 1993. *How to Investigate Drug Use in Health Facilities: Selected Drug Use Indicators.* Geneva: WHO/DAP. <http://whqlibdoc.who.int/hq/1993/WHO_DAP_93.1.pdf>

WHO/HAI Global (World Health Organization/Health Action International Global). 2008. *Measuring Medicine Prices, Availability, Affordability and Price Components.* 2nd ed. Geneva: WHO.

WHO/PSM and EPN (World Health Organization Department of Medicines Policy and Standards and Ecumenical Pharmaceutical Network). 2006. *Multi-Country Study of Medicine Supply and Distribution Activities of Faith-Based Organizations in Sub-Saharan African Countries.* Geneva: WHO. <http://whqlibdoc.who.int/hq/2006/WHO_PSM_PAR_2006.2_eng.pdf>

★ WHO/TCM and DACP (World Health Organization/Technical Cooperation for Essential Drugs and Traditional Medicine and WHO Boston Collaborating Center on Pharmaceutical Policy). 2006. *Using Indicators to Measure Country Pharmaceutical Situations: Fact Book on WHO Level I and Level II Monitoring Indicators.* Geneva: WHO/TCM. <http://www.who.int/medicines/publications/WHOTCM2006.2A.pdf>

Williams, H. A., D. Durrheim, and R. Shretta. 2004. The Process of Changing National Malaria Treatment Policy: Lessons from Country-Level Studies. *Health Policy and Planning* 19(6):356–70.

World Bank. 1993. *World Development Report 1993: Investing in Health.* New York: Oxford University Press. <http://files.dcp2.org/pdf/WorldDevelopmentReport1993.pdf>

CHAPTER 37

Managing pharmaceutical programs

SUMMARY

Although management means different things in different contexts, all managers are responsible for the activities and accomplishments of their organization. Good management is about ensuring reliable operations that serve clients, staff, and other stakeholders in their efforts to reach common goals. As a result of the manager's actions, the organization successfully and consistently does what it is supposed to do.

Managers must balance their time among the four activities of crisis management, routine administration, control and supervision of operations, and long-term program development. They are called upon to fulfill the roles of—

- Leader: providing direction, motivating staff, maintaining liaison with other organizations
- Coach: using a coaching style of interaction to improve employee performance
- Communicator: maintaining networks of formal and informal contacts, disseminating information, serving as spokesperson
- Decision maker: allocating resources, deciding on program change and development, solving problems, negotiating

Organizations need good leadership to move toward a better future and good management to make sure that current operations run smoothly and efficiently, and produce the intended results. Leading means enabling others to face challenges and achieve results under complex conditions. By using their adaptive skills, managers who lead are able to achieve results even when conditions are very difficult and resources scarce.

Effective managers require technical, analytical, and interpersonal skills. They set priorities based on the urgency, relevance, effect, future consequences, and growth of competing issues. They follow systematic processes for decision making and problem solving. Necessary skills can be acquired through formal management training programs and practiced in formal and mentoring situations.

The management process, which is at the hub of the pharmaceutical management framework, consists essentially of three basic functions—

- Planning (see Chapter 38)
- Implementation
- Monitoring and evaluation (see Chapter 48)

Improvements in pharmaceutical systems involve change; leading well requires continuously adapting to changing conditions in the environment and helping others to do the same. To manage change effectively, managers who lead must understand the forces driving internal and external change, the sources of resistance to change, and the principles for successfully managing change.

37.1 Managing and leading a pharmaceutical program to produce results

Part III of this manual, Management Support Systems, takes a look at the knowledge, values, practices, and skills required to manage organizations, finances, information, and people and to successfully lead change efforts to improve current operations. The preceding sections on selection, procurement, distribution, and use presented the technical core of the pharmaceutical management framework. Management support systems form the hub of this framework (Figure 37-1). This chapter explores the requirements for creating a strong hub for pharmaceutical management.

Failing programs and organizations have demonstrated that neither abundant resources nor excellent technical skill can guarantee success. If management or leadership or both are not well executed, the organization will not be able to fulfill its mission or will do so with unnecessary effort and significant waste of resources. Although managing and leading are critical organizational functions, they are often taken for granted. This chapter provides new and experienced managers with a practical framework for assessing and improving their own and others' management and leadership practices and skills.

Managing for performance

As a prerequisite to receive funding, an increasing trend in performance-based development aid requires health programs to establish and meet measurable objectives (see Chapter 14). Such results, in pharmaceutical management as in any other specialized area of management, must be directly linked to improved delivery of services to the population, always with a view toward improved health for all people in the country or in the population served by the public health program.

Achieving results in pharmaceutical management by meeting program objectives requires action by individual staff members as they work together as a team toward common objectives. Establishing individual performance-based

Figure 37-1   Pharmaceutical management framework

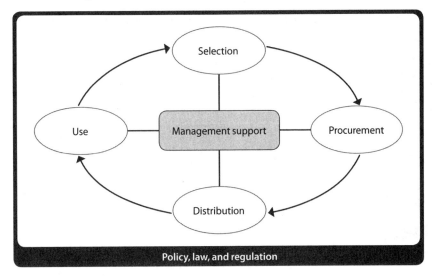

Source: CPM/MSH 2011.

objectives is a participatory process in which managers and staff members set goals that are then used to periodically assess performance. Using performance-based objectives provides the link between overall program implementation activities and individual staff performance. Section 37.3 covers monitoring individual objectives in more detail.

To provide the desired level and quality of services, organizations or programs need to make sure that—

- Management systems are well designed, fully operational, and maintained by appropriately trained people. Management systems are the structures, processes, and procedures that managers develop to help staff do their work. Managers use systems to inform, organize, and track progress in performing these tasks.
- The work climate is positive and promotes staff motivation and dedication to produce intended results. Work climate refers to the prevailing mood of a workplace or what it feels like to work there. It is the environment related to staff motivation, including working conditions, managerial support, acknowledgment, and encouragement.
- The organization or program is able and prepared to continually adapt to changing circumstances, which includes the ability to anticipate and adapt to changing conditions in the internal or external environment. This capacity relies on staff resilience, empowerment, optimism, openness to learning, creativity, and ability to communicate with partners from other ethnic, social, gender, and organizational groups.

The manager's role is to make sure that these three conditions are met in the workplace. A positive work climate,

strong management systems, and openness to learning all foster an organization's capacity to respond to a changing world (Figure 37-2).

Managers and leaders

People often refer to one person or another as a good manager or a good leader. Such statements are usually intuitive, and when pressed to describe the difference between leading and managing, many people find it hard to do so. What exactly is the difference? *Managing* means organizing the internal parts of the organization to implement systems and coordinate resources to produce reliable performance. *Leading* means enabling others to face challenges and achieve results under complex conditions. Modern organizations and the increased understanding of how people function have led to a different concept of management methods. Table 37-1 contrasts the attitudes and style of traditional and modern methods.

People who manage well are good at planning and organizing. They make sure that processes and procedures, staff, and other resources are used in an efficient and effective manner. Good management is about ensuring reliable operations that serve clients, staff, and other stakeholders in their efforts to reach common goals. As a result of a good manager's actions, the organization successfully and consistently does what it is supposed to do—it is trustworthy to its clients, supporters, and suppliers. Trustworthiness helps the organization maintain its funding flows, goodwill from supporters, and reputation for reliable results. Although good management and the establishment of sound management systems form the foundation for the organization's work, they do not always guarantee the desired results.

Figure 37-2   Leading and managing for results model

How do management and leadership contribute to improved service delivery?

Source: MSH 2005a.

Managers with new tools and systems often get the same outcomes as before, unless they *lead* others to use these systems well, periodically adapt tools and systems to meet changing needs, and manage the organizational context.

Leading well requires continuously adapting to changing conditions in the environment and helping others do the same. By using their adaptive skills, managers who lead are able to achieve results even when conditions are very difficult and resources scarce. They make sure that they are always well informed about opportunities and threats. They continually inquire into their own, their organization's, and their staff members' strengths and weaknesses. They are able to develop a compelling vision, get key stakeholders to buy into that vision, and then focus organizational efforts on achieving it. They mobilize people, resources, and goodwill around the vision and keep everything moving in the right direction. They inspire and encourage staff to overcome obstacles that obscure the vision, recognize the contributions of everyone, celebrate successes, and learn from mistakes.

Pharmacists as professional leaders

Pharmacy professionals, because of their technical training and unique expertise in systems management, have much to offer in public health policy making and leadership, especially as part of the global effort to increase access to medicines and scale up major public health programs, such as antiretroviral therapy. Although representatives from all health professions—medical, nursing, pharmacy, health administration—should be involved with public health planning and implementation, often the pharmacy profes-

sion does not play as strong a leadership role as it could in public health decision making, whether at the national, regional, or facility level. Although pharmacy staff are valued for their role in supply management, the contributions of the profession to patient care and to promoting the rational use of medicines is often unrecognized and underresourced, and the pharmacy staff members' clinical skills are often underused. The International Pharmaceutical Federation recommends that "governments and international organizations with a focus on health should recognize the unique contribution pharmacists can make, through their technical expertise, to improving access to medicines for people in developing countries" (FIP 2005). More important, however, pharmacy professionals, themselves, through their professional organizations as well as through individual efforts, should work toward strengthening their role as leaders at all levels of the health care system, mentor the next generation of leaders in the profession, work to improve access to medicines through use of ancillary dispensers, and, when appropriate, position the pharmacy profession at the forefront of public health policy development and implementation.

37.2 What makes a successful manager who leads?

Organizations need both good leadership to move toward a better future and good management to make sure that current operations run smoothly, efficiently, and produce the intended results. The notion of "managers who lead" makes sure that both areas are covered.

Table 37-1   Comparison of traditional and modern managers

Traditional manager	Modern manager
Acts as authoritarian figure, critic	Acts as facilitator, coach
Is concerned about structure and procedures	Is concerned about objectives and results
Tries to succeed alone	Succeeds through the success of the team
Pushes staff to focus on manager's needs and concerns	Encourages staff to focus on the program's needs and concerns
Gives little feedback	Gives positive feedback and constructive negative feedback
Is critical; discourages individual initiative	Is supportive; coaches staff to take initiative
Uses threats to control staff	Uses encouragement and support to motivate staff
Uses one-way, top-down communication	Uses two-way communication
Is secretive	Shares information
Knows all the answers	Recognizes the expertise of other team members
Holds decision-making authority; makes decisions single-handedly	Involves staff in decision making
Decides not only what should be done but also how it should be done	Allows staff to participate in deciding what should be done and defining how they can best do it
Resists change; views change as a threat	Welcomes change as a source of improvement
Is concerned with punishing people for doing a bad job	Helps people do a better job
Creates fear, which discourages staff from asking questions and making suggestions	Creates a sense of security; staff ask questions and make constructive suggestions

Sources: Adapted from Ivancevich et al. 1994; Rees 2001.

The tasks of a manager

Managers in every part of the world have something in common: their days are filled with four quite different sets of tasks, all of which require their attention—

- Crisis management
- Routine administration
- Control and supervision of operations
- Long-term program development

Crisis management—or "fighting fires"—can consume entire days or sometimes entire weeks: an overdue proposal to a donor, a shipment of emergency medicines stuck at the port, an outbreak of meningitis in one part of the country, a break-in or robbery at the regional store in another part of the country. Many such crises are actually preventable through better management of activities, but learning to respond quickly and decisively—and not to overrespond or to overcommit scarce resources—is an important part of becoming an effective manager.

Routine administration includes the whole range of day-to-day activities involved in receiving reports, managing staff, making decisions, and generally conducting the business of the organization or program. These activities are necessary but can often be managed more efficiently through delegation and other skills described in other management support chapters.

Control and supervision of operations is the formal or even legal responsibility of the manager. He or she must ensure that the work is done in compliance with national or institutional regulations and requirements. Controlling and supervising is a true balancing act. Too much supervision and too much control will discourage employees from developing initiative and resourcefulness, which creates a fearful and demoralized workforce. Too little control and too little supervision nearly always produce unnecessary crises and leave employees feeling abandoned, create opportunities for leakage and graft, and risk noncompliance, thus leaving the manager and the organization vulnerable to sanctions.

Long-term program development concerns a task that is important, even critical, to long-term survival and program success. Because it is never urgent at any particular moment, long-term program development always receives less attention than the urgent and important tasks. Nevertheless, failure to plan and implement needed changes often increases the number of management "fires" and makes even routine administration less efficient and more time-consuming than it should be. Unfortunately, many managers are so consumed by the first three tasks that they make little time for long-term program development.

An effective manager who leads must balance attention to these four tasks—responding promptly to crises, efficiently handling routine administrative work, and exerting the right amount of control and supervision while still attending to the long-term growth and development of the program or organization.

The practices of a manager who leads

A study of successful public health managers who lead (MSH 2005b) showed that, despite differences in style and personality, they all did similar things: they continually scanned, they focused, they aligned and mobilized, and they inspired. These are the particular practices of good leaders. They also planned, organized, implemented, and monitored and evaluated. These are the practices of good managers. Effective managers who lead constantly and consistently use these eight practices to produce intended results. The leading and managing practices described in the leading and managing framework (Figure 37-3) offer specific practices to improve organizational performance and sustain performance over time.

The skills of a manager who leads

Most health program managers have climbed up through the ranks and have been promoted because of their technical skills and knowledge. Technical skills, therefore, are rarely an area of weakness. Nevertheless, any health program manager has to have a certain minimum amount of practical and theoretical knowledge as well as a set of practical skills in the professional discipline relevant to his or her job. These skills may relate to pharmaceuticals, medicine, logistics, accounting, epidemiology, public health, infectious diseases, and so on.

Because all managers have responsibility over budgets, they have to be familiar with the basics of financial management, such as preparing, managing, and monitoring budgets; assessing value for money in people and projects; and doing a cost-benefit analysis. They should also be able to read, understand, and manipulate financial data pertaining to their program or organization.

Managers who lead need another set of skills, however, unrelated to their level of technical expertise in their area. The following skills become increasingly important as the scope of a manager's authority, influence, and responsibility increases—

Priority setting: Focusing attention and action among multiple options and interests
Managing time: Making good use of time to align personal and organizational goals
Problem solving and decision making: Using analytical abilities, pragmatism, and other tools to resolve complex problems and make the right decision in a variety of contexts
Coaching: Mastering a comfortable coaching style and using it strategically to improve performance

Communicating: Communicating both orally and in writing and relating to a broad range of people within and outside of the organization
Negotiating: Arriving at understandings and agreements with a broad range of people inside and outside the organization or program
Managing change: Adapting to and thriving in times of internal or external change

In addition, computer skills have become indispensable. Managers who lead should be comfortable using word-processing, spreadsheet, database, presentation, and other software applications that are relevant to their work. They should be able to use the potential of the Internet to its fullest, for both research and communication. The skills listed here are discussed in more detail in Sections 37.4 and 37.5.

The values of a manager who leads

Values guide the manager who leads as he or she makes choices about how to serve staff, clients, and partners. Positive leadership has a strong ethical component that is missing from negative leadership. Those who lead with an eye on the common good are sustained by their values; positive leaders communicate their values frequently, and those values are visible in all their actions. In contrast, negative leadership draws on people's fears. It uses reward and punishment and depends on including some people and excluding others in the exercise of power and authority and in the distribution of rewards.

Managers who demonstrate positive values gain the respect of their staff, and they easily attract others to join them in pursuit of a vision of success as they display these values in their everyday life—

Integrity and commitment: People respect leaders for their ethics and personal commitment. People who are honest and ethical are credible to others who value integrity. A manager who leads who strongly believes in serving a greater good can avoid the temptations that often come with power.
Respect and trust: Respecting others means being willing to listen to their points of view and their needs. Respect builds trust over time, and trust is the foundation for developing productive relationships. Successful managers who lead nurture respectful work relationships with subordinates, colleagues, and superiors. They create new connections to broaden their own network and spend time improving existing relations that are problematic.
Courage: One job of leaders is to set an example for taking calculated risks that do not endanger the organization, its mission, or individuals. People who lead do not give up if they fail; they find the courage to reengage. Supported by their networks of trusting relationships, they find

Figure 37-3   Leading and managing framework: Practices that enable work groups and organizations to face challenges and achieve results

Leading	Managing
Scanning • Identify client and stakeholder needs and priorities • Recognize trends, opportunities, and risks that affect the organization • Look for best practices • Identify staff capacities and constraints • Know yourself, your staff, and your organization—values, strengths, and weaknesses **ORGANIZATIONAL OUTCOME** Managers have up-to-date, valid knowledge of their clients, the organization, and its context; they know how their behavior affects others	**Planning** • Set short-term organizational goals and performance objectives • Develop multiyear and annual plans • Allocate adequate resources (money, people, and materials) • Anticipate and reduce risks **ORGANIZATIONAL OUTCOME** Organization has defined results, assigned resources, and an operational plan
Focusing • Articulate the organization's mission and strategy • Identify critical challenges • Link goals with the overall organizational strategy • Determine key priorities for action • Create a common picture of desired results **ORGANIZATIONAL OUTCOME** Organization's work is directed by well-defined mission, strategy, and priorities	**Organizing** • Ensure a structure that provides accountability and delineates authority • Ensure that systems for human resource management, finance, logistics, quality assurance, operations, information, and marketing effectively support the plan • Strengthen work processes to implement the plan • Align staff capacities with planned activities **ORGANIZATIONAL OUTCOME** Organization has functional structures, systems, and processes for efficient operations; staff are organized and aware of job responsibilities and expectations
Aligning/Mobilizing • Ensure congruence of values, mission, strategy, structure, systems, and daily actions • Facilitate teamwork • Unite key stakeholders around an inspiring vision • Link goals with rewards and recognition • Enlist stakeholders to commit resources **ORGANIZATIONAL OUTCOME** Internal and external stakeholders understand and support the organization goals and have mobilized resources to reach these goals	**Implementing** • Integrate systems and coordinate work flow • Balance competing demands • Routinely use data for decision making • Coordinate activities with other programs and sectors • Adjust plans and resources as circumstances change **ORGANIZATIONAL OUTCOME** Activities are carried out efficiently, effectively, and responsively
Inspiring • Match deeds to words • Demonstrate honesty in interactions • Show trust and confidence in staff, acknowledge the contributions of others • Provide staff with challenges, feedback, and support • Be a model of creativity, innovation, and learning **ORGANIZATIONAL OUTCOME** Organization displays a climate of continuous learning and staff show commitment, even when setbacks occur	**Monitoring and Evaluating** • Monitor and reflect on progress against plans • Provide feedback • Identify needed changes • Improve work processes, procedures, and tools **ORGANIZATIONAL OUTCOME** Organization continuously updates information about the status of achievements and results, and applies ongoing learning and knowledge

Source: MSH 2005a.

support and courage to take necessary chances, make tough decisions, and face criticism or personal failure. By example, they encourage others to take calculated risks as well.

Openness to learning: Effective managers who lead are open to learning and inspire others to do the same. Their open minds are evident in their eagerness to continually learn and acquire knowledge and information. They initiate approaches to learning with others. This openness to learning and anticipation of the need to change allows a nimble response when the time comes to change old habits or long-standing practices.

The attitudes of a manager who leads

Effective managers who lead are recognizable by their mind-set. A *mind-set* is a habitual way of interpreting and responding to situations, which results from beliefs that are shaped by personal history and the surrounding culture. Such beliefs may be about the power of an individual to change a situation, the innate goodness or trustworthiness of others, or the assumption that the value of a person depends on his or her position in society.

For example, if a manager believes that people have something to contribute, he or she will find ways to encourage participation and shared learning. If a manager believes that individuals can make a difference, he or she will look for opportunities for thinking and working creatively together to achieve common goals.

By changing his or her view and interpretation of a situation, or by questioning deeply held beliefs, a manager may see new avenues for action that were hidden before. Therefore, being flexible enough to change one's viewpoint may reveal new possibilities for action and for success. These capacities are particularly important for managers who lead. These "leader shifts" are fundamental to effective leadership. Each of the following five leader shifts represents a series of changes in perspective that occur when people deepen their understanding of themselves, others, and the environment—

- From a belief in heroic actions to a preference for collaborative action that builds on the strength of a group of individuals to produce sustainable results
- From a state of despair or cynicism, where problems and obstacles appear to be insurmountable, to a place of hope and dreams, where multiple possibilities present themselves to make things better
- From a tendency to blame others for problems or failure to take the initiative, taking ownership of challenges, and working together to do something about them
- From frantic days filled with unrelated activities carried out for their own sake to purposeful work directed toward achieving results that matter

- From a preoccupation with oneself and ways to satisfy one's own needs to a concern with the greater good and a sense of responsibility toward others and society as a whole

These shifts are not easy to make or sustain, because a person's own needs, habits, and worries can interfere at any time. By being mindful of these issues, managers who lead can make corrections when they see that they are becoming busy but unproductive or are being drawn into a state of despair. They can stop themselves when they feel the urge to blame someone else or when their own needs begin to overshadow the greater good.

37.3 The management cycle and leading and managing practices

Program management activities are cyclical. To move from idea to result, the manager has to complete a set of activities through a series of phases: the planning phase, the implementation phase, and the monitoring and evaluation phase. This loop is continuous, because each evaluation contains the seeds for a new plan, and each plan is only as useful as it is feasible and implemented. Implementation is only successful if program goals and objectives are met, which is determined through monitoring and evaluation.

To make sure that the activities related to the management cycle are well managed and led, the manager draws on a particular set of management and leadership practices for each phase of the cycle (Figure 37-4).

Planning phase

In this phase, all major decisions regarding the use of human, financial, and other resources have to be made. During this phase, indicators are established that will allow later monitoring and evaluation. Although all managing and leading practices are required during this phase, the most critical practices are—

- *Scanning* to ensure that relevant and critical information about the current situation, key actors, strengths, weaknesses, threats, and opportunities is available, understood, and analyzed
- *Focusing* to set priorities among the many competing needs and interests and to identify key stakeholders and major variables, so that the best program approaches, broad goals, and strategies can be established
- *Planning* to set specific objectives and targets, determine implementation strategies, define activities and tasks, assign responsibilities, and allocate the resources needed to implement the plan and reach objectives

Figure 37-4   The management cycle

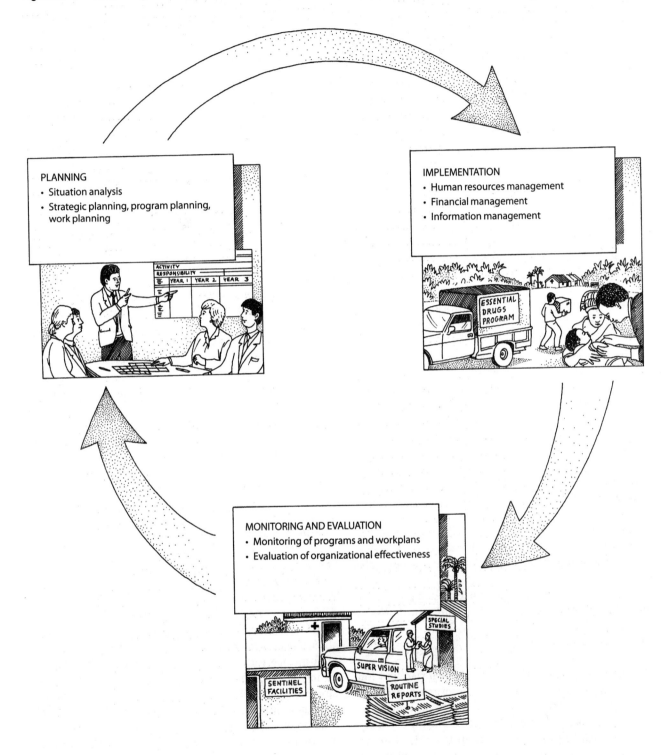

In all health programs, three main levels of planning exist, differing in purpose, time frame, and level of detail—

1. *Strategic planning:* This is planning with a long-term focus, usually more than five years and possibly as much as twenty-five years into the future. Such plans are concerned with the overall effectiveness and direction of the program or organization, and they establish or confirm a common vision of what the organization or program is meant to achieve. National development plans, national health policies, and national pharmaceutical policies are forms of strategic planning.
2. *Program planning:* This is planning with a medium-term focus, and it seeks to establish major objectives, activities, and resources needed for a specific program or organization over a three- to five-year period. Essential medicines program master plans and most large, multiyear project proposals are forms of program planning.
3. *Work planning:* This is planning with a short-term focus (usually six to twelve months), indicating for each major objective the specific target outputs, required tasks, individual responsibilities, schedule, and budget. Work planning also includes operational planning, such as that required to produce a national formulary manual, renovate a medical store, or conduct a major educational campaign on rational medicine use. Strategic plans and program plans that lack workplans are of little practical use.

To maximize the chance of success, those who will be involved in implementing a plan must be involved in formulating the plan. For strategic plans, senior ministry or program officials may have to be involved. For program plans or annual workplans, the staff of the program, department, and units involved should participate in plan formulation.

Chapter 38 describes in detail the planning process, the three levels of planning, and various planning methods.

Implementation phase

During the implementation phase, the plans are put into action. This phase usually requires most of a manager's time and energy. The work that is done during the planning phase provides the foundation for implementation; the better and more realistic the plan, the more likely that this phase will start well. The true test of a good plan is in its implementation: can the manager transform money, information, people's energy and skills, and other resources into the intended outcome?

The following managing and leading practices are particularly important during the implementation phase—

- *Aligning and mobilizing* to make sure key stakeholders are engaged and all possible resources are fully mobilized toward the planned activities
- *Organizing* to make sure that the right resources are available and usable at the right time at the right place and that people have the skills to use them
- *Implementing* to ensure the smooth progress of activities, coordinate with others, solve problems, remove obstacles, and make timely decisions
- *Inspiring* to create and support the commitment that sustains and nurtures people's efforts over time, especially when they are encountering setbacks or problems in their work

The effective functioning of the various management systems is especially important during the implementation phase. Specific aspects of implementation are discussed in other chapters of this manual, including—

- *Organizational structure for pharmaceutical supply* (Chapter 8): alternative models for pharmaceutical supply, centralization versus decentralization of pharmaceutical supply systems
- *Human resources management* (Chapter 51): staff selection, job descriptions, support and supervision, communication, delegation, motivation, and discipline
- *Financial management* (Chapter 41): budgeting, cash planning, costing, accounting, financial control, and reporting
- *Information management* (Chapter 49): information needs, information systems, and use of information for decision making

Monitoring and evaluation phase

The next phase in the management cycle is monitoring and evaluation. Although closely related, monitoring and evaluation are two distinct activities.

Monitoring starts during the implementation phase and is, in fact, an integral part of it. *Monitoring* is the process of observing implementation activities and comparing actual performance with plans. Objective indicators, developed during the planning phase, help track performance against targets. Objectives should be SMART—specific, measurable, appropriate to the individual or unit, realistic, and time-bound. They should also be written down. Objective indicators may specify performance levels for ongoing activities or plans to complete new tasks.

Examples of individual performance objectives within an essential medicines program would be—

- For the training officer: ensure that ongoing education programs contain a module on rational medicine use

- For the chief supplies officer: ensure that stock record–keeping is properly maintained
- For the district pharmacist: ensure that appropriate data, such as consumption rates for individual medicines, overstocks, and shortages, are collected and used for decision making

Methods of monitoring these performance activities may include carrying out random stock and record checks or requiring submission of quarterly reports on pharmacy data.

Monitoring allows the manager to take action when a discrepancy occurs. Program monitoring is done through supervisory visits, routine reporting, the use of sentinel reporting sites, and special studies (see Chapter 48). In addition, the staff members or units and supervisors should review individual progress on a regular basis. The review should assess progress toward each target, identify implementation problems, make any required changes in the targets, and suggest additional inputs required to achieve the targets. Actions may include providing corrective feedback, reallocating staff or other resources, adjusting plans and targets, or requesting additional information.

Evaluation is a periodic assessment of progress toward achieving long-term objectives and goals. Whereas monitoring is concerned with whether activities are being implemented as planned, evaluation is concerned with the overall relevance, effectiveness, efficiency, sustainability, effect, and future of the program. Evaluation builds on information gathered for monitoring purposes, but it requires additional information. Evaluation methods are also useful in pharmaceutical sector assessment for project planning (see Chapter 36).

In this phase, all the leading and managing practices are required. If the monitoring activities show that progress is being made, and if evaluation indicates that objectives and goals have been reached, the practice of inspiring becomes easier because nothing inspires people as much as being successful. The manager who leads needs to acknowledge all contributions to the success.

Chapter 48 describes monitoring and evaluation methods, the use of indicators, common pitfalls, and ways of using the monitoring system to improve performance.

37.4 Skills for managers who lead

For most people, training is a significant motivator, and most people look for opportunities to develop and grow professionally and personally. Skill development, whether self-directed or imposed, requires awareness, willingness to learn, training, and practice. Part of the planning phase requires an assessment of whether staff members have the required skills to implement the plan. If training is needed,

adequate resources (time and money) need to be reserved for this purpose.

Those concerned with pharmaceutical management policy increasingly recognize the need to support the strengthening of management and leadership skills. This reinforcement can be done on the job through coaching programs, by giving people assignments that challenge them to go beyond their current skill level, through continuing education schemes, or by participating in formal training programs.

A promising approach to management and leadership skill development is the enrollment of complete work teams in management and leadership development programs. In these programs, which can be face-to-face or Internet based, natural work teams select a real work challenge and learn the skills, practices, and values that will help them overcome the challenge and produce intended results (MSH 2005b).

Setting priorities

Priority setting is the skill of focusing attention and action among multiple options and interests. Devoting time to one problem or decision means that another must wait. All phases of the management cycle require priority setting, and the practice of *focusing* makes this possible.

In the *planning phase*, the manager has to decide what to plan for and what not; in the *implementation phase*, the manager has to make choices about how staff members use time; and in the *monitoring and evaluation phase*, the manager has to decide what to monitor and what to evaluate, because resources will never be enough to monitor and evaluate everything.

Managers are constantly faced with questions about which decision should be made first and which problems should be solved first. How much time and effort should be allocated to a specific problem or decision? What tasks should be delegated to other staff? To set priorities, managers need to ask themselves several questions—

Urgency: Many issues seem urgent, but which ones really have a critical requirement with an absolute deadline or time limit?
Relevance: Which issues are most central to long-term strategic plans and goals?
Impact: Which issues are likely to have the greatest impact on major program activities?
Future consequences: Which issues present the greatest threat to or the greatest opportunity for the future of the program?
Growth tendency: Which issues will get worse if they are not addressed sooner rather than later?

In general, issues should receive high priority if they are urgent, are likely to significantly affect future activities, or are likely to become worse if left unattended. The dilemma is that these high-priority issues are usually also the complex issues that require complex responses that cannot be addressed by the manager alone, whereas the simple, less urgent, or unimportant issues can be easily done and checked off a to-do list, thus giving the illusion of progress and successful action, yet having little or no significant impact.

An important principle for setting priorities is *management by exception*. With this approach, the manager expects staff to handle all decisions, problems, and activities, except for those that are of special importance, have long-term consequences, or are unusual in some way. This system allows the manager to focus on those issues that really need his or her attention. Management by exception is similar in some ways to the 80-20 rule in ABC analysis (see Chapter 40). It allows managers to focus on the most important areas. Management by exception can be applied to a variety of management tasks—

- Program development efforts should focus on the key aspects of pharmaceutical policy implementation that present the greatest difficulties.
- Routine reports should be reviewed to identify districts, facilities, or activities that are doing exceptionally badly (so that corrective action can be taken) or exceptionally well (so that they can be acknowledged and learned from).
- Follow-up supervisory visits should be made to regional depots, districts, or health units that are known from routine reports or other information to be having the most problems.

Management by exception and the key priority-setting questions apply mostly to the allocation of human resources. Chapter 38 discusses setting priorities for financial and other tangible resources as part of the planning process.

Managing time

Staff time and personal time are resources that need to be managed. Wasting time diverts a manager from important tasks. The most frequent time wasters include—

- Random activities ("busy-ness") that do not contribute to specified objectives
- Failure to set priorities
- Absence of deadlines
- Unnecessary or badly structured meetings
- Visitors arriving without appointments
- Telephone or e-mail interruptions
- Too little or too much information
- Attempts to do too much in too little time
- Overemphasis on easier, more routine work at the expense of harder tasks

- Long breaks and social chat
- Inability to say no

To avoid wasting time, the following techniques may be useful—

- Be clear on your own and your team or organization's vision.
- Identify measurable results as milestones toward the vision.
- Clarify objectives by writing them down.
- Establish in the morning at least one good outcome for the day ("this will be a good day if I accomplish . . .") and then focus your attention and effort on achieving it.
- Keep a log of how days are spent, and review it.
- Reserve the best time of the workday to concentrate on the most important task.
- If necessary, negotiate with your supervisor to take work to a quiet place—the unoccupied office of someone on leave, a nearby library, or home—when an assignment must be finished.

Time is one resource that is equally available to everyone and distributed in a finite way; only twenty-four hours are available in a day. When time is frittered away, it is lost forever. A manager who makes good use of time to align personal and organizational goals is investing well in his or her own future as well as the future of the program.

Decision making and problem solving

Decision making is a skill that requires a combination of analytical thinking, pragmatic considerations, and intuition. Many tools are available that can help in this process. Successful management requires prompt, thoughtful responses to the problems that inevitably arise when plans are put into action. This is the art of effective implementation. Some managers are very good at both decision making and problem solving; others defer decisions, avoid problems, or make impulsive responses that create new problems.

Although they are different in some respects, decision making and problem solving can both be approached through a seven-step process, which requires the management and leadership practices of scanning and focusing—

1. Review the basic objective.
2. Define the decision to be made or the problem to be solved.
3. Assess the situation to determine the cause of the problem.
4. Identify alternative solutions.
5. Compare the alternatives, using defined criteria.
6. Select and implement the best decision or solution.
7. Follow up and adjust.

Decision making and problem solving can go wrong at any of the seven steps, but some of the following common mistakes can lead to bad decisions or unworkable solutions.

Losing track of the original objective or solving the wrong problem: The basic problem must be clearly identified. Managers may be presented with a problem of inadequate financing for pharmaceuticals when the real problem is that the procurement unit is wasting money by not following the essential medicines list. Or considerable time and money may be invested in renovating and reorganizing the central warehouse to improve the supply system when the real problem is that staff members are not adequately trained or motivated.

Failure to properly assess the situation or the causes of the problem: If the causes of a problem are thoroughly understood, the solution is often obvious. It is therefore important to identify what additional information is needed to adequately understand the situation. If a stockout of amoxicilline occurs, for example, the manager needs to know whether it is because the medicine was not ordered, not shipped, not delivered, or consumed more rapidly than expected.

Failure to identify all relevant alternatives: Managers who act too quickly may achieve poor results because they have not considered the options or consulted key stakeholders who could have pointed out previously unnoticed issues. Similarly, managers who avoid decisions and problems may do so simply because they have not made the effort to identify reasonable alternatives.

Lack of clear criteria for selecting among alternatives: If what is to be accomplished is clear, the criteria for choosing among alternatives will be easier to define. Sometimes cost is a major factor; sometimes it is time.

Failure to follow up and adjust: Things seldom work out exactly as expected. Managers must be willing to adjust their actions on the basis of experience. Lack of follow-up, leaving people to their own devices when new behaviors are needed, laziness, carelessness, or stubborn unwillingness to adjust to experience are likely to waste resources.

One effective way for managers to improve decision making and problem solving is to ask staff to go through these steps themselves before coming to the manager. They should present the manager not only with a question or a problem but also with a list of alternative courses of action, a recommended course, and the reasons for the recommendation. The manager can then make the final decision. With staff members doing the basic problem solving, the decision is likely to be better and require much less time and effort.

Managers who maintain control by acting as if or believing they are the only source of answers and solutions may resist this approach. But as the quality of decisions—and

with it, program performance—improves, the manager will soon appreciate the benefits of the new approach.

Coaching

Coaching is a conversation in which the coach is committed to the development and success of the person being coached. A coach helps the other person clarify her commitments and intended results, see new possibilities and actions, and expand her range of behavior choices. Coaching also helps the person understand his own contribution to recurrent problems and see the consequences of choices made. Ultimately, coaching is intended to help the other person think more clearly and see new ways of achieving intended results. However, for a person to be coached, he or she has to want to learn and change, be open to feedback from others, and be willing to take responsibility for his or her own actions.

A coach does not evaluate and judge, blame, criticize, scold, or give solutions. An effective coach builds a relationship of trust and support, cares about the person being coached and has his or her growth in mind, listens well, and asks questions to clarify and illuminate a goal or challenge. Some of the questions a coach might ask are—

- What are you committed to achieving?
- What have you achieved so far?
- What obstacles are you facing?
- Why do you think you are stuck?
- If it could turn out exactly as you dreamed, how would it turn out?
- What actions could you take to overcome your obstacles?
- What support do you need from others?
- How can I support you?

Coaching is a good vehicle for the manager to give the underperforming person a warning and a chance to improve. Sometimes poor performance is simply a matter of mismatched expectations or the complete absence of feedback. When no feedback or no adverse reaction results from poor performance, the staff member may conclude that performance is either up to standards or does not matter. Perhaps current policies, procedures, and flow of resources support and reward mediocre performance. And finally, staff may not have the skills to do well.

The manager should prepare for the coaching conversation before meeting with the staff member. Preparation will help the manager avoid being sidetracked from the planned conversation in case strong emotions surface (such as crying, shouting, making threats). Review what happened, separating feelings and thoughts from facts or observations, and then reach a decision with the person that reengages him or her in the task at hand.

By mastering a comfortable coaching style and using it strategically to improve performance, the manager who leads will be able to deal more effectively with difficult personnel issues.

Communicating

The manager who leads is the central focus for receiving and disseminating information. He or she needs to be able to communicate orally and in writing to various stakeholder groups, including not only staff members, peers, and bosses, but also people outside the program or organization.

Disseminating information to staff members helps them in their work. Insecure managers trying to protect their jobs sometimes purposefully withhold relevant information from subordinates. Sadly, by failing to support subordinates in their work, the manager increases the chances that the program will perform poorly, which in turn reflects badly on the manager.

Good communication will permit the manager to build a network of formal and informal contacts. This network is an invaluable source of information for scanning so that the manager can monitor changes, opportunities, problems, or misunderstandings that may affect the work. Networking is especially important in formalized relationships, such as those between ministries (finance and health, for example) or between programs and their donors.

Feedback is an important part of communication. If staff members do not know whether they are performing below standards, they cannot take corrective action. Often, managers avoid giving feedback about poor performance because it makes them uncomfortable. After all, giving someone bad news is not easy. Such avoidance can be devastating for individuals, however, and in the end, an unnecessary delay makes the conversation even more awkward and uncomfortable than it needs to be. The easiest way to give feedback is to alert the person ahead of time; seek a quiet place where the conversation cannot be interrupted, disturbed, or overheard; and review the things that go well, the things that need improvement, and finally, the things that need to stop. If the manager provides feedback in the right manner, an employee will be able to hear it without becoming defensive. Feedback can also become a motivator for change and improve the quality of information submitted to the manager.

Communication skills require an acute awareness of how messages are being transmitted, such as tone of voice, phrasing, and even use of words. Using simple and descriptive language and avoiding jargon are important. Simple and clear language that avoids confusion or double meanings is especially important when communicating with people from other cultures—whether professional, ethnic, or socioeconomic. Many potential misunderstandings are entirely preventable by paying more attention to language.

Senior-level managers often have to serve as spokespersons and present program needs and activities to higher officials, to donor organizations, or to the community. For such written or oral communication, the manager needs to think through the purpose and desired outcome of the report or presentation. Is it for information only or is some sort of action expected? Before composing a written communication, whether for oral presentation or for a report, the manager needs to consider the following questions—

- What is the purpose of the communication?
- Who is the audience?
- What is the expectation that the audience will retain?
- What is the audience, or selected parts of the audience, expected to do as a result of the communication?

Presenters of PowerPoint slides need to follow a few simple rules—

- Use only a few slides and use them as a presentation guide.
- Avoid reading the exact text from a slide.
- Use no more than five lines of five to six words each per slide.
- Distribute dense tables or long lists of statistics as handouts rather than putting them on slides.
- Practice the presentation with people who are likely to give honest feedback.

Negotiating

Negotiations usually happen either to create something new that neither party can produce on its own or to resolve a problem between two parties. Therefore, negotiating is a critical skill for managers who lead. Whatever the reason for the negotiation, managers need to be able to reach understandings and agreements with a broad range of people inside and outside their organization or program.

Each negotiation involves two factors: the substance of the negotiation (what is being negotiated) and the relationship between the two parties. To deal with the substance of the negotiation, the manager needs to present and defend his or her own point of view to establish his or her voice in the negotiation. But the manager also needs to establish and nurture the relationship with the other party in the negotiation. Different negotiating circumstances and partners require different tactics, and the manager has to decide which is more important—the relationship or the substance of the negotiation; sometimes they are equally important.

Pharmaceutical system managers often have little power within their larger organizations, which makes negotiation skills especially important for them. The basis for their power lies mainly in their knowledge and information. Managers need to plan their negotiations carefully by recognizing good opportunities to open a negotiation, thinking about the best timing for negotiations, and presenting good evidence to support the case.

Planning for a negotiation requires three steps related to the leading and managing framework (see Figure 37-3)—

Step 1. Characterize the substance of the negotiation. This step requires the practice of scanning.

- Find out as much as possible about what each party brings to the table (for example, skills, information, experience).
- Recognize factors that make each party vulnerable and plan how to deal with them.
- Develop alternatives to a negotiated agreement.
- Seek fresh perspectives from others.
- Anticipate reactions from the other party to the presented viewpoint and proposals.

Step 2. Attract the other party to the table, which requires the practice of aligning and mobilizing.

- Make sure the other party sees that entering into the negotiation will be of value, and that this value will not be available otherwise.
- Make negotiation unavoidable by showing that no one has an alternative to a negotiated agreement or that not negotiating will result in an undesirable change for the other party.
- Level the playing field by establishing authority and credibility. When the negotiator is lower in status than the other party, getting explicit authorization from a superior is helpful.
- Build support for the agenda by using allies as intermediaries, strategic partners, and promoters of the cause.

Step 3. Make the personal connection, which requires the practices of scanning, focusing, aligning, and mobilizing.

- Invest time and energy in relationship building, participation, and staying engaged.
- Get everyone to take ownership of the problem by pointing out the negative consequences for all of not reaching agreement.
- Take a critical look at your own situation in order to separate fact from fiction or belief.
- Be open to listening to the other person's situation, appreciating his or her feelings, ideas, and need to save face. Look for links between the two situations.

As an example, a hospital pharmacist negotiating for a budget increase to add a computerized information system might need to—

1. Look into what competing priorities for resources the hospital administrators are juggling.

2. Enlist the support of colleagues in other departments, such as clinicians and nurses, whose performances are affected by service in the pharmacy.

3. Present the case for how a computerized pharmacy system will provide information to clinicians on patient adherence levels and adverse drug reactions and information to administrators, who need to compile monthly reports on patient treatment for donors and the ministry of health. Present the case that the computer will not only make a measurable difference in pharmaceutical service quality,v but also will help the hospital meet overall performance objectives.

It is important to recognize, however, that sometimes the other party is playing by different rules and is unwilling to engage in a fair negotiation. The power imbalance between the two parties may simply be too great, turning the negotiation into a win-lose battle. Managers need to recognize this situation and be prepared to cut their losses (and try to do better next time).

37.5 Managing change

Leading is by definition related to change, because leaders take their followers to a place in the future that is different from the current situation. Improvements in managing pharmaceutical systems involve changes in policy, organizations, and individuals. Successful development is in many respects the management of change, and an organization that does not change eventually fails.

Change occurs at different levels and magnitudes, from restructuring the entire supply system to simply introducing a new dispensing register, or from launching a comprehensive national medicine policy to changing generic labeling requirements. Strategic planning may lead to major changes, whereas annual workplans generally involve smaller operational changes.

Effective management of change depends on an understanding of forces for change, resistance to change, and principles for successful change management.

Forces for change

Forces for change may come from within or outside the organization. Internal forces include pressure from individuals genuinely seeking to improve the program, from ambitious individuals pursuing their own ends, or from individuals and groups who are dissatisfied.

Sources of external pressure for change can include parts of the government or society, groups working globally, or specific donors. Such external pressure may arise from economic factors, political forces, or philosophical differences.

External pressure may also arise from trends toward democratization, decentralization, or privatization.

Managers who do not recognize and respond to change forces risk being overwhelmed by them. Many directors of medical services and program managers have lost their positions because they failed to appreciate the need for change and did not exert leadership in managing change.

Resistance to change

Resistance to change is a normal human response that is more likely to interfere with the change process if the change is imposed without any consultation with those most affected by it. Common sources of resistance to change include—

Personal self-interest: People resist change when they perceive it as a threat to their status, power, or personal finance; in short, when the change represents the loss of something that is significant. This situation includes instances where vested interests are being threatened. Anyone who is benefiting from the current situation is likely to resist the proposed change.

Bureaucratic inertia: Bureaucracies develop structures, policies, and procedures of their own: "We've always done it this way." The response to change can be to subvert it with innumerable delays, diversions, and other barriers.

Habit: People resist change in organizations, but they also resist changing themselves. Most people find comfort and safety in the familiar.

Fear and uncertainty: Change generally involves some risk. Although things are supposed to get better, they could become worse if the change is unsuccessful.

Conformity and peer pressure: If new warehouse procedures or computerization of procurement systems is seen as a threat to jobs, co-workers may pressure colleagues to undermine the changes.

Rejection of outsiders: Changes are sometimes designed, proposed, or advocated by outsiders to the system and may bring in new managers or staff. Changes associated with outsiders are often resisted, regardless of the potential benefits of the changes themselves.

Understanding the sources of resistance to change can help identify ways of reducing this resistance, described below in the section on principles for managing change.

Changing management systems

Improving the performance of essential medicines programs often means developing and implementing new management systems or strengthening existing ones and developing the capacities of staff. Examples include the

process for selecting essential medicines and publishing the results; the committee structure, procedures, and forms used for tendering and other procurement activities; and the inventory control system and delivery schedule for distribution.

Effective management systems are rarely developed by people sitting behind a desk, and management systems never implement themselves. Too often, new management systems are designed in isolation and implemented without adequate testing. To increase the chance that the proposed changes are implemented, four key steps are necessary—

Step 1. Assessment of needs: What are the management needs? The procurement system for a program that buys medicines only from a few established international low-cost suppliers is likely to be quite different from one that buys through open international tender.

Step 2. Interactive system design and testing: In an interactive design process, those responsible for developing new systems work closely with operational staff. For example, new district systems can often build on innovations developed by an individual district or several health facilities. Procedures, recording systems, or reporting forms can be tested and revised at selected sites.

Step 3. Implementation training: Training based on general management concepts often has limited impact. But implementation training is an indispensable part of management development and should be as practical as possible and include a visit to facilities that have already implemented the new systems.

Step 4. Focused supervision: Training alone will not ensure implementation of new systems. Considerable follow-up supervision, focused on those units that are having the greatest difficulty, is often needed.

The concept of interactive system design is especially important. Staff members tend to resist centrally designed systems that fail to consider local needs or practical constraints. Most important, experienced operational staff members have clever ideas and solutions of their own to contribute. Interactive system design should not be seen as a totally democratic process in which everyone's ideas are adopted. Instead, it is a creative but pragmatic process in which the most demonstrably useful ideas are incorporated into the final design.

Phased implementation

When new management systems, reporting forms, or other major changes are introduced, the manager needs to make sure that all affected parties are aligned and mobilized around the proposed change. For example, introduction of a new standard treatment manual or ordering system would begin with a national workshop for key staff from provincial hospitals, followed several months later by provincial-level workshops for key district staff within the province. Finally, each district would hold workshops for its staff.

Phased implementation has the following advantages—

- It is more practical than introducing changes at all levels and all sites at the same time.
- It allows some real-world testing and revision of new systems before national implementation.
- It allows the public to adjust to new ideas and provides some flexibility in the timing of expansion to other levels. This gradual introduction is especially important when the proposed change has political ramifications, such as the introduction of user fees.
- It allows time for training and follow-up at one level before moving to the next level; when the new system has become fully functional at the initial level, facilities at that level can serve as training sites for the next level (see Country Study 37-1).
- Senior medical and administrative staff at one level who have become familiar with the new system become more effective advocates and supervisors at the next level.

Phased implementation may start at the central level and move to the provincial or state, district or regional, and local levels; it may also be geographical, thereby completing the introduction of new systems in one area, province, or state before moving to the next.

Force field analysis

Force field analysis is a technique for identifying driving forces, those forces that push toward an objective, and restraining forces, those that stand in the way. The balance of these forces determines the point of equilibrium.

Implementing change or solving problems involves unbalancing the forces and shifting the equilibrium. The analysis has three steps—

1. *Diagnosing:* Identify all driving and restraining forces.
2. *Unfreezing:* Find ways to reduce restraining forces, strengthen driving forces, or find new driving forces.
3. *Refreezing or redefining:* Reestablish the equilibrium at the new target point.

Force field analysis uses a brainstorming technique, which is ideal for management teams. It enables a logical, systematic review of any problem or change situation, facilitates a comprehensive discussion of factors and possibilities, and is a highly participatory planning method that enhances teamwork. See Box 37-1 for more information on force field analysis.

Country Study 37-1
Using learning sites to phase in the implementation of antiretroviral therapy programs in Kenya

An antiretroviral therapy (ART) learning site is a health facility where the facility managers, ART program staff, and partners collaborate to apply, integrate, and maintain best practices in ART pharmaceutical management system and services. The facility staff then serve as leaders and mentors, and the facility serves as a practicum site for training and promoting high standards for health commodity management.

The Coast Provincial General Hospital (CPGH) in Mombasa was the first facility in Kenya that integrated comprehensive HIV care and treatment into existing services, and CPGH became Kenya's first ART learning site as the country began scaling up ART. CPGH's package of services included clinical, pharmaceutical, laboratory, psychosocial, and community linkages.

Arranging site visits to and mentoring relationships with the learning site is an effective strategy to prepare staff who are about to start providing ART pharmaceutical services. The objective is to give pharmacy staff hands-on experience in managing inventory and dispensing antiretroviral medicines, quantifying consumption, and medication counseling and to familiarize them with tools and record keeping. The learning site experience also allows the pharmacy staff members to exchange information on their challenges and lessons learned and to give them a reference point as they make changes at their own sites.

Pharmacy staff from Coast province and other provinces that used CPGH as a resource strengthened their own facilities and then became pharmaceutical management learning sites modeled on CPGH. In addition, the two national teaching and referral hospitals, Kenyatta National Hospital and Moi Teaching and Referral Hospital, adopted the CPGH model for ART pharmaceutical services. Eventually, the success of the learning site model resulted in Kenya's National AIDS/ STD Control Program adopting it in support of the country's goal of providing universal access to HIV care and treatment. Its decentralization strategy for HIV services is anchored in learning sites.

Box 37-1
Force field analysis

Force field analysis is a technique for analyzing the forces in an environment that can drive or restrain change. Force field analysis involves the following steps—

1. Write the objective at the top of a flip chart.
2. Draw a line down the middle of the sheet.
3. Brainstorm and list on the right-hand side all the restraining forces: those factors in the situation that will have a negative influence on the achievement of the objective.
4. On the left-hand side, list all the driving forces: those that will have a positive influence on the achievement of the objective. (It is important to put down only those factors that are actually present in the current situation, not what would be desirable in the future.)

After the force field has been fully set out, strategies for creating change can be developed.

5. Draw a line under the list in the left-hand column and write "Action Points."
6. Analyze the array of forces that has been constructed. Consider how the positive ones can be strengthened or augmented and, more important,

how the negative ones can be eliminated or counteracted. The questions to be asked at this stage are—

- Can any of the restraining forces be reduced?
- Can any of the driving forces be strengthened?
- Can any new driving forces be found?

7. In light of the foregoing analysis, list action points that will be helpful in achieving the objective.

In the accompanying figure, the objective is to move from a current level of 50 percent pharmaceutical availability (vertical bar on the left) to a level of 75 percent pharmaceutical availability (bar on right). The first step is diagnosis—identifying driving and restraining forces. Below are some of the forces that might come out.

Driving forces	Restraining forces
• Political pressure to solve medicine availability problem	• Interference in procurement process
• New pharmaceutical management leadership	• Poor quantification practices
• Up-to-date essential medicines list	• Lax storage and distribution system
• New training on rational use of medicines	• Overprescription by health workers

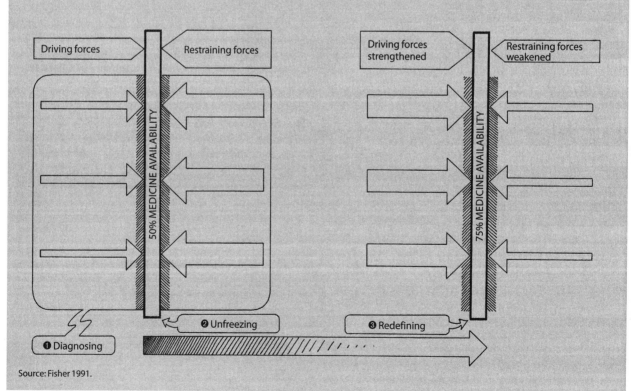

Source: Fisher 1991.

Principles for managing change

Success depends on the magnitude and circumstances of the change as well as on the organizations and people affected by it. It is important to understand the responses people have to change and provide support and encouragement that are appropriate to where people are in their own process (see Figure 37-5). The following suggestions are useful in overcoming resistance to change and in managing change only when a manager has a clear sense of direction and purpose—

Know yourself: Managers should recognize their own reactions to change and their strengths and limitations.
Learn how others feel: Using both direct and indirect channels of communication helps managers assess reactions to change and adjust the change process.
Know the organization: Any organization has both a formal structure of reporting relationships and informal channels of influence. Understanding the organization, often with the help of others, is important to planning and managing change.
Generate "ownership" through participation: The seeds of success or failure for change are sown even before the change has been fully planned or implemented. Involving potential supporters and implementers early in the process generates a sense of ownership.
Use reason: Make the case (as in a legal argument) for the proposed change by pointing out the pros and cons of the change, showing the consequences of not addressing it.
Debunk myths: Directly (but tactfully) challenge myths stemming from long-held beliefs, wrong or outdated ideas, or misinformation passed on by others.
Share the credit: Part of generating a sense of ownership among staff involves sharing the credit. Leaders who capture the credit for themselves are likely to find themselves alone at a critical point in the process.
Look for win-win strategies: Change is more likely to succeed if every interest group benefits in some way. Generic medicine substitution can benefit both customers and retail pharmacists if the pharmacist is allowed to make a higher mark-up on a much less expensive medicine.
Develop a sense of timing: People often expect and want policy and program changes when the leadership changes. New governments and new managers provide an opportunity for change.
Share information and educate: Much of the resistance to change comes from fear and uncertainty. These can be reduced by clear and open communication with staff.
Recognize that people take in information in different ways: Some need to see numbers presented in graphs or tables. Others prefer to see pictures or hear quotations.
Tell a compelling story about the vision and show how the changes are inevitable.

Figure 37-5 Working with people's responses to change

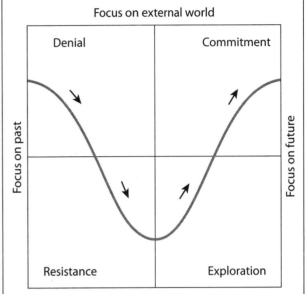

It is important to understand the responses people have to change and provide support and encouragement that is appropriate to where people are in their own process.

When people are in a place of...

Denial. Provide them with more information so that it becomes difficult to stay in denial.

Resistance. Create opportunities for people to express their feelings. Resist the impulse to explain or defend, which will make things worse. Show empathy for and understanding of the losses people experience.

Exploration. Make available opportunities and resources for discovering what is possible in the new situation. Encourage people to get together and support one another.

Commitment. There is no need to "manage" the change process at this point, since people will manage themselves. Get out of the way.

Source: Scott and Jaffe 2010.

Describe the vision in a variety of ways: Provide opportunities for people to "try on" the new vision for themselves.
Facilitate and support: Fear and anxiety can also be reduced if managers listen, show concern, and support staff in their effort to understand and adapt to change.
Be persistent: Change does not happen immediately. Successful change often occurs slowly, step-by-step. A gradual approach, with occasional retreats (two steps forward, one step back), is sometimes the best way to succeed.
Reinforce the desired new behaviors or practices: Provide resources and rewards (which may include publicity, public recognition, awards, extra resources, or

opportunities for growth) to those who apply the new behaviors or practices.

Use force sparingly: Threats of firing, reassignment, loss of privileges, or other forms of coercion may be necessary to manage specific individuals or groups. Such measures should be used selectively, and only when other approaches have not worked; threats that are not carried out soon become hollow. ∎

References and further readings

★ – Key readings.

★ Amonoo-Lartson, R., G. Ebrahim, H. Lovel, and J. Ranken. 1996. *District Health Care: Challenges for Planning, Organisation and Evaluation in Developing Countries.* 2nd ed. Oxford: Macmillan Education.

Brown, L. D. 1993. *Assessing the Quality of Management: User's Guide.* Health Care Management Advancement Program, Module 7. Geneva: Aga Khan Foundation. <http://www.jhsph.edu/delta_omega/Internet_Resources/phcmap-doc.html>

Covey, S. 2004. *The Seven Habits of Highly Effective People: Powerful Lessons in Personal Change.* Rev. ed. New York: Free Press.

CPM/MSH (Center for Pharmaceutical Management/Management Sciences for Health). 2011. *Center for Pharmaceutical Management: Technical Frameworks, Approaches, and Results.* Arlington, Va.: CPM.

FIP (International Pharmaceutical Federation/Fédération internationale pharmaceutique). 2005. *FIP Statement of Policy: Improving Access to Medicines in Developing Countries.* The Hague: FIP. <http://www.fip.org/www/uploads/database_file.php?id=156&table_id=>

Fisher, R., W. Ury, and B. Patton. 1991. *Getting to Yes: Negotiating Agreement without Giving In.* 2nd ed. New York: Penguin Books.

Hilton, M., L. M. Franco, G. Murphy, and M. Francisco. 1993. *Problem-Solving. Primary Health Care Management Advancement Program, Manager's Guide.* Geneva: Aga Khan Foundation. <http://www.jhsph.edu/delta_omega/Internet_Resources/phcmap-doc.html>

Ivancevich, J. M., P. Lorenzi, S. J. Skinner, and P. B. Crosby. 1997. *Management Quality and Competitiveness.* 2nd ed. Chicago: Richard D. Irwin.

Kouzes, J. M., and B. Z. Posner. 2008. *The Leadership Challenge: How to Get Extraordinary Things Done in Organizations.* 4th ed. San Francisco: Jossey-Bass.

McCauley, C. D., and E. Van Velsor, eds. 2003. *The Center for Creative Leadership Handbook of Leadership Development.* 2nd ed. San Francisco: Jossey-Bass.

★ McMahon, R., E. Barton, and M. Piot. 1992. *On Being in Charge: A Guide to Management in Primary Health Care.* 2nd ed. Geneva: World Health Organization. <http://whqlibdoc.who.int/publications/9241544260.pdf>

Millar, M. 1993. *Assessing the Quality of Management: Facilitator's Guide.* Primary Health Care Management Advancement Program, Module 8. Geneva: Aga Khan Foundation. <http://www.jhsph.edu/delta_omega/Internet_Resources/phcmap-doc.html >

MSH (Management Sciences for Health) 2005a. *Leadership Development Program Guide.* Cambridge, Mass.: MSH. <http://www1.msh.org/projects/lms/Documents/loader.cfm?csModule=security/getfile&pageid=13712>

★ ———. 2005b. *Managers Who Lead: A Handbook for Improving Health Services.* Cambridge, Mass.: MSH. <http://www.msh.org/Documents/upload/MWL-2008-edition.pdf>

ASSESSMENT GUIDE

Tasks, practices, skills, values, and mind-sets

- How do managers divide their time between crisis management, routine administration, control and supervision, and long-term program development?
- To what extent do managers use the eight management and leadership practices?
- Are the managers up-to-date on their technical skills?
- To what extent are the managers financially literate and computer literate?
- What are the strengths and weaknesses of senior managers with respect to the essential management and leadership skills (setting priorities, managing time, problem solving and decision making, coaching, communicating, negotiating, managing change)?
- To what extent do managers set priorities based on the urgency, relevance, impact, future consequences, and growth of issues? Do they manage by exception?
- How frequently do managers have contact with operational staff? Do they involve staff in planning, decision making, and problem solving?
- Do managers and staff members jointly set performance targets and use them to monitor performance?

Management cycle

- Can managers articulate the management and leadership practices for each of the three phases in the management cycle?
- What levels of planning take place—strategic planning, program planning, work planning?
- Does the planning process involve staff members who are responsible for implementation?
- Are new management systems designed with input from operational-level staff? Is implementation phased? Are staff trained in the use of new systems?
- Does regular monitoring take place? Are monitoring results used to make corrective adjustments?
- Are evaluations focused on the program or project's relevance, effectiveness, efficiency, sustainability, and impact?

Quick, J. C., J. D. Quick, D. L. Nelson, and J. J. Hurrell. 1997. *Preventive Stress Management in Organizations*. Rev. ed. Washington, D.C.: American Psychological Association.

Rees, F. 2001. *How to Lead Work Teams: Facilitation Skills*. 2nd ed. Hoboken, N.J.: John Wiley & Sons.

★ Reynolds, J., M. Francisco, and S. Gearon. 1993. *Better Management: 100 Tips*. Primary Health Care Management Advancement Program, Manager's Guide. Geneva: Aga Khan Foundation. <http://www.jhsph.edu/delta_omega/Internet_Resources/phcmap-doc.html>

Rifkin, S., and P. Pridmore. 2001. *Partners in Planning: Information, Participation and Empowerment*. Oxford: Macmillan/TALC. (Available online from Teaching-aids At Low Cost (TALC) at http://www.talcuk.org.)

Rogers, E. 2003. *Diffusion of Innovations*. 5th ed. New York: Free Press.

Schein, E. H. 2010. *Organizational Culture and Leadership*. 4th ed. San Francisco: Jossey-Bass.

Scott, C. D., and D. T. Jaffe. 2010. *Managing Personal Change: Stay Positive and Stay in Control*. 3rd ed. Boston: Course Technology/Thomson Learning.

WHO and FIP (World Health Organization and International Pharmaceutical Federation). 2006. *Developing Pharmacy Practice: A Focus on Patient Care*. Geneva: WHO and FIP. <http://www.who.int/medicines/publications/WHO_PSM_PAR_2006.5.pdf>

Glossary

Activity: An action aimed at achieving a particular objective.

Delegation: The assignment by a manager of an activity, task, defined scope of authority, or responsibility to a staff member under the manager's supervision.

Evaluation: A periodic assessment of progress toward achieving long-term objectives and goals. Monitoring and evaluation are the third phase in the management cycle.

Force field analysis: A planning technique used in change management to identify driving forces, those forces that favor a particular change, and restraining forces, those that stand in the way of change.

Goal: The general aim toward which the organization or program is striving.

Implementation: The second phase in the management cycle; the process of putting a plan into action by organizing and directing the work. It involves managing people, money, information, and other resources to achieve intended results.

Indicator: Criterion used to measure changes, directly or indirectly, and to assess the extent to which the targets and objectives of a program or project are being attained. Indicators should meet the criteria of clarity, usefulness, measurability, reliability, validity, and acceptance by key stakeholders.

Information system: The system of records kept at offices, storage facilities, and clinical facilities; forms that are used to communicate supply needs, consumption data, and other information; reports that summarize the data from records and forms for planning and evaluation purposes; and procedures that coordinate the use and flow of these documents.

Management by exception: A technique in which the manager expects staff to handle all decisions, problems, and activities, except for those that are of special importance, have long-term consequences, or are in some way unusual.

Management cycle: The process consisting of the three interconnected phases of planning, implementing, and monitoring and evaluating.

Mission (or mission statement): A brief general description of the type of organization, its main purpose, and its values.

Monitoring: The ongoing process of reviewing the degree to which program activities are completed and objectives are being met, to allow for corrective action to be taken during implementation. Monitoring and evaluation are the third phase in the management cycle.

Objectives: Results that a program or workplan seeks to achieve. A well-formulated objective fits the SMART mnemonic: specific, measurable, appropriate to overall objectives or goals, realistic in terms of available resources, time-bound (there is a deadline).

Participatory management: The process of involving staff in management processes to bring more information, creativity, and experience to planning, decision making, and problem solving, often resulting in better conclusions and better implementation efforts.

Performance target: An objective or desired standard of performance for an individual or unit that is written, specific, measurable, appropriate to the individual or unit, realistic, and time-bound; is in line with overall program goals and objectives; and is used to periodically assess progress.

Planning: The first phase in the management cycle; the process of analyzing the current situation, assessing needs, establishing goals, setting objectives and targets, and determining the strategies, responsibilities, and resources needed to achieve the objectives. Three levels of planning are strategic, program, and work planning.

Program plans: Medium-term plans (three to five years) that specify major objectives, activities, and resources needed for a specific program or organization; examples include master plans and multiyear-project plans.

Sentinel sites: Selected units or facilities from which more detailed information is collected for monitoring purposes, on a more frequent basis than from other units.

Strategic plans: Long-term development plans concerned with the overall effectiveness and direction of a program or organization.

Strategy: A broad plan of action for fulfilling a program's basic purpose and achieving its main goals.

Supervise: To oversee; to provide direction; to guide and instruct with immediate responsibility for performance.

SWOT analysis: An assessment of the internal strengths and weaknesses of an organization or program, as well as external opportunities and threats.

Targets: Measurable, time-limited, intermediate progress points toward objectives; also called milestones.

Task: Specific work to be performed as part of an activity and within a certain time.

Workplans: Short-term plans (usually six to twelve months) that list for each major objective the target outputs, required tasks, individual responsibilities, schedule, and budget.

CHAPTER 38

Planning for pharmaceutical management

SUMMARY

Planning is the process of analyzing the current situation; assessing needs; establishing goals; setting objectives and measurable targets; and determining the strategies, responsibilities, and resources needed to achieve the expected results.

The three levels of planning differ in purpose, time frame, and focus of detail.

Strategic planning is concerned with the long-term future of an organization and its overall effectiveness and direction in light of changing external and internal environments. It includes specific strategies for achieving the organization's mission and a means of tracking progress. A national pharmaceutical policy, for example, may result from a strategic-planning process. New strategies are most useful when—

- Current strategies are not working
- A pharmaceutical sector options analysis has been completed and new strategies are required
- The political or social environment changes dramatically
- There is a crisis

Program planning follows from strategic planning and focuses on medium-term objectives. For each objective, a program or project plan should specify outcomes, responsibilities, time frame, and budget. It is best implemented through operational workplans. Essential medicines programs, for example, should have program plans.

Work planning or operational planning is short-term planning and should involve staff who will be responsible for implementation. Workplans generally specify a limited set of objectives, all major activities, individual responsibilities, timing (at least to the month), indicators for monitoring and measuring progress and results,

budget, and source of funds for each activity or task. Gantt charts are often key features and are useful for monitoring.

Some project-planning methods and tools that can be helpful include the critical path method (CPM) and project evaluation and review technique (PERT), the logical framework approach (LogFrame), and various computer software packages.

Plans may fail to achieve their intended objectives when—

- Problems, root causes, and options have not been well analyzed
- Planning is unrealistic or overly ambitious
- Existing commitments have not been considered
- Implementers have not been involved
- There is inadequate support, funds, staff, or time
- Planning is undertaken for the wrong reasons or at the wrong level
- Plans are poorly presented or overly complicated
- Implementation is not regularly monitored

Planning is a part of every person's life. Similarly, every organization and every program needs to plan in order to be effective. A good plan begins with a realistic and objective assessment of the present situation and asks where the organization or program is going, how it will get there, what resources are needed, and how progress will be monitored and measured. Planning is an essential tool for effective work and overall organizational performance, not a constraint on what can be done.

Planning is the first step in the management framework described in Chapter 37. A well-formulated plan provides direction and inspiration for an organization and is necessary to coordinate implementation efforts, staff activities, and financial operations.

38.1   The planning process

Planning is the process of analyzing the current situation; assessing needs; establishing goals; setting objectives and measurable targets; and determining the strategies, responsibilities, and resources needed to achieve the expected results. Before reviewing in detail the different types of planning, it is important to consider the reasons for planning.

Why plan?

It is always possible to find reasons not to plan: "We're too busy; we have no time for planning." "We have no medicines

and no money; there's nothing to plan with." "Whatever we plan is changed by the higher-ups." Despite such constraints, good planning is essential to the success of any program or organization. When time or money is limited, planning is even more important.

Planning is a process, not simply the creation of a product (the plan). The planning process, as well as the result, is important for achieving at least six purposes—

1. To clearly identify goals: Is the organization addressing the right goals and in the right way? It is easy to continue doing the same things in the same way, but are these the best things to be done and the best way to do them?

2. To assess current needs and problems: What is the current pharmaceutical sector situation? What are the most pressing problems? (See Chapter 36 for a discussion of assessment methods.)

3. To ensure wise use of available human and financial resources: Good planning helps coordinate the use of limited resources and avoid duplication. A plan that has been agreed on becomes a commitment of available resources and gives managers more control and a basis for saying yes or no to unexpected requests.

4. To obtain additional resources: A good plan with clear objectives and expected results is useful in building support among senior officials, board members, and others in authority for obtaining additional staff or funding, and it is usually essential for donor or other external support.

5. To provide a basis for evaluating effectiveness: Without a stated plan, assessing what the organization is achieving is difficult.

6. To align staff priorities and build a sense of teamwork: The planning process can provide a forum for staff and other stakeholders to work together on a shared vision.

Nonetheless, plans can also be used to avoid responsibility for failure, especially where they have been either ill conceived or developed without the full participation of all relevant stakeholders. For similar reasons, ensuring that planning does not become an end in itself is important.

Types of planning

Organizations engage in three types of planning that differ in purpose, time frame, and level of detail: strategic planning, program planning, and work planning (Figure 38-1). These types of planning are discussed in more detail later in the chapter.

Strategic planning. Strategic planning is concerned with the long-term future of an organization and its overall effectiveness and direction in light of changing external and internal environments. This type of planning begins with a clear statement of the mission and vision of the organization. A strategic plan might follow from a comprehensive pharmaceutical sector assessment and options analysis; in any case, a strategic plan must be based on a thorough and objective assessment of the organization's current situation—including its market, organizational strengths and opportunities, priority goals and strategies, and financial plans—and takes into account relevant experience and lessons learned from other countries or other organizations. It includes specific strategies for achieving the organization's mission and a means of tracking progress. Strategic planning takes a long-

Figure 38-1   Levels of planning: The planning pyramid

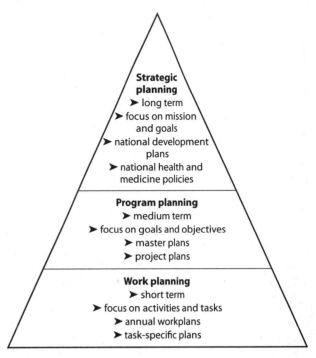

term perspective, usually five years or more, and is less detailed than program or work planning.

Program planning. Program planning, sometimes called tactical-level planning, focuses on clearly defined, medium-term objectives (up to five years) within the organization's overall long-term goals. It specifies major activities that address the objectives, responsibilities (usually by unit, not by individual), and time frame (usually by year or quarter, not by month). The time frame and level of planning are usually used for specific development assistance projects. In such instances, program planning can also serve the needs of project planning. In the context of essential medicines, program plans are sometimes called master plans. Generally, program plans should be tied to activity-specific budgets.

Work planning. Work planning, or operational planning, is short-term planning (usually one year or less). Annual workplans typically specify a limited set of objectives, all major activities, individual responsibilities, time frame (detailed at least to the month), indicators for monitoring and measuring progress and results, and activity-specific or task-specific budgets. Operational planning covers specific tasks, such as producing a national formulary manual for the first time, renovating a medical store, or carrying out a major public education campaign on rational medicine use. The annual workplan should contribute to the organizational mission and to the achievement of the organization's long-term strategies and goals. In this respect, workplans are the organization's annual building blocks.

Planning questions and terms

Whether preparing a strategic plan, a program plan, or a workplan, people engaged in the planning process address four key questions—

1. Where are we now and how did we get here?
2. Where do we want to go?
3. How will we get there?
4. How will we know when we have arrived?

Planning terminology varies considerably among organizations, countries, and programs, even though the questions are similar. What is a "goal" to one person is an "objective" or a "result" to another. Because no universally agreed-upon terminology exists, there can be no right or wrong definitions. For consistency, however, this manual uses planning terms as defined in the following paragraphs, which the reader can adapt to the local setting.

1. Where are we now and how die we get here? All planning begins with an assessment of the current situation and needs, customized for each particular context. As mentioned, Chapter 36 describes pharmaceutical sector assessment and different methods for conducting an assessment.

2. Where do we want to go? Statements of intent describe the expected measurable results of a long- or short-term plan.

This description can be organized based on five levels of breadth and detail—

Mission: The mission, or mission statement, is a brief general description of the type of organization, its main purpose, and its values. The mission of an organization describes why the organization exists and provides the rationale for defining strategies and goals.

Vision: The vision statement describes where an organization wants to be in the future and creates the method for working toward that vision. The vision helps remind the organization why it is doing what it is doing and provides the big picture and the inspiration to keep it going in the face of obstacles as it strives to achieve its stated short- and long-term results (MSH 2005).

Goal: Goals describe the proposed long-term benefits the organization will bring to the people, programs, or other organizations it serves, defined in general terms. In an essential medicines program, for example, one goal might be to ensure access to safe, effective, affordable essential medicines at all public health institutions.

Objectives: Objectives are the anticipated results or outcomes defined by the organization in its long- or short-term plan, described in measurable terms, and indicating a specific period of time during which these results will be achieved (MSH 1996). A well-formulated objective uses the SMART mnemonic—

- Specific—to avoid differences of interpretation
- Measurable—to enable monitoring and evaluation
- Appropriate—in relation to overall organizational mission, strategies, and goals
- Realistic—achievable and meaningful in terms of available human and financial resources
- Time-bound—with a specific time period for achieving them

An objective might be "to ensure that all medicines used in government facilities are prescribed according to national treatment guidelines within two years of introduction."

Expected results: Expected results, or targets, are measurable, time-limited, intermediate progress or anticipated end points; for example, "By 2009, achieve at least 50 percent compliance with national treatment guidelines." Milestones may also apply to process objectives; for example, "Train 600 clinicians (about 33 percent of an estimated 1,800 clinicians) in rational medicine use."

3. How will we get there? Methods for achieving specific objectives and results can also be described by using different levels of breadth and detail—

Strategy: a broad plan of action for fulfilling a program's basic purpose and achieving its main goals; for example, "Promote rational prescribing through strengthening formal education, continuing education, and supervision."

Activity: a specific action aimed at achieving a particular objective; for example, "Conduct a workshop on rational prescribing."

Task: specific work to be performed as part of an activity and within a certain time; for example, "Prepare session notes and overhead transparencies at least four weeks before workshop."

The inputs needed for achieving the desired objectives and results are people, time, and money. Plans should therefore describe responsibilities, schedules, and budgets, with the level of detail depending on the type of plan.

4. How will we know when we have arrived? A key function of effective project management is monitoring and evaluation linked directly to the planning process. Monitoring is a continuous process that focuses on the implementation of specific activities and the achievement of targets or milestones. Evaluation focuses on achievement of objectives and expected results.

Progress toward achieving goals, objectives, milestones, and expected results should be monitored on an ongoing basis. Formal review of program plans should take place at least annually. Progress on workplans should be reviewed monthly or quarterly.

Indicators can help measure changes directly or indirectly and assess the extent to which the results and objectives of a program or project are being attained. As described in Chapter 48, indicators are an integral part of monitoring and make a useful contribution to evaluation.

Who should plan?

The test of a plan is in its implementation; to maximize the chances of success, those involved in implementing a plan should be part of formulating it. Therefore, establishing the planning team at the outset is important. For strategic planning, the team usually consists of policy makers and senior staff members, although organizations should consider involving staff members from other organizational levels and even some beneficiaries. For program and work planning, the team should include all key people in the units concerned. Stakeholders at all levels of the organization should be identified and their roles and responsibilities in the planning process delineated. Depending on the level of complexity of the planning process and the funding available, stakeholders may include ministry of health decision makers or technical staff; development partners, such as donors or technical assistance agencies; health care providers in the public and private sectors; nongovernmental organizations (NGOs) and community groups; and patient representatives.

Planning can be top-down or bottom-up. In top-down planning, major discussions and decisions start at the top. Situation assessment and other planning data are provided by operational units, but setting goals, identifying options, and choosing among options all happen at the senior level. In bottom-up planning, the process starts with each operational unit carrying out its own planning exercise and developing a plan that is then merged with others and revised to form the overall plan.

Bottom-up planning is most appropriate for operational planning, in which the purpose and major goals are already clear. Top-down planning may be more appropriate for strategic planning, in which the basic mission and goals must be defined; however, top-down planning does require input from lower levels as well as acceptance and alignment of a plan throughout the organization after it has been completed.

Planning for pharmaceutical management is too important and specialized to be left to planning experts or outside advisers alone. National planning ministries, although they often maintain population, economic, and other forecasts to estimate program growth, are not experts on pharmaceutical management and cannot fully assess alternative pharmaceutical management strategies and solutions. Nonetheless,

---

Country Study 38-1
Establishing a multisectoral team to plan an HIV/AIDS/TB program in Tanzania

Scaling up national prevention and treatment programs related to HIV/AIDS requires a multisectoral planning process. The government of Tanzania submitted a proposal to the Global Fund to Fight AIDS, Tuberculosis and Malaria on the theme of integrating care and support for HIV/AIDS and tuberculosis (TB). The goal of the five-year program was to decrease morbidity from HIV/AIDS/TB and related opportunistic infections and to stabilize mortality from TB through increased access to care and support for Tanzanians benefiting from voluntary counseling and testing.

The resulting plan was unique because it included such a wide range of partners from around Tanzania—

- National AIDS Control Program
- National TB and Leprosy Control Program
- Ministry of Health facilities at the national, regional, and local levels
- Five faith-based organizations
- One parastatal organization
- Ten nongovernmental organizations
- One private-sector group
- One national association of people living with HIV/AIDS
- Two academic organizations
- Health Services of the Tanzania People's Defense Force

Source: Helfenbein and Severo 2004.

---

planning units and health information units have important roles, because they are usually adept at gathering and analyzing data and presenting the results.

Local or international expert advisers can make important contributions. They can provide a neutral outside perspective, bring skills in organizing and in analyzing perspectives from other countries, and make suggestions for practical alternative strategies that might otherwise be missed. In some cases, however, expert advisers may have their own agendas and may be unfamiliar with the circumstances of the program.

Multisectoral planning brings together organizations from different sectors, such as the ministry of health and ministry of finance in the public sector and a professional organization or community group in the private sector (see Country Study 38-1). It is appropriate for large-scale programs, such as planning and implementing an HIV/AIDS prevention and treatment program at the country level. Multisectoral planning enables participants to understand their interdependence, identify how they can contribute (and make a commitment to contributing), and agree on which functions will be managed in common. The planning process creates the partnerships through which activities will be carried out (Helfenbein and Severo 2004).

Good plans and good opportunities

Good managers are always reviewing their goals, assessing the current situation, considering current strategies, and monitoring the progress and results of their programs. The most effective managers also have a long-term strategic perspective in mind and are constantly watching for, and making the most of, opportunities to progress.

Adapting plans to changing circumstances and opportunities is important. Most enlightened senior officials and donors would prefer to hear that short- or long-term plans should be modified to make better use of limited time and money than to be told eventually that by faithfully following the original plan, opportunities were missed and resources were wasted.

38.2 Strategic planning

Strategic planning is concerned with developing a shared vision of mission or fundamental purpose. It is concerned with the overall effectiveness and direction of the program. Fundamentally, strategic planning asks the question, Is the organization doing the right things? In contrast, program planning is more concerned with the question, Is the organization doing things the right way?

Specific questions that a strategic thinker asks are—

- What are the basic values of the organization?
- Who is meant to benefit from our services?
- What are our priority goals?
- What are the most appropriate strategies for achieving our goals?
- Is the organization appropriately structured for achieving its goals and expected results?

For example, is a goal to provide free medicines for all patients appropriate given the external and internal environments? Is a more appropriate alternative goal to ensure access to medicines for all patients, with only the poorest receiving free medicines and others paying a reasonable fee?

When weighing these goals, consider whether a large, centralized government supply system is the best way to distribute medicines to government health facilities.

When is a strategic plan needed? A strategic-planning exercise is most needed and most useful in the following situations—

When current strategies are not working: Organizational directors or their superiors often accept perpetually marginal or poor results simply because "we've always done it this way" or "nobody has thought of a better way." Strategic planning provides a mechanism for finding better ways. For example, if the current strategy of centralized supply is failing to ensure a regular supply of medicines, the best solution may not be a project to renovate central medical stores but a strategic planning exercise to consider restructuring the supply system.

In response to an assessment: A comprehensive assessment of the pharmaceutical sector can identify problems and their root causes. A consensus-based options analysis can result in the need for a strategic plan to address problems.

When the political or social environment changes dramatically: Changes in government or replacement of senior ministry officials may offer the opportunity or result in the demand for change. The pharmaceutical sector may be affected by prevailing national trends, such as decentralization, civil service reform, or privatization. Strategic planning can help redirect an organization to adapt to such trends and take maximum advantage of opportunities for improved performance.

When a new initiative or restructuring of programs is undertaken: The development of a new essential medicines program, the integration of essential medicines and family planning commodities, or the creation of a division of pharmaceutical services all provide opportunities and challenges for senior officials and program managers. A strategic plan can help them respond to such changes.

When a crisis occurs: Not all crises create the need for a strategic plan—some crises are short-lived and do not reflect underlying deficiencies. But a major currency devaluation, a national disaster such as an earthquake or a flood, or a debt crisis may have long-term consequences that mandate new approaches.

A national pharmaceutical policy (see Chapter 4) represents a government effort to articulate new goals and strategies for the pharmaceutical sector and often results from what is effectively a strategic-planning process.

Strategic planning involves several steps, which are outlined in Box 38-1. Authors may describe these steps differently, but the basic ideas are similar.

Step 1. Create the guiding framework

Who will organize the work of the planning team? Who will be on the planning team? Who else will be consulted, and how will they be consulted? Why is a strategic plan being sought, and how will it be used? All these questions must be answered in establishing the guiding framework for strategic planning.

Box 38-1
Steps in strategic planning

Step 1. Create the guiding framework

- Create the planning team
- Identify stakeholders: the community, patients, beneficiaries, health staff members, national government, politicians, ministry of health, essential medicines program, suppliers (local industry, overseas suppliers)

Step 2. Establish mission and vision of the organization

- Define or clarify mission, long-term goals
- Define or clarify the vision

Step 3. Assess the current situation and environment

- Identify strengths, weaknesses, opportunities, and threats within the context of the organization

Step 4. Establish specific goals

Step 5. Identify strategic options

- Question everything about current structures and operations
- Think creatively

Step 6. Use defined criteria to select specific strategies

- Decide who chooses
- Establish criteria for choice on the basis of information and facts
- Avoid bias and reflexive reactions

Step 7. Transform strategies into operational plans

- Prepare the strategic plan
- Prepare program plans and work or operational plans

Step 8. Assess impact and adjust strategies

Source: Adapted from Helfenbein et al. 1994.

The planning process lays the groundwork of support for implementation and requires identifying the key stakeholders, or those individuals and organizations with an interest in the pharmaceutical sector: ministry of health, treasury, and other ministries; the pharmacy division, the essential medicines program, health facilities, and health care providers; international agencies, bilateral donors, and development banks; local industry, overseas manufacturers, and pharmaceutical suppliers; and patients, the general public, and local communities.

Having identified the stakeholders, the next question is, How will they be involved? That is, will they be full participants, contributors to selected parts of the process, or commentators on draft plans? Chapter 4 describes various ways of seeking advice in formulating a national pharmaceutical policy.

Finally, responsibilities for the planning process must be assigned, a timetable established, and a budget prepared.

Step 2. Establish the mission and vision of the organization

Every organization should have a vision and a mission statement or statement of purpose that addresses at least the following questions: Why does the organization exist and who are its beneficiaries? Policy makers and program managers may assume that they know why a national pharmaceutical policy is necessary or why an essential medicines program exists. Nevertheless, it is useful to ensure that there is agreement on the mission that underlies the policy or the existence of an organization.

The mission statement for the Mission for Essential Drugs and Supplies (MEDS), a church-sponsored supply service in East Africa, for example, states—

> MEDS seeks to promote health for all through the provision of essential drugs, medical supplies, training and other pharmaceutical services, guided by ethical and professional Christian values. In pursuit of this mission, MEDS has two broad objectives: to provide a reliable supply of essential drugs and medical supplies of good quality at affordable prices; and to improve the quality of patient care through training in all aspects of health and general management, with specific emphasis on the essential drugs concept and the rational use of drugs (WHO 2004).

This statement, which clearly describes the purpose and intended beneficiaries of MEDS, is made available to all MEDS staff members and the health units it serves. It mentions the quality of services, the source of funding (there will be a cost to health units), and the services provided (training as well as pharmaceutical supply).

A discussion of the purpose of an organization is needed to formulate a mission statement as well as to create a shared vision among the leadership and senior staff. For example, the following alternative mission statements for a national essential medicines program have very different implications for the management, financing, and operation of the organization—

- The purpose of the national essential medicines program is to ensure the availability, accessibility, and quality of medicines to all members of society.
- The purpose of the national essential medicines program is to provide high-quality essential medicines to the ministry of health facilities, with emphasis on ensuring access for the poor and medically needy members of society.

Mission statements may also include value statements, such as, "The national essential medicines program is based on the belief that provision of a limited list of low-cost, high-quality essential medicines is a highly cost-effective health care intervention." Mission statements need to be communicated throughout the organization as well as to the general public and should be reviewed periodically to ensure that they remain appropriate.

Unlike the mission of the organization, which states why the organization exists, the *vision provides a picture of a desired future*. It describes where the group or the organization wants to be in the years to come and creates the method for working toward that vision. An organizational vision could come from the top level, such as a minister, executive director, or management team; however, a vision is more powerful when a team creates it and shares it. Because people usually are motivated to support what they help to create, organizations should try to create a shared vision that is developed and owned by those who will need to carry it out (MSH 2005).

An example of a vision might be, "Our pharmacy is known for consistently providing excellent medicines and service, and people come from all around to have us dispense their medicines. We make sure that people have the correct medicines at the correct time, and that they understand how to take their medicines properly. As a result, the people in our area are healthier and happier."

Step 3. Assess the current situation and environment

Systematic assessment, as described in Chapter 36, means documenting what is going well and what is not going well and why. Increasingly, this process involves objective indicators that allow comparison of pharmaceutical sector structure, process, and performance with targets, over time, and with other countries. These indicators are important and should be included in any planning process. In the context

---

Box 38-2
Key elements of a strategic plan for an essential medicines program

Mission (overall goal): Improve the health of the population by ensuring the availability and proper use of essential medicines for the treatment, prevention, and diagnosis of common health problems at government health facilities.

Goal: pharmaceutical availability—ensure that safe, effective, high-quality essential medicines are available at all times at all government health facilities.

Objectives

- *Financing*—ensure that financial resources are adequate to meet basic pharmaceutical needs.
- *Procurement*—obtain a regular supply of medicines at favorable prices.
- *Quality assurance*—ensure that procured medicines meet recognized standards of quality and that quality is maintained through the distribution chain.
- *Central storage*—ensure that medicines are properly stored, with minimal expirations or other losses.
- *Delivery*—ensure timely delivery of medicines to health units.
- *Storage at health units*—ensure that medicines are properly stored, with minimal expirations or other losses.

Goal: rational use—ensure that medicines are rationally prescribed, correctly dispensed, and appropriately used by patients.

Objectives

- *Selection*—maintain an up-to-date list and information on safe, effective, affordable essential medicines.
- *Prescribing*—ensure that medicines are prescribed according to local standard treatment guidelines.
- *Dispensing*—ensure that medicines are correctly identified, labeled, and packaged and that patients are clearly instructed on medicine use.
- *Patient use*—ensure that patients consume medicines as prescribed and do not use medicines in an unsafe manner.

---

of strategic planning, however, situation assessment is much broader, in that it looks at the environment surrounding the pharmaceutical sector, including the political, economic, and social environment—the context in which the program is working. A broad-based assessment also identifies options for correcting problems and analyzes their feasibility and implementation costs.

A SWOT analysis considers internal strengths and weaknesses of the organization or program, as well as external opportunities and threats. (*SWOT* is an acronym for strengths, weaknesses, opportunities, and threats.) SWOT analysis is an essential method for assessing the internal and external environment.

For example, a particular essential medicines program's internal strengths may include a well-established medicine selection process, an efficient procurement office, and a series of regular workshops on rational medicine use. Internal weaknesses may include poor central and regional storage facilities and unreliable transport. For the same program, a growing private-sector distribution network may provide external opportunities for contracting out storage and transport functions. But decreasing government revenues caused by an economic downturn may represent an external threat to the program. In this example, SWOT analysis might suggest maintaining the government's role in selecting, procuring, and promoting the rational use of

medicines, but decentralizing warehousing, contracting out distribution, and encouraging local financing.

Step 4. Establish specific goals

The goals of a program or organization should follow from its mission and the functions central to achieving that mission. A strategic plan for the pharmaceutical sector may have goals related to pharmaceutical availability in government health facilities, rational medicine use, pharmaceutical quality, access to medicines in the private sector, the role of NGOs in expanding access and rational medicine use, control of medicines on the market, and local production. Examples of two goals are shown in Box 38-2.

Step 5. Identify strategic options

Perhaps the most serious mistake in strategic planning is to consider only familiar strategies or those that have been tried in the past. The greatest benefit from planning often comes from identifying practical new options. In generating new ideas, a number of tactics can be useful—

- Talk to people with relevant experience and listen to what they suggest. Although ministries of health, private health care providers, mission health services, and various NGOs work under very different circumstances, many of the problems they face are similar. Strategies that have been successful for one may be useful to another, perhaps with modifications or adaptations.

- Learn about other programs from published reports, project evaluations, or other local sources, and international agencies, such as the World Bank or the World Health Organization's Health Technology and Pharmaceuticals section, and independent organizations, such as Management Sciences for Health.

- Visit other programs through study tours or by arranging short visits as part of regional conferences. Often the most useful lessons—both positive and negative—come from the experiences of neighboring countries. Although some question the benefit of study tours, when the right people are sent to the right places for the right reasons, study tours can be extremely effective in opening up thinking to new ideas and stimulating alternative views of the future.

- Brainstorm within the planning team. Brainstorming helps groups be more creative at all types of planning, decision making, and problem solving. Proven to be highly successful in a wide range of organizations and cultures, brainstorming is neither a free-for-all nor a formal discussion. Chapter 52 provides guidelines.

- Bring in outside expertise. Local or international advisers can be costly but may offer practical suggestions and important ideas that might have otherwise been difficult or impossible to conceive.

Identifying strategic options requires thinking creatively and questioning current strategies, structures, and operations if analysis identifies chronic deficiencies in performance or threats from actual or anticipated changes in the external environment.

Step 6. Use defined criteria to select specific strategies

After the full range of options has been identified, the most promising should be selected for further consideration and carefully evaluated. Final judgments should be based on information and facts, not on unfounded biases or reflexive reactions.

Who should be involved, and how should choices be made? Senior officials and those most central to the implementation process should participate in selecting specific strategies, using established criteria against which each option can be assessed.

Commonly used criteria are—

Potential impact: If the strategy is successful, how large an impact can be expected? For example, would shifting to international competitive bidding reduce prices by 40 to 50 percent, or by only 5 to 10 percent? Whenever possible, the potential impact should be expressed in terms of cost savings or other financial benefits.

Political feasibility: Successful strategy implementation is in large measure a political process. Judgments must be made about expected political support and opposition.

Technical feasibility: Local infrastructure capacity, available human resources, and even the state of pharmaceutical science influence technical feasibility. For example, a demand-based pull system for supplying health centers, although theoretically less wasteful than a push system, may not be feasible when most staff members have only a minimal level of education. Such a system may become feasible, however, as the general level of education and experience rises.

Financial feasibility: Many good ideas may be unaffordable. Financial feasibility may relate to recurrent operating costs or initial implementation costs (see Chapter 40) and may depend in part on donor interest.

Cost-benefit: Cost-benefit (see Chapter 10 for more details) relates the cost of a particular strategy to its potential impact on cost. A total cost analysis exercise during the assessment can help determine cost-effectiveness (Chapter 40). Usually this measurement involves approximate costs and projected, rather than actual, measures of each. Even rough estimates may provide useful insights for planning purposes.

Political will and technical feasibility help define the likelihood of success. Selecting strategies involves weighing the potential impact or benefits, if successful, against the likelihood of success and the costs of success.

Step 7. Transform strategies into operational plans

When strategies have been selected, the strategic plan should be put in writing. Generally, it should cover the following points as succinctly as possible—

- Mission and vision statements of the organization
- Brief assessment of the current situation: strengths, weaknesses, opportunities, threats
- Concise description of each goal for the organization
- Brief summary of each specific strategy for achieving these goals
- Monitoring and evaluation plan, including indicators for each goal

After the strategic plan has been completed, official endorsement is beneficial and is usually required. If all concerned senior officials have been involved in the process and have accepted the plan, a letter of transmittal may be sufficient. In government settings, the plan may need to be presented to a senior ministerial management committee or even to the cabinet. In NGOs and private organizations, strategic plans may need to be endorsed by the governing body or board of directors, which may also have been involved in the planning process.

The benefits of strategic planning are felt only when the plan is implemented. Strategic plans do not include operational detail. Turning the approved strategic plan into action requires short-term planning, such as a three- or five-year program plan or project proposal, or both.

Step 8. Assess impact and adjust strategies

As noted, the true test of any plan is in its implementation—however, the strategic-planning process does not stop with formulation of the plan, or even with its implementation. The strategic-planning process continues through ongoing monitoring and periodic evaluation.

Perform regular assessment of the plan. Are the strategies being turned into programs and workplans? Are they having the intended effect? If not, does the problem lie with the implementation process? Are different people required? Is more time required? Is the basic goal wrong? Should it be revised? Or are the strategies themselves to blame? A strategy that is good in theory but that cannot be implemented is not a good strategy.

38.3 Program planning

Most planning is done at the program, project, and operational levels. Program planning focuses on clearly defined medium-term objectives within a framework of overall, long-term strategic goals. A program plan should follow from a strategic plan, national pharmaceutical policy, or national development plan. Often, however, a program plan is based on historical expectations and assumptions about the role of pharmaceutical management within the government. In addition, if a program was preceded by a pilot project, the full-scale program plan may be developed based on the experiences from its pilot. However, the two plans are not interchangeable, because a pilot plan may not adequately address the challenges of scaling up.

A government essential medicines program, a mission essential medicines service, or any other major pharmaceutical program should have a program plan, regardless of funding sources. A well-formulated plan provides direction and a framework for month-to-month and year-to-year activities; it helps coordinate staff, finances, and other resources. In the context of national essential medicines programs, program plans provide an overview of the sector and a three- to five-year plan of action and are sometimes called five-year implementation plans.

Program plans are more specific than strategic plans with respect to objectives, responsibilities, time frame, and usu-

---

Box 38-3
Program-planning process

Exploration

Step 1. Establish the planning group
Step 2. Confirm long-term goals, strategies, and current objectives
Step 3. Assess the current situation

Formulation

Step 4. Specify objectives for the planning period
Step 5. Set targets for each objective and the monitoring and evaluation plan
Step 6. Determine the resources needed for achieving each objective

Action

Step 7. Prepare the program plan and budget
Step 8. Implement the plan
Step 9. Monitor the plan

---

ally, budget. They are best implemented through detailed annual or semiannual operational workplans (described below).

Program-planning process

Program planning usually involves a three-stage process. In the exploration phase, a planning group is formed, existing long-term goals and strategies are reviewed, and the current situation is assessed. In the formulation phase, objectives for the planning period are specified, targets and indicators are set for each objective, and resource requirements are determined. In the action phase, the program plan and budget are prepared, implemented, and monitored. Each of these three stages has distinctive operational steps, outlined in Box 38-3.

Exploration. The first step in program planning is to establish the planning group, usually the program manager and senior staff and representatives from other organizations, if the program is operating at the regional or national level. Experienced advisers may help guide the planning process. Representatives of international organizations, donors, and development banks often can provide useful input into the planning process, but they are generally not part of the planning team.

If a national pharmaceutical policy, national development plan, or other form of strategic plan for the pharmaceutical sector exists, broad objectives have already been developed. Even in the absence of such a plan, most national programs have some objectives toward which they

Figure 38-2 Five-year program plan for promoting rational medicine use

Goal: Rational use—ensure that medicines are rationally prescribed, correctly dispensed, and appropriately used by patients

Objectives/activities	Output targets (5 year)	Inputs	Budget (U.S. dollars)	Time frame				
				Year 1	Year 2	Year 3	Year 4	Year 5
Selection—*maintain an up-to-date list and information on safe, effective, affordable essential medicines.*								
Essential medicines list (EML)—revise and distribute national essential medicines list every 2 years.	Two revisions of EML	Meeting expenses	2,000	<<—>>				
National formulary manual (NFM)—prepare/revise and distribute national formulary manual at least every 4 years.	First edition of NFM completed and distributed	Meeting expenses, editing services, layout, printing, implementation workshops	32,000		<<—>>			
Prescribing—*ensure that medicines are prescribed according to locally recognized standards of care.*								
Undergraduate training—ensure that all students are trained in essential medicines concept and rational medicine use in basic health curricula (amount of time depends on professional category).	Four curricula designed and implemented (medicine, pharmacy, nursing, paramedical)	Meeting expenses, curriculum materials, books	5,000	<<—>>				
Standard treatment guideline (STG)—develop/revise and distribute standard treatment manual at least every 4 years.	First edition of STG completed and distributed	Meeting expenses, editing services, layout, printing, implementation workshops	48,000	<<—>>				
Continuing education—provide all clinicians with at least 1 week of in-service training on rational medicine use every 3 years.	65% of clinicians trained (1,300 of estimated 2,000)	Workshop costs, short-term training adviser, training materials	42,000		<<—	———	———	—>>
Pharmaceutical information—establish a medicine information center in each teaching and provincial hospital.	Three operational medicine information centers (three of seven hospitals)	Computers, books, software, office materials	21,000			<<—	———	—>>
Self-monitoring—ensure that 70% of health units conduct medicine use self-assessment at least once each quarter.	Self-assessment methods developed and implemented at 50% of health units (150 of 300 units)	Short-term adviser, design workshop, implementation workshop, training materials	28,000			<<—	—>>	
Dispensing—*ensure that medicines are correctly identified, labeled, and packaged and that patients are clearly instructed on medicine use.*								
Packaging and labeling—ensure that at least 80% of patients receive medicines in clearly labeled containers or dispensing envelopes.	Packaging and labeling materials provided, sufficient for 80% of patients	Labels, dispensing envelopes	15,000	<<—>>				
Continuing education—ensure that all staff dispensing drugs receive at least 3 days of refresher training every 4 years.	60% of pharmacy staff trained (240 of estimated 400)	Workshop costs, short-term training adviser, training materials	24,000		<<—	———	———	—>>
Patient use—*ensure that patients consume medicines as prescribed and do not use medicines in an unsafe manner.*								
Undergraduate training—ensure that all students are trained in communication and patient education methods in basic health curricula (amount of time depends on professional category).	Included in prescribing continuing education (see prescribing outputs)	(see above)	(see above)	<<—>>				
Continuing education—include skills for patient education at in-service training workshops.	Included in prescribing training (see prescribing outputs)	(see above)	(see above)					
Patient education materials—ensure that at least 80% of health units have materials for delivering 8 basic medicine-use messages.	Package of 8 basic medicine-use messages prepared; package introduced at 50% of health units (150 of 300 units)	Patient survey, short-term communication adviser, materials design, implementation workshop	18,000				<<—	—>>

have been working. These should be written down and reviewed.

Assessment of the current situation can be rather limited and impressionistic, depending on the resources available to carry it out. Whenever possible, however, assessment of the current situation should be based on monitoring data, indicators, review of progress reports, and other systematic measures described in Chapter 36.

Current problems and constraints can be identified from the systematic assessment. For major problems, a force field analysis (described in Chapter 37) may be useful to identify restraining and driving forces that must be considered if the program plan is to achieve its objectives.

Formulation. The next steps are to specify objectives, set targets, and determine resources needed to achieve each objective. As previously noted, objectives should be SMART: specific, measurable, appropriate, realistic, and time-bound.

Figure 38-2 contains an example of a five-year program plan for promoting rational medicine use. This plan, which follows from the key elements of a strategic plan outlined in Box 38-2, illustrates specific objectives that might be included.

As with problem solving (described in Chapter 37) and strategic planning (described above), one of the most critical steps in the program-planning process is identifying the full range of options. Each option should be analyzed for likely strengths and weaknesses, resource demands, and possible consequences. Country Study 38-2 shows how poor information gathering led planners to an administrative obstacle in a multisectoral plan for HIV/AIDS and tuberculosis.

Action. After objectives, priorities, and activities have been established, a draft plan should be prepared, specifying responsibilities, schedules, budgets, and a monitoring and evaluation plan with indicators, preferably according to activity. Important deadlines should be clearly identified.

First drafts of program plans usually promise too many activities in too short a time for the number of staff and amount of money available. For the plan to have any value, it must be realistic. Making a realistic plan usually means reducing the number of activities and lengthening the time frame to reflect the amount of staff time and money actually available.

The final step is to implement and monitor the plan, as described in Chapter 37, and revise it as needed based on changing circumstances or priorities.

Contents of a program or project plan

A program or project plan should include—

- A summary of the long-term goal
- Major strategies for achieving the goal
- Specific objectives
- Targets for each objective
- Responsibilities for each activity
- A schedule for each objective, in chronological order (usually by year)
- A budget for each objective or area of activity

The written plan usually consists of text and tables. A table showing activities, targets, inputs with budget amounts, and time frame is most useful, as in Figure 38-2.

Although budget figures can be included in the summary table, a separate budget is usually necessary. A program budget should indicate the area of activity (pharmaceutical supply or rational medicine use, for example), the type of expenditure (salary, medicine purchases, per diem,

---

Country Study 38-2
Identifying administrative obstacles in Tanzania

The multisectoral plan for care and support of those affected by HIV/AIDS and tuberculosis called for transferring funds to a variety of government ministries, faith-based organizations, national hospitals, NGOs, and private companies. The plan required a single institution to act as financial manager, holding the funds, transferring them to partners, and reporting on them to the donor in a timely fashion. Having this institution house the coordinating unit for technical execution of the program would also make sense.

One logical option was for the national AIDS commission, TACAIDS, to add these two functions to its existing roles of coordination and resource mobilization.

However, the founding legislation for TACAIDS precludes the commission and its secretariat from managing financial resources other than its own operating budget because it has monitoring authority over all HIV/AIDS activities and institutions in the country. Therefore, a financial manager had to be found elsewhere.

Planners should not assume, on the basis of incomplete information, that a logical or innovative option can be implemented. It is important to first become informed about regulations, legislation, and administrative obstacles that may prevent otherwise good ideas from being realized.

Source: Helfenbein and Severo 2004.

and so forth), whether the expenditure is in local or foreign currency, and the likely source of funding. Chapter 41 contains more detailed information on preparing budgets.

In addition to the summary table, descriptive text is necessary to communicate the goal and rationale of the program, describe specific activities, and justify the budget.

38.4 Work planning

Work planning is the most detailed type of routine planning. A workplan is like a blueprint: it shows each of the smaller steps involved in achieving the larger goal. Effective managers use workplans to keep efforts focused on planned activities and to align and coordinate staff efforts in the achievement of longer-term goals. Workplans are not intended to limit staff members' initiative, but they should help managers and staff members say no to unreasonable and unplanned requests and discourage overly optimistic promises.

A workplan is typically prepared annually to cover a twelve-month period, although some essential medicines programs do operational work planning on a six-month cycle. Compared with program plans, workplans should be more specific with respect to outputs, individual responsibilities, precise time frame, and budget requirements.

The steps for preparing an annual workplan—which are similar but not identical to those for preparing a program plan—follow.

1. Review long-term goals and existing program plans.
2. Define specific objectives for the upcoming year.
3. Set targets for each objective, and define indicators.
4. List major activities for each objective. Prepare monitoring and evaluation plan.
5. Prepare an activity-time (Gantt) chart showing the responsibility and timing for each activity.
6. Review or prepare the annual budget.
7. Revise the plan based on available staff, time, and funds.
8. Implement the plan.
9. Monitor the plan and revise as needed.

For each objective and activity, workplans generally specify major tasks involved, measurable outputs and indicators, responsibilities for each task, timing (at least to the month or quarter), budget, and source of funds for each activity or task.

Under Step 4, considering what activities are necessary for achieving each objective is important, as is not being limited to what was done last year.

Figures 38-3 and 38-4 illustrate two different types of activity-time charts (Step 5).

Step 7 is particularly important. When Steps 1 through 6 have been completed and a draft workplan exists, the plan must be reviewed carefully and finalized according to available staff, time, and funds. A plan that is unrealistic from the start will quickly lose credibility and have little value as a management tool. In addition, a plan may need to be revised several times while progress is being monitored (Step 9).

Work-planning process

Preparation of workplans must involve those who will be implementing them. Because this activity requires a focused effort without interruptions, moving out of the office for a day or more is often useful while preparing the workplan. Participants should be chosen on the basis of their knowledge and expertise as well as their commitment to making contributions. Brainstorming techniques (see Chapter 52) can be useful in generating ideas for specific activities and tasks. In any case, the tone of meetings should encourage the open exchange of ideas and creative thinking. Sometimes, informal discussions preceding the formal work-planning discussion can help staff members reflect on the preceding year, consider the reasons for recent successes and failures, and begin thinking about the next year.

Objectives, targets, activities, and tasks should be consistent with the definitions given earlier in this chapter. Responsibilities for each activity should be listed by unit or office, or sometimes by person or team. The time frame for each activity is usually set by year or quarter rather than by month.

Generally, workplans should be tied to activity-specific budgets that reflect all required inputs, including staff salaries, pharmaceutical costs, vehicle costs, and other operating costs. For government programs, routine, recurrent costs such as salary and utility expenses, may be part of larger divisional budgets and not readily separated. Certainly pharmaceutical costs and major additional costs should be noted separately.

Activity-time chart

At the center of an annual workplan is an activity-time (Gantt) chart, chronogram, or schedule of activities and responsibilities. A Gantt chart provides a clear, concise summary that is invaluable for communicating plans to staff, checking financial and other resource requirements, and monitoring progress.

A Gantt chart groups activities under objectives and usually contains a series of rows for each major activity. Typically, it contains columns for—

- The objectives and activities
- The person or unit responsible for each activity
- The time period in which the activity will occur

Figure 38-3   Annual workplan (Gantt chart), first year of five-year plan

Goal: Rational use—ensure that medicines are rationally prescribed, correctly dispensed, and appropriately used by patients

Objectives/activities	Responsibility	Jan	Feb	Mar	Apr	May	Jun	Jul	Aug	Sep	Oct	Nov	Dec
Selection													
Essential medicines list (EML)—revise and distribute national EML every 2 years.													
Appoint national drug and therapeutics committee (NDTC).	Director, medical services	X											
Call for proposals for additions and deletions to EML.	Chairman, NDTC			X									
Hold NDTC meeting to revise EML.	NDTC						X						
Prescribing													
Undergraduate training—ensure that all students are trained in essential medicines concept and rational medicine use in basic health curricula (amount of time depends on professional category).													
Convene national workshop to outline changes in medical, pharmacy, nursing, paramedical curricula.	Dean, medical school			X									
Organize working groups to prepare detailed core curricula for each health profession.	Individual training institutions			X			X						
Support core groups at institutional level to implement curricula changes.	Individual training institutions									X			X
Standard treatment guidelines (STGs)—develop/revise and distribute standard treatment manual at least every 4 years.													
Appoint committee to coordinate drafting of manual.	Director, medical services	X											
Assign writing responsibilities.	Senior editor/chairperson of editorial committee		X										
Complete draft treatment manual.	Individual authors			X				X					
Distribute draft manual for review.	Essential medicines program (EMP) training officer								X				
Continuing education—provide all clinicians with at least 1 week of in-service training on rational use every 3 years.													
Do needs assessment (identification of major medicine-use problems).	Medical school, clinical pharmacology				X								
Design continuing education (CE) programs.	EMP training officer training consultant					X							
Prepare course materials.	EMP training officer training consultant						X	X					
Conduct first CE workshop.	EMP training officer training consultant									X			
Revise CE program and materials.	EMP training officer training consultant									X	X		
Conduct second CE workshop.	EMP training officer and staff											X	
Dispensing													
Packaging and labeling—ensure that at least 80% of patients receive medicines in clearly labeled containers or dispensing envelopes.													
Review and revise design of dispensing containers and labels.	Pharmacy school	X											
Include dispensing envelopes and labels in medicine tenders.	EMP procurement officer			X									
Prepare circular letter/memorandum to inform dispensing staff.	EMP information officer										X		
Distribute envelopes and labels to health units.	EMP supply officer												X

Figure 38-4   Example of an activity-time chart for a three-year program in East Africa

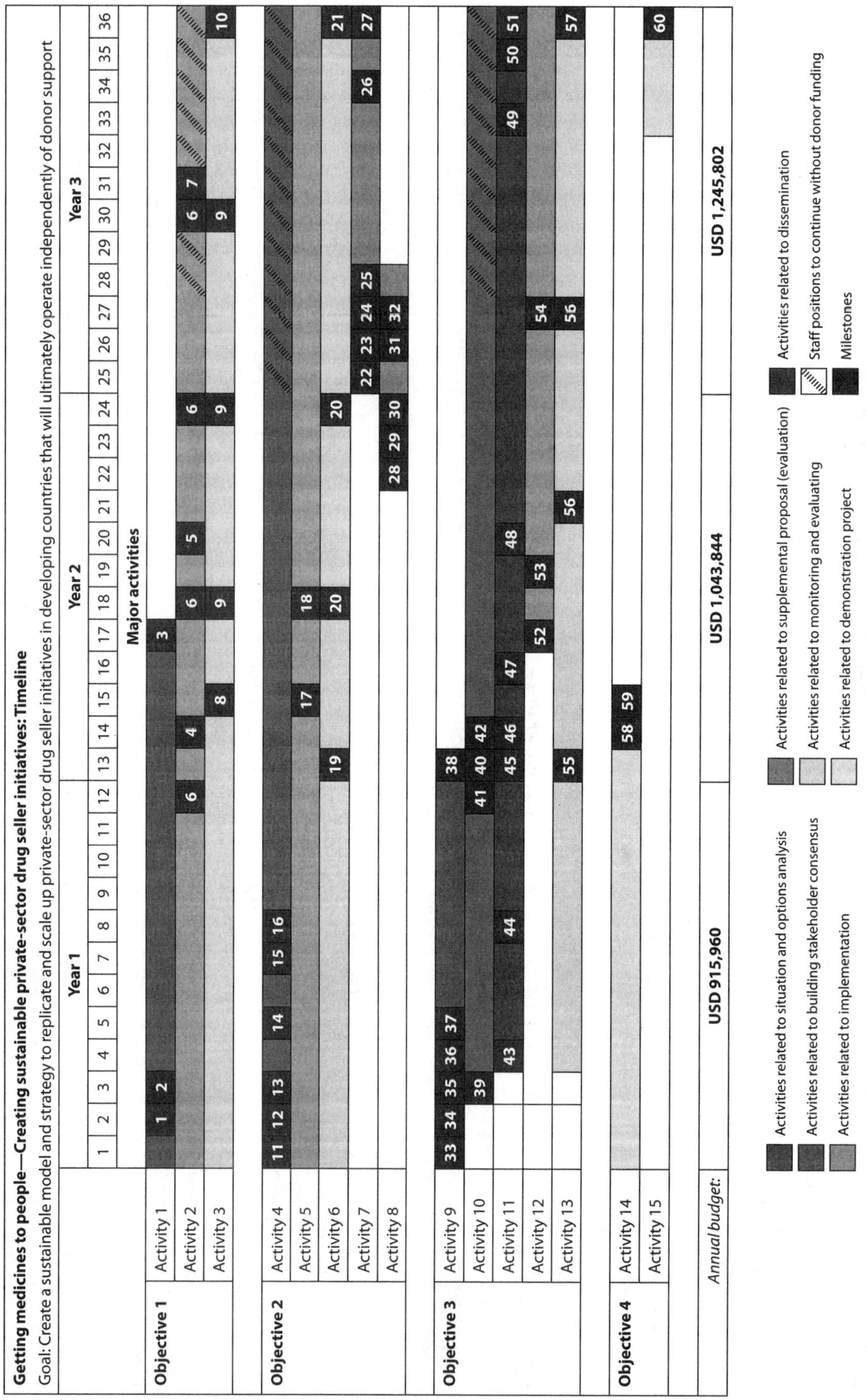

Getting medicines to people—Creating sustainable private-sector drug seller initiatives: Timeline
Goal: Create a sustainable model and strategy to replicate and scale up private-sector drug seller initiatives in developing countries that will ultimately operate independently of donor support

Output targets and performance indicators for each objective may be listed separately or included as a column of the Gantt chart. Budgets should be linked to objectives and sometimes to individual activities. Often, budgets are listed in a separate part of the workplan. However, if specific funds and funding sources are associated with each activity, columns in the Gantt chart can specify the amounts and sources of funds.

Figure 38-3 shows an example of a Gantt chart for an essential medicines program. This example is based on the first year of the program plan shown in Figure 38-2. Figure 38-4 illustrates a simpler activity-timeline with program milestones.

Monthly, weekly, and daily workplans

An annual workplan provides major deadlines and a certain level of detail. Individual units and staff members, however, often prepare their own monthly, weekly, or daily schedules or to-do lists. This activity allows individuals to translate the workplan into short-term tasks and to set priorities to ensure that the most important tasks are being accomplished.

For example, the training officer responsible for the national workshop on undergraduate curriculum listed under "Undergraduate training" in Figure 38-3 may take this activity and prepare a one-page to-do list that contains tasks and target dates for selecting the venue, sending invitations, planning the agenda, obtaining flip charts and other training supplies, and doing other important tasks. Such lists help spread work over the available time so that staff members are not left with a large number of last-minute tasks before a major event.

Using workplans to check progress

To be an effective management tool, workplans must be readily accessible and frequently reviewed by managers and staff members involved in implementing them. Wall charts of the workplan in the office and copies taped to desktops can be used as consistent reminders.

Workplans should be checked regularly. When specific activities are behind schedule, a decision must be made by the concerned manager: reorganize priorities, assign additional staff or provide extra resources to get the activity back on schedule, or accept the delay.

If an annual workplan is well formulated and consistent with long-term program objectives, the performance of a program and its staff can be assessed by the extent to which it adheres to the workplan.

38.5 Project-planning methods and tools

Several planning methods and computer-based tools exist to help managers. These include methods derived from

Figure 38-5 Critical path method (CPM) analysis of plan to upgrade central pharmaceutical supply functions

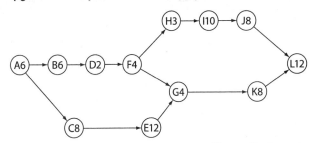

Activity	Activity description	Time (weeks)	Predecessor activity
A	Plan to upgrade central pharmaceutical supply services	6	—
B	Appoint committee to revise essential medicines list	6	A
C	Develop new procurement procedures	8	A
D	Revise essential medicines list, organize by level of care	2	B
E	Prequalify suppliers	12	C
F	Quantify pharmaceutical requirements by level of care	4	D
G	Prepare and distribute tender documents	4	F, E
H	Prepare budget proposal	3	F
I	Obtain budget approval	10	H
J	Ensure availability of funds	8	I
K	Complete tendering and place orders	8	G
L	Receive and pay for medicines	12	J, K

industrial and engineering management science, methods supported by specific donor requirements, and computer programs for project management.

Management science methods

For program and work planning, two commonly used methods from management science are the critical path method (CPM; see Figure 38-5) and the project evaluation and review technique (PERT). Although originally formulated as two distinct methods, their similarities are such that they are commonly referred to collectively as CPM-PERT. The combined method uses a network model to help planners arrange and schedule project activities.

The main steps for CPM-PERT planning are (1) identify all necessary tasks; (2) determine which tasks need to be completed before the next ones are started; (3) estimate the time needed for each task; and (4) combine the information from the first three steps into a diagram of the whole process.

The most important benefits of the CPM-PERT method are that it forces managers to estimate realistically the time

Table 38-1   The logical framework matrix

Narrative summary	Verifiable indicators	Means of verification	Assumptions/risks
Goal	Quantitative ways of measuring, or qualitative ways of judging, achievement of broad objectives	What sources of information exist?	External factors necessary for sustaining objectives in the long term
Purpose	Quantitative measures or qualitative evidence to judge achievement and impacts (estimated time)	What sources of information exist?	External factors affecting movement of purposes toward project goal
Outputs (Outputs to be produced to achieve project purpose)	Performance questions and indicators for each output—output indicators	What sources of information exist?	External factors affecting movement of outputs to purposes
Activities (Activities to be undertaken to accomplish the outputs)	Can Include the needed inputs for activities	What sources of information exist?	External factors affecting movement of activities toward outputs

required for each task or activity and to think carefully about the best sequence of tasks and activities. Full-scale application of the method is most common with complex construction projects, but realistic assessment of time requirements and efficient sequencing of activities should be part of any planning effort.

Each circle on the diagram in Figure 38-5 represents a task or well-defined activity that is part of the project. The number in each circle represents the expected time required to complete the task. Arrows indicate the dependencies of relationships among the tasks and show which tasks must be completed before the next can begin. Adding together all of the task times in Figure 38-5 shows that 83 weeks of work must be completed; however, several tasks can be done simultaneously. For example, when task A has been completed, B and C can be started and worked on concurrently. Therefore, the earliest completion date is estimated by looking at all possible paths through the diagram and choosing the one with tasks requiring the most total time. In this example, the longest, or "critical," path is A–C–E–G–K–L, requiring a total time of fifty weeks.

The LogFrame project-planning method

Most donors have a required series of steps that they follow to identify, plan, implement, and monitor projects (see Chapter 14). The logical framework approach (LogFrame, or LFA) is one such planning method that has broader applications. The LogFrame approach has been used by the U.S. Agency for International Development, Danida, and other donors and organizations. The World Bank (2005) has published a guidebook on the approach.

The LogFrame approach combines all the key components of a project in one place and presents them in a systematic, concise way. LogFrame also ensures a logical inter-relatedness among project elements, highlights the influence of external factors, and provides a systematic basis

for monitoring. However, the approach can lead to an inflexible project design without connection to realities in the field or changing situations. Nevertheless, if the LogFrame analysis is seen not as a final product, but rather is evaluated and updated along the way, it can provide a clear view of needs, objectives, and strategies for all involved on a continuing basis.

The written output of a LogFrame basically appears as a four-by-four matrix (see Table 38-1). Along the horizontal axis are objectives, indicators, means of verification, and assumptions; along the vertical axis are four hierarchical levels of objectives: goal, purpose, outputs, and activities. The matrix summarizes what the project should achieve; the performance questions and indicators that will be used for monitoring and evaluation; how these indicators will be monitored or where the data can be found; and assumptions, such as a secure government or the availability of funds, plus associated risks for the project if assumptions turn out to be incorrect.

Project-planning management software

A number of computer programs based on variations of CPM-PERT and other planning methods can help organize operational planning and monitoring. Planning software can be useful for generating charts and schedules of different levels of detail; for determining when too much has been planned for available human or financial resources; for summarizing tasks by objective, unit, or individual; for preparing and monitoring project budgets; and for reporting on project achievements.

In practice, simple spreadsheet programs are the most commonly used software for program planning. The example in Figure 38-2 is from a spreadsheet model in which each category of essential information (such as objective or target) forms a separate column and each task or activity is given a separate row.

Computers are useful for organizing planning information, but they cannot replace clear thinking about project objectives, substitute for personal monitoring of project activities, or make planning decisions.

38.6 Progress review cycle

Planning represents the beginning of the management cycle. Plans must be implemented, and equally important, implementation must be monitored. When plans are made and implemented, determining how often progress will be monitored is important. The review cycles for strategic plans, program plans, and workplans are different, but they should be linked.

If formal evaluations of progress are carried out (see Chapter 48), they are typically done after two to three years. Such evaluations may focus on long-term strategic plans, program plans, or specific project plans.

Progress toward achievement of the objectives set forth in a program plan should be reviewed at least annually, whether the plan covers a three-year, five-year, or other period. If a strategic plan exists, progress toward achieving long-term goals is generally reviewed at the same time as the program plan is reviewed.

An annual program review should address the following questions—

- What progress has been made toward each objective and expected result or output?
- What are the implementation problems?
- What changes are needed in strategies, objectives, or specific activities?
- What activities should be deleted from the plan?
- What new activities must be added to achieve the original objectives?

Progress toward implementation of annual workplans should be formally reviewed at least quarterly, if not monthly. In general, the questions asked during annual progress reviews also apply to quarterly or monthly reviews of workplans.

38.7 Why plans sometimes fail

Good plans to guide program development and implementation require time and effort. Sometimes, however, plans exist merely on paper: they are made but never actually used. Even well-conceived, well-presented plans can remain unused.

Why are plans not implemented? If implemented, why do plans fail to achieve their intended objectives? There are many reasons, but some of the more common are—

Unrealistic or overly ambitious planning: Planning must be based on a realistic assessment of the current situation, clear objectives for the future, and a practical assessment of what is possible. Planning, particularly in groups, can sometimes become overly optimistic and idealistic. Planning should be forward thinking but should not confuse hopes and wishes with good judgment and decisions about what is possible.

Failure to consider existing resources and commitments: Plans must be made within the context and constraints of existing commitments. Although the opportunity often exists for great progress, progress takes time. Plans that propose too much in too little time may spread everyone's efforts too thinly to accomplish any of the stated objectives or may compromise the work's quality.

Lack of involvement by the implementers: Plans are best made at the levels where they will be carried out. Strategic plans to guide long-term policy must involve policy makers, medium-term program plans must involve program managers and key program staff members, and annual work planning must involve the people whose work is being planned. Without such involvement, plans are likely to lack both the realism and the commitment necessary for effective implementation.

Lack of support: Success also depends on support from others who are not directly involved in implementation. Such support may come from senior staff members and officials of ministries (such as treasury) and other governmental bodies, international organizations such as WHO and UNICEF, donors and development banks, local NGOs, and local professional societies. Selectively involving individuals from such organizations in preparing or reviewing a strategic or program plan can lay a good foundation for future support during implementation.

Planning for the wrong reasons: Some plans are never really meant to be implemented. Examples include plans made only for short-term political gain or to satisfy a condition for receiving a grant or a loan. Whenever possible, however, plans pushed by external needs should also suit the needs of the organization or program. If plans are sometimes made "for appearances only," staff members should understand why this is done so that the experience does not undermine their confidence in the value of good planning.

Lack of funds: Nothing is more frustrating than spending considerable time and effort in planning, only to learn that funds are insufficient to carry out the plan. Planning should be based on a realistic assessment of potential funding sources.

Lack of people or time: Although plans are made for organizations or programs, they depend on people. Ambitious plans require more people and more capable people. But

Strategic planning

- Does a strategic plan exist for the pharmaceutical sector (for example, a national pharmaceutical policy or national development plan)? Does it reflect the current political, social, and economic environment? Are its strategies appropriate and realistic?
- Did the strategic-planning process involve policy makers and senior staff? Which key stakeholders were involved or consulted?
- Did the strategic-planning process actively consider new strategic options, such as strategies used elsewhere or suggested by outside experts?
- Is the strategic plan written? Does it include mission and vision statements; a brief assessment of the current situation, including strengths, weaknesses, opportunities, and threats; a concise description of each goal and measurable results; and a brief summary of each strategy for achieving these goals? Has it been officially endorsed?
- Is the strategic plan reflected in program plans and workplans? To what extent are strategies having the intended impact?

Program planning

- If there is an essential drugs program or other major pharmaceutical program, is there a pharmaceutical master plan, five-year implementation plan, or other program plan?
- Does each program or project plan include a statement of the goal, strategies, objectives, targets or output, responsibilities, schedule, monitoring and evaluation plan, and budget? Does the plan include both descriptive text and summary tables?

- Are program plans implemented through annual or semiannual operational workplans?
- Have program plans been used in presenting arguments for additional funding?

Work planning

- Are workplans prepared annually?
- Do they specify objectives, activities, major tasks, measurable outputs or targets, individual responsibilities, timing (at least to the month), monitoring and evaluation plan, budget, and source of funds for each activity? Are workplans realistic in terms of available staff, time, and funds?
- Do workplan documents include activity-time (Gantt) charts? Are they used for monitoring?
- To what extent are implementing staff involved in the preparation of workplans? Do individual units and staff members prepare, based on the workplan, their own monthly, weekly, or daily schedules or to-do lists?

Planning tools

- What planning methods or computer tools (for example, CPM, PERT, LogFrame) are used to support planning efforts?

Planning as part of the management cycle

- After plans have been established, are they reviewed on a regular basis for implementation progress and problems? Are the review cycles for strategic plans, program plans, and workplans linked?
- Have formal assessments or evaluations been done? If so, have the findings and recommendations been incorporated into revised plans?

even a plan that was realistic at the time it was made may fail if key people are transferred or otherwise become unavailable.

Wrong level of planning: Some managers and staff tend to avoid planning for themselves. They prefer planning for the people below them or making recommendations to the people above them. A fundamental principle of planning, as noted above, is that plans should be developed with the active involvement of those who are central to implementing them.

Poorly presented or overly complicated plans: Often, the clearest, most useful plans are the shortest plans. For example, an annual workplan for a national essential medicines program may consist of a one-page introduction and statement of objectives, a two-page chart of

activities and time frame (Gantt chart), a monitoring and evaluation plan, a one-page budget, and one page of text describing the eight major program components. Plans that are poorly organized or overly complex or that provide excessive detail are difficult to understand, let alone implement.

Lack of follow-up and monitoring: One of the most common management failures is the failure to actually use a plan after it has been prepared. A five-year program plan such as that shown in Figure 38-2 should be reviewed regularly and used to formulate annual workplans. Annual workplans and timelines such as those shown in Figures 38-3 and 38-4 should be checked on a weekly or monthly basis. The program's monitoring system (see Chapter 48) should be linked with organizational and program plans. Without this link, the plan loses its value in guiding implementation.

Thus, for plans to be implemented effectively, they must be realistic, they must be developed with input from the people who will implement them, they must have sufficient support, they must have adequate resources, and they must be clearly presented. ■

References and further readings

★ = Key readings.

AusAid. 2005. AusGuideline: 3.3 The Logical Framework Approach. Canberra: Commonwealth of Australia. <http://www.ausaid.gov.au/ausguide/pdf/ausguideline3.3.pdf>

Blanco-Sequeiros, M. 1994. Health Projects within the Health Care System. In *Health and Disease in Developing Countries*, K. A. Lankinen, S. Bergstrom, P. H. Makela, and M. Peltomaa, eds. London: Macmillan.

Danida (Danish International Development Agency). 2003. *Guidelines for Project Management*. 1st ed. Copenhagen: Danida.

Green, Andrew. 2007. *An Introduction to Health Planning for Developing Health Systems*. Oxford: Oxford University Press.

Helfenbein, S., S. Seims, and D. Ruhe. 1994. Learning to Think Strategically. *Family Planning Manager* 3(1). <http://erc.msh.org/TheManager/English/V3_N1_En_Issue.pdf>

Helfenbein, S., and C. A. Severo. 2004. *Scaling Up HIV/AIDS Programs: A Manual for Multisectoral Planning*. Cambridge, Mass.: Management Sciences for Health. <http://erc.msh.org/newpages/english/health/Scaling_Up_HIV_AIDS_Programs.pdf>

Kam, C. C., G. Goodridge, and R. Moodie. 2001. Strategic Planning, Program Design and Management. In *HIV/AIDS Prevention and Care in Resource-Constrained Settings: A Handbook for the Design and Management of Programs*, P. R. Lamptey and H. D. Gayle, eds. Arlington, Va.: Family Health International. <http://www.fhi.org/NR/rdonlyres/eyp6csam27ofp2peoybfn3so7zpa6scfybenhju4ypq6qqkj5dz526bfod2cciptusbpzov5o5i6zo/PCHandbook1.pdf>

Miller, J., and J. Wolff. 1993. Developing Plans and Proposals for New Initiatives. *Family Planning Manager* 2(4). <http://erc.msh.org/TheManager/English/V2_N4_En_Issue.pdf>

MSH (Management Sciences for Health). 2005. *Managers Who Lead: A Handbook for Improving Health Services*. Cambridge, Mass.: MSH. <http://www.msh.org/Documents/upload/MWL-2008-edition.pdf>

————. 2003. Coordinating Complex Health Programs. *The Manager* 12(4). <http://erc.msh.org/TheManager/English/V12_N4_En_Issue.pdf>

————. 2002. Achieving Functional HIV/AIDS Services through Strong Community and Management Support. *The Manager* 11(4). <http://erc.msh.org/TheManager/English/V11_N4_En_Issue.pdf>

————. 1996. *Family Planning Management Terms: A Pocket Glossary in Three Languages*. Cambridge, Mass.: MSH.

————. 1992a. Developing and Using Workplans. In *The Family Planning Manager's Handbook: Basic Skills and Tools for Managing Family Planning Programs*, J. A. Wolff, L. J. Suttenfield, and S. C. Binzen, eds. West Hartford, Conn.: Kumarian Press. <http://erc.msh.org/mainpage.cfm?file=2.2.3.htm&module=planning&language=English>

————. 1992b. Planning for the Future. In *The Family Planning Manager's Handbook: Basic Skills and Tools for Managing Family Planning Programs*, J. A. Wolff, L. J. Suttenfield, and S. C. Binzen, eds. West Hartford, Conn.: Kumarian Press. <http://erc.msh.org/mainpage.cfm?file=2.1.5.htm&module=planning&language=English>

Örtengren, K. 2004. *The Logical Framework Approach: A Summary of the Theory Behind the LFA Method*. Stockholm: SIDA. <http://www.sida.se/shared/jsp/download.jsp?f=SIDA1489en_web.pdf&a=2379>

★ Seltzer, J. B. 2010. Planning the Work and Working with the Plan. In *Health Systems in Action: An eHandbook for Leaders and Managers*, S. Vriesendorp, L. de la Peza, C. Peabody Perry, J. B. Seltzer, M. O'Neil, S. Reimann, N. Merlini Gaul, et al., eds. Cambridge, Mass.: Management Sciences for Health. <http://www.msh.org/Documents/upload/msh_eHandbook_ch04.pdf>

South African Department of Health. 2003. *Guidelines for District Health Planning and Reporting*. Pretoria: South African Department of Health. <http://www.doh.gov.za/docs/factsheets/guidelines/dhp/index.html>

WHO (World Health Organization). 2004. *Mission for Essential Drugs and Supplies, Kenya: A Case Study*. Geneva: WHO. <http://www.who.int/hiv/pub/prev_care/en/meds.pdf>

★ World Bank. 2005. *The Logframe Handbook: A Logical Framework Approach to Project Cycle Management*. Washington, D.C.: World Bank. <http://www-wds.worldbank.org/external/default/WDSContentServer/IW3P/IB/2005/06/07/000160016_20050607122225/Rendered/PDF/31240b0LFhandbook.pdf>

| Part I: Policy and economic issues | Part II: Pharmaceutical management | Part III: Management support systems |

Planning and administration
36 Pharmaceutical supply systems assessment
37 Managing pharmaceutical programs
38 Planning for pharmaceutical management
39 Contracting for pharmaceuticals and services
40 Analyzing and controlling pharmaceutical expenditures
41 Financial planning and management
42 Planning and building storage facilities
Organization and management
Information management
Human resources management

CHAPTER 39

Contracting for pharmaceuticals and services

SUMMARY

A contract for goods or services is a legally binding agreement between a purchaser and a provider for a specified period of time. In the public sector, the purchaser is usually the government and the provider may be a private-sector company.

Some health systems contract out (outsource) customs clearance, pharmaceutical storage, procurement, and transport. In some cases, a health system may contract out pharmaceutical services through retail or not-for-profit pharmacies. Outsourcing services can, in some cases, reduce costs and improve effectiveness. The decision whether to contract out or to provide services in-house must rely on a careful analysis of the effect on the entire supply chain, including costs, performance, the capacity of the private sector to provide the goods and services in question, and the capacity of the health system to monitor the contract. Outsourcing is most likely to succeed when real competition takes place, the health system is equipped to supervise the contract, and sufficient funds are available to pay the contractor.

This chapter considers—

- *Pharmaceutical procurement contracts:* Careful preparation of specifications and enforcement of contract terms are a must for efficient procurement.
- *Service contracts:* Such arrangements may reduce or eliminate the need to maintain government storage and transport infrastructure. In a supply agency contract, an autonomous private or parastatal agency operates warehousing and transport services on the government's behalf. In a direct delivery contract, the supplier delivers to regional or district stores and hospitals. Under a primary distributor contract, health facilities order from a contracted distributor and pay the manufacturer's contract price for the medicines plus a distribution fee. Pharmacy benefit management programs provide prescription services to designated beneficiaries, either in person at contracted pharmacies or through direct delivery (that is, via mail) from a central location.
- *Service contracting process:* The process of contracting for services has four stages: (1) identify a service that could be provided by contract and establish the feasibility of contracting out; (2) prepare detailed tender specifications and contract terms; (3) short-list suitably qualified contractors, invite formal tenders, and appoint a contractor; and (4) monitor the contractor's and the health system's performance.

39.1 Overview of contracts

A health system is responsible for ensuring a continuous supply of high-quality goods and services to its clients at an affordable cost. This responsibility does not mean, however, that the organization needs to manufacture the supplies or provide all the services itself. Nevertheless, an argument is made—especially in developing countries—that the government should be responsible for the effective and efficient functioning of the entire national supply chain, regardless of whether individual components are managed by government agencies or by the private sector. In most health systems, pharmaceuticals and medical equipment are routinely supplied by private companies. Increasingly, the storage and distribution of these goods are also being contracted out. Industrialized countries often contract out the complete pharmaceutical program to serve designated categories of patients. Box 39-1 describes contracts for prescription services (pharmacy benefit programs). This chapter discusses—

- Contracts for pharmaceutical procurement
- Contracts for the direct delivery of pharmaceuticals by suppliers

- Contracts for nonsupply services such as customs clearance, warehousing, and transport
- Assessment and monitoring of the quality and cost-effectiveness of contracts

Contracting for services is also discussed in Chapters 24 (port clearing), 25 (transport management), and 42 (warehouse construction).

The essential first step in contract management is to decide whether an outside contract is desirable. The authority whose budget will cover the cost of the contract must make this decision, considering its impact on the entire health system—not on only one specific component. For example, in an environment of government inefficiency, outsourcing pharmaceutical distribution to a contractor may actually save costs, but may also justify a higher expenditure, if distribution services are more effective under the contractor and stock levels improve.

Producing supply items such as pharmaceuticals and other health care goods in-house is usually too expensive or impractical. Services, however, are different, and the total cost and performance of an in-house service as compared with a contracted service needs to be assessed. Furthermore, the choice is not a one-time decision. Regular monitoring of

Source: Abt Associates 2010.

Box 39-1
Pharmacy benefit programs

Pharmacy benefit management companies (PBMs) have emerged in industrialized countries as a way to contain health care costs by implementing mechanisms to improve the cost-effectiveness of prescription medicine programs. A PBM contracts with employers, insurers, and others to provide benefits to those groups' members. Often the PBM is paid a fixed amount for which it must provide contracted services, either by itself or by subcontracting with others.

Full-service PBM functions can include the following—

- Establishing networks of pharmacies for use by plan members
- Processing claims electronically and maintaining a database on drug use and cost
- Encouraging the use of generic products
- Managing existing formularies, helping to establish customized formularies, or providing a national formulary

- Encouraging prescriptions for maintenance medications to be filled less frequently with larger amounts, often by mail order
- Negotiating volume-based rebates from manufacturers
- Performing drug-use reviews
- Developing disease management programs based on standard treatment guidelines and assessments of patient outcome

PBM mechanisms for decreasing costs include implementing consumer cost-sharing to encourage the use of generic drugs, requiring prior authorization for certain prescriptions, and establishing multitiered formulary copayments. Although studies have shown that some mechanisms, such as tiered formularies and prior authorization do positively affect costs and medicine usage, little information is available on how these PBM programs affect health outcomes.

the contracted service and annual comparison with an in-house alternative are necessary to confirm that outsourcing remains the most cost-effective option.

A *contract* for the provision of goods or services is a legally binding agreement between a *purchaser* (or buyer) and a *provider* (or seller) for a period of time specified. In the health system context, the purchaser is generally the government or a public or private health care system, and the provider a private-sector company or parastatal entity. The responsibilities and interests of the purchaser and the provider, as well as remedies to address any potential future disagreement between the parties, are defined by the contract terms and conditions. Pharmaceutical contracts should be established in a formal written document.

The contracting process usually starts with the preparation of a *tender document,* which specifies the *technical requirements* of the goods or services required and the *terms and conditions* of the contract. Tenders are then formally invited and evaluated. The service agreement becomes binding after a tender is accepted, a letter of acceptance is issued, the contract is signed by both parties, and, in some special cases, the contract is registered with the appropriate government representative. If either party subsequently fails to comply with the contract, penalties are imposed. Clear and comprehensive technical requirements and contract terms and conditions are essential; otherwise, disputes may arise and the contractor may not perform as expected. Changes to a contract should be authorized only when technical evi-

dence supports the change or when the change will not significantly affect services provided.

The design, implementation, and monitoring of contracts must also take into consideration the issue of corruption. Contracts related to pharmaceutical management, and especially procurement, are susceptible to corruption because the supply chain can be complicated and lack transparency, and because drug volumes are usually large and unit costs high, thereby making such contracts very lucrative for suppliers (Cohen 2002).

Established service contracts should be reviewed to ensure that their terms and conditions continue to address the required scope of work and that they comply with current legislation and that all parties are performing as agreed. Outsourcing may not be cost-effective if the quality of the contracted service cannot be monitored and enforced.

39.2 Critical contract terms in pharmaceutical procurement

The discussion of tender management procedures in Chapter 21 introduced issues related to supply contracts. Tender specifications include many of the conditions of contract performance. Normally, by submitting a bid, the prospective seller is agreeing to the proposed contract terms (unless the seller stipulates otherwise in writing on

Figure 39-1   Contract terms must be fully specified

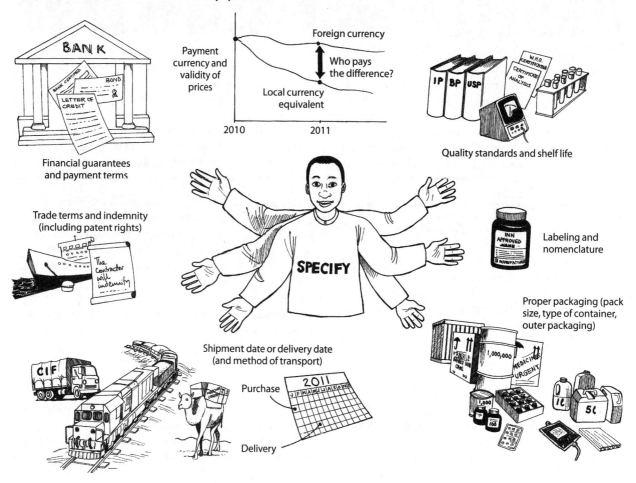

the tender submission). Care should be taken to ensure that the terms of the final contract match the terms specified in the tender or bid document. If any conditions are altered, the desired performance or price may be compromised or losing bidders may feel that they were disadvantaged in the contracting process and take legal action.

Although the tender documents specify the supplies and services expected, the purchaser and the provider should execute a discrete written contract. The most critical contract terms are discussed below (see also Figure 39-1).

Preparing an effective pharmaceutical procurement contract is a specialized function requiring a great deal of care. Critical details include the specification of the medicine; the quality standards required; analyses to be performed; batch records required; certificates of quality assurance that must be issued; the type of packing, documentation, lot numbering, and labeling requirements; return and disposal procedures and obligations; communication requirements; shipment and delivery agreements; the price and payment terms; and the last date of shipment. Again, the contract specifications should be consistent with those pre-

sented in the tender or bid document to ensure the fairness of the process. Failure by the supplier to comply with those requirements can cause substantial loss or extra expense to the buyer. From the supplier's perspective, if the procurement office places a verbal order and subsequently refuses to confirm it or fails to pay for an order as agreed, the supplier will suffer loss or added expense. Thus, all orders should be requested in writing and signed by the authorized contract representative.

An interpretation or clarification of the various terms and conditions contained in a tender should become part of the overall tender document to avoid any ambiguity or conflict that may arise because of different interpretations. Annex 39-1 shows a tender's sample interpretation section. Questions should be solicited from the bidders at the beginning of the bid process. All questions and corresponding answers should be distributed in writing to all prospective bidders, and written confirmation of receipt requested from each. Any additional questions that arise during the bidding process should be addressed in the same manner.

Trade terms

Trade terms are used in pharmaceutical supply contracts to define the division of costs and responsibilities during the shipment of commodities between the supplier and the buyer's stores. Trade terms were standardized by the International Chamber of Commerce in 1953 when it first published *Incoterms*; these standards are reviewed and revised approximately every decade (International Chamber of Commerce 2010). Over the years, more precise definitions and new terms have been created to establish the exact point where the seller's costs and responsibilities end and the buyer's begin. However, old terms are still in common use, so it is important that both parties understand and agree on the contract terms. Table 39-1 summarizes the trade terms most commonly used for government supply programs. Procurement agencies should have a copy of the latest version of *Incoterms*.

The buyer usually specifies the applicable trade terms in the contract or tender document. The buyer must, therefore, understand the implications of various trade terms and the corresponding relative risks assumed by the buyer and the seller in case of loss or damage. Of the trade terms listed in Table 39-1, CIP (carriage and insurance paid) is generally preferable for pharmaceutical supply tenders. These terms make it easier to compare tender offers fairly and to budget for the true cost of products on the tender list. In cost-recovery programs, these terms also make it easier to determine the full replacement cost for each product. When using CIP terms, specifying precisely the final destination to which the cost of transport will be paid by the seller is essential.

In many countries, transportation routes are limited, and economical delivery of goods from overseas requires a detailed knowledge of these routes. If the chosen supplier is unfamiliar with local trade routes but the procurement office is knowledgeable about local routes, FAS (free alongside ship) or FOB (free on board) terms may be preferable, with the buyer making separate arrangements for shipping and insurance. According to FAS terms, the seller pays for packing and delivery to the place of loading. The buyer pays loading costs plus export customs and documentation charges. Under FOB terms, documentation charges are paid by the seller.

Table 39-1   Summary of common trade terms in the 2010 *Incoterms*

Category	Code	Code meaning	Explanation
Any mode of transport	EXW	Ex works. Need to state a named place.	Seller pays for expenses at factory or warehouse. Buyer assumes all onward expenses.
	FCA	Free carrier. Need to state a named place.	Seller pays packing and delivery at the named point into the custody of the carrier and cleared for export.
	CPT	Carriage paid to. Need to state the destination port.	Seller pays freight and charges to named destination port. Buyer pays expenses from this port onward, including foreign customs clearance.
	CIP	Carriage and insurance paid. Need to state the destination port.	Like CPT, but the seller also has to procure and pay for cargo insurance.
	DAP	Delivered at place. Need to state place.	Seller delivers the goods when they are placed at the disposal of the buyer on the arriving means of transport ready for unloading at the named place of destination. Seller bears the responsibility and risks to deliver the goods to the named place.
	DAT	Delivered at terminal. Need to state place.	Seller delivers when the goods have been unloaded and are placed at the disposal of the buyer at a named terminal at the named port or named destination.
	DDP	Delivered duty paid. Need to state place.	Seller pays for all transportation costs and bears all risk until the goods have been delivered and pays the duty.
Waterway transport	FAS	Free alongside ship. Need to state the loading port.	The same as FCA, with the exception that buyer pays for loading. NOT suitable for multimodal sea transport in containers.
	FOB	Free on board. Need to state the loading port.	The same as FCA, but for ocean or inland waterway freight use only. NOT suitable for multimodal sea transport in containers.
	CFR	Cost and freight. Need to state the destination port.	Seller pays all expenses up to arrival at named port of destination, and buyer pays marine insurance.
	CIF	Cost, insurance, and freight. Need to state the destination port.	Same as CFR, except seller also pays for insurance for the buyer.

In general, sea freight cost is about 10 percent, and insurance about 1 percent of the FOB cost. Some buyers require that bidders provide both CIP or CIF and FOB prices to help determine whether shipping and insurance could be managed at a lower cost by the buyer. The eventual contract may also require that the FOB portion remain unchanged but that the CIP price be adjusted for actual freight and insurance costs. By this means the buyer can collect data on actual freight charges and compare costs under the different trade terms.

Financial capability

The bidder must submit documentary evidence demonstrating to the buyer's satisfaction that the bidder has the financial capability to perform its obligations under the supply contract if its bid is chosen. Such documentation should include the bidder's financial accounts for the two most recently completed fiscal years.

Purchase quantities

The buyer may request tenders for either fixed or estimated quantities (see Chapter 21). The contract terms should specify if estimated quantities represent a guaranteed minimum purchase or if there is no guarantee of quantities in the contract. The latter arrangement is standard practice in pharmaceutical group-purchasing contracts in developed countries. From a supplier's perspective, offering a specially discounted price for a quantity that is not a guaranteed purchase would not be beneficial. Price fluctuations of raw materials used in pharmaceuticals are such that suppliers tend to build higher buffers into their pricing structures, depending on the certainty of a purchase and the period over which they are expected to keep their prices valid.

Exchange rates and price comparisons

Often, bidding documents will require that bidders use a specified currency or currencies to express their bids. However, the International Bank for Reconstruction and Development (IBRD) guidelines for procurement (2010) suggest that if bidders are allowed to state their bids in the currency of their choice, in order to compare prices, all bid prices should be converted to a single currency selected by the buyer (local currency or fully convertible foreign currency) and established in the bidding documents. Price comparisons can be based on the official rates of exchange prevailing on the day bids are opened, with the stipulation that if those rates subsequently change, the rates applicable at the time of the award of contract should be used. Table 39-2 illustrates how this rule would be applied to compare bids from four hypothetical suppliers. Whether or not the IBRD guidelines are used, the method for bid comparisons should be stated in the bidding documents.

The currency chosen for comparing bids can be a major influence on the award process. When bid evaluation is done in a currency within a high-inflation economy, price differences at the time of bid opening, the date of award, and the date of payment can be substantial. In such circumstances, requesting bids in U.S. dollars or another commonly accepted currency in international pharmaceutical trade, such as Japanese yen, British pounds, or the euro, may be advisable.

Payment currency

The contract must specify the payment currency, which should be the currency specified in the terms and conditions of the bid. The payment currency may be widely used in international trade or may be the supplier's or buyer's

Table 39-2   Bid comparison according to currency conversion rate

| Supplier | Tender currency | Value of bid in U.S. dollars | | | |
		On date of bid submission	On date of opening bid	On date of award	On date of payment
A	Euro	6.43	7.07	7.07	7.07
B	Japanese yen	6.86	6.86	7.20	7.20
C	U.S. dollar	7.14	7.14	7.14	7.14
D	U.K. pound	7.57	7.57	7.19	6.84

Source: Westring (1985).

Note: Currency conversion rates used to evaluate tenders and guide awards should be consistent with the terms and conditions stipulated in tender/bid documents. The table shows how exchange rates could vary at different times in the bid invitation, submission, award, and payment process. Considering that bidders may submit their bids at different times before the specified closing date and that the buyer may delay the time between the award and the bid opening, the fairest process is to base the value of the bid on the conversion rate prevailing on the date of the bid opening. For example, on the date of bid submission, supplier A offered the lowest price (USD 6.43), but this offer was irrelevant because supplier B had the most favorable price when the bids were opened (USD 6.86). Sellers should not be held responsible for delays experienced on the part of buying agencies in evaluating bids, which can happen if a buying agency takes several months to determine an award. Therefore, although supplier A's bid was the lowest on the date of the award, the value on the date of bid opening is the relevant one for bid selection. It would be purely speculative to attempt to anticipate changes in parity, which should be avoided in public procurement. Payment value should be based on the rate on the date of the bid opening, because that is the rate used to determine the award, and this process should be specified in the contract between the buyer and supplier. Problems can be reduced by specifying or limiting the currencies that suppliers can use when bidding.

own currency. If the buyer's currency is used, a speculative risk exists for the supplier if the local currency is not freely convertible or if the conversion rate fluctuates significantly. Many international suppliers either do not accept payment in local currency or include a "contingency factor" that raises prices.

When procurement offices can pay only in local currency, the need for a contingency factor may be avoided if the buyer is able to guarantee that payments will be converted into the supplier's currency at the exchange rate prevailing when the contract was awarded.

Validity of contract prices

The validity period is the period of time after contract signing during which contract prices apply. The length of this period depends on the type of tender and contract. If the tender establishes a specific quantity to be shipped at a certain time, the bid prices are normally valid until the final shipment has been received by the buyer and payment has been made. If the tender is based on estimated quantities with periodic orders, bid prices should be valid for a longer term. The standard in industrialized countries is one year, although shorter and longer terms are sometimes required. As discussed in Chapter 21, in highly inflationary environments, it may be necessary to tender more frequently or include a price-escalation clause in the contract that adjusts prices for inflation at specific intervals (for example, quarterly). Such adjustments should be clearly specified; it may be useful to tie the adjustment to the actual rate of inflation or another economic indicator as reported by the national central bank or other authoritative source.

As previously discussed, the greater the supplier's uncertainty regarding an actual purchase against a tender, the higher the risk factor the supplier builds into its pricing. To best protect themselves in an uncertain purchasing environment, procurement agencies should consider undertaking a Pareto or ABC analysis and base their purchasing strategies on the items that comprise the bulk of their order value, rather than applying one rule for all items they purchase. (See Chapter 40 for an explanation of ABC analysis.)

Payment terms

The contract must specify payment terms. Unless timely and secure payment is guaranteed, obtaining the best prices is difficult. Many public-sector systems are either periodically short of funds or have a slow payment process. Suppliers generally require such supply systems to pay by irrevocable letter of credit, submitted before any shipments are made. Public-sector systems must realize that reputable suppliers conduct a risk analysis before submitting prices and that the supplier will usually build in a larger buffer if its experience shows that the public system has continually delayed payments.

Letter of credit. A letter of credit is an interbank document stating that a certain sum of money is available for the seller to claim from its bank as soon as it ships a consignment and presents the required documents. A letter of credit generally involves a surcharge of 1 to 2.5 percent for the buyer. However, because it reduces the supplier's credit risk, using a letter of credit can facilitate a better contract price offer. Contract agreements often allow for some price fluctuations caused, for example, by changes in freight and insurance costs. Accordingly, a supplementary payment or refund may be necessary at the time of delivery.

Deferred payment (commercial terms). The buyer and the seller may contract for payment at the time of delivery (without a letter of credit), or payment may be deferred for a period of 30, 60, 90, 120, or 180 days. Both options are forms of credit buying, and the procurement office must be careful not to contract for more supplies than it can ultimately afford. If a country defaults on deferred payment terms, it may subsequently be forced to prepay or to pay solely by letter of credit or cash on delivery.

Deferred payment allows the buyer to retain use of funds for a longer period. In addition, it enables the buyer to withhold payment if the supplier provides substandard or incomplete deliveries.

When tenders are being evaluated, the cost of various payment options should be carefully compared. Suppose two suppliers quote the same price. Supplier A requires a letter of credit to be submitted when goods are cleared from the port. Supplier B allows a credit period of 120 days from receipt of goods until payment. If the annual interest rate in the buyer's country is 12 percent, this credit period represents a 4 percent savings compared with supplier A's terms.

Quality standards

The contract terms should state that all pharmaceutical products are to be manufactured in conformity with recognized pharmacopoeial standards. The most commonly used standards in pharmaceutical procurement are the latest editions of the *British Pharmacopoeia* (BP) or the *United States Pharmacopeia* (USP), but others, such as the *European Pharmacopoeia* (EA) or the *International Pharmacopoeia* (IP), may be appropriate in some circumstances. The major pharmacopoeias include specifications for most pharmaceutical products, both raw materials and finished products in their final dosage form, organized by generic name (international nonproprietary name, INN), not by brand name.

As discussed in Chapter 21, the pharmacopoeial standards should be specified in both the tender invitation and the contract. Suppliers should be required to state the pharmacopoeial standard applicable to each product offered. The contract should specify that batch certificates and the World

Health Organization (WHO) certificate of a pharmaceutical product must be supplied for each product (see Chapter 19). In some procurement situations, it may be necessary to require that products and supplies be prequalified by WHO or approved by stringent regulatory authorities.

Manufacturing approvals

For each pharmaceutical product, tender conditions should specify that the bidder must attach the following documentation for evaluation—

- A copy of the product certificate authorizing the source facility to manufacture the particular pharmaceutical product
- A copy of the statement of licensing status, which gives the source facility manufacturing authority
- A copy of the product license as issued for the exporting country
- A copy of the product license as issued for the other countries (up to a maximum of five) in which the pharmaceutical is sold or distributed
- Copies of approval documents from WHO prequalification
- The product information
- A sample of the standard marking or label to be included on each dispensing unit
- An estimate of the percentage of capacity committed to other contracts
- A good manufacturing practices inspection certificate from the regulatory authority in the country of manufacture (although WHO provides guidelines for the certification process, countries implement it through their drug regulatory authorities; therefore, the quality of GMP (Good Manufacturing Practices) certification may be inconsistent)

Some health systems tender with commercial or nonprofit wholesale suppliers rather than manufacturers. The suppliers should provide the information and documentation (described above) required of the manufacturers.

Labeling and nomenclature

Many otherwise identical medicines are marketed under several different brand names by multinational pharmaceutical corporations and by local enterprises (see Chapter 19). To avoid confusion in the selection, procurement, distribution, and use of medicines, contract terms should require standard labeling for all products. General guidelines for labeling are as follows—

- The language for labeling should be clearly specified in the contract.

- All package labels should contain at least the following information—
  - Generic name of the active ingredients
  - Dosage form (tablet, ampoule, vial)
  - Quantity of active ingredient(s) in the dosage form
  - Number of units per package
  - Batch number
  - Date of manufacture
  - Expiry date (in clear language, not in code)
  - Pharmacopoeial standard
  - Instructions for storage
  - Name and address of manufacturer
  - "Not to be sold without a prescription" statement, if appropriate
  - "Keep out of the reach of children" statement

- The label on each ampoule or vial should contain the following information—
  - Generic name of the active ingredient(s)
  - Quantity of the active ingredient
  - Batch number
  - Expiry date
  - Name of manufacturer

- The full package label (as specified above in this list) should appear on the immediate container.
- Directions for use and precautions may be given in leaflets (package inserts). However, leaflets provide supplementary information and are not an alternative to labeling.
- For products requiring reconstitution before use (for example, powder for injection), instructions for the reconstitution should be on the label.

In some countries, unique identifiers are used to reduce theft and also to promote the essential medicines concept (see Chapter 43). However, such measures may increase cost.

Packaging

Proper packaging should be clearly specified in the tender documents and in the supply contract. General packaging guidelines are as follows—

- If pack size is important, it should be clearly specified (for example, tablets and capsules packaged in amounts of 1,000; ampoules and vials packaged in amounts of 100).
- All packaging must be suitable for the climate zone and storage conditions in the destination country.
- Tablets and capsules should be packed in sealed, waterproof containers with replaceable lids that protect the contents against light and humidity. If individual pack-

aging for tablets or capsules is required, this condition must be stipulated. Tampering evidence requirements need to be specified.

- Liquids should be packed in unbreakable, leakproof bottles or containers.
- Ampoules should preferably be one-ended and auto-breakable. Alternatively, packages should include an adequate supply of ampoule files to facilitate breaking. Light-sensitive products, such as ergometrine, should be packed in brown glass ampoules. Individual ampoules should be packed in plastic or in cardboard trays (five to ten ampoules per tray) and trays in outer cartons (for example, 100 trays per carton).
- Containers for all pharmaceutical preparations should conform to the latest edition of an internationally recognized pharmacopoeia (such as BP or USP).
- Outer cartons should be of strong, export-quality material able to withstand rough handling and the prevailing climatic conditions during transport and storage.
- If the receiving warehouse is equipped to handle pallets (see Chapter 44), the contract should require that cartons be shipped on pallets. The preferred pallet size should be specified. Additional security against theft and water damage is provided if pallets are shrink-wrapped in clear plastic.
- Each consignment must be accompanied by a detailed packing list, stating the number of cartons and the type and quantity of medicines in each carton. An outer carton should contain products with the same expiry date; this date should be printed on the carton as well as on the immediate containers. If required, outer cartons should also be labeled with a unique identifier (see Chapter 43), a commodity code, or both.
- Upon delivery, packaging becomes the property of the buyer.
- The supplier is responsible for replacing any packages and products found to be damaged at the point of delivery.

To ensure proper packing and labeling, suppliers—particularly those that are new or unknown—should be instructed to submit samples along with their bids. By assessing and visually checking the samples, buyers may avoid problems caused by poor packaging or labeling. Packaging specifications for medicine kits are discussed in Chapter 26.

Shelf life and expiry date

Pharmaceutical products have varying shelf lives. The expiry date is specified by the manufacturer at the time of manufacture and can range from six months to more than five years.

Supply contracts should specify the required minimum shelf life remaining at delivery for all pharmaceutical products. Because of the length of time required for local distribution, it is advisable to include a general condition that, at the time of arrival, at least two years of shelf life should remain. For products with a shelf life of less than two years, at least 75 percent of the shelf life should remain upon arrival.

Because the same generic products from different manufacturers may have different shelf lives, suppliers should specify the shelf life for every product in their bids so that the procurement office can consider shelf life when evaluating bids.

Bid bonds and performance bonds

In international trade, ascertaining the reliability of suppliers is sometimes difficult. To encourage suppliers to live up to their obligations, financial guarantees may be required.

Bid bonds are earnest money or security deposits in the form of cash, certified check, bank draft, state bond, or other negotiable bank document (equal, for example, to 1 percent of the value of the offered bid) that are provided by the potential supplier at the time a bid is submitted. This security is forfeited if the successful bidder withdraws the offer or refuses to agree to the contract requirements. Bid bonds are refunded when the award is announced and all suppliers have accepted the contract terms. World Bank pharmaceutical standard bidding documents recommend the use of bid bonds and performance bonds (World Bank 2008).

Performance bonds are security deposits in the form of negotiable fiscal documents that may be required at the time a contract is awarded. Their purpose is to guarantee that the supplier fulfills the contract obligations. An amount equivalent to 5 to 10 percent of the contract price is often used for this purpose. The deposit is separate from documentation involved in the letter of credit and is returned only after goods have been received in the country and are found to meet all contractual standards and to be of acceptable quality. The World Bank specifies a performance bond set at an amount stated in the contract, posted as a cashier's check or irreversible letter of credit within twenty-eight days of contract award. The performance bond is released after the contractual requirements have been fulfilled (World Bank 2008).

Both bid and performance bonds provide protection for the buyer against supplier default. The potential financial risk, however, may drive away many potential bidders, including some reliable international companies. For example, when the banking system of the purchasing country is poorly integrated into the international banking system, retrieving a performance bond after the contract is completed may be difficult.

As an alternative to requiring bonds, the risk of supplier default can be reduced by inviting tenders only from suppliers of known reliability. It is not uncommon for pharmaceutical procurement programs to require financial guarantees only from new or previously unreliable suppliers.

Performance bonds are particularly unappealing to suppliers in a tender that calls for "draw-down" by purchasing group members, in which the tender quantity is just an estimate and orders are placed throughout a contract period. In such cases, the supplier would presumably lose access to the performance bond funds for the entire contract period; most established pharmaceutical companies would not be interested in such a contract. Despite these reservations, performance bonds may be warranted in fixed-quantity open tenders with postqualification, where many bidders and suppliers may be largely unknown entities.

Experience

The bidder should provide documentary evidence acceptable to the purchaser—including sales figures for at least three years—to prove that it is a regular supplier of pharmaceuticals to the domestic and international markets under the specific type of tender involved.

Shipment date

For fixed-quantity contracts, the contract and the letter of credit (if used) should specify the last date by which the supplier is to ship the consignment. The implication of this requirement is that the bill of lading (the standard shipping documentation) issued by the shipping company and signed by the master of the carrying vessel must be dated on or before the last date of shipment specified in the letter of credit.

The bank that holds the letter of credit is prohibited from accepting a bill of lading dated after the last date for shipment under the contract unless the buyer has agreed to the delay and the letter of credit has been suitably extended. If orders are covered by import licenses, an extension from the appropriate office may also be needed.

In contracts based on estimated quantities with periodic orders during the contract, the contract should specify the maximum number of days between the receipt of an order by the supplier and the shipment of goods.

Patent provisions

In countries that recognize patent laws, most new pharmaceutical products were originally covered by patent for periods ranging from two to seventeen years. Since 1994, World Trade Organization (WTO) members have been obligated under the Agreement on Trade-Related Aspects of Intellectual Property Rights (TRIPS) to recognize twenty-year patent periods. During this period, no seller may manufacture or market a patented product without the consent of the patent holder.

Each country's policy regarding patent rights is governed by legal, political, and economic considerations, both local and international. If the country is a WTO member, it may be obligated by the TRIPS agreement, or it may be restricted by intellectual property conditions within bilateral trade agreements. The Declaration on TRIPS and Public Health (Doha Declaration) gives developing countries some flexibility in adhering to TRIPS, enabling them to take steps to protect the public health of their populations. Least-developed countries have been given until at least 2016 to comply with pharmaceutical patent requirements. Chapter 3, on intellectual property and access to medicines, details the issues surrounding pharmaceutical patents and the TRIPS agreement.

Purchasing countries must decide which patent laws, if any, will be recognized in the procurement contract. The simplest practice for buyers is to place the responsibility for observance of patent rights in the country of origin on the supplier. Contracts can stipulate that the supplier will indemnify the buyer against all claims that may arise on account of patent rights, trademarks, proprietary designs, or royalties.

Penalties for default

The contract should specify the remedies available to each party in case of default by the other party, and the body of law and court under which disputes will be resolved.

Contracts with domestic suppliers are, of course, subject to the laws of the buyer's country. Contracts with international suppliers may also be written with that provision, but enforcing local law on an international supplier that has no local operations may be difficult. Even if a judgment is obtained, it may be impossible to recover damages.

Contracts are sometimes written providing that disputes will be resolved through arbitration, but this process is also unlikely to produce a favorable solution for a buyer that is injured through the default of an international supplier.

The contract should specify that the buyer will withhold payments in process and/or cancel any outstanding transactions in the event of supplier default. This remedy is suitable only in contracts in which some form of delayed payment applies and when the deliveries and payments are divided. If the contract specifies a single shipment with payment by letter of credit up front, payment will have been made by the time problems are discovered. Annex 39-2 illustrates a typical contract for pharmaceutical supply.

Some countries have a system to delist suppliers who have clearly defaulted on a contract. A delisted supplier could potentially be barred from supplying a national agency for periods ranging from one to three years or more, depending on the nature of the default. Delisted suppliers must undergo a new prequalifying process to be reconsidered as a supplier.

39.3 Contracts for services

For many years, private companies and governments in industrialized countries have used outside contractors to provide specialized services at lower cost and with higher quality than the company or government can achieve in-house. Increasingly, many developing countries' governments are considering this model.

Contracting out, or outsourcing, in health care has traditionally been used for nonclinical services, such as equipment maintenance, laundry, and catering. Outsourcing might be used in the pharmaceutical supply system in many ways. Chapter 8 discusses various ways in which contracts may be used to manage pharmaceutical warehousing and distribution services to the public sector, extending in some cases to total pharmaceutical service provision through the private sector. Chapter 24 points out options for contracting port-clearing services, and Chapter 25 discusses contracts for private-sector transport services.

Successful contracting of services can tap private-sector expertise and efficiency, yet still leave the government in overall control. In some cases, there may be additional benefits; for example, a private transport firm that is awarded the contract to deliver medicines to remote rural locations may be able to offer local agricultural cooperatives a favorable price to carry their produce on the return trip. Contracting out can also reduce the cost to the supply system of wastage and losses due to theft, by making the contractor responsible for losses. However, in considering an outsourcing option, the supply system management must also consider the overall indirect costs and benefits to the entire system, not only compare the direct costs between options. A total cost analysis can inform decisions regarding whether to outsource (see Chapter 40).

The main steps in contracting out nonsupply services are to—

- Identify a single, well-defined service
- Carry out a feasibility study, including a total cost analysis
- Specify the contract terms clearly and precisely
- Use a competitive tender to select the contractor
- Pay the contractor
- Monitor the contract

When considering service contracts, the first step is to determine whether the private sector has the capacity to provide an adequate level of service. If the capacity exists, the next step is to calculate the total cost of providing the service in-house and to establish, by means of a survey or formal tender, what the total cost of contracting or privatizing the service would be. If the private-sector service appears to be more cost-effective and is able to provide at least the same level of service, it should be seriously con-

sidered. The answers to five key questions may determine the feasibility and desirability of contracting for services (McPake and Ngalande-Bande 1994)—

1. *Will real competition take place?* Are multiple providers in the market, or do one or two companies monopolize the service?
2. *Will competition actually promote efficiency?* When the background of the bidders is not known or when the service is new in the market, it may be difficult to assess the bidders' ability to meet the terms of the contract at the price and quality required. If a contractor fails to perform satisfactorily, the health service is left with an interrupted service and with the problem of finding an alternative supplier.
3. *Can the health system effectively supervise the contract?* Are there defined procedures for supervising contracts? Are these procedures included in the terms of the contract? Does the health system staff have the necessary skills, and is the information system able to provide indicators to monitor the contractor's performance?
4. *Will funding be sufficient for the contract?* Budget constraints might make fulfilling payment obligations to contractors impossible. For example, releasing funds regularly or on time may not be possible, which would likely lead to either suspension of services by the provider or less than optimal performance.
5. *Is advocacy sufficient within the government to adopt an outsourced model and will public reaction support the initiative?* Often, many departments within the government must work together to accomplish change, particularly when actions are taken to partner with the private sector. In addition, public sentiment may interfere with the government's willingness to move ahead, especially if outsourcing will result in the loss of government jobs. An effective communications strategy must be prepared to address these critical stakeholder groups.

Before contracting out any service, an options analysis should be conducted, and these questions should be answered.

39.4 Feasibility assessment

Contracting out may be one way of solving the problems of an unsatisfactory service, but only if the process can be managed properly. If it cannot, an unsatisfactory situation may be made worse. Senior health service managers are responsible for ensuring that a contracted service is feasible and cost-effective, that the private sector can offer reliable tenderers that are able to provide good-quality service, and that the contract can be monitored effectively. This

Country Study 39-1
Public-private health services contracting experience in Cambodia

In the mid-1990s, the Cambodian health care system was having difficulty serving an adequate level of the population, especially the poor living in remote, rural areas. Nine rural districts participated in a study comparing the traditional government model of health care with two different models using nongovernmental organizations (NGOs) as contractors. The contracts were awarded through an international competitive bid, based on the technical quality of the proposed services and price. The districts were randomly assigned to one of three models—

- Contracting out: NGO contractors had responsibility for services, including hiring, firing, wage setting, and procuring and distributing essential medicines and commodities.
- Contracting in: NGO contractors worked within the government system to strengthen infrastructure through management support. They could not hire or fire workers, and medicines were distributed through normal government channels.
- Government: Government continued managing and supplying services.

Evaluation indicators were established, and extensive data were collected before and two and a half years after the intervention started. All districts had extremely poor health service coverage at baseline. The contracts included detailed and objectively measurable service coverage and equity goals. The control (government) districts were given the same goals. For example, for immunization, the target was to increase to 70 percent the percentage of children who are fully immunized, while targeting children from the poorest 50 percent of households. The contracts specified financial bonuses for achieving coverage higher than the target and equity rates, as well as penalties if the goals were unmet.

Results showed that contracted-out districts experienced significantly better improvements in virtually every public health service that was analyzed; for example, immunization rates increased by 158 percent in those districts compared with 82 percent and 56 percent increases in contracted-in and control districts, respectively. Additionally, the contracted districts provided more than proportionate benefits to poor households.

The average annual recurrent expenditure per person was USD 3.88 for the contracted-out districts, USD 2.40 for the contracted-in districts, and USD 1.65 for the control districts. Although the direct expenditure was higher in contracted-out districts, many indirect costs were decreased; for example, people in these districts lost 15 percent less work time because of illness and time spent seeking health care, and even more important, their out-of-pocket expenses for health care were significantly reduced. Expenditures by the poorest 50 percent of people fell 70 percent, or USD 35, which is impressive. The addition of out-of-pocket expenses to the government expenditure made contracting out the most cost-effective choice.

On the basis of their experience, the study organizers concluded that successful contracting requires—

- Predetermined and objectively measurable performance indicators, with clear and detailed contract targets
- Government support at the central and local levels
- An allowance for government health care workers to be employed by the contractor for market wage rates
- Contractors to be given the maximum management autonomy to achieve specified contract targets

Sources: Bhushan et al. 2002; Schwartz and Bhushan 2004.

determination requires feasibility assessment, planning, implementation of the tender process, contract monitoring, and review. Again, the entire process must be conducted with transparency, especially if the political or business environment is conducive to corrupt practices.

Four main issues need to be considered to determine the feasibility of contracting out a service. First, the total *cost* of the existing service must be compiled and compared with the total projected cost of alternative forms of provision to determine whether contracting out is potentially cost-effective; second, a *total cost analysis* must be carried out from a broader supply chain perspective; third, the *capacity* of potential contractors to provide an acceptable quality

of service must be assessed; and fourth, the service *performance* required must be clearly defined so that satisfactory tender documents can be prepared.

Comparative cost

In the case of a new contract, the total cost of the in-house service should be accurately assessed before modeling costs with other options and before inviting any tenders. Figures can then be compared realistically with the cost of the tenders received (see also Chapter 21). Usually, two cost models of the in-house service are made, one including the capital cost of improving the service and the other excluding it. In addition, the potential cash benefits and out-of-pocket costs associated with privatization must be considered. On the one hand, income may be generated when buildings and equipment that are no longer needed are sold. On the other hand, severance payments may have to be made to workers whose jobs are eliminated. Another approach to this issue is to require the contractor to take over existing buildings and equipment and to absorb the existing workforce.

In the case of an existing contracted service whose cost-effectiveness is being assessed, an analysis of a suitable comparable noncontracted service in another health unit or province is needed to compare the cost of the in-house service with the price of the contract.

Standard cost-accounting methods should be used, and the cost per unit of service should be computed. Costs need to be assigned to each of the service units. This determination is sometimes difficult when such data are not routinely collected or compiled, or when all expenditures are categorized by line item and not by department or service. In such cases, a special study is required. After the data are analyzed, the cost per unit of service is calculated.

Contracting out may be justified if potential contractors can provide good-quality service at a lower total cost. Keeping the cost of the existing service confidential is essential; otherwise, tenderers may be tempted to underbid those costs without carrying out a proper analysis. They may then find that they are unable to provide an acceptable service at the bid price.

Total cost analysis from the supply chain perspective

Managers tend to look at the immediate gross cost savings rather than net cost savings after considering the value of benefits; however, a careful benefits assessment should not be overlooked. Total cost analysis (Chapter 40) is one approach to analyzing costs and benefits of structured changes in a pharmaceutical supply system.

Outsourcing options are generally considered when the regular distribution system is regarded as ineffective and inefficient or when the organization is shifting the concentration of its core business to an area of activity other than direct distribution. However, the supply chain operation is undermined if a total analysis fails to consider both the costs and benefits to the entire interlinked system, not just the individual sectors whose functions are being outsourced.

Easily measurable effects relevant to the entire system include changes in stock-holding practices and inventory management at holding points, and the amount of wastage. More difficult to measure, but important, effects are related to indirect costs and benefits, such as the level of community satisfaction with health care in terms of the availability of and access to essential medicines and out-of-pocket costs. Country Study 39-1 shows how a contracted service that, at start-up, was more expensive than the in-house service ultimately resulted in cost savings.

Private-sector capacity

Capacities of the private sector can vary significantly between countries and within different regions in the same country. Some countries use a combination of public, private, and nonprofit providers to fulfill varying service needs (see Country Study 39-2). A structured survey of private-sector capacity (see Chapter 36) can be used to assess the capacity and willingness of the private sector to provide the required service. The survey will help managers determine

---

Country Study 39-2
Using innovative contracting to address regional challenges in Papua New Guinea

Around 2005, Papua New Guinea had nineteen provinces and one national capital district. The terrain and poor road conditions in the country made distributing pharmaceuticals and medical supplies to the provinces extremely difficult. The country had 650 health centers: half were accessible by road; 30 percent were accessible only by a combination of road and water; 18 percent had only air access; 2 percent had to be accessed by a combination of road, water, and walking. Certain provinces with especially challenging terrain had problems over the years with ineffective distribution of pharmaceutical and medical supply kits to health centers.

Many provinces did not have enough private-sector contractors with sufficient capacity to efficiently distribute to the entire province. Although local people or small companies did the actual distribution, they did not have the management capacity to meet the contract conditions that would result from a competitive tender. Therefore, larger companies based in the capital, Port Moresby, or the port city of Lae that had the necessary organizational ability joined forces with these experienced local agents to bid for provincial distribution contracts managed by various international nonprofit agencies. Papua New Guinea's innovative contracting successfully combined the talents of the few central companies capable of competing in a tender and managing the conditions of a contract with the local expertise needed to overcome logistical and geographic challenges in the field.

whether there would be competition for the contract, what options are available, and how total costs might vary with each option.

Performance indicators to compare options and monitor contracts

Performance indicators for the service need to be identified for two reasons. First, measuring the performance of the existing service is essential in order to establish where it succeeds and where it fails. Only by doing so can the purchaser prepare a realistic tender specification for the contracted alternative. Second, performance indicators are an essential component of contract monitoring; if the contractor cuts costs, it may be at the expense of quality. After performance indicators for the type of service are identified, a checklist for their assessment is prepared. For example, indicators for the assessment of contracting for the management of essential medicines warehousing and distribution might include—

- Total costs to the public sector (see Chapter 40)
- Service level to lower-level warehouses and health facilities (see Chapter 44)
- Availability of indicator medicines at pharmacies and health facilities
- Average lead time for receiving orders
- Average shelf life remaining upon delivery
- Average percentage of time out of stock for indicator medicines in facilities
- Number of complaints about short shipments or incorrect items shipped
- Number of complaints about damaged or poor-quality goods received

39.5 Developing a contract for services

When contracting has been determined to be feasible and potentially cost-effective, five major steps are involved in developing a service contract—

1. Identifying qualified providers
2. Preparing and completing all internal and public communications
3. Developing and managing the tender for services
4. Adjudicating and awarding contracts
5. Monitoring performance

Identifying qualified providers

A short list should be prepared of contractors adequately qualified to tender for the contract. Depending on the size of the contract and on local tendering regulations, this list may be developed by informal inquiry, through structured interviews and inspections, or by means of a prequalification tender process. This step can be incorporated into the survey of capacity previously discussed. For example, a first step in identifying potentially qualified providers might be through an invitation to submit an expression of interest (EOI). Each EOI response would include information from the provider as to its ability to meet the contract requirements.

A formal set of procedures for identifying and evaluating potential contractors produces more objective results than information gathering that is more subjective and informal. Formal qualification procedures increase the transparency of the contracting process and promote the fair evaluation of all prospective contractors, while decreasing the likelihood of corruption. Questions to consider and to require supporting documentation for include the following—

- Does the company have established experience in providing this type of service?
- Is the company financially sound, and are its accounts satisfactory?
- Does the company's financial accounting comply with government procedures?
- Does the company have the necessary infrastructure and equipment?
- Are sound management systems in place?
- Are internal quality-control measures in place?
- Does the company manage any other government contracts?
- Does the company's management information system produce useful reports on services provided?
- Does the company have an adequate number of trained staff persons to handle the proposed contract?
- Can the company provide documentation of its performance according to the indicators deemed critical for the type of service?
- Are other clients satisfied with services received?
- Do any conflicts of interest, such as family member associations with key government officials, exist that could compromise the initiative or create public concern?

When a short list of qualified service providers has been prepared, the contract can be formally tendered.

Developing the service contract and managing the tender

After the decision to contract out a service has been reached, tender specifications and provisions of the service contract must be drawn up. The tender documents and provisions of the service contract should clearly specify the duties of both contracting parties. The issues to be covered include—

Scope of the service: This section must include a detailed description of the service required and the anticipated workload. For example, in the case of a transport contract, it should include a full definition of the routes, the delivery points, the delivery schedule, and responsibility for loading and unloading. The contractor must agree to work as part of the national or provincial health system and to be supervised by the relevant authorities.

Performance standards and service quality: This section should define the performance and quality standards that have been set for the service, including matters such as service level, response rates, security measures, documentation, and maintenance standards. The duties of the contractor in maintaining and monitoring quality standards should be defined. Restrictions on assignment of the contractor's duties in the event of a change of ownership must be clearly defined to avoid any potential interference with service during such transitions.

Contract management: This section should define the client's and the contractor's responsibilities for overseeing the contract, assessing and monitoring performance, and reporting and payment procedures. Subcontracting requirements or prohibitions should be defined clearly.

Staffing: The contract may specify the qualifications and skills required for key positions needed to manage the contract and how many workers should be assigned to the contract, although the contractor usually has total responsibility for the selection, discipline, and termination of staff. The contract terms should specify how issues such as staffing increases, overtime, working on holidays, and so on will be addressed. In some service contracts, contractors may try to cut costs by paying very low wages. This practice contributes to high staff turnover and poor service. If minimum wage legislation is in force, the contractor should be required to conform to it.

Staff qualifications: Where appropriate, staff qualifications and in-service training requirements should be specified.

Property rights over equipment: In cases in which the contractor takes over the service from the government, existing buildings, equipment, or vehicles may be used by the contractor. The contract should clearly define the ownership and disposal procedures for these assets. A detailed inventory should be attached to the contract describing the assets and their age, condition, and value at transfer. If the property is to be sold to the contractor, terms of reimbursement must be negotiated.

Payment terms: This section should define how payments are to be calculated and when they are to be made. If payments are linked to the exchange rate (or another index), the calculation method should be clearly defined. Generally, payment is made after a unit of service has been completed. This practice provides an incentive for the contractor and protects the government against the contractor's failure to perform. Payment in advance (for example, monthly or quarterly), based on estimated costs, is sometimes acceptable, however, especially when the contractor is a nonprofit organization. Four main payment mechanisms are used for nonsupply contracts—

1. *Cost reimbursement contracts* provide for payment of incurred costs, to the extent described in the contract, in addition to a set fee for the service.
2. *Fixed-price contracts* establish a fixed price for the entire contract. Such an approach may work for the service component of a central medical stores management contract, where medicines and supplies are paid for separately, but not for more variable services such as transport.
3. *Percentage-of-turnover contracts* pay on the basis of a fixed percentage of turnover (for example, a percentage of the value of medicines managed or transported).
4. *Cost per quantity contracts* pay on the basis of some measure of the quantity of medicines handled (for example, pharmaceutical transport may be charged per metric ton per kilometer or per cubic meter per kilometer).

Accounts and reports: The contract should define the reports necessary for effective management of the contract. These might include monthly accounting reports and reports of monthly deliveries.

Budget: The budget submitted by the contractor should be attached to the contract. It will help in the monitoring and auditing of the contract account and in budget planning.

Contract duration: The contract start and completion dates should be specified.

Contract review procedures: Contracts may specify a formal mid–contract period review, to allow problems to be overcome and procedures to be changed by mutual agreement. The health system should in any case review contract performance regularly.

Grounds for contract termination: The grounds and procedures for contract termination by either party must be clearly specified. These grounds should be fair to both parties and defensible in court in the event of a dispute.

Penalties for noncompliance with the contract: These penalties should be clearly defined. For example, the contractor could be penalized for late delivery or loss of pharmaceuticals in transit. The government could be made liable for interest charges in the event of late payments.

Health system indemnity: The contract should indemnify the health system against any claims arising from delayed deliveries, injury to patients or staff of the system or the contractor, drug reactions, product defects, and similar problems caused by the contractor's negligence or inefficiency.

Insurance: The buyer's and the contractor's respective insurance obligations under the contract should be clearly defined. Items to be considered include fire and theft insurance and employer and public liability insurance.

Notices and communication: Procedures for communicating under the terms of the contract should be defined. Generally, all communication should be in writing.

Conducting and adjudicating the tender

The steps for conducting a tender for services are similar to those in Chapter 21 (for pharmaceuticals and supplies) and Chapter 42 (for construction). The procedure for evaluating tenders should be outlined, made known to prospective service providers in advance, and then used to assess the prequalification requirements of providers. The key is to have a transparent process that is free from influence by special interests and to use written criteria to evaluate bids and select the contractor.

Monitoring the contract

After the contract has been awarded, it must be monitored to ensure that both parties comply with its terms and conditions. A contract monitoring office should be designated or set up to perform this task. The cost of running this office should be taken into account as part of the financial evaluation. The duties of the contract monitoring office include—

- Monitoring health system compliance with the contract conditions and correcting any health system performance defects that prevent the contractor from fulfilling the specified duties
- Monitoring the contractor's services to ensure that the standards specified in the contract are maintained and invoking penalty clauses if the contractor fails to achieve the required standards of performance
- Monitoring clients' satisfaction—for example, receiving stores should submit regular reports indicating whether the contractor delivers on time, listing any missing or damaged goods, and documenting other quality-control and service problems (the contractor should be informed whenever problems occur)
- Responding to all complaints and initiating any required investigations or interventions
- Monitoring the contractor's activity reports
- Checking the contractor's invoices and certifying payments due under the contract
- Preparing an assessment of the contractor's overall performance before the contract is reviewed or renewed
- Communicating appropriately—internally and publicly—during the execution of the contract ∎

References and further readings

★ = Key readings.

Abt Associates on behalf of the Academy of Managed Care Pharmacy. Effect of 6 Managed Care Pharmacy Tools: A Review of the Literature. *Journal of Managed Care Pharmacy* 16(6):1–22. <http://www.amcp.org/data/jmcp/JulSuppA.pdf>

Bhushan, I., S. Keller, and B. Schwartz. 2002. *Achieving the Twin Objectives of Efficiency and Equity: Contracting Health Services in Cambodia.* ERD Policy Brief Series 6. Manila: Asian Development Bank. <http://www.adb.org/Documents/EDRC/Policy_Briefs/PB006.pdf>

Cohen, J. C. 2002. *Improving Transparency in Pharmaceutical Systems: Strengthening Critical Decision Points against Corruption.* Washington, D.C.: World Bank.

Downs, D. E., ed. 1992. *Understanding the Freight Business: A Quick Reference Manual for All Those Engaged in the Operational Aspects of Forwarding Cargo from Producer to Customer.* 4th ed. Egham, England: Micor Freight UK.

England, R. 2004. *Experience of Contracting with the Private Sector: A Selective Review.* London: DFID Health Systems Resource Centre. <http://www.nihfw.org/WBI/docs/India%20Flagship%20sessions/Contracting/Exp%20of%20contracting%20with%20pvt%20sector-DFID%20paper.pdf>

———. 2000. *Contracting and Performance Management in the Health Sector: A Guide for Low and Middle Income Countries.* London: DFID Health Systems Resource Centre. <http://www.minsa.gob.pe/ogpp/APP/doc_complementarios/Contracting%20for%20performance%20mgmnt%20in%20health%20UK%20DFID.pdf>

The Global Fund to Fight AIDS, Tuberculosis and Malaria. 2009. *Guide to the Global Fund's Policies on Procurement and Supply Management.* Geneva: The Global Fund. <http://apps.who.int/medicinedocs/en/m/abstract/Js17081e/>

IBRD (International Bank for Reconstruction and Development)/World Bank. 2011. *Guidelines: Procurement of Goods, Works, and Non-Consulting Services under IBRD Loans and IDA Credits & Grants.* Washington, D.C.: IBRD/World Bank. <http://web.worldbank.org/WBSITE/EXTERNAL/PROJECTS/PROCUREMENT/0,,contentMDK:20060840~pagePK:84269~piPK:60001558~theSitePK:84266,00.html>

International Chamber of Commerce. 2010. *Incoterms 2010: ICC Rules for the Use of Domestic and International Trade Terms.* ICC Publication No. 715. Paris: ICC Publishing S.A.

Kadaï, A., F. L. Sall, G. Andriantsara, and J. Perrot. 2006. The Benefits of Setting the Ground Rules and Regulating Contracting Practices. *Bulletin of the World Health Organization* 84(11):897–902. <http://www.who.int/bulletin/volumes/84/11/06-030056.pdf>

Lagarde, M, and N. Palmer. 2009. The Impact of Contracting Out on Health Outcomes and Use of Health Services in Low and Middle-Income Countries. *Cochrane Database System Review* 7(4):CD008133.

Liu, X., D. R. Hotchkiss, and S. Bose. 2008. The Effectiveness of Contracting-Out Primary Health Care Services in Developing Countries: A Review of the Evidence. *Health Policy and Planning* 23:1–13.

———. 2007. The Impact of Contracting-Out on Health System Performance: A Conceptual Framework. *Health Policy* 82(2):200–11.

Loevinsohn, B. 2008. *Performance-Based Contracting for Health Services in Developing Countries: A Toolkit.* Washington, D.C.: The World Bank.

Loevinsohn, B., and A. Harding. 2005. Buying Results? Contracting for Health Service Delivery in Developing Countries. *The*

ASSESSMENT GUIDE

Criteria for evaluating the success of a contract—

- What is the purpose of this contract? Are any documents attached that justify the decision to contract? Was an assessment made of in-house costs for the contracted service?
- What types of services or goods are being contracted? Are they nonclinical (storage, transport, food, linen, laundry, or catering services) or clinical (medicines, immunization patrols, anesthetic services)?
- Who prepared the terms of the contract?
- Does the contract comply with applicable legislation?
- Who signed the contract? At what level was it tendered and signed (national, provincial, district, or local)?
- How were tenderers selected? How was the contract tendered? How many bids were submitted?
- How did bids compare with pre-tender estimates? How did the lowest bid compare with the assessment of in-house costs?

- Are required performance and quality standards and indicators defined? Are they sufficiently precise?
- Are payment terms clearly defined? Are they sufficiently precise?
- Is the contractor paid on time?
- What is the length of the contract period? Is it too short, too long, or indefinite?
- Is the contractor meeting contract standards? What are the penalties for performance failure? Have they been invoked? If yes, why?
- Has this contract been renewed? If yes, by whom and why?
- Has the contract been terminated? If yes, by whom and why?
- What is the cost of the contract? Are there any budget implications? What contract terms ensure accountability for the funds paid to the provider?
- Who monitors the contract? Is the provider required to submit any reports (accounting, productivity, and so forth)? Is the monitor required to prepare reports? Could any of these reports be located?

Source: Adapted from McPake 1993.

Lancet 366:676–81. <http://www.cgdev.org/doc/ghprn/Lancet_harding.pdf>
★ McPake, B., and E. Ngalande-Bande. 1994. Contracting out Health Services in Developing Countries. *Health Policy and Planning* 9:25–30.
McPake, B. 1993. *Contracting Out in Zimbabwe: A Case Study of a Contract between the Wankie Colliery Hospital and the Ministry of Health.* London: Health Policy Unit, London School of Hygiene and Tropical Medicine.
★ Mills, A. 1998. To Contract or Not to Contract? Issues for Low and Middle Income Countries. *Health Policy and Planning* 13(1):32–40. <http://heapol.oxfordjournals.org/cgi/reprint/13/1/32>
Perrot, J. 2006. Different Approaches to Contracting in Health Systems. *Bulletin of the World Health Organization* 84 (11): 859–866. <http://www.who.int/bulletin/volumes/84/11/06-034314.pdf>
Preker, A. S., and J. C. Langenbruner, eds. 2004. *Spending Wisely: Buying Health Services for the Poor.* Washington, D.C.: World Bank.
Schwartz, J. B., and I. Bhushan. 2004. Improving Immunization Equity through a Public-Private Partnership in Cambodia. *Bulletin of the World Health Organization* 82(9):661–7.

Siddiqi, S., T. I. Masud, and B. Sabri. 2006. Contracting but not without Caution: Experience with Outsourcing of Health Services in Countries of the Eastern Mediterranean Region. *Bulletin of the World Health Organization* 84(11):867–75.
Westring, G. 1985. *International Procurement: A Training Manual.* Geneva: International Trade Centre.
WHO (World Health Organization). 1999. *Operational Principles for Good Pharmaceutical Procurement.* WHO/EDM/PAR/99.5. Geneva: WHO. <http://whqlibdoc.who.int/hq/1999/WHO_EDM_PAR_99.5.pdf>
WHO/WPRO (World Health Organization/Regional Office for the Western Pacific). 2002. *Practical Guidelines on Pharmaceutical Procurement for Countries with Small Procurement Agencies.* Manila: WHO/WPRO.
★ World Bank. 2008. *Standard Bidding Documents for Procurement of Health Sector Goods.* Washington, D.C.: World Bank. <http://go.worldbank.org/R557PHPNU0>

Annex 39-1   Sample conditions of bid document from Papua New Guinea

---

1   INTERPRETATION

1.1   Definitions

In these Conditions of Bid, unless a contrary intention appears:

"Acceptable [Country] Bank" means any of [Country] bank, which the Purchaser, at the request of the Bidder, has, prior to the Closing Date, advised the Bidder in writing is acceptable to the Purchaser.

"Acceptance Date" means approximately three weeks after the Closing Date or such earlier date not prior to the Closing Date as the Purchaser may in its sole discretion determine.

"Accounts" means profit and loss accounts and balance sheets together with statements, reports and notes, including a director's report or an auditor's report, attached to or intended to be read with any of those profit and loss accounts or balance sheets.

"Anticipated Delivery Dates" means the dates completed by the Bidder for each of the shipments specified in the Form of Bid.

"Currency nominated" means the lawful currency of [the Country].

"Bid" means the offer to sell made by each Bidder in accordance with the provisions of these Bidding Documents.

"Bid Bond" means a banker's undertaking or bank guarantee which is:

a. issued in favor of the Purchaser by an Acceptable [Country] Bank;

b. for an amount denominated in [country currency] equal to 2.5 percent of the Bid Price;

c. not expressed to expire on a date earlier than 55 days after the Closing Date; and

d. in the form of the Bid Bond Proforma or in such other form as the Bidder has submitted to the Purchaser and the Purchaser has approved before the Bidder has submitted the completed Bid Documents to the Purchaser.

"Bid Bond Proforma" means the document contained in relevant schedule.

"Bidder" means the company submitting the bid as noted in the Form of Bid.

"Bidding Documents" means all of the documents of which these Conditions forms part inclusive of the Invitation to Bid at the commencement of these documents, these Conditions and all Schedules.

"Bid Documents" means the Form of Bid as completed by a Bidder, together with all attachments as required by the terms of the Form of Bid, including the Bid Bond and the Bid Price Schedule.

"Bid Price" means the amount tendered a Bidder as per the bid terms specified (i.e., FOB, CIF, etc.)

"Bid Price Schedule" means the document contained in Schedule 2 in which the Bidder has completed in respect of each Pharmaceutical, with details of the country of origin and the Delivery Price.

"Box" means a container containing multiple Packages, which must comply with the Box Specification.

"Box Specification" means a Box that complies with the following:

a. the Box must

i. be of appropriate strength and porosity and packed in such a way as to protect the Pharmaceuticals that a Box contains from damage or deterioration from rough handling in transit to or storage in the Warehouse (where humidity may be between 75 percent and 100 percent and temperatures may be between 25°C and 35°C), and distribution from the Warehouse by sea, air, or land to remote destinations within the country of purchase;

ii. have sides of at least 275 gsm and top/bottom of at least 150 gsm (or as appropriate and to be completed by the buyer);

iii. be of a thickness of at least 7 mm (or as appropriate and to be completed by the buyer).

b. each Box is sealed in such a way that any tampering with the Box prior to it being opened will be easily detectable;

c. each Box must not exceed 25 kg in weight (or as appropriate and to be completed by the buyer);

d. each Box is clearly labeled or marked in a prominent place:

i. with the words "Department of Health of [Country]";

ii. with the earliest expiry date of any Pharmaceutical that the Box contains.

"Business Day" means any day that is not a Saturday, Sunday, public or bank holiday in the [country of purchase].

"Closing Date" means (buyer to indicate date).

"Competent Authority" of a country means the national authority as identified in the formal letter of acceptance in which that country informs WHO of its intention to participate in the Scheme.

"Conditions" or "Conditions of Bid" means the terms and conditions on which the Invitation to Bid is made comprising these conditions and all of the Schedules.

"Contract Date" means the date of the Notification of Acceptance.

"Contract Price" means the Bid Price set out in the Form of Bid submitted by the successful Bidder to whom the Purchaser gives Notification of Acceptance.

"Delivery Price" means in respect of each Pharmaceutical the amount completed in (relevant column) in the Bid Price Schedule by the Bidder as being the total price required by the Bidder to be paid by the Purchaser for the supply and delivery of the particular Pharmaceutical to the Warehouse.

"Dispensing Unit" means the smallest package or container in which a Pharmaceutical will be supplied by a Bidder (for example, this might consist of a bottle, a plastic container, a grouping of tablets or capsules in a press-out card, a bag, or some other distinct container).

"Form of Bid" means the document set out in appropriate schedule.

"Invitation to Bid" means the page that is headed "Invitation to Bid" located at the commencement of the Bidding Documents.

"Item" means an item of particulars in the Appendix to the Form of Bid.

"Notification of Acceptance" means notice of acceptance of the Bid substantially completed by the Purchaser in accordance with the relevant clause of the Conditions.

"Package" means any parceling together of Dispensing Units of a particular Pharmaceutical.

"Packaging" means the material in which Pharmaceuticals are packed for delivery to the Warehouse, including any material that protects against rough handling, humidity or temperature, the Packages or the Boxes (other than the actual Pharmaceuticals they contain), any tape or other substance used to seal the Boxes, and any other fastenings used to secure each Box.

"Performance Bond" means a banker's undertaking or bank guarantee that is:

a. issued in favor of the Purchaser by an Acceptable [Country] Bank;

b. for an amount denominated in (currency specified) equal to 10 percent of the Contract Price;

c. not expressed to expire on a date earlier than 33 weeks (or as specified) after the Contract Date; and

d. in the form of the Performance Bond Proforma or in such other form as the Purchaser may in its sole discretion approve.

"Performance Bond Proforma" means the document contained in the Bid Document.

"Pharmaceutical" means any one of the items described in the relevant column in the Bid Price Schedule.

"Product Certificate" means in respect of a Pharmaceutical the "Certificate of a Pharmaceutical Product," conforming to the format required by WHO, that is validated and issued for that Pharmaceutical by the Competent Authority of the country in which the Pharmaceutical is manufactured.

"Product Information" means in respect of a Pharmaceutical the product information submitted to a Competent Authority in support of an application for a Product Certificate and that normally consists of information for health professionals and the public (patient information leaflets) as approved in the exporting country and, when available, a data sheet or summary of product characteristics approved by the Competent Authority.

"Product License" means in respect of a Pharmaceutical an official document issued by a competent drug regulatory authority of a country for the marketing or free distribution of that Pharmaceutical and that contains the following:

a. the name of the product (i.e., pharmaceutical);

b. the pharmaceutical dosage form;

c. the quantitative formula (including excipients) per unit dose (using international non-proprietary names where they exist);

d. the shelf life;

e. storage conditions;

f. packaging characteristics;

g. all information approved for health professionals and the public (except promotional information);

h. the sales category;

i. the name and address of the license holder; and

j. the period of validity of the license.

"Purchaser" (indicate purchasing agency).

"Representative" of a person means an officer, employee, contractor, or agent of that person.

"Scheme" means the WHO Certification Scheme on the Quality of Pharmaceutical Products moving in International Commerce as recommended initially at the Twenty-Second World Health Assembly, in resolution WHA 22.56.

"Statement of Licensing Status" means in respect of a Pharmaceutical a statement in the format recommended by WHO issued by the Competent Authority of the country from which the Pharmaceutical is exported that the Pharmaceutical is licensed for use in the exporting country, which statement must include (where issued) the number and the date of issue of the Product License of the Pharmaceutical.

"Supply Contract" means the contract format contained in bid document.

"Warehouse" means the warehouse located at (indicate location).

"WHO" means the World Health Organization.

Annex 39-2   Sample pharmaceutical supply contract

Period of contract. One year.

Trade terms. Prices are CIF or CPT "Warehouse Port, Seatown" unless otherwise specified; however, the invitation to tender requires that cost, insurance, and freight charges be listed separately, along with the total CIF price. The contractor is the sole source of supply for the duration of the contract.

Purchase order. This is issued if there is an uncommitted balance in the country's pharmaceutical account.

Assignment. The contractor shall not bargain, sell, sublet, or dispose of the contract without previous consent of the buyer.

Prices. The contract price is the maximum price of the item packaged and delivered for the duration of this contract and payable in U.S. dollars.

Payment. Payment will be made by irrevocable confirmed letter of credit payable after forty-two days. All shipments will be inspected by an international inspection agency, and letter of credit is payable subject to submission of a clean report of findings.

Quality. All the products on this contract must: (1) meet the requirement of manufacturing legislation in the country of origin and be approved for use in that country; (2) be of USP or BP standard; (3) contain a lot or batch number and expiry date on the label of every dispensing unit; (4) be certified in accordance with the WHO Certification Scheme for Pharmaceuticals Moving in International Commerce (WHO Resolution 28.65B). This certificate should be issued by the health authorities of the country of original manufacture. Certificates of analysis shall be provided within one month of request for microbiological and pharmacological tests. Tests for each batch actually shipped should be sent as well and should reach this office before final arrival of the goods. Samples must be submitted in the case of a new supplier or new tendered item, product with changed presentation or formulation, or upon request by the buyer.

Labeling. Labels should be in English. All internal and external containers should be labeled with the INN for the active ingredient and should contain at least the following additional information: quantity of active ingredient, dosage form, number of units per pack, batch number, date of manufacture, expiry date, pharmacopoeial standard, instructions for storage, name and address of manufacturer, directions for use.

Specifications. Supplies should conform to the specifications indicated in the tender document. No alterations, unless confirmed in writing, are acceptable.

Cold storage. Items requiring cool storage and transport (for example, vaccines) should be shipped by air with proper insulating packing, ensuring product remains below 8°C for at least forty-eight hours. A written pre-advice with exact shipment details should be sent at least five days before the actual arrival of the consignment.

Performance bond. The successful tenderer may be called upon, within one week after acceptance of the tender, to deposit with the buyer an amount equal to 2.5 percent of the total value of the contract. This amount will be forfeited if the contract is not completed within the time limit and to the satisfaction of this office.

Default. Should the supplier fail to—
- deliver the supplies by the specified date or to the specified port; or
- replace, within one month, any rejected supplies; or
- comply with each and every other condition of this contract;

the government may do any or all of the following—
- after notice to the supplier, nullify this contract without compensation and obtain needed supplies from other suitable sources;
- recover from the supplier any losses sustained by this office resulting from supplier's failures;
- delist the supplier from the "preferred list of suppliers."

Delivery. Shipment shall be made as specified in the invitation to tender, unless an alternative delivery date has been agreed upon in writing. For each consignment the supplier shall send a shipment advice, clearly indicating date of shipment, name of the vessel, and estimated time of arrival in "Port Seatown." No purchase order shall be completed by more than two (2) partial shipments. Payments for goods requested shall be made when total order is received in the purchasing country.

Indemnity. The supplier shall indemnify this government against all claims and shall bear the costs of defending such claims that are related to patent rights, trademarks, designs, and royalties.

Packaging. Supplies must be packed in immediate and external export containers, suitable to withstand rough handling in transit and storage under tropical conditions where humidity may be between 75 and 100 percent and temperatures between 25 and 30°C. On arrival at their ultimate destination, supplies should be free from damage. Containers should be sealed in a manner that makes tampering with the pack during transit easily detectable. The supplier shall be liable for all losses, damage, or expense due to insufficient or unsuitable packing. A clear packing list should be sent for all consignments, showing the individual content and including expiry dates of each carton.

Expiry date. Unless otherwise specified, all items should have at least two years and/or 75 percent of their shelf life remaining from the date supplies are received by this office. Expiry dates should be clearly stated on all internal and external containers.

Unique identifiers. All immediate and external containers should bear the words Ministry of Health together with the WHO logo. Application for exemption from this requirement should be made at the time offers are submitted.

Import documents. The supplier is responsible for providing this office with all documents necessary for taking possession of supplies and clearing them. The supplier shall be held responsible for any expenses or losses incurred by incorrect, incomplete, or late provision of documents.

CHAPTER 40

Analyzing and controlling pharmaceutical expenditures

SUMMARY

This chapter focuses on identifying and controlling excess costs in the selection, procurement, distribution, and use of medicines. Several analytical tools are presented that help managers quantify costs and identify areas where costs can be reduced; the information provided is also essential in designing and monitoring interventions to control costs.

Total cost analysis compiles information on variable costs associated with purchasing and inventory management to help managers consider options for change in terms of their impact on total costs. It is a key tool for pharmaceutical system assessments. The other analytical tools discussed in this chapter may be used as part of a total cost analysis, or they may be used individually for special purposes.

The VEN system categorizes pharmaceuticals by their relative public health value. It is useful in setting purchasing priorities, determining safety stock levels and pharmaceutical sales prices, and directing staff activities. The categories in the original system are vital (V), essential (E), and nonessential (N) (sometimes called VED—vital, essential, and desirable). Some health systems find a two-category system more useful than the three-tiered VEN; for example, the categories might be V and N, differentiating between those medicines that must always be in stock and other medicines.

ABC analysis examines the annual consumption of medicines and expenditures for procurement by dividing the medicines consumed into three categories. Class A includes 10 to 20 percent of items, which account for 75 to 80 percent of expenditures. Class B items represent 10 to 20 percent of items and 15 to 20 percent of expenditures. Class C items are 60 to 80 percent of items but only about 5 to 10 percent of expenditures. ABC analysis can be used to—

- Measure the degree to which actual consumption reflects public health needs and morbidity
- Reduce inventory levels and costs by arranging for more frequent purchase or delivery of smaller quantities of class A items
- Seek major cost reductions by finding lower prices on class A items, where savings will be more noticeable
- Assign import and inventory control staff to ensure that large orders of class A items are handled expeditiously

Therapeutic category analysis considers the use and financial impact of various therapeutic categories of medicines and then compares cost and therapeutic benefit to select the most cost-effective medicines in each major therapeutic category. This analysis can be done to select medicines for a formulary or procurement list.

Price comparison analysis compares pharmaceutical prices paid by different supply systems as one measure of procurement efficiency. The analysis can also compare supply system acquisition and selling prices with local private-sector prices to gauge the cost-effectiveness of in-house pharmaceutical services and to assess price elasticity for cost recovery.

Lead-time analysis is a systematic approach to tracking procurement lead times, determining the points at which lead time can be reduced, and adjusting safety stock appropriately. Payment time should also be analyzed (when delayed payment to suppliers is feasible).

Expiry-date analysis examines levels of stock on hand and their expiry dates and compares this information with average rates of consumption to assess the likelihood of wastage (and to develop appropriate countermeasures).

Hidden-cost analysis examines supplier performance to identify any hidden costs incurred because of problems such as late deliveries and short shipments. Hidden costs may make one supplier considerably more expensive than a competitor that offers a higher unit price but better performance.

40.1 Tools for analyzing costs

The two largest centers of recurrent costs in most public pharmaceutical systems are personnel expenses and pharmaceutical purchases. Controlling personnel costs usually means reducing staff, which may be politically difficult. However, policies may be reformed so that the pharmaceutical supply system does not employ extra staff members who contribute to lowered productivity and increased losses from wastage and theft.

This chapter concentrates on techniques for analyzing costs in the pharmaceutical supply system so that managers can identify major costs, losses, and opportunities for savings. All these techniques have been cited in earlier chapters. Here, the focus is on how to perform each analysis and how to use the results. The techniques considered are—

- Total cost analysis
- VEN system
- ABC analysis
- Therapeutic category analysis
- Price comparison analysis
- Lead-time and payment-time analysis
- Expiry-date analysis
- Hidden-cost analysis

Although these analyses can be carried out manually, the process is very time consuming, except in small supply systems that use relatively few pharmaceutical products. Using a computer to perform these analyses is much easier. Expensive computers and customized software are not required—all the analyses in this chapter can be done with commercial spreadsheet software.

40.2 Total cost analysis

In pharmaceutical supply systems, the total cost of operating the supply system is the sum of pharmaceutical purchase cost, inventory-holding cost, ordering cost, and shortage cost. Total cost analysis compiles the values of these various costs on one data sheet. The manager's objective is to identify strategies that will minimize the total cost. If an intervention will reduce ordering costs but drive up inventory-holding costs by an amount that produces a net increase in the total cost, it is not worthwhile. Alternatively, a strategy to increase ordering frequency might drive up the costs associated with purchasing, but the net savings in inventory-holding costs might be far greater than the incremental purchasing cost.

Analyzing and controlling costs

Total cost analysis has two basic applications: (1) analyzing current costs to find opportunities for cost reduction and (2) modeling the cost impact of potential changes in the supply system.

Table 40-1 shows a summary sheet for a total cost analysis. In the table, costs and inventory are shown for an illustrative warehouse and purchasing office in a Latin American country. Inventory and costs are found at all levels of the system; in a supply system with several regional warehouses, the inventory (and associated costs) may be considerably higher in the aggregate at the regional level than at the central warehouse. This result is also true for supply systems in which health facilities hold significant quantities of stock. For the most complete picture, total costs should be calculated for each significant level of the supply system; however, for simplicity's sake, this example focuses on one central warehouse.

The manager's objective is to identify apparently excessive costs in one or more cost categories and then to devise strat-egies to minimize the total cost. A review of the compiled data in Table 40-1 might yield several ideas for reducing costs—

- Reduce the average inventory from the current five months of stock (which would reduce holding costs) by more frequent ordering.
- Reduce the cost of pharmaceutical purchases through more efficient tendering, potentially adding therapeutic subcategory tendering.
- Cut down on losses.
- Consider whether the number of employees (and salary costs) can be reduced without harming efficiency.
- Cut down on emergency purchases through better stock management.

Meeting any of these objectives would require trade-offs—when one cost component is reduced, another is likely to increase. For example, suppose that a country has the total cost profile in Table 40-1 and uses annual purchasing almost exclusively. Changing the purchasing system from an annual system to a combination of annual and biannual tenders (see Figure 23-4, in Chapter 23) might possibly reduce the average inventory value by half, but result in two annual tenders, thereby increasing the costs related to purchasing.

Holding costs and purchasing costs basically oppose each other. Frequent ordering in small quantities drives up the average cost of placing an order (or managing a tender), because the procurement and accounting offices must go through all the steps on multiple occasions. However, more frequent orders should reduce average stock levels and thus reduce holding costs. Annual ordering in large quantities tends to increase the average inventory level and holding costs but decreases the average annual ordering costs.

Usually an inverse relationship exists between shortage costs and holding costs. The shortage costs in a supply system are likely to be low when stock levels (and holding costs) are high, and vice versa.

Using the data from Table 40-1, one can model the effects of switching from an annual to a biannual tender. For example, pharmaceutical acquisition costs are projected to be the same as they were in Table 40-1. Average inventory value decreases by half to 2.9 million U.S. dollars (USD), with an associated decrease in some incremental holding costs: opportunity cost down to USD 290,000; losses down to USD 370,000. This decrease suggests a net savings of USD 660,000 in holding costs, but what are the likely increased costs? Assuming that the additional tender can be managed by existing staff, the additional purchasing costs should be limited to increases in supplies, communications, and other tendering costs. Assuming that these costs double (in the worst case), the extra incremental purchasing costs would be USD 117,000, resulting in a net savings of USD 443,000.

Table 40-1   Total cost analysis summary

Cost category	Total (USD)	Incremental (USD)	Predictable (USD)
Pharmaceutical acquisition costs			
(Includes supplier shipping charges and duty)	14,000,000	14,000,000	
Inventory-holding costs			
Average inventory, central warehouse			
(beginning value plus year-end value, divided by two)	5,800,000	5,800,000	
Financial opportunity cost			
(10% average interest rate)	580,000	580,000	
Losses from inventory			
Expiry	69,000	69,000	
Spoilage/wastage	18,000	18,000	
Loss during repacking	200	200	
Short shipments from suppliers	500	500	
Obsolete medicines—no longer used	12,000	12,000	
Unexplained losses	640,000	640,000	
Subtotal	739,700	739,700	
Operating costs—storage and stock management			
Salaries	665,000		665,000
Space and utilities	117,000		117,000
Communications	4,000		4,000
Supplies	650,000	650,000	
Other direct costs	3,700		3,700
Depreciation	46,900		46,900
Administrative overhead	NA	NA	NA
Subtotal	1,486,600	650,000	836,600
Transport costs—to operating units			
Salaries	115,000		115,000
Supplies (gas, etc.)	112,000	112,000	
Other direct costs	700	700	
Depreciation	8,100		8,100
Administrative overhead	NA	NA	NA
Subtotal	235,800	112,700	123,100
Total holding cost	3,042,100	2,082,400	959,700
Holding cost as percentage of average inventory	52%		
Percentage incremental and predictable		68%	32%
Purchasing costs			
Salaries	72,000		72,000
Space and utilities	11,000		11,000
Communications	2,000		2,000
Supplies	70,000		70,000
Other direct costs	400		400
Depreciation	5,000		5,000
Administrative overhead	NA	NA	NA
Subtotal	160,400		160,400
Total additional costs of annual tender	45,000		45,000
Total purchasing cost	205,400		205,400
Shortage costs			
(Estimate 20% emergency purchases at 20% premium)	560,000	560,000	
Total cost	17,807,500	16,642,400	1,165,100
Percentage incremental and predictable		93%	7%

Note: Data are based on a composite from Latin America and do not represent any specific country. NA = not applicable; USD = U.S. dollars.

Of course, the increases would largely be in visible expenditures, and the decreases would be in hidden costs, but a real net savings to the system would occur.

Modeling the effect of alternatives for changing the supply system

Suppose that the supply system is considering three options for warehousing and distribution in the future: (1) keeping all services in-house (the current system); (2) keeping warehousing in-house but contracting out transport; and (3) contracting out both warehousing and distribution. Each of the possible new models implies significant changes in personnel needs and operating costs at the various levels of the supply system. Total cost analysis provides a convenient format to project how the supply system's operating costs would change with each option.

The basic steps in total cost modeling are the same, whatever the options being considered. The total cost is compiled for the most recent year for which data are available (as illustrated in Table 40-1), for one or several levels of the supply system, and adjusted for inflation and expected changes in use, to estimate the total cost with the current system in the year or years in which change would be implemented. Then, for each of the alternate supply system models, the percentage increase or decrease for each major total cost component is estimated and applied to the baseline cost, again adjusting for inflation and changes in use in subsequent years.

The resulting models are not exact but do predict the relative cost effect of the alternatives being considered. Sometimes the exercise identifies viable interventions that had not been previously considered. For example, in one Latin American country a total cost–modeling exercise showed that total costs could be reduced by consolidating storage at the regional level and privatizing transport and that still greater savings could be gained by contracting out for all warehousing and transport (assuming that the system could be managed). However, the models also showed that a far greater savings in total cost could result from improved medicine selection—if it produced only a 10 percent reduction in pharmaceutical acquisition costs—than could be achieved even by closing all warehouses and contracting out all storage and distribution functions.

The typical annual inventory-holding cost for a commercial firm is no more than 25 to 35 percent of the average inventory value, but the percentage could be much higher for a public pharmaceutical supply program. For example, during a multicountry assessment of inventory management practices in the Caribbean region, one country was found to have an *average* inventory of twelve months' consumption. The manager of this supply system was very proud of his stock levels, saying that he had no problem with stockouts. Of course, he had not given adequate consideration to the costs of holding inventory, which in this

case equaled half the entire annual pharmaceutical purchasing budget.

Costs may be either predictable or incremental. If the cost remains the same no matter how many transactions or how much inventory is involved, it is a predictable cost (sometimes called a fixed cost—see Chapter 41). If the cost increases directly with the number of purchases or volume of inventory, it is an incremental cost. In most accounting systems, incremental costs are termed variable costs, but for this analysis, all the costs are variable. By their nature, pharmaceutical acquisition costs, many inventory-holding costs, and shortage costs are incremental; most purchasing costs tend to be predictable, but they are likely to have incremental components. Although the difference between predictable and incremental costs can be important, most data from developing countries are insufficient to differentiate between the two. In these cases, the focus should be on identifying and addressing the major overall contributors to excessive costs, whether they are predictable or incremental.

Compiling the total cost

Many of the costs discussed in this section are visible, in that they are actual budget expenditures; others are hidden, in that the costs are not expenditures but represent reductions in available resources. Managers should understand that both visible and hidden costs are real.

In most supply systems, data gaps make assembling all this information difficult, but the effort should yield a real understanding of where expenses are concentrated and what sorts of interventions may yield substantial cost savings.

The total cost is made up of four components, which are compiled in one table—

- Pharmaceutical acquisition costs (totally incremental)
- Inventory-holding costs (predictable and incremental)
- Purchasing costs (predictable and incremental)
- Shortage costs (primarily incremental)

Pharmaceutical acquisition costs. These costs are the net cost of all pharmaceutical purchases, including shipping and insurance charges from the manufacturer and any duty or customs fees. They are an incremental cost. Data can be obtained from purchasing records, stock records, or supplier invoices.

Inventory-holding costs. The inventory-holding cost has several subcomponents, some of which are incremental and some of which are predictable.

The first entry under "inventory-holding costs" in Table 40-1 is the average inventory value (which is used to calculate the percentage of holding costs). The standard basis for valuing inventory is the original net purchase cost rather than the selling price. Four standard methods can be used for determining the original purchase cost for all items in inventory: actual value, first-in/first-out (FIFO), last-in/ first-out (LIFO), and average value. As discussed in Chapter 41, most pharmaceutical supply systems are unable to accurately track actual value and should use either the average value or the FIFO method.

The key is that the method, once chosen, needs to be applied consistently from one financial year to the next; otherwise, year-to-year comparisons of holding costs and financial performance may be invalid.

The standard components of the inventory-holding cost are the following—

Financial opportunity cost is incremental and varies with the average inventory value; it is obtained by multiplying the average inventory value by the average interest rate paid on money-market accounts in local banks (or sometimes by the average interest rate charged for short-term loans).

Loss from inventory is often an incremental cost, in that losses rise as inventory values increase. The amounts may be broken down as shown in Table 40-1, to the extent that data are available from inventory records. If data are not available, estimate losses as a percentage of the average inventory value, based on local expert opinion.

Deterioration and spoilage costs for medicines are more likely to occur with poor storekeeping practices, but some risk exists in all warehouses. In general, these costs are incremental—the higher the stock levels, the higher the costs of spoilage.

Expiry costs are often 3 to 5 percent of pharmaceutical inventory each year. If this ratio holds, the costs are incremental as inventory value increases. High expiry costs are a reflection of poor inventory control and storekeeping.

Obsolescence costs apply principally to equipment and spare parts, but changes in formulary lists and prescribing practices may make certain medicines obsolete. These may be viewed as predictable costs; they do not necessarily vary with the inventory size or value.

Wastage costs caused by theft, pilferage, and other unexplained losses add considerably to the cost of carrying inventories. As noted in Chapter 23, losses of 10 percent are not unusual in public pharmaceutical supply systems. These are likely to be incremental costs—the total loss increases as the average inventory rises.

Operating costs for storage and stock management are a mixture of predictable and incremental costs. Salaries (which should include benefits), space costs (rent or building depreciation), utilities, communications, other direct costs, and depreciation of equipment are predictable costs unless additional staff, space, or equipment is added to manage a growing inventory. In such a situation, the added costs are incremental. Supplies are primarily incremental, in that more supplies are used as more stock is stored and distributed. In some settings, a predictable component of the supplies cost may possibly be determined. Data should be obtained from financial records or budget books or (if necessary) by estimates from local experts. If administrative overhead is charged as a cost by the supply system, it should be added in the appropriate percentage to operating costs here.

Transport costs to operating units include predictable costs (salaries and benefits for transport personnel, depreciation of vehicles) and incremental costs (gasoline, repairs, and travel expenses for transport personnel). Again, if more drivers or vehicles were added to cope with an increased workload, these costs would be incremental.

The total of all these costs is the total inventory-holding cost, showing predictable and incremental components.

Purchasing costs. Purchasing costs (sometimes called reordering costs) are the costs associated with managing tenders, placing purchase orders, and receiving goods. Like inventory-holding costs, purchasing costs have several components. Salaries (including benefits) should include wages for all staff who are involved in managing tenders, ordering medicines, and receiving them. Note that some staff may be attached to the warehouse rather than the purchasing office, but for this purpose, their costs should be attributed to purchasing. If warehouse staff members have multiple responsibilities, including some that are related to purchasing, attribute a portion of their cost to inventory-holding and a portion to purchasing. Utilities and space costs include rent, basic communications, and all utilities for the purchasing office. Supplies include all forms used in tenders and purchase orders (this might be broken down into predictable and incremental components in a perpetual or scheduled purchasing system). Other direct costs include travel costs and maintenance of building and equipment. Depreciation may be calculated on all valuable equipment and on the building if it is owned by the system. Again, if administrative overhead is charged, it should be added using the current percentage. Additional tender costs include costs that are not included in standard purchasing costs but that are associated with the quantification, tendering, and adjudication processes, including travel, per diem, and other costs associated with committee meetings.

In a public pharmaceutical supply system that uses annual or biannual purchasing, most of these purchasing costs can be considered predictable, assuming the existence of a procurement office with permanent staff and office space. In a perpetual system, or a scheduled system with periodic orders, the costs of communications and supplies such as forms are incremental with each order placed.

Data on the individual component costs may be available from financial records or budget books; once the individual component costs (actual or estimated) are obtained and

Box 40-1
Calculations to fill the pharmaceutical inventory pipeline

The length of the pharmaceutical inventory pipeline is measured in numbers of months. It is determined by the number of levels in the distribution system, the safety stock at each level, and the average working stock (which depends on the delivery interval—see Chapter 23). The diameter of the pipeline is determined by the final outflow—the total value of medicines dispensed per month.

The following example illustrates a pipeline calculation to serve a network of 210 community pharmacies. It includes a central supply agency, district stores, and the community pharmacies.

The pipeline for the proposed pharmaceutical sales program begins with the disbursement of funds for procurement and ends at the point where funds are collected and made available for purchasing replenishment supplies. The pipeline can be broken down into a number of segments, described below and illustrated in the accompanying diagram—

Average monthly sales. The number of low-, medium-, and high-volume community pharmacies and the average monthly sale per pharmacy are estimated in the second table.

Funding requirements. With an average pipeline length of sixteen months and an average consumption for all 210 pharmacies of USD 65,000 per month, total funding requirements would be—

$$16 \times \text{USD } 65,000 = \text{USD } 1,040,000$$

Sources of funding and possible cost savings. Funding can be supplied from various sources: donations could finance the purchase pipeline and safety stock, government allocations could finance the working stock for central and district levels, and community fund-raising efforts could finance the community pharmacy funds. Improved procurement payment terms, more rapid flow of pharmaceuticals through the system (faster turnover), and more efficient bank transfers could shorten the pipeline and reduce funding costs.

Cash and medicines in the pipeline	Months
Purchase pipeline. In this example, about 50 percent of medicines are assumed to be purchased from international sources and 50 percent from local sources. For international purchases, an average of six months will elapse between the provision of a letter of credit and the receipt of the pharmaceuticals at the central supply agency. For domestic purchases, payment will be made upon receipt. Therefore, the average purchase pipeline will be three months.	3
Central supply agency safety stock. A three-month safety stock will be maintained at the central supply agency.	3
Central supply agency working stock. The supply agency will tender once a year but will receive deliveries every four months. This strategy implies a maximum working stock of four months and an average working stock of two months.	2
District safety stock. The district medical stores of the supply agency will maintain a two-month safety stock.	2
District working stock. The district medical stores will receive shipments from the central supply agency every two months, implying a maximum working stock of two months and an average working stock of one month.	1
Community pharmacy safety stock. The community pharmacies will maintain a one-month safety stock.	1
Community pharmacy working stock. The community pharmacies will be resupplied once a month, implying a maximum working stock of one month and an average working stock of half a month.	0.5
Community pharmacy cash on hand. The community pharmacies will use their revenues once a month when they purchase their resupplies from the district medical stores. On average, these funds will have been held half a month by the community pharmacies.	0.5
District to center cash transfer. Money received by the district medical stores will be deposited within the week at the local branch of the national bank. On average, this money will take one month to be credited to the account of the supply agency.	1
Cash on hand. In general, purchases made by the supply agency will represent one-third of its annual turnover. As a result, money will sit in the agency's central account up to four months, or an average of two months, before being used to effect a purchase.	2
Total pipeline	**16**

	Low volume	Medium volume	High volume	Total
Number of community pharmacies	150	50	10	210
Average number of patients per month per pharmacy	500	1,250	2,500	NA
Average cost per pharmaceutical item (USD)	0.20	0.20	0.20	NA
Average items per patient	2	2	2	NA
Average monthly sales per pharmacy (USD)	200	500	1,000	NA
Total monthly sales (pharmaceutical cost; USD)	30,000	25,000	10,000	65,000

Note: NA = not applicable.

recorded, they are summed to produce the total purchasing cost.

Shortage costs. Four potential kinds of shortage or stock-out costs exist: excess cost of emergency purchases, loss of revenue when clients purchase outside the system, increased morbidity and mortality caused by stockouts, and loss of goodwill caused by erosion of confidence in the system. Only the first two can be realistically quantified for a public pharmaceutical supply system.

If good procurement records for both regular and emergency purchases are available, the actual cost of emergency purchases can be calculated by recording the difference between the emergency cost and the regular cost per unit or package and multiplying by the quantity purchased for each emergency purchase. If data are not available for all emergency purchases, a sample may be used to estimate the average percentage price difference and the percentage of purchases attributable to emergency purchases (as was done in Table 40-1).

If the supply system sells medicines from one level to another, itemized data on actual purchases outside the system may be obtained for items that would normally be purchased inside. An estimate can be made for the value of such purchases based on the breakdown between purchases inside and outside the supply system.

Calculating the total cost. The total cost is calculated as the sum of the subtotals for each component. In Table 40-1, the costs total USD 17.8 million. The major component is pharmaceutical acquisition, but holding costs and shortage costs are significant factors; purchasing costs are the lowest component. As discussed earlier, the inventory-holding costs are mostly incremental, and the purchasing costs are mostly predictable.

Structure of the inventory pipeline. To compile a total cost analysis, one must consider the structure of the supply system to determine where costs are incurred. As discussed in Chapter 22, the inventory management system is similar to a pipeline, with warehouses and health facilities that function as reservoirs where stock is held. To ensure a continuous supply of medicines to patients, the pipeline must be filled; once filled, consumption must be matched by purchases. Box 40-1 illustrates the calculations used to determine pipeline funding and expenditures.

One of the single-most important decisions in terms of cost and efficiency of the distribution system is the number of storage levels in the system. Chapter 22 discusses options for selecting the best structure and considering setup, operating, and inventory-holding costs.

Generally, more levels in the supply system create higher inventory levels and inventory costs, but the increase is not

---

Country Study 40-1
Analyzing pharmaceutical supply system total costs and options in Costa Rica

In Costa Rica, the health care services of almost 90 percent of the population are covered under the government's social insurance scheme, the Costa Rica Social Security Fund (CCSS). As part of a health-sector reform project, the CCSS board of directors expressed an interest in addressing issues related to medicine stockouts and a large increase in warehouse costs. Management Sciences for Health (MSH) conducted an assessment of the CCSS distribution system to analyze pharmaceutical supply system costs and identify intervention options to reduce costs through improved efficiency.

The analysis showed the following annual costs in the CCSS system—

- Warehouse operations (USD 2.1 million)
- Lease for one regional warehouse (USD 3.6 million)
- Inventory losses (USD 779,000)
- Financial opportunity cost (USD 7.3 million)

By sector within the distribution system, 58 percent of the costs were associated with the main CCSS warehouse, 41 percent of the costs with system pharmacies, and 1 percent of the costs with the regional warehouses.

MSH analyzed four options to address the issues related to warehouse and distribution costs: (1) strengthening the current system; (2) implementing a direct delivery system, where the pharmaceutical supplier would be responsible for storage and distribution; (3) implementing a primary distributor system, which would outsource supply logistics; or (4) implementing a mixed system that combines elements of basic models.

As a result of the analysis and recommendations, the government instituted—

- Renewable contracts to reduce the number of pharmaceutical tenders
- An open contract with preselected suppliers to procure emergency supplies
- Direct delivery of large-volume parenterals
- Procurement of slow-moving items (orthopedic supplies) on a consignment basis

The CCSS is also using the postal service to deliver some medicines to patients more efficiently.

always directly proportional. Ordering frequency, average supplier lead time, and policies for safety stock have a major effect on inventory levels. As shown in Figure 22-4, in Chapter 22, a supply system with three levels (regional stores, district stores, and health facilities) might have three times the inventory of a two-level system (district stores and health facilities). However, depending on the inventory management system's operating efficiency, the differences in inventory levels and costs between the two types of systems might be much lower or even greater than that shown in Figure 22-4.

Overstocking at health facilities and lower-level stores can disproportionately affect overall inventory costs. The large number of these units multiplies the impact of overstocking. When conducting an analysis of inventory costs or developing an inventory control policy, the analysis needs to consider costs at each level of the system and identify options for rationalizing order frequency and safety stock levels to achieve desired services with the lowest possible total inventory in the supply system.

Country Study 40-1 describes a total cost and options analysis in Costa Rica.

Standard performance indicators and ratios

When the total cost has been compiled, several ratios calculated from total cost components can serve as basic indicators for comparing operating efficiency among different parts of the current supply system (or with alternative models). Standard ratios include—

- Holding cost as a percentage of average inventory, calculated by dividing the total holding cost by the average inventory value and expressing the result as a percentage. In commercial firms, the inventory-holding cost is usually between 25 and 35 percent of average inventory value; in a public pharmaceutical supply system, the percentage may be considerably higher, although it need not be with good inventory management.
- Purchasing costs as a percentage of pharmaceutical acquisition costs, to compare how efficiently the purchasing function is managed.
- Average inventory turnover (the total value of medicines purchased or distributed, divided by the average inventory value), discussed in Chapter 23.
- Personnel costs, space costs, transport costs, other direct operating costs, each as a percentage of total holding costs, showing the relative proportion of total costs attributable to each category.
- Total holding cost as a percentage of the value of medicines distributed or the value of receipts, giving an indication of the cost-effectiveness of maintaining in-house services rather than contracting out some or

Figure 40-1 Efficiency indicators in the supply systems of four Latin American countries

a. Stock-turnover ratio

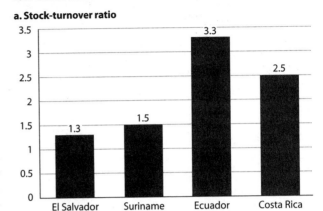

Note: The ratio represents the total value of medicines purchased or distributed, divided by the average inventory value.

b. Inventory-holding costs

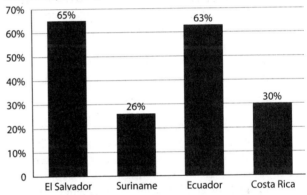

Note: The percentage represents holding cost as a percentage of average inventory, calculated by dividing the total holding cost by the average inventory value.

all aspects of storage and distribution. A variation of this ratio is total cost to value of medicines distributed or received.

Figure 40-1 illustrates two efficiency indicators in four Latin American countries.

40.3 VEN system

The VEN system sets priorities for selection, procurement, and use according to the potential health impact of individual medicines. VEN assigns each pharmaceutical product on the formulary or essential medicines list to one of the following three categories—

V: vital medicines are potentially lifesaving, have significant withdrawal side effects (making regular supply mandatory), or are crucial to providing basic health services.

Table 40-2   Sample guidelines for VEN categories

Characteristic of medicine or target condition	Vital	Essential	Nonessential
Occurrence of target condition			
Persons affected (percent of population)	Over 5	1–5	Less than 1
Persons treated (number per day at average health center)	Over 5	1–5	Less than 1
Severity of target condition			
Life-threatening	Yes	Occasionally	Rarely
Disabling	Yes	Occasionally	Rarely
Therapeutic effect of medicine			
Prevents serious disease	Yes	No	No
Cures serious disease	Yes	Yes	No
Treats minor, self-limited symptoms and conditions	No	Possibly	Yes
Has proven efficacy	Always	Usually	May or may not
Has unproven efficacy	Never	Rarely	May or may not

E: essential medicines are effective against less severe but nevertheless significant forms of illness but are not absolutely vital to providing basic health care.

N: nonessential medicines are used for minor or self-limited illnesses, are of questionable efficacy, or have a comparatively high cost for a marginal therapeutic advantage.

Assignment to the nonessential category does not mean the medicine is no longer on the system's formulary or essential medicines list; in many cases, medicines for minor illnesses are included on the essential medicines list but may be considered a lower priority for procurement than other medicines.

The classification of medicines should not be a one-time exercise. As the national formulary or essential medicines list is updated, and as public health priorities change, the VEN or VN categories should be reviewed and updated. Any new medicines added to the list should be categorized appropriately, and category assignments for older medicines should be reviewed and changed if needed.

The VEN system was developed in Sri Lanka, where it was first applied to importations by the State Pharmaceuticals Corporation. All pharmaceuticals procured by the corporation were reviewed by a clinical pharmacologist and assigned to one of the three categories. Since the first edition of this book in 1981, the VEN approach has been adapted and used in other countries around the world.

Some supply systems may find maintaining and updating the three-tiered VEN system difficult; they may find deciding how to classify certain medicines hard. An alternative is a two-tiered VN system, in which vital medicines are those that should be available at all times, and nonessential medicines, although still on the formulary, are of lower priority and should be purchased only after the need for all vital medicines is satisfied.

Either system—two or three categories—will work if the system is maintained; the main objective is an ongoing system to give priority to essential, lifesaving medicines as opposed to expensive nonessential items.

Performing VEN analysis

Because of its broad implications for procurement and use, classification of medicines into VEN or VN categories is probably best done by a designated expert committee, such as a national formulary committee. The classification should be determined primarily on the basis of the public health impact of individual medicines. Unit prices should be a secondary consideration, and popularity of medications should have minimal influence on the process. Table 40-2 provides sample guidelines for establishing VEN categories. Examples of medicines classified under this method are given in Table 40-3.

Applications of VEN analysis

The major uses of VEN analysis are assigning priorities for medicine selection, procurement, and use in a supply system; guiding inventory management activities; and determining appropriate medicine prices.

Selection: Vital and essential medicines should be given priority in selection, especially when funds are short.
Procurement: A medicine's VEN classification may affect the following—

- Order monitoring: Orders for vital and essential medicines should be monitored closely, as shortages in these items require expensive air shipment of supplies.
- Safety stock: Safety stocks should be higher for vital and essential items. Inventory savings can be realized by

Table 40-3   Examples of medicines classified by the VEN system

	Vital	Essential	Nonessential
Criteria	• Potentially lifesaving • Significant withdrawal side effects • Major public health importance	• Effective against less severe but nevertheless significant forms of illness	• Used for minor or self-limited illnesses • Questionable efficacy • High cost for marginal therapeutic advantage
Health center	• Phenobarbitone sodium tablet, 30 g • Phenoxymethylpenicillin tablet, 250 mg • Co-trimoxazole tablet, 480 mg • Nystatin pessaries, 100,000 units • Artemether-lumefantrine tablet, 20 mg + 120 mg • Ferrous sulfate/folic acid tablet, 200 mg/0.5 mg • Adrenaline injectable, 1/1,000, 1 mL ampoule • Oral rehydration salts (ORS) powder, 1 liter (WHO) • Gentamicin injectable, 40 mg/mL, 2 mL vial • Condoms with spermicide • Measles vaccine, live injectable, 10-dose (5 mL) vial • Ergometrine maleate injectable, 500 mcg/mL, 1 mL ampoule • Salbutamol sulfate tablet, 4 mg • Vitamin A capsule, 200,000 IU	• Lignocaine HCl injectable 1%, 25 mL vial • Praziquantel tablet, 600 mg • Gentian violet paint, aqueous 0.5%, 500 mL • Benzyl benzoate application, 25%, 100 mL • Magnesium trisilicate complex tablet, chewable • Chlorpromazine HCl tablet, 25 mg • Aminophylline tablet, 100 mg • Vitamin B complex tablet • Aluminum acetate eardrops, 13% • Zinc oxide ointment, 15% • Mebendazole tablet, 200 mg • Ferrous sulfate mixture, pediatric, 60 mg/5 mL • Chlorpheniramine maleate tablet, 4 mg • Lidocaine + adrenaline dental cartridge 2% + 1/80,000	• Lignocaine + adrenaline injectable, 1% + 1/200,000 • Aspirin tablet, pediatric, 75 mg • Suramin sodium injectable, 1 g vial, powder for reconstitution • Nystatin tablet, 500,000 units • Amodiaquine tablet, 200 mg base • Migril tablet • Ferrous sulfate tablet, 200 mg • Propranolol HCl tablet, 10 mg • Magenta paint, 20 mL • Anti-snakebite serum injectable, 10 mL amp • Ergometrine maleate tablet, 500 mcg • Vitamins, multiple pediatric drops • Thymol mouthwash solution tablet
District hospital	• Diazepam injectable, 5 mg/mL, 2 mL ampoule • Atropine sulfate injectable, 600 mcg/mL, 1 mL ampoule • Nalidixic acid tablet, 500 mg • Isoniazid + thiacetazone tablet, (HT3) 300 mg/150 mg • Digoxin tablet, 250 mcg	• Diazepam tablet, 5 mg • Paracetamol tablet, 500 mg • Codeine phosphate tablet, 15 mg • Amoxicilline elixir, 125 mg/5 mL • Erythromycin suspension, 125 mg/5 mL	

reducing safety stocks of nonessential items.
• *Order quantities:* If funds are short, the VEN system should be used to ensure that enough quantities of vital and essential medicines are bought first.
• *Supplier selection:* Only reliable suppliers should be used for vital and essential medicines. Quality and service for new and unknown suppliers can be tested by awarding them contracts for nonessential medicines.

Use: Review of usage by VEN categories may suggest underuse of vital or essential items or overuse of nonessential items. VEN or VN categories can be compared with ABC analysis and therapeutic category analysis (see following sections) to monitor how well actual use compares with priorities.
Pricing in pharmaceutical sales programs: Higher prices on popular but marginally useful items, such as cough and cold remedies, can be used to subsidize immunizations and antibiotics.

Stock control: Special attention should be paid to stock levels of vital and essential items to avoid stockouts.
Assignment of staff: Stock clerks and other inventory control staff who are more experienced or more skilled should be assigned to keep track of vital and essential items.

Country Study 40-2 describes the application of the VEN system.

Using the VEN system to guide purchases

The VEN (or VN) system helps minimize distortions in the pharmaceutical procurement process and thus maximizes the health effect of available funds. When procurement quantities must be reduced, these steps can be taken—

Step 1. Classify all medicines on the national essential medicines list as V, E, or N (or V or N): If the funding shortage is temporary, consider options for limiting individual order quantities (and increasing order frequency) for high-turnover V and E medicines, as determined by ABC analysis (see Section 40.4).

Step 2. Reconsider the proposed purchase quantities to make sure they are justified: Check assumptions, order formulas, and the accuracy of calculations. Particular attention should be paid to V and E medicines, because they will be the last eliminated from the list.

Step 3. Try to find additional funds: A clear and well-documented presentation of a system's requirements may result in increased pharmaceutical budget allocations or additional funds from donors. Introduction of a cost-recovery or a cost-sharing system may be an alternative source of additional funds in the long term (see Chapter 13).

Step 4. Remove from the procurement list any N medicines for which no clear therapeutic need exists: Then reassess funds in relation to revised estimates. If a funding gap still exists, proceed to Step 5.

Step 5. Reduce quantities of or eliminate other N items, and reassess the estimated procurement cost for remaining items: If requirements still exceed the available budget after all N items are eliminated, proceed to Step 6.

Step 6. Limit therapeutic duplications: If the list of V and E items (or V items in a VN system) contains more than one medicine with a similar therapeutic effect, some tendering by therapeutic subcategory may be possible (see Chapters 18 and 21). If certain medicines are usually purchased in more than one strength, it may be possible to limit such duplication and reduce total quantities for the medicines in question. If these sorts of adjustments are not feasible, or if they do not produce the necessary cost reductions, proceed to Step 7. Therapeutic category analysis (Section 40.5) may be useful to identify opportunities for limiting duplication.

Step 7. Reduce the quantities of medicines that must be purchased using the "preferential weighting" or "equal misery" approach: With a VN system, this step applies to all remaining medicines on the list. With a VEN system, one option is to purchase the entire quantity of V medicines and allocate remaining funds among E medicines. The alternative is to reduce quantities of both V and E medicines.

Country Study 40-2
An example of the VEN analysis process

A country's ministry of health (MOH) felt the need to further prioritize the medicines on its essential medicines list (EML) for procurement for the public sector because its limited resources prevented the central medical stores (CMS) from ensuring the continuous availability of all products on the EML.

The national medicines committee (NMC), the committee responsible for selecting medicines and updating the EML, started planning its review of the list as part of an ongoing review process to prioritize items on the list using VEN principles. In preparation for a two-day national meeting, all members of the NMC received information on amendments to the EML proposed by various health workers (along with scientific evidence backing up the proposals). Members also received a draft protocol for the VEN allocation exercise, clarifying both the rationale for the exercise (continuous availability of the most important medicines) and the proposed therapeutic criteria for allocation to V, E, or N categories. In addition, they received a list of all medicines on the EML by level of use and therapeutic group, with a suggested VEN allocation prepared by the NMC secretariat, with assistance from selected clinicians.

At the start of the meeting, participants agreed that in view of the economic circumstances, all items of limited therapeutic benefit (N medicines) should be removed from the list. They then used the VEN system to allocate medicines to V or E according to therapeutic relevance.

Early on during the meeting, it became clear that the NMC had to reinterpret the VEN criteria to reach consensus. For example, according to the original criteria, paracetamol did not qualify as a vital medicine. However, the majority of the committee members believed that because of the public health implications (that is, paracetamol is an antipyretic and also used for nonspecific complaints), it should be a V item.

In addition to allocation by therapeutic relevance, the NMC allocated all items by level of use (H, health center; D, district hospital; and C, central hospital) and by expected consumption (A for high- and B for low-consumption medicines).

The NMC agreed with the CMS that the CMS's first responsibility should be to ensure the continuous availability of vital high-consumption items (especially HVA items). Procurement of all other medicines would depend on the availability of additional funds. In addition, the CMS would not routinely stock low-consumption (especially DEB and CEB) items. Finally, clients (hospitals and districts) would be responsible for ordering all B items well in advance (for example, once a year at the beginning of the financial year).

The preferential weighting strategy protects one or more classes of medicines or one or more classes of facilities.

In one variation, the highest-priority classes are exempted from the cuts, and quantities of remaining medicines (or facility estimates) are reduced until the procurement budget balances with estimated purchases. Another option is to reduce quantities for the highest-priority classes less than for the lower-priority classes.

The equal misery strategy for reducing quantities is sometimes applied to pharmaceuticals or facilities. If it is applied to a single list of medicines, all medicine quantities are reduced by an equal percentage until the necessary cost reductions are achieved. If equal misery is applied to individual health facility estimates, all health facility estimates are reduced by the same percentage. Equal misery is not recommended for general use in the public pharmaceutical supply system—in most situations, preference should be given to certain medicines (and sometimes to certain types of health facilities).

40.4 ABC analysis

A well-known fact in supply chain management is that a relatively small number of items account for most of the value of annual consumption. The analysis of this phenomenon is known as Pareto analysis or, more commonly, ABC analysis.

In any supply system, analyzing consumption patterns and the value of total consumption for all items is useful; in all but the smallest systems, inventory items can be classified into three categories (A, B, and C) based on the value of their annual usage. Related tools such as therapeutic category analysis and price comparison analysis build on the basic ABC analysis, and the data for these analyses can be compiled as the ABC analysis is constructed by adding data columns to the spreadsheet.

A, B, and C categories are not assigned categories like VEN categories; each line item is categorized based on the result of a particular ABC analysis. If use patterns change, the item may fall into a different category the next time ABC analysis is performed.

Applications of ABC analysis

ABC analysis is an extremely powerful tool, with uses in selection, procurement, management of distribution, and promotion of rational medicine use.

Selection. Review of class A medicines may uncover high-use items for which lower-cost alternatives are available on the formulary or in the marketplace. The ABC analysis also helps managers identify purchases made for items that are not on the formulary or essential medicines list or not approved for use in the supply system.

In a West African country, analyses of consumption in a sample of twenty health facilities showed that three of the facilities (15 percent) continued to use and stock ampicillin suspension regularly, although it had been deleted from the national formulary five years earlier in favor of amoxicilline.

Procurement. ABC analysis can be useful to facilitate procurement-related activities, such as determining sources for lower-priced products, assuring procurement is in line with public health priorities, and assessing how order frequency affects overall supply—

Determining order frequency: Ordering class A items more often and in smaller quantities should lead to a reduction in inventory-holding costs. Note that order frequency and quantity influence supply activities in at least six ways: (1) they determine average inventory (higher order quantity means higher inventory levels); (2) they determine procurement workload (higher order quantity means a lower number of orders, and vice versa); (3) they determine safety stock (more frequent ordering means less inventory and less safety stock); (4) they influence bulk prices (larger orders mean more special bulk rates); (5) they determine storage space requirements for medicines; and (6) they influence the likelihood of losses to expiry (less frequent bulk purchasing may lead to more expired medicines).

Seeking lower-cost sources for class A items: The procurement office should concentrate on getting lower prices for class A items by looking for cheaper dosage forms or cheaper suppliers. Price reductions for items classified as A products in the analysis can lead to significant savings.

Monitoring order status: Emphasis should be placed on monitoring the order status of class A items, because an unexpected shortage may lead to expensive emergency purchases.

Monitoring procurement priorities: As mentioned in the VEN system discussion, ABC analysis can help monitor procurement patterns in comparison with health system priorities. For example, an ABC analysis of Kenya's consumption of antiretrovirals showed the high proportion of the budget dedicated to nevirapine. After switching to procurement of generic nevirapine, its value shifted significantly—from representing 40 percent of the antiretroviral budget in 2005 to about 9 percent in 2007.

Comparing actual and planned purchases: ABC analysis can be used to compare actual and planned purchases in a public-sector supply system. For example, in one Latin American ministry of health supply system, the original procurement budget for the year specified that 97 items would be purchased through tender at an estimated cost of USD 2.5 million. ABC analysis of the year's two tenders showed that 124 items were actually purchased, at a total cost of USD 3.36 million. Of the

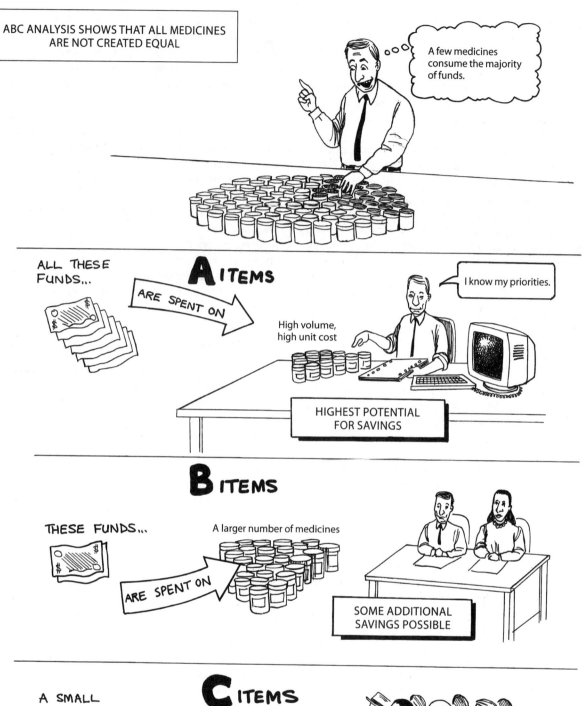

ABC ANALYSIS SHOWS THAT ALL MEDICINES ARE NOT CREATED EQUAL

A few medicines consume the majority of funds.

A ITEMS

ALL THESE FUNDS...

ARE SPENT ON

High volume, high unit cost

I know my priorities.

HIGHEST POTENTIAL FOR SAVINGS

B ITEMS

THESE FUNDS...

A larger number of medicines

ARE SPENT ON

SOME ADDITIONAL SAVINGS POSSIBLE

C ITEMS

A SMALL FRACTION OF FUNDS...

ARE SPENT ON

HIGH MANAGEMENT INPUT REQUIRED FOR PRACTICALLY NO COST REDUCTION

The majority of inventory

124 items purchased, 61 (nearly half) did not appear on the original procurement plan, and 34 of the medicines that had been on the plan were not purchased. The cost of the unplanned medicines was USD 1.17 million. Senior health system managers were unpleasantly surprised to learn of these discrepancies, and reforms in quantification and procurement procedure were devised for the procurement office.

Distribution and inventory management. In addition to selection and procurement, ABC analysis can also help with distribution and inventory management activities such as the following—

Monitoring shelf life: Emphasis should be given to class A items to minimize waste caused by medicines exceeding their shelf lives.

Delivery schedules: Even when all medicines are ordered only once a year, divided deliveries of class A items can lead to increased shelf lives.

Stock count: As discussed in Chapter 23, cyclic stock counts should be guided by ABC analysis, with more frequent counts for class A items.

Storage: Improving control for the issuance and storage of class A medicines at user points, such as hospitals and health centers, can minimize waste, pilferage, and organized theft of medicines.

Use. Review of high-use items by health officials, practicing physicians, and other health workers may suggest areas of overuse and underuse as exemplified in a Kenya hospital (Country Study 40-3).

Performing ABC analysis

ABC analysis can be applied to total annual consumption, to consumption during a short period, or to a particular tender or set of tenders; the basic methodology is the same no matter which data are used. The basic steps are also the same whether the ABC analysis is done manually or by computer, although the process is much easier with a computer.

The process is described in eight steps and illustrated in Tables 40-4 and 40-5 and Figure 40-2; the example used in the illustrations comes from an essential medicines program in Central Asia in 2010. The values shown are for part of one tender and do not represent annual pharmaceutical consumption in the country.

Step 1. List all items purchased or consumed and enter the unit cost: The cost is for one basic unit of an item (column 3 of Table 40-4). The basic unit should be the same as the issue unit tracked on stock records, except when a smaller basic unit such as a milliliter or a gram is needed to incorporate several different bottle, tube, or vial sizes

---

Country Study 40-3
Using ABC analysis to control antimicrobial resistance in Kenya

The Drug and Therapeutics Committee (DTC) at Aga Khan University Hospital in Nairobi established a multidisciplinary antimicrobial subcommittee to focus on interventions to contain antimicrobial resistance. The DTC did an ABC analysis of 793 medicines for 2005 and found that the top four products were antimicrobials, accounting for almost 10 percent of the medicine budget. Meropenem, an expensive, broad-spectrum carbapenem, had the highest consumption by value.

Top five medicines by value in ABC analysis for 2005

Medicine	Quantity	Cumulative percentage of budget
Meropenem, injectable, 1 g	3,346	3.44
Tazocin, injectable, 4.5 g	3,056	5.62
Augmentin, injectable, 1.2 g	15,212	7.70
Zinnat, tablets, 500 mg	48,422	9.60

The results of a retrospective drug use evaluation on Meropenem from 100 inpatient records reinforced the need for its rational use: only 40 patients received the standard treatment regimen (5–7 days); 35 received it despite inappropriate indications; 27 patients got a subtherapeutic dose; and 27 patients were given a 7–14-day regimen without valid justification.

In response, the DTC endorsed the development of an order sheet that restricted the use of Meropenem and six other antimicrobials. The antimicrobial order sheet was piloted in the intensive care unit and in surgical and medical wards. It was subsequently refined and launched hospitalwide. The DTC also endorsed the subcommittee recommendation that the microbiologist be involved in intensive care unit rounds, where the threat of antimicrobial resistance is high. Health care providers received information on the correct use of Meropenem and other antibiotics. The ABC analysis was repeated for 2006, and the results showed a 62 percent decrease in Meropenem consumption compared with 2005.

Source: Shah, Konduri, and Gunturu 2007.

Table 40-4   How to perform an ABC value analysis, using 2010 data from a Central Asian country (steps 1–4)

1	2	3	4	5	6
Product description	Basic unit	Unit tender price (local currency)	Total units purchased over twelve months	Value (local currency)	Percentage of total value
Acyclovir 200 mg	Tablet	5	3,700	18,500	0.95
Amikacin 100 mg	Ampoule	50	340	17,000	0.87
Amino acid 500 mL	Bottle	80	425	34,000	1.75
Amoxicilline 250 mg	Capsule	3	6,000	18,000	0.93
Amoxicilline 500 mg	Capsule	4	5,760	23,040	1.18
Ampicillin 1 g	Vial	22	6,270	137,940	7.09
Ampicillin 500 mg	Vial	18	11,930	214,740	11.04
Atropine sulfate 0.5 mg	Ampoule	8	1,205	9,640	0.50
Benzathine benzylpenicillin 1.2 M IU	Vial	20	1,475	29,500	1.52
Calcium D3	Bottle	30	400	12,000	0.62
Cefazolin 1 g	Vial	40	805	32,200	1.65
Cefotaxime 1 g	Vial	40	512	20,480	1.05
Ceftazidime 1 g	Vial	50	250	12,500	0.64
Ceftriaxone 1 g	Vial	40	905	36,200	1.86
Ceftriaxone 2 g	Vial	60	200	12,000	0.62
Chloramphenicol 1 g	Vial	22	720	15,840	0.82
Ciprofloxacin 250 mg	Tab	5	5,000	25,000	1.29
Cloxacillin 500 mg	Tablet	3	5,000	15,000	0.77
Diclofenac 75 mg/3 mL	Ampoule	10	1,557	15,570	0.80
Dopamine 200 mg	Ampoule	63	770	48,510	2.50
Erythromycin 250 mg	Tablet	2.5	34,860	87,150	4.48
Gentamicin 80 mg	Ampoule	20	8,549	170,980	8.79
Glucose 1,000 mL	Bottle	25	5,186	129,650	6.67
Glucose 500 mL	Bottle	25	1,195	29,875	1.54
Ketamine 500 mg	Vial	110	2,348	258,280	13.28
Metronidazole 400 mg	Tablet	40	440	17,600	0.91
Mix 500 mL	Bottle	35	1,320	46,200	2.37
Morphine 10 mg	Tablet	110	100	11,000	0.56
NaCl 1,000 mL	Bottle	25	4,720	118,000	6.07
Penicillin crystal 1 million IU	Vial	8	3,200	25,600	1.32
Penicillin procaine 2 million IU	Vial	10	1,900	19,000	0.98
Phenobarbital 100 mg	Ampoule	45	349	15,705	0.81
Polyvitamin	Tablet	2	9,000	18,000	0.93
Povidone iodine 450 cc	Bottle	85	656	55,760	2.87
Ringer's lactate 1,000 mL	Bottle	35	4,337	151,795	7.80
Ringer's lactate 500 mL	Bottle	35	670	23,450	1.20
Silver sulfadizine 1%	Tube	60	315	18,900	0.97
Total				**1,944,605**	

IU = international units.

for the same item. See Chapter 50 for a discussion of issue units, basic units, and pack sizes.

Ideally, the actual CIF (cost, insurance, and freight) acquisition unit cost for all items should be used, but this cost is difficult to track when multiple purchases of an item have been made at different prices. The most accurate alternatives are a weighted average or a FIFO average, as discussed in Chapter 41. In Table 40-4, the unit cost of one basic unit (tablet) of acyclovir was 5 units of the local currency, which is the equivalent of USD 0.012.

Step 2. Enter consumption quantities: Enter the number of basic units consumed or purchased during the period under review. Make sure that the same review period is used for all items to avoid invalid comparisons. Table 40-4 shows that for acyclovir, 3,700 tablets were purchased over the twelve months under review.

Step 3. Calculate the value of consumption: Multiply the unit cost by the number of units consumed or purchased to obtain the total value for each item. In Table 40-4, column 5 shows that for acyclovir, the total value of purchases was 18,500 local currency, or USD 430. After this amount is calculated for each item, add up the total value of all items at the bottom of column 5.

Step 4. Calculate the percentage of total value represented by each item: Divide the value of each item by the total value of all items. Enter the results for each item under the heading "Percentage of Total Value," as shown in column 6 of Table 40-4. At this point, any ABC list will look something like Table 40-4; in the example, amikacin (the second item) represented 0.87 percent of total value. (Carrying the percentage to two decimal places is useful because several items may be close together in value and many may represent less than 1 percent of total value. The data are easier to understand when these items are clearly differentiated with two decimal places.)

Step 5. Rearrange the list: Rank the items in descending order by total value (column 5), starting at the top with the highest value. For example, in Table 40-4, the highest-value item was ketamine, which now becomes item 1; ampicillin 500 mg moves to second place, and so forth. This rearrangement yields a list that is also ordered by percentage of total value, as in Table 40-5.

Step 6. Calculate the cumulative percentage of total value for each item: Beginning with the first item at the top of Table 40-5, add the percentage in column 6 to that of the item below it in the list (creating column 7). For example, ketamine represented 13.28 percent of total procurement value. Ampicillin 500 mg represented 11.04 percent; the cumulative percentage of the two items was 24.32 percent (rounded) of total procurement value.

Step 7. Choose cutoff points or boundaries for class A, B, and C medicines: In general, the following boundaries are

Figure 40-2   How to perform an ABC value analysis (step 8)

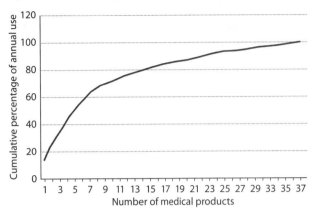

used: A items have the highest annual usage, with 10 to 20 percent of the items usually accounting for 75 to 80 percent of the funds spent. B items represent another 10 to 20 percent of the items and use 15 to 20 percent of the funds, and C items account for 60 to 80 percent of the items but only 5 to 10 percent of the value of annual consumption.

These boundaries are somewhat flexible; for example, class A status might be given to items that cumulatively account for 70 percent of the funds. The decision depends on how volume and value are dispersed among items on the list and how the results of the ABC analysis are going to be used. If class A items are going to be managed more intensively than class B and C items, allocation of items to class A must be based on management capacity. Using the suggested boundaries with the Central Asian example would result in only two products in the A category; therefore, cumulative value might be the more appropriate way to categorize in this instance.

Step 8. Present the results graphically: Plot the percentage of the total cumulative value (column 7) on the vertical or y axis against the item number on the horizontal or x axis. Figure 40-2 shows a graph of the sample ABC analysis. The number of items in the medicine list influences the slope of the ABC curve. Figure 40-3 shows the results of ABC analysis for a full year's medicine consumption in two large supply systems; note the difference in the shape of the curves in comparison to Figure 40-2. In Country I, 25 class A items of a total 344 accounted for about 75 percent of the total value. In Country II, which shows a less steep ABC curve, 34 items of 220 total items (15.5 percent) represent nearly 70 percent of the total value. To limit the number of items in class A, a cutoff point was selected that represents a lower proportion of the total value. In general, the steeper the curve, the higher the proportion of the total value that would be included in class A.

Table 40-5 How to perform an ABC value analysis, using 2010 data from a Central Asian country (steps 5 and 6)

	1	2	3	4	5	6	7
	Product description	Basic unit	Unit tender price (local currency)	Total units	Value (local currency)	Percentage of total value	Cumulative percentage of total value
1	Ketamine 500 mg	Vial	110	2,348	258,280	13.28	13.28
2	Ampicillin 500 mg	Vial	18	11,930	214,740	11.04	24.32
3	Gentamicin 80 mg	Ampoule	20	8,549	170,980	8.79	33.11
4	Ringer's lactate 1,000 mL	Bottle	35	4,337	151,795	7.80	40.91
5	Ampicillin 1 g	Vial	22	6,270	137,940	7.09	48.00
6	Glucose 1,000 mL	Bottle	25	5,186	129,650	6.67	54.67
7	NaCl 1,000 mL	Bottle	25	4,720	118,000	6.07	60.74
8	Erythromycin 250 mg	Tablet	2.5	34,860	87,150	4.48	65.22
9	Povidone iodine 450 cc	Bottle	85	656	55,760	2.87	68.09
10	Dopamine 200 mg	Ampoule	63	770	48,510	2.50	70.59
11	Mix 500 mL	Bottle	35	1,320	46,200	2.37	72.96
12	Ceftriaxone 1 g	Vial	40	905	36,200	1.86	74.82
13	Amino acid 500 mL	Bottle	80	425	34,000	1.75	76.57
14	Cefazolin 1 g	Vial	40	805	32,200	1.65	78.22
15	Glucose 500 mL	Bottle	25	1,195	29,875	1.54	79.76
16	Benzathine benzylpenicillin 1.2 million IU	Vial	20	1,475	29,500	1.52	81.28
17	Penicillin crystal 1 million IU	Vial	8	3,200	25,600	1.32	82.60
18	Ciprofloxacin 250 mg	Tablet	5	5,000	25,000	1.29	83.89
19	Ringer's lactate 500 mL	Bottle	35	670	23,450	1.20	85.09
20	Amoxicilline 500 mg	Capsule	4	5,760	23,040	1.18	86.27
21	Cefotaxime 1 g	Vial	40	512	20,480	1.05	87.32
22	Penicillin procaine 2 million IU	Vial	10	1,900	19,000	0.98	88.30
23	Silver sulfadizine 1%	Tube	60	315	18,900	0.97	89.27
24	Acyclovir 200 mg	Tablet	5	3,700	18,500	0.95	90.22
25	Amoxicilline 250 mg	Capsule	3	6,000	18,000	0.93	91.15
26	Polyvitamin	Tablet	2	9,000	18,000	0.93	92.08
27	Metronidazole 40 mg	Tablet	40	440	17,600	0.91	92.99
28	Amikacin 100 mg	Ampoule	50	340	17,000	0.87	93.86
29	Chloramphenicol 1 g	Vial	22	720	15,840	0.82	94.68
30	Phenobarbital 100 mg	Ampoule	45	349	15,705	0.81	95.49
31	Diclofenac 75 mg/3 mL	Ampoule	10	1,557	15,570	0.80	96.29
32	Cloxacillin 500 mg	Tablet	3	5,000	15,000	0.77	97.06
33	Ceftazidime 1 g	Vial	50	250	12,500	0.64	97.70
34	Calcium D3	Bottle	30	400	12,000	0.62	98.32
35	Ceftriaxone 2 g	Vial	60	200	12,000	0.62	98.94
36	Morphine 10 mg	Tablet	110	100	11,000	0.56	99.50
37	Atropine sulfate 0.5 mg	Ampoule	8	1,205	9,640	0.50	100.00
	Total				**1,944,605**		

IU = international units.

Figure 40-3 Typical ABC analysis for two pharmaceutical supply programs

	Country I – ABC class				Country II – ABC class			
	A	B	C	Total	A	B	C	Total
Number of items	25	34	285	344	34	35	151	220
Percentage of all items	7.3	9.9	82.8	100	15.5	15.9	68.6	100
Value of annual consumption (USD)	11,151,270	2,197,600	1,438,274	14,787,144	6,401,593	1,415,641	1,401,088	9,218,322
Percentage of total annual consumption	75.4	14.9	9.7	100	69.4	15.4	15.2	100

40.5 Therapeutic category analysis

Therapeutic category analysis reviews the volume of use and the value of various therapeutic categories and subcategories of medicines. This technique builds on ABC analysis, sorting the ABC list into therapeutic categories (based on the cumulative volume and value of the individual medicines in those categories). Table 40-6 shows a summary therapeutic category analysis, using data from a Caribbean country. Table 40-7 provides details on the top three therapeutic categories in Table 40-6.

Applications of therapeutic category analysis

The applications of therapeutic category analysis are similar to those of ABC analysis. Managers should focus cost-control efforts on the therapeutic categories that show the highest consumption and greatest expenditures.

Selection. Therapeutic category analysis can be used to choose the most cost-effective products for essential medicines lists and formularies and find opportunities for therapeutic substitution. For example, in Table 40-7, look at the comparison between methyldopa and atenolol. If all hypertensive patients in the sample were converted from methyldopa to atenolol, the health system would save about USD 33,440—over 20 percent of the

total expenditures for pharmaceutical purchases in this country.

In addition, therapeutic category analysis can help provide information for pharmacoeconomic analysis. Pharmacoeconomic analysis is the process of comparing cost, therapeutic efficacy, and safety. Two techniques are most commonly used in comparing treatment regimens: cost-minimization and cost-effectiveness analysis. Other pharmacoeconomic techniques such as cost-utility and cost-benefit analysis are less appropriate for comparing treatment regimens (see Chapter 10). Cost minimization is the simpler of the two techniques—it is used when two therapeutic options are the same in terms of therapeutic benefit and safety but one is less expensive. As discussed in Chapter 10, cost-effectiveness is used to compare the costs and benefits of therapeutic alternatives when cost minimization alone is not appropriate. (For more information on pharmacoeconomic analysis, see Bootman, Townsend, and McGhan 2005.)

Procurement. As discussed in Chapters 18 and 21, some supply systems tender for certain therapeutic subcategories (for example, first-generation cephalosporins) rather than for individual medicines. A therapeutic category analysis would show managers how many different products in a subcategory are being purchased. If duplications exist—for example, two oral products are being purchased—tenders

Table 40-6   Therapeutic category analysis summary

	Formulary code	Formulary category	Number of products	Category total cost (USD)	Percentage of total cost	Cumulative percentage of total cost
1	8.12	Antibacterial/antifungal agents, systemic	30	46,053	19.17	19.17
2	68.20	Antidiabetic agents	5	36,175	15.06	34.23
3	24.08	Hypotensive agents	8	31,006	12.91	47.13
4	40.12	Replacement solution/agents	10	14,834	6.17	53.31
5	84.04	Topical anti-infectives	4	14,302	5.95	59.26
6	40.20	Caloric agents (dextrose solutions)	6	12,480	5.19	64.46
7	28.08	Analgesics/antipyretics	10	11,835	4.93	69.38
8	36.00	Diagnostic strips	1	6,496	2.70	72.09
9	86.00	Anti-asthmatic medicines	8	6,195	2.58	74.66
10	4.00	Antihistamines	5	4,892	2.04	76.70
11	38.00	Disinfectants	3	4,846	2.02	78.72
12	28.16	Psychotherapeutic agents (antipsychotic/antidepressant)	14	4,574	1.90	80.62
13	88.28	Multiple vitamins	3	4,318	1.80	82.42
14	20.04	Iron preparations	3	3,207	1.33	83.75
15	56.40	Miscellaneous gastrointestinal medicines	4	3,039	1.26	85.02
16	8.08	Anthelmintics	2	2,663	1.11	86.13
17	92.00	Dispensing envelopes	1	2,643	1.10	87.23
18	68.04	Adrenal hormones	4	2,246	0.93	88.16
19	48.00	Antitussive/anti-expectorant	2	2,240	0.93	89.09
20	56.04	Antacids	2	1,781	0.74	89.84
21	28.04	General anesthetics	3	1,693	0.70	90.54
22	84.05	Topical antifungals	4	1,633	0.68	91.22
23	88.08	Vitamin B preparations	5	1,547	0.64	91.86
24	28.12	Anticonvulsant agents	5	1,465	0.61	92.47
25	92.00	IV administration sets	1	1,300	0.54	93.02
26	12.20	Skeletal muscle relaxants	3	1,283	0.53	93.55
27	52.04	Eye, ear, nose, and throat (EENT) anti-infectives	4	1,283	0.53	94.08
28	40.28	Diuretics	5	1,248	0.52	94.60
29	8.16	Antitubercular agents	5	1,212	0.50	95.11
30	24.04	Cardiotonic and antiarrhythmic agents	6	1,119	0.47	95.57
31	52.08	EENT anti-inflammatory agents	2	1,113	0.46	96.04
32	12.08	Anticholinergic agents	4	925	0.39	96.42
33	56.12	Laxatives	5	886	0.37	96.79
34	84.07	Scabicides/pediculocides	1	765	0.32	97.11
35	76.00	Oxytocics	3	718	0.30	97.41
36	20.12	Anticoagulants and coagulants	2	691	0.29	97.70
37	52.20	Miotics	1	534	0.22	97.92
38	56.22	Anti-emetics	3	531	0.22	98.14
39	84.36	Miscellaneous topical preparations	2	515	0.21	98.35
40	72.00	Local anesthetics	6	491	0.20	98.56
41	8.32	Antitrichomonal agents (metronidazole)	3	481	0.20	98.76
42	84.06	Topical anti-inflammatory	2	363	0.15	98.91

	Formulary code	Formulary category	Number of products	Category total cost (USD)	Percentage of total cost	Cumulative percentage of total cost
43	52.36	EENT miscellaneous	2	358	0.15	99.06
44	28.24	Anxiolytics, sedatives, hypnotics	3	356	0.15	99.21
45	88.12	Vitamin C	1	345	0.14	99.35
46	68.36	Thyroid/antithyroid preparations	2	246	0.10	99.45
47	88.24	Vitamin K-1	1	201	0.08	99.54
48	24.12	Coronary vasodilators	2	189	0.08	99.61
49	12.12	Adrenergic agents	1	188	0.08	99.69
50	64.00	Antidotes/metal antagonists	1	149	0.06	99.75
51	28.10	Narcotic antagonists	1	135	0.06	99.81
52	12.16	Adrenergic blocking agents	1	85	0.04	99.85
53	8.36	Urinary anti-infectives	2	82	0.03	99.88
54	40.08	Alkalinizing agents	1	79	0.03	99.91
55	12.04	Cholinergic agents	1	74	0.03	99.94
56	52.10	Carbonic anhydrase inhibitor	1	63	0.03	99.97
57	40.40	Antigout agents	1	60	0.02	100.00
58	52.24	Mydriatic/cycloplegic	1	12	0.00	100.00
		Total	**222**	**240,241**		

could specify only "oral first-generation cephalosporins." Review of Table 40-7 does not yield obvious candidates for subcategory tendering.

Use. Therapeutic category analysis can help promote rational medicine use by identifying potential problems of irrational use: for example, managers can compare information from the summary (Table 40-6) and the detailed analysis (Table 40-7) with known patterns of morbidity to see how well use matches the patterns. For example, in Table 40-7, note that 7,467 courses of therapy (COTs) of chlorpropamide were used; the manager might ask how that corresponds with the incidence of diabetes that would justify the use of chlorpropamide. Note that the use of chlorpropamide was almost three times greater than the use of glibenclamide (and chlorpropamide's unit cost was seven times higher). Are these patterns rational for the situation? Table 40-7 does not have enough information to make that determination, but a small, well-targeted study of prescribing might be used to find out (as described in Chapter 28).

In addition, this type of analysis can identify overprescribing and leakage by comparing the number of COTs that theoretically should have been provided against patient contact data—for example, are the numbers of diabetic patients treated consistent with the number of COTs?

Performing therapeutic category analysis

Therapeutic category analysis is divided into two phases: the summary analysis and the detailed analysis. The sum-

mary analysis starts with the same steps taken as part of an ABC analysis, then includes a classification by therapeutic category. The detailed analysis is a more in-depth look at the high-cost categories identified in the summary phase.

Summary therapeutic category analysis. The summary analysis consists of five steps—

Steps 1–3: Follow the first three steps in ABC analysis (see Section 40.4) to produce a list of medicines, with the volume and value of use calculated for each medicine.

Step 4: Add a column and assign each of the medicines to a therapeutic category, as discussed in Chapter 16. The key requirement is a standard formulary coding system. The system can be simple (with relatively broad categories) or complex (with many subcategories). Commonly used coding systems include the World Health Organization (WHO) Model List of Essential Medicines and the American Hospital Formulary Service (AHFS) Pharmacologic-Therapeutic Classification. More detailed, multilayered schemes are the Anatomical, Therapeutic, Chemical Classification System with Defined Daily Doses of the WHO Collaborating Centre for Drug Statistics Methodology and the U.S. Department of Veterans Affairs Drug Classification System.

Step 5: Rearrange the list into therapeutic categories by sorting according to the formulary codes. The values and percentages for the various therapeutic categories are then summed from the results for the individual items in

Table 40-7   Therapeutic category analysis—detail with defined daily dose comparisons

Product name	Strength	Basic unit	Basic unit price (USD)	Total use (basic units)	Value of annual use (USD)	Defined daily dose (number of comparison units)	Defined daily dose cost (USD)	Standard COT (days)	Basic units per COT	Annual number of COTs	Cost per COT (USD)
Antibacterial/antifungal agents, systemic / USD 31,543 / 20.1% of total											
Ampicillin	250 mg	Tablet	0.0218	237,000	5,167	8	0.1744	10	80	2,963	1.74
Ampicillin	500 mg	Tablet	0.0428	31,500	1,348	4	0.1712	10	40	788	1.71
Ampicillin sodium injection	500 mg	Ampoule	0.1332	3,120	416	4	0.5328	5	20	156	2.66
Ampicillin suspension 100 mL	125 mg/ 5 mL	Bottle	0.48	6,951	3,336	0.4	0.192	10	4	1,738	1.92
Benzathine benzylpenicillin injection	2.4 million IU	Ampoule	0.3664	1,848	677	1	0.3664	5	5	370	1.83
Cephadrine injection	500 mg	Ampoule	0.1153	3,050	352	4	0.4612	5	20	153	2.31
Cefalexin	250 mg	Tablet	0.0538	5,200	280	8	0.4304	10	80	65	4.30
Cefalexin suspension 100 mL	125 mg/mL	Bottle	0.68	909	618	0.4	0.272	10	4	227	2.72
Chloramphenicol	250 mg	Tablet	0.0162	2,100	34	8	0.1296	10	80	26	1.30
Chloramphenicol injection	1 g	Ampoule	0.36	400	144	3	1.08	5	15	27	5.40
Chloramphenicol suspension 100 mL	125 mg/ 5 mL	Bottle	0.64	120	77	0.4	0.256	10	4	30	2.56
Cloxacillin sodium injection	500 mg	Vial	0.1616	2,000	323	4	0.6464	5	20	100	3.23
Cloxacillin suspension 100 mL	125 mg/ 5 mL	Bottle	0.75	1,798	1,349	0.4	0.3	10	4	450	3.00
Cloxacillin	250 mg	Tablet	0.0209	9,100	190	8	0.1672	10	80	114	1.67
Co-trimoxazole IV injection 5 mL	80/16 mg/ mL	Ampoule	1.326	100	133	5	6.63	5	25	4	33.15
Co-trimoxazole suspension 100 mL	200/40 mg/5	Bottle	0.42	679	285	0.3	0.126	10	3	226	1.26
Co-trimoxazole	400/80 mg	Tablet	0.0101	75,000	758	2	0.0202	10	20	3,750	0.20
Erythromycin suspension 100 mL	200 mg/ 5mL	Bottle	2.7	1,452	3,920	0.25	0.675	10	3	484	8.10
Erythromycin	250 mg	Tablet	0.0267	96,000	2,563	4	0.1068	10	40	2,400	1.07
Gentamicin injection 2 mL	40 mg/mL	Ampoule	0.0948	5,470	519	3	0.2844	5	15	365	1.42
Griseofulvin	125 mg	Tablet	0.0168	3,000	50	4	0.0672	10	40	75	0.67
Griseofulvin	500 mg	Tablet	0.0491	31,000	1,522	1	0.0491	10	10	3,100	0.49
Nystatin oral suspension 60 mL	0.1 million IU/mL	Bottle	1.578	494	780	0.25	0.3945	10	3	165	4.73

Product name	Strength	Basic unit	Basic unit price (USD)	Total use (basic units)	Value of annual use (USD)	Defined daily dose (number of comparison units)	Defined daily dose cost (USD)	Standard COT (days)	Basic units per COT	Annual number of COTs	Cost per COT (USD)
Nystatin oral	.5 MU	Tablet	0.0514	1,100	57	3	0.1542	10	30	37	1.54
Penicillin G sodium injection	1 MU	Vial	0.0864	2,250	194	5.76	0.497664	5	29	78	2.51
Penicillin G sodium injection	5 MU	Vial	0.256	1,300	333	1.15	0.2944	5	6	217	1.54
Penicillin VK suspension 100 mL	125 mg/5 mL	Bottle	0.71	2,257	1,602	0.4	0.284	10	4	564	2.84
Penicillin VK	250 mg	Tablet	0.018	72,000	1,296	8	0.144	10	80	900	1.44
Procaine penicillin G injection	4.8 mg	Vial	0.4157	3,269	1,359	1	0.4157	5	5	654	2.08
Tetracycline HCl	250 mg	Tablet	0.0107	174,000	1,862	4	0.0428	10	40	4,350	0.43
Antidiabetic agents / USD 83,112 / 52.9% of total											
Chlorpropamide	250 mg	Tablet	0.0292	336,000	9,811	1.5	0.0438	30	45	7,467	1.31
Glibenclamide	5 mg	Tablet	0.0041	152,000	623	2	0.0082	30	60	2,533	0.25
Insulin (soluble) injection, 10 mL	100 IU/mL	Vial	8.018	385	3,087	0.04	0.32072	30	1.2	321	9.62
Insulin lente, 10 mL	100 IU/mL	Vial	9.65	6,568	63,381	0.04	0.386	30	1.2	5,473	11.58
Insulin lente human injection, 10 mL	100 IU/mL	Vial	11.585	536	6,210	0.04	0.4634	30	1.2	447	13.90
Antihypertensive agents / USD 42,205 / 26.9% of total											
Atenolol	100 mg	Tablet	0.0076	29,000	220	1	0.0076	30	30	967	0.23
Hydralazine	50 mg	Tablet	0.04	86,000	3,440	2	0.08	30	60	1,433	2.40
Hydralazine injection	20 mg/mL	Ampoule	1.6592	410	680	2	3.3184	5	10	41	16.59
Methyldopa	500 mg	Tablet	0.083	443,500	36,811	4	0.332	30	120	3,696	9.96
Nifedipine	10 mg	Tablet	0.0116	7,000	81	3	0.0348	30	90	78	1.04
Propranolol HCl	40 mg	Tablet	0.0055	70,000	385	4	0.022	30	120	583	0.66
Propranolol	80 mg	Tablet	0.0231	5,000	116	2	0.0462	30	60	83	1.39
Reserpine	.25 mg	Tablet	0.016	29,500	472	2	0.032	30	60	492	0.96
Three category totals: USD 156,860											

IU = international units.

the category and cumulative percentages are calculated, producing a summary therapeutic category analysis (see Steps 4–6 under ABC analysis).

In the summary therapeutic category analysis in Table 40-6, fifty-eight different therapeutic categories are represented; this country uses the Organisation of Eastern Caribbean States' Pharmaceutical Procurement Service formulary coding system (OECS/PPS 2006), which has seventy-four possible therapeutic categories. The system is based on the AHFS system, with minor modifications.

Note that seven of the categories were responsible for nearly 70 percent of total expenditures. This grouping resembles class A in ABC analysis, and the principle is the same—a relatively small number of therapeutic categories often consume most of the funds in a supply system. To reduce costs, managers should look first at these high-cost therapeutic categories.

Detailed therapeutic category analysis. The second phase of the analysis focuses on the high-cost categories identified in the summary phase. The goal is to identify possible changes in therapeutic strategy that might prove to be cost-effective. This analysis compares the cost for a defined daily dose (DDD) of the medicines (the average daily dose for all patients) and the cost of a defined COT.

This stage of the analysis starts with the detailed list of medicines for important therapeutic categories assembled in phase 1. The list of medicines within the categories can be sorted either alphabetically (which is probably easiest for additional data entry) or by value. Data fields (columns) are added to the list to enter the number of basic units per DDD, the annual use in DDDs, the cost per DDD, the standard COT in days, the annual number of COTs, and the average cost per COT (see Box 40-2).

After the standard COT is determined, the final step in constructing the detailed therapeutic category analysis is multiplying the DDD cost by the COT and dividing the annual number of DDDs by the COT (see Table 40-7 for examples).

40.6 Price comparison analysis

Procurement prices can be compared with prices from other systems, and sales prices can be compared with local private-sector prices. These comparisons can help managers set prices for cost-sharing programs and understand whether continuing with current in-house pharmaceutical services is cost-effective.

Acquisition price comparison

Acquisition price comparison analysis tells the manager whether the system is getting the maximum benefit from

---

> **Box 40-2**
> **Determining DDDs and COTs**
>
> The DDD can be obtained from at least two sources; the official list is published periodically by the WHO Collaborating Centre in Oslo, Norway (WHOCC 2011), and the Management Sciences for Health *International Drug Price Indicator Guide* (MSH 2010) includes the DDD for selected essential medicines. Note that the DDD in Table 40-7 is listed in terms of comparison units; in the references cited here, the DDD is specified in grams and International Units, so they must be converted to comparison units. For example, the DDD for ampicillin is 2 grams, which converts to eight capsules of 250 mg, four capsules of 500 mg, and four ampoules of 500 mg for the injection. The official DDD for ampicillin suspension would be 80 mL (0.8 bottles of 100 mL), but the official DDD does not differentiate between adult and pediatric dosages. For the various pediatric suspensions in Table 40-7, the DDD was assumed to be 40 mL. The annual number of DDDs is obtained by dividing total annual consumption by the DDD; the cost per DDD is calculated by multiplying the comparison unit price by the DDD.
>
> The average COT will differ according to local policy and custom; for example, some health systems might specify a standard course of ten days for outpatient antibiotic therapy, and other systems might say five or seven days. The COT for chronic medications can be set at thirty days (for ease of comparison). The COT for inpatient medicines might be set at five days (again, for ease of comparison).

---

available procurement funds, and if not, how much might be saved with alternative procurement practices.

Applications. The obvious application of price comparison analysis is to measure procurement performance and to focus efforts on obtaining better prices. The comparison of average tender prices with international prices can be used as a routine indicator of procurement system performance.

The analysis can also identify certain medicines that should be considered for alternative methods of procurement. For example, if a supply system is currently purchasing all medicines from local suppliers, the price comparison analysis may indicate some medicines that could be obtained for a significantly lower price through international tender or even through direct procurement from one of the international nonprofit agencies.

Country Study 40-4 shows the results of a 2009 price comparison analysis from a Latin American country.

Country Study 40-4
Price comparison analysis

In this analysis, 2009 prices from local suppliers in a Latin American country were compared with the Organisation of Eastern Caribbean States' Pharmaceutical Procurement Service (OECS/PPS) prices, based on information from the MSH *International Drug Price Indicator Guide*.

The Latin American country received a better or the same price locally as the OECS/PPS did internationally for twelve of thirty products—in some cases, particularly for solutions, the local price was better than the international price (largely because shipping costs are a major component of the international price). OECS/PPS international prices were better on eighteen of thirty products. Certain items, in particular, made a difference; for example, items that had higher local prices combined with large order quantities, such as chloramphenicol suspension, halothane liquid, lidocaine solution, and rifampicin tablets. The country could have saved over USD 143,000 by purchasing only those four items internationally. The accompanying table shows the format for the price comparison analysis.

Description	Strength	Form	Comparison unit	Total units purchased, two tenders	Total USD at country tender price	Total USD at OECS/PPS tender price	Country price as percentage of OECS/PPS price
Acetazolamide	250 mg	Tablet	Tablet	3,000	200.40	60.00	334.0
Allopurinol	100 mg	Tablet	Tablet	15,000	171.00	300.00	57.0
Benzathine penicillin	2.4 million IU	Solution	Ampoule	60,000	30,840.00	36,000.00	85.7
Bisacodyl	5 mg	Tablet	Tablet	30,000	3,486.00	2,700.00	129.1
Cephalexin	500 mg	Capsule	Tablet	500,000	32,250.00	32,050.00	100.6
Chloramphenicol	1 g	Solution	Ampoule	25,000	12,857.50	25,000.00	51.4
Chloramphenicol	125 mg/5 mL	Suspension	100 mL bottle	125,000	110,000.00	58,750.00	187.2
Co-trimoxazole	80 mg+40	Tablet	Tablet	2,000,000	28,800.00	28,800.00	100.0
Co-trimoxazole	240 mg/5 mL	Suspension	100 mL bottle	110,000	56,100.00	50,600.00	110.9
Dextrose in NaCl, 1 L	5%/0.9% mg	Solution	Ampoule	110,000	80,300.00	99,000.00	81.1
Diazepam	5 mg	Tablet	Tablet	200,000	2,420.00	1,700.00	142.4
Erythromycin	250 mg	Tablet	Tablet	500,000	29,800.00	19,550.00	152.4
Furosemide	40 mg	Tablet	Tablet	50,000	500.00	290.00	172.4
Gentamicin	80 mg/2 mL	Solution	Ampoule	200,000	18,000.00	12,760.00	141.1
Halothane	250 mL	Liquid	Bottle	2,000	92,620.00	60,000.00	154.4
Hydralazine	50 mg	Tablet	Tablet	10,000	373.00	250.00	149.2
Insulin NPH, 10 mL	40 units/mL	Solution	Ampoule	8,000	40,448.00	43,840.00	92.3
Ketamine (10 mL)	50 mg/mL	Solution	Ampoule	4,000	9,220.00	9,600.00	96.0
Lidocaine (50 mL)	2% sin epi	Solution	Ampoule	8,000	35,120.00	4,240.00	828.3
Methyldopa	500 mg	Tablet	Tablet	100,000	9,380.00	4,400.00	213.2
Metronidazole	250 mg	Tablet	Tablet	3,000,000	44,400.00	15,300.00	290.2
Oral rehydration salts	—	Powder	Packet	200,000	31,040.00	46,400.00	66.9
Oxytocin	10 U/mL	Solution	Ampoule	25,000	1,365.00	8,250.00	16.5
Phenytoin	100 mg	Capsule	Capsule	270,000	10,989.00	5,832.00	188.4
Propranolol	40 mg	Tablet	Tablet	150,000	1,740.00	1,275.00	136.5
Propranolol	80 mg	Tablet	Tablet	50,000	1,305.00	1,000.00	130.5
Quinidine sulfate	200 mg	Tablet	Tablet	60,000	7,800.00	8,082.00	96.5
Rifampicin	300 mg	Capsule	Tablet	1,600,000	221,600.00	126,720.00	174.9
Sodium chloride, 1 L	0.9%	Solution	Ampoule	70,000	39,200.00	62,300.00	62.9
Vitamin B complex	120 mL	Solution	Bottle	100,000	49,000.00	21,000.00	233.3
Average tender price as percentage of international price							175.2%
Standard deviation—average tender price/international price							144.81%
Weighted average percentage—tender price/international price							127%

Note: — Not applicable; IU = international units.

Pharmaceutical price comparison analysis. One potential source for comparative procurement information is a list of prices from a neighboring supply system. Another is the MSH *International Drug Price Indicator Guide* (available online or in a CD-ROM version that allows the user to enter local prices and compare them with the international prices that are already in the system). In addition, Health Action International and WHO have developed a methodology to assess medicine prices; the website (http://www.haiweb.org/medicineprices) includes survey data from many countries as well as resources for many other sources of medicine prices.

When the comparison prices have been entered for each medicine, divide the local price by the comparison price, which calculates the local price as a percentage of the comparison price. After doing this, all these percentages are totaled and divided by the number of medicines to get the average percentage.

A manager can also determine how much overall difference exists for a certain volume of purchases (the weighted average percentage) in a manner similar to the ABC analysis. Total annual values are calculated for each item for both local prices and comparison prices, based on annual consumption. The values at local prices and the values at comparison prices are totaled at the bottom of the respective columns. Then the weighted average percentage is calculated by dividing the total value for all items at local prices by the total value at comparison prices. The weighted average is useful because large differences may exist for individual medicines that skew the simple average comparison.

When using the MSH indicator prices for comparison, it is important to understand that the international reference prices reflect a combination of actual tender prices paid by selected countries' procurement programs and prices from international nonprofit suppliers such as Supply Chain Management System and the IDA Foundation; the reference prices are not actual prices. When a wide range of prices makes up the average, the average may be much higher or lower than actual prices from any of the individual suppliers or tendering programs listed. Therefore, the guide shows the median prices, which controls for skewing that may occur with price averaging.

The prices being compared must refer to the same year; the pharmaceutical products being compared must be the same generic products in the same or comparable dosage forms, and the comparison units must be the same. If all these points are not addressed correctly, the price comparison analysis will be invalid.

Comparison of supply system prices and private-sector prices

This analysis compares acquisition and selling prices against local private-sector wholesale and retail prices.

Applications. The analysis provides useful information for cost-recovery programs. Note in Table 40-8 that CMS sales prices at a 30 percent markup were, on average, 84 percent of the private-sector wholesale prices for the same medicines (47 percent of the average retail sales price) and 92 percent of the sales prices from the local nongovernmental organization (NGO) warehouse. This finding might seem to indicate that the CMS could increase prices somewhat. However, this simple comparison is not enough to make a determination, because the key issue is how much services are valued by patients. If public pharmaceutical services are not valued as highly as private-sector medicines and services, there may be no room at all for price increases.

The most useful application of this type of analysis is to indicate the cost-effectiveness of in-house pharmaceutical services. If supply system procurement acquisition prices are higher than or nearly as high as the private-sector sales prices, and procurement system improvements are unlikely to be able to significantly reduce acquisition prices, further investigation is warranted—for example, serving public-sector patients through contracts with private pharmacies may be more cost-effective.

Doing the analysis. This analysis demands some extra effort to get comparative information. Information on average wholesale or retail prices may be available from the local pharmacy association, but if it is not or if it is not reliable, prices in local wholesale and retail outlets can be obtained through a simple survey, focusing on a limited list of essential medicines (see MSH/RPM 1995). If a wide range of prices is obtained in the survey, using the simple median retail price rather than an average of the prices may be best.

This analysis is set up in the same way as the preceding price comparison analysis, building on the list used for ABC analysis and adding columns of comparative prices from the private sector. If the public supply system is selling medicines from one level to the next or to the public, columns should be provided for both acquisition and selling prices. Again, a percentage comparison is made for both individual medicines and an overall average. To show the private-sector price as a percentage of the supply system prices, the retail price is divided by the supply system price. To show the supply system prices as a percentage of the private-sector prices, supply system prices are divided by private-sector prices.

Table 40-8 illustrates a comparison between CMS prices and local wholesale prices.

40.7 Lead-time and payment-time analysis

Lead time is defined as the interval between submitting an order and receiving the goods. In many countries, most pharmaceuticals purchased by the public sector are imported, and lead times are frequently long and variable.

Table 40-8   Price comparison: CMS 30 percent markup compared with private-sector wholesale and retail prices and NGO prices

Description	Strength	Issue unit	Projected CMS 30 percent markup on 2009 cost	Wholesale average price	CMS price as percentage of average wholesale price	Retail average price	CMS price as percentage of average retail price	NGO May 2009 unit price	CMS price as percentage of NGO price
Acetylsalicylic acid	325 mg	Tablet	0.0030	0.0037	81	0.0096	31	0.0033	90
Amodiaquine	200 mg	Tablet	0.0118	0.0219	54	0.0423	28	—	NA
Amoxicillin	125 mg/5 mL	60 mL bottle	0.4758	0.5874	81	0.7674	62	0.3473	137
Amoxicilline	250 mg	Tablet	0.0291	—	NA	—	NA	0.0313	93
Chloramphenicol	250 mg	Tablet	0.0208	0.0245	85	0.0353	59	0.0184	113
Chloroquine	150 mg	Tablet	0.0251	0.0374	67	0.0597	42	—	NA
Chlorpheniramine	4 mg	Tablet	0.0025	0.0036	68	0.0075	33	0.0030	83
Co-trimoxazole	480 mg	Tablet	0.0144	0.0166	87	0.0225	64	0.0129	112
Diazepam	5 mg	Tablet	0.0043	0.0075	57	0.0187	23	0.0069	62
Ferrous sulfate	60 mg iron	Tablet	0.0098	0.0106	92	0.0244	40	0.0091	107
Folic acid + iron	0.25 mg/60 mg	Tablet	0.0027	0.0303	9	0.0455	6	—	NA
Furosemide	40 mg	Tablet	0.0068	0.0169	40	0.0338	20	0.0111	61
Mebendazole	100 mg	Tablet	0.0059	0.0585	10	0.1463	4	0.0195	30
Metronidazole	250 mg	Tablet	0.0065	0.0081	80	0.0159	41	0.0078	83
Multivitamin	NA	Tablet	0.0099	0.0059	168	0.0154	64	0.0069	144
Oral rehydration salts	NA	Sachet	0.1573	0.1748	90	0.2537	62	0.1873	84
Paracetamol	500 mg	Tablet	0.0059	0.0049	119	0.0087	67	0.0049	119
Penicillin procaine	4 million IU	Vial	0.4194	0.4415	95	0.6553	64	—	NA
Penicillin, benzyl	5 millionn IU	Vial	0.4940	0.2041	242	0.3293	150	—	NA
Reserpine	0.25 mg	Tablet	0.0538	0.1455	37	0.3166	17	0.0828	65
Averages—30% CMS markup as % of other					**84.13%**		**47.25%**		**92%**

Note: — Not applicable; NA = not available; IU = international units.

Table 40-9   Lead-time analysis

Purchase order	Contract lead time	Actual lead time	Shipment days overdue	Contract payment time	Actual payment time	Payment days overdue
KIT-8001	45	57	12	45	43	0
LUC-8001	45	27	0	45	112	67
LUC-8001	45	119	74	45	20	0
MON-801	45	30	0	45	63	18
VIN-8000	45	21	0	45	96	51
Average lead time		50.8 days		Average pay time		66.8 days
Percentage of orders overdue		50%		Percentage of late payments		75%
Average delay when overdue		43 days		Average delay when payment overdue		45 days

Source: Data come from the Caribbean pooled procurement program.
Note: LUC-8001 was shipped in two partial shipments, one on time, the other not.

Payment time is defined as the interval between receipt of goods at the warehouse and payment to the supplier. This interval is of concern in supply systems that have delayed payment terms with suppliers; in such systems, monitoring and controlling payment time is of paramount importance if the system wishes to continue to pay on delayed terms.

An analysis of lead times and payment times for purchases by an international pooled procurement program is presented in Table 40-9. It shows the variability that occurs in practice and illustrates how to construct a lead-time and payment-time analysis table. Note that the supplier was late in delivering half of this small sample of orders. The average lead time for all shipments was more than fifty days, compared with the contractual forty-five days, but the average delay nearly doubled the contract lead time, adding forty-three days on average. In the same table, the procurement agency paid within the contracted forty-five days for only two of the five shipments. The average payment time was sixty-seven days (rounded up), and for those payments that were overdue, the average was double the contract requirement.

These results have two major implications. First, this supplier has a highly variable lead time, and the procurement office needs to either adjust safety stock to cope with the worst case or switch suppliers. Second, the purchaser may have little choice if payment time is not improved—the supplier may refuse to ship without prior payment. The payment delays may also be affecting the supplier's interest in delivering on time.

When evaluating supplier offers and planning orders and deliveries, managers need to use the expected delivery date based on past performance rather than the promised delivery date. Many supply systems take the simple average actual lead time from past deliveries and assume that it is the expected lead time. Thus, for the supplier in Table 40-9, the expected lead time would be fifty-one days (rounded up) instead of the promised forty-five days. A variation of

six days would probably be acceptable in most situations, but two of five shipments were delayed longer than fifty-one days (much longer in one case). Chapter 23 discusses options for adjusting the simple average lead time to cover substantial variation; one of these methods should be used for this supplier.

40.8 Analysis of expiry dates

Analysis of expiry dates compared to inventory levels is useful for determining how much stock is at risk of wastage. Table 40-10 shows the results of an expiry-date analysis in an illustrative country.

The analysis is done for each medicine by determining the average monthly consumption during the past year (adjusted for periods out of stock), and dividing the quantity in stock by the average monthly consumption to determine the stock position in months. Then the number of months remaining until expiry is calculated.

If the months until expiry are greater than the stock position in months, the risk of wastage should be limited. If the stock position is higher than the months until expiry, some risk exists. Multiply the months until expiration by the average monthly use to get the projected use before expiry; subtract this total from the stock on hand to obtain the quantity of stock at risk. The unit acquisition price, multiplied by the quantity at risk, yields the value of stock at risk.

Options to solve the problems identified in this analysis include increasing the use of some of the items at risk by substituting them for other commonly used items (with the consent of prescribers and dispensers). It may be possible to return some of the items to the supplier for credit, or perhaps a barter arrangement can be negotiated with another warehouse or supply system.

In the example from Table 40-10, substantial quantities of stock would clearly have been lost to expiry unless

Table 40-10 Illustrative expiry-date analysis (January 2010)

Name, strength, and form	Issue unit	Issue unit cost (USD)	Average monthly use	Current stock position (units)	Current stock position (months)	Expiry date	Months until expiry	Projected use	Quantity of stock at risk	Value of stock at risk (USD)
Cephalexin 125 mg/ 5 mL suspension	100 mL bottle	1.26	4	60	13.5	June 2010	5	22	38	47.88
Cephalexin 250 mg	Tablet	0.0526	333	8,200	24.6	August 2010	7	2,333	5,867	308.60
Chlorhexidine gluconate 5% solution	5 L bottle	30.5	1	45	45	April 2012	15	15	30	915.00
Chlorpheniramine 2 mg/5 mL elixir	1 L bottle	3	8	140	16.8	September 2011	8	67	73	219.00
Codeine 30 mg	Tablet	0.0555	52	104	2	November 2011	22	18	40	2.22
Dexamethasone injection, 4 mg/mL, 5 mL	5 mL vial	0.425	17	290	17.4	February 2010	1	17	273	116.03
Diazepam injection, 10 mg/2 mL	2 mL ampoule	0.1116	150	1,300	8.7	August 2011	7	1,050	250	27.90
Erythromycin base salts 250 mg	Tablet	0.0342	333	6,000	18	November 2011	10	3,333	2,667	91.21
Lidocaine 2% jelly	15 g tube	1.035	20	640	32	June 2012	17	340	300	310.50
Naloxone HCl injection, 0.02 mg/mL, 2 mL	2 mL ampoule	0.406	3	110	44	December 2011	11	28	83	33.70
Pancuronium bromide injection, 2 mg/mL	2 mL ampoule	1.148	4	50	12	December 2011	11	46	4	4.59
Penicillin G benzathine injection, 2.4 million IU	Ampoule	0.3228	39	1,990	50.5	June 2012	29	1,143	847	273.41
Penicillin G Na injection, powder, 1 MU	Vial	0.1399	33	1,000	30	May 2012	16	533	467	65.33
Phytomenadione injection, 1 mg/1 mL	Ampoule	0.1807	83	2,000	24.2	December 2011	11	909	1,091	197.14
Water for injection, 10 mL	Vial	0.06	117	400	3.4	April 2010	3	350	50	3.00
Total value at risk										**2,615.52**

IU = international units.

action was taken. Note that for cephalexin tablets and injections, action was needed quickly because of the rapidly approaching expiration date. It was already too late to use up dexamethasone or water for injection. The chlorhexidine gluconate presented the highest financial risk (almost one-third of the total value at risk).

For some of the items at risk, increasing use through substitution might be feasible. For example, cephalexin tablets could be substituted for erythromycin. Penicillin injection might replace cephalosporins (if they are commonly used). Substitution would be a less appropriate solution for medicines such as codeine, diazepam, or phytomenadione; probably the best solution for these items (and for most overstocks) would be a barter arrangement with a neighboring supply system.

The real value of expiry-date analysis is that, if used regularly, it can help avoid a situation like the one illustrated by detecting potential wastage problems before they are insoluble.

40.9 Hidden-cost analysis

The concept of hidden costs was introduced in Chapter 18. Hidden costs are those costs that occur because of poor supplier performance; they are not obvious in the invoice price.

The total cost of purchasing an item from a specific supplier is the sum of the quoted price, any shipping and handling costs, and any hidden costs. In comparing quotations from different suppliers, procurement officers should consider the expected hidden costs for each supplier, based on past performance. One way to do this is to calculate the hidden cost ratio (hidden costs divided by visible costs). Visible costs are the sum of cost, insurance, and freight (CIF) for all past orders. Hidden costs are the sum of the following—

- Commissions for local agents
- Cost of late deliveries (including air freight for emergency needs, use of more expensive alternatives, higher cost for emergency replacements, and so forth)
- Cost of delivery errors (sum of costs incurred because of short shipments, incorrect medicines shipped, shipments delivered to wrong port, additional port costs because of lack of proper documents, and so forth)
- Value of losses caused by poor packaging
- Replacement cost of unusable medicines (short shelf lives, disintegrated medicines, and so forth)

The value of cost-saving contributions (deferred payment terms, suggestions for less expensive dosage forms, and so forth) is subtracted from this total.

In the example illustrated in Figure 40-4, assume that Supplier A has provided pharmaceuticals to a supply system at a net CIF cost of USD 100,000 (the visible cost). A review

Figure 40-4   Impact of hidden cost on total cost

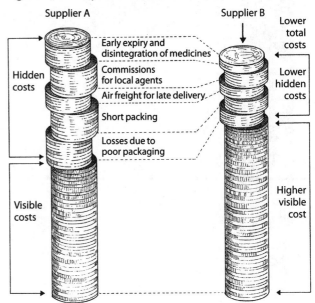

TOTAL COST = VISIBLE COST + HIDDEN COST

of the procurement office's records might show that for these purchases, the following hidden costs were incurred—

- Unusable medicines (replacement cost for tablets that disintegrated in transit; expired products not replaced by supplier) = USD 6,000
- Commission for local agents (3 percent) = USD 3,000
- Late deliveries (air freight and higher price for temporary emergency stocks) = USD 9,000
- Delivery errors (2 percent average short packing) = USD 2,000
- Losses from poor packaging (not covered by insurance) = USD 3,000

Based on this experience with Supplier A, the procurement office calculates a hidden cost ratio of 23 percent, derived from (USD 6,000 + USD 3,000 + USD 9,000 + USD 2,000 + USD 3,000) / USD 100,000. This information can then be used to project total costs of later orders for comparison with competing suppliers. A hidden cost ratio of 23 percent for Supplier A means that the total cost for the pharmaceutical supply system will be about USD 1.23 for every USD 1.00 quoted by Supplier A for a product. If Supplier A quotes a CIF price of USD 100 for an item, the total expected cost would be USD 123. If Supplier B quotes a CIF price of USD 110, but Supplier B has an estimated hidden cost ratio of only 5 percent, the expected total cost (USD 115) would make Supplier B the most cost-effective choice.

Precision in calculating hidden cost estimates is rarely possible, but criteria for reviewing supplier performance might include hidden costs as one aspect of comparison. If large differences in hidden cost ratios exist between two suppliers, based on past performance, this might be a deciding factor in the choice. As discussed in Chapter 18, if hidden costs are to be considered in evaluating supplier offers, this fact should be clearly specified in procurement evaluation criteria and in tender documents. ∎

References and further readings

★ = Key readings.

★ Bootman, J. L., R. J. Townsend, and W. F. McGhan, eds. 2005. *Principles of Pharmacoeconomics*. 3rd ed. Cincinnati, Ohio: Harvey Whitney Books.

Bragg, S. M. 2004. *Inventory Best Practices*. Hoboken, N.J.: John Wiley & Sons.

★ Creese, A., and D. Parker, eds. 1994. *Cost Analysis in Primary Health Care: A Training Manual for Programme Managers*. Geneva: World Health Organization. <http://www.who.int/immunization_financing/data/methods/en/caphc_creese.pdf>

Freund, D. A., and R. S. Dittus. 1992. Principles of Pharmacoeconomic Analysis of Drug Therapy. *Pharmacoeconomics* 1(1):20–31.

MSH (Management Sciences for Health). 2010. *International Drug Price Indicator Guide, 2009 Edition*. (Updated annually.) Cambridge, Mass.: MSH. <http://erc.msh.org>

MSH/RPM (Management Sciences for Health/Rational Pharmaceutical Management Project). 1996. *Prescription Analysis Software System—User's Manual*. Washington, D.C.: MSH/RPM.

★ ———. 1995. *Rapid Pharmaceutical Management Assessment: An Indicator-Based Approach*. Arlington, Va.: MSH/RPM. <http://erc.msh.org/toolkit/Tool.cfm?lang=1&TID=197>

OECS/PPS (Organisation of Eastern Caribbean States' Pharmaceutical Procurement Service). 2006. Formulary 06/07. Castries, St. Lucia: OECS/PPS.

Shah, S., N. Konduri, and R. Gunturu. 2007. *Taking Action on Antimicrobial Resistance: Experience of Pharmacy and Therapeutics Committee in a Kenyan Hospital*. Presentation at the 67th FIP World Congress "From Anecdote to Evidence: Pharmacists Helping Patients Make the Best Use of Medicines," Beijing, China, September 3.

USP (United States Pharmacopeia). 2010. *USP Dictionary*. (Updated annually.) Rockville, Md.: USP.

WHOCC (WHO Collaborating Centre for Drug Statistics Methodology). 2011. Anatomical therapeutic chemical/defined daily dose (ATC/DDD) classification index. (Updated regularly.) Oslo: WHOCC. <http://www.whocc.no/atcddd/>

Glossary

ABC analysis: Classification of inventory items into three categories (A, B, and C) according to the value of their annual use, which is useful for analyzing medicine consumption and use, comparing actual versus planned purchases, justifying procurement budgets, guiding procurement patterns, and setting priorities for stock management.

Analysis of expiry dates: The analysis of stock position compared to expiry dates in the supply system inventory to avoid or minimize losses caused by wastage.

Lead-time analysis: The analysis of supplier lead time (interval between decision to order and receipt of stock), to help in selecting the best suppliers for future procurements, and payment lead time (interval between receipt of goods and payment to supplier), to monitor procurement office compliance with contracts.

Pipeline analysis: Analysis of the logistics system to identify the optimal location and quantities of stock in the distribution network, which serves as the basis for devising more efficient ordering and stock-keeping policies and procedures.

Price comparison analysis: The comparison of a supply system's costs and prices to those of other programs or systems; for example, comparison of procurement prices to those paid by neighboring supply systems or obtainable internationally, or of sales prices to prices in the local private and NGO sectors.

Technical efficiency: Using inputs to achieve the greatest output for a given cost or to achieve a given output at the lowest cost. For pharmaceutical management, this includes therapeutic efficiency (selection and use) and operational efficiency (management of procurement and distribution):

Therapeutic category analysis: The analysis of expenditures by therapeutic category, for comparison with morbidity patterns and public health priorities, as a means of focusing cost control efforts:

VEN system: A system of categorizing medicines by their public health value (vital, essential, and nonessential), which can be useful in setting purchasing priorities, determining safety stock levels, and directing staff activities.

ASSESSMENT GUIDE

Indicators related to analytical techniques

- Numbers of medicines and value of average consumption for medicines in classes A, B, and C from ABC analysis
- Value of unplanned purchases (items not on original quantification list) as a percentage of value of total purchases
- Average supply system acquisition price as a percentage of average international price for indicator medicines
- Average medical stores sales price as a percentage of local wholesale sales price for indicator medicines—private and NGO sectors
- Average public-sector pharmacy sales price as a percentage of local retail pharmacy sales price for indicator medicines
- Ratio of net sales (or value of distributed medicines) to inventory—also called "inventory turnover"
- Operating margin on total sales—the value of total sales, minus the cost of goods sold, divided by the total sales
- Inventory-holding costs as percentage of average inventory value
- Purchasing costs as a percentage of average inventory value
- Average lead time and payment time for each major supplier
- Value of medicines at risk of expiry as a percentage of inventory value

Total cost analysis

Data elements that contribute to a total cost analysis include—

- Availability of expenditure reports or budget estimates of operating costs in warehouses and purchasing offices
- Value of accounts receivable from patients and from other facilities
- Value of bad-debt write-offs
- Value of total purchases and total sales (or value of medicines distributed)
- Value of cost of goods sold (or distributed)
- Beginning and ending inventory value for the fiscal year for major warehouses and health facilities, and average inventory value
- Inventory shrinkage: the sum of beginning inventory value plus purchases, minus the sum of cost of goods sold plus ending inventory value

- Value of any donations received or stock returns from clients
- Value of operating costs—predictable and incremental—for stock management functions (ideally at each major level of the system)
- Value of expired or wasted stock removed during the year and any such stock remaining
- Value of operating costs associated with pharmaceutical transport
- Value of operating costs—predictable and incremental—for purchasing functions
- Value of incremental costs associated with managing tenders
- Value of incremental costs of emergency purchases to cover shortages
- Value of lower-level purchases outside supply system (for centralized procurement systems)

Analytical capacity in supply system

- Which departments or offices in the supply system are responsible for analyzing recurrent costs and developing cost-control strategies?
- What kinds of analyses and reports are produced (and how frequently are they produced)?
- Are computers and spreadsheet software available for analyzing costs in the pharmaceutical supply system?
- What kinds of software with analytical and reporting capacity, in addition to spreadsheets, are available?

VEN analysis

- Does a two- or three-tier system exist for prioritizing procurement according to public health value (similar to VEN or VN)?
- If no formal system exists, how are priorities determined when funds are insufficient to purchase all medicines requested?

ABC analysis

- Has an ABC analysis been done recently of medicine consumption or purchases (and if not, does the system have the data and the capacity needed to do this analysis)?
- How do use and expenditures compare with health priorities?
- How is information from ABC analysis used to improve purchasing and inventory management?

Therapeutic category analysis

- Have recent efforts been made to analyze consumption and expenditures by therapeutic category (and if so, how is the information used)?
- How are the merits of one pharmaceutical product compared with those of other products in medicine selection and procurement?
- Does the purchasing office sometimes tender by therapeutic category or subcategory rather than for specific medicines?

Price comparison analysis

- What sources of data are available for price comparison analysis? (See also price comparison indicators above.)

Lead-time and payment-time analysis

- How are lead times and payment times tracked and used by the purchasing office?

Expiry-date analysis

- How does the supply system track expiration dates? Are reports prepared on the expiry status of medicines in stock?
- What is done about stock that will likely expire before it can be used?

Hidden-cost analysis

- Are hidden costs calculated for regular suppliers to the supply system, and if not, are records adequate to compile the information?

CHAPTER 41

Financial planning and management

SUMMARY

Effective financial planning and management are vital for the successful generation, safekeeping, and use of funds to achieve program objectives.

Many government budgeting and accounting systems operate on a cash basis, recording a transaction only when cash is involved. Private-sector or semi-autonomous government programs, including many revolving drug funds (RDFs), use an accrual system, which also records noncash transactions such as medicines issued. Public-sector managers can complement government accounting systems with elements of an accrual system to support more effective and efficient program management.

Long-range financial plans include projections of funding and expenditures over several years and thus facilitate long-range planning for health services. For an RDF, a long-range plan can project the point in the future when revenues from medicine sales will be sufficient to cover medicine program expenses. The realization of projected revenues depends on the development and implementation of detailed pricing strategies for medicines.

The first-year figures from a "rolling" long-range plan provide the basis for an annual budget, which is used to plan and control spending for the current year. Whereas government budgets may be based on fixed funding, an RDF budget is flexible, with the level of expenditure dependent on sales revenue. A cash flow forecast helps ensure the availability of sufficient cash to cover anticipated obligations each month. Cost analysis is used to measure program efficiency and to help set prices.

Principles for effective financial control include—

- Dividing duties among different individuals
- Regulating transactions through the use of written procedures, budgets, and purchase-request systems
- Recording and monitoring all transactions
- Instituting both random and scheduled third-party auditing

The accounting system should produce the following standard reports on a monthly and annual basis—

- Budget performance report
- Income and expense statement
- Cost-center expense reports
- Balance sheet
- Summary of accounts payable and receivable

41.1 Introduction

Government allocations continue to be a major source of financing for pharmaceutical supply in many countries. Although ministries of finance and of planning (see Chapter 11) traditionally have made public-expenditure decisions, program managers can often lobby for more funding for their programs and activities. They are better able to do so if they understand the issues involved in public-sector resource allocation, can argue effectively for greater investments in health, and can demonstrate responsible and efficient use of existing resources. However, the trend in many resource-limited countries has been to decentralize health services, including pharmaceutical management. In a decentralized environment, local governments and health facilities become more responsible for managing services and mobilizing resources, with the role of the central government focusing more on regulation.

With public financing of pharmaceutical supply, managers of pharmaceutical programs are responsible for ensuring that resources are used in the best way possible, with the goal of achieving program objectives. Financial management is vital to this role. Managers need to plan, control, and monitor the generation, safekeeping, and use of funds, and they must be able to provide appropriate financial reports to government authorities and donors. This chapter is designed to provide managers with a working knowledge of key financial management concepts and skills.

Pharmaceutical programs generally define their objectives in terms of services provided. However, financial objectives are becoming increasingly important as programs try to maintain or expand services, often in the face of reduced funding. Programs need to seek increased government and donor funding, generate additional revenues from cost sharing, and be efficient and cost-effective in providing services. To achieve these objectives, program managers must be able to—

- Prepare long-range plans to project the need for services, devise the most cost-effective way of providing them, outline the resources needed, and help secure government and donor funding
- Prepare and communicate program policies and procedures
- Set sales prices that are affordable, competitive, and meet program cost-sharing goals (discussed in Chapter 9)
- Prepare and use budgets to plan and contain expenses

- Prepare cash flow forecasts to ensure the availability of cash to cover anticipated financial obligations
- Analyze costs to assess cost-effectiveness and monitor efficiency
- Control and manage the collection, safekeeping, and spending of funds
- Keep proper accounting records and prepare reports for management, government, and donors

Public-sector financial management systems, as traditionally designed, are often less than ideal for managing pharmaceutical programs—especially with regard to collection of sales revenue, which is often a new and unfamiliar task for government ministries. Given such limitations, managers of government programs may need to develop and use complementary systems to help them manage their resources effectively. New directions in public health–sector management also include decentralizing health care services, and adapting the traditional central medical store (CMS)—traditionally operated as part of the ministry of health—to serve as an autonomous or semi-autonomous supply organization operating on a commercial, but non-profit, basis (see Chapter 8). In addition, governments more often incorporate private-sector options in pharmaceutical supply management, such as contracting out specific services, which must be accounted for within the budgeting and financial planning system.

This chapter describes both how to get the best results with existing government financial management systems and how to develop complementary procedures to enhance

efficiency. A system that combines both approaches should provide a good basis for effective financial management. The chapter presents sample budgets and reports based on the hypothetical case of a government pharmaceutical program that is beginning to sell and account for medicines, as in an autonomous revolving drug fund (see Chapter 13). These examples are each inter-related, and the figures can therefore be followed from one to another.

41.2 Getting the best from a government finance system

In recent years, many government departments have begun to follow the private-sector principle of demonstrating "value for money" through the effective and efficient use of resources. They have often been hampered, however, by the limitations of budgeting and accounting systems designed only to control spending. In addition, a changing public-sector environment, featuring health care reforms such as decentralized responsibilities and autonomous management, greatly affects how a country carries out its health-sector financial management.

For example, vertical health programs that focus on targeted health interventions, such as HIV/AIDS or tuberculosis control, are usually financed by donors and operate in parallel to the government pharmaceutical supply system. Governments have recognized the inherent inefficiency in this parallel system and have made integrating vertical health programs into the government system a priority

---

Country Study 41-1
Negotiating prices for services to vertical programs in East Africa

A revolving drug fund frequently subsidizes vertical health programs when they operate in parallel. Often, storage space and other resources consumed by vertical programs are 50 percent of the total, whereas they pay only a minimal fee for those services. For example, in the recent experience of a national central medical store (CMS) revolving drug fund in East Africa, vertical programs used 60 percent of storage space but paid fees of only 6 to 10 percent of the value of their supplies to the CMS. This situation meant that on the remaining 40 percent of activities, the CMS had to charge a 50 percent markup to cover costs.

Vertical programs often deliver supplies to the CMS without giving distribution details, resulting in supplies that take up space for months or years. A monthly storage-fee invoice to the vertical programs should help alleviate this practice. Also, vertical programs should

meet the full cost of disposing of their expired stock. To avoid the inequalities between resources used by vertical programs and what they pay for those resources, the CMS needs to negotiate a realistic memorandum of understanding (MOU) with the vertical health programs, supported by reliable, up-to-date activity costs for the following—

- Procurement
- Clearing and forwarding
- Storage
- Distribution
- Disposal of expired stock

The MOU should be based on vertical program contributions to the CMS that are relative to the resources they consume, and the charges must be specified in detail.

Source: Rational Pharmaceutical Management Plus Program/ Management Sciences for Health.

objective. Resource-intensive functions such as procurement, quality assurance, storage, and physical distribution may be integrated under the essential medicines program, whereas financing, quantification, and monitoring may stay under the control of the vertical program. Progress on integration has been mixed. In some cases, cost savings and efficiency gains have been higher than anticipated, but frequently, integrating health programs has been restricted by program-level resistance and perceived weaknesses in government management of the system. Integration can provide savings and benefits, but is reliant on strong government commitment to the process and the willingness of programs to give up some or all of their activities (see Country Study 41-1).

Government pharmaceutical programs generally suffer from the same problem: the accounting system keeps track of expenditures for pharmaceutical procurement, but it does not record the value of medicines distributed or lost. The main problem is usually that the government accounting system operates on a cash basis, recording a transaction only when cash is received or spent. Under such a system, medicines purchased on credit are not recorded in the accounting records until payment is made, and medicine issues are not recorded at all if cash is not received. A cash-based system does not record donated medicines or equipment, medicines issued free of charge, medicine losses, purchases and sales on credit, accounts receivable, accounts payable, or depreciation, nor does it maintain an accounting record of the stock of medicines. Without such information, managing a program properly is almost impossible.

A private-sector program, or a semi-autonomous government program such as an RDF, is more likely to use an accrual-basis accounting system. Such a system records all transactions at the time they are made. For example, a purchase of pharmaceuticals on credit is recorded when the products are received, increasing the balance in the pharmaceutical stock account and creating a liability to the supplier. When the supplier is paid, the liability is canceled and the cash balance is reduced. All noncash transactions, such as donations of medicines, depreciation, and stock write-offs, are also recorded.

Figure 41-1 compares a traditional government budget (cash basis) with an RDF budget (accrual basis). The two budgets are based on the same events, except that the RDF budget includes noncash transactions. The government budget for 2005 shows pharmaceutical purchases of 230,000 U.S. dollars (USD) as an input to the system but shows no figure for services delivered as an output. The RDF budget, however, shows the projected cost of pharmaceuticals issued (USD 250,000) as a measure of program output; the USD 230,000 of pharmaceutical purchases is recorded in a separate pharmaceutical stock account.

Unlike the government budget, the RDF budget also takes into account the value of income received from vertical programs, the cost of expired or lost medicines, and depreciation of fixed assets. In the government cash budget, for example, operating income is shown as USD 260,000 (based on a government allocation of USD 135,000 plus projected sales revenue of USD 125,000), which will be used to purchase pharmaceuticals valued at USD 230,000 and to pay expenses of USD 30,000. Total operating income in the RDF budget, however, includes income received from services provided through vertical programs (USD 185,000) and sales revenue of USD 125,000, for a total of USD 310,000; this operating income will be used to distribute USD 250,000 worth of medicines (cost of medicines issued), cover stock losses of USD 12,500 (cost of expired medicines), pay operating expenses of USD 30,000, fund depreciation of USD 10,000, and generate an operating surplus (income less expenses) of USD 7,500. The assets that represent that surplus and the reserve of USD 10,000 for depreciation appear as an increase of USD 17,500 in pharmaceutical stock from the previous year (see closing balance in the pharmaceutical stock account in Figure 41-1).

Note also that the format of the RDF budget provides more useful management information by grouping categories; for example, showing the deficit created by buying and selling the medicines in the pharmaceutical account. In both the government and the RDF formats, the actual income and expenses for the previous year are shown next to the budget figures for comparison.

When possible, an accrual basis (which recognizes receivables and payables without a cash exchange) should always be used. However, if a cash basis must be used because of government rules, elements of an accrual system should be used to complement the government accounting figures and provide more complete information. Priority should be given to those elements that, when adjusted, would have the greatest effect on the overall figures. The most important element is generally maintaining complete accounts for pharmaceutical transactions.

In order to track pharmaceutical transactions on an accrual basis, accounts should be opened for stock, accounts payable, and accounts receivable. This double-entry system reflects each transaction in two accounts. The pharmaceutical stock account starts with the stock balance and all subsequent pharmaceutical transactions are reflected in the account, so that at any given time the balance reflects the value of stock on hand. Medicines bought on credit increase the stock balance in the stock account and create a liability in accounts payable. Medicines received as donations (valued at the equivalent local cost) increase the stock balance in the stock account and are credited to a donations-in-kind account. The cost of lost, damaged, or expired medicines reduces the stock balance in the stock account and is debited to a medicine losses account. The cost of pharmaceuticals issued or sold reduces the stock balance in the stock account and is debited to

Figure 41-1 Comparison of traditional government and RDF budgets

CENTRAL MEDICAL STORES Traditional Government Budget (Cash Basis)	Latest Estimate* 2004	Budget 2005
RECURRENT BUDGET		
EXPENDITURES		
Salaries	18,000	19,000
Vehicle operations	2,500	2,700
Other transport	1,500	1,600
Packaging and labeling	3,000	3,300
Utilities	2,000	2,200
Office supplies	1,000	1,200
Pharmaceutical purchases	160,000	230,000
GROSS EXPENDITURES	188,000	260,000
APPROPRIATIONS IN AID		
Sales revenue	0	125,000
NET EXPENDITURES	188,000	135,000
(Government allocation)		
CAPITAL BUDGET		
Equipment	5,000	10,000
Other transport	1,500	1,600

CENTRAL MEDICAL STORES Revolving Drug Fund (Accrual Basis)	Latest Estimate* 2004	Budget 2005
OPERATING BUDGET		
INCOME FROM VERTICAL PROGRAMS		
Procurement	25,740	16,650
Clearing and forwarding	51,480	33,300
Storage	57,200	37,000
Distribution	151,580	98,050
Total income (A)	286,000	185,000
PHARMACEUTICAL ACCOUNT		
Sales revenue	0	125,000
Less cost of medicines issued	240,000	250,000
	(240,000)	(125,000)
Less cost of expired medicines, etc.	15,000	12,500
Surplus/deficit on pharmaceutical account (B)	(255,000)	(137,500)
EXPENSES		
Salaries	18,000	19,000
Vehicle operations	2,500	2,700
Other transport	1,500	1,600
Packaging and labeling	3,000	3,300
Utilities	2,000	2,200
Office supplies	1,000	1,200
Total operating expenditures	28,000	30,000
Depreciation	0	10,000
Total expenses (C)	28,000	40,000
INCOME LESS EXPENSES (A + B – C)	3,000	7,500
CAPITAL BUDGET		
Equipment	5,000	10,000
PATIENT VOLUME	520,000	500,000

PHARMACEUTICAL STOCK ACCOUNT	2004	2005
Opening balance	85,000	88,000
Purchases	160,000	230,000
Donations	98,000	50,000
	343,000	368,000
Less cost of issues	240,000	250,000
Less medicine losses	15,000	12,500
Closing balance	88,000	105,500

* Because the budget must usually be completed before the end of the current year, a latest estimate of the current year is made for comparison purposes. The latest estimate for the current year is typically compiled from actual figures for the first nine months and a revised estimate for the last three months.

a cost-of-medicines-issued or cost-of-sales account. All transactions are valued at the purchase cost, and the balance in the stock account therefore equals the cost of stock on hand. An average cost should be used in the stock account for items purchased from multiple suppliers at different prices or from the same supplier at different times and for donated goods. Sales prices are normally based on these average costs. Also, stock in transit and in quarantine should be identified separately from stock on hand to avoid overstatement of availability.

Although the cost of expired medicines is often a small percentage of the total budget, the cost of disposing of expired and damaged pharmaceuticals can be enormous because of regulatory requirements and lack of disposal facilities. In addition, there is usually a hidden—but substantial—cost for storing expired medicines. Government regulations often fail to recognize medicine expiry as an integral part of pharmaceutical management; for example, the same regulations authorize writing off medicine expiry as writing off other losses (such as truck tires). Also, RDFs frequently do not include an allocation for the physical disposal of expired medicines. In such circumstances, disposal of expired medicines often has very low priority, and expired stock tends to accumulate in the storage area for months or even years. As a result, if storage is limited, it may become necessary to rent additional space to accommodate new supplies.

The cost of pharmaceuticals issued can be calculated by recording the cost of each medicine at the time of issue, but this procedure usually requires a computerized inventory system. The figure can be calculated manually, however, by adding the cost of pharmaceuticals purchased and donated to the cost of the opening pharmaceutical stock and deducting the cost of the closing pharmaceutical stock. Provided that the same method is used to value both opening and closing stocks, the resulting figure represents the cost of medicines used plus the cost of expired, missing, and damaged medicines.

The other adjustments that can be made to produce an accrual-based report from a government account relate to depreciation and operating expenses. However, because a government usually replaces fixed assets through capital budgets, these adjustments are probably not worth making unless the program will have to replace assets from self-generated resources in the future. Also, bringing operating expenses, such as salaries or electricity, onto an accrual basis may not be worthwhile if the amounts are relatively small and the expenses are paid on a regular basis.

The remaining sections of this chapter describe other elements of good financial management that should be in place, whether a program is governmental or autonomous. Some of these elements relate to the planning and management of sales revenues, which apply only to those programs that currently sell pharmaceuticals or plan to in the future.

41.3 Long-range financial planning

It is important to have a long-range view of both program objectives and activities and the resources needed to carry them out. A long-range plan for any program must include a realistic financial plan showing what funding is anticipated and how it will be spent. Without a financial plan, unachievable objectives may be set. A long-range plan might cover five years and should be a "rolling" plan—updated each year for a new five-year period beginning with the current year. The plan is broken down to show what activities will be carried out each year, as well as each year's estimated funding and expenditures. Program planning and financial planning are inseparable, and both program and financial managers must be involved in developing the financial plan.

A long-range plan is just as necessary for a grant-funded pharmaceutical program as it is for an RDF. With a grant-funded program, a long-range plan attempts to forecast services based on estimated levels of fixed funding and, at the same time, to justify additional funding. With an RDF, it is a plan for both revenue generation and services, with each being completely dependent on the other. Often, a program is funded through a mixture of grant and revenue monies. For example, administration could be covered by a grant, whereas the purchase of medicines is funded from revenue. With decentralization, funding usually goes to the health facilities to buy supplies from the CMS. Often, sales prices must cover all operating expenses and capital expenditures. Donors may finance some capital expenditures.

In summary, long-range financial planning is important because it results in—

- A documented summary of results compared with the previous year's plans and objectives
- An assessment of resources required for necessary services
- A review of the financial feasibility of plans and a determination of whether more funds will be needed or activities will have to be reduced
- A plan for long-term resource generation and investment
- Greater ability to seek funding successfully
- Prioritization of essential program activities
- A plan to obtain resources when they are needed
- A tool that can be used to set periodic programmatic and financial benchmarks

Figure 41-2 shows an example of a long-range financial plan for a grant-funded government pharmaceutical program that is to be converted to a revenue-funded RDF over a three-year period. The structure of the plan serves both types of program equally well. All long-range financial plans must build in a factor for annual inflation, as this example does. For expenditures on imported goods, changes in exchange rates

Figure 41-2   Five-year financial plan

CENTRAL MEDICAL STORE
Five-Year Financial Plan 2009–14
OPERATING STATEMENT (USD)

	2009 Actual	%	2010 Planned	%	2011 Planned	%	2012 Planned	%	2013 Planned	%	2014 Planned	%
SALES												
Medicines	805,000	81.0	901,600	81.3	1,000,800	83.0	1,180,900	83.4	1,393,500	83.7	1,644,300	84.1
Equipment	189,000	19.0	207,900	18.7	205,000	17.0	235,800	16.6	271,100	16.3	311,800	15.9
TOTAL SALES	994,000	100.0	1,109,500	100.0	1,205,800	100.0	1,416,700	100.0	1,664,600	100.0	1,956,100	100.0
Less: Cost of goods sold*	825,000	83.0	930,000	83.8	1,016,900	84.3	1,211,800	85.5	1,430,000	85.9	1,698,000	86.8
Less: Cost of expired medicines, etc.	12,400	1.2	9,800	0.9	9,900	0.8	8,000	0.6	8,500	0.5	9,600	0.5
GROSS MARGIN	156,600	15.8	169,700	15.3	179,000	14.8	196,900	13.9	226,100	13.6	248,500	12.7
Other income	19,800	2.0	22,200	2.0	24,900	2.1	31,200	2.2	43,000	2.6	53,500	2.7
	176,400	17.8	191,900	17.3	203,900	16.9	228,100	16.1	269,100	16.2	302,000	15.4
Less: Packing materials	5,000	0.5	5,000	0.5	7,800	0.6	8,800	0.6	9,900	0.6	12,000	0.6
Less: Distribution costs	34,800	3.5	38,800	3.5	41,200	3.4	49,000	3.5	56,000	3.4	68,900	3.5
CONTRIBUTION	136,600	13.8	148,100	13.3	154,900	12.8	170,300	12.0	203,200	12.2	221,100	11.3
GENERAL EXPENSES												
Personnel	69,700	7.0	74,000	6.7	79,600	6.6	89,000	6.3	98,000	5.9	107,000	5.5
Board of trustees	1,300	0.1	1,600	0.1	2,400	0.2	2,600	0.2	3,000	0.2	3,400	0.2
Training & recruitment	3,500	0.4	3,600	0.3	4,100	0.3	4,500	0.3	5,200	0.3	5,800	0.3
Services & utilities	17,900	1.8	19,500	1.8	20,100	1.7	21,500	1.5	24,900	1.5	27,000	1.4
Office & general	16,900	1.7	18,300	1.6	19,500	1.6	22,000	1.6	25,600	1.5	28,900	1.5
Depreciation	19,900	2.0	22,500	2.0	23,200	1.9	24,900	1.8	32,000	1.9	47,000	2.4
TOTAL GENERAL EXPENSES	129,200	13.0	139,500	12.6	148,900	12.3	164,500	11.6	188,700	11.3	219,100	11.2
NET OPERATING RESULT	7,600	0.8	8,600	0.8	6,000	0.5	5,800	0.4	14,500	0.9	2,000	0.1
CAPITAL PLAN												
Buildings	0		0		1,500		4,500		9,200		8,500	
Vehicles	6,000		3,000		0		3,000		4,800		4,800	
Equipment	2,300		3,600		1,400		1,600		2,100		3,300	
TOTAL	8,300		6,600		2,900		9,100		16,100		16,600	
FUNDING												
Revolving fund	2,300		3,600		2,900		4,300		6,800		8,500	
Donors	6,000		3,000				4,800		9,300		8,100	
TOTAL	8,300		6,600		2,900		9,100		16,100		16,600	

* Cost of goods sold is expected to increase with volume from additional facilities served by the CMS and with inflation—estimated at 5 percent annually.

over time must be considered as well. Box 41-1 gives further details on adjusting for price levels and exchange rates.

The long-range financial plan shown in Figure 41-2 projects increased year-to-year sale of medicines. The price markup is calculated to cover all costs (including cost of medicines, packing, distribution, medicine expiry, and general expenses) and leave a nominal net operating profit. To meet nonprofit criteria, the net profit would normally not exceed 1 percent of sales revenues. Although general operating expenses will increase over time, the rate of increase should be less than the growth in sales revenue because administrative costs are composed of fixed or semivariable components. For example, whereas personnel costs increase from USD 69,700 in 2009 to USD 107,000 in 2014, the percentage of personnel costs in relation to sales falls from 7.0 percent in 2009 to 5.5 percent in 2014. By limiting the increase in general expenses to a rate below the increase in sales, the CMS can progressively reduce the gross margin charged (from 15.8 percent in 2009 to 12.7 percent in 2014) and increase the percentage of revenues spent on pharmaceutical supplies (cost of goods sold) from 83.0 percent in 2009 to 86.8 percent in 2014.

Box 41-1
Adjusting for price levels and exchange rates

Any comparison of funding amounts at different points in time requires consideration of the possible effect of inflation and changes in the exchange rate. Such situations include budgeting and forecasting future expenditure needs, pricing in revolving drug funds, and analyzing expenditure trends.

Inflation

Inflation can arise when the cost of imported goods rises because of rising world prices or exchange rate depreciation. Inflation also arises when the growth in a country's expenditure or consumption of goods and services exceeds the growth in its supply or production of goods and services.

Changes in the price level make the comparison of expenditures in different years more complicated: the purchasing power of a given budget depends on the price level during that year. Expenditures that are not adjusted to account for changes in the price level are called nominal or current-price expenditures; when they are adjusted to reflect changes in the price level, they are called real or constant-price expenditures. To compare expenditures in different years, they can be translated into the same "price units" using a gross domestic product (GDP) deflator series, which is usually available from the ministry of economic planning or another central government agency. In these series, one year is chosen as the base year, and other years are expressed as values relative to the base year.

The accompanying figure shows the evolution of health expenditures in an illustrative country, Kenya, over time, in both current prices and constant prices. Using current prices, expenditures appear to increase from 2005 to 2010. However, when expenditures are translated into constant dollars, in this case using 2007 as the base year, it becomes clear that the real value of expenditures has

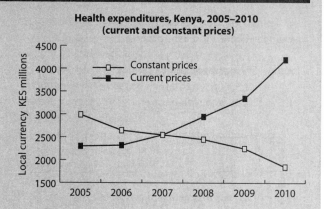

Health expenditures, Kenya, 2005–2010 (current and constant prices)

actually fallen from 3,000 million of the local currency in 2005–06 to 1,800 million in 2009–10.

Exchange rates

The exchange rate is the price of foreign currency that equalizes the balance of payments. It is the price at which the inflow of foreign currency from exports and foreign aid is equal to the demand for foreign currency to purchase imports. The exchange rate may be fixed (determined by the government) or flexible (determined in foreign exchange markets).

Changes in the exchange rate over time can make expenditure projections more complicated when a significant proportion of total expenditures is on imported goods (such as medicines). That is often the case in countries undergoing structural adjustment, where the exchange rate may be experiencing large, somewhat unpredictable changes. In those circumstances, it is often useful to separate the local currency and foreign currency items in the budget, so that the foreign currency costs can be updated more easily in response to new information. The ministry of health or planning may be able to provide assistance in making projections about the exchange rate.

41.4 Costing

Cost analysis is an important management tool that allows managers to measure the efficiency of their programs and price products and services equitably to their clients. Efficiency can be understood as getting the most output for a given quantity of resources (for example, purchasing more pharmaceuticals with a constant budget) or achieving a given level of output at minimum cost (such as treating a bacterial infection at lowest cost). Efficiency concepts are discussed in more detail in Chapter 10. By determining the cost of each unit of output (which, in a pharmaceutical supply system, is the cost of medicines and services provided), managers can evaluate the efficiency of their programs over time or make comparisons with other organizations. Cost figures can also be used to estimate the financial effect of serving various patient volumes, different patient types, or different disease types, as well as to set prices. Total cost analysis is a good tool for assessing all costs in an entire pharmaceutical system (Chapter 40).

The starting place in determining medicine costs is the original purchase price of each medicine. Price varies over time, depending on the supplier, the date of purchase, the unit of purchase, and the volume of purchase. The costing method depends on the purpose of the exercise: an average cost can be used for making comparisons, and the cost of the most recent purchase should be used for setting a sales price. If significant transport costs are involved for imported medicines, they should be added to the purchase cost of the particular medicines supplied.

Other costs, including the transport charges for in-country distribution, are best allocated evenly over the total number of dispensing outlets, particularly if the cost information is used to set prices. Adding high transport costs to the cost of medicines sent to remote places is not equitable, especially because the patients in those areas are often poor.

If the total operating costs of the pharmaceutical supply system amount to 10 percent of the total cost of the medicines distributed, the total cost of each medicine is its purchase price plus its in-country transport costs (for imported medicines) plus 10 percent. A charge for depreciation, expiry, and obsolescence losses should be included in the total.

If medicines are being repackaged, the cost of such procedures may be attributed to the specific medicines as direct costs. However, if the overall costs are low (say, less than 10 percent of the total medicine costs), allocating them to individual medicine prices may not be worthwhile because such costing can be complicated and lengthy. Donated resources should be included at the equivalent local cost so that the full cost of each medicine is calculated. Finally, for costing and pricing to work properly, the accounting system should be on an accrual basis, or all bills must be paid promptly; otherwise, cost calculations will not be accurate.

Figure 41-3 Break-even analysis: 2004 prices for different volumes

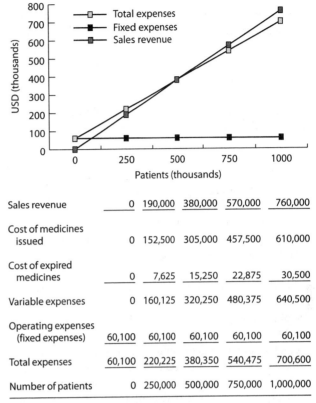

Sales revenue	0	190,000	380,000	570,000	760,000
Cost of medicines issued	0	152,500	305,000	457,500	610,000
Cost of expired medicines	0	7,625	15,250	22,875	30,500
Variable expenses	0	160,125	320,250	480,375	640,500
Operating expenses (fixed expenses)	60,100	60,100	60,100	60,100	60,100
Total expenses	60,100	220,225	380,350	540,475	700,600
Number of patients	0	250,000	500,000	750,000	1,000,000

Note: Break-even point is where number of patients is approximately 500,000.

Figure 41-2 shows that certain costs are direct and others indirect. *Direct costs* are those that can be attributed directly to the items being costed (for instance, the purchase price of the medicine). *Indirect costs* are those that cannot be attributed directly, such as medicine losses and general operating expenses. The easiest way to allocate indirect costs is to treat them as percentage additions to the direct cost of each medicine.

Costs are often divided into fixed (predictable) and variable (incremental) costs (Chapter 40). Rent for a warehouse would be a fixed cost, because it would not vary with the quantity of pharmaceuticals held. Packing materials would be a variable cost, because materials needed vary directly with the quantity of medicines issued. This division between fixed and variable costs is useful when determining the break-even point (the production or service volume at which sales revenue equals expenses). Figure 41-3 shows a graph of the revenue and expenses with various patient volumes, using 2004 prices and expenses. Sales prices set must be sufficient to cover the fixed and variable costs, as well as the need for reserves, at the expected volume of sales. In the figure, this point is achieved with a volume of about 500,000 patients.

In practice, many costs are semivariable; this factor should be taken into account when using break-even analysis data. Salaries are an example of a semivariable cost. With increasing activity, additional staff will probably be needed, but unlike the proportional cost increase shown in Figure 41-3, the increase in staff costs should be considerably less than the increase in patient volumes. Even warehouse rents are not always a fixed cost. Often, as product volumes increase, they can be accommodated in the existing warehouse, but when the warehouse is full, additional volume can only be accommodated by renting more warehouse space.

41.5 Setting prices for pharmaceutical sales and services provided

The development and implementation of detailed pricing strategies are key to realizing the projected revenues from pharmaceutical sales that are part of a long-range financial plan.

Building on the long-range plan shown in Figure 41-2, Figure 41-4 presents an example of price setting to achieve the pharmaceutical sales revenue of USD 457,531 projected for 2005. The example is simplified—including only four medicines and two geographic regions—but it shows how prices can be set based on each medicine's cost. The example is for the year in which sales revenue is projected to exceed total expenses in the five-year plan. In this analysis, net sales revenue of USD 457,531 is shown under (3) Summary Forecast. Gross sales revenue is projected at USD 481,688, with an anticipated total volume of social discounts or waivers valued at USD 24,157.

Projected purchase costs for each medicine, together with total operating costs, determine the medicines' full cost. Pharmaceutical sales prices are then established, based on these total costs, with various markups added and adjustments made as necessary to achieve a program's social as well as financial objectives. Adjustments for social discounts and regional equity should take into account willingness and ability to pay. If pharmaceutical use estimates are available by region, revenue contributions by medicine and by region can be calculated. Price adjustments are then made as needed to ensure that the sum of revenue contributions will equal the overall projected sales revenue. For example, in Figure 41-2, the 2005 figures have been produced by forecasting sales, other income, cost of sales, packing expenses, distribution expenses, and general costs, which together produce a small operating surplus (net operating result) of USD 8,600. Perhaps several drafts of the financial plan were necessary to achieve an acceptable operating result within revenue and cost parameters. For pricing purposes, the focus should be on the USD 930,000 cost of goods sold. The gross-margin target is USD 169,700 plus the expired medicine cost of USD 9,800, for a total of USD 179,500. The markup needed to earn USD 179,500 on cost of sales of USD 930,000 is 19.3 percent. So the default pricing markup for 2005 should be 19.3 percent. Pricing for RDFs is discussed in more detail in Chapter 13.

41.6 Budgeting

In addition to a long-range financial plan, it is necessary to have a detailed budget to plan and control spending for the current year. An annual budget should be based on the first-year figures from the current rolling long-range financial plan and should reflect the activities programmed for the year.

The budgeting process must begin well before the start of the year, because it takes time for budgets to be approved. Approving government budgets, in particular, can be a lengthy process, where a predetermined schedule exists for submitting a draft budget to the ministry of health, which then forwards the budget to the ministry of finance. If the budgeting is decentralized, the process will take even longer and will have to start earlier.

The budget should show funding sources as well as expenses. A grant-funded government budget is a fixed budget, or a zero-balance budget, where funding is known and the objective is to make sure that expenditures do not exceed the funding level. If any income comes from sales revenue, the budget is flexible, since the level of expenditure will depend on the level of income.

Budget detail

All the resources to be obtained should be shown in the budget, including resources that are to be donated, so that the budget reflects the total resources needed to carry out planned activities. Separate budgets are prepared for operating (recurrent) funds and capital (development) funds.

The operating budget covers the cost of all items consumed during the year, including salaries, allowances, medicines, transport, travel, postage, telephone, office supplies, heat, electricity, water, and office rent. Any donated items, such as medicines or office supplies, should be shown and identified in relation to a specific funding source. When assets are to be replaced from sales revenue, depreciation should be included here as an expense.

The capital budget must show all land and buildings to be bought or built, as well as vehicles and equipment to be purchased. All assets that have a long life (more than one year) or a significant value should be included. The definitions of life and value should be in accordance with government regulations or with current accounting standards, if not covered by regulations. A donated item, such as a vehicle, should be shown in the capital budget and identified in relation to a specific funding source.

Figure 41-4   2005 price structure and forecast

CENTRAL MEDICAL STORES REVOLVING DRUG FUND
2005 Price Structure and Forecast

(1) PRICE STRUCTURE	Drug 1	Drug 2	Drug 3	Drug 4
A Purchase price[a]	1.00	2.00	3.00	4.00
B Inward freight, duty, etc.[b]	0.05	0.00	0.15	0.20
C Direct cost	1.05	2.00	3.15	4.20
D Stock losses[c] (C x 5.00%)	0.05	0.10	0.16	0.21
E Overhead expenses[c] (C x 16.42%)	0.17	0.33	0.52	0.69
F Full cost	1.27	2.43	3.83	5.10
G Stock replenishment reserve[c] (C x 2.00%)	0.02	0.04	0.06	0.08
H Profit [c,d] (C x 1.61%)	0.02	0.03	0.05	0.07
I Standard price	1.31	2.50	3.94	5.25
J Drug use policy adjustment[e]	0.13	-0.25	0.43	-0.42
K Adjusted price	1.44	2.25	4.37	4.83
L Markup to cover social discount[f] (C x 6.60%)	0.07	0.13	0.21	0.28
	1.51	2.38	4.58	5.11
Regional equity adjustment				
Adjusted regional price, Region 1[g]	1.21	1.91	3.66	4.09
Adjusted regional price, Region 2[g]	1.66	2.62	5.04	5.62

(2) FORECASTED REVENUE BY MEDICINE AND BY REGION	Drug 1	Drug 2	Drug 3	Drug 4	Total
Sales volume					
Expected number of units sold, Region 1	14,070	12,665	12,665	9,999	49,399
Expected number of units sold, Region 2	28,144	25,335	25,335	20,001	98,815
Expected number of units sold, total	42,214	38,000	38,000	30,000	148,214
Revenue contribution by medicine					
Cost of medicines issued	42,214	76,000	114,000	120,000	352,214
Inward freight, duty, etc.	2,111	0	5,700	6,000	13,811
Direct cost	44,325	76,000	119,700	126,000	366,025
Stock losses	2,216	3,800	5,985	6,300	18,301
Overhead expenses	7,278	12,479	19,654	20,689	60,100
Total cost	53,819	92,279	145,339	152,989	444,426
Stock replacement reserve	886	1,520	2,394	2,520	7,320
Profit	713	1,222	1,925	2,026	5,886
Net sales revenue	55,418	95,021	149,658	157,535	457,632
Medicine use policy adjustment	5,542	(9,502)	16,462	(12,603)	(101)
	60,960	85,519	166,120	144,932	457,531
Markup to cover social discount	2,925	5,016	7,900	8,316	24,157
Gross sales revenue	63,885	90,535	174,020	153,248	481,688
Regional equity adjustment					
Adjusted sales revenue, Region 1	17,034	24,140	46,401	40,862	128,437
Adjusted sales revenue, Region 2	46,852	66,396	127,621	112,387	353,256
Total	63,886	90,536	174,022	153,249	481,693

(3) SUMMARY FORECAST	% of Cost	Income & Exps
Sales revenue		481,688
Less social discounts	6.60	24,157
Net sales revenue		457,531
Cost of medicines issued		366,025
		91,506
Less: stock losses	5.00	18,301
Gross profit		73,205
Less: overhead expenses	16.42	60,100
Operating profit	3.58	13,105
Less: stock replacement reserve	2.00	7,320
Net profit		5,785

Notes: In a decentralized program, the field programs would use the sales price of the central program as the purchase price for their program. The other costs added to the transfer price would be those incurred at the field level. If reserves are managed at the central level for the whole program, they would not also be maintained at field levels.

[a] Use the price of the most recent purchase.

[b] Drug 2 is manufactured locally. Freight and duty costs for other medicines were estimated as a percentage.

[c] All other costs and markups for reserves are allocated as a percentage of direct costs, based on the annual budget.

[d] A nonprofit organization would not have a profit markup but would have markups for building necessary reserves to cover a bad year or a disaster (such as major stock damage), assuming insurance is not available.

[e] This adjustment relates to a cross-subsidy from nonessential medicines (here drugs 2 and 4 are essential).

[f] An average of 5 percent of services are provided free over both regions. The higher level of social discounts in Region 1 is not borne only by the full payers in that region.

[g] This cross-subsidy is from the richer Region 2 to the poorer Region 1. Region 2 is assumed to have twice the volume of sales of each medicine as Region 1.

Budgeting method

In government programs, although budgets are prepared according to program needs, the amounts approved generally follow a historical basis: that is, the previous year's budget is adjusted by a percentage to reflect the expected change in overall government funding and, to some degree, shifting program priorities. Resource-allocation decisions may also be affected by political and other external forces, as discussed in Chapter 11.

The main purpose of budget preparation is to determine and obtain the level of funding needed to provide services. After the amount of funding is decided, the job of the manager is to use those funds to achieve approved program objectives in the most cost-effective way. This task is not easy when the distribution of funds among line items is inefficient and cannot be changed.

In programs that have some autonomy and that have funding from donors or from sales, the budget is prepared more as a planning tool, with a relationship among program activities, expenditures, and income. For example, in the 2005 RDF budget shown in Figure 41-1, the ability to purchase and distribute medicines valued at USD 250,000 depends on the ability to recover half the cost in sales revenue. After the budget is approved, the manager has some autonomy to reduce or increase expenditures, depending on funding levels, or to shift funds among line items to achieve maximum efficiency.

Whichever method of budgeting is used, the preparation involves identifying, quantifying, and costing the resources needed; determining the level of available funding; and adjusting expenditures to the expected level of funding.

Identify, quantify, and cost the resources needed. Each activity in the workplan must be examined, and the staff time, supplies, and equipment needed to carry it out must be quantified. For example, a CMS manager must decide how many staff are needed to properly handle and record the medicines, what types of equipment (such as forklifts or computers) are needed, what it takes to operate them, and what supplies are needed. (See the discussion of quantification of pharmaceutical needs in Chapter 20.) After each resource needed has been quantified, the cost can be estimated. If any of the resources are to be purchased long after the budget is prepared, a percentage for inflation should be added to the current price.

Determine the level of available funding. Funding may include government allocations, donor grants, and sales revenues. It is important to show each funding source separately and to show the relationship between any dedicated funding source and the expenditures to which it relates. Not all the government funding may materialize—sometimes only salaries are maintained at the budgeted level. The budget should be prepared as if the whole government allocation will be provided, but managers should antici-pate that some funds may not arrive and pace spending accordingly.

In the case of revenue generated from sales, managers should be conservative when preparing estimates because of the risk that such revenues might not be forthcoming (for instance, because of collection problems). Sales revenues depend on the forecasted volume of sales for each medicine and its price. From this revenue it is necessary to deduct the sales value of medicines to be provided free (either for poor clients or for exempt services) and the value of any estimated losses—such as those due to leakage, deterioration, theft, or expiration.

Adjust expenditures to the expected level of funding. This adjustment is cyclical. Activities are originally determined in accordance with needs and with an optimistic view of funding. As the actual level of funding becomes clear, if it is less than hoped, activities are reduced or made less costly. Setting priorities among activities is useful so that it is known in advance which activities will be cut if funding is lacking.

The budget must always show the basis for each line item. For example: Fuel for transporting medicines—USD 16,000 (four vehicles at 20,000 miles per year, 10 miles per gallon, USD 2 per gallon). A budget that clearly relates financial estimates to activities is easier to justify and provides a stronger basis for obtaining the required funding. The RDF budget example in Figure 41-1 shows the number of patients to be served, which is useful to include. Types of patient (children), disease (malaria), and geographical areas to be covered could also be included.

41.7 Cash planning

Even though there may be sufficient funds in the budget, there may be times when not enough cash is available to pay the bills, especially if funding is irregular or large payments must be made (such as for a bulk purchase of pharmaceuticals). A cash flow forecast helps ensure sufficient cash to cover all anticipated financial obligations each month. An example of a cash flow forecast is given in Figure 41-5.

The cash flow forecast should be prepared from the workplan and budget. The process is simple: start with the anticipated cash balance (cash in hand and at the bank), and add receipts and deduct payments in the months when they are expected to fall. In the example shown in Figure 41-5, grants are expected to be received periodically, in January, April, July, October, and December. Sales revenue is expected to vary only slightly each month. A loan of USD 50,000 will be available in January. Capital purchases, receipts, and payments relating to accounts receivable and payable should be included in the cash flow forecast, but items that do not result in cash receipts or payments (depreciation, stock losses) can be omitted.

Figure 41-5 Cash flow forecast

CENTRAL MEDICAL STORES REVOLVING DRUG FUND
Cash Flow Forecast 2005

	Cash Budget 2005	Jan	Feb	Mar	Apr	May	Jun	Jul	Aug	Sep	Oct	Nov	Dec
							Monthly Allocation						
RECEIPTS													
Grants	145,000	33,750			33,750			33,750			33,750		
Sales revenue	125,000	10,000	10,250	10,500	10,500	10,750	11,000	10,750	10,500	10,500	10,000	10,250	10,000
Loan	50,000	50,000											
Total receipts	320,000	93,750	10,250	10,500	44,250	10,750	11,000	44,500	10,500	10,500	43,750	10,250	20,000
PAYMENTS													
Drug purchases	230,000	57,500			57,500			57,500			57,500		
Salaries	19,000	1,583	1,583	1,584	1,583	1,583	1,584	1,583	1,583	1,584	1,583	1,583	1,584
Vehicle operations	2,700	225	225	225	225	225	225	225	225	225	225	225	225
Other transport	1,600	134	133	133	134	133	133	134	133	133	134	133	133
Packaging and labeling	3,300	275	275	275	275	275	275	275	275	275	275	275	275
Utilities	2,200	183	184	183	183	184	183	183	184	183	183	184	183
Office supplies	1,200	100	100	100	100	100	100	100	100	100	100	100	100
Total payments	260,000	60,000	2,500	2,500	60,000	2,500	2,500	60,000	2,500	2,500	60,000	2,500	2,500
Receipts less payments	60,000	33,750	7,750	8,000	−15,750	8,250	8,500	−15,500	8,000	8,000	−16,250	7,750	17,500
Less capital expenditures	10,000			4,000									6,000
Net cash flow	50,000	33,750	7,750	4,000	−15,750	8,250	8,500	−15,500	8,000	8,000	−16,250	7,750	11,500
Add opening cash balance	0	0	33,750	41,500	45,500	29,750	38,000	46,500	31,000	39,000	47,000	30,750	38,500
Closing cash balance	50,000	33,750	41,500	45,500	29,750	38,000	46,500	31,000	39,000	47,000	30,750	38,500	50,000
Patient volume	500,000	40,000	41,000	42,000	42,000	43,000	44,000	43,000	42,000	42,000	40,000	41,000	40,000

If the balance at the end of any month is negative, funds will be insufficient that month. When this happens, either activities or funding schedules will have to be changed, or credit will have to be obtained. If a significant surplus exists, putting the funds into a deposit account at the bank to earn interest may be desirable, but speculative risks should not be taken to earn higher returns.

In circumstances where an additional sales markup is made on pharmaceuticals to cover replacement cost, it may be appropriate to put the additional funds generated into a separate bank account so that they will be available when the time comes to replace the pharmaceuticals. Likewise, the depreciation fund could be put into a separate bank account as a special reserve. Payments to such special-reserve accounts should be treated as cash payments in the cash flow forecast so that these funds are not perceived as being available to cover operating costs. In the month when they will be used to replace pharmaceuticals or a fixed asset, the funds should be shown as incoming revenue. Because such procedures are not considered best practice in modern financial management, however, they should be considered only by programs with limited financial management capacity.

Failure to predict cash flow accurately can result in cash shortages, which can mean problems in paying salaries (resulting in demoralization of staff), replenishing pharmaceutical stocks, keeping vehicles operational, or replacing equipment. Any one of those problems can prevent a program from achieving its objectives.

41.8 Controlling and managing resources

Good financial controls and a sound accounting system are the basis for effective financial management. Although financial managers and accountants are responsible for establishing and maintaining the control and accounting systems, the general manager must know enough about the system to supervise staff members and to detect any problems.

The first principle of cost control is that the benefit of control efforts should exceed their costs—measured in money, time, or effort. Some government-based controls are so cumbersome and bureaucratic that they prevent the organization from meeting its objectives. For example, the use of multistage, paper-based procedures for controlling goods received has resulted in delays of weeks and months in processing supplies following delivery, preventing customers from being supplied, even though supplies were physically available. Process flows should be analyzed and modified to avoid such a scenario.

Standardized financial controls and accounting procedures help ensure that resources are generated and used properly and that a complete and accurate financial picture

of operations, assets, and liabilities can be obtained. See Box 41-2 for a financial control checklist.

The three main principles of an effective financial control system are to—

1. Divide duties among individuals so that no one person can control all phases of a transaction. For example—
   - Tasks of requesting payment, authorizing payment, and issuing checks should each be carried out by a different person.
   - The person who prepares a bank reconciliation should not handle or record receipts or payments.
   - The person making purchases and the person paying for them should be different, and they should report to different supervisors.

2. Use financial control procedures to regulate transactions. For example—
   - Issue preprinted, serially numbered receipts for all inflows of cash.
   - Deposit all cash receipts in the bank and make deposits promptly.
   - Minimize the use of cash and require detailed expense reports with receipts for such transactions.

3. Use the accounting system to record and monitor all transactions and assets. For example—
   - Record all issues of medicines in the accounting records and include the value of stocks in the accounting system.
   - Produce monthly income and expenditure statements from the accounting system and review the figures for stocks, sales, and waivers.

Usually, government systems require extensive approval procedures before funds can be spent. Managers still must ensure, however, that the funds have been spent wisely and well. The first step is to have a strict approval process for expenditures. This process includes keeping good records of uncommitted fund balances for each line item (with separate amounts for each donor, if necessary) and approving expenditures only after ensuring that they are within the budget and that adequate cash is currently on hand. If the spending follows the current budget and the budget has been regularly reviewed so that it is in line with program needs, the use of the funds can be approved.

Reviewing prices paid for services or products is important to ensure that the best price and quality were obtained, and to check that the services or products were actually received. For example, before paying a bill for painting a storeroom, the manager should visit the storeroom to see whether the job was done well. Before paying for a batch of medicines, the manager should go to the store and see whether they are on the shelves and shown in the stock

Box 41-2
Manager's checklist for good financial control

Controlling receipts

- Issue prenumbered receipts for all cash received.
- Keep all original receipts and copies of canceled checks.
- Control all receipt books in use and in stock, and lock up all unused receipt books.
- Keep all cash and checks received separate from other funds. Do not use them as a source for payments, and bank them promptly.
- Reconcile the bank balance every month.
- Use a register to record all checks received.
- Do not cash personal checks from petty cash.
- Use a register to record all donations of supplies or fixed assets, showing the value.

Controlling assets

- Maintain up-to-date inventory records and reconcile balances each month with the accounting records.
- Physically check a sample of inventory balances each month.
- Maintain a fixed assets register.
- Keep up-to-date maintenance and inspection records.
- Put permanent identification tags, numbered sequentially and recorded in the asset record, on all equipment.
- Make a photographic or video record of all equipment and assets.
- Protect against loss or theft of assets with appropriate security and insurance.
- Keep usage records for equipment and vehicles (for example, log books).
- Monitor advances and accounts receivable and make sure that they are cleared within a prescribed period.
- Make arrangements for recovering overdue staff advances from salaries.
- Place cash reserves in low-risk, interest-earning investments (such as bank savings accounts).

Controlling expenditures

- Establish detailed procurement procedures.
- Obtain written bids or quotes for all purchases above a specified limit and file them with the purchase order.
- Use a local purchase order for all local purchases.
- Check that goods and services purchased are received and recorded (pharmaceuticals must be entered in inventory records).
- Check that the quality, quantity, and price of goods

or services received correspond to purchase specifications.
- Make all payments for goods or services by check.
- Require supporting documentation for all purchases.
- Make sure that all expenditures are genuine, reasonable, and in line with program plans and budgets.
- Check the proposed expenditure against the budget and ensure that the budget is up-to-date regarding donor contributions and sales revenue.
- Check that funds are available.
- Check that the petty cash balance is maintained at the agreed level of imprest.
- Control liabilities
- Manage supplier accounts so that balances are paid promptly when they are due for payment.
- Maintain control over suppliers' invoices, know what supplies have been paid for and when they will be delivered, and monitor date of receipt.

Many programs use computerized management information systems that carry out or support these controls. Such computerized systems can greatly improve the level of financial control by providing regular, up-to-date information, data analysis, and report generation with levels of detail that are not possible using manual systems. These systems, however, bring their own control challenges, which are best addressed before and during the implementation phase. They include—

- Conducting a thorough review when planning a computerized system. The system should be designed to make the most of the computer's functionality and should not just mimic the previous manual system.
- Completing a review of system rights and privileges and incorporating those attributes as well as any changes in the new system. System rights and privileges specify who can change the system, change data, edit master files, enter and confirm different transactions, and has read-only access. The review team needs to include senior management and the internal auditor (if there is one); the review should not be left solely to information technology staff.
- Reviewing software license agreements to ensure all aspects of the program are included and sufficient flexibility exists to support potential evolution of the program.
- Establishing a system security policy.
- Establishing a data backup policy.
- Ensuring that internal and external audit staff members are qualified to audit computerized systems.

Figure 41-6   Budget report

CENTRAL MEDICAL STORES REVOLVING DRUG FUND
Operating Budget Report March 2005

	Budget 2005	Budget Year-to-Date	Budget Month	Actual Year-to-Date	Actual Month	Variance Year-to-Date
INCOME FROM GRANTS						
Grants	135,000	33,750	0	33,000	0	(750)
Donated medicines	50,000	12,500	4,167	15,000	5,000	2,500
Total grants	185,000	46,250	4,167	48,000	5,000	1,750
MEDICINES ACCOUNT						
Sales revenue	125,000	31,250	10,417	30,000	9,000	(1,250)
Less cost of medicines dispensed	250,000	62,500	20,833	64,000	21,000	(1,500)
	(125,000)	(31,250)	(10,416)	(34,000)	(12,000)	(2,750)
Less cost of expired medicines, etc.	12,500	3,125	1,042	3,500	1,500	(375)
Surplus/deficit on medicines account	(137,500)	(34,375)	(11,458)	(37,500)	(13,500)	(3,125)
EXPENSES						
Salaries	19,000	4,750	1,583	4,800	1,600	(50)
Vehicle operations	2,700	675	225	700	240	(25)
Other transport	1,600	400	133	390	120	10
Packaging and labeling	3,300	825	275	800	300	25
Utilities	2,200	550	183	600	150	(50)
Office supplies	1,200	300	100	296	110	4
Total operating expenditures	30,000	7,500	2,499	7,586	2,520	(86)
Depreciation	10,000	2,500	833	2,500	833	0
Total expenses	40,000	10,000	3,332	10,086	3,353	(86)
Income less expenses	7,500	1,875	(10,623)	414	(11,853)	(1,461)
Patient volume	500,000	41,667	125,000	40,997	123,489	(1,511)

records. Checking a few of the items purchased should be sufficient.

To avoid spending the entire available budget during the first few months, program managers may establish a monthly spending limit, requiring special approval of any expenditure in excess of that limit. However, to avoid lengthy approval delays, financial managers may want to establish special procedures to accommodate known fluctuations caused by planned outlays for annual rents or capital improvements. Because the expenditure budget is based on a particular level of funding, updating the budget is vital if any significant variation in funding is expected (anything over 5 percent would be significant). For example, if a donor that was going to provide 10 percent of the pharmaceutical supply can now provide only 5 percent, the budget must be revised. If additional funding is generated, the expenditure budget can be increased accordingly or the surplus reserved for unidentified future requirements.

The accounting and reporting system must provide fast, accurate information in terms of funds received and expenditures made so that budget adjustments can be made promptly. With increased use of computers in program management, budgeting tasks can be handled more quickly and more accurately, but manual record keeping is still the norm in many places. If computer-based systems are used, making regular backup files or printing hard-copy reports periodically is a good practice. In either case, a budget report must be produced every month. This report shows the budgeted and actual figures for each revenue and expense category for the month and for the year to date and also shows the variance between the year-to-date budget and the year-to-date actual figures. All significant variances must be investigated and appropriate action taken. A sample budget report is shown in Figure 41-6.

Cash and bank movements and balances should be reviewed daily to make sure that receipts and payments are as expected and that funds are sufficient to meet obligations. A statement should be obtained from the cashier each morning showing the opening balance, cash received by source, payments made, closing balance for the previous day, and payments due that day.

Usually, imported supplies will be paid for in foreign currency (often U.S. dollars). To protect against currency fluctuations, maintaining a U.S.-dollar bank account to hold funds for future procurement is sensible, when this is possible. The U.S. dollar is also the currency frequently used for donated funds. When such funds are provided for procurement purposes, donors should be persuaded to pay in U.S. dollars deposited to the CMS dollar account. This procedure not only preserves procurement capacity of the funds against exchange-rate movements, but also avoids commissions charged by banks to exchange dollars into local currency and then back into U.S. dollars.

It is also important to have an annual external audit, which helps ensure that controls are operating properly and that transactions are being properly recorded. This institutional audit should cover both donor funds and the organization's own funds. Separate audits of individual donor funding should be discouraged because they do not provide a complete picture and consume excessive amounts of management time. Instead, managers should attempt to persuade donors to share in the cost of the institutional audit.

41.9 Accounting and reporting

An autonomous pharmaceutical program can normally establish its own accounting and reporting procedures, provided they are in accordance with generally accepted accounting principles. However, a government program usually must follow uniform accounting procedures. As described in Section 41.2, standard government accounting systems may not provide adequate information on transactions or assets and may not allow performance to be measured accurately. In order to satisfy management needs, supplementary records must be kept and additional reports produced. The following books, or subsidiary ledgers, are usually required for a complete accounting and reporting system—

- Cash-received book showing the date and source of receipts (such as donor, government, or sales point) and when and where the cash was deposited
- Cash-paid book showing payee, purpose, funding source, and bank account
- Petty cash book for small cash payments
- Accounts receivable ledger with accounts for people who owe money to the organization
- Accounts payable ledger with accounts for people who are owed money by the organization
- Journals showing purchases and sales made on credit,

transfers between accounts, and donations in kind
- General ledger with income, expense, asset, and liability accounts
- Salary book showing details of staff salaries and allowances
- Inventory records showing the quantity and cost of all medicines received, issued, and on hand by type of medicine
- Fixed assets register showing the quantity and cost of all fixed assets bought, sold, and on hand

Some of these ledgers may be consolidated in an integrated, computerized accounting package.

The chart of accounts, which sets out the accounts structure, lists all accounts—with a unique code for each. The code is used primarily to identify the type of asset, liability, revenue, or expense (for example, bank account, medicine sales, or salaries), but it can also be used to identify a responsibility center (such as a regional distribution center) or donor fund (such as a tuberculosis program). For the accounting system to provide the control and information required, the accounts must be structured appropriately. For example, in order to readily produce a report showing expenses for each regional center, each expense item must be coded by regional center and posted to a separate account. The coding structure should be detailed enough to provide needed managerial information but not so complex that excessive effort or skill is required to code and process transactions accurately.

Transactions must be recorded and processed promptly and accurately. For example, if all pharmaceutical issue records are not up-to-date in the accounting books, it will be impossible to reconcile the inventory balances in the accounting department with those shown on the warehouse stock cards.

The accounting system should produce a number of basic reports that provide all the information needed to review financial progress and status. In particular, the reports should indicate clearly if the program is—

- Meeting its financial objectives—for example, covering costs or generating a surplus
- Operating efficiently and effectively
- Looking after its assets
- Generating and using resources properly
- Meeting donor requirements

Reports should be produced both monthly and annually. The most common standard reports are as follows—

Budget performance report: This monthly report compares budgeted and actual revenue/expenses (see Figure 41-6).
Income and expense report: This report, produced monthly and annually, shows all income and expenses to date

and the cumulative surplus or deficit (Figure 41-7). For comparative purposes, actual figures for the previous year and budget figures for the current year are shown. A key figure is the deficit or surplus in medicines funding as a percentage of the cost of medicines issued or the cost of sales. This figure shows the extent to which medicine costs are being recovered. For the 2005 figures shown in Figure 41-7, the deficit of USD 138,000 represents 57 percent of the cost of medicines issued (USD 242,000). This deficit means that 43 percent of the cost of medicines is being recovered, taking into account stock losses. In Figure 41-2, the projected surplus (contribution line) of USD 170,300 for 2007 represents 14 percent of the USD 1,211,800 cost for medicines sold. These percentages are a measure of effective pricing, revenue collection efficiency, and control over stock losses.

Balance sheet: This report, produced monthly and annually, shows the soundness of the program at one point in time. It shows the balances at the end of the period for all assets, liabilities, reserves, and fund balances (Figure 41-8). Certain key ratios help managers to evaluate the program's financial health. The ability of the program to meet its current liabilities in the short term is measured by comparing the cash balance with the accounts payable (in 2003, this would be USD 4,520 compared with USD 4,230). The same measure in the medium term compares the total current assets with the total current liabilities (USD 62,650 compared with USD 7,246 in the same example). When assessing the ability of a program to meet its liabilities, it is vital to be sure that the amounts for pharmaceutical stock and accounts receivable are realistic—that is, that they will result in cash income that can be used to meet those liabilities. Note that a strong balance sheet can be a misleading indicator of an organization's financial health. For example, abundant long-term assets cannot satisfy immediate short-term liabilities. Provisions should be made to account for obsolete and slow-moving medicine stocks and for old accounts receivable in the balance sheet.

Pharmaceutical stock account: It is important to prepare a summary of the pharmaceutical stock account as an attachment to the income and expense report (see Figure 41-7). This summary shows the total figures for pharmaceuticals received and issued, as well as opening and closing balances, and it provides a picture of the movements in that account. If a computerized accounting program is used, the program should be able to produce a similar report for each pharmaceutical, a feature that is useful for measuring sales frequency and months of stock on hand. Chapter 40 discusses a number of analyses that can help managers understand and control inventory costs.

Accounts payable and receivable: These additional reports support the figures shown in the balance sheet and show the balance for each debtor and creditor, with a

Figure 41-7   Income and expense report

CENTRAL MEDICAL STORES REVOLVING DRUG FUND Income and Expense Statement 2005			
	Actual 2004	*Budget 2005*	*Actual 2005*
INCOME FROM GRANTS			
Grants	188,000	135,000	130,000
Donated medicines	98,000	50,000	50,000
Total grants	286,000	185,000	180,000
MEDICINE ACCOUNT			
Sales revenue	0	125,000	120,000
Less cost of medicines issued[a]	240,000	250,000	242,000
	(240,000)	(125,000)	(122,000)
Less cost of expired medicines, etc.	15,000	12,500	16,000
Surplus/deficit on medicines	(255,000)	(137,500)	(138,000)
EXPENSES			
Salaries	18,000	19,000	20,000
Vehicle operations	2,500	2,700	2,876
Other transport	1,500	1,600	1,745
Packaging and labeling	3,000	3,300	2,908
Utilities	2,000	2,200	2,190
Office supplies	1,000	1,200	1,186
Total operating expenditures	28,000	30,000	30,905
Depreciation	0	10,000	10,000
Total expenses	28,000	40,000	40,905
Total income less expenses	3,000	7,500	1,095
Patient volume	520,000	500,000	490,346

[a]PHARMACEUTICAL STOCK ACCOUNT		
	Actual 2004	*Actual 2005*
Opening stock	85,000	88,000
Purchases	160,000	230,000
Donations received	98,000	50,000
	343,000	368,000
Less cost of medicines dispensed	240,000	242,000
	103,000	126,000
Less cost of medicines expired, etc.	15,000	16,000
Closing stock	88,000	110,000

breakdown of the balance by month of origin. The older a receivable item is, the less likely the funds are to be collected; a procedure should be in place to account for uncollectible debts. In addition, old accounts payable may be an indication of poor management or cash flow issues.

Certain reports, such as the income and expense report, can be prepared for different responsibility centers, such as regional distribution centers. If different funding agencies

Figure 41-8   Balance sheet

CENTRAL MEDICAL STORES
REVOLVING DRUG FUND
Balance Sheet as of December 31, 2003

	31 Dec 02	31 Dec 03
ASSETS		
Fixed assets		
Cost	40,000	53,000
Depreciation	17,000	21,000
Net fixed assets	23,000	32,000
Current assets		
Cash and bank	2,356	4,520
Accounts receivable	7,560	8,330
Pharmaceutical stocks	43,780	49,800
Total current assets	53,696	62,650
LIABILITIES AND CAPITAL		
Current liabilities		
Accounts payable	3,456	4,230
Advance payments	2,540	2,760
Accruals and provisions	245	256
Total current liabilities	6,241	7,246
Working capital	47,455	55,404
Total net assets	70,455	87,404
FINANCED BY		
Loans		
Long-term loan	8,900	8,100
Equity		
Capital	500	500
Capital fund	24,560	29,800
Revenue reserves	12,310	13,200
New working capital	3,000	3,000
Donor grants	21,185	32,804
Total equity	61,555	79,304
Total long-term loans and equity	70,455	87,404

require separate reports, the reports can be prepared by funding source, provided that this capability is built into the account structure. Producing reports by responsibility center or funding source is easy if the accounting system is computerized. However, with a manual accounting system, the accounts can be set up in only one way—by responsibility center or by funding source. The decision should be based on the relative importance of each kind of analysis and the ease of extracting information from the accounting system. For example, if regional sales are of interest, these data can be extracted from the monthly regional reports.

Where a pharmaceutical sales program is in place, it is important to record and report revenue lost because of free distribution of medicines. Waivers for sales to the poor and exemptions applicable to special age groups or other categories should be recorded using special receipts. Such transactions should be authorized by the manager. They should be put into the books as sales and debited to a special account for free issues. They will then appear as an expense in the income and expense report.

In order to measure a program's output in terms of pharmaceuticals issued or the surplus or deficit from pharmaceutical sales, it is necessary to record the cost of pharmaceuticals issued. This process is an accounting transfer from the pharmaceutical stock account to a cost-of-issues account. The pharmaceuticals issued are valued at the cost of purchase—that is, at the same value at which they entered into the pharmaceutical stock account.

When quantities of a pharmaceutical in stock have been bought at different prices, there are different ways to value the quantity issued and, at the same time, the value of stock on hand. See Box 41-3 for a comparison of the three common methods. It is important to remember that the accounting method used determines how much surplus or deficit is shown in the income and expense report and how much stock value is shown in the balance sheet. Consistency is most important—the same method should be used each year. If a change is made in the methodology used, it must be disclosed in the organization's financial statements.

The average method is recommended because it is the easiest to understand. Calculating the average cost is simple: the financial balance in the stock account is simply divided by the number of units on hand. The average cost is updated every time a new purchase is made. Issues are then charged out at the average cost of the items in stock.

In the case of high inflation or large exchange fluctuations, where a computerized accounting program is used, keeping stock records in a stable foreign currency may be useful. Local currency records must still be kept, however.

In an autonomous RDF, generating sufficient revenue to replace stocks is extremely important. This is best done by creating a reserve for the purchase of replacement stocks. For example, if the replacement cost is expected to be 20 percent above the current cost, an extra 20 percent markup should be added to pharmaceutical sales prices, and an amount equivalent to that 20 percent for all sales for the month should be added to the reserve set aside to replace the stocks (see Section 41.5 and Chapter 13). ∎

References and further readings

★ = Key readings.

★ Creese, A., and D. Parker, eds. 1994. *Cost Analysis in Primary Health Care. A Training Manual for Programme Managers.* Geneva: World Health Organization. <http://whqlibdoc.who.int/publications/9241544708.pdf>

Box 41-3
Three methods of accounting for medicines issued

FIFO (first in/first out). Issues are charged out at the purchase cost of the earliest batch in stock. This method charges less to cost of sales and values stock higher.

LIFO (last in/first out). Issues are charged out at the purchase price of the latest batch in stock. This method charges more to cost of sales and values stock lower.

AVG (average). Issues are charged at the average price of the items in stock; the average is updated every time a new purchase is made. This puts the same value on issues and stocks.

LIFO is the most conservative method because it puts the lowest value on stocks and the highest value on issues. The average method is somewhat conservative, and the FIFO method is the least conservative. With both FIFO and LIFO, record keeping is more complicated, because it is necessary to keep track of how much balance remains from each purchase, and issues may have to be charged out at two or more prices.

Example of the effect of the three methods of accounting for medicines issued

	# Units	Unit price (USD)	FIFO (USD)	LIFO (USD)	AVG (USD)	Avg. unit cost (USD)[a]
Bought January 1	100	1	100	100	100	
Bought February 1	100	2	200	200	200	
Balance February 1	200		300	300	300	1.50
Issued February 22[b]	120		140	220	180	
Balance February 28	80		160	80	120	
Bought March 1	100	3	300	300	300	
Balance March 1	180		460	380	420	2.33
Issued March 26	80		160	240	186	
Balance March 31	100		300	140	234	

[a] Average unit cost changes with new purchase.
[b] The figures for the February 22 issues are calculated as follows:
‰ FIFO—100 units at 1 USD and 20 units at USD 2;
‰ LIFO—100 units at 2 USD and 20 units at USD 1;
‰ AVG—120 units at the average unit cost of USD 1.50 (total cost of USD 300 divided by total quantity purchased of 200).

★ Dropkin, M., J. Halpin, and B. La Touche. 2007. *The Budget Building Book for Nonprofits: A Step-by-Step Guide for Managers and Boards.* 2nd ed. San Francisco: Jossey-Bass.

★ Glynn, J. J. 1993. *Public Sector Financial Control and Accounting.* 2nd ed. Oxford: Blackwell Publishers.

Goodman, H., and C. Waddington. 1993. *Financing Health Care.* Oxford: Oxfam Publishing.

★ Herkimer, A. G., Jr. 1989. *Understanding Health Care Accounting.* Rockville, Md.: Aspen Publishers.

———.1986. *Understanding Hospital Financial Management.* 2nd ed. Rockville, Md.: Aspen Publishers.

Jones, R., and M. Pendlebury. 2010. *Public Sector Accounting.* 6th ed. Upper Saddle River, N.J.: Financial Times/Prentice Hall.

MSH (Management Sciences for Health). 2004. *FIMAT: The Financial Management Assessment Tool.* Boston: MSH. <http://erc.msh.org/mainpage.cfm?file=5.12htm&module=toolkit&language=English>

———. 2003. "Assessing Your Organization's Capacity to Manage Finances." *The Manager* 12(2):1–22. <http://erc.msh.org/newpages/english/finance/V12_N2_EN_ISS.pdf>

———. 1998. *Cost Revenue Analysis Tool Plus* (CORE Plus). Boston: MSH. <http://erc.msh.org/mainpage.cfm?file=5.10.htm&module=toolkit&language=English>

★ ———. 1991. "Managing Your Finances." In *The Family Planning Manager's Handbook: Basic Skills for Managing Family Planning Programs.* Boston: MSH. <http://erc.msh.org/mainpage.cfm?file=handbook2.htm&module=enhancement%20other&language=English>

Shepard, D. S., D. Hodgkin, and Y. E. Anthony. 2000. *Analysis of Hospital Costs: A Manual for Managers.* Geneva: WHO. <http://whqlibdoc.who.int/publications/2000/9241545283.pdf>

Waddinton, C. 2006. *Economics and Financial Management: What Do District Managers Need to Know?* Geneva: World Health Organization. <http://whqlibdoc.who.int/hq/2006/WHO_EIP_healthsystems_2006.3_eng.pdf>

Vian, T. 1993. Analyzing Costs for Management Decisions. *Family Planning Manager* 2(2):1–18.

ASSESSMENT GUIDE

Current pharmaceutical budget and expenditures

- What is the ministry of health's (MOH) per capita budget or total expenditure on pharmaceuticals, in U.S. dollars?
- What was the value of the public pharmaceutical budget spent per capita in the last year, out of the average value of the same budget during the past three years?
- How much of the public pharmaceutical budget was spent, of the public pharmaceutical budget allocated?
- During the last fiscal year, how much did the central medical store spend on fuel for transport, maintenance, administration, hired labor, warehouse space (rent, telephone, utilities), or other costs (describe)?

Accounting system

- Is the pharmaceutical program's accounting system on a cash basis or an accrual basis?
- Do accounts exist for stock? What accounting method is used to value pharmaceutical stocks and issues—first in/first out (FIFO), last in/first out (LIFO), or average costing?
- Are records kept on the value of donated medicines? The cost of expired or lost medicines? Depreciation of fixed assets?
- Are records maintained for accounts payable? Accounts receivable?
- Does a chart of accounts exist? Is it structured to provide necessary management information?

Financial planning, budgeting, and cash planning

- Is there a long-range financial plan projecting both funding and expenditures for the next five years, and maintained on a rolling basis? Is a factor for inflation built into the plan?
- If pharmaceutical sales are anticipated, have pricing strategies been determined? Does the plan project the point at which revenues will cover expenses?
- Which offices are responsible for developing and approving budgets? (List steps and persons or offices responsible.) What information is used in developing budget requests?
- What information and supporting documents are submitted with budget requests?
- How does the MOH access budgeted funds for routine procurement—by scheduled allocation or access whenever needed?
- What approvals are required for expenditures?

- How does the MOH access funds for emergency procurement?
- What is the average lead time for MOH approval of procurement allocation (for both routine and emergency procurements) and for approval of foreign exchange allocation?
- How does the MOH access foreign exchange for procurement?
- Is the annual budget based on the first-year figures from the long-range financial plan? Are there separate operating and capital budgets?
- Does the budget relate financial estimates to activities in terms of the number of patients to be served, types of patients, diseases, and/or geographical areas to be covered?
- Has a cash flow forecast been developed to support the budget?

Costing

- Are the costs of in-country transportation, repackaging, medicine losses, and other operating expenses included in total pharmaceutical costs?
- Are analyses performed with regard to the cost of serving different patient volumes, different patient types, or different disease types?
- For an RDF, has a break-even point been projected?
- What method is used to value inventory?

Financial control and reporting

- Are duties divided among individuals so that no one person can control all phases of a transaction?
- Are preprinted, serially numbered receipts issued for all inflows of cash? Are cash receipts deposited promptly?
- Is there a budget approval process by which expenditures are approved only after ensuring that funds are available?
- Is the budget revised when funding is greater or less than anticipated?
- Is a budget report produced every month, showing budgeted and actual figures and variances for each revenue and expense category? Are causes of variances analyzed and addressed?
- Are income and expense reports, balance sheets, summaries of the pharmaceutical stock account, and reports on accounts payable and receivable prepared monthly and annually?
- Is an annual institutional audit performed by external auditors?

| Part I: Policy and economic issues | Part II: Pharmaceutical management | Part III: Management support systems |

Planning and administration
36 Pharmaceutical supply systems assessment
37 Managing pharmaceutical programs
38 Planning for pharmaceutical management
39 Contracting for pharmaceuticals and services
40 Analyzing and controlling pharmaceutical expenditures
41 Financial planning and management
42 Planning and building storage facilities
Organization and management
Information management
Human resources management

CHAPTER 42

Planning and building storage facilities

SUMMARY

This chapter describes methods for developing effective storage facilities, a process in which supply system managers play a key role.

Storage facilities are of three basic types—

- Mechanized warehouses rely on the use of mechanical handling equipment. They are appropriate where most goods are stored in bulk on pallets.
- Manual warehouses are appropriate where goods are stored in smaller quantities, mostly on shelves.
- Storerooms are fitted with shelves, refrigerators, and a secure cupboard or safe. Every facility needs a location where medicines and medical supplies can be stored safely.

Satisfactory storage accommodation may be obtained by reorganization or renovation of an existing facility, lease or purchase of a commercial warehouse, or putting in a new building. A new building may involve ground-up construction or the erection of a prefabricated building that is purchased and assembled on the preferred site. Most of the chapter focuses on managing traditional construction.

There are six stages in the procurement and construction process—

1. *Inception:* conducting a needs assessment; setting up a project team; appointing consultants
2. *Feasibility:* carrying out a feasibility study; obtaining a budget allocation
3. *Site selection and acquisition:* selecting a site or building; obtaining the site or building
4. *Design:* preparing a detailed design brief; selecting storage methods and choosing materials-handling equipment; planning space; designing the building
5. *Tender and project planning:* selecting a procurement method; drawing up a contract; conducting the tender process; planning the project
6. *Construction and commissioning:* managing the construction contract; commissioning the facility

Following procurement and construction, building and equipment maintenance adds an ongoing stage to the process.

42.1 Types of storage facilities

Well-located, well-built, well-organized, and secure storage facilities are an essential component of a pharmaceutical supply system. An effective building provides the correct environment for the storage of medicines and commodities and assists the efficient flow of supplies. Storage facilities designed with these factors in mind will help maintain pharmaceutical quality and reduce operational costs. Storage facilities fall into three categories: mechanized warehouses, manual warehouses, and storerooms.

Mechanized warehouses are designed around modern methods of storage and materials handling. A mechanized warehouse typically has tiers of pallet racks. Mechanical handling equipment is used to unload and store goods received and often to load outgoing goods onto delivery vehicles. Mechanized warehouses can range from very simple buildings using manually operated handling equipment and manually operated stock control systems to highly complex operations that are entirely automatic and computer controlled. Mechanized medical warehouses are most likely to be primary stores at the national or regional level. Typically, they are located close to major transport routes.

Manual warehouses may also hold some stock on floor pallets, but most items are stored on shelves and are moved without mechanical assistance. Medical supply warehouses at the regional or district level are usually manual warehouses. They are often attached to a hospital, which they also serve.

Storerooms are needed in every health facility to store medicines and medical supplies safely. The smallest facilities may need only a medicine cupboard, but most facilities require a room fitted with shelves and refrigerators, along with a secure cupboard or safe for controlled drugs.

This chapter provides guidelines to help managers make rational choices about designing and constructing warehouses. This material focuses on management of construction from the ground up. There are six stages in the process: inception, feasibility, site selection and acquisition, design, tender and project planning, and construction and commissioning (see Table 42-1). Following the planning and construction process is the continuing activity of building and equipment maintenance, which lasts throughout the life of the building.

In recent years, options have emerged for purchasing prefabricated warehouses and placing them at prepared sites rather than going through a new construction process (see Box 42-1).

This chapter is not a comprehensive technical manual and is not intended to be a substitute for the advice of a specialist. In most cases, specialist staff or outside consultants will be needed to deal with design and construction management issues. The day-to-day management of medical stores is covered in Chapter 44.

Table 42-1   Steps to plan and build a storage facility

Stages and tasks	Principal responsibility of—
Inception stage	
State the aim of the project (needs assessment)	Supply system
Establish the project team and appoint consultants	Supply system
Feasibility stage	
Identify quantity and type of storage space needed	Project team
Review options for reorganizing existing warehouse space	Project team
Consider leasing or purchasing an existing building	Project team
Determine whether a building is needed. If so—	Project team
• Establish operational requirements and prepare outline brief	Project team
• Assess financial, material, and personnel resources required	Project team
• Contact relevant authorities	Project team
• Survey regulatory requirements	Project team
• Assess availability of incentives	Project team
• Establish outline budget and obtain budget allocation	Project team
• Establish a program for the design and construction stages	Project team
Selection/acquisition of site stage	
Short-list and evaluate potential sites and buildings	Project team
Select and acquire site or building	Supply system
ESTABLISH FEASIBILITY AND PROCEED WITH DESIGN	
Design stage	
Outline proposals	
Develop design brief	Project team
Survey site or building	Project team
Prepare outline proposals showing main dimensions, allocation of space, and construction methods	Project team
Prepare cost estimates	Project team
Select suitable design	Project team
Obtain development consent	Project team
Scheme design and detail design	
Design each room and fix sizes	Project team
Determine needs for storage and handling equipment	Project team
Decide on construction method and all materials	Project team
Make new cost estimate	Project team
Prepare and agree on final design drawings	Project team
DESIGN SHOULD NOT BE CHANGED AFTER THIS POINT	
Production information	
Prepare production drawings, specifications, and bills of quantities, giving all information needed to construct the works	Project team
Select all fittings, fixtures, and equipment	Project team
Obtain approval from building regulations authority	Project team
Make final cost estimate	Project team
Tendering and project-planning stage	
Select method of building procurement	Project team/supply system
Prepare short list of contractors, or prequalification tender	Project team/supply system
Assemble tender documents and invite tenders	Project team/supply system
Analyze bids and select the best	Project team/third-party observer
Make any changes required for cost reasons	Project team/supply system
Agree on contractor's program and procedures	Contractor/project team
Finalize insurances and sign the contract	Contractor/supply system
Tender for and obtain mechanical handling equipment	Project team/supply system
CHANGES BEYOND THIS STAGE WILL COST EXTRA TIME AND MONEY	
Construction and commissioning stage	
Site work	
Supervise work on-site	Project team
Hold regular progress meetings with contractor	Contractor/project team
Prepare valuations and make interim payments	Contractor/project team/supply system
Handover	
Witness tests, inspect the works, and list defects	Contractor/project team
Hold handover meeting and accept keys and building manual	Contractor/project team/supply system
Commissioning and defects period	
Commission building	Supply system
Check that the defects have been rectified	Project team
Settle final account by releasing the retention sum	Contractor/project team/supply system

Source: Adapted from Mein and Jorgensen 1988.

42.2 Inception stage

From a consultant's standpoint, a good client (the supply system) should be knowledgeable and discerning. Most of the key decisions in a building project are made during the inception and feasibility stages, when client input is critical. These decisions fundamentally affect the cost and ultimate effectiveness of the project and should not be made casually. Particularly when resources are limited, careful feasibility planning is necessary to design and build effective warehouses at the lowest cost, while taking future needs into account.

The logistics team should assume responsibility for identifying the most suitable locations for medical stores throughout the country, based on an overall analysis of the distribution system (see Chapter 22). After an individual store location has been selected and outline zoning approval has been obtained from the relevant authorities, the detailed building procurement process can start. This process begins with a broad needs assessment, which guides the decision about whether to procure a prefabricated building or construct a new building and defines the critical operational parameters for the proposed building (see Box 42-2). This needs assessment will form the basis for developing the detailed design brief in conjunction with the project team and technical consultants.

The project team

A project team should be formed as soon as the decision to obtain storage space has been made. A senior pharmaceutical program manager or health official should direct the team. Its composition varies, depending on the size of the project and the project stage. The full team for the implementation stages of a large project such as a new central medical store (CMS) normally includes the lead consultant (usually an architect or engineer), a client representative, the supply system representative, a cost consultant, a structural engineer, a mechanical services engineer, an electrical engineer, an information technology specialist, a quality assurance/regulatory consultant, and a logistics and materials-handling consultant.

A wide range of other people and organizations should be consulted. Broadly based consultation is essential to the development of an appropriate building design. Too often, a project design takes shape without adequate consultation between the people who are to work in the building and the specialists who are designing it.

Box 42-1
Installing a prefabricated warehouse

Prefabricated warehouses offer an alternative to conventional warehouse construction methods. Such warehouses are built using technologically advanced materials, which simplify structure assembly. The kit consists of pre-engineered and prefabricated warehouse modules (framework, panels, doors, and other requested sections) produced to technical specifications in a controlled environment. While the warehouse is being manufactured to the client's design, the concrete slab foundation is poured at the selected site according to predetermined specifications; the slab is the only element that is "constructed." Once the slab is completed and quality tested, the necessary building components are shipped to the site. The manufacturer's staff supervise and certify warehouse assembly. This approach can be used to install any size warehouse facility (central, provincial, district, or health center). The process generally takes three to six months whereas a conventional construction project can take up to thirty-six months.

Advantages of opting for a prefabricated warehouse include—

- There is no need for engineers or architects on site (lower costs).

- Materials are produced by the supplier according to technical specifications.
- The structure can be installed in any location regardless of availability of local construction expertise.
- There is no need for an extensive design process (faster timeline and lower costs).
- Modular design allows for easy extension.
- Having few conventional construction steps results in less materiel loss, lower risk of accidents, and fewer delays.
- Composite materials used for the walls and roof require less repainting and fewer roof repairs, dramatically reducing maintenance and operational costs.
- Materials provide high thermal insulation and class 1 fire resistance.
- The possibility of prequalified suppliers simplifies complex procurement procedures (construction tender process), thus shortening the procurement phase.
- The cost of installation can be 65 percent of conventional construction, and operations and maintenance costs may be halved.

Box 42-2
Conducting a needs assessment for site planning

The needs assessment should consider the following factors—

- Who will own the store—public or private sector?
- Who will operate the store—public or private sector?
- What is to be stored—types of medicines and supplies and approximate annual volumes?
- Who are the major suppliers?
- Who are the major customers?
- In what formats will goods be stored (pallets, cartons, or individual packs)?
- Will bulk packages be "broken" to fulfill individual customer orders?
- What type of materials-handling equipment is likely to be appropriate?

- What are the likely restock and distribution frequencies?
- What temperature and humidity controls will be needed within the store?
- How will goods be protected against fire and theft?
- Will stock control be manual or electronic?
- What are the intended operating hours for the store?
- How many administrators and manual workers will be needed on the staff?
- What facilities should be provided on-site to ensure staff welfare?
- How will staff members reach the site?
- Who will monitor the performance of the store and how will this be done?

Appointment of consultants

If the project is complex, suitably qualified consultants should be appointed at the earliest possible stage for estimating building design costs, cost control, construction site management, and logistics and materials handling. The roles and responsibilities of the consultants are very much dependent upon the chosen procurement route to be followed (see Section 42.6). If the project is small and simple, professional consultants may be appointed after the feasibility stage, when alternative sites or buildings are being considered.

Building design. Professional design assistance is essential to ensure that a building satisfies the design brief and is constructed in accordance with building codes. There are various ways of procuring a design service.

In the *conventional* model, a lead consultant directs the project team; typically this person is an architect, but he or she could be an engineer. The lead consultant is appointed by the client to prepare the design, specifications, and bills of quantities, in liaison with the engineering and cost consultants. In some countries, all other consultants work directly for the lead consultant, and the cost of their services is included in the lead consultant's fee. In other countries, each consultant is appointed separately by the client.

After the contractor is hired, the lead consultant monitors the building work and certifies the payments to be made to the contractor. Finally, the lead consultant certifies when the building is complete and agrees on a final account with the contractor. The principal advantage of this model is that the lead consultant acts as the client's agent throughout, which helps ensure that the finished building is completed to an acceptable standard.

In the *design-and-build* model, the client appoints an architect to prepare a design with an agreed-upon level of detail. The contracting company quotes a fixed price for building this design but is allowed to modify construction details to suit its own working methods. The architect has no executive authority on-site but may continue to act as an observer for the client.

In the *turnkey* model, the client hires a contracting company to provide a complete building product for a fixed price. The contracting company is responsible for appointing the design team, which prepares a scheme in accordance with a design brief that has been agreed upon with the client. A variation on this model is where the contractor supplies a prefabricated building to erect at a client's preferred site. The building may include warehouse equipment and even information systems.

In the *public-private partnership* model, the client contracts out the entire building construction, building operation, and building maintenance process to a private consortium for an extensive time period; in essence, the client pays an annual fee and gets a building and complete pharmaceutical storage service in return. At the end of the contract period, ownership of the building reverts to the client. Preparation of a clear and legally binding contractual agreement is essential.

The principal advantage of the last three models is cost. The principal disadvantage is that quality control is largely in the hands of the contracting company, which has a vested interest in saving money and increasing its profit margin.

Cost control. The cost consultant prepares a preliminary cost estimate for the project. This estimate is updated as the design evolves. This consultant may also contribute to the assessment of contractors' tenders, assist the architect in negotiating any variations in the contract with the contractor, and audit the final account.

Logistics and materials handling. If the project is large and complex and involves extensive mechanical handling equipment, the advice of a specialist is needed at an early stage. Without this advice, an accurate design brief cannot be prepared, and expensive mistakes may be made. Some architects have the appropriate expertise. Alternatively, advice can be obtained from a materials-handling consultant or a supplier of materials-handling equipment.

The appointed consultants should have relevant experience, the resources to manage the project, and a proven ability to complete satisfactory buildings on time and within budget. The selection process should not allow corruption or favoritism; a formal tender helps minimize such problems. The client and project team should prepare a list of qualified firms and invite each to submit a formal proposal for consideration by the team. The proposal should set out the consultant's approach to the project and specify the fee to be charged. Before making a final decision, the project team should visit the offices of the short-listed consultants, view some of their completed projects, and talk to other clients.

42.3 Feasibility stage

The first task of the project team is to establish whether more space is really required. It may be more cost-effective to achieve the desired results by reducing the order interval, by reorganizing stock within existing buildings, or by contracting out for supply chain services. If the team decides that new construction is the preferred option, the feasibility study should establish the following—

- Type of store required
- Approximate size of the store and site
- Options for obtaining space
- Assessment of prefabrication versus new construction
- Regulatory requirements
- Potential development incentives
- Short list of possible sites or buildings for the store
- Staff recruitment and training implications
- Outline budget or cost plan, including an assessment of operational and maintenance costs
- Workplan for project completion
- Site selection and acquisition for new construction

Rebuilding from scratch or buying a prefabricated building may be more cost-effective than renovation. Although it may appear at first that renovating an existing building would save money, such "savings" are often offset by lost opportunities for improving efficiency. Chances are that if the current structure is not adequate, a renovation alone would not be the best solution.

Identify type of store required

A mechanized warehouse is required if a large percentage of products will be received and stored on pallets. This type of warehouse requires powered forklift trucks and other equipment capable of moving pallets within the store. Pallets may be stored on the floor (pallet standing/ block stacking) or on pallet racks. Pallet standing—especially block stacking—can be very space efficient, but limits the ability to handle goods on a FIFO (first-in, first-out) or FEFO (first-expiry, first-out) basis. Pallet racking generally makes the most efficient use of space consistent with FIFO or FEFO handling. If pallet racking is chosen, the number of tiers determines the internal height of the store. This critical decision of how to design the pallet storage needs to be made at an early stage; it is dictated largely by the type of handling equipment used. A mechanized warehouse should not be considered unless an effective supply and service network exists for mechanical handling equipment. Preferably, several sources of such equipment should be available. If battery-powered mechanical handling equipment will be used, building space estimates will need to include a battery-recharging area.

A manual warehouse is appropriate if the majority of products will be received and stored in packages that can be moved around by hand or with the assistance of trolleys. A manual store may also require some floor pallets. If pallets are to be handled, manual pallet trucks will be needed to offload them from the delivery vehicles and move them around the store. Most items in a manual warehouse are likely to be stored on shelving units with a top shelf not more than 1.7 meters high and with no package weighing more than 25 kilograms, which means that the internal height of the store is not a critical factor.

Establish approximate size of store and site

The final size of the warehouse and the detailed site layout are established during the design stage. It is essential, however, for the project team to establish approximate sizes during the feasibility stage for three reasons—

- To short-list suitable sites or buildings
- To establish a realistic design brief
- To prepare a budget estimate

Determining store size is complex, because the size of the store is affected by many factors. The most important factors are—

- The volume of individual items
- The maximum stock level for each item
- The way in which goods are stored (floor pallets, pallet racking, or shelves)

DE-JUNK OR EXPAND

- The efficiency of the inventory control and store-keeping systems
- The type of storage required (for example, climate control, refrigeration)
- Quarantine or isolation requirements
- Environmental regulatory and emergency response requirements
- Subdivision of the administrative facilities, if there are multiple users of the store

Stock volume can be estimated from calculations based on volume of past shipments, by analysis of shipping volumes for specific items, or by using item-by-item analysis.

Calculations based on the overall order value and volume of past shipments. If the total value and volume of a shipment are known, it is possible to calculate the value per cubic meter of mixed medicines and other medical supplies and to use this figure as a basis for store sizing. Adjustments may have to be made for inflation if the data are drawn from different periods. This method is most appropriate for calculating volumes at the CMS and other primary stores when a strict annual or periodic ordering system is used and the stock is "topped up" at known intervals.

Analysis of shipping volumes for specific items. For instance, 1 million aspirin, 300 mg, in tins of 1,000, in cartons, from a current supplier might occupy about 1.6 m³. A computer program (spreadsheet or database) can use this type of information for store sizing. This method is retrospective. It does not take account of differences in bulk for similar items from other sources.

Item-by-item analysis using average volumes taken from a range of suppliers. The WHO publication *How to*

Estimate Warehouse Space for Drugs (Battersby and Garnett 1993) provides a method for making an item-by-item analysis. This type of approach applies mainly to specialist areas, such as vaccine stores, where storage equipment costs (for example, cold rooms and freezer rooms) are high, and the risk of underestimating the specialized storage space has severe programmatic implications.

Whichever method of estimating stock volume is used, the store size and type are determined by—

- Maximum net volume of goods to be stored
- How goods are to be stored and handled (floor pallets, pallet racking, or shelving)
- Type of stock location system used (see Chapter 44)
- Climatic conditions
- Area of ancillary spaces, including loading bays; cold rooms; packing areas; locations for storing hazardous materials, climate and air management, and materials-handling equipment maintenance; offices; sanitary facilities; and staff lounges

Finally, the required site size is determined by—

- Size and type of store—a tall, mechanized warehouse has a smaller "footprint" than a manual warehouse that would handle the same volume of inventory
- Space and clearance needed for ancillary buildings, including those for the storage of fuels and hazardous chemicals—safety considerations determine how far away from other buildings hazardous substances should be stored
- Access and parking for delivery and staff vehicles

- Access for fire engines and other emergency services
- Office space
- Water runoff management
- Site security
- Site area needed for future expansion

Select method of obtaining space

There are seven ways of obtaining necessary storage space—

1. *Erect a temporary building.* These buildings are most suitable for use in emergencies, but erecting a temporary building is a rapid and effective solution to a short-term storage problem. A number of excellent temporary warehouse buildings are now available. Their main problem is that because they are fabric-clad, they are inherently less secure than a permanent building.
2. *Reorganize, renovate, or extend an existing health system warehouse.* This approach can be the quickest and cheapest, but only if suitable buildings are available.
3. *Lease a suitable commercial building.* This approach has the advantage of speed and avoids a large capital investment, but nevertheless there will be costs to outfit the space to suit the specific needs of a medical warehouse.
4. *Buy a suitable commercial building.* Again, this approach has the advantage of speed, assuming funds are available, but there will be fitting-out costs.
5. *Build a standard building.* Many countries have standard designs for health service buildings. Advantages of this approach are that design lead time is reduced, cost is more certain, and the design should be proven. The disadvantage is that the performance of standard designs has often not been evaluated effectively. Poor designs may be perpetuated.
6. *Build a purpose-designed building on an existing site, or obtain and develop a new site.* This approach is likely to have the longest lead time and may be the most expensive, but this may not necessarily be so, especially if the government already owns the land. It should ensure the closest fit to the specified requirements.
7. *Purchase a prefabricated building to install at the preferred site.* Assuming a vendor is able to accommodate design requirements, this may be more cost-effective than new construction.

Regulatory requirements

Before searching for potential sites, a review of the federal, regional, and local regulatory requirements that apply to stores facilities is essential. Zoning restrictions, water management laws, and permit or license requirements may all affect the viability of a particular site. In some cases, air or noise emissions or the impact of increased traffic within the area need to be considered. These issues may require an environmental impact assessment; overlooking the implications to the project of such issues could have devastating consequences.

Potential incentives

Often, development incentives exist within territorial areas. Such incentives may include funding of employee training, project financing, land donation, tax reductions and deferrals, and assumption of some operational costs. Incentives can often be more important than logistics benefits when siting the store, particularly if the project has an element of private-sector ownership or operations. A ministry of health may even be able to defer operational or construction costs to other funding sources in the government.

Identify possible sites or buildings

When the sizes of the store and the site have been established, a short list of suitable sites or buildings should be prepared.

Identify staff recruitment and training implications

An assessment of personnel needs should be made at an early stage so that salaries and wages can be budgeted for and a recruitment and training program planned.

Establish an outline budget and obtain a budget allocation

Funding may be obtained from government sources, donor agencies, or commercial sources. The cost consultant should prepare a budget for submission to the funding authority (see Figures 42-1 and 42-2). The budget should include estimated costs for site acquisition, consultants' fees, and construction or installation costs. It should also include an assessment of annual operational and maintenance costs; if these items are not considered and budgeted for, the facility may not be sustainable. After funding is approved, site selection can begin.

The feasibility stage ends with the preparation of a detailed workplan for the design phase, setting out the tasks and timelines for the participants. An outline workplan for the construction phase should also be prepared.

42.4 Site selection and acquisition for new construction

When a budget allocation has been obtained, the project team should recommend the most suitable site or building from the short list.

Figure 42-1   Budget outline for constructing a medical stores from the ground up

Name of project:	
Date of budget:	Anticipated construction start:
Net area:	Gross area:

Capital costs
1. Site acquisition: total cost + commission and fees
2. Construction
   a. Off-site infrastructure (access roads, utilities, etc.)
   b. On-site infrastructure (roads, utilities, walks, paving, landscaping, security fencing, water management, etc.)
   c. Building (structure and works to 1.5 meters outside exterior walls)
   d. Fixed equipment (shelving, pallet racking, climate control and air management, refrigeration, water treatment, water storage for firefighting, etc.)
   e. Materials-handling equipment (forklifts, pallet trolleys, etc.)
   f. Information technology equipment (computers, bar-code readers, etc.)
   g. Furniture and other loose items
3. Professional services (surveys, soil analysis, water analysis, planning, architecture, regulatory licenses/permits and engineering)
4. Miscellaneous costs (utility connection fees, plan approval fees, legal fees)
5. Inspection and testing (job inspection, material testing)
6. Contingencies (cost escalation contingency, construction contingency)
7. Financing (loan fee, interim and permanent financing costs, bond legal fees)

Recurrent costs
8. Annual operational costs (staff salaries and overheads, insurance, equipment maintenance, security, communications, utilities)
9. Average annual maintenance costs (repairs and renewals)

Figure 42-2   Budget outline example for a prefabricated warehouse

- Steel frame
- Gable and cladding
- Chromadek sheeting
- Personnel doors x 2
- Roller shutter doors x 8
- Plans and engineer's certificate
- Estimated concrete floor cost
- Erecting the building
- Storerooms for flammables and corrosives
- Office block
- Dock levelers
- Cold room
- Fitting out and contingency

Selection

In some countries, zoning laws completely prohibit development in certain areas and allow only buildings of a particular type in other areas. Other regulations may limit the size and position of buildings on a chosen site. A suitable site must satisfy all the regulatory requirements, be economical to build on, have convenient and unrestricted access for vehicles and staff, be adequately served by utilities and communications, be secure, and have potential for future expansion. The Assessment Guide at the end of this chapter lists some criteria for site selection.

Acquisition

A site and the buildings on it, or both, may be purchased outright or leased on a long-term or short-term basis. Use of government land or outright purchase is the conventional route for government projects. Leasing may be a suitable method for an agency such as a nongovernmental organization (NGO) whose needs are limited in time. Whichever method is chosen, it is essential that the transfer of ownership or leasehold title be legally correct to avoid later disputes.

42.5 Design stage

There are four stages in the design for new construction. At the end of each stage, the project should be reviewed and a formal decision made to proceed to the next stage. The stages are—

1. *Preliminary proposals:* Preliminary design proposals are prepared and costed. An acceptable scheme is selected. If the building is to be procured on a turnkey or public-private partnership basis, the contractor may be chosen at this stage.
2. *Schematic design:* The design is developed in sufficient detail to enable the client to approve basic spatial

arrangements, materials, and appearance. A more detailed cost estimate is prepared. Mechanical handling equipment suppliers should be consulted where appropriate. At this stage, it may be necessary to obtain formal permission to build from the relevant government authority and seek agreement on the scheme with the fire department. The layout of the building and basic method of construction should not be altered after this stage.

3. *Detailed design:* The construction details are worked out. The cost estimate is refined. Specialist subcontractors and suppliers (such as cold-room manufacturers) are consulted, and quotations are obtained. Formal application is made for approval under local building regulations. If a design-and-build contract is to be used, the contractor is typically selected at this point. Major construction details should not be altered after this stage.

4. *Production information:* Final construction drawings are prepared, together with specifications and bills of quantities. These should be sufficiently detailed to enable contractors to tender for the project.

Client's role

Although executive responsibility for building design and monitoring of the construction contract rests with the project team, the client is responsible for establishing the initial project brief and for raising the necessary funds to cover design and construction costs. In addition, the client's representative on the project team has a project management role to play in the following areas—

- Attending meetings of the project team and monitoring progress
- Developing the brief
- Formally reviewing and approving the scheme as each design stage is completed (altering major decisions made at a previous stage is extremely disruptive and may cause delays and increase costs)
- Ensuring that communications within the team are timely, clear, and accurate
- Scheduling periodic and ad hoc reviews with the client as required
- Arranging payment of fees for planning and building control applications
- Arranging payment of consultants' fees
- Attending meetings with prospective contractors

If the project is large, the client may choose to employ a professional project manager to undertake some or all of these tasks.

All members of the project team, in turn, should ensure that the client is kept fully informed of progress and is pro-

vided with copies of drawings, correspondence, and other documentation.

Some of the general design features that should be considered during the design stages are outlined below. Note that most of these points apply to both ground-up construction and prefabricated building installation.

Detailed project brief

The detailed project brief is the key design document. It should be developed in discussion with the people who will operate, use, and regulate the building. The brief is not a fixed document. It will change and expand as the design develops in response to input from the client and from the project team. Typical elements of a brief are outlined in Table 42-2.

Store and site planning

Storage buildings and site layouts should be planned to allow for future expansion with minimal disturbance to existing building elements, roads, and other physical infrastructure. Air-conditioning, other climate-control elements, and fire management systems are often significant expenditures and dictate building design.

Storage buildings should be planned for maximum flexibility of use. The layout of shelving, racking, and ancillary spaces is certain to change during the life of the building, and the building's future uses will be either enhanced or limited based on the initial investment and design. Buildings with widely spaced columns (wide-span structures) are generally easier to reorganize than those with closely spaced columns. Wide-span structures are more expensive to build, but their long-term advantages are likely to justify the extra expense in all but the simplest manual stores. An alternative approach in "high-bay" warehouses is to use the racking system as part of the building structure. In such cases, the storage system is effectively fixed for the life of the building.

Stores that have a relatively square plan are generally cheaper to build and more efficient to operate than stores that are long and narrow. In a large store, cross aisles should be provided at reasonable intervals to reduce travel time from aisle to aisle. The most appropriate spacing depends on picking frequency. A rule of thumb is a cross aisle every 10 to 20 meters. When assigning storage locations, it is good practice to place slow-moving product lines in long aisles and fast-moving product lines in short aisles (see Figure 42-3).

Storage methods

Goods can be stored in four basic ways: shelves, floor pallets (pallet standing), pallet block stacking, and pallet racks. The choice of storage method depends on the form in which goods arrive: in bulk on prepacked or store-packed

Table 42-2   Typical elements of a project brief ("functional program")

Brief	Elements
Operational brief	• Inventory management and stock control systems and stores management procedures • Description of major activities, including flow of goods and paperwork • Type of stock to be accommodated • Environmental and security (zoning) requirements for different types of stock (see Chapter 43) • Quality control and regulatory requirements • Approximate volumes of stock to be accommodated in each zone • Approximate throughput of store (maximum cubic meters per day received and dispatched) • Operational requirements for shipping goods to other countries (if relevant) • Type of store required (mechanized, manual, or manual to be upgraded) • Schedule of staff • Types and number of delivery vehicles • Number of staff and visitor vehicles to be accommodated • Phasing and program expansion
Site development brief	• Site development restrictions • Access and parking for vehicles and access for pedestrians • Access for emergency services • Water supply and water storage, including water storage for firefighting • Site security and lighting, including gatekeeper's accommodation and barriers • Landscaping • Schedule of individual buildings (main store, flammables store, fuel store)
Building accommodation brief	• Storage – Loading bay – Incoming goods area (for checking, inspecting, sorting, unpacking, and palleting, including power outlets for refrigerated vehicles) – General storage areas (ambient, controlled temperature, controlled security) – Isolation and quarantining of goods – Order assembly and dispatch area, including secure storage for assembled orders – Handling equipment storage, including charging points for electric vehicles – Ancillary storage (office consumables, packing materials, waste) – Battery charging area (if required) – Generator room (if required) • Administration – Detailed schedule of accommodation and facilities required for record keeping (including computers, bar-code readers, RFID readers, and other IT equipment as appropriate), communications, pharmaceutical information, product testing, training • Staff welfare – Sanitary facilities and changing rooms – First-aid room – Lounges and cafeteria or lunchroom

pallets, or as smaller packages. The four storage methods are discussed more fully in Chapter 44. Figure 42-4 illustrates the major dimensional constraints of pallet racking. Figure 42-5 illustrates the major dimensional constraints of shelf storage.

Environmental control and energy conservation

Opportunities for energy conservation exist in all aspects of warehouse design, construction, and operation, from site selection to equipment selection. A well-designed store can significantly moderate internal temperatures in a passive way. Passive design works with the site's microclimate by using trees for shade and shelter, orienting the building correctly for natural lighting and ventilation, and selecting appropriate building materials and methods to control internal temperatures.

In hot, dry climates, good construction and night-time ventilation can maintain daytime temperatures several degrees below ambient temperatures. In hot, humid climates, effective cross-ventilation is required. In cold climates, storage buildings should be well insulated. Mechanical systems such as air-conditioning need to be chosen with a view to future maintenance. Sophisticated systems may not be sustainable.

Adequate electrical lighting is required throughout the store. Bright sunlight and fluorescent lighting affect some pharmaceuticals, and stores should be designed to prevent such damage.

A building design should always consider water management. Rainwater runoff from the site may require special permits or isolation and treatment. Sprinkler systems or fire water may need to be contained, sampled, or treated prior to release to a public system. Regulations should be reviewed carefully and requirements included in the site design.

In tropical climates especially, close attention should be paid to design measures that reduce or eliminate damage by pests, such as termites, reptiles, and rodents.

Figure 42-3   Options for layout of store aisles

Shelving

Arrangement for frequent access

Very frequent access

Assembly area

Frequent access

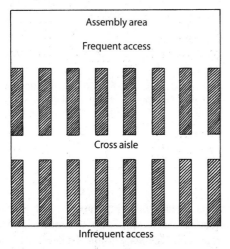

Combined arrangement for frequent and infrequent access

Assembly area

Frequent access

Cross aisle

Infrequent access

Arrangement for infrequent access

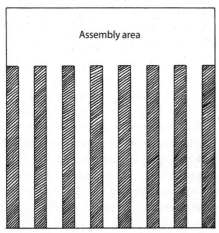

Assembly area

Telecommunications and information technology

Good telecommunications and access to information technology (IT) are increasingly vital components of a pharmaceutical store. Modern IT equipment is already being used for stock control in remote areas, and reliable Internet connections will soon be an essential requirement for effective supply chain management. The pharmaceutical industry has used bar coding for many years. Radio frequency identification devices (RFID) are likely to supplant bar coding on products within the next decade, and their use should greatly improve the accuracy and speed of stock control operations (see Chapter 49 on pharmaceutical management information systems). Buildings should be enabled and ready to exploit this technology when it becomes available locally.

Special storage conditions

The building must provide specific storage conditions for different types of pharmaceuticals. Quarantine and isolation requirements must be incorporated into the design. The quality assurance consultant should provide detailed requirements. See Chapters 19 and 44 for more details.

Ancillary accommodations and loading bays

The design and sizing of ancillary accommodations should be carefully considered. These spaces include offices; staff rooms for rest, recreation, and eating as well as sanitary facilities and changing rooms; receiving and packing areas; and storage space for pallets and other packing materials. Chapter 44 details these requirements.

The vehicle loading bay area is particularly important. It must be protected from the weather and large enough to receive the maximum number of vehicles expected at any one time. In larger stores, the loading bay should be raised so that the floor of the vehicle is level with the floor of the warehouse. Dock-leveling devices are available to suit vehicles of different heights, but vehicles often do not have appropriate structures to be secured to the dock leveler.

Guidelines for security

Pharmaceuticals are small, valuable, and therefore prone to theft (see Chapter 43). The warehouse complex should be designed with security in mind.

- Unsupervised access from the loading bay to the store itself should not be possible. The main storage area where order picking takes place needs to be especially secure. The drivers' waiting area should be isolated from any area containing products and also from administrative offices.

- Ideally, the office area should have windows overlooking the loading bays and the warehouse access.
- The staff rest area, sanitary facilities, and changing rooms should not have direct access to the warehouse or from the outside.
- Visitors and drivers should have separate sanitary facilities.
- Staff parking should be well separated from the loading area.
- Adequate perimeter fencing and external lighting should be provided.
- Emergency evacuation doors should be alarmed to the main office.

Mechanical equipment specifications

The storage systems and mechanical equipment needed to operate the store effectively, including shelving, should be specified in the design. Some of this equipment will be supplied and installed as part of the building contract, but some may be supplied under a separate "fitting-out" contract.

Fire protection and emergency response

All sections of the warehouse should have adequate fire-detection equipment and be well supplied with firefighting appliances. Smoke alarms are inexpensive to install and provide warning in case of fire. The design should satisfy local building codes and the requirements of insurers in the following respects.

Site and building layout and construction. Key aspects of design planning for fire safety include—

- Accessibility by the fire department
- Adequate escape routes and emergency doors with locks that do not prevent staff from leaving the building in an emergency (such as push bars with doors opening outward)
- Compartmentalized buildings to reduce the risk of a fire's spreading
- Isolation doors with appropriate fire ratings between bays
- Electrical connections, wiring, and devices meeting fire safety codes
- Noncombustible building construction materials

Fire-detection and firefighting equipment. Essential components of a fire safety system include—

- Adequate provision of smoke alarms, heat detectors, and fire alarm sounders to ensure that fires are detected as soon as possible
- Correctly positioned fire hydrants and hose pipes with an adequate and reliable supply of water

Figure 42-4   Pallet racking: Dimensional constraints

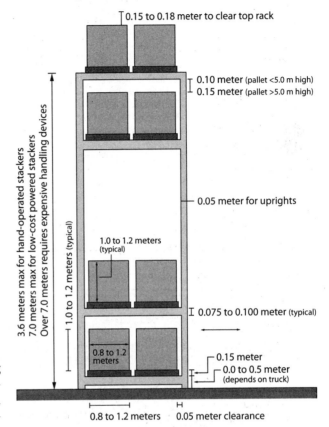

Clearance for lights, sprinklers, etc.

0.15 to 0.18 meter to clear top rack

0.10 meter (pallet <5.0 m high)
0.15 meter (pallet >5.0 m high)

0.05 meter for uprights

1.0 to 1.2 meters (typical)

0.075 to 0.100 meter (typical)

0.15 meter

0.0 to 0.5 meter (depends on truck)

0.8 to 1.2 meters

3.6 meters max for hand-operated stackers
7.0 meters max for low-cost powered stackers
Over 7.0 meters requires expensive handling devices

1.0 to 1.2 meters (typical)

0.8 to 1.2 meters

0.8 to 1.2 meters   0.05 meter clearance

- Correctly designed sprinkler systems (because if a poorly designed system is set off by accident, water may ruin some stock; or if there is a fire, the system may soak stock that is well away from the core of the fire); choice of a dry or wet system must be made with the building managers and the insurers of both the building and its contents
- Adequate numbers and types of fire extinguishers suitable for chemical fires (so staff can extinguish small fires before they spread)
- An automatic or manual telephone link to the fire service

Construction standards

The method and standard of construction required should be agreed on as part of the project brief–development process or spelled out in prefabricated warehouse tender documents. These decisions are important because they affect the initial cost of the building and largely determine how long it will last and how much it will cost to maintain. The government may have standard equipment and construction requirements for all buildings of a particular type.

Figure 42-5   Shelving: Optimal layout with ergonomic considerations

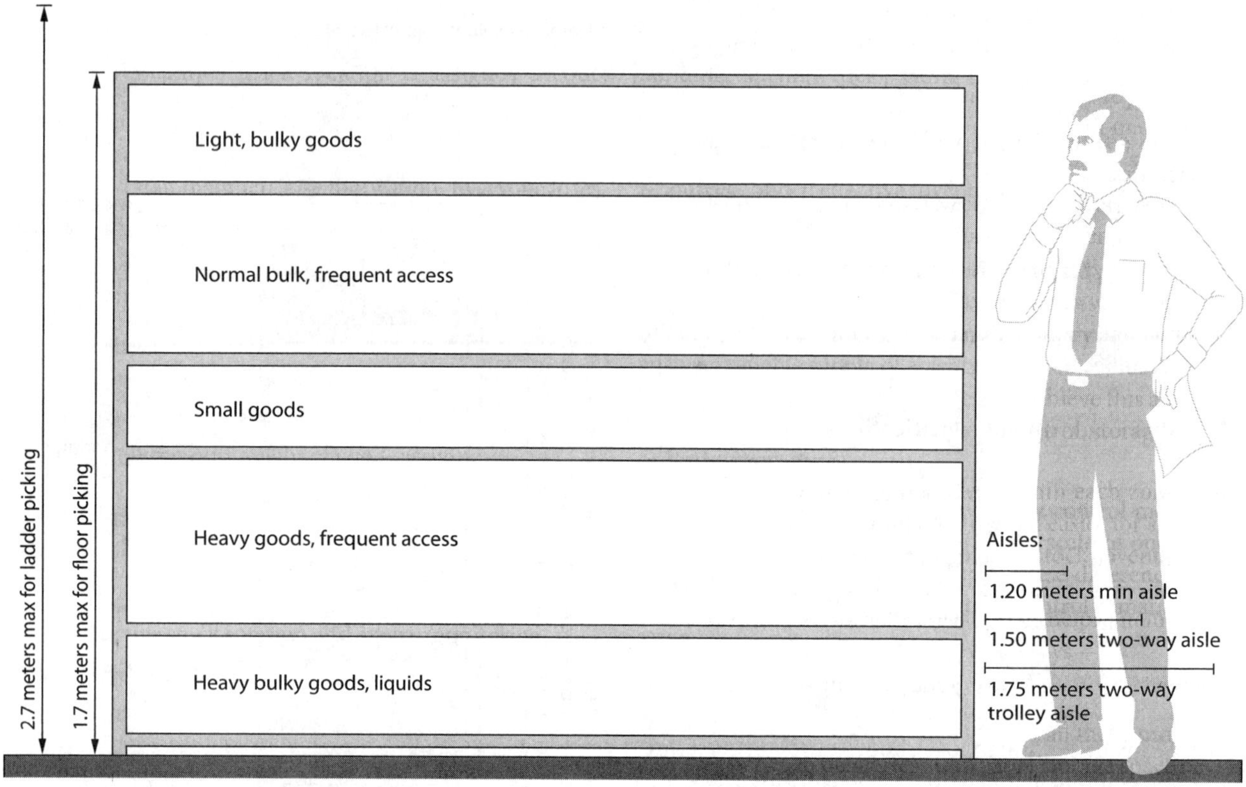

Standardized requirements help simplify maintenance and reduce costs.

Before finalizing the design, it is essential to check that it complies with all relevant engineering and health and safety standards. Failure to do so could create many operational problems after the storage facility is completed.

42.6 Tender and project-planning stage

The tender stage marks the transition point between the design and construction phases. The five procurement routes described below illustrate a range of tendering possibilities. Variations exist, and the project team should recommend the most appropriate method.

Conventional procurement

In conventional procurement, tenderers submit bids based on a set of tender documents complete enough to enable the building to be constructed. There are variations on this method. In a "fast-track" contract, the contractor is appointed as early as possible in the design process and starts work on-site before the design work has been completed. The aim of this approach is to build more quickly by overlapping the design and construction stages.

Fast-track procurement should be considered only if all parties to the contract are experienced and extremely well organized.

Design-and-build procurement

In a typical design-and-build procurement, tenderers are provided with design drawings and specifications. The tender submission is a fixed-price offer to build the tendered design. The successful tenderer is free to change construction details within the limits set in the tender documentation. The client may appoint a professional representative in a monitoring role to report on the activities of the contractor and to ensure that the client's requirements continue to be met as the scheme develops. Alternatively, or in addition, the successful design-and-build contractor may "take over" the client's design team, which will then develop the design for construction.

Turnkey procurement and procurement of prefabricated buildings

In turnkey procurement and procurement of prefabricated buildings, the tender documents consist of a performance specification or schedule of requirements. Tenderers are required to submit preliminary design proposals as part of their bid submissions. The successful tenderer then prepares a fully worked-out design for approval by the client before construction begins. Again, the client may appoint a professional representative to monitor the contractor's activities.

Public-private partnership procurement

A relatively new approach to building procurement is the public-private partnership model, which is essentially a long-term agreement that uses private financing for public services. Under this arrangement, tenderers are invited to bid not just for construction and outfitting of the building, but also for its day-to-day maintenance and operation for a defined period—typically thirty years. In the case of a medical store, the service agreement could include all aspects of inventory management, up to and including ordering and distributing medicines and commodities. The successful contractor charges an annual fee that covers the amortized cost of the building, its operation costs, and the contractor's profit. The contractor's performance is monitored against a set of predefined indicators, with financial penalties in the event of service failure. At the end of the contract period, the building and its equipment are handed back to the client organization in satisfactory condition, as defined in the original contract.

The contract

There should be a formal building contract for all building projects, however small. Informal arrangements lead to disaster. Various forms of contracts are in use, ranging in complexity from a simple letter of agreement to a complex document. Contracts are often country or organization specific. A few are widely used internationally.

The contract is the legal agreement that commits the contractor to carry out work for the building owner according to the drawings, bills of quantity, and materials specifications within a specified time. A financial penalty may be imposed if the building is not completed on time. The contracting agency (client) agrees to pay the contractor a specified sum of money at agreed-upon stages during the course of the work or upon satisfactory completion. Following completion, the contractor has an obligation to rectify any defects that arise within an agreed period after the handover date, which is typically six months or one year. The total contract sum may be varied if the nature or extent of the work changes. Under conventional procurement, the architect is a third party to the contract and can both represent the owner and act as arbiter in case of contractual disputes.

Tendering

A competitive tender is usually the best method of selecting a building contractor or source of a prefabricated building.

Negotiation with one contractor may be applicable when only one company is suitable for the job or when a government building agency (for instance, the ministry of works) is to undertake the project. In all other cases, the tender short list should be drawn up after careful screening. A list of each contractor's projects should be requested and verified. Commercial and bank references should be obtained. Previously completed projects should be visited, and it is helpful to talk with the architects and owners of these buildings about how the contractor performed.

Government clients generally have strict tendering procedures designed to prevent corruption and ensure accountability. There are three basic systems—

1. *Open tendering:* Under this arrangement, any suitably qualified contractor can submit a bid. The tender board then considers bids.
2. *Prequalification tendering:* The contract is advertised, and interested contractors make formal prequalification submissions. The tender board meets and agrees on a short list of contractors. They are invited to submit bids, which are considered by the tender board.
3. *Short-list tendering:* A short list of tenderers is drawn up by the project team or the client. Bids from this list are then considered by the tender board. This method is adopted by most private-sector and NGO clients. A minimum of three contractors should be invited, but the rules may require a larger number.

The tender instructions specify the date for the return of the bid, how it should be presented, and when bids will be opened. It is helpful to ask a trusted third-party observer, such as a bank official or lawyer, to observe the bid-opening process. The witness's testimony will be valuable in any future disputes from unsuccessful bidders. After the bid opening, the bids are analyzed by the project team, and the most economically advantageous one is selected. An economically advantageous bid is not necessarily the cheapest; all aspects of the bid require consideration, including time to completion and contractor reputation and reliability. A comprehensive and carefully constructed bid analysis template is absolutely essential in the case of the unconventional procurement routes described at the beginning of this section. If cost reductions need to be made, they should be negotiated before the contract is signed.

Project planning

Discussions are held with the successful contractor, and a construction or installation program is worked out, including site-access management and construction site security. All contractual matters, including the property and liability insurance obligations of the client and the contractor, are finalized and checked by both parties. If a performance bond is required, it is finalized (see Chapter 39). Facilities for construction workers should meet appropriate standards, with special attention given to site safety and to providing welfare facilities. Injury and other health-related work stoppages or interruptions can significantly delay a project.

The client finalizes funding arrangements so that payments can be made to the contractor on time and at the agreed-upon stages. The contract is then signed.

42.7 Construction and commissioning

The contractual role of the client during the construction phase is largely confined to making payments to the contractor, approving any changes in the cost of the project, and attending formal site meetings. The contract supervising officer (usually the architect) is responsible for the day-to-day administration of the contract. The client should never issue direct instructions to the contractor; instructions should always be channeled through the supervising officer. The supervising officer should regularly provide the client with the following—

- Minutes of the site meetings
- Reports on the contractor's progress and changes in the program
- Reports on significant contractual or construction problems
- Reports on labor issues, including health-related or injury incidents
- A photographic record of the site preparation and construction, which may be carried out by the contractor's staff
- Payment valuations
- Details of changes to the design or specifications (variation orders)
- Details of changes in the cost of the project (cost reports)

In addition, the client must prepare to take over and commission the building. Staff must be allocated, recruited, and trained; equipment, furnishings, and stationery must be purchased; contract arrangements must be made with utility companies; and management systems for the new facility must be drawn up. Transport arrangements need to be established. These tasks are demanding and time-consuming, and adequate resources should be allocated to them.

Supervision

The supervising officer should carry out regular site inspections, preferably once a week, to ensure that the contractor is following the drawings and specifications. If the project is large, a full-time site architect or a site monitor or clerk of works may be appointed by the client. The site monitor has no executive authority. His or her role is to act as the project team's "eyes" on-site and to report to the project team and the supervising officer.

Valuations and payments

The contractor's work should not be paid for until it has been approved by the supervising officer. Any unsatisfactory work must be corrected before it is included in a valuation. Typically, valuations and payments are periodic (often monthly), based on a measurement of work actually completed. Alternatively, for simple projects, they may be made in defined amounts at defined construction stages (for example, 10 percent of the total contract sum when the floor slab has been laid). Payment is made against a certificate issued by the architect. A percentage (usually 5 to 10 percent) of the value of the certificate is retained by the client until the contractor has rectified all defects after the end of the specified defects-liability period. The defects-liability period usually extends for six or twelve months after handover.

Handover

The building is handed over to the client after the design team has fully inspected the completed building and witnessed satisfactory tests of the water supply, drainage, fire protection, and mechanical and electrical services, and after the contractor has corrected any problems. A few outstanding items may remain to be finished, but the list should be short and completion should not interfere with the client's use of the building. The client should attend the pre-handover inspection and should not accept the building unless satisfied. The supervising officer then certifies that the contractor has achieved practical completion.

The contractor hands over all keys to the building and provides the client with instructions on the use of mechanical and electrical equipment. The design team provides a building manual containing a complete set of "as-built" record drawings (drawings revised to show changes made during construction) and general guidance on maintenance. The client's building maintenance officer should be briefed at this stage so that he or she gets to know the building during the defects-liability period.

Commissioning

The client or operator moves into the building and commissions it. At this stage, various "growing pains" can be expected. Some of these will be operational, and some will be caused by building defects. Building problems should be resolved by the contractor and the project team.

Defects liability

During the defects-liability period, the project team, the client, and the contractor agree on the final account. At the end of the defects-liability period, the supervising officer inspects the building again and instructs the contractor to rectify any defects that have arisen. The contractor should be given reasonable access to the building to do so. When all defects have been corrected, a final certificate is issued, and final payment is released to the contractor. If a major contractual dispute has arisen, the issuance of the final certificate (and payment) must be delayed until this dispute is resolved according to the terms of the contract.

Building or renovating a new medical stores facility is a major expense. The temptation to profit personally from the project by bribery or kickbacks is a reality that must be tackled head-on by the project team. Strict controls should be in place to prevent this problem. Advance payments should never be made to the contractor. The client should pay only for work that has been correctly completed and certified.

If the construction process runs into serious problems, a dispute may arise that the parties are unable to resolve. Arbitration is a method of settling such disputes without the need for legal proceedings. Informal hearings are held under the control of an arbitrator, whose judgment is final and binding on the parties to the dispute. This procedure is quicker and less expensive than judicial proceedings. However, arbitration may not be adequate if significant differences of opinion exist as to the quantity or quality of work performed. The type of arbitration procedure and scope of its application should be clarified in the initial contract.

42.8 Building and equipment maintenance

A building and its equipment will not continue performing satisfactorily unless both are regularly maintained. Buildings need both emergency and routine maintenance, but buildings and equipment rarely fail if they are looked after and serviced in a systematic way. A planned cycle of routine maintenance should include general cleaning, replacing lightbulbs, drain clearing, and maintaining fire extinguishers, mechanical equipment, and similar items. Similarly, there should be a planned cycle for periodic maintenance, including painting and replacing life-expired elements such as mechanical equipment and roof finishes. The client should have adequate recurrent and capital budgets and the human resources necessary to carry out these tasks over the life of the building. ■

References and further readings

★ = Key readings.

Alternatives Technologie Pharma, Inc. 2009. A Global Approach to Good Storage and Distribution Practices for the Storage and Distribution of Pharmaceutical Products. *Next Generation Pharmaceutical: eMagazine.* Issue 7. <http://www.ngpharma.eu.com/article/A-global-approach-to-good-storage-and-distribution-practices-for-the-storage-and-distribution-of-pharmaceutical-products/>

Battersby, A., and A. Garnett. 1993. *How to Estimate Warehouse Space for Drugs.* Geneva: World Health Organization Action Programme on Essential Drugs. <http://whqlibdoc.who.int/hq/1993/WHO_DAP_93.3.pdf>

BuyerZone. Steel Buildings Buyer's Guide. <http://www.buyerzone.com/industrial/steel_buildings/bg1-steel-buildings-introduction.html>

★ De Chiara, J., and M. J. Crosbie, eds. 2001. *Time-Saver Standards for Building Types.* 4th ed. New York: McGraw-Hill Professional.

★ Drury, J., and P. Falconer. 2003. *Buildings for Industrial Storage and Distribution.* 2nd ed. Oxford: Architectural Press.

John Snow, Inc./DELIVER in collaboration with the World Health Organization. 2003. *Guidelines for the Storage of Essential Medicines and Other Health Commodities.* Arlington, Va.: John Snow, Inc./DELIVER, for the U.S. Agency for International Development. <http://deliver.jsi.com/dlvr_content/resources/allpubs/guidelines/GuidStorEsse_Pock.pdf>

★ Littlefield, D. 2008. *Metric Handbook Planning and Design Data.* 3rd ed. Oxford, UK: Architectural Press.

Mein, P., and T. Jorgensen. 1988. *Design for Medical Buildings: A Manual for the Planning and Building of Health Care Facilities under Conditions of Limited Resources.* Nairobi: Kenya National Federation of Co-operatives, Ltd. (with support from the Housing Research and Development Unit, University of Nairobi).

★ Mulcahy, D. 1993. *Warehouse Distribution and Operations Handbook.* New York: McGraw-Hill Professional.

★ Murphy, P. R., and D. F. Wood. 2007. *Contemporary Logistics.* 9th ed. Upper Saddle River, N.J.: Prentice Hall.

———. 2003. *Guide to Good Storage Practices for Pharmaceuticals.* Annex 9 to the *WHO Expert Committee on Specifications for Pharmaceutical Preparations: Thirty-seventh Report.* Geneva: WHO. <http://apps.who.int/medicinedocs/pdf/s6156e/s6156e.pdf>

———. 2002. *Guideline for Establishing or Improving Primary and Intermediate Vaccine Stores.* Geneva: WHO Vaccines and Biologicals. <http://whqlibdoc.who.int/hq/2002/WHO_V&B_02.34.pdf>

Glossary

Commissioning: The process of preparing a building for operation. It includes adjusting the heating, ventilating, and air-conditioning systems; establishing security procedures; and training occupants.

Contract sum: The total amount payable by the owner to the contractor for performing the contracted work. Depending on the contract terms, this amount may be adjusted at the end of the contract, to take account of variations approved during construction.

ASSESSMENT GUIDE

Is additional space really required, or can existing space be maximized by—

- Changing delivery intervals?
- Disposing of damaged and expired drugs?
- Reorganizing space within an existing warehouse?
- Contracting out for supply chain services?

If additional space is required, establish availability of funds and consider building procurement. What type of warehouse operation is required?

- Mechanical? If yes, are the necessary equipment and servicing infrastructure available?
- Manual? If yes, will this decision unduly limit future program development?
- Manual, upgradable to mechanical? If yes, are funds available to ensure that the building is designed and built to be suitable for upgrading?

What is the most practical and cost-effective way to obtain additional storage space?

- Erect a temporary building?
- Renovate an existing warehouse?
- Lease a commercial warehouse?
- Buy a commercial warehouse?
- Build a standard warehouse?
- Build a purpose-designed warehouse?
- Purchase a prefabricated warehouse?

What is the most cost-effective method of building procurement?

- Conventional design service?
- Design and build?
- Turnkey or prefabricated package?
- Public-private partnership?

Compare short-listed sites or buildings against the following criteria—

Site development potential

- Will the relevant authorities allow the site to be developed as intended?
- Is the site large enough to satisfy current and expected future needs?
- Is the existing building on the site suitable, or will it have to be demolished?
- Does a risk of contamination or interference exist from neighboring operations?
- Do rights-of-way, liens, and underground rights affect the development potential of the site?
- Is the site well drained? Is there any risk of flooding or other weather-related risk?

- Is the site protected from landslides, earthquakes, avalanches, and other natural hazards?
- Are ground conditions suitable for building economically?
- Will regulatory requirements (for example, environmental, labor, licenses, taxation) affect the development potential of the site?
- Can the site be developed at an acceptable cost?
- Are any fiscal or other incentives available to help fund the project?
- Are there any community issues that could affect the development potential of the site?

Access

- Is the site close to the relevant transport links?
- Do local access routes suffer from vehicle congestion?
- Is the site well served by public transport? (Public transport is needed by staff.)
- Are routes to the site accessible year-round by all types of vehicles?
- Is there adequate access for vehicles and space for parking?

Utilities and communications

- Does the site have a reliable main electricity supply?
- Does the site have a main water supply, borehole, or other reliable source of clean water?
- Is the water supply sufficient for firefighting?
- Does the site have main drainage? If not, are ground conditions suitable for a septic tank or other autonomous system?
- Is there an existing standby generator? If so, is it powerful enough to supply the cold rooms and refrigerators in the new store?
- Does the site have access to reliable telephone, Internet, and postal services?

Security

- Is the site likely to invite intrusion or vandalism?
- Can the site be properly monitored and supervised outside normal working hours?
- Is the site easily accessible by the fire department, police, and ambulance services?

Future conditions

- Will access to the site and the security of the electricity, water drainage, and communications systems be adversely affected by future development in the area?
- Will adequate resources be available to maintain the building and equipment over the life of the building?

Design-and-build procurement: In this method, the contractor takes responsibility for the detailed design and construction of a building based on an agreed-upon preliminary design.

Final account: A financial reconciliation prepared at the end of a building contract, in which the contract sum is adjusted to take account of all variations that have occurred during the construction process. (These variations include design changes by the client, design changes as a result of site conditions, claims for extra payment by the contractor for delays that are not its responsibility, and counterclaims by the owner for damages caused by the contractor's failure to keep to the program.)

Final certificate: A document issued by the architect or contract supervisor that states the amount of money owed by the client to the contractor (or vice versa) at the end of the contract.

Program or brief: A written statement of the owner's conditions and requirements for the project.

Public-private partnership procurement: A method in which the client pays an annual fee for complete building construction, maintenance, and drug storage service over an extended time period.

Record drawings: Drawings revised to show changes made during construction.

Retention: A sum (typically 5 percent) withheld from each payment made to the contractor during the course of construction. This money is usually released to the contractor after all defects have been rectified and the final certificate is issued.

Subcontractor: One who has a contract with the primary contractor to perform a portion of the work.

Turnkey procurement: A method in which the client hires a contracting company to provide a complete building product for a fixed price.

| Part I: Policy and economic issues | Part II: Pharmaceutical management | Part III: Management support systems |

Planning and administration
Organization and management
  43 Security management
  44 Medical stores management
  45 Hospital pharmacy management
  46 Pharmaceutical management for health facilities
  47 Laboratory services and medical supplies
Information management
Human resources management

CHAPTER 43

Security management

SUMMARY

Security breaches include theft, bribery, and fraud. They can have a substantial, and sometimes disastrous, economic and health effects. A comprehensive security system includes—

- Analysis of the sources of security breaches
- Determination of methods to improve security
- Consideration of costs and savings
- Implementation of security measures

Security breaches can be found through a mix of informal and formal investigations, independent inventory counts, consumption comparisons, and surveys of medicine outlets. The conditions that lead to theft often include—

- Shortage of the products in the market or at service-provision points
- High product demand
- High product value and hence a good open market for the product
- Economic conditions that lead people to market stolen products
- Weak security measures that make theft easy

Theft prevention may require—

- Providing unique identifiers for all pharmaceutical supplies
- Dealing with the sources of theft
- Closing the outlets for stolen medicines
- Improving record keeping and instituting a perpetual inventory control system
- Improving salaries for staff members who handle medicines
- Controlling access to the storage facility

Controlling bribery requires mechanisms to prevent suppliers from influencing the choice of medicines, purchase quantities, and selection of suppliers.

Fraud control requires close attention to quality assurance procedures and routine stock control procedures. Security measures may be expensive, but they are often very cost-effective.

43.1 Introduction

Theft, bribery, and fraud can interfere with the effective functioning of national pharmaceutical supply systems. In some countries, security breaches can be the single most devastating problem for pharmaceutical programs. A strong security system can—

- Minimize shortages
- Minimize abuse or misuse
- Contribute to accurate record keeping on medicine consumption and disease prevalence

In one Central African country, a hospital pharmacist routinely allowed for losses of 80 to 90 percent on certain medicines when she placed her orders to ensure that she received enough supplies to treat hospital patients. In an extremely poor Southeast Asian country, losses caused by theft are estimated to be more than 30 percent of the total pharmaceutical supply, despite theoretically strict accounting requirements for medicines. The government medical store in an East African country is reported to have placed an order for more than 100,000 U.S. dollars' (USD) worth of pharmaceutical cocaine, which vanished from the wharf when it arrived.

Pharmaceutical pilferage was a problem in a facility in one West African country. Managers took measures to make pilferage difficult, including reinforcing doors and windows, clearly and systematically shelving medicines, putting into place a perpetual inventory system for fast-moving and high-demand pharmaceutical products, and limiting unauthorized access to the store. Despite those measures, medicines still disappeared. Suspecting that the facility's storekeeper might be involved, the managers announced a plan that denied their own free access to the store and gave the storekeeper the authority to search the managers when they exited the store. In addition, the managers made the storekeeper financially responsible for any future losses, which prompted him to voluntarily quit his job, indicating that the storekeeper was comfortable working there only as long as he was able to pocket some of the medicines. Most losses or thefts are caused by employees working alone or in collusion with others.

Other examples can be cited. In a Central American country, inventory records showed that stock levels of oral ampicillin, antibiotic eye ointment, and dozens of other products were intentionally overstocked—enough for three, five, ten, and up to thirty years—because government buyers received special "commissions" for their purchase. Theft of antibiotics for black market sale and treatment of sexually transmitted infections is common in many countries. Hospitals in the United States have a difficult time controlling staff pilferage, and several incidents in recent years have involved theft and resale of significant quantities of public-sector medicines. In a scandal involving pharmaceutical suppliers and airport personnel, a consignment of antiretroviral medicines (ARVs) headed to an African country from a European country was flown back to Europe before it even reached the store.

Security breaches can and should be confronted. Theft and wastage are caused by a mixture of cultural, political, and economic factors. Nevertheless, even when bribery and theft are coordinated or condoned at high levels, countries have been able to reduce these activities when supply system managers have made a strong commitment to do so.

Improving security involves analyzing the sources and nature of security breaches, developing methods for improving security, and comparing the costs of security measures with the financial and public health costs of inadequate security. Country Study 43-1 shows how Ethiopia assessed and addressed security concerns before introducing a new antiretroviral therapy (ART) program.

In 2004, the World Health Organization (WHO) launched a Good Governance for Medicines program to—

- Raise awareness of the impact of corruption in the pharmaceutical sector
- Increase transparency and accountability in medicine regulatory and supply management systems
- Promote individual and institutional integrity in the pharmaceutical sector
- Institutionalize good governance in pharmaceutical systems by building national capacity and leadership

The program website (http://www.who.int/medicines/ggm) offers many resources that relate to the issues covered in this chapter.

43.2 Analysis of security breaches

Security breaches include theft, bribery, and fraud, and they can occur at all levels of the pharmaceutical supply cycle, including procurement, storage, and distribution. Shortages caused by these activities can lead to suffering and death.

Country Study 43-1
Securing antiretrovirals from theft: Ethiopia's experience

In 2005, Ethiopia started its first large-scale public program to distribute ARVs free to patients with HIV/AIDS through selected public hospitals. Previously, ARVs were only available from private pharmacies to patients who could afford their cost. Because the initial phase of the treatment program was limited, the government gave first priority to clinically eligible patients with low or no income and to special groups, such as children and pregnant women. When the availability of ARVs increased, a policy of universal access replaced screening patients based on income. Because the demand for ARVs outweighed the supply, and because ARVs are high-value and high-demand products, preserving the limited supply of ARVs through secure storage was of paramount importance.

Following an assessment conducted by Management Sciences for Health's Rational Pharmaceutical Management Plus (RPM Plus) Program, a parastatal pharmaceutical procurement and distribution organization called PHARMID was given responsibility for clearing, storing, and distributing ARVs at the central level. RPM Plus evaluated and recommended PHARMID based on the availability of separate storage space; security of the premises (strong walls, secure ceiling, metal doors, barred windows, armed guards); limited access to storage spaces; adequate record keeping and inventory control; history of security breaches; measures against culprits; availability

of insurance on products and safe transport; and presence of a dedicated store manager for ARVs.

RPM Plus also assessed the public hospitals that were to distribute ARVs to patients and found that all aspects of the storage capacity, security, and record keeping were weak. Because putting ARVs into such a vulnerable environment would be risky, RPM Plus helped the facilities address security concerns through a number of interventions, including renovating the physical infrastructure (improve storage space; reinforce walls, ceilings, doors, and windows); providing lockable storage cabinets and dispensing booths; developing information system tools for inventory control, reporting, and auditing; and developing standard operating procedures and training staff members in how to use them.

Now, the public hospitals store ARVs in separate bins and monitor their movement weekly. Specific staff members are assigned to manage ARVs, and access to the medicines is limited to these people. The treatment register that is maintained for all patients in the program gives a running total of patients and the medicines they have taken. The register makes it easy to calculate the number of medicines dispensed, which ensures that the inventory status is reliable. The register is an important monitoring tool that helps minimize the vulnerability of ARVs from theft and pilferage.

Figure 43-1 shows the main types of security breaches and the levels at which they occur.

Some factors that promote theft are—

- Shortages of essential medicines
- High demand for medicines in the private sector
- Poor physical security in stores
- Weak inventory records
- Unlimited access to stores by unauthorized people
- Paying staff members salaries that are significantly lower than necessary for self-support
- Access by underpaid staff members to high-value products
- Inadequate legal systems for dealing with thieves

Politically motivated thefts can be a form of sabotage that creates generalized shortages and discredits the government, or they can be a means of financing political operations through the sale of stolen pharmaceuticals.

Stolen medicines find their way to four major types of outlets. They may be exported to adjacent countries through legitimate or illegitimate trade routes; sold to local private warehouses, pharmacists, or physicians for subsequent retail sale; sold directly to the public through street vendors; or distributed to family and friends.

43.3 Searching for security breaches

Identifying major security breaches and the places where they usually occur is the first step in controlling them. Several methods exist for uncovering theft, bribery, and fraud—

- Taking unannounced physical inventory counts
- Checking consumption using inventory records
- Monitoring and reviewing patient records
- Surveying suspected sales outlets
- Gathering anonymous, informal information

Informal channels (such as informants, spot checks, and ad hoc staff meetings) may be one way of determining whether a problem exists. Pharmacists, physicians, politicians, and other officials often know of, or at least suspect, diversion. Large stocks of unissued and unusable medicines at medical stores, the overnight disappearance of large quantities of medicines, systematic failure of deliveries to reach their final destinations, and frequent shortages at well-supplied facilities indicate a security problem. Responding vigorously to informal reports of diversion can be quite effective.

Unannounced physical inventory counts can uncover security breaches at all levels. The results of a surprise stock count should be compared with medicine receipts and

issues. Sampling only a selection of facilities at various levels may be sufficient to determine the extent of the problem; certainly, any facilities where problems are suspected should be included in the sample.

Consumption comparisons using inventory records can sometimes be revealing. For example, in one Central American country, theft of significant quantities of medical supplies, equipment, and food was uncovered by comparing the stock issued to each facility with the past consumption patterns at that facility. This comparison suggested that certain hospitals were ordering suspiciously large quantities of supplies. The hospitals and departments involved were then carefully examined, and security breaches were identified. A similar approach has been helpful in other countries. This system depends on the presence of an up-to-date record-keeping system. An organized group involved in stealing will intentionally make the record-keeping system non-functional, so that the control system will not be effective.

Surveys of suspected private outlets for black market sales are often effective. When government-purchased pharmaceuticals can be distinguished by capsule type, batch number, packaging, or some other identifier, a survey of street vendors, pharmacies, and physicians' supplies can identify pharmaceuticals from government sources. Tanzania is one country that has labeled packaging for artemisinin-based combination therapy differently for the public and private sectors, to track leakage.

43.4 Controlling theft

Three common forms of theft are—

1. Slow, sustained, small-scale leakage that may go unnoticed for a long time. Staff members with access to the medicines storage area are usually responsible for such losses.
2. Large-scale robbery that may involve people both inside and outside the pharmaceutical supply system. For example, groups that conduct clandestine actions, such as political groups involved in guerilla warfare, may raid warehouses to meet their pharmaceutical supply needs.
3. Diverting a shipment before it reaches its destination, which may involve people in responsible positions with access to information on the movement of goods.

When the major sources of losses have been identified, methods to control theft, bribery, and fraud should be implemented. Theft can be tackled by prevention and control measures that include installing physical barriers (closing outlets for stolen goods; reinforcing doors and windows); using human and electronic security guard systems; providing adequate storage and shelving; enforcing

Figure 43-1   Summary of common security breaches

Suppliers (manufacturers, foreign suppliers, importers)
- Intentional short packing
- Intentional omission of expensive active ingredients
- Shipping of products near their expiration date
- Dilution and repacking of liquid medications
- Delivery of incomplete orders and billing for full amounts

Wharf/Airport
- Off-loading of government shipments directly onto vessels bound for nearby countries
- Petty theft by port workers
- Major theft from wharves, customs warehouses, airport fields, and elsewhere

Purchasing Office
- Acceptance of bribes in return for purchase of unnecessary types of medicines, purchase of excessively large quantities of medicines, or purchase from specific suppliers
- Intentional overpurchasing to obtain quantities sufficient for systematic diversion into the black market while maintaining legitimate government distribution

Medical Stores (central, regional, and hospital)
- Major theft through breaking and entering
- Major systematic theft by employees
- Acceptance of bribes from suppliers for intentional overordering of specific items
- Intentional underordering by government pharmacists or storekeepers, so that shortages will arise, followed by compensatory purchasing from local pharmacists who offer illegal "commissions"

Transportation
- Selling of medicines by drivers and at markets along the delivery route
- Consumption of preparations containing alcohol by delivery staff, who then refill bottles with water
- Systematic diversion of large quantities for black-market sale
- Theft of large quantities by nursing staff for use in their own unofficial private practices

In Hospitals
- Petty theft by delivery staff, nurses, and doctors for personal and family use
- Drinking of spirited preparations by hospital staff, who refill bottles with water
- Systematic diversion of large quantities for black-market sale
- Theft of large quantities by nursing staff for use in their own unofficial private practices

Outpatient Departments
- Patients faking illness to obtain medicines for resale
- Visits by patients to several clinics to obtain multiple prescriptions for antibiotics, analgesics, and other popular resale items
- Writing of multiple prescriptions by physicians—to the same person or to false names—in return for a share of resulting black-market sales

Health Centers/Village Health Workers
- Pilfering of health center supplies by government physicians and health workers for use in their private practices
- Popular black-market items overordered from medical stores and diverted by physicians, nurses, dispensers, or laborers

Figure 43-2 Unique identifiers

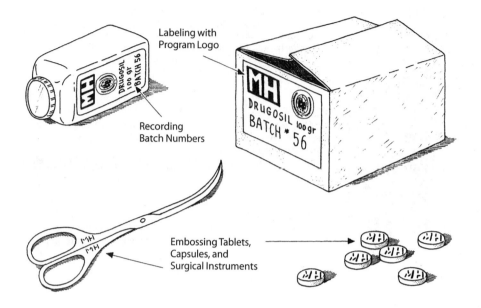

Labeling with Program Logo

Recording Batch Numbers

Embossing Tablets, Capsules, and Surgical Instruments

correct and regular record keeping and inventory audits, and maintaining an active procurement and shipment tracking system; improving working conditions of personnel, including salary increases; educating staff and increasing their moral awareness and responsibility; involving other stakeholders and the community as watchdogs; and taking disciplinary or legal measures against the thieves and their collaborators.

A hotel in Harare, Zimbabwe, had problems with guests' missing property and came up with the idea of writing "thou shalt not tempt" on visible places, such as ashtrays, toilets, mirrors, and doors. The message to the guest is to keep valuables in a safe place and not to leave them in the open. Keeping high-value and high-demand products out of public view and limiting access to authorized personnel will minimize theft.

The private sector can be more successful at preventing theft and pilferage because it uses the enumerated measures systematically and consistently.

Inventory control

Good inventory management and stock control systems are essential for detecting and controlling theft (see Chapter 23). At each level in the supply system, records should indicate how much of each type of medicine was received and issued, who received or issued the medicines and verified the amounts, the source of medicines received, and the destination of every issue. Such information provides an audit trail for the purchase, distribution, and consumption of medicines. The records also provide a basis for comparing medicine consumption with use of services and a starting

point for tracing security breaches. Such recorded transactions will have great value if they are documented and reported monthly and if feedback is provided to the reporting facility.

A good information system alone is often not enough, and additional deterrent measures are needed.

Unique identifiers

An individual or group caught with medicines believed to be stolen may claim that the medicines were purchased. Theft is difficult to prove unless medicines have unique identifiers, as shown in Figure 43-2. A country can require suppliers to identify medicines in one or more of the following ways—

- Imprint all containers (bottles, boxes, foil packages) and external packing (cartons, crates) with a unique client seal or monogram.
- Register batch numbers on all immediate containers and external packing and (if purchase quantities are large) agree not to sell products from the same batch to any other buyer in the country or in adjacent countries.
- Emboss tablets and print capsules with a unique client monogram.
- Color code tablets and capsules.
- Use electronic tagging devices. The latest technologies involve electronic identifiers detectable through GPS (global positioning systems), which can trace the location of a tagged product. This option, however, is expensive and may not be feasible in resource-limited environments.

Unique identifiers have been introduced in many pharmaceutical programs. They can, however, increase medicine prices significantly, and this economic disincentive has led to the discontinuation of the program in some countries. Whether identifiers should be used depends on the following factors: the types and quantities of medicines purchased, the capacity and willingness of suppliers to provide identifiers, the incremental expense of doing so, the speed with which deliveries are needed, and the source and extent of pharmaceutical theft.

Imprinting containers and packaging. Container imprinting is the most common type of identifier. The immediate container and the external packing are imprinted with the name or initials of the government program, the seal of the government, or some other symbol. In one South American country, individual foil packets as well as external boxes contain the program title "Medicamentos Básicos," and all are printed with the same color code. In Sri Lanka, all container labels are required to bear the national seal. In Malaysia, containers are labeled as ministry of health property.

Imprinted containers can be used to identify stolen pharmaceutical products only when thieves keep the products in their original containers. If large numbers of pills are packaged in plastic-lined containers, culprits can easily remove the inner lining and destroy the identifying imprint. They will have to take much more time and effort to remove pills from individual foil packets or blister packages. In some countries, the business is so lucrative that thieves produce their own packing materials or containers to elude such preventive measures.

Container imprinting adds extra time and cost to the packing process. A requirement to imprint all immediate and external containers may delay shipments, increase the price, or dissuade some suppliers from bidding. One solution is to require imprinting only for orders that exceed a set minimum quantity or order value.

Batch number registration. The use of batch numbers as unique identifiers is less obvious to thieves than imprinted containers. By forbidding contract suppliers to sell products with the same batch numbers anywhere else in West Africa, one country was able to identify stolen goods and close several major black market wholesale and retail outlets, recovering thousands of dollars' worth of stolen government medicines.

Because the unique batch number requirement does not add time to the manufacturing process, it is less likely to add to the cost or delivery time. However, suppliers may not be willing to restrict sales of a batch unless the requesting supply system purchases all or most of the batch. Thieves who are aware of the system can still remove the label or discard the container. Furthermore, the use of batch numbers as unique identifiers is effective only if the contractual requirement is monitored and enforced.

Tablet embossing and capsule imprinting. Imprinting individual tablets and capsules with the pharmaceutical program's initials or seal provides the most effective protection against diversion for resale in the private sector. However, it is also the option most likely to increase medicine prices. Country Study 43-2 gives an example of this practice in Southeast Asia. The embossing and imprinting process is easiest to implement in state-owned factories. With commercial suppliers, lead times may increase and prices may greatly increase because of the embossing requirement. The pricing gap may decrease if imprinting is required only for large-quantity orders.

See Chapter 19 for additional information on using product identification technology to ensure the integrity of the pharmaceutical product and to deter theft and counterfeiting.

Country Study 43-2
Tablet and capsule embossing in Southeast Asia

In one successful government pharmaceutical supply program, contracts with suppliers specified that tablets and capsules in quantities greater than 500,000 units had to be embossed with the Ministry of Health initials. All tablets produced by the government pharmaceutical plant also had to be embossed.

Theft of attractive items such as diazepam, paracetamol, antibiotics (used extensively for sexually transmitted infections), and other medicines was a steady, if small-scale, drain on supplies in major hospitals. Individual ampicillin and tetracycline tablets, which cost the government less than USD 0.04, were sold for USD 0.50 to USD 1.00 each on the black market.

The embossing of tablets did not stop these thefts, but it substantially reduced large-volume theft and subsequent sale to commercial pharmacies and physicians. In one year, losses caused by theft during the wharf-clearing and delivery process amounted to 5 to 10 percent. A thorough investigation of pharmacies and doctors' offices in the capital city uncovered several places that dealt in stolen pharmaceuticals. This investigation led to a rapid reduction in thefts. Without the embossing on the tablets and capsules, proving that the medicines had come from government stores would have been difficult, if not impossible.

Good management

One principle of theft control is to provide secure storage places with limited access at all points in the distribution system. A weak physical infrastructure predisposes itself to easy break-ins. Cheap locks, glass windows without metal bars, poor lighting inside and outside the stores, weak walls and doors, and congested and disorganized storage that makes taking inventory difficult all provide a weak link in the security system. If security guards exist, they are often not supervised well, nor are they well trained or equipped to protect the property. In urban locations where private security companies have strong monitoring and support systems, outsourcing external security is cost-effective. Country Study 43-3 describes a pilot project for improving inventory control in Sierra Leone.

A second principle is active use of the information system to detect theft and trace the point where it occurred. The best inventory system is useless unless periodic physical stock counts are compared with recorded stock levels, and unfortunately, many record-keeping systems are not well monitored, and information is not updated regularly. The transaction between stores and dispensaries in many places is recorded only in bulk quantities and not by individual pharmaceutical products. Claiming a product as issued when, in fact, most of it is diverted, is very easy. Detailed record keeping and a patient treatment register with specifics on prescribed quantities can ensure that every product is accounted for. Record tampering and excuses of lack of staff for handling record keeping can be cover-ups for potential corruption.

Although designing a system that prevents theft at every point in the flow of medicines from port to patient is probably not possible, measures can be implemented to attack the problem at its major sources—

- Strengthen physical storage facilities with solid doors and windows, and reinforce with bars.
- Introduce systematic and orderly shelving.
- Use unique product and container identifiers.
- Strengthen inventory-control systems at all levels.
- Maintain a perpetual inventory system with regular physical counts.

Country Study 43-3
Experience in improved inventory control in Sierra Leone

The Sierra Leone Ministry of Health introduced improved security measures as a pilot project. At the time, the supply system lacked proper storage and inventory control, and essential medicines were in short supply. More than USD 1 million in medicines had been stolen the previous year. The project's main aims were to enforce accountability, strengthen security, and provide training in store and pharmaceutical management at central medical stores and selected district, hospital, and peripheral health unit levels.

Improvements were made at the hospital level. First, the hospital store was renovated. Wooden doors were replaced with reinforced double-lock steel doors, windows were fitted with steel bars, and the ceiling was reinforced to prevent access from adjacent rooms. A large lockable shelf was provided for expensive, fast-moving items. All other items were kept in sealed boxes on pallets. A storekeeper was appointed. The hospital pharmacy was cleaned, obsolete items were removed, and shelves and medicine cabinets were constructed. The pharmacy was divided into two parts: a mini-store and a dispensing room equipped with a small lockable cabinet. The mini-store supplied the dispensing room. Replenishment was made with a special requisition form only after previous receipts had been accounted for. The dispenser or pharmacist issued medicines by official prescription to patients through a dispensing window. Access to the store was limited to the storekeeper in charge. At the end of the day, the storekeeper, the dispenser, and the cashier audited the day's transactions and tallied the money received against the supplies issued. The money was then deposited in a special revolving drug fund that was used to replenish medicines. The strict physical and inventory record control and the weekly perpetual inventory of selected fast-moving medicines improved security.

Worries existed, however, about the system's integrity. Several creative methods of pilfering were discovered. In one of the stores, the containers all appeared to be in place when viewed from floor level; when viewed from a height (the supervisor climbed a ladder), empty spaces could be seen where medicines had been removed. It was also discovered that medicines had been removed from their containers and the empty containers replaced on the shelves. After these thefts were discovered, the storekeepers were held responsible. Subsequently, such pilfering techniques were abandoned.

The security system was effective for a few years, but ultimately, the system broke down as major economic and social problems engulfed the country.

Source: G. Daniel, unpublished data, Africare, 1994.

- Insist on perpetual record checking with discrepancy reporting.
- Concentrate security measures on fast-moving, popular, and expensive items.
- Assign responsibility for security to one person.
- Limit store access to accountable staff members only.
- Disallow individual prescription filling from the store.
- Improve staff salaries and working conditions.

When corruption and theft are prevalent in a supply system, extremely low staff salaries are often a contributing factor. Increasing salaries to a level comparable to local private-sector salaries for similar positions is expensive but may be cost-effective if losses can be controlled.

Many of those responsible for handling valuable and expensive ARVs are government employees. Constraints relating to the civil service that might hinder good security management include—

- Compulsory rotation (may apply to trained staff)
- Exposure to recruitment embargoes/vagaries
- No hiring/firing responsibility
- No control over remuneration
- Lack of resources
- Government security personnel (only) on duty at key sites; they may be military staff, for example, untrained for the job required

Some physical security measures that can be used at all levels in the supply chain include—

- Improved external and internal lighting
- Alarm systems
- Watchdogs
- Private security agents
- Secure fencing
- Double locks
- Strong, lockable delivery boxes and containers
- Closed delivery vans

Narcotics and controlled medicines require special security management practices. Special procedures may include restricting who can access information regarding purchases and shipments and planning for increases in usual product volume that might occur when, say, a country is introducing or scaling up methadone maintenance programs as a way to decrease the spread of HIV. Methadone products are generally low cost; however, their street value may be much higher, making them valuable targets for thieves. Managers need to consider ways to mitigate risk; for example, in Vietnam, providers add a low-temperature caramelizing agent to the liquid methadone preparation, which makes it impossible to concentrate—adding heat will quickly give the product a tarry consistency that makes it impossible to inject.

The United Nations (2007) has developed guidelines on procuring controlled substances for dependency treatment.

Box 43-1 provides a sample of techniques used in various parts of the world. Unfortunately, the comparative effectiveness of the various methods has not been tested and is likely to vary from country to country, depending on the commitment of individuals and on political, cultural, and economic circumstances.

Law enforcement and closing of outlets

When the major outlet for stolen goods is black market sale within the country, the incentive to steal is reduced greatly by closing black market outlets. This step is more easily taken if the outlets can be readily identified and if pharmaceutical products carry unique identifiers.

Governments that condone the presence of open-market drug peddlers are often victims themselves, because the medicines sold in these illegal outlets are often products stolen from government programs. Eliminating unauthorized outlets is a first step in controlling theft and irrational medicine use.

Unfortunately, police may be unwilling or unable to spend time on such activities. To solve this problem, the pharmaceutical section of one Southeast Asian ministry of health managed to obtain authority from the police department for its own staff to investigate and prosecute violations, which improved enforcement efforts. Such a solution would not work, however, if theft were coordinated or condoned at the upper levels of the supply system.

When stolen pharmaceuticals are sold through a multitude of street vendors, closing the outlets may not be feasible because they are difficult to identify and locate. In those instances, control can be exerted more effectively at the sources of theft rather than at the outlets.

43.5 Bribery

Illegal payments from suppliers to purchasing officials can occur at all levels and in any country. The supplier may try to use bribery to influence which medicines are bought, how much is purchased, or which suppliers are selected. A determined supplier can influence decisions in most supply systems. Bribery is made more difficult if separate mechanisms are established for making each of those three decisions and if all decisions are made by a committee rather than by an individual.

Measures that can discourage bribery include making sure the system is transparent; identifying the parties involved; bringing the culprits to justice through an anticorruption or similar mechanism; and instituting court action. If bribery is considered a major issue in an organization, using covert techniques can help identify the individuals or the network.

Box 43-1
Techniques for theft control

Monitor selected items

Monitoring should be targeted at those products that are most likely to disappear—those that are fast moving, chronically in short supply, in high demand by consumers, expensive, lifesaving, and easy to hide or disguise. A simple way to monitor targeted medicines is to—

1. Select a drug product that is particularly likely to be pilfered or that may be misused (prescribed inappropriately), for example, tetracycline tablets.
2. Check pharmacy or storeroom inventory records to determine consumption during a specified period (example: 8,000 tablets were issued during a three-month period).
3. Check medical charts or prescription ledgers and count the number of treatment courses over the same period (example: 101 adults were dispensed fifty-six tetracycline tablets each).
4. Convert treatment courses to dose units (example: 5,656 tablets).
5. Compare this figure with the stock issued from the storage area. If the difference is significant, further investigation and possibly punitive action are warranted.

A system of supervision that incorporates scheduled and unscheduled visits to facilities will deter theft and fraud. A monthly audit system and report on stock status coupled with on-the-spot physical counts of selected items will indicate foul play. Such preventive measures will help minimize losses and ensure that the problem is identified and addressed before large losses occur.

At the port

Containerization. If the port is equipped to handle containers, containerization reduces both major and petty theft because containers are physically secure (although entire containers can be stolen).

Rapid port clearance. Inadequate and inefficient port-clearing procedures can lead to long delays, providing opportunities for theft if security is weak. Increased efficiency in port clearing reduces theft. Ensure that all necessary documents for clearance (airway bill, invoice, certificate of analysis, certificate of free sales) are ready.

At the medical stores

Limited access. Access to medicine storage areas should be limited to the store's staff members only. Hospital pharmacies should not be accessible on evenings or

weekends or when the pharmacist or dispenser is not present. Limited extra supplies for emergency rooms and wards should be entrusted to medical officers or nurses when the pharmacy is closed. Their distribution should be accounted for and monitored by pharmacy staff.

Secure locks and doors. These physical barriers are essential to good security. Country Study 43-3 describes improvements that can be made.

Unannounced searches of medical stores and hospital staff and security staff. In some countries, the pharmacist or medical director personally supervises periodic, unannounced searches.

Independent stock count. Staff members from the central pharmaceutical supply office should visit all major medical stores periodically to perform either a complete or a sampling stock count and an audit of receipt and issue records.

During transport

Document verification. A selected staff member should be responsible for checking receipts against the packing slip. A separate invoice should be sent from the issuing store, and the receiving form should be verified against this invoice. This control measure shows where shipments have partially or completely disappeared in transit. A waybill used during any delivery (that records the date of travel, destinations, driver, particulars of the vehicle, products transported, date of arrival, and signature by the dispatcher and the person in-charge at the destination) is an important tracking measure.

Packing seals. Shrink-wrapped pallets and tape, wax seals, and wire seals used to close cardboard boxes or other transport containers make tampering obvious to see.

Strongboxes. When large shipments are made to small numbers of facilities, portable strongboxes or built-in compartments with padlocks or tamper-proof strings should be used. One key should remain at the issuing store and the other at the receiving store.

In hospitals

Pharmaceutical accounting. Ward and outpatient staff should record all pharmaceuticals received and dispensed. These records should be checked periodically (monthly or bimonthly) against pharmacy issue records. A daily treatment register that keeps a record of all patients treated, by age, gender, diagnosis, and prescribed quantities, can give a running total of medicines that can be linked with stock status.

Issue-consumption verification. For dangerous and controlled medicines, and for medicines that are frequently stolen, a consumption report showing the time, date, patient, patient's number, dose, and remaining stock levels should be submitted to the pharmacist with each order for additional stocks.

Presentation of prescriptions for ward issue. For selected expensive or frequently abused medicines, the hospital pharmacy should be provided with a copy of the signed prescription to be filed with the pharmacy before medicines are issued to the ward.

Rotating stock containers. Wards can keep a limited number of labeled containers for each medicine they stock. When the containers are empty, they must be returned to the pharmacy for replenishment, along with the dispensary record for the medicine. The containers allocated for each medicine should hold enough stock for several days. Excessive replenishment of stock is cause for suspicion.

Locked transport boxes. The pharmacy can issue medicines in wooden or metal boxes with padlocks. Each ward should have its own box. The pharmacist should have a key for all ward boxes, and the head nurse should have the second key for that ward's box.

Upgrading of transport staff. In several countries, security has improved when nursing students, dispensers, or nurses, rather than laborers, collect medicines from the pharmacy. When the pharmacy establishes and adheres to an appropriate issuing schedule for wards, nursing staff are able to allocate time to collect medicines.

Upgrading of pharmacy staff. Gradual replacement of untrained dispensary staff with trained pharmacists and dispensers has been credited with reducing theft in some countries. A combination of more careful screening of individuals, professional socialization, and higher pay may explain this observation.

In outpatient departments and health centers

Maximum dispensing quantities. Setting a maximum quantity prevents patients from altering prescriptions to obtain large amounts of medicines and prevents collaborating physicians from writing excessively large prescriptions.

Recording of individual prescriptions. This measure is recommended to increase the dispenser's accountability. A patient treatment register serves as a prescription record of all medicines issued, corresponding to the disease. The register makes any discrepancy in prescription amount, overprescription, incompatibilities, or evidence of irrational medicine use easy to see.

Influencing choice of medicines

In Chapter 16, it was noted that the participation of a panel of respected physicians, pharmacists, and public officials often improves the appropriateness of medicine selection and makes the process more credible and therefore more acceptable. Another advantage of involving multiple participants is that it lends greater visibility to the selection process. A supplier will find it more difficult to persuade a whole group to buy an unnecessary type or brand of medicine than to influence one or two individuals.

Influencing order quantities

When inventory control is poor, purchasing officers usually have to estimate rather than calculate the amounts to purchase. If no consumption data are available to compare with these estimates, order quantities can be inflated by bribe-seeking purchasing officers without great risk of detection. In contrast, when inventory control and forecasting are effective, when a systematic method of calculation is used to determine order quantities, or both (see Chapters 20 and 23), the supplier or a purchasing officer will have much more difficulty influencing the amounts ordered.

Influencing supplier selection

Suppliers in many countries attempt to influence the selection of the supplier for a particular order. As discussed in Chapter 21, a transparent tender process and tender awards made by a broad-based committee are the best ways of combating this problem.

43.6 Fraud

Manufacturers and importers may dilute liquid preparations, omit or reduce the quantity of expensive active ingredients, or short-pack their shipments. Some suppliers may even provide counterfeit or spurious products. This type of fraud can be uncovered by proper quality assurance practices (Chapter 19) and thorough checking of receipts by the receiving clerk at the medical store or pharmacy (Chapters 44 and 46).

Specialists from the Ethiopian Ministry of Health paid visits to selected winners of tenders and found that although many suppliers claimed to meet the criteria for bidding on tenders, they failed to meet even the basic requirements. Their visit to India showed that over 80 percent of forty-

Investing in strengthening security in the pharmaceutical sector can result in major cost savings and overall health benefits to the population. Theft of medicines and other medical products directly disrupts health system services by denying health providers and patients the means of addressing illnesses. Effective medical practice demands that pharmaceuticals are available in the quantity prescribed and when needed, and averted thefts mean more medicines are reliably available for initiating or continuing treatment. Strengthening security will ensure that not only high-value products such as ARVs are protected from theft, but also all other essential medicines in the facility.

The following table demonstrates the cost-benefit scenario from Ethiopia's HIV/AIDS treatment program in 2004. The scenario is based on—

- Strengthening physical security measures at the health facility level (drug store and dispensing pharmacy)
- Using local materials and labor
- Employing two security guards for one year
- Treating patients with first-line combination ARVs for one year

Expense	Cost
Cost of one-time physical security reinforcement: • Metal doors and locks (3) • Metal windows (5) • Steel bars for windows (5) • Flood lighting • Lockable storage cabinets (6)	USD 1,800
Cost of security guards for one year (2)	USD 1,440
Total estimated cost of security	**USD 3,240**
Estimated Cost of ARVs Cost of first-line ARVs for five patients for one year	USD 3,000

The table illustrates that a small one-time capital investment for physical reinforcement of USD 1,800 and a recurrent annual cost of security guards for one year of USD 1,440 are equivalent to the cost of treating five patients with ARVs for one year. If the facility has a patient load of 500, the theft of one year's worth of ARVs will cost the system USD 300,000. This figure does not take into account the inestimable loss of life or interruption of treatment.

Physical security measures need to be complemented by other management and inventory control actions, but this case in Ethiopia illustrates that a small investment in security can have high returns.

five pharmaceutical suppliers to the Ethiopian government medical store failed to meet several basic quality assurance standards.

Falsifying transaction records, such as invoices and receipt and issue vouchers, is a major type of fraud that does not involve the physical product. Many phony suppliers forge official documents—such as WHO or national government certifications, quality control data, or free trade papers—and pass off the counterfeit or stolen pharmaceutical products as genuine to countries with weak regulatory systems. These transnational and international practices can be curbed with close collaboration between countries, WHO, the World Trade Organization, and consumer interest groups.

The supplier should be held accountable both for intentional errors, such as fraud, and for mistakes in formulation or packing. Fraudulent product ingredients have caused deaths, and suppliers have been prosecuted accordingly. Precise specification of product requirements and rigid enforcement of contracts are essential, as described in Chapter 39.

Temptations and pressures always exist that may lead personnel in responsible positions to commit fraud, so constant monitoring is required.

43.7 The cost of security

In some cases, no additional costs are specifically attributable to security control. Several methods for preventing security breaches serve a dual purpose, because they are also necessary for the effective procurement and distribution of pharmaceuticals: establishment of a pharmaceutical selection committee, quality assurance, inventory control and forecasting, and checking of receipts.

Other security measures may be quite costly but are worth the investment. Imprinting containers, embossing tablets and capsules, hiring special security staff, constructing secure warehouses and storerooms, and regularly monitoring and auditing stock records all can be expensive. Those expenses must be weighed against the potential savings in resources and in health from reduced theft, bribery, and fraud (see Country Study 43-4).

Breaches in security can have substantial medical as well as financial costs. Fraud may have serious and even life-threatening medical consequences if the supplier uses insufficient amounts of active ingredients. Theft raises costs by increasing the volume of pharmaceuticals that have to be purchased; it also has medical costs resulting from shortages

ASSESSMENT GUIDE

Prevalence of leaks

- Is pharmaceutical leakage a problem?
- What are the annual losses as (1) absolute value and (2) percentage of total annual pharmaceutical purchases?
- Where do leaks occur: at ports, at primary and intermediate stores, at health facilities, during transport?
- What types of leaks are experienced in each setting: petty pilferage, major thefts, diversion of shipments, bribery and corruption, supplier fraud? Which are the most significant?
- What are the products targeted?
- Are high-value and disposable items, such as ARVs, always receiving priority attention?

Security systems

- Does an effective inventory control system exist?
- Are special procedures in place for narcotics and other controlled medicines?
- What systems are used to control theft? Have thefts been detected in the past year? What measures were taken after detection?
- What systems are used to control bribery and corruption? Is a committee system used? Has bribery or corruption been detected in the past year? What measures were taken after detection?
- Are physical security systems in buildings and vehicles adequate or inadequate?
- Are doors and windows secure?

- Are stock/bin cards used and completed regularly? Is there regular internal auditing?

Theft detection

- How is theft detected: informers, physical inventory count, consumption comparisons, surveys of selected outlets?
- Are the police cooperative?
- Are junior staff members cooperative?
- Are senior managers cooperative?

Fraud detection

- What systems are used to control supplier fraud? Has fraud been identified in the past year? What measures were taken after detection?
- Are product and packaging specifications adequate?
- Do supplier contracts specify penalties in the event of fraud?
- How is fraud detected: visits to suppliers, receiving inspections, or assays?
- Are any laws or regulations in place for controlling fraud?

Bribery

- Where and at what level and in what form is bribery taking place?
- Is the procurement system transparent enough to prevent bribery in all its forms?
- Has the organization experienced bribery in the past? What measures have been taken?

---

and the use of inappropriate medicines. Bribery and corrupt procurement can be particularly costly. Traditionally, in one South American country, 7 to 10 percent of the procurement value is paid to procurement officials. This corruption "tax" adds up to several hundred thousand U.S. dollars each year because these bribes are added to the medicine's price. ■

References and further readings

John Snow, Inc./DELIVER in collaboration with the World Health Organization. 2003. *Guidelines for the Storage of Essential Medicines and Other Health Commodities.* Arlington, Va.: John Snow, Inc./ DELIVER, for the U.S. Agency for International Development. <http://www.who.int/3by5/en/storage_pocketguide.pdf>

Ritter, L., J. Barrett, and R. Wilson. 2006. *Securing Global Transportation Networks.* New York: McGraw-Hill.

Seiter, A. 2005. *Pharmaceuticals: Counterfeits, Substandard Drugs and Drug Diversion.* HNP brief #2. Washington, D.C.: World Bank.

<http://apps.who.int/medicinedocs/documents/s16755e/s16755e.pdf>

Sweet, K. M. 2006. *Transportation and Cargo Security: Threats and Solutions.* Upper Saddle River, N.J.: Pearson/Prentice Hall.

United Nations Office on Drugs and Crime (UNODC) Regional Centre for East Asia and the Pacific. 2007. *A 'Step-by-Step' Algorithm for the Procurement of Controlled Substances for Drug Substitution Treatment.* Internal document no. 3/2007. Thailand: UNODC. <http://www.who.int/hiv/amds/step_by_step_procure_subs_treat.pdf>

WHO (World Health Organization). 2010. "Medicines: Spurious/ Falsely-Labelled/ Falsified/Counterfeit (SFFC) Medicines" Fact sheet no. 275. Geneva: WHO. <http://www.who.int/mediacentre/factsheets/fs275/en>

———. 1999. *Guidelines for the Development of Measures to Combat Counterfeit Drugs.* Geneva: WHO. <http://whqlibdoc.who.int/hq/1999/WHO_EDM_QSM_99.1.pdf>

WHO/IMPACT (World Health Organization/International Medical Products Anti-Counterfeiting Taskforce). 2008. *Counterfeit Drugs Kill!* Geneva: WHO/IMPACT. <http://www.who.int/impact/FinalBrochureWHA2008a.pdf>

Part I: Policy and economic issues	Part II: Pharmaceutical management	Part III: Management support systems

Planning and administration
Organization and management
   43 Security management
   44 Medical stores management
   45 Hospital pharmacy management
   46 Pharmaceutical management for health facilities
   47 Laboratory services and medical supplies
Information management
Human resources management

CHAPTER 44

Medical stores management

SUMMARY

This chapter discusses medical stores management at central-level stores and at regional or district-level stores that are independent from health facilities. This supply model represents the traditional top-down system that is operated by a governmental or parastatal entity or a nongovernmental organization; however, a number of countries have now decentralized many of their pharmaceutical sector operations, including stores management. Chapter 8 discusses supply chain options, including the trend toward decentralization. In addition, many supply systems contract out certain operations to private-sector companies. Managing contracts requires skills such as defining and monitoring performance indicators and negotiating payment and service terms. See Chapter 39 for more information on contracting. The tenets of this chapter, therefore, apply to stores operating in either the public (often called central medical stores) or nonpublic sectors.

Medical stores management should assist both the flow and reliability of supplies from source to user as economically and reliably as possible, and without significant wastage, loss of quality, or theft. The primary purpose of a store is to receive, hold, and dispatch stock. This materials management process is implemented through inventory control and warehouse management systems, which may be manual or computer based. The primary purpose of inventory control is to manage stock and ensure the smooth flow of goods by determining what, how much, and when to order stock. Consequently, it provides essential information for procurement management. Warehouse management comprises the physical movement of stock into, through, and out of a medical store warehouse. The systems should also be designed to provide information for performance monitoring.

The following are characteristics of a well-managed stores operation—

- The store should be divided into zones that provide a range of environmental conditions and degrees of security.
- There should be an appropriate zone to suit every item to be stored.
- Stock should be arranged within each zone according to some orderly system.
- Stock should be stored off the floor on pallets, on pallet racks, or on shelves. Each of these systems requires specific types of handling equipment.
- Good housekeeping—cleaning and inspection, the disposal of expired and damaged stock, recording of stock movements, and the management of security—should be maintained.
- The management structure should be clearly defined.
- Staff should be appropriately qualified, trained, disciplined, and rewarded.
- Clearly written procedures and handbooks should be available.
- To promote efficiency, staff should have good working conditions and facilities.
- Stock should be verified regularly and periodic audits should be conducted.

Although the essential characteristics of materials management are the same for all systems, the level of sophistication of medical stores varies widely, and each store approaches its system and documentation differently. Therefore, the basic features presented in this chapter are adaptable, depending on the complexity of the medical stores management operation.

44.1 Information for materials management

The goals of medical stores management are to protect stored items from loss, damage, theft, or wastage and to manage the reliable movement of supplies from source to user in the most economical and expeditious way. Effective management of information is the key to achieving these goals. The integrated process is known as materials management. A fully developed system has three key components—

1. An *inventory control system* ensures that the right goods are acquired, in the correct quantities, monitors their quality, and minimizes the total variable cost of operations (see Chapter 23).

2. A *warehouse management system* monitors the physical flow of goods within the system, such as receipts, storage, and issues.

3. A *performance monitoring system* checks that the systems are operating effectively.

Information is essential to management (see Chapter 49). Collecting, processing, and disseminating information may seem costly, but the cost of developing and maintaining an information system should be balanced against the costs of ineffective inventory control (see Chapter 23). The design of the information system is important, but its success depends primarily on well-trained, organized, and supervised staff. Country Study 44-1 describes some of the inventory control system challenges to the central medical stores in Namibia.

Manual versus computerized systems

The information system must include data on products entering and leaving the warehouse, products in stock, products on order, and ways to monitor the progress of orders in the supply pipeline. Key elements of the system are well-designed forms, computerized information systems, and clearly defined procedures.

Two decades ago, most public supply systems relied completely on manual stock records, but now, many programs have changed to computerized systems. Even with computerization, however, many countries still maintain a manual system, such as bin cards, as a backup, especially during the transition to computerization. There is a widely held belief that computerization solves the problem of inventory control. This belief is misguided. A computer is not a substitute for trained staff; it is simply an additional tool for staff to use (see Chapter 50). Both manual and computerized systems perform the same fundamental information-processing tasks: data input, data storage, data processing, data retrieval, and data dissemination. The difference is that a computerized system enables some tasks

to be accomplished more rapidly, accurately, economically, and flexibly. Even with a computerized system, data must be entered, manipulated, and interpreted by skilled and knowledgeable staff.

Procurement information

The procurement process (Chapters 18–21) involves medical stores input at all levels of the distribution system. These inputs are described below.

Procurement can be handled from a department within the medical stores or from an external unit. The medical stores unit provides the (internal or external) procurement unit with a list of the types and quantities of medicines needed for its operation. After a supplier is selected and a purchase order is placed, the procurement unit informs the medical stores unit about suppliers, unit prices, the quantities on order, the expected arrival dates of shipments, and other vital information.

The procurement unit tracks information on inventory status, new shipments received and taken into stock, issues made to health facilities, expired medicines, damaged medicines, and audit data from physical stock checks.

The medical stores unit also tracks issues to individual health facilities, noting methods of transport, delivery

---

Country Study 44-1
Central medical stores inventory control system operations in Namibia

Namibia operates a classic central medical stores (CMS) distribution system with a CMS and two regional medical stores. Administratively, the regional stores do not have any links with the CMS—the relationship between them is one of customer and client. The CMS distributes medicines and supplies to the two regional medical stores, all district hospitals, and local hospitals and clinics in the surrounding regions, while the regional stores and district hospitals are responsible for distributing to other facilities within their geographic jurisdictions.

Facilities are expected to order products from CMS every six weeks, and it usually takes CMS about four weeks to process and deliver the order. An assessment of the CMS distribution showed, however, that stock records were not adequately maintained and physical inventory counts did not correspond with either stock records or computerized records. Because the regional stores and health facilities had no effective systems for deciding when, what, or how much to order, most facilities ended up placing many emergency orders within the six-week order period, which stretched the capabilities of the already overburdened CMS.

A computerized inventory control system had been installed at the CMS several years earlier, but most of the staff members who were initially trained to use it had left the public service; remaining staff members, therefore, were not using the system to its full advantage. Many functions that could have been handled by the system were done manually or with spreadsheets. Moreover, management personnel reported that they did not have enough time to acquire the additional skills that would help them use the system.

As a result of the CMS assessment, a number of recommendations to improve the inventory control system were made: conduct complete physical inventory counts at all levels and use the results to update or introduce stock records; develop standard operating procedures for store management; and train staff on how to maintain stock records and use the computerized inventory control system to their best advantage.

Source: Management Sciences for Health/Rational Pharmaceutical Management Plus Program.

times, and confirmation of receipts from user units. This tracking should generate information on the monthly and annual value of total issues, issue quantities, details of specific products, and how budget allocations are used.

After an order has been placed, its progress should be monitored until it is received at the central medical stores (CMS). A good monitoring system makes it possible to estimate realistic delivery times and to decide whether any supplementary or emergency orders are needed, well before a stockout occurs.

Both manual and computerized systems should identify milestones during the lead-time period to facilitate communication with suppliers and to prompt corrective action if required. Important milestones of the procurement lead time are—

- Order initiating date
- Date of award to supplier (for tenders)
- Letter of credit information
- Shipment information and date
- Arrival at port
- Port-clearing date
- Date of issuing a receiving report

An effective supplier information system should include general information on suppliers and products, lead times, merit ratings, value of purchases, product quality, payment methods, and prequalification based on good manufacturing practices. Information about supplier performance should be compiled throughout the procurement cycle to assist in choosing future suppliers. Chapter 21 discusses the features of a procurement information system in more detail.

Stock records

Stock records contain information about suppliers, customers, prices, stock receipts, stock issues, stock losses, and stock balances. These data are essential for planning distribution.

A stock record (manual or computerized) must be maintained for each item in the inventory. The stock record documents all transactions relating to an item. It may contain information about reorder level, reorder interval, reorder quantity, lead time, stock on order, and estimated consumption rate. Many stores also maintain bin cards for each product in each storage area to record information on issues, receipts, and stock balances. In some stores, this bin card is the most current and accurate record of inventory movement.

The design of stock cards and bin cards depends on the choice of inventory control system. For details regarding the design, selection, and use of different types of inventory control systems, see Chapter 23; examples of a stock record card and a bin card are provided in Annexes 44-1 and 44-2.

When a shipment of medicines is received at the CMS, it is inspected to ensure that it meets the specifications in the supply contract. If the shipment is satisfactory, the receiving section of the warehouse produces a receiving report (see Annex 44-3). This report brings the procurement lead-time period to an end.

Individual health facilities are the end users of medical supplies. Maintaining information from health facilities is essential in order to monitor consumption, forecast pharmaceutical requirements, and make other management decisions. Many medical stores information systems also keep general information on facility location, facility status, population served, method of distribution, delivery schedule, value of issues, and extent of current budget utilization.

Performance monitoring and reporting

A store should monitor and evaluate its operations to identify problems in the system that need to be addressed. Record-keeping and reporting systems should be designed to make the collection of data for routine monitoring as simple as possible (see Chapter 48). Stock records are a vital source of information on how effectively the distribution system is being managed; therefore, maintaining these records accurately and keeping them up-to-date is vital. They provide detailed evidence of how products flow through the system and can be used to identify where problems are occurring so that corrective action can be taken. Operational indicators can track progress at two critical levels: from the supplier to the store, or "upstream," and from the store to clients, or "downstream." Upstream information includes lead-time from supplier to the store, number of medicines procured, and monthly stock status reports. At the downstream level, the store should collect routine lead-time information; distribution information by facility, district, and product; client satisfaction and consumption data; and order-fill rate. Box 44-1 shows a list of sample indicators. The medical stores should prepare regular reports on stock and order status, such as those described in Chapter 23, and send them to relevant parties such as the ministry of health, public health programs, donors, lower-level warehouses, and health facilities.

Communications

The medical stores must maintain effective communications with suppliers, with procurement and inventory control units, with lower-level warehouses and health facilities, and with managers from the ministry of health. Periodic meetings with the staff members of client facilities can help ensure good communications and a more effective supply system.

> **Box 44-1**
> **Examples of monitoring and evaluation targets and indicators**
>
> - Number of sites to which medicines are distributed
> - Quarterly report delivered on time
> - Payment voucher processing time
> - Number of patients receiving treatment
> - Percentage of medicines that are wasted (as a result of breakages, expiries, pilferage) as a proportion of overall stocks
> - Time elapsed from order receipt by store until shipment receipt by client
> - Order processing time within the store
> - Lead time between the supplier and the store
> - Lead time between the store and the client
> - Forecast for store commodities completed
> - Percentage of commodities out of stock in service delivery sites
> - Percentage of products tested for which a quality problem was detected
> - Percentage of shipments to service delivery sites that are consolidated
> - Percentage of cost savings as a result of price negotiations

44.2 Flow of stock and information

Stock, and the information that accompanies it, should flow through the warehouse in an orderly manner. This process has six stages—

1. *Receiving:* Goods that arrive in the receiving room are quarantined, inspected, and if found to be acceptable, entered into the stock-recording system. Receiving reports are prepared.
2. *Storage:* Accepted goods are moved to their allocated storage positions in the warehouse, where they are stored in first-in/first-out (FIFO) or first-expiry/first-out (FEFO) order. Records for stocks on hand and on order are adjusted.
3. *Allocation of stock:* In most medical stores, the manager determines whether to allocate the complete quantities requested when a requisition is received. The decision can be made in collaboration with the requesting facility but generally depends on stock status, a review of facility consumption patterns, and, in some cases, budget status.
4. *Order picking:* An order-picking list is prepared (this may be the original requisition form rather than a separate list). Workers use this list to identify and col-

lect the allocated items from the warehouse.

5. *Order assembly:* Individual orders are assembled and checked in the packing area. They are then packed for delivery. Delivery documentation is prepared.
6. *Dispatch and delivery:* The packed goods are held in designated secure areas pending shipment, then loaded onto the transport and dispatched, accompanied by the necessary documentation, including a packing list recording all items and quantities. Ideally, an invoice showing unit costs of medicines and total value should accompany the shipment. Signed delivery notes are checked when the vehicle returns. If errors or damage have been reported, appropriate action is taken.

Formal and informal physical stock counts should be taken regularly to ensure that stock is being correctly handled and that losses and inaccuracies are properly accounted for.

Stock receipt

Importation and port clearing are described in Chapter 24. The procedure outlined here assumes that those tasks are carried out by an import unit attached to the CMS. Port clearing may, however, be contracted to a clearing agent or made the responsibility of the supplier. In such cases, the goods are delivered directly to the CMS or are collected from the agent's warehouse. Final responsibility for inspection remains with the CMS.

With the exception of locally purchased items, multiple copies of the supplier's shipping documents and supplier's invoice should be received by the CMS before supplies arrive at the port of entry. This information is recorded on a manual or computerized form to track each purchase order. In addition, the import unit should record the arrival information. This advisory is clipped to the purchase order in the supplier's file to await the arrival of the shipment.

When notice is received of a shipment's arrival at the port, the necessary customs forms are completed. It is always necessary to visit the port to arrange for the release of the shipment.

Containers are inspected against the supplier's shipping document. The first part of the receiving report is completed (Annex 44-3). Any apparent damage and missing shipping cases are noted and reported to the port authorities, insurance agents, and customs officials.

When the shipment arrives at the warehouse receiving area, contents should be quarantined until they have been checked (Figure 44-1). The receiving clerks systematically check the cases and their contents against the supplier's invoice. Discrepancies, variations, and damage are noted on the invoice. A prompt and thorough inspection based on predefined criteria is essential to quality assurance and as a

Figure 44-1   Checking received goods

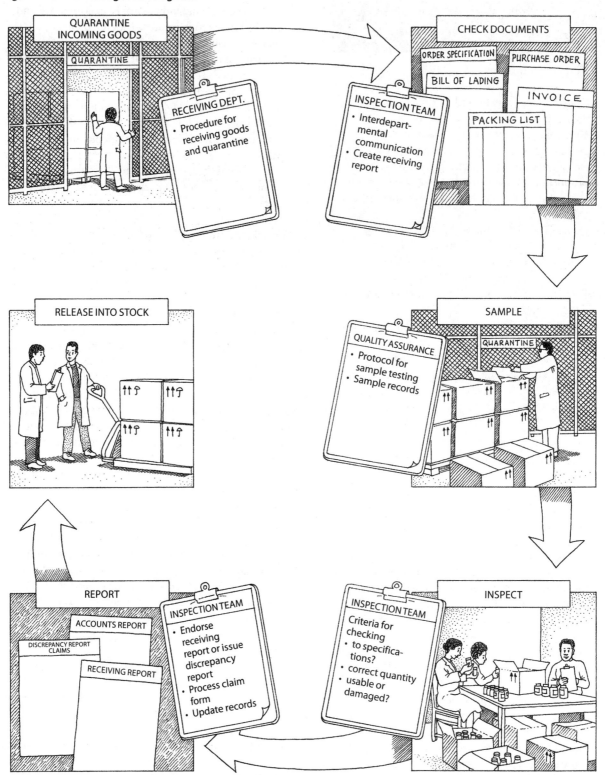

precursor to any insurance claim. Table 44-1 is a checklist with sample inspection criteria.

The annotated invoice is signed and dated by a senior staff member. Observations are summarized on the second part of the receiving report.

One copy of the receiving report is filed according to the purchase order number to which it corresponds. The other copy and the annotated supplier's invoice are passed to the stock control section. In some warehouses, a separate copy goes to the accounting department.

The items are then entered on their respective stock record cards (Annex 44-1). The new stock on hand and on order totals are calculated, as well as the average cost per unit for each item. If a computerized system is used, receipts are entered into the system as prescribed in the software manual.

Planning for space requirements

As mentioned in other chapters, the massive increase in funding for pharmaceuticals from global health initiatives such as the Global Fund and the U.S. President's Emergency Plan for AIDS Relief has increased the storage and distribution volume needed in some countries by two- or threefold. In addition, managing these "strategic" stocks can be challenging; for example, in the case of what to do with "dead" stock that never gets issued. Stores, therefore, need to work carefully with their clients to communicate about scale-up of initiatives such as antiretroviral therapy and distribution of bed nets to prevent malaria that will affect space and distribution planning and to develop policies on managing strategic stock.

Stock storage

After incoming stock has been checked and approved, it is formally released from the receiving area and moved to the warehouse to be stored in the appropriate zone. New stock may be stored on floor pallets, pallet racks, or shelves. If a fluid or semifluid location system is used (see Section 44.4), the exact location of each item must be recorded. If a bin card system is in use, receipts should be entered on the bin card when the items are transferred to the storage area.

Table 44-1   Inspection checklist for medicine receipts

Product	Notes	Checklist
All shipments	Compare the goods with the supplier's invoice and original purchase order or contract. Note discrepancies on the receiving report. Take a sample for testing (if preacceptance sampling is a standard procedure).	❏ Number of containers delivered is correct ❏ Number of packages in each container is correct ❏ Quantity in each package is correct ❏ Drug is correct (do not confuse generic name and brand name) ❏ Dosage form is correct (tablet, liquid, other) ❏ Strength is correct (milligrams, percentage concentration, other measurement) ❏ Unique identifiers are present, if required (article code, ministry of health stamp, other code) ❏ No visible evidence of damage (describe if present)
Tablets	For each shipment, tablets of the same drug and dose should be consistent.	❏ Tablets are identical in size ❏ Tablets are identical in shape ❏ Tablets are identical in color (shade of color may vary from batch to batch) ❏ Tablet markings are identical (scoring, lettering, numbering) ❏ There are no defects (check for spots, pits, chips, breaks, uneven edges, cracks, embedded or adherent foreign matter, stickiness) ❏ There is no odor when a sealed bottle is opened (except for flavored tablets and those with active ingredients normally having a characteristic odor) ❏ There is no odor after tablets have been exposed to room air for 20 to 30 minutes
Capsules	For each shipment, capsules of the same drug and dose should be consistent.	❏ Capsules are identical in size ❏ Capsules are identical in shape ❏ Capsules are identical in color (shade of color may vary from batch to batch) ❏ Capsule markings are identical ❏ There are no defects (check for holes, pits, chips, breaks, uneven edges, cracks, embedded or adherent foreign matter, stickiness) ❏ There are no empty capsules ❏ There are no open or broken capsules
Parenterals	Parenterals are all products for injection (IV liquids, ampoules, dry solids for reconstitution, suspensions for injection).	❏ Solutions are clear (solutions should be free from undissolved particles, within permitted limits) ❏ Dry solids for use in injections are entirely free from visible foreign particles ❏ There are no leaking containers (bottles, ampoules)

Stock control using FIFO and FEFO

In order to avoid accumulation of expired and obsolete stock, items should be stored and issued on a FIFO or FEFO basis, according to the following guidelines.

The stock control system must record the expiry date and the date of receipt. Stock must be stored so that earliest-expiring or first-delivered batches can be picked and issued first. When small quantities are involved, this goal can be achieved by placing the newly received stock at the back of the shelf behind the existing stock. When larger quantities are involved—for example, several pallet loads—the newly received items can be placed on the upper levels of the pallet racking. They remain there until the older stock has been issued. The picking stock is kept in an accessible position, assuming that orders are picked by hand in relatively small quantities. In warehouses where whole pallet loads are picked for distribution to lower-level stores, accessibility is less of a concern because mechanical transporters are used.

Newly arrived stock sometimes has an earlier expiry date than a previously received batch of the same item. If a FEFO system is used, this stock should be "promoted" so that it is issued before later-expiring stock. Making this adjustment is particularly important with products that have short shelf lives, such as vaccines.

Note that the system for stock rotation may be determined by the scheme for price increases, if medicines are sold to clients. If pricing is done on a FIFO basis, this system should also be used for stock management, except when newer stock will expire before it can be used under a FIFO rotation.

Order allocation

Under a pull distribution system, lower-level stores and health facilities submit requests, or requisitions, for supplies. At most medical stores, a designated official is responsible for reviewing requisitions and allocating stock based on inventory levels at the requesting facility and in the issuing warehouse as well as on past consumption at the facility. In many countries, facilities use a set formula for quantification based on their inventory control system to prevent over- or underordering. Usually, the order quantity is rationed at the warehouse level only if there are insufficient funds or stock. The requesting facilities may have budgets that must be considered in making allocations. After the allocation has been made, the order can be picked.

Order picking

The allocated quantities form the order-picking list. This list is passed to the storekeeper. In a large store—especially one that uses a fluid location system (see Section 44.4)—the picking list often needs to specify the exact position of the items to be selected. In a small store, the storekeeper prob-

ably knows where everything is. The listed items are taken from stock in strict FIFO or FEFO order and transported to the packing area, where order assembly takes place.

In large stores, it is common to use separate zones or rooms for storing specific types of products, such as antiretrovirals, which must be locked up. A specific storekeeper is also assigned the responsibility of managing these products. In such instances, it may be necessary to divide the picking list for a given customer into several smaller picking lists, according to the number of separate storerooms or areas in use. A similar approach would be needed when generating goods received notes and transferring fresh supplies to individual storage areas.

If bin cards are used, the stock issued should be recorded on the bin card as it is pulled from the storage area.

Order assembly

At a secured shipping location, the supplies are arranged in the order in which they appear on the picking list or requisition voucher. The order is double checked by the storekeeper or shipping clerk before the items are packed, sealed, and labeled for delivery. Some items, such as vaccines and controlled substances, require special packing and handling.

Order dispatch and delivery

In the most commonly used in-house delivery system, supplies are generally distributed according to a fixed delivery schedule. In some instances, a collection system may be used, whereby representatives from health facilities collect supplies from the store. The shipping clerk completes a delivery voucher (Annex 44-5). The voucher lists the number and type of shipped packages. Their specific content is not identified unless the items require special handling, such as vaccines, loose items (such as bulk germicides), and medical gas tanks. The voucher is signed by the driver, who takes two copies with him, together with two copies of the invoice or completed requisition form. The third copy of the delivery voucher remains bound in the delivery vouchers book, which is maintained by the shipping clerk.

When the delivery arrives at the receiving facility, the driver and the facility's receiving officer count and inspect the containers. Any apparent loss or damage is noted on the delivery voucher. The receiving officer and the driver sign both copies; each keeps one copy. Ideally, the received parcels should be opened and verified against the requisition form in the presence of the driver. Because of time constraints, however, immediate inspection is not always possible.

The signed delivery voucher certifies that the driver has safely delivered the supplies. The receiving store retains the two copies of the completed requisition form. One is signed and dated and returned to the delivering store. Any differences between the contents of the delivery and the requisition form are reported on the requisition form, and an investigation takes place if there are discrepancies.

The driver returns the signed copy of the delivery voucher to the inventory clerk, who signs and dates it and also signs and dates the permanent copy in the delivery vouchers book. That copy (now bearing the signatures of the driver, the receiving officer, and the inventory clerk, with the respective dates) is placed with the file copy of the completed requisition form.

Some supply systems require that the receiving facility send a written notification of receipt. In such cases, the receiving facility should return a signed copy of the completed requisition form to the CMS before the facility's next requisition date. The date of its return is entered in the register of requisitions (stores issues ledger; see Annex 44-6). If the receiving facility does not submit this "certified received" copy, the supplying store may refuse to fill the next requisition. The copy is filed in the individual requisitioner's file by date. If any discrepancies have been noted and subsequently verified, all relevant records, including the inventory card, must be adjusted. Again, all these records can be computerized, with file copies maintained.

Inventory taking

The bin card (Annex 44-2) and the stock record card (Annex 44-1), the computer file, or both provide a continuous record of each supply item in stock. The filed copies of the purchase orders and the verified copies of suppliers' invoices are used to document additions to the inventory.

The medical stores unit must regularly take physical counts of stock on hand to check that the stock balance on perpetual inventory records is correct. The government or stores audit office should also periodically certify that the recorded transactions and net totals are accurate. The audit is carried out by examining procurements and requisitions and is verified by a physical stock count. As discussed in Chapter 23, the cyclic stock count is now preferred to the traditional annual count. The cyclic count is easier to manage and is more likely to allow reconciliation of discrepancies between records and physical stock.

Both active and safety stock in all locations should be counted as scheduled and compared with the numbers on the respective cards (or computerized records). Inventory verification, at every location where supplies are stocked, should be planned to—

- Enforce procedures and regulations designed to prevent loss and wastage
- Ensure that security measures are adequate
- Provide an additional form of evaluation that may reveal defects in the warehousing system

- Provide regular evaluation of storage conditions and the adequacy of storage facilities, layout, and stock arrangement
- Identify surplus, expired, and obsolete stock

44.3 Zoning stock within the store

Medicines and essential medical supplies must be located in a part of the store with the correct combination of temperature and security. This initial zoning process is the most basic way in which supplies are arranged.

A zone can be a separate building or room, a locked cupboard, a refrigerator, a freezer, or a cold room. Table 44-2 indicates several possible combinations of temperature and security and illustrates how to classify items according to their storage requirements. Thus, an item classified "2B" in this scheme would be stored at +15 to +25–30°C in a secure store.

The product manufacturer's storage instructions should be followed to the extent possible. If these instructions cannot be followed, the product must be kept in the most suitable conditions available and used as quickly as possible. The product manufacturer should be consulted before violating recommended storage conditions, to determine how long the product will remain safe and effective under the actual storage conditions.

If no specific storage instructions are given, "normal storage conditions" apply. Normal storage conditions for medicines have been defined as "storage in dry, well-ventilated premises at temperatures of +15°C to +25°C, or, depending upon climatic conditions, up to +30°C" (WHO 2003). Each storage zone should have at least one thermometer, and temperatures should be recorded daily at the hottest time of day.

Table 44-2   Temperature and security zones

Category	A Normal security	B High security	C Flammable	D Corrosive
1: Uncontrolled temperature	X	X	X	X
2: +15 to +25–30°C (controlled humidity)	X	X		
3: 0 to +8°C	X			
4: –20°C	X			

Notes: The +15 to +25–30°C zone is assumed to be air-conditioned and therefore humidity controlled. In temperate climates, this temperature range can be achieved without air-conditioning, but humidity control may still be necessary.

Cells marked X are commonly required temperature and security zones. Other combinations may be required for specific products. For example, zones "3B" and "4B" may be needed for vaccines if the vaccines have a black-market value—for instance, hepatitis B—or there is a particular problem with security for refrigeration equipment.

Storage at uncontrolled room temperature

Many products can be safely stored at uncontrolled room temperature. However, the temperature in the upper part of a store can exceed +40°C even in temperate climates. In cold climates, temperatures will drop below freezing in unheated stores. Such temperature extremes may damage some items. Chapter 19 discusses items known to be sensitive to extreme storage conditions.

Storage at controlled temperature and humidity

In hot climates, it is necessary to store many items in air-conditioned rooms. In humid climates, dehumidifiers are useful for preventing moisture damage. In cold climates, stores may need to be heated in winter to protect products that are damaged by freezing.

Cold storage

The potency of vaccines, sera, test kits, and many other items depends on cold storage. Vaccines, in particular, are temperature-sensitive and must be kept at precisely controlled temperatures from the point of manufacture to the point of administration.

Cold-chain defects are a frequent cause of problems in immunization programs. The World Health Organization's (WHO) Department of Immunization, Vaccines and Biologicals publishes comprehensive advisory material on designing and implementing a cold chain (see the WHO Immunization, Vaccines and Biologicals website). This material should be referred to for detailed technical advice. Table 44-3 summarizes the requirements for an effective cold chain.

National and regional vaccine stores should be equipped with standby generators; ideally, district vaccine stores should have them as well. Having backups ensures that vaccines and other products are protected in the event of a power failure.

Secure storage

Narcotics and other controlled substances should be kept in a secure room or in a safe. Ideally, a red warning light or warning bell that will activate when the door is unlocked should be fixed close to the store. The keys to the secure store should be kept in a safe.

Entry to the store must be controlled. No more than two assigned officers should have access. Typically, one should be the director of the store, the most senior pharmacist, or the most senior storekeeper (see also Chapter 43). Such precautions may also be needed for non-narcotic medicines that are frequently stolen. For example, many stores keep expensive products, such as antiretrovirals, in a secured space.

Flammables

Flammables, such as alcohol and ether, must be stored in special buildings or rooms. A separate building is best because it greatly reduces the risk of a fire's spreading to the main store. The flammables store must be well ventilated and fireproof. It must be fitted with an "explosion hatch," which may be part of the roof or part of a wall.

Fuel must never be stored in or near a medical store. Fuel tanks should be placed inside a locked compound to prevent theft. There should be a continuous earth bank or low wall around the tanks. The area enclosed should be sufficient to hold the total potential volume of fuel stored to ensure that fuel is contained if a major spill occurs. With these precautions, if a fire occurs, the risk of its spreading will be reduced.

44.4 Stock location within a zone

Within each zone, stock may be located in fixed, fluid, or semifluid locations. Fixed location systems are the simplest to manage, because each stock item is always stored in the same place, but they waste space. Fluid location systems make better use of available space, but require sophisticated stock management, because the location of each stock item varies over time. Semifluid systems combine features of both systems.

Fixed location

In a fixed location system, each stock item is allocated to specific shelves, pallet racking, or an area of floor. A fixed location system is like a house in which each family member has his or her own room. A room is left empty if a person is not at home.

For a fixed location system to work well, the store has to be large enough to accommodate the maximum possible level of stock for every item, including safety stock. As stock is used up, the storage location is emptied and left vacant until a new shipment of the item is received.

With a fixed location system, stock administration is relatively easy. Goods can always be found in the same place. However, this system has certain disadvantages—

- Fixed location systems are inflexible. If there is a change in the quantity ordered or a change in packaging, the assigned location may become too large or too small.
- If a new item is ordered, there may be no place to store it.
- Theft may increase because all store staff are familiar with the locations of valuable items.
- Storage space may be wasted, because at times it is largely empty.

Table 44-3   Typical requirements for an effective cold chain

Level and staff functions	Management activities	Supplies and equipment needed
National Management • National program coordination • Epidemiology • Logistics • Transport management • Training • Procurement • Budget and finance • Data analysis Central store • Storekeeping • Delivery Maintenance • Equipment care and maintenance	Program planning • Demographic/epidemiological data • Administrative structures • Logistic systems Program monitoring • Disease surveillance • Immunization coverage • Cold-chain and transport operations • Supplies usage • Program costs Supplies management • Procurement, storage, delivery • Refrigeration monitoring • Transport management Also— • Independent evaluations • Staff recruitment and training • Supervision of operations	Cold-chain equipment • +4°C cold room: twin refrigeration units, recording thermometer, alarm • −20°C freezer room equipped as above • Ice packs and cold boxes unless refrigerated vehicles are used • Standby power supply Working and safety stocks • Vaccines and injection equipment • Stationery and forms • Cold-chain monitoring cards • Cold-chain equipment and spare parts Also— • Transport and fuel • Special facilities • Vaccine control laboratory (where feasible)
Regional/provincial Management • Regional program • Epidemiology • Logistics and transport • Training • Data analysis and reports Regional store • Storekeeping • Delivery Maintenance • Equipment care and maintenance	Program monitoring • Disease surveillance • Immunization coverage • Cold-chain and transport operations • Supplies usage Supplies management • Requisitioning, storage, delivery • Refrigeration monitoring • Transport management Also— • Staff recruitment and training • Supervision of district operations	Cold-chain equipment • +4°C cold room or vaccine refrigerators, thermometers, alarm • Vaccine freezers, thermometers, alarm • Ice packs and cold boxes unless refrigerated transport is used • Standby power supply Working and safety stocks • Vaccines and injection equipment • Stationery and forms • Spare parts Also— • Transport and fuel
District Management • District program • Data analysis and reports District store • Storekeeping • Delivery Maintenance • Equipment care and maintenance	Program monitoring • Disease reporting • Immunization reporting • Cold-chain and transport operations • Supplies usage Supplies management • Requisitioning, storage, delivery • Refrigeration monitoring • Transport management Also— • Supervision of health facilities	Cold-chain equipment • Vaccine refrigerators, thermometers, alarm • Vaccine freezers, thermometers, alarm • Ice packs and cold boxes • Standby power supply Working and safety stocks • Vaccines and injection equipment • Stationery and forms • Spare parts Also— • Transport and fuel
Health facility • Giving immunizations • Storekeeping • Reporting • Equipment care and maintenance	Supplies management • Requisitioning and storage • Refrigerator monitoring • Transport management Reporting of— • Disease incidence • Immunizations given • Refrigerator defects • Transport mileage and defects • Stock on hand	Cold-chain equipment • Vaccine refrigerator with ice-making compartment and thermometer • Cold boxes for outreach sessions • Vaccine carriers Working and safety stocks • Vaccines and injection equipment • Stationery and forms Also— • Transport and fuel

Fluid location

In a fluid location system, the store is divided into many designated locations. Each location is assigned a code. Individual items are stored wherever space is available at the time of delivery. A fluid location system is like a hotel. Rooms are assigned only when guests arrive.

A fluid location system uses available space efficiently, but it requires sophisticated stock administration. Experience suggests that a store using a fluid location system can be 20 to 25 percent smaller than one using a fixed location system.

The administration of a fluid location system works as follows—

- The procurement unit provides information on the type, volume, and weight of goods arriving.
- The storekeeper assesses which locations will be empty when the new stock arrives and assigns an appropriate location. These data are recorded in the stock control system.
- If insufficient space is available, other goods may be moved to create more space.
- The stock control location records are updated.

Fluid location systems require a classification system that allocates a unique identifier code to each stock item and to each location. Also, the stock record for each batch of each item must always indicate the physical location of the item in the store. In a fluid location system, different batches of a particular item may be stored in several different places. For example, if item number 150-050-48 is 500 mg amoxicilline, 150-050-48: B1-B could be a batch of this product stored in aisle B, bay 1, cell B, and 150-050-48: C2-B could be another batch of the same product stored in aisle C, bay 2, cell B.

Fluid location systems benefit immensely from the use of a computerized bin location and storage system, which improves productivity and optimizes storage capacity. Such systems identify not only locations of items, but also the best location for storing an incoming consignment within storage areas.

Semifluid location

A semifluid location system is a combination of the fixed and fluid systems. It is like a hotel that has regular guests. Regular guests are always given the same room. Casual guests are given any room that is available.

In a semifluid location system, each item is assigned a fixed space for picking stock. When an order is prepared, the order-picking staff members know where to find each item. The remainder of the store is filled on the fluid location principle. When the picking stock runs low, the fixed locations are restocked using items from the fluid locations.

A semifluid location system is not as space-efficient as a fluid location system. However, picking stock is stored at a convenient height, eliminating the need for mechanical handling during order picking in stores that issue in relatively small quantities.

Another feature is that picking stock is always kept in the same place. Unlike in a fixed location system, however, less risk exists that changing requirements will disrupt the system. If demand increases for a particular item, the picking stock can be replenished more frequently. As new products are introduced, picking bays may be subdivided to provide sufficient space.

44.5 Stock classification

Items should be clearly organized within each zone of the store. Such organization makes it much easier for store personnel to control stock, take periodic stock inventory, and pick orders.

In stores that use the fixed location principle, items can be physically organized in one of several ways—

- Therapeutic or pharmacological category
- Alphabetical order
- Dosage form
- Random bin
- Commodity code

In a fluid location system, clear organization and unique product identification are absolutely essential to the success of the system. Otherwise, items get lost. Coding by any one of the first four methods is inappropriate for a fluid location system, because the position of a particular stock item will vary over time. For example, if antipyretics are randomly distributed about the store in a fluid location system, organizing the store on the basis of therapeutic class is not feasible.

However, therapeutic or pharmacological class, alphabetical order, and classifications may be used as ways of organizing the stock records, whatever stock location system is used. One of the advantages of a computerized stock control system is that records can be sorted in a variety of ways for different management purposes; for instance, according to therapeutic classes or in alphabetical order.

Therapeutic or pharmacological category

Therapeutic or pharmacological classification may be an effective way of organizing medicines in smaller stores and in the dispensaries of small clinical facilities where the storekeeper is also the dispenser. It is not an advantage in larger stores.

Alphabetical order

Alphabetical order (by generic name) is also attractive in peripheral stores that keep a small number of items. However, each change in the national (essential) medicines list or in the level-of-use list requires reorganization of the stores themselves and of the stock administration system. This method may not result in optimal use of available space.

Dosage form

A system based on dosage form is commonly used in smaller warehouses. Tablets and capsules are stored together, with separate areas for oral liquids, injections, creams and ointments, and topical liquids. Within each dosage-form area, products may be stored in a fixed, fluid, or semifluid manner and further organized by any of the other systems described in this section. The main advantages are that the forms are easy to recognize when receiving goods and this system allows optimal use of space.

Random bin

The random bin is a unique storage space identified by a code. For example, a shelving unit can be divided vertically and horizontally into cells, each with a unique location code. A unit of shelving might be labeled "B," its bays "B1" and "B2," and its shelves "A," "B," and "C." A unique cell would be identified, for example, as B1-B (see Figure 44-2). This cell is called a bin.

The random bin storage method can combine the methods previously described. For example, items are placed alphabetically within therapeutic classifications. Generic names are used throughout. If there is more than one brand of the same generic drug preparation, all are stored in the bin for that type.

Commodity code

Commodity coding is an abstract organizational system. It offers maximum flexibility and can be used equally well in small and large stores.

This system is based on a unique article code combined with a unique location code. Examples of article codes include WHO technical specifications or UNICEF stock codes. Article codes can be designed to specify therapeutic class, clinical indication, level of use, or any other relevant data. In systems that use article coding and location coding, storekeeping staff do not need to have specific knowledge of pharmaceutical names and therapeutic uses.

Changes in the national medicines list can easily be introduced by assigning unique article codes to new products. Article coding works well in a computerized system. Tender contracts may require that only the article code be marked on the bulk packaging as well as on the smaller units of supply. This method increases security but still allows the goods to be identified by those staff members who have access to the coding key.

The location code is totally independent of the article code and is similar to the random bin principle. Codes can be designed to incorporate any number of characteristics, including—

- Correct storage temperature for the product
- Correct security level for the product
- Whether the product is flammable
- The building where the product is located
- Pack size
- Pharmaceutical form

44.6 Stock storage and handling

Within each temperature and security zone, products must be stored so that they are easily accessible and protected against damage. There are four basic systems of storage: shelves, floor pallets, block-stacked pallets, and pallet racks. Direct storage of cartons on the warehouse floor should be avoided because their contents may be damaged by moisture. The choice of system depends on the following factors—

- Total quantity of products to be stored
- Average volume of each product
- Internal height of the storage building
- Local availability of mechanical handling equipment and the skills to use and maintain it

Pallets are generally used at the national and regional levels, where products are stored in bulk. At the district level and below, storage on shelves is most common. The fundamental rule for pallet storage is that each pallet should be used for only one product line. Pallets have the following advantages—

- They keep goods together and impose a disciplined method of storage.
- Large loads can be moved easily using mechanical handling equipment.
- Pallets are easy to transship because they do not require any unpacking and repacking.
- Pallets isolate goods from floors, which may be damp.
- If goods are supplied by the manufacturer on shrink-wrapped pallets, it is easy to see when tampering has occurred.
- Inspection for damage and for short shipments is easy to perform.
- When stock rearrangement is necessary, it is much easier to move pallets with mechanical handling

Figure 44-2   Storage and load-handling equipment

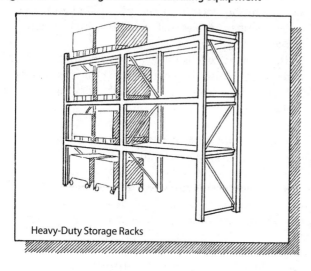

Heavy-Duty Storage Racks

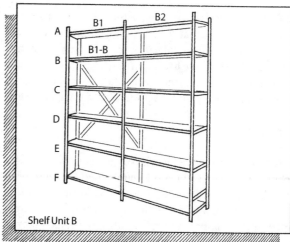

Shelf Unit B

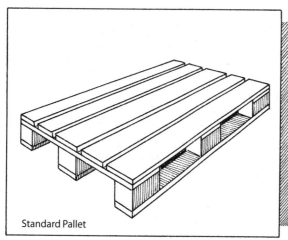

Standard Pallet

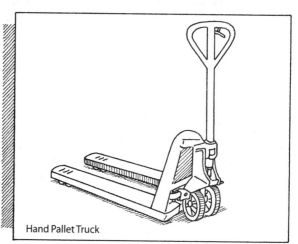

Hand Pallet Truck

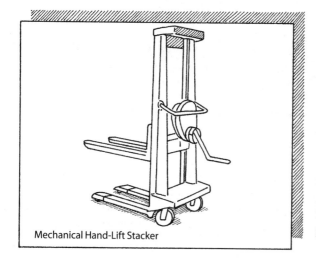

Mechanical Hand-Lift Stacker

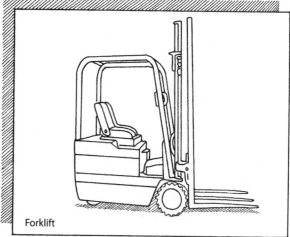

Forklift

equipment than it is to move a large volume of loose stock that has been placed on shelves.

Packaging specifications

Appropriate packaging specifications reduce the risk of damage during handling. Floor pallets and pallet racks must be laid out to suit a selected pallet module. Pallets come in a range of sizes, and the size and weight of pallets affect the layout of the store and the choice of mechanical handling equipment. Although it may be difficult in practice due to the range of pallets that may be available, whenever feasible, a standard pallet size should be adopted throughout the distribution system, and all contracts with suppliers should include this specification.

Shelving

Storage on shelves does not require mechanical handling equipment and is a good choice when—

- The volume and weight of individual items are too small to justify pallets.
- The internal height of a building is not large enough for multitier pallet racking, and shelving can be used on its own or in combination with floor pallets or two-tier racking.
- Manual goods handling is locally more reliable or economical than mechanical handling.

If shelving is used in a warehouse more than 4.5 meters high, it may be possible to install an independent mezzanine flooring system supporting a second tier of shelving. This system can increase the available shelving volume by up to 100 percent, at the expense of some inconvenience in materials handling. Obviously, if a mezzanine is added, high-quality construction is critical to avoid injury to staff and damage to stored goods.

Floor pallets

Floor pallets are a good solution in warehouses with ceiling heights of less than 3 meters and in stores where the cost of pallet racking and forklift trucks cannot be justified. Many heavy or bulky items, such as rolls of cotton, medicine kits, or large hospital equipment, require floor locations. Floors should be marked to indicate pallet and aisle positions.

Block-stacked pallets

Pallets containing light goods may be stacked on top of one another in blocks. Block-stacked pallets should be used only for items without expiry dates or with very high turnover, because the first-in items are at the bottom of the stack.

Block stacking is a cheap and space-efficient method of storage, and no racking is required.

Pallet racking

Simple pallet racks generally have two or three tiers. Two tiers of racking require a clear height of about 3 meters, and three tiers require a clear height of about 4.5 meters. It is possible to have several more tiers, but sophisticated mechanical handling equipment is then required.

The benefits of shelving and pallet racking can be combined. The bottom tier of racking may be used to store the working stock. This tier is at a convenient height for manual order picking. Alternatively, a special picking shelf can be placed immediately above the bottom tier of pallets. In both cases, the upper tiers can be used to store safety stock.

Load handling

Each of the four storage systems described above requires suitable handling equipment and appropriate organization of stored goods. Appropriate handling equipment reduces the risk of injury to workers and damage to goods. Careful stock organization on shelves and pallets reduces unnecessary lifting and ensures easy access to goods during order picking.

Shelving. In order to reduce manual handling, goods should be transported to and from the shelves on trolley carts. Heavy items should be stored on the lower shelves. Whenever possible, other items should be organized so that frequently picked items are at waist height. Safety stock may be stored at a higher level.

Pallets. Loaded pallets can be moved only by using mechanical equipment. Hand-operated hydraulic pallet trucks and pallet lifts are suitable for floor pallets and for pallet racking up to three tiers high. Operations that have pallets stored at higher levels or turn over large volumes of stock must use powered forklift trucks. Figure 44-2 illustrates some typical storage and handling equipment.

44.7 Housekeeping

Housekeeping tasks for a store include cleaning and pest control, a regular inspection system for issues such as temperature and roof leaks, disposal of stock, precautions against fire, and strict security measures.

Cleaning and pest control

The store should be kept tidy and should be cleaned at minimum two or three times a week; a busy store should be cleaned once a day. Most warehouses have adequate personnel available for scheduled cleanups, and adequate cleaning

Figure 44-3   Good stores management

Figure 44-4   Poor stores management

equipment should be made available. Figures 44-3 and 44-4 illustrate good and bad stores management.

Pest control can be difficult, but to avoid possible contamination and physical damage to stock, insects, mice, and other pests must be kept out of the storage area. If needed, pest control measures such as poison should be implemented, with proper precautions. One of the chief reasons pests become a problem is the consumption of food in storage areas; therefore, this practice should be strictly avoided.

Inspection

Senior staff should inspect the store regularly. The chief storekeeper must make sure that storeroom employees check the shelves and pallets daily for signs of theft, pests, or water damage and for deterioration caused by climatic conditions. Storekeepers should open suspect containers and report problems to managers.

Buildings and equipment need both emergency and routine maintenance, but a regular building and equipment inspection and maintenance program prevents major failures and saves costs overall (see Chapter 42).

Disposal of expired or damaged stock

Damaged or expired stock should be placed in a designated salvage area to await authority for disposal. A written record of all stock consigned to this area should be maintained. It

is recommended that each item be valued at its acquisition cost. The responsible authority should be informed in writing that stock is to be written off. Disposal may be delayed if a committee decision is required, and substantial storage space may be needed for junk stock. When destruction is authorized, the inventory control clerk must adjust the stock records. All medicines and other potentially toxic products should be disposed of in accordance with local regulations in a manner that does not pose a risk to public health.

Fire precautions

Flammable trash, such as cartons and boxes, must not be allowed to accumulate in the stores. Smoking must be strictly forbidden, with "No Smoking" signs posted throughout the store. Senior staff must obey the rule as strictly as junior staff, and penalties should be imposed on those who ignore the rules. A smoking area outside the warehouse should be designated. Management must ensure that fire-detection and firefighting equipment are regularly inspected and that staff members receive adequate training in firefighting techniques and emergency action. Regular fire drills should be held to reinforce that training.

Staff should check frequently for fire, but management is ultimately responsible. Night watchmen can serve the dual purpose of responding to fire alarms and protecting against theft.

Security

Ideally, the chief storekeeper's office should have windows that overlook the loading bay, the compound entrance, and the store itself. A storekeeper who sits behind a closed door with the curtains drawn cannot observe what is happening at the site.

No vehicles should be allowed into the store compound unless they are authorized by the chief storekeeper or another senior staff member. A list of authorized vehicles should be prepared for the compound's gatekeeper.

Pedestrian access to the storage buildings should be strictly controlled. Visitors should report to the storekeeper's office and should not be allowed into the store area except on business. Visits by friends and family of staff should be discouraged. Business visitors should always be accompanied by a senior staff member. (See Chapter 43 for further discussion of security measures.)

44.8 Human resources management in medical stores

The organization of a typical central medical store is illustrated in Figure 44-5. The organizational structure at an intermediate store is generally a compressed version of this structure.

Medical stores managers are encouraged to review Chapters 51 and 52, which discuss human resources management in more detail.

Staff training and the medical stores procedures manual

Every worker should receive appropriate job training and refresher training, as appropriate. Most warehouse jobs are nontechnical, and in-service training and supervision of staff are likely to be the most effective approach. A written manual of standard operating procedures should cover the following—

- General management policy
- Management structure
- Job descriptions
- Reporting procedures
- Stock control and other record-keeping procedures
- Operational procedures
- Health and safety procedures
- Security

The manual should include visual aids that clarify operations. These documents are normally used by the director and section chiefs to train new staff and to settle procedural questions. Table 44-4 gives a sample contents list.

Each work area should have a copy of the manual. The contents of the document should be reviewed and explained in group presentations. The manual should be available to every employee, and staff members should be encouraged to use it in performing their duties. The manual should also be regularly reviewed and updated to reflect changes in operations or the introduction of new systems or procedures.

Staff supervision and discipline

The supervisory hierarchy should be clearly described to all workers. Personnel problems should be solved at the appropriate level. Section heads who do not supervise their workers regularly and effectively should be replaced.

Positive feedback and encouragement are essential. Minor lapses in performance should be kept in perspective. Major problems, such as proven cases of theft or reckless driving, should be handled through established ministry or organizational regulations. Regular staff meetings can help maintain a sense of shared purpose and ensure that all staff members understand their responsibilities.

Career development

Workers in the logistics system often have low status. They are frequently badly paid, work under poor conditions, and are not motivated. These problems result in low levels of performance.

An effective store relies on staff members who want to perform their jobs correctly. When staff members perform well, they should be rewarded and praised. Although it is difficult to do in many government supply systems, improving salary grades and promoting staff who show ability and commitment will help the organization retain good staff. Staff members are also motivated by participating in training programs and other opportunities for personal development. Frequent transfers of personnel from one site to another should be avoided, if possible. Chapter 51 discusses employee satisfaction and motivation.

If stores staff are treated badly by management, they will look for other jobs, and their experience will be lost. A stores operation that relies on casual labor is more likely to suffer from theft, breakages, and distribution errors.

44.9 Staff facilities

Good staff facilities encourage cleanliness, protect workers against occupational injuries, and contribute to good staff morale. Just as medicines are susceptible to damage from excessive heat or cold, staff performance and motivation suffer in these conditions.

Figure 44-5   Medical stores organizational chart

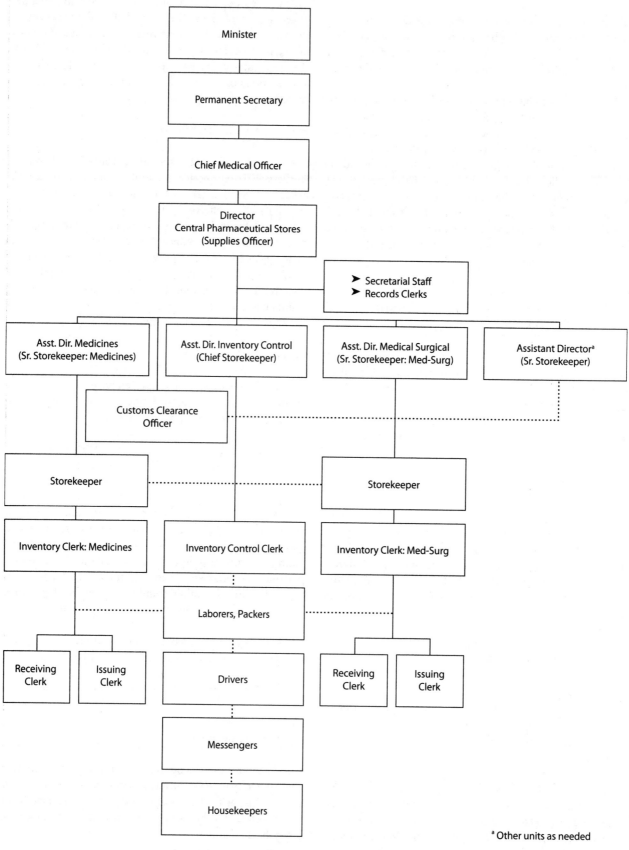

ᵃ Other units as needed

Table 44-4   Contents of a procedures manual for a central pharmaceutical supply system

Content unit	Typical structure
Statement of operational policy	• Central level
Organizational staffing pattern	• Regional level • District level • Community level • Lines of authority
Overview of sequence of tasks and activities in supply management process (with discussion of objectives)	• Job descriptions (all personnel by level, each level treated separately) • Logistics information system • Flow chart of central, regional, and district information • Supply operations forms (purchase order, receiving report, inventory card, requisition/issue form, issues ledger by item and facility, delivery voucher) • Accounting system and procedures • Inventory control system and procedures • Security system and regulations • Computerized information systems • Supply system administration • Operating budget (utilities, salaries, maintenance, supplies, miscellaneous) • Maintenance procedures (for buildings and equipment) • Special operating instructions • Cold-chain storage procedures • Quality-control procedures • Shipping and packaging procedures

Sanitary facilities

Personal cleanliness is essential among workers who handle medical supplies. The store needs well-maintained sanitary facilities for staff and visitors. Sanitary accommodations should be located on the perimeter of the building to allow natural ventilation and keep the drains outside the building.

Staff rest areas

A separate rest area, with a kitchen, toilet, and pantry for preparing and storing food, improves staff morale and reduces fire hazards and the risk of vermin infestation in the warehouse. It also improves efficiency by segregating resting staff from working staff.

First aid

Adequately trained personnel with first-aid equipment and dressings should be available to treat workers who suffer injuries on the job. Emergency washing facilities should be provided in case a staff member comes into contact with a corrosive or toxic agent. Installing emergency showers may be necessary. Eye-washing sprays should also be provided. Local health and safety regulations should always be followed. ∎

References and further readings

★ = Key readings.

★ Battersby, A., and A. Garnett. 1993. *How to Estimate Warehouse Space for Drugs.* Geneva: World Health Organization. <http://whqlibdoc.who.int/hq/1993/WHO_DAP_93.3.pdf>

Dalberg Global Development Advisors and the MIT-Zaragoza International Logistics Program. 2008. *The Private Sector's Role in Health Supply Chains: Review of the Role and Potential for Private Sector Engagement in Developing Country Health Supply Chains.* New York: The Rockefeller Foundation. <http://apps.who.int/medicinedocs/documents/s16323e/s16323e.pdf>

Ghiani, G., G. Laporte, and R. Musmanno. 2004. *Introduction to Logistics Systems Planning and Control.* West Sussex, England: John Wiley & Sons. <http://wileylogisticsbook.dii.unile.it>

★ John Snow Inc./DELIVER. 2005. *Guidelines for Warehousing Health Commodities.* Arlington, Va.: John Snow, Inc./DELIVER, for the U.S. Agency for International Development. <http://deliver.jsi.com/dlvr_content/resources/allpubs/guidelines/GuidWareHealComm.pdf>

★ John Snow, Inc./DELIVER in collaboration with the World Health Organization. 2003. *Guidelines for the Storage of Essential Medicines and Other Health Commodities.* Arlington, Va.: John Snow, Inc./DELIVER, for the U.S. Agency for International Development. <http://deliver.jsi.com/dlvr_content/resources/allpubs/guidelines/GuidStorEsse_Pock.pdf>

★ Mulcahy, D. 1994. *Warehouse Distribution and Operations Handbook.* New York: McGraw-Hill Professional.

WHO (World Health Organization). 2009. *WHO Expert Committee on Specifications for Pharmaceutical Preparations.* 43rd Report. Geneva: WHO. <http://www.who.int/medicines/publications/pharmprep/pdf_trs953.pdf>documents

ASSESSMENT GUIDE

General description

- How are goods received, stored, and supplied?
- What facilities are served? How often is each supplied? What methods of transport are used? Is a delivery, collection, or mixed system in use?

Stores management and staffing

- Does an operations manual adequately describe current procedures and responsibilities?
- Are staff positions described by category, listing the positions approved to be filled and those that have been filled?

Receiving

- Are procedures for receiving and checking medicines observed? Are standard checklists used?
- What medicines were returned during the past year, and why?
- How are complaints concerning product quality handled?

Communications and reporting

- What reports are regularly issued from medical stores, for whom, and how often?

Stock control

- What stock control system is used?
- Are random and periodic stock checks carried out? Is a stock auditing system in place?
- What percentage of stock records (and bin cards) corresponds with physical counts?

Stock management

- Is stock location fixed, fluid, or semifluid?
- Are medicines issued by FIFO or FEFO?

- What was the average stockout duration over the last year?
- How many expired medicines are in stock? What is their value?
- What was the value of inventory at the beginning and end of the last fiscal year?

Storage conditions

- Are medicines zoned in correct combinations of temperature, humidity, safety, and security?
- How are medicines organized within each zone?
- Are vaccines stored and monitored in accordance with the recommendations of the WHO Expanded Programme on Immunization?
- Is the store neat, and are effective pest control procedures in place?

Buildings and equipment

- Is storage space too small, adequate, or excessive?
- Are the loading bay, receiving area, packing area, administrative area, staff rest area, and sanitary facilities adequate?
- What is the condition of roofs, walls, floors, ceilings, firefighting equipment, windows, doors, locks, burglar bars, and water supply and drainage equipment and infrastructure?
- What storage systems are used (shelving, floor pallets, pallet racking)?
- What are the conditions of mechanical handling equipment, electricity supply, and telephones?
- What computer hardware and software systems are employed and are they adequate to support inventory control needs?
- Is there direct access to international communications?

———. 2007. WHO *New Product Information Sheets (PIS) Since 2000 Edition*. Geneva: WHO. <http://www.who.int/immunization_standards/vaccine_quality/new_sheets_intro/en/index.html>

★ ———. 2003. Guide to Good Storage Practices for Pharmaceuticals. Annex 9 to the *WHO Expert Committee on Specifications for Pharmaceutical Preparations*. 37th Report. Geneva: WHO. < http://apps.who.int/medicinedocs/pdf/s6156e/s6156e.pdf>

———. 2002. *Guidelines for Establishing or Improving Primary and Intermediate Vaccine Stores*. Geneva: WHO. <http://whqlibdoc.who.int/hq/2002/WHO_V&B_02.34.pdf>

———. 2000. *WHO/UNICEF Product Information Sheets, 2000 Edition*. Geneva: WHO.

———. No date. "Performance, Quality and Safety (PQS)." <http://www.who.int/immunization_standards/vaccine_quality/pqs_prequalified_devices_e13/en/>

WHO/EPN (World Health Organization/Ecumenical Pharmaceutical Network). 2006. *Multi-Country Study of Medicine Supply and Distribution Activities of Faith-Based Organizations in Sub-Saharan African Countries*. Geneva: WHO/EPN. <http://whqlibdoc.who.int/hq/2006/WHO_PSM_PAR_2006.2_eng.pdf>

Annex 44-1   Sample stock record card

STOCK RECORD CARD

Generic Name: Metronidazole   Strength: 200 mg   Dosage Form: tab

Code No.: 8022   Unit of Issue: tab   Unit Price: 0.3400

                                   Class: B

	Exp.		Order Date	Purchase Order No.	Order Qty.	From whom Rec./Issu.	Qty. Rec.	Rec. Date	Qty. Issu.	Balance	Remarks	Signature
Avg. Usage			1/3/08			Inventory				100,000	Exp. 9/2010	
Mar	11,000		2/3/08			PHC I			5,000	95,000		
Feb	5,000		3/3/08			PHC II			6,000	89,000		
Jan	21,000		7/4/08			PHC I			10,000	79,000		
Dec	5,000		20/4/08			PHC III			5,000	74,000		
			21/4/08			PHC I			3,000	71,000		
Nov	5,000		2/5/08	08-015	50,000	IDA	50,000	2/12/08		121,000	Exp 5/2011	
Oct	5,000		7/5/08			PHC II			1,000	120,000		
			8/5/08			HOSP			10,000	110,000		
Sep	7,000		8/7/08			HOSP			10,000	100,000		
Aug	6,000		15/7/08			PHC I			5,000	95,000		
			31/7/08			PHC III			2,000	93,000		
Jul	17,000		3/8/08			PHC I			1,000	92,000		
Jun	0		30/8/08			PHC II			5,000	87,000		
			30/9/08			PHC I			7,000	80,000		
May	11,000		5/10/08			PHC III			2,000	78,000		
			8/10/08			PHC I			3,000	75,000		
Apr	18,000		1/11/08			HOSP			5,000	70,000		
			7/12/08			PHC I			3,000	67,000		
Fiscal Year			15/12/08			PHC II			2,000	65,000		
FY: 07/08	1		1/1/09			PHC I			5,000	60,000		
			13/1/09			PHC III			6,000	54,000		
FY:			14/1/09			PHC II			10,000	44,000		
			2/2/09			HOSP			4,000	40,000		
			3/2/09			HOSP			1,000	39,000		

Pharmacy _____

Annex 44-2   Sample bin/stock card

Ministry of Health
Department of Medical Supply
BIN/STOCK CARD

Description: <u>Paracetamol tabs 500 mg</u>   Unit of issue: <u>1,000 tabs</u>

Stock No.: <u>02-4600</u>

Date 2007	Document/ Number	Received From/ Issued To	Units Received	Units Issued	Balance	Initials
Mar 5	BALANCE BROUGHT FORWARD				1,665	PF
5	IV 98534	PHC 42		10	1,655	RS
5	IV 98541	PHC 44		10	1,645	RS
6	IV 98543	HOSP 6		200	1,445	BJ
6	IV 98546	PHC 55		16	1,429	BJ
6	IV 98561	PHC 53		10	1,419	PF
6	IV 98562	PHC 52		12	1,407	BJ
6	IV 98565	PHC 54		10	1,397	PF
6	IV 98567	HOSP 7		150	1,247	PF
6	IV 98570	PHC 63		5	1,242	PF
6	IV 98572	PHC 64		5	1,237	BJ
7	IV 98573	PHC 66		5	1,232	RS
7	IV 98575	PHC 62		5	1,227	RS
7	IV 98574	PHC 68		5	1,222	RS
7	IV 98579	PHC 61		5	1,217	PF
7	IV 98601	PHC 65		5	1,212	PF
7	IV 98600	PHC 69		5	1,207	RS
7	IV 98603	PHC 67		5	1,202	PF
8	RN 98166	NOVAPHARM	10,000		11,202	BJ
8	IV 98605	HOSP 9		200	11,002	BJ
8	IV 98604	HOSP 8		200	10,802	BJ
8	IV 98609	PHC 71		10	10,792	BJ
8	IV 98611	PHC 75		12	10,780	RS
8	IV 98613	PHC 78		10	10,770	RS
8	IV 98614	PHC 72		15	10,755	RS

Annex 44-3   Sample receiving report

Ministry of Health
Department of Medical Supply
Central Pharmaceutical Stores
RECEIVING REPORT

Supplier: Apotex Inc.

P.O. No.: DMS—116/07

Port of entry: Port St. Philip

Date received at port of entry: 5/12/08

Number of shipping cartons/containers: 3

Invoice No.: 686033

Carrier: Fast Forwarders

Date Cleared: 05/17/08

Certified that from external inspections, all containers appear to be suitable and without damage except as follows:

Nil

Gavaza H.	05/18/08
Clearing officer	Date

Certified that all items on the invoice and the purchase order (specified above) were received and, after inspection, released for removal to shelving except as follows (or as marked on the invoice):

Check Muvuro	05/22/08	Usopero M.	05/22/08
Receiving clerk	Date	Chief storekeeper	Date

Annex 44-4   Sample requisition/issue voucher

Ministry of Health
Department of Medical Supply
REQUISITION/ISSUE VOUCHER

Requisition no.: PHC63-98-3-23

Health facility: Utano H.C.

Authorized by: Mukuru, DNO.

Date: March 4, 2008

Supply period: April to May 2008

Status of requisition:
- ☑ regular
- ☐ interim
- ☐ emergency

Item No.	Stock Number 1	Description 2	Unit of Issue 3	Stock on Hand 4	Quantity Requested 5	Quantity Approved 6	Quantity Issued 7	Amount ($) 8	Notes 9
1	02-0500	Aspirin tabs 300 mg	1000T	12	18	18	18	165.60	
2	02-2200	Metronidazole 150 mg	1000T	3	5	5	5	61.00	
18	02-4600	Paracetamol tabs 500 mg	1000T	6	8	8	8	209.60	
19	02-4800	Phenoxymethyl tabs 250 mg	1000T	3	4	4	2	81.40	short
20	02-4850	Piperazine tabs 500 mg	1000T	1	1	1	1	11.20	

15:00 March 4, 2008	11:00 March 26, 2008
Hour and date requisition received	Hour and date shipment received

CLEARANCES:

Mutamba, SO	Kaeke, Dir.	Mhanda, PT	Mundandishe, PT
1. Shipping and receiving review	2. Director of medical stores	3. Inventory control unit	4. Medical stores
Mufawatamba, SO	Mugari	Tinoda, SRN	
5. Shipping and receiving	6. Driver or custodian accepts shipment	7. Recipient, acknowledgment of receipt of shipment	

Annex 44-5   Sample delivery voucher

Ministry of Health
Department of Medical Supply
DELIVERY VOUCHER

Deliver to: _Utano HC_

Requisition no.: _PHC 63-98-3-2R_   Issue voucher no.: _98570_

Received from Central Pharmaceutical Stores __3__ sealed cartons and __2__ containers described below:

| 3 x cartons |
| 1 x 5L disinfectant |
| 1 x bale of sanitary pads |

for delivery to the above-named requisitioner/facility.

| _Mufawatamba_ | _Mugari_ | _09:00 Mar 26, 2008_ |
| Stores issuing officer | Driver/custodian of shipment | Date and time |

Received by requisitioner from the above-named custodian of shipment, the containers and/or items stated above in good order, except as follows:

| 1 carton damaged by leakage | _Mugari_ |
| 1 container missing | _Mugari_ |

| _Tinoda (TINODA, SRN)_ | _11:00 Mar 26, 2008_ |
| Receiving officer of requisitioning facility | Date and time |

IF ANY DISCREPANCY IS RECORDED BY THE RECEIVING OFFICER, THIS DELIVERY VOUCHER IS TO BE INITIALED BY THE CUSTODIAN OF THE SHIPMENT AS WELL.

Annex 44-6   Sample register of requisitions

Ministry of Health
Department of Medical Supply
REGISTER OF REQUISITIONS
(STORES ISSUES LEDGER)

Stores Issue No.	Date	Requisition No.	Issue Voucher No.	Value of Issues ($)				Certified
				Drugs	Med-Surg.	Other	Total	
001	Mar 5	98-3-2R	PHC42 98534	2412.60	836.50	—	3249.10	Mariyacho
002	Mar 5	98-3-2R	PHC44 98541	2933.50	1078.50	—	4012.00	Mariyacho
003	Mar 5	98-3-4R	HOSP6 98543-45	28364.20	6517.60	937.50	35819.30	Mariyacho
023	Mar 8	98-3-2R	PHC75 98611	3545.30	948.60	—	4493.90	Zvinodura
024	Mar 8	98-3-2R	PHC78 98613	2266.40	592.30	—	2858.70	Zvinodura
025	Mar 8	98-3-2R	PHC72 98614	2947.70	876.10	—	3823.80	Zvinodura

Part I: Policy and economic issues	Part II: Pharmaceutical management	Part III: Management support systems

Planning and administration
Organization and management
  43 Security management
  44 Medical stores management
  45 Hospital pharmacy management
  46 Pharmaceutical management for health facilities
  47 Laboratory services and medical supplies
Information management
Human resources management

CHAPTER 45

Hospital pharmacy management

SUMMARY

Appropriate medicine use in the hospital setting is a multidisciplinary responsibility that includes—

- Selection and formulary management by a multi-disciplinary committee
- Prescribing by the physician
- Procurement, storage, medication order review, and preparation and dispensing by the pharmacy department
- Medication administration by nurses or other health care professionals
- Monitoring the effect of medicines on the patient by all members of the health care team

The drug and therapeutics committee (DTC) is responsible for developing policies and procedures to promote rational medicine use. Its functions include—

- Management of the approved medicine list or hospital formulary
- Ongoing drug use review
- Adverse drug event reporting and implementation of safe medication practices

Members of the DTC should include representatives from the medical, pharmacy, and nursing staffs; hospital administrators; and the quality assurance coordinator. Subcommittees are often formed for in-depth analysis of particular issues.

The pharmacy department, under the direction of a qualified pharmacist, is responsible for the procurement, storage, and distribution of medications throughout the hospital. In larger hospitals, satellite pharmacies may bring the pharmacist closer to patient care areas, facilitating interactions between pharmacists and patients. In some settings the pharmacist is used as a resource for medicine information and specialized medication therapy management.

Medications may be distributed in bulk, in courses of therapy, or in unit doses. Unit-dose distribution is optimal for patient care but requires initial capital outlay for repackaging equipment and medication cabinets. Recent technological advances, such as computerized dispensing machines and bar coding, are now available to further promote safe medication practices.

Additional mechanisms for inpatient medicine management include—

- Patient medication profiles, maintained in the pharmacy department
- Medication administration records, maintained by nurses
- Periodic inspection of medicine storage areas
- Procedures for strict control of dangerous drugs and controlled substances
- Responsible disposal of pharmaceutical waste
- Procedures for after-hours pharmacy service

Small-scale pharmaceutical production often is not cost-effective and should be evaluated by the DTC.

The control of narcotics is of particular concern in the hospital setting and requires a systematic approach for the prevention and detection of abuse.

A hospital exists to provide diagnostic and curative services to patients. Pharmaceuticals are an integral part of patient care. Appropriate use of medicines in the hospital is a multidisciplinary responsibility shared by physicians, nurses, pharmacists, administrators, support personnel, and patients. A medical committee, sometimes called the drug and therapeutics committee, pharmacy and therapeutics committee, or the medicine and therapeutics committee, is responsible for approving policies and procedures and monitoring practices to promote safe and effective medicine use. The pharmacy department, under the direction of a qualified pharmacist, should be responsible for controlling the distribution of medicines and promoting their safe use. This task is challenging because medicines are prescribed by physicians, administered by nurses, and stored throughout the hospital.

This chapter covers hospital-specific pharmaceutical management issues, such as pharmacy department organization and alternative pharmaceutical distribution systems. Several functions of the DTC are discussed, with an emphasis on formulary management. Other important issues relevant to hospital pharmaceutical management are treated in Chapter 17 on treatment guidelines and formulary manuals, and Chapters 28 and 29 on investigating medicine use and on promoting rational prescribing, respectively. Chapter 35, "Pharmacovigilance," discusses adverse drug reaction monitoring and medication error management.

45.1 Responsibilities of hospital staff

The hospital pharmacist should be an expert on medicines who advises on prescribing, administering, and monitoring, as well as a supply manager who ensures that medicines are available through procurement, storage, distribution, inventory control, and quality assurance. The balance between these two roles varies, depending on the individual's background and the work setting. A pharmacist may assume a prominent clinical role in settings where his or her knowledge of clinical pharmacology and capacity to provide expert advice have earned the acceptance of hospital medical and nursing staff.

The responsibility for establishing policies and procedures related to medication selection, procurement, distribution, and use often lies with the DTC. Because the medicine use process is multidisciplinary, the committee should include representation from all functional areas involved: medical staff, nursing, pharmacy, quality assurance, and hospital administration.

Purchasing and stock management

In some hospitals, a separate department manages all hospital purchasing (pharmaceuticals, medical supplies, equipment, and so forth); this department may be called medical stores or materiel management. In such cases, the chief pharmacist prepares an annual budget request for pharmaceutical purchases and places orders for medicines through the medical stores.

In other settings, the pharmacy department manages pharmaceutical purchasing directly. No single individual should have total control of pharmaceutical procurement. A designated committee should review and approve all purchases; either a special purchasing committee or the DTC (see below) may manage this function.

Procedures for procurement and inventory management should be written in a manual that has been approved by hospital administration and the appropriate committees; the procedures for purchasing should follow guidelines provided in Chapters 18 and 23. Stock management procedures are determined by the facility's size and whether a warehouse is attached to the hospital (see Chapters 44 and 46).

Medication use

The medication-use process can be divided into four components—

1. *Prescribing.* The physician has overall responsibility for the care of the patient, prescribing or ordering medications as part of the treatment plan. The mechanisms to ensure appropriate prescribing within the hospital customarily fall within the purview of the medical staff committees, usually including the DTC. The DTC may establish protocols or procedures that allow pharmacists or nurses to prescribe within specific guidelines.

2. *Preparation and dispensing.* The pharmacy department, under the direction of a registered pharmacist, is responsible for preparing and dispensing medications. Policies and procedures for these functions should be approved by the DTC. The chief pharmacist reports to hospital administration.

3. *Medication administration.* Administering medications is generally the responsibility of the nursing staff. The chief nursing officer oversees all nursing functions. In some cases, physicians may administer medicines such as anesthetic agents. Other health care professionals may administer medicines within the scope of their practice (for example, midwives attending deliveries).

4. *Monitoring the effect of medications on the patient and ordering appropriate changes in therapy.* Monitoring activities are primarily the responsibility of the physician. However, observation and reporting are required from the person who administered the medication (usually the nurse) and from other members of the health care team involved in the patient's therapy. In some settings, a clinical pharmacist or pharmacologist monitors medication therapy in the hospital and consults on medication therapies that require special expertise to ensure safety and efficacy; for example, total parenteral nutrition, anticoagulation, or treatment with aminoglycoside antibiotics.

Government agencies and licensing boards regulate medications through laws and professional practice standards. The laws and regulations usually specify that the chief pharmacist be the person responsible for the control of medications within a hospital, including procurement, storage, and distribution throughout the facility.

Although the chief pharmacist is responsible for the pharmaceutical budget and the control of medications, he or she does not supervise those who prescribe or administer the medications. In addition, in some hospitals, purchasing, receiving, and storing of medications are handled by a medical stores department that is not under the supervision of the pharmacist.

These varying responsibilities illustrate the complexity of pharmaceutical procurement, storage, and use in the hospital. Efforts to improve the system should respect this complexity and include multidisciplinary representation and involvement. Coordination is required at the policy level through the DTC, at the management level (beginning with hospital administration), and through the different branches of the organizational tree.

45.2 Organization of hospital pharmacy services

In organizing hospital pharmacy services, both the way in which the staff is organized and the physical layout of the building must be considered.

Personnel

Hospital pharmacy personnel can be divided into three major categories—

1. *Management.* Management includes the chief pharmacist and sometimes deputy chief pharmacists, who are responsible for procurement, distribution, and control of all pharmaceuticals used within the institution and for management of personnel within the pharmacy department.
2. *Professional staff.* These professionals are qualified pharmacists who procure, distribute, and control medications and supervise support staff for these activities. In some facilities, pharmacists provide clinical consulting services and medicine information.
3. *Support staff.* The support staff category often includes a combination of trained pharmacy technicians, clerical personnel, and messengers.

The smallest hospitals may have only two or three pharmacy staff members, with the chief pharmacist as the only pharmacist. Larger teaching hospitals that provide extensive pharmaceutical distribution and clinical services may have more than 100 staff members.

The cornerstone for a well-functioning medication system is an up-to-date manual of policies and procedures. Staff members should be familiar with the manual and adhere to it.

Physical organization

The extent of the pharmacy's physical facility is determined by the size of the hospital and the services provided. A large pharmacy department might have the following sections within one physical space or in separate locations throughout the hospital—

- Administrative offices
- Bulk storage
- Narcotic or dangerous drug locker
- Manufacturing and repackaging
- Intravenous solution compounding
- Inpatient and outpatient dispensing
- Medicine information resource center
- After-hours pharmacy
- Emergency medicine storage

Inpatient dispensing is sometimes done from satellite pharmacies throughout the hospital. In larger hospitals, satellite pharmacies are beneficial because they enable a shorter turnaround time for individual medication orders, especially in distribution systems that dispense medications packaged for individual patients. Satellites also increase the pharmacist's presence in the patient care area, facilitating interactions with medical staff, nursing staff, and patients, and thus ultimately improving patient care.

With satellite pharmacies, there is reduced need for ward stocks. However, each satellite requires a certain minimum inventory level of pharmaceuticals. A system with multiple satellites most likely has a higher total inventory level than that of a central pharmacy system. The higher inventory and additional personnel costs needed to staff satellite pharmacies may be justified by reductions in pharmaceutical supply costs (because there is less wastage) and improvements in patient care. Whether or not multiple satellite pharmacies serve inpatients, separate pharmacies often serve inpatients and outpatients. Figure 45-1 illustrates how a hospital pharmacy with separate inpatient and outpatient departments is organized in one African country.

45.3 Hospital drug and therapeutics committee

Most commonly, the committee designated to ensure the safe and effective use of medications in the hospital is the DTC. The American Society of Health-System Pharmacists' guidelines on DTCs state that "medication use is an inherently complex and dangerous process that requires constant evaluation. Organizations need to implement tools and processes necessary to meet the goals of using medications effectively and safely" (ASHP 2008).

Purpose and functions

The DTC promotes the rational use of medication through the development of relevant policies and procedures for medication selection, procurement, distribution, and use and through the education of patients and staff. Country Study 45-1 lists the functions of the DTC in an Afghan hospital.

In some hospitals, the DTC becomes overwhelmed with the difficulty of obtaining an adequate supply of medications. Members are caught up in routine decisions about which medicines to buy, how much, and from whom, rather than focusing on long-term planning, policies, and programs for improving the safe and cost-effective use of medications. As discussed, in most settings, daily purchasing decisions can be handled by the chief pharmacist, with supervision by the DTC or another committee responsible for procurement.

Figure 45-1   Multiple-department pharmacy system

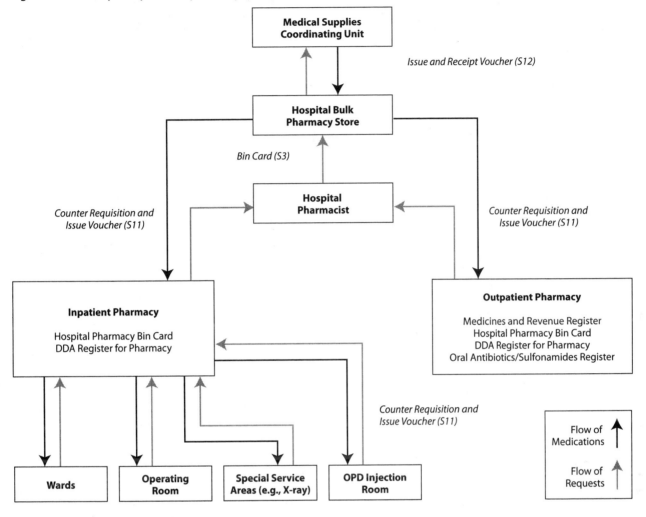

Source: Ministry of Health, Government of Kenya, 1994.

DDA = Dangerous Drugs Act.

Note: Forms and registers for wards, operating room, special areas, and outpatient department (OPD) injection room are the same as for the central pharmacy system.

Membership

An effective DTC requires that members participate in meetings and assist with other committee activities. Membership should include representation from—

- Medical staff (including representation from each department)
- Pharmacy (the chief pharmacist often serves as the secretary)
- Nursing
- Hospital administration
- Quality assurance staff

The committee should have broad representation but be sufficiently small and manageable to conduct business effi-ciently: a membership of eight to fifteen members often ful-fills these criteria. The committee may occasionally invite a specialist to make a presentation or provide advice on a particular issue. For example, a cardiologist may attend a committee meeting to advise members regarding a for-mulary decision on a new cardiac medication. DTCs often have subcommittees to address particular issues, such as antibiotic use, drug use evaluations, or medication errors. Subcommittees can manage specific tasks without consum-ing a large portion of the DTC's meeting time.

Hospital formulary management

The hospital formulary is the cornerstone of medication management in the hospital, and it should be the princi-pal concern of the DTC. The issues related to medication

> **Country Study 45-1**
> **Functions of a hospital drug and therapeutics committee in Afghanistan**
>
> Facility-based DTCs will be set up by the steering bodies of the individual health facilities in association with the National Pharmaceutical and Therapeutic Committee.
>
> The DTCs' basic functions include—
>
> - Establishing local policies and procedures on the use of medicines
> - Ensuring that the national essential medicines list and local formularies are used appropriately in the facility
> - Disseminating national standard treatment guidelines (STGs) and developing local STGs for common diseases and medical conditions
> - Conducting medicine use evaluations in the facility
> - Conducting facility-based pharmacovigilance activities
> - Monitoring medicine use at the health facility
>
> - Providing education to local health care providers on the appropriate use of medicines
>
> The members will be appointed according to their positions and responsibilities within the health facility. The DTC member numbers will be defined based on the health facility level. In the majority of heath facilities, the DTCs will include the following members—
>
> - One representative from each specialized medical service of health facility (senior physician)
> - One representative from the nursing department
> - One representative from the pharmacy department
> - One representative from the administration and finance department
> - Other members appointed according to their personal expertise (specialists in pharmaceutical information or quality assurance)
>
> Source: Ministry of Public Health, Government of Afghanistan, 2009.

selecttion for formularies are treated in detail in Chapter 17; the following list provides general guidelines for the hospital setting.

- Limit the formulary list to conserve resources—stocking all medicines on the national formulary is usually not necessary.
- Eliminate generic duplication—only one brand or label of each generic medicine should be routinely stocked.
- Minimize the number of strengths stocked for the same medication; multiples of lower strengths can be used for infrequently needed higher strengths.
- Select medications for the formulary based on diseases and conditions treated at the facility.
- Specify formulary medicines of choice for common therapeutic indications. Medicines of choice should be selected by comparing efficacy, safety, toxicity, pharmacokinetic properties, bioequivalence, and pharmaceutical and therapeutic equivalence. Cost-effectiveness and availability should be primary considerations, evaluating alternatives as described in Chapters 10 and 17. After medicines of choice are selected, they form the basis for standard treatment guidelines and for therapeutic substitution programs (see below).
- Include second-line alternatives to medicines of choice as needed, but minimize therapeutic duplication.

- Ensure that the hospital formulary corresponds with any national or regional standard treatment guidelines that have been formally approved by the health system.

In addition to the basic formulary process, many hospitals add two more features—therapeutic substitution and use restrictions for certain medications in the formulary.

Therapeutic substitution (sometimes called therapeutic interchange) is based on the hospital formulary. The DTC provides guidelines for substituting specific formulary medicines for specific nonformulary medicines (or a specific category of medications), usually for specific disease conditions. Whenever a prescription is written for a nonformulary medicine that is covered by the therapeutic substitution policy, the designated formulary product is automatically substituted by the pharmacy department (or nurse). Note that this substitution is not generic—the two products are chemically different.

The DTC should develop formal written policies specifying which medicines (or categories of medications) are suitable for automatic therapeutic substitution. These programs usually start with relatively noncontroversial medication categories, such as antacids and vitamins, and progress over time to other therapeutic groups, such as antibiotics and certain cardiac medications, as physicians become comfortable with therapeutic exchange. Two main arguments are used to justify therapeutic substitution programs. One is that such programs ensure that only the most cost-effective products are routinely used, a policy that has obvious benefits in terms of controlling both actual purchase costs and inventory-holding costs (see Chapter 23). In settings where funds are limited, the more limited the list of medications that are routinely stocked, the more likely that all those medications will always be available. The other justification is that the DTC has presumably spent considerable effort selecting medications that offer the best therapeutic value for the conditions covered by therapeutic substitution. An ancillary benefit is that hospital staff will be more familiar with the proper methods for handling, reconstituting, and administering the formulary products.

Therapeutic substitution is often resisted by staff physicians, but almost 90 percent of hospitals in the United States (a stronghold of physician independence) have substitution policies in place (Pederson et al. 2008). Therapeutic substitution is often practiced informally and unintentionally in hospitals where stockouts are common—if the prescribed medicine is out of stock, another must be substituted. Physicians who practice in such settings are likely accustomed to the concept.

Normally, the therapeutic substitution policy allows escape clauses for specific patients. The physician can submit a special form that justifies the use of a specific nonformulary medicine for a specific patient (as discussed below).

Use restrictions are most often applied in larger hospitals where specialist physicians are on staff. Restrictions may apply to certain individual formulary medicines or to certain categories of medicines; the principle is that restricted medicines can be prescribed only by certain specialists or can be used only on certain wards. Such restrictions are generally applied to particularly expensive medications (such as anticlotting medications) or particularly toxic medications (such as cancer chemotherapy); however, some hospitals go further, requiring specialist consultation on many different categories of medications. Restrictions should be carefully considered; they decrease the use of medicines involved (which may or may not be desirable), increase the demand on specialists (and potentially the cost of services), and increase administrative burdens for nurses and pharmacists who must manage the process.

Methods to promote formulary adherence include the following—

- Review and take action on all nonformulary medicine use.
- Prohibit use or distribution of samples of nonformulary products.
- Establish procedures and approved product lists for therapeutic substitution.
- Provide easy access to the formulary list (copies at each medication ordering location and in pocket manuals).
- Involve medical staff in all impending formulary decisions.
- Advertise and promote formulary changes.

Requests to use nonformulary medicines should be monitored by the DTC. If many nonformulary medicine requests come from a particular physician, or if requests are frequent for a particular nonformulary medicine, the committee should take action. Actions may include adding the medicine to the formulary, educating physicians on the rationale for the nonformulary status of the medicine, or banning the medicine from use in the hospital. Country Study 45-2 is an example of a procedure for nonformulary medicine use in a hospital in the United States.

Drug use review

Drug use review (DUR) is a tool to identify such common problems as inappropriate product selection, incorrect dosing, avoidable adverse drug reactions, and errors in medication dispensing and administration. DUR may then be used to implement action plans for change. DUR is an ongoing, planned, systematic process for monitoring, evaluating, and improving medicine use and is an integral part of hospital efforts to ensure quality and cost-effectiveness. More appropriate and more effective use of medicines ultimately results in improved patient care and more efficient use of resources.

Chapter 28 provides an overview of the concepts and approaches for investigating medication use. Chapter 29 contains the specific methodologies for developing a hospital DUR program.

45.4 Inpatient medication management

In general, the issues presented in Chapter 30 for good dispensing practices are relevant to the hospital setting. Patient education and medication counseling are described in Chapter 33 and are also applicable in hospitals. The purchasing and inventory strategies described in Chapter 23 should be applied in the hospital setting.

Medication distribution systems

Medication distribution has long been the primary function of hospital pharmacy services.

Four basic types of medication distribution systems exist—

1. Bulk ward stock replenishment
2. Individual medication order system
3. Unit-dose system
4. Automated medication dispensing

Variations of each exist, and all four systems may be in use in the same facility, depending on the strategy developed. For example, a facility may use the bulk ward stock system for high-volume, low-cost medicines (aspirin, paracetamol, and antacids) that do not require a high level of control for preventing theft or medication errors. Individual medication order systems or unit doses can be used for medicines requiring a higher level of control (see Table 45-1). In addition, automated dispensing systems are now frequently used in developed countries and will become more common in the future.

Bulk ward stock

In a ward stock system, the pharmacy functions as a warehouse and dispenses bulk containers on requisition without reviewing individual patient medication orders for appropriateness. The main advantage is shorter turnaround time between prescribing and administering the medication. The

use of ward stock medications should be minimized, but it is appropriate and desirable for certain situations—

- In emergency departments and operating rooms, medications are usually required immediately after the physician prescribes them. Unless a pharmacy satellite is located in these emergency areas, dispensing medications according to individual patient orders is not possible. Unfortunately, medicines used in these situations are often expensive, and control is always a challenge for the pharmacy department.
- In life-threatening emergency situations, medications need to be kept in patient care areas as a time-saving measure.
- High-volume, low-cost medicines can be dispensed from ward stock if the patient safety risk is low.

Individual medication order system

The individual medication order system closely resembles dispensing to outpatients: a course of therapy is dispensed according to a written prescription for an individual patient. Compared with ward stock distribution, the advantages are that the pharmacist can review the appropriateness of ther-

---

Country Study 45-2
Procedure for the use of nonformulary medicines in a U.S. hospital

A limited formulary of medicines may not satisfy all individual or unique patient needs. A physician may request use of a nonformulary medicine on a one-time (one course of therapy), one-patient basis.

The physician requesting the nonformulary medicine or the pharmacist receiving the medicine order must fill out the nonformulary medicine request form. The pharmacist receiving the request must inform the physician of alternative medicines that may be used. The pharmacist must also indicate how long it will take before the medicine will be available. The physician and pharmacist should avoid obtaining the medicine by special delivery or borrowing from another hospital if possible.

Nonformulary medicines will be stocked in the nonformulary section of the pharmacy only during the individual patient's course of therapy. The pharmacy will track expenses related to nonformulary medicines and report to the drug and therapeutics committee.

Nonformulary Medicine Request Form (For One-Time/One-Patient Use)

Patient: _____   Room #: _____   Date: _____

Medicine name/strength/dosage form: _____

Current formulary alternatives (suggested by pharmacist): _____

Why is this agent preferable to the formulary alternatives suggested? _____

Was this medicine request prompted by a manufacturer's representative? ❑ yes ❑ no

Are you requesting permanent addition of the medicine to the medication formulary? ❑ yes ❑ no

If so, will you be present at the next pharmacy and therapeutics committee meeting to discuss the advantages of this medicine? ❑ yes ❑ no

If accepted, what formulary medicines do you recommend for deletion? _____

_____

Prescribing doctor: _____
Signature: _____

Table 45-1   Comparison matrix for pharmaceutical distribution system

Factor	Bulk ward stock	Individual medication order	Unit dose	Automated dispensing
Material and supply costs	Low	Medium–low	High	Very high
Pharmacy labor costs	Low	Medium	High	High
Nursing labor costs	Medium–low	Low	Low	Low
Pilferage risk	High	Medium	Low	Very low
Medication error risk	High	Medium–low	Low	Low

apy, a patient-specific medication profile can be maintained, pharmacy charges to patients are facilitated, and closer control of inventory is possible. This system can limit the time intervals for dispensing: for example, an individual supply for three days of therapy is sent initially; if therapy is continued beyond three days, the empty container is returned to the pharmacy to be refilled.

Unit-dose medicine distribution

A preferred system from a patient care perspective is the unit-dose system, which has a lower possibility for error. Medications are dispensed in unit-dose packages (each dose is separately packaged) in separate bins or drawers for each patient. Commonly, a twenty-four-hour supply is provided. Medications returned to the pharmacy can be put back in stock without concern for identity or contamination. This system is efficient but requires a large initial capital outlay for the purchase of repackaging machines and medication cabinets with individual patient drawers. The cost per delivered dose is higher than with bulk packaging, but this increased expense may be offset by reduced wastage and easier detection of leakage. Hospitals in some countries have found innovative ways of adapting local technologies to construct their own fixtures and equipment.

Automated medication dispensing

Technology-based interventions have been investigated as a mechanism to improve medication distribution and reduce medication errors that lead to adverse drug reactions. The use of automated dispensing machines has become commonplace in many hospitals, but cost remains a big deterrent for implementation in resource-limited settings. The mechanism is founded on a computer interface between the hospital pharmacy computer terminals and the dispensing machines at the clinical ward. This system electronically controls and tracks the dispensing of unit doses for each patient based on individual medication profile. The dispensing machines allow medicines to be stored on the ward and to be more conveniently accessed by the clinical staff. (See chapter 11 in AHRQ 2001 for an overview.)

Patient medication profiles

Patient medication profiles are necessary if hospital pharmacists are to monitor inpatient medication therapy. Each profile contains data on the patient's current and recent pharmaceutical therapy, allergies, diagnosis, height, weight, age, and sex. Profiles work best in conjunction with unit-dose medicine distribution or automated dispensing systems but can be used with the individual medication order system.

A pharmacy profile allows the pharmacist to review all the medications that a patient is taking before dispensing the first dose and with each new medication order. Problems with pharmaceutical therapy, such as allergies, duplicate therapy, medicine-medicine interactions, medicine-disease interactions, inappropriate length of therapy, and inappropriate dosing, can be detected and avoided or corrected.

Computerized pharmacy systems display the patient's medication profile on the screen, and the pharmacist edits the screen with each new order. Medication interactions, dosage ranges, and other monitoring functions can be programmed into the computer. In developed countries, information technology advances now provide linkages to patient-specific information from laboratory and clinical monitoring.

Medication treatment record

Also known as the medication administration record (MAR), the medication treatment record helps the nurse schedule treatments for each patient and provides a permanent record of the medications administered. It also allows nurses to review the patient's pharmaceutical regimen and provides a way to compare quantities of medications dispensed from, and returned to, the pharmacy with quantities administered to the patient. Physicians review MARs to verify current therapy and as part of their routine rounds. The trend is toward computerizing MARs; in the United States, over two-thirds of hospital pharmacies surveyed in 2005 used computer-generated or electronic records (Pedersen et al. 2006). Country Study

45-3 describes the procedure for completing a medication treatment record used in Kenya.

Ward and department inspections

The pharmacy department should undertake periodic inspections of medication storage areas throughout the hospital to ensure appropriate levels of properly stored medications, to monitor expiration dates, and to remove unnecessary stock. Figure 45-2 is a sample ward inspection record. When problems are detected in inspections, pharmacy and nursing staff must develop methods to correct the situation.

Dangerous drugs and controlled substances

Controlled substances require greater attention in the hospital setting than other medications, just as they do outside the hospital. The various definitions and categories of controlled drugs all relate to abuse and addiction potential.

Procedures specific to the procurement, reception, storage, dispensing, and administration of controlled drugs should establish a readily retrievable trail of accountability for each individual drug unit. The records should document ordering, receiving, dispensing, administration, and wastage. Perpetual inventory records should be used at all storage sites, and controlled drug stocks should be counted and reconciled against the records daily, with unexplained losses reported to the pharmacy. Controlled substances stored throughout the hospital should be securely double locked within a well-constructed storage area, with the pharmacy department in control of the distribution and duplication of keys.

Methadone maintenance therapy (MMT) programs, which some countries are endorsing as a way to prevent the spread of HIV/AIDS, can significantly impact a hospital's ability to manage controlled drugs. In general terms, hospitals are already familiar with handling largely injectable narcotics, typically in 2 to 5 mL vials, along with other

---

Country Study 45-3
Kenya medication treatment record

Purpose

Each inpatient has a medication treatment sheet (see opposite) on which all medications prescribed are recorded by the consultant, medical officer, or clinical officer, and on which all medications administered are recorded by the nursing staff. In addition, individual prescriptions are required for Dangerous Drugs Act (DDA) drugs and specific other medicines designated by the hospital drug and therapeutics committee.

Procedure

1. At the time of admission, a medication treatment sheet is completed by the clinician with the following information—

   - Patient's complete name (all names must be included to ensure proper identification)
   - Medication allergies
   - Inpatient number
   - Ward and bed number
   - Age and sex

2. For easy access during hospitalization, the treatment sheet is kept at the foot or head of the patient's bed with the observation sheet. (Because of this accessibility, the diagnosis should not be written on the treatment sheet.)

3. All medication orders must be written on the medication treatment sheet by an authorized prescriber (doctor or clinical officer). The order should include the date and time the order was written; the medication name, strength, dose, route of administration, frequency, and duration; a legible official name; and the signature of the prescriber.

4. In addition, for DDA medicines and specific other medicines designated by the hospital drug and therapeutics committee, individual prescriptions are required; entries for DDA medicines must be in red ink.

5. When a medication is administered to a patient, the nurse or clinician administering the medicine writes the date and time of administration and signs in the appropriate place on the medication treatment sheet.

6. When an ordered medicine cannot be administered for any reason, the nurse writes in the patient's nursing notes the name of the medicine, the date, and time the medicine was to be administered, and the reason that the medicine could not be administered (patient not on ward, unavailability, any other reason).

7. The nursing officer should regularly review medication treatment sheets to ensure that they are being used properly on all wards and that all required information is being recorded.

Ministry of Health
Medication Treatment Sheet

Patient _____ Allergies _____
Inpatient Ward _____ Age _____
Bed No. _____ Sex _____
                                  Name of Institution _____

Note: Use RED pen for DDA. Enter your own signature for every medicine given.

TO BE COMPLETED BY CLINICIAN		TO BE COMPLETED BY NURSING STAFF					
			DATES AND SIGNATURE				
DATE	MEDICATIONS	TIME					
		3 AM					
		9 AM					
		3 PM					
		9 PM					
		3 AM					
		9 AM					
		3 PM					
		9 PM					
		3 AM					
		9 AM					
		3 PM					
		9 PM					
		3 AM					
		9 AM					
		3 PM					
		9 PM					
		3 AM					
		9 AM					
		3 PM					
		9 PM					
		3 AM					
		9 AM					
		3 PM					
		9 PM					
		3 AM					
		9 AM					
		3 PM					
		9 PM					
		3 AM					
		9 AM					
		3 PM					
		9 PM					

STAT, PRN, AND PRE-OP MEDICATIONS

TO BE COMPLETED BY CLINICIAN		TO BE COMPLETED BY NURSING STAFF			
DATE	MEDICATIONS		DATES, TIMES, AND SIGNATURE		

Source: Ministry of Health, Government of Kenya, 1994.

Figure 45-2   Sample ward inspection record

Nursing ward: _____Inspection date: _____

Check each item that complies with standards:
- ❏   Medication storage area orderly and clean
- ❏   Internal use/injectable medications separated from disinfectants and toxic medications
- ❏   Medications properly secured from theft
- ❏   No unlabeled or mislabeled medicines present
- ❏   No unauthorized floor stock
- ❏   No excessive floor stock quantities
- ❏   No expired products in stock
- ❏   Medication refrigerator temperature maintained within limits (see temperature log)
- ❏   Narcotics properly secured and records complete
- ❏   Approved emergency medicines in stock
- ❏   Concentration, date, and time mixed written on reconstituted injectables
- ❏   Medication formulary list available

Pharmacist's comments on areas of nonadherence to standards:
_____
_____
_____

Action recommended:
_____
_____
_____

Pharmacist: _____
Nurse in charge: _____

small-volume preparations, but because of the dilute nature of the products used in methadone maintenance therapy for oral administration (typically 1 to 10 mg/mL) and daily treatment regimens (typically 70 mL per day), large physical volumes of products can be required. Even a small MMT program can dramatically increase the need for narcotic product secure storage space and handling of bulk products in facilities that are designed to handle much lower volumes (see Country Study 45-4). Methadone programs can also force the facilities' pharmacy service departments to take on unwanted small-scale production responsibilities.

After-hours pharmacy

Although the need for medications is continuous, many hospitals cannot justify staffing a pharmacy department twenty-four hours a day. If medications must be obtained while the pharmacy is closed, either an on-call pharmacist

can come in or a nursing supervisor can dispense medications. Medication dispensing by nonpharmacists should be limited, however, to preserve the system of checks and balances and to prevent medication errors. To minimize the risk of incorrect dispensing, the following measures can be taken—

- Establish procedures for after-hours pharmacy service.
- Require training or in-house certification of nurses before they undertake dispensing responsibility.
- Prohibit after-hours access to most of the pharmacy. A limited formulary of prepackaged and labeled medicines can be provided in a separate, locked night cabinet.
- Require completion of dispensing records by the nurse and subsequent review by the pharmacist.

45.5 Small-scale hospital pharmaceutical production

The several types of pharmaceutical production that exist have varying levels of complexity (see Chapter 7). The type of small-scale production of pharmaceuticals in a hospital pharmacy could include secondary production from existing raw materials that are usually imported and the packaging or repackaging of finished goods into smaller dispensing packs and course-of-therapy (COT) packages (tertiary production). Small-scale production can be further divided into nonsterile and sterile production or compounding. Most hospitals repackage medications in smaller unit-dose containers and may compound specialty items such as creams with special formulations; however, hospitals should evaluate the feasibility of producing any pharmaceutical products based on the availability of qualified staff, adequate facilities, sufficient equipment, and all the other necessary resources (see Country Study 45-5).

The following sections examine some of the management issues for each type of production, in order of increasing complexity.

Repackaging and course-of-therapy packaging

Repackaging and COT packaging are relatively simple forms of local pharmaceutical production. They require the ability to provide adequate packaging, labeling, and control of the final product.

Repackaging is usually considered when the product can be purchased in bulk quantities at a favorable price and then repackaged locally, where labor costs are lower, and when local-language labeling may be important. In addition to the cost savings, a more convenient package size can be made available to small health centers and individuals, as Table 45-2 illustrates.

Country Study 45–4
Scaling up methadone maintenance therapy in Vietnam

In an attempt to curtail the spread of HIV among injecting drug users in Vietnam, the government piloted the country's first community-based methadone program in seven clinics in Hai Phong, Ho Chi Minh City, and Ha Noi City in 2008. HIV prevalence is higher in injecting drug users (30 percent) than any other subpopulation in Vietnam. By 2010, about 1,800 clients had received free MMT along with basic health care services and HIV care and treatment, including antiretroviral therapy.

In planning for the program, the national Pharmacy and Therapeutics Committee chose a base of 10 mg/mL of methadone solution for the therapy. This decision made it necessary to transport large volumes of narcotics around the country—typically 2.5 liters per patient year—and to squeeze large, secure storage cabinets into already overcrowded hospital pharmacies. Then the pharmacies had to dilute the solution to 1 mg/mL to dispense to patients, a procedure which, because of the regulations on handling narcotics, is fairly onerous.

This system of providing methadone therapy product can be contrasted to the United Kingdom's methadone maintenance program, which distributes 1 g vials of methadone powder to dispensing sites, for a total of only 2.5 1 g vials per patient year. These 1 g powder vials fit more easily into existing narcotics storage cabinets, and a single vial is simply dissolved into commercially available 1 liter bottles of simple syrup at the dispensing site to produce the appropriate 1 mg/mL dose to dispense to patients.

As a result of positive pilot program results, the Ministry of Health in Vietnam plans to expand methadone maintenance therapy to cover 80,000 clients in thirty provinces. This will require moving 204,000 liters of narcotic product per year and assuring the capacity for its secure storage.

While many factors go into choosing the most appropriate preparations to use, physical storage and distribution sizes should not be neglected. The Pharmacy and Therapeutics Committee may need to reconsider its choice of methadone formulation in order to facilitate large-scale program expansion.

Sources: *Thanh Nien News* 2010; Family Health International 2010.

Many types of glass and plastic are used, with the choice often depending on what is being packaged. For instance, acids, solvents, and corrosive materials must be packaged in glass, with lids that can be firmly closed. Fortunately, the majority of simple liquids, solids, and tablets can be packaged in rigid plastic bottles or resealable polyethylene bags of various sizes and thicknesses, usually with a write-on panel for labeling or handwritten instructions to the patient.

Nonsterile production

Nonsterile production of topical ointments and oral or topical liquids is more difficult and complex than repackaging but less demanding than sterile production. If the facility plans to carry out only nonsterile production, resource requirements can be simplified. However, standard written instructions for batch preparation and packaging must be followed, and quality control must be closely monitored for each aspect of the process.

Every product requires a well-designed production control worksheet (also called a batch documentation sheet). It clearly specifies the production formula (the detailed recipe that the pharmacist must follow precisely) and the instructions for preparation. It includes spaces to verify packaging, labeling, and other control procedures. Figure 45-3 shows a sample pharmacy production and control worksheet.

The chief pharmacist of the facility is usually responsible for developing the master production formulas and instructions, as well as for training production staff. The staff should always work from copies of the master production and control worksheet, with a unique control number preassigned by the pharmacist in charge. Any changes to that formula, such as scaling down quantities to make a smaller batch, should be made only by a qualified pharmacist.

A pharmacy preparation, no matter how simple, should never be made from memory. The working copy of the pharmacy production control worksheet should be readily available or posted in the production area for easy reference and initialing of each production step and control procedure.

Sterile production

Sterile production is the most demanding type, and it must be carried out in strict compliance with current good manufacturing practices (GMPs). Depending on need and capacity, sterile products that can be manufactured include eyedrops, small-volume injections, and large-volume injections (or parenteral products).

Country Study 45-5
Assessing the feasibility of small-scale pharmaceutical production in the Catholic Diocesan Hospital Pharmacies of Ghana

The Diocesan Hospital Pharmacies (DHPs) were originally established in 1976 to provide pharmaceuticals and medical supplies to National Catholic Health Service facilities in Ghana. The DHP produced their own products such as infusions, injections, ointments, and drops to supply their clients more economically. Beginning in 1976, however, both the economy and the pharmaceutical market in Ghana expanded, and many competing pharmaceutical products became available from local and international sources. Furthermore, little additional funding was available to make capital improvements, which limited the DHPs' ability to accommodate increasing demands for improved quality assurance. In 2004, an assessment investigated the utility of the DHP to continue small-scale pharmaceutical production for thirty-three hospitals and sixty-six clinics in the context of the changing pharmaceutical market.

The assessment concluded that the DHPs—

- Should stop producing terminally sterilized products, for example, intravenous solutions, due to the high capital, personnel, and production costs, in addition to the associated risk to patients if the

requirements for sterile operations are not adequately met.
- Could continue to produce non-terminally sterile products, such as ophthalmic items, as long as they made several facility upgrades.
- Have a role in the compounding of non-sterile products, such as oral syrups, for their clients. The assessment recommended several production modifications to assure uniformity and efficiency.
- Should develop pharmacovigilance systems to identify and report adverse drug reactions and medicine product quality problems.

Overall, the assessment recommended that the DHPs focus their production on non-sterile products for which there was an increasing demand. Moreover, they should stop the production of other products that require more technical expertise and oversight due to quality and safety concerns. To ensure the supply of these sensitive products, the DHPs could consider developing a partnership with a local manufacturer or buy from international sources.

Source: RPM Plus 2004.

From a production process perspective, intravenous (IV) fluids are among the easiest products to make. The standard pharmacy production and control worksheet, including the sterility quality-control aspects, is used (see Figure 45-3). From a technical perspective, however, the production of IV fluids is very demanding on resources and personnel. Special (often quite expensive) equipment, facilities, techniques, and quality-control procedures need to be in place, along with the means to ensure continuous production with adequate reserves of ingredients and supplies, regular maintenance of equipment, and refresher training for production staff. The demands on supervisory personnel, who must ensure the high quality of the final product, are also much greater. Contaminated or incorrectly prepared IV fluids administered to very sick people can just as easily kill patients as help them.

Medications produced by the pharmacy must have adequate process and finished-product controls to ensure identity, strength, purity, and quality. A hospital pharmacy may have difficulty achieving the same cost efficiencies as a pharmaceutical manufacturer specializing in a particular product line. The DTC needs to evaluate the costs and benefits of producing such special preparations as compared to

purchasing commercial products. Chapter 7 includes more details on assessing the feasibility of small-scale pharmaceutical production.

45.6 Pharmaceutical disposal

Hospitals and other health care facilities generate all sorts of hazardous waste, from sharps to materials contaminated with bodily fluids to expired or damaged pharmaceuticals. Improper disposal of pharmaceuticals can result in contaminated water supplies, the resale of poor-quality medicines, and polluted air from improper incineration.

Often, hospitals can return products to the facility from where they were obtained. However, when that option is not available, a disposal plan should be in place and should be regularly monitored. Depending on the properties of the pharmaceutical waste, incineration, land disposal, and inertization (where the product is mixed with cement) can all be appropriate methods for disposal. Special care must be taken with certain classes of pharmaceuticals, such as narcotics, or toxic drugs, like anticancer medicines. Before a disposal technique is instituted, any government laws and

Table 45-2   Pharmaceutical repackaging

Product type	Name of product	Bulk package size	Repackaged size
Liquids	Denatured alcohol	20 L	500 mL
Solids	Talcum powder	50 kg	1 kg
Tablets	Aspirin 300 mg	1,000	100
	Aspirin 300 mg	1,000	12
	Co-trimoxazole 480 mg	1,000	10 (bid for 5 days)
	Mebendazole 100 mg	1,000	6 (bid for 3 days)

regulations relevant to health care waste management and environmental protection should be reviewed.

45.7   Controlling leakage and drug abuse

Chapter 43 discusses systematic approaches for detecting, analyzing, and preventing pharmaceutical losses caused by theft, bribery, and fraud. Those approaches are applicable to hospitals and other health facilities.

The control of narcotics is of particular concern in a hospital because it may be the only type of institution regularly stocking, dispensing, and administering them. Drug addiction among physicians, pharmacists, and nurses is quite common. To avoid drug abuse and prevent leakage—

- Be alert to changes in performance, injuries, and mood swings in workers.
- Ensure double-witness and double-signature procedures for wastage of narcotics.
- Limit access to narcotic storage areas.
- Check patient charts and medication administration records for patterns of consumption; be suspicious if patients receive noticeably more narcotics during a particular shift.
- Ask patients if they received the medications.
- Use locked boxes or wire cages to ensure security for medications moved from the pharmacy to the wards.
- Issue individual narcotics boxes to each anesthesiologist daily, and make sure that the box is returned to the pharmacy at the end of the day with a written record of quantities used for each patient.
- Count narcotic stocks daily and reconcile with inventory records.

The same procedures followed for narcotics are sometimes used for antibiotics and other medicines that are easily resold and commonly lost to theft, such as antiretrovirals to treat HIV/AIDS. ■

References and further readings

★ = Key readings.

★ AHRQ (Agency for Healthcare Research and Quality). 2001. *Making Health Care Safer: A Critical Analysis of Patient Safety Practices.* Evidence Report/Technology Assessment no. 43, AHRQ Publication no. 01-E058. Rockville, Md.: AHRQ. <http://www.ahcpr.gov/clinic/ptsafety>

★ ———. *Best Practices for Health-System Pharmacy, 2009–2010.* (Updated annually.) Bethesda, Md.: ASHP.

Family Health International. 2010. "USAID/FHI-supported Methadone Programs Achieve Results: A New Era of Drug Treatment in Vietnam. Country Profiles." <http://www.fhi360.org/en/CountryProfiles/Vietnam/res_Methadone.htm>

Joint Commission on Accreditation of Healthcare Organizations (JCAHO). 2009. *A Guide to JCAHO's Medication Management Standards.* 2nd ed. Oakbrook Terrace, Ill.: JCAHO.

———. 2010. *Comprehensive Accreditation Manual for Hospitals: The Official Handbook (CAMH).* (Updated annually.) Oakbrook Terrace, Ill.: JCAHO.

Ministry of Health, Government of Kenya. 1994. *Good Management of Hospital Drugs and Medical Supplies.* Nairobi: Ministry of Health.

Ministry of Public Health/General Directorate of Pharmacy Affairs, Government of Afghanistan. 2009. *Memorandum on the Creation of Drug and Therapeutic Commitees.* Kabul: Ministry of Public Health.

Mittmann, N., and S. Knowles. 2009. A Survey of Pharmacy and Therapeutic Committees across Canada: Scope and Responsibilities. *Canadian Journal of Clinical Pharmacology* 16:1:e171–e177. <http://www.cjcp.ca/pdf/CJCP08027e171-e177_mittmann.pdf>

Pedersen, C. A., P. J. Schneider, and D. J. Scheckelhoff. 2008. National Survey of Pharmacy Practice in Hospital Settings: Prescribing and Transcribing—2007. *American Journal of Health-System Pharmacy* 65(9):827–43.

———. 2006. ASHP National Survey of Pharmacy Practice in Hospital Settings: Dispensing and Administration—2005. *American Journal of Health-System Pharmacy* 63:327–45.

Prüss, A., E. Giroult, and P. Rushbrook, eds. 1999. *Safe Management of Wastes from Health-Care Activities.* Geneva: World Health Organization. <http://whqlibdoc.who.int/publications/9241545259.pdf>

Rational Pharmaceutical Management (RPM) Plus Program. 2007. Drug and Therapeutics Committees Training Course. Arlington, Va: Management Sciences for Health. <http://www.msh.org/projects/rpmplus/Resources/TrainingInitiatives/All-DTC-Training-Guides.cfm>

———. 2004. *Assessment of Production Cost and Quality Assurance Processes in the Catholic Diocesan Hospital Pharmacies of Ghana.* Arlington, Va: Management Sciences for Health.

Figure 45-3   Pharmacy production and control worksheet

Ministry of Health
Department of Medical Supply
PHARMACY PRODUCTION AND CONTROL WORKSHEET

Name of the preparation: Sodium Chloride 0.9%   Control number: _97-03-20-A_

Formula Source of formula: USP/NF (1995), page 1418	Quantity	Raw Material Lot Number	Prepared by	Check by
Sodium chloride	540.0 g	HCI 1052	AL	SD
Water for injection, freshly prepared q.s. to make	60.0 L	—	AL	SD

Instructions:
1. Prepare all required equipment and packaging materials according to standard protocols.
2. Weigh the sodium chloride using a precision balance.
3. Mix and make the solution in a closed, graduated, stainless-steel mixing vessel.
4. Filter the solution under air pressure through a 0.45-micron prefilter and a 0.2-micron final filter into previously cleaned and sterilized bottles.
5. Stopper and cap the bottles.
6. Autoclave the batch immediately according to standard protocols.
7. After cooling, label the bottles.
8. Perform all the required quality-control checks.
9. Hold in quarantine until batch is released by Quality Control.

Packaging
Done by: ___GL___
Bottle used/size: DIN Class I 500 mL IV bottle
Closure used: Chlorobutyl rubber stopper
Theoretical yield: 120 bottles
Actual yield: ___115___
Special storage required: None
Expiration date: 1 year
Checked by: ___TK___

Quality Control / Sterile
Sterilizer used: Uniclave 88
Time: from _10:30_ hour to _10:50_
Temperature: _121°C_ Pressure: _1.2 Bar_ By: _AB_
Clarity Test: Yes _√_ No _____ By: _JR_
Sterility Test: Yes _√_ No _____ By: _DA_
Pyrogen Test: Yes _√_ No _____ By: _DH_
Analytical Test: Yes _√_ No _____ By: _PR_
Checked by: _ML_ Released from quarantine by: _KK_

Product Label
Made by: ___HE___   Attached by: ___DW___
Sample Label (attach below):

Sodium Chloride 0.9%
1,000 mL
Intravenous Infusion
310 mOsm/L
Store Below 25°C
Sterile and Pyrogen-Free
Do Not Use If Solution Contains Particles

Batch No: _97-03-20-A_   Manufactured by:
Exp. Date: _3/20/08_   Central Pharmacy
                                 Sterile Production Unit

Final Disposition of Production
Accepted: _√_   Rejected: _____
Date: _3/28/07_

Quantity added to inventory: _112_
Received by: _JB_
Signature of pharmacist (or delegated person):
   R.L. Watt

ASSESSMENT GUIDE

Organization

- Which department and individuals are responsible for ordering medicines and managing inventory?
- What systems are used to manage inventory and procure pharmaceuticals?
- Apart from the central pharmacy, are there satellite pharmacies? If so, how many?
- How are medicines distributed to wards?
- Does a hospital formulary exist? If so, how many items are listed? When was it last updated?
- Is there an after-hours pharmacy? How is it managed?
- Does a pharmacy and therapeutics committee exist? If yes, how many meetings were held in the past year? What percentage of members attended? What issues were discussed?

Staffing

- How many pharmacy staff members—professional and support—are employed?
- What is the educational level of professional staff?
- What refresher training or continuing education have the professional pharmacy staff members received in the past two years?
- How do the professional pharmacy staff members spend their workdays—divided among clinical advice, preparation and dispensing, ward supervision, and administration?

Operation

- How many patients were admitted last year?
- What is the average number of prescriptions per day dispensed by pharmacies to inpatients? To outpatients?

- Among outpatients, what is the average dispensing communication time? What percentage of medicines dispensed are adequately labeled? What is the level of patient understanding?
- How often are ward storage areas inspected?
- Are the medication records accurately filled in?
- How many items are stocked in the central unit, satellite units, and ward stocks?
- How much does the hospital spend annually on pharmaceuticals?
- Does the hospital have procedures in place to dispose of expired or damaged pharmaceutical products?

Other pharmacy responsibilities

- Are preparations manufactured in the hospital? If so, how many? What quality-control measures exist?
- Is there a need for COT or special packaging for facility use? Are sufficient equipment, supplies, and personnel available for this type of production? Is it possible to ensure that packaging, labeling, and quality control are adequate?
- Are there any special regulations in effect that govern local manufacturing by a hospital pharmacy? Are these regulations being adequately enforced?
- Have drug use review activities occurred during the past year? If yes, who reviews the reports? What actions or improvements have occurred as a result of DUR?
- Is a system in place to track adverse drug reactions and medication errors? What actions or improvements have occurred as a result of this activity?

Rich, D. S. 2004. New JCAHO Medication Management Standards for 2004. *American Journal of Health-System Pharmacists* 61:1349–58.

Thanh Nien News. 2010. "Methadone Makes Impressive Debut in Vietnam." April 18. <http://www.thanhniennews.com/2010/Pages/20100418134811.aspx>

USP (United States Pharmacopeia). 2008. USP <797> Guidebook to Proposed Revisions: Pharmaceutical Compounding—Sterile Preparations. Revised version. Rockville, Md.: USP.

WHO (World Health Organization). 2003. *Drug and Therapeutics Committees: A Practical Guide.* Geneva: WHO, in collaboration with Management Sciences for Health. <http://whqlibdoc.who.int/hq/2003/WHO_EDM_PAR_2004.1.pdf>

WHO/DAP (World Health Organization/Action Programme on Essential Drugs). 1996. *Good Pharmacy Practice (GPP) in Community and Hospital Pharmacy Settings.* Geneva: WHO/DAP. <http://whqlibdoc.who.int/hq/1996/WHO_PHARM_DAP_96.1.pdf>

| Part I: Policy and economic issues | Part II: Pharmaceutical management | Part III: Management support systems |

Planning and administration
Organization and management
  43 Security management
  44 Medical stores management
  45 Hospital pharmacy management
  46 Pharmaceutical management for health facilities
  47 Laboratory services and medical supplies
Information management
Human resources management

CHAPTER 46

Pharmaceutical management for health facilities

SUMMARY

Health facilities are the last component of the pharmaceutical supply chain. Managing pharmaceutical supply at the facility level directly affects the quality of health care. If medicines are consistently unavailable, patients suffer and staff members lose motivation. Everyone loses confidence in the health system, and patient attendance decreases. A constant pharmaceutical supply promotes effective care, inspires confidence in the health facility, and contributes to job satisfaction and self-esteem among staff.

Every health facility, however large or small, needs to store and manage its medicine stocks. Systems must be in place to ensure—

- Secure storage
- Storage in correct environmental conditions
- Accurate record keeping
- Effective reordering
- Effective stock rotation and expiry monitoring
- Effective fire and theft prevention

Health workers and managers often believe that inventory control is possible only when resources are plentiful. This is not the case. Inventory control is about managing and using the resources available. There will be "sufficient resources" only if effective inventory control is implemented.

Good inventory control makes ordering and pharmaceutical management easier. Essential medicines programs place a high priority on improving inventory control to ensure a reliable supply of essential medicines, vaccines, and other items at health facilities. To achieve this aim, staff need to be trained in inventory control, storage, and ordering procedures.

The choice of an appropriate inventory control method varies according to the type of facility, scale of operations, and staff capabilities. Despite these differences, the principles of effective inventory control remain the same.

46.1 Managing medicines at health facilities

The purpose of inventory control at the facility level is to—

- Prepare effective orders
- Maintain sufficient safety stock levels within budget limits
- Maintain records in accordance with local requirements
- Adjust inventory levels to respond to new morbidity trends and changes in standard treatment guidelines
- Provide appropriate, safe, and secure storage
- Prevent expiry of medicines

HIV/AIDS is changing the picture of pharmaceutical supply management in many facilities because of the lifelong nature of the treatment. However, the ultimate goal of inventory control is to ensure that the right medicines are kept in the right quantities and are available at the right time.

Benefits of a successful inventory control system at the facility level

Maintaining a sufficient stock of items at a health facility has many benefits. Patients receive medicines promptly, and stockouts can be prevented even when deliveries are delayed. Supplies can be replenished at scheduled intervals, saving on administrative costs and transport time. Patients have confidence in the facility and seek help when they are ill. In addition, an effective inventory control system keeps track of and ensures accountability for supplies.

Problems arising from poor stock control

When inventory control fails, problems occur. A patient's condition may worsen or antimicrobial resistance may develop because of a delay in treatment; a patient may even die if a lifesaving medicine is out of stock. If medicines are not available in rural facilities, patients may have to make long and expensive journeys to obtain treatment. If medicine availability at the secondary level is better than at the primary level, the community will lose confidence in primary health care and seek hospital treatment instead. When a medicine is out of stock, a less suitable alternative may be prescribed. Frequent stockouts may establish or reinforce poor prescribing habits. Emergency orders, which are expensive for the purchaser and inconvenient for the supplier, may be required.

Staff commonly resist the implementation of inventory control systems. The reasons should not be ignored but rather brought out into the open for discussion. Common reasons for resistance are a perceived lack of time for record keeping or a feeling that "this is not my job." Lack of appropriate training may also play a major role in resistance to new systems. An advocate on staff can demonstrate that the time spent on inventory management activities is time well spent. Patients also need to understand that the time health care staff spend to maintain records ensures that their medicines will be available during their next visit.

Cost of maintaining stock

Stocking a new health facility can account for a significant amount of the facility's total annual budget. If stock is managed well, however, future expenses will be consistent with use. An efficient inventory control system saves money. Poor inventory control leads to wastage or increased costs for holding stock—

- Overstocking of certain items may tie up a substantial portion of the pharmaceutical budget, leaving insufficient funds for other important, perhaps life-saving, medicines.
- Overstocked medicines often expire; for example, some antiretrovirals (ARVs) have only a six-month shelf life.
- Poor storage conditions may result in spoiled stock (for example, dressings may be soaked by a leak in the roof, or injectable medicines may lose potency if the storeroom is too hot).
- Poor stock records and poor security make theft easier.
- A change in prescribing policy or practice may make a medicine obsolete. Without good inventory control, such changes may result in excessive wastage.

46.2 Managing the storage area

Good inventory control requires careful thought about the dimensions and design of the storage space, appropriate conditions for storage of different types of supplies, and the importance of stock rotation and systematic arrangement of stock, as well as attention to cleanliness, fire-prevention measures, and security within the store (see Figure 46-1).

Dimensions and design of the store

Storage should be located in a dry, weatherproof building. Stock should be organized and easily accessible on an adequate amount of good-quality shelving (most items in health facilities can be kept on shelves). Space and cold-chain equipment should be provided for the refrigeration of vaccines and other items. Temperature and humidity levels should be controlled within appropriate limits, and the space should be well ventilated. Pharmaceuticals and medical supplies should be segregated from linens, food, and other nonmedical items. The building should be physically secure.

Sizing. Product and packaging innovations, as well as fear of blood-borne infections, such as HIV and hepatitis B, have increased the use of disposable medical sundries. These items require more storage space. In addition, large global funding initiatives, particularly for HIV/AIDS, tuberculosis, and malaria, have dramatically increased the volume of medicines that facilities have to handle. For example, treatment kits, such as those used for tuberculosis, and blister packs of artemisinin-based combination therapies take up much more space than bulk bottles of tablets, for example. Designers of new facilities frequently underestimate storage requirements, and older facilities are often very short of space, with supplies stored in corridors and blocking work areas. Appropriate adjustable shelving and handling equipment are often lacking. Health facilities need to be aware of possible increases in space requirements due to public health program scale-up and plan accordingly.

Hospital stores are more difficult to size because they vary with the range of services offered and the organization of services. Stock levels and lead times also need to be considered in the estimate. However, the general rule is that 1 square meter per hospital bed can be used for initial planning and costing, assuming that supplies are received every month.

Receiving bay. A weather-protected area designated for receiving supplies should be close to the storage area and preferably linked to it by a covered walkway. A pharmacy or medical stores department in a hospital may have its own delivery bay, which is often raised above ground level to facilitate unloading from large delivery vans. Smaller facilities have a single receiving bay providing access to ambulances and small delivery trucks. Designating one area of the actual storeroom as the receiving area may be necessary, if no space exists for a separate receiving bay.

Storage of supplies

Most pharmaceuticals and medical supplies can be kept at uncontrolled room temperature. If the product has no special instructions, normal storage conditions apply. These conditions mean storage in dry, clean, well-ventilated premises at temperatures of +15 to +25°C or, depending on climatic conditions, up to +30°C.

Less stable medicines must be stored in specific conditions to maintain their effectiveness and prevent contamination. Storage instructions are product-specific. Different brands of the same generic drug may have different storage requirements because their packaging or formulation differs slightly. The manufacturer's recommendations should be followed. The expiry date provided by the manufacturer assumes that products are stored under ideal conditions. The following categories of medicines require special storage facilities—

- Products that must be kept frozen (usually vaccines and sera)

Figure 46-1   Tips for managing stock in the pharmaceutical storeroom

Security

Secure the storeroom
- double doors/double locks on entrance
- burglar bars on windows

Use extra precaution for "attractive items"

No lockable cupboards?
Then improvise: secure using
wire mesh, latch, and padlock

Bulk Storage

Store bulk off the floor

Allow air circulation

Limit the height of stacks to prevent crushing

No pallets?
Then improvise: construct
a wood frame

Orderly Arrangement

Provide sufficient shelving

Use a system for arrangement: by order code/
drug category or alphabetic by generic name

Guard against spoilage: lightweight items
higher up; heavy fluids, fragile items lower

Arrange neatly and label shelf for each item

No shelves?
Then improvise: support planks with
bricks or crates; use strong cartons
and other empty containers

Accountability

Restrict access and check stock frequently

Maintain a stock card for each item if possible
- keep stock card next to item
- fasten stock card to shelf

No stock cards?
Then improvise: make your own
or use a book

Stock Rotation

When receiving, place containers
according to expiry date
- later expiry at back
- earlier expiry at front

When issuing
- take the container with the earliest
  expiry date

What about items without expiry date?
Use FIFO

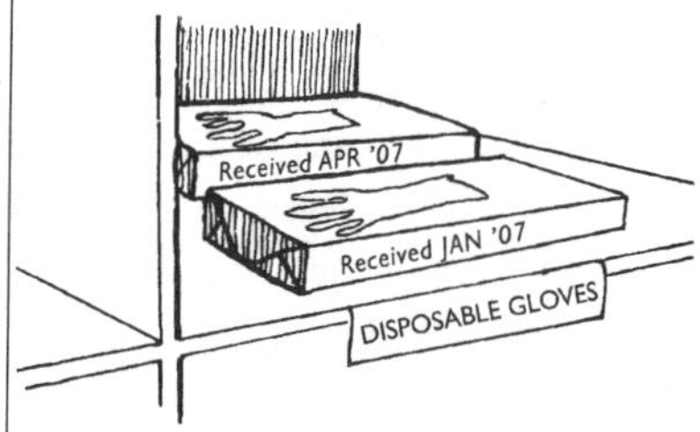

- Products sensitive to heat that require refrigeration
- Products that have a reduced shelf life at uncontrolled room temperature and need mechanical ventilation or air-conditioning
- Flammable products that require separate, fireproof premises
- Products prone to theft or misuse (see Chapter 43)

Items needing storage in a controlled environment. The usable shelf life of the following products may be reduced if stored at uncontrolled humidity or at room temperature in hot climates—

- Some injectable products (for example, adrenaline). Most injectable preparations are less stable than solid oral forms (tablets and capsules). Injectable preparations in solution are particularly unstable, whereas freeze-dried powder preparations (for reconstitution) are less degradable. Many injectables require protection from light as well as from heat.
- Some suspensions, such as the ARV stavudine, which has a shorter shelf life than the capsule form.
- Intravenous fluids (particularly if purchased in plastic containers).
- Some suppositories, pessaries, creams, and ointments. These products may melt at temperatures greater than 30°C. If they do melt, they should not be used because the active ingredient in the formula may become unevenly distributed.
- X-ray films and chemicals. Manufacturers typically recommend storage of X-ray film at a maximum of 21°C. Opened packages are also affected by humidity. A humidity range of 30 to 50 percent is advisable. X-ray film should be handled carefully to avoid staining, creasing, buckling, and friction.
- Products containing rubber, latex, cellulose, or some plastics. Condoms, most sterile disposable medical devices, and surgical products such as syringes, needles, and catheters require protection from excessive humidity, cold, and strong light. Any of these conditions may make products brittle, stained, malodorous, and unusable. Sterility cannot be ensured if packaging is damaged.

In hot climates, these items should be stored in the coolest place possible, preferably with air-conditioning or air-circulation fans. When preparing essential medicines lists (see Chapter 16), taking account of the stability of medicines and the type of storage facilities available is important.

Items needing freezing or refrigeration. Vaccines, blood products, and some other medicines lose potency if kept, even briefly, at temperatures outside the recommended range. For those products, the cold chain must be maintained at every stage. (See Table 44-3 and References and Further Readings for literature on cold-chain management.)

All cold-chain equipment should meet WHO standards. Top-loading refrigerators and freezers are the most appropriate choice. Electric refrigerators of the ice-lined type have good "hold-over" characteristics in the event of a power failure. Front-loading types should be used only in places where the electricity or fuel supply is completely reliable, because they have very poor hold-over characteristics and temperature control.

Having a contingency plan in place before a refrigerator breaks down is essential. Rural health facilities are often so small and so isolated that no other source of refrigeration is available. Larger facilities frequently have more than one refrigerator and can use another refrigerator to store vaccines for short periods. Alternatively, an arrangement can be made to move the contents to a private refrigerator elsewhere in the community or to obtain a regular supply of ice packs until the defect is rectified.

Performing routine monitoring and maintenance is also important, as well as organizing an effective repair system. The temperature in each appliance must be monitored and recorded routinely at least once a day. Any breakdown must also be recorded, including the period during which the medicines were exposed to uncontrolled temperatures. Medicines are then kept or discarded, depending on the program guidelines or the manufacturer's advice. Cold-chain monitor cards and devices in or on packages that change color or otherwise alert staff to potential damage assist in monitoring.

Freezing is as damaging as high temperatures for some items, including injectable contraceptives, ergometrine, insulin, adrenaline, and the DPT, DT, TT, and hepatitis B vaccines. Frozen toxoids can be detected by the "shake test" (if the contents clump or fail to resuspend after vigorous shaking). Evidence from Eastern Europe shows that vaccines can freeze inside a refrigerator during winter months when heat in a building is inadequate. Refrigerators incorporating a heating circuit are available to overcome this problem. Loss of potency in ergometrine injection has frequently been found in field studies, and may also be detected visually. If the solution appears colored when compared with water, the injection has less than 90 percent of stated content and should be discarded.

Short periods at room temperature (during transportation or local distribution, for instance) are acceptable for many products (such as ergometrine and insulin), even though such exposure can, to some extent, reduce shelf life. Other items, such as vaccines, should always be transported in cold boxes.

Controlled drugs. Narcotics (for example, pethidine injection, morphine preparations) and other specified medicines that may be abused are governed by special legislation and regulations that control import, export, production, supply, possession, prescribing, record keeping, and retention of documents.

The following security measures are suggested in the pharmacy and at each user level—

- A safe or reinforced, double-locked cabinet fitted with a light (preferably with a red bulb) that comes on when the door is opened
- A special register recording details of each receipt or issue with two signatures, physical counting after each entry, and signatures at "handover-takeover"
- Independent audit (by supervisors and national pharmaceutical inspectors)

Attractive items. Some noncontrolled items are particularly prone to theft, abuse, or misuse. They include expensive medicines (cimetidine, praziquantel, ARVs); certain antibiotics; psychotropics; equipment such as scissors, safety razors, and hypodermic needles; and sundries, such as rolls of cotton. Such items should be stored in a separate, locked area or cupboard, where they can be supervised.

These items require stricter record keeping and more frequent stock taking than other items. Periodic audits should be made of consumption (issues) against actual recorded use (outpatient registers, prescription records, or ward stock records) to expose any theft or misuse. Embossing packaging or the pharmaceutical products themselves with a unique identifier can deter the diversion of pharmaceuticals into the private sector (see Chapter 19).

Flammables and corrosives. Flammable liquids commonly found in health facilities fall into three categories, according to United Nations hazard classifications—

1. Flash point of −18°C (for example, acetone, anesthetic ether)
2. Flash point of −18 to +23°C (such as alcohols before dilution)
3. Flash point of +23 to +61°C (for example, kerosene)

Bulk supplies of flammable substances require a separate outdoor store located away from the main buildings and pathways. Even small stocks of category-1 flammables should be kept in an outbuilding designed specifically for that purpose (AHRTAG 1994). Firefighting equipment should be readily available.

A small working stock of flammables may be kept in a steel cabinet in well-ventilated premises, away from open flames and electrical appliances. The cabinets should be marked "highly flammable liquid" and bear the international hazard symbol. The cabinet shelves should be designed to contain spillage.

Corrosive or oxidant substances (such as trichloracetic acid, glacial acetic acid, concentrated ammonia solutions, silver nitrate, sodium nitrite, and sodium hydroxide pellets) should be stored away from flammables, ideally in a separate steel cabinet. Appropriate industrial-type protective gloves should be used when handling these substances.

Stock rotation and expiry monitoring

The first-expiry/first-out (FEFO) rule ensures stock rotation and prevents wastage through expiry. In this system, the stock with the longest life should be placed farthest to the back (or, if shelving makes such placement impossible, farthest to the left). Stock should be issued only from the front or from the right-hand side. The expiry dates of medicines should be checked at the time of receipt and noted on the stock record. Stock nearing expiry should not be accepted unless it can be used before expiry. Facilities should regularly monitor expiry dates, and expired medicines should be removed immediately from stock. In most cases, they must be destroyed. There should be an agreed-upon procedure for disposal that protects public health. A written record is necessary, and in some countries, a committee decision is required.

Health professionals sometimes have to decide whether to use an expired medicine or withhold treatment. The medicine may still be usable and could save a life, but an expired medicine might actually kill a patient. Such decisions have ethical and legal consequences. The only legal procedure for using expired medicines is to test them, transmit the test results to the manufacturer, and have the manufacturer extend the expiry date.

No guarantee exists of a medicine's effectiveness after the expiry date. In exceptional circumstances, when expired medicines might have to be used, a pharmacist who is experienced in quality assurance must be involved and the clinician must be informed. Medicines usually expire because they have been overordered or the FEFO rule has not been observed. In well-run stores where orders are placed regularly and stock is rotated, wastage caused by expiry should not occur. When it does, the supervisor should find out why and take corrective action.

Expired or damaged products should be disposed of following written standard procedures that conform to country laws or regulations related to hazardous waste.

Arrangement of stock

Organizing stock systematically saves time when ordering or locating items and prevents stock from being lost. Chapter 44 discusses various systems for organizing stock (see Section 44.5). The systems most often used in health facilities are organization by therapeutic category, clinical indication, or dosage form, with products arranged alphabetically within those categories.

Treatment rooms and medicine trolley carts should arrange medicines by therapeutic class (for example, antibiotics, antiasthmatics, or antihypertensives) or consistently follow another approved classification.

Liquids for internal use must be kept separate from those for external use throughout the supply chain, but particularly in treatment areas. Products for external use are often poisons. If kept with medicines for oral use, they may be accidentally swallowed, which could be fatal. To avoid risk, observe the following labeling conventions—

- External-use products should be properly labeled according to the country's pharmaceutical control legislation. Warning labels in red are recommended.
- All internal-use medicines should be labeled according to national or local requirements.

Cleaning

A clean, tidy store is easier to manage than one that is dirty, untidy, and filled with waste. A cleaning schedule with clear designation of staff responsibilities should be established.

Fire prevention

Fire-prevention measures should include a strict no-smoking rule, careful disposal of combustible waste materials, and careful handling of flammables. Firefighting equipment should be regularly checked and maintained, and staff members should be trained with regular fire drills.

Security

Access to storage areas should be restricted for security reasons. All staff members who handle supplies should be accountable for their actions. One or two responsible and trustworthy people should be accountable for the keys, and one set should be available on the premises at all times. The person in charge of the health facility is ultimately held responsible.

All storeroom windows should have burglar bars, and doors must be fitted with security locks. Work areas such as the pharmacy or dispensary should have double locks (see Chapter 43).

46.3 Inventory control within health facilities

Every facility needs an inventory management system—and written procedures—to deal with ordering supplies, receiving and storing stocks, and recording and accounting for stocks.

In larger facilities, inventory management requirements are greater. At large hospitals, pharmacists or other specialized staff members usually manage supplies. Separate facilities may exist for the various activities and types of stock. At

smaller facilities, such as health centers, activities tend to be integrated, and a single person may have multiple responsibilities. Even in a small facility, however, stocks of food and linen should be separated from medical supplies to maintain hygiene standards and to allow nonprofessional staff easy access to the food and linen.

Keeping records and ordering stock

Chapter 23 outlines the principles of inventory management, which are equally relevant for small health facilities and large stores. Their application may be different, but the underlying methods are the same.

Keeping records. The most important record is the stock card or ledger. The examples in Chapter 44 (see Annexes 44-1 and 44-2) contain most of the features that are likely to be required, but many variations are possible. At a minimum, space should exist for a description of the item and its stock number, the unit of issue (for example, 500-tablet jar, tablet, or mL), and expiry date, if applicable. Columns and rows to document receipt and issue of stock should appear below this standard information. In addition to the stock card kept next to the items on the shelf, a stock book may be used that maintains a duplicate record of each transaction. Some larger facilities may use a computerized record-keeping system for inventory management.

Ordering stock. Most health facilities use a requisitioning system to order supplies. Staff must assess the rate at which individual items are used and have a clear understanding of the safety stock concept. Various methods of calculating order quantity exist, but all are based on monthly consumption. Monthly consumption can be determined from the stock card or from the monthly stock check.

Various ways of calculating safety stocks and order quantities are described in Chapter 20. One simple system of ordering for health facility use is the imprest, or "topping up," system to the maximum stock level. This system is particularly suitable for hospital wards and small health facilities that receive supplies frequently. In the imprest system, no running stock records are kept. The only stock control document is a preprinted sheet that describes each item and gives its stock number, unit of issue, and imprest level—the recommended maximum stock level for that item. The amount ordered is the difference between the stock on hand and the imprest level.

Another effective system is ordering based on consumption versus maximum stock levels, typified by the approach used in the Eastern Cape Province in South Africa (see Box 46-1).

Box 46-1
Calculating how much stock to order using the maximum stock approach

The maximum stock approach consists of replenishing stock to an optimal maximum stock level every time an order comes in. Determining the maximum stock factor can simplify the calculation. The maximum stock factor varies with the frequency of orders and the lead time, according to the following table. The lead time and the order frequency are known from experience (or from an order schedule).

Maximum stock factor table

Order frequency	Lead time			
	1 Week	2 Weeks	4 Weeks	6 Weeks
Once a week	0.05	1		
Every 2 weeks	1	1	2	
Once a month	1.5	2	3	4
Every 6 weeks	2	3	4	5
Every 2 months	3	4	5	6
Every 3 months	4	5	6	7

To identify the maximum stock factor, one should draw two imaginary lines: one horizontal line on the corresponding order frequency row and one vertical line on the lead-time column. The meeting point of those two lines indicates the maximum stock factor. For example, if supplies are ordered once a month and the lead time from the source is equal to four weeks (or one month), then the maximum stock factor is equal to three.

After the maximum stock factor is identified, the next step is calculating the maximum stock using the following formula—

$$\text{Maximum stock (in issue units)} =$$
$$\text{average monthly consumption} \times \text{maximum stock factor}$$

The next step is comparing this maximum stock to the current stock balance of usable stock (without any expired items)—

- If the current stock balance is greater than or equal to the maximum stock, no order needs to be placed.

- If the current stock balance is smaller than the maximum stock, then an order must be placed unless the product is discontinued or its use is influenced by some external factors, such as the end of a season, the end of a public health campaign, or modification of the essential medicines list.

After the reorder factor is identified, the next step is calculating the quantity to order using the following formula—

$$\text{Quantity to order (in issue units)} =$$
$$\text{maximum stock} - \text{stock on hand}$$

Note: If the result is too small (not enough needed to place an order), an order might be placed only on the next scheduled date. In some cases, if the demand for this product is related to a particular season and the season is over, the quantity to order is decreased or nothing is ordered.

These formulas should only be used as guidelines in estimating order quantities. A modification to any one of the components of the procurement cycle (time of delivery, expiration date, disease outbreak, new physician, and so on) will influence the entire system. The requisitioning officer's individual experience as well as the nature of each product are essential considerations in arriving at a final decision.

Example

Product A's average monthly consumption equals 45 units. This product is ordered every two weeks, and the lead time is equal to four weeks. The current stock is 60 units. If an order has to be placed, how much has to be ordered?

1. The maximum stock factor has to be calculated. In this case, it is equal to two. Therefore, the maximum stock is equal to 90. The current stock balance is 60, so an order has to be placed.

2. The quantity to order is calculated using the recommended formula—

$$\text{Quantity to order} =$$
$$90 \text{ (maximum stock)} - 60 \text{ (stock on hand)} = 30$$

Source: Eastern Cape Department of Health 2000.

After the order quantity is calculated, orders are sent to the issuing store on a requisition/issue voucher (see Annex 44-4). The facility and the issuing store should always keep copies of the requisition voucher or imprest forms. Those forms should be compared to the stock cards to monitor consumption and prevent overordering.

Receiving stock

A clear procedure for receiving stock should be in place. If goods are not checked into the store on arrival, chaos occurs. The person in charge should be responsible, whether or not he or she personally undertakes the task.

All deliveries should be formally received, whether they arrive inside or outside normal working hours. The number of packages delivered should be noted in a register and signed for by both the person receiving and the person delivering the goods.

Unpacking and checking stock

Supplies should be unpacked and checked next to the storage area, which may also be used for assembling stock for distribution. Two people should perform these activities, to provide a witness in case supplies are damaged or differ in type or quantity from what was ordered (or from what is shown on the packing list). Supplies should be individually checked using a checklist like the one in Chapter 44 and their receipt recorded on the supply documents (packing list or returned requisition form). The copy of the original requisition form should always be compared with documents from the issuing facility to prevent later disputes.

The issuing store should be notified of any discrepancies (using a form like the one in Figure 46-2), including—

- Missing boxes or cartons
- Open boxes or cartons
- Missing items
- Quantity different from the one shown on the packing list
- Wrong items (items not ordered)
- Damaged, broken, or poor-quality items

Staff members should see checking not simply as counting the units delivered but as part of the quality assurance system. This process includes visually inspecting the packaging, the integrity of containers, and the completeness and legibility of labels (approved medicine name, strength, any special storage instructions, expiry date). The expiry date should be checked to ensure that adequate shelf life remains (see Chapter 19).

Packaging is an important factor in maintaining the quality of medicines and other supplies when stability is a consideration. Good packaging protects the product from light and air. Packaging should be removed only after careful consideration of the effect on pharmaceutical quality.

Finally, the delivery documents should be signed and filed for reference; they should usually be kept for a minimum of two years (or the time specified in regulations).

46.4 Distributing stock from the storeroom

Medicines and supplies need to be moved from the facility store to the places where they are used, such as treatment areas, wards, or outpatient facilities. The procedures are similar, whatever the size of the facility.

Small health facilities

Small facilities may not have a separate pharmacy, but they should have a medicine storeroom or cupboard and a dispensing and treatment area. A working stock (often a single container) of common medications should be kept in the treatment area. Oral medication should be stored in a lockable trolley cart or cupboard. A small stock of common injectable medicines should be kept on a tray in the treatment room. A separate area usually exists for cleaning and dressing wounds, where an appropriate range of items should be kept on trolley carts and in lockable cupboards. These working stocks are replenished from the storeroom daily. Working-stock containers must be kept closed except when they are actually being used, to avoid deterioration and loss of therapeutic value.

Hospital pharmacy departments

The movement and control of stocks are more complex in larger facilities where medical, surgical, and maternity care are provided. Each type of ward should have its own stock list to facilitate control and misuse, and separate storerooms may be needed. The hospital pharmacy should be responsible for restocking all medicine storage areas and may also dispense to individual inpatients and outpatients. The volume of outpatient prescriptions may justify an outpatient dispensary separate from the main pharmacy.

As HIV/AIDS programs scale up, one option for hospitals that offer antiretroviral therapy is to refer established patients to local health facilities for their medications, which reduces the time and cost of travel for patients. Country Study 46-1 shows how a South African hospital has expanded its system to include other patients with chronic health conditions.

The hospital pharmacy may have working stock from which it dispenses medications to inpatients, and upon their discharge, to outpatients, and to wards, departments, and emergency trays. A "want list" should be compiled throughout the day, for daily replenishment from the storeroom.

Figure 46-2   Discrepancy report

Ministry of Health
Department of Medical Supply
DISCREPANCY REPORT

Health facility: Utano HC

1. Received by: Tinoda SRN
2. Witnessed by: Jayuguru SRN

Date: Mar 26, 2008
No. of cartons received: 3
No. of other containers received: 1

DETAILS OF SHIPMENT

3. Issue voucher no./s: 98570
4. Transporter: DMS Driver
5. Name of driver: Mugari
6. List of cartons rcvd.: 3 cartons

Vehicle reg. no.: 25TCE176
Transporter shipment note: MUG65
List of cartons not rcvd.: 1 container 5 Liter

DETAILS OF DISCREPANCIES

7. Breakages (if any):

Issue voucher no.	Item Description	Code No.	Unit	Quantity Broken
98570	Chloroquine syrup	03-2500	Bottle 500 mL	2

8. Items missing:

Issue voucher no.	Item Description	Code No.	Unit	Quantity Missing
98570	Chlorhexidine solution 2%	04-1650	5 Liter	1

9. Items issued in error:

Issue voucher no.	Item Description	Code No.	Unit	Quantity Tampered With

10. Any other discrepancies/comments:

PLEASE CREDIT BREAKAGES AND RESUPPLY ANY MISSING ITEMS

11. Signature: Tinoda (TINODA)
    Office held: SRN

Country Study 46-1
Improving treatment for chronic conditions with a computerized referral system in South Africa

Cecilia Makiwane Hospital is located in Mdantsane, Eastern Cape Province, one of the largest townships in South Africa. The hospital implemented the national *Comprehensive Plan for the Treatment and Care of HIV and AIDS* in October 2004, and a year later, more than 800 patients had been enrolled on antiretroviral therapy (ART). All patients collect their medication regularly at the hospital; after a patient has been stabilized and the patient demonstrates his or her ability to adhere to treatment, the doctor prescribes a repeat of the medication for five months. However, frequent trips to the hospital can be a burden. In some cases, patients may pay as much as 120 South African rands (19 U.S. dollars) for transportation to pick up their medication. This expense strains patients' already low income and can affect treatment adherence. Furthermore, these patients can overburden the hospital's pharmaceutical service, where staff also need to deal with new or complicated cases on a daily basis.

To maximize patients' access to ART, Management Sciences for Health's Rational Pharmaceutical Management Plus (RPM Plus) Program looked at innovative approaches for dispensing repeat prescriptions to established patients. The result is a fully integrated computerized program, RxSolution, designed to support pharmaceutical care activities at the facility level. RxSolution includes a referral module that optimizes dispensing of chronic medicines by shifting ART care to primary health care facilities in the local communities.

In collaboration with the provincial pharmacy team, RPM Plus staff visited all community referral clinics to ensure that the conditions and facilities required to deliver high-quality and safe medications were in place.

As one of the clinic nurses said, "We also had to ensure that not a single client misses a single dose as that would affect treatment outcomes."

After receiving training on the computer system, the pharmacy staff of the Cecilia Makiwane Hospital record patient details in the RxSolution database. As stable ART patients are recruited into the program, they are given appointment cards with the date of their next visit and told at which referral clinic to collect their medication. Using RxSolution, hospital staff members group all prescriptions by referral clinic and create a prescription pick list, a set of medication and address labels, and a patient accountability checklist. Prescriptions are checked, packaged in cartons, sealed, grouped according to the referral clinics, and dispatched by courier.

At the referral clinic, the nurse signs the distribution list, which is returned to the hospital. During scheduled patient visits, the nurse reviews progress and gives medications to the patient, with both the nurse and the patient signing that this interaction has taken place. The list is then returned to the hospital along with any uncollected medication. The hospital staff uses this information to monitor the patient adherence at each referral clinic. During the last visit at the referral clinic, the patient is reminded of his or her next clinical assessment at the hospital.

Referring patients from hospitals to primary health care facilities has always been a challenge. Although the RxSolution system was developed to support patients on ART, it has successfully been extended to other chronic conditions, thereby strengthening the delivery of quality health care to all levels.

This responsibility should rest with a limited number of individuals on a rotational basis.

Prepacking for outpatient dispensing. To save time for both staff and patients in busy facilities with high prescription volumes, prepacking commonly dispensed oral medications in appropriate quantities for standard treatment courses is useful. This packing can be done at quiet times of the day or week. Prepacking is also necessary when quantities smaller than the original pack are needed for ward stocks (see Chapters 30 and 45). In some countries, purchasing commonly used medicines commercially prepacked in "unit-of-use" (course-of-therapy) containers may be cost-effective. Important considerations when repacking medicines are to—

- Use containers suited for maintaining pharmaceutical quality.
- Avoid contaminating or mixing different batches of medicines.
- Label containers appropriately and assign a new "use-by" date.

Supplying inpatients. As discussed in Chapter 45, three basic techniques exist for hospital pharmaceutical distribution to inpatients: bulk ward stock, individual medicine orders, and unit-dose distribution. The bulk ward stock system is still used in many countries. The imprest or topping-up system is a common method for supplying wards with bulk stock. Empty containers are returned for refilling (the "full-for-empty" method) at weekly or twice-weekly intervals. Each ward should have a box that can be locked by both pharmacy and ward staff. Stricter security procedures should be applied for antibiotics, "attractive items," and narcotic drugs.

In a ward stock system, the pharmacy should provide a schedule indicating on which day each ward or department is to be supplied and specifying the category of supplies. Pharmacy, stores, and ward staff must decide together about the types and quantities of medicines required, and pharmacy staff members must monitor ward stock storage and record keeping.

Emergency trays. A selection of medicines and equipment for emergencies should be placed in wards and outpatient departments. The contents should be recorded on a list and checked regularly. Whenever an item is used, it should be restocked immediately. The emergency tray should not be used for routine supplies. Box 46-2 is an example of an emergency tray at a health post in Timor-Leste.

Supplying community-based health workers. Community health workers usually have a very limited selection of items. The topping-up system can be used to replenish stocks as long as requirements are small and the health center is reliably stocked. A monthly supply interval is usually adequate.

Home-based care kits. The family is usually the source of long-term care for chronic conditions such as HIV/AIDS and tuberculosis. Home-based care kits can be supplied to community health workers to distribute to caregivers. Kits should be designed according to the individual condition, but at a minimum should contain appropriate essential medicines, such as painkillers and antidiarrheals, as well as supplies such as gloves, soap, and disinfectant. Basic care information written in local languages and using diagrams and drawings should be included. The kit contents should be restocked from the supplies at dispensaries and health centers.

46.5 Staff training

Staff members who handle supplies should be trained in the following subjects—

- Setting up a storeroom and good storage practices
- Use of stock control forms, including requisitions, stock records, and prescriptions
- Cold-chain procedures, including the use and maintenance of refrigerators
- Security and theft control

Chapter 52 discusses the design and management of appropriate training programs for supply system staff and resources for available courses. ■

Box 46-2
Medicines for an emergency tray at a health post

Ampicillin powder for injection, 1 g (as sodium salt) in vial

Atropine injection, 1 mg (sulfate) in 1 mL ampoule

Calcium gluconate injection, 100 mg/mL in 10 mL ampoule

Charcoal, activated powder for oral suspension, bottle, 50 g

Chloramphenicol powder for injection, 1 g (sodium succinate) in vial

Diazepam injection, 5 mg/mL in 2 mL ampoule (intravenous or rectal)

Epinephrine/adrenaline injection, 1 mg (as hydrochloride or hydrogen tartrate) in 1 mL ampoule

Ergometrine injection, 200 μg (hydrogen maleate) in 1 mL ampoule

Gentamicin injection, 40 mg (as sulfate)/mL in 2 mL vial

Glucose injectable solution, 5% in 1 L bag

Glucose injectable solution, 50% hypertonic

Hydrocortisone powder for injection, 100 mg (as sodium succinate) in vial

Phytomenadione (vitamin K1) injection, 10 mg/mL in 1 mL ampoule (adult)

Promethazine injection, 25 mg (as hydrochloride)/mL in 2 mL ampoule

Magnesium sulfate injection, 500 mg/mL in 10 mL ampoule for use in eclampsia and severe preeclampsia and not for other convulsant disorders; available for trained midwives

Magnesium sulfate powder

Nifedipine scored tablet, 10 mg

Quinine injection, 300 mg (as dihydrochloride)/mL in 2 mL ampoule

Salbutamol injection, 50 μg (as sulfate)/mL in 5 mL ampoule

Sodium lactate, compound solution injectable solution, 1 L bag

Source: Timor-Leste Ministry of Health 2004.

ASSESSMENT GUIDE

See Chapter 23 for indicators of stock control performance. Also, see Annex 46-1 for a supervisory checklist to assess pharmaceutical management activities at the facility level.

Inventory control system

- Is there a standard inventory control system at health facilities?
- Are stock cards or stock books used for every movement of stock in or out of the facility storeroom?
- Are pharmaceuticals reordered according to a consumption-based system?
- Is the minimum or safety stock level set according to the frequency of delivery and average consumption?
- Are used stock cards, ledgers, or regulation books kept for a defined period?
- Do stock records correspond with physical stock for a sample of commonly used medicines?

Staff training in inventory management

- Have the staff responsible for ordering, storing, or distributing pharmaceuticals been formally trained in inventory management?
- Are procedures manuals for inventory management available in the health facility?

Stock storage facilities

- Have the stock storerooms been sized according to any formula?
- Will public health program expansion create a need for more storage space?
- Is there a receiving area? Is there an unpacking area?
- Is there a discrepancy report form? Over the past year, has it been used?
- Is the storeroom dry, clean, well ventilated, and between +15 and +25°C?
- Is there a refrigerator? Is its temperature regularly recorded?

Storeroom management

- When medicines or supplies are unpacked, are they stored according to FEFO or FIFO order?
- Over the past year, have expired medicines been used?
- Are there expired drugs in stock now?
- Are liquids for internal use kept separate from liquids for external use?

References and further readings

★ = Key readings.

AHRTAG (Appropriate Health Resources and Technologies Action Group). 1994. *How to Manage a Health Centre Store.* 2nd ed. London: AHRTAG.

John Snow, Inc./DELIVER in collaboration with the World Health Organization. 2003. *Guidelines for the Storage of Essential Medicines and Other Health Commodities.* Arlington, Va.: John Snow, Inc./DELIVER. <http://apps.who.int/medicinedocs/en/d/Js4885e/1.html>

Eastern Cape [Province] Department of Health. 2000. *Managing Drug Supply for Health Institutions.* Pretoria, South Africa: Management Sciences for Health/The Equity Project.

Timor-Leste Ministry of Health. 2004. Essential Medicines List for East Timor: Complete List. 2nd issue. Ministerio da Saude, Republica Democratica de Timor-Leste. <http://www.searo.who.int/LinkFiles/Essential_Drugs_and_Medicines_TLS.pdf>

WHO (World Health Organization). 2009. Stability Testing of Active Pharmaceutical Ingredients and Finished Pharmaceutical Products. Annex 2 to the *Forty-third Report of the WHO Expert Committee on Specifications for Pharmaceutical Preparations.* Geneva: WHO. <http://www.who.int/medicines/publications/pharmprep/pdf_trs953.pdf#page=101>

———. 2005. *Manual on the Management, Maintenance and Use of Blood Cold Chain Equipment.* Geneva: WHO. <http://whqlibdoc.who.int/hq/2005/9241546735.pdf.>

———. 2004. Stability Testing for Hot and Humid Climates. *WHO Drug Information* 18(2):113–6. <http://whqlibdoc.who.int/druginfo/18_2_2004.pdf>

———. 1999. *Guidelines for Safe Disposal of Unwanted Pharmaceuticals in and after Emergencies.* Geneva: WHO. <http://whqlibdoc.who.int/hq/1999/WHO_EDM_PAR_99.2.pdf>

WHO/AFRO (World Health Organization/Regional Office for Africa). 2004. *Management of Drugs at Health Centre Level: Training Manual.* Brazzaville: WHO/AFRO. <http://apps.who.int/medicinedocs/en/d/Js7919e/>

WHO/QSM (World Health Organization/Quality Assurance and Safety of Medicines). 2003. Guide to Good Storage Practices for Pharmaceuticals. Annex 9 to the *Thirty-seventh Report of the WHO Expert Committee on Specifications for Pharmaceutical Preparations.* Geneva: WHO/QSM. <http://whqlibdoc.who.int/trs/WHO_TRS_908.pdf>

Annex 46-1   Supervisory checklist to assess pharmaceutical management activities at the facility level

CLINIC: _____   DATE: _____

Infrastructure conditions: How does your store match up to the ideal store?   [✓] **Check if statement is TRUE**

- The store is separate from the dispensary.
- Medicines are dispensed only from the dispensing area.
- The store is large enough to keep all supplies.
- The store is kept locked at all times when not in use.
- The store has no cracks, holes, or sign of water damage.
- The store has a ceiling that is in good condition.
- Air moves freely in the store; fans and screens are in good condition.
- The windows are painted in white (or have curtains) and are secured with grilles.
- There are no signs of pest infestations in the store (e.g., cockroaches, rats).
- The store is tidy; shelves are dusted, the floor is swept, and walls are clean.
- Supplies are stored neatly on shelves or in boxes.
- Shelves and boxes are raised off the floor, on pallets or on boards and bricks.
- No supplies are in direct contact with the floor.

Storage procedures: How well is your store organized?

- Supplies are systematically classified on the shelves (i.e., by dosage forms or therapeutic class).
- Supplies are arranged on the shelves in alphabetical order by generic name within each category.
- Tablets and other dry medicines (e.g., ORS) are stored in airtight containers.
- Liquids, ointments, and injectables are stored on the middle shelves.
- Supplies, such as surgical items, condoms, and bandages, are stored on the bottom shelves.
- Items are grouped in amounts that are easy to count.
- No expired medicines are in the store.
- Medicines with shorter expiry dates are placed in front of those with later expiry dates (FEFO).
- Supplies with no expiry or manufacture date are stored in the order received (FIFO).
- Supplies with a manufacture date only are stored in chronological order.
- No damaged containers or packages are on the shelves.
- No overstocked or obsolete items are on the shelves.
- The disposal of medicines is recorded in a separate register and includes the date, time, witness, value, quantities, and reason(s).
- Narcotics and psychotropic drugs are in a separate, double-locked storage space.
- Items are checked regularly for potential deterioration (i.e., bad odor or discolored tablets).
- Temperature-sensitive items are stored in a refrigerator.
- The refrigerator is in working condition.
- No staff food is in the refrigerator.
- A temperature record is available and up-to-date.

Stock card: How are the stock cards used in your facility?

• Does each item in the store have a stock card?	Y	N
• Is the stock card kept on the same shelf as the item?	Y	N
• Is all information on the stock card up-to-date?	Y	N
• Is information recorded on the stock card at the time of movement?	Y	N
• Is an accurate running tally kept in the **balance** column?	Y	N
• Does the physical count match the balance column? (Check 10 items.)	Y	N
• Is a physical count made at regular intervals, such as once a month?	Y	N

CLINIC: _____   DATE: _____

Ordering supplies: If delivery schedule changes

• How often do you place an order?		
• What is your average lead time?		
• What is your facility's reorder factor?		
• Do you know how to calculate the Average Monthly Consumption (AMC)? Ask/check formula.	Y	N
• Do you take into consideration stockout period when calculating the AMC?	Y	N
• Do you calculate the Maximum Stock by multiplying the AMC by the Maximum Stock Factor?	Y	N
• Has the Maximum Stock been calculated for each item in the store?	Y	N
• Is the Maximum Stock recorded on each item's stock card (in pencil)?	Y	N
• When was the last time that the Maximum Stock was reviewed?		
• When you order, do you use the Quantity to Order formula? Ask/check formula.	Y	N
• Is a standard order form used at all times?	Y	N
• Is the order costed?	Y	N
• Is the requisition book kept at the facility?	Y	N
• Is all information on the requisition form accurate and clearly written?	Y	N

Receiving supplies: How are supplies received at your store?

• Are deliveries received by a health worker in person?	Y	N
• Are deliveries inspected by a health worker before acceptance?	Y	N
• Are supplies received checked against the items listed on the packing slip/delivery form?	Y	N
• Are deliveries acknowledged and recorded on the prescribed forms?	Y	N
• Does the delivery person sign the form before he leaves the facility?	Y	N
• Have you ever sent back items to the supplier? If so, ask for the reason.		
• Are the expiry dates of all items checked before final acceptance?	Y	N
• Does the health worker check for poor-quality items, such as		
- poorly packaged refrigerated items?	Y	N
- discoloration of medicines, vaccines, and suspicious product settlement?	Y	N
- broken containers and supplies spoiled by leakage?	Y	N
- unsealed and unlabeled items?	Y	N
• As soon as the supplies are checked, are all receipts recorded on the stock cards?	Y	N
• If poor-quality products are suspected, does the health worker check for		
- unusual odors of tablets and capsules?	Y	N
- damaged containers?	Y	N
- injectables with small particles that reflect light?	Y	N
- suspension with broken glass?	Y	N
• Do you accept expired or short date or poor-quality items?	Y	N
• Are all discrepancies documented?	Y	N

| Part I: Policy and economic issues | Part II: Pharmaceutical management | Part III: Management support systems |

Planning and administration
Organization and management
  43 Security management
  44 Medical stores management
  45 Hospital pharmacy management
  46 Pharmaceutical management for health facilities
  47 Laboratory services and medical supplies
Information management
Human resources management

CHAPTER 47

Laboratory services and medical supplies

SUMMARY

The management of medical and laboratory supplies and equipment shares many similarities with the management of pharmaceuticals and is just as important in providing effective health services. Although the value of supplies and equipment may equal a substantial proportion of what governments spend on pharmaceuticals, such items are rarely given enough attention. Each country's ministry of health is responsible for ensuring that commodity management standards are set and followed by instituting quality assurance mechanisms and monitoring evaluation and reporting systems.

Problems associated with supplies and equipment include lack of policies, absence of dedicated government budgets, and lack of standardization. Countries should develop a national list of medical and laboratory supplies and equipment, based on expected types of tests, treatments, and interventions to be delivered at different levels of health care. Such a national list is useful to—

- Define priority items and help ensure that the most essential items are available where needed
- Promote cost-effective use of scarce financial resources
- Reduce the number of items through standardization
- Serve as the basis for training staff and technicians

The four main criteria in selecting equipment are (1) local possibilities for servicing and spare parts; (2) local availability of essential supplies (such as chemicals and filters); (3) a well-established brand name and a simple and sturdy design; and (4) local possibilities for training staff in equipment use and maintenance.

Finding good data on the consumption and cost of medical supplies is a challenge, especially on individual items. The number of different items and brands is much larger than the average number of essential medicines, and the specifications are much less standardized. Another problem comes from the records used to compile data: Are different sizes of X-ray films or all sizes of syringes regarded as one item? In some countries, medicines and other medical supplies and laboratory supplies come under different management structures or different budgets, which makes intercountry comparisons difficult.

Before procuring medical and laboratory supplies and equipment, specifications should be defined in close collaboration with technical staff. These specifications are needed for the procurement department and for claims in case of faulty products.

Donations of commodities and equipment to laboratories and health facilities must be handled carefully, including the assurance that donations are based on need expressed by the recipient country. When donors provide medical and laboratory supplies and equipment, problems related to the lack of standardization and to maintenance may arise.

47.1 Introduction

Clinical laboratory services are a critical, yet often neglected component of essential health systems in resource-limited countries. Laboratories play a central role in public health, in disease control and surveillance, and in individual patient diagnosis and care, yet many millions of people still do not have access to reliable, basic, diagnostic laboratory services (Petti et al. 2006).

Effective laboratory leadership and management are often lacking—many countries still do not have a national laboratory policy, a strategic plan, or a dedicated budget for laboratories. Fundamental weaknesses in the overall management of laboratory services, together with a lack of human and financial resources and poor infrastructure, prevent the efficient operation and delivery of accessible, quality-assured laboratory services to support national public health programs, including malaria and tuberculosis (TB) control and treatment and the delivery of antiretroviral therapy (ART). A greater realization of the laboratory's role combined with advocacy from global health initiatives such as the U.S. President's Emergency Plan for AIDS Relief to build capacity for laboratory systems has resulted in encouraging signs that suggest a gradual increase in focus. Country Study 47-1 describes a successful program to build leadership in laboratories in Uganda.

If laboratory services are to support health care effectively, they need to provide reliable, valid, and timely results. Functioning, good-quality equipment and uninterrupted supplies of test kits, reagents, and other consumables are mandatory. Yet many countries have given little attention to the particular needs of laboratories and what is required to create an effective commodity management system. Governments and donors responsible for procuring and managing laboratory equipment and other commodities often lack updated standard international guidance. Consequently, stockouts occur when large quantities of materials that are inadequate, inappropriate, or of poor quality are procured, and resources are wasted.

Like laboratory services and commodities, medical supplies and equipment are rarely given enough attention. Recognizing the important role of this category of products, the World Health Assembly adopted a resolution in 2007 that covers the need to establish priorities in the selection and management of health technologies, specifically medical devices. The World Health Organization (WHO) defines a *medical device* as "an article, instrument, apparatus or machine that is used in the prevention, diagnosis or treatment of illness or disease, or for detecting, measuring, restoring, correcting or modifying the structure or function of the body for some health purpose" (WHO/EHT 2011b, 4). The term *equipment* refers to a medical device that requires calibration, maintenance, repair, user training, and decommissioning. According to

WHO's definition, medical equipment excludes implantable, disposable, or single-use medical devices (WHO/EHT 2011b). Items that have traditionally been categorized as "supplies," including bandages and gloves, are considered devices under WHO's taxonomy. This chapter and the rest of the book recognize the new definition of *device* but continue to refer to such nonpharmaceutical items as supplies and commodities to reflect common understanding and usage.

As a result of the 2007 World Health Assembly resolution, WHO launched the Global Initiative on Health Technologies to make core health technologies available at an affordable price, particularly to resource-limited communities. Through the initiative, WHO and its partners have developed a series of reference documents for countries,

---

Country Study 47-1
Strengthening laboratories to expedite the countrywide scale-up of the ART program in Uganda

With funding from the U.S. President's Emergency Plan for AIDS Relief, Management Sciences for Health (MSH) partnered with the Joint Clinical Research Centre (JCRC) and the Ugandan Ministry of Health (MOH) to design and implement the Laboratory Performance Improvement Program for laboratory management teams from selected MOH regional referral hospitals that support the national ART rollout program. Traditionally, laboratory support has focused on providing equipment and supplies and training staff in test methods but has ignored underlying management issues. Before this program, many regional hospital laboratories in Uganda were unable to provide quality-assured basic services to manage treatment of those infected with HIV/AIDS and TB.

MSH helped bring together multidisciplinary laboratory management teams, comprising the medical superintendent, the hospital administrator, a doctor, a nurse, laboratory staff, and local staff from the JCRC-TREAT Program (Uganda's national ART program). As part of the program process, each team took responsibility for improving laboratory performance at its own hospital by managing the resources and developing effective work processes to produce quality laboratory test results. During the program, the teams received support from a central JCRC-TREAT-MOH team of experts, including the principal technologist at the central public health laboratory.

Through a series of five workshops spread over one year, the teams learned leadership and management skills and how to work together more effectively. They learned how to apply the performance improvement process to narrow the gap between the specific results they wanted to

achieve and their actual results, created a vision of how well their laboratory could operate in the future, and then committed themselves to realizing this vision by developing and implementing an action plan. Critical to their progress were the activities that each team implemented between workshops to use existing resources to improve laboratory performance. These efforts led to the first hospital monthly budget allocation for laboratory supplies, additional space for key laboratory functions, improved laboratory staff morale, and increased productivity resulting in more essential tests being performed in a timely manner. Early in the program, MSH worked with the teams to develop a laboratory performance monitoring tool that was appropriate for their local needs. Teams used the tool at the beginning of the program and again at the end of the program to review their progress and pinpoint remaining challenges.

At the end of the program, the executive director of JCRC stressed what the Laboratory Performance Improvement Program had demonstrated—

> The laboratories are critical for the quality and safety of the TREAT Program . . . There is such a huge need because the [Laboratory Performance Improvement] Program started almost from scratch as far as up-country laboratories were concerned. Only a tiny group of leaders and professionals were involved, and they almost unanimously expressed great appreciation for the importance of laboratory training, especially in management. It has exposed a big gap.

Source: MSH n.d.

covering areas such as policy, regulations, management, and innovation. The document series and other information can be found at WHO's website on medical devices: http://www. who.int/medical_devices/en.

With the increased emphasis on the importance of effective laboratory services to a country's public health, this chapter focuses particularly on issues related to laboratories. It provides guidance for procuring and managing equipment and other supplies that health facilities and laboratories use.

47.2 Using national policies to guide equipment and supply management

Sound national policies on laboratories and medical equipment with lists of related essential supplies can simplify supply issues, reduce costs, and promote efficient provision of health care and rehabilitation; however, only 33 percent of low-income countries in a 2010 survey had national policies covering health technologies (WHO/ EHT 2011b). Policies should specify which medical equipment and supplies should be used in which types of medical tests, interventions, and operations. Because different medical procedures are carried out at different levels of health care, and different tests are performed at different levels of laboratory service, the policies define the sets of supplies and equipment that will be needed at each of these levels.

National laboratory policy, strategic plan, and budget

A national laboratory policy provides a framework for ensuring that health laboratory services adequately support the efficient delivery of a country's health care package. National laboratory policies usually support regional and global health goals and priorities; for example, the 2008 Maputo Declaration on Strengthening of Laboratory Systems in Africa recognizes the challenges and limitations of scaling up services for TB, malaria, and HIV/AIDS and calls on national governments, donors, and partners to integrate support to improve laboratory systems (WHO/ AFRO 2008b). In addition, achieving the three millennium development goals of reducing child mortality; improving maternal health; and fighting HIV/AIDS, malaria, and other diseases requires efficient national laboratory systems.

Implementation of a national laboratory policy requires a strategic plan that provides clear guidance on the actions needed to improve laboratory systems as well as insight into implementation and budget implications for translating policy into practice. The plan and budget guide the mobilization of needed resources and help the government and stakeholders identify areas to target.

Aligning laboratory services with packages of health care

A national laboratory policy usually contains objectives to ensure the availability of appropriate functional equipment and adequate supplies of test kits, reagents, and consumables for laboratories at all levels. It may also outline strategies for ensuring an effective supply chain, national standardization of equipment and supplies, registration by the appropriate regulatory authority, equipment maintenance and servicing, management of donations, and safe disposal of obsolete equipment and expired supplies. However, neither the laboratory policy nor the strategic plan usually specifies the actual list of equipment and other laboratory commodities because these may change with technology development and innovation.

National policies and decisions on public health priorities and health care should indicate which essential laboratory tests and services each level of health care will provide and which resources the laboratory needs to deliver these services. This approach stems from the "basic package" health care concept that was developed to increase the efficient allocation and use of limited resources (World Bank 1993). A basic (or essential) package of health care includes limited and proven cost-effective interventions that focus on health conditions and service gaps that disproportionately affect the poor and address a country's major causes of morbidity and mortality. The elements of a country's basic package of care provide a foundation for determining which types of clinical and public health services, treatments, and medicines will be provided at each health care level and the rationale for referrals to the next level of care. This information is critical for compiling the essential list of laboratory tests and services required to implement the interventions, and it contributes to the management of each target disease or condition.

Developing a national list of essential laboratory supplies and equipment

Once the ministry of health has established a list of essential laboratory tests and services that each level of health care will provide, the next step is to nationally adopt the methods or technologies needed to provide each test and service, including the most appropriate types and makes of equipment. All of these steps need to be completed before compiling the lists of essential equipment and the test kits, reagents, and commodities needed to run the equipment or perform tests. Many central medical stores do not have a national laboratory supplies list, and staff members do not know which items or how much of a particular item is required to carry out essential laboratory tests. As a result, many products may not be stocked or even available in the country. Therefore, the develop-

---

Box 47-1
Steps for preparing a national list of essential laboratory equipment and supplies

- Review national health plans and policies on priorities for service provision and essential health care packages to identify target diseases and conditions.
- Review standard treatment and diagnostic protocols for each disease or condition for each health care level to identify where laboratory support is required.
- For each level of health care provision, make a list of all the priority disease areas and conditions in the health care package.
- Next to each disease area, list the essential tests required at that level of health care. (Note that some tests will appear against several conditions.)
- Use this information to summarize the list of laboratory tests and services to be provided at each level.
- Obtain a consensus on the technologies and test methods to be used at each level of health care.
- Identify and come to an agreement on the capital equipment items best suited to deliver these technologies and test methods.
- Write technical specifications for each item of capital equipment.

- Identify manufacturers or vendors to supply the capital equipment.
- Prepare a capital equipment list, specifying make, model number, and so on for the national catalog.
- Identify all proprietary consumables, test kits, and reagents required to operate and perform quality control for the equipment.
- Identify all nonproprietary consumables, test kits, reagents, and minor equipment items required to deliver essential laboratory tests and services.
- Compile a capital equipment list.
- Compile a list of laboratory consumables and supplies, disaggregating proprietary and nonproprietary items.
- Come to consensus with national medical stores on VEN/ABC classification for all laboratory items in the national stores catalog.
- Prepare guidelines for administrative and laboratory staff on how to use the catalog for ordering, including explanation of VEN/ABC classification.
- Print and distribute catalogs, or where feasible, maintain an online catalog.
- Update lists annually.

---

ment of a standardized list is essential for laboratories to function properly.

A national committee of experts should combine the lists for each level of care into one national list of essential laboratory supplies and equipment. Similar to the list of essential medicines, this list should form the basis for standardizing procurement and distribution of supplies and equipment, as well as for training. Box 47-1 summarizes the steps to prepare such a list.

The list of essential laboratory supplies and equipment should contain a complete and clear description of each item, including stock number, type, standard pack size, and the most recent unit price. With more laboratories improving availability and use of automated analyzers for hematology, clinical chemistry, and immunology, combining the complete list of all proprietary items needed to operate each analyzer is useful because the items need to be procured and supplied to each laboratory as a complete package. Nonproprietary items should be grouped either by laboratory specialty (for example, microbiology, hematology, blood transfusion, chemistry, and immunology) or by category (for example, chemicals, culture media, test kits, antibiotics, glassware, minor equipment, safety items, and disposables), and use the stock or catalog number to identify the category.

Standardization of equipment and devices

The absence of equipment policy guidelines and lack of standardization of supplies can lead to wasteful overstocking. In many supply organizations, the number of different items of equipment and other commodities can be greater than the number of essential medicines. Although equipment is not generally subject to expiration, many examples are available of accumulating stocks of outmoded analyzers, instruments, and spare parts that have been ordered but that are no longer required or are not compatible with newer types of equipment.

The world is still not harmonized in several important areas, such as electrical and measurement systems. There are at least four different types of electrical plugs; two voltage systems, with 110 or 220 volts and 50 or 60 cycles per second; three different weight and volume measurement systems; and instructions in dozens of languages. In addition, for equipment such as gauges on gas containers, different companies may use different internal standards. These variations create immense problems for countries that have not managed to standardize their equipment or that receive equipment from a number of different donors.

The obvious strategy for tackling this problem is to standardize equipment and devices as much as possible. When the standard types and brands have been chosen, a list of standard equipment with specifications should be prepared to serve as a guideline for the procurement department and for donations.

Countries without an equipment standardization policy will often have several brands of the same piece of equipment on hand, which creates difficulties in procuring spare parts, arranging for service contracts, or providing training for staff to use the equipment. For example, a survey of laboratories in Malawi identified ninety microscopes from sixteen different manufacturers, 63 percent of which had been procured by donors (Mundy, Kahenya, and Vrakking 2006). Although 50 percent of the microscopes in use were reported to be in good condition, none had ever received professional service or repair, and in fact, were ineffectual because of mechanical faults and fungal growth on the lenses, although unsupervised staff used them for malaria microscopy.

47.3 Laboratory and medical commodity management systems

Efficient laboratory and medical commodity management ensures that appropriate commodities of adequate quality are reliably available, so technicians can perform laboratory tests for individual patient care and health care staff can treat patients appropriately. Managing commodities in any setting (public or private sector) and at any level (local, regional, provincial, or national) requires appropriate—

- Selection
- Quantification
- Procurement
- Quality assurance
- Distribution
- Inventory management
- Disposal

The following section deals with the practical aspects of managing these components, which, although similar in many ways to how pharmaceuticals are managed, have distinct differences.

Selecting diagnostics and supplies

As indicated in Section 47.2, ensuring availability of essential commodities requires that health managers and policy makers seek input from users (health care providers and laboratory staff) and review current information on national health policies and plans and budgetary constraints. The

---

Box 47-2
Developing guidelines for diagnosing HIV

Standard guidelines or algorithms for HIV testing must be developed and periodically updated at the national level. HIV testing guidelines should address the range of service delivery models to be used and the settings in which they are to be deployed.

Diagnosing HIV infection involves two different types of tests—both based on detecting HIV antibodies in the blood: (a) screening or initial tests and (b) confirmatory or supplemental tests. Initial tests identify antibody-positive specimens, whereas supplemental tests confirm whether specimens found reactive with a particular screening test contain antibodies specific to HIV. A variety of simple, instrument-free initial tests are now available. The test kits contain testing devices and all other supplies needed to perform the test. Specimens and reagents are often added by means of a dropper to the test device. The results are read visually. Most of these tests can be performed in less than twenty minutes and are therefore called rapid assays. In general, these tests are most suitable for use in testing and counseling centers and laboratories that have limited facilities and process low numbers of specimens daily.

The Joint United Nations Programme on HIV/AIDS (UNAIDS) and WHO recommend three testing strategies to maximize accuracy while minimizing cost. The choice of the most effective strategy depends on the prevalence of HIV in the sample population; the sensitivity and specificity of the test; and the objectives for performing the test—surveillance, diagnosis, or blood screening purposes.

One of two testing algorithms is part of the strategy. In a *parallel* testing algorithm, blood samples are simultaneously tested using two assays. In the *serial* algorithm, all specimens are tested by a first test that is highly sensitive. If the result is negative, the specimen is considered a true negative. Positive specimens are retested with a second assay that has a high specificity. If the second assay is also positive, the sample is considered a true positive. In both algorithms, discordant samples are retested immediately using the same tests to rule out error. If they remain discordant, the client is advised to come back in two weeks for another test to rule out HIV infection.

Sources: CDC/UNAIDS/WHO 2009; Walkowiak and Gabra 2008; WHO 2010a; WHO/EHT and UNAIDS 2009.

selection process involves reviewing the health problems or conditions to be prevented, tested for, and treated at facilities in line with the country's basic health care package; developing a list of commodities by level of health care; choosing appropriate packaging or unit sizes; and basing the selection process on relevance, proven efficacy and safety, performance in a variety of settings, quality, cost-benefit ratio, previous experience, location of manufacturer, and capacity of laboratory or facility staff.

WHO is creating model lists of devices and equipment for different levels of health facilities, from health posts to specialized hospitals, (http://www.who.int/medical_devices/innovation/health_care_facility/en/index1.html).

Diagnostics. Standard guidelines for disease testing must be developed at the national level, and national and local guidelines should be developed or updated in accordance with international recommendations. The responsible coordinating body (for example, the national AIDS control committee in the case of HIV diagnosis) may need to work with the national essential medicines committee to update the existing national essential medicines list, formulary, or both to include the diagnostic needs for a public health program. Box 47-2 describes different strategies for approaching HIV testing.

Selecting a limited range and type of diagnostic commodity can lead to better availability, better staff knowledge (from buying reagents that staff are familiar with), more appropriate use, and lower costs. As with pharmaceutical selection (Chapter 16), sensible commodity and equipment selection is one of the most effective ways to save costs because it has both clinical and economic implications. The WHO Prequalification of Diagnostics Programme's recommendations should be followed to ensure that laboratories purchase affordable diagnostic commodities of assured quality that are appropriate for use in resource-limited settings (WHO/DLT 2011).

Ensuring safe and effective use of diagnostic services and commodities entails a range of interventions, including incorporating laboratory testing into diagnostic and treatment guidelines, developing and implementing standard operating procedures, and using job aids and other appropriate behavior-change interventions targeted at clinicians, diagnostic service providers, and care-seekers in the community.

Box 47-3 highlights the high cost of using an unapproved diagnostic test for TB.

Disposable and reusable items. The national policy on the use of disposable or reusable items may differ from one country to another. Table 47-1 lists important factors to consider in making a choice. If reusable products are chosen, buying products that can be autoclaved is essential. When buying disposable components for special equipment, ensuring that what is purchased will actually fit the equipment is important. Some equipment uses standard

Box 47-3
WHO urges a ban on inaccurate blood tests for tuberculosis

In 2011, in an unprecedented move, WHO issued an explicit "negative" policy recommendation against a widely used diagnostic practice and is urging countries to ban the use of commercial blood tests to diagnose active TB. These tests, which are manufactured in North America and Europe, have not been approved by any regulatory authorities yet are widely used in developing countries. Expert analysis shows that the tests produce either false-positive or false-negative results at least half the time, which obviously puts individual patients at great risk and negatively affects public health overall.

WHO estimates that more than a million of these inaccurate blood tests are carried out every year to diagnose active TB, especially in India and China. The tests are costly for patients, who can pay up to 30 U.S. dollars for them. "Blood tests for TB are often targeted at countries with weak regulatory mechanisms for diagnostics, where questionable marketing incentives can override the welfare of patients," said Dr. Karin Weyer, coordinator of TB diagnostics and laboratory strengthening for the WHO Stop TB Department. "It's a multimillion-dollar business centered on selling substandard tests with unreliable results."

Source: WHO 2011.

disposables; other equipment requires product-specific supplies.

In countries with limited funds for medical supplies, challenges with using disposable syringes and needles have been expensive and have caused stockouts. As a result, facilities sometimes sterilize disposable supplies and reuse them, which creates two problems: first, disposables are not meant to be sterilized, and the practice can result in air leakage and compromised performance; second, the method of sterilization is often inadequate. It is common to see a few "disposable" needles and syringes floating in a pan of water, with or without a lid, which may or may not have been boiling for some time. Boiling only disinfects; it does *not* sterilize. The same applies for soaking disposables in a disinfectant solution. Where stockouts are a problem, every health facility should probably keep a few reusable syringes and needles in reserve. This implies that a national policy for using only disposable or only reusable materials is not always practical.

The United Nations Children's Fund (UNICEF) and WHO tackled the problem of disposable reuse by creating "auto-disable" disposable syringes, which are made so

Table 47-1 Advantages and disadvantages of disposable and reusable items

Disposables	Reusables
Advantages	**Advantages**
• No sterilizer or running costs	• Cheaper to purchase
• No labor cost	• Need less storage space
• Safer; less risk of disease transmission (if not reused)	• Less waste
Disadvantages	**Disadvantages**
• Usually more expensive	• Need sterilizing equipment, running costs, and continuous supply of bags, autoclave control tape, and glove powder
• Bulky	• Time-consuming to sterilize
• Waste problem	• Less safe; risk of transmitting disease if not cleaned and sterilized properly
• Unsafe if reused (cannot be sterilized)	

they can be used only once. Although originally more expensive than ordinary disposables, auto-disable disposable syringes are now produced in such large numbers that the price difference has disappeared. The carton in which they are supplied serves as a safe disposal box, with an inner lining that can be burned easily. The plastic melts all needles and syringes into one block, which can be safely discarded. The WHO–UNICEF–United Nations Population Fund policy on injection safety states that all countries should use only auto-disable syringes for immunization (WHO 2006a).

Kits. Pharmaceutical and supply kits contain selected medicines and medical supplies in predefined quantities (Chapter 26). The quantity, range, and purpose of kits vary according to situation. Some comprise essential medicines and supplies targeting health care delivery at various levels. Others comprise special products to meet specific program needs or emergency situations. UNICEF offers a number of different supply and equipment kits, including surgical instruments and basic sterilization and resuscitation equipment. For example, the UNICEF obstetric surgery kit for health facilities to handle 100 deliveries includes instruments and equipment for fifty deliveries with complications and surgery and a midwifery kit that contains basic medicines, renewable medical supplies, medical equipment, and basic sterilization and resuscitation equipment. UNICEF considers its basic surgery set as the minimum investment for a health facility performing basic surgical activities such as simple appendectomies. Box 47-4 contains the list of medical supply items in the basic surgery set.

Diagnostic kits are also available; for example, the Global Drug Facility (GDF) supplies diagnostic TB test kits to facilitate and promote DOTS expansion in countries with a high TB burden. In many of these countries, much of the rural population has limited access to reliable microscopy services; therefore, the kits were designed specifically to meet the needs of lower-level laboratories at the periphery of the health system. Such laboratories often do not have reliable electricity or water supplies or the expertise, equipment, and materials required to prepare good-quality stains. Receiving

> **Box 47-4**
> **Contents of UNICEF's Basic Surgical Instruments Supply Kit**
>
> 4 Clamp, towel, Backhaus, 130 mm
> 2 Forceps, tissue, Allis, 150 mm
> 6 Forceps, artery, Halst-Mosq, 125 mm, cvd
> 1 Forceps, artery, Kocher, 140 mm, str
> 1 Forceps, dressing, standard, 155 mm, str
> 1 Forceps, tissue, Collin, 160 mm
> 1 Forceps, tissue, standard, 145 mm, str
> 1 Forceps, dressing, Cheron, 250 mm
> 1 Needle holder, Mayo-Hegar, 180 mm, str
> 1 Probe, double-ended, 145 mm
> 1 Retractor, Farabeuf, d-e, 120 mm, pair
> 1 Scalpel handle, no. 4
> 1 Scissors, Metzembaum, 140 mm, cvd, b/b
> 1 Scissors, Mayo, 140 mm, cvd, b/b
> 1 Bowl, stainless steel, 180 mL
> Source: UNICEF 2011.

all the supplies required for performing TB microscopy in one box facilitates easier ordering and distribution and ensures the availability of a complete set of standardized, high-quality commodities. Box 47-5 has more information about the GDF TB test kit.

WHO has starter kits for laboratories that want to introduce CD4+ or viral load testing technology that include equipment, reagents, controls, installation, training, and a maintenance contract. WHO also sells reagents and control kits to laboratories with existing CD4+ or viral load equipment.

Quantification

Both stockouts and expired items occur because of poor monitoring and quantification nationally and at the facility level. Regular monitoring of the consumption of supplies and equipment is necessary to plan for future requirements, allocate supplies, identify facilities that have higher-than-expected consumption of particular items, and avoid stockouts of other items.

Effective quantification helps—

- Avoid stockouts and ensure continuous availability of essential supplies
- Avoid waste caused by overstocking
- Make the best use of scarce resources and budget within the laboratory's means
- Facilitate central bulk purchasing
- Increase the effectiveness of an existing laboratory supply program budget

- Prepare and justify a budget
- Plan for new or expanding programs and policies
- Calculate emergency needs
- Resupply an existing supply network that has become depleted of supplies
- Estimate how much space, including refrigerated space, might be needed in the future

Three primary methods exist for quantifying how much to order—consumption, adjusted consumption, and morbidity (Chapter 20). The *consumption method* employs historical data on use that should be readily available in both the central medical store and individual laboratories. This method can be applied only to products that have been used in the past or to their direct replacements (for example, one test kit being replaced by an equivalent). In the *adjusted consumption method,* data from a laboratory service with a similar workload and numbers of patients is used as the basis of the quantification. The *morbidity method* is useful when reliable

---

Box 47-5
Global Drug Facility TB diagnostic kits

Although medicines are essential to TB prevention and cure, their proper use depends on the availability of reliable, quality-assured laboratory diagnosis of TB. Sputum-smear microscopy for TB diagnosis, an integral component of the DOTS strategy, is a relatively simple laboratory procedure but is often hampered by the lack of appropriate diagnostic equipment and sustainable supplies of high-quality laboratory consumables. Supplying kits to low-income countries, those undergoing health-sector reforms, or those in postconflict situations could facilitate procurement and control of laboratory supplies for TB microscopy. As a result of this initiative, the kits are now regularly available through the StopTB Partnership's GDF.

The GDF designed and field-tested four kits—

Consumables kit. Each kit contains 5 × 1 liters of methylene blue plus other consumables, such as slides, filter paper, immersion oil, and lens-cleaning tissue, sufficient to process and stain 1,000 sputum specimens.

Sputum collection containers. Each pack contains 1,000 screw-capped, leak-proof, disposable sputum collection containers. The kit is distinct from the laboratory consumables to permit independent ordering and direct distribution to health facilities for collection of sputum specimens. Specimens are then forwarded to the nearest microscopy center.

Equipment starter kit. The equipment starter kit is for setting up new microscopy sites or for equipping existing sites that do not have the basic requirements. Each kit contains minor equipment items (for example, slide storage boxes, a staining rack, forceps, spirit lamp, slide drying rack) required to process and stain sputum specimens for acid-fast bacilli. This kit plus the consumables kit provides a sufficient set of materials to set up a new microscopy center.

Microscope kit. Many countries have unreliable or intermittent power supplies. Therefore, the microscope kit contains one binocular microscope suitable for use both with a country's main electricity supply and with a mirror and external light source. Accessories in the kit include a 12-volt battery, a battery charger, a mirror unit, an external lamp for use with the battery and mirror unit, a surge protector, and spare bulbs. The battery can be charged either from the main electricity supply or from a solar panel.

The consumables kit is packed in two boxes compatible with the safety regulations for the different classes of chemical reagents. The other three kits are each packed in a single box, which facilitates easy handling, storage, and transport because the total volume of each kit is less than the collective volumes if all the items were purchased individually.

Source: Mundy, Kahenya, and Vrakking 2006.

laboratory data on workload and consumption are not available. A modification of the morbidity method can be used to calculate the quantity of laboratory supplies required for TB microscopy. This method helps national TB programs accurately forecast requirements for laboratory consumables based on simple TB case data that the program already collects.

Over time, use indicators can be developed along the lines of those that exist for medicines. An example of a use indicator would be the number of milliliters of stain needed for 100 TB sputum-smear tests or the number of rolls of cotton per month per 100 medical admissions. Such an indicator becomes a useful tool for comparing consumption among laboratories or facilities and for planning future requirements.

Procurement

Procurement of laboratory and medical supplies is not substantially different from procurement of pharmaceuticals (see Chapters 18–21). Good procurement practices depend on reliable and accurate quantification of needs, transparency in selection of suppliers and in management of bids or contracting, and quality assurance of commodities. For example, bidders should have sufficient knowledge of equipment maintenance, rather than being mere equipment traders. Equipment installation and maintenance training in addition to user training should be a condition of the sales contract.

Health managers often set priorities for the selection, procurement, distribution, and use of pharmaceuticals to analyze and control costs (see Chapter 40). A limited number of items are usually responsible for a large proportion of the budget, and these can be identified by ABC analysis. These "A" items should be procured through tender, and as with medicines, the tender should be restricted to prequalified suppliers to ensure quality. The same classifications used for pharmaceuticals can be adapted and applied to laboratory and medical supplies, not only to control costs, but also as a means to ensure that all vital items are supplied in a timely manner to minimize avoidable stockouts and service disruption. VEN categories (vital, essential, nonessential) are also useful for identifying those items that should never be allowed to run out of stock. Classifying items appropriately requires a detailed analysis. Uganda, for example, is developing the country's first lists of essential laboratory and medical supplies, which include level of health care categories and VEN classification to facilitate ordering and procurement (Table 47-2).

Table 47-3 gives examples of how cost analysis tools for pharmaceuticals can be adapted for laboratory consumables and reagents.

For several items, such as cotton and dressing materials, local procurement may be more attractive than importation.

For example, both of these items are easy to manufacture and bulky to transport. In addition, they take up enough storage space to make frequent deliveries cost-effective; local producers can provide such deliveries more easily and cheaply. However, capital equipment for laboratories is specialized and invariably has to be imported from an industrialized country—purchasing inexpensive local alternatives is *not* advisable. Service contracts should be arranged at the time of purchase and their cost included in the total procurement cost—an important point because many ministries of health do not have funds available to service equipment.

In addition to the few items that are needed in large quantities, other items are needed in small quantities only. Many of these have to be imported, but neither their cost nor their volume makes putting them through the tender process worthwhile. In those cases, buying these items through international nonprofit suppliers such as the IDA Foundation and UNICEF is usually much more cost-effective.

Requests will always come to procure items that are not on the national list of essential supplies and equipment. For these items or for new items that have not yet been included on the list, or for new items with an expected low turnover, the procurement manager should ask the following questions before placing an order—

- Is the item really necessary? Can and will it be used in the place for which it is being ordered?
- Is a feasible, local alternative available?
- Are spare parts or a way to maintain the item consistently available?

Quality assurance

The quality specifications of pharmaceuticals and laboratory reagents are usually available in pharmacopoeias or from WHO. Unfortunately, such standardization rarely exists for supplies and equipment, making the preparation of detailed specifications for each item important. Many medical supplies (for example, gloves, catheters, and sutures) come in various sizes and materials. One of the most difficult aspects of managing supplies is to ensure that the specifications for the items (size, material, pack size) are all correct.

A national quality assurance system should ensure that products meet international quality and safety standards and technical specifications. In addition to a catalog or list of essential items, a separate set of technical specifications for the items must be developed. Technically qualified personnel must prepare these specifications, which must be as accurate and precise as possible. Accurate specifications are essential for the procurement department or tender board to be able to ensure the quality of the items. Without them, issuing the tender, evaluating bids, and claiming any damages in case of faulty products are difficult. Box 47-6 gives an example of technical specifications for one item.

Table 47-2   Example from the Ugandan Ministry of Health's Essential Health Supplies List

Item code	Description	Specification	Unit	Level of care	VEN
S3	**Bandages and dressings**				
S3.1	Adhesive tape	2.5 cm × 5 m	1	HC2	N
S3.2	Bandage, cotton W.O.W. hydrophilic	75 mm × 4 m	1	HC3	N
S3.3	Bandage, P.O.P	100 mm × 2.75 m	1	H	E
S3.4	Bandage, P.O.P	150 mm × 2.75 m	1	H	E
S3.5	Bandage, triangular cotton	136 × 96 × 96 cm	1	HC3	N
S3.6	Bandage, crepe, stretched	100 mm × 4.5 m	1	HC2	E
S3.7	Gauze, absorbent, ribbon	25 mm × 12 m	1	HC4	E
S3.8	Gauze bandage	7.5 cm × 3.65–4 m	12	HC4	E
S3.9	Gauze bandage	10 cm × 3–4 m	12	HC4	N
S3.10	Gauze pads, nonsterile	10 × 10 cm	100	HC4	N
S3.11	Gauze pads, sterile	10 × 10 cm	45	HC4	N
S3.12	Gauze pads, sterile	10 × 10 cm	100	HC4	N
S3.13	Gauze pads, sterile	10 × 10 cm	1	HC4	N
S3.14	Gauze swabs, abdominal	30 × 50 cm, nonsterile	10	HC4	V
S3.15	Gauze, hydrophilic	90 cm × 50 m, X-ray detectable	1	HC4	E
S3.16	Gauze, paraffin	10 × 10 cm	36	HC4	E
S3.17	Gauze, paraffin, medicated	10 × 10 cm	10	HC4	E
S3.18	Gauze, W.O.W, hydrophilic	90 cm × 50 m	1	HC2	V
S3.19	Plaster, adhesive elastic	100 mm × 4.5 m	1	HC4	N
S3.20	Plaster, adhesive elastic	75 mm × 4.5 m	1	HC4	E
S3.21	Plaster, adhesive, zinc oxide	75 mm × 5 m	1	HC2	V
S3.22	Wool, cotton	500 g	1	HC2	V
S3.23	Wool, cotton	200 g	1	HC2	N

HC = health center; H = hospital; V = vital; E = essential; N = nonessential; P.O.P. = plaster of paris; W.O.W. = woven without edges.

Regulatory agencies in resource-constrained countries often lack the capacity to conduct dossier evaluation of diagnostics, and many countries recognize efficacy and safety evaluations by another drug regulatory authority as "proxy evaluations," particularly countries participating in the International Conference on Harmonization. To help resource-limited countries make decisions related to procuring diagnostic supplies, WHO evaluates the quality and operational characteristics of diagnostics for HIV/AIDS, malaria, and hepatitis B and C (WHO/DLT 2011). Manufacturers of acceptable assays are then eligible to tender for procurement through UN programs. This scheme makes quality-assured diagnostic-related reagents, consumables, and laboratory equipment, such as microscopes, available to purchasers in member countries at reasonable prices.

Countries are also using resources from the Global Fund to Fight AIDS, Tuberculosis and Malaria to purchase diagnostic and laboratory supplies and equipment to support the control of the three diseases (GFATM 2009). In addition, organizations can use AIDS Medicines and Diagnostics Services, which is based at WHO, as a source of information and assistance related to procurement and supply management for HIV-related medicines and diagnostics, including HIV antibody test, CD4 cell count, and HIV viral load count. WHO also maintains a list of prequalified health equipment (http://www.who.int/medical_devices/innovation/en).

Chapter 19 includes more information on quality assurance systems.

Distribution

Items are often supplied to laboratories and health facilities because they happen to be in stock rather than because they are actually needed. When stock is adequate, identical quantities of an item may be sent to all laboratories or facilities without considering their particular needs, workload, or past consumption. As a result, some laboratories experience stockouts and cannot provide testing services while others have excess stock, eventually resulting in expired

Table 47-3   Adapted codes for cost analysis of laboratory supplies

Category		Pharmaceuticals	Laboratory consumables, test kits, and reagents
Level-of-use code: Indicates the level of health institution at which the item would normally be permitted for use			
H	Health center level	Items for use through the health system at health center, district hospital, and central hospital levels. For all practical purposes, hospital outpatient departments will be regarded as H level.	Items for use through the health system at health center, district hospital, and referral (regional/central hospitals) levels.
D	District hospital level	Items for use at district hospital and referral hospital levels only.	Items for use at district hospital and referral (regional/central hospitals) levels only.
C	Central hospital level	Items for use at referral hospital level only.	Items for use at referral (regional/central hospitals) levels only.
Therapeutic priority code/diagnostic priority code: Identifies the therapeutic or diagnostic importance of each item using the VEN system			
V	Vital items	The items— • Are potentially *lifesaving*, • Have *significant withdrawal side effects*, making regular supply mandatory • Are of major public health importance (for example, needed by many patients for treatment of serious or contagious diseases, needed to control epidemics, and so on)	The items— • Are required to perform the tests listed in the essential test list to support the implementation of the basic health care package or ART monitoring • Are required to ensure that essential tests are performed in a quality manner (according to agreed standard operating procedures), making regular supply mandatory • Are required for tests used to diagnose, treat, or control diseases of major public health importance (as defined in the basic health care package and national health plan)
E	Essential items	The items— • Are effective against less severe, but nevertheless significant forms of illnesses	The items— • Are normally used to perform essential tests in the basic health care package or ART monitoring; however, absence of the item does not necessarily prevent the test from being performed
N	Nonessential items	The items— • Are used for minor or self-limiting illnesses • Are of questionable efficiency • Have a high cost for a marginal therapeutic advantage	The items— • Are used for additional tests not classified as essential for delivering the basic health care package or ART monitoring • Have a high cost for a marginal therapeutic advantage
Procurement system code: Specifies how items will be procured by national medical stores and by the user units			
A		The items— • Are generally required for large numbers of patients • Will routinely be procured and stocked by national medical stores • Include all H-level medicines Where funds for procurement are insufficient, first priority will be given to the procurement and supply of **V**(ital) **A**-list items. If funds remain after securing such **VA** items, procurement of **E**(ssential) **A**-list items will then be initiated. Thus, ensuring the availability of A-list items is primarily the responsibility of national medical stores.	The items— • Are generally required for large numbers of tests or patients • Will routinely be procured and stocked by national medical stores • Include all H- and D-level laboratory items Where funds for procurement are insufficient, first priority will be given to the procurement and supply of **V**(ital) **A**-list items. If funds remain after securing such **VA** items, procurement of **E**(ssential) **A**-list items will then be initiated. Thus, ensuring the availability of A-list items is primarily the responsibility of national medical stores.
B		The items— • Are generally required for limited numbers of patients • Will not be routinely procured and stocked by national medical stores • Require estimates of annual needs to be made well in advance by the hospitals and submitted as appropriate to national medical stores according to a preagreed time schedule • Require that payment be made in advance before procurement by national medical stores and subsequent supply to the hospitals Thus, procurement of B-list items is primarily the responsibility of the user units.	The items— • Are generally required for limited numbers of tests or patients • Will not be routinely procured and stocked by national medical stores • Require estimates of annual needs to be made well in advance by the hospitals and submitted as appropriate to national medical stores, according to a preagreed time schedule • Require that payment be made in advance before procurement by national medical stores and subsequent supply to the hospitals Thus, procurement of B-list items is primarily the responsibility of the user units.

items and waste. Stockouts of HIV test kits or other essential equipment such as syringes and needles to draw blood may require clients to return another day or go to another clinic. However, many clients who are turned away will not come back, and an opportunity for testing is lost. Country Study 47-2 shows how Zambia dramatically scaled up the distribution of HIV test kits in a few years.

Preprinted standard requisition lists of laboratory and medical supplies organized by service level are useful tools to simplify the distribution of supplies and promote the rational use of limited resources. Such lists indicate to the end user the range of items that are available within the system, with specifications, pack sizes, and stock numbers. The lists can also include current unit prices. In addition, such lists facilitate checking procedures for ensuring that facilities order and supply only approved items. The lists should specify the maximum amounts of all critical items to be kept in the health facility or laboratory. The amount ordered would then be the difference between the stock on hand and this maximum quantity. For facilities with four shipments per year, the maximum amount could reflect three months' use; for hospital wards or departments, a two-week supply is probably reasonable (see Chapter 23).

Putting together a requisition form that is clear to everybody remains a challenge: Should it list single units or packages (for example, one syringe or a box of 100, one bandage or a pack of twelve)? How should the list be organized—strictly alphabetically or by class? Should an alphabetical list

---

Box 47-6
Sample product specifications

Tricot tubular bandage

- *Elasticity:* Three or four times the original width. Good resistance to lading in both directions. Keeps elasticity after washing or stretching.
- *Components:* Knitted jersey tube, without seam.
- *Material:* 100 percent cotton, unbleached.
- *Size selected:*
- Bandage, tricot, tubular.
- Width: approx. 5 cm.
- Length: approx. 25 m.
- Disposable.
- Nonsterile.

Packaging and labeling:
- Primary packaging: Unit of use.
- One tricot bandage in a plastic bag.
- Labeling on the primary packaging:
- Name and/or trademark of the manufacturer.
- Manufacturer's product reference.
- Type of product and main characteristics. If the packaging is not transparent, it must bear a diagram (preferably actual size) showing the essential parts of the product and indicating the position of the product in the packaging.
- Lot number prefixed by the word "LOT" (or equivalent harmonized symbol) (if applicable).
- Expiry date by year and month, prefixed by the word "EXP" (or equivalent harmonized symbol) (if applicable).
- The words "for single use" (or equivalent harmonized symbol).
- The words "destroy after use" (if space allows).
- Number of units per primary packaging (if applicable).

- Information for particular storage conditions (temperature, pressure, light, humidity, etc.), as appropriate (or equivalent harmonized symbol).
- Manufacturer's instruction for use.
- Alternatively, the instruction for use can be indicated on a separate insert.

Secondary packaging: Protected unit.
- Ten tricot bandages in a plastic bag.
- Labeling on the secondary packaging:
- Labeling to be the same as primary packaging.
- Extra information required:
- Number of units per secondary packaging.

Weight/volume/dimensions:
- Estimated weight: 0.500 kg
- Estimated volume: 2 cdm

Instructions for use:
- Tubular bandage applied under plaster of Paris bandage to protect the skin.
- This dressing should fit the limb snugly but not tightly and without any fold.
- If needed, it can be used as a sterile item in surgery after steam sterilization.
- This size has been chosen as being the most commonly used.
- Provision for hospitals that constantly use this item (see plaster of paris).

Conditions for stock:
- Keep under dry conditions.

Source: UNICEF 2011.

Country Study 47-2
Scaling up HIV testing in Zambia

The objectives of the Zambia Voluntary Counseling and Testing Services (ZVCTS) are to coordinate the implementation of voluntary counseling and testing (VCT) services, train adequate numbers of VCT staff, review and harmonize HIV testing protocols, streamline information systems, improve tracking of specimens sent for testing, and continue research activities with the virology laboratory.

Zambia has scaled up its HIV testing and counseling services substantially since 1999; ZVCTS reports that the number of VCT sites had increased from 22 to 650 by the end of 2006. ZVCTS data show that the number of clients tested increased from 27,348 in 2002 to 337,760 in 2006—representing a twelvefold increase in the number of test kits that needed to be stored and distributed in just four years.

In 2000, six different rapid HIV test kits were used in Zambia because of the lack of harmonization across donors and facilities. Some donated test kits were either not included in the national HIV testing protocol or were inappropriate for the technical capacity and local situation. In 2001, after a literature review and consultation with kit users, stakeholders, and regional laboratory technicians, the country adopted a nationwide testing protocol. In the absence of reliable information, each newly established VCT site estimated how many new kits it needed; these numbers were consolidated and adjusted based on population, epidemiological data, and projected coverage.

ZVCTS and the Ministry of Health recognized early on that building capacity at the district level is essential to support scale-up of HIV testing and counseling services and to sustain programs in the long term. Strategies to transfer technology and skills to the district level and build local ownership began in 2002 and included estab-

lishing a pull system for ordering, developing tools as part of the commodity management information system, and training staff to quantify their commodity needs and prepare accurate reports. The information system is actually maintained at the district level; the district officer is responsible not only for aggregating data and generating and forwarding reports to ZVCTS, but also for providing feedback to facilities on a monthly basis. This monthly report compares each site's activities with other similar facilities and aims to motivate staff to maintain or improve their performance.

Facilities no longer need to collect their test kits and supplies from the Medical Stores Limited (the central medical store), because it delivers directly to the HIV counseling and testing sites. A long-established system is used for returning short-dated stock for redistribution. In 2005, mobile HIV testing and counseling units began offering services, and demand for services is reportedly high, with some sites reporting that mobile services are contributing more than 50 percent of the clients tested. Building the commodity management capacity of districts has been key to supporting the rollout of this new service delivery model, because mobile units get their commodities from and report consumption to the district level.

In 2006, stakeholders, including the National AIDS Council, the Zambia HIV/AIDS Prevention, Care and Treatment Partnership, and the Ministry of Health, developed and approved a new national HIV testing algorithm. The new standard test kit does not require refrigeration and is easier to use. The phased implementation of the new algorithm began in 2007 with support for managing the new commodities coming from new forms, standard operating procedures, and training.

Source: Walkowiak and Gabra 2008.

---

mention *Bandage, crepe,* or *Crepe bandage*? If the list is by class, should all plastics be listed together or classed as disposables, nondisposables, or something else?

The best solution for the central store and highest-level health facilities is a full list of items organized in groups and using the common pack size of items as the counting unit. For the lower levels of the health care system or for individual hospital wards, a short alphabetical list and standard order form can be used, with single items as the counting unit. Whatever the system, it needs to be logical, and the form should be tested with some end users.

Inventory management

Good management of storage and inventory involves monitoring expiration dates, inventory levels, unexplained losses (leakage), and storage conditions such as light, temperature, and sanitation, which are particularly critical for test kits and diagnostic reagents (Chapter 44). Computerized or manual records are required to control inventory effectively. These records include basic records such as stock or bin cards, monthly consumption records, inventory control forms, and a list of expired supplies (Chapter 23). The process should be supported by an information system for performance monitoring (Chapter 49).

The following conditions need to be considered when storing supplies, especially for the laboratory—

- Restricted access to the laboratory to authorized staff
- Cleanliness of benches and shelves
- Appropriate methods for disposal of waste
- Humidity
- Temperature requirements and monitoring
- Adequate refrigerated space maintained at optimal temperatures (+2 to +6°C)
- Adequate freezer space (at -20°C and -70°C)
- Emergency power supply
- Lighting (for example, store out of direct sunlight)
- Appropriate shelving and cupboards

Safe disposal

The safe disposal of laboratory waste and other contaminated materials is of prime importance.

Although most medical and laboratory waste is similar to domestic waste, 10 to 25 percent is infectious or hazardous. These items represent dangers to both laboratory and health facility staff and the community. In addition, the uncontrolled dumping of solid, liquid, chemical, and biological medical and laboratory waste threatens the environment.

Laboratory and medical waste includes—

- Sharps
- Chemical waste—expired reagents and consumables
- Human anatomical waste
- Blood and body fluids
- Solid waste such as cotton wool, tissue paper, culture plates with used media, used blood-giving sets, empty blood packs, used test tubes, and used glass slides
- Laboratory specimens
- Equipment effluent

Incineration is the most widely used technology to dispose of medical waste, but other methods are available and may be more appropriate depending on the context. WHO has published detailed guidelines on medical waste management (Prüss, Giroult, and Rushbrook 1999) and has a website with information on disposing of hazardous medical and laboratory waste (http://www.healthcarewaste.org/en/115_overview.html).

47.4 Equipment management

Countries should develop an equipment policy that includes a maintenance plan, a budget for equipment maintenance (that is, for repairs and spare parts), and guidance on equip-

ment donations. Laboratory or health facility managers must have technical oversight of equipment management and monitor related activities. They should assign responsibilities and ensure all staff members are trained on basic equipment management requirements.

Criteria for selecting equipment

Managers must select capital laboratory and other equipment based on the proposed use of the equipment, the equipment's fit with the service provided, its performance characteristics, facility and infrastructural requirements, cost, availability of reagents and consumables, ease of operation, and input from users such as health care providers and laboratory staff. In addition to input from users, equipment should be selected in consultation with maintenance staff.

WHO's Regional Office for Africa and partners published a document that provides equipment specifications that may be useful when selecting equipment (WHO/AFRO 2008a). In addition, WHO has published a list with fact sheets of core medical equipment (WHO/EHT 2011a).

Equipment acquisition

Equipment may be acquired through direct purchase, lease, or rental. Expertise is required for the purchase and maintenance of medical equipment. Consulting experts at an early stage of the procurement process may prevent problems later.

Procuring equipment centrally is often best. If many of the same items are required, then bulk procurement may be the most cost-effective and practical approach. Regardless of how the equipment is acquired, laboratories and health facilities must consider the responsibilities of the manufacturer or distributor and the conditions of the sales contract, customer support plan, and maintenance contract.

The manufacturer or distributor must guarantee—

- Provision of all reagents, consumables, and culture materials at an affordable and sustainable price (distributors usually offer reduced prices for high-consumption items, so bulk or central ordering may be an advantage)
- A reasonable expiration date on all reagents and consumables
- Acceptable shipment conditions and assistance with customs logistics to avoid damage to equipment or deterioration of the reagents
- Installation of the equipment, staff training, and ongoing technical support
- Provision of a parts manual and an operator's manual
- A trial period for the equipment, after which it can be returned if it is not deemed suitable

- Ongoing maintenance and repairs, including emergency services

The sales contract must be reviewed carefully before completing the purchase. The contract should clearly stipulate all of the preceding manufacturer or distributor responsibilities, and a customer support plan and maintenance contract should be available for all capital equipment. Maintenance contracts are essential for all automated equipment, such as hematology and chemistry analyzers, CD4 counters, automated blood culture and liquid TB culture systems, such as the Mycobacteria growth indicator tube and Cepheid GeneXpert® TB assay, and biosafety equipment, which should also include maintenance contracts for biological safety cabinets.

Before installation, confirm who is responsible for installation and verify that physical requirements have been met, including safety checks of electrical connections, space, ventilation, water supply, and ambient temperature. Upon equipment receipt, verify package contents. The new equipment should not be used before it has been properly installed; the manufacturer should install capital equipment.

Equipment inventory management

The basis for effective inventory management is an up-to-date and complete list of all equipment in a health facility's inventory. The minimum information to be on the list includes the manufacturer, the model, the identification number, the power requirements, and the equipment's physical location in the facility. Other minimum information is listed in WHO's manual on the topic (WHO/EHT 2011c).

After the inventory list has been compiled, it needs to be updated whenever information changes, such as purchase of a new piece of equipment or movement of an existing item. In addition, the facility engineer, or whoever is responsible, should conduct an annual audit to make sure the list is accurate. The inventory list can then be used as a resource to develop budgets, identify human resource and training needs, and manage service contracts, among other activities (WHO/EHT 2011c).

Equipment maintenance and service

After installation, establish an inventory record for the equipment; define the conditions for the equipment's use; develop and implement protocols for calibration, performance verification, and operating procedures; establish a maintenance program; and provide training for all operators. New equipment must be validated and calibrated before use.

Equipment maintenance programs ensure equipment safety, fewer work interruptions, lower repair costs, longer equipment life, and greater confidence in the reliability of test results. Maintenance involves systematic and routine cleaning and adjustment or replacement of instrument and equipment parts. Maintenance should be performed daily, weekly, or monthly, depending on the equipment. Laboratory or facility managers should schedule regular service for all key equipment by the manufacturer or representative. Having all items of the same model (for example, microscopes) serviced at the same time is efficient. Local biomedical service technicians can maintain basic equipment items such as water baths.

If a piece of equipment malfunctions, users should check the manufacturer's instructions, determine the source of the problem—which could be, for example, the sample, the reagent, the equipment, the electrical supply, or the water supply—and make one change at a time to try to diagnose the source of the problem.

Retire equipment when experts indicate the item cannot be repaired or is outmoded and should be replaced with a new model. Updating equipment prevents inaccurate test results, frees up valuable space, and reduces hazards. Any usable parts from the old equipment can be salvaged, taking into account any biohazards. Safety disposal procedures must be followed for any parts that cannot be reused.

47.5 Donations of equipment and other commodities

Donations of commodities and equipment to laboratories and health facilities must be handled carefully, ensuring that donations are based on need expressed by the recipient country. When donors are involved in providing medical supplies and equipment, problems related to the lack of standardization and to maintenance may arise. First, many donors want to buy the equipment, leaving the recipient to solve the problem of paying for installation, maintenance, and recurrent costs. Second, many donors are not sensitive to the recipient's technical requirements. Therefore, storerooms in many countries have equipment that has never been used or has broken down and cannot be repaired because of a lack of spare parts and local service facilities or a lack of instructions in the local language. Third, a donor's policy may differ from the national policy, for example, in relation to the use of disposable syringes. In general, donated equipment contributes to the lack of equipment standardization in developing countries.

All donated capital equipment and diagnostic commodities must comply with the quality standards of both the donor and the recipient country, and insisting that donated diagnostic commodities have a shelf life of at least one year is reasonable. Any instructions should be in English or in the country's national language that is easily understood by laboratory or facility staff. Whenever possible, the donor agency pays for international and local transport, warehousing, and port clearance as well as a maintenance contract. Adequate supplies of consumables should accompany donations of capital equipment.

Most of the principles of pharmaceutical donations, as presented in Chapter 15, apply equally to supplies and equipment. Nevertheless, a few specific issues regarding equipment donations should be kept in mind (WHO/EHT 2011d). Governments should develop local policy, guidelines, and regulations to govern health care equipment donations, if they do not already exist. The most important issue is the provision for maintenance and spares. As mentioned, it should be the first criterion used in choosing equipment for procurement; it should also be the first argument for acceptance of a proposed donation.

In its guidelines on health care equipment donations, WHO (2000) outlined the four core principles of equipment donations—

- A health care equipment donation should benefit the recipient to the maximum extent possible.
- A donation should respect the wishes and authority of the recipient and conform to existing government policies and administrative arrangements.
- No double standard should exist in quality: if the quality of an item is unacceptable in the donor country, it is also unacceptable as a donation.
- The donor and the recipient should communicate effectively, with all donations resulting from a need expressed by the recipient and following a plan formulated by both parties. ∎

References and further readings

CDC/UNAIDS/WHO (U.S. Centers for Disease Control and Prevention, Joint United Nations Programme on HIV/AIDS, and the World Health Organization). 2009. *Guidelines for Using HIV Testing Technologies in Surveillance: Selection, Evaluation and Implementation—2009 Update.* Geneva: WHO. <http://www.who.int/hiv/pub/surveillance/hiv_testing_technologies_surveillance.pdf>

CDC/WHO/AFRO (U.S. Centers for Disease Control and Prevention and African Regional Office of the World Health Organization). 2004. *Guidelines for Appropriate Evaluations of HIV Testing Technologies in Africa.* Geneva: WHO. <http://whqlibdoc.who.int/afro/2002/a82959_eng.pdf>

GFATM (Global Fund to Fight AIDS, Tuberculosis and Malaria). 2009. *Guide to the Global Fund's Policies on Procurement and Supply Management.* Geneva: Fund to Fight AIDS, Tuberculosis and Malaria.

IDA Foundation. No date. *Webcatalogue.* Amsterdam: IDA Foundation. <http://www.idafoundation.org/we-offer/web-catalogue.html>

MSH (Management Sciences for Health). No date. "Strengthening Laboratories in Uganda." <http://www.msh.org/news-bureau/strengthening-laboratories-in-uganda-14-102005.cfm>

Mundy, C., G. Kahenya, and H. Vrakking. 2006. *Support to the Global TB Drug Facility: Design and In-Country Evaluation of TB Diagnostic Laboratory Kits Initiative, 2004–2006.* Submitted to the Global TB Drug Facility and the United States Agency for International Development by the Rational Pharmaceutical Management Plus Program. Arlington, Va.: Management Sciences for Health. <http://www1.msh.org/projects/rpmplus/Documents/upload/TB-Diagnostic-Lab-Kits-Report_2006.pdf>

Mundy, C., M. Ngwira, G. Kadewele, I. Bates, B. Squire, and C. Gilks. 2000. Evaluation of Microscope Condition in Malawi. *Transactions of the Royal Society of Tropical Medicine and Hygiene* 94:1–2.

Petti, C. A., C. R. Polange, T. C. Quinn, A. R. Ronald, and M. A. Sande. 2006. Laboratory Medicine in Africa: A Barrier to Effective Health Care. *Clinical Infectious Diseases* 42:377–82.

Prüss, A., E. Giroult, and P. Rushbrook, eds. 1999. *Safe Management of Wastes from Health-Care Activities.* Geneva: WHO. <http://www.who.int/water_sanitation_health/medicalwaste/itoxiv.pdf>

RPM Plus/CPGH/MoH, Kenya (Rational Pharmaceutical Management Plus Program, in collaboration with the Laboratory Department, Coast Provincial General Hospital, and Ministry of Health, Kenya). 2004. *Standard Operating Procedures for Laboratory Services.* Prepared for Antiretroviral Therapy (ART) Programme, Coast Provincial General Hospital. Arlington, Va.: Management Sciences for Health. <http://www.msh.org/Documents/upload/SOPs_for_Laboratory-1.pdf>

Tayler, Y., ed. 2004. *Battling HIV/AIDS: A Decision Maker's Guide to the Procurement of Medicines and Related Supplies.* Washington, D.C.: World Bank. <http://www.who.int/hiv/amds/WB_battlingaids.pdf>

UNICEF (United Nations Children's Fund). 2011. *Supply Catalogue.* Copenhagen: UNICEF. <https://supply.unicef.org>

Vandepitte, J., J. Verhaegen, K. Engbaek, P. Rohner, P. Piot, and C. C. Heuck. 2003. *Basic Laboratory Procedures in Clinical Bacteriology.* 2nd ed. Geneva: WHO.

Walkowiak, H., and M. Gabra, with G. Sangiwa and Y. D. Mukadi. 2008. *A Commodity Management Planning Guide for the Scale-Up of HIV Counseling and Testing Services.* Submitted to the U.S. Agency for International Development by the Rational Pharmaceutical Management Plus Program. Arlington, Va.: Management Sciences for Health. <http://www1.msh.org/projects/rpmplus/Documents/upload/HIV-Testing-Commodity-Guide-VCT_final.pdf>

Wang, B., E. Furst, T. Cohen, O. R. Keil, M. Ridgway, and R. Stiefel. 2006. Medical Equipment Management Strategies. *Biomedical Instrumentation & Technology* 40(3):233–7.

WHO (World Health Organization). 2011. "WHO Warns Against the Use of Inaccurate Blood Tests for Active Tuberculosis: A Substandard Test with Unreliable Results." News release, July 20. Geneva:WHO. <http://www.who.int/mediacentre/news/releases/2011/tb_20110720/en/index.html>

————. 2010a. *Delivering HIV Test Results and Messages for Re-Testing and Counselling in Adults.* Geneva: WHO. <http://whqlibdoc.who.int/publications/2010/9789241599115_eng.pdf>

————. 2010b. *Fluorescent Light Emitting Diode (LED) Microscopy for Diagnosis of Tuberculosis: Policy Statement.* Geneva: WHO. <http://www.who.int/tb/laboratory/who_policy_led_microscopy_july10.pdf>

————. 2010c. *Non-Commercial Culture and Drug-Susceptibility Testing Methods for Screening of Patients at Risk of Multi-Drug Resistant Tuberculosis: Policy Statement.* Geneva: WHO. <http://www.stoptb.org/wg/gli/assets/documents/WHO%20policy%20on%20non%20commercial%20culture%20and%20DST%20methods_Rev%20Nov%202010.pdf>

————. 2010d. *Same-Day-Diagnosis of Tuberculosis by Microscopy: Policy Statement.* Geneva: WHO. <http://www.who.int/tb/laboratory/whopolicy_same-day-diagnosis_bymicroscopy_july10.pdf>

ASSESSMENT GUIDE

Management

- Does a national laboratory policy exist?
- Have national lists of essential medical supplies and equipment been officially adopted and distributed countrywide?
- Is there an official committee whose duties include updating the lists?
- Have the lists been updated and distributed country-wide in the past five years?

Selection

- How many items does the list of essential medical and laboratory supplies and equipment contain? How are the items classified?
- Is the list divided into levels of health care? How many items exist for each level?
- What equipment, testing kits, reagents, consumables, and specimen collection supplies are needed to perform specific diagnostic tests, such as HIV diagnosis, monitoring of HIV treatment, TB diagnosis, identification of drug resistance, and so on?
- Does the laboratory equipment require unique commercial brands of testing reagents or kits?
- Does the equipment need specialized preventive maintenance and repair?
- Are the parts accessible?
- Does a service agreement exist?

Procurement and distribution

- Is procurement in the public sector limited to items on the list?
- What is the ratio of the value of items from the list procured in the public sector to the total value of laboratory supplies and equipment procured in the same sector?
- What mechanisms for procuring laboratory reagents, test kits, and consumables currently exist at the national level, the facility level, or both?

- If no system exists, can procurement be integrated into the existing medicine or laboratory supply system?
- If the procurement of laboratory supplies and diagnostics is to be decentralized to lower levels, do the staff have the skills, finances, managerial support, and information to carry out procurement functions successfully?
- Do equipment and supply donations comply with the national lists?
- Do any of the commodities have special storage requirements? Is the freezer, refrigerated, or cold storage space adequate? Is the electricity supply reliable?
- Is a procedure in place for a cold chain to maintain and monitor special storage temperatures from delivery of the commodity to storage and use? Are supplies to transport heat-sensitive commodities, including cooler boxes and icepacks, adequate? What system is in place to monitor freezer, refrigerator, and storeroom temperatures regularly?
- How much room is needed to store all the commodities between deliveries? Can more storage space be found or more frequent deliveries be scheduled? If scaling up is planned, where will additional commodities be stored?

Human capacity

- Are staff trained to handle specimens, equipment, reagents, test kits, and other consumables safely and appropriately?
- Do they need training updates for new tests or procedures? Are approved, written standard operating procedures available and followed for (1) use and maintenance of each item of equipment, (2) preparation of reagents, (3) procedures for performing each test, and (4) safety practices?
- Are supplies available to safeguard the health and safety of the staff performing HIV testing?

———. 2010e. "WHO Endorses New Rapid Tuberculosis Test: A Major Milestone for Global TB Diagnosis and Care." News release, December 10. Geneva: WHO. <http://www.who.int/mediacentre/news/releases/2010/tb_test_20101208/en/index.html>

———. 2008. *Molecular Line Probe Assays for Rapid Screening of Patients at Risk of Multidrug-Resistant Tuberculosis (MDR-TB): Policy Statement.* Geneva: WHO. <http://www.who.int/tb/laboratory/lpa_policy.pdf>

———. 2007a. "Definition of a New Sputum Smear-Positive TB Case, 2007." WHO Policy: TB Diagnostics and Laboratory Strengthening. Geneva: WHO. <http://www.who.int/tb/laboratory/policy_sputum_smearpositive_tb_case/en>

———. 2007b. "Reduction of Number of Smears for the Diagnosis of Pulmonary TB, 2007." WHO Policy: TB Diagnostics and Laboratory Strengthening. Geneva: WHO. <http://www.who.int/tb/laboratory/policy_diagnosis_pulmonary_tb/en>

———. 2007c. "The Use of Liquid Medium for Culture and DST, 2007." WHO Policy: TB Diagnostics and Laboratory Strengthening. Geneva: WHO. <http://www.who.int/tb/laboratory/policy_liquid_medium_for_culture_dst/en>

———. 2006a. "Injection Safety." Fact Sheet no. 231. Geneva: WHO. <http://www.who.int/mediacentre/factsheets/fs231/en/index.html>

———. 2006b. *The Interagency Emergency Health Kit 2006.* 3rd ed. Geneva: WHO. <http://whqlibdoc.who.int/hq/2006/WHO_PSM_PAR_2006.4_eng.pdf>

———. 2006c. *The Role of Laboratory Diagnosis to Support Malaria Disease Management: Focus on the Use of Rapid Diagnostic Tests in Areas of High Transmission. Report of a WHO Technical Consultation, 25–26 October 2004.* Geneva: WHO.

———. 2005. *WHO Consultation on Technical and Operational Recommendations for Scale-Up of Laboratory Services and Monitoring HIV Antiretroviral Therapy in Resource-Limited Settings.* Geneva: WHO. <http://www.who.int/hiv/pub/meetingreports/labmeetingreport.pdf>

———. 2004. *Laboratory Biosafety Manual.* 3rd ed. Geneva: WHO. <http://www.who.int/csr/resources/publications/biosafety/WHO_CDS_CSR_LYO_2004_11/en>

———. 2003a. *Manual of Basic Techniques for a Health Laboratory.* 2nd ed. Geneva: WHO.

———. 2003b. *Medical Device Regulations: Global Overview and Guiding Principles.* Geneva: WHO. <http://www.who.int/medical_devices/publications/en/MD_Regulations.pdf>

———. 2003c. *Surgical Care at the District Hospital.* Geneva: WHO. <http://whqlibdoc.who.int/publications/2003/9241545755.pdf>

———. 2002. "Aide-Memoire for National Medical Device Administrations." *Safe Medical Devices.* Geneva: WHO. <http://www.who.int/medical_devices/publications/en/AM_Devices_EN.pdf>

———. 2000. *Guidelines for Health Care Equipment Donations.* Geneva: WHO. <http://www.who.int/medical_devices/publications/en/Donation_Guidelines.pdf>

———. 1998. *Laboratory Services for Primary Health Care: Requirements for Essential Clinical Laboratory Tests.* Geneva: WHO.

———. 1986. *Methods Recommended for Essential Clinical Chemical and Haematological Tests for Intermediate Hospital Laboratories.* Geneva: WHO.

———. No date. "TB Diagnostics and Laboratory Strengthening." *Tuberculosis.* Geneva: WHO. <http://www.who.int/tb/laboratory/en>

WHO/AFRO (World Health Organization/Regional Office for Africa). 2008a. *Consultation on Technical and Operational Recommendations for Clinical Laboratory Testing Harmonization and Standardization.* Meeting, January 22–24, Maputo, Mozambique. <http://www.who.int/diagnostics_laboratory/3by5/Maputo_Meeting_Report_7_7_08.pdf>

———. 2008b. The Maputo Declaration on Strengthening of Laboratory Systems. January 24, Maputo, Mozambique.

WHO/CDC (World Health Organization/U.S. Centers for Disease Control and Prevention). 2005. *Guidelines for Assuring the Accuracy and Reliability of HIV Rapid Testing: Applying a Quality System Approach.* Geneva: WHO. <http://www.who.int/diagnostics_laboratory/publications/HIVRapidsGuide.pdf>

WHO/DLT (World Health Organization/Diagnostics and Laboratory Technology). 2011. *Overview of the Prequalification of Diagnostics Assessment Process: Prequalification of Diagnostics.* Geneva: WHO. <http://www.who.int/diagnostics_laboratory/evaluations/110322_pqdx_007_pq_overview_document_v4.pdf>

WHO/EHT (World Health Organization/Department of Essential Health Technologies). 2011a. *Core Medical Equipment.* Geneva: WHO. <http://whqlibdoc.who.int/hq/2011/WHO_HSS_EHT_DIM_11.03_eng.pdf>

———. 2011b. *Development of Medical Device Policies.* WHO Medical Device Technical Series. Geneva: WHO. <http://whqlibdoc.who.int/publications/2011/9789241501637_eng.pdf>

———. 2011c. *Introduction to Medical Equipment Inventory Management.* WHO Medical Device Technical Series. Geneva: WHO. <http://whqlibdoc.who.int/publications/2011/9789241501392_eng.pdf>

———. 2011d. *Medical Device Donations: Considerations for Solicitation and Provision.* WHO Medical Device Technical Series. Geneva: WHO.

———. 2011e. *Procurement Process Resource Guide.* WHO Medical Device Technical Series. Geneva: WHO.

———. 2010. *Medical Devices: Managing the Mismatch: An Outcome of the Priority Medical Devices Project.* Geneva: WHO. <http://whqlibdoc.who.int/publications/2010/9789241564045_eng.pdf>

———. 2005. "Basic Operational Framework for Diagnostics and Laboratory Technology." Basic Operational Frameworks (BOF) for Essential Health Technologies. Geneva: WHO. <http://www.who.int/eht/frameworks/en>

———. No date. *Towards a WHO Model List of Essential Medical Devices.* Geneva: WHO. <http://www.who.int/eht/en/MedicalDevices.pdf>

WHO/EHT and UNAIDS (World Health Organization/Department of Essential Health Technologies and Joint United Nations Programme on HIV/AIDS). 2009. *HIV Assays: Operational Characteristics; Report 16, Rapid Assays.* Geneva: WHO. <http://whqlibdoc.who.int/publications/2009/9789241597692_eng.pdf>

———. 2008. *Policy Guidance on Drug-Susceptibility Testing (DST) of Second-Line Antituberculosis Drugs.* Geneva: WHO. <http://www.who.int/tb/publications/2008/who_htm_tb_2008_392.pdf>

———. 2004a. *HIV Assays: Operational Characteristics (Phase 1); Report 14, Simple/Rapid Tests.* Geneva: WHO. <http://www.who.int/diagnostics_laboratory/publications/hiv_assays_rep_14.pdf>

———. 2004b. *HIV Assays: Operational Characteristics (Phase 1); Report 15, Antigen/Antibody ELISAs.* Geneva: WHO. <http://www.who.int/diagnostics_laboratory/publications/en/HIV_Report15.pdf>

WHO/Stop TB (World Health Organization/Stop TB Partnership). 2007. *New Technologies for Tuberculosis Control: A Framework for Their Adoption, Introduction and Implementation.* Geneva: WHO. <http://whqlibdoc.who.int/publications/2007/9789241595520_eng.pdf>

WHO/StopTB GLI (World Health Organization/Stop TB Partnership Global Laboratory Initiative). 2011. *Rapid Implementation of the Xpert MTB/RIF Diagnostic Test: Technical and Operational "How-to" Practical Considerations.* Geneva: WHO. <http://whqlibdoc.who.int/publications/2011/9789241501569_eng.pdf>

———. 2010. *Framework for Implementing New Tuberculosis Diagnostics.* Geneva: WHO. <http://www.stoptb.org/wg/gli/assets/documents/WHO%20Policy%20Framework%20FINAL%20July%202010_%20Rev%20Nov%202010.pdf>

WHO/TDR (World Health Organization on behalf of the Special Programme for Research and Training in Tropical Diseases). 2009. *Good Clinical Laboratory Practice (GCLP).* Geneva: WHO. < http://whqlibdoc.who.int/publications/2009/9789241597852_eng.pdf>

WHO/UNAIDS (World Health Organization and Joint United Nations Programme on HIV/AIDS). 2005. *CD4+ T-Cell Enumeration Technologies: Technical Information.* Geneva: WHO.

WHO/WPRO (World Health Organization Western Pacific Region). 2006. *The Use of Malaria Rapid Diagnostic Tests.* 2nd ed. Manila: WPRO.

———. 2003. *Quality Assurance of Sputum Microscopy in DOTS Programmes: Regional Guidelines for Countries in the Western Pacific.* Manila: WPRO.

World Bank. 2007. *An Overview of Medical Device Policy and Regulation.* HNP Brief no. 8. Washington, D.C.: World Bank. <http://siteresources.worldbank.org/HEALTHNUTRITIONANDPOPULATION/Resources/281627-1109774792596/HNPBrief8.pdf>

———. 1993. *World Development Report 1993: Investing in Health.* New York: Oxford University Press.

Part I: Policy and economic issues	Part II: Pharmaceutical management	Part III: Management support systems

Planning and administration
Organization and management
Information management
  48 Monitoring and evaluation
  49 Pharmaceutical management information systems
  50 Computers in pharmaceutical management
Human resources management

CHAPTER 48

Monitoring and evaluation

SUMMARY

Monitoring refers to the ongoing review of the progress toward completing program activities and achieving objectives. It allows corrective action during program implementation. Monitoring systems focus on inputs and short-term outputs and should be an integral part of day-to-day management.

Fully developed monitoring systems, which may be established in phases, typically consist of a combination of four methods—

1. Supervisory visits for continual, informal monitoring of workplan implementation and progress toward program plans
2. Routine reporting of selected data through the pharmaceutical management information system (PMIS)
3. Sentinel sites for more detailed reporting when new initiatives or rapid expansion requires more intensive monitoring
4. Special studies whenever an implementation problem or planning question requires specific additional information

Performance indicators can facilitate tracking a program's progress toward established performance targets or milestones and help compare this progress to that of other programs. Indicators should meet the criteria of clarity, usefulness, measurability, reliability, and validity, as well as acceptance by key stakeholders.

To be effective in improving program performance, monitoring requires—

- Clear communication of plans and targets
- Regular review and sharing of monitoring results
- Follow-up to provide feedback and take corrective action

Evaluation is commonly discussed along with monitoring as part of an overall strategy. It refers to the periodic analysis of a program's progress toward meeting established objectives and goals. Evaluations fall into three categories, which differ in timing and purpose—

- Needs assessment (situation analysis, see Chapter 36)
- Formative evaluation (midterm review)
- Summative evaluation (final evaluation)

Evaluations use data collected through the ongoing monitoring system, supplemented by document review, interviews, additional data collection, and field surveys using standard pharmaceutical assessment indicators. Strategies for monitoring and evaluation are normally developed in parallel to ensure a comprehensive, unified evaluation strategy.

48.1 Definitions of monitoring and evaluation

Monitoring refers to reviewing, on a continuous basis, the degree to which program activities are completed and performance targets or milestones are being met. Typically, monitoring focuses on tracking program inputs such as funding, staff, facilities, supplies, and training. As such, monitoring is part of the operational management of a program. Monitoring also tracks outputs such as availability of medicines and supplies, number or percentage of trained staff, and quality of services. Systematic monitoring of inputs and outputs can help identify potential problems and corrective actions to be taken during program implementation.

Evaluation refers to analyzing progress toward meeting established objectives, goals, or results. It provides feedback on the outcomes of activities, such as changes in prescribing behavior and health care–seeking behavior, whether plans have been met, and the reasons for success or failure. Evaluation should also provide direction for future programmatic plans. Evaluation methods may be used to carry out a situation analysis or a needs assessment as the first step in designing an appropriate intervention to improve program performance. Evaluation takes a longer-term perspective and concentrates on the strengths and weaknesses of the program strategies.

Country Study 48-1 illustrates the monitoring and evaluation system put into place for pharmacy and laboratory services in a new antiretroviral therapy (ART) program in Kenya.

This chapter is concerned mostly with monitoring pharmaceutical supply systems. Monitoring is closely linked with the pharmaceutical management information system, described in Chapter 49. Evaluation, which is closely linked with systematic assessment (Chapter 36), is discussed briefly at the end of this chapter.

48.2 Monitoring issues

Systematic and ongoing monitoring is essential for ensuring that program performance is on track, for improving performance, and for achieving long-term program goals and results. Unfortunately, during program implementation, attention can easily get focused on specific technical activities at the expense of monitoring activities. Too often, monitoring is done casually, without a clear plan, without a clear link to program objectives and targets, and without any effort to use monitoring results to improve program performance.

Monitoring should be an integral part of the day-to-day management of pharmaceutical supply systems. Managers of pharmaceutical supply programs are concerned with getting the most out of scarce resources. Meeting this goal means making the program as efficient and as effective as possible. Therefore, managers need to generate current, reliable information to use in making decisions on program performance and operations.

The monitoring system should center on key program activities and objectives. To operate efficiently, it must focus on a small number of specific, clearly formulated monitoring issues that are directly related to performance and are generally taken from program plans, objectives, and targets.

Monitoring is intended to—

- Determine whether activities are being carried out as planned
- Measure achievement of targets
- Identify implementation problems to initiate corrective action
- Identify and reinforce good performance
- Identify and strengthen weak performance
- Help target supervision toward problem areas
- Assess whether activities are having their expected effect
- Assess long-term trends
- Contribute to reviewing and revising program priorities and plans

Funding agencies and donors may impose their particular reporting requirements for their own monitoring and reporting purposes. For the most part, these reporting requirements do not deviate much from standard reporting needs. The advent of international funding initiatives, such as the Global Fund to Fight AIDS, Tuberculosis and Malaria, has been accompanied by increased attention to the issue of ensuring accountability in the use of funds and achievement of program goals (see References and Further Readings). Unfortunately, specific reporting requirements, performance indicators, and targets may differ significantly between donors and funders, thereby increasing the monitoring and reporting burden of funding recipients.

Ultimately, monitoring is meant to improve the long-term performance of the program and individual staff members.

48.3 Monitoring methods

How are monitoring activities organized, and where does monitoring information come from? Information required for monitoring can be obtained through a combination of four formal and informal methods: supervisory visits, routine reporting, sentinel reporting systems, and special studies.

Supervisory visits

Supervisory visits support the performance of individual staff or health care workers, provide some on-site, in-service training, and represent an important method for informal but direct monitoring of program implementation (see Chapter 51).

Supervisory visits should reinforce routine reporting requirements. Such visits may include checking the quality of entries on standard reporting forms, such as inventory management forms (for example, stock cards). Visits sometimes involve the collection of information, such as the availability of specific medicines, for special studies.

Routine reporting

The core of a monitoring system for pharmaceutical supply programs is the routine reporting that is accomplished through the pharmaceutical management information system. A PMIS consists of record-keeping documents; data reporting forms; feedback reports; and procedures that govern the availability, use, and flow of information up and down the system, including tracking the availability and use of medicines.

Chapter 49 provides a practical overview and specific guidance on designing an effective PMIS. It emphasizes the need to build on existing recording and reporting systems, to involve users in developing the system, to use appropriate data collection methods, to integrate the PMIS with other information systems, to take advantage of practical analysis methods, and to communicate information promptly and clearly.

Depending on the program's objectives, routine reporting focuses on the availability of supplies at different levels in the system, finances, procurement and supplier performance, training, quality assurance, and medicine use. Clear presentation of reported information, feedback to those providing the information, and follow-up action contribute to the effectiveness and usefulness of the reporting system. Reports should include both quantitative information and brief descriptions of processes, key problems, and proposed follow-up actions. Some countries are now using mobile telephones to transmit routine monitoring data to a central location for timely analysis or even analyzing data at remote locations. For example, the National Malaria Control Program in Malawi is using a mobile phone–based tool to collect and analyze data on malaria commodity availability and case management indicators during supervisory visits to facilities. This method allows supervisors to identify and address problems quickly.

Country Study 48-1
Developing a monitoring and evaluation component for a new ART program in Mombasa, Kenya

In countries that are introducing and scaling up ART programs, a challenge is improving ART access quickly while at the same time working to strengthen systems that support long-term quality care. In 2002, the government of Kenya, with technical assistance from various partners, initiated an ART program in four health facilities in Mombasa. The overall goal of the Mombasa ART program was to reduce HIV/AIDS-related morbidity and mortality and to improve the quality of life of people living with HIV/AIDS and their families in the Mombasa district. The program's specific objectives were to—

- Improve the capacity of HIV/AIDS clinics, laboratory, and pharmacy services in selected public health facilities in Mombasa to provide HIV/AIDS comprehensive care, including ART
- Provide ART to 300 patients over a period of five years in accordance with eligibility criteria
- Sensitize communities and strengthen support groups' knowledge of comprehensive HIV/AIDS care, including ART

A monitoring and evaluation system was incorporated into the program design to provide quality information to help decision makers take timely corrective actions and ensure that the program is achieving its goal and objectives.

The key features of the system were to—

- Encourage analysis and use of information by using well-defined indicators rather than *only* reporting. The system stresses the use of data at the point where data are collected.

- Monitor all aspects (input, process, output, and quality) of the program, including support systems (for example, availability of human resources and enhancement of their capacities).
- Build on the existing information system to minimize the additional burden on service providers.
- Integrate feedback mechanisms at all levels.
- Ensure system simplicity to facilitate staff training on its modification and use.
- Make sure the system is functioning manually before computerizing it.

The diagram opposite illustrates the processes and timing of the monitoring and evaluation system throughout the life of the program (five years).

Baseline status: Result of the pre-implementation assessment formed the baseline status.

Activity monitoring: Pharmacist and laboratory staff responsible for the ART program monitored the activities during the week and reported to their supervisors at the end of *each week*.

Supportive auditing: At the *end of each month*, the supervisor, together with the respective responsible staff members, performed an audit of the activities and resources and discusses problems and solutions.

Review with pharmacy/laboratory technical partner: At the end of each quarter, all staff related to ART (pharmacy and laboratory) and technical partner staff jointly reviewed the activities and progress and discussed problems and solutions. Quarterly indicators were used as a basis for discussion.

The biggest failures in routine reporting systems are overdesign and underimplementation. Collecting too much data usually results in too little analysis. Also, reporting systems that are overly complex result in poor compliance with reporting requirements. Implementing an information system takes time and money. Moreover, the more complex the system is, the greater is the need for qualified and trained staff, time, and money to make it function.

Therefore, the content of routine reporting systems should be limited to the minimum amount of information that the typical reporting unit can reasonably be expected to provide and that can routinely be analyzed for decision making and feedback purposes. Identification of key data requirements is the result of a prioritization exercise that considers the critical information needs of all components of the pharma-

ceutical supply cycle. The simple rule is: do not collect what you cannot use.

Sentinel reporting systems

When routine reporting systems are properly collecting only the minimal essential information, a great deal of potentially useful information is not included. To supplement routine reporting, sentinel reporting systems can be useful.

A sentinel reporting system consists of a carefully selected sample of health facilities or dispensaries that are given greater recording and reporting responsibilities. For example, in a country with forty districts, six districts may be selected as sentinel districts. Within each district, a sample of health facilities from each level may be selected. Sentinel

Review with all technical partners: All technical assistance partners participated in the biannual review. Quarterly indicators were used as a basis for discussion.

Midterm evaluation: The technical partner conducted a midterm review of activities related to pharmacy and laboratory and also participated in the midterm evaluation jointly conducted by all the partners with the Kenyan Ministry of Health (MOH). Quarterly indicators were used as a basis for discussion.

Final evaluation: The pharmacy/laboratory partner conducted a program-end review of related activities and participated in the final evaluation jointly conducted by the other technical assistance partners and the MOH.

Source: Bhattarai and Walkowiak 2005.

	Weeks	1	2	3	4	1	2	3	4	1	2	3	4	...	1	2	3	4	...	1	2	3	4	...	1	2	3	4
Processes	**Months**	1				2				3				...	6				...	30				...	60			
Baseline status		•																										
Activity monitoring		•	•	•	•	•	•	•	•	•	•	•			•	•	•	•		•	•	•	•		•	•	•	•
Supportive auditing				•					•				•					•					•					•
Review with pharmacy/laboratory technical partner													•					•					•					•
Review with all technical partners																		•										•
Midterm evaluation																							•					
Final evaluation																												•

reporting differs from routine reporting in the amount of information collected, the frequency or promptness of report submission, and the level of accuracy demanded.

Sentinel reporting is common in disease control programs such as HIV/AIDS prevention, control of diarrheal disease, and treatment of sexually transmitted diseases. Sentinel sites provide a relatively economical means of collecting up-to-date, detailed information on disease incidence, antimicrobial resistance, and responses to program interventions.

Need for sentinel reporting. A sentinel reporting system is most useful when a system is undergoing rapid or substantial change, such as when a new treatment or public health intervention is being introduced. Sentinel reporting helps assess the implementation and short-term effect of changes or interventions such as—

- Introduction of a major new computerized stock management system
- Transition from a central medical stores system to a decentralized system
- Introduction or scale-up of a treatment program, such as ART or artemisinin-based combination therapy

Sentinel reporting is particularly important for new or expanded HIV/AIDS treatment programs where donors may have many new record-keeping requirements and where many unknowns may exist regarding how the patients will be integrated into the health system. Policy makers and managers can recognize and react more quickly to unexpected or undesirable issues related to program implementation, and information on the availability of antiretrovirals, patient adherence to medication regimens, and other key variables may be collected and rapidly reported.

Whereas the routine reporting system answers only the questions it asks, a sentinel reporting system can be useful to detect unexpected or unintended outcomes. However, recording and reporting formats developed for sentinel sites sometimes prove sufficiently useful and convenient to be incorporated into routine reporting.

Selection of sentinel sites. The level and number of health units in a sentinel system depend on the organization of the health and pharmaceutical management systems, the monitoring objectives, and the overall diversity within the country. If, for example, a country has only one central medical store and a handful of regional stores, they would all be included in sentinel reporting requirements. Generally, at least six units should be included within each level. For example, a sentinel system could include six districts, six district hospitals, and six health centers within each district (thirty-six health centers total). Larger numbers of units are needed in more populous, more organizationally complex, or more diverse countries.

Selection of specific districts, locations within districts, or health facilities is generally purposeful, not random. Selection is aimed at achieving diversity rather than statistical representativeness. The selected sites should represent the range of facilities that serve culturally, linguistically, and geographically diverse groups; the distribution of ministry and nongovernmental facilities; and accessibility.

Staffing levels at sentinel sites should be sufficient to handle additional recording and reporting requirements, which may mean hiring extra staff at some sites. Extra incentives are sometimes given for prompt, complete, accurate reporting, although this practice should be avoided. Prompt feedback of information can be sufficient to motivate staff to respond quickly and reliably. Because cost is a consideration, relatively inaccessible sites are usually chosen as sentinel sites, even at the price of omitting cultural or geographic diversity; however, if these inaccessible sites are particularly likely to suffer shortages of medicines and delayed delivery, including some of them in the sentinel system may be worth the effort, especially if there is an intent to make changes in the system to address these deficiencies.

Information required from sentinel sites. Sentinel sites may differ in the amount of information recorded, the amount of information routinely reported, or the speed at which the information is processed. Additional recording and reporting requirements should be based on the reasons that the sentinel system was established, such as monitoring a new stock management system, assessing transition to a supply agency system, or evaluating the effect of a user-fee program.

Most of the principles used in designing a PMIS apply to sentinel reporting: being selective in deciding which indicators to collect, choosing appropriate data collection methods, and building on existing recording and reporting systems whenever possible. In some instances, putting in computers at sentinel sites may be appropriate (or choosing sites that already have computer capability), even if national computerization is not currently foreseen.

Working with sentinel sites. Establishing a system of sentinel sites nearly always requires training key staff at the sites and making frequent supervisory visits, especially in the beginning. Sites may require additional forms, registers, stock records, and other materials.

Finally, a system of sentinel sites is generally maintained for a specified period of time, perhaps for the first several years of a transitional program. After that, these sites may revert to normal reporting status.

Special studies

Sometimes managers and planners need to gather information that is not available from routine or sentinel reporting. Examples of topics that may warrant a special study include—

- Names, dosage forms, and values of medicines purchased by individual health units
- Names, dosage forms, and value of recently expired medicines
- Reasons for expiration of pharmaceuticals
- Average percentage of essential medicines available

- Level of patient adherence to prescribed treatment
- Level of prescriber adherence to standard treatment protocols

Facility or population-based survey and research methods are typically used to obtain this type of information. These methods may involve expenses that are not considered in regular recurrent operating costs and may require specialists to design and carry out, but many questions can be answered with relatively simple methods and at little additional cost. For example, Chapter 40 describes how ABC analysis, lead-time analysis, expiry-date analysis, and pipeline analysis can help improve performance and reduce costs.

Both managers and staff should be involved in the design and implementation of these studies, as well as in the analysis and interpretation of results. However, it is also the manager's role to identify when additional information is needed and to use experts to help design and conduct these special investigations, so that resources are not wasted on a useless effort.

In-depth interviews, structured observation, focus group discussions, or other qualitative methods (see Chapter 28) can be used to explore behavior, attitudes, practices, and causal factors.

Rapid assessments are small-scale studies that include a survey of sample facilities, use of selected core indicators, and interviews with key informants. Rapid assessments typically are designed and conducted within one month (see MSH/RPM et al. 1995).

Country Study 48-2 describes how these four approaches were combined and how the system evolved for monitoring medicine and treatment fees in one East African country.

48.4 Designing the monitoring system

The principles for designing a monitoring system are to focus on key monitoring questions and indicators; keep data collection to a minimum; develop practical procedures for managing monitoring information; and consider the need to make comparisons between performance of similar programs, performance of different facilities within the program, and performance over time. Design should also consider how information will be available for timely feedback and follow-up action. The "KISS" concept should be applied: keep it simple and straightforward (or keep it short and simple).

When time pressures, financial resources, and staff members' inexperience with monitoring methods are limiting factors, phasing the design and implementation may make sense. Initial monitoring efforts can focus on issues of selection and procurement. Medical stores data, for example, are often easy to collect. As the program develops, the monitoring system and core indicators can be expanded to cover medicine distribution and use. Regardless of the approach taken, the design of the monitoring system must be based on a sound understanding of how the system works, including the relationships between system inputs, outputs, and desired outcomes.

Managers can often benefit by designing a monitoring system that allows comparison of the performance of vari- ous health units or facilities. When a facility is introducing or phasing in a new activity, practice, or program, it can be matched to a control site that has not yet been introduced to the new practice or program. The control site should be as similar to the program site as possible, so that any changes can be more reliably attributed to the new pro- gram. If no control site is available to use as a comparison,

---

Country Study 48-2
Monitoring the introduction of medicine fees in Kenya

The Kenyan Ministry of Health introduced a new user-fee program. After early implementation problems, the ministry initiated a program of management improvement and regular fee adjustments. An outpatient medicine and treatment fee was introduced in phases. To assess the effect of the program—in particular the medicine treatment fee—a comprehensive monitoring system was implemented. The system consisted of targeted field supervision, routine reporting, a sentinel system of indicator districts, and special studies.

Targeted field supervision: Supervisory staff from the MOH health financing program made regular supervisory visits to each part of the country. Information from routine reporting and other sources was used to identify problem districts and problem facilities. These were visited more often. Gradually, the role of headquarters staff evolved from primary supervision (directly visiting districts and facilities themselves) to secondary supervision: teaching supervisory skills to provincial and district staff by making visits with counterparts.

Routine reporting: Routine reporting used the financial information system (FIS) and the health information system (HIS). The FIS was developed specifically for the user-fee program and consisted of reports from districts and hospitals covering collections, expenditures, insurance claims, exemptions, and bank balances. The existing HIS was adapted to support additional information needs of the user-fee system.

Indicator districts: The routine reporting system was kept to a minimum for reasons of feasibility, cost, and staff availability. Therefore, a system of six indicator districts was developed to provide additional details on the implementation of user fees. Districts were selected to achieve rural/urban and socioeconomic diversity. Specialized information gathering in the indicator districts included (a) outpatient use data from all MOH levels as well as selected mission and private facilities; (b) rapid household surveys before and after major fee changes to assess care-seeking patterns and knowledge

of fees; (c) outpatient and inpatient surveys to assess patients' perceptions of the fee system and quality changes; and (d) a quality-of-care checklist to assess the availability of critical patient care inputs.

Special studies: During implementation, questions arose that could not be answered through either routine reporting or the indicator district system. Special studies were, therefore, conducted on the planning and expenditure process for the use of revenue; on fee preferences, to assist in expanding the fee schedule; on exemptions, to assist in adjusting exemptions to balance equity and revenue needs; and on revenue losses caused by non-collection of inpatient fees.

Uses of monitoring information: Supervision and routine reporting information were used to identify districts and facilities that were performing poorly and to strengthen their performance. Supervisory visits corrected misunderstandings of the new management systems. In some cases, staff members were intentionally flouting new rules for personal gain, and disciplinary action was taken. Districts and facilities that were performing well were identified and publicly recognized. Data from the indicator districts were used to guide decisions about the type, level, and timing of fee changes. Results from special studies were used to correct management problems and to revise management systems.

Evolution of the monitoring system: As the new user-fee system matured over a five-year period, the nature of the monitoring system evolved. Supervision was decentralized to the provincial and district levels. Routine reporting requirements were simplified to focus on the few critical FIS and HIS reports that most facilities could generate regularly. Data from indicator districts were important for monitoring major fee changes, but subsequent fee adjustments were having less and less effect, so little information was being gained from the indicator districts. Efforts were then concentrated primarily on effective local use of targeted supervision and routine reports.

In Zimbabwe, training pharmaceutical technicians and health workers in medicine management resulted in significant improvements in inventory management and rational medicine use, but the achievements were not sustained. A monitoring program based on two supervisory visits every three months was instituted in district-level health facilities to determine whether progress in managing medicines could be maintained.

The study compared three different groups—

1. Twenty-three facilities receiving supervision on using standard treatment guidelines
2. Twenty-one facilities receiving supervision on inventory management
3. A control group of eighteen facilities receiving no supervision in either area

The evaluation measured performance using a range of indicators relating to medicine availability, use of stock cards and books, and monthly ordering, as well as adherence to the standard treatment guidelines.

The results showed that after supervision, overall inventory management and adherence to standard treatment guidelines improved significantly when compared with the control and comparison groups. In addition, supervisory visits had a positive effect on improving staff performance in other areas besides just inventory management and rational medicine use.

Source: Trap et al. 2004.

mance of the overall system. A well-defined indicator is clearly linked to an important input, process, or outcome. A well-selected indicator will help managers quickly identify potential problems in critical areas. Indicators are extremely helpful to communicate important performance gains and losses to other stakeholders of the pharmaceutical supply system. Indicators can be developed for different levels of the supply system.

Managers should be aware that well-established indicators exist for measuring the performance of the different components of the pharmaceutical supply system (for example, WHO 2007). However, because systems can be organized in different ways, managers should adapt or modify internationally recognized indicators to reflect the realities of their own system if necessary.

Applications of indicators

When used to make measurements at one point in time, indicators allow a manager to compare a program's performance with a target level of performance (or with another program's performance) and to identify areas of relative strength and weakness. Applied over time, such indicators can be used to set and monitor performance improvement targets, such as—

- Monitoring implementation of program plans and workplans
- Evaluating achievement of long-term goals
- Assessing the performance of individual units
- Identifying relative strengths and weaknesses in current policies and systems
- Measuring the effect of new policies or management systems
- Self-monitoring to improve performance
- Demonstrating needs to treasury, donors, or other funders
- Reporting on progress to senior officials, donors, or other interested parties

For program management purposes, whether at the national or facility level, performance indicators should tie directly to program plans and annual workplans and to a general performance improvement process. One way to view the management process is that it takes *inputs* (for example, human and financial resources, equipment, policies) and the implementation of certain management and clinical *processes* (meetings, trainings, development of materials) to create specific service or activity *outputs* (number of staff trained or clients served, new management system), which have immediate *outcomes* (change in practices, improved services), which lead to a desirable long-term *impact* on health status (change in disease rates, change in birth rates). This process is illustrated in Figure 48-1.

baseline data can be collected to use as a basis for assessing development after the program is started at the site. If more than one facility is initiating a program, the different facilities can serve as comparison groups to monitor how well each group is progressing. Country Study 48-3 details the effects of supervisory visits using both comparison and control groups.

48.5 Using indicators for monitoring and evaluation

Indicators are variables that measure change. They may be numerical and expressed in terms of numbers, percentages, or averages. They may also be expressed as binomials such as "yes" and "no." Indicators are useful tools for managers to track the performance of particular aspects or activities of the pharmaceutical supply system as well as the perfor-

Figure 48-1 The health management process and illustrative indicators

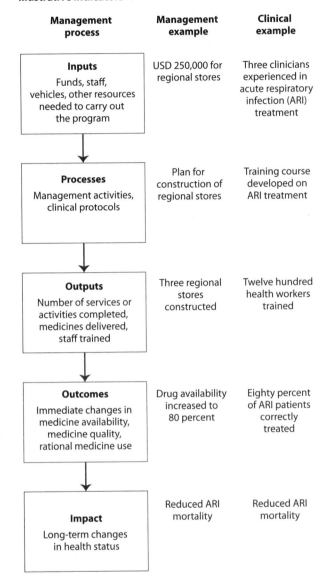

Management process	Management example	Clinical example
Inputs Funds, staff, vehicles, other resources needed to carry out the program	USD 250,000 for regional stores	Three clinicians experienced in acute respiratory infection (ARI) treatment
Processes Management activities, clinical protocols	Plan for construction of regional stores	Training course developed on ARI treatment
Outputs Number of services or activities completed, medicines delivered, staff trained	Three regional stores constructed	Twelve hundred health workers trained
Outcomes Immediate changes in medicine availability, medicine quality, rational medicine use	Drug availability increased to 80 percent	Eighty percent of ARI patients correctly treated
Impact Long-term changes in health status	Reduced ARI mortality	Reduced ARI mortality

Types of indicators

Indicators can be developed for each point in the health management process to monitor specific inputs, processes, and outputs associated with both management and clinical activities. Similarly, pharmaceutical supply system managers can identify input, output, and outcome measures for each major component of the pharmaceutical supply cycle. Table 48-1 lists commonly used indicators that correspond to the components of selection, procurement, distribution, use, policy, and management support.

Managers of pharmaceutical supply systems will note that many of their management activities focus on inputs such as financing, human resources, and the existence of

policies and standard operating procedures. Examples of corresponding indicators include—

- Existence of a national medicine policy updated within the last three years
- Percentage of total health program budget dedicated to procuring pharmaceuticals

Managers are also concerned with activities or processes such as procurement, stock keeping, and prescribing and their outputs. Examples of related indicators include—

- Percentage of the pharmaceutical budget spent on essential medicines
- Average supplier lead time from order to delivery (in days)
- Average inventory turnover
- Number of prescribers trained on standard treatment guidelines

Important outcome indicators for pharmaceutical management focus on aspects of availability and affordability of key medicines, quality issues, and the appropriate use of medicines. Indeed, these indicators are typically the most visible and most commonly cited in evaluating how successfully a supply system is functioning. Examples of outcome indicators include—

- Average number of days of stockouts (of key medicines and supplies)
- Average number of items out of stock at a given point in time
- Average number of medicines prescribed to a patient for a given condition

Selecting indicators

Five necessary criteria for selecting appropriate performance indicators are—

- Clarity: the indicator is easily understood and calculated.
- Usefulness: the indicator reflects an important aspect of performance.
- Measurability: the indicator can be defined in quantitative terms and used within existing constraints on information quality and availability.
- Reliability: the indicator permits consistent assessment over time and among different observers.
- Validity: the indicator is a true measure of what it is meant to measure (see Chapter 36). Validity must also be based on the indicator's acceptance by key stakeholders and the consistency of interpretation among different stakeholders.

Table 48-1   Examples of performance indicators and performance targets

Objective and performance indicator	Performance target
Overall performance	
Central stores: indicator pharmaceuticals available (unexpired)	90%
District stores: indicator pharmaceuticals available (unexpired)	90%
Health units: indicator pharmaceuticals available (unexpired)	90%
Health units: average stockout duration for indicator pharmaceuticals	10 days
Financing—ensure that financial resources are adequate to meet basic pharmaceutical needs	
Per capita government pharmaceutical expenditure	USD 1.20
MOH budget allocation for pharmaceuticals	15%
Actual pharmaceutical expenditures as a percentage of budgeted allocation for pharmaceuticals	85%
Medicine costs covered by user fees	60%
Procurement—obtain a regular supply of pharmaceuticals at favorable prices	
Total value of MOH medicines purchased through competitive tender	95%
Total value of MOH purchases on essential medicines list	98%
Average ratio of unit prices of indicator pharmaceuticals to international prices	0.9 to 1.1
Average lead time for external suppliers	50 days
Average lead time for local suppliers	20 days
Quality assurance—ensure that procured pharmaceuticals meet recognized standards of quality and that quality is maintained throughout the distribution chain	
Number of medicines/batches tested of number of medicines/batches procured	1 of 4
Number of medicines/batches that failed quality control testing, of number of medicines/batches tested	0
Central storage—ensure that medications are properly stored, with minimal expiration and other losses	
Medicines for which stock records and physical counts agree (all medicines)	100%
Average difference between stock records and physical count (all medicines)	Less than 5%
Drugs for which stock records, procurement records, and physical counts agree (indicator pharmaceuticals)	100%
Value of expired medicines as a percentage of total pharmaceutical purchases last year	Less than 3%
Delivery—ensure timely delivery of pharmaceuticals to health units	
Average lead time from central medical stores to health units, routine monthly orders	30 days
Average lead time from central medical stores to health units, emergency orders	5 days
Storage at health units—ensure that medicines are properly stored, with minimal expiration or other losses	
Health units using stock cards correctly	75%
Stock records correspond with physical counts	90%
Health units with expired items	25%
Health units practicing first-expiry/first-out (FEFO)	90%

In selecting indicators, considering how data will be collected is also important. Indicators may rely on generally available information from routine reporting, or they may require special surveys or other sources of information. The sources and the cost of collecting and processing these data must be carefully considered in selecting indicators.

Some indicators may be routinely available from standard recording and reporting systems (such as percentage of indicator pharmaceuticals available), whereas other indicators may require a special survey (for example, percentage of pharmaceutical costs covered by user fees or percentage of health units using stock cards correctly). Some indicators represent annual summary measures (per capita government pharmaceutical expenditure or percentage by total value of pharmaceuticals purchased through competitive tender).

It may be useful to distinguish core performance indicators, for which data are routinely reported and monitored, from complementary performance indicators, for which data may be collected only at sentinel sites or in special studies or that may be used only for periodic evaluation purposes.

The indicator examples in this chapter draw on five useful sets of internationally recognized indicators, some of which are described in greater detail in Chapter 36 (Brudon, Rainhorn, and Reich 1999; CPM 2003b; MSH/ RPM et al. 1995; WHO 2007). By using internationally defined indicators for national pharmaceutical policy (Brudon, Rainhorn, and Reich 1999), pharmaceutical management (MSH/RPM et al. 1995; WHO 2007), and medicine use (Nachbar et al. 2003; WHO 2007; WHO/ DAP 1993), countries can compare their performance against that of other countries.

Setting performance targets

A performance target is a desirable and—in principle— attainable standard of performance. For example, the impact indicator may be the percentage of ten indicator pharmaceutical products in stock, and the performance target may be 80 percent availability at each level for this list of indicator pharmaceuticals. Performance targets should be set for each indicator. Table 48-1 presents illustrative targets for the indicators listed.

A widely used guide to developing performance targets is SMART (MSH/LMS 2008). A SMART result is—

Specific (S): The performance target is clearly written to avoid different interpretations.
Measurable (M): The target allows a team to monitor and evaluate progress toward achieving its result.
Appropriate (A): It is in line with the scope of a team's program or work activities, so that it can have influence or make changes.
Realistic (R): The target is achievable within the time allowed.
Time-bound (T): The performance target has a specific time period for completion.

Performance indicators can be compared with agreed-upon performance standards over time within the same health unit, among health units of the same level, or across countries. Initially, comparisons among health units may help set realistic performance standards, which can be adjusted upward as the system develops.

When setting targets, managers should keep in mind that costs are associated with reaching their targets, and therefore, they should consider budget and staff limitations. For example, attaining a 100 percent service level (in essence, completely filling every order for medicines in one delivery) may not be possible or practical, even though it may be theoretically desirable. Therefore, the target should be set at an appropriate level, and the manager's challenge is to have a strategy to ensure that shortfalls in the pharmaceutical service level do not jeopardize the facility's ability to provide quality care.

Formulation of indicators

If indicators are variables that measure change, they can be counted. Indicators can be in the form of counts (400 health workers trained), rates (two workshops per year), ratios (USD .90 per tin versus USD .60 per tin equals a ratio of 3:2), proportions (400 of 1,200 health workers trained equals one-third), or percentages (400/1,200 health workers trained equals 33 percent). Indicators can also require a "Yes" or "No" response ("Yes, there is a national pharmaceutical policy," or "No, standard treatment guidelines have not been updated in the last three years").

When defining a numerical indicator, considering the availability of information is important. Proportions and percentages require that the size of the whole (the denominator) be reliably known; if not, then actual counts may be more useful. For example, if the number of health workers in a district is not precisely known, specifying a count (400 health workers trained) is preferable to a percentage that cannot be verified.

Indicator pharmaceuticals and supplies

Several of the performance indicators listed in Table 48-1, mentioned in Chapter 36, or included in some of the chapter assessment guides are based on the availability, prices, and accuracy of stock records for a list of indicator pharmaceuticals and supplies.

Indicator pharmaceuticals and supplies are a small number of representative items, which are also known as tracer or index medicines. Economists use a market basket of common goods and services to measure inflation through the consumer price index. Similarly, the list of indicator medicines is sometimes called a basket of medicines (WHO 2006). The advantage of using a list or basket of items for indicators is that data collection and analysis are simplified.

Selecting which items to include on a tracer list is based on preestablished criteria and should include input from important stakeholders. The items should be on the national essential medicines list or national medicine formulary, therapeutically important, widely used, appropriate for the level of care where measurements will be made, and commonly available internationally (if the study includes multinational comparisons). In principle, these items should be available at all times (target 100 percent). For this reason, inclusion of medicines that are not commonly used, that are difficult to obtain, or that have other unusual characteristics influencing how they should be managed is not practical.

Table 48-2 provides a list of medicines, grouped by therapeutic category, that was used to assess the pharmaceutical supply system in Tanzania. Depending on the purpose and uses of the indicators, distinguishing a list of fifteen core indicator medicines to use as indicators for all levels of the health system and a supplementary list of ten additional

Table 48-2   Example of a list of indicator pharmaceuticals and supplies

Pharmaceutical/supply	Form, dosage
Analgesics/antipyretics	
Acetylsalicylic acid (aspirin)	Tablet, 300 mg
Paracetamol	Tablet, 500 mg
Antihelminthics	
Mebendazole	Chewable tablet, 100 mg
Anesthetic	
Ketamine	Vial, 50 mg/mL
Antibacterials	
Amoxicilline	Tablet, 250 mg
Metronidazole	Tablet, 450 mg
Benzylpenicillin sodium	Vial, 5 MU
Sulfamethoxazole/trimethoprim (co-trimoxazole)	Tablet, 400 mg + 80 mg
Ciprofloxacin	Tablet, 500 mg
Doxycycline	Tablet, 100 mg
Erythromycin	Tablet, 250 mg
Gentamycin	Ampoule, 40 mg/mL
Rifampicin + isoniazid	Tablet, 150 mg/100 mg
Antimalarials	
Sulfadoxine/pyrimethamine	Tablet, 500 mg/25 mg
Quinine dihydrochloride	Ampoule, 300 mg/mL
Cardiovascular medicines	
Propranolol	Tablet, 40 mg
Hydroclorothiazide	Tablet, 25 mg
Gastrointestinal medicines	
Oral rehydration salts	Sachet
Minerals	
Ferrous sulfate + folic acid	Tablet, 200 mg/0.25 mg
Ophthalmological preparations	
Oxytetracycline eye ointment 1%	Tube, 5 mg
Vaccines	
Polio vaccine	Vial

Source: CPM 2003a.

of ten or twenty medicines usually suffices. For calculating rates and percentages, using a number that divides easily into 100 (for example, 10, 20, or 25) is convenient. Larger or more diverse lists of indicator pharmaceuticals may be needed for specific purposes. When first introducing performance indicators and indicator items, however, it is probably wise to keep to a core list such as that shown in Table 48-2.

48.6 Using the monitoring system to improve performance

A monitoring system gives managers a way to identify potential problems with program and staff performance and to improve performance. A formalized monitoring system facilitates the development of improvement plans and performance targets, all of which must be clearly communicated at all levels of the pharmaceutical management system. For the monitoring system to be useful, managers should review and share the results regularly and take timely action to follow up. For example, Country Study 48-4 shows how a psychiatric hospital instituted a monitoring system that included regular feedback to psychiatrists to improve prescribing habits. The ongoing monitoring activities will determine if follow-up actions achieved the desired results.

Communicating plans and targets

Program plans and workplans are sometimes viewed simply as documents for fund-raising or for "the people above." To the contrary, they should be blueprints to guide the day-to-day work of staff at all levels, who need to be aware of the plans as well as of output and performance targets. Managers should communicate plans and targets both in writing and face-to-face: memoranda or circular letters alone are usually insufficient. Often, staff members need some education or training to understand why indicators were selected, how they are measured, and how results will be used.

Reviewing progress

A schedule is needed to review program progress, with the review period depending on the nature of the plan and the specific indicators. Managers should review implementation progress for a five-year program plan, for example, at least once a year. During the review, key staff members meet to systematically assess each objective, each activity, and each output target. For an annual workplan, reviewing progress each month or at least each quarter is important. New programs should also be reviewed often as they are getting off the ground.

In a progress review, actual outputs and performance are compared against the established targets; when discrepancies exist between the expected results and actual perfor-

medicines to use at central storage facilities and hospitals may be helpful. The supplementary list of items might include other dosage forms, such as injections and topical preparations, and additional therapeutic categories, such as cardiovascular medications and contraceptives. Items to consider for the core list include oral rehydration solutions, procaine penicillin injections, paracetamol tablets, tetracycline eye ointment, iodine, gentian violet or a local alternative, benzoic acid and salicylic acid ointment, or retinol (vitamin A) (WHO 2007).

To facilitate measurement calculations and consistency, the number of items on the list should be kept small: a list

mance, further discussion or investigation is needed. When progress has exceeded expectations, managers should ask whether positive lessons can be learned and whether specific people should be recognized for their work. Table 48-3 provides an example of a progress review based on a workplan to promote rational medicine use.

When progress is less than expected, it is even more important for managers to ask the reasons why. For instance—

- Were necessary funds, materials, or other inputs lacking?
- Were two units unable to communicate their expectations to each other or to coordinate their actions?
- Did key staff simply fail to take the plans and performance targets seriously?
- Is failure to achieve a specific planned output a reflection of overly ambitious plans?

A well-designed, well-implemented monitoring system can usually provide information on *what* happened or did not happen. Information about *why* things happened—or did not happen—may come from the monitoring system or may require management follow-up.

Giving feedback

No monitoring system is complete without feedback. Giving feedback to individual units or staff members tells them how well they have done the reporting and how useful the information is. Feedback also demonstrates the value and importance of the reports. As such, it represents one of the most powerful tools for motivating staff. Feedback also improves the quality of data by breaking the "bad data cycle" (see Chapter 49).

Direct, action-oriented feedback involves presenting staff with some of the problems and successes identified in the monitoring or evaluation reports—

- Discuss the achievement of specific performance targets.
- Identify weak performers for more intensive supervision or training.
- Identify and congratulate successful districts and facilities.
- Identify policy or program weaknesses and how to strengthen them.

Always check to see whether the information has been used, how it has been used, and what action has been taken.

Taking action

Effective use of the monitoring system requires prompt follow-up action. A manager can take at least five types of action—

- Provide positive feedback to high-performing units or staff to encourage continued good performance.

Country Study 48-4
Monitoring the use of neuroleptic medicines in a psychiatric hospital in Ṭatarstan, Russia

Neuroleptic drugs, such as chlorpromazine, can help control symptoms related to schizophrenia, but overuse, polypharmacy, and medicine interactions can contribute to dangerous adverse effects, such as irreversible movement disorders. The Clinical Psychiatric Hospital in the Republic of Tatarstan, Russia, implemented a monitoring system to measure the use of neuroleptic drugs and related adverse effects and to institute regular feedback to hospital psychiatrists aimed at decreasing the use of neuroleptic medicines and improving overall prescribing habits.

The hospital used standardized medicine-use indicators developed by the World Health Organization (WHO) to track the outcomes related to the monitoring program. Results showed that implementing medicine-use monitoring helped psychiatrists improve their prescribing habits for schizophrenic patients, although adding an educational intervention component to regular monitoring might result in additional gains.

Source: Ziganshina et al. 2004.

		WHO medicine use indicators[a]			
Year	Number of medicines/patient	Percentage of cases prescribed generic medicines	Percentage of cases including antibiotics	Percentage of medicines on formulary	Percentage of cases prescribed injections
1[b]	8.3	56.7	32.2	63.5	40.8
2	5.8	69.1	10.6	99.0	38.8

[a] WHO/DAP 1993.
[b] Before monitoring system was implemented.

Table 48-3   First-year progress review for promoting rational medicine use

Objectives/activities	Outputs		Budgets		Expenditures	Balance	Comments
	Target	Actual	Five-year budget (USD)	First-year budget (USD)	First-year actual (USD)	First year (USD)	
Selection							
Essential medicines list (EML): Revise and distribute national EML at least every two years.	Revision of EML completed	Done	4,000	2,000	2,850	850	Required additional workshop to finalize
Prescribing							
Undergraduate training: Ensure that all students are trained in essential medicines concept and rational medicine use in basic health curricula (amount of time depends on professional category).	Curricula designed for medicine, pharmacy, nursing, paramedical training	Initial workshop held, curricula not completed	5,000	5,000	2,670	2,330	
Standard treatment guidelines (STGs): Develop/revise and distribute standard treatment manual at least every four years.	First edition of STGs completed and distributed	Manual completed and printed, not distributed	96,000	48,000	39,860	8,140	
Continuing education: Provide all clinicians with at least one week of in-service training on rational medicine use every three years.	Sixty-five percent of clinicians trained (1,300 of estimated 2,000)	Training designed, first workshop held	84,000	42,000	4,830	37,170	
Dispensing							
Packaging and labeling: Ensure that at least 80 percent of patients receive medications in clearly labeled containers or dispensing envelopes.	Packaging and labeling materials provided, sufficient for 80 percent of patients	Materials ordered, not received	15,000	3,000	0	3,000	Materials order placed too late
Patient use							
Undergraduate training: Ensure that all students are trained in communications and patient education methods in basic health curricula (amount of time depends on professional category).	Combined with essential medicines training for prescribing	See above	See above	0	0	0	
Continuing education: Include skills for patient education at in-service training workshops.	Combined with essential medicines training for prescribing	See above	See above	0	0	0	
Total			204,000	100,000	50,210	49,790	

- Provide corrective feedback to staff or units that have not met expectations, but that should be able to take specific steps to improve their performance; many problems can be corrected through supervision and retraining.
- Reallocate resources or reassign staff to achieve a better fit between the task to be accomplished and the resources or staff available.
- Make plans and targets more realistic based on actual experience.
- Request additional information to further define a specific performance problem and the reasons for the problem.

Country Study 48-5 illustrates how indicators can be used to improve performance through self-monitoring.

Whatever actions are taken after a progress review, the effects of these actions should be considered at the next progress review.

48.7 Evaluation

Whereas monitoring focuses on program activities, evaluation focuses primarily on assessing progress toward achieving goals by fulfilling program objectives—taking a step back to look at the program as a whole. An evaluation is carried out at a specific time and should have a clear purpose.

Evaluation questions

Depending on the timing and purpose, evaluations may be of three types (Table 48-4)—

1. Needs assessment (situation analysis)
2. Formative evaluation (midterm review)
3. Summative evaluation (final evaluation)

A needs assessment or situation analysis is meant to appraise the pharmaceutical system or essential medicines program and to identify areas of strength and weakness (see Chapter 36). The purpose is to design a project to address major weaknesses in the system.

Formative and summative evaluations are more programmatic and concerned with answering some or all of the following questions—

- Is the program relevant? Are its goals and objectives appropriate to the present circumstances of the country and the pharmaceutical system?
- Is the program effective? Is it achieving satisfactory progress toward its stated goals and objectives? What are the reasons for success or failure?
- Are monitoring results representative? Do the results

Table 48-4   Types of evaluation

Type	Project stage	Purpose
Needs assessment (initial analysis)	Design	• Assess current situation • Develop program/project plan • Acquire baseline for comparison
Formative evaluation (midterm review)	Implementation	• Focus on implementation process • Assess progress toward goals and objectives • Improve program/project implementation
Summative evaluation (final evaluation)	Follow-up	• Assess program/project outputs • Measure impact of program/project • Demonstrate program/project impact to donors • Recommend future actions

Source: Adapted from García-Núñez 1992.

from the program's monitoring system reflect the actual situation?
- Is the program efficient? Are the effects of the program being achieved at an acceptable cost compared with alternative approaches to providing the same services?
- Is the program sustainable? Financially and institutionally, can the program continue with present levels of local inputs? If external financial and technical assistance is involved, can the program continue after it has stopped?
- Is the program having the intended impact? Does the program appear to be achieving or will it achieve its intended long-term health care benefits?
- What future changes should be made? What recommendations can be made for program development, new plans, or project assistance? Are new goals or objectives needed?

In practice, needs assessments, formative evaluations, and summative evaluations sometimes overlap. For example, the final evaluation for one project may also serve as the needs assessment for the next project.

Conducting an evaluation

Chapter 36 describes three approaches to assessment: self-assessment, limited assessment, and structured assessment. Structured assessment is the most comprehensive but requires the most resources. The choice of assessment approach depends on available financial and human resources, timing, sponsorship, and intended uses of the results.

Health program and health project evaluations are sometimes limited assessments, consisting primarily of

Country Study 48-5
Use of indicators for self-monitoring in rural Java

The twenty-nine health centers and 109 subcenters of Gunungkidul district in Java, Indonesia, suffer from periodic shortages of medicines, as do other health facilities. These shortages are caused by limited resources; increasing patient demand; and overprescribing of injections, antibiotics, and other medicines. To address this problem, the district health team in Gunungkidul undertook a series of activities to improve and control medicine use.

The team first surveyed medicine use with three prescribing indicators. Results showed extensive polypharmacy (4.2 medicines per case), a high percentage of patients receiving antibiotics (63 percent), and a very high percentage receiving injections (76 percent). The team explored these issues in randomly selected health centers using in-depth interviews, observation, focus group discussions, and questionnaires (see Chapter 28). From this information, a self-monitoring system was developed, pilot-tested, and implemented in all health centers in the district.

Each health center completes a monitoring form each month, based on a survey of thirty cases in each health center and subcenter. Results are discussed locally and forwarded to the District Health Office for review. Data

from the four subcenters under Widoyo Health Center are compared with those from the previous month (see the accompanying figure). Using this form, health center staff can easily determine whether each indicator has increased or decreased in each facility.

The continuity of the self-monitoring process is sustained by—

- Weekly staff meetings of the district team at which results are discussed
- Monthly district-level meetings for the heads of all health centers
- Regular feedback and occasional supervisory visits to health centers by members of the district team

After two years, an evaluation showed substantial improvements in all three indicators. Despite these changes in practice, the number of attendances at health centers had remained constant. Interviews with health workers showed improved attitudes toward the use of standard treatments, willingness to improve skills, and increased communication among health workers and the district team.

Source: Sunartono and Darminto 1995.

Local area monitoring form

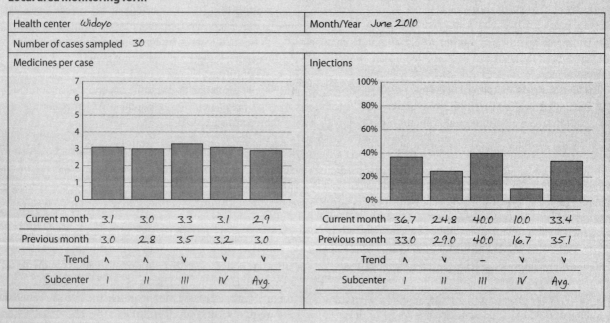

interviews, secondary analysis of existing monitoring and other data, and review of available documents. Increasingly, however, evaluations are expected to contain performance data indicating what services and outcomes are resulting from the program. The starting point for an evaluation should be the data collected through the monitoring system, but field surveys using standard pharmaceutical sector assessment indicators (WHO 2007) will contribute to a much more objective, credible, and useful evaluation.

Evaluation methods and tools

An evaluation is much like a research project. The usual considerations of research design apply, including defining the scope and questions for the evaluation, choosing evaluation methods, developing and testing data collection instruments, managing data collection, collating and analyzing data, interpreting results, and presenting the findings.

Methods of obtaining information include document review, key informant interviews, data collection from existing records, and prospective surveys. These methods and the steps involved in a structured assessment are discussed in detail in Chapter 36.

Knowledge, skill, and experience are required to design and execute a credible, comprehensive evaluation. See References and Further Readings for several sources that provide practical guidance on evaluation methods.

Who should evaluate?

When individuals involved in a program carry out an evaluation, they have the advantage of understanding its aims and design; however, such evaluations can be subjective and may miss important lessons. Therefore, outsiders are frequently asked to perform evaluations. Because they are disinterested, outsiders may be more objective and may bring fresh ideas. Outside evaluators might come from local universities, local nongovernmental organizations, international organizations, or organizations in other countries.

Combined insider and outsider evaluations have many advantages. The outsider, being ignorant of the local situation, can ask the difficult questions, and the insider often knows whether the true answer is being given. Having the insider view the program or project through the eyes of the outsider is also useful. The outsider benefits because the insider knows where the answers are to be found.

Resources required

Evaluation is an activity that goes beyond routine monitoring and requires staff, time, and funds to be earmarked for it. In the case of a specific program, funds for evaluation should be built into the original proposal. Careful costing should be performed, taking into account all proposed activities.

The budget should be prepared early in the planning process. A template presented in Table 48-5 can be used to develop a budget. It should be updated as additional information becomes available, such as personnel daily rates and the cost of translators, if needed. Some key considerations for the budget include—

- Team member time
  - Planning time—technical lead and administrative/logistics support
  - Team member time—preparatory, fieldwork, and report preparation
- Travel costs (as needed)
  - Airfare
  - Per diem
  - Visa costs
  - Telecommunications costs (phone/Internet access)
- Contracted services (as needed)
  - Local consultant
  - Translator(s)
  - Driver(s) and car(s)
  - Conference room facilities for the stakeholder workshop (room charge, food costs, and equipment rental)
- Miscellaneous charges
- Photocopies—reference materials, reports, etc.
- Postage (mailing documents prior to visit, for example)

48.8 Some common pitfalls in monitoring and evaluation

Although monitoring and evaluation are two distinct activities, they share certain common pitfalls—

Failure to identify the basic questions: All monitoring and evaluation activities should start with a clear statement of the questions they intend to answer. Without this, the information gathering has no focus.

Overambitiousness: Collecting too much information is perhaps the most common failing. A basic rule is that more information means greater expense, less accuracy, more time spent managing the data, less time spent interpreting the data and providing feedback, and less time for using the data.

Complexity: Monitoring systems should be as practical and streamlined as possible. Cumbersome systems have often been designed from the top down, with insufficient testing and input from staff involved in generating and using monitoring information.

Lack of integration with planning and implementation: Monitoring and evaluation activities should follow directly from program plans, link closely with ongoing

Table 48-5   Sample assessment budget template

Line Item		Rate (USD)	Unit	Quantity	Total (USD)
Labor (add lines for as many people as needed)					
Name	Title		/day	# days	
Name	Title		/day	# days	
Name	Title		/day	# days	
Name	Title		/day	# days	
Name	Title		/day	# days	
Subtotal U.S. Labor					Subtotal
Travel					
Travel – airfare	Destination		/trip	# fares at that rate	
Travel – airfare	Destination		/trip	# fares at that rate	
Travel – airfare	Destination		/trip	# fares at that rate	
Per diem	Destination		/days	# days	
Per diem	Destination		/days	# days	
Per diem	Destination		/days	# days	
Other costs – local travel	Destination		/trip	#	
Other costs – visa			/trip	#	
Other costs – misc.			/trip	#	
Subtotal travel					Subtotal
Subcontracts/outside services					
Conference room	Stakeholder workshop		/day	# days	
Coffee service	Stakeholder workshop		/person	# people	
Audiovisual equipment	Stakeholder workshop		/day	# days	
Driver and car			/day	# days	
Translators			/day	# days	
Subtotal subcontracts					Subtotal
Other costs					
Postage					
Communications					
Other					
Subtotal other					Subtotal
Total assessment budget					(Sum of subtotals)

implementation activities, and lead logically into the next round of planning.

Failure to build on existing systems: Existing information systems are never perfect, but considerable resources can be squandered trying to build a separate system instead of building on and strengthening existing systems.

Inadequate resources: Both monitoring and evaluation require considerable financial and human resources. It is generally better to seek additional resources or narrow the scope of assessment rather than try to gather too much information with too few resources.

Lack of objectivity: Management indicators introduce some objectivity into the assessment process; assessments based only on subjective information are less credible and less useful.

Jumping to wrong conclusions: Well-designed monitoring and evaluation systems allow some cross-checking of findings. Taken out of context, individual monitoring reports and evaluation observations can be misleading.

Lack of comparison data: Observations must be compared over time, against agreed-upon performance standards, among health units at the same level, or across countries. Good baseline data against which changes can be compared are especially useful, but to be valid, they must come from the same sources and have the same measures as the follow-up data. If the sources or measures are altered, it is difficult to say whether apparent changes (good or bad) are real or are a result of the assessment process.

Other common problems are failure to analyze data promptly, lack of feedback mechanisms to apply results, evaluations that do not gather new information, and monitoring done for the wrong reasons. Inappropriate reasons for monitoring and evaluation include doing the activity because of tradition or donor requirements and using the activity to try to resolve conflicts between donors and recipients or to get information to punish certain staff members. ∎

References and further readings

★ = Key readings.

Bhattarai, H. R., and H. Walkowiak. 2005. *Mombasa Antiretroviral Therapy Program: Monitoring and Evaluation Plan for Pharmaceutical and Laboratory Capacity Building Activities, February 2004.* Arlington, Va.: Management Sciences for Health, Rational Pharmaceutical Management Plus Program.

★ Brudon, P., J.-D. Rainhorn, and M. R. Reich. 1999. *Indicators for Monitoring National Drug Policies.* 2nd ed. Geneva: World Health Organization. <http://whqlibdoc.who.int/hq/1999/WHO_EDM_PAR_99.3_pp1-114.pdf>

CPM (Center for Pharmaceutical Management). 2003a. *Access to Essential Medicines: Tanzania, 2001.* Prepared for the Strategies for Enhancing Access to Medicines Program. Arlington, Va.: Management Sciences for Health. <http://www.msh.org/seam/reports/CR022304_SEAMWebsite_attach1.pdf>

★ ———. 2003b. *Defining and Measuring Access to Essential Drugs, Vaccines, and Health Commodities: Report of the WHO-MSH Consultative Meeting, Ferney-Voltaire, France, December 11–13, 2000.* Prepared for the Strategies for Enhancing Access to Medicines Program. Arlington, Va.: Management Sciences for Health. <http://www.msh.org/seam/reports/Access_Meeting_Ferney_Voltaire_1.pdf>

Federal Ministry of Health, Nigeria. 2010a. *Access to and Rational Use of Medicines at the Facility Level.* Abuja: Federal Ministry of Health. <http://apps.who.int/medicinedocs/documents/s16886e/s16886e.pdf>

———. 2010b. *Access to and Rational Use of Medicines at the Household Level.* Abuja: Federal Ministry of Health. <http://apps.who.int/medicinedocs/documents/s16887e/s16887e.pdf>

Fresle, D. A., A. Hardon, and C. Hodgkin. 2004. *How to Investigate the Use of Medicines by Consumers.* Geneva: World Health Organization and University of Amsterdam. <http://apps.who.int/medicinedocs/pdf/s6169e/s6169e.pdf>

García-Núñez, J. 1992. *Improving Family Planning Evaluation.* West Hartford, Conn.: Kumarian Press.

Global Fund to Fight AIDS, Tuberculosis and Malaria. 2006. *Monitoring and Evaluation (M&E) Toolkit: HIV/AIDS, Tuberculosis and Malaria.* 2nd ed. Addendum March 2008. <http://www.info.gov.za/issues/hiv/global_fund08_toolkit.pdf>

Global Partnership to Roll Back Malaria, Monitoring and Evaluation Reference Group. 2005. *Malaria Indicator Survey: Basic Documentation for Survey Design and Implementation.* Geneva: World Health Organization. <http://whqlibdoc.who.int/publications/2005/9241593571_eng.pdf>

LeMay, N. 2010. "Managing Information: Monitoring and Evaluation." In *Health Systems in Action: An eHandbook for Leaders and Managers,* S. Vriesendorp, L. de la Peza, C. P. Perry, J. B. Seltzer, M. O'Neil, S. Reimann, N. M. Gaul, et al., eds. Cambridge, Mass.: Management Sciences for Health. <http://www.msh.org/resource-center/health-systems-in-action.cfm>

MSH (Management Sciences for Health). 2001. Using Evaluation as a Management Tool. *The Manager.* Vol. 9. Boston: MSH. <http://erc.msh.org/mainpage.cfm?file=2.1.1.htm&language=english&module=info>

MSH/LMS (Management Sciences for Health/Leadership, Management and Sustainability Program). 2008. *From Vision to Action: A Guide on Monitoring and Evaluation for Facilitators of Leadership Development Programs.* Cambridge, Mass.: MSH/LMS.

Nachbar, N., J. Briggs, O. Aupont, L. Shafritz, A. Bongiovanni, K. Acharya, S. Zimicki, S. Holschneider, and D. Ross-Degnan. 2003. *Community Drug Management for Childhood Illness: Assessment Manual.* Arlington, Va.: Management Sciences for Health. <http://erc.msh.org/toolkit/toolkitfiles/file/C-DMCI%20Assessment%20Manual%20English.pdf>

Rational Pharmaceutical Management Plus Program (RPM Plus). 2009. *A Guide for Implementing the Monitoring-Training-Planning (MTP) Approach to Build Skills for Pharmaceutical Management.* Arlington, Va.: Management Sciences for Health.

★ Rational Pharmaceutical Management Project/Management Sciences for Health (MSH/RPM), Latin American and Caribbean Health and Nutrition Sustainability Project/University Research Corporation, and Regional Program on Essential Drugs/Pan American Health Organization. 1995. *Rapid Pharmaceutical Management Assessment: An Indicator-Based Approach.* Arlington, Va.: MSH/RPM. <http://erc.msh.org/newpages/english/toolkit/rpma.pdf>

ASSESSMENT GUIDE

Monitoring methods and systems

- Does a program or unit exist to monitor and evaluate pharmaceutical services? Who is responsible for monitoring and evaluation?
- Is monitoring based on program objectives and linked to specific activities? Are these objectives, along with output targets and performance targets, clearly communicated to concerned staff?
- Which of the following methods are used as sources of monitoring information: supervisory visits, routine reporting, sentinel reporting, special studies?
- How often are data collected? How are they used?
- Are monitoring results regularly reviewed and shared? How and with whom? Is feedback provided to concerned staff?
- What actions are taken when problems are detected through monitoring and evaluation?

Indicators

- Have performance indicators been established? If so, how were they established, and who was involved?

Do they include process, output, and impact indicators? Are they both qualitative and quantitative? Have performance targets been set?
- Have indicator pharmaceuticals been identified for indicators requiring medicine-specific information?

Evaluation

- Is progress toward achievement of program goals and objectives periodically assessed through formal evaluation?
- Does the evaluation begin with a clear statement of its basic question? Is this question used as a focus for information gathering?
- Which of the following methods are used to obtain information—review of existing monitoring reports, additional data collection, document review, interviews, field surveys using standard pharmaceutical assessment indicators?
- How is the evaluation team determined? Does it include insiders, outsiders, or both?

Sunartono, Y., and B. Darminto. 1995. From Research to Action: The Gunungkidul Experience. *Essential Drugs Monitor* 20:21–2.

Trap, B., C. H. Todd, H. Moore, and R. Laing. 2004. *Impact Assessment of Supervision on Medicines Management.* Presentation to the International Conference on Improving Use of Medicines, March 30–April 2, Chiang Mai, Thailand.

UNAIDS (Joint United Nations Programme on HIV/AIDS). 2002. *Monitoring and Evaluation Modules.* Geneva: UNAIDS. <http://data.unaids.org/Topics/M-E/me-modules-a4_en.pdf>

UNFPA (United Nations Population Fund). *The Programme Managers Planning, Monitoring and Evaluation Toolkit.* <http://www.unfpa.org/monitoring/toolkit.htm>

U.S. President's Emergency Plan for AIDS Relief (PEPFAR). 2009. *The President's Emergency Plan for AIDS Relief: Next Generation Indicators Reference Guide.* Version 1.1. Washington, D.C.: PEPFAR. <http://www.pepfar.gov/documents/organization/81097.pdf>

Valadez, J. J., W. Weiss, C. Leburg, and R. Davis. 2002. *Assessing Community Health Programs: A Participant's Manual and Workbook; Using LQAS for Baseline Surveys and Regular Monitoring.* Washington, D.C.: Child Survival Collaborations and Resources Group, CORE. <http://www.coregroup.org/storage/documents/Workingpapers/LQAS_Participant_Manual_L.pdf>

World Bank. 2004. *Monitoring and Evaluation: Some Tools, Methods and Approaches.* Washington, D.C.: World Bank. <http://go.worldbank.org/1K0M1NHOQ0>

★ WHO (World Health Organization). 2010. *Country Pharmaceutical Situations: Fact Book on WHO Level 1 Indicators, 2007.* Geneva: WHO. <http://apps.who.int/medicinedocs/documents/s16874e/s16874e.pdf>

★ ———. 2007. *WHO Operational Package for Assessing, Monitoring and Evaluating Country Pharmaceutical Situations: Guide for Coordinators and Data Collectors.* Geneva: WHO. <http://apps.who.int/medicinedocs/documents/s14877e/s14877e.pdf>

★ ———. 2006. *Using Indicators to Measure Country Pharmaceutical Situations: Fact Book on WHO Level I and Level II Monitoring Indicators.* Geneva: WHO. <http://www.who.int/medicines/publications/WHOTCM2006.2A.pdf>

———. 2004a. *Compendium of Indicators for Monitoring and Evaluating National Tuberculosis Programs.* Geneva: WHO. <http://whqlibdoc.who.int/hq/2004/WHO_HTM_TB_2004.344.pdf>

———. 2004b. *National AIDS Programmes: A Guide to Monitoring and Evaluating HIV/AIDS Care and Support.* Geneva: WHO. <http://www.who.int/hiv/pub/epidemiology/en/Care&SupportGuideE.pdf>

WHO/DAP (World Health Organization/Action Programme on Essential Drugs). 1993. *How to Investigate Drug Use in Health Facilities: Selected Drug Use Indicators.* Geneva: WHO/DAP. <http://whqlibdoc.who.int/hq/1993/WHO_DAP_93.1.pdf>

WHO/HAI (World Health Organization and Health Action International). 2008. *Measuring Medicine Prices, Availability, Affordability and Price Components.* 2nd ed. Geneva: WHO/HAI. <http://www.haiweb.org/medicineprices/manual/documents.html>

Ziganshina L. E., A. V Kuchaeva, F. F. Gatin, and L. M. Minnetdinova. 2004. *Pharmacoepidemiological Monitoring Helps in Reducing Neuroleptic-Induced Extrapyramidal Disorders at the Psychiatric Clinical Hospital in Tatarstan.* Presentation to the International Conference on Improving Use of Medicines, March 30–April 2, Chiang Mai, Thailand. <http://www.icium.org/icium2004/agenda.asp?keyword=Tatarstan>

Part I: Policy and economic issues	Part II: Pharmaceutical management	Part III: Management support systems
		Planning and administration
		Organization and management
		Information management
		48 Monitoring and evaluation
		49 Pharmaceutical management information systems
		50 Computers in pharmaceutical management
		Human resources management

CHAPTER 49

Pharmaceutical management information systems

SUMMARY

The planning process for a new or revised pharmaceutical supply system should include a pharmaceutical management information system (PMIS). The PMIS is an organized system for collecting, processing, reporting, and using information for decision making. Information for each subsystem is collected by means of—

- Record-keeping documents, a combination of registers, ledgers, and filing systems that typically are not circulated
- Information reporting forms, such as periodic status reports, that transmit data to other departments or levels for use in making management decisions
- Feedback reports, also called analytical reports, that are usually provided to the units that collected the data

Design or revision of a PMIS should be based on the differing information needs of users at each level of the system and should build on existing forms, reports, and procedures as much as possible. Any forms should be designed through a participatory process and field-tested with staff who will use them.

Other issues to consider include—

- Selection of indicators to monitor system performance and intended results (discussed in Chapter 48)
- Integration of the PMIS with other data collection systems
- Computerization at appropriate levels

A successful PMIS requires effective use of the information generated, which includes—

- Efficient data processing to reduce large amounts of data to a manageable number of key indicators, often in summary tables
- Presentation of information in graphic form to simplify interpretation
- Interpretation of information to identify trends and potential problems
- Appropriate use of technology (for example, e-mail, websites) to present and share information with a wider audience in less time
- Action in response to both positive and negative results
- Effective mechanisms to provide and receive feedback

49.1 Importance of a pharmaceutical management information system

A good PMIS provides the necessary information to make sound decisions in the pharmaceutical sector. Effective pharmaceutical management requires policy makers, program managers, and health care providers to monitor information related to patient adherence, drug resistance, availability of medicines and laboratory supplies, patient safety, postmarket intelligence, product registration, product quality, financing and program management, among other issues.

Coordinating the elements of a pharmaceutical supply system requires relevant, accurate, and timely information. Increased funding for HIV/AIDS, tuberculosis, and malaria programs has contributed to the need for accurate and timely information on a variety of parameters that affect the ability to conduct accurate quantification, procurement planning, budgeting, resource mobilization, and program management. In addition, multiple donors require different data reports, complicating program management. Because a pharmaceutical supply system uses many forms and other documents, managers often feel as if they are buried under mountains of data and that filling in the forms and producing reports ends their responsibility. They are unable to analyze and use many of these data for improved decision making. Many factors affect the usability of these data, including data quality and quantity (for example, missing or incomplete data or too much data to analyze effectively) or a manager's lack of analytical skill. Therefore, many managers find themselves making decisions based not on information but on intuition.

This chapter focuses on the practical aspects of organizing and managing a routine pharmaceutical management information system. It should be read in conjunction with Chapters 48 and 50. Chapter 48 puts information management into the broader context of monitoring and evaluating program performance against long-term goals and objectives and against medium-term workplans and targets. Chapter 50 presents a variety of tools for analyzing data produced by the PMIS.

Definition of a pharmaceutical management information system

The PMIS integrates pharmaceutical data collection and the processing and presentation of information that helps staff at all levels of a country's health system make evidence-based decisions to manage pharmaceutical services.

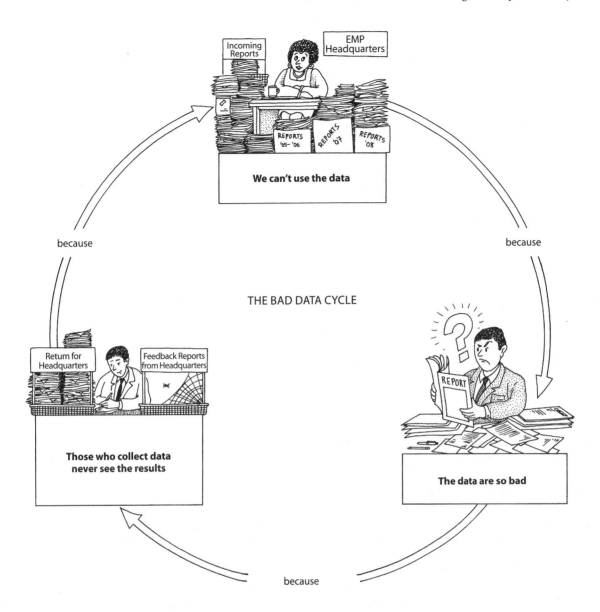

The features that distinguish a PMIS from a logistics management information system include—

- The incorporation of patient-specific data in addition to product-centered data
- A focus on decision making for pharmaceutical services, not just resupply
- Information on outcomes related to medicine use, such as adherence, adverse drug reactions, and pharmacovigilance, that affect pharmaceutical policy and selection decisions, including individualized treatment options
- Overarching information about the pharmaceutical sector, such as a summary of available professionals/personnel, outlets, legislation status, and distribution of personnel and facilities
- Varied data sources from the whole pharmaceutical sector, not just activities related to procurement and inventory management
- The ability to triangulate consumption data with clinical and patient-specific data

Functions of a pharmaceutical management information system

An effective PMIS is able to synthesize the large volume of data generated by pharmaceutical management operations. It then processes the data into information for use in planning activities, estimating demand, allocating resources, and monitoring and evaluating pharmaceutical management operations. This information is often in the form of a few key indicators. Indicators should be targeted toward staff at all levels so that they can monitor both their own performance and that of the units for which they are responsible.

Another important function of a PMIS is to improve accountability. Much of the recording and reporting in a PMIS is intended to create an audit trail for products as they enter or leave a pharmaceutical supply system.

Data and information

An understanding of the distinction between data and information is necessary to appreciate how a management information system functions. *Data* represent real-world observations or measurements. Data, in and of themselves, often have little value and take on meaning only after they are processed into a more usable form. *Information* is a meaningful aggregation of data that can be interpreted for a specific use. In other words, information is processed data that contains sufficient context to make it meaningful. The tools in Chapter 40 are intended primarily to aggregate data into useful information.

For example, data from a health center reveal that 3,000 co-trimoxazole tablets were distributed last month. Is this consumption level abnormal? Without analysis, this question would be difficult to answer. The data can be converted to information by comparing the 3,000 tablets distributed with the number distributed the previous month, say 1,000. This interpretation could then be expressed as a 300 percent increase in co-trimoxazole distribution. But information is indicative, not prescriptive. The manager must analyze the complete context and make decisions.

In a PMIS, data are routinely collected on a common set of indicators, usually expressed as proportions or rates. Some of these indicators measure performance toward objectives, whereas others may measure process efficiency.

The information systems pyramid

Viewing information systems as a pyramid may be helpful (Figure 49-1). At the base of the pyramid are operational systems. These include subsystems—procurement, distribution, financial management, medicine use—that handle data at the transactional level. Every item that moves in and out of inventory must be tracked, and decisions must be made about how much to supply to a health facility, when to reorder, and how much to bill. This level is characterized by a high volume of data that must be recorded and processed, usually daily and at the time of transaction. Data recording accuracy is very important at this level because every unit of medicine matters.

The next level of the pyramid is formed by management information systems (MIS). These systems typically provide summaries of operational data on a periodic basis (for example, monthly or quarterly) to help managers of specific departments monitor the performance of their units. Annual reports often summarize information on key indicators from many different operational subsystems, such as

Figure 49-1 The information systems pyramid

procurement, personnel, financial management, or stock control (see the sample report format in Annex 49-1). Information provided by the MIS helps managers answer questions such as the following—

- How do expenditures compare with the budget at a given level of operation?
- How effective is the inventory control system in eliminating stockouts and cutting stock losses?
- What is the delivery performance over the last period?
- Are the trends generally favorable, or are indicators worsening?

Information at this level may demonstrate reduced accuracy because errors might be introduced during the consolidation of data, so a certain level of variation is normal.

The highest level of the information systems pyramid is the executive level. At this level, the system further summarizes management information for use in strategic planning and policy making. The executive level of the MIS typically generates program-wide information on how effective the organization is in accomplishing its mission. Systems at this level track a limited number of indicators, less frequently. They provide users with the tools, such as total cost analysis and price comparison analysis (see Chapter 40), to perform periodic queries on data at every information-system level, either to investigate the causes of problems or to perform "what if" analyses to test the effect of changes in strategy. Some of the strategic questions that can be answered with executive-level information include the following—

- Should the transport and delivery function be contracted out?

Table 49-1   Information users and information needs

Level and function	Users	Information needs
National		
Selection	National essential medicines committee	Morbidity patterns
		Standard treatment strategies
Procurement	Procurement unit	Medicine-use rates
		Lead times
		Supplier performance
		Prices
		Funds available for procurement
Medicine-use education	Training unit	Number of staff trained in essential medicines use
		Number of public education messages developed and campaigns conducted
Financial management	Finance unit	Operating costs
		Revenues
		Value of inventory
		Stock turnover rates
		Stock fund growth or loss
Provincial/district		
Warehousing	Medical stores manager	Medicine-use rates
		Maximum and minimum stock levels
		Lead times for requisitions from the national level
		Shelf life
		Warehouse maintenance and equipment needs
		Stock losses
Distribution	Logistics manager	Distribution schedules
		Vehicle-use records
		Maintenance and fuel costs
Facility		
Use	Medical director, pharmacist	Prescription patterns
		Patient adherence
		Pharmaceutical availability
		Patient load
Inventory control	Storekeeper	Maximum and minimum stock levels
		Lead times for requisitions
		Prices
		Medicine-use rates
		Shelf life
		Cold-storage temperature variations

- Could savings be obtained by combining orders with those of another large buyer?
- Which districts are the best served?
- Would targeting underserved areas with more marketing and training be worthwhile?

49.2 Meeting the information needs of users with different requirements

Staff at every level and position use information to make decisions that affect the overall functioning of a pharmaceutical supply system. For example, a storekeeper can monitor the temperature chart on a vaccine refrigerator and save thousands of dollars' worth of vaccine from spoiling when the refrigerator begins to malfunction. The chief pharmacist may be unaware that large quantities of a medicine are due to expire in the warehouse. But if the pharmacist had information about expiration dates and could match that

information with data on the stock levels in health facilities, medicines could be dispatched to facilities that are running low, thereby averting waste of money and medicines.

A good PMIS alerts staff to problems and triggers critical actions at all levels. Usually, this systemwide usage means that a strict separation does not exist between data collectors and information users. Analysis and use of data are encouraged at every level of the system (see Country Study 49-1). Table 49-1 summarizes key information users and some of their most important information needs at each level of the system.

49.3 Typical components of a pharmaceutical management information system

The operational systems level of a PMIS can be examined further using the analogy of the information systems pyramid. This level typically contains four subsystems: selection,

Country Study 49-1
Using the Electronic Dispensing Tool to manage pharmaceutical information at different levels of the health care system

Although all medicines need to be carefully managed, antiretrovirals (ARVs) need special attention because they are expensive and because health care professionals in developing countries lack long-term experience with them. As part of a lifetime treatment regimen, patients must be carefully monitored for their adherence to the medicines. To maintain an uninterrupted supply of ARVs, pharmacy staff must collect timely information on medicine consumption and patient characteristics so they can accurately forecast the amount of medicines needed.

As antiretroviral therapy (ART) programs began scaling up in developing countries, assessments showed that pharmacies in ART centers did not have adequate systems in place to gather the needed data. What record keeping existed was done through manual registers that were impractical. This lack of adequate systems prevented staff from maintaining a patient's medicine consumption history and compiling the information on medicines and patients needed to support management decisions. In addition, the cost of these expensive medicines is often shared by multiple donor agencies that require different reports at different times.

The Rational Pharmaceutical Management Plus Program developed a simple, Microsoft Access–based electronic tool for pharmacy staff to use to track patients and inventory. The Electronic Dispensing Tool maintains the basic patient profile, a history of medicines dispensed, and other information that is relevant to the patient, such as adverse drug reactions. The tool also maintains consumption records that are needed to quantify pharmaceutical needs and to make other program management decisions.

Summary of data and reports

Commodity management
- ARV and opportunistic infections medicine inventory, stock consumption, short-dated stock

Dispensing
- Medication dispensing history
- Patient characteristics (other medicines, allergies)
- Change of regimen

Patient management
- Basic patient profile with contact address
- Patient schedule of visits
- List of patients (for example, by different donor support, by age, by gender)
- Current status of patient (e.g., active, lost to follow-up, deceased)

- Number of active patients by regimen
- Number of new patients by regimen
- Age, weight, sex distribution of patients
- Patient enrollment trend

Examples

The tool is used at different levels of the health care system to manage inventory and patient information in multiple countries in Africa and the Caribbean. Below are examples of three levels of use in Kenya—

- Many ART centers use the tool in adherence monitoring by regularly printing out the list and contact information of the patients who missed their scheduled appointments. Pharmacy staff, social workers, or nurses can then check up on the patients. Facilities also track various trends in the ART program, such as the rate of patients starting ART and the rate of patient attrition. ART sites use this information as a basis for decision making and for developing interventions; for example, Kenyatta Hospital in Nairobi changed its protocol after data identified that 63 percent of inpatients started on ARVs were dropping out of the ART program.
- The Eastern Deanery AIDS Relief Program, a faith-based organization in Nairobi, has nine satellite ART sites serving more than 5,000 patients but manages the inventory on one personal computer, using the Electronic Dispensing Tool. Each satellite site has a person responsible for record keeping; drivers pick up the previous day's data every morning, and the data are entered into the database at the central data management office. Using the tool, the data management team is able to create different reports for management and for monitoring and evaluation; in addition, the organization must submit different reports to the Ministry of Health and to donors. Once a month, the data are reconciled with the pharmacy inventory. Eventually, each site will have its own computer for individual data entry.
- The Mission for Essential Drugs and Supplies (MEDS) provides medicines and supplies to facilities serving tens of thousands of patients on ART all over Kenya. RPM Plus Kenya closely monitors MEDS ARV distribution activities by using the tool to help track pharmaceutical consumption, which is needed to quantify orders for all of its client sites. In addition, this tool has been used to create reports needed for monitoring and evaluation efforts.

procurement, distribution, and use. Information is necessary within each of these subsystems to efficiently manage finances, pharmaceutical stocks, and personnel.

The documents that form the basis of the information system can be grouped into three areas: record-keeping documents, information-reporting forms, and feedback reports.

Record-keeping documents

A combination of registers, ledgers, and filing systems (manual, computerized, or both) is used to maintain data about the activities of a specific organizational unit. Normally, records stay in one place and are not circulated to other departments or levels. An efficient record-keeping system enables its users to quickly retrieve information about activities and simplifies the job of aggregating data for reporting purposes.

Data compilation/aggregation tools

These tools are in specially designed formats (manual or computerized) that facilitate data processing. Examples include tally sheets, summary registers, and computer programs to compile data.

Data-reporting forms

Forms for reporting information differ from the data records described above because they are designed for transmission to other parts of an organization. Copies of forms filed at various points in the distribution network help establish the audit trail for tracking the flow of pharmaceuticals and funds. These forms typically include requisition/ issue vouchers to document stock transfers and periodic status reports, such as monthly or annual reports (see Annex 49-1). Status reports can be descriptive and principally qualitative forms, or they can be standardized, quantitative forms designed to transmit data on specific indicators to others. In a standardized reporting chain, individual health facilities typically report to district offices. These, in turn, report to provincial offices, which report to the central office to project future pharmaceutical needs, revise budgets, and assess medicine use at the central level.

Feedback reports

Analytical reports are produced from data reported by other units. These feedback reports have two main purposes: to address issues highlighted by status reports, and to analyze how each reporting unit has performed relative to other similar units. The reports are usually fed back to the units that first collected and provided the data. Experience has shown that regular and corrective feedback is one of the best ways to improve data quality and reporting compliance.

When staff members see that their data are being used, they become much more conscientious about data collection and reporting.

A good information system also includes procedures to govern the use and flow of information up and down the pharmaceutical supply network. These procedures typically include details about how and when to collect data, the schedule for report preparation, and to whom the documents should be sent. Figure 49-2 illustrates the flow of documents in a basic PMIS, and Table 49-2 describes the types of documents prepared and maintained.

If parts of the information system are computerized, clear guidelines must exist for the entry, maintenance, and archiving of data, as well as for the preparation and distribution of standard feedback reports. In addition, procedures are often needed for conducting periodic analyses and sharing data among different levels of the organization.

Data collection methods can take various forms in a PMIS. Although routine collection of data from all levels and facilities for monthly, quarterly, or annual reports is most common, sample surveys, rapid assessment techniques, and sentinel reporting systems are also important (see Chapter 48). In many cases, these collection methods provide data for decision-making support that are more reliable than routine data.

49.4 Steps in designing or revising a pharmaceutical management information system

When a new pharmaceutical supply program is started or an old program is revised, the basic planning should include establishing a complete information system. All necessary forms should be available, and all staff should be trained to use these forms before pharmaceuticals start moving through the system. Without this preparation, recording of pharmaceutical consumption and forecasting of medicine needs quickly breaks down. The principal steps in designing or revising a PMIS are shown in Box 49-1.

A PMIS should be based on the information needs of the users at each level. To the extent possible, it should build on existing forms, reports, and procedures. Adding as few new forms and data elements as possible and removing unnecessary forms and reports will simplify the system and increase the chances that information will be reliably recorded and reported. In some cases, worksheets may need to be developed to facilitate the collation of data from records into summary report forms.

Users need to be empowered through procedures and training to perform appropriate data analysis, understand key trends within their own units, and use information for decision making at the local level. Depending solely on feedback reports from higher levels may not be effective because

Figure 49-2   Flow of documents in a basic supply system PMIS

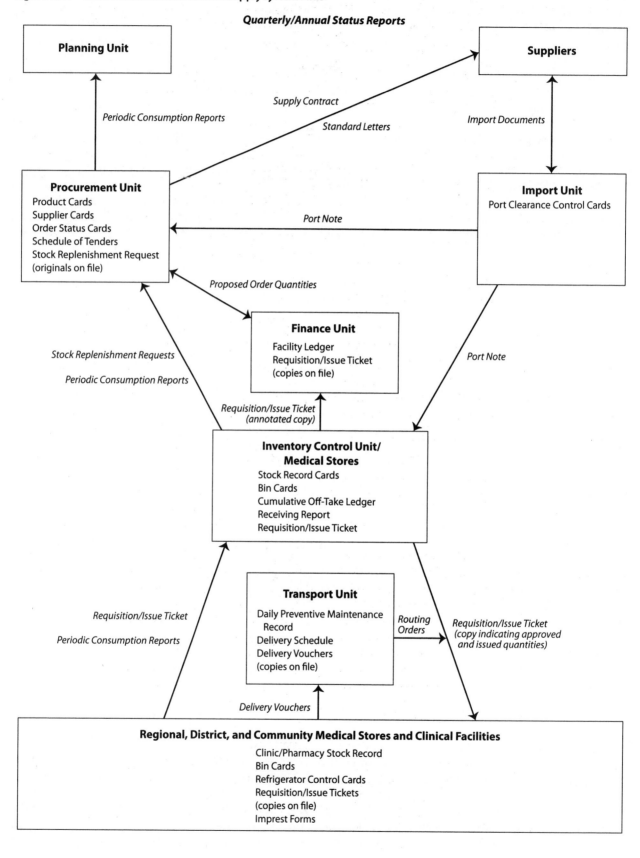

Table 49-2   Forms and records for a basic supply system PMIS

Type of document	Originated/maintained by
Forms	
Supply contract—statement of the terms of supply, usually publicized with the call for offers, specifying exact pharmaceutical requirements, dosage forms, quality standards, labeling and packaging, delivery date, and other supply details	Procurement unit
Standard letters—form letters used in correspondence with suppliers to provide and obtain information regarding outstanding orders	Procurement unit
Import documents—used to confirm the supply contract, guarantee payment, and certify the quantity and quality of shipment contents, and to provide other types of trade information	Procurement, supplier, shipper, banks
Port note—notification from import unit to procurement and medical stores that a specific shipment has arrived and has been cleared from port	Import unit
Receiving report—notification to inventory control that a specific shipment has been received; indicates damages, short shipments, and other problems	Medical stores
Requisition/issue ticket—request for specific quantities of standard items from medical stores; amended by inventory control if stocks are low; orders filled by medical stores; copies provide audit trail; return copy is packing slip	Medical stores, health facilities
Stock replenishment request—request to procurement to begin the procurement cycle for specific items; sent at reorder level or reorder interval	Inventory control
Proposed order quantities—proposed order quantities for a single procurement cycle; finance unit estimates cost and adjusts if needs exceed available funds	Procurement
Routing order—delivery order for drivers; provides a record of vehicle movements, indicates the order of deliveries (planned to minimize travel)	Transport unit
Delivery voucher—signed receipt indicating that a specific shipment of pharmaceuticals has been delivered intact	Medical stores, health facilities
Imprest forms—simplified supply requisitions for use by smaller clinical facilities and individual health workers	Health centers and workers
Records	
Product cards—product specifications and supplier history for each item; used to prepare bid specifications and select suppliers	Procurement unit
Supplier cards—record of experiences with individual suppliers, including delivery record, adherence to contract, pharmaceutical and packaging quality, and other performance factors; used in supplier selection	Procurement unit
Order status cards—used to monitor the status of outstanding orders to reduce lead times, supplier defaults, and port delays	Procurement unit
Schedules of tenders—summaries of offers from each supplier on each product in a tender purchase	Procurement unit
Port clearance control cards—used for a manual control system to monitor port-clearing activities and thereby shorten port delays	Import unit
Stock record cards—cards or a ledger used to record stock balances, issues, receipts, and outstanding orders; essential in inventory decisions such as when and how much to order	Medical stores, health facilities
Bin cards—similar to stock record cards but kept in medical stores with the physical stock to record supply movement in and out of the stores	Medical stores
Facility ledger, cumulative off-take ledger—records indicating the quantity and cost of pharmaceuticals issued to individual facilities; used for budgeting, billing, and/or estimating future needs	Finance unit, inventory control
Daily preventive maintenance record—checklist of daily vehicle maintenance activities; used to promote preventive maintenance	Transport unit
Delivery schedule—monthly timetable for requisitions and deliveries; prepared for maximum staff and vehicle efficiency	Transport unit
Refrigerator control cards—temperature and maintenance log to ensure proper cold-chain storage	Clinical facilities
Reports	
Quarterly and annual status reports—to national level	
Feedback reports—from national level to warehouse/facilities	

> **Box 49-1**
> **Steps in designing or revising a PMIS**
>
> 1. Identify information users.
> 2. Identify information needs for each user, including selected indicators (see Chapter 48).
> 3. Review existing record-keeping and reporting procedures.
> 4. Match existing information with information needs to identify overlaps, gaps, and items that can be deleted.
> 5. Draft record-keeping and reporting procedures to fill the gaps.
> 6. Develop tools and procedures to help users do simple data analysis and present key trends.
> 7. Prepare or modify the instruction manual.
> 8. Field-test any newly designed or revised records and report forms, including instruction manuals.
> 9. Make modifications to record-keeping forms, reporting forms, and/or the instruction manual, based on field-test results.
> 10. Develop procedures for preparing feedback reports.
> 11. Train information users at all levels in data collection, reporting procedures, and use of information.
> 12. If the PMIS is computerized, provide training for staff in general computer use and specific applications.
> 13. Monitor the system's implementation, including the quality and regularity of reporting.
> 14. Adapt the records, report forms, and software as information needs evolve.
> 15. Continuously monitor the relevancy and sufficiency of the existing PMIS and make necessary changes through a participatory process.

of delays and a lack of local context. For example, a storekeeper may wish to maintain a graph of the average number of days out of stock of selected products to see whether stock control is improving or getting worse rather than wait for someone at a higher level to send graphs drawn from local data.

It is essential to field-test any newly designed records and report forms with staff from the units that will eventually use the new system. Staff at actual work sites can almost always suggest better ways of doing things, as well as point out places where the new forms or procedures are unclear. Computerized procedures and feedback report formats should also be field-tested and revised. Chapter 50 contains more information about computerization.

49.5 Key issues in designing or revising a pharmaceutical management information system

Overall, political support for making changes is crucial. Many other key issues need to be considered to ensure the success and sustainability of the PMIS.

Involve users in design and pilot testing. The usefulness and sustainability of a PMIS increase with user involvement. To embrace the system, users need to know how the PMIS can answer their questions and solve their problems. In addition, users should be trained to manage the system's evolution.

Be selective in choosing indicators. To save time and money, use proxy indicators when they make data collection more efficient and are likely to be accurate. For example, although knowing the average number of days each medicine is out of stock would be useful, reporting the number of pharmaceuticals out of stock at a particular moment may be more practical. Chapter 36 introduces the concept of performance indicators, and Chapter 48 discusses their use in monitoring. In general, indicators should be designated in areas such as selection, procurement efficiency, product and service quality, distribution efficiency (stockouts, overstocks), rational use, financial management, human resources management (training activities, for example), and reporting compliance with the PMIS. Table 49-3 illustrates a set of indicators for rational medicine use and the associated information for data collection for a PMIS in Namibia.

Strive for representativeness, not comprehensiveness. A comprehensive set of data appears to provide more accurate information, but, in fact, a statistically representative set of data can provide equally good information for less cost and in a shorter time. Representativeness can be achieved by using sentinel data collection systems or sampling methodologies either to select subsets of facilities to survey or to monitor lot quality to focus on the best- and worst-performing service units.

Choose appropriate data collection methods. When possible, use available data sources and rapid assessment methods to collect information on medicine use at the health service and household levels. Qualitative data collection methods include focus group discussions, in-depth interviews, structured observation, questionnaires, and simulated patient surveys (see Chapter 28). Use supervisors to gather observational data, complete checklists, and

**Table 49-3   Proposed PMIS indicators for building a pharmaceutical supply system in Namibia:
Rational use of medicines and quality of care**

Indicator	Numerator/denominator	Data collector	Where data collected	Tool	Level	Frequency
Percentage of vital reference materials available in the pharmacy	Number present/total number	Pharmacy assistant (PA)/hospital pharmacist	Reference books	Tally sheet 1	District, regional, national	Annually
Percentage of essential reference materials available in the pharmacy	Number present/total number	PA/hospital pharmacist	Reference books	Tally sheet 1	District, regional, national	Annually
Average number of medicines per outpatient prescription	Number of medicines prescribed/number of outpatient prescriptions	PA/hospital pharmacist	30 outpatient prescriptions	Tally sheet 3	District, regional, national	6 months
Percentage of generic names per outpatient prescription	Number of medicines prescribed generically/number of medicines prescribed	PA/hospital pharmacist	30 outpatient prescriptions	Tally sheet 3	District, regional, national	6 months
Percentage of outpatient prescriptions with an antibiotic	Number of prescriptions with an antibiotic/number of prescriptions	PA/hospital pharmacist	30 outpatient prescriptions	Tally sheet 3	District, regional, national	6 months
Percentage of therapeutics committee meetings held and minuted out of number planned	Number of therapeutics committee meetings held and minuted/number of therapeutics committee meetings planned	PA/hospital pharmacist	Therapeutics committee meeting minutes		District, regional, national	Quarterly
Percentage of patients returning on time to collect refill prescriptions (ART)	Number of patients returning on time for refill/number of patients expected to collect refill	PA/hospital pharmacist	ART records		District, regional, national	Quarterly

Source: Lates 2005.

provide immediate feedback and support to staff. Finally, use sentinel systems to generate higher-quality but fewer data from a subset of health facilities (see Chapter 48).

Common errors at different points in the recording and reporting process are noted in Table 49-4, which also describes common sources of problems and possible solutions.

Integrate the PMIS with other data collection systems. System integration is particularly important in the health sector when information about service delivery is being collected. Health workers are often overburdened by multiple or vertical reporting systems for immunizations, family planning, disease control programs, and so on. In this case, try to collect data through existing reporting systems or other means, such as medical record reviews and sample surveys, rather than by introducing additional routine reports.

One important factor for computerization is the adoption of standard coding systems for medicines, health facilities, diseases, and geographic areas. A uniform coding system is essential to ensure efficient aggregation across facilities or geographical regions. In addition, standard data file structures often need to be developed to promote compatibility among different software programs in use (see Chapter 50).

Develop practical analysis methods to facilitate data interpretation and use. Users should be taught the graphics techniques described in Section 49.7 for use with two to four key indicators and should use them to monitor their own performance. Worksheets can help staff aggregate data and calculate indicators manually from existing records.

Computerize at appropriate levels. Achieving the right mix of computer and manual systems is critical, as is ensuring that they are fully integrated so that units without computers can produce their reports manually. Keep in mind the adage: "If you can do it by hand, the computer might make it more efficient, but if you can't, the computer is likely to make it worse." Decisions about computerization should take the following factors into account—

- Availability of a dependable source of electricity, secure physical space, and adequate consumables (for example, paper, ink, CD-ROMs, backup media).
- Local human resources to support computer hardware and software installation, maintenance, and training.
- Volume of data to be processed. If the volume of data is manageable manually, computerization will only add to the cost. Computers are useful if storage

Table 49-4   Improving recording and reporting accuracy

Kinds of problems	Sources of problems	Possible solutions
Errors in recording	Too many data items are on a single page	Limit number of data items per page Use checklists wherever possible
	Data items are not clearly labeled	Label data items in large letters
	No instructions exist for data entry	Provide instructions for each data entry
	Data need to be recopied several times on different forms	Use carbons if multiple copies are necessary
	Data are not verified for accuracy	Make periodic checks on the validity and accuracy of data
Errors in deciphering	Entries are illegible	Use checklist to avoid illegible handwriting
	Data entries are abbreviated because of insufficient entry space	Leave sufficient space to avoid abbreviations
Errors in tabulating	Columns are too long	Add summary lines in long columns
	A single page has too many columns	Limit number of columns to five per page
	There is no place to tally page summaries	Add a sheet for page summaries

and retrieval or compilation of a large database is required.

- Complexity of analysis required. Computers are excellent tools that can be used to solve complex mathematical problems and produce various analytical reports, including graphical representations.

Use software appropriate for needs. The software needs of a PMIS will depend on the size of the data set and complexity of analysis. For example, a spreadsheet program may be adequate, or a database application may be the better choice, depending on the size of the data set and the types of reports needed. A spreadsheet is simpler to set up and navigate, but it is primarily designed for manipulating numbers and making calculations. Spreadsheets are very useful for doing "what if" analyses and generating graphs and are more straightforward to understand. However, a spreadsheet usually requires more redundancy in data entry, which becomes increasingly difficult to handle as the number of records increases. In addition, querying data sets is difficult in a spreadsheet. Keep in mind, however, that data can be converted from a spreadsheet to a database and vice versa.

A database program is designed for collecting, storing, and organizing data. It is more complex to set up, but data entry is generally easier and can be better controlled and validated than in a spreadsheet. A database program has more powerful querying features, which facilitate the manipulation of complex data. Modern databases, usually called relational databases, have improved techniques to efficiently store data that are complexly related. Getting the database structure right is critical to having an effective system, so expert advice may be necessary.

Any system needs to be able to create graphics, such as charts (as discussed in Section 49.7). A Web-based system, as shown in Country Study 49-2, allows many different facilities at different levels of the health care system to access needed information and other resources easily. Software can be an off-the-shelf package or a package custom designed in-house or by consultants. Developing software in-house is a tempting option when an off-the-shelf package does not appear to meet all needs. However, developing software in-house or through a consultant is a difficult task that requires very careful planning. In most cases, using an off-the-shelf package and compromising on some of the desired functions may be a better solution.

Ensure that information is communicated effectively. Key decisions need to be made about what, how, and with what frequency data will be communicated to higher levels. Do all data need to be transmitted and analyzed at a higher level, or only summary data? Do raw data need to be reviewed by line managers before being submitted for analysis, or can line managers rely on analyzed feedback from a central information clearinghouse? For computerized systems, can some data be entered in decentralized computer centers and transmitted in batches, using disks, or through the Internet? Can parts of the system be designed for online use from remote locations? However data are transmitted, careful attention must be paid to setting up and monitoring reporting schedules so that timely information can be produced.

Hire or train staff with appropriate skills. Hiring and keeping knowledgeable and skilled human resources to maintain a PMIS is a challenge; skilled staff members may take positions in the private sector, where remuneration is generally better. Knowledge and understanding of the health system in general and the pharmaceutical management system in particular are important attributes in someone who is designing or overseeing a PMIS. The level of technological expertise needed will depend on the system, but the person should have a good understanding of information system design principles. Being able to communicate with decision makers to determine the information requirements is more important than simply being a computer expert.

If the required expertise is not available in-house, contracting out the development of a PMIS and computer system may be the best option. Employees already working in pharmaceutical management should also participate in the design of the PMIS; however, some people are reluctant to learn a computerized system, which may be a constraint. Box 49-2 reproduces a job description, including the qualifications and skills, for a PMIS manager in Kenya.

49.6 Implementing a pharmaceutical management information system

Implementation of PMIS changes should be more successful with proper field-testing, phased implementation, flexibility, and adequate training. Field-testing should involve not only the well-performing sites but, more important, the average or worse-performing sites.

A modular approach may be useful. Develop stand-alone modules that can be applied and tested as they are completed, rather than developing the entire system from start to finish before the users ever see it. These modules can later be integrated to form the complete system.

Flexibility is also important. Build in flexibility to add or reduce data elements, or change reporting formats, data entry screens, and feedback reports. Staff members need to

---

Country Study 49-2
Building a data management information system for MDR-TB surveillance in Brazil

In Brazil, the Hélio Fraga National TB Reference Center, the National TB Program, and the Rational Pharmaceutical Management Plus Program developed a new data management information system as part of a larger effort to decentralize surveillance of multi-drug-resistant tuberculosis (MDR-TB) to the states. The PMIS tracks treatment of MDR-TB patients—diagnosis, case management, and pharmaceutical provision and distribution—including second-line medicines.

The process of creating the PMIS included a stakeholder working group with representatives from decentralized sites that developed and field-tested standardized procedures, defined indicators, and implemented epidemiological and operational reporting. The information

system is Internet-based, so all tools and reports are available online, making information available to users at all levels of the system (see figure below). The MDR-TB surveillance PMIS was designed to integrate into existing governmental health surveillance systems.

The Internet-based components of the PMIS include—

- Case notification data sheet
- Quarterly follow-up data sheet
- Follow-up data sheet after treatment success
- Request for MDR-TB medicines
- Quarterly report on stock turnover for MDR-TB medicines
- Customized reports
- Data extraction tool

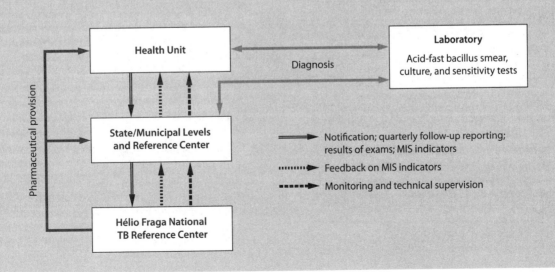

Box 49-2
Job description for a pharmaceutical management information officer in Kenya

Overall responsibilities

The Pharmaceutical Management Information Officer provides assistance to selected Ministry of Health (MOH) divisions in planning and coordinating information on reproductive health and HIV/AIDS commodities for health facilities in line with the Kenya Health Sector Strategic Plan. The Pharmaceutical Management Information Officer assists in strengthening the capacity of pharmacy and laboratory staff in terms of information management for medicines and commodities at both the national and service delivery levels. The Pharmaceutical Management Information Officer also assists with the monitoring of project activities, including collecting and analyzing data related to key indicators established within the MIS, identifying and reporting problems, implementing solutions in coordination with other members of staff, and writing periodic activity reports.

Specific responsibilities

1. Act as the commodity information management liaison to MOH and Rational Pharmaceutical Management Plus (RPM Plus) staff.
2. Support RPM Plus staff to perform the commodity information management functions, which includes but is not limited to the following—

   a. Receive and collate commodity consumption data and assist with analyzing data related to key indicators established within the MIS
   b. Identify and report problems; implement solutions in collaboration with staff from the divisions
   c. Support activities to ensure quality of data
   d. Develop reports that will inform commodity resupply to sites, stock status audits, and quantification
   e. Support the database reporting routines for reporting to stakeholders
   f. Mentor division staff in their monitoring and evaluation (M&E) and MIS roles

3. Participate in commodity distribution planning for and in collaboration with MOH divisional counterpart staff.
4. Participate in commodity management systems strengthening and training activities that target staff in the public health sector–assisted sites. Troubleshoot problems and facilitate progress as necessary.

5. Support the MOH staff in the adaptation, updating, implementation, and dissemination of commodity management standard operating procedures and MIS and M&E tools with the goal of ensuring the effective ordering, storage, distribution, and use of pharmaceuticals and commodities in support of selected priority health care delivery programs.
6. Participate in supportive supervision, M&E, and site assessment activities as conducted by staff of the public-sector program divisions and RPM Plus staff.
7. Participate in the development and submission of appropriate monthly and other ad hoc technical and progress reports, achievements, and challenges faced in implementing the MIS to stakeholders on a timely basis.
8. Assist in the implementation and documentation of Kenya public health sector program activities with specific reference to the information management of the pharmaceutical and laboratory commodities.

Qualifications

1. Graduate degree in public health, pharmacy, or other health-related field or relevant equivalent experience.
2. Experience in pharmaceutical and commodity management systems is preferred.
3. Knowledge and skills in pharmaceutical and commodity management for ART is an added advantage.
4. Long-term working resident experience in Kenya with an understanding of the Kenya public health system.
5. Demonstrated ability to write lucid technical reports.
6. Experience in strengthening pharmaceutical management systems, including pharmaceutical policy development and implementation, supply chain management, dispensing pharmaceuticals, and counseling patients, is preferred.
7. Excellent interpersonal skills and demonstrated ability to interact professionally with a diverse staff, clients, and consultants.
8. Proficiency in English and Kiswahili, including reading, writing, and speaking skills, is preferred.
9. Computer skills, including spreadsheet, database, word processing, presentation, and electronic mail; Microsoft Office preferred. Knowledge of other graphics packages is an added advantage.
10. Ability and willingness to travel extensively in Kenya.

adapt a PMIS and perform ad hoc analyses as information needs evolve.

Many electronic tools exist that can be used in implementing a PMIS; for example, personal computers are now being used in even the most resource-limited settings, and special software packages are being developed to facilitate data analysis and reporting in pharmaceutical management (Country Study 49-1). In addition, other technologies such as personal digital assistants and geographic information systems are being used as tools in MIS (see Chapter 50).

Finally, staff at all levels need sufficient training for their roles in the information system, which may include design and development of an MIS, data collection, computerized data processing, and use of data.

49.7 From information to action

The most fundamental element of a successful PMIS is the effective use of the data generated by the system. Figure 49-3 illustrates the process of transforming data into information and interpreting them for use in decision making. The key steps are processing data, presenting information, interpreting information, and taking action.

Processing data

Data processing can take many forms, ranging from simple data aggregation by district, calculation of averages, or trend analysis over time to the use of sophisticated statistical techniques such as analysis of variance. The objective of data processing is to reduce large amounts of data to a manageable amount, often using summary tables. It is important to remember that a computer is not necessary for data processing. Tally sheets can be developed to help users gather data from many sources and to compute totals, counts, and averages.

Presenting information

Some people have difficulty interpreting information presented in tables. Simple techniques for graphing tabular data can help simplify interpretation. However, complex tables with many elements are not good candidates to present graphically. A computer spreadsheet or graphics program can make creating these presentations easier and clearer. Some common graph types and their uses are—

- Bar graphs: comparison of values for different items or for the same item at different physical locations
- Line graphs: presentation of trends over time
- Pie charts: demonstration of the relationships among the parts of a whole
- Maps: demonstration of the geographic distribution of indicators

Figure 49-4 illustrates some common graph styles and their key uses.

Figure 49-3 PMIS information stages

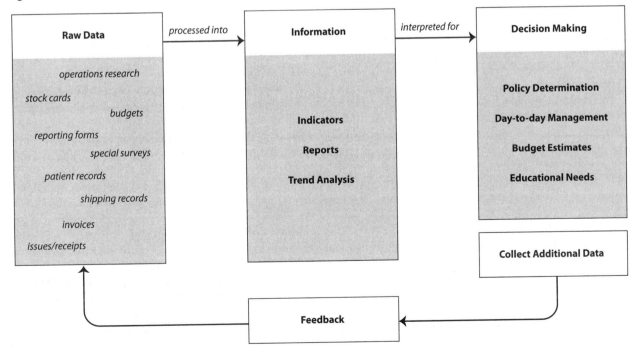

Figure 49-4   Graph styles

Bar Graph

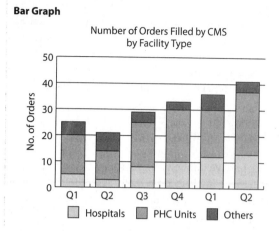

Pie Chart

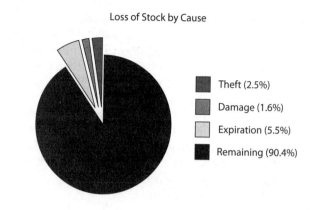

Line Graph

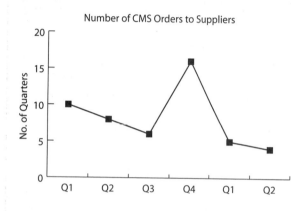

Map

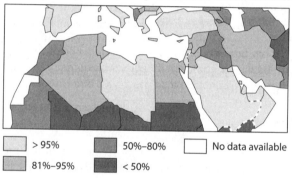

Interpreting information

Interpreting the information is often the most interesting part of using data. Interpretation is based on context, so creating detailed guidelines for interpreting data is not possible. However, listed below are some of the points to consider in this process.

Are the data correct? If the sources (registers, for example) were reviewed again, would the same figures result? Were the calculations made correctly? Procedures for validating the data should be in place to ensure their accuracy and completeness; for example, pharmaceutical inventory data should be periodically reconciled with physical stock counts. Because verifying all the data may not always be possible, periodic verification based on sampling would greatly improve data quality.

Are the data representative? Ensure that aggregation and analysis are based on a representative sample of data by ensuring that a majority of units are reporting on time. If only the best-performing units are reporting, the data interpretation may be misleading.

Do any of the figures seem improbable? In absolute terms—without making any calculations—do any num-

bers seem strange? Do expenditures seem too high or too low? Are too many essential medicines out of stock? Are too few orders from facilities being filled? Does the number of emergency purchases seem too high? (Small variations from month to month may be insignificant and should be disregarded.)

How do the figures compare with previous figures? Is a trend toward improvement evident although the figures may not seem good in absolute terms? For example, even though some revolving drug fund decapitalization may exist, is it lower than the previous year's? Using a simple graph or a wall chart can help identify such trends.

How do the figures for different geographic areas compare? Are some districts more successful than others? Do some need extra help building up their clientele or reevaluating procurement or quantification methods? Does more targeted training, education, and communication work need to be done for staff or clients?

What might be the causes of problems identified in reports? Could external factors (such as clients' economic problems or seasonal variations) be responsible for problems? What could their internal causes be (for example, poor estimation of pharmaceutical requirements or delays

Box 49-3
Example of information interpretation and use

Year	Essential medicines program price	World price	World price index
2003	3,600	3,000	120%
2004	3,300	3,100	106%
2005	3,800	3,050	125%
2006	2,800	3,000	93%

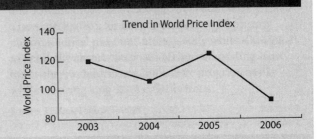

Observation: The difference between the price that the Essential Medicines Program (EMP) has been paying for its pharmaceuticals and the world price has been decreasing steadily, except in 2005.

Possible interpretations	Possible actions
An increasing proportion of central medical stores' pharmaceuticals are being purchased in bulk competitive tenders.	The overall trend is very positive. Ensure that procurement officers are congratulated for a job well done.
A greater share of the priority pharmaceuticals are now manufactured within the country, so the costs of transport and clearance are decreasing.	Continue to focus on identifying local manufacturers to bid for large orders.
The jump in price in 2005 was caused by serious delays in the arrival of major international orders. As a result, the EMP had to replenish stocks with emergency purchases from local pharmacies.	Get more information about why the large procurement was delayed. If the delay was caused by vendor performance, look for a different vendor. If caused by poor planning within the EMP, set earlier deadlines or order more stock so that the pipeline can be shortened.

in processing orders or clearing items through the ports)? Use a table similar to the one in Box 49-3 to list possible interpretations of the information on key indicators.

Taking action

Interpretations of the information provide possible courses of action for each scenario.

Discuss reports with colleagues. When reports are first prepared, discuss them in a staff meeting. Other staff members may offer useful insights into why specific indicators are getting better or worse, and they may have helpful suggestions about changes that could be made.

Provide feedback. When reports are sent from other units, simple feedback can be given, such as acknowledging receipt of the report and providing a response on any issues that require action. Better yet, a routine mechanism can be developed to provide some analysis of data on key indicators in reports received from all reporting units. This analysis should help people compare their performance with that of other units. Automating the preparation of feedback reports is an important use for computers in a PMIS.

For each interpretation, identify possible actions. Note that action should not be limited to dealing with problems; focusing on positive results is also important. If one quarter had especially good results, see what can be learned from

staff about what went right and try to share it with others and replicate it (see Box 49-3).

Gather more data. If reports based on routine data indicate that a problem might exist, confirmation can be obtained through an alternative data collection method, such as a survey or a special supervisory visit.

Correct the problem. Many problems can be corrected through supervision and retraining, but situations may occur in which sanctions and disciplinary action are required. The survival of the program may depend on it. ∎

References and further readings

★ = Key readings.

Chaulagai, C. N., C. M. Moyo, J. Koot, H. B. Moyo, T. C. Sambakunsi, F. M. Khunga, and P. D. Naphini. 2005. Design and Implementation of a Health Management Information System in Malawi: Issues, Innovations and Results. *Health Policy and Planning* 20(6):375–84.

Eldis Health & Development Information Team. No date. *Health Management Information Systems.* Brighton, U.K.: Eldis Programme. <http://www.eldis.org/go/topics/resource-guides/health-systems/key-issues>

Fraser, H. S., P. Biondich, D. Moodley, S. Choi, B. W. Mamlin, and P. Szolovits. 2005. Implementing Electronic Medical Record Systems in Developing Countries. *Informatics in Primary Care* 13(2):83–95.

Fraser, H. S., D. Jazayeri, P. Nevil, Y. Karacaoglu, P. E. Farmer, E. Lyon, M. K. Fawzi, F. Leandre, S. S. Choi, and J. S. Mukherjee. 2004. An

Information System and Medical Record to Support HIV Treatment in Rural Haiti. *BMJ* 329(7475):1142–46.

Lates, J. 2005. *Report of the Pharmacy Management Information System National Consensus Building Workshop, April 5–6, 2005.* Submitted to the U.S. Agency for International Development by the Rational Pharmaceutical Management Plus Program. Arlington, Va.: Management Sciences for Health.

Lates, J., C. Ouma, V. Muthiani, D. Mabirizi, D. Tjipura, and J. Nwokike. 2009. *Implementation of a National Pharmacy Management Information System in Namibia.* Arlington, Va.: Management Sciences for Health, Strengthening Pharmaceutical Systems Program. <http://pdf.usaid.gov/pdf_docs/PNADS166.pdf>

Millar, M. 1993. "Assessing Information Needs" (Facilitator's Guide, Module 1). In *Primary Health Care Management Advancement Program.* Geneva: Aga Khan Foundation. <http://www.jhsph.edu/delta_omega/Internet_Resources/phcmap-doc.html>

MSH (Management Sciences for Health). 1991. "Managing and Using Information." In *The Family Planning Manager's Handbook: Basic Skills and Tools for Managing Family Planning Programs,* J. A. Wolff, L. J. Suttenfield, and S. C. Binzen, eds. West Hartford, Conn.: Kumarian Press.

★ Reynolds, J. 1993. "Assessing Information Needs" (User's Guide, Module 1). In *Primary Health Care Management Advancement Programme.* Geneva: Aga Khan Foundation. <http://www.jhsph.edu/delta_omega/Internet_Resources/phcmap-doc.html>

★ Tomasi, E., L. A. Facchini, and F. Maia Mde. 2004. Health Information Technology in Primary Health Care in Developing Countries: A Literature Review. *Bulletin of the World Health Organization* 82(11):867–74.

★ WHO (World Health Organization). 2004. *Developing Health Management Information Systems: A Practical Guide for Developing Countries.* Manila: WHO Regional Office for the Western Pacific. <http://www.wpro.who.int/NR/rdonlyres/3A34C50D-C035-425A-8155-65E8AD3CB906/0/Health_manage.pdf>

ASSESSMENT GUIDE

Information system design

- Does the overall plan for the pharmaceutical supply program include an information management plan?
- Does the information management plan support strategic, program, and work-planning needs? Does it support monitoring and evaluation for assessing the implementation of these plans?
- Have key information users been identified at all levels? Have their needs for information related to management decisions been specified?
- Are data-reporting forms, such as periodic status reports, designed to be easily completed from existing registers, ledgers, and filing systems?
- Have key indicators been defined? Are their uses understood by staff at all levels?
- Is there at least one indicator for each key area of activity?
- Is the PMIS integrated with other information systems? If not, how much duplication of data exists between systems?
- If computerized systems exist, are they integrated with manual systems?
- Is the PMIS well documented? Is there an instruction manual on how to use the system? In computerized systems, are data structures and dictionaries documented?
- Are there enough trained staff? Do entry-level and in-service training schemes exist? Do staff have the capability to adapt the PMIS if necessary?

Data collection, reporting, and use

- Is an institution/unit(s) responsible for managing any health information systems? What type of information is collected and compiled by these systems?
- Are any of the systems automated? Which levels are automated and which levels are manual?
- Does the same system cover more than one vertical program (for example, tuberculosis, HIV/AIDS, immunization)?
- Are data collection methods appropriate for the types of data being collected?
- How long do staff take to fill in the reporting forms each month, quarter, and year? Can these times be reduced?
- Are report forms standardized? Are instructions available for filling them in?
- Is the quality of data entered into forms validated?
- Do any overlaps exist in the data being reported at different intervals? Are any types of data collected that are never used?
- Do staff use any data to complete report forms before sending the forms on to higher levels?
- Where does data get aggregated and/or compiled?
- What type of reports exist?
- Are feedback reports provided routinely to the units that collected the data? Do they incorporate graphical as well as tabular information?
- Does a schedule exist for report preparation, data transmission, and feedback reporting? What percentage of facilities reports information in a timely manner?
- Is a supervisory system in place that oversees the quality of management information?
- Is the information generated by the PMIS used for management decisions? Who are the key users of data on pharmaceutical management? Have their needs for information related to management decisions been specified? What are the examples of information being used in decision making?

Computers and communication of data

- Are any pharmaceutical management data entered or compiled using a computer? At what levels of the system is a computer used (for example, hospital, clinic, warehouse)?
- What kind of software is used to enter or analyze data?
- Do any facilities lack access to reliable electricity? Telephone connections?
- Is Internet access available to facilities if desired? Are there any issues related to Internet access?
- Can computers and communication systems be locally maintained? If not, what arrangements can be made?

Annex 49-1 Sample annual EMP status report

A. Identification

1. Year of report	
2. EMP office name	
3. State	

B. Staffing positions in EMP units

Location	No. Approved	No. Filled	No. Transferred
a. EMP office			
b. CMS			
c. Total			

C. Procurement

	Number	Value
1. Contracts awarded this year:		
a. Competitive tender		
b. Restricted tender		
c. Others		
d. Total contracts awarded		
2a. Contracts awarded to local manufacturers		
2b. Percent of total procurements (2a/1d) x 100		%
3. World price index for selected priority medicines		%

D. Training

Workshop Course Type	Number Held	Total Days	No. of Participants		
			Professional	Paraprofessional	Other
1. Rational procurement					
2. Stores management					
3. Quality assurance					
4. Financial management					
5. MIS/computers					
6. Rational use					
7. Information, education, and communication					
8. Training of trainers					

E. Inventory control (from inventory audit report)

	Value	% of Total
1. Average lead time for filling stock requisitions from district stores and health facilities (days)		
2. Total value of stock at end of year inventory		
3. Stock lost due to:		
a. Expiration		
b. Damage		
c. Theft		

F. Comments

G. Signatures

CMS manager	Date
Financial accountant	Date
EMP project manager	Date

H. Local supplier performance for deliveries completed this year

Name of Local Supplier	No. of Deliveries Completed	Total Value	Value of Rejected Medicines	Avg. Lead Time	Avg. Delay of Deliveries
Average lead time for local suppliers (sum of avg. lead times/no. of local suppliers)					

I. Foreign supplier performance for deliveries completed this year

Name of Foreign Supplier	No. of Deliveries Completed	Total Value	Value of Rejected Medicines	Avg. Lead Time	Avg. Delay of Deliveries
Average lead time for foreign suppliers (sum of avg. lead times/no. of foreign suppliers)					

J. Financial management

1. Expense summary	Amount	% of Total
a. Stock procurement		%
b. Transport costs		%
c. Workshops and IE&C		%
d. Fellowships and ext. training		%
e. Supplies and equipment		%
f. Maintenance and repairs		%
g. Other expenses		%
Total expenses		100%
2. Income summary		
a. Sales of CMS stock		%
b. Other income		%
Total income		100%

3. Financial data	
a. Total value of stock issues (from J2a)	
b. Total operating costs (1b +1c +1d +1e +1f)	
c. Total value of stock at end of year (from E2)	
d. Value of prepaid pipeline orders	
e. Other debts	
f. Stock fund value at end of previous year	

4. Financial indicators	
a. Operating costs as % of sales ((3b/3a) x 100)	
b. Number of stock turns (3a/((3c +3f)/2))	
c. Stock fund value at end of last year (3c +3d − 3e)	
d. Stock fund growth ((4c − 3f)/3f x 100)	

| Part I: Policy and economic issues | Part II: Pharmaceutical management | Part III: Management support systems |

Planning and administration
Organization and management
Information management
  48 Monitoring and evaluation
  49 Pharmaceutical management information systems
  50 Computers in pharmaceutical management
Human resources management

CHAPTER 50

Computers in pharmaceutical management

SUMMARY

Users should first define what functions or tasks computers will be used for, identify appropriate software for those functions, and then select hardware that is capable of using the software efficiently.

A computerization process is easier when—

- Efficient manual procedures exist
- Staff members are capable of, and interested in, learning to use computers
- Funds have been allocated for training, maintenance, and equipment upgrades
- A reliable power supply exists

Pharmaceutical management programs should usually begin with basic word processing and spreadsheet applications. Users can then gain experience and develop support systems for supplies, repairs, and security. Specialized pharmaceutical management programs are often used for quantification of pharmaceutical requirements, procurement, inventory management, or medicine-use analysis.

Medicine information is increasingly available through electronic communications systems. Most pharmaceutical supply systems have access to Internet communications. Two main options are available: e-mail and World Wide Web browsers. Use of the Internet for international communications has become increasingly important.

Central to most pharmaceutical management applications is a product master file, including product name, strength, dosage form, therapeutic category, route of administration, and packaging. A coding system with a unique identifier for each drug product must be developed.

Personal computers, or PCs, can be used in all aspects of the pharmaceutical management cycle. Hardware refers to the computer's electronic and mechanical parts, which include—

- A microprocessor chip
- Memory chips (RAM, for random-access memory)
- Input devices (keyboard, flash drive, mouse, scanner)
- Storage devices (hard disk drive, CD-ROM, magnetic tape)
- Output and peripheral devices (monitor, printer, modem, network card, speakers)

Software refers to instructions that can be understood and executed by the computer. Categories include—

- The operating system, which coordinates and directs information for the microprocessor
- General-purpose software, such as word processing, spreadsheets, and database management software
- Special-purpose software, such as presentation graphics, project management, and accounting software
- Utility programs, such as antivirus, file backup, and data recovery programs
- Specialized pharmaceutical management software, often a custom-programmed database application

When used effectively, computer systems save money, promote efficiency, and improve the quality of services. However, poorly conceived or implemented computer systems waste money, decrease efficiency, and distract attention from other management improvements.

This chapter discusses the uses of computers in pharmaceutical management and examines special issues in computerizing pharmaceutical management information. It also includes specifications for computer applications in pharmaceutical management, considerations for hardware selection, and requirements for maintaining and supporting computers. Preparing data for computerization is discussed, along with coding systems and definitions of units. This chapter focuses on personal computers because they are the most widely used by essential medicines programs. Instructing users in particular software programs or making recommendations for the purchase of a specific piece of hardware or software is beyond the scope of this chapter.

The question today is usually not whether but rather how and how much to computerize. Even more important, however, is how to computerize efficiently. This chapter provides guidelines to help decision makers computerize their operations effectively.

50.1 Uses of computers in pharmaceutical management

Computers can be used in all aspects of the pharmaceutical management cycle, from selection to use. Using communication devices, users can exchange or share information with other computers at the same site through a local area network (LAN) or with computers anywhere in the world. The term *computers* here also encompasses devices such as personal digital assistants (PDAs) and handheld and pocket devices such as "smartphones." Table 50-1 summarizes some of the many current computer applications for pharmaceutical management.

50.2 When and how to computerize

Computer technology changes quickly, with machines continually becoming faster, more capable, and less expensive. The benefits of computers in managing pharmaceuticals depend on the choice of tools, the commitment to using the tools, and the ability to overcome the hurdles involved in incorporating computers into the organization. No standard formula exists for successful computerization in pharmaceutical management, but rather a mix of elements applies; the right mix can yield great benefits.

Benefits and limitations of computerization

Some of the benefits of computerization are to—

- Simplify and speed up complex tasks
- Increase accuracy by checking spelling, calculations, and data integrity
- Update and access information quickly
- Automate repetitive tasks
- Provide management information for decision making
- Allow organizations to expand operations
- Streamline administrative processes
- Generate timely reports without repetition

Nevertheless, computers do have limitations. They cannot assume responsibilities, make decisions, define problems, set objectives, improve the basic data available, or make a person more organized. They cannot fulfill needs if appropriate hardware and software are not chosen, and they are not a one-time expense: funds are required for upgrades, training, and support over time for both hardware and software.

Conditions in an organization that support computerization include—

- Efficient existing manual procedures
- Other departments that have computerized successfully

Table 50-1   Computer applications for pharmaceutical management

Area of activity	Uses
Project planning	• Workplans • Simulation programs • Annual reports
Selection	• Preparation of essential medicines lists • Literature searches
Requirements planning	• Quantification of pharmaceutical needs • ABC analysis • Weight and volume analysis of kits
Financing	• Budget management • Pharmaceutical sales monitoring • Accounting • Financial analysis
Procurement	• Tender document preparation • Tender monitoring • Bid analysis • Preparing purchase orders and receiving reports • Monitoring of order status
Inventory control	• Monitoring of stock positions • Monitoring of expiry dates • Prediction of reorder dates and quantities • Invoicing
Transport	• Vehicle routing and scheduling • Weight and volume calculation • Transport voucher preparation
Pharmaceutical registration and control	• Database of registration data • Adverse reaction reporting • Medicines recalls
Medicines information	• Formulary preparation • Literature searches • Data storage and transfer • Pharmaceutical bulletin production • Training material preparation
Rational use	• Formulary • Standard treatment schedule • Calculation of WHO medicine-use indicators • Survey analysis • Training (simulation games)
Personnel management	• Training software • Personnel records • Supervision monitoring • Payroll calculations
Health statistics	• Population data • Morbidity data • Mortality data
Use	• Health care coverage calculations • Medicine consumption analysis
Presentation	• Graphs and charts • Overhead transparencies or slide shows for training
Communication	• Fax • E-mail • Mailing

Box 50-1
Key steps in the computerization process

1. Identify the tasks or the system to be computerized with a detailed analysis of needs compared to current systems.

2. Survey the environment and consider integrating with other systems to the extent feasible. (What software and hardware are being used by other departments? Does an institutional computer policy exist? What equipment is already available?)

3. Evaluate the staff situation (actual versus needed).

4. Select software before hardware.

5. Identify whether the software needed is available in the local language and to which original version it is equivalent (non-English-language versions are sometimes not as current as English versions).

6. Ensure the availability of supplies and maintenance.

7. Select the hardware and software suppliers that provide the most support.

8. Plan progressive implementation (one step at a time) and involve current and future users in the design and implementation process.

Box 50-2
Illustrative phases in computerization

Phase I: Convenience computing

This phase includes tasks that could be done with a typewriter and calculator but are easier on the computer. If the computer "goes down" (temporarily stops working), the work can still be done. Examples are—

- Word processing
- Simple databases (for example, an address list)
- Simple budgets

Phase II: Periodic analyses and special activities

These tasks would be extremely difficult to do by hand but could be delayed for a few days or weeks if the computer were down. Examples are—

- Quantification exercises
- Complex project budgets
- Survey analysis

Phase III: Essential daily activities

These tasks involve large volumes of data handled daily or almost daily. If the computer went down, the work would be seriously impaired. Examples are—

- Inventory control
- Accounting
- Pharmaceutical registration

- Staff capable of, and interested in, operating computers
- A reliable power supply
- Adequate funds to support maintenance, training, and equipment upgrades

Conditions that can impede computerization include—

- Hardware or software not suited to the task
- Not enough trained operators
- Lack of a maintenance plan
- Lack of reliable power (voltage surges ruin computers and databases)
- Inadequate supply of storage media, paper, or printer ink and toner
- Unsuitable physical environment (exposure to dust, heat, or magnets, which can damage hardware and software)

Starting the computerization process

Begin with the basic questions: What will the computer be used for? Who will use it? Where will it be used? What is the budget for equipment, software, and maintenance? What special functions may be required? Will data need to be shared? Will a network be necessary? The key steps are listed in Box 50-1.

In computerization, users should walk before they try to run. Trying to do everything at once increases failure rates, so organizations often computerize in phases (see Box 50-2). This strategy enables computer operators to handle increasingly demanding tasks, permits support systems for supplies and repairs to develop, and allows security systems to be put in place to protect against electrical damage, computer viruses, theft, and other hazards.

Perhaps most important, a phased approach to computerization allows users to develop a clearer concept of what computers can do, what kind of information they want from the computerized system, and which modifications they need to make in reporting and management systems to obtain that information. Computerization must be planned carefully so that implementation occurs smoothly, with a minimum of interruption and dislocation in the organization's work. Country Study 50-1 provides some examples of good and bad computerization experiences.

Computer software: options and guidelines

Software is always becoming more powerful, and upgraded versions appear regularly. Upgrades may mean that the software packages require upgraded hardware resources (such as additional hard disk space, processor power, and memory) to run effectively. This factor is the main argument for choosing software before hardware and for including hardware upgrades in the budget.

Computer magazines (and their websites, which are often free) are a valuable source of comparison articles on software and hardware. "After-market" software books published by companies such as Sybex or Que are often easier to use than the manual provided by the software company.

Three broad categories of computer software are useful in pharmaceutical management: general purpose, special purpose, and utility programs.

General-purpose software

General-purpose software programs (such as word processing, desktop publishing, presentation management, spreadsheets, and commercial database programs) perform routine daily activities or periodic analyses. Software suites that combine individual programs in one software package are designed to allow easy exchange of information among the different programs, such as linking spreadsheet figures in a text document. Standard suites usually contain a word processor, spreadsheet, and presentation program, while "professional" suites also contain a database program. The most important factor in choosing general-purpose software is access to local support. Some questions to consider are: Which package is the most common locally? Is local training available? What software is used in other local offices with which our office interacts?

Country Study 50-1
Sample computerization experiences

Poor planning. The central medical store (CMS) in a sub-Saharan African country was computerized as part of a program to strengthen the computer capacity of the Ministry of Health. Unfortunately, the firm chosen to do the work did not realize that two previous attempts at computerization had failed because of internal organizational issues that had little to do with computers. The firm repeated many of the previous mistakes, because it believed that the introduction of technology could establish organizational systems and controls, and it did not examine the organization's existing structure.

An ambitious plan to computerize inventory and financial accounts within three months was devised. What resulted was hardware that could not be serviced locally and inadequate training of staff. Only a few poorly attended meetings were held with CMS management, and for many reasons, the data entered into the software were never accurate or up-to-date.

After nine months, the main CMS computer was stolen. No data backup had been made for more than three months because no diskettes were available. The last four months of data were lost, and no one thought that the system should be revived. No maintenance budget had been set aside for recurring costs, such as printer toner, diskettes, and systems maintenance, and the computers were being used only for word processing.

Computer integration issues. In a rapidly developing South Asian country, problems have occurred in the integration and transfer of data. Many departments have computerized, and data collection and processing overlap because responsibilities have not been clearly defined. In addition, incompatible software packages have been used; coding of key data, such as locations and medicine names, has not been consistent; and data linking has been very difficult. Many of the problems could have been avoided by clear definitions of responsibilities, a software policy, and a common coding system for key data.

Well-planned computerization. A Southeast Asian country has undertaken the process of computerizing slowly. Initially, data on medicine consumption, procurement, supply, and health statistics were collected manually. Computers were first used to enter these data in a spreadsheet program. Although this system worked well initially, the amount of data to be processed eventually overloaded the system, and the decision was made to upgrade it. Appropriate software and a systems developer were carefully selected. Training of local staff by expatriate staff was very successful and is still important for maintenance of the system. Computerization has helped provide useful management data for consumption analysis, pharmaceutical procurement and supply, and reallocation of supplies among health facilities. A computerized registration system is planned. Computerization has been relatively successful in this country because a step-by-step approach was used, starting from manual systems and developing the system with end users to meet their information needs.

Word processing. Word processing programs have long replaced the typewriter. For most offices, 80 percent of computing time is spent on word processing. It is usually the easiest task to learn, because the input and output are obvious even to a novice. These programs are mainly used for correspondence and for producing documents. Features such as graphics capabilities, spelling checkers, search-and-replace functions, and generators for tables of contents make producing documents easier.

Desktop publishing. This software has word processing features but is more powerful for handling graphics, large documents, and production of files to be used by a printer for newsletters, bulletins, training materials, or books. Newsletters can also be produced using a word processing program.

Spreadsheet. A spreadsheet is a worksheet consisting of horizontal and vertical lines that define a matrix of rows and columns. It is modeled after an accountant's ledger, and data are entered in cells identified by coordinates in the matrix. Any type of data (text or numbers) can be entered in these cells, and sophisticated calculations and analyses (such as those discussed in Chapter 40) can be performed.

A major advantage of spreadsheets is their ability to revise totals, percentages, and other calculations immediately after any number or set of numbers is changed, allowing experimentation with "what if" alternatives. They can be linked to allow consolidation of accounts and can produce graphics and charts of the data entered.

In pharmaceutical management, spreadsheets are used for budgeting, financial analysis, quantification of pharmaceutical requirements, ABC analysis, price comparisons, pricing models, and creating or revising national essential medicines lists, as discussed in other chapters.

Presentation. A simple graph often has more visual impact than a complex table, so presentation graphics packages can be useful for preparing effective and attractive reports, funding proposals, overhead transparencies, and presentations.

Database. A database is like an electronic filing cabinet. Data (characters, numbers, dates, formulas, or memos) are stored in fields. The combination of fields forms a record, the records together constitute a table, and a group of tables constitutes a database. Database software can store and manipulate large amounts of data quickly. Databases are used in many business applications, allowing users to—

- Sort data in any order using multiple sorting keys
- Establish relationships between databases and generate sophisticated consolidated reports
- Improve data consistency by allowing or requiring data to be entered according to defined choices
- Quickly retrieve data according to specific criteria
- Develop complex applications using powerful programming languages
- Import and export data

In pharmaceutical management, databases are used in data-intensive tasks, such as inventory control, procurement, tender management, detailed analyses of prescriptions, accounting, and drug product registration. Databases are superior to spreadsheets for this type of application because they store more data in smaller files with less need for duplicating entries. A common field can link separate records in the database, limiting the need for duplication of data entry and facilitating data retrieval and reporting. The structure of databases permits easy data manipulation for access and reporting, and they can be designed to check the data entered for consistency with previously entered data. A relational database is particularly useful in pharmaceutical management because it allows multiple records for the same basic item (helpful for inventory management, tender analysis, or medicine-use analysis).

Special-purpose commercial software

Pharmaceutical management systems often need special-purpose commercial software packages, such as programs for presentation graphics, project management, statistics, accounting, bibliographic data, and communications.

Project management. Project management software organizes and tracks project tasks to be accomplished according to a defined schedule and shows potential conflicts in the use of resources. Budgeting information can also be included.

Statistical. Although spreadsheets and databases have standard statistical functions, using a dedicated statistical package is sometimes preferable. Epi Info, developed and distributed by the World Health Organization (WHO) and the U.S. Centers for Disease Control and Prevention (CDC), integrates basic word processing, data entry, statistical, and database functions. It is particularly useful for processing survey data and tabulating data stored in standard database programs.

Accounting. Accounting programs are available with a wide range of capabilities. Basic bookkeeping can be done with spreadsheets, but a dedicated accounting package is often more appropriate. Selection depends on local factors: What can the bookkeeper use? What does a donor use? What support is available? What bookkeeping technique is used? Is the accounting format compatible with local regulations? Increasingly, reputable local accounting firms can advise which accounting programs are most suitable for an organization.

Bibliographic. Bibliographic software greatly facilitates storing, searching for, retrieving, and manipulating bibliographic information on books, journals, training materials, and government and project documents. This kind of software requires staff to keep the database up-to-date.

Utility programs

Programs called *utilities* help manage and maintain computers and stored data. Common utilities include antivirus, file management, file backup, file exchange, data recovery, data compression, firewall, and network software. Because operating systems now include many of the commonly needed utilities, checking the capabilities of a particular operating system is advised before buying a separate utility.

A current antivirus program is absolutely vital for computer units that handle essential day-to-day functions, such as inventory control, drug product registration, accounting, or maintenance of national health statistics. It is also essential for any system that receives data from outside sources, including branch offices within the country. A firewall program is equally necessary for any computer that connects to the Internet. The firewall protects the network from unauthorized access.

Network software

Establishing an office-based computer network may be useful. A LAN (local area network) connects the computers and printers in a single location. A wide area network (WAN) connects computers in separate locations. A LAN can be established with or without a server, although a server may be required for certain purposes, such as running centralized inventory software. If the network has a server, it must be protected in a secure, climate-controlled room and its data must be backed up regularly.

A network is helpful if a number of computers in the office need to easily share resources, such as a printer or an Internet connection. A network is essential if multiple computer users need to simultaneously access the same software program, such as an inventory program running on the server. Installing the inventory program on the server means that all of the program's data is stored in one central location (a secure server room) and that other computers on the network can access the data from various locations, such as the accounts department or the warehouse, if the appropriate permissions have been granted.

Although the cabling and configuration of the network are often done by an outside firm, someone on the office staff should know at least the basics of network troubleshooting and maintenance so that downtime is minimized if system problems occur. If physically cabling the computers together is problematic, a wireless network can also be an option.

Wireless networks can also be used to connect computers in separate locations over a WAN. Some countries have decentralized pharmaceutical operations such as distribution so that work is done at the provincial or district level rather than the central level. Using a WAN, the lower levels of the system can connect to a server at the central level to manage inventory distribution. Maintaining the information in a central location allows users from all levels to easily share data and coordinate work. Because the data are pooled in one location, management reports are easier to produce and use in a timely fashion.

Custom software

Development of custom-built software, such as an inventory program, is a complex and time-consuming task. Although the idea of custom-built software is attractive, purchasing software that has already been written and tested by others is usually preferable, unless a suitable program cannot be found. If new software does need to be developed, approach this task in a step-by-step fashion—

- Define the system requirements.
- Choose the software and tools for developing the custom program.
- Design a system.
- Develop and program the system.
- Test and debug the system.
- Implement the system through data entry and training.
- Develop system documentation and a complete user's manual.
- Provide system support, revision, and upgrades.

Frequently, lack of time, money, or expertise results in the development of unusable software. Developing custom software always takes longer than expected and often goes over budget. Users should explore all alternatives carefully before choosing to develop software themselves. Annex 50-1 contains advice on developing a product master file for pharmaceutical management database software.

Open source software

Open source software emerged when individuals inventing programming code as part of the software development process shared their inventions with other networked users. Because any user could modify any part of this code and then share it with the network, the phrase *open source software* became a natural way of describing it. Open source software differs from proprietary software because its programming code is available for inspection, modification, reuse, and distribution by others. Although open source software can be free of charge, it can also be purchased; but once attained, it is freely modified. Today, open source software is used by individuals and organizations in the public and private sectors worldwide and is gaining popularity. Linux is one of the best examples of open source software—in this case, to control the computer's operation.

Table 50-2   Computer hardware specifications

Hardware	Indicator	Significance
Hard drive	Gigabyte (GB)	The number of gigabytes describes the storage capacity of the hard drive—how much data and software it can contain.
Processor chip	Chip type, with speed in gigahertz (GHz)	The chip type and speed determine how quickly the computer can make calculations, run software, and function. Any chip sold today should be sufficient for most office uses. The type and speed are more important for computers that will be used as network servers.
RAM (random-access memory)	Megabyte (MB) or gigabyte (GB)	The amount of RAM in a system determines how many tasks the computer can run at once and how complicated a program it can handle. A gigabyte is approximately 1,000 megabytes.
Monitor	Size (inches or centimeters)	The LCD (liquid-crystal display) monitors sold today vary primarily in their physical size and can be selected on that basis and on price, unless they will be used for highly graphics-intensive work.
Printer	Characters per second (CPS), pages per minute (PPM), dots per inch (DPI)	Dot matrix printers are judged in CPS, and laser and inkjet printers in PPM. Both are important when producing large amounts of output. Printer quality is measured in DPI and is important when producing high-quality output.
Modem	Baud	The baud rate is how much information a modem can send in a second and controls how long it takes to send a file over a telephone line.
Ethernet card	Speed	The speed of the Ethernet card determines how quickly it can send and receive data on a network.
CD-ROM or DVD-ROM drive	Speed	The speed of a CD-ROM or DVD-ROM drive describes how quickly it can access and read information from a CD-ROM or DVD-ROM.
CD-RW or DVD-RW drive	Speed	The speed of a CD-RW or DVD-RW drive describes how quickly it can write information to a CD-ROM or DVD-ROM. These drives can also read information from CD-ROMs and DVD-ROMs.

Program decision makers need to evaluate a number of issues when considering the use of open source software, including—

- A definition of program needs
- The types of open source applications available for the needs
- A review of open source and proprietary software alternatives, including differences in costs
- The availability of resources to support the open source approach
- The functionality and usability of the open source application
- The availability of professional support skills

A good resource on the use of open source software in developing countries is available (Dravis 2003).

Computer hardware: options and guidelines

The size and speed of computer hardware continue to change so quickly that specific recommendations about what a user should buy are impossible to make. When purchasing computers and peripheral devices such as printers, the important issues are processing, storage, memory, and output capacities. Always buy the most powerful equipment that the budget will allow, especially if a new computer cannot be purchased for a few years. Hardware generally improves so rapidly that a computer should not be purchased until shortly before it will be used. Delaying a purchase for even a month or two can mean a lower price or greater capabilities for the same price. Table 50-2 describes different types of computer hardware. In general, larger numbers are better for the indicators listed.

The use of handheld computers called personal digital assistants (PDAs) is increasing in the health care field and in pharmaceutical management, because they are a convenient way both to access and record information while away from the office. Country Study 50-2 discusses different ways that PDAs are being used by various country programs.

Geographic information systems

A geographic information system (GIS) is a computer system that captures, stores, analyzes, and displays information that is identified according to a specific location. In other words, it provides an interface between all kinds of data and a map. GIS allows data sets from different sources to be brought together in spatial context to reveal relationships and patterns that are not necessarily obvious otherwise. In public health, for example, GIS technology can combine demographic, environmental, and health data with satellite maps to determine endemic or epidemic disease patterns.

A GIS can use digitized maps or coordinates from global positioning system (GPS) receivers to determine spatial relationships. In Tanzania and Uganda, Management Sciences for Health's (MSH's) East African Drug Seller Initiative is using GPS to map the locations of public- and private-sector clinics and drug shops to determine gaps in health care coverage in remote areas.

Country Study 50-2
Using handheld computers in pharmaceutical management

The increased technological ability and convenience of handheld computers or personal digital assistants (PDAs) or smartphones have made them popular tools in the health care field, including pharmaceutical management. Many information sources have been adapted for use on PDAs, including the National Library of Medicine's MEDLINE database and pharmaceutical-specific resources, such as the *British National Formulary*. Some of these resources are free and others are subscription-based.

In addition to providing easy access to health information, PDAs and smartphones are also being used to collect, analyze, and report data more accurately and efficiently in a number of countries.

Canada. In British Columbia, PDAs are being used as part of a quality-management program in a 285-bed hospital that requires the collection and analysis of quality indicators for pharmacy services. An electronic form was custom designed based on the pharmacists' data needs for process and outcome indicators, including adverse drug reactions and medication cost savings. The resulting electronic patient care form was installed on four PDAs and each pharmacist received a two-week orientation before switching from paper-based logs. The PDA data were downloaded daily to a single PC into a common database program, where it could be easily analyzed and used for reports. Users of the PDAs found that they were able to double the number of patients they counseled, and much less time was needed to collect, analyze, and report the data.

Source: Collins 2004.

Tanzania. In an effort to improve the effectiveness of its drug product and premises inspection programs, the Tanzania Food and Drugs Authority (TFDA) worked with Management Sciences for Health to introduce the use of PDAs in data collection and management. The TFDA inspectors collect data on a wide range of product- and site-specific information, which previously had been handwritten on paper forms, then transferred to a database. The program's PDAs include forms for port-of-entry inspections, premises inspections, and postmarket surveillance in a format that guides inspectors through the data-gathering process. Collected data are sent monthly to TFDA by public mail/transport or by hand delivery to the TFDA central office. Also, updated product references needed by the inspectors in the field are uploaded to the PDAs monthly. The new system makes analyzing data and creating reports easier, and it improves the accuracy of inspection records through design controls and by increasing inspector accountability.

Uganda. The Uganda Health Information Network is using PDAs that are connected through the local GSM cellular telephone network to help expand access to health and medical information and support data collection and analysis. Health workers in the field use PDAs to send and receive information and data via "jacks," which are relay devices that contain a GSM cellular transceiver and a data cache. The jack then communicates with a main server in Kampala. When users connect to the jack, information is both uploaded and downloaded. In the pilot of this program, the PDA system was used primarily for collecting and disseminating field data, such as weekly disease surveillance reports and broadcasting medical education material.

Source: UHIN 2004.

50.3 Specialized software for pharmaceutical management and control

Pharmaceutical systems that successfully computerize usually begin with basic word processing and spreadsheet applications and then seek specialized applications for inventory management, procurement, pharmaceutical regulation, or medicine-use analysis. This section provides an overview of types of specialized software for various tasks and guidelines to consider when evaluating alternatives. Examples of specific types of programs are given, and others are listed in the references at the end of the chapter.

Quantification of pharmaceutical requirements

Quantification of pharmaceutical requirements (see Chapter 20) is complex, and a computer can greatly speed up the process. Spreadsheets can be used if limited data are involved. Worksheets can be set up to forecast requirements using consumption data; formulas can be entered into the spreadsheet for estimates based on different scenarios. Spreadsheets can be linked, or a single spreadsheet can be divided into sections (one to record the morbidity profile, one to organize the standard treatments, and one to summarize pharmaceutical requirements within therapeutic

Figure 50-1   Summary of illustrative integrated pharmaceutical supply management software and characteristics

Management component		Uses
1.	**Accounting**	Accounting manages the financial aspects of pharmaceutical management activities.
1.1	Accounts Payable/Purchasing	Tracks and processes bills and payments and provides complete checking account management functions.
1.2	Accounts Receivable/Billing	Tracks all customer histories and accounts.
1.3	Job Costing and Cost Accounting	Job costing and cost accounting provide a method for collecting, analyzing, and reporting all costs associated with a particular job.
1.4	General Ledger	General ledger maintains the Chart of Accounts and provides the basis for all other financial functions.
1.5	Financial Reporting	
1.6	Accounting Standards	
2.	**Distribution**	Distribution addresses selling and providing pharmaceuticals to other facilities.
2.1	Client Orders/Sales Orders	Receives and processes client and sales orders.
2.2	Consumption Reporting	Reports the distribution of items in stock.
2.3	Delivery	Supports processes and methods of delivering ordered items to others.
2.4	Kit Management	Addresses putting together and breaking apart stock items for distribution.
2.5	Push System	Provides facilities with predetermined types and quantities of stock.
2.6	Repackage into Dispensable Units	Addresses breaking apart large quantities of stock into smaller packages.
2.7	Reporting	
3.	**Tender Management**	Tender management manages the competitive bid process.
4.	**Inventory Control**	Inventory control manages the stock and inventory.
4.1	Receiving	Adds stock to the inventory database.
4.2	Supplier Performance Monitoring	
4.3	Maintaining History of Transactions	Stores and archives transactions for future reference.
4.4	Selling Inventory over the Internet	E-commerce associated with selling inventory over the Internet.
4.5	Establish and Maintain Inventory Records	
4.6	Reporting	
4.7	Forecasting and Order Planning	Forecasting and order planning supports methods and processes used to estimate the quantities of pharmaceuticals needed for your organization.
5.	**Procurement**	Procurement manages the acquisition of pharmaceuticals.
5.1	Purchase Requisitions	Collects and disseminates information about requested items.
5.2	Purchase Orders	Creates and tracks information about a sales transaction.
5.3	Group Purchasing/Pooled Procurement	Manages the procurement for a group with similar purchasing needs.
5.4	Perpetual Purchasing	Manages the procurement of stock-based designated or calculated reorder points.
5.5	Scheduled Purchasing	Manages the procurement of stock on a predetermined purchasing cycle.
5.6	Ordering Online over the Internet	
5.7	Supplier Management	Tracks supplier information.
5.8	Reporting	
6.	**Vehicle and Equipment Management**	Vehicle and equipment management deals with tracking and monitoring the assets in the organization.
6.1	Vehicle Management	
6.2	Equipment Management	
6.3	Cold-Chain Equipment Management	
6.4	Load Building	
6.5	Route Planning	
6.6	Transport Personnel Management	
6.7	Transport Personnel Assignments	
6.8	Vehicle Allocation/Vehicle Tracking	
6.9	Reporting	
7.	**Warehouse Management**	Warehouse management deals with managing the physical stock, whether it is in-house or located in another warehouse.
7.1	Bar Coding and Related Technologies	
7.2	Managing Multiple Warehouses	Manages multiple physical or virtual warehouses.
7.3	Stock Location Tracking	Tracks the physical location of inventory items.
7.4	Reporting	
7.5	Picking	

Management component		Uses
8.	**Transfunctional**	Transfunctional includes requirements that span the entire range of functions and includes some miscellaneous requirements.
8.1	Currency	Supports multiple currencies.
8.2	Languages	Supports multiple languages.
8.3	Interface with WHO Drug Registration Software (SIAMED)	Imports drug registration data from a SIAMED export.
8.4	Master Drug File (from WHO)	Imports the master drug file.
8.5	User Customization	
8.6	Custom Reporting	
8.7	Indicators	Addresses custom thresholds and acceptable ranges for monitoring system.
9.	**Technical**	Technical requirements describe the architectural characteristics of the system.
9.1	Multitier Organizational Structure	Operates in a three- and four-level organizational hierarchy.
9.2	Single-User Environment	Operates in a single-user, single workstation environment.
9.3	Multiuser Environment	Operates in a multiuser, networked environment.
9.4	Software Platform: Microsoft Windows	
9.5	Security	Addresses user authentication and data security.
9.6	System Maintenance	Backs up and archives data.
9.7	Data Exchange	Supports importing and exporting data with other applications.
9.8	System Architecture	
10.	**User Support**	User support deals with technical support facilities you may require for this type of software.
10.1	Online Help	
10.2	User's Manual	

categories). Linking spreadsheets requires an advanced level of proficiency with spreadsheets.

Quantimed is a database tool for forecasting that has been developed by MSH. Users enter consumption data (past and forecasted use) and/or morbidity data (number of expected cases for each age range and for each health problem). When standard treatments are defined, Quantimed generates a table that compares the medicines needed, using both consumption and morbidity methods (see Chapter 20). Quantimed also produces a number of other reports, including some that can help with budgeting and comparing costs among different products and treatment regimens.

Basic data analysis and production of formulary manuals

Basic commercial software can be used for many pharmaceutical management purposes, such as data analysis and publication of formulary and therapeutics manuals.

Data analysis. Spreadsheets are ideal tools for developing a medicines list, because they allow easy manipulation of both text and numbers. Creating a spreadsheet that lists medicines and data on price, consumption, lead time, and formulary category is very easy. Formulas can then be added to perform various analyses, such as ABC analysis, price comparison analysis, and therapeutic category analysis (see Chapter 40).

Formulary manuals. A word processing program can be used to develop a formulary manual with treatment guidelines (see Chapter 17). A desktop publishing program can produce documents ready for printing.

Procurement and inventory management

Spreadsheets can automate aspects of procurement and inventory management, but they are not ideal for processing large amounts of data. Database software is more appropriate for this purpose. Using the same database program for procurement, inventory management, and accounting is preferable, because these activities are interconnected.

Inventory management is often part of a commercial accounting software package, but such packages typically focus on accounting and lack features specific to pharmaceutical management, such as the ability to track multiple products for the same code number, or to track items by lot number and expiry date. The ability to track issues by lot number is important for medicine recalls.

Database programs have been developed by MSH and others specifically to manage procurement and inventory control in public pharmaceutical systems (see References and Further Readings and Box 50-3). Figure 50-1 provides a summary of pharmaceutical supply management software requirements and characteristics. Box 50-4 lists standard reports that should be produced by such software. Country Study 50-3 illustrates how software for inventory management and procurement has been used to improve pharmaceutical management for an HIV/AIDS treatment program in Haiti.

Hospital pharmacy management software

Specialized hospital pharmacy software can support various aspects of a hospital pharmacy (Chapter 45), including—

---

tBox 50-3
RxSolution

RxSolution is an integrated computerized pharmaceutical management system. The system is used to manage inventory; process purchase orders; handle issues to wards, out/inpatient pharmacy, and satellite clinics; dispense medication to patients; and prepare repeat prescriptions for down-referral at the facility level (down-referral occurs when a higher-level health care facility such as a hospital transfers all or part of a patient's care to a lower-level facility that is more convenient for the patient). RxSolution supports best practices for procurement, storage, distribution, and dispensing of pharmaceuticals and medical supplies, helping to ensure availability of critical products at all times. Users record information on products, suppliers, clients, prescribers, dispensers, and patients.

The program has modules for—

- Budgeting
- Procurement
- Receipts
- Requisitions
- Dispensing
- Down-referrals

Any or all of these modules may be used, depending on the needs of the site and user restrictions. The program includes a wide range of clinical and management reports, which help improve pharmaceutical use, stock availability, and financial and logistic accountability.

RxSolution is currently being used in more than 120 sites in southern Africa. Examples of how facilities are using the software include the following—

- Staff in one South African hospital can now produce the monthly tracer list report for the provincial office with one click, rather than taking a day to count stock and write up the information. They can also track expenditures to come in on budget, and easily determine the amount spent on antiretroviral medicines, which they are required to report. Store management reports now include much more financial information.

- The director of pharmacy services for a South African city reports that RxSolution allows the staff to better manage their system and cost centers, because they can more easily track budgets and monitor clinics. The main depot receives 90 to 95 facility orders each month and can complete all of the orders within two weeks.

- Installing and using RxSolution in eleven hospitals and health centers in Swaziland met the Global Fund's requirements for a reliable antiretroviral tracking system. These facilities use the system to produce regular stock, patient, and prescribing reports for national-level managers. As a result of the successful installation and use of RxSolution, the Global Fund authorized funds for Swaziland to purchase antiretrovirals.

- The chief pharmacist at a South African hospital uses RxSolution to produce ABC analysis reports for the wards and the hospital to support his pharmacy and therapeutics committee work.

See http://www.msh.org/projects/sps/Resources/Software-Tools/RxSolution.cfm for more information.

- Patient medication profile
- Records of intravenous therapy
- Management of total parenteral nutrition
- Unit-dose management
- Medication administration record
- Order entry and inventory management
- Medication interaction checking
- Allergy checking
- Food and medicine interactions
- Duplicate therapy checking
- Laboratory value monitoring
- Outpatient prescriptions
- Patient billing
- Patient adherence

Accounting and financial management

Most public-sector supply systems must abide by government accounting regulations, which differ from country to country. Commercial accounting software is widely available, but it may require modification to correspond with local regulations. If a specialized pharmaceutical management software program is used for inventory control, the inventory software and the accounting software should be modified to communicate with each other.

Learning how to perform basic spreadsheet analysis is now a must for the essential medicines program manager. Spreadsheets can be used for both simple and sophisticated analyses of program finances. See Chapter 41 for examples.

Box 50-4
Standard reports for supply management software

Supply management software should generate standard reports to support decision making, such as the following.

Inventory reports

Stock status report: lists all products in the product master file, including product code and description, unit of measure, quantity in stock, quantity on order, quantity reserved, quantity available.

Reorder report: lists all products that are below the reorder level, with reorder quantity.

Overstock report: lists all products exceeding the maximum level.

Inventory valuation report: lists the current value of the inventory, based on the chosen valuation method (last-in, first out [LIFO], first-in, first-out [FIFO], average).

Expired or soon-to-expire stock report: lists the products that are presently expired or will expire within a defined period.

Order reports

Open order report: lists orders from customers that have been entered and not yet shipped.

Back order report: lists all unshipped back orders.

Order history report: reports on all orders (shipped and nonshipped) on file.

Product reports

Catalog report and price list: lists all products in the product master file. Can contain pricing information and be used as a price list.

Product history report: lists by stock item total quantities and sales values for each fiscal period.

Sales analysis and forecasting reports

Customer analysis report: lists sales made to each customer in a specified period.

Ranked customer analysis report: same as above, but ranked by sales volume, with cumulative percentages.

Functional lists/outputs printed by the system

List of "picking tickets"

List of delivery notes/invoices

List of stock count sheets

Multilocation reports

(If using a system that tracks stock in multiple locations)

Transfer advice report: a reorder advice report that lists products that are over the maximum or under the reorder level. This report makes it possible to determine whether a product that is unavailable or understocked in one location is available in another location.

Financial reports

(If linked to financial information)

Credit hold orders report: lists orders that are on hold because the customer is over the credit limit.

Debtors and creditors report: lists those who owe and are owed money.

Tender reports

Bid evaluation report: for each product in a tender, lists all suppliers that offered bids, with information on the supplier (country, delivery time) and on the quoted product (unit cost, quoted unit price, bid converted to base currency, manufacturer, quality of sample, and any other details).

Supplier performance report: lists, for a given supplier, details of all previous quotations, orders, and deliveries, including both a comparison between date promised and date delivered and the condition of products.

Product quotation record: for each product, lists previous bids, with details of the supplier and the quoted prices. If an order was made, this is indicated with supply timeliness and quality information.

Database listings: lists suppliers and products. The supplier listings can also be available as mailing labels and for mail-merging into a word-processed letter.

Country Study 50-3
Creating an Internet-based information system for HIV treatment in Haiti

The daily administration of several different antiretroviral medicines as part of antiretroviral therapy (ART) requires that each patient is monitored for health status, that results of laboratory tests are tracked and communicated to doctors, and that pharmaceutical supplies are reliably available at each treatment site. Zanmi Lasante, a nongovernmental organization that operated a successful ART site in Haiti's central plateau, was funded to scale up its program to five additional sites. In rural Haiti, where doctors are few, roads are almost nonexistent, and electricity is spotty, creating and maintaining such an information system among disparate sites would be challenging.

On the basis of its experience, Zanmi Lasante decided that the cheapest and most flexible communication strategy would be to establish a small satellite connection to the Internet in each of the five new sites. Instead of placing servers in each clinic, one shared server could be guaranteed a secure environment with stable power and a reliable data backup system. Using Web-based electronic records allows data collection and review from the remote sites, and with one server, the most recent data are accessible to all. The Web-based electronic medical record system in Haiti is built with standard, open source software.

Clinic staff members enter all clinical and medication data using a standardized Web-based patient form. To facilitate data entry, the form has an electronic checklist of patient management items, including requests for laboratory tests, details of treatment regimens, and lists of standard ART medicines. Doctors can check the medicines, doses, and administration schedules. As the medicines are entered into the form, they are cross-checked to the patient record for allergies, inappropriate doses, and incompatible medicine combinations. The system displays warnings about problems—for example, if zidovudine and stavudine are prescribed together. When the form is completed, the user can print out an order for the pharmacy. As new patient information (for example, laboratory results) is added that indicates additional treatment, e-mails are automatically sent to all clinicians with links to the medical records of patients who require follow-up.

Staff members also enter warehouse stock data into Web forms, and those figures are analyzed and monitored against expected use patterns from the treatment regimens in the system.

Source: Fraser et al. 2004.

Drug use reviews

Simple analyses of medicine-use patterns can be done with spreadsheets and commercial database software. Commercial software is available for analyzing data on medicine use from large databases. These software programs are usually fairly expensive (thousands of U.S. dollars [USD] per installation).

Pharmaceutical product registration

Pharmaceutical product registration software can help the drug regulatory authority track the hundreds or thousands of registered products. Registration data can be tracked in a manual card system, sorted by product name or company, but retrieving data needed for specific purposes is very time-consuming. Database programs can automate this procedure, retrieving records meeting specific criteria almost instantaneously. SIAMED, a software program for pharmaceutical product registration, is available from WHO. Computers can greatly facilitate pharmaceutical registration by improving access to information, but they do not provide the enforcement capacity needed to give registration

meaningful impact. A legal framework for pharmaceutical registration and a flexible and efficiently functioning drug regulatory authority are prerequisites to successful computerization of drug product registration. Table 50-3 presents the features needed in pharmaceutical registration software.

50.4 Electronic communications and medicine information

Communications and medicine information are discussed together because medicine information is increasingly available through electronic communication systems. An enormous amount of reference information on medicines is available on the Internet. In addition, many organizations now create their own websites to share information internally or to show their progress and activities to the outside world.

Electronic communications

Computers are powerful and relatively cheap communication tools. Computer-based communication is possible

Table 50-3   Select features of registration software

Names and identifications	Pharmacological information	International information	Quality assurance	Administrative tracking
• Registration of products by vendor and manufacturer	• Pharmacopoeial standards applicable to product	• Country of origin	• Certification by regulatory agency in country of origin (WHO certification scheme)	• Duration of license, dates of approval and renewal (or denial)
• Identification by International Nonproprietary Name (INN) and brand name	• Dosage strength and dosage form	• Product status and regulatory action in other countries	• Dates and results of quality tests and assays	• Dates of receipt and action on registration application
• Identification of alternative generic names (U.S. Adopted Name [USAN], British Approved Name [BAN])	• Quantities and functions of active and inactive ingredients	• Variable handling of applications from suppliers based in the registering country	• Summary of results of clinical trials	• Dates and results of agency hearings and regulatory actions regarding products, vendors, and manufacturers
• Cross-indexing between generic and brand names, active ingredients, and authorized vendors and manufacturers • Records of imports and foreign exchange applications and authorizations related to products, vendors, and manufacturers	• Shelf life and storage conditions		• Results of good manufacturing practices or other inspections • Details of inspection program based on user-defined criteria, such as geographical area, company activity, type of products, characteristics of inspectors • Registration and licensing of wholesale suppliers, licensed pharmacies, and other licensed pharmaceutical outlets	• Records of payments and dues regarding application and marketing authorization fees • Variable length of authorization for marketing • Records of price agreements and price control categories and decisions (as applicable)

Source: WHO 2004.

through electronic mail (e-mail), the World Wide Web, computer-to-computer modem connection, or fax.

If a good telephone line is available, computers equipped with a fax-modem can send and receive fax messages or complete documents in just a few seconds. Modern word processing software can send fax messages directly from the computer. The transmission speed and quality depend on the quality of the telephone line, but error protection protocols can help ensure the integrity of the transmitted data.

The most comprehensive computer-based communications medium is the Internet. Most countries have local connections to the Internet, which can send any data (including e-mail messages or computer files) for only a fraction of the cost of a telephone connection. Once the connection is established, Internet use is relatively inexpensive, especially for universities and governments. Increasingly, Internet cafés provide access in many locations. Locations with inadequate telephone-line infrastructure are having success with wireless Internet connections, which do not rely on traditional wires and cables. Other Internet connections are made through satellite and radio transmission.

In recent years, discussion groups have formed to exchange information over the Internet. For example, E-Drug is a discussion group that uses regular e-mail to exchange information on essential medicines management

issues. PharmWeb is a website that offers information on worldwide pharmacy and pharmaceutical management issues and organizations. PharmWeb links the user to various websites maintained by organizations active in the field. See References and Further Readings for contact information for E-Drug and PharmWeb. Web-based discussion groups can be helpful sources of information on a wide range of subjects, from computer problems to pharmaceutical information.

Medicine information

Traditional sources of information on medicines are journals and textbooks, such as those listed in Chapter 34. Maintaining an up-to-date library of texts and journals is costly, however, and information is not always easily accessed by users in remote areas.

Computers can greatly facilitate access to pharmaceutical information. For example, PubMed, a nonprofit service of the U.S. National Library of Medicine, provides access to millions of articles from more than 4,800 medical journals on the Web (http://www.ncbi.nlm.nih.gov/sites/entrez). PubMed can also be accessed with a PDA. The more commonly used and readily available computer databases for medicine information are listed and discussed in more detail in Chapter 34.

CD-ROM is relatively inexpensive technology that can store about 680 megabytes of data on one compact disc. DVD-ROMs are similar to CD-ROMs, but they hold about four gigabytes of data. Many products are now available on DVD. It is important that new computers be able to read DVD products.

Through powerful indexing routines and huge storage capacity, CD-ROMs and DVDs permit very fast access to medicine information. Books such as the *British National Formulary* and *USP Drug Information* are available in CD-ROM format. CD-ROMs with medication information or advice for poisoning treatment are used in many pharmacies and medicine information centers in industrialized countries, and their use is spreading quickly around the world as computers become more widely available.

Plenty of websites offer biased information on and questionable sales of medical products, including medications, but reliable, independent information on the quality, regulation, and rational use of pharmaceutical products is lacking. Learning to evaluate website content for accuracy, bias, and timeliness is an important skill. Chapter 34 has more information. See also the list of references in this chapter for some useful websites.

Developing a website

If an organization has information that it needs to communicate, it may wish to consider developing its own website. Websites can be used to disseminate information to the public or can be designed specifically for an organization's internal use (intranet). Although the design and development of the site can be contracted out if staff members do not have the necessary skills, staff should be involved in the review and approval of material for the site, because it represents the organization. Many Internet service providers (ISPs) offer hosting services for websites and can house the necessary files on their servers to make them available on the Internet.

An organization can use an intranet to share information and data if a WAN cannot be established. For example, users can access an intranet to view or submit inventory data for procurement or distribution purposes. An intranet can also be used to share files or disseminate organizational information, such as standard policies and procedures. The intranet site can be maintained at the central level of the system but accessed by other levels in the system as long as the other levels have Internet access and the proper permissions. The intranet allows pooling and sharing of information in a system without requiring a direct connection among the different levels of the system. (See Country Study 50-3.)

A website developer should consider the following criteria when creating a site to ensure that it is useful and informative (WHO 2001).

General criteria to consider for every site include—

- *User-friendliness:* The first impression should include an attractive design and logical organization of information.
- *Site map:* The site map indicates logical links and organization of the site and explains how to navigate through the content.
- *Navigability:* This characteristic allows the user to find information easily.
- *Speed:* The pages should be displayed within four to five seconds.
- *Search function:* The site should have its own search engine.
- *Update:* The website should include its creation date and when the pages were updated. Information should be updated regularly.

Specific criteria to consider for an organization or program site may include—

- Mission statement
- Contact information
- Organizational structure (or management hierarchy)
- Services offered
- News, events, and meetings
- Forms to download
- Hyperlinks to other useful resources
- Publications

Answering the questions in Box 50-5 can help in making a decision about whether and how to develop a new website.

50.5 Maintenance and support requirements

Using computers, like using any electronic tool, requires access to reputable repair services and supplies. Even more important, however, is a reliable, adequately trained staff.

Staff recruitment and training

Discussions about computerization often focus only on software and hardware, but computers are useless without competent staff to run them. Recruitment and training are key in maintaining good computer services, particularly when day-to-day operations such as inventory management and accounting are computerized. Investing in training staff members to use computers effectively is quite worthwhile.

Experienced typists interested in learning new skills can be recruited for word processing and data entry tasks. Computer courses are available in many countries. The cost of courses should be built into computerization budgets, along with sufficient funds each year to train new staff and retrain existing staff in new software. Online courses are also available if one has an Internet connection. For example, Microsoft offers free, self-paced courses for most of its Office products at http://office.microsoft.com/en-us/training/default.aspx.

When specialized pharmaceutical management programs are installed by an outside organization, the vendor must provide adequate training that is spread out over time so that staff members can raise their own questions as they become familiar with the new system.

Provisions need to be made for staff changes. At least two people need to be familiar with each specific computer program and operation so that sickness, annual leave, or job changes will not bring the computer unit to a halt. Additional training may be necessary from the vendor if personnel leave the unit.

A highly computerized operation that uses software to support critical operations, such as procurement or inventory management, should have the support of an information technologist on-site, if at all possible. If computer hardware or software is disabled by a problem that interferes with the daily business operations of an organization, the problem needs to be resolved as soon as possible. An information technology support unit serves to ensure that the organization's hardware and software remain functional through proper maintenance and prompt attention to errors.

Protecting data

Data in a computer are stored on magnetic media, such as a hard disk, CD-ROM, DVD, or flash drive. Unfortunately, magnetic storage media can lose data, so other precautions must be taken. The computer, along with all data on the hard

---

Box 50-5
Developing a website or posting materials to the Web

Here are some questions that will be useful to think about to effectively plan for, develop, and maintain a website.

Vision

- What is the purpose for developing a website or for posting materials to the Web?
- What do you hope to achieve?
- What are the intermediate and long-term goals or objectives?
- Do you see this activity as part of an existing website or something new?
- Is it important for this site to have a unique URL or Web address?

Audience

- Who are your primary and secondary audiences?
- What is the anticipated size of your audiences?
- Where are your audiences located?
- What are the information and/or learning needs of your audiences?
- What is the audience's level of comfort and experience using Internet?
- What is the audience's level of Internet access?
- What is the audience's level of computer proficiency?
- Do you anticipate this site being public or private/restricted?

Content

- What type of content do you anticipate for this site?
- What content currently exists?

- What new content needs to be written?
- How often will content be updated?
- In what languages will content be presented?
- Is any of the content proprietary, or is use restricted by any parties?
- Do any donors or partners need to approve posting of content?

Functionality

- What tasks do you want users to perform when they come to the site?
- What specific functions would you like to include on the website (for example, information database, online message boards)?

Marketing

- How will you reach your audience?

Evaluation

- How will you know when you have achieved your goals?
- What evaluation methods will you use (for example, e-mail survey, phone interviews)?

Roles

- Who will develop content?
- Who will update content over time?
- Who will market the site?
- Who will provide technical support to users?

drive, might be stolen or could be harmed by dust or high-voltage electrical spikes.

Data can also be damaged by a computer virus when programs or data are exchanged between computers or when an infected e-mail attachment is opened. This risk increases when illegally copied (pirated) software is used. A virus can result in anything from harmless messages appearing unexpectedly on the computer screen to complete loss or theft of data on the hard drive. To avoid getting a computer virus, accept files only from users who take precautions against viruses, do not open unknown attachment files from e-mail senders, use virus-check software that automatically scans the computer's hard drive every day, and check any media, such as flash drives or CD-ROMs, used to share data . Regular updates of virus protection programs are needed because new viruses are created continually.

CD-ROMs and DVDs can be damaged by magnetic fields (from loudspeakers, telephones, and metal detectors), and by moisture, particles, and scratches. Thus, having only one copy of data is risky, and the importance of making backup copies cannot be overemphasized. Basic rules for maintaining backups are—

- Make at least one backup copy of all important work when it is created.
- Back up routine work daily with separate sets of CDs, DVDs, or external drives used in rotation for extra security, especially for large databases such as inventory control systems.
- Ideally, store backups off-site to guard them from fire or theft. Consider saving and archiving an entire set of data at the end of each month or quarter.

Access to computers should be restricted to authorized staff; most computer operating systems and software can be protected with passwords, which are required to enter the system (and which allow managers to track use of the computer).

Maintaining computers

Computers are adversely affected by humidity, static electricity, power surges, extreme temperatures, dust, cigarette smoke, and food or liquid spilled on the keyboards. Computers are also vulnerable to frequent switching on and off, sudden physical movements while the hard disk is running, misuse by untrained staff, and unprofessional repair attempts. To protect computers—

- Make sure that a reliable firm (or department) is under contract to support hardware and software.
- Train all operators in proper computer handling.

Box 50-6
Lessons for successful computerization

- Assess what software is needed before choosing hardware.
- Ensure software and hardware compatibility.
- Secure local support for hardware and software.
- Have a well-functioning manual system.
- Provide adequate staff training and involve staff in the computerization process.
- Computerize in phases, allowing sufficient time for each step.
- Establish and enforce strict procedures for data and equipment protection, using backups, virus checkers, restricted access, surge suppressors, and so on.
- Set aside adequate funds in each year's budget for hardware and software maintenance, supplies, and staff training.
- Plan and budget for timely hardware and software upgrades.

- Protect the computer room with air-conditioning—if possible—against excess heat, humidity, and dust.
- Do not eat or drink near the computer or smoke in the computing room.
- Protect keyboard, monitor, and computer with covers.
- Always use spike/surge protectors (for computer, printer, monitor, and fax) and an uninterruptible power supply. Car batteries with an inverter or a separate fuel generator may also provide safe electrical power.
- Move the computer only when it is switched off.
- Use reliable maintenance and repair services.

50.6 Lessons for successful computerization in pharmaceutical management

Successful computerization in pharmaceutical management can greatly increase an organization's efficiency, productivity, and capabilities, but it must be carefully planned. Expensive mistakes are easy to make through a lack of knowledge or forethought, hindering rather than helping a project. Following the list in Box 50-6 and considering the issues raised earlier in this chapter will help a manager to avoid or prevent such mistakes. The information presented in this chapter should enable a manager to ask the right questions and effectively plan the computerization of an organization. ■

ASSESSMENT GUIDE

Use of computers in pharmaceutical management

- In which phases of pharmaceutical management will computerization be most useful: medicine selection and formulary development, registration, quantification of pharmaceutical requirements, procurement, inventory control, prescription analysis, other areas?
- Does a product master file exist? Has a coding system been developed to uniquely identify pharmaceutical products? Is the ICD or other coding system used to identify health problems?

Readiness for computerization or expansion

- Are computers currently used for producing correspondence, newsletters, reports? Preparation of tables, graphs, charts? Budgets and other spreadsheet applications? Electronic communications?
- Do good manual systems exist for pharmaceutical management functions?
- Are staff members capable of and interested in learning to operate computers?
- Are resources available for staff training? Supplies such as CDs and DVDs, paper, and printer ink and toner? Computer support and periodic upgrades, as needed?

Computerization planning

- Have needs been identified and the specific tasks, functions, and systems to be computerized carefully analyzed?
- Has appropriate software been identified, for example, for word processing, spreadsheets, database management, and special functions such as presentation graphics, project management, accounting, or electronic communications?
- Is training available for each software package? Are manuals or other instruction books available?
- Have hardware specifications been defined in terms of operating system, microprocessor speed, available RAM, storage capacity, monitor, printer, modem, uninterruptible power supply? Is this hardware capable of running the software identified?
- Has the computerization process been planned in phases, so that experience with computer applications will develop in parallel with broad systems development?
- Have procedures been developed for data and equipment protection, such as restricted access, use of an uninterruptible power supply and surge suppressors, virus checking, backing up data files, and storing backups off-site?

Hardware and software support and maintenance

- Is there a firm in the country or area that sells software and provides support? Does this firm provide training in use of the software?
- Is there a firm in the country or area that sells and maintains computer hardware?
- Is there a government agency or department that can provide support services to the supply system?
- Has someone on the staff been trained, at minimum, in the basics of computer troubleshooting?

References and further readings

General

Camara, G., and F. Fonseca. 2007. Information Policies and Open Source Software in Developing Countries. *Journal of The American Society for Information Science and Technology* 58(1):121–32.

Collins, M. F. 2004. Measuring Performance Indicators in Clinical Pharmacy Services with a Personal Digital Assistant. *American Journal of Health-System Pharmacy* 61(5):498–501.

Dravis, P. 2003. *Open Source Software: Perspectives for Development.* Washington, D.C.: Dravis Group, *info*Dev, and World Bank Group. <http://www.infodev.org/en/Publication.21.html >

Enders, S. J., J. M. Enders, and S. G. Holstad. 2002. Drug-Information Software for Palm Operating System Personal Digital Assistants: Breadth, Clinical Dependability and Ease of Use. *Pharmacotherapy* 22(8):1036–40.

Fraser, H. S. F., D. Jazayeri, P. Nevil, Y. Karacaoglu, P. E. Farmer, E. Lyon, M. K. Fawzi, et al. 2004. An Information System and Medical Record to Support HIV Treatment in Rural Haiti. *BMJ* 329:1142–6.

Gookin, D. 2007. *PCs for Dummies.* 11th ed. Hoboken, N.J.: John Wiley & Sons.

Harindranath, H., W. G. Wojtkowski, J. Zupancic, D. Rosenberg, W. Wojtkowski, S. Wrycza, and J. A. A. Sillince, eds. 2002. *New Perspectives on Information Systems Development: Theory, Methods, and Practice.* New York: Springer.

Healthlink Worldwide, AfriAfya, and the Institute for Sustainable Health Education and Development. 2006. *Improving Health, Connecting People: The Role of ICTs in the Health Sector of Developing Countries.* Working Paper No. 7. Washington, D.C.: *info*Dev. <www.infodev.org/en/Document.84.pdf>

Keplar, K. E., and C. J. Urbanski. 2003. Personal Digital Assistant Applications for the Healthcare Provider. *Annals of Pharmacotherapy* 37:287–96.

McFadyen, J. 2003. *Pharmaceutical Management Logistics Software Evaluation Report.* Prepared for the Strategies for Enhancing Access to Medicines Program. Arlington, Va.: Management Sciences for Health.

Miller, M. 2009. *Absolute Beginner's Guide to Computer Basics*. 5th ed. Indianapolis, Ind.: Que Corp.

MSH (Management Sciences for Health). 2000. E-Learning for Program Managers through Global Information Resources. *The Manager* 9:(1&2). <http://erc.msh.org/TheManager/English/V9_N1/V9_N1_En_Issue.pdf>

UHIN (Uganda Health Information Network). 2004. *Technical Report: September 2003–October 2004*. Prepared for The International Development Research Centre. (Available at http://pda.healthnet.org.)

WHO (World Health Organization). 2004. *Setting up a Computerized Drug Registration and Allied Information System*. Geneva: WHO. <http://whqlibdoc.who.int/publications/2004/9290610646.pdf>

———. 2001. Improving the Quality and Usefulness of Drug Regulatory Authority Websites. *WHO Drug Information* 15(3 and 4):163–7.

Coding systems

AHFS (American Hospital Formulary Service) Drug Information. (Online updates.) Bethesda, Md.: American Society of Health-System Pharmacists. <http://www.ahfsdruginformation.com>

WHO (World Health Organization). 2010. *International Nonproprietary Names (INN) for Pharmaceutical Substances*. (Updated regularly.) Geneva: WHO. <http://www.who.int/medicines/publications/druginformation/innlists/RL63.pdf>

———. 2007. *International Classification of Diseases (ICD-10-CM)*. Geneva: WHO. <http://www.who.int/classifications/icd/en>

———. No date. "INN Stems." (Updated regularly.) <http://www.who.int/medicines/services/inn/stembook/en/index.html>

WHO Collaborating Centre for Drug Statistics Methodology. ATC/DDD Index 2010. (Updated annually.) Oslo: WHO Collaborating Centre for Drug Statistics Methodology/Norwegian Institute of Public Health. <http://www.whocc.no/atcddd>

Pharmaceutical-related computer applications

British Medical Association and Royal Pharmaceutical Society of Great Britain. *British National Formulary* (BNF). (Updated every six months; website updated more frequently.) Paperback, CD-ROM, or online. <http://www.bnf.org>

The Electronic Dispensing Tool is a software application for managing essential medicines stock and monitoring details on dispensing to individual patients. The tool was designed to be used by a dispensing pharmacist. Contact cpm@msh.org for more information.

Epi Info is a series of microcomputer programs for word processing, data management, and epidemiological analysis, designed for public health professionals. The software can be downloaded free from a number of websites, including the following: <http://www.cdc.gov/epiinfo>

INRUD (International Network for Rational Use of Drugs). *Medicines Use Bibliography*. (Updated regularly.) <http://www.inrud.org>

The Inventory Management Assessment Tool (IMAT) is a user-friendly, Excel-based instrument designed to collect and calculate indicators of effective pharmaceutical inventory management. <http://erc.msh.org/toolkit>

The Inventory Tracking Tool aids in managing ARV stocks at higher levels than the facility (program, district, or national). The tool monitors aggregated medicine consumption and compares it with projected consumption. Contact cpm@msh.org for more information.

Logistics Support System (WHO/PAHO Supply Management System). Supply management project software for use in disaster relief efforts. PAHO. <http://www.lssweb.net>

The Medical Letter. Adverse Drug Interactions Program. (Updated regularly.) Available for Windows-based PCs, PDAs, and in CD-ROM format. The Medical Letter also has a number of other software products. <http://secure.medicalletter.org/subscriptions_products#5>

PubMed provides access to citations from biomedical literature, including MEDLINE, the U.S. National Library of Medicine's bibliographic database covering the fields of medicine, nursing, dentistry, veterinary medicine, the health care system, and the preclinical sciences. PubMed is accessible online through the National Library of Medicine Database via Datastar, Dialog, or NLM. CD-ROM version through Silver Platter. Contact the PubMed help desk at custserv@nlm.nih.gov or 888-346-3656. <http://www.ncbi.nlm.nih.gov/entrez/query.fcgi?db=PubMed>

Quantimed is a quantification database tool that facilitates the generation of realistic estimates of pharmaceutical needs at the facility, regional, or national level, using morbidity and/or consumption data. Contact cpm@msh.org for more information.

RxSolution is designed to manage pharmaceuticals and medical supplies, from procurement to dispensing to patients. Contact cpm@msh.org for more information.

SIAMED: Model System for Computer-Assisted Medicine Registration. <http://www.who.int/medicines/areas/quality_safety/regulation_legislation/siamed/en/index.html>

WHO Model Web Site for Medicines Regulatory Agencies. A tool to help the drug regulatory agencies in WHO member states to develop or review their own websites. <http://www.who.int/medicines/areas/quality_safety/regulation_legislation/model_site/en/index.html>

Vigibase Services is a unique collection of international drug safety data available through WHO's Uppsala Monitoring Centre. <http://www.umc-products.com/DynPage.aspx?id=4910&mn=1107>

PDA-specific applications and resources

Dalhousie University College of Pharmacy. "Drug- and Pharmacy-Related Mobile Technology" <http://dir.pharmacy.dal.ca/pda.php>

Johns Hopkins Point of Care Information Technology (POC-IT). <http://www.hopkinsmedicine.org/poc-it>

University of Kansas Medical Center. Dykes Library. Mobile Resources. <http://library.kumc.edu/m/index.html>

Internet resources

E-Drug (Essential Drugs English) and other global discussion groups in various languages on pharmaceutical issues. See http://www.healthnet.org for information on subscribing to any e-mail forum.

Eldis is an Internet-based information service presenting development information through the Web and e-mail. The Eldis ICT for Development Resource Guide has information and resources specific to using information technology in developing countries. <http://www.eldis.org/go/topics/resource-guides/ict-for-development>

The Information and Communication Technology (ICT) for Development Gateway shares information and promotes ideas on how information and communication technologies can be used to address socioeconomic needs in developing countries, with a special focus on achieving the Millennium Development Goals. <http://ict.zunia.org>

The Information for Development (*info*Dev) Program works to promote better understanding, and effective use, of information and communication technologies as tools of poverty reduction and broad-based, sustainable development. <http://www.infodev.org>

InterConnection works to make Internet technology accessible to nonprofit organizations in developing countries. <http://www.inter connection.org>

Management Sciences for Health (MSH), Center for Pharmaceutical Management (CPM). View the website at http://www.msh.org/cpm. To send an e-mail message, write to cpm@msh.org. MSH freely makes available electronic products for the practice of international health at the Manager's Electronic Resource Center. <http://erc.msh.org>

The Open Source Initiative is an organization that promotes the use and distribution of open source software. <http://www.opensource.org>

PharmWeb is a website with pharmacy-related information and links to other sites maintained by organizations active in pharmaceutical management. PharmWeb sponsors a number of discussion groups and pharmaceutical information mailing lists. View the website and find instructions for subscribing to the lists. <http://www.pharmweb.net>

SATELLIFE is a nonprofit telecommunications organization dedicated to providing health care workers around the world with affordable access to critical health information through the HealthNet network and other communications services. <http://www.healthnet.org>

The World Health Organization's (WHO's) Essential Medicines and Pharmaceutical Policies (EMP) website provides information on EMP's political and administrative components, including its mandate, management approach, and worldwide projects, and on its technical components and services. These include national medicine policies, indicators, medicine information and documentation, rational medicine use, training courses, and publications. Selected documents and publications can easily be downloaded from the EMP website. <http://www.who.int/medicines>

The WHO Medicine Information System Web page lists a number of resources related to pharmaceutical-related information systems. <http://www.who.int/medicines/services/medicines_etools/en/index.html#ED>

Glossary

Apple: Company that made one of the first desktop computers. It now makes the Mac line of computers and iPhones (smartphones).

Backup: An extra copy of software or data, normally kept on file in case the original program or information is damaged or lost.

Baud: A measure of the speed at which data travels (normally between a computer and a peripheral).

Bit: A binary digit (1 or 0).

Bug: A flaw or problem in a software program.

Byte: A sequence of bits that represents a single character. In most small computers, a byte is eight bits.

CD-ROM (compact disc read-only memory): A medium for storing large amounts of data that can be accessed quickly and selectively using a CD-ROM drive. CD-ROMs are less vulnerable to damage than diskettes, which are seldom used anymore.

Chip: A generic term for an integrated circuit, a single package holding thousands of microscopic electronic components. The processor of a computer is one.

CPU (central processing unit): The "brain" of the computer, which directs and processes input and output.

Data: Numerical or verbal representations of facts that are processed to produce information.

Database: A collection of related data that can be retrieved and manipulated by a computer.

Debug: To go through a software program to remove mistakes.

Density (double, high): Describes how much information can be stored on a storage medium.

Disk: A round piece of magnetic-coated material used to store data.

Disk drive: Part of a computer that reads data from, or writes data to, a disk.

Dot matrix printer: A printer that produces lower-quality output than a laser printer. This type of printer is the best for printing on multiple kinds of paper.

Downtime: Any period when a computer is not available or not working.

DVD (digital video [or versatile] disc): A medium for storing large amounts of data that can be accessed quickly and selectively by using a DVD drive. DVDs hold more data than CD-ROMs.

Field: In a database, the basic column unit, in which the same type of information appears.

File: An organized collection of bytes stored on disk, maintained by the operating system, and referenced by name.

Hard disk: A fast-spinning, rigid piece of equipment made of stainless steel with a magnetic layer, which stores huge amounts of data inside a computer.

Hardware: The physical equipment of a computer system, such as the computer, monitor, and printer. Useless without software.

Inkjet printer: A type of printer with print quality between that of a dot matrix printer and a laser printer.

Laptop/notebook/netbook: Small computer that incorporates the CPU, monitor, and keyboard in one unit and can run on batteries. A notebook computer is smaller than a laptop, and a netbook is smaller than either.

Laser printer: A type of printer that uses laser technology to produce very high print quality.

Mainframe: Big, powerful, expensive computer, usually used by universities and the military. Usually not necessary for managing pharmaceutical supplies.

Memory: Circuitry and devices that hold the bits the computer can access. Examples are RAM (random-access memory) and ROM (read-only memory).

Minicomputer: Smaller than a mainframe but still too big or costly for an individual; may be useful for storing large amounts of data in a central medical store.

Modem: An electronic device that allows computer equipment to send and receive information through telephone lines.

Monitor: A TV-like display used with most computers to show the information being input and output.

Motherboard: The board containing the computer's circuitry, onto which all other parts of the CPU are attached.

Mouse: A small, mobile manual device that controls movement of the cursor and selection of the function on a computer display.

Network: An interconnected system of computers. The components do not have to be physically close to one another—they can be connected by telephone, data lines, or without wires.

Operating system: Software that oversees the overall operation of a computer system. It enables other software to communicate with the hardware and must be present for the computer to function. An example is Windows, used by PCs, and OS X, used by Macs.

PC (personal computer): Any general-purpose computer for individual use. Microsoft and Intel dominate the PC operating system market. Today's PCs evolved from PCs standardized by IBM

Annex 50-1   Building a product master file in a database

This section describes essential concepts for building the main reference file (that is, the product master file) in pharmaceutical management database software.

Product master file

Common to nearly all forms of database management is a master file, which includes features for pharmaceutical management, such as product name, strength, dosage form, and therapeutic category. For procurement and inventory control systems, the product master file usually has supplementary information on cost and pack size. The full description of a product can be split into database fields to sort and classify the data.

The following table briefly describes the information commonly contained in a basic product master file. The development of this file should be carefully planned around several issues, including product coding systems, definition of units, and identification of supplier-specific products.

Product master file code

A computer program must be able to identify each product quickly and without confusion. After a coding system has been chosen, it must be maintained without ambiguity, or duplication will occur. Many options exist for coding systems. The simplest system is the "dummy" code, which has no intrinsic meaning—for example, *12345* is assigned to the first item entered in the list, *12346* for the second, and so on. With this system, the only question is how many digits are needed; the key point is that the code should be unique. In most systems, a five-digit code is sufficient for many years. If a large number of different items exist, a six-digit code might be prudent.

A more complex option is an "information-bearing" code, in which each digit has significance—for example, ampicillin 500 mg capsules might be coded as *AMP500C*. In some countries, formal information-bearing codes have been developed at the national level for pharmaceutical products. An example is the nine-digit National Drug Code in the United States, in which the first four digits signify the manufacturer or labeler, the next three digits show the product, and the last two show the package size.

Arguments exist favoring each of these coding options, as well as others. Data entry errors are reduced with more complex coding schemes, but the time required to enter data may be greater. An information-bearing coding scheme takes more time to develop and maintain than a simple numeric code for products. Note that a separate coding scheme will be needed for therapeutic categories. Several international coding systems for medicine categories are discussed in Chapter 16.

Health problem coding

Health problem information must be coded for diagnosis-specific medicine-use analysis and morbidity quantification of pharmaceutical requirements. The accepted standard is the WHO *International Classification of Diseases* (ICD-10), a hierarchical classification based on major and minor disease categories, which is available online, on CD-ROM, and for PDAs and smartphones. Most information systems are now based on the ICD system, although local adaptations often result in different groupings of individual health problems.

Definition of units

When computerizing medicines systems, considerable confusion can arise over the definition of units. For example, in the preliminary quantification exercise for a large essential medicines project, requirements for benzyl benzoate (a topical preparation for skin infestations) were calculated in milliliters, whereas the essential medicines list specified liters. This discrepancy led to a 1,000-fold error that increased estimated pharmaceutical requirements by USD 1 million.

Defining the basic unit, issue unit, defined daily dose unit, pack size, and minimum order can help avoid major mistakes.

Basic or comparison unit. The basic unit is the smallest unit in which a drug product can be conveniently dispensed or administered. It is also used to compare prices of different sized bottles or vials. The total number of basic or comparison units is equal to one issue unit. For example, 100 tablets make up one bottle, with the tablet as the basic unit and the bottle as the issue unit.

Issue unit. The issue unit is used to count and distribute the stock. It allows the comparison of items of different pack sizes

---

in the 1980s, except for Apple Corporation products, which are not considered to be PCs.

Peripherals: Equipment (usually hardware) that is external to the computer itself. Examples are tape drives and speakers.

Personal digital assistant (PDA): Handheld computing device that can record and store data to synchronize with a desktop computer.

Power spikes/surges: Major fluctuations in electrical current that can disrupt the computer's internal operation and damage hardware.

Printer: A device to produce hard-copy output.

RAM (random-access memory): The main type of memory used in computers, also known as read/write memory because data in RAM can be easily changed.

Record: One entry, or row, in a database.

ROM (read-only memory): Memory where information is perma-nently stored and cannot be altered. This form of memory is also random access.

Scanner: A piece of hardware that reads information from text or images and converts it into digital form for a computer to use.

Server: The main computer on a network; provides storage and processing capabilities for client computers.

Smartphone: A mobile phone that offers more-advanced computing ability and connectivity than a basic mobile phone. Smartphones allow the user to install and run more-advanced applications and transmit data easily.

Software: Programs or segments of programs.

Spreadsheet: A program for calculating and linking numbers.

Virus: An undesirable program that displays bizarre messages or destroys data on the computer. Transferred mainly by sharing files without testing them first with antivirus software or by opening infected attachments to e-mail messages.

but the same issue unit. The total number of issue units per pack is equal to one pack size.

Pack size. In procurement, the pack size is used to request bids. Suppliers usually give the product cost for a pack size.

See the table on the following page for more examples of units. Individual computer systems may handle these concepts differently, but managers of pharmaceutical programs must be thoroughly familiar with the problems of defining pharmaceutical units. Unambiguous local definitions must be established, and everyone involved in recording, entering, verifying, or using the computer data must be trained to use these definitions.

Standard information in a master product data file

Description	Example	Explanation
Product code	AMP250C	Each entry in the product data file must have a unique code. (See text for discussion of coding options.)
Generic name	Ampicillin	The official International Nonproprietary Name (INN) is generally preferred. The WHO Model List of Essential Medicines, which is regularly updated, uses the INN.
Strength	250 mg	The International System of Units (SI), with related SI abbreviations, should be used. "Strength" can be split into "strength number" (250, for example) and "strength unit" (such as mg), but this method often creates unnecessary confusion and coding difficulties.
Route of administration	PO	Standard abbreviations should be used. For example, PO = per os (oral), IV = intravenous, TOP = topical.
Dosage form	CAP	Standard abbreviations should be used. For example, CAP = capsule, TAB = tablet.
Issue unit	CAP	The issue unit is the smallest unit by which a drug product can be conveniently distributed. (See text for further explanation.)
Defined daily dosage (DDD)	4	The DDD represents the usual total daily therapeutic dosage for an adult. In computer systems, it is best defined in terms of issue unit per DDD.
DDD unit	g	The unit in which the DDD is measured.
National essential medicines list (EML)/formulary status	Y	Is the medicine listed in the national EML or formulary? Y = yes, N = no.
Therapeutic class	44:29	Categorizing medicines by therapeutic or pharmacologic class can be useful. Several systems exist, including the ATC, BNF, AFHS, and PAHO systems, and that used for the WHO Model List of Essential Medicines. (See Chapter 40 for further discussion of therapeutic category systems.)
Prescription status	POM	Status for retail sales. For example, POM = prescription-only medicine, OTC = over-the-counter.
Level of care	A	National EMLs may categorize medicines according to level of care. For example, A = all levels, B = all levels except dispensary, and so forth.
ABC classification	A	Classification of a product as A, B, or C according to the volume consumed and unit cost. (See Chapter 40 for discussion of ABC analysis.)
VEN classification	V	Classification of a product as V, E, or N, according to its therapeutic value as vital, essential, or nonessential. (See Chapter 40 for discussion of the VEN system.)
WHO status	M	Is the medicine on the WHO Model List of Essential Medicines? This entry can be listed as Y (yes) or N (no). It can also be listed as M (main), C (complementary), E (therapeutically equivalent), or N (not on the list).

Annex 50-1   Building a product master file in a database (continued)

Units in pharmaceutical management

Code	Description	Strength	Form	Comparison units per issue unit	Comparison unit	Issue units per pack size	Issue unit	Pack size units per minimum order	Pack size	Pack size cost	Minimum order cost	Cost per issue unit	Cost per comparison unit
				Issue unit		Pack size		Miniumum order					
AMP250T	Ampicillin	250 mg	Tablet	1	Tab	1,000	Tablet	5	Bottle	34.00	170.00	0.0340 per tab	0.0340 per tab
PIL2OD	Pilocarpine	2%	Drops	15	mL	12	Dropper	1	Box	17.52	17.52	1.4600 per dropper	0.0973 per mL
BNTOT	Bacitracin + neomycin	USP	Ointment	3.5	g	100	Tube	1	Box	100.00	100.00	1.0000 per tube	0.2857 per g
NACL09I	Sodium chloride	0.9%	Injection	1,000	mL	12	Vial	10	Box	1.56	15.60	0.1300 per vial	0.0001 per mL
AMP500I	Ampicillin	500 mg	Injection	1	Vial	100	Vial	1	Box	30.00	30.00	0.3000 per vial	0.3000 per vial
PEN5MI	Penicillin	2 MU	Injection	1	Vial	12	Vial	6	Box	6.00	36.00	0.5000 per vial	0.5000 per vial
COD0S	Codeine	USP	Syrup	500	mL	1	Bottle	6	Box	7.00	42.00	7.0000 per bottle	0.0140 per mL
SAL200S	Salbutamol	100 mcg per dose	Inhaler	200	Doses	1	Inhaler	100	Box	2.70	270.00	2.7000 per inhaler	0.0135 per dose
COND0L	Condom	—	Disp	1	Condom	100	Condom	10	Box	1.50	15.00	0.0150 per condom	0.0150 per condom
BIS10S	Bisacodyl	10 mg	Suppository	1	Suppository	12	Suppository	10	Box	10.00	100.00	0.8333 per supp	0.8333 per supp
AL90L	Alcohol	95%	Liquid	1	Liter	210	Liter	1	Drum	100.00	100.00	0.4762 per liter	0.4762 per liter
JELOJ	Jelly, lubricating	BP	Gel	142	g	12	Tubes	1	Box	100.00	100.00	8.3333 per tube	0.0587 per g
GLOV7D	Glove	7	Disp	2	Glove	50	Pair	1	Box	100.00	100.00	2.0000 per pair	1.0000 per glove
NED21G	Needle	21 g	Disp	1	Needle	100	Needle	10	Box	10.00	100.00	0.1000 per needle	0.1000 per needle

| Part I: Policy and economic issues | Part II: Pharmaceutical management | Part III: Management support systems |

Planning and administration
Organization and management
Information management
Human resources management
   51 Human resources management and capacity development
   52 Designing and implementing training programs

CHAPTER 51

Human resources management and capacity development

SUMMARY

Human resources are central to planning, managing, and delivering health services, including pharmaceutical services. In most countries, personnel account for a high proportion of the national budget for the health sector—often 75 percent or more. Despite the critical importance of human resources to the functioning of pharmaceutical management programs, few concerted efforts have addressed the severe staff shortages facing the health sector in many countries. The HIV/AIDS pandemic has intensified this already serious situation.

In addition to staffing shortages, the health system faces many human resources challenges, including human resources planning, recruitment, deployment, training, staff motivation, and staff development. The root causes of these issues can be traced to years of neglect, low salaries, poor workplace climate, and limited capacity to train and update staff skills. Interventions needed to alleviate the human resources crisis include short-term actions, such as task shifting, while in the long term, countries need to expand their capacity to train enough staff to fill needs. Some issues need to be addressed at the national level (for example, compensation), but many can be addressed through better leadership and human resource management (HRM) at the facility level. In the pharmaceutical sector, the goal of HRM is to develop and sustain an adequate supply of skilled professionals who are motivated to provide a high level of pharmaceutical care.

Effectively addressing human resources challenges requires improved leadership and management at all levels. An expanded HRM role, especially at the facility level, is needed to transform the outdated view of human resources as mainly an administrative function to one where the human resources staff work closely with managers to support the health goals of the organization and to ensure that the right staff with the right skills are in place to meet these goals.

Managing people is an important and challenging task for any manager. Employees are motivated by many factors that can be affected by management. Receiving effective supervision, perceiving they are fairly treated, understanding their job priorities, getting feedback, feeling valued and appreciated, and having opportunities for professional development can all help staff perform better.

Developing and maintaining a fair, equitable, and effective HRM system can motivate staff and increase their level of job satisfaction and efficiency, which can result in improved service quality. An important part of a long-term strategy is creating an organizational and management structure for HRM that is implemented by managers and staff at all levels. A human resources partnership between senior managers, supervisors, human resources professionals, and individual staff members is what makes an HRM system work.

51.1   Recognizing the crisis in human resources for health

Countries throughout the world, especially developing countries, have long suffered from a severe lack of skilled health workers and managers. The delivery of health services is labor intensive, and the workforce is the primary determinant of health system effectiveness, yet strategies and systems for human capacity development in most ministries of health are inadequate to meet the needs of the population. In addition, the lack of health staff, including trained pharmacy staff, has compromised health care in rural areas. Moreover, the demands of scaling up antiretroviral treatment (ART) programs and the related time-consuming care have overburdened already weak systems for human resources development and management and drained personnel from other health services. Absenteeism and low morale are widespread, and work-related stress reduces health workers' productivity.

Countries with a high prevalence of HIV/AIDS that cannot address acute shortages in the short term are unable to deliver effective services. In these countries, staff attrition rates are rising because of HIV infection, illness, and death as well as the migration of staff to urban areas or other countries. Vacancy rates in public-sector organizations are also rising, while the pool of skilled candidates to fill positions is still not deep enough. Results from a twelve-country survey showed that the problem is so serious that countries simply do not have the human resources capacity to absorb, deploy, and use additional funds that they are receiving to improve health (Kinfu et al. 2009). Estimates cited in the survey indicate that workforces in the most-affected countries would need to increase by up to 140 percent to attain health development targets.

The pharmaceutical personnel situation in many countries is dire; for example, countries such as Benin and Mali have less than one pharmaceutical worker for every 100,000 people, whereas France, in comparison, has more than 100 per 100,000 (Table 51-1). Uganda has an estimated 30 percent of the pharmacists it actually needs (Matsiko and Kiwanuka 2003). Some industrialized countries also have pharmacy staff shortages; many areas of the

Table 51-1 Pharmaceutical personnel,[a] density per 100,000 population in selected countries, 2007–08

Country	Density
Benin	< 1
Niger	< 1
Senegal	1
Burkina Faso	2
Malawi	2
Uzbekistan	3
Bhutan	4
Ghana	7
Liberia	8
Nigeria	13
Turkey	33
Albania	39
Israel	76
Bahrain	86
France	118

Source: WHO Department of Human Resources for Health 2008.

[a] Pharmaceutical personnel include pharmacists, pharmaceutical technicians, and pharmaceutical technologists.

United States have some difficulty filling pharmacist positions (FIP 2009).

The dynamics of entry and exit from the health workforce in many countries remains poorly understood, and many reasons—such as lack of investment in training, illness, and premature retirement and death—contribute to the shortage. This lack of understanding inhibits countries and development partners from developing and implementing appropriate interventions. Several factors, however, are recognized as important contributors to the shortage of trained pharmacy personnel and other health care workers, including—

Migration of health personnel: Migration contributes significantly to the loss of health workers from many countries. For example, almost two-thirds of Ghana's 140 pharmacy school graduates in 2003 migrated to a different country; between 2001 and 2004, Zimbabwe had about 150 new pharmacy graduates, while 100 Zimbabwean pharmacists registered to work in the United Kingdom during the same period (FIP 2006). Even relatively well-off countries like South Africa are losing trained health professionals to richer economies (FIP 2006).

Staff leaving the public sector: Health staff members leave the public sector to work for donor-funded projects that are flourishing from the large influx of money into Africa; in addition, health workers often choose to work in the private sector, where remuneration is often better.

For example, in Kenya, 58 percent of health facilities are in the public sector, whereas 86 percent of the pharmaceutical workforce is employed in the private sector (FIP 2009). Country Study 51-1 shows how a public-private partnership in Namibia, where pharmacists prefer private-sector employment, successfully recruited and pharmacy professionals into public-sector service.

Poor distribution of staff: The predominance of health workers is in urban areas—where they earn more and have access to better opportunities—meaning that rural areas often suffer from acute shortages of trained workers. Uganda is a country that has less than one pharmacist per 100,000 people in its population, but almost 90 percent of the existing pharmacists are located in the Central region, while the other 10 percent are divided among the other four regions in the country (FIP 2006).

Insufficient preservice training: Many countries lack the ability to train enough pharmaceutical professionals to fill their needs; they may have no or only one accredited school of pharmacy, for example. Increasing the number of skilled workers requires capacity in the educational system—enough teachers, updated curriculum, and adequate infrastructure—which takes time to build. Even when graduates are available, retention is difficult unless good management exists to absorb, train, and support them.

51.2 Addressing the crisis in the short and long terms

Global action is required not only to address high-priority infectious diseases but also to meet the long-term human resources needs of health systems in developing countries. The greatest challenge is to begin addressing shortages of health personnel in an integrated and comprehensive fashion. Responses to the challenge must meet both the short-term necessities of providing lifesaving treatment and the long-term human resources needs of the health sector (see Country Study 51-1).

Short-term responses include implementing aggressive retention policies, such as improving terms and conditions of service for health workers, providing ART to health workers who need it to preserve their health and productivity, and encouraging temporary regional migration of workers from countries with surplus workers to countries with deficits. For example, Kenya has bilateral agreements with Namibia, Southern Sudan, and Lesotho to send nurses to work on short-term contracts in those countries.

Task shifting has been used extensively and often effectively to fill gaps in health care worker shortages, including in pharmacies (WHO Maximizing Positive Synergies Collaborative Group 2009). Often, lower-level pharmacy workers, such as pharmacy technicians, or other cadres,

Country Study 51-1
Using partnerships to improve human resources capacity to deliver pharmaceutical services in Namibia

Human resources crisis in pharmacy

According to the World Health Organization's Global Atlas of the Health Workforce, in 2004, Namibia had fourteen pharmacists per 100,000 people, or half of South Africa's twenty-eight pharmacists per 100,000. Namibia's pharmacists are also poorly distributed—80 percent work in the private sector, leaving priority public health programs short of qualified staff. About half the pharmacists working in the public sector are located in Khomas region, particularly in Windhoek city, leaving the other twelve regions short of qualified personnel. Pharmacist assistants in most district hospitals occupy positions meant for more highly skilled pharmacists.

In 2006, of the forty-eight public-sector pharmacy posts available, only fourteen were filled—four of these were filled by Namibians.

Challenges in filling positions in Namibia

- Foreigners on two-to-three-year contracts fill 90 percent of pharmacist positions. Knowledge of local languages is critical; English speakers usually need translators to communicate with patients, while the many Cuban pharmacists have a hard time because of a lack of Spanish translators.
- No pharmacy school exists in Namibia, and an inadequate number of Namibian students pursue a pharmacy degree abroad. Those who do return from abroad choose careers in the private sector.
- Of 515 students pursuing health and social welfare training at the University of Namibia during 2003–04, only two were enrolled in the prepharmacy program.
- The Namibia National Health Training Center trained only about eight pharmacist assistants in a year.
- The public-sector recruitment process was time consuming; therefore, engaging pharmacists—particularly those from abroad—took a long time.

A partnership to expedite the recruitment of pharmacy staff

The Ministry of Health and Social Services (MoHSS) and the Rational Pharmaceutical Management Plus (RPM Plus) Program developed an intervention with the goal of increasing the number of facilities with qualified pharmaceutical staff. The partnership model comprised the following components—

- RPM Plus worked with the MoHSS to develop a mechanism to expedite the hire of pharmacists and pharmacist assistants for priority positions in the public sector; all target positions were identified and aligned with MoHSS priorities.
- Job descriptions for temporary staff were made commensurate with those in the public sector; work standards were set according to MoHSS policies.
- The MoHSS led the interview and selection process.
- Remuneration for recruited staff was set in accordance with the MoHSS scale.
- A local human resources company, Potentia Namibia Recruitment Consultancy, recruited successful personnel and managed their remuneration and benefits.
- The MoHSS directly supervised and evaluated the performance of recruited personnel.
- The MoHSS mobilized its own resources and systems to progressively absorb the newly appointed personnel into the government personnel structure.

Results of the partnership

In two years, twenty-eight pharmaceutical staff members (eleven pharmacists, one network administrator, and sixteen pharmacy assistants) were recruited; 64 percent of the staff positions have been absorbed into the public service (46 percent of the pharmacists and 81 percent of the pharmacy assistants). Despite Namibia's lucrative private sector, no pharmacist that the partnership recruited and supported has been lost to the private sector. Vacancy rates have been reduced by more than half, and evidence suggests that the quality of pharmaceutical care and services has improved. According to the Kunene regional director, "There is better ordering of pharmaceutical items and stock management has improved. The compilation of consumption pattern has been done, and it is easier to forecast needs of certain pharmaceutical items. The Regional and District Therapeutic Committees have been resuscitated and have begun to look more closely at pharmaceutical issues in the region and districts."

Lessons learned

The time and resources needed to manage staff before they were absorbed into the public sector proved higher than RPM Plus expected. Thus, contracting with a local human resources company to manage the seconded staff on behalf of the MoHSS and RPM Plus proved vital to the partnership's success. Additional steps that were critical to the process included working closely with the MoHSS to identify its needs, complying with MoHSS policies and standards, and recruiting pharmacy assistants as they graduate and before they slip into the private sector.

Innovative partnerships between the public and private sectors can help national programs expand their human resources base more quickly; however, the success of such partnerships relies heavily on the explicit commitment of each partner, including the host government, the donor, and the technical assistance team. Human capac-ity–building interventions should be based on existing government systems to ensure their eventual integration and sustainability. This innovative collaboration created a new mechanism for the government to fill priority pharmaceutical positions more quickly while allowing it to gradually absorb the positions into its existing struc-ture—thereby addressing immediate program needs while ensuring long-term contributions.

Source: Tjipura-Tjiho et al. 2007.

such as nurses, are given the responsibility of running an entire dispensing site because no fully trained pharmacist is available to do so. Some countries are training community health workers to dispense certain medicines, especially for childhood illnesses. Country Study 51-2 illustrates how Kenya supported pharmaceutical management task shifting to support ART scale-up. The World Health Organization (WHO), the U.S. President's Emergency Plan for AIDS Relief, and the Joint United Nations Programme on HIV/AIDS (WHO, PEPFAR, and UNAIDS 2008) have also collaborated on guidelines for task shifting in the health sector.

To address the lack of pharmaceutical workers in rural or peri-urban areas, countries such as Vietnam require students receiving government scholarships to work in underserved areas upon graduation. Vietnam also allows pharmacy schools to accept students from underserved provinces and rural areas without a competitive examination (FIP 2009). Other countries use financial incentives to boost recruitment in rural areas, but this strategy may not be sustainable if it relies on outside funds. Australia is tackling its shortage of pharmacists through a series of strategies known as the Rural Pharmacy Program. The framework is based on the belief that a combination of incentives to address these multiple factors is more likely to be successful than a single intervention and that the synergy among the interventions can improve both recruitment and retention (FIP 2009). Table 51-2 shows examples of the types of strategies the program uses.

Countries are also enacting policies and incentives to recruit and retain more pharmaceutical personnel in the public sector. In Kenya, for example, improved policies and terms of service in the public sector have led to higher retention of pharmacy staff—from 433 in 2005 to 609 in 2008—and Sudan now requires pharmacist graduates to spend one year in government health institutions, which has increased the number of pharmacists in the public sector, particularly in rural areas (FIP 2009). Sudan has also created opportunities for postgraduate study to minimize attrition from the public sector (FIP 2009). WHO launched an initiative to increase access to health workers in remote and rural areas through improved retention (see http://www.who.int/hrh/migration/expert_meeting/en/index.html).

Long-term solutions require national-level planning and strategies. Governments should work with professional organizations, regulatory bodies, training institutions, unions, and employers to develop long-term workforce plans. Strategies should strive for self-sufficiency rather than rely on foreign workers or educational institutions. Governments also need to ensure that legislation and regulations keep up with capacity-building strategies. For example, Sudan's Ribat University opened a new school and approved a three-year curriculum for pharmacy technicians; however, the pharmacy technician cadre was not defined in any policy or legislation, and how the cadre differs from that of pharmacy assistant or what its role is in pharmacy practice is unclear (FIP 2009).

More educational and preservice training opportunities are the key to solving long-term staffing problems. WHO and the International Pharmaceutical Federation (FIP) have established a task force to examine issues related to addressing pharmacy education as a means of increasing the number of pharmacists. Box 51-1 includes the task force's plan of action. Namibia addressed its lack of pharmaceutical training capacity by expanding the ability of the National Health Training Centre to train pharmacy assistants by renovating classrooms and offices, revising curriculum, and providing tutors and training consultants. As a result, the center increased its yield of pharmacy assistant graduates by 100 percent in one year—from nine in 2009 to eighteen in 2010, with sixty more in line to graduate by 2012. The 2010 graduates were all recruited into the public sector.

In addition to using public institutions to help build pharmaceutical sector human resources, providing technical assistance to academic institutions in resource-limited countries and fostering regional collaboration are efficient ways to build institutional capacity. The Regional Technical Resource Collaboration for Pharmaceutical Management, described in Country Study 51-3, is an example of such a regional approach to capacity building.

Box 51-2 presents a human resources for health (HRH) framework that promotes a comprehensive and integrated

Country Study 51-2
Supporting task shifting to build HR capacity in pharmaceutical management in Kenya

Only 38 to 45 percent of those in need have access to ART in Kenya. Because of the severe shortage of pharmaceutical professionals, Kenya's adoption of decentralized ART has resulted in other health cadres being used to manage pharmaceuticals; however, these other health care providers lack skills in pharmaceutical management, thus limiting ART scale-up.

The Strengthening Pharmaceutical Systems (SPS) Program collaborated with the National AIDS and STI Control Programme (NASCOP), training institutions, and other government agencies to develop and implement short- and long-term measures that support decentralization and task shifting, thereby strengthening human resources capacity and sustainability. Key interventions included training more than 1,500 health providers in pharmaceutical management and implementing a mentorship program. Training of trainers increased the pool of regional experts and created a mechanism to provide ongoing supervision.

SPS developed eleven job aids and eleven pharmaceutical standard operating procedures (SOPs) and guidelines,

which NASCOP adopted and disseminated to more than 400 ART sites to improve services and standardize practices. Decentralization of ART pharmaceutical services has been implemented successfully in more than 300 satellite sites. In addition, more than 2,500 public and private practitioners attended continuing professional development courses in pharmaceutical management. Advocacy for incorporating pharmaceutical management into preservice curricula culminated in 162 students at middle- and tertiary-level educational institutions receiving training. SPS is developing a pharmaceutical management orientation package for new providers at all levels of care and working with institutions to include pretested pharmaceutical management modules in preservice training curricula to promote sustainability.

Systematically implemented task shifting strategies that combine pre- and in-service training programs, job aids, reference guides, and SOPs have alleviated human resources challenges in a context of decentralized ART.

Source: MSH/SPS-Kenya 2009.

Table 51-2   Australia's rural pharmacy program strategies to increase pharmacy staff in underserved areas

Strategies	Type of disincentive addressed			
	Economic	Professional	Educational	Family
Recruitment of pharmacists to rural areas				
Undergraduate scholarship scheme	√		√	
Placement (internship) allowance	√		√	
Pharmacist academic positions at university departments of rural health		√	√	
Administrative support to pharmacy schools			√	
Rural pharmacy promotion campaign			√	
Rural pharmacist preregistration incentive allowance	√	√		
Retention of pharmacists in rural areas				
Emergency locum service	√	√		√
Continuing pharmacy education allowance	√	√	√	
Rural pharmacy newsletter		√		

Source: FIP 2009.

Box 51-1
FIP, UNESCO, and WHO Pharmacy Education Taskforce Action Plan 2008–10

- To define pharmacy service competencies across all settings and levels of the health system
- To set educational objectives aligned with competencies and develop a framework that considers the entire pharmacy education continuum from undergraduate education through to continuing professional development at the postgraduate level
- To develop a global framework for quality assurance and the development of accreditation systems (e.g., development of standards for educational institutions and programs) in pharmacy education
- To gather and analyze data on the academic/faculty workforce, and review and develop capacity development strategies that meet local, regional, or global needs

- To guide stakeholders toward an accepted holistic vision for the entire continuum of pharmacy education at the global, regional, and local levels
- To provide advocacy and technical guidance to country-level stakeholders and educational institutions
- To establish a global platform for ongoing dialogue; sharing of evidence, practices, lessons learned, resources, and tools for pharmacy education; and workforce planning

FIP = International Pharmaceutical Federation; UNESCO = United Nations Educational, Scientific and Cultural Organization; WHO = World Health Organization.

---

approach to developing strategies to tackle both immediate and longer-term HRM challenges. The framework examines six components of planning and managing the workforce so that appropriately trained personnel are available in the right places at the right time: HRM, policy, finance, education, partnerships, and leadership. HRM systems are at the center of the diagram because of their importance in integrating all the other components. Country Study 51-4 illustrates how the results of an HRM assessment of the pharmaceutical sector in Namibia were organized using the HRH framework.

51.3 Understanding the role of HRM at all levels of the health care system

Human resources management is the integrated use of systems, policies, and management practices to recruit, maintain, and develop employees so the organization can meet its desired goals (MSH 1999). Effective HRM should help managers make plans and hire trained staff, and help employees find meaningful work with avenues for career development. A comprehensive HRM system provides managers with a framework and tools to better plan, recruit, hire, deploy, motivate, and retain employees. At the national level, HRM involves developing health-sector strategies, policies, and practices to ensure a workforce that is balanced in numbers of staff, qualifications, and placement.

Initiatives such as the Global Fund to Fight AIDS, Tuberculosis and Malaria and the President's Emergency Plan for AIDS Relief, while adding more financial resources, are also putting pressure on human resources. Sometimes such initiatives can be an opportunity to advocate for better

salaries and working conditions, but these benefits must be equitable for all staff.

Even as policy makers adjust policy and regulatory frameworks at the national level, managers of district health services, nongovernmental organizations, public hospitals, or pharmacies can still do much to strengthen the HRM system. At the organizational level, where most program managers function, HRM involves linking management and development of human resources to an organization's strategic plan, goals, and objectives. Establishing these links is an essential management strategy.

An essential part of the overall management strategy should be to consider how HRM can help the organization fulfill its goals. Often people view HRM as having a limited, administrative role focused on documenting staff personnel actions. Although this administrative role is very important, the role of human resources should not be limited to these activities. In light of the new global initiatives resulting in scaled-up public health treatment programs for diseases such as HIV/AIDS and malaria, human resources should—

- Be a strategic partner in developing and attaining the goals of global initiatives
- Align human resources needs with the demand for new and old services
- Assess the need for task shifting and new job descriptions
- Develop incentives for staffing hard-to-reach areas
- Keep all employees informed about the changes taking place
- Create opportunities for staff to contribute ideas
- Encourage teamwork and team spirit

Box 51-2
The human resources for health framework

The World Health Organization and the U.S. Agency for International Development invited thirty-five representatives from various agencies, donor countries, nongovernmental organizations, and academia to draft a common technical framework to help governments and national planners understand the complex problems of human resources for health.

Meeting participants agreed that the framework should be scientifically based, tested in the field, and useful in a multisectoral and multistakeholder context. It had to capture the content and processes involved in develop-

ing and implementing a national strategy for human resources for health; be simple but comprehensive; and show the interdependencies among the various players, institutions, and labor markets involved in the health workforce.

The following figure and table illustrate and explain the final framework. Additional information on the development of the framework and how it can be used to develop a national strategy can be found in the publication *Tools for Planning and Developing Human Resources for HIV/ AIDS and Other Health Services* (MSH/WHO 2006).

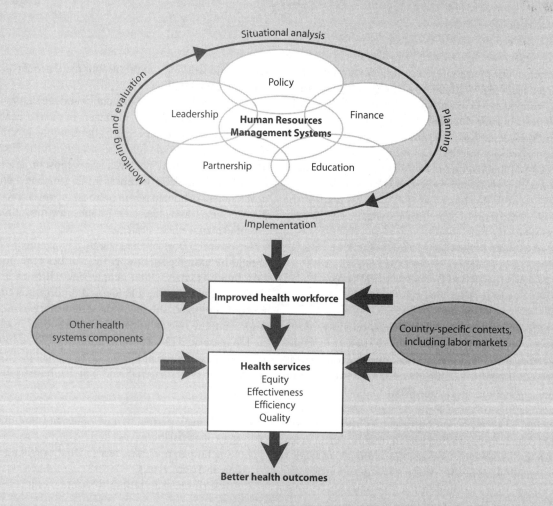

Framework components		
Component	**Goal**	**Factors in achieving the goal**
HRM systems	HRM systems are in place that result in adequate and timely staffing, staff retention, teamwork, effective planning, and good performance.	• HRM capacity in health facilities, local governments, and local health offices • Effective personnel systems: planning, recruitment, hiring, transfer, promotion, firing • Staff retention strategies • Training aligned with job requirements • Human resources information systems • Workplace programs for HIV prevention
Policy	Employment process in government is streamlined; appropriate HR policies are in place and enforced.	• National civil service rules • Government policies and structure for HRM (such as centralized hiring and firing) • Authorized scopes of practice for health cadres
Finance	Approved budget is adequate to sustain projected health workforce requirements. Allocation authority is aligned with technical and management planning and decision making.	• Health expenditures • Salary structures • Incentives to prevent migration of health staff • Support for preservice and in-service training • Administrative costs for recruitment, hiring • Supervision • Accountability
Education	Preservice training institutions have the capacity to meet demand for essential health workers and to adapt curricula as needed for new content requirements.	• Enough institutions to train all required health cadres • Adequate number of lecturers and tutors who meet quality standards for both content and teaching capacity • Training programs that match demand for health cadres and include essential content (clinic management, health management information systems, etc.) • Availability of equipment and supplies needed for preservice training
Partnerships	Planned links among sectors; districts; and nongovernmental, community, and religious organizations increase human capacity.	• Effective links among public-sector, private-sector, and community networks • Collaboration between ministry of health and ministries of finance and education
Leadership	Managers at all levels demonstrate that they value health workers and provide staff with leadership to face challenges and achieve results.	• Visionary leadership • Advocacy for reform of human resources policies • Leadership development for managers at all levels

Source: MSH/WHO 2006.

Furthermore, a strong and comprehensive HRM system has many benefits for managers and employees at all levels in both public- and private-sector organizations. Such a system can help ensure that staff members deliver quality health and pharmaceutical services to their client communities. Box 51-3 lists the benefits of establishing a strong HRM system.

51.4 Assessing the strength of HRM in the organization

HRM is perhaps the most misunderstood and poorly used management system in the health sector. As a result, determining an organization's view of its human resources and how it should strengthen its systems can be a challenging task. One of the most important actions in establishing a strong, comprehensive HRM system is gathering the information that will help plan for and implement the system. To do this, management needs to assess the organization's existing areas of strength and the areas that need strengthening. After it has identified the areas that require strengthening, management should prioritize them and develop an HRM action plan to address them.

By asking the following questions, a manager can begin to think about some of the issues involved and begin the process of establishing an HRM system that improves productivity and helps provide quality services—

• Do employees understand how their work specifically contributes to the mission and goals of the organization?
• Do employees view performance appraisals as an opportunity to learn about their skills and competencies and to discuss plans?

- Is the supervisor's role valued and supported by the organization?
- Are job descriptions up-to-date and readily available to all employees?
- Are employees routinely considered for job vacancies and other opportunities for promotion?
- Do employees understand the organization's policies on salaries and benefits and consider them fair and equitable?
- Can the organization engage in long-range planning, knowing it has or can develop the human resources required?
- Does the organization have strategies to provide meaningful jobs?
- Does the organization have a spirit of achievement and high performance?
- Do employees come to work on time and work productively for the full workday?

- Do managers spend less than 10 percent of their time dealing with grievances?
- Can the organization take on new objectives or tasks with cooperation from everyone?

Assuming the assessment identifies gaps that indicate the need to establish a stronger HRM system in the organization, several key issues should be considered, which include—

- Encouraging human resources leadership at the organizational level
- Assessing staffing requirements
- Developing and maintaining a performance management system
- Establishing a responsive supervisory system
- Improving staff motivation and performance through better human resources practices

---

Country Study 51-3
Using a regional resource to build capacity in pharmaceutical management

In addition to helping public institutions build pharmaceutical-sector human resources, providing technical assistance to academic institutions in resource-limited countries and fostering regional collaboration are efficient ways to build institutional capacity. The Regional Technical Resource Collaboration (RTRC) for Pharmaceutical Management comprises groups from Makerere University in Uganda, Muhimbili College of Health Sciences in Tanzania, the University of Nairobi in Kenya, and the National University of Rwanda. These institutions are leading in-country initiatives for building the capacity of health care workers to manage medicines by developing and adapting training materials, training health care workers, and developing effective approaches for skills building in low-resource settings.

Over a period of two years, the RTRC assessed pharmaceutical supply management systems and practices in Kenya, Rwanda, Tanzania, and Uganda. In a 2006 workshop in Uganda, the RTRC contributed to the development of comprehensive HIV/AIDS pharmaceutical management training materials, which are now widely available in all four countries. In Tanzania and Uganda, the RTRC has been involved with the training of more than 100 health care workers in HIV/AIDS pharmaceutical management. In Kenya, Tanzania, and Uganda, the RTRC has been conducting operations research to find solutions to those countries' skills-shortage problems.

A number of junior members of the academic staff within the mentioned institutions were targeted for

capacity building. This training allowed the system to build a significant pool of professionals with skills and competences in pharmaceutical supply management. At Tanzania's Muhimbili University College of Health and Allied Health, ten members of the academic staff— three senior staff members and seven junior staff members— have developed competences and skills in pharmaceutical management. Makerere University in Uganda has thirteen staff members who have developed competences in pharmaceutical management.

Following the development of training materials and the training of a number of academic staff members in pharmaceutical supply management, Makerere University's Department of Pharmacy has now adapted various components into its preservice pharmacy curriculum. In addition, the schools of pharmacy in both Tanzania and Uganda have plans to develop master of science programs in pharmaceutical supply management that draw largely from the initiative. In Rwanda, the Department of Pharmacy at the National University has revised its preservice curriculum to include components of pharmaceutical supply management.

The skills acquired by local institutions can be incorporated into both preservice and in-service teaching curricula to ensure long-term availability of skills in-country. The ability of trained institutions to mobilize their own resources for skills-building activities is crucial for the success and sustainability of these programs.

Source: Matowe et al. 2004.

Box 51-3
Benefits of establishing a strong HRM system

Benefits to the organization

- Increases the organization's capacity to achieve its goals
- Increases the level of employee performance
- Uses employee skills and knowledge efficiently
- Saves costs through the improved efficiency and productivity of workers
- Improves the organization's ability to manage change

Benefits to the employee

- Improves equity between employee compensation and level of responsibility
- Helps employees understand how their work relates to the mission and values of the organization
- Helps employees feel more highly motivated
- Increases employee job satisfaction

These HRM areas are relevant in any organization, regardless of its size, purpose, and degree of complexity, and whether it is public or private. Carrying out a comprehensive HRM assessment will help address policy, planning, training, and management in an integrated way.

51.5 Encouraging human resources leadership at the organizational level

Many organizations treat HRM in a piecemeal fashion. Human resources leaders link all components of human resources to create one, integrated HRM system. When an organization's leaders create this type of integrated system, the effect on organizational performance can be profound. In supporting human resources by giving it a prominent and strategic role, managers and leaders are also sending a message to all staff that the organization will treat them fairly and will respect their contribution to its success. Table 51-3 lists the components that contribute to developing a human resources system.

Every organization or program needs leadership at the highest level to support human resources. To take a leadership role in HRM, a manager should—

- Create a positive climate for human resources
- Create a management structure for human resources
- Define what needs to be done
- Forge new organizational arrangements that foster employee participation, teamwork, and growth
- Ensure that human resources activities are integrated throughout the organization
- Involve staff at all levels and from all departments in HRM
- Dedicate staff and budget to building human resources capacity within the organization
- Make learning an organizational priority
- Provide a link between internal HRM and external stakeholders

Table 51-3   Human resources development components

Component	Sample elements
HRM capacity	• HRM budget • HRM staff
HRM planning	• Organizational mission and goals • HRM planning
Personnel policy and practice	• Job classification system • Compensation and benefits system • Recruitment, hiring, transfer, and promotion • Orientation program • Policy manual • Discipline, termination, and grievance procedures • Relationships with unions • Labor law compliance
HRM data	• Employee data • Computerization of data • Personnel files
Performance management	• Job descriptions • Supervision • Work planning and performance review
Training	• Staff training • Management and leadership development • Links to external preservice training

- Influence health policy makers
- Influence the curricula offered by preservice training organizations

51.6 Assessing staffing requirements

Determining the staffing requirements of a pharmaceutical program means taking into account factors such as the size of the program and its goals, its geographic location, and its place within the agency of which it is a part. Three interrelated questions can be used for an initial determination of staffing requirements—

Country Study 51-4
Assessing Namibian pharmaceutical sector capacity to support the scale-up of HIV/AIDS programs

The burden of HIV/AIDS on Namibia's health service delivery system and human resources is enormous. For example, in 2005, a referral hospital had 2,570 people on ART who must see the pharmacist every month. At that time, the ART pharmacy served approximately eighty people per day, staffed by one pharmacist and one pharmacist assistant. Staff had no computer system to track patients and no telephone or transport to find the patients who had started on ART but then stopped coming. Staff members at this hospital were barely coping with the demand; how they were going to be able to scale up ART services without additional pharmacy help was hard to imagine.

In 2005, an assessment in the Namibian pharmaceutical sector was the first step in identifying and implementing both short-term and long-term solutions to the shortage of pharmacists and pharmacist assistants in scaling up HIV/AIDS services in the national health system. The assessment and the resulting recommendations were seen as the first move toward strengthening the capacity of pharmaceutical personnel for the scale-up of HIV/AIDS as well as the delivery of health services in general.

Assessment team activities

- Reviewed all relevant human resources data and pre-service statistics
- Reviewed HIV/AIDS operational strategy, and identified the numbers and types of cadres required to implement it
- Conducted interviews with health staff, especially those linked to pharmacy, using a participatory tool and instrument with questions
- Held meetings and focus group discussions with a diverse range of human resources stakeholders in all sectors of the national health system
- Met with selected training institutions and interviewed managers and faculty
- Used the HRH framework to assess and analyze data collected in the assessment
- Formulated both short- and long-term recommendations and cost elements
- Debriefed stakeholders on draft findings and recommendations

Assessment results

Despite the different approaches used in establishing ART programs as rapidly as possible, the assessment showed that the pharmaceutical services in all of the hospitals had human resources constraints that compromised their delivery of ART services. These constraints included—

- Vacant positions
- Reliance on foreign pharmacists, creating language barriers
- Small number of trained pharmacists and pharmacist assistants coming from the educational system
- Limited opportunities for in-service training and career mobility for pharmacists and pharmacist assistants
- Difficulty in retaining pharmacists and pharmacist assistants in the public sector
- Inability of pharmacists and pharmacist assistants to perform efficiently

Short- and long-term recommendations

The assessment team used the HRH framework as an approach to capture the recommendations made in their report (see Box 51-2). The HRH framework is based on the understanding that an integrated and comprehensive response is needed to address the global priority of scaling up HIV/AIDS treatment. Short-term solutions are needed to address emergency staffing issues, but longer-term strategies are critical to ensure an effective and sustainable health workforce over time.

HRM systems

In the short term—

- Contract a marketing firm to develop and implement a marketing campaign to recruit more candidates for the pharmacy program.
- Increase the number of pharmacist assistants being trained. Restart the program at another location.
- Contract with an outside recruitment firm to secure more foreign pharmacists. Provide a central-level monitoring mechanism.
- Implement the HIV/AIDS workplace program developed by the MoHSS.
- Use pharmacist assistants to counsel ART patients.
- Review the role pharmacists play in hospital pharmacy to make optimum use of the limited resources.
- Reconsider the staffing mix at medical stores to include more management skills.

In the long term—

- Provide a leadership development program for managers at all levels.
- Ensure that trained human resources professionals are in place throughout the health system.

Policy and financial

In the short term—

- Establish a minimum of ten bursaries or grants for students pursuing a pharmacy degree and two for pharmacist assistants.
- Develop a two-year community service requirement, in lieu of bonding.
- Permit part-time employment for pharmacists.
- Create a new cadre of pharmaceutical technician as promotional step for pharmacist assistants.
- Finalize a policy to permit pharmacists to work in both the private and public sectors.
- Increase the number of pharmacist assistant students that a pharmacist may supervise.
- Install computer tracking systems at ART sites.

In the long term—

- Streamline the employment process, and improve human resources links between the central and regional levels.

Education

In the short term—

- Install Internet facilities in all district hospitals to enhance learning.
- Review in-service training to improve availability and meet the needs of pharmacy staff.
- Introduce a best practices program for pharmacists and pharmacist assistants to share knowledge.

- Provide intensive English-language training for Cuban pharmacists.

In the long term—

- As a long-term measure, the MoHSS should introduce distance learning and computer-aided instruction to its in-service training capacity.

Leadership

In the short term—

- Implement leadership development programs to create a climate of teamwork and support at all ART sites.

In the long term—

- Improve multisector collaboration for strengthening human resources capacity in all areas of health.

Partnerships

In the short term—

- Partner with the Pharmaceutical Society of Namibia to market pharmacy and support more students in training.
- Enlist assistance of district councils to develop formal partnerships with community groups that can provide needed human capacity in ART.

In the long term—

- Work with the two education ministries and the University of Namibia to improve science education at the secondary level.

- What is the scope of the services to be offered in relation to the selection, procurement, distribution, and use of pharmaceuticals?
- What different types of workers are required at each level of the system?
- What is the optimal number of employees needed to deliver these services in the most efficient and effective manner?

Administrative arrangements can vary considerably, even within one agency or government. For example, medicine selection and use may fall under the purview of the ministry of health, whereas procurement and distribution may be handled by a different ministry, responsible for supplies. Also, many options exist in linking with pharmaceutical supply sources. If pharmaceutical procurement and distribution are provided directly by a government agency, then all jobs may be performed by government staff. If the central procurement office is limited to negotiating with commercial suppliers for direct delivery to health facilities, then

most of the importation, bulk inventory control, and bulk storage occur within the private sector.

An example of a large-scale human resources challenge is the integration of ART for HIV/AIDS into existing pharmacy services, which can easily double the volume of pharmaceutical products the staff handles and dramatically increase the number of patients served at the pharmacy. Pharmacy staff that dispenses antiretroviral drugs must spend more time counseling patients, especially new patients. In addition, because patients continue therapy for a lifetime, they need regular monitoring for treatment adherence, which adds to staff responsibility.

An analysis of information on human resources requirements for ART showed that the number of pharmacy staff needed depended on how dispensing and counseling activities were divided among different cadres; however, the average number of pharmacy staff was estimated at one to two per 1,000 ART patients (Hirschhorn et al. 2006). In Kenya, ART managers have addressed the shortage of pharmacists by developing a cluster of facilities that share the services

Box 51-4
Recruitment action checklist

1. Review staff requirements

Take a broad view of your staffing needs and consider whether you really have a vacancy. For example, if an employee is leaving a clinic that you feel is already over-staffed, review the workload at that facility and decide whether a full-time permanent replacement is needed or whether an alternative option would be more appropriate. For example, would a part-time or temporary worker be sufficient? Should the job be restructured? What would the staffing implications of a restructured position be?

2. Consult with those involved

Always be sure to take any organizational policies and procedures into account. Authorization for a replacement or a new appointment may be needed from senior management, or in the case of most health ministries, from another government agency. Consult with your personnel or human resources department if you have one, because they will have expertise in this area.

3. Specify the sort of person you are looking for

List the duties, responsibilities, and relationships involved in the job role, and define the level of authority the post holder will have. Decide what qualifications and skills are required, what type and length of experience are needed, and which personal attributes will be important. This information will enable you to create an up-to-date job description and role specification. State the geographic location of the vacancy (hospital, clinic, etc.) and set a target start date.

4. Research the labor market

Depending on the nature of the job, you may want to review the job description and role specification and ask yourself whether you are likely to find what you are looking for in one person. If so, undertake some research to gauge the pay and benefits package you will need to offer. Salary surveys are usually expensive, but they are often summarized in the press at the time of publication. Monitoring job advertisements and net-working with employers in your area and sector can also give you an idea of current pay rates for certain common job categories.

5. Comply with local labor laws and other legal requirements

In most countries, recruitment activities are covered by a growing body of legislation and codes of practice designed to exclude favoritism, discrimination, and unfair treatment. As such, the entire recruitment team needs to be aware of and keep up-to-date with the latest developments to ensure that they follow good practice and do not infringe on the regulations.

6. Plan how to find and attract candidates

Again, depending on the position you want to fill, you may want to start within your organization. Are any employees suitable for promotion or reassignment? Even if you are doubtful, advertising internally as a courtesy to staff who may wish to apply is important, and keep in mind that they may have friends or relations who will be interested in the position.

Refer to your existing database of previous applicants, whether unsolicited or otherwise. Draw on any appropriate contacts.

Decide whether to use the services of a recruitment agency to identify and short-list candidates for you, weighing the costs incurred against the time and expertise at your disposal.

Consider whether electronic recruitment techniques, using either a government website (as in Kenya) or an online recruitment service, would be appropriate.

7. Decide where to advertise

If you decide to advertise independently rather than use an agency, think through the options and decide which is most likely to reach the kinds of candidates you have in mind: local or national press, bulletin boards of professional associations, Internet recruitment sites, or mailing lists. Research the costs involved, and decide what you can afford.

8. Write the advertisement

Decide if you or other staff members have the skills and knowledge required to draft an advertisement. If your organization has a human resources department, they will probably take on this task, but ensure that you are involved throughout the process. In the case of a senior post, or if you are recruiting in large numbers, you may wish to hire an advertising agency to draft the advertisement and place it appropriately. Naming your organization in the advertisement is preferable to using a box number unless you have particular reasons for secrecy. Ensure that the advertisement provides the following details clearly and succinctly—

- Duties and responsibilities of the job
- Qualifications and experience required
- Personal qualities sought
- Location
- Some indication of the salary range
- Form of reply you require (i.e., CV and covering letter, copies of relevant certificates, and testimonials)
- Deadline for the submission of applications and where the application should be sent

If you are asking applicants to complete an application form, check that it requests all the details you will need to help you assess the candidates. Asking a colleague to complete the form from the perspective of a candidate can also be helpful to ensure that the form is clear.

Source: Society for Human Resources Management (http://www.shrm. org).

of one ART-trained pharmacist, who floats among the clustered sites, while technicians or nurses take care of the routine responsibilities.

Calculating and justifying the number of pharmaceutical management staff needed can be difficult. The *norms approach*, which specifies a standard staffing level, or norm, for each staff cadre, quickly breaks down in practice. For example, a norm that says that each regional store needs three supplies officers will result in overstaffing at small regional stores and understaffing at busier stores.

The *workload approach* to staffing is based on the activities, volume of work (workload), and activity standards for each type of staff at each level. This is known as the WISN, or workload indicator of staffing need, approach (Shipp 1998). The WISN method is generally a much more realistic approach for determining staffing needs than the norms approach. Because it is based on actual workload, results from the WISN method are more readily explained and defended.

No matter how the organizational structure and contractual arrangements are defined, all the tasks and related jobs must be performed if the pharmaceutical supply system is to operate reliably and expeditiously. An organizational chart describing the relationships among different staff positions is very useful.

51.7 Recruiting and hiring needed workers

Effective recruitment processes are vital in ensuring that a ministry of health or any other health organization has the people it needs to implement its strategy and meet its objectives. Recruitment can be expensive, but so too is the appointment of an employee who is inadequately qualified, fails to perform well, or leaves the organization before he or she has been able to make a significant contribution. The time and effort invested in planning the process of recruitment carefully can help get the right person for the job, reduce turnover, build a strong team, and enhance organizational performance.

Recruitment is the process of attracting, assessing, selecting, and employing people to carry out the work activities

required by a health facility or organization. Box 51-4 has a recruitment action checklist that focuses on planning and undertaking the initial stages of the process. In addition to assessing the need for additional or replacement staff, the process involves identifying the tasks to be carried out, specifying the kind of person needed, finding a pool of suitable candidates, drawing up a short list, conducting interviews, hiring, inducting the new hires, and deploying them.

Country Study 51-5 describes how implementing emergency administrative reform allowed Kenya to fast-track recruitment and hiring into the public-sector health services.

51.8 Developing and maintaining a performance management system

One of the most important tasks for a manager is to support the establishment of an organization-wide performance management system that connects strategic and operational plans with performance measures for organizational units and for individuals. This system helps employees understand how their work contributes to the success of the organization, which may make them feel more motivated and be more productive. When implemented in a systematic way, performance management has the potential to improve both group and individual performance and to make organizations more successful.

Human resources elements of a performance management system include—

- A written job description for each position in the organization
- Defined supervisory relationships
- Regular work-planning meetings between supervisors and their staff
- Periodic performance review meetings
- Opportunities for training and staff development

Regular work planning is a key element in an effective performance management system. To do work planning, the supervisor and the employee jointly develop the employee's workplan objectives for a designated period, often six months. They derive these objectives in part from the organization's annual workplan objectives. They should write the employee's workplan down and sign it. At the end of the designated period, they meet again to review the employee's performance against his or her performance objectives and to develop a workplan for the next period.

Work planning helps the staff member understand his or her work objectives and understand that he or she is accountable for achieving them. If an employee is unable to perform at a satisfactory level, a good HRM system provides personnel procedures for the supervisor to follow in providing opportunities to learn needed skills or in taking corrective actions.

Accountability, or being responsible for achieving agreed-upon work objectives, is an important element in a performance management system. A core set of people-centered values does not mean a lack of employee accountability. A human resources leader shows respect for people by building a performance management system that provides for assessing employee performance in an objective and constructive way and holds employees accountable for work-planning objectives. (See References and Further Readings for a list of performance management tools.)

As a way to promote accountability and deter unethical behavior in public servants or employees, some countries and organizations establish codes of conduct based on moral values and ethical principles. As part of its Good Governance for Medicines program, WHO (2006) has laid out the framework for a code of conduct for public-sector employees—

- A public service is a trust that requires a public servant to place faithfulness to his/her moral contract with society and obedience to the laws and ethical principles above private gain.
- A public servant shall fulfill his/her lawful obligations to the government and the public with professionalism and integrity.
- A public servant shall perform his/her official duties with justice, truthfulness and with a spirit of service to the common good (public interest).
- A public servant shall perform his/her official duties with honesty, transparency, and accountability.
- A public servant shall respect the rights of the public and of his/her colleagues.
- A public servant shall disclose unethical practice and corruption to appropriate authorities.
- A public servant shall avoid any actions that may create the appearance of violating the law or ethical principles promoted by this code of conduct.

In addition, codes of conduct can specify actions that the employee must avoid to adhere to the code, such as avoiding conflicts of interest, not giving preferential treatment to an organization or person, or not engaging in private activities that would reflect poorly on the government or organization of employment.

Country Study 51-5
Instituting an emergency hiring plan in Kenya

Despite a large pool of unemployed health workers in Kenya, staffing levels at most facilities were only 50 percent, and poor geographic distribution of existing staff left many people without access to ART and other essential health services. Because filling vacant positions in the public sector can take one to two years, even when funding is available, an emergency approach was needed to fast-track the hiring and deployment process. Management Sciences for Health staff designed the Kenya Emergency Hiring Plan and led the difficult negotiations with senior health-sector leaders that eventually allowed the plan's successful implementation.

The emergency hiring plan incorporated a nongovernmental outsourcing mechanism to rapidly hire, train, and deploy workers on short-term contracts. Deloitte & Touche, Kenya, was selected to carry out most business functions, such as screening, recruitment, and benefits management, while the African Medical and Research Foundation, the Kenya Medical Training College, and the Kenya Institute of Administration worked together to ensure that the newly hired health staff had the necessary knowledge and skills to provide appropriate services.

In the first six months, 890 health providers, including 129 pharmacy technologists, were hired for positions in critically underserved public-sector health facilities. The new hires were given three-year contracts after which they will become permanent government staff. After experiencing the initial success, the public health sector fully embraced the concept, and consequently, 3,000 health workers are working in rural health facilities on various kinds of contracts funded by both the government and donors.

Source: Adano 2008.

51.9 Establishing a responsive supervisory system

The role of the supervisor in an effective human resources system is critical because he or she provides the bridge between the organization and the employee. The supervisor communicates the larger goals of the organization to the employee and, through the work-planning process, guides the work of the employee to directly support these goals. The supervisor needs to be aware of gaps in job readiness and to support the development of employee skills and capacity as needed. The supervisor must also be aware of problems in employee performance that cannot be solved through training or development activities and make decisions about how to address them in a positive and constructive manner.

Several characteristics are likely to define supervisors who are concerned about the developmental as well as the disciplinary aspects of supervision. These supervisors are—

- Knowledgeable and enthusiastic about the jobs they are supervising
- Sensitive to staff members' needs and feelings
- Capable of supporting and guiding without harassment
- Skilled in communication—good listeners, approachable, and open-minded about ideas that conflict with their own
- Ready to praise good work and quick to support their staff
- Willing, whenever possible and appropriate, to involve staff in making decisions, especially about matters directly affecting their own work
- Able to preserve harmony within the team and the workforce by minimizing personal jealousies and conflicts
- Able to organize effectively and to mobilize staff
- Able to allow staff to complete assigned duties without interference
- Willing to delegate tasks
- Scrupulous in making regular supervisory visits and punctual in keeping appointments
- Capable of appraising staff without bias and writing reports on the basis of work performance rather than hearsay or favoritism

Managers must allow supervisors adequate time to meet with and develop their supervisees for the supervisory process to be effective in meeting the needs of the staff and of the organization. In addition, the organization must fully integrate the supervisory process with other HRM components, such as performance management and personnel policy.

At all levels of the organization, supervisors in pharmaceutical management and other areas of the health sector contribute to the delivery of high-quality health services to clients. They do so in two ways: through both individual and team supervision. For either supervisory approach, the role of the supervisor is to facilitate the work of individual employees or employee teams so they can effectively perform their job responsibilities. Staff members respond positively when they are given interesting and challenging work assignments by supervisors who are themselves clearly working hard toward fulfilling the organization's objectives.

Individual supervision involves supervising the performance of an individual employee on a one-to-one basis. It also involves periodic joint work planning and performance review meetings between the supervisor and the staff member. It can also involve day-to-day guidance, mentoring, and problem solving.

In team supervision, supervisors build and support a clinic team whose members work together to analyze and solve problems on an ongoing basis. A team approach to supervision emphasizes individual performance only as it relates to the ability of the team to achieve common goals. By using a team approach to supervision and by placing an emphasis on team problem solving, supervisors can overcome many of the shortcomings of traditional supervision, which can focus more narrowly on vertical programs or individual performance and may not be as supportive or facilitative (see MSH's Improving Supervision: A Team Approach in References and Further Readings).

An effective supervisory system—

- Describes all supervisory roles in writing
- Ensures that all supervisors and employees are aware of the system and the procedures
- Makes clear all individual performance objectives and also overall clinic objectives and desired results or outcomes
- Trains supervisors
- Provides adequate time and resources for supervisors and supervisees to meet and work together
- Fully integrates the supervisory system with the overall strategies and goals of the organization and the other components of the HRM system

51.10 Improving motivation, retention, and productivity through HRM

If staff members were asked to brainstorm on all the factors that affect their attitudes about work, the resulting "pressure map" might look something like Figure 51-1. If staff members are then asked to say whether each of these pressures is positive or negative, they are likely to find more negatives than positives on the chart. Most will feel that they are poorly paid and are expected to handle heavy workloads with limited resources. Because advancement frequently

Figure 51-1   Staff pressure map

depends on formal educational qualifications or on "affiliations" rather than on the quality of work done, many may feel that they have low promotion prospects. Supervision is often constrained by lack of transport and other resources. If a staff member has extensive family responsibilities, he or she will be tempted to look outside the job for opportunities to increase income. In such circumstances, motivating staff members to perform their best may be difficult. Many of these factors are not within the control of individual managers. Some of these problems relate to a general lack of funds for running health services; other obstacles cannot easily be overcome within the constraints of typical budgeting and civil service procedures.

Conventional motivational approaches often rely on reward schemes, improved working conditions, or competition for promotions and pay increases. These approaches are not always easy to apply in resource-constrained settings. Although people need fair compensation, money alone does not improve performance. Meaningful work that is integral to the goals of the organization, has the respect of fellow employees, and provides opportunities to develop individual skills results in a more sustained level of employee performance. For example, senior staff from eleven pharmaceutical supply organizations in sub-Saharan Africa reported that the main factors contributing to staff motivation were team-building exercises, bonus schemes, staff appraisal systems, staff meetings, and church fellowship–related activities (WHO/EPN 2006).

As part of a joint initiative of several international health professional councils, including the FIP, the Global Health

Workforce Alliance (2008) commissioned a publication that extensively describes incentive plans for health workers. The guidelines include nonfinancial incentives, such as career development and positive working environments, as well as financial incentives, such as performance-linked payments. Such performance-based incentive plans are receiving increasing attention as successful mechanisms to improve service quality and worker satisfaction. Country Study 51-6 describes how a performance-based financing scheme has affected health services in Rwanda.

A human resources system that integrates performance management with organizational goals will ensure that employees understand how their work relates to and contributes to the mission of their organization.

A carefully planned and implemented human resources system addresses the kinds of employee concerns that can affect motivation. These concerns are reflected in questions that employees frequently ask about their workplace, including—

- Am I being treated fairly?
- What am I supposed to do?
- How well am I doing it?
- Does my work matter to the organization?
- How can I develop myself within the organization?

HRM responsibility for fairness in the workplace

A major factor in employee motivation is people's perception of fairness, which is especially important regarding salary and compensation. An employee may begin to develop his or her perception of fairness in the organization starting with the hiring process. Perceptions of fairness relate to the day-to-day application of personnel policies, the distribution of tasks and responsibilities among employees, the organization's salary policies, and the organization's support for and recognition of employees.

One important managerial responsibility is making sure that all managers and staff apply personnel policies on a day-to-day basis and distribute tasks and responsibilities fairly and equitably among employees. When developing an integrated HRM system, a manager should review the organization's job classifications and related salary scales to ensure that salaries are appropriate to the level of responsibility and are competitive when compared with local economic conditions. In some cases, correcting salary imbalances may be difficult, but every effort should be made to take corrective action internally to ensure that all staff members receive fair and equitable compensation.

A manager should also review the organization's personnel policies, update them as needed, and make the updated information available to all staff. In addition, all supervisors and managers should be informed about the new personnel policy and apply the rules fairly and equitably to all employees.

HRM responsibility for setting work priorities

People want to know exactly what is expected of them in their work. In many cases, job descriptions are not clear, supervisors have not specified their expectations, or managers who have hired people for a specified job ask them to perform other duties. If employees do not understand their work priorities or if their supervisor changes their work priorities on a regular basis, employees find maintaining a consistent level of productivity and a sense of self-worth in the organization difficult.

One of the steps that can strengthen an HRM system is to make sure that all staff members have an up-to-date job description that provides them with information about their general duties and responsibilities. The description should clearly describe all job responsibilities and the supervisory relationship. The job description gives the supervisor a starting place in developing a workplan with the employee. See Section 51.12 for more detail on how to develop job descriptions.

Because the job description is general, it does not describe the specific responsibilities or performance objectives for which a supervisor may hold an employee accountable in a certain period. Most employees do not perform all the duties listed in their job description all the time, even if the job description is up-to-date, because work and organizational priorities change. As stated earlier, a supervisor and a staff member should conduct work-planning and performance review meetings on a semi-annual basis to allow them to jointly and systematically plan the specific performance objectives for which the employee will be responsible in a given six-month period. This joint work-planning process also helps the supervisor identify in a timely way the skills and resources that the employee needs to successfully perform the tasks required to meet his or her work objectives.

Country Study 51-6
Using performance-based financing to increase worker retention and service quality in Rwanda

Although most health workers recognize and appreciate the intrinsic rewards of providing quality services, historically, low wages and lack of resources have tended to make recruiting, retaining, and motivating health workers challenging. In Rwanda, Management Sciences for Health worked with health-sector leaders and the government of Rwanda to design and implement a groundbreaking performance-based financing (PBF) model. By decentralizing administrative structures and budgets and paying PBF funds directly into health facility accounts, facility directors and their teams at all levels of the system were empowered to improve performance. PBF starts with contracts that define the obligations of the government, development partners (the purchasers), and health care facilities (the providers). Health centers receive payment based on the number of health services they deliver, multiplied by the fee set for those services, and adjusted by a quality score. Access to data monitoring and verification systems promotes accuracy, accountability, trust, and collaboration among all parties.

Since the introduction of PBF in 2005, the health workforce has grown by 250 percent and retention has improved. A World Bank evaluation of the scheme in 2008 showed that PBF also fostered teamwork and health worker participation in problem solving and improved quality of care. These improvements led to greater support from the community and increased use of health services. The result has been a self-sustaining process leading to improved health outcomes for the Rwandan people.

Source: Management Sciences for Health/Rwanda HIV/Performance-Based Financing Project 2009.

HRM responsibility for providing feedback on performance

Employees need ongoing feedback about their job performance. Anxiety about not performing well can directly affect an employee's motivation and productivity. This anxiety often results in denial and avoidance of responsibilities and in other work behaviors that reduce productivity.

An important element of a work-planning and performance review system is holding work-planning and performance review meetings on a regular basis. As discussed, the supervisor and employee agree on specific performance objectives during these meetings. These agreed-upon objectives become the basis of the next performance review. This system allows both the supervisor and the employee to evaluate performance and to plan for training or other career development activities, if needed. A work-planning and performance review system can improve individual performance and increase staff motivation. If the system is used for creating a staff development plan, it will also help align staff development efforts more closely with the organization's goals. Ongoing supervision between the semi-annual work-planning and performance review meetings is also key.

HRM responsibility for providing meaningful work

When employees feel that their work is meaningful to their organization and important to the people they serve, they work more productively. For many people, having skills and competencies and performing well is not motivating if the result does not contribute to the success of the organization. Therefore, communicating to employees that their work matters is an important element in an HRM strategy. Engaging in systematic planning and taking steps to make sure that people's day-to-day work directly supports the priorities of the organization is critical in meeting the organization's objectives. These objectives represent the strategic areas in which the organization has decided to focus in a given year, as identified during the organization's annual planning process. These objectives may vary on an annual basis, depending on changing organizational priorities.

A supervisor can link the work-planning and performance review process to the organization's annual work-planning cycle by using organization, department, or unit priorities as the basis of joint work planning with his or her staff. Such linkage will help ensure that the work of each person matters and that each person understands how his or her work is important to the organization.

HRM responsibility for professional development of staff

People feel motivated and challenged when they have opportunities to learn, develop new competencies, and assume new responsibilities, and when they believe that their efforts will strengthen their careers. Providing these opportunities can also be an important way to recognize employees. Participating in training and other activities where people share learning and value each other's experience increases staff collaboration and teamwork and can increase overall performance and productivity.

Health organizations devote a significant portion of their funds and staff time to training, with the goal of improving the effectiveness and efficiency of their staff and their programs. Often, however, health organizations have designed and implemented this training without adequately diagnosing or planning for the needs of the organization or their employees, who hope that training will further their career development and credentials. As a result, whether the training has either solved individual performance problems or contributed to improving the organization's performance overall is not always clear. Furthermore, many health organizations are becoming reluctant to pay for expensive training until they see more tangible benefits to employees, the organization, and the community.

Making staff development a priority is an important component of a comprehensive HRM system. Posting job opportunities within the organization and supporting internal candidates will send a signal that the current experience of the staff is valued. A well-managed program of training and staff development can broaden the skills and competencies of staff and reap many payoffs. Formal, organized training, which is discussed below, is only one vehicle for staff development. Other staff development strategies include—

- On-the-job learning through mentoring relationships
- Cross-functional assignments
- Membership in task forces and committees
- Additional job assignments
- Technical presentations and discussions at staff meetings

These strategies can all provide the challenge and opportunity needed for personal and professional growth, as well as increase the knowledge that people have in common and expose them to new ways of thinking and doing.

Technology is also opening up a range of new ways to transfer knowledge. If staff have access to computers and the Internet, a variety of electronic training and educational resources is available that employees can use to develop skills without leaving their work site. Although these technologies have the potential to increase staff competency in some areas, how staff members can use these technologies in a productive and cost-efficient way is not always clear. As with traditional training programs, a manager should first determine the training needs and integrate training planning into the overall HRM system. Doing so will allow the effective use of electronic training to solve individual perfor-

Table 51-4   Comparison of communication channels

Channel	Examples	Positive aspects	Negative aspects
Controlling—used when telling someone what to do, giving an order, or making a criticism	"Do it this way." "No, not that way, silly!"	Can provide necessary direction	Can result in inflexible dictating
Caring—used when expressing concern for someone's welfare	"How are you today, Aziz?" "Don't worry—it will be OK."	Can be nurturing	May become smothering
Computing—used when giving, processing, or exchanging information; when reasoning, measuring, calculating; when thinking as opposed to feeling	"If we allow too many exemptions, the revolving drug fund will collapse." "On average, how many patients attend this health center per day?"	Necessary calculations may provide an objective viewpoint	May come across as thoughtless lack of feeling or compassion
Complying—used in "editing" what we say; when conforming to the wishes of another person; when adapting our behavior in light of the likely reactions of the other person	"Would you mind if I ...?" "I'm sorry, I won't do it again."	May be polite accommodation	May be undignified subservience
Expressing—used when spontaneously expressing feelings of pleasure or pain; having fun, expressing humor, sharing a joke	"Great—that was really great!" "Ouch!"	Displays honest emotions	May result in selfishness and egotistical behavior

mance problems and contribute to improving the organization's performance.

51.11   Using channels of communication

The previous sections on management and leadership imply that effective managers have good communication skills, but no set formula will work every time. Five main channels used in interpersonal communication are set out, with their positive and negative aspects, in Table 51-4.

Choosing the channel

The key factor in communication is deciding which of the five channels should be used in any given situation. Two basic skills help in communicating with others: the ability to use all five channels and the sensitivity to choose the most appropriate channel on any particular occasion.

Nonverbal communication

Effective communicators have the ability to alternate among the five channels like nimble telephone switchboard operators. However, unlike using the telephone, where only the voice is important, interpersonal communication involves both words and body language. Therefore, a good manager must be aware of factors such as posture, gestures, and facial expressions.

Improving communication

A manager can improve communication with staff in a number of ways—

Clarify ideas before attempting to communicate them: Good communication depends on clear thinking. Think about how best to express the idea and what format to use (for example, a formal circular, an informal memo, or a talk), and try to assess its likely impact.

Follow up on any communication: Good communication depends on feedback. Ask questions and encourage reactions.

Be a good listener: Good communication also depends on good listening. Careful attention to what people say helps one know what is best to say to them.

Feedback skills

Good managers try to provide feedback as a regular feature of the work experience. Done well, feedback both enhances individual performance and improves teamwork.

When giving feedback, consider the following recommendations—

- Deal only with what is known for certain.
- Describe actual behavior ("You did not attend the last two meetings") rather than making judgmental comments ("You are irresponsible").
- Start with positive feedback before giving negative feedback.
- Do not exaggerate.
- Listen as well as talk.

Techniques found to be successful in prompting discussion of problem areas include the following—

- Ask open rather than closed questions, avoiding those that can be answered with a simple yes or no. ("What is your experience in this matter?")

- Present possible scenarios that encourage concrete descriptions. ("If you were faced with such a problem, how would you tackle it?")
- Rephrase the speaker's words. ("You are saying that you feel that you are not trusted, because you are not allowed to handle the finances for the workshops—am I right?")
- Acknowledge the other person's feelings. ("You seem to be very worried about this matter—am I right?")
- Concentrate on what is being implied as well as what is being said. People are much more willing to talk if they are convinced that they are really being heard.

Clearly, such techniques go well beyond simple criticism or interrogation.

The rest of this chapter addresses some of the common functions of human resources management—developing job descriptions, disciplining staff, resolving conflict, and conducting meetings—in light of what has been said about leadership and communication.

51.12 Preparing job descriptions

One of the most important functions of a pharmaceutical supplies manager is to ensure that the tasks of the organization are distributed equitably. This involves matching the jobs that need to be done with the skills and abilities of the individuals who make up the workforce. Each position should have a written job description and a summary of duties and responsibilities.

Job descriptions are important management tools. They are helpful in—

- Determining job qualifications, because the tasks to be performed in a particular job determine the necessary skills and experience
- Orienting new employees, because the written job description explains basic duties to new employees
- Establishing performance expectations and supervising staff

Job descriptions have no fixed format, but most have five distinct sections—

Job title: The title gives only the briefest information needed to identify the job, for example, "director of pharmaceutical services" or "chief supplies officer."
Job summary: A brief paragraph summarizes the main responsibilities of the job.
Duties and responsibilities: The core of the job description is a more detailed description of the work to be performed and the activities for which the employee is responsible.

Qualifications: This section comprises a statement of the qualifications and requirements necessary for satisfactory job performance, including education, experience, knowledge, skills, and abilities.
Reporting relationship: The person's supervisor should be listed. Adding a chart that indicates the structure of the organization can be useful, particularly if it shows reporting relationships.

Developing a job description

When a job description is outdated or nonexistent, the situation can be remedied by compiling and analyzing information, writing a job description, assigning time allocations, and obtaining agreement on the job description among the employee doing the job, the supervisor, and others who may have a say, such as the human resources manager.

Compile information. The information needed to build a job description can be obtained in several ways—

- Having the employee complete a questionnaire about key aspects of the job
- Observing and interviewing the employee while various tasks are being performed
- Conducting a group interview when a number of employees perform the same job
- Having the employee keep a daily record of work done, in the form of a log or diary

Analyze information. Identify the major tasks and related clusters of minor ones. Review each cluster to ensure that it accurately represents the tasks to be performed. Arrange the main tasks and related minor ones in a logical sequence, to give a clear overview of the job.

Write the job description. Group activities related to one duty, such as planning, budgeting, or supervising. In writing the descriptive statements, use active verbs and be concise. Try to avoid any ambiguity or vagueness. If someone is responsible for signing the pharmaceutical supplies order, state "signs the supply order" rather than "approves the supplies order."

Each statement should describe one functional element of the job and be able to stand by itself. Normally, duties should be arranged in order of priority.

Obtain agreement. In updating a current employee job description, as part of good management practice, the immediate supervisor should review the job description with the employee to ensure that the listed duties and responsibilities are mutually understood and accepted. The job description form should include space for both the supervisor's and the employee's signatures to formalize this process.

An example of a job description for a chief pharmaceutical supplies officer is presented in Figure 51-2.

Staff orientation

Every organization has its own culture; set of goals and expectations, policies and procedures; and norms and standards. Sometimes these are not made explicit, and a written job description alone can never convey all the nuances of a job. It is only one tool in the broader process of orientation and training.

New managers especially need to become familiar with the organization they have joined. Three essential steps help accomplish this—

1. Explore the new work environment. This step means getting acquainted with staff members (both senior and junior) as well as the physical location of job sites, outreach services, and training facilities.
2. Review the mission and strategy of the organization. This step involves acquiring a sound understanding of the long- and short-term goals; the organizational structure and general mode of operation; and the roles, responsibilities, and functions of the individual members of the workforce.
3. Identify training needs and opportunities. Managers need to do this for themselves and for their subordinates.

Before questioning others, good managers need to ask the following questions of themselves—

- Do I have a job description?
- Have I discussed it with my supervisor?
- Am I clear about the objectives of the organization? Can I explain them to others?
- How does my department relate to other departments? Can I explain how they relate to mine?
- What resources do I have at my disposal to achieve the organizational objectives? Consider buildings, facilities, transport, utilities, medical supplies, finances, and personnel.
- Do I have a staff development plan and a personal development plan?

Staff procedures handbook

The regulations and rules governing work should be gathered in a staff handbook that is regularly updated and includes information on—

- Organizational purpose and objectives
- Organizational structure
- Activities
- Address and telephone lists
- Safety and health policies
- Personnel classifications
- Hours of work

- Personnel policies, including recruitment, performance planning, and review of records
- Ethical standards
- Grievance, disciplinary, and termination policies
- Salary policies, including overtime
- Vacation, holidays, and other leave
- Pension and insurance benefits
- Administrative procedures, including communication, travel, procurement, and parking

Producing a handbook takes time and effort, but both supervisors and staff need to know the policies and procedures of the organization, and the handbook may be essential backup when disputes arise.

51.13 Disciplining staff

A good manager should not shirk the responsibility of disciplining staff when necessary. However, in a pharmaceutical supply program within a ministry of health or as part of a larger nongovernmental organization or private operation, a manager may be able to do little beyond submitting a report to higher authorities recommending disciplinary action. Measures such as indictment, suspension, transfer, or dismissal are normally outside the powers of a program manager. Nevertheless, maintaining fairness and dignity is important in coping with situations that might lead to making disciplinary recommendations. The following guidelines are suggested—

- If taking disciplinary action is necessary (whether a verbal warning, a written warning, or a report to higher authorities), the action should be immediate. Discipline that follows soon after the offense is more likely to be associated with the offense itself than with the manager. A delayed action can lead to resentment and a lack of trust.
- Advance warning should be given. Unexpected discipline is usually regarded as unfair. Staff members are more likely to understand and accept the need for disciplinary action if they are given a clear presentation of the rules, followed by a warning that disciplinary measures will be taken if the rules are infringed.
- Discipline should be consistent. If it is imposed differently under the same conditions, staff will be confused or frustrated, and the manager will quickly lose staff respect.
- Discipline should be impartial. It should be clear that a particular behavior is being challenged and not the personality of the individual staff member.

Of course, dealing with problematic situations before they become crises that call for formal disciplinary proce-

Figure 51-2   Sample job description for a chief pharmaceutical supplies officer

JOB DESCRIPTION

JOB TITLE: Chief pharmaceutical supplies officer, Pharmaceutical Service, Ministry of Health

JOB SUMMARY: Responsible for the overall operation of the central medical stores unit; ordering and distributing medicines, medical
supplies, and other related products; supervising stock control; providing technical inputs to the national formulary
committee and tender board; and preparing reports on all aspects of the operation of the service

DUTIES AND RESPONSIBILITIES: (In order of priority)

1. Provide medicines, medical supplies, and other products to all government health institutions by
   - Estimating requirements for medicine and nonmedicine products
   - Supervising preparation of medicine orders
   - Monitoring distribution of medicines and other supplies
   - Preparing monthly, quarterly, and annual reports on the status of the service

2. Supervise the control of medicines and other supplies to ensure continuous availability by
   - Maintaining an up-to-date inventory-control system
   - Continually evaluating the logistics management system
   - Implementing stock management guidelines and procedures
   - Liaising with a drug testing laboratory to monitor medicine quality

3. Provide technical inputs to management, as well as other agencies involved in monitoring the supply of medicines and
   other products, by
   - Functioning as a standing representative of the central traders' committee
   - Serving as a member of the national formulary committee
   - Providing technical information to these committees as required

4. Administer the dangerous drug component of the pharmaceutical supplies program by
   - Issuing import certificates covering dangerous drugs
   - Ordering, distributing, and monitoring psychotropic and narcotic drugs for government institutions
   - Preparing monthly, quarterly, and annual reports on the use of these medicines

QUALIFICATIONS:
Education:
   - Pharmacy degree
   - Certificate in management

Knowledge and experience required:
   - Pharmaceutical principles and practices
   - Pharmaceutical supplies management
   - Sources of supply for medical and nonmedical drugs
   - Procedures for the estimation and importation of narcotic drugs

Abilities required:
   - Forecasting pharmaceutical supply requirements
   - Coordinating pharmaceutical supply services
   - Monitoring the quality of work of others
   - Using computers

Working conditions:
   - Work is performed at the central medical stores department.

REPORTING RELATIONSHIP: Responsible to the director of pharmaceutical services

SIGNATURES:

Incumbent: _____   Date: _____

Director of pharmaceutical services: _____   Date: _____

dures is always preferable. If someone is making mistakes, a good manager takes that person aside for a talk. Criticizing someone's behavior is perhaps one of the most difficult tasks a manager faces. The challenge is to remain objective and avoid blaming. The manager must—

- Present the perceived problem clearly
- Ask for the other person's point of view and listen when it is given
- Avoid expressing anger or frustration and remain calm and firm
- Focus on possible solutions rather than dwell on mistakes
- Discuss ways to resolve the issue and how such problems might be avoided in the future

51.14 Handling conflict

Conflicts can occur when employees feel that their needs are not being met or their concerns are being ignored. Conflicts inevitably occur in the struggle to secure adequate resources for effective pharmaceutical supply systems. This section reviews conflict resolution strategies that harmonize with the consultative, participatory approaches emphasized in this chapter.

Two forces determine how conflicts play out—

1. *Assertiveness:* the extent to which a person attempts to satisfy his or her own needs
2. *Cooperation:* the extent to which a person attempts to satisfy the needs of others

Individuals or groups manage conflict using a number of styles, but each can be understood as an interplay between these two driving forces. The two dimensions of assertiveness and cooperation define a model that provides a framework for describing various styles of conflict management and for assessing their relative strengths and weaknesses.

Competing style

The competing style involves maximum assertiveness and minimum cooperation. Competitors try to satisfy their own needs at the expense of other parties, using whatever powers are at their disposal. They try to gain power through direct confrontation or manipulation. A competitive style is not necessarily bad; it depends on the circumstances. In situations where life is threatened (an outbreak of cholera, for example, where quick decision making can save lives), a manager might need to take quick and decisive action, even if it means riding roughshod over those who challenge his or her policies.

Strengths. A competitive strategy might be appropriate when—

- Quick, decisive action is vital
- An unpopular decision needs to be made
- No doubt exists about the right course of action
- Defensive measures are urgently required

Weaknesses. A competitive strategy can lead to—

- Lost opportunities for collaboration or compromise
- Degeneration into stubborn opposition
- Low morale among employees, who may feel they have no input in decision making

Accommodating style

Accommodation is at the opposite pole from competition; it is characterized by unassertive and totally cooperative behavior. Accommodation means putting the other party's needs above one's own.

Strengths. Accommodation is an appropriate strategy when—

- The other party is clearly in the right
- Preserving harmony is the most important consideration
- Gaining goodwill is the most important outcome

Weaknesses. Too much accommodation can lead to—

- Reduced influence, respect, and recognition (someone who earns the label "accommodator" will always be expected to give in)
- People taking advantage of a perceived weakness

Avoiding style

Avoiding is characterized by zero assertiveness and zero cooperation—it means choosing not to engage. The avoider evades the issue, withdraws from the discussion, and never bothers to press for a resolution. Avoiding can sometimes be used effectively as an interim strategy.

Strengths. Avoidance may be appropriate when—

- Discussions become overheated and a cooling-off period is advisable
- A conflict should be delayed until more information is gathered or a closer analysis can be made
- The issue is relatively unimportant
- There is not enough time to come to a resolution
- The issue is identified as only a symptom of a substantial and extensive problem that needs to be dealt with later

Weaknesses. An inappropriate use of avoidance procedures can lead to—

- Communication breakdown, as when staff "left in the dark" stop taking initiatives
- Reduced effectiveness, as decisions are made by default
- Conflicts persisting and then flaring up later

Collaborating style

In the collaborating style, maximum use is made of both assertiveness and cooperation. Those using this style seek to satisfy the needs of all parties concerned. Collaboration is the best way to develop consensus solutions to problems and achieve a commitment to those solutions. Neither side feels that it has lost out in any way, so this is an ideal management style.

Strengths. The collaborating style is most effectively used when—

- The needs and concerns of the parties are sufficiently important to warrant the time and energy it takes to collaborate properly
- All parties agree to combine resources and efforts for a more effective outcome

Weaknesses. This is the most time-consuming and energy-sapping style. It can result in—

- Relatively unimportant matters getting too much attention
- The establishment of cumbersome procedures, which may lead to frustrating delays in making decisions and taking action

Compromising style

Compromise is an intermediate strategy, midway between competition and collaboration, avoidance and accommodation. The objective is to find a solution that partly satisfies both parties—by "splitting the difference."

Strengths. Compromise solutions are appropriate when—

- The parties are strongly committed to mutually exclusive goals, and it is clear that no solution will be wholly satisfactory to both of them
- The goals of both parties are important but not worth the effort needed for collaboration
- Temporary solutions are sought for complex issues because the time for decision making is short

Weaknesses. If compromises are made too readily or casually—

- Important principles may be disregarded
- The value of the enterprise may be diminished

In conflict situations, the best approach to take depends on the circumstances. A good manager is in command of all the channels of communication, is sensitive to the needs of the situation, and can select the correct approach. Unfortunately, what tends to happen is that individual managers and groups become locked into one preferred style of conflict management and use it in almost every situation.

Collaboration and compromise are the styles that match the consulting, all-channels-open, problem-solving management approaches explored in this chapter.

51.15 Delegating

Effective delegation enables managers to become much more productive and, therefore, more successful. Unfortunately, many managers have never learned how to delegate effectively. A sure sign of trust between manager and staff is the manager's willingness to delegate responsibilities. If delegation happens consistently and properly, the effectiveness of a team can be greatly enhanced.

Delegation is more than simply assigning tasks to subordinates. Delegation skills involve the following steps—

1. *Selecting the right person for the job.* Delegation works well only when the person to whom work is being delegated is capable of handling the task. Delegating to the wrong person invites failure.
2. *Clearly specifying the assignment being delegated.* Unless the assignment is clear, the staff member may do too much or too little.
3. *Defining the level of authority being delegated.* Is the staff member being asked to investigate a problem and then report back to the manager for a decision and action? Is the staff member to investigate, see the manager for a decision, and then act? Or is the staff member to investigate, decide, and act—informing the manager afterward? Both manager and staff member risk anger or frustration if the level of authority is not made clear.
4. *Informing concerned parties.* Unless other staff members are informed of what assignments have been delegated and to whom, they may feel that a staff member's actions are inappropriate. They may think that the staff member is trying to take over the manager's job rather than acting on the manager's behalf.
5. *Monitoring without meddling.* Once an assignment has been delegated, monitoring progress is important. The manager may need to advise the staff member of possible problems. But if the manager intrudes, short-circuits, undercuts, goes around, or otherwise

meddles in the assignment, the staff member will lose interest in doing a good job. Accepting that the assignment will probably be done differently from the way the manager would have done it is part of delegating. Different is not necessarily worse. Staff members often have more time or other insights that allow them to do the task better than the manager would have.

6. *Completing the delegation neatly.* When the assignment has been completed, the staff member should brief the manager. Necessary follow-up actions should be identified. Most important, the staff member should receive positive feedback if the assignment went well and clear and direct negative feedback if the assignment did not turn out well. The manager should suggest specific corrective action.

When these basic steps are not followed, the result is often confusion, poor decision making, mistrust, and frustration. Managers are afraid to delegate because "the staff will mess it up," and staff are afraid to take the initiative because "the boss will tell me I messed up."

Directing managers have trouble delegating because they do not like to give up control. Avoiding managers have trouble delegating because they do not provide clear guidance and feedback. Consulting managers generally do the best job of delegating.

Delegation has three main benefits. First, it provides subordinates with the opportunity to accumulate valuable experience and develop new skills. Second, delegation prevents managers from being overworked, a condition that can cause delays in decision making. Finally, delegation frees senior managers to concentrate on long-term planning activities.

51.16   Conducting meetings

Properly run meetings can be vital to the effectiveness of an organization: they are forums for gathering information, reviewing progress, discussing ideas, planning actions, and resolving conflicts. Improperly run meetings can be a colossal waste of time.

Meetings are appropriate if—

- An issue affecting the work team needs to be clarified
- Concerns should be shared with a group
- The group needs to be involved in a problem-solving and decision-making activity
- A group has asked for a meeting

Meetings are inappropriate if—

- The decisions have already been made

- The calendar says that a meeting is due, but no urgent matters need discussion

Conditions for effective meetings

However informal and lively the interaction, effective meetings are usually the result of careful planning. The following are some of the most important factors that contribute to a meeting's success—

Purpose: The objectives of the meeting should be clear to all participants.
Preparation: The members should be knowledgeable about the topics under discussion. Relevant papers may need to be circulated beforehand.
Control: The chairperson should be in authority but not *the* authority and responsible for the conduct of the meeting but not the only decision maker in the group.
Size: The group should be small enough for everyone to make a contribution, unless the meeting is merely a gathering for dispensing information.
Setting: The seating should be arranged so that everyone has eye contact with everyone else.
Atmosphere: The climate should be such that participants feel free to offer ideas and to challenge and be challenged.
Summary: The meeting should end with a statement of what has been achieved.
Record: Taking accurate minutes of the meeting is important so that efficient monitoring can take place and those responsible for arranged actions can be held accountable.
Time: The meeting should begin on time and last for a predetermined length of time.

Skills of chairing

The success of meetings depends on the kind of control exercised by the chairperson. Some of the main techniques used to facilitate open and purposeful discussion and decision making are—

Initiating: Start by ensuring that all members know the objectives and agenda of the meeting.
Seeking opinions: Invite participation by bringing members in when you know that they will have something to contribute.
Clarifying: Rephrase or illustrate points so they can be understood by all members.
Steering: Bring the discussion back on track when it veers off course.
Summarizing: Pull together the ideas that have been expressed and sum up the conclusions that have been reached.
Keeping time: End the meeting on time.

ASSESSMENT GUIDE

In addition to the HRM system assessment questions in Section 51.4, the following questions can be used to assess an organization's human resources components—

- Do experienced HRM staff in your organization maintain human resources functions?
- Does an annual human resources plan exist? Is it monitored?
- Is a human resources information system in place to gather employee data that can be used in human resources planning and forecasting?
- Do personnel files exist for all staff? Do staff members have access to these files?
- Is a job classification system in place?
- Is a system in place to determine salaries and to determine upgrades and merit awards?

- Is orientation offered to all new employees?
- Does an updated personnel policy manual exist? Is it used by managers and supervisors to address employment questions?
- Are formal procedures in place for addressing discipline and termination issues?
- Does an organizational chart of staffing positions and relationships exist? When was it last revised?
- Do job descriptions exist for these positions? When were they last revised? Does each staff member have a copy of his or her job description?
- Is a training plan in place? Does it include a plan for management and leadership development?
- Does the organization have links to preservice training institutions?

Finally, the conclusions of most meetings can be encapsulated in a brief plan of action, recording what is to be done, by whom, and by when. ■

References and further readings

★ = Key readings.

Adano, U. 2008. The Health Worker Recruitment and Deployment Process in Kenya: An Emergency Hiring Program. *Human Resources for Health* 6:19. <http://www.human-resources-health.com/content/6/1/19>

Adano, U., J. McCaffery, P. Ruwoldt, and B. Stilwell. 2008. Human Resources for Health: Tackling the Human Resource Management Piece of the Puzzle. Technical Brief 14. Chapel Hill, N.C.: Capacity Project. <http://www.capacityproject.org/images/stories/files/techbrief_14.pdf>

Anello, E. 2008. *A Framework for Good Governance in the Pharmaceutical Sector.* [Working draft for field testing and revision, October.] Geneva: World Health Organization. <http://www.who.int/medicines/areas/policy/goodgovernance/GGMframework09.pdf>

Chen, L. C. 2010. Striking the Right Balance: Health Workforce Retention in Remote and Rural Areas. *Bulletin of the World Health Organization* 88:321–400. <http://www.who.int/bulletin/volumes/88/5/10-078477/en/index.html>

Dambisya, Y. M. 2007. *A Review of Non-financial Incentives for Health Worker Retention in East and Southern Africa.* Regional Network for Equity in Health in East and Southern Africa Discussion Paper No. 44. Harare: EQUINET (Network on Equity in Health in Southern Africa). <http://www.equinetafrica.org/bibl/docs/DIS44HRdambisya.pdf>

FIP (International Pharmaceutical Federation). 2006. *Global Pharmacy Workforce and Migration Report: A Call for Action.* The Hague: FIP.

★ ———.2009. *2009 FIP Global Pharmacy Workforce Report.* The Hague: FIP. <http://www.fip.org/www/index.php?page=programmesandprojects_pharmacyeducationtaskforce_human-resources>

★ Global Health Workforce Alliance (International Council of Nurses, International Hospital Federation, International Pharmaceutical Federation, World Confederation for Physical Therapy, World Dental Federation, World Medical Association). 2008. *Guidelines: Incentives for Health Professionals.* Geneva: World Health Organization. <http://www.who.int/workforcealliance/knowledge/publications/alliance/Incentives_Guidelines%20ENG%20low.pdf>

Hawthorne, N., and C. Anderson. 2009. The Global Pharmacy Workforce: A Systematic Review of the Literature. *Human Resources for Health* 7:48. <http://www.human-resources-health.com/content/7/1/48>

Helfenbein, S., and C. A. Severo. 2004. *Scaling Up HIV/AIDS Programs: A Manual for Multisectoral Planning.* Boston, Mass.: Management Sciences for Health. <http://erc.msh.org/newpages/english/health/Scaling_Up_HIV_AIDS_Programs.pdf>

Hirschhorn, L. R., L. Oguda , A. Fullem, N. Dreesch, and P. Wilson. 2006. Estimating Health Workforce Needs for Antiretroviral Therapy in Resource-limited Settings. *Human Resources for Health* 26 (4):1. <http://www.human-resources-health.com/content/4/1/1>

Hongoro, C., and C. Normand. 2006. "Health Workers: Building and Motivating the Workforce." In *Disease Control Priorities in Developing Countries,* 2nd ed. D. T. Jamison, J. G. Breman, A. R. Measham, G. Alleyne, M. Claeson, D. B. Evans, P. Jha, A. Mills, and P. Musgrove (eds). New York: Oxford University Press. <http://www.dcp2.org/pubs/DCP/71/>

★ Joint Learning Initiative. 2004. *Human Resources for Health: Overcoming the Crisis.* Cambridge, Mass.: The President and Fellows of Harvard College. <http://www.healthgap.org/camp/hcw_docs/JLi_Human_Resources_for_Health.pdf>

Kinfu, Y., M. R. Dal Poz, H. Mercer, and D. B Evans. 2009. The Health Worker Shortage in Africa: Are Enough Physicians and Nurses Being Trained? *Bulletin of the World Health Association* 87(3):161–244.

Management Sciences for Health/Rwanda HIV/Performance-Based Financing Project. 2009. *A Vision for Health: Performance-Based Financing in Rwanda.* Cambridge, Mass.: MSH. <http://www.msh.org/resource-center/publications/upload/Rwanda-EOP-11-10-09_spreads.pdf>

Marchal, B., G. Kegels, and V. De Brouwere. 2004. Human Resources in Scaling Up HIV/AIDS Programmes: Just a Killer Assumption or in

Need of New Paradigms? *AIDS* 18:2103–5.

Matowe, L., M. Duwiejua, and P. Norris. 2004. Is There a Solution to the Pharmacist Brain Drain from Poor to Rich Countries? *Pharmaceutical Journal* 272(7283):98–9.

Matsiko, C. W., and J. Kiwanuka. 2003. A Review of Human Resources for Health in Uganda. *Health Policy and Development* 1(1):15–20.

McCaffery, J. A., and U. Adano. 2009. *Strengthening Human Resources Management: Knowledge, Skills and Leadership.* Capacity Project Knowledge Sharing Legacy Series no. 11. <http://www.capacity project.org/images/stories/files/legacyseries_11.pdf>

MSH (Management Sciences for Health). 1999. Human Resources: Managing and Developing Your Most Important Asset. *The Manager* 8(1). <http://erc.msh.org/TheManager/English/V8_N1_En_Issue.pdf>

———. 1998. *Developing a Performance Planning and Review System.* Cambridge, Mass.: MSH. <http://erc.msh.org/mainpage.cfm?file=2.8.0.htm&module=hr&language=English#toptop>

———. Various. *The Manager: Management Strategies for Improving Health Services.* <http://erc.msh.org/TheManager/index.cfm>
- Assessing the Impact of Training on Staff Performance
- Creating a Work Climate That Motivates Staff and Improves Performance
- Developing Managers Who Lead
- Exercising Leadership to Make Decentralization Work
- Human Resources: Managing and Developing Your Most Important Asset
- Improving Supervision: A Team Approach
- Leading Changes in Practices to Improve Health
- Managing Performance Improvement of Decentralized Health Services
- Planning for Leadership Transition
- Tackling the Crisis in Human Capacity Development for Health Services
- Using Evaluation as a Management Tool
- Strengthening Human Resources to Improve Health Outcomes

MSH/SPS (Management Sciences for Health/Strengthening Pharmaceutical Systems Program)–Kenya. 2009. *SPS Info Kenya: Strengthening Pharmaceutical and Supply Systems Newsletter* 1 (January–July). Arlington, Va.: MSH/SPS.

MSH/WHO (Management Sciences for Health/World Health Organization). 2006. *Tools for Planning and Developing Human Resources for HIV/AIDS and Other Health Services.* Cambridge, Mass.: MSH.

Pedler, M., J. Burgoyne, and T. Boydell. 2002. *A Manager's Guide to Self-Development.* 4th ed. New York: McGraw-Hill.

Shipp, P. J. 1998. *Workload Indicators of Staffing Need (WISN): A Manual for Implementation.* Geneva: World Health Organization/Division of Human Resources Development and Capacity Building. <http://whqlibdoc.who.int/hq/1998/WHO_HRB_98.2.pdf>

Tjipura-Tjiho, D., D. Mabirizi, K. Lazell, J. Nwokike, S. Saleeb, and C. Dennis. 2007. *A Partnership Model to Improve Human Resource Capacity to Deliver Pharmaceutical Services in Namibia.* Poster presented at HIV/AIDS Implementers Meeting, June 16–19, Kigali, Rwanda.

Viberg, N., G. Tomson, P. Mujinja, and C. S. Lundborg. 2007. The Role of the Pharmacist—Voices from Nine African Countries. *Pharmacy World & Science* 29:25–33.

WHO (World Health Organization). 1997. *The Role of the Pharmacist in the Health Care System: Preparing for the Future Pharmacist.* Vancouver: WHO Consultative Group on the Role of the Pharmacist in the Health Care System. <http://whqlibdoc.who.int/hq/1997/WHO_PHARM_97_599.pdf>

———. 2006. *The World Health Report 2006—Working Together for Health.* Geneva: WHO. <http://www.who.int/whr/2006/en/index.html>

WHO (World Health Organization) Department of Human Resources for Health. 2008. *Global Atlas of the Health Workforce.* <http://apps.who.int/globalatlas/default.asp>

WHO/EPN (World Health Organization and Ecumenical Pharmaceutical Network). 2006. *Multi-Country Study of Medicine Supply and Distribution Activities of Faith-Based Organizations in Sub-Saharan African Countries.* Geneva: WHO and EPN. <http://whqlibdoc.who.int/hq/2006/WHO_PSM_PAR_2006.2_eng.pdf>

WHO/FIP (World Health Organization and International Pharmaceutical Federation). 2006. *Developing Pharmacy Practice: A Focus on Patient Care.* WHO/PSM/PAR/2006.5. Geneva: WHO and FIP. <http://www.who.int/medicines/publications/WHO_PSM_PAR_2006.5.pdf>

WHO (World Health Organization) Maximizing Positive Synergies Collaborative Group. 2009. An Assessment of Interactions between Global Health Initiatives and Country Health Systems. *Lancet* 373:2137–69.

WHO, PEPFAR, and UNAIDS (World Health Organization, U.S. President's Emergency Plan for AIDS Relief, and Joint United Nations Programme on HIV/AIDS). 2008. *Task Shifting: Rational Redistribution of Tasks among Health Workforce Teams: Global Recommendations and Guidelines.* Geneva: WHO.

Yumkella, F. 2009. Worker Retention in Human Resources for Health: Catalysing and Tracking Change. Technical Brief 15. <http://www.capacityproject.org/images/stories/files/techbrief_15.pdf>

HRM online tools and resources

HRH (Human Resources for Health) Global Resources Center <http://www.hrhresourcecenter.org/>

HRM Resources Kit <http://erc.msh.org/mainpage.cfm?file=2.8.0.htm&module=hr&language=English>
- Organizing and Staffing the HRM Office
- Developing a Job Classification System
- Developing a Salary Policy
- Guidelines on Recruitment and Hiring
- Guidelines on Staff Orientation
- Developing a Personnel Policy Manual
- Developing a Workplace Prevention Program (HIV/AIDS)
- Developing a Performance Planning and Review System
- Supervisory Competency Self-Assessment Inventory
- Supervision Manual
- Conducting a Training Needs Assessment
- Developing an Annual Training Plan
- Assessing Trainer Competency
- Contracting Out for Training

Human Resources Management Rapid Assessment Tool for HIV/AIDS Environments: A Guide for Strengthening HRM Systems <http://erc.msh.org/newpages/english/toolkit/hr_hiv_assessment_tool.pdf>

Human Resources Management Rapid Assessment Tool for Private- and Public-Sector Health Organizations: A Guide for Strengthening HRM Systems <http://erc.msh.org/newpages/english/toolkit/hrd.pdf>

Human Resources for Health journal <http://www.human-resources-health.com>

Performance Management Tool <http://erc.msh.org/newpages/english/toolkit/pmt.pdf>

Supervisor Competency Self-Assessment Inventory <http://erc.msh.org/newpages/english/toolkit/supervis.pdf>

Workgroup Climate Assessment (WCA) Tool and Guide for Facilitators <http://www.msh.org/resource-center/workgroup-climate-assessment-tool-and-guide-for-facilitators.cfm>

World Health Organization Tools and guidelines for human resources for health <http://www.who.int/hrh/tools/en/>

| Part I: Policy and economic issues | Part II: Pharmaceutical management | Part III: Management support systems |

Planning and administration
Organization and management
Information management
Human resources management
  51 Human resources management and capacity development
  52 Designing and implementing training programs

CHAPTER 52

Designing and implementing training programs

SUMMARY

Training is any planned activity to transfer or modify knowledge, skills, and attitudes through learning experiences. Personnel may require training for a variety of reasons, including the need to maintain levels of competence and respond to the demands of changing circumstances and new approaches and technologies. Training by itself cannot solve structural, organizational, or policy problems within an organization, although supportive supervision and the use of motivational strategies can help sustain performance improvement derived from training.

The first step in the design of training involves an assessment of training needs. The assessment comprises—

- Observing workers performing normal duties
- Interviewing workers and others
- Studying routine reports or performance reviews, along with job descriptions
- Identifying performance problems

The second step involves defining the training program's learning objectives. The learning objectives, which are derived from the needs assessment, specify the observable, measurable actions that each learner will be able to demonstrate as a result of participating in the training activities.

The third step is the creation and implementation of a training program to improve performance, taking into account the experience and educational levels of the personnel and the time and resources available for training. Options range from short courses to long-term placements in academic institutions in the country, in the region, or overseas, and non–classroom-based interventions, such as on-the-job training, coaching, and mentoring. All options must be weighed against the immediate operational needs of the program or institution, because facilities may not have enough personnel to operate when staff members go for training.

The learning outcomes that must be achieved, along with the training environment, audience characteristics, and the experience of the trainer, all determine the mix of learning methods and media that will achieve maximum effectiveness. Methods and media may include lecture, discussion, case study, role-playing, group exercise, simulation games, brainstorming, and demonstration. If no published training materials—including audiovisual aids—are available, the trainer must develop them.

Development of the training program also includes design of the training evaluation, which is carried out during the course as well as at its conclusion. During the course, trainers monitor learner progress and satisfaction to identify where they may need to make adjustments to the training program. At the end of the course, trainers should collect data on how well the learners achieved the course objectives and how satisfied they were with the training experience. Whenever possible, the trainer should follow up with participants after they return to their work situations to assess the impact of training on performance. Data collected during follow-up can help identify the need for additional training or reinforcement of newly acquired skills, as well as inform review and revision of the training materials.

In some countries, availability of basic training and continuous professional development programs is limited; therefore, many health workers lack access to formal training opportunities and new ideas and approaches that can improve their work performance. Well-designed in-service training programs can help fill this need.

Training should be put into a context of continuous performance improvement. Changing and improving practices require an environment conducive to work, the appropriate learning resources, and the continuous use of motivational strategies. Training should be based on competencies: the abilities required to do work to the standards expected. Therefore, training should result in changes in work behavior that lead to an improved, efficiently functioning pharmaceutical management system. At the same time, training alone is unlikely to change overall supply system performance unless the environment and supervisory systems support change (see Chapter 37) and unless individuals are encouraged to maintain changes (see Chapter 51).

Learning requires active involvement. People prefer to learn in different ways—through visual stimuli, verbal interactions, and learning by doing. Therefore, offering a variety of training opportunities and training techniques is usually more effective than using only one approach. Training can be formal or informal, academic or applied, guided or self-directed, or provided in public agencies or private institutions.

Training alone is often not sufficient to change behavior or improve performance. Improved performance, changed attitudes, and new skills acquired during training may need to be complemented by and maintained through continuing education, supportive supervision, and adequate motivational incentives. In many cases, structural changes, such as workspace improvements and increased access to supplies and equipment may be needed to support improved performance.

Figure 52-1   Capacity-building framework

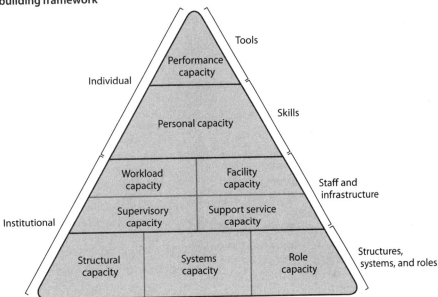

Source: Adapted from Potter and Brough 2004.

52.1 Objectives of training

The training of personnel in pharmaceutical management has four major objectives—

1. Increase knowledge about the special considerations related to pharmaceutical systems
2. Improve attitudes about the importance of pharmaceutical management, thus improving the environment for change
3. Build and strengthen skills in the specific tasks to be completed for efficient functioning of the pharmaceutical system
4. Improve work behavior, so that people function better at assigned activities and fulfill their potential

The goal of these objectives is to increase access to quality pharmaceutical products and services.

Training should address the needs of three levels of personnel, because it takes all three groups to effect sustainable change—

1. Policy makers, who are responsible for creating the environment needed for improved pharmaceutical management
2. Midlevel managers, who are responsible for planning and supervising activities required in the management and use of medicines
3. Line or operations-level personnel, who are responsible for carrying out the work of pharmaceutical management

A country's national pharmaceutical program alone is not in a position to handle comprehensive training for policy makers and midlevel managers; many of their learning objectives are best handled through general management training. However, it is still possible and necessary to reorient this group on pharmaceutical policies and issues through information exchange, reports, and seminars. Training for operations-level personnel is critical because they often lack the basic knowledge and skills necessary to be effective at their jobs.

Finally, training alone will not result in significantly improved performance unless it is linked to an enabling institutional environment. This is illustrated by Figure 52-1, which is a conceptual framework for building in-country capacity for pharmaceutical management services. It illustrates the concept that health structures, systems, and roles, staff and infrastructure, skills, and tools must all be addressed to strengthen a country's ability to effectively provide pharmaceutical services.

52.2 Developing a comprehensive training program

A training program is composed of a schedule of activities with training goals, learning objectives, subject areas, methods, trainers, trainees, methods of assessment, and locations. A good training program is designed to address performance problems, such as long delays in getting medicines from suppliers to the main stores, delays in distributing medicines from midlevel stores to end-user units, or

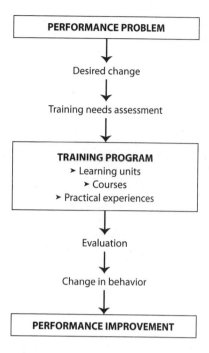

Figure 52-2   The training process for improved performance

```
┌─────────────────────────────┐
│     PERFORMANCE PROBLEM     │
└─────────────────────────────┘
              │
              ▼
        Desired change
              │
              ▼
    Training needs assessment
              │
              ▼
┌─────────────────────────────┐
│      TRAINING PROGRAM       │
│      ➤ Learning units       │
│         ➤ Courses           │
│    ➤ Practical experiences  │
└─────────────────────────────┘
              │
              ▼
         Evaluation
              │
              ▼
      Change in behavior
              │
              ▼
┌─────────────────────────────┐
│   PERFORMANCE IMPROVEMENT    │
└─────────────────────────────┘
```

failure to ensure quality of medicines. Figure 52-2 shows how a training program is developed, proceeding from problem identification, through needs assessment, training, and evaluation, to a change in behavior that results in better performance.

The key elements of a training program include needs assessment, course work, learning tasks, and practical application. Facilitators introduce new information to trainees through course work or lectures. Learning tasks or activities, such as case studies or role-plays, provide individuals with opportunities to work with the new information in a small-group setting. Practical experiences and application give the trainees the opportunity to apply the knowledge and skills learned in a real-life or simulated situation.

The current level of the trainees' skills will guide decisions on developing a training program specifically for the group. For example, the objectives and goals for a program to train new employees will differ dramatically from those for a program geared toward experienced technicians learning a new technique.

Conducting needs and knowledge assessments

A training needs assessment and a pretraining knowledge and skills assessment are required to help plan an effective training program. The needs assessment should encompass the overall working environment, including the supervisory structure and the level of employee motivation. Pharmaceutical management training will be effective only if all areas of the pharmaceutical supply system are assessed frankly and carefully.

A knowledge and skills assessment evaluates the participants' level of prior knowledge, as well as previous training and experience, in the area of interest. The results of this assessment are used to develop the training learning objectives, and ultimately, the content.

Methods for assessing training needs are outlined below. The optimal method depends on the goals of the assessment and the cadre of the individuals being assessed.

A knowledge assessment can be based on observation of a worker performing routine duties. This review uncovers both strengths and weaknesses, but the presence of an observer may influence the behavior observed. For example, a clinical worker examining a patient is likely to be more thorough than usual if someone is watching. Specific training needs can be determined more clearly by using well-established indicators, such as those on performance monitoring and evaluation described in Chapter 48, and observation methods, such as those described in Chapter 28.

Interviews with supervisors, administrators, users of services, and workers can help determine where performance problems might exist and what skills need to be taught or improved. If workers fear reprisals from management, reassurances about confidentiality of information will be necessary to obtain good data. In some situations, a training needs analysis can be done by conducting a group interview in which the staff are invited to identify competencies in terms of knowledge, attitudes, and skills. Staff members rate themselves on a graph in relation to each of a set of competencies. Exit interviews with workers leaving their jobs can also be useful. Finally, interviews with users of the services can help in assessing levels of satisfaction.

Analyses of job and task descriptions may reveal special training needs. Self-administered, anonymous questionnaires for both managers and workers can also be valuable.

Several types of reports are useful needs assessment tools—

- Organizational reports, for an overview of the performance of the organization and personnel
- External evaluation or appraisal reports, for an outsider's view of the organization and its training needs (and performance)
- Annual or semiannual performance reviews

Selecting subject areas and setting learning objectives

A training needs assessment should indicate which subject area, topic, or target group should be given priority (Table 52-1). In many countries, some subject areas require more attention than others, but certain basics must be provided: the selection process needs to be well managed and par-

Table 52-1 Subject areas, training topics, and target groups

Subject area	Training topics	Target groups
Selection	• Essential medicines lists • Public formulary • Sources of information • Safety and efficacy • Cost comparisons • Levels of use • Hospital formularies • National pharmaceutical policy	• Policy and decision makers in ministry of health (MOH), ministry of finance (MOF), other ministries • Service providers: doctors, nurses • Auxiliary personnel • Pharmacists and dispensers • Hospital administrators
Procurement	• Procurement cycle • Purchasing methods • Quantification of pharmaceutical needs • Scheduling of purchases • Terms of payment • Selection of suppliers • Payment mechanisms • Organization of procurement services • Quality assurance • Make-or-buy decisions • Shipment specifications • Contracting	• Division of planning, MOH • Division of finance, MOH • Division of administration or purchasing, MOH • MOF • Central procurement service (if it exists) • Central laboratories, MOH • Pharmaceutical quality laboratories • Drug regulatory bodies • Senior MOH/MOF officials for policy decisions (such as make-or-buy)
Distribution	• Distribution cycle • Information system • Port clearing • Warehouse operations • Packaging and repackaging • Transportation • Security	• Division of planning, MOH • Division of administration, MOH • Operations personnel in port and warehouses (central, regional, and district) • Transportation
Use	• Promotion of appropriate therapy • Training of health workers • Dispensing practices • Patient education • Information systems • Patient adherence • Rational-medicine-use indicators	• Program directors • Program supervisors • Doctors • Nurses • Pharmacists • Dispensers • Auxiliary and community health workers • Drug sellers • Patients and clients

ticipatory; procurement officers need training in efficient purchasing methods and quantification of pharmaceutical needs; distribution—proper storage, efficient transportation, and security of medicines—is a continuing concern; and rational use is becoming a major focus of many pharmaceutical programs.

In addition to these basic pharmaceutical management skills, staff will benefit from training in other areas, including—

- General management
- Financial management, budgeting, and accounting
- Computer systems and information management
- Training program development and management
- Training materials development
- Patient and public communications
- Personnel planning and management
- Program planning, monitoring, and evaluation
- Proposal development and writing

Pharmaceutical supply systems often run into difficulty not because they lack staff members with technical expertise but because they lack staff members who have critical management skills. Thus, when considering subject areas, thinking broadly about which skills are most needed to improve the performance of the organization is important.

After determining which tasks and competencies are required by staff for a particular situation, training goals should be established and learning objectives should be set. Goals will be broad statements about what the training intends to achieve: for example, "This course aims to provide medical stores personnel with the knowledge and skills to accurately estimate quantities of medicines and related commodities to order."

Objectives, on the other hand, should clearly state what the participant must be able to do at the end of the training. They must be clear, concise, relevant, easily understood, and measurable—in other words—SMART (specific, measurable, achievable, realistic, and time-bound) (CDC 2009).

They are, in fact, indicators by which course output and performance can be assessed. For example—

On completion of the course, participants should be able to—

- State the rationale and uses for quantification of pharmaceuticals and other related commodities
- Describe the attributes, uses, and limitations of various quantification methods
- Identify the data required for each of the quantification methods

Because objectives must be measurable, terms such as "understand" or "know" are not acceptable.

Learning methods

A variety of learning experiences can be used in training, including—

Brainstorming: Members of a small or large group are encouraged to contribute any suggestion that comes into their heads on a given subject, initially with no criticism, but later with a sifting and assessment of all ideas. (Because brainstorming is such a versatile but sometimes misunderstood method, it is described in detail in Box 52-1.)

Case study: A real situation is presented in a brief paper or presentation, then analyzed by participants.

Demonstration: The facilitator shows learners how and what should be done while explaining why, when, and where an action is taken; participants then perform the action.

Discussion: A method in which the participants learn from one another, usually with guidance from a facilitator.

Distance learning: A system designed to build knowledge and skills of learners who are not physically on-site to receive training. Facilitators and students may communicate at times of their own choosing by exchanging printed or electronic media or through technology that allows them to communicate in real time.

Box 52-1
Brainstorming: A versatile technique for training, planning, and problem solving

Brainstorming is a group technique that is useful in training situations. It also helps work groups be more creative in decision making and problem solving. The basic process is easy. The facilitator writes the topic or questions on a flip chart, whiteboard, or blackboard. Group members are asked to call out their ideas in short phrases that can be written down readily. To keep the discussion moving, a tight time limit is usually set—typically, five to ten minutes. The facilitator should be prepared to stimulate brainstorming with a few examples or prompting questions.

The creativity of brainstorming is enhanced by giving the group the following short set of guidelines before starting—

No idea is a bad idea: No matter how odd, unconventional, or silly an idea may seem, no idea should be ignored.

No discussion of ideas is allowed: Discussion of ideas can come later. Grimaces, groans, and other nonverbal judgments discourage creative thinking and should be avoided.

Everybody is encouraged to contribute: The facilitator should try to get everyone to make at least one suggestion.

Go for quantity: This encourages the maximum contribution and discourages people from screening out potentially good ideas before suggesting them.

Build on other people's ideas: Although discussion of ideas is discouraged, generating new ideas from those already suggested is fine.

After the brainstorming session, ideas are usually typed up, organized in some way, and brought back to the group for discussion.

Although brainstorming can generate many creative ideas, it is not always successful. Some people may be discouraged from contributing, and inhibitions may exist about raising certain ideas. Brainstorming may also be dominated by certain individuals or get stuck on one part of the topic. Sticking to the preceding guidelines will help. In addition, methods to make brainstorming more productive include—

- Prepare a broad range of prompts that can be used to direct the group's thinking into new areas if suggestions consistently concern one area.
- Begin by asking each person to brainstorm individually for a few minutes and write down ideas.
- Divide the group into several smaller groups to brainstorm on the same topic. Then compile and discuss the topics in a larger group.
- Limit the number of suggestions by an individual group member. Generally, this degree of directness should be reserved for situations in which one group member dominates the brainstorming session.

e-learning: Participants interact with facilitators through the use of some of the many electronic, computer-based learning materials that are now available, ranging from CD-ROMs to Web-based systems.

Group exercise: A number of participants undertake an activity together, followed by a critical analysis of the process involved.

Lecture: A direct talk with or without learning aids but without group participation.

Role-playing: Participants act out the roles of those represented in a given situation.

Self-paced: Participants are allowed to learn anywhere, anytime, and at a pace that suits their levels of skills, knowledge, and aptitudes.

Simulation game: A more advanced version of a case study, where participants are given more detailed information on a situation, including data sets to analyze. On the basis of their analyses, participants develop and defend a plan of action.

Worksheet: A step-by-step approach to identifying problems or solutions through written questions or problems, with space provided for answers.

The uses, advantages, disadvantages, and trainers' role for some of these methods are summarized in Table 52-2. Some of the methods are more suitable for adult participatory training, and others work well in formal academic settings (such as lectures or seminars). Most people learn better in an active rather than a passive fashion. A combination of methods is likely to be more effective than the exclusive use of one method.

Sequencing topics. *Sequencing* means arranging topics in a logical order during training. In doing so, bear in mind that most people prefer to learn in easy and progressive stages. Adults, especially experienced trainees, usually prefer to start with an overview of the whole course before concentrating on particulars. The best approach is to sequence topics to build on previously completed content and learning experiences. In addition, *spiraling* the curriculum revisits the basic concepts repeatedly, while building on them. The trainer should, however, be aware of training fatigue and not leave the most complex topic for the end of the course, when learners are likely to be more tired.

Developing teaching materials. Training materials may not be available for the kind of in-service training that would best suit a particular pharmaceutical management program. Many countries, however, have developed their own teaching materials using a number of approaches. These materials can be requested and used as is or can be adapted to suit specific needs. Materials from international sources are listed in Annex 52-1.

Manuals. Many countries have training manuals that are not being used effectively by their health workers, often

---

Box 52-2
Outline of trainers' and participants' guides for workshops

Trainers' guides

Summary

- Learning objectives and content of the unit
- Preparations that the trainer must make
- Supplementary reading material

Unit outline and session plan

- Prerequisites for participation in the session
- Components of the session and the estimated time
- Visual aids to be used

Teaching notes

- Technical background
- Instructions for activities

Visual aids (which can be copied onto transparencies or redrawn on flip charts)

Participants' guides

Session guide

- Learning objectives and content of the unit
- Basic information the participant must have before attending the session
- Additional reading materials

Session notes (containing basic technical information, including definitions of essential terms)

Session activities (with worksheets and instructions)

---

because the workers were not involved or consulted in developing them. A better approach is to ask knowledgeable persons to write on one or two topics; circulate drafts among selected end users; and develop the final version in a workshop involving end-users, the authors, and national pharmaceutical management program officers. This approach creates a sense of ownership, which leads to increased acceptance and use of the materials developed. The topics can be compiled inside one cover or distributed as a series of individual modules.

Trainers' and participants' guides. Training materials should include guides for both trainers and participants, as well as audiovisual aids. Some of these materials may be obtained from established programs. Typical contents of trainers' and participants' guides are outlined in Box 52-2. Both provide structured but adaptable notes and exercises for each unit. The participants' guide should contain the technical content for the unit, including definitions of all

Table 52-2   Comparison of training methods

Method	Useful for	Advantages	Disadvantages	Trainer's role
Lecture	• Passing on information and facts • Giving specific information related to occupation, job, or task	• Allows much material to be delivered in a short time • Handles a large number of participants • Permits lecturer to be in full control	• Learner is passive • Little of what is said is remembered • Lecturer receives little feedback	• Provide information • Answer questions
Discussion	• Stimulating interest and thought • Generating possible solutions to problems • Consolidating other types of learning • Developing consensus	• Stimulates learners' interest • Involves learners actively • Allows sharing of learners' experiences with others	• Time-consuming • Requires learners to have facts about the topic • Needs to be well controlled to have value • Can be dominated by a few active persons	• Establish small groups early in course • Help groups select moderators and rapporteur • Clearly specify tasks for each group • Assign time limits for each task and enforce them
Case study	• Solving problems • Changing attitudes • Building analytical skills	• Involves learners actively • Allows sharing of learners' experiences with others • Stimulates ideas and discussions of concrete subject	• Time-consuming to prepare • Not easy to validate • Discussion may focus on areas different from those intended by trainer	• Carefully prepare or read case and relevant material • Ask provocative questions to provide key issues for discussion • Guide discussion to achieve analysis, possible solution, recommendations for action
Role-playing	• Developing interactive knowledge and modifying attitudes • Introducing humor and liveliness into training	• Stimulates interest • Is fun • Is active • Uses participants' experiences	• Time-consuming to prepare • Observers may be passive • Some key points may not be addressed • Those engaged in role-playing may learn more than observers	• Choose a suitable story to illustrate key points • Debrief (discuss insights gained from role-playing)
Group exercise	• Team building • Developing interactive skills • Studying group dynamics	• Facilitates high participation of motivated learners	• Trainer's skills required to guide the exercise • Takes time for group to work in harmony	• Prepare carefully to ensure that everything is organized
Brainstorming	• Stimulating creative thinking • Generating possible solutions • Consolidating past learning • Providing diversion	• Promotes active participation of learners • Uses learners' experiences and ideas	• Time-consuming • Some learners may be passive • Requires high-level trainers' skills	• Record suggestions • Reorganize into groups • Lead discussion at end
Demonstration	• Showing correct procedures and required standards	• Stimulates a lot of interest • Can be used for large groups	• Takes effort to produce • Good viewing by learners is difficult in a large group	• Arrange for demonstration materials in advance • Do demonstration alone to ensure that everything works • Observe participant demonstrations • Correct mistakes promptly • Encourage slow learners
Worksheet	• Performing quantitative exercises requiring calculations • Working out solutions for issues of case studies	• Helps learners relate their general learning to some specific area of their work	• Time-consuming • Difficult to prepare	• Prepare a worksheet based on real situations to show difficulties and successes • Guide the learners but leave most responsibility with participants
E-learning	• Individual study • Passing on information and facts • Showing correct procedures • Working out quantitative exercises requiring calculations	• Allows materials to be passed on quickly • Allows participants to study at their own locations, at their own pace • Some Web-based systems allow for communication between participants working on the same module at the same time	• Expensive and time-consuming to prepare • Participants may not have computer equipment or communications links capable of handling some forms of electronic platforms (e.g., Web-based)	• Provide backup support for tutoring, coaching through various means, including telephone, chat room, and Listserv

essential terms and concepts. The trainers' guide should provide guidance on how the session should be taught.

Audiovisual aids. Audiovisual aids are useful because they stimulate the trainee and help reinforce the ideas presented. However, poor visual aids can confuse participants.

Common visual aids include posters, wall charts, chalkboards, flip charts, overhead projections, and computer-projected presentation slides. CDs and tapes are common audio aids. Videotapes, DVDs, and films are good audiovisual aids, but their expense often makes them impractical. The equipment and technology support required for some of these approaches may limit their use in certain settings. If relying on equipment or technology that requires electricity, having a backup option that does not need electricity is an important consideration.

52.3 Implementing a training program

There are two basic approaches to implementing a training program: one is centered on the trainer, who controls learning contents and experiences; the other is centered on the learner, with the trainer acting as a guide and providing resources. This approach assumes that people are able and willing to learn if they are given the proper materials in an atmosphere that is conducive to learning. This method is preferred because it is participatory, learners' experiences are shared, and participants have more freedom to learn at their own speed.

An important aspect to include in a training package is follow-up support to the participants and evaluation of the training outcome. This support, which should be included in the training budget, may be in the form of supervision, coaching, mentoring, setting up a network support group, or simply providing a source of ongoing information. Follow-up activities may be conducted in person but may also be provided by telephone or e-mail. Country Study 52-1 shows how a follow-up plan is used to track participants' progress in developing drug and therapeutics committees.

Strategies

Training strategies must be appropriate to the educational level of personnel being trained and to the resources available in the country, feasible in terms of the amount of time and travel involved, and relevant to the job. In some countries, governments often place officials in jobs that require a higher degree of technical capacity than they possess. In such cases, managers and trainers need to work together to close the gap between requirements and ability.

Training programs must consider the resources available. For example, an individual working in a central medical store that uses a simple card system for inventory control

THE PROFESSIONAL WORKSHOPPER

should be trained in the operation of that system rather than a computerized system that may never be installed.

Training programs must be feasible. Governments may not be able to allow a senior official to take an extended training leave, regardless of potential long-term benefits. Some officials may not be able to be absent from work for more than one week. Similarly, health care providers may not be able to be away from the patient population they serve if no backup staff support is available. This factor is of particular concern in the private sector, where having staff away from work will result in facilities' losing revenues and in providers' losing income.

Preservice training is conducted at established training institutions and is often a prerequisite for hiring. In-service training may be offered in a classroom setting or in the work environment, either as part of a planned staff development program or after an assessment of deficiencies has determined what training is needed at the workplace.

Continuing professional development allows cadres of professionals to maintain and improve their knowledge and professional competence throughout their careers. Professional associations often develop and sponsor continuing professional development courses and accreditation. A recognized credential can be a powerful incentive for seeking professional development; for example, Tanzania created a new cadre of private-sector drug dispenser, who may earn a license to work in a government-accredited drug dispensing outlet after completing a training program and examination.

The decision about the kind of training program to use depends on the issues raised in Table 52-3, as well as the criteria of appropriateness, feasibility, and relevance. A comprehensive training program is likely to include a combination of long- and short-term training, observation trips,

Country Study 52-1
Follow-up activities to support a drug and therapeutics committee course for professionals in developing countries

Drug and therapeutics committees (DTCs) are effective in promoting rational medicine use, but DTCs have been underused in developing countries. The Rational Pharmaceutical Management (RPM) Plus Program and World Health Organization (WHO) designed a course, training materials, and a manual to train health care providers and administrators who would be involved in DTC activities in developing countries. The course includes fifteen training modules and a field trip to hospitals where participants assess the hospital DTCs, conduct medicine use evaluations, and review the formulary process. The course ends with each participant making a workplan for future DTC-related activities.

A common problem with training courses is that when participants go back to their places of work, they may have difficulty maintaining their new skills without ongoing support. The RPM Plus follow-on program, Strengthening Pharmaceutical Systems (SPS), addresses that issue through an innovative follow-up program designed to help participants carry out their DTC workplans and become DTC advocates. The workplans developed in the training are made available on a DTC Learning Center website. The follow-up program provides specific technical assistance and support for all DTC course participants and local organizations to implement a DTC and related activities. Participants' activities are monitored on the website and through regular e-mail follow-up and support. Technical assistance and support for implementing their workplan activities are made available to all participants, and through this post-training support mechanism, participants can share the problems they encounter in their work and brainstorm possible solutions.

Between 2001 and 2010, 24 courses were conducted in Asia, Africa, Latin America, and Eastern Europe for 945 people from 70 countries. Follow-up e-mail contact with participants showed that they initiated almost 400 activities based on the training.

The RPM Plus/SPS process for promoting and supporting DTCs through training and follow-up of course participants has paid measurable dividends in many countries. The following examples show the wide range of accomplishments by course participants and other in-country stakeholders—

- Reduced the percentage of outpatients receiving antibiotics at each visit from 90 to 60 percent (Kenya)
- Established a system that monitors prescribing patterns for certain high-use antibiotics (Malaysia)
- Developed a generic substitution policy that allows the pharmacy to substitute equivalent products, which decreased the average prescription cost by 20 percent (Kenya)
- Created an adverse drug reaction reporting system (Pakistan)
- Analyzed cost of pneumonia treatment, resulting in institution of new standard treatment guidelines and medical records review to assess physician adherence (Paraguay)
- Performed ABC analysis, resulting in changes in the formulary and in the suppliers of several drugs (India)

Training courses can promote the use of DTCs and related activities in developing countries, but increased support at the country level plus post-training support and technical assistance are needed to help course participants achieve their objectives. In addition, more intensive course follow-up appears to produce enhanced results in a very short period.

Source: MSH/SPS 2010.

conferences and seminars, and in-country counterpart training.

Long-term training. Long-term training is often obtained in an institution of higher learning (sometimes in overseas institutions). Such training, whether in academic or nonacademic settings, is most useful for highly technical areas, such as research and development of new drugs, quality assurance, pharmaceutical production, improved manufacturing practices, or advanced areas of patient care. The provision of fellowships for doctors, pharmacists, industrial engineers, and other technical professionals is most appropriate here.

This approach is limited because a pharmaceutical program does not have the specific duty to provide basic training, and most programs cannot afford to have top personnel away for a long time. In addition, if personnel fail to return to their job, the costs for training new personnel can be high.

Short-term training. Short-term training is usually conducted over a period of one to three months in an academic or nonacademic setting. To work effectively, the trainee

Table 52-3   Issues to consider when designing training programs

Audience	Mode	Length	Location	Funding source

• Trainers to be trained
• Senior government officials
• Administrators in government ministries
• Managers of donor programs, nongovernmental organizations
• Managers of facilities in decentralized settings
• Line or operations-level personnel
	• Preservice training
	• On-site job training, counterpart training
	• Classroom (off-site, in-service training)
	• Tours, observational trips
	• Workshops and seminars
	• Courses (short or long term)
		• Seminar (two weeks or less)
		• Short-term course (two weeks to three months)
		• Long-term course (six to twenty-four or more months)
			• Local college or university
			• National management institute (where one exists)
			• International sponsor (for example, WHO, UNICEF, USAID, Danida, SIDA, KfW, and GTZ)
			• Business
			• Independent private group
			• Government agency
				• Government
				• Private organizations
				• Industry
				• University
				• Self
				• Donors
				  – International organizations
				  – National government donor agencies
				  – Foundations
				  – Private charity, such as a church group

needs to be separated from everyday work responsibilities. Sometimes, when staff members have difficulty getting away for an entire week, training may occur on a series of Saturdays.

This approach is appropriate for most training needs in pharmaceutical management, especially for top- and middle-level personnel. Prerequisites for effective short-term training include—

- A sufficient supply of people with appropriate background or education
- Courses available in the language of the participants
- Course design that uses training modules to allow for flexible curricula to meet the needs of target groups
- Intensive, practical training so that participants gain a good mix of information and skills in a short time
- Adequate follow-up of graduates, including provision of continuing education programs, to ensure that they continue to function effectively

In addition to training the target groups outlined in Table 52-1, this type of program is suitable for the training of trainers (often referred to by the acronym TOT) who will return to their jobs and train others in the techniques and skills they have learned. Thus, short-term training should include pedagogical and leadership skills and provide some institution-building capacities. Annex 52-2 provides further information on workshop logistics and evaluation.

An example of an innovative type of training is the monitoring-training-planning (MTP) methodology, which puts into place an ongoing process to deal with individual training issues in the short term. MTP puts the tools and responsibility for training into the hands of local staff, who tackle specific problems in concise, monthly sessions. See Country Study 52-2 for an introduction and example of the MTP methodology being used in the Lao People's Democratic Republic (P.D.R.).

A number of institutions have developed training materials and can provide training at the regional or international level. Some private nongovernmental institutions in the United States, such as Management Sciences for Health, and quasi-governmental institutions, such as the Eastern and Southern African Management Institute in Arusha, Tanzania, offer training in individual countries. In addition, some institutions are beginning to develop regional training centers in management; Country Study 52-3 illustrates a regional approach to technical assistance and capacity building in East Africa.

Observation trips. Countries that do not have formal training programs but have successfully implemented essential medicines programs can offer useful and practical examples for personnel from other countries. In addition, some multinational and national pharmaceutical manufacturers have regional or local warehouses, manufacturing plants, and laboratories that are good sites for visits. Observation trips work best when combined with short-term training, to reinforce in a practical way the skills learned. Such programs can benefit both the visitors and the institution visited, especially if the trainer accompanies the trainees.

Conferences and seminars. Standardized curricula prepared by an international institution can be used to present at regional conferences and seminars. This approach works well for focusing on particular components, such as pharmaceutical distribution or use. It is also an effective way to promote longer training programs, information sharing among developing-country personnel, desire for improvement, and general sensitization of policy makers to the importance of pharmaceutical management.

In-country counterpart training. An outside consultant with expertise in an aspect of pharmaceutical management, such as computerized inventory, can train counterparts by working on-site for a period of weeks or months. Short-term consultancies work best when they are focused on a specific activity (for example, a pharmaceutical packaging process or the development of an operations manual). Longer periods (from two to four years) are required for overall systems renovation. Meaningful improvements in pharmaceutical management systems can be made using long-term, on-site consultants. The major limitations are—

Expense: International agencies characteristically spend a significant amount of money a month to support an in-country consultant.

Lack of regional effect: Only the individual country benefits, although participants in a program could train others.

Lack of appropriate institutional capacity building: The host country may not be able to continue innovations after the departure of the consultant.

Assistance for the design and implementation of training courses

Ideally, training courses are best developed by educators skilled in instructional design who have a solid background in and knowledge of the topic areas. However, the skills

---

Country Study 52-2
Using the MTP methodology in Lao P.D.R.

The monitoring-training-planning methodology uses a sequence of steps involving techniques to implement a sustainable health project or program. MTP places the tools and responsibility for programs in the hands of local staff, who learn how to mobilize their own resources, carry out the MTP program, and improve pharmaceutical management in their health facilities. Central- and regional-level managers accompany and monitor the staff as they implement the new pharmaceutical management programs.

The MTP tool relies on the following principles—

- The program is continuous, stepwise, and implemented in a structured fashion.
- Every implementation step is planned in advance and detailed in the instructions and materials.
- The programs lead to concrete products that are shared among peers.
- Because MTP participants are usually volunteers, the institution should recognize their efforts.
- Work is spread among the team of participants so that everyone takes part.
- Supervision by all participants of each other's responsibilities and tasks increases accountability and improves problem-solving skills.
- Sessions must be short and punctual so time and travel commitments are minimized.
- Materials and approach should allow for adaptation to the particular needs of each locale.

MTP is unique in that it incorporates monitoring, training, and planning into a single monthly session that achieves tangible results. For one day or less on a monthly basis, participants first review achievements from the previous session, analyze information about their own situation, study how to take action, and then plan short-term activities. Each segment sets the stage for the succeeding segment; the planning segment of one module flows into the monitoring section of the next. For example, if an organization launches a program to improve warehouse management at the local level, the program designers may organize a session on evaluating storerooms, one on improving storage conditions, and another on inventory control. Each session begins with a report on the planned activities from the previous month; contains a concrete product, such as an evaluation, correct storage practices, or an operating inventory system; and ends with participants knowing their responsibilities and tasks for the next month.

The Lao P.D.R. National Drug Policy Program promotes rational medicine prescribing in hospitals through the activities of Drug and Therapeutics Committees; however, when some problems did not respond well to that approach, MTP was implemented to handle small-scale training issues. The use of the MTP approach in the Lao P.D.R. involved a series of small-group discussions among prescribers in individual hospital departments. After being trained in the MTP methodology, these groups defined their problem of interest, selected targets they wanted to achieve, applied a problem-solving approach, and monitored indicators to observe the response. By using MTP, groups frequently met defined targets within two to three monthly training cycles. For example, within three months, Vientiane Hospital reduced postoperative antibiotic prescription from 60 percent to 49 percent, close to its goal of 45 percent; Mittaphap Hospital reduced intravenous fluid use for gastritis from 78 percent to 46 percent and antibiotic use from 40 percent to 20 percent; and Oudomxay Hospital reduced antibiotic use in outpatients from 60 percent to 45 percent. Initially implemented in eleven provincial hospitals, the MTP methodology has been extended to fourteen provincial and fourteen district hospitals and will be extended to all hospitals in the country.

Source: Sisounthone, Luanglath, and Phanyanouvong 2004.

As a result of major global funding initiatives, countries in Africa have experienced a tremendous increase in the volume of pharmaceuticals and health commodities to manage. However, the weakness in the region's pharmaceutical management has required interventions to help build in-country and regional capacity to support the scale-up of treatment programs.

With help from the Rational Pharmaceutical Management (RPM) Plus Program, the Makerere University in Uganda began coordinating a network of institutions from Uganda, Kenya, Tanzania, and Rwanda to develop capacity for pharmaceutical management. The idea behind the Regional Technical Resource Collaboration (RTRC) for Pharmaceutical Management initiative is to create a collaborative group that offers regional and country advisers with expertise in the supply, management, and use of antiretrovirals and other medicines. Each country core group is multidisciplinary and includes pharmacists, social scientists, and representatives from academic institutions, ministries of health, and nonprofit organizations. In the long term, the RTRC plans to incorporate institutions from other countries, such as Ethiopia and Zambia.

Each country's core group assumes a role in the country's national pharmaceutical management activities. For example, by conducting national assessments of the pharmaceutical sectors, each group identified key areas in which to develop and consolidate specific skills in the supply, management, and use of medicines in their countries. The country groups then take a regional lead in a specific area and offer assistance to other groups related to this area of expertise. In addition, the groups consult with ministries of health and other stakeholders regarding research activities and the monitoring and evaluation of pharmaceutical management initiatives.

The RTRC's first activity was to assess management of HIV/AIDS pharmaceuticals and commodities in each of the four countries. The assessments identified many problems, among them inadequate human resource capacity to handle the basic functions of pharmaceutical management, such as selecting, quantifying, and distributing AIDS-related commodities, including rational prescribing. As a result, the RTRC has placed priority on training health care workers on how to manage AIDS-related pharmaceuticals.

As a next step, RPM Plus developed generic HIV/AIDS pharmaceutical training materials that can be easily adapted to train pharmacists, pharmaceutical technologists and technicians, pharmacist assistants, nurses, and storekeepers. The training materials were developed with a diverse audience in mind, with content that is neither too complicated nor too basic. The training process is as practical as possible to help trainees apply the lessons learned in their daily work. The RTRC countries are also incorporating the monitoring-training-planning approach in their training programs (see Country Study 52-2).

involved in designing and implementing a training program can be learned by observing good trainers and paying attention to how they use different methods. Many pharmaceutical programs rely on outside organizations, such as Management Sciences for Health, i+Solutions (previously the International Dispensary Association), and WHO to help them develop local training programs or provide training opportunities for staff (see Annex 52-1). Training-of-trainers courses are also frequently offered by local, regional, or international training institutes.

Another valuable resource for a training program is the practical experience of organizations and institutions in the pharmaceutical supply process. Among these are international organizations, governmental and nongovernmental organizations, universities, developing-country institutions, and programs already operating in developing countries.

With few exceptions, however, these organizations have made technical assistance rather than training their highest priority. Training programs have usually been established on an ad hoc basis to fulfill a specific need rather than in a systematic and comprehensive way. But some programs address specific areas for a particular level in the supply system or for multiple levels in a vertical disease control program.

Annex 52-1 lists selected organizations that have practical experience in the design or implementation of training programs, or both. These organizations are invaluable resources for the development of many types of training programs.

Training and presentation skills

A trainer is expected to be knowledgeable, possess excellent communication skills, and be able to communicate at the level and in the language of the participants (consecutive or simultaneous translation may be appropriate for certain situations). To be effective, the trainer should take into account

Figure 52-3   Seating arrangements for various training applications

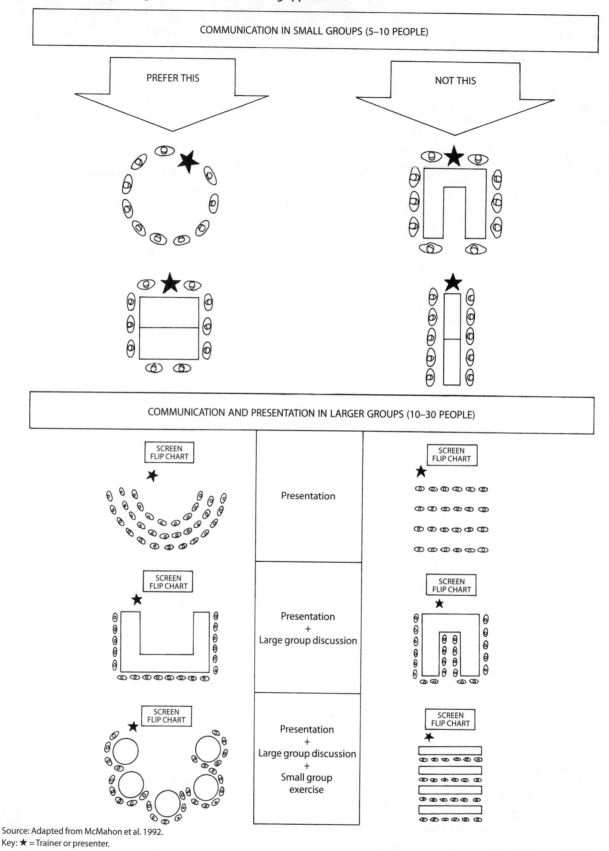

Source: Adapted from McMahon et al. 1992.
Key: ★ = Trainer or presenter.

Country Study 52-4
Measuring the effect of training on pharmaceutical supply management at primary health care clinics in South Africa

Training in pharmaceutical supply management was introduced as part of the Essential Drugs Program in Mpumalanga province in South Africa. To study the effect of the training, a pre- and post-intervention study was conducted comparing six randomly chosen primary health care clinics that received training to six primary health care clinics that did not receive training. The three-day workshop was part of a provincial pharmaceutical supply management training cascade.

The evaluation included a pre-intervention survey, the training workshop for staff of the study group clinics, a post-intervention survey one month after the training, and a second survey three months after the training. The study measured not only supply management outcomes,

such as organization of supplies, record keeping, ordering and stock control, labeling of medicines, but also rational-medicine-use indicators, such as patient knowledge and advice received from staff and appropriate use of the essential medicines list. The results of the evaluation showed significant improvements across the range of outcome measures in the intervention group, and the improvements were sustained and even increased in some instances from the first to the second post-intervention survey. The pharmaceutical supply management training not only affected the pharmaceutical management indicators, but also improved patient care and raised the level of use of the essential medicines list.

Source: Summers and Kruger 2004.

the nature of the target group or audience (who are they? are they senior or line managers?) and their level of knowledge and skill (have participants been trained in the subject to be presented or related subjects?).

Preparation. Time used in preparation is time well spent. On average, the amount of time spent preparing the first presentation of a course or training session by a person knowledgeable on the topic equals four times that spent presenting it. So a one-week course would require four weeks of preparation. After looking up information and consulting manuals and other resources that are relevant to the subjects (identified in the needs assessment), the trainer chooses appropriate learning methods and puts together a session plan. He or she takes steps to acquire or prepare appropriate participants' guides and audiovisual aids well in advance of the targeted training date. The trainer should have the draft materials peer reviewed by someone who is technically competent in the subject area. Also, if possible, the trainer should rehearse the presentation before colleagues, keeping in mind issues of time and clarity.

Presentation. The trainer should always come to the training venue and the session early to check out the room, the seating arrangements, and the audiovisual equipment (Figure 52-3). A friendly chat with participants before the session creates a more comfortable environment.

Formal introductions should take place at the beginning of the first session. One way to do this is to ask pairs of participants to interview each other; then each presents the other to the group or records the information on a wall chart for all to see.

The actual session should begin with the trainer presenting the objectives of the course or session and summarizing

its main points. These main points are then expanded using the chosen learning methods. At the end of the session, the trainer should always summarize the discussion, making sure to allow time for questions and clarification.

In developing visual aids, the following points should be kept in mind—

- Use only one idea per visual aid to avoid crowding.
- Use large letters and clear drawings.
- Do not include too much information on one slide (seven lines with seven words per line is a maximum guideline).
- Do not use multiple fonts, sizes, and colors.
- Allow plenty of time for preparing the visual aids and time for obtaining and testing the equipment.
- Test the materials in a rehearsal before the session, preferably in front of critical colleagues.

When using visual aids, the trainer should take care to—

- Check the visual aids and equipment a few minutes before the session begins.
- Always face the audience, without obstructing their view, and use a pointer.
- Switch off the equipment during discussions.

Trainers' personal style. Personal appearance and style can make a difference in keeping participants' interest during a session. The trainer should maintain eye contact with the group and make sure that his or her voice is clear and can be heard by everybody. When interest appears to be flagging, the trainer needs to be flexible and willing to change the schedule, perhaps by introducing a role-play or arranging a short field visit or by inserting an unscheduled break to allow participants to stretch or get refreshments. A good story or joke can help revive interest. In a session in which participants are divided into small groups, having the trainer move from group to group stimulates interest. During a long course, allocating time for dinners and other social activities is important.

Monitoring and evaluation

Monitoring and evaluation to assess the performance and progress of the participants is one of the trainer's key roles. These assessments should be done as formative evaluations while the course is in progress (for midcourse adjustments and fine-tuning), as summative evaluations at the end of the course (to make the course better in the future), and as periodic follow-ups after the training is over to monitor outcomes and assess the continuing performance of the trainees. The training outcomes should be measurable, performance-based, and directly related to the objectives of the training program. For example, if the goal of the training is for the participants to be able to institute a post-exposure prophylaxis program in their workplaces, a relevant outcome measure would be the completion of this activity within a reasonable time frame. Curriculum mapping is a method to evaluate the links between course content and outcomes (Plaza et al. 2007).

Country Study 52-4 details a study designed to assess the effect of pharmaceutical management training on clinics in South Africa.

In training, formative assessment is important, because the aim of the course is to improve performance, not to grade the participants. The trainer can help them learn more quickly and more completely by providing them with constructive criticism during the course. The trainer can also use the feedback from evaluations to adjust the content and methods of the training to better meet participants' needs. ∎

References and further readings

★ = Key readings.

Abbatt, F. R. 2004. *Teaching for Better Learning: A Guide for Teachers of Primary Healthcare Staff.* 2nd ed. Geneva: World Health Organization.

★ Bienvenu, S. 2000. *The Presentation Skills Workshop: Helping People Create and Deliver Great Presentations.* New York: American Management Association.

CDC (U.S. Centers for Disease Control and Prevention). 2009. *Writing Smart Objectives.* Atlanta: CDC. <http://www.cdc.gov/HealthyYouth/evaluation/pdf/brief3b.pdf>

Ho, S., D. Kember, C. Lau, M. Au Yeung, D. Leung, and M. Chow. 2009. An Outcomes-Based Approach to Curriculum Development in Pharmacy. *American Journal of Pharmaceutical Education* 73(01):

14. <http://www.ajpe.org/view.asp?art=aj730114&pdf=yes>

Klatt, B. 1999. *The Ultimate Training Workshop Handbook.* New York: McGraw-Hill.

Lucas, R. W. 2005. *Conducting a Training Needs Assessment, Developing an Annual Training Plan, Assessing Trainer Competency, Contracting Out for Training.* In Human Resource Management Resource Kit. <http://erc.msh.org/mainpage.cfm?file=2.8.0.htm&module=hr&language=English>

—————. 2003. *Creative Training Idea Book: Inspired Tips and Techniques for Engaging and Effective Learning.* New York: American Management Association.

McMahon, R., E. Barton, and M. Piot. 1992. *On Being in Charge: A Guide to Management in Primary Health Care.* 2nd ed. Geneva: World Health Organization.

★ MSH/RPM Plus Program (Management Sciences for Health/Rational Pharmaceutical Management Plus Program). 2009. *A Guide for Implementing the Monitoring-Training-Planning (MTP) Approach to Build Skills for Pharmaceutical Management.* Arlington, Va.: MSH/RPM Plus. <http://www.msh.org/Documents/upload/MTP-Tool-for-Pharma-Mgmt.pdf>

MSH/SPS Program (Management Sciences for Health/Strengthening Pharmaceutical Systems Program). 2010. *Promoting Rational Medicines Use and Drug and Therapeutics Committees.* Arlington, Va.: MSH/SPS Program.

★ Nimmo, C. M. 2000. *Staff Development for Pharmacy Practice.* Bethesda, Md.: American Society of Health-System Pharmacists.

Pike, R. W. 2003. *Creative Training Techniques Handbook: Tips, Tactics, and How-Tos for Delivering Effective Training.* 3rd ed. Amherst, Mass.: HRC Press.

Plaza, C. M., J. R. Draugalis, M. K. Slack, G. H. Skrepnek, and K. A. Sauer. 2007. Curriculum Mapping in Program Assessment and Evaluation. *American Journal of Pharmaceutical Education* 71(02):20. <http://ajpe.org/view.asp?art=aj710220&pdf=yes>

Potter, C., and R. Brough. 2004. Systematic Capacity Building: Hierarchy of Needs. *Health Policy and Planning* 19(5):336–45.

Sisounthone, B., S. Luanglath, and A. Phanyanouvong. 2004. *Using Monitoring-Training-Planning (MTP) to Reduce Irrational Use of Drugs in Hospitals in Lao PDR.* Abstract, International Conference on Improving Use of Medicines 2004, March 30–April 2, Chiang Mai, Thailand.

★ Stolovitch, H. D., and E. J. Keeps. 2002. *Telling Ain't Training.* Alexandria, Va.: American Society for Training and Development.

Summers, R. S., and C. H. Kruger. 2004. *Impact of Training in Drug Supply Management (DSM) on DSM, Dispensing Practices, and Patient Knowledge and Care at Primary Health Care (PHC) Clinics.* Abstract, International Conference on Improving Use of Medicines 2004, March 30–April 2, Chiang Mai, Thailand.

Trap, B., C. H. Todd, H. Moore, and R. Laing. 2001. The Impact of Supervision on Stock Management and Adherence to Treatment Guidelines: A Randomized Controlled Trial. *Health Policy Planning* 16(3):273–80.

WHO/EMRO (World Health Organization Regional Office for the Eastern Mediterranean). 2006. *Training Manual for Community-Based Initiatives: A Practical Tool for Trainers and Trainees.* Cairo: WHO/EMRO. <http://www.emro.who.int/dsaf/dsa736.pdf>

ASSESSMENT GUIDE

Training programs

- Was a needs assessment conducted before the training programs were developed?
- Were performance indicators established? If so, how were they established and who was involved?
- Do the performance indicators include process, output, performance, and impact indicators? Are they both quantitative and qualitative?
- What training programs have been held?
- How many people of each target group have been trained? What percentage is that of the total target number?
- What methods were used for the training?
- What feedback did the participants give on the training?
- What were the evaluation results for knowledge change? Work performance change?
- How much money has been spent on training activities (if possible, compare budget to actual expenditures)? What percentage of the overall program budget is this?

Sites and institutions

- Which institutions provide training for staff working in the pharmaceutical sector?
- Over the past two years, where has training occurred? For whom?

Trainers

- At each of the institutions identified, how many trainers are there?
- How many of these people have been formally trained as trainers?
- In the courses undertaken, what were the evaluation ratings of the trainers?

Materials

- What training materials were used for the training courses?
- Where and how were the materials developed? When were they last updated?
- How widely available are the training materials?
- Do the training materials correspond with current policies?

Annex 52-1   Sources of assistance for training programs to improve pharmaceutical management

The following organizations and institutions offer training in selected activities relevant to the pharmaceutical supply process. This listing is not exhaustive, nor is it an endorsement of these training programs. For details, these organizations should be contacted directly.

International organizations are listed first, followed by national and private organizations and institutions. Also included is a list of short courses on pharmaceutical policy, pharmaceutical management, rational medicine use, and related subjects.

International organizations

World Health Organization (WHO), 20 Avenue Appia, CH 1211 Geneva 27, Switzerland; telephone: 41 22 791 21 11

Department of Essential Medicines and Pharmaceutical Policies; website: http://www.who.int/medicines

Assists member states in the development and implementation of pharmaceutical policies, the supply of essential medicines of good quality at the lowest possible cost, and the development of training in the rational use of medicines. Works closely with WHO collaborating centers on pharmaceutical regulation and quality assurance and control. Provides training in product registration and computerization of drug regulatory data, as well as good manufacturing practices (GMPs), analytical control, and preparation of chemical reference substances.

WHO's medicines department provide training programs to support policy makers, ministry of health officials, nongovernmental organizations (NGOs), professional associations, and other stakeholders in managing medicines supply and rational pharmaceutical management. WHO participates in regional and national training courses for drug regulators.

WHO/EMP maintains a list of training resources on its website at http://www.who.int/medicines/training/en.

United Nations Children's Fund (UNICEF), Supply Division, UNICEF Plads, Freeport, 2100 Copenhagen Ø, Denmark; telephone: 45 3527 3527; fax: 45 3526 9421; website: www.unicef.org/supply

The Supply Division conducts training on vaccine forecasting at regional immunization meetings and has developed a complete suite of training modules on supply chain management. Through its Procurement Services, the Supply Division can arrange for training in procurement and supply upon request.

United Nations Institute for Training and Research (UNITAR), International Environment House, 11–13 Chemin des Anemones, CH 1219 Chatelaine Geneva; telephone: 41 22 917 84 00; fax: 41 22 917 80 47; website: http://www.unitar.org

Conducts training and workshops on many areas, including social and economic management, although not specific to pharmaceuticals. Offers a number of online training courses.

National and private organizations and institutions

Commonwealth Pharmacists Association, 1 Lambeth High Street, London SE1 7JN, United Kingdom; telephone: 44 20 7572 2364;

fax: 44 20 7572 2508; e-mail: admin@commonwealth pharmacy.org; website: www.commonwealthpharmacy.org

Offers the Management of Pharmaceutical Supply, a distance learning program for all pharmacist and nonpharmacist managers involved with pharmaceutical supply procurement and management, especially at the regional level. The course does not require the student to take leave from his or her employment.

Crown Agents, St. Nicholas House, St. Nicholas Road, Sutton, Surrey, SM1 1EL United Kingdom; telephone: 44 20 8710 6771; fax: 44 20 8770 0479; e-mail: TrainingEnquiries@crownagents.co.uk; website: http://www.crownagents.com/Training/CrownAgentsTraining.aspx

Crown Agents offers a number of short courses on general management and finance topics and in procurement and supply management, including a Certificate in Health Supply Chain Management. Courses are held in the United Kingdom and in a number of other countries, including some in Africa and Asia.

Fédération Internationale Pharmaceutique/International Pharmaceutical Federation (FIP), P.O. Box 84200, 2508 AE, The Hague, The Netherlands; telephone: 31 70 302 1970; fax: 31 70 302 1999; e-mail: fip@fip.org; website: www.fip.org

Provides contact information on more than 900 pharmacy schools worldwide as well as an extensive list of organizations offering continuing education and online and distance learning courses on pharmacy topics. The FIP Foundation for Education and Research provides a certain number of scholarships, fellowships, and grants every year to assist in the development of individuals or groups in the fields of pharmacy practice and pharmaceutical science.

Eastern and Southern Africa Management Institute (ESAMI), P.O. Box 3030, Arusha, Tanzania; website: http://www.esami-africa.org

A regional institution that was designated by the UN Economic Commission for Africa as the African Centre of Excellence in Management Development, ESAMI has nine program areas, including training in general financial management and health management. Clients come from governments, parastatals, the private sector, NGOs, and national and regional institutions in Africa.

i+Solutions, Westdam 3b, 3441 GA Woerden, The Netherlands; telephone: 31 34 848 9630; fax: 31 34 848 9659; e-mail: info@ iplussolutions.org; website: http://www.iplussolutions.org

i+Solutions is a not-for-profit organization specializing in pharmaceutical supply chain management for low- and middle-income countries. i+Solutions offers a variety of courses and training programs in pharmaceutical management.

Mahidol University, Faculty of Pharmacy, Sri-ayudhaya Road, Rajadhevi, Bangkok 10400, Thailand; telephone: 66 02 644 8677 91, ext. 1301; fax: 66 02 354 4326; website: http://www.pharmacy. mahidol.ac.th/eng

Offers short courses on pharmaceutical management, including use of essential medicines, GMP training, and pharmaceutical economics. Organizes professional meetings, conferences, and symposia as a means of professional continuing education.

Management Sciences for Health (MSH), 784 Memorial Drive, Cambridge, Mass. 02139-4613 USA; telephone: 1 617 250 9500; fax: 1 617 250 9090; website: www.msh.org

Center for Pharmaceutical Management, 4301 North Fairfax Drive, Suite 400, Arlington, Va. 22203 USA; telephone: 1 703 524 6575; fax: 1 703 524 7898; e-mail: cpm@msh.org

Offers short-term courses in multiple languages on rational medicine use and other aspects of pharmaceutical management and on other topics, including pharmacovigilance, management information systems, and disease-specific pharmaceutical management—such as HIV/AIDS, malaria, and tuberculosis. In more than thirty years, thousands of health professionals have participated in MSH courses in the United States and other countries.

Robert Gordon University, School of Pharmacy, Schoolhill, Aberdeen AB10 1FR, Scotland, United Kingdom; telephone: 44 1224 262 502; website: www.rgu.ac.uk/pharmacy

The School of Pharmacy offers postgraduate distance learning courses and certificates for health care professionals to develop an advanced therapeutic knowledge base and the necessary practical skills to ensure rational prescribing.

Swiss Tropical and Public Health Institute, Course Secretariat, Socinstrasse 57, CH 4002, Basel, Switzerland; telephone: 41 61 284 82 80; fax: 41 61 284 81 06; website: http://www.sti.ch

Offers the two-week course Rational Management of Medicines—A Focus on HIV/AIDS, Tuberculosis and Malaria. Conducted in English. Other courses in international health include Health Care and Management in Tropical Countries.

University of Heidelberg, Institute of Public Health, Course information: Im Neuenheimer Feld 365, 69120, Heidelberg, Germany; telephone: 49 62 21 56 50 48; fax: 49 62 21 56 49 18; website: http://www.klinikum.uni-heidelberg.de/Short-Courses.109912.0.html

Offers short courses in international health. Most of the courses are post graduate, advanced level, one- and two-week long programs conducted in English. The institute also offers a one-year master's of science in international health.

Annex 52-2   Workshop logistics

Workshop and support checklist

Advance planning

- Goals
- Objectives, expected outcomes
- Needs assessments
- Content, topics, session
- Length, time frame
- Number of participants
- Implementation approach (e.g., small-group interaction versus large-group presentations)
- Materials, including prereading for the participants, participants' and facilitators' guides, handouts
- Participant list
- Short-term consultants, facilitators or presenters (choosing the best people to present each topic)
- Budget, including materials, travel, accommodations
- Venue: reservations, deposit, other concerns
- Invitations to participants and follow-up phone calls

Workshop material

- Ruled writing pads, pens, pencils with erasers
- Document binders
- Flip charts, pens, and markers
- Blank overhead transparencies and pens
- Masking tape and transparent tape
- Stapler and staples
- Hole punch
- Photocopying paper
- Computer paper, printer ribbon, blank diskettes, multiplug adapter
- Letterhead stationery and envelopes
- Paper clips, scissors, Post-it pads, rubber bands, Wite-out, glue
- Calculator
- Name badges

Workshop support responsibility

- Logistics: supervision of conference site, meals, breaks, and accommodations
- Finances: payment of cash food allowances, paperwork, and reimbursement for transportation expenses
- Secretary for word processing
- Vehicle and driver
- Messenger and photocopier

Workshop support facilities

- Telephone access (incoming and outgoing) for facilitators
- On-site (or easily accessible) photocopy machine (with toner and paper) for low-volume copies
- Photocopy service site for high-volume copies
- Computer and printer
- Overhead projector, extra bulb, extension cord of adequate length
- LCD projector and projection screen
- Sound system and microphones (if needed)

Setup of main meeting room

- Opening session and plenary sessions: horseshoe versus classroom-style seating with extra chairs
- Tables for small group work

- Break room(s) or area(s)
- Groups of approximately equal size
- Overhead and slide projector check: screen that all participants can see, projector proper distance and angle from screen, sufficiently long electric cord, extra bulb
- Transparencies and pens
- Flip charts and pens available for plenary and small groups

Daily preparation of meeting room

- Projectors: position, cord, spare bulb, transparencies, pens
- Blackboard or whiteboard: cleaner, pens
- Flip charts: location, paper, pens

Workshop administration checklist

- Upon arrival at the training site, make sure that the conference room is arranged properly and note any changes that need to be made. Find out if additional rooms are available for small-group discussions. Set up a registration desk near the entrance and a working table where appropriate. Arrange the handouts on a separate table where they are readily accessible.
- Set up the projector and test it. Make sure that the projection screen can be seen easily by all participants.
- Put the writing pads, pens, and programs into document binders and place them on the tables.
- Inform the management of the site about all the practical arrangements.
- Put up a signboard at reception displaying the location of the conference room and registration time.
- Using the list of participants, prepare the name tags and spread them out on the registration desk so that the participants can collect them as they register. This step can be done either the evening before or in the morning before registration begins.
- Give a copy of the program to the management so that they know when to serve tea or coffee and meals.
- During the introductory session, make administrative announcements: when allowances will be paid (night-out allowances are normally paid at the end of day one; reimbursements for travel expenses are normally paid at the break on the last day, upon presentation of receipts as documentation).
- As soon as the last person has registered, type out the participant list and start preparing the receipts for participants to sign when receiving allowances. Use a duplicate receipt book with a carbon. Mark the receipt number against the participant's name on the list to make paying easier.
- Type out a separate list for reimbursing transport expenses and make out payment receipts. Fuel and other travel receipts can be collected on day one when paying out allowances.
- Give a copy of the participant list to hotel management, indicating the participants who are not staying at the site so that they know how many extra teas and lunches to charge for. Also, give management the names of the people who are settling their own bills (facilitators, secretaries) so that they will not be included in the main bill.
- On the last day, have the hotel management prepare the detailed bill and check it against the participant list.

Index

Peace through Health: How Health Professionals Can Work for a Less Violent World

Edited by Akshaya Neil Arya and Joanna Santa Barbara

"Neil Arya, Joanna Santa Barbara, and the community of experts they have gathered in this book not only subject the causes of war to a rigorous public health analysis, but also explore a radically different model for preventing armed conflict: primary prevention in a social framework, in service of the common good. 'Peace through health' may sound like a slogan, but readers of this book will learn that it is a profound and practical vision of a social compact in which war has no place."

—John Loretz, Program Director
International Physicians for the Prevention of Nuclear War

"A well-written, easily accessible resource for the growing field of peace studies and conflict resolution."

—Choice

We typically define and talk about wars using the language of politics, but what happens when you bring in a doctor's perspective on conflict? Can war be diagnosed like an illness? Can health professionals participate in its mitigation and prevention? The contributors to *Peace through Health: How Health Professionals Can Work for a Less Violent World* engage with these ground-breaking ideas and describe tools that can further peace once war is understood as a public health problem.

An Imprint of Stylus Publishing

22883 Quicksilver Drive, Sterling, VA 20166-2102

Subscribe to our e-mail alerts: **www.kpbooks.com**